THE ANNUAL DIRECTORY OF

American and Canadian Bed & Breakfasts

1995 Edition

THE ANNUAL DIRECTORY OF

American and Canadian Bed & Breakfasts

1995 Edition

Julia M. Pitkin, *Editor*

RUTLEDGE HILL PRESS
NASHVILLE, TENNESSEE

Published in Nashville, Tennessee, by Rutledge Hill Press, Inc., 211 Second Avenue North, Nashville, Tennessee 37219. Distributed in Canada by H. B. Fenn and Company Ltd., 1090 Lorimar Drive, Mississauga, Ontario L5S 1R7.

Cover design and book design by Harriette Bateman

Printed in the United States of America.

1 2 3 4 5 6—97 96 95 94

Contents

A Message from the Editor

It has been my pleasure to compile the 1995 edition of *The Annual Directory of American and Canadian Bed & Breakfasts*. With each issue, the participation of Canadian inns has increased, leading us to introduce our new name last year. This year the number of Canadian inns has jumped dramatically, a pleasure we hope will continue in further issues.

When we began the directory in 1989, Rutledge Hill Press hoped it would be the most comprehensive and authoritative reference of bed and breakfast inns published. I believe the book has met these expectations, and I'm proud to have been associated with it from the beginning.

My hearty thanks go to all of the innkeepers who participated in this volume. Their helpfulness and interest in their profession have helped me understand why many travelers prefer to stay at bed and breakfast inns. My own experiences have been positive. When I have traveled, I have always found the hosts to be attentive, thoughtful, and professional.

Julia M. Pitkin

Introduction

Another year, another directory, you're thinking. Not so. The 1995 edition of *The Annual Directory of American and Canadian Bed & Breakfasts* is one of the most comprehensive directories on bookstore shelves today.

Whether you are planning your honeymoon, a family vacation or reunion, or a business trip (many bed and breakfasts provide conference facilities), you will find what you are looking for at a bed and breakfast. From the restored sea captain's home in Maine to the antebellum plantation in Mississippi. From the adobe hideaway in Santa Fe to the working farm in Iowa. From the lavish Victorian in San Francisco to the rustic cabin near the glaciers in Alaska. They are all here just waiting to be discovered.

Once you have chosen your destination, look for it, or one close by, to see what is available. Each state has a general map with city locations to help you plan your trip efficiently. There are listings in all 50 states, Canada, Puerto Rico, and the Virgin Islands. Don't be surprised to find a listing in even the remote spot you thought only you knew about. Even if your favorite hideaway isn't listed, you're sure to discover a new one.

How to Use This Guide

The sample listing below is typical of the entries in this directory. Each bed and breakfast is listed alphabetically by city and establishment name. The description provides an overview of the bed and breakfast and may include nearby activities and attractions. Note: The descriptions were written by the hosts. The publisher has not visited these bed and breakfasts and is not responsible for inaccuracies.

Following the description are notes that are designed for easy reference. Looking at the sample, a quick glance tells you that this bed and breakfast has four guest rooms, two with private baths (PB) and two that share a bath (SB). The rates are for two people shar-

GREAT TOWN _____

Favorite Bed and Breakfast

123 Main Street, 12345
(800) 555-1234

This quaint bed and breakfast is surrounded by five acres of award-winning landscaping and gardens. There are four guest rooms, each individually decorated with antiques.

It is close to antique shops, restaurants, and outdoor activities. Breakfast includes homemade specialties and is served in the formal dining room at guests' leisure. Minimum stay of two nights.

Hosts: Sue and Jim Smith
Rooms: 4 (2 PB; 2 SB) $65-80
Full Breakfast
Credit Cards: A, B
Notes: 2, 5, 8, 10, 11, 12, 13

ing one room. Tax may or may not be included. The specifics of "Credit Cards" and "Notes" are listed on the bottom of each page. For example, the letter A means that the hosts accept MasterCard. The number 10 means that tennis is available on the premises or within 10 to 15 miles.

In many cases, the bed and breakfast name is listed with a reservation service that represents several houses in one area. This service is responsible for bookings and can answer other questions you may have. They also inspect each listing and can help you choose the best place for your needs.

Before You Arrive

Now that you have chosen the bed and breakfast that interests you, there are some things you need to find out. You should always make reservations in advance, and while you are doing so you should ask about the local taxes. City taxes can be an unwelcome surprise. Make sure your children will be welcome. If you have dietary needs or prefer nonsmoking rooms, find out if these requirements can be accommodated. Ask about check-in times and cancellation policies. Get specific directions. Most bed and breakfasts are readily accessible, but many are a little out of the way.

When You Arrive

Remember that in many cases you are visiting someone's home. Be respectful of their property, their schedules, and their requests. Don't smoke if they ask you not to, and don't show up with pets without prior arrangement. Be tidy in shared bathrooms, and be prompt. Most places have small staffs or may be run single-handedly and cannot easily adjust to surprises.

With a little effort and a sense of adventure you will learn firsthand the advantages of bed and breakfast travel. You will rediscover hospitality in a time when kindness seems to have been pushed aside. And with the help of this directory, you will find accommodations that are just as exciting as your traveling plans.

The staff of *The Annual Directory of American and Canadian Bed & Breakfasts* would like to hear from you about any experiences you have had or any inns you wish to recommend. Please write to us at:

The Annual Directory of American and Canadian Bed & Breakfasts
211 Seventh Avenue North
Nashville, Tennessee 37219

THE ANNUAL DIRECTORY OF

American and Canadian Bed & Breakfasts

1995 Edition

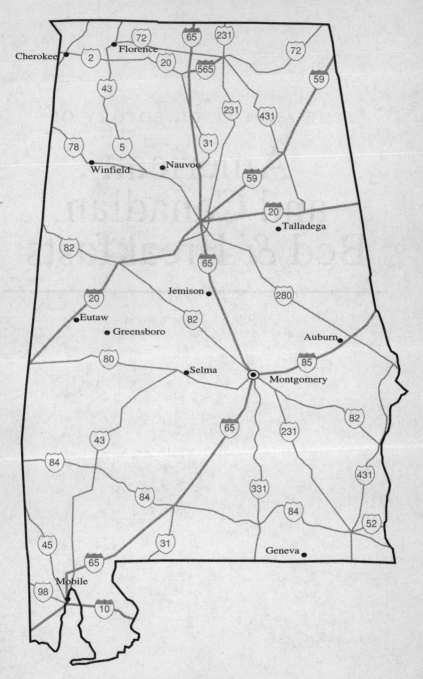

Alabama

Alabama

The Crenshaw Guest House

AUBURN

The Crenshaw Guest House

371 North College Street, 36830
(334) 821 1131

A gracious bed and breakfast in Auburn's historic district, rich in history and late Victorian detail. Spacious rooms include private baths, touch-tone telephones, cable TV, VCR, and clock/radio cassette players. Gleaming porcelain, brass, and ornately carved mantels provide the perfect setting for a collection of comfortable antiques. Suite or kitchenette units available. Room service breakfast. Just a short drive to world-class golf, three blocks to campus, downtown, and restaurants. AAA-rated three diamonds. Easy access from I-85.

Hosts: Fran and Kash Verma
Rooms: 5 (PB) $50-70
Continental Breakfast
Credit Cards: A, B, C
Notes: 2, 5, 8, 9, 10, 11, 12, 14

CHEROKEE

Natchez Trace Reservation Service

P.O. Box 193, Hampshire, TN 38461
(615) 285-2777; (800) 377-2770

CHE-01. Just three miles from the trace and four miles from the Tennessee River and Pickwick Lake, this home was burned during the Civil War, rebuilt at the turn of the century, and recently refurbished. Guests love the charm of this old home with its antique furnishings. Relax on the porch or stroll around the 12 acres of giant, old cedar trees. $55-65.

Kirkwood, 1860

EUTAW

Kirkwood, 1860 Bed and Breakfast

111 Kirkwood Drive, 35462
(205) 372-9009

Come enjoy this bed and breakfast in an antebellum plantation home. There are many

NOTES: Credit cards accepted: A MasterCard; B Visa; C American Express; D Discover Card; E Diner's Club; F Other; 2 Personal checks accepted; 3 Lunch available; 4 Dinner available; 5 Open all year; 6 Pets welcome; 7 Smoking allowed; 8 Children welcome; 9 Social drinking allowed; 10 Tennis available; 11 Swimming available; 12 Golf available; 13 Skiing available; 14 May be booked through travel agents.

antebellum homes in this small town. Kirkwood's construction began in 1857 and was completed in 1860. The Swayzes purchased the home in 1972, and 15 years were spent in restoration work.

Host: Mary B. Swayze
Rooms: 2 (SB) $75
Full Breakfast
Credit Cards: None
Notes: 2, 5, 8, 10, 11

Lincoln Ltd.

P.O. Box 3479, Meridian, 39303
(601) 482-5483; (800) 633-MISS (reservations)
FAX (601) 693-7447

89. This Federal Greek Revival, circa 1840, has been owned by the family now occupying it since 1914 and owned by only two families in over 150 years. The home has the original wide heart-pine flooring upstairs, rife quartersawed pine flooring downstairs, pillared mantels, and 18 paned windows. Rock on the front porch and enjoy a step back in time! One guest room available. $75.

FLORENCE

Riverview Bed and Breakfast

Route 7, Box 123G, 35630
(205) 757-8667

On the banks of the beautiful Tennessee River between Wilson and Wheeler dams with a spectacular view of each dam and the river. Recently constructed contemporary home was architecturally designed and professionally decorated to blend with the surrounding wooded area and lake view. Guest rooms have decks and patios, offering panoramic views of sailboats a few feet away.

Hosts: Edith and Buddy Meeks
Rooms: 2 (PB) $75-95
Full Breakfast
Credit Cards: A, B
Notes: 2, 5, 10, 12, 14

Wood Avenue Inn

658 North Wood Avenue, 35630
(205) 766-8441

Exquisite Queen Anne mansion built in 1887 in the historic district. Within walking distance of fine restaurants, museums, antique shops, and old downtown. Enjoy 18th-century furnishings or relax in wicker rockers and observe the variety of birds in the wisteria garden. The Victorian elegance pampers each guest with fine china, stemware, silver tea sets, and candlelight breakfasts. Become captivated by the yesteryears of the heart of Dixie!

Hosts: Gene and Alvern Greeley
Rooms: 5 (PB) $55-85
Full Breakfast
Credit Cards: A, B
Notes: 5, 10, 11, 12

Live Oaks of Geneva

GENEVA

Live Oaks of Geneva

307 South Academy Street, 36340
(205) 684-2489

Beautifully restored 1918 home one block from downtown in southeast Alabama, this bed and breakfast offers comfortable bedrooms, private baths, and TVs. Enjoy the large porch, sunroom, and living room as a family member. A guest entrance allows visitors to come and go as they wish. Smoking is restricted to the porch. No pets in bedrooms. Children welcome.

Hosts: Horace and Pamela Newman
Rooms: 3 (PB) $40
Continental Breakfast
Credit Cards: None
Notes: 2, 5, 8, 12

GREENSBORO

Blue Shadows Bed and Breakfast Guest Home

Rural Route 2, Box 432, 36744
(205) 624-3637

Country setting on 320 acres offers elegant accommodations. Enjoy the nature trail, private fish pond, bird sanctuary, and formal garden. Afternoon tea and sherry served by request. Nearby attractions include historic sites, Marion Military Institute, Judson College, University of Alabama, Tuscaloosa Indian Mounds, antique shops, and beautiful churches. Come and enjoy Southern hospitality! Reservations a must!

Hosts: Janet and Thaddeus May
Suite: 1 (SB) $65
Continental Breakfast
Credit Cards: None
Notes: 7 (limited)

JEMISON

Horse Shoe Bunk House

356 County Road 164, 35085
(205) 646-4109

This three-bedroom home is right off I-65 between Birmingham and Montgomery, in the peach country of central Alabama. Decor is cowboy, Indian, and Oriental (in one bedroom). Pet the horses, fish in the lake, or just relax. Full country breakfast is served. No pets. No smoking. Christian atmosphere.

Host: Kay Red Horse
Rooms: 3 (1 PB; 2 SB) $45-50
Full Breakfast
Credit Cards: None
Notes: 2, 3, 4, 5, 8 (over 15), 14

MOBILE

Malaga Inn

359 Church Street, 36602
(205) 438-4701

The Malaga Inn, in the historic district of downtown, is the only hotel of its kind in the state. Originally the two townhouses were built in 1862 by two brothers-in-law when the Civil War was going well for the South. The two homes have been lovingly restored around a quiet patio garden. All rooms are furnished with a great deal of individuality, reminiscent of the finest Southern tradition. The friendly and courteous attention afforded to each guest, the convenient location next to the Civic Auditorium, and all the historic sites of Mobile have attracted those who relish the inn's Old Town atmosphere for many years. Restaurant and pool on the premises. Breakfast not included in the rates.

Host: Julie Beem
Rooms: 40 (PB) $69-79
No Breakfast
Credit Cards: A, B, C, D
Notes: 2, 3, 4, 5, 7, 8, 9, 11, 12, 14

Mallory Manor

Mallory Manor

1104 Montauk Avenue, 36604
(205) 432-6440

6 Pets welcome; 8 Children welcome; 9 Social drinking allowed; 10 Tennis available; 11 Swimming available; 12 Golf available; 13 Skiing available; 14 May be booked through travel agents.

Experience the charm of the Old South in this comfortably elegant setting in the heart of Mobile's historic districts. The City Museum, Fort Conde, and USS *Battleship Alabama* are minutes away. Participate in the excitement of Mardi Gras; it all began right here in Mobile in 1711. Within easy walking distance of the parade routes. Comfortable rooms with queen-size bed and single sleeper, sitting room, and private bath are available year-round.

Hosts: Don and Joan Seeley
Rooms: 2 (1 PB; 1 SB) $65
Full Breakfast
Credit Cards: A, B
Notes: 2, 5, 8, 7 (limited), 9

The Lattice Inn

MONTGOMERY

The Lattice Inn Bed and Breakfast

1414 South Hull Street, 36104
(334) 832-9931; (800) 525-0652
FAX (334) 264-0075

The Lattice Inn is Montgomery's quiet way to relax in Southern comfort. In the historic garden district, this turn-of-the-century home, built in 1906, has been lovingly restored to provide a wonderful and comfortable retreat for today's traveler. The shady front porch has just enough lattice to provide privacy while reading or lounging on its swing. The pool and decks in the back yard provide a restful place to unwind.

Host: Michael Pierce
Rooms: 5 (PB) $55-70
Full Breakfast
Credit Cards: A, B, C, D
Notes: 2, 5, 7 (limited), 9, 10, 11, 12, 14

Red Bluff Cottage

551 Clay Street, P.O. Box 1026, 36101
(334) 264-0056; FAX (334) 262-1872

The Waldos built Red Bluff Cottage in 1987 high above the Alabama River in the historic Cottage Hill District. A raised cottage, all guest rooms are on the ground floor, with easy access to off-street parking, gazebo, and fenced play yard. Upstairs, guests will enjoy pleasantly light and airy public rooms, including dining, living, music (piano and harpsichord), and sitting (TV) rooms. A deep porch overlooks downtown, the state capitol, and river plain.

Hosts: Ann and Mark Waldo
Rooms: 4 (PB) $65
Full Breakfast
Credit Cards: A, B, D
Notes: 2, 5, 8, 9, 14

NAUVOO

The William Cook House

William Cook Parkway, 35578
(205) 272-1972; (205) 697-5792

Scottish-immigrant, coal-mining pioneers built this home, circa 1900, in the heart of the Alabama Highlands' booming coal-mining district. Furnished with original heirloom pieces, it is on the Alabama Register of Historic Places and convenient to other tourist attractions. Comfortable rooms, circular porches, and Continental breakfast. Victorian atmosphere adds to the romance of the home.

Hosts: Jean Dillon and Frances Vance
Rooms: 2 (SB) $45-55
Continental Breakfast
Credit Cards: None
Notes: 2

NOTES: Credit cards accepted: A Master Card; B Visa; C American Express; D Discover Card; E Diner's Club; F Other; 2 Personal checks accepted; 3 Lunch available; 4 Dinner available; 5 Open all year;

SELMA

Grace Hall
Bed and Breakfast Inn

506 Lauderdale Street, 36701
(334) 875-5744

This antebellum mansion, circa 1857, is on The National Register of Historic Places. Restoration certified by the Department of Interiors. The Evans, Baker, and Jones' families have occupied this home for the past 110 years. There are many original antiques to view while taking a tour: admission is $5 for adults, $3 for students, no charge for children under six. Group rates for the tour are available. Dinner and lunch available for parties of ten or more.

Hosts: Joey and Coy Dillon
Rooms: 6 (PB) $80-110
Full Breakfast
Credit Cards: A, B, C
Notes: 2, 3, 4, 5, 6 and 14 (by arrangement), 7, 8 (over 5), 9, 10, 11, 12

TALLADEGA

Grace Hall

The Governor's House
500 Meadowlake Lane, 35160
(205) 763-2186

The Governor's House, built in 1850 by a former governor of Alabama, is on a knoll overlooking Logan Martin Lake and part of the cattle farm. It was moved to the farm and furnished with antiques from the hosts' families. There is a Horse Barn Galleries Antique shop and a wicker-furnished broad front porch. Come enjoy quiet, peaceful country living at its best and slow it down. Just two miles south of Exit 165 on I-20 in Lincoln. A full breakfast is served in the dining room or on the front porch. Air-conditioned. Ceiling fans throughout. Tennis courts on the premises. Golf 15 miles away.

Hosts: Mary Sue and Ralph Gaines
Rooms: 3 (1 PB; 2 SB) $60-70
Full Breakfast
Credit Cards: None
Notes: 2, 3, 4, 5, 8 (over 12), 9, 10, 12

WINFIELD

White Oaks Inn

Route 5, Box 32, 35594
(205) 487-4115

White Oaks Inn is a restored 1918 family home built by the Pearce family. The inside has been completely renovated to include a private bath for each guest room. All rooms have TVs and telephones. A large-screen TV and VCR are available in the den for movies and sporting events. A pool and hot tub are available for guests. The large front porch with swing and rockers invites guests to relax. Two cabins are also available. In a dry county, no alcoholic beverages permitted.

Hosts: Linda and Roger Sanders
Rooms: 5 (PB) $60
Cabins: 2 $50-60
Credit Cards: A, B, C, D
Notes: 2, 5, 10, 11

6 Pets welcome; 8 Children welcome; 9 Social drinking allowed; 10 Tennis available; 11 Swimming available; 12 Golf available; 13 Skiing available; 14 May be booked through travel agents.

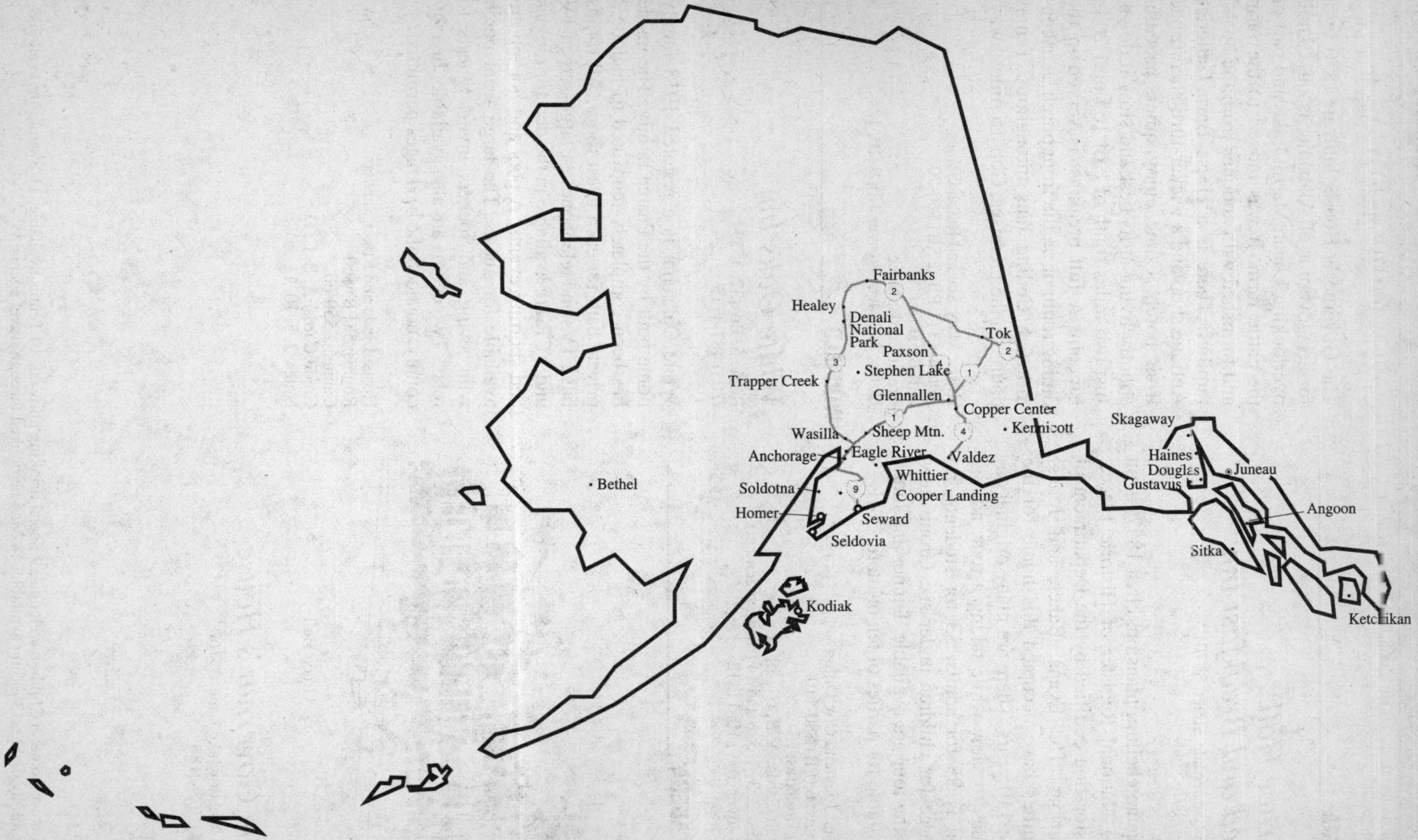

Ketchikan

Angoon

Juneau

Sitka

Skagaway

Haines

Douglas

Gustavus

Kennicott

Copper Center

Tok

Valdez

2

Stephen Lake

Whittier

Fairbanks

Paxson

1

Glennallen

Cooper Landing

Denali
National
Park

Sheep Mtn.

Eagle River

2

Healey

Seward

3

Trapper Creek

Wasilla

Seldovia

Anchorage

9

Soldotna

Kodiak

Homer

Bethel

Alaska

Alaska

ANCHORAGE

Alaskan Frontier Gardens Bed and Breakfast

1011 East Tudor Road, #160, 99503
(907) 345-6556; FAX (907) 562-2923

Elegant accommodations on a scenic three-acre landscaped wooded setting. Come enjoy Alaskan hospitality with 30-year resident. In Anchorage's peaceful hillside area near the Chugach State Park, 20 minutes from downtown. Spacious rooms and luxury suite with Jacuzzi, sauna, and fireplace. Great for honeymooners. Museum-like environment with exceptional comfort. Truly Alaska's finest. Gourmet breakfast. Laundry service.

Host: Rita Gittins
Rooms: 5 (2 PB; 3 SB) $100-225
Full Breakfast
Credit Cards: A, B, C
Notes: 2, 5, 7 (limited), 8, 9, 11, 12, 13, 14

Arctic Loon Bed and Breakfast

P.O. Box 110333, 99511
(907) 345-4935

Elegant accommodations in this exquisite 6,500-square-foot Scandinavian home in the hillside area of south Anchorage. Breathtaking, spectacular views of Mount McKinley and Anchorage Bowl. An eight-person Jacuzzi, sauna, and rosewood grand piano provide relaxation after a full gourmet breakfast. Fully licensed, this bed and breakfast has a quiet mountain setting near golf course, zoo, and Chugach State Park hiking trails.

Hosts: Janie and Lee Johnson
Rooms: 3 (1 PB; 2 SB) $75-90
Full Breakfast
Credit Cards: A, B
Notes: 2, 5, 8, 9, 10, 11, 12, 13, 14

Coastal Trail Bed and Breakfast

3100 Iliamna Drive, 99517
(907) 243-5809

Coastal Trail Bed and Breakfast invites guests to a comfortable Alaskan homestay. The three-room suite is furnished for comfort and includes telephone, TV, and VCR. Enjoy the outdoor hot tub. Be amazed at the beauty and rarity of flowers in the gardens. Hunting and fishing are spoken here by traditional Alaskan hosts. In the center of a gracious neighborhood, Coastal Trail adjoins an urban walking trail where guests may enjoy wildflowers, migratory birds, whales, and views of Denali. Full breakfast served. No smoking.

Hosts: Sherry and Derek Tomlinson
Suite: 1 (PB) $75
Full Breakfast
Cards: None
Notes: 2, 5, 10, 13, 14

A Homestay at Homesteads

Box 771283, Eagle River, 99577
(907) 272-8644

A1. The crossroads of life in a residential area. Within walking distance to town, coastal trail access for skiing in the winter

NOTES: Credit cards accepted: A MasterCard; B Visa; C American Express; D Discover Card; E Diner's Club; F Other; 2 Personal checks accepted; 3 Lunch available; 4 Dinner available; 5 Open all year; 6 Pets welcome; 7 Smoking allowed; 8 Children welcome; 9 Social drinking allowed; 10 Tennis available; 11 Swimming available; 12 Golf available; 13 Skiing available; 14 May be booked through travel agents.

A Homestay at Homesteads
(continued)

and biking, skating, and walking in the summer. Hosts are a professional family. Nonsmoking. Private and shared baths. Full breakfast. $65-90.

A2. The owners have converted an apartment complex to accommodate folks who like the freedom of their own kitchen. Studio, one-, and two-bedroom suites in the heart of downtown. Depending on the season and space guests want, enjoy this Eighth Avenue place for $80-140.

A3. Great older home where guests can choose the attic or the basement. In the heart of downtown, all the bus lines are at the doorstep including McKinley Tours' early one-day adventure. Fresh pastry provided. Families welcomed. $65-98.

A4. Just at the tree line with a great trail across the creek lies this delightful home. In the winter ski from the porch. In the summer climb the mountains surrounding this unique getaway. A wood stove provides the warmth. Homemade quilts. No smoking. Full breakfast. $65-95.

ANGOON

Favorite Bay Inn
P.O. Box 101, 99820
(907) 788-3123

Nestled in a clearing on the beach overlooking Favorite Bay, the inn offers a most comfortable, convenient, and relaxing way to enjoy real Alaska at its best. Built in 1937, it is well appointed with four guest rooms, two baths, a large family room, dining room, sitting room, library, and deck. An atmosphere of oak, leather, brass, lace, and crystal allows guests to indulge their sense of romance. Enjoy world-class scenery and spectacular wildlife viewing. Superb fresh-water and saltwater fishing.

Hosts: Richard and Sharon Powers
Rooms: 5 (SB) $59-119
Full Breakfast
Credit Cards: A, B
Notes: 2, 3, 4, 5, 8, 14

BETHEL

Bentley's Porter House Bed and Breakfast
624 First Avenue, P.O. Box 529, 99559
(907) 543-3552; (907) 543 5923
FAX (907) 543-3561

On the beautiful Kuskokwim River in southwest Alaska, offering comfortable rooms with cable TV. Full, elegant breakfast. Special dietary accommodations can be arranged with prior notice. Reasonable rates at a downtown location. Guests call it their home away from home. Reservations advisable; brochure available.

Host: Millie Bentley
Rooms: 18 (SB) $95
Full Breakfast
Credit Cards: A, B, C, D, E
Notes: 2, 5

COOPER LANDING

A Homestay at Homesteads
Box 771283, Eagle River, 99577
(907) 272-8644

CL. Need one huge room? Comes with two queen-size beds, one twin, and lots of floor mats. Fishing parties, hikers, and families all love to stay here. Private. Transportation available, but not included. $150.

CL1. This inn is rustic! Founded in an original log house that still has the best restaurant around. The cabins have two double beds and private baths. The rug is warm, and the place is open year-round. Also, one

NOTES: Credit cards accepted: A MasterCard; B Visa; C American Express; D Discover Card; E Diner's Club; F Other; 2 Personal checks accepted; 3 Lunch available; 4 Dinner available; 5 Open all year;

with a kitchenette. Meals available, but not included. From $65.

Red Salmon Guest House

Mile 48.2 Sterling Highway, P.O. Box 725, 99572
(907) 595-1 RED

On the banks of a wild and curving salmon river, the Upper Kenai, these rooms and Alaskan cabins have spectacular views. Go world-class fishing or scenic river rafting right from the Guest House, take a wonderful day hike to nearby Exit Glacier and the Russian River Falls, or relax on the deck and watch the water peacefully roll by while moose visit, eagles fish, and sheep graze on the mountain. An Alaskan breakfast is often the highlight as guests gather together in the beautiful dining room overlooking the river.

Hosts: Patti and George Heim
Rooms: 4 (2 PD; 2 SB) $69-129
Full Breakfast
Credit Cards: A, B
Notes: 2, 8, 9, 14

COPPER CENTER

A Homestay at Homesteads

Box 771283, Eagle River, 99577
(907) 272-8644

CC1. In the original dog team and carriage stop—a two-story building. Some of the rooms are still slightly warped, but the hosts are upgrading the baths and rooms more each year. Travelers come from miles around for "out to dine" in the formal dining room. Meals available, but not included. Some private baths, some shared. Homey and historic place to rest overnight and to enjoy during the day. $55-75.

DENALI NATIONAL PARK

A Homestay at Homesteads

Box 771283, Eagle River, 99577
(907) 272-8644

D1. How about a nice hot tub at the end of the day? The hosts do not serve breakfast but do offer guests a spectacular view in individual log cabins on the side of the mountain above the hustle and bustle of the tourists. Private baths. Walk to the best restaurants. $115-140.

D2. These cabins fit lots of budgets, from the central bath and shower units to full family cabins with private baths. Right on the Parks Highway, with marvelous wooded pathways between the cabins. No breakfast served, but the shuttle will take guests to the park's entrance or to good restaurants. $80-130.

Kantishna Roadhouse

P.O. Box 130, 99755
(907) 683-1475; (800) 942-7420

Kantishna Roadhouse is a modern, full-service lodge with all the amenities guests would expect from a first-class wilderness resort. Packages include transportation to and from Kantishna, three home-cooked meals a day, and a wide range of activities. Open June 5 through September 10.

Host: Roberta Koppenberg
Cabins: 27 (PB)
Full Breakfast
Credit Cards: A, B
Notes: 2, 3, 4

DOUGLAS

Windsock Inn
Bed and Breakfast

P.O. Box 240223, 99824-0223
(907) 364-2431

Only three families have owned and occupied this historic home. Built in 1912 in the heart of Douglas, the inn overlooks Mount Roberts and the Gastineau Channel. On the city bus line and five minutes from the capital city of Juneau. Pioneer Alaskan hosts cater to seniors, teachers, and foreign trav-

6 Pets welcome; 8 Children welcome; 9 Social drinking allowed; 10 Tennis available; 11 Swimming available; 12 Golf available; 13 Skiing available; 14 May be booked through travel agents.

elers with affordable rates. Two bedrooms, plus sitting room, cable TV, full breakfast, handicap access, and shared bath. Courtesy transportation to airport and ferry with visits exceeding two nights.

Hosts: Julie and Bob Isaac
Rooms: 2 (SB) $50-55
Full Breakfast
Credit Cards: None
Notes: 2, 8, 10, 11, 12, 14

EAGLE RIVER

A Homestay at Homesteads

Box 771283, 99577
(907) 272-8644

ER1. Surrounded by wilderness. Ski from the porch or hike across the creek on the wilderness trail. Wonderful wood stove and fireplace to relax in Alaskan style. Enjoy the lifestyle here, seven tree-lined miles up the dirt road with two glaciers "back valley" and Denali framed in the window "down valley." Nonsmoking. Full Alaskan-style breakfast at Heaven Crest. $65-90.

ER2. The hosts built their own home in this wilderness-surrounded area. Their big dogs get first choice on the davenport, but guests may join the hosts at the cooking bar for great food and shared stories. Birders will enjoy the activity summer and winter. Smoking permitted. Double with private bath and a complete, immaculate Airstream trailer for families. Full breakfast is served, of course, at the Birdhouse. $65-120.

ER3. Here at Chickadee, there is a new all-glass addition to the living room, so guests can watch it snow in the winter and all the birds can see inside. This family is 4H and homemaker-minded. The hosts have built their own home in the high wilderness area. Only eight miles to the main highway, bringing guests back to the reason Alaskans

stay here. The hosts love to cook full breakfasts. Private entrance to the suite of rooms downstairs with a private patio. $80-120.

FAIRBANKS

A Homestay at Homesteads

Box 771283, Eagle River, 99577
(907) 272-8644

F1. Nestled in the hills of town, this secluded neighborhood is the perfect area to watch birds and take walks on dirt roads. The hosts catch and release birds as a banding unit for birding count. Berries grow almost wild in the garden. Special places for special people. Private bath. Full breakfast upstairs with hosts. Nonsmoking. $65-90.

7 Gables Inn

7 Gables Inn

P.O. Box 80488, 99708
(907) 479-0751

Historically, Alaska's 7 Gables Inn was a fraternity house within walking distance to the UAF campus, yet near the river and airport. This spacious 10,000-square-foot Tudor-style home features a floral solarium, antique stained glass in the foyer with an indoor waterfall, cathedral ceilings, a wedding chapel, wine cellar, and rooms with dormers. A gourmet breakfast is served daily. Other amenities include cable TV and telephone in each room, laundry facilities, Jacuzzis, bikes, and canoes.

Hosts: Paul and Leicha Welton
Rooms: 12 (PB) $50-110
Full Breakfast
Credit Cards: A, B, C, D, E
Notes: 2, 5, 8, 9, 11, 12, 13, 14

GLENNALLEN

Evergreen Lodge
HC 01, Box 1709, 99588
(907) 822-3250

Evergreen Lodge is one of the oldest lodges at Lake Louise. This nonsmoking bed and breakfast lodge has modern rooms, private baths, summer cabins, large lounge, and deck overlooking the lake. Small house bar and sauna. Vacation packages including meals are also available.

Host: Jack Hansen
Rooms: 4 (PB) $85
Cabin: 1 (SB)
Full Breakfast
Credit Cards: None
Notes: 2, 14

GUSTAVUS (GLACIER BAY)

Glacier Bay Country Inn
P.O. Box 5-AD, 99826
(907) 697-2288; FAX (907) 697-2289
Winter: P.O. Box 2557, Saint George, UT 84771
(801) 673-8480; FAX (801) 673-8481

Peaceful storybook accommodations away from the crowds in a wilderness setting. Cozy comforters and warm flannel sheets. Superb dining features local seafood, garden-fresh produce, home-baked breads, and spectacular desserts. Enjoy fishing, whale watching, sightseeing, hiking, bird watching, photography, and Glacier Bay boat and plane tours. Rates include three meals, airport transfers, and use of bicycles. A second inn, the Whalesong Lodge, offers bed and breakfast rooms, condominium rentals, and full meal packages as well.

Hosts: Al and Annie Unrein
Rooms: 9 (8 PB; 1 SB) $144-228
Full Breakfast
Credit Cards: None
Notes: 2, 3, 4, 8, 9, 14

Glacier Bay Country Inn

Good Riverbed and Breakfast
P.O. Box 37, 99826
(907) 697-2241

Enjoy a warm welcome in this bright, spacious log home with comfortable beds, patchwork quilts, and two modern bathrooms. A hearty breakfast of homemade breads, granolas, wildberry, and jams. Bikes are complimentary, and tours are arranged. Hiking, fishing, kayaking, whale watching, flight seeing, and more are available at this Glacier Bay access.

Host: Sandy Burd
Rooms: 5 (S2B) $50-75
Continental Breakfast
Credit Cards: None
Notes: 2, 8, 14

Gustavus Inn
Box 60, 99826
(907) 697-2254; FAX (907) 697-2255

Glacier Bay's historic homestead, newly renovated, full-service inn accommodates 26. Family-style meals, seafood, garden produce, wild edibles. Boat tours of Glacier Bay, charter fishing, and air transportation from Juneau arranged. Kayaking and hiking nearby. Bikes and airport transfers included

6 Pets welcome; 8 Children welcome; 9 Social drinking allowed; 10 Tennis available; 11 Swimming available; 12 Golf available; 13 Skiing available; 14 May be booked through travel agents.

in the daily rates. Lunch and dinner included. American Plan only. Closed September 20 through May 1

Hosts: David and Jo Ann Lesh
Rooms: 13 (11 PB; 2 SB) $130
Full Breakfast
Credit Cards: A, B, C
Notes: 2, 3, 4, 7, 8, 9, 14

Gustavus Inn

A Puffin's
Bed and Breakfast Lodge

1/4 Mile Logging Road, Box 3, 99826
(907) 697-2260

Guests stay in their own modern cottage on a five-acre, partially wooded homestead carpeted in wildflowers and berries. Full country breakfast served in new picturesque lodge with private meeting room. Covered picnic area with barbeque. Coin-operated laundry. Lunch and dinner available within walking distance. Special diets accommodated. Hike beaches or bicycle miles of country roads. See marine life from a charter cruiser or kayak. Courtesy transportation: Glacier Bay tours and travel services available. Special rates for children and senior citizens. Closed September 30 through May 1.

Hosts: Chuck and Sandy Schroth
Cottages: 3 (PB) $50-100
Full Breakfast
Credit Cards: A, B
Notes: 6, 7 (limited), 8, 9 (cabins), 14

HAINES

A Homestay at Homesteads

Box 771283, Eagle River, 99577
(907) 272-8644

H1. The flower box is always full. Hosts have one room to share with travelers. If traveling on the ferry, better call early as all the rooms in town are full. A nice place to visit. Breakfast is served. $65.

HEALEY

A Homestay at Homesteads

Box 771283, Eagle River, 99577
(907) 272-8644

D3. A short drive toward Fairbanks brings visitors to the tiny town of Healey and out of the tourist traffic. An original carriage and dog team stop, this old hotel is all charm. Wood floors. Some shared baths. Wonderful restaurant next door. An inexpensive stop over. Smoking and nonsmoking areas. $40-100.

HOMER

A Homestay at Homesteads

Box 771283, Eagle River, 99577
(907) 272-8644

H1. This beach house is like no other. A two-story contemporary with all-glass in the ocean side. Because of the elegant floors and rugs, guests are asked to leave their shoes at the door. Private and shared baths. Gourmet cooking is the hosts' specialty. $70-120.

H2A. The oldest and the only place to stay at the end of the Homer split. Walk from here to catch fishing charters, day boat tours, or fish from the beach while watching the boats come and go. Rooms with private

---

NOTES: Credit cards accepted: A MasterCard; B Visa; C American Express; D Discover Card; E Diner's Club; F Other; 2 Personal checks accepted; 3 Lunch available; 4 Dinner available; 5 Open all year;

baths. Breakfast is not served. When making reservations, please specify smoking or nonsmoking. $75-140.

H2B. Cross the creek on the walking bridge to get here! Nonsmoking retreat with retired, longtime Alaskans. Out of town, in the hills, but worth it! $85.

H3. Join all of the guests for a huge homemade typical Alaskan breakfast at the glass-rimmed dining area. These hosts were the first to entertain bed and breakfast guests, and years later they would not change their hospitality for anything. Cozy rooms in the house or family spaces in the "out" buildings. Everyone joins for breakfast. The hosts can get guests the best in fishing, touring boats, and travel, too! Guests do need transportation to get to this hilltop home with a panoramic view. $75-90.

JUNEAU

A Homestay at Homesteads

Box 771283, Eagle River, 99577
(907) 272-8644

J1. These hosts have got the view and know the ferry is a long way out of town. If guests need a rental car, they arrange it, and if guests want to be picked up they can do that, too! Breakfast included (most of the time). The inn is booked to assist the legislature when in session, otherwise they will welcome guests. Laundry, cooking, sauna, and picnic area. Nonsmoking. $65.

The Lost Chord

2200 Fritz Cove Road, 99801
(907) 789-7296

The hosts' music business has expanded to become a homey bed and breakfast on an exquisite private beach. Breakfast is with the proprietors, who have been in Alaska

since 1946. In the country 12 miles from Juneau; a car is suggested.

Hosts: Jesse and Ellen Jones
Rooms: 4 (1 PB; 3 SB) $40-75
Full Breakfast
Credit Cards: None
Notes: 2, 5, 6 (by arrangement), 7 (limited), 8, 9, 10, 11, 12, 13, 14

Pearson's Pond Luxury Bed and Breakfast

4541 Sawa Circle, 99801
(907) 789-3772

Relax in style at this welcome retreat tucked in the forest amid spectacular scenery and abundant wildlife. Soothe cares in a steaming spa on the banks of a natural pond left by the retreating Mendenhall Glacier nearby. Enjoy every imaginable amenity in guests' own private studio. Kitchenettes, barbecue, freezer, rowboat, poles, and bikes. Guests will be away from the crowds, yet close to major attractions. Year-round weekly and monthly rates. Be sure to book far in advance for summer visits. Guests say it's the highest combination of beauty, comfort, privacy, and warmth. AAA-rated three stars, ABBA-rated three crowns; excellence awards from both AAA and the ABBA.

Hosts: Steve and Diane Pearson
Rooms: 2 (SB) $69-149
Suite: 1 (PB)
Continental Breakfast
Credit Cards: A, B, C, E, F
Notes: 2, 5, 8 (over 3), 9, 10, 11, 12, 13, 14

Silverbow Inn and Restaurant

120 Second Street, 99801
(907) 586-4146; FAX (907) 586-4242

The Silverbow Inn and Restaurant, built in 1890, is in the heart of downtown. Each individually decorated room has a touch-of-home coziness and queen-size beds. The inn is AAA approved and Fodor's

6 Pets welcome; 8 Children welcome; 9 Social drinking allowed; 10 Tennis available; 11 Swimming available; 12 Golf available; 13 Skiing available; 14 May be booked through travel agents.

choice for southeast Alaska. Top off an evening with dinner in the award-winning restaurant. Antique furnishings, good music, and a friendly, knowledgeable staff will add to an evening's enjoyment. When in Juneau, stay here and let the hosts provide special memories.

Hosts: Richard and Chava Lee
Rooms: 6 (PB) $79-109
Full Breakfast
Credit Cards: A, B, C
Notes: 3, 4, 5, 8, 9, 10, 11, 13, 14

KENNICOTT

A Homestay at Homesteads

Box 771283, Eagle River, 99577
(907) 272-8644

A newly made antique. When the old hotel burned to the ground, the hosts took the original plans (updating the baths) and built a new "old" hotel. Just waiting for adventurous souls to enjoy the gourmet dining and tales of the mining days. Share baths as in the olden times. Day rates vary with the size of the traveling group, but calculate $105 per person with meals. Overnight with no meals also available. Plan to spend at least two nights; the hosts and the area are worth it. Most people drive in, but guests may fly in (weather permitting).

KETCHIKAN

A Homestay at Homesteads

Box 771283, Eagle River, 99577
(907) 272-8644

K. On the only road north of the ferry terminal, guests will need a car (rentals available) to find this secluded beach-side home in Ward Cove. Join the hosts with the wilderness all around and the lapping waters to put one to sleep. Nonsmoking. $75.

KODIAK

Kodiak Bed and Breakfast

308 Cope Street, 99616
(907) 486-5367; FAX (907) 486-6567

Visitors enjoy a spectacular view of Kodiak's busy fishing fleet in a location just above the boat harbor. Mary's home is easy walking distance from a historic Russian church, art galleries, Baronof Museum, air charters, and downtown restaurants. Enjoy this fishing city with its Russian heritage, stunning beaches, cliffs, and abundant fish and bird life. Fresh local fish is often a breakfast option.

Host: Mary A. Monroe
Rooms: 16 (13 PB; 3 SB) $60-72
Full Breakfast
Credit Cards: A, B, C
Notes: 2, 5, 6, 8, 9, 14

PAXSON (DENALI HIGHWAY)

A Homestay at Homesteads

Box 771283, Eagle River, 99577
(907) 272-8644

McClaren River in the heart of the Denali Highway produces fishing, hiking, wilderness skiing, hunting, and a wonderful old lodge. Some cozy rooms upstairs with some cabins outside. Come linger with the year-round pioneering owners. Full breakfast included. Other meals available. Specify smoking or nonsmoking rooms. $40-90.

SELDOVIA

A Homestay at Homesteads

Box 771283, Eagle River, 99577
(907) 272-8644

SL1. Come dance with the eagles at this lodge over the water where the tide marches in and out. The hosts have kayaks to rent, as well as bikes. Nice cozy hot tub (most of the time) and rooms inside the house as

NOTES: Credit cards accepted: A MasterCard; B Visa; C American Express; D Discover Card; E Diner's Club; F Other; 2 Personal checks accepted; 3 Lunch available; 4 Dinner available; 5 Open all year;

well as the self-contained cabin by the hot tub. Flexible and fun-loving hosts. Closed for the winter so as not to freeze the pipes, but the inn plans to be open May 15 through September 15. From $50.

SEWARD

A Homestay at Homesteads

Box 771283, Eagle River, 99577
(907) 272-8644

S1. Guests' very own log cabin nestled in the trees next to a rushing salmon spawning stream. Fresh pastries, fruit, and juice delivered to the door. Lounge in bed and watch the wilderness from the picture windows. So the pipes do not freeze in the winter, there is a year-round heated central bath and shower. There are camping spots, too. Creekside is a treat worth waiting for. Families welcome. Just off the highway on the road to Exit Glacier. $90-130.

S2. These hosts have a big family and an even bigger white house just across the creek on the way into Seward. Guest rooms are separate, nonsmoking with shared or private baths. In the guest space is a nice kitchen stocked with breakfast goodies to share with the other guests. Visit winter or summer. $65-90.

S3. If guests like their mornings calm, they will enjoy a full breakfast with these hosts in their typical two-story split-level home. Within walking distance to town and the boat harbor where guests can catch the tours into the Kenai Fjords National Park. Close to the train, and the bus will let guests off at the corner. $65-80.

S4. Smell the fresh cinnamon buns upon awakening in the morning. Enjoy sitting with other guests at the formal dining room table. Just out of town and down the lane

enough to know where the real Alaskans live, breathe, and enjoy life. $65-80.

The White House Bed and Breakfast

P.O. Box 1157, 99664
(907) 224-3614

Nestled in a mountain panorama. The home's intrigue is country charm—quilts and handcrafts abound. Breakfast is self-serve buffet in guest kitchen. Cable TV in guest common area. Attractions close by: Resurrection Bay, Kenai Fjords National Park, historical Iditarod Trail (cross-country skiing or dog mushing), and Exit Glacier.

Hosts: Tom and Annette Reese
Rooms: 5 (3 PB; 2 SB) $56.10-76.50
Continental Breakfast
Credit Cards: A, B
Notes: 2, 5, 8, 13 (cross-country), 14

The White House

SHEEP MOUNTAIN

A Homestay at Homesteads

Box 771283, Eagle River, 99577
(907) 272-8644

SM. Make these log cabins home. Most have private baths. Dorm rooms are available with central bath. Finest meals around with homemade pastries and pies available, but not included. $75-90.

---

6 Pets welcome; 8 Children welcome; 9 Social drinking allowed; 10 Tennis available; 11 Swimming available; 12 Golf available; 13 Skiing available; 14 May be booked through travel agents.

SITKA

A Homestay at Homesteads

Box 771283, Eagle River, 99577
(907) 272-8644

ST1. After stepping off the ferry, walk right across the street and up the hill to this home. The rooms have the finest views around. The hosts have been here for years and love to talk about their adventures. Breakfast is included. Shared bath. $55.

SKAGWAY

Gold Rush Lodge

P.O. Box 514, 6th and Alaska streets, 99840-0514
(907) 983-2831; FAX (907) 983-2742

The Gold Rush Lodge is within walking distance of historic district and local sights and trails. Ground level, private entrances. All rooms have private baths, cable TV, telephones, and heat control. Courtesy shuttle to and from ferry terminal, train depot, and airport. Twelve clean and tastefully decorated rooms. Nonsmoking.

Hosts: Harry and Vickie Bricker
Rooms: 12 (PB) $50-90
Continental Breakfast
Credit Cards: A, B, D
Notes: 5, 6, 9, 10, 13, 14

SOLDOTNA

Posey's Kenai River Hideaway Bed and Breakfast Lodge

P.O. Box 4094-ABB, 99669
(907) 262-7430; FAX (907) 262-7430

On the bank of the Kenai River with its world-record king salmon. Good, wholesome breakfast served before fishing. Will arrange guided salmon or halibut charter, also fly-out fishing or sightseeing trips. After catching fish, relax on the sun deck built out over the river and swap fish stories. Will freeze and pack fish for the return trip home.

Hosts: Ray and June Perry
Rooms: 10 (3 PB; 7 SB) $110-130
Full Breakfast
Credit Cards: A, B
Notes: 2, 3, 4, 5, 7, 9, 12, 13, 14

STEPHEN LAKE

A Homestay at Homesteads

Box 771283, Eagle River, 99577
(907) 272-8644

SL. The hosts will pick up guests in their plane and fly them to the dock in front of the main house. Great fishing in the stream nearby. The hosts love to cook gourmet meals; all meals are included. Because of the flight time, guests stay for an unforgettable experience for two or more nights (three or more days). Non-hunting or non-fishing guests may receive reduced rates. Fly out cabins available; hosts will bring meals out to guests. Call for rates.

TOK

Cleft of the Rock Bed and Breakfast

Sundog Trail, Box 122, 99780
(907) 883-4219

Three miles west of Tok. Enjoy friendly Christian hospitality in the guest rooms or cabins. An Alaskan hearty breakfast. Year-round service.

Hosts: John and Jill Rusyniak
Rooms: 5 (3 PB, 2 SB) $60-95
Full Breakfast
Cards: A, B
Notes: 2, 5, 6, 8, 9 (limited)

The Stage Stop

P.O. Box 69, 99780
(907) 883-5338

For horses and people, this charming log home offers a private cabin and two large rooms with king- and queen-size beds. Full country breakfast. New log barn and corrals

NOTES: Credit cards accepted: A MasterCard; B Visa; C American Express; D Discover Card; E Diner's Club; F Other; 2 Personal checks accepted; 3 Lunch available; 4 Dinner available; 5 Open all year;

for horses. New room with private bath. Quiet location just off Tok Cutoff Highway.

Host: Mary Dale Underwood
Rooms: 3 (1 PB; 2 SB) $45-75
Full Breakfast
Credit Cards: None
Notes: 2, 5, 6, 8, 9, 14

TRAPPER CREEK

McKinley Foothills Bed and Breakfast

P.O. Box 13089, 99683
(907) 733-1454; FAX (907) 733-1454

Great view of Mount McKinley. Secluded, rustic, and comfortable log cabins completely furnished with kitchenettes and accommodations for four people. Home-cooked meals featuring omelets and sourdough waffles. Special meals available with notice prior to arrival. King-salmon fishing, snow machining, cross-country skiing, and dog mushing. Pets and children welcome. No smoking

Hosts: Bob and Vilma Anderson
Rooms: 3 (PB and SB) $75-85
Full Breakfast
Cards: A, B
Notes: 3, 4, 5, 6, 8, 13 (cross-country)

North Country Bed and Breakfast

P.O. Box 13377, 99683
(907) 733-3981

North Country is nestled on a lake with a spectacular view of Mount McKinley, the tallest mountain in North America. Hosts offer four rooms with private baths, and there is also a master suite with private bath, jetted tub, and sitting room. All five rooms have TV and private outside entries. The cabin on the lake sleeps two adults. There is a recreation room where the guests go to have Continental breakfast, relax, and socialize.

Hosts: Mike and Sheryl Uher
Rooms: 5 (PB) $85-120
Cabin: 1
Continental Breakfast
Credit Cards: A, B
Notes: 5, 8, 11, 14

VALDEZ

Alaskan Flower Forget-Me-Not Bed and Breakfast

P.O. Box 1153, 99686
(907) 835-2717

Prince William Sound hospitality at its best. Guests will enjoy their visit as they relax in one of the luxurious guest rooms. Enjoy the complimentary, informal breakfast served from 6:30 to 9:00A.M. Walk to nearby cruise ships, the ferry, and the downtown area.

Host: Betty Schackne
Rooms: 4 (1 PB; 3 SB) $60-75
Continental Breakfast
Credit Cards: None
Notes: 2, 5, 8, 9, 13, 14

A Homestay at Homesteads

Box 771283, Eagle River, 99577
(907) 272-8644

V1. If guests want the best of all bed and breakfasts, it is right here! Since the hosts have enjoyed travelers in their home for years, they decided to add on just the right rooms for guests. Private or shared baths. Taking the ferry? It is always early or late, so the hosts will keep the coffee pot hot! Full breakfast. $60-80.

V2. Down home-style Continental breakfast is served so guests can take advantage of whatever their next adventure brings. The hosts' cocker will greet guests, yet prefers not to have other four-footed competition as guests. No smoking. Three rooms share two baths. $60-80.

6 Pets welcome; 8 Children welcome; 9 Social drinking allowed; 10 Tennis available; 11 Swimming available; 12 Golf available; 13 Skiing available; 14 May be booked through travel agents.

A Homestay at Homesteads
(continued)

V3. Guests cannot put a boat next to the house, but this inn is within walking distance of the water! Hosts teach during the school year so they will only be available during the summer months. Shared baths. Breakfast is served. $75-90.

V4. If guests have a family looking for the perfect stop, the hosts have the right rooms with doubles and bunk beds. What a joy to find a fun family stop that loves and welcomes well-behaved kids as well as their parents. Need a hickory stick? The hosts might be able to find that, too. Families and large groups are welcomed. From $85.

WASILLA

Yukon Don's
1830 East Parks Highway, Suite 386, 99654 (mail)
2221 Yukon Circle, 99654
(907) 376-7422

When traveling in Alaska, guests do not want to miss staying at Yukon Don's. All rooms are decorated with authentic Alaskana. Stay in the Iditarod, Fishing, Denali, and Hunting rooms, or in the suite. Guests are pampered by relaxing in the Alaska room, complete with Alaskan historic library, video library, pool table, cable TV, and gift bar. The all-glass-view room on the second floor offers the grandest view in the Matanuska Valley. Hosts also offer telephones in each room, Yukon Don's own expanded Continental breakfast bar, sauna, and exercise room.

Host: Yukon Don and Kristan Tanner
Rooms: 5 (1 PB; 4 SB) $63-105
Continental Breakfast
Credit Cards: A, B
Notes: 2, 5, 8, 9, 10, 11, 12, 13

WHITTIER

A Homestay at Homesteads
Box 771283, Eagle River, 99577
(907) 272-8644

World-class view of the spectacular fjord at this warm water port where two-thirds of the population live in the high-rise built for troops during the second world war. The ferry leaves from the docks below. Plenty of winter skiing, summer hiking, and kayaking, and hosts' small boat will carry guests to wilderness fishing and glacier and shrimping areas. Nonsmoking. Boat not included. $40-90.

Arizona

Bed and Breakfast Inn Arizona

P.O. Box 11253, Glendale, 85318-1253
(602) 561-0335; FAX (602) 561-2300

AJ001. This stately guest house from the mid-1920s has been totally renovated and is now peaceful and relaxing. Close to Organ Pipe Cactus National Monument. Spectacular desert scenes. Call for rates.

AJ101. The old mine manager's home, built at the turn of the century. Completely renovated in styles of the period. Breakfast is lavish. There is a guest library, sunroom, small gift shop, and a spa. Golf course nearby. All rooms have private baths; only one room allows smoking. No pets or children. Modest to deluxe rates.

Mi Casa Su Casa

P.O. Box 950, Tempe, 85281
(602) 990-0682; (800) 456-0682

291. Near Organ Pipe Cactus National Monument and 50 minutes from Mexico. Originally built in 1925 to accommodate visiting company officials for Phelps Dodge, this inn has six guest rooms, queen-size and twin beds, five private baths, a reputation for warm hospitality, and excellent breakfasts. The furnishings reflect the rich traditions of Arizona. Children welcome. No smoking. Roll away bed available for an extra ten-dollar charge. $55-69.

Bed and Breakfast Inn Arizona

P.O. Box 11253, Glendale, 85318-1253
(602) 561-0335; FAX (602) 561-2300

AJ102. A ranch family used this guest ranch as the main headquarters for their cattle operation in the White Mountains. These are hospitable country folk who have been written about as far away as Europe, and they know how to provide true hospitality. Individual cabins with private baths. Enjoy breakfast in the main house. Gift shop full of Western goodies. Horseback riding can be arranged nearby. Smoking permitted. Superior rates.

AJ104. Experience the Sonoran Desert at its finest, yet stay within an easy drive of the amenities of the Phoenix metro area in this rugged native stone and siding second-floor guest house. The Majestic Mountain Room has a queen-size bed and queen-size Hide-a-bed, private bath, picture window, sitting area, and TV. The Valley View Room has a queen-size bed and a trundle (makes into double or twin beds), private bath, and deck. Both rooms have small refrigerators, microwave ovens, and coffee makers. No children. Rugged terrain and stairs not suitable for handicapped. Deluxe rates include Continental breakfast.

6 Pets welcome; 7 Smoking allowed; 8 Children welcome; 9 Social drinking allowed; 10 Tennis available; 11 Swimming available; 12 Golf available; 13 Skiing available; 14 May be booked through travel agents.

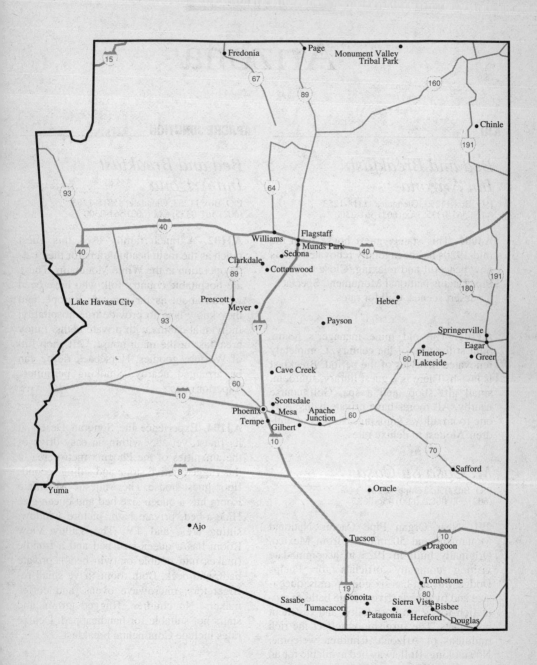

Arizona

BISBEE

Bed and Breakfast Inn Arizona

P.O. Box 11253, Glendale, 85318-1253
(602) 561-0335; FAX (602) 561-2300

BE001. Beautifully appointed mansion has linens, lace, crystal chandeliers, canopied beds, and fireplaces. Call for rates.

BE002. Spanish-style original mining company VIP guest house. Grandly spacious rooms with antique furnishings. Leaded-, beveled-glass windows. Call for rates.

BE005. In the center of Bisbee atop Castle Rock, a 1906 restored mansion with exceptional views. A relaxing and inspiring atmosphere. Handicapped accessible. All amenities. Call for rates.

BE106. The delightful host couple is steeped in the lore and tradition of the area and welcomes guests as family. Breakfasts, usually served in the sunroom, feature delicious fresh breads and goodies of choice. The spacious home, built in 1912, faces a park with tennis and golf only a few steps away. TV and library. All fully restored bedrooms are upstairs. Two rooms have private baths, and two share a bath. Deluxe and modest rates. No children or pets; there is a friendly resident cat.

The Inn at Castle Rock

112 Tombstone Canyon Road, P.O. Box 1161, 85603
(602) 432-4449; (602) 432-7195

An old Victorian miner's boarding house in central historic Bisbee features antiques, original art, gardens, and three parlors. Each of the rooms and suites has its own unique decor, original art, and bath. The top floor is an art gallery, and the first floor has the Indian Spring. Breakfast includes a healthy fare of fresh fruit, juices, homemade muffins, coffees, and teas. Bisbee has a rich history and is elevated 5,300 feet into the Mule Mountains. Near wild country and nature conservancy areas.

Host: Jim Babcock
Rooms: 15 (PB) $50-60
Continental Breakfast
Credit Cards: A, B
Notes: 2, 5, 8, 11

Mi Casa Su Casa

P.O. Box 950, Tempe, 85281
(602) 990-0682; (800) 456-0682

255. A first glimpse of historic Bisbee seems to turn the clock back a century. Cradled in a valley in the Mule Mountains 90 miles from Tucson is this 1920s 5,000-square-foot two-story Mediterranean-style home. The host couple are Bisbee natives and extend a casual Western welcome to guests. All guest rooms are on the second floor. Room one has a queen-size bed and private bath. Room two has a queen-size waterbed and private bath. Room three has a king-size bed or twin beds. Room four has a double bed. Rooms three and four have balconies and share a hall bath. Full breakfast. Children welcome. Resident cat. Smoking allowed outside. Visa and MasterCard accepted. $40-60.

2552. Newly restored and decorated home built around the turn of the century and in the Warren area. Step back in time while enjoying the art collection and antiques. All guest rooms are on the second floor. The master guest room has a queen-size bed, private bath, and a two-night minimum stay. Two other guest rooms have queen-size beds and share a bath. A family room with TV, VCR, many books, and a sunroom decorated in antique wicker and green plants are available for relaxing and reading. Full breakfast. No children. Resident dog and cat. Smoking outside. $50-65.

2553. This bed and breakfast inn, built in 1906 by a mining company, is a fine example of Craftsman architecture. It offers the privacy of eight suites and rooms furnished in antiques, private baths, and claw-foot tubs. Most baths have showers. Kitchens are stocked, and freshly baked muffins are delivered each day. Original billiard room with pool table and TV. Guest patio has a barbecue area. Air-conditioned. Two-night minimum stay. Nonsmoking. Fifteen dollars for additional person. $75-125.

Old Pueblo Homestays

P.O. Box 13603, Tucson, 85732
(800) 333-9 RSO

Park Place Bed and Breakfast. No visit to Arizona is complete without seeing the historical old mining town of Bisbee, some 25 miles from Tombstone. Cool in the summer and far enough south to have mild winters. Park Place is a 1920s well-cared-for two-story Mediterranean-style home with spacious bedrooms, balconies, terraces, library, and sunroom. Two guest rooms have queen-size beds and adjoining baths. Two other bedrooms share hall bathroom. Minimum stay is two nights. $50-70.

School House Inn

818 Tombstone Canyon, P.O. Box 32, 85603
(602) 432-2996; (800) 537-4333

An old schoolhouse built in 1918 and converted into lovely large rooms and suites with 12-foot ceilings and private baths. High up Tombstone Canyon, the 5,600-foot elevation provides spectacular scenery, clean air, and a relaxing retreat. A full breakfast is served on the shaded patio or in the spacious family room. The inn is close

to mine tours, art galleries, antique shops, hiking, bird watching, and much more.

Hosts: Marc and Shirl Negus
Rooms: 9 (PB) $40-60
Full Breakfast
Credit Cards: A, B, C, D, E
Notes: 2, 5, 11, 12

CAVE CREEK

Mi Casa Su Casa

P.O. Box 950, Tempe, 85281
(602) 990-0682; (800) 456-0682

233. Spacious, comfortable ranch-style home rests on ten acres of virgin desert adjacent to state land and the scenic foothills. Hike and become surrounded by the lush and undisturbed wonders of the Sonoran Desert. Enjoy the panoramic view of sunrises and midnight constellations from the deck. This ranch is ideal for the scenic Prescott/Jerome/Sedona day-trip loop. Private guest wing has guest room with queen-size bed, TV, sitting/game room, private bath with shower, and private entrance. Main kitchen privileges. Full breakfast. Smoking outside. Children are welcome. Horses boarded. $50-65.

286. Large rustic home on five acres. Guest accommodations are in one section of the house. Large suite has own living room, TV, large bedroom with queen-size bed, double bed, twin bed, and connecting full bath. The second bedroom is smaller and has a double bed and a hall bath. The apartment has a private entrance, bath, kitchenette, and two rooms each with a double bed. Pool available. Cookouts, barbecues, and hay rides available by appointment. Continental breakfast weekdays, and full breakfast on weekends. Resident dog. Smoking outside only. Ten-dollar charge for well-behaved children over ten years of age. $40-65.

CHINLE

Bed and Breakfast Inn Arizona

P.O. Box 11253, Glendale, 85318-1253
(602) 561-0335; FAX (602) 561-2300

CN002. Historic lodge in spectacular, scenic Navajo land near Canyon de Chelly National Monument. Charming restaurant inside original 1896 trading post. Private baths. Call for rates.

CLARKDALE

Mi Casa Su Casa

P.O. Box 950, Tempe, 85281
(602) 990-0682; (800) 456-0682

145. Ideal for all who love and appreciate nature. All accommodations have Arizona country decor. A separate guest house is nestled under majestic old cottonwood trees. It has a queen-size bed, private bath with shower. The country condo is separate but attached to the main house. It has a private entrance, porch, bedroom with queen-size bed, an extra-large double shower, and a full kitchen with microwave oven. There is a comfortable sofa in the living/dining room where a third person could sleep. There is also a guest room in the main house which has a private entrance, a double bed, and private hall bath. Full breakfast. Children are welcome. Smoking outside. Guest pet with permission. $65-75.

COTTONWOOD

Bed and Breakfast Inn Arizona

P.O. Box 11253, Glendale, 85318-1253
(602) 561-0335; FAX (602) 561-2300

CW103. This rustic cottage is a romantic hideaway for two, complete with queen-size bed, private bath, country decor, and outside hot tub. This hostess enjoys serving sun-ripened fruit (in season) from her organic garden with a country breakfast. In the main house is an additional bedroom with queen-size bed, private hall bath, and a second bedroom for children. Only ten minutes from Clarkdale train. Outside dog and cat. Modest to deluxe rates.

CW104. Magnificent views of Mingus Mountain, the Verde Valley, the red rocks of Sedona, and on clear days, the San Francisco Peaks. This friendly host couple makes sure guests are comfortable, and they serve a wonderful country-style full breakfast. Spa and a choice of the Sunrise Room, with queen-size bed, private hall bath, TV in room; or the Guest House, with queen-size bed, private, connecting bath, wood-burning stove, and kitchenette, ecorated in Early American style. Dogs and cats on premises. Children over five are welcome. Modest to deluxe rates.

DOUGLAS

Mi Casa Su Casa

P.O. Box 950, Tempe, 85280-0950
(602) 990-0682; (800) 456-0682

1628. This ranch is on the northeastern slope of the Chiricahua Mountains near many historic sites, museums, and old Mexico. Daily trail rides are available for four to 20 people, and the ranch can supply pack animals for heavy packs. One- or two-room bunk houses have baths; an apartment includes a kitchenette and private patio. Camper and trailer hook-ups nearby. Swimming pool and three-acre catfish pond on premises. Rates include room, three daily meals, and horse. $85-160.

---

6 Pets welcome; 7 Smoking allowed; 8 Children welcome; 9 Social drinking allowed; 10 Tennis available;
11 Swimming available; 12 Golf available; 13 Skiing available; 14 May be booked through travel agents.

DRAGOON

Mi Casa Su Casa

P.O. Box 950, Tempe, 85281
(602) 990-0682; (800) 456-0682

307. This bed and breakfast offers spectacular views and the opportunity to enjoy country living. Both the main house and the separate guest house are rammed earth, passive solar structures. The guest house has two bedrooms, one with a queen-size bed and the other with twin beds. The hall bath with shower is shared. Guest rooms have electric heaters and electric blankets. The sitting area is warmed by a potbelly stove, and the small kitchen has a coffee maker, sink, microwave oven, toaster oven, electric skillet, and small refrigerator. Private sun deck and gas grill available. Children over 12 are welcome. Full breakfast. Smoking allowed outside only. Spa in main house. $45-55.

EAGAR

Bed and Breakfast Inn Arizona

P.O. Box 11253, Glendale, 85318-1253
(602) 561-0335; FAX (602) 561-2300

EA101. Step back into time in this wonderfully restored historic landmark home from the early 1900s, built in the Colonial Revival style. Four luxurious rooms, each with private bath, plus a deluxe breakfast, make this a quaint getaway worth the trip in winter for skiing, or summertime to escape the desert heat. Three rooms with double beds, one suite with a double bed in one room, and twin in the other. The guest parlor has an old-fashioned soda fountain. Swimming and tennis nearby. Deluxe rates.

Mi Casa Su Casa

P.O. Box 950, Tempe, 85281-0950
(602) 990-0682

390. Large, luxurious, and rustic home in the pines. The huge, hand-peeled logs came from the Apache reservation on the back of Mount Baldy. The log home is self-sufficient, using solar panels, battery storage backed by generator, radio-telephone, and purified creek water. Two second-floor guest rooms feature private baths, king-size beds, walk-in closets, and unique decor. First-floor guest room includes queen-size bed, private bath, and whirlpool tub. Spacious great room with fireplace and large loft with pool table. No children. Resident dog. No pets. Two-night minimum. $80.

FLAGSTAFF

Arizona Mountain Inn

685 Lake Mary Road, 86001
(602) 774-8959

The Old English Tudor-style inn and cottages are about three miles from Flagstaff. There are 13 wooded acres surrounded by national forest. The rooms are decorated in antiques, crystal, and lace in a beautiful mix of European charm and classic Southwestern elegance.

Hosts: The Wanek family
Rooms: 3 (PB) $70-100
Continental Breakfast
Credit Cards: A, B, D
Notes: 5, 9, 13

Bed and Breakfast Inn Arizona

P.O. Box 11253, Glendale, 85318-1253
(602) 561-0335; FAX (602) 561-2300

FS001. Premier, extreme trilevel contemporary amongst the pines. Quiet, close to downtown and park. Views of the San Francisco peaks. Full breakfast. Call for rates.

FS003. The charming, quaint, and comfortable ambience here is unsurpassed. Previ-

NOTES: Credit cards accepted: A MasterCard; B Visa; C American Express; D Discover Card; E Diner's Club; F Other; 2 Personal checks accepted; 3 Lunch available; 4 Dinner available; 5 Open all year;

ously a stately family residence. Full breakfast. Call for rates.

FS112. Three cozy little cottages in the heart of old Flagstaff are the ultimate for privacy. The hostess will greet guests and show them to a private two-bedroom cottage and leave the first morning's breakfast for guests to self-cater. Built in the 1920s, the cottages have been furnished in the spirit of those times. Laundry facilities, TV, and telephone. Playground nearby—great for families. No pets. Some traffic noise can be heard in two of the cottages on the road to the canyon. Superior rates.

Birch Tree Inn

824 West Birch Avenue, 86001
(602) 774-1042

The Birch Tree Inn, circa 1917, offers comfortable surroundings amidst authentic period furnishings in one of the city's finest historic old homes. The parlor offers guests a place to read, converse, or relax in front of a roaring fire. Each bedroom features its own comfortable atmosphere: antiques, heirlooms, Southwestern or wicker, with specially chosen linens and wall coverings to add the perfect finishing touches. Off-street parking. A full breakfast is prepared and served in the sunny dining room or outside on the veranda, while early morning coffee is served in the upstairs hall. Afternoon refreshments are served in the parlor. "A wonderfully relaxing time to meet other interesting guests or plan the evening."

Hosts: Sany and Ed Znetko;
   Donna and Roger Pettinger
Rooms: 5 (3 PB; 2 SB) $50-80
Full Breakfast
Credit Cards: A, B, C
Notes: 2, 5, 9, 10, 11, 12, 13, 14

Dierker House

423 West Cherry Street, 86001
(602) 774-3249

Charming old house with spacious antique-filled rooms, private entrance, sitting room, and guest kitchen. An excellent breakfast is served at 8:00 A.M. in the downstairs dining room; Continental breakfast for late risers.

Host: Dorothea Dierker
Rooms: 3 (SB) $45
Full and Continental Breakfasts
Credit Cards: None
Notes: 2, 5, 9, 10, 11, 12, 13

The Inn at 410

410 North Leroux Street, 86001
(800) 774-2008

The Inn at 410 offers guests four seasons of hospitality in a charming 1907 home. Elegantly furnished with antiques, this inn has stained glass and touches of the Southwest. The spacious, sunny living room and lovely garden gazebo provide a peaceful ambience in which to relax. Each guest is pampered with a personal touch that includes oven-fresh cookies, healthy breakfasts, and recommendations of day trips to the Grand Canyon, Indian ruins, and hiking or skiing.

Hosts: Howard and Sally Krueger
Rooms: 9 (7 PB; 2 SB) $70-85
Full Breakfast
Credit Cards: A, B, C
Notes: 2, 5, 7, 8, 12, 13, 14

Mi Casa Su Casa

P.O. Box 950, Tempe, 85281
(602) 990-0682; (800) 456-0682

The Inn at 410

---

6 Pets welcome; 7 Smoking allowed; 8 Children welcome; 9 Social drinking allowed; 10 Tennis available; 11 Swimming available; 12 Golf available; 13 Skiing available; 14 May be booked through travel agents.

100. Very nice split-level house built in 1967 on a sloping mountain lot in a pretty residential neighborhood. The guest rooms are on the first level, several steps down from the front door. The host couple live on the second floor. Both guest rooms have king-size beds. Full hall bath. Recreation room has cable TV, VCR, refrigerator, fireplace, and a double sofa bed. Only one party accepted at a time. Perfect for families. Crib available. Full breakfast. Resident dog. Smoking allowed outside. Infants stay at no charge. Five dollars for children under five years of age and $10 for children over five. Twenty-five dollars for additional adults. $55-65.

247. Contemporary, trilevel home in the forest has multiple spacious decks, views, and extra-large rooms with tongue-in-groove wood ceilings. The house is decorated with Grand Canyon and Navajo art. Host couple and son live on second and third levels. The guest area on the first level has a private entrance, king-size bed, double-size futon, small flip chair, playpen, and private full hall bath. Also on the first level is a very large family room with a wet bar, microwave, small refrigerator, TV, VCR, private telephone, and a wood-burning stove. Full breakfast. Resident dog and cat. Smoking allowed outside only. Perfect for families. Five dollars for children under five years of age and $10 for children over five. Infants free. Fifteen dollars for additional adult. $55-65.

364. Private home with spacious suite, private entrance, deck, and one small guest room. Chemically and environmentally sensitive surroundings feature ionizing air cleaners, natural non-perfumed soaps and non-toxic cleansers, unscented toilet paper and facial tissue, non-toxic paints, tile floors, and linens washed with biodegradable detergent. Suite has bedroom with king-size bed, living room, TV, twin beds, kitchen, and private bath. The second room

has a double bed and shares a hall bath. Continental-plus breakfast. Children over nine welcome. No pets. No smoking. Open May 1 through November 1. A two-night minimum preferred. $55-85.

Old Pueblo Homestays
P.O. Box 13603, Tucson, 85732
(800) 333-9 RSO

Hakatai House Bed and Breakfast. In northern Arizona about 75 miles from the Grand Canyon, this bed and breakfast is close to ski areas, Sunset Crater, and other points of interest. This three-story home has a large king-size bedroom with private bath. The first-floor family room has a double futon and a twin bed. There is also a wet bar, microwave, TV, VCR, and fireplace for guests' convenience. Select breakfast from a menu. Two resident outside cats and a dog. Five dollars each child under five and $10 for children over five. $75.

Starlit Farm Bed and Breakfast
8455 Koch Field Road, 86004
(800) 484-7389 code 5759

Nestled in a valley with an amazing view of the mountains, this contemporary bed and breakfast is five miles northeast of Flagstaff. This home rests on over seven acres of land and is convenient to many places of interest such as the Grand Canyon, Meteor Crater, Lowell Observatory, and Sedona. Guests are welcome to use the hot tub, watch a movie, view the stars through the telescope, enjoy billiards and pinball, and ride mountain bikes. Dog run and RV parking.

Hosts: Tobie and Bernie Trejo
Rooms: 2 (PB) $55-75
Full and Continental Breakfast
Credit Cards: A, B, C
Notes: 2, 3, 12, 13, 14

NOTES: Credit cards accepted: A MasterCard; B Visa; C American Express; D Discover Card; E Diner's Club; F Other; 2 Personal checks accepted; 3 Lunch available; 4 Dinner available; 5 Open all year;

FOUNTAIN HILLS

Bed and Breakfast Inn Arizona

P.O. Box 11253, Glendale, 85318-1253
(602) 561-0335; FAX (602) 561-2300

FH106. Just minutes from Scottsdale, Saguaro Lake, and some of the finest golf in the Phoenix area. Lovely guest suite with private entrance, spa, and sitting room. A queen-size bed, private bath, and sitting room Hide-a-bed, all done in Southwestern style, has an uninterrupted view of the mountains and desert sunrise. Join the family for a full breakfast. Visit "Out of Africa," a nearby wildlife park. Because of the pool, only children ten and older are welcome. No smokers. Superior rates.

FH107. A stunning multilevel private home bed and breakfast built into the side of a small canyon with private entrances for each room. Charming, professional hosts serve full breakfasts in the main part of the house; or a Continental breakfast can be delivered to the suites. Explore the Verde River or laze around the pool in the sunshine. The Linger Longer suite is an eclectic mix of Victorian and Southwestern, with a queen-size bed, private bath, and an efficiency kitchen. Second room has twin beds, private hall bath. Both rooms have French doors opening onto a lovely patio overlooking the pool. Dog in residence. Children are welcome by prior arrangement. Modest to deluxe rates.

FREDONIA

Mi Casa Su Casa

P.O. Box 950, Tempe, 85281
(602) 990-0682; (800) 456-0682

340. Built in the early 1900s, this two-story house was one of the first homes in Fredonia, a town within one and one-half hours of the North Rim of the Grand Canyon, Zion and Bryce national parks, Lake Powell, and numerous other sites. Five guest rooms, double and queen-size beds, and two baths. Guests are welcome to use the TV in the living room. Continental-plus breakfast. Smoking outside. $40-45.

GILBERT

Mi Casa Su Casa

P.O. Box 950, Tempe, 85281
(602) 990-0682; (800) 456-0682

283. Twenty minutes from the airport, handsome ranch home has a quiet rural-park setting with large mature trees, Arabian horses, peacocks, cats, and dogs. In season, an orchard supplies some of the fruit for a full breakfast. The hostess is an expert on quilting, and the host couple are knowledgeable about local history. The guest room has king-size or twin beds and a private hall bath. Resident dogs and cats. Smoking allowed outside. Two-night minimum stay required. $65.

GLOBE

Bed and Breakfast Inn Arizona

P.O. Box 11253, Glendale, 85318-1253
(602) 561-0335; FAX (602) 561-2300

GL101. A wonderful modern guest house on a working horse farm (horses are not for hire). The kitchen window overlooks Besh Ba Gowah Archaeological Park, a partially reconstructed Salado Indian ruin, and Pinal Mountains. Two bedrooms, one with queen-size bed and private bath (shower only); and one with two twin or king-size beds with private bath (shower and tub). Self-catered Continental breakfast. Children over 12 welcome. Deluxe rates.

6 Pets welcome; 7 Smoking allowed; 8 Children welcome; 9 Social drinking allowed; 10 Tennis available; 11 Swimming available; 12 Golf available; 13 Skiing available; 14 May be booked through travel agents.

Mi Casa Su Casa

P.O. Box 950, Tempe, 85281
(602) 990-0682; (800) 456-0682

302. Handsome brick ranch-style home has separate guest house with a large living room/full kitchen, and two guest rooms, each with private bath. Room one has a queen-size bed and room two has twin beds. The hostess raises Paso Fino horses and the host is an attorney and a volunteer firefighter. Their seven-acre horse farm is at the edge of town with a panoramic view of the nearby Pinal Mountains and is near a famous archeological site. The breakfast is self-catering as the kitchen is stocked with breakfast items. Two-night minimum. Children 12 and older are welcome. Smoking allowed outside. $65.

GREER

Bed and Breakfast Inn Arizona

P.O. Box 11253, Glendale, 85318-1253
(602) 561-0335; FAX (602) 561-2300

GR001. Southwestern hospitality in a 100-year-old farmhouse. Nestled in remote mountain valley. Special home-made breakfast offerings. Selected full housekeeping cabins also available. Call for rates.

Mi Casa Su Casa

P.O. Box 950, Tempe, 85281
(602) 990-0682; (800) 456-0682

303. Meadowview is a ten-room house that combines the feel of a traditional log cabin with modern convenience and luxury. The master suite on the first floor includes a queen-size bed, fireplace, and full bath with Jacuzzi tub. Private entrance to large front deck with a view of beautiful Greer Valley. A second bedroom is on the second floor and has a king-size bed and two trundle twin beds with private hall bath. Continental

breakfast. Children eight and older are welcome. Smoking allowed outside. $10 each for additional person in room two. $55-75.

HEBER

Mi Casa Su Casa

P.O. Box 950, Tempe, 85281
(602) 990-0682; (800) 456-0682

258. A rustic home surrounded by ponderosa pines and adjoining the Sitgreaves National Forest. Extra-large guest suite on the first level. Suite includes king-size bed, queen-size sofa bed, private bath, private entrance, private deck, microwave, refrigerator, satellite TV, VCR, washer/dryer, outside cooker, and combination wood-burning stove/fireplace. Near many attractions and recreational facilities. Resident dog. Children are welcome. No smoking. Four dollars for additional child or adult. Special rates for senior citizens. $35-55.

HEREFORD

Ramsey Canyon Inn

31 Ramsey Canyon Road, 85615
(602) 378-3010

Capture the romantic spirit of country living with a warmth and graciousness that is traditionally Arizona. In the Huachuca Mountains at an elevation of 5,400 feet, Ramsey Canyon is truly a hummingbird haven, with 15 species on record. Nestled by a winding mountain stream and surrounded by sycamore, maple, juniper, oak, and pine trees, wildlife is abundant. The average summer temperature is 75 degrees. One-bedroom cottages are also available. Come and discover the rich history of Cochise County.

Hosts: Ronald and Shirlene DeSantis
Rooms: 6 (PB) $90-105
Cottages: 2
Full Breakfast
Credit Cards: F
Notes: 2, 5, 7 (limited), 9, 10, 11, 12

NOTES: Credit cards accepted: A MasterCard; B Visa; C American Express; D Discover Card; E Diner's Club; F Other; 2 Personal checks accepted; 3 Lunch available; 4 Dinner available; 5 Open all year;

Ramsey Canyon Inn

LAKE HAVASU CITY

Bed and Breakfast Inn Arizona

P.O. Box 11253, Glendale, 85318-1253
(602) 561-0335; FAX (602) 561-2300

LH001. Friendly resort inn, lake view rooms, suites, fireplaces, pool, and Jacuzzi. Call for rates.

MAYER

Bed and Breakfast Inn Arizona

P.O. Box 11253, Glendale, 85318-1253
(602) 561-0335; FAX (602) 561-2300

MA001. Victorian setting in old mining town. Pool, Jacuzzi, private entrance. Close to Prescott, Sedona, Verde Valley, and Jerome areas. Call for rates.

MESA

Bed and Breakfast Inn Arizona

P.O. Box 11253, Glendale, 85318-1253
(602) 561-0335; FAX (602) 561-2300

ME103. This delightful Mediterranean-style guest house has a queen-size bed, private entrance, pool, and lakeside frontage in the midst of citrus trees and flowers. Small refrigerator, microwave oven, coffee maker, electric skillet, and private bath. Gazebo next to lake for eating or relaxing. Weekdays, Continental breakfast; weekends, full breakfast. Ideal for family, with the best of both privacy and a bed and breakfast host. Children are welcome. Deluxe rates.

ME104. A fantastic adult community with a homey atmosphere, this bustling retirement resort boasts everything for the visitor, with breakfast plus the choice of second meal daily in their restaurant, cable TV, 24-hour staffing, crafts, game and exercise rooms, heated pool and spa, and even an in-house parlor. Fully furnished apartments available by the day, week, or month include a living room, bedroom, bath, and furnished kitchen. The younger crowd is welcome for shorter visits. Superior rates.

Mi Casa Su Casa

P.O. Box 950, Tempe, 85281
(602) 990-0682; (800) 456-0682

001. Country living in the city. Twenty minutes from Tempe and Scottsdale. These two accommodations are nestled in a large citrus grove. The guest room in the main house offers a room with twin beds, cable TV, private hall bath, and full breakfast. The self-contained guest cottage, built in 1975 to match the handsome main house, has a living room with TV and phone, complete kitchen, bedroom with queen-size bed, dressing room, full bath, and enclosed garage. No children. No resident pets. No smoking. Special weekly and monthly rates available. $45-75.

002. Friendly, busy host couple welcome guests to their casual, happy home. Their

6 Pets welcome; 7 Smoking allowed; 8 Children welcome; 9 Social drinking allowed; 10 Tennis available; 11 Swimming available; 12 Golf available; 13 Skiing available; 14 May be booked through travel agents.

Mi Casa Su Casa
(continued)

very large, contemporary Spanish home on one acre is close to shopping, golf, and spring baseball training. Guest suite has private entrance, living room with double bed, double Hide-a-bed, private bath, dining area, sink, refrigerator, and TV. Casual breakfasts might include homemade breads and jams and fresh eggs produced on the premises. Pool. Resident dog. Handicapped possible. Children over nine are welcome. Smoking outside. Ten dollars extra for children. $35-45.

220. Friendly, caring Scandinavian host couple from Minnesota welcome guests to a spacious Spanish-style home. In a quiet, handsome neighborhood, it is one mile to the golf course, three miles to baseball spring training, and an easy drive to Superstition Mountains and Apache Trail. Decor is traditional with Scandinavian touch. Room one has a queen-size bed, room two has a double bed; they share a hall bath. Only one party accepted at a time. Laundry facilities are available. Continental-plus breakfast. Children 12 and older are welcome. No smoking. Weekly rates are available. $35-45.

230. Outgoing hostess of Irish background enjoys bed and breakfast guests. She has a three-bedroom, two-bath home. Friendly accommodating atmosphere. Near golf courses, two miles from the Chicago Cubs spring training, 15 miles to Indian reservation and gambling. Near public transportation. Master bedroom has queen-size bed and private bath. A smaller guest room has twin beds and a shared bath. Guests are welcome to use family room with TV and fireplace. Full breakfast. Kitchen privileges. Children under 12 are welcome. No resident pets. Small guest pet possible. Smoking allowed outside. $35-45.

236. This spacious stucco Mediterranean-looking home has beautiful landscaping and a view of the Superstition Mountains. The hostess, an outstanding cook, enjoys fixing gourmet breakfasts and evening snacks. Three guest rooms are available in private guest wing that has one bath. Only one party at a time. Room one has a king-size bed or a pair of twin beds, room two has a double bed, and room three has one twin bed. Guests are welcome to use the family room with stereo and fireplace or living room that has cable TV and VCR. Pool. Small resident dog. Smoking allowed outside. Fifteen-dollar extra for children over ten. $45-55.

358. In east Mesa, near Apache Junction, the Superstition Mountains, and the Apache Trail, is this contemporary home on an acre of land. Two guest rooms have queen-size beds and share a hall bath. Guests are welcome to swim in the solar-heated swimming pool or to relax by the living room fireplace. Full breakfast. Children are welcome. Pre-arranged baby-sitting available. Resident cat. Smoking allowed outside. Special rates for long stays. $50.

381. Large, handsome home in quiet residential neighborhood on a cul-de-sac in citrus growing area. Guest suite is very private. The guest room has a king-size bed. The private full bath in hall has two sinks. The guest sitting area has a TV and double sofa bed for a third person. Crib available. Infants only. No pets. No smoking. $55-70.

MONUMENT VALLEY TRIBAL PARK

Bed and Breakfast Inn Arizona

P.O. Box 11253, Glendale, 85318-1253
(602) 561-0335; FAX (602) 561-2300

NOTES: Credit cards accepted: A MasterCard; B Visa; C American Express; D Discover Card; E Diner's Club; F Other; 2 Personal checks accepted; 3 Lunch available; 4 Dinner available; 5 Open all year;

MV001. Lodge and trading post open since 1924. Adjacent to Navajo tribal park, motor inn-type accommodations, attractively furnished, Southwestern-style rooms, panoramic views, some on hillside level with balconies and patios. Indoor heated pool. Call for rates.

MR001. Discover the Navajo Nation. Southwestern/Navajo-style rooms with TV, private bath, and restaurant with traditional Navajo dishes and Southwestern-style foods. Personalized tours of Navajo Nation available. Call for rates.

MUNDS PARK

Mi Casa Su Casa
P.O. Box 950, Tempe, 85281
(602) 990-0682; (800) 456-0682

342. Sociable couple have a two-story country cottage in a heavily wooded area. Built in the 1960s, the house is in a country club area 17 miles south of Flagstaff, which offers an 18 hole golf course, tennis, heated pool, bingo, and bridge. The second floor has two bedrooms that share a full hall bath. Room one has a king-size bed, and room two has twin beds. Only one party accepted at a time. Guests are welcome to use the living room, which has cable TV. The couple has a suite on the first floor. Full healthy breakfasts. Resident dog. No smoking. No children. Open May 15 through September 15. $65.

ORACLE

Bed and Breakfast Inn Arizona
P.O. Box 11253, Glendale, 85318-1253
(602) 561-0335; FAX (602) 561-2300

OR001. Spanish-style hideaway. Private entrances off the courtyard. Spacious rooms with fireplaces and private baths. Close to prehistoric cliff dwellings and Biosphere 2. Call for rates.

OR101. An original homestead ranch with three separate cottages, plus a romantic suite in the main house. Guests enjoy breakfast with the gracious hosts in the spacious country kitchen of the 100-year-old ranch house. The Hill House has three bedrooms, living room, fully equipped kitchen, bath with antique tub/shower, and porch. The Guest House is an adobe with queen-size bedroom/sitting room, private bath, and a screened sleeping porch. The Forman's House is secluded, with two bedrooms, a full kitchen, private bath, and screened porch. The Trowbridge Suite, in the main house, is a romantic hideaway with a queen-size bed, fireplace, sitting area, private bath, rose arbor entrance, and private patio. Children welcome. Deluxe rates.

Mi Casa Su Casa
P.O. Box 950, Tempe, 85281
(602) 990-0682; (800) 456-0682

376. Near Biosphere 2, this home in a country-desert setting has four guest rooms, all with private baths and private entrances onto a courtyard. Guests enjoy the distant mountain views and the hiking. Near Catalina Park, 35 minutes from Tucson, eight miles to Peppersauce Canyon, 30 minutes to Aravaipa Canyon. Two queen-size beds, one double bed, and one pair of twin beds. Full breakfast. No resident pets. Children over 12 are welcome. Ten dollars for third person in same room. Weekly and monthly rates available. $45-50.

Old Pueblo Homestays
P.O. Box 13603, Tucson, 85732
(800) 333-9 RSO

Villa Cardinale. A Spanish hideaway with red-tile roofs and courtyard with fountain. Just 35 minutes from Tucson but a world

6 Pets welcome; 7 Smoking allowed; 8 Children welcome; 9 Social drinking allowed; 10 Tennis available;
11 Swimming available; 12 Golf available; 13 Skiing available; 14 May be booked through travel agents.

away from the city's fast pace. Catalina Mountain country with spectacular views and clear, starry nights. Spacious rooms, private entrance, fireplace, baths. A full country breakfast is included as part of every stay. Minimum stay is two nights. Children over 16. $55.

PAGE

Bed and Breakfast Inn Arizona

P.O. Box 11253, Glendale, 85318-1253
(602) 561-0335; FAX (602) 561-2300

PG001. This full-service miniresort features Southwestern Indian-designed architecture. Private bath and bedrooms with two double beds or king-size beds. Pool. Call for rates.

PG002. Lodge overlooking spectacular lake. Pool, restaurants, and TV available. Housekeeping units. Call for rates.

PG103. Home with a modern setting. Hosts are outdoor enthusiasts and river-raft runners. Landscaped patio and garden. Private entrance, bath. Breakfast. Call for rates.

Mi Casa Su Casa

P.O. Box 950, Tempe, 85281
(602) 990-0682; (800) 456-0682

359. Spacious home on edge of Page with sunken courtyard and formal garden. Homes here are ranchette style on lots no smaller than two acres. The large guest room has air conditioning, queen-size bed, cable TV, walk-in closet, sink, telephone, and Southwest decor. There is one folding cot available. Private full hall bath. The breakfast possibilities include Western specialties, or a buffet is set, depending upon the scheduled river trips. The hosts enjoy activities in the many nearby national parks,

reading, theater, and gardening. Resident cats. Smoking allowed outside. $60-70.

Old Pueblo Homestays

P.O. Box 13603, Tucson, 85732
(800) 333-9 RSO

A Place Above the Cliff. In northern Arizona, this two-story home has a large room on the second floor with French doors leading to a balcony overlooking Lake Powell. The room has a queen-size bed and private bath with marble shower. An air bed is available for children. Continental breakfast is served. A grand piano and cable TV are available. Smoking allowed outside only. No pets. $75.

PATAGONIA

Bed and Breakfast Inn Arizona

P.O. Box 11253, Glendale, 85318-1253
(602) 561-0335; FAX (602) 561-2300

PA001. Turn-of-the-century Adobe miners' apartments. Private entrances. Full breakfast, beautiful sunsets, and scenery. Call for rates.

PA002. Guest house. Private and relaxing atmosphere. Close to the Mexican border. Patio, fireplace, private baths. Full breakfast. Golf, hiking, and shopping close by. Call for rates.

PA003. In town and within walking distance of all activities. Full breakfast. Close to San Rafel Mountains, ghost towns, and silver mines. Call for rates.

Little House

P.O. Box 461, 341 Sonoita Avenue, 85624
(602) 394-2493

NOTES: Credit cards accepted: A MasterCard; B Visa; C American Express; D Discover Card; E Diner's Club; F Other; 2 Personal checks accepted; 3 Lunch available; 4 Dinner available; 5 Open all year;

In the heart of southeast Arizona's birding and naturalist area at a comfortable 4,000 feet, Little House offers two rooms in a private adobe guest house. Both queen-size bedrooms and twin bedrooms have patios, fireplaces, private baths, and sitting areas. The gourmet breakfast features homemade breads, sausages, and eggs from local hens. Always fresh fruit and juices accompany select teas and freshly ground coffees.

Hosts: Don and Doris Wenig
Rooms: 3 (PB) $50-60
Full and Continental Breakfast
Credit Cards: None
Notes: 2, 5, 7 (limited), 9

Mi Casa Su Casa

P.O. Box 950, Tempe, 85281
(602) 990-0682; (800) 456-0682

356. Hostess and son welcome guests to historic turn-of-the-century adobe home on the square, which was originally miners' apartments. The home is decorated with original artwork by area artists. Suite one has a bedroom with twin beds and connecting bath. The sitting room has two twin beds. Suite two is decorated with period antiques, including a wood-burning stove, and has a bedroom with a queen-size bed, connecting bath with claw-foot tub and pedestal sink. The sitting room has twin beds. Resident dog. Children are welcome. Full breakfast. Smoking allowed outside. Handicapped access possible. Twenty dollars for additional adults. Between $5 and $15 for children. $65.

363. This guest house is near many scenic natural sites. Originally built in the 1930s, this bed and breakfast is a frame house in the bungalow style, much like an English cottage. There are many trees, flowers, and vines. The interior is light and airy with antique and contemporary furnishings. It has a living room, full kitchen, two bedrooms, each with a double bed, a full hall bath, and private patio. Only one party accepted at a time. The kitchen is stocked, and breakfast is self-serve. Bicycles available for guests' use. Children over 12 are welcome. Smoking outside. Ten dollars for each additional person. $75.

1624. Warm host couple have separate guest cottage in a pretty flower garden. Room one has a king-size or twin beds and private bath. Room two has a queen-size bed and private bath. Many guests ask for recipes after having the full breakfast here, which is served in the main house. Up to two children over eight are welcome if family takes whole house. Handicapped accessible. Resident cat. Smoking allowed outside only. $55-65.

Old Pueblo Homestays

P.O. Box 13603, Tucson, 35732
(800) 333-9 RSO

The Duquesne House. On the original main street of Patagonia, this turn-of-the-century adobe structure was originally built as miners' apartments when it was a thriving mountain town. Sixty miles south of Tucson and 20 miles east of Nogales near the US Border, Patagonia is known for its scenic beauty and diversity of birds and plant life. Each accommodation has a private entrance and consists of a sitting room with a twin bed, a bedroom and private bath with two twin/queen-size beds. Full breakfast. Smoking permitted outside only. No pets. Fifteen dollars for den with twin bed. $65.

PAYSON

Bed and Breakfast Inn Arizona

P.O. Box 11253, Glendale, 85318-1253
(602) 561-0335; FAX (602) 561-2300

PY001. Ranch lodge rooms and cabins. Pool, sauna, fireplaces, stables. Lounge and restaurant. Just off the banks of the Tonto Creek "Zane Grey Territory." Call for rates.

PY002. Beautiful quality lodging, Bedrooms with queen- or king-size beds and Jacuzzi suites. Call for rates.

PY103. This treetop hideaway in Payson is ideal for a family escape from the desert heat—or a fast weekend getaway. It is a little guest house, completely equipped with full kitchen, TV in living room with single sofa sleeper, and a bedroom with a private bath. This hospitable family will leave breakfast fixings the night before, so guests can eat at leisure in the morning. Children are welcome. Hosts have ten-year-old and toddler boys, an eight-year-old girl, a dog, chickens, and a guinea pig. A comfy, homey, down-home host family will make guests comfortable while giving the privacy of a separate guest house. Deluxe rates.

Mi Casa Su Casa

P.O. Box 950, Tempe, 85280-0950
(602) 990-0682; (800) 456-0682

47. Three miles south of Payson, a very large A-frame house adjoins the national forest. Queen-size bedroom with private full bath and a large balcony with trundle beds overlooking the living room. Easy drive to Mogollon Rim, Zane Grey's cabin, and Tonto Natural Bridge. Continental breakfast. Two-night minimum stay is required. No smoking. No alcoholic beverages allowed. $45-50.

346. Enthusiastic retired host couple welcome guests to their large two-story Swiss chalet-style home in the pines in a quiet neighborhood. Room one is on the first floor and has a queen-size bed, one twin bed, and a private bath. Rooms two and three are on the second floor. Each has one queen-size bed and one twin bed, and they share a hall bath. Guests have enjoyed see-ing the llamas raised in the vicinity. Full breakfast. No resident pets. Children are welcome. No smoking. Ten dollars for third person in room. $65.

PHOENIX

Bed and Breakfast Inn Arizona

P.O. Box 11253, Glendale, 85318-1253
(602) 561-0335; FAX (602) 561-2300

PX001. Superb location at the base of Camelback Mountain, this former estate has magnificent grounds and gardens. Swimming pools, tennis, and golf amid date palms. Call for rates.

PX105. Minutes from the downtown area, this Spanish-style home is a beautifully preserved tribute to a bygone era. Built in 1937, it is decorated in English antiques, with beamed living room ceiling and arched doorways lending quaint charm. Warm, friendly hosts who like to cater to their guests. Room has queen-size bed, English lace curtains, and a view of the garden, yard, and gazebo. Private hall bath with shower. Extra room with single-size bed. Traditional full American breakfast, which can be prepared to accommodate dietary needs. No children; no pets. Modest to deluxe rates.

PX108. Gracious second-generation bed and breakfast hostess will make sure of guests' comfort in this quiet stucco home in a peaceful Phoenix neighborhood. Pool and patio where one can watch the hummingbirds feed, nice views of Camelback Mountain, and very convenient to Sky Harbor, downtown, and Scottsdale, it's a real bargain! Bedroom with one queen-size bed, private bath, telephone, and TV. Delicious full breakfast. Children over eight are welcome. Modest rates.

NOTES: Credit cards accepted: A MasterCard; B Visa; C American Express; D Discover Card; E Diner's Club; F Other; 2 Personal checks accepted; 3 Lunch available; 4 Dinner available; 5 Open all year;

PX111. An airily decorated guest house in the heart of north central Phoenix on an expansive old homesite, where guests will be served a gourmet breakfast in the summerhouse. Two double beds, bath, living room, and kitchen make this second-story bed and breakfast a perfect stop over for comfort. With pool and patio, citrus trees, large lawn, off-street parking; in a central location for easy access to all parts of the city. Professional hosts and their children will make any stay a comfortable one. Children over five welcome. Deluxe rates.

PX115. Don't be fooled by the quiet, plain exterior of this tract home—inside, it is a never-never-land filled with stained glass and antiques. Warm, gracious hostess is a tour guide at the Phoenix Art Museum and a gourmet chef; host creates stained-glass windows. Breakfast of choice. Back yard with gazebo, open-pit fireplace, and Jacuzzi—an oasis in the midst of the urban crush. Double bedroom with private bath down the hall. Child with a single parent welcome. Deluxe rates.

PX116. A quiet townhome guest room at the top of a spiral staircase, with queen-size bed and private hall bath, is convenient to the airport, downtown, and Scottsdale. Retired librarian hostess and artist husband are world travelers and assure guests a warm welcome. Join them at a delicious full breakfast, then relax by the pool or on the patio. Ideal for the business traveler. Lovely Burmese cat in residence. Children over ten welcome. Modest to deluxe rates.

PX124. This lovely condominium is hosted by a professional artist/decorator who has filled the house with an eclectic mixture of antiques and art pieces. Room with twin beds, private bath, and a small "Arcadia" garden, plus a Continental breakfast with the hosts, makes this the perfect base for business or pleasure in the center of the city. Only a mile to the Arizona Center. No children. Deluxe rates.

PX125. Quiet, immaculate home with retired host couple who welcome guests. Hostess bakes homemade cinnamon and pecan rolls, bread, and jams with full breakfast. Close to Metro Center, Western International University, Sun City, and easy access to I-17 to travel south to the airport and Tucson, and north to Sedona and the Grand Canyon. Hosts will be very helpful in orienting guests to the area. One bedroom with twin beds, one with double bed, share a hall bath with each other. Sunny yard with fountain. Modest rates.

PX134. Near the interstate, Metro Center, and North Mountain Park, this suite with private entrance, kitchenette, private bath, and king-size or two twin beds is a real find for the bed and breakfast guest. The hosts are avid hikers and hikers and know all about the great places to see in Arizona. Plus, they will (by appointment) take guests on overnight jaunts in their motor home to those hidden back roads or day trips to the Superstition Mountains, etc. It is perfect for a longer stay, too, with a bus line nearby. Full breakfast weekends; fixings left in the kitchen weekdays. Modest rates.

PX136. Numerous awards winner! Casual, but sophisticated luxury casita townhouse bed and breakfast with Southwestern decorations and design. Private petite patio, queen-size bed, private bath, TV, VCR, telephone, and FAX. Hearty Southwestern breakfast, country club privileges. On the golf course; pool, health club, tennis, and more! Call for rates.

PX139. If visitors want a sophisticated getaway in the heart of uptown, this luxury home is perfect. Savor a Continental breakfast in the privacy of one's own suite, join

---

6 Pets welcome; 7 Smoking allowed; 8 Children welcome; 9 Social drinking allowed; 10 Tennis available; 11 Swimming available; 12 Golf available; 13 Skiing available; 14 May be booked through travel agents.

Bed and Breakfast Inn Arizona
(continued)

the host and hostess on the sunny back deck, enjoy the Jacuzzi, or relax next to the fireplace inside. The Library Suite has a four-poster king-size bed, private connecting bath, and private deck entrance. The library has a desk and a sofa sleeper for a third person. The Victorian Suite has a sitting room and private bath. Private entrances and private baths in the remaining three suites. Deluxe and superior rates.

PX141. Featuring 35 individual casitas, ranging from single bedrooms to villas with full kitchens that can sleep up to eight. All are decorated in classic Spanish/Mexican style for privacy and pleasure. Nestled on six acres of beautifully landscaped desert, where a pool, Jacuzzis, tennis courts, and handcrafted details throughout reflect the old Phoenix of days gone by. Although breakfast is not included, most rooms have kitchenettes, a restaurant is being restored on the property, and there are plenty of nearby eateries. Children are welcome. Smoking allowed. Deluxe to superior rates.

PX142. In the Biltmore area of Phoenix, this home has magnificent gardens and a pool, and it blends into the impeccably kept gardens creating an island of serenity. Join the hosts for a full breakfast, then relax in the lovely surroundings. There are four suites all with private entrances, mini-refrigerators, microwave ovens, TVs, and private baths. No children, please; the pool and fountain are not child-proof. Superior rates.

PX143. Historic inn with guest house built of adobe and other natural, local materials. Private entrances, pool. Full breakfast. Nestled near the solitude of the Squaw Peak Mountain Preserve. Call for rates.

The International Bed & Breakfast Club, Inc.
504 Amherst Street, Buffalo, NY 14207
(800) 723-4262; FAX (716) 873-4462

A deluxe private resort offering country club privileges, such as golf, tennis, and Olympic pool. Guests are greeted with casual Western comfort, class, and privacy. Six rooms with private baths. Full breakfast. $49-122.

Maricopa Manor
15 West Pasadena Avenue, 85013
(602) 274-6302

Five luxury suites, spacious public rooms, patios, decks, and the gazebo spa offer an intimate Old World atmosphere in an elegant urban setting. Maricopa Manor is in the heart of the Valley of the Sun, convenient to shops, restaurants, museums, churches, and civic and government centers. The Spanish-style manor house, built in 1928, houses beautiful art, antiques, and a warm Southwestern hospitality. Advance reservations required.

Hosts: Mary Ellen and Paul Kelley
Suites: 5 (PB) $79-129
Continental Breakfast
Credit Cards: A, B, C, D
Notes: 2, 5, 7, 8, 9, 10, 11, 12, 14

Mi Casa Su Casa
P.O. Box 950, Tempe, 85280-0950
(602) 990-0682; (800) 456-0682

82. Handsome, large home near Biltmore has an extra-large yard with a pool. Separate guest wing has a large bedroom with a king-size bed, private bath with a shower, sitting and writing area, and a private entrance. A full breakfast is served. Minimum stay is three nights. $60-65.

155. In the historic district of Phoenix, this Spanish-style home was built circa 1930 and has been renovated and furnished in 1930s style. Beamed living room ceilings and arched doorways lend quaint charm. The guest room, overlooking the garden and gazebo, has a private hall bath, a queen-size bed, and lace curtains from England. Full breakfast. Minimum stay is two nights. $60-70.

165. Spanish-style house in a residential neighborhood sits at the foot of a mountain. Ten minutes from downtown and 20 minutes from downtown Scottsdale. Large bedroom has extra-long twin beds or king-size bed, bath with Roman tub and shower, small refrigerator, microwave oven, TV, telephone, dressing room, and sitting area with a private entrance. Continental breakfast. Minimum stay is three nights. $50-60.

207. On a street known for large houses, yards, and old trees, this old Spanish-style home has been restored and furnished with English Victorian antiques. Three guest rooms offer a choice of king-, queen-size, or twin beds, and all are equipped with full baths. Pool and spa available. An abundant breakfast includes fresh-squeezed orange juice from two acres of citrus trees adjoining the property. $45-65.

226. Condominium in the Biltmore area has two bedrooms, two baths, and overlooks the golf course from a balcony. The hostess lives in one of the bedrooms, and the guest room has a queen-size bed, cable TV, and connecting full bath. Two heated swimming pools, Jacuzzi, four tennis courts, and an exercise room are available to guests. Continental breakfast. Minimum stay is two nights. $45-55.

268. Gracious hostess welcomes guests to a very large Southwestern stucco ranch-style home. This house was built beside a golf course in a handsome neighborhood with large trees. Two guest rooms have a queen-size bed and full hall bath; another guest room has twin beds, TV, and shares the full hall bath. Only one party is accepted at a time. Guests are welcome to use the large living room with fireplace, cable TV, VCR, or pool. Full breakfast. Smoking allowed outside. No resident pets. Ten dollar charge for children between ten and 16. Those 16 and older pay full rate. $50-70.

269. Large immaculate home is near many activities including a large shopping mall, golf courses, tennis, art galleries, and Arabian horse farms. Large master bedroom has a queen-size bed, sitting area, TV, and glass doors to back yard. The second guest room has a queen-size bed and a shared hall bath. Light kitchen and laundry privileges, RV and/or boat parking, bicycles, large living room with sofa bed, TV, and fireplace available. No resident pets. Continental breakfast served. No smoking. Minimum stay is two nights. Twenty-dollar charge for children over five. $45-60.

270. Traditional ranch home with 3,200-square feet is in the "green belt" of central Phoenix. Private guest wing has two large guest rooms with king-size beds, TVs, and telephones. One guest room has a connecting bath with a shower, and the other guest room has a private, full hall bath. Hostess is professional cake decorator; host is in food sales business. Full breakfast on weekends, Continental on weekdays. $75.

282. This 1955 ranch-style home is in a beautiful older neighborhood with large, mature trees. Near a mall, public transportation, and the freeway. Photographic exhibit is in the sunroom. The guest room has a queen-size bed with private hall bath. It has a private entrance opening to the patio and pool. Hosts are knowledgeable about their city and state. Resident dog. Full, heart-healthy breakfasts. $50-55.

6 Pets welcome; 7 Smoking allowed; 8 Children welcome; 9 Social drinking allowed; 10 Tennis available; 11 Swimming available; 12 Golf available; 13 Skiing available; 14 May be booked through travel agents.

Mi Casa Su Casa
(continued)

293. This 500-square-foot attractive guest house at the base of Camelback Mountain has a private entrance and faces a heated pool, attractive back yard, and a dramatic view of the mountain. Twenty minutes from downtown, Scottsdale, or the airport. The living room has a fireplace, cable TV, VCR, small refrigerator, microwave, and dining table. King-size or twin beds in bedroom, full bath, and private phone line with answering machine. Refrigerator is stocked so guests can eat when they choose. Smoking allowed outside. Minimum stay is three nights. $75-85.

313. Recently remodeled home with patio, swimming pool, and view of Camelback Mountain. Twenty minutes from downtown Phoenix, Scottsdale, and the airport. Enthusiastic, friendly host couple receives happy evaluations from their guests. They enjoy classical music, travel, and the Phoenix Suns. Hosts have been Arizona residents for over 40 years—giving suggestions about places to visit. Award-winning Southwestern-design guest room has a queen-size bed, TV, phone, and connecting bath with shower. Full breakfast featuring home-baked bread. No resident pets. Smoking allowed outside only. Two-night minimum stay preferred. $45-50.

315. Contemporary two-story townhouse in a small complex in a grapefruit grove. Near Camelback Mountain, twenty minutes from downtown Phoenix, Scottsdale, and airport. Near public transportation. Guests write glowing evaluations about their visits. The host couple has lived worldwide and enjoys talking with guests. Guest room is up a spiral staircase onto second floor and has a pleasant Southwestern decor, queen-size bed, private bath, phone, and TV. The pool

is next door. Two nights preferred. Full breakfast. No smoking. Resident cat. $65.

319. Helpful, warm-hearted host couple has a large architect-designed home, built in 1987 in a very nice neighborhood. Spanish-style with stucco exterior and a tile roof. There are two large rooms and bath over the two-car garage. One room is used for storage; the other is the guest room. It has a queen-size bed, TV, private entrance with exterior stairs, private hall bath, and telephone. Pool. Full breakfast is served in the main house and often includes homemade breads. Two-night minimum. Crib and portable crib available. No smoking. Children up to age six only, and they stay free of charge. Weekly and no-breakfast rates are available. $55-65.

337. This gracious 1920s adobe home and two guest cottages are on three acres. Chosen as the Designer Show House in October 1991 by *Phoenix House and Garden* magazine. The house has many arched doorways and French doors opening onto five formal gardens. Very large diving pool. All suites have private baths, TVs, and private entrances. The Conservatory Suite in the main house has a queen-size, four-poster bed and a sitting room with fireplace. One separate guest house has a library with fireplace and two suites. Each has a king-size bed and minikitchen. The second guest house is light and airy with a king-size bed, minikitchen, and views of a garden. No resident pets. Two-night minimum preferred. A full breakfast is served. Smoking allowed outside only. No children. $150.

338. Guests will enjoy the acre of flowering shrubs, palm, citrus, and pomegranate. The main house was built in 1924, and the guest cottage was built in the 1950s. The second-story "cottage" offers a kitchenette, a bedroom with two double beds, a living room

NOTES: Credit cards accepted: A MasterCard; B Visa; C American Express; D Discover Card; E Diner's Club; F Other; 2 Personal checks accepted; 3 Lunch available; 4 Dinner available; 5 Open all year;

with TV, a private bath with claw-foot tub, and a porch with a view of the pool. Ten minutes from the Heard Museum, twenty minutes from the airport, and two blocks from Central Avenue. Breakfast is self-catering. Smoking allowed outside only. Children over six who can swim are welcome. Discount rates for longer stays. $75.

341. Retired, friendly host couple were farmers in the Midwest. Active in the Mennonite church, they enjoy hiking, bowling, and spectator sports. Modest home in residential neighborhood. Room one has a double bed, TV, and shares a full hall bath with room two, which has twin beds and TV. Near public transportation. Full breakfast with homemade breads and pecan rolls is served in the dining room or on the patio in pretty back yard. No resident pets. Children are welcome. No smoking. Weekly stay receives a ten-percent discount. $30-40.

352. Handsome two-story home near the Hilton Pointe Tapatio. Sociable host couple enjoy horseback riding, hiking, hunting, and fishing. The couple's room and bath are on the second floor. Room one on the first floor has a queen-size bed and private hall bath. Room two on the second floor has a double bed and private hall bath. Queen-size sofa bed is also available on the second floor. Balcony available. Heated pool, tennis, golf course, and stables are nearby. Spanish spoken. Continental breakfast weekdays, full breakfast on weekends. Older, friendly resident dog. Children nine and older are welcome. Smoking allowed outside. Two-night minimum. Ten-dollar charge for children. $55-65.

368. Rambling brick four-bedroom, three-bath home is surrounded by mature trees filled with birds in a quiet, convenient neighborhood near Phoenix College. One block from the Phoenix College Library. Handsome, contemporary decor with fireplaces, fine art, wide assortment of books, magazines, and travel guides. Guests welcome in large living room and covered patio, front and back lawns. Walk to bike paths, tennis, park, golf, shopping, and churches or temple. Guest room one is romantic Victorian with double bed. Second room is Southwestern with twin beds. Rooms share spacious bath with shower. Cable TV and VCR. Distilled water. Computer, printer, and modem available. Grapefruit tree on property provides fresh fruit or marmalade for homemade bread. Resident cat and dog. Minimum stay is two nights. Special weekly rates available. $45-60.

385. Pretty, spacious, and comfortable ranch-style house built in 1959 in very quiet, up-scale neighborhood "near everything." Many birds in vicinity, near Camelback Mountain. Some antiques, ec-lectic decor. Air-conditioned. Room one has a king-size bed and a crib and shares the full bath with room two which has twin beds. Only one party accepted at a time. A real find for the bed and breakfast traveler, guests are welcome to use the pool table in the family room, the TV in the den with fireplace, or the large covered patio. Fenced, unheated diving pool in the nice back yard. No resident pets. Minimum stay is two nights. Special rates for children. $75.

Old Pueblo Homestays

P.O. Box 13603, Tucson, 85732
(800) 333-9 RSO

Arrowzona Bed and Breakfast. This luxurious casita townhouse features a deluxe guest room with a queen-size bed, private bath, courtesy bathrobes, bath toiletries, morning paper, TV, private phone, mini-refrigerator, and microwave. Savor a delicious breakfast on the deck and patio overlooking the 11th green of a golf course. The hostess can give suggestions about sightseeing and dining. Guests have complete usage of country club facilities. Smoking outside only. Two resident cats. No children. No pets. $49-98.

PINETOP-LAKESIDE

Bed and Breakfast Inn Arizona

P.O. Box 11253, Glendale, 85318-1253
(602) 561-0335; FAX (602) 561-2300

PT103. This little log home in the pines, done in rustic frontier style, is a wonderful escape into the White Mountains during the summer. There are two bedrooms. The Indian Room Suite has an antique double bed in one room and two studio beds in the adjoining room. The Cowboy Room has handmade log twin beds. Both share a hall bath. Feast on a full country breakfast and enjoy afternoon tea on the old log porch. Children over 12 are welcome. Available Memorial Day through Labor Day.

PT104. A deluxe getaway in the Mogollon Rim country, this executive retreat boasts five self-contained cabins, tennis courts, sauna, private lakes, a gazebo, fitness center, and peace and quiet! Each cabin has a fully stocked kitchen with staples (coffee, tea, sugar) and cookware provided, but guests bring their own goodies. Breakfast is not provided. The Cheyenne Cabin has three bedrooms; the Santa Fe has two bedrooms; the Honeymoon has one bedroom; the Barn has two bedrooms; and the Pueblo Lodge can accommodate up to 14 people. Minimum two-night stay. Children welcome. No pets. Superior rates.

PRESCOTT

Bed and Breakfast Inn Arizona

P.O. Box 11253, Glendale, 85318-1253
(602) 561-0335; FAX (602) 561-2300

PR001. Nestled amid shade trees in the center of the Mount Vernon historic district, Arizona's largest Victorian neighborhood. Various deluxe accommodations offered. Full breakfast and afternoon refreshments. Call for rates.

PR002. Secluded country elegance overlooking the creek and mountains. Private baths, hot tubs, and decks. A big farm-fresh breakfast is served. Close to city amenities. Call for rates.

PR104. This meticulously restored lodging house is near the courthouse square. Original oak planking is refinished, and walls are covered with period wallpapers. Bedrooms with twin or queen-size beds, private baths, and ceiling fans. Continental breakfast is served. Smoking permitted. One- or two-room suites. This facility is suitable for large parties, such as weddings. Deluxe to superior rates.

PR106. A stunning, modern, but very comfortable home built on, and actually into, a mountain above Prescott. The twin or king-size bed master bedroom has a private bath, floor-to-ceiling windows with a breathtaking view of Prescott and of the fabulous rock hillside. A second bedroom (not available separately) has a queen-size bed and shares bath with suite. Watch the wildlife while eating a lavish breakfast on the second-floor deck. Hostess is a superb cook and can cook for special diets if asked. Resident dog. Children eight or older are welcome. Deluxe rates.

PR109. A lovely, completely renovated old home dating from the turn of the century. There are four beautifully decorated rooms with private baths, afternoon refreshments, and full or Continental breakfast. The elegant downstairs Terrace Suite has a queen-size bed, sofa bed in sitting room, bath, and

NOTES: Credit cards accepted: A MasterCard; B Visa; C American Express; D Discover Card; E Diner's Club; F Other; 2 Personal checks accepted; 3 Lunch available; 4 Dinner available; 5 Open all year;

private covered terrace; enough room for two couples. All other rooms are upstairs. The Pine View Suite has a queen-size bed, bath, fireplace, and sofa sleeper. The Garden Room has a queen-size bed, bath, and wicker furnishings. The Coventry Room has twin beds, private hall bath, and lovely views of the mountains. Children over ten welcome. Superior rates.

Hassayampa Inn

122 East Gurley Street, 86301
(602) 778-9434; (800) 322-1927

Nestled in the pines of mile-high Prescott is the majestic Hassayampa Inn. Locally known as "Prescott's Grand Hotel," the inn offers 67 graciously appointed rooms, a full-service restaurant, and lounge. Built in 1927 and completely renovated in 1985, the lobby is acknowledged as one of the most beautiful in Arizona. Featuring tile floors, Oriental rugs, oversize easy chairs, and potted palms. The focal point, however, is the beamed ceiling decorated with Spanish and Indian motifs. The renowned Peacock Room serves breakfast, lunch, and dinner and boasts a combination of tapestry print booths and etched Deco-style glass with ambience and Prescott's finest cuisine. Overnight rooms include daily breakfast and an evening cocktail.

Hosts: Bill and Georgia Teich
Rooms: 67 (PB) $85-140
Full Breakfast
Credit Cards: A, B, C, D, E
Notes: 2, 3, 4, 5, 7, 8, 10, 11, 12, 14

Mi Casa Su Casa

P.O. Box 950, Tempe, 85281
(602) 990-0682; (800) 456-0682

1063. Join the host couple on the veranda of a magnificently restored turreted Queen Anne Victorian in Arizona's first capital. A short walk to the courthouse, museums, galleries, restaurants, and antiquing. The two-bedroom Ivy Suite on the first floor has a private bath. Three guest rooms are on the

second floor. The Tea Rose has a queen-size bed and private bath in the hall. The Princess Victoria has a queen-size bed, a view of the southern mountains, and a private bath with an 1800s bathhouse-style copper tub. The Queen Anne Suite has a king-size bed, turret sitting room, white wicker, and a private bath. Rates include afternoon refreshments and a full breakfast. Resident dog. Smoking allowed outside. Visa and MasterCard accepted. $70-120.

1064. A wonderfully romantic bed and breakfast! Rural luxury and scenic views on a 25-acre wooded, hilly property. The two guest cottages each have two suites. Features antique or western decor. King- and queen-size beds. Can take up to 12 guests. Decks, spas, hiking, and volleyball. In the large main house, there are exotic birds. Families welcome. Children enjoy seeing the farm animals. Smoking outside. Full country breakfasts are served in the main house. Fifteen dollars for additional adult. Ten dollars for children. $95-125.

1065. Contemporary redwood home with open floor plan and three decks is in a setting of granite boulders, rolling hills, and forests. Easy drive to various local activities and recreation. One guest room has a king-size bed, or two twins, with a private bath, a microwave oven, and an adjacent covered patio. Another room has a queen-size bed and is ideal for a third or fourth party sharing a bath with the other guest room. Full breakfast. $30-70.

1067. In historic downtown, a hostess and her son welcome guests to a two-story bed and breakfast inn built in 1906. On the first floor, the two-room Terrace Suite has a bedroom with private deck. Upstairs, there are three guest rooms. The two-room Pine View Suite has a bedroom with a king-size bed, sitting room with queen-size sofa bed, and fireplace. The Garden room has a

6 Pets welcome; 7 Smoking allowed; 8 Children welcome; 9 Social drinking allowed; 10 Tennis available; 11 Swimming available; 12 Golf available; 13 Skiing available; 14 May be booked through travel agents.

queen-size bed and private bath. The Coventry has twin beds and private bath in the hall. Full breakfast and afternoon refreshments are served. Available for seminars, meetings, and weddings. Smoking allowed outside only. Well-behaved children are welcome. $70-120.

SAFFORD

Bed and Breakfast Inn Arizona

P.O. Box 11253, Glendale, 85318-1253
(602) 561-0335; FAX (602) 561-2300

SA001. Western Colonial Revival-style architecture in a rural setting. Spectacular scenery, hot springs, fishing, and hiking are found nearby. Full breakfast. Call for rates.

Mi Casa Su Casa

P.O. Box 950, Tempe, 85280-0950
(602) 990-0682; (800) 456-0682

322. Western Colonial-style brick house built in 1890 has wide verandas that run across the front of the house. Three large, old-fashioned guest rooms all share a large hall bath. One room has a double bed, a twin bed, and an old-fashioned pedestal sink. Another room has a double bed, dressing room, and a large window that overlooks two old, large pecan trees. A third room has an antique armoire, double bed, French doors to the balcony, and two 12-foot pocket doors to the sitting room. A guest cottage is also available. Full breakfast is served. No smoking. Visa and MasterCard. $65.

SASABE

Mi Casa Su Casa

P.O. Box 950, Tempe, 85280-0950
(602) 990-0682; (800) 456-0682

1627. Reaching 3,800-feet high in the Sonoran Desert, this fascinating 250-year-old ranch is one of the last great Spanish haciendas still standing in the United States. There are 16 full modernized guest rooms, each with its own private bath and fireplace. Heated pool, spa, hot tub, variety of recreational activities on site, including horseback riding. Three meals are served a day. Horseback riding packages. $60-105.

SCOTTSDALE

Bed and Breakfast Inn Arizona

P.O. Box 11253, Glendale, 85318-1253
(602) 561-0335; FAX (602) 561-2300

SD002. This elegant inn features luxurious suites, original artwork, and antiques. Southwestern Santa Fe style. Fireplaces and balconies. Continental breakfast is served. Call for rates.

SD003. These designer-decorated casitas and luxury villas are nestled in the foothills of the Sonoran Desert. Featuring gourmet dining, romantic lounge, and fitness center. Call for rates.

SD106. Attached guest house with kitchenette, private entrance, king-size bed, private bath, and French doors opening onto a patio. Pool and citrus trees. Pool can be heated except in January and February. TV and his and her golf clubs available. The hosts have tickets for guests to watch the baseball Giants train. Near downtown Scottsdale. Breakfast is served only on the first day. Deluxe rates.

SD107. Very friendly Scottsdale home where host and hostess always get rave reviews. Interesting couple has traveled widely and knows how bed and breakfast is supposed to be done. Full breakfast served.

NOTES: Credit cards accepted: A MasterCard; B Visa; C American Express; D Discover Card; E Diner's Club; F Other; 2 Personal checks accepted; 3 Lunch available; 4 Dinner available; 5 Open all year;

Light, airy ambience in king-size bed master suite with private bath. Has pool, bicycle, and golf clubs. Seven golf courses are only five minutes away. Deluxe rates.

SD127. Trilevel Scottsdale townhouse with swimming pool, in walking distance from Fashion Square and art galleries. Hostess will prepare anything guests want for breakfast, within reason. Cool, lower-level studio with sitting area, king-size or two twin beds, small refrigerator, cable TV, and stereo. Sitting area with couch, a small table where snacks, coffee, and the like may be enjoyed. Private bath with shower. Refreshments before bed, if guests wish. Hide-a-bed for third person available. Private carport parking. Modest to deluxe rates.

SD132. Just for the larger party or longer stay, this set of suites in the heart of downtown Scottsdale offers classic resort amenities: heated pools, Jacuzzis, tennis, gas-fired grills, and putting green. The Arizona Canal provides jogging out the back door, and there are sun decks, horseshoes, and croquet. Each spacious suite has two bedrooms with twin, double, or queen-size bed available, two baths, living room, fully appointed kitchen, cable TV, and telephone. Guests are on their own for breakfast. Children are welcome; cribs available. No pets. Superior rates.

SD135. This beautiful adobe-style guest house boasts privacy, elegance, and quiet surroundings, yet is within walking distance of over a dozen restaurants and the most exclusive shopping in Scottsdale. Charming hostess puts first-day Continental breakfast fixings in guests' kitchen. Relax on the queen-size bed or in the sitting area, enjoy the stereo, and wake to fresh coffee in the morning. Queen-size sofa bed in same room for additional guest. Dog in main residence. Deluxe rates.

SD136. A quiet home just south of McCormick Ranch is a real find for the bed and breakfast traveler. Artist hostess is antique collector and has a house full of lovely pieces. Master bedroom with queen-size bed is decorated in 1820s country antiques, has connecting private bath with shower. Family room with TV, pool and patio, and bikes available. Hostess prepares guests' choice of breakfast. Children 12 and over welcome. Resident cat. Modest rates.

SD137. A modest rock-walled guest house faces the pool in this northern-area bed and breakfast, only 15 minutes to the Mayo Clinic and Westworld (horseworld). King-size or twin beds, private bath, and complete kitchen make it the ideal haven for quiet relaxation. Continental breakfast self-catered with goodies left by the hostess. Private guest parking, private entrance, kitchen, TV, and patio. A short drive to shopping, restaurants, and golf. The pool is unfenced; no children or pets. Deluxe rates.

SD139. Lovely home on quiet street, convenient to downtown Scottsdale with all its art galleries, wonderful restaurants, and shopping. The hostess serves a full breakfast while guests enjoy the scenery of the lovely pool and private back yard. The guest bedroom has a double bed with private adjoining bath with tub and shower. Second bedroom for additional guests in same party has private hall bath. Outdoor hot tub (must be reserved in advance). Older teens and adults only; cat and dog in residence. Modest to deluxe rates.

Inn at the Citadel

8700 East Pinnacle Peak Road, 85255
(602) 585-6133; (800) 927-8367

Enjoy the splendor of the Sonoran Desert's enchantment. Private, intimate suites are appointed with antiques and original artwork. Fireplaces, terraces, and spectacular

6 Pets welcome; 7 Smoking allowed; 8 Children welcome; 9 Social drinking allowed; 10 Tennis available;
11 Swimming available; 12 Golf available; 13 Skiing available; 14 May be booked through travel agents.

views are woven together into a tapestry of unequaled ambience. Fine dining, shopping, and salons await at the Citadel. A deluxe Continental breakfast is served.

Host: Kelly Keyes
Rooms: 11 (PB) $135-265
Continental Breakfast
Credit Cards: A, B, E
Notes: 2, 3, 4, 5, 6 (by arrangement), 7, 8, 9, 10, 11, 12, 14

Mi Casa Su Casa

P.O. Box 950, Tempe, 85281
(602) 990-0682; (800) 456-0682

66. Near McCormick Ranch, this patio home is near golf courses, Hilton Village, Borgata, and a short walk to lighted tennis courts, spa, and pool. Very nice hostess is a real estate agent who is very knowledgeable about the area. Guest room is small and comfortable with a double bed and private hall bath. Guests are welcome to use the living room and patio. A Continental-plus breakfast is served. Resident poodle. Hostess smokes; smokers are welcome. Weekly stays receive discount. $40-45.

134. *Hafod-y-Gwynt* means "shelter from the wind" in Welsh. This is the place to experience quiet desert living. On ten acres with mountains in every direction, the 600-square-foot guest apartment with private entrance is connected to the main house and is in a remote, scenic area. Air-conditioned. Comfortable 20' x20' combined living room and bedroom with twin beds, TV, and traditional decor. Bathroom has shower. Fully equipped kitchen stocked for first few days' breakfasts. Resident pets include horses, dogs, and one cat. Closed May 15 through October 15. Three-night minimum stay is required. $65.

204. Contemporary ranch-style house is minutes from PGA driving range, world-class golf courses, and paths by the canal for jogging or walking. Master guest suite with king-size bed, dressing area and sitting

area with TV, telephone, and private bath. Bicycles and golf clubs available; gas grill on the porch. Full country breakfast and complimentary refreshments. $45-55.

227. Architect-designed New Mexico-style luxury, spacious home on two desert-landscaped acres with panoramic views of the McDowell Mountains. Comfortable, contemporary furnishings. Conveniently near Carefree, Taliesin West, Mayo Clinic, Rawhide, fine dining, and several golf courses. Sociable hostess is gourmet cook; host is excellent golfer. Guest room has a pair of twin beds with handmade quilts, TV, private, full hall bath, private exit to the pool, patio, and parking areas. Full gourmet breakfast. No smoking. Minimum stay is two nights. $55-65.

245. Attractive ranch-style house is on one acre of tall palms, pines, and native plants. Lush resort landscaping surrounds the pool. Large, private guest suite includes a sitting room, office area with a FAX, private bath with a shower, and smaller second bedroom with a twin bed. Private tennis/health club facilities accessible (for a small extra fee). Breakfast and complimentary refreshments are served. $65-75.

273. This excellent hostess invites guests to luxurious, comfortable Spanish ranch-style home in neighborhood with homes on one-acre or larger lots. Tropical back yard with pool, lawn, palms, citrus trees, and roses. Contemporary interior with a few antiques. Room one has a king-size bed, large private bath, sitting area, and French doors to pool. Room two is a medium-size room with an extra-long double bed and a large, private hall bath. Room three has a queen-size bed. There is a bathroom between rooms three and four. Room four, which has twin beds, can have a private bath at the opposite end of the house. Full breakfast. German spoken. Smoking allowed outside. No resident pets. Well-behaved children over 12 (swimmers) are welcome. Two-night minimum stay is required. $75-85.

278. In a handsome neighborhood on an acre in north central Scottsdale is a charming guest house with a bedroom/living room with queen-size bed, sofa bed, fully equipped kitchen, and full bath. Arcadia doors to pool. Contemporary furniture. Guests enjoy jogging or hiking along the nearby scenic canal. Walk to Hilton Village, public transportation. For short stays, breakfast items are stocked in the kitchen. For longer stays, self-catering. Smoking allowed outside only. Laundry facilities available. Children six and older who can swim are welcome. Two-night minimum stay is required. Ten dollars for each additional guest. $75.

301. Stone-front cozy guest cottage built in 1985 is opposite the main house with the pool in between. Full kitchen, private bath with shower, white tile floors, contemporary furniture, and well-maintained yard with flowering bushes. Twin beds or king-size bed and TV. Kitchen stocked with breakfast items first morning. Self-catering. Phone, water purifier, and air purifier. Near shopping centers and aquatic center. No smoking. Weekly, monthly, and summer rates are available. $70.

312. Enthusiastic, interesting, and lighthearted host couple invite guests to a luxury home, which has a beautifully landscaped back yard with a pool and citrus trees and is in the McCormick Ranch area of Scottsdale. The guest suite is at one end of the house with total privacy. The suite has a sitting area, queen-size bed, a large private luxury bath, and cable TV. From the sitting area, French doors open to a private patio with chaise lounges for relaxing. A full breakfast is served. No resident pets. Smoking allowed outside. German spoken. Minimum stay is two nights. $85.

327. A luxury 7,500-square-foot contemporary adobe home with panoramic mountain views in a quiet desert setting. The owner has spared no expense with this beautiful home and two guest casitas. Green lawns and palm trees surround the pool area. There is also a tiled, outdoor spa and private tennis court. Guest casita one has a bedroom with a king-size bed, a living room with TV and kiva fireplace, private bath, and kitchen. Guest casita two has a bedroom with a king-size bed, a living room with big screen TV and kiva fireplace, private bath, kitchen, and a steam room. The main house has two bedrooms, each with a queen-size bed and private bath. Full breakfast. No resident pets. Smoking allowed outside. One child ten or older is welcome in main house. Two-night minimum stay is required. $100-175.

328. Host welcomes guests to this spacious, contemporary luxury home near a lake on McCormick Ranch. Ultramodern decor. Guest rooms are at one end of the house. Host has a suite at the opposite end. Room one has a king-size bed and private bath. Room two has a queen-size bed and private bath. Private entrance through enclosed garage. Two pools are available: a lap pool and a game pool. Continental-plus breakfast is served. No resident pets. No children. No smoking. $100-150.

331. Handsome home with Southwestern decor in upscale area. Quiet, but close to shopping and restaurants. Near tennis courts, canal bank for jogging. Sociable couple enjoy the outdoors. Host knows Arizona well as he has explored little-known back roads and canyons. Hostess is a potter, using Native American methods of collecting clay and firing. The guest room has a queen-size bed and private bath. Guests are welcome to use large living room with TV. Host couple area is at opposite end of house. Full, healthy breakfasts. Resident dog. No smoking. No children. Open October 15 through May 1. $85.

6 Pets welcome; 7 Smoking allowed; 8 Children welcome; 9 Social drinking allowed; 10 Tennis available; 11 Swimming available; 12 Golf available; 13 Skiing available; 14 May be booked through travel agents.

Mi Casa Su Casa
(continued)

347. On a beautiful lake and golf course in well-maintained McCormick Ranch, this stucco home with red tile roof was built in 1977 with many windows looking out to the lake. Very large master guest room has lake view, four-poster queen-size bed with luxurious linens, private bath, walk-in closet, private entrance, cable TV, CD player, stereo, and telephone. Paddle boat available. Full breakfast. No resident pets. Smoking allowed outside. Minimum two nights. Ten percent discount for seniors staying a week. $75-85.

348. A homey, quiet, and comfortable bed and breakfast for guests who appreciate American country antiques. The hostess is an artist who always has great guest reviews. The guest room has a queen-size bed and private, full hall bath. Guests are welcome to use the family room with TV. Pool and laundry facilities are available. Hostess prepares guests' choice of breakfast. Friendly cat. Smoking allowed outside only. Children over 11 welcome. $45-55.

379. Hostess from New Zealand welcomes guests to the tranquil atmosphere and hospitality of this home in a quiet neighborhood near famous Camelback Mountain. This "home away from home" is convenient to downtown where art galleries, theaters, wonderful restaurants, and shopping abound. Breakfast is served in the lovely dining room overlooking the pool and yard. Enjoy waffles with strawberry sauce, delicious muffins and breads and/or cereals, omelets, fresh fruit, and natural health foods, all lovingly prepared. Room one has a double bed with private adjoining bath that includes a tub and shower. Room two has one twin bed with a private hall bath. Please reserve outdoor hot tub in advance for heating. Quiet surroundings make this a delightful break from the busy Scottsdale scene. Resident cat and dog. Two night minimum. $45-55.

380. Four-level condominium with white interior in a very nice complex one mile from Scottsdale Fashion Square. Room one has sitting area and private bath. Room two has a shared full bath. Community pool is heated except December through February. Full breakfast served. Two-night stay preferred. Children over nine. No pets. Outside smoking. $65-75.

384. This Santa Barbara-style home was built in 1993 in a quiet, gated residential community at the foot of scenic McDowell Mountains. Master bedroom is very large and has 11-foot cathedral ceilings, queen-size bed, white tile shower, and separate tub. Bedroom two is moderate size with queen-size bed and private bath. Living room with TV, light kitchen and laundry privileges. Heated swimming pool and spa at clubhouse. Full breakfast served. Two-night stay preferred. No children. No pets. No smoking. $75-125.

386. This spacious, trilevel condominium in a nice complex is in a parklike setting "close to everything." Furnishings are traditional and antique. Two blocks from large city park with bike and hiking trails. Near art galleries, Fifth Avenue, and Scottsdale Fashion Square. Air-conditioned. Room one is large bedroom/sitting room on first floor with private full bath eight steps up from bedroom level. King-size or twin beds, large walk-in closet, cable TV, and phone. Compact refrigerator, microwave in snack corner. Community pool is heated except in December, January, and February. FAX available. Full breakfast. Pets accepted with prior approval. $55-60.

Valley O' the Sun Bed and Breakfast

P.O. Box 2214, 85252
(602) 941-1281

In the college district of Tempe but still close enough to Scottsdale to enjoy the

---

NOTES: Credit cards accepted: A MasterCard; B Visa; C American Express; D Discover Card; E Diner's Club; F Other; 2 Personal checks accepted; 3 Lunch available; 4 Dinner available; 5 Open all year;

glamour of its shops, restaurants, and theaters. Valley O' the Sun Bed and Breakfast offers clean, comfortable rooms at reasonable and affordable rates.

Host: Kathleen Curtis
Rooms: 3 (1 PB; 2 SB) $35-40
Full and Continental Breakfast
Credit Cards: None
Notes: 5, 7, 8 (over 9), 9, 10, 11, 12, 13, 14

SEDONA

Bed and Breakfast Inn Arizona

P.O. Box 11253, Glendale, 85318-1253
(602) 561-0335; FAX (602) 561-2300

SE001. Charming cottages along the banks of Oak Creek. Quiet, soothing atmosphere. Full breakfast. Call for rates.

SE002. Elegant French-style country inn. Retreat to understated luxury and tranquility of genteel country life. Full breakfast. Call for rates.

SE003. This bed and breakfast has quiet and relaxing, award-winning architecture. Overlooks waterfalls. Beautiful antique furnishings. Scrumptious breakfast creations. Call for rates.

SE005. Old West ambience. Western movie location. Jacuzzi, fireplaces. Full breakfast and snacks. Call for rates.

SE006. Cabins amid the pines in Oak Creek Canyon. Magnificent scenery. Hiking and fishing. Call for rates.

SE007. Farmhouse nestled in the pines between the Sedona red rocks and Wild Horse Mesa. Bridle paths, hiking. Horse accommodations available. Full breakfast. Call for rates.

SE008. These deluxe cabins amid a lush forest setting feature private decks and kitchens. Magnificent scenery of the Oak Creek Canyon area. Call for rates.

SE009. Bed and breakfast near Red Rock Crossing. Swimming, hiking, and fishing. Breakfast included. Call for rates.

SE010. Elegant and rustic bed and breakfast. Handicapped accessible. Full breakfast and evening refreshments are served. Call for rates.

SE012. This new-age Sedona bed and breakfast features a hot tub and an outdoor BBQ. Gourmet breakfast is served. Quiet and casual atmosphere. Call for rates.

SE013. This rambling country inn with magnificent red rock views features a private deck. Full breakfast. Call for rates.

SE014. This cozy inn with country French antique decor features private entrances for the guest rooms and a convenient location. Call for rates.

SE015. Unique and elegant. Pool, spa, and private balconies with dramatic views of red rock country. Gourmet breakfast is served. Call for rates.

SE114. An artists' and photographers' favorite! Half-century-old historic ranch estate with magnificent red rock views. Beautiful gardens with spa and pool. Hostess serves a lavish Continental breakfast. Late afternoon refreshments are served, and a homemade goody is provided with turndown. View Suite has superb views, a canopied queen-size bed, rock fireplace, dressing room, and private bath. Rose Garden Room has king-size or twin beds, marble-topped nightstands, cozy rock fireplace, private bath, and

6 Pets welcome; 7 Smoking allowed; 8 Children welcome; 9 Social drinking allowed; 10 Tennis available; 11 Swimming available; 12 Golf available; 13 Skiing available; 14 May be booked through travel agents.

French doors opening onto a walled rose garden. Special occasion packages available. Two small resident dogs. Two-night minimum stay is required. Superior rates.

SE120. If one is looking for luxury in a commercial-style bed and breakfast, look no further than this exquisite ten-room gem between Sedona and Oak Creek. This Spanish-style home has private connecting bath with whirlpool tubs, private balconies or patios, and unrestricted views of the red rocks in each room. The gracious hosts provide a full breakfast, then treat guests to late afternoon refreshments by the pool. Can accommodate small parties. Special honeymoon packages. No pets. Children over ten welcome. No smoking. Superior rates.

SE121. Extraordinary bed and breakfast. A haven for relaxation, hospitality, and fantastic red rock views. Hearty Southwestern breakfast. Call for rates.

SE122. Ranch-style setting. Superb views. Queen-size beds, sitting rooms with fireplaces, and private baths. At the base of Castle Rock. Convenient location to golf, shops, and restaurants.

Briar Patch Inn

H-C 30, Box 1002, 86336
(602) 282-2342

Nestled in Oak Creek Canyon on nine lush creekside acres, this oasis is described by guests as a paradise. Summer mornings guests can breakfast by the creek with Bach and Mozart played by resident musicians. In the winter, cozy up to a favorite fireplace with a good book. Handcrafted cabins, Southwestern furnishings, and Native American crafts create relaxing and memorable moments. Discover Sedona's unique beauty: Indian ruins, hiking, galleries, and vortex energy. Close to the Grand Canyon and Navajo and Hopi Indians. A real gem!

Hosts: JoAnn and Ike Olson
Rooms: 16 (PB) $135-215
Full Breakfast
Credit Cards: A, B
Notes: 2, 5, 8, 9, 11, 12, 14

Canyon Villa Bed and Breakfast Inn

125 Canyon Circle Drive, 86351
(602) 284-1226; (800) 453-1166

Nestled among the red rocks of Sedona, this AAA four-diamond award bed and breakfast offers ten luxurious guest rooms with fantastic views and relaxing whirlpool tubs. Enjoy the gourmet breakfasts, fireplaces, and heated pool.

Hosts: Chuck and Marion Yadon
Rooms: 11 (PB) $95-175
Full Breakfast
Credit Cards: A, B
Notes: 2, 5, 10, 11, 12, 14

Casa Sedona

Casa Sedona

55 Hozoni Drive, 86336
(602) 282-2938; (800) 525-3756

Casa Sedona offers fabulous red-rock views from each of its 15 terraced guest rooms. Individually appointed to please and pamper guests, the rooms are spacious, luxurious, and include private baths, spa tubs, and a delightful fireplace. Guests are served a hearty Southwestern breakfast in a smoke-free environment (inside and out). On an acre of wooded grounds, Casa Sedona offers a tranquil, serene experience.

Hosts: Lori and Misty Zitko; Dick Curtis
Rooms: 15 (PB) $95-150
Full Breakfast
Credit Cards: A, B, D
Notes: 2, 5, 9, 10, 11, 12, 13, 14

The Cozy Cactus

80 Canyon Circle Drive, 86351-8678
(602) 284-0082; (800) 788-2082

Cozy Cactus Bed and Breakfast is at the foot of Castle Rock between Sedona's red rock cliffs and Wild Horse Mesa. Cozy Cactus is a ranch-style home comfortably furnished with family heirlooms and theatrical memorabilia. Each room has a private bath, and each pair of bedrooms shares a sitting room with a fireplace. Breakfasts are served in the great room. Guests have direct access into Coconino National Forest for hiking, bird watching, and photography.

Hosts: Bob and Lynne Gillman
Rooms: 5 (PB) $80-95
Full Breakfast
Credit Cards: A, B, C, D
Notes: 2, 5, 8, 9, 10, 11, 12, 13, 14

The Graham Bed and Breakfast Inn

150 Canyon Circle Drive, 86351
(602) 284-1425; (800) 228-1425
FAX (602) 284-0767

The Graham Inn is an impressive, contemporary Southwest inn with huge windows providing views of Sedona's famous red rock formations. Six guest rooms with private bath, TV, VCR, and balconies with red rock views. Some rooms have fireplaces and whirlpool tubs. Enjoy wonderful breakfasts, afternoon refreshments, pool, and Jacuzzi. Innkeepers give orientation program after breakfast.

Hosts: Roger and Carol Redenbaugh
Rooms: 6 (PB) $99-209
Full Breakfast
Cards: A, B, D
Notes: 2, 5, 8, 9, 10, 11, 12

The Lodge at Sedona

125 Kallof Place, 86336
(602) 204-1942; (800) 619-4467

"It's the nearest to heaven you'll come at 4,500 feet," wrote The Arizona Republic, when naming this lodge "Arizona's Best Bed and Breakfast Inn" in 1993. Elegantly rustic, it offers secluded privacy on two and one-half wooded acres with eleven guest rooms, two suites, and ample common rooms for guests' pleasure. The two-story lodge, accented with earthy, country pine antiques and red rock views, provides a comfortable and nurturing ambience. Some rooms have decks; one suite has a double Jacuzzi. A full gourmet breakfast is served on the morning porch, which offers peaceful outdoor views.

Hosts: Barb and Mark Dinunzio
Rooms: 13 (PB) $95-175
Full Breakfast
Credit Cards: A, B
Notes: 2, 5, 8, 10, 11, 12, 13, 14

Mi Casa Su Casa

P.O. Box 950, Tempe, 85281
(602) 990-0682; (800) 456-0682

309. Experience the ever-changing red rock vistas that surround this five-bedroom inn. Built in 1983, the inn is a triplex ranch-style house at the foot of Castle Rock. All bedrooms have large windows, queen-size beds, private baths, and their own unique furnishings and artwork. Each pair of bedrooms shares a sitting room featuring a fireplace and small kitchen. The fifth bedroom is in the main part of the triplex and has a private bath. Full breakfasts served in the great room at a large knotty pine table with view. Two small resident dogs. School-age children are welcome. Smoking allowed outside. Handicapped possible. Special rates for large groups. $70-90.

357. The hostess invites guests into her large one-story home where she has a suite on one side of the house. The Honeymoon Suite is entered from the living room and has a king-size bed; windows with a view of the red rocks, patio, and gardens; flagstone floor and private bath with a whirlpool tub. Entered from a hall near the front door are two guest rooms. Room two is decorated with Native American and Mexican arts and crafts, has a queen-size bed and connecting bath. Room three has twin beds, a small private balcony, family heirlooms, and a full hall bath. A full breakfast features gourmet recipes. Children ten and older are welcome. Smoking allowed outside. $90-115.

375. Contemporary stucco and tile home nestled into a rock slope. Built in 1993, it is in a peaceful, residential neighborhood with breathtaking views of the red rocks. Separate apartment with private entrance, deck, and sitting room. The bedroom, with its glorious views, has a queen-size bed and a lounging sofa. Featuring a well-stocked, fully equipped kitchen and laundry, full private bath, cable TV, and telephone. Two-night minimum stay. No children. No pets. No smoking. $70-75.

Rose Tree Inn

376 Cedar Street, 86336
(602) 282-2065

"The best kept secret in Sedona." Small, quaint, private, and quiet. Three units with fully furnished kitchenettes. Beautiful property in a lovely English garden environment. Within walking distance of Old Town. One hundred miles north of Phoenix; two and one-half hours to the Grand Canyon. Reservations a must.

Host: Rachel Gillespie
Rooms: 4 (PB) $82-116
Coffee and Tea in room
Credit Cards: A, B
Notes: 2, 5, 9, 10, 12, 14

Slide Rock Lodge and Cabins

Star Route 3 Box 1141, 86336
(602) 282-3531

Six miles north of Sedona in Oak Creek Canyon. Parklike setting against red rock cliffs. Family owned and operated. Twenty rustic, well-maintained rooms with showers; some have fireplaces. Four special cabins for couples only with kitchen, fireplaces, and whirlpool tubs. Cabins are nonsmoking inside and out. No TV, phones, or pets. Picnic area with grills. Creek swimming. Away from bustle of Sedona but close enough to enjoy all town benefits. The hostess goes out of her way to plan guests' stay. Nonsmoking rooms are available in the lodge.

Host: Milena Pfeifer
Rooms: 20 (PB) $55-80
Cabins: 4 (PB) $115-125
Continental Breakfast
Credit Cards: A, B
Notes: 2, 5, 7, 8, 9, 10, 11, 12, 13

A Touch of Sedona Bed and Breakfast

595 Jordan Road, 86336
(602) 282-6462; FAX (602) 282-1534

In historic uptown, this California ranch-style inn is within easy walking distance of shops, galleries, restaurants, and the Sedona Art Center, and playhouse. The eclectic elegance features stained glass, antiques, and contemporary furnishings and art. Beautiful red rock views and sensational stargazing from the deck. Private baths. Generous hospitality, multi-course gourmet breakfasts with home-baked goodies. Quiet, residential area is also near forest service trails. Smoke-free environment. No pets. AAA three-diamond rating. ABBA three-crown rating.

Hosts: Bill and Sharon Larsen
Rooms: 5 (PB) $85-135
Full Breakfast
Credit Cards: A, B
Notes: 5, 9, 10, 11, 12, 14

NOTES: Credit cards accepted: A MasterCard; B Visa; C American Express; D Discover Card; E Diner's Club; F Other; 2 Personal checks accepted; 3 Lunch available; 4 Dinner available; 5 Open all year;

SIERRA VISTA

Mi Casa Su Casa
P.O. Box 950, Tempe, 85281
(602) 990-0682; (800) 456-0682

362. This bed and breakfast is a secluded two-story ranch house and separate guest casita on five acres in a quiet, rural area within walking distance of the historic San Pedro River. The Casita Room has Mexican decor, is across the patio from the main house, and has a large room with a private entrance, queen-size bed, private bath, microwave, and refrigerator. Guests are welcome to use the common room to read, watch TV, play cards, or use the pool table. There is a shaded courtyard, walled patio area, hot tub, and pool. Two additional guest rooms are also available. Full breakfast. Resident outside dog. Children 12 and older are welcome. Smoking allowed outside. Guests preferred Friday through Monday, but exceptions can be made. Roll away bed available. Seven dollars for third person. $60-65.

Old Pueblo Homestays
P.O. Box 13603, Tucson, 85732
(800) 333-9 RSO

San Pedro Bed and Breakfast. This secluded two-story ranch house with a separate guest casita is in a quiet, rural area on five acres surrounded by rolling hills and towering cottonwood trees. Perfect setting for bird watching, hiking, or sightseeing. The guest house has a private entrance, queen-size bed, bath with shower only, microwave, and refrigerator. The common room provides a TV/VCR, pool table, card table, and small library. Shaded garden courtyard, walled patio area, pool, and spa. Southwestern breakfast. Minimum two nights. No pets. Children over 12 welcome. No smoking inside. Seven dollars each additional person. $60-65.

SONOITA

Bed and Breakfast Inn Arizona
P.O. Box 11253, Glendale, 85318-1253
(602) 561-0335; FAX (602) 561-2300

SN001. Luxurious accommodation on a working cattle ranch. In a land of beautiful views. Pool, tennis court. Continental breakfast. Call for rates.

Mi Casa Su Casa
P.O. Box 950, Tempe, 85280-0950
(602) 990-0682; (800) 456-0682

1623. This working ranch offers luxury accommodations in Arizona's high grass country. There are facilities for 16 people in both the main house and guest house, and sizes of beds range from king-size to twin. For those wanting more privacy, the entire house can be rented. Ranch is next to the National Forest, foothills, and Santa Rita Mountains. Guests are not waited on hand and foot, because the hosts believe that most people want privacy, seclusion, and the freedom to choose their own mealtimes. Kitchen privileges, partial maid service, bed linens, pool, and tennis court are all available. Self-serve Continental breakfast. Minimum stay is two nights. $75-300.

SPRINGERVILLE

Mi Casa Su Casa
P.O. Box 950, Tempe, 85280-0950
(602) 990-0682; (800) 456-0682

325. Carefully restored Colonial Revival home circa 1910 allows a visitor to step back in time. Enjoy antiques such as an original soda fountain, two old, operable jukeboxes, and Coca-Cola signs. Four bedrooms with private baths are furnished with antiques, handmade quilts, and goosedown pillows. Full breakfast is served with antique crystal, china, and table linens. Smoking outside only. $65-75.

TEMPE

Bed and Breakfast Inn Arizona

P.O. Box 11253, Glendale, 85318-1253
(602) 561-0335; FAX (602) 561-2300

TE104. This gentle, old home is in the heart of Tempe, close to the airport and ASU. The hosts have created a new addition to their 50-year-old home with guests' comfort in mind. Twin or king-size beds, private entrance, and private, connecting bath. There is also a sitting area with sofa bed for extra guest. French door opens onto a patio. Citrus trees on the property mean fresh juice in season with gourmet breakfast. Library wall, TV, small refrigerator, and microwave oven available. Sweet, old dog in house. Infants or children over seven welcome. Deluxe rates.

Mi Casa Su Casa

P.O. Box 950, 85250-0950
(602) 990-0682; (800) 456-0682

131. Comfortable home in nice, quiet neighborhood minutes from ASU, Mesa Community College, large shopping malls, and adult recreation centers. Near restaurants, churches, and public transportation. Large, sunny master bedroom has king-size bed, connecting bath, TV, VCR, glass doors to the pool, and patio area. Second bedroom has double bed, shares hall bath with host couple. Full breakfast might include homemade bagels and muffins. Children over eight who can swim are welcome. Smoking allowed outside. No resident pets. Ten dollars for children. Rates for stays over two weeks are negotiable. $45-65.

290. Single-family residence near public transportation to Phoenix, Mesa, and ASU. Many golf courses, tennis and handball courts, and fitness centers in the vicinity. One room has a queen-size bed, TV, and private hall bath. Another room features a double bed and shares a bath with the other room. The lower-level family room has a sofa bed and private bath for use. Full breakfast is served. No smoking. Minimum stay is two nights. $40-55.

314. This bed and breakfast is in an older, quiet, well-kept neighborhood two blocks from ASU and downtown Tempe. The main house was built in 1939 and is typical of the "cottage" architecture of that time. A new 475-square-foot addition with a private entrance onto the patio blends well with the old house. This area consists of large, open space with sitting room/bedroom with TV, VCR, microwave, and small refrigerator. The private bath has a whirlpool tub. King-size or twin beds, and queen-size sofa bed. Resident outside dog who is willing to share fenced area with a guest dog. Smoking allowed outside. Infants are welcome; Port-a-crib available. Minimum stay is two nights. Ten dollars for third and fourth persons. $65.

TOMBSTONE

Bed and Breakfast Inn Arizona

P.O. Box 11253, Glendale, 85318-1253
(602) 561-0335; FAX (602) 561-2300

TM102. This 1880 Adobe house is in the heart of Old Tombstone. Rooms furnished with antiques and collectibles. Hearty breakfast in country kitchen. Call for rates.

Mi Casa Su Casa

P.O. Box 950, Tempe, 85281
(602) 990-0682; (800) 456-0682

NOTES: Credit cards accepted: A MasterCard; B Visa; C American Express; D Discover Card; E Diner's Club; F Other; 2 Personal checks accepted; 3 Lunch available; 4 Dinner available; 5 Open all year;

330. Personable, friendly host couple have carefully restored these historic buildings built around 1880. There are two white stucco buildings: the main house and the "miner's cabin." The hardwood floors have been refinished and each room is decorated in a simple, authentic 1890 western motif. The parlor is furnished in Victorian style and has a baby grand piano and a TV. There are six guest rooms in the main house, each with a private entrance. The seventh room is in the miner's cabin. Most rooms have private baths. A full breakfast is served in a large dining room. Well-behaved children are welcome. No resident pets. Smoking allowed outside. $45-65.

Old Pueblo Homestays

P.O. Box 13603, Tucson, 85732
(800) 333-9RS0

Priscilla's Bed and Breakfast. This is Tombstone's only remaining two-story clapboard country Victorian house, built in 1904. Immaculately restored, the house has all the original wood and still has some of the original gas lighting fixtures as well as a large oak staircase. The three rooms upstairs are tastefully decorated to fit the era reminiscent of grandma's house. The Primrose, Violet, and Rose rooms have double beds, sinks, and vanities. Breakfast is served on a lace-covered oak table, and home-baked breads complete the atmosphere of earlier days. Across the street from Arizona's first Protestant church, built in 1876. Smoking is limited. $35-55.

Tombstone Boarding House. Two 1880 adobe houses surrounded by an 1880-style picket fence. The first house, built by the town's first banker, was remodeled and enlarged in early 1930. The second house was the original Barrows House where legend has it that in the 1880s the notorious Buckskin Frank Leslie roomed. In the 1930s renowned artist H.E. Wenck built a studio addition with a large picture window and a

spectacular view of the surrounding mountains and Sheep's Head. A hearty breakfast is served in a sunny, antique-filled country kitchen. Each of six rooms furnished with antiques features a private entrance and bath. Children are welcome. Smoking permitted outside only. $45-75.

TUCSON

Bed and Breakfast Inn Arizona

P.O. Box 11253, Glendale, 85318-1253
(602) 561-0335; FAX (602) 561-2300

TU002. This ranch inn sits on the slopes of the Tucson Mountains. Extensive natural desert grounds and 30 acres of pristine chaparral country. Fantastic amenities including pool and spa. Close to all attractions. Continental breakfast. Call for rates.

TU003. Adobe home in the quiet central foothills of Tucson. Private entrances, Jacuzzi, and Continental breakfast. Great mountain views. Call for rates.

TU004. Unique inn with massive beams. Great for nature lovers. Kitchens, patios, and pools. Close to Arizona-Sonora Desert Museum and Old Tucson. Call for rates.

TU006. This Southwestern hacienda features private, scenery, and solitude. Pool, courtyard with fountain, and beautiful views. Full breakfast is served.

TU007. In quiet residential neighborhood encompassing Santa Fe-style decor, this bed and breakfast was built in 1930 as Clark Gable's getaway home. Features king-size beds, spa, and a Continental breakfast. Call for rates.

6 Pets welcome; 7 Smoking allowed; 8 Children welcome; 9 Social drinking allowed; 10 Tennis available; 11 Swimming available; 12 Golf available; 13 Skiing available; 14 May be booked through travel agents.

Bed and Breakfast
Inn Arizona
(continued)

TU010. Unique territorial inn, whose innkeeper and host is a retired travel agent with extensive knowledge of who, what, when, and where. Walking distance to shopping, museums, etc. Gourmet breakfast. Call for rates.

TU011. Elegant inn built in the 1902s in the heart of the city. Walking distance to University of Arizona and University Hospital. Call for rates.

TU102. Luxurious, contemporary 1,100-square-foot guest house with solar-heated pool, patio, and gorgeous views of the Santa Catalina Mountains. Near golf course. Full kitchen, breakfast bar, stone fireplace, king-size bed, one twin bed, TV, and own telephone. Private bath and entrance. Garage space for guest vehicle. Wheelchair accommodations. Full breakfast served on weekends by Swedish hostess. Hostess works outside the home, so weekday breakfast fixings are left in guest kitchen. Cat in residence. Deluxe to superior rates.

TU109. Enjoy the mountain views while soaking in the Jacuzzi or pool; these can be heated for additional charge. Two suites, which may be used together for large party. One suite has washer/dryer, kitchen stocked with groceries for guests to fix their own breakfast. Private entrance, hall bath with shower. Bedroom with king-size bed, twin bed in the Arizona Room, and queen-size Hide-a-bed in living room. Children over 16 accepted in this suite with parents. Smoking is allowed in this suite. The second suite has Continental breakfast. Private entrance, two bedrooms with double beds, hall bath with tub and shower. No smoking

in this suite. Resident dog and cat; guest pets are welcome. Deluxe rates.

TU114. This small ranch high in the Sonoran Desert foothills above the city is a bird watcher's paradise, and home to fowl, horses, well-behaved dogs, and peaceful cats. Enjoy a full ranch breakfast on the patio with fountain and birds. Private guest room with Ben Franklin stove, private bathroom (shower), and patio. Sleeping accommodations include a queen-size bed, two twins, and a single roll away if needed for children. Crib also available. Color TV, radio, tape player, phone, snack refrigerator, books, and games. Jacuzzi and pool. Children are welcome. Deluxe rates.

TU119. A Southwestern-style home in downtown Tucson with a choice of three rooms: the Cabana, which has a double bed and private bath; the Studio, which is a private apartment with double bed and complete kitchen; and the Governor's Room, which has a queen-size antique bed, private bath, and sitting area with fireplace. Pool and patio. Full breakfast, racquet club privileges, and a sophisticated, warm atmosphere make this well worth the rates. Dog and cats in residence. Superior rates.

TU120. This fascinating rammed-earth pueblo-style home with a stupendous view of the Santa Catalina Mountains in the northern part of the city is hosted by a tour guide. Grandmother's heirloom guest room has a queen-size bed, private hall bath, and guests are welcome to the great room with TV and VCR. Second bedroom is available for additional guests in same party, but they will need to share hall bath with first bedroom. Redwood deck for relaxing and watching the wildlife, and a hot tub will complete the stay. If guests cannot escape work, there is a desk and telephone available. Continental breakfast. Two small dogs. No children. Deluxe rates; weekly rates for longer stays.

TU121. Tucson's premier corporate retreat, nestled on over four acres against the Santa Catalina Mountains. Each room reflects host's favorite international hotels. Heated pool, patio, magnificent views, and polished, professional service make this a most sophisticated, yet comfortably intimate bed and breakfast. Full breakfast. Each room has a private bath, TV, VCR, phone, terry-cloth robes, and all the amenities one would expect in a world-class bed and breakfast. The Oriental Room has a queen-size bed, private Jacuzzi, and Oriental furnishings. The Regent has a queen-size bed and French doors that open onto the patio. The Four Seasons has a queen-size canopied bed and warm mahogany furnishings. The Cannaught has Chippendale furniture and an accent non-working fireplace. Closely supervised children welcome. Minimum two-night stay is required. Superior rates.

TU122. This private home is a real classic in the Craftsman tradition. The sparkling hostess presides over a full breakfast. There is a guest parlor with TV and VCR. Pool and patio in the back. Off-street parking available. The home is decorated with antique furnishings. The Amethyst Room has an antique queen-size bed, the original Victorian wallpaper, and a private hall bath with original claw-foot tub. The Saguaro Room is decorated with a lodgepole queen-size bed, armoire, table and chairs, cozy fireplace, and private bath. The Spanish Room has a queen-size bed and private bath. The Rose Quartz Room has one twin and one double bed, a private bath, and French doors that open onto the living room area (some traffic noise in this room). No children. Deluxe to superior rates.

TU123. Privacy, magnificent views, pool, patio, and desert surroundings in this delightful Southwestern-style guest house. Two bedrooms (only one guest party at a time), full kitchen and bath, and private entrance into a finely detailed, handcrafted guest house complete with handpainted Mexican tiles and custom Southwestern cabinetry. The Catalina Room has a queen-size bed, desk, sitting area; the Patio Room has twins, rustic rawhide table and chairs, and French doors onto the patio. Telephones, TV, and VCR are all in the guest house, and the hostess leaves full breakfast fixings for guests to self-cater when they feel like getting up. Bikes available for the adventurous. No children under five. Dog and cats in main house. Two-night minimum stay. Superior rates.

Casa Alegre
Bed and Breakfast Inn

316 East Speedway, 85705
(602) 628-1800

This distinguished 1915 home is between the University of Arizona and downtown Tucson. A scrumptious full breakfast is served in the formal dining room or poolside on the serene patio. Casa Alegre allows easy access to Tucson's many historic, cultural, and recreational attractions, state and national parks, as well as great shopping and fantastic eateries.

Host: Phyllis Florek
Rooms: 4 (PB) $70-95
Full Breakfast
Credit Cards: A, B, D
Notes: 2, 5, 9, 10, 11, 12, 14

Casa Tierra Adobe
Bed and Breakfast Inn

11155 West Calle Pima, 85743
(602) 578-3058

Casa Tierra is on five acres of beautiful Sonoran desert 30 minutes west of Tucson. This secluded area has hundreds of saguaro cactus, spectacular mountain views, and brilliant sunsets. The rustic adobe house features entryways with vaulted brick ceilings, an interior arched courtyard, Mexican furnishings, and a Jacuzzi overlooking the desert. Great hiking and birding. Near Arizona-Sonora Desert Museum, Saguaro National Monument, and Old Tucson.

Hosts: Karen and Lyle Hymer-Thompson
Rooms: 3 (PB) $75-85
Full Breakfast
Credit Cards: None
Notes: 2, 8, 9

Catalina Park Inn

309 East First Street, 85705
(602) 792-4541; (800) 792-4885
FAX (602) 792-0838

Overlooking Catalina Park, this historic residence affords you an environment of understated elegance. All rooms are handsomely furnished with antiques. Some have private porches. All have a private bath. Perfect for a romantic getaway, honeymoon, or just for a chance to relax. A sumptuous extended Continental breakfast is delivered to the room. Enjoy our lush Mediterranean garden. Superb location in the West University Historic District, just blocks from the University of Arizona and Fourth Avenue's eclectic shops and restaurants. Minimum stay requirements during some periods.

Hosts: Mark Hall and Paul Richard
Rooms: 3 (PB) $67.50-130
Continental Breakfast
Cards: A, B
Notes: 2, 5, 7 (limited), 8 (over 10), 9, 10, 11, 12, 13, 14

June's Bed and Breakfast

3212 West Holladay Street, 85746
(602) 578-0857

This Tucson Mountain hideaway features a magnificent view and a friendly hostess who is an artist.

Host: June Henderson
Rooms: 3 (1 PB; 2 SB) $45-55
Continental Breakfast
Credit Cards: None
Notes: 2, 5, 9, 10, 11, 12, 13

The Lodge on the Desert

306 North Alvernon Way, 85711
(602) 325-3366; (800) 456-5634
FAX (602) 327-5834

A small resort hotel providing the finest in food and accommodations. The lodge has been under the same family ownership for more than 50 years. Close to golf, tennis, and shopping. One-half hour from Arizona-Sonora Desert Museum, Old Tucson movie location, Coronado National Forest. Three miles from the University of Arizona. Pool on the premises.

Host: Schuyler W. Lininger
Rooms: 40 (PB) $58-177
Continental Breakfast
Credit Cards: A, B, C, D, E
Notes: 2, 3, 4, 5, 6 (by arrangement), 7, 8, 9, 10, 11, 12, 14

Mi Casa Su Casa

P.O. Box 950, Tempe, 85281
(602) 990-0682; (800) 456-0682

038. Townhouse in a quiet area with attractive desert trees, plants, and mountain and city views. Near La Paloma, Sabino Canyon. Guest room has a king-size bed, TV, and private bath. Pool adjacent to the house is available during the summer and a nearby pool is heated in the winter. Near tennis courts and resort golf courses. Continental-plus breakfast. No resident pets. Smoking allowed outside. No children. Two-night minimum. $45-65.

142. Guests describe this architect-designed 1,100-square-foot guest cottage as a home away from home. Next to 127 acres of natural desert, and near the Catalina Mountain Foothills and Sabino Canyon. The guest house has a patio, comfortable living room with a double sofa bed, TV, and private phone. There is a full kitchen, washer and dryer, and dining area. The bedroom has twin beds and connecting bath. The kitchen is stocked for short stays. For longer stays, breakfast is not included.

NOTES: Credit cards accepted: A MasterCard; B Visa; C American Express; D Discover Card; E Diner's Club; F Other; 2 Personal checks accepted; 3 Lunch available; 4 Dinner available; 5 Open all year;

Smoking allowed outside. Children over eight who are swimmers welcome. Fifteen dollars for third person. Special weekly and monthly rates. Three-night minimum stay is required. $65-75.

175. Built in 1886 amid other historic mansions, this inn has been featured in books and articles. The charming Carriage House has a living room/kitchen, bedroom with queen-size bed, and private bath. In the main house, the Gate House suite has a living room/bedroom with a queen-size bed, Pullman kitchen, private bath, and private entrance. The Victorian Suite has a bedroom with queen-size bed, private bath, and a large sitting room. The Quilt Room has a double bed and private bath. Full gourmet breakfasts. Smoking allowed outside. No resident pets. Children age 15 and older are welcome. Two-night minimum stay with exception of the Carriage House, which has a three-night minimum stay. $65-105.

212. Attached but separate architect-designed, very large, charming guest cottage with private patio in the Catalina Mountain Foothills. Many windows look out on the beautiful pool and yard. The furnishings include contemporary furniture with Southwestern and Scandinavian accents. Living room/bedroom has fireplace, king-size bed, one twin bed, full kitchen, and large private bath. For short stays, the kitchen is stocked, and guests serve themselves during the week. Full breakfasts are served on the weekends. Well-behaved children who can swim are welcome. Three-night minimum. Resident dog in main house. Smoking allowed outside. Monthly rate available. Weekly rates do not include breakfast. $85.

223. Imagine being able to ski on Mt. Lemmon in the morning and sun by the pool in the afternoon! Tranquil home and separate guest house have panoramic view of the city and the mountains surrounding Tucson. Two guest rooms in main house have private baths and TVs. One has a queen-size bed, the other has a pair of extra-long twin beds. Guests are welcome to use large living room. The three-room guest cottage has a living room with queen-size sofa bed, TV, fireplace, bedroom with queen-size bed, hall bath, full kitchen, and private courtyard. Full breakfast is served in the main house. Two small resident dogs. Smoking allowed outside. No children. Three-night minimum stay in guest cottage. $85-120.

243. Brick house built in 1947 has an eclectic, comfortable decor. In a quiet neighborhood about two miles from University of Arizona and three miles from downtown business district. Room one has a king-size bed, private bath, and private entrance. Room two has a queen-size bed and a shared hall bath. Continental-plus breakfast served. Infants welcome. Pets welcome with prior approval. Resident cats live in hosts' area. Outside smoking. $45-65.

276. An adobe bed and breakfast with central courtyard and rustic charm reminiscent of haciendas found in central Mexico. Join the hosts in their serene desert living, birding, and hiking. The three guest rooms have queen-size beds, private baths, private entrances, and patios. Two nights preferred. Full breakfast is served. Resident dogs and cats. Smoking allowed outside only. Children are welcome. Roll away and crib available for $10. $60-75.

277. Handsome two-level home in the Catalina Foothills is near Sabino Canyon with its spectacular mountain tram tour. Four guest rooms are decorated with American antiques and Southwestern furnishings, and all have their own entrance coming from the pool-patio area. Private and shared baths. Continental and full breakfast. $55-65.

6 Pets welcome; 7 Smoking allowed; 8 Children welcome; 9 Social drinking allowed; 10 Tennis available; 11 Swimming available; 12 Golf available; 13 Skiing available; 14 May be booked through travel agents.

Mi Casa Su Casa
(continued)

280. This charming hostess welcomes guests to her Santa Fe-style patio home, built in 1993, in a quiet north central area. Beautiful, unobstructed views of the mountains. Landscaped back yard with desert plantings. Access to community pool. Room one has twin beds, private hall bath, and private patio. Available for two-week or longer stays is the master bedroom with a queen-size bed, connecting private bath, and private patio. Guests are welcome to enjoy the living room with fireplace. Laundry privileges. Enclosed garage. Full breakfast served. Smoking allowed outside. Children over three are welcome. $45-60.

304. Luxury townhouse in a beautifully landscaped green area is near malls, theaters, good restaurants, and 20 minutes from the university. One very large room has a king-size bed, TV, phone, and a connecting full bath. Heated pool, spa, and tennis court in complex. Complimentary refreshments and Continental breakfast. No resident pets. No smoking. Three-night minimum. $90.

310. Panoramic view of the ever-changing Catalina Mountains in a quiet country setting. Many articles have been written about this spacious, passive-solar environmentally designed Santa Fe-style home. All homes in the area are on one- or two-acre lots, so guests might see roadrunners, hummingbirds, or quail. Golf and tennis nearby. Room one has a queen-size bed. Room two has twin beds or king-size bed. Full hall bath is private to guests. The master bedroom has a view, fireplace, queen-size bed, and private bath. Spa. Continental breakfast. Two small, resident dogs. Smoking allowed outside. No children. $60-85.

316. Warm, outgoing hostess welcomes guests to a delightfully restored two-story home built around 1900 in a quiet, well-kept neighborhood near the University of Arizona. On the first floor, room one has a queen-size bed, sitting area, and a private bath. Room two on the second floor has a canopied double bed and shares the hall bath. Light kitchen privileges available. Near public transportation. Continental-plus breakfast is served. No resident pets. Children welcome. $45-65.

326. Host couple welcome guests to their large stucco home built in 1990 in a resort community north of the Catalina foothills. The back yard adjoins state open range, which is nice for hiking and bird watching. Twenty-four miles from downtown Tucson. Available are a club house with restaurant, tennis courts, 18-hole golf course, two heated swimming pools, driving range, health club with spa. Guests have private use of the living room with fireplace, dining room, and den. Room one has a king-size bed or twin beds and a private full bath. Room two has a queen-size sofa bed for additional members of the party and shares the hall bath. Full breakfast is served. No resident pets. Children welcome. Guest pets welcome by arrangement. Smoking permitted. Weekly rates are available. Closed May 1 through October 1. $35-75.

343. Near the University of Arizona is a 1915 Craftsman-style bungalow with mahogany and leaded glass, built-in cabinetry, and hardwood floors. The hostess enjoys helping guests discover the special offerings of the region. The four guest rooms have private baths and their decor reflects facets of Tucson's history. One guest room has twin beds. Tasty, full breakfasts. Restful patio and pool. No resident pets. Children ten and older are welcome. Smoking allowed outside. Discount rates June 1 through September 1. $65-80.

NOTES: Credit cards accepted: A MasterCard; B Visa; C American Express; D Discover Card; E Diner's Club; F Other; 2 Personal checks accepted; 3 Lunch available; 4 Dinner available; 5 Open all year;

351. Enjoy the unobstructed spectacular views of the Saguaro National Monument East and a sweeping valley going up to the mountains. Near the airport and downtown Tucson. Separate but attached apartment has a private entrance, living room with trundle beds that can be made into two single beds or a king-size bed, TV, and VCR. Bedroom with queen-size bed has a full bath. In the large main house, the guest room has a queen-size bed and private hall bath. Apartment has enclosed patio with spa. For short stays, the kitchen is stocked. For longer stays, self-catering. Children over nine welcome. Smoking allowed outside. Resident cat and dog. French spoken. Apartment rented by the month. $55-65.

354. At the northeastern edge of Tucson is a mini-ranch of five acres with wonderful views of the Catalina Mountains. The main house and guest area are separated by a patio. Nearby are the Coronado and the Saguaro national forests. Guest area has a private entrance, queen-size bed, two single (trundle) beds, private bath, refrigerator, TV, library of bird and western lore, private patio. Pool and spa. Full ranch breakfast. Children two and older welcome. Smoking allowed outside. Ten dollars additional for children. $45-55.

355. Guests are welcome to use common room with cable TV, VCR, and fireplace. Light kitchen privileges, grill, outside spa, laundry facilities, and cordless telephones in rooms. Roll away and cot available for small additional fee. The Quail's Nest Honeymoon Suite has views, private porch, queen-size bed, TV, fireplace, and private bath with double whirlpool tub. The Cactus Wren has views, double bed, private bath with whirlpool tub, and TV. Continental-plus and full breakfasts. Well-behaved children are welcome. Smoking allowed outside only. Resident pets. Handicapped possible. Two-night minimum. $65-85.

361. Host couple welcome guests to this luxury, contemporary home with 80-mile views in northeast Tucson. Location offers the quiet of the desert, but is convenient to all of Tucson's cultural activities and superb restaurants. Inside, guests will find terra cotta tiles, Oriental rugs, fresh flowers, and a sense of serenity. Private guest suite has a bedroom with queen-size bed, spacious private bath, separate reading room with sofa, desert library, TV, and telephone. Full breakfast. No resident pets. No children. No smoking. $95.

371. Secluded desert setting on over three acres of native plants and trees with panoramic mountain views of the Catalinas and Rincons. Private guest wing has two bedrooms, a sitting room with TV, telephone, and a utility room with washer and dryer. Both rooms have queen-size beds and private baths. Exercise room and pool available. Traditional breakfasts are featured, as well as low-fat, gluten free, and vegetarian diets. Children over six welcome. No pets. Smoking allowed outside only. $75-85.

372. This beautiful, spacious adobe-style home in fashionable north Tucson offers mountain views and an overview of Tucson. Large room has a king-size bed, plus a sofa that converts to a double bed. Large bath with walk-in closet. Sliding glass doors lead to garden and pool. Continental-plus breakfast provided. Two-night stay preferred. Children over ten welcome. No pets. Smoking allowed outside only. $65-70.

378. This home is decorated in an eclectic style, incorporating African carvings and art, American Indian arts and crafts, an art collection, and antique china—reflecting years of world travel. Private, newly remodeled guest area has two rooms. Room one has a double pull-down bed. Room two is a sitting room that has two trundle beds.

6 Pets welcome; 7 Smoking allowed; 8 Children welcome; 9 Social drinking allowed; 10 Tennis available; 11 Swimming available; 12 Golf available; 13 Skiing available; 14 May be booked through travel agents.

Mi Casa Su Casa
(continued)

There is a shared bath. Private entrance with small garden, private telephone, and laundry facilities available. Room three is very large with a queen-size bed, library, and private hall bath. Full breakfast is served. Well-behaved children welcome. Resident cat. Small pet with prior approval. No smoking. $45-65.

388. Handsome, extra-large ranch-style home in quiet, residential neighborhood. Guest suite with three rooms has private entry, sitting room, bedroom with queen-size bed, and private bath. Guest house has private entrance, large living/dining/sleeping room, kitchenette, and bathroom. Two-night minimum in guest house. Children in guest house only. Pets with prior approval. No smoking or alcohol. $55-75.

1625. Here at this guest and working ranch, some activities include cookouts, rodeos, team-roping, and steer wrestling. Riding instruction is also available. The heated pool and the indoor redwood hot tub are also popular with guests. Children will enjoy the petting zoo. Rates include all meals, hayrides, and all ranch activities. All rooms have private baths, and most rooms have double beds. Deluxe suites have a fireplace, whirlpool tub, king-size bed, and roll away bed is available. Laundry facilities. Families are welcome. No smoking in dining room. Free airport transportation. Closed May 1 through October 1. Four-night minimum. Children under two stay at no charge. Seventy-nine dollars for third person in room. $125-134.

Natural Bed and Breakfast

3150 East Presidio Road, 85716
(602) 881-4582

At Natural Bed and Breakfast, the word "natural" is true in all senses of the word. Attention is paid to a natural, non-toxic and non-allergenic environment. For example, this home is water cooled rather than air-conditioned, and only natural foods are served. Shoes are not worn inside. The natural home environment is very nurturing. Professional massage is available. Guests are invited to share the large, homey living room with fireplace.

Host: Marc Habermon
Rooms: 3 (2 PB; 1 SB) $55-65
Full Breakfast
Credit Cards: None
Notes: 2, 5, 8, 9, 10, 11, 12, 13, 14

Old Pueblo Homestays

P.O. Box 13603, 85732
(800) 333-9 RSO

Adobe House. This home is in the foothills between the Santa Catalina Mountains and midtown Tucson. Private bath and sitting room with TV and radio. Outside is a covered porch complete with swing and a patio. Beautiful mountain views can be enjoyed during the day. Continental breakfast served outside, weather permitting, including freshly squeezed juice. Minimum stay is two nights. No children. Smoking outside only. $60.

The Antik House Bed and Breakfast. This lovely territorial home in northeast Tucson reflects the travels of the hosts in the Orient and in Europe. Enjoy mountain views with pool-side full or Continental breakfast. One room with king-size bed overlooking pool/patio area with radio, color TV, and private bath and entrance. Other room with twin beds, radio, and shared hall bath. Close to a bus stop, Sabino Canyon, Restaurant Row, shopping, and hiking. Bicycles available. Hosts have two small poodles. Two-night minimum. Smoking outside only. Children over 12 welcome. No pets. $45-65.

NOTES: Credit cards accepted: A MasterCard; B Visa; C American Express; D Discover Card; E Diner's Club; F Other; 2 Personal checks accepted; 3 Lunch available; 4 Dinner available; 5 Open all year;

Bonnie's Bed and Breakfast. A large ranch decorated in traditional and romantic style offers a three-room suite and a fully-furnished guest cottage. The suite has a queen-size bed, private bath and entrance, and close parking. The one-room guest cottage has a double bed and two twin beds, and a kitchenette. A full breakfast is served in front of the fireplace, in the back yard, or in guests' room. Within walking distance of a mall, church, library, business district, and restaurants. Christian videos, books, and tapes available. Children and pets welcome in cottage only for a five-dollar charge. No single men accepted. Smoking outside only. $45-75.

Car-Mar's Southwest. Attractive bed and breakfast in a quiet country setting with courtyards and pathways accentuated by native desert landscaping and wildlife feeders. There are four suites, each uniquely and romantically inspired by the rustic charm of lodgepole and saguaro rib furniture. Perfect setting for weddings and parties. Pool, spa, TV/VCR, refrigerator, microwave, and barbecue patio. Full breakfast. Smoking outside only. Inquire about children. No pets. $65-125.

La Casita. Townhouse set in lush desert growth area. Hostess is a former travel agent. One room with a king-size waterbed and private bath. Pool adjacent to the house for enjoyment in the hot summer, and another pool is heated during the winter. Jacuzzi is heated year-round. Continental breakfast. Near La Paloma, Vantana Canyons, and resort golf courses. Minimum stay is two nights. $55-65.

The Cat and Whistle Bed and Breakfast. Newly remodeled block home built in the late 1950s in a quiet east side neighborhood. In addition to decorations in quasi-Southwestern fashion, the home incorporates African- and Native American carvings and art. The suite features a double Murphy bed, a trundle bed in the sitting room for children, air conditioneing, private bath, and separate entrance. There is a queen-size bedroom in the residence, cooled by evaporative cooler. A full breakfast is served. Walking distance of a church and excellent restaurants. Resident cat. No smoking. Children over three welcome. Children charged an additional rate, as well as pets placed in the kennel. Weekly rates also available for the suite. $45-70.

Cloud House. Southwestern Territorial home nestled in the Catalina foothills above the city. A blend of Southwestern furnishings tastefully decorate the three bedrooms. TV and VCR in the family room. The stereo is by the fireplace in the living room. The Quails Nest Master Honeymoon Suite includes private porch, queen-size bed, down comforter, and fireplace. The Cactus Wren Bedroom has city lights and double bed with Jacuzzi tub. The Coyote's Den is a secluded private studio with a separate entry, queen-size bed, three-quarter bath with large shower, and a minikitchen with a refrigerator and microwave oven. Guests can enjoy their breakfast in the dining room or privately in their own quarters. A Continental-plus breakfast served weekdays; full breakfast served weekends. No smoking. Children are welcome. Friendly dog and cat. $65-85.

The Desert Yankee. Family residence is in a quiet neighborhood. Five rooms, all with private baths, offer a variety of bed sizes. Lovely courtyard, great room, and pool available. Continental breakfast served in the dining room or courtyard. Within walking distance of the university. Smoking on the patio only. Two cats in residence, but more pets welcome. Children $10. $65-85.

The Desert Yankee-Too. This modest home has a suite with private entrance, king-size bed, and private bath. The circu-

6 Pets welcome; 7 Smoking allowed; 8 Children welcome; 9 Social drinking allowed; 10 Tennis available; 11 Swimming available; 12 Golf available; 13 Skiing available; 14 May be booked through travel agents.

Mi Casa Su Casa
(continued)

lar drive provides adequate parking in a quiet neighborhood. Relax outside in an enclosed garden with well established cactus and desert plants. Continental-plus breakfast. Close to bus stop with easy access to the Convention Center and downtown shopping, the downtown arts district, Tucson Art Museum, shops, and restaurants. Two-night minimum. Smoking allowed outside only. Children and pets are welcome. $55-65.

Double K Ranch. Bird watcher's paradise! Private guest facility with Ben Franklin stove, private shower, and patio. Color TV, radio, tape player, telephone, western books, and games. Jacuzzi and pool available. Experience splendid bird watching, explore ancient Hohokam sites on private trail, or venture off on nearby national forest trails. The ranch is home to many animals. Tennis is five minutes away, and bicycles are loaned to guests. Children are welcome. $55.

Elizabeth's Bed and Breakfast. This modest, attractively decorated home with an Arizona room for relaxing with a book is within walking distance of a bus stop, regional park, golf course, and driving range. The guest bedroom has a queen-size bed, large closet and dresser space, TV, radio, and telephone. Limited kitchen and laundry privileges. Continental breakfast. No children. No pets. Smoking outside only. Two-night minimum. Five-dollar charge for full breakfast. $45-55.

The Elysian Grove Market Bed and Breakfast. Built in the 1920s as a corner market in one of Tucson's historic Barrios, this adobe building is filled with antiques and folk art. The great room has a fireplace, books, music, etc. There are two guest

rooms with double beds that share a tiled bath. There is also a lower-level room. Guests may relax outside in an enclosed garden with desert plants. European breakfast is served. Close to the downtown art district, Tucson Art Museum, shops, restaurants, and the Convention Center. Children welcome. No pets. Smoking allowed outside only. $55-65.

Ford's Bed and Breakfast. A warm welcome awaits guests at this nonsmoking, air-conditioned home in a residential cul-de-sac on Tucson's northeastern side. Guests enjoy a bird's-eye view of the mountains from their own private patio. Suite consists of two bedrooms, small sitting room with TV, refrigerator, private bath, and separate entrance. Expanded Continental breakfast served. Visit Saguaro Monument East, Sabino Canyon, Colossal Cave, and scenic drives. Minimum stay is two nights. Children over 12 are welcome. $50.

Fort Escalante. A mile from Saguaro National Monument, this French Chateau-styled home offers guests a breathtaking, unobstructed view of the beautiful Sonoran Desert. Guest quarters feature a furnished living room with a TV, satellite, VCR, radio, telephone, full bath, separate bedroom with a double bed, and a sofa that will turn into a king-size bed or two twin beds. Also available in the main house is a bedroom decorated in blue with a king-size bed. Smoking limited to the patio. No pets. Children over 12 are welcome. $35-60.

The Gable House. The picturesque style of Santa Fe Pueblo Indian with Mexican influence is found throughout this home, which was built in 1930. Clark Gable lived in this house in the early 1940s. Air conditioning. Southwestern decor throughout. Hostess is a licensed massage therapist; massage is available on the premises. Continental-plus breakfast is served in the dining room or on the patio. Hosts are vegetarians but try to accommodate guests. There are three guest rooms: one room has shared bath and a TV; the second has shared bath, TV, and VCR; and the third has a private bath, fireplace, and TV. All rooms have telephone service. No smoking. Children ten and older are welcome. $50-70.

Horizons Bed and Breakfast. This elegant modern Western adobe home is on three and one-half acres on the edge of the Coronado National Forest and the Catalina Mountains. The private guest suite has two rooms with queen-size bed and couch, writing alcove, and private bath. A full breakfast is served on the upper pool patio or in the dining room; special diets are accommodated cheerfully. Enjoy evening tea or coffee in front of a fire. Children welcome. No pets. Two resident mini-Dachshunds. No smoking. Fifteen dollars each additional person. $95.

Jane Cooper House. This historic, fashionable two-story fired red brick building with its second-story balcony built in 1905 has four bedrooms, each furnished with country antiques. Three rooms upstairs, one queen-size with canopied and a sitting room with twin, one king-size with balcony (these two rooms share a common bath). The third room is an apartment with a double bed and private bath, a kitchenette, and a queen-size sofa bed. Downstairs is a queen-size suite with private bath. A full breakfast is served in either the sunny dining room or outside in the garden; guests may also have breakfast served in their room. Relax in the shade of the garden or in the private hot tub. A certified massage therapist may be requested. Smoking permitted outside only. Children are welcome. $50-65.

Katy's Hacienda. Charming home filled with antiques. Hostess entertains with home privileges. Colorful, restful back yard. A

choice breakfast is served. Within walking distance of Park Mall, theaters, and many fine restaurants. Close to bus line. One room with private bath. Resident dog. Minimum stay is two nights. Children over 12 welcome. $45-55.

The Mariposa Inn. Formerly the Brimstone Butterfly, this adobe home is loaded with antiques, stained glass, tile, attractive gardens, patios, and pool. Near the pool is a separate guest house with a double bed and sitting room, also a separate suite with a kitchenette and a queen-size bed. There is another bedroom in the main house with a king-size bed and private bath. The hostess, a former dancer and choreographer, massage therapist, and realty agent, takes pride in her gourmet breakfast. A pet dog and two cats on the premises. Two-night stay minimum. Smoking permitted outside only. Children under one year old and over 12 are welcome. $95.

Melissa's Desert Classic. A three-story home loaded with antiques, tile floors, attractive desert landscaping, patio, spa, and pool. There is a separate guest house with two bedrooms, large living room, and full kitchen. On the top floor of the main house is a bedroom suite with king-size bed and private bath. A queen-size bedroom with large private bath is on the lower level. There are also two rooms that share a bath. Enjoy the large great room with cable TV. Full breakfast. Inquire about children. No pets. Smoking outside only. Two-night minimum. $40-75.

Mesquite Retreat. Offering desert quiet near the base of Mount Lemmon, yet easy access to the city—five minutes to fine dining. This spacious ranch-style home is decorated with a blend of traditional and many antiques. Two guest rooms feature antique beds and share a bath. Living area shared with host has TV and fireplace. Mountain

6 Pets welcome; 7 Smoking allowed; 8 Children welcome; 9 Social drinking allowed; 10 Tennis available; 11 Swimming available; 12 Golf available; 13 Skiing available; 14 May be booked through travel agents.

Old Pueblo Homestays
(continued)

view patio with pool and spa. Full or light breakfast served. Resident dog. Children over 12. $50.

Mountain Views Bed and Breakfast. This spacious territorial adobe home is on a little over three acres with unobstructed scenic views of the Catalina Mountains. Each of the guest quarters in a dedicated wing has a queen-size bed, private bath, sitting room with TV, writing desk, and reading material. A utility room with washer and dryer is available for guest use. Breakfast menu will cater to low-cholesterol, low fat, gluten-free diets, but not exclusively. Picnic lunches available on order, and quiet romantic dinners are available on special request. Children welcome. Pets welcome. No smoking. $75-85.

Las Naranjas. Restored Spanish Colonial, circa 1900, is in the West University area close to Fourth Avenue and city bus lines. The Rebecca Room and the Canopy Room feature exquisite antiques and private baths. Enjoy the working fireplace, covered front porch, breakfast room with large bay window, laundry and kitchen facilities, and Edgar, the bed and breakfast cat. Continental breakfast features lots of homemade goodies, and the hostess stocks a cookie jar full of homemade chocolate chip cookies. Smoking allowed; children and some pets allowed. $45-65.

Paz Entera: Bed, Breakfast, and Beyond. A secluded two-story adobe and rock ranch house built in 1937 with hardwood floors and spectacular views on 30 acres. Enjoy the library, piano, fireplace, TV, and telephone. Guest casitas and bunk houses, large patio, pool, Jacuzzi, hammocks, and hiking and walking trails. Meeting rooms, indoor and outdoor locations for weddings, reunions, workshops, barbecues, etc. Continental Breakfast Buffet is served. Arrangements for group-event lunch and dinner may be made. Two-night minimum. Children over ten are welcome. No pets. Smoking outside only. Ten dollars additional for an extra child. $75-120.

Quail's Vista. Panoramic view of the Catalina Mountains makes this Santa Fe-style, rammed-earth solar structure home give guests the feeling of true desert living. Guest room has a queen-sized bed with private full hall bath. Swim-stream spa, and hostess' membership at private country club with golf, tennis, and aerobics available to guests. Continental breakfast is served. Smoking allowed outside only. No pets or children. $60-85.

Redbud House. In a quiet neighborhood within walking distance to parks, shops, and good restaurants, as well as transportation. Cozy atmosphere with mountain views, use of living room with fireplace. Two cheerful bedrooms with private bath and TV. Full or light breakfast offered. Use of barbecue, patio, books, games, and bicycles. Minimum stay is two nights. $50.

Rimrock West. A Southwestern hacienda of two talented artists on 20 acres in the foothills of the Santa Catalina Mountains, two miles from city limits. Two rooms in the main house with private baths open onto a courtyard with fountain. Separate adobe guest house near pool area has living room, full kitchen, bedroom. Breakfast is informal and plentiful, including freshly baked muffins and interesting conversation. Minimum stay is two nights. $85-120.

The Tillinghast Place. In a world-class resort community known as Saddlebrooke. Clubhouse with a restaurant, tennis courts,

NOTES: Credit cards accepted: A MasterCard; B Visa; C American Express; D Discover Card; E Diner's Club; F Other; 2 Personal checks accepted; 3 Lunch available; 4 Dinner available; 5 Open all year;

18-hole golf course, two swimming pools (heated), driving range, practice putting green, and health club. Guests may hike in the desert or just sit in the back yard with a beautiful view of the Catalina Mountains and observe the wildlife. Guests have private use of the living room with fireplace, dining room, and den. Private bath. Only one couple with children or two couples traveling together. $40-75.

Timrod. Desert living at its best. Beautiful home set in a lovely rural area with mountain vistas. A self-contained four-room suite. Private bath, full kitchen, separate entrance. Hostess stocks refrigerator with breakfast foods. Second suite with two bedrooms and bath. Pool is heated at additional charge. Pottery lessons available by hostess. Resident dog. Minimum stay is two nights. Children over 15. $60-80.

Tucson Mountain. This home offers a relaxed, friendly atmosphere. Three rooms with shared bath. Queen-size bedroom with private bath. Hostess sets out a very special Continental breakfast. Easy access to desert and mountain trails, community center, downtown Tucson, and the University of Arizona. Share family room, TV, and pool. Minimum stay is two nights. Children over 12 welcome. $45-55.

View Point. This lovely two-level home in the Catalina foothills has four large bedrooms and a beautiful blend of antique and Southwestern furniture. Large bedrooms surround inviting great room opening onto a solar pool. Refrigerator, microwave oven, toaster, coffee maker, TV, VCR, fireplace, and small library. Convenient to everything. Continental to a full breakfast served in the dining room or on the poolside patio. Private entrance into great room. No smoking. Children over 16 are welcome. $50-65.

Peppertree Bed and Breakfast Inn
724 East University Boulevard, 85719
(602) 622-7167

A 1905 Victorian Territorial house just two blocks west of the main gates of the University of Arizona. The house, which is furnished with family antiques, is within easy walking distance of the university, museums, shops, restaurants, theaters, and downtown. There are three guest rooms with private baths, and two two-bedroom guest houses. Each guest house contains a living room, dining room, full kitchen with washer/dryer, and private patio. They are ideal for families or couples traveling together. The hostess is a published cookbook author and is renowned for her gourmet breakfasts.

Host: Marjorie Martin
Rooms: 5 (1 PB; 4 SB) $65-80
Full Breakfast
Credit Cards: A, B, D
Notes: 2, 5, 8, 9, 12, 13, 14

La Posada Del Valle
1640 North Campbell Avenue, 85719
(602) 795-3840

An elegant 1920s inn nestled in the heart of the city. Five guest rooms with private baths and outside entrances. Mature orange trees perfume the air as guests enjoy a gourmet breakfast and sip tea each afternoon on the patio overlooking the garden. Full breakfast served weekends only.

Hosts: Tom and Karin Dennen
Rooms: 5 (PB) $90-125
Full and Continental Breakfasts
Credit Cards: A, B
Notes: 2, 5, 8 (over 12), 9, 10, 11, 12, 13, 14

El Presidio Bed and Breakfast
297 North Main Street, 85701
(602) 623-6151

6 Pets welcome; 7 Smoking allowed; 8 Children welcome; 9 Social drinking allowed; 10 Tennis available; 11 Swimming available; 12 Golf available; 13 Skiing available; 14 May be booked through travel agents.

A Victorian adobe, this inn is a splendid example of American-Territorial style and is listed on the National Register of Historic Places. Close to downtown and within walking distance of the best restaurants, museums, and shopping. Guests enjoy true Southwestern charm in spacious suites, two with kitchens that open onto large courtyards and gardens, fountains, and lush floral displays. A tranquil oasis with the ambience of Old Mexico. Three-star rating from Mobil and AAA.

Host: Patti Toci
Rooms: 4 (PB) $70-110
Full Breakfast
Credit Cards: None
Notes: 2, 5, 9, 10, 11, 12, 14

The Swedish Guest House Bed and Breakfast

941 West Calle Dadivoso, 85704
(602) 742-6490

At the beginning of the Catalina Foothills, this spacious guest house offers 1,100-square-foot quarters. Fireplace, telephone with private number, TV, radio, air conditioning, parking in garage, own patio overlooking the swimming pool. Plush bathroom has bathtub and an extra large shower. Nearby are golf courses, hiking, horseback riding. Eighteen minutes from the University of Arizona. Hosts are transplanted Swedes from Stockholm and Tucson residents since 1977. Smoking outside only. Weekly rates available. *Valkommen!* Full breakfast served on weekends only. Self-serve during the week. Closed July.

The Swedish Guest House

Hosts: Lars and Florence Ejrup
Guest house: 1 (PB) $85
Full Breakfast
Credit Cards: None
Notes: 9, 11, 14

TUMACACORI

Old Pueblo Homestays

P.O. Box 13603, Tucson, 85732
(800) 333-9 RSO

The Old Mission Store. The building was constructed in the late 1920s and served as a grocery store, post office, and gathering place until the 1960s. Adjacent to the Demano Gallery, featuring work by local and regional artists. Guests are near the ruins of an old Spanish Colonial Mission and the Tumacacori National Historical Park, three miles south of Tubac and 21 miles north of U.S. border at Nogales, Arizona. The south wing consists of a breakfast/sitting room, bedroom, private bath, additional sleeping room, and private entrance and patio. Resident feline named Buddy. No smoking. Children are welcome. $60.

WICKENBURG

Mi Casa Su Casa

P.O. Box 950, Tempe, 85280-0950
(602) 990-0682; (800) 456-0682

1626. Homesteaded at the turn of the century and a guest ranch since 1926, this working ranch is listed on both the state and national historic registers. The handmade adobe buildings are snuggled close by the Hassayampa River, and the food is worth a letter home. Three meals a day are included, and guests can choose from a variety of lodging choices. Horseback riding and heated pool. Two-night minimum stay is required. Visa and MasterCard accepted. $95-355.

NOTES: Credit cards accepted: A MasterCard; B Visa; C American Express; D Discover Card; E Diner's Club; F Other; 2 Personal checks accepted; 3 Lunch available; 4 Dinner available; 5 Open all year;

WILLIAMS

Bed and Breakfast Inn Arizona

P.O. Box 11253, Glendale, 85318-1253
(602) 561-0335; FAX (602) 561-2300

WM002. Convenient and charming setting in small Arizona town. Continental breakfast. Grand Canyon National Park, Grand Canyon Restored Historic R.R. Excursion are only a whistle away! Queen-size and double beds, private baths. Call for rates.

WM003. This log bed and breakfast deluxe home. Private baths, cozy beds, daily hospitality hour, and breakfast. Gateway to the Grand Canyon. Call for rates.

The Johnstonian Bed and Breakfast

321 West Sheridan Avenue, 86046
(602) 635-2178

As guests cross the threshold of this century-old, two-story Victorian home, the hosts will welcome them into a relaxed family atmosphere in keeping with the same spirit of hospitality that pervaded the Victorian era. Guests' senses will transport them to the turn-of-the-century when they see the quaint rooms furnished with an-

tiques and smell fresh bread baking. Enjoy breakfast in the dining room at the round oak table.

Hosts: Bill and Pidge Johnston
Rooms: 4 (1 PB; 3 SB) $50-65
Full Breakfast
Credit Cards: None
Notes: 2, 5, 8, 9, 10, 12, 13, 14

Mi Casa Su Casa

P.O. Box 950, Tempe, 85280-0950
(602) 990-0682; (800) 456-0682

1631. This two-story inn is convenient to the center of Williams, two blocks from the Grand Canyon Railroad Station. Each of the nine rooms is decorated differently. Continental-plus breakfast. $45-75.

YUMA

Mi Casa Su Casa

P.O. Box 950, Tempe, 85281
(602) 990-0682; (800) 456-0682

110. This handsome adobe home is on large lot in quiet older neighborhood. Eclectic, charming interior. Guest room has fine antiques, double bed, and private hall bath. Full attractive breakfasts served on fine china and table linens. Sociable hostess is a native of Yuma. Smokers are welcome. Pool. $50-55.

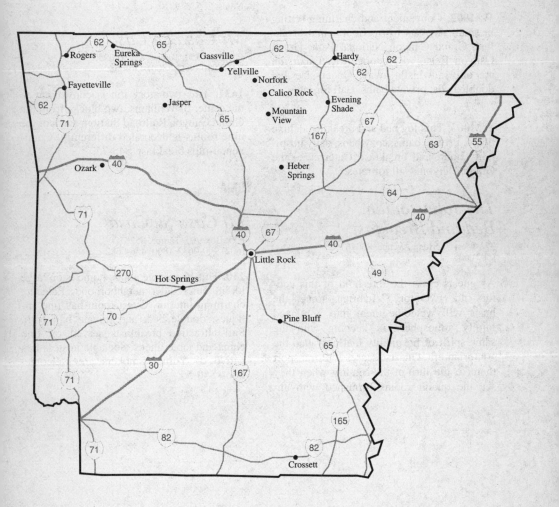

Arkansas

Arkansas

CALICO ROCK

Arkansas and Ozarks Bed and Breakfast

HC 79, Box 330A, 72519
(800) 233-2777

A. Two log cabins surrounded by the Ozark National Forest, decorated with the past in mind but offering modern comforts. A sleeping loft in each cabin sleeps two; downstairs has a Hide-a-bed and wood stove in the living area, kitchen, and bath. The cabins are unhosted for maximum privacy but are provided with coffee, milk, cereal, and homemade fruit bread. Relax on the front porch and enjoy a panoramic view of the river, forest, and ever-present wildlife. Minutes from town, antique shops, live music shows, dinner theaters, Blanchard Springs Caverns, and the Ozark Folk Center. $48.

B. Original 1923 hotel within walking distance of two boat docks, one block from Main Street. Continental breakfast provided. Furnishings include antiques and collectibles of the 1920s. Handmade jewelry shop on premises. $35-50.

C. Forest home lodge is perched on a 300-foot bluff overlooking the beautiful, clear White River. A large country breakfast, including homemade breads and a hearty main dish, is served on a deck outside guests' room. The contemporary home, decorated with stained glass, has a large three-keyboard organ, satellite TV, and video games in the spacious living room for the guests' enjoyment. The Ozark Folk Center, Blanchard Caverns, craft shops, antique shops, and hiking trails are only minutes away. $45.

D. This large, modern house with balconies overlooks a national forest. Acres of mixed woods with caves, springs, and waterfalls distinguish this area, near both White River for great trout fishing and Lake Norfolk for boating, swimming, and fishing. Breakfast, served on the deck or in the dining room, includes wild blueberries, huckleberries, and blackberries. Call for rates.

CROSSETT

The Trieschmann House Bed and Breakfast

707 Cedar, 71635
(501) 364-7592; (800) TRIESCH

Built in 1903 for an official of the Crossett Company, this lovely bed and breakfast is nine miles from the Felsenthal Refuge for good fishing and hunting. Front porch with wicker swing and furniture; common room with a wood-burning stove, cable TV, and games. Full breakfast is served in the kitchen, and the home is furnished with furniture from the past. The hosts invite guests to travel back in time with them.

NOTES: Credit cards accepted: A MasterCard; B Visa; C American Express; D Discover Card; E Diner's Club; F Other; 2 Personal checks accepted; 3 Lunch available; 4 Dinner available; 5 Open all year; 6 Pets welcome; 7 Smoking allowed; 8 Children welcome; 9 Social drinking allowed; 10 Tennis available; 11 Swimming available; 12 Golf available; 13 Skiing available; 14 May be booked through travel agents.

Hosts: Pat and Herman Owens
Rooms: 3 (1 PB; 2 SB) $40-45
Full Breakfast
Credit Cards: A, B, C
Notes: 2, 5, 8, 10, 12, 14

EUREKA SPRINGS

Arbour Glen
Bed and Breakfast
Victorian Inn

7 Lema, 72632
(501) 253-9010

Circa 1896, on Eureka Springs historic district loop and trolley route, with downtown shops and cafes only a five-minute walk. Completely renovated with guests' comfort in mind, the Arbour Glen still retains its Victorian charm, elegance, and romance. On the veranda relax and enjoy the picturesque setting of the tree-covered hollow for an unforgettable experience. Hosts offer Jacuzzis for two, antique furnishings, private baths, color cable TV, gourmet breakfasts, smoke-free suites, and a nature trail.

Rooms: 3 (PB) $65-95
Full Breakfast
Credit Cards: A, B
Notes: 2, 5, 8, 9, 10, 11, 12

Arsenic and Old Lace

60 Hillside Avenue, 72632
(501) 253-5454; (800) 243-LACE

Arsenic and Old Lace

An elegant and luxurious Queen Anne Victorian inn complete with wraparound verandas and tower has antiques and original pieces of art. Enjoy the Jacuzzis, fireplaces, TV/VCRs, and fresh flowers. A full gourmet breakfast is served in the morning room overlooking the English perennial garden. Ideal location on a trolley stop in the historic district, and within easy access of all major tourist attractions.

Hosts: Gary and Phyllis Jones
Rooms: 5 (PB) $90-150
Full Breakfast
Credit Cards: A, B
Notes: 2, 5, 7 (limited), 9, 10, 11, 12, 14

Bed and Breakfast
Reservation Services

11 Singleton Street, 72632
(501) 253-9111

Travelers may choose from 30 charming inns and cottages. Reservations for the Passion Play and the Dinner Train can be arranged.

Bonnybrooke Farm
Atop Misty Mountain

Route 2, Box 335A, 72632
(501) 253-6903

If guests' hearts are in the country—or long to be—the hosts invite them to come share in the sweet quiet and serenity that awaits them in their place to come home to. Five cottages, distinctly different in their pleasures to tempt guests: fireplace and Jacuzzi for two, full glass fronts, mountaintop views, shower under the stars in the glass shower, wicker porch swing in front of the fireplace, and a water fall Jacuzzi. Guests are gonna love it!

Hosts: Bonny and Josh
Cottages: 5 (PB) $85-125
Credit Cards: None
Notes: 2, 5, 9, 11, 14

NOTES: Credit cards accepted: A MasterCard; B Visa; C American Express; D Discover Card; E Diner's Club; F Other; 2 Personal checks accepted; 3 Lunch available; 4 Dinner available; 5 Open all year;

Bridgeford House Bed and Breakfast

263 Spring Street, 72632
(501) 253-7853

Nestled in the heart of Eureka Springs' historic residential district, Bridgeford House is an 1884 Victorian delight. Outside are shady porches that invite guests to pull up a chair and watch the world go by on Spring Street. Each room has a private entrance, antique furnishings, and private bath. Fresh coffee in the suite, a selection of fine teas, color TV, air conditioning, and a mouth-watering breakfast.

Hosts: Michael and Denise McDonald
Rooms: 4 (PB) $85-95
Full Breakfast
Credit Cards: A, B
Notes: 2, 5, 7 (limited), 8, 9, 10, 11, 12, 14

Brownstone Inn, Inc.

75 Hillside, 72632
(501) 253-7505

The inn was built in 1895 and for 70 years served as the site of the Ozarka Water Co. The limestone structure maintains the original facade, while the interior has been converted to two large suites and two smaller units, all with private baths. All are decorated in unique Victorian fashion and filled with many antiques. The inn sits directly across the street from the ES&NA Railroad steam train depot. The inn is in a cool valley surrounded by a brick patio on the ground level and wood terrace for the upper level. Come and enjoy a personal touch from the hosts.

Hosts: Marvin and Donna Shepard
Rooms: 4 (PB) $85-105
Full Breakfast
Credit Cards: A, B
Notes: 2, 5, 9, 14

Cliff Cottage and The Place Next Door— A Bed and Breakfast Inn

42 Armstrong Street, 72632
(501) 253-7409

First mayor of Eureka's Eastlake Victorian home and the only bed and breakfast in the heart of historic downtown. Guest rooms and suites with Jacuzzi, one with shower, refrigerators, complimentary champagne, fresh flowers, and scented linens. Sumptuous breakfasts delivered bedside. Candlelight gourmet dinners also available. Victorian picnic lunch available aboard skippered 24-foot pontoon boat sailing to romantic coves. Sunset cruises. Extensive fine wine cellar. Golf, tennis, and swimming privileges available at Holiday Island Resort.

Hosts: Sandra CH Smith
Rooms: 5 (PB) $70-135
Full Breakfast
Cards: A, B
Notes: 2, 3, 4, 5, 7 (limited), 8 (over 12), 9, 10, 11, 12, 14

Crescent Cottage Inn

211 Spring Street, 72632
(501) 253-6022

Premier-class 1881 Victorian "painted lady" on the national register. Built for the first governor of Arkansas after the Civil War. Oldest, most historic and photographed bed and breakfast with beautiful gardens and panoramic views. Walk to town and trolley stop. Queen-size beds, some private double Jacuzzis and verandas, and antiques. Newly redecorated. Featured in magazines and books, and nationally rated. Great breakfasts! Area known for wonderful music, arts, crafts, lakes, forests, and Passion Play.

Hosts: Ralph and Phyllis Becker
Rooms: 4 (PB) $75-115
Full Breakfast
Credit Cards: A, B, D
Notes: 2, 5, 7 (limited), 8 (over 13), 9, 10, 11, 12, 14

6 Pets welcome; 7 Smoking allowed; 8 Children welcome; 9 Social drinking allowed; 10 Tennis available; 11 Swimming available; 12 Golf available; 13 Skiing available; 14 May be booked through travel agents.

Dairy Hollow House

515 Spring Street, 72632
(501) 253-7444; (800) 562-8650

Welcome to Dairy Hollow House, a tiny, irresistible country inn and restaurant nestled
in a serene, wooded valley. Just one mile
from historic downtown, there are two
houses, each with the prettiest rooms and
suites imaginable. Waiting for guests are
fireplaces, landscaped hot tub, fresh flowers, regional antiques, and Ozark wildflower soaps. Uncle Ben's "Best Inn of the
Year," 1989, 1990, and 1991. Mobil two-
star inn. There are also murder mystery
weekends four times each year. The restaurant serves a *prix fixe* "Nouveau 'Zarks
Haute Country Cuisine" dinner Thursday
through Monday nights at 7:00 P.M. Hosts
are members of BBAA and PAII.

Hosts: Crescent Dragonwagon and Ned Shank
Rooms: 6 (PB) $125-165
Full Breakfast
Credit Cards: A, B, C, D, E
Notes: 2, 4, 5, 8, 9, 10, 11, 12, 14

Dr. R.G. Floyd House

246 Spring Street, 72632
(501) 253-7525

This 1892 authentically restored Queen
Anne is surrounded by award winning terraced gardens in a wooded area. Eureka's
finest home is on the historic loop within
easy walking distance of the galleries,
shops, and restaurants. All rooms are appointed with Victorian wall and ceiling papers, carpeting, beautiful woodwork, period
antiques, and meticulous attention to detail.
Guest quarters include a two-bedroom
suite. Each day begins with a gourmet
breakfast served in the privacy of guest's
room or on the veranda.

Hosts: Georgia Rubley and Bill Rubley
Rooms: 2 (PB) $90-155
Cottage: 1 (PB)
Full Breakfast
Credit Cards: A, B, D
Notes: 2, 5, 7 (limited), 9, 11, 12

Enchanted Cottages

18 Nut Street, 72632
(800) 862-2788

In a secluded park-like setting in the historic district, Enchanted Cottages are romantic and private. Just two-and-a-half
blocks to shops and restaurants. These storybook cottages are surrounded by woods
frequently visited by a neighborhood family
of deer. Each cottage has either an indoor
Jacuzzi for two or a private outdoor hot tub.
Accommodations include king- or queen-
size beds, antique furnishings, cable TV,
kitchens, and patios with grills. Special
honeymoon and anniversary packages!

Hosts: Barbara Kellogg and David Pettit
Rooms: 3 (PB) $75-129
Continental Breakfast
Credit Cards: A, B
Notes: 2, 5, 9, 14

Evening Shade Inn

Route 1, Box 446, Highway 62 East, 72632
(501) 253-6264; (800) 992-1224 (reservations)

Relax in elegantly decorated luxury rooms
in the tranquil mountain woodlands, or sit
on the porch and enjoy the view and
wildlife. The privacy of a motel, and the
service and hospitality of a bed and breakfast inn. Large, immaculate rooms with remote color cable TV and HBO. Slip into a
private Jacuzzi for two. Breakfast is
brought to the room whenever guests
choose. Near the center of Eureka Springs
and exciting attractions, but secluded and
quiet with ample parking. In-room telephones. On the trolley route.

Hosts: Ed and Shirley Nussbaum
Rooms: 5 (PB) $100-150
Continental Breakfast
Credit Cards: A, B, C, D, E, F
Notes: 2, 5, 9, 14

The Gardener's Cottage

11 Singleton, 72632
(501) 253-9111; (800) 833-3394

NOTES: Credit cards accepted: A MasterCard; B Visa; C American Express; D Discover Card; E Diner's
Club; F Other; 2 Personal checks accepted; 3 Lunch available; 4 Dinner available; 5 Open all year;

Tucked away in a wooded area in the historic district, this private cottage features charming country decor with romantic touches and a Jacuzzi for two. This cozy retreat with beamed cathedral ceiling, skylights, full kitchen, TV, ceiling fan, and air conditioning is within walking distance of the galleries and cafes. Guests can relax on the spacious porch with its swing and hammock while listening to the bubbling stream just yards away. Discounts for five days or more. Open April through November. Breakfast is not included, but can be prearranged for $12 when space is available at Singleton House.

Host: Barbara Gavron
Cottage: 1 (PB) $95-125
No Breakfast
Credit Cards: A, B, C, D
Notes: 2, 11, 12, 14

Harvest House

104 Wall Street, 72632
(501) 253-9363

This turn-of-the-century Victorian house is filled with antiques, collectibles, and family favorites. The guest rooms have private entrances and private baths. In the historic district of Eureka Springs, Harvest House is a step off the beaten path yet close to the bustle of downtown. A full breakfast is served in the dining room, or weather permitting, in the screened-in gazebo overlooking pine and oak trees. Bill is a native Arkansan and knows all the hidden treasures of the area. Patt is the shopper with a particular interest in antiques and the local attractions. A non-smoking inn.

Hosts: Bill and Patt Carmichael
Rooms: 5 (4 PB; 1 SB) $60-90
Full Breakfast
Credit Cards: A, B, D
Notes: 2, 5, 6, 9, 14

Heart of the Hills Inn

5 Summit Street, 72632
(501) 253-7468; (800) 253-7468

This historic home was built in the 1800s and offers three rooms with air conditioning, refrigerator, and TV. Private baths and tubs with showers, and one suite has a two-person Jacuzzi with shower. There is also a completely equipped cottage with deck overlooking the woods. Eureka Springs is noted for its Passion Play, restaurants, fine museums, and trolley system.

"Heartstone Inn", Eureka Springs, AR

The Heartstone Inn

Host: Jan Jacobs Weber
Rooms: 3 (PB) $69-119
Cottage: 1 (PB)
Full Breakfast
Credit Cards: A, B
Notes: 2, 8, 9, 10, 11, 13, 14

The Heartstone Inn and Cottages

35 Kings Highway, 72632
(501) 253-8916

In the historic district, this Victorian house combines nostalgic charm with 20th century convenience. Guest rooms are inviting with antiques, fresh flowers, beautiful linens, private entrances, bath, cable TV, and air conditioning. The adjacent Victoria house has ten-foot ceilings, fireplace, and two large bedrooms, or choose the cozy Country Cottage for two. Relax on the verandas or in the gazebo surrounded by flowers and shade trees. Experience the treat of a revitalizing, therapeutic massage. Stroll down tree-lined streets to parks, shops, and restaurants. Mobil, AAA, and ABBA approved. Mini-

6 Pets welcome; 7 Smoking allowed; 8 Children welcome; 9 Social drinking allowed; 10 Tennis available; 11 Swimming available; 12 Golf available; 13 Skiing available; 14 May be booked through travel agents.

mum-stay requirements for weekends and holidays. Closed during Christmas.

Hosts: Iris and Bill Simantel
Rooms: 10 (PB) $67-118
Cottages: 2 (PB)
Full Breakfast
Credit Cards: A, B, C, D
Notes: 2, 9, 11, 12, 14

Hillside Cottage Bed and Breakfast

23 Hillside Avenue, 72632
(501) 253-8688

Turn-of-the-century gingerbread house, two blocks from historic downtown shopping and dining area. Surrounded by sloping lawn, flower beds, and 100-year-old trees, peaceful country ambience is evident. An inveterate antiquer, the hostess has embellished Hillside Cottage with treasures collected over the years. Enjoy breakfast in the eclectic dining room, experience a cup of exotic-blend coffee, and stroll through the garden while listening to the songs of the birds. Come and relax!

Host: Barbara Kessler
Rooms: 4 (PB) $70-90
Full Breakfast
Credit Cards: A, B
Notes: 2, 8, 9, 10, 11, 12, 13 (water), 14

The Inn at Rose Hall

56 Hillside, P.O. Box 386, 72632
(501) 253-5405; (800) 828-4255

Hospitality begins here with romantic elegance and gracious service. Perfect for Victorian weddings, receptions, and honeymoons. Enjoy every romantic amenity including Jacuzzis and showers for two, Victorian gazebo, secluded garden and courtyard, windows of stained glass, dramatic tower, and fireplaces. The Inn at Rose Hall is for guests who wish to experience the ambience of luxury.

Host: Sandy Latimer
Rooms: 5 (PB) $110-150
Full Breakfast
Credit Cards: A, B, C, D, E
Notes: 2, 5, 9, 11, 12, 14

Red Bud Manor

Number 7 Kingshighway, 72632
(501) 253-9649

Friendly hospitality awaits at this Victorian inn. Rediscover romance in a charming historic atmosphere. Sit on the porch swings and watch the world go by or walk to historic Old Town attractions and restaurants. Turn-of-the-century furnishings, fresh flowers, soft music, gourmet breakfasts, queen-size beds, private baths, private Jacuzzis for two, private outside entrances, cable TVs, refrigerators, and off-street parking are among the amenities.

Hosts: Tandy and Shari Bozeman
Rooms: 3 (SB) $65-105
Full Breakfast
Credit Cards: A, B
Notes: 2, 5, 9, 14

Scandia Bed and Breakfast Inn

33 Avo, Highway 62 West, 72632
(501) 253-8922; (800) 523-8922

Set in the pines on the quiet side of town, Scandia offers quaint 1940s cottages featuring designer linens and draperies. Elegant

NOTES: Credit cards accepted: A MasterCard; B Visa; C American Express; D Discover Card; E Diner's Club; F Other; 2 Personal checks accepted; 3 Lunch available; 4 Dinner available; 5 Open all year;

breakfasts are served daily in the breakfast room where guests will find the tables festively adorned with fresh flowers, china, silver, and folded linen napkins. A romantic hot tub gazebo under the dogwoods awaits at any hour. Evening room service and boat excursions on beautiful Beaver Lake are optional. Water-skiing, canoeing, horseback riding, wedding services, honeymoon suite for two with Jacuzzi, and fantasy grapevine and ivy arbor are all available for guests to enjoy.

Hosts: Cynthia Barnes and Marty Lavine
Rooms: 7 (PB) $69-99
Full Breakfast
Credit Cards: A, B, C, D
Notes: 2, 5, 8, 9, 10, 11, 12, 13 (water)

Singleton House Bed and Breakfast

11 Singleton Street, 72632
(501) 253-9111; (800) 833-3394

This country Victorian home is an old-fashioned place with a touch of magic. Each guest room is whimsically decorated with a delightful collection of antiques and folk art. Breakfast is served on the balcony overlooking the fantasy wildflower garden below, with its goldfish pond and curious birdhouse collection. A honeymoon cottage with a Jacuzzi at a separate location is also available; however, no breakfast is served. In the historic district. Guests park and walk a scenic, wooded pathway to Eureka's shops and cafes. Innkeeper apprenticeship program available.

Host: Barbara Gavron
Rooms: 5 (PB) $55-95
Cottage: 1 (PB) $95
Full Breakfast
Credit Cards: A, B, C, D
Notes: 2, 5, 8, 9, 11, 12, 14

Sunnyside Bed and Breakfast Inn

5 Ridgeway, 72632
(501) 253-6638; (800) 554-9499

Lovingly restored, circa 1880 Victorian home in the historic district. Beautifully appointed, air-conditioned rooms. Quiet and restful surroundings are smoke and alcohol free. Honeymoon suite has a Jacuzzi. View the wilderness from the deck. Walking distance to downtown.

Host: Gladys Rose Foris
Rooms: 5 (PB) $80-125
Full Breakfast
Credit Cards: A, B
Notes: 2, 5, 8, 14

EVENING SHADE

Arkansas and Ozarks Bed and Breakfast

HC 79, Box 330A, Calico Rock, 72519
(800) 233-2777

This modern home on 19 rolling, wooded acres has cool breezes and tranquil surroundings. Guests enjoy a wraparound porch and a large deck. The home features air conditioning, ceiling fans, and queen-size beds. Near antique and craft shopping, country music, and the Spring River for canoeing and swimming. Call for rates.

FAYETTEVILLE

Eton House

1485 Eton, 72703
(501) 443-7517

This buff-brick ranch-style home has a cathedral ceiling and is furnished in delicate pastels, Victorian wicker, and more staid European pieces. Guests are welcome to relax in the living room by a cozy fireplace during winter months, but the screened-in patio overlooking a parklike setting is a spring and summer delight. A gazebo can be used for weddings. Walton Arts Center, donated by the late Sam Walton of Wal-Mart fame, is just three miles away. The

6 Pets welcome; 7 Smoking allowed; 8 Children welcome; 9 Social drinking allowed; 10 Tennis available; 11 Swimming available; 12 Golf available; 13 Skiing available; 14 May be booked through travel agents.

area is rich in arts, crafts, and southern hospitality. Fayetteville is the home of the University of Arkansas.

Host: Patricia Parks
Rooms: 3 (PB) $45
Continental Breakfast
Credit Cards: None
Notes: 5, 7, 9, 12, 14

Hill Avenue Bed and Breakfast

131 South Hill Avenue, 72701
(501) 444-0865

In a residential neighborhood, this home is the only licensed bed and breakfast in Fayetteville. It is near the University of Arkansas, Walton Art Center, and the town square. Guests will find immaculate, comfortable, nonsmoking accommodations. A hearty country breakfast is served in the dining room or on the large porch.

Hosts: Dale and Cecelia Thompson
Room: 1 (PB) $40
Suite: $60
Full Breakfast
Credit Cards: None
Notes: 5

GASSVILLE

Lithia Springs Lodge

Route 1, Box 77-A, Highway 126, 72365
(501) 435-6100

A lovingly restored former lodge with an additional gift shop, featuring many of the host's own handcrafts. A full breakfast is served on the large screened front porch or in the dining room. On 39 acres of meadows and woods, it reflects the original character of the lodge. World-class fishing can be found in the nearby White and Buffalo rivers, with canoeing, hiking, and boating in or near Bull Shoals or Norfork Lake.

Hosts: Paul and Reita Johnson

Rooms: 5 (3 PB; 2 SB) $45-50
Full Breakfast
Credit Cards: A, B
Notes: 2, 5, 10, 11, 12, 14

HARDY

Arkansas and Ozarks Bed and Breakfast

HC 79, Box 330A, Calico Rock, 72519
(800) 233-2777

This newly renovated stone house used as a boarding house in the Great Depression is only a short walk from handicraft and antique shops and the Spring River. The rock formations in its walls and fireplace provide an interesting background for its antiques, collectibles, and locally handcrafted decor. Music shows, golf, tennis, horseback riding, and canoeing are available nearby. $55.

Olde Stonehouse Bed and Breakfast Inn

511 Main Street, 72542
(501) 856-2983; (800) 514-2983

Native Arkansas stone house with large porches lined with jumbo rocking chairs is comfortably furnished with antiques and features central heat and air, ceiling fans, queen-size beds, and private baths. One block from Spring River and the shops of old Hardy town. Three country music theaters, golf courses, horseback riding, canoeing, and fishing nearby. Local attractions include Mammoth Spring State Park, Grand Gulf, Evening Shade, and Arkansas Traveller Theater. Two-room "special occasion" suites are in a separate 1905 cottage.

Host: Peggy Johnson
Rooms: 5 (PB) $55-85
Full Breakfast
Credit Cards: A, B, D
Notes: 2, 5, 9, 10, 11, 12, 14

NOTES: Credit cards accepted: A MasterCard; B Visa; C American Express; D Discover Card; E Diner's Club; F Other; 2 Personal checks accepted; 3 Lunch available; 4 Dinner available; 5 Open all year;

HEBER SPRINGS _____

Arkansas and Ozarks Bed and Breakfast

HC 79, Box 330A, Calico Rock, 72519
(800) 233-2777

Originally constructed as a theater in the 1800s, used as a school, doctor's clinic, and, since 1915, as a hotel, this interesting inn has 16 individually decorated rooms. Country antiques are featured, with ceiling fans and private baths. The parlor room, with a large native stone fireplace and delicious breakfast, creates a warm, relaxed atmosphere for guests' visits. Across from the city park and a short drive to Greers Ferry Lake and Little Red River, guests can enjoy the antique and crafts shops. $52-65.

HOT SPRINGS NATIONAL PARK _____

The Gables Inn

318 Quapaw Avenue, 71901
(501) 623-7576; (800) 625-7576

A 1905 Victorian bed and breakfast with some of the original chandeliers, stained-glass windows, wood floors, and woodwork. In President Clinton's boyhood home town, where visitors can still experience the luxury of hot mineral springs baths and massages in historic bath houses. Walk downtown to art galleries, shops, and restaurants, or relax on the spacious porch. All guest rooms have private baths and handmade quilts. A full breakfast is served in the turn-of-the-century dining room.

Hosts: Shirley and Larry Robins
Rooms: 4 (PB) $55-75
Full Breakfast
Credit Cards: A, B, C
Notes: 2, 5, 9, 12, 14

Vintage Comfort Bed and Breakfast Inn

303 Quapaw, 71901
(501) 623-3258

Vintage Comfort Bed and Breakfast is an elegant, two-story Victorian home with warmth, graciousness, and comfort as its key ingredients. A full breakfast is served, and guests are pampered with old-fashioned hospitality. The inn is within easy walking distance of Hot Springs Bathhouse Row, art galleries, restaurants, shops, and Hot Springs National Park.

Host: Helen R. Bartlett
Rooms: 4 (PB) $60-85
Full Breakfast
Credit Cards: A, B, C, E
Notes: 2, 5, 8 (over 5), 9, 10, 11, 12, 14

Wildwood 1884 Bed and Breakfast

808 Park Avenue, 71901
(501) 624-4267

Peach and ivory Victorian mansion on one acre of grounds. There is a carriage turn-around in the front of the mansion. Beautiful cherry, walnut, and mahogany woodwork, all made of Arkansas native trees. Visiting Wildwood 1884 is like stepping back somewhere in time. Listed on the National Register of Historic Places.

Hosts: Randy and Karen Duncan
Rooms: 5 (PB) $85-95
Full Breakfast
Credit Cards: A, B, D
Notes: 2, 5, 10, 11, 12, 14

JASPER _____

Brambly Hedge Cottage

HCR 31, Box 39, 72641
(501) 446-5849; (800) BRAMBLY

Breakfast above the clouds at this mountaintop home right on Scenic Highway 7. Gorgeous view "clear to Missouri" overlooks

6 Pets welcome; 7 Smoking allowed; 8 Children welcome; 9 Social drinking allowed; 10 Tennis available; 11 Swimming available; 12 Golf available; 13 Skiing available; 14 May be booked through travel agents.

Buffalo River Valley. Country French-Victorian elegance in the rugged Ozarks. "Absolutely charming," says *National Geographic Traveller*. Thick-walled living room is a homestead log cabin. Bodywork relaxations available. Minutes from Buffalo National River float trips, hiking trails, and craft shops; short distance to Eureka Springs; Branson, Missouri; major lakes. Less than five miles south of Jasper.

Host: Jacquelyn Smyers
Rooms: 3 (PB) $55-75
Full Breakfast
Credit Cards: None
Notes: 2, 5, 9

MOUNTAIN VIEW

The Inn at Mountain View

West Washington Street, 72560
(800) 535-1301

On the National Register of Historic Places, the inn has been a traditional stopping place for folks since 1886. The inn has ten guest suites, each with private bath. All rooms are furnished with antiques and air conditioning. Breakfast is a hearty meal of homemade biscuits, sausage, gravy, eggs, Belgian waffles, fresh fruit compote, raspberry ambrosia, bacon, homemade peach and apple butters, juice, and lots of coffee. Mountain View is the world capital of folk music, with the National Folk Center just one mile from the inn. The caverns at Blanchard Springs are about nine miles from the inn. White River trout fishing is five miles away, and the Buffalo River, noted for its canoe and float trips, is a short drive.

Hosts: Bob and Jenny Williams
Rooms: 10 (PB) $55-91
Full Breakfast
Credit Cards: A, B, D
Notes: 2, 5, 9, 10, 12

Wildflower Bed and Breakfast

On the Square, P.O. Box 72, 72560-0072
(501) 269-4383; (800) 591-4879 (reservations)

The Wildflower Bed and Breakfast is on the historic courthouse square, where local musicians gather to play old-time music. Offering affordable European-style accommodations in a restored 1918 Craftsman-style inn listed on the National Register of Historic Places. Attractive without being pretentious, the rooms include handmade curtains, dust ruffles, original dressers, and iron bedsteads. The home of the award-winning HearthStone Bakery, as well as a modest bookshop. Guests are urged to come with an appetite for relaxation, entertainment, conversation, and good food.

Hosts: Todd and Andrea Budy
Rooms: 8 (6 PB; 2 SB) $41-70
Continental Breakfast
Credit Cards: A, B, D
Notes: 2, 3, 8, 10, 11, 12

NORFORK

Arkansas and Ozarks Bed and Breakfast

HC 79, Box 330A, Calico Rock, 72519
(800) 233-2777

A mountain retreat with a country club setting, this lodge sits on the banks of the White River and overlooks the beauty and serenity of the Ozark National Forest. In the large, antique-furnished dining room, family-style home-cooked meals include hand selected meats, fowl, fish, vegetables, freshly baked breads, and European desserts. A complete breakfast is included with lodging. The bedrooms have their own entrances into an open-air courtyard. $67.50.

NOTES: Credit cards accepted: A MasterCard; B Visa; C American Express; D Discover Card; E Diner's Club; F Other; 2 Personal checks accepted; 3 Lunch available; 4 Dinner available; 5 Open all year;

OZARK

Arkansas and Ozarks Bed and Breakfast

HC 79, Box 330A, Calico Rock, 72519
(800) 233-2777

A. This 1800s Victorian-style inn is beautifully restored, with original wood floors, stained glass, crystal chandeliers, and a winding staircase. A hammered dulcimer and piano add to the enjoyment. A luxurious breakfast is served with china, crystal, and silver. Evening desserts are also available. The romantic honeymoon/anniversary suite offers a candlelight dinner (included in room rate) served in the guests' room. Selected pieces of the lovely furnishings are for sale. $45-75.

B. This spacious brick home overlooking the Arkansas River provides queen-size beds, TV, and private baths in each lovingly decorated room. Enjoy a full breakfast in the large, fireplaced family room or relax in the hot tub. The River View Suite is available, with dinner served in the room. The window wall provides a full view of the barge and river traffic. $35-75.

PINE BLUFF

Margland II, III, and IV Bed and Breakfast Inns

703 West Second Street, 71601
(501) 536-6000; (800) 545-5383

Southern hospitality as it was meant to be— each suite is carefully furnished for the perfect combination of atmosphere and comfort. Guests may savor breakfast in the garden or in the formal dining room. Cable TV, private baths, VCRs, FAX, and Jacuzzis. Twin, full, or queen-size beds; conference rooms; exercise room. Margland II is handicapped accessible. All buildings are equipped with sprinkler fire protection system. Lunch and dinner reservations are required for groups of eight or more.

Host: Wanda Bateman
Rooms: 17 (PB) $65-95
Full Breakfast
Credit Cards: A, B, C, D, E
Notes: 2, 3 and 4 (by reservation), 5, 7, 8, 9, 10, 11, 12, 14

ROGERS

Arkansas and Ozarks Bed and Breakfast

HC 79, Box 330A, Calico Rock, 72519
(800) 233-2777

This country charmer is nestled among oak, dogwood, and redbud trees for adult travelers. Queen-size beds, private baths, fruit, and homemade candy are just a few of the features. A full breakfast is served in the spacious country dining room or on the veranda where birds, wildlife, and natural beauty may also be enjoyed. The hosts delight in providing special arrangements for birthdays, anniversaries, and other occasions. Only minutes from boating, fishing, swimming, golf, and a variety of shopping and craft areas. $44-48.

YELLVILLE

Arkansas and Ozarks Bed and Breakfast

HC 79, Box 330A, Calico Rock, 72519
(800) 233-2777

A. This elegant Victorian home is beautifully and lovingly restored to its stately charm. There are seven rooms in this spacious inn, including a honeymoon suite for those special celebrations. Also available are porches, sitting rooms, and extensive grounds. MasterCard and Visa accepted. No smoking indoors. Children over six welcome. $45-75.

6 Pets welcome; 7 Smoking allowed; 8 Children welcome; 9 Social drinking allowed; 10 Tennis available; 11 Swimming available; 12 Golf available; 13 Skiing available; 14 May be booked through travel agents.

B. This unhosted, two-bedroom home has a full kitchen, dining room, guest parlor, and family room. Piano, books, games, TV, and high chair provided. Surrounded by forests and wildflower meadows, guests can enjoy a variety of birds and the possible early-morning sighting of deer and wild turkey. Within walking distance to a floating and swimming stream and a short drive to Buffalo National River and Bull Shoals Lake. A rewarding change of pace. $68.

C. This modern log home on a working ranch is three miles from the Buffalo National River. Four bedrooms have private bath. The balcony offers a beautiful Ozark view. A large country breakfast is served daily. Near Mountain View, Blanchard Springs, and the Ozark Folk Center, with several canoe and float outfitters also nearby. Call for rates.

California

ALAMEDA

Garratt Mansion

900 Union Street, 94501
(510) 521-4779

This 1893 Victorian makes time stand still
on the tranquil island of Alameda. Only 15
miles to Berkeley or downtown San Francisco. The hosts will help maximize vacation plans or leave guests alone to regroup
Rooms are large and comfortable, and
breakfasts are nutritious and filling.

Hosts: Royce and Betty Gladden
Rooms: 7 (5 PB; 2 SB) $75-125
Full Breakfast
Credit Cards: A, B, C, E
Notes: 2, 5, 8, 11, 12, 14

ALBION

Albion River Inn

P.O. Box 100, 95410
(707) 937-1919

This romantic inn and restaurant offers
beauty, serenity, and luxury in New England-style cottages with garden entrances,
cliftop ocean views, wood-burning fireplaces, decks, Jacuzzis, and double tubs.
Each room is individually decorated. Complimentary wine, morning newspaper, fresh
coffee, and delicious full breakfast. The celebrated coastal cuisine of Chef Stephen
Smith is served nightly in the restaurant,
paired with the award-winning wine list and
entertainment on weekends. Weddings are
welcomed!

Hosts: Flurry Healy and Peter Wells
Rooms: 20 (PB) $160-250

Full Breakfast
Credit Cards: A, B, C
Notes: 2, 4, 5, 8, 9, 10, 11, 12

Fensalden Inn

Box 99, 95410
(707) 937-4042; (800) 959-3850

This restored 1860s stagecoach way station
has antique furnishings, and several units
have fireplaces. Quiet country setting with
pastoral and ocean views. Enjoy strolling
country lanes where grazing deer share the
crisp morning air, or the evening panorama
of the setting sun over a crimson-stained
ocean. Minimum-stay requirements weekends and holidays.

Hosts: Frances and Scott Brazil
Rooms: 8 (PB) $85-130
Full Breakfast
Credit Cards: A, B
Notes: 2, 5, 8 (over 11), 9, 10, 11, 12, 14

ANAHEIM

Bed and Breakfast International

P.O. Box 282910, San Francisco, 94128-2910
(415) 696-1690; (800) 872-4500
FAX (415) 696-1699

501. Perfect location for visiting Disneyland,
Knott's Berry Farm, and other tourist attractions in Southern California. This is a large
two-story home that is ideal for a family.
Guest room has a queen-size bed and private
bath, plus a queen-size sofa bed in an adjacent
sitting room with a fireplace and balcony.
Breakfast at this house lasts all day. $55.

---

6 Pets welcome; 7 Smoking allowed; 8 Children welcome; 9 Social drinking allowed; 10 Tennis available;
11 Swimming available; 12 Golf available; 13 Skiing available; 14 May be booked through travel agents.

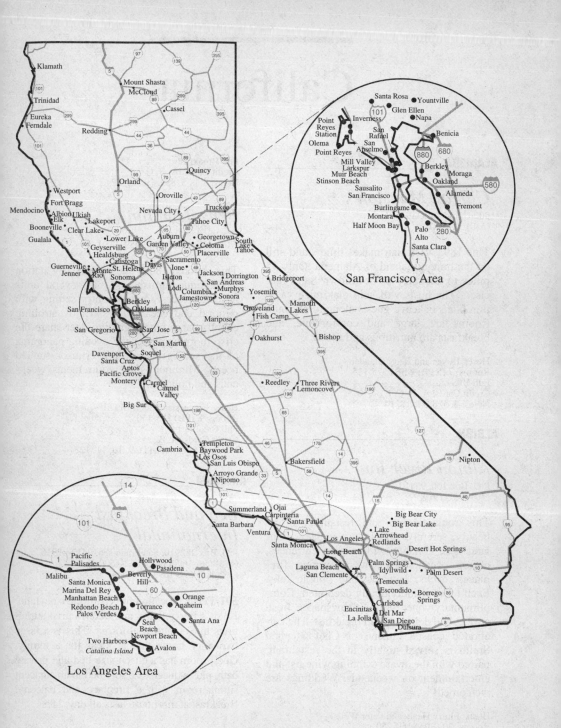

Klamath

Mount Shasta
McCloud

Trinidad
Eureka
Ferndale

Cassel

Redding

Westport
Fort Bragg
Mendocino
Albion **Ukiah**
Elk
Booneville **Clear Lake**
Gualala

Quincy

Orland

Oroville

Nevada City

Tahoe City

Truckee

Lakeport
Lower Lake
Geyserville
Healdsburg
Calistoga
Guerneville **St. Helena**
Jenner **Monte**
Rio
Sonoma

Auburn
Garden Valley
Coloma
Placerville
South Lake Tahoe

Davis
Ione
Isleton
Lodi

Sacramento

Jackson
San Andreas **Dorrington**
Columbia **Murphys**
Jamestown **Sonora**

Bridgeport

Yosemite

Berkley
Oakland
San Francisco
San Gregorio **San Jose**

Groveland
Fish Camp

Mamoth Lakes

Mariposa

Oakhurst

Bishop

San Martin
Davenport **Soquel**
Santa Cruz **Aptos**
Pacific Grove
Montery **Carmel**
Carmel Valley
Big Sur

Reedley **Three Rivers**
Lemoncove

Cambria
Templeton
Baywood Park
Los Osos
San Luis Obispo
Arroyo Grande
Nipomo

Bakersfield

Nipton

Summerland **Ojai**
Carpinteria
Santa Barbara **Santa Paula**
Ventura

Los Angeles
Santa Monica **Long Beach**

Laguna Beach
San Clemente

Big Bear City
Big Bear Lake
Lake Arrowhead
Redlands **Desert Hot Springs**

Palm Springs
Idyllwild **Palm Desert**
Temecula
Escondido **Borrego Springs**
Carlsbad
Encinitas **Del Mar**
La Jolla **San Diego**
Dulsura

San Francisco Area

Santa Rosa **Yountville**
Glen Ellen
Inverness **Napa**
Point Reyes Station **San Rafael** **Benicia**
Olema **San Anselmo**
Point Reyes
Mill Valley
Larkspur
Muir Beach
Stinson Beach **Berkley**
Sausalito **Moraga**
San Francisco **Oakland**
Alameda
Burlingame **Fremont**
Montara
Half Moon Bay
Palo Alto
Santa Clara

Los Angeles Area

Pacific Palisades
Malibu **Hollywood**
Santa Monica **Pasadena**
Beverly Hill
Marina Del Rey
Manhattan Beach
Redondo Beach **Torrance** **Orange**
Palos Verdes **Anaheim**
Santa Ana
Seal Beach
Two Harbors **Newport Beach**
Catalina Island **Avalon**

California

Eye Openers Bed and Breakfast Reservations

P.O. Box 694, Altadena, 91003-0694
(213) 684-4428; (818) 797-2055
FAX (818) 798-3640

AN-A91. Beautifully restored and decorated, this 1910 Princess Anne Victorian, now a friendly bed and breakfast, is surrounded by lovely gardens and is in a residential area convenient to most Orange County attractions with local bus service. Hearty breakfast and afternoon refreshments. No smoking. Nine guest rooms with private and shared baths. $65-120.

AN-P3. This bed and breakfast, with its country kitchen and full breakfast, offers comfort, convenience, economy, and good location near restaurants and public transportation. Bicycles, hot tub, and complimentary transport to Disneyland are available. Children welcome. Two guest rooms with private and shared baths. $35-55.

GG-04. Convenient to Orange County attractions, this home features large comfortable rooms, full breakfast, and TV room with fireplace. Four guest rooms with private and shared baths. $40-55.

OR-C3. Enjoy a delicious country-style breakfast in this contemporary wood-and-glass bed and breakfast. Relax in the pool, Jacuzzi, living room, or interesting family room. Convenient to Disneyland, Anaheim Convention Center, and Stadium. Handicapped accessible with adaptive equipment. No smoking. Three guest rooms available. $60.

SA-W1. This 1930s Renaissance cottage with antiques and country French decor features one guest room with French doors that open onto a deck overlooking a garden and pond. Choice of breakfast. It has a queen-size bed and private bath. Near South Coast Plaza, Orange County Airport, and major freeways. No smoking. $60-70.

Kids Welcome

3924 East 14th Street, Long Beach, 90804
(310) 498-0552; (800) 383-3513

7-5. The guest wing of this spacious house in Anaheim has room for the entire family, with a living room with a fireplace, balcony, kitchen, and private bath. Living room couch converts to a bed for the kids. Two downstairs guest rooms share a bath. Enjoy the spa and patio, as well as the full country breakfast. Pets welcome. Affordable rates. $60.

ANGWIN

Forest Manor

415 Cold Springs Road, 94508
(707) 965-3538; (800) 788-0364

Secluded 20-acre English Tudor estate tucked among forest vineyards in famous Napa wine country. Described as "one of the most romantic country inns. A small exclusive resort." Fireplaces, verandas, 53-foot pool, spas, spacious suites (one with Jacuzzi), refrigerators, coffee makers, home-baked breakfast. Close to more than 200 wineries, ballooning, hot springs, and a lake.

Hosts: Harold and Corlene Lambeth
Rooms: 3 (PB) $99-199
Full Breakfast
Credit Cards: A, B
Notes: 2, 5, 9, 10, 11, 14

APTOS

Apple Lane Inn

6265 Soquel Drive, 95003-3117
(408) 475-6868

NOTES: Credit cards accepted: A MasterCard; B Visa; C American Express; D Discover Card; E Diner's Club; F Other; 2 Personal checks accepted; 3 Lunch available; 4 Dinner available; 5 Open all year; 6 Pets welcome; 7 Smoking allowed; 8 Children welcome; 9 Social drinking allowed; 10 Tennis available; 11 Swimming available; 12 Golf available; 13 Skiing available; 14 May be booked through travel agents.

Apple Lane Inn is a historic Victorian farm-house restored to the charm and tranquility of an earlier age. It is just south of Santa Cruz on two and one-half acres of grounds, with gardens, a romantic gazebo, and fields. Explore the many miles of beaches within walking distance. Golf, hiking, fishing, shopping, and dining are all nearby.

Hosts: Doug and Diana Groom
Rooms: 5 (3 PB; 2 SB) $70-175
Full Breakfast
Credit Cards: A, B, D
Notes: 2, 5, 6, 7 (limited), 8, 9, 10, 11, 12, 14

Mangels House

570 Aptos Creek Road, Box 302, 95001
(408) 688-7982

A large southern Colonial on four acres of lawn and orchard, and bounded by a 10,000-acre redwood forest, is less than a mile from the beach. The five large, airy rooms are eclectic in decor and European in feel, reflecting the owners' background. Closed December 24 through 26.

Hosts: Jacqueline and Ronald Fisher
Rooms: 5 (PB) $105-135
Full Breakfast
Credit Cards: A, B, C
Notes: 2, 5, 6 and 7 (limited), 8 (over 8), 9, 10, 11, 12, 14

Mangels House

ARROYO GRANDE

Arroyo Village Inn

407 El Camino Real, 93420
(805) 489-5926

Romantic, award-winning Victorian offer-ing a delightful blend of yesterday's charm and hospitality with today's comforts and conveniences. Spacious suites are decorated with Laura Ashley prints and antiques with private baths, window seats, and balconies. In the heart of California's Central Coast, halfway between Los Angeles and San Francisco. Near beaches, wineries, mineral spas, San Luis Obispo; less than one hour to Hearst Castle. "The best kept secret on the Central Coast" says the *Los Angeles Times.*

Host: Gina Glass
Rooms: 7 (PB) $95-165
Full Breakfast
Credit Cards: A, B, C, D, E
Notes: 2, 5, 8, 9, 10, 11, 12, 14

AUBURN

Power's Mansion Inn

164 Cleveland Avenue, 95603
(916) 885-1166

This magnificent mansion was built from a gold fortune in the late 1800s. It has easy access to I-80 and off-street parking. Close to gold country, antiquing, water sports, hiking, horseback riding, skiing, balloon-ing, and restaurants.

Owners: Arno and Jean Lenieks, Tony and Tina Verhaart
Rooms: 11 (PB) $69-149
Full Breakfast
Credit Cards: A, B, C
Notes: 2, 5, 8, 9, 10, 11, 12, 13, 14

AVALON

Gull House

344 Whittley Avenue, Box 1381, 90704
(310) 510-2547

NOTES: Credit cards accepted: A MasterCard; B Visa; C American Express; D Discover Card; E Diner's Club; F Other; 2 Personal checks accepted; 3 Lunch available; 4 Dinner available; 5 Open all year;

For honeymooners and those celebrating anniversaries. AAA-approved contemporary house with swimming pool, spa, barbecue, gas-log fireplaces, morning room with refrigerator, color TV. Close to bay beaches and all water activities. Deposit or full payment in advance reserves taxi pickup and return. Ask about the guest rooms. Two-night minimum stay is required.

Hosts: Bob and Hattie Michalis
Suites: 2 (PB) $125-135
Continental Breakfast
Credit Cards: F
Notes: 2, 8, 10, 11, 12, 13, 14

Gull House

Zane Grey Pueblo

199 Chimes Tower Road, P.O. Box 216, 90704
(310) 510-0966

Zane Grey's home built in 1926. A Hopi Indian-style pueblo on a bluff overlooking the breathtaking ocean view. Quietest hotel in town. Each room is different, and all are named after Zane Grey's novels, which are available for guests to borrow from the office. No TVs or telephones in rooms. The living room does have cable TV, a grand piano, a fireplace, and a deck that overlooks the ocean. There is also a pool in the shape of an arrowhead. Complimentary pick up at the boat dock on arrival and to and from the hotel six times a day.

Host: Karen Baker
Rooms: 17 (PB) $55-125
Continental Breakfast
Credit Cards: A, B, C
Notes: 2, 5, 8, 9, 10, 11, 12, 14

BAKERSFIELD

Bed and Breakfast Inn Arizona

P.O. Box 11253, Glendale, AZ 85318-1253
(602) 561-0335; FAX (602) 561-2300

NE-001. Built on historic Route 66 in early 1930s, this bed and breakfast has a totally restored unique center court, charming park-like court patio, and antique and classic period furnishings. Private bath, full and queen-size beds. Forty miles from Lake Havasu. Call for rates.

BAYWOOD PARK

Baywood Bed and Breakfast Inn

1370 2nd Street, 93402
(805) 528-8888

The Baywood Bed and Breakfast is on Morro Bay on the central California coastline, 12 miles west of San Luis Obispo in a small neighborhood on a tiny peninsula. The inn is close to kayaking, golf, hiking, bicycling, and picnicking. Beautiful Montano De Oro State Park and Hearst Castle are minutes away. The inn features 15 highly decorated theme suites. All have bay views, cozy seating areas, wood-burning fireplaces, and private baths. Guests are treated to afternoon wine and cheese, room tours, and breakfast in bed.

Hosts: Edie Havard; Pat and Alex Benson
Rooms: 15 (PB) $80-160
Full Breakfast
Credit Cards: A, B
Notes: 2, 3, 4, 5, 8, 9, 11, 12, 14

6 Pets welcome; 7 Smoking allowed; 8 Children welcome; 9 Social drinking allowed; 10 Tennis available; 11 Swimming available; 12 Golf available; 13 Skiing available; 14 May be booked through travel agents.

BENICIA

Captain Walsh House

235 East L Street, 94510
(707) 747-5653

The Captain Walsh House commands a distinguished place in California's history. The house was built in Boston, dismantled, shipped around the Horn, and erected in Benica in 1849. Only two blocks from Benicia's charming First Street, where guests can visit California's first State Capitol. Within walking distance, guests will find quality tennis courts, a 50 meter swimming pool, and a wide variety of shops and restaurants. Only 40 minutes from San Francisco and 20 miles from Napa, Benicia is an ideal place for an uncomplicated and relaxing weekend getaway. Whatever guests desire, they can come and enjoy a warm and enchanting stay at Captain Walsh House.

Hosts: Reed and Steve Robbins
Rooms: 4 (PB) $110-125
Full Breakfast
Credit Cards: B, C
Notes: 2, 3, 4, 5, 9, 10, 11, 12

Union Hotel

401 First Street, 94510
(707) 746-0100

Built in 1882 and active as a 20-room bordello until the early 1950s, the Union Hotel was completely renovated in 1981 into a 12-room hotel and bed and breakfast. Each of the 12 rooms is decorated with a theme and named accordingly. Each room has a queen- or king-size bed, individual room-temperature controls, Jacuzzi, and TV. The superb stained-glass picture windows in the bar and dining room are worth a trip on their own. Restaurant on premises. Twenty minutes from the wine country, 45 minutes from San Francisco, and 20 minutes from the ferry to Fisherman's Wharf.

Host: Stephen Lipworth
Rooms: 12 (PB) $74-135

Continental Breakfast
Credit Cards: A, B, C, D, E
Notes: 3, 4, 5, 7, 9, 10, 12, 14

Hillegass House

BERKELEY

Hillegass House

2834 Hillegass Avenue, 94705
(510) 548-5517; (800) 400-5517

Built at the turn of the century amidst much greenery, the Hillegass House is in a quiet, refined neighborhood near the university and just two blocks from many of the excellent shops and restaurants for which Berkeley is famous. The large guest rooms with king- or queen-size beds are furnished with antiques, and all have telephones. San Francisco is a short ride on public transportation, and the wine country is less than an hour's drive. Midweek and long-term discount offered. A sauna is available.

Host: Richard Warren
Rooms: 4 (PB) $80-90
Full Breakfast
Credit Cards: None
Notes: 2, 5, 8, 9, 10, 11, 14

BEVERLY HILLS

Eye Openers Bed and Breakfast Reservations

P.O. Box 694, Altadena, 91003-0694
(213) 684-4428; (818) 797-2055
FAX (818) 798-3640

NOTES: Credit cards accepted: A MasterCard; B Visa; C American Express; D Discover Card; E Diner's Club; F Other; 2 Personal checks accepted; 3 Lunch available; 4 Dinner available; 5 Open all year;

BH-N1. In the heart of Beverly Hills, guest cottage in garden area of host home offers privacy and comfort. Cottage has twin beds, private bath, microwave, refrigerator, and choice of continental or full breakfast. Public transportation available. $50-55.

BH-W2. Charming canyon cottage behind the Beverly Hills Hotel provides a large suite and smaller guest room with private baths. One has king-size bed, the other has a queen-size bed. Convenient to UCLA, Hollywood, and Studio City. Host is biographer, theatre critic, and UCLA instructor. No smoking. Three-night minimum stay. $65-85.

BIG BEAR CITY

Bed and Breakfast, L.A.
3924 E. 14th Street, Long Beach, 90804
(310) 498-0552; (800) 383-3513

Festive Big Bear Victorian. On the southern shore of Big Bear Lake, this four-room Victorian focuses on beautiful surroundings and creature comforts. Rooms are large and well decorated, and all have private baths. Breakfast in the sunny dining room features "exclusive culinary creations." Afternoons feature teatime or a wine and cheese fest. $90-125.

BIG BEAR LAKE

Knickerbocker Mansion
P.O. Box 3661, 869 South Knickerbocker Road, 92315
(909) 866-8221

Built in the 1920s with old-country charm, Knickerbocker Mansion is nestled in the national forest on a hill overlooking Big Bear Lake. Just blocks to the village where guests can find shops and restaurants. In the summer there is boating, fishing, swimming, waterskiing, and parasailing; in the winter, Nordic and downhill skiing. All-season weddings, indoor or outdoor, are welcomed. Hosts cater to groups, corporate meetings, and family reunions. Picnic lunches and Saturday dinners available.

Hosts: Clee Langley and Karen Bowers
Rooms: 11 (6 PB; 5 SB) $110-225
Full Breakfast
Credit Cards: A, B, C, D
Notes: 2, 3, 4, 5, 8 (limited), 9, 10, 11, 12, 13, 14

BIG SUR

Ventana Inn
Highway 1, 93920
(408) 667-2331; (800) 628-6500

Deluxe romantic inn on 243 acres above Pacific, 35 miles from Monterey airport. Decorator-designed accommodations in 12 buildings with king- or queen-size bed, terrace, air conditioning, and telephone; most with fireplace, some with wet bar and hot tub. All with TVs and VCRs. Three townhouse suites. Wheelchair accessibility. Complimentary continental breakfast and afternoon wine and cheese are served. Highly regarded restaurant and fireside lounge. Two heated pools, sauna, massage, two Japanese hot baths, horseback riding, and hiking. Country store and gallery. Beach nearby.

Host: R.E. Bussinger
Rooms: 60 (PB) $195-370
Continental Breakfast
Credit Cards: A, B, C, D, E
Notes: 2, 3, 4, 5, 7 (limited), 9, 11, 14

BISHOP

1898 Chalfant House
213 Academy, 93514
(619) 872-1790

Turn-of-the-century inn standing between towering mountains just one block off Highway 395. Each of seven guest rooms has private bath, antiques, and handmade quilts and comforters. The wood-burning

6 Pets welcome; 7 Smoking allowed; 8 Children welcome; 9 Social drinking allowed; 10 Tennis available; 11 Swimming available; 12 Golf available; 13 Skiing available; 14 May be booked through travel agents.

stove in the antique-filled sitting room creates a cozy ambience to be enjoyed while reading, watching TV, or visiting with other guests. A full gourmet breakfast is generously served on china and silver service. Old-fashioned ice cream sundaes are a delightful complimentary treat in the evenings between eight and nine.

Hosts: Fred and Sally Maneche
Rooms: 6 (PB) $60-90
Suites: 3
Full Breakfast
Credit Cards: A, B, C
Notes: 2, 5, 8, 9, 12, 13

The Matlick House

1313 Rowan Lane, 93514
(619) 873-3133

A 1906 ranch house, completely renovated, at the base of the eastern Sierra Nevada Mountains. Close to year-round fishing, hiking, skiing, and trail rides. Telephones, air conditioning, wine and hors d'oeuvres; antiques throughout.

Host: Ray and Barbara Showalter
Rooms: 5 (PB) $79-89
Full Breakfast
Credit Cards: A, B
Notes: 2, 5, 7 (limited), 8 (over 14), 9, 10, 11, 12, 13

BOLINAS (MARIN COUNTY)

Bed and Breakfast, L.A.

3924 East 14th Street, Long Beach, 90804
(800) 383-3513

This cabin is on a spit of land surrounded by Bolinas Bay. Point Reyes National Park is on one side; Stinson Beach and Mount Tamalpais on the other side. Two bedrooms, a living room, full kitchen, and a bathroom. The cabin is well stocked, including charcoal for the barbecue. $125.

BOONVILLE

Boonville Hotel

14050 Highway 128, 95415
(707) 895-2210

This eight-room hotel is simply decorated with Shaker Southwestern furnishings, and features a popular California-style restaurant and bar serving dinner Wednesday through Monday night. In a small town in Anderson Valley, the wine growing region and apple farming area. Just a 30-minute drive from the Mendocino coast. Closed January.

Hosts: John Schmitt and Jeanne Eliades
Rooms: 8 (PB) $70-145
Continental Breakfast
Credit Cards: A, B
Notes: 2, 4, 8, 10

BORREGO SPRINGS (DEATH VALLEY)

Bed and Breakfast, L.A.

3924 E. 14th Street, Long Beach, 90804
(310) 498-0552; (800) 383-3513

Watch the wildflowers bloom at this perfectly restored desert resort. All rooms have private baths, TVs and a panoramic view of the valley. Sun yourself at the pool or take advantage of the many hiking trails and canyons. Grounds include indoor and outdoor restaurant areas at reasonable prices. Affordable to luxury rates.

BRIDGEPORT

The Cain House

11 Main Street, 93517
(619) 932-7040; (800) 433-CAIN

In a small valley with a view of the rugged eastern Sierras, the Cain House has blended European elegance with a western atmos-

---

NOTES: Credit cards accepted: A MasterCard; B Visa; C American Express; D Discover Card; E Diner's Club; F Other; 2 Personal checks accepted; 3 Lunch available; 4 Dinner available; 5 Open all year;

phere. Every amenity has been provided for, including wine and cheese in the evenings. After breakfast, the pristine beauty of the valley, lakes, and streams await for a day of hiking, boating, fishing, hunting, and cross-country skiing. Three-diamond AAA and Mobil approved.

Hosts: Chris and Marachal Gohlich
Rooms: 7 (PB) $80-135
Full Breakfast
Credit Cards: A, B, C, D, E
Notes: 2, 9, 10

BURLINGAME

Burlingame Bed and Breakfast

1021 Balboa Avenue, 94010
(415) 344-5815

Boating, swimming, fishing (bay and ocean), running, golf, hiking, art, entertainment, sports. Near Stanford, other colleges, and transportation.

Hosts: Joe and Elnora Fernandez
Room: 1 (PB) $40-50
Continental Breakfast
Credit Cards: None
Notes: 2, 5, 7 (limited), 8, 10, 11, 12

CALISTOGA

Bed and Breakfast, L.A.

3924 E. 14th Street, Long Beach, 90804
(310) 498-0552; (800) 383-3513

Garden Serenity. Walk to downtown Calistoga from this private, quiet three-room cottage featuring a large bedroom, kitchenette, and bath. Enjoy a continental breakfast in the quaint outdoor eating and lounge area under a 150-year-old oak tree. Antique furnishings, including an iron and brass bed, are a reminder of the slower pace of old California. Call for rates.

Brannan Cottage Inn

P.O. Box 81, 109 Wapoo Avenue, 94515
(707) 942-4200

A charming Victorian country cottage built in 1863 right in town. On the National Register of Historic Places. Six bright and airy guest rooms, all with private baths and entrances. Oak floors harmonize with antique pine furniture, creating a pleasant old-world ambience. Rates include a full buffet breakfast and a welcome decanter of wine. Hot springs, massages, mud-baths, gliders, and wine and champagne tasting nearby.

Host: Dieter Back
Rooms: 6 (PB) $110-160
Full Breakfast
Credit Cards: A, B, C
Notes: 2, 5, 9, 10, 11, 12, 14

Calistoga Country Lodge

2883 Foothill Boulevard, 94515
(707) 942-5555

This 1917 farmhouse is set among 100-year-old oaks and has been restored in a Southwestern style. Rooms feature whitewashed pine floors, custom lodgepole furnishings, and one of a kind Navajo rug wall hangings. A large, stone fireplace and Georgia O'Keefe-style artifacts draw guests to the spacious common area. A colorful breakfast buffet overlooks the patio and heated pool, where guests can relax and enjoy the view.

Host: Rae Ellen Fields
Rooms: 6 (4 PB; 2 SB) $95-125
Continental Breakfast
Credit Cards: A, B, C
Notes: 2, 10, 11, 12, 14

Calistoga Wayside Inn

1523 Foothill Boulevard, 94515
(707) 942-0645; (800) 845-3632

6 Pets welcome; 7 Smoking allowed; 8 Children welcome; 9 Social drinking allowed; 10 Tennis available;
11 Swimming available; 12 Golf available; 13 Skiing available; 14 May be booked through travel agents.

A 1920s Spanish-style home in a parklike setting with fountains and gardens. Full breakfast served in dining room or on lower patio. King- and queen-size beds. Private baths. Near hiking, golfing, tennis, shopping, wineries, restaurants, and glider and balloon rides. Wine and cheese served in the afternoon. Sherry and snack served in the evening. No smoking. In-week specials. Walking distance to town.

Rooms: 3 (PB) $95-135
Full Breakfast
Credit Cards: A, B, C
Notes: 2, 5, 8, 9, 10, 11, 12, 14

Christopher's Inn

1010 Foothill Boulevard, 94515
(707) 942-5755

An architect created this country inn with exceptional landscaped grounds close to the center of historic Calistoga. Elegant formality and privacy with English country ambience is created with fine antiques and Laura Ashley matching comforters, balloon drapes, wallpaper, and fluffy pillow covers. Play croquet beneath ancient cedar trees. Step across the road to a romantic spa that creates the ultimate bath experience, especially for couples. Then return to the guest room, private bath, secret gardens, fresh flowers, and breakfast in bed while snuggling by a cozy, private fireplace.

Hosts: Christopher and Adele Layton
Rooms: 10 (PB) $120-170
Continental Breakfast
Credit Cards: A, B, C
Notes: 2, 5, 8 (by arrangement), 9, 10, 11, 12, 14 (weekdays)

"Culvers," A Country Inn

1805 Foothill Boulevard, 94515
(707) 942-4535

A lovely Victorian residence built in 1875, filled with antiques and offering a full country breakfast. Jacuzzi and seasonal pool, indoor sauna. Within minutes of wineries, mud baths, and downtown Calis-

toga. Lovely view of St. Helena mountain range from the veranda. Sherry and hors d'ouvres are offered in the afternoon, with an afternoon beverage and baked treats offered upon arrival. Closed December 24 through 26, Thanksgiving, and New Year's.

Hosts: Meg and Tony Wheatley
Rooms: 6 (SB) $105-125
Full Breakfast
Credit Cards: For deposit only
Notes: 2, 8 (over 16), 9, 10, 11, 12, 14

The Elms
Bed and Breakfast Inn

1300 Cedar Street, 94515
(707) 942-9476; (800) 235-4316

This 1871 French three-story Victorian is one-half block from town next to a park on the Napa River. It is very quiet and peaceful, yet within walking distance of restaurants, spas, gliders, bike rentals, golf, and tennis. The rooms are very romantic—decorated with antiques. All have private baths, coffee makers, bathrobes, chocolates, and ports for after dinner. The feather beds are piled high with pillows and down comforters. Some rooms have fireplaces, TV, and spa tubs. A huge three-course gourmet breakfast is served, and wine and cheese is served in the afternoon.

Host: Stephen and Karla Wyle
Rooms: 7 (PB) $110-175
Full Breakfast
Credit Cards: A, B
Notes: 5, 11, 12, 14

Foothill House

3037 Foothill Boulevard, 94515
(707) 942-6933; (800) 942-6933

"The most romantic inn of the Napa Valley," according to the *Chicago Tribune* travel editor. In a country setting, Foothill House offers spacious suites individually decorated with antiques, each with private bath and entrance, fireplace, and small refrigerator. Two suites offer Jacuzzi tubs. Complimentary wine and hors d'ouevres each evening, and free turndown service. Private elegant cottage also available.

Hosts: Doris and Gus Beckert
Rooms: 3 (PB) $115-220
Full Breakfast
Credit Cards: A, B, C
Notes: 2, 5, 9, 10, 11, 12, 14

Foothill House

Hillcrest

3225 Lake County Highway, 94515
(707) 942-6334

Breathtaking view of Napa Valley country side. Hiking, swimming, and fishing on 40 acres. Family-owned since 1860. Hilltop modern country home decorated with heirlooms from family mansion. Rooms have balconies. Fireplace and grand piano, rare art work, silver, crystal, china, and Oriental rugs. Family photo albums date back to 1870s. Breakfast is served weekends on a 12-foot antique table fit for a king. Outdoor spa and large pool.

Host: Debbie O'Gorman
Rooms: 4 (1 PB; 3 SB) $45-90
Continental Breakfast
Credit Cards: None
Notes: 2, 5, 6, 7, 9, 10, 11, 12, 14

Mountain Home Ranch

3400 Mountain Home Ranch Road, 94515
(707) 942-6616

In the hills above the Napa Valley, the 300-acre vacation facility has been in the same family since 1913. Quiet, restful, rejuvenating. Pool, tennis, lake fishing, wilderness walking trails. Fifteen minutes to the heart

of the wine country with its hot air ballooning, spas, and golf. Closed mid-December through the end of January.

Host: Kimo Fouts
Rooms: 14 (PB) $60-125
Continental Breakfast
Credit Cards: A, B
Notes: 2, 6, 7, 8, 9, 10, 11, 12, 14

The Pink Mansion

1415 Foothill Boulevard, 94515
(707) 942-0558

A 119-year-old Victorian in the heart of the Napa Valley wine country. Within biking distance of several wineries; walking distance to Calistoga's many spas and restaurants. Fully air-conditioned; complimentary wine and cheese. Each room has a wonderful view and private bath. Two-night minimum stay required for weekends and holidays.

Host: Jeff Seyfried
Rooms: 5 (PB) $105-165
Full Breakfast
Credit Cards: A, B, C
Notes: 2, 5, 8 (over 12), 9, 10, 11, 12, 14

Quail Mountain

Quail Mountain Bed and Breakfast Inn

4455 North St. Helena Highway, 94515
(707) 942-0316

Quail Mountain is a secluded luxury bed and breakfast on 26 wooded and vineyard acres. Three guest rooms, each with king-size bed, private bath, and private deck.

6 Pets welcome; 7 Smoking allowed; 8 Children welcome; 9 Social drinking allowed; 10 Tennis available; 11 Swimming available; 12 Golf available; 13 Skiing available; 14 May be booked through travel agents.

Complimentary wine, pool, spa. Full breakfast. Close to Napa Valley wineries and restaurants. A two-night minimum stay weekends and holidays is required.

Hosts: Don and Alma Swiers
Rooms: 3 (PB) $100-125
Full Breakfast
Credit Cards: A, B
Notes: 2, 5, 9, 10, 11, 12, 14

Trailside Inn

4201 Silverado Trail, 94515
(707) 942-4106

A charming 1930s farmhouse in the country with three very private suites. Each suite has its own entrance, porch or deck, bedroom, bath, fireplace, and air conditioning. Fresh home-baked breads provided in the fully equipped kitchen.

Hosts: Randy and Lani Gray
Suites: 3 (PB) $120
Continental Breakfast
Credit Cards: A, B, C, D
Notes: 2, 5, 7, 8, 9, 10, 11, 12, 14

Zinfandel House

1253 Summit Drive, 94515
(707) 942-0733

Zinfandel House is in a wooded setting on a western hillside with a spectacular view of the famous Napa Valley vineyards. Halfway between St. Helena and Calistoga. Choose from three tastefully decorated rooms with a private or shared bath. Breakfast is served on the deck or in the solarium.

Hosts: Bette and George Starke
Rooms: 3 (PB or SB) $70-100
Full Breakfast
Credit Cards: None
Notes: 2, 5, 9, 10, 11, 12

CAMBRIA

Bed and Breakfast, L.A.

3924 E. 14th Street, Long Beach, 90804
(310) 498-0552; (800) 383-3513

Watch the ocean from the hot tub. The entire lower level of this luxury home in Cambria is designed for bed and breakfast pampering. There is a bedroom with queen-size bed, living room with fireplace, stereo and TV systems, dining area, fully equipped kitchen (including goodies!), and two decks—both with ocean view and one with guests' own hot tub. British hostess bakes fresh scones as part of every gourmet breakfast. Walking distance to town. There is even a secret, private entrance. $110.

Eye Openers Bed and Breakfast Reservations

P.O. Box 694, Altadena, 91003-0694
(213) 684-4428; (818) 797-2055
FAX (818) 798-3640

CA-B51. Contemporary A-frame bed and breakfast inn on the beach has antique furnishings, ocean views, and outdoor decks. Continental breakfast. No smoking. Five guest rooms. Private bath. $120-150.

CA-D2. Friendly, comfortable bed and breakfast in wooded area offers a peak at the ocean and quiet surroundings. Two guest rooms with double and twin beds. Private bath. No smoking. Full breakfast. $35-60.

CA-061. Each of the six guest rooms in this 1873 Greek Revival-style historic inn is decorated differently, but all have antiques from the 1800s. Full breakfast. No smoking. Six guest rooms. Private bath. $85-125.

CA-P31. Just south of Hearst Castle at the ocean, this bed and breakfast features rooms with fireplaces, private patios, and bath ensuite. A full breakfast is served with an ocean view. No smoking. Three guest rooms. Private bath. $85.

NOTES: Credit cards accepted: A MasterCard; B Visa; C American Express; D Discover Card; E Diner's Club; F Other; 2 Personal checks accepted; 3 Lunch available; 4 Dinner available; 5 Open all year;

The Pickford House Bed and Breakfast

2555 MacLeod Way, 93428
(805) 927-8619

Only eight miles from Hearst Castle, Pickford House is decorated with antiques reminiscent of the golden age of film. Eight rooms have king- or queen-size beds, private baths, fireplaces, and a view of the mountains. Parlor with an 1860 bar is used for wine and tea bread at 5:00 P.M. TV in rooms. All have claw-foot tubs and showers in rooms. Extra person is $20.

Host: Anna Larsen
Rooms: 8 (PB) $85-125
Full Breakfast
Credit Cards: A, B
Notes: 2, 5, 7 (limited), 9, 11

CARLSBAD

Pelican Cove Inn

320 Walnut Avenue, 92008
(619) 434-5995

Pelican Cove Inn features two rooms with spa tubs, feather beds, fireplaces, private entries, private baths, lovely antiques, a sun deck, balconies, and a gazebo. Walk to the beach and restaurants. Palomar Airport and Amtrak pick-up. Beach chairs, towels, picnic baskets available. Beautiful gardens. Two-night minimum stay is required for weekends and holidays.

Hosts: Kris and Nancy Nayudu
Rooms: 8 (PB) $85-175
Full Breakfast
Credit Cards: A, B, C
Notes: 2, 5, 8 (over 9), 9, 10, 11, 12, 14

CARMEL

Bed and Breakfast International

P.O. Box 282910, San Francisco, 94128-2910
(800) 872-4500; (415) 696-1690
FAX (415) 696-1699

203. Large contemporary home with several decks surrounded by hills ten minutes from Carmel. There is a studio guest house with a queen-size lodgepole pine bed, wood-burning fireplace, and private entrance. There is a hot tub on one of the decks for guests to use. Breakfast is brought to the guest house by the host. $88.

205. Spacious modern home has four fireplaces and is very contemporary in design. Just minutes from downtown Carmel. The guest room has a charming and cozy decor with professional decorator touches. There is a private entrance, fireplace in the room, private bath, and view of Point Lobos. Breakfast is prepared by the host in the main house. $98.

207. Contemporary townhouse with fine art and tasteful furnishings on the east side of Highway 1, five minutes from Carmel Beach. The guest room is large and has a queen-size bed and private bath. There is a pool available for guests' use. $78.

Bed and Breakfast, L.A.

3924 East 14th Street, Long Beach, 90804
(800) 383-3513

Carmel Ocean View. These hosts have one room with double bed and shared bath, partial ocean view at a great Carmel location, and they will also make their whole house available (two bedrooms, two baths) by the week. Complete ocean view with a fully equipped kitchen. Breakfast is full and the hosts allow full use of the house—even their bicycles! $70.

Carmel-2. Oceanview suite in Carmel. Walk to the beach from this private bed and breakfast, with two guest suites, both with private entrances, full bath, and ocean view. One has a four-poster bed, sitting area, and deck. The other has sitting area, loft, and can

6 Pets welcome; 7 Smoking allowed; 8 Children welcome; 9 Social drinking allowed; 10 Tennis available;
11 Swimming available; 12 Golf available; 13 Skiing available; 14 May be booked through travel agents.

sleep four people. Sumptuous breakfast included, and only a five-minute drive into town. Moderate rates.

Carriage House Inn
Junipero between 7th and 8th, 93921
(800) 433-4732

Fresh flowers and country inn flavor. Continental breakfast and newspaper delivered to the room each morning. Wood-burning fireplaces, down comforters. Spacious rooms, many with open-beam ceilings and sunken tubs. Wine and hors d'oeuvres each evening in the library. Carmel's AAA four-diamond inn. A romantic getaway! Two-night minimum stay required for weekends and holidays.

Host: Raul Lopez
Rooms: 13 (PB) $145-250
Continental Breakfast
Credit Cards: All Major
Notes: 2, 5, 7, 11, 12, 14

Eye Openers Bed and Breakfast Reservations
P.O. Box 694, Altadena, 91003-0694
(213) 684-4428; (818) 797-2055
FAX (818) 798-3640

CA-251. This country inn offers 25 large, nicely decorated guest rooms with fireplace, full breakfast, afternoon and evening refreshments. Convenient to all Carmel area attractions. No smoking. Private bath. $105-180.

CA-V11I. Fireplaces and mini-refrigerators in all rooms in a lovely English Tudor-style inn built around a courtyard. Eleven guest rooms and suites with king-, queen-size, or double beds; private baths. Walking distance to beaches. Some suites have kitchenettes. A continental breakfast is served. $80-110.

CA-D12I. Rustic bed and breakfast near Carmel shops offers twelve rooms and

suites with fireplaces. Queen-, king-size, or twin beds and private baths. Continental breakfast. $75-110.

Holiday House
P.O. Box 782, Camino Real at 7th Avenue, 93921
(408) 624-6267

Built in 1905, this comfortable inn is a brown-shingled house on a hillside amid a colorful, well-maintained garden. Six quaint rooms, four with private baths, offer refuge and relaxation. All rooms are furnished with antiques, complimenting the slanted ceilings and dormer windows looking out onto ocean or garden. A full breakfast is served buffet-style daily. Three blocks to beach and one block off Carmel's main street. A cozy get-away right in the heart of charming Carmel.

Hosts: Dieter and Ruth Back
Rooms: 6 (4 PB; 2 SB) $100-125
Full Breakfast
Credit Cards: A, B, C
Notes: 2, 5, 9, 10, 11, 12

San Antonio House
P.O. Box 3683, 93921
(408) 624-4334

A romantic seaside country inn capturing the charm of early Carmel. One block from Carmel Beach and four blocks from town. Four comfortably furnished rooms with private entrances, patios, and wood-burning fireplaces offer that restful place to get away from the hectic pace of the world. Beautiful gardens surround the inn. Close to golf courses.

Hosts: Sarah and Rick Lee
Rooms: 4 (PB) $110-150
Continental Breakfast
Credit Cards: A, B
Notes: 2, 5, 12, 14

The Sandpiper Inn-at-the-Beach
2408 Bay View Avenue, 93923
(408) 624-6433; (800) 633-6433

NOTES: Credit cards accepted: A MasterCard; B Visa; C American Express; D Discover Card; E Diner's Club; F Other; 2 Personal checks accepted; 3 Lunch available; 4 Dinner available; 5 Open all year;

Within sight and sound of beautiful Carmel Beach. Quiet comfort and luxury in a relaxed atmosphere. Rooms and cottages are filled with antiques and fresh flowers; all have private baths. Some have glorious ocean views, others have fireplaces. Buffet breakfast and complimentary afternoon beverages are served in the comfortable lounge. Perfect for celebrating anniversaries and special occasions.

Hosts: Graeme and Irene Mackenzie
Rooms: 16 (PB) $100-180
Continental Breakfast
Credit Cards: A, B, C
Notes: 2, 5, 9, 10, 11, 12, 14

Sea View Inn

P.O. Box 4138, 93921
(408) 624-8778

The Sea View Inn, a simple country Victorian, has been welcoming guests for more than 70 years. A quiet, cozy bed and breakfast, the Sea View has eight individually decorated rooms, six with private baths. Near the village and the beach, the Sea View provides a welcoming retreat. A generous continental breakfast and afternoon tea are complimentary.

Host: Diane Hydorn
Rooms: 8 (6 PB; 2 SB) $80-115
Continental Breakfast
Credit Cards: A, B
Notes: 2, 5, 9, 10, 11, 12

Vagabond's House Inn

P.O. Box 2747, 93921
(408) 624-7738; (800) 262-1262 (US reservations);
(800) 221-1262 (CA reservations)

In the heart of the village, this inn surrounds a Carmel-stone courtyard dominated by large oak trees, plants, ferns, and flowers in profusion. The 11 unique guest rooms are appointed with a combination of collectibles and antiques in a mixture of European elegance and country tradition.

Hosts: Honey Spence and Jewell Brown
Rooms: 11 (PB) $85-145
Continental Breakfast
Credit Cards: A, B, C
Notes: 2, 5, 6, 7 (limited), 9, 10, 11, 12, 14

CARMEL VALLEY

The Valley Lodge

Carmel Valley Road and Ford Road, P.O. Box 93, 93924
(408) 659-2261; (800) 641-4646

This quiet country inn is on three beautifully landscaped acres in picturesque Carmel Valley, the sunbelt of Monterey Peninsula. Relax and unwind in a garden patio room, a fireplace suite, or a cozy one- or two-bedroom fireplace cottage with a kitchen. Enjoy the heated pool, hot spa, sauna, fitness center, and games area. Walk to fine restaurants and quaint shops in the village, or just "listen to your beard grow."

Host: Peter Coakley
Rooms: 31 (PB) $95-135
Continental Breakfast
Credit Cards: A, B, C
Notes: 2, 5, 6 (fee), 7, 8, 9, 10, 11, 12, 14

CARPINTERIA

Carpinteria Beach Condo

1825 Cravens Lane, 93013
(805) 684-1579

In a lush flower-growing valley and across the street from "the world's safest beach."

6 Pets welcome; 7 Smoking allowed; 8 Children welcome; 9 Social drinking allowed; 10 Tennis available; 11 Swimming available; 12 Golf available; 13 Skiing available; 14 May be booked through travel agents.

Unit has mountain view. Tropical island decor has a sunset wall mural, fully furnished kitchen, queen-size bed, and color cable TV. Pool, spa, and gas barbecue on complex. Self-catering with beverage provided and fruit from host's ranch. Sleeps four. Eleven miles south of Santa Barbara. Hosts available for tennis, bridge, or tour of their semitropical fruit ranch. No smoking.

Hosts: Bev and Don Schroeder
Suite: 1 (PB) $60-65
Continental Breakfast
Credit Cards: None
Notes: 2, 5, 8, 9, 10, 11, 12

D&B Schroeder Ranch Bed and Breakfast

1825 Cravens Lane, 93013
(805) 684-1579

Nestled in the foothills of Carpinteria one mile from Highway 101 with an ocean view, the Schroeder ranch produces avocados and semi-tropical fruit. The guest accommodation has a separate entrance, queen-size bed, color TV, small refrigerator, and private bath. There are decks for viewing the Pacific Ocean, Channel Islands, and gorgeous sunsets. Guests may enjoy strolling around the ten acres, discovering fruit trees and a year-round creek. There is a spa in a lush tropical setting to soothe weary travelers. The "world's safest beach' is two miles away. Santa Barbara is twelve miles away. The hosts are ready for a bridge game or tennis. Nonsmokers.

Hosts: Bev and Don Schroeder
Room: 1 (PB) $60-65
Full Breakfast

CASSEL

Clearwater House

Cassel Road, 96016
(916) 335-5500

Clearwater House is a quiet country inn on Hat Creek at the heart of California's finest wild trout fishing. Within minutes are the renowned Fall River, the McCloud River, the Pit, and the Sacramento. Catering exclusively to the fly fishers for over ten years, Clearwater is a handsome turn-of-the-century farmhouse offering seven bedrooms and baths. The staff is friendly and professional, and the meals and service are first class. Private guiding and fly-fishing schools for anglers of all levels are available. Guests can arrange wade and float trips from April through November. Biking, hiking, and driving tours are available. Tennis courts on the grounds. Five-hour drive from San Francisco; one hour from the airport in Redding. Open April 30 through November 15.

Hosts: Dick Galland and Lynn Bedell
Rooms: 7 (PB) $210-260
Full Breakfast
Credit Cards: A, B
Notes: 2, 3, 4, 8, 9, 10, 11, 12, 13, 14

CATALINA

Bed and Breakfast, L.A.

3924 E. 14th Street, Long Beach, 90804
(310) 498-0552; (800) 383-3513

Canyon Resort on Catalina. This elegant resort "on the island" is in a quaint canyon overlooking Avalon. Rooms include king- or queen-sized beds, private baths, TVs, and phones. Heated pool, Jacuzzi, and sauna. Hosts provide complimentary shuttles to and from town. Accommodations do not include breakfast. Special midweek rates. $55-135.

CLEAR LAKE

Muktip Manor

12540 Lakeshore Drive, 95422
(707) 994-9571

Suite consisting of one bedroom, bath, kitchenette, sitting room, TV, and deck. Private beach on the largest lake in California, with canoes and bicycles available. Several golf

NOTES: Credit cards accepted: A MasterCard; B Visa; C American Express; D Discover Card; E Diner's Club; F Other; 2 Personal checks accepted; 3 Lunch available; 4 Dinner available; 5 Open all year;

courses are in the county. Hiking, biking, and rock hounding. One-hundred and ten miles north of San Francisco, near five wineries.

Hosts: Jerry and Nadine Schiffman
Room: 1 (PB) $65
Full Breakfast
Credit Cards: None
Notes: 2, 5, 6, 9, 10, 11, 12

COLOMA

Coloma Country Inn

345 High Street, Box 502, 95613
(916) 622-6919

Surrounded by the 300-acre Gold Discovery State Park, this 1852 farmhouse provides quiet comfort and close access to Sutter's Mill, museum, and attractions. White water rafting and ballooning with hosts. Featured in the June 1988 issue of *Country Living* magazine.

Hosts: Cindi and Alan Ehrgott
Rooms: 5 (3 PB; 2 SB) $89-155
Cottage Suites: 2
Full Breakfast
Credit Cards: None
Notes: 2, 5, 8, 9, 14

Columbia City Hotel

Box 1870, 95310
(209) 532-1479

In the heart of a historic Gold Rush town preserved and protected by the state of California, this impeccable inn is surrounded by relics of the past. All rooms have been restored to reflect the 1850s. Downstairs, the highly acclaimed restaurant and always inviting What Cheer Saloon provide a haven for travelers seeking comfort and gracious hospitality. All rooms have half-baths; hall showers. Closed Christmas Eve and Christmas Day.

Host: Tom Bender
Rooms: 10 (PB) $70-90
Continental Breakfast
Credit Cards: A, B, C
Notes: 2, 3, 4, 5, 7 (limited), 8, 9, 10, 11, 12, 13, 14

Columbia City Hotel

Fallon Hotel

Washington Street, 95310
(209) 532-1470

Since 1857, the historic Fallon Hotel has provided a home away from home to countless visitors. Authentically restored to its Victorian grandeur, most of the furnishings are original to the inn. Several rooms have private balconies, and all rooms have half-baths. Baskets of toiletries, robes, and slippers are provided for the showers off the hallway. One handicapped room available. In the heart of a state-restored Gold Rush town. Adjacent to the Fallon Theatre, which provides year-round productions. Call or write for price information.

Host: Tom Bender
Rooms: 14 (SB) $55-95
Continental Breakfast
Credit Cards: A, B, C
Notes: 2, 5, 8, 9, 10, 11, 12, 13, 14

COSTA MESA

Bed and Breakfast, L.A.

3924 E. 14th Street, Long Beach, 90804
(310) 498-0552; (800) 383-3513

6 Pets welcome; 7 Smoking allowed; 8 Children welcome; 9 Social drinking allowed; 10 Tennis available; 11 Swimming available; 12 Golf available; 13 Skiing available; 14 May be booked through travel agents.

This lovely country-style home has one guest room and a shared bath. Huge yard and garden. Hosts will pick up at John Wayne Airport and provide full country breakfast. $50-55.

DAVENPORT

New Davenport Bed and Breakfast

31 Davenport Avenue, 95017
(408) 425-1818; (408) 426-4122

Halfway between Carmel-Monterey and San Francisco, on Coast Highway 1. Small, rural, coastal town noted for whale watching, wind surfing, Ano Nuevo Elephant Seal State Reserve, hiking, bicycling, and beach access. Wonderful restaurant and gift store with unusual treasures and jewelry.

Hosts: Bruce and Marcia McDougal
Rooms: 12 (PB) $65-115
Full Breakfast
Credit Cards: A, B, C
Notes: 2, 3, 4, 5, 8, 9

DAVIS

University Inn Bed and Breakfast

340 A Street, 95616
(916) 756-8648

Adjacent to the University of California-Davis, this country inn offers a charming escape from a busy college town in a home-like setting. Each room has a private bath, telephone, refrigerator, cable TV, and microwave oven. There are complimentary chocolates, beverages, and flowers. A generous continental-plus breakfast is served.

Hosts: Lynda and Ross Yancher
Rooms: 4 (PB) $55
Continental Breakfast
Credit Cards: A, B, C, D, E
Notes: 2, 5, 6 and 7 (limited), 8, 9, 10, 11, 12, 14

DEL MAR

The Blue Door

13707 Durango Drive, 92014
(619) 755-3819

Enjoy New England charm in a quiet Southern California setting. Lower-level two-room suite with king-size bed, private bath, and cozy sitting room opening onto bougainvillaea-splashed patio with open vista of Torrey Pines Reserve Canyon. Only 20 miles north of San Diego. Creative full breakfast.

Hosts: Bob and Anna Belle Schock
Suite: 1 (PB) $50-60
Full Breakfast
Credit Cards: None
Notes: 2, 5, 8 (over 16), 9, 10, 11, 12

Eye Openers Bed and Breakfast Reservations

P.O. Box 694, Altadena, 91003-0694
(213) 684-4428; (818) 797-2055
FAX (818) 798-3640

DM-R101. Romantic getaway in a lovely seaside village just north of San Diego offers a choice of ten rooms, many with an ocean view and one with a fireplace. Enjoy an extended continental breakfast, afternoon refreshments, a walk on the beach, or a trip to the racetrack or nearby renowned flower-growing areas. Private and shared bath. $80-145.

NOTES: Credit cards accepted: A MasterCard; B Visa; C American Express; D Discover Card; E Diner's Club; F Other; 2 Personal checks accepted; 3 Lunch available; 4 Dinner available; 5 Open all year;

Gull's Nest

P.O. Box 1056, 92014
(619) 259-4863

Gull's Nest rustic hideaway is a contemporary wood home surrounded by pines with a beautiful ocean and bird sanctuary view from two upper decks. There is a third deck on the studio apartment. Home is decorated with many paintings, mosaics, and wood carvings. Fifteen minutes from La Jolla and five minutes from Del Mar. Close to I-5, and just 20 minutes from the San Diego Zoo and airport.

Hosts: Michael and Constance Segel
Rooms: 2 (PB) $65-85
Full Breakfast
Credit Cards: None
Notes: 2, 5, 8 (over 5), 9, 10, 11, 12

DESERT HOT SPRINGS

Travellers Repose

66920 First Street, P.O. Box 655, 92240
(619) 329 9584

Bay windows, gingerbread trim, and stained glass decorate this two-story Victorian home. The interior is color coordinated throughout, blending natural woods and wallpapers. The three individually decorated bedrooms are spacious and all have queen-size beds. Guests enjoy the view of desert floor and mountains rising to 11,000 feet. Amenities include a patio, gardens, pool, and spa. Desert Hot Springs is famous for its natural hot mineral waters. Palm Springs is only minutes away, with its museums, shopping, famous restaurants and celebrities, golf tournaments, tennis tournaments, and theaters and stage shows.

Hosts: Marian and Sam Relkoff
Rooms: 3 (1 PB; 2 SB) $55-75
Continental Breakfast
Credit Cards: None
Notes: 2, 9, 10, 11, 12, 14

DORRINGTON

Dorrington Hotel and Restaurant

3431 Highway 4, P.O. Box 4307, 95223
(209) 795-5800

This 1860 hotel was originally a stage coach stop and served as a depot for stockmen and as a summer resort. Restored, the hotel provides a gracious and relaxing atmosphere. Cozy homemade quilts, brass beds, and handsome antiques fill the five comfortably elegant rooms. Fresh fruit and other amenities will make one feel at home. A full breakfast of choice is served in the dining room; newspapers left outside the door. Enjoy a tastefully prepared lunch or dinner in the casual elegance of the northern Italian-style restaurant.

Hosts: Bonnie and Arden Saville
Rooms: 5 (2 SB) $85
Full Breakfast
Credit Cards: A, B
Notes: 2, 3, 4, 5, 10, 11, 12, 13

Dorrington Hotel

DULZURA

Brookside Farm Bed and Breakfast Inn

1373 Marron Valley Road, 91917
(619) 468-3043

6 Pets welcome; 7 Smoking allowed; 8 Children welcome; 9 Social drinking allowed; 10 Tennis available; 11 Swimming available; 12 Golf available; 13 Skiing available; 14 May be booked through travel agents.

A country farmhouse furnished with collectibles, handmade quilts, and stained glass. Tree-shaded terraces by a stream, farm animals, gardens, hot tub in the grape arbor. Perfect for country walks. Close to Tecate, Mexico, and 35 minutes from San Diego. Two-night minimum stay required for holidays and in some rooms.

Hosts: Edd and Sally Guishard
Rooms: 10 (PB) $55-115
Full Breakfast
Credit Cards: A, B, C, D
Notes: 2, 4 (weekends), 5, 9, 10, 12, 14

ELK

Elk Cove Inn

6300 South Highway 1, 95432
(707) 877-3321; (800) 275-2967

The Elk Cove Inn is an 1883 lumber baron's oceanfront estate on the Mendocino coast, with a front porch, gazebo, gardens, and private steps down to the beach. Hosts offer antique-filled rooms and king- and queen-size beds piled high with down comforters and lots of pillows. Some rooms have fireplaces and/or canopied beds. All rooms have coffee makers, bathrobes, private baths, and bedtime port and chocolates. The rooms are very large with rocking chairs and views. The house has common rooms with TV, VCR, books, and games. Afternoon tea and wine and cheese are complimentary. A sumptuous full breakfast is served in the oceanfront dining room. Wineries, redwoods, unique shops, and gourmet restaurants are just minutes away.

Host: Elaine Bryant
Rooms: 10 (PB) $108-198
Full Breakfast
Credit Cards: A, B
Notes: 2, 5, 9, 10, 11, 12, 14

ENCINITAS

Eye Openers
Bed and Breakfast
Reservations

P.O. Box 694, Altadena, 91003-0694
(213) 684-4428; (818) 797-2055
FAX (818) 798-3640

EN-S4I. In this renowned flower-growing area in Southern California, this family-run bed and breakfast with ocean views, Southwestern decor, and a relaxed atmosphere has large rooms, an apartment, and penthouse with Jacuzzi. They have queen- or king-size beds and private baths. Continental-plus breakfast and afternoon refreshments are served. Walking distance to the ocean. No smoking. $75-150.

SeaBreeze
Bed and Breakfast

121 North Vulcan Avenue, 92024
(619) 944-0318

Encinitas' first bed and breakfast. A true find, squeaky clean. "An absolute treasure," said KABC talk radio. Features in this contemporary two-story oceanview home are three bedrooms all with private baths, downstairs that has common sitting room with a fireplace and kitchenette, done in southwest custom-designed handcrafted furnishings and decor. A new addition to the inn is the penthouse, a true "boudoir," with a king-size bed, cable TV and VCR, whirlpool tub and shower, plus an eight-foot spa on an ocean-view balcony. Also, an upstairs one-bedroom apartment with fireplace, kitchen, and double soaking tub equipped with bubble bath and champagne. There is a lovely sun deck in the front yard with a waterfall and fish pond. Intimate wedding grotto available. Make reservations early.

NOTES: Credit cards accepted: A MasterCard; B Visa; C American Express; D Discover Card; E Diner's Club; F Other; 2 Personal checks accepted; 3 Lunch available; 4 Dinner available; 5 Open all year;

Host: Kirsten Richter
Rooms: 5 (PB) $75-150
Continental Breakfast
Credit Cards: A, B, D
Notes: 2, 5, 7, 8, 9, 10, 11, 12, 14

ESCONDIDO

Eye Openers Bed and Breakfast Reservations

P.O. Box 694, Altadena, 91003-0694
(213) 684-4428; (818) 797-2055
FAX (818) 798-3640

DD-P2. Japanese ambience characterizes this two-bedroom guest house and outdoor areas. Views of nearby mountain lakes and surrounding mountains can be enjoyed from the decks, living room with fireplace, and upstairs bedroom. Indoor hot tub, choice of full or continental breakfast. Twenty minutes inland from San Diego near Escondido, and only a short drive to several beach cities. No smoking. $75-115.

EUREKA

Carter House/Hotel Carter

301 L Street/1033 Third Street, 95501
(707) 444 8062; (707) 445-1390

These spectacularly re-created landmark Victorians are in scenic Old Town, near the famed Carson Mansion. Original art and antique appointments. Bay and marina vistas, fireplaces, whirlpool baths, featherbeds, truly elegant dining. Dinners featured in *Bon Appetit.* "Best breakfast in California," says *California* magazine.

Hosts: Mark and Christi Carter
Rooms: 30 (PB) $95-285
Full Breakfast
Credit Cards: A, B, C, E, F
Notes: 2 (limited), 4, 5, 8 (over 8), 9, 10, 11, 12, 14

"An Elegant Victorian Mansion"

1406 C Street, 95501
(707) 444-3144; (707) 442-5594

"Victorian opulence, grace, grandeur—the most elegant house in Eureka," says *The New York Times* of this national historic landmark. Features sauna, massage, croquet, Victorian ice cream sodas, French gourmet breakfasts, secured garage parking, laundry service, vintage classic movies, bicycles, antique cars, and world-famous custom-made mattresses. Near redwood parks, fishing, boating, cultural events, carriage and train rides, bay cruises. In a quiet Victorian neighborhood near Old Town. Recommended by Mobil and AAA. English, French, and Dutch spoken.

Hosts: Doug and Lily Vieyra
Rooms: 4 (2 PB; 2 SB) $75-135
Full Breakfast
Credit Cards: A, B
Notes: 2, 5, 9, 10, 12, 13

Heuer's Victorian Inn

1302 E Street, 95501
(707) 442-7334

This Queen Anne Victorian was built in 1893 and restored to its present splendor in 1980. Just like being transported back in time to an earlier era. For that quiet, relaxing time, it's a must.

Hosts: Charles and Ausbern Heuer
Rooms: 3 (1 PB; 2 SB) $75
Continental Breakfast
Credit Cards: A, B, C, D, E, F
Notes: 2, 5, 9, 10, 12

Old Town Bed and Breakfast Inn

1521 Third Street, 95501
(707) 445-3941; (800) 331-5098
FAX (707) 445-8346

6 Pets welcome; 7 Smoking allowed; 8 Children welcome; 9 Social drinking allowed; 10 Tennis available;
11 Swimming available; 12 Golf available; 13 Skiing available; 14 May be booked through travel agents.

The uniquely Victorian seaport of Eureka is the setting for this 1871 Greek Revival Italianate two-story Victorian. A short stroll to Humboldt Bay brings nostalgic memories of the great fleets of sailing ships that once carried loads of redwood lumber to San Francisco and the world and brought the bounty of the fishing fleets home. Only two blocks from lumber baron William Carson's famous mansion. Teak hot tub, evening wine and fruits, and homemade cookies. Bring cameras and appetites.

Hosts: Leigh and Diane Benson
Rooms: 6 (4 PB; 2 SB) $75-150
Full Breakfast
Credit Cards: A, B, C, D, E
Notes: 2, 5, 8 (over 10), 9, 10, 11, 12, 14

Upstairs at the Waterfront

102 F Street, 95501
(707) 443-9190

Upstairs at the Waterfront, offering a beautiful bay view, was built in 1892 and restored in 1992. The upstairs, a brothel in the 1950s, has been completely rebuilt as a 1,500-square-foot salon which is rented as a two-bedroom, two-bath bed and breakfast. The space is ideal for two couples traveling together or can be completely private for two separate parties. The downstairs Cafe Waterfront offers a friendly relaxed atmosphere and some of the best food in Humboldt County. Breakfast is served downstairs.

Host: Diane Smith
Rooms: 2 (PB) $75-250
Full Breakfast
Credit Cards: A, B, D
Notes: 2, 3, 4, 5, 9, 10, 12

A Weaver's Inn

1440 B Street, 95501
(707) 443-8119

A Weaver's Inn, the home and studio of a fiber artist and her husband, is a stately Queen Anne Colonial Revival house built in 1883 and remodeled in 1907. Placed in a spacious fenced garden, it is airy and light, but cozy and warm when veiled by wisps of fog. Visit the studio, try the spinning wheel before the fire, or weave on the antique loom before having refreshments.

Hosts: Bob and Dorothy Swendeman
Rooms: 4 (2 PB; 2 SB) $65-85
Full Breakfast
Credit Cards: A, B, C, D
Notes: 2, 5, 6, 8, 9, 14

FERNDALE

The Gingerbread Mansion

400 Berding Street, 95536
(707) 786-4000

The Gingerbread Mansion bed and breakfast inn is well known as one of America's most photographed homes. Its striking Victorian architecture trimmed with gingerbread, its colorful peach and yellow paint, and its surrounding English gardens all make the Gingerbread Mansion a photographer's delight. It is an understatement to say that the interiors are also spectacular.

Host: Ken Torbert
Rooms: 9 (PB) $85-205
Full Breakfast
Credit Cards: A, B, C
Notes: 2, 5, 9, 10, 12, 14

Shaw House
Bed and Breakfast Inn

703 Main Street, 95536
(707) 786-9958; FAX (707) 786-9958

An 1854 carpenter Gothic built by the founders of Ferndale, Shaw House is on an acre in a tranquil parklike estate with Victorian gardens. Guests can enjoy the gazebo, bicycles, and croquet. Coffee or tea at check-in and before a full breakfast in the morning. The hosts also offer umbrellas, robes, slippers, and much more. Within walking distance of shops and restaurants, and a half hour from the Avenue of the Giants. Three-crown rating from ABBA, and three-star rating from Northern California Best Places.

NOTES: Credit cards accepted: A MasterCard; B Visa; C American Express; D Discover Card; E Diner's Club; F Other; 2 Personal checks accepted; 3 Lunch available; 4 Dinner available; 5 Open all year;

Hosts: Norma and Ben Bessingpas
Rooms: 6 (PB) $75-135
Full Breakfast
Credit Cards: A, B, C
Notes: 2, 5, 10, 14

FISH CAMP

Karen's Bed and Breakfast Yosemite Inn

1144 Railroad Avenue, P.O. Box 8, 93623
(209) 683-4550; (800) 346-1443

Experience the splendor of each season in Yosemite National Park. Only two miles from the south entrance, Karen's is open year-round offering cozy country comfort. Nestled amid the towering pines and whispering cedars at 5,000 feet, it blends contemporary and country living. The innkeepers will assist in planning the ultimate visit while in the Yosemite area.

Hosts: Karen Bergh and Lee Morse
Rooms: 3 (PB) $85
Full Breakfast
Credit Cards: None
Notes: 2, 5, 8, 10, 11, 12, 13, 14

Scotty's Bed and Breakfast

1223 Hwy 41, P.O. Box 82, 93623
(209) 683-6936

Guests will enjoy a cozy room with a private entrance and bath, full or queen-size bed, river rock fireplace, color TV, stereo, microwave, continental breakfast, beautiful yard, barbecue, creek-side view, fishing, golf, skiing, historical train ride, back country hiking, biking, and stables. All of this and more is only two miles from Yosemite National Park.

Host: Scott B. Sanders
Rooms: 2 (1 PB; 1 SB) $55-75
Continental Breakfast
Credit Cards: None
Notes: 5, 8, 9, 10, 11, 12, 13

FORT BRAGG

Avalon House

561 Stewart Street, 95437
(707) 964-5555; (800) 964-5556

A 1905 Craftsman house, built completely of redwood and extensively remodeled in 1988, Avalon House is furnished with a mix of antiques and willow furniture. The emphasis here is on luxury and comfort: fireplaces, whirlpool tubs, down comforters and pillows, good bedside lights, as well as mood lights to create a romantic ambience. The inn is in a quiet residential area three blocks from the Pacific Ocean and one block from Highway 1. The Skunk Train depot is two blocks away.

Host: Anne Sorrells
Rooms: 6 (PB) $70-135
Full Breakfast
Credit Cards: A, B, C, D
Notes: 2, 5, 8, 9, 14

Grey Whale Inn

615 North Main Street, 95437
(707) 964-0640; (800) 382-7244 (reservations)

Handsome four-story Mendocino Coast landmark since 1915. Cozy rooms to expansive suites, all private baths. Ocean, garden, or hill and city views. Some have fireplaces and/or TVs; one has whirlpool tub; all have telephones. Recreation area: pool table, books, fireside lounge, and TV theater. Conference room seats 16 people. Friendly, helpful staff. Buffet breakfast features Colette's Blue-ribbon coffeecakes. Relaxed seaside charm, five blocks from beach. Celebrate a special occasion at the fabled Mendocino Coast! Mobil three-star rating. ABBA three crowns. Limited facilities for children.

Host: Colette Bailey
Rooms: 14 (PB) $80-150
Full Breakfast
Credit Cards: A, B, C, D
Notes: 2, 5, 9, 10, 11, 12, 14

6 Pets welcome; 7 Smoking allowed; 8 Children welcome; 9 Social drinking allowed; 10 Tennis available; 11 Swimming available; 12 Golf available; 13 Skiing available; 14 May be booked through travel agents.

FREMONT

Lord Bradley's Inn

43344 Mission Boulevard, 94539
(415) 490-0520

This Victorian is nestled below Mission Peak, adjacent to the Mission San Jose. Numerous olive trees on the property were planted by the Ohlone Indians. Common room, garden, patio. Parking in rear. Take the bus or Bay Area Rapid Transit to San Francisco for a day.

Hosts: Keith and Anne Bradley Medeiros
Rooms: 8 (PB) $65-75
Continental Breakfast
Credit Cards: A, B, E, F
Notes: 2, 5, 9, 10, 14

GARDEN GROVE

Kids Welcome

3924 East 14th Street, Long Beach, 90804
(310) 498-0552; (800) 383-3513

7-4. Kids are really welcome in this lovely older home near Disneyland. There are three guest rooms; one has a fireplace and a balcony, and another one has a TV and small refrigerator. All have private baths. The hostess is a weaver and doll collector. Full breakfast is served. Special rates for four people. $55.

Rent-A-Room

11531 Varna Street, 92640
(714) 638-1406

This is a referral service that books private homes between Los Angeles and San Diego. No inns are on this list; these bed and breakfasts are in the British tradition. Most of the offerings are close to southern California attractions, such as Disneyland, Knott's Berry Farm, San Diego Zoo, Sea-World, Universal Studios, Anaheim Convention Center, and beaches. One to three guest rooms in each home. All rooms have private baths. Full breakfast is served in all bookings. $45-65.

GARDEN VALLEY

Mountainside Bed and Breakfast

5821 Spanish Flat Road, 95633
(800) 237-0832

Between Placerville and Georgetown, this old country home is in the center of 80 acres with a 180-degree view. There are three guest rooms with private baths and a large attic with bath and deck that can sleep eight. A country breakfast is served in the dining room or sunny breakfast room. Guests can enjoy the cozy parlor with fireplace and piano, or spa after a day of river rafting, hiking, or fishing.

Hosts: Paul and Mary Ellen Mello
Rooms: 4 (PB) $70-75
Full Breakfast
Credit Cards: A, B
Notes: 2, 5, 7 (limited), 9, 14

GEORGETOWN

American River Inn

Orleans Street, Box 43, 95634
(916) 333-4499; (800) 245-6566 (CA)

In the heart of Gold Country nine miles off Highway 49 between I-80 and I-50, this "Jewel of the Mother Lode" is a totally restored 1853 miners' boarding house. Each room is individually decorated with Victorian and turn-of-the-century antiques. Gorgeous natural gardens, a refreshing mountain stream pool and Jacuzzi, a dove aviary, and bicycles. Enjoy a full breakfast in the morning, local wines and treats in the evening. Antique shop on the premises. Facilities for the handicapped. Other amenities include a croquet field, putting green,

NOTES: Credit cards accepted: A MasterCard; B Visa; C American Express; D Discover Card; E Diner's Club; F Other; 2 Personal checks accepted; 3 Lunch available; 4 Dinner available; 5 Open all year;

and mini-driving range. Georgetown is a Sierra foothills village with real flavor and only six miles from Gold Discovery Park in Coloma.

Hosts: Will and Maria
Rooms: 25 (12 PB; 13 SB) $78-108
Full Breakfast
Credit Cards: A, B, C, D, E
Notes: 2, 5, 8, 9, 10, 12, 13, 14

GEYSERVILLE

Campbell Ranch Inn

1475 Canyon Road, 95441
(707) 857-3476

A thirty-five-acre country setting in the heart of Sonoma County wine country. Spectacular view, beautiful gardens, tennis court, swimming pool, hot tub, and bicycles. Five spacious rooms, one with fireplace, private baths, king-size beds, balconies, fresh flowers, and fruit. Air-conditioned. Refreshments and homemade evening dessert. Full breakfast served on the terrace. Teenagers welcome. Color brochure available. Minimum-stay requirements for weekends.

Hosts: Mary Jane and Jerry Campbell
Rooms: 5 (PB) $100-165
Full Breakfast
Credit Cards: A, B
Notes: 2, 5, 7 (limited), 9, 10, 11, 14

Isis Oasis Lodge

20889 Geyserville Avenue, 95441
(707) 857-3524

A classic lodge of 12 rooms, lounge with fireplace, meeting room, and game area. A pool spa and sauna in a secluded garden. Acres of land with exotic birds and animals to play with. A honeymoon cottage with fireplace and private hot tub. The Retreat House, Vineyard House, and Tower House in addition to yurts, a tipi, and a wine barrel room give guests a variety of options. Wine and country breakfasts. Group rates.

Hosts: Loreon Vigne and Paul Ramses
Rooms: 23 (7 PB; 16 SB) $50-100
Full Breakfast
Credit Cards: A, B, C
Notes: 2, 3, 4, 5, 11

GLEN ELLEN

Glenelly Inn

5131 Warm Springs Road, 95442
(707) 996-6720

Charming country inn in the Sonoma wine country near Jack London Park. Restored turn-of-the-century inn with spacious garden, in-ground spa, and oak trees. Boutique wineries and good restaurants nearby. One hour north of San Francisco.

Hosts: Kristi and Ingrid Hallamore
Rooms: 8 (PB) $95-130
Full Breakfast
Credit Cards: A, B
Notes: 2, 5, 7 (limited), 8 (by arrangement), 9, 10, 11, 12, 14

Glenelly Inn

JVB Vineyards

14335 Sonoma Highway, P.O. Box 997, 95442
(707) 996-4533

Two private little Spanish-style adobe haciendas overlooking the vineyard. Queen-size beds, hot tub, beautiful patio. Great waffles for breakfast. Thirty-seven wineries and champagne cellars in historic Sonoma Valley. Site of raising of the Bear Flag, author Jack London's Wolf House, last mission on the California trail, and home of General Vallejo.

Hosts: Beverly and Jack Babb
Rooms: 2 (PB) $95-115
Full Breakfast
Credit Cards: None
Notes: 2, 5, 9, 11, 12, 14

GROVELAND

Berkshire Inn

19950 Highway 120, P.O. Box 207, 95321
(209) 962-6744

This beautiful 12,000-square-foot house sits on 20 acres of pine- and oak-covered mountains. Massive open beam construction, loungers, breakfast area, and breathtaking views create a warm and cozy environment. Offering large bedrooms, all with private baths, private entrances, queen-size beds, and wooden decks. An extended continental breakfast is served. Just minutes away from Yosemite National Forest. Near boating, water and snow skiing, white-water rafting, golf courses, and historical towns and landmarks.

Hosts: Carl, Dody, Kim, Mike, and Christopher Yates
Rooms: 6 (PB) $79
Continental Breakfast
Credit Cards: A, B, D
Notes: 2, 5, 7 (limited), 8, 9, 10, 11, 12, 13, 14

The Groveland Hotel

18767 Main Street, P.O. Box 289, 95321
(209) 962-4000; (800) 273-3314
FAX (209) 962-6674

Yosemite National Park is 23 miles away, on Highway 120. The two buildings, an 1849 adobe and a 1914 frame building, have been completely restored. They house 17 guest rooms, a seasonal gourmet restaurant, and a conference room. Furnishings are European antiques and down com-

forters. Each room has terrycloth robes, upscale linens, and very Victorian decor. There are also three suites with fireplaces and Jacuzzis. The courtyard is a garden setting for weddings, parties, and outdoor dining. Golf, tennis, swimming, fishing, hiking, skiing, and world-class white-water rafting are minutes away. The conference room is available for meetings of up to 25 people. Complimentary wine is served in the evenings.

Hosts: Peggy and Grover Mosley
Rooms: 17 (PB) $85-165
Continental Breakfast
Credit Cards: A, B, C, D, E, F
Notes: 2, 4, 5, 6, 8, 9, 10, 11, 12, 13, 14

GUALALA

North Coast Country Inn

34591 South Highway 1, 95445
(707) 884-4537; (800) 959-4537

A cluster of rustic redwood buildings with ocean views. Rooms feature queen-size beds, fireplaces, kitchenettes, private baths, decks, and private entries. The inn has a hot tub and gazebo. Full breakfast is served in guest rooms. Golf, hiking, horseback riding, fishing, and beaches are nearby. Minimum stay requirements for weekends and holidays.

Hosts: Loren and Nancy Flanagan
Rooms: 4 (PB) $148.50
Full Breakfast
Credit Cards: A, B, C
Notes: 2, 5, 9, 10, 11, 12, 14

GUERNEVILLE

Bed and Breakfast International

P.O. Box 282910, San Francisco, 94128-2910
(415) 696-1690; (800) 872-4500
FAX (415) 696-1699

304. An estate among rolling hills in one of Northern California's most beautiful wine country areas. Very peaceful atmosphere, high quality decor, and full breakfasts. Nine rooms, all with private baths, and furnished in antiques and other fine pieces. Lots of fresh flowers. Swimming pool and hot tub are available. $115-150.

Ridenhour Ranch House Inn

12850 River Road, 95446
(707) 887-1033

A 1906 inn on two and one-quarter acres of trees, gardens, and meadow in the Russian River area of Northern California. Each room is decorated in country English and American antiques, quilts, plants, and fresh flowers. The area has many restaurants, and dinner can be arranged at the inn.

Hosts: Diane and Fritz Rechberger
Rooms: 8 (PB) $95-130
Full Breakfast
Credit Cards: A, B, C
Notes: 2, 4, 5, 8 (over 10), 11, 12, 14

Santa Nella House

Pocket Creek Canyon, 12130 Highway 16, 95446
(707) 869-9488

Santa Nella is nestled in a redwood forest where quiet and beauty prevail. Enjoy a short walk to the Russian River and Korbel Champagne Cellars when the summer bridge is in. The house is a bucolic Country Victorian, circa 1870, with a grand wrap-around veranda and restored turn-of-the-century guest rooms—all with wood-burning fireplaces. A well-stocked library is available for guests to enjoy, and a large country kitchen with wood-burning stove and a bay window, as well as a parlor/music room, provide a pleasant atmosphere for friendly conversation. Large country breakfasts consisting of fresh fruits, juices, freshly ground and brewed coffee, various egg dishes, waffles, and homemade cakes are served in the dining room or on the veranda and gazebo on warm mornings.

Hosts: Ed and Joyce Ferrington
Rooms: 4 (PB) $90-100
Full Breakfast
Credit Cards: A, B, C
Notes: 2, 9, 10, 12, 14

HALF MOON BAY

Cypress Inn on Miramar Beach

407 Mirada Road, 94019
(415) 726-6002

Cypress Inn is 26 miles south of San Francisco and two miles north of Half Moon Bay. All eight luxury ocean-front rooms have a private deck, fireplace, and bathroom. The unique architecture and Mexican folk art decor are a perfect compliment to the beachfront location. Breakfast is outstanding, and tea is served every afternoon. Many activities and fine dining nearby.

Owner: Suzie Lankes
Rooms: 8 (PB) $160-225
Suite: $250
Full Breakfast
Credit Cards: A, B, C
Notes: 2, 3, 4, 5, 9, 10, 11, 12, 14

Old Thyme Inn

779 Main Street, 94019
(415) 726-1616

This lovingly restored 1899 Queen Anne Victorian is on historic Main Street in Old Town. Seven unique rooms with lovely antiques, whimsical stuffed bears, fresh flowers, cozy fireplaces, and/or luxurious whirlpool tubs. Private suite has TV, VCR, stereo, and refrigerator. Delicious breakfasts are served in the parlor. Walking distance to beaches, art galleries, local shops, and gourmet restaurants. Local activities include hiking, bird watching, surfing, golf, horseback riding, and whale watching.

Hosts: George and Marcia Dempsey
Rooms: 7 (PB) $65-210
Full Breakfast
Credit Cards: A, B
Notes: 2, 5, 9, 10, 11, 12, 14

6 Pets welcome; 7 Smoking allowed; 8 Children welcome; 9 Social drinking allowed; 10 Tennis available; 11 Swimming available; 12 Golf available; 13 Skiing available; 14 May be booked through travel agents.

Zaballa House

324 Main Street, 94019
(415) 726-9123

The first house built in Half Moon Bay (1859), standing at the entrance to historic Main Street, has been carefully restored into a bed and breakfast. The inn is set in a garden across the street from shopping and two fine restaurants. Guests enjoy the Victorian decor in rooms with high ceilings and antiques, some with double-wide whirlpool tubs and fireplaces. The friendly innkeeper provides drinks in the evening and a wonderful breakfast in the morning.

Host: Kerry Pendergast
Rooms: 9 (PB) $65-165
Full Breakfast
Credit Cards: A, B, C, D
Notes: 2, 5, 6, 9, 10, 12, 14

HEALDSBURG

Bed and Breakfast San Francisco

P.O. Box 282910, San Francisco, 94128-2910
(415) 479-1913; FAX (415) 921-BBSF

16. Jane's place is in the heart of wine country, just minutes from some of California's finest wineries. Close to the Russian River beaches and resorts, and only 30 minutes from the Pacific coast. Three quaintly furnished rooms with private baths on an estate overlooking vineyards. Home-cooked breakfast. $85.

Frampton House

489 Powell Avenue, 95448
(707) 433-5084

A stately 1908 Victorian in the heart of Sonoma wine country, Frampton House offers personalized service and privacy. Ping Pong, pool, spa, sauna, fireplace, wine. Custom-made tubs for two. Relax in any season. Rooms have sky lights with views and air-conditioning.

Host: Paula Bogic
Rooms: 3 (PB) $77-99
Full Breakfast
Credit Cards: A, B
Notes: 2, 5, 7 (limited), 8 (over 14), 9, 10, 11, 12, 14

Grape Leaf Inn

539 Johnson Street, 95448
(707) 433-8140

A magnificently restored 1900 Queen Anne Victorian home with seven bedrooms, each with private bath. Five have whirlpool tubs for two. All the rooms are air-conditioned and have king- or queen-size beds. Second-floor bedrooms and baths have skylights. A full country breakfast is served. Premium local wines and cheeses are offered each afternoon. Convenient to Healdsburg town center, the Russian River, Lake Sonoma, and 65 wineries.

Hosts: Terry and Karen Sweet
Rooms: 7 (PB) $95-150
Full Breakfast
Credit Cards: A, B, D
Notes: 2, 5, 9, 10, 11, 12, 14

Haydon Street Inn

321 Haydon Street, 95448
(707) 433-5228

The Haydon Street Inn is an intimate bed and breakfast in a quiet residential neighborhood within walking distance of downtown shops and restaurants. Each of the six rooms in the main house is beautifully decorated with French and American antiques affording each room its own distinctive personality. The inn also includes two romantic rooms in a storybook Victorian cottage, each with double whirlpool tubs and other special appointments. Full breakfast served daily at 9:00 a.m. Closed December.

Innkeeper: Joanne Claus
Rooms: 8 (4 PB; 4 SB) $75-150
Full Breakfast
Credit Cards: A, B
Notes: 2, 9, 11, 12

NOTES: Credit cards accepted: A MasterCard; B Visa; C American Express; D Discover Card; E Diner's Club; F Other; 2 Personal checks accepted; 3 Lunch available; 4 Dinner available; 5 Open all year;

Healdsburg Inn
on the Plaza

110 Matheson Street, P.O. Box 1196, 95448
(707) 433-6991

This 1900 brick Victorian, formerly a Wells Fargo stagecoach express station, has been restored and is now elegantly furnished as a bed and breakfast. Features include bay windows with a view of the Plaza, fireplaces, and central heat/air. Solarium/roof garden for afternoon snacks, popcorn, wine, music. Coffee and cookies available all day. Champagne breakfasts on weekends. TV, VCR, telephone, and gift certificates. Family owned and operated; close to everything. Midweek and winter rates are discounted 20 to 30 percent.

Hosts: Genny Jenkins and Dyanne Celi
Rooms: 9 (PB) $135-175
Full Breakfast
Credit Cards: A, B
Notes: 2, 5, 9, 10, 11, 12

Madrona Manor,
A Country Inn

1001 Westside Road, 95448
(707) 433-4231; (800) 258-4003
FAX (707) 433-0703

This 21-room inn in a national historic district is distinguished by its sense of homey elegance that combines the graciousness one might feel at a friend's home with luxurious European amenities: thick terry-cloth robes, an expansive breakfast buffet, stately furniture, elegant decor. Nationally acclaimed restaurant.

Hosts: John and Carol Muir
Rooms: 21 (PB) $135-225
Full Breakfast
Credit Cards: A, B, C, D, E
Notes: 2, 3, 4, 5, 6 (limited), 7, 8 (limited), 9, 10, 11, 12, 14

The Raford House

10630 Wohler Road, 95448
(707) 887-9573

This 1880s Victorian summer house overlooks award-winning vineyards and is listed as a Sonoma County historical landmark. Surrounding the inn are towering palm trees and old-fashioned flower gardens. The seven guest rooms are furnished with turn-of-the-century antiques. A full breakfast is served in the dining room. The sunroom and front porch entice guests to the splendid view and complimentary wine and hors d'oeuvres in the evening. Near many fine wineries, restaurants, historical points of interest, the Russian River, and the rugged Northern California coast.

Hosts: Carole and Jack Vore
Rooms: 7 (5 PB; 2 SB) $85-135
Full Breakfast
Credit Cards: A, B, D
Notes: 2, 5, 9, 10, 11, 12, 14

HOLLYWOOD

Bed and Breakfast, L.A.

3924 E. 14th Street, Long Beach, 90804
(310) 498-0552; (800) 383-3513

Cottages around the pool in West Holly wood. The owner of this inn has bought all the little houses in the neighborhood to set up housekeeping for singles and couples in this great mid-City location. Rooms range from studios with shared kitchens and baths to whole apartments. Continental breakfast is served by the pool. $65-120.

Eye Openers
Bed and Breakfast
Reservations

P.O. Box 694, Altadena, 91003-0694
(213) 684-4428; (818) 797-2055
FAX (818) 798-3640

HH-G1. Savor a panoramic view of the Los Angeles basin from this Hollywood Hills bed and breakfast. One guest room with king-size or twin beds and private baths. Ten minutes from Westwood or Beverly

---

6 Pets welcome; 7 Smoking allowed; 8 Children welcome; 9 Social drinking allowed; 10 Tennis available; 11 Swimming available; 12 Golf available; 13 Skiing available; 14 May be booked through travel agents.

Hills. A full breakfast is served. No smoking. $90-100.

HO-N1. Historic West Hollywood neighborhood is the setting for very private self-hosted one-bedroom guest house with kitchen, living room, private bath, double bed, and pool. Central to most tourist attractions, and good public transportation is available. No smoking. $85–100.

HH-C1. Enjoy a quiet canyon view from this Hollywood Hills private guest house with fireplace, kitchen, private bath, and terrace. King-size or twin beds. Extended continental breakfast. No smoking. $85.

LA-G2. This 1910 California bungalow on a quiet palm-lined street close to Hollywood's well-known attractions offers two second-floor guest rooms, one with a sun deck overlooking the spacious garden. Well-traveled hosts speak several languages. Continental breakfast. Good public transportation. Resident dog and cat. No smoking. Private bath. $40–45.

Hollywood, California Bed and Breakfast

1616 North Sierra Bonita Avenue, 90046
(213) 876-5715; FAX (213) 851-6243

This 1910 Californian bungalow is on a palm-lined street in Hollywood convenient to public transportation and many tourist attractions. Two uptairs guest rooms, one has private sundeck, bathtub with shower, coffee maker, and sitting area. Both rooms have private bath, refrigerator, color cable TV, queen-size beds, and air conditioning. Hosts speak French, German, Russian, Hebrew, Spanish, and Italian and welcome overseas guests. Hosts offer tour of Hollywood and great restaurant and sightseeing recommendations. Families welcome.

Hosts: Avi and Elaine Gilboa
Rooms: 2 (PB) $40-50
Continental Breakfast
Credit Cards: None
Notes: 2, 4, 6, 8, 9, 10, 12, 14

Kids Welcome

3924 East 14th Street, Long Beach, 90804
(310) 498 0552; (800) 383-3513

2-2. Kids, dogs, and cats live downstairs, and guests live upstairs in this home near Sunset Boulevard. Hosts speak many languages. Affordable rates.

2-3. Cute three-bedroom, two-bathroom bungalow can be rented by the room or the entire house. West Hollywood location includes living room with fireplace, dining room, and kitchen. Hostess brings a full breakfast from the house next door. $60.

Wilkum Inn

IDYLLWILD

Wilkum Inn

Box 1115, 92549
(909) 659-4087

Sheltered by pines and cedars, this two-story shingle-style inn offers that "at home" feeling. Warm hospitality and innkeepers' attention to detail are enhanced by handmade quilts and family antiques, as comfort combines with nostalgia in an ambience of yesteryear. Enjoy the pine-forested mountain village with unique shops, excellent restaurants, and fine and performing arts. Create memories hiking under clear skies or just by relaxing in front of the fireplace with a good book.

Hosts: Annamae Chambers and Barbara Jones
Rooms: 4 (2 PB; 2 SB) $75-95
Continental Breakfast
Credit Cards: None
Notes: 2, 5, 9, 14

INVERNESS

Bed and Breakfast, L.A.

3924 East 14th Street, Long Beach, 90804
(310) 493-6837; (800) 383-3513

These hosts have thought of everything for the perfect rural vacation. This farmhouse has a bedroom, loft, living room, fireplace, fully equipped kitchen, bath, private garden (with a pond), kids' playhouse and swing, deck-top hot tub (with ocean view), barnyard animals, TV, stereo, VCR (with movies), library, typewriter, guitar, and teddy bears. $125.

Dancing Coyote Beach

P.O. Box 98, 94937
(415) 669 7200

Four charming cottages set on a private beach surrounded by Point Reyes National Seashore, each with kitchen, fireplace, decks, and bay views. Stroll along the beach, linger over breakfast in the morning sun on the private deck, walk to the village of Inverness, or simply relax by the fire.

Rooms: 4 (PB) $95-125
Full Breakfast
Credit Cards: None
Notes: 2, 5, 9

IONE

The Heirloom

214 Shakeley Lane, 95640
(209) 274-4468

Travel down a country lane into a romantic English garden where a petite Colonial mansion (circa 1863) is shaded by century-old trees and scented by magnolias and gardenias. Fireplaces and balconies. Breakfast has a French flair. Enjoy gracious hospitality. Closed Thanksgiving, Christmas Eve, and Christmas Day.

Hosts: Patricia Cross and Melisande Hubbs
Rooms: 6 (4 PB; 2 SB) $60-92
Full Breakfast
Credit Cards: A, B, C
Notes: 2, 8 (over 10), 9, 10, 11, 12, 14

ISLETON

Delta Daze Inn

20 Main Street, P.O. Box 607, 95641
(916) 777-INNS

This historic bed and breakfast offers relaxation with fun. Boat and bus tours, free bikes, or just sitting by the river are all part of the Delta experience. After guests have browsed through the boutiques and art galleries, relax in the parlor, or have a Delta Delite from the old-fashioned ice cream parlor while listening to music from the 1920s on a hand-crank Grafanola. It's all part of living, Delta style.

Host: Shirley Russell
Rooms: 12 (PB) $90-125
Full Breakfast
Credit Cards: A, B, C
Notes: 2, 5, 7 (limited), 8, 9, 11, 12, 13, 14

JACKSON

Court Street Inn

215 Court Street, 95642
(209) 223-0416

An 1872 Victorian inn with four rooms and a two-room cottage. All rooms feature private baths and the suite offers a whirlpool tub. Three rooms have fireplaces, as well as the parlor and cottage. A full breakfast is served. Guests can enjoy the patio and rose garden, or relax on the porch swing or in the

6 Pets welcome; 7 Smoking allowed; 8 Children welcome; 9 Social drinking allowed; 10 Tennis available; 11 Swimming available; 12 Golf available; 13 Skiing available; 14 May be booked through travel agents.

outdoor hot tub. Near wineries, restaurants, and shopping. Skiing one hour away.

Hosts: Janet and Lee Hammond; Gia and Scott Anderson
Rooms: 8 (7 PB) $90-130
Full Breakfast
Credit Cards: A, B, C
Notes: 2, 5, 8, 9, 10, 11, 12, 13, 14

Gate House Inn

Gate House Inn

1330 Jackson Gate Road, 95642
(209) 223-3500; (800) 841-1072

Charming turn-of-the-century Victorian in the country on an acre of garden property with a swimming pool. Rooms are decorated with Victorian and country furnishings and feature an angel theme. One has a fireplace, and the private cottage has a wood stove. Walk to fine restaurants and historic sites. Three-star Mobil rating. Angel gift shop on the premises.

Hosts: Keith and Gail Sweet
Rooms: 5 (PB) $85-120
Full Breakfast
Credit Cards: A, B, D
Notes: 2, 5, 8 (over 12), 9, 10, 11, 12, 14

The Wedgewood

11941 Narcissus Road, 95642
(209) 296-4300; (800) 933-4393

Charming Victorian replica tucked away on wooded acreage. Antique decor, afternoon refreshments, porch swing, balcony, wood burning stoves, full gourmet breakfast. In the heart of the gold country, close to excellent dining, shopping, and sightseeing. Gazebo and terraced English gardens. Mobil travel guide three stars. AAA three diamonds.

Hosts: Vic and Jeannine Beltz
Rooms: 6 (PB) $85-140
Full Breakfast
Credit Cards: A, B, C, D
Notes: 2, 5, 7 (limited), 8 (over 12), 9, 12, 13, 14

JAMESTOWN

The National Hotel

Box 502, 95327
(209) 984-3446

The historic National Hotel bed and breakfast, an 11-room Gold Rush hotel built in 1859. Fully restored, with an outstanding restaurant and the original saloon. Classic cuisine and gracious service are only part of the charm.

Hosts: Stephen and Pamela Willey
Rooms: 11 (5 PB; 6 SB) $65-80
Continental Breakfast
Credit Cards: A, B, C, D, E
Notes: 2, 3, 4, 5, 6 and 8 (by arrangement), 7, 9, 10, 11, 12, 13, 14

Royal Hotel

18239 Main Street, P.O. Box 219, 95327
(714) 835-8787

Gold Rush Victorian theme, English antiques, Axminister carpeting, honeymoon cottage in second oldest gold mining town in the West. Nostalgic items and book shop specializing in Coca-Cola, WWI, WWII, Hollywood, transportation, and cookbooks. Two-story, on one-half acre, four cottages, and four-unit miner's shack. Main building built in 1922. Impeccably clean. Town of 1,200 people and one long block of restaurants, antique shops, and memorabilia.

Hosts: Joyce and Don Chitty
Rooms: 19 (10 PB; 9 SB) $35-80
Continental Breakfast
Credit Cards: A, B, C
Notes: 5, 8, 9, 12, 13, 14

NOTES: Credit cards accepted: A MasterCard; B Visa; C American Express; D Discover Card; E Diner's Club; F Other; 2 Personal checks accepted; 3 Lunch available; 4 Dinner available; 5 Open all year;

JENNER

Murphy's Jenner Inn

Coast Highway 1, Box 69, 95450
(707) 865-2377

Coastal cottages and rooms decorated with antiques, wicker, houseplants, and love. Idyllic setting at the end of the Russian River with ocean and river views. All rooms have private baths and entrances. Most have private decks. Fireplaces, hot tubs, and kitchens are available. Area activities: beachcombing, whale and seal watching, bird watching, hiking, bicycling, and canoeing. Close to Armstrong State Redwood Reserve, historic Russian Fort Ross, and more than 50 wineries. Conference and wedding facilities.

Rooms: 13 (PB) $65-165
Continental Breakfast Plus
Credit Cards: A, B, C
Notes: 3, 4, 5, 8, 11, 12, 14

KERNVILLE

Bed and Breakfast, L.A.

3924 E. 14th Street, Long Beach, 90804
(310) 498-0552; (800) 383-3513

At the Colorado River. Old fashioned hospitality and great river views are this inn's claim to fame. Reasonably priced rooms include private bath, king- or queen-size brass beds, fireplaces, and whirlpool tubs. Full breakfast and afternoon snacks help prepare you for days of white-water rafting, kayaking, fishing, and hiking. And don't forget Kernville's antique shops. Moderate rates.

Historic restoration at the Kern. This amazing house was first built in Kernville in 1878 but fell into decline and disuse for over 100 years. Hosts lovingly dismantled, moved, and reconstructed it in 1989. Four rooms, two with private bath, two shared, all with down comforters and antique furnishings. Take a deep bath in the claw-foot tub, try the player piano, doze by the fire,

browse in the library, or hike or raft in the Kern River Valley. Call for rates.

Kern River Inn
Bed and Breakfast

119 Kern River Drive, P.O. Box 1725, 93238
(619) 376-6750; (800) 986-4382

A charming country riverfront bed and breakfast on the wild and scenic Kern River in the quaint little town of Kernville within Sequoia National Forest and the southern Sierra Mountains. Six individually decorated theme rooms reflect the charm of the Kern River Valley. All have river views, private baths, and either king- or queen-size brass beds. Some rooms feature fireplaces or whirlpool tubs. A full breakfast features giant home-baked cinnamon rolls, stuffed French toast, homemade granola with yogurt, sweetheart waffles, fresh fruit, and lots more. Walk to restaurants, parks, museums, and antique shops. For the adventuresome, the Kern River offers white water rafting, kayaking, and fishing. Hiking and biking trails nearby offer a chance to explore the surrounding mountains and view beautiful vistas, giant redwood trees, spring wildflowers, and fall foliage. Golf and skiing nearby.

Hosts: Jack and Carita
Rooms: 6 (PB) $79-89
Full Breakfast
Credit Cards: A, B
Notes: 5, 8, 9, 10, 11, 12, 13

KLAMATH

Requa Inn

451 Requa Road, 95548
(707) 482-8205; FAX (707) 482-0844

This inn is on the majestic Klamath River, 60 miles north of Eureka in the heart of the Redwood National Park. Near hiking trails and beaches—a nature lover's paradise. Relax in the front parlor overlooking the river, or treat yourself to an unforgettable dinner in the dining room. Closed January.

Hosts: Sue Reese and Leo and Melissa Chavez
Rooms: 10 (PB) $70-95
Full Breakfast
Credit Cards: A, B, C, D
Notes: 3, 4, 8, 9

LAGUNA BEACH

The Carriage House

1322 Catalina Street, 92651
(715) 494-8945

The Carriage House features all private suites with living room, bedroom, bath, and some kitchen facilities. Two-bedroom suites available. All surround a courtyard of plants and flowers, two blocks from the ocean. Close to art galleries, restaurants, and shops. Minimum-stay requirements for weekends and holidays.

Hosts: Vern, Dee, and Tom Taylor
Suites: 6 (PB) $95-150
Continental Breakfast
Credit Cards: None
Notes: 2, 5, 8, 11, 12, 14

Casa Laguna Inn

2510 South Coast Highway, 92651
(714) 494-2996; (800) 233-0449
FAX (714) 494-5009

A Spanish mission-style inn in an ocean-view hillside setting with tropical gardens and courtyards, heated pool, aviary, observation bell tower, and cozy library. Two cottages with fireplaces. Complimentary afternoon tea, wine, and hors d'oeuvres. A five-minute stroll to the beach. Near Los Angeles and Disneyland.

Host: Louise Gould
Cottages/Rooms/Suites: 21 (PB) $79-205
Continental Breakfast Plus
Credit Cards: A, B, C, D, E
Notes: 2, 5, 7, 8, 9, 10, 11, 12, 14

Eiler's Inn

741 South Coast Highway, 92651
(714) 494-3004

In the heart of Laguna, just a few steps from the Pacific Ocean. Tennis, shops, and restaurants are within walking distance. The inn offers elegant yet casual sophistication, with all rooms furnished in antiques, ocean views from the sun deck, fireplaces, and flower-scented brick courtyard with bubbling fountain.

Hosts: Henk and Annette Wirtz
Rooms: 12 (PB) $100-175
Full Breakfast
Credit Cards: A, B, C
Notes: 2, 5, 9, 10, 11, 12, 14

Eye Openers Bed and Breakfast Reservations

P.O. Box 694, Altadena, 91003-0694
(213) 684-4428; (818) 797-2055
FAX (818) 798-3640

LA-J1. Sitting room, bedroom, private bath, private entrance, and large deck with panoramic ocean views make up this suite. Sitting room has a refrigerator, microwave, TV, and VCR. Full breakfast served. Walk to the beach. No smoking. $95.

LG-B2. Hilltop bed and breakfast has an ocean view. European hostess can accommodate up to eight guests. Full or continental

NOTES: Credit cards accepted: A MasterCard; B Visa; C American Express; D Discover Card; E Diner's Club; F Other; 2 Personal checks accepted; 3 Lunch available; 4 Dinner available; 5 Open all year;

breakfast is served. Resident dog. Two guest rooms. Private and shared baths available. No smoking. $65-75.

LG-B3. Spacious bed and breakfast with ocean view in the hills above Pacific Coast Highway. Full Breakfast. $75.

LG-C201. Charming Spanish-style bed and breakfast inn with unique guest rooms and suites provides a generous buffet breakfast and evening refreshments in the library or poolside. Nineteen guest rooms and one cottage. Private bath. $95-155.

LG-E121. Rooms in lovely continental-style bed and breakfast in the heart of Laguna are set around a courtyard. Guests may enjoy breakfast and lounging near the fountain, flowers, tables, and chairs. The beach is just outside the back gate. No smoking. Eleven guest rooms and one suite. Private bath. $100-165.

LG-S2. Contemporary seaside getaway in Laguna offers expansive view from an outdoor deck. Self-hosted apartment. Bedroom and living room with small kitchen have ocean views. Quiet area of bustling renowned seaside art colony. Self-catered breakfast. No smoking. Weekly rates.

LA JOLLA

The Bed and Breakfast Inn at La Jolla

7753 Draper Avenue, 92037
(619) 456-2066

Offering deluxe accommodations in 16 charmingly decorated rooms, the Bed and Breakfast Inn at La Jolla is listed as Historical Site 179 on the San Diego registry. Fireplaces and ocean views are featured in many rooms, and every bedroom offers ei-

ther a queen-size bed, a pair of twin beds, or one king-size bed. Fresh fruit, sherry, fresh flowers, and terry-cloth robes await in each guest room. Savor a large breakfast in the dining room, on the patio, the sun deck, or the bedroom. A picnic basket to add the finishing touch to the day is also available.

Hosts: Pierette Timmerran
Rooms: 16 (15-PB; 1-SB) $85-225
Full Breakfast
Credit Cards: A, B, D
Notes: 2, 5, 7, 8, 9, 10, 11, 12

Bed and Breakfast, L.A.

3924 E. 14th Street, Long Beach, 90804
(310) 498-0552; (800) 383-3513

This Mediterranean-style home is set in an exclusive area with a stunning view of the Pacific. Hosts have two rooms, both with twins or a king-size bed, and both with private bath. Hosts are an architect and a retired teacher who also collect modern art. They love entertaining and serve a full breakfast on the terrace by the pool. $85.

Eye Openers Bed and Breakfast Reservations

P.O. Box 694, Altadena, 91003-0694
(213) 684-4428; (818) 797-2055
FAX (818) 798-3640

LJ-S2. Tastefully decorated contemporary bed and breakfast designed by the architect/host in La Jolla features views of San Diego and beaches from the pool and Jacuzzi. Two guest rooms feature king- or twin beds with private baths and private entrances. A full breakfast is served. No smoking. $65-70.

LAKE ARROWHEAD

The Carriage House Bed and Breakfast

6 Pets welcome; 7 Smoking allowed; 8 Children welcome; 9 Social drinking allowed; 10 Tennis available; 11 Swimming available; 12 Golf available; 13 Skiing available; 14 May be booked through travel agents.

472 Emerald Drive, P.O. Box 982, 92352
(714) 336-1400

New England-style house hidden in the woods, with views of Lake Arrowhead. Country decor, with feather beds and down comforters. Three rooms, each with private bath. Beverages and snacks in afternoon. Large sunroom and deck. Close to lake and wonderful walking trails. Returning guests rave about the warmth and hospitality of the hosts and the great breakfasts.

Hosts: Lee and Johan Karstens
Rooms: 3 (PB) $95-120
Full Breakfast
Credit Cards: A, B, D
Notes: 2, 5, 9, 11, 13

Chateau du Lac
Bed and Breakfast Inn

911 Hospital Road, 92352-1098
(909) 337-6488; FAX (909) 337-6746

Chateau du Lac is nestled on a bluff with a spectacular view of beautiful Lake Arrowhead. Enjoy breakfast on the balcony during the summer or by a crackling fire in the dining room during the winter. Lake Arrowhead is a mile high and offers the four seasons in a rare mountain setting. About a two-hour drive from Los Angeles/Orange County areas, Lake Arrowhead is in the forest of the San Bernardino Mountains.

Hosts: Jody and Oscar Wilson
Rooms: 6 (4 PB; 2 SB) $95-215
Full Breakfast
Credit Cards: A, B, C, D, E
Notes: 2, 5, 9, 13, 14

Eagle's Landing

12406 Cedarwood, 92317
P.O. Box 1510, Blue Jay, 92317 (mail)
(909) 336-2642

The interesting Mountain Gothic architecture, tower, stained glass, 26-foot ceilings, and walls of glass with grand views of Lake Arrowhead make Eagle's Landing a landmark, but the warmth, fun, and hospitality

of the hosts are what guests return for. The three beautiful rooms are decorated with art, antiques, and crafts collected from around the world. The suite is cabin-like and done in Early California style.

Host: Dorothy Stone
Rooms: 4 (PB) $95-195
Full Breakfast
Credit Cards: A, B, D
Notes: 2, 5, 9, 10, 11, 13, 14

Storybook Inn

P.O. Box 362, 28717 Highway 18, Skyforest, 92385
(714) 336-1483

Nine elegantly decorated rooms, all with baths, and a separate rustic three-bedroom, two-bath cabin with stone fireplace. The inn has a spectacular 100-mile view. Full home-cooked breakfast is served in the guest room on white wicker trays with Bavarian china, silverplate, and crystal or in the elegant dining room with its fantastic view and fine furnishings. Nightly social hour includes complimentary wines and hors d'oeuvres. Hot chocolate chip cookies are served before bed. Conference room, nearby hiking trails, and private picnics.

Hosts: Kathleen and John Wooley
Rooms: 9 plus cabin (PB) $98-200
Full Breakfast
Credit Cards: A, B, D
Notes: 2, 3 and 4 (limited), 5, 8, 9, 10, 11, 12, 13, 14

LAKEPORT

Forbestown Inn

825 Forbes Street, 95453
(707) 263-7858

The peace, solitude, and charm of Forbestown Inn will please the senses. Built in 1869 when Lakeport was known as Forbestown, it is furnished with unique American oak antiques. Enjoy the beautiful gardens, swimming pool, and outdoor spa. Full, hearty breakfast; afternoon tea; baked goods; or wine, cheese, and crackers. The inn is one block from Clear

Lake, boating, Jetski, water skiing, parasailing, bicycling, fishing, wineries, antique hunting, gold mines, geothermal steam wells.

Hosts: Nancy and Jack Dunne
Rooms: 4 (1 PB; 3 SB) $75-110
Full Breakfast
Credit Cards: A, B, C
Notes: 2, 5, 7 (limited), 8 (over 12), 9, 10, 11, 12, 13 (water), 14

LAKE TAHOE

Bed and Breakfast, L.A.

3924 E. 14th Street, Long Beach, 90804
(310) 498-0552; (800) 383-3513

Country Inn in Tahoe. On the west shore of the Lake, this 1930s inn features a gourmet quality breakfast, a restaurant and bar for other meals, a huge stone fireplace, bed and breakfast rooms, and five cottages nestled in the pine trees. Take a quick hike to Sugar Pine State Park or drive to Emerald Bay. Guests are welcome to use the pool, spa, horseshoes, and Ping Pong tables. Bike paths and discount lift tickets are available, and the inn will tailor food and recreational activities to parties' needs. Kids and pets welcome. $80-125.

Eye Openers Bed and Breakfast Reservations

P.O. Box 694, Altadena, 91003-0694
(213) 684-4428; (818) 797-2055
FAX (818) 798-3640

LT-C3. This lakefront 1928 Tahoe-style stone house bed and breakfast has contemporary decor with antique accents. Continental or full breakfast. Three rooms and a suite. Private. No smoking. $100-115.

LT-C71. This 1938 Old Tahoe-style with European pine furniture offers cottage

suites and large rooms, full breakfast, afternoon refreshments, private beach with a dock, and winter ski packages. Private bath. No smoking. $100-160.

LT-R41. This inn decorated with Laura Ashley fabrics has pine walls and lake view. Full breakfast. Four guest rooms. Private bath. $100-200.

LARKSPUR

Bed and Breakfast San Francisco

P.O. Box 420009, San Francisco, 94142-0009
(415) 479-1913; FAX (415) 921-BBSF

Nestled beneath Mount Tamalpais, Barbara offers an entire floor with living room, grand piano, two bedrooms, bath, and a wonderful, private patio. During the warm summer months, guests are welcome to the pool. Marin County offers a wealth of wonderful activities, from shopping the small town of Sausalito to hiking and biking. Muir Woods, Stinson Beach, and the rugged California coast are just a short drive away. Full breakfast. $85-115.

Eye Openers Bed and Breakfast Reservations

P.O. Box 694, Altadena, 91003-0694
(213) 684-4428; (818) 797-2055
FAX (818) 798-3640

4. The hostess offers guests an entire floor with a living room, two bedrooms, bath, and a wonderful private patio. Pool available during the summer months. Muir Woods, Stinson Beach, and the rugged California coast are just a short drive away. Full breakfast. $95-115.

LODI

Wine and Roses Country Inn

2505 West Turner Road, 95242
(209) 334-6988; FAX (209) 334-6570

Converted to a romantic country inn with ten elegant suites filled with handmade comforters, antiques, and fresh flowers, this 1902 estate is secluded on five acres of towering trees and old-fashioned flower gardens. Amenities include afternoon tea and cookies, evening wine, delightful continental breakfast available from 6:00 to 9:00 A.M. and a full breakfast served at 9:00 A.M., library, and "wine country" dining. An easy walk to the lake, with swimming, boating, and fishing. Five minutes to wine-tasting, golf, tennis, health club. The 1,000-mile Delta waterway is 15 minutes away; museums, performing arts, Sacramento, and gold country within 30 minutes. Full restaurant which serves lunch Tuesday through Friday, dinner Wednesday through Saturday, and brunch on Sunday. Cocktails and full bar also available. San Francisco 90 minutes away; Lake Tahoe and Yosemite two and one-half hours away.

Hosts: Kris Cromwell; Del and Sherri Smith
Rooms: 10 (PB) $76-145
Full and Continental Breakfast
Credit Cards: A, B, C, D
Notes: 2, 3, 4, 5, 8, 9, 10, 11, 12, 14

LONG BEACH

Bed and Breakfast, L.A.

3924 East 14th Street, 90804
(800) 383-3513

Bluff Park Bed and Breakfast. This perfectly restored 1912 Craftsman home has two big guest rooms and one smaller one: perfect for a family. On a quiet residential street, just two blocks from the beach. Antique furnishings are simple and serene.

Breakfast is sumptuous on weekends, self-serve during the week. $65.

The Painted Lady. Deep pastels swathe this 1903 home on a hill in Long Beach. Two guest rooms (one with kids' beds, and toys!) share one and a half baths, a large wooden deck, a hot tub and old-fashioned garden—and it's all less than a mile from the airport or the beach. Full breakfast. $55.

Eye Openers Bed and Breakfast Reservations

P.O. Box 694, Altadena, 91003-0694
(213) 684-4428; (818) 797-2055
FAX (818) 798-3640

LB-H3. A 1912 California bungalow in historic Bluff Park area is close to beaches, park, and museum. Helpful hosts, comfortable airy guest rooms, and inviting common rooms. A full breakfast awaits guests. Dog in residence. No smoking. $55-65.

LB-M1. This bed and breakfast is three short blocks from the beach, with a second-floor guest room and suite with kitchen. Continental breakfast. Weekly rates available. Private bath. $50-75.

Lord Mayor's Inn Bed and Breakfast

435 Cedar Avenue, 90802
(213) 436-0324

This elegantly restored 1904 home of the first mayor of Long Beach invites guests to enjoy the ambience of years gone by. Recipient of awards in 1991 for restoration and beautification, the inn's rooms have ten-foot ceilings and are tastefully decorated with period antiques. Each unique bedroom has a private bath and access to a large sun deck. A full breakfast is prepared by the hosts and served in the dining room or on the deck overlooking the garden area. Convenient to beaches, the convention center, civic center, and theaters.

Hosts: Laura and Reuben Brasser
Rooms: 5 (PB) $85-105
Full Breakfast
Credit Cards: A, B, C
Notes: 2, 5, 7 (limited), 8, 14

LOS ANGELES

Bed and Breakfast, L.A.

3924 East 14th Street, Long Beach, 90804
(310) 498-0552; (800) 383-3513

Art Nouveau in Old LA. Atop a hill in Hancock Park, this stately 1929 mansion features feather beds, fresh flowers, crystal, and lace—and a full old-fashioned breakfast. Five guest rooms. The elegant Masters Suite has a private bath. The others share two baths. Perfect for sightseeing or business. Also close to downtown and convention center. $75-100.

A. This Craftsman cottage is perfect for a family of three. The turn-of-the-century decor, king-size bedroom, single bed in the living room, full bath, and kitchen make it a real home. The hostess brings breakfast to the door. Affordable to moderate rates.

B. Country-style cottage near the airport in Westchester has one guest room. Close to restaurants, tennis, and golf. Transportation from the airport is available. $55.

Eye Openers Bed and Breakfast Reservations

P.O. Box 694, Altadena, 91003-0694
(213) 684-4428; (818) 797-2055
FAX (818) 798-3640

LA-B1. Five minutes from the Marina and LAX and walking distance to parks, tennis courts, golf, and restaurants, this cozy bed and breakfast is also near public transportation. Continental breakfast. No smoking. One guest room. Shared bath. $35-45.

LA-B4. At the foot of the Hollywood Hills near West Hollywood restaurants and attractions, this Mediterranean-style house with a music room, interesting artifacts, and antiques offers four guest rooms with queen-size, double, or twin beds and private or shared baths. Amenities include a full breakfast, patio areas, hot tub, and off-street parking. Good public transportation is available. No smoking. $50-70.

LA-C2. Beautifully restored Craftsman-style house on the National Register of Historic Places is close to USC and civic and convention centers. Two comfortable guest rooms, lovely gardens, and patio are available for guests to enjoy. No smoking. Shared and private baths. $40-50.

LA-D1. Spacious apartment with elegant hospitality, interesting artifacts, and a location near most West Side destinations makes this a good bed and breakfast at a modest price. Swimming pool available. Continental breakfast. No smoking. Two guest rooms. Private bath. $50-55.

HA-D2. Convenient to L.A. International Airport, this comfortable, homey bed and breakfast with two spacious guest rooms has full exercise equipment room and hearty American breakfast. Hosts speak Spanish. No smoking. Private and shared baths. $40-45.

LA-P1. Walk to Westwood and UCLA from this attractive Wilshire Boulevard bed and breakfast. Enjoy an ample continental breakfast on the balcony prepared by French-speaking host. No smoking. Good public transportation nearby. One guest room with private bath. $60.

6 Pets welcome; 7 Smoking allowed; 8 Children welcome; 9 Social drinking allowed; 10 Tennis available;
11 Swimming available; 12 Golf available; 13 Skiing available; 14 May be booked through travel agents.

Eye Openers
Bed and Breakfast
Reservations
(continued)

LA-S1. This convenient and spacious 800-square-foot, three-room apartment with patios is a good location for vacationing sightseers, business people, and people interested in relocating to the Los Angeles area. Breakfast is self-catered. Weekly rates are available. No smoking. $65-75.

LA-S3. Two-story, Art Deco-style, architect-designed bed and breakfast nestled in the beautiful Los Feliz Hills of near Griffith Park and the Greek Theatre. Offering a quiet, comfortable setting convenient to fine restaurants, entertainment, and tourist attractions. Two guest rooms with private bath. Public transportation available. $55-60.

LA-S51. This antique-decorated, restored 1908 Craftsman home provides the setting and mood of an earlier era. Features a marvelous full gourmet breakfast and evening refreshments. Convenient to the University of Southern California, Civic Center, Hollywood, and tourist attractions. Five guest rooms. Shared and private baths. $65-95.

LA-T51. Close to the Los Angeles Convention Center, this stately 1902 inn with period furnishings offers a lovely setting. Full breakfast and afternoon tea or wine is served in the parlor or library. No smoking. Five guest rooms. Private bath. $75-105.

WLA-C2. French country decor and collectibles throughout this lovely, spacious apartment hosted by interior decorator. Two guest rooms with queen-size or twin beds and private baths. Convenient to LAX, beach cities, freeways, and many tourist attractions. Enjoy an extended continental breakfast on balcony. Garage parking. No smoking. $50-60.

WW-P2. English country decor fills this lovely home within walking distance of UCLA. Two guest rooms have queen-size or twin beds with private or shared baths. Continental-plus breakfast served. Good public transportation available. Resident dogs. No smoking. $62-70.

Kids Welcome
3924 East 14th Street, Long Beach, 90804
(310) 493-6837; (800) 383-3513

3-5. This retired couple lives in a quiet neighborhood and have two guest rooms and one bath in an upstairs suite. Toys, crib, and TV. Guests can walk to Universal Studios. Affordable rates. $60.

LOS OSOS

Gerarda's
Bed and Breakfast
1056 Bay Oaks Drive, 93402-4006
(805) 534-0834

The ideal place to stop between San Francisco and Los Angeles. On the coast with ocean and mountain views. Close to Hearst Castle, Morro Bay, and San Luis Obispo. Area activities include golf, tennis, hiking, and shopping. Dutch hospitality; host speaks several languages.

Host: Gerarda Ondang
Rooms: 3 (1 PB; 2 SB) $45
Full Breakfast
Credit Cards: None
Notes: 2, 5, 8, 9, 10, 11, 12

NOTES: Credit cards accepted: A MasterCard; B Visa; C American Express; D Discover Card; E Diner's Club; F Other; 2 Personal checks accepted; 3 Lunch available; 4 Dinner available; 5 Open all year;

LOTUS (COLOMA)

Golden Lotus

P.O. Box 830, 1006 Lotus Road, 95651
(916) 621-4562

This 1857 pre-Victorian is surrounded by herb and flower gardens and has frontage on the American River. Escape from the ordinary, and discover the special world awaiting guests in any one of the special rooms: the Secret Garden with a private entrance, Wish-Upon, Pirates Cove, Orient Express, Westward Ho, and Tranquility. Relax in the library. Guests can enjoy fishing and gold panning in the river. One mile to Coloma Gold Discovery Park. Ten to fifteen miles from tennis, swimming, and golf. One hour from skiing. Restaurant in 1855 brick building. Separate antique store and tea room. White-water rafting. Reiki available.

Hosts: Bruce and Jill Smith
Rooms: 6 (PB) $75-95
Full Breakfast
Credit Cards: A, B
Notes: 2, 3, 4, 5, 6 (by arrangement), 8 (over 6), 10, 11, 12, 13, 14

LOWER LAKE

Big Canyon Inn

P.O. Box 1311, 95457
(707) 928-5631; (707) 928-4892

Secluded and peaceful home on a hilly 12 acres of pines and oaks beneath Cobb Mountain. Guests stay in a bedroom suite with private porch and entrance, private bath and kitchenette. The suite is cozy in winter with its own wood stove and comfortable in summer with air conditioning.

Hosts: John and Helen Wiegand
Rooms: 2 (PB) $65
Continental Breakfast
Cards: None
Notes: 2, 5, 8, 9, 11, 12, 14

MALIBU

Bed and Breakfast, L.A.

3924 E. 14th Street, Long Beach, 90804
(310) 498-0552; (800) 383-3513

Topanga Canyon Hideaway. This amazing estate has been a boys school, a convent, and a brothel. Now it is owned by a gentleman who spent years restoring its original handcrafted character. Two guest rooms look out to the pool and over an acre of gardens. One room is huge, all white and round, with historic chandelier and massive marble bath fixtures. The Tower Room is shaped like an octagon and features an antique double bed that looks like a throne. Truly hidden in the hills. $100-125.

Casa Larronde

Box 86, 90265
(213) 456-9333

This is the area of the "famous," so the locals call this beach "Millionaires' Row." The Ocean Suite has 40 feet of windows adjoining its deck. Features include TV, telephone, fireplace, kitchenette, ceiling fan over a king-size bed, floor-to-ceiling three-way mirrors in the dressing room, and a large bathroom with twin basins. Cocktails are offered in the evening, and a full American breakfast is served leisurely in the morning. Closed July through mid-October.

Host: Charlou Larronde
Rooms: 2 (PB) $110-125
Full Breakfast
Credit Cards: None
Notes: 2, 8 (by arrangement), 9, 10, 11

Malibu Beach Inn

22878 Pacific Coast Highway, 90265
(310) 456-6444; (800) 4 MALIBU

Malibu, a tiny and exclusive coastal strip just north of Los Angeles, famous for its beaches, breaking surf, natural beauty, and casual but elegant lifestyle. That's exactly

6 Pets welcome; 7 Smoking allowed; 8 Children welcome; 9 Social drinking allowed; 10 Tennis available; 11 Swimming available; 12 Golf available; 13 Skiing available; 14 May be booked through travel agents.

what guests find at the the beautiful Malibu Beach Inn. Built on the beach, the Inn offers the ultimate "California Dreamin' " experience. Accommodations are designed to create the feeling of being in one's own private cottage on the beach and features private oceanfront balconies, fireplaces, Jacuzzis, and a full range of amenities.

Host: Lorraine Irving
Rooms: 47 (PB) $125-195
Continental Breakfast
Credit Cards: A, B, C, E
Notes: 3, 4, 5, 7, 8, 9, 10, 11, 12, 14

Malibu Country Inn

6506 Westward Beach Road, 90265
(310) 457-9622; (800) FUN-N-SURF

An enchanting country inn nestled on a bluff above one of the world's most beautiful beaches. Guests will find intimate accommodations in the midst of a private, three-acre, lush garden setting. Each room is provided with a thoughtful array of amenities: refrigerator, coffee maker, remote control television, telephone, private patio, and snack basket. A heated swimming pool overlooks both the ocean and mountains. Complimentary continental breakfast is served; full breakfast is available at an additional cost. Paradise awaits guests!

Hosts: Charity Dailey and Rosie Lambremont
Rooms: 16 (PB) $95-175
Continental Breakfast
Credit Cards: A, B, C, E
Notes: 5, 6, 8, 9, 10, 11, 12, 14

MANHATTAN BEACH

Eye Openers
Bed and Breakfast
Reservations

P.O. Box 694, Altadena, 91003-0694
(213) 684-4428; (818) 797-2055
FAX (818) 798-3640

MB-C2. Walk to the beach, shops, and restaurants from this restored beach bungalow. Ocean view from upstairs guest room. Continental breakfast and other amenities available. No smoking. Two guest rooms. Private and shared bath. $50-75.

MB-L2. Beachfront Bed and Breakfast is the entire first floor of this lovely home on the Strand. Private entrance, living/dining room area with fireplace, wet bar, and guest parking are some of the amenities offered. Continental breakfast. No smoking. Two guest rooms. Private bath. $75-85.

MARINA DEL REY

Eye Openers
Bed and Breakfast
Reservations

P.O. Box 694, Altadena, 91003-0694
(213) 684-4428; (818) 797-2055
FAX (818) 798-3640

MR-M40I. French country decor is featured in this large bed and breakfast inn close to the beach, good restaurants, and shopping. Forty guest rooms have queen-size or twin beds and private baths. A continental breakfast is served. No smoking. $80-130.

MR-Z1. Large self-hosted one-bedroom apartment offers privacy and comfort, contemporary decor, full kitchen, living/dining room area, and self-catered continental breakfast. Walk to the beach, and short ten minutes from LAX. Weekly rates available. No smoking. Private bath. $55-85.

PL-D2. Set on a hillside near the beach, this three-story tudor-style bed and breakfast offers the first story as guest quarters with two bedrooms, living room and patio.

NOTES: Credit cards accepted: A MasterCard; B Visa; C American Express; D Discover Card; E Diner's Club; F Other; 2 Personal checks accepted; 3 Lunch available; 4 Dinner available; 5 Open all year;

Gourmet, continental, or full breakfast served. No smoking. Private bath. $60-80.

MARIPOSA

Oak Meadows, too.

5263 Highway 140N, Box 619, 95338
(209) 742-6161

In a historic Gold Rush town, this bed and breakfast has turn-of-the-century charm. New England architecture. Guest rooms are decorated with handmade quilts, wallpaper, and brass headboards. Close to Yosemite. Home of the California State Mining and Mineral Museum.

Hosts: Frank Ross and Kaaren Black
Rooms: 6 (PB) $59-89
Continental Breakfast
Credit Cards: A, B
Notes: 2, 5, 14

MARIPOSA

The Pelennor

3871 Highway 49 South, 95338
(209) 966-2832

Country atmosphere about 45 minutes from Yosemite National Park. Four guest rooms, featuring twin, double, and queen-size beds. After a day of sightseeing, guests may want to take a few laps in the pool, unwind in the spa, enjoy the available games, relax in the sauna, and listen to an occasional tune played on the bagpipes.

Hosts: Dick and Gwen Foster
Rooms: 4 (SB) $35-45
Full Breakfast
Credit Cards: None
Notes: 2, 5, 6, 8, 9, 11

MAMMOTH LAKES

Tamarack Lodge Resort

Twin Lakes Road, P.O. Box 69, 93546
(619) 934-2442; (800) 237-6879 (CA only)

Historic lodge and cabins on six wooded acres on the shore of Mammoth's Twin Lakes. Housekeeping cabins have kitchens and baths, and range in size from studio to a three-bedroom. Lodge rooms have private or European-style shared bath. On-premises dining at the regionally acclaimed Lakefront Restaurant, serving hearty breakfasts and gourmet dinners. Tamarack Lodge Resort operates year-round offering fishing, hiking, boating, horseback riding, and sightseeing in summer; cross-country skiing in winter. Forty-five minutes from Yosemite National Park, and two and one-half miles from Mammoth Mountain ski area. Full and continental breakfast available at additional cost.

General Manager: Courtney McGrale
Rooms: 36 (31 PB; 5 SB) $45-155
Credit Cards: A, B, C
Notes: 2, 3, 4, 5, 8, 9 (wine and beer), 10, 11, 12, 13, 14

McCLOUD

McCloud Guest House

606 West Colombero Drive, 96057
(916) 964-3160

Built in 1907, this beautiful old country home is nestled among stately oaks and lofty pines on the lower slopes of majestic Mount Shasta. On the first floor is one of Siskiyou County's finer dining establishments. The second floor has a large parlor surrounded by five guest rooms, each individually decorated. Two-night minimum stay required for holidays.

Hosts: Bill and Patti Leigh; Dennis and Pat Abreu
Rooms: 5 (PB) $75-90
Continental Breakfast
Credit Cards: A, B
Notes: 4, 5, 11, 12, 13

MENDOCINO

Agate Cove Inn

11201 Lansing Street, Box 1150, 95460
(707) 937-0551; (800) 527-3111

6 Pets welcome; 7 Smoking allowed; 8 Children welcome; 9 Social drinking allowed; 10 Tennis available; 11 Swimming available; 12 Golf available; 13 Skiing available; 14 May be booked through travel agents.

Agate Cove Inn is on an ocean bluff with dramatic views of the Pacific and rugged coastline. There are individual cottages, each with an ocean view, a Franklin fireplace, and a private bath. A full country breakfast served in the main 1860s farmhouse. Hiking, golf, and tennis are close by.

Hosts: Sallie McConnell and Jake Zahavi
Rooms: 10 (PB) $75-175
Full Breakfast
Credit Cards: A, B, C, D
Notes: 2, 5, 9, 10, 12

Brewery Gulch Inn
9350 Coast Highway 1, 95460
(707) 937-4752

An authentic country bed and breakfast farm on the rugged coast, just one mile from the village of Mendocino. The lovely old white farmhouse is furnished in the Victorian style with queen-size beds, homemade quilts, and down pillows. Each guest room window provides views of the gardens and meadows beyond.

Hosts: Linda and Bill Howarth
Rooms: 5 (3 PB; 2 SB) $75-130
Full Breakfast
Credit Cards: A, B
Notes: 2, 5, 10, 11, 12

John Dougherty House

DeHaven Valley Farm
39247 North Highway 1, 95488
(707) 961-1660

The inn, a Victorian farmhouse built in 1875, is on 20 acres of meadows, hills, and streams, across from the Pacific Ocean.

Guests enjoy various farm animals, exploring tide pools, and soaking in the hot tub. Restaurant serves delicious four-course dinners complemented by home-grown herbs and vegetables. The inn is convenient for visiting the gigantic redwoods 25 miles to the north, or the artist colony of Mendocino 25 miles to the south. Closed January.

Hosts: Jim and Kathy Tobin
Rooms: 8 (6 PB; 2 SB) $85-135
Full Breakfast
Credit Cards: A, B, C
Notes: 2, 4, 8, 9

The Headlands Inn
Box 132, 95460
(707) 937-4431

The Headlands Inn is an 1868 Victorian, within Mendocino village on California's scenic north coast minutes from redwoods and wineries. Full gourmet breakfasts are served in the room. All rooms have woodburning fireplaces and private baths. Two rooms have spectacular ocean views overlooking an English-style garden. King- or queen-size feather beds. Two parlors, many antiques. Afternoon tea service with mineral waters, cookies, and mixed nuts. Minimum-stay requirements for weekends and holidays.

Hosts: Sharon and David Hyman
Rooms: 6 (PB) $85-180
Full Breakfast
Credit Cards: None
Notes: 2, 5, 10, 11, 12

John Dougherty House
571 Ukiah Street, P.O. Box 817, 95460
(707) 937-5266

Historic John Dougherty House was built in 1867 and is one of the oldest houses in Mendocino. On land bordered by Ukiah and Albion streets, the inn has some of the best ocean and bay views in the historic village; steps away from great restaurants and shopping, but years removed from 20th-century reality. The main house is furnished with period country antiques taking guests back to

1867. Enjoy quiet, peaceful nights seldom experienced in today's urban living.

Hosts: David and Marion Wells
Rooms: 6 (PB) $95-165
Continental Breakfast
Credit Cards: A, B, D
Notes: 2, 5, 9, 12, 14

Joshua Grindle Inn

44800 Little Lake Road, P.O. Box 647, 95460
(707) 937-4143

On two acres in a historic village overlooking the ocean, the Joshua Grindle Inn is a short walk to the beach, art center, shops, and fine restaurants. Stay in the lovely two-story Victorian farmhouse, a New England-style cottage, or a three-story water tower. Six rooms have fireplaces; all have private baths, antiques, and comfortable reading areas. Enjoy a full breakfast served around a ten-foot 1830s harvest table.

Hosts: Jim and Arlene Moorehead
Rooms: 10 (PB) $90-160
Full Breakfast
Credit Cards: A, B, C
Notes: 2, 5, 9, 10, 12

Kids Welcome

3924 East 14th Street, Long Beach, 90804
(310) 498-0552; (800) 383-3513

16-7. These hosts raised a total of 12 children in this Victorian home before taking in bed and breakfast guests. Four guest rooms, all with private baths. The house has plenty of activities for kids and includes all the necessities a parent could ask for. Kids stay free in parents' room. Breakfast is not included. Affordable rates.

MacCallum House Inn

45020 Albion Street, P.O. Box 206, 95460
(707) 937-0289

Unique accommodations that include the Victorian home of Daisy MacCallum, water tower, greenhouse, barn, and English gardens. In the center of the village; walk to

shops, restaurants, beach. Minimum-stay requirements for weekends May through December and during holidays.

Hosts: Melanie and Joe Reding
Rooms: 20 (7 PB; 13 SB) $75-180
Continental Breakfast
Credit Cards: A, B
Notes: 2, 4, 5, 8, 9, 10, 12, 14

Mendocino Farmhouse

Mendocino Farmhouse

Box 247, 95460
(707) 937-0241; FAX (707) 937-1086

Mendocino Farmhouse is a small bed and breakfast with all the comforts of home, surrounded by redwood forest, beautiful gardens, a pond, and meadow. Choose from comfortable rooms decorated with country antiques for a quiet night's rest and enjoy a farmhouse breakfast in the morning. Midweek discounts available.

Hosts: Margie and Bud Kamb
Rooms: 5 (PB) $85-115
Full Breakfast
Credit Cards: A, B
Notes: 2, 5, 8 (by arrangement), 10, 11, 12

Mendocino Village Inn

Main Street, Box 626, 95460
(707) 937-0246

Guests' home on the north coast, complete with lush gardens, frog ponds, fireplaces, and water tower suite. This 1882 Queen

6 Pets welcome; 7 Smoking allowed; 8 Children welcome; 9 Social drinking allowed; 10 Tennis available;
11 Swimming available; 12 Golf available; 13 Skiing available; 14 May be booked through travel agents.

Anne Victorian offers hearty breakfasts, beach trails, and good company. Coastal whimsy, quiet merriment, and repose. Minimum-stay requirements for weekends and some holidays.

Hosts: Bill and Kathleen Erwin
Rooms: 13 (11 PB; 2 SB) $65-190
Full Breakfast
Credit Cards: None
Notes: 2, 5, 9, 10, 11, 12

Stevenswood Lodge

P.O. Box 170, 95460
(707) 937-2810; (800) 421-2810

Distinctive contemporary suites, all hand-crafted, on Mendocino's spectacular coast. Virgin "old-growth" setting off shoreline Highway 1, with beach access and forest trails. Hosts serve a three-course gourmet breakfast. Ocean views, fireplaces, stocked refrigerators, 33-channel remote-control TV, executive conference room, VCR, and art gallery. AAA four-diamond rated.

Hosts: Robert and Vera Zimmer
Room: 1 (PB) $95-115
Suites: 9 (PB) $120-195
Full Breakfast
Credit Cards: A, B, C, D
Notes: 2, 5, 8, 9, 10, 11, 12, 14

Whitegate Inn

Box 150, 499 Howard Street, 95460
(707) 937-4892; (800) 531-7282

Everything travelers look for in a bed and breakfast experience: antiques, fireplaces, ocean views, and private baths. Elegant 1880 Victorian, in the center of the historic preservation village of Mendocino. Shops, galleries, and nationally acclaimed restaurants are just steps away. A perfect setting for romance, weddings, or just rest and relaxation.

Hosts: Carol and George Bechtloff
Rooms: 6 (PB) $95-165
Full Breakfast
Credit Cards: A, B
Notes: 2, 5, 9, 10, 11, 12

MILL VALLEY

Mountain Home Inn

810 Panoramic Highway, 94941
(415) 381-9000

A romantic country inn high atop Mount Tamalpais, offering spectacular views of the Marin Hills and San Francisco Bay. Ten guest rooms, some offer Jacuzzi baths, private decks, and fireplaces. Just outside the front door is Mount Tamalpais State Park, offering miles of hiking trails. Muir Woods National Monument, Muir Beach, and Stinson Beach are a short drive away, with downtown San Francisco only 25 minutes away. Restaurant on premises.

Rooms: 10 (PB) $131-215
Full Breakfast
Credit Cards: A, B
Notes: 2, 3, 4, 5, 7, 8, 9, 10, 11, 12, 14

MONTARA

The Goose and Turrets

835 George Street, Box 937, 94037
(415) 728-5451

A 1908 Italian villa in a quiet garden offers comfort, four-course breakfasts, and afternoon tea. Thirty minutes to San Francisco; 20 minutes from San Francisco airport; one-half mile to the beach. Near restaurants, horseback riding, tide pools, whale watching, aerotours, galleries, and golf. Pick-up at local harbor and airport. French-speaking hosts.

Hosts: Raymond and Emily Hoche-Mong
Rooms: 5 (PB) $85-110
Full Breakfast
Credit Cards: A, B, C, D
Notes: 2, 5, 8, 9, 10, 11, 12, 14

NOTES: Credit cards accepted: A MasterCard; B Visa; C American Express; D Discover Card; E Diner's Club; F Other; 2 Personal checks accepted; 3 Lunch available; 4 Dinner available; 5 Open all year;

MONTEREY

Bed and Breakfast International

P.O. Box 282910, San Francisco, 94128-2910
(415) 696-1690; (800) 872-4500
FAX (415) 696-1699

204. Three homes on the southern end of Monterey, all modestly priced. Two have views of the bay. There are six rooms that offer twin, queen-size, and double beds. All have shared baths. Excellent breakfasts are prepared by experienced hosts. $50-60.

206. Contemporary two-story redwood home in one of Monterey Peninsula's most exclusive areas and one block to the ocean. The home is spacious with much glass. The breakfast room is a glass semicircle extending into the garden. There is a fireplace and a view of the ocean from the living room. Two rooms with private baths. $98

Bed and Breakfast, L.A.

3924 East 14th Street, Long Beach, 90804
(800) 383-3513

Carmel-3. Easy family travel. This 19-room inn has rooms with fireplaces, living room suites, and two-bedroom units, and it is in the heart of Monterey. There is a heated pool. Continental breakfast is served. There is no charge for a child in adult's room. Affordable rates.

Del Monte Beach Inn

1110 Del Monte Avenue, 93940
(408) 649-4410

The only one of its kind on the Monterey Peninsula, the Del Monte Beach Inn offers guests all of the charm and comfort of a quaint European bed and breakfast at comfortably affordable rates in an ideal location. Walk across the boulevard to the beach and the biking and walking trail. Only minutes from Fisherman's Wharf, Cannery Row, historic Monterey, and the Aquarium.

Host: Ellen Lankford
Rooms: 18 (2 PB; 16 SB) $40-75
Continental Breakfast
Credit Cards: A, B, C, D
Notes: 2, 5, 8, 9, 10, 11, 12, 14

The Jabberwock

598 Laine Street, 93940
(408) 372-4777

Alice's Wonderland just four blocks above Cannery Row and Monterey Bay Aquarium. The Jabberwock has one-half acre of lush gardens and waterfalls overlooking the bay. Each room has down pillows and comforters. Hors d'oeuvres at 5:00 P.M. and cookies and milk at bedtime.

Hosts: Jim and Barbara Allen
Rooms: 7 (3 PB; 4 S2B) $100-180
Full Breakfast
Credit Cards: A, D
Notes: 2, 5, 9, 10, 11, 12

MONTE RIO

Huckleberry Springs

P.O. Box 400, 95462
(707) 865-2683; (800) 822-2683

This upscale relaxed country inn on 56 acres offers five unique cottages with private decks and baths. Spring water spa and pool. Regional gourmet dining. Breakfast included in the rates.

Host: Suzanne
Rooms: 5 (PB) $145
Full Breakfast
Credit Cards: A, B
Notes: 2, 4, 9, 10, 11, 12, 14

MORAGA

Hallman Bed and Breakfast

309 Constance Place, 94556
(415) 376-4318

6 Pets welcome; 7 Smoking allowed; 8 Children welcome; 9 Social drinking allowed; 10 Tennis available; 11 Swimming available; 12 Golf available; 13 Skiing available; 14 May be booked through travel agents.

Bed and breakfast on a quiet cul-de-sac in the beautiful Moraga Valley. Bed down in one of the tastefully appointed rooms; one in the Victorian manor and the second as contemporary as California itself. Awake refreshed with breakfast on the delightful terrace or comfortable dining room. Take off and "do" San Francisco or any other bay area attractions. Return in time for a refreshing dip in the pool or a relaxing time in the Jacuzzi spa, which is available May through September. There are many fine restaurants nearby for an enjoyable dinner. There are two guest rooms available, each with a comfortable queen-size bed. Shared bath. Both rooms are used only when guests are in the same party.

Hosts: Frank and Virginia Hallman
Rooms: 2 (SB) $60
Full Breakfast
Credit Cards: None
Notes: 2, 5, 8, 9, 11

MOUNT SHASTA

Mount Shasta Ranch

1008 W. A. Barr Road, 96067
(916) 926-3870

This Northern California historic two-story ranch house offers affordable elegance. There are four spacious guest rooms in the main house, each with private bath. Carriage house accommodations include five rooms. Two-bedroom vacation cottage available year-round. Guests are invited to enjoy the rec room with Ping Pong, pool table, and piano. Relax in the Hot-Spring® spa. Close to lake, town, and ski slopes. Full country-style breakfasts each morning.

Hosts: Bill and Mary Larsen
Rooms: 9 (4 PB; 5 SB) $55-95
Cottage: 1
Full Breakfast
Credit Cards: A, B, C, D
Notes: 2, 5, 8, 9, 10, 11, 12, 13, 14

MUIR BEACH

Bed and Breakfast San Francisco

P.O. Box 282910, San Francisco, 94128-2910
(415) 479-1913; FAX (415) 921-BBSF

22. A lovely bedroom suite with private entrance, fireplace, and private bath overlooking the ocean and beach. Muir Beach is a quiet community 45 minutes from downtown San Francisco. Full breakfast. $95.

MURPHYS

Dunbar House, 1880

271 Jones Street, 95247
(209) 728-2897

Explore Gold Country during the day and enjoy a glass of lemonade or local wine on the wide porches in the afternoon. Inviting fireplaces and down comforters in antique-filled rooms. The Cedar Room has a two-person whirlpool bath. All rooms have TVs, VCRs, and a classic video library. Breakfast may be served in the room, in the dining room, or out in the century-old gardens. Two-night minimum stay required for weekends.

Hosts: Bob and Barbara Costa
Rooms: 4 (PB) $105-145
Full Breakfast
Credit Cards: A, B, C
Notes: 2, 5, 8 (over 10), 9, 10, 11, 12, 13, 14

NAPA

Arbor Guest House

1436 G Street, 94559
(707) 252-8144; (800) 707-8144

This gracious 1906 Colonial transition home and carriage house are furnished with

NOTES: Credit cards accepted: A MasterCard; B Visa; C American Express; D Discover Card; E Diner's Club; F Other; 2 Personal checks accepted; 3 Lunch available; 4 Dinner available; 5 Open all year;

antiques and separated by trumpet vine covered arbor. Bask in the spa tubs in the Winter Haven or Autumn Harvest rooms while enjoying the warmth of a crackling fire. Rose's Bower provides an intimate getaway with fireplace. Afternoon refreshments and delicious full breakfasts are served by thoughtful host/owners fireside or in the garden. Near wineries, gourmet restaurants, Wine Train, ballooning, golf, and shopping. All rooms feature private baths and queen-size beds.

Hosts: Bruce and Rosemary Logan
Rooms: 5 (PB) $85-145
Full Breakfast
Credit Cards: A, B
Notes: 2, 5, 8, 9, 10, 12, 14

Beazley House
1910 First Street, 94559
(707) 257-1649

Guests sense the hospitality as they stroll the walk past verdant lawns and bright flowers. The landmark 1902 mansion is a chocolate brown masterpiece. Visitors feel instantly welcome as they are greeted by a smiling innkeeper. The view from each room reveals beautiful gardens. And all rooms have a private bath; some a private spa and a fireplace. Napa's first bed and breakfast and still its best!

Hosts: Carol and Jim Beazley
Rooms: 11 (PB) $105-185
Full Breakfast
Credit Cards: C
Notes: 2, 5, 9, 10, 11, 12, 14

Bed and Breakfast International
P.O. Box 282910, San Francisco, 94128-2910
(415) 696-1690; (800) 872-4500
FAX (415) 696-1699

303. Guests cannot go wrong when choosing this location. The fabulous architecture in the 101-year-old home is modeled after an English country estate. Great hosts, antiques galore, and one of the best prices in the wine country. $79-149.

Bed and Breakfast, L.A.
3924 East 14th Street, Long Beach, 90804
(310) 498-0552; (800) 383-3513

15-3. This 1900 farmhouse overlooks Napa Valley's best vineyards. One room has a fireplace and wet bar. Breakfast is served by the pool, and wine and cheese is served in the afternoon. Moderate rates.

La Belle Epoque
1386 Calistoga Avenue, 94559
(707) 257-2161

Historic Queen Anne Victorian bejeweled in stained glass. Six guest rooms furnished in period antiques, each with private bath, two with fireplaces, and one with a spa tub. Join the hosts in the charming wine-tasting room/cellar for evening tastings and hors d'oeuvres. Within walking distance of the Wine Train Depot, restaurants, shops, and riverfront. Wineries nearby, as well as hot-air ballooning, mud baths, tennis, swimming, and golf.

The Blue Violet Mansion
443 Brown Street, 94559-3348
(707) 253-BLUE (2583)

An 1886 Queen Anne Victorian mansion on one acre, this inn is listed on the National Register of Historic Places. King- and queen-size beds. Two rooms with balcony and fireplaces; two with spas. Antique furnishings and Oriental carpets. Complimentary use of bicycles and kites. Picnic baskets. Candlelight champagne breakfast, dinner, and massage services are available in guests' room. Evening wine service and late night desserts. Full breakfast served in the dining room. In historic Old Town near shops, Napa Wine Train, hot air balloons, and wine tastings.

6 Pets welcome; 7 Smoking allowed; 8 Children welcome; 9 Social drinking allowed; 10 Tennis available; 11 Swimming available; 12 Golf available; 13 Skiing available; 14 May be booked through travel agents.

Hosts: Bob and Kathy Morris
Rooms: 6 (PB) $115-195
Suite: 1
Full Breakfast
Credit Cards: A, B, C
Notes: 2, 3, 4, 5, 8, 9, 10, 11, 12, 14

Cedar Gables Inn

486 Coombs Street, 94559
(707) 224-7969

In Old Town Napa, this 100-year-old home is styled after English country manors of the 16th century. Antique furnishings are throughout the house. Some rooms have fireplaces and whirlpool tubs. A huge family room with large fireplace and big-screen TV is also available for guests. Minutes from wineries, restaurants, and the Napa Valley Wine Train.

Hosts: Margaret and Craig Snasdell
Rooms: 6 (PB) $89-159
Full Breakfast
Credit Cards: A, B, C
Notes: 2, 5, 9, 14

Churchill Manor Bed and Breakfast Inn

485 Brown Street, 94559
(707) 253-7733

A magnificent 1889 mansion resting on an acre of beautiful gardens, Churchill Manor is listed on the National Register of Historic Places. Elegant parlors boast carved-wood ceilings and columns, leaded-glass windows, Oriental rugs, brass and crystal chandeliers, four fireplaces, and a grand piano. Ten guest rooms are individually decorated with gorgeous antiques. Guests enjoy afternoon fresh-baked cookies and lemonade, evening wine and cheese reception, and a full gourmet breakfast served in a mosaic-floored sunroom. Complimentary tandem bicycles and croquet.

Host: Joanna Guidotti and Brian Jensen
Rooms: 10 (PB) $75-145
Full Breakfast
Credit Cards: A, B, C, D
Notes: 2, 5, 9, 10, 11, 12, 14

Eye Openers Bed and Breakfast Reservations

P.O. Box 694, Altadena, 91003-0694
(213) 684-4428; (818) 797-2055
FAX (818) 798-3640

NA-C91. Bed and breakfast in the heart of wine country is offered in the 1889 mansion that has been designated a national historic landmark. Each room is individually decorated. Enjoy an extended continental breakfast, and relax on the veranda with evening refreshments. No smoking. Nine guest rooms. Private bath. $75-160.

Hennessey House

Hennessey House

1727 Main Street, 94559
(707) 226-3774

Queen Anne Victorian in downtown Napa, the gateway to the historic wine country. Main house and carriage house. All rooms are furnished with antiques and have private baths. Selected rooms have fireplaces and whirlpool tubs. Full breakfast is served in unique dining room, which features a beautiful hand-painted, stamped tin ceiling. Listed on National Register of Historic Places. Sauna and bike rentals on premises. Complimentary wine in the evening.

NOTES: Credit cards accepted: A MasterCard; B Visa; C American Express; D Discover Card; E Diner's Club; F Other; 2 Personal checks accepted; 3 Lunch available; 4 Dinner available; 5 Open all year;

Hosts: Andrea LaMar and Lauriann Delay
Rooms: 10 (PB) $85-155
Full Breakfast
Credit Cards: A, B, C
Notes: 2, 5, 9, 12, 14

The International Bed and Breakfast Club, Inc.

504 Amherst Street, Buffalo, NY 14207
(800) 723-4262; FAX (716) 873-4462

This elegant 1886 Queen Anne home, in the historic district of Napa, was built for Emanuel Manasse, an executive at the Sawyer Tannery. His innovative leather tanning techniques are still in use today. Evidence of his craft remains in the embossed leather wainscoting adorning the main foyer. This mansion has been lovingly restored and offers a blend of country living and Victorian elegance to ensure visits are pleasurable experiences. Relax in the Victorian ambience of the parlors, outside in the garden gazebo, or on the veranda or shaded deck. Nine rooms with private baths. Gourmet breakfast. $115-195.

Napa Inn

1137 Warren Street, 94559
(707) 257-1444

The Napa Inn is a beautiful Queen Anne Victorian on a quiet tree-lined street in the historic section of the town of Napa. Furnished with turn-of-the-century antiques, the inn features six guest rooms, a large parlor, and formal dining room. Each spacious bedroom has its own private bath, and two suites feature fireplaces. The inn is convenient to the Napa, Sonoma, and Carneros wine regions. Also many other activities: hot air ballooning, gliding, biking, hiking, golf, tennis, many fine restaurants, and the Napa Valley Wine Train. Closed Christmas Day.

Hosts: Doug and Carol Morales
Rooms: 6 (PB) $120-170
Full Breakfast
Credit Cards: A, B
Notes: 2, 10, 12, 14

Oak Knoll Inn

2200 East Oak Knoll Avenue, Napa Valley, 94558
(707) 255-2200

Tall French windows, rustic stone walls, and vaulted ceilings distinguish the four spacious guest rooms at this luxurious inn, set well off the bustle of the main roads and surrounded by 600 acres of Chardonnay vineyards. The rooms have king-size brass beds, marble fireplaces, private baths, and sitting areas with overstuffed chairs and sofas. A full breakfast is served at guests' leisure in the room, dining room, or on the veranda surrounding the heated pool, spa, and magnificent views.

Hosts: Barbara Passino and John Kuhlmann
Rooms: 4 (PB) $175-250
Full Breakfast
Credit Cards: A, B
Notes: 2, 5, 10, 11 (on premises), 12, 14

The Old World Inn

1301 Jefferson Street, 94559
(707) 257-0112

For a holiday of romance and plentiful gourmet delights, plan a stay at this charming Victorian inn. Relax in the outdoor spa or choose a room with a sunken spa tub. Guests are pampered with home-baked treats from morning until bedtime: they start the morning with a gourmet breakfast, feel at home with the afternoon tea, unwind during the wine and cheese social, and are treated to a chocolate lover's dessert buffet.

Host: Diane Dumaine
Rooms: 8 (PB) $105-140
Full Breakfast
Credit Cards: A, B, C, D
Notes: 2, 5, 9, 12, 14

La Residence Country Inn

4066 St. Helena Highway, 94558
(707) 253-0337

Accommodations, most with fireplaces, are in two structures: a Gothic Revival home, decorated in traditional American antiques,

6 Pets welcome; 7 Smoking allowed; 8 Children welcome; 9 Social drinking allowed; 10 Tennis available;
11 Swimming available; 12 Golf available; 13 Skiing available; 14 May be booked through travel agents.

and the "French barn," decorated with European pine antiques. Two acres of grounds with hot tub and a heated swimming pool are surrounded by a gazebo and trellis. Wine is served each evening.

Hosts: David Jackson and Craig Calussen
Rooms: 20 (18 PB; 2 SB) $85-190
Full Breakfast
Credit Cards: A, B, E
Notes: 5, 8, 9, 10, 11, 12, 14

Sybron House

7400 St. Helena Highway, 94558
(707) 944-2785

Victorian inn on a hilltop in the middle of the Napa Valley with magnificent view of surrounding wineries and vineyards. Private tennis court. Excellent restaurants nearby, as well as ballooning, biking, hiking, and mud baths. Closed December and January.

Host: Cheryl Maddox
Rooms: 4 (PB) $120-160
Full Breakfast
Credit Cards: A, B, C
Notes: 2, 9, 10, 12, 14

Downey House

NEVADA CITY _____

Downey House Bed and Breakfast

517 West Broad Street, 95959
(916) 265-2815; (800) 258-2815

Eastlake Victorian, circa 1870, restored to its original elegance with lovely garden and water falling into a lily pond by new arbor with tables where guests may eat breakfast. One block from fine shops and restaurants, live theater, museums, art galleries, and horse-drawn carriages. Near historic gold mines, lakes, streams, tennis, golf, skiing, horseback riding, and more.

Host: Miriam Wright
Rooms: 6 (PB) $75-100
Full Breakfast
Credit Cards: A, B
Notes: 2, 5, 8, 10, 11, 12, 13, 14

Emma Nevada House

528 East Broad Street, 95959
(916) 265-4415

A 19th-century opera star Emma Nevada, who lived in this charming 1856 Victorian home as a child, would be proud of the inn that bears her name. The newly restored and elegantly decorated home sparkles from an abundance of antique windows, one of many architectural details. Spacious living areas and porches allow guests to relax or observe horse-drawn buggies touring the Victorian neighborhood. A gourmet breakfast is served overlooking the forest-like setting behind the inn.

Host: Ruth Ann Riese
Rooms: 6 (PB) $100-150
Full Breakfast
Credit Cards: A, B, C
Notes: 2, 5, 9, 10, 11, 12, 13, 14

The Parsonage Bed and Breakfast

427 Broad Street, 95959
(916) 265-9478

This home, dating back to 1885, offers six guest rooms with private baths. Each guest room honors a California pioneer ancestor of the owner. The entire home is furnished with family antiques that date back to the 1850s. A continental breakfast including fresh baked muffins and croissants, homemade jam, yogurt, fresh fruit, juice, and coffee, is served at a table with line-dried and hand-pressed linens. In every way, the hosts like to transport their guests back 100 years to a gentler era where people cared about each other.

Host: Deborah Dane
Rooms: 6 (PB) $65-115
Continental Breakfast
Credit Cards: A, B
Notes: 2, 5, 6 and 8 (limited), 13, 14

NEWPORT BEACH

Bed and Breakfast, L.A.
3924 E. 14th Street, Long Beach, 90804
(310) 498-0552; (800) 383-3513

Balboa Island Cottage. The owner of this cute island cottage lives upstairs and makes the downstairs available for bed and breakfast visitors. Accommodations include bedroom alcove, living room, full kitchen, and bath. The private entrance opens out to a fenced garden courtyard, and breakfast comes with a coupon for the little restaurant next door. $95-125.

Lido Island Waterfront. The architect-owners of this beautiful home love to take visitors out on their boat. They have two guest suites, one with an incredible ocean view and both with queen-size bed and private bath. Breakfast is fresh and bountiful. Beautiful setting and Lido Island is convenient to restaurants, shops, and attractions. $90-115.

Doryman's Inn Oceanfront Bed and Breakfast
2102 West Oceanfront, 92663
(714) 675-7300

Romance, luxury, and resounding elegance await at this exquisite oceanfront bed and breakfast. Capture picture-perfect sunsets on the Pacific Ocean, sip champagne on the a bayview patio, or have any one of the world-class concierges draw a bath with rose petals and chilled grapes. All rooms come with a complimentary bottle of champagne and a French breakfast in the morning. All rooms have imported Italian marble bathrooms with sunken tubs and French-Victorian style decor.

Hosts: Michael D. Palitz and Fi Laing
Rooms: 10 (PB) $135-275
Continental Breakfast
Credit Cards: A
Notes: 2, 4, 5, 7, 8, 9, 10, 11, 12, 14

Eye Openers Bed and Breakfast Reservations
P.O. Box 694, Altadena, 91003-0694
(213) 684-4428; (818) 797-2055
FAX (818) 798 3640

NP-D2. Crow's nest with 360-degree view tops this trilevel beach home. The third level is a large guest deck with barbecue and refrigerator. Stained glass is featured throughout the house. Perfect for beach and bay activities; bicycle and beach chairs available. Full or continental breakfast and afternoon refreshments. Two guest rooms. Private baths. $50-75.

NP-D101. A very special beachfront bed and breakfast inn has spacious antique-decorated guest rooms, each with its own fireplace and some with ocean views and Jacuzzis. Delicious full breakfast is served in the room, on the patio, or in the parlor. Ten guest rooms. Private baths. $135-275.

NP-W2. Stunning, well-decorated bed and breakfast on the water's edge has two guest rooms, private baths, a guest den with retractable roof, lounge chairs, refrigerator, and grassy yard for sunbathing. Take the shuttle or bike to unique shops and restaurants. Continental breakfast. Minimum stay is two nights. Resident dog. $80-85.

6 Pets welcome; 7 Smoking allowed; 8 Children welcome; 9 Social drinking allowed; 10 Tennis available; 11 Swimming available; 12 Golf available; 13 Skiing available; 14 May be booked through travel agents.

Chateau du Sureau

NIPOMO

Kaleidoscope Inn Bed and Breakfast

130 East Dana Street, P.O. Box 1297, 93444
(805) 929-5444

This 1886 Victorian is furnished with antiques and offers beautiful gardens, delicious full breakfasts, a Jacuzzi in one bath, and a king-size bed in one guest room. Halfway between Los Angeles and San Francisco, this bed and breakfast is near local attractions, golf, beach, lakes, hot springs, great dining, theater, horseback riding, and wind surfing. The owner loves to spoil guests.

Host: Patty Linane
Rooms: 3 (PB) $80
Full Breakfast
Credit Cards: A, B, C
Notes: 2, 5, 9, 10, 11, 12, 14

NIPTON

Hotel Nipton

72 Nipton Road, 92364
(619) 856-235

Hotel Nipton, originally built in 1904, was restored in 1986. In the east Mojave scenic area soon to become Mojave National Park, 65 miles southwest of Las Vegas between the Grand Canyon and Death Valley. Enjoy the beautiful panoramic views of Ivanpah Valley and New York Mountains. Outside Jacuzzi for star gazing. Only bed and break- fast in this historic mining town with a population of 60.

Hosts: Jerry and Roxanne Freeman
Rooms: 4 (SB) $49.05
Continental Breakfast
Credit Cards: A, B, E
Notes: 5, 7, 8, 9, 11, 14

OAKHURST

Chateau du Sureau

P.O. Box 577, 48688 Victoria Lane, 93644
(209) 683-6860

On the rim of Yosemite National Park commanding extraordinary views of the Sierra Nevada sits this seven and one-half acre French country estate. An enchanting, authentic European castle, the hotel offers nine exquisite guest rooms, all lovingly decorated with period antiques, king-size canopied beds, wood-burning fireplaces, CD and stereo systems, and gorgeous baths with lots of hand-painted French tile and deep Roman tubs large enough for two. A sumptuous full breakfast is served by warm and friendly personnel in the breakfast room, starting the day with a smile. On the grounds, pathways meander through wild-flower gardens, a European pool, and an outdoor chess and checkers court.

Host: Erna Kubin-Clanin
Rooms: 9 (PB) $260-360
Full Breakfast
Credit Cards: A, B, C
Notes: 3, 4, 5, 8, 10, 11, 12, 13, 14

NOTES: Credit cards accepted: A MasterCard; B Visa; C American Express; D Discover Card; E Diner's Club; F Other; 2 Personal checks accepted; 3 Lunch available; 4 Dinner available; 5 Open all year;

OCCIDENTAL

The Inn at Occidental

3657 Church Street, 95465
(707) 874-1047; (800) 522-6324 (reservations)
FAX (707) 874-1078

In a charming village near the spectacular Sonoma coast and wine country, The Inn at Occidental is a completely renovated 1877 Victorian with European ambience. With antique furnishings and goose-down comforters, each room features original art, antiques, fresh flowers, and a private bath. Amenities include a courtyard garden, fireplaces, afternoon refreshments, and sumptuous breakfast. Two-night minimum stay required for weekends and holidays.

Rooms: 8 (PB) $95-195
Full Breakfast
Credit Cards: A, B, C, D
Notes: 2, 5, 8 (over 9), 9, 10, 11, 12, 14

OJAI

Kids Welcome

3924 East 14th Street, Long Beach, 90804
(310) 498-0552; (800) 383-3513

Orchard in Ojai. This homey bed and breakfast is nestled among the oaks outside of town, with the mountains as a picturesque backdrop. Drink fresh orange juice from the orchard while sitting on the side patio that has a fountain. Features three sunny guest rooms sharing a bath, with plantation style decor and mahogany furnishings. Very, very peaceful. $75.

OLEMA

Point Reyes Seashore Lodge

10021 Highway 1, P.O. Box 39, 94950
(415) 663-9000; (800) 404-LODGE
FAX (415) 663-9030

A re-creation of a turn-of-the-century lodge offers 18 designer-coordinated rooms and three suites, many with whirlpool tubs and fireplaces. A great base for exploring the Point Reyes National Seashore Park, bird or whale watching, hiking, and biking.

Hosts: Jim and Pat Huffman
Rooms: 22 (PB) $75-250
Continental Breakfast
Credit Cards: A, B, C, D
Notes: 2, 5, 8, 9, 10, 11, 12, 14

ORANGE

Country Comfort Bed and Breakfast

5104 East Valencia Drive, 92669
(714) 532-2802

In a quiet residential area, this house has been furnished with comfort and pleasure in mind. It is handicapped accessible with adaptive equipment available. Amenities include a swimming pool, cable TV and VCR, atrium, fireplace, piano, and the use of bicycles, one built for two. Breakfast often features delicious Scotch eggs, stuffed French toast, hash, fruits and assorted beverages. Vegetarian selections also available. Six miles to Disneyland and Knott's Berry Farm.

Hosts: Geri Lopker and Joanne Angell
Rooms: 4 (2PB; 2SB) $50-60
Full Breakfast
Credit Cards: None
Notes: 2, 5, 7 (limited), 8, 9, 10, 11, 12, 14

ORLAND

The Inn at Shallow Creek Farm

4712 Road DD, 95963
(916) 865-4093

A gracious two-story farmhouse offering spacious rooms furnished with antiques—a blend of nostalgia and comfortable country living. Three miles off I-5. The inn is known for its orchard and fresh garden pro-

6 Pets welcome; 7 Smoking allowed; 8 Children welcome; 9 Social drinking allowed; 10 Tennis available; 11 Swimming available; 12 Golf available; 13 Skiing available; 14 May be booked through travel agents.

duce. Breakfast features old-fashioned baked goods and local fruits and juices.

Hosts: Kurt and Mary Glaeseman
Rooms: 4 (2 PB; 2 SB) $55-75
Full Breakfast
Credit Cards: A, B
Notes: 2, 5, 9, 11, 12, 14

OROVILLE

Jean's Riverside Bed and Breakfast

45 Cabana Drive, P.O. Box 2334, 95965
(916) 533-1413

This romantic waterfront bed and breakfast has individualized rooms and suites, some with private Jacuzzis and Franklin fireplaces. Fishing, swimming, gold panning, bird watching, badminton, and croquet are all on the property. Quaint shops with antiques and local handcrafts, excellent restaurants, Oroville Dam and Lake, fish hatchery, historic sites, hiking, and scenic drives are nearby.

Host: Jean Pratt
Rooms: 15 (PB) $55-115.50
Full Breakfast
Credit Cards: A, B, C, E
Notes: 2, 5, 9, 10, 11, 12, 14

PACIFIC GROVE

Eye Openers Bed and Breakfast Reservations

P.O. Box 694, Altadena, 91003-0694
(213) 684-4428; (818) 797-2055
FAX (818) 798-3640

PG-C20I. This century-old Victorian boarding house is now a refurbished award-winning bed and breakfast inn. Beautifully decorated rooms, delicious breakfast, and afternoon refreshments. Shared and private baths. $80-185.

PG-G08I. This 1884 Victorian with ocean view has been renovated and opened its doors in 1990 to become a Pacific Grove bed and breakfast inn close to the beach. Each room is uniquely decorated and features views or sundecks. Delicious full breakfast and afternoon refreshments are provided. No smoking. Private bath. $110-150.

PG-G11I. This 1888 Queen Anne-style mansion-by-the-sea has a panoramic view of Monterey Bay. Delicious breakfast and afternoon refreshments. Shared and private baths. $100-160.

PG-G21I. Beautifully preserved 1887 Victorian on the National Register of Historic Places can now be enjoyed as a bed and breakfast inn. Wonderful breakfast, afternoon hors d'oeuvres, and wine or tea served. $85-150.

Gatehouse Inn Bed and Breakfast

225 Central Avenue, 93950
(800) 753-1881

Built in 1884, the historic Gatehouse Inn is a seaside Victorian home with distinctive rooms, stunning views, private baths, fireplaces, patios, delicious breakfasts, and afternoon wine and hors d'oeuvres. Walk to the ocean, Cannery Row, Monterey Bay Aquarium, shops, and restaurants. Just ten minutes to Carmel, Pebble Beach, and world-renowned golf courses.

Hosts: Lois DeFord
Rooms: 8 (PB) $110-150
Full Breakfast
Credit Cards: A, B, C
Notes: 2, 5, 8, 9, 10, 11, 12, 14

The Martine Inn

255 Oceanview Boulevard, 93950
(408) 373-3388; (800) 852-5588

NOTES: Credit cards accepted: A MasterCard; B Visa; C American Express; D Discover Card; E Diner's Club; F Other; 2 Personal checks accepted; 3 Lunch available; 4 Dinner available; 5 Open all year;

Surpassed only by the beauty of Monterey Bay, the Martine Inn compliments the rugged terrain with a timeless sense of graciousness. Don and Marion Martine have filled this Victorian-turned-Mediterranean mansion, built in the 1890s, with an extensive collection of antiques. The all-private bath bedrooms offer richness in history and tradition, many of which have incredible ocean views or a wood-burning fireplace. Enjoy the spectacular bay vistas, while breakfast, evening wine, and hors d'oeuvres are served on Old Sheffield silver, fine china, and crystal.

Hosts: Marion and Don Martine; Tracy Harris
Rooms: 19 (PB) $125-230
Full Breakfast
Credit Cards: A, B, C
Notes: 2, 3, 5, 9, 10, 11, 12, 14

The Old St. Angela Inn

321 Central Avenue, 93950
(408) 372-3246; (800) 748-6306

The Old St. Angela's Inn began as a country home in 1910, converted to a rectory and then a convent in 1920, and is now a cozy bed and breakfast inn overlooking the natural beauty of the Monterey Bay. Within this historic Cape Cod home are rooms of distinctive individuality and warmth to provide guests with comfort and serenity. Country pine furniture, little teddy bears, and other pleasant surroundings provide a relaxing, informal, and home-away-from-home atmosphere. Mingle with fellow guests by the fireplace in the living room and enjoy an afternoon wine, tea, or coffee and cookies. Relax in the garden patio amidst beautiful flowers, butterflies, and sunshine. Just 100 yards from the water and only minutes from excellent restaurants and shopping areas, and other activities.

Host: Kathy Pedullà
Rooms: 11 (8 PB; 3 SB) $90-150
Full Breakfast
Credit Cards: A, B, C
Notes: 5, 9, 10, 11, 12, 14

Seven Gables Inn

555 Ocean View Boulevard, 93950
(408) 372-4341

It is difficult to imagine a more scenic and dramatic spot than the rocky promontory occupied by Seven Gables Inn overlooking Monterey Bay. This century-old mansion is furnished with elegant Victorian antiques. All guest rooms have panoramic ocean views and private baths. A generous, full, sit-down breakfast and 4:00 P.M. high tea are included. Smoking permitted in the garden areas only. Seven Gables is easily accessible to the Monterey Aquarium, Cannery Row, 17-Mile Drive, Carmel, and numerous other scenic sites in the Monterey area.

Hosts: The Flatley family
Rooms: 14 (PB) $105-205
Full Breakfast
Credit Cards: A, B
Notes: 2, 5, 10, 11, 12

PACIFIC PALISADES

Bed and Breakfast, L.A.

3924 E. 14th Street, Long Beach, 90804
(310) 498-0552; (800) 383-3513

Ellen's Bed and Breakfast. Between Santa Monica and Malibu is this quiet condominium. It has a bedroom with two beds and private bath. Accommodations include pool, sundeck, Jacuzzi, sauna, and a fully equipped exercise room. Tennis courts, picnic areas, and a playground are within walking distance. Hostess is the president of a non-profit organization helping worldwide environmental efforts, and her home is adjacent to Will Rogers Historic Park and the J. Paul Getty Museum.

Jane's House is a sprawling home in luxurious Pacific Palisades with five guest rooms, three with private baths, several with views of the garden and pool. One Victorian-style suite includes a perfect kid-sized attic room. Breakfast is full of fresh homegrown fruit. On the bluffs not far from the ocean. $50-65.

Eye Openers
Bed and Breakfast
Reservations

P.O. Box 694, Altadena, 91003-0694
(213) 684-4428; (818) 797-2055
FAX (818) 798-3640

PP-H1. Large, sunny condominium one-half mile from the ocean offers a good location, friendly hospitality, and pool. The guest room has twin beds and private bath. Continental breakfast. No smoking. Resident cat. $50-55.

PP-A4. Relax in a family-style bed and breakfast in beautiful, serene Pacific Palisades close to beaches, Santa Monica, and West Los Angeles. Four guest rooms have double or twin beds with private or shared baths. An extended continental breakfast is served by the pool and Jacuzzi. No smoking. $60-90.

PALM DESERT

Bed and Breakfast, L.A.

3924 E. 14th Street, Long Beach, 90804
(310) 498-0552; (800) 383-3513

Blue Desert Skies. In the heart of Palm Desert, Tres Palmas features lovely rooms uniquely decorated in the Southwestern style. Indulge in specialty coffees and teas as part of a special continental breakfast in the dining room, around the pool, or in the privacy of the room. Hosts of this cozy bed and breakfast offer individual attention as they help make stays a pleasant experience. Call for rates.

Eye Openers
Bed and Breakfast
Reservations

P.O. Box 694, Altadena, 91003-0694
(213) 684-4428; (818) 797-2055
FAX (818) 798-3640

PD-B4. New contemporary-style bed and breakfast features Southwestern decor, a welcome, delightful atmosphere, many amenities, pool, and spa. Four guest rooms have queen- or king-size beds with private baths. An extended continental breakfast is served, and refreshments are available during the day. It is walking distance to El Paseo with its boutiques, galleries, and restaurants and to other entertainment areas. No smoking. $90-140.

Tres Palmas
Bed and Breakfast

73135 Tumbleweed Lane, 92260
(619) 773-9858

Tres Palmas is only one block south of El Paseo, the "Rodeo Drive of the Desert," where guests will find boutiques, art galleries, and fine restaurants. Guests can choose to stay "home" to relax and enjoy the desert sun in and around the pool and spa. The guest rooms feature queen- or king-size beds, climate controls, and TVs and are uniquely decorated in Southwestern style. Lemonade and iced tea are always available. Snacks are provided in the late afternoons.

Hosts: Terry and Karen Bennett
Rooms: 4 (PB) $90-140
Continental Breakfast
Credit Cards: A, B
Notes: 2, 5, 9, 10, 11, 12, 14

NOTES: Credit cards accepted: A MasterCard; B Visa; C American Express; D Discover Card; E Diner's Club; F Other; 2 Personal checks accepted; 3 Lunch available; 4 Dinner available; 5 Open all year;

PALM SPRINGS

Casa Cody
Bed and Breakfast
Country Inn

175 South Cahuilla, 92262
(619) 320-9346

Romantic, historic hideaway in the heart of Palm Springs village. Beautifully redecorated in Santa Fe decor, with kitchens, wood-burning fireplaces, patios, two pools, and a spa. Close to the Desert Museum, Heritage Center, and Moorten Botanical Gardens. Nearby hiking in Indian canyons, horseback riding, tennis, golf. Polo, ballooning, helicopter, and desert Jeep tours. Near celebrity homes, date gardens, and Joshua Tree National Monument.

Hosts: Therese Hayes and Frank Tysen
Rooms: 17 (PB) $45-175
Continental Breakfast
Credit Cards: A, B, C, E
Notes: 2, 5, 6, 7, 8, 9, 10, 11, 12, 13, 14

Eye Openers
Bed and Breakfast
Reservations

P.O. Box 694, Altadena, 91003-0694
(213) 684-4128; (818) 797-2055
FAX (818) 798-3640

PA-C3. New Japanese-style inn and decor create a relaxed bed and breakfast stay. Shoji windows open to the pool. Three guest rooms have queen-size or twin futons with shared or private baths. Shiatsu massage, kimonos, and additional amenities available. Choice of continental or full Japanese breakfast. No smoking. $55-75.

PS-H3. This former home of a glamorous 1930-40s movie star is now a unique bed and breakfast with a suite and two additional guest rooms. Queen-size or twin beds

and private baths. Wonderfully decorated with period pieces and appointed antiques, this bed and breakfast has warm and gracious hospitality. Extended continental breakfast served by the pool, patios, or dining room. No smoking. $60-100.

PALO ALTO

Adella Villa

P.O. Box 4528, 94309
(415) 321-5195; FAX (415) 325-5121

Exclusive luxury villa on a secluded acre. Electronic gates, pool, fountains, and barbecue. The 4,000-square-foot residence has five bedrooms, five private baths (two with Jacuzzi tubs), and a grand piano in the music foyer. Breakfast is cooked to order. Complimentary sherry and white wine are served. Bicycles are available. Thirty minutes from San Francisco.

Host: Tricia Young
Rooms: 5 (PB) $95-110
Full Breakfast
Credit Cards: A, B, C, E
Notes: 2, 5, 8 (over 12), 9, 10, 11, 12, 14

Hotel California

2431 Ash Street, 94306
(415) 322-7666

A unique bed and breakfast inn ideal for visiting professionals, out-of-town guests, and many foreign academic visitors. One of the most reasonably priced places to stay. Twenty comfortable rooms, each with private bathroom, attractively furnished with turn-of-the-century pieces. A great and convenient place to stay when visiting Stanford University. Close to shops. Breakfast is served downstairs in the bakery.

Hosts: Andy and Michelle Hite
Rooms: 20 (PB) $53-60
Continental Breakfast
Credit Cards: A, B, C, D, E, F
Notes: 5, 14

6 Pets welcome; 7 Smoking allowed; 8 Children welcome; 9 Social drinking allowed; 10 Tennis available; 11 Swimming available; 12 Golf available; 13 Skiing available; 14 May be booked through travel agents.

The Victorian on Lytton

555 Lytton Avenue, 94301
(415) 322-8555

Special amenities include down comforters, Battenberg lace canopies, botanical prints, Blue Willow china, and claw foot tubs. Wander through the English country garden with over 900 perennial plants. Five king-size and five queen-size beds available. Relax with a picture book or novel in the parlor with a cup of tea while listening to classical music.

Hosts: Maxwell and Susan Hall
Rooms: 10 (PB) $98-175
Continental Breakfast
Credit Cards: A, B, C
Notes: 2, 5, 9, 10, 11, 12, 14

PALOS VERDES

Bed and Breakfast, L.A.

3924 East 14th Street, Long Beach, 90804
(800) 383-3513

This house on the Palos Verdes Peninsula has a sweeping view of the ocean and a road to a private beach and surfing cove. Two guest rooms are available, both with TVs and private baths. One bath is connecting, and the other bath is down the hall. Hosts provide fresh robes. Affordable rates.

Eye Openers
Bed and Breakfast
Reservations

P.O. Box 694, Altadena, 91003-0694
(213) 684-4428; (818) 797-2055
FAX (818) 798-3640

PV-B2. Ocean breezes, a panoramic view of the Pacific, and private beach facilities are offered by this homey bed and breakfast with two guest rooms and a private bath. Extended continental breakfasts are served in the dining area or on the deck by well-traveled host. No smoking. $55-60.

Kids Welcome

3924 East 14th Street, Long Beach, 90804
(310) 498-0552; (800) 383-3513

View of the Ocean. Sprawling over the hillside, this house in colorful Palos Verdes offers three rooms with private baths. One room has a crib. Try a visit to the tidepools a few blocks from the door. Special rates for four people. $60.

PASADENA

Eye Openers
Bed and Breakfast
Reservations

P.O. Box 694, Altadena, 91003-0694
(213) 684-4428; (818) 797-2055
FAX (818) 798-3640

AL-C2. A special 1926 French Normandy farmhouse in a lovely neighborhood has two-story living room and open-hearth fireplace. Enjoy an elegant continental breakfast in the garden patio or dining room. Good hiking trails, museums, and libraries nearby. Short drive to Los Angeles. No smoking. Two guest rooms. Private and shared baths. $55.

AL-J1. This pool house with small kitchen offers privacy and comfort. On a cul-de-sac across from golf course. With queen-size sofa bed, twin bed, and private bath. Good local hiking, but only 15- to 20-minute drive to LA Civic Center or to Hollywood. Continental breakfast is served. No smoking. $45-55.

AL-L1. Pool house bed and breakfast hosted by multi-lingual hosts is near the mountains and hiking trails but close to Old Town and Los Angeles tourist attractions. Guest cottage has twin beds and private bath. Continental breakfast. No smoking. $50-55.

NOTES: Credit cards accepted: A MasterCard; B Visa; C American Express; D Discover Card; E Diner's Club; F Other; 2 Personal checks accepted; 3 Lunch available; 4 Dinner available; 5 Open all year;

AL-M2. Large Mediterranean-style home with mountain views offers two large guest rooms with twin or king-size beds and private baths. Beautiful neighborhood with good hiking areas, yet seven minutes to Old Town and 20 minutes to Los Angeles. Resident dog and cat. No smoking. $50.

AL-P8. Enjoy an extended continental breakfast near the fountain in this beautifully landscaped, walled garden of a stately, Spanish-style home, hosted by a yoga teacher and amateur astronomer. No smoking. Two guest rooms. Shared bath. $50-55.

AL-R2. Large, contemporary home with Old World wine cellar has Angeles National Forest as its back yard. Enjoy a continental or full breakfast on the deck overlooking pool and view of the valley. Host teaches wine classes and is a gourmet cook. No smoking. Two guest rooms. Private baths. $55-60.

AL-S1. This large, well-landscaped yard in a quiet residential community is a wonderful retreat at the end of the day. A delicious continental breakfast is served. No smoking. One guest room. Private bath. $50-55.

AL-W2. Cape Code-style bed and breakfast appointed with early American antiques is on one of Altadena's loveliest streets and hosted by horse enthusiasts. Two guest rooms have twin or double beds and private baths. Large yard with pool. Continental breakfast. No smoking. Resident dogs. $50-55.

AR-P2. Horseracing and garden enthusiasts will be close to Santa Anita Racetrack and the Los Angeles County Arboretum while enjoying the hospitality at this large, well-decorated, contemporary home. Enjoy a continental breakfast by the pool or in the family room. Two guest rooms. Private and shared baths. $45-50.

AR-W2. This home sits on a quiet cul-de-sac near the Santa Anita Racetrack, Los Angeles County Arboretum, Huntington Library, golf courses, and the beautiful San Gabriel Mountains. Host loves to garden, hike, and travel. Enjoy a continental breakfast on the pool patio. No smoking. Two guest rooms with private and shared baths. $35-45.

PA-A2. Pasadena neighborhood known for its spacious homes, large lawns, and yards is the setting for this bed and breakfast offering warm hospitality and continental breakfast. Two guest rooms have twin or double beds and private baths. No smoking. Resident cats. $45-50.

PA-A3. Japanese-hosted bed and breakfast is in the center of the city. Three guest rooms have queen-size or double futons with private and shared baths. Continental breakfast. No smoking. $45-55.

PA-H1. Near the historic Huntington Hotel, now the Ritz-Carlton, this contemporary bed and breakfast is hosted by a retired school administrator. Enjoy the lovely garden room, where an ample continental breakfast is served. Convenient to all local tourist attractions. Resident cat. No smoking. One guest room with private bath. $55-50.

PA-L1. Dramatic contemporary bed and breakfast within walking distance to the Rose Bowl offers a quiet setting near most tourist attractions. The guest room has queen-size bed and a shared bath. Continental breakfast is served in the dining area or pool side. No smoking. $85.

PA-O1. In renowned residential area known as Bungalow Heaven, this comfortable bed and breakfast offers friendly hospitality, continental breakfast, and an interesting host who works in the movie industry. The guest room has a double bed and private bath. No smoking. $45-50.

6 Pets welcome; 7 Smoking allowed; 8 Children welcome; 9 Social drinking allowed; 10 Tennis available; 11 Swimming available; 12 Golf available; 13 Skiing available; 14 May be booked through travel agents.

Eye Openers
Bed and Breakfast
Reservations
(continued)

PA-P2A. Sprawling ranch-style house in Colonial style has a large living room and book-lined library, both with a fireplace. A full scrumptious breakfast is served on the sunny patio or formal dining room. Host is concert pianist, organist, and harpsichordist. Close to Los Angeles and most tourist attractions. No smoking. Two guest rooms. Private and shared baths. $65.

PA-P2B. This craftsman-style house near Orange Grove's historic millionaire's row offers gracious surroundings and well-traveled hosts. Two guest rooms with twin or queen-size beds have private and shared baths. Walk to Old Town, restaurants, and concert hall. Continental breakfast. No smoking. $45-75.

PA-R3. Short walk to Pasadena Civic and Convention Center, this bed and breakfast is an older, well-kept California bungalow with first-floor guest accommodations, as well as a separate, private apartment. Hosts who enjoy traveling have lived abroad and speak Swedish. Continental or full breakfast. No smoking. Private and shared baths. $35-75.

PA-S9. Gracious hosts interested in art offer very private guest quarters, which make up the entire first floor of this contemporary hillside home, with guest living room and patio. Garden and pool lend an Oriental atmosphere, and a delicious full breakfast served along with a view of the city make this bed and breakfast a special place for guests to stay. No smoking. Two guest rooms; shared bath. $65-75.

PA-V1. Decorated with European antiques, this lovely bed and breakfast in a charming area near the Ritz-Carlton offers a full gourmet breakfast in dining room or patio. The guest room has twin beds and private bath. No smoking. $50-55.

PA-W2. Half-timbered Tudor-style home was designed and built by the host, who is a magician, yoga enthusiast, and vegetarian gourmet cook. Lovely community with good hiking is close to museums and tourist attractions. No smoking. One guest room with private bath. $55-60.

SM-S1. Very private guest house set in nicely landscaped yard of quiet, lovely neighborhood near the Huntington Library. Small kitchen, twin beds, and private bath. No smoking. Special weekly and monthly rates available. $50-60.

SP-A4I. This 1895 Victorian farmhouse has been refurbished and decorated to recall the heritage of the home and city. Full breakfast and afternoon refreshments. Four guest rooms with double, queen- or king-size beds and private baths. No smoking. $90-100.

SP-B3I. Restored elegant Victorian on the National Register of Historic Places close to Old Town, museums, and restaurants. Host offers gracious hospitality, lovely grounds, and a full breakfast served in the dining room or patio areas. Three guest rooms have queen-size beds and private baths. No smoking. $100-150.

SP-P1. A 400-square-foot redwood guest house shares patio and Jacuzzi with host's home, which faces Arroyo Seco natural recreation area. Horse stable, par three golf course, racquetball, and tennis courts are within walking distance. Cottage has cooking facilities and TV. Twelve-minute drive to Los Angeles. No smoking. Private bath. $55-75.

NOTES: Credit cards accepted: A MasterCard; B Visa; C American Express; D Discover Card; E Diner's Club; F Other; 2 Personal checks accepted; 3 Lunch available; 4 Dinner available; 5 Open all year;

PETALUMA _____

Cavanagh Inn
10 Keller Street, 91606
(707) 765-4657

Step back into the romantic past and enjoy the warmth and charm of Petaluma's first bed and breakfast. Appreciate the rare redwood heart paneling in both of these turn-of-the-century homes. The fireplace-warmed parlors and library are stocked with books and games. Guests may help themselves to fresh cider, lemonade, and cookies. Cavanagh Inn is a short walk from historic downtown Petaluma, the Petaluma River, and in close proximity to wineries, Bodega Bay, San Francisco, and the beautiful Sonoma coast.

Host: Billie Erkel
Rooms: 7 (5 PB; 2 SB) $55-105
Full Breakfast
Credit Cards: A, B, C
Notes: 2, 5, 8, 10, 11, 12, 14

PLACERVILLE _____

Combellack–Blair House
3059 Cedar Ravine, 95667
(916) 622-3764

This gracious Queen Anne Victorian home has stood as a landmark to travelers and residents alike for nearly a century. When guests enter the front door they will enjoy the magnificent sight of a spiral staircase that is a work of art. The front parlor is a collection of period furnishings, recalling the 1890s. The rooms are decorated in a Victorian manner. This truly is a historic home, now a bed and breakfast to enjoy.

Hosts: Al and Rosalie McConnell
Rooms: 2 (PB) $89-99
Continental Breakfast
Credit Cards: A, B
Notes: 5, 10, 11, 12, 13

The Chichester–McKee House
800 Spring Street, 95667
(916) 626-1882; (800) 831-4008

This elegant 1892 home was built by lumber baron D.W. Chichester. Enjoy fireplaces, fretwork, stained glass, antiques, and relaxing hospitality. A "special" full breakfast is served in the dining room, and three air-conditioned guest rooms with private baths and robes are available. Downtown near Apple Hill and Gold Discovery Site.

Hosts: Doreen and Bill Thornhill
Rooms: 3 (PB) $75-85
Full Breakfast
Credit Cards: A, B, C, D
Notes: 2, 5, 8, 9, 10, 11, 12, 13, 14

The Chichester–McKee House

River Rock Inn
1756 Georgetown Drive, 95667
(916) 622-7640

Welcome to Gold Country. The River Rock Inn offers comfortable rooms furnished with antiques (two with half-baths), a hot tub on the deck, and an uninterrupted view of the river. Go exploring, fishing, gold panning, white-water rafting, or hot air ballooning. Tour an old gold mine, visit Marshall State Park, or enjoy friendly shops, antique stores, restaurants, and wineries that are all just minutes away. It's all here to enjoy.

Host: Dorothy Irvin
Rooms: 4 (2 PB; 2 SB) $72-85
Full Breakfast
Credit Cards: None
Notes: 5, 8, 12, 13, 14

6 Pets welcome; 7 Smoking allowed; 8 Children welcome; 9 Social drinking allowed; 10 Tennis available; 11 Swimming available; 12 Golf available; 13 Skiing available; 14 May be booked through travel agents.

POINT REYES STATION

The Country House

P.O. Box 98, 94956
(415) 663-1627

California ranch house on an acre overlooking Point Reyes Station. Two separate, private suites with queen-size beds and private baths. Fireplaces, antiques, beautiful views, and good food. Apple orchards and cottage flower garden. Walk to village; easy drive to Point Reyes National Seashore. Minimum-stay requirements for holidays and weekends. Deposit required. Entire house suitable for vacation rentals for conferences or families.

Host: Ewell H. McIsaac
Suites: 3 (PB) From $100
Credit Cards: None
Notes: 2, 5, 8, 9, 11, 14

Ferrandos Hideaway

12010 Highway 1, 94956
(415) 663-1966

Rich and homey bed and breakfast one mile north of Point Reyes Station. Private cottage with fully equipped kitchen. Two rooms in main house. Hot tub, private baths, wood-burning stoves, vegetable garden, chickens. Close to Point Reyes National Seashore, hiking, biking, birding, horseback riding, whale watching, and miles of sandy beaches.

Hosts: Greg and Doris Ferrando
Rooms: 2 (PB) $95-120
Cottage: 1
Full Breakfast
Credit Cards: None
Notes: 2, 5, 8, 12

Horseshoe Farm
Bed and Breakfast Cabin

39 Drake's Summit, P.O. Box 332, 94956
(415) 663-9401

Private, cozy, and charming cabin, with sunny deck, fireplace, and private hot tub in the peaceful, quiet woods of Inverness Ridge. Adjacent to the scenic wonders of 65,000-acres in Point Reyes National Seashore. Ocean beaches, hiking trails, whale watching, year-round bird watching. Great restaurants nearby.

Host: Paki Stedwell-Wright
Rooms: 2 (PB) $115-145
Full Breakfast
Credit Cards: None
Notes: 2, 5, 7

Jasmine Cottage

Jasmine Cottage

11561 Coast Route One, 94956
(415) 663-1166

This charming guest cottage was built in 1879 for the original Point Reyes schoolhouse. Secluded, romantic cottage sleeps four, has a library, fireplace, full kitchen, beautiful pastoral views, private patios, and garden hot tub. Five-minute walk down the hill to town; five-minute drive to spectacular Point Reyes National Seashore. A crib and highchair are available.

Host: Karen Gray
Cottage: 1 (PB) From $115
Full Breakfast
Credit Cards: A, B
Notes: 2, 5, 6, 8, 9, 11, 14

Marsh Cottage Bed and Breakfast

Box 1121, 94956
(415) 669-7168

The privacy of a peaceful bayside retreat near Inverness and the spectacular Point Reyes National Seashore. Exceptional location and views, tasteful interior, fireplace, fully equipped kitchen, complete bath. Breakfast provided in the cottage. Ideal for romantics and naturalists. Hiking nearby. Two-night minimum stay required for weekends and holidays

Host: Wendy Schwartz
Room: 1 (PB) $95-110
Full Breakfast
Credit Cards: None
Notes: 2, 5, 8, 9, 11

Terri's Homestay

P.O. Box 113, 94956
(415) 663-1289; (800) 969-1289

High atop the Inverness Ridge this sunny, secluded trailside bed and breakfast offers magnificent views. Private bath, entrance, and deck. Natural fiber bedding and colorful central-American decor. Step outside and enjoy the extensive network of Point Reyes National Seashore Trails. Relax in the ozone-purified hot tub that uses 95 percent less chlorine. Health-oriented, supportive staff also provides professional massage, which couples can receive simultaneously. Approximately an hour-and-a-half's drive north of San Francisco; detailed map provided with reservation.

Hosts: Terri Elaine, and Richard Lailer
Rooms: 2 (PB) $85-115
Continental Breakfast
Credit Cards: A, B, C
Notes: 2, 5, 8, 9, 10, 11, 14

Thirty-nine Cypress

Box 176, 39 Cypress Road, 94956
(415) 663-1709

This small redwood inn overlooking a 500-acre ranch, marshlands, and the upper reaches of Tomales Bay offers spectacular views for guests to enjoy. Furnished with family antiques, Oriental rugs, original art, and an eclectic library, each of the rooms opens onto its own private patio. An outdoor spa overlooking the views is available, and this is a favorite spot for bird watchers. Near Point Reyes National Seashore, with its splendid beaches and 140 miles of hiking trails.

Host: Julia Bartlett
Rooms: 3 (SB) $95-125
Full Breakfast
Credit Cards: A, B, C
Notes: 2, 5, 6, 9, 11, 14

The Tree House

P.O. Box 1075, 73 Drake Summit, 94956
(415) 663-8720; FAX (415) 663-8120

On the Inverness Ridge with a view of Point Reyes Station, and direct access to the National Seashore Park. The Tree House sits close to the beaches, the lighthouse, hiking trails; this is also a bird watcher's paradise all year round. Whale watching from December until April. Horseback riding available.

Host: Lisa P. Patsel
Rooms: 3 (PB) $90-110
Full or Continental Breakfast
Credit Cards: A, B, C
Notes: 2, 5, 6, 7, 8, 9, 14

QUINCY

The Feather Bed

542 Jackson Street, P.O. Box 3200, 95971
(916) 283-0102

The Feather Bed is a country Victorian, circa 1893, in a small community town in the high Sierras. All seven guest rooms have private baths, queen-size beds, and private entrances. An abundant country breakfast is served each morning in the charming dining room and, during the summer months, on the Victorian patio. Guests can enjoy hiking, swimming, picnicking, and other outdoor activities nearby. Enjoy a stroll through historic downtown Quincy, dine in one of the fine restaurants, or relax on the old-fashioned veranda.

Hosts: Bob and Jan Janowski
Rooms: 7 (PB) $70-120
Full Breakfast
Credit Cards: A, B, C, D, E
Notes: 2, 5, 8, 10, 11, 12, 14

REDDING

Palisades Paradise Bed and Breakfast

1200 Palisades Avenue, 96003
(916) 223-5305; (800) 382-4649

Guests will love the breathtaking view of the Sacramento River, the city, and surrounding mountains from this beautiful contemporary home with its spa, fireplace, wide-screen TV, VCR, and homelike atmosphere. Palisades Paradise is a serene setting for a quiet hideaway, yet one mile from shopping and I-5, with water skiing and river rafting nearby. Inspected, rated, and approved by the ABBA. Full breakfast is served only on the weekends.

Host: Gail Goetz
Rooms: 2 (SB) $55-85
Continental and Full Breakfasts
Credit Cards: A, B, C
Notes: 2, 5, 7 (limited), 9, 10, 11, 12, 13, 14

Palisades Paradise

REDLANDS

Morey Mansion Bed and Breakfast Inn

190 Terracina Boulevard, 92373
(909) 793-7970

Built in 1890 by David Morey, a retired shipbuilder, this Queen Anne Victorian with a Russian dome is a landmark in historical Redlands. There are five guest rooms available, four with a private bath, and a continental breakfast is served in the morning. The downstairs area, as well as the veranda and lawn, are available for weddings, receptions, and teas.

Host: Dolly Wimer
Rooms: 5 (3 PB; 2 SB) $109-185
Continental Breakfast
Credit Cards: A, B, C, D, F
Notes: 2, 5, 8, 9, 10, 11, 12, 13, 14

REDONDO BEACH

Bed and Breakfast, L.A.

3924 E. 14th Street, Long Beach, 90804
(310) 498-0552; (800) 383-3513

Eagan House. Hosts have remodeled their home to include a guest suite with private bath. Quiet, residential neighborhood, close to LA Interntaional Airport but not far from the beach or tourist attractions. Hosts are both teachers and serve full breakfast on weekends and in the summer. $60-70.

Ocean Breeze Bed and Breakfast

122 South Juanita Avenue, 90277-3435
(310) 316-5123

Near the beach, between Los Angeles and Long Beach, close to freeways. Private entry, spa bathtub, and hospital beds with plush mattress covers. Remote TV, microwave oven, refrigerator, toaster, and coffee maker in large luxurious rooms.

NOTES: Credit cards accepted: A MasterCard; B Visa; C American Express; D Discover Card; E Diner's Club; F Other; 2 Personal checks accepted; 3 Lunch available; 4 Dinner available; 5 Open all year;

Additional room with twin beds. Special rates for two or more nights and for seniors.

Hosts: Norris and Betty Binding
Rooms: 2 (PB) $30-50
Continental Breakfast
Credit Cards: None
Notes: 2, 5, 7, 8 (over 5), 9, 10, 11, 12

REEDLEY

The Fairweather Inn
Bed and Breakfast
259 South Reed Avenue, 93654
(209) 638-1918

This Craftsman home was built in 1914 and has 3,500 square feet. It was refurbished over a period of four years to bring it back to the early 1900s. The inn has been beautifully restored and decorated. All furniture, light fixtures, tubs, sinks, etchings, etc., have been collected all over the country. This charming early California home will make guests feel like the clock has been turned back to an earlier era.

Host: Vi Demyan
Rooms: 4 (2 PB; 2 SB) $75-85
Full Breakfast
Credit Cards: A, B, C
Notes: 5, 11, 12, 13, 14

SACRAMENTO

Abigail's Bed and Breakfast
2120 G Street, 95816
(916) 441-5007; (800) 858-1568

Quiet elegance and old Sacramento charm in historic district. Walking distance to restaurants and the state capitol. Award-winning breakfasts, large airy rooms with king- or queen-size beds, private baths. One bathroom has a whirlpool tub. Hot tub in secluded garden. Telephones, a refrigerator, and TV available. Knowledgeable innkeepers. Resident cats. Sacramento's loveliest bed and breakfast.

Hosts: Susanne and Ken Ventura
Rooms: 5 (PB) $95-155
Full Breakfast
Credit Cards: A, B, C, D, E
Notes: 2, 5, 9, 10, 11, 12, 14

Amber House
Bed and Breakfast
1315 22nd Street, 95816
(916) 444-8085; (800) 755-6526
FAX (916) 447-1548

Just eight blocks from the capitol, on a quiet street of historic homes, Amber House offers the perfect blend of elegance, comfort, and friendly hospitality. In both the cozy hideaway and in the spectacular mini-suite with elegant marble bath and Jacuzzi tub for two, a delicious gourmet breakfast is served, in-room if so desired. Early morning coffee tray, evening beverages, and all of the personal attention wanted. Phones, TVs, and in-room Jacuzzis.

Hosts: Michael and Jane Richardson
Rooms: 9 (PB) $85-195
Full Breakfast
Credit Cards: A, B, C, D, E, F
Notes: 2, 5, 9, 10, 11, 14

Bed and Breakfast
International
P.O. Box 282910, San Francisco, 94128-2910
(415) 696-1690; (800) 872-4500
FAX (415) 696-1699

402. Historic Victorian home close to the capitol, Old Town, museums, and restaurants. It is on the Sacramento Old House Tour and is furnished with antiques. There is an upstairs sitting room with a fireplace. One guest room with private bath; one with shared bath. $60-65.

Hartley House
Bed and Breakfast Inn
700 22nd Street, 95816
(916) 447-7829; (800) 831-5806

6 Pets welcome; 7 Smoking allowed; 8 Children welcome; 9 Social drinking allowed; 10 Tennis available; 11 Swimming available; 12 Golf available; 13 Skiing available; 14 May be booked through travel agents.

A stunning turn-of-the-century mansion, surrounded by majestic elm trees and stately old homes of historic Boulevard Park in midtown. Offering exquisitely appointed rooms, the inn is near the capitol, Old Town, the convention center, and the city's finest restaurants, and coffee and dessert cafes. The host also has a cookie jar filled with freshly baked cookies!

Host: Randy Hartley
Rooms: 5 (PB) $95-135
Full Breakfast
Credit Cards: A, B, C, D, E, F
Notes: 2, 5, 9, 10, 11, 12, 13, 14

ST. HELENA

Ambrose Bierce House

1515 Main Street, 94574
(707) 963-3003

Built in 1872, this house combines history, romance, and pampering. Queen-size beds, claw-foot tubs, and armoires decorate the former home of the writer Ambrose Bierce. Suites are named for historical figures whose presence touched Bierce and Napa Valley in the late 1800s. Convenient location; walking distance to restaurants, shops, and wineries. A gourmet continental breakfast is complimentary, as is the hospitality.

Host: Jane Gibson
Rooms: 3 (PB) $99-139
Continental Breakfast
Credit Cards: None
Notes: 2, 5, 9, 14

Bartels Ranch and Country Inn

1200 Conn Valley Road, 94574
(707) 963-4001; FAX (707) 963-5100

In the heart of the world-famous Napa Valley wine country, this secluded, romantic, and elegant country estate overlooks a "100-acre valley with a 10,000-acre view." The honeymoon suite features a sunken Jacuzzi, sauna, shower, stone fireplace, TV, VCR, and stereo. The Blue Valley Room, the Sunset Room, and the Brass Room have various amenities, including a deck, Jacuzzi, refrigerator, coffee maker, and microwave oven. Fireplaces and FM stereos available in all rooms. Expansive entertainment room, pool table, fireplace, library, and terraces overlooking the vineyard. Bicycles, refrigerator, TV, and telephone available. Wineries, lake activities, golf, tennis, fishing, boating, and mineral spas nearby. Limousine, hot air balloons, and helicopter available. Wine seminars with a tailored itinerary are a house special.

Host: Jami Bartels
Rooms: 4 (PB) $115-275
Continental Breakfast
Credit Cards: A, B, C, D
Notes: 2, 3, 4, 5, 7 (limited), 8, 9, 10, 11, 12, 14

Bartels Ranch and Country Inn

Cinnamon Bear Bed and Breakfast

1407 Kearney Street, 94574
(707) 963-4653

This classic Arts and Craft house, built in 1910, is furnished in that style with lots of bears. Guests are close to downtown shops and restaurants. Air-conditioned. Afternoon socializing with snacks, beverages, TV, telephone. Family-owned and operated. Midweek and winter discounts available.

Host: Genny Jenkins
Rooms: 3 (PB) $135-155
Full Breakfast
Credit Cards: A, B
Notes: 2, 5, 9, 10, 11, 12

NOTES: Credit cards accepted: A MasterCard; B Visa; C American Express; D Discover Card; E Diner's Club; F Other; 2 Personal checks accepted; 3 Lunch available; 4 Dinner available; 5 Open all year;

Creek-side Inn

945 Main Street, 94574
(707) 963-7244

Creek-side is a beautiful and quiet country cottage in the heart of St. Helena, yet peacefully sheltered from the hustle and bustle of town by ancient oaks and the murmurs of White Sulphur Creek rippling past its secluded rear garden patio. When guests walk through the door from the outside world, they enter the private world that is Creek-side.

Hosts: Jean Nicholson and Virginia Toogood
Rooms: 3 (SB) $75-95
Full Breakfast
Credit Cards: A, B, C
Note: 2

Elsie's Conn Valley Inn

726 Rossi Road, 94574
(707) 963-4614

An authentic European-style bed and breakfast nestled in the Napa Valley foothills. Enjoy lush gardens with vineyard and forested hill views. Peaceful, romantic getaway. Refrigerator in room with complimentary Napa Valley wine, cheese, crackers, and a basket of fruit.

Host: Elsie Asplund Hudak
Rooms: 3 (1 PB; 2 SB) $95-110
Full Breakfast
Cards: A, B, C
Notes: 2, 5, 8, 9, 10, 11, 12, 14

Eye Openers
Bed and Breakfast
Reservations

P.O. Box 694, Altadena, 91003-0694
(213) 684-4428; (818) 797-2055
FAX (818) 798-3640

SH-D3I. Secluded in a forest above vineyards, yet near town, this small bed and breakfast offers a peaceful, rustic retreat. Guest room has private entrance and fireplace. Carriage Room and two-room cottage are decorated with antiques and very private. Queen- or king-size beds and private baths. An extended continental breakfast is served. No smoking. $105-125.

Hilltop House
Bed and Breakfast

9550 St. Helena Road, P.O. Box 726, 94574
(707) 944-0880

Poised at the very top of a ridge that separates the famous wine regions of Napa and Sonoma, Hilltop House is a country retreat with all the comforts of home and a view that must be seen to be believed. The hosts built this contemporary home with this mountain panorama in mind, and the vast deck allows guests to enjoy it at leisure with a glass of wine in the afternoon, with breakfast in the morning, or with a long soak in the hot tub. From this vantage point sunrises and sunsets are simply amazing. Guests will cherish the natural setting, caring hospitality, and prize location.

Host: Annette Gevarter
Rooms: 4 (PB) $115-175
Full Breakfast
Credit Cards: A, B, C
Notes: 2, 5, 8, 9, 10, 11, 12, 14

Shady Oaks Country Inn

399 Zinfandel Lane, 94574
(707) 963-1190

Secluded and romantic on two acres, nestled among the finest wineries and restaurants in Napa Valley. Wine and cheese are served each evening, and the full champagne breakfast is known as "the best in the valley." The inn's reputation has been built on warm, sincere hospitality with all comforts in mind. Each immaculate room is spacious and furnished with antiques; elegant ambience and country tranquility. Off-season and midweek rates available.

Hosts: John and Lisa Wild-Runnells
Rooms: 4 (PB) $125-165
Full Breakfast
Credit Cards: None
Notes: 2, 5, 9, 10, 11, 12, 14

6 Pets welcome; 7 Smoking allowed; 8 Children welcome; 9 Social drinking allowed; 10 Tennis available; 11 Swimming available; 12 Golf available; 13 Skiing available; 14 May be booked through travel agents.

Villa St. Helena

2727 Sulphur Springs Avenue, 94574
(707) 963-2514

This secluded hilltop Mediterranean villa combines quiet, country elegance with panoramic views of Napa Valley. Romantic antique-filled rooms, private baths, entrances, and fireplaces in some. A private world on a wooded 20-acre estate; walking trails, spacious courtyard, cozy library. World-class wine tasting, dining, and shopping nearby. Convenient to tennis and golf. Complimentary wine and an exclusive continental breakfast.

Rooms: 3 (PB) $145-225
Continental Breakfast
Credit Cards: A, B
Notes: 2, 5, 9, 10, 11, 12, 14

The Wine Country Inn

1152 Lodi Lane, 94574
(707) 963-7077

Perched on a knoll overlooking manicured vineyards and the nearby hills, this country inn offers 25 individually decorated guest rooms. The hosts used family-made quilts, local antiques, fireplaces, and balconies to create an atmosphere of unparalleled comfort. Closed Christmas.

Hosts: Jim Smith and Diane Horkheimer
Rooms: 25 (PB) $140-170
Continental Breakfast
Credit Cards: A, B
Notes: 2, 7, 9, 10, 11, 12, 14

SAN ANDREAS

Robin's Nest

247 West Saint Charles Street, P.O. Box 1408, 95249
(209) 754-1076

This Victorian, built in 1895, retains its dramatic character and Old World charm with modern conveniences. The inn is on an acre of grass and fruit trees. Nearby activities include California Caverns, art and antique shops, Big Trees State Park, wine tasting, boating, fishing, water-skiing, and cross-country skiing.

Hosts: George and Carolee Jones
Rooms: 9 (7 PB; 2 SB) $55-95
Full Breakfast
Credit Cards: A, B, C
Notes: 2, 5, 8, 10, 11, 12, 13, 14

Robin's Nest

SAN ANSELMO

Bed and Breakfast Exchange of Marin

45 Entrata, 94960
(415) 485-1971

This spacious, separate guest suite features a private bath, TV, and private kitchen. Walk to town, fine restaurants, hiking trails, and a lake. It is 45 minutes to wine country and 15 minutes north of San Francisco. Children are welcome. Special rates available for longer stays. $75.

SAN CLEMENTE

Bed and Breakfast, L.A.

3924 E. 14th Street, Long Beach, 90804
(310) 498-0552; (800) 383-3513

Casa Tropicana. Lovingly built by owner-operators, this perfect little bed and breakfast

---

NOTES: Credit cards accepted: A MasterCard; B Visa; C American Express; D Discover Card; E Diner's Club; F Other; 2 Personal checks accepted; 3 Lunch available; 4 Dinner available; 5 Open all year;

looks out on the ocean and the San Clemente pier. Seven rooms have tropical, jungle, or country French motifs. All have ocean views. Several have Jacuzzis and fireplaces. Hosts serve an elegant full breakfast on guests' very own private deck. $120-325.

A. This majestic estate on the San Clemente Bluffs was built in the 1930s by the Campbells Soup family. This sprawling estate features four guest rooms, all with private bath. Three open out to a glass breezeway with views of pool, spa, gardens, and ocean. The fourth has two bedrooms, a bath, and full kitchen! Decor includes original art and tile work. Hosts serve fruit, wine, and cheese upon arrival and a fresh continental breakfast in guest room or garden. $85-100.

Casa de Flores Bed and Breakfast

184 Avenue La Cuesta, 92672
(714) 498-1344

San Clemente's best-kept secret. Midway between Los Angeles and San Diego sits this beautiful 5,500-square-foot Spanish home, offering two two-room suites and a spectacular view of the ocean and Dana Point Harbor. One suite features a fireplace in the bedroom and a spa in its own private enclosed patio; the other has a double sofa bed in the sitting room for two additional people at an extra charge. Both suites offer TV/VCRs and in-room coffee. Beach chairs and towels, more than 450 videos, pool table, washer, dryer, and iron available. Complimentary beverages. Turn-down service. Beautiful beaches and fine restaurants within one mile. Inspected and approved by the Automobile Club of Southern California. Two-night minimum stay required for holidays and weekends.

Hosts: Marilee and Robert Arsenault
Suites: 2 (PB) $75-100
Full Breakfast
Credit Cards: None
Notes: 2, 5, 7 (limited), 8, 9, 10, 11, 12, 14

SAN DIEGO

The Balboa Park Inn

3402 Park Boulevard, 92103
(619) 298-0823; (800) 938-8181

One of San Diego's most romantic settings—a guest house in the heart of the city. The affordable difference is a suite for the price of a room. Within walking distance of the San Diego Zoo, Old Globe Theatre, museums, and restaurants, and only ten minutes to the beach.

Host: Ed Wilcox
Suites: 26 (PB) $80-190
Continental Breakfast
Credit Cards: A, B, C, D, E, F
Notes: 5, 7, 8, 9, 10, 11, 12, 14

Bed and Breakfast International

P.O. Box 282910, San Francisco, 94128-2910
(415) 696-1690; (800) 872-4500
FAX (415) 696-1699

503. San Diego does not get any better than this. A gorgeous plantation-style home with ocean views from the pool and spa. Lots of art work, European decor, and hospitality. Classy and inviting. $75-85.

Bed and Breakfast, L.A.

3924 E. 14th Street, Long Beach, 90804
(310) 498-0552; (800) 383-3513

This classic Victorian in a private park in Old San Diego is a perfectly restored mansion with seven guest rooms and a huge family cottage. Four rooms share baths; the rest are private. The cottage has two bedrooms, one with a king-size four-poster bed, the other with twins. Also a wonderful marble bath with double sunken tub. Hosts provide elegant afternoon snacks and a full buffet breakfast. Definitely the best in San Diego! $90-225.

6 Pets welcome; 7 Smoking allowed; 8 Children welcome; 9 Social drinking allowed; 10 Tennis available; 11 Swimming available; 12 Golf available; 13 Skiing available; 14 May be booked through travel agents.

Blom House Bed and Breakfast

1372 Minden Drive, 92111
(619) 467-0890

Blom House is a charming cottage in a quiet residential neighborhood less than ten minutes from downtown, the zoo, airport, beach, and all local tourist attractions. The 65-foot deck features a spa and a superb view of Hotel Circle lights and the I-163 and I-8 interchange below. All accommodations have 14-foot ceilings, antique furnishings, TV, VCR, phones, refrigerators with complimentary wine and cheese, bathrobes, and private baths. A two-bedroom suite with private bath is also available for families or two couples.

Hosts: Bette and John Blom
Rooms: 3 (PB) $59-75
Full Breakfast
Credit Cards: None
Notes: 2, 5, 8, 9, 10, 11, 12, 14

Carole's Bed and Breakfast Inn

3227 Grim Avenue, 92104
(619) 280-5258

Historic 1904 two-story Craftsman home built by the city's mayor is furnished with antiques and a piano; a rose garden is on the grounds. Swimming pool, hot tub, and gas barbecue. Less than one mile to zoo. Close to all major attractions. Expanded continental breakfast served in guest room or dining area. Refreshments served in the evening. Dinner is available, but not included in the rate. Smoking allowed outside. Senior rates are available. Reservation deposit is required. Traveler's checks are accepted.

Hosts: Carole Dugdale and Michael O'Brien
Rooms: 6 (2 PB; 4 SB) $65-85
Continental Breakfast
Credit Cards: None
Notes: 2, 4, 5, 8, 9, 10, 11, 12, 14

The Cottage

3829 Albatross Street, 92103
(619) 299-1564

Between the zoo and SeaWorld, The Cottage is a quiet retreat in the heart of a downtown residential neighborhood. The turn-of-the-century furnishings throughout evoke visions of a bygone era. Each morning guests will be served a breakfast of freshly baked bread, juice, and beverage.

Hosts: Robert and Carol Emerick
Rooms: 2 (PB) $55-85
Continental Breakfast
Credit Cards: A, B, C
Notes: 2, 5, 8, 9, 10, 11, 12, 14

Erene's Inn

3776 Hawk Street, 92103
(619) 295-5622

This charming, circa 1900, Mission Hills home close to Balboa Park, Gaslamp District, and Old Town beaches welcomes guests with its pillared porch and French doors. Original paintings, enamels, and ceramics complement Greek antiques, English armoires, Oriental wares, and Turkish rugs. Coffee and tea around the fireplace or on the sunny deck, fresh flowers on the breakfast table, and tiny surprises upon departure are some of the cordial gestures guests enjoy. Full breakfast served on the weekends.

Host: Erene Rallis
Rooms: 2 (1 PB; 1 SB) $40-50
Full and Continental Breakfasts
Credit Cards: None
Notes: 2, 4, 5, 6 and 7 (limited), 8, 9, 10, 12, 14

Eye Openers Bed and Breakfast Reservations

P.O. Box 694, Altadena, 91003-0694
(213) 684-4428; (818) 797-2055
FAX (818) 798-3640

NOTES: Credit cards accepted: A MasterCard; B Visa; C American Express; D Discover Card; E Diner's Club; F Other; 2 Personal checks accepted; 3 Lunch available; 4 Dinner available; 5 Open all year;

FA-B2. Large country French chateau is nestled on a working avocado ranch. Relax and unwind poolside in a peaceful hilltop setting. Antiques are throughout this pretty bed and breakfast, and the guest room overlooks the garden. Full breakfast. Wineries, antique shops, and golf courses are nearby. Resident cats and dogs. No smoking. Two guest rooms with private and shared baths. $60-75.

SD-B2. Pacific beach bed and breakfast is a short walk to the ocean or to Mission Bay. The two guest rooms have queen-size and double beds with a shared bath. Enjoy the relaxed beach atmosphere and the homemade full breakfast served in the dining room or on the private, walled patio. No smoking. $65-75.

SD-B4. Ten minutes from downtown, beaches, and local tourist attractions. Relax and enjoy views from the 75-foot deck with spa. Four guest rooms have twin, queen- or king-size beds and private baths. Robes, minirefrigerator, TV, and VCR are provided, as well as a gourmet breakfast and afternoon refreshments. No smoking is allowed. $75-95.

SD-E1. Separate guest house with turn-of-the-century furnishings assures privacy in central San Diego and offers a bedroom, sitting room with wood-burning stove, and dining area where a delicious continental breakfast is served. Additional guest room in the house is available. Private bath. $55-75.

SD-E21. Newly built bed and breakfast less than a block from the beach offers friendly hospitality and a wonderful convenient location. Cape Cod-style architecture. An extended continental breakfast is served. Seven guest rooms offer queen-size beds and private baths. No smoking. $85.

SD-H61. This trilevel bed and breakfast inn has a harbor view and garden. Near Balboa Park, Sea World, and the zoo. Continental breakfast. All six guest rooms have private baths. $65-95.

SD-H91. This 1889 Victorian antique-furnished bed and breakfast inn is in a restored village convenient to tourist attractions. Full breakfast, candlelight dinners, and special amenities available. No smoking. Nine guest rooms. Private baths. $85-130.

SD-P1. Condominium bed and breakfast near San Diego Jack Murphy Stadium with excellent freeway access to all tourist attractions. Continental breakfast, swimming pool, Jacuzzi, kitchen, and laundry facilities. One room with private bath. No smoking. $75.

SD-Q21. Converted San Diego trolley-car cottage and two-room guest suite with kitchen, all beautifully restored and decorated with memorabilia and antiques. In a natural setting on the edge of a canyon in central San Diego close to Balboa Park. They have queen-size beds and private baths. Lushly landscaped patios are a quiet retreat after a busy day of sightseeing. Self-hosted continental-plus breakfast and afternoon refreshments are provided. No smoking. $75-80.

SD-Y1. Pacific beach cottage includes pool and garden. It has a double bed and private bath. Walk to tourist attractions along Mission Bay. Public transportation available. Continental breakfast. No smoking. Weekly rates available. $75.

Harbor Hill Guest House

2330 Albatross Street, 92101
(619) 233-0638

---

6 Pets welcome; 7 Smoking allowed; 8 Children welcome; 9 Social drinking allowed; 10 Tennis available; 11 Swimming available; 12 Golf available; 13 Skiing available; 14 May be booked through travel agents.

Overlooking the San Diego Harbor is the ideal location for business, weekend get-aways, honeymoons, and family reunions. Accommodates 16 adults. The Carriage House is a separate hideaway for two. Private baths. Continental breakfast. Each level has a semi-private entry. A kitchen is on each level.

Rooms: 5 (PB) $65-90
Continental Breakfast
Credit Cards: A, B
Notes: 2, 5, 7, 8, 9, 10, 11, 12, 14

Vera's Cozy Corner

2810 Albatross Street, 92103
(619) 296-1938

This crisp white Colonial with black shutters sits in a quiet cul-de-sac overlooking San Diego Bay. Comfortable guest quarters consist of a separate cottage with private entrance across a flower-filled patio. The hostess offers freshly squeezed orange juice from her own fruit trees in season as a prelude to breakfast, which is served in the dining room. The house is convenient to local shops and restaurants, beaches, and is one mile from the San Diego Zoo.

Host: Vera V. Warden
Room: 1 (PB) $45-50
Continental Breakfast
Credit Cards: None
Notes: 2, 5, 9, 10, 11, 12, 14

SAN FRANCISCO

Alamo Square Inn

719 Scott Street, 94117
(415) 922-2055; (800) 345-9888

Alamo Square Inn affords a variety of rooms and suites, from cozy single or double guest rooms to the luxurious, Oriental-influenced suites overlooking a sweeping skyline and the imposing pines and cypresses of Alamo Square. Rates include a full breakfast (which usually consists of omelets, pastry, fresh fruit, and fresh-squeezed orange juice) and free off-street parking. Enjoy the late afternoon tea and wine. The inn can accommodate receptions, meetings, or other small groups.

Hosts: Wayne Corn and Klaus May
Rooms: 13 (PB) $85-275
Full Breakfast
Credit Cards: A, B, C, E
Notes: 2, 5, 8, 10, 11, 12, 13, 14

Archbishops Mansion Inn

1000 Fulton Street, 94117
(415) 563-7872; (800) 543-5820

On a beautiful park surrounded by much-photographed Victorian homes. All the interesting areas of the city are only minutes away. Every guest room is custom designed to create a personalized atmosphere reminiscent of the last century. Amenities include exquisite antiques, embroidered linens, and comfortable sitting area. Most rooms have fireplaces. Lovely private baths, stacks of towels, French-milled soaps, and private telephones. Complimentary evening wine service.

Host: Rick Janvier
Rooms: 15 (PB) $115-385
Continental Breakfast
Credit Cards: A, B, C
Notes: 2 (deposits), 5, 7 (limited), 8, 9, 10, 11, 12, 14

Art Center and Bed and Breakfast Suites, Wamsley

1902 Filbert Street, 94123
(415) 567-1526; (800) 821-3877

The best residential area—Marina, Cow Hollow—where history stands still. Just a 20-minute walk to Fisherman's Wharf. A French New Orleans inn with privacy, kitchens, canopied queen-size beds, fireplaces, and whirlpool suite. Shopping on Union Street and jogging at the marina. Day tours of Northern California's charms, nearby theater, music, cruising, and dancing on the bay—all within easy reach. Business travelers and families welcome. Commercial discounts, art classes, and gallery.

NOTES: Credit cards accepted: A MasterCard; B Visa; C American Express; D Discover Card; E Diner's Club; F Other; 2 Personal checks accepted; 3 Lunch available; 4 Dinner available; 5 Open all year;

Hosts: George and Helvi Wamsley
Rooms: 5 (PB) $75-120
Continental Breakfast
Credit Cards: A, B, C, D, E, F
Notes: 2, 5, 8, 9, 10, 12, 14

Bed and Breakfast International

P.O. Box 282910, 94128-2910
(415) 696-1690; (800) 872-4500
FAX (415) 696-1699

101. Location, location, location. This charming two-bedroom apartment in a Victorian home is a stone's throw from cable cars, Fisherman's Wharf, Ghiradelli Square, North Beach, and the bay. Private quarters by the bay. $95-150.

102. Second-floor home in a modernized Victorian building near the North Beach area on Telegraph Hill. Walking distance to Fisherman's Wharf and many restaurants. Cable car is three blocks away. Two rooms share a bath. $55-68.

103. Three-story turn-of-the-century home that has been pictured in *Sunset* magazine. Favorite spot for many returning guests. Only 15 minutes from Union Square and an equal distance to Ocean Beach. Within walking distance to Golden Gate Park, the Presidio, and the many shops and restaurants on Clement Street. One room with sitting area and private bath. Two rooms with shared bath. $60-70.

104. Exceptionally clean and well-decorated guest room, studio, or carriage house in the back garden of an 1880 Victorian home. Room has a double bed, private bath, and private entrance. Studio has queen-size bed, fireplace, fully equipped kitchen, and deck. Two-story carriage house has fireplace, grand piano, formal dining room, and fully equipped kitchen. Continental breakfast items are left for guests. $65-175.

105. This 1876 Victorian is "eccentrically, eclectically, and very tastefully decorated." This home is truly San Francisco and is close to shops and restaurants in popular Pacific Heights. There is a guest room with private bath, minikitchen, and sitting room. In the back garden, a guest cottage affords privacy and opens onto the patio. $85-95.

106. Combine elegance, location, lots of space, and a view of the bay in the heart of the city in this Russian Hill 1908 Italianate Victorian. Two bedrooms, a sunroom, living room with fireplace, and fully equipped kitchen. Gorgeous! $150-200.

107. Four homes all built around the 1920s furnished with antiques and near many interesting shops and restaurants on Haight Street. All homes have back decks. About 15 minutes from downtown and walking distance to Golden Gate Park. Ten rooms with all types of bed sizes. All have shared baths. Host prepares breakfast. $50-65.

Bed and Breakfast, L.A.

3924 East 14th Street, Long Beach, 90804
(800) 383-3513

A. This hostess offers two guest rooms, one with twins and the other with a queen-size bed. Bath between the two is shared. On Knob Hill, Chinatown is only three blocks away. $75.

B. This 1920 Edwardian home is near the University of California Medical Center and Golden Gate Park. Four guest rooms which share two baths are available. Cribs are also available. Continental breakfast is self-serve. $60.

6 Pets welcome; 7 Smoking allowed; 8 Children welcome; 9 Social drinking allowed; 10 Tennis available; 11 Swimming available; 12 Golf available; 13 Skiing available; 14 May be booked through travel agents.

C. This classic inn, a "painted lady," was one of San Francisco's original golden-era mansions. Built in 1878, it has quaint rooms with shared baths, more spacious ones with private baths, and several elegant suites that can sleep up to five. Afternoon goodies and full buffet breakfast are provided. Parking is available. Guests will enjoy the bonus—big, old-fashioned hot tub in the garden. $70-175.

D. This fairy-tale Victorian has just one elegant suite: bedroom with brass bed and down comforter, sitting room with kitchenette, and a private bath. Popcorn, drinks, and fresh flowers abound. A different gourmet breakfast is served every morning. Hosts are there to pamper. $85.

E. This great, old Victorian home just north of Golden Gate Park has three guest rooms with double beds and one with private bath. Hostess serves a full breakfast and specializes in turning visitors into friends. $55-70.

Bed and Breakfast San Francisco

P.O. Box 420009, 94142-0009
(415) 479-1913; FAX (415) 921-BBSF

1. A wonderful warm San Francisco neighborhood. Lots of excellent local shops and restaurants on 24th Street. This lovely bed and breakfast is on the J-Church streetcar line only 20 minutes from downtown. Full breakfast; shared bath. $55.

2. Pines Mews, a Victorian treasure, sits in San Francisco's most prestigious neighborhood, Pacific Heights. The three accommodations, the Carriage House, the Studio, and the Guest Quarter, have been splendidly restored, and some modern amenities have been added. Full breakfast is provided. $65-200.

3. A new, private addition onto a charming old San Francisco home. If guests prefer privacy this unhosted, charming, and quiet bed and breakfast is most enjoyable. Large bedroom has a view of North Beach; excellent Italian restaurants in the neighborhood. Fisherman's Wharf and Chinatown are a short walk. Full breakfast. Crib available. Ten to fifteen dollars additional charge for children. $125.

5. High atop charming Russian Hill sits a two-bedroom Victorian flat with a beautiful view of San Francisco Bay. This is a great place for two couples or a family. Off the living room is a sunny solarium, a full kitchen, and a bath. One bedroom has a double bed, and the other bedroom offers a queen-size bed. A futon is available. The living room has a TV, fireplace, and telephone. Cable cars are just around the corner, and Fisherman's Wharf is just a short distance away. Special rates for stays longer than seven days. $125-175.

6. A scenic location with a panoramic view. Three guest rooms, each facing west, providing a lovely sunset overlooking the Glen Canyon Park and its beautiful eucalyptus grove. Mount Davidson towers majestically over the canyon in full view from each guest room. Guests have a choice of twin beds, a room with a queen-size bed, or a large family room accommodating up to four people. Each room has a TV. Two guest baths; ample street parking; full breakfast. $55-95.

7. In one of San Francisco's most beautiful neighborhoods, Jays Place sits atop the Broadway tunnel. Just a short walk down the steps to North Beach Italian restaurants, Fisherman's Wharf, and Chinatown. Cable cars are only one block away. This exclusive, quiet location offers San Francisco sights just minutes away. Jays offers one

---

NOTES: Credit cards accepted: A MasterCard; B Visa; C American Express; D Discover Card; E Diner's Club; F Other; 2 Personal checks accepted; 3 Lunch available; 4 Dinner available; 5 Open all year;

guest room with a private bath. Private patio; full breakfast. $85-95.

8. The true charm of San Francisco. The hostess offers her wonderful, charming, and recently renovated Victorian bed and breakfast. There are four guest rooms, three with bay views. At the bottom of Lombard Street where guests are within walking distance of Fisherman's Wharf, North Beach restaurants, and cable cars. Excellent parking; private bath; full breakfast. $85-125.

9. One of San Francisco's most enjoyable neighborhoods. Noe Valley is a local treasure of restaurants and shops. Bill and Marie have beautifully renovated their charming home and included a bed and breakfast suite. The suite has a private entrance, king-size bed, and a full kitchen. A full breakfast is served. Transportation to the center of downtown (15 minutes away) is excellent. $65-95.

12. In the exclusive St. Francis woods area, Pam offers her large Spanish-style home for bed and breakfast. Three luxurious guest rooms plus a family suite. All rooms have private bath. The garden surrounds an enclosed pool and pool house, which has a shower and sauna as well as a living room. Full breakfast served. $95-125.

13. In the heart of San Francisco, the Richmond district offers a wealth of wonderful things to do from bike riding and walking trails to excellent restaurants. Its ethnic diversity makes it one of the city's most interesting neighborhoods. JoAnn offers one guest room with queen-size bed, TV, VCR, and private bath. The living room has a fireplace and ocean view. The world-famous Cliff House restaurant, Seal Rocks, and Ocean Beach are just a few blocks away. Transportation to downtown is excellent; an express bus travels to Union Square in 15 minutes. Full breakfast served. $65-75.

14. Originally built in 1895 as a candy store, Cathy's bed and breakfast is a beautifully renovated Victorian at the very top of Ashbury Terrace. She offers a beautiful main-floor apartment completely furnished in heirloom antiques in a Scandinavian motif. It consists of a living room with a garden view, bedroom with queen-size bed, full kitchen, and large bath. The area is not far from the city center and is close to Golden Gate Park and the University of California Medical Center. Full breakfast provided. $100.

15. A beautifully restored Victorian just a few blocks from Golden Gate Park. Learn the intricacies of restoring an 1880s Victorian. George bought his bed and breakfast about a year ago. He has lovingly spent a lot of time and money renovating his home to its original splendor. The three guest rooms are furnished in family antiques. The Asian Art Museum, Steinhart Aquarium, the Japanese Tea Garden, and jogging and bike trails are close by. Full breakfast served. $75-85.

Casa Arguello

225 Arguello Boulevard, 94118
(415) 752-9482

These comfortable rooms are in a cheerful, spacious flat 20 minutes from the center of town. In a desirable residential neighborhood near Golden Gate Park and the Presidio. Continental-plus breakfast is served. Restaurants and shops within walking distance. Excellent public transportation close by.

Hosts: Emma Baires and Marina McKenzie
Rooms: 5 (2 PB; 3 SB) $42-72
Continental Breakfast
Credit Cards: None
Notes: 2, 5, 8, 9, 10, 11, 12

6 Pets welcome; 7 Smoking allowed; 8 Children welcome; 9 Social drinking allowed; 10 Tennis available; 11 Swimming available; 12 Golf available; 13 Skiing available; 14 May be booked through travel agents.

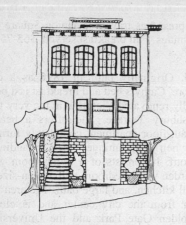

Casa Arguello

Country Cottage
Bed and Breakfast

5 Dolores Terrace, 94110
(415) 479-1913; (800) 452-8249
FAX (415) 921-2273

A cozy country-style bed and breakfast in the heart of San Francisco. The four guest rooms are comfortably furnished with antiques and brass beds. The house is at the end of a quiet street, away from the city noise. There is a small patio with trees and birds. A full breakfast is served in the sunny kitchen.

Hosts: Susan and Richard Kreibich
Rooms: 4 (S2B) $65
Full Breakfast
Credit Cards: A, B, C
Notes: 2, 5, 8, 9, 10, 11, 12, 14

Dockside Boat and Bed

Pier 39, 94133
(415) 392-5526
77 Jack London Square, Oakland, 94607
(510) 444-5858

Spend a romantic evening on a yacht! Luxurious private yachts for overnight dockside accommodations allow fantasy to become reality. The boats range in size from 35 to 68 feet in length, and several are available for charter with a captain. Romantic candle-light catered dinners add to the fantasy of living the life of the "rich and famous."

Host: Rob Harris
Yachts: 10 (PB) $95-275
Continental Breakfast
Credit Cards: A, B, C
Notes: 2, 4, 5, 7, 8, 9, 14

Eye Openers
Bed and Breakfast
Reservations

P.O. Box 694, Altadena, 91003-0694
(213) 684-4428; (818) 797-2055
FAX (818) 798-3640

SF-A3. Victorian with Old World decor offers friendly hospitality and excellent location in the Marina District. Good public transportation. Continental breakfast. Three guest rooms and studio. Shared and private baths. $75-85.

SF-B1. Unique small cottage to the rear of the host home atop one of San Francisco's highest points near Golden Gate Park. Fireplace and kitchen. Continental breakfast is self-catered. Car essential. Minimum stay is three nights. Private bath. $75-85.

SF-K51. This Victorian bed and breakfast features three guest rooms with fireplace, rooftop deck with Jacuzzi, and full breakfast. Excellent location with good transportation to all tourist attractions and business meetings. Five guest rooms. Private and shared baths. $75-125.

SF-L1. This convenient Victorian condo is well decorated with period pieces and offers privacy in lovely surroundings. Continental breakfast. Five guest rooms. Self-hosted apartment. No smoking. $125.

SF-M1. Upstairs guest room in a well-maintained garden apartment is in a quiet neighborhood three miles from Golden Gate Park, five miles from downtown, and provides a continental-plus breakfast. No smoking. One guest room with shared bath. $40-45.

SF-M301. This four-story Victorian hotel, now a Marina District bed and breakfast inn, features four-poster beds and modern amenities. Continental breakfast is served. Thirty guest rooms. Private baths. $65-85.

SF-P261. Sister inns, one French Country and the other formal English, are two blocks from Union Square and offer beautifully appointed rooms, hospitality, afternoon refreshments, and wonderful breakfast. Twenty-six guest rooms. Private bath. $110-250.

SF-P3. Hilltop home in Diamond Heights area has glorious view of the bay and city from the two-story living room. Enjoy a full breakfast in the Scandinavian dining area. Each of three guest rooms has a balcony. Two baths. $35-45.

The Golden Gate Hotel

775 Bush Street, 94108
(415) 392-3702; (800) 835-1118

The ambience, location, and price make the Golden Gate Hotel an extraordinary find in the heart of San Francisco. Dedicated to a high standard of quality and personal attention, the hosts keep fresh flowers in all the rooms. The continental breakfast includes fresh croissants and the city's strongest coffee.

Hosts: John and Renate Kenaston
Rooms: 23 (14 PB; 9 SB) $55-89
Continental Breakfast
Credit Cards: A, B, C, E, F
Notes: 2 and 6 (by arrangement), 5, 8, 9, 10, 11, 12, 14

The Grove Inn

890 Grove Street, 94117
(415) 929-0780; (800) 829-0780

The Grove Inn is a charming, intimate, and affordable bed and breakfast. Close to public transportation, it has two suites for the convenience of families with children. The owners and managers are always available for information, help in renting cars, booking shuttles to the airport, and city tours. Free parking. Closed December.

Hosts: Klaus and Rosetta Zimmermann
Rooms: 18 (14 PB; 4 SB) $50-80
Continental Breakfast
Credit Cards: A, B, C
Notes: 2, 5, 8, 9, 10, 11, 12, 14

The Inn at Union Square

440 Post Street, 94102
(415) 397-3510; (800) 288-4346

An elegant, small European-style hotel in the heart of San Francisco's financial, theater, and shopping districts. Each floor has an intimate lobby and fireplace where guests enjoy complimentary continental breakfast in the morning, afternoon tea, and wine and hors d'oeuvres in the evening. Rooms are individually decorated with beautiful fabrics and comfortable Georgian furniture, and terry-cloth robes are provided. Penthouse accommodations include a cozy sauna, whirlpool bath, fireplace, and wet bar. Personalized service and attention to detail.

Host: Mr. Brooks Bayly
Rooms: 30 (PB) $110-400
Penthouse: 1 (PB) $400
Continental Breakfast
Credit Cards: A, B, C, E, F
Notes: 2, 3, 4, 5, 8, 9, 10, 11, 14

The Inn San Francisco

943 South Van Ness Avenue, 94110
(415) 641-0188; (800) 359-0913
FAX (415) 641-1701

Restored historic Italianate Victorian mansion, circa 1872. Ornate woodwork, Oriental carpets, marble fireplaces, and period antiques are combined with modern hotel conveniences. Full buffet breakfast provided. Relax in the redwood hot tub in the garden or reserve a room with a private spa

6 Pets welcome; 7 Smoking allowed; 8 Children welcome; 9 Social drinking allowed; 10 Tennis available; 11 Swimming available; 12 Golf available; 13 Skiing available; 14 May be booked through travel agents.

tub—the perfect romantic escape! Two-night minimum stay required for weekends and holidays.

Hosts: Marty Neely and Connie Wu
Rooms: 22 (17 PB; 5 SB) $75-195
Full Breakfast
Credit Cards: A, B, C, D, E, F
Notes: 2, 5, 7 (limited), 8, 9, 10, 11, 12, 14

Jackson Court

2198 Jackson Street, 94115
(800) 872-4500

Jackson Court is a unique ten-room inn in one of San Francisco's most picturesque areas, Pacific Heights. Converted from a historic mansion, each room has special amenities and a delightfully different decor. There are two suites and eight other rooms, all with private baths.

Rooms: 10 (PB) $108-150
Continental Breakfast
Cards: A, B, C
Notes: 5, 9, 14

Kids Welcome

3924 East 14th Street, Long Beach, 90804
(310) 498-0552; (800) 383-3513

14-1. Walk to Golden Gate Park from this three-story Victorian that is geared toward traveling families. Two guest rooms share one bath on each floor. Full breakfast is provided, and guests are welcome to use the kitchen, fireplace, and even the playpen. Host's teenage daughter is willing to babysit. Family rates are available.

The Monte Cristo

600 Presidio Avenue, 94115
(415) 931-1875; FAX (415) 931-6005

The elegantly restored Monte Cristo was originally built in 1875 as a saloon and hotel. It has served as a bordello, a refuge after the 1906 earthquake, and a speakeasy. Only two blocks from Victorian shops, restaurants, and antique stores on Sacramento Street; ten minutes to any other point in the city. Two-night minimum stay required for weekends and holidays.

Host: George
Rooms: 14 (11 PB; 3 SB) $63-108
Continental Breakfast
Credit Cards: A, B, C, D, E
Notes: 5, 7, 8, 14

No Name Victorian Bed and Breakfast

847 Fillmore Street, 94117
(415) 479-1913; (800) 452-8249
FAX (415) 921-2273

This bed and breakfast is in one of the city's most photographed areas, the historic district of Alamo Square. Close to the civic center, opera house, Davies Symphony Hall, Union Square, and all the sights that make the city famous. Three of the guest rooms have fireplaces. In the evening, guests can help themselves to wine and relaxation in the hot tub, where many a guest has had a surprise visit from the neighborhood resident, Nosey the raccoon.

Hosts: Susan and Richard Kreibich
Rooms: 5 (3 PB; 2 SB) $75-125
Credit Cards: A, B, C
Notes: 2, 5, 8, 9, 10, 11, 12, 14

Petite Auberge

863 Bush Street, 94108
(415) 928-6000

A French country inn in the heart of San Francisco. Each room is individually decorated; many have fireplaces. Guests enjoy a full buffet breakfast, afternoon wine and hors d'oeuvres, valet parking, fresh fruit, and homemade cookies. Truly romantic.

Host: Celeste Lytle
Rooms: 26 (PB) $110-220
Full Breakfast
Credit Cards: A, B, C
Notes: 2, 5, 8, 9, 10, 12, 14

The Queen Anne Hotel

1590 Sutter Street, 94109
(415) 441-2828

NOTES: Credit cards accepted: A MasterCard; B Visa; C American Express; D Discover Card; E Diner's Club; F Other; 2 Personal checks accepted; 3 Lunch available; 4 Dinner available; 5 Open all year;

An 1890 landmark that has been beautifully restored with 49 individually designed rooms and suites, many of which include bay windows, fireplaces, and turn-of-the-century antiques. The Queen Anne Hotel is on the corner of Sutter and Octavia streets in lower Pacific Heights. Easy access to downtown, civic center, and Fisherman's Wharf. Complimentary continental breakfast, morning limousine to downtown (weekdays), and nightly tea and sherry are only a few of the amenities provided.

Host: Steven L. Bobb
Rooms: 49 (PB) $99-275
Continental Breakfast
Credit Cards: A, B, C, E
Notes: 2, 5, 8, 14

The Union Street Inn

2229 Union Street, 94123
(415) 346-0424; FAX (415) 922-8046

In the heart of San Francisco's most fascinating shopping and dining area, the Union Street Inn and its delightful English garden offers a haven of elegant tranquility. Experience warm European hospitality in this charming Edwardian inn. All rooms feature antique furnishings, down comforters, fresh flowers, and fruit. Breakfast is a superb culinary treat.

Host: Jane Bertorelli
Rooms: 6 (PB) $125-225
Full Breakfast
Credit Cards: A, B, C
Notes: 2, 5, 8, 9, 14

Victorian Inn on the Park

301 Lyon Street, 94117
(415) 931-1830; (800) 435-1967

Queen Anne Victorian near Golden Gate Park and decorated with Victorian antiques. Many rooms have fireplaces, and the Belvedere Room features a private balcony overlooking the park. The inn features fireplaces, dining room with oak paneling, and a parlor with fireplace. Complimentary

wine served nightly; fresh breads baked daily. Parking available.

Hosts: Lisa and William Benau
Rooms: 12 (PB) $99-159
Continental Breakfast
Credit Cards: A, B, C, D, E
Notes: 2, 5, 7, 8, 9, 10, 11, 12, 14

Victorian Inn on the Park

The Washington Square Inn

1660 Stockton Street, 94114
(415) 981-4220; (800) 388-0220
FAX (415) 397-7242

The Washington Square Inn is in the heart of San Francisco's historic North Beach area just one block from Telegraph Hill. Continental breakfast, afternoon tea, wine and hors d'oeuvres are served. With only 15 rooms, the inn is special for those who care about quiet and comfort with dashes of elegance. The staff has time to concentrate on the guests' individual needs and wants. No smoking.

Host: Brooks Bayly
Rooms: 15 (10 PB; 5 SB) $85-180
Continental Breakfast
Credit Cards: A, B, C, E, F
Notes: 2, 5, 8, 9, 14

White Swan Inn

845 Bush Street, 94108
(415) 775-1755

6 Pets welcome; 7 Smoking allowed; 8 Children welcome; 9 Social drinking allowed; 10 Tennis available; 11 Swimming available; 12 Golf available; 13 Skiing available; 14 May be booked through travel agents.

In the heart of San Francisco, a bit of London resides. Each oversize guest room has a fireplace, wet bar, sitting area, color TV, radio, bath robes, fresh fruit, and soft drinks. Enjoy a full breakfast, afternoon wine and hors d'oeuvres, newspaper, valet parking, concierge, laundry, FAX machine, living room, library, and gracious service.

Host: Celeste Lytle
Rooms: 26 (PB) $145-250
Full Breakfast
Credit Cards: A, B, C
Notes: 2, 5, 8, 9, 10, 12, 14

SAN GREGORIO

Rancho San Gregorio

5086 San Gregorio Road, P.O. Box 21, 94074
(415) 747-0810

Five miles inland from the Pacific off Highway 1 in a rural valley, Rancho San Gregorio welcomes travelers to share relaxed hospitality. This country getaway has 15 acres, an old barn, creek, gardens, decks, and gazebo. Full country breakfast features home-grown specialities. Forty-five minutes from San Francisco, Santa Cruz, and the bay area.

Hosts: Bud and Lee Raynor
Rooms: 4 (PB) $70-105
Suite: $145
Full Breakfast
Credit Cards: A, B, C, D
Notes: 2, 5, 7 (limited), 8, 9, 11, 12, 14

SAN JOSE

The Hensley House

456 North Third Street, 95112
(408) 298-3537

Three-story Queen Anne with square witches cap tower, 40-foot living room with hand-painted beam ceilings and walls, ten-foot fireplace, antique crystal and brass chandeliers, and hand-painted and gilded walls and ceilings. Queen-size beds with down comforters, European feather beds, TV, VCR, telephones, and air conditioning.

Two rooms have whirlpool baths, while one room features a fireplace and bar. Gourmet breakfasts are served in the dining room or on the patio. Lunch and dinner are available upon request. Refreshments are served in the afternoon. Downtown historical district nearby, with restaurants, museums, and theaters also close.

Hosts: Sharon Layne and Bill Priest
Innkeeper: Raili Hartihainen
Rooms: 5 (PB) $82.50-174.50
Full Breakfast
Credit Cards: A, B, C, D, E
Notes: 2, 3, 4, 5, 9, 10, 11, 12, 14

The Hensley House

SAN LUIS OBISPO (ARROYO GRANDE)

Eye Openers
Bed and Breakfast
Reservations

P.O. Box 694, Altadena, 91003-0694
(213) 684-4428; (818) 797-2055
FAX (818) 798-3640

LO-03. This well-traveled, multilingual host offers comfortable accommodations. Living room has a view of Morro Rock. A delicious breakfast is served. No smoking. Three guest rooms. Shared and private baths. $35-50.

PB-S301. Contemporary inn on the beach in the midst of 23 miles of unspoiled sand and surf. Continental breakfast delivered to

NOTES: Credit cards accepted: A MasterCard; B Visa; C American Express; D Discover Card; E Diner's Club; F Other; 2 Personal checks accepted; 3 Lunch available; 4 Dinner available; 5 Open all year;

the guest room. Twenty-five guest rooms. Private bath. $75-165.

Garden Street Inn

1212 Garden Street, 93401
(805) 545-9802

In a celebrated California community, the grace and simplicity of yesteryear prevail at this 1887 Italianate Queen Anne home. Classic Victorian decor in nine guest rooms and four suites appointed with antiques, fireplaces, Jacuzzis, and historic, cultural, and personal memorabilia. Homemade full breakfast, spacious outside decks, and well-stocked library. One block from a 1772 mission and the old-fashioned downtown. Close to Hearst Castle, Pismo Beach, Morro Bay, and Cambria.

Hosts: Dan and Kathy Smith
Rooms: 9 (PB) $90-160
Suites: 4
Full Breakfast
Credit Cards: A, B, C
Notes: 2, 5, 9, 10, 11, 12, 14

SAN MARTIN

Country Rose Inn Bed and Breakfast

455 Fitzgerald Avenue E, 95046
(408) 842-0441

Featured in *Country Inns,* Country Rose Inn Bed and Breakfast is nestled at the base of Santa Clara Valley between Morgan Hill and Gilroy. The 1920s Dutch Colonial manor offers comfort and relaxation in rural grandeur. Surrounded by farmland, guests get a sense of old California in this natural and beautiful setting. A full gourmet breakfast is served. There are spacious common areas for relaxing. Nearby activities include wineries, hot-air ballooning, outlet shopping, hiking, Hecker Pass Theme Park, and Henry Coe State Park. Conference facilities.

Host: Rose Hernandez
Rooms: 5 (PB) $89-169

Full Breakfast
Credit Cards: A, B
Notes: 2, 5, 9, 12, 14

SAN RAFAEL

Bed and Breakfast Exchange of Marin

45 Entrata, San Anselmo, 94960
(415) 485-1971

Stay in this lovingly restored Victorian brown shingle in the Dominican College area of Old San Rafael. Rooms have various bed sizes, private tile bathrooms, and white robes. Hot tub in the garden. Breakfast served on deck or in dining room with fire in winter. Fifteen minutes north of San Francisco. Call for rates.

SANTA ANA

Bed and Breakfast, L.A.

3924 E. 14th Street, Long Beach, 90804
(310) 498-0552; (800) 383-3513

Built in the early 1920s, this registered historic home has been decorated for beauty and romance. One private guest suite features queen-size bed, private bath, French doors to the deck, garden, and Koi pond. Full gourmet breakfast is served in the guest room or on the deck. Host is an artist with an eye for sunshine and perfection. $75.

SANTA BARBARA

Bath Street Inn

1720 Bath Street, 93101
(805) 682-9680; (800) 788-2284

An 1890 Queen Anne Victorian in the heart of historic Santa Barbara. Scenic downtown is within walking distance. Rooms have views, balconies, and private baths, and two feature fireplaces and Jacuzzis. Breakfast is served in the dining room or in the garden;

6 Pets welcome; 7 Smoking allowed; 8 Children welcome; 9 Social drinking allowed; 10 Tennis available; 11 Swimming available; 12 Golf available; 13 Skiing available; 14 May be booked through travel agents.

bikes are available; evening wine and afternoon tea.

Host: Susan Brown
Rooms: 10 (PB) $75-150
Full Breakfast
Credit Cards: A, B, C
Notes: 2, 5, 8, 9, 10, 11, 12, 14

The Bayberry Inn Bed and Breakfast

111 West Valerio Street, 93101
(805) 682-3199

A bit of paradise. The Bayberry Inn has been warmly welcoming guests since 1981. A quiet haven from the excitement and bustle of the West Coast's most popular resort city. The Bayberry Inn is the perfect departure point for a tour to the wine country, a sunny day at the beach, or a walking tour of the unique shops that have made this town a shopping mecca.

Host: Keith Pomeroy
Rooms: 8 (PB) $95-155
Full Breakfast
Credit Cards: A, B, C, D
Notes: 2, 5, 6 (by arrangement), 10, 11, 12, 14

Casa Del Mar Inn

18 Bath Street, 93101
(805) 963-4418; (800) 433-3097
FAX (805) 966-4240

A unique Mediterranean-style inn less than a block from the beach and harbor in Santa Barbara. Walk to shopping and fine restaurants. Twenty rooms offer a variety of accommodation options ranging from one- or two-bedroom bungalow-style family suites with full kitchens and fireplaces to cozy rooms with one king- or queen-size bed. One room is newly remodeled for full handicapped access. All rooms feature private baths, telephones, and color remote-control TV. Amenities include a garden, courtyard spa and sun deck, buffet-style breakfast, evening wine and cheese social hour, and kind attention from caring innkeepers and staff. A best value at a prime location.

Hosts: Mike and Becky Montgomery
Rooms: 20 (PB) $59-199
Continental Breakfast
Credit Cards: A, B, C, D, E
Notes: 2, 5, 6, 7, 8, 9, 10, 11, 12, 14

Cheshire Cat Inn

36 West Valerio Street, 93101
(805) 569-1610

Victorian elegance in a Southern California seaside village. The Cheshire Cat is near theaters, restaurants, and shops. Decorated exclusively in Laura Ashley papers and linens, the sunny guest rooms have private baths; some with fireplaces, spas, and balconies. Collectibles, English antiques, and fresh flowers enhance any stay in beautiful Santa Barbara. Special midweek rates are available.

Hosts: Christine Dunstan
Rooms: 14 (PB) $125-269
Full Breakfast
Credit Cards: A, B
Notes: 2, 5, 7 (limited), 9, 10, 11, 12, 14

Eye Openers Bed and Breakfast Reservations

P.O. Box 694, Altadena, 91003-0694
(213) 684-4428; (818) 797-2055
FAX (818) 798-3640

SB-B1. Convenient and filled with country charm, this inn's beautiful grounds provide a feeling of seclusion. Delicious full breakfast and evening refreshments. Bicycles available. No smoking is allowed. Eight rooms. Private and shared bath. $85-165.

SB-C110. Luxurious Victorian inn with a wide choice of uniquely decorated guest rooms is convenient and offers an excellent breakfast. No smoking allowed. Eleven rooms. Private bath. $108-250.

SB-O61. Delicious, elegant breakfasts, comfortable rooms, and friendly hospitality can be found at this convenient inn near

NOTES: Credit cards accepted: A MasterCard; B Visa; C American Express; D Discover Card; E Diner's Club; F Other; 2 Personal checks accepted; 3 Lunch available; 4 Dinner available; 5 Open all year;

beaches and mission. 1904 Craftsman-style bungalow with individually decorated rooms, several with private decks. Beach towels and chairs provided. Six rooms and one guest cottage. Private bath. $105-155.

SB-R1. This architect-designed contemporary home is nestled among oaks near Santa Barbara Mission and five minutes to the beach and shopping. Choice of full or continental breakfast. One room. Private bath. No smoking. $45-50.

SB-R51. This 1886 restored Victorian inn decorated with antiques is close to the mission and shops. Continental breakfast with homemade breads. Bikes available. Five guest rooms. Private and shared baths. No smoking allowed. $95-120.

Glenborough Inn

1327 Bath Street, 93101
(805) 966-0589

Experience the ultimate in romance. Full gourmet breakfast served to guests' room, parlor fireside, or in the lush gardens. Elegant fireplace suites. Secluded spa for private use. Evening social hour including hors d'oeuvres and late night desserts and beverages. Stocked guest refrigerator. Two bicycles. Walk three blocks to fine shops, restaurants, and theaters. Regular electric shuttle bus to and from the beach daily.

Hosts: Michael, Steve, and Ken
Rooms: 11 (5 PB; 6 SB) $75-170
Full Breakfast
Credit Cards: A, B, C, D, E
Notes: 2, 5, 10, 11, 12, 14

Long's Seaview Bed and Breakfast

317 Piedmont Road, 93105
(805) 687-2947

Overlooking the ocean and Channel Islands. In quiet neighborhood of lovely homes. Breakfast usually served on huge

patio. Convenient to beach, Solvang, and all area attractions. Large bedroom furnished with antiques and a king-size bed. Private entrance, private bath. Local information and maps provided. No smoking.

Host: LaVerne Long
Room: 1 (PB) $75-79
Full Breakfast
Credit Cards: None
Notes: 12

Montecito Inn

1295 Coast Village Road, 93108
(805) 969-7854; (800) 843-2017

Built in 1928 by Charlie Chaplin as a sanctuary for the stars of the silver screen. Two blocks from the beach, the inn has 53 Provincial-style rooms and suites with floral prints, hand-painted tiles, and ceiling fans. Complimentary continental breakfast, room service available. Heated outdoor pool, spa, sauna, and exercise room. Free sightseeing trolley passes and use of touring bicycles. Charlie Chaplin video library, cable TV with Showtime. New conference facility. Valet parking.

Host: Linda Davis
Rooms: 52 (PB) $245
Continental Breakfast
Credit Cards: A, B, C, D, E
Notes: 2, 3, 4, 5, 7, 8, 9, 10, 11, 12, 14

Ocean View House

P.O. Box 3373, 93130-3373
(805) 966-6659

A wonderful location in Santa Barbara in a quiet, private home within walking distance of the ocean. Two rooms with antique charm, TV, interesting books, and collections. Oranges, apples, and melons are presented from the garden with breakfast on the patio. Two-night minimum stay is required.

Host: Carolyn Canfield
Rooms: 2 (PB) $60
Continental Breakfast
Credit Cards: F
Notes: 2, 5, 6, 8, 9, 10, 11, 12, 14

6 Pets welcome; 7 Smoking allowed; 8 Children welcome; 9 Social drinking allowed; 10 Tennis available; 11 Swimming available; 12 Golf available; 13 Skiing available; 14 May be booked through travel agents.

Old Mission Inn

435 East Pedregosa, 93103
(805) 569-1914

This is a Craftsman house built in 1895. The rooms are spacious, and all contain fireplaces. Within walking distance of the Santa Barbara Mission, the Museum of Natural History, and downtown. A continental breakfast is served featuring baked goods, fresh fruit, juice, and coffee—all in a comfortable homelike atmosphere.

Host: Marie Miller
Rooms: 2 (1 PB; 1 SB) $50-65
Continental Breakfast
Credit Cards: None
Notes: 2, 5, 9, 10, 11, 12

The Old Yacht Club Inn

431 Corona Del Mar Drive, 93103
(805) 962-1277; (800) 549-1676 (CA)
(800) 676-1676 (US)

The Old Yacht Club Inn has nine guest rooms in two houses: a 1912 California Craftsman and a 1920s Early California-style building. The inn opened as Santa Barbara's first bed and breakfast in 1980 and is now world-renowned for its hospitality and warmth in comfortable surroundings and for its fine food. Within a block of the beach, the inn is close to tennis, swimming, boating, fishing, and golf. Evening wine, bikes, and beach chairs included. Dinner is available Saturdays.

Hosts: Nancy Donaldson, Lu Caruso, Sandy Hunt
Rooms: 9 (PB) $90-150
Full Breakfast
Credit Cards: A, B, C, D
Notes: 2, 4, 5, 8, 9, 10, 11, 12, 14

The Olive House

1604 Olive Street, 93101
(805) 962-4902; (800) 786-6422
FAX (805) 899-2754

Enjoy the quiet comfort and gracious hospitality of an owner-occupied, lovingly restored 1904 Craftsman-style house in a quiet residential neighborhood near the Mission and downtown. Ocean and mountain views, terraced garden, large sundeck, and off-street parking. Gracious living room replete with redwood paneling, bay windows, fireplace, and studio grand piano. Private decks and hot tubs. A delicious breakfast is served in the large, sunny dining room. Afternoon wine, evening tea, sherry, and treats.

Host: Lois Gregg
Rooms: 6 (PB) $105-175
Full Breakfast
Credit Cards: A, B, C, D
Notes: 2, 5, 9, 10, 11, 12, 14

The Secret Garden Inn (FORMERLY Blue Quail Inn)

1908 Bath Street, 93101
(805) 687-2300; (800) 676-1622 (US);
   (800) 549-1622 (CA)

Relax and enjoy the quiet garden that surrounds the main house and cottages. Linger over a delicious full breakfast, including home-baked goods, served on the patio or in the main house dining room. Take a picnic lunch and the inn's bicycles for a day of adventure, then return for afternoon wine and light hors d'oeuvres. Sip hot spiced apple cider in the evening before enjoying a restful sleep in a cottage, suite, or guest room. Near town and beaches.

Host: Jack C. Greenwald
Rooms: 9 (PB) $95-165
Full Breakfast
Credit Cards: A, B, C
Notes: 2, 5, 9, 10, 11, 12, 14

Simpson House Inn

121 East Arrellaga, 93101
(805) 963-7067; (800) 676-1280

Beautifully restored 1874 Victorian estate secluded on an acre of English gardens. Only a five-minute walk to historic downtown, restaurants, and shopping. Cottages, suites, and rooms elegantly furnished with antiques and Oriental rugs feature private patios with fountains, fireplaces, and Jacuzzis. Rates include afternoon beverages, evening wine, bicycles, and croquet.

Minimum-stay requirements for weekends and holidays.

Hosts: Gillean Wilson, Glyn and Linda Davies
Rooms: 13 (PB) $105-275
Full Breakfast
Credit Cards: A, B, C, D
Notes: 2, 5, 7 (limited), 9, 10, 11, 12, 14

The Upham Hotel and Garden Cottages

1404 De la Vina Street, 93101
(800) 727-0876

Established 1871, this beautifully restored Victorian hotel is on an acre of gardens. Guest rooms and suites feature period furnishings and antiques. Continental breakfast and afternoon wine and cheese. Walk to museums, galleries, historic attractions, shops, and restaurants downtown.

Host: Jan Martin Winn
Rooms: 49 (PB) $115-325
Continental Breakfast
Credit Cards: A, B, C, D, E, F
Notes: 3, 4, 5, 7, 8, 9, 10, 11, 12, 14

SANTA CLARA

Madison Street Inn

1390 Madison Street, 95050
(408) 249-5541; (800) 491-5541
FAX (408) 249-6676

Just ten minutes from San Jose airport and five minutes from Santa Clara University, this elegant Victorian sits peacefully in the heart of Silicon Valley. Telephones in rooms.

Hosts: Ralph and Theresa Wigginton
Rooms: 6 (4 PB; 2 SB) $60-85
Full Breakfast
Credit Cards: A, B, C, D, E
Notes: 2, 3, 4, 5, 8, 9, 10, 11, 12, 14

Babbling Brook Inn

1025 Laurel Street, 95060
(408) 427-2437; (800) 866-1131
FAX (408) 427-2457

Waterfalls and a meandering brook are in the gardens of this 12-room inn with French decor. Each room has a private bath, telephone, TV, fireplace, private deck, and private entrance. Two have deep soaking bathtubs, while two feature bathtubs "for two." Walk to beaches, the boardwalk, a garden mall, or tennis. Full breakfast and complimentary wine and cheese. Romantic garden gazebo available for weddings. Historic water tower. Two-night minimum stay required for weekends.

Host: Helen King
Rooms: 12 (PB) $85-150
Full Breakfast
Credit Cards: A, B, C, D, E
Notes: 2, 5, 8 (over 12), 9, 10, 11, 12, 14

Babbling Brook Inn

Bed and Breakfast, L.A.

3924 East 14th Street, Long Beach, 90804
(800) 383-3513

Santa Cruz-1. Majesty on the cliffs. Santa Cruz is the home of this beautiful mansion overlooking the ocean. Eight rooms, mostly with semi-private bath, are filled with unusual antiques and artwork. Guests can busy themselves by the great room fireplace, visit the Boardwalk, or walk through the redwoods.

Santa Cruz-2. Vacation home in the redwoods. This 1,600-square-foot home was built to blend with the breathtaking natural

6 Pets welcome; 7 Smoking allowed; 8 Children welcome; 9 Social drinking allowed; 10 Tennis available; 11 Swimming available; 12 Golf available; 13 Skiing available; 14 May be booked through travel agents.

environment, just ten minutes from the Santa Cruz beaches. Two bedrooms, both with private bath and spa robes, a fully equipped kitchen, cable TV, VCR, stone fireplace, and redwood deck with hot tub—even a piano. The hosts stock the refrigerator with a sumptuous full breakfast, and a welcoming bottle of wine. $125.

Bed and Breakfast San Francisco

P.O. Box 420009, San Francisco, 94142-0009
(415) 479-1913; FAX (415) 921-BBSF

21. This Frank Lloyd Wright-designed home is in the beautiful Santa Cruz mountains only seven miles from the popular Santa Cruz beach. One bedroom has a mountain view, private entrance, and private bath. Another bedroom has mountain view and shared bath. Full breakfast. Minimum stay is three nights. $65-75.

26. A fantasy in the forest. One guest room, with a queen-size bed, private bath, fireplace, TV, and VCR, looks out into the forest. The second guest room, with a queen-size bed, private bath, fireplace, TV, and VCR, is fixed up like an old-fashioned barn loft or chicken coop, and filled with antiques. Ice cream treats are served in the evenings. Ten acres of forest for hiking; two ponds. Full breakfast. $100-125.

Chateau Victorian

Chateau Victorian, A Bed and Breakfast Inn

118 First Street, 95060
(408) 458-9458

Chateau Victorian was built in the 1880s as a family home. Only one block from the beach and Monterey Bay. Opened in June 1983 as an elegant bed and breakfast inn, each room features a private bathroom, fireplace, queen-size bed, carpeting, and an individual heating system. Expanded continental breakfast is served. Each room is furnished in Victorian style. Chateau Victorian is within walking distance to downtown, the municipal wharf, the Boardwalk amusement park, and fine dining.

Hostess: Alice June
Rooms: 7 (PB) $110-140
Continental Breakfast
Credit Cards: A, B, C
Notes: 2, 5, 9

The Darling House— A Bed and Breakfast Inn By the Sea

314 West Cliff Drive, 95060
(408) 458-1958

A 1910 oceanside architectural masterpiece designed by William Weeks, lighted by the rising sun through beveled glass, Tiffany lamps, and open hearths. The spacious lawns, rose gardens, citrus orchard, towering palms, and expansive oceanview verandas create colorful California splendor. Stroll to secluded beaches, lighthouse, wharf, and boardwalk. Soak in the hot tub spa, and fall asleep securely to the serenade of seals and surf.

Hosts: Darrell and Karen Darling
Rooms: 8 (2 PB; 6 SB) $95-225
Continental Breakfast
Credit Cards: A, B, C, D
Notes: 2, 5, 8, 9, 10, 11, 12, 14

NOTES: Credit cards accepted: A MasterCard; B Visa; C American Express; D Discover Card; E Diner's Club; F Other; 2 Personal checks accepted; 3 Lunch available; 4 Dinner available; 5 Open all year;

Downeyland Bed and Breakfast

4205 Vine Hill Lane, 95065
(408) 425-8065

Redwoods surrounding Downeyland provide serenity, yet it is a short distance from Santa Cruz and Monterey Bay. The charming house is filled with antiques, a parlor for gatherings. The large Rose Camilla Room has a classical queen-size bed, fireplace, TV and its own entrance. The Sweetheart Room, a Victorian cottage bedroom has a double bed, TV. Breakfast, which includes the hosts' famous banana-nut, persimmon, and cinnamon breads, can be served on the attractive porch while wild birds, deer and cottontails entertain. The redwood grove has picnic tables. Lounge furniture is available. Guests are personally guided to local culinary and sightseeing locations.

Hosts: Leah and Jim Downey
Rooms: 3 (2 PB) $60-80
Full Breakfast
Credit Cards: None
Notes: 2, 3 (picnic), 5, 8 (limited), 9, 10, 11, 12

Jasmine Cottage

731 Riverside Avenue, 95060
(408) 429-1415

Charming home with all amenities, private entrance, and fresh foods cooked to individual taste. Double beds and private baths. Deposit required to confirm booking.

Host: Dorothy Allen
Room: 1 (PB) $45-60
Full Breakfast
Credit Cards: A, B
Notes: 2, 5, 9, 10, 11, 14

Pleasure Point Bed and Breakfast

2-3665 East Cliff Drive, 95062
(408) 475-4657

This beachfront home overlooks the beautiful Monterey Bay. Guest rooms have ocean views and private baths. Forty-foot motor yacht for fishing or cruising daily. Within walking distance of Capitola Beach and three miles to the Santa Cruz Beach boardwalk. Innkeepers love to share their inn with guests.

Hosts: Barbara and Gary Dasquini
Rooms: 3 (PB) $100-135
Continental Breakfast
Credit Cards: A, B
Notes: 5, 8, 9, 10, 11, 12

SANTA MONICA

Bed and Breakfast International

P.O. Box 282910, San Francisco, 94128-2910
(415) 696-1690; (800) 872-4500
FAX (415) 696-1699

502. Designer-built addition with a deck on the second floor of a renovated 1920 California bungalow. Contemporary furnishings in blue and white and natural wood. Close to the Venice boardwalk and one mile to Santa Monica pier, two blocks to the beach. Beach chairs, equipment, and towels are available. $75.

Channel Road Inn

219 West Channel Road, 90402
(310) 459-1920

Elegant inn one block from the beach in Santa Monica. "One of the most romantic places in Los Angeles," says *LA* magazine. Views and bicycles. Guests are two miles from the J. Paul Getty Museum.

Hosts: Kathy Jensen and Susan Zolla
Rooms: 14 (PB) $85-225
Full Breakfast
Credit Cards: A, B
Notes: 2, 5, 8, 9, 10, 11, 12, 14

6 Pets welcome; 7 Smoking allowed; 8 Children welcome; 9 Social drinking allowed; 10 Tennis available; 11 Swimming available; 12 Golf available; 13 Skiing available; 14 May be booked through travel agents.

Eye Openers
Bed and Breakfast
Reservations

P.O. Box 694, Altadena, 91003-0694
(213) 684-4428; (818) 797-2055
FAX (818) 798-3640

SM-C14I. Near Santa Monica Canyon and the beach, this 1910 shingle-clad Colonial Revival inn offers gracious hospitality and an excellent location. It has 14 guest rooms with double, queen- or king-size beds and private baths. Some of the amenities provided are a spa, bicycles, and a full breakfast. No smoking. $95-200.

SM-H1. This economically priced bed and breakfast offers large guest room. Hosts have interesting collection of folk instruments and a large library. Good public transportation nearby. Continental breakfast. Resident cat and dog. Private bath. No smoking. $40-45.

VE-V101. This turn-of-the-century beach estate is now a lovely bed and breakfast inn. Guest rooms and suites are individually decorated with antiques and hand-detailed furnishings. Large continental breakfast and evening refreshments are served. Ten guest rooms. Shared and private bath. No smoking. $90-150.

SANTA PAULA

Bed and Breakfast, L.A.

3924 East 14th Street, Long Beach, 90804
(800) 383-3513

Cen Coast-3. House Beautiful in Santa Paula. Once home to the town doctor and his (abundant) family, this stately Spanish mansion has four guest rooms, all with private bath. Well-kept gardens surround the heated pool. Breakfast is ample, decor is soothing and tasteful, and the little town of Santa Paula is perfect for a stroll. $95-125.

SANTA ROSA

Pygmalion House
Bed and Breakfast

331 Orange Street, 95407
(707) 526-3407

Pygmalion House, one of Santa Rosa's historic landmarks, is a fine example of Queen Anne Victorian architecture. Each morning a bountiful breakfast is served in the country kitchen. Throughout the day, complimentary bottled spring water and soft drinks are available. In the evening, guests may enjoy coffee, sparkling cider, or tea while relaxing around the fireplace.

Host: Lola L. Wright
Rooms: 5 (PB) $60-70
Full Breakfast
Credit Cards: A, B, C
Notes: 2, 5, 9, 10, 12, 14

Vintners Inn

4350 Barnes Road, 95403
(707) 575-7350; (800) 421-2584

Amid a 50-acre vineyard in the Sonoma wine country, this four-diamond, 44-room, European-styled inn features antique furnishings, modern private baths, fireplaces if desired, balconies or patios, vineyard and plaza views, along with a complimentary breakfast. Beautiful sun deck and Jacuzzi. Also the home of the nationally acclaimed John Ash & Co. Restaurant.

Hosts: John Duffy and Cindy Young
Rooms: 44 (PB) $127.44-199.80
Continental Breakfast
Credit Cards: A, B, C, E
Notes: 2, 3, 4, 5, 8, 9, 10, 11, 12, 14

SAUSALITO

Bed and Breakfast
Exchange of Marin

45 Entrata, San Anselmo, 94960
(415) 485-1971

NOTES: Credit cards accepted: A MasterCard; B Visa; C American Express; D Discover Card; E Diner's Club; F Other; 2 Personal checks accepted; 3 Lunch available; 4 Dinner available; 5 Open all year;

Stay on a houseboat! Enjoy this picturesque lifestyle for one night or a week. You are the only occupants. Houseboat has kitchen, bath, TV, VCR. At end of flower-filled dock affording uninterrupted views of Mount Tamalpais. Bird book and binoculars. Self-catered breakfast. $100.

Bed and Breakfast International

P.O. Box 282910, San Francisco, 94128-2910
(415) 696-1690; (800) 872-4500
FAX (415) 696-1699

108. Try a new way to stay at a bed and breakfast. Three houseboats docked in Sausalito, five minutes north of the Golden Gate Bridge and close to interesting shops and restaurants in downtown Sausalito. Two have beautiful views of the bay from the decks, and all are beautifully furnished in fine furniture and art. Two are unhosted for optimum privacy. The third comes with a home-cooked breakfast. $105-150.

Bed and Breakfast San Francisco

P.O. Box 420009, San Francisco, 94142-0009
(415) 479-1913; FAX (415) 921-BBSF

04. The picturesque village of Sausolito in Marin County offers wonderful restaurants, quaint shops, and romantic views of San Franscisco. Stay aboard a houseboat, a permanently moored home on the bay. Decks on three sides, living room with a fireplace, king-size bed in the bedroom, full kitchen, and a full bath. The home is unhosted, but all breakfast items are in the kitchen for a self-catered breakfast. Enjoy a glass of wine while watching the city lights come on and the sun slip behind Mount Tamalpais. $125.

The Butterfly Tree

P.O. Box 790, 94966
(415) 383-8447

At Muir Beach, guests are within easy walking distance to the Pacific Ocean, Muir Woods, and the Golden Gate National Recreation Area. A secluded, fragile environment good for nature buffs, lovers, hikers, and bird watchers. Only 30 minutes from San Francisco; 20 minutes to the Sausalito ferry, shopping, and excellent dining.

Host: Karla Andersdatter
Rooms: 2 (PB) $115
Full Breakfast
Credit Cards: None
Notes: 5, 8 (limited), 9, 11

SEAL BEACH

Eye Openers Bed and Breakfast Reservations

P.O. Box 694, Altadena, 91003-0694
(213) 684-4428; (818) 797-2055
FAX (818) 798-3640

SB-D2. Large villa on the sand with colorful gardens beach-side beckons guests to indulge in water sports, sun on the dunes, or relax on an enclosed balcony with an ocean view. Indoor Jacuzzi. Continental-plus breakfast. Two guest rooms. Private bath. No smoking. $75.

SB-S241. A bed and breakfast inn with the look and ambience of an elegant European inn is surrounded by lovely gardens. Inn has a brick courtyard, pool, library, and a gracious dining room for large continental breakfasts and evening refreshments. Twenty-four guest rooms all have individual decor and private baths. This lovely, quiet beach community is a well-kept secret. $108-235.

Seal Beach Inn and Gardens

212 Fifth Street, 90740
(310) 493-2416

6 Pets welcome; 7 Smoking allowed; 8 Children welcome; 9 Social drinking allowed; 10 Tennis available; 11 Swimming available; 12 Golf available; 13 Skiing available; 14 May be booked through travel agents.

An elegant country inn by the sea, with a classic French Mediterranean appearance. The accommodations are appointed in handsome antique furnishings. Many have sitting areas and kitchens. The inn is surrounded by lush, colorful, gardens, French sculpture, fountains, and ancient garden art An Old World-style bed and breakfast, but far more than that. This is a full-service country inn with all the conveniences, activities, and amenities of a fine hotel.

Host: Marjorie Bettenhausen
Rooms: 23 (PB) $118-185
Full Breakfast
Credit Cards: A, B, C, D, E, F
Notes: 3 and 4 (by arrangement), 5, 9, 10, 11, 12, 13 (water), 14

SEQUOIA NATIONAL PARK _____

Bed and Breakfast, L.A.
3924 East 14th Street, Long Beach, 90804
(800) 383-3513

A. At the foot of the Sequoia is a classic country bed and breakfast with nine guest rooms, four in the main house and three suites in the garden. All have private bath and several include sitting areas and claw-foot tubs. Friendly hosts serve a full country breakfast in the dining room. $70-85.

B. This family cottage in the little town of Three Rivers was built by an architect for beauty and efficiency. It has a bedroom, living room, bath, full kitchen, and redwood deck. The splendor of the wilderness surrounds this cottage. Moderate rates.

Eye Openers Bed and Breakfast Reservations
P.O. Box 694, Altadena, 91003-0694
(213) 684-4428; (818) 797-2055
FAX (818) 798-3640

LE-L9I. Family-run inn near entrance to Sequoia National Park offers gorgeous scenery and friendly hospitality. Ten guest rooms have queen- or king-size beds and private or shared baths. Full breakfast. No smoking. $55-90.

TR-C1. Enjoy an architect-designed cottage with kitchen facilities. Beautiful views of the mountains. Near the entrance to Sequoia National Park. Hot tub available. Private bath. No smoking. $75.

Lemon Cove Bed and Breakfast
33038 Highway 198, Lemoncove, 93244
(800) 240-1466

Near the Sequoia National Park, the Lemon Cove Bed and Breakfast is nestled in the Sierra foothills, just one mile below Lake Kaweah. A bridal suite with fireplace, whirlpool bath, and balcony is one of nine romantic rooms tastefully decorated with antiques and quilts. Off-street parking. Evening refresments served.

Hosts: Pat and Kay Bonette
Rooms: 9 (7 PB; 2 SB) $55-89
Full Breakfast
Credit Cards: A, B, C, D
Notes: 2, 5, 8, 9, 11, 12, 14

SONOMA _____

Bed and Breakfast International
P.O. Box 282910, San Francisco, 94128-2910
(415) 696-1690; (800) 872-4500
FAX (415) 696-1699

301. In the heart of Sonoma, within walking distance to the plaza and wineries, is an old stonecutter's cottage. It has a king/twin bed with bath and large deck. There is a Franklin stove in the cottage. In a garden setting surrounded by countryside studded with giant oaks. Breakfast is served in the main house. $100.

302. Contemporary, Colonial-style, two-story home in the Sonoma Valley wine country. Surrounded by 17 acres, it has views of rolling hills and Mount St. Helena, yet is only three miles from downtown Healdsburg. Guest quarters are in a separate building from the main house and are furnished in antiques, quilts, and Oriental rugs. Both rooms have double beds and private baths. Breakfast is in main house. $80.

Bed and Breakfast, L.A.

3924 E. 14th Street, Long Beach, 90804
(310) 498-0552; (800) 383-3513

Indulge in the peace of a private cottage close to this small town. Artist hosts have decorated these distinctive suites with their original art. Enjoy a continental breakfast in the shadow of a lilac-lined drive leading to a vineyard or mountain view. All rooms feature deluxe queen-size beds, patios, and full baths.

Eye Openers Bed and Breakfast Reservations

P.O. Box 694, Altadena, 91003-0694
(213) 684-4428; (818) 797-2055
FAX (818) 798-3640

HE-C61. This 1869 Italianate Victorian townhouse on one-half acre has landscaped grounds with pool and large antique-filled guest rooms Breakfast with fresh baked breads and afternoon refreshments are served. Six guest rooms. Shared and private baths. $75-135.

HE-F2. Seventy-acre grape ranch in Sonoma County's spectacular Dry Creek Valley near many wineries and restaurants is a family-run bed and breakfast. Enjoy

charming antique decorated guest rooms, tranquil vineyard setting, and walks, swimming pool, garden terrace, and wildlife pond. Full breakfast. Two guest rooms. Private bath. No smoking. $90.

HE-G71. This 1902 Queen Anne Victorian offers an elegant return to a bygone era. Upstairs rooms have roof windows and view of the lovely grounds. Full country breakfast. Seven guest rooms. Private bath. No smoking. $85-130.

The Hidden Oak

214 East Napa Street, 95476
(707) 996-9863

A 1913 two-story Craftsman bungalow restored home in the historic neighborhood of Sonoma, one block from the plaza. The innkeeper has a comfortable warm and private setting for guests who enjoy English and Oriental antiques and books to browse through by the fireside. There are three guest rooms with queen-size beds and private baths, and a luxury three-room suite with private bath, patio, and many other amenities. Full breakfast and complimentary bicycles. Near wineries, shopping, restaurants, art galleries, and historical sites.

Host: Catherine Cotchett
Rooms: 4 (PB) $105-225
Full Breakfast
Credit Cards: C, D
Notes: 2, 8 (by arrangement), 9, 10, 12

Sonoma Hotel

110 West Spain Street, 95476
(707) 996-2996; (800) 468-6016
FAX (707) 996-7014

This beautiful vintage hotel offers accommodations and dining to the discriminating seeker of relaxation and respite from the urban hustle. To spend an evening here is to step back into a romantic period of history. Each antique bedroom evokes a distinct feel

6 Pets welcome; 7 Smoking allowed; 8 Children welcome; 9 Social drinking allowed; 10 Tennis available; 11 Swimming available; 12 Golf available; 13 Skiing available; 14 May be booked through travel agents.

of early California; the emphasis on comfort is European. On a tree-lined plaza, it is within walking distance of famous wineries, beautiful picnic spots, distinctive art galleries, unique shops, and historic landmarks. Guests receive wine on arrival.

Hosts: John and Dorene Musilli
Rooms: 17 (5 PB; 12 SB) $75-130
Continental Breakfast
Credit Cards: A, B, C, E
Notes: 2, 3, 4, 5, 7, 8, 9, 10, 11, 12, 14

Victorian Garden Inn

316 East Napa Street, 95476
(707) 996-5339; (800) 543-5339

Nestled beside Nathanson Creek on an acre of beautiful gardens with private patios and winding paths, this lovely and historic (1870) farmhouse is just one and a half blocks from Sonoma's historic plaza and the Sebastiani Winery. The comfortable and artfully decorated rooms, furnished with antiques, are designed for comfort and have a view of the gardens and secluded swimming pool. A gourmet California breakfast is served in the cheerful dining room, on the patios, or in rooms as requested. Concierge services are provided for the ultimate romantic experience in this sophisticated and gracious environment.

Host: Donna Lewis
Rooms: 4 (3 PB; 1 SB) $79-139
Continental Breakfast
Credit Cards: A, B, C, E, F
Notes: 2, 5, 7, 9, 10, 11, 12, 14

SONORA

Kids Welcome

3924 East 14th Street, Long Beach, 90804
(800) 383-3513

17-2. Play with the llamas at this creek-side guest ranch in the country. Features hot tub and sauna, music room/library with lots of kids' games, and gracious Southern hospitality. Moderate rates.

Lulu Belle's Bed and breakfast

85 Gold Street, 95370
(209) 533-3455; (800) 538-3455

Charming 1886 Victorian with beautiful gardens and a relaxing atmosphere. Each of the five lovely guest rooms features private baths, private entrances, and air conditioning. Enjoy delicious hearty breakfasts and excellent location to explore the "Gold Country." Get-away packages available for dinner/theater, river rafting, steam train excursions, and skiing.

Rooms: 5 (PB) $80-100
Full Breakfast
Credit Cards: A, B, C, D
Notes: 2, 5, 8, 9, 10, 11, 12, 13, 14

Blue Spruce Inn

SOQUEL

Blue Spruce Inn

2815 Main Street, 95073
(408) 464-1137; (800) 559-1137
FAX (408) 475-0608

Spa tubs, fireplaces, and quiet gardens foster relaxation for guests. The Blue Spruce is four miles south of Santa Cruz, one mile inland from Capitola Beach—an ideal location for a romantic getaway, special celebration, business travel, or a special business meeting. Hike in the redwoods.

NOTES: Credit cards accepted: A MasterCard; B Visa; C American Express; D Discover Card; E Diner's Club; F Other; 2 Personal checks accepted; 3 Lunch available; 4 Dinner available; 5 Open all year;

Bike through country fields. Walk to fine dining. Relax in the outdoor hot tub. Professional, personal attention is the hallmark of this inn. Visit soon!

Hosts: Pat and Tom O'Brien
Rooms: 6 (PB) $85-135
Full Breakfast
Credit Cards: A, B, C
Notes: 2, 5, 8, 9, 10, 11, 12, 14

STINSON BEACH

Casa del Mar

37 Belvedere Avenue, Box 238, 94970
(415) 868-2124

A peach-colored Mediterranean villa overlooking the Pacific Ocean and surrounded by terraced gardens and a rock wall. Wind through jacarandas, passion flowers, bananas, by the pond, and up to the inn. Guests can hear the waves break all day long. "One of the most memorable breakfasts [guests will] ever be privileged to experience," says Linda Kay Bristow, author of Bed and Breakfast California.

Innkeeper: Rick Klein
Rooms: 4 (PB) $100-225
Full Breakfast
Credit Cards: A, B, C
Notes: 2, 5, 8, 9, 11, 14

SUMMERLAND

Inn on Summer Hill

2520 Lillie Avenue, P.O. Box 376, 93067
(805) 969-9998; (800) 845-5566

Award-winning 16-room inn adjacent to world-famous Santa Barbara and its attractions in the quaint seaside village of Summerland. English Country decor with European elegance. Rooms have full ocean-island views, fireplaces, canopied beds, private baths, Jacuzzis, VCR, TV, stereo cassette players, robes, and down comforters. Full breakfast, hors d'oeuvres, and dessert included. Two-night minimum re-

quired for weekends; special rates and packages midweek.

General Manager: Verlinda Richardson
Rooms: 16 (PB) $160-275
Full Breakfast
Credit Cards: A, B, C
Notes: 3, 5, 10, 11, 12, 14

Summerland Inn

2161 Ortega Hill Road, P.O. Box 1209, 93067
(805) 969-5225

The Summerland Inn, "where New England meets the Pacific," is a delightful bed and breakfast with ten rooms, private baths, telephones, TV, and breakfast served in guests' room. Summerland has its own beach a short walk from the inn, antique and gift shops, and places to eat.

Host: James R. Farned
Rooms: 11 (PB) $55-140
Continental Breakfast
Credit Cards: A, B, C, D, E
Notes: 2, 5, 8, 12, 14

Chaney House

TAHOE CITY

Chaney House

P.O. Box 7852, 4725 West Lake Boulevard, 96145
(916) 525-7333

Built on the Lake Tahoe shore by Italian stonemasons, Chaney House has an almost medieval quality with its dramatic arched windows, 18-inch-thick stone walls, and enormous fireplace. The private beach and pier beckon guests. Bicycling, hiking, boating, fishing, and 19 ski areas are close at hand. Scrumptious breakfasts are served on the patio overlooking the lake on mild days.

Hosts: Gary and Lori Chaney
Rooms: 4 (PB) $100-115
Full Breakfast
Credit Cards: None
Notes: 2, 5, 9, 10, 11, 12, 13, 14 (off season only)

The Cottage Inn

1690 West Lake Boulevard, P.O. Box 66, 96145
(916) 581-4073; (800) 581-4073

The Cottage Inn Bed and Breakfast is nestled in two acres of pines just steps from the lake and private beach. All cottages feature original knotty pine paneling with unique themes and charming Tahoe appeal. The rooms have private entrances and baths. Rock fireplaces, TV, and VCR. The main lodge, built in 1938, is decorated with old Tahoe-style furnishings, and there is also a rock fireplace. Enjoy a hearty breakfast in the dining room or on the deck in the summer. The sauna is a year-round favorite. A wide variety of four-season outdoor recreation is available.

Hosts: Jerry and Lisa Miles
Rooms: 14 (PB) $90-150
Full Breakfast
Credit Cards: A, B
Notes: 2, 5, 9, 10, 11, 12, 13, 14

Mayfield House

236 Grove Street, P.O. Box 5999, 96145
(916) 583-1001

Snug and cozy 1930s Tahoe home, one-half block from the beach. Premium skiing within five miles. Full breakfast, homemade baked goods. Within walking distance of shops and restaurants in Tahoe City. Off-street parking.

Hosts: Cynthia and Bruce Knauss
Rooms: 6 (SB) $85-115
Full Breakfast
Credit Cards: A, B, C
Notes: 2, 5, 8, 9, 10, 11, 12, 13, 14

Eye Openers
Bed and Breakfast
Reservations

P.O. Box 694, Altadena, 91003-0694
(213) 684-4428; (818) 797-2055
FAX (818) 798-3640

TE-S61. In Southern California's wine country, this lovely bed and breakfast has six uniquely decorated guest rooms. Full country breakfast. No smoking. Private bath. $95-125.

Loma Vista

TEMECULA

Loma Vista
Bed and Breakfast

33350 La Serena Way, 92591
(909) 676-7047

Loma Vista, in the heart of Temecula's wine country, is convenient to any spot in Southern California. This beautiful new mission-style home is surrounded by citrus groves and premium vineyards. All six rooms have private baths; most have balconies. A full champagne breakfast is served. Closed Thanksgiving, Christmas, New Year's days.

Hosts: Betty and Dick Ryan
Rooms: 6 (PB) $95-125
Full Breakfast
Credit Cards: A, B, D
Notes: 2, 9, 10, 11, 12, 14

TEMPLETON

Kids Welcome

3924 East 14th Street, Long Beach, 90804
(310) 498-0552; (800) 383-3513

San Luis-8. Just north of San Louis Obispo
on Highway 101, this quaint inn takes
guests back 100 years. The Country Inn is
perfectly restored, down to the parlor and
veranda. Four guest rooms in pastel colors,
two with private bath, and two sharing.
Low midweek rates available.

TORRANCE

Bed and Breakfast, L.A.

3924 E. 14th Street, Long Beach, 90804
(310) 498-0552; (800) 383-3513

Lovely ranch-style home is about a mile
from the beach. This home features two
guest rooms, both with private bath. One
room has a queen-size bed and a twin bed;
the other has a queen-size bed, a kitchenette, and sliding doors to the deck and
garden. Hostess loves to visit and makes
whatever you want for breakfast! Close to
both LA International Airport and the
southern beaches. $55-65.

TRINIDAD

Bed and Breakfast, L.A.

3924 East 14th Street, Long Beach, 90804
(800) 383-3513

Guests can watch the waves from the hot
tub, while the kids are out berry-picking at
this perfect family vacation spot. Hosts designed this bed and breakfast retreat for
family fun and comfort. Breakfast is big
and nutritious; town is nearby and full of
activity; and scenic trails to tide pools are at
the doorstep. The kids are provided with an
enclosed playground, playhouse, barnyard

animals, and storytelling. Need a night out?
Childcare is available, too. Call for rates.

The Lost Whale
Bed and Breakfast

3452 Patrick's Point Drive, 95570
(707) 677-3425

Unique bed and breakfast on four wooded
acres with a private beach and trail. Wake
to barking sea lions and a spectacular ocean
view. Amenities include outdoor hot tub,
afternoon tea, private baths, and queen-size
beds. Fifteen minutes from Eureka airport
and the largest redwood forests in the
world. Enjoy the gardens, decks, and
gourmet breakfast.

Hosts: Lee Miller and Susanne Lakin
Rooms: 8 (PB) $105-135
Full Breakfast
Credit Cards: A, B
Notes: 2, 5, 8, 11, 14

Trinidad Bed and Breakfast

Trinidad Bed and Breakfast

Box 849, 95570
(707) 677-0840

A Cape Cod-style home overlooking beautiful Trinidad Bay. The inn offers spectacular
views of the rugged coastline and fishing
harbor from two suites, one with a fireplace,
and two upstairs bedrooms, all with private
baths. Surrounded by beaches, trails, and

6 Pets welcome; 7 Smoking allowed; 8 Children welcome; 9 Social drinking allowed; 10 Tennis available;
11 Swimming available; 12 Golf available; 13 Skiing available; 14 May be booked through travel agents.

redwood parks. Within walking distance of restaurants and shops. The suites enjoy breakfast delivered. The other two rooms enjoy breakfast at a family-style table.

Hosts: Paul and Carol Kirk
Rooms: (PB) $90-155
Continental Breakfast
Credit Cards: A, B
Notes: 2, 9, 10, 12

TRUCKEE

The Truckee Hotel

10007 Bridge Street, 96161
(800) 659-6921

This circa 1873 Victorian bed and breakfast is in Truckee's historical district. Begin the day with an expanded continental breakfast, and enjoy the sights and activities that this beautiful Sierra location offers. In-house dining at The Passage offers fine wine and cuisine. Relax fireside in the parlor before turning in for the night. Shopping and dining are moments from the inn, and Amtrak is close by. Come for a visit by train. No smoking. Call for brochure.

Host: Rachelle L. Pellissier
Rooms: 37 (8 PB; 29 SB) $60-115
Continental Breakfast
Credit Cards: A, B, C
Notes: 2, 5, 8, 11, 12, 13

TWO HARBORS (SANTA CATALINA ISLAND)

Banning House Lodge

P.O. Box 5044, 90704
(310) 510-0303

The Banning House Lodge is a refurbished 1910 lodge on the isthmus of the island. Stunning views await guests from the west-facing veranda. Make an afternoon adventure of touring, kayaking, or hiking. Enjoy fine dining at Doug's Harbor Reef before relaxing in front of the fireplace of the Lodge Room. Viewing the star-filled sky is a perfect way to end a perfect day.

Hosts: Elizabeth Devries and Steve Stroud
Rooms: 11 (PB)
Continental Breakfast
Credit Cards: A, B, C
Notes: 3, 4, 5, 9, 10, 11, 14

UKIAH

Bed and Breakfast, L.A.

3924 East 14th Street, Long Beach, 90804
(800) 383-3513

16-8. The champagne baths are the center of attention at this parklike resort at the foot of the Mendocino Hills. Twelve individually decorated rooms with private baths date from the 1860s. The two free-standing cottages, complete with modern kitchens, were built in 1854. Abundant wildlife in the 700 acres of woods, meadows, streams, and falls that surround the ranch. Sailing, windsurfing, Jet skiing, and salmon fishing are all within easy reach, and naturally carbonated hot tubs are at the doorstep. Moderate to luxury rates.

Vichy Springs Resort and Inn

2605 Vichy Springs Road, 95482
(707) 462-9515

Vichy Springs Resort, a delightful two-hour drive north of San Francisco, 12 rooms and two self-contained cottages that have been renovated and individually decorated. Nearby are 14 tubs built in 1860 and used by the rich and famous in California's history. Vichy features naturally sparkling 90-degree mineral baths, a communal 104-degree pool, Olympic-size pool, 700 private acres with a waterfall, trails and roads for hiking, jogging, picnicking and mountain bicycling, and Swedish massage, reflexology, and herbal facials.

Hosts: Gilbert and Marjorie Ashoff
Rooms: 14 (PB) $85-160
Continental Breakfast
Credit Cards: A, B, C, D, E, F
Notes: 2, 3, 4, 5, 8, 9, 10, 11, 12, 14

NOTES: Credit cards accepted: A MasterCard; B Visa; C American Express; D Discover Card; E Diner's Club; F Other; 2 Personal checks accepted; 3 Lunch available; 4 Dinner available; 5 Open all year;

VENTURA

Bella Maggiore Inn
67 South California Street, 93001
(805) 652-0277

This 1920s northern Italian-style inn was designed by A.C. Martin, architect of the Los Angeles City Hall. The home is in the old business district near Mission San Buenaventura. Full breakfast served in the dining room or courtyard. Appetizers with beverages served in the afternoon. Telephone, TV, whirlpool, fireplace, and air conditioning in some rooms.

Hosts: Thomas Wood
Rooms: 27 (PB) $75-150
Full Breakfast
Cards: A, B, C, D, E
Notes: 3, 4, 5, 8, 10, 11, 12, 14

Eye Openers Bed and Breakfast Reservations
P.O. Box 694, Altadena, 91003-0694
(213) 684-4428; (818) 797 2055
FAX (818) 798-3640

VE-B171. Three blocks from the beach, this inn with Mediterranean decor offers comfort and convenience. Full breakfast and afternoon refreshments. Seventeen rooms. Private bath. $75-120.

VE-M5I. Bavarian-style hospitality at this lovely bed and breakfast near the beach. Five guest rooms have queen- or king-size beds and private baths. Walking or biking distance from many shops, restaurants, and attractions. Short commute to Santa Barbara, Ojai, and Santa Ynez Valley. Full breakfast. No smoking. $90-125.

Kids Welcome
3924 East 14th Street, Long Beach, 90804
(310) 498-0552; (800) 383-3513

3-14. This four-acre ranch in Camarillo has stables, fruit trees, a spa, and hiking trails. The two guest wings have a total of five rooms, which is perfect for a large family. Only half an hour to Santa Barbara. $65.

La Mer
411 Poli Street, 93001
(805) 643-3600

Nestled in a green hillside, this Cape Cod-style Victorian overlooks the heart of historic San Buena Ventura and the California coastline. Originally built in 1890 and a historic landmark, La Mer has individually decorated, antique-filled rooms furnished to capture a specific European country, all with private baths and entrances, plus ocean view. Two-night minimum stay required for weekends and holidays.

Host: Gisela Flender Baida
Rooms: 5 (PB) $80-155
Full Breakfast
Credit Cards: A, B, C
Notes: 2, 5, 8, 9, 10, 11, 12, 14

WATSONVILLE

Dunmovin' Bed and Breakfast
1006 Hecker Pass Road, 95076
(408) 728-4154; (408) 722-2810

This 70-year-old Tudor English home on 22 acres overlooks the Watsonville and Monterey Bay area. Tennis court, hot tub, four llamas, six peacocks, a dog, and cat. Redwood trees and wildlife on property. On Highway 152 seven miles from Gilroy (wine tasting) and Watsonville, and a 30-minute drive to Pacific Grove, Monterey, and Santa Cruz. Homemade muffins and cinnamon rolls are freshly baked.

Hosts: Ruth and Don Wakefield
Rooms: 3 (PB) $65-75
Full Breakfast
Credit Cards: None
Notes: 2, 5, 8, 9, 10, 11, 12

6 Pets welcome; 7 Smoking allowed; 8 Children welcome; 9 Social drinking allowed; 10 Tennis available; 11 Swimming available; 12 Golf available; 13 Skiing available; 14 May be booked through travel agents.

WESTPORT

Howard Creek Ranch
Box 121, 95488
(707) 964-6725

A historic 1867 farm on 40 acres, only 100 yards from the beach. A rural retreat adjoining wilderness. Suite and cabins; views of ocean, mountains, creek, or gardens; fireplace/wood stoves; period furnishings; hot tub, sauna, ornamental spring-fed pool, and horseback riding nearby. Gift certificates available.

Hosts: Charles (Sunny) and Sally Grigg
Rooms: 10 (8 PB; 2 SB) $55-145
Full Breakfast
Credit Cards: A, B, C
Notes: 2, 5, 6 and 8 (by arrangement), 7 (limited), 9, 11

YOSEMITE

Eye Openers
Bed and Breakfast
Reservations
P.O. Box 694, Altadena, 91003-0694
(213) 684-4428; (818) 797-2055
FAX (818) 798-3640

YG-C2. Get away to this large A-frame house with open-beamed ceilings on a tree-filled hillside above a private lake 20 minutes west of Yosemite. Loft bedroom/sitting room and two other guest rooms available. Full breakfast served on deck with view of the Sierra Nevadas. Private bath. $60-70.

YO-P3I. Halfway between Yosemite Valley and Wawona is this beautiful, new bed and breakfast with uniquely decorated rooms, each with fireplace and one with Jacuzzi for two. The three guest rooms have double, queen-, and king-size beds and private baths. Outdoor decks offer serenity, views, and a hot tub. Full breakfast. No smoking. $100-150.

YOUNTVILLE

Burgundy House
P.O. Box 3156, 6711 Washington Street, 94599
(707) 944-0889

Solidly built 1890 French Country stone structure. Originally a brandy distillery with 22-inch-thick walls of river-rock and field-stone. Six comfortable rooms, all with private bath, invite guests to settle in and relax. The antique furnishings throughout the house add to the Old World charm and ruggedness. Colorful rose garden and lawn invite guests to picnicking or wine tasting. Full breakfast served buffet-style. In the center of Napa Valley's wine region.

Host: Deanna Roqué
Rooms: 6 (PB) $100-125
Full Breakfast
Credit Cards: A, B, C
Notes: 2, 5, 9, 10, 12, 14

Eye Openers
Bed and Breakfast
Reservations
P.O. Box 694, Altadena, 91003-0694
(213) 684-4428; (818) 797-2055
FAX (818) 798-3640

YO-M13I. Newly renovated 100-year-old inn with French country decor in the heart of the Napa Valley serves a full breakfast. Thirteen guest rooms with queen- or king-size beds and private baths. Relax at the pool and Jacuzzi. Good restaurants nearby. No smoking. $110-190.

Oleander House
7433 St. Helena Highway, 94599
(707) 944-8315

Country French charm at the entrance to wine country. Spacious, high-ceiling rooms done in Laura Ashley fabric, wallpaper, and antiques. Breakfast is served in the large dining room on the main floor. All rooms have fireplaces, private baths, and their own decks. Two-night minimum stay required for weekends and holidays.

Hosts: The Packards
Rooms: 4 (PB) $115-160
Full Breakfast
Credit Cards: A, B
Notes: 2, 9, 10, 11, 12, 14

Vintage Inn

6541 Washington Street, 94599
(800) 351-1133

Vintage Inn in Napa Valley is a contemporary luxury country inn on a historic 23-acre winery estate in the walking town of Yountville. Centered amidst some of Napa Valley's finest vineyards, guests enjoy a unique resort atmosphere with pool, spa, tennis, cycling, and hot air ballooning. A California champagne buffet breakfast of pastries, assorted fruits, cheeses, yogurt, and cereals is included with each guest stay. Superb accommodations for year-round comfort, featuring wood-burning fireplaces, whirlpool baths, compact refrigerators, and many other extras.

Host: Nancy M. Lochmann
Rooms: 80 (PB) $136-216
Continental Breakfast
Credit Cards: A, B, C, D, E, F
Notes: 2, 3, 4, 5, 6, 7, 8, 9, 10, 11, 12, 14

YUBA CITY

Harkey House Bed and Breakfast

212 C Street, 95991
(916) 674-1942

An 1874 Victorian Gothic with queen-size beds, fireplaces, TV/VCR/CD players, and telephones. Breakfast is served in the dining room or on the patio. Spa, basketball court, chess, game table, and library. Air-conditioned. Original art work, piano, and fountains. Near museums, hiking, and fishing. Fresh flowers and down comforters. Complimentary beverage and popcorn. A romantic getaway! Reservation deposit required. Five-day cancellation notice. $10 cancellation fee. Call for business rates.

Hosts: Bob and Lee Jones
Rooms: 4 (PB) $75-100
Continental Breakfast
Credit Cards: A, B, C, D
Notes: 2, 3, 5, 8, 9, 10, 11, 12, 13, 14

6 Pets welcome; 7 Smoking allowed; 8 Children welcome; 9 Social drinking allowed; 10 Tennis available; 11 Swimming available; 12 Golf available; 13 Skiing available; 14 May be booked through travel agents.

Colorado

Colorado

Cottonwood Inn Bed and Breakfast and Gallery

123 San Juan Avenue, 81101
(719) 589-3882

Lovely turn-of-the-century Craftsman-style inn, decorated with antiques and local artwork. Packages availabe with the Cumbres Toltec Railway and golf courses. Near the Great Sand Dunes, wildlife refuges, Adams State College, cross-country skiing, and the Rio Grande. Delicious breakfasts featuring freshly ground coffee, homemade baked goods, and fresh fruit. Famous for green chili strata.

Hosts: Julie Mordecai and George Sellman
Rooms: 7 (4 PB, 3 SB) $58-79
Full Breakfast
Credit Cards: A, B, E
Notes: 2, 5, 8, 9, 10, 11, 12, 14

ARVADA

Bed and Breakfast Agency of Colorado at Vail

P.O. 491, Vail, CO 81658
(303) 949-1212; (800) 748-2666

On Golden Pond. For European hospitality and a relaxing blend of country comfort, come to this romantic retreat on ten acres, with fishing pond, swimming pool, and hot tubs. Only 15 miles from Denver. Enjoy many activities, full breakfast, and after-noon kaffeeklatsch. Five rooms are offered with private baths. No smoking. No pets. $50-100.

ASPEN

Bed and Breakfast Agency of Colorado at Vail

P.O. 491, Vail, CO 81658
(303) 949-1212; (800) 748-2666

Alpine. Welcome to the historic Alpine Lodge, originally built in 1890 to house a successful miner and his family. Enjoy European hospitality, gourmet meals, and a cozy Bavarian setting within walking distance of the center of town. Stay in one of the charming cabins with kitchenette, in the main lodge with private bath, or in one of the rooms with a private European bath. A Continental breakfast is included in summer, and full breakfasts and dinners are available in winter (for a small additional charge). From goosedown comforters to personal home-cooked dinners, the warmth and charm of this inn is something to remember. No smoking. No pets. $59-99.

Ambiance (Carbondale). Enjoy Aspen, Glenwood Springs, and the beautiful Crystal Valley in this spacious chalet-style home, featuring vaulted ceilings throughout. The 1950s ski-lodge decor of the very large Aspen Suite or the Victorian elegance of the Sonoma Room with its romantic four-poster bed are ideal for getaways. The Santa Fe Room is alive with

NOTES: Credit cards accepted: A MasterCard; B Visa; C American Express; D Discover Card; E Diner's Club; F Other; 2 Personal checks accepted; 3 Lunch available; 4 Dinner available; 5 Open all year; 6 Pets welcome; 7 Smoking allowed; 8 Children welcome; 9 Social drinking allowed; 10 Tennis available; 11 Swimming available; 12 Golf available; 13 Skiing available; 14 May be booked through travel agents.

the warmth of the Southwest. All rooms adjoin the library sitting room on the balcony. The Kuauai Room features atmosphere and a two-person Jacuzzi. Full breakfasts. No smoking. $60-80.

Crestahaus. Experience European charm in the heart of the Rockies. Thirty distinctive rooms and one suite feature private baths, telephones, and cable TV; most have mountain views. Lodge amenities include Jacuzzi and sauna, heated pool (summers only), daily housekeeping, complimentary breakfast buffet, and après ski appetizers and drinks (winter only). Choose between rustic-traditional rooms in the main lodge, or deluxe-contemporary rooms. Enjoy two fireplace areas, BBQ/patio area, and year-round hospitality and comfort. Airport transportation and free shuttle downtown (one quarter mile). $50-175.

Heatherbed. High in the mountains, where the roar of the creek below and the rustle of the towering pines soothes the spirit, is a small country inn called the Heatherbed. For over 30 years it has welcomed mountain travelers with its sunny pine, bright copper, fresh wildflowers, and friendly faces. Although it's only two miles from one of the most exciting resorts in the world, this inn's loyal following comes not from its sophistication, but from its European tradition of Alpine hospitality, where the guests are a part of the family. Fifteen rooms with private baths are either creekside or mountainside. Breakfast, hot tub, and pool (seasonal) are just a few of the amenities offered. $75-155.

Main Street. All rooms richly appointed, opening up to a center room lounge. They offer wet bars, refrigerators, cable TV, and telephones. On the premises is a heated pool and Jacuzzi. A river rock fireplace cascades in the lounge, where a Continental breakfast and wine and cheese are served

daily. Great for traveling couples. No smoking. $85-155.

Starry Pines. Wake up to panoramic views of Mount Sopris and the Elk Mountain Range, on 70 private acres in scenic Snowmass Valley. Enjoy a Continental breakfast on the deck overlooking a beautiful mountain fishing stream, just 20 minutes from Aspen. Two rooms and one small apartment. Enjoy the patio outdoor hot tub. No smoking. No pets. $70-100.

Van Horn House (Carbondale). This European cottage with quiet location is 25 minutes from downtown Aspen. Each of the four guest rooms has spectacular views of Mt. Sopris. Country decor with antiques adorn each room. There is an outdoor hot tub. Full breakfast is provided. No smoking. No pets. $60-95.

B&B Reservation Service of Colorado and Vail

P.O. Box 491, 81658
(303) 949-1212; (800) 748-2666

C.C.'s. Hot tub under a star-filled sky warms guests after a long day on the slopes. Hosts are restaurateurs who serve a hearty breakfast. Five minutes to Snowmass Mountain and 15 minutes to downtown Aspen. On bus route. No smoking. $65.

Main Street. All rooms are richly appointed, opening up to a center room lounge. They offer wet bars, refrigerators, cable TV, and telephones. On the premises is a heated pool, Jacuzzi, and parking lot. A river-rock fireplace cascades the lounge where a Continental breakfast and a wine and cheese party are served daily. Great for traveling couples.

What a View! For the feel of being in the mountains with a great view, this is it! A former home that has been renovated into four units, this apartment was the family's patio overlooking Aspen highlands and Maroon Bells. Within walking distance of downtown Aspen, these rooms offer plenty of privacy with a lock-off master bedroom suite and a sunken Japanese tub in the bathroom. A warm, comfortable stay. $65-75.

Boomerang Lodge

500 West Hopkins, 81611
(303) 925-3416; (800) 992-8852

This unique ski lodge in the quiet West End is within walking distance to downtown or the music festival. All guest rooms and fireplace apartments have a sunny patio or balcony, thanks to the handsome design influenced by the owner-architect's teacher, Frank Lloyd Wright. Thoughtful touches include pool, whirlpool, and sauna. Additional winter amenities include afternoon tea and town courtesy van. Discover why devoted guests return to Boomerang.

Hosts: Charles and Fonda Paterson
Rooms: 35 (PB) $93-174
Continental Breakfast
Credit Cards: A, B, C, E
Notes: 2, 5, 8, 11, 12, 13, 14

Crestahaus Lodge

1301 East Cooper Avenue, 81611
(303) 925-7081; (800) 344-3853

Experience European charm in the heart of the Rockies. Thirty-one distinctive rooms and one suite feature private baths, telephones, cable TV, and most have mountain views. Lodge amenities include Jacuzzi and sauna, heated pool (open summers only), daily housekeeping, complimentary breakfast buffet, après ski appetizers, and drinks (winter only). Choose between rustic-traditional rooms in the main lodge, or deluxe-contemporary rooms. Enjoy two fireplace areas, barbecue/patio area, and year-round hospitality and comfort. Airport transportation and free shuttle downtown (one-quarter mile).

Host: Melinda Goldrich
Rooms: 31 (PB) $50-175
Continental Breakfast
Credit Cards: A, B, E
Notes: 2, 5, 6, 8, 9, 10, 11, 12, 13, 14

Little Red Ski Haus

118 East Cooper Street, 81611
(303) 925-3333

Charming 107-year-old Victorian three blocks from the center of town. No TV, but always interesting conversation. One could travel the world just sitting in the living room. The house is very popular with Australians. Exceptionally clean and friendly, especially suited to those traveling alone. Full breakfast only served in the winter. Closed April 10 through May 31.

Hosts: Marge Babcock and Derek Brown
Rooms: 20 (PB/SB) $23-60
Full and Continental Breakfast
Credit Cards: A, B
Notes: 4, 8, 9, 10, 11, 12, 13, 14

Sardy House
Hotel and Restaurant

128 East Main Street, 81611
(303) 920-2525; (800) 321-3457

One of Aspen's finest historic residences, now an elegant hotel, beautifully restored and graciously appointed in the Victorian tradition. Winner of the Mobil four-star award. "Outstanding...a special trip." Blue-green spires of Colorado spruce, among them the tallest in Aspen, rise above the hotel's landscaped grounds. Amenities include a heated pool, spa, sauna, and concierge. Fine dining is offered in the Victorian dining room.

Host: Jayne Poss
Rooms: 14 (PB) $160-550
Suites: 6
Full Breakfast
Credit Cards: A, B, C, E
Notes: 2, 4, 5, 8, 9, 10, 12, 13, 14

6 Pets welcome; 7 Smoking allowed; 8 Children welcome; 9 Social drinking allowed; 10 Tennis available; 11 Swimming available; 12 Golf available; 13 Skiing available; 14 May be booked through travel agents.

Snow Queen Victorian Lodge Bed and Breakfast

124 East Cooper Street, 81611
(303) 925-8455; (303) 925-6971

This quaint, family-operated Victorian ski lodge was built in the 1880s. The charming parlor has a fireplace and color TV for guests. There is a variety of rooms with private baths, plus two kitchen units. The lodge is in town, within walking distance of restaurants, shops, and the ski area. A nice outdoor hot tub is available. Lower rates are available during off-season and summer. Closed April 15 through May 15.

Hosts: Norma Dolle and Larry Ledingham
Rooms: 5 (PB) $65-138
Continental Breakfast
Credit Cards: A, B, C
Notes: 2, 7, 8, 9, 10, 11, 12, 13, 14

BASALT

Altamira Ranch Bed and Breakfast

23484 Highway 82, 81621
(303) 927-3309

Beautiful ranch 15 minutes from Aspen on the Roaring Fork River, a gold medal trout stream. Enjoy quiet, peaceful country atmosphere adjacent to skiing, hiking, river sports, and famous Glenwood Hot Springs. Antique shop on the premises. Guests' home away from home.

Host: Martha Waterman
Rooms: 2 (SB) $65
Full Breakfast
Credit Cards: A, B
Notes: 2, 5, 8 (over 6), 9, 13, 14

Shenandoah Inn

600 Frying Pan Road, Box 578, 81621
(303) 927-4991

Contemporary western Colorado bed and breakfast is on two riverfront acres on the Frying Pan River, one of North America's premier trout streams, in the heart of the White River National Forest. Twenty minutes from Aspen and Glenwood Hot Springs; year-round access to the best of Colorado outdoors. Enjoy the riverside hot tub, warm, friendly atmosphere, and exceptional cuisine.

Hosts: Bob and Terri Ziets
Rooms: 4 (2SB; 2 PB) $70-90
Full Gourmet Breakfast
Credit Cards: None
Notes: 2, 5, 9, 10, 12, 13, 14

BOULDER

Bed and Breakfast Agency of Colorado at Vail

P.O. 491, Vail, CO 81658
(303) 949-1212; (800) 748-2666

Greenwood. There is a bright sunny feeling in this home, which has been decorated with a Southwest contemporary flair. The second floor is just for guests; the bedrooms have a great view of the mountains, and guests can relax in the private sitting room. The hostess, a Colorado native who also designed the home, serves a Continental breakfast. Lovely garden for warm weather enjoyment. One block from bus. No smoking. $50-60.

Bed and Breakfast at Sunset House

1740 Sunset Boulevard, 80304
(303) 444-0801

Two rooms offered with shared bath and a private entrance. The family room has a cozy fireplace, small library, and a TV. Outside patios overlook the city to the south and the Flatirons to the west. Bicycles are available for use on Boulder's nearby bike paths. The Pearl Street Mall is a ten-minute walk away. Taikoo, a Shih Tzu mix is the resident dog. Sunset House is a nonsmoking environment.

Hosts: Phyllis and Roger Olson
Rooms: 2 (SB) $60
Full Breakfast

NOTES: Credit cards accepted: A MasterCard; B Visa; C American Express; D Discover Card; E Diner's Club; F Other; 2 Personal checks accepted; 3 Lunch available; 4 Dinner available; 5 Open all year;

Credit Cards: None
Notes: 2, 5, 9

The Boulder Victoria Historic Bed and Breakfast

1305 Pine Street, 80302
(303) 938-1300

Downtown Boulder's exquisitely renovated Victorian inn offers seven unique guest rooms that feature antique furniture, private baths, telephone, and TV. Enjoy tea and scones in the elegant parlor, luxuriate in a private steam shower, or enjoy breakfast in the bay-windowed dining room. Soak in Boulder's sun on the spacious patio. Convenient to downtown, campus, and mountain activities.

Hosts: Kristen Peterson and Zoe Kircos
Rooms: 7 (PB) $114-164
Continental Breakfast
Credit Cards: A, B, C
Notes: 2, 5, 9, 10, 11, 12, 13, 14

The Castle House

977 Ninth Street, 80302
(303) 444-2340

This historic home with two guest rooms specializes in personal attention and is perfect to enjoy the best of Boulder on University Hill. It has been lovingly restored by the owners and reflects their desire to provide guests with an elegant retreat. Lovely grounds with resident dog and two cats. Fresh flowers, silver and china, refreshments, and great breakfasts make for a memorable visit. No pets. No children. No smoking.

Hosts: Pam and Bill Schlenzig
Rooms: 2 (PB) $75
Full Breakfast
Cards: None
Notes: 2, 5, 9, 10, 11, 12, 13, 14

Creekside Bed and Breakfast

1125 Gapter Road, 80303
(303) 494-5022

Creekside is a charming and welcoming home within minutes of central Boulder. This comfortable inn sits on two wooded acres with a beautiful creek running amidst lush gardens. Creekside is a lovely natural setting. Each of the three rooms includes queen-size beds, soft flannel sheets, and handmade quilts. One private bath. No pets. No children. No smoking.

Hosts: Jennifer McKeown and Alice Defler
Rooms: 3 (1 PB; 2 SB) $65-120
Full Breakfast
Cards: A, B
Notes: 2, 5, 9, 10, 11, 12, 13

The Magpie Inn on Mapleton Hill

1001 Spruce, 80302
(303) 449-6528

The Magpie Inn employed nine local interior designers to refurbish the mansion. Each room was given special and unique attention from one of the designers, with the focus being romance with a Victorian theme. The result is a collection of antiques, custom furniture, and softly-hued fabrics to elicit memories of an elegant home. Visual delights abound from marble fireplaces and fine paintings, to old photographs and prints of Boulder.

Rooms: 7 (5 PB; 2 SB) $88-135
Credit Cards: A, B
Notes: 2, 5, 9, 11, 12, 13

Pearl Street Inn

1820 Pearl Street, 80302
(303) 444-5584; (800) 232-5949

The Pearl Street Inn blends the privacy and service of a country bed and breakfast with the amenities of a luxury hotel. The rooms, which encircle a garden courtyard, have antique furniture, full bath, fireplace, and cable TV. The inn is three blocks from a famous pedestrian mall and only a few minutes from the University of Colorado.

6 Pets welcome; 7 Smoking allowed; 8 Children welcome; 9 Social drinking allowed; 10 Tennis available; 11 Swimming available; 12 Golf available; 13 Skiing available; 14 May be booked through travel agents.

Host: Cynthia Dunken
Rooms: 7 (PB) $72-128
Continental Breakfast
Credit Cards: A, B, C, D
Notes: 2, 4, 5, 9, 10, 11, 12, 13, 14

Pearl Street Inn

BRECKENRIDGE

Allaire Timbers Inn

9511 Highway 9, South Main Street, 80424
(303) 453-7530

This award winning mountain inn combines contemporary Southwestern and rustic log furnishings in a newly constructed
log setting. Guest rooms have private bath
and deck with mountain views. Suites offer
private fireplace and hot tub. Great room
with fireplace, sunroom, loft, and outdoor
spa all have spectacular views of the
Colorado Rockies. Hearty breakfast and
afternoon happy hour included daily.
Wheelchair accessible. In Breckenridge,
Colorado's oldest Victorian mountain town,
offering an abundance of year-round activities. Nonsmoking inn.

Hosts: Jack and Kathy Gumph
Rooms: 10 (PB) $115-250
Full Breakfast
Credit Cards: A, B, C, D
Notes: 2, 5, 9, 10, 11, 12, 13, 14

Bed and Breakfast Agency of Colorado at Vail

P.O. 491, Vail, CO 81658
(303) 949-1212; (800) 748-2666

Cotton House. Cozy 1886 Victorian in
Historic District with three beautiful turn-
of-the-century rooms. Full breakfast, fresh-
ground coffee, and afternoon refreshments
in a friendly environment. All attractions
within walking distance. Common room
with mountain view offers a home-away-
from-home atmosphere. $50-90.

Fireside Inn. This inn, housed in an 1880
building, is only two blocks from Main
Street in the National Historic District of
the town. The inn offers a variety of accommodations: a suite, rooms with private
baths, or dorm facilities with shared baths.
A hot tub and parlor with open-hearth fireplace are on the property. Breakfasts include Sourdough French toast, eggs, and
buttermilk pancakes. Ski and golf packages
available. $45-90.

Hummingbird House. Enter through the
private entrance reserved for guests and
enjoy a beautiful mountain view. Hand-
painted chairs and knickknacks, stenciled
ducks, and bears decorate the home and
breakfast nook. A kitchenette with microwave and refrigerator is available. Two
suites with private bath are offered. Outside
hot tub. Full breakfast served. Smoking permitted unless other guests object. $49-89.

Wellington Inn. Upscale luxury Victorian
Inn, with spectacular mountain views of the
ski area from balconies off each of the four
guest rooms with Jacuzzi tubs. Complimentary sherry in the rooms. Full hearty breakfast; afternoon tea or wine-and-cheese. No
smoking. $99-199.

Williams House. Enjoy a romantic get-away in a beautifully restored mining home and private Victorian cottage, furnished in fine antiques. Two parlors graced with mantled fireplaces are in the main house. The lovely cottage has fireplace, Jacuzzi, and parlor. Outdoor hot tub. Great breakfasts. $69-200.

B&B Reservation Service of Colorado and Vail

P.O. Box 491, 81658
(303) 949-1212; (800) 748-2666

Breckenridge Inn 1. Two blocks from downtown shops and restaurants on the free shuttle bus during ski season, this inn offers free parking and ski storage. In the historic section of this Victorian mining town, this inn offers guests comfortable accommodations and use of a central living room with TV, games, books, and fireplace. Summer activities include hiking, backpacking, bicycling, four-wheeling, sailing, horseback riding, golf, and rafting. If meeting people and spending time with travelers who want a true bed and breakfast experience is appealing, guests will enjoy staying at this inn.

Mountain Crest. This lovely, contemporary cedar home sits in a large, peaceful forest one and one-half miles south of the Breckenridge ski area. With a private entrance, guests have a large sitting room with a full-size pool table, color TV, and wood-burning stove. Full breakfast on weekends; Continental on weekdays. Cross-country skiing available from the front door in winter; hiking trails to lakes in summer. No smoking. $80-85.

Cotten House

102 South French Street, P.O. Box 387, 80424
(303) 453-5509

In the heart of beautiful historic Breckenridge, the Cotten House is a restored 1886 Victorian with a full view of the ten-mile range. Three clean, fully decorated rooms with flowers await guests. A hearty seven-day menu breakfast and afternoon refreshments are served. Winter activities are available at the front door on the free bus. Evening activities and restaurants are two blocks away. Spring, summer, and fall events, and sports make this area unforgettable. AAA approved.

Hosts: Pete and Georgette Contos
Rooms: 3 (1 PB; 2 SB) $50-90
Full Breakfast
Credit Cards: None
Notes: 2, 5, 8, 9, 10, 11, 12, 13

Muggins Gulch Inn

4023 Tiger Road
P.O. Box 3756, 80424
(303) 453-7414

The inn is a unique post-and-beam lodge on 160 secluded acres surrounded by the Arapaho National Forest. Hiking and biking on the Colorado Trail from the doorstep. Golf is four miles away; snowmobiling, skiing, and the excitement of Breckenridge just minutes away. Two charming rooms with private baths. Two spacious suites. Enjoy the great-room with huge fireplace. Hearty breakfast and afternoon snack. No pets. No children. No smoking.

Hosts: Bethanne and Tom Hossley
Rooms: 4 (PB) $65-195
Full Breakfast
Cards: A, B
Notes: 2, 5, 9, 12, 13, 14

Swan Mountain Inn

P.O. Box 2900, Denver; 16172 Highway 9, Breckenridge, 80435
(800) 578-3687

The Swan Mountain Inn strives to combine a warm, cozy environment with luxury and

---

6 Pets welcome; 7 Smoking allowed; 8 Children welcome; 9 Social drinking allowed; 10 Tennis available; 11 Swimming available; 12 Golf available; 13 Skiing available; 14 May be booked through travel agents.

pampering to give its guests the perfect Colorado getaway. Exceptional fireside dining for breakfast and dinner, a full-service bar, private and starlit hot tubs, TV/VCR, movies, and beautiful decor. The location is less than ten minutes to four of the hottest Colorado ski areas and golf courses. On the bike path, next to the Blue River and Lake Dillon. No pets. Children welcome. No smoking.

Rooms: 4 (3 PB; 1 SB) $40-135
Full Breakfast
Cards: A, B, D
Notes: 2, 3 (summer), 4, 5, 8, 9, 10, 11, 12, 13, 14

The Walker House

103 South French Street, Box 509, 80424
(305) 453-2426; (800) 365-6365

A small restored log home in the historic district. Original 100–year–old furnishings. Walking distance to town and ski slopes. Two bedrooms; one private bath, one shared bath. Vegetarian-style breakfast, light snacks, coffee, and tea. Very quiet rooms without TV. Near large indoor recreation center with swimming pools. Two- and three-day minimum. No pets. No children. No alcohol. No smoking.

Host: Sue Ellen Strong
Rooms: 2 (1 PB; 1 SB) $89-112
Full Breakfast
Cards: A, B, C, D, E
Notes: 3 , 4, 10, 11, 12, 13, 14

Williams House, Circa 1885, and Willoughby Cottage, Circa 1880

303 North Main Street, P.O. Box 2454, 80424
(303) 453-2975; (800) 795-2975

Restored historic mining home furnished with fine antiques. Two romantic parlors, each with mantled fireplaces, are available for guests' use, and bedrooms have private baths. Hearty miners' breakfast with homemade baked goods is served each morning, and refreshments are served each afternoon.

Enjoy an outdoor hot tub and mountain views. Adjacent Victorian cottage for two has a large Jacuzzi, fireplace, and sitting room. In the historic district on the trolley route. Approved by Bed and Breakfast Innkeepers of Colorado.

Hosts: Diane Jaynes and Fred Kinat
Rooms: 4 (PB) $69-136
Cottage: 1 (PB) $165-225
Full Breakfast
Credit Cards: C
Notes: 2, 3, 5, 9, 10, 11, 12, 13, 14

BUENA VISTA

Bed and Breakfast Agency of Colorado at Vail

P.O. 491, Vail, CO 81658
(303) 949-1212; (800) 748-2666

Buena Vista Inn. This original 1890 boarding house has been totally refurbished by its new owners and offers four rooms and a cabin. Decorated with country furnishings and antiques. Wake up and enjoy a full breakfast. Cakes and goodies are offered throughout the day, with a variety of teas and coffees. Satellite TV, video library, and three common areas for relaxing. No smoking. No pets. $65-75.

CARBONDALE

The Ambiance Inn

66 North 2nd Street, 81623
(303) 963-3597

Enjoy Aspen, Glenwood Springs, and the beautiful Crystal Valley from this spacious chalet-style home featuring vaulted ceilings throughout. The 1950s ski lodge decor of the very large Aspen Suite or the Victorian elegance of the Sonoma Room featuring a romantic four-poster bed are ideal for getaways. The Santa Fe Room is alive with the warmth of the Southwest. All rooms adjoin the library-sitting room on the balcony. The

Kauai Room features atmosphere and a two-person Jacuzzi.

Hosts: Norma and Robert Morris
Rooms: 4 (PB) $60-80
Full Breakfast
Credit Cards: A, B, C
Notes: 2, 5, 9, 10, 11, 12, 13, 14

COLORADO SPRINGS

Holden House—1902 Bed and Breakfast Inn

1102 West Pikes Peak Avenue, 80904
(719) 471-3980

A 1902 storybook Victorian and a 1906 carriage house filled with antiques and heirlooms. Immaculate accommodations in a residential area near historic district and central to the Pikes Peak region. Enjoy the parlor, living room with fireplace, or veranda with mountain views. Guest rooms boast queen-size beds, down pillows, and private baths. Honeymoon suites with tubs for two, fireplaces, and more! Complimentary refreshments. Friendly resident cats named "Muffin" and "Mingtoy." "Experience the Romance of the Past with the Comforts of Today." AAA and Mobil approved. One room is handicapped accessible. Minimum-stay requirements for holidays, special events, and during high season.

Hosts: Sallie and Welling Clark
Rooms: 2 (PB) $70-75
Suites: 4 (PB) $95-105
Full Breakfast
Credit Cards: A, B, C, D, E
Notes: 2, 5, 9, 10, 11, 12, 14

Hughes Hacienda

12060 Calle Corvo, 80926
(719) 576-2060

Hughes Hacienda is a Colorado country bed and breakfast on 19 secluded acres at the foot of Blue Mountain, with magnificent views of the mountains, the Red Rock Valley, and the twinkle of city lights in the dis-

tance at night. There are hiking trails, and a hot tub to relax in. The hosts serve a gourmet Southwestern-style breakfast. Twenty minutes from downtown Colorado Springs and the airport.

Hosts: Wayne and Carol Hughes
Rooms: 1 (PB) $85-100
Full and Continental Breakfast
Credit Cards: A, B, D
Notes: 2, 5, 9, 10, 11, 12, 13, 14

Our Hearts Inn Old Colorado City

2215 West Colorado Avenue, 80904
(719) 473-8684; (800) 533-7095

This 100–year–old Victorian, two blocks from the heart of historic Old Colorado City, unique restaurants, and shops Hand-stenciled inn, with original, unusual plaster detail, and arched nine-foot ceilings. Furnished with antiques and a "rocker for every room." Cottage has a western-theme, catering to families and week long stays with a small kitchen facility. Full breakfast served. Desserts and coffee in the evening. Children welcome. No smoking.

Hosts: Pat and Andy Fejedelem
Rooms: 3 (PB) $60-90
Full Breakfast
Cards: A, B, D
Notes: 2, 5, 8, 10, 11, 12, 14

The Painted Lady Bed and Breakfast Inn

1318 West Colorado Avenue, 80904
(719) 473-3165

This restored 1894 Victorian home is complete with gingerbread trim, wraparound porches, coach lights, and wonderful mountain views. Inside, guest rooms feature lace curtains and period furnishings. One room includes a claw-foot tub for two. Common rooms are bright and inviting. A hearty breakfast is served. Convenient to Pike's Peak, shopping, and historic Old Colorado City. Skiing only two hours away. Resident cat on hand to greet you. No guest pets. Children over ten. No smoking.

Hosts: Valerie and Zan Maslowski
Rooms: 4 (2 PB; 2 SB) $55-75
Full Breakfast
Cards: A, B, D
Notes: 2, 5, 8 (over 10), 9, 10, 11, 12, 14

CREEDE

Creede Hotel

Box 284, 81130
(719) 658-2608

The hotel is a landmark in Creede, dating back to the wild days of the silver boom. Four rooms, all with private baths, have been individually restored. The hotel dining room is open to the public and noted for its delicious food. Guests love Creede and the hotel! "Warm hospitality. . . capturing the lure of the 1890s."

Hosts: Cathy and Rich Ormsby
Rooms: 4 (PB) $59-69
Full Breakfast
Credit Cards: A, B, D
Notes: 2, 3, 4, 9

CRESTED BUTTE

Bed and Breakfast Agency of Colorado at Vail

P.O. 491, Vail, CO 81658
(303) 949-1212; (800) 748-2666

Inn at Crested Butte. An inviting inn where the charm of the past and the amenities of the present can be found. Features 17 rooms, each with private bath, pine bed, armoire, and warm down comforters. The views from these rooms of the surrounding mountains are spectacular. Enjoy the deluxe Continental breakfast by the fireplace in the spacious great room, stroll on the second-floor sun deck or relax in the Jacuzzi. For guests requiring special assistance, all ADA requirements are met and elevator service is available to all rooms. No smoking.

Purple Mountain Lodge

Box 897, 81224
(303) 349-5888

Guests enjoy sharing their adventures and discussing plans in the living room by a fire in the massive stone fireplace. If conversation slows, cable TV is available. The spa in the sunroom offers welcome relief to tired muscles. Crested Butte is 8,885 feet above sea level in an open valley surrounded by the Elk Mountains. It has many trails and roads to explore by foot, mountain bike, horseback, or four-wheel-drive automobile. Nearby mountain lakes and streams provide canoeing, kayaking, rafting, and fishing.

Hosts: Walter and Sherron Green
Rooms: 5 (3 PB; 2 SB) $55-90
Full Breakfast
Credit Cards: A, B, D, E
Notes: 2, 5, 6, 8, 9, 10, 12, 13, 14

CRIPPLE CREEK

Bed and Breakfast Agency of Colorado at Vail

P.O. 491, Vail, CO 81658
(303) 949-1212; (800) 748-2666

Cripple Creek Hospitality House. The host has completely renovated this 1900 former hospital to create an award-winning building with 18 guest rooms. Outside, relax in the gazebo hot tub; watch the world (and the gamblers) go by from either of two enclosed porches. On-site amenities include a beauty parlor, game room, playground, and campground. Many casinos are within walking distance. $49-99.

CORTEZ

Bed and Breakfast Agency of Colorado at Vail

P.O. 491, Vail, CO 81658
(303) 949-1212; (800) 748-2666

NOTES: Credit cards accepted: A MasterCard; B Visa; C American Express; D Discover Card; E Diner's Club; F Other; 2 Personal checks accepted; 3 Lunch available; 4 Dinner available; 5 Open all year;

Lost Canyon Lake Lodge. This gateway to the San Juan Mountains, is 20 minutes from Mesa Verde and 40 miles from Durango. Built on a lake in 1983, it features five bedrooms, two overlooking the lake. Offers a full breakfast and afternoon refreshments. Hot tub. No smoking allowed. $60-90.

DENVER

Bed and Breakfast Agency of Colorado at Vail

P.O. 491, Vail, CO 81658
(303) 949-1212; (800) 748-2666

The Tree House. A charming guest house in the middle of a ten-acre forest, with 60-foot oaks and maples all around. Balconies on the front and back provide a perfect spot for breakfast or afternoon tea. Five bedrooms each have private baths; four have wood-burning fireplaces. Full breakfasts. Guests are welcome to use the kitchen and laundry facilities. No smoking. No pets. $65-95.

Castle Marne

1572 Race Street, 80206
(303) 331-0621; (800) 92 MARNE

Come, fall under the spell of one of Denver's grandest historic mansions. Built in 1889, the Marne is on both the local and national historic registers. Guests' stay is a unique experience in pampered luxury. Minutes from the finest cultural, shopping, sightseeing attractions, and the convention center, 12 minutes from Stapleton International Airport. Ask about the candlelight dinners.

Castle Marne

Hosts: The Peiker family
Rooms: 9 (PB) $85-190
Full Breakfast
Credit Cards: A, B, C, E
Notes: 2, 5, 9, 10, 11, 12, 13, 14

Haus Berlin

1651 Emerson Street, 80218
(303) 837-9527

Haus Berlin, a newly renovated Victorian townhouse in a historic district, is on a quiet tree-lined street just minutes from downtown Denver. Three bedrooms and one suite have either queen- or king-size beds. All the bed and bath linens are superior 100-percent cotton and the decor is a beautiful eclectic mix of the old and the new. Come and enjoy. Hosts are urban, friendly, and comfortable, just like their guests.

Hosts: Christiana and Dennis Brown
Rooms: 4 (PB) $85-120
Continental Breakfast
Credit Cards: A, B, C
Notes: 5, 9, 10, 12, 13

The Oxford Hotel

1600 17th Street, 80202
(303) 628-5400

Built in 1891, the landmark Oxford Hotel is celebrating its 102nd birthday. Renovated in 1983, the rooms are furnished with 19th-century French and English antiques. Amenities include complimentary coffee service, sherry service, shoe shine, turndown with chocolates, morning newspaper, and limousine service. Adjacent health club and European city spa. In historic lower downtown less than one block from Union train station and close to shopping, dining, and the arts complex.

6 Pets welcome; 7 Smoking allowed; 8 Children welcome; 9 Social drinking allowed; 10 Tennis available; 11 Swimming available; 12 Golf available; 13 Skiing available; 14 May be booked through travel agents.

Host: Jill Johnson
Rooms: 81 (PB) $95-275
Continental Breakfast
Credit Cards: A, B, C, D, E
Notes: 2, 3, 4, 5, 7, 8, 9, 14

The Queen Anne Inn

The Queen Anne
Bed and Breakfast Inn

2147 Tremont Place, 80205
(303) 296-6666; (800) 432-INNS (out of state)
FAX (303) 296-2151

Experience history, elegance, and warm
hospitality in side-by-side Victorians facing
a park on a quiet street that is within walking distance of downtown Denver's pedestrian mall, state capitol, shops, museums,
restaurants, theaters, convention center, and
businesses. Enjoy a full breakfast, period
furnishings, private baths, chamber music,
fresh flowers, telephones, and off-street
parking. Choose from 14 individually decorated rooms, including four "gallery suites"
dedicated to artists Remington, Rockwell,
Audubon, and Calder. The inn has been
named among the ten most romantic across
the country, the ten best nationally, Best of
Denver, and is AAA and Mobil rated.

Host: Tom King
Rooms: 14 (PB) $75-155
Full Breakfast
Credit Cards: A, B, C, D, E
Notes: 2, 5, 9, 10, 12, 14

Victoria Oaks Inn

1575 Race Street, 80206
(303) 355-1818

The warmth and hospitality of Victoria
Oaks Inn is apparent the moment guests
enter this historic restored 1896 mansion.
Elegant original oak woodwork, tile fireplaces, and dramatic hanging staircase replete with ornate brass chandelier set the
mood for a delightful visit.

Hosts: Clyde and Rie
Rooms: 9 (1 PB; 8 SB) $55-85
Continental Breakfast
Credit Cards: A, B, C, E, F
Notes: 2, 5, 6, 7, 8, 9, 10, 11, 12, 14

DILLON

Bed and Breakfast Agency
of Colorado at Vail

P.O. 491, Vail, CO 81658
(303) 949-1212; (800) 748-2666

Annabelle's. This quiet home provides
comfortable and economical accommodations convenient to an area full of activity.
It offers four large bedroom suites, with
private bath, daily maid service, TV, telephone, laundry facilities, and storage
space for skis. Swimming, Jacuzzi, and
sauna are available, as is parking. Continental plus breakfast includes homemade
coffeecakes, bagels, fruits, yogurt, coffee,
tea, espresso, or cappucino. No smoking
and no pets. $45-100.

Home and Hearth. This large, warm, and
comfortable home, decorated with antiques, offers a choice of double, twin, or
bunk rooms. Good food and company
abound. Home away from home. Outside
hot tub. $45-85.

NOTES: Credit cards accepted: A MasterCard; B Visa; C American Express; D Discover Card; E Diner's
Club; F Other; 2 Personal checks accepted; 3 Lunch available; 4 Dinner available; 5 Open all year;

Paradox Lodge

35 Montezuma Road, 80435
(303) 468-9445

Paradox Lodge is a secluded 37-acre Alpine location surrounded by Arapahoe National Forest providing picturesque views of mountain peaks and forests along the Continental Divide. Guests may have a choice of a comfortable, completely furnished cabin that can sleep five or a room for two in the main lodge. A wood-fired outdoor hot tub is available for guest use.

Hosts: George and Connie O' Bleness
Rooms: 7 (3 PB; 4 SB) $50-120
Continental Breakfast
Credit Cards: A, B, C, D, E
Notes: 2, 5, 6 and 7 (limited), 8, 12, 13, 14

DOLORES

Historic Rio Grande Southern Hotel

101 South 5th Street, P.O. Box 516
(303) 882-7527

This historic railroad hotel was built in 1893. On the town square, it is within walking distance to the Dolores River and McFee Reservoir. Within driving distance are Mesa Verde National Park, Anasazi Heritage Center, Crow Canyon, and golfing. Fishing, skiing, hunting, backpacking, and bicycling are available in the area. Ski Telluride half-price program available. Open year-round. There is a suite available as well.

Hosts: Cathy and Fred Green
Rooms: 9 (3 PB; 6 SB) $45-120
Full Breakfast
Credit Cards: A, B
Notes: 2, 3, 4, 5, 7, 8, 9, 10, 11, 12, 13, 14

Mountain View Bed and Breakfast

28050 County Road P, 81323
(303) 882-7861

Mountain View is in the "four corners area," and is one mile from the gateway to the San Juan Skyway, a nationally designated 238-mile scenic loop, and 12 miles from the entrance to Mesa Verde National Park. Mountain View includes 22 acres with walking trails, cottonwood-lined stream, and canyon. On the west slope of the San Juan Mountains at an elevation of 6,500 feet overlooking the beautiful Montezuma Valley.

Hosts: Brenda and Cecil Dunn
Rooms: 8 (PB) $49-59
Full Breakfast
Credit Cards: A, B
Notes: 2, 5, 8, 11, 12, 13, 14

DURANGO

B&B Reservation Service of Colorado and Vail

P.O. Box 491, 81658
(303) 949-1212; (800) 748-2666

Country Sunshine. Nestled below rocky bluffs, there's a spectacular view of the San Juan Mountains from this spacious ranch home. Enjoy the sound of the Animas River flowing or the sight of abundant wildlife from the deck. The bed and breakfast has spacious common areas and private baths, serves full hearty breakfasts, and is central to many area attractions. $77.

Gable House Bed and Breakfast

805 5th Avenue, 81301
(303) 247-4982

This Queen Anne Victorian mansion was built in 1892. A beautifully restored three-story home, with turret, balconies, and wraparound front porch, all overlooking a manicured private yard and gardens. Each room is intimate and elegantly appointed with antiques and unusual art pieces. A full breakfast is served in the formal dining

6 Pets welcome; 7 Smoking allowed; 8 Children welcome; 9 Social drinking allowed; 10 Tennis available; 11 Swimming available; 12 Golf available; 13 Skiing available; 14 May be booked through travel agents.

room on Blue Willow china and antique silver. This lovely historic home is five blocks from downtown Durango. Open June, July, and August.

Hosts: Heather and Jeffrey Bryson
Rooms: 3 (S2B) $65-85
Full Breakfast
Credit Cards: A, B
Notes: 2, 9, 10, 11, 12, 14

The Leland House Bed and Breakfast Suites Hotel

721 East Second Avenue, 81301
(303) 385-1920; (800) 664-1920; fax (303) 385-1967

Lovingly restored 1920s brick craftsman-style apartment house. Six rooms are actually three-room suites: kitchen, living room, and bedroom with private bath. Breakfast served in theVictorian cottage restaurant next door. Rooms are decorated with Southwestern and Cowboy Victoriana antiques. No pets. Children welcome. No smoking.

Hosts: Diane, Kirk, and Kara Komick
Rooms: 10 (PB)
Full Breakfast
Cards: A, B
Notes: 2, 3, 5, 8, 9, 13, 14

River House Bed and Breakfast

495 Animas View Drive, 81301
(303) 247-4775; (800) 544-0009

River House is a large, sprawling, Southwestern home facing the Animas River. Guests eat in a large atrium filled with plants, a water fountain, and eight skylights. Antiques, art, and artifacts from around the world decorate the seven bedrooms, snooker, and music room. Enjoy a soak in the hot tub before retiring to the living room to watch a favorite video on the large screen TV, and enjoy the warmth of the fire in the beautiful stone and brass fireplace. Comfort, casualness, and fun are themes.

Host: Crystal Carroll, and Kate and Lars Enggren
Rooms: 7 (PB) $70-95
Full Breakfast
Credit Cards: A, B, D
Notes: 2, 5, 8, 9, 10, 11, 12, 13, 14

Rochester Hotel

726 East Second Avenue, 81301
(303) 385-1920; (800) 664-1920; fax (303) 385-1967

Luxury accommodations in the Wild West! Western movies, made in the four-corners area, were the inspiration for the decor in this newly renovated 1890s hotel. Tall ceilings, wide hallways, and a beautifully landscaped courtyard add to the elegance. Cowboy Victoriana furnishings and antique accessories make the Rochester unique. Continental plus breakfast provided. No pets. No children. No smoking.

Hosts: Diane Komick and son Kirk
Rooms: 15 (PB) $112-185
Continental Breakfast
Cards: A, B
Notes: 2, 3, 5, 9, 12, 13, 14

Scrubby Oaks Bed and Breakfast Inn

P.O. Box 1047, 81302
(303) 247-2176

On ten acres overlooking the spectacular Animas Valley and surrounding mountains. Three miles from downtown Durango and one-half hour from Purgatory ski resort. Rooms are spacious and furnished with antiques, art works, and good books. Beautiful gardens and patios frame the inn outside, with large sitting areas inside for guest use.

Host: Mary Ann Craig
Rooms: 7 (3 PB; 4 S2B) $65-75
Full Breakfast
Credit Cards: None
Notes: 2, 5, 8, 9, 10, 11, 12, 13, 14

Strater Hotel

699 Main Avenue, 81301
(303) 247-4431; (800) 247-4431

NOTES: Credit cards accepted: A MasterCard; B Visa; C American Express; D Discover Card; E Diner's Club; F Other; 2 Personal checks accepted; 3 Lunch available; 4 Dinner available; 5 Open all year;

Built in 1887, the historic Strater Hotel surrounds its guests with one of the world's largest collections of Victorian walnut antiques which assures that each of the 93 guest rooms is unique. Visit the restaurant which features specialty cuisine and local favorites for breakfast, lunch, and dinner. There is a lounge offering live honky-tonk piano and costumed staff. Enjoy live music, light food, and libations at the Pelican's Nest. The Strater Hotel is in the heart of historic downtown shopping.

Host: Rod Barker
Rooms: 93 (PB) $54-145
Credit Cards: A, B, C, D, E
Notes: 2, 3, 4, 5, 7, 8, 9, 10, 11, 12, 13, 14

EMPIRE

Mad Creek Bed and Breakfast

167 West Park Avenue (US40); P.O. Box 404,
   80438
(303) 569-2003

1881 Victorian cottage filled with antiques, family heirlooms, original artwork, unique artifacts and old mountain charm. Relax in front of the rock fireplace, peruse the library filled with local lore, or plan adventures with the numerous Colorado guides and maps. At 8600 feet, Empire's picturesque valley is 42 miles west of Denver. Six major ski areas within 15 to 45 minutes. Rafting, hiking, biking, horseback riding, mine and train tours, fishing, and shopping. Hot tub available. No pets. No children. No smoking.

Hosts: Heather and Mike Lopez
Rooms: 3 (1 PB; 2 SB) $49-69
Full Breakfast
Cards: A, B
Notes: 2, 5, 9, 10, 11, 12, 13, 14

The Peck House

83 Sunny Avenue, P.O. Box 428, 80438
(303) 569-9870

Built in 1862, the Victorian rooms of this Colorado hotel abound with antiques, some

original. Denver and gambling in Central City and Black Hawk are conveniently close, as are many historic districts and landmarks. Rated five-star by a Colorado restaurant guide, the Signature restaurant of the owner/chef is considered one of the finest in Colorado. A finalist for Uncle

The Peck House

Ben's 1992 Ten Best Country Inns of the Year award. Lunch is available in the summer only.

Hosts: Gary and Sally St. Clair
Rooms: 11 (9 PB; 2 SB) $45-80
Continental Breakfast
Credit Cards: A, B, C, D, E, F
Notes: 2, 3, 4, 5, 7, 8, 9, 13, 14

ESTES PARK

Aspen Lodge at Estes Park

6120 Highway 7, 80517
(303) 586-8133; (800) 332-MTNS

This magnificent 3000-acre, year-round ranch resort celebrates Colorado's largest log lodge and cozy cabins with fantastic food, and recreation. Enjoy the incredible views and wildlife of the surrounding Rocky Mountain National Park, plus a multitude of activities. Enjoy the Sports Center, nearby golf and an exciting Children's program, as well as extensive winter activities, including snowmobiling and cross-country skiing. Advanced open- country horseback

6 Pets welcome; 7 Smoking allowed; 8 Children welcome; 9 Social drinking allowed; 10 Tennis available; 11 Swimming available; 12 Golf available; 13 Skiing available; 14 May be booked through travel agents.

riding on 36,000 acres that will stir the soul. Tennis and swimming. No pets. Children welcome. No smoking.

Hosts: Tom and Jill Hall
Rooms: 59 (PB) $99 ($240 including meals)
Full and Continental Breakfast
Cards: A, B, C, D, E
Notes: 2, 3, 4, 5, 8, 9, 10, 11, 12, 14

Big Horn Guest House

P.O. Box 4486, 80517
(303) 586-4175; (800) 734-0473

Big Horn Guest House is a lovely and intimate hideaway. Enjoy the gracious hospitality and warmth that abounds in this 1923 home, decorated with antiques that add to the relaxing and traditional atmosphere. Home-baked treats and goodies await, along with a scrumptious full Rocky Mountain breakfast (special diets are honored with advance notice) in the sunny breakfast area overlooking natural rock outcroppings. TVs in each guest room. Relax in the comfortable living room with its wood-burning fireplace, TV, and VCR, or just sit back and read or enjoy music. Some guests may even thrill to the sight of elk and deer that frequent the yard and neighborhood. Close to horseback riding, open air concerts, trolley tours, and the various other activities Estes Park has to offer.

Host: Calla Ferrari Haack
Rooms: 2 (SB) $60-75
Full Breakfast
Credit Cards: A, B
Notes: 2, 5, 10, 11, 12, 13 (cross-country), 14

Black Dog Inn
Bed and Breakfast

650 South St. Vrain Avenue; P.O. Box 4659, 80517
(303) 586-0374

Built in 1910, the Black Dog Inn was one of the earliest homes in Estes Park. It is snuggled among towering pine and aspen on a rolling acre with expansive view of the Mummy Range and Estes Valley. The inn consists of four comfortable rooms decorated with family antiques, private baths,

and tubs-for-two. Full breakfast served, refreshments, common areas, books, and movies will make you feel right at home. Cross-country skiing and snowshoeing. No pets. Children over 15. No smoking.

Hosts: Pete and Jane Princehorn
Rooms: 4 (PB) $70-130
Full Breakfast
Cards: A, B
Notes: 2, 5, 8 (over 15), 9, 10, 11, 12, 13 (cross-country), 14

Eagle Cliff
Bed and Breakfast

2383 Highway 66, Box 4312, 80517
(303) 586-5425

A warm and friendly facility nestled in ponderosa pines at the base of Eagle Cliff Mountain. Relax in the comfort of soft colors native to Southwestern decor, combined with the beautiful woods used in American antiques, to create warmth and hospitality. Enjoy the enticing aromas of a hearty country breakfast served in our bright and sunny breakfast nook Tender homemade breads and rolls and fresh fruit each morning. The abundant breakfast and "never empty" cookie jar keep guests ready for a full day of activities in the heart of Colorado's most spectacular landscapes.

Hosts: Nancy and Mike Conrin
Rooms: 3 (PB) $65-95
Full Breakfast
Credit Cards: None
Notes: 2, 5, 8, 9, 10, 11, 12

EVERGREEN

The Inn at Soda Creek

32163 Soda Creek Drive, 80439
(800) 670-3798

The Inn at Soda Creek is conveniently 30 miles west of Denver, almost halfway between Denver and the Continental Divide and less than one hour from the finest skiing in the world. Amenities of the inn include: commercial steam room, dry sauna, hot tub, exercise room and hiking area. Five guest rooms with beautiful decor. Private and shared baths. No children. No pets. Smoking outside only.

Host: Cyndi Gilliland
Rooms: 5 (3 PB; 2 SB) $75-120
Full Breakfast
Cards: A, B
Notes: 2, 5, 7 (limited), 10, 11, 12, 13, 14

FRISCO

Bed and Breakfast Agency of Colorado at Vail

P.O. 491, Vail, CO 81658
(303) 949-1212; (800) 748-2666

Finn Inn. This Frisco Country house welcomes guests with a beautiful mountain view from the large open living room and wraparound deck. The two bedrooms and bath downstairs can form a suite. A third bedroom upstairs has one double bed and one twin, with a private half-bath. The hot tub is on the outside deck; inside, there's a huge moss rock fireplace. Full and hearty country breakfast. $59-89.

Naomi's Nook. This home in a quiet neighborhood offers a one-bedroom suite with private entrance and bath. It accommodates up to four people with pullout bed, sitting room, TV, refrigerator, and laundry facilities. The entire floor is reserved for guests, although the hosts enjoy visiting and are happy to let visitors cuddle up to their wood-burning stove. Breakfast is served in suite or in the main living room. Hosts have lived in the area for over 20 years. $45-95.

Open Box H. Central in Summit County, just one-half block west of the Frisco Elementary School, close to six downhill ski areas, cross-country skiing, bikepaths, hiking, fishing, and sailing. All units are non-smoking and have private baths.

Homemade jams and goodies are offered for breakfasts before a hard day on the slopes or hiking. Outside hot tub. $49-99.

Frisco Lodge

321 Main Street, P.O. Box 1325, 80443
(303) 668-0195; (800) 279-6000

The Frisco Lodge, built in 1885, is the longest ongoing lodging facility in Summit County. It was a stagecoach stop as well as a facility serving train passengers on the D&RGW Railroad. The lodge is convenient to all the finer shops and restaurants in town. Outdoor hot tub, ski and bicycle tuning, storage room, free movies, and telephones. Great location near the extensive 50-plus mile paved bike path network. Central to all the Summit ski areas.

Host: Susan Wentworth
Rooms: 18 (10 PB; 8 SB) $30-90
Full Breakfast
Credit Cards: A, B, C, D
Notes: 2, 5, 8, 9, 10, 11, 12, 13, 14

Galena Street Mountain Inn

P.O. Box 417; 106 Galena Street, 80443
(303) 668-3224; (800) 248-9138

A wonderful combination of old world charm and mid-western comfort reminiscent of the Arts and Crafts movement of the 1920s, the Galena Street Mountain Inn is simplicity at its most luxurious. Striking Neo-mission style furnishing, down comforters, and window seats with stunning mountain views enhance each of the inn's 14 rooms. Amenities include gourmet breakfast, private baths, phones, cable TV, hot tub, sun deck, private porches, meeting rooms, complimentary beverages, and home baked treats.

Host: Brenda McDonnell
Rooms: 14 (PB) $79-150
Full Breakfast-Winter
Continental Breakfast-Summer
Credit Cards: A, B, C, D, E
Notes: 2, 5, 9, 10, 11, 12, 13, 14

---

6 Pets welcome; 7 Smoking allowed; 8 Children welcome; 9 Social drinking allowed; 10 Tennis available; 11 Swimming available; 12 Golf available; 13 Skiing available; 14 May be booked through travel agents.

MarDei's Mountain Retreat

221 South 4th Avenue, 80443
(303) 668-5337

MarDei's chalet architecture is influenced by and features European design interior. Guest rooms have twin, queen-, and king-size beds with down comforters. Hot tub and fireplaces available, and the inn is in the center of four ski areas. Bicycle trails, rafting, fishing, and sailing are also nearby.

Hosts. Carmen Abare and Jack Galbraith
Rooms: 5 (2 PB; 3 SB) $35-100
Full Breakfast
Credit Cards: None
Notes: 2, 5, 8, 9, 13

GEORGETOWN

The Hardy House Bed and Breakfast

605 Brownell, P.O. Box 0156, 80444
(303) 569-3388

This Victorian house, built in 1880, has four delightful rooms. There are TV/VCRs in all rooms, gas fireplace in one room, a parlor with potbellied stove for all guests to use, and a hot tub in the back yard. A full candlelight breakfast is served each morning. Historic Georgetown is within close proximity of seven major ski areas; Denver is only 45 minutes away; hiking and fishing locally; and beautiful shops and restaurants housed in some of the 200 Victorian homes and buildings. Carriage rides upon request. Guests are living the 1800s here in Georgetown.

Hosts: Carla and Mike Wagner
Rooms: 4 (PB) $73-102
Full Breakfast
Credit Cards: A, B (for guarantee only)
Notes: 2, 5, 8 (over 13), 9, 13, 14

Hillside House

1034 Main Street, P.O. Box 266, 80444
(303) 569-0912

High in the Colorado Rockies in the beautifully restored Victorian mining town of Georgetown, guests will find the Hillside House bed and breakfast. Enjoy the warmth of cathedral-planked floors and stained glass windows. Sit on the veranda in the evening and drink in the beauty of the majestic mountains. Choose the warm, cozy Rose Room overlooking the flower-filled garden and close mountains, or the Columbine suite with dormed ceiling, beautiful woodwork, and four-poster queen-size bed.

Hosts: Ken and Marge Acker
Rooms: 2 (PB) $60-75
Full Breakfast
Credit Cards: None
Notes: 2, 5, 8, 9, 13, 14

KIP on the Creek

1205 Rose Street, 80444
(800) 821-6545

On the banks of Clear Creek, in historic Georgetown, less than an hour's drive from Denver. The inn offers old-fashioned hospitality with hearty breakfasts and modern amenities. Decorated in antique oak and wicker, it exemplifies country teddy-bear warmth and charm.

Hosts: Sue and Terry Yordt
Rooms: 3 (PB) $60-80
Full Breakfast
Credit Cards: A, B
Notes: 2, 5, 7, 9, 13

GLENWOOD SPRINGS

Back In Time

927 Cooper, 81601
(303) 945-6183

A wonderful 1903 Victorian lovingly restored by owners. The spacious home is filled with antiques, family quilts, and clocks. Two bedrooms filled with antiques, down comforters, and quilts are available. A full breakfast is served in the dining room. Enjoy skiing in the winter, swimming and rafting in the summer. Within walking distance to shopping, dining, and the world's largest hot springs. Forty miles from Aspen. No children. No pets. No smoking.

Hosts: June and Ron Robinson
Rooms: 2 (PB) $55
Full Breakfast
Cards: A, B
Notes: 2, 5, 10, 11, 12, 13, 14

The Kaiser House

932 Cooper Avenue, 81601
(303) 945-8827; FAX (303) 945-8826

In the center of the "Spa of the Rockies," The Kaiser House features turn-of-century charm with 20th-century conveniences. On the corner of 10th Street and Cooper, The Kaiser House features seven bedrooms, each with attached baths, and each uniquely decorated in Victorian style. In the winter, before hitting the ski slopes, enjoy a gourmet breakfast in the spacious dining room or the sunny breakfast area. In the summer, enjoy brunch on the private patio. It's an easy walk to parks, shopping, and fine restaurants, and to the Hot Springs Pool and Vapor Caves.

Hosts: Ingrid and Glen Eash
Rooms: 7 (PB) $55-115
Full Breakfast
Credit Cards: A, B, D
Notes: 2, 5, 9, 10, 11, 12, 13, 14

GOLDEN

Antique Rose
Bed and Breakfast

1422 Washington Avenue, 80401
(303) 277-1893

The Antique Rose, a renovated 1880s Queen Anne Victorian home, features four tastefully appointed guest rooms, two with private baths, two with private whirlpool

baths. Rates include a full, formal American-style breakfast. Room occupancy is limited to two people; however, adjoining rooms can be booked to accommodate larger parties. Just 13 miles west of Denver near the Coors Brewery. Within easy access to major highways into the mountains and the gaming casinos of Blackhawk and Central City. Brochure available.

Innkeeper: Sharon Bennetts
Rooms: 4 (PB) $75-115
Full Breakfast
Credit Cards: A, B, C
Notes: 2, 5, 8, 9, 10, 11, 12, 13, 14

Bed and Breakfast Agency of Colorado at Vail

P.O. 491, Vail, CO 81658
(303) 949-1212; (800) 748-2666

Talmar. Enjoy elegant executive suites or champagne honeymoon weekends in these cozy country rooms. Fifteen minutes from downtown shops, and 20 minutes from casino, opera, and hot jazz. Fabulous full breakfasts include filet mignon and eggs Benedict. Horseback riding with lessons is also available on-site. The suite has private entrance, deck, and balcony, with sunken tub. You will leave this property wanting to return soon. $45-150.

The Dove Inn

711 14th Street, 80401-1906
(303) 278-2209

Charming Victorian inn in the foothills of west Denver, yet in the small-town atmosphere of Golden. Close to Coors tours, Rocky Mountain National Park; one hour to ski areas. No unmarried couples, please.

Hosts: Sue and Guy Beals
Rooms: 6 (4 PB; 2 SB) $48-70
Full Breakfast
Credit Cards: A, B, C, E
Notes: 2, 5, 8 (limited), 10, 11, 12, 13, 14

6 Pets welcome; 7 Smoking allowed; 8 Children welcome; 9 Social drinking allowed; 10 Tennis available;
11 Swimming available; 12 Golf available; 13 Skiing available; 14 May be booked through travel agents.

GRAND JUNCTION

The Cider House Bed and Breakfast

1126 Grand Avenue, 81501
(303) 242-9087

The Cider House Bed and Breakfast is at home in a 1907 frame house refurbished and decorated with wallpaper and lots of lace. Antiques and French doors carry out the Victorian theme. The guest rooms are queen-size with lots of light and quiet. A full breakfast is served in the formal dining room. The hostess enjoys entertaining and welcomes the opportunity to make the guests' travel experiences memorable.

Host: Helen Mills
Rooms: 4 (1 PB; 3 SB) $38-45
Full Breakfast
Credit Cards: A, B, C
Notes: 2, 3, 4, 5, 7 (limited) , 8, 10, 11, 12, 13

Junction Country Inn Bed and Breakfast

861 Grand Avenue, 81501
(303) 241-2817

The elegance of a turn-of-the-century show house, mixed with the comforts of home, awaits guests at Junction Country Inn. Four beautifully decorated rooms, with both private and shared baths. Hosts will gladly help with trip-planning. A delicious full breakfast and afternoon snack are served in the parlor and dining room. Children welcome. No pets. No smoking.

Hosts: The Bloom Family
Rooms: 4 (2 PB; 2 SB) $35-69
Full Breakfast
Cards: A, B, C
Notes: 2, 5, 8, 9, 10, 11, 12, 13, 14

GREELEY

Bed and Breakfast Agency of Colorado at Vail

P.O. 491, Vail, CO 81658
(303) 949-1212; (800) 748-2666

Sterling House. Enjoy the comfort and charm of this recently renovated 100-year-old Victorian, once the home of one of Greeley's pioneers. Two rooms, both decorated with antiques, are available with queen-size beds and private baths. Many amenities for the business traveler. Full gourmet breakfast. No pets. Smoking on the back-porch only. Children over 10 welcome. $45-55.

GREEN MOUNTAIN FALLS

Outlook Lodge

P.O. Box 5, 6975 Howard Street, 80819
(719) 684-2303

Built in 1889 as the parsonage for the church in the Wildwood, Outlook Lodge sits nestled in the pines of the scenic mountain town of Green Mountain Falls. Nearby hiking to the town's two waterfalls, close to horseback riding, fishing, swimming, and tennis. Short drive to Colorado Springs and its attractions. Lodge furnished with period antiques as well as local art. Large veranda. Delicious full gourmet breakfast. Open year-round. BBIC approved.

Hosts: Hayley and Patrick Moran
Rooms: 8 (6 PB; 2 SB) $45-70
Full Breakfast
Credit Cards: A, B
Notes: 2, 5, 8, 9, 10, 11, 12, 14

NOTES: Credit cards accepted: A MasterCard; B Visa; C American Express; D Discover Card; E Diner's Club; F Other; 2 Personal checks accepted; 3 Lunch available; 4 Dinner available; 5 Open all year;

GUNNISON

Mary Lawrence Inn

601 North Taylor Street, 81230
(303) 641-3343

Make this Victorian home the center of excursions through Gunnison County. The mountains, rivers, and lakes are extraordinary. Golf, swimming, rafting are accessible. The inn is furnished with antiques and collectibles. Breakfasts are bountiful and imaginative. Special fly fishing weekends. Great ski package offered for Crested Butte skiing.

Host: Jan Goin
Rooms: 3 (PB) $69
Suites: 2 (PB) $85
Full Breakfast
Credit Cards: A, B
Notes: 2, 5, 8, 10, 11, 12, 13, 14

IDAHO SPRINGS

Glacier House
Bed and Breakfast

603 Lake Road, 80452
(303) 567-0536

This unique homestay-style bed and breakfast, in a pine-nestled modern mountain chalet, offers guests very personal service, yet complete privacy. One large suite, with private entrance on the first floor, features a living area with large hot tub, a bedroom with queen-size cherry wood post bed and down comforter, and a full bath with shower massager. The living area is equipped with queen-size futon couch-bed, reading area, dinette, refrigerator, and coffee and tea makings. A full hearty breakfast is prepared for weekend guests. Continental breakfast is served on weekdays.

Host: Howard J. Cole
Rooms: 1 (PB) $65-75
Full Breakfast
Credit Cards: None
Notes: 2, 5, 9, 13

St. Mary's Glacier
Bed and Breakfast

336 Crest Drive, 80452-9709
(303) 567-4084

Enjoy majestic views of the Continental Divide, a waterfall and lake, from the deck of this handhewn-log mountain retreat. The guest rooms have brass king- or queen-size beds fit with electric blankets and covered with a handmade quilt. Private baths, Jacuzzi tubs, antiques, private balconies, afternoon refreshments, and a decanter of sherry to greet guests. Hiking and cross-country skiing are right outside the door. In the evening, return to a romantic suite or enjoy a roaring fire in the parlor, browse in the library, or relax in the hot tub. Breakfast is served near a cozy fireplace with spectacular views of the Rockies.

Hosts: Jackie and Steve Jacquin
Rooms: 5 (PB) $75-150
Full Breakfast
Credit Cards: A, B
Notes: 2, 4, 5, 9, 13, 14

LEADVILLE

Bed and Breakfast Agency
of Colorado at Vail

P.O. 491, Vail, CO 81658
(303) 949-1212; (800) 748-2666

Apple Blossom Inn. Originally built in 1879, this former banker's home features beautiful stained-glass windows, Victorian fireplaces, and hardwood floors. Eight rooms are available, with luscious brass and four-poster feather beds. It is in a historic district. Suite with kitchenette is also available. Delicious breakfasts. $55-115.

Historic Delaware Hotel

700 Harrison Avenue, 80461
(719) 486-1418; (800) 748-2004

Enjoy the ambiance of this historic hotel, circa 1886. Each of the 36 rooms features

6 Pets welcome; 7 Smoking allowed; 8 Children welcome; 9 Social drinking allowed; 10 Tennis available; 11 Swimming available; 12 Golf available; 13 Skiing available; 14 May be booked through travel agents.

antique furnishings and heirloom-style bedspreads. Each room features a private bath and TV. A Jacuzzi, Callaway's Restaurant, and Victorian lobby and lounge are also available for guests to enjoy.

Rooms: 36 (PB) $55-90
Full Breakfast
Credit Cards: A, B, C, D, E
Notes: 2, 3, 4, 5, 8, 9, 10, 11, 12, 13, 14

LOVELAND

The Lovelander
Bed and Breakfast Inn

217 West 4th Street, 80537
(303) 669-0798

Nestled against the Rocky Mountain foothills, minutes from Rocky Mountain National Park, The Lovelander is a rambling Victorian-style inn. Its beauty and elegance are characteristic of the turn of the century, when the home was built. Near restaurants, shops, museums, and art galleries, the Lovelander is a haven for business and recreational travelers and romantics. Meeting and reception facilities are available.

Hosts: Marilyn and Bob Wiltgen
Rooms: 11 (PB) $69-125
Full Breakfast
Credit Cards: A, B, C, D
Notes: 2, 5, 8 (over 10) , 9, 11, 12, 14

MANITOU SPRINGS

Gray's Avenue Hotel

711 Manitou Avenue, 80829
(719) 685-1277

This bed and breakfast is in the Manitou Springs Historic Preservation District. It was built in 1886 and opened as the "Avenue Hotel," one of the original seven hotels in this resort town. Within minutes of most tourist attractions and walking distance to shops and restaurants. Children over ten, please. One suite is available in addition to the rooms.

Hosts: Tom and Lee Gray
Rooms: 9 (3 PB; 6 SB) $40-65
Full Breakfast
Credit Cards: A, B, C
Notes: 2, 5, 8 (over 10), 10, 11, 12, 14

Onaledge
Bed and Breakfast

336 El Paso Boulevard, 80829
(719) 685-4265; (800) 530-8253

Built on a hill overlooking Manitou Springs, this 1912 English Tudor rock home speaks of romance. At the foot of Pikes Peak near all attractions. Lovely honeymoon suite featuring a private hot tub and all amenities. Lovely gardens and patios. Although within walking distance of Garden of the Gods and downtown Manitou Springs, Onaledge retains the seclusion of an English country inn.

Hosts: Mel and Shirley Podell
Rooms: 4 (PB) $75-125
Full Breakfast
Credit Cards: A, B, C, D
Notes: 2, 5, 7 and 8 (limited), 9, 10, 11, 12, 14

Prickly Pear Cottage
Bed and Breakfast

124 Via Vallecito, 80829
(719) 685-5899

A private fantasy cottage with hand-painted furniture and stenciled walls. At the edge of the Garden of the Gods. This hideaway with skylights, fireplace, kitchen, private baths, and gourmet breakfasts served in the courtyard garden, is the perfect getaway in the foothills at the base of Pike's Peak. Tennis, swimming, and golf nearby. Children welcome. No pets. No smoking. $15 per additional person

NOTES: Credit cards accepted: A MasterCard; B Visa; C American Express; D Discover Card; E Diner's Club; F Other; 2 Personal checks accepted; 3 Lunch available; 4 Dinner available; 5 Open all year;

Hosts: Suzanne Murphy and Brooks Fountain
Cottage (PB) $85-95
Full Breakfast
Cards: None
Notes: 2, 5, 8, 9, 10, 11, 12, 14

Red Crags Bed and Breakfast

302 El Paso Boulevard, 80829
(719) 685-1920

Get lost "Somewhere In Time" in this magnificent four-story Victorian mansion built in the 1870s. The house, over 7000 square feet, dominates the two–acre estate. Great views, with beautifully landscaped grounds and herb gardens. Watch the ducks in the gurgling brook or relax in the outdoor Jacuzzi. Inside, sit in the parlor filled with antique furniture, or lounge in the solarium on a sunny day. A gourmet breakfast awaits each morning. Children over ten. No pets. No smoking.

Hosts: Howard and Lynda Lerner
Rooms: 6 (PB) $75-150
Full Breakfast
Cards: A, B, C, D
Notes: 2, 5, 8 (over 10), 9, 10, 11, 12, 14

Red Eagle Mountain Bed and Breakfast Inn

616 Ruxton Avenue, 80829
(800) MTN-VU01; (719) 685-4541

This charming, century-old Victorian mountain home offers four individually decorated guest rooms, featuring floral fabrics, lace curtains, stenciling, and antique furnishings. Amenities include fireplaces, tub-for-two, sauna, and outdoor hot tub. Hearty gourmet breakfasts and afternoon snacks. Quiet location offers great hiking, and nature- and bird-watching opportunities. Close to shops, restaurants, and attractions. Pets welcome. Children welcome. No smoking.

Hosts: Stacie and Don LeVack
Rooms: 4 (PB) $70-85
Full Breakfast

Cards: A, B
Notes: 2, 5, 6, 8, 9, 10, 11, 12, 13

Victoria's Keep A Bed and Breakfast Inn

202 Ruxton Avenue, 80829
(719) 685-5354; (800) 905-KEEP

Victoria's Keep, an antique, gourmet inn, was built in 1892. The inn is housed in a fully restored Queen Anne Victorian home complete with two fireplaces, nine stained-glass windows, period wall coverings and wainscoting, a wraparound porch, and a turret. Each of the 18 rooms is decorated with period antiques. The four guest rooms are all large, one with Jacuzzi tub. Twenty-four-hour beverages, spa, bicycles, and wine are also offered.

Hosts: Marvin and Vicki Keith
Rooms: 4 (PB) $65-120
Full Breakfast
Credit Cards: A, B, C, D
Notes: 2 (in advance), 5, 9, 10, 11, 12, 13, 14

MINTURN

Eagle River Inn

145 North Main Street, Box 100, 81645
(303) 827-5761; (800) 344-1750

This lovely 12-room inn is decorated in the Southwestern style. Enjoy a gourmet breakfast in the sunny breakfast room; in the evenings, relax in front of the fireplace while enjoying wine, appetizers, and classical music, or experience the outdoor hot tub overlooking the Eagle River. Seven miles from Vail and Beaver Creek ski resorts. Seven-night minimum stay required during Christmas. Closed during May.

Hosts: Jane Leavitt and Richard Galloway
Rooms: 12 (PB) $89-200
Full Breakfast
Credit Cards: A, B, C
Notes: 2, 8 (over 12) , 9, 10, 11, 12, 13, 14

6 Pets welcome; 7 Smoking allowed; 8 Children welcome; 9 Social drinking allowed; 10 Tennis available;
11 Swimming available; 12 Golf available; 13 Skiing available; 14 May be booked through travel agents.

NATHROP

Streamside Bed and Breakfast
18820 County Road 162, 81236
(719) 395-2553

This high-country home on beautiful Chalk Creek is deep within Colorado's 14,000 foot Collegiate Peaks mountain–range, in San Isabel National Forest. Three guest rooms with private baths. Full breakfast served. Hiking, climbing, fishing, and wildlife-viewing opportunities abound; in winter, cross-country and downhill skiing are readily available. White-water rafting, horseback riding, and hot-springs pools are all a ten-minute drive. No pets and no smoking.

Hosts: Denny and Kathy Claveau
Rooms: 3 (PB) $60-65
Full Breakfast
Cards: None
Notes: 2, 5, 8 (limited), 9, 11, 12, 13

OURAY

Bed and Breakfast Agency of Colorado at Vail
P.O. 491, Vail, CO 81658
(303) 949-1212; (800) 748-2666

The Manor. Nestled 7800 feet high in the San Juan mountains, this 1890 manor house offers polished Victorian charm in a quiet setting, one block from Ouray's unique shops and restaurants. Relax in the natural hot springs pool. Off-roading tours, hiking, backpacking, cross-country skiing, skating, and ice climbing are all nearby. Parlor with TV and fireplace; balcony, patio, croquet courts, and manicured grounds. Buffet-style Continental breakfast. Outdoor hot tub. In winter, half-priced tickets to Telluride ski mountain. $75-85.

Main Street Bed and Breakfast
322 Main Street, P.O. Box 641, 81427
(303) 325-4871

Two superbly renovated, turn-of-the-century residences offer three suites, three rooms, and a two-story cottage. All accommodations have private baths, queen-size beds, and cable TV. Five of the units have decks with spectacular views of the San Juan Mountains. Three units have fully equipped modern kitchens. Guests who stay in rooms without kitchens are served a full breakfast on antique china. Guests who stay in kitchen suites are provided with supplies for a hearty breakfast.

Hosts: Lee and Kathy Bates
Rooms: 7 (PB) $58-90
Full Breakfast
Credit Cards: A, B
Notes: 2, 8, 9, 11

St. Elmo Hotel
426 Main Street, P.O. Box 667, 81427
(303) 325-4951

Listed on the National Register of Historic places and established in 1898 as a miners' hotel. Now fully renovated with stained glass, antiques, polished wood, and brass trim throughout. An outdoor hot tub and aspen-lined sauna are available, as well as a cozy parlor and a breakfast room.

Hosts: Sandy and Dan Lingenfelter
Rooms: 9 (PB) $60-94
Full Breakfast
Credit Cards: A, B, C, D
Notes: 4, 5, 8, 9, 10, 11, 13, 14

PAGOSA SPRINGS

Echo Manor Inn
3366 Highway 84, 81147
(303) 264-5646

NOTES: Credit cards accepted: A MasterCard; B Visa; C American Express; D Discover Card; E Diner's Club; F Other; 2 Personal checks accepted; 3 Lunch available; 4 Dinner available; 5 Open all year;

Beautiful country Dutch Tudor manor with towers, turrets, and gables. Set in the majestic San Juan Mountains and described by many as a "fairy tale castle," this lovely bed and breakfast offers a honeymoon suite, country breakfast, hot tub, horseback riding, rafting, snowmobiling, fishing, hunting, and boating. Across the street from beautiful Echo Lake. Guests are invited to enjoy cozy wood stoves and fireplaces.

Hosts: Sandy and Ginny Northcutt
Rooms: 10 (6 PB; 4SB) $49-125
Suite: 1
Full Breakfast
Credit Cards: A, B, D
Notes: 5, 6, 7, 8, 9, 10, 11, 12, 13, 14

Royal Pine Inn

Royal Pine Inn

56 Talisman 4002, 81147
(303) 731-4179

This inn is an eight-year-old building designed in the old Tudor fashion. Offering five bedrooms, three with private baths. Two bedrooms share an extra large full bath with a half-bath across the hall. Bedrooms are large and spacious and decorated in Laura Ashley-style. All rooms have their own TV and breathtaking views. The hosts serve a full breakfast of waffles, French toast, and eggs to order, with freshly baked pastries, jams, fresh fruit, and cold cereal.

Hosts: Kathy and Roy
Rooms: 5 (3 PB; 2 SB) $49-65
Full Breakfast

Credit Cards: A, B
Notes: 5, 7 (limited), 8, 10, 11, 12, 13

Abriendo Inn

PUEBLO

Abriendo Inn

300 West Abriendo Avenue, 81004
(719) 544-2703

A classic bed and breakfast on the National Register of Historic Places, in the heart of Pueblo and one mile off the interstate. Bask in the comfort, style, and luxury of the past in rooms delightfully decorated with antiques, crocheted bedspreads, and brass and four-poster beds. Restaurants, shops, galleries, golf, tennis, and other attractions are all within five minutes of the inn.

Host: Kerrelyn Trent
Rooms: 7 (PB) $56-89
Full Breakfast
Credit Cards: A, B, C, E
Notes: 2, 5, 8 (over 7) , 9, 10, 11, 12, 13, 14

REDSTONE

Avalanche Ranch Country Inn and Cabins

12863 Highway 133, 81623
(303) 963-2846

The 1913 farmhouse has been restored to a country inn bed and breakfast and antiques shop. The inn is decorated with an eclectic

6 Pets welcome; 7 Smoking allowed; 8 Children welcome; 9 Social drinking allowed; 10 Tennis available; 11 Swimming available; 12 Golf available; 13 Skiing available; 14 May be booked through travel agents.

collection of early country antiques and folk art. Eleven cozy log cabins feature different amenities. Each cabin is fully equipped with a kitchen and bathroom. Avalanche Ranch provides an ideal setting for romantic getaways, family reunions, and weddings. In accordance with emphasis on health, smoking is not permitted in any ranch buildings. While the hosts have taken great care to create an interesting yet comfortable atmosphere for their guests, it is their philosophy that "The ornament of a house is the friends who frequent it"—Emerson.

Avalanche Ranch

Hosts: Sharon and Jim Mollica
Rooms: 4 (2 PB; 2 SB) $80-95
Cabins: 11 (PB) $75-125
Continental Breakfast
Credit Cards: A, B, D
Notes: 2, 5, 6 and 8 (limited), 9, 10, 11, 12, 13, 14

Cleveholm Manor: The "Historic" Redstone Castle

0058 Redstone Boulevard, 81623
(303) 963-3463; (800) 643-4837

Cleveholm Manor is a majestic 42-room manor home built at the turn of the century by coal and steel baron John Cleveland Osgood. The finest quality craftsmanship, furnishings, and decoration lend charm and grace to transport a guest back in time to an era of solitude and serenity. Cleveholm operates today as a bed and breakfast mountain inn, and as a host for special events, retreats, weddings, concerts, elegant dinners most Friday and Saturday evenings, and conferences.

Hosts: Rose Marie Johnson and Cyd Lange
Rooms: 16 (8 PB; 8 SB) $95-180
Continental Breakfast
Credit Cards: A, B, C
Notes: 2, 4, 5, 6, 7 (limited), 8, 9, 14

SILVERTON

Alma House

220 East 10th Street, 81433
(303) 387-5336

A totally restored European-style hotel with Victorian decor. Step back in time and experience the gracious charm of yesteryear. Superb cuisine served in Christine's fine-dining restaurant. Enjoy fine wines and relax in the splendor of a time gone by. Room service is available, Continental breakfast is served. Pets welcome. Children welcome.

Host: Christine Alicia Payne
Rooms: 10 (2 PB; 8 SB) $45-80
Continental Breakfast
Cards: A, B, C, D
Notes: 3, 4, 5, 6, 8, 9, 10, 13, 14

Christopher House Bed and Breakfast

821 Empire Street, P.O. Box 241, 81433
(303) 387-5857 (June-Sept)
(904) 567-7423 (October-May)

Traditional Irish bed and breakfast hospitality amid the scenic splendor of the Rocky Mountains. The charming 1894 Victorian home features original woodwork and fireplace with sturdy antiques. Comfortable, carpeted rooms with mountain view and fresh flowers. Within walking distance of shops, restaurants, riding stable, stage coach, and narrow-gauge train station. Closed September 16 through May 30. Reasonable rates.

Hosts: Eileen and Howard Swonger
Rooms: 4 (1 PB; 3SB) $42-52

NOTES: Credit cards accepted: A MasterCard; B Visa; C American Express; D Discover Card; E Diner's Club; F Other; 2 Personal checks accepted; 3 Lunch available; 4 Dinner available; 5 Open all year;

Full Breakfast
Credit Cards: None
Notes: 2, 8, 9, 10, 14

STEAMBOAT SPRINGS _____

Bed and Breakfast Agency of Colorado at Vail

P.O. 491, Vail, CO 81658
(303) 949-1212; (800) 748-2666

Easy Access. Simply decorated and affordable, this is a great place for skiers seeking comfortable accommodations. It is within walking distance of downtown shops and restaurants, and three miles from the ski area. Amenities include in-room TV, whirlpool, a fully stocked library, bumper pool, and movies. $89-95.

Inn Town. In the heart of downtown, with restaurants, shops, and mineral springs within walking distance. Each room has unique decor. Telephone, TV with HBO. Kids stay FREE. Continental breakfast, $60-119.

Steamboat Valley Guest House. Spectacular views and warm hospitality await you at this beautiful log home. Unique comfortable bedrooms have Old World flavor. Quiet. Hot tub. Covered parking. Walk to shops and restaurants. Hot springs, for which Steamboat is famous, are only minutes away. No smoking. No pets. $60-135.

B&B Reservation Service of Colorado and Vail

P.O. Box 491, 81658
(303) 949-1212; (800) 748-2666

Easy Access. TV in rooms, whirlpool, a fully stocked library, bumper pool, or movie watching are just a few of the amenities offered here. Simply decorated and affordable, this is great for skiers wanting comfortable accommodations. Within walking distance to downtown shops and restaurants, this bed and breakfast is three miles from the ski area.

The Log Cabin

47890 County Road 129, 80487
(303) 879-5837

The spectacular Elk River Valley is the setting for this small guest cabin, uniquely constructed of whole logs and river rock. Its queen-size bed, large shower, wood stove, library, microwave, and mini-refrigerator ensure comfort and privacy for two. Full breakfast served in main house. Only 15 minutes from the Steamboat ski area and close to national forest, and wilderness area. Resident cat, dog, and horses.

Hosts: Ann and Bill Root
Cabins: 1 (PB) $63-75
Full Breakfast
Credit Cards: None
Notes: 2, 5, 9, 10, 11, 12, 13, 14

Vista Verde Ranch

P.O. Box 465, 80477
(303) 879-3858; (800) 526-7433

This small, highly regarded Western guest and cattle ranch provides a secluded, picturesque setting and active summer program of riding, hiking, fly fishing, rock climbing, and rafting. In winter, enjoy ski touring, sleigh rides, dog sledding, as well as riding. In both seasons savor superbly prepared cuisine served in the new lodge. Relax in the elegantly furnished log rooms or log cabins with fireplaces, or in the hot tubs and sauna. Minimum stays are required by season.

Rooms: 3 (PB) $300-400
Cabins: 8
Full Breakfast
Credit Cards: None
Notes: 2, 3, 4, 8, 9, 10, 11, 12, 13, 14

6 Pets welcome; 7 Smoking allowed; 8 Children welcome; 9 Social drinking allowed; 10 Tennis available;
11 Swimming available; 12 Golf available; 13 Skiing available; 14 May be booked through travel agents.

TELLURIDE

Alpine Inn
Bed and Breakfast

P.O. Box 2398, 440 West Colorado Avenue, 81435
(303) 728-6282

Enjoy the charm and spectacular views from this restored Victorian inn in the historic district of Telluride. The inn is within walking distance of ski lifts, hiking trails, and festivals. Each room captures a Victorian serenity with antiques and handmade quilts. Enjoy breakfast views from the sunroom or sundeck. Relax on the porch with the wildflower garden, read a good book by the fire, or enjoy sunset views from the hot tub.

Hosts: Denise and John Weaver
Rooms: 8 (6 PB; 2 SB) $50-220
Full Breakfast
Credit Cards: A, B
Notes: 2, 5, 9, 10, 12, 13, 14

Bear Creek
Bed and Breakfast

221 East Colorado, P.O. Box 1797, 81435
(303) 728-6681; (800) 338-7064

A charming European-style bed and breakfast. On Telluride's historic Main Street, guests are only steps away from dining, shopping, hiking, ski slopes, Town Park, and summer festivals. Private telephones and cable TV with HBO. Complimentary après ski. Other amenities include a central fireplace, sauna, steam room, and a roof deck with its stunning 360-degree view of the mountains. The inn is closed April 12 through May 6, and October 25 through November 18.

Hosts: Tom and Colleen Whiteman
Rooms: 8 (PB) $55-145
Full Breakfast
Credit Cards: A, B
Notes: 2, 5, 9, 10, 11, 12, 13, 14

Johnstone Inn

403 West Colorado, Box 546, 81435
(303) 728-3316

A true, 100-year-old restored Victorian boarding house in the center of Telluride and the spectacular San Juan Mountains. Rooms are warm and romantic with Victorian marble and brass private baths. Full breakfast is served. Winter season includes apres ski refreshments. A sitting room with fireplace and outdoor hot tub complete the amenities. Nordic and Alpine skiing, hiking, Jeep tours, and loafing are within walking distance of the inn.

Hosts: Bill Schiffbauer
Rooms: 8 (PB) $80-140
Full Breakfast
Credit Cards: A, B, C
Notes: 2, 5, 9, 10, 12, 13, 14

San Sophia

330 West Pacific Avenue, P.O. Box 1825, 81435
(800) 537-4781

Elegant, luxurious accommodations for the discriminating traveler. Indoor and outdoor dining areas, huge bathtubs for two, brass beds, handmade quilts, and a dramatic view of the surrounding 13,000-foot mountains. Common areas include an observatory, library, and gazebo with Jacuzzi. "One of the most luxurious and romantic inns in America," according to *Inside America*. Complimentary refreshments each afternoon. Closed April 10 through May 14 and October 20 through November 24.

Hosts: Dianne and Gary Eschman
Rooms: 16 (PB) $95-195
Full Breakfast
Credit Cards: A, B, C
Notes: 2, 9, 10, 11, 12, 13, 14

TWIN LAKES

Twin Lakes Mountain Retreat

129 Lang, Box 175, 81251
(719) 486-2593

NOTES: Credit cards accepted: A MasterCard; B Visa; C American Express; D Discover Card; E Diner's Club; F Other; 2 Personal checks accepted; 3 Lunch available; 4 Dinner available; 5 Open all year;

This clean and relaxing country inn is tucked away in one of Colorado's last unspoiled high mountain valleys. Come see the real Colorado and experience bright sunny mornings, delicious country breakfasts, unlimited activities, homemade bakery goods with quiet relaxing evenings in front of the fire. The inn sits at the base of Colorado's highest peak and across from the breathtaking beauty of Twin Lake. All of these features combine to make a visit to Twin Lakes Mountain Retreat truly unforgettable.

Hosts: Roger and Denny Miller
Rooms: 5 (3 PB; 2 SB) $64-73
Full Breakfast
Credit Cards: A, B
Notes: 2, 4 (by arrangement), 5, 8, 10, 11, 12, 13, 14

VAIL

Bed and Breakfast Agency of Colorado at Vail

P.O. 491, Vail, CO 81658
(303) 949-1212; (800) 748-2666

Alpine Creek. This beautiful house is on Alpine, just minutes from downtown. Two rooms with private baths are offered in this home. Elegantly decorated with European flair. Guests wake up to the rippling sound of the creek and the smell of fresh-brewed coffee. A delicious breakfast starts off each day of winter skiing or summer recreation. $85-125.

Bagels n' Grits. This self-contained apartment is perfect for parties of four or more. A fully stocked kitchen, fireplace, TV/VCR, and ski storage are available. The creekside property is less than five minutes from downtown Vail on the FREE bus service. Call for rates.

Colorado Comfort. For peace and quiet, only minutes from the active world, this inn is the place. Guest suite has a private entrance, TV, fireplace, fully stocked kitchenette, spectacular views, and gracious hosts. Breakfast is prepared and offered early, so rise and enjoy the splendor of the Vail Valley year-round. The outside patio is on the golf course for long leisurely summer breakfasts or cross-country ski jaunts in the winter. A deluxe accommodation for golfers or skiers. $95-155.

European Splendor. Hostess has a knack for entertaining. This home nestled in the aspen and pine trees welcomes any guest year-round. Cross-country skiing is moments away, as is Vail Mountain. On the FREE bus route. Great morning breakfasts are offered with a European flair. $70.

Heather Inn. Just east of downtown Vail, this one-bedroom property with private entrance is like walking into the past. Decorated with a 100-year-old Queen Anne four-poster bed and various antiques and quilts, its comfort and warmth are unending. Guest room is spacious, with an Empire chair and dresser that converts to a desk. Breakfast is served in the dining room overlooking the stream and beaver-pond. Resident dog. No smoking. $65.

Hilltop. This townhouse features impeccably decorated rooms with wonderful views from each. Nestled in the trees on a hillside, it is less than ten minutes from downtown. Exercise equipment and a large steamroom are available. Full breakfasts feature fresh homemade breads. $65-125.

Just Relax. If relaxing in a private apartment sounds appealing, then this home is perfect. Joint entry leads to newly renovated garden-level unit, with private bedroom and bath, living room with fireplace, TV, and pullout couch, and fully stocked kitchenette. This unit is perfect for a small family or two couples traveling together. On the golf course, so cross-country or

6 Pets welcome; 7 Smoking allowed; 8 Children welcome; 9 Social drinking allowed; 10 Tennis available; 11 Swimming available; 12 Golf available; 13 Skiing available; 14 May be booked through travel agents.

snowshoe just off the deck; or downhill ski at Vail or Beaver Creek, minutes away. Continental plus breakfast is provided in the morning. $75-150.

M&M's. This showcase home is fabulous. Selected bedrooms have a queen-size bed, private bath, double-sink, walk-in closet, and balcony. Guests have full use of kitchen, washer and dryer, Jacuzzi, and fireplace. Two resident dogs. With so many amenities, guests will return many times annually. $65-150.

B&B Reservation Service of Colorado and Vail

P.O. Box 491, 81658
(303) 949-1212; (800) 748-2666

Alpen Haus. This Austrian-flavored home is one bus stop from Vail village on the golf course. Great views from each bedroom, one overlooking the Gore Range and Vail Village; the other looks out on tall pines and aspens. Common gathering room available for après ski with TV, VCR, and library. Kitchenette with microwave oven and refrigerator. No smoking. $105-115.

Aspen Haus. If guests would like to be pampered, then this is the house. Set on a hillside, surrounded by trees, the guest suite has a delightful, homey feeling with a great view. There is a TV, telephone, and large couch to snuggle into and relax. The bath is in the suite for extra privacy. Breakfast is served upstairs in the European decorated home. High ceilings and wonderful German artifacts grace the sunny kitchen area. The hosts offer a ski locker in town at the base of the the mountain, as well as an athletic club membership, discounted parking tickets, and ski tickets (limited availability). Wine and cheese served each afternoon. $125.

Base Cabin. This single-family home is hidden away creekside only minutes from Beaver Creek. The owner, who built this log house, is a world-traveled climber, adventurer, and Himalayan guide. The artifacts collected from his travels make the home seem like a minimuseum, and of course there is a great story behind each item. Sherpa, the resident cocker spaniel and master of mischief, is always eager to greet guests and discuss his toys. Base Camp is a little off the beaten path but well worth the effort. No place else in the valley offers privacy like this. Guests will love it if they do not mind the short drive and would like to save some money. No smoking and no pets. $50-65.

BB Inn. This inn is everything guests would expect from a Rocky Mountain getaway. On Gore Creek, this handcrafted log inn with an enormous main room has a cozy fire, great views, and warmth beyond compare. Breakfast features baked breads, rolls, muffins, fruits in season, and a daily gourmet creation. Après ski snacks and appetizers are also served daily. $80-175.

Bluebird. This wonderful mountain home offers warmth and charm to all guests who stay here. The hostess offers quaint rooms, each with its own decor. Additional children are welcome in the room or on the futon for an extra $10-15. Microwave oven and refrigerator are available for guests to use. Views of Vail and surrounding mountains are spectacular. In summer, relax on the outside sunny deck while feasting on breakfast. Bus stops at the end of the street, and free shuttle to downtown. $80-95.

Chalet Chamonix. If privacy is needed in a bed and breakfast, then this self-contained apartment suite will meet that need. The small, intimate property has kitchenette, private bath, living room, TV, and private entrance. A Continental breakfast is served each day. On the free bus route; however, hosts suggest that guests use their cars because it is a bit of a walk to the bus stop. No smoking and no pets. $85-125.

Colorado Comfort. This comfortable two-story townhouse offers beautiful views of Aspen and the pine trees while overlooking a challenging golf course. Guest rooms feature high vaulted ceilings with electric blankets, humidifiers, TVs, and bathrooms in the room. Cross-country ski outside the back door in the winter, and golf in the summer. Guests are welcome to relax in the home when shopping and touring are finished. $8-11 discount lift tickets and Vail parking is available (excluding Christmas and New Year's). $80-85.

Creekside Retreat. This comfortable suite features a bedroom, private bath, kitchenette, living room, and dining area. A spacious, sunny, high-vaulted room has a private entrance and offers privacy to those guests who prefer to be separate from hosts. Hosts live in next-door unit and provide breakfast each morning. Relax at own pace each day with the TV and VCR or hop on the free shuttle to Vail for skiing and recreation. This home is perfect for couple wanting space and quality, and a kitchen for additional meals. $125-150.

Dave's Domain. On Vail's free bus shuttle, this self-contained apartment is perfect for two traveling couples or a family of four. Full kitchen, private entrance, TV, small living room. Host lives upstairs. Five minutes from downtown Vail and close to shopping and skiing. $90-125.

Elk View. This gorgeous townhome nestled on the hillside of Beaver Creek boasts five levels with a breathtaking view of Beaver Creek Mountain. Beautifully decorated, each room has a charm of its own, and the

house is impeccably furnished. In summer, breakfast can be enjoyed on one of the three outside decks, and in the winter, after a long day of skiing, relax in the outside hot tub. This property is perfect for honeymoon couples and guests wanting to relax with the locals. $85.

Fairway House. This beautiful rustic mountain home lies very close to the ski mountain. The guest room is cozy, with a stucco fireplace and magnificent view of Gore Range. Adjoining living room with fireplace, TV, VCR, wet bar, library, pool table. Two blocks from free bus route. Continental breakfast. $100.

Family Home. This young family's cozy home is set up with other young families in mind. The hosts have playpens and toys with many additions so that children are very welcome. A full breakfast is served. There is a membership to a health club with a pool, weights, tennis, and exercise equipment. A TV, VCR, radio, and queen-size sofa bed will enhance guests' stay. Please contact the office for more details.

Game Creek House. Between Vail and Beaver Creek, this private home is on nine acres and is surrounded on three sides by forest service land. Near four local favorite restaurants. Refrigerator, laundry, fireplace, TV, VCR. Many outdoor activities. Breakfast is served in the kitchen with beautiful mountain view. $75.

Kay's Corner. This new home, nestled in a corner lot, offers a great view and serenity. Bedroom is spacious with TV, refrigerator, and a great view. Host is a ski instructor. Continental breakfast. $80.

Matterhorn. TV's in rooms, telephone nearby, snow tires suggested for driveway. Enjoy a hearty breakfast with a magnifi-

6 Pets welcome; 7 Smoking allowed; 8 Children welcome; 9 Social drinking allowed; 10 Tennis available; 11 Swimming available; 12 Golf available; 13 Skiing available; 14 May be booked through travel agents.

B&B Reservation Service of Colorado and Vail (continued)

cent view of the Gore Valley. A European family (all speak German—daughter is bilingual) offers a comfortable, cozy home. Box lunch is provided for early rising convention attendants. Great for single travelers. $60-75.

Lover's Haven. Few bed and breakfasts in America or the Vail area can offer the serenity and mountain views guests experience here. This beautiful Southwestern adobe home makes guests feel like they are in Santa Fe. The decor is impeccable, breakfasts are superb and are served in a glassed-in room overlooking the Vail Valley, and terry robes are offered should guests forget their own robes. The hostess is supreme in hosting people—this is a bed and breakfast guests will not forget. Smoking permitted on the patios only. $100-125.

Mountain Chalet. Ski out the front door to cross-country terrain, or summers, just walk on the Vail Golf Course. This beautiful Bavarian mountain chalet is wonderfully decorated with antiques. Large moss-rock fireplace and sitting room with TV and stereo. On bus route. Full breakfast. Rate includes two rooms. $185.

Mountain Hideaway. Bring bathing suits to sooth weary bones in the hot tub while sipping a glass of wine or cappuccino while enjoying aprés-ski refreshments. On a wooded lot overlooking a creek, this spacious mountain home beckons travelers. Newly renovated with high vaulted ceilings and a beautiful glassed-in kitchen nook, guests will find countless hours of relaxation here. Close to the village on the free bus route, the host family's hospitality is incomparable. Discounted Vail parking is available. $90-125.

Mountain Retreat. If one is looking for an out-of-the-way spectacular home with an unsurpassed view, this bed and breakfast will meet those needs. Travelers will need a car to get there, because it is not on any of the bus routes, but once they arrive, they will never want to leave. The hostess pampers every need with breakfast served on fine china and crystal. A hot tub room is available while enjoying the views of Beaver Creek and Arrowhead mountains. Guest room is impeccably decorated and offers another great view. $100-125.

Outdoorsman. Overlooking a lake and the majestic mountains, this beautifully appointed condo is decorated with an abundance of antiques and special color blends. Full breakfast. No smoking. $65-75.

Powder Stash. Even though this property is in a condo unit, it offers all the amenities of being in a private home and then some. There is a pool and Jacuzzi on-site and a balcony off the living room with a magnificent view of Beaver Creek. The hosts are avid skiers and can describe the mountain well, and in summer they know as much about activities as a concierge. Guests will love the hospitality from this couple. The kitchen is available for additional meals. $50-89.

Private Homestay. Less than one mile to the base of Beaver Creek, this private lock-off offers privacy, yet the host is on-site to provide breakfast and meet the needs of guests. Many amenities are available to make guests' stay a most pleasant one. The guest room has a coffee maker, microwave, refrigerator, and color TV. Each morning the host brings a gourmet Continental breakfast to the door for a relaxing morning meal. This house is perfect for a couple who likes additional privacy within a central location. No smoking. No pets. $55-89.

NOTES: Credit cards accepted: A MasterCard; B Visa; C American Express; D Discover Card; E Diner's Club; F Other; 2 Personal checks accepted; 3 Lunch available; 4 Dinner available; 5 Open all year;

Sportsman's Haven. Surrounded by pine trees and nestled on a creek, this home is a warm, spacious mountain home that beckons guests to snuggle in in during the winter, or lounge on the sunny, private sun decks in summer. The hosts offer a ski home with two rooms. One is bright and cheery with pine trees outside every window, and the downstairs room has a private bath with a sauna and offers an adjoining family room with TV, pool table, shuffleboard, and fireplace. The home is within easy walking distance to the free bus. Discounted parking tickets available if guests should decide to drive. $70-80.

Streamside. This townhouse is conveniently just a few minutes west of Vail Village. The bus stop is only a few steps away so guests don't even need a car. The hosts are a young couple and avid skiers, and are eager to share their life in Vail with guests. On cold afternoons, visitors can look forward to a warm or cold après-ski drink, heat some popcorn from the microwave oven, or store drinks in the refrigerator. Upstairs, relax by the fire in the main living room to watch TV or read a book. This property is perfect for two couples traveling together or a young family. $70-85.

Taste of Vermont. The hosts, who have been in Vail business for many years as a local restaurateur and ski instructor, open this newly built spacious home to guests. For a taste of New England charm, the suites boasts a logged frame, tweed sheets, private bath, TV, and a view of the mountains that is incomparable. Each morning breakfast is served in the great room with homemade delight. Each afternoon enjoy self-serve hot chocolate, and après ski refreshments. This welcoming home has a large living room where guests may enjoy conversation with the hosts. The suite is a perfect room to snuggle while relaxing. Great views from each room help to understand how special it is living in the mountains. $100-125.

Tortilla Flats. Bordered by forest land with a spectacular view of Meadow Mountain, this bed and breakfast has immediate access to cross-country, hiking, and mountain biking trails. This cozy suite features a sitting room and bedroom with a private bath and is furnished with antique oak and brass. An extra day bed is also available for a family with a child. Continental breakfast is served in the private dining area. Within walking distance to Minturn's restaurants and galleries. Private parking and entrance allow for secluded, quiet retreat. $85.

Valley View. For affordable luxury, this home on an 18-hole golf course welcomes guests summer or winter. It is perfect for golfers, and in the winter, cross-country skiing is right out the back door. The guest rooms have a sitting room with TV, refrigerator, microwave, and dry bar right outside the door. Guests look forward to returning each season to sample the hospitality that reigns in this comfortably formal home. Breakfasts are unbeatable! Beaver Creek and Arrowhead Mountains are minutes away. $100-125.

Village Artist. Central, on the free bus route, right in the heart of Vail. Within walking distance of the village, slopes, Vail's nightlife, Vista Bahn, and Lionshead Gondola. Share the living area, TV, fireplace, and kitchen with hostess. Full or Continental breakfast. $75.

Whiskey Hill. If a quiet, secluded, romantic bed and breakfast room is desired, it can be found here at Whiskey Hill. The guest room on a private floor has a rock fireplace and private bath and entrance. Near shops, restaurants, and close to Beaver Creek. Continental breakfast. No smoking. $80.

6 Pets welcome; 7 Smoking allowed; 8 Children welcome; 9 Social drinking allowed; 10 Tennis available; 11 Swimming available; 12 Golf available; 13 Skiing available; 14 May be booked through travel agents.

Columbine Chalet
Bed and Breakfast of Vail

P.O. Box 1407, 81658
(303) 476-1122; fax (303) 476-8515

Experience mountain living at this Austrian-style chalet nestled in the pines of an exclusive neighborhood at the edge of the Vail golf course. Enjoy a hearty breakfast, afternoon refreshments, and outdoor hot tub. A recreation path outside the front door serves cross-country skiers in the winter and bicyclists and hikers in the summer. Just one stop away on the FREE Vail bus are the award-winning ski slopes. Come revitalize in the Rockies!

Host: Pat Funk
Rooms: 3 (PB) $50-175
Full Breakfast
Credit Cards: A, B, D
Notes: 2, 5, 8, 9, 10, 12, 13, 14

WINTER PARK

Alpen Rose
Bed and Breakfast

244 Forest Trail, P.O. Box 769, 80482
(303) 726-5039

Surrounded by aspen and pine trees with a spectacular view of the front range. In a sporting paradise, two miles from nation's fifth largest ski area and 40 minutes from Rocky Mountain National Park, the Alpen Rose reflects the owners' love of Austria and feels like an Austrian chalet. Five rooms with Austrian furnishings, down puffs, and handmade quilts make guests feel at home. A memorable breakfast with Austrian specialties awaits in the morning; crackling fire, hot tea, and cookies beckon travelers home after an enjoyable day in the Rockies.

Hosts: Robin and Rupert Sommerauer
Rooms: 5 (PB) $65-95

Full Breakfast
Credit Cards: A, B, C, D
Notes: 2, 5, 9, 10, 11, 12, 13, 14

AngelMark
Bed and Breakfast

P.O. Box 161, 80482
(303) 726-5354; (800) 424-2158

A beautiful mountain home in a forest setting provides guests with a safe, quiet stay. African or cowboy collections decorate the roomy suites with kitchenette and fireplace. The White Satin Room is perfect for honeymoons or anniversaries. Enjoy the hot tub, sun deck, and picnic area. Gourmet breakfasts are served, as well as complimentary hors d'oeuvres. The area offers all the amenities of a small winter/summer mountain resort town. Top-of-the-line accommodations and hospitality.

Hosts: Bob and Jeanenne Temple
Rooms: 3 (PB) $80-95
Full Breakfast
Credit Cards: A, B, C, D
Notes: 2, 5, 9, 10, 11, 12, 13

WOODLAND PARK

Hackman House
Bed and Breakfast

P.O. Box 6902, 602 West Midland Avenue, 80866
(719) 687-9851

This 1887 country Victorian home is in a small, sunny mountain town 20 miles west of Colorado Springs, at the foot of Pikes Peak. Within walking distance to many conveniences, gift shops, hiking/biking trails, horseback riding, and many special events. Therapeutic massages available. A quiet, peaceful, and refreshing atmosphere await guests.

Hosts: Laurie Glauth and Jan Greene
Rooms: 4 (4 PB; 2 shared showers) $57-75
Full Breakfast

NOTES: Credit cards accepted: A MasterCard; B Visa; C American Express; D Discover Card; E Diner's Club; F Other; 2 Personal checks accepted; 3 Lunch available; 4 Dinner available; 5 Open all year;

Credit Cards: A, B, D
Notes: 2, 5, 9, 10, 11, 12, 13, 14

YELLOW JACKET _____

Wilson's Pinto Bean Farm

House No. 21434, Road 16, Box 252, 81335
(303) 562-4476

The Wilson's farm is in Montezuma County, 40 miles from the Four Corners where the four western states join. Accommodations include three rooms with double beds and shared baths. Waving wheat, fragrant alfalfa, pinto beans, and mountains are visible in every direction. The farmhouse sits among elm trees, with orchards and gardens around. There are farm animals to enjoy, home-cooked meals, eggs to hunt, and fruits to pick in season. Children of all ages can see the delights of farm animals and country living.

Hosts: Arthur and Esther M. Wilson
Rooms: 3 (SB) $60
Full Breakfast and Dinner
Credit Cards: None
Notes: 2, 3, 4, 6, 8, 9, 11

6 Pets welcome; 7 Smoking allowed; 8 Children welcome; 9 Social drinking allowed; 10 Tennis available; 11 Swimming available; 12 Golf available; 13 Skiing available; 14 May be booked through travel agents.

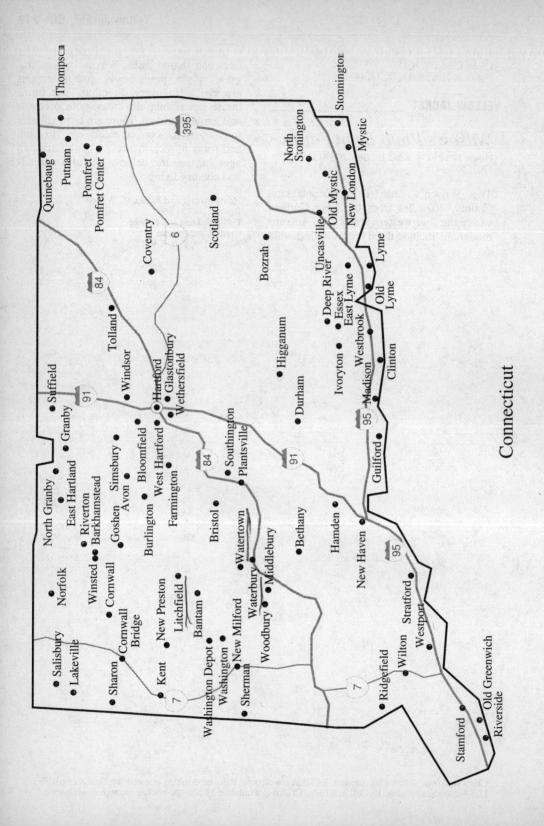

Connecticut

Connecticut

AVON

Nutmeg
Bed and Breakfast
P.O. Box 1117, West Hartford, 06107
(203) 236-6698

414. This bright, spacious contemporary has a solarium, deck, and lovely grounds including a Japanese garden with a pond and a waterfall. One room has a cathedral ceiling and skylight; adjacent studio. Six languages spoken here. Continental breakfast and afternoon tea served. Children welcome; baby-sitting available. No smoking.

BANTAM

Nutmeg
Bed and Breakfast
P.O. Box 1117, West Hartford, 06107
(203) 236-6698

319. Deer Island Guest house on Bantam Lake with a lake view in back, front on road; rustic but comfortable. One bedroom with three twin beds, fireplace, chairs, table for dining in a completely equipped kitchen, bath with a shower; kitchen stocked for breakfast; canoe rentals and restaurant nearby. Continental breakfast; children allowed; no smoking; no pets in the guest house.

BARKHAMSTED

Covered Bridge
P.O. Box 447, Norfolk, 06058
(203) 542-5944

Rustic Victorian lake lodge features fireside concerts on the antique grand piano, wraparound porch with a commanding view of woods, and crystal clear lake. Feel free to borrow the canoe, relax on the private beach, or enjoy a country walk. Three guest rooms, one has balcony overlooking the lake, share a bath and a half. $80-95.

BETHANY

Bed and Breakfast, Ltd.
P.O. Box 216, New Haven, 06513
(203) 469-3260

Normandy French manor house, architecturally fascinating. Woodsy setting, horse country, yet close to Yale. Interesting furnishings. Gregarious hosts. Reservations hours 5:00 until 9:00 P.M. only September through July. Phones available anytime July and August. $85-95.

BLOOMFIELD

Nutmeg
Bed and Breakfast
P.O. Box 1117, West Hartford, 06107
(203) 236-6698

NOTES: Credit cards accepted: A MasterCard; B Visa; C American Express; D Discover Card; E Diner's Club; F Other; 2 Personal checks accepted; 3 Lunch available; 4 Dinner available; 5 Open all year; 6 Pets welcome; 7 Smoking allowed; 8 Children welcome; 9 Social drinking allowed; 10 Tennis available; 11 Swimming available; 12 Golf available; 13 Skiing available; 14 May be booked through travel agents.

450. Hospitality rules here, with a den, refrigerator, and ice. Four guest rooms with private and shared baths. One has connecting playroom with TV and telephone. Convenient to West Hartford and Hartford, and across the road from Penwood State Forest for walking, jogging, or cross-country skiing. Full breakfast served. Children are welcome.

467. This 1958 ranch-style house has spacious rooms, wide hallways, and wheelchair accommodations. There are three rooms with a choice of king-size, double, or single beds. All share a bath. Convenient to the University of Hartford, Loomis Shaffee, the University of Connecticut, and the airport. Three minutes to public transportation; off-street parking available. Continental breakfast served to the room if desired. Children allowed. No smoking.

BOZRAH

Bed and Breakfast, Ltd.

P.O. Box 216, New Haven, 06513
(203) 469-3260

Gorgeous period home. Private baths, fireplaces, canopied beds. Eclectic, elegant furnishings. Near Foxwood Casino and Mystic Seaport. Reservation hours 5:00 until 9:00 P.M. only September through July. Phones available anytime July and August. $85-95.

Covered Bridge

P.O. Box 44, Norfolk, 06058
(203) 542-5944

Circa 1790 farmhouse is set in a vineyard, offering a very special getaway. The four guest rooms all offer private baths, fireplaces, TV, and telephones. A full breakfast is served. $125.

Nutmeg Bed and Breakfast Agency

P.O. Box 1117, West Hartford, 06127-1117
(203) 236-6698; (800) 727-7592

505. Gambral Home circa 1790. Lovely country setting; host grows berries and makes wine; the berries are served in the mouth-watering country breakfast. Twenty minutes from Mystic and Ledyard. The four guest rooms have private baths, TVs, phones, gas fireplaces, beautiful furnishings, ceiling fans; one bath has jet tub. Breakfast is served in glass-enclosed sunroom and guests have use of several sitting rooms. Guest room wing has its own private entrance. No children, no smoking.

BRISTOL

Chimney Crest Manor

5 Founders Drive, 06010
(203) 582-4219

Experience quiet elegance in this splendid 32-room Tudor mansion. Chimney Crest was built in 1930 in the Federal Hill historic district, just minutes away from the Litchfield Hills, where guests will find antiques, wineries, parks, museums, and restaurants. Stay in the spacious suites for pleasure or on business. Guests are treated with warm, attentive hospitality set in the splendor and style of a bygone era. National Historical Register. Mobil Travel Guide three-star rated.

Hosts: Dan and Cynthia Cimadamore
Suites: 5 (PB) $65-125
Full Breakfast
Credit Cards: A, B, C
Notes: 5, 8, 10, 11, 12, 13, 14

Nutmeg Bed and Breakfast

P.O. Box 1117, West Hartford, 06107
(203) 236-6698

411. Bright and spacious English Tudor mansion has a grand foyer, large den, elegant formal dining room, sunroom, and back patio overlooking Farmington Valley and the fountains in the large yard. The ballroom suite contains a large living room with double sofa bed, a full eat-in kitchen, bedroom with double bed, and bath. Also five suites on second floor, including one with two bedrooms and a kitchen. All rooms have ceiling fans and TVs. Full breakfast. Designated smoking area. Children welcome.

433. Visitors to Bristol's clock museum and history lovers will especially enjoy a stay in the Dutch Colonial home of the city historian. Large lawns and gardens surround this home in a residential area. One guest room with private bath. Full breakfast served. No smoking.

BURLINGTON

Nutmeg Bed and Breakfast
P.O. Box 1117, West Hartford, 06107
(203) 236-6698

412. Ten-room Dutch Colonial built around 1930, surrounded by 12 acres of woods crisscrossed with marked paths. First floor guest room with double brass bed and private bath; second floor room with twin beds, private bath. Full breakfast. No children, no smoking.

478. This ranch-style home has a screened porch, pool, and lovely gardens. There is a room with twin beds, private bath, living room, porch, and deck for guests' use. Convenient to Avon Old Farms, Miss Porter's, and the University of Connecticut Medical Center. Full breakfast. No children. No smoking. Dogs on premises.

CLINTON

Captain Dibbell House
21 Commerce Street, 06413
(203) 669-1646

This 1866 Victorian, on a historic residential street, is two blocks from the harbor and features a century-old, wisteria-covered iron truss bridge. Rooms are furnished with a comfortable mix of heirlooms, antiques, auction finds, and a growing collection of original art by New England artists. Bicycles are available. Closed January through March.

Hosts: Helen and Ellis Adams
Rooms: 4 (PB) $80-95
Full Breakfast
Credit Cards: A, B, C, D
Notes: 2, 8 (over 14), 9, 10, 11, 12, 13, 14

COLCHESTER

The Hayward House Inn
35 Hayward Avenue, 06415
(203) 537-5772

A 1767 home on the National Register of Historic Places, this Federal Colonial is furnished with antiques. The Goodspeede Opera House, shops, beaches, golf, biking, and tennis are all within a short distance. Experience small-town New England at its best. Massage therapist on the premises. Lunch, dinner, and tea are served for an extra charge in the inn's tea room.

Hosts: Bettyann and Stephen Possidento
Rooms: 6 (PB) $75-95
Full Breakfast
Credit Cards: A, B
Notes: 2, 3, 4, 5, 8, 9, 10, 11, 12, 13, 14

CORNWALL

Cornwall Inn
Route 7, 06754
(800) 786-6884

Nestled in the northwest hills of Connecticut, an inn for all seasons. Antique-decorated inn rooms and country motel-type rooms all have private baths. Enjoy the pool and patio in the summer or the roaring fireplace in the dining room in the winter.

Hosts: Lois and Emily
Rooms: 12 (11 PB; 1 SB) $50-115
Full Breakfast
Credit Cards: A, B, C, D
Notes: 2, 3, 4, 5, 6, 7, 8, 9, 11, 12, 13, 14

Covered Bridge

P.O. Box 447, Norfolk, 06058
(203) 542-5944

1C. An 1808 Colonial farmhouse set on 20 acres adjoining Mohawk State Forest. The guest living room has a large old Colonial fireplace and wood stove. Breakfast is served in the country kitchen, or in the summer, on the terrace. Three bedrooms decorated in period antiques with shared full and half-baths. $85.

2C. Enjoy warm, quiet hospitality at this custom-designed stone home set on a 64-acre private estate with breathtaking views of the countryside. Hearty full breakfasts are served before the library fireplace or on the terrace. All of the rooms are decorated in antiques. Two guest rooms with private baths. $95.

CORNWALL BRIDGE

Nutmeg Bed and Breakfast

P.O. Box 1117, West Hartford, 06107
(203) 236-6698

344. Recently renovated small inn/motel has five rooms on the second floor of inn; three rooms have private baths, two share and are rented to families or to couples traveling together; also second-floor sitting room with TV, books, and games. Motel rooms have queen- or king-size beds (some have two queen-size beds), private baths,

and TV. Full breakfast included; inn also has restaurant serving lunch and dinner, and a bar. Children allowed (five and under stay free); smoking allowed; dog and cat on premises; pets accepted. Check-in 2:00 P.M.; check-out 11:00 A.M.

COVENTRY

Nutmeg Bed and Breakfast

P.O. Box 1117, West Hartford, 06107
(203) 236-6698

457. This Colonial was built in 1731 and operated as a tavern until 1823. It was used as part of the underground railroad stops for slaves in the mid-1800s. The two guest rooms have queen-size canopied beds, working fireplaces, and a feather mattress for winter warmth. One has a private bath, the other a shared. There is also a cottage with private entrance, queen-size sofa bed, private bath, fireplace, and small kitchen. Hostess will prepare a hearth cooked dinner with advance notice. Full country breakfast on weekends, Continental weekdays. Children ten and over welcome. No smoking. Cat in residence.

458. Pink towered Victorian with a well-traveled hostess who collects antique toys; shop and museum. Bed and breakfast dining area with picture windows and skylights, solarium with potted plants. House is air-conditioned; two guest rooms have private baths, one has a queen-size bed, and the other a pair of twin beds; both have access to large guest balcony overlooking the garden. Another twin bedded room shares a bath with hosts. Full breakfast; children allowed; no smoking; no pets.

463. Fully modernized Colonial home built in 1731 on three and one-quarter acres with a pool, Jacuzzi, maple trees with hammocks, and three fireplaces. Four guest rooms with double beds share one upstairs and one downstairs bath. Rollaway available. Full breakfast. Infants and over five allowed. No smoking. Dog in residence.

DEEP RIVER

Riverwind Inn

209 Main Street, 06417
(203) 526-2014

With its eight wonderfully appointed guest rooms, rambling common areas, and informal country atmosphere, Riverwind is more than just a place to stay; it's a destination. Relax, step back in time, and enjoy a stay amid an enchanting collection of New England and Southern country antiques. Each morning starts with the inn's complimentary Southern buffet breakfast.

Hosts: Barbara Barlow and Bob Bucknall
Rooms: 8 (PB) $85-145
Full Breakfast
Credit Cards: A, B, C
Notes: 2, 5, 7, 9, 10, 11, 12, 14

DURHAM

Nutmeg Bed and Breakfast

P.O. Box 1117, West Hartford, 06107
(203) 236-6698

509. Georgian Colonial built in 1740 with museum-quality restoration. Furnished with antiques. Two second-floor guest rooms with private baths, one twin-bedded room, and one pencil post double canopied rope bed. Both rooms have beautiful non-working fireplaces. Continental breakfast; no smoking. Charming cat on the premises.

EAST HARTLAND

Nutmeg Bed and Breakfast

P.O. Box 1117, West Hartford, 06107
(203) 236-6698

480. Guest house adjacent to Colonial farmhouse built in 1700s. Private entrance to sitting room with working fireplace, double Murphy bed, complete kitchen, full bath, and beautiful setting with horses, stone fences, and hills beyond. Full breakfast served in antique-filled main dining room or in guest house. Only 20 minutes to the airport; hiking, skiing, biking, fishing minutes away. Children allowed. No smoking. No pets in guest house.

EAST LYME

Nutmeg Bed and Breakfast

P.O. Box 1117, West Hartford, 06107
(203) 236-6698

517. This 1760 Colonial has exposed beams, wide oak floor boards, seven fireplaces, a root cellar, an original goose pen, and a host and hostess who bake, and make jelly. One guest room with twin or king-size bed and private bath, and one guest room with a double bed and shared bath. Afternoon tea or apple cider is served in season. Full breakfast is served on the outdoor deck in good weather. No smoking. Resident cat.

ESSEX

Nutmeg Bed and Breakfast

P.O. Box 1117, West Hartford, 06107
(203) 236-6698

508. If guests are boating enthusiasts, this entertaining hostess, whose family shares the passion, would love to trade some sailing stories. This special home, right on the bank of the Connecticut River, is convenient to many attractions of the area, 20 miles from Mystic, and close to Hammonasset public beach in Madison. Theaters and fine restaurants are nearby. Two rooms, one with a double bed and one with

6 Pets welcome; 7 Smoking allowed; 8 Children welcome; 9 Social drinking allowed; 10 Tennis available; 11 Swimming available; 12 Golf available; 13 Skiing available; 14 May be booked through travel agents.

twins, have private baths. Full breakfast can be served on the glass porch overlooking the river. Children welcome.

FARMINGTON

Nutmeg
Bed and Breakfast

P.O. Box 1117, West Hartford, 06107
(203) 236-6698

402. Small inn with traditional country furnishings. Rooms have double, queen-, and king-size beds with private baths, TV, VCR, and telephones. Children under 12 stay free in same room. Continental breakfast served.

406. This elegant estate is now a gracious small inn with beautifully landscaped grounds, pool, tennis court, conference room, and lounge. There are seven rooms with TVs, telephones, and private baths. A short drive from Hartford. Perfect for the business traveler. Continental breakfast. Children welcome.

415. This is a luxurious new inn with suites complete with kitchens, fireplaces, and bathrooms with all the amenities. Enjoy complimentary racquet club privileges with pools and tennis courts. Continental breakfast. Children welcome.

GLASTONBURY

Butternut Farm

1654 Main Street, 06033
(203) 633-7197

An 18th-century architectural jewel that is furnished in museum-quality period antiques. Estate setting with ancient trees, herb gardens, prize dairy goats, barnyard chickens, pigeons, and a goose. Three

Abyssinians inhabit the main house. Ten minutes from Hartford. All of Connecticut is within 90 minutes.

Host: Don Reid
Rooms: 5 (2 rooms, 2 suites, 1 apartment) (PB)
  $68-88
Full Breakfast
Credit Cards: C
Notes: 2, 5, 8, 9, 10, 11, 12, 13

GOSHEN

Covered Bridge

P.O. Box 447, Norfolk, 06058
(203) 542-5944

1GCT. An 1809 Federal Colonial set on 24 acres that has been beautifully restored and decorated with antiques. The couple and their two young children welcome other families to enjoy the special atmosphere at their bed and breakfast. A full breakfast is served in the elegant dining room. There are two guest rooms, one with a fireplace and one with a Jacuzzi. Both rooms have private baths. $100-150.

GRANBY

Nutmeg
Bed and Breakfast

P.O. Box 1117, West Hartford, 06107
(203) 236-6698

442. There is a sophisticated country atmosphere to this stone house. The separate guest wing includes a sitting room with TV, and two guest rooms with private baths. Convenient to Bradley International Airport, state parks, historic Old Newgate Prison, and local attractions. Guests enjoy wine, cheese, and crackers in the afternoon, and a Continental breakfast is served. Horses can be boarded for a nominal fee. Children welcome. No smoking.

NOTES: Credit cards accepted: A MasterCard; B Visa; C American Express; D Discover Card; E Diner's Club; F Other; 2 Personal checks accepted; 3 Lunch available; 4 Dinner available; 5 Open all year;

GUILFORD

Bed and Breakfast, Ltd.

P.O. Box 216, New Haven, 06513
(203) 469-3260

Antique Colonial farmhouse, lovingly restored, antique filled, charming. Close to historic green, near shoreline and many fine antique shops. Delightful hosts. Reservation hours 5:00 until 9:00 P.M. only September through July. Phones available anytime July and August. $65.

HAMDEN

Nutmeg Bed and Breakfast

P.O. Box 1117, West Hartford, 06107
(203) 236-6698

207. A pool and lovely deck add to the enjoyment of this comfortable home. Right outside New Haven, this house has one guest room with shared bath, perfect for the single traveler. Continental breakfast. No smoking.

HARTFORD

Nutmeg Bed and Breakfast

P.O. Box 1117, West Hartford, 06107
(203) 236-6698

453. Lovely Victorian home in an exclusive residential section has a third-floor room with king-size bed, private bath with shower, seating area with sofa which opens into a queen-size bed, TV, clock radio, terry robe, two telephone jacks; second-floor room with double bed and bath shared with hosts, and small TV. Kitchen and laundry privileges for long-term stay. Two-night minimum stay required for weekends from Memorial Day through the end of October.

Continental plus breakfast; no children; smoking allowed; cat and dog in residence.

HIGGANUM

Nutmeg Bed and Breakfast

P.O. Box 117, West Hartford, 06107
(203) 236-6698

521. This Dutch Colonial home is in a very secluded setting on a wooded two-acre lot. There is a second floor king-size bedroom, and a private bath across the hall; a single bed is available in the next room for a child. There is a sauna and shower in the basement. Full breakfast is served. Children are allowed. No smoking. No pets.

The Copper Beech Inn

IVORYTON

The Copper Beech Inn

46 Main Street, 06442
(203) 767-0330

Gracious gardens and rustic woodlands set the stage for this handsome inn. A gallery offers antique Oriental porcelain, and the dining room is noted for fine country French cuisine. Breakfast includes fresh fruit, homemade pastries, breads, cereal, juice, tea, and

6 Pets welcome; 7 Smoking allowed; 8 Children welcome; 9 Social drinking allowed; 10 Tennis available;
11 Swimming available; 12 Golf available; 13 Skiing available; 14 May be booked through travel agents.

coffee. Beautiful countryside, quaint villages, museums, antique shops, theater, and water sports distinguish the area. Two-night minimum stay for weekends and holidays. Closed Mondays, Christmas, and New Year's Day.

Hosts: Eldon and Sally Senner
Rooms: 13 (PB) $117.60-184.80
Continental Breakfast
Credit Cards: A, B, C, E
Notes: 2, 4, 5, 8 (over 8), 10, 11, 12

KENT

Chaucer House

88 North Main Street, 06757
(203) 927-4858

Chaucer House is a Colonial home resting on large lawns amid maple shade trees and is owned by a couple from Kent, England. Guests appreciate being on Main Street and enjoy the short stroll to the Kent galleries, cafes, antiques, shops, and restaurants. Many of western Connecticut's recreation areas and beauty spots are close by, and canoeing, skiing, fishing, hiking, cycling, and picnicking are just some of the local activities.

Hosts: Brenda and Alan Hodgson
Rooms: 4 (2 PB; 2 SB) $75-80
Full Breakfast
Credit Cards: A, B, C
Notes: 2, 5, 9, 10, 11, 13

Covered Bridge

P.O. Box 447, Norfolk, 06058
(203) 542-5944

1K. Charming 18th-century house is one of the oldest in Kent, and is a splendid example of Federal architecture and decor. Living room with fireplace is available for guests; upstairs suite has an ornately carved four-poster canopied bed and private bath. Continental breakfast. $85-120.

2K. This 1860 Colonial set on two acres is close to Kent Falls. The owner, who also

has an antique shop on the grounds, has decorated all of the rooms with period furniture. There is a living room and a den with a fireplace and TV. Continental breakfast. Three guest rooms with shared and private baths. $85-95.

Nutmeg Bed and Breakfast

P.O. Box 1117, West Hartford, 06107
(203) 236-6698

306. This 1790s farmhouse is in the middle of 200 acres of fields and woods. The furnishings are a blend of antique and contemporary. The two first-floor rooms, one double and one queen-size, have private baths. The two rooms on the second floor share a bath—one is a double, the other a single. Continental breakfast; children over three welcome. Several cats in residence.

322. Friendliness awaits guests at this 1860s Colonial bed and breakfast home. Unwind in the romantic Rose Stenciled Room with beamed ceiling or the Country Blue Room with carved Victorian headboard, both with private baths. There is an adjacent cottage with a sitting area, a queen-size room, a private bath, and kitchen. Relax by the fireplace in the cozy den or walk the lovely grounds and view St. John's Ledges. After a Continental breakfast in the charming dining room, visit the adjoining antique shop. Nearby to hiking, skiing, canoeing, museums, and many fine restaurants. Children over 12 welcome. No smoking.

LAKEVILLE

Nutmeg Bed and Breakfast

P.O. Box 1117, West Hartford, 06107
(203) 236-6698

NOTES: Credit cards accepted: A MasterCard; B Visa; C American Express; D Discover Card; E Diner's Club; F Other; 2 Personal checks accepted; 3 Lunch available; 4 Dinner available; 5 Open all year;

328. Set along a lovely lake, this 15-room turn-of-the-century bed and breakfast is filled with antiques and charm. Guests may choose guest rooms with a sleigh or a spool bed, each with its own private bath. After a sumptuous Continental breakfast, enjoy some of the area's many attractions: Lime Rock Park, Music Mountain, and Mohawk Ski Area. Children over eight are welcome. No smoking.

330. High on a peaceful hill, this stately home sits on beautifully landscaped acreage. Guests will find flowers in the room, fresh from the greenhouse, and terry-cloth robes to snuggle in after bathing in an old-fashioned claw-foot tub. The three guest rooms are lovingly furnished with antiques and have private and semi-private baths. Guests have a private entrance and share their own sitting room with fireplace. Children over ten are welcome. No smoking.

331. Dutch Colonial on eight scenic acres overlooking banks of a trout stream. One room with king-size or twin beds, one with single, one with double. All have shared baths. A twin-bedded room can have private bath. Breakfast on enclosed porch overlooking waterfall. Five minutes to Lime Rock, two miles to Salisbury or Hotchkiss Schools. Continental breakfast. Children one and over. No smoking. Cats in residence.

LEDYARD

Applewood Farms Inn Bed and Breakfast

528 Colonel Ledyard Highway, 06339
(203) 536-2022

Five generations of the Galloup family have worked this farm, circa 1826, near Mystic. The classic center chimney Colonial, furnished with antiques and early-American pieces, is on 33 acres of fields and mead-ows. Rooms are light and airy, with braided rugs on wide-board floors and pine and oak antiques. Stone fences meander through the property and many of the original outbuildings remaining are on the National Register, cited as one of the best surviving examples of a 19th century farm in Connecticut.

Hosts: Tom and Frankie Betz
Rooms: 5-1/2 (PB) $115-150
Full Breakfast
Credit Cards: A, B
Notes: 2, 5, 6, 7, 9, 10, 11, 12, 14

Nutmeg Bed and Breakfast

P.O. Box 1117, West Hartford, 06107
(203) 236-6698

515. Casual, informal country inn on six and one-half acres, within walking distance of Foxwoods Casino, and convenient to Mystic and Stonington. Four guest rooms with private baths, two with queen-sizebeds, one with king size water bed, and one with double. Host will provide shuttle service to casino. Full breakfast. Children welcome. Smoking outside only. Two cats in residence.

519. This English Tudor house is set on more than an acre of wooded land with gardens. Near Mystic Seaport, Foxwood Casino, the Coast Guard Academy, Connecticut College, and the sub base. The double room has a private bath. A queen room and a king room share a bath. Full breakfast served; no smoking. Friendly cat in residence.

LITCHFIELD

Covered Bridge

P.O. Box 447, Norfolk, 06058
(203) 542-5944

Pre-Revolutionary War Colonial set on more than 200 acres. In summer, guests can

6 Pets welcome; 7 Smoking allowed; 8 Children welcome; 9 Social drinking allowed; 10 Tennis available; 11 Swimming available; 12 Golf available; 13 Skiing available; 14 May be booked through travel agents.

enjoy a full breakfast overlooking a wooded brook. There are three guest rooms: one on the first floor with a queen-size bed and private bath, and two king-size bedrooms on the second floor with a bath between the rooms. $90.

Nutmeg Bed and Breakfast

P.O. Box 1117, West Hartford, 06107
(203) 236-6698

333. On a quiet country road outside the historic village of Litchfield, this bed and breakfast features: one guest room with queen-size bed and private bath. The house is a pre-Revolutionary Colonial, shaded by century-old sugar maples. Horses and sheep graze in the pasture. Guests will enjoy a full breakfast on the stone terrace or the covered porch in warm weather where they can overlook a view of a wooded brook. Children over 12 welcome.

334. Charming country inn with 31 guest rooms with private baths, some with fireplaces, full service dining room which serves three meals a day. Roll aways are also available. Breakfast at additional charge. Children welcome. Smoking OK.

LYME

Covered Bridge

P.O. Box 447, Norfolk, 06058
(203) 542-5944

1LY. A 1765 Colonial set on four acres and surrounded by stone walls, gardens, and terraces. Relax in the living room with fireplace and the original beehive oven or choose a book from the library. Full breakfast served. Three guest rooms with private bath. $95-110.

2LY. European charm and antiques make this Colonial set on 14 acres a very special retreat. A full breakfast is served in the elegant dining room or in the sitting room that has a wood burning stove and offers a lovely view of the grounds. Several pieces of furniture have been hand-painted by the hostess, reflecting her Swiss heritage. The three queen-bedded guest rooms, each with a private bath, have handmade quilts. $95-110.

Nutmeg Bed and Breakfast

P.O. Box 117, West Hartford, 06107
(203) 236-6698

512. This new center-chimney Colonial is on several acres of woods and has its own walking trail and horseshoe court. Two guest rooms with private baths are accented by family pieces and European furnishings. Convenient to the Old Lyme Art Center, all the shoreline attractions, and many restaurants. Full breakfast. No smoking.

MADISON

Madison Beach Hotel

94 West Wharf Road, 06443
(203) 245-1404

Built in the early 1800s, the Madison Beach Hotel is nestled on a private beach on Long Island Sound. Distinctly Victorian in style and decor. Many rooms have private balconies overlooking the water. Antique oak bureaus, wainscotting, wicker, and rattan furniture, along with old-fashioned wallpaper, complete the Victorian feeling. The hotel's restaurant serves lunch and dinner. Closed January and February.

Hosts: Betty and Henry Cooney; Roben and Kathy Bagdasarian
Rooms: 35 (PB) $55-195
Continental Breakfast
Credit Cards: A, B, C, D, E
Notes: 2, 3, 4, 7, 8, 9, 10, 11, 14

NOTES: Credit cards accepted: A MasterCard; B Visa; C American Express; D Discover Card; E Diner's Club; F Other; 2 Personal checks accepted; 3 Lunch available; 4 Dinner available; 5 Open all year;

Nutmeg Bed and Breakfast

P.O. Box 1117, West Hartford, 06107
(203) 236-6698

520. Lovely center-chimney Colonial about 20-years-old, large living room for guests, lovely dining room, pool, comfortably large eat-in kitchen, fireplace in family room, pool, patio for breakfast on nice days; about five minutes from beach. Two second-floor guest rooms share bath; one has double spool bed, wicker chaise, chest, large closet, shuttered windows overlooking pool; one has twin beds, bedroom chair, chest, large closet. Continental breakfast. No children. No smoking. No resident pets.

MIDDLEBURY

Tucker Hill Inn

96 Tucker Hill Road, 06762
(203) 758-8334

Tucker Hill Inn is a large center-hall Colonial just down from the village green in Middlebury. It was built around 1920 and was a restaurant and catering house for almost 40 years. The period rooms are spacious. Nearby are antiques, country drives, music and theater, golf, tennis, water sports, fishing, hiking, and cross-country skiing. Closed Christmas Day.

Hosts: Richard and Susan Cabelenski
Rooms: 4 (2 PB; 2 SB) $60-90
Full Breakfast
Credit Cards: A, B, C
Notes: 2, 8, 9, 11, 12, 14

MYSTIC

The Adams House

382 Cow Hill Road, 06355
(203) 572-9551; (800) 321-0433

Charming 1790s country home features six rooms with private baths in main house; two rooms have fireplaces. Carriage house has two suites (one with sauna) and kitchenette, accommodates up to eight people. Open year-round. Children welcome. No smoking. No pets.

Hosts: Mary Lou and Gregory Peck
Rooms: 7 (PB) $95-185
Full Breakfast
Credit Cards: A, B, C, D
Notes: 2, 5, 8, 11, 12

Comolli's House

36 Bruggeman Place, 06355
(203) 536-8723

Ideal for vacationers touring historic Mystic or the business person who desires a homey respite while traveling. This immaculate home, on a quiet hill overlooking the Mystic Seaport complex, is convenient to Olde Mistick Village and the aquarium. Sightseeing, sporting activities, shopping, and restaurant information is provided by the hosts. Off-season rates are available.

Host: Dorothy M. Comolli
Rooms: 2 (PB) $65-95
Continental Breakfast
Credit Cards: None
Notes: 2, 5

Covered Bridge

P.O. Box 447, Norfolk, CT, 06058
(203) 542-5944

1MYCT. This restored 150-year-old Victorian farmhouse is on two acres of lovely, landscaped grounds with old stone walls, fruit trees, and an outdoor eating area for the enjoyment of guests. A full breakfast is served in the dining room and a Scottish tea is served in the afternoon. There are six guest rooms, one with fireplace and all with private baths. Room rates are $85-120.

6 Pets welcome; 7 Smoking allowed; 8 Children welcome; 9 Social drinking allowed; 10 Tennis available; 11 Swimming available; 12 Golf available; 13 Skiing available; 14 May be booked through travel agents.

Harbour Inne and Cottage

15 Edgemont Street, 06355,
(203) 572-9253

This inn is on the banks of the Mystic River
in the heart of downtown Mystic. Each
room has a double bed, air conditioning,
cable, and private bath. Cottage with fireplace, kitchen, private bath, air conditioning, cable, and outside hot tub. Pets
allowed. Walking distance of shopping.
One mile from the seaport, two miles from
Olde Mystic Village, and 30 minutes from
beaches in Rhode Island and the Foxwoods
Casino. Kitchen privileges for guests.
Guests are encouraged to make reservations. $10 for pets.

Host: Charles Lecouras, Jr.
Rooms: 7 (PB) $55-200
No Breakfast
Credit Cards: None
Notes: 2 (in advance), 5, 6, 8, 9, 10, 11, 12, 14

Nutmeg Bed and Breakfast

P.O. Box 1117, West Hartford, 06107
(203) 236-6698

513. Built in 1837, this large farmhouse is
surrounded by fruit trees and strawberry
beds. Five guest rooms have private baths;
two have fireplaces. There is also a spacious
dining room and a warm family room. The
home-cooked breakfast with specialty
muffins is amply satisfying. Full breakfast.
Children welcome. Cat and dog in residence. No smoking.

522. Lovely, bright house convenient to
downtown Mystic and Seaport but in a nice
residential neighborhood. Guest bedroom
on the first floor with double spool bed, private full bath. Small upstairs room available
for child. Living room available for guests.
Continental breakfast. Children allowed.
No smoking. Cat in residence.

Steamboat Inn

73 Steamboat Wharf, 06355
(203) 536-8300; (800) 364-6100

On the river, romantic and luxurious, quiet
and elegant in the heart of downtown Mystic. Eight beautiful rooms, all with antique
and custom furnishings, TV, telephones,
and individually controlled heat and air
conditioning. Six rooms feature wood-burning fireplaces, along with two dock-level
semi-suites with double whirlpools. A Continental breakfast is included, featuring pastries and muffins daily. Many shops,
restaurants, and boats within walking distance.

Host: Kitty Saletnik
Rooms: 8 (PB) $95-185
Continental Breakfast
Credit Cards: A, B, C
Notes: 2, 5, 11, 12, 14

NEW HAVEN

Bed and Breakfast, Ltd.

P.O. Box 216, New Haven, 06513
(203) 469-3260

Elegant Italianate home circa 1849. On National Register and shown on historic house
tours. Four-room suite with Victorian bedroom. Private everything! Romantic and
gorgeous. Five minutes to Yale. Reservation hours 5:00 until 9:00 P.M. only September through July. Phones available anytime
July and August. $95.

Nutmeg Bed and Breakfast

P.O. Box 1117, West Hartford, 06107
(203) 236-6698

208. Catch a game at the Yale Bowl or the
bus downtown from this bed and breakfast
in the Westville section. This English Tudor
has two double bedded guest rooms with
shared bath. Guests help themselves to

Continental breakfast. Children welcome. Smoking restricted. Dog in residence.

210. Walk to Yale from this gracious Victorian home set in the residential section of New Haven. A newly decorated third-floor suite consists of a bedroom with a large private bath and a smaller bedroom. A guest room is also available on the second floor. Continental breakfast. Children welcome. Cats in residence.

215. This home near Yale is a 1910 Dutch Colonial with a private garden and deck. Two guest rooms are on the second-floor, one has a double bed and the other has twin beds; both share a bath. Baby equipment available. The house is just over one block from the bus. Continental breakfast; infants welcome. No smoking. Dog in residence.

NEW LONDON

Lighthouse Inn

6 Guthrie Place, 06320
(203) 443 8411

For an exceptionally different experience, come enjoy the Victorian-style rooms, refurbished far beyond their original 1902 grandeur. No two are alike in size or style. Gracious dining further enhances the visit, with the award-winning chef and in-house baker preparing foods for breakfast, lunch, dinner, and Sunday brunch. A varied menu in the lounge is complimented by the Lighthouse Inn jazz series, continuing every Friday and Saturday evening. The inn knows no season, and guests enjoy a private beach and many year-round tourist attractions.

Host: Richard Hamilton
Rooms: 50 (PB) $90-205
Continental Breakfast
Credit Cards: A, B, C, E
Notes: 2, 3, 4, 5, 7, 8, 9, 11, 12, 14

NEW MILFORD

Covered Bridge

P.O. Box 447, Norfolk, 06058
(203) 542-5944

1NM. Vista for viewing, woods for walking, hills for cross-country skiing, streams for fishing, flower gardens, and a pool are some of the attractions of this sprawling estate three miles outside of town. First-floor guest room with private bath and an upstairs guest room. $60-95.

The Homestead Inn

5 Elm Street, 06776
(203) 354-4080; FAX (203) 354-7046

Enjoy warm hospitality in this charming Victorian inn near the village green in the heart of the Litchfield Hills. Stroll to the village and enjoy the shops, restaurants, and movie theater. Eight inn rooms and six motel rooms, all recently redecorated. All have country antiques, private bath, color TV, air conditioning, and telephone. AAA and Mobil approved.

Hosts: Rolf and Peggy Hammer
Rooms: 14 (PB) $72-95
Continental Breakfast
Credit Cards: A, B, C, D, E, F (Carte Blanche)
Notes: 2, 5, 7, 8, 9, 10, 11, 12, 13 (cross-country), 14

Nutmeg Bed and Breakfast Agency

P.O. Box 1117, West Hartford, 06127-1117
(203) 236-6698; (800) 727-7592

A charming home built with wood from a reverse wood tobacco barn, this bed and breakfast is delightfully landscaped with a pool. First floor room with separate entrance to deck has twins or king-size bed and private bath. Second floor room with twin beds and shared bath. One small bedroom on second floor is suitable for a child. Continental breakfast includes home-grown berries, homemade jams, popovers, and muffins prepared by a former chef. Children welcome. Smoking in designated area only. Dog in residence.

NEW PRESTON

Atha House Bed and Breakfast

Box 2015, 06777
(203) 355-7387

Cozy Cape Cod cottage in the rural Washington, Connecticut area offers year-round beauty and solitude. Two comfortable rooms, each with private bath, tastefully appointed sitting room, and living room with fireplace and grand piano. Substantial Continental breakfast. Convenient to historic sites, nature trails, galleries, and antique shops. No smoking. Pets accommodated.

Host: Ruth Pearl
Rooms: 3 (2 PB; 1 SB) $70-85
Continental Breakfast
Credit Cards: None
Notes: 2, 5, 6, 8, 11

NORFOLK

Bed and Breakfast, Ltd.

P.O. Box 216, New Haven, 06513
(203) 469-3260

Near Tanglewood and the Litchfield Hills. Romantic getaway in historic inn. Charming and tranquil atmosphere in a country setting. Reservation hours 5:00 until 9:00 P.M. only September through July. Phones available anytime July and August. $95-125.

Blackberry River Inn

Route 44, 06058
(203) 542-5100

This beautiful 231-year-old Colonial inn, built in 1763, is listed on the National Register of Historic Places. On 27 scenic rural acres, surrounded by the colorful Berkshires, three white Williamsburg buildings house 19 guest rooms including two suites, fireplaces, plus a separate honeymoon suite. Nearby hiking, horseback riding, tennis, lakes for swimming, rivers for trout fishing, flat and whitewater canoeing, rafting, downhill and cross-country skiing, sleigh rides, carriage, hayrides, auto racing at Lime Rock Park, Tanglewood and Norfolk music, festivals, antique shops, autumn foliage, and county fairs. Generous breakfast.

Host: Jeannette Angel
Rooms: 20 (11 PB; 9 SB) $75-150
Continental Breakfast
Credit Cards: A, B, C
Notes: 5, 6, 8, 10, 11, 12, 13, 14

Covered Bridge

P.O. Box 44, Norfolk, 06058
(203) 542-5944

2N. Romantic 1880 Victorian on 11 acres of woods, gardens, and a brook is just steps from the village green. A full breakfast is served on one one of the lovely porches, in the dining room, or in one of the four enchanting guest rooms. All have private baths, two with Jacuzzis. $110-140.

Greenwoods Gate Bed and Breakfast Inn

105 Greenwoods Road East, 06058
(203) 542-5439

Warm hospitality greets guests in this beautifully restored 1797 Colonial home. Small and elegant with four exquisitely appointed guest suites, each with private bath and one with Jacuzzi. Fine antiques, fireplaces, and sumptuous breakfasts to indulge guests. *Yankee* magazine calls this "New England's most romantic Bed and Breakfast." *Country Inns Bed and Breakfast* magazine calls it "A Connecticut Jewel." Join in on the new Deanne Raymond renowned romantic

---

NOTES: Credit cards accepted: A MasterCard; B Visa; C American Express; D Discover Card; E Diner's Club; F Other; 2 Personal checks accepted; 3 Lunch available; 4 Dinner available; 5 Open all year;

cooking classes; call for details. Afternoon tea; early evening refreshments served.

Hosts: George and Marian Schumaker
Suites: 4 (PB) $150-215
Full Breakfast
Credit Cards: None
Notes: 2, 5, 8 (over 12), 9, 10, 11, 12, 13, 14

Manor House

Manor House

Maple Avenue, P.O. Box 447, 06058
(203) 542-5690

Victorian elegance awaits guests at this historic Tudor/Bavarian estate. Antique decorated guest rooms; several with fireplaces, canopies, balconies, a two-person Jacuzzi, and a two-person soaking tub offer a romantic retreat. Enjoy a sumptuous breakfast in the tiffany-windowed dining rooms or treat yourself to breakfast in bed. Designated Connecticut's Most Romantic Hideaway, and included in *Fifty Best Bed and Breakfast's in the USA.*

Hosts: Hank and Diane Tremblay
Rooms: 9 (PB) $85-160
Full Breakfast
Credit Cards: A, B, C
Notes: 2, 5, 8 (over 12), 9, 10, 11, 12, 13, 14

Nutmeg Bed and Breakfast

P.O. Box 1117, West Hartford, 06107
(203) 236-6698

302. This 18th-century inn has Victorian furnishings throughout. There are seven guest rooms, two with shared baths, while the others have private baths. The dining room is open to the public for dinner. Full breakfast. Children welcome.

317. Lovingly restored Victorian has common room with original Tiffany windows, grand foyer, and huge fieldstone fireplace. Eight guest rooms with double, queen- or king-size beds and private baths. Full breakfast. Children over 12. Smoking designated area only. One cat in residence.

336. 1898 house on main street of town features handmade rugs and comfortable furnishings. Opposite Norfolk Chamber Music Festival and near three state parks for hiking and cross-country skiing. Four guest rooms share two full baths. Full breakfast. Children welcome. No smoking. Cat in residence.

Weaver's House

58 Greenwoods Road West, 06058
(203) 542-5108; (800) 283-1551

Turn-of-the-century home on Main Street overlooks the estate of the Norfolk Chamber Music Festival. Host couple offers simple hospitality. Guest rooms are enhanced with handwoven curtains and rag rugs made by the hostess. Full breakfast features home baking and good coffee. Tanglewood is nearby, Music Mountain, Lime Rock Park, skiing, antiquing, swimming, boating, fine dining, and more. German spoken. No smoking.

Hosts: Arnold and Judy Tsukroff
Rooms: 4 (SB) $43-48
Full Breakfast
Credit Cards: A, B, C
Notes: 2, 5, 9, 11, 13

6 Pets welcome; 7 Smoking allowed; 8 Children welcome; 9 Social drinking allowed; 10 Tennis available; 11 Swimming available; 12 Golf available; 13 Skiing available; 14 May be booked through travel agents.

NORTH GRANBY

Nutmeg Bed and Breakfast

P.O. Box 1117, West Hartford, 06107
(203) 236-6698

401. A contemporary home on five acres sits near a three-quarter-acre pond. There are many hiking trails, and three bridges span the stream. A guest suite has a bedroom with a queen-size bed, sitting area, private bath with sauna, wood-burning stove, and a deck. The other room has a double Hide-a-bed and private bath. Continental breakfast; children welcome. Resident cat.

NORTH STONINGTON

Covered Bridge

P.O. Box 447, Norfolk, 06058
(203) 542-5944

1NS. Two 1861 and 1820 Victorian houses are linked by a courtyard and set in a charming, historic seacoast town close to Mystic. The hosts furnished their home in the Georgian manner with formal antique furniture and accessories, many of which are offered for sale. The four guest rooms in the 1861 house have four-poster canopied beds. Full English breakfast served. $90-185.

Nutmeg Bed and Breakfast

P.O. Box 1117, West Hartford, 06107
(203) 236-6698

506. This beautiful village Victorian, built in 1861, has a covered porch and lovely flower and herb gardens. The rooms are beautifully furnished, and a gourmet breakfast is served in the elegant dining room with silver and china. There are four guest rooms; two with private baths, and some with four-poster canopied beds. Mystic Seaport is just ten minutes away; Rhode Island beaches are close by, as are Stonington Village and local vineyards. Full breakfast. No smoking.

OLD GREENWICH

Harbor House Inn

165 Shore Road, 06870
(203) 637-0145

A lovely bed and breakfast by the beach. Harbor House Inn is filled with "old world" charm. One mile from a charming New England village. Close to the train station.

Hosts: Dolly Stuttig and Dawn Browne
Rooms: 23 (17 PB; 6 SB) $70-125
Continental Breakfast
Credit Cards: A, B, C, D
Notes: 5, 8, 9, 10, 11, 12, 14

Nutmeg Bed and Breakfast

P.O. Box 1117, West Hartford, 06107
(203) 236-6698

120. On Long Meadow Creek, an open, airy beach house with a dock on the tidal inlet off Greenwich Cove. Walking distance to the village and train to New York City, and about a mile off I-95. First floor room with queen-size sofa bed (open when guests arrive), wicker sofa, TV, private bath with shower. Full breakfast. Ask about children. No smoking. Resident cats.

OLD LYME

Janse Bed and Breakfast

11 Flat Rock Hill Road, 06371
(203) 434-7269

Large room with sitting areas, antiques, air conditioning, TV, and private bath. This custom saltbox, decorated in Williamsburg-style, is on a quiet road with century-old maples, a large yard with gardens, and vintage stone walls. Just three miles from I-95. Near family-style and four-star dining, shops, theaters, and recreational areas. Thirty minutes to Mystic seaport, Indian Casino, and historic areas. In-room bouquets and snacks.

Hosts: Helen and Donald Janse
Room: 1 (PB) $75
Full Breakfast
Credit Cards: A, B, C
Notes: 2, 5, 7, 8 (over 10), 9, 10, 11, 12

Old Lyme Inn

Old Lyme Inn

85 Lyme Street, P.O. Box 787, 06371
(203) 434-2600; FAX (203) 434-5352

Outside, wildflowers bloom all summer; inside, fireplaces burn all winter, beckoning guests to enjoy the romance and charm of this 13-room Victorian country inn with an award-winning, three-star New York Times dining room. Within easy reach of the state's attractions, yet tucked away in an old New England art colony. Closed first two weeks in January.

Host: Diana Field Atwood
Manager: Fran McNulty
Rooms: 13 (PB) $98-144
Continental Breakfast
Credit Cards: A, B, C, D, E
Notes: 2, 3, 4, 6, 7, 8, 9, 10, 11, 12, 14

OLD MYSTIC

Covered Bridge

P.O. Box 447, Norfolk, 06058
(203) 542-5944

1OMCT. This 1800s Colonial village setting offers a quiet retreat only minutes from the center of Mystic. There is a pleasant living room with a fireplace and a large dining room where a full breakfast is served. There are four guest rooms in the main house, three with fireplaces, and four guest rooms in the carriage house, two with whirlpool tubs. All rooms have queen-size beds and private baths. $98-135.

PLAINFIELD

French Renaissance House

550 Norwich Road, 06374
(203) 564-3277

This lovely historic home, built in 1871 by a wealthy Victorian gentleman, is one of the finest examples of French Renaissance Second Empire architecture in Connecticut. It is near Plainfield Greyhound Park, within reasonable driving distance of Mystic Seaport, Hartford, Providence, Newport, and Sturbridge Village, Massachusetts. Near Foxwood Indian Casino. Winter rates available.

Host: Lucile Melber
Rooms: 4 (1 PB; 3 S2B) $50
Full Breakfast
Credit Cards: A, B, E
Notes: 2, 5, 8, 9, 10, 12

French Renaissance House

6 Pets welcome; 7 Smoking allowed; 8 Children welcome; 9 Social drinking allowed; 10 Tennis available; 11 Swimming available; 12 Golf available; 13 Skiing available; 14 May be booked through travel agents.

PLANTSVILLE

Nutmeg Bed and Breakfast

P.O. Box 1117, West Hartford, 06107
(203) 236-6698

465. This 11-room central-chimney Colonial circa 1740 is on a beautifully landscaped acre with a pool and surrounded by centuries-old maple trees. There are four fireplaces and a Dutch oven in the great room. One guest room has a king-size bed and a private bath; another has queen-size bed, private bath, and working fireplace. Both rooms are air-conditioned. Full breakfast is served. Children are allowed; smoking is restricted; cat and dog on the premises.

Clark Cottage

POMFRET

Clark Cottage at Winter Green

354 Pomfret Street, Routes 44 and 169, 06259
(203) 928-5741

A spacious 1880 Victorian cottage in a quiet, private area with 100-year-old trees down long driveway. Cottage to former Clark Estate consisting of 18 rooms. Next to Pomfret School, and less than a mile from Rectory School, both private boarding schools. Near restaurants.

Hosts: Doris and Stanton Geary
Rooms: 4 (3 PB; 2 SB) $60-75
Continental Breakfast
Credit Cards: A, B
Notes: 2, 8, 7, 9, 11, 12

Covered Bridge

P.O. Box 447, Norfolk, 06058
(203) 542-5944

Set on over six acres, this 18-room Victorian cottage offers a very secluded country getaway. All of the common rooms and guest rooms are exquisitely decorated with Oriental rugs and antiques. There is a large living room with a fireplace and a very elegant dining room. There are two guest rooms with private baths and a two-bedroom suite with a bath. Several rooms also have fireplaces. A full breakfast and afternoon tea are served. $75-110.

POMFRET CENTER

Nutmeg Bed and Breakfast

P.O. Box 1117, West Hartford, 06107
(203) 236-6698

413. 1730 Cape secluded in middle of 23 acres has ideal country setting with birds galore and abundant wildlife. Two guest rooms with double beds and antique furnishings share a bath. Convenient to Pomfret and Rectory Schools. Full breakfast. Children welcome. No smoking. One dog and two cats on premises.

421. This Victorian sits on six acres with flower and vegetable gardens. The formal dining room and sitting room have fireplaces. There are two queen-size rooms with private baths, and a twin- and queen-size room with a shared bath. Full breakfast. No smoking. Children welcome. Dog in residence.

NOTES: Credit cards accepted: A MasterCard; B Visa; C American Express; D Discover Card; E Diner's Club; F Other; 2 Personal checks accepted; 3 Lunch available; 4 Dinner available; 5 Open all year;

PUTNAM

The Felshaw Tavern

Five Mile River Road, 06260
(203) 928-3467

Built as a tavern in 1742, this noble white center-chimney Colonial served the Revolutionary militiamen, notably Israel Putnam of Bunker Hill fame. In 1982, its present owners opened it as a bed and breakfast. Convenient to Boston, Hartford, Providence, and Worcester, it is three and one-half hours from New York. Two guest rooms, furnished in antiques, offer private baths and working fireplaces. Quiet rural setting on three acres.

Hosts: Herb and Terry Kinsman
Rooms: 2 (PB) $80
Full Breakfast
Credit Cards: None
Notes: 2, 5, 9, 10, 11, 12, 13, 14

Nutmeg Bed and Breakfast

P.O. Box 1117, West Hartford, 06107
(203) 236-6698

424. A 1742 two-story tavern with an oak-paneled den and antique furnishings in the guest rooms. Each room has a private bath, working fireplace, and queen-size bed. There is a smaller room with a double bed for a child. Continental breakfast. Children welcome. No smoking.

QUINEBAUG

Captain Parker's Inn at Quinebaug

32 Walker Road, 06262
(203) 935-5219; (800) 707-7303

Captain Parker's Inn at Quinebaug is a new bed and breakfast in the quiet northeastern corner of Connecticut. The home features beautiful varied hardwoods throughout. Although the ocean is about an hour away, the decor portrays a nautical theme. A fine house with Victorian flare and an elegant atmosphere. The inn lends itself to romantic getaways and small weddings. Each guest room features a different hardwood flooring and trim, and most have a bathroom en-suite. The more-than-ample common areas include a library with a wood stove, a large foyer with a baby grand piano, a relaxing entertainment room, a formal dining room with a fireplace, and a pretty, hospitable kitchen. No smoking permitted inside.

Host: David J. Parker
Rooms: 6 (PB)
Full Breakfast

RIDGEFIELD

Nutmeg Bed and Breakfast

P.O. Box 1117, West Hartford, 06107
(203) 236-6698

301. Combine a trip into history with the pleasures of an active getaway at this 200-year-old bed and breakfast. Complimentary tickets to Keeler Tavern, the historical society's showcase, and bicycles for a tour of the nearby nature trails. Two guest rooms with a shared bath. Wine and cheese served upon arrival. Robes, heated spa, and Jacuzzi provided. Children welcome.

West Lane Inn

22 West Lane, Route 35, 06877
(203) 438-7323

The West Lane Inn offers Colonial elegance in overnight accommodations. Special attention is paid to detail and the individual. Also close to shopping, museums, and points of interest.

Host: M.M. Mayer
Rooms: 20 (PB) $120-165
Continental Breakfast
Credit Cards: A, B, C, E
Notes: 5, 7, 8, 10, 11, 12, 13, 14

6 Pets welcome; 7 Smoking allowed; 8 Children welcome; 9 Social drinking allowed; 10 Tennis available; 11 Swimming available; 12 Golf available; 13 Skiing available; 14 May be booked through travel agents.

RIVERSIDE

Nutmeg Bed and Breakfast

P.O. Box 1117, West Hartford, 06107
(203) 236-6698

105. These active hosts have decided to share this lovely country-style Cape home. Guest room has private bath. New York City is only one hour away. Full breakfast. Children welcome. No smoking.

RIVERTON

Old Riverton Inn

Route 20, P.O. Box 6, 06065
(203) 379-8678

Experience the Litchfield Hills hospitality for the hungry, thirsty, and sleepy since 1796. Originally a stagecoach stop on the Hartford to Albany route. On the west branch of the Farmington River, with the Hitchcock Chair Factory Outlet and Museum. Listed on the National Register of Historic Places.

Rooms: 12 (PB) $65-150
Full Breakfast
Credit Cards: A, B, C, D, E
Notes: 3, 4, 5, 8, 9, 10, 11, 12, 13, 14

SALISBURY

Covered Bridge

P.O. Box 447, Norfolk, 06058
(203) 542-5944

1S. An 1810 Colonial set on two private, landscaped acres in the center of town. There is a large living room with a fireplace and a study with a TV for guests. A full breakfast is served. Two guest rooms. $95.

Nutmeg Bed and Breakfast Agency

P.O. Box 1117, West Hartford, 06127-1117
(203) 236-6698; (800) 727-7592

324. Among the oldest in Salisbury, this attractive home overlooking a lovely lake is a fine example of early Federal period architecture. Two guest rooms, one with queen-size and one with double bed, share a bath. A king-bedded suite faces the lake and has a private bath. A twin-bedded lakefront room and a queen-bedded room share a bath, but only one is booked unless a family is traveling together. Full breakfast is served in the dining room. Picnic baskets are available for extra charge. Sorry, no children. No smoking. Dog and cats on premises.

337. This 1813 Colonial is in the historic district of Salisbury, one of Connecticut's most charming villages. There are two guest rooms with private baths. Breakfast in dining room or on the stone terrace in warm weather. Walk to fine restaurants, shopping, and antiquing. Convenient to Lime Rock. Children welcome. No smoking. Pets on premises.

SCOTLAND

Nutmeg Bed and Breakfast

P.O. Box 1117, West Hartford, 06107
(203) 236-6698

454. A 1797 Colonial-style country inn with a large sitting room for guests, keeping room, and kitchen for breakfast. Also a TV room with fireplace, double bedroom, and queen-size bedroom with fireplace. Both share a bath. Full breakfast. Children over 10 allowed. No smoking. Resident cat.

SHARON

Covered Bridge
P.O. Box 447, Norfolk, 06058
(203) 542-5944

1SH. Beautifully nestled in a secluded setting, this lovely contemporary home is decorated throughout with antiques. Guests are welcome to enjoy the large living room, sun porch, and deck. Within walking distance of the village green and the Sharon Playhouse. Reserve a suite or just ask for the bedroom. $85-125.

2SH. An 1890 Colonial on the main street in Sharon is set on beautifully landscaped grounds. There is a large living room and sun porch for guests. A large lake is nearby for swimming, and several areas for skiing in the winter. Four guest rooms with private baths; two with microwave and refrigerator. Full breakfast. $95-105.

3SH. Set on ten acres and surrounded by a land trust of 100 acres, this 1770s Colonial is a special country getaway. All of the common rooms are decorated with antiques as well as the three guest rooms, two with private baths and one with a fireplace. A Continental breakfast is served in the dining room. $90-145.

4SH. Two hundred-year-old Colonial offers a spacious and relaxed country getaway. There are two guest rooms in the main house, one with a Jacuzzi and a private balcony and a guest cottage next to the pool. A full breakfast is served on the sun porch. $95-145.

5SH. Close to the center of town and the Audobon Center, this beautifully restored Colonial is landscaped with terraces, gardens, a stream, and woods. A Continental breakfast is served. There is a two-bedroom guest suite. $95-170.

SHERMAN

Covered Bridge
P.O. Box 447, Norfolk, 06058
(203) 542-5944

1SHR. Circa 1835, this restored bed and breakfast was a rest stop for travelers throughout the 1800s. There is a pleasant living room for guests' use and a Jacuzzi on the deck overlooking the secluded grounds. Acres of woods and fields for hiking or cross-country skiing. Three guest rooms with private baths. Full breakfast. $85-95.

Nutmeg Bed and Breakfast
P.O. Box 1117, West Hartford, 06107
(203) 236-6698

321. This superbly restored 1835 Colonial farmhouse has three air-conditioned guest rooms which are furnished with antiques and have private baths. A king-size and a twin bedroom share a bath. After a full country breakfast, guests are invited to enjoy the outdoor Jacuzzi, game room, or sitting room with TV. One mile from Candlewood Lake, boating, fishing, swimming, and cross-country skiing nearby. Children over ten are welcome. No smoking. Dog and cat in residence.

SIMSBURY

Nutmeg Bed and Breakfast Agency
P.O. Box 1117, West Hartford, 06127-1117
(203) 236-6698; (800) 727-7592

6 Pets welcome; 7 Smoking allowed; 8 Children welcome; 9 Social drinking allowed; 10 Tennis available; 11 Swimming available; 12 Golf available; 13 Skiing available; 14 May be booked through travel agents.

425. Small inn listed on the National Register of Historic Places. All rooms have private baths, TV, phone, and amenities. Full service dining room. Wedding and banquet facilities. Country Continental breakfast. Children welcome. Smoking allowed.

Simsbury 1820 House

731 Hopmeadow Street, 06070
(203) 658-7658

Elegant country inn and restaurant featuring 34 unique guest rooms with private baths. Antique-furnished with modern amenities of today. Highly acclaimed restaurant offers lunch, dinner, and Sunday brunch. Seasonal fireplaces and outdoor dining on scenic veranda. Country Continental breakfast served in dining room each morning. Seasonal discounts available.

Host: Wayne Bursey
Rooms: 34 (PB) $85-125
Suite: 1 (PB) $135
Continental Breakfast
Credit Cards: A, B, C, D, E
Notes: 2, 3, 4, 5, 7, 8, 9, 10, 11, 12, 13, 14

SOUTHINGTON

Nutmeg Bed and Breakfast

P.O. Box 1117, West Hartford, 06107
(203) 236-6698

461. A two-story Colonial-style farmhouse with a large wraparound pillared veranda, 70 acres of grounds with a fish pond, pine grove, and rolling hills. Traditional furnishings in two upstairs bedrooms, each with double beds and shared full bath at the end of the hall. Full Continental or low-calorie breakfast, also special diets are accommodated if necessary. Long term preferred. Children allowed.

SOUTH WINDSOR

Cumon Inn

130 Buckland Drive, 06074
(203) 644-8486; (800) CUMON INN

This beautiful old farmhouse is hosted by Krawski Klan, a speciality building material business owner, a working farmer and a former fighter pilot. This bed and breakfast is open year-round. Relax in any of the eight guest rooms with six shared baths in this saltbox Colonial on 20 acres. Featured in House Beautiful.

Host: Krawski Klan
Rooms: 8 (SB) $75-100
Full Breakfast
Credit Cards: A, B
Notes: 3, 5, 7, 8, 9, 11, 12, 14

STAMFORD

Nutmeg Bed and Breakfast

P.O. Box 1117, West Hartford, 06107
(203) 236-6698

116. This Nantucket Colonial has a water view on a sandy beach. Breakfast is served on the sun porch. One guest room has built-in twin beds, while one has a single bed and both share a bath. The third room has a queen-size bed and private bath. Full breakfast; children welcome. No smoking.

117. This 1960s ranch-style inn has a family room with fireplace, a country kitchen, and a screened porch. The first-floor bedroom trundle bed can be single or double. Private bath and TV. Continental breakfast. No children. No smoking. One dog on premises.

NOTES: Credit cards accepted: A MasterCard; B Visa; C American Express; D Discover Card; E Diner's Club; F Other; 2 Personal checks accepted; 3 Lunch available; 4 Dinner available; 5 Open all year;

STONINGTON

Covered Bridge

P.O. Box 44, Norfolk, 06058
(203) 542-5944

1890s home and cottage set in historic village only a block from the harbor. The cottage has a sitting and dining area with a woodstove, four-poster queen-size bed and its own terrace. $120

Nutmeg
Bed and Breakfast

P.O. Box 1117, West Hartford, 06107
(203) 236-6698

502. This Greek Revival, circa 1830-1850, is just a five-minute walk to the water and within walking distance to many fine restaurants. The private entrance goes into the guest parlor and a non-working marble fireplace. The upstairs room has a double bed and private bath. There are antique furnishings throughout. Continental breakfast. Dog in residence. No smoking.

STRATFORD

Bed and Breakfast, Ltd.

P.O. Box 216, New Haven, 06513
(203) 469-3260

Out of *House Beautiful*. Elegant antique farmhouse, fully restored. Peaceful, serene setting. Fireplaces. Charm everywhere. Near hiking and fine restaurants. Reservation hours 5:00 until 9:00 P.M. only September through July. Phones available anytime July and August. $85-95.

SUFFIELD

Nutmeg
Bed and Breakfast

P.O. Box 1117, West Hartford, 06107
(203) 236-6698

427. This large, custom-built ranch house about a mile from Suffield Academy is immaculate in a quiet location with an attentive, hospitable hostess. Private, spacious first-floor guest room with bath, TV, telephone, and private entrance. Full breakfast. Fruit and snacks always available.

474. An 1825 Federal Colonial near the town green on Main Street; it is a five-minute walk to the grocery, library, pharmacy, movies, and restaurants. There is a choice of a bedroom with attached bath with tub and shower, double four-poster bed, chest, easy chair, and a large built-in closet, or a bedroom not attached to bath with old Victorian double bed, princess dresser, easy chair, bookcase, two closets, and sink. Will rent either room but not both; guests have use of living room, dining room, kitchen, and yard. There is a TV with HBO in one room. It is ten minutes to Bradley; host will provide transportation to and from airport with advance notice. Long term only. No children. No smoking. No resident pets.

THOMPSON

Lord Thompson Manor

Route 200, P.O. Box 428, 06277
(203) 923-3886

Set on 62 acres, Lord Thompson Manor, once a private estate, offers eight guest rooms, four of which are luxury suites, each with an inviting fireplace and private bath.

6 Pets welcome; 7 Smoking allowed; 8 Children welcome; 9 Social drinking allowed; 10 Tennis available; 11 Swimming available; 12 Golf available; 13 Skiing available; 14 May be booked through travel agents.

For romance, Lord Thompson Manor offers guests private candlelight dining, gourmet picnic basket dinners, and romantic candlelight bubble baths. Explore the grounds and gardens landscaped by the renowned Frederick Law Olmstead. For breakfast, enjoy fresh-squeezed orange juice, fresh ground coffee, fresh fruit, waffles, pancakes, and sausages.

Rooms: 8 (4 PB; 4 SB) $75-120
Full Breakfast
Credit Cards: A, B
Notes: 2, 3, 4, 5, 8, 9, 10, 11, 12, 13, 14

Nutmeg Bed and Breakfast

P.O. Box 1117, West Hartford, 06107
(203) 236-6698

468. A new post-and-beam two-story home in a wooded area with lake frontage, three acres, a picnic and swimming area, and within walking distance to convenience store and antique furnishings. The inn offers cable TV, VCR, and telephone. One double-size bedroom and one with twin beds, share a bath and large sitting room, and each has a private entrance. Queen-size Hide-a-bed in the sitting room. Rollaways, and a refrigerator available to guests. Convenient to Sturbridge Village, Woodstock Fair, Thompson Raceway. Pets welcome. Full breakfast. Children welcome. No smoking. Resident dogs.

470. Lovely Cape-style house built in 1780, fully modernized with "touch of Ireland" decor throughout. Completely separate guest quarters with queen-bedded room overlooking back patio with private bath, TV, telephone; second upstairs studio with whirlpool tub in shared bath (this room perfect for children), third queen-bedded room has half-bath and shares Jacuzzi bath with second room if that room is booked. Charming sitting room and dining room for guests, but most prefer breakfast in the family dining room or the sun porch overlooking the back patio and gardens. Full breakfast served. Children ten and over welcome. No smoking.

A Taste of Ireland

47 Quaddick Road, 06277
(203) 923-2883

Country cottage on the National Registry. Sitting room with fireplace, collection of Irish literature, and Celtic music. Full breakfast served with imported foods and beverages from Ireland. Quiet country setting with perennial gardens and lovely stone walls.

Hosts: Jean and Elaine Chicoine
Rooms: 3 (PB) $60-70
Full Breakfast
Credit Cards: None
Notes: 2, 5, 6, 8, 9, 10, 11, 12, 13

TOLLAND

The Tolland Inn

63 Tolland Green, 06084-0717
(203) 872-0800

Built in 1800, the inn stands on Tolland's historic village green, less than one mile north of I-84 Exit 68. Seven guest rooms decorated with antiques and furniture made by the host. Two suites with queen-size canopied beds. One with fireplace, one with kitchen and sitting room. The first floor room has a queen-size canopied bed, fireplace, and a sunken hot tub. Three beautiful common rooms and a fireplace complete the picture. Convenient to Brimfield Fair, Old Sturbridge, and the University of Connecticut.

Hosts: Susan and Stephen Beeching
Rooms: 7 (5 PB; 2 SB) $56-78.40
Suites: $78.40-100.80
Full Breakfast
Credit Cards: A, B, C, D, E
Notes: 2, 5, 8 (over 10), 9, 10, 11, 12, 14

UNCASVILLE

Nutmeg
Bed and Breakfast

P.O. Box 1117, West Hartford, 06107
(203) 236-6698

523. A 90-year-old Dutch Colonial near Mystic, Foxwood Casino, and New London. Four guest rooms, all with private baths, separate entrances, and queen-size beds. Each also has cable TV and telephones. Continental breakfast. Children welcome. One room can accommodate smoking.

WASHINGTON

Covered Bridge

P.O. Box 447, Norfolk, 06058
(203) 542-5944

1WA. Cozy Cape Cod cottage surrounded by woods and fields in nicely landscaped setting. There is a living room with a grand piano and a sitting room with a TV for guests. Two guest rooms with private baths. Continental breakfast. $85.

WASHINGTON DEPOT

Nutmeg
Bed and Breakfast

P.O. Box 1117, West Hartford, 06107
(203) 236-6698

348. A lovely contemporary home overlooking lawns, fields, woodlands, and a small pond has a completely private guest house with nicely furnished sitting room (cable TV and VCR), spacious double bedroom, private bath with shower, separate sleeping alcove with built-in single bed, and small porch. There is a small refrigerator in the guest house and picnic table in pine grove next to the pond. Continental breakfast. Children allowed. Smoking outside only. Cat on premises.

WATERBURY

Covered Bridge

P.O. Box 447, Norfolk, 06058
(203) 542-5944

1WAT. An 1888 Victorian house on the National Register of Historic Places set on an acre in a historic district. There are several common rooms, including an antique-decorated living room with a fireplace. All guest rooms are decorated with antiques. Full breakfast and high tea are served. $75-150.

WATERTOWN

The Clarks   c/osed

97 Scott Avenue, 06795
(203) 274-4866

The Clarks is a 1939 Cape-style home three blocks from Taft Preparatory School and convenient for travelers on Routes 8 and 84. Two guest rooms, one with a double bed and one with twin beds, have ceiling fans. Guests are welcome to use the entire house including porches, barbecue grill, and laundry facilities. The hosts are active in Lions Club, community, and church, and provide a warm family atmosphere.

Hosts: Richard and Barbara Clark
Rooms: 2 (SB) $40-45
Continental Breakfast
Credit Cards: None
Notes: 2, 8, 9

WESTBROOK

Binder's Farm

593 Essex Road, 06498
(203) 399-6407

Since 1928, three generations of Binders have lived on and worked this land. Now

6 Pets welcome; 7 Smoking allowed; 8 Children welcome; 9 Social drinking allowed; 10 Tennis available; 11 Swimming available; 12 Golf available; 13 Skiing available; 14 May be booked through travel agents.

the hosts offer their home to share with vacationers and travelers from all over the globe. The 1820 home was built by a sea captain at a time when everyone was a farmer. The hosts still grow corn and pumpkins. Have eggs from the farm, homemade jams and jellies, and fresh baked breads for breakfast. One mile from I-95; close to town beach and convenient to many local attractions.

Hosts: Ed and Anna Binder
Rooms: 3 (1 PB; 2 SB) $85-95
Full Breakfast
Credit Cards: None
Notes: 2, 8, 9, 11

Talcott House
Bed and Breakfast

161 Seaside Avenue, P.O. Box 1016, 06498
(203) 399-2500

The host invites guests to join her at Talcott House, a beautifully restored 1890 home on Long Island Sound. Comfort is assured in any of the four spacious oceanfront suites, one with its own veranda. All have private baths, and each is decorated to reflect the warmth and tradition of the house. An efficiency apartment is also available. Cozy fireplaces encourage relaxation in the living room. Enjoy the adjacent beaches for a refreshing swim or a walk at sunset. Relax and enjoy the scenic water views from the spacious lawn. For boating enthusiasts, Pilots Point Marina is just a short half-mile walk away.

Host: Allson
Rooms: 4 (PB) $125-135
Full Breakfast
Credit Cards: A, B
Notes: 2, 10, 11

Welcome Inn
Bed and Breakfast

433 Essex Road, 06498
(203) 399-2500

Originally a strawberry farm, the Welcome Inn was built around 1897 and retains its country charm. It is convenient to everything the Connecticut River Valley and seashore has to offer. There are three lovely guest rooms. The house and rooms are decorated with antiques, fine reproductions, lace, and family heirlooms. A complimentary full breakfast is served from 8:00 A.M. to 9:30 A.M. daily with delicious homemade goodies and special coffee. Relax in the parlor with a crackling fire, a glass of sherry and a good book, or in the garden (weather permitting). Hosts can assist guests with arranging restaurant reservations, tours, and other activities.

Hosts: Alison and Robert Bambino
Rooms: 3 (SB) $85-110
Full Breakfast
Credit Cards: None
Notes: 2, 3 and 4 (by arrangement), 8 (over 11), 11, 12

WEST HARTFORD

Nutmeg
Bed and Breakfast

P.O. Box 1117, 06127-1117
(203) 236-6698; (800) 727-7592

405. Colonial-style home with large living room, formal dining room, and two guest rooms on second floor. One has queen-size bed, one has twins; both are nicely decorated. Queen room has private bath; twin has shared bath. Continental breakfast. Children welcome. No smoking.

441. The single-story home is furnished with a blend of modern, traditional, and antique. One guest room with TV has twin or king-size bed and private bath. Continental breakfast. Hungarian spoken. Children welcome. No smoking.

NOTES: Credit cards accepted: A MasterCard; B Visa; C American Express; D Discover Card; E Diner's Club; F Other; 2 Personal checks accepted; 3 Lunch available; 4 Dinner available; 5 Open all year;

455. This center hall colonial has a year-round sunroom. On the bus line and within walking distance to the University of Connecticut, West Hartford branch, and St. Joseph's College. Small child in house. Second floor bedroom with double bed and bath shared with the family. Long term preferred. Continental breakfast. Children allowed. No smoking. No pets.

462. This charming home in a convenient location has a second floor room facing lovely gardens with a double canopied bed and private bath. The third floor suite has a double bed, desk, sitting room, private bath. Continental breakfast. Children welcome. No smoking. Resident dog and cat.

473. This apartment, on the first floor in back of the house with private entrance, offers a bedroom with two closets and queen-size bed, sitting room with TV, table for dining, fully equipped kitchen with storage, bath with tub and shower, and small hallway. Central air, weekly laundering of linens, periodic cleaning with cleaning fee. Long-term only. No breakfast, no children. No smoking. No pets on premises.

482. Ranch-style home with facilities for handicapped. Guest bedroom with private bath, attractive furnishings, three windows, carpeted, queen-size bed, ample storage; second bedroom with twin beds, a full bath (both used for a family traveling together). Continental breakfast (full on request). Children allowed. No smoking. No pets on premises.

WESTPORT

Destinnations New England

P.O. Box 1173, Osterville,MA 02655
(508) 428-4600; (800) 333-4667 (reservations)
FAX (508) 420-0265

The 15-room inn, recently named "Inn of the Month" for *Country Inns* magazine, is one of the most lavishly decorated inns in New England and is reminiscent of Europe's elete manor houses. Each common area, hallway, guest chamber is, in itself, a unique work of art. All rooms are hand-painted and stenciled in a remarkable collaboration of workmanship, architecture, and artistic vision. Some guest chambers feature soaring ceilings, balconies, and expansive windows with sweeping river views. Each room features television with VCR, telephone, and refrigerator. Bathrooms are luxurious with sunken or enthroned tub with superb amenities. *Trompe l'oeil* abounds throughout the inn, and its superb collection of antiques, *objets d'art,* fine paintings, and truly unique touches make one's stay here a most unforgettable experience. If one can bear to leave the building, the Connecticut shoreline's vast array of sights and attractions are nearby. There is a fine restaurant on-site offering contemporized French and Italian cuisine. Open all year. Children welcome. No pets. No smoking. $195-450.

Nutmeg Bed and Breakfast

P.O. Box 1117, West Hartford, 06107
(203) 236-6698

104. Georgian Colonial with pool has second floor guest room with twins or king-size bed, wicker furnishings, private bath with shower. Convenient to railroad station. Full breakfast. Children welcome. No smoking. Dog in residence.

111. Breathtaking setting overlooking Long Island Sound, this home combines rural beauty with metropolitan sophistication. Guest wing is private with its own sitting room, fireplace, and entrance. Three guest rooms with private and shared bath. Enjoy the beach during summer. Continental

---

6 Pets welcome; 7 Smoking allowed; 8 Children welcome; 9 Social drinking allowed; 10 Tennis available; 11 Swimming available; 12 Golf available; 13 Skiing available; 14 May be booked through travel agents.

breakfast. Children welcome. No smoking. $60 plus.

114. A large Colonial surrounded by many old trees on a hilly, wooded acre just outside of town. The original part of the house was built in 1740; guest quarters with separate entrance, bedroom with separate sitting room, double bed, a Hide-a-bed in sitting room. Full private bath; parking in front lot. Pool and spa for guests, dog pen available. Continental breakfast. Children allowed. No smoking. Dogs on premises.

WETHERSFIELD

Chester Bulkley House Bed and Breakfast

184 Main Street, 06109
(203) 563-4236

Chester Bulkley House is a Greek Revival-style house built in 1830. Come and enjoy the New England charm of this historic village settled in 1634. Walk to shops, restaurants, museums, and church. Take a stroll along the cove at sunset. The newly renovated inn boasts warm and friendly hospitality, period antiques, fireplaces, five large guest rooms, and generous full breakfast. Suites are available upon request. Conveniently between New York and Boston, and only a few minutes from Hartford. The hosts hope to anticipate guests' every need and make a stay at the Chester Bulkley House as luxurious and exciting as possible.

Hosts: Frank and Sophie Bottaro
Rooms: 5 (3 PB; 2 SB) $65-85
Full Breakfast
Credit Cards: A, B, C
Notes: 2, 5, 8, 9, 10, 11, 12, 13, 14

Nutmeg Bed and Breakfast

P.O. Box 1117, West Hartford, 06107
(203) 236-6698

408. Nestled in the historic village of Old Wethersfield, this classic Greek Revival brick house has been lovingly restored to provide a warm and gracious New England welcome to all travelers. Built in 1830, it boasts five airy guest rooms furnished with period antiques. Three rooms have private baths; two rooms share a bath. Fresh flowers, cozy living room and parlor; afternoon tea and elegant full breakfast. Children over 11 welcome.

429. This attractive Colonial home is rich in the history of the town. The hostess, a member of the historical society, offers one guest room with private bath. A small room suitable for a child available. Close to a park and safe for walking. Full breakfast. Children welcome. Smoking restricted.

WILTON

Nutmeg Bed and Breakfast

P.O. Box 1117, West Hartford, 06107
(203) 236-6698

119. Contemporary cottage with Oriental architectural accents beside a rushing stream and two small waterfalls. The guest room has a living room/bedroom with two glass walls overlooking the stream and two pull-out queen-size beds. The kitchen has a deck beside the waterfall. Private bath in cottage; guests have use of the heated spa/sunroom. Full breakfast. Children allowed. Smoking allowed. No resident pets. Dogs welcome.

WINDSOR

Bed and Breakfast, Ltd.

P.O. Box 216, New Haven, 06513
(203) 469-3260

NOTES: Credit cards accepted: A MasterCard; B Visa; C American Express; D Discover Card; E Diner's Club; F Other; 2 Personal checks accepted; 3 Lunch available; 4 Dinner available; 5 Open all year;

Fabulous Queen Anne complete with wrap-around porch! Like out of a magazine. Four rooms with private baths and beautiful antiques. Baby grand piano, period furnishings. Minutes to downtown Hartford. Reservation hours 5:00 until 9:00 P.M. only September through July. Phones available anytime July and August. $75.

Covered Bridge

P.O. Box 447, Norfolk, 06058
(203) 542-5944

1WINCT. This 1860 Queen Anne Victorian rests in Connecticut's oldest town, and is furnished with exquisite period antiques and William Morris wallpapers. Guests are welcome to relax in the living room or music room with a grand piano and a century-old music box. The three guest rooms, one with a fireplace, have private baths. $75-100.

Nutmeg Bed and Breakfast

P.O. Box 1117, West Hartford, 06107
(203) 236-6698

469. Charming Victorian home dating to 1860s, renovated with an addition in 1890. Lovely antique furniture, large front porch, three second floor bedrooms, two with extra-long double beds, one with extra-long twin beds, all with private baths. Convenient to airport, University of Hartford, and Loomis Chaffee. Full breakfast. Children over 12. No smoking. Dog on premises.

WINSTED

Nutmeg Bed and Breakfast Agency

P.O. Box 1117, West Hartford, 06127-1117
(203) 236-6698; (800) 727-7592

326. French Provincial style home featuring unique oak carvings, oak paneling, and lovely open staircase. All rooms are air-conditioned. Second floor sitting room with cable TV, fully equipped kitchen for guest snacks. All six guest rooms have either double, twin, or king-size beds and share two baths. Continental breakfast. Children welcome. Designated smoking area.

WOODBURY

Covered Bridge

P.O. Box 447, Norfolk, 06058
(203) 542-5944

1WOCT. This 1789 Colonial set on four acres, is in a town which has been described as the Antique Capital of Connecticut. Many of the original features of the house, such as the large covered porch, wide oak floorboards, and fireplaces, have been preserved. A grand living room with a fireplace and a library are available for guest use. A full country breakfast is served in the dining room or on the south porch. There are five lovely bedrooms and suites. $80-100.

Curtis House

506 Main Street, 06798
(203) 263-2101

Connecticut's oldest inn has been in operation since 1754 in this quaint New England town famous for antique shops. The inn features canopied beds and a popular restaurant serving regional American fare, amply portioned and moderately priced. Closed Christmas Day and Monday lunch.

Host: The Hardisty family
Rooms: 18 (12 PB; 6 SB) $30-70
Continental Breakfast
Credit Cards: A, B
Notes: 2, 3, 4, 5, 7, 9, 10, 11, 12, 13, 14

6 Pets welcome; 7 Smoking allowed; 8 Children welcome; 9 Social drinking allowed; 10 Tennis available; 11 Swimming available; 12 Golf available; 13 Skiing available; 14 May be booked through travel agents.

Nutmeg Bed and Breakfast Agency

P.O. Box 1117, West Hartford, 06127-1117
(203) 236-6698; (800) 727-7592

345. 1789 Colonial on three acres, carefully restored and tastefully furnished with antiques. Two guest rooms have double beds and shared bath; combined they make a suite. Remaining three guest rooms all have private baths. They have either twin, king-, or queen-size beds. Full breakfast. Children five and over welcome. No smoking. Resident cat.

Delaware

LAUREL

Amanda's Bed and Breakfast

1428 Park Avenue, Baltimore, MD, 21217
(410) 225-0001; (800) 899-7533
FAX (410) 728-8957

217. Peaceful country setting. This 18th-century manor house is listed on the National Register of Historic Places. Ideal for experiencing the flavor of the Eastern Shore. Full breakfast. $65-85.

MILTON

Amanda's Bed and Breakfast

1428 Park Avenue, Baltimore, MD, 21217
(410) 225-0001; (800) 899-7533
FAX (410) 728-8957

313. Built by shipbuilders around the middle of the 19th century. On a street with many charming houses. Simple but elegant charm complemented by attractive gardens and a sun porch with afternoon tea. Each room with a private bath and queen-size bed. Full breakfast.

NEW CASTLE

Jefferson House Bed and Breakfast

The Strand at the Wharf, 19720
(302) 325-1025; (302) 322-8944

Packed with charm and history, Jefferson House is an elegant 200-year-old river-front hotel-residence. On a cobblestone street in the center of the historic district, just a few feet from all the historic buildings, museums, shops, and parks. Antique furnishings, hot tub, air conditioning, fireplace, screened porch, efficiencies (long or short term). Private parking. Brochure available.

Host: Martha Rispoli
Rooms: 3 (PB) $49-85
Continental Breakfast
Credit Cards: A, B
Notes: 2, 3, 5, 7, 8, 9, 10, 12, 14

William Penn Guest House

206 Delaware Street, 19720
(302) 328-7736

Choose one of four rooms in this beautifully restored 1682 guest house in the center of historic New Castle, 20 minutes from museum and public gardens.

Hosts: Richard and Irma Burwell
Rooms: 4 (SB) $45
Continental Breakfast
Credit Cards: None
Notes: 2, 5, 8 (over 12), 9, 10

REHOBOTH BEACH

Barry's Gull Cottage

116 Chesapeake Street, Dewey/Rehoboth Beach, 19971
(302) 227-7000 (May to October); (302) 227-0547

A "very special place" for those who want to get away. Gull Cottage, decorated in wicker and offering modern conveniences, centers around pampering its guests. The beaches and bay are within walking dis-

---

6 Pets welcome; 7 Smoking allowed; 8 Children welcome; 9 Social drinking allowed; 10 Tennis available; 11 Swimming available; 12 Golf available; 13 Skiing available; 14 May be booked through travel agents.

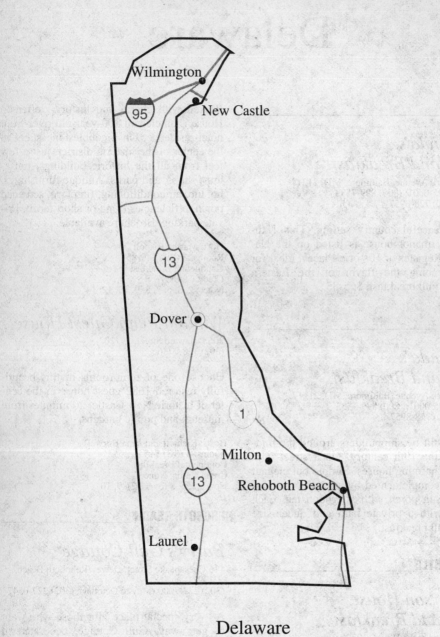

Delaware

tance, and guests can plan the day while enjoying a healthy gourmet breakfast overlooking the lake. Nearby shopping includes a large number of factory outlets and antique malls, as well as dining, ranging from French cuisine to the eastern seaboard's finest seafood. Fresh fruits and vegetables abound in nearby orchards and farmers' markets. Afternoon tea, hot tub by candlelight, and free parking are among the many amenities. Minimum-stay requirements for weekends and holidays. Reservations required. Weekday package discounts.

Innkeepers: Bob and Vivian Barry
Rooms: 5 (3 PB; 2 SB) $85-125
Full Breakfast
Credit Cards: None
Note: 2, 9, 10, 11, 12

The Royal Rose Inn Bed and Breakfast

41 Baltimore Avenue, 19971
(302) 226-2535

A charming and relaxing 1920s beach cottage, this bed and breakfast is tastefully furnished with antiques and a romantic rose theme. A scrumptious breakfast of homemade bread, muffins, egg dishes, and much more is served on a large, screened porch. Air-conditioned bedrooms, guest refrigerator, and off-street parking are real pluses for guests. One and a half blocks from the Atlantic Ocean and boardwalk. Midweek special; weekend packages; gift certificates. Open May through October.

Hosts: Kenny and Cindy Vincent
Rooms: 7 (3 PB; 4 SB) $35-115
Continental Breakfast
Credit Cards: None
Notes: 2, 9, 10, 11, 12

Tembo Bed and Breakfast

100 Laurel Street, 19971
(302) 227-3360

Seven hundred fifty feet from the beach in a quiet, residential area, Tembo offers a casual atmosphere with warm hospitality. Relax among Early American furnishings, antiques, oil paintings, waterfowl carvings, and Gerry's elephant collection. Air-conditioned bedrooms offer firm beds. Minimum-stay requirements for weekends and holidays.

Hosts: Don and Gerry Cooper
Rooms: 6 (1 PB; 5 SB) $60-125
Continental Breakfast
Credit Cards: None
Notes: 2, 5, 6 (limited), 8 (over 12), 9, 10, 11, 12

WILMINGTON

The Boulevard Bed and Breakfast

1909 Baynard Boulevard, 19802
(302) 656-9700

This beautifully restored city mansion was originally built in 1913. Impressive foyer and magnificent staircase leading to a landing complete with window seat and large leaded-glass windows flanked by 15-foot columns. Breakfast is served on the screened porch. Close to the business district and area attractions.

Hosts: Charles and Judy Powell
Rooms: 6 (4 PB; 2 SB) $60-75
Full Breakfast
Credit Cards: A, B, C
Notes: 2, 5, 8, 9, 10, 12

NOTES: Credit cards accepted: A MasterCard; B Visa; C American Express; D Discover Card; E Diner's Club; F Other; 2 Personal checks accepted; 3 Lunch available; 4 Dinner available; 5 Open all year; 6 Pets welcome; 7 Smoking allowed; 8 Children welcome; 9 Social drinking allowed; 10 Tennis available; 11 Swimming available; 12 Golf available; 13 Skiing available; 14 May be booked through travel agents.

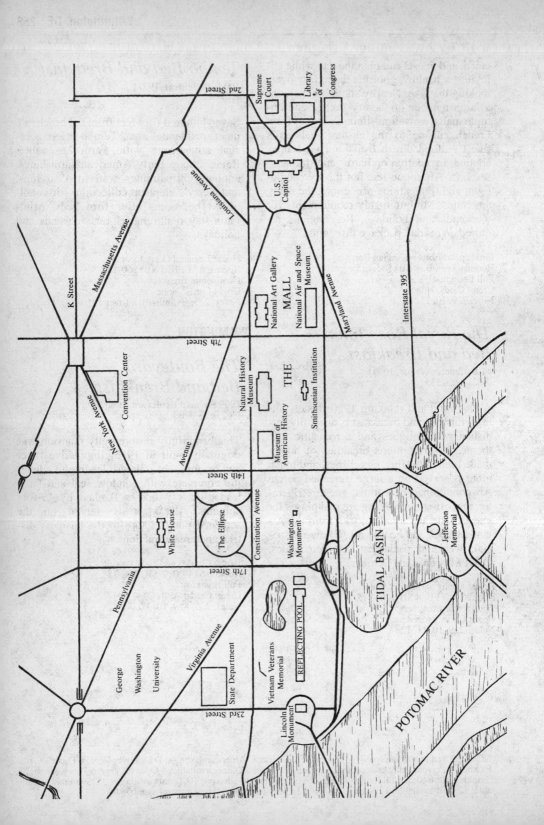

District of Columbia

Adams Inn

1744 Lanier Place, NW, 20009
(202) 745-3600

Convenient, comfortable, home-style atmosphere in a neighborhood with over 40
ethnic restaurants to choose from. Near the
bus lines, shopping, Metro, museums, government buildings, and convention sites.
Economical for the tourist and business
traveler. Both private and shared rooms
available.

Hosts: Gene and Nancy Thompson; Anne Owens
Rooms: 25 (12 PB; 13 SB) $55-95
Continental Breakfast
Credit Cards: A, B, C, D, E
Notes: 2, 5, 8, 14

Adams Inn

Amanda's Regional Reservation Service for Bed and Breakfast

1428 Park Avenue, Baltimore, MD 21217
(410) 225-0001; (800) 899-7533
FAX (410) 728-8957

227. A lovely home near Dupont Circle
Metro on a tree-lined street. Leave the car at
home. Convenient to area restaurants and
shops. Relax in the garden after sightseeing
downtown. Uniquely furnished. Continental breakfast. $71.50.

230. Art deco urban inn with continental
breakfast. All rooms have private baths,
color TV, and telephones. Walk to Metro
for connections around Washington. Ethnic
restaurants in neighborhood. Parking limited. $79-129.

Bed and Breakfast Accommodations, Ltd.

P.O. Box 12011, 20005
(202) 328-3510; FAX (202) 332-3885

108. This turn-of-the-century three-story
bayfront was completely renovated from
1990 to 1992. It boasts central air conditioning, fireplaces, books, and plants galore. Hosts offer two large guest rooms with
private baths, ceiling fans, king-size beds,
comfortable chairs, and televisions. Guests
are also invited to enjoy the living room, library, and back patio. This is a nonsmoking
household. $90-110.

NOTES: Credit cards accepted: A MasterCard; B Visa; C American Express; D Discover Card; E Diner's Club;
F Other; 2 Personal checks accepted; 3 Lunch available; 4 Dinner available; 5 Open all year; 6 Pets welcome; 7
Smoking allowed; 8 Children welcome; 9 Social drinking allowed; 10 Tennis available; 11 Swimming avail-
able; 12 Golf available; 13 Skiing available; 14 May be booked through travel agents.

Bed and Breakfast Accommodations, Ltd.
(continued)

111. On General's Row, a row of town-houses constructed in the late 1880s. This house is just three blocks from Dupont Circle, second only to Georgetown as a neighborhood for the trendy. Dupont Circle offers good restaurants, boutiques, and theaters, and the Dupont Circle Metro Subway is three blocks away. Four guest rooms have either double or a pair of twin beds, and both shared and private baths are available. The hostess is an artist with a MA from the University of Alabama. Resident cat. $60-75.

120. This upper northwest Washington residence is tastefully appointed with crafts, flowers, and comfortable furniture. The fashionable neighborhood offers elegant shopping, close access to all the attractions in downtown Washington, and other major activity areas in Maryland. This host family has lived in Washington D.C. for 25 years, and he is an urban planner, which makes him an excellent source on Washington's attractions. $55-65.

123. Designed in 1891 by famous Washington architect Franklin Schneider, this house was recently renovated by its present owner, an attorney who has traveled all over the United States, Europe, and the Far East. Accommodations include a queen-size reproduction of a Victorian iron and brass bed, private hall bath, and separate sitting room. There is also a front study with extensive bookcases and a sun porch that guests are welcome to use. $75-85.

125. This Victorian townhouse was built in 1990 and is filled with an eclectic mix of period pieces, Oriental, and contemporary art. Four gracefully appointed bedrooms

share two baths on the second floor. A third-floor suite adjoins a private bath and can accommodate up to four people. In the heart of the city, this home is one mile north of the White House and six blocks of Dupont Circle Metro stop on the red line. No smoking; no children. $65-75.

126. This house is a Georgian-style brick Colonial with a slate roof. On a wide, tree-lined avenue in a residential neighborhood, Tenley Circle is between Georgetown and Chevy Chase, Maryland. Guests have easy access to downtown business areas and major bus routes, and within two blocks are many restaurants, shops, movie theaters, tennis courts, and an indoor pool. Two large guest rooms each have a private bath with a tiled shower. Dog and cat in residence. Guest pets and smoking are not permitted. $70-80.

129. This red-brick, former schoolhouse, circa 1880, was converted about four years ago into condominiums. It features enormous windows and 15-foot ceilings. Four and one-half blocks from Union Station. The guest room was designed by the hostess, an avid collector of antiques. It has an Old World-style bed built into an existing alcove, and an entertainment center and appliances are all operated by remote control so that a tired guest can prop himself against a pillow and never have to move. Walking distance to charming cafes and restaurants that line Massachusetts Avenue. $60, single only.

133. A beautifully restored Victorian home built in 1859. The house is full of lovely antiques, including antique beds in the guest rooms and features a lovely garden area with Koi pond and fountain, which has been the site of several weddings. One guest room has a white iron and brass queen-size bed, antique armoire, ceiling fan, stained-glass window, dressing room, and private

NOTES: Credit cards accepted: A MasterCard; B Visa; C American Express; D Discover Card; E Diner's Club; F Other; 2 Personal checks accepted; 3 Lunch available; 4 Dinner available; 5 Open all year;

bath with a large walk-in double shower. The other guest room has a large Victorian double bed and antique furnishings, including handmade rugs from North Carolina. The room is decorated in Laura Ashley wallpaper, linens and fabrics, and has a private attached bath. $85-100.

136. This unhosted apartment on a quiet residential street of three-story townhouses is only a few blocks away from Metro stops to the White House, Woodley Park/Zoo, excellent area shops and restaurants, and the Sheraton Washington and Connecticut Avenue. This completely self-contained one-bedroom apartment occupies one floor of the townhouse. It has been professionally decorated, has a queen-size bed, full bath, fully equipped kitchen, and living room with cable TV, VCR, stereo, and private patio. Roll-away bed, laundry facilities, and weekly maid service available. $90-100.

137. Seven blocks behind the Capitol, walking distance to the Supreme Court and Library of Congress, and a ten-minute walk to both Eastern Market Metro and Union Station. This house, built in 1902, has been restored to its present condition by the owner, a fashion designer whose renovations have been featured in *Better Homes and Gardens* and the *Washington Post*. Two guest rooms are available, each with a double bed, color TV, telephone, and shared bath. $65-75.

137A. This furnished two bedroom apartment in the entire English basement of a three-story, 100-year-old Victorian townhouse. Seven blocks from the US Capitol, Library of Congress, House of Representatives, and Senate. One bedroom has an antique queen-size bed; the other has double bed. A queen-size fold-out sleeper sofa is in the living room. Fully equipped kitchen, color TV, clock radio, telephone, and win-

dow air conditioning. No off-street parking. No smoking. $100.

139. This spacious five-bedroom house was designed by famed Washington architect Harry Wardman, who developed this elegant, tree-lined district adjacent to Rock Creek Park. One guest room has twin beds, a sitting room, and a private bath. The second guest room has a twin bed and shared bath. There is an enclosed garden in the back where parking is available. $60-75.

146. Built in 1926, this semi-detached residence is part of the larger three-story rowhouse developments of beautiful North Cleveland Park in northwest Washington, yet is still quaint like Georgetown. On a tree-lined street, the house is recessed from the road. The guest rooms are on the second floor. The Green room can either have twin beds or a sumptuous king-size bed, and includes a comfortable loveseat, an antique writing table, extra large closet, and a shared bath with shower/tub. The Mauve room is furnished with a down covered king-size bed, dressing room/office, television, and private bath with shower. Private telephone line and TV/VCR. Airport/station pick-up or drop-offs can be arranged.

149. This one bedroom apartment has a dining area, screened-in back porch, queen-size bed and sleeper sofa, telephone, ceiling fans, air conditioning, fully equipped kitchen, and color TV. Easy walk to Capitol, Library of Congress, and the House of Representatives. Metro is a few blocks away and buses even closer. National monuments and the Smithsonian Institute are nearby. $85.

155. A 19th-century inn in historic Virginia just 45 minutes from downtown, the inn has been lovingly restored as a beautiful, cozy bed and breakfast. There are 14 unique

6 Pets welcome; 7 Smoking allowed; 8 Children welcome; 9 Social drinking allowed; 10 Tennis available; 11 Swimming available; 12 Golf available; 13 Skiing available; 14 May be booked through travel agents.

Bed and Breakfast Accommodations, Ltd. *(continued)*

rooms furnished with antiques and reproductions, and each is named for a noteworthy Virginian. The dining room was inspired by Belvoir, the home of William Fairfax. Gardens designed to reflect the era when the inn was constructed have been added to both the front and back of the building. Full breakfast and high tea are both served. $115-250.

158. A three-story brick townhouse at Tiber Island is right in the heart of the city on Washington's waterfront. Guests have an easy stroll to the Smithsonian Institute, the Jefferson Memorial, and the Tidal Basin. Accommodations include a queen-size bed, private hall bath, kitchen, dining/living room, and music/video room. $85.

168. This exceptional Victorian bay-front was built in 1881 and has been featured on the Capitol Hill House Tour. Guests are just five blocks from the Capitol, the Library of Congress, Supreme Court, and the Mall. The Blue/Orange Metro line is less than a ten-minute walk. The guest suite has a private bath, sitting room, queen-size reproduction of a Victorian iron bed, color TV, VCR, and telephone. Outside smoking only. $80.

170. The house is a beautifully restored Victorian retaining most of the original architectural details. It faces Pennsylvania Avenue and is furnished with American antiques throughout. Guests are invited to use the Florida room where breakfast is served, as well as the Florentine room and garden. There are two large guest rooms sharing a bath, one with a period antique double bed and one with a queen-size bed. $65-80.

175. This beautiful old federal front rowhouse built in 1885, just twenty years after the Cilvil War, is furnished with lovely pieces from the 30's and 40's which gives guests the feeling of grandmother's house. There are two bedrooms with private baths. The living room features a working fireplace and guests are invited to use the beautiful French Quarter-style patio and enjoy the fountains and fish pond, directly off the living room. Off-street parking is available. No smoking in the house. $70-90.

180. This fully equipped one bedroom English basement apartment is just five blocks from Union Station, which is a major stop for the Old Town trolley and the Tourmobile. The apartment is also convenient to all sites on Capitol Hill. Accommodations include a double bed, queen-size sofa bed, living room, dining room, fully equipped kitchen, TV, telephone, and air conditioning. $65.

190. A spacious two bedroom English basement apartment decorated with original art, new European-style modern furnishings, and a fully equipped kitchen with dishwasher and disposal. There is a private patio entrance to the living room, security doors at the front and rear, and windows throughout. Color TV, stereo/radio/cassette sound system, and central heat and air. There is a fireplace in the living room, but it can only be used by special arrangement with the owner. $80-115.

195. Washington's Foggy Bottom/West End is the setting for this spacious, two-level, modern, one-bedroom apartment. The Metro is only three blocks away. Accommodations include a living room with a queen-size sleeper sofa, fireplace, color TV with cable, telephone, central heat and air conditioning, and an eat-in kitchen. A separate bedroom features a queen-size bed and a modern bath with tub/shower. $100.

NOTES: Credit cards accepted: A MasterCard; B Visa; C American Express; D Discover Card; E Diner's Club; F Other; 2 Personal checks accepted; 3 Lunch available; 4 Dinner available; 5 Open all year;

200. Each of the 54 guest rooms and suites are unique. Many contain historical features. Each guest room is individually decorated with original art work and authentic period furnishings complimented by custom design and hand-crafted pieces. Guest room features include: maid service twice a day, including turn-down service; convenient in-room bar and refreshments; baths with marble vanities and personal toiletries; many rooms with bay windows and some with porches; individually controlled heating and air conditioning; telephones, computer access data ports; color TV and in-room movies; and AM/FM radios. Valet parking is available. Special weekly rates. $135-185.

Capitol Hill Guest House

101 Fifth Street Northeast, 20002
(202) 547-1050

The Capitol Hill Guest House is a 19th-century Queen Anne-style row house only three blocks behind the U.S. Supreme Court on historic Capitol Hill. There are ten moderately priced rooms with the flavor of a bygone era when all visitors to the nation's capital stayed in the many guest houses that dotted Capitol Hill.

Host: Mark Babich
Rooms: 10 (SB) $45-85
Continental Breakfast
Credit Cards: A, B, C, D
Notes: 5, 9, 10, 11, 14

Embassy Inn

1627 16th Street Northwest, 20009
(202) 234-7800; (800) 423-9111

A European-style inn nine blocks north of the White House and within short walking distance to Metro subway transportation. Features a charming and relaxed atmosphere, personalized service, and extras such as continental breakfast, evening sherry, and snacks each day. Economical rates in a nice neighborhood.

Host: Susan Stiles
Rooms: 38 (PB) $69-99
Continental Breakfast
Credit Cards: A, B, C, E, F
Notes: 5, 7, 8, 9, 14

Henley Park Hotel

926 Massachusetts Avenue, Northwest, 20001
(202) 638-5200; FAX (202) 638-6740

An intimate 96-room luxury property reminiscent of a traditional European country inn specializes in personalized services, such as mini-bars, and 24-hour room service. The restaurant offers award-winning cuisine, and has been named in the top five most romantic restaurants, with its sun-filled atrium. Marley's lounge offers live jazz. The Wilkes Room has a traditional tea with scones and Devonshire cream in a cozy atmosphere of fresh flowers and a fireplace. Complimentary breakfasts with certain packages. Near Union Station, the Capitol, Smithsonian Museums, and the Metro.

General Manager: Michael Rawson
Rooms: 96 (PB) $185-350
Credit Cards: A, B, C, D, E
Notes: 2, 3, 4, 5, 7, 8, 9, 12, 14

Hereford House

604 South Carolina Avenue Southeast, 20003
(202) 543-0102

A 1915 brick townhouse with original parquet flooring. On a wide tree-lined street on historic Capitol Hill, one block from the Metro. The U.S. Capitol, Congressional Library, Smithsonian, and many restaurants are all within easy walking distance, making Hereford House the perfect location for Washington visitors. Bountiful English breakfast served by British hostess. Guests will want to return again to their new home away from home after experiencing the hospitality.

Host: Ann Edwards
Rooms: 4 (SB) $40-65
Full Breakfast
Credit Cards: None
Notes: 2, 5, 8 (over 12), 9, 10, 11

6 Pets welcome; 7 Smoking allowed; 8 Children welcome; 9 Social drinking allowed; 10 Tennis available; 11 Swimming available; 12 Golf available; 13 Skiing available; 14 May be booked through travel agents.

Kalorama Guest House at Kalorama Park

1854 Mintwood Place Northwest, 20009
(202) 667-6369

A charming Victorian inn in a quiet downtown residential neighborhood, only a short stroll to the underground Metro and a potpourri of ethnic restaurants and shops. Enjoy the hospitality of the innkeepers, a complimentary continental breakfast, and evening aperitif. Just ten minutes from the mall, White House, and most attractions. Economical rates bring guests back again and again.

Hosts: Tami, John, and Carlotta
Rooms: 30 (12 PB; 18 SB) $45-95
Continental Breakfast
Credit Cards: A, B, C, E
Notes: 2, 5, 7, 8, 9, 14

Morrison–Clark Inn

Massachusetts and L Street, 20001
(202) 898-1200

The restored Morrison-Clark Inn preserves the elegance of Victorian design and creates the feel of an elegant turn-of-the-century Washington home. The guest rooms and suites are individually decorated with authentic period furnishings. Breakfast, lunch, and dinner are served in the restaurant, one of the best in Washington. The inn is just six blocks from the White House near downtown shopping, Chinatown, and the convention center. Weekend rates are available.

Host: Michael Rawson
Rooms: 54 (PB) $125-195
Continental Breakfast
Credit Cards: A, B, C, D, E
Notes: 2, 3, 4, 5, 7, 8, 9, 10, 11, 12, 14

The Reeds

P.O. Box 12011, 20005
(202) 328-3510

A 100-year-old Victorian mansion that has been carefully and extensively restored. Original wood paneling, stained glass, chandeliers, and porch. Each room has a color TV and telephone; laundry facilities are available. Adjoins Logan Circle Historic District, with excellent transportation and easy parking. This beautiful home was selected as a part of the "Christmas at the Smithsonian" festivities, and was featured in the Washington Post in December when it was decorated for Christmas. Ten blocks from the White House. The hosts speak English and French.

Hosts: Charles and Jackie Reed
Rooms: 5 (SB) $55-82.50
Continental Breakfast
Credit Cards: A, B, C, E
Notes: 2 (in advance), 5, 8, 9

Windsor Inn

1842 16th Street Northwest, 20009
(202) 667-0300; (800) 423-9111

A charming inn 11 blocks from the White House in the heart of Washington, D.C. Features a relaxing and friendly atmosphere as well as personalized service from the staff. A complimentary continental breakfast, evening sherry, and snacks are available. Economical rates, suites, and a nice neighborhood.

Host: Susan Stiles
Rooms: 46 (PB) $62.55-168
Continental Breakfast
Credit Cards: A, B, C, E, F
Notes: 5, 7, 8, 9, 14

NOTES: Credit cards accepted: A MasterCard; B Visa; C American Express; D Discover Card; E Diner's Club; F Other; 2 Personal checks accepted; 3 Lunch available; 4 Dinner available; 5 Open all year;

Florida

AMELIA ISLAND

The Amelia Island Williams House

103 South 9th Street, 32034
(904) 277-2328

This 1856 antebellum mansion was built in the grand style by a wealthy Boston banker. The town's most historic home has some of the most outstanding architectural details in Fernandina Beach. The perfect setting for the owner's extensive Oriental art and antique collection dating from the 1500s. Four superb guest rooms, including an exceedingly elegant bridal suite with Napoleonic antiques. All rooms have private baths. Breakfast is served in opulent red and gold dining room. Children over 12. No smoking.

Hosts: Dick Flitz and Chris Carter
Rooms: 4 (PB) $95-135
Continental plus Breakfast
Cards: A, B
Notes: 2, 5, 8 (over 12), 9, 10, 11, 12, 14

The Fairbanks House

227 South Seventh Street, 32034
(904) 277-0500; (800) 261-4838

The Fairbanks House is an Italianate villa, built in 1885 and listed on the National Register of Historic Places. It has ten rooms, suites, or cottages, all with private baths, telephones, and TVs. Four-poster king, queen, or twin beds are available with claw foot tubs, showers, or Jacuzzis. The Fairbanks House has been completely restored. Furnishings are done in antiques, period-pieces, and Oriental rugs. Enjoy the piazzas, swimming pool, and beautiful gardens. A gourmet Continental breakfast and complimentary afternoon refreshments are included.

Hosts: Mary and Nelson Smelker
Rooms: 10 (PB) $85-150
Full Breakfast
Credit Cards: A, B, C, D
Notes: 2, 5, 8, 9, 10, 11, 12, 14

ARCADIA

Bed and Breakfast Scenic Florida

P.O. Box 3385, Tallahassee, 32315-3385
(904) 386-8196

FL46. Built in the 1890s, this Southern Double Porch Colonial home has a 1914 addition. Public rooms include the formal dining room and parlor. Upstairs porches are furnished with wicker and overlook the grounds. Guests may choose from three second-floor rooms with double beds, fireplaces, shared or private baths, including a claw-foot tub and shower. The home is also centrally heated and air-conditioned. Breakfast includes homemade muffins and is served in the formal dining room from 8:00 to 10:00 A.M. No smoking. $60-75.

BIG PINE KEY

The Barnacle

Route 1, Box 780A, 33043
(305) 872-3298

Enjoy the ambience of a homestay bed and breakfast, along with every amenity. A

6 Pets welcome; 7 Smoking allowed; 8 Children welcome; 9 Social drinking allowed; 10 Tennis available; 11 Swimming available; 12 Golf available; 13 Skiing available; 14 May be booked through travel agents.

29

10

Niceville

Pensacola Holley
Destin
Santa
Rosa
Beach

98

231

Quincy
Tallahassee

10

319

Wakulla Springs

98

St. Teresa
Beach

19

27

19

Monticello

75

27

High Springs

Gainesville
Micanopy

301

San Mateo

Ocala

75

Cedar Key

Cedar Key

27

1

Fernandina Beach
Amelia Island

Jacksonville
Orange Park

10

301

St. Augustine
Crescent City

1

Daytona Beach

Edgewater

4

95

Mount Dora

Longwood
Orlando

TPK

Lake Buena Vista

Kissimmee

Cocoa

19

Holiday
Tarpon Springs
Palm Harbor

Treasure Island
St. Pete Beach
Terra Verde

Holmes Beach
Bradenton
Cortez

Venice

Lakeland
Tampa

4

60

St Petersburg

Palmetto
Sarasota

75

Haines City

Lake Wales

TPK

Palm Bay

Indialantic

60

Zolfo Springs

Fort Pierce

95

Tequesta

Jupiter

Palm Beach
Gardens

80

Wellington
Harbour Pointe

27

80

Lake Park
West Palm Beach
Lake Worth
Lantana
Delray Beach
Boca Raton
Deerfield Beach

TPK

75

41

Hollywood
Miami

1

Key Largo
Plantation

1

Marathon
Big Pine Key

Key West

Florida

unique experience on the ocean, surrounded by lush, verdant foliage, where guests can enjoy peace and quiet, yet be only 30 miles from the attractions of Key West.

Hosts: Wood and Joan Cornell
Rooms: 4 (PB) $75-100
Full Breakfast
Credit Cards: None
Notes: 2, 5, 7, 9, 11

The Barnacle

Canal Cottage
P.O. Box 430266, 33043 0266
(305) 872-3881

Relax in the private apartment of this quaint, natural-wood stilt home. Nestled in the treetops, cooled by island breezes and Bahama fans. Enjoy the bicycles, cable TV, gas grill, and fully furnished kitchen. Private club privileges for pool, tennis, raquetball. Weekly discounts.

Hosts: Dean and Patti Nickless
Rooms: 2 (PB) $85
Continental Breakfast
Credit Cards: None
Notes: 2, 5, 7, 8, 9, 11, 14

Deer Run
Long Beach Road, Box 431, 33043
(305) 872-2015; (305) 872-2800

Deer Run is a Florida Cracker-style house nestled among lush native trees on the ocean. Breakfast is served on the large veranda overlooking the ocean. Dive at Looe

Key National Marine Sanctuary, fish the Gulf Stream, or lie on the beach. A nature lover's paradise and a bird watcher's heaven. Two-night minimum stay required.

Host: Sue Abbott
Rooms: 2 (PB) $85-110
Full Breakfast
Credit Cards: None
Notes: 2, 5, 9, 11

BOCA RATON

Bed & Breakfast Co.
P.O. Box 262, South Miami, 33243
(305) 661-3270; FAX (305) 661-3270

BR064. This conventional suburban ranch home in Boca Raton offers a variety of personal touches that reflect the hosts' interests in needlework, gardening, and flowers. In a pleasant neighborhood, near ten golf courses, two miles to a large mall, and seven miles to the beach. Two comfortable bed and breakfast rooms available with double bed and shared bath. Very hospitable hosts. $40.

Open House Bed and Breakfast Registry
P.O. Box 3025, Palm Beach, 33480
(407) 842-5190

Suburban Ranch. A comfortable home west of Florida's Turnpike, near mall restaurants and shopping. Guests are welcome to use the barbecue and refrigerator on the patio. From the pool, relax and enjoy looking at the lush greens of a local golf course. Choose between a corner queen-size bedroom or a single bedroom. $40-60.

BRADENTON

Bed & Breakfast Co.
P.O. Box 262, South Miami, 33243
(305) 661-3270; FAX (305) 661-3270

NOTES: Credit cards accepted: A MasterCard; B Visa; C American Express; D Discover Card; E Diner's Club; F Other; 2 Personal checks accepted; 3 Lunch available; 4 Dinner available; 5 Open all year; 6 Pets welcome; 7 Smoking allowed; 8 Children welcome; 9 Social drinking allowed; 10 Tennis available; 11 Swimming available; 12 Golf available; 13 Skiing available; 14 May be booked through travel agents.

BB275. Renovated Victorian home built in the late 1800s was moved by barge in 1946 along the Manatee River to its present location, across the street from the gulf beach. Interesting antique furnishings in the guest room and one-bedroom apartment. A delightful, low key, restful spot for the tourist or professional who wants to relax. Gracious hostess serves speciality breakfast favorites. $60-75.

B&B Suncoast Accommodations

8690 Gulf Boulevard, St. Pete Beach Island, 33706
(813) 360-1753

6. This home offers a pool, spa, king-size bed, and private bath to guests. On the Canal, the Gulf beach is ten minutes away. Seventh night free. $65-85.

CEDAR KEY

Bed and Breakfast Scenic Florida

P.O. Box 3385, Tallahassee, 32315-3385
(904) 386-8196

FL48. Dating to 1859, this home is listed on the National Register of Historic Places. Public rooms include lounges and second-floor porch with paddle fans and eclectic furnishings. No TVs or room telephones intrude. Ten guest bedrooms are upstairs and have a mix of private in-suite baths, private hall baths, and shared baths. Rooms have ceiling fans and window air conditioners. Guests have access to cozy bar and gourmet dinners served in the dining room or adjoining porch. A full American breakfast is available from 8:00-11:00 A.M. No children. No smoking. $75-85.

The Island Hotel

P.O. Box 460, 32625
(904) 543-5111

A pre-Civil War building with Jamaican-style architecture. Rustic and authentic, with much of the original structure. On the National Rigister of Historic Places. Gourmet seafood dining room, serving local Cedar Key specialties. Like stepping back in time, with muraled walls, paddle fans, French doors, and a wide wraparound porch which catches gulf breezes. A cozy lounge bar completes a perfect place to get away from it all.

Hosts: Tom and Alison Sanders
Rooms: 10 (6 PB; 4 S2B) $75-95
Full Breakfast
Credit Cards: A, B, C
Notes: 2, 4, 5, 7 (limited), 8 (by arrangement), 9, 10, 11, 12, 14

COCOA

FMH Bed and Breakfast

809 Clearlake Road, 32922
(407) 632-7060

The hosts welcome guests to their modern modular private homes. Enjoy a private kitchen, bath, two bedrooms, living room, patio, etc. Walk to shopping centers. Public golf courses and recreation, fishing, etc. are within five miles; Space Center is within 15 miles; and beaches are within ten miles. Disney World, MGM, Epcot, Universal Studio, and Sea World are within a one-hour drive. $5 per additional person.

Hosts: Bill and Joyce Frey
Rooms: 5 (PB) $55
Continental Breakfast
Credit Cards: A, B
Notes: 5, 8

CORAL SPRINGS

Bed & Breakfast Co.

P.O. Box 262, South Miami, 33243
(305) 661-3270; FAX (305) 661-3270

CS276. Luxury home in Coral Springs, a unique, relatively new community west of Pompano Beach, well-known for its excel-

NOTES: Credit cards accepted: A MasterCard; B Visa; C American Express; D Discover Card; E Diner's Club; F Other; 2 Personal checks accepted; 3 Lunch available; 4 Dinner available; 5 Open all year;

lent community services, schools, theater, etc. This is a spacious ranch home with large rooms, expensive contemporary and traditional furnishings throughout. Large screened pool-patio, nicely landscaped yard with fruit trees. Delightful hostess does hand-painting of china as hobby. $50.

CORTEZ

B&B Suncoast Accommodations

8690 Gulf Boulevard, St. Pete Beach Island, 33706
(813) 360-1753

7. This home offers two guest rooms, both of which have a private bath. Pool on premises, and ten minutes to the beach. Seventh night free. $55-70.

CORTEZ VILLAGE

Bed & Breakfast Co.

P.O. Box 262, South Miami, 33243
(305) 661-3270; FAX (305) 661-3270

SA320. Picturesque fishing village between Sarasota and Bradenton on the bay. This bed and breakfast offers a rare glimpse of Florida life as natives of the area have always known it. It is operated by descendants of Captain Billy Fulford, one of Cortez's original settlers. It combines an eclectic mixture of Southern hospitality and New England charm. Antique furnishings; a suite for three; a king-size room with private bath. Relax around the pool or on the docks. $55.

CRESCENT CITY

Bed and Breakfast Scenic Florida

P.O. Box 3385, Tallahassee, 32315-3385
(904) 386-8196

FL 26. Within easy driving distance of Atlantic beaches, this 1892 Steamboat Gothic home is shaded by moss-draped oaks. All rooms and suites are on the second floor, have private baths, and are air-conditioned. Most have TVs. Choices include three rooms with double beds, two suites with queen-size beds, and a third suite that is large and modern. A full gourmet breakfast is served in the full service restaurant. Lunch and dinner are also available, and diners come from surrounding communities. No children. No smoking. $50-125.

Sprague House Inn and Restaurant

125 Central Avenue, 32112
(904) 698-2430

This 103-year-old inn, with wraparound porches and a view of Crescent Lake, is in a quiet fishing town. Each room has a private bath and sitting room, with two newly renovated deluxe suites. A full gourmet breakfast is served in the award-winning restaurant. Relax among the shady oaks while the hosts prepare gourmet meals and desserts.

Hosts: Terry and Vena Moyer
Rooms: 6 (PB) $50-125
Full Breakfast
Credit Cards: A, B
Notes: 3, 4, 5, 9, 10

DAYTONA BEACH

Bed & Breakfast Co.

P.O. Box 262, South Miami, 33243
(305) 661-3270; FAX (305) 661-3270

DB263. This two-story suburban home is on a new golf course development just off I-4. Guest bedroom with queen-size bed; private bath is on the second floor. Retired hosts are gracious. $40.

6 Pets welcome; 7 Smoking allowed; 8 Children welcome; 9 Social drinking allowed; 10 Tennis available;
11 Swimming available; 12 Golf available; 13 Skiing available; 14 May be booked through travel agents.

Coquina Inn

544 South Palmetto Avenue, 32114
(904) 254-4969; (800) 727-0678

Luxurious historic inn just off the beaten
path. Romantic guestrooms feature private
baths, fireplaces, and soaking tubs. Garden
Jacuzzi. Gourmet full breakfast, in bed if
desired. Sunset sailing and bicycles available. Minutes to the beach. Walk to fine
dining. Three-diamond AAA rating.

Hosts: Jerry and Susan Jerzykowski
Rooms: 4 (PB) $85
Full Breakfast
Credit Cards: A, B, C
Notes: 2, 9, 10, 11, 12, 14

DAYTONA BEACH SHORES

Bed & Breakfast Co.

P.O. Box 262, South Miami, 33243
(305) 661-3270; FAX (305) 661-3270

DB323. Super luxury in a townhouse development on A1A across from the ocean. All
appointments throughout guest room and
home are top quality, harmonious, and
comfortable. King-size bed in guest room
with double convertible in den for third person. Par-three golf course, tennis, pool, fitness equipment available at no cost. Walk
to restaurants, shops, and public transportation to mall, race track, etc. Children over
eight welcome. $75.

DEERFIELD BEACH

Open House Bed and Breakfast Registry

P.O. Box 3025, Palm Beach, 33480
(407) 842-5190

Parkland. A country home in the suburbs
on one and one-quarter acres invites guests
to sun by the pool or stroll across the
grounds to the private pond. A footbridge
and waterfall are part of the garden landscape. Some French is spoken by the hosts,

a professional couple. They will prepare
extra breakfast treats on weekends. A small
dog will greet guests. $45-55.

DE FUNIAK SPRINGS

Bed and Breakfast Scenic Florida

P.O. Box 3385, Tallahassee, 32315-3385
(904) 386-8196

FL14. This Queen Anne Victorian home
was the residence of Florida Governor Sidney J. Catts and dates back to the 1880s.
Porches provide a place to relax, and the atmosphere reflects the era. A third-floor
common room provides TV, VCR, and
reading alcove. A collectible shop is also on
the third floor. Three guest rooms are available. Guests may choose a full-size bed
with large private bath, a full-size bed with
hot tub, or king-size bed with claw-foot tub
and shower. All rooms have ceiling fans
and carpeting. Wake-up coffee or tea pre-
cedes a full breakfast in the formal dining
room that includes special offerings. No
children. No smoking. $75.

DELRAY BEACH

Bed and Breakfast Co.

P.O. Box 262, South Miami, 33243
(305) 661-3270; FAX (305) 661-3270

DB045. In a modest and quiet residential
area of Delray Beach is this typical ranch
home with pool. Contemporary, attractive,
quality furnishings throughout. Bed and
breakfast room has two twin beds, private
hall bath adjoining; offers excellent privacy
in one wing of the home. Three miles from
the ocean. Three dogs in residence. Hostess
has an interior design business. $50.

DB39601. Cruise and snooze, or a bedroom
for landlubbers in this bed and breakfast

waterway home. The 44-foot sloop can sleep ten, has two baths, and is completely entertainment equipped. Special Snooze and Cruise packages include wine and hors d'oeuvres, desert with champagne, dinner aboard, overnight stay and breakfast. Bedroom also available in lovely ranch home. $40-250.

Open House Bed and Breakfast Registry

P.O. Box 3025, Palm Beach, 33480
(407) 842-5190

Petit Salon. The name accurately describes this artist's home. The hostess' talents carry through to her lush tropical garden. Double or twin bedrooms, each with a private bath, are available. One and one-half miles from the beach. Children welcome; bikes provided; resident cats. Continental breakfast. $55

Henderson Park Inn

DESTIN

Henderson Park Inn— A Beachside Bed and Breakfast

2700 Highway 98E-Beach Route, 32541
(800) 336-4853

Destin's first and only beachside bed and breakfast combines the charm of a Queen Anne-style inn with the amenities of a modern resort. Perfect for couples and romantics; rooms are decorated with cozy impressionistic themes, antique handcrafted reproductions, high ceilings, some rooms have fireplaces and four-poster canopied beds, fine linens, and private balconies and baths, some of which have Jacuzzis. Villas are perfect for families up to six. Southern beachside breakfast, beach service, maid service, turndown service, evening social receptions, heated pool, veranda, palm grove, and restaurant. Dedicated conference/meeting facilities for up to 60.

Host: Susie Nunnelley
Rooms: 20 (PB) $54-210
Villas: 18
Full Breakfast
Credit Cards: A, B, C, D
Notes: 2, 3, 4, 5, 8, 9, 10, 11, 12, 14

EDGEWATER

The Colonial House

110 East Yelkca Terrace, 32132
(904) 427-4570

On Florida's east coast between Daytona Beach and Cape Canaveral. Guests enjoy fine European hospitality in a quiet family atmosphere. Rooms have air conditioning, TV, refrigerator, and private bath. Enjoy solar-heated swimming pool and Jacuzzi. Nearby beaches, golf, deep-sea fishing, the Space Center, and Disney World. Two-night minimum stay is required.

Host: Eva Brandner
Rooms: 3 (PB) $52
Full Breakfast
Credit Cards: None
Notes: 2, 5, 8 (over 4), 9, 10, 11, 12, 14

FERNANDINA BEACH (AMELIA ISLAND)

The Bailey House

P.O. Box 805, 32034
(904) 261-5390

Completed in 1895, this fine old home is an outstanding example of the Queen Anne style. The owners have filled the home with

The Bailey House

a vast collection of carefully chosen period antiques collected across the nation. The large, comfortable and elegant guest rooms are furnished with authentic antique furniture and decorator pieces, yet offer the modern conveniences of a private bath. For guests, a complimentary expanded Continental breakfast is served each morning in the main dining room. The Bailey House has central heat and air for year-round comfort. Near Ft. Clinch State Park, horseback riding, and beautiful beaches. In consideration of all guests, the hosts must say no to pets and children under ten years of age. No smoking. Come enjoy the charm and history of this beautiful turn-of-the-century home and relax in the ambience of a bygone era.

Host: Thomas W. Bishop, Jr.
Rooms: 5 (PB) $75-105
Continental Breakfast
Credit Cards: A, B, C
Notes: 2, 5, 7 (limited), 8 (over 10), 11, 12, 14

Bed & Breakfast Co.

P.O. Box 262, South Miami, 33243
(305) 661-3270; FAX (305) 661-3270

FB210. This beach house is just across the road from the ocean. Large, two-story frame home with two suites; one with full kitchen, TV, and video collection; the other has a sitting room, microwave, and refriger-ator. An outstanding collection of books, magazines, and adult activity items. $65.

Elizabeth Pointe Lodge

98 South Fletcher Avenue, 32034
(904) 277-4851

Seaside lodge of an 1890s Nantucket shingle-style architecture. Large porches, with rockers and lemonade, overlook the ocean. Great room with fireplace and library. Oversize tubs, remote color cable TV, fresh flowers, and newspaper delivered to room. Wine at 6:00 P.M. Homemade snack and desserts always available. Baby-sitting, laundry room service, and concierge assistance. Historic seaport of Fernandina nearby. Bikes available for touring the island.

Hosts: David and Susan Caples
Rooms: 20 (PB) $95-150
Full Breakfast
Credit Cards: A, B, C
Notes: 2, 3, 4, 5, 7, 8, 9, 10, 11, 12, 14

Elizabeth Pointe Lodge

The Phoenix' Nest

619 South Fletcher Avenue, 32034
(904) 277-2129

On Amelia Island, a seaside retreat in the bed and breakfast tradition. Suites 150 feet from the Atlantic. Wide, unobstructed ocean views. Beautiful, private, gracious, and rich in color and texture. Fascinating books and magazines spanning 250 years are so enthralling guests may hope it rains. Bicycles, hammock, surf fishing gear, and videos from Chaplin to Napoleon, Koko to O'Keefe.

Host: Harriett Johnston Fortenberry
Suites: 6 (PB) $65-90
Continental Breakfast
Credit Cards: A, B, C
Notes: 2, 5, 7, 8, 9, 10, 11, 12, 14

The 1735 House

584 South Fletcher Avenue, 32034
(904) 261-5878; (800) 872-8531

An oceanfront country inn. Antique nautical decorations enhance the private ocean view. Full suites, private bath, freshly baked pastries, and morning newspaper. One suite in a lighthouse, with two bedrooms, bath, galley, working light, and observation deck.

Hosts: Gary and Emily Grable
Suites: 6 (PB) $75-150
Continental Breakfast
Credit Cards: A, B, C, D
Notes: 2, 5, 7, 9, 10, 11, 12, 14

FORT PIERCE

Bed and Breakfast Co.

P.O. Box 262, South Miami, 33243
(305) 661-3270; FAX (305) 661-3270

FP33901. Guests fish for grouper and trout off the bank of the river when they stay in this 80-year-old duplex along the Intra-coastal Waterway. Lots of antiques, collectibles, and excellent art collection. The home sits atop a small hill with a lovely view of the river. Three bedrooms with private baths. Outside cat. Smoking outside. $45.

GAINESVILLE

Bed and Breakfast Scenic Florida

P.O. Box 3385, Tallahassee, 32315-3385
(940) 386-8196

FL20. The historic district is home to this 1885 French Second Empire Victorian guest house. All six guest rooms have gas fireplaces, ceiling fans, and are decorated in period pieces. Guests have a choice of rooms on two stories. Accommodations include double bed and daybed, queen-size bed, double iron bed, a four-poster queen-size bed, a bridal chamber with a canopied double bed, and a suite with a queen-size bed. Baths include both private and shared facilities, some with claw-foot tub and shower. A breakfast of specialties is served in the dining room. No children. No smoking. $60-90.

HAINES CITY

Holly Garden Inn

106 First Street South, 33844
(813) 421-9867

Romantic bed and breakfast in a historic small town in the heart of central Florida's citrus groves. This 1924 home has been lovingly restored to recapture the grand elegance of the old south. Just 20 miles from Walt Disney World and most central Florida attractions, it is a perfect spot for that romantic getaway, family vacation, wedding or small meeting. Escape to a place where the flag still waves and Southern hospitality is a way of life. Lunches served Monday through Friday.

Hosts: Camilla and Wesley Donnelly
Rooms: 5 (4 PB; 1 SB) $79-89
Full Breakfast
Credit Cards: A, B, C
Notes: 2, 3, 5, 8, 9, 12, 14

6 Pets welcome; 7 Smoking allowed; 8 Children welcome; 9 Social drinking allowed; 10 Tennis available; 11 Swimming available; 12 Golf available; 13 Skiing available; 14 May be booked through travel agents.

HARBOUR POINTE

Open House Bed and Breakfast Registry

P.O. Box 3025, Palm Beach, 33480
(407) 842-5190

Ten minutes from Wellington and west of Florida's Turnpike. This townhouse is located in a private resort colony. Swimming pool, health club, and tennis are available. Activities available include Scrabble, bridge, and Canasta. Double-bed suite features TV and private bath. Continental breakfast served on screened porch overlooking pond. $55-60.

HAVANA

Gaver's Bed and Breakfast

301 East Sixth Avenue, 32333
(904) 539-5611

Circa 1907 restored house with a screened porch, cable TV, central air conditioning, ceiling fans, 12-foot ceilings, and fireplaces in each room with queen-size beds. Licensed by the state of Florida and the town of Havana. Off-street, lighted parking. In the center of town, two blocks from 30 antique shops. Twelve miles north of I-10 and Tallahassee on U.S. 27.

Hosts: Shirley and Bruce Gaver
Rooms: 2 (PB) $65-75
Continental Breakfast
Credit Cards: None
Notes: 2, 5, 9, 12

HIGH SPRINGS

Bed and Breakfast Scenic Florida

P.O. Box 3385, Tallahassee, 32315-3385
(940) 386-8196

FL21. This two-story Victorian home was built in 1906. Guests may enjoy the common areas, including the formal parlor, glassed sunroom with TV and stereo, deck, gazebo, and porches. Three guest rooms have double beds and a large shared bath with claw-foot tub and shower. Instructional packages for scuba diving are available, and gear may be stored securely on the grounds. Breakfast is served buffet style. No children. No smoking. $70-85.

FL 36. A deep, shady porch distinguishes this 1917 Craftsman bungalow. Guests may enjoy the front parlor or the game room. A canoe and bicycles are also available. Accommodations include a guest room with an antique iron double bed and three suites with queen-size, king-size, and double beds. Twin beds may be requested, and a daybed accommodates a third person. A modern bath is available, as well as period claw-foot tubs and a tin tub. A buffet breakfast is served indoors or on the porch. No smoking. $69-79.

HOLIDAY

Oakridge House

P.O. Box 3773, 34690-0773
(813) 372-8444; (800) 554-0085

Spacious country home in picturesque setting on one and one-half acres of attractively landscaped grounds. The bedrooms are newly decorated with handmade quilts, ceiling fans, and Early American heirlooms. Guests are welcome to enjoy the screened patio with 20' x 40' pool or relax in the comfortable TV room or parlor. Shopping and gulf beaches are minutes away. Breakfast, evening meal, and personal laundry service are complimentary.

Host: Karen Pflanzer
Rooms: 2 (SB) $35-50
Full Breakfast
Credit Cards: None
Notes: 2, 3, 5, 6, 8, 9, 10, 11, 12, 14

NOTES: Credit cards accepted: A MasterCard; B Visa; C American Express; D Discover Card; E Diner's Club; F Other; 2 Personal checks accepted; 3 Lunch available; 4 Dinner available; 5 Open all year;

HOLLEY

Bed and Breakfast Co.

P.O. Box 262, South Miami, 33243
(305) 661-3270; FAX (305) 661-3270

Guest house is two-story spanish home on
the bay. Heated pool, screened porch, efficiency kitchen, private entry. Ten minutes
to Sugar Beach on the Gulf. Living Room
with sleeper sofa; bedroom with two twin
beds. Full breakfast available. Retired hosts
are former business man and artists. Children over 12. No smoking. $50-60.

HOLLYWOOD

The International Bed & Breakfast Club, Inc.

504 Amherst Street, Buffalo, NY 14207
(800) 723-4262; FAX (716) 873-4462

Stunning contemporary with Oriental decor.
Easy access and easy living in this one-story
ranch home. Two bedrooms with shared
bath. Full breakfast served. Tropical garden
and in-ground swimming pool. Fifteen minutes from shopping center and Fort Laud
erdale airport; ten minutes from beach.
Renting by the week only. Open November
through May. Smoking permitted. $65-70.

HOLMES BEACH

Harrington House Bed and Breakfast

5626 Gulf Drive, 34217
(813) 778-5444

The charm of old Florida architecture and
the casual elegance of beachfront living are
beautifully combined at the Harrington
House, a one-of-a-kind bed and breakfast
guest house on Anna Maria Island. Built in
1925, this lovingly restored home has seven
charming bedrooms, each with private bath.

Most rooms have French doors leading to
balconies overlooking the pool, the beach,
and the blue-green Gulf of Mexico. Guests
are served a full breakfast in the dining
room as they enjoy stimulating conversation with other guests. Relax by the pool,
take a moonlit stroll on the beach, or listen
to the surf. AAA rated; Mobil Guide rated;
ABBA rated.

Hosts: Frank and Jo Adele Davis
Rooms: 8 (PB) $59-149
Full Breakfast
Credit Cards: A, B, C
Notes: 2, 5, 9, 11, 14

INDIALANTIC

Bed & Breakfast Co.

P.O. Box 262, South Miami, 33243
(305) 661-3270; FAX (305) 661-3270

IN340. This ranch-style home is only one
and one-half blocks from the beach in Indi-
anlantic, a quiet community bordering the
ocean just east of Melbourne. Thirty miles
from the Space Center and about two hours
from Orlando. Three miles to downtown
Melbourne with its restaurants, stores, and
antique shops. Two roomy, comfortable
bedrooms (queen-size and double beds)
share a bath. There is a queen-size convertible available in the study. $40-45.

JACKSONVILLE

Bed and Breakfast Scenic Florida

P.O. Box 3385, Tallahassee, 32315-3385
(904) 386-8196

FL 27. Built in 1903 in the vernacular balloon style, this inn is in the historic Springfield area and recognized by *The Miami
Herald* as one of the ten best inns in the
state. The many common rooms include a
formal parlor, sitting rooms, and porches.
Four rooms, all with private baths, offer
double beds, extra daybed, TV, and

6 Pets welcome; 7 Smoking allowed; 8 Children welcome; 9 Social drinking allowed; 10 Tennis available;
11 Swimming available; 12 Golf available; 13 Skiing available; 14 May be booked through travel agents.

porches. A separate carriage house has a private porch, double bed, and upstairs loft. A bountiful breakfast is served in the formal dining room and includes homemade breads and other specialties. Afternoon wine, soft drinks, cheese, and fruit are complimentary. Business and social events can be arranged. No children. No smoking. $63-70.

FL 29. This Prairie-style home built in 1914 is in Jacksonville's Riverside area, which is part of the National Historic District. It is just minutes from the convention center and a few steps from the St. John's riverbank. Guests may enjoy two distinct living areas, one with TV and comfortable couches, and three porches. Two upstairs rooms have queen-size beds and may connect for family use. A large bath has both walk-in shower and deep pedestal tub. A full Continental breakfast with homemade breads may be served in the dining room, on the porch, or in the guest's room. No children. No smoking. $60.

FL 30. This three-story Mediterranean Revival home built in 1925 fronts the St. John's River and overlooks the well-landscaped swimming pool. Guests may choose from two rooms: one with antique twin beds, full bath and refrigerator; and the other with double bed plus daybed, private bath with tub and shower, and a refrigerator. A full breakfast is served in the formal dining room and includes specialties. No children. Smoking is limited. $75-80.

House on Cherry Street

1844 Cherry Street, 32205
(904) 384-1999; FAX (904) 981-2998

Historic restored home on the St. Johns River near downtown Jacksonville, featuring antiques, elegant breakfasts, wine, snacks, and bicycles for guest use.

Host: Carol Anderson
Rooms: 4 (PB) $77.05-81.20
Full Breakfast
Credit Cards: A, B
Notes: 2, 5, 8 (over 9), 9, 10, 12, 14

JUPITER

Innisfail

134 Timber Lane, 33458
(407) 744-5905

A contemporary ranch framed by palm trees is the home gallery of the VanNoorden sculptors. While guests don't have to be art lovers to visit, it helps to be a pet lover, as the four-footed family consists of three dogs and two cats. Enjoy a relaxing poolside Continental breakfast before exploring the lovely beaches of Jupiter and the many sights and activities of the Palm Beach area.

Host: Katherine Van Noorden
Room: 1 (PB) $50-60
Continental Breakfast
Credit Cards: None
Notes: 2, 4, 5, 6, 8, 9, 10, 11, 12

KEY LARGO

Bed & Breakfast Co.

P.O. Box 262, South Miami, 33243
(305) 661-3270; FAX (305) 661-3270

LK260. Romantic one-bedroom apartment that opens onto a sand beach, the ocean, and a pool. Also a protected patio and grassy area for lounging. An L-shaped area where bedrooms are closed off from sitting area. Hosts live on the second level and have a child and two dogs. Lovely breeze. Continental breakfast supplies in the kitchen. $125.

Jules' Undersea Lodge

Key Largo Undersea Park
51 Shoreland Drive, 33037
(305) 451-2353; FAX (305) 451-4789

NOTES: Credit cards accepted: A MasterCard; B Visa; C American Express; D Discover Card; E Diner's Club; F Other; 2 Personal checks accepted; 3 Lunch available; 4 Dinner available; 5 Open all year;

Dive, dine, and dream at five fathoms in "the world's first and only underwater hotel," where guests scuba dive to their rooms. Resort courses available for non-certified divers, packages for $195 to $295 per person. Includes dinner, breakfast, unlimited diving, refreshments, 42-inch windows, TV, VCR, stereo sound system, and telephone.

Hosts: Neil Monney and Ian Koblick
Rooms: 2 (SB) $195-590
Full Breakfast
Credit Cards: A, B, D
Notes: 3, 4, 5, 11, 14

KEY WEST

Andrew's Inn

Zero Walton Lane, 33040
(305) 294-7730

Central Old Town Key West and down a shaded lane off Duval Street. Each queen-size or king-size deluxe room is distinctive and beautiful. All have private entrances, full bath, remote control TV, air conditioning, and telephone. Guests will be served a hot, full breakfast each morning, and cocktails are on the house. Overlooking the Hemingway estate.

Hosts: Tim Gatewood and Andrew Cleveland
Rooms: 9 (PB) $98-148
Full Breakfast
Credit Cards: A, B, C, D
Notes: 2, 5, 6, 7, 8, 9, 11, 12, 14

The Banyan Resort

323 Whitehead Street, 33040
(800) 225-0639; FAX (305) 294-1107

A lush Caribbean estate on half a block in the heart of Old Town Key West. Extensive botanical gardens, fruit trees, two swimming pools, Jacuzzi, and Tiki bar. Thirty-eight modern suites with all amenities in eight elegant Victorian homes, of which five are on the National Register of Historic Places. Kitchen in each room. Coffee by the pool. Weekly rates available. No pets.

Host: Martin J. Bettercourt
Rooms: 38 (PB) $115-265
Credit Cards: A, B, C, D
Notes: 2, 3, 5, 7, 9, 11, 14

Bed & Breakfast Co.

P.O. Box 262, South Miami, 33243
(305) 661-3270; FAX (305) 661-3270

KW42. The hostess is a well-known artist who graciously opens her home to guests from October through April. The two bedrooms and baths have designer touches that help make a visit memorable. Delightful patio with colorful plants and tropical foliage adjoins the kitchen. Walk to the center of the village for unique shopping, attractions, historic sites, beaches, and an unbelievable choice of restaurants. Do not miss a ride on the Conch Tour Train or Old Town Trolly. $70.

Chelsea House

707 Truman Avenue, 33040
(305) 296-2211; (800) 845-8859

Beautifully restored Victorian mansion. All rooms have been tastefully appointed with period pieces and Caribbean ambience. Breakfast is served poolside, with cooking facilities available. Off-street parking. Easy walking to all attractions in Old Town Key West. It's truly paradise!

Hosts: Jim, Gary, and Robb
Rooms: 14 (PB) $78-148
Continental Breakfast
Credit Cards: A, B, D
Notes: 5, 6, 7, 9, 10, 11, 14

Duval House

815 Duval Street, 33040
(305) 294-1666; (800) 22 DUVAL

Restored century-old Victorian house with charm and deluxe amenities. Large swimming pool and quiet tropical gardens. Walk to restaurants and all attractions. AAA and Mobil Travel Guide approved.

Host: Richard Kamradt
Rooms: 28 (25 PB; 3 SB) $80-195
Continental Breakfast
Credit Cards: A, B, C, D, E
Notes: 5, 7, 9, 10, 11, 12, 14

Duval House

Eden House

1015 Fleming Street, 33040
(800) 533-KEYS

A charming 1924 Art Deco hotel in Key West. Features air conditioning, pool, Caribbean Jacuzzi, garden cafe, and a tropical garden. Come experience the feeling of Old Key West. Wicker furniture, balconies, private parking lot, and complimentary happy hour. Call for rates.

Host: Stephen Clement
Rooms: 42 (22 PB; 20 SB)
No Breakfast
Credit Cards: A, B
Notes: 3, 4, 5, 6 (limited), 7, 8, 9, 10, 11, 12

Garden House of Key West

329 Elizabeth Street, 33040
(305) 296-5368; (800) 695-6453
FAX (305) 292-1160

In the historic district and within walking distance to everything. Tropical gardens, spa with waterfall, and sun deck. Air-condi-

tioned rooms with both private and shared bath. Complimentary Continental buffet breakfast and wine hour daily under the covered patio.

Hosts: John and Helene Montagu
Rooms: 10 (8 PB; 2 SB) $66-125
Continental Breakfast
Credit Cards: A, B, C
Notes: 5, 6, 7, 8, 9, 11, 12, 14

Heron House

512 Simonton Street, 33040
(305) 294-9227

Heron House consists of three homes. One, built in 1856, represents the few remaining classic conch houses. Location is in the very heart of the historic district, one block from the main tourist street and three blocks from the nearest beach.

Host: Fred Geibelt
Rooms: 17 (PB) $83.25-249.75
Continental Breakfast
Credit Cards: A, B, C
Notes: 2 (deposit), 5, 7, 9, 10, 11, 12, 14

Heron House

The Island City House Hotel

411 William Street, 33040
(305) 294-5702; (800) 634-8230

The Island City House Hotel is three historic Victorian guest houses offering 24 one- and two-bedroom suites with tropical gardens and red brick walkways winding throughout. Enjoy a complimentary breakfast buffet of fruits, breads, and coffee on a secluded patio, or relax on the deck in our crystalline pool and Jacuzzi in this lush tropical paradise.

Hosts: Stanley and Janet Corneal
Rooms: 24 (PB) $95-210
Continental Breakfast
Credit Cards: A, B, D, E
Notes: 5, 7, 8, 9, 10, 12, 14

Key West Bed and Breakfast: The Popular House

415 William, 33040
(305) 296-7274; (800) 438-6155

A classically restored turn-of-the-century three-story Victorian. Built by Bahamian shipbuilders and on a quiet tree-shaded street. The house is decorated in a Caribbean style. Four porches, sun deck, tropical gardens, Jacuzzi, and sauna for immediate relaxation. In the heart of the historic preservation district within walking distance to restaurants, beaches, and shops.

Host: Jody Carlson
Rooms: 8 (4 PB; 4 SB) $59-200
Continental Breakfast
Credit Cards: A, B, C, D, E
Notes: 2, 5, 7, 9, 10, 11, 12, 14

Lime House Inn

219 Elizabeth Street, 33040
(305) 296-2978

An "island within an island," this guest house for men is in the heart of the historic Old Town. It is the most private and friendly place to stay in Key West. Enjoy life in the old conch mansion or lounge in the pool or hot spa. Most rooms have kitchenettes, TVs, air conditioning, and telephones. Just steps from the waterfront, two blocks off Duval Street with its shops and night life.

Hosts: Jim and Godfrey
Rooms: 7 (PB) $55-130
Continental Breakfast
Credit Cards: A, B, C, D
Notes: 5, 7, 9, 10, 11, 14

Marquesa Hotel

600 Fleming Street, 33040
(305) 292-1919; (800) 869-4631
FAX (305) 294-2121

This exquisitely restored Victorian home in Old Town is six blocks from the Gulf of Mexico, three miles from the airport. All rooms have air-conditioning, remote-control cable TV, telephone, bathrobes, and security safe. Small gourmet restaurant, two pools, concierge, and turndown service with Godiva chocolates. AAA four-diamond award.

Host: Carol Wightman
Rooms: 27 (PB) $115-260
Full Breakfast
Credit Cards: A, B, C, E
Notes: 4, 5, 7, 8, 9, 10, 11, 12, 14

Merlinn Guest House

811 Simonton Street, 33040
(305) 296-3336

Lush tropical gardens, decks, and pool in the heart of Old Town. Freshly baked breakfast served among exotic birds in the secluded garden. Evening cocktails and appetizers. Eighteen rooms and apartments with private baths, TV, and air conditioning. Also handicapped accessible unit with private garden. The staff can arrange a day on the water—snorkeling, fishing, sailing, or playing. Guests never want to leave! Three-night minimum stay during holidays.

Host: Pat Hoffman
Rooms: 18 (PB) $65-150
Full Breakfast
Credit Cards: A, B, C, D
Notes: 2 (deposit), 5, 6, 8, 9, 11, 14

Nassau House

1016 Fleming Street, 33040
(305) 296-8513; (800) 296-8513

6 Pets welcome; 7 Smoking allowed; 8 Children welcome; 9 Social drinking allowed; 10 Tennis available; 11 Swimming available; 12 Golf available; 13 Skiing available; 14 May be booked through travel agents.

In the heart of Old Town, Nassau House is a century-old Conch house which offers rooms and suites with air conditioning, telephones, cable TV, private baths, comfortable queen-size beds, and charming wicker furnishings. Four suites have kitchens. Guests may relax on the large and airy front porch, enjoy the tropical lagoon-style pool/Jacuzzi, or bask on the tri-level sun deck. The shops and excitement of Duval Street, Mallory Square, and Key West's beaches are all within walking distance. Bicycle and scooter rentals available nearby. Minimum stay during holidays.

Hosts: Damon Leard and Bob Tracy
Rooms: 7 (PB) $59-139
Continental Breakfast
Credit Cards: A, B, C
Notes: 5, 6, 9, 10, 11, 12, 14

Seascape

420 Olivia Street, 33040
(305) 296-7776

Listed on the National Register of Historic Places, with heated pool-spa nestled under crimson bougainvillaea, tropical garden, and sun decks. All rooms feature private bath, air conditioning, Bahama fan, cable TV, and a queen-size bed. Complimentary Continental breakfast and wine hour (in-season). In the heart of Old Town. Minutes to the Atlantic Ocean and the Gulf of Mexico. Steps away from the finest shops and eating and drinking establishments. "Sparkling"—*New York Times.*

Host: Alan Melnick
Rooms: 5 (PB) $69-114
Continental Breakfast
Credit Cards: A, B, C, D
Notes: 5, 7, 9, 10, 11, 12, 14

Treetop Inn Historic Bed and Breakfast

806 Truman Avenue, 33040
(305) 293-0712; FAX 294-3668

Built in 1902, Treetop Inn has been restored (1993) to provide modern comforts in a 1900s setting. It received the 1994 Key West Chamber of Commerce's Business for Beauty award. In central Old Town, Treetop Inn is within walking distance of beaches, restaurants, and shops. Breakfast is provided on the pool deck amid lush tropical gardens. The hosts are knowledgeable about all Key West activities. Spacious rooms are graciously furnished and include cable TV and air conditioning.

Hosts: Sue and Fred Leake
Rooms: 3 (1 PB; 2 SB) $78-148
Full Breakfast
Credit Cards: A, B, D
Notes: 5, 7 (limited), 9, 10, 11, 12

The Watson House

525 Simonton Street, 33040
(305) 294-6712; (800) 621-9405

The Watson House, circa 1860, is a distinctively furnished small guest house in the historic preservation district. Received 1986 award for excellence in rehabilitation from Historical Florida Keys Preservation Board. Swimming pool, heated Jacuzzi, patio, decks, and gardens. All units have their own distinct style, private baths, color TV, air conditioning, and telephone; larger suites have fully equipped kitchens. Privacy prevails; adults only; no pets. Brochure available.

Hosts: Joe Beres and Ed Czaplicki
Suites: 3 (PB) $95-360
Continental Breakfast
Credit Cards: A, B, C
Notes: 5, 7, 9, 10, 11, 12, 14

Whispers Bed and Breakfast Inn

409 William Street, 33040
(305) 294-5969; (800) 856-SHHH

The owner-managers take great pride in the service, hospitality, and the romance of their historic 1866 inn. Each room is unique and appointed with antiques. Included in the room rate is a full gourmet breakfast served in the tropical gardens and membership at a local beach club and health spa.

Host: John Marburg
Rooms: 7 (5 PB; 2SB) $69-175
Full Breakfast
Credit Cards: A, B, C, D
Notes: 2, 5, 7 and 8 (limited), 9, 10, 11, 12

KISSIMMEE

The Unicorn Inn

8 South Orlando Avenue, 34741
(407) 846-1200

The only Colonial-style bed and breakfast inn in historic downtown Kissimmee off Broadway, the inn comprises six rooms, plus two adjoining rooms or two suites, all with private baths. British owned and run. Hosts' only rule is that guests make themselves at home. Only 300 yards from the famous bass fishing Lake Tohopekalegia and from Amtrak; 150 yards from Greyhound. Close to golf courses, Disney World, Sea World, and Wet 'n Wild. Airport pickups, and shuttle to and from attractions are available at a nominal fee.

Hosts: Fran and Don Williamson
Rooms: 6 (PB) $55
Full Breakfast
Credit Cards: None
Notes: 2, 5, 8, 9, 11, 12, 14

LAKE BUENA VISTA

Bed and Breakfast Scenic Florida

P.O. Box 3385, Tallahassee, 32315-3385
(904) 386-8196

FL 42. Within minutes of the heart of Disney World, this home is on a secluded 20-acre parcel of land. Completed in 1990, the home has been designed to offer comfort to single travelers and families. Four guest rooms have private entrance to the grounds, convenient parking, private bath with combination tub and shower, ceiling fans, TV,

telephone, and central heat and air conditioning. Choices include queen- and king-size beds with space for a crib. The great room is a gathering place for guests. An extended, self-service Continental breakfast is available. Children are welcome. No smoking. $65.

LAKELAND

Bed and Breakfast Scenic Florida

P.O. Box 3385
Tallahassee, FL 32315-3385
(904) 386-8196

FL 43. This fully restored country inn is a blend of Victorian and Colonial Revival architecture, and it is listed on the National Register of Historic Places. Four rooms with common parlors have twin, double, or queen-size beds. Privacy screens complement claw-foot tubs and furnishings reflect Oriental, French, and Queen Anne decor. TV is available. Evening wine and cheese or desserts are served in the formal parlor. Breakfast features Southern breads and other specialties; at lunch the tearoom opens to the public with a full menu. No smoking. $95.

LAKE PARK

Open House Bed and Breakfast Registry

P.O. Box 3025, Palm Beach, 33480
(407) 842-5190

Classic Comfort. In suburban community seven miles north of West Palm Beach and five minutes from the beautiful ocean beaches of Singer Island, this comfortable bungalow offers a standard double bedroom, or a twin bedroom. The hosts serve freshly squeezed orange juice from citrus

---

6 Pets welcome; 7 Smoking allowed; 8 Children welcome; 9 Social drinking allowed; 10 Tennis available;
11 Swimming available; 12 Golf available; 13 Skiing available; 14 May be booked through travel agents.

trees on the premises with a Continental breakfast. Children over four welcome. Family rates available. $45.

LAKE WALES

Chalet Suzanne Country Inn and Restaurant

3800 Chalet Suzanne Drive, 33853-7060
(813) 676-6011; (800) 433-6011

Discover Europe in the heart of Florida. This historic country inn is on 70 acres surrounded by orange groves. It has 30 charming guest rooms with private baths; award-winning dining overlooking Lake Suzanne. It is just 45 minutes southwest of the Orlando area.

Hosts: Carl and Vita Hinshaw
Rooms: 30 (PB) $125-185
Full Breakfast
Credit Cards: A, B, C, D, E, F (JCB)
Notes: 2, 3, 4, 5, 6, 7, 8, 9, 10, 11, 12, 14

LAKE WORTH

Open House Bed and Breakfast Registry

P.O. Box 3025, Palm Beach, 33480
(407) 842-5190

College Park. This is a corner property on a quiet, residential street near shopping, restaurants, and the beach. Two efficiency suites each with private entrance. Double or king-size beds, private bath, telephone, and TV. Each also includes a fully equipped kitchen and dining area. Special features are the 15' x 30' swimming pool and a sauna. Lounge or dine on the poolside terrace. Complete privacy is assured in these unhosted accommodations. Weekly and monthly rates available. $60-65.

LANTANA

Open House Bed and Breakfast Registry

P.O. Box 3025, Palm Beach, 33480
(407) 842-5190

Lagoon Setting. Twenty minutes south of Palm Beach International airport and west of I-95, this sprawling ranch home is secluded yet near good restaurants and ten minutes from the ocean. If traveling with family or friends, guests will have a choice of double, king-size, or twin bedrooms. Children over five welcome. Family rates. Relax on the screened patio and by the pool. Continental breakfast. $55.

LONGWOOD

Bed & Breakfast Co.

P.O. Box 262, South Miami, 33243
(305) 661-3270; FAX (305) 661-3270

OR309. Sprawling, luxurious ranch home in exclusive suburban development north of Orlando, on three-fourths acre. The home opens to garden areas and a large screened pool area. The family room has a double-shot basketball game. About a 15-minute drive to Orlando, 40 minutes to Disney World. Two bedrooms with private baths. Hospitable hostess and teacher. $55-60.

MARATHON

Hopp-Inn Guest House

500 Sombrero Beach Road, 33050
(305) 743-4118; FAX (305) 743-9220

In the heart of the Florida Keys. Every room has a water view. Families welcome in villas.

NOTES: Credit cards accepted: A MasterCard; B Visa; C American Express; D Discover Card; E Diner's Club; F Other; 2 Personal checks accepted; 3 Lunch available; 4 Dinner available; 5 Open all year;

Host: The Hopp family
Rooms: 5 (PB) $50-150
Villas: 4 (PB)
Full Breakfast
Credit Cards: A, B
Notes: 10, 11, 12

MIAMI

Bed & Breakfast Co.

P.O. Box 262, South Miami, 33243
(305) 661-3270; FAX (305) 661-3270

MI08. Spacious ranch home in prestigious residential area of Key Biscayne. There is a private entrance to two bedrooms that open onto the screened pool area. Walk or bike to beautiful sand beach. The Seaquarium, Ocean World, and state park are nearby, with other Miami attractions just across the causeway. $45-80.

MI14. Exclusive residential area near Kings Bay Country Club and Biscayne Bay, about ten miles south of the downtown area. Charming home with two private-bath bedrooms; screened pool area. These delightful hosts enjoy entertaining guests. $40.

MI016. Spacious estate in "horse country," southwest Dade County. Large ranch home on a property where horses are boarded; an equestrian school is across the street. Rent riding horses nearby. Relax in the country atmosphere while being only a 10-20-minute drive away from the city and airport! Three bedrooms, one with private deck, and private baths with whirlpool tubs. One studio apartment with full kitchen and one one-bedroom apartment which sleeps four. Hostess is a gourmet cook who also operates a cat boarding facility at the rear of the estate. $40-60.

MI018. Casual, comfortable, and exceptionally attractive small home designed to integrate the garden areas into the living space. Excellent location, close to shops, restaurants, entertainment, and local transportation, including metro-rail. Near Coral Gables and University of Miami. Shared bath. Single only. $38.

MI25. An unusual, contemporary two-story home on a quiet tree-lined street that goes down to the bay. An iron spiral staircase extends from ground level to the third-level crow's nest where guests can sun and see across the bay to Key Biscayne. Guest room with queen-size bed and private bath is on the first level and opens on to a deck and the waterway. Walk to the village shops, restaurants, sidewalk cafes, sailboat and bike rental, or explore the beautiful side streets throughout the grove.

MI034. Spend memorable days in a Miami Beach mansion on a private residential island in Biscayne Bay. Furnishings reflect the Old World charm of this Danish family. They are expert sailors and love travel and the arts. Host is a harbor pilot; hostess, a nurse. Swim in an ecologically balanced pool—no chemicals, only fish and plants, and luxuriate in the hot tub. Three rooms with private baths. Children welcome. $80.

MI058. This large ranch home is one mile west of the renowned Dadeland Mall; one-half mile from the metrorail, bus, other shops, and restaurants. A traditional home, attractively furnished. Bed and breakfast room is large with king-size bed, and private bath with tub and shower. Hospitable, charming hosts. $40.

MI077. Nestled in a large, deep lot with many trees and plants is this ranch home in South Miami. Comfortably furnished with traditional and antique pieces, accessorized with interesting collectibles from the hostess' extensive travels. Walk to the University of Miami, metrorail, shops, restaurant, and movies. Bus is a half block away. High-

6 Pets welcome; 7 Smoking allowed; 8 Children welcome; 9 Social drinking allowed; 10 Tennis available; 11 Swimming available; 12 Golf available; 13 Skiing available; 14 May be booked through travel agents.

rise bed, private bath adjoining in hall. Single occupancy only. $40.

MI219. Luxury home on the shore of the Intracoastal Waterway. Near Bal Harbor and the exclusive shops and the ocean. Enjoy the pool and hot tub. Three bedrooms with private baths, two rooms with water view. Hosts are retired executives who enjoy travel, golf, and gourmet cooking. Children welcome. $60-75.

MI236. This exceptional multilevel home is in one of Coconut Grove's finest residential areas. Large two-bedroom apartment available for bed and breakfast guests on the first floor. Complete with living and music room with piano, large bath with two lavatories, private landscaped patio for al fresco lounging or dining. Queen-size bed in first bedroom, double and single in second. $80-120.

MI244. Perfect spot for exploring all the facets of Miami Beach's "South Beach Art Deco District," from the ocean and beach itself to the many restaurants, sidewalk cafes, trendy shops, historic architecture, and more! This studio efficiency has a view of the ocean, and has two double beds that fold into the wall, thus providing ample living space. Full kitchen, eating area, and bath. Unhosted. Parking on city block one and one-half blocks away. $85.

MI246. Ultra luxury, private one-bedroom apartment in a spectacular tropical setting in Coconut Grove! Within a lush walled estate also containing main house. Grounds are beautifully landscaped with specimen tropical plantings, splashy colored bromeliads, and natural pool with fountain. Apartment completely equipped for a permanent home with full kitchen, cable TV, VCR, phone—all the creature comforts. Double bed and sofa can be used for additional guest. $100.

MI281. Luxury home in Coconut Grove on the bay. Completely contemporary, with Spanish tile floors and simple, but stunning, uncluttered modern furnishings. See through house from entry, across the pool (with whirlpool) and to the bay. Large deck on third floor for an expansive view of entire area. Bed and breakfast room is upstairs with queen-size bed and well-equipped private bath. $80

MI293. A unique experience guaranteed by this bed and breakfast. A 36-foot luxury trawler yacht with all the comforts and conveniences of home. Sleeps six. Has two staterooms, two full baths, TV with VCR, stereo, completely equipped kitchen. Basically a charter boat, with most business in the afternoon; available for bed and breakfast in the evenings and when not booked for a charter. Also featuring a Cruise and Snooze option. This includes a one hour cruise on the Intercoastal, dinner aboard ship, and bed and breakfast. $95-250.

MI316. This exceptional pool home in South Miami on a large corner lot has an adjoining cabana with a private garden entrance available for bed and breakfast guests. It opens onto a beautiful garden and pool area. Comfortable and airy, with king-size bed, private bath, and refrigerator. Close to Metrorail, shops, and restaurants. Hosts are antique dealers. $80.

MI348. Contemporary one-room pool cottage in tranquil, tropical, private setting (separated from main house by garden and foliage). Sliding glass doors which open to the pool form a window wall; the feeling of light and spaciousness further enhanced by skylights. Kitchenette—host provides breakfast foods in refrigerator. Simple, custom-designed contemporary furnishings. Two oversize single beds at right angles form major seating area. Close to Coral Reef Yacht Club. Walk to Coconut Grove Village. $85.

NOTES: Credit cards accepted: A MasterCard; B Visa; C American Express; D Discover Card; E Diner's Club; F Other; 2 Personal checks accepted; 3 Lunch available; 4 Dinner available; 5 Open all year;

MI371. Lovely luxury cottage on Coconut Grove private one-acre estate with electronically controlled security. Mansion listed in historic registry. Walk five blocks to Coconut Grove Village with its trendy sidewalk cafes, restaurants, boutiques, and shops. Fireplace, efficiency kitchen, antique furniture, and elegant accessories. Opens to private covered patio and large pool. Queen-size bed. Suite with twin beds is also available in the main house. $125.

MB40501. Very large efficiency apartment in Miami Beach's Art Deco area. Balcony with fantastic view of the ocean. Full kitchen, two double beds, luxury condo with all the amenities. Unit is just below the penthouse. Convenient walk to convention center and sidewalk cafes. $135.

MI28501. Charming two-room suite with sleeper sofa in sitting room and an extra bedroom if desired. In choice area of the Grove, near Vizcaya and the bay. Fifteen minute walk to the village; fifteen minute drive to downtown, port, or airport. Queen-size bed in suite bedroom, private entry, large bath with stall shower. A small cottage with stall shower suitable for single is also available. Beautifully landscaped grounds with fruit trees and hibiscus. $45-70.

MICANOPY

Bed and Breakfast Scenic Florida

P.O. Box 3385, Tallahassee, 32315-3385
(940) 386-8196

FL18. This Classical Revival mansion was built over the original 1845 structure and reflects the wealth of the family in 1915. Ten rooms and suites and the first-floor parlor are available. Private baths, large windows, ceiling fans, and period decor are common to all rooms. Choices include a canopied king-size bed, cast iron double

bed, a brass and copper double bed, and a queen-size bed. Baths include both modern and period facilities. One suite has a Jacuzzi, and a restored cottage offers added privacy and a kitchenette. Guests may choose an early, full Continental breakfast or a formal, seated breakfast at 9:00 A.M. No smoking. $60-140.

FL25. Open porches and stained glass make this new structure reminiscent of yesteryear. Five guest rooms and suites with private baths and TVs are available. Choices include queen-size beds, four-poster beds, and a king-size water bed. Baths may be modern or period with clawfoot tub. Stained glass art classes are available. The full breakfast may be hearty Southern or gourmet and is served in the dining room. Room service is also available. No smoking. $75-125.

Herlong Mansion

Herlong Mansion

402 Northeast Cholokka Boulevard
P.O. Box 667, 32667
(904) 466-3322

"Micanopy is the prettiest town in Florida. The Herlong Mansion is its crown jewel"— *Florida Trend*, November 1989. The brick Greek Revival structure has four Corinthian columns, ten fireplaces, six different types of wood, and is decorated in period antiques. Built in 1845 and 1910, the three-story house has 11 bedrooms, all with private baths, on two acres with moss-draped oaks, pecans, dogwoods, and magnolias.

Host: H. C. (Sony) Howard, Jr.
Rooms: 11 (PB) $70-130
Full Breakfast
Credit Cards: A, B
Notes: 2, 5, 8, 9, 14

Shady Oak

Shady Oak
Bed and Breakfast

203 Cholokka Boulevard, 32667
(904) 466-3476

The Shady Oak stands majestically in the center of historic downtown. A marvelous canopy of old live oaks, quiet shaded streets, and store fronts offer visitors a memorable connection to Florida's past. This three-story 19th-century-style mansion features beautifully spacious suites and porches, Jacuzzi, Florida room, and widow's walk. A country breakfast is served weekdays, with a gourmet breakfast on weekends. Local activities include antiquing, bicycling, canoeing, bird watching, and much more. "Playfully elegant accommodations, where stained glass, antiques, and innkeeping go together as kindly as warm hugs with old friends."

Host: Frank James
Concierge: Nancy Hale
Rooms: 5 (PB) $75-125

Full Breakfast
Credit Cards: A, B, D
Notes: 2, 3, 4, 5, 7, 8, 9, 14

MONTICELLO

Bed and Breakfast
Scenic Florida

P.O. Box 3385, Tallahassee, 32315-3385
(940) 386-8196

FL 47. Old live oak trees surround this stately Classical Revival home, which was built in 1836. It is listed on the National Register of Historic Places and is the oldest home in the county. The formal parlor, glassed sunrooms, and an open porch are all public areas. Four guest bedrooms are individually heated and air-conditioned and have private baths. Two rooms have antique canopy beds, one double and one queen-size. Other rooms have four-poster double beds. Telephone and TV are available. Breakfast is casual and served in the sun-room. Weekday fare is deluxe Continental; weekend meal is expanded with traditional items. No smoking. $70.

MOUNT DORA

Farnsworth House
Bed and Breakfast

1029 East 5th Avenue, 32757
(904) 735-1894

On one and one-half acres in the historic town of Mount Dora with its many boutiques and antique shops. Built in 1886 with three suites and two efficiencies each decorated in a unique theme with private baths and kitchens. Guests can enjoy the large screened porch, living and dining room, and hot tub enclosed within a screened gazebo.

Hosts: Dick and Sandy Shelton
Rooms: 5 (PB) $75-95
Credit Cards: A, B
Notes: 2, 5, 9, 10, 11, 12, 14

NOTES: Credit cards accepted: A MasterCard; B Visa; C American Express; D Discover Card; E Diner's Club; F Other; 2 Personal checks accepted; 3 Lunch available; 4 Dinner available; 5 Open all year;

NICEVILLE

The International Bed & Breakfast Club, Inc.

504 Amherst Street, Buffalo, NY 14207
(800) 723-4262; FAX (716) 873-4462

The Bluewater Bay resort offers Northwest Florida's number one ranked golf course says *Golfweek*; one of the top 50 tennis resorts says *Tennis* magazine; and one of America's top ten vacation resorts says *Family Circle*. Easy drive from Atlanta, Nashville, New Orleans, and Dallas. Private bayside beach, casual and fine dining, and a natural deep-water marina with four swimming pools. Park areas, nature and biking trails are also available. Residence provides suite with private bath. Full breakfast served. $85.

OCALA

Bed and Breakfast Scenic Florida

P.O. Box 3385, Tallahassee, 32315-3385
(904) 386-8196

FL 34. Built as a family home in 1888, this three-story Queen Anne Victorian inn is one of *Southern Living* magazine's six best bed and breakfast inns. Seven rooms and suites are individually decorated. Choices include twin, double, queen-size, and king-size beds. Some are canopied, iron, or four-poster beds. Baths include both modern facilities and period claw-foot tubs. A full breakfast is a gourmet affair with special items. No children. No smoking. $105-135.

Seven Sisters Inn

820 Southeast Fort King Street, 34471
(904) 867-1170; FAX (904) 732-7764

The Seven Sisters Inn is an elegant yet cozy retreat recently rated as one of the top ten restorations in the United States. This *Country Inns* magazine award winner is nestled in the heart of the historic district and thoroughbred horse country. Seven beautifully appointed Victorian rooms each have a private bath, some with deep soaking tubs. Amenities include full gourmet breakfast, murder mystery weekends, candlelight dinners, and romantic rendezvous packages. Close to famous Silver Springs glass-bottom boats, horse farm tours, unique antique shops, and the unspoiled Ocala National Forest. The inn has been featured in *Southern Living* magazine, *Country Inns*, *Conde Neste Traveler*, *National Geographic*, Mobil Travel and Fodor's guides. Dinner prepared for special occasions. Pet sitter is available.

Hosts: Ken Oden and Bonnie Morehardt
Rooms: 7 (PB) $105-135
Full Breakfast
Credit Cards: A, B, C, D, E
Notes: 2, 4 , 5, 6, 8 (over 11), 9, 10, 11, 12, 13 (water), 14

ORANGE PARK

Club Continental Suites

2143 Astor Street, 32073
(904) 264-6070; (800) 877-6070

The Club Continental Suites is a Mediterranean-style inn overlooking the broad St. Johns River, featuring romantic Continental dining with "old Florida charm." The Club, built in 1923 as the Palmolive family estate, now hosts 22 riverview suites with expansive grounds, giant live oaks, lush gardens, seven tennis courts, three pools, and a pre-Civil War Riverhouse Pub with live entertainment. Sunday brunch available. Lunch and dinner available Tuesday through Friday.

Hosts: Caleb Massee and Karrie Massee
Rooms: 22 (PB) $55-120
Continental Breakfast
Credit Cards: A, B, C
Notes: 2, 3 , 4, 5, 6 (limited), 8, 9, 10, 11, 12, 14

---

6 Pets welcome; 7 Smoking allowed; 8 Children welcome; 9 Social drinking allowed; 10 Tennis available; 11 Swimming available; 12 Golf available; 13 Skiing available; 14 May be booked through travel agents.

ORLANDO

The Courtyard at Lake Lucerne

211 North Lucerne Circle East, 32801
(407) 648-5188; (800) 444-5289

Victorian and Art Deco elegance in a tropical setting in the heart of downtown Orlando. Three separate buildings, each with its own distinctive style, surrounding a luxuriously landscaped brick courtyard with fountains. Complimentary bottle of wine on arrival and expanded Continental breakfast each morning. Award-winning renovation in beautiful surroundings, convenient to everything the area has to offer. One house is nonsmoking.

Hosts: Charles Meiner and Paula Bowers
Rooms: 22 (PB) $65-150
Continental Breakfast
Credit Cards: A, B, C, E
Notes: 2, 5, 7 (limited), 8, 9, 10, 14

Garden Cottage Bed and Breakfast

1309 East Washington Street, 32801
(407) 894-5395; FAX (407) 894-5395

Escape to a relaxed garden atmosphere in historic downtown Orlando. This renovated 1920s home has a cozy cottage adjacent to it, tucked away in a quiet, safe neighborhood. Enjoy beautiful decor, antiques, wicker, fine art, designer linens, tasteful accents, and full kitchen. Sunbathe in the garden courtyard. Stroll to Lake Eola, Church Street Station and Marketplace, unique shops, restaurants, coffee houses, and night clubs. Disney, Epcot, SeaWorld, and Universal Studios nearby. Drive 45 minutes to beaches.

Hosts: Sherry Nelson and Lisa Talmadge
Cottage: 1 (PB) $75
Continental Breakfast
Credit Cards: None
Notes: 2, 5, 7 (limited), 9, 11

The International Bed & Breakfast Club, Inc.

504 Amherst Street, Buffalo, NY 14207
(800) 723-4262; FAX (716) 873-4462

This country estate is nestled in "Disney's backyard." Each of four guest rooms is furnished with a queen-size brass bed or king-size four-poster, with private bath, outside entrance, TV, telephone, and air conditioning. Pool and Jacuzzi are also available. Continental breakfast served. $65-75.

Perri House Bed and Breakfast Inn

10417 State Road 535, 32836
(407) 876-4830; (800) 780-4830

Perri House is a quiet, private, secluded country estate conveniently in the back yard of the Walt Disney World Resort area. Because of its outstanding location, Disney Village is only three minutes away, and EPCOT is only five minutes away. An upscale continental breakfast awaits each morning to start the day. The hosts offer a unique blend of cordial hospitality, comfort, and friendship to all their guests.

Hosts: Nick and Angi Perretti
Rooms: 6 (PB) $69-89
Continental Breakfast
Credit Cards: A, B, C, D
Notes: 2, 5, 8, 9, 10, 11, 12, 14

The Rio Pinar House

532 Pinar Drive, 32825
(800) 277-4903

A quiet, spacious, private home equipped with filtered air and water, furnished with antiques, and featuring an outdoor hot tub and breakfast porch overlooks a yard of trees and flowers. Convenient to the airport, Citrus Bowl, and downtown Church Street Station. Less than an hour from the Space Coast. Only a few blocks from the East-West Expressway that accesses Disney

NOTES: Credit cards accepted: A MasterCard; B Visa; C American Express; D Discover Card; E Diner's Club; F Other; 2 Personal checks accepted; 3 Lunch available; 4 Dinner available; 5 Open all year;

parks, Universal Studios, Sea World, and the convention center.

Hosts: Delores and Vic Freudenburg
Rooms: 3 (PB) $45-50
Full Breakfast
Credit Cards: None
Notes: 2 (in advance), 5, 8, 9, 12

The Spencer Home Bed and Breakfast

313 Spencer Street, 32839
(407) 855-5603

The suite with private entrance consists of one or two bedrooms with a queen-size and double bed and living room with queen-size sofa bed. TV, swimming pool, kitchen, laundry are all available. Con-vention center and most of Central Florida's attractions are within 15 to 30 minutes away. Brochure available. Two-night minimum stay is required.

Hosts: Neal and Eunice Schattauer
Rooms: 2 (PB) $50-100
Continental Breakfast
Credit Cards: None
Notes: 5, 8, 9, 11

Casa Del Sol

PALM BAY

Casa Del Sol

Country Estates, 232 Rheine Road Northwest, 32907
(407) 728-4676

An award winning home on Florida's central east coast. Breakfast is served on the lanai, with breathtaking foliage. From here see a spaceship launched. Enjoy the luxury of a Roman tub. Minutes away from the space pad, all Disney attractions, and the Marlins' winter quarters. Closed April 16 through November 7.

Host: Stanley Finkelstein
Rooms: 3 (1 PB; 2 SB) $55-125
Full Breakfast
Credit Cards: None
Notes: 2, 6, 8, 9, 10, 11, 12, 13, 14

PALM BEACH

Bed & Breakfast Co.

P.O. Box 262, South Miami, 33243
(305) 661-3270; FAX (305) 661-3270

MI369. Luxurious contemporary estate on a canal in Palm Beach Gardens. Common areas include a sunken living room with stone fireplace; a den with TV, VCR, and fireplace; sunken dining room; second-floor central foyer and balcony; pool; patio with Jacuzzi; deck with boat slips; and beautiful landscaped grounds. Four rooms are available for bed and breakfast with private entrances and baths, and small refrigerator. Full-size double beds in three rooms, king-size bed in fourth bedroom. There are also two staterooms available on a yacht. $80-100.

Open House Bed and Breakfast Registry

P.O. Box 3025, Palm Beach, 33480
(407) 842-5190

Palm Beach. This world-renowned enclave of the rich and famous offers a choice of small historic inns or a cottage colony. From the cottages walk one block to the beach. These one- or two-bedroom hideaways have porches or balconies surrounded by lush tropical foliage; a truly Caribbean flavor. Full kitchens, but breakfast provided for short stays. Children and pets welcome. $95.

Palm Beach Historic Inn
365 South County Road, 33480
(407) 832-4009

A historic landmark building, beautifully restored to preserve its original integrity and stately elegance; every modern convenience. Thirteen guest rooms and suites, tastefully and individually appointed, private baths and showers, air conditioning, cable TV and telephones. Guests will be served a complimentary deluxe Continental breakfast in their rooms. Walk one block to the beach and two blocks to the world-famous Worth Avenue shopping. Perfect for weekend getaways, family vacations, relaxing retreats, business trips, and romantic weekends.

Innkeepers: Barbara and Harry Kehr
Rooms: 9 (PB) $75-150
Suites: 4 (PB) $125-250
Continental Breakfast
Credit Cards: A, B, C, D, E
Notes: 2, 9, 10, 11, 12, 14

PALM BEACH GARDENS

Bed and Breakfast Co.
P.O. Box 262
South Miami, FL 33243
(305) 661-3270; FAX (305) 661-3270

PB-369-01. Key West-style living in a five-bedroom, five-bath home on two Intracoastal Waterway acres between West Palm Beach and Jupiter. Designed for relaxing and enjoying the dramatic pool and spa. Dock is protected by small tropical island. Hosts' 48-foot Sport Fisherman is docked there; however, there is space for guest boats. Longer staying guests are usually treated to a cruise. Property is ideally suit-

able for special occasions and celebrations. $75-110.

Open House Bed and Breakfast Registry
P.O. Box 3025, Palm Beach, 33480
(407) 842-5190

Decorator's Town House. Whether viewing the surroundings from the bedroom's private balcony or relaxing on the sequestered patio, guests will find it hard to believe that they are a short walk to a shopping mall with a choice of restaurants, even the movies. The location is convenient to the interstate. The colorfully stylish twin-bedded guest room has a private bath. Full breakfast. Cat in residence. $45-55.

Heron Cay. Water, boats, sun, and fun describe this unique hideaway on two acres facing the Intracoastal Waterway. Explore the Private island or hop into the pool or hot tub. Weekly guests may enjoy a cruise on the host's 48-foot Sportsfisherman. Inside, relax by the stone fireplace in the Victorian parlor, or guests may try their luck on the pinball machine in the game room. Guest rooms have either a king-size or double bed with balconies for a beautiful view of the inlet. Full breakfast; dinner served at extra charge. Resident dog and cats. Dockage available. $80-125.

Windermere Villa. This is a luxurious contemporary villa on the grounds of a renowned national resort and spa. There are miles of walking and bike trails. Take a short stroll to one of the swimming pools. Sophisticated dining and shopping are on the premises, plus the European Health Spa. The balcony of the king-size bedroom overlooks an expansive garden landscape. Ultra-modern double room has private bath. Choose to have your full breakfast served on the screened terrace. Available December through May. $85.

PALMETTO (BRADENTON)_____

Five Oaks Inn

1102 Riverside Drive, 34220
(813) 723-1236; (800) 658-4167

Magnificent Southern estate with river views. Tastefully decorated with period antiques, giving each room its own special flavor. Wraparound porch, oak staircase, beamed ceilings, and window seats add to the elegance and grace, as well as a fully stocked library and bar. Cool nights sitting by the fireplace in the living room sipping hot cider or curling up with a good book takes guests back in time to a more relaxing life. Not five miles from the gulf and its powdery sand and calming waves for sun worshippers. Hospitality guaranteed.

Hosts: Bette and Chet Kriessler
Rooms: 4 (PB) $65-100
Full Breakfast
Credit Cards: A, B, C, D
Notes: 2, 3, 7, 9, 10, 11, 12, 14

PALM HARBOR_____

Bed and Breakfast of Tampa Bay

126 Old Oak Circle, 34683
(813) 785-2342

An Art Deco look invites guests to enjoy paintings, artifacts, and statues from all over the world. Two miles from the Suncoast white sand beaches, golf, tennis, boating, and fishing are all a short distance away. Ninety miles to Disney World and Seaworld. Busch Gardens, Adventureland, Dali Museums, and historic Tarpon Springs are all within a day's visit. Bus lines, shopping malls, ice skating, and fine restaurants nearby. AAA building for travel assistance within walking distance. A Jacuzzi and swimming pool are available for guests to use, and color TV and telephone are in every room.

Hosts: Vivian and David Grimm
Rooms: 4 (2 PB; 2 SB) $45-75
Full Breakfast
Credit Cards: None
Notes: 2, 5, 8, 9, 11, 12

PENSACOLA _____

Bed and Breakfast Scenic Florida

P.O. Box 3385, Tallahassee, 32315-3385
(904)386-8196

FL39. This Victorian residence was built in 1904 and is within the sixteen-block historic district. Recent renovation in the 1980s has preserved the original gas lighting and the beauty of the wood staircase and floors. The first-floor parlor, dining room, and glassed side porch are available for business or social functions. Amenities include TV, VCR with large tape selection, coffee maker, small refrigerator, and private phone. Guests are treated to breakfast, lunch, or dinner (their choice) at the famous landmark, The Hopkins Boarding House, where Southern home-cooked meals have been served family style since 1948. The spacious guest suite has a queen-size bed tucked into an alcove and a Pauley Island hammock for relaxing. The bath is modern with a walk-in shower. No smoking. $70.

PLANTATION_____

Bed & Breakfast Co.

P.O. Box 262, South Miami, 33243
(305) 661-3270; FAX (305) 661-3270

PL068. In Plantation (west of I-95, eight miles from the ocean), this bed and breakfast is in an upscale community of ranch-style homes. Bed and breakfast room with two single beds and private hall bath. Furnishings are attractive, comfortable, and conventional. Community is north of Nova University. Lots of tennis available (home

6 Pets welcome; 7 Smoking allowed; 8 Children welcome; 9 Social drinking allowed; 10 Tennis available; 11 Swimming available; 12 Golf available; 13 Skiing available; 14 May be booked through travel agents.

is across the street from a community pool and tennis court). $40.

QUINCY

Bed and Breakfast Scenic Florida

P.O. Box 3385, Tallahassee, 32315-3385
(940) 386-8196

FL23. This Classic Revival Raised Cottage was built in 1843. A major renovation in 1990 resulted in five rooms on two levels. Guests may choose two double beds, individual double beds, or one king-size bed. All have private baths, including some with claw-foot tub and shower. All rooms have TV and telephone with a laundry, small kitchen, and refrigerator available for guests' use. An extended Continental breakfast is served in the upstairs parlor, and trays permit guests to return to their rooms if they prefer. No smoking. $69.90.

ST. AUGUSTINE

Carriage Way Bed and Breakfast

70 Cuna Street, 32084
(904) 829-2467

An 1883 Victorian in the historic district, within walking distance of the waterfront, shops, restaurants, and historic sites. Complimentary cordials, newspaper, cookies, bicycles, and breakfast. The atmosphere here is leisurely and casual.

Hosts: Bill and Diane Johnson
Rooms: 9 (PB) $49-105
Full Breakfast
Credit Cards: A, B, D
Notes: 2, 5, 9, 10, 11, 12, 14

Casablanca Inn on the Bay in Old St. Augustine

24 Avenida Menendez, 32084
(800) 826-2626

Casablanca Inn features elegant suites and rooms with fine antiques, panoramic bayfront views, private entrances and baths; some with Jacuzzis. A hearty full breakfast is served on the grand front porches overlooking the bay. Wines and sweets included. Bicycles available. In the historic district; restaurants, shopping, and all historic points are within walking distance.

Hosts: Tom and Janet Murry
Rooms: 12 (PB) $59-155
Credit Cards: A, B, C, D
Notes: 2, 5, 9, 10, 11, 12, 14

Casa de la Paz

22 Avenida Menendez, 32084
(904) 829-2915

Mediterranean-style inn overlooking the Matanzas Bay in the historic district. Elegant furnishings and imported fine linens. From the guest rooms or from a second-story veranda, enjoy a view of Matanzas Bay. From the veranda an open stairway leads to a beautiful walled garden courtyard. The inn is central to all historic sites, fine restaurants, and miles of ocean beaches. Complimentary sherry; full breakfast.

Host: Jan Maki
Rooms: 6 (PB) $65-125
Full Breakfast
Credit Cards: A, B
Notes: 2, 5, 9, 10, 11, 12, 14

Castle Garden

15 Shenandoah Street, 32084
(904) 829-3839

Stay at the Castle and be treated like royalty! Relax and enjoy the peace and quiet of royal treatment at this newly restored 100-year-old castle of Moorish Revival

---

NOTES: Credit cards accepted: A MasterCard; B Visa; C American Express; D Discover Card; E Diner's Club; F Other; 2 Personal checks accepted; 3 Lunch available; 4 Dinner available; 5 Open all year;

design, where the only sound to hear is the occasional roar of a cannon shot from the old fort 200 yards to the south, the creak of the original solid wood floor, or the chirping of birds. The unusual coquina stone exterior is interesting to see, while the interior of this former Warden Castle Carriage House has been completely renovated and features two magnificent and romantic honeymoon suites with sunken bedrooms, in-room Jacuzzis, and cathedral ceilings. Amenities include complimentary wine, chocolates, bikes, and fenced parking.

Hosts: Joyce Kloeckner and Bruce Kloeckner
Rooms: 6 (PB) $55-150
Full Breakfast
Credit Cards: A, B, C, D
Notes: 2, 3, 4, 5, 8, 10, 12, 14

The Cedar House Inn

79 Cedar Street, 32084
(904) 829-0079; (800) CEDAR-INN

Capture romantic moments at this 1893 Victorian home in the heart of the ancient city. Escape into an antique-filled bedroom with private bath and claw-foot tub or enjoy the grand parlor with its fireplace, player piano, and antique Victrola. Elegant full breakfast, complimentary beverages, evening snack, convenient on-premises parking, Jacuzzi spa, and bicycles. Walk to all historic sites. Easy drive to I-95, Atlantic Ocean beaches, tennis, and golf.

Hosts: Nina and Russ Thomas
Rooms: 6 (PB) $65-125
Full Breakfast
Credit Cards: A, B, D
Notes: 2, 4, 5, 9, 10, 11, 12, 14

The Kenwood Inn

38 Marine Street, 32084
(904) 824-2116

Local maps and early records show the inn was built between 1865 and 1885, and was functioning as a private boarding house as early as 1886. In the historic district, the inn is within walking distance of many fine restaurants and all historic sights. One block from the Intracoastal Waterway, with its passing fishing trawlers, yachts at anchor, and the classic Bridge of Lions. Beautiful ocean beaches are just across the bridge.

Hosts: Mark Kerrianne and Caitlin Constant
Rooms: 14 (PB) $65-95
Continental Breakfast
Credit Cards: A, B, C
Notes: 2, 5, 9, 10, 11, 12

The Kenwood Inn

Old City House Inn and Restaurant

115 Cordova Street, 32084
(904) 826-0113

In the heart of town, within walking distance of all the sites sits the Old City House, a classic example of St. Augustine Colonial Revival architecture. Restored in 1990, the premises include five bed and breakfast rooms and a full-service award-winning restaurant. It commands a view of some of the most beautiful historic architecture in northeastern Florida. Enjoy wine on the veranda in the afternoons. Queen-size beds, private baths, cable TV, air conditioning, private entrances, and a full breakfast. Special weekday rates are available.

Hosts: Bob and Alice Compton
Rooms: 5 (PB) $60-105

6 Pets welcome; 7 Smoking allowed; 8 Children welcome; 9 Social drinking allowed; 10 Tennis available; 11 Swimming available; 12 Golf available; 13 Skiing available; 14 May be booked through travel agents.

Old City House

Full Breakfast
Credit Cards: A, B, C, E
Notes: 2, 3, 4, 5, 9, 10, 11, 12

Old Powder House Inn

38 Cordova Street, 32084
(904) 824-4149; (800) 447-4149

High ceilings, wraparound verandas, and elaborate woodwork distinguish this Victorian home built in 1899 on the site of an 18th-century Spanish powder magazine. Cordova Street is in the heart of the historic area with horse and buggies trotting right past the house. Restaurants, antique stores, and quaint shops are within easy walking distance. Full gourmet breakfast, tea and pastries in the afternoon, and sparkling juice, wine, and hors d'oeuvres each day. Bicycles and tandems. In-ground Jacuzzi and parking on the premises.

Hosts: Al and Eunice Howes
Rooms: 9 (PB) $59-109
Full Breakfast
Credit Cards: A, B, D
Notes: 2, 5, 9, 10, 11, 12, 14

St. Francis Inn

279 St. George Street, 32084
(904) 824-6068; (800) 824-6062

The St. Francis Inn, in the historic district of St. Augustine, was built as a private home for a Spanish soldier in 1791. Originally known as the Garcia-Dummett House, it began operating as an inn in 1845. It is a Spanish Colonial structure with a private

courtyard, fireplaces, balconies furnished with rocking chairs, and the modern amenity of a swimming pool. The inn has a wide variety of accommodations ranging from single rooms, to two- and three-room suites, to an entire cottage. The warmth and peacefulness of the inn itself, its location, and the kind of guests it attracts are all strong assets.

Hosts: Stan and Regina Reynolds
Rooms: 14 (PB) $49-115
Continental Breakfast
Credit Cards: A, B
Notes: 2, 5, 9, 10 ,11, 12, 14

Westcott House

146 Avenida Menendez, 32084
(904) 824-4301

One of St. Augustine's most elegant guest houses overlooking Matanzas Bay. Circa 1890, restored in 1983, in the historic area and within walking distance to historic sites. All rooms have private baths, king-size beds, cable TV, private telephone, and are furnished in antiques. Year-round climate control. Complimentary bottle of wine upon arrival. One-half block from the city's yacht pier.

Hosts: Sherry and David Dennison
Rooms: 8 (PB) $95-150
Continental Breakfast
Credit Cards: A, B
Notes: 2, 5, 8, 9, 10, 11, 12, 14

Westcott House

NOTES: Credit cards accepted: A MasterCard; B Visa; C American Express; D Discover Card; E Diner's Club; F Other; 2 Personal checks accepted; 3 Lunch available; 4 Dinner available; 5 Open all year;

ST. PETE BEACH ISLAND

B&B Suncoast Accommodations

8690 Gulf Boulevard, 33706
(813) 360-1753

2. Rooftop sun deck, spa, dock, and fabulous sunsets characterize this bed and breakfast. Guest accommodations include queen-size bed, private bath, TV, telephone, refrigerator, and microwave. See the dolphins swim by the breakfast table. Second room available for families. Seventh night free. $50-80.

ST. PETERSBURG

B&B Suncoast Accommodations

8690 Gulf Boulevard, St. Pete Beach Island, 33706
(813) 360 1753

3. Live bird aviary in an artist's home. Five minutes to the beach. Guest room includes king-size bed and a private bath. Second room available for families. Seventh night free. $50-65.

Bed and Breakfast Scenic Florida

P.O. Box 3385, Tallahassee, 32315-3385
(904) 386-8196

FL45. Located downtown, this 1904 Southern home is near Busch Gardens and Weeki Wachee. Guests enjoy mingling in the first-floor sitting room with fireplace and piano or on the porch and patio. Five guest rooms and a separate carriage house room have private baths, ceiling fans, and sitting areas. Choices include one room with twin beds and five with queen-size beds, all with central heat and air conditioning. A substantial English breakfast that features Welsh cakes and home fries is served from 8:00-9:30 A.M. in twin dining rooms. No children. No smoking. $60-65.

Bayboro House Bed and Breakfast

1719 Beach Drive Southeast, 33701
(813) 823-4955

Turn-of-the-century Queen Anne home furnished in antiques. Old-fashioned porch swing to enjoy sea gulls and sailboats on Old Tampa Bay. Minutes from the Dali Museum, Pier, Suncoast Dome, Bayfront Center, and Al Lange Stadium. Many fine restaurants in the area. Personal suite available on request.

Hosts: Gordon and Antonia Powers
Rooms: 4 (PB) $75-85
Continental Breakfast
Credit Cards: A, B
Notes: 2, 5, 7 (limited), 9, 10, 11, 12, 14

Beach Haven Villas

4980 Gulf Boulevard, 33706
(813) 367-8642

Directly on the sparkling Gulf of Mexico, Beach Haven hearkens back to the days when much of Florida offered vacationers colorful Art Deco-style motels. Still in pink, Beach Haven retains its charming personality, while providing updated interiors and furnishings. Close to shopping, dining, and entertainment. Add the peaceful setting, a gulf front pool, and a sandy beachfront setting and guests will know why Beach Haven is so popular.

Hosts: Jone and Millard Gamble
Rooms: 18 (PB)
Continental Breakfast
Credit Cards: A, B
Notes: 5, 8, 10, 11, 12, 14

The Heritage Hotel

234 3rd Avenue North, 33701
(813) 822-4814; (800) 283-7829

6 Pets welcome; 7 Smoking allowed; 8 Children welcome; 9 Social drinking allowed; 10 Tennis available;
11 Swimming available; 12 Golf available; 13 Skiing available; 14 May be booked through travel agents.

The Heritage Hotel is downtown St. Petersburg's finest hotel, featuring gracious hospitality and Southern charm. The Heritage Hotel combines the glamour and exuberance of the early 1920s architecture and furniture, with luxurious, comfortable rooms and suites. On site is the Heritage Grill, which combines excellent cuisine with one of Tampa Bay's finest art galleries.

Host: Stan Ockwig
Rooms: 70 (PB) $58-90
Full Breakfast
Credit Cards: A, B, C, E
Notes: 2, 3, 4, 5, 7, 8, 9, 10 (close by), 11, 12 (close by), 14

Inn on the Beach

1401 Gulf Way, 33706
(813) 360-8844

The perfect combination of miles of sugar sand beaches and Old-World charm, in a National Historic District. Tastefully remodeled, professionally decorated, with modern kitchens and baths, decks, courtyards, tile floors, antiques, new beds, designer sheets and spreads, wooden shutters, cable TV, and telephones. Bicycles, beach chairs, beautiful sunsets, local restaurants, and shops. Continental breakfast provided. Children welcome.

Hosts: Woody and Ellen Miller
Rooms: 14 (PB) $45-150
Continental Breakfast
Cards: A, B
Notes: 2, 5, 7, 8, 9, 10, 11, 12, 14

Mansion House

105 5th Avenue Northeast, 33701
(813) 821-9391

Charming turn-of-the-century Southern home recently renovated. Wood floors, stained glass, fireplace, sitting porches, and soft furnishings add to the relaxing ambience. Hearty breakfast served with Welsh hospitality. Walking distance to marina, pier, museums, restaurants, theaters, beach, pool, tennis, sailing, and other Bay Shore amenities.

Hosts: Suzanne and Alan Lucas
Rooms: 6 (PB) From $60
Full Breakfast
Credit Cards: A, B
Notes: 2, 5, 9, 10, 11, 12, 13, 14

SAN MATEO

Bed and Breakfast Scenic Florida

P.O. Box 3385, Tallahassee, 32315-3385
(904) 386-8196

FL44. This three-story 1889 Victorian home is less than an hour from the Atlantic beaches. Public rooms include the parlor with TV, music and game room, and a formal dining room. One two-bedroom suite and four guest rooms are on the second floor. The suite features queen-size beds and a private bath with claw-foot tub and shower. The other rooms offer double, queen, and king-size beds with modern or period baths. A full gourmet breakfast is served and features homemade breads. $45-100.

SANTA ROSA BEACH

Bed and Breakfast Scenic Florida

P.O. Box 3385, Tallahassee, 32315-3385
(904) 386-8196

FL38. This antebellum plantation-style home was built in 1990 as a bed and breakfast. It is just steps from the beach and has a deep, wide porch where guests can relax on wicker furniture. The home is fully heated and air-conditioned. The guest parlor provides a TV, stereo, ice maker, and fireplace. Four guest rooms and a carriage house have private entrances and private baths with tub and shower combinations. Guests may choose rooms with queen-size or double four-poster beds or the carriage house, which has a king-size bed and queen-size sleeper. A dining area includes a microwave, toaster, coffee maker, small refrigerator, glassware, and dishes. A TV is also

NOTES: Credit cards accepted: A MasterCard; B Visa; C American Express; D Discover Card; E Diner's Club; F Other; 2 Personal checks accepted; 3 Lunch available; 4 Dinner available; 5 Open all year;

provided. Breakfast is served in the formal dining room and features a variety of unique items. No smoking. Special rates December through February. $83-105.

ST. TERESA BEACH

Bed and Breakfast Scenic Florida

P.O. Box 3385, Tallahassee, 32315-3385
(940) 386-8196

FL32. This two-story beach house was built in the early 1980s. The location is ideal for shelling, sunning, and swimming at the beach. The common parlor has TV, VCR, a fireplace, and wicker furnishings. Three bedrooms are available. One has a double bed, ceiling fan, and a bath with shower. Two other rooms have double beds and a shared bath with combination tub and shower. A Southern breakfast is served in the common room. No children. No smoking. $75.

TALLAHASSEE

Bed and Breakfast Scenic Florida

P.O. Box 3385, Tallahassee, 32315-3385
(904) 386-8196

FL17. This Federal style two-story brick home sits among stately oaks in a quiet residential area, which is near the downtown capital complex, restaurants, and shops. Two guest rooms have private baths; one has a queen-size bed and a twin bed in an adjoining room. A casual first floor sitting room has a TV for guests' use. A cozy breakfast for two may be served, or a larger group may use the formal dining room. A fresh fruit platter, quality breads, jams and beverages are served. Business meetings and social events can be arranged. Wine and flowers are available for special occasions. No Smoking. $75-90

Governors Inn

209 South Adams Street, 32301
(904) 681-6855

The Governors Inn combines original woodwork, exposed beams, and brilliant skylights to create a French country environment. The 41 guest rooms and suites are furnished with antique armoires and English pub tables. No two rooms are alike. Some have French four-poster beds and framed prints. Others have loft bedrooms and fireplaces, spiral staircases, and clerestory windows. The Spessard Holland suite has a wet bar and vaulted ceilings. Conferences for up to 75 people can be arranged. One-half block from the state capitol.

Rooms: 41 (PB) $99-229
Continental Breakfast
Credit Cards: A, B, C, D, E
Notes: 5, 7, 8, 9, 12, 14

Governors Inn

TAMPA

Gram's Place Bed and Breakfast Guest House

3109 North Ola, 33603
(813) 221-0596; (813) 292-1415 (pager)

Named in honor of singer/songwriter Gram Parsons, this artists' retreat and music lovers' paradise appeals to all with its relax-

6 Pets welcome; 7 Smoking allowed; 8 Children welcome; 9 Social drinking allowed; 10 Tennis available; 11 Swimming available; 12 Golf available; 13 Skiing available; 14 May be booked through travel agents.

ing, laid back atmosphere and provides a taste of Amsterdam and Key West. Guests are encouraged to bring their favorite music from classical, jazz, blues, rock, country, folk, and gospel. Oversized Jacuzzi, tropical courtyard and bar, waterfall, and sun deck. Skylights throughout the house and a fireplace. Continental-plus breakfast served. Two miles northwest of historic Ybor City and downtown Tampa. Open 24 hours.

Host: Mark Holland
Rooms: 10 (3 PB; 7 SB) $45
Continental Breakfast
Credit Cards: A, B, C
Notes: 3, 4, 5, 6, 7, 8, 9, 11, 14

TARPON SPRINGS

East Lake Bed and Breakfast

421 Old East Lake Road, 34689
(813) 937-5487

Private home on two and one-half acres, on a quiet road along Lake Tarpon. Bedroom and adjoining private bath are at the front of the house, away from the family quarters. Twenty-four hour access. Room has color TV and telephone. The hosts are retired business people who enjoy new friends and are well informed about the area. A full home-cooked breakfast is served.

Hosts: Marie and Dick Fiorito
Room: 1 (PB) $35-40
Full Breakfast
Credit Cards: None
Notes: 2, 5, 9, 10, 11, 12

Inn on the Bayou

P.O. Box 1545, 34688
(813) 942-4468

Guests will stay in a beautiful, modern, contemporary home on a quiet bayou. Fish for a big old red, or watch blue herons and pelicans in a bird sanctuary behind the inn. Enjoy a swim in the solar heated pool or relax in a whirlpool spa. Just minutes to a white-sand beach and breathtaking sunsets. Take a stroll through the famous sponge docks or go antiquing on Main Street. Busch Gardens and Adventure Island are close by. Private tours with transportation are available.

Hosts: Al and Chris Stark
Rooms: 3 (PB & SB) $45-50
Continental Breakfast
Credit Cards: None
Notes: 2, 4, 5, 8, 9, 11, 12

TEQUESTA

Open House Bed and Breakfast Registry

P.O. Box 3025, Palm Beach, 33480
(407) 842-5190

County Line. Just north of Jupiter and 35 minutes from Palm Beach International Airport, this new home, designed for bed and breakfast travelers, is on a residential cul-de-sac. The private sun decks of single, double, and family bedrooms overlook the pool and hot tub. Continental breakfast. Additional people $10 each. $55.

TERRA VERDE

B&B Suncoast Accommodations

8690 Gulf Boulevard, St. Pete Beach Island, 33706
(813) 360-1753

5. Two queen rooms in a bayfront home with a pool and private baths is less than five minutes to the beach. Nonsmoking, non-drinking home. Seventh night free. $75-90.

TREASURE ISLAND

B&B Suncoast Accommodations

8690 Gulf Boulevard, St. Pete Beach Island, 33706
(813) 360-1753

NOTES: Credit cards accepted: A MasterCard; B Visa; C American Express; D Discover Card; E Diner's Club; F Other; 2 Personal checks accepted; 3 Lunch available; 4 Dinner available; 5 Open all year;

1. Walk to the Gulf of Mexico from this home. King-size bed and private bath. Waterfront with a dock and outside tiki bar. Fantastic views from the second floor. Seventh night free. $75-85.

VENICE

The Banyan House

519 South Harbor Drive, 34285
(813) 484-1385

Experience the Old World charm of one of Venice's historic Mediterranean homes, circa 1926, on Florida's Gulf Coast. Fully-equipped efficiencies are tastefully decorated, each with its own character. Large shaded courtyard with pool and Jacuzzi. Close to beaches, restaurants, golf, and fishing. Complimentary bicycles. Nonsmoking.

Hosts: Chuck and Susan McCormick
Rooms: 9 (7 PB; 2 SB) $59-99
Continental Breakfast
Credit Cards: None
Notes: 2, 5, 8 (over 12), 9, 10, 11, 12

WAKULLA SPRINGS

Wakulla Springs Lodge

One Spring Drive, 32305
(904) 224-5950

Wakulla Springs Lodge is a 27-room lodge, with imported marble, rare Spanish tile, and paint and wrought iron work by artisans—a most unique retreat. Standing today as it did then, changed only for improvements in modern conveniences and fire safety, the Wakulla Springs Lodge attracts guests worldwide and guarantees the need for return visits to all who venture just 15 miles south of Florida's Capitol in Tallahassee. Full restaurant, snack bar, and gift shop in lobby. On the National Register of Historic Places. In Edward Ball Wakulla Springs State Park. Glass-bottom and riverboat cruises. Open year-round.

Hosts: William Roberts, General Manager
Rooms: 27 (PB) $54-70
Full Breakfast
Credit Cards: A, B
Notes: 2, 3, 4, 5, 8, 9, 11, 14

WELLINGTON

Open House Bed and Breakfast Registry

P.O. Box 3025, Palm Beach, 33480
(407) 842-5190

Polo Country. Antique buffs will love this charming home. It is embellished with 19th-century English pine and sporting art. Only five minutes from the world-famous Palm Beach Polo grounds, as well as the famous Florida Rowing Center at Lake Wellington. Other activities, such as the Palm Beach Trap and Skeet Club and the Winter Equestrian Festival, are open to guests. The hostess may invite guests to join in a shopping tour of quality antique districts in the county. Children and pets welcome. Continental breakfast. $50-65.

WEST PALM BEACH

Mount Vernon Motor Lodge

310 Belvedere Road, 33405
(407) 832-0094

Enjoy the best of everything here at Mount Vernon Motor Lodge. There are 46 single and double occupancy rooms and a lovely large pool on the premises. Breakfast is served. Only 60 miles from Miami, and one and one-half miles from the airport. Intracoastal water is within walking distance, and shopping centers and restaurants are within a quarter mile. City is famous for its beaches in addition to Worth Avenue, the exclusive market of the United States.

Host: Parish Kanu
Rooms: 46 (PB) $39-59

6 Pets welcome; 7 Smoking allowed; 8 Children welcome; 9 Social drinking allowed; 10 Tennis available; 11 Swimming available; 12 Golf available; 13 Skiing available; 14 May be booked through travel agents.

Credit Cards: A, B, C, D, E
Notes: 5, 8, 9, 10, 11, 12, 13, 14

Open House
Bed and Breakfast
Registry

P.O. Box 3025, Palm Beach, 33480
(407) 842-5190

Cosmopolitan. Near Flagler Drive and the Intracoastal Waterway, this is an easy walk across the bridge to Palm Beach.Guests may wine and dine in one of many renowned restaurants, and can enjoy celebrity-watching from the sidewalk cafes. Convenient to shops, beach, and airport. King-size bedrooms, private bath, and Continental breakfast. Resident dog and cat. $40-50.

Old Northwood Historic District. Near the Intracoastal Waterway, several charming early century homes, restored to their original splendor, are featured in an annual Holiday Candlelight House Tour. Swimming pools available. Ten minutes to the beach and airport. Breakfast is special. Choice of accommodations, including unhosted, separate studio efficiencies with weekly or monthly rates. $60-90.

Lake Clarke Shores. The suburban ranch style home is just west of I-95. Enjoy quiet relaxation on the large screened porch overlooking the picturesque canal. Walk out on the dock and watch the boats go by on their way to Lake Osborne. Children welcome. Continental breakfast and/or kitchen privileges. Family and weekly rates. $40-55.

West Palm Beach
Bed and Breakfast

419 32nd Street, 33407
(407) 848-4064; (800) 736-4064
FAX (407) 842-1688

A cozy Key West-style cottage built in the 1930s with all today's conveniences: private baths, air conditioning, paddle fans, and cable TV. The hosts have retained the charm of old Florida with white wicker furniture in a colorful Caribbean decor; sun by the lush tropical pool, ride complimentary bicycles, or just relax! In the Old Northwood Historic District, just one block from the waterway, and minutes to the tropical waters of the Atlantic or Palm Beach.

Host: Dennis Keimel
Rooms: 3 (PB) $55-115
Continental Breakfast
Credit Cards: A, B, C, E
Notes: 2, 5, 7, 9, 10, 11, 12, 14

ZOLFO SPRINGS

Double M Ranch
Bed and Breakfast

Route 1, P.O. Box 292, 33890
(813) 735-0266 (after 6:00 P.M.)

The Mathenys welcome guests to this 4,500-acre working cattle and citrus ranch in the heart of agricultural Florida. There are numerous recreational opportunities nearby, including fishing, golf, canoeing, and a state park. Accommodations include approximately 1,000 square feet of space and a private entrance. A ranch tour is an option most guests enjoy taking. If guests want to see a part of Florida most tourists miss, come out to the ranch! Two-night minimum stay required.

Hosts: Mary Jane and Charles Matheny
Rooms: 2 (1 PB; 1 SB) $60
Continental Breakfast
Credit Cards: None
Notes: 2, 5, 9, 11, 12, 14

NOTES: Credit cards accepted: A MasterCard; B Visa; C American Express; D Discover Card; E Diner's Club; F Other; 2 Personal checks accepted; 3 Lunch available; 4 Dinner available; 5 Open all year;

Georgia

ANDERSONVILLE

A Place Away Cottage

110 Oglethorpe Street, 31711
(912) 924-1004; (912) 924-2558

Country-style guest cottage with polished
pine floors, private baths, TV, coffee maker,
and small refrigerator in each room, front
porch with rocking chairs, and back deck
overlooking yard with barbecue grills and
picnic tables. Common room with round
pine table is where breakfast is served.

Hosts: Peggy and Fred Sheppard
Rooms: 2 (PB) $45 50
Continental Breakfast
Credit Cards: None
Notes: 2, 5, 7, 8, 9, 10

ATLANTA

Atlanta's Woodruff Inn

223 Ponce de Leon Avenue, 30308
(404) 875-9449

Southern hospitality and charm await
guests at this historic, beautifully restored
bed and breakfast inn. In midtown Atlanta
and convenient to everything. Lots of antiques. A full Southern breakfast cooked by
the on-site owners is a real treat.

Hosts: Joan and Douglas Jones
Rooms: 13 rooms $69-295
Full Breakfast
Credit Cards: A, B, C, D
Notes: 2, 5, 8, 9

Bed and Breakfast Atlanta

1801 Piedmont Avenue, Suite 208, 30324
(404) 875-0525; (800) 96PEACH
FAX (404) 875-9672

A1. This early 1900s neighborhood is on
the historic register and has special appeal
for walkers and joggers. Nearby are the
Woodruff Arts Center, High Museum,
Botanical Gardens, Piedmont Park, and
Colony Square with many appealing restaurants and shops. Public transit is excellent.
Host couple resides in Dutch Colonial
home with private cottage in rear. Bright,
cheery, spacious unit has bedroom alcove
with double bed and desk. The living-dining space has a double sleep sofa, chair, and
breakfast table. New full bath and galley
kitchen. Cable TV and telephone available.
Self-catered breakfast. No smoking. $88-
100.

A2. This bed and breakfast in Midtown,
two to three miles to downtown, has excellent public transportation in a historic
neighborhood of winding streets and parks.
Private entry guest unit offers a bedroom
with twin beds, adjacent sitting room with
cable TV, private shower-only bath, and
special amenities for minor cooking such as
a small refrigerator, coffee maker, toaster
oven, and a microwave oven. Breakfast
provisions are stocked for self-catering.
Host welcomes nonsmokers. $68-80.

A3. A Georgian-style brick building in
Midtown (Ansley Park) offers one bed and
breakfast room in a large second-floor
owner-occupied apartment. Small, attractive room has twin beds, telephone, TV, and
private bath off the hall. A small sitting
room and den with a single bed is available
for parties traveling together with a willing-
ness to share the bath. Computer available.
Nonsmokers only. Continental breakfast.
$48-56.

---

6 Pets welcome; 7 Smoking allowed; 8 Children welcome; 9 Social drinking allowed; 10 Tennis available;
11 Swimming available; 12 Golf available; 13 Skiing available; 14 May be booked through travel agents.

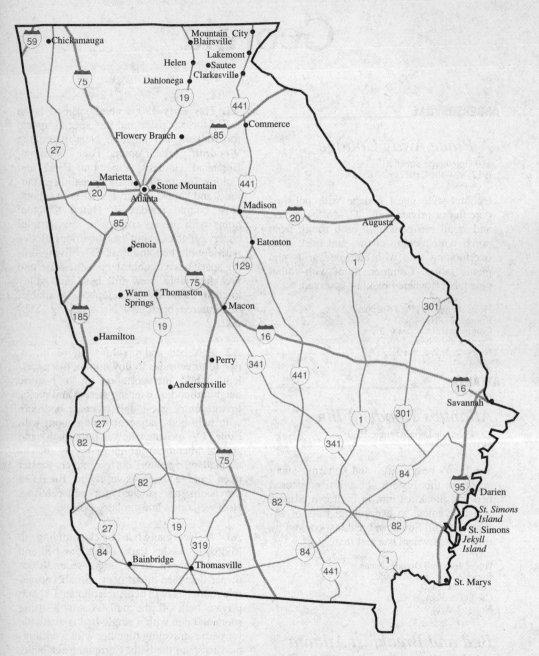

Georgia

Bed and Breakfast Atlanta (continued)

A4. In one of the few contemporary residences in this interesting close-in historic area. Guest suite has a private entrance, living room, kitchen, bedroom, full bath, separate heating and air conditioning system, private telephone line, stereo, and cable TV. FAX is available. Kitchen has a refrigerator stocked for self-catered breakfast, microwave oven, toaster, coffee maker, etc. Within walking distance to Woodruff Art Center or the Botanical Gardens. $72-88.

A5. This bed and breakfast is a few miles from downtown. Excellent public transportation. Architecturally interesting home built about 1910; neighborhood is on the Historic Register. There are two large guest rooms with a shared full bath. One bedroom offers a king-size bed and sitting area. The other room has twin beds. Interesting mixture of contemporary and antique furniture. Continental-plus breakfast is served in glassed breakfast area which features beautiful outdoor viewing and bird watching. Hosts readily share their love of Atlanta and a vast well of information about the city. Nonsmokers only. Both rooms are used only with party traveling together. $80.

B1. Secluded privacy in "The Cottage," a guest house in Buckhead, one of Atlanta's loveliest residential areas. Expansive guest house, nestled behind large residence on four acres, offers two spacious bedrooms, full bath, living room, dining area with adjacent deck, and a small, well-equipped kitchen. Breakfast provisions are stocked daily for self-catering. Washer/dryer, private phone line, TV, VCR, central heating and air system, pool, and croquet. $120–180.

B2. Charming, newly renovated two-story brick traditional home offers delightful vistas of lush green trees, beautifully landscaped yard and a golf course across the street. Two upstairs bedrooms are offered with one full bath. Both rooms are used only when party is traveling together. King room has a small refrigerator and large desk. Upstairs is private to guests. Continental breakfastserved. A resident cat. $68–80.

B3. Rambling Cape Cod-style home is in a beautiful residential area near Peachtree Road. Private entry to the guest room is through a welcoming patio next to the swimming pool. Upstairs room has dormer windows which look out over lush greenery and lovely homes. Traditional furnishings include twin beds, chairs, and a round table suitable for breakfast in the room if desired. Breakfast is also served in a downstairs dining area or on the patio. Nonsmokers. $60–68.

D1. An intimate bed and breakfast just a few blocks off the square in Decatur, the house was built in 1937. There are two bedrooms for guests. The gourmet breakfasts include homemade breads, muffins, fresh fruit or fruit smoothies, freshly ground coffee, imported tea, and sweet, dark honey gathered from hives in the lower garden. There is a hot tub and a nearby pool available to guests. The city of Decatur is one of Atlanta's most historic and well maintained neighborhoods. It is less than six miles from downtown Atlanta and three miles from Emory University, the CDC, and the American Cancer Society. $60-72.

D3. A cream-colored Victorian brick house with convenient access to MARTA public transportation. Enter the private-entry suite from a large front porch with rocking

NOTES: Credit cards accepted: A MasterCard; B Visa; C American Express; D Discover Card; E Diner's Club; F Other; 2 Personal checks accepted; 3 Lunch available; 4 Dinner available; 5 Open all year; 6 Pets welcome; 7 Smoking allowed; 8 Children welcome; 9 Social drinking allowed; 10 Tennis available; 11 Swimming available; 12 Golf available; 13 Skiing available; 14 May be booked through travel agents.

Bed and Breakfast Atlanta
(continued)

chairs. Suite offers an elegant library and sitting room with fireplace, large bedroom with antique double bed and adjoining new stall-shower bath. There is also a second-floor bedroom with private bath. Full or Continental breakfast served in formal dining room, contemporary kitchen or on the rear deck overlooking garden, pool, and hot tub. Bicycles are available. Smoking allowed in outdoor areas only. Resident dogs and cats. $80-120.

E1. This traditional two-story house with swimming pool is on 12 beautifully wooded acres in Druid Hills. Two guest rooms, each with queen-size bed, share one bath. One room has handmade quilts and an antique doll collection. The other provides a wonderful view of the pool, woods, and flowers. An expanded Continental breakfast is served in the charming downstairs dining room. One of the hosts builds beautiful reproduction furniture; an impressive silver chest in the front entry is evidence of his skill. $60-72.

E2. Lovely 1930s brick bungalow houses a bed and breakfast that is walking distance to Emory University. Excellent public transportation for downtown meetings as well. This bright, cheerful room has an antique double bed; adjacent den with TV is private to guests. The full bath and dressing area has been totally renovated. Gracious Continental breakfast is served each morning in a large, modern kitchen with views of the lovely patio on the rear of the house and numerous birdfeeders. Nonsmokers only. $60-72.

E3. This very special private guest cottage in Druid Hills includes a living room with a love seat that opens into a twin bed, fully equipped kitchen, bedroom with full-size

brass bed, and bath. Furnishings are over-stuffed vintage, with beautiful linens, down comforters, and ample breakfast provisions for self-catering. Hosts share their enthusiasm for Atlanta's sights. No smoking. Weekly and monthly rates upon request. $100-140.

I1. Small inn overlooks Springvale Park in the historic Victorian neighborhood, Inman Park. Two guest rooms, each with double bed and private bath, are offered. In addition, the Garden Suite is a private apartment on the terrace level with its own entrance, lawn, and parking. The suite has a living room with sleep sofa, bedroom with queen-size bed, full bath, and a totally equipped kitchen. Cable TV, washer/dryer, and private phone are included. Garden Suite guests may enjoy breakfast in the upstairs dining room or self-cater. Weekly and monthly rates available. Two resident cats. No smoking. $60-100.

I3. The Santa Fe Suite is a private full upstairs living unit in Atlanta's only Victorian neighborhood, Inman Park. Suite includes huge bedroom, queen-size bed, sitting area with sofa and TV, kitchen, and breakfast area and office. Totally new bath adjoining the bedroom, has a stall shower, dressing room, and washer/dryer. In addition there are two first-floor bedrooms, each with double bed. Bath is shared. Secured parking. Excellent public transit. Nonsmokers only. Resident cat. $60-88.

K1. Fully renovated, spacious 1960s brick ranch-style home offers one sunny antique-furnished double with adjoining bath and one spacious and bright twin-bed room with private bath down the hall. A single-bed studio room with full view of the patio and garden is sometimes available. Host couple serves nutritious breakfasts featuring home-baked breads, and lively hospitality complete the picture as a bed and breakfast

NOTES: Credit cards accepted: A MasterCard; B Visa; C American Express; D Discover Card; E Diner's Club; F Other; 2 Personal checks accepted; 3 Lunch available; 4 Dinner available; 5 Open all year;

winner. Within walking distance of Emory University. Kosher dietary laws observed. No smoking. $68-80.

M1. A 60-year-old Colonial brick home in Morningside. Excellent public transportation. Walk to shops, restaurants and points of interest. Spacious, light-filled bedroom on the second floor has queen-size brass bed and adjoining shower-only bath. Third-floor guest suite affords total privacy with a large living room with cable TV, bedroom with queen-size bed and adjoining bath with shower. Guests enjoy sitting areas downstairs and a lovely rear terrace overlooking walled yard. The smell of fresh baking completes the picture. Continental or full breakfast. No smoking. Resident dog and cat. $72-88.

M2. Private entry apartment in 1920s neighborhood called Morningside offers easy access to downtown, Midtown, Emory University, CDC, and Virginia-Highland. This immaculately kept second-floor guest suite offers a bedroom with queen-size bed, spacious living room, well-equipped kitchen, and full bath. A second guest room with an antique sleigh bed across the hall from the suite is used only when needed by the same party. Beautiful, eclectic furnishings. Individual heating, air conditioning, TV, and telephone. Host sets in provisions for self-catered breakfast. $80-160.

O3. Large, quiet apartment near Perimeter Center offers a private entrance with off-street parking and a patio overlooking wooded area. This is a luxury, contemporary one-bedroom unit has 1,100-square feet. The bedroom has a queen-size bed and full bath. Spacious living and dining area has queen-size sleep sofa, love seat, and table and chairs. Kitchen is totally equipped. Cable TV, washer/dryer, and telephone are available. Ample provisions for self-catered

breakfast and wonderful guidance for local attractions provided. $80-100.

V1. Private garden cottage behind large home is in Virginia-Highland. This neighborhood allows walks to unique shops, diverse entertainment, and wonderful restaurants. Bed and breakfast offers a living room with sofa, TV, table and chairs, bedroom with double iron bed, bath, and well-equipped kitchen. Guests also enjoy small rear patio. Private telephone line and provisions for self-serve catered breakfast. No smoking. $68-76.

Beverly Hills Inn

Beverly Hills Inn

65 Sheridan Drive, 30305
(404) 233-8520

A charming city retreat one-half block from public transportation, one and one-half miles from Lenox Square, and five minutes from the Atlanta Historical Society. Full kitchens, library, free parking, color TV, and Continental breakfast.

Host: Mit Amin
Rooms: 18 (PB) $74-160
Continental Breakfast
Credit Cards: A, B, C, E
Notes: 2, 5, 7, 8, 9, 10, 11, 12, 14

Enchanted Forest Bed and Breakfast

955 Canter Road Northeast, 30324
(404) 262-9753

6 Pets welcome; 7 Smoking allowed; 8 Children welcome; 9 Social drinking allowed; 10 Tennis available; 11 Swimming available; 12 Golf available; 13 Skiing available; 14 May be booked through travel agents.

Just steps from shopping, restaurants and rail transportation. Nestled deep within two wooded acres. Rooms are spacious and comfortable. Glass enclosed living and dining rooms bring nature indoors. Get cozy by the fireplace, breakfast outdoors under the forest canopy, or watch wildlife from the bridge overlooking the stream. Deluxe breakfast including delicious homemade banana bread and gourmet coffees. If not for the ultra-convenient city locale, guests would think they were in the country. Children welcome. No smoking.

Host: Linda A. Verrill
Rooms: 4 (SB) $50-80
Continental Breakfast
Credit Cards: A,B
Notes: 2, 3, 4, 5, 8, 9, 10, 11, 12, 14

Inman Park
Bed and Breakfast

100 Waverly Way NE, 30307
(404) 688-9498

The honeymoon cottage of Robert Woodruff, Atlanta's famous anonymous donor and soft-drink magnate. Totally restored Victorian in historic Inman Park. One block from the subway station, close to dining. Its 12-foot ceilings, heart-pine woodwork, fireplaces, antiques, screened porch, and private garden are to enjoy.

Host: Eleanor Matthews
Rooms: 3 (PB) $65-85
Continental Breakfast
Credit Cards: A, B, C
Notes: 2 (deposit), 5, 8, 9, 10, 11, 12, 14

King-Keith House

889 Edgewood Avenue Northeast, 30307
(404) 688-7330

This 1890 Queen Anne Victorian home is in a National Register of Historic Places neighborhood. Ideal for walking and jogging, this home is close to Atlanta's most popular in-town shopping, restaurant, and theater districts. Two miles to downtown Atlanta. Two-and-a-half blocks to MARTA

(subway) with direct connections to the airport as well as all sporting and cultural events. Unusually spacious guest rooms, with high ceilings, filled with antiques. Private upstairs balcony. One of Atlanta's most photographed historical homes.

Hosts: Jan and Windell Keith
Rooms: 3 (2 PB; 1 SB) $75-95
Continental Breakfast
Credit Cards: A, B, C
Notes: 2, 5, 8, 9, 14

Little Five Points
Bed and Breakfast

466 Seminole Avenue, 30307

The Little Five Points Bed and Breakfast is a 1905 Craftsman cottage with 12-foot ceilings, pool, Jacuzzi, and a beautiful large guest room with adjoining private bath. Guests can also enjoy a private media room with movie library. In the famous Little Five Points shopping district. Fifteen restaurants are within 300 yards of this renovated classic. Walk to MARTA. Georgia Dome, Omni, Fulton County Stadium, World Congress Center, and Inforum are within three miles.

Hosts: Andy and Jane Fillo
Room: 1 (PB) $65-85
Continental Breakfast
Credit Cards: A, B, C
Notes: 2, 5, 9, 14

Oakwood House
Bed and Breakfast

951 Edgewood Avenue Northeast, 30307
(404) 521-9320

Oakwood House is a classic 1911 home in historic Inman Park just outside downtown Atlanta. Guests will find original woodwork, stained glass, front porch swing, and hundreds of books. The hosts live next door, offering traditional hospitality and privacy. Whirlpool and family suites. A short walk to Little Five Points for ethnic dining, theater, and shopping. The Carter Presidential Library and Martin Luther

King Historic District are nearby. Walk to the subway for downtown's Underground, World Congress Center, and CNN. Continental-plus breakfast. Fresh baked muffins and a bottomless cookie jar. All the comforts of a home—only better. No smoking indoors.

Hosts: Robert and Judy Hotchkiss
Rooms: 5 (PB) $65-175
Continental Breakfast
Credit Cards: A, B, C
Notes: 2, 5, 8, 9, 14

Shellmont Bed and Breakfast Lodge

821 Piedmont Avenue Northeast, 30308
(404) 872-9290

Impeccably restored 1891 mansion in midtown—Atlanta's theater, restaurant, and cultural district. Independently listed on the National Register of Historic Places and designated a City of Atlanta Landmark Building. A virtual treasure chest of stained, leaded, and beveled glass, intricately carved woodwork, hand-painted stenciling, and an authentic "Turkish Corner." Guest rooms are furnished with antiques, Oriental rugs, and period wall treatments. Wicker-laden verandas overlook manicured lawns and gardens, including a Victorian fish pond.

Hosts: Ed and Debbie McCord
Rooms: 5 (PB) $77-97
Continental Breakfast
Credit Cards: A, B, C, E
Notes: 2, 5, 8 (limited), 9, 14

AUGUSTA

Into the Woods Bed and Breakfast

176 Longhorn Road, Hephzibah, 30815
(706) 554-1400

This house was built in the late 1800s and completely restored and furnished with antiques of the period. Relax in the Victorian parlor, step out onto one of the porches, or pull up a rocker and have a cookie from the kitchen. All of the guest rooms have good firm beds. Guests can take a short drive to Augusta for for a lovely walk on the Riverwalk along the Savannah River, or visit the restaurants and shops. Guests will enjoy breakfast in the sunny dining room after a good night's rest.

Hosts: Mr. and Mrs. Robert L. Risser
Rooms: 4 (2 PB; 2 SB) $55-75
Full Breakfast
Credit Cards: A, B
Notes: 2, 5, 8, 12

Oglethorpe Inn

836 Greene Street, 30901
(706) 724-9774

Named after Augusta's founder, General James Oglethorpe, Oglethorpe Inn is Augusta's only historic bed and breakfast. Shaded by 100-year-old magnolias, it is in the very heart of the central business district. It is within walking distance of Augusta's new Riverwalk, the Civic Center, and other historic sites. All rooms have been carefully renovated to include all of the modern conveniences the lodging guest requires. Some with fireplaces and whirlpool tubs.

Host: Fran Upton
Rooms: 19 (PB) $85-125
Full Breakfast
Credit Cards: A, B, C, D, E
Notes: 5, 8, 9, 10, 11. 12, 14

Oglethorpe Inn

6 Pets welcome; 7 Smoking allowed; 8 Children welcome; 9 Social drinking allowed; 10 Tennis available; 11 Swimming available; 12 Golf available; 13 Skiing available; 14 May be booked through travel agents.

The Perrin Guest House Inn

208 LaFayette Drive, 30909
(706) 731-0920, FAX (706) 731-9009

The Perrin Place is an old cotton plantation home established in 1863. The plantation has long since become the Augusta National Home of the Masters, while the three acres of the homeplace remain a little spot of magnolia haven surrounded by shopping, golfing, and fine dining. The guest house has beautifully redecorated bedrooms that feature fireplaces, Jacuzzis, antiques, and comforters. Enjoy the private fireplaces in spacious accommodations; or share the pleasure of a front porch rock, the comfort of a cozy parlor, or the cool of a scuppernong arbor with other guests. Weddings, receptions, and other social functions become treasured events when held at the Perrin. Inn is available by reservation only.

Hosts: Ed and Audrey Peel
Rooms: 10 (PB) $70-120
Continental Breakfast
Credit Cards: A, B, C
Notes: 2, 5, 8, 9, 10, 11, 12, 14

BAINBRIDGE

Bed and Breakfast Scenic Florida

P.O. Box 3385
Tallahassee, FL 32315-3385
(940) 386-8196

FL41. Built in the mid-1800s, this Southern Colonial home was restored in the 1980s. Guests are only 45 minutes north of Tallahassee and have local access to Lake Seminole. Modern amenities include full baths, central heat and air conditioning, room telephones, and a pool and gazebo. The parlor and second-floor gallery and library serve as common room for guests. Three individually decorated guest rooms are available. Guests may choose queen-size four-poster bed with private shower and bath or twin beds and antique double bed that share a large bath with walk-in shower. Continental

breakfast with specialty breads is served in the large formal dining room or at poolside. No children and no smoking allowed. $40-45.

BLAIRSVILLE

Seven Creeks Housekeeping Cabins

5109 Horseshoe Cove Road, 30512
(706) 745-4753

One- to three-bedroom cabins surrounded by dogwoods and meadows in a 70-acre hideaway. Each with fireplace, fully equipped kitchen, private bath, telephone, TV, washer/dryer and grill. Swim or fish in the stocked, spring-fed lake or nearby trout streams. Hike the Appalachian Trail, explore Vogel State Park and Brasstown Bald, Georgia's tallest peak. Two hours from Atlanta, Chattanooga, Asheville or Greenville.

Hosts: Marvin and Bobbie Hernden
Cabins: 6 (PB) $45-55
No Breakfast
Credit Cards: A, B, C, D
Notes: 2, 5, 6, 7, 8, 9, 10, 11, 12, 13

CHICKAMAUGA

Gordon-Lee Mansion Bed and Breakfast Inn

217 Cove Road, 30707
(706) 375-4728; (800) 487-4728

Circa 1847. Step back in time and enjoy this beautifully restored antebellum plantation house, set on seven acres with formal gardens and furnished with museum-quality period antiques in the atmosphere of early southern aristocracy. Used as a Union headquarters and hospital. Near the Chickamauga Battlefield and 15 miles from Chattanooga, Tennessee. Continental-plus breakfast served in the elegant dining room.

NOTES: Credit cards accepted: A MasterCard; B Visa; C American Express; D Discover Card; E Diner's Club; F Other; 2 Personal checks accepted; 3 Lunch available; 4 Dinner available; 5 Open all year;

Civil War artifacts museum. Private baths. National Register of Historic Places.

Host: Richard Barclift
Rooms: 5 (PB) $70-100
Continental Breakfast
Credit Cards: A, B
Notes: 2, 5, 9, 10, 12, 14

CLARKESVILLE

The Charm House Inn

108 North Washington Street, 30523
(706) 754-9347

This beautiful Southern mansion, circa 1907, is listed in the National Register of Historic Places. Large, cheerfully decorated rooms. Air conditioning and private baths. Elegant dining for guests by reservation 6:00-10:00 P.M. Thursday through Sunday. Enjoy golf, horseback riding, antiquing, sightseeing, or just pass the time visiting with other guests on the veranda. Two-night minimum stay is required for holidays.

Hosts: Mary and Fred Newman
Rooms: 5 (PB)
Full Breakfast
Credit Cards: A, B, C
Notes: 2, 4, 5, 7, 9, 10, 11, 12, 13, 14

COMMERCE

The Pittman House

81 Homer Road, 30529
(706) 335-3823

This house is a grand 1890 Colonial completely furnished with period antiques. Wraparound porch just waiting to be rocked on. In the northeastern Georgia foothills near many interesting places. One hour northeast of Atlanta just off I-85. Tennis, golf, discount shopping mall, fishing, antiquing, and watersports all nearby.

Hosts: Tom and Dot Tomberlin
Rooms: 4 (2 PB; 2 SB) $50-65
Full Breakfast
Credit Cards: A, B
Notes: 2, 5, 8, 10, 11, 12, 14

DAHLONEGA

Mountain Top Lodge at Dahlonega

Route 7, Box 150, 30533
(706) 864-5257

Share the magic of a secluded bed and breakfast inn surrounded by towering trees and spectacular views. Enjoy antique-filled rooms, cathedral ceiling, great room, spacious decks, and heated outdoor spa; some rooms with fireplaces, whirlpool tubs, and porches. Deluxe room accommodations also available. Generous country breakfast with homemade biscuits. Two-night minimum stay required for holidays.

Host: Karen Lewan
Rooms: 13 (PB) $60.50-137.50
Full Breakfast
Credit Cards: A, B, C
Notes: 2, 5, 8 (over 11), 9, 14

The Smith House

202 South Chestatee Street, 30533
(706) 864-3566

Experience country hospitality in an 1884 inn. Old-time charm combined with modern comforts. All rooms have cable TV, telephones, and private baths. Outdoor pool for hotel guests. Enjoy famous family-style meals, including three meats and eight to ten vegetables served daily. Visit the country store and browse the many unique collectibles. Special winter hours. Closed Christmas Day and on Mondays.

Hosts: Fred, Shirley, Chris, and Freida Welch
Rooms: 16 (PB) $45-80
Continental Breakfast
Credit Cards: A, B, C, D
Notes: 3, 4, 5, 7, 8, 10, 11

DARIEN

Open Gates Bed and Breakfast

Vernon Square National Historic District, 31305
(912) 437-6985

6 Pets welcome; 7 Smoking allowed; 8 Children welcome; 9 Social drinking allowed; 10 Tennis available; 11 Swimming available; 12 Golf available; 13 Skiing available; 14 May be booked through travel agents.

Explore untrammeled barrier islands and the Altamaha River Delta via a scenic byway one and one-half miles east of I-95. Open Gates was an 1876 timber baron's home; it has been featured on the cover of *Southern Homes*, in *Georgia Off the Beaten Path*, *Fodor's: Bed and Breakfasts*, and *Country Inns*. Family heirlooms, a superb library of coastal material, locally produced caviar, and hostess knowledgeable about Georgia's second oldest town and environment enhance guests' stay. Ecological and historical tours. Bicycles and canoeing. Sailing school nearby. Birding groups.

Host: Carolyn Hodges
Rooms: 4 (2 PB; 2 SB) $48-53
Full Breakfast
Credit Cards: None
Notes: 2, 5, 7 (limited), 9, 11, 14

The Crockett House

EATONTON

The Crockett House

671 Madison Road, 31024
(706) 485-2248

Nearly a century of good living has given the Crockett House a mellow ambience. A stately and gracious turn-of-the-century antebellum home on Georgia's historic Antebellum Trail offers a warm welcome and comfortable accommodations year-round. Just minutes from Lake Oconee, Georgia's second largest lake, and surrounded by Oconee National Forest. The large cozy bedrooms are thoughtfully decorated with heart-of-pine floors, 12-foot ceilings, fireplaces, and private baths. Rates include a full breakfast with lots of homemade goodies.

Hosts: Christa and Peter Crockett
Rooms: 6 (PB) $55-75
Full Breakfast
Credit Cards: A, B
Notes: 2, 5, 8 (over 10), 9, 10, 11, 12, 14

FLOWERY BRANCH

Whitworth Inn

6593 McEver Road, 30542
(404) 967-2386

Contemporary country inn on five wooded acres offers relaxing atmosphere, 11 uniquely decorated guest rooms, and two guest living rooms with TVs. Full country breakfast served in large sunlit dining room. Meeting and party space available. Thirty minutes northeast of Atlanta at Lake Lanier. Nearby attractions and activities include boating, golf, beaches, and water parks. Close to Road Atlanta and Chateau Elan Winery and Golf Course. Easily accessible from major interstates. Three-diamond AAA rating.

Hosts: Ken and Chris Jonick
Rooms: 8 (PB) $55-65
Full Breakfast
Credit Cards: A, B
Notes: 2, 5, 8, 10, 11, 12, 14

HAMILTON

Wedgwood Bed and Breakfast

P.O. Box 115, 31811
(706) 628-5659

Beautiful 1850 home decorated in Wedgwood blue with white stenciling, just five and one-half miles south of Callaway Gardens and 18 miles from Roosevelt's Little

White House. Enjoy the piano in the living room or a classic movie on the VCR in the den. Swing on the screened porch or doze in the hammock. Fine dining nearby.

Host: Janice Neuffer
Rooms: 3 (PB) $65-75
Full Breakfast
Credit Cards: None
Notes: 2, 5, 8, 9, 10, 11, 12, 14

HELEN

Chattahoochee Ridge Lodge and Cabins

P.O. Box 175, 30545
(706) 878-3144; (800) 476-8331

Perched on a wooded ridge a mile from Alpine Helen, each new unit has cable TV, air conditioning, refrigerator, coffee maker, free phone, and large Jacuzzi. Some have a full kitchen, extra bedroom, and fireplace. There is also a gas grill on the back deck. Hosts are "earth friendly" with double insulation and back-up solar heating. Everything guests need is furnished and on the premises, including hosts who can fill guests in on attractions. Chalets in the woods are also available, please inquire.

Hosts: Bob and Mary Switt
Rooms: 5 (PB) $45-70
Continental Breakfast
Credit Cards: A, B, C, D
Notes: 2, 5, 8, 9, 10, 11, 12

Habersham Hollow Bed and Breakfast and Cabins

Route 6, Box 6208, Clarkesville, 30523
(706) 754-5147

This elegant country home is nestled in the northeast Georgia mountains. Five minutes from Alpine Helen. Spacious rooms; a suite with a fireplace, sitting room, and its own covered porch. King-size beds, terry robes, and TV are all included. Relaxed, casual, and friendly atmosphere. Cozy cabins with

fireplaces on the grounds where well-behaved children and pets are welcome.

Hosts: C. J. and Maryann Gibbons
Rooms: 4 (PB) $85
Full Breakfast
Credit Cards: A, B
Notes: 2, 5, 6, 8, 9, 10, 11, 12, 13

JEKYLL ISLAND

The Jekyll Island Club Hotel

371 Riverview Drive, 31527
(912) 635-2600

The historic Jekyll Island Club Hotel, on a beautiful barrier island off Georgia's coast, offers full resort amenities including 63 holes of golf; miles of beach, bicycle and nature trails; water sports and tennis. Built in the late 1880s, this Victorian beauty has rooms and suites furnished with reproduction pieces of the era. Some have Jacuzzis, balconies, and river views.

Host: Kevin Runner
Rooms: 134 (PB) $90-130
No Breakfast
Credit Cards: None
Notes: 2, 3, 4, 5, 7, 8, 9, 10, 11, 12, 14

LAKEMONT

Lake Rabun Hotel

Lake Rabun Road, P.O. Box 10, 30552-0010
(404) 782-4946

An original mountain inn built in 1922. A Rabun County landmark. Antique mountain furnishings, rustic, charming; huge fieldstone fireplace in downstairs great room. Has 15 rooms, shared baths. Honeymoon Room with fireplace upstairs. Third-generation guests now visit.

Hosts: Rosa and Bill Pettys
Rooms: 16 (2 PB; 13 SB) $60-70
Continental Breakfast
Credit Cards: A, B, D
Notes: 2, 3, 8, 9, 10, 11, 12, 13, 14

6 Pets welcome; 7 Smoking allowed; 8 Children welcome; 9 Social drinking allowed; 10 Tennis available; 11 Swimming available; 12 Golf available; 13 Skiing available; 14 May be booked through travel agents.

MACON

1842 Inn

353 College, 31201
(912) 741-1842; (800) 336-1842 (reservations)

Four Diamond Award winner for seven consecutive years. Elegant antebellum Greek Revival Tara in heart of beautiful historic district. In-room complimentary breakfast, evening hors d'oeuvres and light piano music, plus concierge turndown service. Restaurant and museum houses within walking distance. Exit 52 I-75 five blocks.

Hosts: Phillip Jenkins and Richard Meils
Rooms: 21 (PB) $95-125
Continental Breakfast
Credit Cards: A, B, C
Notes: 2, 5, 7, 9, 10, 11, 12, 14

MADISON

The Brady Inn

250 North Second Street, 30650
(706) 342-4400

Two Victorian cottages linked together by an extended porch filled with rockers welcome guests to this bed and breakfast. All rooms have private baths, heart-pine floors, and antiques. Come enjoy Southern hospitality and see "the town Sherman refused to burn."

Hosts: C.G. and L.J. Rasch
Rooms: 6 (PB) $50-70
Full Breakfast
Credit Cards: A, B
Notes: 2, 3, 4, 5, 6, 7, 8, 9, 10, 11, 12

Burnett Place

317 Old Post Road, 30650
(706) 342-4034

Burnett Place, circa 1830, is a Federal-style house typical of the Piedmont region of Georgia. It is conveniently in the historic district of Madison, one hour east of Atlanta. Within easy walking distance of shops and restaurants, museums and gal-leries, the Madison-Morgan Cultural Center, and Heritage Hall. The house and guest rooms harmoniously blend nineteenth century ambience with twentieth century comforts.

Hosts: Leonard and Ruth Wallace
Rooms: 3 (PB) $75
Full Breakfast
Credit Cards: A, B
Notes: 2, 5, 6, 7, 8, 9, 10, 11, 14

MARIETTA

Bed and Breakfast Atlanta

1801 Piedmont Avenue NE, Suite 208, 30324
(404) 875-0525

O4. This French Regency-style Victorian house in Marietta, circa 1872, was saved from demolition in 1990 and restored by the current owners. There are front and rear porches where breakfast is served when the weather permits, as well as a downstairs sitting room. Gourmet breakfast is served in the dining room, with careful attention given to low-fat ingredients and special dietary needs. Four guest rooms are available, one with king-size bed and three with queen-size beds, all with private baths. $76-120.

MOUNTAIN CITY

The York House

P.O. Box 126, 30562
(800) 231-YORK

A lovely 1896 bed and breakfast inn with a country flair and listed on the National Register of Historic Places. It is nestled among the beautiful north Georgia mountains and is close to recreational activities. Completely renovated, the 13 guest rooms are decorated with period antiques and offer private baths and cable TV. Guests begin their day with a full Continental breakfast served in their rooms on a silver tray. Between Clayton and Dillard one-quarter mile off Highway 441 on the York House Road.

Owners: Joe and Angela Smith
Hosts: Phyllis and Jimmy Smith
Rooms: 13 (PB) $64-79
Continental Breakfast
Credit Cards: A, B, C, D
Notes: 2, 5, 7 (limited), 8, 9, 10, 11, 12, 13, 14

PERRY

Swift Street Inn

1204 Swift Street, 31069
(912) 988-4477

Step back 137 years to a time of Southern charm, romance, and luxury. A gourmet breakfast, deluxe service, and spacious guest rooms, each with its own unique character and all filled with antiques, await. Come experience the elegance and warm feeling of a small inn in a growing Southern town. The hosts take pride in making guests' stay restful, pleasant, and memorable.

Hosts: Dennis and Carolyn Lovejoy
Rooms: 4 (PB) $65-85
Full Breakfast
Credit Cards: A, B, C
Notes: 2, 5, 6, 12, 14

Goodbread House

ST. MARYS

Goodbread House

209 Osborne Street, 31558
(912) 882-7490

The Goodbread House is a carefully restored Victorian home. The high ceilings, fireplaces, wide pine floors, and original wood trim add to its ambience. Each antique-filled bedroom has its own fireplace and private bath, as well as ceiling fans and air conditioning. The ferry to Cumberland Island National Seashore is only a block away. Restaurants within walking distance.

Hosts: Betty and George Krauss
Rooms: 4 (PB) $50-60
Full Breakfast
Credit Cards: F
Notes: 2, 5, 9, 12, 14

Historic Spencer House Inn

Osborne at Bryant Street, 31558
(912) 882-1872

A charming Victorian inn in the heart of St. Marys historic district, and only one block from the Cumberland Island ferry, features 14 rooms filled with antiques and beautiful reproductions. Enjoy the three verandas overlooking the quiet streets of this historic village. The Spencer House Inn is within short driving distance to Georgia's Golden Isles, Okefenokee Swamp, Amelia Island, and Jacksonville, Florida. St. Marys is in the coastal corner of Georgia, and is the gateway to beautiful Cumberland Island.

Hosts: Dale and Donna Potruski
Rooms: 14 (PB) $55-100
Continental Breakfast
Credit Cards: A, B, D
Notes: 2, 5, 8, 9, 10, 11, 12, 14

ST. SIMONS

Little St. Simons Island

P.O. Box 1078, 31522
(912) 638-7472

6 Pets welcome; 7 Smoking allowed; 8 Children welcome; 9 Social drinking allowed; 10 Tennis available; 11 Swimming available; 12 Golf available; 13 Skiing available; 14 May be booked through travel agents.

Privately owned, 10,000-acre barrier island retreat with six miles of pristine beaches. Comfortable accommodations, bountiful regional meals with hors d'oeuvres and wine, horseback riding, fishing, boating, canoeing, bird watching, and naturalist expeditions. A unique experience in an unspoiled, natural environment. Day trips and full island rentals available. Open for individuals February through November.

Host: Debbie McIntyre
Rooms: 12 (10 PB; 2 SB) $300-400 FAP
Full Breakfast
Credit Cards: A, B
Notes: 2, 3, 4, 7, 8, 9, 11, 14

SAUTEE

The Stovall House

1526 Hwy 255 North, 30571
(706) 878-3355

This 1837 farmhouse beckons to guests for a country experience in the historic Sautee Valley near Helen. The award-winning restoration and personal touches here will make one feel at home. Enjoy mountain views in all directions. The restaurant, recognized as one of the top 50 in Georgia, specializes in regional cuisine with a fresh difference.

Host: Ham Schwartz
Rooms: 5 (PB) $75
Continental Breakfast
Credit Cards: A, B
Notes: 2, 4, 5, 7 (limited), 8, 9, 10, 11, 12

SAVANNAH

Ballastone Inn and Townhouse

14 East Oglethorpe Avenue, 31401
(912) 236-1484; (800) 822-4553
FAX (912) 236-4626

A beautifully restored Victorian mansion dating from 1838 in the heart of the city's historic district, the Ballastone Inn is the epitome of gracious Southern hospitality. The guest rooms reflect a distinct Victorian flavor. Added touches include flowers and fresh fruit, terry-cloth robes, fireplace, TV with VCR, and some Jacuzzis. There is a beautifully landscaped courtyard and a full-service bar. In the mornings, a Continental breakfast is served in guests' room, the parlor, or the courtyard. Sherry, coffee or tea, fruit, and pastries are available in the front parlor. Nightly turndown service includes robes, chocolates, and brandy. The inn is recommended by the *New York Times*, *Brides*, *Glamour*, *Atlantic*, and *Gourmet* magazines.

Hosts: Richard Carlson and Tim Hargus
Rooms: 22 (PB) $95-200
Continental Breakfast
Credit Cards: A, B, C
Notes: 2, 5, 6, 7, 9, 10, 11, 12, 13, 14

The Forsyth Park Inn

The Forsyth Park Inn

102 West Hall Street, 31401
(912) 233-6800

Circa 1893 Queen Anne Victorian mansion with 16-foot ceilings and 14-foot doors. Ornate woodwork, floors, stairways, fireplaces, antiques, whirlpool baths, and courtyard cottage. Faces a 25-acre park in large historic district. Complimentary wine, social hour;

NOTES: Credit cards accepted: A MasterCard; B Visa; C American Express; D Discover Card; E Diner's Club; F Other; 2 Personal checks accepted; 3 Lunch available; 4 Dinner available; 5 Open all year;

fine dining, tours, museum homes, river cruises, and beaches all nearby.

Hosts: Virginia and Hal Sullivan
Rooms: 10 (PB) $89-175
Continental Breakfast
Credit Cards: A, B, C, D
Notes: 2 (in advance), 5, 7, 8, 9, 10, 11, 12, 14

Habersham at York Inn

130 Habersham Street, 31401
(912) 234-2499

Here, gentle manners still prevail. Habersham at York Inn is on the garden floor of a handsomely restored Italianate residence constructed in 1884 on the northeast corner of Columbia Square. Features a bubbling fountain, fragrant gardens, and a private entrance to bed and breakfast. Fresh flowers, turndown service, and surprise snack. Convenient walk to excellent restaurants. Complimentary wine/champagne for special occasions. Intimate setting, a great place for anniversaries and honeymoons. Continental-plus breakfast, served in room, lounge, or garden, includes freshly squeezed orange juice and fresh breads.

Host: M. B. Rossini
Rooms: 2 (PB) $135
Continental Breakfast
Credit Cards: None
Notes: 2, 5, 8, 9, 10, 11, 12, 14

The Jesse Mount House

209 West Jones Street, 31401
(912) 236-1774

An 1854 Greek Revival townhouse with four luxurious suites. All have gas-log fireplaces, canopied beds, and private baths, some with whirlpools. The house is furnished with many rare antiques and an eclectic art collection. Access to a private courtyard with fountains. Garden suite features a full kitchen. Complimentary turndown service, wine and sweets. Bicycles available.

Host: Sue Dron
Suites: 4 (PB) $125-155
Continental Breakfast
Credit Cards: A, B, D
Notes: 5, 7, 8, 9

Joan's on Jones Bed and Breakfast

17 West Jones Street, 31401
(912) 234-3863

In the heart of the Historic District, two charming bed and breakfast suites distinguish the garden level of this three-story Victorian private home. Each suite has private entry, off-street parking, bedroom, sitting room, kitchen, bath, private telephone, and cable TV. Note the original heart-pine floors, period furnishings, and Savannah grey brick walls. Innkeepers Joan and Gary Levy, former restaurateurs, live upstairs and invite guests on a tour of their home if they are staying two nights or more.

Host: Joan Levy
Suites: 2 (PB) $95-110
Continental Breakfast
Credit Cards: None
Notes: 2, 5, 6 (by arrangement), 8, 9, 10, 11, 12

Lion's Head Inn

120 East Gaston Street, 31401
(912) 232-4580; (800) 355-LION

A stately 19th-century home in a quiet neighborhood just north of picturesque Forsyth Park. This lovely 9,200-square-foot mansion is filled with fine Empire antiques. Each guest room is exquisitely appointed with four-poster beds, private baths, period furnishings, fireplaces, TVs, and telephones. Each morning enjoy a deluxe Continental breakfast, and in the evening enjoy wine and cheese on the sweeping veranda overlooking the marbled courtyard.

Host: Christy Dell'Orco
Rooms: 6 (PB) $75-125
Continental Breakfast
Credit Cards: A, B, C
Notes: 2, 5, 8, 9, 10, 11, 12, 14

Presidents' Quarters
(A Premier Historic Inn)

225 East President Street, 31401
(912) 233-1600; (800) 233-1776
FAX (912) 238-0849

Four-diamond award-winning inn in the heart of historic district offers suites with TVs and VCRs, Jacuzzis, fireplaces, balconies overlooking secluded courtyard. Private parking. Physically challenged facilities available. Daily amenities include full afternoon tea and nightly turndown with cordial; fruit and wine in suite upon arrival. Continental-plus breakfast. An inn fit for a president.

General Manager/Innkeeper: Muril Broy
Rooms: 16 (PB) $97-157
Continental Breakfast
Credit Cards: A, B, C, D, E
Notes: 2, 5, 7, 8, 9, 10, 11, 12, 14

Pulaski Square Inn

203 West Charlton Street, 31401
(800) 227-0650

This elegant home, built in 1853, is in Savannah's historic district, only a 15-minute walk from the Savannah River. It is completely restored with original wide-pine floors, chandeliers, and marble mantles. It is furnished with antiques and traditional furniture throughout. Modern luxury baths with gold-plated fixtures.

Hosts: Hilda and J. B. Smith
Rooms: 10 (8 PB; 2 SB) $48 plus
Continental Breakfast
Credit Cards: A, B, C
Notes: 2, 5, 7, 8, 9, 10, 11, 12, 14

Remshart-Brooks House

106 West Jones Street, 31401
(912) 234-6928

Enjoy casual Southern hospitality at this historic Savannah home built in 1853. The guest accommodations are furnished with comfortable country antiques. Share the garden for a Continental breakfast. Private off-street covered parking is free.

Host: Anne E. Barnett
Suite: 1 (PB) $65
Continental Breakfast
Credit Cards: None
Notes: 2, 5, 9, 10, 11, 12

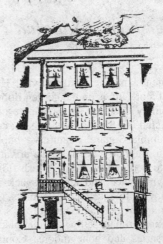

Remshart-Brooks House

RSVP Savannah B&B

9489 Whitfield Avenue, Box 49, 31406
(800) 729-7787 (Mon.-Fri. 9:30 A.M.-5:30 P.M.)

The Carlton House. An 1853 Victorian home. One private bedroom with queen-size bed is available. Continental breakfast is included. No smoking. $75.

The Haslam-Fort House. Savannah's earliest bed and breakfast since 1979. This is an 1872 brick Victorian townhouse offering guests one entire suite of rooms consisting of a living room with fireplace, a king- and queen-size bedroom, private bath, and fully stocked country kitchen for self-serve breakfast. TV, VCR, and telephone. Guests have private entrances, off-street parking, garden patio, and terraces. Handicapped accessible. Children welcome. From $100.

NOTES: Credit cards accepted: A MasterCard; B Visa; C American Express; D Discover Card; E Diner's Club; F Other; 2 Personal checks accepted; 3 Lunch available; 4 Dinner available; 5 Open all year;

Stoddard House. In Savannah's historic district, guest accommodations include a second-floor queen-size bedroom with full private bath. No smoking. $125.

Sullivan House. In a historic Savannah district, this garden-level suite includes a living room, fireplace, sofa bed, kitchen, bedroom, full bath, and sunroom. Enclosed garden and parking. No smoking. $88.

02. An 1890s townhouse offers a second-floor bedroom with twin beds and full private bath. Guests share the house with the host. Private parking. $60.

05. This is an 1853 inn with 22 rooms, each with either king- or queen-size four-poster beds. Guests can enjoy the beautiful courtyard and fountain in this historic district. $88-108.

07. This charming inn is in an 1845 restored warehouse. Twenty-eight rooms are available, with either single or queen-size beds. Evening refreshment and private parking. $98.

08. A circa 1854 warehouse for tobacco, rice, or cotton has been converted into a spectacular 44-room inn. Rooms face the Savannah riverfront or park. Some rooms have balconies. $109.

10. This riverfront warehouse has been converted to full efficiency suites with kitchens, living rooms, and bedrooms. Ideal for families or two couples traveling together. Lovely river views. Ice cream and snacks served at bedtime. $95.

11. This 1883 Empire Victorian home has six rooms available for guests. Continental breakfast served. No smoking. From $100.

12. Guests may choose from two suites in this Victorian townhouse. Continental breakfast is served. Smoking permitted on patio. From $95.

13. Antiques and huge rooms make this Queen Anne Victorian mansion attractive. Nine rooms and whirlpool baths are available. From $95.

14. This 1863 Regency Italiante home has 13 rooms. Whirlpool and hot tub are available. Full breakfast included. No smoking. From $125.

15. Southern charm and antiques highlight this 20-room Regency mansion circa 1852. Whirlpool baths are available. Continental breakfast included. No smoking. From $95.

17 Hundred 90 Inn and Restaurant

307 East President Street, 31401
(912) 236-7122; (800) 487-1790
FAX (912) 236-7123

Enjoy exquisite luxury and Old South charm here where the hosts offer 14 splendidly appointed guest rooms. The furnishings in every room will please the history buff and delight the antique lover. Fireplaces provide that extra charm that couples love. Above all else, gracious service distinguishes the inn. Guests enjoy a complimentary bottle of wine and Continental breakfast. Later in the day, the restaurant and lounge at the inn will add an exciting dimension to the stay. Lunch is available Monday through Friday.

Host: Darline Lehmkohl
Rooms: 14 (PB) $89-129
Continental Breakfast
Credit Cards: A, B, C
Notes: 2, 3, 4, 5, 6 (small), 8, 9, 10, 12, 14

6 Pets welcome; 7 Smoking allowed; 8 Children welcome; 9 Social drinking allowed; 10 Tennis available; 11 Swimming available; 12 Golf available; 13 Skiing available; 14 May be booked through travel agents.

SENOIA

Culpepper House

35 Broad Street, 30276
(404) 599-8182

Step back 120 years to casual Victorian elegance at the Culpepper House. Share a special evening in a four-poster canopied bed next to a fireplace, with sounds of the night coming through the window. Wake to a gourmet breakfast then take a tandem bike ride through the historic town, visit area shops and picturesque countryside, or just sit on the porch and rock. Only 30 minutes from Atlanta.

Hosts: Maggie Armstrong and Barb Storm
Rooms: 3 (1 PB; 2 SB) $75
Full Breakfast
Credit Cards: A, B
Notes: 2, 5, 7, 9, 10, 11, 12, 13

The Veranda

252 Seavy Street, P.O. Box 177, 30276-0177
(404) 599-3905; FAX (404) 599-0806

Beautifully restored spacious Victorian rooms in a 1907 hotel on the National Register of Historic Places. Just 30 miles south of Atlanta airport. Freshly prepared Southern gourmet meals by reservation. Unusual gift shop featuring kaleidoscopes. Memorabilia and 1930 Wurlitzer player piano pipe organ. One room has a whirlpool bath; all have private baths and air conditioning.

Hosts: Jan and Bobby Boal
Rooms: 9 (PB) $90-110
Full Breakfast
Credit Cards: A, B, C
Notes: 2, 3, 4, 5, 8, 10, 12 (all by arrangement), 14

STONE MOUNTAIN

Bed and Breakfast Atlanta

1801 Piedmont Avenue NE, Suite 208, 30324
(404) 875-0525

O2. This authentic 1830s white two-story farmhouse in Stone Mountain was moved and carefully reassembled on this site in 1984. The house has porches on all sides. In the main house there is a terrace room with a private entry, king-size poster bed, antique furniture, a fireplace, and a large full bath. The carriage house has a suite with a large living room, dining room with a wet bar, undercounter refrigerator, and microwave, and a large screen TV. The bedroom features a king-size canopied bed and more interesting antiques. The private bath has a shower only. There is a queen-size sleep sofa in the living room, and a Porta-Crib is available. $72-92.

THOMASTON

Woodall House

324 West Main Street, 30286
(706) 647-7044

The interior "gingerbread" is original in this restored Victorian home built by the county physician at the turn of the century. Private baths with individual air conditioning and cable TV. One-half block from beautiful old courthouse square, ten miles from Flint River, 40 miles from Roosevelt's Little White House and Andersonville Confederate Cemetery, and 60 miles from Plains, Georgia, home of former President Jimmy Carter. Only 50 miles from Atlanta, Columbus, and Macon. "Home away from home" is the management philosophy.

Hosts: Bill and Charlene Woodall
Rooms: 3 (PB) $46
Full Breakfast
Credit Cards: None
Notes: 2, 5, 8, 9, 10, 11, 12

THOMASVILLE

Deer Creek

1304 Old Monticello Road, 31792
(912) 226-7294

In historic town on two scenic acres with wall-to-wall windows to view woods. Guests can enjoy the fireplace, piano, cable TV, full breakfast, and large private bath.

NOTES: Credit cards accepted: A MasterCard; B Visa; C American Express; D Discover Card; E Diner's Club; F Other; 2 Personal checks accepted; 3 Lunch available; 4 Dinner available; 5 Open all year;

Decorator decor with fine antiques and rare items. The 30-foot treetop deck and terrace are private to guests. Exclusive single-party booking. Extra charge for children. Two-night minimum on travel agent bookings.

Hosts: Gladys and Bill Muggridge
Rooms: 2 (1 PB) $65-75
Full Breakfast
Credit Cards: None
Notes: 2, 5, 8, 9, 10, 12, 14

Evans House
Bed and Breakfast

725 South Hansell Street, 31792
(912) 226-1343; (800) 344-4717
FAX (912) 226-0653

In the Parkfront Historical District, this restored Victorian home is directly across from the 27-acre Paradise Park near fine downtown antique shops and dining. Featuring four guest rooms with private baths. Full breakfast served in the country kitchen. Bikes and many other amenities.

Hosts: Lee and John Puskar
Rooms: 4 (PB) $65-115
Full Breakfast
Credit Cards: None
Notes: 2, 5, 8, 9, 12, 14

Quail Country
Bed and Breakfast, Ltd.

1104 Old Monticello Road, 31792
(912) 226-7218; (912) 226-6882

1. This quaint Williamsburg-style guest house is next to the pool. Twin beds, private bath, dressing room, and full kitchen. The eighteenth-century garden overlooks other dependencies. Children welcome. $50.

2. Surrounded by natural woodland of oaks and pines, this charming country French Provincial house is near shopping center and restaurants. Excellent area for walking and bird watching. $40.

3. In a lovely residential area, this second-story garage apartment overlooks a beautiful swimming pool. Two bedrooms, bath, equipped kitchen, and living area. Crib available. The owner is an antique car enthusiast. $50.

4. Built in 1900 in pecan groves, this Neo-classical-style house features porches with large columns on three sides of the house. Each bedroom has its own bath and fireplace. The floors throughout the house are heart pine, and the rooms are furnished with antiques. $40.

5. Twenty-five-year-old bungalow in a lovely residential neighborhood has a bedroom with twin beds and private bath. $40.

THOMSON

Four Chimneys

2316 Wire Road Southeast, 30824
(706) 597-0220

Early 1800s plantation-plain-styled country house. Original hand-planed pine board floors, walls, and ceilings. Furnished with antiques and reproductions; all guest rooms have fireplaces and four-posters. Beautiful grounds with Colonial-style herb and flower garden. Equestrian events, golf, and antique shops are nearby. Easy access to I-20 and Augusta. Two miles to town and restaurants.

Hosts: Maggie and Ralph Zieger
Rooms: 4 (2 PB; 2 SB) $40-50
Continental Breakfast
Credit Cards: A, B
Notes: 2, 5, 7, 9, 10, 12

6 Pets welcome; 7 Smoking allowed; 8 Children welcome; 9 Social drinking allowed; 10 Tennis available; 11 Swimming available; 12 Golf available; 13 Skiing available; 14 May be booked through travel agents.

WARM SPRINGS

Hotel Warm Springs Bed and Breakfast

P.O. Box 351, 17 Broad Street, 31830
(706) 655 2114

Relive history and the Roosevelt era. Visit this 1907 hotel, restaurant, and gift shops. Authentically restored, beautifully decorated with Roosevelt furniture and family antiques. Featured are cable TV, the ultimate honeymoon suite with heart tub, and king-size bed, social hour, and individual heat and air conditioning. Nestled in quaint Warm Springs Village—a shopper's paradise. Home of FDR's Little White House, 14 miles from Callaway Gardens, and one hour south of Atlanta.

Hosts: Lee and Geraldine Thompson
Rooms: 11 (PB) $60-160
Suites: 3
Full Breakfast
Credit Cards: A, B, C, D
Notes: 2, 3, 4, 5, 7, 8, 9, 10, 11, 12, 13 (water), 14

NOTES: Credit cards accepted: A MasterCard; B Visa; C American Express; D Discover Card; E Diner's Club; F Other; 2 Personal checks accepted; 3 Lunch available; 4 Dinner available; 5 Open all year;

Hawaii

Adrienne's
Bed and Breakfast

85-4577 Mamalahoa Highway 8E, 96704
(808) 328-9726; (800) 328-9726
FAX (808) 328-9787

This custom cedar home has an unobstructed view of the ocean from the hot tub
on the lanai where a continental breakfast is
served. All rooms king- or queen-size beds
with private baths, entrances, TV, VCR
(over 1,000 movies), and refrigerator.
Marie, the host, shares information on
restaurants, snorkel and swimming places,
and hiking trails. Flashlights, ice chests,
boogie boards, and snorkel gear are avail
able. On-premises swimming on the lanai.
Near beaches and Place of Refuge.

Host: Marie Miller
Rooms: 4 (PB) $50-80
Continental Breakfast
Credit Cards: None
Notes: 2, 4, 5, 7, 8, 9, 10, 11, 12, 13, 14

Bed and Breakfast Hawaii

P.O. Box 449, Kapaa, 96746
(808) 822-7771; (800) 733-1632

H53. Host offers getaway for those travelers looking to get away where the order of
the day is tranquility. A Hawaiian-style residence on an acre of botanical gardens with
an unbelievably panoramic view of more
than 40 miles of coastline, including
Kealakekuna Bay and the Captain Cook
Monument. Two miles below is the famous
bay with world-class snorkeling, scuba diving, kayak rentals and more. Part of the res-

idence, but with complete privacy and separate entrances, are two one-bedroom apartments. The upper apartment has a large
bedroom with two double beds, full tile
bath, living room-kitchen combination, and
outside dining lanai overlooking the view.
Kitchen includes a full refrigerator, range,
oven, microwave, and sink. Also included
is a color TV, VCR, and telephone. The
lower apartment has all of the above with a
smaller bedroom with one queen-size bed.
The lower apartment has a small refrigerator. Amenities include a large deep-water
swimming pool with waterfall spilling
down into a smaller pool, a large heated
spa, sundeck, and shower room. A lily
pond, picnic area, film and book library,
and unsurpassed quiet and seclusion complete the picture. Three night minimum. No
smoking. $65-90.

Bed and Breakfast Hawaii

P.O. Box 449, Kapaa, 96746
(808) 822-7771; (800) 733-1632

H63. This host home is at 1500 feet alti-
tude, three miles from Hawi on a gentle
slope of the Kohala Mountains. The view is
unobstructed to the ocean and across
Alenuihaha channel to the Haleakala peak
on Maui. The location is secluded and about
1/2 mile from the highway; thus it is very
quiet and relaxing. The bed and breakfast
unit has private access, living room area,
fully equipped kitchenette, and bedroom
with queen-size bed and private bath. Two
night minimum. $65.

6 Pets welcome; 7 Smoking allowed; 8 Children welcome; 9 Social drinking allowed; 10 Tennis available; 11
Swimming available; 12 Golf available; 13 Skiing available; 14 May be booked through travel agents.

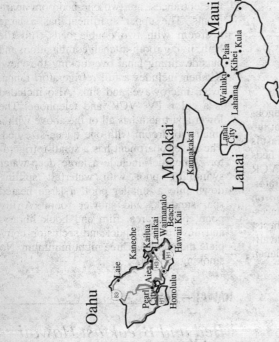

HAWAII—HILO

Affordable Paradise Bed and Breakfast Reservations

226 Pouli Road, 96734
(808) 261-1693; (800) 925-9065
FAX (808) 261-7315

Heuhilo. This home is on Hilo Bay directly overlooking the water. It is about five minutes from downtown Hilo. The hostess enjoys gardening and has a large, green, grassy garden where guests can sit outside and relax. Host has two bedrooms in her home. Both rooms share a bath between the two. Host serves a rich breakfast. Many of the guests discuss the abundant breakfast menu. $45.

Keg. This home is uphill from Hilo town. It is about a five minute drive to downtown Hilo. Host has two rooms available. One room has a twin bed. The other has a king-size bed. The rooms share a bath between them and share a common sitting room. There is a small refrigerator and coffeemaker available for guests. Home has a nice view of Hilo and Hilo Bay. $50-60.

Bed and Breakfast Hawaii

P.O. Box 449, Kapaa, 96746
(808) 822-7771; (800) 733-1632
FAX (808) 822-2723

H1. A large Hawaiian-style house about two miles north of Hilo overlooking Hilo Bay, this home has a yard so private that if guests decide to take a swim in the pool, only the birds will know. There are two bedrooms available to guests, each with a pair of twin beds, one which converts to a king-size bed, if desired. The yard is beautifully landscaped around the pool and a lovely mile walk past the surfing beach meanders through a tropical forest. $55.

H2. Hale Paliku, which means "house against the cliff," is the name of this home originally built in the 1930s. Three blocks from downtown Hilo. Guests share the TV, tape deck, microwave, and refrigerator. Two rooms with shared bath are available, one with ocean view and private balcony. Each room has down pillows, comforters, shuttered windows, and a table for two. Hosts live downstairs. $55-65.

H3. Relax on a grand scale in this large, modern, Hawaiian-style home surrounded by nearly four acres of parklike setting on an oceanfront bluff. With a spectacular view of Wailea Bay, this is the perfect spot for a peaceful haven. A tennis court and a municipal beach park are within walking distance, and the world-famous Akaka Falls is a short drive away. A spacious one-bedroom apartment includes bedroom, private bath, fully equipped kitchenette, and living room with cable TV, radio, piano, and day beds. Children over eight welcome. $75.

H3A. A charming little beachfront cottage surrounded by swaying coconut palms awaits guests. There is a nice beach and boat launch for guests to explore in a quiet, private setting. Guests can enjoy sitting out on the big lanai with ocean view or sitting on the rocks dangling their toes in the water while watching fishermen and sailboats. Two guest rooms with private bath. Resident dog. Two-night minimum stay. $75.

H5. This beautiful Hilo home has been renovated to provide guests with a wonderful bed and breakfast experience similar to the traditional inns of the world. Your hosts offer three exceptional rooms for guests along with common area for lounging, breakfast served each day in dining area, library, and lanai with superb coastal viewing. Two of the bedrooms offer views of the ocean and town of Hilo and one bedroom

NOTES: Credit cards accepted: A MasterCard; B Visa; C American Express; D Discover Card; E Diner's Club; F Other; 2 Personal checks accepted; 3 Lunch available; 4 Dinner available; 5 Open all year; 6 Pets welcome; 7 Smoking allowed; 8 Children welcome; 9 Social drinking allowed; 10 Tennis available; 11 Swimming available; 12 Golf available; 13 Skiing available; 14 May be booked through travel agents.

Bed and Breakfast Hawaii (continued)

looks out to one of the many garden areas. The Garden Room is ground level and offers a double bed and Bill Blass motif, country garden ambience, reading area, and private bath. Ehu Noe offers king-size or twin beds with Laura Ashley decor, sitting area in antique wicker, ocean and herb garden view, and private bath. Hono Kuhio offers an antique four-poster bed in Ralph Lauren motif, dressing room, sitting area, ocean view, and private bath. All rooms have a private entrance. Your hosts want to make your vacation unforgettable. Three night minimum. No smoking. $75-80.

H7. Right on a bluff overlooking the ocean, the home offers an oceanfront pool with Jacuzzi and a view of a popular surfing beach. Large, covered, comfortably furnished decks face the ocean where guests can watch the whales and cruise ships. This modern home is just two miles from downtown Hilo but quiet and private. Three guest rooms with private baths are separated by a family room with TV, VCR, and a private entrance to the pool. The master suite is sometimes available. Minimum stay is three nights. $95-120.

H8. Paradise Place is the name of this accommodation on a rural acre just one-half mile from the ocean in Keaau. Accommodations are downstairs with a private entrance and consist of a two-room suite with a double bed in the bedroom, sofa sleeper in the living room, and private bath with a shower. This area also has a TV with VCR, microwave, small refrigerator, and table where host puts all the fixings for a leisurely breakfast served on a quiet landscaped patio. This area is a central location for a guest to explore the fresh lava flows and Volcano National Park. Seventh night is free. $65.

H12. Relax in charming downtown Hilo's only bed and breakfast. Across from Hawaii's famous Lyman Museum in the center of historic Hilo town, quaint shops and restaurants await your discovery. This 1922 five-bedroom home is uniquely decorated in vintage Hawaiian. The first steps onto the old style lanai, will transport guests to a lifestyle for visitors seeking true Hawaiiana. All rooms are furnished with queen-size beds. One private bedroom with full bath includes a private lanai area. Four of the bedrooms have a half-bath that is private and a shared large shower. Color TV, VCR, and tapes are available for guests along with a library of Hawaiian books. Breakfast is served each morning. Two night minimum stay. $75-89.

H33. A rain forest retreat just south of Hilo is waiting next to an orchid nursery. The hostess tends the orchids and boards horses on her property as well as accommodating bed and breakfast guests. A private studio complete with a king-size bed, private bath, and light cooking appliances (refrigerator, hot plate, and toaster oven). Guests are welcome to use the hot tub. This retreat is only 30 minutes away from Hilo and Volcano National Park. $60-70.

H63. A detached studio apartment has a private bath and kitchenette. Hosts own an eight-acre lot at 1,500-foot elevation above and three miles from Hawaii. The view of the ocean is unobstructed, and guests have access to the Alenuihaha Channel to Halaekala on Maui. The main house and the guest house are on the property. The guest house is furnished with a sofa bed and a double bed, color TV, and radio. Sliding glass doors overlook the view of the ocean. The kitchen is fully equipped for preparing all meals, and breakfast fixings are stocked in the refrigerator. Another studio attached to the main house has a separate entrance and private bath. $65-75.

NOTES: Credit cards accepted: A MasterCard; B Visa; C American Express; D Discover Card; E Diner's Club; F Other; 2 Personal checks accepted; 3 Lunch available; 4 Dinner available; 5 Open all year;

Bjornen

111 Honolii Pali, 96720
(808) 935-6330

A beautiful four-star bed and breakfast on the bluff facing the ocean, surfing beach, and Hilo Bay. Two miles from downtown Hilo, yet quiet and private. Hale Kai-Bjornen offers a swimming pool and Jacuzzi, large deck, and bar room. All rooms face the ocean and offer private baths and cable TV. Three miles away are Rainbow Falls and Botanical Gardens; nine miles away is Akaka Falls and 30 miles away are the volcanoes and Waipo Valley. The hostess and host are very friendly and ready to help direct guests. Excellent restaurants nearby and guest cottage with kitchen facilities are also available.

Hosts: Evonne Bjornen and Paul Tallett
Rooms: 5 (PB) $80-98
Full Breakfast
Credit Cards: None
Notes: 2, 5, 7 (limited), 8 (over 12), 9, 11, 12, 14

Go Native •• Hawaii

P.O.Box 11418, 65 Halaulani Place, Hilo, 96721
(808) 935-4178; (800) 925-9065
FAX (808) 935-4178

Haili House Inn is across from Hawaii's famous Lyman Museum in the center of historic Hilo town. This five-bedroom home, circa 1922, is decorated in Hawaiian eclectic decor. Accommodations include queen-size beds, ceiling fan, full or half-baths, and a private lanai. Other amenities include color TV, VCR and tapes, stereo, and complimentary breakfast. Children six and older accepted. Additional charge for extra person(s). $75-99.

Hale Paliku. "House against the cliff" is a kamaaina home built in the 1930s just three blocks from the downtown area. Guests are greeted with spectacular view of the Pacific at Hilo Bay. Explore historic old Hilo, starting at the Lyman Museum two blocks away. A short stroll brings guests to shops, restaurants, art galleries, and Kalakaua Park, while a short drive takes them to gorgeous waterfalls and the scenic Hamakua coastline. House is 45 minutes away from Volcanoes National Park. Two guest rooms, one mountainside and one oceanside, contain down pillows, comforters, Laura Ashley prints, and "happi coats" (bathrobes). $55-100

Keoni's Macadamia Nut House is on the lower slopes of Mauna Kea, only five miles from downtown Hilo. The home was built in 1993 and has two bedrooms, two private baths, private lanai, queen-size bed, color TV, ceiling fan, and refrigerator. Both rooms have private entrances. Breakfast includes fresh island fruits, and dietary restrictions are respected. Volcanoes National Park is 35 miles away. $65.

HI 1135. This private guest studio is just five minutes above downtown Hilo. Accommodations include a self-contained kitchenette, bath, cable TV, VCR, stereo and air conditioning. Hosts provide a continental breakfast each morning. The studio is only minutes away from Rainbow Falls, Lyman House Museum, and Hilo Farmer's Market. Children are welcome. Weekly rates are available. Additional charge for extra person. No smoking. $65.

HAWAII—HOLUALOA

Bed and Breakfast Above the Kona Coast

P.O. Box 197, 96725
(808) 322-3295

A newly built house on seven and one-half acres is designed with the guests' needs in mind. A large lanai encircles the main house where guests can have breakfast while enjoying the expansive view of the ocean. Breakfast includes fresh fruits and juices, homemade tropical jellies, muffins, and fresh

Kona coffee. A grass courtyard separates the main house from the guest buildings. Each of the rooms has a private entrance, color TV, queen-size and twin bed, full bath, and angled high windows that act as skylights. Each day fresh fruit and flowers are placed in guests' room to enhance the beautiful atmosphere. Between the two guest buildings is the hot tub where one can sit and relax in the evening under an umbrella of stars.

Host: Patricia Barlow
Rooms: $50-65

HAWAII—HONOKAA

Bed and Breakfast Hawaii

P.O. Box 449, Kapaa, 96746
(808) 822-7771; (800) 733-1632
FAX (808) 822-2723

H11. The hostess of this large plantation estate enjoys having guests share its beauty and tranquility. With ocean views on three sides, the estate is built on an ocean point at the 1,200-foot level just outside of Honokaa. The main house offers three guest accommodations: a large suite with fireplace, an adjoining bedroom, private lanai, and private bath; a queen room with private bath, 12-foot ceilings, and tongue-and-groove woodwork. There are also two cottages on the property. Lighted tennis courts, gazebo, macadamia orchard, fruit trees, and lush tropical flowers throughout the estate. $75-200.

H21. Enjoy privacy and relaxation when staying at this unique, cozy cottage surrounded by lush foliage above the city of Kailua Kona where it is cooler and quiet. Use the fully equipped kitchen which includes breakfast treats to prepare a leasurely breakfast. The bathroom features a shower and the living room a color TV/VCR plus telephone. The bedroom has a queen-size bed and a spectacular panoramic view of the Kona coastline. Awaken each morning to the songs of the cardinals and smaller birds. In the late afternoon enjoy a relaxing soak in the hot tub while viewing a beautiful Kona sunset. Two night minimum. Outside smoking only. $60.

HAWAII—KAILUA-KONA

Adrienne's Casa Del Sol Bed and Breakfast Inn

77-6335 Alii Drive, 06740
(808) 326-CASA (2272); (800) 395-2272
FAX (808) 326-2272

This beautiful over 6,000-square-foot Mediterranean-style home has wrought iron throughout, sweeping arched private oceanfront/view lanais from every room and suite. Breakfast buffet is served poolside or by oceanview spa. A personal chef is available for lunch and dinner. All rooms have king- or queen-size beds; suites have full kitchens, living rooms, dining rooms, and private entrances. Less than five minutes to world class golf, tennis, skin diving, fishing charter (best marlin tournaments), surfing, snorkeling, beaches, restaurants, and shopping. Between Kailua-Kona and resort community of Keauhou in the heart of the resort community. The true Aloha spirit is shared with all guests.

Hosts: Adrienne and Reginald Batty
Rooms: 2 (PB)
Suites: 2
Continental Breakfast
Credit Cards: A, B
Notes: 2, 3, 4, 5, 7 (limited), 8, 9, 10, 11, 12, 13, 14

Affordable Paradise Bed and Breakfast Reservations

226 Pouli Road, 96734
(808) 261-1693; (800) 925-9065
FAX (808) 261-7315

DeKona. This home is in Kona about five minutes from Kona town. The hosts are very friendly and offer many suggestions on what to see and do in Kona. This home has three different accommodations. Two studios, each with a private entrance, private bath, refrigerator, coffeemaker, and hot plate. Breakfast is not served. Then there is a large two bedroom apartment, one bath, kitchen, and living room area. Breakfast is not served, but the cooking area is provided so that guests may prepare light meals. There is an additional charge for extra persons. $45-65.

Toya. This is a nice, comfortable, one bedroom cottage. It is about a 15 minute drive from Kona town. Unit has a kitchen area but host feels this is not really adequate cooking for large meals. Prepare light and simple meals. There is a small living room, separate bedroom and bathroom. $65.

Rowils. A Swiss hostess makes sure you have an enjoyable stay in Kona. Her accommodation is a large two bedroom downstairs unit. There is a kitchen, living room, and one bath. Breakfast is not served, but guests may prepare light meals in the kitchen. The home is about five minutes from downtown Kona. Additional charge for extra persons. $60.

Bed and Breakfast Hawaii

P.O. Box 449, Kapaa, 96746
(808) 822-7771; (800) 733-1632
FAX (808) 822-2723

H10. These warm-hearted hosts have a spacious home surrounded by tropical foliage about a five-minute drive from the ocean. The downstairs accommodation includes a private lanai with an ocean view and a separate entrance through glass doors to the bedroom. The room is large and has a minirefrigerator, a microwave, TV, and telephone. A tasty continental breakfast is served. No smoking. Two-night minimum stay. $70.

H23. Guests are invited to share the magnificent panoramic view from this hillside home. Bed and breakfast guests can choose between the Hula Room, with queen-size bed and large, private lanai, and the Garden Room, with two twin beds. Both have TV, microwave, and small refrigerator. Smoking outside only. $65-75.

H26. Escape to the peaceful hillside of Hualalai Mountain overlooking the Kona coast. The interior of this lovely 2,500-square-foot home is meticulously furnished. The guest quarters are on the first level and have two bedrooms, with one bath, and a kitchen and living area. There is a large deck for guests' exclusive use. Breakfast fixings are provided. Three-night minimum stay. $65.

H32A. Right on the beach in Kona is this luxurious and comfortable oceanfront home. Two rooms are available: one is oceanfront with a queen-size bed, and the other is oceanview with a queen-size bed. Both have full private baths and a color TV. Hostess loves to play tennis and meet new people. No smoking. $95-115.

H34. Just 12 minutes from the airport and 15 minutes from Kailua Village in the cool Kaloko Mauka area is this beautiful new home on five acres. It offers an attractive separate apartment at garden level with two bedrooms, bath, and sitting room with TV and limited cooking facilities. Guests may choose to breakfast with their hosts or on their own. After a busy day of sports, shopping, or sightseeing, sit on the lanai high above the Kona coast and enjoy the magnificent sunset. Resident dog, cats, and llamas. Three-night minimum stay. No smoking. $75.

H44. A charming cottage awaits guests very near Kailua Bay and village. Relax in the pri-

6 Pets welcome; 8 Children welcome; 9 Social drinking allowed; 10 Tennis available; 11 Swimming available; 12 Golf available; 13 Skiing available; 14 May be booked through travel agents.

Bed and Breakfast Hawaii (continued)

vate courtyard with a lovely garden view. Through sliding glass doors, the one-bedroom cottage offers a bedroom with queen-size bed and private bath, TV, VCR, and stereo. The kitchenette offers a full refrigerator, microwave, coffee pot, toaster oven, and blender. Great for a small family. Hosts have two children and welcome families with children. Beach equipment is available, and tennis courts are close by. Two-night minimum stay. Special weekly rates. $65.

H46. Elegant, brand new, with an ocean view. Guests will enjoy this accommodation in Kona separate from the main house. One bedroom with a queen-size bed and full bathroom, plus a sitting area with TV, is decorated in off-white with rose-colored accents. There is also a dining area with a refrigerator and wet bar. Private deck. No smoking. Two-night minimum stay. $80.

H50. This bed and breakfast has a private entrance on the lower level of this beautiful, brand-new, two-story Art Deco home. Guests have a choice of two large bedrooms, with access to the gardens that offer a beautiful ocean view. A special Aloha breakfast is served in the family room that is furnished with a piano, pool and Ping Pong tables, and big-screen TV. A great location for two couples traveling together. $50-80.

H59. Guests can experience one of the many breathtaking sunsets from this bed and breakfast overlooking the coastline just above Kona Village. On a three-acre estate, the accommodations for guests are private and self-contained. A separate apartment features one bedroom with a queen-size bed, living room with a fold-out sofa, private bath, kitchen, TV, private entrance, and lanai with a barbecue. A queen-size futon is also available. The building is designed like a dome with open beam ceilings. Smoking outside only,. $80-95.

H60. For the traveler who enjoys the comforts of luxurious accommodations, this Kailua plantation house offers oceanfront and oceanview suites, all of which have a private lanai that overlooks the ocean, spa, and pool. The house is elegantly decorated and air-conditioned. Each of the five guest rooms is unique and offers a variety of bed sizes, and one guest room has a whirlpool tub and bidet. All the rooms have a TV, telephone, small refrigerator, and daily maid service. $120-175.

H70. This longtime favorite bed and breakfast is on the west side of the Big Island, 18 miles south of Kailua Kona. The accommodation is on the garden level of the host home with a private entrance. An unobstructed ocean view is great for catching those famous Kona sunsets. The bedroom has a king-size bed, private full bath, refrigerator, coffee pot, microwave, and TV. Your hosts serve a continental breakfast on your private lanai. This accommodation is only five minutes from the closest beaches to enjoy the best snorkeling and swimming on the island. Three night minimum stay. $50-70.

H71. Your hosts, landscapers by trade, show off their talents on this beautiful property above Kailua Kona. Their large home is just six miles from the airport and three miles from the beach and offers beautiful ocean views. A private suite, decorated with antique oak furniture throughout, offers a queen-size bed and large, private bath with shower. Kitchenette is available, including a microwave and refrigerator. Sitting area with TV, lanai, washer-dryer, and a lap pool with cabana and waterfall are also available for guests. A continental breakfast is served. Outside smoking only. Minimum stay is two nights. $75-85.

H72. A large, private studio is made-to-order for short and long stays. Guests will enjoy this studio on the hillside in a quiet, residential neighborhood. The bedroom has a queen-size bed and an additional double futon is available. A full kitchen for guests along with private full bath. Guests are welcome to use an outside covered lanai with BBQ, TV, and phone. The hosts welcome children. Smoking outside only. Two night minimum stay. $55-65.

H73. Tucked away above Kailua Kona these hosts have a one-bedroom apartment on the ground floor of their home. A queen-size bed in the bedroom plus a double futon for a third person is available. Kitchenette for light cooking includes refrigerator and microwave. There is a private full bath. The unit will be stocked with breakfast goodies. From the lanai guests may BBQ and enjoy an ocean view and the fabulous sunsets of Kona. Smoking outside only. Children ten years and older. $65-70.

Go Native • • Hawaii

P.O.Box 11418, 65 Halaulani Place, Hilo, 96721
(808) 935-4178; (800) 925-9065
FAX (808) 935-4178

Hale Malia A spacious, modern home built in the old plantation-style. Whether guests choose the oceanfront bedroom or the partial ocean view, they will enjoy a private bath and a queen-size bed, TV and lots of charm. Two miles south of picturesque Kailua-Kona on the ocean and just minutes away from scuba-diving, snorkeling, fishing, kayaking, golf, tennis, and biking. Kilauea, erupting continuously since 1983, is a major attraction. Come share the Aloha spirit! $75-95

Luna Kai. Choice accommodations in either a self-contained cottage or delightful studio. The cottage is nestled in a tropical garden, is designer-decorated, and has king-size bed, private bath, and outside lanai. A studio is below the main house. A wonderful continental breakfast is served on a carpeted open lanai with a 180° view of Kailua Bay and the Kona coastline. $80.

Puanani Bed and Breakfast. Nestled in a quiet hillside on a cul-de-sac, these three-room private suites provide spectacular views of the Pacific. The grounds are beautiful, with indigenous landscaping to encourage bird-watching. Amenities include antiques, private entrance, queen-size bed, large sitting room, kitchenette, and lanai. There is also an exercise-weight room, a 40-foot lap pool with waterfalls, and a fish pond with water lilies and hyacinths. A tropical paradise. $70-85

Hale Maluhia Bed and Breakfast

76-770 Hualalai Road, 96740
(800) 559-6627; (808) 329-5573
FAX (808) 326-5487

Gracious up-country plantation living in the heart of the Kona Recreational Paradise. Nestled in beautiful Holualoa coffee land. Enjoy large bedrooms, private baths, good beds, and stone spa. Old Hawaii living with native woods, open beam ceilings, koa cabinets, big lanais, four common areas, and a stream with waterfalls as the central focus. Full breakfast includes fresh breads, fruits, juices, eggs, granola, teas, and pure Kona coffee. Just three miles from the Kailua-Kona Village with easy airport access. Smoking permitted outside only. Beach and snorkeling equipment available. Wheelchair friendly.

Hosts: Ken and Ann Smith
Rooms: 5 (3 PB; 2 SB) $55-75
Cottages: 3 (PB) $110-220
Full Breakfast
Credit Cards: A, B, C, D
Notes: 2, 5, 6, 8, 9, 10, 11, 13, 14

6 Pets welcome; 8 Children welcome; 9 Social drinking allowed; 10 Tennis available; 11 Swimming available; 12 Golf available; 13 Skiing available; 14 May be booked through travel agents.

Three Bears' Bed and Breakfast

72-1001 Puukala Street, 96740
(808) 325-7563; (800) 765-0480

Three Bears' Bed and Breakfast features comfortable, friendly accommodations and a spectacular ocean view of the Kona coastline on the Big Island of Hawaii. This bed and breakfast is just a short drive to Kailua town and the many beaches on the Kona coast. A terrific extended Continental breakfast is served each morning on the lanai, and complimentary beach chairs, coolers, boogie boards, and snorkel gear are provided. The hosts can also help guests find places to stay on the other Hawaiian Islands. German is spoken.

Hosts: Ann, Art and Nanette Stockel
Rooms: 2 (PB) $65-75
Continental Breakfast
Credit Cards; A, B
Notes: 5, 8, 9, 10, 11, 12, 14

HAWAII—KAMUELA

Bed and Breakfast Hawaii

P.O. Box 449, Kapaa, 96746
(808) 822-7771; (800) 733-1632
FAX (808) 822-2723

H27A. The host and hostess have a 4,000-square-foot home and have used about 800 square feet of it for a completely separate apartment for guests. Guest quarters include a bedroom, private bath, and living room with a sink and small refrigerator. The home borders a stream and has a 360 degree view of the Kohala Mountains, Pacific Ocean, the famous Mauna Kea and Mauna Loa. Three-night minimum stay. $80-90.

H41. In the historic area of North Kohala just about seven miles from lush Pololu Valley and the rugged coastline of beautiful Hawaii, guests can enjoy the rural atmosphere and cooler climate. The home is set back from the road and is a modified A-frame. Accommodations include a self-contained studio under the main house with a separate entrance, limited kitchenette, private bath, and double bed. No smoking. Two-night minimum stay. $50.

H62. This bed and breakfast is part of a beautiful Swiss chalet-style home just three and one-half miles from Kamuela and 12 minutes from Hapuna Beach. Accommodations consist of a two bedroom apartment, and each bedroom has a queen-size bed. Full bath, a living room with a fireplace, TV, and telephone included. Enjoy views of Mauna Kea and the ocean from the private sun deck. $65-75.

H67. A large, three-story Victorian home in Kamuela is the site of this bed and breakfast for those travelers looking for an out-of-the-way vacation site. This home has lush, tropical landscaping featuring waterfall and hot tub. On the ground floor a large bedroom with queen-size bed and additional single bed in living room is offered to guests. The unit has private bath along with kitchenette that includes refrigerator, microwave, toaster oven. The home has wonderful mountain and ocean views from decks surrounding the home. Breakfast is provided in the unit. Near the heart of Waimea, close to parks, with open markets nearby on Saturdays. Hosts will accept children. Smoking outside please. Two nights minimum stay. $10 each additional guest. $65-85.

Go Native ·· Hawaii

P.O.Box 11418, Hilo, 96721
(808) 935-4178; (800) 662-8483

Kamuela's Mauna Kea View. Private suites with panoramic views of Parker Ranch and majestic Mauna Kea. Suites modeled after Swiss chalets are just three minutes from restaurants and shopping, and only 15 minutes from the Big Island's best beaches. Hosts are 14-year residents and invite guests to enjoy amenities like private entrances, two bedrooms, cozy fireplaces, relaxing sun decks, and colorful gardens. Close to hiking, horseback riding, golf, tennis, skiing, and more. $55-65

Kamuela Inn

P.O. Box 1994, 96743
(808) 885-4243; FAX (808) 885-8857

Comfortable, cozy rooms and suites with private baths, with or without kitchenettes, all with color cable TV. Continental breakfast served in a sunny lanai each morning. In a quiet, peaceful setting near shops, parks, museums, and restaurants. Hawaii's white sand beaches, golf, and valley and mountain tours are only minutes away.

Host: Carolyn Cascavilla
Rooms: 31 (PB) $54-165
Continental Breakfast
Credit Cards: A, B, C, D, E
Notes: 2, 5, 7, 8, 14

HAWAII—KEAAU

Bed and Breakfast Hawaii

P.O. Box 449, Kapaa, 96746
(808) 822-7771; (800) 733-1632

H69. The hosts have retired to Hawaii and look forward to sharing their home with bed and breakfast guests. Twenty minutes from the Hilo airport, this accommodation is for those who want to spend their vacation in rural Hawaii. The area is great for hiking and biking while only 15 minutes from beaches, shopping, restaurants, volcanoes, and golf courses. The guest rooms offered are very private, each with a private entrance and bath. There is a covered porch area with refrigerator, microwave, and BBQ. Breakfast is served. Minimum stay is two nights. Outside smoking only. $40.

Na Hala O Ke Kai
(The Hala Trees by the Sea)

HCR 2 Box 9591, 96749
(808) 966-4384

Aloha! This beautiful oceanfront home is furnished with antiques and family heirlooms. The bed and breakfast lodging is downstairs, with direct access to the shoreline, pounding surf and black lava cliffs. Studio apartment with private entrance and bath, efficiency kitchen, and dining and sitting areas. Guests enjoy a gourmet breakfast on the deck overlooking the coastline while watching for dolphins, turtles, and whales.

Hosts: Pedar and Eileen Wold, and Randi Wold-
  Brennon
Room: 1 (PB) $75
Continental Breakfast
Credit Cards: None
Notes: 2, 5, 8, 9, 11, 12, 14

Ohia Cottage

HCR 2, Box 9591, 96749
(808) 966-4384

This charming plantation-style cottage was built in the 1930s and is on the National Register of Historic Places. It is the ideal getaway for families. Furnished for comfort, Ohia Cottage has three bedrooms, shared bath, full kitchen, fireplace, and is wheelchair-accessible. Just a half-mile from Hawaii Volcanoes National Park, guests may explore the unbelievable beauty of the world's most active volcano. Golf courses are less than 30 minutes away. Continental breakfast is provided.

Hosts: Pedar and Eileen Wold, and Randi Wold-
  Brennon
Rooms: 3 (SB) $75
Continental Breakfast
Credit Cards: None
Notes: 2, 5, 8, 9, 12, 14

HAWAII—KEALAKEKUA

Bed and Breakfast Hawaii

P.O. Box 449, Kapaa, 96746
(808) 822-7771; (800) 733-1632
FAX (808) 822-2723

H38. This is an unusual and beautifully designed home with hardwood floors, decks, and lots of windows with screens. This two-story home is just 200 yards from Napoopoo Bay, a great area for swimming and snorkeling. Downstairs, two separate bedrooms with private baths and queen-size beds share a sitting room with a covered deck that views the ocean. $75.

HAWAII—NAALEHU

Bed and Breakfast Hawaii

P.O. Box 449, Kapaa, 96746
(808) 822-7771; (800) 733-1632

H55. This bed and breakfast is in the most Southern community in the United States and is unique in its attraction. Sixty-four miles from Hilo, 56 miles from Kona, Naalehu offers exploration of the site of the first Polynesian landings on the island, spectacular views of the cliffs and shoreline and green sea turtles in Punalu'u State Park. The home is a 50-year-old plantation house with multiple rooms available. A full breakfast is served. Room one features a queen-size bed and private bath. Room two features two double beds and private bath with shower. Room three features a queen-size bed with shared bath. $45-65.

HAWAII—PAHOA

Kalani Honua by the Sea

Rural Route 2, Box 4500, 96778
(808) 965-7828; (800) 800-6886

Guests may treat themselves to the beauty of a rare coastal Hawaiian paradise. Kalani Honua, meaning "Harmony of Heaven and Earth," is the ideal location for rest and relaxation. Accommodations include private guest cottage units with an ocean view. Guests are welcome to join for the three gourmet meals served each day, take an ongoing class, enjoy a massage or relax at the spa. Nearby are many natural wonders including a black-sand beach and warm springs.

Hosts: Richard Koob and Dottie Kaiser
Rooms: 30 (11 PB; 19 SB) $52-97
Full Breakfast
Credit Cards: A, B, C, E, F
Notes: 3, 4, 5, 7 (limited), 8, 9 10, 11, 14

Kalani Honua

HAWAII—PUAKO

Bed and Breakfast Hawaii

P.O. Box 449, Kapaa, 96746
(808) 822-7771; (800) 733-1632

H54. Right on the beach! New studios on the beachside of Puako Beach Drive between Mauna Kea and Mauna Lani Resorts. On second story with surrounding deck to take advantage of partial ocean view, the Queen Studio offers a full-size kitchen, queen-size bed, living room with TV and VCR, and private full bath. There is an oceanside gazebo with BBQ for guests in this tropical beach setting. The King Room offers either twin- or king-size bed for guests along with a kitchenette and private full bath. The two rooms have solid, double adjoining doors that can be open for parties traveling together. Also available is a fully furnished, brand-new cottage that is able to sleep five people. Queen-size bed in a bedroom plus a queen-size sofa sleeper and twin bed in the living room area which is very large. A full kitchen and private bath along with deck overlooking the ocean. All three accommodations are just one mile from beautiful Hapuna beach, 25 minutes from the airport, and 20 minutes to Parker Ranch. Smoking outside only. Some staples supplied in units; no breakfast served. Three night minimum stay for the studios. Five night minimum for the cottage. Studios: $95-105; Cottage: $145.

HAWAII—VOLCANO

Affordable Paradise Bed and Breakfast Reservations

226 Pouli Road, 96734
(808) 261-1693; (800) 925-9065
FAX (808) 261-7315

There are many accommodations available in the Volcano area. This host has bedrooms, cottages and complete houses. The house is a complete two bedroom home. There is a kitchen, living room, and bath room. It is decorated very nicely and is surrounded by two and one-half acres of rain forest. Host requests a three day minimum and charges $75 per night for the complete house. Please check with us for more detailed descriptions of the home in the Volcano area.

Bed and Breakfast Hawaii

P.O. Box 449, Kapaa, 96746
(808) 822-7771; (800) 733-1632
FAX (808) 822-2723

H18. This cottage in Volcano Village is a charming, cozy plantation-style cottage surrounded by giant cedars, native koa and ohia trees, and hapu'u ferns. The perfect place for a quiet vacation stay disturbed only by the native birds. Ideal for families or golf weekends, the cottage includes three bedrooms, two double rooms and one single room. The bath is shared by all three rooms. A fully equipped kitchen is available. The cottage also features a fireplace for those cooler nights, cable TV, and a ramp entrance. Continental breakfast is provided. Can be rented by the room (shared bath) or the entire cottage for up to five guests. Two night minimum. Children welcome. No smoking. $55-150.

H51. Just two miles from Volcanoes National Park at 3,500-foot elevation. Helpful hosts offer a king-size bedroom with its own entrance and private bath. A futon can be put down for a third person. Great breakfasts are served every morning to get guests off to a good start for exploring the park. $70.

H51A. Also available in H51 are three cottages. Guests check in with hosts and receive keys. The refrigerator and kitchen are stocked with breakfast foods ample for a week's stay. Choose from one of three cottages: The Dome, Grand Cedar, or Cedar One. All are plush and beautifully furnished with fireplaces, TV with VCR, and stereos. $85-125.

Chalet Kilauea-The Inn at Volcano

P.O. Box 998, 96785
(808) 967-7786; (800) 937-7786)
FAX (808) 967-8660

This inn, at 3500 feet amid the lush splendor of a tropical rain forest, is near Hawaii Volcanoes National Park. Choose from superior theme rooms and suites including the Treehouse Suite and separate spacious vacation homes. Awaken to a candlelit, two-course full gourmet breakfast featuring international and local cuisine. Enjoy afternoon tea in the guest's living room filled with stunning and fascinating art from around the world or outside on the huge covered veranda complete with its own fountain. All units have private entrance, and private bath, some featuring marble Jacuzzi tubs. Other features include fireplaces, outside Jacuzzi, TV, VCR, and a video, music, and book library. The am-

6 Pets welcome; 8 Children welcome; 9 Social drinking allowed; 10 Tennis available; 11 Swimming available; 12 Golf available; 13 Skiing available; 14 May be booked through travel agents.

biance of Chalet Kilauea is both exquisitely tasteful and reassuringly comfortable.

Hosts: Lisha and Brian Crawford
Rooms: 11 (PB) $75-225
Full Breakfast
Credit Cards: A, B, C, D, F
Notes: 2, 5, 8, 9, 11, 12, 14

Kilauea Lodge

P.O. Box 116, 96785
(808) 967-7366; FAX (808) 967-7367

Charming mountain lodge one mile from Volcanoes National Park. Full service dining room with excellent wine list. Full breakfast readies guests for an active day of hiking and viewing the wonders of Pele, the volcano goddess. All private baths. Twelve rooms: six rooms with fireplace; common area.

Rooms: 12 (PB) $90-120
Full Breakfast
Credit Cards: A, B
Notes: 2, 4, 5, 8, 9, 12

Kilauea Lodge

Volcano Bed and Breakfast

P.O. Box 998, 96785
(808) 967-7779; (800) 736-7140
FAX (808) 967-8660

Volcano Bed and Breakfast offers a peaceful setting and safe haven that draws visitors from all over the world. All five rooms in the three-story turn-of-the-century home look out onto tree ferns, fragrant ginger, and native ohia forest. Various activities nearby include golf, black sand beaches, and Volcanoes National Park's hiking trails and spectacular lava flows. Host provides an abundance of information and are known for their great breakfasts.

Host: Saul Rollason
Rooms: 5 (SB) $55-75
Full Breakfast
Credit Cards: A, B, C, D, F
Notes: 2, 5, 8, 10, 11, 12, 14

KAUAI—ANAHOLA

Bed and Breakfast Hawaii

P.O. Box 449, Kapaa, 96746
(808) 822-7771; (800) 733-1632
FAX (808) 822-2723

K67. Wake up in beautiful tropical surroundings at Anahola Beach abundant with flowers, fresh fruit, singing birds, and sounds of the ocean. Enjoy beautiful views and beach atmosphere in this bright studio with private yard and entrance, full bath, and breakfast facilities. The home is across the street from a beach great for swimming, snorkeling, boogie boarding, and wind surfing. Convenient to all Kauai attractions. Tropical continental breakfast fixings provided. Two-night minimum stay. $75.

KAUAI—HANALEI

Bed and Breakfast Hawaii

P.O. Box 449, Kapaa, 96746
(808) 822-7771; (800) 733-1632
FAX (808) 822-2723

K13. The hosts' brand new and beautiful house is built on one and one-half acres. The community offers a 45-hole golf course, clubhouse, athletic club, tennis, swimming, and driving range just minutes away. Breakfast is served in the dining room or on the decks overlooking the Pacific. All rooms have private entrances, ceiling fans, refrigerators, and color TVs. Choose from three rooms—one a honeymoon suite with whirlpool tub, one a penthouse with whirlpool and balcony. Two-night minimum stay. $85-190.

NOTES: Credit cards accepted: A MasterCard; B Visa; C American Express; D Discover Card; E Diner's Club; F Other; 2 Personal checks accepted; 3 Lunch available; 4 Dinner available; 5 Open all year;

K21. This hostess offers to share her beach house right on Anini Beach with visitors. She is a world traveler and has a natural affinity for travelers. Her home is halfway between Kilauea and Hanalei, and the room offered has a double bed, and shared bath. There is a large covered porch for relaxing and viewing the sunsets of the Northshore. Two-night minimum stay. $50.

K32. A newly remodeled home just 150 yards from Hanalei Bay offers guests a fully equipped top-floor apartment with a loft bedroom overlooking Hanalei Bay. A full kitchen, laundry facilities, living room with TV are also included. There is a queen-size bed in the bedroom. No breakfast is served or provided in the apartment. For short or long stays, guests may enjoy the Hanalei experience between the beautiful mountains and the bay. The hostess will offer monthly rates. Five night minimum. No smoking. $100.

K45. This bed and breakfast accommodation is 100 yards from the gorgeous Hanalei Bay. Perfect for hiking, watersports, sightseeing, golf, sunbathing, or just long walks in a quaint, unpretentious town. Sunsets from the lanai are breathtaking. A two-story home with 1,000 square feet of deck surrounding the second floor and providing a partial ocean view and a mountain view of waterfalls. A continental breakfast of fresh island fruit, juice, and breads is served on the second-story lanai. $65-85.

K46. This spacious new country home and guest quarters offer comfort and a spectacular view of the Hanalei Valley. Enjoy the sunsets, the mountain waterfalls, and the peace of this special location. The guest bedroom has a king-size bed, a microwave, sink, refrigerator, and private bath. On five and one-half acres. Three-night minimum stay. $70.

K83. This Hanalei cottage has it all for short or long vacation stays. Just two blocks from Hanalei Bay and Hanalei Town is this lovely separate guest house that can sleep four comfortably. The bedroom has twin beds that convert to king-size and there is a queen-size sofa bed in the living area. Private full bath, complete kitchen, washer/dryer, and private lanai available for guests. Light breakfast fixings are available in the cottage. Three night minimum. Outside smoking only. $85.

Go Native • • Hawaii

65 Halaulani Place, P.O. Box 11418, Hilo, 96721
(808) 935-4178; (800) 662-8483

This house is stylish, tastefully designed three-story building with a lanai surrounding the second floor. Accommodations include two rooms, one studio, one apartment, and one honeymoon suite. All have queen-size beds, private baths, and three kitchens. Guests may boat, canoe, wind-surf, swim, snorkel, hike, picnic, or fish in the town of Hanalei. Within walking distance of markets, restaurants, shopping, and local art displays. Continental breakfast served. Well-behaved children only. Outside smoking only. $60-80.

KAUAI—KALAHEO

Affordable Paradise Bed and Breakfast Reservations

226 Pouli Road, 96734
(808) 261-1693; (800) 925-9065
FAX (808) 261-7315

Heart. The view from the backyard is unforgettable. There is a wide, beautiful waterfall which captures attention. Lush tropical plants and trees surround the little valley of this home. The bed and breakfast accommodations are downstairs from the main home. The hosts and guests share the main entrance but each has their own privacy. The accommodations include two bedrooms, which are only rented together for guests traveling together, bathroom, living room, and small bar area. Breakfast is not served. There is a sun deck and Jacuzzi in the backyard where guests can enjoy the beautiful area around them. $65-125.

Bed and Breakfast Hawaii

P.O. Box 449, Kapaa, 96746
(808) 822-7771; (800) 733-1632
FAX (808) 822-2723

K17. This complete one-bedroom apartment looks out toward the spectacular ocean and mountain scenery of the sunny south shore. Just up the hill is the Kukuiolono Golf Course known for its stunning vistas and beautiful gardens. Central and just 15 minutes from beaches, 25 minutes from the airport. The hosts offer a studio with private entrance and bedroom housing a queen-size bed, full private bath, living area including full-size pull-out couch, TV and kitchenette. Guests are welcome to lounge outside on their private lanai. No breakfast is served. Two night minimum. Outside smoking only. $65.

K19. Three bedrooms open onto a swimming pool flanked by flowering hibiscus, gardenias, and bougainvillaeas in this home nestled in the hills of South Kauai. A second-story wooden porch overlooks sugar cane fields, jungle, and the National Botanical Gardens. It is only a seven- to 20-minute drive to beaches. All rooms have private baths, and one room is handicapped accessible. The hostess is proud of her breakfast that includes homemade bread and hot muffins, Hawaiian fruits, and Hawaiian coffee. No smoking. $55-75.

K27. In quaint, quiet old Kalaheo town, this is a modern, executive-style home over-looking Poipu with distant mountain and ocean views. The large home offers several rooms for guests. Guests may plan favorite activities over Hawaiian continental breakfast served each morning. Two master suites are available for guests. Makai offers a large room with king-size bed and private bath with Jacuzzi. Mauka suite offers a queen-size bed with private bath. Also, two bedrooms, one with a double bed and the other with twin beds, share a bath with tub and shower plus additional shower. This is a great place for large parties to share the bed and breakfast experience. Two night minimum. Children over 16. No smoking in bedrooms. $50-85.

K85. Mango Hills Cottage is on two and one-half acres in Kalaheo overlooking the ocean and many acres of coffee fields. The hostess is an interior designer, and her attention to details inside the cottage is apparent. The living room has a pull-out queen-size sofa bed, cable TV, and an adjoining full kitchen with counter seating. The bedroom has a mountain view and a queen-size bed with adjoining bath. Hosts invite guests to swim in their pool or relax in a hammock under flowering trees. Minimum stay is three nights. $80.

Go Native •• Hawaii

P.O.Box 11418, 65 Halaulani Place, Hilo, 96721
(808) 935-4178; (800) 925-9065
FAX (808) 935-4178

South Shore Vista. South Shore Vista is ten minutes from the Poipu Beach resort area and ten minutes from beaches to the west. Accommodations include a bedroom with queen-size bed, private full bath, living area, and kitchenette. Beautifully decorated, this one-bedroom ohana has an ocean view and looks out toward the spectacular mountain scenery of Kauai's sunny south shore. Sleeps up to four. Children over four welcome. $75.

KAUAI-KALIHIWAI

Bed and Breakfast Hawaii

P.O. Box 449, Kapaa, 96746
(808) 822-7771; (800) 733-1632

K34. As guests eyes wander from a spectacular lush green country hillside lanai out to the blue Pacific, experience a relaxing, peaceful feeling. Come share in the experience of watching whales splash in the distance or enjoy a quiet walk down to our freshwater stream. In Kalihiwai Valley, this relaxing home is only minutes away from Princeville. The hosts offer an accommodation with private entrance, a fully equipped kitchen, two queen-size beds, private shower, washer/dryer, and TV. The perfect setting for a Northshore stay. Three night minimum. No smoking. $75.

KAUAI—KAPAA

Affordable Paradise Bed and Breakfast Reservations

226 Pouli Road, 96734
(808) 261-1693; (800) 925-9065
FAX (808) 261-7315

Kabark. This bed and breakfast home has been operating for many years. It is one of the most established on the island. The house has five bedrooms and a cottage and is about a five to ten minute drive uphill from Kapaa town. Each bedroom has a private bath. Guests join together for breakfast which is served daily. The cottage has a private entrance, private bath, little sitting area outside and inside. $50-60.

Santak. A cute little cottage awaits guests in Kapaa. It is about a five to ten minute drive uphill from Kapaa town. The cottage has its own private driveway which is lined with flowers. This short drive to the unit leads up to a definite feeling of entering a "home away from home". There is a private entrance, private bath, living room, and kitchen. It is decorated nicely and the accommodations are very comfortable. The hosts definitely have the Aloha spirit and make guests feel right at home. Breakfast is not served. $75.

Bed and Breakfast Hawaii

P.O. Box 449, 96746
(808) 822-7771; (800) 733-1632
FAX (808) 822-2723

K1. A secluded oceanfront home on beautiful Anahola Bay where guests can enjoy a large studio apartment detached from the main house. Accommodations include queen-size bed and private bath with a garden shower, color cable TV, and a kitchenette. Breakfast fixings are provided for the first three days. Occasionally a honeymoon room with a deep Jacuzzi is available. Enjoy the oceanfront amenities and privacy of the property. Three-day minimum stay. Weekly rates. $95-125 honeymoon room.

K3A. Cloud Nine Holiday is a spacious apartment that is completely private with its own entrance. It comes equipped with a color cable TV, a microwave, a small refrigerator, and all the breakfast fixings. The lanai overlooks a beautifully landscaped "bird of paradise" tropical garden perfect for romantic sunrise or sunset strolls. Near the beach and public tennis court. No smoking. $60-100.

K6. These three fresh and comfortable accommodations overlook a horse pasture skirted by Opaekaa Stream. Waterfalls are often visible in the distance from the lanai. Private entrances to all suites decorated in wicker and rattan. All rooms feature king- or queen-size beds, kitchen areas, and private baths. Smoking outside only. $60-100.

6 Pets welcome; 8 Children welcome; 9 Social drinking allowed; 10 Tennis available; 11 Swimming available; 12 Golf available; 13 Skiing available; 14 May be booked through travel agents.

Bed and Breakfast Hawaii (continued)

K16. Three rooms on the coconut coast of Kauai, just two blocks inland from the beach. Two rooms in the main house have private baths. A third room is separate from the main house. Enjoy breakfast with the hosts or choose to self-cater. All the rooms have hand-painted art done by the hostess. No smoking in rooms. $55.

K78. This one-bedroom condo with an ocean view is not really a bed and breakfast, but since the hosts live nearby, breakfast can be arranged easily if desired. Queen-size bed in the bedroom and private bath, plus the living room can sleep two more on the double Murphy bed. Full kitchen and private lanai with an ocean view, and the beach is only a few steps away. Guests are welcome to the pool, Jacuzzi on premises, and restaurants and shops are within easy walking distance. Weekly rates available. Minimum stay is three nights. $75.

K82. Hosts built an extra two-story house on their mountain view plateau property just for bed and breakfast guests. Accommodations for guests are two separate units downstairs. One unit has a queen-size bed, private bath, living area with queen-size sofa bed, color TV, wet bar, refrigerator, and microwave. Another larger unit includes a bedroom with a pair of twin beds, spacious living area with a queen-size sofa bed, large private bath, color TV, wet bar, refrigerator, and microwave. Each area has its own lanai and entrance. Breakfast is served upstairs in the breakfast nook, and a gazebo with a sauna and Jacuzzi is on premises. $75-105.

Go Native •• Hawaii

P.O.Box 11418, Hilo, 96721
(808) 935-4178; (800) 925-9065
FAX (808) 935-4178

Winters Guest House. This guest house sits behind the hosts' home with a view of Queen's Acres and Sleeping Giant. One bedroom has king-size or twin beds, an over-sized bath, queen-size Hide-a-bed in the great room, and a sleeping loft for two additional guests. Other amenities include a combination tub/shower, color TV with cable, and full kitchen help. A generous Aloha continental breakfast is stocked in the kitchen and replenished daily, including fruits and specialty breads. $80

Winters Mac Nut Farm and Inn. This two-bedroom accommodation is in a tranquil country setting with beautiful mountain views, including Mount Waialeale and Sleeping Giant. Beaches, golf, tennis, shopping, and dining are three miles away. Accommodations include king-size bed, queen-size bed, color TV with cable, refrigerator, and shared bath with ceramic tub and shower. Hawaiian continental breakfast is served, including tropical fruits and specialty breads. Rooms are rented to single party of two couples or family. $50.

Kay Barker's Bed and Breakfast

P.O. Box 740, 96746
(808) 822-3073; (800) 835-2845

The home is in a lovely garden setting, in a quiet rural area, with pastoral and mountain views. There is a large living room, TV room, extensive library, and lanai for guests to enjoy. Brochures are available.

Host: Gordon Barker
Rooms: 5 (PB) $49.05-76.30
Continental Breakfast
Credit Cards: A, B
Notes: 2, 5, 7, 8, 9, 10, 11, 12, 14

KAUAI—KILAUEA

Bed and Breakfast Hawaii

P.O. Box 449, Kapaa, 96746
(808) 822-7771; (800) 733-1632
FAX (808) 822-2723

NOTES: Credit cards accepted: A MasterCard; B Visa; C American Express; D Discover Card; E Diner's Club; F Other; 2 Personal checks accepted; 3 Lunch available; 4 Dinner available; 5 Open all year;

K31. A private, Northshore of Kauai guest house is the perfect setting for getting away from it all. Accommodations include a light cooking area, full bath, queen-size bed, and a sitting area. Overlooking the beautiful Kilauea River and "rainbow valley," named for the brilliant rainbows that stretch from the lush recesses of the valley floor to the ocean. A private hiking trail takes guests down to a secluded, semiprivate sandy beach. The main house has a pool available to guests. $115.

KAUAI—KOLOA

Affordable Paradise Bed and Breakfast Reservations

226 Pouli Road, 96734
(808) 261-1693; (800) 925-9065
FAX (808) 261-7315

Kobou. This is a wonderful upstairs private accommodation. It is in Koloa which is about a 15 minute drive to Poipu beach. The unit is newly built and is decorated very comfortably. There is a living room, kitchen, separate bedroom, and private bath. Breakfast is not included, but kitchen is large enough for guests to prepare wonderful breakfasts or meals. $60.

Naka. Koloa town and Poipu beach are both a short five minute drive from this bed and breakfast home. One guest room is attached to the house but has its own private entrance. There is a small kitchen area, private bathroom, and a small outdoor sitting area. The studio is separate from the main home with private entrance and bath, TV, refrigerator, and hot plate. $40-45.

Bed and Breakfast Hawaii

P.O. Box 449, Kapaa, 96746
(808) 822-7771; (800) 733-1632

K88. The location on the sunny shore of Kauai is perfect for this host and hostess who operate a scuba and snorkel charter. A cozy studio with a private entrance and decorated with a Hawaiian flair is perfect for a couple or young family. The studio has a king-size bed and there is an additional full-size Hide-a-bed. Private full bathroom, dining area, living room with TV and telephone, and complete kitchenette provide a comfortable living area for long or short term. A large deck has mountain and distant ocean views. Two night minimum. Smoking outside only. $65.

KAUAI—LAWAI

Victoria Place Bed and Breakfast

P.O. Box 930, 96765
(808) 332-9300

Perched high in the hills of southern Kauai, overlooking the lush jungle, cane fields, and the Pacific, Victoria Place is an oasis of pampered comfort and privacy. With only three guest rooms and a studio apartment with private entrace, cable TV and laundry privileges, the hillside inn looks out to the poolside deck, filled with gardenia, bougainvillaea, ginger, and hibiscus. The hearty continental breakfast includes homemade breads and four or five tropical fruits. Vacationers receive personal attention from the gregarious proprietor who steers them to little-known restaurants, beaches, and scenic hideaways. Poipu beaches are only ten minutes away. Just five minutes to golf course, boutiques, restaurants. Rental cars, helicopter tours, and horseback riding nearby. One room is handicapped accessible.

Host: Edee Seymour
Rooms: 4 (PB) $55-95
Continental Breakfast
Credit Cards: None
Notes: 2, 5, 7 (limited), 9, 10, 11, 12, 14

---

6 Pets welcome; 8 Children welcome; 9 Social drinking allowed; 10 Tennis available; 11 Swimming available;
12 Golf available; 13 Skiing available; 14 May be booked through travel agents.

KAUAI—NORTHSHORE

Bed and Breakfast Hawaii

P.O. Box 449, Kapaa, 96746
(808) 822-7771; (800) 733-1632
FAX (808) 822-2723

K01. This suite is surrounded by what the hosts call "real Hawaii." The river that adjoins the property has been beautifully landscaped, has its own waterfalls, and is perfect for a swim. Two outdoor hot tubs, eight-person Jacuzzi, and massage are also available to guests. The accommodation is a private guest house with a loft bed, kitchen, and queen-size brass bed on the main level. Living area has a VCR and stereo CD/cassette player. Indoor and outdoor showers also available. $105-130.

K39A. On the north shore of Kauai in Kalahiwai, hosts offer a room with a private entrance and adjoining bath. This home with three acres, horses, and golden retrievers, adjoins a 600-acre guava orchard. The accommodations are elegant, large, and sound-proofed, and include a king-size bed, double-head tiled shower, color TV, VCR, and a bay window that overlooks the grounds. Hosts encourage guests to explore the quiet, uninhabited grounds with waterfalls and streams that surround their lovely home. No smoking. Minimum three-night stay. $90.

K45. This bed and breakfast accommodation is perfect for guests who enjoy hiking, water sports, sightseeing, golf at Princeville, sunbathing, or long walks in a quiet unpretentious Hawaiian-style town. The house is a stylish two-story home on grounds abundant with coconut, plumeria, and papaya trees, and the views from the 1,000-square-foot deck and the lanai are breathtaking. Guests will instantly feel at home in one of the rooms, which all feature queen-size beds and private baths. Continental breakfast of fresh fruit, juice, and warm breads is served each morning on the second-story lanai that views Mt. Waialeale. $65-85.

K64. This private, handcrafted redwood cottage is carefully and comfortably equipped for any length of stay. It includes a kitchenette, a private full bath, queen-size bed in the bedroom, and a living room with a large futon couch. French doors open to deck that offers distant mountain, ocean and sunset views, and the area surrounding the cottage is full of thoroughbred horse farms and organic fruit, flower, and vegetable farms. No smoking inside. Children welcome. $85.

K74. A slightly rustic accommodation on a working farm is a great way to relax in Kauai. Hosts have added onto their barn by building a bedroom, efficiency kitchen, and private bath on the second story. Comfortable king-size bed and double sofa bed furnish the room. Grounds have a pineapple patch and orchid greenhouse that guests are welcome to explore. Children welcome. $80.

K81. This full apartment in Hanalei town is just 200 feet from the bay. Hostess lives in the upstairs half of a new two-story house across the street from the ocean. The whole downstairs portion of the house is for guests to enjoy. Guests have a private entrance, queen-size bed in the bedroom, private bath with tub and shower, fully equipped kitchen, and cozy living room. No breakfast is served here. Minimum stay is three nights. $90.

KAUAI—POIPU

Bed and Breakfast Hawaii

P.O. Box 449, Kapaa, 96746
(808) 822-7771; (800) 733-1632
FAX (808) 822-2723

NOTES: Credit cards accepted: A MasterCard; B Visa; C American Express; D Discover Card; E Diner's Club; F Other; 2 Personal checks accepted; 3 Lunch available; 4 Dinner available; 5 Open all year;

K22. Bed and breakfast is available in this plantation house with two lovely rooms with private baths. Relax in the screened-in lanai or in the common living room. Tropical continental breakfast is served in the formal dining room or on the lanai. Two-night minimum is preferred. Smoking outside. $70-75.

K24. Poipu Plantation is not really a bed and breakfast accommodation because 20 people can be accommodated in the small inn. Nine rooms feature a variety of bed sizes, face the garden or ocean, and have their own telephone lines. Two of the units are two-bedroom, two-bath suites. Guests are welcome to pick any fruit in season, and a barbecue, sunning area, and laundry facilities are available to guests. $80-125.

K25. This unhosted property is a two-bedroom condo at Makahuena. The complex is on the oceanfront at Makahuena Point but has no ocean view. Two bedrooms, two baths, fully equipped kitchen, TV, telephone, swimming pool, and tennis courts make this a perfect spot for families. Walk along the cliffs to Shipwreck Point or down the street to Poipu Beach Park. No breakfast is served. $85.

K29. Brand-new one-bedroom apartment overlooking the shore of Kauai is just minutes from the beach and in O'mao. Hosts have lived in Kauai over 15 years and can share information about beaches, dining, and shopping. The apartment is upstairs through a private entrance and has a kitchen, telephone, cable TV, queen-size bed in the bedroom, private bath, and sofa bed in the living room. Guests can enjoy ocean view from their private deck; and breakfast fixings are in the refrigerator. Smoking outside only. Minimum stay is three nights. $60.

K38. These special hosts visited Kauai and decided this is the place to live. Gail purchased this home with bed and breakfast in mind. She has designed and decorated each room for guests with beauty and comfort her primary goal. Just two blocks from the beaches and golf courses in Poipu, Michael and Gail offer two rooms for guests. Each room has a private entrance. Room one has a king-size bed and private bath with stall shower, TV/VCR, refrigerator, and microwave. There is a private outside lanai in a fenced back yard. Room two has a queen-size bed, private bath with shower and tub, along with a sitting room, TV/VCR, refrigerator, and microwave. This room also offers a private backyard sitting area. Breakfast is served each morning either in the room or on the lanai. Guests also have swimming pool and tennis court privileges in Poipu Kai. Two night minimum. No smoking. $65-75.

K43. This bed and breakfast offers one of the most spectacular views of Kauai's South Shore and Poipu. The three suites offer all the comforts of home with daily linen service, private bath, color TV, plush carpeting, private entrance, and continental breakfast. One suite offers a living room and a kitchenette. Home is very private but close to Garden Island. Kokee Mountain and Waimea Canyon are two of Kauai's "don't miss" attractions, and are only 20 miles west. $65-75.

K61. Enjoy a quiet, relaxing stay in lush surroundings on the South Shore of Kauai in a beautifully furnished room with a king-size bed, reading area, and breakfast nook with a coffee maker, small refrigerator, and microwave for light snacking. The bedroom is cool and airy with an adjoining private bath, and the home is within walking distance of the National Tropical Botanical Gardens. The host is a third-generation-born Hawaiian. $65.

6 Pets welcome; 8 Children welcome; 9 Social drinking allowed; 10 Tennis available; 11 Swimming available; 12 Golf available; 13 Skiing available; 14 May be booked through travel agents.

Gloria's Spouting Horn Bed and Breakfast

4464 Lawai Beach Road, 96756
(808) 742-6995

Oceanfront rooms are just steps from the surf, and hammocks under swaying palm trees overlook a secluded beach. This beachhouse is nestled between the sea and acres of sugarcane. Walk to the Spouting Horn, the natural wonder a few houses away, or to Poipu Beach, where swimming and snorkeling are at their best year round. Extended tropical continental breakfast.

Hosts: Bob and Gloria Merkle
Rooms: 3 (PB) $100-125
Continental Breakfast
Credit Cards: A, B
Notes: 2, 5, 9, 10, 11, 12

KAUAI—POIPU BEACH

Poipu Bed and Breakfast Inn and Vacation Cottages

2720 Hoonani Road, Poipu Beach, 96756
(808) 742-1146; (800) 22 POIPU
FAX: (808) 742-6843

Oceanside, in the heart of Poipu Beach, set amid lush tropical gardens and within walking distance of restaurants, shops, beaches, golf, and the Kiahuna Tennis Club and pool (complimentary to guests). All rooms have garden views, private baths (most with whirlpools), color cable TV/VCR, free videos, ceiling fans, and most have king-size beds. Also, three oceanfront luxury suites have private lanais, sitting areas, whirlpool tubs for two, and kitchenettes. One suite is air-conditioned and handicapped accessible. The main plantation house was built in 1933 and exquisitely renovated, winning a National Trust for Historic Preservation award. The cottages in Poipu and Kalaheo, from studio to four-bedroom, have kitchens and telephones. A tropical breakfast is served. All have guest laundry facilities. Weekly discounts.

Hosts: Dotti Cichon and Audry Nokes
Suites/cottages: 10 (PB) From $60
Continental Breakfast
Credit Cards: A, B, C, D, E, F
Notes: 2, 5, 8, 10, 11, 12, 14

KAUAI—PRINCEVILLE

Bed and Breakfast Hawaii

P.O. Box 449, Kapaa, 96746
(808) 822-7771; (800) 733-1632

K66. The Princeville area is known for the magnificent views, and this host home is on the famous golf course with distant ocean and mountain views all around. Just one mile from the Princeville Hotel, the host offers a studio on the ground floor of her two-story home. The bedroom has a king-size bed and additional futons are available. Private bath with tub and shower and kitchenette for light cooking. Three French doors lead to the outside lanai area. Very good for honeymoon couple or small family. This hostess really enjoys meeting visitors and helping them explore the beautiful Northshore. Two night minimum. No smoking. $80.

Go Native • • Hawaii

P.O.Box 11418, Hilo, 96721
(808) 935-4178; (800) 925-9065
FAX (808) 935-4178

Hale Ho'o Maha. This bed and breakfast's name means "House of Rest". It is on Kauai's famous Northshore, a five-minute drive from Lauai's most beautiful beaches and rivers. Panoramic view of the Kalalau mountain range and ocean can be seen from every window of the house. Guest accommodations include the Pineapple Room, with private entrance and full private bath and king-sized bed, and the Mango Room with a shared bath, cable TV, and double bed. $55-70.

Hale 'Aha—Bed and Breakfast in Paradise

Box 3370, 96722
(808) 826-6733; (800) 826-6733

NOTES: Credit cards accepted: A MasterCard; B Visa; C American Express; D Discover Card; E Diner's Club; F Other; 2 Personal checks accepted; 3 Lunch available; 4 Dinner available; 5 Open all year;

Newly built on one and one-half acres of golf resort property, this gracious home offers the serenity of 480 feet of fairway frontage overlooking the ocean and mountains of Kauai. Hale 'Aha hospitality also offers honeymoon privacy with separate decks and entrances. The 1,000-square-foot fabulous Penthouse Suite has its own balcony, with open beams and 360-degree views, including "Bali Hai" where *South Pacific* was filmed.

Hosts: Herb and Ruth Bockelman
Rooms: 4 (PB) $85-210
Continental Breakfast
Credit Cards: A, B
Notes: 2, 5, 9, 10, 11, 12, 14

Hale 'Aha

KAUAI—WAILUA

Bed and Breakfast Hawaii

P.O. Box 449, Kapaa, 96746
(808) 822-7771; (800) 733-1632
FAX (808) 822-2723

K5B. Makana Inn offers two separate units. A one-bedroom guest cottage with private bath and light cooking facilities has a private lanai overlooking Mount Waialeale and green pastures. The apartment is downstairs in the main house and has a bedroom, sitting area, private bath, and kitchenette. A generous continental breakfast is stocked in the kitchen upon arrival. Three miles from beach, golf, tennis, shopping, and dining. Two-night minimum stay. $95.

K14. This accommodation, tucked in the mountains above the town of Kapaa, is just right for those travelers looking for the tranquility of the lush mountains and valleys overlooking the Wailua River. Over 4,000-square-foot Japanese-style home offers two bed and breakfast rooms for guests. Guests may enter through the main house or through a private entrance off their lanai. The garden view room offers a queen-size bed and large private bath with tub and shower. Just down the hallway, glass doors lead to the multi-level deck with pool and hot tub. The master bedroom offers a queen-size bed and private full bath featuring dual showers. This room faces the deck and opens up to the pool. Futons may be provided for children ten years or older. Guests are served continental breakfast each morning and are welcome to use refrigerator, microwave, and toaster. Three night minimum. No smoking. $70-85.

K30. The Fern Grotto Inn is on the only private property in the middle of the Wailua River State Park. Breakfast is served on elegant English china in the Plantation Dining Room with its many windows providing a view of the Wailua River. Drift off to sleep in one of the three bedrooms on queen-size beds with designer sheets and comforter and piled high with white goose down pillows. European down/feather beds are provided for added comfort and luxury. Elegant adjoining private bath. $70-100.

K47. A spectacular 360 degree view of the ocean, Sleeping Giant, and Mount Waialeale can be seen from this bilevel cottage that sleeps up to six people. The bedroom has a queen-size bed, and there is a queen-size sofa bed in the living room. A private bath, living room, large screened-in lanai, and loft complete the accommodations. The hosts live in the main house. Children welcome. Baby equipment is available. Three-night minimum stay. $80.

6 Pets welcome; 8 Children welcome; 9 Social drinking allowed; 10 Tennis available; 11 Swimming available; 12 Golf available; 13 Skiing available; 14 May be booked through travel agents.

Bed and Breakfast Hawaii
(continued)

K50. Guests will be enthralled with this contemporary tropical elegant residence in Wailua Hui Hoani, the most desirable and sacred area of ancient Kauai, into which a commoner entered only at the behest of royalty. The view of the Wailua River from cliffside is gorgeous and Mount Waialeale provides a mystical backdrop. Opaekaa Falls and the Sleeping Giant (Nonou Forest Reserve) are opposite. Opportunities abound for reveling in nature. The host will escort guests down to the picturesque Waileileinani Falls if desired. Two bright, comfortable rooms are available, both with ceiling fans, garden views, and spacious tiled baths. One room has a queen-size bed and the other twin beds. Pamper body and soul each morning with breakfast on the lanai. Central to the entire island. A locked-off special-occasion suite is also available for five night minimum stays. This upstairs portion features a small private lanai with an expansive view, a spacious tiled bath, walk-in closet, and king-size bed. A mini kitchenette is downstairs. Three night minimum for rooms. No smoking. $65-75.

K62. The Orchid Hut is a modern cottage on a bluff overlooking the north fork of the Wailua River. The front door opens into a sitting room with color TV and kitchenette. Dine at the outdoor table or just relax and enjoy the scenic view of nature and the meticulously landscaped tropical garden. Perfect for couples and honeymooners, this beautifully furnished unit is just three minutes from the mouth of the Wailua River for water skiing, the beach, restaurants, and shopping. Nonsmoking adults only. Three-night minimum stay. $85.

K63. A private, cool, mountain bed and breakfast nestled behind Sleeping Giant

Mountain. The entrance takes guests into a cozy and comfortable recreation room with a fully equipped kitchen plus a fireplace. Three bedrooms have private adjoining baths. A continental breakfast is served at guests' wake-up time. Laundry service available. Enjoy fresh fruit right off the trees on a lovely, landscaped half acre. On Kauai with a scenic drive past Opaeka'a Falls and only five minutes from Wailua Bay. $50-55.

K70. For those travelers looking for the peace, tranquility, and isolation that the mountains above the town of Kapaa can provide, consider this private cottage secluded on the mountaintop above the town of Kapaa. Step out and the mountains embrace you, the lush green valley with small streams is all yours. The cottage consists of living room, kitchen, bedroom with king-size bed and full private bath. Simple country living. The host lives next door and is pleased to meet guests at the airport to be a guide to the mountain hideaway. No breakfast is served, although fresh fruits are provided when available. A sofa bed is available for an older child. Three night minimum. No smoking. $85.

KAUAI—WAIMEA

Bed and Breakfast Hawaii
P.O. Box 449, Kapaa, 96746
(808) 822-7771; (800) 733-1632
FAX (808) 822-2723

K42. In the heart of old Waimea and within walking distance of the store, pier, restaurants, and shops, this home is perfect for those who want to hike the Waimea Canyon and explore Kokee State Park. There is a private entrance into the cozy bedroom, sitting area, and light cooking area. Private bath. Three-night minimum stay. $60.

NOTES: Credit cards accepted: A MasterCard; B Visa; C American Express; D Discover Card; E Diner's Club; F Other; 2 Personal checks accepted; 3 Lunch available; 4 Dinner available; 5 Open all year;

LANAI—LANAI CITY

Bed and Breakfast Hawaii

P.O. Box 449, Kapaa, 96746
(808) 822-7771; (800) 733-1632
FAX (808) 822-2723

L1. Two of the bedrooms in this retired nurse's home are available for guests visiting the small, fairly remote island of Lanai. One room offers a double and single bed, while the other has a queen-size bed. There is a full and a half-bath shared by both hostess and guests. Both of the bedrooms are good-size and well-furnished. Hostess is an artist and has a fascinating collection of bottles and shells. $55-75.

MAUI—HAIKU

Affordable Paradise Bed and Breakfast Reservations

226 Pouli Road, 96734
(808) 261-1693; (800) 925-9065
FAX (808) 261-7315

N.D. This is a large one-bedroom cottage. Full kitchen, washer and dryer, bathroom, living room, separate bedroom. Cottage is completely separate from the host home. Private driveway for guests' convenience. Accommodations are in Haiku, a town near the mountains about a ten minute drive from the famous windsurfing beach, Hookipa. Haiku is about a 25-30 minute drive from Kahului airport. Paia town is nearby where there are wonderful restaurants and shops. Additional charge for extra persons. $65.

Bed and Breakfast Hawaii

P.O. Box 449, Kapaa, 96746
(808) 822-7771; (800) 733-1632

M7. This studio is on a quiet, secluded two-acre horse ranch among tropical flower gardens and banana orchards where vistas of Mount Haleakala and the ocean await you. The hosts offer a two-bedroom studio with one queen-size bed and one double bed, kitchen, dining, and living room. The living area has TV/VCR, stereo, and guests have use of washer/dryer. The hostess does not serve breakfast, but she will provide a welcome basket of fresh island fruits, bagels or muffins, coffee, tea, and juice. Three night minimum. Children welcome. No smoking. $70-80.

M34. This cottage is on a private estate in the lower slopes of upcountry Maui. Along the spectacular road to Hana in Haiku this bed and breakfast is central to all of Maui's bounty: 15 minutes from Paia's Baldwin Beach; ten minutes from Twin Falls and Hookipa Beach; and thirty minutes from the airport. The estate is on seven acres of totally unobstructed, panoramic ocean views through forests and pastures and is perfect for those travelers searching for the real and pristine Hawaii. The plantation cottage is newly renovated and decorated with antiques and art work in keeping with the rural area. Queen-size bed, private full bath, full kitchen, living room with TV/VCR, and private lanais. No breakfast is served. Guests are provided a welcome basket of on-site grown fruit together with breakfast items to enjoy at guests' convenience. The hosts live in a separate house on the estate and are available for assistance and recommendations. One night stays for $10 premium. Weekly rate available. $70-80.

M71. Experience bed and breakfast off the beaten path in upcountry Maui. Enjoy a continental breakfast with fresh island fruits, German breads and homemade pastries. This accommodation has a unique European charm and is decorated with antiques collected as the hosts traveled around the world. Three bedrooms, each furnished with a queen-size bed topped with down comforters, shared 1-1/2 bath for

Bed and Breakfast Hawaii (continued)

guests only and small refrigerator in each room. The hosts also offer a squash court in their home with 30 minutes of free court time a day. Two night minimum. Outside smoking only. $60-65.

M66. The hosts offer two accommodations on Huelo Point in upcountry Maui with spectacular views all the way up the coast to Hana and the summit of Haleakala. Each unit offers privacy and the opportunity to enjoy the natural beauty of Hawaii. At the main house a suite is offered on the ground floor with a private entrance. The large bedroom offers spectacular views and a queen-size bed. The bedroom opens onto a large covered deck and the kitchenette also opens to a deck—a special place for sunset teas. The large private bath has an elegant tiled tub looking into its own tropical garden—big enough for two. The cottage was originally a fisherman's cottage and then a barn. Now completely renovated, it sits amongst coconut palms on an acre of land and looks out through greenery to views on all sides: rolling pastures, the ocean, and the slopes of Haleakala. Here, guests can pick bananas a few feet from their door. Upstairs is a large bedroom and study area. Downstairs a full kitchen plus sitting room and solarium with a deck extending into the garden. Private bath includes a restored Victorian bathtub with glass all around. If guests prefer, an outdoor shower hot or cold surrounded by palms is available. A pull-out sofa is downstairs for a second couple. Two night minimum. Children only in cottage. No smoking. $95-125.

M79. A great escape awaits on the northshore of Maui at Huelo Point overlooking Waipio Bay. The hosts offer two rooms each with a queen-size bed, private bath, small refrigerator, toaster oven, and coffee maker. Rooms are decorated with wicker furniture and open to a private lanai. Separate from the main house, hosts offer a private two-bedroom cottage with queen-size bed and two twin beds along with a private bath. There is a full kitchen and laundry facilities available. The cottage is spacious with open beam ceiling and glass throughout. Mount Haleakala is the backdrop. Guests are welcome to enjoy the swimming pool and hot tub overlooking Waipio Bay. This secluded location is 30 minutes from Kahului airport and 20 minutes from restaurants and stores in Paia and world-class wind surfing at Hookipa Beach Park. Two night minimum for room. Three night minimum for cottage. $85-125.

Go Native·· Hawaii

P.O.Box 11418, Hilo, 96721
(808) 935-4178; (800) 925-9065
FAX (808) 935-4178

Hamakualoa. A tea-house cottage in a peaceful, unspoiled environment on the lush north shore of Maui. Here in the center of a tropical jungle is a pleasant bed and breakfast with views of both the ocean and mighty Haleakala. The lovely cottage is tastefully furnished with antiques and Oriental rugs. Bedroom, living room, kitchenette, and screened lanai. A unique feature—requiring a bit of adventure—is the free-standing bathhouse and outhouse, both to modern standards. Continental breakfast. $75.

Halfway to Hana House

P.O. Box 675, 96708
(808) 572-1176; FAX (808) 572-3609

A truly delightful bed and breakfast with exquisite ocean and mountain views, Halfway to Hana House is peaceful and quiet. The clean, airy studio has a separate entrance, spacious private bath, and covered patio. Its minikitchen has a microwave, hot plate, toaster, coffee maker, and refrigerator. The exotic tropical breakfast is served outdoors in a colorful, breezy setting of bamboo and palms overlooking the sea. Off the beaten path and on the way to Hana, in the proximity of freshwater pools and waterfalls, this is a memorable hideaway. Continental-plus breakfast.

Host: Gail Pickholz
Room: 1 (PB) $60-85
Continental Breakfast
Credit Cards: None
Notes: 5, 8 (over ten), 9, 11, 12, 14

MAUI—HANA

Affordable Paradise Bed and Breakfast Reservations

226 Pouli Road, 96734
(808) 261-1693; (800) 925-9065
FAX (808) 261-7315

G.S. There is one accommodation in Hana. This is a large, five bedroom home across the street from the ocean. House has full kitchen, living room, three bathrooms. Rates are flexible depending on the number of bedrooms used. Begin at $125.

S. and F. These accommodations are on the road to Hana. It is about a 30-40 minute drive from the airport. Guests must travel on some small, rock roads but it is worth every minute of travel. The view is something seen once in a lifetime!! It is absolutely incredible!! The house is directly on the ocean but about 300 feet above on a cliff. Look down the cliff into deep, blue waters. This is also a place where many whales are born and where guests should spend most of their time. There is a pool for the guests. The accommodations include a small, glass studio. There is a Japanese futon bed in the room, coffeemaker, hot plate, and toaster oven. The accommodations are small, but beauty is everywhere. There is a private, outdoor shower and small bathroom. The hosts also rent their home which is a two-three bedroom house

with a full kitchen and a bathroom with sunken tub. Glass windows which open to the ocean. Recommended for a few days there and a few nights on the other side of the island to do some touring. Breakfast is not served. $75-250.

Hana Plantation Houses

P.O. Box 249, 96713
(808) 248-7049; (800) 228-HANA
FAX (808) 248-8240

Discover Hana, the other Maui with waterfalls, secluded beaches, and hiking in bamboo jungles just steps from the tropical and beachfront cottages. Home to many celebrities, Hana offers exotic black-sand beaches, and natural sparkling pools once known only to Hawaiian royalty. Many of the homes feature spas, color TV, and kitchens. A cafe is in the botanical gardens.

Hosts: Blair Shurtleff and Tom Nunn
Rooms: 18 (PB) $60-185
Full and Continental Breakfasts
Credit Cards: A, B, C
Notes: 2, 3, 5, 8, 9, 10, 11, 14

Kaia Ranch Bed and Breakfast

P.O. Box 404, 96713
(808) 248-7725

Kaia Ranch Bed and Breakfast is in a tropical, botanical 27-acre garden setting. Two studios with queen-size beds and kitchens. Quiet and relaxing atmosphere. There is also a chalet on the big island of Hawaii. Near Volcano National Park. There are three rooms with queen-size and twin beds, and sitting room/kitchen. Two-night minimum stay. Host resides next door. No smoking.

Host: JoLoyce Kaia
Rooms: 5 (PB) $50-75
Continental Breakfast
Notes: 2, 5, 11, 12, 14 (ten percent)

6 Pets welcome; 8 Children welcome; 9 Social drinking allowed; 10 Tennis available; 11 Swimming available; 12 Golf available; 13 Skiing available; 14 May be booked through travel agents.

MAUI—KIHEI

Affordable Paradise Bed and Breakfast Reservations

226 Pouli Road, 96734
(808) 261-1693; (800) 925-9065
FAX (808) 261-7315

Ilse. Ilse has a very nice, clean, large one bedroom unit. Her property is in a new neighborhood but does back onto the highway. Guests love her place because of the friendly atmosphere and all that is available to them. She does not serve breakfast but usually keeps the refrigerator stocked with items to prepare yourself. There is a separate bedroom, living room, kitchen area, bathroom, and private entrance. Her home is about a five minute drive to Wailea Beach. German–speaking host. Unit can sleep up to four persons. Additional charge for extra people. Guests welcome children. $55.

Ulla. This home is in Maui Meadows in Kihei. This is about a five to ten minute drive to Wailea Beach. This unit is a cottage with living room, kitchen, bathroom, and separate bedroom. German-speaking host. Nice accommodations for the price. $65.

W.W.H. This house is beautifully designed and on the hills above Wailea in an area call Maui Meadows. The home has four different accommodations available. There is a pool in a very tropical setting for all the guests. Breakfast is served on the large lanai which overlooks the ocean and two other smaller islands. Breakfast is served Monday through Friday only for all guests. There are two bedrooms, one faces the mountains and the other faces the ocean. Each room has a private entrance and TV. The rooms share a bath between the two. The studio is on the lower level of the house. There is a kitchen area with stove, refrigerator, and coffeemaker. The studio has a TV, private entrance, and private bath. Lush, tropical surroundings. Small lanai to sit outside. There is also a cute, very original, Hawaiian–style cottage. The cottage is in the back of the property surrounded by very lush, tropical landscape. There is a small kitchen area, living area, bathroom, and sleeping in a loft above the main floor. $65-85.

Bed and Breakfast Hawaii

P.O. Box 449, Kapaa, 96746
(808) 822-7771; (800) 733-1632

M10. This unhosted one-bedroom condo on the ground floor of a small complex does not offer breakfast, but it is available for guests at an attractive rate. The condo is fully furnished, has all the appliances for cooking, including a dishwasher, color TV, and washer/dryer. There are two pools and a tennis court for guests to enjoy, and the unit could easily accommodate a family. A white sandy beach is across the street. $55.

M11. Come linger in the land of continuous summer in the island of Maui. Stay at a private cozy island cottage that sits at the base of Mount Haleakala, just three minutes from the beautiful beaches of Wailea, golf courses, and endless shopping. Tucked away from the crowds, this separate cottage is a sanctuary of complete peacefulness. The cottage is 600 square feet and newly remodeled, decorated with flares of Hawaii and Bali. It sleeps one to three comfortably with a full kitchen looking out onto the pool area. The refrigerator is stocked with fresh fruits grown on the property. Other amenities are cable TV, VCR, stereo with CD player, telephone, fans, barbecue, pool, private back yard, and washer/dryer. The bedroom features a queen-size bed, and an additional queen-size sofa bed is in the living room. No breakfast is served or provided. Three night minimum. Smoking outside only. $75.

M16. This a large home on the edge of of Ulapalakua Ranch is totally surrounded by decks. Breakfast is served on the upper deck, which provides a great place to whale-watch, and accommodations include two bedrooms decorated with Japanese antique furnishings. Both share a bath across the hall, and one has an ocean view, while the other views a tropical garden. A studio with a kitchenette, private entrance, and private bath, and a cottage with one bedroom both offer more room and more privacy for families. $65-85.

M17. Tennis buffs could not ask for a better place to vacation than sunny Kihei, with courts available right outside their door. The accommodation is a full apartment with one bedroom, private bath, kitchenette, living/dining room, cable TV. The home has an ocean view and is a short drive to beaches, golf, and restaurants. Three-night minimum stay. $65-100.

M22. This hideaway sits at the top of a hill overlooking the beautiful south beaches of Maui only two blocks from the beach. The hostess offers two accommodations for guests. The Pink Shell room is a spacious bedroom with a king-size bed and private full bath across the hall. The room is air-conditioned, has ceiling fans, telephone, and TV. The Blue Ocean room offers guests a private entrance, queen-size bed, private bath and private lanai, phone, TV, and ceiling fans. Continental breakfast is served on the lanai each morning surrounded by palm trees and bougainvillea. Guests are welcome to use the large Ohana room including kitchen area, dining, and living room. Two night minimum. No smoking. $55.

M24. In sunny Kihei on a half-acre in Maui Meadows, these hosts offer guests the opportunity to pick fruit from trees outside the door or swim in the black-bottom pool surrounded by tropical flowers. The accommo-dation is on the ground floor and has a private entrance and lanai area. The bedroom has a queen-size bed, and an additional queen-size sofa bed is in the living room. A fully equipped kitchen, washer/dryer, TV, VCR, stereo, and hot tub make this a great vacation spot for short or long stays. Three night minimum. Children over 12. Outside smoking only. $55-65.

M28. Luxuriate in the privacy of one of three guest rooms in this large home. One accommodation is a suite with two bedrooms, queen-size beds, minikitchen, and one and one-half baths. A third bedroom has a king-size bed that can convert to twins, and a loft bed, private entrance, and private bath with a huge all-tile sunken tub. Minimum stay is three nights. $85-110.

M30. In Maui Meadows only one mile from the beach resort area of Wailea and two miles from the shops and restaurants of Kihei. A separate cottage decorated in soft tropical colors is completely furnished with a queen-size bed, additional sofa bed, full kitchen, private bath, TV/VCR, telephone, and deck with view of the ocean and the island of Lanai. Outdoor barbecue also available for guest use. Guests will enjoy short or long stays on the sunny shore of Maui. No breakfast is served. Three night minimum. Children over 12. Outside smoking only. $85.

M32. This beautiful home offers a bedroom with a private bath and private entrance off the deck. The room has a queen-size bed and color TV. Another single bedroom is next door. Breakfast is usually served on the lanai where guests can enjoy a view of a well-landscaped tropical garden. The hostess loves to treat her guests to some delicious breakfast treats. Three-night minimum stay. $55.

6 Pets welcome; 8 Children welcome; 9 Social drinking allowed; 10 Tennis available; 11 Swimming available; 12 Golf available; 13 Skiing available; 14 May be booked through travel agents.

Bed and Breakfast Hawaii (continued)

M32A. This accommodation is a large garden-level apartment with fully equipped kitchen and two bedrooms with one bath. Ideal for a small family. The unit has lots of windows affording guests an excellent ocean view. The hostess serves breakfast on the lanai upstairs. One-week minimum stay. $80.

M38. This bed and breakfast accommodation offers two bedrooms on the second level of this oceanfront home. Each bedroom has a private entrance, private full bath, small refrigerator, color TV, and a queen-size bed. Breakfast is served downstairs, and guest rooms share a covered deck that overlooks the ocean and islands of Kahoolawe and Molokini. Minimum stay is three nights. No smoking. Children over 12. Resident dog. $70.

M75. This 350-square-foot studio is just one mile from the ocean and 12 miles from the airport. Guests can have it all. Oceanview, pool, and hot tub along with kitchenette that includes a refrigerator and microwave. Guest accommodation has a private entrance, private bath with shower, and king-size bed. Hosts are happy to stock the unit with homemade breads and fresh island fruits. Three night minimum. No smoking. $75.

Go Native•• Hawaii

P.O.Box 11418, Hilo, 96721
(808) 935-4178; (800) 925-9065;
FAX (808) 935-4178

365. Whale Watch House. This Hawaiian pole house in on a hill at the edge of Ulapalakua Ranch. Five minutes by car from the beach and resort areas of Wailea and Kihei. Four separate units, including two guest rooms with private baths. A private

"Ohana" studio on the garden level, has private entrance, queen-size beds, refrigerator, cable TV, and access to a poolside deck, separate kitchen, living area, bath, king-size bed, and ocean views. A thatched room cottage is an ideal honeymoon hideaway with private entrance, separate kitchen, living area, queen-size bed, optional Hide-a-bed, bath, and poolside deck. Each unit has access to a natural swimming pool with waterfall. $65-85.

MAUI—KULA

Bed and Breakfast Hawaii

P.O. Box 449, Kapaa, 96746
(808) 822-7771; (800) 733-1632
FAX (808) 822-2723

M52. A lovely home with two rooms in Kula awaits guests. The master bedroom has a private adjoining bath. The second room shares the bath in the hall. Lovely landscaping and large decks with magnificent views can be enjoyed here. Breakfast is served in the dining area. $55.

M53. Enjoy an elegant and comfortable stay with charming, gracious hosts. Up on the slopes of the dormant volcano, Haleakala, guests can enjoy two separate bedrooms with private baths and separate entrances to the sunny courtyard where breakfast is served. The home is new and specially designed with a bed and breakfast in mind. About 30 minutes by car to the beaches and 40 minutes to the airport, this is truly a quiet, relaxing place to enjoy Maui. Three-night minimum stay. $57.

Kula View Bed and Breakfast

140 Holopuni Road, P.O. Box 322, 96790
(808) 878-6736

Glorious sunrise and sunsets, sweeping ocean, mountain and garden views from every window of the guests' rooms nestled in "up-country" Maui makes a stay in Kula magical. Raised 2,000 feet above sea level, on the slopes of the dormant volcano, Haleakala. Kula View is surrounded by two acres of lush greenery, fruits, flowers, banana and coffee trees, and yet is close to the Kahului airport, shopping centers, hiking parks, and beaches. The upper-level suite awaits with a private entrance, deck, and private bath luxuriously appointed with a queen-size bed, reading area, wicker breakfast nook and mini-refrigerator. Kula View offers visitors personal old-fashioned Maui up-country-style hospitality. Two-night minimum stay.

Host: Susan Kauai
Room: 1 (PB) $75
Continental Breakfast
Credit Cards: None
Notes: 2, 5, 9, 11, 12, 14

Kula View

MAUI—LAHAINA

Bed and Breakfast Hawaii

P.O. Box 449, Kapaa, 96746
(808) 822-7771; (800) 733-1632
FAX (808) 822-2723

M2. A new ocean-front room is offered for guests at Oceanfront Bed and Breakfast. The private entrance room features a queen-size bed, private bath, TV, private lanai, and small refrigerator. Great snorkeling and beautiful swimming beaches are just minutes away both up and down the coast. Shopping and dining are minutes away in Lahaina and Kaanapali. Enjoy the sound of the surf as it breaks on shore and the rustling of palm trees as they sway to and fro in the balmy tropical breeze. Two night minimum. No smoking. $65.

M2A. An attached cottage, Ohana House, just 50 feet from the ocean. The cottage has a kitchenette and private bath and entrance. The refrigerator will be stocked with fresh fruit and juice. Two-night minimum stay. $60-85.

M5. This guest house is a private home created for those who appreciate a restful, relaxed holiday. Every guest room offers optimum privacy with color TV, refrigerator, ceiling fan, and air conditioning. All rooms have private baths, and one includes a Jacuzzi tub. The shared family room has a VCR, and the living room has a 350-gallon marine aquarium. A short walk to shops and restaurants as well as the beach, or relax beside the pool at the guest house. $75-95.

M44. This B&B is the exclusive hideaway choice for the discerning visitor in Lahaina, the gem of the West Side of Maui, with a large selection of shops, restaurants, and a mecca of art galleries. The host offers an elegant private home furnished in exquisite taste with artistic appointed details. Relax in a beautiful setting two blocks from Wahikuli Beach in guests' choice of a one-bedroom accommodation or studio with full access to a sparkling swimming pool and hot tub. Full wet bar and barbecue are also available. The light and airy one-bedroom apartment offers spacious living/dining room, queen-size bed plus queen-size Hide-a-bed, TV/VCR, fully equipped kitchen, and sliding glass door leading to pool and garden. The studio offers a queen-size bed,

6 Pets welcome; 8 Children welcome; 9 Social drinking allowed; 10 Tennis available; 11 Swimming available; 12 Golf available; 13 Skiing available; 14 May be booked through travel agents.

Bed and Breakfast Hawaii (continued)

TV/VCR, fully equipped kitchenette, private entrance and bath, and glass door to a private landscaped courtyard. Two night minimum. Children 12 and over. Outside smoking only. $95-125.

M78. Just two blocks from the beach in Lahaina, the hosts offer two accommodations for guests visiting the Valley Isle. A 475 square foot garden studio sits on a 1/4 acre lot with private deck and ocean view. Inside the cottage the bedroom has a queen-size bed and an additional queen-size sofa sleeper in the sitting area along with TV. There is a full private bath and kitchenette also available for guests. Just right for a small family or three traveling together. The studio is air-conditioned and hosts offer laundry facilities. In addition to their cottage, hosts offer a bed and breakfast room for guests. The bedroom has a queen-size bed and private bath and guests are treated to a continental breakfast in the morning. Two night minimum for B&B Room. Three night minimum for studio. No smoking. $50-95.

Go Native ·· Hawaii

P.O.Box 11418, Hilo, 96721
(808) 935-4178; (800) 925-9065;
FAX (808) 935-4178

Blue Horizons. A new (1994) inn, one block from the ocean between Kaanapali and Kapalua. Accommodations include three suites with living rooms, private kitchens and baths. Two guest rooms are also available. Color TV and air conditioning are included. A common living room and gourmet guest kitchen serve all guests. Pool, barbecue, and washer/dryer. $75-95.

Lahaina Guest House. In the heart of Lahaina, only one block from the beach, an el-

egant tropical-style home with delightful, easy-living appointments. Offers four personalized guest rooms, all with private baths and Jacuzzis, a spacious family room, and a relaxing living room. Full use of kitchenette stocked with gourmet cooking utensils and spices. Guests prepare own snacks, picnics, or meals. Continental breakfast is provided. $95.

Laha 'Ole. A wonderful oceanfront home in Lahaina right at the water's edge. Hosts offer one bedroom delightfully appointed with a queen-size day bed, TV, private bath, and ocean view. Accommodates two. Within walking distance of shops, restaurants, and entertainment. A delightful welcome awaits guests in the tradition of Aloha. Continental breakfast. $65.

Old Lahaina House

P.O. Box 10355, 96761
(808) 667-4663; (800) 847-0761
FAX (808) 667-5615

This convenient, relaxing place from which to visit Maui allows guests to enjoy the romantic, secluded ambience of a private pool in a tropical courtyard. Only steps from a serene beach and convenient walking distance to dining and shopping in historic Lahaina Town, a culturally rich and diverse old whaling town. Old Lahaina House is a home away from home, a special retreat, or an intimate piece of paradise!

Hosts: John and Sherry Barbier
Rooms: 4 (2 PB; 2 SB) $60-95
Continental Breakfast
Credit Cards: A, B, C
Notes: 2, 5, 8, 9, 10, 11, 12, 14

MAUI—PAIA

Bed and Breakfast Hawaii

P.O. Box 449, Kapaa, 96746
(808) 822-7771; (800) 733-1632
FAX (808) 822-2723

NOTES: Credit cards accepted: A MasterCard; B Visa; C American Express; D Discover Card; E Diner's Club; F Other; 2 Personal checks accepted; 3 Lunch available; 4 Dinner available; 5 Open all year;

M1. Million-dollar views of west Maui, the ocean, and two islands surround this house perched on top of a dormant volcano Hawaiians call the House of the Rising Sun. Breakfast is brought up each morning and served either on the private deck or in the room. The large studio has its own entrance, queen-size bed, wicker furniture, and private bath. There is a counter, sink, and refrigerator, so that picnic lunches can be prepared, but no cooking is possible. No smoking. Minimum two-night stay. $75.

M4A. This charming inn was built in 1850 for Maui's first doctor who came with the pineapple cannery. Newly refurbished, it sits among nearly one and one-half acres of pineapple fields and pine trees. Just 700 feet above sea level and just down the road from Hookipa Beach, this bed and breakfast includes full breakfast, twin or queen-size beds, and private baths in all rooms. Four rooms. $80.

M12. Right on the beach and convenient for sightseeing all of Maui, this large plantation-style home is in an exclusive neighborhood adjacent to the Maui Country Club. It offers a large guest room with a private bath. There is no ocean view from the home, but a short walk will take guests to a stretch of white, sandy beach good for walking. Usually the hosts' friendly dog will accompany guests. No smoking inside. $70.

Go Native ·· Hawaii

P.O.Box 11418, Hilo, 96721
(808) 935-4178; (800) 925-9065;
FAX (808) 935-4178

Huelo Point Flower Farm. Bed and breakfast on a two-acre stunning oceanfront estate set high on the edge of a cliff overlooking Waipio Bay on Maui's rugged north shore. Only one-half hour from Kahului, this breathtaking site offers bed and breakfast in the marvelous gazebo with queen-size futon, wicker furnishings, color TV, small refriger-

ator, hot plate, and many other amenities. The cliffside views from the outside hot tub are unforgettable. $95.

MAUI—UPCOUNTRY

Bed and Breakfast Hawaii

P.O. Box 449, Kapaa, 96746
(808) 822-7771; (800) 733-1632
FAX (808) 822-2723

M9. A delightful bed and breakfast with an ocean view setting, this studio is attached to the host's home in a quiet and private setting. The accommodation offers a separate entrance and is furnished with rattan furniture. Unit includes a double bed, private bath, ceramic tile floors, and a mini kitchen with a microwave, toaster, coffee maker, and refrigerator. The host serves a delicious Aloha-style breakfast on the patio that has an exquisite ocean view. $65.

M15. For the free-spirited, this glass gazebo is perched on the cliff overlooking Waipio Bay on Huelo Point. Inside is fully carpeted with a futon on the floor; nicely appointed with a stereo, small refrigerator, and coffee maker. The half-bath is hidden behind all-glass sliding doors. The hot/cold shower is outside in the newly landscaped gardens, and the large cement patio includes a hot tub shared with the hosts who live in the main house. Hosts rent the entire home when they are away. Three-night minimum stay. $95.

M26. Named Halemanu, which is Hawaiian for birdhouse, this home is perched 3,500 feet above the town of Kula and provides an awesome view of the island of Maui. The home is new and has lots of windows and decks. The guest room has its own private deck, private full bath, and queen-size bed. Breakfast is served in a sunny spot on the deck or in the dining area. $75.

6 Pets welcome; 8 Children welcome; 9 Social drinking allowed; 10 Tennis available; 11 Swimming available; 12 Golf available; 13 Skiing available; 14 May be booked through travel agents.

M55. Real island-style living can be enjoyed while staying here, just five minutes from Hookipa, the windsurfing beach of Maui. Overlooking pineapple fields, this studio has a separate entrance and sun deck with tropical flowers and fruit trees. The artwork was done by a famous Maui artist. Three-night minimum stay. $55.

MAUI—WAILUKU

Bed and Breakfast Hawaii
P.O. Box 449, Kapaa, 96746
(808) 822-7771; (800) 733-1632
FAX (808) 822-2723

M14. This comfortable home is only a few minutes from the Kahului airport. Two bedrooms, each with private entrance and shared bath. Outdoor patio is shared and includes a pool. No children. No smoking. Two-night minimum stay. $60.

M41. A modern-style home a quarter mile from the ocean and four miles from the airport. The main-floor bedroom has a separate deck with views of the ocean and Haleakala. The room has a king-size bed and private spa, bath, and shower. Host serves continental breakfast in the dining room or on the deck. Accommodation is close to golf course, and tee times are available with a two-day notice. Two night minimum. $45-55.

M70. Just a short distance from the airport and only two blocks from the beach makes this bed and breakfast perfect for those who want to explore Maui. The host offers a room furnished with twin beds that may convert to king-size and private full bath. Guests have use of a beautiful deck area with ocean view, a small kitchenette, and washer-dryer. Children over ten are welcome. Outside smoking only. Two night minimum stay. $60-75.

MOLOKAI—KAUNAKAKAI

Bed and Breakfast Hawaii
P.O. Box 449, Kapaa, 96746
(808) 822-7771; (800) 733-1632

MO2. Across the road from Father Damien's historic St. Joseph Church, lies Kamalo Plantation, a five-acre tropical garden and lime orchard at the foot of Mount Kamakou. Ancient Hawaiian stone ruins beside the plantation offer a unique sense of peace and tranquility. Stay at the country cottage with a fully equipped kitchen or, in the main house that has two rooms and a shared bath available. Enjoy a healthy Aloha breakfast including fresh tropical fruits and freshly baked bread (no breakfast in cottage). Experience Hawaiian living, plantation style. Three night minimum. No smoking. $65-75.

MO5. On two acres, this rustic cottage is for those guests who really want to get away from the hustle and bustle. A two-bedroom cottage is available for guests 30 miles from the airport and five miles from the ocean. There is ocean and mountain view. Full kitchen and bath with shower. No TV or telephone. No breakfast is served, however, coffee and tea are provided for guests. Two night minimum. Outside smoking only. $100.

Go Native •• Hawaii
P.O.Box 11418, Hilo, 96721
(808) 935-4178; (800) 925-9065;
FAX (808) 935-4178

Kamalo Plantation. A cozy cottage with accommodations on the grounds of the main house. Only ten miles east of Kaunakakai and across from the Father Damien Church. Lovely setting with mountains in background and cascading waterfall. Features studio accommodations with cooking facilities, twin beds, bath, and self-catered continental breakfast. Two adults maximum. Three-night minimum stay. $70.

OAHU—AIEA

Pearl Harbor View/ Pacific–Hawaii B&B

99-442 Kekoa Place, 96701
(808) 486-8838; (808) 487-1228; (808) 486-3187;
    (800) 999-6026
FAX (808) 261-6573; FAX (808) 487-1228

Home away from home. Convenient location. Complete two-bedroom upstairs apartment with kitchen and living room, in a private home. View to Pearl Harbor and a yard full of orchids and tropical flower and fruit trees. Beautifully furnished with valuable oriental antiques. King-size and single beds. Cable TV, phone, and more. Best value for the money. Five-day minimum stay. Also a reservation service for more than 400 bed and breakfasts across all islands of Hawaii. Monthly rates available.

Host: Doris Epp-Reichert
Suite: 1 (PB) $65
No breakfast
Credit Cards: A, B
Notes: 2, 5, 6, 8, 9, 14

OAHU—HAWAII KAI

Bed and Breakfast Hawaii

P.O. Box 449, Kapaa, 96746
(808) 822-7771; (800) 733-1632
FAX (808) 822-2723

O19. The hosts, mother and daughter, are from England and combine Old World charm with New World Aloha to make sure their guests have a good time. In this home there is a spacious, airy bedroom with private bath, color TV, and sliding door leading to the swimming pool. Breakfast with the hosts in the dining room No smoking. Two-night minimum stay. $60.

O26. Stay in this beautiful home in the best part of town, and enjoy a spectacular ocean view from this hillside setting. The whole downstairs level of the house is devoted to bed and breakfast and accommodates up to six people. Sliding glass doors facing the ocean run the length of each room. No smoking. Two-night minimum stay. $60.

OAHU—HONOLULU

Bed and Breakfast Hawaii

P.O. Box 449, Kapaa, 96746
(808) 822-7771; (800) 733-1632
FAX (808) 822-2723

O22. Outstanding views characterize this home on the edge of the beach and near local tourist attractions. Two upstairs suites with private baths and lanai are available for bed and breakfast guests. The Mauka Suite has an antique bed and a view of Diamond Head; the Makai Suite has two double beds and view of the garden. $75-100.

O30. This large family home is on the hillside of Manoa Valley. It is quiet, cool, and surrounded with birds. The guest room has a queen-size bed, futon, and shared bath. Breakfast is served in the dining room with a wraparound view of Waikiki, Honolulu, and Manoa Valley or on the spacious and sunny front deck. Close to bus stop. Smoking outside. $45.

O53. Built on a hillside about one-fifth of a mile from the University of Hawaii at Manoa, this home has two bed and breakfast rooms available for guests. Guests are encouraged to sit on the large deck and enjoy the city's skyline and ocean below. One room offers a queen-size bed and a private bath with a shower. The other room offers extra-long twin beds and a private half bath and shared shower. Smoking outside only. Children over ten years old. Minimum three-night stay. $55-65.

O53. The downstairs of this lovely home offers a peaceful, two-bedroom retreat ten minutes from Waikiki and Ala Moana

6 Pets welcome; 8 Children welcome; 9 Social drinking allowed; 10 Tennis available; 11 Swimming available; 12 Golf available; 13 Skiing available; 14 May be booked through travel agents.

Bed and Breakfast Hawaii (continued)

Shopping Center. No breakfast is served here, but 1,150 square feet of living space provides a family with a perfect vacation accommodations. The sleeping porch area has a queen-size bed, and the two bedrooms have double beds. Area includes living room, dining room, fully equipped kitchen, and full bath. Smoking outside only. Minimum stay is three nights. Discount for weekly stay. $95.

O54. Spectacular bird's-eye views of Diamond Head and the entire Honolulu coastline can be seen from the deck of this little studio. The studio has its own private entrance, and sliding glass doors off the lanai open into an air-conditioned bedroom with a king-size bed and a private bath. The hosts stock the mini-fridge with breakfast fixings. Smoking outside only. Preferred minimum stay is three nights. $65.

The Manoa Valley Inn

2001 Vancouver Drive, 96822
(800) 634-5115

An intimate country inn in lush Manoa Valley just two miles from Waikiki Beach. Furnished in antiques, each room is individually decorated to enhance its charm and personality. Continental breakfast buffet; fruits and cheese served evenings on the shady veranda. Call for rates.

Host: Lisa Hookano-Holly
Rooms: 8 (SB)
Continental Breakfast
Credit Cards: A, B, C, D, E
Notes: 2, 5, 14

OAHU-KAHALA

Bed and Breakfast Hawaii

P.O. Box 449, Kapaa, 96746
(808) 822-7771; (800) 733-1632

066. Guests will enjoy this beautiful Kahala home just two blocks from Wialae Golf Course, the beach, and the Kahala Hilton Hotel. The hosts, a kamaaina couple of several generations, will be happy to help with outing suggestions. There are two units available. The one-bedroom apartment on the ground floor is stylishly furnished with beautiful antiques. There is a queen-size bed and private bath. Full kitchen stocked with breakfast items and french doors that open to a covered lanai where guests may barbecue. There is a living room with TV and private phone. The upstairs two-bedroom apartment has a view of the golf course. The master bedroom has king-size bed; second bedroom has queen-size bed. A beautiful bath has tub and separate shower. Living area has TV, private phone, and full kitchen. Both apartments are air-conditioned and guests have use of swimming pool with some restricted family hours. No smoking. Three night minimum. No children. $125-225.

OAHU—KAILUA

Affordable Paradise Bed and Breakfast Reservations

226 Pouli Road, 96734
(808) 261-1693; (800) 925-9065
FAX (808) 261-7315

Beachlane B&B. This property is on the windward side of the island, a few steps from Kailua Beach, 30 minutes from the airport or Waikiki, and a 15-20 minute walk from Kailua town. Two bedrooms each have queen-size beds, TV and shared bath, with breakfast served daily. The studio has a private entrance and bath, king-size bed, kitchen area and TV, as well as outdoor furniture; no breakfast is served for studio guests. $45-65.

Garden Getaways. About a five-minute drive from Lanikai Beach, this property offers two accommodations. The Garden Cottage has a private entrance, private bath, small kitchen area, separate queen-size bedroom, futon sofa-bed and large TV. The Coconut Studio is attached to the main home, and has a private entrance, kitchen and sitting areas, TV, microwave, private bath and a small deck. No breakfast is served. $45-55.

Hamai. This home is just off Kailua Beach, and a 15-20 minute walk to town. The studio has a queen-size bed, private entrance and bath, small cooking area, TV and a large deck. An additional bedroom features a choice of king-size or twin beds, a private entrance and bath, and small cooking facilities (no specific kitchen-area). No breakfast for either accommodation. $45 60.

Kailua Beach B&B. This home is about a 15-20 minute walk from Kailua Beach, and on a bus line. The front bedroom has a private bath, TV and full-size bed; the pool bedroom opens onto the pool, and shares a bath with hosts. The hosts speak German and serve a wonderful breakfast (for bedroom guests only) each morning. The studio has its own entrance, king-size or twin beds, a private bath, TV, and small kitchen and sitting areas; there is also an outside barbecue area. $45.

All Islands Bed and Breakfast

823 Kainui Drive, 96734-2025
(808) 263-2342; (800) 542-0344
fax (808) 263-0308

Experience the real Hawaii! Over 475 private guest accommodations available on all Hawaiian islands. Excellent car rental and inter-island air fares. Rooms, studios and cottages available.

Rooms: $75-260
Cards: A, B, C
Notes: 2, 5, 7, 8, 9, 10, 11, 12, 14

Bed and Breakfast Hawaii

P.O. Box 449, Kapaa, 96746
(808) 822-7771; (800) 733-1632
FAX (808) 822-2723

O8A. Within walking distance of Kailua Beach on the canal, this studio apartment is perfect for longer stays. The bedroom area has a queen-size bed, there is a kitchenette for light cooking, and the bathroom has a two-person Jacuzzi. Share the pool with the host family. The hostess enjoys interaction with guests. Five-night minimum stay. Special weekly rates. $65.

O12. This accommodation allows guests to lounge by the swimming pool and enjoy a leisurely breakfast or sit in the hot tub after a day of sightseeing. One mile from Kailua Beach, this home gives guests their choice of two rooms with a shared bath between them. One room has a double bed, and the other has a twin bed. Guests are welcome to use the host's refrigerator to keep light snacks, and a crib is available. One-night stays have an extra $5 surcharge. $55.

O16. A gracious home on a private access road one-half block from a safe swimming beach. There are two large bedrooms with adjoining bath. This is ideal for couples traveling together. Two covered lanais surrounded by tropical foliage and a separate refrigerator are for guests. A neighborhood shopping center and restaurants are within walking distance. Adults only. $65.

O27. This home has easy access to the expansive Kailua Beach. The hosts offer an attractive studio apartment with a new screened-in lanai. The interior is furnished with twin beds and a loft. It has light kitchen facilities and an outdoor barbecue. Continental breakfast includes coffee, tea, fresh fruit, rolls, and juice. Resident pets. Three-night minimum stay. $60.

6 Pets welcome; 8 Children welcome; 9 Social drinking allowed; 10 Tennis available; 11 Swimming available; 12 Golf available; 13 Skiing available; 14 May be booked through travel agents.

Bed and Breakfast Hawaii (continued)

028. Just three blocks from the beach in Kailua, the host and hostess offer two rooms for guests. Each room has a private entrance, private bath/shower, air conditioning, cable TV, private phone, laundry, and kitchenette. The hostess enjoys providing all the little touches to make guests' stay very special. The Maile bedroom offers a king-size bed and the Banyon bedroom offers a queen-size bed. A lanai area with barbecue is available for guests. This accommodation is very close to a bus line. Upon arrival the hostess will provide three days breakfast fixings including juice, coffee, tea, creamer, and fresh fruit. Breakfast is not served. Three night minimum. No smoking. $60-65.

O31. An elegant oceanfront home opens in front on a large pool with Jacuzzi and in back opens to the ocean. The home is spacious and has comfortable areas for guests to relax after a day of sightseeing. Bedrooms have private bath and private entrance from the pool/courtyard area. Each is decorated with an antique and tropical mixture. A deluxe continental breakfast is served. $120.

O32. This bed and breakfast apartment is attached to the host's home, but has a private entrance and private porch with a two-person swing. The unit consists of a living room, bedroom with a queen-size bed, and a private full bath. The unit also has a microwave, refrigerator, toaster, coffee maker, TV, and radio. Kailua Beach is a five-minute drive. No breakfast is included in this accommodation. $55.

O42. A block away from Kailua Beach, guests have two newly remodeled bedrooms available with private baths, TV, microwave, and refrigerator, plus use of the swimming pool. Breakfast supplies for three days are stocked to use at leisure. Three-night minimum stay. $55-65.

042C. This brand new, completely self-contained cottage is available for guests looking for a vacation rental cottage. Manu Mele is a 642-square-foot cottage with a full kitchen and bath. It is in Enchanted Lakes, Kailua, a five-minute drive to the beach. Decorated in the modern style, the cottage has ceramic floor tile throughout the living room, dining room, kitchen, and bedroom. Bedroom features a queen-size bed. Parking and laundry facilities are also available. No breakfast is served. Five night minimum. No smoking. $75.

O44. One block from Kailua Beach, hosts offer three sets of accommodations. The first is a separate one-bedroom cottage with a complete kitchen, two double beds, color TV, and a private bath and patio area. The second accommodation is a studio attached to the house with a kitchenette, private bath, private patio, and private entrance. The third and newest studio can sleep only two in a double bed and also has a light kitchenette and color TV. Minimum four-night stay. No breakfast is served. $55-75.

O57. Within walking distance from Kailua Beach is this two-bedroom apartment on the ground level of a two-story home. Two bedrooms, a private bath, and complete kitchenette. The living room is complete with TV and rattan furniture, and has sliding glass doors to the patio and fenced yard. Perfect for a family of four. Smoking outside. $75; $100 for four.

O63. This complete studio cottage is separate from the main house and one block from Kailua Beach. It is well kept and nicely furnished with tropical rattan. The cottage sits on the edge of the swimming pool as well as an attractive gazebo. There is a queen-size bed, full bath, TV, table and chairs, light cooking area, and telephone. Smokers accepted. No children. Minimum three-night stay. $65.

Go Native • • Hawaii

P.O.Box 11418, Hilo, 96721
(808) 935-4178; (800) 925-9065;
FAX (808) 935-4178

HI 251. This accommodation is a garden level, two-bedroom facility just four blocks from Kailua beach. Guests will have a complete kitchen, outside lanai with grill, TV, telephone and washer/ dryer. A queen-size bed, twin beds, and one bath are available. Continental breakfast supplies are provided. Additional charge for extra person(s). No smoking. $100.

Papaya Paradise

395 Auwinala Road, 96734
(808) 261-0316

Private, quiet, tropical, and near all attractions. Swim in the 20' by 40' pool. Relax in the Jacuzzi. Stroll Kailua Beach. Enjoy breakfast on the lanai surrounded by Hawaiian plants, trees, and flowers with Mount Olomana in the background. Rooms with private bath, private entry, refrigerator, air conditioning, and TV. Tennis, golf, and all kinds of water sports nearby. Just 20 miles from Waikiki and the Honolulu airport. Minimum three-night stay.

Hosts: Bob and Jeanette Martz
Rooms: 2 (PB) $65-75
Continental Breakfast
Credit Cards: None
Notes: 2, 5, 7, 8, 9, 10, 11, 12

Bed and Breakfast Hawaii

P.O. Box 449, Kapaa, 96746
(808) 822-7771; (800) 733-1632
FAX (808) 822-2723

O56. This bed and breakfast is a luxuriously furnished private home with beautiful views of Kanehoe Bay from the living room, dining room, and swimming pool area. The hosts offer two bedrooms, each of which has a private bath. One room offers twin beds with a bath across the hall, and the other room offers a double bed and has an adjoining bath. Ample, relaxed breakfasts are served each morning. Tea is served in the late afternoon. $55-60.

Emma's Guest Rooms

47-600 Hui Ulili Street, 96744
(808) 239-7248; FAX (808) 239-7224

Modern spacious home in beautiful Temple Valley on Oahu's lush windward shore. This beautiful valley, guarded by high mountains and filled with songbirds, surrounds guests with peace and tranquility. Features include a private guest entrance, kitchenette, TV lounge, and dining area. Color brochure available upon request.

Hosts: Stanley and Emma Sargeant
Rooms: 3 (PB) $95/night
No Breakfast
Notes: 5, 8, 9, 10, 11, 12, 14

Go Native • • Hawaii

P.O.Box 11418, Hilo, 96721
(808) 935-4178; (800) 925-9065;
FAX (808) 935-4178

Windward. A spacious and delightful tropical home with continental ambience. In the bedroom community of Kaneohe, it features two guest bedrooms with private baths. It is beautifully furnished with antiques and has a swimming pool and library. It overlooks Kaneohe Bay and ancient

Heeia fish pond. Continental breakfast and afternoon tea are served. $55-60.

OAHU—LAIE

Bed and Breakfast Hawaii
P.O. Box 449, Kapaa, 96746
(808) 822-7771; (800) 733-1632

046-LAIE. For those who wish to experience life on the Northshore of Oahu, this is the perfect B&B. On the beautiful beach of Laie Bay, this is the perfect example of Hawaiian paradise where all ocean sports are available and sun bathing on the white sand beach is a sensual delight. A large studio is offered for guests with separate entrance, private bath, and lanai with Jacuzzi. A double bed plus queen-size sofa bed are available. Use of the main kitchen is available for light cooking. The hosts want guests to feel like this is a home in the islands. Three night minimum. No smoking. $60.

OAHU—LANIKA

Bed and Breakfast Hawaii
P.O. Box 449, Kapaa, 96746
(808) 822-7771; (800) 733-1632

035. Lanikai Beach is one of the most photographed beaches in Hawaii. Not only is the view magnificent, this beach is great for swimming. The hostess offers two rooms at her home 20 feet from the ocean. One bedroom offers a queen-size bed with private bath and the other a smaller room with a double bed and shared bath. The hostess is an artist and her home reflects her casual lifestyle. Guests may use the kitchen for light food preparation and a refrigerator is available. Organic gardens provide fresh greens for guests and the hostess will serve breakfast. Three night minimum. No smoking. $60-75.

OAHU—PEARL CITY

Bed and Breakfast Hawaii
P.O. Box 449, Kapaa, 96746
(808) 822-7771; (800) 733-1632
FAX (808) 822-2723

O1A. This bed and breakfast home is just eight miles from Honolulu International Airport and offers an outstanding accommodation for its guests. The home is near the Pearl City Golf Course. The unit is a garden-level apartment with a separate entrance and private bath. A large pool is just outside the door. Children who know how to swim are welcome. $65.

OAHU—WAIMANALO BEACH

Go Native • • Hawaii
P.O.Box 11418, Hilo, 96721
(808) 935-4178; (800) 925-9065;
FAX (808) 935-4178

Orchid Row. A charming hideaway bordered by the majestic Koolau Mountain Range at the footstep of Mount Olomana in the quiet countryside of Waimanalo (14 miles outside Waikiki). On an orchid farm, this marvelous apartment-studio features a private bath, queen-size bed, cable TV, cozy kitchenette, and is perfectly decorated. Only minutes away from the best beaches on Oahu. Here is bed and breakfast with the peace and privacy of Old Hawaii. Continental breakfast. $65.

Idaho

Idaho Heritage Inn

BOISE

Idaho Heritage Inn

109 West Idaho, 83702
(208) 342-8066

This inn was a former governor's mansion and home to the late Senator Frank Church. In the historic Warm Springs District, the inn enjoys the convenience of natural geothermal water. It is surrounded by other distinguished turn-of-the-century homes, but it is also within walking distance of downtown, beautiful parks, museums, and Boise's famous Greenbelt River walkway. All rooms have been comfortably and charmingly appointed with private baths, period furniture, and crisp linens.

Hosts: Phyllis and Tom Lupher
Rooms: 6 (PB) $59-89
Full Breakfast
Credit Cards: A, B, C, D
Notes: 2, 5, 9, 10, 11, 12, 13, 14

COEUR D'ALENE

Cricket on the Hearth

1521 Lakeside Avenue, 83814
(208) 664-6926

Al and Karen Hutson have brought the beauty of Coeur d'Alene indoors and added a touch of country living, giving the inn an aura of "down home." The five guest rooms, three with private baths, are delightfully decorated to carry out a theme, setting the mood for a perfect getaway.

Hosts: Al and Karen Hutson
Rooms: 5 (3 PB; 2 SB) $50-80
Full Breakfast
Credit Cards: None
Notes: 2, 5, 9, 10, 11, 12, 13, 14

Greenbriar Inn

315 Wallace, 83814
(208) 667-9660

Built in 1908, the Greenbriar is Coeur d'Alene's only nationally registered inn. Just four blocks from downtown and five blocks from the lake, the Greenbriar reflects the residential charm of years gone by.

Greenbriar Inn

6 Pets welcome; 7 Smoking allowed; 8 Children welcome; 9 Social drinking allowed; 10 Tennis available; 11 Swimming available; 12 Golf available; 13 Skiing available; 14 May be booked through travel agents.

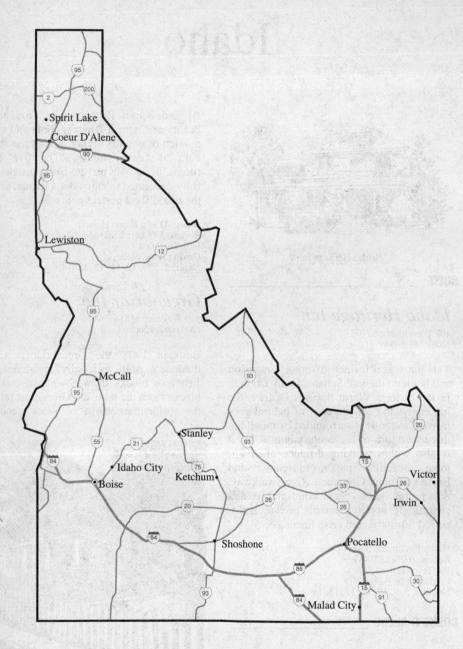

Idaho

Surrounded by 40-foot-high maples, guests enjoy the spa outside, the wine and tea hour late in the afternoon, and a famous three-course gourmet breakfast in the morning.

Host: Kris McIlvenna
Rooms: 8 (6 PB; 2 SB) $55-95
Full Breakfast
Credit Cards: A, B, C, D
Notes: 2, 4, 5, 8, 9, 10, 11, 12, 13, 14

Gregory's McFarland House Bed and Breakfast

601 Foster Avenue, 83814
(208) 667-1232

Surrender to the elegance of this award-winning historical home, circa 1905. Breakfast is gourmet to the last crumb, and the cookie jar is always full. Guests will find an ideal blending of beauty, comfort, and clean surroundings. Jerry Hulse of the *Los Angeles Times* says, "Entering Gregory's McFarland House is like stepping back 100 years to an unhurried time when four-posters were in fashion, and lace curtains fluttered at the windows." Private baths and air conditioning. Weddings. Resident minister and professional photographer available.

Hosts: Winifred, Carol, and Stephen
Rooms: 5 (PB) $75-120
Full Breakfast
Credit Cards: A, B
Notes: 2, 5, 10, 11, 12, 13, 14

Katie's Wild Rose Inn

E. 5150 Coeur d' Alene Lake Drive, 83814
(208) 765-WISH (9474)

Katie's welcomes all who enjoy a cozy, warm atmosphere. The house is decorated country cottage-style, offering four guest rooms. The suite includes a view of the lake, large spa bathtub, and queen-size bed. Three and one-half miles east of Coeur d'Alene, it is on the projected Centennial Trail for hikers and bicyclists. Relax and enjoy the library, TV, or a game of pool. Weddings are a specialty; there is a resident minister.

Hosts: Lee and Joisse Knowles
Rooms: 4 (2 PB; 2 SB) $55-95
Full Breakfast
Credit Cards: A, B
Notes: 2, 5, 10, 11, 12, 13

Katie's Wild Rose Inn

Someday House Bed and Breakfast

790 Kidd Island Bay, 83814
(208) 664-6666

Quiet and relaxed, this sophisticated home, decorated with simple country charm, was designed by the innkeeper's husband. It commands a 180-degree view of Lake Coeur d'Alene, the city, and surrounding mountains. Breakfast is a treat to be enjoyed on the patio or dining room overlooking the lake. Five cozy rooms have choice of Jacuzzi tub or shower. Private beach one mile down the hill. Twelve miles south of town—truly a country inn bed and breakfast.

Host: Sue Fall
Rooms: 5 (3 PB; 2 SB) $55-85
Full Breakfast
Credit Cards: None
Notes: 2, 5, 8 (over 12), 9, 11, 12, 13

NOTES: Credit cards accepted: A MasterCard; B Visa; C American Express; D Discover Card; E Diner's Club; F Other; 2 Personal checks accepted; 3 Lunch available; 4 Dinner available; 5 Open all year; 6 Pets welcome; 7 Smoking allowed; 8 Children welcome; 9 Social drinking allowed; 10 Tennis available; 11 Swimming available; 12 Golf available; 13 Skiing available; 14 May be booked through travel agents.

IDAHO CITY

Idaho City Hotel

215 Montgomery Street, P.O. Box 70, 83631
(208) 392-4290

Completely renovated since its turn-of-the-century construction, this tiny hotel has retained its quaint charm and rustic flavor, while providing modern-day comfort. Each of the five rooms offers one double bed, phone, cable TV, and private bath with shower. The hotel is in the heart of historic Idaho City—an old gold mining town in the mountains near Boise.

Hosts: Don and Pat Campbell
Rooms: 5 (PB) $35-46.50
Credit Cards: A, B, C, D, E
Notes: 2, 5, 6, 7, 8, 9, 11, 13

IRWIN

Swan Valley Bed and Breakfast

535 Swan Lane, P.O. Box 115, 83428
(800) 241-SWAN; (208) 483-4663

In scenic Swan Valley, Idaho, on the bank of the beautiful south fork of the Snake River. Guests can enjoy world-famous trout fishing, bicycle riding, hiking, floating, snow skiing, and much more. Only 55 minutes from Jackson Hole, Wyoming, or Idaho Falls. Spacious accommodations are offered with private bath, river view, comfortable common area, and a spa overlooking the river. Full breakfast is provided. Children welcome. Outside smoking only.

Rooms: 4 (PB) $65-85
Full Breakfast
Cards: A, B, C, D
Notes: 2, 5, 7 (limited), 8, 9, 11, 12, 13, 14

KETCHUM

The Idaho Country Inn

134 Latigo Lane, 83340
(208) 726-1019

The Idaho Country Inn is on a lofty knoll halfway between Ketchum and Sun Valley. Designed with a love of Idaho, the inn features ten spacious guest rooms, each named and decorated with a different Idaho theme. The large living room with river-rock fireplace gives spacious yet cozy ambience. A full breakfast is served each morning including "something healthy" and "something decadent." Each room has a spectacular view, and the view from the large outdoor hot tub is breathtaking. ABBA four-crown rating.

Rooms: 10 (PB) $85-185
Full Breakfast
Credit Cards: A, B, C
Notes: 2, 5, 9, 10, 12, 13, 14

LACLEDE

Mountain View Farm Bed and Breakfast

P.O. Box 0150, 83841
(208) 265-5768; (800) 254-5768

On eight picturesque acres, this circa 1900 Victorian farmhouse welcomes its guests with four seasonal theme guest rooms, complete with country antiques, hand-stenciled walls, and Victorian craft accessories. A full breakfast featuring farm-fresh eggs and home-baked goodies is served in the dining room by candlelight. Only 15 minutes from Sandpoint and within walking distance to the Pend Oreille River. Come on back to where quiet can still be heard.

Host: Toni Brown
Rooms: 4 (S2B) $55-65
Full Breakfast
Credit Cards: A, B
Notes: 2, 5, 8, 10, 11, 12, 13, 14

River Birch Farm

P.O. Box 0280, 83841
(208) 263-3705; (800) 700-3705

Imagine gazing from the parlor windows of a large turn-of-the-century home, and visualize a panoramic view of a wide river surrounded by meadows, forests, and mountains. Experience a fun-filled summer holiday swimming and canoeing from the dock facilities. Relax in the Jacuzzi. Capture the rich history of the area during a colorful autumn weekend. Spend a quiet winter evening relaxing by the fireplace after skiing. Look for spring wildflowers during a leisurely vacation. Come stay for any occasion and enjoy the scenic serenity, friendly people, and special hospitality of northern Idaho.

Hosts: Charlie and Barbro Johnson
Rooms: 5 (4 SB; 1PB) $65-130
Full Breakfast
Credit Card: A, B
Notes: 2, 5, 9, 11, 12, 13, 14

River Birch Farm

LEWISTON

Shiloh Rose
Bed and Breakfast

3414 Selway Drive, 83501
(208) 743-2482

The Shiloh Rose, decorated in a warm, country/Victorian-style, offers a spacious three-room suite as a home away from home. Lace curtains, fragrant potpourri, and fresh roses in season invite guests to linger. Have morning coffee in the sitting room with a real wood-burning stove. Browse through the overflowing bookshelves, enjoy the TV/VCR, or the grand piano. A com-

plete gourmet breakfast is served in the dining room or on the deck overlooking the valley. The views are fantastic. Guests will love it here.

Suite: 1 (PB) $70-75
Full Breakfast
Credit Cards: A, B
Notes: 2, 5, 9, 10, 11, 12, 13

MALAD CITY

Chantilly

63 South Main, 83252
(208) 766-4961

A turn-of-the-century, country-Victorian house in a small town in southwest Idaho. The charming rooms are decorated with antiques and furnished to offer a comfortable stay.

Hosts: Joyce and Richard Mizrahi
Rooms: 5 (1 PB; 4 SB) $50-60
Full Breakfast
Credit Cards: A, B, D
Notes: 2, 8, 9, 11, 12

McCALL

Northwest Passage

P.O. Box 4208, 201 Rio Vista Boulevard, 83638
(208) 634-5349; (800) 597-6658

Originally built in 1938 for the crew of the film *Northwest Passage* starring Spencer Tracy, this beautiful pine lodge is nestled in tall ponderosa pines. Six guest rooms with private baths and a guest apartment that sleeps up to 12 with a kitchen, fireplace, and TV. Area activities: water sports on Payette Lake, fishing, snowmobiling, skiing, hunting, golf, tennis, mountain biking, and hiking. Groups of up to 22 welcome!

Hosts: Steve and Barbara Schott
Rooms: 6 (PB) $70-80
Apartment: 1 $150
Full Breakfast
Credit Cards: A, B, D
Notes: 2, 4, 5, 6, 7, 8, 9, 10, 11, 12, 13, 14

6 Pets welcome; 8 Children welcome; 9 Social drinking allowed; 10 Tennis available; 11 Swimming available; 12 Golf available; 13 Skiing available; 14 May be booked through travel agents.

POCATELLO

Liberty Inn—A Victorian Bed and Breakfast

404 South Garfield, 83204
(208) 232-3825

The hosts have taken an elegant turn-of-the-century Victorian home in historic Pocatello and created an exceptional lodging experience. Built in 1893, the inn combines the spirit of yesterday with the comforts of today. Appointed with original furnishings, guest rooms reflect grand turn-of-the-century living. Liberty Inn is in the historic district and within walking distance of many fine shops and restaurants.

Hosts: Scott and Linda Murry
Rooms: 4 (PB) $55
Full Breakfast
Credit Cards: A, B, C
Notes: 2, 12, 13

SHOSHONE

Governors Mansion Bed and Breakfast Inn

315 South Greenwood, 83352
(208) 886-2858

First occupied in 1906, the Governor's Mansion was built by the Gooding family. It was owned by Thomas Gooding, older brother of Frank Gooding, once Governor of Idaho. Come to a small-town atmosphere 55 miles from Sun Valley and near many Idaho attractions, including Shoshone Falls and the Craters of the Moon. Hosts offer a friendly, home-like atmosphere and breakfast to guest's order. Open year-round. Air-conditioned.

Host: Edith Collins
Rooms: 7 (2 PB; 5 SB) $45-65
Full Breakfast
Credit Cards: None
Notes: 2, 5, 6, 7, 8, 9

SPIRIT LAKE

Fireside Lodge

P.O. Box 445, 83869
(208) 623-2871

The Fireside Lodge, built in 1907, was one of the first buildings in Spirit Lake. The lodge is right on the banks of Spirit Lake with a great northwestern view which includes wildlife on certain days and great fishing; guests can use a canoe. The upstairs rooms are decorated in country-Victorian with lots of unique visiting and resting areas. A restaurant and gift shoppe are on the main floor with unusual decor and unique dinner music. Guests will enjoy the warm atmosphere.

Hosts: Rod and Nancy Erickson
Rooms: 4 (SB) $45-50
Full Breakfast
Credit Cards: A, B
Notes: 2, 3, 4, 11, 12, 13

STANLEY

Idaho Rocky Mountain Ranch

HC 64, Box 9934, 83278
(208) 774-3544

One of Idaho's oldest and finest guest ranches, offering comfortably decorated lodge and cabin accommodations. Beautiful mountain vistas from the front porch. Delightful meals served by a friendly staff. Hiking, fishing, horseback riding, mountain biking, rafting, cross-country skiing, wildlife viewing, and much more, both on and off the ranch. Fifty miles north of Sun Valley in the Sawtooth National Recreation Area and on Highway 75. Brochure available; weekly rates available. Closed April 15 through May 31 and September 15 through November 25.

Hosts: Bill and Jeana Leavell
Rooms: 21 (PB) $85-210
Credit Cards: A, B
Notes: 2, 3, 4, 8, 9, 11, 13

NOTES: Credit cards accepted: A MasterCard; B Visa; C American Express; D Discover Card; E Diner's Club; F Other; 2 Personal checks accepted; 3 Lunch available; 4 Dinner available; 5 Open all year;

VICTOR

Moose Creek Ranch

Box 350, 215 East Moose Creek Road, 83455
(208) 787-2784; (800) 676-0075
FAX (208) 787-2284

Come and enjoy the natural wonders of
Teton-Yellowstone Country from the secluded comfort of the Moose Creek Ranch.
A traditional Dude Ranch in the
summer, only 35 minutes from either Teton

Village or Grand Targhee ski resorts and
Nordic skiing right out the cabin door. Full
sit-down breakfast. Hot tub and sauna, and
use of the lodge for fireplace viewing (no
television).

Hosts: Kelly and Roxann Van Orden
Rooms: 9 (PB)
Credit Cards: A, B, C
Notes: 2, 3, 4, 8, 9, 13, 14

6 Pets welcome; 8 Children welcome; 9 Social drinking allowed; 10 Tennis available; 11 Swimming available;
12 Golf available; 13 Skiing available; 14 May be booked through travel agents.

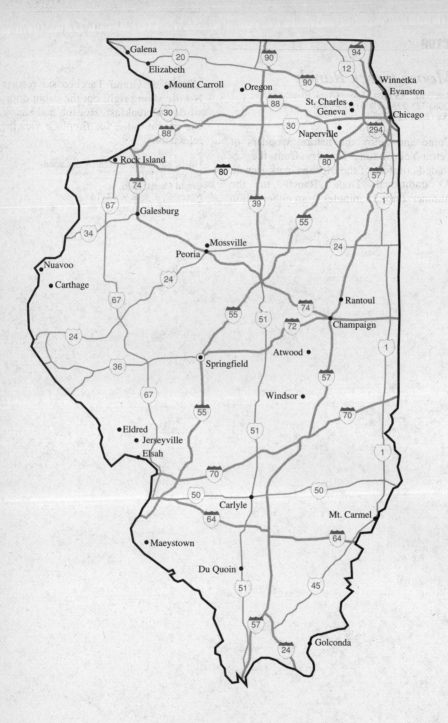

Illinois

Illinois

ATWOOD

Harshbarger Homestead

Rural Route 1, Box 110, 61913
(217) 578-2265

A casual, quiet, and comfortable country home amid central Illinois prairie. Ten miles from Illinois' largest Amish community. Many craft and antique shops. Visitors will enjoy beautiful herb and flower gardens, interesting coveys of collectibles throughout the house, and a 150-year-old log cabin displaying antiques with family history. Special playroom and sleeping quarters for children. Fun for all ages. Tent and camping accommodations and family rates are available.

Host: Shirley Harshbarger
Rooms: 3 (S2B) $45
Continental Breakfast
Credit Cards: F
Notes: 2, 8, 9

CARLYLE

Country Haus

1191 Franklin, 62231
(618) 594-8313; (800) 279-4486

1890s Eastlake bed and breakfast. Country hospitality makes a stay in one of five guest rooms, each with a private bath, a special memory. Full breakfast is served in the dining room, robes are provided for the trip to the hot tub, and a well-stocked library with TV is here for guests to enjoy. Only 55 miles east of St. Louis.

Hosts: Ron and Vickie Cook
Rooms: 5 (PB) $45-55
Full Breakfast
Credit Cards: A, B, C, D, E
Notes: 2, 5, 10, 11, 12, 13 (water), 14

CARTHAGE

The Wright Farmhouse

Rural Route 3, 62321
(217) 357-2421

Comfortable, quiet rooms with period furnishings in a restored 19th-century home on a working farm. Country charm plus private baths, air conditioning, and private guest entrance. Nearby attractions include historic town square and courthouse and the scenic Mississippi River.

Hosts: John and Connie Wright
Rooms: 4 (PB) $31.80 58.30
Continental Breakfast
Credit Cards: A, B
Notes: 8, 9, 10, 11, 12

CHAMPAIGN

Barb's Bed and Breakfast

606 South Russell, 61821
(217) 356-0376

This cozy cottage is in a quiet, attractive neighborhood with quick access to the University of Illinois. The comfortable guest rooms feature antiques, ceiling fans, and handmade quilts, and they share a parlor with a fireplace. Delicious breakfasts are served in the dining room. The twin cities and nearby communities offer a wide variety of things to

NOTES: Credit cards accepted: A MasterCard; B Visa; C American Express; D Discover Card; E Diner's Club; F Other; 2 Personal checks accepted; 3 Lunch available; 4 Dinner available; 5 Open all year; 6 Pets welcome; 7 Smoking allowed; 8 Children welcome; 9 Social drinking allowed; 10 Tennis available; 11 Swimming available; 12 Golf available; 13 Skiing available; 14 May be booked through travel agents.

see and do. Antique shops, theaters, museums, an outlet mall, fishing lakes, swimming, and golf are all nearby.

Hosts: Barbara and Merle Eyestone
Rooms: 2 (SB) $45
Continental Breakfast
Credit Cards: None
Notes: 2, 9, 10, 11, 12

The Golds
Bed and Breakfast

2065 County Road 525 East, 61821
(217) 586-4345

Restored 1874 farmhouse with antique furnishings, just off I-74 west of Champaign, surrounded by farm fields. Antique shopping, golf, university, and parks nearby. Continental breakfast includes homemade coffeecake, muffins, jam, fresh fruit, and juice. Enjoy a cool beverage on the deck. The hosts will strive to make the stay an enjoyable bed and breakfast experience. Call or write for a descriptive brochure.

Hosts: Rita and Bob Gold
Rooms: 3 (P1/2B; SB) $45
Continental Breakfast
Credit Cards: None
Notes: 2, 5, 9, 12, 14

The Golds

Grandma Joan's Homestay

2204 Brett Drive, 61821
(217) 356-5828

This comfortable, contemporary home features two fireplaces, multilevel decks, Jacuzzi, screened-in porch, and collection of modern and folk art. Ten minutes from the University of Illinois. Grandma pampers guests with cookies and milk at bedtime and with a healthy breakfast in the morning. Closed December 20 through January 10. Let this be a home away from home.

Host: Joan Erickson
Rooms: 3 (1 PB; 2 SB) $50-70
Full Breakfast
Credit Cards: None
Notes: 2, 9, 10, 11, 12, 14

CHICAGO

Bed and Breakfast/
Chicago, Inc.

P.O. Box 14088, 60614-0088
(312) 951-0085; FAX (312) 649-9243

2. This historic Kenwood home was recently restored by the architect/owner and her co-host who is a public TV producer. Its Prairie-style architecture is wonderfully harmonized with antique furniture for an Old World European charm. $75.

3. This self-contained one-bedroom garden apartment is in a renovated frame building. Recently decorated, it is furnished with a four-poster queen-size bed and sleeper sofa and offers kitchen and private bath. There is a lovely garden for guests to sit in and have breakfast, weather permitting. The host family lives upstairs; he is a TV reporter and she owns Bed and Breakfast/Chicago, Inc. Air conditioning and TV. $95.

4. This spacious, self-contained, one-bedroom apartment is in a vintage highrise building in the north part of the Gold Coast. It has a king-size bed, full bath, living room, and kitchen. It is within walking distance of the Magnificent Mile. There is a cafe in the building. Air-conditioned. TV. $95-125.

5. A traditionally furnished three-story townhouse offers an extra guest room with twin beds and a shared bath with host. Guests are welcome to enjoy the family room, fireplace, and other homey comforts provided. The host has been with Bed and Breakfast/Chicago for over six years. Easily accessible to public transportation. Air conditioning and TV. $75.

8. This renovated Victorian brick building offers several possibilities. There are both guest rooms and self-contained apartments available. There is a twin guest room with a private bath available in the apartment of the owner. Other guest rooms include queen-size and double rooms with a shared bath. Guests also have access to living room and kitchen. This unit can also be rented as a self-contained two-bedroom apartment. The owner has just redone a one-bedroom unit with twins or a king-size bed, sleeper sofa in the living room, and a Jacuzzi. Air-conditioning and TV. $75-145.

9. This self-contained one-bedroom garden apartment has been recently decorated and offers a queen-size bed, bath, full kitchen, and a living room. Air conditioning and TV. No smoking. $95.

12. This renovated mansion in prime Lincoln Park offers two double-bedded guest rooms with a private, unattached bath. The Victorian home has been redone to maintain the original feeling with antiques, wicker furniture, etc. Also available is a self-contained one-bedroom apartment on the third floor of the home. This unit is a large loft-like space with light wood floors, an island kitchen, and more contemporary furnishings. $75-135.

17. Relax and enjoy the modern comforts of this 40-year-old home renovated by an architect and brightly decorated in Southwest style. Downstairs guest room, on same level as the hosts' bedroom, offers double bed and private bath (shower and tub). Upstairs guest room offers queen-size futon on frame, private attached bath with bathtub (hand-held shower) and sitting area. Pleasant, outdoor deck off front of house offers excellent place for lounging. Air conditioning and TV. The hostess is in advertising/public relations and the host does research in cancer at Northwestern University Medical School. $75-85.

27. This beautifully rehabbed Victorian Queen Anne, built in the late 1800s offers charm, original woodwork, hardwood floors, two fireplaces, and at the same time provides the best in modern comforts. The guest room offers a double bed, private hall bath, and sitting area. Air conditioning and TV. No smoking. $85.

29. This high-rise apartment offers a guest room in the spacious condominium of a public relations professional. The guest room in this stylish, contemporary home is furnished with a double bed and has a private bath. The building has a health club. Air conditioning and TV. $75-85.

34. This single-family home has just been redone. The host, who has traveled extensively and loves staying in bed and breakfasts, lives in a coach house behind this accommodation. Three guest rooms with private baths offered. Breakfast is self-serve from the kitchen. This is an ideal arrangement for groups traveling together or visitors in Chicago for an extended time who want to settle in and feel they have found a home away from home. Air conditioning and TV. Weekly and monthly rates are available. $75-85.

6 Pets welcome; 8 Children welcome; 9 Social drinking allowed; 10 Tennis available; 11 Swimming available; 12 Golf available; 13 Skiing available; 14 May be booked through travel agents.

Bed and Breakfast/ Chicago, Inc. (continued)

35. This convenient accommodation is just two blocks from Northwestern University, Kendall College, and the Chicago "el" (elevated train). Only five minutes away, downtown Evanston and Lake Michigan are also easily accessible. This second-floor apartment offers two comfortable guest rooms, one with twin beds (placed together), and the other with a single bed. Enjoy a welcoming glass of sherry, assorted contemporary magazines, classical music, TV, and VCR in a tastefully decorated environment. Terry bathrobes and other amenities add to the homey feeling. Shared bath. Continental breakfast consists of seasonal fruits or juices, and delectable scones, muffins, or croissants from Evanston's premier bakers. No smoking. $85.

37. Elegantly furnished country French home on three-quarters of an acre offers charm and sophistication in a beautiful area just ten blocks from Lake Michigan. This home has been written up in several local and city publications and features beautiful gardens, Olympic-size swimming pool, large game room with a 50-inch TV, marble entryway, and many antiques. Three guest rooms are offered: king-size bed with private hall bath, queen-size bed with private attached bath with Jacuzzi, and twin beds with private attached bath with Jacuzzi. Air conditioning. No smoking. Deluxe breakfast. $90-100.

41. This ground-floor, self-catering apartment in a two-flat building comes fully equipped for a short or long-term stay (three-night minimum), and consists of two bedrooms, one bath, living room, dining room, eat-in kitchen, porch, and private telephone line. On a quiet residential street, it is close to public transportation in south-

east Evanston. For short-term stays, self-serve Continental breakfast is provided. The hosts, a retired professor and a teacher, live downstairs in separate apartments. Weekly and monthly rates available. $85.

54. Spacious, self-contained one-bedroom garden apartment, one block from St. Francis Hospital in Evanston, offers queen-size bed in bedroom plus a trundle bed in living room, a kitchen, and a private bath/shower. Air conditioning. No smokers. The hosts, an employee of the federal government and a vice president of education/training in health care, live on the premises in their own apartment. $85.

56. This Victorian home in Evanston's Lake Shore historic district is one mile south of Northwestern University and a short walk from fine restaurants and public transportation. Featured in several local and national magazines, it is furnished with a blend of lovely antiques and art. One double room and one single room are available on the third floor. Shared bath when other guest room is occupied. A generous Continental breakfast is provided. No smokers. Individuals or married couples only. $75.

Annie's. This comfortable, completely furnished studio apartment has a private entrance, fully equipped kitchen, queen-size bed and private bath. Close to some of Chicago's best restaurants, live theater, and fine shopping. Air conditioning and TV. $85.

City View Inn. This lovely 22-room property was originally a private club. On the 40th floor of a building in the financial district, all rooms have king-size beds, marble baths, and gorgeous views. Included in the rate is use of the first-class health club in the building. Parking and Continental breakfast. This is ideal for small group meetings. $137.50-176.

NOTES: Credit cards accepted: A MasterCard; B Visa; C American Express; D Discover Card; E Diner's Club; F Other; 2 Personal checks accepted; 3 Lunch available; 4 Dinner available; 5 Open all year;

Hyde Park House

5210 South Kenwood Avenue, 60615
(312) 363-4595

This is a Victorian house with a veranda, porch swing, rear deck, two grand pianos, and attic greenhouse. Near the University of Chicago, the Museum of Science and Industry, and 15 minutes from downtown by bus along the Lake Michigan shore. Also within walking distance are excellent sushi, Thai, Cantonese, Greek, Italian, and Continental restaurants, gift shops, and art galleries.

Host: Irene Custer
Rooms: 3 (1 PB; 2 SB) $55-70
Continental Breakfast
Credit Cards: None
Notes: 2, 5, 6, 7, 8, 9, 10, 11, 12, 13, 14

DU QUOIN

Francie's Bed and Breakfast Inn

104 South Line Street, 62832
(618) 542-6686

A quiet getaway in a restored 1908 orphanage. Four lovely air-conditioned guest rooms (two of which are suites) with a full breakfast served on the balcony, to the guest room, or in the dining room. Perfect accommodations for group seminars or retreats. Meeting rooms and meals are available for 15-60 persons. Hosts will arrange a murder mystery weekend for a group or five couples. Call for information or reservations.

Hosts: Tom and Francie Morgan
Rooms: 4 (PB) $60-80
Full Breakfast
Credit Cards: A, B
Notes: 2, 5, 9, 10, 11, 12

ELDRED

Bluffdale Vacation Farm

Rural Route 1, 62027
(217) 983-2854

This new hideaway cottage in the woods is cozy and secluded. Its lovely accommodations include a wood-burning rock fireplace, inside and outside private whirlpool spas, a cathedral ceiling with native log rafters and beams, and wide plank floors. On the side of the bluffs, it has a large deck with sheltering trees growing through it and a magnificent view of the Illinois River Valley. An adjoining bedroom with its own private bath can sleep up to four children.

Hosts: Bill and Lindy Hobson
Rooms: 9 (PB) $62-80
Full Breakfast
Credit Cards: None
Notes: 2, 3, 4, 8, 9, 11, 12, 14

ELIZABETH

Ridgeview Bed and Breakfast

8833 South Massbach Road, 61028
(815) 598-3150

A 1921 country schoolhouse and former residence of author/artist Thomas Locker overlooks ten miles of Rush Creek Valley. Three large, unique rooms and one loft suite, all with their own individual character, offer easy access to a Mississippi River town and other historic towns in the Galena/Jo Daviess County area. A great place to enjoy the outdoors and ride bikes on the hard-top roads along the ridges. Romantic getaway packages available.

Host: Betty Valy
Rooms: 4 (PB) $69-89
Continental Breakfast
Credit Cards: A, B, C
Notes: 2, 5, 6 (call), 7 (limited), 8 (call), 11, 12, 13, 14

ELSAH

Green Tree Inn

P.O. Box 96, 15 Mill Street, 62028
(618) 374-2821; FAX (615) 244-2978

6 Pets welcome; 8 Children welcome; 9 Social drinking allowed; 10 Tennis available; 11 Swimming available; 12 Golf available; 13 Skiing available; 14 May be booked through travel agents.

Mississippi River's most romantic 19th century village, 1850s-style inn and general mercantile. Ten rooms with private baths and access to balconies. Nearby water related activities, bike trail, horseback riding, golf and American Bald Eagle sightings January through March. Over 100 antique shops are within a 30-minute radius. Amenities include cocktails, bicycles built for two and gourmet breakfast.

Hostess: Mary Ann Pitchford
Rooms: 10 (PB) $69-105
Full Breakfast
Credit Cards: A, B
Notes: 2, 3 (call), 5, 8 (over 12), 9, 11, 12, 13, 14

EVANSTON

The Margarita European Inn

1566 Oak Avenue, 60201
(708) 869-2273

Originally a women's private club, this Georgian mansion north of Chicago has been reopened as a bed and breakfast inn with an Italian ristorante, Va Pensiero, Zagat Guide's number one Italian ristorante in Chicagoland. Choose from 34 rooms, half with newly decorated private baths. Relax in the spacious parlor which features a molded fireplace and floor-to-ceiling arched windows. A rooftop garden, paneled library, and party rooms are also available. Continental breakfast includes muffins, pastries, and fresh fruit. Lunch and dinner are available in the restaurant. Facilities for weddings and meetings are available.

Hosts: Barbara and Tim Gorham, Owners; Judith Baker, Innkeeper
Continental Breakfast
Credit Cards: A, B, C
Notes: 2, 3, 4, 5, 8, 9, 10, 14

GALENA

Aldrich Guest House

900 Third Street, 61036
(815) 777-3323

The Aldrich House combines the elegance of the 19th century with all the amenities of the 20th century. Period furnishings and wall coverings. Five queen-size beds and one twin, central air conditioning, screened porch, and a library with books, TV, and video tapes, all for the guests' pleasure. A full breakfast is served in the dining room. Both hosts are dedicated to sharing the warmth and charm of their home. Two blocks from Grant's house and downtown Galena. Golf, swimming, skiing, and many gourmet restaurants are all within a couple of miles.

Hosts: Sandy and Herb Larson
Rooms: 5 (PB) $70-95
Full Breakfast
Credit Cards: A, B, D
Notes: 2, 5, 9, 10, 11, 12, 13

Aldrich Guest House

Amber Creek's Chicago Connection

1260 North Dearborn, P.O. Box 5, 61036
(815) 777-9320

Charming apartment on Chicago's Gold Coast in a quiet, secure building only one-half block from the Ambassador Hotel. Tastefully decorated, spacious living room with nice views, including lake. Full kitchen and bath. Romantic bedroom with king-size bed, down quilts, and extra pillows. Linens and towels provided. Walk to lake, Water Tower, and Michigan Avenue shopping. Half block to airport limousine and public transportation. Parking garage next door. Ideal for one couple. Queen-size futon provides sleeping for additional guests.

Host: Kate Freeman
Apartment: 1 (PB) $75-125
Continental Breakfast
Credit Cards: A, B, C, D
Notes: 2, 3, 4, 5, 8, 9, 11, 14

Avery Guest House

606 South Prospect Street, 61036
(815) 777-3883

Within Galena's historic district, this pre-Civil War home is a short walk from antique shops and historic buildings. Enjoy the scenic view from the porch swing; feel free to play the piano or just visit. Breakfast is served in the sunny dining room with a bay window overlooking the Galena River valley. Two-night minimum stay required for weekends and holidays.

Hosts: Flo and Roger Jensen
Rooms: 4 (S2B) $40-60
Continental Breakfast
Credit Cards: A, B
Notes: 2, 5, 8, 9, 10, 11, 12, 13

Belle Aire Mansion Guest House

11410 Route 20 West, 61036
(815) 777-0893

Belle Aire Mansion is a pre-Civil War home set on 11 beautiful acres just minutes from Galena. Three of the rooms feature gas fireplaces, and one suite has a double whirlpool. Two-night minimum stay for weekends is required. Closed Christmas. Guests say, "It's just like visiting friends." The hosts say, "Welcome home—to our home."

Hosts: Jan and Lorraine Svec
Rooms: 5 (PB) $70.85-147.15
Full Breakfast
Credit Cards: A, B, D
Notes: 2, 8, 9, 11, 12, 13

Brierwreath Manor

Brierwreath Manor Bed and Breakfast

216 North Bench Street, 61036
(815) 777-0608

Circa 1884 Queen Anne house with wrap-around porch only one short block from historic Main Street. Cable TV, early morning coffee buffet, and full breakfast are only a few of the comforts guests will experience. The manor has three large suites with sitting areas, gas log fireplaces, and private baths. Each is furnished with an eclectic blend of antiques and modern comforts. Special packages available.

Hosts: Mike and Lyn Cook
Suites: 3 (PB) $85-90
Full Breakfast
Credit Cards: None
Notes: 2, 5, 9, 11, 12, 13

Craig Cottage

505 Dewey Avenue, 61036
(815) 777-1461

This restored two-story brick-and-limestone house sleeps two to five and is within walking distance of Galena's downtown. Enclosed porch, patio, grill, fireplace with wood supplied, washer/dryer, color cable TV, telephone, microwave oven, air conditioning, and antique furnishings and decor.

6 Pets welcome; 8 Children welcome; 9 Social drinking allowed; 10 Tennis available; 11 Swimming available; 12 Golf available; 13 Skiing available; 14 May be booked through travel agents.

Coffee and wine included. The house over-looks a wooded valley. Discounts for mid-week or multiple-night reservations are available. A very private and unique stay.

Hosts: Charles and Katherine Marsden; Mark Van Osdol
Cottage: 1 (PB) $72-120
Credit Cards: A, B
Notes: 2, 5, 6, 7, 8, 9, 11, 12, 13

DeSoto House Hotel

230 South Main, 61036
(815) 777-0090; (800) 343-6562

Historic DeSoto House Hotel is in scenic downtown Galena. Originally opened April 9, 1855. Listed on the National Register of Historic Places. Notable past guests include Abraham Lincoln, U.S. Grant, Theodore Roosevelt, Susan B. Anthony, and Mark Twain. Hotel offers 55 Victorian-style guest rooms with private baths and modern amenities. Features two restaurants and complimentary enclosed parking. Close to historic sites and shops. Bed and breakfast package available upon request; however, breakfast is not included in regular rates.

Rooms: 55 (PB) $69-238
Full Breakfast
Credit Cards: A, B, C, D, E
Notes: 2, 3, 4, 5, 8, 9, 10, 11, 12, 13, 14

The Goldmoor

9001 Sand Hill Road, 61036
(815) 777-3925; (800) 255-3925

South of Galena, this is the only inn on the bluffs overlooking the Mississippi River. Specializing in the romantic getaway, and anniversary and honeymoon packages. The suites include fireplaces, whirlpools (some overlooking the Mississippi), and galleys with mini-refrigerators. Full gourmet breakfast. Spacious landscaped grounds, complimentary bikes for the use of guests. Riverboat casino packages are available. Midweek discounts. Three-crown rating by the ABBA.

Host: James C. Goldthorpe
Rooms: 6 (PB) $95-225
Full Breakfast
Credit Cards: A, B, D
Notes: 2, 5, 6, 7, 8, 10, 11, 12, 13, 14

Grandview Guest Home

113 South Prospect Street, 61036
(815) 777-1387; (800) 373-0732

A 123-year-old brick traditional on Quality Hill, overlooking the city and countryside. Victorian furnishings. Hearty Continental breakfast featuring home-baked goods and European coffees. Two blocks from Main Street shops, museums, and restaurants.

Hosts: Harry and Marjorie Dugan
Rooms: 3 (1 PB; 2 SB) $65-80
Full Breakfast
Credit Cards: A, B, C, D
Notes: 2, 5, 7, 8, 10, 11, 12, 13, 14

Park Avenue Guest House

Park Avenue Guest House

208 Park Avenue, 61036
(815) 777-1075; (800) 359-0743

An 1893 Queen Anne "painted lady," with wraparound screened porch and shaded garden with gazebo. Original woodwork, queen-size beds, and antique furniture. Central air conditioning. In-room fireplaces. Second parlor has cable TV. Walk to town; ample parking.

Host: Sharon Fallbacher
Rooms: 4 (PB) $60-95
Continental Breakfast
Credit Cards: A, B, D
Notes: 2, 5, 9, 10, 11, 12, 13

Pine Hollow Inn

4700 North Council Hill, 61036
(815) 777-1071

On a 110-acre Christmas tree farm one mile
north of Galena. "Helping make it one of
the best are spacious rooms with fireplaces,
skylights, private baths, and whirlpools,
plus some superb scenery." Rooms at the
inn are very large. Each is appointed with
beautiful country furnishings. One of the
unique qualities of the area is the peaceful
solitude that is especially nice when enjoyed from the large porch surrounding the
house.

Hosts: Larry and Sally Priske
Rooms: 5 (PB) $75-105
Continental Breakfast
Credit Cards: A, B, D
Notes: 2, 5, 9, 10, 11, 12, 13

Queen Anne Guest House

200 Park Avenue, 61036
(815) 777-3849

Restored 1891 Queen Anne Victorian nestled in a quiet residential neighborhood of
historic Galena. Four romantically furnished rooms with private baths, claw-foot
tubs, ceiling fans, twin-, queen- and king-
size beds, antiques, and period furnishings.
Library, double parlors, wraparound porch,
and delicious breakfasts. Short stroll to antique shopping, museums, and fine restaurants in historic downtown district. Minutes
to skiing, golf, riverboat excursions, and
casino boats.

Hosts: Frank Checchin and Diane Thompson
Rooms: 4 (PB) $75-95
Continental Breakfast
Credit Cards: A, B, D
Notes: 2, 5, 9, 10, 11, 12, 13

Queen Anne Guest House

GALESBURG

Seacord House
Bed and Breakfast

624 North Cherry Street, 61401-2731
(309) 342-4107

This 1890s Eastlake Victorian is lovingly
furnished in period decor with family antiques. Enjoy a landmark house filled with
traditional comfort, hospitality, and charm.
Guests may use the parlors for conversation or reading, or relax on the patio. Books
and games are always on hand. The inn is
close to Knox College, the Sandburg Birthplace, Bishop Hill, and Spoon River Country. The expanded Continental breakfast
includes special recipe muffins or waffles
made from scratch daily. Inspected and approved by the Illinois Bed and Breakfast
Association.

Hosts: Gwen and Lyle Johnson
Rooms: 3 (SB) $40
Continental Breakfast
Credit Cards: A
Notes: 2, 5, 8, 9

GENEVA

Oscar Swan Country Inn

1800 West State Street, 60134
(708) 232-0173

6 Pets welcome; 8 Children welcome; 9 Social drinking allowed; 10 Tennis available; 11 Swimming available;
12 Golf available; 13 Skiing available; 14 May be booked through travel agents.

A mansion on eight acres and filled with antiques. The gardens are like paradise—cool, crisp, and refreshing. A swimming pool also beckons. The city offers art, history, beauty, and relaxation. The quietest times are Sunday through Thursday.

Hosts: Nina and Hans Heymann
Rooms: 8 (6 PB; 2 SB) $88-149
Full Breakfast
Credit Cards: A, B, C
Notes: 2, 5, 7, 8, 10, 11, 12, 14

Oscar Swan Country Inn

GOLCONDA

Marilee's Guest House

Washington and Monroe Streets, P.O. Box 627, 62938
(618) 683-2751; (800) 582-2563

Attractive bungalow, warmly furnished, comfortable; telephone, air conditioners, TV, refrigerator, snacks, wood-burning fireplace, and spacious rooms with open-beam ceilings. Near the beautiful Ohio River, two blocks from the marina at Smithland Pool. The deer capital of Illinois, near the Shawnee National Forest. Deer hunting, bass fishing, wild turkey, and quail country. Children welcome.

Host: Marilee Joiner
Rooms: 3 (1 PB; 2 SB) $45
Full Breakfast
Credit Cards: None
Notes: 2, 5, 8, 9, 11, 13

JERSEYVILLE

The Homeridge Bed and Breakfast

1470 North State Street, 62052
(618) 498-3442

Beautiful, warm, brick 1867 Italianate Victorian private home on 18 acres in comfortable country atmosphere. Drive through stately iron gates and pine tree-lined driveway to the 14-room historic estate of Senator Theodore Chapman. Beautiful, expansive pillared front porch. Handcarved stairway to spacious guest rooms and third floor. Large swimming pool. Central air conditioning. Between Springfield, Illinois, and St. Louis, Missouri.

Hosts: Sue and Howard Landon
Rooms: 4 (PB) $65
Full Breakfast
Credit Cards: A, B
Notes: 2, 5, 10, 11, 12

MAEYSTOWN

Corner George Inn

P.O. Box 103, Main and Mill, 62256
(618) 458-6660; (800) 458-6020

A frontier Victorian structure built in 1884, the Maeystown Hotel and Saloon is now the Corner George Inn. Forty-five minutes south of St. Louis, the inn has seven painstakingly restored, antique-filled guest rooms, two sit-

Corner George Inn

ting rooms, a wine cellar, and an elegant ballroom. Maeystown is a quaint, 19th-century village with shops and a restaurant. Nearby are Fort de Chartres, Fort Kaskaskia, and the scenic bluff along the Mississippi.

Hosts: David and Marcia Braswell
Rooms: 5 (5 PB; 2 SB) $65-95
Full Breakfast
Credit Cards: A, B
Notes: 2, 5, 12, 14

MOUNT CARMEL

The Poor Farm Bed and Breakfast

Poor Farm Road, 62863-9803
(800) 646-FARM (3276)

From 1857 to 1949, the Poor Farm served as a home for the homeless. Today, it is home for the traveler who enjoys a warm, friendly atmosphere, authentic country charm, and an abundance of local history. Guests experience a gracious glimpse of yesteryear as they enter the 35 room stately brick structure. Enjoy luxury in one of the four-room suites or spacious double rooms, all with private baths. Within walking distance are golf, tennis, swimming, and two parks with fishing. In three minutes guests can be on the banks of the historic Wabash River, and in the spectacular Beall Woods Nature Preserve in 15 minutes. Red Hill State Park is only one half hour away. Come enjoy!

Hosts: Liz and John Stelizer
Rooms: 4 (PB) $50-95
Credit Cards: A, B, C, D
Notes: 2, 5, 8, 9, 10, 11, 12, 14

MOUNT CARROLL

Prairie Path Guest House

1002 Lowden Road, 61053
(815) 244-3462

This Victorian home, built in 1876, sits at the edge of historic Mount Carroll. Country and Victorian rooms are available where guests are treated to warm hospitality and a full country breakfast of homemade breads and other specialities. Make this a home away from home. Private and shared baths are available, and the house has central air conditioning. There is a unique quilt and antique shop on the premises with old-fashioned ambience! Full advance deposit is required or credit cards may be used to guarantee a reservation.

Rooms: 3 (1 PB; 2 SB) $60-70
Full Breakfast
Credit Cards: A, C

NAPERVILLE

Harrison House Bed and Breakfast

26 North Eagle Street, 60540
(708) 420-1117

Harrison House Bed and Breakfast, circa 1904, is 25 miles west of Chicago in historic Naperville. Hosts offer five antique-filled, air-conditioned guest rooms with private baths, one with Jacuzzi. Walk to downtown restaurants, historic sites, quaint shops, and Centennial Beach. Homemade chocolate chip cookies, fresh flowers, gourmet coffee, and scrumptious breakfast. Friendly atmosphere. Business or pleasure, relax and be pampered.

Hosts: Neal and Lynn Harrison
Rooms: 5 (3 PB; 2 SB) $68-138
Full Breakfast
Credit Cards: A, B, C
Notes: 2, 5, 9, 10, 11, 12, 13, 14

NAUVOO

Mississippi Memories

Rural Route 1, Box 291, 62354
(217) 453-2771

Gracious lodging on the Mississippi riverbank. Elegantly served full homemade

6 Pets welcome; 8 Children welcome; 9 Social drinking allowed; 10 Tennis available; 11 Swimming available; 12 Golf available; 13 Skiing available; 14 May be booked through travel agents.

breakfasts; quiet wooded setting. Five minutes from restored Mormon city, "the Williamsburg of the Midwest." From two decks watch spectacular sunsets, abundant wildlife, and barges drifting by. Excellent geode hunting. Air conditioning, fireplaces, piano, fruit, and flowers in rooms. River boat cruises only two miles away. AAA rated three stars.

Hosts: Marge and Dean Starr
Rooms: 5 (3 PB; 2 SB) $45
Full Breakfast
Credit Cards: A, B
Notes: 2, 5, 10, 11, 12, 13

Mississippi Memories

OREGON

Pinehill
Bed and Breakfast

400 Mix Street, 61061
(815) 732-2061

On the National Register, this 1874 Italianate Country villa is also the "home" of the (edible) decorated fudge wreaths. Complete with marble fireplaces in guest rooms, central air conditioning, feather, king-, and queen-size beds, private baths, and Jacuzzi. A library of books, and rockers are everywhere. Guests are invited to sleep late, linger over afternoon tea, and indulge at breakfast—all included. Private chocolate tea parties a tradition! Yard games. Porch events.

Host: Sharon Burdick
Rooms: 5 (PB) $75-165

Full Breakfast
Credit Cards: None
Notes: 2, 5, 8, 9, 10, 11, 12, 14

PEORIA (MOSSVILLE)

Old Church House Inn
Bed and Breakfast

1416 East Mossville Road, 61552
(309) 579-2300

Come take sanctuary from the cares of life in this 1869 renovated "one-room country church," where sleeping is encouraged! Nestled in central Illinois, guests delight in the plush warmth of a Victorian era where attention to detail radiates. Stroll through colorful flower gardens, capture memories by the fireplace, and sink into queen-size featherbeds for a restful night's sleep. Continental-plus breakfast is served. No smoking.

Hosts: Dean and Holly Ramseyer
Rooms: 2 (1 PB; 1 SB) $69-99
Continental Breakfast
Credit Cards: A, B
Notes: 2, 3, 5, 10, 11, 12, 13

RANTOUL

Better 'N Grandma's
Overniters

102 South Meyers Street, 61866
(217) 893-0469

This 110-year-old Victorian has a varied decor: Mexican hallway, a touch of country, and the Orient in other areas. At $10 per person per night, Better 'N Grandma's is an economical bed and breakfast in downtown Rantoul, near the former Chanute Air Force Base with its air museum and only miles north of Champaign-Urbana and the University of Illinois.

Host: Janet Anderson
Rooms: 3 (SB) $20
Continental Breakfast
Credit Cards: None
Notes: 2, 5, 7, 10, 11, 12

NOTES: Credit cards accepted: A MasterCard; B Visa; C American Express; D Discover Card; E Diner's Club; F Other; 2 Personal checks accepted; 3 Lunch available; 4 Dinner available; 5 Open all year;

ROCK ISLAND

The Potter House

1906 7th Avenue, 61201
(309) 788-1906; (800) 747-0339

Enjoy a full breakfast in a 1907 solarium with arched windows framed by columns and a marble-tile floor. On the National Register and in a historic neighborhood. Outstanding architectural features include stained glass, leather wall covering, six fireplaces, and grand staircase. Amenities include refreshments, in-room cable TV, and telephones. Walk to casino boat, dinner theater, and restaurants. Five-room historic guest cottage sleeps four in two bedrooms and has complete kitchen facilities. AAA three-diamond rating.

Hosts: Gary and Nancy Pheiffer
Rooms: 5 (PB) $65-95
Cottage: 1
Full Breakfast
Credit Cards: A, B, C, D, E
Notes: 2, 5, 9, 10, 11, 12, 13, 14

Top o' the Morning

1505 19th Avenue, 61201
(309) 786-3513

Sam and Peggy welcome guests to this brick mansion on the bluffs overlooking the Mississippi River. Fantastic view day or night. Three-acre wooded estate with winding drive, orchard, and gardens. Air-conditioned bedrooms, whirlpool tub, and natural fireplaces.

Hosts: Sam and Peggy Doak
Rooms: 3 (PB) $50-60
Full Breakfast
Credit Cards: None
Notes: 2, 5, 7, 8, 9, 10, 11, 12, 13

Victorian Inn
Bed and Breakfast

702 20th Street, 61201
(309) 788-7068

Light from the windows of the stained-glass tower welcomes guests to the Victo-

rian Inn Bed and Breakfast. In the Broadway historic area near riverboat gambling and festival attractions. Antiques adorn the five spacious guest rooms with private baths. Close to Augustana College. Built with Old World charm in 1888. Step back in time to gracious living in this home listed on the National Register of Historic Places.

Hosts: David and Barbara Parker
Rooms: 6 (PB) $55-75
Full Breakfast
Credit Cards: A, B
Notes: 2, 5, 7 (limited), 8, 10, 11, 12, 13, 14

ST. CHARLES

Charleston Guest House

612 West Main Street, 60174
(708) 377-1277

St. Charles's only bed and breakfast is conveniently within walking distance of many St. Charles attractions—antique shops, bike trails, parks, and restaurants. Close to festivals and world-famous Kane County Flea Market. Built in 1892, this Queen Anne-style home has three comfortable guest rooms on the second floor. Because the hosts reside on the premises, personal attention, information, and conversation are readily available.

Hosts: Bill and Judy Schultz
Rooms: 3 (PB) $69-89
Continental Breakfast
Credit Cards: A, B, D
Notes: 2, 5, 7, 9, 12

SPRINGFIELD

Glenmar Plantation

2444 Valley Hill Road, 40069
(606) 284-7791; (800) 828-3330

Guests repeatedly travel to the Plantation, circa 1785, to enjoy the serenity and country grandeur of this National Historic setting. The plantation features a 250-acre working horse farm, English gardens,

6 Pets welcome; 8 Children welcome; 9 Social drinking allowed; 10 Tennis available; 11 Swimming available;
12 Golf available; 13 Skiing available; 14 May be booked through travel agents.

walking paths, gazebos, and exotic animals. Designed for families or romantics. Meeting room available. Evening dessert provided.

Host: Kenneth Mandell
Rooms: 7 (4 PB; 3 SB) $75-150
Cottage: 1
Full Breakfast
Credit Cards: A, B, C
Notes: 2, 5, 6, 8, 9, 11, 12

Chateau des Fleurs

WINDSOR

Deerfield Bed and Breakfast

Rural Route 1, Box 994, 61957
(217) 459-2750

The Deerfield is a two-story log cabin at the entrance to Wolf Creek State Park. The inn has four upstairs bedrooms that share a common bath, and one large room with a private bath. Coffee and muffins are served on the porch at 7:30 A.M. during the summer; a full breakfast is served in the dining room at 8:30 A.M. The inn is a quiet retreat to make guests feel restful and relaxed. No smoking.

Hosts: Larry and Mary Bodine
Rooms: 4 (1 PB; 3 SB) $50-70
Full Breakfast
Credit Cards: None
Notes: 2, 5, 9, 11, 12

WINNETKA (CHICAGO)

Chateau des Fleurs

552 Ridge Road, 60093
(708) 256-7272

Chateau des Fleurs is an elegant respite from the world that welcomes guests with light, beauty, warmth, and lovely views of magnificent trees, gardens, and a swimming pool. A French country home filled with antiques, four fireplaces, 50-inch TV, and a grand piano. By a private road for jogging or walking; only four blocks from shops and restaurants and a 30-minute train ride to Chicago's Loop. Ten minutes from Northwestern University. Minimum stay of two nights.

Minimum stay of two nights
Host: Sally H. Ward
Rooms: 3 (PB) $90-95
Full Breakfast
Credit Cards: None
Notes: 2, 8 (over 11), 9, 10, 12, 13, 14

NOTES: Credit cards accepted: A MasterCard; B Visa; C American Express; D Discover Card; E Diner's Club; F Other; 2 Personal checks accepted; 3 Lunch available; 4 Dinner available; 5 Open all year;

Indiana

ANGOLA

Sycamore Hill Bed and Breakfast

1245 Golden Lake Road, 46703
(219) 665-2690

This two-story Colonial, pillared home was built in 1963 by master craftsmen. Tucked away amid 26 acres of rolling hills and woods. Great for bird watching. Shady back yard with two picnic tables at guests' disposal. Sumptuous breakfast. Gas grill in the back yard.

Host: Betsey Goranson
Rooms: 4 (1 PB; 3 SB) $40-60
Full Breakfast
Credit Cards: A, B
Notes: 2, 5, 8, 10, 11, 12, 13

AURORA

The Aurora Inn

220 Fourth Street, 47001
(812) 926-4412

The Aurora Inn, an elegant 100-year-old Queen Anne home, is in a quaint river town on the banks of the Ohio. A wraparound veranda is filled with wicker, rocking chairs, and a swing for relaxing. Enjoy a bountiful breakfast in the bright, airy sunroom. Walk to restaurants, shops, and historic sites. Close to skiing and boating. Six miles from I-275 exit. Forty minutes from west Cincinnati. Near I-71, I-74, and I-75.

Hosts: Bev and Steve Reynolds
Rooms: 4 (S2B) $49-59
Full Breakfast
Credit Cards: A, B, C
Notes: 2, 5, 8 (over ten), 9, 11 ,12, 13, 14

BEVERLY SHORES

Dunes Shore Inn

33 Lake Shore County Road, Box 807, 46301
(219) 879-9029

A casual bed and breakfast in secluded Beverly Shores is surrounded by the Indiana Dunes National Lakeshore. Only one block to Lake Michigan and one hour to Chicago. Miles of trails and beaches, spectacular sunrises and sunsets, and an ever-changing lake await guests. No smoking. Minimum stay weekends and holidays: two nights.

Hosts: Rosemary and Fred Braun
Rooms: 12 (S4B) $50-60
Continental Breakfast
Credit Cards: None
Notes: 2, 5, 8, 9, 10, 11, 12, 13

BLOOMINGTON

Scholars Inn

801 North College Avenue, 47404
(812) 332-1892

The Scholars Inn is a restored, elegant brick mansion blending the past with the present for a warm and comfortable atmosphere. This 100-year-old styled mansion includes the finest in amenities. Five bedrooms feature either king- or queen-size beds with pillow top mattresses. Private baths, two bathrooms feature Jacuzzi-style tubs.

Host: Nickky Jackson
Rooms: 5 (PB) $69-135
Continental Breakfast
Credit Cards: A, B, C, E
Notes: 2, 5, 9, 10, 11, 12, 13

6 Pets welcome; 7 Smoking allowed; 8 Children welcome; 9 Social drinking allowed; 10 Tennis available; 11 Swimming available; 12 Golf available; 13 Skiing available; 14 May be booked through travel agents.

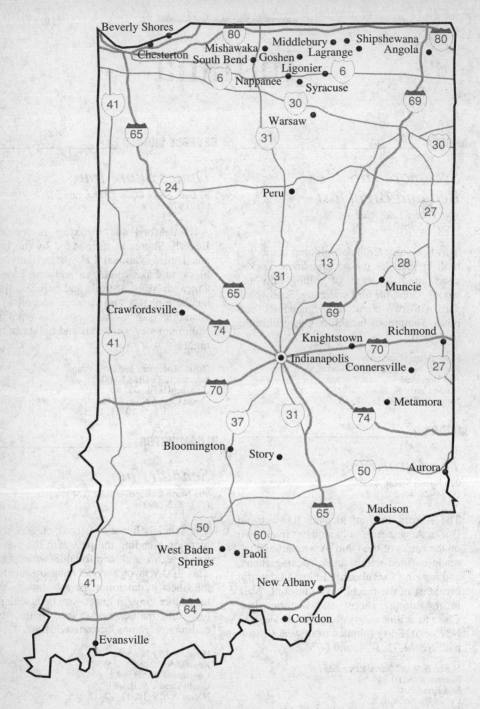

Indiana

Gray Goose Inn

CHESTERTON

Gray Goose Inn

350 Indian Boundary Road, 46304
(219) 926-5781; (800) 521-5127

English-style country house on 100 wooded acres overlooking a private lake. Walking trails, paddleboat, rowboat, and bikes are available for guests. Minutes from Dunes State and National Lake Shore parks; 50 minutes from Chicago.

Hosts: Tim Wilk and Chuck Ramsey
Rooms: 8 (PB) $80-135
Full Breakfast
Credit Cards: A, B, C, D
Notes: 2, 5, 7, 8 (over 12), 9, 10, 11, 12, 13, 14

Indian Oak Resort

558 Indian Boundary Road, 46304
(219) 926-2200; (800) 552-4232

Nestled among tall oaks on private Lake Chubb, forty-five minutes from Chicago, just off the intersection of Interstates 94 and 49, close to Lake Michigan, Indiana Dunes State Park, and Indiana National Lakeshore Park. Exceptional restaurants, hiking trails, dramatic sunsets, exquisite gardens, and more. Lovely woodside and lakeside rooms, professionally licensed full-service salon, fitness center with pool and

whirlpool, live entertainment, and comedy club. Meeting and conference space available. Something for everyone!

Host: Catherine Chubb
Rooms: 100 (PB) $64-124
Continental Breakfast
Credit Cards: A, B, C, D
Notes: 2, 3, 4, 5, 7, 8, 9, 10, 11, 12, 13, 14

CONNERSVILLE

Maple Leaf Inn Bed and Breakfast

831 North Grand Avenue, 47331
(317) 825-7099

The Maple Leaf Inn blends the old with the new, offering warm hospitality and boasting much of its original craftsmanship from the mid-1860s. Four bedrooms with private baths. Nearby are antique shops, two state parks, and an old canal town with unique shops.

Hosts: Angel and Cindy Perez
Rooms: 4 (PB) $55-65
Continental Breakfast
Credit Cards: A, B
Notes: 2, 5, 7, 8, 11, 12, 14

Maple Leaf Inn

CORYDON

Kintner House Inn

101 South Capitol Avenue, 47112
(812) 738-2020

NOTES: Credit cards accepted: A MasterCard; B Visa; C American Express; D Discover Card; E Diner's Club; F Other; 2 Personal checks accepted; 3 Lunch available; 4 Dinner available; 5 Open all year; 6 Pets welcome; 7 Smoking allowed; 8 Children welcome; 9 Social drinking allowed; 10 Tennis available; 11 Swimming available; 12 Golf available; 13 Skiing available; 14 May be booked through travel agents.

Completely restored inn, circa 1873, a national historical landmark, with 15 rooms, each with private bath, furnished in Victorian and country antiques. Serves full breakfast. Unique shops, fine restaurants, antique malls, historic sites, museums, art glass factory, and excursion train all within walking distance of the inn. Sports available. Rated AAA and Mobil. A hideaway for romantics.

Host: Mary Jane Bridgwater
Rooms: 15 (PB) $39-89
Full Breakfast
Credit Cards: A, B, C, D, E
Notes: 2, 5, 8, 9, 10, 11, 12, 14

CRAWFORDSVILLE

Sugar Creek's Queen Anne Bed and Breakfast

901 West Market, P.O. Box 726, 47933
(317) 362-4095

A cozy, warm atmosphere, surrounded by beautiful flowers and shrubs. Built in 1900, this home features Victorian decor, with statues throughout. Four rooms with private bath. Jacuzzi room also available. Honeymooner's suite includes flowers and non-alcoholic champagne in the room. Afternoon tea available by arrangement and includes international pastries. Each visit includes limousine sightseeing tour of historic Crawfordsville, including Lane Place, Lew Wallace Study, Old Jail Museum, and Doll Cottage.

Hosts: Mary Alice and Hal Barbee
Rooms: 4 (PB) $55
Continental Breakfast
Credit Cards: A, B
Notes: 2, 5, 8

EVANSVILLE

The River's Inn

414 Southeast Riverside Drive, 47713
(812) 428-7777; (800) 797-7990

A delightful 18th-century guest house tastefully restored with period antiques. The

The River's Inn

flower-bordered balconies overlook the Ohio River in downtown Evansville. A full breakfast offers gourmet dining freshly prepared each morning and served in the formal dining room in view of the Victorian garden. The guest rooms feature beds constructed in the 1800s with complementary pieces, Oriental rugs, lace, and fine linens. Bridal chambers available. Airport service, FAX and copier service, private entrance, and off-street parking. Across the street from the museum in the historic district.

Hosts: Marsha and Allan Trockman
Rooms: 5 (PB) $75-95
Full Breakfast
Credit Cards: A, B, C
Notes: 2, 5, 7, 10

GOSHEN

The Checkerberry Inn

62644 County Road 37, 46526
(219) 642-4445

At the Checkerberry Inn, in the heart of northern Indiana Amish country, guests will find a unique atmosphere, different from anywhere else in the Midwest. Each individually decorated room has a breathtaking view of the unspoiled countryside. Outdoor

---

NOTES: Credit cards accepted: A MasterCard; B Visa; C American Express; D Discover Card; E Diner's Club; F Other; 2 Personal checks accepted; 3 Lunch available; 4 Dinner available; 5 Open all year;

pool, tennis court, and croquet green. Cycling, jogging, and walking area. Shopping and golf within 10 to 15 minutes. Award-winning restaurant. Closed January.

Hosts: John and Susan Graff
Rooms: 14 (PB) $130-300
Continental Breakfast
Credit Cards: A, B, C
Notes: 2, 3, 4, 8, 9, 10, 11, 12, 14

GRANDVIEW

The River Belle

P.O. Box 669, 47615
(812) 649-2500; (800) 877-5165

Come to the River Belle for a little bit of southern charm in southern Indiana on the Ohio River. Guests may choose from one of three accommodations: an 1866 white-painted brick steamboat-style, an 1890 red-brick Italianate, or the "little house under the pecan tree"—an 1860 cottage with full kitchen. Guests may choose to walk along the river or sit quietly and watch the white squirrels play among the magnolias, pecan trees, and azaleas. Within 20 miles of the Lincoln Boyhood National Memorial, Lincoln State Park, Lincoln drama, and Holiday World—the nation's oldest amusement park.

The River Belle

Hosts: Don and Pat Phillips
Rooms: 6 (2 PB; 4 SB) $45-65
Continental Breakfast
Credit Cards: A, B
Notes: 2, 8

INDIANAPOLIS

Boone Docks on the River

7159 Edgewater Place, 46240
(317) 257-3671

A 1920s English Tudor home on the White River, just north of Broad Ripple Village, Boone Docks is a resort-like setting overlooking the river. Enjoy the comforts and charm of the River Room Suite, gracefully decorated in blue, white eyelet, and lace. A hearty breakfast is enjoyed seasonally in the sunroom or on the deck. Convenient to dining, entertainment, shopping, museums, antiquing, and many downtown attractions.

Hosts: Lynne and Mike Boone
Room: 1 (PB) $65
Full Breakfast
Credit Cards: C
Notes: 2, 5, 7, 8

Le Chateau Delaware

1456 North Delaware Street, 46202
(317) 636-9156

This bed and breakfast inn combines the elegance and charm of a turn-of-the-century manor with the modern convenience of today. The hosts welcome the opportunity to be the hosts for an overnight or extended stay, special parties, receptions, or executive conferences. Emphasis is on graciousness, comfort, and service.

Host: Mignon Wyatt
Rooms: 5 (1 PB; 2 SB) $75-175
Full Breakfast
Credit Cards: A, B
Notes: 5, 11, 12, 14

The Hoffman House Bed and Breakfast

545 East 11th Street, P.O. Box 906, 46206-0906
(317) 635-1701; FAX (317) 635-1701

6 Pets welcome; 8 Children welcome; 9 Social drinking allowed; 10 Tennis available; 11 Swimming available; 12 Golf available; 13 Skiing available; 14 May be booked through travel agents.

The Hoffman House is a 1903 American Four Square in downtown Indianapolis. This bed and breakfast homestay provides affordable elegance featuring oak woodwork, antiques, and period reproductions. Two comfortable guest rooms are on the second floor. Rooms feature antique double beds with handmade quilts. A Continental plus breakfast is served on a lace tablecloth with blue and white china and cobalt blue glassware. Two cats and a dog in residence.

Host: Laura A Arnold
Rooms: 2 (SB) $60-90
Continental Breakfast
Credit Cards: A, B
Notes: 2, 8, 9, 14

KNIGHTSTOWN

Old Hoosier House

7601 South Greensboro Pike, 46148
(800) 775-5315

Old Hoosier House, circa 1840, offers high ceilinged, air-conditioned, tastefully furnished rooms. Easily accessible from I-70 or U.S. 40. Close to Indianapolis and is in the heart of Indiana's antique alley. Next door is one of Indiana's finest Scottish-style 18-hole golf course. Guests play better golf, shop more astutely, and travel more comfortably after one of the hosts' delightful breakfasts.

Hosts: Jean and Tom Lewis
Rooms: 4 (3 PB; 1 SB) $57-67
Full Breakfast
Credit Cards: None
Notes: 2, 5, 8, 9, 12, 14

LAGRANGE

The 1886 Inn

212 Factory Street, 46761
(219) 463-4227

The 1866 Inn bed and breakfast is filled with historical charm and elegance and glows with old-fashioned beauty in every room. Finest lodging area, yet affordable,

this inn is ten minutes from Shipshewana Flea Market.

Hosts: Duane and Gloria Billman
Rooms: 4 (PB) $79
Continental Breakfast
Credit Cards: A, B
Notes: 2, 5, 10, 12

Weaver's Country Oaks

0310N US 20, 46761
(219) 768-7181

This home, just seven minutes from Shipshewana, offers four tastefully decorated guest rooms with private baths. On three acres of well landscaped, shady countryside, it is next to Amish farms. Open year-round to accommodate off-season shopping and many country attractions.

Hosts: Rocky and Catherine Weaver
Rooms: 4 (PB) $65-75
Full Breakfast
Credit Cards: A, B
Notes: 2, 5, 7 (limited), 12

Solomon Mier Manor

LIGONIER

Solomon Mier Manor

508 South Cavin Street, 46767
(219) 894-3668

This Italian/Queen Anne Renaissance home was built in 1899. It has four guest rooms completely furnished in antique furniture of the period. Each room has its own private bath. This home is on the edge of Ligonier's business district, which is in an area that has been placed on the National Register of Historic Places. It contains some of the grandest architecture to be seen. It is minutes away from the Shipshewana flea market, Nappanee Amish Acres, Auburn-Cord Dusenburg Museum, Das Essenhause at Middlebury, and much more. Air conditioning. Two dollar charge per additional person in room.

Hosts: Ron and Doris Blue
Rooms: 4 (PB) $55
Continental Breakfast
Credit Cards: A, B
Notes: 2, 5, 12

MADISON

Main Street Bed and Breakfast

739 West Main Street, 47250
(812) 265-3539; (800) 362-6246

Graceful, classic, Revival home built circa 1843. Offering three tastefully decorated guest rooms, all with private baths. Elegant atmosphere, yet relaxed and friendly. Within the historic district of Madison. A gentle walk to shops, restaurants, and the Ohio River. A perfect base for sampling southern Indiana and refreshing one's soul.

Hosts: Mark and Mary Balph
Rooms: 3 (PB) $85-135
Full Breakfast
Credit Cards: A, B
Notes: 2, 5, 7 (restricted), 10, 11, 12, 14

METAMORA

The Thorpe House Country Inn

Clayborne Street, P.O. Box 36, 47030
(317) 647-5425; (317) 932-2365

Visit the Thorpe House in Metamora where the steam engine still brings passengers and the gristmill still grinds cornmeal. Spend a relaxing evening in this 1840 home, only one block from the historic Whitewater Canal. Homey, cozy rooms are tastefully furnished with antiques and country accessories. Enjoy a hearty breakfast before exploring over 100 shops in this quaint village. Public dining room. Special packages are available. Between Indianapolis and Cincinnati. Open April through the middle of December

Hosts: Mike and Jean Owens
Rooms: 5 (PB) $60-100
Full Breakfast
Credit Cards: A, B, D
Notes: 2, 3, 4, 6, 7, 8, 9, 11, 12, 14

MIDDLEBURY

Bee Hive Bed and Breakfast

Box 1191, 46540
(219) 825-5023

Come home to the farm. Enjoy country life, snuggle under a handmade quilt, and wake to the smell of freshly baked muffins. In the heart of Amish country. Enjoy the shops, flea markets, and antique stores in the area. Right off the Indiana Turnpike. Guest cottage available.

Hosts: Herb and Treva Swarm
Rooms: 4 (1 PB; 3 SB) $52-68
Full Breakfast
Credit Cards: A, B
Notes: 2, 5, 8, 10, 11, 12, 13

The Lookout Bed and Breakfast

14544 County Road 12, 46540
(219) 825-9809

A perfect place to renew, unwind, or just relax in Northern Indiana's Amish Country. Serene and comfortable country setting with swimming pool and walking trails. Enjoy a country breakfast in the sunroom with a panoramic view of surrounding farm country and wooded areas. Close to shops,

6 Pets welcome; 8 Children welcome; 9 Social drinking allowed; 10 Tennis available; 11 Swimming available; 12 Golf available; 13 Skiing available; 14 May be booked through travel agents.

good restaurants, and Shepshiwana Action and Flea Market.

Rooms: 5 (3 PB; 2 SB) $55-70
Full Breakfast
Credit Cards: A, B
Notes: 2, 5, 8, 9, 11, 12, 13

Varns Guest House

205 South Main Street, P.O. Box 125, 46540
(219) 825-9666; (800) 398-5424

A circa 1898 house built by the innkeeper's great-grandparents, this home has been in the Varns family for over 90 years. Recently restored, it is in the heart of Amish country just three miles south of the Indiana toll road's Middlebury exit. There are five air-conditioned guest rooms, each with private bath and individually decorated and named after the hosts' ancestors. Relax on the wraparound porch or snuggle before a wood-burning fireplace in the parlor during cold weather. Area attractions include giant Shipshewana flea market, Amish communities, fine shops, and restaurants.

Hosts: Carl and Diane Eash
Rooms: 5 (PB) $69
Continental Breakfast
Credit Cards: A, B, D
Notes: 2, 5, 8, 9, 10, 11, 12, 14

Varns Guest House

MISHAWAKA

The Beiger Mansion Inn Fables Gallery, Inc.

317 Lincoln Way East, 46544
(219) 256-0365; (800) 437-0131
FAX (219) 259-2622

The 22,000-square-foot inn offers gracious accommodations for travelers who appreciate its blend of historic and cultural personality. The romance and nostalgia of the mansion appeal to travelers, whether on holiday or business trip. Listed on the National Register of Historic Places. Close to South Bend and Notre Dame. Gift and art gallery on main level. Gourmet dining weekends; lunch Tuesday-Saturday.

Hosts: Ron Montandon and Phil Robinson
Rooms: 8 (PB) $65-175
Full Breakfast
Credit Cards: A, B, C, D, E, F
Notes: 2, 3, 4, 5, 9, 10, 11, 12, 14

MUNCIE

Ole Ball Inn Bed and Breakfast

1000 West Wayne, 47303
(317) 281-0466

A beautiful three-story Southern Colonial restored home is near Ball statue. Featuring fireplaces, five bedrooms all with private baths, TVs, telephones, FAX service, and elegant dining room. Guests enjoy homemade snacks by the fireplace in the living room or swinging on the old porch swing on the veranda. A suite with large open deck and fireplace will be long remembered. Many nearby attractions.

Hosts: Don and Sharon Green, Kathie and Larry Lewis
Rooms: 5 (PB) $75-95
Full Breakfast
Credit Cards: A, B, C
Notes: 2, 5, 7 (limited), 8, 9, 10, 11, 12

NOTES: Credit cards accepted: A MasterCard; B Visa; C American Express; D Discover Card; E Diner's Club; F Other; 2 Personal checks accepted; 3 Lunch available; 4 Dinner available; 5 Open all year;

NAPPANEE

Market Street Bed and Breakfast

253 East Market Street, 46550
(800) 497-3791

The red-brick house on the corner nestled among the tall maples in Amish country, 45 minutes from Notre Dame campus, close to the Dunes and Lake Michigan recreation, art festivals; nationally famous flea market area. Home-baked cookies offered as refreshment on arrival. Amish dinner reservation service; special packages available. A full breakfast is served.

Host: Sharon Bontrager
Rooms: 5 (3 PB; 2 SB) $55-75
Full Breakfast
Credit Cards: A, B
Notes: 2, 5, 10, 11, 12

NEW ALBANY

Honeymoon Mansion

1014 East Main Street, 47150
(800) 759-7270

Honeymoon Mansion is a lovely Victorian antebellum home. It was built in 1850 and is a national historic landmark. The beautiful interior combined with Southern charm lets guests enjoy the serenity and romance of yesteryear. Six beautiful bedrooms, each with a lovely bath, await guests' enjoyment. Three suites have large marble Jacuzzis with eight-foot high marble columns. One suite has a fireplace and private entrance. The Ohio River can be seen from the penthouse suite. Ten minutes from Louisville.

Hosts: Franklin and Beverly Dennis
Rooms: 6 (PB) $68-135
Full Breakfast
Credit Cards: F
Notes: 2, 5, 7 (limited), 9, 10, 11, 12, 13, 14

PAOLI

Braxtan House Inn Bed and Breakfast

210 North Gospel, 47454
(812) 723-4677; (800) 6-BRAXTAN

Braxtan House is a 21-room Queen Anne Victorian, lovingly restored and furnished in antiques. The inn overlooks the historic courthouse square and is near Paoli Peaks ski resort, Patoka Lake, and antique and craft shops in picturesque southern Indiana hill country.

Hosts: Duane and Kate Wilhelmi
Rooms: 6 (PB) $55-65
Full Breakfast
Credit Cards: A, B, C, D
Notes: 2, 5, 7 (limited), 8, 9, 10, 11, 12, 13, 14

Braxtan House Inn

PERU

Rosewood Mansion Inn

54 North Hood, 46970
(317) 472-7151

Step back in time. The Rosewood Mansion is a beautiful Victorian home in the heart of Peru, a town rich in railroad and circus history. Built in 1872, it showcases an open grand staircase of tiger oak, beautiful stained-glass windows, gorgeous natural woodwork, large windows and bays over-looking beautiful grounds, an oak-paneled library, and antique furnishings. Enjoy the quiet, comfortable elegance, warm hospitality, and delicious breakfasts.

Hosts: Lynn and David Hausner
Rooms: 8 (PB) $55-80
Full Breakfast
Credit Cards: A, B, C, D
Notes: 2, 5, 8, 9, 10, 11, 12, 14

RICHMOND

Norwich Lodge and Conference Center

920 Earlham Drive, 47374
(317) 983-1575

Surrounded by 400 acres of woods and streams, Norwich Lodge is open year-round and provides the ideal getaway for anyone who wants to escape life's daily routine. Outside the lodge, a choice of paths leads guests on a fascinating escapade through one of nature's most scenic and beautiful playgrounds. Hike along winding creeks, pause to watch the wildlife, or spot a variety of birds that inhabit the surrounding country.

Hosts: Melissa Bickford and Lois Hood
Rooms: 15 (PB) $35-45
Continental Breakfast
Credit Cards: A, B
Notes: 2, 5, 8, 10, 11

SHIPSHEWANA

Morton Street Bed and Breakfast

140 Morton Street, P.O. Box 775, 46565
(219) 768-4391; (800) 447-6475

In the heart of Amish country, guests will find themselves within walking distance of all kinds of shops and the famous Shipshewana flea market. Special winter and week-end rates available. Full breakfast Monday through Saturday, Continental breakfast on

Sunday, and lunch and dinner available at the restaurant next door.

Hosts: Joel and Kim Mishler and Esther Mishler
Rooms: 10 (PB)
Full and Continental Breakfasts
Credit Cards: A, B, D
Notes: 2, 3, 4, 5, 8 (limited), 12, 14

SOUTH BEND

The Book Inn

508 West Washington Street, 46601
(219) 288-1990

Second Empire home in downtown South Bend. Designers' showcase—every room beautifully decorated. Fresh flowers, silver, fine china, and candlelight. The hosts emphasize service for the business person as well as leisured guests. The inn also houses a quality used bookstore, and guest rooms include the Louisa May Alcott, Jane Austen, and Charlotte Brontë rooms. Corporate rates available.

Hosts: Peggy and John Livingston
Rooms: 5 (PB) $65-80
Continental Breakfast
Credit Cards: A, B, C
Notes: 2, 5, 9, 10, 11, 12, 14

Queen Anne Inn

Queen Anne Inn

420 West Washington Street, 46601
(219) 234-5959; (800) 582-2379

The Queen Anne Inn, an 1893 Victorian home listed on the historic register, is fa-

mous for the Frank Lloyd Wright bookcases and leaded glass. Antiques are used
throughout the house. The inn is three
blocks from downtown South Bend, near
Notre Dame and Oliver House Museum.
Relax and step back into the past.

Hosts: Bob and Pauline Medhurst
Rooms: 5 (PB) $65-100
Full Breakfast
Credit Cards: A, B, C
Notes: 2, 5, 8, 10, 11, 12, 13, 14

STORY

Story Inn

6404 South State Road 135, Nashville, 47448
(812) 988-2273; FAX (812) 988-6516

Situated on the southern edge of the Brown
County State Park, this historic Dodge City-
style general store is now a country inn
housing a critically acclaimed full-service
restaurant. Overnight lodgers can stay upstairs or in the surrounding village cottages.
Rooms are furnished with period antiques,
original artwork, fresh flowers, private
baths, and all rooms are air conditioned.
Reservations required.

Hosts: Bob and Gretchen Haddix
Rooms: 11 (PB) $71-104
Full Breakfast
Credit Cards: A, B, D, E, F (Carte Blanche)
Notes: 3, 4, 5, 8, 9, 10, 11, 12, 13

SYRACUSE

Anchor Inn
Bed and Breakfast

11007 North State Road 13, 46567
(219) 457-4714

Anchor Inn is a turn-of-the-century, two-
story home filled with period furniture and
antiques. Features of the home include claw-
foot tub, pier mirror, transomed doorways,
hardwood floors, and a large, inviting front
porch that overlooks the greens of an 18-
hole public golf course. Halfway between
South Bend and Fort Wayne in Indiana's

Anchor Inn

lake region and directly across the highway
from Lake Wawasee (Indiana's largest natural lake). Nearby attractions include the
Amish communities of Nappanee and Shipshewana, several antique shops, flea markets, two live theater groups, stern-wheeler
paddleboat rides, 101 lakes in Kosciusko
County, and a 3,400-acre game preserve.
Air-conditioned for guests' comfort.

Hosts: Robert and Jean Kennedy
Rooms: 8 (5 PB; 3 SB) $50-65
Full Breakfast
Credit Cards: A, B
Notes: 2, 5, 11, 12

WARSAW

Candlelight Inn

503 East Ft. Wayne, 46580
(219) 267-2906; (800) 352-0640

The Candlelight Inn is in a small town
where guests can enjoy two lakes within
walking distance as well as one of Indiana's
finest gardens down the block. The inn is
decorated in warm Victorian style with antiques, comfortable beds, and private baths
in each room. Warm cookies, a turned-
down bed, and soft, glowing candles await
guests as they return to their rooms each
night. Breakfast is served in the dining
room in elegant fashion with delicious
homemade creations. The inn serves the
visitor on vacation or corporate guests.

6 Pets welcome; 8 Children welcome; 9 Social drinking allowed; 10 Tennis available; 11 Swimming available;
12 Golf available; 13 Skiing available; 14 May be booked through travel agents.

Telephones and TV in each room, along with a FAX for the business traveler.

Hosts: Bill and Debi Hambright
Rooms: 10 (PB) $69-130
Full Breakfast
Credit Cards: A, B, C
Notes: 2, 5, 9, 10, 11, 12, 14

WEST BADEN SPRINGS_____

E. B. Rhodes House
Bed and Breakfast

Box 7, 47469
(812) 936-7398

A spacious first edition home built in 1901 with beautiful hand-carved woodwork and stained-glass windows. Two large porches complete with rockers to enjoy southern Indiana vistas and just plain relaxing. Entertainment for all seasons and tastes include gracious dining, historical tours, antiquing, steam locomotive rides, museums, and theater. For the more adventurous there is water or snow skiing, nearby state parks, and caving.

Hosts: Tom and Tina Hilgediek,
    Frank and Marlene Sipes
Rooms: 2 (PB) $35-45
Full Breakfast
Credit Cards: A B
Notes: 2, 5, 8, 10, 11, 12, 13

Iowa

The Shaw House

ANAMOSA

The Shaw House

509 South Oak, 52205
(319) 462-4485

Enjoy a relaxing step back in time in this three-story, 1866 Italianate mansion on a hilltop overlooking scenery immortalized in the paintings of native son Grant Wood. Special rooms include porch with panoramic countryside view, two-room tower suite, and ballroom. The mansion is on a 45-acre farm within easy walking distance of town. State park, canoeing, and antiques are nearby.

Hosts: Connie and Andy McKean
Rooms: 4 (3 PB; 1 SB) $40-65
Full Breakfast
Credit Cards: None
Notes: 2, 3, 4, 5, 8, 9, 10, 11, 12, 13, 14

ATLANTIC

Chestnut Charm Bed and Breakfast

1409 Chestnut Street, 50022
(712) 243-5652

An enchanting 1898 Victorian historic mansion with serene surroundings. Experience beauty, pleasure, and fantasy with someone special or enjoy a wonderful respite in a busy travel schedule. Relax and enjoy the tranquility! Elegant guest rooms with private baths. Exquisite gourmet meals with advance reservations. Awaken to the aroma of gourmet coffee and home baking. Air-conditioned. Experience gracious Iowa hospitality. Short drive to the famous bridges of Madison County. One suite is available.

Host: Barbara Stensvad
Rooms: 5 (PB) $60-90
Full Breakfast
Credit Cards: A, B
Notes: 3 and 4 (by reservation), 5, 10, 11, 12, 14

6 Pets welcome; 7 Smoking allowed; 8 Children welcome; 9 Social drinking allowed; 10 Tennis available; 11 Swimming available; 12 Golf available; 13 Skiing available; 14 May be booked through travel agents.

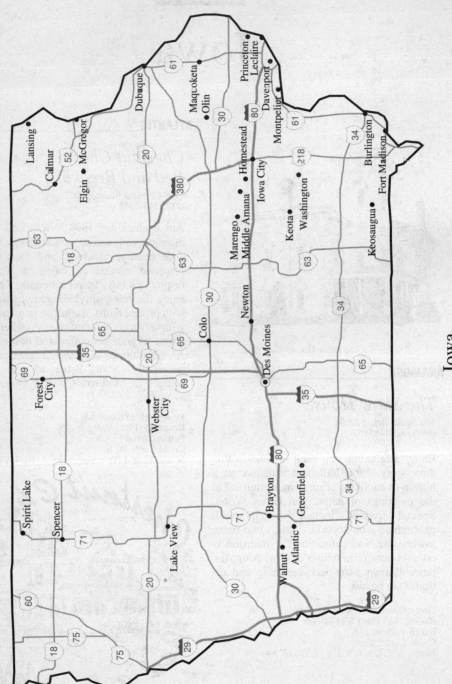

Iowa

BRAYTON

Hallock House

3265 Jay Avenue, P.O. Box 19, 50042
(712) 549-2449; (800) 945-0663 (reservations)

Victorian country home. Enjoy warm hospitality, fresh air, beautiful sunsets. Relax on the porch swing. Awaken to the sound of roosters crowing and the aroma of muffins baking. Full country breakfast served in the dining room. Gas grill available on the deck for those wishing to prepare lunch or dinner. Facilities available for overnight stabling of horses. Near Walnut, the Antique City of Iowa, and Elk Horn, the home of the National Danish Museum.

Hosts: Guy and Ruth Barton
Rooms: 2 (PB) $40
Full Breakfast
Credit Cards: A, B
Notes: 2, 5, 6 and 7 (limited), 8, 9, 10, 12

The Schramm House

BURLINGTON

The Schramm House
Bed and Breakfast

616 Columbia Street, 52601
(319) 754-0373

Step into the past when entering this restored 1870s Victorian in the heart of the historical district. High ceilings, parquet floors, original oak woodwork, wainscoting, and antique furnishings create the mood of an era past. Experience Burlington hospitality while having lemonade on the porch or tea by the fire with the gracious hosts. Walk to the Mississippi River, antique shops, restaurants, and more. An architectural masterpiece awaits guests in the city of Steeples.

Hosts: Sandy and Bruce Morrison
Rooms: 2 (PB) $75
Full Breakfast
Credit Cards: A, B
Notes: 2, 5, 7 (limited), 9, 10, 11, 12

CALMAR

Calmar Guesthouse

Rural Route 1, Box 206, 52132
(319) 562-3851

Newly remodeled Victorian home in northeast Iowa with many antiques, near Luther College and the newly accredited NICC (Northeast Iowa Community College, formerly Northeast Iowa Technical Institute). Close to world-famous Bily Clocks in Spillville, Niagara Cave, Lake Meye. Air-conditioned. Wake up to a fresh country breakfast. Good variety of restaurants in the area. Bike trail one block away.

Hosts: Art and Lucille Kruse
Rooms: 5 (1 PB; 4 SB) $35-45
Full Breakfast
Credit Cards: A, B
Notes: 2, 5, 7 (limited), 8, 9, 10, 11, 12, 13

COLO

Martha's Vineyard
Bed and Breakfast

620 West Street, 50056
(515) 377-2586

Just 15 minutes east of US 35, this bed and breakfast is a working farm on the edge of town. Homemade and homegrown food is served. The hostess is a retired home economics teacher. This fourth-generation 1920 family home has been lovingly restored and is furnished with antiques and collectibles throughout. A wildlife area and an old-fashioned flower garden add quiet beauty. Open May through October. Just like a visit to grandma's house.

Hosts: Norb and Martha Kash
Rooms: 2 (PB) $40-45
Full Breakfast
Credit Cards: None
Notes: 2, 8, 9, 10, 11, 12, 14

DAVENPORT _____

Fulton's Landing Guest House

1206 East River Drive, 52803
(319) 322-4069

The old Fulton mansion is a large Italianate stone residence built in 1871 by Ambrose Cowperthwaite Fulton. Listed on the National Register of Historic Places, the home offers a majestic view of the Mississippi River and is only minutes away from all area attractions. Five bedrooms are available for guests. A full breakfast is served in the dining room. Two large porches overlook the river, one on the main floor, and the other on the second floor with easy access from all the bedrooms. On Route 67 near downtown Davenport.

Hosts: Pat and Bill Schmidt
Rooms: 5 (3 PB; 2 SB) $55-100
Full Breakfast
Credit Cards: A, B, C
Notes: 2, 5, 8, 9, 12

River Oaks Inn

1234 East River Drive, 52803
(319) 326-2629

Overlooking the Mississippi River, River Oaks Inn has five guest rooms with private baths in an 1858 restored Victorian listed on the National Register of Historic Places.

Gazebo and large deck for relaxing river watching. Three-bedroom, two-bath carriage house with hot tub room on property. Close to area attractions. Full breakfast served. Children welcome. No smoking.

Hosts: Bill and Mary Jo Pohl
Rooms: 5 (PB) $55-125
Full Breakfast
Credit Cards: A, B, D
Notes: 2, 5, 8, 9, 11, 12, 14

DES MOINES _____

Carter House Inn

640 20th Street, 50314
(515) 288-7850

Built in the late 1870s, this Italianate was moved from its original site in 1988 to save it from demolition. In the Sherman Hill historic district, this bed and breakfast features original stenciling and faux marble fireplaces. Guest rooms have private or shared baths with claw-foot tubs. Breakfast is served in the formal dining room.

Host: Penny Schlitz
Rooms: 4 (2 PB; 2 SB) $50-60
Full Breakfast
Credit Cards: A, B
Notes: 2, 4, 5, 12, 14

Ellendale Bed and Breakfast

5340 Ashworth Road, 50266 (W.D.M.)
(515) 225-2219

Ellendale combines Old World Scandinavian decor and hospitality with established old farmstead setting and gardens. A short distance from I-80 and I-35, Ellendale is conveniently near Living History Farms, historic and creatively restored Valley Junction (Iowa's antique capital), and a major mall. Des Moines offers many cultural events, beautiful parks and churches, botanical art, and historical centers. Three-room suite plus fireplace and garden room.

NOTES: Credit cards accepted: A MasterCard; B Visa; C American Express; D Discover Card; E Diner's Club; F Other; 2 Personal checks accepted; 3 Lunch available; 4 Dinner available; 5 Open all year;

Hosts: Ellen and Dale Jackson
Rooms: 2 (PB) $55-70
Full Breakfast
Credit Cards: None
Notes: 2, 5, 8, 10, 11, 12

DUBUQUE

Juniper Hill Farm

15325 Budd Road, 52002
(319) 582-4405; (800) 572-1449
FAX (319) 583-6607

Beautiful country setting on 40 acres of woods with walking trails and a stocked pond. Adjacent to Sundown Ski Area (the only bed and breakfast in Iowa where guests can ski to the front door); ride to Heritage Bicycle Trail. Comfortably and restfully appointed with country atmosphere, some antiques. All rooms have private baths, one with whirlpool, and all rooms have access to an eight-foot outdoor hot tub.

Hosts: Ruth and Bill McElhiney
Rooms: 3 (PB) $65-140
Full Breakfast
Credit Cards: A, B, D
Notes: 2, 5, 8, 9, 12, 13, 14

The Richards House

The Richards House Bed and Breakfast

1492 Locust Street, 52001
(319) 557-1492

Relax in this 1883 stick-style Victorian mansion with original interior, over 80 stained-glass windows, eight fireplaces and eight varieties of varnished woodwork, embossed wall coverings, period furnishings, and more. Most rooms include working fireplaces, concealed TVs, and telephones. A full breakfast is served in the formal dining room. Easy access with plenty of parking.

Host: Michelle Delaney
Rooms: 5 (4 PB; 1 SB) $40-85
Full Breakfast
Credit Cards: A, B, C, D, E
Notes: 2, 5, 8, 9, 10, 11, 12, 13, 14

ELGIN

Country Swiss Guest House

404 Mill Street, 52141
(319) 426-5594

The Country Swiss Guest House is a classic home overlooking a Swiss settlement in a river valley and streams stocked with trout. Nearby is a conservation park with skiing, canoeing, hiking trails for the blind, and deer, pheasant, and wild turkey hunting. Amish stores and antique shops nearby.

Hosts: Ray, Sue, and Cathleen Crammond
Rooms: 2 (1 PB; 1 SB) $45-50
Full Breakfast
Credit Cards: None
Notes: 2, 5, 8, 10, 12, 13

FOREST CITY

1897 Victorian House Bed and Breakfast and Antiques

306 South Clark, 50436
(515) 582-3613

The 1897 house is a Queen Anne Victorian style, furnished in period furniture, much of which is for sale. Air conditioning has been added. The aroma of coffee and a four-course breakfast awaken guests each morn-

6 Pets welcome; 8 Children welcome; 9 Social drinking allowed; 10 Tennis available; 11 Swimming available; 12 Golf available; 13 Skiing available; 14 May be booked through travel agents.

ing. House is available for weddings, showers, dinners, teas, and weekend retreats.

Hosts: Richard and Doris Johnson
Rooms: 7 (3 PB; 4 SB) $60-80
Full Breakfast
Credit Cards: A, B
Notes: 2, 3, 4, 5, 11, 12, 14

1897 Victorian House

FORT MADISON

Kingsley Inn

707 Avenue H on Highway 61
(319) 372-7074; (800) 441-2327

Yesterday's charm and today's luxury describe this historic Victorian inn on the Mississippi River. Enjoy lunch and dinner at Alpha's, the unique in-house theme restaurant. Walk to the faithfully restored 1808 Old Fort Madison, Train Depot Museum, Steam Engine, unique shops, the Flood Museum, the Riverboat Casino, and galleries. Stately 19th-century residential district is nearby, and guests are a ten-minute drive to historic Nauvoo, Illinois, which has been called the "Williamsburg of the Midwest," with 40 restored 1840s shops and homes. Rooms have private baths, some of which are whirlpools. CATV, air conditioning, telephones, sprinklers, and alarms. Elevator and FAX machine available.

Host: Myrna Reinhard
Rooms: 14 (PB) $65-105
Continental Breakfast
Credit Cards: A, B, C, D, E
Notes: 2, 3, 4, 5, 9, 14

GREENFIELD

The Wilson Home

Rural Route 2, Box 132-1, 50849
(515) 743-2031

A huge indoor pool nestled in the Iowa countryside, only minutes from the bridges of Madison County, makes this bed and breakfast one of the most unique in America. Each spacious guest room opens directly onto the pool deck areas that are beautifully furnished with wicker and wrought iron. Breakfast is served in the adjacent 1918 antique-filled farm home. Perfect for honeymooners, hunters, vacationers, and business or escape weekends!

Hosts: Wendy and Henry Wilson
Rooms: 2 (PB) $68-90
Full Breakfast
Credit Cards: None
Notes: 2, 5, 6, 7 (limited), 8, 9, 10, 11, 12, 14

HOMESTEAD (AMANA COLONIES)

Die Heimat Country Inn

Main Street, Homestead, 52236
(319) 622-3937

Die Heimat, German for "the home place," is a century-old 1854 historic inn with 19 rooms, all furnished with Amana walnut and cherry furniture, private baths, TVs, and air conditioning. Colony heirlooms are found throughout the inn. Some rooms have Amana walnut canopied beds. Nature trail, golf course, wineries, woolen mills, and restaurants are all nearby. Murder mystery evenings available. Cash, traveler's checks, or personal checks preferred.

Hosts: Warren and Jacki Lock
Rooms: 19 (PB) $42.95-65.95
Full Breakfast
Credit Cards: A, B, D
Notes: 2, 5, 6, 7 (limited), 8, 9, 10, 11, 12,
   13 (cross country)

NOTES: Credit cards accepted: A MasterCard; B Visa; C American Express; D Discover Card; E Diner's Club; F Other; 2 Personal checks accepted; 3 Lunch available; 4 Dinner available; 5 Open all year;

IOWA CITY

Bella Vista Place Bed and Breakfast

2 Bella Vista, 52245
(319) 338-4129

The hostess has furnished this lovely 1920s home with antiques and artifacts she acquired on travels in Europe and Latin America. Downtown Iowa City and the University of Iowa are within walking distance of Bella Vista Place. The Hoover Library, Amana Colonies, and the Amish center of Kalona are all nearby. Breakfast consisting of coffee, tea, juice, fresh fruit, croissants, muffins, bagels, and eggs is served in the dining room's unique antique setting. Tennis courts and a pool are nearby in city park.

Host: Daissy P. Owen
Rooms: 3 (1 PB; 2 SB) $55-65
Full Breakfast
Credit Cards: None
Notes: 2, 5, 9, 10, 11, 14

Bella Vista Place

The Golden Haug

517 East Washington Street, 52240
(319) 338-6452

Elegance and whimsy decorate this 1920 arts and crafts house. Guests can retreat to one of four suites with in-room private bath or enjoy camaraderie of other guests. A full breakfast is served family-style. Relax on the porch swing, munch on sweets from the candy bowl, soak in the whirlpool or birthday bath, and enjoy tasty evening dessert in air-conditioned comfort. In the heart of Iowa City within a couple of blocks of the University of Iowa, eateries, and shopping.

Hosts: Nila Haug and Dennis Nowotny
Suites: 4 (PB) $65-90
Full Breakfast
Credit Cards: None
Notes: 2, 5, 8, 9, 10, 11, 12, 14

Haverkamps' Linn Street Homestay

619 North Linn Street, 52245
(319) 337-4363

A large and comfortable 1908 Edwardian-style home filled with antiques and collectibles. Wonderful front porch with old-fashioned swing. Walking distance to University of Iowa campus and the downtown area. Only a short drive to the Amana Villages, Kalona, Hoover Museum in West Branch, and Cedar Rapids. One mile south of I-80 at Exit 244.

Hosts: Clarence and Dorothy Haverkamp
Rooms: 3 (SB) $30-45
Full Breakfast
Credit Cards: None
Notes: 2, 5, 8, 9, 10, 11, 12, 14

KEOSAUQUA

Mason House Inn of Bentonsport

Route 2, Box 237, 52565
(319) 592-3133

The Mason House Inn was built in 1846, the year Iowa became a state, by Mormon craftsmen making their famous trek to Utah. It is the oldest steamboat river inn still serving overnight guests in the Midwest. The inn has the only fold-down copper bathtub in the state. Oral tradition has it

6 Pets welcome; 8 Children welcome; 9 Social drinking allowed; 10 Tennis available; 11 Swimming available; 12 Golf available; 13 Skiing available; 14 May be booked through travel agents.

that John C. Fremont, Abraham Lincoln, and Mark Twain slept here. The entire village is on the National Register of Historic Places. Guests will find a full cookie-jar in every room.

Hosts: Sheral and William McDermet III
Rooms: 9 (5 PB; 4 SB) $49-74
Full Breakfast
Credit Cards: A, B
Notes: 2, 3, 4, 5, 8, 9, 11, 12

Elmhurst

KEOTA

Elmhurst

305 County Line Road North, 52248
(515) 636-3001

This 1905 Victorian mansion was built with no expense spared by Thomas Singmaster. The family was the world's largest importer of draft horses. The mansion retains much of its original grandeur: prismed stained-glass and curved windows, circular solarium, parquet floors, beamed ceilings, Italian marble fireplace mantels, third floor ballroom, beveled plate-glass windows, two grand stairways, leather wall coverings, and more. The house is filled with history and antiques. Golf course, swimming, and 14-mile nature trail nearby. Closed January.

Host: Marjie Schantz-Koehler
Rooms: 5 (SB) $42
Full Breakfast
Credit Cards: None
Notes: 2, 3, 4, 7 (limited), 9, 10, 11, 12

LAKE VIEW

Marie's Bed and Breakfast

969 7th Street, P.O. Box 817, 51450
(712) 657-2486

This modern, all brick ranch-style home with nice view is just one block from the 900-acre beautiful Black Hawk Lake. Two bedrooms; one with a queen-size bed and private bath, and the other with an extra-long double bed and shared bath. The city of Lake View has a truly relaxing atmosphere with several parks, numerous sports, and other activities. A must-see is the annual Water Carnival which takes place the third weekend of July. Breakfast is choice of full or Continental. Seasonal and weekly rates available. Wheelchair accessible.

Hosts: Roy and Marie Werkmeister
Rooms: 2 (1 PB; 1 SB) $35-45
Full and Continental Breakfasts
Credit Cards: None
Notes: 2, 3, 4, 5, 6, 8, 10, 11, 12

LANSING

FitzGerald's Inn Bed and Breakfast

160 North 3rd Street, 52151
(319) 538-4872

Antique-filled Victorian home built in 1863. Five bedrooms and four baths (one large suite). Spacious grounds rise to a bluff-top screened gazebo overlooking the Mississippi River at one of its most beautiful stretches. A delicious full breakfast is served each morning and features home-baked goods, fresh fruit, and various breakfast items. Whole house rental available. In scenic northeast Iowa.

Hosts: Marie and Jeff FitzGerald
Rooms: 5 (3 PB; 2 SB) $60-75
Full Breakfast
Credit Cards: None
Notes: 2, 5, 7, 8, 9, 10, 11, 12, 13, 14

NOTES: Credit cards accepted: A MasterCard; B Visa; C American Express; D Discover Card; E Diner's Club; F Other; 2 Personal checks accepted; 3 Lunch available; 4 Dinner available; 5 Open all year;

LECLAIRE

Monarch
Bed and Breakfast Inn

303 South Second Street, 52753
(319) 289-3011; (800) 772-7724

Overlooking the mighty Mississippi River, the Monarch was built in the late 1850s. It boasts wood floors and high ceilings and is decorated with antiques and mementos from Europe. Enjoy the enclosed porch and deck. Leclaire is a quaint historical town and is the birthplace of Buffalo Bill. Two-day river cruises are available May through October. Two miles north off I-80 Exit 306. French and Polish also spoken.

Hosts: David and Emilie Oltman
Rooms: 7 (4 PB; 3 SB) $45-65
Full and Continental Breakfasts
Credit Cards: None
Notes: 2, 3, 4, 5, 8, 12, 14

MAQUOKETA

Squiers Manor
Bed and Breakfast

418 West Pleasant, 52060
(319) 652-6961

Awaken to the aroma of homemade goodies and elegant entrees in this historic 1882 Queen Anne brick mansion with period furnishings. Six elegant guest rooms including bridal suite. Single and double whirlpools. Candlelight evening dessert. Crackling fireplace. All this in a quiet, romantic and friendly atmosphere.

Hosts: Virl and Kathy Banowetz
Rooms: 6 (PB) $65-95
Full Breakfast
Credit Cards: A, B, C
Notes: 2, 5, 8, 9, 10, 11, 12, 13, 14

MARENGO

Loy's Farm
Bed and Breakfast

2077 KK Avenue, Rural Route 1, 52301
(319) 642-7787

In the heartland of an Iowa farm town, this corn and hog farm has a recreation room and outdoor enjoyment with play equipment for all ages. Full breakfast with homemade products. Close to colonies, Iowa City, and Cedar Rapids. Designer outlet mall and golf courses nearby. Close to I-80.

Hosts: Loy and Robert Walker
Rooms: 3 (1 PB; 1 SB) $50-60
Full Breakfast
Credit Cards: None
Notes: 2, 4, 5, 6 (limited), 8, 9, 10, 11, 12, 14

McGREGOR

River's Edge
Bed and Breakfast

112 Main Street, 52157
(319) 873-3501

McGregor's premiere waterfront location. Cozy comfortable rooms overlooking the Mississippi River. Fully equipped kitchen and dining room for guest use. Each guest room has a private bath and cable TV. Spacious family room, patio, screened porch, and a second-level deck. Central air. Unique antique shopping, quaint restaurants, riverboat gambling, and various recreational activities can be found in this area. Come for a special getaway.

Host: Rita Lange
Rooms: 3 (PB) $50
Continental Breakfast
Credit Cards: A, B
Notes: 2, 5, 8, 9, 10, 11, 12, 13

6 Pets welcome; 8 Children welcome; 9 Social drinking allowed; 10 Tennis available; 11 Swimming available; 12 Golf available; 13 Skiing available; 14 May be booked through travel agents.

MIDDLE AMANA

Dusk to Dawn Bed and Breakfast

Box 124, 52307
(319) 622-3029

An invitation to relax in a peaceful, comfortable atmosphere, in a house decorated with beautiful Amana antiques. In historic Middle Amana. A touch of the past is accented with a greenhouse, spacious deck, and Jacuzzi.

Hosts: Bradley and Lynn Hahn
Rooms: 7 (PB) $43.05
Continental Breakfast
Credit Cards: A, B, C, D
Notes: 2, 5, 7, 8, 9, 10, 11, 12, 14

MONTPELIER

Varners' Caboose Bed and Breakfast

204 East 2nd, P.O. Box 10, 52759
(319) 381-3652

Stay in a real Rock Island Lines caboose. Set on its own track behind the hosts' house, the caboose is a self-contained unit, with bath, shower, and complete kitchen. It sleeps four, with a queen-size bed and two twins in the cupola. There is color TV, central air and heat, plus plenty of off-street parking. A fully prepared country breakfast is left in the caboose kitchen to be enjoyed by guests whenever they choose. On Route 22, halfway between Davenport and Muscatine.

Hosts: Bob and Nancy Varner
Room: 1 (PB) $55
Full Breakfast
Credit Cards: None
Notes: 2, 5, 6, 8, 14

NEWTON

La Corsette Maison Inn

629 First Avenue East, 50208
(515) 792-6833

La Corsette Maison Inn

This opulent, mission-style mansion built in 1909 by Iowa state senator August Bergman maintains the charm of its original oak woodwork, art nouveau stained- glass windows, brass light fixtures, and even some original furnishings. Despite the addition of contemporary comforts, the bedchambers' original features have been retained—the bevelled glass windows in the penthouse and the French country decor in the renovated servant's quarters. Down-filled pillows and comforters are available. Enjoy Kay's special hot spiced wine in front of one of three fireplaces. Be prepared for a delectable breakfast served in the gracious tradition of La Corsette.

Host: Kay Owen
Rooms: 9 (PB) $70-185
Full Breakfast
Credit Cards: A, B, C
Notes: 2, 4, 5, 6 and 8 (call), 7 (limited), 9, 10, 11, 12, 14

OLIN

LampPost Bed and Breakfast

101 East Cleveland Street, 52320-0027
(319) 484-2925 (evenings)

A restored 1892 Victorian home in Jones County, Iowa, which is famous for artist Grant Wood, painter of *American Gothic*. Enjoy the small town tranquility, a bit of the past, and hold onto a few precious mementoes with the antiques and wicker restora-

NOTES: Credit cards accepted: A MasterCard; B Visa; C American Express; D Discover Card; E Diner's Club; F Other; 2 Personal checks accepted; 3 Lunch available; 4 Dinner available; 5 Open all year;

tion shop available on site. Central air, golf, fishing, boat dock, and hunting close by.

Hosts: Vicki and Ronald Conley
Rooms: 3 (SB) $35-45
Full Breakfast
Credit Cards: None
Notes: 2, 3 and 4 (by reservation), 5, 7, 8, 9, 12

PRINCETON

The Woodlands

P.O. Box 127, 52768
(319) 289-3177; (319) 289-4661

A secluded woodland escape that can be as private or social as guests wish. The Woodlands bed and breakfast is nestled among pines on 26 acres of forest and meadows in a private wildlife refuge. Guests delight in an elegant breakfast by the swimming pool or by a cozy fireplace while viewing the outdoor wildlife activity. Boating and fishing on the Mississippi River, golf, cross-country skiing, and hiking are available. A short drive to the Quad City metropolitan

The Woodlands

area, shopping, art galleries, museums, theater, restaurants, and sporting events.

Hosts: Betsy Wallace and E. Lindebraekke
Rooms: 3 (2 PB; 1 SB) $75-115
Full Breakfast
Credit Cards: A, B
Notes: 2, 3, 4, 5, 7 (limited), 8, 9, 10, 11, 12, 13, 14

SPENCER

Hannah Marie Country Inn

Rural Route 1, Highway 71 South, 51301
(712) 262-1286; (712) 332-7719

This lovingly restored farm home offers a hearty gourmet breakfast. Guests are pampered with private baths, air conditioning, evening dessert, whirlpools, or claw-foot tubs. Lunches Tuesday through Saturday. Iowa Great Lakes 20 miles away. Large herb garden and croquet court. Closed December through April.

Hosts: Mary and Dave Nichols
Rooms: 4 (PB) $55-85
Full Breakfast
Credit Cards: A, B, C, D
Notes: 2, 3, 4, 6 and 7 (limited), 8, 10, 11, 12, 14

SPIRIT LAKE

Moorland Country Inn

Rural Route Box 7313, 51360
(507) 847-4707; (800) 544-1148

Moorland is an English country estate built at the turn of the century. Much of the Moore family furnishings have been returned to the five-bedroom main house. Also on the estate is a three-bedroom carriage house and the gate house suite. Guests are treated to a formal breakfast served either in the main dining room or on the front sun porch.

Host: Kevin Joul
Rooms: 0 (PB) 070 150
Full Breakfast
Credit Cards: A, B
Notes: 2, 3, 5, 9, 11, 12, 13, 14

WALNUT

Antique City Inn
Bed and Breakfast

P.O. Box 584, 400 Antique City Drive, 51577
(712) 784-3722

6 Pets welcome; 8 Children welcome; 9 Social drinking allowed; 10 Tennis available; 11 Swimming available; 12 Golf available; 13 Skiing available; 14 May be booked through travel agents.

This 1911 Victorian home has a wrap-around porch, beautiful woodwork, French doors, butler pantry, and dumbwaiter ice box. One block from antique shops with 250 antique dealers, turn-of-the-century brick streets, storefronts, globed street lights, historical museum, and a restored opera house. Home of a country music museum and Iowa's Country Music Hall of Fame.

Host: Sylvia Reddie
Rooms: 5 (1 PB; 4 SB) $40
Full Breakfast
Credit Cards: A, B, C
Notes: 2, 3, 4, 5, 8 (over 12), 9

Roses and Lace

WASHINGTON

Roses and Lace Bed and Breakfast

821 North 2nd Avenue, 52353
(319) 653-2462

Capture the ambience of Victorian living in this restored 1893 Queen Anne home that boasts Eastlake woodwork, beaded spandrels, pocket doors, and original chandeliers. All 11 rooms have antique furnishings. Relax in the parlor in front of a cozy fire in the winter, or enjoy a glass of lemonade on the inviting wraparound porch in the summer. Guests may use bicycles to ride the Kewash Nature Trail. Enjoy the county's many antique shops.

Hosts: Milt and Judi Wildebuer
Rooms: 2 (PB) $55
Full Breakfast
Credit Cards: None
Notes: 2, 5, 8, 10, 11, 12, 13

WEBSTER CITY

Centennial Farm Bed and Breakfast

1091 220th Street, Rural Route 2, 50595-7571
(515) 832-3050

Built in 1869, parts of the original homestead and barns have been incorporated into the air-conditioned farmhouse, which is among fields of corn and soybeans. The hosts are fourth-generation farmers here, and Tom was born in the downstairs bedroom. Guests can see the farm operation and Tom's 1929 Model A Ford pickup. Close to golf, tennis, swimming, antiques, parks, and fine dining. Just 22 miles west of I-35 at exit 142 or 144.

Hosts: Tom and Shirley Yungclas
Rooms: 2 (SB) $35
Full Breakfast
Credit Cards: None
Notes: 2, 5, 7, 8, 9, 10, 11, 12

Kansas

Balfours' House

940 1900 Avenue, 67410
(913) 263-4262

Gilbert and Marie Balfour welcome guests
to this modern, cottage-style home set on a
hillside. The house is on just over two
acres, and has a spacious yard. Guests
have their own private entrance into the
family room, which includes a fireplace,
piano, and TV. The main attraction of the
house is a hexagonal recreation room that
has a built-in swimming pool, spa, and
dressing area with shower. A separate
Southwestern-style bungalow is also available. The hosts will gladly direct guests to
the Eisenhower Museum, Greyhound Hall
of Fame, and old historic mansions.

Hosts: Gil and Marie Balfour
Suites: 2 (PB) $65
Continental Breakfast
Credit Cards: A, B
Notes: 2, 5, 6, 8, 9, 11

Balfours' House

Bedknobs and Biscuits

15202 Parallel, 66007
(913) 724-1540

A little bit of country close to Bonner
Springs and Kansas City. A warm, inviting
beamed gathering room; walls covered in
handpainted vines. Stenciling throughout
the house, lovely quilts, cookies in the
evening, and a huge country breakfast in the
morning. Three country Victorian bedrooms with two shared baths. The hosts
want to pamper their guests!

Host: Sonie Mance
Rooms: 3 (SB) $50-70
Full Breakfast
Credit Cards: None
Notes: 2, 5, 12

Windmill Inn

1787 Rain Road, 67431
(913) 263-8755

Windmill Inn is a prairie-style, four-square
home built in 1917. Surrounded by acres of
farm ground and nestled near historic Abilene, Kansas, this bed and breakfast inn
recreates the charm of a bygone ear. Special
attention has been given to every detail of
the restoration, down to the beautiful oak
woodwork and brilliant stained and beveled
glass in the common areas. The wraparound
front porch lures guests to enjoy the sights
and sounds of country life while relaxing in
a porch swing or rocking chair.

6 Pets welcome; 7 Smoking allowed; 8 Children welcome; 9 Social drinking allowed; 10 Tennis available; 11
Swimming available; 12 Golf available; 13 Skiing available; 14 May be booked through travel agents.

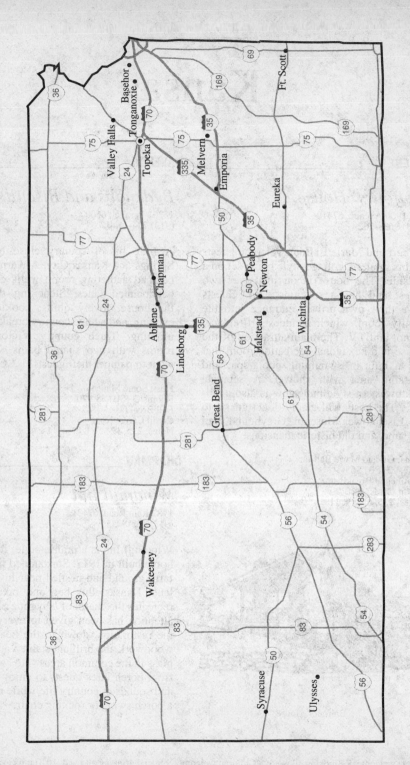

Kansas

Hosts: Deb and Tim Sanders
Rooms: 4 (PB) $55-69
Full Breakfast
Credit Cards: A, B, D
Notes: 2, 4, 5, 8 (over 8), 9, 10, 11, 12, 14

EMPORIA

Plumb House Bed and Breakfast

628 Exchange Street, 66801
(316) 342-6881

Step back in time for a restful stay in the restored Victorian home of early day Emporians, George and Ellen Plumb. Experience the elegance of beveled glass windows, pocket doors, lace curtains, and antique furnishings, combined with 1990s convenience. Guests will awaken to the smell of fresh bread and home cooking! Morning coffee or afternoon tea may be taken on the balcony, or front porch, or in the garden.

Host: Barbara Stoecklein
Rooms: 5 (3 PB; 2 SB) $55-75
Full Breakfast
Credit Cards: A, B
Notes: 2, 5, 8, 9, 10, 11, 12

EUREKA

123 Mulberry Street Bed and Breakfast

123 South Mulberry Street, 67045
(316) 583-7515

This Victorian-era house nestled in the heart of the Flint Hills in quiet, rural Eureka, Kansas, is the perfect setting for a honeymoon, anniversary weekend, or mini-vacation. One hour east of Wichita on Highway 54, this 1912 home features a choice of uniquely decorated rooms in "Victorian Dreams," "Country Charm," or "Rosemeade." A cozy parlor with wide screen TV and a hot tub under the stars complete the picture for a relaxing break from everyday life. The peaceful, scenic landscape of the Flint Hills is always a delight. Guided driving tours of historic spots are available. Enjoy the natural beauty of the Fall River Reservoir and Wildlife Area. Horseback riding, golfing, and antique hunting.

Hosts: Jay and Linda Jordan
Rooms: 3 (1 PB; 2 SB) $50-60
Full Breakfast
Credit Cards: A, B
Notes: 5, 9, 11

FORT SCOTT

The Chenault Mansion

820 South National Avenue, 66701
(316) 223-6800

At the gracious home built by Edwin Chenault, little has changed since 1887. Take a step back in the time when graciousness was routine. Visit in the Victorian parlor, sleep in a period room, and enjoy a full breakfast under one of the crystal chandeliers. The elegant interior features curved glass windows, stained and leaded glass, ornate cherry, gum, ash, and oak woodwork, pocket doors, and fireplaces. The home is furnished with antiques, as well as a large china and glass collection. All rooms include private baths, queen-size beds, and central air conditioning for guests' comfort. Hospitality is not just the hosts' business, it's their way of life.

Hosts: Bob and Elizabeth Schafer
Rooms: 5 (PB) $70-85
Full Breakfast
Credit Cards: A, B, D
Notes: 2, 4 (by reservation), 5, 8, 9, 10, 11, 12, 14

GREAT BEND

Peaceful Acres Bed and Breakfast

Route 5, Box 153, 67530
(316) 793-7527

NOTES: Credit cards accepted: A MasterCard; B Visa; C American Express; D Discover Card; E Diner's Club; F Other; 2 Personal checks accepted; 3 Lunch available; 4 Dinner available; 5 Open all year; 6 Pets welcome; 7 Smoking allowed; 8 Children welcome; 9 Social drinking allowed; 10 Tennis available; 11 Swimming available; 12 Golf available; 13 Skiing available; 14 May be booked through travel agents.

This sprawling farmhouse has a working windmill, small livestock, chickens, and guineas. Five miles from Great Bend and close to Cheyenne Bottoms and Quivira Wet Lands, Ft. Larned, Pawnee Rock, Wilson Lake, Lake Kanopolis, and Santa Fe Trail. Enjoy hospitality and the quiet of the country in this farmhouse furnished with some antiques. Homegrown and homemade foods. Full country breakfast is served. Kitchen available.

Hosts: Dale and Doris Nitzel
Rooms: 2-3 (SB) $30
Full Breakfast
Credit Cards: None
Notes: 2, 5, 6, 8, 10, 11, 14

HALSTEAD

Heritage Inn

300 Main Street, 67056
(316) 835-2118

Heritage Inn is an extraordinary 1922 bed and breakfast inn in the heart of Kansas. The moment guests step through the doors of the Heritage Inn, they will feel the comfort and relaxed charm of the 1920s, but will enjoy the convenience of the 1990s.

Hosts: Jim and Gery Hartong
Rooms: 5 (PB) $29
Full Breakfast
Credit Cards: A, B
Notes: 2, 3, 4, 5, 7, 8, 9, 10, 11, 12, 14

LINDSBORG

Swedish Country Inn

112 West Lincoln Street, 67456
(913) 227-2985; (800) 231-0266 out of state

Lindsborg is a lovely Swedish community in the center of Kansas. The inn is furnished with Swedish pine furniture, and all of the beds have hand-quilted quilts. A delicious full Scandinavian breakfast is served, and all rooms have private bath and TV. No smok-

Swedish Country Inn

ing or guest pets allowed. Near Bethany College, where Handel's *Messiah* is performed on Palm and Easter Sundays.

Hosts: Gene and Helen Van Amburg
Rooms: 19 (PB) $45-75
Full Breakfast
Credit Cards: A, B, D
Notes: 2, 5, 8, 10, 11, 12

MELVERN

Schoolhouse Inn

106 East Beck, 66510
(913) 549-3473

Built in 1870 as Melvern's first schoolhouse, this two-story limestone structure sits on an acre-and-a-half lot with shade trees. The four upstairs guest rooms are furnished with antique and contemporary furnishings. The inn is away from busy streets, making it an ideal place for a weekend getaway. A full breakfast is served at a large dining table. Three miles from Melvern Lake where guests can enjoy all types of water sports. No smoking.

Hosts: Rudy and Alice White
Rooms: 4 (2 PB; 2 SB) $50-60
Full Breakfast
Credit Cards: A, B
Notes: 2, 5, 8, 11

NOTES: Credit cards accepted: A MasterCard; B Visa; C American Express; D Discover Card; E Diner's Club; F Other; 2 Personal checks accepted; 3 Lunch available; 4 Dinner available; 5 Open all year;

NEWTON

Hawk House
Bed and Breakfast

307 West Broadway, 67114
(316) 283-2045

In the heart of wheat country. A three-story Victorian home with massive oak staircase and spacious common rooms accented by oak floors and stained glass. Each guest room is fully furnished with antiques, linens, and appointments. Guests are surrounded with elegance and hospitality. Air conditioning.

Hosts: Lon and Carol Buller
Rooms: 4 (1 PB; 3 SB) $50-60
Full Breakfast
Credit Cards: A, B
Notes: 2, 5, 10, 11, 12

Jones Sheep Farm

PEABODY

Jones Sheep Farm
Bed and Breakfast

Rural Route 2, Box 185, 66866
(316) 983-2815

Enjoy a turn-of-the-century home in a pastoral setting. On a working sheep farm "at the end of the road," the house is furnished in 1930s style (no telephone or TV). Quiet and private. A wonderful historic small town is nearby. The full country breakfast features fresh farm produce.

Hosts: Gary and Marilyn Jones
Rooms: 2 (SB) $45
Full Breakfast
Credit Cards: None
Notes: 2, 5, 6, 10, 11, 12

SYRACUSE

Braddock Ames
Bed and Breakfast

201 North Avenue B and Main Street, 67878
(316) 384-5218; (316) 384-7603

This senior-citizen residential hotel was built in 1930 and features three bed and breakfast rooms and three apartments, all with private bath, TV, and refrigerated air conditioning. Two large lobbies have been renovated and restored, and home-cooked food is served for breakfast, while dinner can be served if requested ahead of time. No-cholesterol breakfasts are available. The sport of tanking on the Arkansas River originated here, and a ride can be arranged in advance. The Wizard of Odds shop is in the downstairs lobby and open to guests. Decorated by Marjorie Hallsten.

Host: Lois Jacobs
Rooms: 3 (PB) Apartments: 3 $45-65
Full Breakfast
Credit Cards: F
Notes: 2, 4, 5, 8 (over 12), 11, 12

TONGANOXIE

Almeda's Bed
and Breakfast Inn

220 South Main Street, 66086
(913) 845-2295

In a picturesque small town designated a historic site in 1983, the inn dates back to World War I. Sip a cup of coffee at the stone bar once used as a bus stop in 1930. In fact, this room was the inspiration for the play *Bus Stop*. Close driving distance to

Kansas City International Airport, Kansas City Country Club Plaza, the Renaissance Festival, the "Sandstone" Amphitheater, Woodlands Racetrack, the National Agriculture Hall of Fame, the University of Kansas, Weston and Snow Creek skiing, Topeka State Capitol, and antique shops.

Hosts: Almeda and Richard Tinberg
Rooms: 7 (PB and SB) $40-65
Continental Breakfast
Credit Cards: None
Notes: 2, 5, 9, 11, 12

TOPEKA

Heritage House

3535 Southwest 6th Street, 66606
(913) 233-3800

A charming country inn, listed on the National Register of Historic Places, situated near the zoo, park, and museum. Twelve tasteful, designer-decorated rooms with private baths, telephones, and TVs. The sunroom/dining room is well known for its outstanding Continental cuisine.

Host: Chad Marsh
Rooms: 12 (PB) $60-145
Full Breakfast
Credit Cards: A, B, C, D, E
Notes: 2, 3, 4, 5, 8, 9, 14

ULYSSES

Fort's Cedar View

1675 West Patterson, 67880
(316) 356-2570

Fort's Cedar View is in the heart of the world's largest natural-gas field. It is on the Santa Fe Trail, eight miles north of famed Wagon Bed Springs, the first source of water after crossing the Cimarron River west of Dodge City, which is 80 miles northeast.

Host: Lynda Fort
Rooms: 5 (2 PB; 3 SB) $35-55
Full Breakfast
Credit Cards: None
Notes: 2, 5, 7 (limited), 10, 11, 12

VALLEY FALLS

The Barn Bed and Breakfast Inn

Rural Route 2, Box 87, 66088
(913) 945-3225

In the beautiful rolling hills of northeast Kansas a 101 year old barn waits for guests. Where once cattle and horses bedded down, people now sleep. In place of straw, king-size beds and private baths greet the guest. The room rate includes supper as well as a full breakfast. A large indoor heated pool is enjoyed year-round. Guests appreciate our two large glassed-in living rooms overlooking the countryside.

Hosts: Tom and Marcella Ryan and Patricia Miller
Rooms: 19 (PB); $71.62-83.38
Full Breakfast
Credit Cards: A, B, C, D
Notes: 2, 3, 4, 5, 8, 9, 10, 11, 12, 13, 14

WAKEENEY

Thistle Hill Bed and Breakfast

Route 1, Box 93, 67672
(913) 743-2644

A comfortable, secluded cedar farm home situated midway between Kansas City and Denver along I-70. Experience farm life and visit Castle Rock. Self-guided wildflower walks through a 60-acre prairie restoration project. Enjoy a hearty country breakfast by the fireplace or on the summer porch overlooking the herb garden.

Hosts: Dave and Mary Hendricks
Rooms: 4 (2 PB; 2 SB) $55-65
Full Breakfast
Credit Cards: None
Notes: 2, 5, 6 and 7 (limited), 8, 9, 10, 11, 12

WICHITA

Inn at the Park

3751 East Douglas, 67218
(316) 652-0500; (800) 258-1951

NOTES: Credit cards accepted: A MasterCard; B Visa; C American Express; D Discover Card; E Diner's Club; F Other; 2 Personal checks accepted; 3 Lunch available; 4 Dinner available; 5 Open all year;

Elegant Old World charm and comfort in a completely renovated mansion. Twelve distinctive suites, ten in the main house and two in the carriage house. Some of the features include fireplaces, whirlpool bath, private courtyard, hot tub, and many spacious three-room suites. A preferred hideaway among people looking for a romantic retreat or convenient base of operation for corporate guests. The Inn at the Park was named one of the top ten outstanding new inns in the country by *Inn Review* newsletter in 1989.

Host: Michelle Hickman
Rooms: 12 (PB) $75-135
Continental Breakfast
Credit Cards: A, B, C, D
Notes: 2, 3, 4, 5, 7 (limited), 8, 9, 10, 14

Max Paul...an Inn

3910 East Kellogg, 67218
(316) 689-8101

Rooms are furnished with feather beds, European antiques, cable TV, and private baths. Executive suites have vaulted ceilings, wood-burning fireplaces, and features such as skylights and private balconies. There is a Jacuzzi/exercise room. Weekends, breakfast may be served in the room or in the garden. Centrally situated for the airport, downtown, shopping, and local attractions. Closed Christmas Day.

Host: Roberta Eaton
Rooms: 14 (PB) $69-149
Full Breakfast
Credit Cards: A, B, C, D, E, F
Notes: 2, 5, 7, 9, 10, 12

6 Pets welcome; 8 Children welcome; 9 Social drinking allowed; 10 Tennis available; 11 Swimming available; 12 Golf available; 13 Skiing available; 14 May be booked through travel agents.

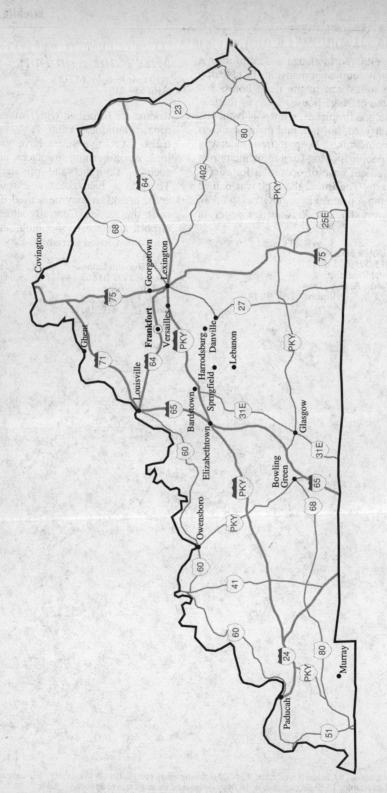

Kentucky

Kentucky

Amber Le Ann
Bed and Breakfast

209 East Stephen Foster Avenue, 40004
(502) 349-0014; (800) 828-3330

Charm and relaxed comfort in a unique Victorian setting. Elegant guest rooms and beautiful decor await guests in this newly remodeled home. King-size beds and private baths. In the center of town within walking distance of most attractions. Full breakfast and evening desserts provided. No pets. No children. No smoking.

Host: Kenny Mandell
Rooms: 5 (PB) $85-125
Full Breakfast
Credit Cards: A, B, C
Notes: 2, 5, 9, 10, 12, 14

Bruntwood Inn

714 North Third Street, 40004
(502) 348-8218

This 1830 antebellum mansion and adjacent cottage provide eight bedrooms furnished in antiques and lovely linens. The mansion, listed on the national register, features dental molding, stained glass, ash floors, grand entrance foyer, and an ash and cherry staircase that spirals up three floors. A full plantation breakfast is included in the stay.

Hosts: Susan and Zyg Danielak
Rooms: 8 (6 PB; 2 SB) $70-140
Full Breakfast
Credit Cards: None
Notes: 2, 5, 8, 9, 14

Jailer's Inn

111 West Stephen Foster Avenue, 40004
(502) 348-5551

In 1819, Jailer's Inn was originally constructed for use as a jail. In 1874 it was turned into the jailer's residence. This complex was the oldest operating jail in the Commonwealth of Kentucky until 1987. Large rooms, completely renovated and furnished with heirlooms and antiques. One room resembles a cell, with two of the original bunk beds plus a waterbed; decorated in prison black and white. One room has a Jacuzzi. A deluxe Continental breakfast is served. Closed January. Call for rates.

Hosts: Challen and Fran McCoy
Rooms: 6 (PB)
Continental Breakfast
Credit Cards: A, B, C, D
Notes: 8, 9, 10, 11, 12, 14

The Mansion
Bed and Breakfast

1003 North 3rd Street, 40004
(502) 348-2586; (800) 399-2586

A beautiful Greek Revival mansion, circa 1851, on the National Register of Historic

NOTES: Credit cards accepted: A MasterCard; B Visa; C American Express; D Discover Card; E Diner's Club; F Other; 2 Personal checks accepted; 3 Lunch available; 4 Dinner available; 5 Open all year; 6 Pets welcome; 7 Smoking allowed; 8 Children welcome; 9 Social drinking allowed; 10 Tennis available; 11 Swimming available; 12 Golf available; 13 Skiing available; 14 May be booked through travel agents.

Places. On more than three acres of land with magnificent trees and plantings, it reminds one of more genteel times. The Mansion is on the site where the first Confederate flag, the Stars and Bars, was raised in Kentucky for the first time. The rooms feature period antiques, hand-crocheted bedspreads, dust ruffles, and shams.

Host: Joseph D. Downs
Rooms: 8 (PB) $75-85
Continental Breakfast
Credit Cards: A, B, D
Notes: 5, 7 (restricted), 9, 14

BOWLING GREEN

Alpine Lodge

5310 Morgantown Road, 42101-8201
(502) 843-4846

Alpine Lodge is a Swiss chalet on the outskirts of Bowling Green. There is a guest cottage, two suites that sleep up to six people, two bedrooms with private baths, and lots of flowers, gardens, and a nature trail with five deer stands. This cottage boasts a pool, gazebo, deck, and screened-in porch. The honeymoon suite has a canopy bed, refrigerator, and private bath. The lodge serves a big country breakfast and is near Mammoth Cave, Opryland USA, Horse Cave Theater, Steeplechase horse race track, Shakertown, and the Corvette plant.

Hosts: Dr. and Mrs. David Livingston
Rooms: 7 (3 PB; 4 SB) $40-150
Full Breakfast
Credit Cards: None
Notes: 2, 5, 6, 7, 8, 9, 11, 12, 14

Walnut Lawn
Bed and Breakfast

1800 Morgantown Road, 42101
(502) 781-7255

This is a restored Victorian house, part of which was built in 1805. It is furnished with family antiques of the period. On a farm three miles from the center of Bowling Green and just off Green River Parkway

and I-65. The place has been in the family for 125 years. Walnut Lawn requires reservations and serves a Continental breakfast. No smoking.

Host: George Anna McKenzie
Rooms: 4 (3 PB; 1 SB) $50
Continental Breakfast
Credit Cards: None
Notes: 2, 5, 9

COVINGTON

Amos Shinkle Townhouse
Bed and Breakfast

215 Garrard Street, 41011
(606) 431-2118

This restored mansion, circa 1854, has won several preservation awards. It features a Greco-Italianate facade with a cast-iron filigree porch. Inside there are lavish crown moldings, Italianate mantels on the fireplaces, 16-foot ceilings, and Rococo Revival chandeliers (Carnelius/Baker). Guest rooms boast four-poster or massive Victorian-style beds and period furnishings. Here Southern hospitality is at its finest. Just a 15-minute walk to downtown Cincinnati, Ohio.

Hosts: Harry (Don) Nash and Bernie Moorman
Rooms: 7 (PB) $70-125
Full Breakfast
Credit Cards: A, B, C, D, E
Notes: 2, 5, 7, 8, 9, 14

DANVILLE

Twin Hollies
Bed and Breakfast

406 Maple Avenue, 40422
(606) 236-8954

Fine old antebellum home features spacious rooms, elegant antiques and genuine Southern hospitality in the heart of Kentucky's Bluegrass region. Twin Hollies, known as the Bridges-Fox House, is on the National Register of Historic Places and has been

NOTES: Credit cards accepted: A MasterCard; B Visa; C American Express; D Discover Card; E Diner's Club; F Other; 2 Personal checks accepted; 3 Lunch available; 4 Dinner available; 5 Open all year;

designated a Kentucky landmark. Full breakfast provided. No children. Outside smoking only.

Hosts: Mary Joe and John Bowling
Rooms: 3 (1 PB; 2 SB) $75
Full Breakfast
Credit Cards: None
Notes: 2, 5, 7 (on porch), 9, 12, 14

ELIZABETHTOWN

The Olde Bethlehem Academy Inn

7051 St. John's Road, 42701
(502) 862-9003; (800) 662-5670

Once the stately home of Gov. John LaRue Helm and a girls' academy, the Olde Bethlehem Academy Inn offers nine large bedrooms and private baths. Comfortably furnished with antiques, brass, and reproduction pieces. The rich history surrounding this lovely bed and breakfast enhances its beautifully restored setting. There are 20 areas for entertaining, including a second-floor chapel that is perfect for receptions, weddings, social gatherings, or a formal ball. A true testament to the 19th century, the Olde Bethlehem Academy Inn invites guests to step back in time and enjoy the artifacts that remain from its significantly rich past. The restaurant, "Magnolia Place," is now in the grand salon, and dinner is served from 5:00 to 9:00 P.M.

Hosts: Ric and Viviana
Rooms: 9 (6 PB; 3 SB); $75-95
Full Breakfast
Credit Cards: A, B
Notes: 2, 3, 4, 5, 6, 7, 8, 9, 10, 11, 12, 14

GEORGETOWN

Log Cabin Bed and Breakfast

350 North Broadway, 40324
(502) 863-3514

Enjoy this Kentucky log cabin, circa 1809, with its shake roof, chinked logs, and pe-

riod furnishings. Completely private. Two bedrooms, fireplace, and fully equipped kitchen. Only five miles to Kentucky Horse Park and 12 miles north of Lexington. Children welcome.

Hosts: Clay and Janis McKnight
Cabin: (PB) $75
Continental Breakfast
Credit Cards: None
Notes: 2, 5, 6, 7, 8, 9, 10, 11, 12

GHENT

Ghent House Bed and Breakfast

411 Main Street (US 42), P.O. Box 478, 41045
(502) 347-5807 (weekends)

Ghent House is a gracious reminder of the antebellum days of the "Old South." Federal-style with a beautiful fantail window, two slave walls, rose and English gardens, gazebo, crystal chandeliers, fireplaces, and whirlpool. Ghent House has a spectacular view of the Ohio River, and one can almost visualize the steamboats. Go back in time and stay at the Ghent House. Come as a guest—leave as a friend.

Hosts: Wayne and Diane Young
Rooms: 3 (PB) $60-90
Full Breakfast
Credit Cards: A, B, C
Notes: 2, 5, 7 (restricted), 8, 9, 10, 11, 12, 13, 14

GLASGOW

Four Seasons Country Inn

4107 Scottsville Road, 42141
(502) 678-1000

Charming Victorian-style inn built in 1989. All rooms have queen-size, four-poster beds, private baths, remote-equipped TVs with cable. Continental breakfast served in inviting lobby with wood-burning fireplace. Some rooms open out to spacious deck or large front porch. Swimming pool. Near Mammoth Cave National Park and Barren River Lake State Park.

6 Pets welcome; 8 Children welcome; 9 Social drinking allowed; 10 Tennis available; 11 Swimming available; 12 Golf available; 13 Skiing available; 14 May be booked through travel agents.

Host: Henry Carter
Rooms: 17 (PB) $52-62
Continental Breakfast
Credit Cards: A, B, C, D, E
Notes: 2, 5, 7, 8, 9, 11, 12, 14

Four Seasons Country Inn

HARRODSBURG

Bauer Haus
Bed and Breakfast

362 North College Street, 40330
(606) 734-6289

Savor the craftsmanship of the past in this 1880s Victorian home listed on the National Register of Historic Places and designated a Kentucky landmark. Nestle in the sitting room, sip tea or coffee in the dining room, repose in the parlor, or ascend the staircase to a private room for a relaxing visit. In Kentucky's oldest settlement, Bauer Haus is within walking distance of Old Fort Harrod State Park and historic Harrodsburg.

Hosts: Dick and Marian Bauer
Rooms: 4 (2 PB; 2 SB) $50-65
Full Breakfast
Credit Cards: None
Notes: 2, 5, 9, 12, 14

Canaan Land Farm
Bed and Breakfast

4355 Lexington Road, 40330
(606) 734-3984

On Highway 68 near Shakertown, Canaan Land Farm Bed and Breakfast is a working sheep farm where guests may enjoy a variety of barnyard animals. Lambing season is

March and April. This circa 1795 historic home was recently designated Kentucky historic farm and is listed on the national register. Filled with antiques, quilts, and feather beds. Features private baths, large swimming pool, hot tub, and hammocks in the shade. The host is a shepherd/attorney, and the hostess is a handspinner/artist. Step back in time nearly 200 years, and enjoy true Southern hospitality.

Hosts: Fred and Theo Bee
Rooms: 3 (PB) $65-75
Full Breakfast
Credit Cards: None
Notes: 2, 5, 9, 11

Inn at Shaker Village
of Pleasant Hill

3500 Lexington Road, 40330
(606) 734-5411

The Shaker Village of Pleasant Hill offers a one-of-a-kind guest experience. Its 80 guest rooms in buildings where Shakers once lived and worked are simply and beautifully furnished with Shaker-crafted furniture. A national historic landmark set on 2,700 acres of rolling bluegrass farmland, the village offers tours, daily exhibitions of Shaker crafts, and hearty country dining. Riverboat excursions from April through October.

Host: Christopher Brassfield
Rooms: 80 (PB) $55-100
Full and Continental Breakfast
Credit Cards: A, B
Notes: 2, 3, 4, 5, 7, 8, 12, 14

LEBANON

Myrtledene

370 North Spalding Avenue, 40033
(502) 692-2223

Four rooms in the heart of Kentucky, Myrtledene is a place to go back in time; to slow down; to unwind. Make this gracious Georgian home, built in 1833 and furnished in period antiques, the headquarters for travel-

NOTES: Credit cards accepted: A MasterCard; B Visa; C American Express; D Discover Card; E Diner's Club; F Other; 2 Personal checks accepted; 3 Lunch available; 4 Dinner available; 5 Open all year;

ing to area attractions. Come, stay a while, and experience the rich heritage of an area noted for its Southern hospitality.

Rooms: 4 (S2B) $60
Full Breakfast
Credit Cards: None
Notes: 2, 5, 7 (limited), 8, 9, 10, 11, 12, 14

LEXINGTON

Gratz Park Inn

120 West Second Street, 40507
(606) 231-1777; (800) 227-4362

Grantz Park Inn is in downtown Lexington in a historical district. The building is on the National Register of Historic Places. Each room is unique with fine antique reproduction furniture and four-poster beds. Hosts offer complimentary breakfast and limousine service in the evenings to downtown restaurants, as well as airport transportation. Turndown service includes fresh flowers and home-baked cookies each evening. Hosts deliver *USA Today* right to guests' room door.

Rooms: 44 (PB) $95-250
Continental Breakfast
Credit Cards: A, B, C, D, E
Notes: 5, 9, 10, 11, 12, 14

LOUISVILLE

Inn at the Park

1332 South Fourth Street, 40208
(502) 637-6930

This Victorian mansion was built in 1886, as a premier example of Richardsonian Romanesque architecture. The inn is elegantly furnished in Victorian antiques and antique reproductions. Very spacious with 14-foot ceilings, eight fireplaces, picturesque porches overlooking Central Park, and rich hardwood floors. Many guests are awestruck upon their first entrance into the foyer—the grand, sweeping staircase is magnificent! Appropriate for special occasions and the very particular guest. Enjoy

cocktails on any of five porches, or an evening stroll in the park. Personal attention from the innkeepers and an excellent full breakfast makes guests' visit complete.

Hosts: Theresa and Bob Carskie
Rooms: 6 (4 PB; 2 SB) $60-95
Full Breakfast
Credit Cards: A, B, C
Notes: 2, 5, 7, 8, 9, 10, 11, 12, 14

Kentucky Homes Bed and Breakfast Inc.

1219 South Fourth Avenue, 40203
(502) 635-7341

A reservation service for Louisville and Kentucky offers approximately 45 rooms, priced from $55-85.

Rooms: 45 approx. (PB) $55-85
Full and Continental Breakfast
Credit Cards: A, B, C
Notes: 2, 5, 8, 10, 14

Old Louisville Inn

Old Louisville Inn

1359 South Third Street, 40208
(502) 635-1574; FAX (502) 637-5892

Wake up to the aroma of freshly baked popovers and muffins when staying in one of the 11 guest rooms or suites. Centrally situated between downtown and the airport. Stay for a romantic getaway or relax on a

6 Pets welcome; 8 Children welcome; 9 Social drinking allowed; 10 Tennis available; 11 Swimming available; 12 Golf available; 13 Skiing available; 14 May be booked through travel agents.

business trip with the special packages and consider this inn " home away from home."

Host: Marianne Lesher
Rooms: 11 (6 PB; 3 SB; 1 two-bedroom suite) $65-195
Continental Breakfast
Credit Cards: A, B
Notes: 2, 5, 8, 9, 10, 12, 14

The Red Room Bed and Breakfast

(502) 458-7197

Spacious condo just five minutes from mid-city. Tree-lined street in an older established neighborhood. One block from Bardstown Road and its wall-to-wall antique shops and restaurants. Queen and twin bedrooms with private baths. Smokers welcome.

Rooms: 2 (PB) $50-60
Full Breakfast
Credit Cards: None
Notes: 2, 5, 7, 9

The Victorian Secret Bed and Breakfast

1132 South First Street, 40203
(502) 581-1914

In historic old Louisville guests will find a three-story brick mansion appropriately named the Victorian Secret Bed and Breakfast. Its 14 rooms offer spacious accommodations, high ceilings, 11 fireplaces, and original woodwork. Recently restored to its former elegance, the 110-year-old structure provides a peaceful setting for enjoying period furnishings and antiques.

Hosts: Nan and Steve Roosa
Rooms: 3 (1 PB; 2 SB) $53-78
Continental Breakfast
Credit Cards: None
Notes: None

Welcome House Bed and Breakfast

1613 Forrest Hill Drive, 40205
(502) 452-6629

Gracious Colonial home in a lovely suburban neighborhood offers two queen, one double, and two single bedrooms with three baths. Off the beaten path, but convenient to antique shops, shopping malls, and the expressways.

Rooms: 4 (2 PB; 1 SB) $35-60
Full Breakfast
Credit Cards: None
Notes: 2, 5, 6, 7, 8, 9, 12, 14

MURRAY

Diuguid House Bed and Breakfast

603 Main Street, 42071
(502) 753-5470

This beautiful home, listed on the National Register of Historic Places, features a sweeping oak staircase, comfortable and spacious rooms, and a generous guest lounge area. This bed and breakfast is in town near the university, lake area, and many antique shops. Full breakfast is included in the reasonable rates, and the area has the reputation for being a top rated retirement area.

Hosts: Karen and George Chapman
Rooms: 3 (SB) $40
Full Breakfast
Credit Cards: A, B
Notes: 2, 5, 8, 14

OWENSBORO

Friendly Farms

5931 Highway 56, 42301
(502) 771-4723; FAX (502) 771-4723

A country cottage with queen-size bed three miles west of Owensboro on Highway 56. Guests may enjoy indoor/outdoor tennis, Nautical fitness, and sauna. Country-style breakfast served at indoor club on property. Enjoy pool in the summer, large fireplace in the winter. Air-conditioned. Stables available to guests for lesson or trail riding. Two

NOTES: Credit cards accepted: A MasterCard; B Visa; C American Express; D Discover Card; E Diner's Club; F Other; 2 Personal checks accepted; 3 Lunch available; 4 Dinner available; 5 Open all year;

bedroom trailer with two baths at lesser charge. Also available is a deluxe two-bedroom cottage furnished with antiques. Fully equipped kitchen with stocked refrigerator and breakfast fixings, on Highway 45, three miles west of Rockport, Inc., and ten minutes north of Owensboro, Kentucky. Patio with gas grill overlooks horse pasture and woods. Air-conditioned. Stables available to guests for lessons or trail riding.

Host: Joan G. Ramey
Cottages: 2 (PB) $35-75
Trailer: 1 (PB)
Full Breakfast
Credit Cards: A, B
Notes: 2, 5, 6, 7, 8, 9, 10, 11, 12

PADUCAH

Ehrhardt's Bed and Breakfast

285 Springwell Lane, 42001
(502) 554-0644

This brick Colonial home is just one mile off I-24, a highway noted for its lovely scenery. The hosts strive to make guests feel at home in antique-filled bedrooms and a cozy den with a fireplace. Nearby are the beautiful Kentucky and Barkley lakes and the famous Land Between the Lakes area.

Hosts: Eileen and Phil Ehrhardt
Rooms: 3 (SB) $30-35
Full Breakfast
Credit Cards: None
Notes: 2, 5, 8, 11, 12

The 1857's Bed and Breakfast

P.O. Box 7771, 127 Market House Square, 42002-7771
(502) 444-3960; (800) 264-5607

This three-story brick building is listed on the National Register of Historic Places, and has a warm, friendly Victorian atmosphere. The first floor houses Cynthia's Ristorante; the second floor houses two guest rooms; and the third floor houses the family

room and game room with hot tub and billiards table. This home is in the downtown historic district, with antique stores, carriage rides, quilt museum, restaurants, and the Market House Cultural Center within walking distance. The entire second floor with private bath may be booked for $85; two-night minimum stay.

Hosts: Deborah and Steve Bohnert
Rooms: 2 (SB) $55-85
Continental Breakfast
Credit Cards: A, B
Notes: 2, 5, 8, 9, 11, 12, 13, 14

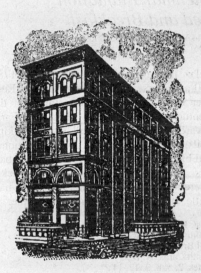

Paducah Harbor Plaza

Paducah Harbor Plaza Bed and Breakfast

201 Broadway, 42001
(502) 442-2698; (800) 719-7799

A warm, friendly atmosphere in the restored turn-of-the-century, five-story bed and breakfast overlooking the Ohio River in downtown Paducah. Antiques abound, and the family antique quilt collection complements the New Quilters Museum built by the American Quilters Society, one block from the bed and breakfast. Paducah is known as "Quilt City, USA." Museum, shops, and an-

6 Pets welcome; 8 Children welcome; 9 Social drinking allowed; 10 Tennis available; 11 Swimming available; 12 Golf available; 13 Skiing available; 14 May be booked through travel agents.

tique stores are accessible via a brick promenade along the river. Nostalgia is created with songs of the past played on a 1911 player piano. Sing-alongs are encouraged by the Harrises.

Hosts: Beverly and David Harris
Rooms: 4 (SB) $55-125
Continental Breakfast
Credit Cards: A, B, C
Notes: 2, 5, 11, 12, 13, 14

SPRINGFIELD

Glenmar Plantation Bed and Breakfast

2444 Valley Hill Road, 40069
(606) 284-7791; (800) 828-3330

Relax in a romantic setting on this 1785 250-acre horse farm. On the National Register of Historic Places. Recipient of the Kentucky Commenitive Historic Farm Award. Guests may stroll along walking trails, go riding, walking, cycling. Antiques and historic buildings including slave quarters and oldest buildings in Kentucky. There are animals including horses, llamas, cattle, and sheep. Children are welcome.

Host: Kenny Mandell
Rooms: 8 (6 PB; 2 SB) $75-150
Full Breakfast
Credit Cards: A, B, C
Notes: 2, 5, 8, 9, 12, 14

Maple Hill Manor

2941 Perryville Road, 40069
(606) 336-3075

Under construction for three years, this 14-room antebellum mansion, circa 1851, is listed on the National Register of Historic Places. On 14 tranquil acres in the Bluegrass region. The honeymoon hideaway has a canopy bed and Jacuzzi. One hour from Louisville and Lexington, close to the Stephen Foster Home and Perryville Battle-

field. Complimentary dessert and beverages served in the evenings. Bro-chure. No smoking.

Hosts: Kay and Bob Carroll
Rooms: 7 (PB) $65-85
Full Breakfast
Credit Cards: A, B
Notes: 2, 5, 8, 9, 10, 12, 14

Shepherd Place

VERSAILLES

Shepherd Place

US 60 and Heritage Road, 40383
(606) 873-7843

Marlin and Sylvia invite guests to share their pre-Civil War home, built between 1820 and 1850. The house has windows that go all the way to the floor, crown moldings, hardwood floors, and large rooms with private baths, as well as a parlor and front porch swing for relaxation. Stroll up to the barn and meet the resident ewes, or ride through the bluegrass horse farms.

Hosts: Marlin and Sylvia Yawn
Rooms: 2 (PB) $65
Full Breakfast
Credit Cards: A, B
Notes: 2, 5

NOTES: Credit cards accepted: A MasterCard; B Visa; C American Express; D Discover Card; E Diner's Club; F Other; 2 Personal checks accepted; 3 Lunch available; 4 Dinner available; 5 Open all year;

Louisiana

CARENCRO

La Maison de Campagne, Lafayette

825 Kidder Road, 70520
(318) 896-6529

This Victorian home, circa 1900, is in a beautiful country setting with 200-year-old oak trees on nine acres. Come enjoy life the way it used to be. The inn offers private baths, antique-furnished rooms, a swimming pool in season, and great Cajun restaurants and attractions five minutes away. A full Cajun country gourmet breakfast is served with the hospitality of the award-winning chef/hostess. Enjoy early morning or late afternoon walks or just relax on the sweeping wraparound galleries or the upstairs balcony. Guests will want to come back again and again. Just 15 minutes north of downtown Lafayette.

Hosts: Joeann and Fred McLemore
Rooms: 4 (PB) From $90
Full Breakfast
Credit Cards: A, B
Notes: 5, 11

HOUMA

New Orleans Bed and Breakfast

P.O. Box 8163, New Orleans, 70182
(504) 838-0071

Acadian Country. Here are several marvelous hosts who share their charming modern homes, food, and stories with guests. Full breakfast. $55-60.

UP11. Guests in this historic 1840 home enjoy a suite which has a sitting room overlooking the pool, a spacious bedroom with a king-size bed, two marble bathrooms, and a wet bar. The sitting area is furnished with a day bed which accommodates two singles or another couple. $75-85.

UP11A. Adjoining this property is another newly restored small home. Here are two bedrooms, each with a private bath and a common sitting room. Suitable for two congenial couples or a family. Continental breakfast is served in the dining room of the main house or on the veranda. $65.

UP12. Near the historic streetcar line, a cozy guest house is often available for the enjoyment of the guests. There is a living room, kitchen-dining area, bedroom with queen-size bed, and bath. Breakfast is in the refrigerator for guests' convenience. $85-95.

UP13. In a varied 1800 neighborhood shaded by ancient oaks is a restored camelback double—a lovely single home to a professional couple. Here the guest has traditional well-appointed bedroom and bath. Breakfast is served in the room. There is off-street parking, a patio, and living room for the guests' enjoyment. $85-95.

UP14. Near Audubon Park and the University area, a delightful hostess shares her home with our guests. The guest room has either two twin beds or one king-size bed, and a private bath. A Continental breakfast is served. $65-75.

6 Pets welcome; 7 Smoking allowed; 8 Children welcome; 9 Social drinking allowed; 10 Tennis available; 11 Swimming available; 12 Golf available; 13 Skiing available; 14 May be booked through travel agents.

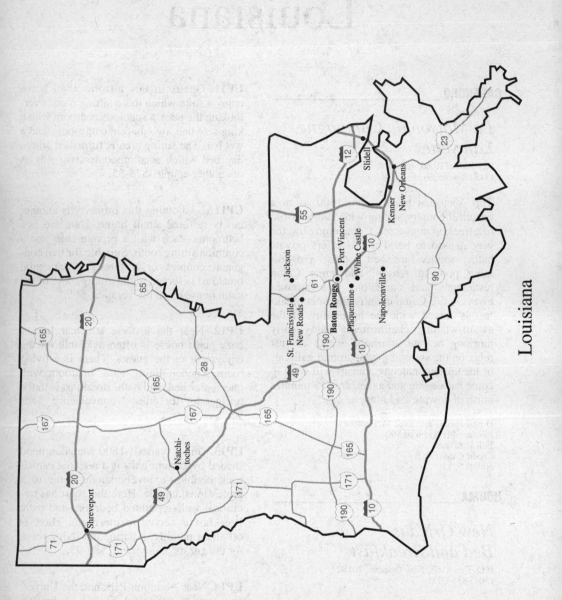

Louisiana

JACKSON

Milbank

3045 Bank Street, 70748
(504) 634-5901

Built in 1836, Milbank is a romantic antebellum mansion with irresistible charm. Come and spend quiet time in this small historic town. Sleep in a queen-size canopied mallard bed. Museum, winery, churches, houses, golf, and walking tour.

Hosts: Paul and Margurite Carter
Rooms: 3 (PB) $75
Suite: 1 (SB) $125
Full Breakfast
Credit Cards: A, B
Notes: 2, 5, 8, 9

KENNER (NEW ORLEANS)

Seven Oaks Plantation

2600 Gay Lynn Drive, 70065
(504) 888-8649

This 10,000-square-foot West Indies-style home overlooking the lake is convenient to the airport and is 20 minutes from the New Orleans French Quarter. Guest rooms open into a large living room and into 12-foot galleries. A full plantation breakfast is served and the entire home can be toured. Antiques and Mardi Gras memorabilia are found throughout. Seven Oaks offers Southern hospitality and will make guests' visits full of warm, pleasant memories.

Hosts: Kay and Henry Andressen
Rooms: 2 (PB) $95-115
Full and Continental Breakfast
Credit Cards: A, B
Notes: 2, 5, 7, 9, 12, 14

LAFAYETTE

New Orleans Bed and Breakfast

P.O. Box 8163, New Orleans, 70182
(504) 838-0071

Acadian City. Stay in a turn-of-the-century home. Listen to stories the hosts tell of the families whose lives revolved around this home. Choose any one of the four memento filled rooms and imagine life there 90 years ago. Enjoy a full breakfast and afternoon refreshments. $100-125.

Tante Da's A Bed and Breakfast

2631 Southeast Evangeline Throughway, 70508-2168
(318) 264-1191

In the heart of "Cajun Country," Tante Da's is characterized by the gracious hospitality of its innkeepers. After completing a three-and-a-half year restoration of this turn-of-the-century Victorian cottage, the hosts opened their home to the weary traveler. They give generously of themselves, making every guest feel comfortable, at ease, and at home. Fresh cut flowers and wonderful aromas from the kitchen give the feeling of visiting grandma's house. At the end of the day, guests can slip into one of the huge antique claw-foot tubs, sip a glass of wine in the parlor, or just relax on one of the swings on the front porch or rear patio.

Hosts: Tanya and Douglas Greenwald
Rooms: 4 (PB) $75-150
Full Breakfast
Credit Cards: A, B, C, D
Notes: 2, 3, 4, 5, 7 (outside only), 9, 10, 12, 14

NAPOLEONVILLE

Madewood Plantation House

4250 Highway 308, 70390
(504) 369-7151

A national historic landmark, Madewood is a stately Greek Revival mansion on Bayou Lafourche about 75 miles from New Orleans' French Quarter. Set on 20 acres in front of a

---

NOTES: Credit cards accepted: A MasterCard; B Visa; C American Express; D Discover Card; E Diner's Club; F Other; 2 Personal checks accepted; 3 Lunch available; 4 Dinner available; 5 Open all year; 6 Pets welcome; 7 Smoking allowed; 8 Children welcome; 9 Social drinking allowed; 10 Tennis available; 11 Swimming available; 12 Golf available; 13 Skiing available; 14 May be booked through travel agents.

working sugar cane plantation, Madewood is furnished with antiques. Bedrooms have canopied beds. Guests dine by candlelight, family-style, after a wine and cheese party in the library. Featured in *Vogue*, *Country Home*, *Country Inns*, *Innsider*, the *Los Angeles Times*, BBC radio, and many more. In cottage, Continental breakfast; in mansion, full breakfast, and dinner for two.

Hosts: Keith and Millie Marshall; Dave D'Aunoy
Rooms: 9 (PB) $165
Full Breakfast
Credit Cards: A, B, C, D
Closed major holidays
Notes: 2, 4, 5, 8, 9, 14

Madewood Plantation House

NATCHITOCHES

Breazeale House Bed and Breakfast

926 Washington Street, 71457
(318) 352-5630

Built for Congressman Phanor Breazeale in the late 1800s, Breazeale house is within walking distance of the historic downtown district. This Victorian house features 11 fireplaces, 12-foot ceilings, nine stained-glass windows, a set of servants' stairs, three balconies, eight bedrooms, and three floors with over 6,000 square feet of living space. President Taft slept here, and this house can be seen in *Steel Magnolias*.

Hosts: Willa and Jack Freeman
Rooms: 5 (2 PB; 3 SB) $50-75
Full Breakfast
Credit Cards: A, B
Notes: 2, 5, 8, 9, 10, 11, 12, 13 (water), 14

Fleur de Lis Bed and Breakfast Inn

336 Second Street, 71457
(318) 352-6621; (800) 489-6621

This grand old Victorian house is in the oldest settlement in the Louisiana Purchase and is listed on the National Register of Historic Places. Guests at the inn may expect a warm welcome, a room tastefully decorated with king- or queen-size beds, private baths, make-up vanities, sitting area, as well as the many amenities one expects in a friend's home. Delicious full breakfast with rich Louisiana coffee and orange juice.

Hosts: Tom and Harriette Palmer
Rooms: 5 (PB) $60-100
Full Breakfast
Credit Cards: A, B, C
Notes: 2, 5, 8, 9, 10, 11, 12, 14

Martin's Roost

1735 1/2 Washington Street, 71457
(318) 352-9215

Comfortable contemporary home with country atmosphere. Patios, pool, and deck with panoramic view of former Red River roadbed. Arts, crafts, plantation doll houses, and needlework. Home of background props filmed in *Steel Magnolias*. Gourmet breakfast; dinner du jour. Certified tour guide to enchanting history of oldest settlement in Louisiana Purchase.

Hosts: Ronald and Vicki Martin
Rooms: 2 (PB) $55
Full Breakfast
Credit Cards: A, B
Notes: 2, 3, 4, 5, 7, 9, 11, 14

NEW IBERIA

The Inn at leRosier

314 East Main Street, 70560
(318) 367-5306

NOTES: Credit cards accepted: A MasterCard; B Visa; C American Express; D Discover Card; E Diner's Club; F Other; 2 Personal checks accepted; 3 Lunch available; 4 Dinner available; 5 Open all year;

LeRosier, an 1870 country inn complete with rose gardens and gourmet breakfast, is a perfect getaway for romantics. There are four guest rooms furnished with lovely antiques and elegant appointments. Each room has its own stocked refrigerator, bath, telephone, and television. Cozy parlors, fireplaces, world-class dining, and personal service at acclaimed leRosier restaurant. In historic district New Iberia across from Shadows-on-the-Teche, a National Trust owned property. Completely smoke-free environment.

Hosts: L. Hallman and Mary Beth Woods
Rooms: 4 (PB) $100
Full Breakfast
Credit Cards: A, B, C
Notes: 2, 3, 4, 5, 9, 14

New Orleans Bed and Breakfast

P.O. Box 8163, New Orleans, 70182
(504) 838-0071

Country Estate. A modern plantation mansion with all the beauty, comfort, serenity, and interest one could wish for. "Enchanting . . . flowers, trees, pond, peacocks and swans . . . . A personification of luxury!" Enjoy the pool, gym, steam room, billiard room in this most luxurious home. Deluxe $85-95.

NEW ORLEANS

Beau Séjour Bed and Breakfast

1930 Napoleon Avenue, 70115
(504) 897-3746

This turn-of-the-century mansion is uptown on the Mardi Gras parade route and near the historic streetcar that carries guests to the French Quarter, convention center, Superdome, aquarium, and universities. Beau Séjour boasts a casual, tropical atmosphere with spacious rooms, queen-size beds, and antiques, embodying the charm and ambience of old New Orleans.

Hosts: Gilles and Kim Gagnon
Rooms: 5 (PB) $75-125
Continental Breakfast
Credit Cards: None
Notes: 5, 7, 8, 9, 10, 11

Bed and Breakfast Inc.

1021 Moss Street, Box 52257, 70152-2257
(504) 488-4640; (800) 729-4640
FAX (504) 488-4639

Architectural Gem. Remaining true to the original design of this wonderful guest cottage has been of primary concern to the owners. They have overseen the renovation project from top to bottom, paying careful attention not to disturb the historic detail of this building. Thick exposed brick walls and three brick fireplaces, used in the 1830s as the kitchen facilities for the main house, reflect the authenticity of this historic restoration. Uniquely designed private baths adjoin each of the two cozy bedrooms. Self-serve Continental breakfast is provided for leisurely enjoyment. $75-150.

Bayou St. John Home. This home is of the "box step cottage" design that is typical of the architectural style of this area. Its street is named after scenic Bayou St. John which passes close by. Set in a charming neighborhood of historic properties, several small French cafes, specialty coffee shop, and gourmet grocery-deli are just a stroll away. Along the banks of Bayou St. John is City Park, the home of the New Orleans Museum of Art set amongst giant oaks in one of America's largest metropolitan parks. Friendly hosts are both nurses and enjoy collecting everything from Mardi Gras memorabilia to antique match books. Ask them for unique and out-of-the-way restaurant suggestions. Dining out is one of their fondest passions. Bus to the French Quarter and downtown in under 15 minutes (five minutes by car) where convention centers are nearby. Continental breakfast.

6 Pets welcome; 8 Children welcome; 9 Social drinking allowed; 10 Tennis available; 11 Swimming available; 12 Golf available; 13 Skiing available; 14 May be booked through travel agents.

Bed and Breakfast Inc.
(continued)

Bourbon Street Suite. Guests enjoy this private, first-floor suite opening onto world-famous Bourbon Street. The host is a New Orleans native and shares his vast knowledge of the special spots not to miss. One bedroom; private bath; Continental breakfast. $75-100.

Creole Cottage. This quaint Creole cottage was built in 1902. The home is minutes away from major New Orleans attractions. The historic Saint Charles Avenue streetcar line makes the famous restaurants, jazz clubs, art galleries, and antique shops accessible. Two bedrooms; Continental breakfast on silver service. $50-70.

Dauphine Street Suite. In the heart of the residential part of the French Quarter, this guest suite is nestled in the courtyard of an 1840s Creole cottage. The second-story suite is off the charming brick courtyard and has a private entrance, horse-hair double bed, and bath. Self-serve Continental breakfast is provided. $75-100.

Designer Guest Cottage. Originally the studio of a famous Southern sculptor, the cottage displays his artistic creativity while preserving its historic past. A short streetcar ride to galleries, antiques, restaurants, and the French Quarter. One bedroom with private bath; Continental breakfast. $95-135.

Desmond Place. This Mediterranean Villa-style home with blue tile roof and terrazzo entryway typifies 1940s New Orleans. In a quiet neighborhood and surrounded by live oak trees, the home is furnished with antiques and artifacts collected by the hosts. Relax after a day of sightseeing or conventions in the inviting pool and patio area. The hosts enjoy dining out, so ask them for out-of-the-way and unique restaurant suggestions. A traditional bed and breakfast, hosts offer two guest bedrooms, each with its own private bath. The French Quarter, Garden District, and Uptown are only minutes away by car or taxi. Off-street parking available. Continental breakfast.

Desoto Suite. Built in the 1880s, this raised Victorian home displays the architectural charm so typical of New Orleans cottages. Set in an area of ongoing restorations, several small French restaurants, specialty coffee shop, and gourmet grocery-deli are just a stroll away. Along the banks of Bayou St. John, which passes close by, is City Park, the home of the New Orleans Museum of Art set amongst giant oaks in one of America's largest metropolitan parks. From this home, the bus takes guests to the French Quarter and downtown to conventions in under 15 minutes (five minutes by car). The host, whose private living quarters are also in the same house, is warm and welcoming. A New Orleans native, he gladly shares his extensive knowledge of the city. Feel free to ask him for restaurant and tour suggestions. Your lovely guest suite is spacious with its own separate entrance, living room-bedroom, bath, and kitchenette. Self-serve Continental breakfast.

Galleried Home. Historians delight in this French Plantation-style home with its lovely antiques. The guest suite is just off the host's living room and opens onto the front balcony. The suite offers a sitting room, bedroom with four-poster double bed, and bath. The garden below provides a tropical setting. Continental breakfast. $95-110.

Garden District Building. Right on the streetcar line, a fun ride to downtown and the French Quarter is less than 15 minutes. Guests will be sharing the host's lovely condominium and will have access to the swimming pool. One bedroom with private bath; Continental breakfast. $50-70.

Garden District Guest Suite. Three lovely antique twin beds grace a nicely decorated suite. Comfortably spacious with a living room and kitchen. Enjoy the special flavors of New Orleans-style cooking at the nearby famous bistros. Two bedrooms with private bath; Continental breakfast supplies provided. $50-80.

Greek Revival Home. Nestled in a historic community just across the Mississippi River from the French Quarter, this imposing Greek Revival home offers guests a private apartment overlooking the swimming pool. Walk or drive to the free ferry for a brief romantic ride. One bedroom with private bath; Continental breakfast. $50-80.

Guest Atelier. In the heart of the French Quarter's antique and art gallery district, this guest suite features natural brick walls and original artworks. A narrow staircase leads guests to a cozy third floor studio apartment, whose windows overlook a walkway famous for fencing masters of the past. Guests enjoy strolling to well-known restaurants and jazz clubs and to nearby downtown convention centers. A minibus and riverfront antique streetcar are available for those who prefer to ride. The personable owner of the property, an artist, is just downstairs. The apartment has a bedroom with sitting area, kitchenette, and private bath.

Guest Suite in Greek Revival Cottage. Greek Revival cottage offers a well-appointed guest apartment with its own private entrance overlooking the swimming pool. Hosts have tastefully decorated their home. The streetcar ride to downtown is just ten minutes. A short walk takes guests

to other attractions. One bedroom with private bath; Continental breakfast. $50-90.

Home Near Audubon Park. Guests can ride the streetcar to the interesting Riverbend with specialty shops and to French coffee houses, art galleries, antiques, famous restaurants, music clubs, and more. This 1950s brick home is set in a lovely historic neighborhood. One bedroom with hall bath; Continental breakfast. $35-50.

La Maison Marigny. In the French Quarter, this petite bed and breakfast inn was just completely renovated down to window dressings and dust ruffles. Each of the three guest rooms has a private entrance and modern bath. Enjoy a Continental breakfast downstairs or outside in the traditional walled garden and patio. $75-100.

The Lanaux House

The Lanaux House. The historic Lanaux House was constructed in 1879 and has been restored by the hostess. A private entrance leads to the second-floor guest suite. Guests enjoy their own lovely living room, bedroom with antique brass double bed, bath, and kitchenette. Self-serve Continental breakfast. $100-150.

La Petite Suite. This stylish guest suite, in the courtyard of an 1850s Creole cottage,

6 Pets welcome; 8 Children welcome; 9 Social drinking allowed; 10 Tennis available; 11 Swimming available; 12 Golf available; 13 Skiing available; 14 May be booked through travel agents.

Bed and Breakfast Inc (continued)

offers the romance and history that is the ambience of New Orleans. The second-floor suite has a private entrance off the charmingly landscaped courtyard area. Once inside, guests enjoy the comfort of a four-poster bed, bath, and kitchenette. Continental breakfast. $75-100.

Le Garconiere Guest Suite. A charming couple welcomes guests to their historic home in the French Quarter. Antique shops, restaurants, and jazz clubs are just a short walk from this quiet neighborhood. The private, two-story guest cottage overlooks the tropical courtyard with a balcony and full kitchen. Experience the streetcar along the Mississippi River. Continental breakfast. $75-100.

Mallard Suite. This historic Italianate-style home was constructed in 1879. It is a favorite background for movies filmed in New Orleans. The extensive restoration of the home includes the return of original pieces and warrants the high regard it receives. Guests are invited to a tour of the home. The second-floor guest suite is a spacious sitting room and bedroom combination. It is graced with authentic antique pieces including Morris Henry Hobbs etchings, Royal Bokara oriental rugs, and early Victorian rosewood bed in the style of Mallard circa 1840. At their leisure, guests enjoy Continental breakfast in privacy of their own suite.

The Orleans Cottage. In the French Quarter area, this 1890s historic Victorian cottage was recently renovated. One bedroom with private bath; Continental breakfast. $75-110.

Prytania Street Suite. The designer of this 19th-century home modeled it after an Austrian manse. Guests enjoy a lovely apartment that includes two bedrooms, full kitchen, and one and one-half baths. Just one block from the St. Charles Avenue streetcar line, this suite is convenient to all. Continental breakfast. $75-125.

Quaint Guest Cottages. A special place filled with romance. Flavored with antiques and architectural details, the cottages look onto a patio and antique swing. The streetcar is downtown at the French Quarter in just 15 minutes. Guests enjoy antiques, famous bistros, and music nearby. Two cottages with private baths; Continental breakfast. $60-125.

Quaint Guest Cottages.

Queen Anne Victorian Home. Recently renovated, this home, with its original artwork and fabric-dressed walls, shows the special touches of the hostess, an interior designer. The Garden District mansions of the past are just steps away, as are restaurants, antiques, and art galleries. Three bedrooms with shared hall bath; Continental breakfast. $45-70.

NOTES: Credit cards accepted: A MasterCard; B Visa; C American Express; D Discover Card; E Diner's Club; F Other; 2 Personal checks accepted; 3 Lunch available; 4 Dinner available; 5 Open all year;

St. Charles Avenue Home. Hosts love sharing their enthusiasm for New Orleans in a historic, homespun setting. Walking distance to the interesting Riverbend area with its specialty shops, coffee houses, and popular restaurants. The host was born in this house that boasts some of the original antiques. Two bedrooms with hall bath; Continental breakfast. $50-60.

University Area Home. A welcoming couple provides a comfortable, homey flavor in this raised cottage. University campuses, restaurants, specialty shops, and music clubs are nearby. A pleasurable 40-minute streetcar ride will take guests downtown. One bedroom with private bath; Continental breakfast. $30-70.

The Uptown Home. Guests enjoy this residential neighborhood, with its shady trees and historic homes. Close to universities, restaurants, antique shops, art galleries, and the streetcar line, which can take guests to many attractions. Each of the three bedrooms has a double bed and shared bath. Great for the budget-minded. Continental breakfast. $40-60.

Vendome Place. In a quiet neighborhood and surrounded by live oak trees, this home offers two beautifully decorated private entrance rooms, each with newly renovated private bath. Guests love to relax after a day of sightseeing or conventions in the inviting pool and patio area. Charming hosts love to give tour and restaurant suggestions. The French Quarter, Garden district, and Uptown are only minutes away by car or taxi. Off-street parking available. Continental breakfast.

Victorian Cottage. The host has lovingly restored this home. It offers peaceful, intimate guest rooms, comfortably furnished, and has a private bath and private entrance onto the patio. Nearby is the old French Market and Mississippi River Walk. Continental breakfast is served on the patio, which has a wet bar. $55-70.

Victorian Manse. An authentic bejeweled crown and scepter, recalling Mardi Gras balls of the past, rest regally on the front parlor mantel of this beautifully restored 100-year-old Victorian home. Just around the corner from charming boutiques, delightful restaurants, and French coffee houses in the hub of the established Historic Uptown District. Designer-decorated guest bedroom and bath are on the second floor. Continental breakfast is served in the country kitchen. $60-70.

Benachi-Torre-Derbes House—"Rendezvous des Chasseurs"

2257 Bayou Road, 70119
(504) 525-9538; (504) 944-7484

The quintessential charm of 19th-century New Orleans awaits guests in this graceful Southern mansion. It has been lovingly restored and furnished by the hosts. Gardens and fountains, oaks and syca-mores, and parlors and grand dining room—all in period antiques. Walk to the French Quarter, City Park, and gourmet restaurants. Three-

Benachi-Torre-Derbes House

6 Pets welcome; 8 Children welcome; 9 Social drinking allowed; 10 Tennis available; 11 Swimming available; 12 Golf available; 13 Skiing available; 14 May be booked through travel agents.

room suite with sitting room and shared bath; other private rooms and baths. Continental-plus breakfast. Gracious hospitality. Secure parking.

Host: James G. Derbes
Rooms: 4 (2 PB; 2 SB) $76-126
Continental Breakfast
Credit Cards: A, B
Notes: 2, 7, 9, 10, 12, 14

The Columns Hotel

3811 St. Charles Avenue, 70115
(504) 899-9308

One of the stateliest remaining examples of turn-of-the-century Louisiana architecture, the Columns Hotel offers a return to former elegance. Despite its elegance, the Columns is affordable and comfortable. Its 19 rooms range from very simple to very grand. Each features some small delight for the experienced traveler: unique fireplace, armoires, and claw-foot tubs. Sunday brunch and private parties are hosted here where guests can expect impeccable service. Convenient to many restaurants, the French Quarter, and Audubon Park. Listed on the National Register of Historic Places. Featured in *Good Housekeeping, Elle,* the *New York Times, Esquire,* on *"Good Morning America,"* and others.

Hosts: Claire and Jacques Creppel
Rooms: 19 (10 PB; 9 SB) $60-150
Continental Breakfast
Credit Cards: A, B, C
Notes: 5, 6, 7, 8, 9, 14

The Cornstalk Hotel

915 Royal Street, 70116
(504) 523-1515

This early 1800s home is central to the sights, sounds, gourmet foods, and night life of old New Orleans. In perhaps the most distinctive and most photographed of the small inns of the French Quarter, guests will have a unique experience of Victorian charm in the Vieux Carré. Glowing crystal chandeliers, antique furnishings, stained-glass windows, fireplaces, Oriental rugs, canopy beds, and complimentary morning newspaper set the mood of quiet comfort during any stay.

Hosts: David and Debi Spencer
Rooms: 14 (PB) $75-150
Continental Breakfast
Credit Cards: A, B, C
Notes: 5

The Cornstalk Hotel

818 Bourbon Street

818 Bourbon Street, 70116
(504) 524-2551

Two lovely apartments in an old historic French Quarter home. Each apartment has queen-size beds, kitchen, private bath, and central heating and cooling. Continental breakfast is provided. No smoking.

Hosts: Tom Redding and Blaine Dorr
Rooms: 2 (PB) $95
Continental Breakfast
Credit Cards: None
Notes: 2, 5

The Glimmet Inn

1631 Seventh Street, 70115
(504) 897-1895

This restored 1891 Victorian home features 12-foot cove ceilings, Cypress woodwork, side and front galleries, wraparound porch, and enclosed brick patio. Across the street from the garden district, just a half block to St. Charles streetcar, and easy access to French Quarter and Audubon Park and Zoo. A private carriage house is also available. All rooms are air-conditioned. Continental-plus breakfast served.

Hosts: Sharon Agiewich and Cathy Andros
Rooms: 6 (1 PB; 5 SB) $65-85
Continental Breakfast
Credit Cards: None
Notes: 2, 5, 9, 10, 12, 14

The Historic French Market Inn

501 Rue Decatur, 70130
(504) 561-5621

In the heart of the French Quarter, close to all major attractions, this historic inn, renowned for its relaxing ambience and Southern hospitality, offers 60 rooms and suites centered around a beautifully land-scaped courtyard. Complimentary Conti nental breakfast and evening cocktail.

Rooms and suites: 60; $79-200
Continental Breakfast
Credit Cards: A, B, C, D, E, F
Notes: 2, 5, 7, 8, 9, 10, 11, 12, 13, 14

Hotel Ste. Helene

508 Chartres, 70130
(504) 522-5014; (800) 348-3888

Hotel Ste. Helene's traditional setting is New Orleans. Courtyards and gardens cre- ate a romantic and relaxing atmosphere. The 24 guest rooms feature 18th-century antiques. Join the hosts in the breakfast room overlooking the pool or have break- fast brought to guest room door. Enjoy champagne during happy hour. Jackson Square and the mighty Mississippi are a few steps away.

Rooms: 16 (PB) $120-185
Continental Breakfast

Credit Cards: A, B, C, D, E
Notes: 2, 5, 7, 8, 11, 14

Hotel St. Pierre

911 Burgundy Street, 70116
(504) 524-4401

Hotel St. Pierre embodies the architecture and ambience of the 18th-century French Quarter. The 74 guest rooms and suites are beset among courtyards and swimming pools. Each morning, complimentary Con- tinental breakfast awaits guests in the Louis Armstrong breakfast room. Two blocks off Bourbon Street and all that jazz!

Host: James Millican
Rooms: 74 (PB) $89-129
Continental Breakfast
Credit Cards: A, B, C, D, E
Notes: 2, 3, 4, 5, 6, 7, 8, 9, 11, 14

Lafitte Guest House

1003 Bourbon Street, 70116
(504) 581-2678; (800) 331-7971

This elegant French manor house, in the heart of the French Quarter, is meticulously

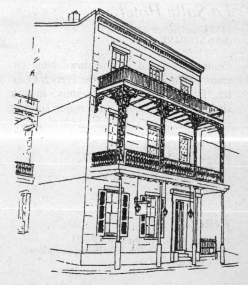
Lafitte Guest House

restored to its original splendor and furnished in fine antiques and reproductions. Every modern convenience, including air conditioning, is provided for guests' comfort. Complimentary Continental breakfast, wine, and hors d'oeuvres at cocktail hour, on-site parking, and a daily newspaper.

Host: Dr. Robert Guyton
Rooms: 14 (PB) $79-165
Continental Breakfast
Credit Cards: A, B, C, D
Notes: 5, 7, 8, 9, 14

Lamothe House

621 Esplanade Avenue, 70116
(504) 947-1161

Elegantly restored Victorian mansion. All rooms have private baths, color TV, telephones, and air conditioning. Some have high ceilings. Jackson Square, French Market, many jazz clubs, and fine restaurants just a stroll away.

Rooms: 20 (PB) $79
Continental Breakfast
Credit Cards: A, B, C
Notes: 5, 9, 10, 12, 14

La Salle Hotel

1113 Canal Street, 70112
(800) 521-9450

Centrally situated in downtown New Orleans within one block of the French Quarter, famous restaurants, theaters, historic sites, exclusive shops, and major sporting events.

Host: Roland Bahan
Rooms: 57 (45 PB; 12 SB) $57-90
Continental Breakfast
Credit Cards: A, B, C, D, E, F
Notes: 5, 7, 8, 14

Lincoln Ltd.

P.O. Box 3479, Meridian, MS 39303
(601) 482-5483; (800) 633-MISS (reservations)
FAX (601) 693-7447

7. Lovely historic home furnished in antiques. Six beautifully appointed bedrooms

with private baths. Situated conveniently close to the Garden District and public transportation. Continental breakfast served. $105-125.

Macarty Park Guest House/Historic Homes

3820 Burgundy Street, 70117-5708
(504) 943-4994; (800) 521-2790

Feel right at home in this century-old classic Victorian guest house and cottages just five minutes from the French Quarter. Step out of your room into lush tropical gardens and jump into the sparkling swimming pool. Our rooms are tastefully decorated in antique, reproduction, or contemporary furnishings, each with private bath, TV, and air conditioning. Free parking and Continental breakfast available.

Host: John Maher
Rooms: 8 (PB) $39-350
Continental Breakfast
Credit Cards: A, B, C
Notes: 5, 7, 14

Mechling's 1860's Mansion

2023 Esplanade Avenue, 70116
(504) 943-4131

This 1860s historical mansion is on beautiful Esplanade Avenue. Come and experience the Victorian era and all the elegance and comforts of a grand mansion. Guests are just a stroll away from the French Quarter and City Park. Spacious, beautifully decorated rooms with private baths. Complimentary breakfasts and airport pickups. Afternoon tea is served in parlor, veranda, or dining room. Public transportation right outside the door. Guests' comfort is the hosts' pleasure.

Hosts: Claudine, Keith, Kelly, and Taina Mechling
Rooms: 6 (PB) $95-155
Full Breakfast
Credit Cards: A, B, C
Notes: 2 (in advance), 5, 9, 14

NOTES: Credit cards accepted: A MasterCard; B Visa; C American Express; D Discover Card; E Diner's Club; F Other; 2 Personal checks accepted; 3 Lunch available; 4 Dinner available; 5 Open all year;

Melrose Mansion

937 Esplanade Avenue, 70116
(504) 944-2255

The Melrose is an 1884 Victorian mansion
that has been completely restored to perfection. This opulent, galleried mansion features eight antique-filled guest rooms with
luxurious private baths, spacious heated
pool and tropical patio, whirlpools, and wet
bars with refrigerators in the rooms. Complimentary airport pick-up and delivery
with house limousine, open bar at cocktail
hour, and a full Creole breakfast. New Orleans grandeur at its very finest.

Hosts: Melvin and Rosemary Jones
Rooms: 8 (PB) $225-425
Full Breakfast
Credit Cards: A, B, C
Notes: 2, 5, 9, 11, 14

New Orleans
Bed and Breakfast

P.O. Box 8163, 70182
(504) 838-0071; FAX (504) 943-3417

BD1. Very friendly hosts have converted a
commercial building into a comfortable, attractive home and offer two guest rooms
with bath in between. Two other smaller
rooms with double beds share a hall bath.
Off-street parking is available. No smoking;
no small children. $40-50.

CP1. Situated in the historic district of the
city and to the rear of an 1890 Creole cottage is a spacious efficiency apartment with
double bed, double sofa bed, private bath,
kitchenette, and private entrance. Walking
distance to the Museum of Art, St. Louis
Cemetery, plantation homes, and the beautiful 150-year-old oaks in City Park. Continental breakfast. $55-70.

CP2. A comfortable one-bedroom apartment,
completely private with twin beds and a fully
furnished kitchen. A double sofa bed is in liv-

ing room. Walk to activities in City Park or
catch a bus to the French Quarter. No smoking; Continental breakfast. $55-70.

GE1. On this tree-shaded boulevard, one
large brick house has three bedrooms. The
master bedroom is done in rose and black,
has five tall windows, king-size bed, and
private bath. Two other rooms share a bath.
Continental breakfast. $55-70.

GE2. A pretty garage apartment has double
bed and a trundle bed in the living area;
kitchen, bath, and loads of off-street parking. Continental breakfast. $55-70.

LK1. A West Indies-style plantation home
built from remains of a long-ago plantation
mansion and filled with antiques, Mardi
Gras mementoes, and giant Audubon prints.
Two bedrooms, private baths, and breezeway on the second floor. On the levee,
guests can jog, ride bikes, or stroll hand-in-
hand. A full plantation breakfast is served
in the family dining room. Near the airport,
25 minutes by car to the French Quarter.
$95-125.

LV1. One large, friendly home has two upstairs bedrooms with common den and independent bath. Great for family or two
couples. Continental breakfast. $55-70.

LV2. In a delightful lake-view subdivision,
a cozy bungalow offers one bedroom with
twin beds and private bath, private entrance, and off-street parking. The guests
will find a restful den and lovely back yard
garden. Continental breakfast. $55-70.

UP2. This friendly, relaxed home has a
cozy patio, spacious bedrooms, some with
private baths, and double or queen-size
beds. Guests have full use of the kitchen facilities. The hostess is a licensed tour guide

6 Pets welcome; 8 Children welcome; 9 Social drinking allowed; 10 Tennis available; 11 Swimming available;
12 Golf available; 13 Skiing available; 14 May be booked through travel agents.

New Orleans Bed and Breakfast (continued)

and speaks both Spanish and French. Continental breakfast is served. $40-70.

UP4. One moderately priced, luxurious home is near first-class restaurants. One bedroom with private bath. Hostess loves to travel. Continental breakfast. From $70.

UP6. In a lovely uptown home with serene atmosphere is a large two-bedroom and bath suite, one with king-size bed and the other with a queen-size bed. Deluxe antiques, private entrance. Just steps away from St. Charles Avenue streetcar. Continental breakfast. $75.

UP10. This renovated historic uptown residence was once a plantation home. It consists of five bedrooms, each with a private bath. Built in 1840, the house is furnished with antiques or reproductions of antiques, and all bedrooms have queen-size beds except one, which has a double Edwardian bed. Situated near the streetcar line and many fine restaurants. Continental breakfast. $70 plus.

New Orleans Guest House

1118 Ursulines Street, 70116
(504) 566-1177; (800) 562-1177

An 1848 Creole cottage with lush courtyard where a complimentary Continental breakfast is served each morning. Private baths, free parking, tastefully decorated with antiques or contemporary furnishings, air conditioning, and TV. Three blocks to famous Bourbon Street.

Hosts: Ray and Alvin
Rooms: 14 (PB) $69-79
Continental Breakfast
Credit Cards: A, B, C
Notes: 5

Nine-O-Five Royal Hotel

905 Royal Street, 70116
(504) 523-0219

In the heart of the French Quarter. Within walking distance to everything.

Rooms and Suites: 10 (PB) $65-120
Credit Cards: A, B
Notes: 5, 8

Old World Inn

1330 Prytania Street, 70130
(504) 566-1330

The Old World Inn is built in traditional New Orleans French cafe-style, with pressed tin ceiling and tile floors in the breakfast room. Guest rooms are simple, furnished in turn-of-the-century oak. All rooms are air-conditioned. In the Lower Garden District, five minutes from French Quarter on the streetcar line. The second inn is called The Hideaway. It is an old New Orleans mansion with a small number of elegantly furnished guest rooms. Marble fireplaces in every room, high ceilings, and antique furniture. Originally built for a Creole gentleman, there have been lurid moments in the history of this house, including some years when the third floor was a bordello reached by a secret stairway. Front desk serves both inns. Multi-lingual, excellent concierge. World-wide clientele.

Hosts: Jean and Charlie Matkin
Rooms: 20 (10 PB; 10 SB) $40-65
Continental Breakfast
Credit Cards: A, B, F
Notes: 5, 7, 9, 10, 12, 14

The Prytania Inn

1415 Prytania Street, 70130
(504) 566-1515

Restored to its pre-Civil War glory and situated in the historic district, the inn received the 1984 Commission Award. Tender care; full gourmet breakfast. Patio, slave quarters, 18 rooms with private baths, and most with kitchen facilities or microwave and refrigerators. Five minutes to the French Quarter and one-block walk to St. Charles Avenue and the streetcar. Free parking. Hosts speak German.

Hosts: Sally and Peter Schreiber
Rooms: 18 (PB) $35-55
Full Breakfast
Credit Cards: A, B, C, D, E, F
Notes: 5, 6, 7, 8

Rue Dumaine

Rue Dumaine

731 Dumaine Street, 70116
(504) 581-2802

Guests' private entranceway leads through a lush, secluded patio to a hideaway in the heart of the bustling French Quarter. Built in 1824, these completely renovated slave quarters have every amenity, including central air and heat, ceiling fans, working fireplace, balcony, private bath, telephones, intercom, and kitchenette with microwave and refrigerator. Have a great time on Bourbon Street just one-half block away and yet sleep soundly in the quiet of an exclusive retreat. Twin beds only.

Host: Clydia Davenport
Room: 1 (PB) $90-150
Continental Breakfast
Credit Cards: D
Notes: 2 (in advance), 5, 9, 14

St. Charles Guest House Bed and Breakfast

1748 Prytania, 70130
(504) 523-6556

A simple, cozy, and affordable European-style pension operating in the lower Garden District for over 40 years. On streetcar line. Minutes to downtown and all attractions. Complimentary Continental breakfast, pool, and decks enjoyable almost year-round. Favored by writers, artists, performers, and world travelers; over 4,000 guests per year. Charming, eclectic, uniquely "Old New Orleans," low tech, and relaxing, from backpacker rooms at $30 to antiques and queen-size beds at $75. Historic district. In guidebooks worldwide.

Hosts: Joanne and Dennis Hilton
Rooms: 38 (26 PB; 12 SB) $30-85
Continental Breakfast
Credit Cards: A, B, C
Notes: 2 (in advance), 5, 7, 8, 9

Soniat House

1133 Chartres Street, 70116
(504) 522-0570; (800) 544-8808
FAX (504) 522-7208

Hidden in a quiet residential section of New Orleans' French Quarter, Soniat House was built in 1829 as a town home for the large family of Joseph Soniat Dufossat, a wealthy plantation owner. Typical of the period, the Creole house incorporates classic Greek Revival details. A wide carriageway entrance leads to a quiet and beautiful courtyard; galleries are framed by lace ironwork, and open spiral stairs lead to the two upper floors. All rooms are tastefully furnished with fine antiques, hand-carved bedsteads, and the work of contemporary New Orleans artists. The Soniat House was recognized as the French Quarter's best restoration on the 50th anniversary of the Vieux Carré Commission. Member of the National Historic Hotels since 1990.

Hosts: Rodney and Frances Smith
Rooms: 24 (PB) $135-550

6 Pets welcome; 8 Children welcome; 9 Social drinking allowed; 10 Tennis available; 11 Swimming available; 12 Golf available; 13 Skiing available; 14 May be booked through travel agents.

Continental Breakfast
Credit Cards: A, B, C
Notes: 5, 14

Terrell House Mansion

1441 Magazine Street, 70130
(504) 524-9859; (800) 878-9859

Terrell House was built in the Classical Revival style in 1858. Restored and opened as an inn in 1984, it has a large following of guests from around the country and abroad. The main mansion guest rooms feature balconies, galleries, and authentic furnishings. Each overlooks the courtyard. The original carriage house has been converted to four guest rooms, each furnished with period antiques and decorated with its own style. The lower Garden District is the oldest purely residential neighborhood outside the French Quarter. The real New Orleans!

Rooms: 9 (PB) $65-110
Continental Breakfast
Credit Cards: A, B, C, D, E
Notes: 2, 9, 12, 14

NEW ROADS

Lincoln Ltd.

P.O. Box 3479, Meridian, MS 39303
(601) 482-5483; (800) 633-MISS (reservations)
FAX (601) 693-7447

38. This attractive Creole cottage is wonderful for a weekend getaway or a special fishing trip. Group accommodations by special request. The hostess is knowledgeable about the history of this Mississippi River town and can offer many ideas about special places to see (plantation homes, fishing, etc.). A Continental breakfast is served each morning by the hostess/owner. Six guest rooms. $45.

New Orleans Bed and Breakfast

P.O. Box 8163, New Orleans, 70182
(504) 838-0071

Country. Across the River (via ferry) is "French Country." Here is a 100-year-old farm cottage on spacious grounds facing False River. Explore the area, go boating, go antiquing, and visit plantations.

PLAQUEMINE

Old Turnerville Bed and Breakfast

23230 Nadler Street, 70764
(504) 687-5337; (504) 687-6029

Antique-furnished guest bedroom with private bath in Miss Louise's house, a century-old raised cottage in Old Turnerville, an 1800s village on the Mississippi. Wide front gallery with swing and rockers. Separate guest cottage. Continental breakfast. Tour of two Old Turnerville house museums includes tariff. Antique shop. Heart of plantation country. Twenty miles south of Baton Rouge.

Host: Brenda Bourgoyne Blanchard
Room: 1 (PB) $65
Cottage: 1 (PB) $85
Continental Breakfast
Credit Cards: A, B
Notes: 2, 5, 7, 8, 9

PORT VINCENT

Tree House in the Park

16520 Airport Road, Prairieville, 70769
(504) 622-2850; (800) LE CABIN

A Cajun cabin in the swamp. Two bedrooms with private entrances off the front porch, each with private bath, queen-size waterbed, private hot tub on sun deck, and pool on lower deck (heated May-October). Boat slip, fishing dock, and double kayak float trip on Amite River. Three acres of ponds, bridges, cypress trees, ducks, and geese. Complimentary supper on arrival. Very peaceful.

Hosts: Fran and Julius Schmieder
Rooms: 2 (PB) $110-150

NOTES: Credit cards accepted: A MasterCard; B Visa; C American Express; D Discover Card; E Diner's Club; F Other; 2 Personal checks accepted; 3 Lunch available; 4 Dinner available; 5 Open all year;

Full Breakfast
Credit Cards: A, B, C
Notes: 2, 4, 5, 9, 11, 14

ST. FRANCISVILLE

Barrow House Inn

9779 Royal Street, Box 700, 70775
(504) 635-4791

Sip wine in a wicker rocker on the front porch while enjoying the ambience of a quiet neighborhood of antebellum homes. Rooms are all furnished in antiques from 1840-1870. Gourmet candlelight dinners are available, as is breakfast in bed. A cassette walking tour of the historic district is included for guests. Closed December 23 through Christmas Day.

Hosts: Shirley and Lyle Dittloff
Rooms: 3 (PB) $85-95
Suites: 3 (PB) $100-125
Full or Continental Breakfast
Credit Cards: A, B
Notes: 2, 4, 5, 7, 8, 9, 12, 14

Green Springs Plantation Bed and Breakfast

7463 Tunica Trace, 70775
(800) 457-4978

Sprawling country estate in Tunica Hills nature area. Peaceful garden setting with butterflies, flowers, birds, creek, natural spring, and Indian mound. Gracious Southern home of area native. Spacious, beautifully decorated rooms with queen-size or twin beds and private baths. Antique furnishings, and modern plumbing. Hot plantation breakfast cooked by creator of "spinach Madeline." Near antebellum homes, Civil War battlefield, antique shops, Mississippi River ferry, and golf course. Biking and hiking are also available.

Hosts: Madeline and Ivan Nevill
Rooms: 3 (PB) $85
Full Breakfast
Credit Cards: A, B, D
Notes: 2, 5, 8, 9, 12, 14

New Orleans Bed and Breakfast

P.O. Box 8163, New Orleans, 70182
(504) 838-0071

Would a cozy cottage under the tall trees be enticing for a romantic or relaxing weekend? If so, details of several separate cottages in quiet country areas can be supplied. Or would the companionship of congenial hosts who serve a special breakfast and whose veranda has rocking chairs and a swing to while away lazy hours be preferred? There are wooded paths to explore on premises and unusual terrain nearby to also explore. $95-125.

SHREVEPORT

Fairfield Place Bed and Breakfast

2221 Fairfield Avenue, 71104
(318) 222-0048

Built before the turn of the century, Fairfield Place has been beautifully restored to bring guests all the charm of a bygone era. Conveniently situated near downtown, I-20, the medical centers, and Louisiana Downs. Within walking distance of fine restaurants and unique shops. Breakfast includes rich Cajun coffee and freshly baked croissants, served in the privacy of guests' rooms, the balcony, porch, or courtyard.

Host: Jane Lipscomb
Rooms: 9 (PB) $95-135
Full Breakfast
Credit Cards: A, B, C
Notes: 2, 5, 9, 10, 11, 12

Twenty-four Thirty-nine Fairfield— A Bed and Breakfast

2439 Fairfield Avenue, 71104
(318) 424-2424; FAX (318) 424-3658

6 Pets welcome; 8 Children welcome; 9 Social drinking allowed; 10 Tennis available; 11 Swimming available; 12 Golf available; 13 Skiing available; 14 May be booked through travel agents.

A 1905 Victorian mansion in historical district surrounded by landscaped English gardens with Victorian swing, gazebo, and fountains. Each room has a private balcony complete with rocking chair and swings. The guest rooms each have private baths with whirlpools, designer linens, Amish quilts, and down comforters. An English breakfast is served in the morning room consisting of eggs, Canadian bacon, sausage, homemade breads, selected cheeses, and imported teas and coffee.

Hosts: Jimmy and Vicki Harris
Rooms: 4 (PB) $95-150
Full Breakfast
Credit Cards: A, B, C, D, E
Notes: 2, 5, 9, 10, 12, 14

SLIDELL

Lincoln Ltd.

P.O. Box 3479, Meridian, MS 39303
(601) 482-5483; (800) 633-MISS (reservations)
FAX (601) 693-7447

73. I-10, Highway 155, 30 minutes from Canal Street: 45 minutes from New Orleans Airport. Circa 1895, a 16-room Queen Anne Revival mansion offering guests the convenience of New Orleans with the ambience of a historic home on four landscaped acres. Furnished with antiques. $75-95.

Salmen-Fritchie House Bed and Breakfast

127 Cleveland Avenue, 70458
(504) 643-1405; (800) 235-4168

Built before the turn of the century by one of the founders of this city, this Victorian mansion is listed on the National Register of Historic Places. Just 30 minutes from New Orleans' famous French Quarter. Beautiful grounds with 300-year-old trees. Several bedrooms have fireplaces. All have private baths, telephones, and TVs. Beautiful period antique furnishings with huge poster beds.

Hosts: Sharon and Homer Fritchie
Rooms: 5 (PB) $85-95
Full Breakfast
Credit Cards: A, B, C
Notes: 2, 5, 8 (over 10), 9, 10, 12, 14

WHITE CASTLE

Nottoway Plantation Inn and Restaurant

P.O. Box 160, Louisiana Highway 1, 70788
(504) 545-2730

Nottoway, circa 1859, is a Greek Revival and Italianate mansion built for a wealthy sugarcane planter just before the Civil War. The home is situated beside the Mississippi River and surrounded by large oak and pecan trees. Rooms are also available in a restored 150-year-old overseer's cottage.

Hosts: Cindy Hidalgo and Faye Russell
Rooms: 13 (PB) $125-250
Full Breakfast
Credit Cards: A, B, C, D
Notes: 2, 3, 4, 5, 8, 9, 10, 11, 14

Maine

Clover Hill Farm
Bed and Breakfast

Rural Route 1, Box 241A, 04002
(207) 490-1105

Unwind on this peaceful, organic farm. Pet the animals. Gather own eggs. Enjoy a bountiful breakfast. Hosts are happy to accommodate special dietary requirements. Hike or ski on 100 acres of rolling hills and woodland or drive a short distance for beaches, fishing, outlet shopping, and a great variety of other activities. Just one-and-a-half hours from Boston, six hours from New York City, and 30 minutes from ocean beaches and Kennebunkport.

Host: Margit Lassen, Ph.D.
Rooms: 3 (SB) $65-85
Full Breakfast
Credit Cards: A, B, D
Notes: 2, 5, 8, 10, 11, 12

BAILEY ISLAND

Captain York House
Bed and Breakfast

Route 24, P.O. Box 32, 04003
(207) 833-6224

Enjoy true island atmosphere on scenic Bailey Island, an unspoiled fishing village accessible by car over the only cribstone bridge in the world. Near Brunswick, Freeport, and Portland. Former sea captain's home tastefully restored to original charm, furnished with antiques. Informal, friendly atmosphere and ocean views from every room. From the deck, enjoy sights of local lobstermen hauling traps and sunsets to remember. Nearby fine dining/summer nature cruise. Oceanview apartment rental also available.

Hosts: Charles and Ingrid Di Vita
Rooms: 4 (2 PB; 2 SB) $60-80
Full Breakfast
Credit Cards: None
Notes: 2, 5, 9, 11, 14

Captain York House

Katie's Ketoh

P.O. Box 105, 04003
(207) 833-7785

Bailey Island, a lobster/fishing community, is connected to the mainland by the only cribstone bridge in the world. The host is a retired lobsterman who carves duck decoys as he enjoys mugs of hot coffee with guests. The hostess will prepare a

6 Pets welcome; 7 Smoking allowed; 8 Children welcome; 9 Social drinking allowed; 10 Tennis available; 11 Swimming available; 12 Golf available; 13 Skiing available; 14 May be booked through travel agents.

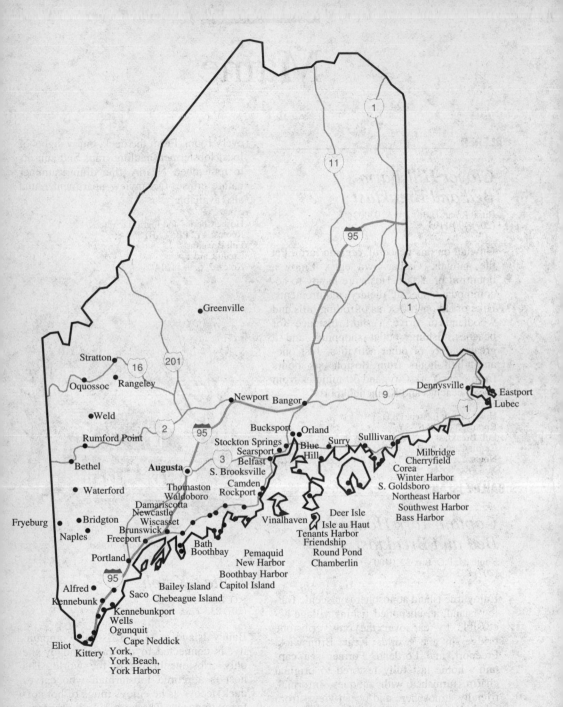

Maine

tasty breakfast for guests. Swimming, hiking, sailing, beachcombing, and ferry rides are available.

Hosts: Albert and Catherine (Katie) Johnson
Rooms: 2 (1 PB; 1 SB) $60-70
Full Breakfast
Credit Cards: None
Notes: 2, 8, 11, 12

The Lady and The Loon Bed and Breakfast

P.O. Box 88, 04003
(207) 833-6871

Restored 1800 Maine Island inn on the ocean. Breakfast served on the bluff overlooking the Casco Bay Islands. Stairs lead down to private stone beach, a haven for naturalists and artists. Homemade cooking includes freshly baked muffins and fresh fruit. Hostess is an artist who teaches landscaping and painting classes in afternoon. Three hours from Boston, Massachusetts; one hour from Portland, Maine; three hours from Bar Harbor.

Host: Gail Sprague
Rooms: 3 (PB) $75-85
Full Breakfast
Credit Cards: A, B
Notes: 11

BANGOR

Bangor's Historic Phenix Inn

20 Broad Street, West Market Square, 04401
(207) 947-3850

The Phenix Inn, a bed and breakfast on the National Register of Historic Places, circa 1873, has been tastefully decorated to offer the finest in historical charm, comfort, and quality accommodations. Guests are invited to enjoy the elegant surroundings, warm, professional staff, and convenient location. Bangor's commercial and financial center, shops, restaurants, and cultural attractions are within walking distance of the inn. All rooms have heating/air conditioning, private bath, telephone, and TV. Free parking.

Host: Kimberly M. Hauen
Rooms: 37 (PB) $35-75
Continental Breakfast
Credit Cards: A, B, C, D, E
Notes: 5, 6, 7, 8, 9, 10, 11, 12, 13, 14

BAR HARBOR

Black Friar Inn

10 Summer Street, 04609
(207) 288-5091

This comfortably restored and rebuilt Victorian house with antiques is on a quiet side street. Six guest rooms with queen-size beds and private baths. Rates include delicious full breakfast, late afternoon refreshments, and rainy day teas. Easy access to Acadia National Park. Short walk to waterfront, shops, and restaurants. Ample parking. Two-night minimum July 1 through mid-October. Sorry, no cots or roll away beds; rooms can accommodate one or two people only. Open May-November.

Hosts: Barbara and Jim Kelly
Rooms: 6 (PB) $85-105
Full Breakfast
Credit Cards: A, B
Notes: 2, 8 (over 11), 9, 10, 12

Breakwater-1904

45 Hancock Street, 04609
(207) 288-2313; (800) 238-6309

Indulge in the luxury of Breakwater-1904, an English Tudor estate on the shores of Frenchman's Bay in Bar Harbor, Maine. Six grand individually appointed bed chambers with fireplaces and private baths await guests' arrival. Relax on the veranda with afternoon tea or evening refreshments and watch the yachts sail by. Listed on the National Register of Historic Places. Full

NOTES: Credit cards accepted: A MasterCard; B Visa; C American Express; D Discover Card; E Diner's Club; F Other; 2 Personal checks accepted; 3 Lunch available; 4 Dinner available; 5 Open all year; 6 Pets welcome; 7 Smoking allowed; 8 Children welcome; 9 Social drinking allowed; 10 Tennis available; 11 Swimming available; 12 Golf available; 13 Skiing available; 14 May be booked through travel agents.

breakfast is included. Nonsmoking bed and breakfast, not appropriate for young children or pets. Inquire about off-season rates.

Rooms: 6 (PB) $175-295
Full Breakfast
Credit Cards: A, B, C
Notes: 2, 9, 10, 11, 12, 13 (cross-country), 14

Canterbury Cottage

12 Roberts Avenue, 04609
(207) 288-2112

Canterbury Cottage, a delightful Victorian shingled structure built in 1900, is family owned and operated. The cottage offers guests a cozy and comfortable alternative to the big inns. It is on a quiet side street, a short two-block walk to the many village and harbor activities. Only five minutes to Acadia National Park and the Nova Scotia ferry terminal.

Hosts: Rick and Michele Suydam
Rooms: 4 (2 PB; 2 SB) $65-85
Continental Breakfast
Credit Cards: None
Notes: 2, 10, 11, 12

Castlemaine Inn

39 Holland Avenue, 04609
(207) 288-4563; (800) 338-4563

Castlemaine Inn is nestled on a quiet side street in the village of Bar Harbor, which is surrounded by the magnificent Acadia National Park. The rooms are well appointed, with canopied beds and fireplaces. A delightful Continental buffet-style breakfast is served. Open May-October

Hosts: Terence O'Connell and Norah O'Brien
Rooms: 13 (PB) $98-148
Continental Breakfast
Credit Cards: A, B
Notes: 2, 8 (over 13), 9, 10, 11, 12

Cleftstone Manor

92 Eden Street, 04609
(207) 288-4951

Cleftstone Manor is a distinguished 33-room Victorian "cottage," set on a hill amid formal gardens, offering gracious accommodations in one of nature's magnificent meetings of land and sea, Mount Desert Island. The manor offers cozy fireside chats, a library, games, a lavish full breakfast buffet, and the peace of country living. Complimentary afternoon tea and evening refreshments. Closed November-March.

Hosts: Don and Pattie Reynolds
Rooms: 16 (PB) $95-198
Full Breakfast
Credit Cards: A, B, D
Notes: 2, 8 (over 7), 10, 11, 12

Graycote Inn

40 Holland Avenue, 04609
(207) 288-3044

This painstakingly restored light and airy 1881 Victorian was completely renovated in 1986. Twelve extra-large rooms or suites with king- or queen-size beds; all private baths, some fireplaces, sun porches, or balconies. Peaceful one-acre village lot with lawns, trees, and off-street parking. Five-minute walk to shops, restaurants, and water activities. Five minute drive to the pristine beauty of Acadia National Park with 120 miles of hiking trails and 50 miles of carriage roads used for hikers or bikers, but not motorized vehicles.

Hosts: Joe and Judy Losquadro
Rooms: 12 (PB) $85-145
Full Breakfast
Credit Cards: A, B, D
Notes: 2, 9, 10, 12

Hearthside

7 High Street, 04609
(207) 288-4533

Built at the turn of the century as the residence for Dr. George Hagerthy, Hearthside is now a cozy and comfortable bed and breakfast. Hearthside is on a quiet side street in Bar Harbor. All of the newly decorated rooms have queen-size beds and private baths; some have private porches, whirlpool tubs, or working fireplaces. Some rooms are air-conditioned. Each morning a

NOTES: Credit cards accepted: A MasterCard; B Visa; C American Express; D Discover Card; E Diner's Club; F Other; 2 Personal checks accepted; 3 Lunch available; 4 Dinner available; 5 Open all year;

Hearthside

lavish breakfast buffet is served, and lemonade and homemade cookies are offered each afternoon. Off-season rates and spring packages available.

Hosts: Susan and Barry Schwartz
Rooms: 9 (PB) $75-115
Full Breakfast
Credit Cards: A, B, D
Notes: 2, 5, 9, 10, 11, 12

The Kedge
Bed and Breakfast

112 West Street, 04609
(207) 288-5180; (800) 597-8306

The Kedge, built in 1870, has a peaceful beauty that is full of light and comfortable elegance. In town across the street from Frenchman Bay, this bed and breakfast rests on a double lot and has beautiful gardens. The dream room is 18 by 22 feet, has a king-size brass bed, fireplace, and whirlpool tub. In the historical district. Smoke free. Full breakfast. AAA.

Hosts: Leo and Cheryl Higgins
Rooms: 5 (PB) $55-150
Full Breakfast
Credit Cards: A, B, C, D
Notes: 2, 5, 8 (seven and older), 9, 10, 11, 12, 13

Long Pond Inn

Box 361, Mount Desert, 04660
(207) 244-5854

On the shore of beautiful Long Pond near the quaint village of Somesville, this inn offers one of the quietest choices of country lodging on Mount Desert Island. The inn is the hosts' year-round home. The four guest rooms are charmingly appointed featuring queen-size beds and private baths, one with a Jacuzzi tub. The stay includes a hearty Continental breakfast of fresh seasonal fruits and homemade muffins. After breakfast, stroll the inn's lavish vegetable, herb, and flower gardens, enjoy a swim, or paddle on Long Pond in one of the rental canoes. Within 15 minutes of Long Pond; Inn in any direction is all that Mount Desert Island has to offer. Resident springer spaniels. No guest pets.

Rooms: 4 (PB) $75-95
Continental Breakfast
Credit Cards: A, B
Notes: 2, 9, 11, 12

Manor House Inn

106 West Street, 04609
(207) 288-3759; (800) 437-0088

This beautiful 1887 Victorian summer cottage is listed on the National Register of Historic Places. Near Acadia National Park. Within walking distance of downtown Bar Harbor and waterfront. Enjoy the acre of landscaped grounds and gardens.

Manor House Inn

Minimum stay July, August, and holidays is two nights. Closed November through mid-April.

Host: Mac Noyes
Rooms: 14 (PB) $55-165
Full Breakfast
Credit Cards: A, B, C
Notes: 2, 8 (over 8), 10, 11, 12

The Maples Inn

16 Roberts Avenue, 04609
(207) 288-3443

Built in early 1900, the Maples Inn originally housed the wealthy summer visitors to Mount Desert Island. It is on a quiet, residential, tree-lined street. Guests will be away from the traffic of Bar Harbor, yet within walking distance of attractive boutiques, intimate restaurants, and the surrounding sea. For the perfect romantic getaway, reserve the White Birch Suite, complete with a blue and white tiled fireplace. Palates will be treated to host's personal breakfast recipes, some of which have been featured in *Bon Appetit* and *Gourmet* magazines. Enjoy the beauty of Acadia National Park and Mount Desert Island year-round.

Host: Susan Sinclair
Rooms: 6 (PB) $60-140
Full Breakfast
Credit Cards: A, B, D
Notes: 2, 3 (picnic), 5, 9, 10, 11, 12,
13 (cross country)

The Maples Inn

Pachelbel Inn

Pachelbel Inn

20 Roberts Avenue, 04609
(207) 288-9655

Join Russell and Helene Fye, along with their children Russ and Samantha, in this comfortable Victorian home. Central to town. Easy walking to shops, restaurants, and the harbor. Five-minute drive to the Blue Nose Ferry Terminal and one mile to Acadia National Park. Smoking on front porch only. People remember the Fyes for their great breakfasts and warm hospitality. All children welcome.

Hosts: Russ and Helene Fye
Rooms: 6 (4 PB; 2 SB) $55-105
Full Breakfast
Credit Cards: A, B
Notes: 2, 5, 7 (limited), 8, 10, 11, 12, 13

Stratford House Inn

45 Mount Desert Street 460-9
(207) 288-5189

Stratford House Inn features English Tudor architecture with a likeness to Queen Elizabeth's summer home. Beautiful bedrooms;

NOTES: Credit cards accepted: A MasterCard; B Visa; C American Express; D Discover Card; E Diner's Club; F Other; 2 Personal checks accepted; 3 Lunch available; 4 Dinner available; 5 Open all year;

each with its own individual decor. Easy walk to stores, restaurants, or the waterfront. Acadia National Park is nearby with beautiful scenery and activities for everyone. Minimum stay on weekends and holidays is two nights. Closed November through May.

Hosts: Barbara and Norman Moulton
Rooms: 10 (8 PB; 2 SB) $75-150
Continental Breakfast
Credit Cards: A, B
Notes: 2, 7, 8, 9, 10, 11, 12,

Stratford House Inn

Thornhedge Inn

47 Mount Desert Street, 04609
(207) 288-5398; (800) 580-0800

Built in 1900 by the publisher of Little Women, this Queen Anne-styled shingled cottage is in the historic corridor district, one block from the main restaurant and shopping area. There are 13 spacious guest rooms as well as many common areas including a dining room with original furnishings, three parlor areas with fireplaces, and a spacious porch with wicker furniture. All rooms provide a private bath, color cable TV, and most have a queen-size bed. Some

rooms also have a fireplace with Sterno logs. Continental breakfast of homemade breads and muffins, orange juice, and coffee or tea is served each morning. No smoking. No pets. Seasonal May 15 through October 15.

Host: Elinor G. Geel
Rooms: 13 (PB) $80-140
Continental Breakfast
Credit Cards: A, B, C
Notes: 9, 10, 11, 12

The Tides

119 West Street, 04609
(207) 288-4968

Oceanfront estate in the historic district of Bar Harbor. Elegant Greek Revival architecture featuring expansive wraparound veranda with fireplace and filled with wicker furniture; a great spot to enjoy breakfast while watching the boating activities. The Tides offers two-room suites, each with queen-size bed, private bath, and full oceanfront views. Private parlors have cable TV. Some suites have working fireplaces. Within walking distance of leisure activities, refreshments, and shops. Very close to Acadia National Park entrance.

Host: Margaret Eden
Rooms: 3 (PB) $195-235
Full Breakfast
Credit Cards: A, B
Notes: 2, 9, 10, 12, 13 (cross-country), 14

BASS HARBOR

Bed and Breakfast Inns of New England

128 S. Hoop Pole Road, Guilford, CT, 06437
(203) 457-0042; (800) 582-0853

ME-853. Once a sea captain's home during Colonial times, this bed and breakfast offers six guest rooms, two with private baths, a large sitting room with TV, large deck with water views, and a large screened porch with hammock, a relaxing

6 Pets welcome; 8 Children welcome; 9 Social drinking allowed; 10 Tennis available; 11 Swimming available; 12 Golf available; 13 Skiing available; 14 May be booked through travel agents.

swing chair, and the best spot to view the unforgettable sunsets. Decor of nautical accents and comfortable furnishings. Walk on nature trails; climb nearby mountains; and fish, swim, or canoe in the lakes. No smoking. Children ten and older are welcome. Resident cat; no guest pets. Two-night minimum stay on weekends July through October. $65-85. $10 additional during summer peak season. $15 for third person.

Pointy Head Inn

Route 102A, 04653
(207) 244-7261

Relax on the quiet side of Mount Desert Island near Acadia National Park in an old sea captain's home. On the shore of a picturesque harbor where schooners anchor overnight. Haven for photographers and artists. Minutes to lighthouse, trails, restaurants, stores.

Hosts: Doris and Warren Townsend
Rooms: 6 (2 PB; 4 SB) $60-85
Full Breakfast
Credit Cards: None
Notes: 2, 8 (over 10), 9, 10, 11, 12

BATH

Fairhaven Inn at Bath

Rural Route 2, Box 85, 04530
(207) 443-4391

Where eagles soar, birds sing, and tidal river meets meadow. This comfortable, quiet 1790 Colonial is renowned for its breakfast, and is the perfect midcoast base from which to enjoy all that Maine's coast has to offer. Hiking and cross-country skiing on property. Beaches and Maritime Museum nearby.

Hosts: George and Sallie Pollard
Rooms: 9 (PB and SB) $53.50-74.90
Full Breakfast
Credit Cards: A, B, C
Notes: 2, 5, 6 (limited), 7 (restricted), 8, 9, 10, 11, 12, 13, 14

Glad II

60 Pearl Street, 04530
(207) 443-1191

A comfortable Victorian home, circa 1851, near the center of town and convenient to Maritime Museum, beaches, Freeport shopping, L.L. Bean, and Boothbay Harbor. The host and her four-legged concierge, Nicholas, love to welcome new friends. Two night minimum stay weekends and holidays.

Host: Gladys Lansky
Rooms: 2 (SB) $50 plus tax
Continental Breakfast
Credit Cards: A, B, C
Notes: 2, 8 (over 12), 9, 10, 11, 12, 13

BELFAST

Bed and Breakfast Inns of New England

128 S. Hoop Pole Road, Guilford, CT, 06437
(203) 457-0042; (800) 582-0853

ME-840. This Greek Revival house was built around 1845 during Belfast's period of great architectural activity. Guests are welcome to use the beautiful formal living room with ornate tiled fireplace. Three large bedrooms with pine floors and a variety of bed sizes are available. All bedrooms have private baths. There is a screened and glassed-in porch overlooking a garden where breakfast is usually served. Complimentary afternoon wine is served in the living room. No pets, but children over ten are welcome. No smoking. $45.

Frost House

6 Northport Avenue, 04915
(207) 338-4159

A turn-of-the-century Victorian with two porches on an acre lot with water views. There are four public rooms where guests may relax. Two bedrooms have queen-size beds, one has California king-size. The

NOTES: Credit cards accepted: A MasterCard; B Visa; C American Express; D Discover Card; E Diner's Club; F Other; 2 Personal checks accepted; 3 Lunch available; 4 Dinner available; 5 Open all year;

house has carved woods, stained-glass parlor windows, and is light and airy. Within walking distance of the harbor and town. Fifty-five miles to Bar Harbor and 20 minutes from Camden. Breakfast is served on porches, weather permitting. A tandem bike and a picnic basket are available for the day. The Frost House has received a triple crown inspection rating from the ABBA which AAA recommends.

Hosts: Joan and John Lightfoot
Rooms: 3 (PB) $64.20-85.60
Full Breakfast
Credit Cards: B
Notes: 2, 9, 10, 11, 12, 14

The Jeweled Turret Inn

16 Pearl Street, 04915
(207) 338-2304; (800) 696-2304 (in state)

Step back into a time when lace, elegant furnishings, and afternoon tea were everyday necessities. The inn is named for the grand staircase that winds up the turret, lighted by stained- and leaded-glass panels with jewel-like embellishments. Lots of woodwork, fireplaces, public rooms, and two verandas available for relaxation. Mornings welcome visitors with gourmet breakfasts, and afternoon tea is served with dessert; off-season November through May. In the historic district; shops, restaurants, and waterfront close by.

The Jeweled Turret Inn

Hosts: Carl and Cathy Heffentrager
Rooms: 7 (PB) $65-85
Full Breakfast
Credit Cards: None
Notes: 2, 5, 9, 10, 11, 12, 13, 14

The Thomas Pitcher House

5 Franklin Street, 04915
(207) 338-6454

Thomas Pitcher built this handsome intown Victorian in 1873. An airy Italian ceramic tile foyer provides access to the common areas. Large bay windows and marble fireplace accent the bright and inviting parlor. Hearty breakfasts are served in the large Chippendale dining room. Guest rooms and common areas feature original Victorian architecture and offer a blend of antiques and reproduction pieces. Convenient to Acadia National Park and other mid-coast Maine attractions.

Hosts: Fran and Ron Kresge
Rooms: 4 (PB) $55-80
Full Breakfast
Credit Cards: None
Notes: 2, 5, 10, 11, 12, 13

BETHEL

Abbott House

P.O. Box 933, 04217-0933
(207) 824-7600; (800) 240-2377

The Abbott House offers four rooms with two shared baths in an 18th-century Cape Cod on two-and-a-half acres. Hot tub, pool, and massage therapy are available. Relax near the perennial gardens. Hosts will serve dinner on request. Near Sunday River Skiway and White Mountains. Murder mystery weekends, golf, and multi-day packages are available. Open year-round.

Hosts: Joe Cardello and Penny Bohac
Rooms: 4 (S2B) $50-65
Full Breakfast
Credit Cards: A, B, C
Notes: 2, 3, 4, 5, 8 (over 5), 9, 10, 11, 12, 13

6 Pets welcome; 8 Children welcome; 9 Social drinking allowed; 10 Tennis available; 11 Swimming available; 12 Golf available; 13 Skiing available; 14 May be booked through travel agents.

The Bethel Inn and Country Club

On the Common, 04217
(207) 824-2175

The Bethel Inn and Country Club is a traditional new England resort with fireplaces, candelight dinners, music on the Steinway, and a casual relaxed atmosphere. But along with this more traditional charm are 200 acres of up-to-date resort amenities. A modern health club, championship golf, and nearby activities answer the needs of today's vacation traveler.

Rooms: 70 (PB) $130-300
Full Breakfast
Credit Cards: A, B, C, D, E
Notes: 2, 3, 4, 5, 6, 8, 9, 10, 11, 12, 13, 14

The Douglass Place

HCR 61, Box 90, 04217
(207) 824-2229

This four-season, 19th-century, Early American/Victorian home is between two major ski areas and the White Mountains of New Hampshire. Marvelous area for antiquing, summer sports, and hiking. Gardens and gazebo in summer; game room, cozy fireplace in winter. Two-night minimum stay required for weekends and holidays. Closed Christmas and for two weeks in April.

Hosts: Dana and Barbara Douglass
Rooms: 4 (SB) $58.85
Continental Breakfast
Credit Cards: C
Notes: 2, 6, 7, 8, 9, 10, 11, 12, 13

Sudbury Inn

Box 369, Main Street, 04217
(800) 395-7837; (207) 824-2174

Near Sunday River ski area, the inn has 18 rooms with private baths. Full breakfast; outstanding dining is available, as well as the famous Suds Pub, with entertainment on weekends. Area attractions include an 18-hole, 6,800-yard golf course, White Mountain National Forest, Grafton Notch State Park, hiking, biking, canoeing, golf, swimming, skiing, shopping, lakes, streams, and gorgeous landscapes.

Host: Jack Cronin
Rooms: 18 (PB) $60-100
Full Breakfast
Credit Cards: A, B, C
Notes: 2, 4, 5, 6, 8, 12, 13, 14

BLUE HILL

Blue Hill Farm Country Inn

Route 15, P.O. Box 437, 04614
(207) 374-5126

This old Maine farmhouse and barn sit on 48 acres at the foot of Blue Hill Mountain. Nature trails, ponds, and assorted ducks, geese, and goats surround the area. Spacious common areas are available. Two miles from the center of the village, guests are close to a number of coastal villages and less than one hour from Acadia National Park.

Hosts: Jim and Marcia Schatz
Rooms: 14 (7 PB; 7 SB) $68-78
Continental Plus Breakfast
Credit Cards: A, B
Notes: 2, 5

Mountain Road House

Rural Route 1, Box 2040
Mountain Road, 04614
(207) 374-2794

Mountain Road House

This 1894 farmhouse is on the only road that traverses the face of Blue Hill Mountain. It offers views of the bay while only one mile from the village. Choose twin, double, or queen-size bedrooms; each with private bath. Early bird coffee/tea available at 7:00 A.M., then breakfast with hot entree, fresh fruit, and muffins. Enjoy antiquing, galleries, bookstores, musical events, fine dining, coastal vistas and villages, and of course, Acadia National Park.

Hosts: Carol and John McCulloch
Rooms: 3 (PB) $55-75
Full Breakfast
Credit Cards: A, B
Notes: 2, 5, 8, 14

Kenniston Hill Inn

BOOTHBAY

Kenniston Hill Inn

Route 27, P.O. Box 125, 04537
(207) 633-2159; (800) 992-2915

Step back two centuries in time at Kenniston Hill Inn, a 1786 Colonial home with six working fireplaces and ten rooms, each with private bath. A delicious full breakfast is included. Fireside dining by reservation. On four beautiful acres, the inn is the oldest in Boothbay. Open all year.

Hosts: David and Susan Straight
Rooms: 10 (PB) $65-110
Full Breakfast
Credit Cards: A, B
Notes: 2, 5, 9, 10, 11, 12, 14

BOOTHBAY HARBOR

Anchor Watch Bed and Breakfast

3 Eames Road, 04538
(207) 633-7565

Islands, fir trees, and lobster boats provide the setting for this cozy bed and breakfast on the prettiest shore of the Harbor. Country quilts and stenciling set the style inside. Breakfast features a baked cheese omelet, or baked orange French toast. Enjoy a table for two or sit with others at an oceanview window. The lawn slopes down to water and ends with a private pier and float. Five-minute walk to shops, boat trips, Monhegan ferry, and fine dining. One hour to beaches, lighthouse museums, and Free-port shopping. It is lovely here in all seasons. Closed January and February.

Hosts: Diane and Bob Campbell
Rooms: 4 (PB) $65-105
Full Breakfast
Credit Cards: A, B
Notes: 2, 9, 10, 11, 12, 14

The Atlantic Ark Inn

64 Atlantic Avenue, 04538
(207) 633-5690

An intimate bed and breakfast inn, offering lovely views of the harbor and only a five-minute stroll to town over a historic footbridge. This 100-year-old Maine home has been lovingly restored and tastefully furnished with antiques and Oriental rugs. Guest rooms are adorned with fresh flowers, floor-length drapes, queen-size poster beds, and private baths, including one with double Jacuzzi and another with Greek tub. Each morning a full breakfast features home-baked goods and a specially prepared entree. Recommended by Stephen Birnbaum in *Good Housekeeping* magazine, August 1990.

Host: Donna Piggott
Rooms: 6 (PB) $65–215
Full Breakfast
Credit Cards: A, B, C
Notes: 2, 9, 10, 11, 12

Bed and Breakfast Reservations

P.O. Box 35, Newtonville, MA 02160
(617) 964-1606; FAX (617) 332-8572

Boothbay B&B. This cozy Colonial home on a quiet street on the ocean has four guest rooms, all with private baths. Three rooms have an ocean view. A delicious homemade full breakfast is served each morning in the sunny breakfast room. Relax on the back yard patio, or stroll to the water's edge with private pier and float. Guests are a five-minute walk from unique shops and restaurants. No smoking. $85-99.

Gull and Gardens B&B. This cozy 1850 New England Cape home, surrounded by perennial gardens, is a short walk from the shops and restaurants of the Harbor. The master guest room has a full, detached private bath, with the option of king-size or two single beds. A two-room guest suite has double beds and shared bath, perfect for families or small groups; a single room in the suite may be taken at private-bath rates. A fabulous full breakfast is served daily. No smoking. Children over 14 welcome. Open year-round. $65-85.

Five Gables Inn

P.O. Box 75, Murray Hill Road, East Boothbay, 04544
(207) 633-4551; (800) 451-5048

Five Gables Inn is a completely restored Victorian, circa 1865, on Linekin Bay. All rooms have an ocean view and five have fireplaces. A gourmet breakfast is served in the large common room or on the spacious wraparound veranda. Minimum stay requirements for weekends and holidays. Closed November 16 through May 15.

Hosts: Ellen and Paul Morissette
Rooms: 15 (PB) $80-130
Full Breakfast
Credit Cards: A, B
Notes: 2, 8 (over 12), 9, 10, 11, 12

Harbour Towne Inn

71 Townsend Avenue, 04538
(207) 633-4300; (800) 722-4240

"The Finest Bed and Breakfast on the Waterfront." A short stroll from the historic coastal village, with scenic harbor views and outside decks in a quiet location on Boothbay Harbor, the boating capital of New England. All rooms have private baths in this refurbished Victorian townhouse that has been updated in traditional style. Also available is a luxury penthouse that will sleep six in absolute privacy. Walk to fascinating shops, art galleries, restaurants, churches, library, dinner theaters, boat trips, and fishing. One to two hour drive to ski-

Harbour Towne Inn

NOTES: Credit cards accepted: A MasterCard; B Visa; C American Express; D Discover Card; E Diner's Club; F Other; 2 Personal checks accepted; 3 Lunch available; 4 Dinner available; 5 Open all year;

ing. Reservations recommended. Special off-season getaway packages.

Host: George Thomas
Rooms: 12 (PB) $49-225
Continental Breakfast
Credit Cards: A, B, C, D
Notes: 2, 5, 8 (limited), 9, 10, 11, 12, 13, 14

The Howard House Motel Bed and Breakfast

Route 27, 04538
(207) 633-3933; (207) 633-6244

Each spacious room has a private bath, color cable TV, and its own balcony. Early American furnishings, high-beamed ceilings, and natural wood walls. Shopping, sightseeing, boating, island clam bakes, seal and whale watches, and fine restaurants are nearby. AAA three diamond and *Mobil Travel Guide* approved.

Hosts: Jim and Ginny Farrins
Rooms: 15 (PB) $55-80
Full Breakfast
Credit Cards: None
Notes: 2, 7 (limited), 8, 9, 10, 11, 12, 14

The Seafarer Inn

38 Union Street, 04538
(207) 633-2116; (800) 531-0065

Captain George T. Murray's stately Victorian home, circa 1880, welcomes guests onto its inviting wraparound porch where breakfast is often served when the weather permits. It is the only inn which can boast of an unobstructed view of Boothbay Harbor and its footbridge. Five charming rooms all tastefully decorated in keeping with the period. A hearty and healthful Continental breakfast with homemade muffins and breads is served. A two-minute walk to the village and other points of interest around the harbor.

Host: Olga F. Carito
Rooms: 5 (3 PB; 2 SB) $65-95
Continental Breakfast
Credit Cards: None
Notes: 2, 3 (call), 8, 9, 10, 11, 12, 14

The Noble House

BRIDGTON

The Noble House Bed and Breakfast

37 Highland Road, P.O. Box 180, 04009
(207) 647-3733

Romantic turn-of-the-century manor, set amid stately old oaks and towering pines. Secluded lake frontage on scenic Highland Lake. Barbecue, canoe, foot-pedal boat, and hammock for guests' use. Experience Shaker village, antique and craft shops, museums, and chamber music festival in summer. Cross-country and downhill skiing close at hand in winter. One hour inland from Portland, and one hour from the White Mountains. Sump-tuous full breakfast. Whirlpool baths and family suites.

Hosts: Jane and Dick Starets
Rooms: 8 (5 PB; 3 SB) $70-115
Full Breakfast
Credit Cards: A, B, C
Notes: 2, 7 (restricted), 8, 9, 10, 11, 12, 13, 14

Tarry-A-While Bed and Breakfast Resort

Rural Delivery 2, Box 68, Highland Ridge Road, 04009
(207) 647-2522

6 Pets welcome; 8 Children welcome; 9 Social drinking allowed; 10 Tennis available; 11 Swimming available; 12 Golf available; 13 Skiing available; 14 May be booked through travel agents.

On Highland Lake, with three sandy beaches in a protected cove. Schloss-Victorian house and gasthaus, more than 100 years old, serves a large buffet breakfast with a view of the lake. Cottages with four bed and breakfast units in each. Air-conditioned, with individually controlled heat. Large recreation hall. Free canoes, rowboats, pedal boats, tennis, and bicycles. Water skis, wind surfers, sailboats, and small motors are available for rent. Clean, quiet lake. Three housekeeping units also available. Many restaurants nearby. Open June 12-Labor Day.

Hosts: Hans and Barbara Jenni
Rooms: 34 (26 PB; 8 SB) $80-120
Full Breakfast
Credit Cards: None
Notes: 2, 7, 8, 9, 10, 11, 12

BRUNSWICK

Bethel Point Bed and Breakfast

2387 Bethel Point Road, 04011
(207) 725-1115

Peaceful oceanside comfort in 150-year-old home. Perfect view of ocean birds, seals, and lobster boats. Opportunities for ocean swimming and shoreline walks to explore the local coast. An easy drive to points of interest such as Bowdoin College, Popham Beach, L.L. Bean, and local restaurants featuring seafood specialties.

Hosts: Peter and Betsy Packard
Rooms: 2 (SB) $60-70
Full or Continental Breakfast
Credit Cards: None
Notes: 2, 5, 8, 9, 11

Brunswick Bed and Breakfast

165 Park Row, 04011
(800) 299-4914

The Brunswick Bed and Breakfast is a Greek Revival house overlooking the town green. On the main level, the twin front parlors offer guests the inviting warmth of two fireplaces for wintertime comfort or the wraparound front porch for summer leisure. The guest rooms are decorated with antique furnishings, unique accessories, and quilts. Within walking distance of local restaurants, museums, and shops. Convenient, allowing guests to easily explore mid-coast Maine harbors and coastline.

Hosts: Mercie and Steve Normand
Rooms: 6 (4 PB; 2 SB) $69-89
Full Breakfast
Credit Cards: A, B
Notes: 2, 5, 8, 10, 12

The Samuel Newman House

7 South Street, 04011
(207) 729-6959

Adjoining the Bowdoin College campus, this handsome Federal house was built in 1821 and is comfortably furnished with antiques. Hearty Continental breakfast includes freshly baked muffins/pastry and homemade granola. Brunswick is a culturally rich college town just ten minutes north of Freeport.

Host: Guenter Rose
Rooms: 7 (SB) $48.15-69.55
Continental Breakfast
Credit Cards: A, B
Notes: 2, 8, 9, 10, 11, 12

BUCKSPORT

The Old Parsonage Inn

P.O. Box 1577, 04416
(207) 469-6477

An 1809 Federal home, formerly the Methodist parsonage, one-half mile from Route 1. Private guest entrance, winding staircase, and original architectural features. The third floor was a Masonic meeting hall. Short walk to restaurants and the waterfront. Close to Fort Knox, Acadia National Park, and Penobscot Bay.

Hosts: Brian and Judith Clough
Rooms: 3 (1 PB; 2 SB) $40-60
Continental Breakfast
Credit Cards: A, B
Notes: 2, 8, 9, 10, 11, 12

NOTES: Credit cards accepted: A MasterCard; B Visa; C American Express; D Discover Card; E Diner's Club; F Other; 2 Personal checks accepted; 3 Lunch available; 4 Dinner available; 5 Open all year;

The River Inn

The River Inn Bed and Breakfast

210 Main Street, P.O. Box 1657, 04416-1657
(207) 469-3783

Spacious old sea captain's home on the Penobscot River in historic Bucksport. Conveniently at the northern tip of Penobscot Bay, Bucksport offers easy access to east and west bay tour areas. Antiquing, auctions, crafts, golf, water, and winter sports are some of the activities available for guests. Public boat launch is nearby, as are mooring rentals. Large deck offers panoramic river views, and a rare player grand piano will interest guests. Breakfast features fruit plates. Children over 12. No smoking.

Hosts: The Stone family
Rooms: 4 (2 PB; 2 SB) $35-60
Full Breakfast
Credit Cards: None
Notes: 2, 5, 6, 9, 10, 11, 12, 13, 14

CAMDEN

Abigail's Bed and Breakfast Inn

8 High Street, 04843
(207) 236-2501, (800) 292-2501

This Greek Revival home built in 1847 is completely furnished in antiques. Rooms have queen-size poster beds, sitting areas with good reading lights, fluffy robes, full bath, and crisp linens. Guests meet for breakfast in the sunny dining room and enjoy a varying menu of fresh juices, fruit, souffles, quiches, waffles, scones, muffins, or coffee cakes. Walk to harbor, shops, restaurants, and galleries.

Hosts: Donna and Ed Misner
Rooms: 4 (PB) $65-125
Suites: 2
Full Breakfast
Credit Cards: A, B
Notes: 2, 5, 8, 9, 10, 11, 12, 13, 14

Camden Harbour Inn

83 Bayview Street, 04843
(207) 236 4200

This historic landmark inn with 22 rooms offers spectacular panoramas of the harbor, bay, and mountains. All rooms have private baths and water views from either the room, balcony, patio, or deck. Canopied beds and fireplaces create a romantic ambience in an elegant but casual country inn atmosphere. Enjoy the friendly service, excellent lodging, food, and spirits that have made Camden Harbour Inn a favorite with travelers and diners for over a century.

Camden Harbour Inn

6 Pets welcome; 8 Children welcome; 9 Social drinking allowed; 10 Tennis available; 11 Swimming available; 12 Golf available; 13 Skiing available; 14 May be booked through travel agents.

Hosts: Sal Vella and Patti Babij
Rooms: 22 (PB) $95-195
Full or Continental Breakfast
Credit Cards: A, B, C, D
Notes: 4, 5, 7, 9, 10, 11, 12, 13, 14

Castleview by the Sea

59 High Street, 04843
(207) 236-2349; (800) 272-VIEW

Spectacular glass-walled rooms overlooking Camden's only two castles and the sea, right from your bed! Count the stars across the bay and wake up to inspiring Maine views found nowhere else. Bright and airy charm of classical 1856 cape architecture, wide pumpkin-pine floors, beamed ceilings, claw-foot tubs, skylights, ceiling fans and stained glass. Five-minute walk to harbor. Video and reading libraries. Healthy breakfast. Pets welcome. Children welcome. No smoking.

Host: Bill Butler
Rooms: 4 (PB) $95-130
Full or Continental Breakfast
Credit Cards: A, B
Notes: 2, 5, 6, 8, 9, 10, 11, 12, 13, 14

Hawthorn Inn Bed and Breakfast

9 High Street, 04843
(207) 236-8842

This elegant, turreted Victorian mansion overlooks the Camden harbor with spacious grounds, bright and airy rooms, large deck, lovely antiques throughout, full buffet breakfast, and friendly innkeepers. A three-minute stroll through the back garden to town amphitheater and harbor park leads to shops and restaurants. Carriage house rooms have full harbor views, private decks, and double Jacuzzis. Recommended by *Yankee, Glamour,* and *Outside* magazines. Featured in *Minneapolis Star Tribune* and *Chicago Tribune.*

Hosts: Abigail and Ken Stern
Rooms: 10 (PB) $75-170
Full Breakfast

Credit Cards: A, B
Notes: 2, 5, 8 (over 10), 9, 10, 11, 12, 13, 14

A Little Dream

66 High Street, 04843
(207) 236-8742

Sweet dreams and little luxuries abound in this lovely white Victorian with wraparound porch. Noted for its lovely breakfast, beautiful rooms, and charming atmosphere. A Little Dream's English country-Victorian decor has been featured in *Country Inns* magazine, and in *Glamour,* "40 Best Getaways Across the Country." In the historic district just a few minutes from shops and harbor, it is listed on the National Register of Historic Places. Some rooms have either a private deck, view, or fireplace. All have special touches such as imported soaps and chocolates, and a hostess who will do her very best to please.

Hosts: Joanna Ball and Bill Fontana
Rooms: 5 (PB) $95-139
Full Breakfast
Credit Cards: A, B, C
Notes: 2, 5, 10, 11, 12, 13

Maine Stay

Maine Stay

22 High Street, 04843
(207) 236-9636

A comfortable bed, a hearty breakfast, and three friendly innkeepers will be found in this 1802 Colonial home in Camden's historic district. Take a short walk to the harbor, shops, restaurants, and state park. Recommended by the *Bangor Daily News*, *Miami Herald*, *Boston Globe*, *Harper's Bazaar*, *Country Inns*, *Glamour,* and *Country Living* magazines.

Hosts: Peter and Donny Smith; Diana Robson
Rooms: 8 (4 PB; 4 SB) $65-115
Full Breakfast
Credit Cards: A, B, C
Notes: 2, 5, 8 (over 8), 9, 10, 11, 12, 13, 14

The Swan House

49 Mountain Street, 04843
(207) 236-8275; (800) 207-8275

This fine Victorian home dates from 1870 and has been renovated to offer six spacious guest rooms—all with private baths. Some offer private sitting areas as well. A creative and generous full breakfast is served each morning on the sun porch. Landscaped grounds and a gazebo are available for guests to enjoy. A hiking trail leading to Camden Hills State Park starts right behind the inn. Off busy Route 1, Swan House is a short walk to Camden's beautiful harbor, shops, and restaurants. Seasonal rates.

Hosts: Lyn and Ken Kohl
Rooms: 6 (PB) $65-120
Full Breakfast
Credit Cards: A, B
Notes: 2, 5, 8, 9, 10, 11, 12, 13, 14

Victorian Bed and Breakfast

P.O. Box 528, 04843
(207) 236-3785; (800) 382-9811

The hosts welcome guests to come relive the charm and romance that only the Victorian era had. The special inn has a unique setting on the picturesque coastline of Maine and only minutes from the bustling village of Camden, which offers a peaceful escape. Quiet serenity with romance, candlelight, crackling fireplaces, beautiful gardens, a gazebo, and a wraparound porch overlooking breathtaking water views that take guests back to a day gone by. Dinner available in winter.

Hosts: Marie and Ray Donner
Rooms: 6 (PB) $65-125
Full Breakfast
Credit Cards: A, B
Notes: 2, 4, 5, 8 (over 7), 9, 10, 11, 12, 13, 14

Windward House

Windward House

6 High Street, 04843
(207) 236-9656

A historic 1854 Greek Revival on stately High Street above picturesque Camden Harbor. Seven tastefully appointed guest rooms are furnished with period antiques and have private baths. Several common rooms, gardens, full gourmet breakfast. Only a short walk to shops, restaurants, and the harbor.

Hosts: Jon and Mary Davis
Rooms: 7 (PB) $65-125
Full Breakfast
Credit Cards: A, B, C
Notes: 2, 7 (outside), 9, 10, 11, 12, 13

CAPE NEDDICK

Ye Olde Perkins Place

749 Shore Road, 03902
(207) 361-1119

Ye Olde Perkins Place is a charming pre-Revolutionary Colonial home and attached guest house with ocean view. Just a short walk to a picturesque pebble beach and

---

6 Pets welcome; 8 Children welcome; 9 Social drinking allowed; 10 Tennis available; 11 Swimming available; 12 Golf available; 13 Skiing available; 14 May be booked through travel agents.

cove for sunbathing and swimming. Close to gift shops, restaurants, and boating at Perkins Cove and Marginal Way, a one-and-a-half mile ocean walk. Golf 10 miles away. Quiet, peaceful atmosphere. Open late June to Labor Day.

Hosts: Prim and Dick Winkler
Rooms: 6 (SB) $55-65
Continental Breakfast
Credit Cards: None
Notes: 2 (for deposit), 7, 9, 10, 11, 12

Albonegon Inn

CAPITOL ISLAND

Albonegon Inn

Capitol Island, 04538
(207) 633-2521

Perched on the rocks of a private island four miles from Boothbay Harbor, the Albonegon offers spectacular views of outer islands, wildlife, and boating traffic. Built in the 1880s, the inn is one of the last original Maine Island stays. It is simple and charming—a great place to relax and unwind.

Hosts: Kim and Bob Peckham
Rooms: 14 (3 PB; 11 SB) $65-115
Continental Breakfast
Credit Cards: None
Notes: 2, 10, 11, 12

CHAMBERLAIN

Ocean Reefs on Long Cove

Route 32, 04541-3530
(207) 677-2386

Watch the waves break over the reefs, lobstermen hauling in traps, or the shoreline between tides. Hike or bicycle on the roads along the rocky coast. Pemaquid Beach, Pemaquid Lighthouse, Fort William Henry, and the boat to Monhegan Island are all within five miles. Two-night minimum stay required during July and August. Closed September 30 through Memorial Day.

Rooms: 4 (PB) $66
Continental Breakfast
Credit Cards: None
Notes: 2, 7, 9, 10, 11, 12

CHEBEAGUE ISLAND

Chebeague Island Inn

Rural Route 1, Box 492, 04017
(207) 846-5155

Quiet island inn with 170-foot wraparound porch overlooking golf course and Casco Bay. The inn is accessible by passenger ferry only. Near Portland and L. L. Bean. The hosts offer a great room with fieldstone fireplace and 21 guest rooms with 15 private baths. Antiques throughout. Four-star dining; full liquor license. Lovely beaches. Special weekday rates available.

Hosts: Jan and Dick Bowden
Rooms: 21 (15 PB; 6 SB) $75-125
Full Breakfast
Credit Cards: A, B, D
Notes: 2, 3, 4, 8, 9, 11, 12

CHERRYFIELD

Ricker House

Park Street, Box 256, 04622
(207) 546-2780

NOTES: Credit cards accepted: A MasterCard; B Visa; C American Express; D Discover Card; E Diner's Club; F Other; 2 Personal checks accepted; 3 Lunch available; 4 Dinner available; 5 Open all year;

Selected as one of the top 50 inns in America. Comfortable 1802 Federal Colonial, on the National Register of Historic Places, borders the Narraguagus River and offers guests a central place for enjoying the many wonderful activities in Down East Maine including scenic coastal area, swimming, canoeing, hiking, and fishing.

Hosts: William and Jean Conway
Rooms: 3 (SB) $48.15-53.50
Full Breakfast
Credit Cards: None
Notes: 2, 5, 9, 10, 11, 12, 13

Ricker House

COREA

The Black Duck on Corea Harbor

Crowley Island Road, P.O. Box 39, 04624
(207) 963-2689

Overlooking Down East Lobster Harbor and open ocean in a tranquil fishing village. Explore the 12 acres and discover hidden salt marshes and a private bay. Curl up in front of a fireplace to read or find a sunny rock outcrop and watch the gulls soar overhead, and maybe spot a bald eagle. Rooms furnished in antiques of various periods. Children over ten are welcome. Low-fat, but elegant breakfast in the antique- and art-filled dining room.

Hosts: Barry Canner and Robert Travers
Rooms: 5 (3 PB; 2 SB) $60-90
Full Breakfast
Credit Cards: None
Notes: 2, 5, 9, 11, 12, 14

DAMARISCOTTA

Brannon-Bunker Inn

HCR 64, Box 045X, 04543
(207) 563-5941

Intimate, relaxed, country bed and breakfast in an 1820 Cape, 1880 converted barn, and 1900 carriage house. Seven rooms furnished in themes reflecting the charm of yesterday with the comforts of today. Ten minutes to lighthouse, fort, beach, antiques, and craft shopping. Antique shop on the premises.

Hosts: Jeanne and Joe Hovance
Rooms: 7 (4 PB; 3 SB) $58.85-69.55
Continental Breakfast
Credit Cards: A, B, C
Notes: 2, 5, 8, 9, 10, 11, 12, 13, 14

The Down Easter Inn

Bristol Road, Route 129/130, 04543
(207) 563-5332

A unique example of Greek Revival architecture, the Down Easter Inn is one mile from downtown Damariscotta, in the heart of the rocky coast of Maine. The inn is fronted by a two-story porch with magnificent Corinthian columns. It is minutes from swimming, fishing, boating, and golf. Listed on the National Register of Historic Places, it features 22 rooms with private baths and TVs. Complimentary Continental breakfast served from 8:00-10:00 A.M.

Hosts: Robert and Mary Colquhoun
Rooms: 22 (PB) $65-85
Continental Breakfast
Credit Cards: A, B
Notes: 2, 7, 8, 9

Mill Pond Inn

Rural Free Delivery 1, Box 245, Newcastle, 04553
(207) 563-8014

Whimsical and cozy, this bed and breakfast in a 1780 home offers an excellent atmosphere to view the wonders of Maine's wildlife. The breakfast room has a view of the pond, complete with loons, otters, beavers, herons, resident bald eagles, and breathtaking Maine wildflowers. The complimentary canoes can be paddled from the pond in the back yard directly into Damariscotta Lake (15.5 miles long), to within 20 feet of a bald eagle's nest! Two mountain bikes are available for guest use, or take a dip in the pond. The host is also a registered Maine guide and guided fishing trips are another added feature to this lovely inn. Nestled in the little 1800s village of Damariscotta Mills. Boothbay Harbor, Camden Hills, Pemaquid Lighthouse, Bath-Brunswick area, and the rugged coast of midcoast Maine await.

Hosts: Bobby and Sherry Whear
Rooms: 6 (PB) $60-70
Full Breakfast
Credit Cards: None
Notes: 2, 5, 7, 8, 9, 10, 11, 12

DEER ISLE

Pilgrims Inn

Main Street, 04627
(207) 348-6615

Gracious and warm country inn, circa 1793. All rooms have a water view and antique furnishings. Beautiful surroundings. Swimming, sailing, golf, and tennis nearby. Close to Haystack School of Crafts and many fine galleries. Bicycling and hiking on the island. Excursion boats to other islands. Open mid-May until mid-October. MAP; outstanding food and drink. Price includes dinner. Full liquor license. Outside diners welcome. Listed on the National Register of Historic Places.

Hosts: Jean and Dud Hendrick
Rooms: 14 (9 PB; 5 SB) $130-180
Full Breakfast
Credit Cards: None
Notes: 2, 4, 9, 10, 11, 12, 14

DENNYSVILLE

Lincoln House Country Inn

Routes 1 and 86, 04628
(207) 726-3953

The centerpiece of northeastern coastal Maine. Two lovingly restored Colonials on 100 acres bordering beautiful Cobscook Bay. Eagles, osprey, and seals can be seen from the front door; whale watching, island hopping from nearby Eastport. Excellent hiking, choice accommodations, and unusual hospitality. Rates include breakfast and dinner.

Hosts: Mary and Jerry Haggerty
Rooms: 10 (6 PB; 4 SB) $160-180 MAP
Full Breakfast
Credit Cards: A, B, C
Notes: 2, 4, 7, 8 (over 10), 9, 10, 11, 12, 13, 14

Lincoln House Country Inn

EASTPORT

Weston House

26 Boynton Street, 04631
(207) 853-2907

This imposing 1810 Federal-style house overlooks Passamaquoddy Bay across to Campobello Island. Listed on the National Register of Historic Places; in a lovely Down East coastal village. Grounds include an lawn suitable for croquet and a flower garden for quiet relaxation. Picnic lunches available.

Hosts: Jett and John Peterson
Rooms: $58.85-74.90
Full Breakfast
Credit Cards: None
Notes: 2, 3, 4, 5, 9, 10

NOTES: Credit cards accepted: A MasterCard; B Visa; C American Express; D Discover Card; E Diner's Club; F Other; 2 Personal checks accepted; 3 Lunch available; 4 Dinner available; 5 Open all year;

ELIOT (KITTERY)

The Farmstead Bed and Breakfast

379 Goodwin Road, 03903
(207) 439-5033; (207) 748-3145

Come and step back in time and enjoy the hospitality that Farmstead offers its guests. Awake to the aroma of coffee, bacon/ sausage, and blueberry pancakes on the griddle. Inspect the 1704 Cape and the "new" floor built in 1896. Explore the two and one-half acres, swing under the pear tree, or have an early morning cup of coffee on the glider after a quiet restful night. All rooms have private bath, mini-refrigerator, and microwave oven. Picnic facilities and gas grill available.

Hosts: Col. and Mrs. John Lippincott
Rooms: 7 (PB) $54
Full Breakfast
Credit Cards: A, B, C, D
Notes: 5, 8, 9, 10, 11, 12, 14

High Meadows

High Meadows Bed and Breakfast

Route 101, 03903
(207) 439-0590

High Meadows, on a hill four and one-half miles from US 1 and I-95, has been in operation as a bed and breakfast since 1982. The original Colonial structure, circa 1736, houses five guest rooms, a large den, porch, and patio for guests' use. Outlet shopping malls are close by, sandy beaches, and harbor cruising. Open April through October. Children over 12 are welcome. Smoking allowed on the terrace only. Wines and iced tea are served in the afternoon.

Host: Elaine Raymond
Rooms: 5 (3 PB; 2 SB) $55-70
Full Breakfast
Credit Cards: None
Notes: 2, 9, 11, 12

FREEPORT

The Bagley House

Route 139, 04222
(207) 865-6566; (800) 765-1776

Peace, tranquility, and history abound in this magnificent 1772 country home. Six acres of fields and woods invite nature lovers, hikers, berry pickers, and cross-country skiers. The kitchen's hand-hewn beams and enormous free standing fireplace with beehive oven inspire mouth-watering breakfasts. A warm welcome awaits guests.

Hosts: Suzanne O'Connor and Susan Backhouse
Rooms: 5 (PB) $80-100
Full Breakfast
Credit Cards: A, B, C, D
Notes: 2, 5, 8, 9, 10, 11, 12, 13, 14

Bayberry Bed and Breakfast

8 Maple Avenue, 04032
(207) 865-1868; (207) 865-6021

The Bayberry Bed and Breakfast is in the village district, one block north of L. L.

6 Pets welcome; 8 Children welcome; 9 Social drinking allowed; 10 Tennis available; 11 Swimming available; 12 Golf available; 13 Skiing available; 14 May be booked through travel agents.

Bean and all the fine shops and restaurants. The Bayberry has been recently restored preserving the early charm of the 1853 Federal home. All rooms have private baths and are tastefully decorated. Choose between king-, queen-size, double, or twin beds. A delicious full breakfast, prepared with fresh local produce, is served daily in the dining room. Relax in the bright and sunny sitting room with TV, VCR, books, games, or good conversation. Several telephones in the hall and guest rooms are available for free local or long distance calls. Freeport has a beautiful coastline with spectacular views, harbor cruises, sailing, fishing, golfing, hiking, etc.

Hosts: The Frank family
Rooms: 5 (PB) $55-95
Full Breakfast
Credit Cards: A, B
Notes: 2, 5, 8, 11, 12, 13, 14

Captain Josiah Mitchell House

188 Main Street, 04032
(207) 865-3289

Famous, historic ship captain's home, circa 1779. The 1866 miraculous survival-at-sea story of Captain Mitchell of the ship *Hornet* is a classic. Mark Twain, then a young newspaperman, wrote about it. Restored more than 25 years ago by the present owners, the house is filled with antiques. Beautiful grounds and only a five-minute walk to L. L. Bean. Eleventh year as an inn. Off-season rates available. No smoking.

Hosts: Alan and Loretta Bradley
Rooms: 6 (PB) $78-85
Full Breakfast
Credit Cards: A, B
Notes: 2, 5, 10, 11, 12, 13, 14

Country at Heart Bed and Breakfast

37 Bow Street, 04032
(207) 865-0512

Enjoy staying in a cozy 1870 country home with handmade crafts, antiques, and reproduction furnishings. Choose one of the country-decorated rooms, the Shaker Quilt or Teddy Bear. A full breakfast is served on an eight-foot oak dining table. After breakfast, browse through Primitive Pastimes, a gift shop with country crafts and antiques. Park and walk to more than 100 outlet stores, restaurants, and L. L. Bean just two blocks away.

Hosts: Rogert and Kim Dubay
Rooms: 3 (PB) $65-75
Full Breakfast
Credit Cards: None
Notes: 2, 5, 8, 9, 12, 14

Country at Heart

Harraseeket Inn

162 Main Street, 04032
(207) 865-9377; (800) 342-6423
FAX (207) 865-1684

An elegant 54-room country inn two blocks north of L. L. Bean in the village of Freeport. Antiques, 23 fireplaces, Jacuzzi tubs, air conditioning, cable TV, lovely gardens, and two restaurants. Steps from 110 upscale factory outlets; three miles from waterfront. Afternoon tea included. Open year-round. AAA four diamond rating.

Hosts: The Gray family
Rooms: 54 (PB) $95-225
Full Breakfast
Credit Cards: A, B, C, D, E
Notes: 3, 4, 5, 8, 9, 11, 12, 14

NOTES: Credit cards accepted: A MasterCard; B Visa; C American Express; D Discover Card; E Diner's Club; F Other; 2 Personal checks accepted; 3 Lunch available; 4 Dinner available; 5 Open all year;

181 Main Street Bed and Breakfast

181 Main Street, 04032
(207) 865-1226

Comfortably elegant, antique-filled 1840 Cape. Just a five-minute walk to L. L. Bean and Freeport's luxury outlets. Hosts provide a renowned breakfast, New England hospitality, and information on all that Maine has to offer—on and off the beaten path. In-ground pool; ample parking. Featured in *Country Home* magazine. ABBA and AAA approved.

Rooms: 7 (PB) $75-95
Full Breakfast
Credit Cards: A, B
Notes: 2, 5, 9, 11, 12, 13, 14

White Cedar Inn

178 Main Street, 04032
(207) 865-9099

Historic Victorian home stands just two blocks north of L. L. Bean. Antique-furnished rooms, all with private baths, are spacious and cozy. Full country breakfast served in the sunroom overlooking beautifully landscaped grounds. A nonsmoking inn. Air-conditioned, AAA inspected.

Hosts: Phil and Carla Kerber
Rooms: 6 (PB) $75-95

White Cedar Inn

Full Breakfast
Credit Cards: A, B
Notes: 5, 9, 10, 12, 13

FRIENDSHIP

The Outsiders' Inn Bed and Breakfast

Box 521A, Corner of Routes 97 and 220, 04547
(207) 832-5197

The Outsiders' Inn is in the center of the village of Friendship, a short walk from the harbor, the home of historic Friendship Sloops and scores of lobster boats. This inn features five comfortable guest rooms with double beds; private and semi-private baths. Efficiency cottage also available. Full breakfasts served daily. Sea kayak rentals and guided tours available. Friendship Sloop charters and dinners are also available by prior arrangement. Country furnishings, delicious food, friendly folks. Come enjoy midcoast Maine.

Hosts: Debbie and Bill Michaud
Rooms: 5 (1 PB; 4 SB) $45-65
Full Breakfast
Credit Cards: A, B
Notes: 2, 5, 8, 9, 11

FRYEBURG

Admiral Peary House

9 Elm Street, 04037
(207) 935-3365

This home was once the residence of Arctic explorer Admiral Robert E. Peary. It has been lovingly restored for guests' comfort, with air-conditioned rooms and private bathrooms, country breakfast, and billiards. The clay tennis court is framed by spacious lawns and perennial gardens. Use one of the bicycles to explore the village and nearby sights. Spend a few hours or a day canoeing and swimming the Saco River. Top it off with a leisurely soak in the outdoor spa. "We look forward to your visit and hope

6 Pets welcome; 8 Children welcome; 9 Social drinking allowed; 10 Tennis available; 11 Swimming available; 12 Golf available; 13 Skiing available; 14 May be booked through travel agents.

you'll enjoy the admiral's home as much as we do," say the hosts.

Hosts: Ed and Nancy Greenberg
Rooms: 4 (PB) $70-108
Full Breakfast
Credit Cards: A, B
Notes: 2, 5, 10, 11, 12, 13, 14

The Oxford House Inn

105 Main Street, 04037
(207) 935-3442

This stately turn-of-the-century inn has a gourmet restaurant on premises with shopping, skiing, hiking, canoeing, tennis, and antiquing nearby. Open year-round, the comfortable, charming guest rooms are decorated with old-fashioned elegance, and some have mountain views. King, queen, double, and twin rooms are available, and a full gourmet breakfast is served in a dining room with a view of the mountains. Dinner and room reservations required.

Hosts: John and Phyllis Morris
Rooms: 5 (PB) $75-95
Full Breakfast
Credit Cards: A, B, C, D, E
Notes: 2, 4, 5, 8, 9, 10, 11, 12, 13, 14

Greenville Inn

GREENVILLE

Greenville Inn

P.O. Box 1194, Norris Street, 04441
(207) 695-2206

This 1895 Victorian lumber baron's mansion is on a hill overlooking Moosehead Lake and Squaw Mountain. A large, leaded-glass window decorated with a painted spruce tree is the focal point at the landing of the stairway. Gas lights, embossed wall coverings, carved fireplace mantels, and cherry and oak paneling grace the inn. In the elegantly appointed dining rooms, diners may savor fresh Maine seafood, glazed roast duckling, grilled chops, or steaks. Whether relaxing by a cozy fire or sipping cocktails on the veranda at sunset, the evening hours are most enjoyable.

Hosts: The Schnetzers
Rooms: 9 (7 PB; 2 SB) $75-95
Continental Breakfast
Credit Cards: A, B, D
Notes: 2, 4, 5, 7, 8, 9, 10, 11, 12, 13

The Sawyer House

P.O. Box 521, Lakeview Street, 04441
(207) 695-2369

The Sawyer House bed and breakfast overlooks Moosehead Lake, just a short walk to shops, restaurants, and local attractions. Relax, make yourself at home in the restored steamship captain's home, circa 1849. All rooms have king- or queen-size beds and private baths. Enjoy the view of Moosehead Lake from one of the outside porches, or relax in the parlor with cable TV.

Hosts: Pat and Hans Zieten
Rooms: 3 (PB) $55-65
Full Breakfast
Credit Cards: A, B, D
Notes: 2, 5, 9, 10, 11, 12, 13

ISLE AU HAUT

The Keepers House

Isle Au Haut, 04645
(207) 367-2261

Remote island lighthouse station in the undeveloped wilderness area of Acadia National Park. Guests arrive on the mail boat from Stonington. No telephones, cars, TV,

The Keepers House

or crowds. Osprey, seal, deer, rugged trails, spectacular scenery, seclusion, and inspiration. Three elegant meals included in rate. Minimum stay July-August: two nights. Closed November 1-April 30.

Hosts: Jeff and Judi Burke
Rooms: 6 (SB) $250, includes meals
Credit Cards: None
Notes: 2, 3, 4, 8, 9, 11

KENNEBUNK

Arundel Meadows Inn

P.O. Box 1129, 04043-1129
(207) 985-3770

This 165-year-old farmhouse, two miles north on Route 1 from the center of town, combines the charm of antiques and art with the comfort of seven individually decorated bedrooms with sitting areas. Two of the rooms are suites, three have fireplaces,

Arundel Meadows Inn

some have cable TV, and all have private bathrooms and summer air conditioning. Full homemade breakfasts and afternoon teas are prepared by co-owner Mark Bachelder, a professionally trained chef. Open year-round.

Hosts: Mark Bachelder and Murray Yaeger
Rooms: 7 (PB) $75-110
Full Breakfast
Credit Cards: A, B
Notes: 2, 5, 9, 11, 12, 14

Bed and Breakfast Inns of New England

128 S. Hoop Pole Road, Guilford, CT, 06437
(203) 457-0042; (800) 582-0853

ME-810. Step back in time to this 1756 farmhouse set on six acres of rolling hills. Common rooms, including a Colonial kitchen, are furnished with period antiques, stenciled walls, pumpkin pine floors, and six fireplaces. Continental breakfast is served on the sun porch each morning. Three rooms with double beds are available, two include private baths, and one has a fireplace. Resident pets, but no guest pets. Children over 14 are welcome. No smoking. $75.

The Ellenbergers' Guest House Bed and Breakfast

154 Port Road, Route 35 Lower Village, 04043
(207) 967-3824

This home features two bedrooms, living room with fireplace, and private bath for guests. A full breakfast is served. The guest house next door has accommodations with kitchen, and hosts will provide guests with breakfast in the main house dining room on request at an additional cost.

Hosts: Cathy and Roger Ellenberger
Rooms: 2 (SB) $55-85
Full Breakfast
Credit Cards: A, B, C
Notes: 2, 5, 8, 9, 10, 11, 12, 13, 14

6 Pets welcome; 8 Children welcome; 9 Social drinking allowed; 10 Tennis available; 11 Swimming available; 12 Golf available; 13 Skiing available; 14 May be booked through travel agents.

English Meadows Inn

141 Port Road, 04043
(207) 967-5766

English Meadows is an 1860 Victorian farmhouse that has been operating as an inn for more than 80 years. Within a five- or ten-minute stroll past interesting shops and galleries to the village of Kennebunkport, English Meadows offers its guests a peaceful taste of country living and the many unique attractions of the area. Antique appointed guest rooms, deliciously full breakfasts, and convivial hosts add further pleasure for visitors at this wonderful inn.

Host: Charlie Doane
Rooms: 13 (9 PB; 4 SB) $75-95
Full Breakfast
Credit Cards: A, B
Notes: 2, 5, 8 (over 9), 10, 11, 12

Lake Brook Guest House Bed and Breakfast

Lower Harbour Village
57 Western Avenue, 04043
(207) 967-4069

Charming rooms with paddle fans, fresh-cut flowers, and a great full breakfast. Lovely perennial garden. Rooms overlook a salt marsh and tidal brook. Lake Brook is only one-half mile from downtown Kennebunkport with its shops, restaurants, galleries. Just over one mile to the beach.

Host: Carolyn A. McAdams
Rooms: 5 (PB) $80.25-96.30
Suite: 1
Full Breakfast
Credit Cards: None
Notes: 2, 5, 8 (call), 9, 10, 11, 12, 13, 14

Sundial Inn

P.O. Box 1147, 48 Beach Avenue, 04043
(207) 967-3850

Unique oceanfront inn furnished with turn-of-the-century Victorian antiques. Each of the 34 guest rooms has a private bath, telephone, color TV, and air conditioning. Sev-

Sundial Inn

eral rooms also offer ocean views and whirlpool baths. Visit Kennebunkport's art galleries and studios, museums, and gift shops. Go whale watching, deep-sea fishing, or hiking at the nearby wildlife refuge and estuary. Golf and tennis are nearby. Continental breakfast features muffins and coffeecakes. Handicapped accessible.

Hosts: Larry and Pat Kenny
Rooms: 34 (PB) $60-148
Continental Breakfast
Credit Cards: A, B, C, E
Notes: 5, 10, 11, 12

KENNEBUNKPORT

Captain Fairfield Inn

P.O. Box 1308, 04046
(207) 967-4454; (800) 322-1928

A gracious 1813 sea captain's mansion in Kennebunkport's historic district, only steps to the village green and harbor. A delightful walk to sandy beaches, Dock

Captain Fairfield Inn

Square Marina, shops, and excellent restaurants. On the corner of Pleasant and Green streets. Gracious and elegant, the bedrooms are beautifully decorated with antiques and period furnishings which lend an atmosphere of tranquility and charm. Several bedrooms have fireplaces, and guests are welcome to relax in the living room, study, or enjoy the tree-shaded grounds and gardens. Guests will awaken to birdsong, fresh sea air, and the aroma of gourmet coffee. Come and enjoy a refreshing, comfortable, and memorable stay.

Hosts: Bonnie and Dennis Tallagnon
Rooms: 9 (PB) $85-160
Full Breakfast
Credit Cards: A, B, C, E
Notes: 2, 5, 8 (over six), 9, 10, 11, 12, 14

The Captain Jefferds Inn

Pearl Street, P.O. Box 691, 04046
(207) 967-2311

An elegant antique-appointed inn with 12 quiet guest rooms and three large suites with kitchens. A *House Beautiful* cover story. Well known for gourmet breakfasts and afternoon tea. Breakfast is different each day, featuring such favorites as Eggs Benedict, blueberry crepes, frittata, and New England "flannel." Open most of the year, the inn is just 300 feet from the picturesque harbor, and a few minutes walk from shops, restaurants, and galleries.

Host: Warren Fitzsimmons
Rooms: 18 (PB) $85-145
Full Breakfast
Credit Cards: A, B
Notes: 2, 6, 8, 9, 10, 11, 12

The Captain Lord Mansion

P.O. Box 800, 04046
(207) 967-3141; (800) 522-3141

The Captain Lord Mansion is an intimate 16-room luxury country inn, at the head of a sweeping lawn, overlooking the Kennebunk River. The inn is famous for its warm, friendly hospitality, attention to cleanliness, and hearty breakfasts served family-style in the big country kitchen.

Hosts: Bev Davis and Rick Litchfield
Rooms: 16 (PB)
Full Breakfast
Credit Cards: A, B, D
Notes: 2, 5, 9, 10, 11, 12, 14

Cove House

11 South Maine Street, 04046
(207) 967-3704

This cozy bed and breakfast is an Early Colonial home in a quiet residential area on a cove with views of the water from the yard. Decorated with antiques and a collection of Flow Blue, it offers charm with authentic bed and breakfast hospitality. A hearty breakfast is served each morning in the dining room. A short walk from the village and beach.

Hosts: The Jones Family (Kathy, Bob, and Barry)
Rooms: 3 (PB) $70
Full Breakfast
Credit Cards: A, B
Notes: 2, 5, 8, 9, 10, 11, 12, 14

1802 House

P.O. Box 646-A, 15 Locke Street, 04046-1646
(207) 967-5632; (800) 932-5632

1802 House is a 19th-century inn tucked away in a quiet section of the quaint seaside village of Kennebunkport. The inn is bounded by the Cape Arundel Golf Club, nestled along the 15th green, yet is only a ten-minute walk to bustling Dock Square. Each of the six guest rooms is furnished with antiques, all have private bathrooms, and two guest rooms offer working fireplaces. One room has a two-person whirlpool bathtub. A full gourmet breakfast awaits.

Hosts: Ron and Carol Perry
Rooms: 6 (PB) $65-145
Full Breakfast
Credit Cards: A, B, C
Notes: 2, 5, 9, 10, 11, 12, 14

6 Pets welcome; 8 Children welcome; 9 Social drinking allowed; 10 Tennis available; 11 Swimming available; 12 Golf available; 13 Skiing available; 14 May be booked through travel agents.

The Green Heron Inn

The Green Heron Inn

P.O. Box 2578, Ocean Avenue, 04046
(207) 967-3315

This 10-room bed and breakfast offers the best breakfast in town, according to local folks. Each guest room is air-conditioned and has cable TV. Homey, comfortable, and clean. Most guests return year after year, which adds to the charm and character of the inn. Reservations are limited in the winter.

Hosts: Charles and Elizabeth Reid
Rooms: 10 (PB) $50-120
Full Breakfast
Credit Cards: None
Notes: 2, 5, 6 (call), 7, 8, 9, 10, 11, 12

The Inn on South Street

South Street, P.O. Box 478A, 04046
(207) 967-5151

The Inn on South Street

Now approaching its 200th birthday, this stately Greek Revival house is in the historic district. There are three beautifully decorated guest rooms and one luxury suite. Private baths, fireplaces, a common room, afternoon refreshments, and early morning coffee. A sumptuous breakfast is served in the large country kitchen with views of the river and ocean. On a quiet street within walking distance of restaurants, shops, and the water.

Hosts: Jacques and Eva Downs
Rooms: 4 (PB) $85-185
Suite: 1
Full Breakfast
Credit Cards: A, B
Notes: 2, 10, 11, 12, 13, 14

The Kennebunkport Inn

One Dock Square, P.O. Box 111, 04046-0111
(207) 967-2621; (800) 248-2621;
FAX (207) 967-3705

The Kennebunkport Inn was originally built by a sea captain in the late 1800s. Today it has 34 rooms with private baths and color TVs. In the center of town, just a skip from Dock Square, but set back from the hubbub. Near shops, the historic district, and the harbor area. A small outdoor pool overlooks the river, and there is a turn-of-the-century bar with a piano player on weekends. Package plans available. Restaurant serves breakfast and dinner May-October; (Rooms only November-April). Continental breakfast on weekend.

Hosts: Rick and Martha Griffin
Rooms: 34 (PB) $59.50-179
Full Breakfast
Credit Cards: A, B, C
Notes: 4, 5, 8, 10, 11, 12, 14

Kylemere House 1818 "Crosstrees"

South Street, Box 1333, 04046-1333
(207) 967-2780

Tucked into a quiet corner of Kennebunkport's historic district is this beautifully restored, 1818 Federal-style inn on the Na-

NOTES: Credit cards accepted: A MasterCard; B Visa; C American Express; D Discover Card; E Diner's Club; F Other; 2 Personal checks accepted; 3 Lunch available; 4 Dinner available; 5 Open all year;

tional Register of Historic Places. Surrounded by spacious, shaded grounds, lovely perennial gardens, and a sparkling pond. Guests come to relax and feel refreshed. Inside are four guest rooms decorated individually with antiques and period furniture, private baths, one with fireplace, and queen, king, or twin beds. Guests enjoy early morning coffee and afternoon refreshments in the guest parlor or on the porch. A delicious breakfast is served in the dining room overlooking the gardens. A quiet haven just a short walk from shops, galleries, marinas, restaurants, and the ocean. Closed mid-December through April.

Hosts: Ruth and Helen Toohey
Rooms: 4 (PB) $80-135
Full Breakfast
Credit Cards: A, B
Notes: 2, 8 (over 12), 9, 10, 11, 12, 14

Maine Stay Inn

Maine Stay Inn and Cottages

Box 500 A, 04046
(207) 967-2117; (800) 950-2117

Elegant rooms and delightful garden cottages in the quiet historic district surroundings of Kennebunkport. Complimentary breakfast, afternoon tea, New England desserts. Color cable TV, private baths, fireplaces. Easy walking distance to restaurants, galleries, shops, and harbor. One mile to beach and golf.

Hosts: Lindsay and Carol Copeland
Rooms: 17 (PB) $85-185
Full Breakfast
Credit Cards: A, B, C, D
Notes: 5, 8, 9, 10, 11, 12, 14

White Barn Inn

Beach Street, P.O. Box 560C, 04046
(207) 967-2321; FAX (207) 967-1100

This 1850s farmhouse and its signature white barn have been transformed into a sophisticated inn and award-winning restaurant. Twenty-four elegant accommodations all with private baths and lovely antiques, many with whirlpool baths and fireplaces. A five-minute walk to the beach or to downtown Kennebunkport. Member Relais and Chateaux. AAA five-diamond dining. Selected among the top 12 inns for the year 1992.

Hosts: Mr. Laurie Bongiorno and Ms. Laurie Cameron
Rooms: 24 (PB) $140-275
Continental Breakfast
Credit Cards: A, B, C
Notes: 2, 4, 5, 9, 10, 11, 12, 14

KITTERY

Bed and Breakfast Inns of New England

128 S. Hoop Pole Road, Guilford, CT, 06437
(203) 457-0042; (800) 582-0853

A romantic ambience and elegant antique furnishings await guests at this 1890 Princess Anne Victorian bed and breakfast. Enjoy a full breakfast of gourmet coffees, omelets, and pastries in the garden or on the sun deck. Six guest rooms are available with double and queen-size beds, shared and private baths. Resident pets, and guest pets are welcome. Children are welcome. No smoking. $79-100.

Enchanted Nights
Bed and Breakfast

29 Wentworth Street, Route 103, 03904
(207) 439-1489

An 1890 Princess Anne Gothic Victorian between Boston and Portland. Three minutes to
dining and dancing in Portsmouth, historic
homes, scenic ocean drives, and the
renowned Kittery outlet malls. Convenient
day trips to neighboring resorts. For the romantic at heart who delight in the subtle elegance of yesteryear; for those who are
soothed by the whimsical charm of a French
country inn. Gourmet coffee, omelets, and
pastries. Enjoy the suite with whirlpool for
two.

Hosts: Nancy Bogenberger and Peter Lamandia
Rooms: 6 (5 PB; 1 SB) $42-135
Full Breakfast
Credit Cards: A, B, C, D
Notes: 2, 5, 6, 8, 9, 10, 11, 12, 14

LUBEC

Breakers by the Bay

37 Washington, 04652
(207) 733-2487

One of the oldest houses in the 200-year-old
town of Lubec, a small fishing village. Three
blocks to Campobello Island, the home of
Franklin D. Roosevelt. All rooms have refrigerators, TVs, hand-crocheted tablecloths,
hand-quilted bedspreads, and private decks
for viewing the bay. All rooms that share a
bath have their own washstands.

Host: E. M. Elg
Rooms: 5 (4 PB; 1 SB) $64.20
Full Breakfast
Credit Cards: None
Notes: 2, 10, 12

MILBRIDGE

Bed and Breakfast
Inns of New England

128 S. Hoop Pole Road, Guilford, CT, 06437
(203) 457-0042; (800) 582-0853

ME-855. This large Victorian has outstanding views of the bay and Narraguagus
River. Common rooms include a sitting
room, formal living room, dining room, and
sun porch. This bed and breakfast is in a
rural village with restaurants, light shopping, and an inexpensive movie theater a
short walk from the doorstep. Full breakfast
includes a bottomless cup of coffee or tea.
Six guest rooms with a variety of bed sizes;
shared and private baths are available. Children over 12 are welcome. No guest pets.
Smoking outside only. $45-55.

MOUNT DESERT

MacDonald's
Bed and Breakfast

P.O. Box 52, 04660
(207) 244-3316

This 1850 home, listed in the National Register of Historic Places, offers the pleasure
of village living without summer crowds. In
Somesville, Mount Desert Island's first permanent settlement. Surrounded by Acadia
National Park and eight miles from Bar
Harbor and surrounding mountains. Full
breakfast features fresh fruit, homemade
breads, muffins, blueberry pancakes, and
crêpes.

Hosts: Stan and Binnie MacDonald
Rooms: 3 (1 PB; 2 SB) $50-75
Full Breakfast
Credit Cards: A, B
Notes: 2, 5, 8 (over 5), 9, 11, 12, 13, 14

Reiber's Bed and Breakfast

P.O. Box 163, 04660
(207) 244-3047

Handsome Colonial homestead on four
acres with tidal creek and meadow is on
outskirts of historic village on scenic Mount
Desert Island. A short drive to Bar Harbor
and Acadia National Park. Full breakfast

served with home-baked breads. Screened porch in summer and snapping fires in winter. Non-smokers are preferred.

Hosts: Gail and David Reiber
Rooms: 2 (1 PB; 1 SB) $60-70
Full Breakfast
Credit Cards: A, B, C
Notes: 2, 5, 8, 9, 10, 11, 12, 13 (cross-country)

NAPLES

The Augustus Bove House

Rural Route 1, Box 501, 04055
(207) 693-6365

Guests are always welcome at the historic 1850 hotel. Originally known as Hotel Naples, it is restored for comfort and a relaxed atmosphere at affordable prices. Guest rooms have elegant yet homey furnishings, some with views of Long Lake. Both shared and private baths. An easy walk to the water, shops, and recreation in a four-season area. Open all year, with off-season and midweek discounts. Air conditioning, TV, and VCR. Coffee or tea anytime. AAA approved.

Hosts: David and Arlene Stetson
Rooms: 11 (7 PB; 2+2 SB) $49-95
Full Breakfast
Credit Cards: A, B, D
Notes: 2, 4 (limited), 5, 6, 8, 9, 10, 11, 12, 13, 14

Inn at Long Lake

P.O. Box 806, 04055
(207) 693-6226

Inn at Long Lake

Enjoy romantic elegance and turn-of-the-century charm at the Inn at Long Lake, nestled amid the pines and waterways of the beautiful Sebago Lakes region. The inn has 16 restored rooms with TVs, air conditioners, and private baths. One minute's walk from the Naples Causeway. Four-season activities and fine dining nearby. This three-diamond AAA facility is worth the trip. Midweek discounts available. Open year-round. Named one of the top ten bed and breakfasts in the United States in a video competition by Innovations, Inc. of Cranford, New Jersey.

Hosts: Maynard and Irene Hincks
Rooms: 16 (PB) $59-120
Continental Breakfast
Credit Cards: A, B, D
Notes: 2, 5, 8, 9, 11, 12, 13, 14

Lamb's Mill Inn

Lamb's Mill Inn

Box 676, Lamb's Mill Road, 04055
(207) 693-6253

A charming country inn in the foothills of Maine's western mountain and lake region. Romantic country atmosphere on 20 acres of fields and woods. Five rooms with private baths and a full country breakfast. Hot tub available. Near lakes, antique shops, skiing, and canoeing.

Hosts: Laurel Tinkham and Sandra Long
Rooms: 5 (PB) $75-85
Full Breakfast
Credit Cards: A, B
Notes: 2, 5, 9, 10, 11, 12, 13, 14

6 Pets welcome; 8 Children welcome; 9 Social drinking allowed; 10 Tennis available; 11 Swimming available; 12 Golf available; 13 Skiing available; 14 May be booked through travel agents.

NEWCASTLE

Glidden House

Rural Route 1, Box 740, Glidden Street, 04553
(207) 563-1859

A lovely mansard-roof Victorian (Second Empire) overlooking the Damariscotta River. A memorable house that is attractively furnished, comfortable, and quiet. Excellent breakfast. Within walking distance of restaurants, shops, galleries, and historic sites.

Host: Doris E. Miller
Rooms: 3 (PB) $50-55
Apartment: $70
Full Breakfast
Credit Cards: A, B
Notes: 2, 5, 7 (limited), 8, 9, 10, 11, 12, 13 (cross-country)

The Newcastle Inn

River Road, 04553
(800) 832-8669; (207) 563-5685

A country inn of distinction on the Damariscotta River. All 15 rooms have private baths, most have river views, and some have canopied beds. Enjoy the changing tide while sitting on the glassed and screened sun porch. In the dining room, elegant four-star candlelight dinners and multi-course breakfasts are served. Featured in *Food and Wine*.

Hosts: Ted and Chris Sprague
Rooms: 15 (PB) $70-105
Full Breakfast
Credit Cards: A, B
Notes: 2, 4, 5, 10, 11, 12, 13, 14

NEW HARBOR

Gosnold Arms

HC 61, Box 161, Route 32, 04554
(207) 677-3727

On the harbor, the Gosnold Arms Inn and cottages, all with private baths, most with water view. A glassed-in dining room overlooking the water is open for breakfast and dinner. The Gosnold wharf and moorings accommodate cruising boats. Within a ten-mile radius are lakes, beaches, lobster pounds, historic sites, boat trips, golf, antiques, shops, and restaurants.

Host: The Phinney family
Rooms: 26 (PB) $79-124
Full Breakfast
Credit Cards: A, B
Notes: 2, 4, 8, 9, 11, 12

NEWPORT

Lake Sebasticook Bed and Breakfast

P.O. Box 502, 8 Sebasticook Avenue, 04953
(207) 368-5507

Take a step back in history in this 1903 Victorian home on a quiet street. Relax on the second-floor sun porch or comfortable wraparound porch and enjoy the sounds of ducks and loons on Lake Sebasticook. Take a short walk to the lake park, or play tennis at the city park a block away. In the morning, savor a full country breakfast including homemade breads. Closed from November to May 1.

Hosts: Bob and Trudy Zothner
Rooms: 3 (SB) $55
Full Breakfast
Credit Cards: C
Notes: 2, 10, 11

NORTHEAST HARBOR

Harbourside Inn

Northeast Harbor, 04662
(207) 276-3272

Peace and quiet, flower gardens at the edge of the forest, and woodland trails into Acadia National Park add to the delights of this genuine 1888 country inn. Spacious rooms and suites, all with private baths, many with king- or queen-size beds. Beautiful antiques, working fireplaces in all first- and second-floor rooms. Guests can walk or drive into nearby Acadia National Park. Sailing, deep-

Harbourside Inn

sea fishing, and carriage rides in the park. All rooms are nonsmoking. Reservations accepted for two nights or more.

Hosts: The Sweet family
Rooms: 11 plus 3 suites (PB) $85-210
Continental Breakfast
Credit Cards: None
Notes: 2, 10, 11, 12

OGUNQUIT

The Beachmere Inn

Box 2340, 03907
(207) 646-2021; (800) 336-3983;
FAX (207) 646-2231

A Victorian inn owned by the Merrill family since 1937, the Beachmere was built at the turn of the century and features accommodations with kitchenettes; most with decks, some with working fireplaces. Rooms overlook the Little Beach, manicured lawns, and gardens to the Marginal Way. Close to trolley route and village activities. Open April to mid-December. Off-season packages. AAA, Mobil Travel Guide.

Host: Louesa Mace
Rooms: 44 (PB) $50-180
Continental Breakfast
Credit Cards: A, B, C, D, E
Notes: 2, 7 (limited), 8, 9, 10, 11, 12, 14

Beauport Inn

102 Shore Road, P.O. Box 1793, 03907
(207) 646-8680

Cozy nonsmoking bed and breakfast furnished with antiques offers four rooms, all of which have private baths. Pine-paneled living room with a fireplace and piano. Baked goods by the host. Antique shop on the premises. Closed January and February.

Host: Dan Pender
Rooms: 4 (PB) $75-85
Continental Breakfast
Credit Cards: A, B, C
Notes: 2, 8 (over 12), 9, 10, 11, 12

Gorges Grant Hotel

P.O. Box 2240, U.S. Route 1, 03907
(207) 646-7003

A modern inn of 56 luxury units with full-service restaurant and lounge. Heated indoor pool and Jacuzzi, heated outdoor pool, large patio/poolside area. A beautiful lobby featuring a fireplace and sitting areas. The restaurant, "Raspberries," is open for breakfast and dinner. Bed and breakfast plan, Modified American Plan, and European packages are available. Ogunquit features one of the world's best beaches, a seacoast walkway called Marginal Way, and picturesque Perkins Cove. Nearby are former President Bush's Kennebunkport home and L. L. Bean. Rated AAA three diamonds.

Hosts: Karen and Bob Hanson
Rooms: 56 (PB)
Full Breakfast
Credit Cards: A, B, C, D, E
Notes: 2, 4, 7, 8, 9, 10, 11, 12

Hartwell House

118 Shore Road, P.O. Box 393, 03907
(207) 646-7210; (800) 235-8883

In the tradition of fine European country inns, Hartwell House offers rooms and suites tastefully furnished with Early American and English antiques. A gourmet breakfast is served daily. Perkins Cove, Ogunquit Beach, and the Marginal Way are

6 Pets welcome; 8 Children welcome; 9 Social drinking allowed; 10 Tennis available; 11 Swimming available; 12 Golf available; 13 Skiing available; 14 May be booked through travel agents.

all within walking distance. Seasonal package arrangements; conference and banquet space available year-round. Minimum one- to three-night stay weekends and holidays.

Hosts: Jim and Trisha Hartwell;
    Alec and Renée Adams
Rooms: 16 (PB) $80-175
Full Breakfast
Credit Cards: A, B, C, D
Notes: 2, 5, 8 (over 10), 9, 10, 11, 12, 13, 14

Holiday Guest House

P.O. Box 2247, 03907
(207) 646-5582

Fully restored 1814 Colonial close to beaches, restaurants, antique shops, outlets, and nature trails. Guest accommodations have private baths and refrigerators. Open year-round.

Hosts: Lou and Rose LePage
Rooms: 2 (PB) $35-65
Continental Breakfast
Credit Cards: A, B, C, D
Notes: 2, 5, 8, 9, 10, 11, 12

Puffin Inn

233 U.S. Route 1, P.O. Box 2232, 03907
(207) 646-5496

Puffin Inn is in a small picturesque village by the sea. The inn, an old sea captain's house, exudes a special warmth and charm of days gone by. Each of the ten rooms has heat, air conditioning, private bath, and refrigerator. A generous homemade breakfast is served each morning on the enclosed porch. Relax and enjoy fresh sea breezes on the open veranda or in the back yard. Five-minute walk to center of village, shops, art galleries, and restaurants. Ten-minute walk to three miles of pristine white sand beach. Open March through November.

Hosts: Maurice and Lee Williams
Rooms: 10 (PB) $60-90
Continental Breakfast
Credit Cards: A, B
Notes: 2 (advance), 7, 8, 10, 11, 12

Scotch Hill Inn

175 Main Street, P.O. Box 87, 03907
(207) 646-2890

Each day begins with a memorable Scotch Hill Inn breakfast. After the beach, indulge in afternoon tea. Rooms are cozy yct amply sized. Reminders of Ongunquit's beauty are to be found in each room; potpourri and fine English soap are included on each vanity to let the guests know how much they are valued. The adjoining Carriage House has four bedrooms, a comfortable parlor, spacious dining room and kitchen. There is horse back riding nearby. Families with

children accommodated in the Carriage House and studios.

Hosts: Donna and Dick Brown; Maggie and Murray Light
Rooms: 13 (1 PB; 12 SB) $50-95
Full Breakfast
Credit Cards: A, B
Notes 2, 5, 8 (limited), 10, 11, 12, 14

The Trellis House

2 Beachmere Place, P.O. Box 2229, 03907
(207) 646-7909

A turn-of-the-century beach house, completely restored and appointed with an eclectic blend of antiques. All rooms have private baths. Breakfast consists of fresh fruits, muffins and breads, juices, coffee, tea, and special entree. The Trellis House is just a short walk to all that is special in Ogunquit.

Hosts: Pat and Jerry Houlihan
Rooms: 4 (PB) $65-100
Continental Breakfast
Credit Cards: A, B
Notes: 2 (limited), 5, 7 (limited), 9, 10, 11, 12

OQUOSSOC

Oquossoc's Own Bed and Breakfast

Rangeley Avenue, P.O. Box 27, 04964
(207) 864-5584

NOTES: Credit cards accepted: A MasterCard; B Visa; C American Express; D Discover Card; E Diner's Club; F Other; 2 Personal checks accepted; 3 Lunch available; 4 Dinner available; 5 Open all year;

Family home built in 1903 with 16 beds available in five guest rooms. On the snow-machine trail for winter sports and just five minutes to golf. Within walking distance of tennis and two lakes. Large yard and porches for relaxing. The hostess has been in the bed and breakfast and catering business since 1980. Group rates available.

Host: Joanne Conner Koob
Rooms: 5 (1 PB; 4 SB) $30-55
Full Breakfast
Credit Cards: A, B, D
Notes: 2, 3, 4, 5, 8, 9, 10, 11, 12, 13

The Sign of the Amiable Pig

ORLAND

The Sign of the Amiable Pig
P.O. Box 237, Route 175, 04472-0232
(207) 469-2561

The Sign of the Amiable Pig is in Orland Village just off Route 1. The house, named for the delightful weathervane which tops the garage, was built in the 18th century. Furnished with interesting antiques and Oriental rugs, the house has six working fireplaces, including the large cooking fireplace with its built-in bake oven in the keeping room. Full breakfast is served in either the dining room or the keeping room. Skiing in Camden or Acadia.

Hosts: Charlotte and Wes Pipher
Rooms: 3 (1 PB; 2 SB) $55

Full Breakfast
Credit Cards: None
Notes: 2, 5, 8, 9, 11, 12, 13

PEMAQUID

Apple Tree Inn
Snowball Hill Road, P.O. Box 485, New Harbor, 04554
(207) 677-3491

Informal, homey atmosphere in cozy old Cape. Two upstairs rooms share a bath. Both have queen-size beds. One has fireplace and sitting area. First-floor room has private bath, twin beds, and a large sunny window. Expanded Continental breakfast. Easy walk to Pemaquid Beach, Little Beach, and Fort William Henry. Quick drive to Pemaquid Point's Lighthouse Park, New Harbor, and Chamberlain's Long Cove, site of the Rachel Carson Salt Pond Preserve. Restaurants and shops nearby, too. Older children are welcome.

Host: Pat Landry
Rooms: 3 (1 PB; 2 SB) $55-70
Continental Breakfast
Credit Cards: None
Notes: 2, 5, 8, 11, 12

PORTLAND

Andrews Lodging Bed and Breakfast
417 Auburn Street, 04103
(207) 797-9157

On over an acre of beautifully landscaped grounds on the outskirts of the city of Portland, this 250-year-old Colonial home has been completely renovated for year-round comfort. Hosts offer modern baths, one with whirlpool, a completely applianced guest kitchen, a library, and a solarium overlooking beautiful gardens or pristine snow in the winter. Guests can expect refreshments in the refrigerator, turndown service, and warm hospitality from the host family as they share their home. Close to

6 Pets welcome; 8 Children welcome; 9 Social drinking allowed; 10 Tennis available; 11 Swimming available; 12 Golf available; 13 Skiing available; 14 May be booked through travel agents.

ocean, lakes, golf, skiing, and the mountains. ABBA rated two and one-half crowns in 1994.

Hosts: Elizabeth and Douglas Andrews
Rooms: 6 (1 PB; 5 SB) $60-125
Continental Breakfast
Credit Cards: A, B, C
Notes: 2, 5, 6, 8 (limited), 9, 12, 14

Inn on Carleton

46 Carleton Street, 04102
(207) 775-1910; (800) 639-1779

Inn on Carleton, a graciously restored 1869 Victorian townhouse in Portland's historic West End, is on a quiet, tree-lined street in a unique residential district. It is a short walk to the Portland Museum of Art and the Performing Arts Center. Nearby are Casco Bay's Calendar Islands, the international ferry to Nova Scotia, and the Old Port with its cobbled streets, colorful shops, and fine restaurants.

Hosts: Philip and Sue Cox
Rooms: 7 (3 PB; 4 SB) $49-95
Full Breakfast
Credit Cards: A, B, D
Notes: 2, 5, 8, 10, 11, 12, 13

West End Inn

146 Pine Street, 04102
(207) 772-1377

A very special place where the elegance and charm of yesteryear has been preserved and blended with the amenities and convenience of today. All rooms are uniquely decorated and provide private baths, cable TV, and phone access. Breakfast is cooked to order and reflects the quality of this establishment. The staff creates an atmosphere of relaxation and enjoyment throughout a stay and are quick to assist with travel tips or dinner reservations.

Host: John Leonard
Rooms: 5 (PB) $75-139
Full Breakfast
Credit Cards: A, B, C
Notes: 2, 5, 8, 9, 10, 11, 12, 13, 14

RANGELEY

Northwoods

P.O. Box 79, Main Street, 04970
(207) 864-2440

A historic 1912 home of rare charm and easy elegance, Northwoods is in Rangeley Village. Features spacious rooms, a lakefront porch, expansive grounds, and private boat dock, Northwoods provides superb accommodations. Golf, tennis, hiking, water sports, and skiing are a few of the many activities offered by the region.

Hosts: Carol and Robert Scofield
Rooms: 4 (3 PB; 1 SB) $60-75
Full Breakfast
Credit Cards: None
Notes: 2, 9, 10, 11, 12, 13, 14

ROCKPORT

Sign of the Unicorn Guest House

P.O.Box 99, 191 Beauchamp Avenue, 04856
(207) 236-8789; (800) 789-8789

This is the twentieth year as a bed and breakfast on a quiet lane overlooking Rockport Harbor. The beds, breakfasts, and ambience are great. Near all sports, sailing, antiquing, wildlife refuge, hiking or biking, concerts, restaurants, and lobster. Senior guests and long-stay rates. Pet accommodations are available at a nearby kennel. Groups can have as many as twelve people, and there are a variety of bed sizes available.

Hosts: Winnie and Howard Jones
Rooms: 5 (2 PB; 3 SB) $50-120

NOTES: Credit cards accepted: A MasterCard; B Visa; C American Express; D Discover Card; E Diner's Club; F Other; 2 Personal checks accepted; 3 Lunch available; 4 Dinner available; 5 Open all year;

Full Breakfast
Credit Cards: None
Notes: 2, 4, 5, 7 (limited), 8, 9, 10, 11, 12, 13, 14

Bed and Breakfast Marblehead and North Shore

P.O. Box 35, Newtonville, 02160
(617) 964-1606; (800) 832-2632
FAX (617) 332-8572

Harbor House Bed and Breakfast. This exquisite bed and breakfast overlooks Rockport Harbor, just a few miles south of Camden, Maine. It has two private balconies and a large deck, offering spectacular views of the harbor and Camden Hills. Three sun-filled guest rooms are available, some with private baths, some with skylights, fireplaces, and Jacuzzi. All open onto balconies or terraces on the harbor. Full breakfast. Private pier where the host's 30-foot sloop awaits charter by day or week. Resident cats. Open June through November. Two-night minimum on weekends. Smoking on decks only. Children over 12 are welcome. $90-150.

ROUND POND

The Briar Rose

Route 32, P.O. Box 27, 04564
(207) 529-5478

Escape to an unspoiled fishing village close to the Pemaquid Lighthouse, beaches, Monhegan Island boat service, and other recreational facilities. The 150-year-old home faces Round Pond Harbor and offers large, airy rooms filled with comfortable antique furnishings and collectibles. Relax in the gardens, enjoy walks in the village, visit local antique shops, country stores, studios, and galleries. Older children welcome; reservations recommended.

Hosts: Anita and Fred Palsgrove
Rooms: 3 (1 PB; 2 SB) $55-70
Full Breakfast

Credit Cards: None
Notes: 2, 5, 8, 9, 11, 12

RUMFORD POINT

The Last Resort

Box 12, 04279
(207) 364-4986

A Colonial Cape in Rumford Corner, nestled in the foothills of western Maine. Country comfort, charm, and good home cooking are a specialty. Skiing within minutes; two state parks and golf courses in the area. Fishing, hunting, hiking, and boating by the back door. Children are welcome. Plenty of wide-open space for outside activities.

Host: Joan A. Tucker
Rooms: 3 (SB) $50
Full Breakfast
Credit Cards: None
Notes: 2, 3 (picnic extra), 5, 7, 8, 9, 10, 11, 12, 13

SACO

Crown 'n' Anchor Inn

121 North Street, P.O. Box 228, 04072-0228
(207) 282-3829

This beautiful, two-story Greek Revival house was built circa 1827. The ornate Victorian furnishings, double parlors with twin mirrors, and bountiful country breakfast afford many memories for guests. All rooms at the inn are furnished with period antiques, many collectibles, and private facilities. Nearby attractions include the York Institute Museum, Thornton Acad-emy, the Dyer Library, Maine State Aqua-rium, and several ocean beaches.

Hosts: John Barclay and Martha Forester
Rooms: 5 (PB) $65-85
Full Breakfast
Credit Cards: A, B
Notes: 2, 5, 6 (call), 8 (over 12), 9, 10, 11, 14

6 Pets welcome; 8 Children welcome; 9 Social drinking allowed; 10 Tennis available; 11 Swimming available; 12 Golf available; 13 Skiing available; 14 May be booked through travel agents.

SEARSPORT

Brass Lantern Inn

Route 1, P.O. Box 407, 04974
(207) 548-0150; (800) 691-0150

Nestled at the edge of the woods, this gracious Victorian inn, circa 1850, overlooks Penobscot Bay. All of the comfortable guest rooms have private baths. Enjoy a hearty breakfast with friendly hospitality. A train shop on the premises, as well as an extensive doll collection. On the National Register of Historic Places. "Open all year, the Brass Lantern will be lit in welcome!"

Hosts: Pat Gatto; Dan and Lee Anne Lee
Rooms: 4 (PB) $50-75
Continental Breakfast
Credit Cards: A, B
Notes: 2, 5, 8, 10, 11, 12, 14

Homeport Inn

Box 647, East Main Street, Route 1, 04974
(207) 548-2259; (800) 742-5814

Homeport, listed on the National Register of Historic Places, is a fine example of a New England sea captain's mansion on beautiful landscaped grounds, with flower gardens and pond that extend to the ocean. This elegant home is furnished with family heirlooms and antiques. There are ten guest rooms, six with private baths. A Victorian cottage is also available. A visit offers a rare opportunity to vacation or be an overnight guest in a warm, homey, hospitable atmosphere without the customary traveler's commercialism.

Hosts: Edith and George Johnson
Rooms: 10 (6 PB; 4 SB) $55-75
Cottage: $470
Full Breakfast
Credit Cards: A, B, C, D, F
Notes: 2, 5, 7 (limited), 8, 9, 10, 11, 12, 13, 14

Thurston House
Bed and Breakfast Inn

8 Elm Street, P.O. Box 686, 04974
(207) 548-2213; (800) 240-2213

Beautiful circa 1830 Colonial home with well and carriage house. Built as a parsonage for Stephen Thurston, uncle of Winslow Homer. Now guests can visit in a casual environment. Quiet village setting is steps away from Penobscot Marine Museum, beach park on Penobscot Bay, restaurants, tavern, galleries, and antiques. Relax in one of four guest rooms, and enjoy the "forget about lunch" breakfasts.

Hosts: Carl and Beverly Eppig
Rooms: 4 (2 PB; 2 SB) $45-60
Full Breakfast
Credit Cards: A, B
Notes: 2, 5, 8, 9, 10, 11, 12, 13, 14

Watchtide

190 West Main Street, 04974
(207) 548-6575

Watchtide is a wondrous, New England-style Cape circa 1795 with a barn attached. Watch ships sail by on the Penobscot Bay while enjoying a full gourmet breakfast served on the wicker-furnished magnificent sun porch. Established as the College Club Inn in 1917 and serving such notables as Eleanor and Franklin Roosevelt. Enjoy birds and wildlife, artwork, antique furnishings, sweeping lawns and gardens, and the Angels to Antiques shoppe. The hosts love to spoil their guests with special treats and treatment. Mid-coast with exceptional antiquing, museums, parks, historical sites, and accessible to most everything. Open year-round. Dinner available off-season.

Hosts: Nancy-Linn and Jack Elliott
Rooms: 4 (2 PB; 2 SB) $55-85
Full Breakfast
Credit Cards: None
Notes: 2, 4, 5, 9, 11, 12, 13, 14

SOUTH BROOKSVILLE

Buck's Harbor Inn

P.O. Box 268, Steamboat Wharf Road, 04617
(207) 326-8660

NOTES: Credit cards accepted: A MasterCard; B Visa; C American Express; D Discover Card; E Diner's Club; F Other; 2 Personal checks accepted; 3 Lunch available; 4 Dinner available; 5 Open all year;

Charming country inn on Buck's Harbor, Penobscot Bay, a famed yachting and boating center. Halfway between Acadia National Park/Bar Harbor and Camden. Historic Deer Isle, Castine, Blue Hill are just a short drive away. Seasonal restaurant (The Landing) next door. Remote, beautiful, comfortable, Brooksville is just the way Maine should be experienced.

Hosts: Peter and Ann Ebeling
Rooms: 6 (SB) $60
Full Breakfast
Credit Cards: A, B
Notes: 2, 5, 8, 9, 11, 12

SOUTH GOULDSBORO

The Bluff House Inn and Restaurant

Route 186, P.O. Box 169, 04607
(207) 963-7805

Resting high above Frenchman Bay, the Bluff House offers everything necessary for a relaxing and enjoyable stay any time of the year. Explore Schoodic Peninsula and all the splendors of the Frenchman Bay area. Kayak or canoe from the shore, hike, bike, cross-country ski, or just relax by the fireside. The hosts provide a million dollar view and a stress-free way of life.

Hosts: Joyce and Don Freeborn
Rooms: 8 (PB) $45-75
Continental Breakfast
Credit Cards: A, B, C, D, E
Notes: 4, 5, 9

SOUTHWEST HARBOR

Harbour Cottage Inn

P.O. Box 258, 04679-0258
(207) 244-5738

This elegant but informal inn is in the heart of Acadia National Park. Private baths offer either whirlpools or steam showers and hair dryers. Harbor-facing guest rooms have individual heat and ceiling fans. Hikers, bikers, boaters, skiers,

and tourists are welcome to enjoy the warm, friendly hospitality.

Hosts: Ann and Mike Pedreschi
Rooms: 8 (PB) $60-135
Full Breakfast
Credit Cards: A, B, C, D
Notes: 2, 9, 10, 11, 12, 13, 14

Harbour Cottage Inn

Harbour Woods

P.O. Box 1214, 04679
(207) 244-5388

Across from Hinckley Great Harbor Marina is this 1800s Maine farmhouse. Enjoy the retained charm and character of days gone by such as family keepsakes, antiques, flowers, and soft glowing oil lamps. Breakfast is a dining experience of the finest kind. Stumble across evening tea and cookies, and the guest refrigerator is always stocked with complimentary soft drinks. Enjoy guest rooms with queen-size beds, evening mints and candy, telephones, and private baths with luxurious towels and a selection of rich soaps. Each room is decorated with its own distinctive personality. Privately reserve the indoor spa which awaits to refresh and relax after a full day of activities in Acadia National Park.

Hosts: Joe and Christine Titka
Rooms: 3 (PB) $65-125
Cottage: 1 (PB) $55-95
Credit Cards: A, B
Notes: 2, 5, 9, 10, 11, 12, 13

6 Pets welcome; 8 Children welcome; 9 Social drinking allowed; 10 Tennis available; 11 Swimming available; 12 Golf available; 13 Skiing available; 14 May be booked through travel agents.

The Island House

The Island House

Box 1006, 04679
(207) 244-5180

Relax in a gracious, restful seacoast home on the quiet side of the island. Island House favorites such as blueberry coffeecake and sausage/cheese casserole are served for breakfast. Charming, private loft apartment available. Acadia National Park is just a five-minute drive away. The house is across the street from the harbor with swimming, sailing, biking, and hiking nearby.

Host: Ann Bradford
Rooms: 5 (1 PB; 4 SB) $55-100
Full Breakfast
Credit Cards: A, B
Notes: 2, 5, 8 (over 5), 9, 10, 11, 12

Island Watch
Bed and Breakfast

Freeman Ridge Road, P.O. Box 1359, 04679
(207) 244-7229

Overlooking the harbors of Mount Desert Island and the village of Southwest Harbor, Island Watch sits atop Freeman Ridge on the quiet side of the island. The finest panoramic views, privacy, and comfort. Walk to Acadia National Park and the fishing village of Southwest Harbor. Private baths, full breakfasts, and a smoke-free environment.

Host: Maxine M. Clark
Rooms: 6 (PB) $75
Full Breakfast
Credit Cards: F (travelers checks)
Notes: 2, 9, 10, 11, 12, 13

The Kingsleigh Inn

100 Main Street, Box 1426, 04679
(207) 244-5302

In the heart of Acadia National Park overlooking the picturesque harbor is a romantic, intimate inn that will surround guests with charm the moment they walk through the door. Many rooms enjoy spectacular harbor views, and all are tastefully decorated.

Hosts: Tom and Nancy Cerelli
Rooms: 8 (PB) $55-155
Full Breakfast
Credit Cards: A, B, D
Notes: 2, 5, 8 (over 12), 9, 11, 12, 13 (cross-country)

The Lambs Ear Inn

Clark Point Road, P.O. Box 30, 04679
(207) 244-9828

The inn is a stately old Maine house, circa 1857. Comfortable and serene, with a sparkling harbor view. Have sweet dreams on comfortable beds with crisp, fresh linens. Start the day with a memorable breakfast. Spend pleasant days here filled with salt air and sunshine. Please visit this special village in the heart of Mount Desert Island surrounded by Acadia National Park.

Hosts: George and Elizabeth Hoke
Rooms: 6 (PB) $65-125
Full Breakfast
Credit Cards: A, B
Notes: 2, 9, 10, 11, 12, 14

Penury Hall

Main Street, Box 68, 04679
(207) 244-7102

On the quiet side of Mount Desert, 14 miles from Bar Harbor, is Penury Hall, where guests enjoy a breakfast of eggs Benedict, blueberry pancakes, cinnamon waffles, or popovers. Guests are welcome to use the

NOTES: Credit cards accepted: A MasterCard; B Visa; C American Express; D Discover Card; E Diner's Club; F Other; 2 Personal checks accepted; 3 Lunch available; 4 Dinner available; 5 Open all year;

canoe or sail aboard Abaco Rage, a 21-foot daysailer. The sauna is relaxing after a hard day of hiking or cross-country skiing.

Hosts: Toby and Gretchen Strong
Rooms: 3 (SB) $45-60
Full Breakfast
Credit Cards: None
Notes: 2, 5, 9, 10, 11, 12, 13

The Hichborn Inn

STOCKTON SPRINGS

The Hichborn Inn

Church Street, P.O. Box 115, 04981
(207) 567-4183

This romantic Victorian inn is listed on the National Register of Historic Places. Quiet area just off Route 1. Period furnishings, beds appointed with fine linens and down comforters, sumptuous full breakfasts, which may feature crepes made with the inn's own raspberries. Penobscot Marine Museum, numerous antique shops, and fine dining nearby. Advance reservations recommended. No smoking.

Hosts: Nancy and Bruce Suppes
Rooms: 4 (2 PB; 2 SB) $55-80
Full Breakfast
Credit Cards: None
Notes: 2, 5, 11, 14

STRATTON

The Widow's Walk

171 Main Street, P.O. Box 150, 04982
(207) 246-6901; (800) 943-6995

The Steamboat Gothic architecture of this Victorian home led to a listing in the National Register of Historic Places. Nearby Bigelow Mountain, the Appalachian Trail, and Flagstaff Lake present many opportunities for boating, fishing, and hiking. In the winter, Sugarloaf USA, Maine's largest ski resort, offers both alpine and cross-country skiing, as well as dogsled rides. Dogs and cats in residence.

Hosts: Mary and Jerry Hopson
Rooms: 6 (SB) $30-46
Full Breakfast
Credit Cards: A, B
Notes: 2, 5, 8 (limited), 9, 11, 12, 13

SULLIVAN

Islandview Inn

Route 1, HCR 32, Box 24, 04664
(207) 422-3031

Turn-of-the-century summer cottage is just off Route 1, 15 minutes from Ellsworth and 35 minutes from Bar Harbor. Choose from seven guest rooms, five with private bath. Each room features original furniture and detailed restoration work, picturesque views of Frenchman's Bay and Mount Desert Island. Private beach, sailing, canoe and dinghy are available.

Host: Evelyn Joost
Rooms: 7 (5 PB; 2 SB) $45-75
Full Breakfast
Credit Cards: A, B, D
Notes: 2, 8, 9, 10, 12

SURRY

The Surry Inn

P.O. Box 25, 04684
(207) 667-5091

6 Pets welcome; 8 Children welcome; 9 Social drinking allowed; 10 Tennis available; 11 Swimming available; 12 Golf available; 13 Skiing available; 14 May be booked through travel agents.

Two gracious buildings on sprawling grounds provide warmth, comfort, and exceptional dining. The main house, built in 1834, served as lodging for stage and steamship passengers in the last century. The expansive grounds have shore walks and a beach with the warmest saltwater bathing in the area. There is croquet, horseshoes, a canoe, and a rowboat. Midway between Mount Desert Island and lovely Deer Island.

Host: Peter Krinsky
Rooms: 13 (11 PB; 2 SB) $48-62
Full Breakfast
Credit Cards: A, B
Notes: 2, 4, 5, 7 (limited), 8 (over 5), 9, 10, 11, 12, 13, 14

TENANTS HARBOR

The East Wind Inn

P.O. Box 149, 04860
(207) 372-6366; (800) 241-VIEW

This authentic country inn at water's edge is owned and operated by a native of Tenants Harbor. Life slows to a comfortable pace in this tiny seaside village, and the natural harmony is evident inside the inn as well. Antique-filled guest rooms and a dining room that serves New England country cooking offer spectacular views of the harbor. Bookshelves, rich with Maine stories, and a staff that is genuinely friendly will make guests feel like they have found a safe haven. The inn and Meeting House with complete conference facilities are available year-round.

Host: Tim Watts
Rooms: 26 (12 PB; 14 SB) $60-130
Full and Continental Breakfast
Credit Cards: A, B, C, E
Notes: 2, 4, 6 (call), 7, 8, 9, 10, 11, 12, 13, 14

THOMASTON

Cap'n Frost's Bed and Breakfast

241 West Main Street, 04861
(207) 354-8217

This 1840 Cape Cod cottage is furnished with country antiques, some for sale. If travelers are visiting the midcoast area, this is a comfortable overnight stay, close to Monhegan Island and a two-hour drive to Acadia National Park. Reservations are helpful.

Hosts: Arlene and Harold Frost
Rooms: 3 (1 PB; 2 SB) $40
Full Breakfast
Credit Cards: A, B, D
Notes: 2, 9

VINALHAVEN

Bed and Breakfast Inns of New England

128 S. Hoop Pole Road, Guilford, CT, 06437
(203) 457-0042; (800) 582-0853

ME-830. Stay at this comfortable, affordable bed and breakfast in a fishing village by Carver's Harbor. Explore uncrowded woodlands, visit seaside nature preserves and parks, and feast on Maine's freshest seafood caught daily in the surrounding waters. Each morning starts with a Continental breakfast, and guests can prepare a picnic in the guest kitchen for the day's adventures. Available are six guest rooms, all with shared baths. Children over ten are welcome. Resident dog, no guest pets. No smoking. $40-60.

Fox Island Inn

Carver Street, P.O. Box 451, 04863
(207) 863-2122

Discover the unspoiled coastal Maine island of Vinalhaven. This comfortable, affordable bed and breakfast is in the quaint fishing village nestled around picturesque Carver's Harbor. Enjoy swimming in abandoned granite quarries and exploring seaside nature preserves by foot or bicycle. State-operated car ferry from Rockland runs six times daily. Island activities include flea markets, church suppers, and wonderful local restaurants.

NOTES: Credit cards accepted: A MasterCard; B Visa; C American Express; D Discover Card; E Diner's Club; F Other; 2 Personal checks accepted; 3 Lunch available; 4 Dinner available; 5 Open all year;

Host: Gail Reinertsen
Rooms: 6 (SB) $40-60
Continental Breakfast
Credit Cards: None
Notes: 2, 9, 11

Libby House

P.O. Box 273, 04863
(207) 863-4696

The Libby House was built in 1869 by T. E. Libby, part-owner of the Libby-Lane Fish Company of Vinalhaven, Maine. The house has the details of the 1800s and the conveniences of today. Vinalhaven is an island with a K-12 school and a community off the mainland of Maine. A 90-minute ride on the state ferry from Rockland, Maine to the island of Vinalhaven. The island has two beautiful fresh-water swimming quarries and a very rich history. The natural beauty of Vinalhaven is well worth the visit.

Host: Philip Roberts
Rooms: 3 (2 PB; 1 SB) $55-100
Continental Breakfast
Credit Cards: None
Notes: 2, 11, 12

WALDOBORO

Bed and Breakfast Inns of New England

128 S. Hoop Pole Road, Guilford, CT, 06437
(203) 457-0042; (800) 582-0853

ME-815. This lovely 1830 inn is handsomely decorated with Victorian furnishings. There is a sun deck and shade garden with a hammock. The inn features a delicious full breakfast, and tea or sherry is served each afternoon. Five guest rooms include a variety of bed sizes, along with shared and private baths. Children over 12 are welcome. No guest pets. Smoking limited. $45-70.

ME-816. Built in 1905, this bed and breakfast features classic woodwork, tin ceilings, two fireplaces, and a large screened porch. Explore the flower and vegetable gardens

or the gallery and gift shop in the barn. Coffee, tea, or hot chocolate is brought to guests' rooms upon awakening, and a full breakfast is served in the dining room. Special diets can be accommodated. Four guest rooms are available with shared and private baths, with a variety of bed sizes. Children welcome. No guest pets. No smoking. $55-65.

Broad Bay Inn and Gallery Bed and Breakfast

Box 607, 1014 Main Street, 04572
(207) 832-6668; (800) 736-6769

Lovingly restored 1830 inn, handsomely appointed with Victorian furnishings, canopied beds, paintings, art and theatrical library, and foreign films. Breakfast banquet feasts and afternoon tea or sherry on the deck. Established art gallery in the barn. Walk down to the river, to tennis, the theater, and antique shops. A short drive to the lighthouse, Audubon sanctuary, and fishing villages. Send for a free brochure.

Hosts: Jim and Libby Hopkins
Rooms: 5 (S3B) $45-75
Full Breakfast
Credit Cards: A, D
Closed January
Notes: 2, 7 (limited), 8 (over 10), 9, 10, 11, 12, 13, 14

Broad Bay Inn

6 Pets welcome; 8 Children welcome; 9 Social drinking allowed; 10 Tennis available; 11 Swimming available; 12 Golf available; 13 Skiing available; 14 May be booked through travel agents.

The Roaring Lion

Box 756, 04572
(207) 832-4038

A 1905 Victorian home with tin ceilings; elegant woodwork throughout. The Roaring Lion caters to special diets and serves miso soup, sourdough bread, homemade jams and jellies. Hosts are well traveled and lived for two years in West Africa. Their interests include books, gardening, art, and cooking. Gallery and gift shop on premises.

Hosts: Bill and Robin Branigan
Rooms: 4 (1 PB; 3 SB) $58.85-69.55
Full Breakfast
Credit Cards: None
Notes: 2, 5, 8, 10, 11, 12, 13, 14

WATERFORD

Kedarburn Inn

Route 35, 04088
(207) 583-6182

Nestled in the foothills of the White Mountains this beautiful white frame house was built in 1858 and is set beside the flowing Kedar Brook which runs to the shores of Lake Keoka. Whether guests come for outdoor activities such as golf, sailing, swimming, or simple enjoyment of the countryside, they are pampered by the hosts in a relaxed atmosphere.

Hosts: Margaret and Derek Gibson
Rooms: 6 (4 PB; 2 SB) $69-88
Full Breakfast
Credit Cards: A, B
Notes: 2, 5, 6, 8, 9, 11, 12, 13, 14

Lake House

Routes 35 and 37, 04088
(207) 583-4182; (800) 223-4182 outside ME

Lake House is one of 21 buildings in Waterford "Flat" listed on the national historic register. The inn was established in the 1790s. For much of the 19th century it served as the Maine Hygienic Institute for Ladies. From the 1890s to 1940, it was operated as a hotel.

Hosts: Michael and Suzanne Uhl-Myers
Rooms: 5 (PB) $79-130
Full Breakfast
Credit Cards: A, B, C
Notes: 2, 4, 5, 8, 9, 10, 11, 12, 13, 14

The Parsonage House Bed and Breakfast

Rice Road, P.O. Box 116, 04088
(207) 583-4115

The Parsonage House, built in 1870 for the Waterford Church, overlooks Waterford Village, Keoka Lake, and Mount Tirem. In a four-season area, it provides many opportunities for outdoor enthusiasts. The Parsonage is a haven of peace and quiet. Double guest rooms or private suite available. A full breakfast is served on the screened porch or in the large farm kitchen beside a glowing wood stove.

Hosts: Joseph and Gail St. Hilaire
Rooms: 3 (1 PB; 2 SB) $50-75
Full Breakfast
Credit Cards: None
Notes: 2, 3, 5, 8, 11, 12, 13

The Waterford Inne

Box 149, Chadbourne Road, 04088
(207) 583-4037

Escape to country quiet in an inn offering the elegance of a fine country home. Ten uniquely decorated guest rooms and carefully furnished common rooms provide a fine setting for four-star dining in historic Waterford. Near mountains and coastline; water and woodland activities nearby. Closed March and April.

Hosts: Barbara and Rosalie Vanderzanden
Rooms: 10 (7 PB; 3 SB) $75-100
Full Breakfast
Credit Cards: C
Notes: 2, 4, 6 (call), 7, 8, 9, 10, 11, 12, 13

NOTES: Credit cards accepted: A MasterCard; B Visa; C American Express; D Discover Card; E Diner's Club; F Other; 2 Personal checks accepted; 3 Lunch available; 4 Dinner available; 5 Open all year;

WELD

Kawanhee Inn Lakeside Lodge

Webb Lake, Mt. Blue, Box 119, Weld, 04285
(207) 585-2000
7 High Street, Farmington, 04938–in winter

Kawanhee Inn is on Webb Lake. "Webb Beach, one of the top ten beaches of New England," says U.S. Air Magazine, May, 1994. Early morning excursions by canoe will allow guests to see moose feeding by the water's edge and the sun rising over the western mountains. Have breakfast before climbing Tumbledown Mountain or going gold panning in the Swift River. Bring a mountain bike, tennis rackets, or golfing equipment for a game at nearby course. Before dinner on the screened porches, swim the private, sandy beach. Seasonal May 15 to October 15.

Host: Martha Strunk
Rooms: 9 (5 PB; 4 SB) $60-85
Continental Breakfast
Credit Cards: A, B
Notes: 4, 8, 9, 10, 11, 12

WELLS

Purple Sandpiper Guest House

Rural Route 3, Box 226C, 04090
(207) 646-7990

The guest house is on Route 1, just minutes from the beach. Rooms are comfortably furnished with private baths, cable TVs, and refrigerators. Continental breakfast includes freshly baked muffins and coffeecakes. Miniature golf, tennis, and restaurants are within walking distance. Closed mid-October to mid-May.

Hosts: Paul and Sandi Goodwin
Rooms: 6 (PB) $36-67
Continental Breakfast
Credit Cards: A, B, C, D
Notes: 2, 7, 8, 9, 10, 11, 12

WINTER HARBOR

Main Stay Inn

P.O. Box 459, 04693
(207) 963-5561

Restored Victorian home overlooking Henry's Cove. Housekeeping units with fireplaces. Walk to restaurants, post office. A quiet village within a mile of Acadia, hiking, biking, and local activities.

Hosts: Pearl and Roger Barto
Rooms: 3 plus 2 units (PB) $45
Credit Cards: A, B
Notes: 2, 5, 7, 8, 9, 11, 12

WISCASSET

The Squire Tarbox Inn

Rural Route 2, Box 620, 04578
(207) 882-7693

Clean, casual, comfortable, and all country, this is a historic Colonial farmhouse on a back road near midcoast Maine harbors, beaches, antique shops, museums, and lobster shacks. The inn offers a proper balance of history, quiet country, good food, and relaxation. Serves a delicious fresh goat cheese by the fire before dinner. Known primarily for rural privacy and five-course dinners.

Hosts: Karen and Bill Mitman
Rooms: 11 (PB) $75-160
Full Breakfast
Credit Cards: A, B, C, D
Notes: 2, 4, 7 (limited), 8 (over 14), 9, 14

YORK

The Cape Neddick House

1300 Route 1, P.O. Box 70, Cape Neddick, 03902
(207) 363-2500

In the historic coastal community of York, this 1800s Victorian farmhouse is central to beaches, boutiques, antique shops, wildlife sanctuaries, boat cruises, factory outlets, and historical and cultural opportunities.

6 Pets welcome; 8 Children welcome; 9 Social drinking allowed; 10 Tennis available; 11 Swimming available; 12 Golf available; 13 Skiing available; 14 May be booked through travel agents.

Sleeping on antique high-back beds, snuggled under handmade quilts, guests are assured of pleasant dreams. No alarm clock needed, as the fragrant smells of cinnamon popovers, apple almond tortes, or ham and apple biscuits drift by, gently waking guests. Reason enough to return time and again. All private baths. Two-room suite with fireplace available.

Hosts: John and Dianne Goodwin
Rooms: 5 (PB) $55-90
Full Breakfast
Credit Cards: None
Notes: 2, 4 (call), 5, 7 (limited), 9, 10, 11, 12, 13
   (cross-country)

Dockside Guest Quarters

Harris Island Road, Box 205, 03909
(207) 363-2868

The Dockside Guest Quarters is a small resort on a private peninsula in York Harbor. Panorama of ocean and harbor activities. Spacious grounds with privacy and relaxing atmosphere. Beaches, outlet shopping, and numerous scenic walks close by. Accommodations are in an early seacoast inn and modern, multi-unit cottages. Full service marina, wedding facilities, and restaurant on site. Minimum stay requirements. Closed October 22 to May 1.

Host: The Lusty family
Rooms: 21 (19 PB; 2 SB) $55-129
Continental Breakfast
Credit Cards: A, B
Notes: 2, 3, 4, 5, 7, 8, 9, 10, 11, 12, 14

YORK BEACH

Homestead Inn Bed and Breakfast

8 South Main Street (Route 1A), 03910
(207) 363-8952

A converted 1905 summer boarding house, the inn is at Short Sands Beach. Individually decorated rooms have ocean views. Walk to beach, enjoy sunsets; visit local Nubble Lighthouse. Historic landmarks;

fine restaurants. Relax, be pampered, and let the seashore entertain.

Hosts: Dan and Danielle Duffy
Rooms: 4 (S2B) $49-59
Continental Breakfast
Credit Cards: None
Notes: 2, 9, 10, 11, 12

YORK HARBOR

Bell Buoy Bed and Breakfast

570 York Street, 03911
(207) 363-7264

At the Bell Buoy, there are no strangers, only friends who have not met. Open year-round and minutes from US 95, Route 1, and the Kittery outlet malls. We are a short walk to sandy beaches, or guests may relax on our large porch or in the guests-only living room with fireplace. A full homemade breakfast will be served in the dining room or on the porch, as desired.

Hosts: Wes and Kathie Cook
Rooms: 3 (1 PB; 2 SB) $60-85
Full Breakfast
Credit Cards: None
Notes: 2, 5, 7, 9, 11, 12

York Harbor Inn

Box 573, Route 1A, 03911
(207) 363-5119; (800) 343-3869

Coastal country inn overlooking beautiful York Harbor, in an exclusive residential neighborhood. There are 32 air-conditioned rooms with antiques, ocean views, and seven working fireplaces. Fine dining year-round. An English pub on the premises with entertainment. The beach is within walking distance; and boating, fishing, antique shops are all nearby.

Hosts: Joe, Jean, Garry, and Nancy Dominguez
Rooms: 32 (PB) $79-139
Continental Breakfast
Credit Cards: A, B, C
Notes: 2, 3, 4, 5, 7, 8, 9, 10, 11, 12, 14

NOTES: Credit cards accepted: A MasterCard; B Visa; C American Express; D Discover Card; E Diner's Club; F Other; 2 Personal checks accepted; 3 Lunch available; 4 Dinner available; 5 Open all year;

Maryland

ANNAPOLIS

Amanda's Bed and Breakfast

1428 Park Avenue, Baltimore, 21217
(410) 225-0001; (800) 899-7533
FAX (410) 728-8957

112. Among beautiful trees on the cove of Severn River, this charming 1850 barn has been renovated with a taste of country, including antiques and old quilts. Historic Annapolis, U.S. Naval Academy, and sailing schools are all nearby. Convenient snack bar. Children welcome. Continental breakfast or farm breakfast. One queen-size bed with private half-bath; one double bed with private half bath and deck. $70.

124. Quiet Annapolis suburb near Quiet Waters Park, just four miles from historic Annapolis. Five rooms, each with a private bath. Full breakfast. $75-85.

127. Charming suite, ground floor of cottage with water access. About five minutes from downtown Annapolis. Newly constructed, spacious room with sitting area, bedroom, bath, and kitchen. Garden view. Short-term rates available. $100.

127A. Newly finished spacious and light studio apartment. Ground floor with skylights, separate bedroom, sitting area with kitchen, garden, air conditioning, and access to water with dock. Canoe. Self-catered. $100.

139. Choose from four historic locations in downtown Annapolis that accurately reflect early architecture. Some include dining rooms, taverns, and conference space. Continental breakfast. $85-250.

141. Nestled between the U.S. Naval Academy and St. John's College, this beautifully decorated historic district townhome features a private apartment suite with fireplace and ivy-covered courtyard. Another suite occupies the entire third floor of the main house. Continental breakfast. Two-night minimum. $120-140.

163. This ten-room bed and breakfast is on the main street in downtown Annapolis, just steps away from the docks, shops, and historic buildings. All rooms have private baths. As the inn is above a famous deli, breakfast may be chosen from a special menu. Full breakfast. $65-85.

182. This beautiful, modern condo on the water looks out onto a marina. Just 15 minutes (three miles) from downtown historic Annapolis. Continental breakfast. One queen-size bed. Private bath. $85.

200. This fully furnished historic home is very close to the docks and the historic district of Annapolis. Feel free to walk to restaurants, shops, and the Naval Academy. Special features include modern kitchen, three working fireplaces, four bedrooms, three baths, TV, a washer/dryer, and central heat and air conditioning. Whole house rental. Sleeps six to ten people. $300.

6 Pets welcome; 7 Smoking allowed; 8 Children welcome; 9 Social drinking allowed; 10 Tennis available; 11 Swimming available; 12 Golf available; 13 Skiing available; 14 May be booked through travel agents.

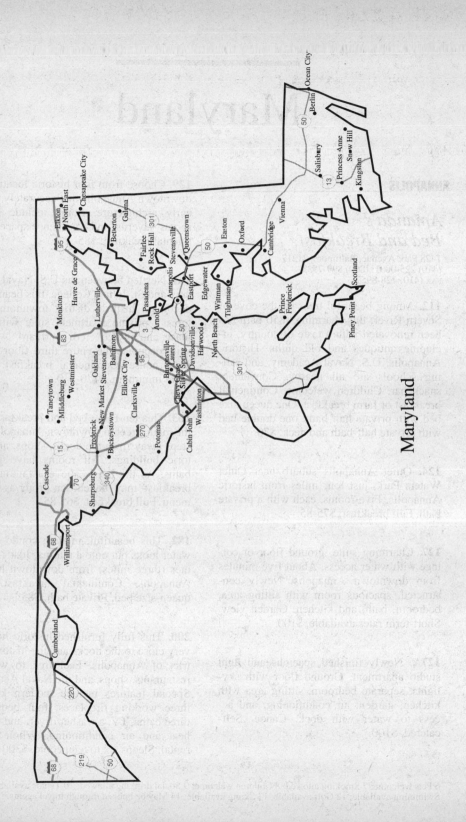

Maryland

Amanda's
Bed and Breakfast
(continued)

218. Two older homes and a newer addition are in the heart of the historic district of Annapolis. There are a total of 20 guest rooms. Parlors, dining and meeting rooms are all lovingly furnished with beautiful antiques. $72-120.

234. An unusual octagon-shaped house on a wooded lot overlooking the South River. Newly created suite with water view, private bath, and sitting area. A fireplace for cool weather enjoyment. Breakfast options available. $125.

258. A luxury 55-foot motor yacht on a lovely creek has every amenity. Put worries to rest in the lounging area that adjoins the master stateroom. A spacious aft deck and fly bridge are also included for your enjoyment. Historic Annapolis city docks and restaurants are just minutes away with the help of a water taxi. Private bath. Continental breakfast. $125-150.

295. Lighthouse replica, built by the water with a beautiful view of the bay. Unique and private. Each of the three rooms has a private bath. Parking and Continental breakfast. A view to be enjoyed. $85.

306. A former corner store, now decorated with a European country flavor. Walk to everything in Annapolis: restaurants, historic sites, naval academy, and shops. Four rooms, two with private baths. Full breakfast. $75-95.

316. Nestled in the woods on the water about five minutes from downtown Annapolis. A charming cottage with one room and private bath. Double hammock by the water. Full breakfast. $100.

322. Downtown Annapolis within walking distance to historic sites, shops, restaurants, and Naval Academy. Lovely antiques; newly decorated. One room with private bath; and one suite with private bath. Full breakfast. $95-150.

334. Just north of the city in a quiet wooded area. A ranch-style home built by the owners. Inside some furniture made by the "men" of the family. A private en-trance wing with queen-size bed and sitting area overlooking dogwood garden. Walking trail just behind the house. Full breakfast. $75.

355. Only ten minutes from downtown Annapolis. Enjoy the water and a pool at this small, comfortable cottage set off from the main house. Private entrance. Double bed. Full breakfast. $85-100.

American Heritage
Bed and Breakfast

108 Charles Road, 21401
(410) 280-1620

Built around 1862, this charming home is in the middle of the historic district of Annapolis. Within easy walking distance of the U.S. Naval Academy, fine restaurants, and local attractions, this inn is filled with antiques and heirlooms that render a feeling of warmth and pleasant memories of the past. Wake to a full breakfast featuring family recipes, homemade breads, jellies, and jams. Enjoy a soothing massage, by appointment, at this bed and breakfast.

Hosts: Bob and Adria Smith
Rooms: 2 (PB) $90-100
Full Breakfast

NOTES: Credit cards accepted: A MasterCard; B Visa; C American Express; D Discover Card; E Diner's Club; F Other; 2 Personal checks accepted; 3 Lunch available; 4 Dinner available; 5 Open all year; 6 Pets welcome; 7 Smoking allowed; 8 Children welcome; 9 Social drinking allowed; 10 Tennis available; 11 Swimming available; 12 Golf available; 13 Skiing available; 14 May be booked through travel agents.

Credit Cards: None
Notes: 2, 5, 9, 14

The Barn
on Howard's Cove

500 Wilson Road, 21401
(301) 266-6840

Bed and breakfast in a restored 1850s barn on a secluded cove off the Severn River, two miles from the center of this historic state capital, sailing center of the United States, and home of the U.S. Naval Academy. Convenient to Baltimore and Washington, D.C. Beautiful gardens, rural setting. Country decor with antiques and handmade quilts. One room has a deck and a loft. Breakfast is served in the flower-filled solarium or on the large deck overlooking the river.

Hosts: Dr. and Mrs. Graham Gutsche
Rooms: 2 (P1/2B, SFB) $70
Full Breakfast
Credit Cards: None
Notes: 2, 5, 8, 10, 11, 12, 14

Bed and Breakfast
of Maryland/Traveller
in Maryland, Inc.

P.O. Box 2277, Annapolis, 21494-2277
(410) 269-6232; FAX (410) 263-4841

105. This ranch-style contemporary is on a quiet residential street within walking distance of the Naval Academy football stadium and a hearty walk to the historic district and waterfront. The home, being built by the owners themselves, is comfortably furnished in contemporary pieces and has a real sense of home and relaxation. The two guest rooms, one with a king-size bed and the other with a queen-size bed, are on the second floor and share a bath. A living room, den (TV), and an outdoor deck are welcome areas for guests. Resident cat. No smoking. Continental breakfast. $50-55.

107. This Victorian Italianate villa, circa 1864, is a charming piece of architecture nestled in the central historic district. At the entry a circular staircase flows up to the second-floor guest room area. Furnished with period antiques, some reproductions, and numerous objects d'art. There are three guest rooms. One with a queen-size bed, fireplace, and private bath. The second has a double bed, TV, telephone, and private hall bath with shower and separate Jacuzzi. The third has a single bed and may be used with either room for an additional person. Resident cats in owners' private wing, only. No smoking. Full breakfast. $50-85.

109. This turn-of-the-century home is on Spa Creek and convenient to all attractions in the historic district. It is filled with antiques and family heirlooms. Has a second-floor sun porch, nice yard, and a terrace where guests can watch the sailboats quietly slip by. There are four guest rooms that have private or shared baths. No smoking. Full breakfast. $60-70.

111. This charming, old home, dating from the 1690s and early 1700s, is one of Annapolis' two oldest residences. It is a Registered Historic Landmark still occupied by descendants of the original owners. In the Historic District and furnished in elements of the original colonial structure. There are three guest rooms. One with a double bed, fireplace, and private bath. The second has a double bed, and shares a bath with the third room with twin beds. Resident cat and dog. No smoking. Continental breakfast. $65-95.

113. This two-story waterfront home has prominent views of the South River, and is a ten minute drive to the Historic District. Family room contains TV, fireplace, and large windows that offer guests the world outside. The rear yard has a tiled patio with a panoramic view. There are three guest rooms with double or king-size beds and private baths. Resident cat. Restricted smoking. Full breakfast. $65-75.

119. This restored horse barn, circa 1860, is nestled on a secluded cove off the Severn River. Plank flooring, working fireplace, handmade quilts, farm tools, workpieces, and open views of the woodlands and water grace this home. The two guest rooms, with double or king-size beds, have private half-baths and share a shower-tub room that connects to each half-bath. No smoking. Full breakfast. $55-65.

121. This unhosted, three-story, 1900s home is in the Historic District. The first floor has a living room with queen sofa bed and center dining room with large rear kitchen. Rear brick patio surrounded by a ten-foot high brick wall adds privacy. Second floor has two bedrooms with double beds. One with sitting area and full bath. Second room contains half-bath. Resident dog. No smoking. Three night minimum stay. $275.

123. This contemporary townhome is on the fringe of the Historic District overlooking Spa Creek. With eclectic furnishings, it has a nice water view from the dining and living rooms. The two guest rooms have water front balconies, one with double and one with twin beds. They share a hall bath. Central air conditioning. Restricted smoking area. Continental breakfast. $60-65.

127. This Victorian bed and breakfast is in the Historic District three blocks from the city waterfront and walking distance to fine restaurants, shopping, the historic sites, and the United States Naval Academy. Furnished with antiques and family collectibles. Rear yard with brick patio. The guest suite has a queen-size bed and separate living room with TV. Private bath. Air

conditioning. No smoking allowed. Continental breakfast served. $90.

129. This Georgian-Revival brick home furnished in family collectibles is in the Historic District and within three blocks of the waterfront. The owner-operator, Naval Academy graduate and retired Naval officer, has hosted Academy guests over the years. The first guest room has a double bed and private hall bath. The second has king-size or twin beds, fireplace, and private bath. The third has a double bed, two trundle beds, and private bath. Can easily accommodate a family. Garden patio provides a relaxing sit on seasonal days where a full breakfast is served. Restricted smoking area. Children are welcome. Extra person $15 each. $70-85.

131. This unique grey and white eight-sided home sits on a two-acre wooded lot 100 feet from the South River. The hills are full of dogwood trees just minutes from a major shopping district, ten minutes from downtown Annapolis, and 35 minutes from downtown Washington, D.C. Eclectic furnishings. There are two guest rooms, one with a queen-size bed and the other with an antique bedroom suite of twin beds. Private and/or shared bath. Your host holds a Master Coast Guard License. Guest, may arrange a one- to three-hour private cruise on a 44-foot trawler for an additional fee, directly with your host. No smoking. Outside dogs. Full breakfast. $63-68.

139. A recently renovated 70-year-old corner store features three guest rooms that combine yesteryear (original tin ceiling and oak counter) with contemporary conveniences (in-room coffeemakers, televisions). Decorated in west coast pastels, turn-of-the-century furnishings along with art accents from Europe and South America. The three guest rooms have double, queen- or king-size beds and private baths.

6 Pets welcome; 8 Children welcome; 9 Social drinking allowed; 10 Tennis available; 11 Swimming available; 12 Golf available; 13 Skiing available; 14 May be booked through travel agents.

Bed and Breakfast of Maryland/Traveller in Maryland, Inc.
(continued)

Two-minute walk from city dock and Naval Academy. Off-street parking at modest cost. No smoking. Extended Continental breakfast. $75-90.

141. This contemporary, waterfront home is within a swift five to eight minutes of the Historic District by auto. Covered waterview deck and small dock facility on the property. This converted fishing bungalow is furnished with a comfortable country decor and feel. The first guest room has a queen-size bed and private hall bath. The second is a ground-floor accommodation with private entrance, living room with working fireplace, bedroom with queen-size bed, private bath, a butler's kitchen with microwave, no stove. Cats in residence (main house). No smoking. Full breakfast. $65-90.

147. This elegant brick townhouse features eclectic decor with a flair including antiques, contemporary pieces, and a collection of oriental which cover the mirror-finished antique softwood floors. Accommodations include two entire floor suites nestled between the USNA and St. Johns College. One guest suite is a completely private garden apartment with separate entrance offering full kitchen, sitting area with fireplace, TV, VCR, telephone, double bed, and private bath. The second suite is on the third floor with sitting room, TV, VCR, double bed and private bath. No smoking. A "breakfast-out" option is available. Continental breakfast. $130-150.

149. This restored four-square home built in 1908 is in the Historic District of Annapolis

and offers its guest a combination of Victorian elegance and quiet splendor. The inn is carefully furnished in genuine antiques and period reproductions. There are five distinctively appointed guest rooms with queen-size beds. Semi-private and private baths. A well behaved dog is in residence. Air-conditioned. No smoking. Full buffet breakfast. $75-140.

151. This restored pre-revolutionary Georgian Colonial was built in 1747 as a forensic club by William Paca and associates and is also on the National Register of Historic Places. Amble out the back door to Main Street shopping and restaurants, the city waterfront, and the Naval Academy. Three guest rooms are beautifully decorated with period colonial reproductions, antiques, museum prints, and floral arrangements. All have private baths and either queen- or king-size beds. Cat in residence (Muffin). No smoking. Continental breakfast. $100.

153. This Historic District home is decorated with Colonial and English flair, including antiques and fishnet canopied beds. Oriental and braided rugs adorn pine floors. Special touches as baskets filled with toiletries and bathrobes are provided. Three guest rooms with twin, double, or queen-size canopied bed share a hall bath with shower. No smoking. At breakfast time, serve yourself from the Sheraton sideboard laden with seasonal morning fare. $60-80.

155. A Victorian Historic District home, circa 1858, blended with the comforts of Laura Ashley decor, working fireplaces, antiques, and crafted quilts. Seven guest rooms have queen- or king-size beds and private baths. Two-room suite has a queen-size bed and private bath with whirlpool and cable One-half block from the Naval Academy and the waterfront area. TV. No smoking. Continental breakfast. $70-120.

Chez Amis
Bed and Breakfast

85 East Street, 21401
(410) 263-6631

Renovated 70-year-old corner store offers four guest rooms combining yesteryear ambience with today's conveniences—air conditioning, TVs, and beverage centers. The 19th-century American antiques, original oak store counter, tin ceilings, and Georgia pine floors blend with European and country decor. In historic district one block from city dock, state capitol, and the U.S. Naval Academy. Enjoy romance and warm hospitality in America's sailing capital at "The House of Friends."

Hosts: Don and Mickie Deline
Rooms: 4 (2PB, 2SB) $75-95
Full Breakfast
Credit Cards: A, B
Notes: 2, 5, 10, 11, 14

College House Suites

One College Avenue, 21401-1603
(410) 263-6124

This elegant brick townhouse, nestled between the U.S. Naval Academy and St. John's College, features two suites: the Annapolitan Suite has a fireplace, Laura Ashley decor, and private entrance through the ivy-covered courtyard; the Colonial Suite has superb Oriental rugs, antiques, and

views of Naval Academy grounds. Fresh flowers, bathrobes, toiletries, fruit baskets, and special chocolates enhance the romantic atmosphere. A "breakfast-out" option is available at a $25 rate reduction. Minimum stay: 2 nights.

Hosts: Don and Jo Anne Wolfrey
Suites: 2 (PB) $160
Continental Breakfast
Credit Cards: A, B
Notes: 5, 9, 10, 11, 14

The International
Bed & Breakfast Club, Inc.

504 Amherst Street, Buffalo, NY 14207
(800) 723-4262; FAX (716) 873-4462

In the historic district of Annapolis. Renovated 70-year-old home which had been the site of a corner store; architecturally interesting because of the building's unusual wedge shape and its positioning at the convergence of two streets. Perfect for events at the U.S. Naval Academy and boat shows in "America's Sailing Capital." Guests enjoy the host hospitality, convenient central location, and charming decor. Three guest rooms with private or shared baths. Children welcome. Nonsmoking. Continental plus breakfast. $75-90.

Riverwatch

145 Edgewater Drive, Edgewater, 21037
(410) 974-8152

A spectacular waterfront panorama to remember for a lifetime. Luxurious accommodations include queen- and king-size beds, private baths, waterfront balconies, pool, hot tub, boat dock, and Oriental/contemporary decor. Ample off-street parking. Just minutes from historic Annapolis. Continental-plus breakfast.

Hosts: Karen Dennis and Donald Silawsky
Rooms: 2 (PB) $68-84
Continental Breakfast
Credit Cards: None
Notes: 2, 9, 10, 11, 12, 14

6 Pets welcome; 8 Children welcome; 9 Social drinking allowed; 10 Tennis available; 11 Swimming available; 12 Golf available; 13 Skiing available; 14 May be booked through travel agents.

William Page Inn

8 Martin Street, 21401
(410) 626-1506; (800) 364-4160

Built in 1908, this dark brown, cedar shingle, frame structure was the local Democratic party clubhouse for more than 50 years. Today, its wraparound porch, furnished with Adirondack chairs and striped canvas awnings, presents a distinctive appearance. There are five distinctively appointed guest rooms, with either semi-private or private baths. The entire third floor is a spacious light-filled room, with dormer windows, each with window seat, skylight, sitting area with sofa bed, cable TV, and private bath with whirlpool tub and separate shower. All accommodations include queen-size bed, sitting area, daily housekeeping, central heat and air, and full buffet breakfast. Off-street parking is available at no additional charge. No smoking.

Hosts: Rob Zuchelli and Greg Page
Rooms: 5 (3 PB; 2 SB) $85-150
Full Breakfast
Credit Cards: A. B
Notes: 2, 5, 9, 10, 11, 12, 14

ARNOLD

Bed and Breakfast of Maryland/Traveller in Maryland, Inc.

P.O. Box 2277, Annapolis, 21494-2277
(410) 269-6232; FAX (410) 263-4841

125. A lovely, professionally decorated, two-story home elegantly furnished in antiques and beautiful accessories. Ten-minute drive from Annapolis and Historic District. This home offers a large, formal living room, family room, screened porch, and in-ground swimming pool. The first guest room has a king-size bed and private bath. The second guest room has a double bed and private hall bath. The third has a single bed and may be shared with the sec-

ond guest room. Central air conditioning. No smoking. Full breakfast. $50-80.

BALTIMORE

Admiral Fell Inn

888 South Broadway, 21231
(410) 522-7377; (800) 292-INNS
FAX (410) 522-0707

This charming historic inn on the waterfront has 38 guest rooms that are uniquely appointed with Federal period reproductions. The restaurant features New American cuisine and seafood specialities in an intimate atmosphere, as well as light fare and spirits in the casual English-style pub. Specially catered meetings, receptions, and banquets up to 125 people are also available.

Host: Dominik Eckenstein
Rooms: 38 (PB) $98-165
Continental Breakfast
Credit Cards: A, B, C, D
Notes: 3, 4, 5, 7, 8, 9, 10, 12, 14

Amanda's Bed and Breakfast

1428 Park Avenue, 21217
(410) 225-0001; (800) 899-7533
(410) 728-8957

102. A four-story row house in historic Mt. Vernon neighborhood has a king-size bed and private bath. Only minutes away from the Inner Harbor, shopping, and restaurants. Ride the new Light Rail to Oriole Park at Camden Yards and Inner Harbor. Continental breakfast. $75.

109. A colorful 18th-century community, Fell's Point is the location for this wonderfully renovated urban inn at the water's edge. All rooms feature private baths and are individually designed and decorated with antiques and period reproductions. Other attractions include an English pub and elegant dining room. $85-up.

NOTES: Credit cards accepted: A MasterCard; B Visa; C American Express; D Discover Card; E Diner's Club; F Other; 2 Personal checks accepted; 3 Lunch available; 4 Dinner available; 5 Open all year;

110. Tudor-style guest house, near Johns Hopkins University Homewood campus, is just minutes from the Inner Harbor, convention center, and stadium. The neighborhood is bordered by two parks and a lake. Biking, fitness track, and public golf course are all within walking distance. Full breakfast. One queen-size. Private bath. $70.

111. Federal-style townhouse offers two delightful guest rooms and is within walking distance of Inner Harbor. Convention center, other meeting centers, financial district, sports arena, Harbor Place, galleries, museums, theaters, and restaurants are all nearby. One double; one twin. Shared baths. $50-60.

117. Restored 18th-century townhouse in historic Fell's Point, a waterfront community with unique shops and restaurants. Inner Harbor is just one mile away either by walking, water taxi, or trolley. Continental breakfast. Three doubles. Private baths. $80-95.

119. Elegant Victorian mansion is decorated with imported antiques and is in historic Mt. Vernon near Antique Row. All 15 guest rooms/suites offer private baths, kitchenettes, and meeting facilities. Ride the Light Rail to Camden Yards and Inner Harbor or walk to the harbor just ten blocks away. Fine dining is nearby. Continental breakfast. $85-105.

131. Downtown historic neighborhood townhouse is furnished with antiques and is on a quiet street facing a park. Public transportation, cultural center, and churches are all nearby. The guest room is a large king-size suite with all the amenities and with private kitchenette. Swimming pool privileges. $85.

186. Restored Victorian townhouse nestled in the Union Square historic district and just minutes away from the Inner Harbor, convention center, and the new sports complex in Camden Station. The rooms, with double beds and private baths, are decorated with period furnishings. Full breakfast. $80-120.

190. Charmingly historic, intimate waterfront retreat is in Fell's Point. This bed and breakfast is listed on the National Register of Historic Places. Includes English garden, marina, and period furnishings. Restaurants and shops are within walking distance and a water taxi is available from May to October. Smoke-free. Continental breakfast. All rooms have private baths, some have a water view. $110-150.

195. An attractive Federal Hill row house, just one and one-half blocks from the science center and Inner Harbor, within walking distance to sites, attractions, restaurants, and shopping. Water taxi is available for rides around harbor. The guest room has a queen-size bed, private bath, and is bright and airy. Great breakfast. $85.

201. Waterfront Manor house built in 1900 with large light-filled room, decorated with antiques and collectibles. Docking privileges, swimming pool, excellent seafood restaurants, and quiet setting. Master suite with fireplace and Jacuzzi. Full breakfast. $75-125.

225. In Charles Village near Johns Hopkins University. The decor spans a century of styles, from the Victorian to the contemporary. All rooms have brass fixtures, English soaps, amenities, hair dryers, alarm clocks, air conditioning, and color televisions. Continental breakfast served to room. Double beds; private baths. $69-129.

226. Built in 1897, the official guest house of the city of Baltimore is comprised of three townhouses in historic Mt. Vernon. Guests are treated to personalized service, private baths, ornate and unusual decor.

6 Pets welcome; 8 Children welcome; 9 Social drinking allowed; 10 Tennis available; 11 Swimming available; 12 Golf available; 13 Skiing available; 14 May be booked through travel agents.

Amanda's Bed and Breakfast *(continued)*

Great location with guest parking. Continental breakfast. $100-125.

236. Enjoy a relaxing time by the fireplace in the guest parlor, walk to the Inner Harbor, snooze in queen-size bed with private bath, and start the day with a satisfying breakfast. A sunny Federal Hill row house, open spiral staircase. $110.

265. This Federal-style townhouse was built in 1982. Features include three stories, patio, garden in back, fireplace in den and living room. Two rooms with double beds. A springer spaniel, Rocky, loves people. Continental breakfast is served in the dining room. $65-75.

312. Restored carriage house in historic Charles Village, near Johns Hopkins University. Also convenient to the Inner Harbor. Parking on premises. King-size or double bed, bath, washer/dryer. Self-catered breakfast. $100.

330. Historic Bolton Hill just two blocks from the Light Rail to Camden Yards or the Inner Harbor. Primarily a residential neighborhood with tree-lined streets, marble steps, and large early 19th-century row houses. One room with private bath with Jacuzzi tub. $95.

346. Federal Hill, a residential/commercial area on the south side of the Inner Harbor. Walk to the many activities, restaurants, and shops at the harbor. Also walk to Oriole Park at Camden Yards. Private little house with two bedrooms. Self-catered breakfast. $125-165.

Bed and Breakfast of Maryland/Traveller in Maryland, Inc.

P.O. Box 2277, Annapolis, 21494-2277
(410) 269-6232; FAX (410) 263-4841

157. Experience the charm and character of these recently restored and renovated two-hundred-year-old townhomes a half-block off the waterfront of historic Fell's Point. Great care went into preserving much of the original woodwork and fireplace mantles. Eleven original fireplaces, one of which is in the large bathroom on the third floor. Walking distance to several restaurants and pubs. Main house features two guest rooms: one has a fireplace, double rope bed, and private bath; the other has twin beds and a private bath. A third guest room is on the second floor of the annex with a double bed and private bath. The fourth accommodation is a two-room suite with sitting area, fireplace, bedroom with double bed and private bath. Private patios are to the rear of each townhome. No smoking. Continental breakfast. $80-95.

159. A Federal-period townhouse built in 1830, which later took on an Italianate appearance with the addition of a fourth floor and additional cornice work to the exterior during the Victorian period. On the first floor there is a sitting room with grand piano, comfortable chairs, sofa, and fireplace. Two guest rooms with double beds and a shared hall bath. The dining room features a banquet table, circa 1790, with 12 matching chairs, where a full sumptuous breakfast is served daily. No smoking. $75.

161. This small urban inn is an exciting combination of European charm of the bed and breakfast and the warm hospitality of the American country inn. Walking distance of "Antique" and "Boutique" rows, which are continuous avenues of antique shops and galleries. Surrounding the inn are the Meyerhoff Symphony Hall, the 1904 Lyric Opera House, Maryland Institute College of Art, the Theatre Project, and the School of Performing Arts. On-site bar and restaurant. Fifteen guest accommodations with private baths, tastefully decorated with rich Baltimorean artwork, antique furniture, brass beds, and fresh flowers. Restricted smoking area. Continental breakfast. $90-140.

Betsy's Bed and Breakfast

1428 Park Avenue, 21217-4230
(800) 899-7533

This four-story "petite" estate in downtown Bolton Hill is on a tree-lined street with white marble steps and brass rails. This spacious home features a hallway laid in alternating strips of oak and walnut, ceiling medallions, six marble mantels, and a center staircase that rises to meet a skylight. The expansive walls are hung with handsome brass rubbings and family heirloom quilts. Guests may relax in a hot tub shaded by a large pin oak tree in season.

Host: Betsy Grater
Rooms: 2 (PB) $75
Full Breakfast
Credit Cards: A, B, C, D
Notes: 2, 5, 9, 11

Celie's Waterfront Bed and Breakfast

Historic Fell's Point, 1714 Thames Street, 21231
(410) 522-2323; (800) 432-0184
FAX (410) 522-2324

On Baltimore Harbor. Ideal for business or pleasure. Seven air-conditioned guest rooms, one wheelchair accessible, others also accessible to a private garden and harbor view roof deck. Some with whirlpools, fireplaces, private balconies, and harbor views, in a relaxed atmosphere. Private telephones, FAX, TV, marina close by. Minutes to Harbor Place, central business district, and Orioles Stadium by water taxi.

Host: Celie Ives
Rooms: 7 (PB) $100-160
Continental Breakfast
Credit Cards: A, B, C, D
Notes: 2, 5, 8 (over 10), 9, 14

Mr. Mole Bed and Breakfast

1601 Bolton Street, 21217
(410) 728-1179

Selected a "romantic hideaway" by *Discerning Traveler,* and "decorated like a designers' showcase home." Amid quiet, tree-lined streets in historic district, Bolton Hill, two miles north of Inner Harbor. This 1870 row house has 14-foot ceilings and some two-bedroom suites. Private phone and bath, garage parking (with automatic garage door opener), and large Continental breakfast included. Near symphony, opera, museums, art galleries, Antique Row, Johns Hopkins University, and Orioles Park. Member of the Maryland Bed and Breakfast Association, AAA approved.

Hosts: Collin Clarke and Paul Bragaw
Rooms: 5 (PB) $95-125
Continental Breakfast
Credit Cards: A, B, C, D
Notes: 2, 5, 9, 14

The Paulus Gasthaus

2406 Kentucky Avenue, 21213
410-467-1688

Guests have described the Paulus Gasthaus as the best little bed and breakfast within the eastern American corridor. This European Tudor home is four and a half miles from Inner Harbor, very close to Johns Hopkins, theaters, and best seafood restaurants, and convenient to all major highways. Lovely residential neighborhood. The hosts offer quality accommodations and full American or German breakfast. Fluent German and some French spoken. Lots of Gemuetlichkeit (personal service). Within walking distance to public golf, tennis courts, and fitness trails.

6 Pets welcome; 8 Children welcome; 9 Social drinking allowed; 10 Tennis available; 11 Swimming available; 12 Golf available; 13 Skiing available; 14 May be booked through travel agents.

Hosts: Lucie and Ed Paulus
Rooms: 2 (1 PB; 2 SB) $70
Full Breakfast
Credit Cards: A, B, C
Notes: 2, 5, 9, 10, 12, 14

Twin Gates

Twin Gates
Bed and Breakfast Inn

308 Morris Avenue, Historic Lutherville, 21093
(301) 252-3131; (800) 635-0370

A peaceful Victorian mansion and gardens, just minutes from Baltimore's attractions: the National Aquarium, Harbor place, and Maryland hunt country. Friendly hosts, wine and cheese, and gourmet breakfasts. Two-night minimum stay weekends and holidays.

Hosts: Gwen and Bob Vaughan
Rooms: 6 (PB) $95-135
Full Breakfast
Credit Cards: A, B, C
Notes: 2, 5, 9, 10, 12, 14

BERLIN

Amanda's
Bed and Breakfast

1428 Park Avenue, 21217
(410) 225-0001; (800) 899-7533
(410) 728-8957

164. Spacious grounds, quiet peaceful setting near great restaurants and the ocean. Beautifully restored early 19th-century Victorian with wraparound porch. All rooms are decorated with quality antiques. Honeymoon suite with Jacuzzi. Full breakfast. $125-150.

Atlantic Hotel
Inn and Restaurant

2 North Main Street, 21811
(301) 641-3589

Restored Victorian hotel with 16 period-furnished rooms. A national register building in the historic district. Elegant dining and piano lounge on the premises. Eight miles west of Ocean City and Assateague Island National Seashore. Walk to nearby antique shops, gallery, and museum.

Host: Stephen T. Jacques
Rooms: 16 (PB) $65-135
Full Breakfast
Credit Cards: A, B
Notes: 2, 3, 4, 5, 8, 9, 10, 11, 12

Bed and Breakfast
of Maryland/Traveller
in Maryland, Inc.

P.O. Box 2277, Annapolis, 21494-2277
(410) 269-6232; FAX (410) 263-4841

171. This faithfully restored 1895 Victorian inn was placed on the National Register of Historic Places in 1980. Carefully restored to its former elegance and grandeur, it is in the center of Berlin's Historic District; eight miles from Ocean City and Assateague National Seashore. All sixteen guest rooms have private bath, air conditioning and direct dial telephones. Each room is furnished with antiques and is unique in its decor. Restricted smoking area. Continental breakfast. $60-108.

Merry Sherwood Plantation

8909 Worchester Highway, 21811
(410) 641-2112; (800) 660-0358

NOTES: Credit cards accepted: A MasterCard; B Visa; C American Express; D Discover Card; E Diner's Club; F Other; 2 Personal checks accepted; 3 Lunch available; 4 Dinner available; 5 Open all year;

Merry Sherwood Plantation, circa 1859, was listed on the National Register of Historic Places in 1991. A wonderful blend of Greek Revival, Classic Italianate, and Gothic architecture, this elegant 27-room mansion has nine Victorian-style fireplaces, private baths, ballroom, 19 acres of 19th-century landscaping, and authentic period antiques. Convenient to Ocean City and many historic and resort attractions.

Host: Kirk Burbage
Rooms: 8 (6 PB; 2 SB)
Full Breakfast
Credit Cards: A, B
Notes: 2, 5, 10, 11, 12, 14

Merry Sherwood Plantation

BETTERTON

Amanda's Bed and Breakfast

1428 Park Avenue, Baltimore, 21217
(410) 225-0001; (800) 899-7533
FAX (410) 728-8957

162. The mouth of the Sassafras River and the headwaters of the Chesapeake Bay open up to this restored 1904 Victorian inn in the resort town of Betterton. In the heart of goose and duck hunting country, this inn is one block from the beach, biking, boating, and wildlife refuges. Full breakfast. Seven rooms, private and shared baths. $60-85.

Lantern Inn

115 Ericsson Avenue, 21610
(410) 348-5809; (800) 499-7265

A restored 1904 inn in a quiet town on Maryland's Eastern Shore. One and one-half blocks to a nice sand beach on Chesapeake Bay. Near historic Chestertown, hiking trails, and three wildlife refuges. Miles of excellent biking roads, with detailed maps provided. Antiquing and good seafood restaurants abound.

Hosts: Ken and Ann Washburn
Rooms: 13 (4 PB; 9 SB) $68-85
Full Breakfast
Credit Cards: A, B
Notes: 2, 5, 9, 10, 11

BUCKEYSTOWN

The Inn at Buckeystown

3521 Buckeystown Pike, 21717
(301) 874-5755; (800) 272-1190

An award-winning, full service country inn occupies this 1897 Victorian mansion and an 1884 Gothic church in the heart of a village listed on the National Register of Historic Places. Furnished with period art and antiques. Opened in 1981, it is noted for food, hospitality, and luxury. Sixty to 70 percent of the guests are repeats; holidays and the changing seasons are celebrated with gusto, and meals are always special occasions. Dinner, dinner tax, and tip are included in the rates.

Hosts: Daniel R. Pelz, Chase Barnett, Rebecca E. Smith
Rooms: 7 (PB) $167-272
Full Breakfast
Credit Cards: A, B, C
Notes: 2, 4, 5, 9, 10, 11, 12, 13, 14

BURTONSVILLE

Amanda's Bed and Breakfast

1428 Park Avenue, Baltimore, 21217
(410) 225-0001; (800) 899-7533
FAX (410) 728-8957

176. The contemporary charm of the guest house features an airy living/dining area highlighted by a yellow pine interior, cathedral ceilings, and an expansive picture window with a spectacular view. Join in the harmony of nature and hospitality. Two queen suites with private bath, and one king suite with private bath. $80-110.

Bed and Breakfast of Maryland/Traveller in Maryland, Inc.

P.O. Box 2277, Annapolis, 21494-2277
(410) 269-6232; FAX (410) 263-4841

204. The contemporary charm of this guest house features an airy living/dining area highlighted by a yellow pine interior, cathedral ceilings, and an expansive picture window offering an uninterrupted view of the natural surroundings. Guests can enjoy sunny mornings on the outdoor deck, afternoon tea in the greenhouse, or cool nights by the fireplace. Come enjoy life on a working horse farm and equestrian center, tour the 18th-century log cabin with herb and flower gardens, stroll along the miles of wooded trails bordering the Rocky gorge reservoir, and get a glimpse of the deer, waterfowl and other natural wildlife occupying more than 1000 acres of adjacent wooded watershed. The two guest rooms have private baths and are furnished with a unique sleep system that allows guests to achieve their own comfort level by adjusting the firmness of the mattress. No smoking. Full breakfast. $75-105.

CABIN JOHN

The Winslow Home

8217 Canaway Street, 20818
(301) 229-4654

Guests may enjoy the best of two worlds while staying at the Winslow Home. This comfortable home is in a lovely residential section of Bethesda, just 20 minutes from downtown Washington, D.C. Imagine touring the Capital with some extra pocket money saved on high hotel costs. Guests are welcome to use the kitchen, laundry facilities, and piano. Georgetown and George Washington and American universities are close by. There is a $5 surcharge for one-night stays.

Host: Janie Winslow
Rooms: 2 (SB) $45
Full Breakfast
Credit Cards: None
Notes: 2, 8, 12

CAMBRIDGE

Bed and Breakfast of Maryland/Traveller in Maryland, Inc.

P.O. Box 2277, Annapolis, 21494-2277
(410) 269-6232; FAX (410) 263-4841

175. The "Cottage" is a gracious suite in a garden setting, with a spacious living and dining room with a view of its own fountain. Complete kitchen, fully equipped. Bedroom has either twin or king-size bed and the sitting room a queen-size sofa sleeper. TV, phone, and air conditioning provided. The "Carriage House" is in a country setting, with fully equipped kitchen, bedroom with twin canopied beds, a spacious living room with double sofa sleeper, TV, phone, and air conditioning. Relax after a fun-filled day of exploring the local by-ways on your patio under great old trees overlooking the broad sweep of gardens. Easy access to ocean and other interesting attractions such as fishing, hunting, bird watching, biking, antique shopping, and Blackwater National Wildlife Refuge. No smoking. Stocked Continental breakfast. $75-85.

Sarke Plantation Inn

6033 Todd Point Road, 21613
(410) 228-7020

Sarke Plantation Inn

An Eastern Shore waterfront property of 27 country acres with a spacious house that is furnished tastefully with many antiques. There is a large pool room with a regulation table, and the living room has a large fireplace, a good stereo system, and a grand piano for guests' enjoyment. Closed New Year's Eve.

Host: Genevieve Finley
Rooms: 5 (3 PB; 2 SB) $50-90
Continental Breakfast
Credit Cards: A, B, C
Notes: 2, 5, 6, 7, 8 (over 10), 9, 11

CASCADE

Amanda's Bed and Breakfast

1428 Park Avenue, Baltimore, 21217
(410) 225-0001; (800) 899-7533
FAX (410) 728-8957

261. Visit the Blue Ridge Summit and Cascade, the undiscovered summer hideaway. Explore Gettysburg or Frederick, ski, or hike. This elegant 1900 manor house on the Mason Dixon line offers gracious old-fashioned porches, luxury, and beauty. Four rooms available. Fireplace. Jacuzzi. $95-125.

CHESAPEAKE CITY

Bed and Breakfast of Maryland/Traveller in Maryland, Inc.

P.O. Box 2277, Annapolis, 21494-2277
(410) 269-6232; FAX (410) 263-4841

190. Relax on three porches or meet other guests in two comfortable parlors of this Georgian-style inn. The inn was built in 1844 and was occupied by renowned author Jack Hunter during the period in which he wrote his famous book *The Blue Max*, the story of the highest honor in the German air force. Six comfortably furnished guest accommodations with private baths. Families welcome. No smoking. No pets. Continental breakfast. $65-85.

Inn at the Canal

104 Bohemia Avenue, P.O. Box 187, 21915
(410) 885-5995

This elegant 1870 Victorian inn sits in the midst of the quaint historical district on the banks of the busy Chesapeake and Delaware Canal. Private baths, six antique-filled rooms, a full breakfast, and some of the best ocean-going and pleasure boat watching are all to be found at the inn.

Hosts: Mary and Al Ioppolo
Rooms: 6 (PB) $70-105
Full Breakfast
Credit Cards: A, B, C, D, E
Notes: 2, 5, 9, 10, 11, 12, 14

Inn at the Canal

6 Pets welcome; 8 Children welcome; 9 Social drinking allowed; 10 Tennis available; 11 Swimming available; 12 Golf available; 13 Skiing available; 14 May be booked through travel agents.

CHESTERTOWN

Amanda's Bed and Breakfast

1428 Park Avenue, Baltimore, 21217
(410) 225 0001; (800) 899-7533
FAX (410) 728-8957

136. The inn sits on the Chester River, four miles below town. The original part of the house was built in the 1830s and was completely renovated prior to its opening as an inn in 1985. Five acres of waterfront make up the grounds, and a marina offers deepwater slips. Five rooms, all with private baths, are available. Continental breakfast. $85-115.

204. This Victorian inn was built in 1877 and is in the heart of town. Restored to its original charm, the dining room and double parlor feature plaster moldings. Walk to historic Washington College and shops. Five rooms, all with private baths, are available. Continental breakfast. $75-135.

205. Lovely brick Georgian manor house sitting at the mouth of the Fairlee Creek and the Chesapeake Bay. Twelve acres of landscaped grounds. Golfing, swimming, and tennis accessible. Small conferences. Eleven rooms, each with a private bath. $80-165.

Bed and Breakfast of Maryland/Traveller in Maryland, Inc.

P.O. Box 2277, Annapolis, 21494-2277
(410) 269-6232; FAX (410) 263-4841

192. Built in 1877, this beautifully restored inn is one of the finest Victorian houses in Chestertown. Only a short walk to the historic Washington College and the shops of High Street. All seven guest rooms are dec-

orated in period furnishings and have private baths. Restricted smoking area. Continental breakfast. $50-110.

The Parker House

108 Spring Avenue, 21620
(410) 778-9041

The Parker House is a charming bed and breakfast in the historic district of historic Chestertown, Maryland. The warm conviviality created by the Parkers has drawn warm praise from satisfied guests. The 1876 house is one of the most famous in Chestertown.

Hosts: Marcy and John Parker
Rooms: 3 (1 PB; 2 SB) $80-110
Continental Breakfast
Credit Cards: None
Notes: 5, 6, 8, 9, 10, 11, 12

The River Inn at Rolph's Wharf

1008 Rolph's Wharf Road, 21620
(410) 778-6347; (800) 894-6347

The River Inn is an 1830s Victorian inn on the scenic Chester River, just three miles south of Chestertown, Maryland. All guest rooms have private baths and a view of the river. Light breakfast is served with fresh squeezed orange juice, and a restaurant is on premises for lunch or dinner. A boat ramp, ice, bait, and a pool are also available. The view is terrific!

Rooms: 6 (PB), $65-115
Continental Breakfast
Credit Cards: A, B, C, D
Notes: 2, 3, 4, 5, 7, 8, 9

The White Swan Tavern

231 High Street, 21620
(301) 778-2300

The White Swan has been a landmark in Chestertown since pre-Revolutionary War days. A quiet, elegant place nestled on Maryland's Eastern Shore, with a history that goes

---

NOTES: Credit cards accepted: A MasterCard; B Visa; C American Express; D Discover Card; E Diner's Club; F Other; 2 Personal checks accepted; 3 Lunch available; 4 Dinner available; 5 Open all year;

back to before 1733, it was returned to its original purpose in 1978: "A comfortable tavern or Public House...situated in the center of business...with every attention given to render comfort and pleasure to such as favor it with their patronage."

Host: Mary Susan Maisel
Rooms: 6 (PB) $100-150
Continental Breakfast
Credit Cards: None
Notes: 2, 5, 7, 8, 9, 10, 11, 12, 14

Widow's Walk Inn

402 High Street, 21620
(301) 778-6455; (301) 778-6864

This restored Victorian home, circa 1877, in the historic district features elegant decorations. In the heart of the Eastern Shore, famous for crabs and geese. Only 90 minutes from Baltimore, Philadelphia, and Washington, D.C. Everyone's dream of old-fashioned family warmth and charm. Weekday and business rates are available.

Hosts: Don and Joanne Toft
Rooms: 5 (1 PB, 4 SB) $85-110
Suites: 2
Continental Breakfast
Credit Cards: F
Notes: 2, 5, 9, 10, 11, 12

Widow's Walk Inn

CHEVY CHASE

Chevy Chase Bed and Breakfast

6815 Connecticut Avenue, 20815
(301) 656-5867

Enjoy gracious hospitality and the convenience of being close to the sights of Washington, D.C., in a charming beamed-ceiling, turn-of-the-century house and garden in historic Chevy Chase. Furnished with rare tapestries, Oriental rugs, and native crafts from around the world. Special breakfasts of homemade breads and muffins, jams, cheeses, fresh fruits, and a special blend of Louisiana coffee.

Host: S. C. Gotbaum
Rooms: 2 (PB) $55-70
Full Breakfast
Credit Cards: None
Notes: 2, 5, 8, 10, 11, 12, 14

CLARKSVILLE

Amanda's Bed and Breakfast

1428 Park Avenue, Baltimore, 21217
(410) 225-0001; (800) 899-7533
FAX (410) 728-8957

350. A renovated antique shop in an old barn. Pleasantly created space with sitting and eating area with kitchenette. Separate bedroom and bath. Plank floors and beamed ceilings. Double bed. Furnished with country antiques. Scenic trails and picnic by pond. $125.

CRISFIELD

Amanda's Bed and Breakfast

1428 Park Avenue, Baltimore, 21217
(410) 225-0001; (800) 899-7533
FAX (410) 728-8957

290. Lovingly restored and decorated with antiques, this Queen Anne-style home has grandeur and charm. In town, walk to docks and touring boats. Four rooms, each with a private bath. $85.

CUMBERLAND

Bed and Breakfast of Maryland/Traveller in Maryland, Inc.

P.O. Box 2277, Annapolis, 21494-2277
(410) 269-6232; FAX (410) 263-4841

210. This inn is an established classic country inn offering its guests charming and comfortable accommodations in either the 1820 Cowden House or the 1890 Dent House. Within walking distance of historical landmarks and museums. Cowden House has eight rooms. The Dent House has five rooms. All guest accommodations have either a private or shared bath facility. The inn offers two parlors and a television room for all overnight guests. No smoking. Full breakfast. $70-100.

Inn at Walnut Bottom

120 Greene Street, 21502
(301) 777-0003; (800) 286-9718

Traditional country inn bed and breakfast in the city of Cumberland, Maryland. Twelve guest rooms and family suites, two parlors, gift shop, private parking. 1815 and 1890 buildings beautifully refurbished. Private telephones and color TVs in guest rooms. Full breakfast served with overnight lodging. The Oxford House Restaurant serves traditional and gourmet food to inn guests and the public daily. Walk to the Scenic Railroad, the Historic District, and live theater. Bicycle rentals for C&O Canal Towpath nearby.

Inn at Walnut Bottom

Host: Sharon Ennis Kazary
Rooms: 12 (8 PB; 4 SB) $60-95
Suites $95-120
Full Breakfast
Credit Cards: A, B, C, D
Notes: 3, 4, 5, 8, 11, 12, 13, 14

DAVIDSONVILLE

Bed and Breakfast of Maryland/Traveller in Maryland, Inc.

P.O. Box 2277, Annapolis, 21494-2277
(410) 269-6232; FAX (410) 263-4841

135. This rambling country-style home is situated on three acres of rolling knolls in Anne Arundel Counties horse raising community on the outskirts of Annapolis. The eclectic furnishings blend well with the seasoned traveler. Living room and den with TV. Outdoor deck. A great pivot point for Annapolis, Baltimore, and Washington, D.C. sightseeing. Two guest rooms, double or twin beds, have private hall baths. No smoking. Full breakfast. $50-55.

NOTES: Credit cards accepted: A MasterCard; B Visa; C American Express; D Discover Card; E Diner's Club; F Other; 2 Personal checks accepted; 3 Lunch available; 4 Dinner available; 5 Open all year;

EASTON

Amanda's Bed and Breakfast

1428 Park Avenue, Baltimore, 21217
(410) 225-0001; (800) 899-7533
FAX (410) 728-8957

118. This charming 1890 Victorian bed and breakfast is registered in the historic section of Easton, the Colonial capital of Maryland's Eastern Shore. Within walking distance of historical points of interest, restaurants, and antique shops, this inn has a wraparound porch and offers seven guest rooms, all with private baths. Continental breakfast. $70-85.

235. A lovely 60-acre estate with a large Georgian plantation home built in 1760. Several original dependency buildings are also on the property. A romantic getaway. Great for weddings, small conferences, or retreats. Dock, pool, chipping course, croquet, and walking trails.

Bed and Breakfast of Maryland/Traveller in Maryland, Inc.

P.O. Box 2277, Annapolis, 21494-2277
(410) 269-6232; FAX (410) 263-4841

177. The roots of this urban inn go back over 265 years when the Talbot County Courthouse was moved here from Oxford. In 1891, a new frame inn was erected on the site of the present day establishment. The inn met its fate by fire in 1947. But, like the phoenix, a new inn took flight. In 1948 the inn reopened to a reception of over 4000 persons. Today, as in the early 1700s, hospitality lives once again. 114 beautifully decorated guest accommodations and suites with private baths, TV, and telephone. Full service restaurant and professional staff await. Restricted smoking area. Continental breakfast. $114-295.

179. This charming Victorian home is registered in the historic section of Easton, colonial capital of Maryland's Eastern Shore. Built circa 1890, the inn has a high octagonal tower, a hipped roof with dormers and a southern wraparound porch for a relaxing afternoon or evening rest. All seven guest accommodations are spacious and bright. Each accommodation is equipped with air conditioning, ceiling fans, and a choice of private or shared bath. No smoking. Resident cat. Continental breakfast. $70-85.

The Bishop's House Bed and Breakfast

214 Goldsborough Street, P.O. Box 2217, 21601
(410) 820-7290; (800) 223-7290

This Victorian home, circa 1880, is within three blocks of boutiques, antique shops, and restaurants; within ten miles of historic Oxford and St. Michaels. Romantically furnished in period style, the Bishop's House features air conditioning, whirlpool tubs, working fireplaces, private off-street parking, secured overnight storage for bicycles, route maps for cycling, and sumptuous breakfasts. Prearranged transportation to and from local marinas and Easton Airport provided at no additional charge. Small business group retreats/planning sessions or private social functions welcome.

Hosts: Diane M. Laird-Ippolito and
   John B. Ippolito
Rooms: 6 (4 PB; 2 SB) $75-110
Full Breakfast
Credit Cards: None
Notes: 2, 5, 10, 12, 14

6 Pets welcome; 8 Children welcome; 9 Social drinking allowed; 10 Tennis available; 11 Swimming available; 12 Golf available; 13 Skiing available; 14 May be booked through travel agents.

The Tidewater Inn and Conference Center

101 East Dover Street, 21601
(410) 822-1300; (800) 237-8775

In Easton, the Colonial capital of the eastern shore, the Tidewater Inn is the perfect setting for a weekend hideaway or sojourn through history. The guest rooms and living rooms are beautifully furnished with fine antique reproductions and fabrics from the 18th century. Guests can relax at the outdoor pool in the summer or enjoy the cozy fireplace during the cold months. Only one hour away from Washington, D.C. Complimentary newspaper and coffee are included; breakfast is available.

Hosts: William N. Quinn Jr.
Rooms: 114 (PB) $139-295
Credit Cards: A, B, C, E
Notes: 3, 4, 5, 6 (limited), 8, 10, 11, 12, 14

EASTPORT

Bed and Breakfast of Maryland/Traveller in Maryland, Inc.

P.O. Box 2277, Annapolis, 21494-2277
(410) 269-6232; FAX (410) 263-4841

133. This contemporary townhouse offers uncomplicated and comfortable furnishings. Walking distance to several sailing schools and Historic District. Ground transportation may be by water taxi to and from the city dock. One guest room with twin beds and private hall bath. Dog in residence. No smoking. Continental breakfast. $55-60.

EDGEWATER

Bed and Breakfast of Maryland/Traveller in Maryland, Inc.

P.O. Box 2277, Annapolis, 21494-2277
(410) 269-6232; FAX (410) 263-4841

115. The views from this three-story waterfront contemporary are spectacular! Nicely decorated with contemporary furnishings and Oriental pieces. Comfortable living room with fireplace and open views of the South River. Wooden deck, hot tub, and inground swimming pool. Two guest rooms have queen- or king-size beds with private baths. Two resident cats. No smoking. Continental breakfast. $65-75.

145. Untroubled lifestyle and tranquility abound in this contemporary home nestled on the banks of Church Creek, a small tributary off of the South River. Gardens are landscaped for seclusion. Two water-view bedrooms with queen-size beds have a private or shared bath. Separate living room with television, VCR, and telephone makes an entire level private to the guest. Upper-level family room and deck are also available for guests. Outdoor cat. No smoking. Full breakfast. $75.

ELKTON

The Garden Cottage

234 Blair Shore Road, 21921
(410) 398-5566

In a setting with an early plantation house, including a 400-year-old sycamore, the Garden Cottage nestles at the edge of a meadow flanked by herb gardens and an old barn with gift shop. It has a sitting room with working fireplace, bedroom, and bath. Freshly ground coffee and herbal teas are offered with the full country breakfast. Longwood Gardens and Winterthur Museum are 50 minutes away. Historic Chesapeake City is seven minutes away.

Hosts: Bill and Ann Stubbs
Cottage: 1 (PB) $85
Full Breakfast
Credit Cards: A, B
Notes: 2, 5, 8, 9, 12. 14

NOTES: Credit cards accepted: A MasterCard; B Visa; C American Express; D Discover Card; E Diner's Club; F Other; 2 Personal checks accepted; 3 Lunch available; 4 Dinner available; 5 Open all year;

ELLICOTT CITY

Bed and Breakfast of Maryland/Traveller in Maryland, Inc.

P.O. Box 2277, Annapolis, 21494-2277
(410) 269-6232; FAX (410) 263-4841

170. A stately Federal-period stone farmhouse situated on two acres with a pond near the historic mill town of Ellicott City. Continuing the tradition of a lighted candle in each window, indicating the availability of rooms, the candles remain lighted as a nostalgic reminder of the inn's past. In the winter months a fire in the parlor fireplace, or the fireplace in the adjoining music room, may encourage guests to linger over a game of chess or checkers. Four guest accommodations with double and queen-size beds. Two have private baths and the two remaining rooms share a hall bath. No smoking. Continental breakfast. $70-90.

FAIRLEE

Bed and Breakfast of Maryland/Traveller in Maryland, Inc.

P.O. Box 2277, Annapolis, 21494-2277
(410) 269-6232; FAX (410) 263-4841

186. This historic Georgian waterfront manor is situated on the Chesapeake Bay. A regal 25-room mansion featuring a spectacular view and twelve acres of luxurious lawns and gardens. A private footpath leads to a quaint, sunny beach with gazebo. Guests have use of a swimming pool, tennis courts, nine-hole golf course and yacht charter service. Nine guest rooms or suites are well-decorated, spacious, and bright with private baths. No smoking. Continental breakfast. $85-165.

FREDERICK

Amanda's Bed and Breakfast

1428 Park Avenue, Baltimore, 21217
(410) 225-0001; (800) 899-7533
FAX (410) 728-8957

106. This inn's 26-acre grounds include a picturesque garden and henhouse. Each room offers a delightful 19th-century ambience, and all rooms have private baths and air conditioning. A stone fireplace, stained-glass windows, and skylights highlight the keeping room where guests can relax. Four rooms, all of which have private baths, are available. Continental breakfast. $95.

Middle Plantation Inn

9549 Liberty Road, 21701
(301) 898-7128

A rustic bed and breakfast built of stone and log. Drive through horse country to the village of Mount Pleasant. Several miles east of Frederick, on 26 acres. Each room has furnishings of antiques with private bath, air conditioning, and TV. Nearby are antique shops, museums, and many historic attractions.

Hosts: Shirley and Dwight Mullican
Rooms: 4 (PB) $85-95
Continental Breakfast
Credit Cards: A, B
Notes: 2, 5, 8 (over 14), 9, 10, 11, 12, 14

Middle Plantation Inn

---

6 Pets welcome; 8 Children welcome; 9 Social drinking allowed; 10 Tennis available; 11 Swimming available;
12 Golf available; 13 Skiing available; 14 May be booked through travel agents.

Turning Point Inn

3406 Urbana Pike, 21701
(301) 874-2421

Turning Point Inn is a 1910 Edwardian estate home with Georgian features. Less than an hour from Washington, D.C., Baltimore, Gettysburg, and Antietam, this inn is situated for getaway weekends of sightseeing, shopping, antiquing, hiking, or exploring historic towns and battlefields.

Host: Charlie Seymour
Rooms: 5 (PB) $75-85
Cottages: 2 (PB) $100-150
Full Breakfast
Credit Cards: A, B, D
Notes: 2, 3 and 4 (limited),5, 8, 9, 10, 11, 12

Turning Point Inn

GAITHERSBURG

Amanda's Bed and Breakfast

1428 Park Avenue, Baltimore, 21217
(410) 225-0001; (800) 899-7533
FAX (410) 728-8957

120. This is a comfortable luxury home in a planned community, with ample parking, a large screened-in porch, close proximity to restaurants and Washington, D.C. Two rooms, both with private baths, are available for guests. Full breakfast. $65-100.

Bed and Breakfast of Maryland/Traveller in Maryland, Inc.

P.O. Box 2277, Annapolis, 21494-2277
(410) 269-6232; FAX (410) 263-4841

198. This two-story, red brick, contemporary, private homestay is furnished in family pieces and has the comfort of the guest in mind. Restaurants, shopping, recreation, and the community lake are nearby. Residential streets provide quiet walks around the lake. Two beautifully furnished guest rooms extend a feeling of warmth and homeyness and share a private hall bath. No smoking. Full breakfast. $55.

Gaithersburg Hospitality Bed and Breakfast

18908 Chimney Place, 20879
(301) 977-7377

In Montgomery Village near restaurants, shopping, and recreation, this luxury home is ideally situated in a residential neighborhood, offers all amenities, and is a 30-minute ride to Washington, D.C. via the car or Metro. It is conveniently situated near I-270 for a drive north to Harpers Ferry, Gettysburg, and Antietam. Hosts delight in catering to travel needs with home cooking and spacious cozy comfort.

Hosts: Joe and Suzanne Danilowicz
Doubles: (PB) $55
Singles: (PB) $45
Full Breakfast
Credit Cards: None
Notes: 2, 8, 10, 11, 12, 14

GALENA

Rosehill Farm Bed and Breakfast

13842 Gregg Neck Road, 21635
(410) 648-5334

NOTES: Credit cards accepted: A MasterCard; B Visa; C American Express; D Discover Card; E Diner's Club; F Other; 2 Personal checks accepted; 3 Lunch available; 4 Dinner available; 5 Open all year;

On 100 scenic acres, Rosehill Farm is close to marinas, excellent restaurants, and historic towns (Chestertown, Easton, and St. Michaels). On the grounds is a working greenhouse which grows miniature roses and ivy topiary. Wildlife abounds with guests frequently seeing fox, deer, geese, ducks, and blue heron, among others. Children, not infants, are welcome. Dog runs available. Guests will experience a thoroughly relaxing visit.

Host: Marie Jolly
Rooms: 3 (PB) $60-70
Continental Breakfast
Credit Cards: None
Notes: 2, 5, 7 (limited), 10, 11, 12

HAGERSTOWN

Amanda's Bed and Breakfast

1428 Park Avenue, Baltimore, 21217
(410) 225-0001; (800) 899-7533
FAX (410) 728-8957

156. An 1890 Queen Anne Victorian on a tree-lined street of grand old homes. Furnished in antiques providing a tranquil setting. Three rooms, one with a private bath. Full breakfast. $75-95.

Beaver Creek House Bed and Breakfast

20432 Beaver Creek Road, 21740
(301) 797-4764

A turn-of-the-century country home filled with family antiques and memorabilia. Five central air-conditioned guest rooms. A full country breakfast is served on the screened porch or elegantly decorated dining room. The parlor with fireplace is the setting for afternoon tea. A sitting room has reading material of local interest. Guests can enjoy a country garden with fish pond and fountain. Visiting historic sites, hiking, biking, skiing, golf, and antiquing are popular recreational pursuits.

Hosts: Don and Shirley Day
Rooms: 5 (3 PB; 2 SB) $75-85
Full Breakfast
Credit Cards: A, B, C, D
Notes: 2, 5, 9, 10, 11, 12, 13, 14

Beaver Creek House

Blue Ridge Bed and Breakfast

Route 2, Box 3895, 22611
(703) 955-1246

A. Large 1890 Victorian filled with beautiful antiques. A culinary delight. Close to downtown shopping. Corporate rates and packages available. $65-75.

B. Turn-of-the-century farmhouse filled with antiques and collectibles in the middle of 125 acres, 40 of which are woods. Hosts speak Spanish, German, and Italian. Close to I-70 and I-81, Antietam battlefield, C & D Canal, Crystal Grottoes Caverns, Potomac River, outlet stores, and antique shops. Children are always welcome. $40-68.

Lewrene Farm Bed and Breakfast

9738 Downsville Pike, 21740
(301) 582-1735

Spacious Colonial country farmhome near I-70 and I-81. Large living room, fireplace, piano, and antique family heirlooms. Deluxe bedrooms with canopied poster beds and other antique beds. Bedside snacks, shared

6 Pets welcome; 8 Children welcome; 9 Social drinking allowed; 10 Tennis available; 11 Swimming available; 12 Golf available; 13 Skiing available; 14 May be booked through travel agents.

Lewrene Farm

and private baths, one of which has a whirlpool. Full breakfast. Home away from home for tourists, business people, families. Children welcome. Peacocks, old-fashioned swing, and a gazebo. Quilts for sale. Antietam battlefield, Harpers Ferry, C&O Canal, and antique malls nearby. 70 miles to Washington and Baltimore.

Hosts: Lewis and Irene Lehman
Rooms: 5 (2 PB; 3 SB) $50-90
Full Breakfast
Credit Cards: A, B
Notes: 2, 5, 8, 10, 11, 12, 13

Spencer Silver Mansion

200 South Union Avenue, 21078
(410) 939-1097

Built in 1896 the Spencer Silver Mansion has been restored to its turn-of-the-century elegance. The five guest rooms are furnished with Victorian antiques and are quite spacious. The Carriage House suite features a fireplace and whirlpool bath. The parlors and dining room feature stained glass, oak floors, and fabulous woodwork. The lavish full breakfast is served at the guest's convenience. In the historic district, just two blocks from the water. Near shops and restaurants. The inn is just two miles off I-95.

Hosts: Carol and Jim Nemeth
Rooms: 5 (3 PB; 2 SB) $65-120
Full Breakfast
Credit Cards: None
Notes: 2, 5, 8, 9, 10, 11, 12, 14

Sunday's Bed and Breakfast

39 Broadway, 21740
(800) 221-4828

In historic Hagerstown, this romantic 1890 Queen Anne Victorian is distinctively furnished with antiques. Guests may want to explore the national historic parks of Antietam, Harpers Ferry, and the C&O Canal. Antique shops, museums, golfing, fishing, skiing, and shopping outlets are all nearby. Full breakfast, afternoon tea and desserts, evening wine and cheese, late-night cordial and truffle, fruit basket, and more await guests.

Host: Bob Ferrino
Rooms: 3 (1 PB; 2 SB) $65-95
Full Breakfast
Credit Cards: None
Notes: 2, 3, 4, 5, 8, 9, 10, 11, 12, 13, 14

Sunday's

HARWOOD

Amanda's Bed and Breakfast

1428 Park Avenue, Baltimore, 21217
(410) 225-0001; (800) 899-7533
FAX (410) 728-8957

NOTES: Credit cards accepted: A MasterCard; B Visa; C American Express; D Discover Card; E Diner's Club; F Other; 2 Personal checks accepted; 3 Lunch available; 4 Dinner available; 5 Open all year;

158. This guest room has a balcony that overlooks a working farm. Ample parking area for a boat trailer or camper. Two rooms share a bath. Just twenty minutes from Annapolis. Continental breakfast. $75.

HAVRE DE GRACE

Amanda's
Bed and Breakfast

1428 Park Avenue, Baltimore, 21217
(410) 225-0001; (800) 899-7533
FAX (410) 728-8957

302. Explore historic Havre de Grace, the upper Chesapeake Bay region, while spending nights in a turn-of-the-century Victorian house, little changed from its original construction. Visit the Concord Paint Lighthouse, a decoy museum, canal museum, a state park; enjoy local seafood and the bay. $60-75.

KINGSTON

Bed and Breakfast
of Maryland/Traveller
in Maryland, Inc.

P.O. Box 2277, Annapolis, 21494-2277
(410) 269-6232; FAX (410) 263-4841

194. This inn, situated on five waterfront acres and nestled on a sweeping bend of the Chester River, boasts a deep water marina. The original part of the house was built in the 1830s and was completely renovated prior to the inn's opening. The inn offers swimming pool and family restaurant featuring fine Eastern Shore food. All six guest accommodations are furnished in the classic style of the house and equipped with private baths. Restricted smoking area. Continental breakfast. $65-115.

LAUREL

Amanda's
Bed and Breakfast

1428 Park Avenue, Baltimore, MD, 21217
(410) 225-0001; (800) 899-7533
FAX (410) 728-8957

217. Peaceful country setting. This 18th-century manor house is listed on the National Register of Historic Places. Ideally situated to experience the flavor of the Eastern Shore. Full breakfast. $65-85.

LUTHERVILLE

Amanda's
Bed and Breakfast

1428 Park Avenue, Baltimore, 21217
(410) 225-0001; (800) 899-7533
FAX (410) 728-8957

128. Serene elegance surrounds this romantic Victorian mansion. Each room is decorated in a different theme from the owner's favorite places. Charming and spacious with a lavish breakfast; seven rooms, five with private baths; two share a bath. Full breakfast. Ride the Light Rail to Oriole Park. $95-125.

Bed and Breakfast
of Maryland/Traveller
in Maryland, Inc.

P.O. Box 2277, Annapolis, 21494-2277
(410) 269-6232; FAX (410) 263-4841

167. A beautifully appointed Victorian home framed by twin gates and a curved driveway. Furnished with whimsical touches throughout, with cozy nooks and corners in the downstairs living rooms, the wide front porch, the lovely gazebo and flower gardens, or the third-floor library. Upon entering the center hall, guests are greeted by the sights and sounds of "com-

6 Pets welcome; 8 Children welcome; 9 Social drinking allowed; 10 Tennis available; 11 Swimming available; 12 Golf available; 13 Skiing available; 14 May be booked through travel agents.

ing home": soft music, fresh flowers, and the smell of muffins baking. Fireplaces are frequently going, either in the living room or in the cozy greeting room next to the dining room. A wide staircase leads to the seven gracious guest rooms with private or shared baths. Each is decorated in a unique style, from the California Suite and Cape May Room to the Maryland Hunt and Pride of Baltimore Rooms. No smoking. Full breakfast. $75-125.

Bowling Brook Country Inn

MIDDLEBURG

Bowling Brook Country Inn

6000 Middleburg Road, 21757
(410) 848-0353

Steeped in the rich tradition of horse racing, Bowling Brook Country Inn represents the modern evolution of a farmhouse built in 1837. All bedrooms include a private bath and color TV, and several rooms feature a large Jacuzzi and king-size canopied bed. Enjoy the amenities of graceful country living—stroll leisurely through the expansive grounds, partake of afternoon tea, wine, and cheese, and simply gaze at the scenery while taking in the country air.

Hosts: Dave and Ginna Welsh
Rooms: 5 (PB) $95-155
Full Breakfast
Credit Cards: A, B, C
Notes: 2, 4, 5, 8, 9, 12, 13

MONKTON

Amanda's Bed and Breakfast

1428 Park Avenue, Baltimore, 21217
(410) 225-0001; (800) 899-7533
FAX (410) 728-8957

209. Warm hospitality and exceptional accommodations are offered on this working farm. Pond with fishing privileges (catch and throw back), bicycling and hiking trails, and tubing on Gunpowder River. Situated near North Central Railroad, Ladew Gardens, and Amish Country. One room is offered to guests, and it features a private bath and fireplace. Continental breakfast. $85.

NEW MARKET

National Pike Inn

9 West Main Street, Box 299, 21774
(301) 865-5055

The National Pike Inn offers five air-conditioned guest rooms, each decorated in a different theme. Private baths are available, and the large Federal sitting room is available for all guests to use. The private enclosed courtyard is perfect for a quiet retreat outdoors. New Market, founded in 1793, offers more than 30 specialized an-

National Pike Inn

NOTES: Credit cards accepted: A MasterCard; B Visa; C American Express; D Discover Card; E Diner's Club; F Other; 2 Personal checks accepted; 3 Lunch available; 4 Dinner available; 5 Open all year;

tique shops, all in historic homes along Main Street. An old-fashioned general store is everyone's favorite, and Mealey's, a well-known retauran, is a few steps away.

Hosts: Tom and Terry Rimel
Rooms: 5 (3 PB; 2 SB) $75-125
Full Breakfast
Credit Cards: A, B
Notes: 2, 5, 8 (over 10), 10, 12, 13 (cross country)

NORTH BEACH

Amanda's Bed and Breakfast

1428 Park Avenue, Baltimore, 21217
(410) 225-0001; (800) 899-7533
FAX (410) 728-8957

356. Calvent Country offers the pleasures of southern Maryland in an original guest house built in 1903. Eight guestrooms. Near a sandy beach and water activities. Mostly private baths. $65-85.

NORTH EAST

The Mill House Bed and Breakfast

102 Mill Lane, 21901
(410) 287-3532

This circa 1710 mill house is completely furnished with antiques. The extensive grounds include mill ruins, a tidal marsh with a variety of wildflowers, and a lawn down to the North East Creek. North East has antique and specialty shops and good restaurants. Boating and golf are nearby. After a restful night in a canopied bed, let a full breakfast with homemade hot breads get the day off to a good start. Open March 1st through December 1st.

Hosts: Lucia and Nick Demond
Rooms: 2 (SB) $65-75
Full Breakfast
Credit Cards: A, B
Notes: 2, 12, 14

OAKLAND

Amanda's Bed and Breakfast

1428 Park Avenue, Baltimore, 21217
(410) 225-0001; (800) 899-7533
FAX (410) 728-8957

157. Recreation land! Water, ice, and snow for year-round fun. Colonial Revival with a large lawn and mature trees in a historic district. Four rooms. Fireside breakfast in dining room. Relax after sporting day in cozy TV room. $55-80.

The Oak and Apple Bed and Breakfast

208 North Second Street, 21550
(301) 334-9265

Built circa 1915, this restored Colonial Revival sits on a beautiful, large lawn with mature trees and includes a large, columned front porch, enclosed sun porch, parlor with fireplace, and cozy gathering room with TV. Awake to a fresh Continental breakfast served fireside in the dining room or on the sun porch. The quaint town of Oakland offers a wonderful small town atmosphere, and Deep Creek Lake, Wisp Ski Resort, and state parks with hiking, fishing, swimming, boating, and skiing are nearby.

Hosts: Jana and Ed Kight
Rooms: 5 (3 PB; 2 SB) $55-80
Continental Breakfast
Credit Cards: A, B
Notes: 2, 5, 9, 10, 11, 12, 13, 14

OCEAN CITY

Amanda's Bed and Breakfast

1428 Park Avenue, Baltimore, 21217
(410) 225-0001; (800) 899-7533
FAX (410) 728-8957

6 Pets welcome; 8 Children welcome; 9 Social drinking allowed; 10 Tennis available; 11 Swimming available; 12 Golf available; 13 Skiing available; 14 May be booked through travel agents.

170. In old Ocean City near the boardwalk and the beach. Parking available. A 14-room bed and breakfast, originally a rooming house for young women. Current owners are local natives and new caring and decorating are a plus. Some private baths. Enjoy good weather off-season.

OXFORD

The 1876 House

110 North Morris Street, P.O. Box 658, 21654-0658
(410) 226-5496

A meticulously restored 19th-century residence with three guest accommodations with private baths and air conditioning. In historic Oxford, this home features ten-foot ceilings, wide-planked pine floors, and Oriental carpeting. Furnishings are mostly Queen Anne reproductions and decor in the Williamsburg style. A cozy living room with fireplace is a popular gathering place for fall and winter guests. The Continental-plus breakfast is served in a formal dining room from 8:00 A.M. to 9:30 A.M. ABBA inspected and rated; excellent rating.

Rooms: 3 (PB) $92-97
Continental Breakfast
Credit Cards: F
Notes: 2, 5, 7, 9, 10, 11, 12

PASADENA

Amanda's Bed and Breakfast

1428 Park Avenue, Baltimore, 21217
(410) 225-0001; (800) 899-7533
FAX (410) 728-8957

231. A lovely setting on the water, this waterfront community called Sunset Knoll is on one and one-half acres on the Magothy River about 15 minutes from downtown Annapolis. Quiet and convenient to Annapolis, Washington D.C., or Baltimore.

Two rooms, one double, one queen, and private baths are available for guests. Full breakfast. $85.

PINEY POINT

Amanda's Bed and Breakfast

1428 Park Avenue, Baltimore, 21217
(410) 225-0001; (800) 899-7533
FAX (410) 728-8957

199. On the Potomac River with sandy beach in front. A gazebo on the beach has a lovely view of the water, passing boats, and birds. Quiet and peaceful. A 20-minute drive to St. Marys or Solmons Island. Private bath. $75.

POTOMAC

Amanda's Bed and Breakfast

1428 Park Avenue, Baltimore, 21217
(410) 225-0001; (800) 899-7533
FAX (410) 728-8957

198. Early American furnishings compliment the charm of this forested, single-family dwelling situated in Maryland's suburbs of Washington, D.C. Two rooms, both of which have a private bath, are available. Continental breakfast. $65-75.

PRINCE FREDERICK

Amanda's Bed and Breakfast

1428 Park Avenue, Baltimore, 21217
(410) 225-0001; (800) 899-7533
FAX (410) 728-8957

153. This century-old farmhouse with a wraparound porch is in a country setting of fields, woods, and a view of the river. The

---

NOTES: Credit cards accepted: A MasterCard; B Visa; C American Express; D Discover Card; E Diner's Club; F Other; 2 Personal checks accepted; 3 Lunch available; 4 Dinner available; 5 Open all year;

private suite for guests includes a parlor and separate entrance. Situated near Chesapeake Bay, Broomes Island, and Cypress Swamp. A full breakfast is served each morning. $90.

PRINCESS ANNE

Amanda's Bed and Breakfast

1428 Park Avenue, Baltimore, 21217
(410) 225-0001; (800) 899-7533
FAX (410) 728-8957

188. This authentically restored Federal-style home is on the National Register of Historic Places and is on a 160-acre farm near the ocean and bay. A popular activity for guests is crabbing and oystering along a mile-long shoreline on the Manokin River, and shallow draft boats are welcome. Four rooms, plus two cottages, are available. Private baths. Full breakfast. $95-135.

Elmwood Circa 1770 Bed and Breakfast

Route 3, Locust Point Road, 21853
(410) 651-1066

Elmwood Bed and Breakfast, circa 1770, is one of the most distinctive Federal-style plantation houses in Somerset County. It has a grand setting on 160 acres of woods, fields, and lawn, with a mile of waterfront; splendid tranquility. The goal of the innkeepers is to surround their guests with the life-style of the 19th century. Two-night minimum stay. Closed December 20th through January 3rd.

Hosts: Helen and Steve Monick
Rooms: 4 (3 PB; 1 SB) $85-97
Cottage: 1 $125
Full Breakfast
Credit Cards: A, B, C
Notes: 2, 7 and 8 (limited), 9, 10, 11, 12, 14

QUEENSTOWN

Amanda's Bed and Breakfast

1428 Park Avenue, Baltimore, 21217
(410) 225-0001; (800) 899-7533
FAX (410) 728-8957

146. This bed and breakfast has been characterized as "an amazing hodge-podge of a converted telephone exchange merged with a private residence." Charming, comfortable, traditional, and convenient, this is a unique getaway specializing in relaxation, rejuvenation, and recreation. The warm, hospitable hosts offer five rooms with private baths. Continental breakfast. $75.

Bed and Breakfast of Maryland/Traveller in Maryland, Inc.

P.O. Box 2277, Annapolis, 21494-2277
(410) 269 6232, FAX (410) 263-4841

173. On Main Street in a quaint waterfront historic village, with easy accessibility to Annapolis, Washington, Baltimore, Easton, Chestertown, and other areas of the Western and Eastern Shores. Each of the four rooms is comfortably and tastefully decorated, and has a private bath. Large family room is a spacious gathering place for guests to "unwind" and meet new acquaintances. No smoking. No pets. Continental breakfast. $65.

ROCK HALL

Amanda's Bed and Breakfast

1428 Park Avenue, Baltimore, 21217
(410) 225-0001; (800) 899-7533
FAX (410) 728-8957

203. This gracious waterfront manor house on more than 58 acres is one mile south of

Rock Hall. Near the water, wildlife, and hunting. Six rooms, all with private baths, are available in this quiet country setting. Continental breakfast. $75-145.

Bed and Breakfast of Maryland/Traveller in Maryland, Inc.

P.O. Box 2277, Annapolis, 21494-2277
(410) 269-6232; FAX (410) 263-4841

188. This gracious waterfront manor is reminiscent of yesteryear with a huge stone fireplace, beautiful wood floors and cabinetry. Situated on 201 acres of prime waterfront property this inn is only minutes away from Rock Hall, MD, one of the last refuges of Maryland's famous watermen. Five guest accommodations with private baths. Central heat and air conditioning, expansive porches, and pleasant company. No smoking. No pets. Continental breakfast. $75-145.

The Inn at Osprey

20786 Rock Hall Avenue, 21661
(410) 639-2194; FAX (410) 639-7716

Enjoy a relaxing visit on the Eastern Shore of Maryland at this inn on scenic Swan Creek. Choose from five spacious guest rooms, each with private bath. In addition, there are two suites, Escapade, with marble bathroom and Jacuzzi tub, and Bolero, with a cozy fireplace. Elegant gourmet restaurant and bar. Osprey is on 30 acres of spacious grounds with pleasant surroundings, a swimming pool, and picnic areas. Bicycles are available. Close to Chestertown and approximately one and a half hours from Philadelphia, Baltimore, and Washington.

Rooms: 7 (PB) $110-150
Continental Breakfast
Credit Cards: A, B
Notes: 2, 4, 5, 8 (limited), 9, 10, 11, 12

ST. MICHAELS

Amanda's Bed and Breakfast

1428 Park Avenue, Baltimore, 21217
(410) 225-0001; (800) 899-7533
FAX (410) 728-8957

245. This historic house, dating back to 1805 with period furnishings, working fireplaces, and four-poster canopied beds, is in a historic waterman's village on the Eastern Shore of the Chesapeake Bay. Within walking distance of shops, restaurants, and the museum, this inn offers seven rooms and one cottage with private and shared baths. Continental breakfast. $65-105.

351. Late 1880s Colonial home near all of the water activities in St. Michael's. Romantic setting with Jacuzzis and fireplaces. Afternoon tea weekends. Full breakfast. $120-180.

Bed and Breakfast of Maryland/Traveller in Maryland, Inc.

P.O. Box 2277, Annapolis, 21494-2277
(410) 269-6232; FAX (410) 263-4841

182. At this elegant waterfront inn, built just after the war of 1812, English and American antiques are elegantly offset by the understated, classic Laura Ashley fabrics and wallpapers. Luxury which is comfortable and cozy. In addition to pleasant little surprises everywhere, guests will naturally find fresh flowers, fruit, and mineral water in their room. All 19 guest rooms or suites have private baths, cable TV telephone, air conditioning, and daily newspaper. Afternoon high tea and full American breakfast. $195-450.

184. Enjoy lodging and breakfast in this Eastern Shore inn. In historic St. Michaels, just off the main street within walking distance of all the shops, restaurants, harbor, and Maritime Museum. This Georgian home, built in 1805 by shipwright and soldier Col. Joseph Kemp, offers period furnishing, working fireplaces, and balcony. There are six guest rooms in the main house with shared or private baths, and a cottage behind the main house with double bed and full bath. No smoking. No pets. Continental breakfast. $55-95.

The Inn at Christmas Farm

P.O. Box T, 21663
(410) 820-7125

The Inn at Christmas Farm, circa 1800, near St. Michaels, Maryland, is a working farm with a restored main house and chapel. There are four suites elegantly furnished in country and lace fashion. Enjoy a full Continental breakfast either on the porch or in a private sitting room. Waterfowl abound, and guests may see them while relaxing by the pond or strolling to Christmas Cove. Guests will receive a warm and friendly welcome for a getaway weekend or vacation

Hosts: David and Beatrice Lee
Rooms: 5 (4 PB; 1 SB) $125-135
Continental Breakfast
Credit Cards: A, B
Notes: 2, 8 (over 12), 9, 11, 12, 14

Parsonage Inn

210 North Talbot Street, Route 33, 21663
(301) 745-5519; (800) 394-5519

Late Victorian bed and breakfast, circa 1883, lavishly restored in 1985 with seven guest rooms, private baths, king- or queen-size brass beds with Laura Ashley linens. Parlor and dining room in European tradition. Gourmet restaurant receiving rave reviews next door. Two blocks to Chesapeake Maritime Museum, shops, and harbor. Ten percent off midweek for AARP or retired officers. AB&BA approved; Mobil three-star award winner.

Parsonage Inn

Host: Ms. France Goupil
Rooms: 8 (PB) $80-130
Full Breakfast
Credit Cards: A, B
Notes: 2, 5, 8, 9, 10, 12

SALISBURY

Amanda's Bed and Breakfast

1428 Park Avenue, Baltimore, 21217
(410) 225-0001; (800) 899-7533
FAX (410) 728-8957

358. Country bed and breakfast just five miles south of Salisbury on a small bass pond. Fish and paddle. Three rooms. Public golf nearby. One black Lab and two cats also reside on premises. Shared bath. $65.

SCOTLAND

St. Michael's Manor Bed and Breakfast

Box 17A, Route 5, 20687
(301) 872-4025

The land belongs to St. Michael's Manor (1805) and was originally patented to Leonard Calvert in 1637. The house, situated on Long Neck Creek, is furnished with antiques. Boating, canoeing, bikes, a swim-

6 Pets welcome; 8 Children welcome; 9 Social drinking allowed; 10 Tennis available; 11 Swimming available; 12 Golf available; 13 Skiing available; 14 May be booked through travel agents.

ming pool, and wine-tasting are available. Near Point Lookout State Park, Civil War monuments, and historic St. Mary's City.

Hosts: Joseph and Nancy Dick
Rooms: 4 (SB) $45-65
Full Breakfast
Credit Cards: None
Notes: 2, 5, 7 (limited), 8 (call), 9, 10, 11

SHARPSBURG

Amanda's Bed and Breakfast

1428 Park Avenue, Baltimore, 21217
(410) 225-0001; (800) 899-7533
FAX (410) 728-8957

268. This inn sits amidst the hallowed ground of the Civil War's Antietam battlefield. Furnishings of Victorian vintage define a gentler way of life, and the pastoral surroundings of the misty Blue Ridge Mountains can be seen from a wraparound porch. Four rooms have private baths. Continental breakfast. $105-125.

SILVER SPRING

Amanda's Bed and Breakfast

1428 Park Avenue, Baltimore, 21217
(410) 225-0001; (800) 899-7533
FAX (410) 728-8957

325. Easy commute to Washington. Wooded park setting in an older residential neighborhood. Tudor-style home with European antiques. Walk to local restaurants. A suite with queen-size bed and private bath. A twin bedroom. Continental breakfast. $70-85.

Bed and Breakfast of Maryland/Traveller in Maryland, Inc.

P.O. Box 2277, Annapolis, 21494-2277
(410) 269-6232; FAX (410) 263-4841

200. This English Tudor home is built of brick with a steep slate roof. It sits alone on one acre of landscaped gardens, including two patios which overlook the creek and woods below. The home is secluded among 50-foot beech and oak trees with a sweeping view of Sligo Creek. Two guest accommodations are furnished in lovely antiques and family collectibles. One has a private bath; the other a shared hall bath. No smoking. No pets. Continental breakfast. $55-65.

202. This homestay is new Victorian-style, with wraparound porches and decks for sitting or sunning. Backed by a wooded area, the location is so secluded that it is sometimes difficult to realize that Washington, D.C., lies only a short distance away. Two comfortably furnished guest rooms with either a private or a shared bath arrangement. Dogs in residence. No smoking. Full breakfast. $65.

SNOW HILL

Chanceford Hall Bed and Breakfast Inn

209 West Federal Street, 21863
(410) 632-2231

A 1759 Eastern Shore mansion impeccably restored. Listed in *Smithsonian's Guide to Historic America.* All private baths, canopied beds, and Oriental rugs throughout. Ten working fireplaces, centrally air-conditioned. Dinner by prior arrangement. Full breakfast served in formal dining room. Lap pool and bicycles. Ocean beaches 20 miles away. Canoe the famous Pocomoke River two blocks away. Complimentary wine and hors d'oeuvres. "When guests require the finest."

Hosts: Michael and Thelma C. Driscoll
Rooms: 5 (PB) $105-125
Full Breakfast
Credit Cards: None
Notes: 2, 5, 9, 10, 11, 12

NOTES: Credit cards accepted: A MasterCard; B Visa; C American Express; D Discover Card; E Diner's Club; F Other; 2 Personal checks accepted; 3 Lunch available; 4 Dinner available; 5 Open all year;

River House Inn

201 East Market Street, 21863
(410) 632-2722

Casual yet elegant retreat in historic waterfront village. Acres of lawns and gardens back up to the wild and scenic Pocomoke River. Queen-size beds, fireplaces, ceiling fans, and antiques. Main house built in 1860, little house in 1835. Enjoy canoeing, cycling, birding, beaches, and historic district. Golf packages available.

Hosts: Larry and Susanne Knudsen
Rooms: 8 (PB) $85-100
Full Breakfast
Credit Cards: A, B, C
Notes: 2, 5, 8, 9, 10, 11, 12, 14

STEVENSON

Amanda's Bed and Breakfast

1428 Park Avenue, Baltimore, 21217
(410) 225-0001; (800) 899-7533
FAX (410) 728-8957

115. Historic 45-acre estate offers elegant living. 1900s-style fireplaces, whirlpool tub, gourmet breakfast, swimming pool, tennis, woodland trails and streams, flowers and herb gardens make this majestic estate a special place to stay. Five guest rooms, all with private baths and some with fireplaces. Full breakfast. $90-150.

Bed and Breakfast of Maryland/Traveller in Maryland, Inc.

P.O. Box 2277, Annapolis, 21494-2277
(410) 269-6232; FAX (410) 263-4841

165. A majestic estate, quietly nestled on 45 acres in Maryland's splendid Green Spring Valley, provides an elegant lifestyle portrayed in the early 1900s. Guests will enjoy suites with fireplaces, private baths (some with Jacuzzi), expansive porches, pool, and tennis court. Woodland trails, streams,

flower and herb gardens abound on this estate. Abundant history is associated with this house through its builder Alexander J. Cassatt, owner of the Pennsylvania Railroad and brother of Mary Cassat, the American impressionist. Later, it was owned by the Brewster family, descendants of Benjamin Franklin and important in government. In the 1950s it became the Koinonia Foundation, a predecessor of the Peace Corps. Four guest suites with double or king-size beds with private baths. Some suites have separate living room and porches. Nonsmoking. Dog in residence. Full gourmet breakfast. $90-125.

STEVENSVILLE

Amanda's Bed and Breakfast

1428 Park Avenue, Baltimore, 21217
(410) 225-0001; (800) 899-7533
FAX (410) 728-8957

180. This historic manor is situated on Kent Island on the Eastern Shore side of the Bay Bridge. This grand mansion, circa 1820, is on the Maryland Historic Register and surrounded by 226 acres of land. One and one-half miles from the waterfront with rooms decorated in Victorian style that will make any stay here memorable. Restaurant has a four-star rating. Continental breakfast.

TANEYTOWN

Amanda's Bed and Breakfast

1428 Park Avenue, Baltimore, 21217
(410) 225-0001; (800) 899-7533
FAX (410) 728-8957

161. This restored 1844 mansion sits on 24 acres with clay tennis courts, croquet, gardens, a view of the Catoctin Mountains, and gourmet dinners provided with reservations. Winner of "Baltimore's Most Ro-

6 Pets welcome; 8 Children welcome; 9 Social drinking allowed; 10 Tennis available; 11 Swimming available; 12 Golf available; 13 Skiing available; 14 May be booked through travel agents.

mantic Getaway," this inn offers eight rooms, all with private baths, fireplaces, and Jacuzzis. Full breakfast. $150-275.

Bed and Breakfast of Maryland/Traveller in Maryland, Inc.

P.O. Box 2277, Annapolis, 21494-2277
(410) 269-6232; FAX (410) 263-4841

168. A Georgian-style country house with a Victorian-style addition. A hideaway guest house situated on a large working farm, placed in the serene Piedmont countryside of Maryland is a remarkable getaway. The property is part of a 3000-acre tract of land called Runnymeade Enlarged, patented prior to the American Revolution by Dr. Upton Scott, whose home on Shipwright Street in Annapolis is still a landmark. Enjoy the living room setting with a large fireplace, a dining room, and a wraparound porch with rocking chairs overlooking Bear Branch. Each air-conditioned bedroom has a pleasant view of lawns, pastures, creeks, or woods. One suite has a private screened porch. A hundred yards across the wide and shaded lawn lies the guest house with two large bedrooms, a living room, and a kitchenette. The guest house is air-conditioned. Nonsmoking. Full Maryland breakfast. $55-100.

TILGHMAN

Chesapeake Wood Duck Inn

P.O. Box 202, Gibsontown Road, 21671
(410) 886-2070; (800) 956-2070

"Southern hospitality on the Chesapeake Bay" is not merely a marketing theme, but a way of life of owners/innkeepers, Dave and Stephanie. 1890 Victorian, graciously restored, overlooking Dogwood Harbor, home of the last fleet of antique skipjack sailing vessels in North America. According to TV's *Travel, Travel,* "The charming Victorian Wood Duck Inn, is a destination

in itself. Guests enjoy the quiet ambience of yesteryear." Impeccably appointed with period furnishings, oriental rugs, original art, luxurious linens, and fresh flowers. On Maryland's Eastern Shore and the Chesapeake Bay, in a quaint fishing village offering spectacular scenery, serenity, and a forgotten way of life. Within walking distance of restaurants, shops, and water activities. Bikes available.

Hosts: Stephanie and Dave Feith
Rooms: 6 (PB) $115-125
Full Breakfast
Credit Cards: A, B
Notes: 2, 5, 9, 10, 11, 12, 14

Black Walnut Point Inn

Black Walnut Road, P.O. Box 308, 21671
(410) 886-2452

Black Walnut Point Inn is on 57 acres surrounded by water. Some amenities include bayside hammocks, pool, tennis court, rocking chairs, and bicycles. Guests enjoy comfort, privacy, peace, and quiet. The island's most romantic bed and breakfast with Key West sunsets.

Rooms: 7 (PB) $110-140
Continental Breakfast
Credit Cards: A, B
Notes: 2, 5, 9, 10, 11, 12

VIENNA

Amanda's Bed and Breakfast

1428 Park Avenue, Baltimore, 21217
(410) 225-0001; (800) 899-7533
FAX (410) 728-8957

149. On the Nanticoke River in historic Vienna, this authentic Colonial tavern has been carefully restored. This original tavern house shares much of the history of the town, as it was built in 1706. Public tennis courts, boat ramp, and the Blackwater Wildlife Refuge are nearby. Four rooms with a shared bath and fireplace are available for guests. Continental breakfast. $65-75.

Bed and Breakfast of Maryland/Traveller in Maryland, Inc.

P.O. Box 2277, Annapolis, 21494-2277
(410) 269-6232; FAX (410) 263-4841

196. This early Victorian structure was built in 1861 on the banks of the Nanticoke River. Known locally as the "Brick House," being the first home to be built of brick in Vienna. The inn still maintains its original character having twelve-foot ceilings, cornices, medallions, working fireplaces, a beautiful three-story spiral staircase, many windows and doorways accented with wood paneling. All eight guest rooms are furnished in a manner that befits this great home and have shared and private baths. Restricted smoking area. Outdoor cat. Continental breakfast. $75-85.

The Tavern House

Box 98, 21869
(301) 376-3347

A Colonial tavern on the Nanticoke River featuring the simple elegance of Colonial living and special breakfasts that are a social occasion. A glimpse into Michener's Chesapeake for those who love Colonial homes, the peace of a small town, or watching osprey in flight.

Hosts: Harvey and Elise Altergott
Rooms: 4 (SB) $60-70
Full Breakfast
Credit Cards: A, B
Notes: 2, 5, 7, 8 (over 12), 9, 10, 12, 14

WESTMINSTER

Amanda's Bed and Breakfast

1428 Park Avenue, Baltimore, 21217
(410) 225-0001; (800) 899-7533
FAX (410) 728-8957

219. This Victorian inn is a former schoolhouse 45 minutes from northwest Baltimore. All guest rooms have queen-size

beds and Jacuzzis. Hearty breakfast buffet and an athletic club available to guests, which includes swimming, jogging, racquetball, and weight machines. Historic Union Hills Homestead and museums are all nearby. $110-155.

Bed and Breakfast of Maryland/Traveller in Maryland, Inc.

P.O. Box 2277, Annapolis, 21494-2277
(410) 269-6232; FAX (410) 263-4841

208. At the turn of the century this inn was a schoolhouse for children of all ages. Today it has been transformed into one of the most elegant getaway destinations in the region. Furnished in collectibles and antiques, the ambience is truly unique. The thirteen guest rooms have queen-size beds and private baths with Jacuzzis. The use of the on-site, state-of-the-art athletic facility adjacent to the inn is included. The inn also offers a fine dining restaurant for its guests. Smoking restricted. Continental breakfast. $105-155.

WILLIAMSPORT

Bed and Breakfast of Maryland/Traveller in Maryland, Inc.

P.O. Box 2277, Annapolis, 21494-2277
(410) 269-6232; FAX (410) 263-4841

206. This diverse homestay is a recently built log house set on 120 acres of farm and woodland with comfortable and cozy eclectic country furnishings. The totally unique aspect of this farm is its collection of wolves, both full blood and wolf-hybrids; hence the name "Wolf's End Farm," Guests will be serenaded by the wolves' unique howling. Each of the two guest rooms have a private bath and furnishings that allow for comfort. No smoking. Full breakfast. $80-100.

6 Pets welcome; 8 Children welcome; 9 Social drinking allowed; 10 Tennis available; 11 Swimming available; 12 Golf available; 13 Skiing available; 14 May be booked through travel agents.

WITTMAN

Bed and Breakfast of Maryland/Traveller in Maryland, Inc.

P.O. Box 2277, Annapolis, 21494-2277
(410) 269-6232; FAX (410) 263-4841

180. A 50-acre waterfront farm, circa 1800, offers the ultimate in peace and privacy. A comfortably restored Bay hundred farmhouse and St. James church (a property saved through historic preservation by the owners) offers the ambience and serenity of a waterman's retreat. Waterfowl and wildlife abound. Antiquing, boating, biking, bird watching, fine restaurants, and museums are but minutes away. All three guest accommodations are suites with private baths. An array of main house pets (cats and dog) and yard livestock (peacocks, goats). No smoking. Continental breakfast. $115.

Massachusetts

Allen House Victorian Bed and Breakfast Inn

AMHERST

Allen House Victorian Bed and Breakfast Inn

599 Main Street, 01002
(413) 253-5000

An authentic 1886 Queen Anne-style Victorian, this home features spacious bed chambers with private baths and air conditioning. Period antiques, decor, art, and wall coverings are historically and accurately featured. In the heart of Amherst on three scenic acres and within walking distance of the Emily Dickinson House. Amherst College, the University of Massachusetts, fine galleries, museums, theaters, shops, and restaurants are nearby. Free busing throughout the five college area. A full formal breakfast is served. Brochure available. Winner of the 1991 Historic Commission Award.

Hosts: Alan and Ann Zieminski
Rooms: 5 (PB) $45-95
Full Breakfast
Credit Cards: None
Notes: 2, 5, 7 (limited), 8 (over 9), 9, 10, 11, 12, 13

American Country Collection

4 Greenwood Lane, Delmar, NY 12054
(518) 439-7001

120. This convenient in-town Victorian with wraparound veranda for outdoor relaxation is on a quiet tree-lined street within walking distance to the college, university, and downtown. The first-floor suite is actually a self-contained flat with bath and full kitchen with eating area. New second-floor guest quarters contain two bedrooms, shared bath plus kitchen and eating area. Smoking outside only. Children welcome. $55-80.

ATTLEBORO

Anna's Victorian Connection

5 Fowler Avenue, Newport, RI 02840
(401) 849-2489

0012. A casual country interior welcomes guests to this excellent example of Greek Revival architecture. A great getaway for the business or vacation traveler, the inn offers 16 guest rooms with shared or private baths. A hearty breakfast buffet is served daily, and a full tea is served several times a week. The Carriage House is available for conferences, seminars, or special gatherings; lunch, dinner, and special parties can be arranged. Just off I-95 between Boston and Providence, the inn is on the commuter-rail line to Boston and convenient to Great Woods, Cape Cod, and Foxboro Stadium. $42-72.

6 Pets welcome; 7 Smoking allowed; 8 Children welcome; 9 Social drinking allowed; 10 Tennis available; 11 Swimming available; 12 Golf available; 13 Skiing available; 14 May be booked through travel agents.

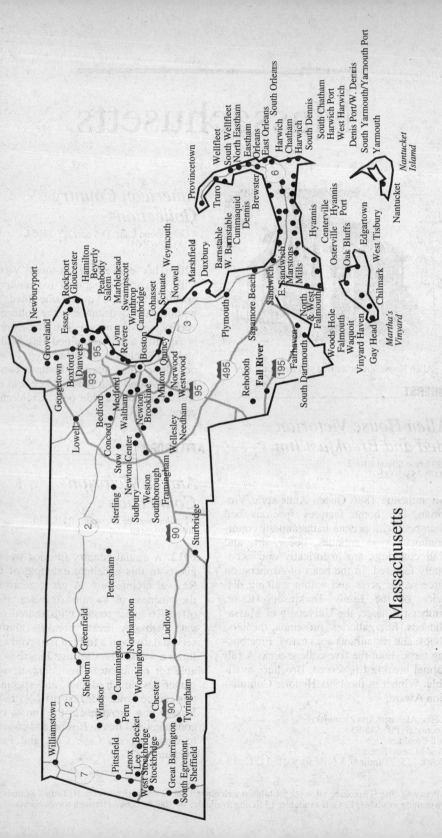

Massachusetts

Newburyport

Rockport
Gloucester
Hamilton
Essex   Beverly
         Peabody
Groveland   Marblehead
Georgetown   Salem   Swampscott
Boxford   Winthrop
Danvers   Lynn   Revere
      95   Cambridge
Lowell   93   Boston
                 Quincy Cohasset
Bedford   Medford Milton Scituate
Concord Waltham Newton Norwell
Stow   Newton Center Brookline Weymouth
Sterling Sudbury Weston Wellesley Marshfield
      Southborough Framingham Needham Duxbury
Petersham   Westwood Westwood
                  Norwood
                      3
                         Plymouth
                              Sagamore Beach
Greenfield   Rehoboth 495
Northampton   Fall River 195
Shelburn   Fairhaven
Cummington Worthington   South Dartmouth
Windsor   Peru   Rehoboth
Williamstown Chester
      Ludlow
Pittsfield   Becket
Lenox Lee Stockbridge
West Stockbridge Great Barrington
South Egremont Tyningham
Sheffield   7   90

Provincetown
Truro
Wellfleet
South Wellfleet
North Eastham
Eastham
Orleans   South Orleans
East Orleans
Brewster Harwich South Orleans
      6   Harwich Port Chatham
Cummaquid Harwich South Chatham
Dennis   Marstons West Harwich
W. Barnstable Mills Denis Port/W. Dennis
Barnstable South Yarmouth/Yarmouth Port
Sandwich Hyannis Yarmouth
E. Sandwich Centerville South Dennis
North & West Hyannis Nantucket
Falmouth Osterville Port
Woods Hole Oak Bluffs Edgartown
Falmouth Vineyard Haven
Waquoit Gay Head West Tisbury
          Chilmark

Nantucket
Nantucket Island

Martha's Vineyard

2

Stockbridge
Sturbridge
90

2

Bed and Breakfast Associates Bay Colony, Ltd.

P.O. Box 57166, Babson Park, Boston, 02157-0166
(617) 449-5302; (800) 347-5088
FAX (617) 449-5958

CW875. Nestled in a quiet country neighborhood, this Colonial reproduction home offers pleasant accommodations for guests attending concerts at Great Woods or visiting Wheaton College, both only ten minutes away. Providence is only a 15-minute drive. Two guest rooms on the second floor share a bath. Full breakfast; children welcome; no smoking. Family and monthly rates available; $70-75.

Ashley Manor

BARNSTABLE (CAPE COD)

Ashley Manor

Box 856, 3660 Old Kings Highway, 02630
(508) 362-8044

Ashley Manor is a very special place, a gracious 1699 mansion on a two-acre estate in Cape Cod's historic district. Romantic rooms and suites feature private baths and fireplaces. Elegant public rooms with antiques and Oriental rugs. Delicious full breakfast in formal dining room or on terrace overlooking parklike grounds and new tennis court. Walk to the beach and village. Prices subject to change.

Hosts: Donald and Fay Bain
Rooms: 6 (PB) $115-175
Full Breakfast
Credit Cards: A, B, C, F
Notes: 2, 5, 8 (over 14), 9, 10, 11, 12, 14

Bed and Breakfast Cape Cod

P.O. Box 341, West Hyannisport, 02672-0341
(508) 775-2772; FAX (508) 775-2884

2. This 1864 sea captain's house is complete with wide board floors, glimpses of Cape Cod Bay, and a gracious rural setting. Two bedrooms are used for one party of guests, assuring a private bath. A child's room with a crib is available in an adjoining guest room. Enjoy a full breakfast on the terrace or in the dining room. Whale-watch boats, the harbor, and fine restaurants are one-half mile away. Three miles to Hyannis and the ferry to Nantucket or Martha's Vineyard. $80.

35. Not many bed and breakfast travelers have a chance to stay in a house built in 1635. This charming old building was part of the Cape Cod designer's tour of homes in 1989. The owner has two bedrooms used for bed and breakfast, with a king-size bed in one room and a pair of twins in the other. The two rooms are let out to one party at a time, thereby assuring a private bath. The grounds are like a rural wooded setting with great trails for walking. A parlor is available on the first floor for guests to use. $70.

39. Built 280 years ago by the founder of Barnstable, this Early American-style home has been painstakingly restored to the original design and decor of the early 1700s. Private baths, period antiques, and four-poster beds are featured in the three bedrooms. Two bedrooms have working fireplaces. A full country breakfast, cooked to order, is served in the common room each morning. $75-95.

Bed and Breakfast Greater Boston and Cape Cod

P.O. Box 35, Newtonville, 02160
(617) 964-1606; (800) 832-2632;
FAX (617) 332-8572

The Corner Inn. An 1830 country barn has been completely and elegantly restored. Three large guest rooms have private baths. A country breakfast is served each morning on the enclosed porch with wicker tables set for two. Guests have an easy walk to many fine restaurants, the Barnstable Harbor whale-watch boat, or the beach. The ferries to Martha's Vineyard and Nantucket are a short ride away in Hyannis. No smoking. Children over 12 welcome. Open year-round. $85-95.

Olde Kings Highway Tavern. Built in 1754 and now fully restored, invites guests to take a step back into history. The three guest rooms are decorated in period antiques; each has a fireplace and a private bath. A hearty Continental breakfast with home-baked breads and pastries is included. Many activities are a short walk away, including fishing, boating, whale-watching, golf, and antiquing. The ferries to Martha's Vineyard and Nantucket are just ten minutes away in Hyannis. No smoking. Children over 12 welcome. $85-100.

DESTINNATIONS New England

P.O. Box 1173, Osterville, 02655
(508) 428-5600; (800) 333-4667 (reservations)
FAX (508) 420-0565;

7209. Set on five majestic acres overlooking Flax Pond, this luxurious Georgian inn, expanded in 1987, includes three elegant rooms furnished with antiques, objects of art, and rich carpets. The building looks out over a parklike setting, which includes a barn and corral for the innkeeper's seven Morgan horses. Nearby are antique and other shops, the village, fine restaurants, beaches, and island ferries. Each of the guest rooms is air-conditioned and handsomely furnished. A deluxe Continental breakfast is included from 8:00 to 9:30 A.M. No smoking, pets, or children. $120-156.

House Guests Cape Cod and the Islands

Box 1881, Orleans, 02653
(508) 896-7053; (800) 666-HOST (reservations)
FAX (508) 896-7054

93030. Built in 1830, this elegantly converted country barn was opened in 1989 as an inn. Guests have exclusive use of the entire second floor, including an expansive enclosed porch with wicker furniture and a large living-dining area with working fireplace. The three spacious, charmingly decorated guest rooms offer queen, king, or twin beds, each with private bath. Hearty Continental breakfast. In the Old King's Highway historic district, this bed and breakfast is less than a mile from Barnstable Harbor and Millway Beach. A non-smoking location. Children 12 and older are welcome. $75-85.

94032. Step back into Colonial days in this elegantly restored tavern house built in 1754. The three romantic guest rooms each have sitting area and private bath; two have working fireplaces. Queen-size and double beds are available, as well as a roll away for an extra person. Guests have use of two common rooms with period antiques and working fireplaces. Restaurants, harbor, and beach are nearby. A hearty Continental breakfast is served. No smoking. Children 14 or older are welcome. Extra fee for additional person. $75-95.

Thomas Huckins House

2701 Main Street, P.O. Box 515, 02630
(508) 362-6379

NOTES: Credit cards accepted: A MasterCard; B Visa; C American Express; D Discover Card; E Diner's Club; F Other; 2 Personal checks accepted; 3 Lunch available; 4 Dinner available; 5 Open all year;

Sleep in canopied beds next to working fireplaces in this restored 1705 house. Breakfast in the antique-filled keeping room; walk to the ocean and village through the historic district on the cape's picturesque and less-crowded North Shore. No smoking.

Hosts: Burt and Eleanor Eddy
Rooms: 3 (PB) $80-105
Suite: 1 (PB) $90-130
Continental Breakfast
Credit Cards: A, B, C, D
Notes: 2, 5, 8 (over 6), 9, 10, 11, 12, 14

Thomas Huckins House

BARNSTABLE VILLAGE

Beechwood

2839 Main Street, 02630
(508) 362-6618

A beautiful example of Queen Anne Victorian restoration. It is furnished with unusual period antiques, including a carved queen-size canopied bed, a hand-painted cottage bedroom set, and a fainting couch. A large suite on the second floor is suitable for three or four people. Tea is served by the fireplace parlor during the winter, and iced tea and lemonade are served on the veranda in the summer. Beechwood is a romantic retreat to the graciousness of the 19th century. A full breakfast is included.

Hosts: Debbie and Ken Trauget
Rooms: 6 (PB) $110-140

Full Breakfast
Credit Cards: A, B, C
Notes: 2, 5, 9, 11, 12, 14

BECKET

Covered Bridge

P.O. Box 447A, Norfolk, CT 06058
(203) 542-5944

1BMA. This totally restored 1790 tavern and stagecoach stop is furnished with antiques and is set on 12 acres. The original ballroom is now a sitting room for guests. There are five guest rooms, all with private baths, and many of the bedrooms have hand stenciling. A full breakfast is served in the dining room. $70-95.

BEDFORD

Bed and Breakfast Folks

48 Springs Road, 01730
(617) 275 9025

Bed and Breakfast Folks offers tourists, business travelers, relocating personnel, or anyone visiting this area an opportunity to experience the warmth and friendliness of a private New England home. Choose from historic, contemporary, or farmhomes. Learn about the charm and history of New England, and experience true hospitality. Near Concord, Lexington, and Boston. Close to lake region, skiing, fall foliage, and much more. $40.

BEVERLY

Bed and Breakfast Marblehead and North Shore

P.O. Box 35, Newtonville, 02160
(617) 964-1606; (800) 832-2632
FAX (617) 332-8572

Beverly Cove Bed and Breakfast. Attractive, immaculate split-level, two-minute

6 Pets welcome; 8 Children welcome; 9 Social drinking allowed; 10 Tennis available; 11 Swimming available; 12 Golf available; 13 Skiing available; 14 May be booked through travel agents.

Bed and Breakfast Marblehead and North Shore
(*continued*)

walk to private beach in quiet, prestigious area close to Endicott College. The hosts are English and enjoy entertaining in the best bed and breakfast tradition. Open year-round. Three guest rooms with private and shared baths. One room has working fireplace. All rooms have TV. Refrigerator for guests. Smoking permitted in common areas. Full breakfast. Children over eight welcome. Cat in residence. $60-75.

Beverly Farms. Enjoy the warmth and charm of an authentic antique Colonial home, dating back to 1839. Three guest bedrooms share a bath, as well as a downstairs common room and half-bath, and an outside deck and back yard. A gourmet Continental breakfast and an afternoon tea are complimentary. This accommodation is within walking distance of town, commuter-rail train to Boston and other parts of the North Shore, including an oceanside beach. No smoking. Children over 12 welcome. $65-75.

Lady Slippers. A charming Dutch Colonial home offering wonderful views from its location opposite a small park and sandy beach. Guests may relax in the sitting room or on the screened porch. Two guest rooms have double beds (one with ocean views) and shared bath. Two guest rooms have twin beds with private/shared bath. The master guest room has queen-size bed, ocean view, and private bath. This is a non-smoking accommodation. Children are welcome. Expanded Continental breakfast. Special rates for long-term guests. $40-75.

Next Door Inn. A beautifully decorated, cozy, Colonial-style home offers guests use of kitchen facilities, color TV in living room, enclosed sun porch, telephone, and off-street parking. There are three attractive guest rooms: a room with a queen-size bed and private bath, another room with a double bed and a fireplace, and a third room with a double and twins. (Second and third rooms share a bath.) In hot weather, common areas have air conditioning, and the guest rooms have fans. Continental breakfast. No smoking. Children welcome. Whole house available for groups of nine or less. $65-75.

Bunny's Bed and Breakfast
17 Kernwood Heights, 01915
(508) 922-2392

Victorian-style bed and breakfast with three bedrooms; one with a fireplace. Cozy living room also has a fireplace. Formal dining room. Off-street parking. Train within walking distance. Made-from-scratch muffins every morning. No smoking. Travelers' checks accepted. Two miles from Salem; restaurants within half a mile.

Hosts: Bunny and Joe Stacey
Rooms: 3 (1 PB; 2 SB) $55-85
Continental Breakfast
Credit Cards: None
Notes: 2, 5, 8, 9, 11

BOSTON

Beacon Hill Bed and Breakfast
27 Brimmer Street, 02108
(617) 523-7376

An 1869 spacious Victorian townhouse overlooking Charles River with large bed-sitting rooms, TV, and air conditioning within an elegant historic neighborhood of brick sidewalks, gas lamps, and tree-lined streets. Boston's best location—two blocks from "Cheers," easy walk to Boston Common, Freedom Trail connecting historic sites, Quincy Market, Filene's Basement, convention center, subway, downtown, public garages, restaurants, and shops. Elevator for luggage.

Host: Susan Butterworth
Rooms: 3 (PB) $115-145
Full Breakfast
Credit Cards: None
Notes: 2 (deposit), 5, 8 (over 10), 9, 14

Beacon Hill

A Bed and Breakfast Agency of Boston

(and Boston Harbor Bed and Breakfast)
47 Commercial Wharf, 02110
(617) 720-3540; (800) 248-9262

Downtown Boston's largest selection of guest rooms in historic bed and breakfast homes including Federal and Victorian townhouses and beautifully restored 1840s waterfront lofts. Also a lovely selection of furnished private studio, one- and two-bedroom condominiums—great for families! Exclusive locations include waterfront, Faneuil Hall/Quincy Market, North End, Back Bay, Beacon Hill, Complex Square, and Cambridge. Yachts and houseboats available. $65-120.

Bed and Breakfast Associates Bay Colony, Ltd.

P.O. Box 57166, Babson Park, 02157-0166
(617) 449-5302; (800) 347-5088
FAX (617) 449-5958

M101. The best view in Boston! This stunning condo overlooks Boston's popular harbor front area from its 30th-floor perch. Watch the sailboards in the harbor or peer down at Quincy Mark/Faneuil Hall and the famous clock tower. One attractive guest room with a twin-king option, contemporary furnishing, and private bath. $125.

M104. Those seeking the charm of an old European hotel will enjoy staying in this prestigious private club with its elegant drawing room and small, gracious dining room. Convenient to Newbury Street shops, historic sites, and the Hynes Convention Center. Four guest rooms, two with private baths. Continental breakfast; elevator service; children welcome. $66-107.

M126. Just three blocks from the Public Garden, country antiques create a charming and comfortable atmosphere in this quiet Beacon Hill home. Stroll along nearby Charles Street and enjoy the fine antique shops, bookstores, and cafes. Three guest rooms with private baths. Generous Continental breakfast; children over ten welcome. $85-120.

M128. This 1835 Federal townhouse has all its original architectural details. Guests enjoy the private use of the entire second floor that consists of a bedroom, sitting room, and bath. The two decorative fireplaces add a warm coziness to this peaceful urban retreat. Continental breakfast served in-room; children welcome; no smoking allowed. $90.

M131. In Boston's prestigious Beacon Hill and adjacent to the historic Massachusetts

6 Pets welcome; 8 Children welcome; 9 Social drinking allowed; 10 Tennis available; 11 Swimming available; 12 Golf available; 13 Skiing available; 14 May be booked through travel agents.

Bed and Breakfast Associates Bay Colony *(continued)*

State House, this inn is a loving restoration of two attached 1830s townhouses. The fine period furnishings include four-poster and canopied beds, decorative fireplaces, and reproduction desks. New private baths throughout, and guests are always welcome to use the kitchen, the dining room, and the parlors. $89-109.

M136. This handsome 46-room mansion at the foot of Beacon Hill is within walking distance of many Boston attractions. Modern amenities have been incorporated into this careful restoration, and rooms include telephone lines, private baths, color TVs, individual climate controls, and some kitchenettes. Elevator and handicapped access is available. The gracious double parlor with working fireplace and period furnishings serves as the lobby, and reproduction furnishings create a warm and elegant atmosphere. Continental breakfast. Laundry and valet. $95-140.

M137. Boston has only one Newbury Street, and it is *the* street for art galleries, designer clothing boutiques, and fine window shopping. This 32-room Newbury Street Inn puts all of this at the doorstep. Opened in 1991, this property is restored and offers warm, comfortable rooms with 19th-century reproductions. The front patio is a perfect spot for people-watching; breakfast is served here when the weather permits. Selectively priced rooms available on all four floors. Reserved parking available in the rear for $10 per day. Two blocks to Copley Square and Hynes Convention Center. $95-155.

M138. In Copley Square, this 64-room inn offers modern business amenities, a gracious lobby, and the best location in the city. All rooms have private bath, queen-size or twin beds, TV, telephone, and individual climate control. Discount on-site parking. $95.

M142. Stay in a true Back Bay mansion! This opulent home defines luxury and in-town convenience. Just two blocks from the renowned shops and cafes of Newbury Street, this bed and breakfast features two lavish guest rooms and a breakfast buffet station. Queen-size canopied beds. In-hall baths are each shared with one tenant. $98.

M143. A Bird's Nest. Atop Beacon Hill, this romantic penthouse studio apartment with its beamed cathedral ceiling has an enchanting decor. In summer, enjoy the marvelous view of Boston from the private balcony with its intricate iron railing and working fountain. In winter, the large fireplace warms guests as they settle in to enjoy the cozy atmosphere. Only three blocks from Charles Street's fine restaurants, antiques, and art. $125-150.

M144. This 1940s New York-style apartment building offers one guest room with private bath for double occupancy, and overlooks Boston's Public Gardens. This immaculate, attractive apartment features both great location and grand views. $99.

M230. On a quiet street of gracious brownstones in Boston's Back Bay, near the Hynes Convention Center, this friendly family offers one very special guest room with queen-size bed, private deck, and private bath en-suite. Fully restored and tastefully decorated. $90.

M240. Lovely Victorian townhouse in the Back Bay just steps from the Prudential Center and Copley Place. This warm and hospitable couple offers their guests full use of their second floor with two charming guest rooms and a bath. They also offer a

NOTES: Credit cards accepted: A MasterCard; B Visa; C American Express; D Discover Card; E Diner's Club; F Other; 2 Personal checks accepted; 3 Lunch available; 4 Dinner available; 5 Open all year;

garden-level efficiency with a new kitchenette and private bath. Continental breakfast served; children welcome; no smoking allowed. $65-80.

M242. Near Boston's famed Symphony Hall, this gregarious hostess offers three attractive bed and breakfast guest rooms in her restored townhouse. With a cheerful country decor parlor and private parking space ($10/night), this is a perfect choice for those wishing to be near the Museum of Fine Arts, Berkley Music College, and the Hynes Convention Center. $85.

M302. A fully furnished one-bedroom apartment with private roof deck in Boston's South End, convenient to Copley Square. Cozy and comfortable, this fourth-floor unit offers one bedroom with queen-size bed, living room with sleep-sofa, fully equipped kitchen, dining area, and bath. Weekly and monthly rates available. $75.

M303. This bed and breakfast host couple offers a wealth of knowledge about Boston along with their kind attention to guest needs. Each of the two guest rooms reflects splendid taste and attention to detail. Near Copley Square, their brownstone townhouse is convenient to Boston's tourist and convention centers. $80.

M304. A furnished one-bedroom apartment with free underground parking is a rarity in central Boston. This contemporary unit is in a converted church building which was recently transformed into stylish condos. Elevator to third floor, queen-size bed, private bath, living-dining room, and fully equipped kitchen. $85.

M306. In a 19th-century townhouse three blocks from Copley Square, guests enjoy the privacy and convenience of this newly decorated studio apartment with a Murphy double bed, futon couch, cooking nook, and private bath. $85.

M308. This 500-square-foot, garden-level suite in a renovated brownstone townhouse is just three blocks from the Boston Common and Copley Square. Guests enjoy a large, brick-walled bedroom with queen-size and twin beds, sitting room, private bath and patio, color TV, stereo, refrigerator, and a laundry. Continental breakfast. Children over 13 welcome. Off-season monthly rates available. $78.

M314. Attention to detail and gracious hospitality are the hallmark of this bed and breakfast. Selected as one of the 100 best bed and breakfasts in the country, this 1863 townhouse is set in the historic district right next to Boston's famed Copley Square. Each impeccable guest room offers unique decorative features that include wide-pine floors, bow windows, marble fireplaces, queen-size brass beds, Chinese rugs, and private baths. Sumptuous breakfast served in the penthouse dining room. $97-125.

M322. This congenial couple offers two lovely guest rooms (one queen-size and one double bed) with charming antique decor, private baths, and central air. Their beautifully restored Victorian bowfront townhouse is on a quiet street with private parking. $80.

M323. This well-kept and appealing 1869 brick townhouse is near the Hynes Convention Center. It features two pretty second-floor guest rooms; one includes a queen-size bed, "decorative" fireplace, delightful antiques, and a bay window breakfast spot. Shared bath. Parking is available on request at $10 per day. $75.

M356. For extended stays, ask about this one-bedroom apartment with a new eat-in kitchenette, queen-size bed, living room with sleep-sofa, color TV, and private bath

6 Pets welcome; 8 Children welcome; 9 Social drinking allowed; 10 Tennis available; 11 Swimming available; 12 Golf available; 13 Skiing available; 14 May be booked through travel agents.

Bed and Breakfast Associates Bay Colony (continued)

in an 1857 townhouse on a quiet street in the South End. Clean and well-maintained. $1200/month.

M359. In Boston's South End, this comfortable Victorian townhouse is near Copley Square and the Hynes Convention Center. The host has thoughtfully furnished two guest rooms which share one full and one half-bath. The studio room has a private attached kitchen and a double bed. The sunrise room has a twins-king option. $75.

M416. In historic Charlestown, one block from the famed Freedom Trail, this 1846 townhouse has been wonderfully restored and attractively furnished with lovely antiques. Two spacious guest rooms, each with private bath. $65-75.

M482. In historic Charlestown, on Boston's famed Freedom Trail, guests enjoy a second-floor suite with deck overlooking gardens and private entrance in this 1847 Greek Revival townhouse. The traditionally furnished guest room has queen-size bed and private bath. A queen-size sleeper-sofa is also available in the attached sitting room. $85.

M510. A wonderful 12-room Victorian in the Jamaica Pond area near the Farber, Children's, and Brigham hospitals. Very large third-floor guest room provides privacy, and its furnishings include a desk and a sofa. A private bath and a full private kitchen adjoin. Drive ten minutes to downtown Boston. Self-serve Continental breakfast; no smoking; monthly rates available. $78.

Bed and Breakfast of Greater Boston and Cape Cod

P.O. Box 35, Newtonville, 02160
(617) 964-1606; (800) 832-2632
FAX (617) 322-8572

Bed and Breakfast Afloat. This completely refurbished yacht in Boston's waterfront district sleeps two to four and offers a galley kitchen stocked with breakfast food, living room with double sofa bed, air conditioning, color TV, separate bedroom with queen-size bed and private bath. By prior arrangement, hosts will cater private boatside parties or dinners. Available May 1 through October 15. $120-180.

The Garden Bed and Breakfast. The perfect place to experience Boston. This Victorian brick row house, built in 1860, is in the largest historic Victorian neighborhood in the United States. The accommodation has a separate private entrance leading to a double parlor; the bedroom has a king-size bed (or two singles), TV, VCR, and air conditioning. There is also a fully equipped efficiency kitchen and a shower bath. No breakfast is provided, but the host will stock the cupboard and refrigerator. Weekly and extended rates. No smoking allowed. $125.

The South End Inn. A small hotel nestled in Boston's South End, a friendly neighborhood of professionals and renovated brownstones. Just two blocks from the train and bus stations, and a short walk to Newbury Street, Copley Place, the theater district, and the convention center. Guest rooms are newly refurbished, all with private bath, color TV, telephones, and air conditioning. Continental breakfast served. Parking available in nearby garage. $74-94.

Bed and Breakfast/Inns of New England

128 South Hoop Pole Road, Guilford, CT 06437
(203) 457-0042; (800) 582-0853

MA-1007. Built in 1894 by a prosperous Boston leather merchant, this late Victorian house was later converted to a retirement home, which it was for more than 70 years. The current owners extensively refurbished the house when they bought it. Spacious rooms, gleaming woodwork, and sparkling stained-glass windows give the house its character. Guests are invited to enjoy the parlor, oak-paneled sitting room with TV, sunny dining room, and breakfast kitchen. A substantial "help yourself" breakfast is provided each morning, and guests are welcome to use the kitchen for snacks or light meals. Six comfortable guest rooms, all with stained-glass windows. Two rooms have private baths; the other four rooms share two additional bathrooms. $50-70.

Chandler Inn

26 Chandler at Berkeley, 02116
(617) 482-3450; (800) 842-3450

Boston's best value! On the edge of the historic Back Bay. Walking distance to Newbury Street, Copley Place, shopping, theaters, and restaurants. All rooms have a private bath, TV, direct-dial telephone, and air conditioning. Continental breakfast included.

Host: Marcia Brown
Rooms: 56 (PB) $74-94
Continental Breakfast
Credit Cards: A, B, C, D, E
Notes: 5, 8, 9, 14

Host Homes of Boston

P.O. Box 117, 02168
(617) 244-1308; FAX (617) 244-5156

Architect's Home. Early Victorian-era townhouse with contemporary furnishings on a quiet street. Bright and private fourth-floor guest room with queen-size bed and roof deck with skyline view. Private bath. Walk to Park Plaza Hotel, restaurants, theaters, Copley Square, and the convention center. No smoking. $75.

Around the Corner. Great location and exceptional decor in this 1826 Federal townhouse. Guest suite has two small single bedrooms, sitting room, TV, and bath. Single guest room with bath on lower level. Near State House, Massachussetts General Hospital, major hotels, MIT, Harvard, and restaurants. No smoking. $85-136.

Bailey's Copley. This typical 1840 Federal townhouse has two guest parlors, a private patio, and cozy atmosphere. Three guest rooms on the second and third floors (king-size or twin beds) share two baths. Self-serve breakfast 7:30-10:00 AM. Resident dogs. Walk to Boston Common, Copley Square, Hynes Convention Center, Amtrak, and subway. Air-conditioned. $68-93.

Coach House. Converted to a private home in 1890, the original structure of this bed and breakfast housed 12 coaches and staff. Here, on a quiet gas-lit street, the host family offers two well-appointed guest rooms on the second (single) and third (queen) floors. Both rooms have private baths. Near Freedom Trail, hotels, restaurants, and "Cheers." Resident cats. $120.

The Nocturne. This 1867 Victorian home in a quiet historic neighborhood has a roof deck and greenhouse. Two third-floor guest rooms (twin beds, or king-size and double with kitchen) with air conditioning and cable TV. Roll away available. Walk to fine restaurants, Back Bay shops, Copley Square, Convention center, Amtrak, and subway. No smoking allowed. Children welcome. $75.

6 Pets welcome; 8 Children welcome; 9 Social drinking allowed; 10 Tennis available; 11 Swimming available; 12 Golf available; 13 Skiing available; 14 May be booked through travel agents.

Host Homes of Boston
(continued)

On the Avenue. Boston Common, Copley Place, convention hotels, and the subway are steps away from 19th-century ambience in private professional club. Dining room; guest parlor. Three spacious doubles have twin beds, telephone, and private bath. Four small singles (one twin bed) share two baths. Roll away: $20. Air conditioning, TV, elevator. $105.

On the Hill. This brick Federal townhouse (1790) on the Hill's loveliest street offers exceptional third-floor quarters—living room, bedroom, modern bath, kitchen, and dining room where breakfast is served. Near Freedom Trail, hotels, State House. Air conditioning; no smoking allowed; TV. $108-115.

On the Park. This 1865 Victorian bowfront in an historic district features antiques and authentic decor. Two fourth-floor guest rooms (king-size and twin beds, or two twins) share a bath. Resident dogs. Four blocks to Copley Square, Hynes Convention Center, Back Bay Orange Line, and Amtrak. No smoking. $75.

Proper Bostonian. Business people like this 1872 townhouse with authentic decor. Spacious third-floor guest room has twin beds, sitting area, and small stocked kitchen where guests make their own breakfast. Another twin room often available, if same party. Busy hosts offer privacy in best area. Four blocks to Copley Square and Hynes Convention Center. Near Boston Commons. Air conditioning; private bath; TV. $85.

Oasis Guest House

22 Edgerly Road, 02115
(617) 267-2262; FAX (617) 267-1920

Two renovated Back Bay townhouses with color TV, telephones, central air, and private baths. Within walking distance of restaurants, museums, and points of interest. This is a great in-town location near the Hynes Convention Center. Enjoy the outside decks. Parking. Fine lodging accommodations in the heart of the city for a price much less than at major hotels. Twelve seasons of mostly repeat and referrals. Call, FAX, or write for more information.

Rooms: 16 (11 PB; 5 SB) $60-78
Continental Breakfast
Credit Cards: A, B, C
Notes: 5, 7, 9, 14

Quincy Adams

Quincy Adams Bed and Breakfast

P.O. Box 158, 02133
(617) 479-6215

Elegant turn-of-the-century Victorian home. Features include canopied beds, fireplaces, and Oriental carpets and furnishings. Sitting room with TV and whirlpool spa. Only 15 minutes from downtown Boston, the Freedom Trail, Faneuil Hall Marketplace, and JFK Library. Walk to historic homes, shops, restaurants, and an ocean beach. Ample parking.

Host: Mary Lee Caldwell
Continental Breakfast weekdays;

Full Breakfast weekends
Rooms: 3 (PB) $60-80
Credit Cards: A, B
Notes: 2, 5, 8, 9, 14

BOURNE

Golden Slumber Accommodations

640 Revere Beach Boulevard, Revere, 02151
(800) 892-3231; (617) 289-1053

103. Charming contemporary Colonial nestled amid a country setting features traditional decor and antique furnishings. Beautifully appointed guest rooms feature twin, double, or queen-size beds and private or shared baths. Scrumptious Dutch-inspired full breakfast served in formal dining room, or enjoy a romantic breakfast in bed featuring fine linen and silver service. Piano, Jacuzzi, fireplace, and laundry facilities. Many additional delightful surprises! Close to island ferries, historic attractions, and private beaches. A rare find! $75-95,

BOXFORD

Bed and Breakfast Marblehead and North Shore

P.O. Box 35, Newtonville, 02160
(617) 964-1606; (800) 832-2632
FAX (617) 332-8572

Day's End. A beautiful architect-designed contemporary home in a country setting with swimming pool on 30 acres. The three guest rooms can be rented individually or as a separate entrance suite. In addition to the efficiency kitchenette and sitting room, the first-floor living room has facilities for entertaining, available for a fee. Open year-round. Continental breakfast. Children welcome. Weekly and monthly rates available. Executive homestays available. No smoking. $55-75.

BREWSTER (CAPE COD)

Bed and Breakfast Associates Bay Colony, Ltd.

P.O. Box 57166, Babson Park, Boston, 02157-0166
(617) 449-5302; (800) 347-5088
FAX (617) 449-5958

CC675. A quiet neighborhood setting, abundant gardens, and an easy drive to the National Seashore await at this cozy little bed and breakfast. Guests will enjoy a full country breakfast with eggs from chickens raised by the hosts. This sparkling fresh and charming home has two guest rooms that share a bath. Full breakfast; no smoking. A two-room suite is available weekly without breakfast. $70.

Bed and Breakfast Cape Cod

P.O. Box 341, West Hyannisport, 02672-0341
(508) 775-2772; FAX (508) 775-2884

17. Along the banks of Cape Cod Bay in historic Brewster is this 1750 sea captain's house. Six hundred yards from the house is a public beach where swimming and fishing are available. A Continental breakfast on the patio with an ocean view is served each morning. Double or twin beds available. Golf, Nickerson State Park, and the village are less than a mile away. $65.

28. This Cape Cod-style house was built in 1739. Today, this lovely old house retains its original appearance and is very well maintained. In a remote area, the birds and plants offer a natural wonderland for sitting or walking in the woods. A two-room suite with a sitting room, double bed, and private full bath is available, and a second guest room on the second floor is also available with a double bed and private bath. Continental breakfast. $85.

33. Perched on a cliff 50 feet above the waters of a beautiful freshwater pond sits a

Bed and Breakfast Cape Cod (continued)

ranch home with two private bath-bedroom suites. On the ground floor, a room with a king-size bed, large sitting area, and a lake view is also available. The hosts serve a Continental breakfast in a lovely, bright dining room, and guests are encouraged to use the parlor. Bring a swim suit and fishing pole, and be prepared to relax in this private setting on the beach. $80.

41. In an antique village, this lovely home was rebuilt in 1973 and has all amenities, including air conditioning, TV, and traditional decor. A short walk takes guests to shops, bay beaches, and other points of interest. A large second-floor private bath-bedroom has a king-size bed, and four other rooms with either double or queen-size beds are also available. Big gourmet breakfast served each morning. $65-125.

Bed and Breakfast of Greater Boston and Cape Cod

P.O. Box 35, Newtonville, 02160
(617) 964-1606; (800) 832-2632
FAX (617) 322-8572

Antique Inn. A restored eighteenth-century sea capain's house and country cottage on seven acres with award-winning gardens. Seven guest rooms with private baths and air conditioning. Each room beautifully decorated with antique furnishings; some rooms have working fireplaces. Full breakfast included. Children over 12 are welcome. $85-135.

The Bramble Inn and Restaurant

2019 Main Street, 02631
(508) 896-7644

The Bramble Inn

Three antique buildings in the heart of the historic district lovingly restored to reflect a bygone era. All 13 rooms with private bath, air conditioning, and breakfast. Chef-owned nationally acclaimed restaurant with five intimate dining rooms, candlelight, antiques, and fresh flowers. Prix fixe four-course dinners by reservation. House specialities include rack of lamb and native seafoods presented with an innovative air. "Best of 1990" *Travel and Leisure* magazine.

Hosts: Cliff and Ruth Manchester
Rooms: 13 (PB) $75-125
Full Breakfast
Credit Cards: A, B, C, D
Notes: 2, 4, 8 (over 7), 9, 10, 11, 12, 14

Brewster Farmhouse Inn

716 Main Street, 02631
(508) 896-3910; (800) 892-3910
FAX (508) 896-4232

Understated elegance and unsurpassed service and amenities. Impeccably furnished gathering room with fireplace, full gourmet breakfasts, creative afternoon teas, heated pool, spa, gardens, and orchard. A country-like setting, yet only a short walk to the beach. Evening turndown with chocolates and sherry. Cozy terry-cloth robes, oversize towels, hair dryers, and fine toiletries. All rooms feature king- or queen-size beds

NOTES: Credit cards accepted: A MasterCard; B Visa; C American Express; D Discover Card; E Diner's Club; F Other; 2 Personal checks accepted; 3 Lunch available; 4 Dinner available; 5 Open all year;

(some with fireplaces), air conditioning, and TV.

Rooms: 5 (4 PB; 1 SB) $65-140
Full Breakfast
Credit Cards: A, B, C, D, E
Notes: 2, 9, 10, 12, 14

Captain Freeman Inn

Captain Freeman Inn

15 Breakwater Road, 02631
(508) 896-7481

Charming old sea captain's mansion offers luxury suites with balcony, private spa, fireplace, canopied bed, TV, and air conditioning. Spacious guest rooms with canopied beds and private baths and rooms with shared bath. Enjoy the wraparound porch, outdoor pool, bikes, and full breakfast. Convenient to Cape Cod's historic north side, walk to beaches, restaurants, and shopping.

Host: Carol Covitz
Rooms: 12 (9 PB; 3 SB) $50-185
Full Breakfast
Credit Cards: A, B, C
Notes: 2, 5, 8 (over 10), 9, 10, 11, 12, 14

High Brewster

964 Satucket Road, 02631
(508) 896-3636; (800) 203-2634

This charming farmhouse, built in 1738, the four cottages, and the main house are on three and a half acres overlooking Lower Mill Pond. The main inn has two rooms; the cottages can accommodate up to six people. High Brewster is a very tranquil and relaxed setting where people come to escape a fast paced lifestyle. The restaurant is one of the area's finest. Guests enjoy American cuisine served in one of three cozy dining rooms. Perfect for a romantic getaway. Children and pets welcome.

Rooms: 8 (PB) $80-190
Continental Breakfast
Credit Cards: A, B, C
Notes: 2, 4, 5, 6, 8, 9, 10, 11, 12, 14

House Guests Cape Cod and the Islands

Box 1881, Orleans, 02653
(508) 896-7053; (800) 666-HOST (reservations)
FAX (508) 896-7054

93100. This beautifully restored bed and breakfast inn was built during the late 1700s. The inn's deceptively small and cozy exterior hides seven spacious and handsomely appointed guest rooms that feature private baths, air conditioning, and queen, king, or twin beds. Some rooms have canopied beds and color cable TV; others have antique hearths with working fireplaces. A full American breakfast is served in the original keeping room or on the deck overlooking several acres of flower gardens, berry patches, and a pond. Children 12 or older are welcome. Smoking is not allowed in the guest rooms. Resident cat. $75-115. $25 for additional person.

93101. In three historic houses in the heart of the historic district, this inn is one-half mile from Cape Cod Bay. The main inn, built in 1861, houses a fine restaurant. Nearby attractions include tennis courts, antique shops, summer theater, bay beaches, and a 17-mile bike trail. Eleven air-conditioned guest rooms feature private baths, period furnishings, and tasteful appointments. Queen, double, and single beds available. The complimentary full breakfasts prepared in the restaurant's kitchen are special treats.

House Guests Cape Cod and the Islands (continued)

Children eight or older are welcome. $75-125. $15-20 for additional person.

93106. A gracious Greek Revival-style home on Route 6A close to the center of town and all mid- and lower-Cape attractions. A guest room with private bath can comfortably accommodate up to three people in a double bed and a single bed. Separate twin and single-bedded guest rooms with adjacent shared bath can be reserved as a suite for three. Guest lounge with refrigerator and TV. Continental breakfast. Smoking limited to designated areas. Open late June through September 30. $48-58. $10 for additional person.

93107. A charming inn built in 1860 with elegant Victorian architectural details. The wraparound porch overlooks the in-ground swimming pool and flower and herb gardens. Fireplace in the common room. Nine romantic guest rooms and luxurious suites, each with private bath and double or queen-size canopied bed. The three suites are air-conditioned and have private whirlpool spas, queen-size canopied beds, TVs, VCRs, telephones, and working fireplaces. On the third floor, three additional guest rooms with double beds and shared bath are available during the warmer months only. Full breakfast served poolside, fireside, or in bed. Children ten or older are welcome. No smoking. $55-185.

93108. Large full-Cape Colonial in a wooded lakeside setting. Every floor has its own deck, so most rooms have deck access and spectacular lake and garden views. Enjoy swimming, sailing, windsurfing, and canoeing from the hosts' dock. The larger of the two very spacious guest rooms has a

double and two twin beds. The other room has a double and one twin bed. The spacious guest bath is shared. Continental breakfast. Children five and older are welcome. A nonsmoking location. Resident dog. $65.

93112. A completely restored three-quarter-Cape home built in 1739. A private guest suite is in a ground-floor wing built in 1950. These comfortable quarters have a bedroom with double bed, a sitting room, private bathroom, and a private entrance. Guests can also be accommodated in a bedroom on the second floor of the original house. It has a double bed and an adjacent large private bath. A third person in party can be accommodated on a roll away bed in the suite. The French-trained host-cook prepares a Continental breakfast. Children 12 and older. No smoking in guest bedrooms. Resident cat. $80-90.

93115. Spacious grounds surround this charming 18th-century Cape farmhouse between two ponds. A peaceful place to rest and relax. The second-floor bedroom has a queen-size bed, private bath with shower, and a lake view. Across the hall, a guest room with double bed and lake view is available for the third and fourth members of a traveling party of four. For children or adults who need separate beds, arrangements can be made to reserve a room with twin single beds and semiprivate bath. A crib is available for infants. Lakeside beach only ten minutes away. Continental breakfast. Children are welcome. Resident cat. Smoking allowed outside. Open May 15 through November 15. Special "Bike or Hike" fall rates available. $65.

93117. Built in 1738 and overlooking one of Brewster's loveliest lakes, this inn and its renowned four-star restaurant are a gleaming tribute to the Colonial past. The main house offers four guest rooms beautifully restored to period country elegance. They feature queen, double, and twin beds, air conditioning, and private and semiprivate baths. There are also three cottages available. Full gourmet breakfasts served. Children are welcome. $40-220.

93118. Less than a mile to Cape Cod Bay from this beautifully restored 1780 vintage bed and breakfast home. On the shore of one of Brewster's lovely lakes, the house has charming guest quarters with private screened porch, private entrance, and water view. There is a queen-size bed and a double pull-out sofa. Private bath with shower. Continental breakfast. Wonderful restaurants and all the attractions of the bayside historic district are nearby. Smoking not permitted in the guest rooms. Resident cat and dog. $68.

93120. A gracious three-story Colonial, once a sea captain's home now an inn, nestled in the heart of Brewster's historic district. Built circa 1800 and lovingly restored by the innkeepers, the inn provides guests with a charming, cozy atmosphere in an antique decor. Each of the nine individually appointed guest rooms has a private bath, air conditioning, and queen-size or double beds. One bedroom has a working fireplace. Complimentary full breakfast. Romantic dining room offers gourmet dinners served by candlelight. Children six and older are welcome. $69-90.

93122. A 150-year-old farmhouse in the historic district and only half a mile from Cape Cod Bay. This impeccably furnished inn features a fireplaced gathering room, heated pool and spa, expansive sun deck, gourmet full breakfasts, afternoon tea, and other unsurpassed services and amenities. There are three guest rooms and a luxurious two-bedroom suite. The guest rooms have king- or queen-size four-poster beds and private baths. One has a private deck conve-

nient to the pool area. Another has a working fireplace. The suite's two queen-bedded rooms share a common bath. The suite can also be reserved as two separate rooms with shared bath. No smoking in guest rooms. Children 16 and older are welcome. $65-155.

Isaiah Clark House

Isaiah Clark House

1187 Main Street, 02631
(508) 896-2223; (800) 822-4001

Built in 1780, this inn was once the mansion of a famous sea captain and is set on five acres of landscaped gardens. All guests enjoy a full American breakfast served on a deck overlooking the gardens. Many guest rooms have working fireplaces; all are air-conditioned. Host was formerly trained as a Swiss hotelier. Special welcome for honeymooners.

Host: Charles Phillipe DiCesare
Rooms: 7 (PB) $95-115
Full Breakfast
Credit Cards: A, B, C
Notes: 5, 7 (limited), 8, 9, 10, 11, 12, 14

Old Sea Pines Inn

2553 Main Street, 02631
(508) 896-6114

Lovely turn-of-the-century mansion, once the Sea Pines School of Charm and Person-

6 Pets welcome; 8 Children welcome; 9 Social drinking allowed; 10 Tennis available; 11 Swimming available; 12 Golf available; 13 Skiing available; 14 May be booked through travel agents.

Old Sea Pines Inn

ality for Young Women, now a newly reno-vated and redecorated country inn. Furnished with antiques, some of the rooms have work-ing fireplaces. On three and one-half acres of land, with a wraparound porch looking out over the lawn, trees, and flowers. Compli-mentary beverage on arrival. Dinner avail-able July and August.

Hosts: Stephen and Michele Rowan
Rooms: 16 (PB) $45-95
Full Breakfast
Credit Cards: A, B, C, E
Notes: 2, 4, 5, 8 (over 8), 9, 10, 11, 12, 14

Orleans Bed and Breakfast Associates

P.O. Box 1312, Orleans, 02653
(508) 255-3824; (800) 541-6226

On Blueberry Hill. Perched on a hill over-looking private Blueberry Pond, this light, open, very contemporary home offers one queen-size and one twin bedroom on a sep-arate level with private entrance. Rooms share a large bath. Enjoy a private patio, or come up to the large deck and screened-in

porch. Swimming in the pond is a must, as is biking on the Cape Cod Bike Trail across the street and down a wooded path. Hostess is a cellist and gourmet cook, has her own jam business, and is an avid gardener and landscaper. $70.

Quail Hollow. Spacious grounds surround this charming 18th-century Cape farmhouse between two ponds. Second-floor bedroom has a queen-size bed and private bath with shower. A single room is available for an-other family member. Both rooms have water view. Breakfast is served on large screened porch. Canoe to lakeside beach for swimming, or walk there in ten minutes. $70.

Stonybrook. A pre-1776 restored Colonial house in a storybook setting next to the old grist mill and famous Stony Brook Herring Run. Private entrance to upstairs large dou-ble room with fireplace, sitting room, small modern kitchenette, and private bath. The suite has a TV and air conditioning. An at-tractive sitting area outside overlooks the mill pond. $60.

BROOKLINE

Beacon Inn

1087 and 1750 Beacon Street, 02146
(617) 566-0088

These turn-of-the-century townhouses have been converted into two of Brookline's most charming guest houses. The original wood-work is reminiscent of their 19th-century construction, and the lobby fire-places offer a friendly welcome to travelers. Large, comfortably furnished, sunny rooms provide pleasant accommodations at a rea-sonable price. The Beacon Inn is minutes away from downtown Boston. The area of-fers a wide variety of restaurants, shops, museums, theaters, and other attractions.

NOTES: Credit cards accepted: A MasterCard; B Visa; C American Express; D Discover Card; E Diner's Club; F Other; 2 Personal checks accepted; 3 Lunch available; 4 Dinner available; 5 Open all year;

Hosts: Dan McMann and Megan Rockett
Rooms: 24 (15 PB; 9 SB) $49-86
Continental Breakfast
Credit Cards: A, B, C
Notes: 5, 8, 9, 14

Bed and Breakfast Associates Bay Colony, Ltd.

P.O. Box 57166, Babson Park, Boston, 02157-0166
(617) 449-5302; (800) 347-5088
FAX (617) 449-5958

M610. This quiet Brookline Hills neighborhood is convenient to the Longwood Medical area as well as the "T" to central Boston. The guest suite is a large room featuring a fully stocked kitchenette, private bath, dining table, and sofa. Continental breakfast; children welcome; no smoking allowed. $75.

M618. Listed on the National Register of Historic Places, this fine brick townhouse has three guest rooms, each reflecting the decorating talents of its gracious hostess. Choice of queen-size or twin beds, with shared bath. Walk to antique shops, bakeries, trolley and bus lines in Brookline Village (or walk to Boston in 30 minutes). Free driveway parking. $55-65.

M644. Close to the medical center (Children's Hospital, Harvard Medical School, Dana-Farber Cancer), this lovingly restored and authentically furnished Victorian home offers exceptional guest privacy. On the third floor, the main guest room is furnished with carved antique twin beds. Lace accents add to the charm. An auxiliary single room is available for parties of three. Driveway parking. $75.

M661. On Beacon Street, between Boston University and Boston College, this historic townhouse dates back to 1894. Fully restored and tastefully furnished with antiques, the guest room has a bird's-eye-

maple four-poster bed and a twin bed, with a private bath in the hall. Free driveway parking. $63-70.

Bed and Breakfast of Greater Boston and Cape Cod

P.O. Box 35, Newtonville, 02160
(617) 964-1606; (800) 832-2632
FAX (617) 322-8572

The Old Manse. This bed and breakfast offers guests a private hall bath and two single beds in a charming six-room apartment decorated with fine art and African artifacts collected by the hostess during her two-year stay in West Africa. Guests are welcome to use the living room, dining room, and eat-in kitchen. Self-serve Continental breakfast. A roll away cot and cradle are available for an extra guest or infant. No smoking. $65-85.

Beech Tree Inn

83 Longwood Avenue, 02146
(617) 277-1620; (800) 544-9660

The Beech Tree Inn is a turn-of-the-century Victorian private home that has been converted to a bed and breakfast. Each room is individually decorated, some with fireplaces, and they vary in size and decor. A Continental breakfast is served, and a fully equipped kitchen is available. The inn is within walking distance of many shops, restaurants, and world-renowned medical centers; and internationally famous academic institutions are only a few blocks away. The nearby subway will take visitors into downtown Boston in 12 minutes. A pleasant interlude for a night, a weekend, or even a week.

Hosts: Kathrine Anderson and Bette Allen
Rooms: 9 (4 PB; 5 SB) $47.17-71.30
Continental Breakfast
Credit Cards: None
Notes: 2, 5, 6, 8

6 Pets welcome; 8 Children welcome; 9 Social drinking allowed; 10 Tennis available; 11 Swimming available; 12 Golf available; 13 Skiing available; 14 May be booked through travel agents.

Greater Boston Hospitality

P.O. Box 1142, 02146
(617) 277-5430

Hundreds of accommodations in outstanding Georgian, Federal, Victorian, and Colonial homes, condos, and inns in the greater Boston area. All include breakfast, many include parking, and others are on excellent transport system. Many are minutes from colleges, medical area, museum, and Freedom Trail. Visit Boston as a native while staying at Greater Boston Hospitality. Write or call today for free brochure.

Manager: Kelly Simpson
Rooms: 125 (100 PB; 25 SB) $47-75
Full and Continental Breakfast
Credit Cards: A, B
Notes: 2, 3, 5, 8, 10, 11, 12, 14

Host Homes of Boston

P.O. Box 117, 02168
(617) 244-1308; FAX (617) 244-5156

Heath House. Country atmosphere close to city in classic Colonial on rolling lawn. English hostess offers two second-floor guest rooms (queen with air conditioning and twins). Children welcome. Near Pine Manor, Boston College, and Longwood medical area. Boston five miles. Green Line-D one-half mile. No smoking. $68.

Sarah's Loft. Bright and spacious third-floor suite with private entrance. Guest quarters include two queen bedrooms. Also, a large living area with skylights, stereo, dining table (where breakfast is served), refrigerator, microwave, and extra sofa bed. Children are welcome. Green Line-C and village two blocks. Fenway Park, Boston one mile. Air conditioning; crib; private bath; TV; no smoking. $75.

Studio Apartment. Colonial home (1620 Salem house replica) on quiet cul-de-sac offers above-ground basement room with double bed, sofa, galley kitchen, patio, and private entrance. Choice of breakfast on tray or self-serve. Five blocks to Green Line-C. Ten minutes to Copley Square. TV; air conditioning; no smoking allowed; private bath. $75.

BROOKLINE HILLS

Host Homes of Boston

P.O. Box 117, 02168
(617) 244-1308; FAX (617) 244-5156

The Tree House. Meg's modern townhouse with traditional decor has a sweeping view from the glass-walled living room and deck. Two second-floor guest rooms (double and twins). Also, in season, a king room with air conditioning and private bath. Two Siamese cats. Near Back Bay, Boston College, and Boston University. Ten minutes to Hynes Convention Center via Green Line-C and D three blocks. Private bath; TV; no smoking. $61-75.

BROOKLINE VILLAGE

Host Homes of Boston

P.O. Box 117, 02168
(617) 244-1308; FAX (617) 244-5156

NOTES: Credit cards accepted: A MasterCard; B Visa; C American Express; D Discover Card; E Diner's Club; F Other; 2 Personal checks accepted; 3 Lunch available; 4 Dinner available; 5 Open all year;

Historic Row. The National Register of Historic Places lists this 1928 Williamsburg attached house. Three large second-floor guest rooms (two queens and twins) each with color TV. Near Boston College, Boston University, Longwood Medical center. Green Line-D three blocks. Ten minutes to Back Bay and convention center. TV; shared bath; no smoking. $64.

BUCKLAND

1797 House

Upper Street-Charlemont Road, 01338
(413) 625-2975

This 18th-century home is in a peaceful, rural area, yet is convenient to many attractions and all points in New England. Large rooms, private baths, down quilts, and a lovely screened porch ensure comfort. A modicum of civilization in an increasingly uncivilized world. Closed December.

Host: Janet Turley
Rooms: 3 (PB) $60-75
Full Breakfast
Credit Cards: None
Notes: 2, 5, 10, 11, 12, 13

CAMBRIDGE

Bed and Breakfast Associates Bay Colony, Ltd.

P.O. Box 57166, Babson Park, Boston, 02157-0166
(617) 449-5302; (800) 347-5088
FAX (617) 449-5958

M804. Near Harvard Yard, this impeccable Philadelphia-style Victorian, circa 1890, is on a quiet street among the finest homes in Cambridge. The two-room suite features a spacious sitting room with sleeper-sofa, fireplace, writing table, TV, and balcony. Continental breakfast; children welcome; no smoking. $85.

M830. On a quiet street near Harvard Law School just north of Harvard Square, this delightful Queen Anne Victorian has two gracious guest rooms, one queen-size and one double, with private baths. Hosts have preserved authentic Victorian details throughout the home. Limited parking. $85-90.

M875. A large home set in a quiet neighborhood adjacent to jogging paths. Just a 20-minute walk from Harvard Square, this home features skylights, sliding doors to deck, many plants, antiques, playroom, and a fenced yard. Three guest rooms with private baths. Full and imaginative breakfast; children welcome. $55; family and monthly rates available.

M885. This congenial hostess, a Boston attorney, shares her cozy Greek Revival home (circa 1853) just outside Harvard Square. Her decor is accented by a refreshing mix of country antiques and her quiet urban neighborhood provides a convenient setting for activities in Boston or Cambridge. Three guest rooms share two full baths. Full breakfast upon request; children welcome; no smoking. $55-66; family and monthly rates available.

M888. Bright, cheerful, and convenient to Harvard Square. This bed and breakfast home has three guest rooms, a guest parlor, and dining room. The third-floor suite has skylights, private bath, twin-king option, and space for queen-size futon for children. Second floor rooms have queen-size beds and share a bath. Free parking on street. $65-78.

M900. This fine bed and breakfast inn is in a Harvard Square neighborhood. The recently completed historic restoration has produced 18 guest rooms with private baths and tasteful decor. Romantics enjoy the second-floor suite with fireplace. Limited reserved parking available. $95-135.

6 Pets welcome; 8 Children welcome; 9 Social drinking allowed; 10 Tennis available; 11 Swimming available; 12 Golf available; 13 Skiing available; 14 May be booked through travel agents.

Bed and Breakfast Associates Bay Colony (continued)

M930. A spectacular decorator-furnished bed and breakfast inn in North Cambridge. Each room has a built-in vanity with sink and color TV. Full breakfast is served in the formal Victorian dining room, and guests are invited to relax in one of the gracious parlors. A lovely carriage house and a nearby guest house have also been restored and are offered as bed and breakfast accommodations. Private baths; children over six welcome; smoking allowed on porch only. $119-169.

A Cambridge House— Bed and Breakfast Inn

2218 Massachusetts Avenue, 02140
(617) 491-6300; (800) 232-9989

Built in 1892 and listed on the National Register of Historic Places, A Cambridge House offers antique-filled guest rooms, many with four-poster canopied beds and private baths, and some with fireplaces. Featured on TV by BBC in Europe and recently on Oprah Winfrey's Dream Vacations, this unique bed and breakfast is considered one of Boston's finest. A five-minute walk to the subway, close to Harvard Square, and minutes from the Freedom Trail. Full breakfast served. Children over six.

Hosts: Ellen Riley and Tony Femmino
Rooms: 14 (10 PB; 4 SB) $89-195
Full Breakfast
Credit Cards: A, B, C
Notes: 2, 5, 8 (over 6), 14

Host Homes of Boston

P.O. Box 117, Boston, 02168
(617) 244-1308; FAX (617) 244-5156

Blue Hawthorne. This 100-year-old Victorian home off Brattle Street is a quiet oasis near bustling Harvard Square. The host offers two first-floor guest rooms (queen and twins) with private baths, telephone, and TV. Shady side garden. Three blocks to the square, Red Line, Charles Hotel, restaurants, and shops. Air conditioning; TV; no smoking. $75.

Cambridge Suite. This large home (1855) is on a quiet road only three blocks from bustling Harvard Square. The first-floor guest suite has a queen bedroom and sitting room with sofa and desk. Breakfast served in the dining room. Near William James Hall and law school. Red Line three blocks. Air conditioning. No smoking. $92.

Near Harvard Square. Just a seven-minute walk to the square, Harvard Yard, Brattle Street, and Red Line. Quiet. Shady location. European decor. Coffee ground fresh for breakfast. Private first-floor guest room with double bed. Air conditioning; TV; shared bath. $68.

True Victorian. Host's Victorian jewel sits on a quiet hill near Massachusetts Avenue between Harvard and Porter squares. Three second-floor guest rooms—two with double bed, TV, and desk; king room. Only two rooms booked at a time. Shared family bath. Hearty breakfast in sunny kitchen, often self-serve on weekdays. Red Line and train at Porter Square three blocks. TV; no smoking. $68.

The Missing Bell

16 Sacramento Street, 02138
(617) 876-0987

This 1883 Queen Anne Victorian is exceptionally beautiful with its unusual hand-carved woodwork, stained-glass windows, and elegant spaces. The spacious guest rooms, carefully furnished with antiques, have private baths, comfortable beds, and air conditioning. Breakfast often gets rave reviews. Served in the dining room, it includes hot-from-the-oven baked goods, a special fruit dish, and freshly ground coffee. Close to Harvard; six blocks to subway at Harvard Square. No smoking permitted.

Hosts: Kristin Quinlan and J. P. Massar
Rooms: 2 (PB) $85
Continental Breakfast
Credit Cards: A, B
Notes: 2, 5, 9

CENTERVILLE

Bed and Breakfast Cape Cod

P.O. Box 341, West Hyannisport, 02672-0341
(508) 775-2772; FAX (508) 775-2884

23. Formerly the home of Cardinal Spellman, this elegant 1830s mansion with grounds designed by Frederick Law Olmstead has been restored in the Victorian splendor of a past era. It offers suites or rooms, all with private baths, a full gourmet breakfast, and a short walk to Craigville Beach. Hyannis is five minutes away. No children. $85-185.

43. This quiet bed and breakfast overlooks Lake Wequaquet, the largest freshwater lake on Cape Cod. The second floor has been set aside for guests, featuring two rooms that share a bath. A first-floor room offers a king-size bed and a private bath. Continental breakfast. $55-65.

52. This property has been featured in *Country Magazine* and is on the National Register of Historic Places. It offers three guest rooms, all with private baths and air conditioning. Full country breakfast served in the dining room. Children over 12 welcome. $80-90.

Bed and Breakfast/Inns of New England

128 South Hoop Pole Road, Guilford, CT 06437
(203) 457-0042; (800) 582-0853

MA-1045. This inn offers the warmth and luxury of a Victorian home in the romantic ambience of an earlier time. Guest rooms have hardwood floors of cherry, maple, and oak, Oriental carpets, and antiques. Privacy is assured, for this 100-year-old home was designed so that no two guest rooms share the same wall. Five suites with private bath (two more with a shared bath), fireplaces, cathedral ceilings, roof deck, and a private library make this inn unique. Garden cottage with queen-size bed, wraparound porch, and private bath also available. $115-135.

Copper Beech Inn

497 Main Street, 02632
(508) 771-5488

Built in 1830 by an intercoastal ship captain, this charmingly restored house is now on the National Register of Historic Places. It stands amid tall trees, including the largest European beech tree on Cape Cod. Interior features include a parlor and a common room for guest use. Walk to Craigville Beach, one of the ten best beaches in the United States. Hyannis, the population center of the Cape, where the ferry to Nantucket and Martha's Vineyard is boarded, is four miles away. Air-conditioned. Two-

Copper Beech Inn

6 Pets welcome; 8 Children welcome; 9 Social drinking allowed; 10 Tennis available; 11 Swimming available; 12 Golf available; 13 Skiing available; 14 May be booked through travel agents.

night minimum stay is required for May 25 through October 10.

Host: Joyce Diehl
Rooms: 3 (PB) $90
Full Breakfast
Credit Cards: A, B, D
Notes: 2, 5, 7 (limited), 9, 10, 11, 12

DESTINNATIONS
New England

P.O. Box 1173, Osterville, 02655
(508) 428-5600; (800) 333-4667 (reservations)
FAX (508) 420-0565

7206. This romantic Victorian mansion, circa 1830, has five rooms and suites and a charming cottage, all with private baths. It sits amidst beautiful landscaping and a Sweetheart Rose Garden in the mid-Cape area. The inn has been restored to its former splendor and features beautiful hardwood floors, Oriental carpets, antiques, and reproductions. A full gourmet breakfast is served in the handsome dining room each morning. It is a short walk to Craigville Beach, and is accessible to the mid-Cape Highway, island ferries, and Boston. No children or pets allowed. Open year-round. $115-185.

The Old Hundred House

1211 Craigville Beach Road, 02632
(508) 775-6166

An old sea captain's home in a quiet country village. Within easy travel of many points of interest, shops, restaurants, churches, etc. Two- to three-minute walk from one of the best beaches on the Cape. Rooms are nicely furnished, airy, and sunny. The great veranda is very popular and gets a constant southwest breeze, keeping it cool.

Hosts: Andrew J. and Marina Downes
Rooms: 6 (SB) $45
Continental Breakfast
Notes: 2, 5, 7, 8, 9, 10, 11, 12

CHATHAM

Bed and Breakfast Associates Bay Colony, Ltd.

P.O. Box 57166, Babson Park Branch,
Boston, 02157-0166
(617) 449-5302; (800) 347-5088; FAX (617) 449-5958

CC475. The hostess invites guests to share this sprawling Cape-style home with its Early American decor. This wooded setting is perfect for country walks. Nearby is the village of Chatham, renowned for its treasure trove of galleries, shops, ice cream parlors, and restaurants in a gracious, old-fashioned, seaside setting. Three guest rooms, some with private baths. Continental breakfast; children welcome; no smoking. $68-83.

Bed and Breakfast Cape Cod

P.O. Box 341, West Hyannisport, 02672-0341
(508) 775-2772; FAX (508) 775-2884

12. This reproduction of an Early American Cape Cod home offers a first-floor room with a private bath, double bed; the second floor offers two rooms with double beds. (These rooms are never rented separately, so they share a "private" bath.) Continental breakfast. A short walk to the village, fish pier, and the beach. $65.

48. This 19-room country inn was built in the 1830s and painstakingly restored in 1989. All guest rooms are air-conditioned, have private baths, and are filled with antiques and tasteful accents. Continental breakfast is served from 8:30-10:00 A.M., and cocktails are served in the Schooner Tavern on the premises. $90-205.

57. In the heart of the residential section of Chatham is an 1860s Colonial house offering three private-bath, queen-size guest rooms. The unique location makes for easy access to the village center, the lighthouse, and the beach. The parklike grounds provide a pleasant place for relaxing. The deck can be used for breakfast or for a beverage in the afternoon. Guest rooms are tastefully done with attention to guest comforts. Breakfasts are a special treat with foods that will surprise and thrill the palate. No smoking. No children under 14. $75-95.

76. The village of Chatham offers something for everyone. This home has three guest rooms with private baths in a quiet residential area. Full Continental breakfast served. Living room with TV as well as a deck that is great for relaxing after a day at the beach or shopping in the village. Immaculate and beautifully decorated.

78. Built in 1985, this lovely host home offers a second-floor suite that has a large bedroom with a double bed and a pair of twins, sitting area, TV, and private bath with a shower. A generous Continental breakfast with homemade breads and muffins is served in the country room or patio, and the home is one-half mile from town and three-quarters of a mile from the harbor. $65-75.

Bed and Breakfast of Greater Boston and Cape Cod

P.O. Box 35, Newtonville, 02160
(617) 964-1606; (800) 832-2632
FAX (617) 322-8572

Classic Cape. Privacy and charm at this classic Cape Cod-style home, close to some of the area's most beautiful beaches and rugged shoreline. Guest accommodation has a separate entrance leading up to a large, sunny room with a double and twins, plus a full private bath. Downstairs there is a guest sitting room with fireplace. A delicious and generous Continental breakfast is served. No smoking; open year-round. Two-night minimum stay. Infants and children over 12 are welcome. $75-85.

The Bradford Inn and Motel

26 Cross Street, P.O. Box 750, 02633
(508) 945-1030; (800) CHATHAM

The Bradford Inn and Motel is a unique complex of 25 rooms in the quaint seaside village of Chatham. Rooms have king- and queen-size canopied beds. Eleven fireplaces, cable TV, air conditioning, and telephones. It is within the historic district, a short stroll from charming shops, theaters, concerts, restaurants, beach, golf, and tennis. Yet the accommodations are in a secluded area away from the hustle of the village proper. Outdoor heated pool. Dinner available from mid-May through October.

Hosts: William and Audrey Gray
Rooms: 25 (PB) $80-175
Full Breakfast
Credit Cards: A, B, C, D
Notes: 2, 4, 5, 7 (limited), 8 (over 8), 9, 10, 11, 12, 14

Carriage House Inn

407 Old Harbor Road, 02633
(508) 945-4688

A small, cozy bed and breakfast with splendid breakfasts! Charming antique home tastefully restored, furnished with antiques and family pieces. Three light and airy bedrooms with queen-size beds and private baths; air-conditioned; three additional rooms will be available in the summer of 1995. Fireplaced living room with piano, farmer's porch, deck, and spacious grounds are all available for guests' enjoyment. Full country breakfast. Guest pantry stocked with beverages and homemade cookies. Easy walk to village and fish pier. Bicycles and beach towels available. Friendly golden retriever, Sadie, in residence. Come relax awhile with these hosts!

6 Pets welcome; 8 Children welcome; 9 Social drinking allowed; 10 Tennis available; 11 Swimming available; 12 Golf available; 13 Skiing available; 14 May be booked through travel agents.

Hosts: Pam and Tom Patton
Rooms: 3 (PB) $75-135
Full Breakfast
Credit Cards: A, B, C
Notes: 2, 5, 8 (over 14), 9, 10, 11,12, 14

Chatham Town House Inn

Chatham Town House Inn

11 Library Lane, 02633
(508) 945-2180; (800) 242-2180

Circa 1881 sea captain's estate-country inn. In the historic district of the village next to the Eldredge Library off Main Street. There are 25 guest rooms and two cottages with fireplaces on two acres of lovely gardens. Air conditioning, telephones, refrigerators, cable color TV, and private baths. Full breakfast each morning served in the gourmet dinner restaurant, Two Turtles. Heated pool and whirlpool spa with the Cabana Grill for lunch. Romantic honeymoon rooms. Within walking distance to all activities and sandy beaches. Nonsmoking restaurant and guest rooms.

Hosts: Russell and Svea Peterson
Rooms: 25 (PB) $100-195
Credit Cards: A, B, C, D, E
Notes: 3, 4, 5, 10, 11, 12, 14

Cranberry Inn at Chatham

359 Main Street, 02633
(508) 945-9232; (800) 332-4667
FAX (508) 945-3769

Chatham's oldest inn, completely renovated. Conveniently in the heart of the historic village district within steps of shopping, dining, and beautiful beaches. Each of the 18 guest rooms is individually appointed and furnished with antiques and reproductions. All private baths; rooms with fireplaces, balconies, and wet bars available. Spacious, deluxe suite available with fireplace and loft. Hospitable hosts and staff. Homemade Continental breakfast is served daily.

Hosts: Jim and Debbie Bradley
Rooms: 18 (PB) $79-205
Continental Breakfast
Credit Cards: A, B, C
Notes: 2, 8 (over 8), 9, 10, 11, 12, 14

The Cyrus Kent House Inn

63 Cross Street, 02633
(800) 338-5368

Comfortably elegant, the inn is an award-winning restoration of a 19th-century sea captain's mansion. Rooms are large, bright, and airy, furnished with antiques. Private baths, telephone, and TV. On a quiet lane in the quaint seaside village of Chatham, a his-

The Cyrus Kent House

toric district. Excellent restaurants and beaches are within steps.

Host: Sharon Mitchell Swan
Rooms: 10 (PB) $90-145
Continental Breakfast
Credit Cards: A, B, C
Notes: 2, 5, 7, 8 (over 12), 9, 10, 11, 12

House Guests Cape Cod and the Islands

Box 1881, Orleans, 02653
(508) 896-7053; (800) 666-HOST (reservations)
FAX (508) 896-7054

93134. A three-quarter Cape Cod-style home in a wooded area close to the beach on Nantucket Sound. This bed and breakfast lodging is ideal for a couple or for a family of four. It consists of a large room with its own private entrance and a private deck. It has a sitting area with color TV and video cassette player, a partially equipped kitchen area, ceiling fan, and a private bath. A trundle bed can be arranged as separate twin beds or a king-size bed, and a sleep-sofa opens to become a double bed. Continental breakfast. Children are welcome. A nonsmoking location. Resident cat. $70.

Orleans Bed and Breakfast Associates

P.O. Box 1312, Orleans, 02653
(508) 255-3824; (800) 541-6226

The Breakaway. This meticulously maintained old house is entered through an attractive front door just a short walk from the famous Chatham Lighthouse. The charming guest parlor with TV is to the right. Upstairs there are three guest bedrooms, two queens and a twin. Two full baths are off the hall. Breakfast in a lovely dining room, or carry coffee onto a large screened side porch. It's less than a mile walk to town with its many boutiques and fine restaurants. Walk to the sea! $80.

Lighthouse View. This pristine traditional Cape Cod house is on a breezy hill with views of Chatham's famous Stage Harbor Lighthouse. Two spacious double-bedded guest rooms share a bath and an upstairs sitting room, decorated with antiques and lace curtains. (One room has a single bed for a traveling companion or child, at $15 extra.) Guests are welcome to sit on the quiet deck or stroll down to the Oyster River. Harding's Beach, on beautiful Nantucket Sound, is a mile away. $70-80.

Salt Marsh House. Fresh breezes ruffle the white curtains in this pristine house to give guests a real feeling of being at the seaside. Only a two-minute walk to Nantucket Sound beach with sailboat and windsurfer rentals and snack bar. Three rooms on second floor; one spacious king-size with private bath; two twin rooms with large shared bath. Buffet-style breakfast. $55-65.

CHESTER

Moses Nickerson House Inn

364 Old Harbor Road, 02633
(508) 945-5859; (800) 628-6972

Quiet, elegant, romantic. Built in 1839 by whaling captain Moses Nickerson, this small inn has seven individually decorated guest rooms featuring canopied beds, fireplaces, Oriental rugs, and private baths. Glass-enclosed breakfast room. Walk to the quaint village of Chatham with its fine shops, galleries, and restaurants, or turn right at the end of the driveway and walk to the beach or fishing pier.

Hosts: Elsie and Carl Piccola
Rooms: 7 (PB) $70-159
Full Breakfast
Credit Cards: A, B
Notes: 2, 9, 10, 11, 12

6 Pets welcome; 8 Children welcome; 9 Social drinking allowed; 10 Tennis available; 11 Swimming available; 12 Golf available; 13 Skiing available; 14 May be booked through travel agents.

CHILMARK (MARTHA'S VINEYARD)

Breakfast at Tiasquam

Rural Route 1, Box 296, 02535
(508) 645-3685

Breakfast at Tiasquam is set among the farms, ponds, woodlands, and rolling pastures of Martha's Vineyard, on the peak of a hill, well off the beaten path. Just minutes away is Lucy Vincent, one of the most beautiful beaches on the entire East Coast. A delicious full country breakfast is served. A beautifully decorated and smoke-free house with attention paid to craftsmanship, privacy, comfort, and quiet. Breakfast at Tiasquam will make every stay on Martha's Vineyard truly unforgettable.

Host: Ron Crowe
Rooms: 8 (2 PB; 6 SB) $70-195
Full Breakfast
Credit Cards: None
Notes: 2, 5, 8, 9, 10, 11, 12, 14

Breakfast at Tiasquam

COHASSET

Bed and Breakfast Cape Cod

P.O. Box 341, West Hyannisport, 02672-0341
(508) 775-2772; FAX (508) 775-2884

81. Enjoy the beautiful harbor, take a swim in the on-premises pool, or play a game of tennis on the host's court. This charming bed and breakfast in a most picturesque village south of Boston offers five bedrooms with private baths. Continental breakfast.

Forty minutes to Boston by watercraft or bus. Children over 11 welcome. $100-135.

Host Homes of Boston

P.O. Box 117, Newton, 02168
(617) 244-1308; FAX (617) 244-5156

Actor's Row. Featured in Colonial Homes, this harborside Colonial (1840) is the ultimate inn, off the beaten path with antiques and manicured grounds. Five renovated guest rooms (four queens and a king-size suite) with private baths. Guest parlor with fireplace. Sculptured pool, Jacuzzi, and tennis court. Walk to Sandy Beach or village, or just relax on the veranda overlooking the harbor with magnificent sunsets. Boston 19 miles. Cape Cod 30-minute drive. A special place. No smoking. Swimming and tennis. $100-135.

CONCORD

Bed and Breakfast Greater Boston and Cape Cod

P.O. Box 35, Newtonville, 02160
(617) 964-1606; (800) 832-2632
FAX (617) 332-8572

1775 Colonial Inn. Just 20 miles west of Boston with easy access to main highways, this meticulously restored Colonial inn offers five guest rooms, all with private baths, color TV, air conditioning, and telephones. Hearty Continental buffet breakfast is served in the mornings, and afternoon tea or sherry is served by the fireplace in the 200-year-old sitting room. Fitness club facilities only a short walk from the inn. $75-85.

Bed and Breakfast/Inns of New England

128 South Hoop Pole Road, Guilford, CT 06437
(203) 457-0042; (800) 582-0853

NOTES: Credit cards accepted: A MasterCard; B Visa; C American Express; D Discover Card; E Diner's Club; F Other; 2 Personal checks accepted; 3 Lunch available; 4 Dinner available; 5 Open all year;

MA-1009. This 1775 center-chimney Colonial has hand-hewn beams, gunstock posts, handsome six-over-six windows, and 18th-century paneling or molding. Guest rooms have double and queen-size beds; all have private bathrooms, direct-dial telephone, color TV, and individual climate control. The inn is two miles from Walden Pond and within a one-minute walk from the Concord Fitness Center, where visitors can stretch, swim, and sauna as a guest of the inn. No smoking. No pets. $65-85.

Colonel Roger Brown

1694 Main Street, 01742
(508) 369-9119; (800) 292-1369

This 1775 Colonial home is on the historic register and close to the Concord and Lexington historic districts, 15 miles west of Boston and Cambridge. Five rooms with air conditioning, private baths, TV, and telephones. Continental breakfast and complimentary beverages at all times. Complimentary use of Concord Fitness Club adjacent to inn. Comfortable and cozy atmosphere.

Host: Sheila Carlton
Rooms: 5 (PB) $65-75
Continental Breakfast
Credit Cards: A, B, C, E
Notes: 2, 5, 8 (over 12), 9, 10, 11, 12, 13, 14

Hawthorne Inn

462 Lexington Road, 01742
(508) 369-5610

Built circa 1870 on land once owned by Ralph Waldo Emerson, Nathaniel Hawthorne, and the Alcotts. Alongside the "battle road" of 1775 and within walking distance of authors' homes, battle sites, and Walden Pond. Furnished with antiques, handmade quilts, original artwork, Japanese prints, and sculpture.

Hosts: G. Burch and M. Mudry
Rooms: 7 (PB) $75-160
Continental Breakfast
Credit Cards: A, B, C, D
Notes: 2, 5, 8, 9, 10, 11, 12, 13, 14

CUMMAQUID

Bed and Breakfast Associates Bay Colony, Ltd.

P.O. Box 57166, Babson Park, Boston, 02157-0166
(617) 449-5302; (800) 347-5088;
FAX (617) 449-5958

CC220. Mid-Cape Barnstable County. On the North Shore of Cape Cod in the oldest historical district in the USA, this quaint Cape-style home has three spotless guest rooms (twin and queen-size), each with private bath. Full breakfast. Walk to Barnstable Harbor or Cape Cod Bay, or just relax on two-and-a-half acres of private grounds. Fine art galleries and restaurants nearby. $80-90.

Bed and Breakfast Cape Cod

P.O. Box 341, West Hyannisport, 02672-0341
(508) 775-2772; FAX (508) 775-2884

61. Just east of Barnstable, this house built in 1930 is a typical Cape Cod-style home with several acres of manicured grounds. Three rooms with private baths are available for guests. Hostess serves a full country breakfast with a Scandinavian flair. Hyannis and the ferry to Nantucket or Martha's Vineyard are four miles away. No smoking. No children. $65-90.

CUMMINGTON

Cumworth Farm

472 West Cummington Road, 01026
(413) 634-5529

A 200-year-old house with a sugar house and blueberry and raspberry fields on the premises. Pick berries in season. The farm raises sheep and is close to Tanglewood, Smith College, the William Cullen Bryant Homestead, cross-country skiing, and hiking trails. Hot tub.

6 Pets welcome; 8 Children welcome; 9 Social drinking allowed; 10 Tennis available; 11 Swimming available; 12 Golf available; 13 Skiing available; 14 May be booked through travel agents.

Hosts: Ed and Mary McColgan
Rooms: 6 (SB) $60
Full Breakfast
Credit Cards: None
Notes: 2, 5, 8, 9, 10, 11, 12, 13

DANVERS

Bed and Breakfast Associates Bay Colony, Ltd.

P.O. Box 57166, Babson Park, Boston, 02157-0166
(617) 449-5302; (800) 347-5088
FAX (617) 449-5958

CN150. This immaculate 200-year-old house has beamed ceilings, beehive fireplaces, a lovely in-ground pool, and private guest quarters. This hostess serves a luscious homemade breakfast on antique pewter. Two guest rooms on the second floor share a bath. Full breakfast; children welcome; smoking downstairs only. $75-90.

Bed and Breakfast Marblehead and North Shore

P.O. Box 35, Newtonville, 02160
(617) 964-1606; (800) 832-2632
FAX (617) 332-8572

The Antique Sleigh. A beautiful 1854 Colonial home on the National Register of Historic Places in an area originally known as "Olde Salem Village." Near Route 95, in the Salem/Marblehead area with easy access to Boston and the North Shore. Kid-friendly and family-friendly accommodations. Many antiques and collectibles throughout, but many kids can also touch and enjoy. Four beautiful rooms with shared baths. Roll aways are available at an additional cost. All rooms are air-conditioned and have color cable TV. Common room with TV and fireplace, and full-sized swimming pool out back. No smoking. $75-85.

Cordwainer Bed and Breakfast

78 Centre Street, 01923
(508) 774-1860

This circa 1854 home is listed on the National Register of Historic Places. It features beamed ceilings, canopied beds, fireplace, kitchen, and family room. The swimming pool is open from June until September. Danvers is 20 miles north of Boston, and five miles west of Salem. New Hampshire is just a 30-minute drive. Continental breakfast provided. Children welcome.

Host: Peggy Blais
Rooms: 3 (1 PB; 2 SB) $55-75
Continental Breakfast
Cards: None
Notes: 8, 11, 12

DENNIS

The Four Chimneys Inn

946 Main Street, 02638
(508) 385-6317

Newly restored, spacious 1881 Victorian home with lovely gardens on Historic Route 6A. Across from Scargo Lake, it's a short walk to Cape Cod Bay beaches, the Cape Playhouse, art museum, restaurants, auctions, concerts, and shops. Golf, tennis, and bike trails within two miles. Central

The Four Chimneys Inn

NOTES: Credit cards accepted: A MasterCard; B Visa; C American Express; D Discover Card; E Diner's Club; F Other; 2 Personal checks accepted; 3 Lunch available; 4 Dinner available; 5 Open all year;

to all of Cape Cod. Closed November through March.

Hosts: Russell and Kathy Tomasetti
Rooms: 8 (6 PB; 2 SB) $40-100
Continental Breakfast
Credit Cards: A, B, C, D
Notes: 2, 7, 8 (over 8), 9, 11, 12, 14

House Guests Cape Cod and the Islands

Box 1881, Orleans, 02653
(508) 896-7053; (800) 666-HOST (reservations)
FAX (508) 896-7054

Isaiah Hall Inn

93043. This cozy home, once a meeting-house for a local church, was built in 1893. Close to Corporation Beach, the Cape Playhouse, fine arts museum, shopping, antique shops, galleries, and restaurants. The friendly hosts will share their extensive knowledge of the area and make guests feel so welcome as they enjoy a Continental breakfast. One guest room has a king-size bed, private bath, sitting area, and color TV; a third person in party can be accommodated in adjoining single-bedded guest room. Smoking not allowed in guest rooms. $62.

93057. This handsome saltbox home features a unique attached bed and breakfast guest wing which predates the main structure by many years. A private entrance leads to the guest room with double bed, color TV, and private bath. Delicious Continental breakfast. Get a real feel of old Cape Cod in these cozy antique surroundings only one and one-half miles from either salt or freshwater beaches. Resident dog. A nonsmoking location. $50-60.

Isaiah Hall Bed and Breakfast Inn

P.O. Box 1007, 152 Whig Street, 02638
(508) 385-9928; (800) 736-0160

Enjoy country ambience and hospitality in the heart of Cape Cod. Lovely 1857 farmhouse tucked away on a quiet historic side-street, within walking distance of the beach and village shops, restaurants, museums, cinema, and playhouse. Nearby bike trails, tennis, and golf. Comfortably appointed with antiques and Orientals. Excellent central location for day trips. Continental-plus breakfast is served. Closed mid-October through April 1.

Host: Marie Brophy
Rooms: 11 (10 PB; 1 SB) $57-107
Continental Breakfast
Credit Cards: A, B, C
Notes: 2, 7, 8 (over 7), 9, 10, 11, 12, 14

DENNIS PORT

House Guests Cape Cod and the Islands

Box 1881, Orleans, 02653
(508) 896-7053; (800) 666-HOST (reservations)
FAX (508) 896-7054

93067. A cozy bed and breakfast, nestled among the pines in a quiet residential area only a few hundred yards from Nantucket Sound. The beach is an easy five-minute walk from private entrance. A bedroom with two single beds and a nonconnecting Florida room are for guests to enjoy. Use the gracious hosts' refrigerator, barbecue, and picnic table, and save money by not eating out. Guests are also welcome to use the hosts' table tennis game. Private bath, TV, and Continental breakfast. This is a

6 Pets welcome; 8 Children welcome; 9 Social drinking allowed; 10 Tennis available; 11 Swimming available; 12 Golf available; 13 Skiing available; 14 May be booked through travel agents.

House Guests Cape Cod and the Islands (continued)

great place for two guys or two girls traveling together. Smoking not allowed. $55.

93070. Salt and freshwater beaches are within a mile of this ranch-cottage-style home. Shops and restaurants are nearby. Two air-conditioned guest bedrooms are accessed by a private entrance. One room has a double bed and the other has twin beds. The full bath is shared only if both rooms are occupied. Private guest parlor with fireplace, TV, and VCR. Continental breakfast. Guests are welcome to use the outdoor grill, and the space available in host's refrigerator. Smoking is not allowed in guest bedrooms. Open late June through Labor Day (available some weekends during off season at reduced rate). Children are welcome. Reduced weekly rate available. $58-68.

The Rose Petal Bed and Breakfast

152 Sea Street, Box 974, 02639
(508) 398-8470

A picturesque traditional New England home complete with picket fence invites guests to share this historic 1872 residence in a delightful seaside resort neighborhood. Stroll past century-old homes to a sandy beach. Home-baked pastries highlight a full breakfast. A comfortable parlor offers TV, piano, and reading. Enjoy queen-size brass beds, antiques, hand-stitched quilts, and spacious and bright baths. Convenient to all Cape Cod's attractions. Open all year. ABBA approved. Minimum stay holidays: two nights.

Hosts: Dan and Gayle Kelly
Rooms: 3 (2 PB; 1 SB) $50-89
Full Breakfast
Credit Cards: A, B, C
Notes: 2, 5, 7 (limited), 8, 9, 10, 11, 12, 14

DUXBURY (PLYMOUTH)

Bed and Breakfast/Inns of New England

128 South Hoop Pole Road, Guilford, CT 06437
(203) 457-0042; (800) 582-0853

MA 1030. This bed and breakfast home is set in a quiet, wooded area. Enjoy the full breakfast on the deck, in the garden, or on the screened porch. The town, on Duxbury Bay, offers many examples of old homes dating from 1637 to 1870. The hosts provide a self-guided written tour of historic Duxbury and shuttle service to the beach. Great restaurants and beach only one mile away. Tennis courts are across the street. Three guest rooms, shared bath, central air, and fresh flowers in each guest room. Two-night minimum during holidays. Children 13 and older are welcome. No smoking and no guest pets. $60-75.

EASTHAM

Bed and Breakfast Cape Cod

P.O. Box 341, West Hyannisport, 02672-0341
(508) 775-2772; FAX (508) 775-2884

72. This 60-year-old beach home is built in the heart of what is now Cape Cod National Seashore Park. Enter from a private entrance to a living room with TV, library, and sitting area. Two bedrooms, one with a queen-size and one with a pair of twins, share the suite's bath. Casual, eclectic decor adds to the relaxed style of this popular beach setting. Continental breakfast from 7:30-9:30 A.M. Ocean view. No smoking. $120.

84. Standing in the midst of a grove of tall pines is a 1983 contemporary home built by the owners. There is a ground floor suite with a king-size bed and a private bath with shower. The sitting area has a TV and sliders to a private porch. The private entrance makes this a quiet place for visitors. The Cape Cod Bike Trail is 100 yards from the house. Continental breakfast. No smoking allowed. $65.

Bed and Breakfast Greater Boston and Cape Cod

P.O. Box 35, Newtonville, 02160
(617) 964-1606; (800) 832-2632
FAX (617) 332-8572

Great Pond House. A beautiful contemporary home in a secluded area of the shores of Great Pond. Only a few miles from the beaches of the bay and ocean. Whale-watching and charter fishing are available from nearby harbors. The large master guest room has a private bath, queen-size bed, and color TV. A second large guest room has a water view, two twin beds, and private hall bath. Guests are invited to relax in the living room, sit on the deck, or simply enjoy the lovely gardens and grounds around the house. Extended Continental breakfast. No smoking allowed. Open May through September. $85.

Bed and Breakfast/Inns of New England

128 South Hoop Pole Road, Guilford, CT 06437
(203) 457-0042; (800) 582-0853

MA 1050. A traditional two-story home in the secluded area on the shore of Great Pond. There is a 1927 Chickering Grand Piano in the music room. The large master bedroom and bath on the second floor has a queen-size bed and color TV. A second large bedroom with pond view has twin beds. A private bathroom is directly across from the bedroom. A Continental breakfast is served on the deck or in the dining room. No children; no smoking; no pets. $75-80.

DESTINNATIONS New England

P.O. Box 1173, Osterville 02655
(508) 428-5600; FAX (508) 420-0565;
(800) 333-4667 (reservations)

7306. This exceptional inn, just a few minutes from Cape Cod National Seashore, has 12 rooms with private baths, including suites and cottage. The inn, circa 1830, has been restored and creatively redecorated with cottage country furniture and wooden and brass beds. It features 19th-century Danish, French, and English antiques with country accents, a brick patio, and splendid gardens. Sitting room provides TV/VCR; living room has fireplace, custom pantry, refrigerator, and icemaker. Full breakfast. No smoking. Children over 12. No pets. $95-165.

House Guests Cape Cod and the Islands

Box 1881, Orleans, 02653
(508) 896-7053; (800) 666-HOST (reservations)
FAX (508) 896-7054

93135. A finely restored Queen Anne Victorian mansion surrounded by elms and oaks The inn has ten bedrooms, complete with brass beds, down comforters, terry-towel robes, and private baths. Afternoon tea and scones served in the Oriental parlor. Bicycles are available. Full breakfast is served. French and Spanish spoken. Children ten and older are welcome. Smoking allowed in designated areas only. Resident dog. $60-115.

93136. A delightful half-Cape-style home with a saltbox addition. In a quiet neighborhood, this bed and breakfast is close to Salt Pond, Visitors' Center, and Nauset Light and Coast Guard beaches. The two guest rooms share a full bath. One room has a king-size bed and the other has a double bed. Both rooms have cozy sitting areas. Delicious Continental breakfast. Guests

6 Pets welcome; 8 Children welcome; 9 Social drinking allowed; 10 Tennis available; 11 Swimming available; 12 Golf available; 13 Skiing available; 14 May be booked through travel agents.

DESTINNATIONS
New England
(continued)

have access to hosts' refrigerator and are invited to share the living room. This is a nonsmoking location. Resident dog. Open February through November. $55-65.

93137. Guests will have ocean views and hear the roar of the pounding surf from the private three-room suite at this secluded hideaway in the National Seashore parklands. Only a short walk to Coast Guard Beach and a short drive to Nauset Light Beach. This bed and breakfast is the perfect spot for beach and nature lovers. There are two bedrooms, one with queen-size bed and the other with twin beds, and a comfortably furnished living room with TV. Private bath, private entrance, and small refrigerator. Continental breakfast. No smoking. Children five and older are welcome. Resident dog and cat. $98. $30 for additional person.

93139. An authentic 18th-century home with bow roof. Built in 1751, the full-Cape-style house was a private residence until the early 1980s, when it was carefully restored, refurbished, and converted to a country inn that retains its Colonial ancestry and charm. Within a mile of beaches. Each of the eleven guest rooms is uniquely furnished creating a relaxed, informal atmosphere. One guest room is a suite with a king-size bed, small refrigerator, and working fireplace. Full country breakfast. Children ten and older are welcome. No smoking in public areas. Resident dog. $60-115.

Orleans Bed and Breakfast Associates

P.O. Box 1312, Orleans, 02653
(508) 255-3824; (800) 541-6226

Bread and Roses. Cozy, sunlit, modern suite. Two bedrooms with skylights, one double and one twin, separated by reading area with color TV. Bath has stall shower. Access to clean, freshwater pond for swimming and canoeing. Breakfast served in dining area or on sunny deck off music room. Artistic, musical hosts and an enchanting Shih Tzu named Muffie will add to guests' pleasure. Ideal for those traveling with children. $65.

Ocean Walk. A wooded path winds past the Three Sisters lighthouses and leads from this comfortable house to the Nauset Light Beach only two-tenths of a mile away. There is a large separate living room for guests with a fireplace, big windows, and deep couches to invite relaxed reading or TV watching. A queen bedroom includes a guest refrigerator and a private bath with an extra-large tub and shower. Hosts leave early to work with the Dolphin Fleet, so a nice Continental breakfast is laid out for guests to enjoy in privacy. $80.

Soft Winds. Staying here is like having a private, comfortable apartment. Guest wing with living room, kitchen, bath, bedroom, and personal deck. Cable TV with HBO. Continental breakfast foods are on hand. On a bike path, convenient to beaches and ponds. $90.

Spindrift. Delightful wing of old house just five-minute walk to Coast Guard Beach. Near bike path. Private entrance into library-sitting room with windows facing ocean. Queen or twin room with private bath. Patio. Interesting hosts offer privacy or great hospitality as guests wish. Breakfast served on dishes made by the host, a potter who maintains a shop in Orleans. $100.

Summertime. Darling Cape Cod house 100 feet from lovely beach on Cape Cod Bay.

NOTES: Credit cards accepted: A MasterCard; B Visa; C American Express; D Discover Card; E Diner's Club; F Other; 2 Personal checks accepted; 3 Lunch available; 4 Dinner available; 5 Open all year;

This is a light, softly decorated, restful environment. On the second floor a charming twin bedroom with a sleeper-sofa and an adjoining double bedroom share bath. TV available in living room and a wide deck for breakfast or relaxing. This is a good location for a family vacation. Convenient to National Seashore. $65.

Sylvanus Knowles House. Magnificent views of Nauset Marsh and leisurely walks on historic Fort Hill surround this impeccably restored 1838 Greek Revival farmhouse. The original house contains two guest rooms furnished with fine antiques. The romantic Emma suite has a private library-sitting room, bedroom with lace-canopied bed, and elegant bathroom featuring an oversized tub and window seat. Upstairs, a quaint, airy double room, Lucille, has its own private bath, hall, and dressing room. Breakfast served in elegant dining room. $90-110.

Tory Hill. An old Cape house with a private entrance into separate guest wing. Twin sitting room with vanity and refrigerator. Full private bath. Guests are invited to share the adjoining family room and lovely patio with hosts. Owners have a specialized antique business in an adjacent barn, and everything reflects their lively interest. Walk to the ice cream parlor from here! It is three-fourths mile to Bay Beach and two miles to the ocean. $75.

Windmill View. An adult-sized doll house just perfect for two or with one small child ($20 extra), with separate entrance and parking space. Exceptionally gracious, hospitable hosts will serve breakfast in the house or on the sunny patio. Spacious double bedroom with TV plus single convertible couch. Fully equipped eat-in kitchen and full bath (as well as warm-water outside shower). This little house sits in a uniquely landscaped garden with grassy

lawn and a path leading to Long Pond for freshwater bathing. A short walk to convenience store and library. Close to National Seashore Visitors' Center. $80.

The Over Look Inn

The Over Look Inn
Cape Cod

3085 County Road, Route 6, 02642
(508) 255-1886

Victorian mansion across from Cape Cod National Seashore offering Scottish hospitality. Antique-filled guest rooms, all with private baths, and the garden room with working fireplace and porch. Victorian parlor for afternoon tea. Winston Churchill library, Hemingway billiard room, and Edward Hopper dining room where a full leisurely breakfast is served each morning. Excellent biking and wildlife sanctuary nearby.

Hosts: The Aitchison Family
Rooms: 10 (PB) $95-125
Full Breakfast
Credit Cards: A, B, C, D, E
Notes: 2, 5, 8, 9, 10, 11, 12, 14

The Whalewalk Inn

220 Bridge Road, 02642
(508) 255-0617

The gracious, welcoming hosts of this inn promise guests an unspoiled environment on outer Cape Cod—one of the country's

6 Pets welcome; 8 Children welcome; 9 Social drinking allowed; 10 Tennis available; 11 Swimming available; 12 Golf available; 13 Skiing available; 14 May be booked through travel agents.

most beautiful areas. On a back road, the site consists of three acres. Only minutes by car or bike to beaches, bike trails, or Orleans Village. This 1830s home has been authentically restored and creatively decorated with handsome antiques. The seven guest rooms and five large suites with full kitchens are furnished with a mix of country antiques, fine linens, and local art. All rooms have private baths; some suites have fireplaces. Breakfast and afternoon hor d'oeuvres are served.

Hosts: Carolyn and Richard Smith
Rooms: 12 (PB) $95-165
Full Breakfast
Credit Cards: A, B
Notes: 2, 9, 10, 11, 12, 14

EAST ORLEANS

Bed and Breakfast Cape Cod

P.O. Box 341, West Hyannisport, 02672-0341
(508) 775-2772; FAX (508) 775-2884

11. This Cape Cod house was built in 1928 and expanded in 1990, adding a lovely ground-floor suite. It offers a private entrance, a large living room with a twin pull-out, a dining area, and a fully equipped kitchen. The bedroom has a queen-size bed and private bath with shower. The location is very convenient to the village and only a mile from Nauset Beach, one of the best beaches on the East Coast. The hostess provides a Continental breakfast each morning. An ideal private accommodation for up to four persons. Queen $100.

25. This Cape Cod-style house offers a second-floor suite with a pair of twin beds that convert to king-size, private bath, and a separate sitting room with studio couch and twin pull-out. The village is one mile away, and the host will pick up and drop off guests at Nauset Beach. Continental breakfast. No smoking. $65.

73. This very special Colonial-style house offers one suite. The honeymoon suite offers queen-size bed, Jacuzzi for two, skylights, private entrance, and Victorian decor. Full breakfast is served each morning. Harbor is one hundred yards away. Children over seven. $150.

Bed and Breakfast/Inns of New England

128 South Hoop Pole Road, Guilford, CT 06437
(203) 457-0042; (800) 582-0853

MA 1048. Built over 170 years ago, this inn is a restored sea captain's home that offers travelers the charm of old-style New England lodging with all the conveniences the modern guest has learned to expect. Guests will enjoy the Continental breakfast that includes homemade breads. Each of the 19 guest rooms is individually decorated in nautical style with special Colonial color schemes and antiques. Some rooms have ocean views, and the master suite has a working fireplace. Children over 12 are welcome. Limited smoking. No guest pets. $50-100.

House Guests Cape Cod and the Islands

Box 1881, Orleans, 02653
(508) 896-7053; (800) 666-HOST (reservations)
FAX (508) 896-7054

94175. A spacious one-bedroom apartment with fully equipped kitchen and bath offers private parking, private entrance, and deck. Cable TV, queen-size bed, single pull-out sofa and a private telephone complete the accommodations. Guests are one mile from Nauset Beach and close to the village center. Host stocks refrigerator with breakfast foods. Special weekly rates and fee for extra person. Children welcome. $95.

Ivy Lodge

194 Main Street, 02643-1195
(508) 255-0119

A guest house since 1910, this smoke-free
1864 Greek Revival home is graced with
family photos and antiques. A morning
"wake-up" breakfast basket is found outside each guest room door, to be enjoyed in-
room or under a shade tree on the spacious
grounds. In beautiful, historic Orleans at the
elbow of Cape Cod. Walking distance to
shops and restaurants. Midway between
ocean and bay beaches. Other amenities
close by.

Hosts: David and Barbara McCormack
Rooms: 3 (1 PB; 2 SB) $56-100
Continental Breakfast
Credit Cards: None
Notes: 2, 5, 8, 9, 10, 11, 12

Nauset House Inn

Nauset House Inn

143 Beach Road, Box 774, 02643
(508) 255-2195

The Nauset House Inn is a place where the
gentle amenities of life are still observed, a
place where sea and shore, orchard and
field all combine to create a perfect setting
for tranquil relaxation. The Nauset House
Inn is ideally near one of the world's great
ocean beaches, yet is close to antique and
craft shops, restaurants, art galleries, scenic
paths, and remote places for sunning, swimming, and picnicking. Continental breakfast
available for lesser rate. Closed November
1 through March 31.

Hosts: Diane and Al Johnson, Cindy and John Vessella
Rooms: 14 (8 PB; 6 SB) $75-115
Full Breakfast
Credit Cards: A, B
Notes: 2, 9, 10, 11, 12

Orleans Bed and Breakfast Associates

P.O. Box 1312, Orleans, 02653
(508) 255-3824; (800) 541-6226

Finlandia. A stunning and immaculate contemporary home, airy and bright, in a
neighborhood ideally suited to bicycling or
walking. Two comfy second-floor bedrooms share a large bath. An open living
room with vaulted ceiling and enormous
windows. Ideal for couples traveling together. Less than two miles from Nauset
Beach. $70.

The Lyttle House. A sunny new apartment
with separate entrance. Living room with
single sofa-sleeper, cable TV, phone. Nice
dining area and full kitchen stocked for
breakfast. A separate queen bedroom and
modern bath with shower. Private deck.
Children welcome ($20 extra per child; crib
provided). Excellent location for biking to
Nauset Beach. $100.

The Red Geranium. From the moment
guests step into this lovely country Cape,
they will feel the warmth of home. Comfortable bedrooms decorated with heirloom
treasures, double or twin beds. Large bath
and cozy sitting room. Guest wing with separate entrance, living room, complete
kitchen, and romantic bedroom with queen-
size bed and private bath. All guest rooms
have individually controlled air conditioning and cable TV. Breakfast is served buffet-style in a beautifully appointed Colonial
dining room in the Main House. A bike ride
to Nauset Beach, walk to East Orleans village and fine dining. $78-110.

6 Pets welcome; 8 Children welcome; 9 Social drinking allowed; 10 Tennis available; 11 Swimming available;
12 Golf available; 13 Skiing available; 14 May be booked through travel agents.

The Parsonage Inn

The Parsonage Inn

202 Main Street, P.O. Box 1501, 02643
(508) 255-8217

Originally a parsonage, circa 1770, this full Cape home is now a cozy, romantic inn only one and one-half miles from one of Cape Cod's most beautiful beaches, Nauset Beach. All eight rooms are uniquely decorated with country antiques, quilts, and stenciling. A bountiful breakfast is served either in the dining room or under sunny skies on the patio. Appetizers are served in the evening in the parlor where guests can mingle while perusing menus of the many fine restaurants.

Hosts: Ian and Elizabeth Browne
Rooms: 8 (PB) $75-105
Continental Breakfast
Credit Cards: A, B, C
Notes: 2, 5, 8 (over 6), 9, 11, 14

Ship's Knees Inn

186 Beach Road, P.O. Box 756, 02643
(508) 255-1312

A 170-year-old restored sea captain's home; rooms individually appointed with their own Colonial color schemes and authentic antiques. Only a three-minute walk to popular sand-duned Nauset. Swimming pool and tennis on premises. Also available three miles away, overlooking Orleans Cove, are an efficiency and two heated cottages.

Rooms: 22 (8 PB; 14 SB) $45-100
Continental Breakfast
Credit Cards: A, B
Notes: 2, 5, 7, 8 (over 12), 9, 10, 11, 12, 14

EAST SANDWICH

DESTINNATIONS
New England

P.O. Box 1173, Osterville, 02655
(508) 428-5600; FAX (508) 420-0565;
(800) 333-4667 (reservations)

7202. This three-room inn sits just off the Olde Kings Highway, on more than seven acres of lawn, gardens, and orchard. The circa 1758 building has been faithfully restored and tastefully blended with modern amenities. The inn is a working farm, with farm-fresh produce (eggs, breakfast meats, and vegetables) from the farm's livestock and gardens. Both main-house guest rooms have private baths and antique furnishings. The Carriage House contains an eclectic mix of antiquity and modern convenience, with private deck, brick patio, luxury bath, kitchen, wood stove, and spiral staircase. A full country breakfast is served each morning. It is but a short country walk to a private ocean beach. Children are welcome; smoking is permitted. Open year-round. $115-150.

Spring Garden

578 Route 6A, P.O. Box 867, 02537
(508) 888-0710

Charming country inn. Tranquil, panoramic views of salt marsh and Tidal Creek from deck or patio. Color cable TV, air conditioning, room telephones, refrigerators, efficiencies, one suite, pool, or walk to private beach. Free generous Continental breakfast. All rooms individually decorated with pillow shams, comforters, dust ruffles, and decorator sheets. Beamed ceilings. No minimum stay. Central to entire Cape, Boston, and Newport.

Hosts: Marvin and Judith Gluckman
Rooms: 11 (PB) $39-65
Continental Breakfast
Credit Cards: A, B, C, D
Notes: 2, 7, 8, 9, 10, 11, 12, 14

NOTES: Credit cards accepted: A MasterCard; B Visa; C American Express; D Discover Card; E Diner's Club; F Other; 2 Personal checks accepted; 3 Lunch available; 4 Dinner available; 5 Open all year;

The Arbor

EDGARTOWN (MARTHA'S VINEYARD)

The Arbor

222 Upper Main Street, P.O. Box 1228, 02539
(508) 627-8137

This turn-of-the-century home was originally built on the adjoining island of Chappaquiddick and moved by barge to its present location. A short stroll to village shops, fine restaurants, and the bustling activity of Edgartown Harbor, The Arbor is filled with the fragrance of fresh flowers. Peggy will gladly direct visitors to the walking trails, unspoiled beaches, fishing, and all the delights of Martha's Vineyard.

Host: Peggy Hall
Rooms: 10 (8 PB; 2 SB) $65-135
Continental Breakfast
Credit Cards: A, B
Notes: 2, 9, 10, 11, 12, 14

Bed and Breakfast Nantucket/Martha's Vineyard

P.O. Box 341, West Hyannisport, 02672-0341
(508) 775-2772; FAX (508) 775-2884

204. This 1840s sea captain's house offers 11 rooms with private baths, some with fireplaces. The decor is Victorian, and a Continental breakfast is served each morning. Transportation to the beach is right outside the door, and a short walk takes guests to the village shops and restaurants. Children over 11 welcome. $110-185.

Captain Dexter House of Edgartown

35 Pease's Point Way, P.O. Box 2798, 02539
(508) 627-7289

This historic inn offers both charm and hospitality. Enjoy beautiful gardens. Savor a home-baked Continental breakfast and evening apéritif. Relax in a four-poster, lace-canopied bed in a room with a working fireplace. Stroll to the harbor, town, and restaurants. Bicycle or walk to the beach. Let the innkeepers make a vacation special! Continental-plus breakfast.

Hosts: Rick and Birdie
Rooms: 11 (PB) $65-190
Continental Breakfast
Credit Cards: A, B, C, E
Notes: 2, 8, 9, 10, 11, 12, 14

The Charlotte Inn

27 South Summer Street, 02539
(508) 627-4751

Fine English antiques and fireplaces in a romantic garden setting with private courtyards and porches. Has 24 impeccably maintained and individually decorated guest rooms. Attention to detail is the Charlotte Inn's trademark. Walking distance to shops, beaches, tennis, and sailing. Excellent French restaurant called l'Étoile in the inn. Serves dinner and Sunday brunch. Member

The Charlotte Inn

6 Pets welcome; 8 Children welcome; 9 Social drinking allowed; 10 Tennis available; 11 Swimming available;
12 Golf available; 13 Skiing available; 14 May be booked through travel agents.

of Relais and Chateaux. Voted one of two "Country House Hotels" of the year—*Andrew Harper's Hideaway Report*.

Hosts: Gery and Paula Conover
Rooms: 24 (PB) $95-550
Full or Continental Breakfast
Credit Cards: A, B, C
Notes: 2, 4, 5, 7, 9, 10, 11, 12

Colonial Inn of Martha's Vineyard

38 North Water Street, P.O. Box 68, 02539
(508) 627-4711

In the heart of historic Edgartown overlooking the harbor, sits the Colonial Inn. It offers 42 newly renovated and lovingly refurbished rooms, all with heat, air conditioning, color TV, telephone, and private bath. Continental breakfast is served daily in the solarium and garden courtyard. Affordable luxury. Closed January through March.

Host: Linda Malcouranne
Rooms: 42 (PB) $50-185

Continental Breakfast
Credit Cards: A, B, C
Notes: 2, 3, 4, 7, 8, 9, 10, 11, 12, 14

The Edgartown Inn

56 North Water Street, 02539
(508) 627-4794

Historic inn built in 1798 as the home for whaling Captain Worth. Early guests included Daniel Webster, Nathaniel Hawthorne, and Charles Summer. Later, John Kennedy stayed here as a young senator. Completely restored over the last 150 years, today it is filled with antiques. Convenient to beaches, harbor, and restaurants. Famous for breakfast, including homemade breads and cakes.

Hosts: Liliane and Earle Radford
Rooms: 20 (16 PB; 4 SB) $85-150
Full and Continental Breakfast
Credit Cards: None
Notes: 2, 9, 10, 11, 12

Governor Bradford Inn

128 Main Street, Box 239, 02539
(508) 627-9510

The atmosphere at this restored 1865 Edgartown home is one of casual elegance. Guests can walk to the many shops and restaurants in Edgartown, bicycle to beaches, or simply relax. Freshly baked treats are served at breakfast and afternoon tea. All guest rooms have private baths and are decorated with a mixture of antiques and reproductions.

Hosts: Ray and Brenda Raffurty
Rooms: 16 (PB) $60-210
Full Breakfast
Credit Cards: A, B, C
Notes: 2, 5, 7, 9, 10, 11, 12, 14

House Guests Cape Cod and the Islands

Box 1881, Orleans, 02653
(508) 896-7053; (800) 666-HOST (reservations)
FAX (508) 896-7054

NOTES: Credit cards accepted: A MasterCard; B Visa; C American Express; D Discover Card; E Diner's Club; F Other; 2 Personal checks accepted; 3 Lunch available; 4 Dinner available; 5 Open all year;

93305. Built in 1830, this friendly, informal inn in the heart of the village offers guests a wide variety of accommodations. The inn has 15 guest rooms with private baths, many with original working fireplaces and ceiling fans, some with canopied four-poster beds, two with air conditioning, and one two-room suite with private entrance and fireplace. Six rooms have French doors opening onto private balconies overlooking the spacious lawns and gardens. Continental breakfast. Within walking distance of fine shops, restaurants, and all attractions of historic seaport village. Guest courtesy card available. Smoking and children welcome. $65-205.

93307. A new contemporary full-Cape-style bed and breakfast home with three stenciled rooms for guests. Built in 1990, this spacious home is halfway between the town center and South Beach. Guests can catch the trolley to the beach from the corner. Each of the oversized rooms has a private attached bath, a sitting area, and queen-size and single beds. One unit features a kitchenette, and guests have magnificent sunset views from its private deck. Continental breakfast. Smoking on the deck only. Children six or older are welcome. Resident cat. Available May through December. $110-125.

93309. Built in 1865, this many-gabled Victorian house offers 16 guest rooms decorated with antiques and reproductions. Each has king-size brass or four-poster bed, private full bath, TV, and ceiling fan. Delicious full breakfast. Afternoon tea with scrumptious sweets. Children 12 and older welcome. $60-195.

Point Way Inn

Box 5255, 02539
(508) 627-8633

This delightful country inn provides a warm, relaxed retreat with working fire-

places in 11 rooms. Tea and scones are provided in the winter; in the summer, lemonade and oatmeal cookies are served in the gazebo overlooking the croquet court and gardens. Complimentary courtesy car available. Minimum stay holidays is two nights.

Hosts: Linda and Ben Smith
Rooms: 15 (PB) $95-235
Continental Breakfast
Credit Cards: A, B, C
Notes: 2, 5, 7, 8, 9, 10, 11, 12, 14

The Shiretown Inn

21 North Water Street, P.O. Box 921, 02539
(800) 541-0090

Shiretown Inn, which is listed in the National Register of Historic Places, is composed of two 1700s Captain's houses, carriage houses, cottage, restaurant, and pub. Some rooms and suites have cable TV, air conditioning, telephones, canopied beds, harbor views, garden views, and decks. On North Water Street in the center of Edgartown one block from the Chappaquiddick Ferry, Town Wharf, and Harbor, it is a short stroll to shops, galleries, and lovely public beaches. Continental breakfast is included; full breakfast is available at an additional cost.

Host: Sonya Lima
Rooms: 34 (PB) $59-259
Continental Breakfast
Credit Cards: A, B, C, D
Notes: 2, 4, 7, 8, 9, 10, 11, 12, 14

EGREMONT

American Country Collection

4 Greenwood Lane, Delmar, NY 12054
(518) 439-7001

138. This 1700s Victorian rural farm is on 500 acres of rolling hills, woods, and fields. It is furnished with antiques and Oriental rugs. There are four guest rooms, two with private baths. Tanglewood, Norman Rockwell Museum, Berkshire Festival, and

6 Pets welcome; 8 Children welcome; 9 Social drinking allowed; 10 Tennis available; 11 Swimming available; 12 Golf available; 13 Skiing available; 14 May be booked through travel agents.

skiing are all within 15 minutes. There is an in-ground pool available for guest use. Full breakfast. Smoking outdoors. Resident dog. Children over 10 welcome. $74-94.

ESSEX

Bed and Breakfast Marblehead and North Shore

P.O. Box 35, Newtonville, 02160
(617) 964-1606; (800) 832-2632;
FAX (617) 332-8572

Essex River Inn. An 1830 Federal-style house built by shipwrights. Six guest rooms have private baths, individual heat and air conditioning, TV and telephones; three have working fireplaces. One suite sleeps four and has a fireplace and balcony; a penthouse suite has a private deck and kitchenette. A delicious full breakfast is included and may be served "in bed" on request. $79-129.

FAIRHAVEN

Edgewater Bed and Breakfast

2 Oxford Street, 02719
(508) 997-5512

Edgewater

A gracious waterfront house in the early shipbuilding area of this historic village. Spectacular views of neighboring New Bedford Harbor so close to the water, guests will think they're riding on a boat. Convenient to historic areas, beaches, and factory outlets. Take a ferry to Martha's Vineyard or Cuttyhunk; five minutes from I-195. Five rooms, each with private bath (two with working fireplaces and sitting rooms).

Host: Kathy Reed
Rooms: 5 (PB) $45-65
Continental Breakfast
Credit Cards: A, B, C
Notes: 2, 5, 7, 8 (over 5), 9, 10, 11, 12, 14

FALMOUTH

Bed and Breakfast Associates Bay Colony, Ltd.

P.O. Box 57166, Babson Park, Boston, 02157-0166
(617) 449-5302; (800) 347-5088;
FAX (617) 449-5958

CC129. Antique house circa 1820 with lovely period furnishings and three guest rooms with private baths. On the village green, just two blocks from the shuttle bus to the ferry to Martha's Vineyard. $80.

Bed and Breakfast Cape Cod

P.O. Box 341, West Hyannisport, 02672-0341
(508) 775-2772; FAX (508) 775-2884

10. This beachfront ranch-style house faces a beautiful saltwater inlet that offers private beach, quiet walks, fishing from the host's property, sailing, and clamming. Two rooms with double beds have private baths and are furnished with antiques. Full country breakfast. Children over 12. $85.

38. Built in 1880, this home on the road to Woods Hole has been restored comfortably, offering four guest rooms with private baths. Guests will enjoy a full breakfast served in the dining room, and a nice parlor for reading or relaxing is also available. The village shops in Falmouth are a mile away, and the ferry is one and one-half miles. No smoking. Children over seven are welcome. $65-85.

42. This gracious Federal Colonial home built in 1822 is on the beautiful village green in Falmouth. Through the years this prominent home has been photographed many times as a reflection of architecture and picturesque New England. Restored some years ago by the hostess, the home now offers two bedrooms with private baths, air conditioning, and canopied four-poster beds. A Continental breakfast is served. Walk to the bus to Martha's Vineyard ferry or stroll across the green to shops and fine restaurants. $65-80.

Capt. Tom Lawrence House

Capt. Tom Lawrence House

75 Locust Street, 02540
(508) 540-1445; (800) 266-8139

Beautiful 1861 Victorian, former whaling captain's residence in the historic village of Falmouth. Central air conditioning throughout the whole facility. Comfortable, spacious, corner guest rooms. Firm beds—some with canopies. Steinway piano and working fireplace. One completely furnished apartment (sleeps four). Gourmet breakfast consists of fresh fruit, breads, pancakes made from freshly ground organic grain, and a variety of other delicious specialties. German spoken. Two-night minimum stay.

Rooms: 6 (PB) $75-104
Full Breakfast
Credit Cards: A, B
Notes: 2, 5, 8 (over 12), 9, 10, 11, 12, 14

DESTINNATIONS
New England

P.O. Box 1173, Osterville, 02655
(508) 428-5600; FAX (508) 420-0565;
(800) 333-4667 (reservations)

7200. Sitting amidst peaceful lawns and gardens, this five-room inn is less than five minutes from the Martha's Vineyard ferry. Four queen-size rooms and one full bedroom, each with private bath, are decorated with unique original art (much of it done by the host), Guest parlor, breakfast room. Host has experience with Woods Hole and the Cape, available on request. Full breakfast. Open year-round. $95-115.

The Elms

P.O. Box 895, 02574
(508) 540-7232

Charming Victorian, built in the early 1800s, features nine beautifully appointed bedrooms, seven private baths, and antique decor throughout. A full Continental breakfast is served. Tour the manicured grounds to survey the flower and herb gardens or relax in the gazebo. In the historic district, walk to restaurants, antique shops, and one-half mile to the ocean.

Hosts: Betty and Joe Mazzucchelli
Rooms: 9 (7 PB; 2 SB) $65-85

6 Pets welcome; 8 Children welcome; 9 Social drinking allowed; 10 Tennis available; 11 Swimming available; 12 Golf available; 13 Skiing available; 14 May be booked through travel agents.

Continental Breakfast
Credit Cards: C, D
Notes: 2, 5, 9, 10, 11, 12

Gladstone Inn

219 Grand Avenue South, 02540
(508) 548-9851

An oceanfront Victorian inn overlooking Martha's Vineyard. Established in 1910. Light, airy guest rooms have period furniture and their own wash stations. Buffet breakfast is served on the glassed-in porch that also provides a cozy place to read, watch cable TV, or relax. Refrigerators, bikes, and gas grill are provided for guests to use. Closed October 15 through May 15.

Hosts: Jim and Gayle Carroll
Rooms: 16 (1 PB; 15 SB) $60-85
Full Breakfast
Credit Cards: A, B
Notes: 2, 7, 8 (over 11), 9, 10, 11, 12

Gladstone Inn

Golden Slumber Accommodations

640 Revere Beach Boulevard, Revere, 02151
(800) 892-3231; (617) 289-1053

124. Enchanting Cape boasts charming European country decor. Bright and spacious rooms feature full or single beds, antiques, cable television, and private bath. Suite available. Large deck and outdoor grill employable in season. Generous full breakfast featuring homemade delicacies is served in the spacious kitchen. Close proximity to Woods Hole and island ferries, in addition to fine dining and shopping. Come enjoy Falmouth's best-kept lodging secret! $65-100.

Grafton Inn

261 Grand Avenue South, 02540
(508) 540-8688; (800) 642-4069
FAX (508) 540-1861

Oceanfront Victorian inn with miles of beautiful beach and breathtaking views of Martha's Vineyard. Sumptuous breakfasts are served on a lovely enclosed porch. Comfortable air-conditioned rooms furnished with period antiques and thoughtful amenities. Bicycles are available, as is ample parking. Short walk to restaurant, shops, and ferry. AAA, Mobil rated.

Hosts: Liz and Rudy Cvitan
Rooms: 11 (PB) $75-135
Full Breakfast
Credit Cards: A, B, C
Notes: 5, 9, 10, 11, 12, 14

House Guests Cape Cod and the Islands

Box 1881, Orleans, 02653
(508) 896-7053; (800) 666-HOST (reservations)
FAX (508) 896-7054

93004. A Cape Cod beach house built in 1911, just one block from the sandy beaches of Vineyard Sound. The sunny guest rooms are "House Beautiful" in decor. Two are furnished with double beds, and the other one has twin beds. The bath is shared. When guests need a break from the sun and surf, relax in the host's spacious parlor, which is graced by high ceilings and a working stone fireplace. Guests will be right on the bike trail to Woods Hole, close to the island ferries, only a block from the ocean, and just a short distance from great restaurants and shopping. Continental breakfast. Smoking not permitted in guest bedrooms. Open April through October. $45-65.

NOTES: Credit cards accepted: A MasterCard; B Visa; C American Express; D Discover Card; E Diner's Club; F Other; 2 Personal checks accepted; 3 Lunch available; 4 Dinner available; 5 Open all year;

93006. Spectacular views of Vineyard Sound can be had from several guest rooms and the enclosed porch of this finely restored Queen Anne Victorian inn. Beach just steps away. Only a six-minute walk to the island ferries and deep-sea fishing boats. Built in the mid-1800s, the inn features a three-story oceanfront turret which houses three guests. Nine of the 11 guest rooms provide full or partial ocean view. Each guest room has a private bath, period antiques, and comfortable beds. Full breakfast served. Children 16 and older are welcome. No smoking. $65-120.

93008. Elegant accommodations, 19th-century charm, and warm hospitality await guests at this gracious Victorian inn on the historic village green. Each spacious and well-appointed guest room offers a queen-size bed and a private full bath. An intimate and romantic two-room suite is the perfect choice for a honeymoon or a respite from a busy lifestyle. The full gourmet breakfast features specialities such as apple-plum crumble or a fresh, tangy ambrosia. Smoking on the porches only. Children age 16 or older are welcome. $75-110.

93009. Built in the 1890s as a summer house, this inn is perched high on a bluff overlooking Vineyard Sound. What a wonderful spot to experience the quaintness and charm of a bygone era on Cape Cod! Within easy walking distance of public beaches, fine restaurants, and other local attractions. Each guest room has a double bed and full or partial ocean view. Altogether there are six guest rooms with private baths. Continental breakfast is served during summer season. Children 12 or older are welcome. $50-90.

The Inn at One Main Street

One Main Street, 02540
(508) 540-7469

The Inn at One Main Street

This elegant 1892 Victorian is in Falmouth's historic district, where the roads to Woods Hole begin. The inn is within walking distance to beaches, bike path, restaurants, shops, and ferry shuttle. Enjoy a romantic getaway in one of six freshly decorated rooms, all with private baths. Whatever wishes guests may have, the hosts will do their very best to ensure an enjoyable stay and send guests home fully refreshed.

Hosts: Karen Hart and Mari Zylinski
Rooms: 6 (PB) $75-105
Full Breakfast
Credit Cards: A, B, C
Notes: 2, 5, 10, 11, 12

The Moorings Lodge

207 Grand Avenue South, 02540
(508) 540-2370

Enjoy homemade breads for buffet breakfast served on a large glassed-in porch with lovely ocean view. This charming old sea captain's home with large airy rooms overlooks Vineyard Sound and Martha's Vineyard Island. Opposite a good family beach and within a short walk to good restaurants and the island ferry.

Hosts: Ernie and Shirley Benard
Rooms: 8 (6 PB; 2 SB) $60-90
Continental Breakfast
Credit Cards: A, B
Notes: 2, 7 (restricted), 9, 10, 11, 12

6 Pets welcome; 8 Children welcome; 9 Social drinking allowed; 10 Tennis available; 11 Swimming available; 12 Golf available; 13 Skiing available; 14 May be booked through travel agents.

Mostly Hall Bed and Breakfast Inn

27 Main Street, 02540
(508) 548-3786; (800) 682-0565

Romantic 1849 Southern plantation-style Cape Cod home with wraparound veranda and widow's walk. Set back from the road on an acre of beautiful gardens with a gazebo. Close to restaurants, shops, beaches, and island ferries. Spacious corner rooms with queen-size canopied beds, central air conditioning, gourmet breakfast, bicycles, and private baths. Minimum stay Memorial Day through Columbus Day is two nights. Closed January through mid-February.

Village Green Inn

Mostly Hall

Hosts: Caroline and Jim Lloyd
Rooms: 6 (PB) $85-110
Full Breakfast
Credit Cards: A, B, C, D
Notes: 2, 9, 10, 11, 12

Village Green Inn

40 West Main Street, 02540
(508) 548-5621

Gracious old Victorian, ideally on historic village green. Walk to fine shops and restaurants, bike to beaches, tennis, and the picturesque bike path to Woods Hole. Enjoy 19th-century charm and warm hospitality in elegant surroundings. Four lovely guest rooms and one romantic suite all have private baths. Also offer bicycles, seasonal beverages, working fireplaces, and beach passes. Open April-December.

Hosts: Linda and Don Long
Rooms: 5 (PB) $85-120
Full Breakfast
Credit Cards: A, B, C
Notes: 2, 9, 10, 11, 12

FRAMINGHAM

Bed and Breakfast Associates Bay Colony, Ltd.

P.O. Box 57166, Babson Park Branch
Boston, 02157-0166
(617) 449-5302; (800) 347-5088
FAX (617) 449-5958

CW625. This is an idyllic country setting at the end of a private road, yet a short walk to Framingham Centre shops and public transportation. The home was once a barn. The contemporary restoration was completed just over 20 years ago but the weathered siding has the rich hues of age. Exit the first-floor suite via French doors to acres of open land. The guest room has a cathedral ceiling and an attached sitting area. Full breakfast; children welcome. Monthly rates available. $68-78.

NOTES: Credit cards accepted: A MasterCard; B Visa; C American Express; D Discover Card; E Diner's Club; F Other; 2 Personal checks accepted; 3 Lunch available; 4 Dinner available; 5 Open all year;

GAY HEAD

Duck Inn

Box 160, 02535
(508) 645-9018

A 200-year-old, five-bedroom farmhouse on eight and one-half acres just a short walk to the beach. Ocean views in most rooms. Watch the sunset over the cliffs and ocean. Fireplaces, decks, piano, hot tub, masseuse, gourmet health breakfasts. Casual and eclectic antique setting. Open year-round with off-season rates.

Host: Elise LeBovit
Rooms: 5 (1 PB; 4 SB) $65-175
Full Breakfast
Credit Cards: A, B
Notes: 2, 5, 7, 8, 9, 11, 12, 14

GEORGETOWN

Bed and Breakfast Marblehead and North Shore

P.O. Box 35, Newtonville, 02160
(617) 964-1606; (800) 832-2632;
FAX (617) 332-8572

The Georgetown Country Manor. A beautiful contemporary Colonial home only 40 minutes from Boston and 15 minutes from historic Newburyport. All rooms have private bath, phone,breakfast is served on weekends; private dining-service available on request. No smoking. Special-occasion packages can be arranged at an additional cost. $100-150.

GLOUCESTER

Bed and Breakfast Associates Bay Colony, Ltd.

P.O. Box 57166, Babson Park, Boston, 02157-0166
(617) 449-5302; (800) 347-5088
FAX (617) 449-5958

NS500. Just steps from the Atlantic, this white frame house in the little village of Lanesville (five miles from Gloucester and Rockport) offers three guest rooms with a shared bath and a separate cottage. Hostess is an energetic woman who has done much of the interior renovation of her attractive New England-style home. Continental breakfast; children over ten welcome; no smoking. $65; family and winter rates available.

NS505. Originally an 1898 Victorian "cottage," this splendid seaside retreat has been completely updated and redecorated. It is on the banks of the Annisquam River, and guests may enjoy watching boats passing from each of the guest rooms, the inviting decks, or the gardens below. There is also a private swimming beach. These three beautifully decorated rooms share two full baths. Continental breakfast; children over 12 welcome. $65-75; family rates available.

Bed and Breakfast Cape Cod

P.O. Box 341, West Hyannisport, 02672-0341
(508) 775-2772; FAX (508) 775-2884

30. This 1899 restoration is the perfect place to watch ships sail by. Decorated with both Victorian and traditional themes, this home offers four carpeted guest rooms that have twin, double, or queen-size beds and share two full baths. All have a view of the water, and each morning a Continental breakfast is served in the dining area or on the one-hundred-foot wraparound porch. $65-75.

Bed and Breakfast Marblehead and North Shore

P.O. Box 35, Newtonville, 02160
(617) 964-1606; (800) 832-2632
FAX (617) 332-8572

Oceanfront Cottage. Small one-bedroom oceanfront cottage in spectacular location, with lawn sloping down to rocky shoreline.

6 Pets welcome; 8 Children welcome; 9 Social drinking allowed; 10 Tennis available; 11 Swimming available; 12 Golf available; 13 Skiing available; 14 May be booked through travel agents.

Small kitchen, living room, and private bath with shower only. Full breakfast in refrigerator which guests prepare themselves. Children welcome. Smoking permitted. No pets. Open mid-May to end of October. $90.

Riverview Bed and Breakfast. An exquisite turn-of-the-century restored waterfront home with 100-foot wraparound porch, perched high above the Annisquam River. Each of the beautifully decorated guest rooms share two full baths. Two front rooms have private decks. The back room has a queen-size brass bed, sink, and water view. The terraced grounds and gardens lead to a private pier. Guests may relax in the sitting room with fireplace. Continental breakfast. $65-85.

GREAT BARRINGTON

American Country Collection

4 Greenwood Lane, Delmar, NY 12054
(518) 439-7001

053. This classic hilltop farmhouse was designed for visitors in 1907 and features wraparound porches with panoramic views of the Berkshire Hills. The dairy barn, renovated in 1987, dates from the 1820s. The main house has five bedrooms decorated with Laura Ashley prints, antique furniture, art, and an extensive book collection. The dairy barn has a hayloft renovation containing two air-conditioned luxury suites with private baths. Guests choose from an extensive country menu for breakfast at any time they wish. Children over 16 welcome. No smoking. Surcharge for in-season weekends, one-night stays. $65-135.

Bed and Breakfast/Inns of New England

128 South Hoop Pole Road, Guilford, CT 06437
(203) 457-0042; (800) 582-0853

MA 1020. A circa 1800 farmhouse built by the Indians early in the last century. It has been added to over the years until it assumed its present rambling shape. There are five brightly furnished guest rooms, each with its own private bath. Bathrobes are found in the bedroom closets for the guests to use. All bedrooms are air-conditioned and equipped with telephones and clock radios. $85-100.

Covered Bridge

P. O. Box 447A, Norfolk, CT 06058
(203) 542-5944

1GBMA. Charming Victorian farmhouse in a rural setting. A full breakfast is served in the dining room. There are three large rooms, each with private bath, cable TV, and air conditioning. Two of the rooms have queen-size beds, and one has twins. A barn on the grounds has also been converted into a two-bedroom cottage. $85-110.

Littlejohn Manor

1 Newsboy Monument Lane, 01230
(413) 528-2882

Victorian charm recaptured in this uniquely personable home. Antiques grace four warmly furnished, air-conditioned guest rooms—one with fireplace. Guest parlor with color TV and fireplace. Full English breakfast and afternoon tea. Set on spacious, landscaped grounds with extensive herb and

Littlejohn Manor

NOTES: Credit cards accepted: A MasterCard; B Visa; C American Express; D Discover Card; E Diner's Club; F Other; 2 Personal checks accepted; 3 Lunch available; 4 Dinner available; 5 Open all year;

flower beds. Scenic views. Close to major ski areas and Berkshire attractions.

Hosts: Herbert Littlejohn Jr. and Paul A. DuFour
Rooms: 4 (SB) $60-85
Full Breakfast
Credit Cards: None
Notes: 5, 7 (limited), 9, 10, 11, 12, 13

Nutmeg Bed and Breakfast Agency

P.O. Box 1117, West Hartford, CT 06107
(203) 236-6698

332. This 100-year-old Victorian with porch, deck, and hot tub has one first-floor room with double bed and private bath; two second-floor rooms with double beds which share a bath; and two other second-floor rooms with private baths. There are sitting areas in all rooms, TV in two of the rooms. Continental breakfast. No children. Smoking OK. Two dogs on premises.

Seekonk Pines Inn

142 Seekonk Cross Road, 01230
(413) 528-4192; (800) 292-4192

This restored 1830s homestead, set amid lovely flower and vegetable gardens, offers a large guest living room with a fireplace and grand piano. A full country breakfast is different every day, and special diets can be accommodated. Convenient to Tanglewood and other cultural events, museums, shops, golf, and hiking. Features antique quilts, stencilling, original artwork, gardens, picnic tables, in-ground pool, and guest pantry. Seen in the *Boston Globe*, *Philadelphia Inquirer*, *Los Angeles Times*, and the August 1992 issue of *Country Inns* magazine.

Hosts: Linda and Chris Best
Rooms: 6 (PB) $75-105
Full Breakfast
Credit Cards: A, B
Notes: 2, 5, 8, 9, 10, 11, 12, 13

The Turning Point Inn

3 Lake Buel Road, 01230
(413) 528-4777

An 18th-century former stagecoach inn. Full, delicious breakfast. Featured in *The New York Times*, *Boston Globe*, *Los Angeles Times*. Adjacent to Butternut Ski Basin; near Tanglewood and all Berkshire attractions. Hiking and cross-country ski trails. Sitting rooms with fireplaces, piano, cable TV. Groups and families welcome.

Hosts: The Yosts
Rooms: 8 (6 PB; 2 SB) $80-100
Full Breakfast
Credit Cards: A, B, C
Notes: 2, 5, 8, 9, 10, 11, 12, 13

GREENFIELD (COLRAIN)

The Brandt House

29 Highland Avenue, 01301-3605
(413) 774-3329; (800) 235-3329; (413) 772-2908

High on a hill just five minutes from historic Deerfield, and a five-minute walk to town, this 16-room estate offers privacy, elegance, and comfort. Private baths, wraparound porches, a clay tennis court, fireplaces, pool table, feather beds, antiques, glowing hardwood floors, fresh flowers, and cozy bathrobes await guests. A sumptuous home-cooked breakfast is included.

Owner/Innkeeper: Phoebe Compton
Rooms: 7 (PB) $50-135
Credit Cards: A, B
Notes: 2, 5, 6 (call), 8, 9, 10, 11, 12, 13, 14

GROVELAND

Bed and Breakfast Marblehead and North Shore

P.O. Box 35, Newtonville, 02160
(617) 964-1606; (800) 832-2632
FAX (617) 332-8572

Seven Acre Farm. A charming country farmhouse, built in 1987, offers two guest rooms. Enjoy the peace and tranquility of quiet walks through the seven acres of land that was once an herb farm. This bed and

6 Pets welcome; 8 Children welcome; 9 Social drinking allowed; 10 Tennis available; 11 Swimming available; 12 Golf available; 13 Skiing available; 14 May be booked through travel agents.

breakfast is furnished with antiques and has beautiful wood floors, Oriental rugs, atrium, skylights, and a cozy wood-burning stove. Guest rooms share one and one-half baths. Easy access to highways leading to Maine, New Hampshire, and Vermont. Generous Continental breakfast. No smoking. Children welcome. $60-75.

HAMILTON

Bed and Breakfast Marblehead and North Shore

P.O. Box 35, Newtonville, 02160
(617) 964-1606; (800) 832-2632
FAX (617) 332-8572

The Country Mannor Inn. This is an exceptional bed and breakfast on 30 acres of land, with eight guest rooms, most of which have private baths. The house is a country Colonial built in 1790 and expanded over the years. There are 12 working fireplaces throughout, as well as several sitting rooms and porches available for guest use. There are beautiful views, wonderful gardens, and a river flowing through the property. Hosts are seasoned bicyclists who will be happy to map out interesting routes throughout the area for guests. Wonderful breakfast. Children are welcome. No smoking. $70-125.

The Elms. Surrounded by tall elm trees, this bed and breakfast offers cozy guest accommodations with the feel of home. Two guest rooms with double and twin beds share a bath and TV-sitting room. Guests may also enjoy daytime use of the downstairs living room, dining area, patio, and gardens. Just a short walk to the commuter-rail line into Boston, and close to the many tourist attractions on the North Shore. A delicious breakfast includes homemade jellies and jams. Children over 12 are welcome. Nonsmoking. Resident cat. $10 additional charge for private bath. $60-75.

Host Homes of Boston

P.O. Box 117, Boston, 02168
(617) 244-1308; FAX (617) 244-5156

Miles River Country Inn. A 200-year-old estate in Cape Ann's horse country near Crane's Beach. The inn is a 24-room vintage Colonial on 30 acres of varied gardens, woods, and wetlands. Eight guest rooms include a suite with twins and a double, and two queens with private baths. Hosts produce eggs, fruit, and honey for breakfast. Thirty minutes from Boston. Resident dogs. $65-90.

HARWICH

Bed and Breakfast Cape Cod

P.O. Box 341, West Hyannisport, 02672-0341
(508) 775-2772; FAX (508) 775-2884

7. This Cape-style home is one hundred yards from a freshwater pond and offers two bedrooms, one with a double bed and the other a pair of twins. The bath is shared, and a full breakfast served in the dining room features home-baked specialities. The pond is available for swimming or fishing, and the beach is close to this pleasant accommodation. No smoking. Children over eight. $60.

47. This Cape-style host home is in a quiet residential section near two freshwater lakes. The house has two guest rooms with either a king-size bed or two twins. A great breakfast is available each morning. It is convenient with easy access to other parts of the Cape, including the beaches on either Cape Cod Bay or Nantucket Sound. This very clean and well-maintained home is excellent for a family or group of up to four people. $60.

NOTES: Credit cards accepted: A MasterCard; B Visa; C American Express; D Discover Card; E Diner's Club; F Other; 2 Personal checks accepted; 3 Lunch available; 4 Dinner available; 5 Open all year;

Bed and Breakfast/Inns of New England

128 South Hoop Pole Road, Guilford, CT 06437
(203) 457-0042; (800) 582-0853

MA-1047. Set on one and one-half acres with flower and vegetable gardens, the main house was built in 1835. A contemporary wing has since been added. Upstairs there are twin beds with a shared bath. Downstairs there is a king-size bed with private bath and entrance. This room boasts five windows and is especially delightful in the summer. An extra small room with a twin bed for a third guest is available, with a shared bath. A Continental breakfast is served each morning. No children; no smoking; resident cat. $30-60.

Cape Cod Sunny Pines Claddagh Inn

77 Main Street, P.O. Box 667, 02671
(508) 432-9628; (800) 356-9628 (reservations)
FAX (508) 432-6039

Irish hospitality in a Victorian ambience. Eight different rooms with private baths, air conditioning, cable TV, and refrigerators. Choose king-, queen-size, or twin. Full Irish breakfast or order off the menu. Served in the Kerry Room. The Claddagh is an authentic Irish pub with a fine dining Irish Art Gallery, The Blarney Room. Enjoy good crack (conversation) with guests and locals while sipping a favorite cocktail or Irish beer. Relax poolside or fireside, depending on the season. Perfect for beach, fishing, golf, biking, hiking, day trips to the islands, Plymouth, Provence Town, and Boston.

Hosts: Jack and Eileen Connell and family
Rooms: 8 (PB) $75-120
Full Breakfast
Credit Cards: A, B, C, D
Notes: 2, 3, 4, 5, 7 (limited), 8, 9, 10, 11, 12, 14

Orleans Bed and Breakfast Associates

P.O. Box 1312, Orleans, 02653
(508) 255-3824; (800) 541-6226

Serendipity. Peace and quiet "on golden pond." Spacious deck overlooking private, sandy beach. Upstairs king bedroom with TV, full bath, lovely water view. Downstairs large room with sliders for private entrance from patio, king-size bed, TV, full bath. Adjacent single room on each floor for another family member ($30). Very private. Minutes to ocean, tennis, and golf. $70.

HARWICH (EAST)

House Guests Cape Cod and the Islands

Box 1881, Orleans, 02653
(508) 896-7053; (800) 666-HOST (reservations)
FAX (508) 896-7054

93140. The house is surrounded by lovely gardens, and there is an in-ground swimming pool and spacious deck for guest use. On the first floor there are two guest rooms with queen-size beds and private baths. One has a private entrance to the deck. A suite with queen-size bed, separate sitting room with queen-size sofa bed, and private bath is in the finished basement. The suite has a private entrance and direct access to the pool and deck through the sliders in the sitting room. Outside shower. Continental breakfast. Children are welcome. Smoking on deck only. Resident cats. Available April through late November. $50-75.

HARWICH (WEST)

House Guests Cape Cod and the Islands

Box 1881, Orleans, 02653
(508) 896-7053; (800) 666-HOST (reservations)
FAX (508) 896-7054

6 Pets welcome; 8 Children welcome; 9 Social drinking allowed; 10 Tennis available; 11 Swimming available; 12 Golf available; 13 Skiing available; 14 May be booked through travel agents.

93151. Built in 1786, this is an inn to be enjoyed by all history buffs. There are five comfortably furnished guest rooms, three of which have private baths. The two remaining rooms make a wonderfully cozy family suite with a private connecting bath. One has a queen-size bed, private entrance, and working fireplace. Guests are invited to use the spacious grounds for lawn games or picnicking. Close to the beach. Children are welcome for stays up to five nights. Crib available. Continental breakfast. Resident dog. Closed October through April. $45-65.

HARWICH PORT (CAPE COD)

Bed and Breakfast Associates Bay Colony, Ltd.
P.O. Box 57166, Babson Park, Boston, 02157-0166
(617) 449-5302; (800) 347-5088
FAX (617) 449-5958

CC360. This luxurious Victorian mansion provides an unforgettable setting for a romantic getaway. Guests can stay in one of five richly appointed guest rooms with fine period furnishings, lovely new baths, and modern amenities. Savor the full gourmet breakfasts and the afternoon hors d'oeuvres in the gracious parlor. Lawn games are provided, as is a guest recreation room. Stroll over to the quaint shopping area and to the nearby beach on Nantucket Sound. Full gourmet breakfast; no children. $165-185.

CC365. This eight-bedroom inn sits just footsteps from the famed sandy beaches of the Cape's South Shore. Guests are delighted by the facilities, which include elegant guest rooms with private baths, welcoming common rooms and romantic decor. Full breakfast provided. $75-155.

CC370. White wicker rocking chairs and hanging geraniums on the wraparound porch beckon guests to this Victorian home one-third mile from the sandy beach. There are five guest rooms with brass beds, fine period furnishings, and pleasing pastel wallpapers. Shops and restaurants are within easy walking distance. Continental breakfast; family and monthly rates are available. $95.

CC371. These hosts offer excellent family accommodations in the relaxed atmosphere of this guest house. All rooms are thoughtfully furnished, spacious, and breezy. A Continental breakfast is served in the dining room, while an outdoor pool awaits just beyond. The beach is less than one-half mile. Children welcome. $95.

Bed and Breakfast Cape Cod
P.O. Box 341, West Hyannisport, 02672-0341
(508) 775-2772; FAX (508) 775-2884

13. This Dutch-style Colonial has served as a small inn for 30 years and is on a private beach on the Nantucket Sound. The house features a large sun porch, living room with fireplace, and a large dining area. A variety of rooms, all of which offer private baths and have queen- and king-size beds, are available. Two apartments with separate entrances are also available. Children over 11 welcome. $105-165.

56. This restored 1860s country Victorian home is very close to Bank Street Beach, village shops, fine restaurants, and two public golf courses. There are two bedrooms available with a shared bath, one with twin beds and the other with a double bed. Ideal private quarters for a couple with two children or two couples traveling together. There is also a guest room with a king-size bed and private bath, and a carriage house efficiency with private bath. Fresh fruit, hot breads, brewed coffee/tea, and cereals included. $65-100.

NOTES: Credit cards accepted: A MasterCard; B Visa; C American Express; D Discover Card; E Diner's Club; F Other; 2 Personal checks accepted; 3 Lunch available; 4 Dinner available; 5 Open all year;

Bed and Breakfast Greater Boston and Cape Cod

P.O. Box 35, Newtonville, 02160
(617) 964-1606; (800) 832-2632
FAX (617) 332-8572

Inn by the Sea. This elegant bed and breakfast inn is only a short walk from a private, sandy beach on Nantucket Sound. Each of the inn rooms offers private bath and king, queen, or twin beds. Some rooms are air-conditioned; several have fireplaces. Two units have separate entrances. There is also a cozy cottage with a fireplace. Full breakfast. The host can also accommodate guests celebrating special occasions with romantic packages, which include champagne, long-stem roses, chocolates, fresh fruit, etc. The inn is open year-round. Children over 12 are welcome. Some smoking rooms are available. $105-165.

Captain's Quarters

85 Bank Street, 02642
(800) 992-6550

A romantic 1850s Victorian with a classic wraparound porch, nostalgic gingerbread trim, and a graceful curving front stairway. Guest rooms have private baths, queen-size brass beds with eyelet lace-trimmed sheets, lace curtains, and comfortable reading chairs. Just a three-minute walk into town and a five-minute walk to an ocean beach. Experience Cape Cod in a relaxed and friendly atmosphere.

Hosts: Ed and Susan Kenney
Rooms: 5 (PB) $65-95
Continental Breakfast
Credit Cards: A, B, C, D
Notes: 2, 5, 9, 10, 11, 12, 14

Country Inn

86 Sisson Road, 02646
(508) 432-2769; (800) 231-1722

An inn of New England tradition set on six country acres. Newly restored guest rooms with color TVs, air conditioning, and romantic bedding offer a perfect setting for a getaway or vacation. Some rooms offer fireplaces. Cozy fireside dining in the fall and winter, and a varied menu features the freshest of native seafood and the finest of meats and poultry. Tennis courts, an in-

Country Inn

ground swimming pool, and walk-to-beach parking provided free of charge (parking is one mile away at the summer family annex, Harbor Breeze).

Hosts: The Dings Family
Rooms: 7 (PB) $75-125
Continental Breakfast
Credit Cards: A, D, C
Notes: 4, 5, 7 (limited), 9, 10, 11, 12

Dunscroft-by-the-Sea

24 Pilgrim Road, 02646
(508) 432-0810

Beautiful, private, mile-long beach on Nantucket Sound. Romantic inn in an exclusive, quiet, residential area. In-town walk to quaint shops, art galleries, and restaurants. King- and queen-size bed chambers, in-room private baths, candlelight, fireplaces, fine linens; sleigh, canopied, and four-poster beds—a romantic interlude by Alyce and Laura Ashley. Full country breakfast. Additionally, there is an enchanted cottage with fireplace which sleeps three.

6 Pets welcome; 8 Children welcome; 9 Social drinking allowed; 10 Tennis available; 11 Swimming available; 12 Golf available; 13 Skiing available; 14 May be booked through travel agents.

Hosts: Alyce and Wally Cunningham
Rooms: 8 (PB) $95-165
Full Breakfast
Credit Cards: A, B, C
Notes: 2, 5, 7 (limited), 8 (over 12), 9, 10, 11, 12, 13 (cross-country), 14

House Guests Cape Cod and the Islands

Box 1881, Orleans, 02653
(508) 896-7053; (800) 666-HOST (reservations)
FAX (508) 896-7054

94165. Just 500 feet from a beautiful private beach on Nantucket Sound, this inn is an easy walk to the quaint shops, restaurants, and art galleries in the village. Eight guest rooms have private baths; three include air conditioning; one has color TV. Twin, king- and queen-size beds are available. Full breakfast is served. Nonsmoking guest rooms are available. Extra fee for additional person. Additionally, a one-bedroom cottage, only steps away from the inn, includes: a king-size bed; a living room with full-size sofa bed, TV, and fireplace; a full kitchen and a private bath. Occupancy is limited to three guests; maid service, linens, and full breakfast are included. Children 12 or older are welcome. Special rates. $85-155.

HYANNIS

The Inn on Sea Street

358 Sea Street, 02601
(508) 775-8030

This elegant 1849 Victorian inn, with ten romantic rooms, plus a carriage house, is just steps from the beach. Features antiques, Persian rugs, and canopied beds in this unpretentious, hospitable atmosphere, where no detail has been overlooked in assuring comfort. Refrigerator and telephone available for guests' use. Full gourmet breakfast of fresh fruit and home-baked delights served at individual tables set with the hosts' finest silver, china, crystal, and fresh flowers. One-night stays are welcome.

Hosts: Lois M. Nelson and J. B. Whitehead
Rooms: 10 (8 PB; 2 SB) $70-110
Full Breakfast
Credit Cards: A, B, C, D
Notes: 2, 9, 10, 11, 12

Sea Breeze Inn

397 Sea Street, 02601
(508) 771-7213

Sea Breeze is a Victorian bed and breakfast close to ferries and the islands. Canopied beds, air conditioning, private baths, and an expanded breakfast of delicious muffins, bagels, and fruit. The beach is just a three-minute walk away. Restaurants and theaters are just a five-minute drive away.

Hosts: Martin and Patricia Battle
Rooms: 14 (PB) $49-95
Continental Breakfast
Credit Cards: A, B, C, D
Notes: 2 (deposit), 5, 7, 8, 9, 10, 11, 12, 14 (10%)

HYANNISPORT

Bed and Breakfast Cape Cod

P.O. Box 341, West Hyannisport, 02672-0341
(508) 775-2772; FAX (508) 775-2884

32. This 200-year-old Colonial-style house is one mile from the center of town, five blocks from the Kennedy compound, two blocks from the ferry to Martha's Vineyard or Nantucket, and less than a mile away from great beaches. One bedroom with a double bed shares a tub and shower with a bedroom that has a pair of twin beds. A Continental breakfast is served each morning, and guests are welcome to use the parlor for relaxing. Children over 12. $55.

The Simmons Homestead Inn

288 Scudder Avenue, 02647
(508) 778-4999; FAX (508) 790-1342

NOTES: Credit cards accepted: A MasterCard; B Visa; C American Express; D Discover Card; E Diner's Club; F Other; 2 Personal checks accepted; 3 Lunch available; 4 Dinner available; 5 Open all year;

An 1820 sea captain's estate that is now one of the nicest inns on Cape Cod. In the country, yet only one-half mile from Hyannis. A very pleasant inn with large porches and huge common rooms, the perfect home base for enjoying the Cape.

Host: Bill Putman
Rooms: 10 (PB) $100-130
Full Breakfast
Credit Cards: A, B, C, D
Notes: 2, 5, 7, 8, 9, 10, 11, 12, 14

LEE

Applegate

279 West Park Street, 01238
(413) 243-4451

A circular driveway leads to this pillared Georgian Colonial home set on six peaceful acres. Applegate is special in every way with canopied beds, antiques, fireplaces, pool, and manicured gardens. Its mood is warm, hospitable, and relaxed. Enjoy complimentary wine and cheese in the living room, complete with a baby grand piano. Continental-plus breakfast is served. New TV room with VCR, small video library, and a Nordic track. Near Norman Rockwell museum and Tanglewood in the heart of the Berkshires.

Hosts: Nancy Begbie-Cannata and Richard Cannata
Rooms: 6 (PB) $80-195
Continental Breakfast
Credit Cards: A, B
Notes: 2, 5, 7 (limited), 8 (over 12), 9, 10, 11, 12, 13

Chambéry Inn

199 Main Street, 01238
(413) 243-2221; (800) 537-4321
FAX (413) 243-3600

Restful, romantic, and rejuvenating; this schoolhouse teaches guests the three "Rs" of travel. Come visit Berkshires' 1885 petite chateau. Built as the country's first parochial school, the inn serves as one of the most spectacular examples of purist restoration. All 400- to 500-square-foot suites are individually decorated with soothing tapestries, fabrics, and colors. Standard features include 13-foot ceilings, eight-foot windows, sitting areas with fireplace, full sparkling and new private baths with whirlpool, air conditioning, decks, phones, and color TV. Choose a king-size canopied or two queen-size beds. Room-delivered breakfast included. Hospitality and facilities—par excellence!

Hosts: Marilyn Kelly and Joseph Toole
Rooms: 8 (PB) $55-195
Continental Breakfast
Credit Cards: A, B, C, D
Notes: 2, 3, 4, 5, 9, 10, 11, 12, 13

LENOX

American Country Collection

4 Greenwood Lane, Delmar, NY 12054
(518) 439-7001

063. This elegant 11-bedroom inn is in the heart of a vibrant Berkshire community. Meticulously restored and on the National Register of Historic Places, this home features large rooms and six fireplaces. Each room has been tastefully furnished to please even the most discriminating traveler. Seven rooms have private baths, two share a bath, and the carriage house has two private suites. Full breakfast includes muffins, omelets, pancakes, French toast, and more. $65-185.

154. A Berkshire tradition since 1780, this gracious country home has 18 guest rooms: seven with jet tubs and private porches, eight with fireplaces, five with air conditioning, and all with private baths. Rooms are cozy and comfortable. The 72-foot swimming pool is available for guest use. A full breakfast is served daily. Children over 12 welcome; smoking permitted. $80-195.

6 Pets welcome; 8 Children welcome; 9 Social drinking allowed; 10 Tennis available; 11 Swimming available; 12 Golf available; 13 Skiing available; 14 May be booked through travel agents.

Birchwood Inn

7 Hubbard Street, 01240
(413) 637-2600; (800) 524-1646

Drive through the village of Lenox, and at the top of the hill stands the historic Birchwood Inn. The first town meeting was held here in 1767. Elegant and beautifully restored, the inn is known for its hospitality throughout the region. Enjoy antiques, fireplaces, library, and wonderful porch. Cultural activities include the Boston Symphony at Tanglewood and performing arts. There is marvelous fall foliage, hiking, and biking. Full breakfast with international specialities daily.

Hosts: Joan, Dick, and Dan Toner
Rooms: 12 (10 PB; 2 SB) $50-195
Full Breakfast
Credit Cards: A, B, C, D, E
Notes: 2, 9, 10, 11, 12, 13

Blantyre

16 Blantyre Road, P.O. Box 995, 01240
(413) 637-3556 (mid-May to early November)
(413) 298-3806

A gracious country house/hotel surrounded by 85 acres of grounds. The hotel has a European atmosphere and exceptional cuisine. Offers tennis, croquet, and swimming as its leisure activities.

Host: Roderick Anderson
Rooms: 23 (PB) $220-550
Full or Continental Breakfast
Credit Cards: A, B, C, E
Notes: 2, 3, 4, 7, 10, 11, 12, 14

Brook Farm Inn

15 Hawthorne Street, 01240
(413) 637-3013

There is poetry here. A lovely century-old Victorian home, nestled in a wooded glen amid gardens and a pool. There is a large library with fireplace, and several guest rooms feature fireplaces and canopied or brass beds. Poetry readings with tea and scones are offered each Saturday. Near

Brook Farm Inn

Tanglewood, theater, ballet, and museums. Enjoy hiking, biking, and wonderful fall foliage. In winter, cross-country and downhill skiing are close by. Relax and enjoy.

Hosts: Joe and Anne Miller
Rooms: 12 (PB) $65-170
Continental Breakfast
Credit Cards: A, B, D
Notes: 2, 5, 7 (limited), 8 (over 14), 9, 10, 11, 12, 13

The Gables Inn

103 Walker Street, 01240
(413) 637-3416

Former home of novelist Edith Wharton. Queen Anne-style with period furnishings, pool, tennis, fireplaces, and theme rooms.

Host: Frank Newton
Rooms: 18 (PB) $60-195
Continental Breakfast
Credit Cards: A, B, D
Notes: 2, 5, 7, 10, 11, 12, 13

Garden Gables Inn

141 Main Street, P.O. Box 52, 01240
(413) 637-0193; FAX (413) 637-4554

A charming 19-room 200-year-old gabled inn in the historic center of Lenox on five wooded acres dotted with gardens, maples, and fruit trees. A 72-foot outdoor swimming pool, fireplaces, and Jacuzzi. Minutes from Tanglewood and other attractions.

Good skiing in winter. In-room phones. Breakfast included.

Hosts: Mario and Lynn Mekinda
Rooms: 14 (PB) $65-180
Full Breakfast
Credit Cards: A, B, C, D
Notes: 2, 5, 10, 12, 13

Host Homes of Boston

P.O. Box 117, Newton, 02168
(617) 244-1308; FAX (617) 244-5156

A Country Home. On a quiet road of local farms, this 1917 Edwardian home occupies two acres. The dining room overlooks a landscaped back garden. Two large second-floor guest rooms (queen-size with air conditioning, twin-size) share the guest bath in the hall. Den with TV. Next to historic Concord. Twelve miles to Boston, four miles to I-95/128 at Waltham, one mile to commuter train. No smoking. Children welcome. $54-61.

Summer Hill Farm

950 East Street, 01240
(413) 442-2057

Comfortable 200-year-old farmhouse and converted-barn guest cottage on 20 acre horse farm. Tastefully furnished with genuine English antiques and Oriental rugs.

Summer Hill Farm

The satisfying country breakfast is served in the dining room or on the sun porch looking out over the gardens and view. The atmosphere is peaceful, relaxed, friendly, and unpretentious. Close to Tanglewood, Jacob's Pillow Dance, museums, galleries, theaters, Hancock Shaker Village, good restaurants, and shops.

Hosts: Michael and Sonya Chassell Wessel
Rooms: 7 (7 PB) $55-160
Full or Continental Breakfast
Credit Cards: None
Notes: 2, 5, 8, 10, 11, 12, 13, 14

LOWELL

Bed and Breakfast Associates Bay Colony, Ltd.

P.O. Box 57166, Babson Park, Boston, 02157-0166
(617) 449-5302; (800) 347-5008
FAX (617) 449-5958

CN300. This beautiful Victorian home with its wraparound porch and stained glass is meticulously maintained and is graced by many authentic architectural details and tasteful period furnishings. Two guest rooms on the second floor share a bath. Expanded Continental breakfast; children welcome, no smoking. $55; family rates available.

LUDLOW

Misty Meadows, Ltd.

467 Fuller Street, 01056
(413) 583-8103

One of Ludlow's oldest, this 200-year-old house has 85 acres on which to wander. A country scenic atmosphere on a working farm that raises "Scottish Highlanders." A scenic patio overlooks the Minechaug Mountain Range. Screened cabana with in-ground pool. Brook fishing nearby. An area with a lot of history and many historical sites less than one-half hour away.

Host: Donna Belle Haluch
Rooms: 2 (SB) $30-50

6 Pets welcome; 8 Children welcome; 9 Social drinking allowed; 10 Tennis available; 11 Swimming available; 12 Golf available; 13 Skiing available; 14 May be booked through travel agents.

Continental Breakfast
Credit Cards: None
Notes: 2, 5, 6, 7, 8, 9, 10, 11, 12, 13

LYNN

Diamond District Bed and Breakfast

142 Ocean Street, 01902-2007
(617) 599-4470; (800) 666-3076
FAX (617) 599-4470

This 17-room architect-designed clapboard mansion was built in 1911. The mansion features a gracious foyer, a grand staircase winding up the three floors, a spacious fireplace in the living room finished in Mexican mahogany and with an ocean view, French doors leading to an adjacent large veranda that overlooks the gardens and ocean, and a banquet-size dining room. Antiques and Oriental rugs fill the house. Other furnishings include an 1895 rosewood Knabe concert grand piano, custom Chippendale dining room table and chairs. Bedrooms offer a custom 1870s Victorian bed and twin beds. Each room boasts the elegance of yesteryear. No smoking.

Hosts: Sandra and Jerry Caron
Rooms: 8 (4 PB; 4 SB) $75-85
Full Breakfast
Credit Cards: A, B, C, D, E
Notes: 2, 5, 6 (limited), 8, 10, 11, 12, 14

MARBLEHEAD

Bed and Breakfast Associates Bay Colony, Ltd.

P.O. Box 57166, Babson Park, Boston, 02157-0166
(617) 449-5302; (800) 347-5088
FAX (617) 449-5958

NS261. Just two blocks to beaches, antique shops, and restaurants, this restored Federal property offers beamed cathedral ceilings and a cozy, charming decor. Two guest rooms on the second floor share a bath. Continental breakfast; children welcome; no smoking. $75-80.

NS262. This friendly couple offers two guest rooms in their charming multilevel hillside home. Both rooms overlook Marblehead Harbor. Two guest rooms share a bath. Generous Continental breakfast; children welcome. Family rates available. $68.

Bed and Breakfast Marblehead and North Shore

P.O. Box 35, Newtonville, 02160
(617) 964-1606; (800) 832-2632
FAX (617) 332-8572

Cobble Court. A decorated carriage house adjacent to the host's 250-year-old historic home. Guests have personal parking spaces (a premium here), modern amenities, fresh flowers, and other surprises. A huge, sunny room with second-level sleeping loft has king-size bed, modern shower-bath, sitting area, sleep-sofa, TV, fans, and air conditioning. Equipment and utensils are available for light meals or snacks. Hosts stock breakfast-foods, or guests may try nearby coffee shop restaurants. No smoking. Open year-round; special rates for weekly/multiple-night stays. Extra fee for additional person. $125.

Marblehead Victorian. This gracious 1890 Victorian home features three guest room, with choice of twin, double, or queen-size beds. All rooms share a full bath in the hall and a half-bath downstairs. A separate-entrance guest suite sleeps two to four people and has a private bath, TV, and refrigerator. Breakfast featuring home-baked bread and muffins is served in breakfast room or country gardens out back. Close to beaches. Recreation room includes pool table. Smoking outside only. Children welcome; portable crib or adult-size cot available for extra fee. Resident dog. Weekly rates available. $108.

NOTES: Credit cards accepted: A MasterCard; B Visa; C American Express; D Discover Card; E Diner's Club; F Other; 2 Personal checks accepted; 3 Lunch available; 4 Dinner available; 5 Open all year;

The Village Nook. A cozy 19th-century bed and breakfast accommodation offering the warmth and comfort of home. Within walking distance to the quaint shops, wonderful restaurants, galleries, and world-renowned harbor of Old Town Marblehead. Accommodations include pretty guest rooms, one queen-size bed and two twin beds, which share a bath. Guests may enjoy the use of the downstairs living room, deck, and hot tub. Nonsmoking. Children are welcome. $75-90.

DESTINNATIONS
New England

P.O. Box 1173, Osterville 02655
(508) 428-5600; FAX (508) 420-0565;
(800) 333-4667 (reservations)

7405. Perched on a seawall above the Atlantic, this six-room classic Tudor inn offers incomparable privacy. Each room is individually decorated in antiques and wicker; most have fireplaces. Each has a private bath; some have ocean views, others face a peaceful street. Continental breakfast in the breakfast room overlooking seascape, or guests may opt to sit in the garden and watch black cormorants and eider ducks swimming in the cove. A short stroll to sandy Preston Beach; a few-minutes drive to Old Town's restaurants, boutiques, galleries, and antique shops. Less than ten minutes from historic Salem; 15 miles north of Boston. Open year-round. No smoking. No children or pets.

The Harbor Light Inn

58 Washington Street, 01945
(617) 631-2186

Premier inn one block from the harbor with rooms featuring air conditioning, TV, private baths, and working fireplaces. Two rooms have double Jacuzzis and sun decks. Beautiful 18th-century period mahogany furniture. Recent acquisition of an adjacent Federalist manor provides more room and

The Harbor Light Inn

amenities, including a conference room and swimming pool.

Hosts: Peter and Suzanne Conway
Rooms: 20 (PB) $85-150
Suites: (PB) $160-185
Continental Breakfast
Credit Cards: A, B, C
Notes: 2, 5, 7, 8, 9, 10, 11, 12

Harborside House

23 Gregory Street, 01945
(617) 631-1032

This handsome 1850 home in the historic district overlooks Marblehead Harbor. Enjoy water views from a fireplaced parlor, period dining room, third-story sun deck, and summer breakfast porch where guests may sample home-baked breads and

Harborside House

muffins. Walk to historic sights, excellent restaurants, and unique shops. Hostess is a professional dressmaker and nationally ranked competitive swimmer. Enjoy quiet comfort and convenience.

Host: Susan Livingston
Rooms: 2 (SB) $85
Continental Breakfast
Credit Cards: None
Notes: 2, 5, 8 (over 10), 10, 11, 14

The Nesting Place

16 Village Street, 01945
(617) 631-6655; (617) 586-5889

This charming 19th-century home is in historic Marblehead and within walking distance of the renowned harbor, beaches, historic homes, galleries, eateries, shops, and famous parks. A relaxing, refreshing home away from home. Two comfortably furnished guest rooms feature a healthful breakfast, outdoor hot tub, and a smoke-free environment. One-half hour from Boston, or one hour from New Hampshire. Day trips by car or bicycle are possible. Seasonal rates available.

Host: Louise Hirshberg
Rooms: 2 (SB) $55-65
Continental Breakfast
Credit Cards: A, B
Notes: 2, 5, 6, 8, 9, 10, 11

Pleasant Manor Inn

264 Pleasant Street, 01945
(617) 631-5843

Pleasant Manor, a fine example of classic Victorian architecture, was built in 1872 and has been a charming inn since 1923. On the bus line 14 miles north of Boston and two miles from Salem. Beaches, restaurants, shops, and historic points of interest are easily accessible from this convenient location. Some features include private baths, TVs, VCRs, air conditioning, tennis court, off-street parking, and immaculate accommodations. Welcome to one of the most beautiful towns in the country.

Hosts: Takami and Richard Phelan
Rooms: 12 (PB) $65-75
Continental Breakfast
Credit Cards: None
Notes: 2, 5, 7, 8, 9, 10, 14

Spray Cliff on the Ocean

25 Spray Avenue, 01945
(508) 744-8924; (800) 626-1530

A marvelous Old English Tudor mansion set high above the Atlantic with views that extend forever. Six guest rooms with private baths, some with fireplaces, most with ocean views. Continental breakfast. Steps from a sandy beach.

Hosts: Richard and Diane Pabich
Rooms: 6 (PB) $95-200
Continental Breakfast
Credit Cards: A, B, C, D, E
Notes: 2, 5, 7, 8, 9, 10, 11, 12, 14

Stillpoint

27 Gregory Street, 01945
(617) 631-1667; (800) 882-3891

Nicely appointed 1840s home is open all year, graciously landscaped, and filled with antiques, fireplace, piano, books, no TV, and quiet, refreshing ambience. Three spacious bedrooms share two full baths (the option of a private bath is available) and a deliciously healthy breakfast is served in the morning on the deck overlooking Marblehead Harbor in good weather. Within walking distance to shops, restaurants, beaches, and public transportation. Twenty miles north of Boston, near Logan airport, and an hour south of Maine/New Hampshire border. Trips to Concord, Lexington, Sturbridge Village, antique stores, and New Hampshire ski slopes are feasible.

Host: Sarah Lincoln-Harrison
Rooms: 3 (1 PB, 2SB) $70-80
Continental Breakfast
Credit Cards: A, B
Notes: 2, 5, 8, 10, 11, 14

NOTES: Credit cards accepted: A MasterCard; B Visa; C American Express; D Discover Card; E Diner's Club; F Other; 2 Personal checks accepted; 3 Lunch available; 4 Dinner available; 5 Open all year;

MARSHFIELD

Bed and Breakfast Associates Bay Colony, Ltd.

P.O. Box 57166, Babson Park, Boston, 02157-0166
(617) 449-5302; (800) 347-5088
FAX (617) 449-5958

SS350. What enthusiasm and hospitality this retired couple brings to hosting! Their New England farm-style home is one block from Marshfield Beach. Built in 1875, it is furnished with warmth and charm; guests will find this bed and breakfast a welcoming retreat. Three guest rooms with private baths. Full breakfast; children welcome; no smoking. $60-70; family rates available.

Bed and Breakfast Cape Cod

P.O. Box 341, West Hyannisport, 02672-0341
(508) 775-2772; FAX (508) 775-2884

77. This two-story home facing the water has two rooms for bed and breakfast, one with a double bed and the other with a pair of twin beds. The bath is shared, and the breakfast is Continental, served between 8:00-9:30 A.M. Convenient to the bus to Boston. Children over 12 welcome. $60.

MARSTONS MILLS

Bed and Breakfast Cape Cod

P.O. Box 341, West Hyannisport, 02672-0341
(508) 775-2772; FAX (508) 775-2884

34. Built in 1986 in a quiet residential neighborhood, this ranch-style house has all the extras one could ask for. One room has queen-size bed, private deck, and private entrance, and another room has a queen-size bed and private bath. The beach is two miles away and the ferry to Martha's Vineyard or Nantucket is three miles away. Children over 12 welcome. No smoking. $75-85.

58. Built in 1790, this beautiful Colonial-style inn sits on three acres of rolling hillside and overlooks a freshwater pond. A working fireplace and country furnishings create a warm, comfortable atmosphere in the first-floor parlor, and a porch with white wicker furniture and fresh floral arrangements looks out onto a swimming pool. A small suite, a carriage house, and three guest rooms offer special appeal. Children over 12. $65-135.

MEDFORD

Bed and Breakfast Associates Bay Colony, Ltd.

P.O. Box 57166, Babson Park
Boston 02157-0166
(617) 449-5302; (800) 347-5088
FAX (617) 449-5958

IN205. On a quiet street near Tufts University, this host couple offers three guest rooms in their ten-room Colonial home, built in 1920. The country decor is cheerful, and the rooms are spacious and sunny; the guest area is apart from the hosts' suite. One half-hour north of downtown Boston. Free parking, near public transit. $68.

MILTON

Host Homes of Boston

P.O. Box 117, Boston, 02168
(617) 244-1308; FAX (617) 244-5156

Historic Country Home. This 1780 country home restored by architect/owners blends heirlooms and modern amenities for a special stay. Second-floor guest room offers a pair of twin beds, and the grounds offer a swimming pool and a barn. Near I-93, Route 128, and I-95. $68.

6 Pets welcome; 8 Children welcome; 9 Social drinking allowed; 10 Tennis available; 11 Swimming available; 12 Golf available; 13 Skiing available; 14 May be booked through travel agents.

NANTUCKET

Bed and Breakfast Nantucket/Martha's Vineyard

P.O. Box 341, West Hyannisport, 02672-0341
(508) 775-2772; FAX (508) 775-2884

102. This 19-room bed and breakfast is close to the harbor in the village. From the widow's walk on the third floor, there is a panoramic view of the Nantucket harbor. All guest rooms have private baths, and two suites are also available. Breakfast is served in the large dining room on the first floor. No smoking. Children welcome. $80-140.

103. In the heart of the village, this guest house has six private-bath bedrooms with queen-size beds and one with twin beds. Each room has a small refrigerator, coffeemaker, and cable color TV. The decor is traditional. No breakfast is served by the host, but several restaurants are only a few steps away. A parlor is also available for guest use. All village points of interest are within a short walk. Combined with its inexpensive cost and complete village convenience, this is an excellent Nantucket accommodation. No smoking. No children under 12. $75-125.

104. A few steps from Main Street in the village, this 1830 Greek Revival-style home offers two bedrooms and a separate cottage for bed and breakfast. Each room has a private bath and king-size bed, and Continental breakfast is served in the dining room. Convenience to the village, a porch, and lovely gardens are several of the amenities this home offers. $100-125.

The Carlisle House Inn

26 North Water Street, 02554
(508) 228-0720

The Carlisle House Inn

Built in 1765, the Carlisle House has been a quality inn for more than 100 years. Just off the center of town, the inn has been carefully restored. Hand-stenciled wallpapers, working fireplaces, inlaid pine paneling, wide-board floor, and rich Oriental carpets. Minimum stay of two nights.

Hosts: Peter and Suzanne Conway
Rooms: 14 (8 PB; 6 SB) $125
Continental Breakfast
Credit Cards: A, B, C
Notes: 2, 5, 7, 8 (over 10), 9, 10, 11, 12, 14

The Carriage House

Five Ray's Court, 02554
(508) 228-0326

Established in 1974, The Carriage House bed and breakfast is lovingly cared for by Jeanne McHugh and son, Haziel. Originally serving as a carriage house for a whaling mansion in the mid-1800s, it is just a half block behind Main Street on one of the prettiest lanes in town. Convenient to museums, shops, restaurants and all the activities of town, yet blissfully quiet and removed from them. The Carriage House is quality-rated in the AAA and *Mobil Travel Guide*. It has been written about in many travel publications including *Yankee Travel Guide, National Geographic,* and the *International Herald Tribune.*

Hosts: Jeanne McHugh and Son
Rooms: 7 (PB) $65-150
Continental Breakfast
Credit Cards: None
Notes: 2, 5, 8, 9, 10, 11, 12, 14

DESTINNATIONS
New England

P.O. Box 1173, Osterville 02655
(508) 428-5600; FAX (508) 420-0565
(800) 333-4667 (reservations)

7206. A short walk from the center of town, this fine inn, with 16 rooms and a two-bedroom apartment, features private baths and distinctive furnishings, including canopied and four-poster beds, working fireplaces, and TV. Sumptuous full breakfast. Bicycles provided for guest use; staff available for planning assistance. Open year-round.

7398. This venerable full-service inn with 60 rooms in six buildings sits atop Broad Street, a short walk from the ferry wharf. Each guest room has private bath; 49 have TV, 30 have refrigerators, ten will accommodate children; two have private entrances. Rooms are furnished with antiques and quality reproductions, each with its own unique charm. The inn has two on-site restaurants, one a pub-style eatery; there are also meeting and banquet rooms available, as well as a catering service. Parking for 20 vehicles on-site. Open year-round. $135-170.

7303. This collection of fine inns, bed and breakfast, and cottages sprawls across Nantucket town with lodgings ranging from a two-bedroom cottage (with TV, kitchen, and private bath) to luxurious guest rooms

with canopied beds and working fireplaces. There are six buildings and over 40 different types and styles of rooms. Most are along Centre Street (a.k.a. Petticoat Row) in the hub of island activity, restaurants, shops, and galleries. One inn has a sunroom with white wicker furniture; another has a parlor with TV. Designated nonsmoking buildings. Children welcome. Open year-round. $45-325.

Eighteen Gardner
Street Inn

18 Gardner Street, 02554
(508) 228-1155

Eighteen Gardner Street Inn

Visitors are warmly welcomed to the circa 1835 home of Captain Robert Joy. Built from the wealth of the whaling era, this island home includes amenities such as fireplaced bedrooms, canopied beds, private baths, and spacious common rooms for the leisure hours of guests' stay. Whether guests choose the cozy Garden Room or a deluxe suite, they will be attended by a courteous staff serving a full Nantucket breakfast and assisting guests with all holiday enjoyment.

Hosts: Roger and Mary Schmidt
Rooms: 17 (PB) $65-185
Full Breakfast
Credit Cards: A, B, C, D
Notes: 2, 5, 8, 9, 10, 11, 12, 14

House Guests Cape Cod and the Islands

Box 1881, Orleans, 02653
(508) 896-7053; (800) 666-HOST (reservations)
FAX (508) 896-7054

93430. A comfortable home on a quiet country lane, less than a mile from the center of Nantucket Town. Hosts can direct guests to area attractions. There are two second-floor bedrooms, one with king-size bed and the other with twin beds, which can be arranged to make a king-size bed. Each room has a mini-refrigerator for storing snacks and beverages. One bath is shared between the two rooms. A window air conditioning unit is available. Continental breakfast. Walk or bike to nearby beaches. Resident dogs. $65. $15 for additional person.

93440. Lovely accommodations in a historic home on a quiet cobblestone street only blocks from the village center, beaches, and the ferry terminal. This 1725 vintage inn has picturesque gardens and offers pleasant views from its five charmingly furnished guest rooms. Each room has a queen-size canopied or four-poster bed and private bath. Home-baked breads and pastries are featured in the hearty Continental breakfast. Children of all ages are welcome. A crib is available for infants. Smoking on sun porch only. $60-140. $20 for additional person.

93450. Just a two-minute walk from Main Street, this friendly and comfortable guest house is in the heart of old Nantucket Town. The six guest rooms feature queen-size and twin beds and private baths. All rooms have air conditioning, color cable TV, small refrigerator, and coffee maker. The friendly hosts invite guests to join them twice weekly for a social get-together with refreshments and conversation on the patio. Breakfast is not offered at this guest house. Children are welcome. Smoking on the patio only. $65-115. $20 for additional person.

93460. Guest comfort is the top priority here, where guests will find an outside shower for beach goers and even on-premise laundry facilities! Choose one of the 16 queen- or twin-bedded rooms or a two-bedroom suite, all with private baths and ceiling fans. Just two minutes from a harbor beach and a ten-minute walk from Main Street. Some guest rooms have a partial water view. The widow's walk (roof deck) offers spectacular harbor views. Children under 12 are welcome in all rooms off-season and in the suite only during peak season. Smoking on the patio only. $80-200.

93465. A lovely Quaker-style 1728 Colonial home in the heart of Nantucket's historic district. Gorgeous gardens. Two spacious guest suites. The largest has a queen-size canopied bed, separate sitting room, and harbor view. The other offers twin beds and a sofa bed in the separate sitting room. Both suites have private baths and come equipped with microwave oven, refrigerator, hot-water kettle, and cable TV. Breakfast is not provided. No smoking. Children 12 and older are welcome. Three-night minimum required. Closed January 1 through May 31. $75-125.

House of Seven Gables

32 Cliff Road, 02554
(508) 228-4706

In the historic district of Nantucket. A Continental breakfast is served in the room. Most rooms in this 100-year-old Victorian have a view of Nantucket Sound.

Host: Suzanne Walton
Rooms: 10 (8 PB; 2 SB) $40-150
Continental Breakfast
Credit Cards: A, B, C
Notes: 2, 5, 7, 8 (over 10), 9, 10, 11, 12

The Martin House Inn

61 Centre Street, P.O. Box 743, 02554
(508) 228-0678

In a stately 1803 mariner's home in the Nantucket historic district, a romantic sojourn awaits guests. A glowing fire in the spacious living room-dining room is the perfect place to read and relax. Large, airy guest rooms with authentic period pieces and four-poster beds and a lovely yard and veranda for peaceful, summer afternoons make sure guests have a memorable stay. A large breakfast featuring homemade breads and muffins, fresh fruits, and granola is served in the dining room.

Hosts: Ceci and Channing Moore
Rooms: 13 (9 PB; 4 SB) $85-140
Continental Breakfast
Credit Cards: A, B, C
Notes: 2, 5, 8, 9 10, 11, 12

The Martin House

76 Main Street

76 Main Street, 02554
(508) 228-2533

All the quiet and subtle beauty is here for guests to explore in comfort. An 1883 Victorian home in the historic district on elm-shaded and cobblestoned Main Street. The host is dedicated to guests' enjoyment of the island and looks forward to accommodating their needs. All rooms are nonsmoking.

Host: Shirley Peters
Rooms: 18 (PB) $120-140
Continental Breakfast
Credit Cards: A, B, C
Notes: 2, 5, 8, 9, 10, 11, 12, 14

Stumble Inne

109 Orange Street, 02554
(508) 228-4482

The Stumble Inne and Starbuck House are on historic Orange Street, a pleasant ten-minute walk to Main Street town center for shops and restaurants. The Stumble Inne has seven double and queen rooms, all with cable TV, and most with bar refrigerators. Some rooms are air-conditioned. The Starbuck House, right across the street, has six double rooms. All rooms in both buildings feature period antiques and Laura Ashley decor.

Hosts: Mary Kay and Mal Condon
Rooms: 13 (11 PB; 2 SB) $65-160
Continental Breakfast
Credit Cards: A, B, C
Notes: 2, 5, 7, 8, 9, 10, 11, 12, 14

Tuckernuck Inn

60 Unions Street, 02554
(508) 228-4886; (800) 228-4886

Tuckernuck Inn is named for the small island just one mile off Nantucket's westernmost tip. Tuckernuck is an Indian word meaning "a loaf of bread." The inn is Colonial in decor and quite comfortable. Amenities include a large back lawn for relaxing and a rooftop widow's walk deck overlooking Nantucket Harbor. Fine dining is offered May through October at the in-house

Tuckernuck Inn

6 Pets welcome; 8 Children welcome; 9 Social drinking allowed; 10 Tennis available; 11 Swimming available; 12 Golf available; 13 Skiing available; 14 May be booked through travel agents.

restaurant. Personal attention for each guest is the primary objective, and many of the guests return year after year. Tuckernuck Inn is recommended by AAA and *Mobil Travel Guide*.

Host: Ken Parker
Rooms: 16 (PB) $80-145
Suites: 2 (PB)
Continental Breakfast
Credit Cards: A, B, C
Notes: 4, 5, 8, 9, 10, 11, 12, 14

The Woodbox Inn

29 Fair Street, 02554
(508) 228-0587

Nantucket's oldest inn, built in 1709, is one-and-a-half blocks from the center of town. The Woodbox offers three double rooms and six suites with working fireplaces, all with private bath. A full breakfast is available along with candlelight gourmet dinners. Voted "Nantucket's Most Romantic Dining Room" and also rated "Nantucket's Finest Dining." Closed mid-October through June 1.

Host: Dexter Tutein
Rooms: 9 (PB) $125-200
Full Breakfast
Credit Cards: None
Notes: 2, 4, 8, 9, 10, 11, 12

NANTUCKET ISLAND

Folger Hotel

P.O. Box 628, 89 Easton Street, 02554
(508) 228-0313

A family resort in a quiet neighborhood, a five-minute walk from downtown, and a short distance to the beaches. The hotel is surrounded with wide verandas which overlook the landscaped grounds and water gardens. A full breakfast is included with the room (in-season), served in the Whale Restaurant.

Hosts: Bob and Barbara Bowman
Rooms: 60 (40 PB; 20 SB) $80-120
Full Breakfast
Credit Cards: A, B, C, D
Notes: 2, 4, 8, 9, 10, 11, 14

NEEDHAM

Bed and Breakfast Associates Bay Colony, Ltd.

P.O. Box 57166, Babson Park, Boston, 02157-0166
(617) 449-5302; (800) 347-5088
FAX (617) 449-5958

IW630. This sweet little Cape-style home epitomizes New England suburban serenity. Convenient to commuter railway, or Boston is only 20 minutes by car. Two guest rooms (large room with double bed or smaller room with twin beds) share a bath on the second floor. Host quarters are on the first floor. Driveway parking. $45-50.

IW638. A delightful multi-level Colonial home with a tasteful and appealing decor. Three guest rooms on the third floor with designer bath. This is a delightful neighborhood! 25 minutes west of downtown Boston. Family rates available. $85.

Host Homes of Boston

P.O. Box 117, Boston, 02168
(617) 244-1308; FAX (617) 244-5156

The Thistle Bed and Breakfast. Typical, cozy Cape Cod on a quiet street has a fireplaced living room for guests and two second-floor guest rooms with doubles or twins and private and shared baths. A few blocks from Route 128/I-95, and guests can walk to the train. $61.

NEWBURYPORT

Bed and Breakfast/Inns of New England

128 South Hoop Pole Road, Guilford, CT 06437
(203) 457-0042; (800) 582-0853

MA-1000. Built in 1806 by Captain William Hoyt, this estate typifies the three-story square style of the Federal period. Among its many fine architectural features

NOTES: Credit cards accepted: A MasterCard; B Visa; C American Express; D Discover Card; E Diner's Club; F Other; 2 Personal checks accepted; 3 Lunch available; 4 Dinner available; 5 Open all year;

are cornices, mantles, balustrades, and a graceful hanging staircase. There are summer and winter porches, a formal front parlor, and library. Many special events are offered throughout the year, including weekend murder mysteries, fashion shows, weddings, and corporate conferences. Just a five-minute walk from downtown Newburyport, a seaport area. There are nine guest rooms on the inn's three floors, all furnished in antiques and some with canopied beds. Children 12 and older welcome. $50-77.

The Windsor House

The Windsor House in Newburyport

38 Federal Street, 01950
(508) 462-3778

Built as a wedding present, this eighteenth-century Federal mansion offers a rare blend of Yankee hospitality and the English tradition of bed and breakfast. Designed as a residence/ship's chandlery, the inn's spacious rooms recall the spirit of an English country house. In a historic seaport near a wildlife refuge. Whale-watching, museums, theater, and antiques. Rates include afternoon tea, English-cooked breakfast, tax, and service.

Hosts: Judith and John Harris
Rooms: 6 (3 PB; 3 SB) $75-125
Full Breakfast
Credit Cards: A, B, C, D
Notes: 2, 5, 6, 8, 10, 11, 12, 13, 14

NEWTON

Bed and Breakfast Associates Bay Colony, Ltd.

P.O. Box 57166, Babson Park, Boston, 02157-0166
(617) 449-5302; (800) 347-5088
FAX (617) 449-5958

IW255. This stately Victorian in a neighborhood of grand 19th-century homes has a private two-room guest suite with light cooking, a charming sitting room, and a dazzling new private bath. Leave the car in the driveway and walk to the express bus for a ten-minute trip to central Boston. Amenities include cable TV, VCR, telephone, a small refrigerator, microwave, built-in sandwich bar, and a Victorian desk and sofa. Ten-to twenty minutes west of Boston. $89.

IW265. The host, a lovely lady, will proudly show guests the distinctive interior and spectacular landscaping of the ranch-style home that her architect husband designed. Large windows afford delightful views of the seasonal splendor. This is one of Boston's best suburban neighborhoods. One guest room with private bath and a single den rented with guest room. Full breakfast; children over ten welcome; no smoking. $80.

Bed and Breakfast Greater Boston and Cape Cod

P.O. Box 35, Newtonville, 02160
(617) 964-1606; (800) 832-2632
FAX (617) 332-8572

Crescent Avenue. In a lovely suburb just west of Boston, with easy access by car and public transportation to Boston and Cambridge. Large, gracious, 12-room Greek Revival home has lovely gardens and an in-ground pool. Beautifully decorated. Two guest rooms with private baths, separate entrance, and parking. Generous Continental breakfast is served in the dining room or on the screened porch. Kitchen area available for guest use. Cat and dog in residence, but they are kept away from guest traffic. No smoking. $75-79.

The Suite at Chestnut Hill. This gorgeous furnished efficiency, in a neighborhood of very beautiful homes, offers easy access by public transportation to Boston/Cambridge. Efficiency has a kitchen area, full bath, color TV, telephone, air conditioning, separate dining and sitting areas, and a queen-size bed. Self-catered breakfast provided. $90.

Host Homes of Boston

P.O. Box 117, Boston, 02168
(617) 244-1308; FAX (617) 244-5156

Alderwood. Guests migrate to the gourmet kitchen in this 1930 Colonial. Second-floor guest room has twin beds. "Pumpkin" the cat lives here. Children welcome. Quiet road near Boston College law campus. One mile to Green Line-D. Ten-minute drive to Boston. Private bath; TV. $68.

Briarwood. This historic district landmark home (1875) combines Early American antiques with modern amenities. Excep-tional guest wing with private entrance and bath, featuring queen-size bed, two twins that double as sofas, skylights, air conditioning, TV, an alcove with dining table, picture window, and light-cooking facilities. Guests prepare own breakfast, food provided. Near restaurants and elegant mall, four blocks to public transit (Green Line-D), one block to Boston College. Boston three miles. No smoking. $81.

The Evergreens. Older Colonial is filled with host's pottery and Mexican art collection. Two second-floor guest rooms share bath. Cozy screened porch. Five-minute walk to Boston College or Green Line-B to

Boston University, Back Bay, and downtown. Air conditioning; shared bath. $61.

Rockledge. Stately 1882 Victorian in prime location. Cordial hosts offer bright, spacious rooms, antiques, trees, and gardens. Three second-floor guest rooms, but only two booked at a time. Ceiling fans. Second-floor guest parlor. Resident cat. Two blocks to lake, village, and subway. Older children welcome. Shared bath; TV; no smoking. $64.

NEWTON CENTER

Bed and Breakfast Associates Bay Colony, Ltd.

P.O. Box 57166, Babson Park
Boston 02157-0166
(617) 449-5302; (800) 347-5088
FAX (617) 449-5958

IW245. This large Victorian home has two pleasant third-floor guest rooms with shared bath. Fully restored and beautifully furnished, this family home is on a quiet street close to shops and public transit. $65-70.

Bed and Breakfast Greater Boston and Cape Cod

P.O. Box 35, Newtonville, 02160
(617) 964-1606; (800) 832-2632
FAX (617) 332-8572

The Park Lane. A large Baronial-style stucco set in a quiet residential area within walking distance of public transit, shops and restaurants. Three rooms on two levels offer double, single with trundle, or queen-size beds. Baths, shared and private, include one Jacuzzi shower/bath. Also available are TV, air conditioning, a sitting room, and a front porch. A generous Continental breakfast is served. Other conveniences include airport pickup, room phones, and visitor T-pass tickets. No smoking. Children welcome. Open year-round. $50-100.

Host Homes of Boston

P.O. Box 117, Boston, 02168
(617) 244-1308; FAX (617) 244-5156

Park Lane. This large Baronial-style stucco (1911) on quiet street has a Victorian motif. Friendly host offers two third-floor guest rooms, one with double-bed and the other with trundle bed (choice of single twins or king-size), second floor with queen-size bed, private bath Jacuzzi, A/C, cable TV. First floor guest parlor with fireplace. Village, public transit (Green Line-D), restaurants all within ten-minute walk. Five miles from Boston. No smoking. Children welcome. $61-115.

NORTH EASTHAM

Bed & Breakfast/Inns of New England

128 South Hoop Pole Road, Guilford, CT 06437
(203) 457-0042; (800) 582-0853

MA-1051. This house, a half-Cape with saltbox addition, is decorated with quilts and collectibles. In a quiet neighborhood less than a mile from Cape Cod National Seashore Visitor's Center, it is minutes from bay beaches, freshwater ponds, and two ocean beaches. Two guest rooms are available, both with shared baths. The first-floor room has a king-size bed, and the upstairs room has a double bed. No smoking. House dog; no guest pets. $50-60.

The Quilted Pineapple

65 Chester Avenue, P.O. Box 89, 02651-0089
(508) 255-3709

For travelers looking for a cozy retreat, yet close to swimming and biking on Cape Cod, the Quilted Pineapple is the place. The charming half-Cape home, in a quiet

neighborhood, is less than a mile from the Cape Cod National Seashore Visitor's Center. Ocean, bay, and freshwater swimming are close by. A substantial Continental breakfast, including homemade breads and muffins, is served in the homey country kitchen.

Hosts: Emily and David Laribee
Rooms: 2 (SB) $55-65
Continental Breakfast
Credit Cards: None
Notes: 2, 5, 8 (over 12), 9, 10, 11, 12

NORTH FALMOUTH

Bed and Breakfast Cape Cod

P.O. Box 341, West Hyannisport, 02672-0341
(508) 775-2772; FAX (508) 775-2884

51. Built in 1793, this Cape Cod Colonial was expanded and fully restored to its original condition and appearance some years ago. Primitive Early American decor and antiques fill this antique dealer's home. Two guest rooms each have a private bath, double canopied beds, fireplaces, and a sitting area where the hostess serves breakfast. $85.

NORTHAMPTON (FLORENCE)

American Country Collection

4 Greenwood Lane, Delmar, NY 12054
(518) 439-7001

016. This large English Tudor home sits on one acre of lovely lawns and overlooks 17 acres of farmland and forest. Full traditional breakfast is served. Although the dining room is elegant and inviting, the hostess finds that guests like to congregate around the kitchen table in the morning. Four guest rooms share two guest baths. Three of the rooms have double beds, and the last room has two twin beds. No smoking. Children over 12 are welcome. Resident cat and dog. $40-50.

6 Pets welcome; 8 Children welcome; 9 Social drinking allowed; 10 Tennis available; 11 Swimming available; 12 Golf available; 13 Skiing available; 14 May be booked through travel agents.

NORWELL

Bed and Breakfast Associates Bay Colony, Ltd.

P.O. Box 57166, Babson Park
Boston 02157-0166
(617) 449-5302; (800) 347-5088
FAX (617) 449-5958

SS330. In the pretty suburban town of Norwell, this country home was built in 1810. The house features beamed ceilings, Oriental rugs, and antiques. Three guest rooms share a bath. Full breakfast; children welcome; no smoking. $68.

NORWOOD

Bed and Breakfast Associates Bay Colony, Ltd.

P.O. Box 57166, Babson Park
Boston 02157-0166
(617) 449-5302; (800) 347-5088
FAX (617) 449-5958

IW560. Just 15-minutes from Boston, this four-bedroom inn was built in 1850, and is authentically furnished with antiques and reproduction pieces. Each room has a private bath, TV, and telephone. $50-60.

OAK BLUFFS (MARTHA'S VINEYARD)

The Beach House Bed and Breakfast

Corner of Seaview and Pennacook Avenue, 02557
(508) 693-3955

A newly renovated 1890s house directly across from large, sandy swimming beach. Friendly, helpful, and relaxed atmosphere. Rooms have brass queen-size beds, ceiling fans, and TV. Close to town, shops, restaurants, ferries, shuttle bus, and tours; moped, car, bike, and boat rentals. Oak Bluffs is a magnificent town for strollers and photographers with its many-hued gingerbread

cottages. It is also home to the Flying Horses, the nation's oldest carousel.

Hosts: Pamela, Calvin, and Justin Zaiko
Rooms: 9 (PB) $55-125
Continental Breakfast
Credit Cards: A, B, C, D, E
Notes: 2, 5, 7, 9, 10, 11, 12, 14

Bed and Breakfast Nantucket/ Martha's Vineyard

P.O. Box 341, West Hyannisport, 02672-0341
(508) 775-2772; FAX (508) 775-2884

201. This 1872 Victorian cottage has seven bedrooms for bed and breakfast and is one city block from the beaches. Bedrooms with private baths and king-size or double beds are available. Continental breakfast is served from 8:00-10:00 AM. Public tennis and public transportation to other parts of the island are two blocks away. $80-130.

House Guests Cape Cod and the Islands

Box 1881, Orleans, 02653
(508) 896-7053; (800) 666-HOST (reservations)
FAX (508) 896-7054

93310. Victorian charm and convenience blend beautifully at this sunny lodging on the harbor. The inn's 19 rooms (some with harbor view) feature private baths, air conditioning, and color cable TV. Two rooms are fully accessible to the handicapped and some can accommodate up to four people in multiple beds. Queen, double, and twin beds are available. After enjoying a Continental breakfast on the gingerbread porch, walk to the beach, the shops, the Flying Horses Carousel, or Cottage City—all within minutes. Children are welcome. Nonsmoking and smoking rooms are available. $65-130. $20 for additional person.

93320. A quaint gingerbread Victorian guest house in a quiet residential neighborhood. The narrow winding corridors and the varying sizes and shapes of the 12 colorful guest rooms reflect the turn-of-the-century origins of this delightful inn. Queen-, double-, and twin-bedded guest rooms are available. Three rooms have private entrances and one has private entrance and a kitchenette. Each unit has a private bath. Enjoy a Continental breakfast on the large porch. It is only three blocks to the ocean beaches and one block to shopping, Cottage City, and the famous Flying Horses Carousel. Children 12 or older are welcome. Open mid-April through mid-October. $50-90. $15 for additional person.

Tivoli Inn

222 Circuit Avenue, P.O. Box 1033, 02557
(508) 693-7928

A newly restored Victorian home which has the island charm and exudes a clean and friendly atmosphere. Walking distance to town shops, restaurants, nightlife, ferries, beach, and public transportation. A great place to stay with all the comforts of home. Each room is charmingly decorated with a Victorian flair. Come visit the treasured island of Martha's Vineyard.

Hosts: Lisa and Lori Katsounakis
Rooms: 6 (3 PB; 3 SB) $50-125
Continental Breakfast
Credit Cards: A, B, C
Notes: 5, 8, 9, 10, 11, 12, 14

Tucker Inn

46 Massasoit Avenue, P.O. Box 2680, 02557
(508) 693-1045

Tucker Inn

The Tucker Inn has the perfect ingredients for a great stay in Oak Bluffs, from its in-town location on a quiet park to its over-size bedrooms, veranda, and inviting living room. The inn is within walking distance of everything. Just down the street are stores, boutiques, theaters, churches, restaurants, clubs, bike and car rental agencies, and the town beach. Public transportation and boat lines are within a five-minute walk.

Innkeepers: Yolanda and Bill Reagan
Rooms: 8 (6 PB; 2 SB) $55-95
Continental Breakfast
Credit Cards: A, B
Notes: 2, 8, 9, 10, 11, 12, 14

ORLEANS

Bed and Breakfast Cape Cod

P.O. Box 341, West Hyannisport, 02672-0341
(508) 775-2772; FAX (508) 775-2884

8. This dramatic, contemporary home is built on high ground and overlooks five acres of wooded land. The large deck is next to an in-ground pool. Interior features include a soaring cathedral ceiling, Oriental carpets, wood burning fireplaces, and spiral staircase. Bedrooms have queen-size beds and private baths, and Nauset Beach is two miles away. A cottage is also available. Full breakfast. No smoking. Children over 11 welcome. $90.

24. Built nearly 78 years ago on land that has been in the host's family for five generations, this is a marvelous house on a private estate. It has an expanded wing, with a suite which includes a king-size bed, a den with fireplace and large deck overlooking the ocean. A marvelously relaxing accommodation with complete suite privacy and a private beach one hundred yards from the house. The village 2.5 miles away features some of the best restaurants on Cape Cod. Full breakfast. No children under 12. No smoking. $100.

6 Pets welcome; 8 Children welcome; 9 Social drinking allowed; 10 Tennis available; 11 Swimming available; 12 Golf available; 13 Skiing available; 14 May be booked through travel agents.

83. The ocean is a few steps away from this home, built in 1954 and later expanded with a private, entrance wing. The double-bed room has a private bath and fireplace. The ocean is visible from the room, offering a view across marshes and the water. Breakfast is served in the first-floor dining room or on the deck. The parlor has a great library, sitting area, and TV. This private setting is a few miles from the center of Orleans. No smoking. No children. $85.

Bed and Breakfast Greater Boston and Cape Cod

P.O. Box 35, Newtonville 02160
(617) 964-1606; (800) 832-2632
FAX (617) 332-8572

Shady Elms. A charming small accommodation within two miles of Nauset Beach. The guest room offers a queen-size and a twin bed, plus a roll away, with private bath, TV, and refrigerator; it is also air-conditioned. A Continental breakfast is also provided in an adjoining room and may be taken to guest room or outdoors. $75.

The Farmhouse

163 Beach Road, 02653
(508) 255-6654

This 19th-century farmhouse has been carefully restored and furnished to provide a unique blend of country life in a

The Farmhouse

seashore setting. Short walk to Nauset Beach, close to sailing, golf, tennis, bike trails, theater, fishing, shopping, museums, and surfing. Some oceanview rooms. Breakfast is served on an oceanview deck. Licensed establishment.

Hosts: The Standishes
Rooms: 8 (5 PB; 3 SB) $32-95
Continental Breakfast
Credit Cards: A, B
Notes: 2, 5, 7 (limited), 8, 9, 10, 11, 12, 14

House Guests Cape Cod and the Islands

Box 1881, Orleans, 02653
(508) 896-7053; (800) 666-HOST (reservations)
FAX (508) 896-7054

94173. Built in 1916, this house overlooks Nauset Harbor and the Atlantic Ocean. A private beach is only steps away from the air-conditioned guest suite, which has a king-size bed, three daybeds, and a sitting room with double sofa bed. Private bath and entrance, deck refrigerator, TV, and a lovely ocean view are included. Continental breakfast is served on the deck. Infants or children 12 and older are welcome. Separate rates for additional persons. No smoking. Resident cats. $90.

Orleans Bed and Breakfast Associates

P.O. Box 1312, 02653
(508) 255-3824; (800) 541-6226

Academy Place. A quaint Cape Cod home with comfortable beds awaits. This 1752 house has many antique charms, post-and-beam construction, wide-pine boards, and period antiques. On the edge of Orleans' shopping district, all the downtown's retail stores and restaurants are a short walk. Atlantic Ocean and Cape Cod Bay beaches only two and one-half miles. $50-70.

Arey's Pond Relais. A very special house filled with warmth, a myriad of delightful details, and intriguing collections. Flower-filled patio serves as private entrance to guest rooms. Queen-size bed with white wicker headboard invites rest. Private bath, small guest refrigerator. Adjacent queen room can accommodate children or other travelers in the group. Breakfast is served on deck overlooking Arey's Pond. $70.

The 1840 House. An 1840 Greek Revival in a residential neighborhood within walking distance of town center, restaurants, galleries, and the Academy of Performing Arts. One twin room, one double room, each with private bath. Sitting room with TV. Breakfast served on fine china. Roll away bed available ($30). $65.

Gray Gables. An enormous old elm shades a secluded yard with lawn furniture set out for guests' pleasure. A private entrance leads to the guest wing of this fine old house with plenty of charm and wonderfully warm hosts. Comfortably spacious, air-conditioned guest room has queen-size and single beds, refrigerator, and TV. Adjacent bath has huge tiled shower. Continental breakfast is set out to enjoy at leisure, in-room or under the elm. Handsome English springer spaniel in residence. $75.

Maison de La Mer. Attractively decorated contemporary country home on Cape Cod Bay, a short, pretty walk to Skaket Beach. Spacious first-floor twin room with private bath. Second-floor bedroom has water view, queen-size bed, and private bath with whirlpool tub. Guests are encouraged to use living room with front entrance. Sunny dining area overlooks seaside garden or enjoy an alfresco meal on the deck. $80-90.

Mayflower House. Handsome reproduction bow roof house on residential dead-end road. Spacious first-floor bedroom with queen-size bed, upstairs bedroom with two double beds; each has private bath, color TV, and air conditioning. Relax or read in first-floor parlor or on secluded deck. Dog-lovers welcome, as hosts have a fat, friendly Doberman. $75.

Morningside. Waterfront suite with private entrance in gracious home overlooking Nauset Harbor and the Atlantic. Private beach. Huge room with king-size bed and sitting area faces the ocean. Private bath. Superb is the only word for it. $100.

Sweet Retreat. A delightful in-town studio. Outside stairs lead to a private deck with view of attractive garden. Enter into kitchenette area with breakfast table. A step down into bedroom with queen-size bed and private bath. Host owns a beautiful patisserie and catering business. Count on good things for breakfast. Bike to beaches and walk to village. $85.

Taffrail. In one of the choicest areas of Orleans and owned by delightful couple. Separate entrance leads upstairs to large room overlooking Nauset Harbor and the Atlantic. Double bed, private bath, and small kitchenette. Living-sitting area with fireplace and TV. Breakfast available in the private guest quarters or on main house patio facing the ocean. Just a short walk to saltwater beach. $85.

Winterwell. Restored 19th-century Cape Cod farmhouse, a short stroll to Skaket Beach yet close to town and bike path, offers two comfortable accommodations. The main house offers a first-floor guest room with separate entrance and private bath. Main living room for occasional reading and TV. A spacious guest wing with separate entrance has bedroom with private bath, sitting room, and kitchen-dining area. All guests enjoy breakfast on enclosed porch overlooking large private yard with busy bird feeder. $75-95.

6 Pets welcome; 8 Children welcome; 9 Social drinking allowed; 10 Tennis available; 11 Swimming available; 12 Golf available; 13 Skiing available; 14 May be booked through travel agents.

OSTERVILLE

Bed and Breakfast Cape Cod

P.O. Box 341, West Hyannisport, 02672-0341
(508) 775-2772; FAX (508) 775-2884

59. Imagine the quintessential New England village, and travelers have found Osterville. This ten-year-old spacious Colonial house offers three guest accommodations, two with double beds and the other with a pair of twin beds. One room has a private bath, and the other two share a bath. No smoking. $52-68.

DESTINNATIONS New England

P.O. Box 1173, Osterville 02655
(508) 428-5600; FAX (508) 420-0565
(800) 333-4667 (reservations)

7411. This lovely inn, circa 1886, is the only lodging in prestigious Osterville. It offers 18 guest rooms, beautifully decorated and tucked beneath a canopy of elms and evergreens. The inn has its own on-site tennis courts, and is a short walk from an ocean beach. Golf, island ferries, and all of the Cape's sights, attractions, and recreation are accessible. Children welcome; no pets. $119-149.

PEABODY

The International Bed & Breakfast Club, Inc.

504 Amherst Street, Buffalo, NY 14207
(800) 723-4262; FAX (716) 873-4462

MA0191PP. Ten minutes from historic Salem, this inn offers three bedrooms, two with twin beds and adjoining bath; one with double bed and shared bath. Continental breakfast and coffee served at all times. Living room fireplace, porch and in-ground pool and patio. $60.

PERU

American Country Collection

4 Greenwood Lane, Delmar, NY 12054
(518) 439-7001

069. Built in 1830 as the town parsonage, this private homestay features the original wide-plank floors and floor-to-ceiling windows that look out onto old stone walls and 13 acres of woods. Guests dine in a sunroom with bay windows and French doors that lead onto a patio. The decor is French country, and the home is furnished with antiques and colorful Waverly and Laura Ashley chintz fabrics. Three excellent cross-country centers and one downhill ski area are within an eight-mile radius. Two bedrooms with private baths and double beds. No smoking. $65.

Chalet d'Alicia

East Windsor Road, 01235
(413) 655-8292

This Swiss chalet-style home offers a private, casual atmosphere. Set in the Berkshire Mountains, it overlooks the beautiful countryside. Fresh homemade breads and muffins round out the full country breakfasts. Three resident cats and one dog make everyone welcome. Tanglewood, Jacob's Pillow, Williamstown Theater, and lots of cross-country skiing are nearby.

Hosts: Alice and Richard Halvorsen
Rooms: 3 (1 PB; 2 SB) $55
Full Breakfast
Credit Cards: None
Notes: 2, 5, 6 (call), 8, 9, 10, 11, 12, 13

PETERSHAM

Winterwood at Petersham

19 North Main Street, 01366
(508) 724-8885

Winterwood at Petersham

An elegant 16-room Greek Revival mansion built in 1842, just off the common of a classic New England town. The inn boasts numerous fireplaces and several porches for relaxing. Cocktails available. On the National Register of Historic Places.

Hosts: Jean and Robert Day
Rooms: 6 (PB) $63.42-84.56
Continental Breakfast
Credit Cards: A, B, C
Notes: 2, 5, 7, 8, 9, 12, 13, 14

PITTSFIELD

Country Hearts Bed 'n' Breakfast

52 Broad Street, 01201
(413) 499-3201

Comfy and casual, this bed and breakfast home is nestled on a quiet residential street well-known for its collection of beautifully restored aristocrats. It is in the center of and easily accessible to all Berkshire attractions. Children always welcome!

Hosts: Jan and Steve Foose
Rooms: 2 (PB) $45-95
Continental Breakfast
Credit Cards: None
Notes: 2, 5, 8, 9, 10, 11, 12, 13

The Olde White Horse Inn

378 South Street, 01201
(413) 442-2512

The Olde White Horse Inn is a charming, spacious Colonial home built around the turn of the century. Centrally in the Berkshires near Tanglewood, it has eight cozy guest rooms, each with a private bath and air conditioner. Guest rooms are tastefully decorated with country charm, fresh flowers, and fluffy comforters on one or two double beds. Wine and cheese are served on Saturday evenings in the parlor. Open May to October.

Hosts: Ron and Paula Virgilio
Rooms: 9 (8 PB; 1 SB) $60-130
Continental Breakfast
Credit Cards: A, B, C
Notes: 2, 10, 11, 12

PLYMOUTH

Remembrance

265 Sandwich Street, 02360
(508) 746-5160

Remembrance is an old, cedar-shingled, Cape style home central in a lovely residential neighborhood one mile from historic Plymouth, Plymouth Plantation, and the expressway; two blocks from the ocean. It is delightfully decorated with antiques, wicker, original art, plants, and flowers. Delicious full breakfasts served at guests' convenience in the greenhouse overlooking the garden and bird feeders. Tea time. Nonsmoking. Gentle resident pets.

Host: Beverly Bainbridge
Rooms: 2 (SB) $65
Full Breakfast
Credit Cards: None
Notes: 2, 5, 9, 11

PROVINCETOWN

Bed and B'fast

44 Commercial Street, 02657
(508) 487-9555

In the quiet west end of Provincetown, this true bed and breakfast contains private-bath rooms and shared-bath rooms. A suite with harbor views and a private deck is available,

6 Pets welcome; 8 Children welcome; 9 Social drinking allowed; 10 Tennis available; 11 Swimming available; 12 Golf available; 13 Skiing available; 14 May be booked through travel agents.

as are fully equipped apartments. The apartments and suites have TV/VCRs, microwave ovens, and refrigerators. Open all year, and special serenity seasonal rates are available.

Hosts: John Fitzgerald and Jack Kosko
Rooms: 7 (4 PB; 3 SB) $40-130
Full Breakfast
Credit Cards: A, B
Notes: 5, 7, 14

Bed and Breakfast Greater Boston and Cape Cod

P.O. Box 35, Newtonville, 02160
(617) 964-1606; (800) 832-2632
FAX (617) 332-8572

The East End Guest House. A lovely historic home, dating back to the 1800s, which offers both rooms and apartments. Six guest rooms arc beautifully decorated; two apartments are fully equipped. A self-service Continental breakfast is available in the common room. Guests may use the microwave, sink and refrigerator, relax watching TV, or use the VCR. (Apartments rent in-season by the week only; off-season, they rent by night with a two-night minimum.) $55-95.

Bradford Gardens Inn

178 Bradford Street, 02657
(508) 487-1616; (800) 432-2334

An 1820 Colonial country inn with rooms offering fireplaces, ceiling fans, and antiques. Fireplaced cottages set in the beautiful gardens. All units have private baths. One block from the ocean and a five-minute stroll to town center for shopping, fine dining, art galleries, and whale-watching.

Host: Susan Culligan
Rooms: 8 (PB); 9 cottages (PB) $69-175
Full Breakfast
Credit Cards: A, B, C
Notes: 2, 5, 7, 9, 10, 11, 12, 14

Elephant Walk Inn

156 Bradford Street, 02657
(508) 487-2543

A romantic Edwardian inn near Provincetown's center. The spacious, well-appointed rooms offer an eclectic mixture of antique furnishings and decorations. All have private bath, color TV, and refrigerator. Enjoy the large sun deck or lounge with morning coffee. Closed November through mid-April.

Host: Len Paoletti
Rooms: 8 (PB) $42-88
Continental Breakfast
Credit Cards: A, B, C, E
Notes: 2 (for deposit), 7, 8 (off-season), 9, 10, 11

Lamplighter Inn

26 Bradford Street, 02657
(508) 487-2529

A sea captain's home with commanding 50-mile vistas of the ocean and Cape Cod. Convenient to shopping, museums, whale-watching, beaches, restaurants, shows, and tours. Clean, airy rooms and suites with private baths await guests' arrival for a memorable stay at the Lamplighter on old Cape Cod.

Hosts: Michael R. Novik and Joseph I. Czarnecki
Rooms: 10 (8 PB; 2 SB) $40-130
Continental Breakfast
Credit Cards: A, B, C, D, E
Notes: 2, 5, 7, 9, 10, 11, 12, 14

Lamplighter Inn

Land's End Inn

22 Commercial Street, 02657
(508) 487-0706

High atop Gull Hill, Land's End Inn overlooks Provincetown and all of Cape Cod
Bay. Large, airy, comfortably furnished living rooms, a large front porch, and lovely
antique-filled bedrooms provide relaxation
and visual pleasure to guests.

Host: David Schoolman
Rooms: 16 (PB) $98-220
Continental Breakfast
Credit Cards: None
Notes: 2, 5, 7, 9, 10, 11, 12

Six Webster Place

Rose and Crown Guest House

158 Commercial Street, 02657
(508) 487-3332

The Rose and Crown is a classic Georgian
"square rigger" built in the 1780s. The
guest house sits behind an ornate iron
fence, and a ship's figurehead greets visitors from her post above the paneled front
door. During restoration, wide floorboards
were uncovered and pegged posts and
beams exposed. An appealing clutter of
Victorian antiques and artwork fills every
nook and cranny.

Host: Sam Hardee
Rooms: 8 (5 PB; 3 SB) $45-110
Continental Breakfast
Credit Cards: A, B, E
Notes: 9, 11

Six Webster Place

6 Webster Place, 02657
(508) 487-2266

A restored 1750s bed and breakfast on a
quiet lane in the heart of Provincetown, the
bed and breakfast is one block from the
Town Hall and Commercial Street and 200
yards from the bay beaches. All rooms have
period furnishings, most offer working fireplaces, and most have private baths. A delicious Continental breakfast is served each

morning; and in the off-season, host serves
tea or a glass of wine by a roaring fire in the
afternoon. Open all year. Three apartments
are available.

Host: Gary Reinhardt
Rooms: 11 (7 PB; 4 SB) $35-95
Continental Breakfast
Credit Cards: A, B, C, D
Notes: 2, 5, 6, 7, 8, 9, 14

Watership Inn

7 Winthrop Street, 02657
(508) 487-0094

Rustic 1820 sea captain's home, with Colonial rooms, private baths, and spacious
lobby. Open year-round, serving Continental breakfast daily. Parking is available, and
a five-minute walk gets visitors to the beach
or to the center of town.

Host: Jim Foss
Rooms: 15 (PB) $26-88
Continental Breakfast
Credit Cards: A, B, C, D
Notes: 5, 7, 9

White Wind Inn

174 Commercial Street, 02657
(508) 487-1526

A white Victorian, circa 1845, across the
street from the beach and a five-minute
walk from almost everything. Continental
breakfast. Write or call for brochure.

6 Pets welcome; 8 Children welcome; 9 Social drinking allowed; 10 Tennis available; 11 Swimming available;
12 Golf available; 13 Skiing available; 14 May be booked through travel agents.

Host: Russell Dusablon
Rooms: 12 (10 PB; 2 SB) $45-110
Continental Breakfast
Credit Cards: A, B, C
Notes: 5, 6 (call), 7, 8, 9, 10, 11

QUINCY

Host Homes of Boston

P.O. Box 117, Boston, 02168
(617) 244-1308; FAX (617) 244-5156

Quincy Adams Bed and Breakfast. This elegant turn-of-the-century home near the ocean has fireplaces, canopied beds, and a den with a TV and hot tub. There are three guest rooms; two have queen-size beds and the third-floor maid's quarters has a double. Near Bayside Expo Center, restaurants, and historic mansions. Boston is 15 minutes away, and the Red Line is one block away. $68-75.

REHOBOTH

Perryville Inn

157 Perryville Road, 02769
(508) 252-9239

This 19th-century restored Victorian on the National Register of Historic Places is on four and one-half wooded acres with a quiet brook, mill pond, stone walls, and shaded paths. Bicycles are available for guests, including a tandem. The inn overlooks an 18-hole public golf course. All

Perryville Inn

rooms are furnished with antiques and accented with colorful handmade quilts. Nearby are antique stores, museums, Great Woods Performing Arts Center, fine seafood restaurants, and an old-fashioned New England clambake. Arrange for a horse-drawn hayride or a hot air balloon ride. Within one hour of Boston, Plymouth, Newport, and Mystic.

Hosts: Tom and Betsey Charnecki
Rooms: 5 (3 PB; 2 SB) $50-85
Continental Breakfast
Credit Cards: A, B, C, D
Notes: 2, 5, 8, 9, 10, 11, 12, 14

REVERE

Golden Slumber Accommodations

640 Revere Beach Boulevard, 02151
(800) 892-3231

Golden Slumber features an unrivaled array of screened accommodations on the seacoast of Massachusetts including Cape Cod, the North and South Shores, and greater Boston. From sprawling oceanfront villas to quaint, country road retreats, gracious historic residences and unique contemporary facilities offer the paramount in Yankee hospitality. Several feature incomparable water views, canopied beds, fireplaces, private entrances, and swimming pools. No reservation fee. Children welcome. Limousine and gift service. Brochure/directory available.

Owner: Leah A. Schmidt
Rooms: 150 (90 PB; 60 SB) $55-220
Full and Continental Breakfasts
Credit Cards: A, B
Notes: 2, 4, 5, 8, 9, 10, 11, 12

ROCKPORT

Addison Choate Inn

49 Broadway, 01966-1527
(508) 546-7543; (800) 245-7543

This charming New England village inn, built in 1851, provides a traditional setting

Addison Choate Inn

for a mix of classic, modern, and antique furnishings and accessories. Complimentary Addison Choate coffee and home-baked Continental buffet breakfast are served in the dining room, which was originally the kitchen of this rambling old house. There is a wraparound porch for fair-weather breakfast overlooking the perennial garden. Parking. Pool. Galleries, shops, restaurants, beaches, and train a short walk away.

Hosts: Knox and Shirley Johnson
Rooms: 7 (PB) $65-110
Continental Breakfast
Credit Cards: A, B, D
Notes: 2, 5, 8, 9, 10, 11, 12, 14

Bed & Breakfast/Inns of New England

128 South Hoop Pole Road, Guilford, CT 06437
(203) 457-0042; (800) 582-0853

MA-1005. An intimate, welcoming guest house open year-round, only one block from Main Street and the T-Wharf, which is full of shops, galleries, and restaurants. Leave the car and walk to everything. A spacious sun deck is reserved for guests. TV, games, magazines, and books are available. Guests have use of their own refrigerator. Seven rooms are available. Children welcome. No smoking. House cat; no guest pets. $58-70.

MA-1006. A small, central inn limited to non-smokers, this 1987 facility is within a five-minute walk from Rockport's art galleries, Headlands beach, restaurants, and shops. Three ground-floor larger-than-average rooms with private bathrooms are available with king- or queen-size beds; all three have private bathrooms. All rooms have controlled air conditioning and heat, cable TV, refrigerators, and microwaves. No children. No smoking. No pets. $80-85.

Bed and Breakfast Marblehead and North Shore

P.O. Box 35, Newtonville, 02160
(617) 964-1606; (800) 832-2632
FAX (617) 332-8572

Rockport Guest House. This guest house is a beautiful 120-year-old home in the quiet South End. Accommodations include a queen-size bedroom with private full bath and two additional rooms which share a shower/bath. Two comfortable sitting areas and several small outside decks are also available to guests. Host prepares a wonderful breakfast every morning and offers personal tours of the area. It is within walking distance to the ocean and sandy beach, and close to the Bearskin Neck tourist area. Open year-round. No smoking. $75-95.

The Inn on Cove Hill

37 Mount Pleasant Street, 01966
(508) 546-2701

A friendly atmosphere with the option of privacy, this painstakingly restored 200-year-old Federal home is just two blocks from the harbor and shops. Meticulously appointed, cozy bedrooms are furnished with antiques, and some have canopied beds. Wake up to the delicious aroma of hot muffins, and enjoy a Continental breakfast at the umbrella tables in the Pump Garden. The fresh sea air is preserved in the non-smoking facility.

6 Pets welcome; 8 Children welcome; 9 Social drinking allowed; 10 Tennis available; 11 Swimming available; 12 Golf available; 13 Skiing available; 14 May be booked through travel agents.

Hosts: John and Marjorie Pratt
Rooms: 11 (9 PB; 2 SB) $48-98
Continental Breakfast
Credit Cards: None
Notes: 2, 9, 11, 12

Lantana House

22 Broadway, 01966
(508) 546-3535

An in-town Victorian guest house open
year-round in the historic district of Rockport, a classic, picturesque, seacoast village.
A short walk takes visitors to the beaches,
art galleries, restaurants, and gift shops.
Rockport is an artist's haven. A nonsmoking inn. Air conditioning available.

Host: Cynthia Sewell
Rooms: 7 (5 PB; 2 SB) $60-75
Continental Breakfast
Credit Cards: None
Notes: 2, 5, 8, 9, 10, 11, 12

Linden Tree Inn

26 King Street, 01966-1444
(508) 546-2494

An 1840 Victorian bed and breakfast inn
with 18 bedrooms with private bathrooms,
12 with air conditioning. Short walk to
beaches, galleries, restaurants, gift shops,
and train to Boston. Come enjoy Penny's
made-from-scratch Continental breakfast,
fresh flowers in the rooms, and lemonade
and cookies in the afternoon. Spectacular
view of the ocean and town from the
cupola. The three resident cats request no
guest pets.

Hosts: Penny and Larry Olson
Rooms: 18 (PB) $85-98
Continental Breakfast
Credit Cards: C
Notes: 2, 7, 8, 9, 10, 11, 12, 14

Peg Leg Inn
and Restaurant

2 King Street, 01966
(800) 346-2352

The original charm of five Colonial New
England homes on the edge of the sea overlooking beautiful Front Beach and Rockport's picturesque shoreline. Panoramic
ocean views from the guest rooms. Each
welcomes with a warm and pleasant atmosphere, including private bath and TV.
Lawns, gardens, and decks for guests' pleasure and relaxation. A short stroll to the
quaint village that abounds in lovely shops
and art galleries. The inn's own oceanview
restaurant is famous for fresh local seafood
and Yankee specialities, and an original
working greenhouse serves as an added dining room.

Rooms: 33 (PB) $65-115
Continental Breakfast
Credit Cards: A, B
Notes: 2, 3, 4, 8, 10, 11, 12, 14

Seacrest Manor

Seacrest Manor

131 Marmion Way, 01966
(508) 546-2211

Decidedly small, intentionally quiet. Gracious hospitality in luxurious surroundings
with magnificent views overlooking woods
and sea. Spacious grounds, lovely gardens,
and ample parking. Famous full breakfast
and afternoon tea included. No pets. Not
recommended for children. Fresh flowers,
cable TV, free daily paper, mints, and turndown. Mobil-rated three stars. Across the
street from the nine-acre John Kieran Na-

NOTES: Credit cards accepted: A MasterCard; B Visa; C American Express; D Discover Card; E Diner's
Club; F Other; 2 Personal checks accepted; 3 Lunch available; 4 Dinner available; 5 Open all year;

ture Preserve. Only an hour north of Boston by car or train. A nonsmoking inn. Closed December through March.

Hosts: Leighton T. Saville and Dwight B. MacCormack
Rooms: 8 (6 PB; 2 SB) $90-124
Full Breakfast
Credit Cards: None
Notes: 2, 11, 12

Seaward Inn and Cottages

62 Marmion Way, 01966
(508) 546-3471

Quietly tucked away on Boston's rocky North Shore, this grand old oceanfront estate offers the perfect respite for weary travelers. Elegant oceanfront dining, expansive grounds and beautiful gardens, active bird sanctuary, putting green, private cottages with fireplaces, spectacular ocean views at every turn, and impeccable service are only the beginning. Short stroll to downtown Rockport (300-year-old fishing village and art colony), shops and boutiques, and wide sandy beaches.

Hosts: Anne and Roger Cameron
Rooms: 38 (PB) $98-138
Full Breakfast
Credit Cards: A, B
Notes: 2, 4, 7, 8, 9, 10, 11, 12, 14

Seven South Street— The Inn

7 South Street, 01966
(508) 546-6708

Built in 1750, the inn has a friendly, informal atmosphere in a quiet setting with gardens, deck, and pool. An ample Continental breakfast is served each morning, after which the guest is free to explore the art galleries and shops within walking distance of the inn.

Host: Aileen Lamson
Rooms: 6 (3 PB; 3 SB) $68-78
Continental Breakfast
Credit Cards: None
Notes: 2, 7, 9, 10, 11, 12

SAGAMORE BEACH

Bed and Breakfast Cape Cod

P.O. Box 341, West Hyannisport, 02672-0341
(508) 775-2772; FAX (508) 775-2884

19. Perched on a cliff 50 feet above Cape Cod Bay, this contemporary home built in 1987 features two suites for guests. The honeymoon suite has a Jacuzzi overlooking the ocean, private bath, king-size bed, and Laura Ashley bed coverings. The second suite has a queen-size bed and ocean view. A ground-floor basement suite offers a parlor with a fireplace, two sleeping rooms, one with a king-size bed and the other with twin beds and small kitchen. $85-125.

SALEM

Amelia Payson House

16 Winter Street, 01970
(508) 744-8304

Built in 1845, this fine example of Greek Revival architecture is in the heart of Salem's historic district. Guest rooms are furnished with canopied or brass beds and antiques. A five-minute stroll to downtown shopping, historic houses, museums, Pickering Wharf's waterfront dining, and train station. Celebrating ten years as a bed and breakfast.

Hosts: Ada and Donald Roberts
Rooms: 4 (PB) $75-85
Continental Breakfast
Credit Cards: A, B, C
Notes: 5, 8 (over 12), 9, 10, 11, 12

Bed and Breakfast Marblehead and North Shore

P.O. Box 35, Newtonville, 02160
(617) 964-1606; (800) 832-2632
FAX (617) 332-8572

6 Pets welcome; 8 Children welcome; 9 Social drinking allowed; 10 Tennis available; 11 Swimming available; 12 Golf available; 13 Skiing available; 14 May be booked through travel agents.

Essex Street Bed and Breakfast. This turn-of-the-century wood frame house is in the McIntyre historic district of Salem. The hosts have lovingly labored to restore their home to its former elegance and charm. One guest room with private bath, separate entrance, and air conditioning is available. Continental breakfast is served. No smoking. Children welcome. $75-85.

The Inn on the Green. In the heart of Salem, this inn is close to many tourist attractions, historic sites, world-famous museums, shopping, and wonderful restaurants. The inn is a Greek Revival-style built in 1846 as a private residence. It has been completely restored to its 19th-century elegance, with modern amenities added. Each of the guest rooms has a queen-size bed, private bath, and color cable TV. There is also a suite with two queen-size beds and adjacent sitting room for families or groups of four. Continental breakfast. Restricted smoking area provided. $75-95.

Suite Dreams. Perfect for a couple or a family with one child, as well as for business travelers. A large ground-level suite in host's ranch-style home has a queen-size bed, private bath and kitchen area, TV, VCR, radio, table and chairs; a cot or roll away can also be added; the kitchen area includes a refrigerator, microwave, coffeemaker, and toaster. For longer stays, a washer/dryer is also available. Extra fee for additional adult or child. Open April-October. No smoking. $85-100.

DESTINNATIONS
New England

P.O. Box 1173, Osterville, 02655
(508) 428-5600; (800) 333-4667 (reservations)
FAX (508) 420-0565

7407. In the heart of town, this 22-room inn and its 11-room sister property across the street offer history-making hospitality. Each room has private bath, color TV, and telephone and is uniquely decorated with charming antiques and reproductions. The sister property is a newly renovated antique classic, offering mini-suites and modern amenities, including some fireplaces and Jacuzzis. There is a bricked courtyard for reading or relaxing. Some family-style apartments are available. Continental breakfast; dinner served at the inn's restaurant. A short stroll from Salem's sights, restaurants, and shops. Salem Trolley stops at the doorstep. Children welcome; no pets. Smoking permitted in main inn; sister property is nonsmoking.

The Inn at Seven Winter Street

The Inn at
Seven Winter Street

7 Winter Street, 01970
(508) 745-9520

Come, be a guest at The Inn at Seven Winter Street! This magnificently restored French Victorian inn is an award winner. Each room finely appointed with period antiques and furnishings. All rooms have something beautifully unique: marble fireplace, canopied bed, Jacuzzi, and sun deck. In a historic area, within a one-minute walk to the waterfront, historic sites, dining, and museums. Evening tea. Off-street parking. No smoking.

NOTES: Credit cards accepted: A MasterCard; B Visa; C American Express; D Discover Card; E Diner's Club; F Other; 2 Personal checks accepted; 3 Lunch available; 4 Dinner available; 5 Open all year;

Hosts: Sally Flint, Jill and D. L. Coté
Rooms: 10 (PB) $75-140
Continental Breakfast
Credit Cards: A, B, C
Notes: 2, 5, 9, 10, 11, 12

The Salem Inn

7 Summer Street, 01970
(508) 741-0680; (800) 446-2995

Elegantly restored 1834 Federal town-house, in the heart of Salem's historic district, has 32 luxuriously appointed rooms with private baths and some working fireplaces. Direct-dial telephones, cable TVs, and air conditioning. Hearty Continental breakfast and lovely rose garden. Jacuzzi suites available.

Hosts: Richard and Diane Pabich
Rooms: 32 (PB) $85-125
Continental Breakfast
Credit Cards· A, B, C, D, E
Notes: 2, 4, 5, 6, 7, 8, 9, 10, 11, 12, 13 (cross-country), 14

Stephen Daniels House

1 Daniels Street, 01970
(508) 744-5709

Built by a sea captain in 1667 and enlarged in 1756, the house is beautifully restored and furnished with antiques. Wood-burning fireplaces in the bedrooms with charming canopied beds. Continental breakfast is served before two huge fireplaces. Walk to all points of interest in Salem.

Host: Catherine Gill
Rooms: 5 (3 PB; 2 SB) $50-95
Continental Breakfast
Credit Cards: C
Notes: 2, 5, 6, 7, 8, 9, 10, 11, 12, 13, 14

Suzannah Flint House

98 Essex Street, 01970
(508) 744-5281; (800) 752-5281

Built around the turn of the 18th century, the Suzannah Flint House was at one time used as a schoolhouse. A fine example of Salem's Federal period architecture, Suzannah now offers four charming guest

rooms year-round. Each spacious room features a private bath, cable color TV, and antique fireplaces. Conveniently in Salem's historic district, adjacent to Salem Commons, and an easy walk to the waterfront wharves, historical attractions, fine shops, and restaurants.

Host: Scott Eklind
Rooms: 4 (PB) $49-109
Continental Breakfast
Credit Cards: A, B, C, D
Notes: 5, 8, 9

SANDWICH

Bay Beach Bed and Breakfast

1-3 Bay Beach Lane, Box 151, 02563
(508) 888-8813

Luxury beachfront bed and breakfast with super amenities in a romantic setting overlooking Cape Cod Bay. Three spacious guest rooms with decks and ocean views, plus a honeymoon suite with a king-size bed and Jacuzzi are available for guests to choose. A two-fireplaced living room and an exercise room with a Lifecycle and Stairmaster are also for guests to enjoy. A full Continental breakfast is served each morning. All rooms have air conditioning, telephones, cable TV, refrigerators, and compact disk players. AAA Four-Diamond Inn. No smoking. Adults only.

Hosts: Emily and Reale Lemieux
Rooms: 5 (PB) $125-195
Continental Breakfast
Credit Cards: A, B
Notes: 2, 10, 11, 12, 14

Bed and Breakfast Associates Bay Colony, Ltd.

P.O. Box 57166, Babson Park, Boston, 02157-0166
(617) 449-5302; (800) 347-5088
FAX (617) 449-5958

CC250. Ten minutes to the Bridge! Private guest house set atop a pretty driveway just steps from the village center, with duck

6 Pets welcome; 8 Children welcome; 9 Social drinking allowed; 10 Tennis available; 11 Swimming available; 12 Golf available; 13 Skiing available; 14 May be booked through travel agents.

pond, famous Cape museums, and tiny cafe. Stylish country decor with cathedral ceiling, skylights, and all-new private bath. Picture-perfect honeymoon suite! $95.

CC255. In the Cape's most enchanting village, this modern home with contemporary decor provides three guest rooms with all the basic comforts and amenities for a pleasant stay, at a most attractive price. Walk to town center and museums. $50-70.

Bed and Breakfast Cape Cod

P.O. Box 341, West Hyannisport, 02672-0341
(508) 775-2772; FAX (508) 775-2884

1. This elegant Victorian-style house was built in 1849 and meticulously restored in 1987. The five guest rooms have private baths and are furnished with antiques. The first-floor common rooms for dining and reading are available for guest use. A full breakfast is served each morning in the dining room. Convenient to many fine restaurants, Heritage Plantation, Sandwich Glass Museum, and the beach. Children over 11 welcome. $75-125.

22. This elegant Victorian-style house in the heart of Sandwich has six bedrooms, most of which offer private baths. In the center of the oldest village on Cape Cod, this inn is within walking distance of fine restaurants, beaches, trails, museums, and parks. A Continental breakfast is served in the large dining room. No smoking. Children over six welcome. $55-90.

27. Built in 1741 in the heart of what is now the center of the village, this lovely restored Colonial-style home is on the National Register of Historic Places. Walk to all village sites, including the pond off the village square. Start the day with a full breakfast, or walk the village streets enjoying the picture of a community not much changed from 200 years ago. The English hosts will treat guests as special visitors, offering a meal in their authentic English tea-room with every reservation. A special place that will give guests memories to cherish. No smoking. $85-95.

31. The design of this 1699 built home reflects the charm of early America. Three bedrooms with private baths are furnished with antiques or furniture with an Early American design. Across the street from a saltwater marsh full of birds, this bed and breakfast is a short walk to many restaurants and shops. A Continental breakfast is served in a keeping room with a bechive oven. No smoking. Children over 12 welcome. $70-85.

Bed & Breakfast/Inns of New England

128 South Hoop Pole Road, Guilford, CT 06437
(203) 457-0042; (800) 582-0853

MA-1040. This 1829 clapboard house reflects the interests of the innkeepers, who have furnished it with Early American pieces and with treasures they have collected from the Orient and the American Southwest. Guests are invited to play the piano, read a book, or play a game in the den. The six guest rooms, four with private baths, are individually painted and stenciled in bright colors; each has a special personality. Furnishings include canopied, spindle, sleigh, and four-poster beds; one room has a fireplace, and another has a claw-foot tub. $50-85.

Capt. Ezra Nye House

152 Main Street, 02563
(508) 888-6142; (800) 388-2278

Comfort and warmth, amid antique-filled rooms, some with fireplaces and canopies, make any stay a treat in this 1829 Federal

Capt. Ezra Nye House

home. Museums, lake, and restaurants within a block. Featured in *Glamour* and *Innsider* magazines, and chosen Best Bed and Breakfast, Upper Cape, by *Cape Cod Life* magazine in 1993 and 1994. "Thank you for opening your hearts and your home to us. . . . You have made our first trip to Cape Cod a memorable one!"

Hosts. Elaine and Harry Dickson
Rooms: 6 (4 PB; 2 SB) $55-90
Suite: 1(PB)
Full Breakfast
Credit Cards: A, B, C, D
Notes: 2, 5, 8 (over 5), 9, 10, 11, 12, 14

DESTINNATIONS New England

P.O. Box 1173, Osterville 02655
(508) 428-5600; FAX (508) 420-0565
(800) 333-4667 (reservations)

7397. This charming, 46-room, full-service country inn in historic Sandwich Village is moments away from quaint shops and attractions. Each room or suite is handsomely furnished with all modern amenities. Some rooms have canopied beds and working fireplaces; all have direct-dial telephones and cable TV. There are two on-site restaurants with renowned cuisine and wine cellar. Additionally, the inn has an outdoor heated swimming pool and bountiful gar-

dens and is near four in-town beaches, seven tennis courts, and four public golf courses. The inn also maintains membership in a fully equipped local health club. Some nonsmoking rooms. Children welcome; no pets. $99-175.

Dillingham House

71 Main Street, 02563
(508) 833-0065

Built circa 1650, the Dillingham House is one of the oldest in the country. It offers its guests an interesting historical experience while providing a quiet and comfortable, natural environment off the beaten path. Sandwich has many historical attractions, as well as quiet beaches for relaxation and a scenic waterfront nearby.

Host: Kathy Kenney
Rooms: 4 (2 PB; 2 SB) $65-75
Continental Breakfast
Credit Cards: None
Notes: 2, 5, 6 (small), 7, 8 (over 12), 9, 10, 11, 12

House Guests Cape Cod and the Islands

Box 1881, Orleans, 02653
(508) 896-7053; (800) 666-HOST (reservations)
FAX (508) 896-7054

93019. Featured in *Country Living* magazine in 1983 and 1986, this is a vintage 1835 Greek Revival-style home which has been beautifully and tastefully restored. Five bedrooms, one with a working fireplace, are imaginatively decorated and appointed to evoke the spirit of the 19th century. King, queen, and twin beds are available, as are private and semiprivate baths. Color TV in guest parlor. Full breakfast. Complimentary English-style afternoon tea daily. Only moments from museums, the Heritage Plantation, and the beach. Children six or older are welcome. Smoking is allowed on the wicker-furnished enclosed sun porch. $10 for additional person. $55-75.

6 Pets welcome; 8 Children welcome; 9 Social drinking allowed; 10 Tennis available; 11 Swimming available; 12 Golf available; 13 Skiing available; 14 May be booked through travel agents.

Isaiah Jones Homestead

165 Main Street, 02563
(508) 888-9115

An intimate Victorian bed and breakfast inn with beautiful antiques, fresh flowers, and candlelight awaits guests. Homemade, freshly baked breakfast and afternoon tea is served daily. Most points of interest are within walking distance. "Superior in every respect—a trip into the past." Minimum stay weekends in season and holidays is two nights.

Host: Shirley Jones Sutton
Rooms: 5 (PB) $75-124
Continental Breakfast
Credit Cards: A, B, C, D
Notes: 2, 5, 10, 11, 12, 14

The Summer House

The Summer House

158 Main Street, 02563
(508) 888-4991

Elegant circa 1835 Greek Revival bed and breakfast featured in *Country Living* magazine, in the heart of historic Sandwich Village, Cape Cod's oldest town (settled 1637). Antiques, hand-stitched quilts, working fireplaces, flowers, large sunny rooms, and English-style gardens. Close to dining, museums, shops, pond, and gristmill; boardwalk to beach. Bountiful breakfast, elegantly served. Afternoon tea in the garden included.

Hosts: David and Kay Merrell
Rooms: 5 (1 PB; 4 SB) $55-75
Full Breakfast
Credit Cards: A, B, C, D
Notes: 2, 5, 8 (over 5), 9, 10, 11, 12, 14

SCITUATE

The Allen House

18 Allen Place, 02066
(617) 545-8221

Sleep comfortably and quietly in a gracious, gabled Victorian merchant's home overlooking an unspoiled New England fishing town and harbor. Only an hour's drive south of Boston. Then wake to classical music and gourmet cuisine. The hosts are English, professional caterers, and cat lovers. On every sunny, warm day expect a full breakfast—and sometimes afternoon tea—on the porch overlooking the harbor.

Hosts: Christine and Iain Gilmour
Rooms: 6 (4 PB; 2 SB) $79-139
Full Breakfast
Credit Cards: A, B, C, D
Notes: 2, 5, 9, 14

Bed and Breakfast Associates Bay Colony, Ltd.

P.O. Box 57166, Babson Park, Boston, 02157-0166
(617) 449-5302; (800) 347-5088
FAX (617) 449-5958

SS250. Just one mile from the ocean, this pretty home affords visitors to the South Shore the opportunity to relax and enjoy nearby tennis, yacht club, pool, and clam digging. The hosts are active tennis players. Two guest rooms, one with private bath. Full breakfast on weekends; children welcome; no smoking. Family and monthly rates available; $50-55.

SS260. Offered by a gourmet caterer and her husband, this circa 1905 home is a scant two-minute walk from Scituate Harbor. They have lovingly remodeled their fine bed and breakfast and filled it with pe-

NOTES: Credit cards accepted: A MasterCard; B Visa; C American Express; D Discover Card; E Diner's Club; F Other; 2 Personal checks accepted; 3 Lunch available; 4 Dinner available; 5 Open all year;

riod furniture, classical music, and English-style hospitality. Guests will surely make themselves comfortable in the cheerful parlor, indulge in the fabulous gourmet breakfast (or ask for a low-cal or "happy heart" diet), relax before the Edwardian fireplace, or gaze out at the yachts in the bustling harbor. A short stroll brings visitors to local shops and seafood restaurants. Three guest rooms, two with private baths. Full breakfast; children over 16 welcome; no smoking. $89-119.

Bed and Breakfast Cape Cod

P.O. Box 341, West Hyannisport, 02672-0341
(508) 775-2772; FAX (508) 775-2884

64. Ocean views and English elegance characterize this 1905 Victorian-style inn. Four guest rooms feature queen-size or double beds and water views; two rooms have a private bath, and two other rooms share a bath. English hosts serve a full gourmet breakfast in the morning, and afternoon tea at 5:00 P.M. each day. Breakfast is served in the Victorian dining room or on a porch overlooking the harbor. No smoking. No children. $69-99.

Rasberry Ink

748 Country Way, 02060
(617) 545-6629

Coastal Scituate is 350 years old, 25 miles southeast of Boston, midway between Boston and Plymouth. It was the home of Thomas Lawson, a copper king in the 1900s. His estate is close by. Rasberry Ink is an early Victorian farmhouse furnished in lace and antiques, in the village. Antique shops nearby; ocean and historic sites.

Hosts: Fran Honkonen and Carol Hoban
Rooms: 2 (SB) $70
Continental Breakfast
Credit Cards: None
Notes: 2, 10, 11, 12, 13 (cross-country)

SHEFFIELD

American Country Collection

4 Greenwood Lane, Delmar, NY 12054
(518) 439-7001

173. An authentic 1840s Colonial barn conversion of hand-hewn beams, plank floors, and stenciled walls nestled on three wooded acres below Mt. Everett in the Berkshire's Taconic Range. Hike from the inn on a connecting trail that runs along a racing stream to the Appalachian Trail via Mt. Race Falls. Thirteen guest rooms in the main house, and three guest rooms in each of two cottages, all different, unique, and individually decorated in a cozy country motif with textured fabrics, quilts, rugs, and stenciling. Several rooms are interconnecting, offering suite arrangements for families with private outside entrances, private baths, and rooms for children. Each cottage room also has its own private bath and entrance as well. A kitchen and laundry are available for guest use. Continental breakfast. No resident pets; well-behaved guest pets with prior arrangements. There is an additional ten percent added to the room rates on high season weekends and holidays. $55-145.

Covered Bridge

P.O. Box 447A, Norfolk, CT 06058
(203) 542-5944

1SHMA. This charming log home, commanding a sweeping view of the Berkshires, is the perfect spot for an idyllic, pastoral retreat. A horse grazes nearby, and it's a short walk across the fields to the swimming pond. A full breakfast is served in the kitchen or on the porch. The host, an actress, has traveled extensively and is also well-informed about area activities. There are two double guest rooms that share a bath. $85.

6 Pets welcome; 8 Children welcome; 9 Social drinking allowed; 10 Tennis available; 11 Swimming available; 12 Golf available; 13 Skiing available; 14 May be booked through travel agents.

2SHMA. This 1771 Colonial set in the village of Sheffield is surrounded by antique shops and close to Tanglewood. There are several common rooms for guests to enjoy as well as a tree-shaded terrace. A full breakfast is served in the dining room. The guest rooms are decorated with antiques. Three rooms share a bath, and one room has a private bath. $80-90.

Ramblewood Inn

Ramblewood Inn

A Unique Bed and Breakfast Inn
Box 729, 01257
(413) 229-3363

This stylish country house, furnished for comfort and romance, is in a beautiful natural setting of mountains, pine forest, and serene private lake for swimming and canoeing. Private baths, fireplaces, central air, lovely gardens, and gourmet breakfasts. Convenient to all Berkshire attractions: Tanglewood, drama/dance festivals, antiques, Lime Rock Racing, skiing, and hiking. Minimum stay requirements for weekends and holidays.

Hosts: June and Martin Ederer
Rooms: 6 (PB) $80-110
Full Breakfast
Credit Cards: A, B
Notes: 2, 5, 8, 9, 10, 11, 12, 13

Stagecoach Hill Inn

Route 41, 01257
(413) 229-8585

In the heart of the Berkshires, the Stagecoach Hill Inn is in a lovely country setting with the Appalachian Trail nearby. This charming, old, country inn has a cozy English pub. All rooms are air-conditioned, and all have telephones. Large screened porch and swimming pool are available for guests' enjoyment. Close to all the popular Berkshire cultural attractions. Continental-plus breakfast.

Host: John Pedretti
Rooms: 9 (PB) $60-85
Continental Breakfast
Credit Cards: A, B, C, D, E
Notes: 2, 8, 9, 10, 12, 13

SHELBURNE

Orchard Hill

Colvain-Shelburne Road, 01370
(413) 625-6802

Orchard Hill is set amid 400 acres of apple orchards. Built before the American Revolution, it is one of few European Capes still in existence, and was restored and renovated after 40 years of neglect. In the western hills of Massachusetts it is accessible to Tanglewood, famous for its music, and to Jacob's Pillow, world-renowned for dance. Within range of Vermont's ski slopes. Guest rooms share bath, but arrangements can be made for private bath.

Host: Joy A. Davenport
Rooms: 3 (SB) $55-60
Full Breakfast
Credit Cards: None
Notes: 2, 5, 8, 9, 11, 12, 13, 14

SOUTHBOROUGH

Host Homes of Boston

P.O. Box 117, Newton, 02168
(617) 244-1308; FAX (617) 244-5156

Apple Tree. Antique charm in 200-year-old homestead in rural setting, with orchards, barn, and country kitchen. First-floor guest room features queen-size bed. Second-floor suite with double and twin beds has connecting bath. Guest parlor with fireplace. Family has cats and Great Dane. Between Boston and Worcester; abutting Framingham and Westboro off Routes 9, I-90 and I-495. No smoking. Children welcome. $87-151.

Bed and Breakfast Associates Bay Colony, Ltd.

P.O. Box 57166, Babson Park, Boston, 02157-0166
(617) 449-5302; (800) 347-5088
FAX (617) 449-5958

CW642. A 200-year-old homestead, lovingly restored with great attention to historical detail. Near Southborough Center, a 40-minute drive from downtown Boston. Three attractive guest rooms, one with a private bath. $80.

SOUTH CHATHAM (CAPE COD) _____

Bed and Breakfast Cape Cod

P.O. Box 341, West Hyannisport, 02672 0341
(508) 775-2772; FAX (508) 775 2884

5. This house was built on Nantucket Island in 1847 and moved to its present location when the island lost its whaling business. Restored five years ago, it is now an inn with five private-bath bedrooms, all decorated in Victorian and traditional decor. Seven-tenths of a mile away are the warm-water beach and the waters of Nantucket Sound. A full Continental breakfast is served each morning in the kitchen or dining area. Shopping, the Chatham fish pier, and recreational activity are all nearby. No children under 8. $65-85.

SOUTH DARTMOUTH _____

Salt Marsh Farm

322 Smith Neck Road, 02748
(508) 992-0980

A 1780 Federal farmhouse with narrow stairs, working fireplaces, antiques, and an interesting library of local and natural history. On a 90-acre nature preserve with trails, stone walls, organic gardens, and laying hens. Bikes available. Scenic coastal community convenient to Martha's Vineyard ferry and day trips to Plymouth, Cape Cod, Newport, Mystic, Boston, and Nantucket. New Bedford Whaling Museum, historic waterfront, and beaches are nearby.

Hosts: Larry and Sally Brownell
Rooms: 2 (PB) $60-85
Full Breakfast
Credit Cards: A, B, C
Notes: 2, 5, 8, 9, 11

SOUTH DENNIS (CAPE COD) _____

Bed and Breakfast Cape Cod

P.O. Box 341, West Hyannisport, 02672-0341
(508) 775-2772; FAX (508) 775-2884

3. Built in 1828, with major additions in 1879, this Cape-style house was changed to Queen Anne Victorian. For many years the house was a private home, before being changed to a guest house. The restoration several years ago now provides an inn with five guest rooms, four with private baths. The full breakfast served in the dining room each morning includes a variety of special house dishes. The 22-mile bike trail is one-half mile away. Some of the best shopping on Cape Cod is within a few miles of the inn. $45-75.

SOUTH EGREMONT _____

Weathervane Inn

Route 23, P.O. Box 388, 01258
(413) 528-9580

This historic inn dating from 1785 has been operated by the Murphy family since 1980. Eleven rooms all with private baths and air conditioning. Full breakfast served every

6 Pets welcome; 8 Children welcome; 9 Social drinking allowed; 10 Tennis available; 11 Swimming available; 12 Golf available; 13 Skiing available; 14 May be booked through travel agents.

morning featuring homemade muffins and breads. In the Berkshires in western Massachusetts, the inn is a mile from the Appalachian Trail and the roads are gentle for bicycling. In the summer guests can enjoy Tanglewood, Berkshire summer theater, Rockwell museum, and antiquing. Downhill and cross-country skiing are nearby in winter. Enjoy the pool in the summer.

Hosts: Anne and Vincent Murphy
Rooms: 11 (PB) $95-115
Full Breakfast
Credit Cards: A, B, C, D
Notes: 2, 4 (weekends), 5, 8 (over 7), 9, 10, 11, 12, 13, 14

SOUTH ORLEANS

Bed and Breakfast Cape Cod

P.O. Box 341, West Hyannisport, 02672-0341
(508) 775-2772; FAX (508) 775-2884

37. The Atlantic Ocean is directly in front of this circa 1780 home that offers three bedrooms with private baths and choice of a king-, queen-size, or twin beds. Enjoy the full breakfast served each morning before walking out to the beach or the host's boathouse on the water. Children over five. $75-90.

80. On high ground above Pleasant Bay, this 1973 Cape Cod-style home offers three bedrooms. One is a large room with a queen-size bed and private bath, and the other two share a bath and have a double bed or a pair of twins. This lovely home is convenient to both Chatham and Orleans shops and restaurants. The deck is great for relaxing after spending the day at the beach. No smoking. $55-70.

Hillbourne House

Route 28, #654, 02662
(508) 255-0780

This charming bed and breakfast was built in 1798 and during the Civil War was part of the Underground Railroad. A circular hiding place is still in evidence beneath the trap door in the Common Room. Enjoy a magnificent view of Pleasant Bay and the great dunes of Outer Beach on the Atlantic. Convenient to all Cape activities. Private beach and dock.

Host: Barbara Hayes
Rooms: 8 (PB) $50-80
Full or Continental Breakfast
Credit Cards: None
Notes: 2, 9, 11, 12

SOUTH WELLFLEET (CAPE COD)

Orleans Bed and Breakfast Associates

P.O. Box 1312, Orleans, 02653
(508) 255-3824; (800) 541-6226

Owl's Nest. Peace and quiet surround this Gothic contemporary home on six acres known as Owl Woods. Charming cathedral-ceilinged living and dining rooms, filled with antiques and collectibles to enjoy. Upstairs a skylighted sitting area separates two queen-size bedrooms which share a large bath. Continental breakfast is served inside or on the 40-foot deck overlooking perennial gardens and pine woods. Walk down a country lane to a picturesque bay beach. It's a short ride to ocean or pond swimming. $75.

The White Eagle. What a neat spot for a Cape visit! Ground-floor private entrance into large room with breakfast table and sitting area, king-size bed, full private bath, TV and wet bar with refrigerator, stocked for breakfast. Sliders open to a pretty patio with comfortable reclining chairs to loaf in and admire the woodsy views. Walk to Bay Beach, or take a short drive to the ocean. $70.

NOTES: Credit cards accepted: A MasterCard; B Visa; C American Express; D Discover Card; E Diner's Club; F Other; 2 Personal checks accepted; 3 Lunch available; 4 Dinner available; 5 Open all year;

SOUTH YARMOUTH (CAPE COD)

Bed and Breakfast Associates Bay Colony, Ltd.

P.O. Box 57166, Babson Park, Boston, 02157-0166
(617) 449-5302; (800) 347-5088
FAX (617) 449-5958

CC380. Contemporary elegance in an antique setting. Ten wonderful guest rooms in this 1845 sea captain's mansion. Every amenity thoughtfully provided in this magnificent restoration. $100-125.

House Guests Cape Cod and the Islands

Box 1881, Orleans, 02653
(508) 896-7053; (800) 666-HOST (reservations)
FAX (508) 896-7054

93091. An 18th-century homestead, circa 1712. The homestead consists of the main residence, the private cottage, the private suite, and an antique carriage house. All just minutes away from the Bass River, fresh and saltwater beaches, the Cape Cod Bike Trail, golf courses, and all mid-Cape attractions. Continental breakfast included in the price of nightly rentals. $55-100. .

STERLING

Sterling Orchards' Bed and Breakfast

60 Kendall Hill Road, 01564-0455
(508) 422-6595; (508) 422-6170

Built in 1740, this Colonial home features many original details such as the 12-foot center chimney, Indian shutters, and wide-pine floors. In a working apple orchard. A full breakfast is served in solarium overlooking lawns and gardens. Many antique stores in the area. No smoking in entire house. Closed January to March. Exit 6 from I-190. Closed January through March.

Hosts: Robert and Shirley P. Smiley
Rooms: 2 (PB) $65-85
Full Breakfast
Credit Cards: None
Notes: 2, 4, 9, 10, 11, 12, 13, 14

Sterling Orchards'

STOCKBRIDGE

Berkshire Thistle Bed and Breakfast

P.O. Box 1227, Route 7 Stockbridge, 01262
(413) 298-3188

This Colonial home is nestled on five acres which offer beautiful gardens, lawns, and a spacious swimming pool. In front is a corral that is home to two thoroughbred horses. There are five rooms of which one is a suite; all are decorated with a feel of elegance, but are simply comfortable and waiting for guests to unwind and enjoy. After a night's sleep, wake up to a full country breakfast served in the dining room or on the large porch in warm weather. Near all area attractions: skiing, Tanglewood, and the Norman Rockwell Museum. Feel welcomed in the heart of the Berkshires by the hosts.

Hosts: Gene and Diane Elling
Rooms: 5 (4 PB; 1 SB) $65-120
Full Breakfast
Credit Cards: None
Notes: 2, 5, 9, 10, 11, 12, 13

6 Pets welcome; 8 Children welcome; 9 Social drinking allowed; 10 Tennis available; 11 Swimming available; 12 Golf available; 13 Skiing available; 14 May be booked through travel agents.

Cherry Hill Farm
Bed and Breakfast

P.O. Box 1245, 24 Cherry Hill Road, 01262
(413) 298-3535; (413) 298-5452

An 1897 Georgian mansion on a large estate one and one-half miles from town on a country road. Fireplaces in bedrooms and grand common rooms. Steinway grand piano. Hosts offer suites (two rooms with connecting door and private bath) to families. Mountain views, tennis court, pond, and cross-country skiing. Full country breakfast served. There are resident pets.

Hosts: The Swanns
Rooms: 4 (2 PB; 2 SB) $60-150
Full Breakfast
Credit Cards: None
Notes: 2, 5, 8, 10, 11, 12, 13

Historic Merrell Inn

1565 Pleasant Street, South Lee, 01260
(413) 243-1794

This 200-year-old brick stagecoach inn in a small New England village along the banks of the Housatonic River is listed on the National Register of Historic Places. Rooms with fireplaces, canopied beds, and antique furnishings. Full breakfast is served in the original tavern room. One mile to Norman Rockwell's beloved Stockbridge.

Hosts: Charles and Faith Reynolds
Rooms: 9 (PB) $65-145
Full Breakfast

Historic Merrell Inn

Credit Cards: A, D
Notes: 2, 5, 9, 13

The Roeder House
Bed and Breakfast

Route 183, Box 525, 01262
(413) 298-4015

A restored 1856 Federal farmhouse with flower gardens, in-ground pool, and patios. Queen-size, four-poster canopied beds, private baths, fine country antique furnishings, and Audubon prints. Full breakfast served on English china. Friday and Saturday summer grill nite served poolside. *Prix fixe.* Winter midweek rates available. Cancellation policy with service charge. Half a mile from Rockwell and Chesterwood museums. Air conditioning and paddle fans. Nonsmoking inn. Brochures available.

Hosts: Diane and Vernon Reuss
Rooms: 6 (PB) $110-195
Full Breakfast
Credit Cards: A, B, C, D
Notes: 2, 4, 5, 8 (over 11), 9, 10, 12, 13

STOW

Bed and Breakfast
Associates Bay Colony, Ltd.

P.O. Box 57166, Babson Park Branch, Boston,
    02157-0166
(617) 449-5302; FAX (617) 449-5958

CW325. Authentic Colonial farmhouse circa 1734 features romantic guest rooms. Honeymoon suite has a sitting room, Jacuzzi in the bath, and queen-size canopied bed. All guest rooms have handmade quilts, decorative fireplaces, and antique furnishings. $80-100.

Bed and Breakfast
Marblehead and
North Shore

P.O. Box 35, Newtonville, 02160
(617) 964-1606; (800) 832-2632
FAX (617) 332-8572

This large gambrel Colonial-style home near Old Sturbridge village offers three beautiful guest rooms and a suite. One queen-size bedroom has a private bath, while a double bed and a twin-single room share a bath. The separate-entrance guest suite features a double bed, half-bath, refrigerator, microwave, and desk. Common areas include a sitting room with TV, a screened porch and a back yard deck. A wonderful full breakfast is served. No smoking. Children welcome. Multiple-night discounts. $80-95.

STURBRIDGE

Colonel Ebenezer Crafts Inn

Fiske Hill Road, P.O. Box 187, 01566-0187
(508) 347-3313; (800)-PUBLICK

The Colonel Ebenezer Crafts Inn was built in 1786 by David Fiske, Esquire, on one of the highest points of land in Sturbridge which offered him a commanding view of his cattle and farmland. The house has since been restored by the management of the Publick House. Accommodations at Crafts Inn are charming. There are two queen-size canopied beds, as well as some four-poster beds. Guests may relax by the pool or in the sunroom, take afternoon tea, or enjoy sweeping views of the countryside. Breakfast includes freshly baked muffins and sweet rolls, fresh fruit and juices, and coffee and tea. Those seeking a more hearty breakfast, lunch, or dinner can stroll down to the Publick House just over a mile away.

Host: Shirley Washburn
Rooms: 8 (PB) $69-150
Continental Breakfast
Credit Cards: A, B, C, E
Notes: 2, 8, 9, 10, 11, 12, 13 (cross-country), 14

1880 Inn

14 Pleasant Street, 01082
(413) 967-7847

Relax in yesterday's charm. This 12-room Colonial is complete with six fireplaces, rustic beams, and hardwood floors. Break-

fast may be served on the porch or in the dining room. Enjoy afternoon tea before the cozy fireplace.

Hosts: Margaret and Stan Skutnik
Rooms: 3; $50-65
Full Breakfast
Credit Cards: None
Notes: 2, 5, 8, 9, 10, 11, 12, 14

Sturbridge Country Inn

530 Main Street, 01566
(508) 347-5503

A historic 1840s inn custom-decorated with Colonial bedrooms. Each room features fireplace and private whirlpool tub. Less than a mile from Old Sturbridge village. Walking distance to restaurants and antique shops.

Host: Kevin MacConnell
Rooms: 9 (PB) $69-135
Continental Breakfast
Credit Cards: A, B, C, D
Notes: 2, 4, 5, 7, 8, 9, 10, 11, 12, 13, 14

SUDBURY

Host Homes of Boston

P.O. Box 117, Boston, 02168
(617) 244-1308; FAX (617) 244-2700

Carousel House. This countryside estate, isolated on a hilltop near Concord offers three guest rooms with outstanding amenities. Second-floor Victorian and Green rooms have queen-size beds, Jacuzzi, and shower baths, and the third-floor Rose room has a pair of twin beds and a shower bath. Grounds include a private golf course and swimming pool, and antique carousel horses artfully blend with traditional decor to make this a special place to stay. No smoking. $95.

Sudbury Bed and Breakfast

3 Drum Lane, 01776
(508) 443-2860

6 Pets welcome; 8 Children welcome; 9 Social drinking allowed; 10 Tennis available; 11 Swimming available; 12 Golf available; 13 Skiing available; 14 May be booked through travel agents.

A large Garrison Colonial home with traditional furnishings on a quiet tree-studded acre. A Continental breakfast is served with homemade muffins and rolls. Close to Boston, Lexington, and Concord. An abundance of outdoor recreation and historical sights nearby. Friendly hospitality for the New England visitor.

Hosts: Don and Nancy Somers
Rooms: 2 (S1.5B) $55-65
Continental Breakfast
Credit Cards: None
Notes: 2, 5, 8, 9, 11, 12

SWAMPSCOTT

Bed and Breakfast Associates Bay Colony, Ltd.

P.O. Box 57166, Babson Park Branch,
Boston, 02157-0166
(617) 449-5302; FAX (617) 449-5958

NS200. Just two and one-half blocks to a sandy beach. This hostess collects antiques, refinishes furniture, and enjoys quilting. As a tour escort around New England, she has a wealth of information to share with her guests. Her small Colonial home in a quiet neighborhood is neat and clean. Three guest rooms share a bath. Full breakfast; children over 12 welcome; no smoking. Family and monthly rates available; $50-60.

Bed and Breakfast Marblehead and North Shore

P.O. Box 35, Newtonville, 02160
(617) 964-1606; (800) 832-2632
FAX (617) 332-8572

Oceanview Victorian. Beautiful turn-of-the-century home offering wonderful views of the ocean. American country decor with hand-stenciled walls in three lovely guest rooms that share two baths. One room has a private half-bath. One oceanfront room has a private deck. Color cable TV and air conditioning. Guest phone and refrigerator in the hallway. In the winter months, relax by the wood stove in the sitting room. Easy access to Boston, Salem, and Marblehead. Airport pickup with prior arrangement. Children over six welcome. No smoking. Continental breakfast. Parking. $75-85.

TRURO

House Guests Cape Cod and the Islands

P.O. Box 1881, Orleans, 02653
(508) 896-7053; (800) 666-HOST (reservations)
FAX (508) 896-7054

93181. Guests will discover the essence of Cape Cod in this 1760 vintage full-Cape-style home set on five lovely acres in the National Seashore parklands. On a rise with a distant view of the ocean, this house is just one-half mile to an ocean beach. There are two guest rooms available. One room, on the first floor, has a double bed and a working fireplace. The other room, on the second floor, has twin beds. The two rooms share a first-floor bath. There is also a cozy room with a twin bed on the third floor which can be reserved for a third person in the party. Resident dog and cats. Smoking not permitted in the bedrooms or dining room. $35 for extra child. $50 for additional adult in separate twin-bedded room. $110 for suite when available. $80-95.

93183. A wonderful old Victorian bed and breakfast inn, built in 1880. There are five comfortable and tastefully appointed guest rooms. One room has a king-size bed, private bath, and adjoining kitchen. Another room, available in-season only, has a king-size soft-sided water bed and private bath. The three remaining rooms have double or single beds and a shared bath. There is also a large three-room apartment with two double beds, private bath, full kitchen, private deck, and air conditioning. Nearby attractions include beaches, Cape Cod Bay, biking and walking trails, and whale-watching cruises. Continental breakfast. Children 13 or older are welcome. $39-99. $250-650 weekly.

94185. Built in 1836 in the Federal style, this inn was originally a farmhouse. Five rooms offer queen- or king-size beds and private tiled baths. The Vintage Suite offers a king-size bed, a two-person Jacuzzi, and an oversized shower. The Cape Cod National Seashore, Highland Golf Course, Cape Cod Lighthouse, whale-watching cruises, and other attractions are easily accessible. No smoking. Children 12 and over are welcome. Resident cat. $55-115.

Orleans Bed and Breakfast Associates

P.O. Box 1312, Orleans, 02653
(508) 255-3824; (800) 541-6226

South Hollow Vineyards Inn. On five picturesque acres, the historic Hughes/Rich Farmstead, circa 1836, remains one of the last working farms on Cape Cod. In 1993, a French vinifera winegrape vineyard was planted on the rolling hills behind the farmhouse, the first of its kind on the Cape. This rambling Federal-style farmhouse has been carefully restored and furnished. Romantic, spacious rooms with queen-size or double poster beds and tiled baths. Sweeping views of the vineyard from the breakfast garden room and adjoining outdoor patio, or from a spacious upstairs sun deck. Sheltered and quiet, the inn is only a mile from Highland Golf Course, Cape Cod Lighthouse and the beaches, and only a short drive from Provincetown. $85-115.

Parker House

P.O. Box 1111, 02666
(508) 349-3358

The Parker House is an 1820 classic full-Cape nestled into the side of Truro Center between the Cobb Memorial Library and the Blacksmith Shop Restaurant. Clean ocean and bay beaches two miles to east or west. Many art galleries and restaurants in Provincetown and Wellfleet ten minutes away by car. Golf, tennis, sailing, and whale watches nearby. The Cape Cod National Seashore and Audubon Sanctuary offer many trails and guided walks. The Parker House offers haven to a limited number of guests who can rest and read or enjoy the many activities nearby.

Host: Stephen Williams
Rooms: 2 (SB) $55
Continental Breakfast
Credit Cards: None
Notes: 2, 5, 9, 10, 11, 12

Parker House

TYRINGHAM

American Country Collection

4 Greenwood Lane, Delmar, NY 12054-1606
(518) 439-7001

202. A hillside overlooking the first Shaker settlement in the Berkshires is the setting for this 250-year-old farmhouse, well-known for the pure maple syrup from nearby trees. Tanglewood, Stockbridge, and the Norman Rockwell Museum are within nine miles. One of two common rooms has couches, chairs, a TV, and a fireplace. Accommodations include one air-conditioned room on the first floor with a private porch, twin beds, and shared bath. Three air-condi-

---

6 Pets welcome; 8 Children welcome; 9 Social drinking allowed; 10 Tennis available; 11 Swimming available; 12 Golf available; 13 Skiing available; 14 May be booked through travel agents.

tioned rooms on the second floor have double beds, twin beds, and a shared bath. An apartment on the second floor has a double bed, an air-conditioned kitchen, a living area, and bath. Full breakfast is served from 8:00-10:00 A.M. in a dining room decorated with Shaker furniture. Intimate dinners are available Thursday-Saturday in late spring, summer, and early fall, served on a side porch at an additional charge. Children are welcome in apartment; in-house age six and older. Smoking outside only. $75-100.

The Golden Goose

Main Road, Box 336, 01264
(413) 243-3008

Small, friendly, 1800 country inn nestled in Tyringham Valley in the Berkshires. Victorian antiques, sitting rooms with fireplaces, homemade breakfast fare. Within one-half hour are Tanglewood, Stockbridge, Jacob's Pillow, Hancock Shaker Village, the Norman Rockwell Museum, Berkshire Theater Festival, skiing, golf, and tennis. The inn is one mile off the Appalachian Trail. Near Butternut, Otis, Jiminy Peak, and Catamount ski slopes.

Hosts: Lilja and Joe Rizzo
Rooms: 6 (4 PB; 2 SB) $70-120
Full Breakfast
Credit Cards: A, B, C, D
Notes: 2, 5, 7 and 8 (limited), 9, 10, 11, 12, 13, 14

The Golden Goose

American Country Collection

4 Greenwood Lane, Delmar, NY 12054
(518) 439-7001

202. On a hillside overlooking the first shaker settlement in the Berkshires is this 250-year-old farmhouse, well-known for the pure maple syrup that comes from nearby trees. Tanglewood, Stockbridge, and the Norman Rockwell Museum are within nine miles. Two lovely common rooms, one with TV and fireplace. Four guest rooms with shared baths. Apartment with kitchen and private bath. Full breakfast served. Intimate dinners are available by arrangement Thursday through Saturday in late Spring, Summer, and early Fall. All children are welcome in the apartment, and children over six are welcome in the house. Smoking outside only. $75-100.

VINEYARD HAVEN (MARTHA'S VINEYARD)_

Bed and Breakfast Greater Boston and Cape Cod

P.O. Box 35, Newtonville, 02160
(617) 964-1606; (800) 832-2632
FAX (617) 332-8572

The Vineyard Haven Guest House. An historic Colonial accommodation, dating back to 1720. There are five guest rooms, with shared and private baths. Guests are just a short walk from the ferry landing. A Continental breakfast and afternoon tea are complimentary. Smoking on outside porch only. $85-165.

Bed and Breakfast/Inns of New England

128 South Hoop Pole Road, Guilford, CT 06437
(203) 457-0042; (800) 582-0853

MA 1070 and 1075. Two historic inns built in two historic towns (#1070 in Vineyard Haven and #1075 in Edgartown), built in

NOTES: Credit cards accepted: A MasterCard; B Visa; C American Express; D Discover Card; E Diner's Club; F Other; 2 Personal checks accepted; 3 Lunch available; 4 Dinner available; 5 Open all year;

the 1840s as sea captains' homes, and have been meticulously restored and furnished to reflect the charm and elegance of that period. Enjoy the Continental breakfast in the elegant dining room or enchanting flower garden. The inns' romantic guest rooms conjure up memories of yesteryear. Each is uniquely different and decorated with fine furnishings. Each has a private bath. Three-night minimum stay on weekends. Two-night minimum stay for some holidays and during high season. Children are welcome. No guest pets. $75-180.

Bed and Breakfast Nantucket/ Martha's Vineyard

P.O. Box 341, West Hyannisport, 02672-0341
(508) 775-2772; FAX (508) 775-2884

202. This wonderful two-acre estate in the village of Vineyard Haven was restored in 1989. It is secluded and romantic, and offers a casual elegance. The luxurious furnishings add to the charm, creating a relaxing getaway. The seven private-bath guest rooms, some with fireplaces, are each unique and beautifully maintained. The special gourmet breakfast is served on the porch or in the dining room. Play the piano or a game of chess while enjoying the warmth of the fireplace in the winter months. This is a very special accommodation. No smoking. No children under 12. $90-189.

205. This home was built nearly 100 years ago as a private home. Later it was used for 40 years as a guest house. It was restored several years ago, and the present owner uses eight rooms for bed and breakfast. Each room has a private bath, and all are clean and bright with tasteful decor. The Continental breakfast is served in a common room where guests meet and greet one another. Walk to all Vineyard Haven shops, stores, and restaurants. Bike rental available on the premises. $75-160.

Captain Dexter House of Vineyard Haven

100 Main Street, Box 2457, 02568
(508) 693-6564

A perfect country inn! Built in 1840, the house has been meticulously restored and exquisitely furnished to reflect the charm of that period. Be surrounded by flowers from the garden and pampered by innkeepers who believe in old-fashioned hospitality. The inn's eight romantic guest rooms are distinctively decorated. Several rooms have working fireplaces (as does the parlor) and four-poster canopied beds. Stroll to town and harbor. Continental-plus breakfast.

Hosts: Rick and Birdie
Rooms: 8 (PB) $55-160
Continental Breakfast
Credit Cards: A, B, C, E
Notes: 2, 5, 8, 9, 10, 11, 12, 14

The Hanover House

The Hanover House

10 Edgartown Road; P.O. Box 2107, 02568
(508) 693-1066; (800) 339-1066 (MA)

Recommended by the *New York Times*, The Hanover House is a large, old inn that has been fully renovated, offering guests modern conveniences while still retaining the quaintness and personalized hospitality of the lovely, old inns of yesteryear. The guest rooms all feature private baths, color cable TV, queen-size or double beds, air conditioning, and individual heat controls. Continental breakfast is served on the sun porch year-round. The inn is within walking distance of the ferry in the town of Vineyard Haven. A nonsmoking inn.

Hosts: Kay and Ron Nelson
Rooms: 15 (PB) $55-158
Continental Breakfast
Credit Cards: A, B, C, D
Notes: 2, 5, 8, 10, 11, 12, 14

House Guests Cape Cod and the Islands

Box 1881, Orleans, 02653
(508) 896-7053; (800) 666-HOST (reservations)
FAX (508) 896-7054

93336. A large turn-of-the-century English-type manor house set on two acres in a quiet residential side street. Exquisite furnishings and lovely accessories set a tone of quiet luxury. The seven spacious guest rooms have private baths and double, queen, or twin beds. Some have four-poster or canopied beds; two have working fireplaces. Delicious expanded Continental breakfast. Children 12 and older are welcome. No smoking. $100-189.

93340. A large antique inn that has been renovated to give the convenience of a modern hotel while still retaining the quaintness and personalized hospitality of the lovely, old inns of yesteryear. Each of the 12 rooms has a private bath, color TV, queen-size bed or two double beds, air conditioning, and individual heat controls. Several rooms have private entrances that open onto spacious sun decks. Continental breakfast during in-season (May through October). Nonsmoking and smoking rooms are available. Cribs are also available. There are also two two-room efficiency units and one studio unit. $15 for additional person in room. $55-158.

93343. A charming Colonial restoration, nestled among the town's historic sea captains' homes. Three guest rooms are in the main house, a fourth is off the porch, and a fifth is a private-entranced room accessed directly from the guest parking area. Each room has its own private bath and amenities such as fresh flowers. Two rooms have working fireplaces and all are air-conditioned. King, queen, double, and twin beds are available. Continental breakfast. Smoking not permitted. $80-180.

93345. A 1906 Victorian farmhouse featuring an enclosed wraparound porch, three sunrooms, and an attached one-bedroom apartment with private entrance, private bath, kitchen, and working fireplace. In addition to the apartment, there are four guest rooms that share a bath. Queen, double, and single beds are available. Two rooms have two double beds. Delicious Continental breakfast. Children five and older are welcome. No smoking. $45-160.

Lambert's Cove Country Inn

Rural Route 1, Box 422, 02568
(508) 693-2298

Once a lovely, old, country estate, Lambert's Cove Country Inn in West Tisbury now offers guest rooms in three charming buildings: the original 1790 residence, a converted 18th-century barn, and a carriage house. The setting is seven and one-half acres of lawn, meadows, gardens, and woodlands, with towering trees, an orchard, and vine-covered stone walls. Each room has its own individual charm. The dining room, which is open to the public, features some of the finest meals available on the island.

Hosts: Russ Wilson and Marchele Kowalski
Rooms: 15 (PB) $85-175
Continental Breakfast
Credit Cards: A, B, C
Notes: 2, 4, 5, 10, 11, 12

NOTES: Credit cards accepted: A MasterCard; B Visa; C American Express; D Discover Card; E Diner's Club; F Other; 2 Personal checks accepted; 3 Lunch available; 4 Dinner available; 5 Open all year;

Lothrop Merry House

Owen Park, Box 1939, 02568
(508) 693-1646

The Merry House, built in the 1790s, overlooks Vineyard Haven Harbor, has a private
beach, expansive lawn, flower-bordered terrace. Most rooms have ocean view and fireplace. All are furnished with antiques and
fresh flowers. Complimentary canoe and
Sunfish for guests' use. Sailing also available on 54-foot ketch Laissez Faire. Close to
ferry and shops. Open year-round.

Hosts: John and Mary Clarke
Rooms: 7 (4 PB; 3 SB) $68-169
Continental Breakfast
Credit Cards: A, B
Notes: 2 (for deposit), 5, 8, 9, 10, 11, 12, 14

Lothrop Merry House

WALTHAM

Bed and Breakfast Associates Bay Colony, Ltd.

P.O. Box 57166, Babson Park, Boston, 02157-0166
(617) 449-5302; (800) 347-5088
FAX (617) 449-5958

IW300. This friendly hostess will welcome
guests to this charming little house with a
white picket fence and a screened porch. It
is in a neighborhood of manicured lawns
just one and one-half miles from I-95,
which circles Greater Boston. Two guest
rooms on the second floor share a bath. Full
breakfast upon request; children welcome.
$55; family rates available.

WAQUOIT

The Wildwood Inn

121 Church Street, 01082
(413) 967-7798

This homey, welcoming, 1880 Victorian
furnished in American primitive antiques,
handmade heirloom and new quilts, and
early cradles. Drive up a maple-canopied
street with stately Victorian homes. Laze in
the hammock swing or rock on the wraparound front porch. Play croquet and frisbee
or sit under the fir trees to read. Try a jigsaw puzzle or board game. Wander in the
110-acre park. Canoe, bike, or ski nearby.
An easy drive to the five-college area, Old
Sturbridge and Old Deerfield, the Basketball Hall of Fame, and I-90. Come try the
"NO-LUNCH" breakfast"!

Hosts: Fraidell Fenster and Richard Watson
Rooms: 7 (4 PB; 3SB) $40-85
Full Breakfast
Credit Cards: A, B, C
Notes: 2, 5, 8 (over 6), 9, 10, 11, 12, 13, 14

WELLESLEY

Bed and Breakfast Associates Bay Colony, Ltd.

P.O. Box 57166, Babson Park, Boston, 02157-0166
(617) 449-5302; (800) 347-5088
FAX (617) 449-5958

IW500. This urbane hostess offers three
guest rooms in this handsome home in
Wellesley's desirable Cliff Estates. The first
floor suite features two rooms and an attached bath set apart from the main living
area of the house. Those wishing designer
decor with French antiques, flowered chintz,
and lace can request the master guest room
and bath. Driveway parking. $68-90.

6 Pets welcome; 8 Children welcome; 9 Social drinking allowed; 10 Tennis available; 11 Swimming available;
12 Golf available; 13 Skiing available; 14 May be booked through travel agents.

Host Homes of Boston

P.O. Box 117, Boston, 02168
(617) 244-1308; FAX (617) 244-5156

Washington Place. A warm welcome awaits guests in this 1920 Colonial near the village. The hostess offers two second-floor guest rooms and parlor with books, TV, and stereo. Route 128 one mile. Boston 12 miles. Just a seven-minute walk to commuter train weekdays. Shared bath; no smoking. $61.

202. This wonderful two-acre estate in the village of Vineyard Haven was restored in 1989. It is secluded and romantic, and offers a casual elegance. The luxurious furnishings add to the charm, creating a relaxing getaway. The seven private-bath guest rooms, some with fireplaces, are each unique and beautifully maintained. The special gourmet breakfast is served on the porch or in the dining room. Play the piano or a game of chess while enjoying the warmth of the fireplace in the winter months. This is a very special accommodation. No smoking. No children under 12. $90-189.

WELLFLEET (CAPE COD)

Orleans Bed and Breakfast Associates

P.O. Box 1312, Orleans, 02653
(508) 255-3824; (800) 541-6226

Aunt Sukie's Bayside Bed and Breakfast. Historic Cape with modern addition, on its own private beach at Wellfleet Bay, overlooking National Seashore lands. The home provides both modern rooms and the ambience of antiques and wood-burning fireplaces, roses, and a perennial garden. Three bedrooms have private balconies and baths; two rooms share a bath, separate entrances, and a guest refrigerator. One mile from town on a warm, sandy beach near golf and tennis. The hosts know Cape Cod and will help plan sightseeing and bicycle routes. A wonderful view of sailing and windsurfing activities from the decks. $100.

Turtle Hill. Tucked away on a hill in the woods is this artists' hideaway. On the patio level are two guest rooms, a king-size and a double, with one private bath. Sliders open onto the guest patio. This is an ideal arrangement for a family, or for two couples traveling together. A back road leads to Wellfleet Center and the Bay. $70.

Cape Cod Claddagh Country Inn

WEST BARNSTABLE

Cape Cod Claddagh Country Inn

77 Main Street, P.O. Box 667, 02671-0667
(508) 432-9628; (800) 356-9628(reservations)

Irish hospitality in a Victorian ambience. Reminiscent of an Irish manor. Eight private suites with air conditioning, TV, and refrigerators. Set on two acres with a pool, Irish art gallery, fine dining courtyard restaurant with homemade fare and fair prices, and Irish pub. Relaxed, friendly atmosphere, comfortable antiques, and designer linens. Perfect location for day trips anywhere on the Cape, Islands, Plymouth, and Boston.

Hosts: Jack and Eileen Connell
Rooms: 8 (PB) $75-120
Full Breakfast
Credit Cards: A, B, C, D
Notes: 2, 3, 4, 5, 7 (limited), 8, 9, 10, 11, 12, 14

NOTES: Credit cards accepted: A MasterCard; B Visa; C American Express; D Discover Card; E Diner's Club; F Other; 2 Personal checks accepted; 3 Lunch available; 4 Dinner available; 5 Open all year;

Honeysuckle Hill

Honeysuckle Hill

591 Main Street, 02668
(508) 362-8414; (800) 441-8418
EMA (800) 696-1397

Charming country inn near the dunes of Sandy Neck Beach. Full country breakfast and afternoon tea. Feather beds, down comforters, and homemade cookies at bedside. English toiletries in private baths. Wraparound screen porch filled with wicker, and a large great room for games and large-screen TV watching make this a perfect spot for any season. Minimum stay on seasonal weekends and holidays is two nights.

Host. Barbara Rosenthal
Rooms: 3 (PB) $90-110
Full Breakfast
Credit Cards. A, B, C, D
Notes: 2, 5, 7, 8 (over 12), 9, 10 ,11, 12, 14

WEST DENNIS

Bed and Breakfast Cape Cod

P.O. Box 341, West Hyannisport, 02672-0341
(508) 775-2772; FAX (508) 775-2884

15. On the warm waters of Nantucket Sound is this 62-year-old beach home that has been restored into a seven-bedroom, private bath, and breakfast accommodation. From all rooms there is an ocean or pond view. The carefully maintained house has a breakfast room overlooking a deck that leads to the 100 yards of private sandy beach. A kitchen on the ground floor is available for guests to cook and eat on the beach. All equipment is available. Conve-

nient to many shops and restaurants, only minutes away from Hyannis. $60-110.

Golden Slumber Accommodations

640 Revere Beach Boulevard, Revere, 02151
(800) 892-3231; (617) 289-1053

156. Immaculate, contemporary, waterfront mansion provides commanding views of the Swan River and nearby Atlantic Ocean. Spacious one-bedroom apartment accessible by elevator or conventional staircase is equipped with kitchenette, queen-size or twin beds, immense private bath, and large dining area with deck overlooking private residential dock. Impressive suspended catwalk leads to two impeccably appointed separate chambers featuring antique double or queen-size beds, deck and private or shared baths. Exquisite! $60-125.

WEST FALMOUTH (CAPE COD)

Bed and Breakfast Cape Cod

P.O. Box 341, West Hyannisport, 02672-0341
(508) 775-2772, FAX (508) 775-2884

70. Built in 1739 and expanded through the years, this lovely, old home is now an accommodation with nine guest rooms. The decor is antique with each room offering special touches of charm. The grounds are beautifully divided into special garden settings. A fabulous breakfast is served each morning in the dining room or on the deck. It is a convenient location, not far from the ferry to Martha's Vineyard. A short walk takes guests to the little village setting of West Falmouth. A popular and historic location. No smoking. No children under 14. $65-85.

DESTINNATIONS New England

P.O. Box 1173, Osterville, 02655
(508) 428-5600; FAX 508-420-0565
(800) 333-4667 (reservations)

6 Pets welcome; 8 Children welcome; 9 Social drinking allowed; 10 Tennis available; 11 Swimming available; 12 Golf available; 13 Skiing available; 14 May be booked through travel agents.

7207. Sitting on a hill overlooking Buzzards Bay, this breathtaking nine-room inn was recently featured in *Country Inns* magazine as a "Cape Cod jewel." Each room has a luxurious marble bath and is beautifully furnished; some have private decks. There is an in-deck pool and tennis court, along with beautiful plantings and a view of Buzzards Bay from the upper levels. Continental breakfast served in the faux marble breakfast room. The inn is also available for weddings and provides catering services. No smoking. No children or pets. Open year-round. $150-185.

WEST HARWICH

Bed and Breakfast Cape Cod

P.O. Box 341, West Hyannisport, 02672-0341
(508) 775-2772; FAX (508) 775-2884

16. This 35-year-old ranch-style home is three blocks from the warm waters of Nantucket Sound. There is one wing set aside for bed and breakfast. The first-floor bedroom has a queen-size bed, private bath, large sitting area, color TV, Oriental carpets, and a small refrigerator for guest use. A marvelous full breakfast is served from 8:00 to 9:30 A.M. Convenient to shopping and restaurants. No smoking. No children. $70.

26. This six-guest-room inn was originally built as a sea captain's home in the 1820s. It features pine-board floors and an original-style "captain's stairs" leading to the second floor. A large pool for guest use is next to the main house. There are six bedrooms with private baths, and some of the suites adjacent to the pool will accommodate up to four persons. A full country breakfast is served in a dining area overlooking the pool. $60-120.

WESTON

Webb-Bigelow House

863 Boston Post Road, 02193
(617) 899-2444

This 1827 elegant Federal house is in an exclusive Boston suburb just 20 minutes from the city, nearby colleges, and historic areas of Lexington and Concord. Furnished with family antiques, this could be a delightful secluded getaway on three acres after a busy day of sightseeing or business meetings. The home-like atmosphere includes a full breakfast, bedroom amenities of hair dryers, terry-cloth robes, and comfortable places to relax. The hosts have updated and restored this spacious house to its prime condition, including air conditioning and a modern pool. Two friendly Aussie dogs in residence.

Hosts: Jane and Robert Webb
Rooms: 3 (2 PB) $85-90
Full Breakfast
Credit Cards: None
Notes: 2, 5, 9, 10, 11, 13 (cross-country), 14

WEST STOCKBRIDGE

American Country Collection

4 Greenwood Lane, Delmar, NY 12054
(518) 439-7001

109. Built in 1830 and recently renovated, this immaculate well-cared-for home boasts shiny hardwood floors, lace curtains, oak dining table, and artwork by the host's father. Guests are welcome to use the living room, dining room, or front porch for relaxation and conversation. Four guest rooms, one private bath, one and one-half shared baths. No smoking. Children over ten years old are welcome. $50-100.

Card Lake Inn

29 Main Street, 01266
(413) 232-0272

NOTES: Credit cards accepted: A MasterCard; B Visa; C American Express; D Discover Card; E Diner's Club; F Other; 2 Personal checks accepted; 3 Lunch available; 4 Dinner available; 5 Open all year;

This Colonial inn is in the heart of the Berkshires, minutes from Tanglewood, Jimmy Pesk, and Butternut ski areas. The atmosphere is warm, comfortable, and casual. An on-premises tavern and restaurant offers good food and drink at reasonable prices. Open year-round.

Hosts: Edward and Lisa Robbins
Rooms: 8 (4 PB; 4 SB) $45-125
Continental Breakfast
Credit Cards: A, B, C, D, E, F
Notes: 2, 3, 4, 5, 8, 9, 10, 11, 12, 13, 14

WEST TISBURY (MARTHA'S VINEYARD)

The Bayberry Inn
Old Courthouse Road, P.O. Box 654, 02575
(508) 693-1984

The Bayberry Inn is on a quiet country lane, surrounded by meadows with horses. It is a short drive to a beautiful, secluded beach. Canopied beds with romantic linens, flowers, and antiques furnish the guest rooms. Memorable breakfasts of Belgian waffles with fresh blueberry sauce or "Dream Boats" (everyone's favorite) are served on the terrace or before the fireplace.

Host: Rosalie Powell
Rooms: 5 (3 PB; 2 SB) $110-150
Full Breakfast
Credit Cards: A, B, C
Notes: 2, 5, 8 (over 12), 9, 10, 11, 12, 14

WESTWOOD

Bed and Breakfast Associates Bay Colony, Ltd.
P.O. Box 57166, Babson Park, Boston, 02157-0166
(617) 449-5302; (800) 347-5088
FAX (617) 449-5958

IW725. This country house and barn are graced by an inviting brick patio with a large in-ground pool. The first floor has been redesigned to provide a view of the grounds through walls of glass. Three guest rooms on the second floor share a bath. A Boston tour guide, this hostess claims there is a "friendly ghost" in the house. Children welcome. $55; family rates available.

IW726. This private hideaway is a converted schoolhouse. A party of five can enjoy the two-story apartment with two bedrooms, two full baths, a kitchen, dining area, living room, and deck. Sleeping space includes an antique double bed, two twins that can be made up as a king, and one single. Children welcome; no smoking. $150 for four adults; $120 for family of four.

Host Homes of Boston
P.O. Box 117, Boston, 02168
(617) 244-1308; FAX (617) 244-5156

Woods Abloom. A tree grows through the roof of this 1958 redwood contemporary in the woods. Stunning blend of antiques, modern art, pottery and porcelain collection. Stone walls and sculptured patio. Both rooms available to same party. Twelve miles southwest of Boston near I-95/128. Air conditioning; private bath; TV; no smoking. $68.

WEYMOUTH

Host Homes of Boston
P.O. Box 117, Boston, 02168
(617) 244-1308; FAX (617) 244-5156

Thayer's Landing. Historic 1696 Colonial on the river that has been restored by the friendly third-generation owners. Guest suite on the second floor with a queen-size and twin beds has a fireplace and a river view. The bright first-floor guest room has a queen-size bed and a river view. Breakfast is served in the dining room or on the porch by the river. Families are welcome. Near Bayside Expo Center and Plymouth. Red Line or water shuttle to Boston. No smoking. $61-108.

6 Pets welcome; 8 Children welcome; 9 Social drinking allowed; 10 Tennis available; 11 Swimming available; 12 Golf available; 13 Skiing available; 14 May be booked through travel agents.

WILLIAMSTOWN

American Country Collection

4 Greenwood Lane, Delmar, NY 12054
(518) 439-7001

022. Set on a knoll with a tri-state view of the mountains and valleys, this home and the surrounding 52-acre farm is the perfect complement to a busy vacation. Swim, row, or fish for trout in the stocked pond. Walk or cross-country ski the five kilometers of trails. Visit the chicks, pigs, cows, and oxen in the barn and pasture. Each of the three guest rooms is furnished with country treasures, oak antique beds, and marble-topped dressers. Breakfast is served in the dining room or on the porch. $60.

029. This 600-acre dairy farm is nestled in the valley, but an energetic guest can hike up the rolling hills to the farm pond to swim, fish, or just feast on the beautiful three-state view. Barn cats and calves delight visiting children. Guests are welcome to join the host family in the living room for conversation, TV, or perhaps playing the piano. The two cozy, paneled guest rooms have comfortable beds and are cool, clean, and quiet. Shared bath. Breakfast is served on antique china and may be enjoyed on the porch on a nice summer day. $45.

167. Accommodations in this newly renovated facility on 350 acres in the Berkshires include cozy rooms with private bath, one-, two-, and three-bedroom suites with living room and fireplace, kitchen, and bedroom with queen-size bed, and secluded fully equipped cottages with one, two, or three bedrooms, each with a fireplace. Heated pool. All are air-conditioned, with telephone and color TV. Children under 16 are welcome and stay free. Pets permitted in cottages. Continental breakfast. Smoking permitted. No resident pets, although there may be guests traveling with pets. $68-188.

Steep Acres Farm Bed and Breakfast

520 White Oaks Road, 01267
(413) 458-3774

Two miles from Williams College and the Williamstown Theatre Festival. A country home on a high knoll with spectacular views of the Berkshire Hills and Vermont's Green Mountains. Trout and swimming pond welcome guests on this farm's 52 acres adjacent to both the Appalachian and Long trails. Short distance to Tanglewood and Jacob's Pillow.

Hosts: Mary and Marvin Gangemi
Rooms: 4 (SB) $45-70
Full Breakfast
Credit Cards: None
Notes: 2, 5, 9, 10, 11, 12, 13

WINDSOR

Windfields Farm

154 Windsor Bush Road, Cummington, 01026
(413) 684-3786

Secluded 100-acre homestead on a dirt road surrounded by gardens, birds, fields, and forests, with swimming pond and hiking trails. Guests have private entrance, book-lined living room, fireplace, piano, and dining room. Family antiques, paintings, and flowers. Organic produce, eggs, maple syrup, raspberries, and wild blueberries enrich the hearty breakfasts. Near Tanglewood, Williams and Smith Colleges, and the new Norman Rockwell Museum. Closed March and April.

Hosts: Carolyn and Arnold Westwood
Rooms: 2 (SB) $45-60
Full Breakfast
Credit Cards: None
Notes: 2, 8 (over 12), 9, 11, 13

The Marlborough

WINTHROP

Bed and Breakfast Associates Bay Colony, Ltd.

P.O. Box 57166 Babson Park, Boston, 02157-0166
(617) 449-5302

IN100. This grand Victorian home has been decorated to reflect the lively good taste of the owner/hostess, a local realty agent. Those wishing to avoid the tunnel traffic leading into Boston from the airport can select this harbor view home on a quiet street just north of the city. Three large, attractive guest rooms provide varied bed sizes. On-street parking. $68.

WOODS HOLE

The Marlborough

320 Woods Hole Road, 02543
(508) 548-6218

The Marlborough is an intimate Cape Cod home with five guest rooms and cozy pool-side cottage, individually decorated with antiques and collectibles, each with private bath and air conditioning. The spacious wooded grounds include a pool and paddle tennis court. One and one-half miles to the Martha's Vineyard ferry. Enjoy easy day trips to Boston, Newport, Plymouth,

Provincetown, and Nantucket. Delightful breakfast. AAA rated three diamonds.

Host: Diana Smith
Rooms: 5 (PB) $85-125
Full Breakfast
Credit Cards: A, B, C
Notes: 2, 5, 9, 11, 14

WORTHINGTON

Hill Gallery

HC 65, Box 96, 01098
(413) 238-5914

On a mountaintop in the Hampshire Hills on 25 acres. Enjoy relaxed country living in an owner-built contemporary home with art gallery, fireplaces, and swimming pool. Self-contained cottage also available. Minimum stay of two nights on holidays.

Hosts: Ellen and Walter Korzec
Rooms: 2 (PB) $60
Full Breakfast
Credit Cards: None
Notes: 2, 5, 8 (over 5), 9, 10, 11, 12, 13

Nutmeg Bed and Breakfast Agency

P.O. Box 1117, West Hartford, CT 06107
(203) 236-6698

347. This Colonial-style, full service, country inn is on 23 wooded acres near the town

6 Pets welcome; 8 Children welcome; 9 Social drinking allowed; 10 Tennis available; 11 Swimming available; 12 Golf available; 13 Skiing available; 14 May be booked through travel agents.

common of a lovely New England village. The five spacious guest rooms each have private baths and are furnished with antiques. A common room for guests has a fireplace and TV. The dining room offers a full breakfast, as well as lunch and candlelight dinners. Picnic baskets and breakfast in bed are available. Hunting, fishing, golf, swimming, and cross-country skiing nearby. Country crafts gift and antique shop on premises. Children over 12 welcome. Smoking restricted.

YARMOUTH (BASS RIVER)

Golden Slumber Accommodations

640 Revere Beach Boulevard, Revere, 02151
(800) 892-3231; (617) 289-1053

Captain Farris House. The ambience of an 1845 sea captain's home graciously offers 1990s amenities. Although one finds antique furnishings around the king- and queen-size beds, the baths are graced with French sinks and Jacuzzi bathtubs. Most rooms offer private entrances; others boast decks and suites. Gourmet breakfasts are served under the chandelier in the dining room or in the open-air courtyard at the center of the house. Other meals are also available to guests. Full breakfast.

House Guests Cape Cod and the Islands

Box 1881, Orleans, 02653
(508) 896-7053; (800) 666-HOST (reservations)
FAX (508) 896-7054

93089. Oceanfront accommodations on a wonderful private beach on Nantucket Sound. The exterior appearance of this lodging establishment resembles a luxury apartment complex; however, each of its bed and breakfast theme rooms is uniquely appointed with fine furnishings. Rooms with full, partial, or no ocean view are available. All rooms have private baths and queen-size or double beds. Continental breakfast. $75-145.

YARMOUTH PORT

Bed and Breakfast Cape Cod

P.O. Box 341, West Hyannisport, 02672-0341
(508) 775-2772; FAX (508) 775-2884

71. This Cape Cod-style house built in 1800 has three bedrooms with private baths, one with a queen-size bed, one with a double, and one with twin beds. A parlor with a TV is available for guests. Enjoy a nice Continental breakfast. Walk to the freshwater pond or to the beach nearby, or simply relax on the pleasant grounds. $65-85.

75. An authentic 1809 Greek Revival host home is available with two bedrooms, each with a queen-size bed and private bath. Restored by its owners several years ago, the house is on the village green in the historic district and is on the National Register of Historic Places. Walk on 1.75 miles of nature trails. Visit the village historical society headquarters next door. Sit on the patio under giant trees and recall what life may have been like here several hundred years ago. Enjoy a great daily breakfast and village convenience, including fine restaurants, shops, and points of historic interest. No smoking. No children under 15. $95.

79. Built in 1710 in the heart of the village, this Cape Cod cottage offers the charm and quaintness that is pure Cape Cod. It is a delightful home offering three private-bath bedrooms, two with doubles and one with a pair of twins. The wonderful full breakfast is served each morning in the dining room or on the terrace. Walk to nature trails, restaurants, village shops, or the ocean on Cape Cod Bay, less than a mile away. Step back into history in this home now on the National Register of Historic Places. No smoking. $85-95.

The Colonial House Inn

Route 6A, 277 Main Street, 02675
(508) 362-4348; (800) 999-3416

NOTES: Credit cards accepted: A MasterCard; B Visa; C American Express; D Discover Card; E Diner's Club; F Other; 2 Personal checks accepted; 3 Lunch available; 4 Dinner available; 5 Open all year;

This registered historic landmark has antique-appointed guest rooms, private baths, and air conditioning. It features gracious hospitality, Old World charm, and traditional New England cuisine. Full liquor license, fine wines, and an indoor heated swimming pool. Lovely grounds, large deck, reading room, TV room, and Victorian living room. Close to nature trails, golf, tennis, antique shops, beaches, and shopping, space for wedding receptions and other functions, up to 135 people.

Rooms: 21 (PB) $50-85
Continental Breakfast
Credit Cards: A, B, C, D
Notes: 2, 3, 4, 5, 6, 7, 8, 9, 10, 11, 12, 13, 14

DESTINNATIONS
New England

P.O. Box 1173, Osterville, 02655
(508) 428-5600; FAX (508) 420-0565
(800) 333-4667 (reservations)

7201. This quintessential New England inn overlooks historic Route 6A, the Olde Kings Highway, one of America's most scenic byways. The Greek Revival building, circa 1812, contains six large guest rooms and suites, featuring wide-board floors, formal country decor, working fireplaces, and exquisite furnishings. All rooms but one have queen-size beds; the other has a double and a twin. Two full suites have private sitting rooms; one has its own screened-in porch, as does one junior suite. All have private bath, period wallpaper, antique quilts, and distinctive paintings. Common room with TV, as well as a dining room with a view of two-plus acres of lawns, gardens, and trees. Full breakfast. Smoking in guest rooms only. Children over ten; no pets. Open year-round. $115-160.

House Guests Cape Cod and the Islands

Box 1881, Orleans, 02653
(508) 896-7053; (800) 666-HOST (reservations)
FAX (508) 896-7054

93093. Built in 1812 as a private residence, this dwelling is the first in Yarmouth Port to have been designed by an architect. In 1983 the entire structure was restored and opened as a bed and breakfast inn. Each guest room has private bath; four have working fireplaces; two are suites and have private screened porches; and the decor and personal amenities in each room exhibit a great deal of attention to detail. Double, queen, and twin bedrooms are available. Full breakfast. No smoking in guest rooms. Children ten or older are welcome. Resident dog. Open year-round. $95-150. $10 for additional person.

Liberty Hill Inn on Cape Cod

77 Main Street, 02675
(508) 362-3976; (800) 821-3977

Billed as "an elegant country inn," Liberty Hill lives up to its claim. The 1825 Greek Revival mansion stands on a rise set back from Route 6A, in an attractive setting of trees and flower-edged lawns. Inside, rooms are large, with tall windows and high ceilings. They are romantically decorated with fine antiques, upholstered chairs, and thick carpets. The third-floor Waterford Room has a king-size bed, an oversized bath, and bay and garden views. Three are air-conditioned.

Hosts: Jack and Beth Flanagan
Rooms: 5 (PB) $75-125
Full Breakfast
Credit Cards: A, B, C
Notes: 2, 3, 4, 5, 7, 8, 9, 10, 11, 12, 14

Olde Captain's Inn

101 Main Street, 02675-1709
(508) 362-4496

Charming restored captain's home, in the historic district. Fine lodgings and superb Continental breakfast. Cable TV. The inn has a truly friendly, elegant atmosphere. Walk to shops and restaurants. No smoking in the guest rooms. Continental-plus breakfast is served. Stay two nights and the third night is free. Suites are available starting at $300 per week.

Hosts: Betsy O'Connor and Sven Tilly
Rooms: 5 (3 PB; 2 SB) $50-100
Continental Breakfast
Credit Cards: None
Notes: 2, 5, 9, 10, 11, 12

One Centre Street Inn

Route 6A and Old Kings Highway, 02675
(508) 362-8910

On the historic north side of Cape Cod, One Centre Street Inn is a short walk or bike ride from Gray's Beach, antique shops, bookstores, and fine restaurants. Newly redecorated in understated elegance, this inn offers guests the perfect combination of comfort and style. A sumptuous breakfast awaits guests with homemade granola, muffins, and scones, and such selections as blueberry lemon yogurt pancakes or Eggs Karina, an original creation of the inn's new owner.

Host: Karen Iannello
Rooms: 4 (2 PB; 2 SB) $75-110
Full Breakfast
Credit Cards: A, B
Notes: 2, 5, 8 (over 11), 11, 12, 14

The Village Inn

92 Main Street, Route 6A, P.O. Box 1, 02675
(508) 362-3182

The Village Inn

This charming sea captain's home built in 1795 has been an inn since 1946. Noted for cordial hospitality and comfortable rooms with private baths. Public rooms, screened porch, and shaded lawn. The inn is within easy walking distance of Cape Cod Bay, excellent restaurants, and antique shops. Nonsmoking.

Hosts: Mac and Esther Hickey
Rooms: 10 (8 PB; 2 SB) $40-85
Full Breakfast or Continental Breakfast
Credit Cards: A, B
Notes: 2, 5, 6, 8, 9, 10, 11, 12, 14

Wedgewood Inn

Wedgewood Inn

83 Main Street, 02675
(508) 362-5157

Situated in the historic area of Cape Cod, the inn is on the National Register of Historic Places and has been featured in *Country Inns of America*. Near beaches, art galleries, antique shops, golf, boating, and fine restaurants. Fireplaces and private screened porches.

Hosts: Milt and Gerrie Graham
Rooms: 6 (PB) $105-145
Full Breakfast
Credit Cards: A, B, C, E
Notes: 2, 5, 7 (limited), 8 (over 10), 9, 10, 11, 12, 14

NOTES: Credit cards accepted: A MasterCard; B Visa; C American Express; D Discover Card; E Diner's Club; F Other; 2 Personal checks accepted; 3 Lunch available; 4 Dinner available; 5 Open all year;

Michigan

The Lodge at Yarrow

10499 North 48th Street, 49012
(616) 731-2090

Rest, relax, retreat, and renew! Yarrow is a unique retreat and conference center on 350 acres of woods, water, and wetlands between Battle Creek and Kalamazoo, Michigan. There are 25 secluded guest rooms, sitting porches, TV with VCR, air conditioning, and private baths. The main lodge overlooks the Potawatomi Valley and was designed to emulate an American Gothic farmhouse. This is where guests gather to converse and dine. The grounds offer hiking trails, biking, canoeing, cross-country skiing, and fishing; golfing nearby.

Rooms: 25 (PB) $99-129
Continental Breakfast
Credit Cards: A, B
Notes: 2, 3, 4, 5, 8 (limited), 9, 11, 12, 13

BATTLE CREEK

Greencrest Manor

6174 Halbert Road, 49017
(616) 962-8633

To experience Greencrest is to step back in time to a way of life that is rare today. From the moment of entrance through iron gates, guests will be mesmerized. This French Normandy mansion on the highest elevation of St. Mary's Lake is constructed of sandstone, slate, and copper. Formal gardens, fountains, and garden architecture. Chosen by Country Inns as one of the "top twelve inns" in North America for 1992. Air=conditioned.

Hosts: Kathy and Tom Van Doff
Rooms: 8 (6 PB; 2 SB) $75-170
Continental Breakfast
Credit Cards: A, B, C
Notes: 2, 5, 8, 9, 10, 12, 13

BAY CITY

Clements Inn

1712 Center Avenue M-25, 48708
(517) 894-4600

This 1886 Queen Anne Victorian home features six fireplaces, magnificent woodwork, an oak staircase, amber-colored glass windows, working gas lamps, organ pipes, two claw foot tubs, and a third-floor ballroom. Each of the six bedrooms includes cable television, telephone, a private bath, and air conditioning. Special features include in-room gas fireplaces, an in-room whirlpool tub, and the 1200 square-foot, fully furnished (including kitchen) Alfred Lord Tennyson Suite.

Hosts: Brian and Karen Hepp
Rooms: 6 (PB) $70-125
Continental Breakfast
Credit Cards: A, B, C, D
Notes: 2, 5, 8, 10, 12, 14

Stonehedge Inn Bed and Breakfast

924 Center Avenue (M-25), 48708
(517) 894-4342

Built by a lumber baron, this 1889 English Tudor home is indeed an elegant journey into the past. Original features include nine fireplaces, stained-glass windows, speaking tubes, and even a warming oven. Its magnificent open foyer with its grand oak stair-

6 Pets welcome; 7 Smoking allowed; 8 Children welcome; 9 Social drinking allowed; 10 Tennis available; 11 Swimming available; 12 Golf available; 13 Skiing available; 14 May be booked through travel agents.

Michigan

Calumet
Laurium
Chassell
26
41
41
Marquette
41
45
2
2
28
2
McMillan
75
Mackinac Island
31
Bay View
Northport
Glen Arbor
Empire
31
Bellaire
Suttons Bay
Elk Rapids
Traverse City
131
Gaylord
23
Black River
West Branch
75
Onekama
Manistee
Ludington
Pentwater
31
Cadillac
Harrison
27
10
Mt. Pleasant
Port Austin
25
Bay City
Saginaw
Frankenmuth
Lexington
94
69
Rochester Hills
75
Wat-ford
96
23
12
Brooklyn
Blissfield
Owosso
69
Lansing
27
94
Hillsdale
12
Mendon
131
Coldwater
Jones
Grand Haven
Holland
196
Saugatuck
Fennville
South Haven
St. Joseph
Union Pier
94
31
Grand Rapids
96
Dimondale
Plainwell
Kalamazoo
Augusta
Battle Creek
131
75
31
Michigan

case leads to eight bedrooms. Ideal for small weddings, parties, and meetings. Corporate rates Sunday through Thursday.

Host: Ruth Koerber
Rooms: 7 (S3B) $75-85
Continental Plus Breakfast
Credit Cards: A, B, C, D
Notes: 2, 5, 8, 9, 14

The Florence

BAY VIEW

The Florence

317 Park Avenue, P.O. Box 1031, 49770
(616) 348-3322

Step back in time in this 1878 summer home overlooking the heart of Bay View, a National Historic Landmark on the shores of Little Traverse Bay. Stroll through winding streets of a village that comes to life only a few months each year. Unwind on the flower-laden wraparound porch and in rooms filled with antiques and colorful charm. Experience an elegant gourmet breakfast and the Bay View Summer Music Festival. Open May through October.

Hosts: Paul and Elizabeth Nelson
Rooms: 8 (PB) $65-120
Full Breakfast
Credit Cards: A, B
Notes: 2, 8, 9, 10, 11, 12, 14

BELLAIRE

Grass River Bed and Breakfast

5615 Grass River Road, 49615
(616) 533-6041

Thirty miles north of Traverse City, this home offers modern comfort in a natural environment. It is tucked in the woods of Antrim County on a chain of lakes, and the house is just steps from its dock on the Grass River. Frequently visited by a variety of wildlife. Soothe aches and pains away in the hot tub or relax in the glass sunroom. Many activities and two ski resorts are just a few miles away. Open May 1 through November 1.

Host: Harriett Beach
Rooms: 3 (PB) $85-95
Continental Breakfast
Credit Cards: A, B, C, D
Notes: 2, 9, 11, 12, 13, 14

BLACK RIVER

Silver Creek Lodge Bed and Breakfast

4361 U.S. 23 South, 48721
(517) 471-2198

On 60 beautiful acres, this comfortably decorated four-bedroom home with cathedral ceilings offers lots of wildlife, hiking, cross-country skiing in winter, and down home hospitality. Just minutes from golfing, swimming, and fine restaurants; there is something for everyone. A full breakfast with homemade bread, muffins, and jams awaits guests.

Hosts: Larry and Gladys Farlow
Rooms: 4 (S2B) $55
Full Breakfast
Credit Cards: None
Notes: 2, 5, 8 (over 5), 9, 10, 11, 12

NOTES: Credit cards accepted: A MasterCard; B Visa; C American Express; D Discover Card; E Diner's Club; F Other; 2 Personal checks accepted; 3 Lunch available; 4 Dinner available; 5 Open all year; 6 Pets welcome; 7 Smoking allowed; 8 Children welcome; 9 Social drinking allowed; 10 Tennis available; 11 Swimming available; 12 Golf available; 13 Skiing available; 14 May be booked through travel agents.

BLISSFIELD

H.D. Ellis Inn

415 West Adrian Street, 49228
(517) 486-3155

This beautifully restored 1883 Victorian red brick house is a Michigan historic site. It is across the street from the 1851 Hathaway House Restaurant. Ellis Inn has four air-conditioned guest rooms with private baths, TV, and phones. All are tastefully appointed in period antiques. Bicycles are provided for exploring the pleasures of Blissfield. Single occupancy business rates available. No smoking.

Hosts: Christine Webster and Frank Seely
Rooms: 4 (PB) $60-80
Credit Cards: A, B, C
Notes: 2, 3, 4, 5, 8, 9, 10, 11, 12, 14

BROOKLYN

The Chicago Street Inn

219 Chicago Street, 49230
(517) 592-3888

An 1880s Queen Anne Victorian, in the heart of the Irish Hills. Furnished with family and area antiques. Antiquing, hiking, biking, swimming, shops, museums, and more are available. Area of quaint villages. Three Jacuzzi suites available.

Hosts: Karen and Bill Kerr
Rooms: 5 (PB) $65-130
Full Breakfast
Continental Breakfast
Credit Cards: A, B
Notes: 2, 5, 7, 9, 10, 11, 12

CADILLAC

American Inn Bed and Breakfast

312 East Cass, 49601
(616) 779-9000

This turn-of-the-century home radiates Cadillac's lumber era with original wood carvings, stained glass, antiques, and hardwood floors. Tastefully appointed guest rooms with private baths, cable TV, hot tub, and sauna. Luxurious suite with private spa and spiral stairway to walk-out deck. Walk to lakes and downtown. Corporate rates.

Hosts: Mike and Cathy Feister
Rooms: 5 (PB) $45-150
Continental Breakfast
Credit Cards: A, B, C
Notes: 2, 5, 8, 9, 10, 11, 12, 13, 14

American Inn

CALUMET

Calumet House

1159 Calumet Avenue, P.O. Box 126, 49913
(906) 337-1936

The Calumet House is on the scenic, historic Keweenaw Peninsula. The house was built by the Calumet and Hecla Mining Company, circa 1895. It features original woodwork and antique furniture. Breakfast is served in the formal dining room, which has the original butler's pantry. Near Michigan Technological University and Suomi College.

Hosts: George and Rose Chivses
Rooms: 2 (SB) $25-30

NOTES: Credit cards accepted: A MasterCard; B Visa; C American Express; D Discover Card; E Diner's Club; F Other; 2 Personal checks accepted; 3 Lunch available; 4 Dinner available; 5 Open all year;

Full Breakfast
Credit Cards: None
Notes: 2, 5, 9, 10, 11, 12, 13

CHASSELL

Palosaari's Rolling Acres Bed and Breakfast

Route 1, Box 354 North Entry Road, 49916
(906) 523-4947

Operating dairy farm where guests can see cows milked and calves fed. Farm is third-generation run. Three comfortable guest rooms are available. Off-road, secure parking. Visit with hosts, or experience the history in the surrounding town. Guests are made welcome with evening coffee and goodies. A full country breakfast is served. Hosts want guests to feel like they are at a home away from home.

Hosts: Evey and Cliff Palosaari
Rooms: 3 (SB) $40
Full Breakfast
Credit Cards: None
Notes: 2, 5, 8, 11, 13

COLDWATER

Batavia Inn

1824 West Chicago Road, US 12, 49036
(517) 278-5146

This 1872 Italianate country inn with original massive woodwork and high ceilings offers a restful charm. Seasonal decorations are a speciality, and an in-ground pool and mini-golf are available for guests to enjoy in the summer. Guests are pampered with evening turn-down and gourmet breakfast. Antique and discount shopping nearby. Recreation and acres of wildlife trails nearby.

Host: E. Fred Marquardt
Rooms: 5 (PB) $59-99
Full Breakfast
Credit Cards: A, B
Notes: 11, 12, 13

Chicago Pike Inn

Chicago Pike Inn

215 East Chicago Street, 49036
(517) 279-8744

Turn-of-the-century renovated Colonial mansion adorned with antiques from the Victorian era. Eight guest rooms with private baths, two with Jacuzzi, individually decorated for pleasure and comfort. Formal dining room, library, and reception room featuring sweeping cherry staircase, parquet floors, and stained-glass window. Full country breakfast and seasonal refreshments served. Come and enjoy the restfulness of the inn.

Host: Rebecca Schultz
Rooms: 8 (PB) $80-165
Full Breakfast
Credit Cards: A, B, C
Notes: 2, 5, 7 (limited), 10, 12, 13

DIMONDALE

Bannick's Bed and Breakfast

4608 Michigan Road, 48821
(517) 646-0224

This large ranch-style home features attractive decor with stained-glass entrances. Almost three rural acres offer a quiet escape from the fast pace of the workaday world.

6 Pets welcome; 8 Children welcome; 9 Social drinking allowed; 10 Tennis available; 11 Swimming available; 12 Golf available; 13 Skiing available; 14 May be booked through travel agents.

On a main highway (M99) five miles from Lansing and close neighbor to Michigan State University.

Hosts: Pat and Jim Bannick
Rooms: 2 (SB) $25-35
Full Breakfast
Credit Cards: None
Notes: 5, 8, 11, 12, 13

ELK RAPIDS

Cairn House
Bed and Breakfast

8160 Cairn Highway, 49629
(616) 264-8994

Built in the style of an 1880s Colonial home, and 15 minutes north of Traverse City, and two miles from Grand Traverse Bay and Port of Elk Rapids. Furnished to make guests feel at home. Full breakfast served in the nook in the all-oak kitchen. Boat trailer parking available. Three rooms with private baths.

Hosts: Roger and Mary Vandervort
Rooms: 3 (PB) $65
Full Breakfast
Credit Cards: None
Notes: 2, 5, 8, 9, 10, 11, 12, 13

EMPIRE

Empire House
Bed and Breakfast

11015 La Core, South, P.O. Box 203, 49630-0203
(616) 326-5524

This 19th-century farmhouse is in the beautiful Sleeping Bear Dunes Lakeshore area. Four rooms with outside entrances are available for guests, and guests are welcome to use the large screened porch. Separate two-bedroom apartment available weekly. A quiet, homey atmosphere, fresh-ground coffee, and wonderful extended continental breakfast make this bed and breakfast worth visiting. Close to the beaches of Lake Michigan, golf, tennis, hik-

ing trails in the summer, and skiing trails in the winter.

Hosts: Harry and Rosemary Friend
Rooms: 4 (1 PB; 3 SB) $46.80-52
Continental Breakfast
Credit Cards: None
Notes: 2, 5, 6 (limited), 10, 11, 12, 13

FENNVILLE

The Crane House

6051 124th Avenue (M-89), 49408
(616) 561-6931

Take a step back in time at the Crane House. A time of simplicity, relaxation, and grandma's featherbeds. This 1870 family farmhouse is elegantly primitive with hand-stenciling, handmade quilts, and antique furnishings. The house sits on a 300-acre family-run fruit farm, and is just minutes from Saugatuck, Holland, and South Haven. Come visit and relax in an atmosphere of yesteryear. Featured in *Country Living*, August 1992.

Hosts: Nancy Crane McFarland and Lue Crane
Rooms: 5 (3 PB; 2 SB) $65-95
Full Breakfast
Credit Cards: A, B, C, D
Notes: 2, 5, 8, 9, 11, 12, 13, 14

The Crane House

Hidden Pond
Bed and Breakfast

5975 128th Avenue, 49408
(616) 561-2491

Hidden Pond Bed and Breakfast is a quiet retreat set on 28 acres. Full gourmet breakfast included. Sunny breakfast porch, fireplace, library, and 60-foot deck for guests' exclusive use. Behind the house is a ravine with a pond, the perfect spot to relax and watch the wildlife. This lovely retreat is near the beaches of Lake Michigan, the boutiques of Saugatuck, and the winery and cider mill in Fennville.

Hosts: Larry and Priscilla Fuerst
Rooms: 2 (PB) $64-110
Full Breakfast
Credit Cards: None
Notes: 2, 5, 9, 10, 11, 12, 13, 14

Hidden Pond

The Kingsley House

626 West Main Street, 49408
(616) 561-6425

An elegant Victorian inn on the edge of Fennville, near Saugatuck, Holland, and South Haven. The guest rooms are decorated in Victorian elegance. Honeymoon suite with Jacuzzi and fireplace. Beaches, shopping, fine dining, and a playhouse theater nearby. The Allegan State Forest, with miles of nature trails, is enjoyable to explore. Bicycles and horse and buggy rides to the lake or winery available. Country lover's delight. Featured in *Innsider* magazine, *Great Lakes Getaway*. Chosen one of the top 50 inns in America by *Inn Times*.

Hosts: David and Shirley Witt
Rooms: 7 (PB) $50-125
Full Breakfast

Credit Cards: A, B, C, D
Notes: 2, 5, 9, 10, 11, 12, 13, 14 (limited)

FRANKENMUTH

Bavarian Town Bed and Breakfast

206 Beyerlein Street, 48734
(517) 652-8057

Beautifully redecorated rooms in a Cape Cod dwelling just three blocks off of Main Street in the most popular tourist town of Michigan. Quiet residential district. Air conditioning. Bilingual hosts are direct descendants of original German settlers of Frankenmuth in 1845. Willing to share hospitality hour and information of Frankenmuth including historic St. Lorenz Lutheran Church. Full breakfast includes fresh fruit, baked goods, and hot entrees. Private toilet and sink. Rooms share a shower. Beautiful yard.

Hosts: Kathy and Louie Weiss
Rooms: 2 (PB) $45-55
Full Breakfast
Credit Cards: None
Notes: 2, 5, 7, 8, 9, 10, 11, 12

Bed and Breakfast at The Pines

327 Ardussi Street, 48734
(517) 652-9019

"Come as a stranger—leave as a friend." Frankenmuth, a Bavarian village, is Michigan's number-one tourist attraction. This

The Pines

6 Pets welcome; 8 Children welcome; 9 Social drinking allowed; 10 Tennis available; 11 Swimming available; 12 Golf available; 13 Skiing available; 14 May be booked through travel agents.

ranch-style home is within walking distance of tourist areas and famous restaurants. Bedrooms tastefully decorated with heirloom quilts, antique accents, and ceiling fans. Enjoy homemade breads and rolls as part of the continental-plus breakfast. Recipes shared. No smoking preferred.

Hosts: Richard and Donna Hodge
Rooms: 3 (1 PB; 2 SB) $30-45
Continental Breakfast
Credit Cards: None
Notes: 2, 5

GAYLORD

Heritage House

521 East Main Street, 49735
(517) 732-1199

Enjoy warmth and hospitality by the fireside in this nearly 100-year-old farmhouse featuring an eclectic collection of old and new furnishings, many handmade. Within walking distance of downtown Gaylord. The old fashioned full breakfast and homemade goodies are served in dining room overlooking the backyard and bird feeder.

Hosts: Patricia Teal and Phyllis Erb
Rooms: 5 (S2B) $55-65
Full Breakfast
Credit Cards: None
Notes: 2, 8, 9, 11, 12, 13

GLEN ARBOR

Sylvan Inn

6680 Western Avenue, 49636
(616) 334-4333

The Sylvan Inn is a beautifully decorated historic landmark building in the heart of the Sleeping Bear Dunes National Lakeshore. Its easy access to Lake Michigan and other inland lakes makes a stay at the Sylvan Inn a unique experience. Closed November, March, and April.

Hosts: Jenny and Bill Olson
Rooms: 14 (7 PB; 7 SB) $60-120
Continental Breakfast

Credit Cards: A, B
Notes: 2, 8 (over 7), 10, 11, 12, 13, 14

Sylvan Inn

GRAND HAVEN

Boyden House Inn Bed and Breakfast

301 South Fifth Street, 49417
(616) 846-3538

Built in 1874, this Victorian-style inn is in the heart of Grand Haven within walking distance to shopping, restaurants, beach, and the boardwalk. Some rooms have fireplaces and balconies. Central air conditioning. Great kitchen and two common rooms are available for guests to use. Full homemade breakfast served in the beautiful dining room.

Hosts: Corrie and Berend Snoeyer
Rooms: 5 (PB) $65-85, Suites + 2 person whirlpool baths $110
Full Breakfast
Credit Cards: A, B, C, D
Notes: 2, 5, 8, 9, 10, 11, 12, 13

Harbor House Inn

114 South Harbor Drive, 49417
(800) 841-0610

Built in 1987, this luxurious Victorian-style inn overlooks Grand Haven's historic Lake Michigan harbor. Seventeen rooms, all offering a private bath and air conditioning.

NOTES: Credit cards accepted: A MasterCard; B Visa; C American Express; D Discover Card; E Diner's Club; F Other; 2 Personal checks accepted; 3 Lunch available; 4 Dinner available; 5 Open all year;

Many rooms have fireplaces and whirlpool tubs. Two common rooms are ideal for meetings. The beach, shops, and restaurants are only a short walk away. Homemade breakfast buffet. A separate cottage is also available.

Hosts: Emily Ehlert, Innkeeper; Tiiu Arrak, Assistant Innkeeper
Rooms: 17 (PB) $85-175
Continental Breakfast
Credit Cards: A, B
Notes: 2, 5, 9, 11, 12, 13

Village Park Bed and Breakfast

60 West Park Street, Fruitport, 49415
(616) 865-6289

Overlooking the welcoming waters of Spring Lake and Village Park where guests can picnic, play tennis, or use the pedestrian bike path and boat launch. Spring Lake with access to Lake Michigan. Relaxing common area with fireplace; guests may also relax on the decks and in hot tub. Historic setting of mineral springs health resort. Tradition continues with "Wellness Weekend" special package including complimentary massage, use of exercise facility, programs on stress management, and creative visualization. Serving the Grand Haven and

Village Park

Muskegon areas. Close to Hoffmaster Park and Gillette Sand Dune Nature Center.

Hosts: John and Virginia Hewett
Rooms: 6 (PB) $50-90
Full or Continental Plus Breakfast
Credit Cards: A, B
Notes: 2, 5, 8, 10, 11, 12, 13, 14

GRAND RAPIDS

Fountain Hill Bed and Breakfast

222 Fountain Northeast, 49503
(616) 458-6621

This 1874 classic Italianate home overlooking downtown Grand Rapids is in the historic Heritage Hill district and cultural center. Architectural elegance, high ceilings, elaborate plaster details, circular staircase set off by wonderful wall coverings, lighting fixtures, and furnishings. Surrounded by delightful gardens, perfect for guests traveling for business or pleasure. Cable TV, VCRs, telephones, air conditioning,, Jacuzzis, copy and FAX machines.

Hosts: Sally Coburn and Chuck Carter
Rooms: 4 (PB) $60-125
Full Breakfast
Credit Cards: A, B, C, E
Notes: 2, 5, 8, 9, 10, 11, 12, 13

HARRISON

Carriage House Inn

1515 Grant Avenue, 48625
(517) 539-1300; FAX (517) 539-5661

The Carriage House Inn is nestled in a 127-acre pine plantation, overlooking Budd Lake, offering guests intimate accommodations. The seven guest rooms are furnished with country classics and antiques. All rooms have private baths, most having whirlpool tubs, color TV/VCR, telephone, coffee maker, refrigerator, and air conditioning. Executive retreat accommodations, private retreats, and reception and training facilities are also available. Amenities and

6 Pets welcome; 8 Children welcome; 9 Social drinking allowed; 10 Tennis available; 11 Swimming available; 12 Golf available; 13 Skiing available; 14 May be booked through travel agents.

attention make the Carriage House Inn a perfect place to spend an "Escape to the North" in any season.

Hosts: John and Connie Mlinarcik
Rooms: 7 (PB) $75-125
Continental Breakfast
Credit Cards: A, B
Notes: 2, 5, 8, 10, 11, 12, 13

HILLSDALE

Shadowlawn Manor Bed and Breakfast

84 Union Street, 49242-1332
(517) 437-2367

A brick Victorian built in 1863, this bed and breakfast has lots of gingerbread trim, a spacious entrance hall, and a small iron fireplace that extends into the parlor providing warm, even heat for the area. Rooms are in various period styles, including Victorian, turn-of-the-century, 1920s, and rattan and white wicker bedrooms. Five blocks from Hillsdale College and three blocks from downtown.

Host: Art Young
Rooms: 4 (PB) $63
Continental Breakfast
Credit Cards: A, B, D
Notes: 2, 5, 9, 11, 12, 14

HOLLAND

Dutch Colonial Inn

560 Central Avenue, 49423
(616) 396-3664

An award-winning Dutch Colonial inn built in 1928 features elegant decor with 1930s furnishings and lovely heirloom antiques. All guest rooms have tiled private baths, some with whirlpool tub for two. Honeymoon suites available for that "special getaway." Attractions include excellent shopping, Hope College, bike paths, ski trails, and Michigan's finest beaches. Business people welcome; corporate rates available. Air conditioning. Open year-round

with special Christmas touches. Dutch hospitality at its finest.

Hosts: Bob and Pat Elenbaas; Diana Klungel
Rooms: 5 (PB) $60-125
Full Breakfast
Credit Cards: A, B, C, D
Notes: 2, 5, 10, 11, 12

Dutch Colonial Inn

JONES

The Sanctuary at Wildwood

58138 M-40 North, 49061
(616) 244-5910

Executive retreat on over 94 acres of woods and meadows in a parklike setting surrounded on three sides by State game area. Sandhill cranes, great blue herons, and lots of deer share the grounds with the guests. Each suite has a private deck, Jacuzzi, TV, and fireplace and a unique decor which incorporates the natural beauty of the surroundings. Public rooms include the gathering room, the library, and the great room. Dining is on the deck overlooking the pond and in the formal dining room. Lavish continental buffet includes fresh-baked breads and homemade preserves. Nearby wineries offer tasting. Arts and crafts malls, and antiques are also nearby.

Hosts: Dick and Dolly Buerkle, Owners; and Judy
  Krupka, Manager
Rooms: 11 (PB) $169-179
Continental Breakfast
Credit Cards: A, B, C, D
Notes: 5, 7, 9, 11, 12, 13 (cross-country), 14

NOTES: Credit cards accepted: A MasterCard; B Visa; C American Express; D Discover Card; E Diner's Club; F Other; 2 Personal checks accepted; 3 Lunch available; 4 Dinner available; 5 Open all year;

KALAMAZOO

Hall House

106 Thompson Street, 49006
(616) 343-2500; FAX (616) 373-5706

Hall House is adjacent to the lovely hillside campus at Kalamazoo College, five blocks from the city. This 1923 Georgian Revival home awaits guests' arrival. Exceptional craftsmanship, warmth, and elegance abound. Spacious rooms with private baths, TV, telephones, robes, and full breakfast weekends. Inquire about special wedding and anniversary packages.

Hosts: Liz and Bob Costello
Rooms: 6 (PB) $69-95
Continental and Full Breakfasts
Credit Cards: A, B, C, D
Notes: 2, 5, 9, 10, 11, 12, 13, 14

LANSING

Maplewood Bed and Breakfast

15945 Wood Road, 48906-1746
(517) 372-7775

Experience the warmth and charm of the Maplewood Bed and Breakfast. Three porches and picnic area offer guests a breathtaking view of the countryside. Maplewood Bed and Breakfast is on three acres of lawn, gardens, and trees. The inn looks back to the turn of the century with its original oak pocket doors and woodwork, French doors, and winding oak stairway to the guest rooms. Close to many activities at the university and downtown.

Host: Pat Bunce
Rooms: 3 (SB) $50-60
Full Breakfast
Credit Cards: A, B
Notes: 2, 5, 8, 9, 10, 11, 12

LAURIUM

Laurium Manor Inn and Victorian Hall

320 Tamarack Street, 49913-2141
(906) 337-2549

Opulent 1908 mansion in the middle of the Keweenaw Peninsula with 42 rooms in 13,000 square feet of accommodations. Some unique features include hand-painted murals; embossed and gilded elephant hide and leather wall coverings; hand-carved oak fireplaces and staircases; built-in wall-size oak, tile, and marble ice box; gilded tile and marble fireplaces; and 1,000 square feet of tiled porch. Activities and attractions nearby include skiing, snowmobiling, scuba diving, cycling, antiques, autumn colors, and ghost towns. Guided tours daily 12:00 to 3:00 P.M., May through November, three dollars..

Hosts: Julie and Dave Sprenger
Rooms: 21 (12 PB; 9 SB) $49-109
Continental Breakfast
Credit Cards; A, B, D
Notes: 2, 5, 8, 9, 10, 12, 13, 14

Laurium Manor Inn

LEXINGTON

Centennial Bed and Breakfast

5774 Main Street, 48450
(313) 359-8762

This 1879 Michigan historic home on Lake Huron features romantic four-poster beds, elegant antique-furnished rooms, and lovely lawn and gardens with fountain. Gourmet breakfast. A stay at Centennial is always special, and great pleasure is taken in sharing a piece of the romantic past.

6 Pets welcome; 8 Children welcome; 9 Social drinking allowed; 10 Tennis available; 11 Swimming available; 12 Golf available; 13 Skiing available; 14 May be booked through travel agents.

Hosts: Dilla and Dan Miller
Rooms: 4 (PB) $60-65
Full Breakfast
Credit Cards: A, B
Notes: 2, 5, 9, 10, 11, 12

LUDINGTON

The Inn at Ludington

701 East Ludington Avenue, 49431
(616) 845-7055

Elegant accommodations in an 1889 Queen Anne Victorian mansion, appointed with treasured antiques and cherished collectibles. Fireplace rooms, bridal suite, and family suite. "On the avenue" close to shopping, fine dining, and miles of Lake Michigan's sandy beaches. Early morning coffee and homemade muffins in the parlor are followed by a sumptuous breakfast in the dining room. Murder mysteries, sweetheart weekend, harvest festival, and a Dickens Christmas weekend in December. Dinner by prior arrangement.

Host: Diane Shields
Rooms: 6 (PB) $60-85
Full Breakfast
Credit Cards: A, B, C
Notes: 2, 3, 5, 7 (limited), 8, 9, 10, 11, 12, 13, 14

MACKINAC ISLAND

Cloghaun

P.O. Box 203, 49757
(906) 847-3885

Cloghaun, a large Victorian home built in 1884, is close to shops, restaurants, and ferry lines. The name *Cloghaun* is Gaelic and means "land of little stones." Built by Thomas and Bridgett Donnelly to house their large Irish family, the Cloghaun represents the elegance and ambience of a bygone era. The house is still owned by their descendants and has undergone recent renovations to bring it back to its original elegance.

Host: James Bond
Rooms: 10 (8 PB; 2 SB) $50-95
Continental Breakfast
Credit Cards: None
Notes: 2, 8, 9, 10, 11, 12

MANISTEE

1879 E.E. Douville House

111 Pine Street, 49660
(616) 723-8654

This Victorian home, completed with lumber from nearby forests, features ornate pine woodwork hand-carved by area craftsman. Interior wooden shutters on windows, a soaring staircase, and elaborate archways with pocket doors are also original to the house. Antiques and collectibles fill the home. Ceiling fans in every room. Manistee Victorian Village, Riverwalk to Lake Michigan, and historic buildings are nearby.

Hosts: Barbara and Bill Johnson
Rooms: 3 (SB) $43-53
Continental Breakfast
Credit Cards: None
Notes: 2, 5, 9, 10, 11, 12, 13

MARQUETTE

Michigamme Lake Lodge

2403 U.S. 41 West, 49855
(906) 225-1393; (906) 339-4400

A historic landmark, this two-story grand lodge is on the shore of Lake Michigamme. Log construction built in 1934, surrounded by birch trees, flower gardens, and the Peshekee River. Large room to gather in with a two-and-one-half-story fireplace. All decorated rooms have down quilts. Gift and antique shop on property. Thirty miles west of Marquette. Sandy beach, swimming, fishing, hiking trails, biking, and guided historical tour of the area available.

Host: Linda Stabile
Rooms: 9 (3 PB; 6 SB) $100-125
Full Breakfast
Credit Cards: A, B
Notes: 2, 8, 10, 11, 12

McMILLAN

Helmer House Inn

Rural Route 3, County Road 417, 49853
(906) 586-3204

The Helmer House, designated a Michigan historic site, was built in the late 1800s by a minister as a mission site for early settlers. It offers five quaint guest rooms furnished with original and authentic antiques. Dining on the old porch specializes in down-to-earth, home-cooked meals. Less than two hours from upper peninsula attractions. Children welcome. Smoking permitted.

Host: Kathleen Plesscher
Rooms: 5 (SB) $40-55
Credit Cards: None
Full Breakfast
Notes: 2, 4, 7, 8, 9, 11, 12, 14

MENDON

Mendon Country Inn
440 West Main Street, P.O. Box 98, 49072
(616) 496-8132

The historic Wakeman House, now known as the Mendon Country Inn, was originally built in 1843 and rebuilt out of brick in 1873 by Adams Wakeman. Eight-foot windows, high ceilings, and spacious rooms complement the walnut spiral staircase in the lobby. There are numerous antique shops, a local Amish settlement, flea markets, golf, and wineries nearby. There is also canoeing at the inn. Hosts endeavor to provide guests with the comforts of home, the friendliness of small-town life, a great continental deluxe breakfast, and a truly enjoyable stay.

Hosts: Dick and Dolly Buerkle
Rooms: 18 (PB) $50-150
Continental Breakfast
Credit Cards: A, B, C, D
Notes: 2, 7 (limited), 8 (over 12), 10, 12, 13, 14

MT. PLEASANT

Country Chalet Bed and Breakfast
723 South Meridian Road, 48858
(517) 772-9259

The Country Chalet is a comfortable Bavarian-style home atop a hill surrounded by rolling wooded farmland, 18 acres of pastures, and woods and ponds that are playgrounds to wild animals and birds. Guests in the three upper level bedrooms share a living/dining room with fireplace, and all guests are welcome to enjoy the chalet's sauna, game room, and fireplace in the lounge. For those who love to watch good college competition, Central Michigan University is less than a ten-minute drive from the chalet.

Hosts: Ron and Carolyn Lutz
Rooms: 3 (SB) $49-59
Full Breakfast
Credit Cards: None
Notes: 2, 5, 8, 9, 10, 11, 12

NORTHPORT

Birch Brook
310 West Third Street, 49670
(616) 386-5188

A charming Colonial-style home set on three well-groomed acres surrounded by a sparkling brook. Tastefully decorated with lovely antiques. Enjoy the view of the brook from all bedrooms and two decks. Eat an extended continental breakfast in the formal dining room or in the adjoining greenhouse. Guided cross-country skiing provided during the winter.

Hosts: Lyn and George Anderson
Rooms: 3 (1 PB; 2 SB) $55-65
Continental Breakfast
Credit Cards: None
Notes: 2, 5, 8, 9, 10, 11, 12, 13

ONEKAMA

Lake Breeze House
5089 Main Street, 49675-0301
(616) 889-4969

Two-story frame house overlooking Portage Lake, where guests share the family bath, living room, and breakfast room. Each room has

6 Pets welcome; 8 Children welcome; 9 Social drinking allowed; 10 Tennis available; 11 Swimming available; 12 Golf available; 13 Skiing available; 14 May be booked through travel agents.

its own special charm of family antiques. Come relax and enjoy the back porch and the sounds of the babbling creek with a full breakfast. Reservations and deposit required.

Hosts: Bill and Donna Erickson
Rooms: 3 (2 shared, 1-½ bath) $55-65
Full Breakfast
Credit Cards: None
Notes: 2, 8, 10, 11, 12, 13

OWOSSO

R&R Farm-Ranch

Hospitality Home
Home Away from Home
308 East Hibbard Road, 48867
(517) 723-3232; (517) 723-2553

A newly remodeled farmhouse from the early 1900s, the Rossman's ranch sits on 150 acres overlooking the Maple River Valley. Rossman's large concrete circular drive and white board fences lead to stables of horses and cattle. Guests may use the family parlor, game room, and fireplace or stroll about the gardens and pastures along the river. Breakfast is served in the dining room or outside on the deck. Children and pets are welcome. No smoking. Central air conditioning.

Hosts: Carl and Jeanne Rossman
Rooms: 2 (SB) $45-55
Continental Breakfast
Credit Cards: None
Notes: 2, 5, 6, 8, 13 (cross-country)

PENTWATER

Historic Nickerson Inn

262 West Lowell, Box 109, 49449
(616) 869-6731

Since 1914, historic Nickerson Inn and Restaurant has been a place of charm and hospitality. Completely renovated in 1991. Ten guest rooms all with private baths and air conditioning, plus two Jacuzzi suites with gas log fireplaces and balconies overlooking Lake Michigan, which is one block away. A quaint village of small shops, four marinas, and beautiful white sandy beaches.

Hosts: Harry and Gretchen Shiparski
Rooms: 12 (PB) $70-150
Serving breakfast, lunch, and dinner
Credit Cards: A, B
Notes: 2, 4, 5, 8 (over 12), 9, 10, 11, 12, 13, 14

Pentwater Inn

180 East Lowell, Box 98, 49449
(616) 869-5909

Lovely 1868 Victorian Inn with English and American antiques in beautifully appointed rooms. Charter boats, marinas, international shopping, the beach on Lake Michigan, and good food and drink all within a few minutes' walk. At the inn, enjoy complimentary drinks and snacks each evening at 6:00 P.M. and a breakfast to remember. Use the hot tub, bikes, or cable TV, or relax on one of the decks. Fishing, cross-country skiing, and golf are close by.

Hosts: Donna and Quintus Renshaw
Rooms: 5 (PB and SB) $60-75
Full Breakfast
Credit Cards: A, B
Notes: 2, 5, 7 (limited), 8, 9, 10, 11, 12, 13

Pentwater Inn

PLAINWELL

The 1882 John Crispe House Bed and Breakfast

404 East Bridge Street, 49080
(616) 685-1293

Museum quality Victorian elegance, elaborate original gaslight fixtures and plaster

12

h Cliff Inn

nn
ren
40-45

an English cottage bed
rlooking Lake Michigan.
ence a soothing relaxation
dations. Each
rated with

st

letely re-
ve an-
and
from

SAUGATUCK

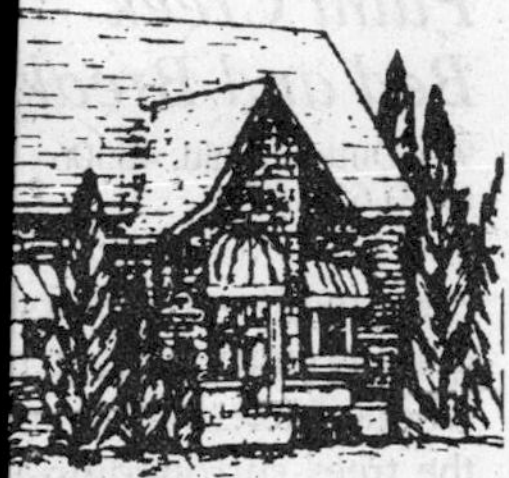

4-Seasons Inn

6068 Blue Star Highway, 49453
(616) 857-1955; (800) 852-1955

Enjoy casual elegance in a charming country setting. Convenient, just minutes from Saugatuck and sandy Lake Michigan beaches, golf courses, hiking trails, boating, cross-country skiing, and fine dining. A perfect place for that relaxing getaway weekend, relax in the hot tub or swim in the indoor pool in a climate controlled room complete with sauna, wet bar, and fireplace. A hearty, healthy continental breakfast is served every morning. Conference facilities available.

Rooms: 11 (PB) $75-150
Continental Breakfast
Credit Cards: A, B
Notes: 2, 5, 9, 10, 11, 12, 13 (cross-country)

Maplewood Hotel

428 Butler Street, P.O. Box 1059, 49453
(616) 857-1771

The Maplewood Hotel architecture is un takably Greek Revival. Some fireplaces and double include a library

The 1882 John Crispe House

moldings complement this home's fine Victorian furnishings. Between Kalamazoo and Grand Rapids, it is within walking distance of some of Michigan's finest gourmet dining and antique districts. The two-and-one-half-acre parklike grounds on the banks of the Kalamazoo River offer a relaxing atmosphere for guests to enjoy.

Host: Ormand J. Lefever
Rooms: 5 (3 PB; 2 SB) $55-95
Full Breakfast
Credit Cards: A, B
Notes: 2, 5, 8, 10, 12, 13

Full Breakfast
Credit Cards: A, B
Notes: 2, 5, 8, 9, 10, 11,

Sou

ST. JOSEPH

South Cliff I
Bed and Bre

1900 Lakeshore Drive
(616) 983-4881

South Cliff Inn is
and breakfast ove
Guests will experie
within the luxurio
room has been i
imported fabric
designed and
room. Parta
the lake
down
mor
the

with Jimmy the dog curled at their feet. Tulip Festival, Victorian Christmas, and Grand Escapes are favorites.

Hosts: Lynda and Joe Petty
Rooms: 8 (PB) $79.50-169.60
Continental Breakfast
Credit Cards: A, B, D
Notes: 2, 5, 7 (limited), 9, 10, 12, 13, 14

The Red Dog Bed and Breakfast

132 Mason Street, 49453
(616) 857-8851

At this comfortable place in the heart of Saugatuck, guests are steps away from shopping, restaurants, art galleries, marinas, and all the year-round activities that have made this harbor village the "Cape Cod of the Midwest." Built in 1879, the Red Dog features a mix of contemporary and antique furnishings. No minimum stay requirement on weekends. Children welcome.

Hosts: Daniel Indurante, Kristine Richter, Gary Kott
Rooms: 7 (5 PB: 2 SB) $55-85
Continental Breakfast
Credit Cards: A, B, C, D, E
Notes: 2, 5, 8, 9, 10, 11, 12, 13, 14

Rosemont Inn

83 Lakeshore Drive; P.O. Box 214, 4
(616) 857-2637

Rosemont Inn

This Victorian home offers 14 delightfu rooms, each with private bath and air conditioning. Lakeview rooms with gas fireplaces. Outdoor heated pool and large indoor spa and sauna in a tropical setting. Public beach on Lake Michigan across the street. Cross-country skiing at the doorstep. Complimentary bicycles. Minimum-stay requirements for weekends and holidays.

Hosts: Joseph and Marilyn Sajdak
Rooms: 14 (PB) $60-145
Full Breakfast
Credit Cards: A, B, C, D
Notes: 2, 5, 9, 10, 11, 12, 13, 14

Sherwood Forest Bed and Breakfast

938 Center Street, P.O. Box 315, 49453
(800) 838-1246

Surrounded by woods, this beautiful Victorian-style house was built in 1900. The guest rooms are decorated with antiques and traditional furnishings. One guest room has a Jacuzzi and another has a fireplace. Central air conditioning. There are also a heated swimming pool, wraparound porch, and separate cottage. The eastern shore of Lake Michigan and a public beach are a half block away, and the charming shop S ugatuck are just two miles a

PORT AUSTIN

Lake Street Manor Bed and Breakfast

8569 Lake Street, 48467
(517) 738-7720

Large bays, high-peaked roof, and gingerbread trim set off this brick Victorian manor house. Continental breakfast served in the gaslight room or guests may have breakfast in bed. The kitchen is open for guests' use. Hot tub for relaxing, fenced yard for picnics, and bikes for a trip to the beach. Color TV and VCRs in all rooms, as well as a selection of movies. Sitting room to socialize and play cards.

Host: Carolyn Greenwood
Rooms: 5 (3 PB: 2 SB) $50-60

and Bre

1631 Brockway Stree
(517) 792-0746

Brockway House stored, using a tiques, reprodu Victorian touches Saginaw's nationa fast. Mackinac Is and Traverse City miles away. Tw guests can find Fest, Birch Run's stores, and Bay with great fishing than 85 miles fro

Hosts: Richard A. Z
Rooms: 4 (PB) $95-

6 Pets welcome; 8 Children welcome; 9 Social drink
12 Golf available; 13 Skiing available; 14 May be boo

6 Pets welcome; 8 Children welcome; 9 Social drinking allowed; 10 Tennis ava
12 Golf available; 13 Skiing available; 14 May be booked through travel agents

Hosts: Michael and Denise Simcik
Rooms: 14 (PB) $68-105.84
Continental Breakfast
Credit Cards: A, B, C, D
Notes: 2, 5, 8 (over 5), 9, 10, 11, 12, 13, 14

Twin Oaks Inn

227 Griffith Street, P.O. Box 867, 49453
(616) 857-1600

Built in 1860, this totally renovated inn offers old English warmth and charm along with all modern amenities. Queen- or king-size beds, and private baths. Air conditioning along with cable TV, VCRs, and a library of more than 700 films, assures a wonderful stay no matter what the weather. Common areas with fireplace and outdoor hot tub along with antiques throughout guarantee a memorable escape. Homemade breakfast and afternoon refreshments daily. Full breakfast served on the weekends only.

Hosts: Nancy and Jerry Horney
Rooms: 6 (PB) $64-94
Cottage: 1
Full and Continental Breakfast
Credit Cards: A, B, D
Notes: 2, 5, 8, 9, 10, 11, 12, 13, 14

SOUTH HAVEN

Arundel House— An English Bed and Breakfast

56 North Shore Drive, 49090
(616) 637-4790

This turn-of-the-century resort has been restored to its former elegance and is registered with the Michigan Historical Society. Guest rooms are individually decorated with antiques. Afternoon tea is available to guests. Walking distance to restaurants, shops, marina, and Lake Michigan Beach. Midweek and off-season rates available.

Hosts: Patricia and Tom Zapal
Rooms: 8 (5 PB; 3 SB) $50-80
Continental Breakfast
Credit Cards: A, B, D
Notes: 2, 5, 10, 11, 12, 13

A Country Place

Bed and Breakfast
79 North Shore Drive North, 49090
(616) 637-5523

This traditional bed and breakfast is an 1860s Greek Revival on five and one-half acres of woodland, two miles from the center of town and one-half block to the beach. The English country theme throughout is created by the use of pretty prints, floral arrangements, and antique furnishings. The cozy common area features a fireplace and entertainment center. Warm days are enjoyed on the spacious deck or gazebo. Leisurely breakfasts feature home-baked goodies and lots of fresh fruit.

Hosts: Art and Lee Niffenegger
Rooms: 5 (PB) $70-85
Full Breakfast
Credit Cards: A, B, C, D
Notes: 2, 5, 9, 10, 11, 12, 13, 14

The Last Resort Bed and Breakfast Inn

86 North Shore Drive, 49090
(616) 637-8943

Built in 1883 as South Haven's first resort inn. Continental breakfast on the deck with view of gardens and lake. Luxury penthouse Jacuzzi suites and historic rooms. There are 14 guest rooms available. The Inn Gallery (on premises) features Mary Hammer's original contemporary artworks. Fishing, boating, golfing, beaches, and Kal Haven Trail are all nearby. Air conditioning. Open May through October.

Host: Mary Hammer
Rooms: 14 (7 PB; 7 SB) $48-185
Continental Breakfast
Credit Cards: A, B
Notes: 2, 7, 8, 9, 10, 11, 12

Ross House

229 Michigan Avenue, 49090
(616) 637-2256

The historic Ross House was built in 1886 by lumber tycoon Volney Ross. It sits on a

NOTES: Credit cards accepted: A MasterCard; B Visa; C American Express; D Discover Card; E Diner's Club; F Other; 2 Personal checks accepted; 3 Lunch available; 4 Dinner available; 5 Open all year;

quiet tree-lined street on the south side of the Black River. Lake Michigan public beaches, downtown shopping area, Kal-Haven Trail, and many fine restaurants are only blocks away.

Hosts: Cathy Hormann and Brad Wilcox
Rooms: 7 (1 PB; 6 S3B) $45-55
Full Breakfast (weekends)
Credit Cards: None
Notes: 2, 5, 9, 10, 11, 12, 13 (cross-country)

Yelton Manor Bed and Breakfast

140 North Shore Drive, 49090
(616) 637-5220

Elegant, gracious Victorian mansion on the sunset shore of Lake Michigan. Seventeen gorgeous rooms, all with private bath, some with Jacuzzi and fireplace. Panoramic lake views, plentiful common area, two salons with fireplaces, cozy wing chairs, floral carpets, four-poster beds, and a pampering staff set the tone for relaxation and romance. Enjoy wonderful breakfasts, day-long treats, and evening hor d'oeuvres. Guests will never want to leave.

Hosts: Elaine and Rob
Rooms: 17 (PB) $95-195
Full Breakfast
Credit Cards: A, B, C
Notes: 2, 5, 9, 10, 11, 12, 13

SUTTONS BAY

Open Windows Bed and Breakfast

613 St. Mary's Avenue, P.O. Box 698, 49682
(800) 520-3722

This 100-year-old home, reminiscent of a bygone era, is beautifully furnished with family heirlooms and antiques, Victorian furniture, and stained glass. Walk the beach, swim, ride hosts' bikes, and visit the unique shops in Suttons Bay, Leland, Northport, and surrounding areas. Relax, enjoy the view, read, rest, or dream while sitting on the front porch. Open year-round. Continental-plus breakfast served.

Hosts: Don and Norma Blumenschine
Rooms: 3 (1 PB; 2 SB) $65-90
Continental Breakfast
Credit Cards: None
Notes: 2, 5, 8, 9, 10, 11, 12, 13, 14

TRAVERSE CITY

Cider House

5515 Barney Road, 49684
(616) 947-2833

Delight in orchard life. Enjoy cider and Scottish shortbread overlooking the apple blossoms in spring and ripe red apples in fall. This contemporary "Bob Newhart Show" inn is only minutes from downtown. Country charm, beautiful oak floors, fireplaces, canopied beds, and great country breakfast. In the fall, guests can pick their own apples. Five guest rooms, all with private baths.

Hosts: Ron and Nan Tennant
Rooms: 5 (PB) $65-70
Credit Cards: None
Notes: 2, 5, 9, 11, 12, 13

Victoriana 1898

622 Washington Street, 49686
(616) 929-1009

Touch a bit of history and take home a memory to be long remembered when staying at this Victorian treasure. Magnificently crafted with tiled fireplaces, oak staircase, gazebo, and carriage house. The home is furnished with antiques and family heirlooms. In a quiet, historic district close to West Bay and downtown. Very special breakfast served.

Hosts: Flo and Bob Schermerhorn
Rooms: 3 (PB) $60-80
Full Breakfast
Credit Cards: A, B
Notes: 2, 5, 9, 10, 11, 12, 13, 14

Warwickshire Inn

5037 Barney Road, 49684
(616) 946-7176

6 Pets welcome; 8 Children welcome; 9 Social drinking allowed; 10 Tennis available; 11 Swimming available; 12 Golf available; 13 Skiing available; 14 May be booked through travel agents.

This stunning turn-of-the-century gem sits on a hill next to an antique shop just minutes from downtown Traverse City. Famous for its family-style breakfast elegantly served on fine Wedgwood china and sterling silver in a dining room overlooking rolling hills. Air conditioning. Private baths.

Hosts: Dan and Roberta Warwick
Rooms: 3 (PB, SB) $55-65
Full Breakfast
Credit Cards: None
Notes: 2, 5, 8, 9, 14

UNION PIER

Gordon Beach Inn

16220 Lakeshore Road, 49129
(616) 469-0800

Take a step back in time at Gordon Beach Inn, a historic inn recently renovated with all of today's modern amenities in a setting reminiscent of days gone by. Take a "culinary world tour" in Jenny's, a restaurant which Jennifer Smith-Drilon, Woman Chef of the Year 1991, calls home. Gordon Beach Inn and Jenny's, a great combination, casual comfortable atmosphere with great food, close to private beach, and antique and art galleries.

Host: Sharon Hawkes
Rooms: 20 (PB) $75-125
Full Breakfast
Credit Cards: A, B
Notes: 2, 3, 4, 5, 7, 8, 9, 10, 11, 12, 14

The Inn at Union Pier

9708 Berrien Street, P.O. Box 222, 49129
(616) 469-4700

Only 90 minutes from Chicago and 200 steps to the beach, The inn caters to both weekend getaways and weekday corporate retreats. Choose from 16 charming guest rooms, many featuring Swedish fireplaces and porches or balconies, and two luxurious whirlpool suites. Unwind in the outdoor hot tub or sauna, or enjoy Michigan wines and popcorn in the Great Room. "Harbor Country" offers diverse dining, antiquing, and wineries, and year-round outdoor activities from biking to cross-country skiing.

Hosts: Joyce Erickson Pitts and Mark Pitts
Rooms: 16 (PB) $105-175
Full Breakfast
Credit Cards: A, B, D
Notes: 2, 5, 7, 9, 10, 11, 12, 13

The Inn at Union Pier

WATERFORD

Bed and Breakfast Reservations of Michigan

4655 Charest, 48327
(810) 682-2665

Bed and Breakfast Reservations of Michigan offers reservation services for over 50 bed and breakfast homes and inns throughout Michigan. All bed and breakfasts are fully inspected to assure guests of cleanliness, location, decor, and ambience. Accommodations are available to suit personal tastes and needs: from simple to elegant, country to urban, and economical to luxurious. Unique settings for anniversaries, weddings, business meetings, romantic getaways, and other special events are offered. Experience four seasons of beauty in Michigan. Enjoy hundreds of scenic lakes, miles of forests, countless of cultural activities and sporting events and hospitality that is unmatched. No fee or service charge for this reservation service.

Rooms: 300 (200 PB; 100 SB) $40-200
Full and Continental Breakfast
Credit Cards: A, B
Notes: 2, 3, 4, 5, 6, 8, 9, 10, 11, 12, 13

WEST BRANCH

The Rose Brick Inn

124 East Houghton Avenue, 48661
(517) 345-3702

This 1906 Queen Anne-style home features a graceful veranda, white picket fence, and cranberry canopy. Tucked in the center two floors of the Frank Sebastian Smith house, the Rose Brick Inn is listed in Michigan's register of historic sites. It is on downtown Main Street in Victorian West Branch. Golfing, hiking, biking, cross-country skiing, snowmobiling, hunting, shopping, and

special holiday events await guests year-round. Jacuzzi. Air conditioning.

Host: Leon Swartz
Rooms: 4 (PB) $48-58
Continental Breakfast
Credit Cards: A, B
Notes: 2, 5, 8, 9, 10, 11, 12, 13

The Rose Brick Inn

Minnesota

Minnesota

ANNANDALE

The Thayer Inn

60 West Elm and Highway 55, 55302
(612) 274-8222; (800) 944-6595

Experience the romance of a bygone era in this charming Victorian inn. Built in 1895 and listed on the National Register of Historic Places, The Thayer Inn offers guests the graciousness of yesterday with all the conveniences of today. Each of the 13, themed, air-conditioned rooms is lovingly furnished with authentic antiques and handmade quilts, plus a private bath with clawfoot tub. A stay is further complemented with a sumptuous Petite Déjeuner served bedside. Minutes from the Twin Cities in the heart of the lakes region. No matter the season, activity abounds. Mystery weekends, packages, and group and corporate rates available.

Hosts: Sharon and Warren Gammell
Rooms: 13 (PB) $69.95-125
Credit Cards: A, B, C, D
Notes: 2, 3, 4, 5, 6 (call), 8, 9, 10, 11, 12, 13, 14

CANNON FALLS

Quill and Quilt

615 West Hoffman Street, 55009
(507) 263-5507; (800) 488-3849

Colonial Revival (1897). Oak woodwork; spacious, airy common areas. Decorated with delicate wallpapers, antiques, and handmade quilts. Four guest rooms. Private baths. One suite with double whirlpool. Full breakfast, evening sweets. Near biking, hiking, skiing, antiquing, and canoeing. Only 35 miles to the Mall of America. Midweek rates; gift certificates.

Hosts: Dennis and Marcia Flom
Rooms: 4 (PB) $45-105
Full Breakfast
Credit Cards: A, B
Notes: 2, 5, 8 (limited), 9, 10, 11, 12, 13, 14

Quill and Quilt

CHATFIELD

Lunds' Guest House

218 Southeast Winona Street, 55923
(507) 867-4003

Two charming houses furnished with 1920s and 1930s furniture. Quaint kitchens, dining rooms, living rooms, one with fireplace, TV, and electric organ or piano. Eight bedrooms and seven and one-half baths available. Large screened front porches and small screened back porches. Central air conditioning. Reasonable rates.

NOTES: Credit cards accepted: A MasterCard; B Visa; C American Express; D Discover Card; E Diner's Club; F Other; 2 Personal checks accepted; 3 Lunch available; 4 Dinner available; 5 Open all year; 6 Pets welcome; 7 Smoking allowed; 8 Children welcome; 9 Social drinking allowed; 10 Tennis available; 11 Swimming available; 12 Golf available; 13 Skiing available; 14 May be booked through travel agents.

Hosts: Shelby and Marion Lund
Rooms: 8 (PB) $55-65
Continental Breakfast
Credit Cards: None
Notes: 2, 5, 7 (limited), 9, 10, 11, 12, 13

CROOKSTON

Elm Street Inn

422 Elm Street, 56716
(218) 281-2343; (800) 568-4476

Lovingly restored 1910 home with antiques, hardwood floors, stained and beveled glass windows, and fireplace. Shared or private bath. Wicker-filled sun porch gift shop. Old-fashioned beds with quilts, terry robes, and fresh flowers. Memorable candlelight breakfast. Intimate dinners, wine service, and bicycles available. Limo to casino. Indoor community pool next door. Excellent birding. Near the University of Minnesota campus. No pets. No smoking. Special murder mystery, quilting, and wine-tasting weekends.

Hosts: John and Sheryl Winters
Rooms: 4 (2 PB; 2 SB) $55-65
Full Breakfast
Credit Cards: A, B, C
Notes: 2, 4, 5, 10, 11, 12, 14

DUNDAS

Martin Oaks Bed and Breakfast

107 First Street, 55019
(507) 645-4644

A Victorian Italianate home listed on the National Register of Historic Places. Near the Cannon River, it was built in 1869 and has been restored and furnished throughout with antiques. Elegant candlelight breakfasts and check-in teas accompanied by storytelling. Golf, hiking, biking, swimming, fishing, antiques, and bookstore browsing nearby.

Hosts: Marie and Frank Gery
Rooms: 3 (SB) $70

Full Breakfast
Credit Cards: A, B
Notes: 2, 4, 5, 9, 10, 11, 12, 13

FERGUS FALLS

Bakketopp Hus

Rural Route 2, Box 187 A (Long Lake), 56537
(218) 739-2915

Lake home ten minutes from I-94 at Exit 50. Spa, fireplace, skylight, vaulted ceilings, natural wood, and windows create a feeling of relaxation. Country French canopied and four-poster beds, decks on the lakeside, and a flower garden patio. Furnished with antiques. State park nearby, as well as nature, ski, snowmobile, and hiking trails. Near antiques, restaurants, golf, and other recreation. A relaxed retreat surrounded by woods and with a hilltop view of the lake. Hear loons call to each other.

Hosts: Judy and Dennis Nims
Rooms: 3 (PB) $60-95
Full Breakfast
Credit Cards: A, B, D
Notes: 2, 5, 8, 9, 10, 11, 12, 13

Bakketopp Hus

HIBBING

Adams House

201 East 23rd Street, 55746
(218) 263-9742

NOTES: Credit cards accepted: A MasterCard; B Visa; C American Express; D Discover Card; E Diner's Club; F Other; 2 Personal checks accepted; 3 Lunch available; 4 Dinner available; 5 Open all year;

The Adams House is a quiet, smoke-free accommodation in the center of the city and its attractions. A brief distance to lakes, woods, golf, and skiing. The English Tudor-style house features antique and chintz decorated bedrooms, a guest lounge with a kitchenette, and a charming flower garden. An English Continental breakfast served in the sunny dining room includes Swedish coffee and warm conversation.

Hosts: Marlene and Merrill Widmark
Rooms: 5 (1 PB; 4 SB) $43-48
Continental Breakfast
Credit Cards: None
Notes: 2, 5, 8, 9, 10, 12

LAKE CITY

Evergreen Knoll Acres Bed and Breakfast

Rural Route 1, Box 145, 55041
(612) 345-2257

This bed and breakfast is on a 160-acre dairy farm with 75 milk cows. It is eight and one-half miles southwest of Lake City and 35 miles north of Rochester. Nearby Lake Pepin provides fishing, sailing, and waterskiing. The large, German-style country home was built in 1919 and is furnished with antiques, country crafts, air conditioning, and a fireplace. A four-bedroom guest cottage is available in a secluded area. Plenty of room for hiking, cross-country skiing, and biking. Open year-round.

Hosts: Paul and Bev Meyer
Rooms: 3 (SB) $55-99
Full Breakfast
Credit Cards: None
Notes: 2, 5, 8, 9, 10, 11, 12, 13

Red Gables Inn

403 North High Street, 55041
(612) 345-2605

Red Gables Inn is in a quiet residential section of Lake City, home of the largest small-boat marina on the Mississippi. A 90-minute drive to the Mall of America, 20 minutes to

A Victorian Bed and Breakfast

the Casino, and 30 minutes to the Mayo Clinic and Rochester. Built in 1865, it displays formal Victorian antiques in the parlor and dining room, while the guest rooms have floral wallpapers and antique Victorian painted iron and brass beds. In the early evening, guests are served beverages. Closed Thanksgiving and Christmas Days. Members of Lake City Chamber of Com-merce, MVP, Minnesota Bed and Breakfast Guild, and the Historic Bed and Breakfast Guild of Minnesota.

Hosts: Mary and Doug DeRoos
Rooms: 5 (PB) $80-99
Full Breakfast
Credit Cards: A, B
Notes: 2, 5, 8 (over 12), 9, 10, 11, 12, 13, 14

The Victorian Bed and Breakfast

620 South High Street, 55041
(612) 345-2167

An 1896 Victorian home where each room has a lake view. Carved woodwork, stained-glass windows, and antique music boxes and furnishings. The Mayo Clinic is 35 miles away; Minneapolis-St. Paul Mall of America 65 miles. Breakfast is served in guests' air-conditioned room or the formal dining room. Enjoy afternoon tea and play the 1800s reed organ.

Hosts: Joel and Sandra Grettenberg
Rooms: 3 (1 PB; 2 HB) $60-75
Continental Breakfast
Credit Cards: None
Notes: 2, 5, 8 (over 10), 9, 10, 11, 12, 13

6 Pets welcome; 8 Children welcome; 9 Social drinking allowed; 10 Tennis available; 11 Swimming available; 12 Golf available; 13 Skiing available; 14 May be booked through travel agents.

LAKE KABETOGAMA

Bunt's Bed and Breakfast Inns

2497 Burma Road, 56669
(218) 875-2691

Three bed and breakfasts one-half mile apart. One inn is on the shores of Lake Kabetogama and Voyageurs National Park. Another on 300 secluded acres. The third is in a converted school and church building. Private baths, full kitchens, fireplaces, whirlpool, Jacuzzis, saunas, many decks, beach, dock, satellite, color TVs, VCRs, and washers and dryers. Truly three touches of class in the midst of the wilderness.

Host: Bob Buntrock
Rooms: 12 (7 PB; 5 SB) $60-120
Continental Breakfast
Credit Cards: A, B, C, D
Notes: 2, 3, 4, 5, 8, 9, 11, 12, 13, 14

Hosts: The Mensings
Rooms: 5 (PB) $55-130
Full Breakfast
Credit Cards: A, B, C, D
Notes: 2, 5, 8, 9, 10, 11, 12, 13, 14

Lindgren's

LANESBORO

Historic Scanlan House Bed and Breakfast

708 Parkway Avenue South, 55949
(507) 467-2158; (800) 944-2158

An 1889 Victorian home on the National Register of Historic Places. Five large bedroom suites furnished with antiques. Original ornate woodwork and beautiful stained-glass windows. Three fireplaces and rooms with private and shared baths. Whirlpool suites available. Six blocks from the Root River, with canoeing, fishing, and tubing, and the 38-mile paved Root River Trail for biking, hiking, walking, rollerblading, and cross-country skiing. Tennis courts, local winery, cheese factory, summer theater, and Amish tours. An exquisite bed and breakfast. Guests will have a feeling of home. Complimentary champagne and chocolates. All rates include a famous five-course breakfast. Seen in the *Chicago Tribune* and the *Minneapolis Star Tribune*.

LUTSEN

Lindgren's Bed and Breakfast

County Road 35, P.O. Box 56, 55612-0056
(218) 663-7450

A 1920s log home in Superior National Forest on walkable shoreline of Lake Superior. Knotty cedar interior decorated with trophies of bear, moose, timber wolf, wild turkey, and fox. Massive stone fireplaces, Finnish sauna, whirlpool, baby grand piano, and color TV/VCR. In center of area known for skiing, golf, stream and lake fishing, skyride, mountain biking, snowmobiling, horseback riding, alpine slide, Superior Hiking Trail, and near Boundary Waters Canoe Area entry point. Spacious manicured grounds. One-half mile off Highway 61 on the Lake Superior Circle Tour.

Hosts: Bob and Shirley Lindgren
Rooms: 4 (PB) $80-110
Full Breakfast
Credit Cards: A, B
Notes: 2, 5, 9, 10, 11, 12, 13, 14

NOTES: Credit cards accepted: A MasterCard; B Visa; C American Express; D Discover Card; E Diner's Club; F Other; 2 Personal checks accepted; 3 Lunch available; 4 Dinner available; 5 Open all year;

MARINE ON ST. CROIX

Asa Parker House

17500 St. Croix Trail North, 55047
(612) 433-5248

The Asa Parker House is a restored lumber-man's home, sitting high on a hill overlook-ing the beautiful St. Croix Valley and the historic village of Marine on St. Croix. Four charming, flower-filled bedrooms, all of which have private baths, period an-tiques, and English fabrics and wallpapers, are available for guests. A wicker-filled porch, gazebo, tennis court, and marina with ca-noes are available for guests to enjoy. Cross-country skiing and bike trails are in the adjacent state park. Scrumptious break-fast awarded four stars. Midweek rates available.

Host: Marjorie Bush
Rooms: 5 (PB) $99-135
Full Breakfast
Credit Cards: A, B, C, D, E
Notes: 2, 5, 9, 10, 12, 13

MINNEAPOLIS

Evelo's Bed and Breakfast

2301 Bryant Avenue South, 55405
(612) 374-9656

This 1897 house is in the Lowry Hill East neighborhood and has a well-preserved Victorian interior. The three guest rooms are on the third floor, each furnished in pe-riod furniture. The entire first floor is done in original dark oak millwork. A small re-frigerator, coffee maker, telephone, and TV are available for guest use. The bed and breakfast is within walking distance of downtown, Lake of the Isles, Upton shop-ping area, Walker Art Center, Guthrie The-atre, and the Minneapolis Art Institute. Established in 1979, it was featured in *Innsider* magazine (June 1989).

Hosts: David and Sheryl Evelo
Rooms: 3 (SB) $50
Continental Breakfast

Credit Cards: A, B, C
Notes: 2, 5, 8, 9, 10, 11, 12, 13

Nan's Bed and Breakfast

2304 Fremont Avenue South, 55405
(612) 377-5118; (800) 214-5118

Comfortable urban 1890s Victorian family home offering guest rooms furnished with antiques. Friendly, outgoing hosts will help guests find their way around town. Near downtown, lakes, theaters, galleries, restau-rants, and shopping. One block from buses.

Hosts: Nan and Jim Zosel
Rooms: 3 (SB) $45-50
Full Breakfast
Credit Cards: A, B, C
Notes: 2, 5, 6, 7, 8, 11, 12

MORRIS

The American House

410 East Third Street, 56267
(612) 589-4054

Victorian home decorated with antiques and country charm. Ride the tandem bike on scenic trails. Within walking distance of area restaurants and shops. One block from the University of Minnesota- Morris campus.

Host: Karen Berget
Rooms: 3 (SB) $35-50
Full Breakfast
Credit Cards: A, B
Notes: 2, 5, 8, 9, 10, 11, 12, 14

PARK RAPIDS

Dickson Viking Huss Bed and Breakfast

202 East Fourth Street, 56470
(218) 732-8089

"Aunt Helen" invites guests to this charm-ing contemporary home with vaulted ceiling and fireplace in the living room that features a watercolor exhibit. Big Continental break-fast. Bicycle or snowmobile the Heartland Trail. Visit Itasca Park and the source of the

6 Pets welcome; 8 Children welcome; 9 Social drinking allowed; 10 Tennis available; 11 Swimming available;
12 Golf available; 13 Skiing available; 14 May be booked through travel agents.

Mississippi or cross-country ski. Unique shop and restaurant attractions. State inspected.

Host: Helen K. Dickson
Rooms: 3 (1 PB; 2 SB) $31.50-44.50
Continental Breakfast
Credit Cards: A, B
Notes: 2, 5, 6 (call), 7 (limited), 8, 9, 10, 11, 12, 13

ST. PAUL

Chatsworth Bed and Breakfast

984 Ashland Avenue, 55104
(612) 227-4288

Elegantly furnished Victorian home in a quiet residential neighborhood. Only 15 minutes from the airport. Near the governor's mansion and numerous restaurants and shops. Easy access to downtown St. Paul and Minneapolis. Two rooms with double whirlpool baths. Licensed. No smoking.

Hosts: Donna and Earl Gustafson
Rooms: 5 (3 PB; 2 SB) $64.20-123.05
Continental Breakfast
Credit Cards: None
Notes: 2, 5, 8, 9, 10, 11, 12, 13

Chatsworth

The Garden Gate Bed and Breakfast

925 Goodrich Avenue, 55105
(612) 227-8430; (800) 967-2703

A large 1906 Victorian duplex in St. Paul's lovely Crocus Hill neighborhood. Newly decorated rooms with individual air conditioning. Therapeutic massages available to guests along with soft cotton sheets and fresh flowers. Two blocks to bus and Grand Avenue's fine restaurants and shops. Easy access to downtown, colleges, airport, and Mall of America. Transportation available on request.

Hosts: Mary and Miles Conway
Rooms: 4 (SB) $50-85
Full Breakfast
Credit Cards: None
Notes: 2, 5, 6 (limited), 8, 9, 10, 11, 12, 13

The Rose Bed and Breakfast

2129 Larpenteur Avenue West, 55113
(612) 642-9417

This 1925 English Tudor is in a large, wooded area between a historic farm museum and a golf course in the center of the Twin Cities metro area. Beside the University of Minnesota-St. Paul campus. Fresh flowers, private tennis court, cross-country skiing, art, books, and privacy or conversation. Full, wonderful breakfasts accommodating any personal dietary preferences or requirements.

Hosts: Carol Kindschi and Larry Greenberg
Suites: 2 (PB) $75-85
Full Breakfast
Credit Cards: None
Notes: 2, 5, 9, 10, 11, 12, 13

SHERBURN

Four Columns Inn

Route 2, Box 75, 56171
(507) 764-8861

Built in 1884 as a stagecoach stop, this lovingly remodeled Greek Revival inn welcomes travelers. Four antique-filled bedrooms, claw-foot tubs, and working fireplaces welcome guests. A library, circular stairway, living room with a grand piano, and a solarium with Jacuzzi make a stay here memorable. A hideaway bridal suite with access to a roof deck with a super view of the countryside is perfect for honeymooners. Full breakfast is served in the formal dining room, on the balcony, in the gazebo, or in the kitchen by the fireplace. Near lakes, antiques, amusement park, and live theater. Two miles north of I-90, between Chicago and the Black Hills.

Hosts: Norman and Pennie Kittleson
Rooms: 4 (3 PB; 1 SB) $50-70
Full Breakfast
Credit Cards: None
Notes: 2, 5, 8 (call), 9 (limited), 11, 12, 13, 14

SIDE LAKE

McNair's Bed and Breakfast

7694 Highway 5, P.O. Box 155, 55781
(218) 254-5878

Luxury accommodations in Minnesota's North Woods. Twenty minutes from Hibbing and Chisholm and 25 minutes from Virginia. Walk to Side Lake, Perch Lake, and Sturgeon Lake chain. Excellent fishing and water sports. Sugar sand beaches. McCarthy Beach State Park. Borders state forest, with breathtaking fall colors. Hiking, biking, picnicking, excellent cross-country skiing, and 2,000 miles of state-maintained snowmobile trails. The perfect pampered retreat or romantic getaway. Elegant spacious view rooms. An eclectic mix of fine furnishings, imported linens, and lace. Accent on comfort and romance. Honeymoon suite with fireplace. Home-made desserts.

Hosts: Don, Louise, and Jessica McNair
Rooms: 5 (PB) $65-125
Full Breakfast
Credit Cards: None
Notes: 2, 5, 9, 11, 13

SPRING VALLEY

Chase's

508 North Huron Avenue, 55975
(507) 346-2850

It's life in the slow lane at this Second Empire mansion. It's flowers, birds, stars, and exploring this unglaciated area. Step back in time with a tour: Amish, Laura Ingalls Wilder, or caves. Enjoy the trails, trout streams, and bike trail. Closed December through February.

Hosts: Bob and Jeannine Chase
Rooms: 5 (PB) $60-75
Full Breakfast
Credit Cards: A, B, D
Notes: 2, 8, 9, 10, 11, 12, 13

Chase's

TAYLORS FALLS

The Old Jail Company

100 Government Road, Box 203, 55084
(612) 465-3112

The historic Taylors Falls Jail Guesthouse and the Cave and Playhouse suites in the Schottmuller Saloon building next door overlook the St. Croix River Valley. Just a few yards from Interstate Park with its ancient glacial potholes and dramatic black rock cliffs. Enjoy swimming, fishing, ca-

6 Pets welcome; 8 Children welcome; 9 Social drinking allowed; 10 Tennis available; 11 Swimming available;
12 Golf available; 13 Skiing available; 14 May be booked through travel agents.

noeing, hiking, riverboat cruises, antiques, potteries, and much more.

Hosts: Julie and Al Kunz
Rooms: 3 (PB) $90-110
Full Breakfast
Credit Cards: None
Notes: 2, 5, 7, 9, 10, 11, 12, 13

WINONA

Carriage House Bed and Breakfast

420 Main Street, 55987
(507) 452-8256

Guests can indulge themselves at Winona's Carriage House Bed and Breakfast. Stay in one of the beautifully decorated rooms, each with its own special charm. Built in 1870, the Carriage House is near the Mississippi River. Enjoy a wonderful breakfast, free tandem bikes, and old-fashioned river town hospitality.

Carriage House

Hosts: Deb and Don Salyards
Rooms: 4 (2 PB; 2 SB) $70-90
Continental Breakfast
Credit Cards: A, B
Notes: 2, 5, 9, 10, 11, 12, 13, 14

NOTES: Credit cards accepted: A MasterCard; B Visa; C American Express; D Discover Card; E Diner's Club; F Other; 2 Personal checks accepted; 3 Lunch available; 4 Dinner available; 5 Open all year;

Mississippi

Lincoln Ltd.

P.O. Box 3479, Meridian, 39303
(601) 482-5483 (information)
(800) 633-MISS (reservations)
FAX (601) 693-7447

79. Overlooking the Mississippi Sound Bay, this turn-of-the-century home welcomes guests to the ambience and quaintness of Bay St. Louis. Enjoy the view from bay windows in the room or rock on the front porch and watch for dolphins playing in the water. All rooms decorated in the taste of their former owners. Seven rooms. Continental breakfast. Children by arrangement. $75-85.

Lincoln Ltd.

P.O. Box 3479, Meridian, 39303
(601) 482-5483 (information)
(800) 633-MISS (reservations)
FAX (601) 693-7447

1. A beautiful 19th-century home completely restored and furnished in the Victorian style with antiques. The host is well known as a decorator and architectural designer. There are four large bedrooms, each with private bath. Dinner is available by special arrangement and reservation. A full breakfast is served. Three guest rooms. $95-110.

Columbus Historic Foundation

P.O. Box 46, Columbus, 39703
(601) 329-3533

Amzi Love (1848). This accommodation in the historic district of town was built in pre-Civil War days. Suites and rooms offer double and/or single beds and private baths; each has an easy chair and TV. The parlor features a working fireplace, games, and card tables. Full Southern breakfast provided. Welcoming refreshments and a narrated guided tour of the house and grounds. $85. (610) 328-5413.

Arcady (1841). This "house-within-a-house" was expanded to a two-story Italianate-design townhouse. The "inner house" survives, completely restored by the owners and operators. There is one bedroom with private bath and oversize double bed, with a tiny adjoining bedroom for children, appealing to families with young children. Full Southern breakfast provided. Welcoming refreshments and a narrated guided tour of the house and grounds. In the heart of historic downtown. $85. (601) 328-7432

Liberty Hall (1832). This Southern planter's home, built by the current owner's great-great-grandfather, has remained in the family for six generations. Nestled in a peaceful country setting, it of-

6 Pets welcome; 7 Smoking allowed; 8 Children welcome; 9 Social drinking allowed; 10 Tennis available; 11 Swimming available; 12 Golf available; 13 Skiing available; 14 May be booked through travel agents.

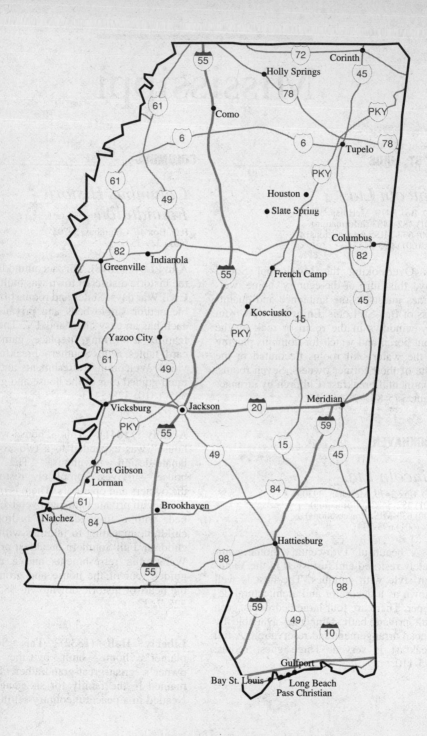

Mississippi

fers a relaxing visit for guests. There is a suite with private bath and dressing room; rooms feature a double-bed and easy chairs, and some have sofas and working fireplaces. There is a sitting room with TV. Enjoy the 600-acre estate, pool, and family cemetery. Full Southern breakfast provided. Welcoming refreshments and a narrated guided tour of the house and grounds. $85. (601) 328-4110

Temple Heights (1837). With its 14 Doric columns, this authentically restored Federal-Greek Revival townhouse allows guests to experience the warmth of Southern hospitality in one of the town's most historic homes. Each room has a double bed, comfortable chairs, and private bath, and is furnished with prized antebellum antiques. Full Southern breakfast provided. Welcoming refreshments and a narrated guided tour of the house and grounds. $85. (601) 328-0599

White Arches (1857). Whether enjoying an early morning cup of coffee on a secluded veranda or relaxing with a book in the gentleman's library, guests will revel in a visit to Victorian times, when simple pleasures were savored and long remembered. Suites and rooms are available, some with queen-size bed, all with comfortable seating. Several rooms include private balcony; each has a private bath. A sitting room with cable TV, VCR, refrigerator, microwave, etc. round out the amenities. Full Southern breakfast provided. Welcoming refreshments and a narrated guided tour of the house and grounds. $85. (601) 328-4568

Cartney-Hunt House (1828). This is the oldest brick house in the northern part of the Magnolia State, and one of the few examples of Federal period architecture in the area. Enjoy authentic Southern hospitality in the heart of the town's acclaimed historic district. Each room has private bath, queen-size bed and comfortable seating. Full Southern breakfast provided. Welcoming refreshments and a narrated guided tour of the house and grounds. $85. (601) 329-3856

Lincoln Ltd.

P.O. Box 3479, Meridian, 39303
(601) 482-5483 (information)
(800) 633-MISS (reservations)
FAX (601) 693-7447

5. This is a Federal-style house and the oldest brick house in Columbus. It was built in 1828, the same year Andrew Jackson was elected president. The house has been completely restored and is furnished with antiques of the period. Three bedrooms, each with private baths. Full breakfast is included. $85.

71. Enjoy this Italian villa-style home built in 1848 and owned by the family of the original builders. Furnished in period antiques and on the National Register of Historic Places. A full Southern breakfast is served. Four guest rooms with private baths. $85.

White Arches Bed and Breakfast

122 7th Avenue South, 39701
(601) 328-4568

Standing among the magnolias in the historic district, White Arches offers gracious accommodations including original period furnishings, sumptuous Southern breakfasts, and a comprehensive tour of the house. Each bedroom is beautifully decorated with private balconies and baths. Built in 1857 and carefully restored to its former elegance, White Arches is listed on the National Register of Historic Places. Shop in restored downtown or leisurely stroll through the historic neighborhood.

Hosts: Ned and Sarah Hardin
Rooms: 5 (PB) $85-125
Full Breakfast
Credit Cards: A, B, C
Notes: 2, 5

COMO

Lincoln Ltd.

P.O. Box 3479, Meridian, 39303
(601) 482-5483 (information)
(800) 633-MISS (reservations)
FAX (601) 693-7447

49. An attractive guest cottage in a delightful small Mississippi town right on I-55 between Memphis and Jackson. There are also accommodations in the main house. A continental breakfast in the guest cottage; full breakfast in the main house. Two guest rooms. One guest cottage. $60.

CORINTH

The Generals' Quarters Bed and Breakfast

924 Fillmore, P.O. Box 1505, 38834
(601) 286-3325

Circa 1870, this fabulous restored home is in the historic district of the old Civil War village of Corinth. It is close to Battery Robinette and a pleasant country ride from the famous Civil War battle area of Shiloh National Military Park. All rooms are fully furnished in period antiques, yet with modern conveniences. There are plenty of shopkeepers offering antiques and flea markets. Beautiful surrounding area for joggers and walkers. Pickwick recreational area is only 15 minutes away. Four rooms feature private baths. A full Southern breakfast is included. Just a short trip from Memphis or Jackson, Tennessee, while en route to perhaps Nashville, Tennessee, or while traveling the Natchez Trace Parkway.

Host: J. L. Aldridge
Rooms: 4 (PB) $75
Full Breakfast
Credit Cards: A, B, C, D, E, F
Notes: 2, 5, 8, 9, 10, 11, 12

Lincoln Ltd.

P.O. Box 3479, Meridian, 39303
(601) 482-5483 (information)
(800) 633-MISS (reservations)
FAX (601) 693-7447

37. A beautiful Victorian home, completely furnished with antiques. Convenient to Memphis, Tennessee, and Shiloh National Military Park, a Civil War battlefield. A full Southern breakfast is served to guests. Lunch and dinner are also available. Four guest rooms. $75.

75. Circa 1869, this Southern-style Colonial house is on two acres of oak and dogwood in the city of Corinth. The host is a native of Oxford, England, and he and his wife are very knowledgeable about the area. Enjoy the original pine floors and walls of two-inch-thick planks. A continental breakfast is served on the back veranda as guests relax in antique wicker furniture. Four guest rooms available. $75.

Natchez Trace Bed and Breakfast Reservation Service

P.O. Box 193, Hampshire, TN 38461
(615) 285-2777; (800) 377-2770

COR-01. Milepost 320. Built circa 1870s. In the historic district of the old Civil War village of Corinth, near Battery Robinette and the site of Fort Williams. Only 22 miles from Shiloh National Military Park; host will be happy to tell guests all about the history of the area. Five rooms with private baths. Full Southern breakfast. $75.

COR-02. Milepost 270, 320, or 320-A. This Southern Colonial-style home, circa

1870, is on two acres of oak trees, dog-woods, boxwoods, and azaleas in historic Corinth. Guests can enjoy breakfast on the back porch, relaxing in antique wicker furniture with veranda ceiling-fans. Complimentary afternoon tea and refreshments are served on arrival. Convenient to Shiloh and Pickwick Lake and State Park. $55-70.

FRENCH CAMP

Lincoln Ltd.

P.O. Box 3479, Meridian, 39303
(601) 482-5483 (information)
(800) 633-MISS (reservations)
FAX (601) 693-7447

59. Enjoy the spacious view of forest and wildlife from the wide windows of this two-story log home. Built with chinked log walls, the home was reconstructed from two log cabins more than 100 years old. Awake to a traditional country breakfast and air scented with cypress and sweet pine. The hosts share their historic home with Southern hospitality and their personal collection of antique tables, books, and quilts. Four guest rooms with private baths. $60.

Natchez Trace Bed and Breakfast Reservation Service

P.O. Box 193, Hampshire, TN 38461
(615) 285-2777; (800) 377-2770

FRC-01. Milepost 181. Two blocks from the Trace, a rustic inn constructed from two century-old log cabins. Known as French Camp, this area is steeped in early Trace history. Enjoy a breakfast of sorghum-soaked biscuits, creamy grits, fresh eggs, crispy bacon, and homemade jams and jellies. Hosts will share the tale of the origin of this historic two-story log cabin and their collection of quilts, antique books, and linens. $60.

GREENVILLE

Lincoln Ltd.

P.O. Box 3479, Meridian, 39303
(601) 482-5483 (information)
(800) 633-MISS (reservations)
FAX (601) 693-7447

48. This antebellum mansion, circa 1856, is one of the finest examples of Italianate architecture in Mississippi. It is on historic Lake Washington and is listed in the National Register of Historic Places. On the River Road just south of Greenville, this lovely home has been restored and decorated with antiques and the personal collections of its owners. The home is surrounded by several acres of beautiful river land. Sit on the front porch and enjoy a lake view, or stroll the grounds, then settle into a room beautifully decorated for guests' comfort. The hosts are Mississip-pians interested in tourism within their state and in their community and will direct visitors to all the special things to do in the Mississippi Delta. Four guest rooms with private baths. $75-95.

GULFPORT

Old South Guest House

1911 Second Street, 39501
(601) 864-7759

The Old South Guest House is of the late Victorian period; a lovely four-square with screened porches and New Orleans courtyard and garden. On a quiet old residential street, just two blocks from the Gulf of Mexico's white beaches. Just minutes to the dazzling new casinos. This home is unique in that guests enjoy a beautifully furnished one-bedroom apartment with fully equipped kitchens and private baths. Apartments can accommodate four guests (with children sleeping on rollaway beds). Continental breakfast. Perfect for romantic getaways. Three-night minimum stay on

6 Pets welcome; 8 Children welcome; 9 Social drinking allowed; 10 Tennis available; 11 Swimming available; 12 Golf available; 13 Skiing available; 14 May be booked through travel agents.

holidays. Rates are for two guests for a two-night minimum stay.

Host: Ellen Reeves
Apartments: 4 (PB) $160
Continental Breakfast
Credit Cards: A, B
Notes: 2, 5, 6 (deposit), 7 (limited), 8, 9, 12, 14 (10 percent)

HATTIESBURG

Lincoln Ltd.

P.O. Box 3479, Meridian, 39303
(601) 482-5483 (information)
(800) 633-MISS (reservations)
FAX (601) 693-7447

78. In the historic neighborhood of Hattiesburg and on the National Register of Historic Places. Guests will enjoy this turn-of-the-century style home with its 11 fireplaces and two-story wraparound porch. Guests are greeted with a complimentary drink and may enjoy the homemade jellies and preserves with their breakfast. Three rooms. $75.

Tally House

402 Rebecca Avenue, 39401
(601) 582-3467

Tally House, a 1907 mansion with 13,000 square feet of floor space in a large National Register district, has been restored to its original grandeur. The Tally House sits on large grounds with formal gardens, fountains, and statuary. Tally House is furnished throughout with antiques. Hosts are avid collectors, therefore Tally House has something of interest to everyone. Antiques, shopping malls, the zoo, three golf courses, the university, and nice restaurants within five minutes.

Rooms: 4 (PB) $60-75
Full Breakfast
Credit Cards: A, B
Notes: 2, 5, 8 (10 years or older), 9, 12, 14

HOLLY SPRINGS

Lincoln Ltd.

P.O. Box 3479, Meridian, 39303
(601) 482-5483 (information)
(800) 633-MISS (reservations)
FAX (601) 693-7447

8. Lovely home furnished with heirloom antiques. Also an antique shop adjoining. Young executive hosts have completely restored this home themselves. Full breakfast is served. Three guest rooms with private baths. $75.

HOUSTON

Lincoln Ltd.

P.O. Box 3479, Meridian, 39303
(601) 482-5483 (information)
(800) 633-MISS (reservations)
FAX (601) 693-7447

39. This Victorian home, completely renovated, is a comfortable stop for travelers on business or pleasure in this small Mississippi town. Just one block from the town square, there are five pleasant bedrooms, all with private bath and TV. Guests can relax and socialize in the downstairs sitting room. A full Southern breakfast is served. $45.

INDIANOLA

Lincoln Ltd.

P.O. Box 3479, Meridian, 39303
(601) 482-5483 (information)
(800) 633-MISS (reservations)
FAX (601) 693-7447

9. Enjoy a full breakfast of country ham and homemade biscuits at this extremely attractive two-story home in the heart of the Mississippi Delta. The hosts, known for their hospitality, will take guests on a tour of the area pointing out crops in season and directing them to well-known area restaurants. One guest room. $60.

NOTES: Credit cards accepted: A MasterCard; B Visa; C American Express; D Discover Card; E Diner's Club; F Other; 2 Personal checks accepted; 3 Lunch available; 4 Dinner available; 5 Open all year;

JACKSON

Lincoln Ltd.

P.O. Box 3479, Meridian, 39303
(601) 482-5483 (information)
(800) 633-MISS (reservations)
FAX (601) 693-7447

50. Circa 1888. Step through the door and step back across 100 years into a graceful world of sparkling chandeliers and finely crafted furnishings in this 19th-century home. Mere moments away from the city's central business and government districts. Convenient to many of Jackson's finest shopping, dining, and entertainment opportunities. The bedrooms are individually decorated, each accompanied by a fully modern private bath. Eleven guest rooms. Single rates available. $85-170.

Natchez Trace Bed and Breakfast Reservation Service

P.O. Box 193, Hampshire, TN 38461
(615) 285-2777; (800) 377-2770

MAD-01. Milepost 110. Just six-and-a-half miles from the Trace, near Madison, and convenient to Jackson, this elegant home features heart-pine floors, antique furnishings, ten-foot ceilings, oriental carpets and porcelains, and expansive grounds. It is a modern home, yet deep Southern authenticity is readily apparent, from its columnar facade to its spacious interior. Rooms with private bath, $75-85; two-bedroom suite $140.

KOSCIUSKO

Lincoln Ltd.

P.O. Box 3479, Meridian, 39303
(601) 482-5483 (information)
(800) 633-MISS (reservations)
FAX (601) 693-7447

63. One of the finest examples of Queen Anne architecture, this historic inn stands as a visual example of the lifestyle and culture of 1884. Four lovely bedrooms, furnished with antiques. Lunch and dinner are available by reservation. Breakfast included. $75-110.

85. This delightful modest home, circa 1837, tells the story of one of Kosciusko's earliest families. Standing on the Natchez Trace, it houses artifacts discovered in or near the home, documenting facts about the Hammond family and the early growth of Kosciusko. Two rooms. $60-90.

Natchez Trace Bed and Breakfast Reservation Service

P.O. Box 193, Hampshire, TN 38461
(615) 285-2777; (800) 377-2770

KOS-01. Milepost 160. Stately two-story structure built in 1884, one of Kosciusko's finest examples of Queen Anne architecture, with a distinctive Victorian multicolor scheme, a three-story octagonal corner tower, and fishscale shingles. Houses a tea room as well, which serves lunch Monday through Friday, dinner Saturday evening from 6:30 P.M. until 9:00 P.M. Only two miles from the Trace. $75.

Redbud Inn

121 North Wells Street, 39090
(601) 289-5086; (800) 379-5086

The Redbud Inn is listed in the National Register of Historic Places. A two-story Queen Anne-style house that travelers have been using as a bed and breakfast since the 1890s. Restaurant and antique shop on premises. Mile marker 160, Natchez Trace Parkway.

Hosts: Maggie Garrett and Rose Mary Burge
Rooms: 5 (4 PB; 1 SB) $75-100
Full Breakfast
Credit Cards: A, B
Notes: 2, 3, 4, 5, 8, 14 (10 percent)

6 Pets welcome; 8 Children welcome; 9 Social drinking allowed; 10 Tennis available; 11 Swimming available; 12 Golf available; 13 Skiing available; 14 May be booked through travel agents.

LONG BEACH

Lincoln Ltd.

P.O. Box 3479, Meridian, 39303
(601) 482-5483 (information)
(800) 633-MISS (reservations)
FAX (601) 693-7447

53. Three-story raised French cottage one and one-half miles south of I-10 at Long Beach on 11 acres of live oaks and magnolias. Features antiques, six fireplaces, and a 64-foot front porch with swings. Gardens, campsites, and cabins are under development. Expanded continental breakfast is served. Four guest rooms with private baths. $54-69.

Red Creek Colonial Inn

7416 Red Creek Road, 39560
(601) 452-3080 (information)
(800) 729-9670 (reservations)

This three-story, raised French cottage is on 11 acres of live oaks and magnolias. The 64-foot porch and six fireplaces add to the relaxing atmosphere of this circa 1899 brick-and-cypress home. English, French, Victorian, and country antiques and working wooden radios and a Victrola are for guests' use. Golf packages available, and casinos are nearby. The inn is just one and one-half miles south of I-10 off Exit 28 and about five miles from Beach Highway 90, via Menge Avenue in Pass Christian to Red Creek Road. Biloxi is about 20 minutes, and New Orleans is about an hour away.

Hosts: Sharon and Denis Crowder
Rooms: 7 (5 PB; 2 SB) $49-69
Continental Breakfast
Credit Cards: None
Notes: 2, 5, 8, 9, 10, 11, 12, 13, 14

LORMAN

Lincoln Ltd.

P.O. Box 3479, Meridian, 39303
(601) 482-5483 (information)
(800) 633-MISS (reservations)
FAX (601) 693-7447

84. Circa 1855, this Italianate Revival home is on a working plantation. It is a wildlife preserve with guided jeep tours of the area, nature trails, and a heated swimming pool. Enjoy a wood-burning fireplace or stove and see wild deer or turkey on a tour or walking the nature trails. A full, seated breakfast and dinner are included in the price. $165.

Natchez Trace Bed and Breakfast Reservation Service

P.O. Box 193, Hampshire, TN 38461
(615) 285-2777; (800) 377-2770

LOR-01. Milepost 30. Completed in 1857 by an architect of Windsor, whose awesome ruins stand nearby. Classic Greek Revival with 14 rooms, 14-foot ceilings, columned galleries, winding stairway, and original slave quarters. Visitors may read in the diary of an early owner of the house about plantation life before and during the Civil War. Even a resident ghost! Rooms are upstairs; canopied beds, private baths, TV, movies, and telephones. Refreshments on arrival, full breakfast, heated pool, and spa. AAA approved. $95-125.

Rosswood Plantation

Rosswood Plantation

Route 552, 39096
(601) 437-4215; (800) 533-5889
FAX (601) 437-6888

NOTES: Credit cards accepted: A MasterCard; B Visa; C American Express; D Discover Card; E Diner's Club; F Other; 2 Personal checks accepted; 3 Lunch available; 4 Dinner available; 5 Open all year;

An authentic antebellum mansion, close to Natchez and Vicksburg, offering luxury, comfort, charm, and hospitality on a serene country estate. Once a cotton plantation, Rosswood now grows Christmas trees. Ideal for honeymoons. A Mississippi landmark; National Register; AAA rated three diamonds.

Hosts: Jean and Walt Hylander
Rooms: 4 (PB) $95-125
Full Breakfast
Credit Cards: A, B, C, D
Closed: January-February
Notes: 2, 7, 8, 9, 11, 14

MERIDIAN

Lincoln Ltd.

P.O. Box 3479, 39303
(601) 482-5483 (information)
(800) 633-MISS (reservations)
FAX (601) 693-7447

13. Restored Victorian home filled with antiques and stands on ten wooded acres within the city limits. Hostess is a noted gourmet cook and by special arrangement will prepare dinner for an additional charge. Full breakfast included. One guest room. $65.

16. A charming guest suite in a home in one of Meridian's historic neighborhoods. Bedroom, bath, and a living area decorated in antiques. Kitchen privileges. Private entrance. Continental breakfast. $65; weekly and monthly rates available.

18. In one of Meridian's loveliest neighborhoods, this home is set among flowering shrubs and dogwood trees. The host and hostess have always been active in civic and cultural activities, both locally and within the state. Attractively furnished, two bedrooms with shared bath (for family or four people traveling together, only) or a double room with private bath. Full Mississippi breakfast. $65-90.

58. A contemporary inn convenient to I-59 and I-20 with 100 beautiful, spacious guest rooms. Meeting space for up to 60 people. Continental breakfast is served. Swimming pool and whirlpool on premises. $39-45; weekly and monthly rates available.

72. Convenient to downtown Meridian, this lovely home is filled with the host's collection of family heirlooms. Sleep in a pre-Civil War mahogany canopied bed. Enjoy the sun porch and patio. The hostess is a Meridian interior designer. $65.

NATCHEZ

Bed and Breakfast Mansions of Natchez

P.O. Box 347, Canal Street Depot, 39121
(601) 446-6631; (800) 647-6742
FAX (601) 446-8687

Camellia Gardens. Elegant Queen Anne Victorian house, circa 1897, in downtown Garden District. Recently restored to exhibit the richness of late Victorian interiors with period decoration. Rare old camellias and swimming pool in the garden. Evening dessert tray, full Southern breakfast. Antique car collection. No smoking.

Elgin. Guests enjoy a plantation experience in the 1853 Guest House. Bedrooms with antique furnishings open onto a private gallery. Downstairs are sitting room, kitchen and dining room where seated breakfast is served. Ten minutes from city center. Featured in *Gourmet*, April 1993. Designated smoking areas.

Glenburnie. Circa 1833. Escape to the charm of history and ambiance of country gardens in a quaint three-room cottage on grounds of Glenburnie. Standing near the heart of downtown Natchez, cottage features beautifully appointed rooms and

6 Pets welcome; 8 Children welcome; 9 Social drinking allowed; 10 Tennis available; 11 Swimming available; 12 Golf available; 13 Skiing available; 14 May be booked through travel agents.

Bed and Breakfast Mansions of Natchez (continued)

caters to the demands of today's traveler with kitchen, washer, dryer. No smoking. Continental breakfast is served.

Glenfield. Charming English Gothic house, circa 1812 and 1845, in a country setting, yet only a short distance from downtown Natchez. Furnished with period antiques. Five generations of the owners family have lived at Glenfield. Guests will enjoy the hospitality of descendants of early Natchez families. Designated smoking area.

Highpoint. Victorian "Country Manor" residence, circa 1890, in lovely Historic District with rare camellias and antique roses. One block from the bluffs and panoramic view of the river. Spacious bedrooms furnished with antiques and period reproductions. Complimentary beverage and snack upon arrival. No smoking.

Lansdowne. Hidden within 100 parklike acres just three miles from downtown Natchez, and still occupied by direct descendants of the builder, it is one of the most authentic houses in the area. Spacious rooms in 1853 dependency are furnished with antiques. Breakfast served in dining room of main house. TV in guest room. Designated smoking areas.

Linden. An imposing Federal Plantation home, circa 1800, in a park-like setting, its front doorway was copied for *Gone with the Wind*. Seven bedrooms furnished with exquisite heirlooms and canopied beds from six generations. Delectable Southern breakfast served in the formal banquet room. AAA three diamond. Designated smoking areas.

Monmouth. On 27 landscaped acres, Monmouth, circa 1818, is a National Historic Landmark. Nineteen rooms and suites. Four Diamond Award; member Small Luxury Hotels of the World. Candlelight dinner served Tuesday through Saturday. Pond, fishing, croquet course and nature walks. Groups and corporate retreats welcome. TV in room.

Mount Repose. A perfect example of a Southern plantation home, circa 1824. Three suites feature treasured heirlooms as eight generations have made this their home. Front and back galleries overlook 27 acres, shaded by ancient live oak trees. Ten minutes from town. Plantation breakfast. Complimentary wine. Designated smoking areas.

Ravenna. Elegant family home, circa 1835, secluded in three acres of an old-fashioned garden a few blocks from downtown Natchez. Known for its three-story elliptical stairway. Three large antique filled bedrooms in main house; one-bedroom guest house by swimming pool. Seated breakfast served in formal dining room.

Shields Town House. Circa 1860. Exclusive bed and breakfast suites in beautiful private setting feature all modern amenities, antique charm, individual landscaped courtyards. Garage parking adjacent to each suite. Main house courtyard features a large three-tier fountain and splendid gardens. Telephone and TV in room. Continental Breakfast is served.

Sweet Olive Tree Manor. Classic Victorian elegance, circa 1880, with period furnishings. Garden District location downtown. Sumptuous gourmet breakfast served in formal dining room and complimentary late afternoon tea hour. Three spa-

NOTES: Credit cards accepted: A MasterCard; B Visa; C American Express; D Discover Card; E Diner's Club; F Other; 2 Personal checks accepted; 3 Lunch available; 4 Dinner available; 5 Open all year;

cious, light and airy bedroom suites. AAA three diamond. No smoking.

Texada. First brick house, circa 1792, in the Mississippi Territory. Elegant townhouse in Spanish Quarter. English and American period antiques with four-poster beds. Four large bedrooms and central sitting room with private entrance. Guest House with sitting room accommodates four. Enclosed landscaped courtyard. Designated smoking areas.

The Wigwam. This antebellum mansion, circa 1836, is noted for its ballroom with decorative hand-painted ceiling, elegant plaster work and arched doorways. Rooms exquisitely furnished with fine period antiques. Two beautiful suites. Guests enjoy use of formal rooms and New Orleans style courtyard. TV in room. Designated smoking areas.

William Harris House. An imposing two-story house, circa 1835, only a few blocks from the center of town. Built by William Harris who was an early planter and civic leader and the father of the Confederate Gen. Nathaniel Harrison Harris. Enjoy elegant period furnishings, New Orleans Courtyard, Pocket Garden. TV in room. Designated smoking areas.

The Briars Inn

31 Irving Lane, 39120
(601) 446-9654

The Briars is on the bluffs overlooking the Mississippi River. There are 19 acres of very interesting gardens. The main house was built in 1812 and was the site of the marriage of Jefferson Davis and Varina Howell in 1843. Large bedrooms, antique-filled spacious private baths, and public areas are open to guests 24 hours a day. Pool, bar, card room, drawing room, and parlor. Cable TV and movies. Four-dia-

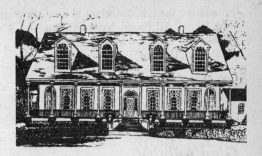

The Briars Inn

mond AAA rating for five years. Easy access to tennis and golf. Riverboat casino gambling and tours of historic Natchez homes and sights. Quiet, private, and relaxing with superior service and hospitality.

Hosts: Nancy Diehl and Christine James
Rooms: 13 (PB) $135-150
Full Breakfast
Credit Cards: A, B, C
Notes: 2, 5, 7 (restricted), 8 (12 and older), 9, 10, 12, 14

The Burn

712 North Union Street, 39120
(601) 442-1344; (800) 654-8859

Circa 1834, three-story mansion especially noted for its semispiral stairway, unique gardens, and exquisite collection of antiques. Overnight guests are pampered with a seated plantation breakfast, tour of the home, and use of the swimming pool. Member of Independent Innkeepers Association.

Host: Ann White
Owners: Larry and Deborah Christensen
Rooms: 7 (PB) $90-125
Full Breakfast
Credit Cards: A, B, C, D, E
Notes: 2, 5, 7, 8, 9, 10, 11, 12, 14

Dunleith

84 Homochitto, 39120
(601) 446-8500; (800) 433-2445

A National Historic Landmark, circa 1856, this picturesque Greek Revival mansion is on a 40-acre landscaped park near downtown Natchez. There are 11 guest rooms;

6 Pets welcome; 8 Children welcome; 9 Social drinking allowed; 10 Tennis available; 11 Swimming available; 12 Golf available; 13 Skiing available; 14 May be booked through travel agents.

three in the main house, eight in the Courtyard Wing. All rooms have working fireplaces. Full Southern breakfast is served in
the Poultry House.

Host: Nancy Gibbs
Rooms: 11 (PB) $85-130
Full Breakfast
Credit Cards: A, B, C, D
Notes: None

Glen Auburn

300 South Commerce Street, 39120
(601) 442-4099; (800) 833-0170

A French Second Empire rarity, recently restored, in the center of antebellum Natchez
offers overnight guests a taste of Victorian
elegance. Choose from four luxurious
suites, several with Jacuzzis, or the eclectic
carriage house. Enjoy evening wine and
cheese, a Southern breakfast in the dining
room, or lounge by the pool. A special
place to make memories or to just get away.

Hosts: Carolyn and Richard Boyer
Suites: 5 (PB) $125-175
Full Breakfast
Credit Cards: A, B
Notes: 2, 5, 9, 10, 11, 12, 14

The Governor Holmes House

207 South Wall Street, 39120
(601) 442-2366

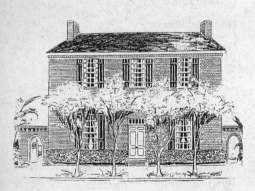

The Governor Holmes House

The Governor Holmes House was built in
1794, one of the oldest and most historic
homes in the Old Spanish Quarter. It was
the home of the last governor of the Mississippi Territory and the first governor of the
state of Mississippi when it became a state
in 1817. The home was also in the painting
of Natchez that Audubon painted in 1823
and is on the National Register of Historic
Places.

Host: Robert Pully, Owner/Manager
Rooms: 4 (PB) $85-115
Full Breakfast
Credit Cards: A, B
Notes: 2, 5, 7 (limited), 9, 10, 11, 12, 14

Hope Farm

147 Homochitto Street, 39120
(601) 445-4848

Four guest rooms furnished with authentic
antiques in the original 1775 house. All
have private baths, air conditioning, and
heat. The main house dates back to 1789.
Breakfast served in the main house dining
room and a tour of Hope Farm takes place
after breakfast.

Host: Ethel G. Banta
Rooms: 4 (PB) $80-90
Full Breakfast
Credit Cards: None
Notes: 2, 5, 7, 8, 9, 10, 12, 14

Lincoln Ltd.

P.O. Box 3479, Meridian, 39303
(601) 482-5483 (information)
(800) 633-MISS (reservations)
FAX (601) 693-7447

19. Circa 1832. This three-story mansion's
outstanding architectural feature is the
semi-elliptical stairway. Horses once trod
where a collection of priceless furnishings
and fine paintings now reside. Listed on the
National Register of Historic Places. Full
breakfast served. Swimming pool on
premises. Ten guest rooms. $90-125.

20. Dating from 1774-89 and surrounded
by old-fashioned gardens, this home was

NOTES: Credit cards accepted: A MasterCard; B Visa; C American Express; D Discover Card; E Diner's
Club; F Other; 2 Personal checks accepted; 3 Lunch available; 4 Dinner available; 5 Open all year;

once the home of a Spanish governor. In keeping with the period of the house, it is charmingly furnished with family heirlooms and other rare antiques. Formerly the home of Mr. and Mrs. J. Balfour Miller. The late Mrs. Miller was the originator of the Natchez Pilgrimage. Listed on the National Register of Historic Places. Full breakfast served. Four guest rooms. $85-105.

21. Circa 1790. Once the home of Thomas B. Reed, first elected U.S. senator from Mississippi, this architectural gem of the Federal period has been occupied since 1849 by the Conner family and its descendants. Listed on the National Register of Historic Places. Full breakfast served. Seven guest rooms. $90-110.

22. Circa 1818. The former home of Gen. John A. Quitman, an early Mississippi governor of Mexican War fame. This antebellum home contains many original Quitman pieces. Listed on the National Register. Fourteen guest rooms; suite available. $85-160.

29. Sleep in a canopied bed or stretch out in a hammock at this historic home hosted by a person who can tell guests all they want to know about Natchez, past and present. A full plantation breakfast is served on the sunny porch. Five guest rooms. $75-100.

30. An outstanding historical home with a panoramic view of the Mississippi River. Furnished with an impressive collection of antiques, including the works of John Belter and P. Mallard. Welcoming beverage, tour of the home, and a large plantation-style breakfast are included. Five guest rooms. $85.

45. Planters Cottage, built in 1836, is on a 500-acre working plantation 13 miles south of Natchez. Owned by descendants of the builders, it was restored in 1986 and retains some original furniture and documents. It is one of the oldest farms in Mississippi and is on the National Register of Historic Places. Pastures and ponds surround the house and provide a peaceful, relaxing setting. Three guest rooms. $90-125.

46. One of the finest examples of early Southern Plantation-style architecture, this lovely home is on a promontory overlooking the Mississippi River. Abounding in history, the antique-filled rooms offer the guest a time to relax and enjoy the very room where Jefferson Davis was married in 1845. All 13 bedrooms are spacious. Private baths available. Full breakfast is served. $130-145.

69. Once owned by the last territorial governor and the first U.S. governor of Mississippi, this home was built in 1794 in the heart of Natchez. Many of the rooms have original 18th-century paneling and are furnished in period antiques. Enjoy the formal drawing room and eat a full plantation breakfast in the elegant dining room or cozy breakfast room. Five guest rooms and one suite available. $85-110.

70. Circa 1853. This beautiful plantation, which is still inhabited by the descendants of the original builders, is on 150 acres of land. Most of the original family antiques still decorate the home. Stay in one of the "Dependencies" and enjoy a full Southern breakfast in the main house. Two guest rooms. $90.

76. An elegant Victorian mansion circa 1880 furnished in antiques. In the Natchez historic district within walking distance of several of the antebellum tour homes. Enjoy a full breakfast served in the formal dining room on fine crystal, silver, and china. Visit

6 Pets welcome; 8 Children welcome; 9 Social drinking allowed; 10 Tennis available; 11 Swimming available; 12 Golf available; 13 Skiing available; 14 May be booked through travel agents.

with the owners over wine, cheese, and tea in the late afternoon or early evening. There are four guest rooms; semi-private and private baths. $110.

Linden

1 Linden Place, 39120
(601) 445-5472

Linden sits on seven landscaped acres and has been in the present owner's family for six generations. It is a Federal-style house furnished in antiques and many heirlooms. All seven bedrooms have four-poster beds and other antiques of the Federal period. The front doorway was copied in *Gone with the Wind*. Early morning coffee, a full Southern plantation breakfast, and a tour of the house are included in the price of a room. Linden is on the famous spring and fall pilgrimages, quality rated by Mobil Guide and three-diamond rated by AAA. The owner welcomes her guests and gives the tour of the home herself.

Host: Jeanette S. Feltus
Rooms: 7 (PB) $90
Full Breakfast
Credit Cards: None
Notes: 2, 5, 7, 8 (over 10), 9, 10, 11, 12, 14

Natchez Trace Bed and Breakfast Reservation Service

P.O. Box 193, Hampshire, TN 38461
(615) 285-2777; (800) 377-2770

NAT-01. Milepost 8. This 1880 Victorian mansion in the historic district is furnished with antiques. A full breakfast is served in the formal dining room; afternoon wine, cheese, and tea is offered in the parlors. Within walking distance of several antebellum homes and other historic sites. No children under 14. Suites with private bath, $110; two-bedroom suite, $160. Inquire about special summer and holiday rates

NAT-02. Milepost 8. Built in 1794, this is one of the oldest and most historic homes in

Natchez, having been the home of the last governor of the Mississippi Territory and first governor of Mississippi. Listed in the National Register of Historic Places, it is beautifully decorated with period furnishings, porcelain paintings, and Oriental carpets. It features suites with private, modern baths. A delicious plantation breakfast is served in the formal dining room or the quaint breakfast room. No small children. Governor's Suite $115; other rooms $85.

NAT-03. Milepost 8. This Natchez home, built between 1774 and 1789, is listed in the National Register of Historic Places and was once owned by the first Spanish governor of the territory. It features exquisite antique furniture from the early 18th century. Each guest room is furnished with a distinctive four-poster bed with draped testers. Private baths. No small children. A large Southern-style breakfast and tour of the home is included. $80-90 double; $20 each extra person.

Oakland Plantation

1124 Lower Woodville Road, 39120
(601) 445-5101; (800) 824-0355

This charming retreat is about eight miles south of Natchez, with 360 acres of pastures, nature trails, fishing ponds, and a tennis court. The guest house dates back to 1785, and guests to this estate include Andrew Jackson and his wife, Rachel. Come for the peace and quiet, and relax in an 18th-century atmosphere.

Hosts: Andy and Jeanie Peabody
Rooms: 3 (2 PB; 1 SB) $65-75
Full Breakfast
Credit Cards: A, B
Notes: 2, 5, 8, 9, 10, 12, 14

Sweet Olive Tree Manor Bed and Breakfast

700 Orleans Street, 39120
(601) 442-1401; (800) 256-INNS

Breakfast in Victorian splendor when guests stay in this mansion furnished in antiques and antique reproductions of the Victorian period. A full gourmet breakfast is served in the formal dining room with fine crystal, silver, and china. Wine, cheese, and teas are served in the early evening. Three blocks from downtown Natchez in the historic garden district. Children over 14 years old are welcome. No smoking. No pets. Stay at Sweet Olive Tree Manor, where Southern hospitality becomes a reality in historic Natchez, Mississippi. Member of Historic Inns of Natchez. Featured in *What's New Down South*. AAA three-diamond rating. Gift certificates available. Special Thanksgiving and Christmas holiday packages

Hosts: Judee McKenna-Brown and Peggy
   McKenna
Rooms: 4 (3 PB; 1 SB) $80-110
Full Breakfast
Credit Cards: None
Notes: 2, 5, 9, 10, 11, 12, 14

Weymouth Hall Inn

Weymouth Hall Inn

1 Cemetery Road, 39120
(601) 445-2304

On the bluff overlooking the mighty Mississippi River, Weymouth Hall stands alone, with its unequaled scenic view. Guests can relax on recessed porches in the late afternoon while delighting in the panoramic view of the river. The outstand-

ing home is completely furnished with an impressive collection of period antiques. Closed January.

Host: Gene Weber
Rooms: 5 (PB) $80-85
Full Breakfast
Credit Cards: A, B
Notes: 2, 7 (limited), 8 (15 and older), 9, 14

PASS CHRISTIAN

Lincoln Ltd.

P.O. Box 3479, Meridian, 39303
(601) 482-5483 (information)
(800) 633-MISS (reservations)
FAX (601) 693-7447

77. Across from Pass Christian Yacht Harbor, this three-story home allows guests to enjoy a harbor view from the front porches with French doors opening onto the porches from all rooms facing the Gulf. As guests stay among the family antiques and art they may enjoy the reception and dining parlors, play cards or billiards in the kitchen or den, or simply enjoy the peaceful harbor view. Five rooms. Children over 14 are welcome. $78-98.

PORT GIBSON

Gibson's Landing

1002 Church Street, Highway 61 South, 39150
(601) 437-3432

Enjoy the small-town charm of Port Gibson! This historic late-Federal/early-Greek Revival mansion was built in 1830 and is known for its spiral staircase that extends two and one-half stories. All five guest rooms are furnished with period antiques and tester beds; all rooms in the main house. Romantic Empire Suite features a Jacuzzi and double shower. Conven-iently to both Vicksburg and Natchez.

Hosts: Trish and Curtley Hayes
Rooms: 5 (PB) $75-120
Full Breakfast

6 Pets welcome; 8 Children welcome; 9 Social drinking allowed; 10 Tennis available; 11 Swimming available; 12 Golf available; 13 Skiing available; 14 May be booked through travel agents.

Credit Cards: A, B
Notes: 2, 5

Lincoln Ltd.

P.O. Box 3479, Meridian, 39303
(601) 482-5483 (information)
(800) 633-MISS (reservations)
FAX (601) 693-7447

26. Enjoy a night in one of the South's most beautiful antebellum mansions. In the National Register of Historic Places, this home is furnished with family heirlooms. Visitors will step back in history to an era of gracious living. Includes a full Southern-style breakfast and a tour of the home. Eleven guest rooms. $85.

66. Circa 1832. This late Federal-style home is noted for its beautiful three-story curved show-off stairway. Once owned by Judge Harry T. Ellet, who drew up the secession paper for the Confederacy. Enjoy one of five guest rooms beautifully decorated or one large suite complete with Jacuzzi. Listed in the National Register of Historic Places. Full Southern breakfast. $75-105.

Oak Square Plantation

1207 Church Street, 39150
(601) 437-4350; (800) 729-0240

Oak Square, circa 1850, is Port Gibson's largest and most palatial Greek Revival antebellum mansion. Visitors experience a quiet retreat into the past. Family heirloom antiques, canopied beds, full Southern breakfast, and a tour of the mansion and grounds. In the National Register of Historic Places and AAA four-diamond rated. Port Gibson is the third oldest town in Mississippi referred to by Gen. U. S. Grant as "the town too beautiful to burn." Area attractions include antebellum homes, churches, a military state park, and Civil War battlefields and museums. Home to the 1800s Spring Festival during the last weekend in March.

Hosts: Mr. and Mrs. William D. Lum
Rooms: 12 (PB) $75-95
Full Breakfast
Credit Cards: A, B, C, D
Notes: 2, 5, 8, 9

SLATE SPRING

The Doler Bed and Breakfast Inn

Dentontown Road, P.O. Box 4605, 38955
(601) 637-2695; (901) 363-0200

This Queen Anne house is on a 150-acre farm where one can walk through the white cotton fields in the fall and the dogwood trails in the spring. Half-tester Victorian beds decorated with lots of lace and heirloom furniture throughout takes one back to the turn of the century. Beautiful Arkansas pine floors and Oriental rugs grace the rooms. A stately nine-foot walnut mantel towers toward 12-foot ceilings. Antique malls and the Natchez Trace Parkway are nearby. Afternoon tea is served on the veranda. A five-course dinner and full breakfast are served to all guests. Lunch available by reservation.

Hosts: Ruth and Lowell Doler
Rooms: 5 (PB) $95-125
Full Breakfast
Credit Cards: None
Notes: 2, 3, 5, 7 (inside), 12, 14

Lincoln Ltd.

P.O. Box 3479, Meridian, 39303
(601) 482-5483 (information)
(800) 633-MISS (reservations)
FAX (601) 693-7447

65. Circa 1890. This lovely old farmhouse with curved staircase has been lovingly restored to its present beauty with half-tester Victorian beds and heirloom antiques. Walk the 150-acre farm with its beautiful wildflowers, colorful birds, and trees. Enjoy a full Southern breakfast and a full-course dinner included in the price. Three guest rooms with private baths. $95.

NOTES: Credit cards accepted: A MasterCard; B Visa; C American Express; D Discover Card; E Diner's Club; F Other; 2 Personal checks accepted; 3 Lunch available; 4 Dinner available; 5 Open all year;

TUPELO

The Mockingbird Inn Bed and Breakfast

305 North Gloster, 38801
(601) 841-0286

Discover the romance of a different place and time in an enchanting getaway in the heart of Tupelo. Each guest room of this 70-year-old home represents the decor from a different area of the world. Cable TV, telephones, truly comfortable queen-size beds, plus pleasant surprises await each guests. Evening refreshments, soft drinks, coffee, and tea are complimentary. Three Civil War battlefields within an hour; five minutes to Elvis' birthplace. Just off the Natchez Trace halfway between Nashville and Natchez. Across the street from two delicious restaurants in lovely old homes.

Hosts: Jim and Sandy Gilmer
Rooms: 7 (PB) $65-95
Full Breakfast
Credit Cards: A, B, C, D
Note: 2, 5, 6, 8 (13 and older), 9, 11, 14

Annabelle

VICKSBURG

Annabelle

501 Speed Street, 39180
(601) 638-2000; (800) 791-2000

Overnight memories are taken from this historic 1868 two-story Victorian home in Riverview, Vicksburg's historic garden district. Elegantly, but comfortably, furnished in beautiful period antiques, Annabelle offers king- and queen-size beds, some with canopies, twelve-foot high ceilings, in-room cable TV, air conditioning, and a beautiful Vieux Carre patio surrounded by crepe myrtles and pecan and magnolia trees. A delicious Southern breakfast is served in the formal dining room. AAA three diamond award.

Hosts: Carolyn and George Mayer
Rooms: 5 (PB) $80-100; Suites: 2 (PB) $135
Full Breakfast
Credit Cards: A, B, C, D, E
Notes: 2, 5, 9, 12, 14

Belle of the Bends Bed and Breakfast

508 Klein Street, 39180
(601) 634-0737; (800) 844-2308

Belle of the Bends is a charming Italianate Victorian three-story home with verandas at two levels that wrap around three sides of the house. From the verandas guests can view the Mississippi River and magnificent gardens. Three large, beautiful guest rooms are decorated in period antiques that are family heirlooms. Each room has individual, central temperature control, radio, cable TV, and private bath. Lace trimmed sheets adorn each bed. This is truly a place to relax and glimpse the elegance of yesteryear with the comforts of today. Full breakfast served in the formal dining room. Tour the house and neighborhood after breakfast.

Hosts: Wally and Jo Pratt
Rooms: 3 (PB) $85-110
Full Breakfast
Credit Cards: A, B
Notes: 2, 5, 8, 9, 14 (10 percent)

Cedar Grove Mansion-Inn

2200 Oak Street, 39180
(800) 862-1300

6 Pets welcome; 8 Children welcome; 9 Social drinking allowed; 10 Tennis available; 11 Swimming available; 12 Golf available; 13 Skiing available; 14 May be booked through travel agents.

Cedar Grove Mansion-Inn

Straight out of *Gone with the Wind* is this 1840 magnificently furnished inn with its four acres of gardens and its fountains, courtyards, gas lights, four-poster beds, and period antiques. Pool, tennis, croquet, lawn and roof garden with a view of the Mississippi River. Jacuzzi and terrace also have a view of the Mississippi River. Piano bar, fine dining, and roof garden. Chosen by the book, *Escape in Style,* as "one of the most romantic inns in the world." Four-diamond rated by AAA and a national historic property.

Rooms: 22 (PB) $85-160
Full Breakfast
Credit Cards: A, B, C, D
Notes: 2, 4, 5, 7 (limited), 8 (over 5), 9, 10, 11, 12, 14

Lincoln Ltd.

P.O. Box 3479, Meridian, 39303
(601) 482-5483 (information)
(800) 633-MISS (reservations)
FAX (601) 693-7447

27. True Southern hospitality in this Federal-style home. Here history combines with every modern amenity, including a hot tub and a swimming pool. Step back in time as guests sleep in an antique-filled bedroom and enjoy a full plantation-style breakfast in the formal dining room. A tour of the home and a welcoming beverage are included. There is one guest room. $125.

32. On six landscaped acres, this outstanding home designed in the Federal style boasts exquisite milled woodwork, sterling silver door knobs, French bronze chandeliers, and a lonely ghost—all echoes of the past. Three lovely guest rooms all furnished in antiques: a Mallard bed, a Heppelwhite tester, or a plantation-style room are here to enjoy. A tour of the home, a plantation breakfast, and mint juleps included. $85.

35. This home, circa 1873, was built as a wedding present from father to daughter. It is an interesting mixture of Victorian and Greek Revival architectural styles. All bedrooms are furnished with antiques and have private baths. Some rooms are available with fireplace and TV. Enjoy a spectacular view of the Mississippi River and valley from a rocking chair on the front gallery. Full plantation breakfast is included. Listed on the National Register of Historic Places. Six guest rooms. $75-130.

36. Lavish antebellum mansion built between 1840 and 1858 as a wedding present from a wealthy businessman to his bride. *Gone with the Wind* elegance that guests won't soon forget. Exquisitely furnished with many original antiques. Enjoy the beautiful formal gardens, gazebos, and fountains. Relax in the courtyard. Pool and spa available. Listed on the National Register of Historic Places. Its 17 guest rooms have private baths. $85-160.

41. Elegant antebellum mansion, circa 1856, in Vicksburg's historic district. It is the best example of Palladian architecture found in Mississippi. Used as a hospital during the Civil War, it was shelled during the siege of Vicksburg. Listed on the National Register of Historic Places. A welcoming beverage, tour of the home, and full breakfast are included. Eight guest rooms. $85-140.

NOTES: Credit cards accepted: A MasterCard; B Visa; C American Express; D Discover Card; E Diner's Club; F Other; 2 Personal checks accepted; 3 Lunch available; 4 Dinner available; 5 Open all year;

73. This historic home, circa 1876, was named after an excursion riverboat and overlooks the Mississippi River. Sit on the porch and watch riverboats pass by, or stroll in the informal gardens. The home is an easy walk to other historic homes, restaurants, and attractions. Enjoy one of the three guest rooms filled with family antiques. $85-95.

Natchez Trace Bed and Breakfast Reservation Service

P.O. Box 193, Hampshire, TN 38461
(615) 285-2777; (800) 377-2770

VIC-01. Milepost 60 or 67. In historic Vicksburg, 15 miles from the Trace, this circa 1873 mansion, built as a wedding present to a daughter, is listed in the National Register of Historic Places. All rooms are furnished with antiques and include TV; some have working fireplaces. There is a 68-foot gallery with a spectacular view of the Mississippi River. Full plantation breakfast is included. $85-105.

Tomil Manor

2430 Drummond Street, 39180
(601) 638-8893

Tomil Manor is a unique house consisting of 32 stained-glass windows, oak, cypress, blue poplar, and fine paneling. Every room has a fireplace except the butler's pantry. Come to the "Red Carpet City" of the South and enjoy true Southern hospitality.

Host: Mildred Kirkland
Rooms: 5 (3 PB; 2 SB) $55-85
Full Breakfast
Credit Cards: A, B
Notes: 5, 8, 14

YAZOO CITY

Lincoln Ltd.

P.O. Box 3479, Meridian, 39303
(601) 482-5483 (information)
(800) 633-MISS (reservations)
FAX (601) 693-7447

70. Twenty miles from Yazoo City. Step back into history and walk among azaleas and spectacular day lilies. This manager's plantation home, built in 1860, offering four bedrooms and tastefully decorated with period antiques, offers an intriguing oasis of privacy for those who wish to get away from the rush of life. Relax in two gazebos and absorb nature's sounds and aromas or slip away to a cozy sitting room upstairs and enjoy a panoramic view of the entire front garden. A full plantation evening meal and breakfast are included. $100-110.

6 Pets welcome; 8 Children welcome; 9 Social drinking allowed; 10 Tennis available; 11 Swimming available; 12 Golf available; 13 Skiing available; 14 May be booked through travel agents.

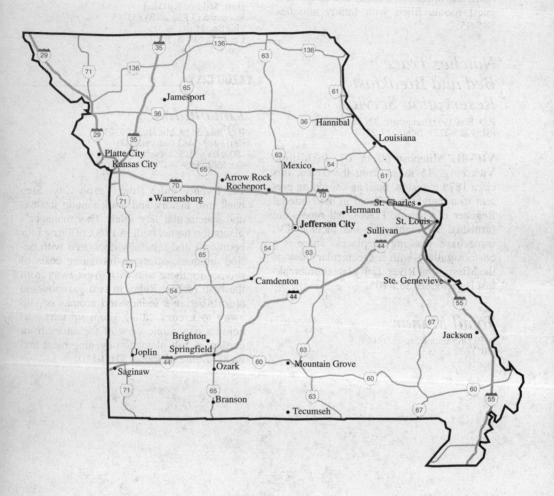

Missouri

Missouri

ARROW ROCK

Borgman's
Bed and Breakfast

706 Van Buren, 65320
(816) 837-3350

The hosts invite guests to experience the historic town of Arrow Rock in the warmth of the century-old home. Choose one of four spacious guest rooms that share three baths, and relax in the sitting room or on the porch. Wind up the old Victrola for a song, choose a game or puzzle, browse through a book, or just sit for a spell, and listen to the sounds of Arrow Rock. In the morning guests will enjoy a family-style breakfast of freshly baked bread, juice or fruit, coffee, and tea.

Hosts: Kathy and Helen Borgman
Rooms: 4 (1 PB; 3 SB) $45-50
Continental Breakfast
Credit Cards: None
Notes: 2, 5, 8

BRANSON

The Barger House
Bed and Breakfast

621 Lakeshore Drive, 65616
(417) 335-2134

Casual country elegance on Lake Taney-como in the beautiful Ozark Hills, the Barger House is a charming version of an 18th-century Colonial home furnished with French and Victorian antiques, and collectibles. A deck with a hot tub and large pool provides a beautiful view of the lake and downtown Branson. Trout fishing off the private boat dock. Delicious multi-course breakfast served in the dining room or on the deck.

Hosts: Ralph and Cathy
Rooms: 3 (PB) $95-125
Full Breakfast
Credit Cards: None
Notes: 2, 5, 10, 11, 12

The Branson Hotel
Bed and Breakfast Inn

214 West Main, 65616
(417) 335-6104

"Branson's Best Lodging," *Southern Living*, April 1994, and winner of AAA four-diamond award 1993 and 1994. History, romance, and elegance await guests at this historical inn which has provided memories to visitors since 1903. Premier location downtown Branson. Cable TVs and in-room phones. Two large verandas overlook downtown. Full breakfast served in the glass-enclosed dining room.

Hosts: Teri Murgina and Susan Jones
Rooms: 9 (PB) $85-105
Full Breakfast
Notes: 2, 8 (over 12), 9, 10, 11, 12, 14

The Branson House
Bed and Breakfast Inn

120 Fourth Street, 65616
(417) 334-0959

Surrounded by rock walls of native field-stone, old oak trees, and country flower gar

---

NOTES: Credit cards accepted: A MasterCard; B Visa; C American Express; D Discover Card; E Diner's Club; F Other; 2 Personal checks accepted; 3 Lunch available; 4 Dinner available; 5 Open all year; 6 Pets welcome; 7 Smoking allowed; 8 Children welcome; 9 Social drinking allowed; 10 Tennis available; 11 Swimming available; 12 Golf available; 13 Skiing available; 14 May be booked through travel agents.

dens, the Branson House sits on a hillside of downtown Branson overlooking the town and the bluffs of Lake Taneycomo. Built in the early 1920s, this spacious home is unique to the area and remains Branson's grandest old home. The English country ambience offers serenity for visitors after a busy day in Branson. Air-conditioned. Open March through mid-December. AAA and Mobil Guide recommended.

Host: Opal Kelly
Rooms: 7 (PB) $65-95
Full Breakfast
Credit Cards: None
Notes: 2, 8 (over 12), 9, 10, 11, 12, 14

Josie's, The Peaceful Getaway

Indian Point Road, HCR. 1, Box 1104, 65616
(417) 338-2978; (800) 289-4125

Three hundred feet of lakefront for guests to enjoy on the shore of Table Rock Lake. Contemporary home with 15-foot-high stone fireplace and cathedral ceilings. Victorian touches which include fresh flowers, china, and stained glass. Forget-me-not suite has private entrance, patio, kitchenette, fireplace, living area, queen-size bed, and whirlpool for two. Blueberry Lace Room features an outdoor Jacuzzi. Veranda with panoramic view. Near marina and Silver Dollar City. Eight miles to country music shows. Celebrate a honeymoon or anniversary in style!

Hosts: Bill and JoAnne Coats
Rooms: 3 (PB) $55-95
Full Breakfast
Credit Cards: A, B
Notes: 2, 5, 9, 11, 12, 14

Red Bud Cove Bed and Breakfast Suite

162 Lakewood Drive (Lake Road 65-48, County Road 65-180), Hollister, 65672
(800) 677-5525

On Table Rock Lake, nine miles south of Branson. Spend the evenings in comfort in the spacious suites with lakefront patio/deck. Seven suites with private entrance have living room (some with fireplace), bedroom with king- or queen-size bed, bathroom (some with spa), fully-equipped kitchenette/dining area, air conditioning, TV, and phones. Full breakfast is served in the dining room in the main house. Boats and dock space are available to rent.

Hosts: Rick and Carol Carpenter
Rooms: 7 (PB) $70-90
Full Breakfast
Credit Cards: A, B, C, D
Notes: 2, 5, 14

Red Bud Cove

BRIGHTON

Eden Bed and Breakfast

Route One, Box 76, 65617
(417) 267-2820

Eden is a 252-acre valley estate 15 miles north of Springfield. Surrounding the main residence and stone guest house are a solar greenhouse of native stone, soft rolling hills, wildflowers, pods, and numerous energizing springs. The guest house offers a fireplace, bath, complete kitchen, and handmade hickory bedstead. The couch could

NOTES: Credit cards accepted: A MasterCard; B Visa; C American Express; D Discover Card; E Diner's Club; F Other; 2 Personal checks accepted; 3 Lunch available; 4 Dinner available; 5 Open all year;

sleep a third person. Pets welcome. Children welcome. Smoking permitted.

Hosts: Neal and Jackie Cohen
Room: 1 (PB) $70-75
Full or Continental Breakfast
Credit Cards: None
Notes: 5, 6, 7, 8, 9, 11, 14

CAMDENTON

Ramblewood Bed and Breakfast

402 Panoramic Drive, 65020
(314) 346-3410 after 5:00 P.M.

This inviting cottage nestles in a grove of oak and dogwood trees. The decor is traditional, touched with Victorian. Guests will be welcomed with tea or lemonade, and homemade goodies. Breakfast is special, beginning with a beautiful fruit plate, followed by tempting dishes and breads. Minutes from the lake, state park, fine restaurants, music shows, and shops.

Host: Mary E. Massey
Rooms: 3 (SB) $50
Full Breakfast
Credit Cards: None
Notes: 2, 5, 9, 10, 11, 12

HANNIBAL

Fifth Street Mansion Bed and Breakfast Inn

213 South Fifth Street, 63401
(314) 221-0445; (800) 874-5661

Historic 1858 Italianate mansion of lifelong friends of Mark Twain combines Victorian charm with contemporary comforts. Period furnishings, original fireplaces, stained glass, and old-fashioned hospitality abound. Walk to historic sites, shops, and restaurants. Inquire about special weekends.

Hosts: Donalene and Mike Andreotti
Rooms: 7 (PB) $60-90
Full Breakfast
Credit Cards: A, B, C, D
Notes: 2, 5, 7 (limited), 8, 9, 10, 11, 12, 14

Garth Woodside Mansion

Garth Woodside Mansion

Rural Route 1, 63401
(314) 221-2789

Stay at this award-winning 1871 Victorian country estate for the ultimate experience. Original furnishings span over 150 years, with potpourri scented air, canopied beds, and nightshirts. Spacious bedchambers are a careful selection of lace, fabrics, and textures chosen to blend with an eye toward every detail and comfort. Stroll on 39 magnificent wooded acres or rock on the veranda. Judged one of the Midwest's "Ten Best Inns."

Hosts: Irv and Diane Feinberg
Rooms: 8 (PB) $65-105
Full Breakfast
Minimum stay holidays: 2 nights
Credit Cards: A, B
Notes: 2, 5, 7 (limited), 8 (over 12), 9, 10, 12

HERMANN

Alice's Wharf Street Bed and Breakfast

206 Wharf Street, 65041
(314) 486-5785

Private first-floor apartment in former Wiedersprecker-Eitzen store constructed in 1840. This building, built of native red brick, has had a long history. At one time it

6 Pets welcome; 8 Children welcome; 9 Social drinking allowed; 10 Tennis available; 11 Swimming available; 12 Golf available; 13 Skiing available; 14 May be booked through travel agents.

was the Masonic Hall; later it was headquarters for supplies for river boats on the Missouri River. In the early 1970s the Leo Jacobsons bought and restored this charming old building that overlooks the Missouri River, Gasconade County Court House, and Missouri River Bridge.

Host: Alice A. Jacobson
Suite: 1 (PB) $65
Full Breakfast
Credit Cards: None
Notes: 2, 8, 9, 10, 11, 12, 14

Trisha's

JACKSON

Trisha's
Bed and Breakfast

203 Bellevue, 63755
(314) 243-7427; (800) 651-0408

Enjoy a gourmet breakfast by candlelight in a 1905 Victorian home in a traditional small town. Tastefully decorated antique bedrooms takes guests back to yesteryear, yet they will enjoy comfortable amenities at reasonable prices. A vintage steam train operates on weekends only three blocks away. Innkeepers impersonate Bonnie and Clyde, Elvira, and other colorful characters aboard the train. Come try hospitality, southeast Missouri-style. Only four miles from I-55.

Hosts: Gus and Trisha Wischmann
Rooms: 4 (3 PB; 1 SB) $65-75
Full Breakfast
Credit Cards: A, B, C
Notes: 2, 4, 5, 8, 10, 11, 12, 14

JAMESPORT

Richardson House
Bed and Breakfast

P.O. Box 227, North Street, 64648
(816) 842-4211

Located in Missouri's largest Amish community, at the end of a quiet lane, this turn of the century Victorian farm house will provide the perfect base for experiencing life in a simpler era. Guests will enjoy the complete privacy and exclusive use of this cozy antique filled house. The house is reserved for one party at a time and sleeps up to eight people. Jamesport features Amish farms and shops, antiques, and festivals all year-round. Children under six free. Country fresh meals served with prior arrangement.

Host: Rebecca Richardson
Rooms: 4 (SB) $67.50-75
Full Breakfast
Credit Cards: A, B
Notes: 2, 3, 4, 5, 8, 9, 14

JOPLIN

Visages

327 North Jackson, 64801
(800) 896-1397

Visages, built in 1898, is named for the faces on exterior masonry walls and family portraits inside. Its beauty is achieved through artistry and ingenuity, not money. Marge and Bill, retired teachers, find guests fascinating and enjoy serving a typical mid-American breakfast.

Hosts: Bill and Marge Meeker
Rooms: 3 (1 PB; 2 SB) $40-60
Full Breakfast
Credit Cards: C, D
Notes: 2, 5, 8, 9, 10, 11, 12, 14

NOTES: Credit cards accepted: A MasterCard; B Visa; C American Express; D Discover Card; E Diner's Club; F Other; 2 Personal checks accepted; 3 Lunch available; 4 Dinner available; 5 Open all year;

KANSAS CITY

Bed and Breakfast Kansas City

P.O. Box 14781, Lenexa, KS 66285
(913) 888-3636

Forty Victorian turn-of-the-century contemporary homes and four inns for great getaways. Accommodations near Country Club Plaza, Kansas City, Independence, or adjacent historic towns. All sizes of beds, all but two with private bath. Some with fireplace, Jacuzzi, pools, hot tubs. Accommodations also available in the country. Full Breakfast. RSO Agent: Edwina Monroe. $40-135.

Doanleigh Wallagh Inn

217 East 37th Street, 64111
(816) 753-2667; FAX (816) 753-2408

A haven for people seeking the ultimate bed and breakfast experience. Guests are invited to make use of the first floor's two living rooms, two dining rooms, and complimentary snack bar in the butler's pantry. Guest rooms have either a king or queen size bed, are individually appointed with European and American antiques, have cable TV and telephone, and some rooms have a porch or fireplace. The hosts help guests find the right activities, restaurants, and shopping to make their stay memorable. Enjoy the beauty that was used for the 1991 Hallmark Keepsakes Christmas poster, Hallmark cards, and settings for Younkers and Jones store advertisements.

Hosts: Carolyn and Edward Litchfield
Rooms: 5 (PB) $80-110
Full Breakfast
Credit Cards: A, B, C
Notes: 2, 5, 7 (limited), 8, 9, 10, 12, 14

Hotel Savoy

219 West 9th Street, 64105
(816) 842-3575

Hotel Savoy

Hotel Savoy is one of the finest European bed and breakfast hotels in the United States. Built in 1888, it offers the opportunity to drift back into time in suites filled with antiques and Victorian decor. Breakfast consists of more than 32 items such as lobster bisque, salmon and caviar, medallions of beef, or even oysters Rockefeller. In the heart of Kansas City's historic garment district. A very romantic getaway.

Host: Dan Lee
Rooms: 110 (PB) $79-120
Full Breakfast
Credit Cards: A, B, C, D, E, F
Notes: 2, 3, 4, 5, 7, 8, 9, 14

Pridewell

600 West 50th Street, 64112
(816) 931-1642

A fine Tudor residence in a residential area on the site of the Civil War battle of Westport. Near the Nelson Art Gallery; University of Missouri, Kansas City; Missouri Repertory Theatre; and Rockhurst College. Adjacent to Country Club Plaza shopping district, including several four-star restaurants, public transportation, public tennis courts, and park.

Hosts: Edwin and Louann White
Rooms: 2 (1 PB; 1 SB) $65-70
Full Breakfast
Credit Cards: None
Notes: 2, 5, 8, 9, 14

6 Pets welcome; 8 Children welcome; 9 Social drinking allowed; 10 Tennis available; 11 Swimming available; 12 Golf available; 13 Skiing available; 14 May be booked through travel agents.

Southmoreland on the Plaza

Southmoreland on the Plaza

116 East 46th Street, 64112
(816) 531-7979

A two-time winner of "Top Bed and Breakfasts in the United States" and awarded "Outstanding Achievement in Preservation" by the Association of American Historic Inns and "Most Romantic New Urban Inn" by *Romantic Hideaways* newsletter, this classic New England Colonial between Country Club Plaza and the Nelson-Atkins Museum of Art has elegant bed and breakfast atmosphere with small hotel amenities. Rooms offer private decks, fireplaces or Jacuzzi baths. Special services designed for business travelers. Sport and dining privileges at a nearby historic private club. Mobil Travel Guide four star winner 1993 and 1994.

Hosts: Penni Johnson and Susan Moehl
Rooms: 12 (PB) $100-145
Full Breakfast
Credit Cards: A, B, C
Notes: 2, 5, 9, 10, 11, 14

LOUISIANA

The International Bed & Breakfast Club, Inc.

504 Amherst Street, Buffalo, NY 14207
(800) 723-4262; FAX (716) 873-4462

This Victorian home with its beautiful stained-glass windows is old enough to be unique, yet modern enough for comfort. It offers two rooms, one with a queen-size bed and the other with a double bed, which share a bath. Amenities include a private patio with a large spa. Continental breakfast and coffee are served. Dinners for guests and small groups are available by appointment. $55-75.

The Orthwein Mansion

2000 West Georgia Street, 63353
(314) 754-5449; (314) 965-4328

In Louisiana, Missouri, a Mississippi River town, enjoy bed and breakfast in an imposing baronial mansion. Polished wood, stained-glass windows, tapestried walls, and hand-painted canvas ceilings offer a charming Old World setting in the serenity guests deserve. Featured in *Midwest Living* and *St. Louis* magazine.

Hosts: Clarence and Dottie Brown
Rooms: 3 (1 PB; 2 SB) $70-90
Continental Breakfast
Credit Cards: None
Notes: 2, 5, 7, 9, 12

MEXICO

Hylas House Inn

811 South Jefferson, 65265
(314) 581-2011

A gracious and elegant bed and breakfast experience. Italianate architecture, magnificent staircase, molded scroll work on staircase, windows with leaded glass, white carpeting, and deep cherry wood. Four bedrooms. Two shared bathrooms. Suite with parlor and lounging balcony with chairs. Cable-remote TV in all rooms with telephones. Rooms redecorated. Gourmet full breakfast includes freshly ground coffee, eggs olé, waffles, and mixed fresh fruits. Museums and antique stores within a ten-minute walk. Spacious lawns and flower beds.

NOTES: Credit cards accepted: A MasterCard; B Visa; C American Express; D Discover Card; E Diner's Club; F Other; 2 Personal checks accepted; 3 Lunch available; 4 Dinner available; 5 Open all year;

Hosts: Tom and Linda Hylas
Rooms: 4 (2 PB; 2 SB) $45-95
Full Breakfast
Credit Cards: A, B,
Notes: 2, 5, 7 (limited), 9, 10, 12, 14

Hylas House Inn

MOUNTAIN GROVE

Cedar Hill Farm

Route Three, Box 83, 65711
(417) 926-6535

Cedar Hill Farm is a fine example of classic Revival architecture, with history and charm. Hosts have eleven acres for guests to enjoy and relax on. The house provides a library and a huge dining room available for weddings and business meetings. The parlor has a cozy fireplace for winter nights, while our front porch is a wonderful place to relax in the summer. Children welcome. No smoking.

Hosts: Stephanie Halford and Myrna Lewis
Rooms: 3 (1 PB; 2 SB) $55-65
Full Breakfast
Credit Cards: None
Notes, 2, 3, 4, 5, 8, 11, 12, 14

OZARK

Bed and Breakfast at Merrywoods

493 Bluff Drive, 65721
(417) 581-5676

Merrywoods is high on the Finley River bluff just north of Ozark. This contemporary bed and breakfast is secluded yet conveniently off Highways 65 and 14, and just 24 miles north of the Branson country entertainment mecca. Bass Pro shop and Wilson Creek Civil War Battlefield are nearby. Constructed in 1980, Merrywood's three spacious suites have private baths. Handicapped visitors accommodated. Walkouts to large deck, fireplaces, fax, modem, and air conditioning. Extended continental breakfast. No smoking. No alcohol. Reservations required.

Hosts: Gail and David Beard
Rooms: 2 (PB) $55-85
Continental Breakfast
Credit Cards: A, B
Notes: 2, 5, 10, 11, 12, 13

PLATTE CITY

Basswood Country Inn Bed and Breakfast

15880 Interurban Road, 64079-9185
(816) 431 5556

Come stay where the rich and famous relaxed and played in the 1940s and 1950s! Most beautiful secluded, wooded, private lakefront accommodations in entire Kansas City area. Try the Truman, Bing Crosby, or Rudy Vallee suites, the 1935 mother-in-law cottage, or country French suites.

Hosts: Don and Betty Soper
Rooms: 7 (PB) $61-125
Cottage: 1 (PB) $96
Continental Breakfast
Credit Cards: A, B, D
Notes: 2, 5, 7, 8, 9, 11, 12, 13, 14

ROCHEPORT (COLUMBIA)

School House Bed and Breakfast

Third and Clark Streets, 65279
(314) 698-2022

6 Pets welcome; 8 Children welcome; 9 Social drinking allowed; 10 Tennis available; 11 Swimming available; 12 Golf available; 13 Skiing available; 14 May be booked through travel agents.

The School House is a three-story brick school building with 13-foot ceilings, black slate chalkboards, and a number nine cast-iron school bell on the front lawn. It is a magical setting for reliving fond school memories or for just getting away. Each of the nine guest rooms is uniquely furnished with beautiful but unassuming antiques. A delicious breakfast is prepared in the turn-of-the-century second-floor classroom. Antique shops and an art gallery; a riverview walking and bicycling corridor; a local winery, cafe, and bistro are all in this historic river town listed on the National Register of Historic Places.

Hosts: Vicki and John Ott
Rooms: 9 (PB) $85-125
Full Breakfast
Credit Cards: A, B
Notes: 2, 5, 8, 9, 10, 12, 14

ST. CHARLES

Boone's Lick Trail Inn

1000 South Main Street, 63301
(314) 947-7000

In the 1840s, this Federal-style building rose where Main Street met Boone's Lick Road. The inn is surrounded by herb and rose gardens, and is decorated with folk art and regional antiques. Delicacies, such as lemon biscuits are served. On the Missouri Riverfront, the inn is within walking distance to the Katy Trail, showboat theater, and casino. Today, guests explore shops, restaurants, and museums along the cobblestone street in Missouri's largest historic district.

Hosts: Vietta Anne and Paul Mydler
Rooms: 5 (PB) $75-135
Full Breakfast
Credit Cards: A, B, D, E
Notes: 2, 5, 8, 9, 10, 11, 12, 14

STE. GENEVIEVE

Inn Ste. Gemme Beauvais

78 North Main, 63670
(314) 883-5744

This magnificent structure has been redecorated and updated this year. It boasts of being the oldest continuously operating inn in Missouri and is in the historic district. Each room has a unique theme and most are two-room suites. A three-course breakfast is served in the elegant Victorian living room, and all historic buildings are within walking distance. Lunch, high tea, and hors d'oeurves are served daily, and dinner is served by special arrangement.

Host: Janet Joggerst
Rooms: 7 (PB) $69-125
Full Breakfast
Credit Cards: A, B
Notes: 2, 3, 5, 8, 9, 10, 11, 12

The Southern Hotel

146 South Third Street, 63670
(800) 275-1412

You are cordially invited to enjoy the fine accommodations of this 200 year old landmark. Step gently into the time when riverboats plied the mighty Mississippi and weary travelers looked forward to the hospitality of this famous hotel. At the Southern Hotel the graciousness of the past is carefully blended with modern comforts to make the guest's stay a very special experience.

Hosts: Mike and Barbara Hankins
Rooms: 8 (PB) $80-110
Full Breakfast
Credit Cards: A, B
Notes: 2, 5, 10, 12

ST. LOUIS

Napoleon's Retreat Guest House Bed and Breakfast

1815 Lafayette Avenue, 63104
(314) 772-6979

Elegantly restored Second Empire Victorian townhouse in historic Lafayette Square. Three spacious guest rooms furnished with period antiques. Each room has a private bath, while one room, a full suite,

Napoleon's Retreat Guest House

has a wet bar, refrigerator, and a view of downtown St. Louis and the Gateway Arch. Telephone and color TV in each room. Beautiful secluded garden and patio. Minutes to downtown, riverfront, Arch, St. Louis Union Station, Busch Stadium, and Missouri Botanical Garden. Full gourmet breakfast.

Host: Michael Lance and Jeff Archuleta
Rooms: 3 (PB) $65-80
Full Breakfast
Credit Cards: A, B
Notes: 2, 5

The Winter House

3522 Arsenal Street, 63118
(314) 664-4399

Nine-room Victorian built in 1897 features pressed-tin ceiling in lower bedroom, a suite with balcony, and decorative fireplace on second floor. Breakfast is served in the dining room using crystal and antique Wedgwood china, and always includes freshly squeezed orange juice. Tea and piano music are available by reservation, with live piano music by Prof. J. Epstein complimentary at breakfast with advance notice. Fruit, candy, and fresh flowers are provided in bedrooms. Nearby attractions include a Victorian walking park on the Na-

tional Register and the Missouri Botanical Garden. Within four miles are the Arch, Busch Baseball Stadium, the new Science Center, zoo, symphony, and Union Station. Walk to fine dining. Reservations required. Additional fee of ten dollars for one night stays.

Hosts: Sarah and Kendall Winter
Rooms: 2 (PB) $65-75
Suite: 1 (PB) $80-90
Continental Breakfast
Credit Cards: A, B, C, D, E
Notes: 2, 5, 8, 9, 10, 11, 12, 14

SAGINAW

Lakeside Cottages and Aviary

P.O. Box 99, 64864
(417) 781-9230

A special place where guests can enjoy the ultimate in romance, luxury, and seclusion, yet just three miles from Joplin, Missouri. Contemporary cottage overlooks a stocked five acre lake for fishing or canoeing. Cottage has a fully equipped kitchenette stocked with breakfast foods, fireplace, TV, VCR, stereo, queen-sized canopied feather bed, and a large Jacuzzi tub for two. Owners breed and raise macaws, parrots and cockatoos.

Hosts: Roberta and Clyde Jeffries
Room: 1 (PB) $95-139
Continental Breakfast
Credit Cards: A, B
Notes: 2, 5, 9, 11, 12

SPRINGFIELD

Mansion at Elfindale

1701 South Fort, 65807
(417) 831-5400

The Mansion, built in the 1800s, features ornate fireplaces, stained-glass windows, and unique architecturally designed rooms. It offers 13 suites, all with private baths, and a full breakfast served in the dining

6 Pets welcome; 8 Children welcome; 9 Social drinking allowed; 10 Tennis available; 11 Swimming available; 12 Golf available; 13 Skiing available; 14 May be booked through travel agents.

room, and prepared by an English chef. Weddings, banquets, or even small business meetings can be accommodated at the Mansion. Come relive the past in Missouri's largest bed and breakfast.

Host: Jef Wells
Rooms: 13 (PB) $70-125
Full Breakfast
Credit Cards: A, B, C, D, E
Notes: 2, 5, 11, 12, 14

Walnut Street Inn

Walnut Street Inn

900 East Walnut, 65806
(417) 864-6346; (800) 593-6346

This award-winning 1894 Queen Anne Victorian inn, in the historic district, invites guests to escape. Friendly innkeepers, flickering fireplaces, European antiques, four-poster beds, feather comforters, thick Turkish bathrobes, Jacuzzis, skylights, and Victorian flower gardens abound. Walk to performing arts centers, theaters, cafes, boutiques, and antique shops. Near Bass Pro shops, Branson music shows, with the glorious Ozark Mountains at the backdoor.

Hosts: Karol and Nancy Brown
Rooms: 14 (PB) $75-150
Full Breakfast
Credit Cards: A, B, C, D, E, F
Notes: 2, 5, 8, 9, 10, 11, 12, 13, 14

TECUMSEH

The Farmhouse

Route 2, Box 207, Highway 160, 65760
(417) 284-3699

The Farmhouse means comfort and relaxation. The hosts love their country atmosphere and enjoy sharing their home and interests, from primitive antiques to their life's travels, with others. A visit here is bound to be a pleasurable one. Sit on the porch swing and watch the parade. There are Belted Galloway cattle, Foxtrotter horses, and even llama to see. Hosts can arrange a float trip on a nearby springfed river in the Ozarks. At the Farmhouse, guests are part of the family!

Hosts: Lynn and Charlotte Taylor
Rooms: 2 (SB) $40
Full Breakfast
Credit Cards: None
Notes: 2, 4, 5, 8, 9, 11

WARRENSBURG

Cedarcroft Farm

431 Southeast "Y" Highway, 64093
(816) 747-5728; (800) 368-4944

Cedarcroft Farm offers old-fashioned country hospitality, country quiet, and more-than-you-can-eat country cooking on an 1867 family farm on the national register. Guests may explore the 80 acres of secluded woods, meadows, and streams, and savor a full country breakfast. Civil War re-enactor hosts demonstrate 1860s soldiers' life. Horseback riding and farm pond fishing nearby.

NOTES: Credit cards accepted: A MasterCard; B Visa; C American Express; D Discover Card; E Diner's Club; F Other; 2 Personal checks accepted; 3 Lunch available; 4 Dinner available; 5 Open all year;

Hosts: Sandra and Bill Wayne
Suite: 1 (PB) $65
Full Breakfast
Credit Cards: A, B, C, D
Notes: 2, 4, 5, 7 (limited), 8, 9, 11, 12, 14

WASHINGTON

Washington House Bed and Breakfast

3 Lafayette Street, 63090
(314) 239-2417; (314) 239-9834

Washington House

Washington House, built circa 1837, is in a National Historic District. This authentically restored inn on the Missouri River features river views, canopied beds, antiques, complimentary wine, and full breakfast. Washington House is in the heart of Missouri's wine country, only 45 minutes west of St. Louis.

Hosts: Chuck and Kathy Davis
Rooms: 3 (PB) $55-75
Full Breakfast
Credit Cards: None
Notes: 2, 5, 8, 9, 10, 11, 12

6 Pets welcome; 8 Children welcome; 9 Social drinking allowed; 10 Tennis available; 11 Swimming available; 12 Golf available; 13 Skiing available; 14 May be booked through travel agents.

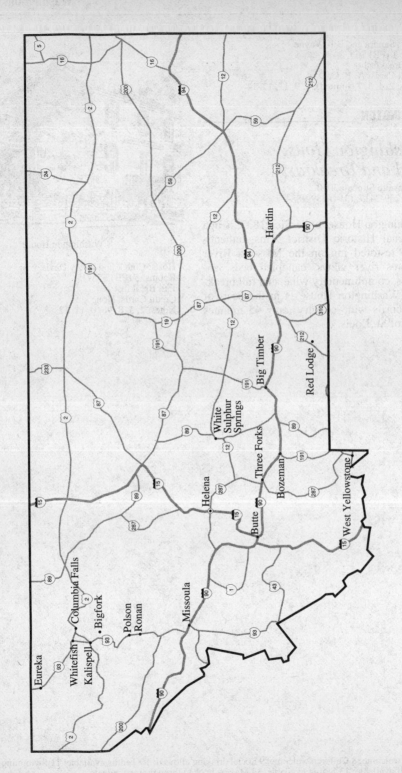

Montana

Montana

O'Duachain Country Inn

675 Ferndale Drive, 59911
(406) 837-6851; (800) 837-7460

Luxurious log lodging with full gourmet
breakfast. On five acres of landscaped soli-
tude. Walking trails, ponds, and wildlife.
One-day junkets include Glacier National
Park, Flathead and Swan lakes and valleys,
Jewel Basin hiking, and National Bison
Range. Golf, swimming, boating, and ski-
ing areas abound.

Hosts: Margot and Tom Doohan
Rooms: 5 (2 PB; 3 SB) $75-95
Full Breakfast
Credit Cards: A, B, C
Notes: 2, 5, 8, 9, 10, 11, 12, 13, 14

Burggraf's Countrylane
Bed 'n' Breakfast
on Swan Lake

Rainbow Drive, 59911
(406) 837-4608; (800) 525-3344
FAX ((406) 837-4608

Log home on seven acres beside Swan Lake
with panoramic view, only 45 minutes from
Glacier National Park. "All-you-can-eat"
breakfast. Complimentary bottle of wine
with fruit and cheese tray upon arrival.
Guest refrigerator and Jacuzzi/whirlpool
tub. All rooms with TVs.

Hosts: Natalie and R. J. Burggraf
Rooms: 5 (PB) $75-85
Full Breakfast
Credit Cards: A, B
Notes: 2, 3 (picnic), 5, 9, 10, 11, 12, 13, 14

The Grand of Big Timber

P.O. Box 1242, 139 McLeod Street, 59011
(405) 932-4459

Built in 1890 and listed on the National
Register of Historic Places, The Grand has
been recently restored to her original dig-
nity and intent: to serve completely. Rooms
are dressed in the Victorian best with high
ceilings, refreshing sunlight, period furnishings and modern conveniences. Full breakfast is provided. Children welcome.
Smoking in bar only.

Host: Lawrence Edwards
Rooms: 10 (4 PB; 6 SB) $55-125
Full Breakfast
Credit Cards: A, B, D
Notes: 2, 3, 4, 5, 7 (limited), 8

Torch and Toes
Bed and Breakfast

309 South Third Avenue, 59715
(406) 586-7285; (800) 446-2138

Set back from the street, it looks much as it
did when it was built in 1906. A tall, trim
brick-and-frame house in the Colonial Revival style. There are just enough lace curtains and turn-of-the-century furniture to
remind guests that this is a house with a
past. Smells of blueberry muffins, coddled
eggs, and fresh fruit will entice guests to
breakfast in the oak-paneled dining room
with the wood-burning fireplace.

NOTES: Credit cards accepted: A MasterCard; B Visa; C American Express; D Discover Card; E Diner's Club;
F Other; 2 Personal checks accepted; 3 Lunch available; 4 Dinner available; 5 Open all year; 6 Pets welcome; 7
Smoking allowed; 8 Children welcome; 9 Social drinking allowed; 10 Tennis available; 11 Swimming avail-
able; 12 Golf available; 13 Skiing available; 14 May be booked through travel agents.

Hosts: Ronald and Judy Hess
Rooms: 4 (PB) $55-70
Full Breakfast
Credit Cards: A, B
Notes: 2, 5, 8, 9, 10, 11, 12, 13, 14

Torch and Toes

Voss Inn Bed and Breakfast

319 South Wilson, 59715
(406) 587-0982

Magnificently restored Victorian inn in the historic district with elegant guest rooms with private baths. A delightful gourmet breakfast is served in the privacy of guests' rooms. Bozeman is 90 miles north of Yellowstone Park, near skiing, fishing, hiking, and snowmobiling. Guided day trips are conducted into Yellowstone and the surrounding area by the hosts. Full afternoon tea. Airport transportation available.

Hosts: Bruce and Frankee Muller
Rooms: 6 (PB) $80-90
Full Breakfast
Credit Cards: A, B, C
Notes: 2, 5, 8 (over 5), 9, 10, 11, 12, 13, 14

BUTTE

Copper King Mansion

219 West Granite, 59701
(406) 782-7580

Step back in time and experience Victorian elegance in this beautiful 34-room brick mansion which was the home of the former multi-millionaire and U.S. Senator William Andrews Clark. It was built in the 1880s, and features stained-glass windows, frescoed ceilings, hand-carved woodwork, and lavish antique furnishings. It is in Historic Uptown Butte, one block west of Montana Street on Granite Street.

Host: Maria Sigl
Rooms: 4 (1 PB; 3 SB) $55-95
Full Breakfast
Credit Cards: A, B, C, D
Notes: 2, 5, 8, 12, 13

COLUMBIA FALLS

Bad Rock Country Bed and Breakfast

480 Bad Rock Drive, 59912
(800) 422-3666

An elegant country home on 30 acres, 15 miles from Glacier National Park. Four luxurious rooms with fireplaces in new log cottages, with Montana hand-made log furniture; three rooms in the home; all with private baths; beautiful Old West antiques. Secluded hot tub with time reserved for each guest. Experience the quiet of the country and the magnificence of "front-yard" mountains. Fantastic breakfasts, superb hospitality. For nonsmoking guests. Children 10 and over. Inspected and approved: AAA, ABBA, MBBA.

Hosts: Jon and Susie Alper
Rooms: 7 (PB) $90-125
Full Breakfast
Credit Cards: A, B, C, D, E
Notes: 2, 3, 5, 8 (over 9), 9, 12, 13, 14

NOTES: Credit cards accepted: A MasterCard; B Visa; C American Express; D Discover Card; E Diner's Club; F Other; 2 Personal checks accepted; 3 Lunch available; 4 Dinner available; 5 Open all year;

EUREKA

Huckleberry Hannah's Montana Bed and Breakfast

3100 Sophie Lake Road, 59917
(406) 889-3381 (for reservations and free brochure)

Nearly 5,000 square feet of old-fashioned charm. Fifty wooded acres, fabulous trout-filled lake, glorious views of the Rockies. This bed and breakfast depicts a quieter time in history, when the true pleasures of life represented a walk in the woods or a moonlight swim, not to mention comfortable sunny rooms and wonderful food. Owned and operated by the author of one of the Northwest's best selling cookbooks, *Huckleberry Hannah's Country Cooking Sampler*. Questions cheerfully answered. Ask about kids and pets. Senior discounts!

Hosts: Jack and Deanna Doying
Rooms: 5 (PB) $40-75
Cottage: 1 (PB)
Full Breakfast
Credit Cards: A, B, D
Notes: 2, 3, 4, 6 (call),7 and 8 (limited), 10, 11, 13, 14

HARDIN

Kendrick House Inn Bed and Breakfast

206 North Custer Avenue, 59034
(406) 665-3035

The Kendrick House Inn was constructed in 1914 by Elizabeth Kendrick to serve as a room and boarding house. In 1943 it became the area's hospital which served the Hardin community until 1945, and later it became private residences. In 1988, the boarding house was purchased and restored, and now the seven guest rooms are filled with antique furniture and period memorabilia. Two glassed verandas and a library and common areas for relaxing. Sinks are provided in each room; baths are shared. Sometimes closed during winter months, so call in advance.

Hosts: Steve and Marcie Smith
Rooms: 7 (S2B) $55
Full Breakfast
Credit Cards: A, B
Notes: 2, 5, 6 (call), 8 (limited), 9, 10, 11, 12, 14

HELENA

The Sanders

Helena's Bed and Breakfast
328 North Ewing, 59601
(406) 442-3309

This 1875 Victorian mansion offers elegant accommodations steeped in Helena's historic past. Appointed with original furnishings, each spacious guest room has a private bath, TV, and telephone. Brass beds, high ceilings, and ornately framed paintings radiate the quiet charm of days past. In the heart of Helena and listed on the National Register, the Sanders combines friendly hospitality with grand turn-of-the-century living.

Hosts: Rock Ringling and Bobbi Uecker
Rooms: 7 (PB) $65-98
Full Breakfast
Credit Cards: A, B, D
Notes: 2, 5, 8, 9, 10, 11, 12, 13

The Sanders

6 Pets welcome; 8 Children welcome; 9 Social drinking allowed; 10 Tennis available; 11 Swimming available; 12 Golf available; 13 Skiing available; 14 May be booked through travel agents.

KALISPELL

Creston Inn

70 Creston Road, 59901
(406) 755-7517; (800) 257-7517

Quiet charm and rural serenity are waiting for guests at this delightful two-story farmhouse with mountain and valley views. The inn's rooms are furnished in old-country style and offer the finest in overnight accommodations. A hearty Montana breakfast is served featuring a colorful fresh fruit plate and never-ending pancakes. Minutes away from Glacier National Park, Flathead Lake, golf, skiing, white-water rafting, antiquing, and theater.

Hosts: Marlene and Tom Brunaugh
Rooms: 4 (PB) $75-85
Full Breakfast
Credit Cards: A, B
Notes: 2, 5, 8 (over 6), 11, 12, 13, 14

MISSOULA

Goldsmith's Inn

809 East Front Street, 59801
(406) 721-6732

This beautiful 1911 brick home is on the banks of the Clark Fork River, only four blocks from downtown Missoula. Guests can enjoy breakfast in the dining room which captures an unparalleled view of the Bitterfoot Mountain and the sparkles of the Clark Fork River as it glistens in the morning sun. Formerly the home for several University of Montana presidents.

Hosts: Jean and Richard Goldsmith
Rooms: 7 (PB) $65-95
Full Breakfast
Credit Cards: A, B, C, E
Notes: 2, 3, 4, 5, 8, 9, 10, 11, 12, 13, 14

POLSON

Ruth's Bed and Breakfast

802 Seventh Avenue West, 59860
(406) 883-2460

There are two guest rooms with portable bathroom facilities. Bath and shower are shared. One room in cottage has a double bed, while the other has a queen-size bed and daveno. Both have TV and are heated.

Host: Ruth Hunter
Rooms: 2 (SB) $28
Full Breakfast
Credit Cards: None
Notes: 2, 5, 8, 9, 10, 11, 12

RED LODGE

Willows Inn

224 South Platt Avenue P.O. Box 886, 59068
(406) 446-3913

Spectacular mountain scenery surrounds this delightful turn-of-the-century inn. Flanked by giant evergreens and colorful flowerbeds, it is reminiscent of a bygone era, complete with white picket fence, gingerbread trim, and a porch swing. Five individually-decorated guest rooms have brass and iron four-poster beds. Delicious home-baked pastries and afternoon refreshments are served. Close to hiking, fishing, and Yellowstone Park. Video movies, books, games, and a large sundeck are available. Two storybook cottages are ideal for families. They have two bedrooms, laundry facilities, and a kitchen and are decorated in cheerful country decor.

Hosts: Kerry, Carolyn, and Elven Boggio
Rooms: 5 (3 PB; 2 SB) $50-75
Continental Plus Breakfast
Credit Cards: A, B, D
Notes: 2, 5, 8 (over 10), 9, 10, 11, 12, 13, 14

RONAN

The Timbers
Bed and Breakfast

1184 Timberlane Road, 59864
(406) 676-4373; (800) 775-4373

Private lodging on 21 acres with magnificent view of the Mission Mountains. Cathedral ceilings, hand-hewn beams, barnwood

NOTES: Credit cards accepted: A MasterCard; B Visa; C American Express; D Discover Card; E Diner's Club; F Other; 2 Personal checks accepted; 3 Lunch available; 4 Dinner available; 5 Open all year;

The Timbers

dining area, and furnishings that hosts have collected give this home a sophisticated yet warm country feel. Elegant two-room suite with private bath can sleep four people. A full country breakfast and use of barbecue are included. Nearby attractions include Flathead Lake, National Bison Range, Glacier National Park, whitewater rafting, horseback riding, art galleries, fishing, local rodeos, and powwows. Additional adult in suite: $35; child over 12 years old in suite: $20.

Hosts: Doris and Leonard McCravey
Rooms and Suite: 2 (1 PB; 2 SB) $95-115
Full Breakfast
Credit Cards: A, B
Notes: 2, 5, 8 (over 11), 9, 10, 11, 12, 13, 14

THREE FORKS

Sacajawea Inn

P.O. Box 648, 5 North Main, 59752
(406) 285-6515

This grand old hotel was founded in 1910 by John Quincy Adams to serve the travelers of the Milwaukee Railroad. Named for Sacajawea, who guided the expeditions of Lewis and Clark in the Three Forks area from 1804 to 1806. Between Yellowstone and Glacier national parks, near hiking, skiing, fishing, hunting, and golf. Graced with rocking chairs, a large veranda welcomes guests to a spacious lobby. Fine dining and comfortable, nostalgic rooms.

Hosts: Jane and Smith Roedel
Rooms: 33 (PB) $49-99
Continental Breakfast
Credit Cards: A, B, C, D
Notes: 2, 3 (summer), 4, 5, 6 (call), 8, 9, 10, 11, 12, 13, 14

WEST YELLOWSTONE

Sportsman's High Bed and Breakfast

750 Deer Street, 59758
(406) 646-7865; FAX (406) 646-9434

Charming accommodations with antique furnishings and a country decor welcome each guest. This haven, with its spectacular mountain views, wildlife, wraparound porch, and acreage of quaking aspen and pines, is conveniently only eight miles from the west entrance to Yellowstone National Park. A stay here is further enhanced by fine amenities such as feather pillows, terry-cloth robes, outdoor hot tub, and a full hot breakfast worth bouncing out of bed for.

Hosts: Diana and Gary Baxter
Rooms: 5 (PB) $65-85
Full Breakfast
Credit Cards: A, B, C
Notes: 2, 5, 10, 11, 12, 13

Sportsman's High

6 Pets welcome; 8 Children welcome; 9 Social drinking allowed; 10 Tennis available; 11 Swimming available; 12 Golf available; 13 Skiing available; 14 May be booked through travel agents.

Castle Bed and Breakfast

Hosts: Jim and Pat Egan
Rooms: 3 (1 PB; 2 SB) $63-98
Full Breakfast
Credit Cards: A, B, D
Notes: 2, 9, 10, 11, 12, 13

WHITE SULPHUR SPRINGS

The Columns

19 East Wright Street, P.O. Box 611, 59645
(406) 547-3666

Recently renovated red brick 1882 private
home with an eclectic blend of yesterday's
charm and today's comfort in the middle of
cow country. Big Sky hospitality at its best.
Delicious ranch-style breakfasts.

Host: Dale N. McAfee
Rooms: 3 (1 PB; 2 SB) $35-50
Full Breakfast
Credit Cards: A, B
Notes: 2, 5, 8 (over 6), 9, 11, 12, 13, 14

WHITEFISH

Castle Bed and Breakfast

900 South Baker, 59937
(406) 862-1257

Enjoy one of three comfortable guest rooms
in this home that is listed on the National
Register of Historic Places. The Castle has
unusual architecture and charm. Breakfasts
are hearty and tempting and include homemade breads and freshly ground gourmet
coffee to complement the featured menu of
the day. The Castle is nine miles from the
Big Mountain Ski Resort and 25 miles from
Glacier National Park.

The Columns

Nebraska

DIXON

The George's

Rural Route 1, Box 50, 68732
(402) 584-2625

Enjoy friendly country hospitality and
hearty breakfasts featuring homemade jellies and jams. This is an opportunity to see a
modern farm operation, some chickens, and
other farm animals. Stay in an air-conditioned, spacious farmhome. Pheasant hunting in season and bird watching anytime.
Just 35 miles west of Sioux City, Iowa;
Ponca State Park and Wayne State College
are within 20 miles.

Host: Marie George
Rooms: 4 (SB) $35-40
Full Breakfast
Credit Cards: None
Notes: 2, 3 and 4 (call), 5, 6, 7 (limited), 8, 9, 14

BARTLEY

Pheasant Hill Farm

HCR 68, Box 12, 69020
(308) 692-3278

Enjoy the good life on this southwest Nebraska farm. Unique family experience. In-
season hunting for dove, quail, pheasant, and
deer. Fish, swim, and boat on area lakes.
Thirty minutes to world-class golf, shopping,
and entertainment. Relax on a porch with
ten-mile vistas. Enjoy country cooking.

Hosts: Max and Dona Nelms
Rooms: 5 (PB) $40
Full Breakfast
Credit Cards: None
Notes: 2, 3, 4, 5, 7, 8, 9, 14

HASTINGS

Grandma's Victorian Inn Bed and Breakfast

1826 West 3rd Street, 68901
(402) 462-2013

Built circa 1886, this Victorian home has an
open staircase and outstanding woodwork.
For guests' comfort, each room has a private bath. Antique furniture is exhibited in
the home with an accent on rocking chairs
and queen-size beds within each room.
Enjoy a lemonade on the beautiful balcony
or relax in the front porch swings. Breakfast
is served in the dining room; breakfast in
bed can be arranged at additional charge.
Return to the memories of yore and "whis-
pers of yesterday."

Manager/Innkeeper: Marilyn DiMartino
Rooms: 5 (PB) $55
Full Breakfast
Credit Cards: A, B
Notes: 2, 5, 8 (over 12), 10, 11, 12

KEARNEY

The George W. Frank, Jr., House

621 West 27th Street, 68847
(308) 237-7545

Built in 1884, this Queen Anne shingle-
style home is packed with history. A night's
stay will transport guests to a time when the
luxuries of peaceful quiet and soft comfort
were abundant. Fall in love with the leaded-
glass windows, spacious rooms, and beautifully carved wood details. Included is a

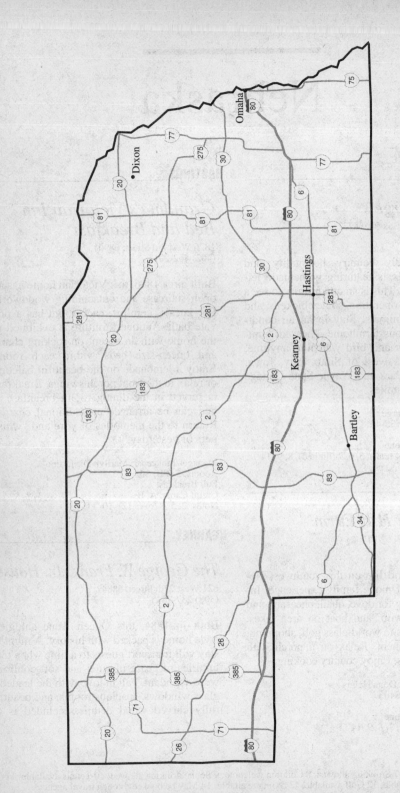

Nebraska

continental breakfast served in the family dining room on heirloom dishes.

Hosts: Ted and Sylvia Asay
Rooms: 2 (SB) $45
Full Breakfast or Continental Breakfast
Credit Cards: None
Notes: 2, 5, 8, 14

OMAHA

The Jones's

1617 South 90th Street, 68124
(402) 397-0721

The Offutt House

Large private residence with deck and gazebo in the back. Fresh homemade cinnamon rolls are served for breakfast. Horse racing nearby in summer as well as several golf courses and Boys Town.

Hosts: Don and Theo Jones
Rooms: 3 (1 PB; 2 SB) $25
Continental Breakfast
Credit Cards: None
Notes: 2, 5, 6, 7, 8, 9, 10, 12

The Offutt House

140 North 39th Street, 68131
(402) 553-0951

This comfortable mansion, built in 1894, is in the section of large homes built around the same time by Omaha's most wealthy residents. Rooms are comfortably spacious and furnished with antiques. Some feature fireplaces. The house is near downtown Omaha and the historic Old Market area, which offers many beautiful shops and excellent restaurants. Full breakfast on Sundays. Reservations required.

Host: Jeannie K. Swoboda
Rooms: 7 (5 PB; 2 SB) $45-85
Full or Continental Breakfast
Credit Cards: A, B, C
Notes: 2, 5, 6, 7, 8, 9, 10, 11, 12, 14

NOTES: Credit cards accepted: A MasterCard; B Visa; C American Express; D Discover Card; E Diner's Club; F Other; 2 Personal checks accepted; 3 Lunch available; 4 Dinner available; 5 Open all year; 6 Pets welcome; 7 Smoking allowed; 8 Children welcome; 9 Social drinking allowed; 10 Tennis available; 11 Swimming available; 12 Golf available; 13 Skiing available; 14 May be booked through travel agents.

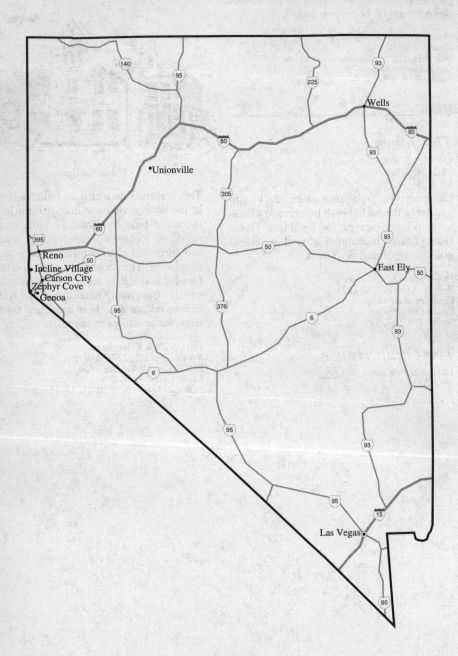

140

95

93

225

Wells

80

80

93

•Unionville

305

93

80

50

395

50

Reno

50

East Ely

•Incline Village

Carson City

Zephyr Cove

•Genoa

376

95

6

93

6

95

95

93

95

15

Las Vegas

95

Nevada

Nevada

Deer Run Ranch

CARSON CITY (WASHOE VALLEY) _____

Deer Run Ranch
Bed and Breakfast

5440 Eastlake Boulevard, 89704
(702) 882-3643

Western ambience in a unique architect-designed ranch house on spacious grounds, between Reno and Carson City. Just minutes from Lake Tahoe and Virginia City. Pond with a boat for summer, skating in winter. Above-ground pool and lots of privacy on 200 acres.

Hosts: David and Muffy Vhay
Rooms: 2 (PB) $75-85
Full Breakfast
Credit Cards: A, B, C
Notes: 2, 5, 9, 11, 12, 13

EAST ELY _____

Steptoe Valley Inn

P.O. Box 151110, 220 East 11th Street, 89315-1110
(702) 289-8687 (June - Sept)
(702) 435-1196 (Oct - May)

Elegantly reconstructed in 1990 from the Ely City Grocery of 1907, this inn is one-half block from the Nevada Northern Railway Museum with its weekend train excursions, and 70 miles from the Great Basin National Park. Its individually decorated guest rooms are on the second floor, and have private balconies with views of the mountains and valley or the gazebo and rose garden. Guests have use of the veranda, Victorian living/dining room, and library. Jeep rental available. Open June through September.

Hosts: Jane and Norman Lindley
Rooms: 5 (PB) $74-80
Full Breakfast
Credit Cards: A, B, C
Notes: 2, 12, 14

Steptoe Valley Inn

GENOA _____

Wild Rose Inn

P.O. Box 256 2332 Main Street, 89411
(702) 782-5697

NOTES: Credit cards accepted: A MasterCard; B Visa; C American Express; D Discover Card; E Diner's Club; F Other; 2 Personal checks accepted; 3 Lunch available; 4 Dinner available; 5 Open all year; 6 Pets welcome; 7 Smoking allowed; 8 Children welcome; 9 Social drinking allowed; 10 Tennis available; 11 Swimming available; 12 Golf available; 13 Skiing available; 14 May be booked through travel agents.

A Queen Anne Victorian set on the eastern foothills of the Sierra Nevada Mountains overlooking the Carson Valley. Guests enjoy comfortable, spacious rooms with lovely views, complimentary use of nearby mineral hot springs, and delicious buffet breakfasts.

Hosts: Joe and Sandi Antonucci
Rooms: 5 (PB) $95-115
Full Breakfast
Credit Cards: A, B, C
Notes: 2, 5, 9, 10, 11, 12, 13

INCLINE VILLAGE

Haus Bavaria

P.O. Box 3308, 89450
(702) 831-6122; (800) 731-6222

Haus Bavaria is a European-style guest house, built in 1980. Each of the five upstairs guest rooms opens onto a balcony, offering a view of the surrounding mountains, while the living room, with its rustic wood paneling and collection of German bric-a-brac, retains the Alpine charm set in place by the original owners. Breakfast is served daily in the cozy dining room downstairs, and includes freshly baked goods, seasonal fruits and juices, freshly ground coffee, and a selection of teas.

Host: Bick Hewitt
Rooms: 5 (PB) $90-110
Full Breakfast
Credit Cards: A, B, C, D
Notes: 2, 5, 9, 10, 11, 12, 13, 14

LAS VEGAS

Mi Casa Su Casa

P.O. Box 950, Tempe, Arizona 85280-0950
(602) 990-0682; (800) 456-0682

334. This large 1950 home with a Southwestern-style exterior is in an established quiet neighborhood within two miles of the Strip. Hostess is an interior designer. Antiques are blended with other lovely furnishings throughout this bed and breakfast. Two guest rooms with two hall baths are available. Bicycles are also on hand for guests to use. Prefer two-night minimum stay on weekends. Full breakfast. Smoking outside only. $50.

RENO

Bed and Breakfast: South Reno

136 Andrew Lane, 89511
(702) 849-0772

Situated just off Highway 395 in South Reno, 12 miles from the airport. The decor is Early American, including poster queen-size beds and beamed ceilings. Landscaped lawns, patios, and decks surround a heated swimming pool. Facing the bed and breakfast are ranch lands, Mount Rose, and Slide Mountain for hiking, sleigh rides, and downhill skiing. Visit Lake Tahoe, Virginia City, or the many Reno casinos. Open year-round.

Hosts: Caroline S. Walters and Robert McNeill
Rooms: 2 (PB) $75-85
Full Breakfast
Credit Cards: C, F
Notes: 2, 5, 8, 9, 10, 11, 12, 13, 14

UNIONVILLE

Old Pioneer Garden

79 Main Street, 89418
(702) 538-7585

The main house includes three guest rooms, and across the field, the Hadley House guest cottage provides six additional bedrooms and a shared library, farm kitchen, and spacious sitting room. The emphasis is on country with all the right touches: brass, iron, and oak beds; fireplaces; old trunks; and window sills filled with baskets of dried flowers. Full breakfast is served at the eight-foot-long wooden table in the large

---

NOTES: Credit cards accepted: A MasterCard; B Visa; C American Express; D Discover Card; E Diner's Club; F Other; 2 Personal checks accepted; 3 Lunch available; 4 Dinner available; 5 Open all year;

kitchen that is warmed by an old-fashioned wood stove. Lots of farm animals. Closed January and February.

Hosts: Lew and Mitzi Jones
Rooms: 9 (3 PB; 6 SB) $65
Full Breakfast
Credit Cards: None
Notes: 2, 3, 4, 6, 8, 9, 12, 14

WELLS

The Big Pillow

730 Fourth Street, Box 205, 89835
(702) 752-3249

Near Interstate 80 and U.S. 93 junction in Wells, Elko County, a friendly small town. One-half hour drive to Angel Lake and wilderness area and mountain lakes on East Humboldt Range of Ruby Mountains. Horseback riding available. Kitchenettes

are available in some accommodations. Meals available at additional cost. Pets Welcome. Children welcome. No smoking.

Hosts: Bob and Claire Morrow
Rooms: 24 (PB) $25-40
Credit Cards: None
Notes: 2, 3, 5, 6, 7, 8, 9, 10, 11, 12, 13, 14

ZEPHYR COVE

Bed and Breakfast International

P.O. Box 282910, San Francisco, 94128-2910
(415) 696-1690; (800) 872-4500
FAX (415) 696-1699

401. Large, attractive Alpine-style house with views of Zephyr Cove near the South Shore of Lake Tahoe. Hosts are extremely accommodating, and it has been said that the breakfasts are wonderful. $75.

6 Pets welcome; 8 Children welcome; 9 Social drinking allowed; 10 Tennis available; 11 Swimming available; 12 Golf available; 13 Skiing available; 14 May be booked through travel agents.

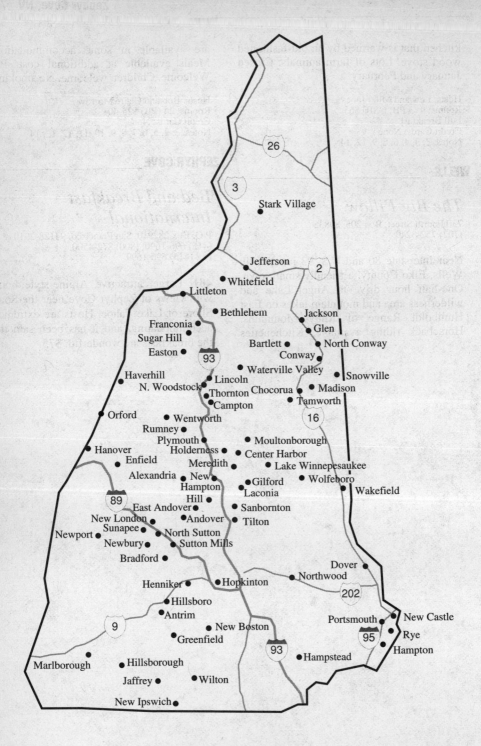

New Hampshire

New Hampshire

ALEXANDRIA

Stone Rest
Bed and Breakfast

652 Fowler River Road, 03222
(603) 744-6066

Contemporary home in a rural setting on 14 acres with 200 feet on a mountain stream with swimming hole. Close to Newfound Lake, Mount Cardigan, Ragged Mountain, shopping, and other major tourist attractions. Adjacent cottage and studio units also available. Hearty country breakfasts. Barbecue grills, picnic tables, horseshoes, and volleyball on grounds. Videos, library, and much more. Individual heat.

Hosts: Dick and Peg Clarke
Rooms: 7 (5 PB; 2 SB) $38-60
Full Breakfast
Credit Cards: None
Notes: 2, 5, 7, 8, 9, 10, 11, 12, 13

ANDOVER

The English House

Box 162, 03216
(603) 735-5987

This home has been renovated and furnished to re-create an English country house. Afternoon tea, as well as a notable breakfast, is served to all guests. All breads, muffins, cakes, jams, jellies, and marmalades are homemade. Minimum stay for foliage and major event weekends is two nights. Closed for two weeks in late March and early April.

Hosts: Gillian and Ken Smith
Rooms: 7 (PB) $60-80
Full Breakfast
Credit Cards: A, B
Notes: 2, 8 (over 7), 9, 10, 11, 12, 13, 14

New Hampshire
Bed and Breakfast

128 South Hoop Pole Road, Guilford, CT 06437
(203) 457-0042; (800) 582-0853

NH306. This turn-of-the-century house built in 1906, was constructed with many fine features of that era, particularly hardwood floors, paneling, and large rooms. It was fully renovated in 1986 and decorated and furnished in the style of an English country home. Afternoon tea and evening sherry are served each day by the hosts. Guests are welcome to use the well-furnished sitting room. Breakfast menus are the choice of the chef, and each morning, guests will awaken to freshly baked breads or muffins, which are always accompanied by fruits in season, homemade cereal, and dishes of distinction. Each of the seven well-appointed bedrooms offers private bath, a lovely view, and the homey touches of caring hosts. Children over eight welcome. No smoking. $55-75.

ANTRIM

The Steele Homestead Inn

Rural Route 1, Box 78, Route 9, 03440
(603) 588-2215

Enjoy warm, personal hospitality in this beautifully restored 1810 home. Lovely

NOTES: Credit cards accepted: A MasterCard; B Visa; C American Express; D Discover Card; E Diner's Club; F Other; 2 Personal checks accepted; 3 Lunch available; 4 Dinner available; 5 Open all year; 6 Pets welcome; 7 Smoking allowed; 8 Children welcome; 9 Social drinking allowed; 10 Tennis available; 11 Swimming available; 12 Golf available; 13 Skiing available; 14 May be booked through travel agents.

decor throughout, and the home is filled with antiques. Three spacious guest rooms with private baths are available; two with fireplace. Friendly, relaxed, smoke-free atmosphere. Healthy gourmet breakfast.

Hosts: Barbara and Carl Beehner
Rooms: 3 (PB) $60-68
Full Breakfast
Credit Cards: A, B
Notes: 2, 5, 8, 9, 11, 12, 13, 14

ASHLAND

Glynn House Victorian Inn

P. O. Box 719, 43 Highland Street, 03217
(603) 968-3775; (800) 637-9599

Step back in time to Victorian yesteryear. A romantic escape in the heart of the White Mountains and *On Golden Pond* lakes region of New Hampshire. Come enjoy the local colors of each season. Gracious seven bedrooms with private baths. Jacuzzi and fireplace amenities. Gourmet breakfast is served. Waterville Valley and Loon Mountain close by. Just two hours from Boston; I-94 exit 24.

Hosts: Karol and Betsy Paterman
Rooms: 5 (PB) $75-135
Full Breakfast
Credit Cards: A, B
Notes: 2, 5, 7 (limited), 8, 9, 10, 11, 12, 13, 14

Glynn House Victorian Inn

The Notchland Inn

BARTLETT

The Notchland Inn

Hart's Location, 03812
(603) 374-6131; (800) 866-6131

A traditional country inn where hospitality hasn't been forgotten. There are 11 guest rooms, all with working fireplaces and private baths. Gourmet dining, spectacular mountain views, hiking, cross-country skiing, and swimming are offered at this secluded mountain estate.

Hosts: Les Schoof and Ed Butler
Rooms: 11 (PB) $120-200
Full Breakfast
Credit Cards: A, B, C, D
Notes: 2, 4, 5, 9, 10, 11, 12, 13, 14

BETHLEHEM

The Mulburn Inn

Main Street, Route 302, 03574
(603) 869-3389; (800) 457-9440

Charming bed and breakfast on historic Woolworth Estate. Spacious warm and comfortable surroundings. Seven elegant rooms, all with private bath. Full breakfast is served. Four-season attractions including hiking, biking, fishing, Storyland, and Santa's Village for Children. Minutes from the scenic beauty of Franconia Notch, Mount Washington, and skiing at Cannon

---

NOTES: Credit cards accepted: A MasterCard; B Visa; C American Express; D Discover Card; E Diner's Club; F Other; 2 Personal checks accepted; 3 Lunch available; 4 Dinner available; 5 Open all year;

Mountain and Bretton Woods. Members of Ski-93. AAA and Mobil approved.

Rooms: 7 (PB) $55-80
Full Breakfast
Credit Cards: A, B, C, D
Notes: 2, 5, 8, 11, 12, 13, 14

New Hampshire Bed and Breakfast

128 South Hoop Pole Road, Guilford, CT 06437
(203) 457-0042; (800) 582-0853

NH135. Built circa 1892, this large Victorian "cottage" is a wonderful example of Victorian ingenuity. Trimmed like a pagoda with bells and dragons and complete with veranda and comfortable rocking chairs, this bed and breakfast has been cited by many home and travel magazines. Each guest room has the welcoming warmth of overstuffed easy chairs, touches of lace and wicker, firm mattresses, and soft, fluffy towels. Throughout the house, family heirlooms and memorabilia mix with pleasing surprises. Relax with morning coffee in room and enjoy a full breakfast that varies from day to day. Seasonal beverages, sherry, and afternoon tea are always available. Four guest rooms with private baths. Two suites and one guest cottage. $50-70.

BRADFORD

The Bradford Inn

Main Street, 03221
(603) 938-5309; (800) 669-5309

The Bradford Inn, a restored 1898 small country hotel, features comfortable lodging and J. Albert's Restaurant, which serves exceptional New England cuisine. Fireplaces, large parlors, wide halls, with antiques and personal mementos. Four-season activity area.

Hosts: Connie and Tom Mazol
Rooms: 12 (PB) $59-79
Full Breakfast
Credit Cards: A, B, C, D, E
Notes: 2, 4, 5, 6, 7, 8, 9, 10, 11, 12, 13, 14

Candlelite Inn Bed and Breakfast

Route 114, Rural Route 1, Box 408, 03221
(603) 938-5571

An 1897 country Victorian inn nestled on three acres in the Lake Sunapee Region. A candlelit breakfast is served in the lovely dining room or in the sunroom overlooking a babbling brook and pond. A gazebo porch is available for guests' enjoyment on a lazy summer day, and on a chilly winter evening, guests can sit by a warm and cozy fire in the parlor. The inn is nonsmoking. Come and enjoy the relaxed and friendly atmosphere of the Candlelite Inn.

Hosts: Les and Marilyn Gordon
Rooms: 6 (PB) $65-75
Full Breakfast
Credit Cards: A, B, D
Notes: 2, 5, 10, 11, 12, 13

Rosewood Country Inn

Pleasant View Road, 03221

Elegant and romantic country inn on a quiet country road, but just minutes away from the lakes and mountains. Cross-country skiing from the front door. Seven tastefully decorated rooms, all with private baths. Drift off to sleep in a canopied or four-poster bed. Mozart and Vivaldi set the mood for the three-course, candlelight and crystal breakfast served before a crackling fire in the dining room, or on one of the lovely sunlit porches. The perfect romantic getaway.

Hosts: Lesley and Dick Marquis
Rooms: 7 (PB) $69-99
Full Breakfast
Credit Cards: A, B
Notes: 2, 5, 7, 8 (over 10), 9, 10, 11, 12, 13, 14

CAMPTON

Campton Inn

Rural Route 2, Box 12, 03223
(603) 726-4449

6 Pets welcome; 8 Children welcome; 9 Social drinking allowed; 10 Tennis available; 11 Swimming available; 12 Golf available; 13 Skiing available; 14 May be booked through travel agents.

In 1836, the Campton Inn was built on Main Street, the same year Campton Village was built. A boarding house and inn since 1880, this classic farmhouse still has its original pine floors, screened porch, large cozy common room with wood stove, and the finest in New England hospitality. A full country breakfast is served. In the heart of the White Mountains with skiing, swimming, biking, hiking, and other recreations found at every corner, or guests can just sit back and relax.

Hosts: Robbin and Peter Adams
Rooms: 6 (1 PB; 5 SB) $50-65
Full Breakfast
Credit Cards: None
Notes: 2, 5, 8, 9, 10, 11, 12, 13, 14

Mountain-Fare Inn

Mad River Road, P.O. Box 553, 03223
(603) 726-4283

Lovely 1840s village home full of the antiques, fabrics, and feel of country cottage living. Flowers and gardens in summer, and foliage in fall; a true skier's lodge in the winter. Accessible, peaceful, warm, friendly, and affordable. Hearty breakfasts. Great local dining. Unspoiled beauty from Franconia Notch to Squam Lake. Wonderful four-season sports, music, theater, and wandering in the "Whites"

Hosts: Susan and Nick Preston
Rooms: 10 (7 PB; 3 SB) $50-90
Full Breakfast
Credit Cards: A, D, E
Notes: 2, 5, 8, 9, 10, 11, 12, 13, 14

New Hampshire Bed and Breakfast

128 South Hoop Pole Road, Guilford, CT 06437
(203) 457-0042; (800) 582-0853

NH116. Just minutes from I-93, the Waterville Valley four-season resort area, the Franconia Notch State Park, and Plymouth. This large, white clapboard farmhouse has gables, a farmer's porch, and a warm hearth. Guests can enjoy the recreational activities in the White Mountains: hiking the marked Appalachian Mountain Club trails, bicycling, snowmobiling, swimming, picnicking, and an excellent selection of alpine and cross-country skiing. The large lawns feature volleyball and croquet sets. Guests are welcome to use the large country living room with fireplace, color cable TV with VCR, games, puzzles, and books. Enjoy a full breakfast and generous seasonal snacks. Eight guest rooms with private baths, three with shared bath. Children welcome. No smoking. $50-85.

Osgood Inn

P.O. Box 419, 03223
(603) 726-3543

The hosts welcome visitors year-round to this warm and gracious village home with four spacious rooms featuring handmade quilts and lovely views. Close to skiing, hiking, golf, shopping, and tourist attractions. Full country breakfast is served in the morning, and afternoon tea is served every day. Charming common room with fireplace, serene gardens, and back porch are available for guests to enjoy. Housekeeping two-bedroom suite available in the Annex. Minutes from I-93.

Hosts: Dexter and Pat Osgood
Rooms: 4 (SB) $50-55
Full Breakfast
Credit Cards: None
Notes: 2, 5, 7 (limited), 8, 9, 12, 13

Osgood Inn

CENTER HARBOR

New Hampshire Bed and Breakfast

128 South Hoop Pole Road, Guilford, CT 06437
(203) 457-0042; (800) 582-0853

NH215. On 75 beautiful acres on Long Island in the center of Lake Winnipesaukee (connected by bridge). The house was built in the 1830s and was established as an inn in 1874. It is now run by a descendant of the original family. Guests enjoy the 75 acres of lawns, fields, and woods which run to the water's edge, either of two private beaches, the lakeside picnic area, and the large living room with fieldstone fireplace. A hearty country breakfast is served in the dining room. Children welcome. No smoking; no pets. Open from the end of June through September. $50.

NH218. Just five-minutes from the center of a pleasant village, visitors can enjoy the amenities of this contemporary ranch style home, yet be surrounded by tall pine trees, singing birds, and a peaceful, wooded setting. Sunbathe or swim at the town beach, take a breakfast cruise on Lake Winnipesaukee, or visit any of the fine craft, antique, and retail shops. Don't miss the region's most expansive quilt shop. Guests enjoy the use of a large screened porch, a living room with fieldstone fireplace, or the den with ample books, magazines, and TV. A Continental breakfast is served each morning in the dining room. No smoking. No pets. Children welcome. $55-60.

Red Hill Inn

Rural Free Delivery 1, Box 99M, 03226
(603) 279-7001

Restored country estate on 60 acres overlooking Squam Lake and the White Mountains. Twenty-one rooms, each with private bath, many with fireplace and Jacuzzi.

Country gourmet restaurant serving all meals; entertainment in the Runabout Lounge. Cross-country skiing (and rentals) on property. Two hours north of Boston.

Hosts: Rick Miller and Don Leavitt
Rooms: 21 (PB) $85-150
Full Breakfast
Credit Cards: A, B, C, D, E
Notes: 2, 3, 4, 5, 7, 8, 9, 10, 11, 12, 13, 14

CHOCORUA

Mt. Chocorua View House

P.O. Box 348, Route 16, 03817
(603) 323-8350

Mt. Chocorua View House is a beautifully renovated 17-room home built 150 years ago in the quaint village of Chocorua in the town of Tamworth. The open-beam ceilings and open staircase add charm to this home that has housed Emily Post, President Franklin D. Roosevelt, and others. The wood-burning Franklin fireplace, paddle fans, and porches make guests feel like they are in a home away from home. Centered in the White Mountains, guests are minutes away from lakes for swimming and canoeing, mountains to ski or hike, shopping outlets, or just plain relaxing. While having breakfast in the dining room or on the porch, the innkeepers are on hand to suggest the right hike or excursion to suite the weather of the day or guests' inclination.

Host: Bill Kern
Rooms: 7 (1 PB; 6 SB) $55-59
Two-room suite: $135
Continental Breakfast
Credit Cards: A, B, C, D
Notes: 2, 5, 7 (limited), 8, 11, 13

New Hampshire Bed and Breakfast

128 South Hoop Pole Road, Guilford, CT 06437
(203) 457-0042; (800) 582-0853

NH107. This spacious hilltop Colonial is on 22 acres of woodlands with majestic views of Mount Chocorua and Ossipee Lake.

6 Pets welcome; 8 Children welcome; 9 Social drinking allowed; 10 Tennis available; 11 Swimming available; 12 Golf available; 13 Skiing available; 14 May be booked through travel agents.

Relax beside the fire in the living room with a good book, play board games, watch TV, or strike up a tune on the piano. Screened porch; tennis court. Hearty country breakfast. Horseshoes, badminton, croquet, and nature walks on premises. Enjoy hiking, boating, swimming, antiquing, auctions, summer theater, and restaurants. Three guest rooms with shared baths. All rooms have spectacular mountain views, hand-stenciled walls, and antique furnishings. A private guest house with fireplace, deck, kitchen, wood-burning stove, and bedding for four guests is also available. Open May through October. $50-75.

CONWAY

Bed and Breakfast Marblehead and North Shore

P.O. Box 35, Newtonville, MA 02160
(617) 964-1606; (800) 832-2632;
FAX (617) 332-8572

This restored Victorian home is furnished with beautiful antiques and collectibles. Three guest rooms offer single, queen- or king-size beds, one with private bath. A wonderful breakfast is served each morning in the formal breakfast room, or in the outdoor nook, weather permitting. The White Mountain National Forest is nearby, and it's just a short ride to the center of Conway Village. Additional fee per person during foliage season. $55-68.

Darby Field Inn

Bald Hill Road, 03818
(603) 447-2181; (800) 426-4147

A charming, out-of-the-way country inn that offers excellent dining, a cozy atmosphere, and spectacular mountain views. An outdoor pool, cross-country ski trails, and a staff that is both friendly and courteous. Reservations recommended. Rate includes

breakfast, tax, and gratuity. Midweek and off-season packages. Minimum stay on weekends is two nights and on holidays is two to three nights.

Hosts: Marc and Maria Donaldson
Rooms: 16 (12 PB; 2 SB) $108-168
Full Breakfast
Credit Cards: A, B, C, E
Notes: 4, 5, 7, 8 (limited), 9, 10, 11, 12, 13, 14

DOVER

New Hampshire Bed and Breakfast

128 South Hoop Pole Road, Guilford, CT 06437
(203) 457-0042; (800) 582-0853

NH410. The charming 100-year-old Queen Anne Victorian offers a special experience for a traveler who wants more than the ordinary. A turned oak staircase and fretwork welcome guests to the turn-of-the-century era. Relax on the tree-shaded porch or enjoy the living room in all seasons. In the seacoast area, convenient to UNH, Portsmouth, Durham, and Maine. Two guest rooms furnished with antiques and a double bed share a full bath. Children over four welcome. No smoking. $45-50.

NH412. A large Victorian country home dating from the mid-19th century, this farm offers comfortable, spacious guest rooms in a unique rural setting. The inn is set among rolling fields with nature trails along the Cacheco River. Guests are welcome to use the antique-filled formal parlor and library. There are horseshoe pits and a volleyball net. Swimming, cross-country skiing, golf, and snowmobiling are available nearby. A full, home-cooked breakfast is complemented by fresh fruits and juices, homemade muffins, breads, scones, and fresh brewed coffee, all served with a touch of Scottish hospitality. Near the seacoast and mountains, near Spaulding Turnpike. Downtown Dover is two miles away and Portsmouth is 15 minutes away. Five guest rooms share two antique baths and are furnished with antiques. No smoking. Children welcome. $45-65.

Silver Street Inn

Silver Street Inn

103 Silver Street, 03820
(603) 743-3000

The inn was once the private home of the Frank B. Williams family of Dover, who decorated it with beautiful imported materials including Spanish mahogany, Austrian crystal doorknobs, Italian slate, and French Caen stone fireplaces. Hosts have installed fire alarm and sprinkler systems. Full breakfast. Rooms have private baths, cable TV, and telephones. Open year-round.

Host: Lorene L. Cook
Rooms: 10 (9 PB; 1 SB) $69-89
Full Breakfast
Credit Cards: A, B, C, E
Notes: 2, 5, 8, 12

EAST ANDOVER

Bed and Breakfast Reservations

P.O. Box 35, Newtonville, MA 02160
(617) 964-1606; (800) 832-2632;
FAX (617) 332-8572

The Lakeside Inn. A Colonial farmhouse dating back to 1800 is in a four-season vacation area. Seasonal activities include fall-foliage hikes, snowmobiling, cross-country skiing, ice-skating and -fishing, boating, fishing, swimming, and golf. Guest rooms include twin, queen- and king-size beds, all with private baths. The Inn is only 23 miles northwest of Concord, and easy to reach from routes 89, 91 or 93. A full breakfast is included. No smoking. Children over eight welcome. $85-100.

Highland Lake Inn

P.O. Box 164, Maple Street, 03231
(603) 735-6426

Built in 1767 and expanded in 1805, this classic building set atop 12 acres overlooks Highland Lake, Tucker, Ragged and Kearsarge mountains. The inn has been recently renovated to include private baths in each of ten spacious guest rooms. A sumptuous and different breakfast is served each morning. Cross-country ski trails on a 21-acre nature conservancy. Downhill skiing, championship golf courses, and antique and outlet shopping nearby. No pets. No children. No smoking.

Hosts: The Petras Family
Rooms: 10 (PB) $85-100
Full Breakfast
Credit Cards: A, B, C
Notes: 2, 5, 9, 10, 11, 12, 13, 14

EASTON

New Hampshire Bed and Breakfast

128 South Hoop Pole Road, Guilford, CT 06437
(203) 457-0042; (800) 582-0853

NH105. In a beautiful meadow setting, only ten minutes from Franconia Notch, an unadorned, restored Victorian farmhouse. Built in 1887, it was considered haunted by some in the 1940s. Guests will appreciate the decorative painting, stenciling, and

6 Pets welcome; 8 Children welcome; 9 Social drinking allowed; 10 Tennis available; 11 Swimming available; 12 Golf available; 13 Skiing available; 14 May be booked through travel agents.

glazing. A full breakfast is served in the common room. Minutes from hiking and cross-country skiing on the Appalachian Trail. A day's trip to the attractions of the White Mountains, the Connecticut River valley, and Vermont. Four guest rooms have shared baths. One room has a private bath. Children are welcome. No smoking allowed. Dog in residence. No guest pets permitted. $40-75.

ENFIELD

Boulder Cottage on Crystal Lake

Rural Route 1, Box 257, 03748
(603) 632-7355

A turn-of-the-century Victorian cottage owned by the family for 70 years, the inn faces beautiful Crystal Lake in the Dartmouth-Sunapee region. Open May through November.

Hosts: Barbara and Harry Reed
Rooms: 3 (2 PB; 1 SB) $45-60
Full Breakfast
Credit Cards: None
Notes: 2, 8, 9, 10, 11, 12

FRANCONIA

Blanche's Bed and Breakfast

Easton Valley Road, 03580
(603) 823-7061

Named for the family dog, Blanche's is a sunny, century-old farmhouse restored to a former glory it probably never had. Quiet, pastoral setting with views of the Kinsman Ridge. In the English bed and breakfast tradition, offering cotton linens, down comforters, comfortable beds, and a great breakfast which might include fresh fruit salad, spinach omelet, or blueberry pancakes (with pure maple syrup) and homemade muffins. Decorative painting throughout; working

studio featuring unusual handmade floorcloths. Close to all outdoor activities.

Hosts: Brenda Shannon and John Vail
Rooms: 5 (1 PB; 4 SB) $60-85
Full Breakfast
Credit Cards: A, B, C
Notes: 2, 4 (for groups), 5, 8, 9, 10, 11, 12, 13, 14

Bungay Jar Bed and Breakfast

P.O. Box 15, Easton Valley Road, 03580
(603) 823-7775

Secluded woodlands with spectacular mountain views, brook, and gardens make memorable this home built from an 18th-century barn. King or queen suites, private balconies, skylights, six-foot soaking tub, sauna, canopied bed. Two-story common area with fireplace for reading, music, and talk. Mountain gaze in the morning sun while breakfasting outside in summer. Small in scale; intimate. Hosts are a landscape architect and a patent attorney, and their young son.

Hosts: Kate Kerivan and Lee Strimbeck
Rooms: 6 (4 PB; 2 SB) $60-110
Full Breakfast
Credit Cards: A, B, C
Notes: 2, 5, 8, 9, 10, 11, 12, 13, 14

Franconia Inn

Easton Road, 03580
(603) 823-5542; (800) 473-5299
FAX (603) 823-8078

A charming inn on 107 acres in the Easton valley, affording breathtaking views of the White Mountains. The inn's 34 rooms are

Franconia Inn

decorated simply, yet beautifully. Elegant American cuisine highlights the inn's quiet country sophistication. Children are welcome. On Route 116. Closed April 1 through May 15

Hosts: The Morris Family
Rooms: 34 (30 PB; 4 SB) $75-110
Full Breakfast
Credit Cards: A, B, C
Notes: 2, 4, 7, 8, 9, 10, 11, 12, 13, 14

The Hilltop Inn

Route 117, 03585
(603) 823-5695; (800) 770-5695

A charming Victorian country inn, built circa 1895. Antique furnishings throughout make each of the six guest rooms unique and the common rooms cozy and inviting. All guest rooms include private baths. Guests are encouraged to enjoy this home. Hosts offer lovely sunset views from the deck, relaxing moments to stroll along quiet country lanes, or to read in comfortable porch rockers or in the Victorian sitting room. Hosts have an assortment of games guests may play, or join the hosts for some friendly conversation by a wood-burning fireplace. Indulge in fine dining and spirits in the intimate candlelit dining room. All room rates include a large country breakfast each morning. Hosts welcome pets if they get along with the resident dog and cats.

Hosts: Meri and Mike Hern
Rooms: 6 (PB) $60-110
Full Breakfast
Credit Cards: A, B, D
Notes: 2, 3, 4 (fall), 5, 6, 7 (limited), 9, 10, 11, 12, 13

The Inn at Forest Hills

P.O. Box 783, Route 142, 03580
(603) 823-9550
(800) 280-9550 (reservations)

This charming, historic 18-room 100-year-old Tudor manor house beguiles guests to enjoy the majestic scenery and year-round attractions of the White Mountains of New Hampshire. Enjoy gracious hospitality in eight comfortable guest rooms, most with

The Inn at Forest Hills

private baths. Relax in country casualness in the sun-filled solarium or by the fireplaces in the living room or alpine room. Savor a gourmet New England breakfast by the fireplace in a fine old country inn!

Hosts: Joanne and Gordon Haym
Rooms: 8 (5 PB; 3 SB) $60-95
Full Breakfast
Credit Cards: A, B
Notes: 2, 5, 9, 10, 11, 12, 13, 14

Lovett's Inn

Route 18, Profile Road, 03580
(603) 823-7761; (800) 356-3802

This circa 1784 inn is on ten country acres in New Hampshire's White Mountains at the entrance to Franconia Notch State Park. On the National Register of Historic Places. Six upstairs guest rooms; four with private baths, two with shared. Enjoy the fireplaced living room, glassed-in sun porch, and three dining rooms on the ground level. Among the evergreens are modern cottages, which add an additional 16 guest rooms. A carriage house is also available offering six upper-level twin rooms with shared baths. The food at Lovett's Inn has been highly rated.

Hosts: Sharon and Anthony Avrutine
Full breakfast and dinner

6 Pets welcome; 8 Children welcome; 9 Social drinking allowed; 10 Tennis available; 11 Swimming available; 12 Golf available; 13 Skiing available; 14 May be booked through travel agents.

Gunstock Country Inn

GILFORD

Gunstock Country Inn

580 Cherry Valley Road, 03246
(603) 293-2021; (800) 654-0180

Nestled in a traditional New England setting with a spectacular view of New Hampshire's Lake Winnipesaukee and surrounding mountains, this country inn has 27 guest rooms furnished with lovely antiques, a health club, and elegant dining room with superior cuisine. Within minutes of golf courses, boating, hiking, skiing, tennis, horseback riding, and area attractions. The health club features an Olympic-size indoor pool, saunas, steam rooms, tanning booths, and fully equipped exercise room.

Rooms: 27 (PB) $63-115
Continental Breakfast
Credit Cards: A, B, C
Notes: 4, 5, 7, 8, 9, 10, 11, 12, 13, 14

GLEN

The Bernerhof Inn

P.O. Box 240, 03838
(603) 383-4414; (800) 548-8007

An elegant Victorian set in the foothills of the White Mountains. The Bernerhof remains true to its European tradition, offering a changing menu of Middle European favorites while the popular tap room offers a lighter fare. Host of "A Taste of the Mountains Cooking School." Most rooms boast an extra large spa tub for true relaxation.

Hosts: Ted and Sharon Wroblewski
Rooms: 9 (PB) $69-139
Suites: 2
Full Breakfast
Credit Cards: A, B, C
Notes: 2, 3, 4, 5, 7 (limited), 8, 9, 10, 11, 12, 13

GREENFIELD

Greenfield Bed and Breakfast Inn

Box 400, Junction Rts 136 and 31, 03047
(603) 547-6327

A romantic Victorian mansion on three acres of lawn in Greenfield, a mountain valley village between Keene and Nashua just 90 minutes from Boston. Enjoy the relaxing mountain view from the spacious veranda. A full hot breakfast is served with crystal, china, and Mozart. Very close to skiing, swimming, hiking, tennis, golf, biking, and bargain antique shopping. A favorite of Mr. and Mrs. Bob Hope and honeymooners of all ages. Senior citizen discount. Two vacation suites are also available.

Hosts: Vic and Barbara Mangini
Rooms: 9 (5 PB; 4 SB) $49-99
Full Breakfast
Credit Cards: A, B
Notes: 2, 5, 6 (call), 7 (limited), 8 (call), 9, 10, 11, 12, 13, 14

HAMPSTEAD

New Hampshire Bed and Breakfast

128 South Hoop Pole Road, Guilford, CT 06437
(203) 457-0042; (800) 582-0853

NH 605. Built by the Ordway family in 1850, this Greek Renaissance Italianate rests on gentle acreage on Main Street in Hampstead. This bed and breakfast boasts three stairways, five chimneys, hardwood floors with Oriental rugs, working wood stoves, and fireplaces. An expanded Continental breakfast is served on the weekdays, and a full, hot, hearty breakfast is served in

NOTES: Credit cards accepted: A MasterCard; B Visa; C American Express; D Discover Card; E Diner's Club; F Other; 2 Personal checks accepted; 3 Lunch available; 4 Dinner available; 5 Open all year;

the formal dining room on weekends. Complimentary wine will greet guests upon arrival, and the cookie jar is always full. Five-minutes to Sunset Lake, and one-half hour from both Manchester and Nashua. Four sets of accommodations are available. Children welcome. No smoking. $60-90.

HAMPTON

The Curtis Field House

735 Exeter Road, 03842
(603) 929-0082

This restored Cape is on five country acres on Route 27-E, three miles from the center of Exeter, seven miles from the ocean, and 50 miles from Boston. Historic Portsmouth and Durham are nearby. A full breakfast is served. The large bedrooms with private baths and air conditioning are decorated with antiques and many lovely reproductions crafted by a descendant of Darby Field. Closed December through March.

Hosts: Mary and Daniel Houston
Rooms: 3 (2 PB, 1 SB) $65
Full Breakfast
Credit Cards: A, B
Notes: 2, 9, 10, 11, 12

New Hampshire Bed and Breakfast

128 South Hoop Pole Road, Guilford, CT 06437
(203) 457-0042; (800) 582-0853

NH421. This restored custom Cape is on five country acres, just over the Exeter line. The large sunny rooms are furnished with many antiques and lovely reproductions that are crafted by a descendant of Darby Field. Enjoy fresh fruit in the air-conditioned guest room and comfortable cozy living room, or enjoy the breeze on the porch. A full country breakfast is served each morning. Three quiet rooms, two of which have private baths, and one of which shares a bath, are air-conditioned and furnished with antiques. Limited smoking. No small children. $65.

The Oceanside

365 Ocean Boulevard, 03842
(603) 926-3542

The Oceanside overlooks the Atlantic Ocean and its beautiful sandy beaches. Each of the ten rooms is tastefully and individually decorated, many with period antiques and all with private baths. The intimate cafe is open for breakfast during July and August and features homemade bread and pastries. At other times a complimentary Continental breakfast is available. This gracious inn is in a less congested part of Hampton Beach within easy walking distance of restaurants, shops, and other attractions. Closed mid-October through mid-May.

Hosts: Skip and Debbie Windemiller
Rooms: 10 (PB) $86-115
Continental Breakfast
Credit Cards: A, B, C, D
Notes: 8 (limited), 9, 10, 11, 12

The Victoria Inn at Hampton

430 High Street, 03842
(603) 929-1437

Comfort and elegance await in this charming century-old guest house. A short walk to sandy beaches and close to good restaurants, factory outlet shopping, theater, art events, and antiquing. Enjoy a full gourmet breakfast in the glassed-in morning room with white wicker furniture and lace. Sit and relax on porches overlooking a picturesque gazebo and gardens. Six rooms are available, all having individual personalities and warm furnishings. Licensed and inspected.

Hosts: Bill and Ruth Muzzey
Rooms: 6 (3 PB; 3 SB) $75-95
Full Breakfast
Credit Cards: A, B
Notes: 2, 5, 8 (over 11), 9, 10, 11, 12, 13, 14

---

6 Pets welcome; 8 Children welcome; 9 Social drinking allowed; 10 Tennis available; 11 Swimming available; 12 Golf available; 13 Skiing available; 14 May be booked through travel agents.

HANOVER

New Hampshire Bed and Breakfast

128 South Hoop Pole Road, Guilford, CT 06437
(203) 457-0042; (800) 582-0853

NH320. This 180-year-old residence is on two acres with handsome red barns and lovely old trees. A former dairy farm, it belonged to a prominent local citizen who entertained President and Mrs. Coolidge and Amelia Earhart. A large formal living room, with beamed ceilings and curved oak staircase, has a wood-burning stove to ward off the chill on winter nights. Lovely private stone terrace. Elaborate Continental breakfast. A variety of rooms with private and shared baths. Children welcome; smoking limited. Two resident dogs, but no guest pets allowed. $100-130.

Stonecrest Farm Bed and Breakfast

119 Christian Street, P.O. Box 504, Wilder, VT 05088
P.O. Box B1163, Hanover, NH 03755
(802) 296-2425; (800) 369-2626

Founded in 1810, this former dairy farm still boasts red barns and spacious grounds in a country setting, but is close to everything. Just three and one-half miles from Dartmouth College, Stonecrest welcomes parents and alumni, plus hikers, bikers, skiers, and visitors from near and far. There are five elegant guest rooms, all with private baths, and antique furnishings throughout. Breakfast offers fresh fruit and homemade scones, muffins, and breads in the dining room where Calvin Coolidge was once a guest. Write for details about the inn-to-inn canoe trip.

Host: Gail Sanderson
Rooms: 5 (PB) $100-115
Continental Breakfast; Full Breakfast on Weekends
Credit Cards: A, B, C
Notes: 2, 5, 8 (over 8), 9, 10, 11, 12, 13, 14

Haverhill Inn

HAVERHILL

Haverhill Inn

Route 10, 03765
(603) 989-5961

This gracious 1810 Colonial home is in the Haverhill Corner historic district. Enjoy hikes in the nearby White Mountains, take walks along country lanes, converse in the parlor, or choose a book and settle in by the fire. Four rooms, all of which have private baths and working fireplaces, are available.

Hosts: Stephen Campbell and Anne Baird
Rooms: 4 (PB) $75
Full Breakfast
Credit Cards: None
Notes: 2, 9, 10, 13

HENNIKER

Henniker House Bed and Breakfast

2 Ramsdell Road, Box 191, 03242
(603) 428-3198

Henniker House, a 19th-century Victorian home with wraparound porches, is bracketed by huge pine trees. The solarium/breakfast room overlooks the Contoocook River; the 50-foot deck overhangs the water.

NOTES: Credit cards accepted: A MasterCard; B Visa; C American Express; D Discover Card; E Diner's Club; F Other; 2 Personal checks accepted; 3 Lunch available; 4 Dinner available; 5 Open all year;

Henniker is the site of New England College, is in the heart of antiquing, and hosts a fiber studio, arts and crafts, quilting, summer music festivals, theater, and symphony. Camping, fishing, skiing, boating, golf, wind surfing, and sailing are all available, or just relax in this little village.

Host: Bertina Williams
Rooms: 4 (2 PB; 2 SB) $55-65
Full Breakfast
Credit Cards: A, B
Notes: 2, 5, 8, 9, 10, 11, 12, 13, 14

Meeting House Inn

35 Flanders Road, 03242
(603) 428-3228

The Meeting House Inn is family owned and operated. It is a renovated country farmstead (established 1982). Hosts seek to provide a relaxed and cozy atmosphere where special attention is paid to the individual comforts of guests. This is a nonsmoking inn. The restaurant serves a delicious selection of individually prepared entrees. Rooms at the inn are filled with family furnishings and antiques, and all have private baths. In the morning, breakfast is served in your room in a country basket. Air-conditioned. AAA approved. Private hot tub and sauna are available.

Rooms: 6 (PB) $65-98
Full Breakfast
Credit Cards: A, B, C, D
Notes: 4, 5, 9, 10, 11, 12, 13, 14

Meeting House Inn

HILL

Snowbound Bed and Breakfast

Rural Route 1, Box 910, Murray Hill Road, 03243
(603) 744-9112

Timberframe home in Cape Cod style on six quiet acres in the Lakes Region of New Hampshire. On a designated New Hampshire scenic road with mountain view. Rooms are furnished with antiques, as is the sunroom, which is also a comfortable sitting area with TV. Breakfast is complete with fruit and home-baked goods. A nonsmoking facility

Hosts: Gayle and Gene Seip
Rooms: 3 (PB) $60
Full Breakfast
Credit Cards: A, B
Notes: 2, 5, 11, 12, 13

HILLSBOROUGH

New Hampshire Bed and Breakfast

128 South Hoop Pole Road, Guilford, CT 06437
(203) 457-0042; (800) 582-0853

NH511. This home is a passive-solar Cape with open concept downstairs. Full southern exposure allows year-round enjoyment of the all-glass breakfast room and patio, which features scenic views of fields, woods, and birds. A full breakfast of bacon and eggs, or waffles, sausage, muffins, and fruits is served. Walk to Gleason Falls and the stone arch bridge, or enjoy the brook and swimming hole nearby. Resident cat. No children. Smoking permitted. $60.

The Inn at Maplewood Farm

P.O. Box 1478, 447 Center Road, 03244
(603) 464-4242

6 Pets welcome; 8 Children welcome; 9 Social drinking allowed; 10 Tennis available; 11 Swimming available; 12 Golf available; 13 Skiing available; 14 May be booked through travel agents.

The simple charm of New England with the elegance of a European country inn. At Maplewood Farm, guest rooms are filled with American and European antiques, an inviting bed, and unique amenities. A four-season getaway, the inn is a great starting point for a retreat of skiing, hiking, swimming, or golfing. In the heart of antique country and on 14 acres of foliage trees. Homemade breakfast every day.

Hosts: Laura and Jayme Simoes
Rooms: 5 (3 PB; 2 SB) $55-65
Full Breakfast
Credit Cards: A, B, C, D
Notes: 2, 3, 5, 8, 9, 10, 11, 12, 13, 14

Windyledge

HOLDERNESS

The Inn on Golden Pond

Route 3, 03245
(603) 968-7269

An 1879 Colonial home on 55 wooded acres. Bright and cheerful setting, breakfast, and game rooms. Close to major ski areas. Nearby is Squam Lake, the setting for the film *On Golden Pond*. Minimum stay on holidays.

Host: Bill and Bonnie Webb
Rooms: 9 (PB) $90-135
Full Breakfast
Credit Cards: A, B, C
Notes: 2, 5, 8 (over 12), 9, 10, 11, 12, 13, 14

HOPKINTON

Windyledge
Bed and Breakfast

1264 Hatfield Road, 03229
(603) 746-4054

This elegant hilltop Colonial is surrounded by nine acres of fields and woods. Bordered by picturesque hills and the White Mountains beyond. The hosts' delicious gourmet apricot-glazed French toast, ricotta souffle, or honey-and-spice blueberry pancakes are served on the airy sun porch or outside on the deck or in the country dining room.

Lakes, golf, skiing, craft shops, and numerous restaurants nearby. After a full day's activities, return "home" to a dip in the pool, wine by the fireside, or good conversation. Come and recapture the romance!

Hosts: Dick and Susan Vogt (pronounced "Vote")
Rooms: 3 (1 PB; 2 SB) $55-75
Full Breakfast
Credit Cards: A, B, D
Notes: 2, 5, 8, 9, 10, 11, 12, 13, 14

JACKSON

Dana Place Inn

Box L, Pinkham Notch, 03846
(603) 383-6822; (800) 537-9276

Century-old inn at the base of Mount Washington on 300 acres along the Ellis River. Dana Place features cozy rooms, fine dining, indoor heated pool, river swimming, Jacuzzi, tennis, hiking, walking trails, fishing, and cross-country skiing on the premises. Golf, outlet shopping, and downhill skiing nearby. Seasonal escape packages available.

Hosts: Harris and Mary Lou Levine
Room: 33 (29 PB; 4 SB) $85-125
Full Breakfast
Credit Cards: A, B, C, D, E
Notes: 2, 3, 4, 5, 6, 7, 8, 9, 10, 11, 12, 13, 14

The Inn at Jackson

P.O. Box 807, Main Street, 03846
(603) 383-4321; (800) 289-8600

NOTES: Credit cards accepted: A MasterCard; B Visa; C American Express; D Discover Card; E Diner's Club; F Other; 2 Personal checks accepted; 3 Lunch available; 4 Dinner available; 5 Open all year;

Guests find this inn on a knoll overlooking the peaceful village of Jackson. In summer, guests can enjoy golf, swimming, tennis, fishing, or just a walk on a quiet mountain trail. In winter, enjoy cross-country skiing, Alpine skiing, sleigh rides, or relax by the cozy fireplace. Spacious guest rooms offer a relaxing atmosphere.

Hosts: R. and Lori Tradewell
Rooms: 9 (PB) $56-100
Full Breakfast
Credit Cards: A, B, C, D, E
Notes: 2, 5, 7, 8, 9, 10, 11, 12, 13, 14

Nestlenook Farm Resort

Dinsmore Road, 03846
(603) 383-9443

Escape into a Victorian past on a 65-acre estate. Seven elegant guest rooms, all of which have two-person Jacuzzis and some of which have parlor stoves, canopied beds, and fireplaces, charming guest kitchen, antiques, and fireplaced gazebo. Horse-drawn sleighs, horseback riding, mountain bikes, rowboats, fishing, and Victorian pool. Savor the romance and step back in time at a gingerbread country inn.

Hosts: Lionel Tetreault
Rooms: 7 (PB) $125-270
Full Breakfast
Credit Cards: A, B
Notes: 2, 4, 5, 9, 11, 12, 13, 14

New Hampshire Bed and Breakfast

128 South Hoop Pole Road, Guilford, CT 06437
(203) 457-0042; (800) 582-0853

NH109. On a birch-covered hill looking towards Mount Washington, this brand-new house has opened recently as a bed and breakfast to rave reviews. The home offers 18th-century antiques, textiles, folk art, handmade quilts, designer sheets, fresh flowers, fruit baskets, and terry-cloth robes. The full gourmet breakfast served on English bone china features sticky buns, shortbread, and fudge. Afternoon tea is served. The living room has a fireplace, TV, and VCR. The deck, hammock, and flower gardens provide splendid mountain views. Three guest rooms with private baths. One room has a private Jacuzzi tub and private deck looking towards Mount Washington. No smoking; no pets. Children over ten welcome. $60-115.

The Village House

The Village House

P.O. Box 359, Route 16A, 03846
(603) 383-6666

Just over the covered bridge is this charming Colonial inn with wraparound porch facing the mountains. In summer, enjoy tennis, swimming, and Jacuzzi on premises; riding, golf, hiking, canoeing, and fine dining nearby. In winter visitors ski from the door of the house onto the 157 kilometers of cross-country trails. Downhill skiing is available at four major nearby mountains. Sleigh rides, ice skating, and snowshoeing are also available. Kitchenettes and family suites available.

Host: Robin Crocker
Rooms: 15 (13 PB; 2 SB) $40-125
Continental Breakfast; Full Breakfast in ski season
Credit Cards: A, B, D, E
Notes: 2, 5, 7, 8, 9, 10, 11, 12, 13, 14

Whitneys' Inn

P.O. Box 822, Route 16B, 03846-0822
(603) 383-8916; (800) 677-5737

---

6 Pets welcome; 8 Children welcome; 9 Social drinking allowed; 10 Tennis available; 11 Swimming available; 12 Golf available; 13 Skiing available; 14 May be booked through travel agents.

Whitneys' Inn

The classic country inn. A lovely pastoral setting in the heart of the White Mountains. Large comfortable rooms grace this restored New England farmhouse, circa 1842. Adjacent to the main inn are cozy fireplace cottages and family suites. The dining room, featuring full country breakfasts and country gourmet dinners, is open to the public. Seasonal on-site activities range from tennis, swimming, and hiking in the summer, to cross-country and downhill skiing during the winter.

Rooms: 29 (PB) $60-110
Full Breakfast
Credit Cards: A, B, C, D
Notes: 2, 4, 5, 7, 8, 9, 10, 11, 12, 13, 14

JAFFREY

Benjamin Prescott Inn

Route 124 East, 03452
(603) 532-6637

Come discover the charm of the past and the comforts of the present within a classic Greek Revival home furnished with antiques. Ten charming guest rooms, each of which has its own private bath, are available for guests, and a full breakfast of hearty country fare is served each morning. Relax and enjoy the surrounding dairy farm, walk the stonewall lined lane, shop, climb Mt. Monadnock, visit local artisans, and eat in excellent restaurants.

Hosts: Jan and Barry Miller
Rooms: 10 (PB) $60-130
Full Breakfast
Credit Cards: A, B, C
Notes: 2, 5, 8 (over 10), 9, 10, 11, 12, 13, 14

The Woodbound Inn

62 Woodbound Road, 03452
(603) 532-8341; (800) 688-7770

The Woodbound Inn is a 40-room country inn/resort set on 160 acres of picturesque New Hampshire. The inn has a nine-hole golf course free to guests. There is also lake swimming, restaurant for all meals, lounge, playbarn, gift shop, and cross-country skiing. Accommodations include 17 rooms in the 100-year-old bed and breakfast, 14 modern rooms, and nine lakefront cabins. This is a perfect place any season for a vacation or business meeting.

Rooms: 40 (33 PB; 7 SB) $65-125
Full Breakfast
Credit Cards: A, B, C

JEFFERSON

Applebrook Bed and Breakfast

Route 115A, 03583-0178
(603) 586-7713; (800) 545-6504

Taste the midsummer raspberries while enjoying spectacular mountain views from this old Victorian farmhouse. Bike, hike, fish, ski, go antiquing, or just relax in the sitting room by the goldfish pool. Near Santa's Village and Six Gun City. Dormitory rooms available in addition to private guest rooms. Brochure available. Try the hot tub under the stars!

Hosts: Sandra J. Conley and Martin M. Kelly
Rooms: 10 (4 PB; 6 SB) $40-60
Dorm Rooms: $20 per person
Full Breakfast
Credit Cards: A, B
Notes: 2, 5, 6, 8, 9, 10, 11, 12, 13, 14

The Jefferson Inn

Route 2, Rural Free Delivery 1, Box 68A, 03583
(603) 586-7998; (800) 729-7908

Among the White Mountains National Forest, the Jefferson Inn offers a 360-degree

NOTES: Credit cards accepted: A MasterCard; B Visa; C American Express; D Discover Card; E Diner's Club; F Other; 2 Personal checks accepted; 3 Lunch available; 4 Dinner available; 5 Open all year;

mountain view. Each room is furnished uniquely, many with themes such as Shaker, Victorian, and New England rooms. With Mount Washington nearby, the inn is an ideal location for hiking, cross-country and downhill skiing. Six golf courses nearby. Afternoon tea is served. Swimming pond. Two family suites and a large family room are available in an isolated wing. Minimum stay foliage weekends and holidays is two nights. Closed November and April.

Hosts: Greg Brown and Bertie Koelewijn
Rooms: 13 (13 PB) $50-80
Full Breakfast
Credit Cards: A, B, C, D
Notes: 2, 8, 9, 10, 11, 12, 13, 14

The Jefferson Inn

New Hampshire Bed and Breakfast

128 South Hoop Pole Road, Guilford, CT 06437
(203) 457-0042; (800) 582-0853

NH125. Built in 1896, this charming Victorian is nestled among the White Mountain National Forest and enjoys 360° mountain views. Look across the Jefferson Meadows to Franconia Notch, Mount Washington, and the northern Presidential Range. See Mount Star King and Waumbek in back of the inn. Each room is furnished with period

antiques and has a character of its own, such as the Victorian and Shaker rooms. Daily afternoon tea is served in the common room. The inn is ideal for hiking, golf, biking, fishing, canoeing, swimming, antiquing, alpine and Nordic skiing, skating, and snowshoeing. Right in town are Santa's Village and Six Gun City attractions. Ten guest rooms, five with private baths. A two-room suite with private bath accommodates families. Children welcome. No smoking; no pets. $55-85.

LACONIA

New Hampshire Bed and Breakfast

128 South Hoop Pole Road, Guilford, CT 06437
(203) 457-0042; (800) 582-0853

NH235. Four blocks from downtown Laconia, this large Victorian home, built in 1903, offers guests a formal living room with fireplace and piano; a den with books, games, and TV; a carpeted front porch with comfortable wicker and cane rockers; and a magnificent two-story solar greenhouse addition with wood-burning stove and tables for board games and puzzles. A full breakfast is served in the formal dining room and there are tea and beverages for afternoon snacks. Two guest rooms with shared bath. Children ages 3-16 are welcome. No smoking in the bedrooms; no pets. $45-50.

NH238. In the local native American tongue, Winnisquam means "smiling water." Guests cannot help but smile at this beautiful setting. The serenity of the lake, mountains, and surrounding woodlands lifts the spirit. This recently built contemporary was expertly designed and finished by the host. All of the wood finish is native oak and pine milled from trees where the house now stands. There is a two-story solarium

6 Pets welcome; 8 Children welcome; 9 Social drinking allowed; 10 Tennis available; 11 Swimming available; 12 Golf available; 13 Skiing available; 14 May be booked through travel agents.

greenhouse overlooking the lake that serves as a wonderful place to read or have a snack. Two sitting rooms have TVs, books, and board games; guests are welcome to use the canoe or sunfish sailboat. Breakfast is an expanded Continental, and three freshly decorated guest rooms are available. Resident dog, but no guest pets. Children welcome. No smoking. $60-85.

Tin Whistle Inn

1047 Union Avenue, 03246
(603) 528-4185

Enjoy gracious hospitality at this charming post-Victorian home. Living room with fireplace, leaded-glass windows, and oak woodwork. Comfortable, spacious bedrooms. View memorable sunsets from the large veranda overlooking Paugus Bay. Minutes to Lake Winnipesaukee attractions and winter skiing facilities. Full, no-need-for-lunch, breakfasts. Closed November.

Host: Maureen Blazok
Rooms: 4 (PB) $45-60
Full Breakfast
Credit Cards: C, D
Notes: 2, 6, 7 (limited), 8, 9, 10, 11, 12, 13, 14

LAKE WINNEPESAUKEE

Host Homes of Boston

P.O. Box 117, Newton, MA 02168
(617) 244-1308; FAX (617) 244-5156

This lakefront townhouse condo sleeps eight, with three bedrooms, three full baths, fireplace, skylights, cathedral ceiling, living and dining rooms, deck and fully equipped kitchen. Linens supplied. Magnificent view of lake. Private beach, near many restaurants. Fifteen minutes to Gunstock/Tenney Mountain; one hour to North Conway and Waterville Valley; less than two hours from Boston. No smoking. No pets. Two-week minimum stay; more information and prices on request.

LINCOLN

Red Sleigh Inn

Pollard Road, P.O. Box 562, 03251
(603) 745-8517

Family-run inn with mountain views. Just off the scenic Kancamagus Highway. One mile to Loon Mountains. Waterville, Cannon, and Bretton Woods nearby. Many summer attractions and superb fall foliage. Shopping, dining, and theater are minutes away. Hiking, swimming, golf, and train rides are available.

Hosts: Bill and Loretta
Rooms: 6 (3 PB; 3 SB) $55-75
Full Breakfast
Credit Cards: A, B
Notes: 2, 5, 11, 12, 13, 14

LITTLETON

The Beal House Inn

247 West Main Street, 03561
(603) 444-2661

For the perfect blend of relaxation and adventure, guests are welcomed to this cheerful 1833 in-village inn! In the heart of the White Mountains, the Beal House offers thoughtful lodging with antique-filled guest rooms, down comforters, and special touches. Fireside breakfast gatherings get guests off to a great start, and gourmet evening dining featuring classic French cuisine and a wine list with more than 250 selections completes the celebration of good things! Game room. Afternoon refreshments.

Hosts: Catherine and Jean-Marie (John) Fisher-Motheu
Rooms: 13 (9 PB; 4 SB) $55-75
Full Breakfast
Credit Cards: A, B
Notes: 2, 4, 5, 8, 9, 10, 11, 12, 13, 14

NOTES: Credit cards accepted: A MasterCard; B Visa; C American Express; D Discover Card; E Diner's Club; F Other; 2 Personal checks accepted; 3 Lunch available; 4 Dinner available; 5 Open all year;

MADISON

New Hampshire Bed and Breakfast

128 South Hoop Pole Road, Guilford, CT 06437
(203) 457-0042; (800) 582-0853

NH110. In a peaceful farm and ranch town on 80 acres of fields and woods, this comfortable farmhouse bed and breakfast is only 15 minutes from the Conways and the Scenic Kancamagus Highway. Guests may enjoy the country kitchen with fireplace and the guest parlor, furnished with antiques. The spacious grounds offer scenic trails for walking, cross-country skiing, and wagon or sleigh rides. A full breakfast is served in the dining room. Children welcome. No smoking in bedrooms. No pets. $45-55.

MARLBOROUGH

Peep-Willow Farm

51 Bixby Street, 03455
(603) 876-3807

Peep-Willow Farm is a working Thoroughbred horse farm that also caters to humans. On 20 acres with a view all the way to the Connecticut River valley. Guests are welcome to help with chores or watch the young horses frolic in the fields, but there is no riding. Flexibility and serenity are the key ingredients to enjoying the stay.

Host: Noel Aderer
Rooms: 3 (SB) $25-45
Full Breakfast
Credit Cards: None
Notes: 2, 5, 6 (call), 8, 9, 13 (cross-country), 14

MEREDITH

New Hampshire Bed and Breakfast

128 South Hoop Pole Road, Guilford, CT 06437
(203) 457-0042; (800) 582-0853

NH211. On the shore of Lake Winnipesaukee, four miles from the center of town, sits this beautiful turn-of-the-century home. Enjoy swimming, boating, canoeing, and badminton outside. Inside, relax on the screened porch or in front of the fireplace in the living room, overlooking the Ossipee Mountains and Lake Winnipesaukee. In town, guests will find shops, galleries, antiques, and restaurants. In the Lakes Region, guests can enjoy such attractions as scenic train and boat rides, amusement centers, golf, tennis, and boat rentals. Full breakfast is served on the porch or on the 80-foot deck. Three guest rooms with shared bath. Children welcome; smoking outdoors; pets accepted. Open May, June, September, and October. $55.

NH212. The closest bed and breakfast to Meredith Bay village. Just a short stroll to the Marketplace of shops, galleries, restaurants, and Lake Winnipesaukee. On a quiet residential lane, it guarantees peaceful days and nights, yet is central to all activities of the Lakes Region. Minutes away from Winnipesaukee Scenic Railroad, the M.S. Mt. Washington cruise ship, Analee's Dolls Gift Shop and Museum, and Weirs Beach. Inside the inn, guests will enjoy an Early American ambience of fluffy quilts, hand-stenciled walls and floors, antique furnishings, and a romantic brick fireplace in the guest parlor. A Continental breakfast is served in the dining room. Evening snacks feature seasonal beverages and freshly baked delights. Five guest rooms, two with private baths. Children welcome. No smoking. Small pets permitted. $50-65.

MOULTONBOROUGH

Olde Orchard Inn

Route 1, Box 256, 03254
(603) 476-5004

This bed and breakfast features five guest rooms, with private baths, in a beautifully

6 Pets welcome; 8 Children welcome; 9 Social drinking allowed; 10 Tennis available; 11 Swimming available; 12 Golf available; 13 Skiing available; 14 May be booked through travel agents.

restored farmhouse. The inn is on 13 acres with a mountain brook and pond. Hosts offer guests a large country breakfast with home-baked goods and all the fixings. Only one mile away from the beautiful Lake Winnipesaukee, and only minutes away from many lakes, regional attractions, and activities. Within one hour's drive, guests will find five major ski areas, or guests may decide to take a cross-country ski tour from the inn's front door. The foliage is stunning in the autumn, but anytime is a delightful time to stay here. Children are welcome. No smoking.

Hosts: The Senner Family
Rooms: 5 (PB) $70-80
Full Breakfast
Credit Cards: A, B, C
Notes: 2, 5, 6 (call), 8, 9, 10, 11, 13, 14

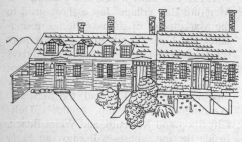

Olde Orchard Inn

NEW BOSTON

Colburn Homestead Bed and Breakfast

280 W. Colburn Road (off Route 136) 03070
(603) 487-5250

This Colonial farmhouse in a country setting is 70 miles from Boston, 20 miles from Manchester, and near many shopping and recreational facilities. Swimming pool available in-season. TVs in all the rooms. Christmas shop with gifts and crafts open year-round.

Hosts: Olive and Robert Colburn
Rooms: 3 (SB) $50-65

Full Breakfast
Credit Cards: A, B
Notes: 2, 5, 7, 8, 11, 12, 13

NEWBURY

The 1806 House

Route 103 Traffic Circle, P.O. Box 54, 03277
(603) 763-4969

In the unspoiled New Hampshire countryside, The 1806 House has beamed ceilings, wide plank floors, and a charming living room complete with candlelight, cozy couches, wing chairs, and a wood-burning stove. Every guest room has been tastefully and individually decorated with period furnishings and modern conveniences. A special breakfast is served every morning, complete with fine china, candlelight, and a Pavarotti aria. A perfect getaway, where Mount Sunapee is the back yard, restaurants abound, skiing, hiking, boating, and swimming are just steps across the road.

Hosts: Lane and Gene Bellman
Rooms: 4 (PB) $79
Full Breakfast
Credit Cards: A, B
Notes: 2, 5, 9, 11, 12, 13, 14

NEW CASTLE

Bed and Breakfast Marblehead and North Shore

P.O. Box 35, Newtonville, MA 02160
(617) 964-1606; (800) 832-2632
FAX (617) 332-8572

Great Islander. A short drive from the downtown area of Portsmouth transports guests to the wonderful island experience of New Castle. Enjoy New Castle's peace and tranquility and lovely beach/park, before heading back to the mainland. This cozy bed and breakfast offers the comforts of home in a two-story traditional Colonial built in the 1700s and fully restored with modern amenities. Two guest rooms share a full bath. Guests may relax in the TV/sitting room. Continental breakfast. No smoking. Open May through October. $75-100.

NEW HAMPTON

New Hampshire Bed and Breakfast

128 South Hoop Pole Road, Guilford, CT 06437
(203) 457-0042; (800) 582-0853

NH240. This 150-year-old antique-filled home with a converted barn is in the heart of the Lakes Region. Common rooms include the living room with a fireplace, den with TV and Nordic Track, and a pool room with pool table, piano, and stereo system. A hearty full breakfast is served, wine will be offered, candy will be in the room, and fruit is always on the table. New Hampton, home to the co-ed prep school by the same name, is an easy stroll from the inn. Four rooms are available. No smoking. Children are welcome. $40-60.

NEW IPSWICH

The Inn at New Ipswich

Porter Hill Road, P.O. Box 208, 03071
(603) 878-3711

Relax awhile in a graceful 1790 home amid fruit trees and stone walls. Cozy fireplaces, front-porch rockers, and large comfortable guest rooms furnished country style. One family suite sleeps four. Refreshments offered upon arrival. Enjoy scrumptious hearthside breakfasts. In the Monadnock region of New Hampshire. Hiking, band concerts, antique auctions, maple sugaring, apple picking, unsurpassed autumn color, cross-country and downhill skiing. No smoking. Children over eight welcome.

Hosts: Ginny and Steve Bankuti
Rooms: 5 (PB) $65
Suite: 1 (PB) $85
Full Breakfast
Credit Cards: A, B
Notes: 2, 5, 8 (over 8), 9, 13

New Hampshire Bed and Breakfast

128 South Hoop Pole Road, Guilford, CT 06437
(203) 457-0042; (800) 582-0853

NH545. Built in 1790, this lovely farmhouse still possesses its early American charm. A classic red barn adjoins the house, and the grounds are bordered by stone walls, gardens, and fruit trees. In summer, guests may enjoy the fresh air on a screen porch full of white wicker furniture. In cooler seasons, guests may play Scrabble by the fire in the parlor or choose a book from the library. Breakfast is served in the keeping room by a crackling fire, and the inn is within short driving distance from a myriad of activities in the Monadnock area. Five guest rooms, two of which share a bath and three of which offer private baths, are available. Resident dog. Children over seven welcome. No smoking. $45-65.

NEW LONDON

Pleasant Lake Inn

125 Pleasant Street, P.O. Box 1030A, 03257
(603) 526-6271; (800) 626-4907

Descending 500 feet from Main Street, visitors will find Pleasant Lake Inn on the shore of Pleasant Lake with Mount Kearsarge as its backdrop. All rooms have been renovated, have private baths, and are furnished with antiques. Five acres of woods, pas-

Pleasant Lake Inn

tures, and gardens surround the inn. Hiking trails nearby. The lake provides swimming and fishing in summer; skiing and skating are equally popular in winter.

Hosts: Margaret and Grant Rich
Rooms: 11 (PB) $75-95
Full Breakfast
Credit Cards: A, B
Notes: 2, 4, 5, 7, 8 (over 6), 9, 10, 11, 12, 13, 14

NEWPORT

The Inn at Coit Mountain

523 North Main Street, 03773
(603) 863-3583; (800) 367-2364

All four seasons provide nature's backdrop to this gracious historic Georgian home which was a summer place for a French family with unlimited income and a lifestyle to match. Some rooms have fireplaces and breakfast is hearty or gourmet, as guests wish. In the Lake Sunapee area, there are outdoor activities year-round with many restaurants and small shops to enjoy.

Hosts: Dick and Judi Tatem
Rooms: 7 (4 PB; 3 SB) $85-140
Full Breakfast
Credit Cards: A, B, C
Notes: 2, 3, 4, 5, 8, 9, 10, 11, 12, 13, 14

NORTH CONWAY

The Buttonwood Inn

Box 1817, 03860
(603) 356-2625; (800) 258-2625 U.S. and Canada
FAX (603) 356-3140

Tucked away on Mount Surprise, the inn is an 1820s Cape. Quiet and secluded, yet only two miles to the village, excellent dining, and tax-free shopping. Nine uniquely appointed guest rooms, pool, and extensive gardens. Enjoy 65 km of groomed cross-country ski trails right from the back door. Full breakfast. Dinners served on Saturdays during foliage season and January and February. Lunch served in the winter. Perfect

spot for romantic getaways, families, groups, reunions, or weddings.

Hosts: Claudia and Peter Needham
Rooms: 9 (PB and SB) $50-100
Full Breakfast
Credit Cards: A, B, C
Notes: 2, 3, 4, 5, 7, 8, 9, 10, 11, 12, 13, 14

Cabernet Inn

Route 16, 03860
(800) 866-4704

Nestled in a grove of towering pines, this 1842 Victorian cottage was refurbished and enhanced into an elegant nonsmoking inn. Deluxe rooms have either Jacuzzis or fireplaces, queen-size beds, and air conditioning. Two guest living rooms with fireplaces open to shaded outdoor patios and provide relaxing ambience. Period lighting and furnishings reflect the innkeepers' passion for antiquing, and when guests step into the large gourmet kitchen, the secrets behind the bountiful breakfasts are revealed.

Hosts: Bruce and Vickie Pantti
Rooms: 9 (PB) $69-169
Full Breakfast
Credit Cards: A, B, C
Notes: 2, 5, 9, 10, 11, 12, 13, 14

The Center Chimney-1787

P.O. Box 1220, River Road, 03860
(603) 356-6788

One of the earliest houses in North Conway is now a cozy, affordable bed and breakfast. Just off Main Street and the Saco River

The Center Chimney-1787

(swim, fish, and canoe). Walk to shops, restaurants, summer theater, free ice skating, and cross-country skiing. Rock and ice climbing on nearby Cathedral Ledge.

Host: Farley Ames Whitley
Rooms: 4 (SB) $44-55
Continental Breakfast
Credit Cards: None
Notes: 2, 5, 7, 8, 9, 10, 11, 12, 13

Cranmore Mt. Lodge

Box 1194, Kearsarge Road, 03860
(603) 356-2044; (800) 356-3596

Cranmore Mt. Lodge, a historic New England country inn, is the perfect place to unwind. The atmosphere is homey, and the accommodations and reasonable rates are ideal for families and groups. Now features a two-bedroom, two-bath, fully equipped townhouse. Formerly owned by Babe Ruth's daughter and visited by him many times. Hiking, rock climbing, skiing, kayaking, canoeing, bicycling, tennis, golf, riding, summer theater, and fine restaurants are just some of the area's attractions.

Hosts: Dennis and Judy Helfand
Rooms: 20 (16 PB; 4 SB) $69-102
Full Breakfast
Credit Cards: A, B, C, D, E
Notes: 2, 4, 5, 7, 8, 9, 10, 11, 12, 13, 14

The Farm

2555 West Side Road, 03860
(603) 356-2694

Since the 1780s, this bed and breakfast has been not just an inn, but a tradition. The Farm has been passed down in one family for 200 years. An award-winning home for sensitive historic preservation, it radiates country charm and hospitality. The ten guest rooms are decorated with family heirlooms. Enjoy the panoramic mountain views while having a full breakfast on the patio. Relax in the historic and pastoral setting on 65 acres of forest and pasture. Two miles from North Conway Village. A place for all seasons; fly fishing, canoeing, swimming, and cross-country skiing on-site.

Hosts: Rick Davis and Charlene Browne
Rooms: 10 (4 PB; 6 SB) $55-90
Full Breakfast
Credit Cards: A, B
Notes: 2, 5, 8, 9, 11, 12, 13 (cross-country), 14

The Forest

The Forest: A Country Inn

Route 16A at the Intervale, 03860
(603) 356-9772; (800) 448-3534

Step into an era of old-fashioned charm and hospitality at the beautifully maintained 1890 Victorian inn set on 25 quiet, wooded acres just minutes from North Conway Village. Eleven lovely rooms with private baths are uniquely furnished with antiques. A romantic stone cottage with fireplaces is the honeymoon hideaway! The guests-only dining room serves country breakfasts each morning. Enjoy the large, screened veranda, heated outdoor pool, tennis, and 60K of cross-country ski trails at the door. A non-smoking inn.

Rooms: 11 (9 PB; 2 SB) $50-125
Full Breakfast
Credit Cards: A, B, C, D
Notes: 2, 5, 8, 9, 10, 11, 12, 13, 14

Isaac Merrill House Inn

P.O. Box 8, 720 Kearsarge Road, 03847
(603) 356-9041; (800) 328-9041

---

6 Pets welcome; 8 Children welcome; 9 Social drinking allowed; 10 Tennis available; 11 Swimming available; 12 Golf available; 13 Skiing available; 14 May be booked through travel agents.

This 220-year-old renovated farm house is in a quiet country setting with spectacular views of Cathedral Ledge and the Moat Mountains. Have a full country breakfast in the dining room with a fireplace, and relax in one of the comfortable sitting areas while enjoying afternoon tea and pastries. Only one mile from downtown and its many fine restaurants, shops, and activities.

Rooms: 22 (18 PB; 4 SB) $50-135
Full Breakfast
Credit Cards: A, B, C, D
Notes: 5, 6, 7, 8, 9, 10, 11, 12, 13, 14

Merrill Farm Resort

428 White Mountain Highway, 03860
(603) 447-3866; (800) 445-1017

Cozy rooms in the main house, all with private baths. Efficiency cottages and spacious loft units with fireplaces. Some nonsmoking rooms. Outdoor pool, canoes on the river, in-room whirlpools, conference facilities. All rooms have cable TV and telephones. Relaxed, informal setting (age 17 and under free). Tax-free outlet shopping in a summer and winter recreation area. Three-diamond AAA rating.

Hosts: Lee and Christine Gregory
Rooms: 60 (PB) $39-139
Continental Breakfast
Credit Cards: A, B, C, D, E
Notes: 5, 7, 8, 9, 10, 11, 12, 13, 14

Nereledge Inn

River Road, 03860
(603) 356-2831

Come and enjoy the charm, warm hospitality, and relaxation of this 1787 traditional bed and breakfast with eleven comfortable guest rooms and views of Cathedral Ledge. Relax by the wood stove in the sitting room, enjoy a game of darts in the English-style pub room, or daydream in a rocking chair on the front porch. A friendly and informal nonsmoking atmosphere awaits guests. A delicious country breakfast includes warm apple crumble with ice cream. Close to hiking trails, rock climbing, skiing, and ice climbing. Walk to the village for shopping, dining, and theater; walk to the river for swimming, canoeing, or fishing.

Hosts: Valerie and Dave Halpin
Rooms: 11 (5.5 PB; 5.5 SB) $60-85
Full Breakfast
Credit Cards: A, B, C
Notes: 2, 5, 8, 9, 10, 11, 12, 13

Scottish Lion Inn and Restaurant

Route 16, Main Street, 03860-1527
(603) 356-6381

At the Scottish Lion guests will find country inn atmosphere with splendid cuisine and comfortable accommodations. All seven rooms have private baths. Five have clan names with corresponding decor. The pride of the Lion is its unique and varied menu of American and Scottish favorites. The inn has the largest selection of single malts and Scotches in New Hampshire, and it is the only inn in New England to serve 100 percent Kona coffee.

Hosts: Chef Michael and Janet Procopio
Rooms: 8 (PB) $49.95-99
Full Breakfast
Credit Cards: A, B, C, D, E
Notes: 3, 4, 5, 7 (limited), 8, 9, 10, 11, 12, 13, 14

The 1785 Inn and Restaurant

3582 White Mountain Highway, P.O. Box 1785,
    03860-1785
(603) 356-9025; (800) 421-1785 reservations
FAX (603) 356-6081

The 1785 Inn has a famous view of Mount Washington popularized by the White Mountain School of Art in the 1800s. The inn was completely refurbished by the current owners and offers romantic accommodations where guests can relax and savor the view while being pampered with fine dining and friendly service. On six pristine acres with swimming pool, skiing, nature trails, 210-year-old fireplaces, hiking, biking, fishing, etc. Free color brochure.

Hosts: Becky and Charlie Mallar
Rooms: 17 (12 PB; 5 SB) $69-159
Full Breakfast
Credit Cards: A, B, C, D, E
Notes: 2, 4, 5, 8, 9, 10, 11, 12, 13, 14

The Stonehurst Manor

Route 16, 03860-1937
(603) 356-3113; (800) 525-9100

A landmark in lodging, food, and spirits for 46 years. The Stonehurst Manor offers a great view, in-room fireplaces, a huge Jacuzzi, the largest pool, all tucked away on 33 acres of grounds. Dining is elegant yet casual, food is presented in a relaxing atmosphere. Watch while the famous wood-fired gourmet pizzas are made in the outdoor or indoor oven ... and yes, this bed and breakfast is affordable (and recommended by *Bon Appetit*)! Free cross-country skiing from the door in the winter. Guided and self-guided walking and hiking vacations in the White Mountains available in the summer. Rates include breakfast and dinner.

Host: Peter Rattay
Rooms: 24 (PB) $96-166
Credit Cards: A, B, C
Notes: 4, 5, 7, 8, 9, 10, 11, 12, 13

Sunny Side Inn

Seavey Street, P.O. Box 557, 03860
(603) 356-6239; (800) 600-6239

Sit back, relax and daydream on the sun-filled, flower-trimmed porches. The comfortable 1850 farmhouse is in a quiet residential setting. Just a five-minute walk to North Conway village with its many fine shops and restaurants to explore. A homey refuge in which to relax and recharge.

Hosts: Peter and Diane Watson
Rooms: 9 (PB) $49-99
Full Breakfast
Credit Cards: A, B, C, E, F (Carteblanche)
Notes: 2, 5, 8, 9, 11, 12, 13, 14

The Victorian Harvest Inn

28 Locust Lane, Box 1763, 03860
(603) 356-3548; (800) 642-0749

Nonsmokers will delight in this 1850s multi-gabled Victorian find. The inn is on a quiet side street, yet is within walking distance to quaint North Conway Village shops and eateries. All rooms have antiques with modern bed and bath comforts in mind. Start a romantic adventure with a full country breakfast and hospitality of New England as it was meant to be. Fireplace, in-ground pool, and air-conditioned. American Bed and Breakfast three-crown rated (A). AAA three-diamond award.

Hosts: Robert and Linda Dahlberg
Rooms: 6 (4 PB; 2 SB) $55-100
Full Breakfast
Credit Cards: A, B, C, D
Notes: 2, 4 (groups), 5, 8 (over 6), 9, 10, 11, 12, 13, 14

The Victorian Harvest Inn

Wildflowers Inn

Route 16, 03860
(603) 356-2224

Return to the simplicity and elegance of yesteryear. With an ideal location and gracefully decorated rooms, this small 1878 Victorian inn specializes in comfort and convenience for the modern-day traveler. From the cheery dining room with fireplace to the porch rockers overlooking the award-winning gardens, Wildflowers will be a welcoming respite on any journey. Closed November through April.

Hosts: Dean Franke and Eileen Davies
Rooms: 6 (2 PB; 4 SB) $54-99.36
Continental Breakfast
Credit Cards: A, B
Notes: 2, 7, 8, 9, 10, 11, 12, 13

Wyatt House Country Inn

Main Street, Route 16, P.O. Box 777, 03860
(603) 356-7977; (800) 527-7978

Experience the charm of an elegant country Victorian inn with panoramic mountain and river views. Six guest rooms are uniquely decorated and furnished with antiques. A candlelit gourmet multi-entree breakfast is served on English Wedgwood and Irish lace. Stroll from the back yard to the Saco River for swimming or fishing. Early morning coffee and muffins are served in the handsome study, as well as afternoon tea and cakes. Village location, and minutes to downhill and cross-country skiing. Tax-free outlet shopping. Smoking limited to Victorian wraparound porch and grounds. Fresh flowers, fruits, and cookie baskets. AAA rated.

Hosts: Bill and Arlene Strickland
Rooms: 6 (4 PB; 2 SB) $65-95
Full Breakfast
Credit Cards: A, B, C, D
Notes: 2, 3, 5, 7 (limited), 8 (over 12), 9, 10, 11, 12, 13, 14

Wyatt House Country Inn

NORTH SUTTON

Follansbee Inn

P.O. Box 92, 03260
(603) 927-4221; (800) 626-4221

An authentic 1840 New England inn with white clapboard and green trim. On peaceful Kezar Lake, with an old-fashioned porch, comfortable sitting rooms with fireplaces, and charming antique furnishings. Nestled in a small country village but convenient to all area activities (four miles south of New London and 95 miles north of Boston). Private pier with rowboat, canoe, paddle boat, and windsurfer for guests. Beautiful walk around the lake during all seasons. Beer and wine license. Healthy nonsmoking inn. Closed parts of November and April.

Hosts: Dick and Sandy Reilein
Rooms: 23 (11 PB; 12 SB) $70-90
Full Breakfast
Credit Cards: A, B
Notes: 2, 4, 8 (over 10), 9, 10, 11, 12, 13

NORTHWOOD

The Aviary

P.O. Box 268, 03261
(603) 942-7755

This secluded, owner-designed lakeside home can accommodate up to six guests in gracious surroundings. Birds and small wildlife are in abundance. Guests may enjoy the deck, private beach, screened porch, lawn games, and other year-round outside activities. The den has a TV, and the living room is well stocked with books and games to enjoy by the fireplace. The Aviary is just minutes away from Northwood's famous antique alley. Accommodations by reservation only.

Hosts: Tad and Georgette Comstock
Rooms: 3 (2 PB; 1 SB) $60-65
Full Breakfast
Credit Cards: None
Notes: 2, 5, 9, 11, 12

NOTES: Credit cards accepted: A MasterCard; B Visa; C American Express; D Discover Card; E Diner's Club; F Other; 2 Personal checks accepted; 3 Lunch available; 4 Dinner available; 5 Open all year;

New Hampshire Bed and Breakfast

128 South Hoop Pole Road, Guilford, CT 06437
(203) 457-0042; (800) 582-0853

NH621. This authentic 18th-century New England Colonial home is on 60 acres in a country setting. Enjoy the character of old beams, original fireplaces, early paneling, and wide-board floors. A full breakfast is served in the keeping room in front of the fireplace. Fields and woods surround the property, and horses graze in the pastures. A short walk down a country lane brings one to a private beach on Jenness Pond, where guests are welcome to swim. Three guest rooms furnished with antiques share a bath. Concord is one-half hour away. Two resident dogs. No smoking. Children are welcome. $45-55.

NORTH WOODSTOCK

New Hampshire Bed and Breakfast

128 South Hoop Pole Road, Guilford, CT 06437
(203) 457-0042; (800) 582-0853

NH117. This 80-year-old inn offers seven personally decorated guest rooms and family suites, each with views of the gardens, Mooselake River, or the south ridge of Loon Mountain. The living room has a fireplace, TV, and games. The spacious front porch is a favorite among guests. Breakfast in the dining room includes apple or cranberry-walnut pancakes with pure New England maple syrup and jugs of freshly ground café au lait. Guests may also choose a Continental breakfast in bed. Close to many parks and resort areas. Children welcome. Smoking limited; no pets. $40-95.

Wilderness Inn Bed and Breakfast

Routes 3 and 112, Rural Free Delivery Box 69, 03262
(603) 745-3890; (800) 200-WILD-200

Built in 1912, the Wilderness Inn is decorated with antiques and turn-of-the-century photographs. Guest rooms offer views of Lost River or the mountains. Avid skiers, canoers, and hikers themselves, the owners are delighted to help guests explore the area. Breakfasts include fresh fruit and juice, home-baked muffins, a choice of apple- or cranberry-walnut pancakes with maple syrup, crepes with sour cream and homemade applesauce, or vegetable omelets.

Hosts: Michael and Rosanna Yarnell
Rooms: 8 (6 PB; 2 SB) $40-90
Full Breakfast
Credit Cards: A, B, C
Notes: 2, 5, 7, 8, 9, 10, 11, 12, 13, 14

ORFORD

The American Country Collection

4 Greenwood Lane, Delmar, NY 12054
(518) 439-7001

178. This is a large country home surrounded by 125 acres of open fields/acres of woods and wonderful views. It has a living room with fireplace, cozy sitting room with wood stove, and a screened veranda. A second-floor sitting room has TV/VCR. Bedrooms have individually-controlled heating and are comfortably furnished with carpets or area rugs, reading lamps, sitting areas, and down pillows and comforters. Children are welcome; 14 and under stay free in the same room as parents, and half price for children under 18 staying in separate room. No resident pets. Smoking permitted outside. Continental breakfast served. $51-85.

PLYMOUTH

Colonel Spencer Inn

Rural Route 1, Box 225, 03264
(603) 536-3438/1944

6 Pets welcome; 8 Children welcome; 9 Social drinking allowed; 10 Tennis available; 11 Swimming available; 12 Golf available; 13 Skiing available; 14 May be booked through travel agents.

Colonel Spencer Inn

The inn is a tastefully restored 1764 Colonial home featuring hewn post and beam construction, wainscoting, paneling, gunstock corners, Indian shutters, and wide pine floors. Seven antique-appointed bedrooms welcome guests with New England warmth and hospitality, and a full country breakfast is served in a fireplaced dining room within view of the White Mountains and the Pemigewasset River. Convenient to lake and mountain attractions, at Exit 27, off I-93, one-half mile south on Route 3.

Hosts: Carolyn and Alan Hill
Rooms: 7 (PB) $45-65
Credit Cards: None
Notes: 2, 5, 8, 9, 10, 11, 12, 13, 14

Crab Apple Inn

Rural Route 4, Box 188, 03264
(603) 536-4476

Nestled at the foothills of the White Mountains, this 1835 brick Federal-style inn offers comfort in its antique appointed guest rooms. A cheery breakfast room and spacious parlor provide ample room to enjoy a gourmet breakfast or the challenge of finishing the ever-present jigsaw puzzle. Spacious grounds and gardens complement this beautiful country inn.

Host: Christine De Camp
Rooms: 5 (3 PB; 2 SB) $60-85
Full Breakfast
Credit Cards: A, B
Notes: 2, 5, 6, 11, 12, 13

PORTSMOUTH

Bed and Breakfast Marblehead and North Shore

P.O. Box 35, Newtonville, MA 02160
(617) 964-1606; (800) 832-2632
FAX (617) 332-8572

On the waterfront in historic Portsmouth is this stately Colonial. The house is furnished traditionally and has seven fireplaces, a beehive oven, handhewn beams, a brick-lined flower garden, and private pier. Three guest rooms with shared bath are perfect for families or small groups traveling together. When available, rooms may also be taken individually at private bath rates. Two of the rooms have water views. A loft suite has a water view, skylights, private bath, kitchen facilities, queen-size bed, and sleep sofa. Generous breakfast served. Smoking is permitted outside. Children over 12 are welcome. $65-150.

Bed and Breakfast Reservations

P.O. Box 35, Newtonville, MA 02160
(617) 964-1606; (800) 832-2632;
FAX (617) 332-8572

The Riverfront Inn. A 19th-century brick building on the Piscataqua River. Ten rooms include queen-size brass beds, reading chairs and full private baths; one extra-large room has an additional queen-size pullout sofa and small refrigerator. A fully equipped two-story, one bedroom condo is also available for 3-night minimum or weekly stays. An expanded complimentary breakfast is served in the sunny breakfast room. The Bow Street Theatre is just next door. FAX service is available on-site. Open year-round. Special rates for extended condo-stay; weekly rate available. No smoking. $89-195.

NOTES: Credit cards accepted: A MasterCard; B Visa; C American Express; D Discover Card; E Diner's Club; F Other; 2 Personal checks accepted; 3 Lunch available; 4 Dinner available; 5 Open all year;

The Bow Street Inn

121 Bow Street, 03801
(603) 431-7760

An attractive alternative for any seacoast tourist, the Bow Street Inn is also irresistible lodging for the traveling professional and visitor. On the Piscataqua River, in downtown Portsmouth, the inn's newly decorated and furnished rooms offer spectacular river views, rooftop views of Portsmouth, telephone, full bath, and color TV. Guests can also enjoy a complimentary Continental breakfast in the breakfast room. The Bow Street Theatre is on the premises. Guests can walk across the city's classic liftbridge into Maine or enjoy the flower gardens at Prescott Park just two blocks away. Other local attractions include 25 restaurants within three blocks and access to waterfront decks and marina.

Host: Liz Hurley
Rooms: 10 (PB)
Continental Breakfast
Credit Cards: A, B
Notes: 2, 5, 9

Governor's House Bed and Breakfast

32 Miller Avenue, 03801
(603) 431-6546

A welcoming warmth is immediately felt as Nancy and John greet guests in this stately Georgia Colonial. A bottomless cookie jar reigns in the dining room with afternoon tea. Each air-conditioned bedroom has a different motif with uniquely private baths that enhance the elegant antique decor. A ten-minute stroll brings guests to the harbor cruises, historic mansions, shops, and fine restaurants. A hidden treasure in Portsmouth.

Hosts: Nancy and John Grossman
Rooms: 4 (PB) $75-140
Full Breakfast
Credit Cards: A, B
Notes: 2, 5, 8 (over 14), 9, 10, 12, 14

Leighton Inn

69 Richards Avenue, 03801
(603) 433-2188

Experience historic Portsmouth in this classic 1806 Federal Colonial home, featuring a three-story suspended stairway and many other superb architectural details. Friendly hospitality greets guests at the door with an orientation to Portsmouth's many acitvities. Spacious, sunny guest rooms with ornamental fireplaces and whimsical decor offer guests comfort and privacy. Enjoy refreshing four o'clock tea and biscuits before strolling downtown. See colorful gardens in summertime. In the winter, tasty breakfast is served "fireside" in cozy, pumpkin-pine paneled dining room at your leisure. Closed Thanksgiving and Christmas.

Hosts: Carvel and Diane Tefft
Rooms: 3 (PB) $90
Suite: 1 $80-160
Continental Breakfast
Credit Cards: None
Notes: 2, 5, 8, 9, 10, 11, 12

Leighton Inn

6 Pets welcome; 8 Children welcome; 9 Social drinking allowed; 10 Tennis available; 11 Swimming available; 12 Golf available; 13 Skiing available; 14 May be booked through travel agents.

RUMNEY

New Hampshire Bed and Breakfast

128 South Hoop Pole Road, Guilford, CT 06437
(203) 457-0042; (800) 582-0853

NH248. This 1790 Early American farmhouse and attached "ell" sit on 125 acres of beautiful fields and woodland, with views of the White Mountains. Gardens, a real sugar house, and a barn all add to the peaceful country setting. Guests will enjoy private sitting areas, games, books, and the full country breakfast in the dining room of the main house. Hiking, walking, or cross-country ski trails are available throughout the property. The sugar house is in operation during March and April of every year. Three guest rooms available. Resident dog. Children welcome. No smoking. $55-75.

RYE

Rock Ledge Manor Bed and Breakfast

1413 Ocean Boulevard, Route 1A, 03870
(603) 431-1413

Gracious traditional seaside manor home (1840-1880) with wraparound porch. All rooms have ocean view. Six-minutes to historic Portsmouth; 20 minutes to University of New Hampshire; 15 minutes to Hampton; within 30 minutes of southern Maine's seacoast attractions. No smoking.

Hosts: Norman and Janice Marineau
Rooms: 4 (2 PB; 2 SB) $70-85
Full Breakfast
Credit Cards: None
Notes: 2, 5, 8 (over 10), 9, 10, 11, 12

SANBORNTON

Ferry Point House

100 Lower Bay Road, 03269
(603) 524-0087

Ferry Point House is a gracious country Victorian built in the early 1800s as a summer retreat on picturesque Lake Winnisquam. The gazebo on the point and 60-foot veranda allow for comfortable, quiet moments with panoramic views. Each morning guests will be treated to a special breakfast that may include stuffed French toast, cheese baked apples, and French breakfast crepes. Snack and beverage upon arrival. Turndown service with mints on pillow. Open Memorial Day through Labor Day, and weekends in September and October.

Hosts: Joe and Diane Damato
Rooms: 6 (PB) $70-85
Full Breakfast
Credit Cards: None
Notes: 2, 8, 9, 10, 11, 12, 14

SNOWVILLE

Snowvillage Inn

Stuart Road, 03849
(603) 447-2818

On a New Hampshire hillside with a sweeping view of the White Mountains, Snowvillage Inn is an ideal romantic getaway. The 18-room inn is a lively blend of New England charm and Alpine flair. All rooms have private baths, comfortable beds, crafts and country antiques, many have views, and some have fireplaces. There are many unique features of the inn, from the llama hikes to the music weekends. So come and see the view, hear the quiet, and feel the romance.

Hosts: Trudy and Frank Cutrone, and
   Tom Spaulding
Rooms: 18 (PB) $38-78
Full Breakfast
Credit Cards: A, B, C, D, E
Notes: 2, 4, 5, 7, 8 (over 7), 9, 10, 11, 12, 13, 14

STARK VILLAGE

New Hampshire Bed and Breakfast

128 South Hoop Pole Road, Guilford, CT 06437
(203) 457-0042; (800) 582-0853

NH130. In historic Stark Village on the banks of the Upper Ammonoosuc River, this large, rambling white farmhouse has been restored and updated to offer guests a large living room with TV and fireplace, a country kitchen with antique wood stove, and a dining room where wonderful breakfasts are served. The inn borders the White Mountains National Forest and is three miles from the Nash Stream Valley Wilderness Area known for some of the best hunting and fishing in New Hampshire. Hiking, swimming, canoeing, bicycling, picnicking, hunting, fishing, cross-country skiing, snowmobiling, and skating are all available. Three guest rooms with private baths. Children welcome. No pets; no smoking. $45-55.

SUGAR HILL

The Homestead Inn

Route 117, 03585
(603) 823-5564

Spanning seven generations, this is one of the oldest family inns in America. its unpretentious atmosphere is relaxing and comfortable, while the local unspoiled beauty and breathtaking mountain views compel many a return visit. Nearby the renowned Franconia State Park and "Old Man of the Mountains." Full country breakfast.

Hosts: Paul and Melody Hayward
Rooms: 19 (9 PB; 10 SB) $50-80
Full Breakfast
Credit Cards: A, B, D
Notes: 2, 5, 6, 7 (limited), 8, 9, 10, 11, 12, 13, 14

New Hampshire Bed and Breakfast

128 South Hoop Pole Road, Guilford, CT 06437
(203) 457-0042; (800) 582-0853

NH133. On the eastern slope of Sugar Hill overlooking Franconia Notch, Mount Washington, and the Presidential Range. Relax on the porch in a comfortable rocker and enjoy views of expansive fields with a backdrop of Mount Washington's snow-capped peak. The surrounding White Mountains region offers year-round recreation and activities, and an on-site tennis court and nearby golf course are available for guests to use. A full country breakfast is served each morning, and three guest rooms, all of which offer private baths, are available. Centrally within a short drive to Franconia Notch State Park, the Robert Frost Homestead, Cannon Mountain Ski Area, and the New England Ski Museum. Resident dog. Children welcome. No smoking. $65-80.

SUNAPEE

New Hampshire Bed and Breakfast

128 South Hoop Pole Road, Guilford, CT 06437
(203) 457-0042; (800) 582-0853

NH302. Nestled in the heart of New Hampshire's Lake Sunapee region, this 18th-century farmhouse sits on six country acres. This bed and breakfast prides itself on warm hospitality, cleanliness, and a hearty homemade breakfast served in a room that overlooks the pond. Fun awaits in the game room where guests will find a pool table, a variety of board games, or a good book or movie. During the winter months, savor the comfort of a crackling fire with a complimentary cup of hot soup or stew. Four guest rooms share two baths. Smoking is allowed downstairs only. Resident dog. Children over six are welcome. $40-50.

SUTTON MILLS

Bed and Breakfast Marblehead and North Shore

P.O. Box 35, Newtonville, MA 02160
(617) 964-1606; (800) 832-2632 outside MA

The Quilt House. This is one of the prettiest bed and breakfasts in the area. It is a 130-year-old Victorian country house over-

---

6 Pets welcome; 8 Children welcome; 9 Social drinking allowed; 10 Tennis available; 11 Swimming available; 12 Golf available; 13 Skiing available; 14 May be booked through travel agents.

looking a quaint village. The hostess runs workshops on quilting, and there are many fine quilts throughout the house. Three guest rooms on the second floor share two baths. Ten minutes away from summer theater, excellent restaurants, fine shopping, and antiquing. Delicious full breakfast; children welcome; no smoking. $50-65.

TAMWORTH

New Hampshire Bed and Breakfast

128 South Hoop Pole Road, Guilford, CT 06437
(203) 457-0042; (800) 582-0853

NH 100. In the center of historic Tamworth Village, this 18th-century Colonial dates back to 1785 and is furnished with period antiques. Exposed beams, wainscoting, stenciled floors, gunstock posts, and fireplaces exude the charm one hopes to find in a country inn. The inn is only a stone's throw from the Swift River for trout fishing; a stroll to summer theater; minutes from AMC hiking trails; and a short drive to North Conway and Mount Washington valley areas. Breakfast is a hearty affair served on antique china in the dining room. Four guest rooms, one with private bath. Children 12 and older welcome. Smoking permitted. No pets. $50-85.

THORNTON

Amber Lights Inn Bed and Breakfast

Route 3, 03223
(603) 726-4077

Lovingly restored 1815 Colonial offering a sumptuous six-course breakfast, homemade bread, and muffins like Grandma made. Queen-size country beds with hand-made quilts and meticulously clean guest rooms. Private and semiprivate baths, Hannah Adams dining room with fireplace, guest

library, and garden rooms. Hors d'oeuvres served nightly. Conveniently between Loon Mountain and Waterville Valley. Close to all White Mountain attractions. Take a stroll through five acres to a private brook. No pets; no smoking. Murder mystery weekends available.

Hosts: Paul Sears and Carola Warnsman
Rooms: 5 (1 PB; 4 SB) $60-75
Full Breakfast
Credit Cards: A, B, C, D
Notes: 2, 3, 5, 8, 9, 10, 11, 12, 13, 14

TILTON

Tilton Manor

28 Chestnut Street, 03276
(603) 286-3457

Tilton Manor, a 16-room turn-of-the-century mansion nestled in a tranquil three and one-half acre setting. Furnished only with antiques and handmade afghans. A full country breakfast is served daily. Awaken to the aroma of home cooking and freshly baked muffins. Dinner is served upon request only. Reservations are requested. Traveler's checks are accepted.

Hosts: Diane and Chip
Rooms: 4 (2 PB; 2 SB) $55-65
Full Breakfast
Credit Cards: C, D
Notes: 2, 4, 5, 6 (call) 7, 8, 9, 10, 11, 12, 13

WAKEFIELD

The Wakefield Inn

Rural Route 1, Box 2185, 03872
(603) 522-8272; (800) 245-0841

Within the historic district of Wakefield Corner. Early travelers arrived by stagecoach. The majestic mountains and cool blue lakes offer unlimited outdoor activities for everyone, or guests can just relax and enjoy the ambience of days gone by. There is a minimum stay requirement of two nights on holidays .

Hosts: Lou and Harry Sisson
Rooms: 7 (PB) $65
Full Breakfast
Credit Cards: A, B
Notes: 2, 5, 8 (over 10), 9, 12, 13 (cross-country)

WATERVILLE VALLEY _____

The Snowy Owl Inn

Box 407, 13215
(603) 236-8383

Rustic country inn in picturesque Waterville Valley. Eighty rooms, some with Jacuzzis and wet bars. Indoor and outdoor pools, saunas, reading porch, and six lobbies with fireplaces. Complimentary wine and cheese party every afternoon, plus free admission to a nearby sports center; golf, tennis, and boating are available nearby.

Host: Tor Brunvand
Rooms: 80 (PB) $49-129
Continental Breakfast
Credit Cards: A, B, C, D, E
Notes: 2, 5, 7, 8, 10, 11, 13, 14

WENTWORTH _____

Hilltop Acres

East Side and Buffalo Road, 03282
(603) 764-5896

Guests can treat themselves to this peaceful country retreat; large pine-paneled recreation room with fireplace, piano, games, and cable TV. Spacious grounds surrounded by pine forest with natural brook; lawn games; peaceful atmosphere. Rooms with private baths; housekeeping cottages. Near White Mountains and Lakes Region attractions. Open May through October.

Host: Marie A. Kauk
Rooms: 4 (PB) $65
Cottages: 2 (PB) $80
Continental Breakfast
Credit Cards: A, B, C
Notes: 2, 6 (limited) 8, 9, 11, 12, 13, 14

New Hampshire Bed and Breakfast

128 South Hoop Pole Road, Guilford, CT 06437
(203) 457-0042; (800) 582-0853

NH120. This charming home, built in the early 1880s, is within an easy drive of both the Lakes Region and Franconia Notch, where guests can enjoy outdoor sports, shops, crafts and art galleries, theater, and fine restaurants. Wentworth offers three natural swimming holes, many hiking trails, fishing streams, and antique shops. The home itself is furnished with antiques. The pine-paneled recreation room is complete with an antique piano, games, an extensive library, and cable TV. Continental breakfast and afternoon teas are served. Six guest rooms, four with private bath. Two housekeeping cottages with kitchen unit, private living room with fireplace, and screened porch available. Children welcome. No smoking; no pets. $65-80.

WHITEFIELD _____

New Hampshire Bed and Breakfast

128 South Hoop Pole Road, Guilford, CT 06437
(203) 457-0042; (800) 582-0853

NH102. One mile down a quaint winding road, surrounded by stone walls and 32 acres of forest and fields, this Victorian home, circa 1860, offers a fireside sitting room, a private library with TV and VCR, movies, and a wraparound porch with outside seating. Horseshoes, volleyball, croquet, and weekend barbecues offered. Only 20 minutes to the White Mountains; fishing and swimming on Burns Pond; white-water rafting and canoeing on the Connecticut River. Choice of breakfast plans. Six guest rooms with shared bath and one two-room suite with kitchenette and balcony. Children welcome. No smoking in bedrooms; no pets. $45-75.

6 Pets welcome; 8 Children welcome; 9 Social drinking allowed; 10 Tennis available; 11 Swimming available; 12 Golf available; 13 Skiing available; 14 May be booked through travel agents.

The Spalding Inn

Mountain View Road, 03598
(603) 837-2572; (800) 368-VIEW

Travel down a winding country road lined
with stone walls to find this historic inn. On
200 acres with glorious mountain views,
warm hospitality awaits guests. This lovely
inn has many amenities including four clay
tennis courts, a nine-hole golf course, and a
heated swimming pool. The inn has large
common rooms and an extensive library. A
variety of accommodations are available in
the main house, the romantic carriage
house, or family cottage. A full country
breakfast is served and guests will not want
to miss dinner; the food is divine.

Hosts: Dione Cockwell and Michael Flinder
Rooms: 36 (PB) $99
Full Breakfast and Dinner
Credit Cards: A, B
Notes: 2, 4, 6, 7, 8, 9, 10, 11, 12, 13, 14

WILTON

Stepping Stones Bed and Breakfast

Bennington Battle Trail, 03086
(603) 654-9048

Rural retreat with peaceful atmosphere 60
miles from Boston. Extensive gardens surround this turn-of-the-century house. Fresh
flowers, handwoven fabrics, and down
puffs in airy, immaculate rooms. Full
breakfast in solar garden room. Books,
games, music, and TV in parlor. Hand-
weaving studio with fabrics available.
Well-behaved children and pets are welcome. Resident dog, cats, and bantams.

Host: Ann Carlsmith
Rooms: 3 (1 PB; 2 SB) $45-50
Full Breakfast
Credit Cards: None
Notes: 2, 5, 6, 8, 9, 12, 13, 14

Tuc' Me Inn

WOLFEBORO

Tuc' Me Inn

118 North Main Street, P.O. Box 657, 03894
(603) 569-5702

This circa 1850 Colonial Federal is within
walking distance of the quaint village of
Wolfeboro, on the eastern shore of Lake
Winnipesaukee, the oldest summer resort in
America. Plan to spend several days here
and enjoy scenic drives, country stores, museums, authentic taverns, fine restaurants,
golf, tennis, horseback riding, cross-country
and downhill skiing, along with a cruise on
the M.S. Mt. Washington. Enjoy high tea in
the Victorian garden room, and relax in the
music room or parlor. After a restful
evening, wake up to a full gourmet breakfast in the elegant dining room or Victorian
garden room.

Hosts: Ernie, Terry, and Tina Foutz; Idabel Evans
Rooms: 7 (3 PB; 4 SB) $59-80
Full Breakfast
Credit Cards: A, B
Notes: 2, 5, 8, 9, 10, 11, 12, 13, 14

NOTES: Credit cards accepted: A MasterCard; B Visa; C American Express; D Discover Card; E Diner's
Club; F Other; 2 Personal checks accepted; 3 Lunch available; 4 Dinner available; 5 Open all year;

New Jersey

The Avon Manor Inn

AVON-BY-THE-SEA _____

The Avon Manor Inn

109 Sylvania Avenue, 07717-1338
(908) 774-0110

Pass through the columned portico and be greeted by a friendly and informal atmosphere in this Colonial Revival home. Furnished with antiques and wicker, the Avon Manor Inn was built in 1907 only one block from the ocean. Enjoy breakfast in the sunny dining room, ocean breezes on the full wraparound veranda, and the charm of this small seaside town. Full breakfast is served on weekends; Continental Breakfast on weekdays. The large living room has a fireplace for cozy winter nights. Rediscover romance at this charming seaside inn.

Hosts: Jim and Kathleen Curley
Rooms: 8 (6 PB; 2 SB) $80-110
Full or Continental Breakfast
Credit Cards: A, B, C
Notes: 2 (deposits only), 5, 8, 9, 10, 11, 12, 14

Cashelmara Inn

22 Lakeside Avenue, 07717
(908) 776-8727; (800) 821-2976

Oceanside/lakefront Victorian inn allow guests to enjoy views of the Atlantic from bed. Rooms decorated in beautiful Victorian antiques and a wicker-filled veranda overlooking the ocean make stays here memorable. A suite with a fireplace is also available. Only 55 minutes from New York City and one hour from Philadelphia. Singles $10 less. Minimum stay summer weekends: three nights; summer holidays: four nights.

Host: Mary E. Wiernasz
Owner: Martin J. Mulligan
Rooms: 12 (PB) $75-165
Suite: 1 (PB)
Full Breakfast
Credit Cards: A, B, C, D
Notes: 2, 5, 8, 9, 10, 11, 12

The Sands
Bed and Breakfast Inn

42 Sylvania Avenue, 07717
(908) 776-8386

The Sands is in a small Victorian town just seven houses from the nicest beach on the Jersey shore. The inn radiates warmth and hospitality. Each of the nine rooms has a paddle fan, and many have sinks and refrigerators. Spend an afternoon on the beautiful white sandy beach, which is just steps away. A lovely breakfast is served each morning in the family dining room or on the porch. A stay at the inn will make guests feel relaxed and refreshed.

Host: Ana Suchecki
Rooms: 9 (SB) $55-75
Full Breakfast
Credit Cards: None
Notes: 2, 8 (over 9), 9, 10, 11, 12

6 Pets welcome; 7 Smoking allowed; 8 Children welcome; 9 Social drinking allowed; 10 Tennis available; 11 Swimming available; 12 Golf available; 13 Skiing available; 14 May be booked through travel agents.

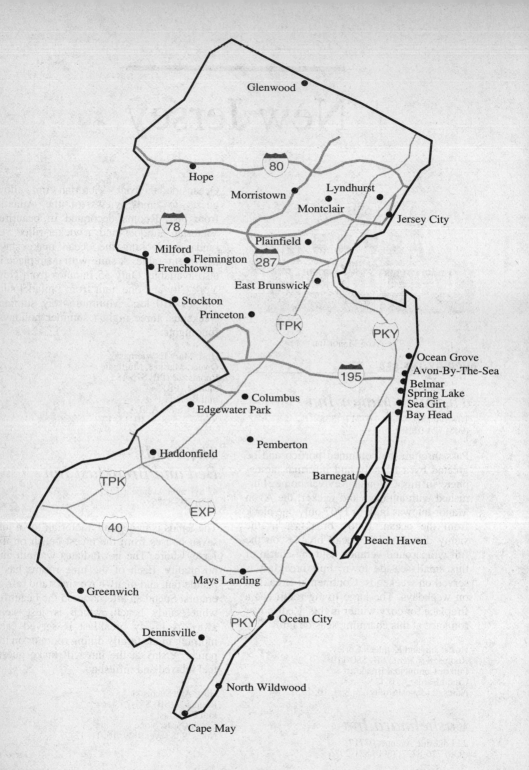

Glenwood

80

Hope

Morristown   Lyndhurst
        Montclair
                    Jersey City

78

Plainfield

Milford
    Flemington
Frenchtown   287

East Brunswick

Stockton
Princeton   TPK   PKY

                              Ocean Grove
                195   Avon-By-The-Sea
                              Belmar
                              Spring Lake
Columbus   Sea Girt
Edgewater Park   Bay Head

Pemberton

Haddonfield   Barnegat

TPK

EXP

40   Beach Haven

Mays Landing

Greenwich

              PKY
Dennisville   Ocean City

North Wildwood

Cape May

New Jersey

The Dynasty

muffins, or coffeecake awakens guests each morning. The full breakfast may feature a savory egg casserole, French toast, or a special blueberry pancake. Enjoy a large collection of original art or swim at the private ocean beaches. Collect seashells and sea glass. Walk to Twilight Lake and feed the ducks or relax in the garden.

Hosts: Carl and Beverly Conover
Rooms: 12 (PB) $85-195
Full Breakfast
Credit Cards: A, B, C
Notes: 2, 5, 9, 10, 11, 12

BEACH HAVEN

The Bayberry Barque

117 Centre Street, 08008
(609) 492-5216

The Bayberry Barque is a tastefully restored Victorian home in Beach Haven's historic district, a half block from the beach. Relax on the wraparound porch. The expanded Continental breakfast features home-baked specialties and is illuminated by the morning sun shining through the unique Oriel stained glass window. The comfortable rooms are individually decorated with period pieces. Walk to Surflight Playhouse, shopping, movies, restaurants, and Atlantic City Cruise Ship. Credit cards accepted in-season only.

Hosts: Tom and Barbara DeSanto
Rooms: 8 (5 PB; 3 SB) $65-125
Continental Breakfast
Credit Cards: A, B, C
Notes: 2, 8 (over 10), 9, 10, 11

BARNEGAT

The Dynasty

Pebble Beach, 248 Edison Road, 08005
(609) 698-1566

A quiet, bayside, air-conditioned home on a peninsula with dock space. Breakfast is served around an award-winning pool amid beautiful foliage. Enjoy a picturesque view of the sunset and wildlife reserve, the warmth of a designer's fireplace, and the ultimate in antiques collected from around the world. Just minutes to the world's largest playground, Atlantic City. Closed October 16 through May 5

Host: Stanley Finkelstein
Rooms: 3 (1 PB; 2 SB) $66-125
Full Breakfast
Credit Cards: None
Notes: 2, 8, 9, 10, 11, 12, 13, 14

BAY HEAD

Conover's Bay Head Inn

646 Main Avenue, 08742
(908) 892-4664

The 12 romantic, antique-filled bedrooms have views of the ocean, bay, marina, or gardens. The aroma of inn-baked biscuits,

The Green Gables
Inn and Restaurant

212 Centre Street, 08008
(609) 492-3553; FAX (609) 492-2507

The Green Gables is a Victorian oceanside inn and restaurant. In the heart of Beach Haven's historic district, Green Gables is

NOTES: Credit cards accepted: A MasterCard; B Visa; C American Express; D Discover Card; E Diner's Club; F Other; 2 Personal checks accepted; 3 Lunch available; 4 Dinner available; 5 Open all year; 6 Pets welcome; 7 Smoking allowed; 8 Children welcome; 9 Social drinking allowed; 10 Tennis available; 11 Swimming available; 12 Golf available; 13 Skiing available; 14 May be booked through travel agents.

included in the National Register of Historic Places. Enjoy the stay on Long Beach Island, strolling on sandy beaches, by the bay, or fishing, crabbing, sailing, and watching the most spectacular sunsets. The Green Gables is also a renowned four-star cuisine restaurant that has been noted as a "real find" by the New York Times. Chosen as the 1994 Best Undiscovered Restaurant in South Jersey by the New Jersey Monthly's 11th Annual Readers' Choice Awards. Also, chosen as the Best Romantic Restaurant by the *Atlantic City* magazine's Best of the Best Awards in 1993.

Hosts: Rita and Adolfo de Matino
Rooms: 8 (1 PB; 7 SB)
Continental Breakfast
Credit Cards: A, B C, E, F
Notes: 3, 4, 5, 8 (over 5), 9, 10, 11, 12, 14

BELMAR

Down the Shore Bed and Breakfast

201 Seventh Avenue, 07719
(908) 681-9023

Off exit 98 on Garden State Parkway, this newly constructed home offers two guest rooms with private baths. Guest parlor with TV, refrigerator, and microwave. Shaded porch for guests to enjoy. Just one block to beach and boardwalk. Midweek special rates.

Hosts: Annette and Al Bergins
Rooms: 3 (PB) $65-75
Full Breakfast
Credit Cards: None
Notes: 2, 5, 9, 11, 12, 14 (10 percent)

CAPE MAY

The Abbey

Columbia Avenue and Gurney Street, 08204
(609) 884-4506

The Abbey consists of two restored Victorian buildings originally in the John McCreary family in the heart of Cape May's

historic district. Line drawings of the main house are on file in the Library of Congress. The cottage is a delightful example of Second Empire Mansard Revival style. All rooms are furnished with period Victorian antiques, have private baths, small refrigerators, and most have air conditioning in season. On-site or remote parking; beach chairs and tags included. Afternoon tea served. Minimum stay June 15-September 30, major holidays and most weekends: three-four nights. Closed from mid-December to March.

Hosts: Jay and Marianne Schatz
Rooms: 14 (PB) $90-185
Full or Continental Breakfast (seasonal)
Credit Cards: A, B, D
Notes: 2 (deposit), 8 (over 12), 9, 10, 11, 12

The Albert Stevens Inn

127 Myrtle Avenue, 08204
(609) 884-4717

Built in 1889 by Dr. Albert G. Stevens for his bride, Bessie, this Queen Anne Victorian home offers its guests a warm, restful visit. Just three blocks from the beach and shopping. A three-course hot breakfast is served each morning with a relaxing tea in the afternoon. Lunch is

The Albert Stevens Inn

available in the off-season. Soak in the 102-degree hot tub before strolling through the unusual Cat's Garden.

Hosts: Curt and Diane Diviney Rangen
Rooms: 9 (PB) $65-155
Full Breakfast
Credit Cards: A, B, C, D
Notes: 2, 4 (off-season), 5, 7, 9, 10, 11, 12, 14

Amanda's Bed and Breakfast

1428 Park Avenue, 21217
(410) 225-0001; (410) 383-1274

168. Built in 1840 and enlarged in 1900, this Victorian mansion retains the ambience and grandeur of the era. Enjoy elegance and comfort, period reproduction wallpapers, and the original furnishings of the Wilbraham family. Heated swimming pool available to guests. Seven accommodations, all with private baths. Full breakfast. $95-185.

Angel of the Sea

5-7 Trenton Avenue, 08204
(800) 848-3369

Angel of the Sea is a national award winning Victorian mansion, just off the beach in historic Cape May. All 26 guest rooms are uniquely furnished and decorated, and all have private baths. Porches and verandas offer guests a panoramic view of the Atlantic Ocean. All rates include a full-serve gourmet breakfast, afternoon tea, sweets, wine and cheese, bicycles, all beach equipment, and private off-street parking.

Hosts: John and Barbara Girton
Rooms: 26 (PB) $135-250
Full Breakfast
Credit Cards: None
Notes: 2, 5, 9, 10, 11, 12, 14

Barnard-Good House

238 Perry Street, 08204
(609) 884-5381

The Barnard-Good House is known for its breakfasts, which were selected as number

one by New Jersey Monthly magazine. The hosts continue to make them even better. Breakfast consists of four courses, all gourmet, and homemade. This purple house caters to happiness and comfort. All rooms have private baths and air conditioning. Minimum stay in-season: three nights; holidays in-season: four nights. Closed November 1 to April 1.

Hosts: Nan and Tom Hawkins
Rooms: 5 (PB) $86-120
Full Breakfast
Credit Cards: A, B (for deposit only)
Notes: 2, 7 (limited), 9, 10, 11, 12

Bed and Breakfast Adventures

Suite 132, 2310 Central Avenue, North Wildwood, 08260
(606) 522-4000; (800) 992-2632

NJ488. An 1877 Victorian home lovingly restored to its original elegance, this inn is a short walk to Washington Street Mall, the ocean promenade and beach, and the area's fine restaurants. All rooms and suites have private baths and in-room refrigerators, and are cooled by ocean breezes and fans or air conditioning. A full buffet breakfast is served each morning. Well behaved children over ten are welcome. Open year-round. Smoking permitted only on the veranda. $75-140.

NJ612. Restored in 1985, this 24-room Victorian Carpenter Gothic inn offers guests a vacation living experience typical of the "Gay Nineties." Accommodations include private and shared baths and a two-room suite with private sitting room. Guests may also enjoy the large pillared living room with fireplace, formal dining room and book-lined library. A delicious breakfast is prepared daily. The inn is within a block of Washington Street Mall, beaches and restaurants. No smoking. Children over 12 welcome. $95-165.

The Brass Bed Inn

The Brass Bed Inn

719 Columbia Avenue, 08204
(609) 884-8075

The restored rooms in this 1872 house boast
a fine collection of 19th-century brass beds,
antiques, lace curtains, and period wall coverings. Bountiful multi-course breakfasts
are served year-round by the hearth. Tea
and refreshments are served in the afternoon. Two blocks to beaches. All rooms are
air-conditioned. Special Christmas tour and
lodging. Closed Thanksgiving and Christmas Day.

Hosts: John and Donna Dunwoody
Rooms: 8 (6 PB; 2 SB) $65-175
Full Breakfast
Credit Cards: A, B
Notes: 2, 5, 9 (moderate), 10, 11, 12

Captain Mey's Inn

202 Ocean Street, 08204
(609) 884-7793

The Dutch heritage is evident from the Persian rugs on table tops to Delft blue china to
European antiques. Guests will marvel at
the Eastlake paneling in the dining room,
leaded-glass bay window, and the restored
fireplace. All guest rooms are air-conditioned. A full country breakfast is served
accompanied by homemade breads, juice,
meats, fresh fruit, and jellies. The meal is

served by candlelight with classical music
in the formal dining room, and in the summer guests may enjoy breakfast on the
lovely wraparound veranda, with antique
wicker and hanging ferns. Cape May offers
a beach, shops, fine restaurants, bicycling,
walking and trolley tours, bird watching,
boating, fishing, and gaslit street.

Hosts: George and Kathleen Blinn
Rooms: 8 (PB) $75-225
Full Breakfast
Credit Cards: A, B
Notes: 5, 8, 9, 10, 11, 14

Cliveden Inn

709 Columbia Avenue, 08204
(609) 884-4516

Enjoy the Cliveden's comfortable and attractive accommodations. All rooms are
spacious and cozy, with period furniture.
Centrally on Cape May's popular Columbia
Avenue in the historic district. Two blocks
from the beach and within easy walking distance to the Victorian Mall and fine restaurants. Afternoon tea and Continental plus
breakfast. Closed November to mid-April.

Hosts: Sue and Al De Rosa
Rooms: 10 (8 PB; 2 SB) $80-105
Continental Breakfast
Credit Cards: A, B, C
Notes: 2, 7 (limited), 8, 9, 10, 11, 12

Duke of Windsor Bed and Breakfast Inn

817 Washington Street, 08204
(609) 884-1355

Queen Anne Victorian house with a 45-foot
tower, built in 1890 and restored with period furnishings. Foyer with three-story,
carved-oak open staircase, and fireplace.
Sitting room, parlor with fireplace, library,
and dining room. Beach tags, hot and cold
outdoor showers, and off-street parking are
available. Air conditioning.

Hosts: Bruce and Fran Prichard
Rooms: 10 (8 PB; 2 SB) $75-165
Full Breakfast

NOTES: Credit cards accepted: A MasterCard; B Visa; C American Express; D Discover Card; E Diner's
Club; F Other; 2 Personal checks accepted; 3 Lunch available; 4 Dinner available; 5 Open all year;

Credit Cards: A, B
Notes: 2, 8 (over 12), 9, 10, 11, 12

Gingerbread House

28 Gurney Street, 08204
(609) 884-0211

The Gingerbread House is a meticulously and elegantly restored 1869 Victorian seaside cottage in the historic district, one-half block from the beach. Period antiques, original Cape May watercolor paintings, classical music, Fred's photographs, and exquisite woodwork combine with friendly service and attention to detail. Breakfast, afternoon tea and goodies, beach passes, fireplace, and guest porch that overlooks the quaint garden.

Hosts: Fred and Joan Echevarria
Rooms: 6 (3 PB; 3 SB) $95-155
Full Breakfast
Credit Cards: A, B
Notes: 2, 5, 8, 9, 10, 11, 12

Gingerbread House

The Humphrey Hughes House

29 Ocean Street, 08204
(609) 884-4428; (800) 582-3634

Nestled in the heart of Cape May's historic section is one of its most authentically restored inns—perhaps the most spacious and gracious of them all. Until 1980 it was the Hughes family home. While the house is filled with magnificent antiques, it still feels more like a home than a museum.

Hosts: Lorraine and Terry Schmidt
Rooms: 10 (PB) $85-210
Full Breakfast
Credit Cards: A, B
Notes: 2, 5, 10, 11, 12

The Inn on Ocean

25 Ocean Street, 08204
(609) 884-7070

Capture the spirit of a bygone era in the cozy splendor of The Inn on Ocean. In the center of Cape May's historic district, the inn offers Victorian ambience with a light touch. The bright and airy suites, some with an oceanview, have private baths, air conditioning, ceiling fans, king- or queen-size beds, cable TV, a wet bar, and refrigerators. Accommoda-tions include a full breakfast and afternoon refreshments.

Rooms: 5 (PB) $95-265 according to season
Full Breakfast
Credit Cards: A, B, C, E
Notes: 2, 5, 10, 11, 12, 14

Leith Hall— Historic Seashore Inn

22 Ocean Street, 08204
(609) 884-1934

Elegantly restored 1880s home in the heart of the historic district. Only one-half block from the beach and three blocks from the mall. The inn features period antiques and wallpapers, ocean views, full gourmet breakfasts, and afternoon English tea. Open year-round. Free parking.

Hosts: Elan and Susan Zingman-Leith
Rooms: 7 (PB) $75-150
Full Breakfast
Credit Cards: None
Notes: 2, 5, 9, 10, 11, 12

6 Pets welcome; 8 Children welcome; 9 Social drinking allowed; 10 Tennis available; 11 Swimming available; 12 Golf available; 13 Skiing available; 14 May be booked through travel agents.

Mainstay Inn

635 Columbia Avenue, 08204
(609) 884-8690

Selected one of the "Five Top Inns for Quality and Value in 1993" by *Zagat Survey*. Spacious rooms and suites with fine antiques, some with fireplaces and private porches. All private baths, some with whirlpool tubs. Luscious breakfasts and afternoon teas.

Hosts: Tom and Sue Carroll
Rooms: 16 (PB) $95-190
Full and Continental Breakfast
Credit Cards: None
Notes: 2, 5, 9, 10, 11, 12

The Manse

The Manse Bed and Breakfast

510 Hughes Street, 08204
(609) 884-0116

The Manse is an elegant turn-of-the-century home ideally in the midst of the historic district of Cape May. It boasts spacious rooms, natural floors, Persian rugs, lace curtains, antiques, and unsurpassed hospitality. Breakfast is a special occasion with homemade specialties served in a formal dining room or on the veranda. One block from the mall or one and one-half blocks to the ocean.

Hosts: Nate and Dorothy Marcus
Rooms: 6 (4 PB; 2 SB) $75-125
Full Breakfast
Credit Cards: None
Notes: 2, 8, 10, 11, 12

The Mason Cottage

625 Columbia Avenue, 08204
(609) 884-3358; (800) 716-2766 reservations

The Mason Cottage was built in 1871 as the summer residence for a Philadelphia entrepreneur and his family. In the historic district, the inn is Second Empire with a concave mansard roof. Within the inn, guests discover elegance, meticulous restoration, and warm hospitality. Guest room accommodations include four suites. Nearby attractions, house tours, antique shops, beaches, and Victorian shopping mall. The inn is within walking distance of most of Cape May's finest restaurants.

Hosts: Joan and Dave Mason
Rooms: 9 (PB) $85-255
Full Breakfast
Credit Cards: A, B
Notes: 2, 9, 10, 11, 12, 14

The Mission Inn

1117 New Jersey Avenue, 08204
(609) 884-8380; (800) 800-8380

A touch of California on the East Coast boasts a latticed open pergola or dining room for breakfast and enclosed porch offer relaxing ambience, with the beach and surf one-half block away. Spacious guest rooms contain king- and queen-size beds. Hollywood stars and Broadway show people stayed here. All rooms have ocean and garden views; just 50 yards from the beach. Guests can restore themselves in this historic inn. All parking on-site. All baths private. All rooms are air-conditioned. Hospitality begins with the guest's call.

Hosts: Diane Fischer and Judith DeOrio
Rooms: 6 (PB) $85-185
Continental Breakfast
Credit Cards: A, B, C
Notes: 2, 7 (limited), 9, 10, 12, 14

NOTES: Credit cards accepted: A MasterCard; B Visa; C American Express; D Discover Card; E Diner's Club; F Other; 2 Personal checks accepted; 3 Lunch available; 4 Dinner available; 5 Open all year;

The Mooring

801 Stockton Avenue, 08204
(609) 884-5425; FAX (609) 884-1357

The Mooring, built in 1882, is one of Cape May's original guest houses. Enjoy the comfortable elegance of this classic Second Empire inn, with its grand entrance hall and wide spiral staircase leading to spacious guest rooms; each with private bath, ceiling fan, and period furnishings; most with air conditioning. Enjoy breakfast and afternoon tea at tables for two in the dining room or on the front veranda. One block from the beach. Open April 1st through New Year's Day.

Host: Leslie Valenza
Rooms: 12 (PB) $75-150
Full Breakfast
Credit Cards: A, B
Notes: 2, 8 (over 6), 9, 10, 11, 12, 14

Perry Street Inn

29 Perry Street, 08204
(609) 884-4590

Built in 1902 in the historic district, the Perry Street Inn is one-half block from the beach and the pedestrian mall with quaint shops and restaurants. Front porch and several guest rooms have ocean views. Furnished with fine antiques. Nutritious breakfast of homemade favorites is served in the airy, sunlit dining room. There is a motel for those desiring modern suites with

Perry Street Inn

kitchen and TV. Free parking on premises. Special events include "Murder Mystery," "Whale and Bird Sightseeing," "Christmas House Tour" weekend packages.

Hosts: John and Cynthia Curtis
Rooms: 10 (7 PB; 3 SB) $45-110
Full Breakfast
Credit Cards: A, B, C
Notes: 2, 3, 5, 9, 10, 11, 12, 14

The Primrose

1102 Lafayette Street, 08204
(609) 884-8288; (800) 606-8288

A delightful blend of yesterday's charm and hospitality with today's comforts and conveniences in this completely restored 1850s home. Breakfast includes home-baked goodies. Enjoy lemonade in the afternoons in the summer. A relaxing getaway four seasons of the year. Guests will fall in love with the Primrose and romantic, historic Cape May.

Hosts: Buddy and Jan Wood, and Sheryl Henry
Rooms: 4 (PB) $80-150
Full Breakfast
Credit Cards: A, B
Notes: 2, 5, 10, 11, 12, 14

The Queen Victoria

102 Ocean Street, 08204
(609) 884-8702

The Wells family welcomes guests as friends and treats them royally with unpretentious service and attention to detail. Three restored buildings furnished with antiques are in the center of the historic district. Nationally recognized for its special Christmas.

Hosts: Dane and Joan Wells
Rooms: 16 (PB) $80-225
Suites: 7 (PB)
Full Breakfast
Credit Cards: A, B, C
Notes: 2, 5, 8, 9, 10, 11, 12

White Dove Cottage

619 Hughes Street, 08204
(609) 884-0613; (800) 321-3683

6 Pets welcome; 8 Children welcome; 9 Social drinking allowed; 10 Tennis available; 11 Swimming available; 12 Golf available; 13 Skiing available; 14 May be booked through travel agents.

This elegant little bed and breakfast, circa 1866, is in the center of the historic district on a quiet tree-lined gaslit street. Five rooms plus one suite offer cheerful accommodations for guests, and bicycle rental, golf course, ocean, and beach are all nearby. Tea and snacks are served every afternoon, and a full breakfast starts the day. AAA, PAII, and NJBBA approved.

Hosts: Frank and Sue Smith
Rooms: 6 (PB) $75-175
Full Breakfast
Credit Cards: None
Notes: 2, 5, 8 (over 10) 9, 10, 11, 12, 14

White Dove Cottage

Wilbraham Mansion

133 Myrtle Avenue, 08204
(609) 884-2046

Antique furnished Victorian mansion with period wallpaper and five magnificent gilded mirrors. A warm, hospitable staff presides over a delicious breakfast and refreshing afternoon tea. Bicycles, beach tags, ten air-conditioned bedrooms and best of all, an indoor heated swimming pool. A glassed front porch abounds with plants and flowers year-round.

Rooms: 10 (PB) $95-185
Full Breakfast
Credit Cards: A, B
Notes: 2, 5, 7 (limited), 10, 11, 12

The Wooden Rabbit

609 Hughes Street, 08204
(609) 884-7293

On one of the prettiest streets in Cape May, the Wooden Rabbit is nestled in the heart of the historic district, surrounded by Victorian cottages, cool, shady trees, and brick walkways. Two blocks from beautiful sandy beaches, one block from Cape May's quaint shopping mall, and within easy walking distance of fine restaurants. Each guest room is air-conditioned, has a private bath, TV, and comfortably sleeps two to four persons. The Wooden Rabbit is also the home of the hosts, comfortable and casual folks, who look forward to sharing their home. Decor is country and relaxed. A full breakfast is served October through May. No smoking. Family atmosphere.

Hosts: Greg and Debby Burow
Rooms: 3 (PB) $85-175
Full or Continental Breakfast
Credit Cards: A, B, D
Notes: 2, 5, 8, 9, 10, 11, 12

Woodleigh House

808 Washington Street, 08204
(609) 884-7123; (800) 399-7123

Victorian, but informal, with off-street parking, beach bikes, comfortable parlor, courtyard, and gardens. Walk to everything: marvelous restaurants, sights galore, nearby nature preserve, dinner theater, and craft and antique shows. Queen-size beds, private baths.

Hosts: Jan and Buddy Wood
Rooms: 4 (PB) $80-150
Continental Breakfast
Credit Cards: A, B
Notes: 2, 5, 8, 10, 11, 12, 14

COLUMBUS (MT. HOLLY)

Bed and Breakfast Adventures

Suite 132, 2310 Central Avenue, North Wildwood, 08260
(606) 522-4000; (800) 992-2632

NOTES: Credit cards accepted: A MasterCard; B Visa; C American Express; D Discover Card; E Diner's Club; F Other; 2 Personal checks accepted; 3 Lunch available; 4 Dinner available; 5 Open all year;

NJ463. This Federal-style home, circa 1845, has been featured in many country magazines. All three third-floor guest rooms are air-conditioned and furnished with period antiques and country decor; one contains a queen-size bed and working fireplace. Bath is private, since host prefers to limit occupancy to one couple at a time, or two traveling together. A full breakfast is served in the formal dining room or the country kitchen. Enjoy nearby racetracks, canoeing, antiquing or nature-walking. A variety of resident pets. $85-100.

DENNISVILLE

Henry Ludlam Inn

Cape May Country, 1336 Route 47,
   Woodbine, 08270
(609) 861-5847

This circa 1760 home, voted "Best of the Shore 1991," offers enchanting rooms, scrumptious gourmet breakfasts, bedroom fireplaces, and fireside picnic baskets. Guests invest in memories here. Mecca for birdwatchers.

Hosts: Ann and Marty Thurlow
Rooms: 5 (3 PB; 2 SB) $75-95
Full Breakfast
Credit Cards: A, B, C, D
Notes: 2, 3, 5, 8 (over 12) 9, 10, 11, 12, 14

EAST BRUNSWICK

Amanda's Bed and Breakfast

1428 Park Avenue, 21217
(410) 225-0001; (410) 383-1274

273. Enjoy a charming and comfortable bed and breakfast experience in this spacious Cape Cod-style home nestled in the privacy of the East Brunswick suburbs. Sumptuous breakfasts served on the screened-in patio. Three guest rooms; shared baths. $60.

EDGEWATER PARK

Historic Whitebriar

1029 Cooper Street, 08010
(609) 871-3859

Historic home nestled on seven acres of miniature horse farm in the center of Edgewater Park. Breakfast is served in an English Conservatory. Just 20 minutes from Liberty Bell. Historic local tours of Burlington, the 300-year-old capital of West Jersey. Pool and spa. Feed the chickens, ducks, turkeys and collect eggs like in bygone days.

Hosts: William, Carole, Carrie, and Lizzie Moore
Rooms: 7 (2 PB; 5 SB) $50-85
Continental Breakfast
Credit Cards: None
Notes: 5, 6, 8, 11

FLEMINGTON

Jerica Hill— A Bed and Breakfast Inn

96 Broad Street, 08822
(908) 782-8234

Be warmly welcomed at this gracious country inn in the historic town of Flemington. Spacious, sunny guest rooms, all with pri-

Jerica Hill

6 Pets welcome; 8 Children welcome; 9 Social drinking allowed; 10 Tennis available; 11 Swimming available; 12 Golf available; 13 Skiing available; 14 May be booked through travel agents.

vate bath and air conditioning, living room with a fireplace, and a wicker-filled screened porch invite guests to relax. A guests' pantry offering beverages and snacks is available 24-hours a day. Champagne hot-air balloon flights are arranged, as well as country picnic and winery tours. A delightful Continental plus breakfast is served. Guest's pantry offering beverages and snacks available 24 hours a day. Corporate and midweek rates available. AAA rated three diamonds. Featured in *Country Inns Bed and Breakfast* and *Mid-Atlantic Country*.

Host: Judith S. Studer
Rooms: 5 (PB) $90-105
Continental Breakfast
Credit Cards: A, B, C
Notes: 2, 5, 9, 10, 11, 12, 14

FRENCHTOWN

Hunterdon House

12 Bridge Street, 08825
(908) 996-3632; (800) 382-0375 (outside NJ)

One-half block from the Delaware River, built in 1864 and noted for its Victorian-Italianate style. Rooms are spacious and furnished with period antiques. Frenchtown is minutes from Bucks County, Pennsylva-nia. A perfect country getaway offering quality galleries, antiques, craft shops, and fine dining. Sports enthusiasts will enjoy fishing, boating, tubing, or skiing and biking on the 60-mile trail running along the river.

Host: Gene Refalvy
Rooms: 7 (PB) $85-145
Full Breakfast
Credit Cards: A, B, C
Notes: 2, 5, 9, 14

GLENWOOD

Apple Valley Inn Bed and Breakfast

Corner Routes 517 and 565, P.O. Box 302, 07418
(201) 764-3735

A Colonial mansion built in 1831 allows guests to relax in the sunroom, formal parlor, or the extensive gardens and in-ground pool. Stroll through the apple orchard or fish the trout stream. Select an antique from the on-premises shop. This picturesque inn is four miles from Action Park and exclusive ski slopes. The inn is on the fall foliage tour. The Appalachian Trail is one mile away. The New Jersey Botanical Gardens, Waterloo Village, and Skylands are a short drive away. West Point and the Hudson Valley make for a wonderful day. Guests start the day with a full country breakfast. Picnic lunches are available.

Hosts: Mitzi and John Durham
Rooms: 6 (1 PB; 5 SB) $60-75
Full Breakfast
Credit Cards: None
Notes: 2, 3, 5, 9, 10, 11, 12, 13

GREENWICH

Bed and Breakfast Adventures

Suite 132, 2310 Central Avenue,
   North Wildwood, 08260
(606) 522-4000; (800) 992-2632

NJ 533. More than two centuries of history and style grace the main house of this Colonial bed and breakfast, which reflects the building styles of 1783, 1930 and 1957. Four guest rooms are furnished in a decor depicting each era of the home's history. Bedrooms have either shared or private baths. The pool has its own cabana with kitchen, bar, and two changing rooms with baths. $75-100.

HADDONFIELD

The Queen Anne Inn

44 West End Avenue, 08033
(609) 428-2195

The only accommodation in south Jersey within walking distance to the hi-speed line

---

NOTES: Credit cards accepted: A MasterCard; B Visa; C American Express; D Discover Card; E Diner's Club; F Other; 2 Personal checks accepted; 3 Lunch available; 4 Dinner available; 5 Open all year;

(17 minutes to Philadelphia, less to the aquarium or Reetgers Camden). No car required—walk to shops and restaurants. Stay in a fully restored Victorian (on the National Register) that is beautifully furnished. In an elegant residential neighborhood in historic Haddonfield. Free local phone calls and free parking. Continental breakfast served Monday-Saturday; full breakfast on Sunday.

Hosts: Nancy Lynn and Frank Dykeman
Rooms: 8 (1 PB; 7 SB) $60
Full or Continental Breakfast
Credit Cards: A, B, C, D
Notes: 4, 5, 8, 9, 10, 11, 12, 14

HOPE

The Inn at Millrace Pond

Route 519, P.O. Box 359, 07844
(908) 459-4884

A gracious country inn restored to Colonial grandeur situated along Beaver Brook in historic Hope. Seventeen individually decorated guest rooms, each with private bath and modern amenities. Scenic location offers hiking, canoeing, tennis, riding, golf, Waterloo Village, craft fairs, wineries, and antique shows. Grist Mill Dining Room open daily for dinner and Sunday from noon until 8:00 P.M. for lunch and dinner. Three stars from Mobil guide. Three diamonds from AAA. Four-crown award from the ABBA.

Hosts: Cordie and Charles Puttkammer
Rooms: 17 (PB) $85-150
Continental Breakfast
Credit Cards: A, B, C, E
Notes: 2, 4, 5, 9, 10, 12, 14

JERSEY CITY

Bed and Breakfast Adventures

Suite 132, 2310 Central Avenue, North Wildwood, 08260
(606) 522-4000; (800) 992-2632

NJ 611. In the heart of the Van Horst Park Historic District, this early 19th-century house supports a garden apartment and a triplex. Accommodations include double beds, period furniture, air conditioning, TV and a shared bath. Guests have access to the parlor and dining room. Breakfast is a variety of fresh fruits, juices and homemade breads, with an assortment of jellies and jams. Well-behaved children and non-smokers are welcome, as are mid-week corporate travelers. $55-75.

LYNDHURST

The Jeremiah J. Yereance House

410 Riverside Avenue, 07071
(201) 438-9457

This 1841 house, a state and national landmark, is five minutes from the Meadow-lands complex and 20 minutes from New York City. The guest rooms in the south wing include a front parlor with fireplace, a central hall, and a small but comfortable bedroom that adjoins the parlor and private bath. The north wing includes a common parlor with three bedrooms that share a bath.

Hosts: Evelyn and Frank Pezzolla
Rooms: 4 (1 PB; 3 SB) $55-75
Continental Breakfast
Credit Cards: C
Notes: 2, 5, 8 (over 12), 9, 10

MAYS LANDING

Bed and Breakfast Adventures

Suite 132, 2310 Central Avenue,
North Wildwood, 08260
(606) 522-4000; (800) 992-2632

NJ595. Just minutes away from the glitter and excitement of the casinos of Atlantic City, this lovely 1860s Victorian mansion offers guests a quiet respite. The three

---

6 Pets welcome; 8 Children welcome; 9 Social drinking allowed; 10 Tennis available; 11 Swimming available;
12 Golf available; 13 Skiing available; 14 May be booked through travel agents.

guest rooms and one two-room suite have queen-size beds, private baths (two with whirlpool tubs), antique furnishings, and a quiet atmosphere. The Victorian parlor provides a pleasant setting for games, reading and conversation. During the summer, tea is served in the English manner on Saturdays and selected weekdays. It is a leisurely stroll to beautiful Lake Lenape, shops, and parks. A short drive to wineries, beaches, and other attractions. Non-smokers, couples and well-behaved children over ten are welcome. $75-125.

MILFORD

Bed and Breakfast Adventures

Suite 132, 2310 Central Avenue,
  North Wildwood, 08260
(606) 522-4000; (800) 992-2632

NJ610. This 200-year-old stone inn is in a quaint village on the Delaware River. Renovated in 1949, this host-home offers a quiet respite for all seasons. Two upstairs bedrooms have double beds and shared bath. Guests enjoy a swimming pool, library, fireplace, TV, and stereo. An extended Continental breakfast is provided. The area has antique shops, wineries, and hot-air ballooning; it is only 30 minutes from New Hope, Pennsylvania. Nonsmokers and children are welcome. $85 and up.

MONTCLAIR

Bed and Breakfast Adventures

Suite 132, 2310 Central Avenue,
  North Wildwood, 08260
(606) 522-4000; (800) 992-2632

NJ617. A country setting awaits guests in this two-story Colonial home in the heart of Montclair's estate section. There are two guest rooms, each with adjoining private

bath. The beds are full-size, and each room has its own sitting area. A full breakfast is served each morning, with the hostess' special recipes. It is convenient to many tourist attractions, including the Meadowlands and the Thomas Edison Home; guests are within minutes of I-280. Nonsmokers and well-behaved children over 12 are welcome. $80.

The Marlboro Inn

334 Grove Street, 07042
(201) 783-5300; (800) 446-6020

A stately 19th-century mansion turned hostelry in 1890, the Marlboro Inn sits on three and one-half tree-shaded acres only minutes from Manhattan. The Inn offers its guests European charm and elegance, with the friendly, casual atmosphere the Calder family cherishes. With a variety of individually decorated rooms and suites, the inn also provides delightful dining, as well as facilities for meetings, banquets and special occasions. Continental breakfast. Children welcome. Smoking permitted.

Hosts: Sandy, Nancy, and Matt Calder
Rooms: 35 (PB) $110-190
Continental Breakfast
Credit Cards: A, B, C, D, E
Notes: 2, 3, 4, 5, 7, 8, 9, 10, 11, 12, 14

MORRISTOWN

Bed and Breakfast Adventures

Suite 132, 2310 Central Avenue,
  North Wildwood, 08260
(606) 522-4000; (800) 992-2632

NJ450. This 22-room Estate Manor House is in the country club area two miles from the city center. Four tastefully decorated rooms are available; amenities include a queen-size bed, sitting area, TV, air conditioning, and a small bar with refrigerator. One room becomes a suite with library and fireplace at an additional charge. Private bath also available. A Continental breakfast

---

NOTES: Credit cards accepted: A MasterCard; B Visa; C American Express; D Discover Card; E Diner's Club; F Other; 2 Personal checks accepted; 3 Lunch available; 4 Dinner available; 5 Open all year;

is served daily. Couples, corporate and non-smoking travelers welcome. $60-100.

NORTH WILDWOOD

Candlelight Inn

2310 Central Avenue, 08260
(609) 522-6200

"There is a quaint haven for those in a vintage romantic mood," wrote the *Philadelphia Inquirer* (July 1988). The Candlelight Inn is a beautifully restored bed and breakfast built at the turn of the century by Leaming Rice. This Queen Anne Victorian structure served as the family home for many years until it was purchased by its present innkeepers in 1985. Within minutes of Cape May and Atlantic City. Special touches and personalized service abound.

Hosts: Paul DiFilippo and Diane Buscham
Rooms: 8 (PB) $75-235
Suites: 2
Full Breakfast
Credit Cards: A, B, C, D
Notes: 2, 5, 9, 10, 11, 12, 14

OCEAN CITY

BarnaGate
Bed and Breakfast

637 Wesley Avenue, 08226
(609) 391-9366

The BarnaGate offers a comfortable, relaxed atmosphere and is decorated with various antiques. The living room offers a common sitting room to watch TV or listen to light music. All rooms are cooled by old-fashioned paddle fans. The five restored visitor's rooms are decorated with country quilts, Victorian antiques, and decorative pillows. Private bath and powder room are available. A sitting room is on the top level, decorated in wicker for comfort. A Continental-plus breakfast is served buffet style. Hosts can provide pamphlets with informa-

BarnaGate

tion about local sights and activities. Full breakfast is served in the winter.

Hosts: Lois and Frank Barna
Rooms: 5 (1 PB; 2 SB) $65-75
Full or Continental Breakfast
Credit Cards: A, B
Notes: 2, 5, 8 (over 9), 9, 10, 11, 12, 14

Beach End Inn
Bed and Breakfast

815 Plymouth Place, 08226
(609) 398-1016

Nestled on a quiet beach-block street in the heart of town, guests are steps from the ocean and boardwalk. Six distinctly decorated and themed guest rooms feature Victorian antiques. Common areas include the parlor room with fireplace, game room, dining room, and front porch. Guests receive complimentary beach tags during the summer. Nightly turndown service. Monthly murder mystery affairs. Minutes from Atlantic City. Bicycling, fishing, water sports, and historical attractions are at hand.

Host: Len Cipkins
Rooms: 6 (3 PB; 3 SB) $55-90
Full Breakfast
Credit Cards: A, B
Notes: 2, 5, 9, 10, 11, 12

New Brighton Inn

519 Fifth Street, 08226
(609) 399-2829

6 Pets welcome; 8 Children welcome; 9 Social drinking allowed; 10 Tennis available; 11 Swimming available; 12 Golf available; 13 Skiing available; 14 May be booked through travel agents.

Magnificently restored 1800s seaside Queen Anne Victorian. Premises comfortably furnished with antiques throughout. Breakfast on sun porch. A romantic, relaxing, charming hideaway close to the beach, boardwalk, tennis courts, restaurants, and fine shops.

Hosts: Daniel and Donna Hand
Rooms: 5 (PB) $70-90
Full Breakfast
Credit Cards: A, B, C, D
Notes: 2 (NJ), 5, 8 (over 10), 10, 11, 12

New Brighton Inn

Northwood Inn
Bed and Breakfast

401 Wesley Avenue, 08226
(609) 399-6071

Beautification award winning 1894 Queen Anne Victorian with 19th-century charm and 20th-century comfort. All eight guest rooms have private baths. Relax in the central air, on the wraparound porch with Carolina rockers, back deck, or roof-top deck. Guests are welcome to use the regulation-size pool table in the billiards room. The library is fully stocked. Three blocks to beach, boardwalk, and downtown shopping. In the historic district of Ocean City. Full breakfast served on the weekends.

Hosts: Marj and John Loeper
Rooms: 8 (PB) $85-145
Full and Continental Breakfasts

Credit Cards: A, B, C
Notes: 2, 5, 8 (over 9), 9, 10, 11, 12

OCEAN GROVE

Cordova

26 Webb Avenue, 07756
(908) 774-3084 summer; (212) 751-9577 winter

The Cordova is a big, century-old Victorian seaside guest house in Ocean Grove. Built in 1885, it is tightly tucked in alongside other summer cottages from the same era, a block from the ocean, white sand beach and boardwalk extending for miles. Ocean Grove is on the National Register of Historic Places. There are 15 guest rooms (including two efficiencies). Here, guests feel a part of an extended family as they use the kitchen, living room, barbecue, and picnic tables. Only an hour-and-a-half bus/ train ride to Manhattan and Atlantic City. The weekly rate gives guests seven nights for the price of five. Open Memorial Day to Labor Day.

Host: Doris Chernik
Rooms: 15 (4 PB; 11 SB) $35-70
Continental Breakfast
Credit Cards: None
Notes: 2, 8, 9, 10, 11, 12, 14

PEMBERTON

Bed and Breakfast
Adventures

Suite 132, 2310 Central Avenue,
  North Wildwood, 08260
(606) 522-4000; (800) 992-2632

NJ613. Built in the mid-1800s, this home underwent high-style Victorian conversion soon after its construction. The inn offers charming and comfortable guest rooms, each with private bath and queen-size bed. There is also a suite with a garden tub in the bath and a sitting area. Breakfast is served each morning. Hosts also offer "Murder Mystery" weekends. Well-behaved children over ten and non-smokers are welcome. Dis-

NOTES: Credit cards accepted: A MasterCard; B Visa; C American Express; D Discover Card; E Diner's Club; F Other; 2 Personal checks accepted; 3 Lunch available; 4 Dinner available; 5 Open all year;

counted rate available for military families and Deborah Hospital visitors. $65-125.

PLAINFIELD

The Pillars
922 Central Avenue, 07060-2311
(908) 753-0922; (800) 37-2REST

Guests may make themselves at home in this restored 1880s mansion. In a secluded acre of trees, The Pillars offers an easy-going, yet elegant ambience. Enjoy the music room, with organ, stereo, and wood fire. Relax in the living room, with library and TV. Use the laundry or raid the refrigerator. A stained-glass skylight illuminates the circular staircase. Close to the shore, with easy access to Newark Airport and New York City. All rooms are air-conditioned and feature private baths. An expanded Continental Swedish breakfast is served. Children under two and over 12 welcome.

Hosts: Tom and Chuck Hale
Rooms: 3 (PB) $65-105
Continental Breakfast
Credit Cards: Call to inquire
Notes: 2, 5, 6 (dogs), 8, 9, 10, 11, 12, 14

PRINCETON

Bed and Breakfast of Princeton
P.O. Box 571, 08542
(609) 924-3189; FAX (609) 921-6271

Bed and Breakfast of Princeton offers homestay accommodations in several local homes and two self-catering apartments. Some accommodations are within walking distance of the town center while others are minutes away by automobile or public transportation. Some homes are nonsmoking. Princeton is the site of many business, research, and academic institutions. Midway between New York and Philadelphia, it

offers a variety of recreational, historical, cultural, and sightseeing opportunities. $50.

SEA GIRT

Holly Harbor Guest House
112 Baltimore Boulevard, 08750
(908) 449-9731; (800) 348-6999 outside New Jersey

Sea Girt is a quiet, residential town 60 miles south of New York City on the Jersey shore. Gracious cedar-shingled house is bordered by holly trees and has a spacious front porch. Only one block from the beach.

Hosts: Bill and Kim Walsh
Rooms: 12 (SB) $75-100
Full Breakfast
Credit Cards: A, B, C
Notes: 2, 5, 8, 9, 10, 11, 12

SPRING LAKE

Ashling Cottage
106 Sussex Avenue, 07762
(908) 449-3553; (800) 237-1877

Under sentinel sycamores since 1877 in a storybook setting, Ashling Cottage, a Victorian seaside inn, has long served as a portal to an earlier time. A block from the ocean and just one-half block from a freshwater lake. Closed January through March.

Ashling Cottage

6 Pets welcome; 8 Children welcome; 9 Social drinking allowed; 10 Tennis available; 11 Swimming available; 12 Golf available; 13 Skiing available; 14 May be booked through travel agents.

Hosts: Goodi and Jack Stewart
Rooms: 10 (8 PB; 2 SB) $70-150
Full Breakfast
Credit Cards: None
Notes: 2, 8 (over 12), 9, 10, 11, 12, 14 (limited)

The Chateau

500 Warren Avenue, 07762
(908) 974-2000

The house may be 101 years old, but it's brand-new inside: air conditioning, color cable TV, HBO, telephones, and refrigerators. Suites and parlors have living rooms, wet bars, paddle fans. Some have fireplaces and facilities for FAX machines and personal computers. VCRs, private porches, and balconies are also available.

Host: Scott Smith
Rooms: (PB) $55-170
Suites: (PB) $75-195
Continental Breakfast
Credit Cards: A, B, C, E
Notes: 2, 5, 7, 8, 9, 10, 11, 12, 14

Hamilton House Inn

15 Mercer Avenue, 07762
(908) 449-8282

The Hamilton House Inn is a newly renovated bed and breakfast. The rooms are spacious, comfortable, and exquisitely decorated. All have queen- or-size beds and each has an individual theme. The in-ground pool is crystal clear and always inviting on a warm day in the summer. Winter and spring offer a quiet season that beckons guests to a vacation with an unhurried pace. Wonderful full breakfasts. Hospitality in the old world tradition.

Hosts: Anne and Bud Benz
Rooms: 8 (PB) $75-195
Full Breakfast
Credit Cards: A, B, C
Notes: 2, 5, 10, 11, 12

Hollycroft

P.O. Box 448, 07762
(908) 681-2254

Hollycroft is a 1908 "Mountain Lodge" at the seashore. Hidden behind a curtain of holly. Two holiday worlds—a quiet, woodsy atmosphere only a few blocks from beach and boardwalk. Country Victorian guest rooms are delightfully furnished and two have their own fireplaces. Spacious common areas invite guests to come and relax. Outdoor breakfast areas in summer and a roaring fireplace in winter make Hollycroft an inn for all seasons.

Hosts: Linda and Mark Fessler
Rooms: 7 (PB) $95-150
Full Breakfast
Credit Cards: C
Notes: 2, 5, 9, 10, 11, 12

Normandy Inn

Normandy Inn

21 Tuttle Avenue, 07762
(908) 449-7172

Less than a block from the ocean, this 1888 Italianate villa has been authentically restored inside and out. Antique-filled guest rooms and parlors invite guests to step back in time to 19th-century elegance. The wide front porch with wicker furniture invites quiet conversation and cool breezes at sunset. A hearty country breakfast awaits visitors in the morning. Explore the wide, tree-lined streets, turn-of-the-century estates, quaint shops, and boutiques. Golf, tennis, horseback riding, and historic villages are nearby. Minimum-stay requirements for March through November weekends, July and August during mid-week, and holidays.

Hosts: Michael and Susan Ingino
Rooms: 17 (PB) $78-146
Carriage House: (PB) $175-220
Full Breakfast
Credit Cards: A, B, C
Notes: 2, 5, 7, 8, 9, 10, 11, 12, 14

Sarann Guest House

209 First Avenue, 07762
(908) 449-9870

Gracious Victorian bed and breakfast guest house in a lovely quiet residential neighborhood, yet within walking distance to village, churches, restaurants, and beach. Guests can relax and enjoy this historical seashore resort on the wraparound porch with other guests in a home-like atmosphere. Convenient to trains and bus lines. Race track nearby.

Hosts: Viola and John Mihalko, Innkeepers
Rooms: 11 (SB) $39-50
Continental Breakfast
Credit Cards: F (travelers cheques)
Notes: 2, 9, 10, 11, 12

Sea Crest by the Sea

19 Tuttle Avenue, 07762
(908) 449-9031

A lovingly restored 1885 Victorian specializes in pampering guests seeking relaxation, romance, or a special fantasy while convenient to both New York City and Philadelphia. Each guest room offers a different fantasy. Choose from the Victorian Rose, the Pussy Willow, the Washington, or the Casablanca. Seven rooms offer fireplaces. The ocean and beach are just a half-block away and there is a stable of bikes for riding. A library with books and games and the porch are convenient places for developing new friendships during a stay. A full breakfast begins at 9:00 A.M. with freshly baked scones and muffins, fruit, and Sea Crest

granola, all served on family china, silver, and crystal.

Hosts: John and Carol Kirby
Rooms: 12 (PB) $92-159
Suite: 1 (PB) $189-239
Full Breakfast
Credit Cards: A, B
Notes: 2, 5, 9, 10, 11, 12

Victoria House

214 Monmouth Avenue, 07762
(908) 974-1882

The Victoria House provides the perfect retreat from today's hustle and bustle. This Eastlake style residence exhibits typical Victorian appeal with its gingerbread accents, stained-glass windows, and Gothic shingles. Come and relax on the spacious wraparound porch and enjoy the cool ocean breezes. Stroll a few steps to the lake or beach or browse through the quaint shops in the village. Spring Lake is easily accessible by car, bus, or train from both New York and Philadelphia.

Hosts: Louise and Robert Goodall
Rooms: 10 (6 PB; 4 SB) $85-150
Full Breakfast
Credit Cards: A, B, C, D
Notes: 2, 5, 8 (over 6), 9, 10, 11, 12

STOCKTON

The Stockton Inn

Main and Bridge Street, 08559
(609) 397-1250

The centerpiece of a small riverside town, the Stockton Inn dates to 1710 and inspired Rodgers and Harts' song "There's a Small Hotel (with a wishing well)." Four buildings house eight suites and three bedrooms, all with private baths, TV, and air conditioning; many boast fireplaces. Full service, three-star restaurant and tavern with six dining rooms; three muraled and five with fireplaces. Alfresco dining in the Garden Pavilions. Enjoy the waterfalls and pond. Three miles to galleries, theaters, and

6 Pets welcome; 8 Children welcome; 9 Social drinking allowed; 10 Tennis available; 11 Swimming available; 12 Golf available; 13 Skiing available; 14 May be booked through travel agents.

plenty of antiquing in Lambertville/New Hope. Closed Christmas.

Hosts: Andrew McDermott and Bruce Monti
Rooms: 11 (PB) $60-165
Continental Breakfast
Credit Cards: A, B, C, D
Notes: 3, 4, 5, 7, 9, 10, 12, 13

Woolverton Inn

6 Woolverton Road, 08559
(609) 397-0802

Woolverton Inn

An elegant stone manor in a pastoral setting, the Woolverton Inn offers the best of past times and the amenities of present comforts. Sitting majestically above the Delaware, the inn features a classic country setting, rooms with fireplaces, Jacuzzi, family antiques, terry-cloth robes, afternoon refreshments, full country breakfast, fireplaced living and dining room, wicker rocking chairs on the porch, horseshoes, croquet, resident sheep, air conditioning. Whether on business, pleasure or celebrating a wedding, come as a guest, but expect to be treated more like a family friend.

Host: Elizabeth and Michael Palmer
Rooms: 11 (PB) $75-150
Suites: 3
Full Breakfast
Credit Cards: A, B
Notes: 2, 5, 9, 10, 11, 12

New Mexico

B&B of New Mexico

P.O. Box 2805, Santa Fe, 87504
(505) 982-3332

402. Beautiful and large single-story adobe home with 18-inch thick walls, brick floors, and viga ceilings. Very private. Surrounded by alfalfa fields, yet close to Albuquerque. Private bath in both rooms. $60.

404. This dramatic pueblo-style home has magnificent mountain views and spectacular sunsets. A generous continental breakfast with freshly ground coffee is served in the guests' room, on the patio, or in the dining area. One room with a king-size bed has a private deck and full hall bath. Twin beds in other room with private bath across living room. $55-60.

Las Palomas Valley Bed and Breakfast

2303 Candelaria Road Northwest, 87107
(505) 345-7228

One of Albuquerque's most beautiful historic adobe estates, this lovely inn occupies three glorious acres of lawns, gardens, and orchards near Old Town. Outdoor hot tub, tennis court, croquet, and bike trails complement the uniquely furnished suites. All rooms have king-size beds, antique furnishings, private bathrooms and lounges, splendid views, and fireplaces. The chef makes fresh breads daily. A full English breakfast is served in the lovely dining room or on the lawns.

Hosts: Lori and Andrew Caldwell
Rooms: 8 (PB) $75-125
Full Breakfast
Credit Cards: A, B, C
Notes: 2, 5, 6, 7 (limited), 8, 9, 10 (on site), 11, 12, 13, 14

Mi Casa Su Casa

P.O. Box 950, Tempe, AZ 85280-0950
(602) 990-0682; (800) 456-0682

1800. Just 20 minutes from downtown Albuquerque, this hostess welcomes guests to a nice Southwestern-style home in a quiet, residential neighborhood. Surrounded by fruit trees with a large vegetable garden in the corner side yard, this bed and breakfast brings a taste of the country to a convenient city location. Three sets of accommodations are available. Full breakfast is served. $35-55.

1810. The only bed-and-breakfast accommodations in Old Town, this spacious mansion with shaded grass and garden courtyard is visible from the Plaza. The Lola Room has a king-size bed, two trundle twin beds, private full bath, and a hand-painted border mural. The Sofia Suite has a king-size bed, an adjacent sunroom with twin beds, private full bath, and sculptured metal ceiling. The romantic Mercedes Room has a queen-size bed and full bath with black jet tub. The mauve marble floors add elegance to this room. Full breakfast. No pets. Smoking outside. Children are welcome. Minimum two-night stay during Balloon Fiesta. $20 per additional adult. $10 per additional child. $49-109.

6 Pets welcome; 7 Smoking allowed; 8 Children welcome; 9 Social drinking allowed; 10 Tennis available; 11 Swimming available; 12 Golf available; 13 Skiing available; 14 May be booked through travel agents.

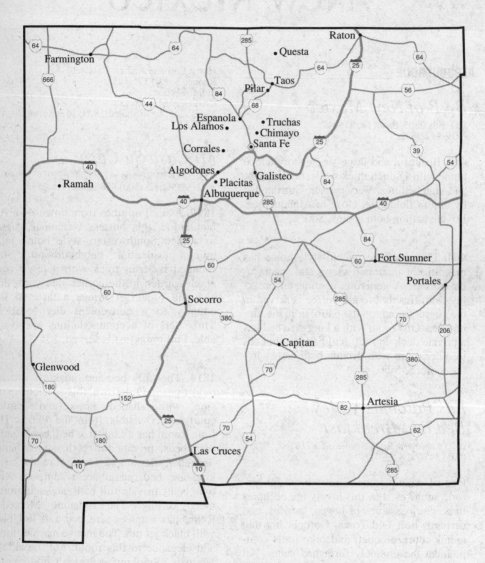

New Mexico

W. E. Mauger Estate

701 Roma Avenue Northwest, 87102
(505) 242-8755

Wonderful 1897 Queen Anne Victorian on the National Register of Historic Places. Eight unique accommodations with private baths, full breakfast, and afternoon refreshments. Within walking distance of Old Town, museums, zoo, Indian Center, shops, restaurants, and the convention center. The beautiful front porch is furnished with wicker. Other features include indoor and outdoor dining rooms. Elegant, gracious, and affordable, this showplace is a must. No smoking. Mobil rated three stars. AAA rated three diamonds.

Hosts: Chuck Silver and Brian Miller
Rooms: 8 (PB) $75-115
Full Breakfast
Credit Cards: A, B, C, E, F
Notes: 2, 5, 6, 8, 9, 12, 14

Old Town Bed and Breakfast

707 Seventeenth Street Northwest, 87104
(505) 764-9144

Old Town Bed and Breakfast is an adobe home on a beautiful, quiet street just two blocks from historic Old Town Plaza, the museums, and a lovely park. The second-floor guest room has a queen-size bed, private bath, private entrance, and provides views of the mountains and tree-lined neighborhood streets. The spacious first-floor guest room has a king-size bed, kiva fireplace, private entrance, and Jacuzzi bath, shared with owner only. Single beds provided upon request. Additional sleeping accommodations in adjacent sitting room. A secluded garden setting is for guests' enjoyment. Generous continental breakfast. Caring hospitality.

Host: Nancy Hoffman
Rooms: 2 (1 PB; 1 SB) $60-75

Old Town Bed and Breakfast

Continental Breakfast
Credit Cards: None
Notes: 2, 5, 8, 9, 14

ALGODONES

B&B of New Mexico

P.O. Box 2805, Santa Fe, 87504
(505) 982-3332

410. This hacienda just 30 miles south of Santa Fe offers the grace and elegance of historic New Mexico. It is decorated with antique furniture. Each room has its own handmade kiva fireplace. The tranquility offered there complements the peace and serenity found in the Hacienda courtyard and garden. The largest room is the Wagner Room with Jacuzzi bathtub, fireplace, sitting area, and queen-size bed. The Peña Room has a queen-size bed. Both the Piñon and Pueblo rooms have full-size beds and private baths. $79-109.

NOTES: Credit cards accepted: A MasterCard; B Visa; C American Express; D Discover Card; E Diner's Club; F Other; 2 Personal checks accepted; 3 Lunch available; 4 Dinner available; 5 Open all year; 6 Pets welcome; 7 Smoking allowed; 8 Children welcome; 9 Social drinking allowed; 10 Tennis available; 11 Swimming available; 12 Golf available; 13 Skiing available; 14 May be booked through travel agents.

Mi Casa Su Casa

P.O. Box 950, Tempe, AZ 85281
(602) 990-0682

1809. A gracious, warm host couple welcome guests to a delightful 200-year-old spacious hacienda. The Hacienda Vargas is full of light, has polished tile floors, Southwestern art, Indian arts and crafts, and a nice mix of antiques. Guests are welcome in the living room or library. The chef presents special full breakfasts. Four guest rooms each have kiva fireplaces, private baths, and private entrances to courtyard or hot tub. The large Wagner Room has a whirlpool tub and a queen-size bed. The Peña Room and the Pueblo Room have queen-size beds. The Piñon Room has a double bed. No resident pets. Smoking allowed outside. Roll away available. $69-129.

ARTESIA

Heritage Inn

209 West Main Street, 88210
(505) 748-2552

The Heritage Inn hosts strive to pamper guests with a delightful and unique home-away-from-home inn experience. There are queen-size beds, private baths, and remote-control color TV. Local calls are free. Newly decorated in country/Victorian. Continental breakfast. Deck. FAX service and conference room available. No smoking. No pets.

Hosts: James and Wanda Maupin
Rooms: 9 (PB) $60-70
Continental Breakfast
Credit Cards: A, B, C, D
Notes: 5

CAPITAN

Catherine Kelly's Bed and Breakfast

311 First Street, 88316
(505) 354-2335

Haste ye' come and experience warm Scottish hospitality and a family atmosphere for parents and children. The host family offers bed and breakfast accommodations to guests with traditional Scots' attention to creature comforts in a rambling ranch house in the heart of the village of Capitan. Enjoy the mountains, rugged landscape, skiing, golfing, hiking, walking, fishing, and other outdoor pursuits summer and winter. Awaken to the smell of fresh-baked bread, hot tea, and fresh-brewed coffee. A generous continental breakfast is served buffet style every morning.

Host: Amanda Tudor
Suites: 2 (PB) $50-125
Continental Breakfast
Credit Cards: A, B
Notes: 2, 5, 6, 8, 12, 13

CHIMAYO

Casa Escondida
A Bed and Breakfast Inn

P.O. Box 142, 87522
(505) 351-4805; (800) 643-7201

Casa Escondida is an intimate New Mexican adobe-style bed and breakfast with a European flair nestled in historic Chimayo between Taos and Santa Fe. Six unique rooms are furnished with antiques, down comforters, some with kiva fireplaces, and all with private Mexican-tiled bathrooms. Enjoy a generous gourmet breakfast and attentive care throughout the stay.

Host: Irenka Taurek
Rooms: 6 (PB) $75-130
Full Breakfast
Credit Cards: A, B
Notes: 2, 5, 8, 9, 13, 14

La Posada de Chimayó

P.O. Box 463, 87522
(505) 351-4605

A cozy, comfortable adobe inn in a traditional northern New Mexico village famous for its tradition of fine Spanish weaving and its beautiful old church, El Santuario. Off

commodations are in individual stone cottages with private baths. A swimming pool, spa, bicycles, and horseback riding are all available. Full breakfast served.

Hosts: Jerry and Tiffany Hagemeier
Rooms: 13 (PB) $65-80
Full Breakfast
Credit Cards: A, B, C, D
Notes: 2, 4, 6 (call), 7, 8, 9, 11

LAS CRUCES

Bed and Breakfast in Arizona

Gally 3 Plaza, 3819 North Third Street, Phoenix,
   AZ 85012
(602) 995-2831; (800) 266-STAY
FAX (602) 263-7762

LC101. Classic adobe architecture and magnificent paintings surround guests in this combination art gallery and bed and breakfast inn in Las Cruces. There is a sparkling fountain and historic antique furniture in the main gallery. The 14 rooms are named after the artist whose work is featured in them, and all have private baths. A lavish continental breakfast is put out in the morning. Children are welcome. Deluxe to superior rates.

B&B of New Mexico

P.O. Box 2805, Santa Fe, 87504
(505) 982-3332

506. Just 11 miles from Las Cruces at the foot of the Organ Mountains. Surrounded by U.S. government land, the area is quiet and beautiful. Horse boarding is available and guests can take their horses for a ride in the mountains. Owners speak German, French, Greek, Spanish, Arabic, and understand Italian. The home has a pool for guests. Two guest rooms are available: one has two twin beds and a private bath; the other has an atrium door that opens onto the deck surrounding the pool, double bed, private bath, and kitchenette. $50-60.

LOS ALAMOS

Casa del Rey

305 Rover Street, 87544
(505) 672-9401

Quiet residential area, friendly atmosphere. In White Rock, minutes from Los Alamos and 40 minutes from Santa Fe. Excellent recreational facilities and restaurants nearby. The area is rich in Indian and Spanish history. Breakfast features homemade granola and breads served on the sun porch overlooking flower gardens, with views of the mountains.

Host: Virginia King
Rooms: 2 (SB) $45
Continental Breakfast
Credit Cards: None
Notes: 2, 5, 8 (8 and older), 9, 10, 11, 12, 13

PILAR

The Plum Tree

Highway 68 at Highway 570, Box B-4, 87531
(505) 758-0090; (800) 999-PLUM

Directly in the spectacular Rio Grande Gorge, The Plum Tree hostel and bed and breakfast is a homey accommodation for the budget-minded traveler. Rooms for singles, couples, and families are decorated with local pottery and paintings. Hostess invites guests to hike the scenic Pilar Ridges with her. Convenient to Taos, Sante Fe, pueblos, ski areas, and Ojo Caliente. Communal kitchen available.

Host: Eva C. Behrens
Rooms: 3 (1 PB; 2 SB) $22-65
Continental Breakfast
Credit Cards: A, B
Notes: 2, 8, 11, 12, 13

Rio Grande Vacation Services

State Road 68, P.O. Box B-4, 87531
(505) 758-0090; (800) 999-PLUM

Rio Grande Vacation Services offers families, groups, couples, and individuals an al-

6 Pets welcome; 8 Children welcome; 9 Social drinking allowed; 10 Tennis available; 11 Swimming available; 12 Golf available; 13 Skiing available; 14 May be booked through travel agents.

ternative experience in northern New Mexico. Specializing in country inns, the service strives to unite guests with rural hospitality and spectacular scenery. The service also books educational and naturalistic vacation adventures. Go off the beaten track and explore New Mexico with Rio Grande Vacation Services. Open year-round. Social drinking allowed. Swimming, golfing, and skiing nearby.

PLACITAS

B&B of New Mexico

P.O. Box 2805, Santa Fe, 87504
(505) 982-3332

415. Guests awaken each morning to the sound of the trickling fountain in the tree-shaded patio. This quiet peaceful spot affords spectacular views of the Sandia Mountains and of the sunsets over the western mesas. The cheery interior of this casita is furnished in Southwestern decor with the owners' original art (both are retired museum directors). The tiled bath opens off a central entryway, providing privacy for both the bedroom and living room. The efficient little kitchen is equipped with all that's needed for light housekeeping. The sofa is a sleeper; the bedroom has a queen-size bed. No smoking. $80 double, $100 for 3 or 4 persons.

PORTALES

The Morning Star Inn and Gift Shop

620 West Second Street, 88130
(505) 356-2994

This classic adobe-style inn was completely renovated in 1993. Hospitality, service, and charming decor, along with fresh fruit, Valencia peanuts, and a guardian angel in every room await guests. A unique option is a romantic dinner flight, a favorite of many.

Whether celebrating a memorable event, traveling on business, or a weekend getaway, the hosts feel every day at the Morning Star is a special occasion.

Hosts: David and Tonya Williams
Rooms: 3 (2 SB) $45-50
Continental Breakfast
Credit Cards: A, B
Notes: 2, 10

QUESTA

B&B of New Mexico

P.O. Box 2805, Santa Fe, 87504
(505) 982-3332

210. Large, cozy, rustic log home is waiting for travelers at the base of the Sangre de Cristo Mountains with three bedrooms, two baths, hot tub, and sauna. Area is quiet and restful with close access to Rio Grande. Wild river hiking, wilderness area, three major ski resorts, wildlife, and shopping in Taos are all at guests' disposal. Continental breakfast, Southwestern style. Rooms are queen, double, and single. $40-70.

RAMAH

Mi Casa Su Casa Bed and Breakfast

P.O. Box 950, Tempe, AZ 85281
(602) 990-0682

1805. Enjoy warm-hearted hospitality on this working cattle ranch owned by a descendant of rancher and writer Evon Vogt. Built in 1915 of rocks from the nearby Anasazi Indian ruins, this old farmhouse has wood floors, Navajo rugs, large enclosed gardens, and big elm trees. Two bedrooms, both of which have Navajo rugs and original artworks, lead off from the large central living room. There is also a separate guest house. No smoking. No pets. Full breakfast. $50-65.

RATON

The Red Violet Inn

344 North Second Street, 87740
(505) 445-9778

Follow the Santa Fe Trail and step back into the past at this appealing 1902 red-brick Victorian home three blocks from Raton's historic downtown. Guests have use of the parlor, dining room, porches, and flower-filled yard. Repeat visitors arrange to be on hand for the classical music and social hour from 5:30 to 6:30 P.M. Full breakfast is served in the formal dining room, accompanied by friendly conversation. A theater and gallery are within a few blocks, and hiking and fishing facilities (Surarite State Park) are just 10 miles away. Other area attractions include a golf course, several antique shops, and a museum Capulin Volcano National Monument is only 30 minutes away. Member of the New Mexico Bed and Breakfast Association. No smoking.

Hosts: Ruth and John Hanrahan
Rooms: 4 (2 PB; 2 SB) $50-65
Full Breakfast
Credit Cards: A, B
Notes: 2, 3, 4, 9, 10, 11, 12, 14

SANTA FE

Adobe Abode

202 Chapelle, 87501
(505) 983-3133 (use for FAX also)

Just three blocks from the Plaza, this is a historic adobe home restored into an inviting and intimate European-style bed and breakfast inn. Decorated with flair and authentic Southwest charm, with private phones and TVs in all rooms. There are two guest rooms and a two-room suite in the main house, plus three detached casitas with fireplaces, private entrances, and landscaped patios, all in pure Santa Fe style. Complimentary sherry, cookies, and morning newspaper in the stylish guest living room with fireplace. A full gourmet breakfast is served.

Host: Pat Harbour
Rooms: 6 (PB) $95-160
Full Breakfast
Credit Cards: A, B, D
Notes: 2, 5, 7, 8, 9, 12, 13, 14

Alexander's Inn

Alexander's Inn

529 East Palace, 87501
(505) 986-1431

For a cozy, romantic stay in Santa Fe, come to a bed and breakfast featuring the best of American country charm. In a lovely residential neighborhood on the town's historic east side, the inn is within walking distance of the downtown Plaza and Canyon Road. Afternoon tea, homemade cookies, and a continental-plus breakfast are served.

Hosts: Carolyn Delecluse and Mary Jo Schneider
Rooms: 7 (4 PB; 2 SB) $75-150
Continental Breakfast
Credit Cards: A, B
Notes: 2, 5, 6, 8 (over 6), 9, 10, 11, 12, 13, 14

B&B of New Mexico

P.O. Box 2805, 87504
(505) 982-3332

101. This private residence provides two guest rooms; one has a queen-size bed and private bath, the other has twin beds and a private bath across the hall. Both have their own telephone. The house is four blocks from downtown Santa Fe, convenient to galleries, shops, and museums. It is one block from the municipal pool, sports complex, and tennis courts, and 14 miles from the Santa Fe

6 Pets welcome; 8 Children welcome; 9 Social drinking allowed; 10 Tennis available; 11 Swimming available; 12 Golf available; 13 Skiing available; 14 May be booked through travel agents.

B&B of New Mexico
(continued)

Ski Basin. Ambience focuses on warmth and friendliness in an artistic atmosphere of quiet and mountain views. No smoking. $65-75.

102. Guests' own adobe casita. In a quiet historic plaza, surrounded by shops, restaurants, and galleries. Three separate casitas can accommodate two to six people per casita. All the casitas have equipped kitchens and telephones. The first is elegant, newly restored, remodeled, and redecorated. High-beamed ceilings, plastered walls, pine and tile floors, air-conditioning, and a front courtyard. Two bedrooms. The second is in the back part of the first casita and also has high beamed ceilings, pine and tile floors. The third is a separate house with pine floors and Mexican tile. Large, well-equipped kitchen, living room and dining room, and two bedrooms. $95-$175.

105. Beautiful two-story home less than one mile from the Plaza. Large downstairs bedroom with queen-size bed, refrigerator, lots of closet space, and a private bath and shower. Upstairs room has twin bed, walls covered with watercolors, private three-quarter bath. Breakfast upstairs in dining room with view of hills filled with piñon trees. Living room has views of Sangre de Cristo Mountains, beamed ceilings, and kiva fireplace. Spanish tile in kitchen and hallways. No smoking. $50-75.

107. Pure Santa Fe! This new adobe-style home has high-beam and rough-sawn ceilings throughout, with 12-inch-thick walls, saltillo tile floors, Mexican tile in baths and kitchen, kiva fireplace, and vigas in the living room. One-half block to historic Canyon Road, one mile to the Plaza. Both rooms are on the second floor and have private baths. One room has its own private

portal, $85. The other has its own private sitting room with twin bed. No smoking. $95 for two; $130 for three in suite .

108. Small, cozy adobe home two blocks from Canyon Road and five blocks from downtown plaza. Kiva fireplace in living room, enclosed courtyard in front. Door from guest room opens onto back garden area. Host very knowledgeable about activities in Santa Fe. Private full bath down the hall and king-size bed. No smoking. $75.

110. Beautiful pueblo-style home in the foothills of the Sangre de Cristo Mountains. Gorgeous sunsets and views of the city lights at night. Jogging trails behind the house. Very quiet except for the sounds of nature. Only 15 minutes to ski basin, ten minutes to the Plaza. Patio for sunning; living room and dining room have high-beamed ceiling with fireplace. Master bedroom has king-size bed, dressing area, walk-in closet, private bath, and views of the foothills. Smaller bedroom has twin beds, large closet, and private bath. Cat in residence. No smoking. $65-80.

115. New Santa Fe pueblo-style home with 15-foot coved ceilings with large vigas and large open rooms. Sunny and cozy half moon banco breakfast nook in which guests can sit and relax. Shepard's fireplace in living room, saltillo tile floors throughout, and carpeted bedrooms. Master suite includes king-size canopied bed, kiva fireplace, TV, huge tiled double-head shower room, and step into tiled whirlpool tub with garden window. Attached but private sitting room with twin bed and TV is available at an additional cost. Cozy room with Santa Fe queen-size bed, TV, and private bath. $80-95.

117. This home has wonderful views of the mountains, city, and sunsets. There is a secluded patio accessible from the living

NOTES: Credit cards accepted: A MasterCard; B Visa; C American Express; D Discover Card; E Diner's Club; F Other; 2 Personal checks accepted; 3 Lunch available; 4 Dinner available; 5 Open all year;

room. Tall entrance hall contains a gallery with dozens of paintings. This home offers three guest rooms: one with two twin beds and adjoining queen-size sleeper (same party only and both rooms share a bath), and the third room has queen-size bed, private bath, and private entrance to flagstone patio. $75-80.

119. From 1867 to 1890 this lovely old adobe was the Santa Fe Meat and Livestock Headquarters. In the heart of the historic district five blocks from the Plaza and one block south of Canyon Road. Parts of the home are believed to date prior to 1846. All of the outside and some of the inside walls are made of adobe, in some cases 30 inches thick; the ceiling of the living room has six inches of dirt on top in spite of the pitched roof. There is a parlor grand piano in the home that guests can use. The bunkhouse can sleep four in two queen-size beds sharing a bath (same party). Queen-size bed, private bath, and private library in the main house. No smoking. $80.

120. This adobe casita has viga ceilings, separate bedroom, small living room with double sleeper/sofa, full bath, and kitchenette. Approximately one and one-half miles from the Plaza. $75-$90.

125. Enjoy the graceful privacy of this Santa Fe location only a five-minute drive from the Plaza. This quiet residence has a completely equipped kitchen, TV, telephone, private patio, bath, and a large living room/dining room, all furnished with tasteful elegance, including antiques and artwork. King-size bed. $80-100.

127. Beautiful, spacious adobe-style home in fashionable northeast Santa Fe, less than two miles from downtown. On a ridge above the city, this home offers a lovely view, spectacular sunsets, and walled back yard. Extensive decks provide summertime relaxation and privacy. Kiva fireplace and beamed ceiling in the den offer winter comfort. Glass-enclosed hot tub feels great at the end of a long day. King-size bed with private bath. Twin beds with private bath next to main room. Breakfast features a variety of homemade breads served in the elegant dining room. No smoking. $65-80.

128. This is a delightful home on the east side, one-half block to Canyon Road and within walking distance of town. It has hardwood floors and some antiques. Enjoy breakfast on the cheerful sun porch. Cable TV is available. There are two rooms to choose from. One is a master bedroom with a private bath and queen size bed; the other has a full-size bed with private three-quarter bath. $75.

136. This private nook is nestled on a hillside, three-quarters of a mile from the heart of the Plaza. The guest room has a separate entrance, off-street parking, and a private garden with mountain view, as well as eating, sunning, and barbecue areas. The unit features a queen-size bed with custom willow bedstead, beamed ceiling, plastered walls, radio, TV, and fireplace. The sitting area has a double futon that can serve as another bed. A microwave kitchen with eating area and telephone completes the area. Windows face west for sunset views. No smoking. $95-105.

139. This home begins with the hostess' music space and ends with the host's painting area. The bedroom corridor gives a warm welcome to visitors. The queen-size bedroom is a comfortable size and overlooks the garden; the single bedroom, though smaller, enjoys the spaciousness of a mountain view and a wall of books to tempt a guest tired from tourist activities. Cat and dog are also on the premises. Both rooms share same bath. $50-65.

6 Pets welcome; 8 Children welcome; 9 Social drinking allowed; 10 Tennis available; 11 Swimming available; 12 Golf available; 13 Skiing available; 14 May be booked through travel agents.

B&B of New Mexico (continued)

142. Romantic guest suite in the heart of Santa Fe's historic eastside. This adobe residence is at the end of a narrow lane, secluded and quiet, surrounded by rock walls, coyote fence, and adobe walls, yet minutes to Canyon Road, galleries, shops, and restaurants. Features include sun-filled bedroom, queen-size four-poster bed, kiva fireplace, vigas, and clerestory windows so guests can watch the stars. Also available are a cozy sitting room and cable TV, with both rooms opening onto patio. $80.

143. This attractive casita is about one and one-fourth miles from the Plaza and is furnished with handcrafted furniture by a leading furniture maker in the Santa Fe tradition. Queen-size and twin beds available with full kitchen and small dining room. $75-85.

145. Decorated in Santa Fe style, this casita has a fully equipped kitchenette, TV, stereo, microwave oven, and king-size bed with convertible sofa. It only takes minutes to get to the Plaza, Santa Fe Ski Basin, and Ten Thousand Waves (a Japanese bath house). $70-80.

146. Simply elegant, this restored 100-year-old spacious adobe features fireplace, hardwood floors, plastered walls, full furnishings, custom kitchen cabinets, washer and dryer, CD, and cable TV. Eight blocks from the Plaza. Queen-size four-poster bed $125 for 2; Queen-size pullout bed. $175 for 4; $225 for 5.

150. On a country road in tree-shaded Tesuque, minutes from downtown Santa Fe, a weathered blue gate opens onto a private patio adjoining a garden with fruit trees. This inviting pueblo-style home features rough-hewn beams, vigas, adobe bancos, and plastered walls. A sunny saltillo-tiled living room offers a comfortable queen-size sleeper sofa and cable TV. The carpeted bedroom with queen-size bed has a kiva fireplace and large bay window-seat overlooking a rock pond with waterfall, shaded by aspen and evergreens. $125 for 2; $175 for 3 or 4.

Bed and Breakfast Texas Style

4224 West Red Bird Lane, Dallas, TX 75237
(214) 298-8586

Spacious Adobe. This bed and breakfast home is in fashionable northeast Santa Fe and hosted by a gracious couple who wish to show their guests the city. Relax in either of two guest rooms or in front of the fireplace in the sitting room. Enjoy the complimentary beverages on arrival and Mexican omelets for breakfast. Lavish gardens and deck invite sun soaking and contemplation. $75-85.

Canyon Road Casitas

652 Canyon Road, 87501
(505) 988-5888; (800) 279-0755

In the historic district behind a walled private courtyard garden on Santa Fe's famous Canyon Road. Built around 1887, the accommodations include a suite with dining room, kitchen, and two separate beds. Fine amenities include duvets, down pillows, imported linens, custom toiletries, pima cotton towels, guest robes, French-roast coffee, with complimentary wine and cheese upon check-in. The finest in Southwestern decor, including kiva fireplace, hand-carved beds, vigas, latillas, original art, and hand-tiled private baths. An award-winning inn.

Host: Trisha Ambrose
Rooms: 2 (PB) $85-169
Continental Breakfast
Credit Cards: A, B, C, D, E
Notes: 2, 5, 8, 9, 14

NOTES: Credit cards accepted: A MasterCard; B Visa; C American Express; D Discover Card; E Diner's Club; F Other; 2 Personal checks accepted; 3 Lunch available; 4 Dinner available; 5 Open all year;

Casa de la Cuma

105 Paseo de la Cuma, 87501
(505) 983-1717

Casa de la Cuma is a beautiful bed and breakfast inn just four blocks from the Santa Fe Plaza, the historic and artistic center of the city. The living room and each of the three bedrooms are richly decorated with Navajo textiles, Mexican antiques, and original art. Friendly, Southwestern hospitality offers afternoon snacks in front of the fireplace or on the guest patio. Vacation rentals (with kitchens) are also available near the Plaza.

Hosts: Art and Donna Bailey
Rooms: 3 (1 PB; 2 SB) $75-115
Continental Breakfast
Credit Cards: A, B
Notes: 2, 5, 9, 10, 11, 12, 13, 14

Don Gaspar Compound

623 Don Gaspar Compound, 87501
(505) 986-8664

Built in 1912 in Santa Fe's Don Gaspar Historic District, the compound is a classic example of Mission and Adobe architecture. Six private suites enjoy a secluded adobe-walled garden courtyard. The soothing sound of falling water from the courtyard's fountain invites guests to wander among the brilliant heirloom flowers or just relax. The compound is a pleasant walk from the Plaza, Canyon Road, art galleries, museums, and fine restaurants. No smoking.

Host: Carrie Blackburn
Rooms: 6 (PB) $95
Continental Breakfast
Credit Cards: None
Notes: 2, 5, 9, 12, 13, 14

Dunshee's

986 Acequia Madre, 87501
(505) 982-0988

A romantic adobe getaway in the historic east side, about a mile from the Plaza. Guests can choose either a two-room suite or a two-bedroom guest house with kitchen. Both units have kiva fireplaces, antiques, folk art, fresh flowers, homemade cookies, phone, TV, pretty linens, private bath, patio, and a great continental-plus breakfast. Two-night minimum stay weekends and holidays.

Host: Susan Dunshee
Rooms: 2 (PB) $110-120
Continental Breakfast
Credit Cards: A, B
Notes: 2, 5, 8, 9, 13

Four Kachinas Inn

512 Webber Street, 87501
(505) 982-2550; (800) 397-2564

Four Kachinas Inn, a short walk from Santa Fe's historic Plaza, offers four rooms with private baths and entrances. The rooms are furnished with Southwestern art and handiwork, including Navajo rugs, Hopi kachina dolls, and handcrafted wooden furniture. Three ground-floor rooms have individual garden patios, while the upstairs room offers a view of the Sangre de Cristo Mountains. A continental-plus breakfast is served in the room. The old adobe guest lounge features afternoon tea and cookies.

Hosts: John Daw and Andrew Beckerman
Rooms: 4 (PB) $85-115
Continental Breakfast
Credit Cards: A, B
Notes: 10, 11, 12, 13

Grant Corner Inn

---

6 Pets welcome; 8 Children welcome; 9 Social drinking allowed; 10 Tennis available; 11 Swimming available; 12 Golf available; 13 Skiing available; 14 May be booked through travel agents.

Grant Corner Inn

122 Grant Avenue, 87501
(505) 983-6678

An exquisite Colonial manor home in downtown Santa Fe. Just two blocks from the historic plaza, the inn nestles among intriguing shops, restaurants, and galleries. Each room is appointed with antiques and treasures from around the world: quilts, brass and four-poster beds, armoires, and art. Private telephones, cable TV, and ceiling fans. Wine is served in the evening.

Hosts: Louise Stewart and Pat Walter
Rooms: 15 (10 PB; 2 SB) $55-130
Full Breakfast
Credit Cards: A, B
Notes: 2, 3, 5, 10, 11, 12, 13, 14

Hacienda Vargas

P.O. Box 307, Algondones, 87001
(505) 867-9115

Romantic, secluded, and historic. Elegantly renovated. Amid the majestic New Mexico Mesas, by the Rio Grande, and lined by cottonwood trees. Four rooms with fireplaces, private baths, and private entrances. One room with two-person Jacuzzi. Barbecue and open-air hot tub area. Few minutes south of Santa Fe and north of Albuquerque. Romance packages available. A place of enchantment in the land of enchantment.

Hosts: Pablo and Julia De Vargas
Rooms: 4 (PB) $69-129
Full Breakfast
Credit Cards: A, B
Notes: 4 (by arrangement for groups), 5, 8 (over 12), 9, 12, 13, 14

Inn of the Animal Tracks

707 Paseo de Peralta, 87501
(505) 988-1546

Inn of the Animal Tracks is a whimsical, warm bed and breakfast inn three blocks east of the Santa Fe Plaza. The best homemade full breakfast in Santa Fe will send guests home full and happy. Two sweet cats and one loving dog are part of the staff. The rooms boast vigas, handmade furniture, feather mattresses and comforters, cable TV, clock radios, and private baths. Shaded, landscaped patio. Fully air-conditioned.

Host: Myrna Wheeler
Rooms: 5 (PB) $90-130
Full Breakfast
Credit Cards: A, B, C, D
Notes: 2, 5, 8, 9, 10, 11, 12, 13, 14

Mi Casa Su Casa

P.O. Box 950, Tempe, AZ 85280-0950
(602) 990-0682; (800) 456-0682

1801. Santa Fe Territory-style accommodations in the Canyon Road Historic District, a mixed zoning area of shops, restaurants, and residences. Guests can choose from two separate accommodations sharing a courtyard behind a shop. The suite consists of a bedroom with a queen-size bed, a sitting room with futon and fireplace, full bath, and kitchenette. The compact casita has a queen-size bed, kitchenette, and bath. Santa Fe furnishings, quality linens and toiletries, original art, and Mexican tile floors. Self-catering continental breakfast. Higher rates during holidays and special area events. $85-169.

1814. Secluded and quiet, this more than 70-year-old adobe home is on a narrow lane in the heart of the historic eastside of Santa Fe. Surrounded by rock walls, a coyote fence, and old gates, it is minutes from Canyon Road art galleries, shops, restaurants, the Plaza, and museums. The host is a retired writer for a major newspaper, and the guest wing is a lovely L-shaped accommodation with a kiva fireplace, private bath, mini-refrigerator, coffee maker, telephone, and daily maid service. Minimum stay is two nights. No children. Continental plus breakfast. $85.

El Paradero

220 West Manhattan, 87501
(505) 988-1177

NOTES: Credit cards accepted: A MasterCard; B Visa; C American Express; D Discover Card; E Diner's Club; F Other; 2 Personal checks accepted; 3 Lunch available; 4 Dinner available; 5 Open all year;

Just a short walk from the busy Plaza, this 200-year-old Spanish farmhouse was restored as a charming Southwestern inn. Enjoy a full gourmet breakfast, caring service, and a relaxed, friendly atmosphere. The inn offers lots of common space and a patio for afternoon tea and snacks.

Hosts: Thom Allen and Ouida MacGregor
Rooms: 14 (10 PB; 4 SB) $40-125
Full Breakfast
Credit Cards: None
Notes: 2, 5, 6, 8 (over 4), 9, 10, 11, 12, 13, 14

El Paradero

Territorial Inn

215 Washington Avenue, 87501
(505) 989-7737

Elegantly remodeled, 100-year-old home just one block north of historic Plaza. Ten rooms, some with fireplaces, cable TV, and telephones. Hot tub in rose garden. Continental-plus breakfast, afternoon treats, and brandy turn-down. Personal service is the hallmark of the hostess.

Host: Lela McFerrin
Rooms: 10 (8 PB; 2 SB) $80-160
Continental Breakfast
Credit Cards: A, B
Notes: 2, 5, 10, 11, 12, 13, 14

SOCORRO

The Eaton House Bed and Breakfast Inn

403 Eaton Avenue, 87801
(505) 835-1067

Thick walls and high ceilings combine comfort with a sense of history in this 1881 adobe. In the formal dining room guests are pampered with a full breakfast of homemade specialties. Rooms open onto the wide brick portal. Relax and enjoy the antics of swarms of hummingbirds. A breakfast basket enhances a morning exploration of the Bosque Del Apache Wildlife refuge. No smoking.

Hosts: Anna Appleby and Tom Harper
Rooms: 5 (PB) $75-120
Full Breakfast
Credit Cards: B, C
Notes: 2, 3, 5, 9, 12

TAOS

American Artists Gallery House

P.O. Box 584, 87571
(505) 758-4446; (800) 532-2041

Charming Southwestern hacienda filled with artwork by American artists. Gourmet breakfasts, adobe fireplaces, private baths, outdoor hot tub, and gardens. Magnificent view of mountains. Minutes from art galleries, museums, restaurants, St. Francis Assisi Church, and ski valley.

Hosts: LeAn and Charles Clamurro
Rooms: 7 (PB) $70-140
Full Breakfast
Credit Cards: A, B
Notes: 2, 5, 9, 10, 11, 12, 13, 14

B&B of New Mexico

P.O. Box 2805, Santa Fe, 87504
(505) 982-3332

6 Pets welcome; 8 Children welcome; 9 Social drinking allowed; 10 Tennis available; 11 Swimming available; 12 Golf available; 13 Skiing available; 14 May be booked through travel agents.

209. This two-story house on a quiet corner is near the Plaza. Two huge rooms with private baths, one upstairs and one downstairs on opposite ends of the house. The living room offers a stone fireplace. There is artwork throughout the house. $85-95.

Hacienda del Sol

The Brooks Street Inn

119 Brooks Street, Box 4954, 87571
(505) 758-1489

Selected as one of the ten best inns of North America for 1988 by *Country Inns* magazine. The atmosphere is casual and fun. Just a short walk from the Plaza. The rambling main house and charming guest house feature fireplaces, reading nooks, skylights, and private baths. Full espresso bar.

Hosts: Carol Frank and Larry Moll
Rooms: 6 (PB) $81.58-104.97
Full Breakfast
Credit Cards: A, B, C
Notes: 2, 5, 8, 9, 11, 12, 13, 14

Casa Encantada

416 Liebert Street, P.O. Box 6460, 87571
(505) 758-7477; (800) 223-TAOS

A few short blocks from the Taos Plaza—in a world of its own—experience Casa Encantada. Peace, beauty, and warm hospitality abound within the adobe walls of this beautiful estate. The ten rooms have private entrances and private baths. Each room and suite is designed for charm and comfort, portraying the diversity of the area. Healthy breakfasts including fruit cereals, home-baked goodies, and Southwest delights are served in a sunny, plant-filled atrium. Information to enhance the Taos experience is generously provided.

Host: Sharon Nicholson
Rooms: 10 (PB) $65-125
Full Breakfast
Credit Cards: A, B, C
Notes: 2, 5, 6 (call), 8 (call), 10, 12, 13, 14

Hacienda del Sol

P.O. Box 177, 87571
(505) 758-0287

A 180-year-old historic, charming, quiet adobe with fireplaces, viga ceilings, and surrounded by century-old trees. Guest rooms have down comforters, carefully selected furnishings, and fine art. Enjoy an unobstructed view of the Taos mountains from the deck of the outdoor hot tub. Generous breakfasts are served by a crackling fire in the winter, or on the patio in the summer. Chosen by *USA Weekend* as one of America's ten most romantic inns. One mile north of Taos Plaza.

Hosts: John and Marcine Landon
Rooms: 9 (PB) $65-120
Full Breakfast
Credit Cards: None
Notes: 2, 5, 8, 9, 10, 11, 12, 13, 14

Mabel Dodge Luhan House

P.O. Box 3400, 87571
(505) 758-9456

The Mabel Dodge Luhan House is a National Historic Landmark. It serves as a bed and breakfast and an educational conference center. The Mabel Dodge Luhan House was a hideaway for some of the most creative people in this century. Now guests can experience some of the same creative environment that inspired such people as D. H. Lawrence, Mary Austin, Carl Jung, and Georgia O'Keeffe.

Rooms: 18 (15 PB; 3 SB) $75-150
Full Breakfast
Credit Cards: A, B
Notes: 2, 5, 8, 12, 13, 14

NOTES: Credit cards accepted: A MasterCard; B Visa; C American Express; D Discover Card; E Diner's Club; F Other; 2 Personal checks accepted; 3 Lunch available; 4 Dinner available; 5 Open all year;

The Mildred and Don Cheek Stewart House

P.O. Box 2326, 87571
(505) 776-2913; (505) 758-1399

Storybook house originally built by an artist as his home and studio. Each room is constructed from materials that are described as reclaimed parts of history. Bedrooms have private baths; many have private patios and fireplaces. A large outdoor hot tub has magnificent sunset and mountain views. Hearty breakfasts are served in the art gallery/common area. Rooms are filled with original artwork. Selected for the 1991, 1992, and 1993 editions of *America's Wonderful Little Hotels and Inns*. Also featured on "Great Country Inns" TV show on the Learning Channel. Converted into an inn in 1989 by owner Mildred Cheek.

Hosts: Mildred and Don Cheek
Rooms: 5 (PB) $75-120
Full Breakfast
Credit Cards: A, B
Notes: 2, 5, 9, 10, 11, 12, 13, 14

Orinda

461 Orinda Lane, 87571
(505) 758-8581

A 50-year-old adobe estate that combines spectacular views and country privacy, yet within walking distance to Taos Plaza. Three bedrooms with private baths and entrances. A hearty continental breakfast is served.

Orinda

Hosts: Cary and George Pratt
Rooms: 3 (PB) $70-90
Continental Breakfast
Credit Cards: A, B
Notes: 2, 5, 9, 10, 11, 12, 13

La Posada de Taos

309 Juanita Lane, Box 1118, 87571
(505) 758-8164; (800) 645-4803

La Posada de Taos, two and one-half blocks from the Taos Plaza, was created out of a turn-of-the-century home in the historic district. Soothing adobe walls lead guests to a shady garden, from where they enter a vaulted-ceiling foyer and living room centered around a traditional adobe fireplace. French doors in the dining room outline the mountains as guests savor a hearty breakfast. The service is highly personal and will draw guests back to Taos again. Minimum-stay requirements for weekends May through October and for holidays.

Hosts: Nancy and Bill Swan
Rooms: 6 (PB) $75-115
Full Breakfast
Credit Cards: None
Notes: 2, 5, 8, 12, 13, 14

El Rincon Bed and Breakfast

114 Kit Carson, 87571
(505) 758-4874

A special bed and breakfast in a historic adobe home, conveniently nestled in the heart of Taos. It boasts a fine art collection distributed throughout. In the summer, breakfast is served on a flower-filled patio. In the winter, it is served near a blazing adobe fireplace. Breakfast is served early to those headed for Taos' fine ski areas. Most rooms have fireplaces, some have refrigerators and VCRs. Hot tub or Jacuzzi available. A lovely blend of old and new.

Hosts: Nina C. Meyers and Paul C. Castillo
Rooms: 12 (PB) $49-109
Continental Breakfast
Credit Cards: A, B, C
Notes: 2, 5, 6, 7, 8, 9, 10, 11, 12, 13, 14

6 Pets welcome; 8 Children welcome; 9 Social drinking allowed; 10 Tennis available; 11 Swimming available; 12 Golf available; 13 Skiing available; 14 May be booked through travel agents.

Salsa del Salto
Bed and Breakfast

P.O. Box 1468, 87529
(505) 776-2422; (800) 530-3097

Designed by world-renown architect Antoine Predock, this beautiful home offers eight guest rooms, each reflecting Southwestern earth tones and pastel colors. All are decorated to tend to the guests' every need, with king-size beds, down comforters, furniture specially designed by local artisans for Salsa del Salto, and original paintngs by Taos artists. As an added treat, all rooms have spectacular views of the mountains and mesas. Breakfast is a gourmet's delight. Hot tub, heated pool, and private tennis court.

Hosts: Dadou Mayer and Mary Hockett
Rooms: 8 (PB) $85-160
Full Breakfast
Credit Cards: A, B
Notes: 2, 5, 8 (over 6), 9, 10 and 11(on premises), 12, 13, 14

The Willows Inn

Corner of Kit Carson Road and Dolan Streets,
  NDCBU 4558, 87571
(505) 758-2558; FAX (505) 758-5445

The Willows Inn is a small bed and breakfast establishment on a secluded acre lot in the heart of Taos. The atmosphere within the adobe-walled buildings and grounds is one of elegance, refinement, and restful contemplation. Each of the inn's five guest rooms has a private entrance and private bath plus a welcoming Kiva fireplace, which is set daily. The rooms are decorated in a variety of themes highlighting the cultures unique to the Taos area. Listed on the national and state historic registries, the property and buildings were once the home and studio of the late E. Martin Hennings. Two-night minimum stay on holiday weekends.

Hosts: Janet and Doug Camp
Rooms: 5 (PB) $95-130
Full Breakfast
Credit Cards: A, B
Notes: 2, 5, 7 (limited), 8, 9, 10, 11, 12, 13, 14

TRUCHAS

Rancho Arriba

Box 338, 87578
(505) 689-2374

A European-style bed and breakfast with an informal and tranquil atmosphere, this traditional adobe hacienda is on a historic Spanish land grant. Spectacular mountain view in every direction, amid Colonial villages featuring traditional arts and architecture. Adobe churches, hand weaving, wood carving, and quilting.

Host: Curtiss Frank
Rooms: 4 (SB) $40-55
Full Breakfast
Credit Cards: A, B, E, F (Mesa Grande, C&B)
Notes: 2, 4, 5, 7 (limited), 8, 9, 13

NOTES: Credit cards accepted: A MasterCard; B Visa; C American Express; D Discover Card; E Diner's Club; F Other; 2 Personal checks accepted; 3 Lunch available; 4 Dinner available; 5 Open all year;

New York

American Country Collection

4 Greenwood Lane, Delmar, 12054
(518) 439-7001

097. This elegant turn-of-the-century Victorian home is on the bus route and just a few minutes' drive from all major area colleges, state buildings, and attractions. Six rooms, two private baths, and four shared baths. All rooms have telephones and air conditioning. Children over 12 welcome. Continental breakfast. Guests can use the TV in the living room. Off-street parking is provided. $49-79.

110. City convenience combined with quiet residential living makes this suburban ranch home an ideal location. Just one block from the bus line. In summer months, a hearty Continental breakfast is served on the screened porch. There's a redwood deck for sunning and a living room with a fireplace. One guest bedroom with shared bath. Double sofa bed also available. Children welcome. $55; $70 for two persons taking both rooms.

111. Once a residence for Albany's earliest extended families, this Victorian bed and breakfast also served as a tavern and grocery store. In the shadow of the Empire State Plaza. Twelve guest rooms with private baths, air conditioning, color cable TV, and telephone. Children are welcome. Smoking permitted. Cat resides in owner's apartment. $95-145.

142. Restored in 1991 as a private bed and breakfast inn, this in-town brownstone is registered as a historic landmark with the Historic Albany Foundation. Completed in 1881, it represents one of the earliest examples of a private building in Albany built in the Neo-Classical style of architecture. Twelve rooms on the second and third floors offer double and single beds, and one suite with two double beds features a working fireplace. Also, four studio suites with complete kitchen, double bed, and private bath. All guest rooms offer a private bath, except for six rooms that have one double bed apiece and share three hall baths. Breakfast includes bread and muffins, seasonal fresh fruit, cereal, juices and beverages, including gourmet tea and coffee. No pets. Children welcome. Smoking permitted. $49-110.

The International Bed and Breakfast Club, Inc.

504 Amherst Street, Buffalo, NY 14207
(800) 723-4262; FAX (716) 873-4462

NY1574PP. This century old Victorian home is in the heart of Pine Hills. Within a 30-minute drive of Saratoga Springs and the Adirondack and Catskill Mountains. Four rooms on the second floor have iron beds with feather mattresses and either shared or private baths. Continental breakfast is served in the large dining room. Off-street parking available. Smoking permitted on the front or back porch. $49-79.

Mansion Hill Inn

115 Philip Street at Park, 12202
(518) 465-2038

6 Pets welcome; 7 Smoking allowed; 8 Children welcome; 9 Social drinking allowed; 10 Tennis available; 11 Swimming available; 12 Golf available; 13 Skiing available; 14 May be booked through travel agents.

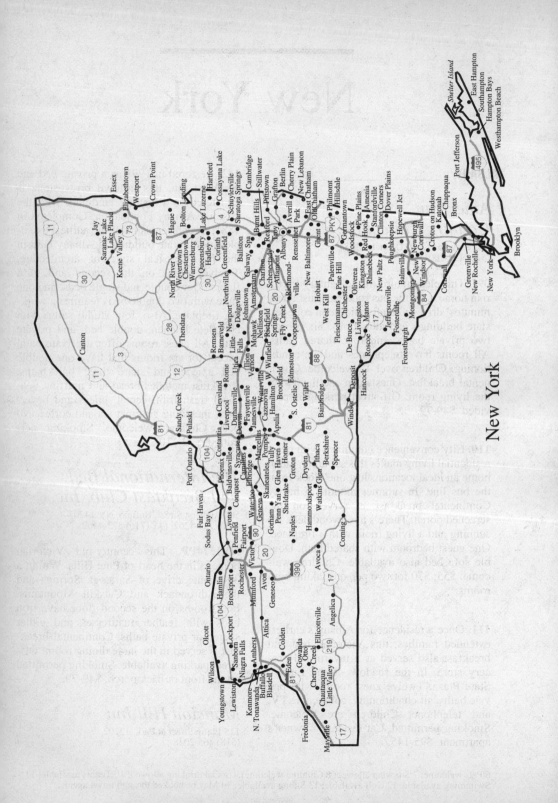

New York

Mansion Hill Inn

An urban inn, around the corner from the New York State Governor's Executive Mansion and Empire State Plaza in a quiet residential neighborhood. The inn is comprised of a complex of Victorian-era buildings centered around a landscaped courtyard. The inn boasts a four-star restaurant, which serves dinner, lunch, and guests' breakfast. All rooms feature individually controlled air conditioning, telephones, color TV, desks, and off-street parking. 1994 Chamber of Commerce Small Business of the Year.

Hosts: Maryellen, Elizabeth, and Steve Stofelano Jr.
Rooms: 8 (PB) $105-145
Full Breakfast
Credit Cards: A, B, C, D, E, F
Notes: 2, 3, 4, 5, 6, 7, 8, 9, 10, 11, 12, 13, 14

ALTAMONT

American Country Collection

4 Greenwood Lane, Delmar, 12054
(518) 439-7001

020. A renovation in 1910 added the large front pillars on the veranda to give the house its southern Colonial flavor, but this impressive home on the site of the first town meeting of Guilderland was actually built in 1765. It first served as a tavern and is now on the state and national historic registers. It is at the base of the Helderburg Mountains on six acres of grounds. Four guest rooms with shared baths. Pets in residence. Children welcome. Crib available. Smoking in common rooms on first floor. Charge for use of in-room fireplaces. Seasonal rates. $55-65.

045. This 75-year-old refurbished Colonial is just 20 miles from the state capitol. It is on 15 acres of well-groomed lawns, old shade trees, a swimming pool, barns, patio, and orchards. Business travelers find this location offers convenient access to both Albany and Schenectady. One third-floor suite has two bedrooms, living room, and private bath. One single room and one room with two twins or a king-size bed on the second floor shares the bath with the owner. Pets in residence. Children welcome. Smoking outdoors only. $40-60.

AMENIA

Covered Bridge

P.O. Box 447 A, Norfolk, CT 06058
(203) 542-5944

2AMNY. Contemporary home set on three acres has been tastefully decorated with antiques and paintings from the owner's gallery. A full breakfast is served in the dining room. The house has central air conditioning. There are four guest rooms, two of which share a bath. Double, twin, queen-, and king-size beds are available. House is available by the week also. $75-95.

Nutmeg B&B Agency

P.O. Box 1117, West Hartford, CT 06107
(203) 236-6698

343. A contemporary home in a 400-acre community offers a double bed and twin bedded room that share a bath. There is also a third-floor loft with a king-size bed and private bath. Close to prep schools and Lime Rock. Continental breakfast; children over eight welcome. Two resident cats.

NOTES: Credit cards accepted: A MasterCard; B Visa; C American Express; D Discover Card; E Diner's Club; F Other; 2 Personal checks accepted; 3 Lunch available; 4 Dinner available; 5 Open all year; 6 Pets welcome; 7 Smoking allowed; 8 Children welcome; 9 Social drinking allowed; 10 Tennis available; 11 Swimming available; 12 Golf available; 13 Skiing available; 14 May be booked through travel agents.

AMHERST

The International Bed and Breakfast Club, Inc.
504 Amherst Street, Buffalo, NY 14207
(800) 723-4262; FAX (716) 873-4462

NY4357PP. This center-entrance Colonial, convenient to downtown Buffalo and minutes from Niagara Falls, is a cozy and comfortable family home in one of Buffalo's most admired areas. Relax on the patio or in the library of this quality inn, minutes from the airport and college campus activities. Five rooms, shared bath. Continental breakfast plus coffee. $50.

AMSTERDAM

American Country Collection
4 Greenwood Lane, Delmar, 12054
(518) 439-7001

118. The guest rooms in this brick Federal Colonial have wide-pine floors, fireplaces, and are decorated with a mix of antiques, country furniture, and treasures found in the home. The history of the house is preserved in photos and mementos displayed throughout the home. Guests are treated to afternoon tea served in the English tradition with light pastries and sweet cakes. Three guest rooms with shared bath. Parakeet in residence. Children welcome. Crib available. No smoking. $35.

ANGELICA

The International Bed and Breakfast Club, Inc.
504 Amherst Street, Buffalo, NY 14207
(800) 723-4262; FAX (716) 873-4462

NY 3295PP. Guests can relax in this elegant mansion built in 1886. Five rooms with private baths are available. Stained-glass windows, crystal chandeliers, lofty ceilings, parquet floors, and oak staircase. Full breakfast is available. Three-diamond rating from AAA of Western New York. $60-70.

APULIA

Elaine's Bed and Breakfast Reservation Service
4987 Kingston Road, Elbridge, 13060
(315) 689-2082

This comfortable old white farmhouse has three guest rooms. Two have queen-size beds, and one has twin beds. Shared bath. The house is updated for convenience and safety and has a wonderful, quiet country setting, yet it's just five minutes from I-81. Full homemade breakfasts on weekends in the kitchen-family room, where guests can play the piano, enjoy the view of the distant hills, relax on the sofa, and stay warm by the wood stove. Close to three Central New York ski areas: Toggenburg, Laborador, and Song Mountain. Thirty minutes south of Syracuse and about 20 minutes north of Cortland. $50.

ATTICA

The International Bed and Breakfast Club, Inc.
504 Amherst Street, Buffalo, NY 14207
(800) 723-4262; FAX (716) 873-4462

NY1573PP. Warm, friendly hospitality in a country setting. This turn-of-the-century home is atop the rolling hills of Wyoming County. Three rooms, shared bath. Spectacular scenery, lovely landscaped grounds, gorgeous fall foliage viewing. Porch, patio, and fireplace. No smoking. Children welcome. Thirty-five miles east of Buffalo, 20 miles from Letchworth State Park. $45.

NOTES: Credit cards accepted: A MasterCard; B Visa; C American Express; D Discover Card; E Diner's Club; F Other; 2 Personal checks accepted; 3 Lunch available; 4 Dinner available; 5 Open all year;

AUBURN

Elaine's Bed and Breakfast Reservation Service
4987 Kingston Road, Elbridge, 13060
(315) 689-2082

A. On Owasco Lake, this magnificent 1910 Adirondack cottage-lodge features two spacious rooms, excellent craftsmanship throughout, solid wood paneling, and built-ins. Each room has picture windows overlooking the lake and double French doors opening onto a large screened porch filled with antique wicker and hung with plants. Each room has private half-bath and shares a full bath. The living room has a large fieldstone fireplace and an ever-changing view of the entire lake. Breakfasts are varied, with homemade hot casseroles, muffins, fruit, juice, coffee, and cold cereal. No smoking. No children under 12. No pets. No credit cards. $85.

B. Restored Victorian in the city, beautifully decorated with antiques and wicker. Five guest rooms, some with private baths. Full gourmet breakfast. $55-95.

AVERILL PARK

Ananas Hus Bed and Breakfast
Rural Route 3, Box 301, 12018
(518) 766-5035

The Tomlinsons' hillside ranch home, in West Stephentown on 30 acres, offers a panoramic view of the Hudson River Valley with its natural beauty and tranquility. Patio dining in summer and the warmth of a fireplace in winter. Skiing and culture abound in nearby western Massachusetts and the capital district of New York state. Closed Christmas Day.

Hosts: Thelma and Clyde Tomlinson
Rooms: 3 (SB) $45-60
Full Breakfast

Credit Cards: B, C
Notes: 2, 5, 8 (over 12), 9, 11, 12, 13

The Gregory House Restaurant and Country Inn
P.O. Box 401, 12018
(518) 674-3774; (800) 497-2977
FAX (518) 674-2977

Built in 1830, The Gregory House provides gracious dining and hospitality and an outstanding wine list. Chef/owner Christopher Miller and wife Melissa add their personal touch. Chris is a graduate of the Culinary Institute of America with a completed one-year apprenticeship in Switzerland. Guest rooms, all with private baths, are decorated in Victorian style. Guests can enjoy the inn's grounds, nearby lakes, golf links, and downhill and cross-country skiing. Excellent location for parents and students visiting the local colleges of Albany, Troy, and New York state's capital district.

Hosts: Melissa and Chris Miller
Rooms: 12 (PB) $80
Continental Breakfast
Credit Cards: A, B, C, E
Notes: 4, 5, 9, 10, 11, 12, 13, 14

The Gregory House

AVOCA

Patchwork Peace Bed and Breakfast
4279 Waterbury Hill, 14809
(607) 566-2443

6 Pets welcome; 8 Children welcome; 9 Social drinking allowed; 10 Tennis available; 11 Swimming available; 12 Golf available; 13 Skiing available; 14 May be booked through travel agents.

Enjoy the sights, sounds, and smells of a real farm. Visit dairy cows and calves. Observe the patchwork of fields in different hues of greens and golds. Take a delightful walk. This 1920 farmhouse with natural floors and woodwork and light, airy bedrooms affords a gentle night's sleep nestled in sun-dried linens. Heirloom quilts throughout. Incredibly quiet. Country breakfast with hosts. Spend a night or a week. Special weekly rates.

Hosts: Bill and Betty Mitchell
Rooms: 3 (1 PB; 2 SB) $40-65
Full Breakfast
Credit Cards: None
Notes: 2, 5, 9

AVON

The International Bed and Breakfast Club, Inc.

504 Amherst Street, Buffalo, NY 14207
(800) 723-4262; FAX (716) 873-4462

NY2838PP. This 30-room mansion, built in 1894, is a private estate on a winding, tree-lined drive. Nestled among 400 acres of Genessee Valley farmland, it features seven rooms, some with private baths. Complimentary cheese and fruit each evening on the veranda or in front of a crackling fire in the library. It's also a perfect setting for special occasions, celebrations, anniversaries, weddings and receptions, retreats, seminars or meetings, showers, rehearsal dinners, or family reunions. In-ground swimming pool. Children welcome. Smoking is limited to porches and living room. $65-125.

BAINBRIDGE

Berry Hill Farm

Rural Delivery 1, Box 128, 13733
(607) 967-8745

A friendly, informal atmosphere. Sunrises, sunsets, stargazing, fresh air, views. Restored 1820s farmhouse on a hilltop sur-

Berry Hill Farm

rounded by vegetable, flower, and herb gardens. On its 180 acres guests can hike, swim, birdwatch, pick berries, skate, cross-country ski, or just sit on the wraparound porch and watch the nature parade. The rooms are furnished with comfortable antiques, and a scrumptious country breakfast is served. A 10-minute drive takes visitors to restaurants, golf, tennis, auctions, and antique centers.

Hosts: Jean Fowler and Cecilio Rios
Rooms: 4 (SB) $60-70
Full Breakfast
Credit Cards: A, B, C
Notes: 2, 5, 7, 8, 9, 10, 11, 12, 13, 13, 14

BALDWINSVILLE

Elaine's Bed and Breakfast Reservation Service

4987 Kingston Road, Elbridge, 13060
(315) 689-2082

Spacious, historic Colonial in the village. The home was built around 1845 and, in keeping with its character, is decorated with many antiques and collectibles. Four guest rooms available, some with private bath and one with working fireplace. The house is on two acres high on a hill, a short walk to stores and the picturesque Seneca River. $50-80.

BALLSTON SPA

American Country Collection

4 Greenwood Lane, Delmar, 12054
(518) 439-7001

NOTES: Credit cards accepted: A MasterCard; B Visa; C American Express; D Discover Card; E Diner's Club; F Other; 2 Personal checks accepted; 3 Lunch available; 4 Dinner available; 5 Open all year;

009. This renovated Second Empire Victorian is the focal point of the historic district of this tiny village. The home is divided into two segments. The rear bed and breakfast section has a private entrance, guest living room with fireplace, dining room, kitchen, and porch for afternoon refreshments. The second floor has two guest rooms, each with a private bath and queen-size bed. Rooms in this section are ideal for family gatherings and groups of four traveling together. There are three additional rooms in the front section, each with a queen-size bed and private bath. Smoking outdoors only. No pets. Children over 11 welcome. Younger children permitted when entire bed and breakfast section is rented to one party. $75-175.

119. This working farm and girls' summer riding academy is on 100 acres of rolling meadows and scenic farmland. Riding lessons are available on the indoor riding arena. A heated swimming pool on the premises is available for guest use. The two guest bedrooms, one with private bath, have air conditioning. There is also a full apartment on the lower level during off-season. No smoking. Children welcome. Crib available, but guests should bring crib linens. Dogs and cats indoors; horses, ducks, geese, goats on the farm. $65-95.

BALMVILLE

The Red Caboose

476 River Road, 12550
(914) 561-1715

An authentic restored New York Central Railroad caboose. It features built-in twin berths with an additional berth over the bathroom, air conditioning, TV, kitchenette, and sitting room with wood-burning stove. Beautiful landscaping overlooking the majestic Hudson River with in-ground pool and cabana. Only 13 miles to West Point, 40 minutes to Hyde Park, and 60 minutes to New York City. Private entrance, unique accommodations, and Continental breakfast. Pets in residence.

Hosts: Doris and Kenneth Sheeleigh
Room: 1 (PB) $70-80
Continental Breakfast
Credit Cards: None
Notes: 2, 6, 7, 8 (over 12), 9, 11, 13, 14

BARNEVELD

Bed and Breakfast Leatherstocking

P.O. Box 53, Herkimer, 13350
(315) 733-0040; (800) 941-BEDS (2337)

001. Grand scale farmhouse from the Victorian era, graciously remodeled and restored with large entrance hall, formal living room, dining room, and informal family rooms and fireplaces. Short ride from Utica. Close to area colleges and ski centers. Network security system in operation, house and grounds surrounded by stockade fencing, private suite with sitting room, one king suite with private bath. Two singles with shared baths. Gourmet breakfasts and fresh flowers daily. $40-90.

BERKSHIRE

The International Bed and Breakfast Club, Inc.

504 Amherst Street, Buffalo, NY 14207
(800) 723-4262; FAX (716) 873-4462

NY4455PP. An elegantly restored 1809 farmhouse on three picturesque acres of manicured lawns and gardens. Four charming guest rooms furnished with antiques and handcrafted rugs, with shared baths. The farmhouse also has a fireplace, patio, whirlpool and private entrance. Full breakfast. $60-80.

6 Pets welcome; 8 Children welcome; 9 Social drinking allowed; 10 Tennis available; 11 Swimming available; 12 Golf available; 13 Skiing available; 14 May be booked through travel agents.

The Sedgwick Inn

BERLIN

The Sedgwick Inn

Route 22, 12022
(518) 658-2334

A historic Colonial inn on 12 acres in the scenic Taconic Valley, beautifully furnished with antiques. The inn is close to the Williamstown Theater, the Tanglewood Festival, other Berkshire attractions, and both downhill and cross-country skiing. There is a renowned restaurant and a small motel unit behind the main house. Pets and children allowed in the motel portion of the inn only.

Hosts: Edith Evans
Rooms: 10 (PB) $65-95
Suite: 1 (PB) $115
Full Breakfast
Credit Cards: A, B, C, D, E
Notes: 2, 3, 4, 5, 6, 7, 8, 9, 10, 11, 13, 14

BLASDELL

The International Bed and Breakfast Club, Inc.

504 Amherst Street, Buffalo, NY 14207
(800) 723-4262; FAX (716) 873-4462

NY8989PP. This quaint bed and breakfast offers homespun hospitality. It features three bedrooms with shared bath and is an ideal setting for families. Continental breakfast served daily. $40.

BOLTON LANDING

American Country Collection

4 Greenwood Lane, Delmar, 12054
(518) 439-7001

056. This 11-room farmhouse was built in 1926 as the caretaker's cottage for a large estate on Millionaire's Row along the west side of Lake George. Two second-floor rooms with shared bath. Third second-floor room has a private bath. Cottage (May to October) has private bath, refrigerator, and full breakfast. Children over four welcome. Pets in residence. Swimming, fishing and ice fishing, skating, parasailing, and boating are available. Just 20-25 miles to Fort Ticonderoga and Great Escape Amusement Park. $50-65.

Hilltop Cottage Bed and Breakfast

Lake Shore Drive, P.O. Box 186, 12814
(518) 644-2492

Clean, comfortable, renovated farmhouse in the beautiful Lake George/eastern Adirondack region. Walk to restaurants, the beach,

Hilltop Cottage

and marinas. Hearty full breakfast, homey atmosphere with helpful hosts.

Hosts: Anita and Charlie Richards
Rooms: 3 (1 PB; 2 SB) $50-60
Full Breakfast
Credit Cards: A, B
Notes: 2, 5, 8, 9, 10, 11, 12, 13

BROCKPORT

The International Bed and Breakfast Club, Inc.

504 Amherst Street, Buffalo, NY 14207
(800) 723-4262; FAX (716) 873-4462

NY0220PP. This historic Greek Revival landmark includes three porches, massive columns, pediments, and a cupola. This 1850 mansion, with three guest rooms and shared bath, is nestled among sycamore, maple, and blue spruce trees. Surprisingly detailed Victorian Continental breakfast served, along with Kettledrum (afternoon tea). Three fireplaces, antiques, chocolates, music-box melodies, and aromatherapy to pamper and exhilarate the spirit. Near colleges, parks, golf courses, lake, antique stores, and shops. Smoking in permitted areas only. No pets. $45-50.

BRONX

Le Refuge Inn Bed and Breakfast

620 City Island Avenue, 10464
(718) 885-2478; FAX (212) 737-0384

The Le Refuge Inn Bed and Breakfast, a 100-year-old Victorian, offers guests six rooms with queen-size beds and shared bath and one suite with private bath. There is also one room with twin beds. In the country just 20 minutes from Manhattan.

Hosts: Pierre and Emmanuelle Saint-Denis
Rooms: 8 (1 PB; 7 SB) $75-125
Continental Breakfast
Credit Cards: C
Notes: 2, 4 5, 8, 9, 10, 11, 12, 14

BROOKFIELD

Gates Hill Homestead

P.O. Box 96, Dugway Road, 13314
(315) 899-5837

A quiet, secluded pioneer-type farmstead, cleared, designed, and built by owners. Unusual saltbox open-beamed construction with massive central fireplace, wide-plank flooring, stenciling, candle chandeliers. Air-conditioned, delicious full breakfasts. Selected in 1987 by *Frommer's Guide to Bed & Breakfasts in North America* as one of the 100 best. Optional entertainment: 70-minute, four-horse stagecoach tour of "the eternal hills," followed by elegant country dinner, all home-cooking, by reservation.

Hosts: Charlie and Donna Tanney
Rooms: 3 (2 PB; 1 SB) $54-74
Full Breakfast
Credit Cards: A, B
Notes: 2, 4, 5, 7, 8, 13

BROOKLYN

Bed and Breakfast on the Park

113 Prospect Park West, 11215
(718) 499-6115

This opulent 1892 limestone Victorian four-story mansion is fully renovated and decorated in period antiques, Oriental rugs, stained-glass windows, and original paintings. Guests enjoy the ambience of gracious living from the turn of the century. Original mantels and woodwork with modern amenities. In Brooklyn just two miles from Manhattan; one-half mile from the Brooklyn Museum and Botanic Gardens; two blocks from shopping and restaurants. Guests keep coming back to this charming Big Apple inn.

Host: Liana Paolella
Rooms: 6 (4 PB; 2 SB) $100-175
Full Breakfast
Credit Cards: A, B
Notes: 2, 5, 7 (limited), 8, 9, 10, 14

6 Pets welcome; 8 Children welcome; 9 Social drinking allowed; 10 Tennis available; 11 Swimming available; 12 Golf available; 13 Skiing available; 14 May be booked through travel agents.

BUFFALO

Bryant House

236 Bryant Street, 14222
(716) 885-1540

Stay in a charming Victorian house, a pleasant and reasonable alternative to commercial accommodations. Five minutes to downtown and the Canadian border: convenient to theaters, boutiques, excellent restaurants, and Niagara Falls. A delicious Continental breakfast is served in the formal dining room or on the multilevel deck, weather permitting. Brochure on request.

Host: John C. Nolan
Rooms: 3 (PB) $50-60
Continental Breakfast
Credit Cards: None
Notes: 2 (for deposit), 5, 8, 9, 14

Bryant House

The International Bed and Breakfast Club, Inc.

504 Amherst Street, 14207
(800) 723-4262; FAX (716) 873-4462

NY0770PP. Find charming accommodations in this Westside Buffalo inn, circa 1870, with an Oriental flavor. It can accommodate up to three persons in its double room and adjoining but separate single room, each with twin beds. Shared bath with tub and shower. Full gourmet breakfast served daily, under skylight in dining area or on the lovely deck overlooking the yard, pool, and garden. Con-veniently minutes from the Peace Bridge to Canada, downtown Buffalo, and historic Allentown. Off-street parking available. Pets considered. $50-60.

NY1428PP. This 1910 Victorian home, designed by well-known architect E. B. Green, features one bright, air-conditioned suite with sauna, porch, and private entrance. It can accommodate up to five adults and includes a double bed, roll away, pullout sofabed and crib, with private bath. TV, refrigerator, and microwave in room. Continental and full breakfasts are served. Blocks from restaurants, shops, colleges, museums, and park; five minutes to downtown Buffalo, ten minutes to Canada. Smoking accepted. Children welcome. Extended-stay discount available. $60-65.

NY1540PP. Stay in a charming Victorian house, a pleasant and reasonable alternative to more commercial accommodations. Offering three rooms with private baths, this lovely house also has antiques, a fireplace, and a patio. Convenient to theaters, boutiques, excellent restaurants, and Niagara Falls; five minutes to downtown Buffalo and Canada. A delicious Conti-nental breakfast is served in the formal dining room or on the multilevel deck. $50-60.

Warnick's Village Bed and Breakfast

328 Wardman Road, 14217
(716) 875-5860

NOTES: Credit cards accepted: A MasterCard; B Visa; C American Express; D Discover Card; E Diner's Club; F Other; 2 Personal checks accepted; 3 Lunch available; 4 Dinner available; 5 Open all year;

The hosts welcome guests to this three-story wood-frame home on a residential tree-lined street just north of the city of Buffalo. Bedrooms are furnished with antiques, and fluffy robes are provided for comfort. The home is just minutes from historical Allentown, antique shops, Albright-Knox Art Gallery, the Buffalo waterfront, and many fine restaraunts. Wake up to the aroma of freshly ground coffee, locally made sausage, homemade muffins, and fresh fruit.

Hosts: Connie and Fred Warnick
Rooms: 2 (SB) $50
Full Breakfast
Credit Cards: None
Notes: 5, 7 (limited), 8, 9, 10, 12

BURNT HILLS

American Country Collection

4 Greenwood Lane, Delmar, 12054
(518) 439-7001

114. The oldest part of this home was built in 1796. The main house, a brick Center Hall Colonial, was completed about 150 years ago. The home is surrounded by trees and old-fashioned flower gardens that abut a 12-acre apple orchard. Two guest rooms with private baths. One guest room opens onto a third room to form a suite. Smoking limited to sitting room and outdoors. Children school-age and over welcome. No pets in residence but may accept guest pet (charge $10). $65-85.

CAMBRIDGE

American Country Collection

4 Greenwood Lane, Delmar, 12054
(518) 439-7001

010. The main house dates from 1896-1903 and features stained-glass windows, ceiling murals, and an Otis brass cage elevator. The carriage house offers a variety of eight suites, each with one to three bedrooms, living room, refrigerator, color TV, and private bath. Smoking permitted. Children welcome. Playpen available; no crib. No pets. $55-65.

CAMILLUS (SYRACUSE)

American Country Collection

4 Greenwood Lane, Delmar, 12054
(518) 439-7001

168. Italianate Colonial inn in a suburban/rural area, completely furnished with antiques and period pieces. Fully restored in 1980, there is also an attached full-service restaurant and pub serving lunch and dinner. Six rooms, all with private bath, air conditioning, and TV. Two of the rooms have a Jacuzzi. Continental breakfast. Children welcome. $60-99.

CANTON

White Pillars Bed and Breakfast

P.O. Box 185, 13617
(800) 261-6292

Experience classic antiquity and modern luxury in this beautifully renovated 1850s homestead. Guest room luxuries include whirlpool tub, marble floor, air conditioning, cable TV/VCR, and expansive windows overlooking 100 acres of meadows. Guests are invited to use the facilities of their hosts' 17-acre estate on Trout Lake, 20 minutes away, where they can enjoy swimming, canoeing, and fishing. Expect to be pampered, appreciated, and valued by the hosts.

Hosts: Donna and John Clark
Rooms: 5 (2 PB; 3 SB) $45-65

6 Pets welcome; 8 Children welcome; 9 Social drinking allowed; 10 Tennis available; 11 Swimming available; 12 Golf available; 13 Skiing available; 14 May be booked through travel agents.

Full Breakfast
Credit Cards: C
Notes: 2, 3, 4, 5, 8, 9, 10, 11, 12, 13

CAZENOVIA

American Country Collection

4 Greenwood Lane, Delmar, 12054
(518) 439-7001

162. Peaceful, quiet retreat directly on the shore of Lake Cazenovia. Unique, modern home furnished with antiques and collectibles from owner's world travels. Large living room with fireplace. Swimming at lake shore and rowboat available. First-floor room with queen-size bed, private deck, and bath. On second floor, one room with a queen-size bed and private bath, one room with twin beds and private bath, and one room with a single bed and shared bath. Continental breakfast is served in the dining room or on the outside patio. Smoking permitted. Handi-capped access. Children welcome. One dog in residence. $50-90.

Brae Loch Inn

5 Albany Street, US Route 20, 13035
(315) 655-3431

The 15 quiet rooms in this inn are on the second floor of the Brae Loch. They feature the old-time charm of antiques, classic luxury of Stickley furniture, and the modern comfort of some king-size beds in selected rooms. All rooms have private baths, and these rooms are so handsome and so reasonably priced that guests will want to visit over and over again.

Hosts: Jim and Val Barr
Rooms: 15 (13 PB; 2 SB) $75-125
Continental Breakfast
Credit Cards: A, B, C
Notes: 2, 4, 5, 7, 8, 9, 10, 11, 12, 13, 14

The Brewster Inn

Route 20 West, P.O. Box 507, 13035
(315) 655-9232

Built in 1890 on the shore of Cazenovia Lake, the Brewster Inn is an elegant country inn known for fine dining, gracious hospitality, and comfortable lodging. Three attractive dining rooms provide a relaxed atmosphere for superb American cuisine and an award-winning wine list. Seventeen hotel rooms offer variety in decor. Each room has a private bath, television, air conditioning, and telephone. Four rooms have Jacuzzis. Cazenovia offers quaint shops, swimming, hiking, golfing, cross-country and downhill skiing, and the impressive Chittenango Falls.

Hosts: Richard and Catherine Hubbard
Rooms: 17 (PB) $65-140
Penthouse: 3 rooms $195
Continental Breakfast
Credit Cards: A, B, D, E
Notes: 2, 4, 5, 8, 9, 10, 11, 12, 13

CHAPPAQUA

Crabtree's Kittle House

11 Kittle Road, 10514
(914) 666-8044

Built in 1790, Crabtree's Kittle House maintains a distinctive blend of country style and comfort. Only 20 miles from New York City, the inn is also a comfortable base from which to explore Van Cortlandt and Philipsburg manors, Sunnyside, and Pocantico Hills. Not to be missed are the dinner specialties of the house, including Dijon herb-crusted loin of free-range lamb and magret of Hudson Valley moulard duck with apricot Armagnac sauce and an award-winning wine list. Live jazz and dancing Thursday through Saturday.

Hosts: John and Dick Crabtree
Rooms: 11, $75-85
Continental Breakfast
Credit Cards: A, B, C, D, E, F
Notes: 2, 3, 4, 5, 7, 8, 9

NOTES: Credit cards accepted: A MasterCard; B Visa; C American Express; D Discover Card; E Diner's Club; F Other; 2 Personal checks accepted; 3 Lunch available; 4 Dinner available; 5 Open all year;

CHARLTON

American Country Collection

4 Greenwood Lane, Delmar, 12054
(518) 439-7001

087. A sense of history prevails throughout this pre-Revolutionary War estate set on 100 acres just a few miles west of Saratoga. One guest room on the first floor has wide-plank pine walls, built-in bookcases, cannonball bed, and comfortable sitting area. A second-floor master suite has a canopied bed and adjacent nursery, and, if needed, a third connecting room with double bed. Both rooms have private bath. Children welcome. Smoking permitted. $65-85.

CHAUTAUQUA

Plumbush

Rural Route 33, P.O. Box 864, 14722
(716) 789-5309

Newly restored, circa 1865, Italian villa on a hilltop surrounded by 125 acres. Just one mile from Chautauqua Institution. Bluebirds and wildlife abound. Bicycles available; cross-country ski trail. Sunny rooms, wicker, antiques, and a touch of elegant charm. As seen in *Victorian Homes,* Summer 1991, *Innsider* magazine, May/June 1990, and *Victoria* magazine, August 1989.

Hosts: George and Sandy Green
Rooms: 5 (PB) $80-95
Full Breakfast
Credit Cards: A, B, D
Notes: 2, 5, 9, 10, 11, 12, 13, 14

CHERRY CREEK

The International Bed and Breakfast Club, Inc.

504 Amherst Street, Buffalo, NY 14207
(800) 723-4262; FAX (716) 873-4462

NY8957PP. Every effort has been made to provide an environment of 19th-century grace, beauty, and comfort in this Italianate inn on 60 acres, with a four-acre stocked pond. Arched windows, multiple roofs, and antiques abound. Five guest rooms are available with private baths. A gourmet breakfast is served daily. Cockaigne Ski Resort is a five-minute drive, and fine cuisine may always be found at the Grainery restaurant. $65-85.

CHERRY PLAIN

Covered Bridge

P.O. Box 447 A, Norfolk, CT 06058
(203) 542-5944

1CPNY. This 1790 Colonial, nestled in the New York Berkshires, is secluded yet minutes from Tanglewood and summer theaters. Hiking trails, cross-country skiing, and a pond for fishing and skating are available on the grounds. Enjoy a full breakfast and dinner, both made with natural foods. The four guest rooms, two with antique canopied beds, have private baths. The rate includes dinner. $110.

CHESTERTOWN

Friends Lake Inn

Friends Lake Road, 12817
(518) 494-4751

In the Adirondacks, overlooking Friends Lake, the fully restored 19th-century inn is 20 minutes north of Lake George, with Gore Mountain Ski Center only 15 minutes away. Breakfast and gourmet dinner are served daily accompanied by an award-winning wine list. Mountain bike, swimming, hiking, and cross-country skiing facilities are on the inn's beautiful grounds.

Hosts: Sharon and Greg Taylor
Rooms: 14 (PB) $120-190
Full Breakfast
Credit Cards: A, B
Notes: 2, 4, 5, 7, 8, 9, 10, 11, 12, 13, 14

6 Pets welcome; 8 Children welcome; 9 Social drinking allowed; 10 Tennis available; 11 Swimming available; 12 Golf available; 13 Skiing available; 14 May be booked through travel agents.

CHICHESTER

Maplewood Bed and Breakfast

c/o Nancy Parsons
6 Park Road, 12416
(914) 688-5433

A lovely Colonial home in the heart of the Catskill Mountains, 12 miles from Hunter or Belleayre Mountain for skiing; close to fishing, tubing, antiquing, and hiking; 20 minutes to Woodstock. Single, double canopied, queen, and king bedrooms share two bathrooms. Each room has a different view of the mountains. Beautiful porch, gardens, and in-ground pool. A full breakfast is served.

Hosts: Nancy and Albert Parsons
Rooms: 4 (SB) $60
Full Breakfast
Credit Cards: None
Notes: 2, 5, 8, 10, 11, 12, 13

CLEVELAND

Bed and Breakfast Leatherstocking

P.O. Box 53, Herkimer, 13350
(315) 733-0040; (800) 941-BEDS (2337)

002. Spacious Victorian on the north shore of beautiful Oneida Lake, within close proximity to Syracuse, Oswego, Utica, Rome, and other central New York locales. In-ground pool. Host offers four double guest rooms with working fireplaces and private baths. Single unit beach house built over the lake boasts dramatic sunrises and moonlit nights with Jacuzzi, kitchenette, two bedrooms, two baths, sun deck, and small bar. Extended stays welcome. $37.50-150.

Elaine's Bed and Breakfast Reservation Service

4987 Kingston Road, Elbridge, 13060
(315) 689-2082

On the north shore of Oneida Lake, guests will find this circa 1820 white Colonial built by an early industrial baron. It has 6,000 square feet of living space. An open porch welcomes guests with antique wicker and a hammock. From the wide center hall, there is a large playroom with billiard table, jukebox, many musical instruments, and the owner's collection of prizes from showing his many antique automobiles. The family room features a large TV, stereo, and beautiful stained-glass leaded window behind the bar. All rooms are large and have working fireplaces and private baths. There is a formal living room full of antiques, a large cheery dining room with a player piano and more than 1,000 rolls. As this is a musical inn, there is an organ and a nickelodeon. A contemporary furnished beach house is also available for $170. Perfect for small conferences. No pets. No smoking. No children under 16. $50-75.

CLINTON CORNERS

American Country Collection

4 Greenwood Lane, Delmar, 12054
(518) 439-7001

181. This modern, air-conditioned, luxurious Greek Revival home is only 90 minutes away from the buzz of Manhattan. Guests enter a large living room with cathedral ceiling, floor-to-ceiling windows, and grand piano. Next comes a dining room decorated in floral patterns, connected to a Blue Stone patio where a full or Continen-tal breakfast is served, weather permitting. Master bedroom has king-size bed, working gas-log fireplace, private porch, and full marble bath with bidet and large Jacuzzi. Leading from the landing on the second floor are the other two spacious guest rooms, each with queen-size bed and private bath. Rhinebeck, the Aerodrome, FDR Home, Vanderbilt Mansion, and Clermont State Historic Site are only 10-15 miles away. $95-125.

NOTES: Credit cards accepted: A MasterCard; B Visa; C American Express; D Discover Card; E Diner's Club; F Other; 2 Personal checks accepted; 3 Lunch available; 4 Dinner available; 5 Open all year;

185. This romantic cottage with plain stucco exterior, only 90 minutes north of New York City, faces directly on a pristine lake. Attached to the cottage and overlooking the lake there is a shaded deck perfect for warm weather dining. Guests enter the cottage to a spacious, beautifully decorated living-dining area, all surrounded by picture windows. Off the living area is a bedroom with queen-size bed, ceiling fan, large walk-in closet, etc. Guests can relax on the deck, swim in the lake, fish for trout (poles provided), canoe, sail, or barbecue. The fridge is stocked with Continental breakfast fare, but for a real treat, guests are encouraged to go to the country store for a full breakfast. Area attractions (Acrodrome, FDR Home, Vanderbilt Mansion, Clermont State Historic Site, etc.) are only 10-15 miles away. $150.

195. Guests relax in a charming country cottage surrounded by colorful flower gardens and a winding brick path, bordering on a pristine lake for swimming, boating, fishing, ice skating, or cross-country skiing. This contemporary lakefront home has a common room with cathedral ceiling, colonial fireplace, and deck overlooking gardens and lake. Guest room is lakeside, with sitting room, TV, skylight, full private bath, and lakeview balcony. Furnishings are a mixture of Colonial and handcrafted Van Hoen furniture. Only 15 miles from Rhinebeck, Millbrook, Culinary Institute, Vanderbilt Mansion, Roosevelt Home and Library, and Hyde Park. $110.

COLDEN

Back of the Beyond

7233 Lower East Hill Road, 14033
(716) 652-0427

A charming country mini-estate in the Boston Hills and ski area of western New York; 25 miles from Buffalo and 50 from Niagara Falls. Accommodations are a separate chalet with three bedrooms, one and one-half baths, fully furnished kitchen, dining/living room, piano, pool table, and fireplace. Stroll through the organic herb, flower, and vegetable gardens; swim in the pond; or hike the woods. Cross-country ski trails on the premises; commercial downhill slopes are only one mile away.

Host: Shash Georgi
Rooms: 3 (SB) $60
Full Breakfast
Credit Cards: None
Notes: 2, 5, 8, 9, 10, 11, 12, 13, 14

The International Bed and Breakfast Club, Inc.

504 Amherst Street, Buffalo, NY 14207
(800) 723-4262; FAX (716) 873-4462

NY 6789PP. Guests will enjoy this scenic rural valley about 25 minutes southeast of Buffalo. The suite has double bed, private bath, living room with queen-size sofa bed, and a small kitchen. Continental breakfast includes home-baked breads and is served in the living area, on the deck, or on the garden table. $65.

CONQUEST

Elaine's Bed and Breakfast Reservation Service

4987 Kingston Road, Elbridge, 13060
(315) 689-2082

On ten private acres, surrounded by hundreds of acres of cornfields in lovely country peace and quiet, and nestled among fruit trees, there is a wonderfully restored old farmhouse with great wide woodwork, fireplaces, and three guest rooms at present (plans for three more plus pool and patio). Shared bath. Full breakfast. Children welcome. Conquest is on Route 38 north of Auburn about 14 miles and south of Fair Haven (on Lake Ontario) about 15 miles. It is not far from the New York State Thruway, I-90. It is a pleasant drive to the Finger Lakes, Oswego, and Syracuse. $45

6 Pets welcome; 8 Children welcome; 9 Social drinking allowed; 10 Tennis available; 11 Swimming available; 12 Golf available; 13 Skiing available; 14 May be booked through travel agents.

single; $55 double; $65 king; $10 per extra person in room.

CONSTANTIA

Elaine's Bed and Breakfast Reservation Service

4987 Kingston Road, Elbridge, 13060
(315) 689-2082

Large, cozy, and warm farmhouse overlooks Oneida Lake. Three guest rooms and bath upstairs, and two rooms with private baths downstairs. Next to restaurant. All freshly remodeled and cheery.

The International Bed and Breakfast Club, Inc.

504 Amherst Street, Buffalo, NY 14207
(800) 723-4262; FAX (716) 873-4462

NY9559PP. This spacious turn-of-the-century farmhouse, recently restored, is on Oneida Lake, 24 miles northeast of Syracuse. It features one queen-size bedroom on the main floor, with private bath and a deck overlooking the pool; on the second floor, two full-size rooms with lake views and one twin room all share a bath. A full breakfast is served in the cheerful dining room overlooking the lake, while Continental breakfast is served poolside. There are several fine restaurants nearby, as well as antique shops, golf courses, a fish hatchery, beaches, cross-country skiing, and shopping centers. $40-65.

COOPERSTOWN

American Country Collection

4 Greenwood Lane, Delmar, 12054
(518) 439-7001

128. Enjoy this rural farmhouse on 7.5 acres just outside historic Cooperstown.

Surrounded by a pond, sugar bush, hills, and meadows, this inn offers travelers a parlor room for relaxing or reading, an air-conditioned breakfast room, and an adjoining room with TV. Three bedrooms are available for guests. One room has two double beds and a private bath, and the other two rooms, with twin and double beds, share a full hall bath. Smoking outdoors only. Full country breakfast. Children are welcome. $45-65.

Angelholm

Angelholm

14 Elm Street, Box 705, 13326
(607) 547-2483; FAX (607) 547-2309

On a quiet residential street within easy walking distance of the Baseball Hall of Fame, museums, shops, restaurants, and other attractions. Angelholm is a gracious 1805 Federal-period home with comfortably elegant furnishings. Five rooms, all with private baths. A full breakfast is served in the formal dining room. Afternoon tea and lemonade are served on the veranda or in the living room. Off-street parking available.

Hosts: Jan and Fred Reynolds
Rooms: 5 (PB) $80-95
Full Breakfast
Credit Cards: A, B
Notes: 2, 5, 9, 10, 11, 12, 14

NOTES: Credit cards accepted: A MasterCard; B Visa; C American Express; D Discover Card; E Diner's Club; F Other; 2 Personal checks accepted; 3 Lunch available; 4 Dinner available; 5 Open all year;

Creekside
Bed and Breakfast

Rural Delivery 1, Box 206, 13326
(607) 547-8203

"A personal favorite," wrote American Express's *Travel & Leisure*. This nationally renowned bed and breakfast, also featured in *Country Inns* magazine, offers beautiful surroundings in an elegant atmosphere. Its elegant Colonial features, bridal suite, honeymoon cottage, and penthouse suite are ideal for honeymooners, reunions, or romantic escapes. Hosts are founders of and performers with Glimmerglass Opera. Four guest rooms all have queen-size beds, private bath, TV/HBO. Five minutes to Baseball Hall of Fame.

Hosts: Gwen and Fred Ermlich
Rooms: 4 (PB) $70-125
Full Breakfast
Credit Cards: A, B, C
Notes: 2, 5, 8, 9, 10, 11, 12, 14

The Inn at Cooperstown

16 Chestnut Street, 13326
(607) 547-5756

The Inn at Cooperstown, built in 1874, continues to provide genuine hospitality within walking distance of all of Cooperstown's attractions. The 17 guest rooms, each with private bath, are simply decorated with the guests' well-being in mind. Enjoy the comfortable beds and the large, thirsty towels.

The Inn at Cooperstown

Relax in a rocking chair on the sweeping veranda shaded by 100-year-old maples or in front of the cozy fireplace in the sitting room. Off-street parking is available behind this award-winning inn. Open year-round.

Host: Michael Jerome
Rooms: 17 (PB) $80-100
Continental Breakfast
Credit Cards: A, B, C, D, E
Notes: 2, 5, 9, 10, 11, 12, 14

Serendipity
Bed and Breakfast

Rural Route 2, Box 1050, 13326
(607) 547-2106

Serendipity is a contemporary home, designed by a student of Frank Lloyd Wright, that offers a friendly, casual atmosphere and panoramic views of Otsego Lake in a quiet, serene setting with guests' own private entrance and deck. Rates include queen-size bed and a low-cholesterol breakfast, while guests enjoy the romantic, natural beauty of the surrounding woods and lake.

Host: Vera A. Talevi
Room: 1 (PB) $75-95
Full Breakfast
Credit Cards: None
Notes: 2, 9, 11, 12

CORINTH

American
Country Collection

4 Greenwood Lane, Delmar, 12054
(518) 439-7001

151. Travelers are graciously invited to share a most unusual country inn at the gateway to the Adirondacks, only minutes away from the villages of Saratoga Springs, Lake George, and Lake Luzerne. Five rooms, all with private baths, and an access ramp for handicapped guests is available. Saratoga, the racetracks, Skidmore College, and SPAC are all within an easy drive.

6 Pets welcome; 8 Children welcome; 9 Social drinking allowed; 10 Tennis available; 11 Swimming available; 12 Golf available; 13 Skiing available; 14 May be booked through travel agents.

Breakfast features a fresh fruit platter, juice selection, muffins with jam, Belgian waffles with cinnamon apples or strawberry blend, coffee, and tea. $50-99.

CORNING

DeLevan House

188 DeLevan Avenue, 14830
(607) 962-2347

Southern Colonial with homelike hospitality. Overlooking Corning. Quiet surroundings, outstanding accommodations, complimentary cool drink served on the beautiful screened porch. Free pick-up from and delivery to the airport. Member of the International Bed and Breakfast Club.

Host: Mary M. DePumpo
Rooms: 3 (1 PB; 2 SB) $55-85
Full Breakfast
Credit Cards: None
Notes: 2, 5, 7, 8 (over 10), 9, 11, 12, 13, 14

1865 White Birch Bed and Breakfast

69 East First Street, 14830
(607) 962-6355

Imagine a friendly, warm atmosphere in an 1865 Victorian setting. Cozy rooms await guests; both private and shared baths. Awake to the tantalizing aromas of a full home-baked breakfast. Walk to museums, historic Market Street, and the Corning Glass Center. Experience it all here.

Hosts: Kathy and Joe Donahue
Rooms: 4 (2 PB; 2 SB) $50-85
Full Breakfast
Credit Cards: A, B, C (deposit)
Notes: 2, 5, 8, 9, 11, 12, 13

The International Bed and Breakfast Club, Inc.

504 Amherst Street, Buffalo, NY 14207
(800) 723-4262; FAX (716) 873-4462

NY2347PP. This brick Colonial is in a quiet, residential neighborhood overlooking the city, one mile from Routes 15 and 17. It features three guest rooms, one with private bath. There are antiques and a small glass museum in the dining room. Full breakfast is served. Airport pick-up available. Private parking in drive. Close to Corning Glass Center, Rockwell Museum, Taylor Wine Company, and Watkins Glen Racetrack. Smoking restricted. Adults preferred; no pets. $55-85.

CORNWALL

American Country Collection

4 Greenwood Lane, Delmar, 12054
(518) 439-7001

184. Historic country estate built in traditional manor style with elegant Greek Revival front, set on seven acres of woodlands and gardens. Guests can step back in time and be surrounded with history and elegance. Play croquet, visit the neighboring farm's craft and gift shop, relax by the goldfish pond, walk through the formal gardens, or explore the rolling hills and mountains. Stay in one of nine sumptuously appointed, color-coordinated rooms or suites, all containing sitting-reading areas, private baths, and air conditioning. Breakfast is served in the breakfast room or the back veranda. Only one mile to the Storm King Art Center and Black Rock Forest hiking trails, five miles to West Point and Brotherhood Winery, and 11 miles to Bear Mountain for swimming and hiking. $105-250.

Cromwell Manor Inn

Angola Road, 12518
(914) 534-7136

An 1820 formal antebellum mansion set on a seven-acre, country-style estate offering nine rooms with private baths. The inn is

NOTES: Credit cards accepted: A MasterCard; B Visa; C American Express; D Discover Card; E Diner's Club; F Other; 2 Personal checks accepted; 3 Lunch available; 4 Dinner available; 5 Open all year;

furnished with antiques and with canopied and poster beds. A wonderful weekend retreat with romance awaits guests at the Manor. One hour north of New York City, and five miles north of historic West Point. Cromwell Manor sits in the Hudson Highland overlooking a 4,000-acre forest preserve with seven mountain lakes. A wonderful place to hike and picnic. Air-conditioned. Open year-round. Two or three-bedroom cottages are available with early booking; please inquire.

Hosts: Dale and Barbara Ohara
Rooms: 13 (12 PB; 1 SB) $95-250
Full Breakfast
Credit Cards: A, B
Notes: 2, 5, 8, 9, 10, 11, 12, 13, 14

COSSAYUNA LAKE

American Country Collection

4 Greenwood Lane, Delmar, 12054
(518) 439-7001

187. Designed and built by the host, this contemporary trilevel home sits on a hillside surrounded by pines on the shore of Lake Cossayuna. Inside, the cathedral ceiling, large rooms with sliding glass doors, and lots of space give the common room a light and airy openness. There is a huge rear deck for relaxing and dining; also for guest use are three fireplaces, a pool table, two TV viewing areas, and a 10-person Jacuzzi. Guests may swim in the adjacent lake fed by hot springs. Breakfast is served either in the kitchen or on the rear deck. Saratoga and Manchester, Vermont are 25 miles away, Willard Ski area is 18 miles; cross-country skiing and snowmobiling can be arranged locally. Deposit. $35-40.

CROTON-ON-HUDSON

Alexander Hamilton House

49 Van Wyck Street, 10520
(914) 271-6737

The Alexander Hamilton House, circa 1889, is a sprawling Victorian home on a cliff overlooking the Hudson. Grounds include a mini-orchard and in-ground pool. The home has many period antiques and collections. Guest accommodations include a queen-bedded suite with fireplaced sitting room, a double-bedded suite with fireplace and small sitting room, two large rooms with queen-size beds, and a bridal chamber with king-size bed, Jacuzzi, entertainment center, pink marble fireplace, and lots of skylights. There is also a new master suite with river view. Nearby attractions include West Point, the Sleepy Hollow Restorations, Lyndhurst, Boscobel, the Rockefeller mansion, hiking, biking, sailing, and New York City just an hour away. No smoking or pets. Children welcome. Off-street parking.

Host: Barbara Notarius
Rooms: 7 (3 PB; 4 SB) $75-250
Full Breakfast
Credit Cards: A, B, C, D
Notes: 2, 5, 8, 9, 11, 12, 14

American Country Collection

4 Greenwood Lane, Delmar, 12054
(518) 439-7001

157. Perfect for vacations, business travel, and romantic getaways, this stately Victorian home, circa 1889, is nestled on a cliff above the Hudson River, only a short walk from the picturesque village of Croton-on-Hudson. Luxurious without being ornate, this bed and breakfast offers three suites, each with a private bath and fireplace, three rooms on the second floor with private baths, and a third-floor suite with a king-size bed, fireplace, and full Jacuzzi. Breakfast offers juice, deep-dish pancakes, stuffed French toast or eggs, coffee, or tea. Smoking outside only. Train station is within close proximity. Children welcome. $95-250.

6 Pets welcome; 8 Children welcome; 9 Social drinking allowed; 10 Tennis available; 11 Swimming available; 12 Golf available; 13 Skiing available; 14 May be booked through travel agents.

CROWN POINT

American Country Collection

4 Greenwood Lane, Delmar, 12054
(518) 439-7001

095. It took three years for a team of Italian craftsmen to complete this 18-room Victorian mansion, circa 1887, on five and one-half acres in the center of this small town. Carved woodwork, doors, and stair railing from oak, cherry, mahogany, and walnut grace the home. Four of the five guest rooms have private baths. In winter, breakfast is served in front of the fireplace in the dining room. Fort Ticonderoga and Fort Crown Point are nearby. Children are welcome. $45-95.

DE BRUCE

De Bruce Country Inn on the Willowemoc

De Bruce Road, 12758
(914) 439-3900

In a spectacular 1,000-acre natural setting within the Catskill forests overlooking the Willowemoc trout stream, the inn offers turn-of-the-century charm and hospitality. Terrace dining, wooded trails, wildlife, pool, sauna, fitness and health center, fresh air, and mountain water. Stays from December 15 through April 1 by special arrangement only.

Hosts: Ron and Marilyn
Rooms: 15 (PB) from $70/person
Full Breakfast
Credit Cards: None
Notes: 2 (deposit), 4, 5 (limited), 6 (call), 7, 8, 9, 10, 11, 12, 13

DEPOSIT

American Country Collection

4 Greenwood Lane, Delmar, 12054
(518) 439-7001

194. Federal Greek Revival-style mansion built in 1820 is furnished with museum-quality antiques, Persian carpets, and hand-carved highboard beds. All rooms have private baths, special linens, air conditioning, TV, and bath amenities. Full breakfast served. King-size, double, and twin beds available. Gourmet dinners are a specialty. $85-135.

Bed and Breakfast Leatherstocking

P.O. Box 53, Herkimer, 13350
(315) 733-0040; (800) 941-BEDS (2337)

194. This 1820 Federal Greek Revival mansion is furnished with museum-quality antiques, persian carpets, and hand-carved highboard beds. All rooms have private baths, special linens, air conditioning, TV, and bath amenities. Smoking outside only. Children welcome. Full breakfast served. Resident cat. Gourmet dinners are a specialty. $85-135.

Chestnut Inn at Oquaga Lake

498 Oquaga Lake Road, 13754
(607) 467-2500; (800) 467-7676;
FAX (607) 467-5911

Built in 1928, the Chestnut Inn at Oquaga Lake is a classic example of architecture and building construction at its best. The inn is almost totally constructed of the now extinct North American chestnut wood. Enjoy the amenities of a lakeside resort. Guests can also enjoy the ultimate dining experience in a relaxed elegance in the main dining room, or casual dining in the lakeside sunroom or on the waterfront terrace. One of the unique pleasures here is the complimentary boat ride in the inn's replica launch, *Pickles*, that once graced the waters of the lake.

Hosts: James Gross (General Manager) and Richard Post (Innkeeper)
Rooms: 31 (7 PB; 20 SB) $69-99

NOTES: Credit cards accepted: A MasterCard; B Visa; C American Express; D Discover Card; E Diner's Club; F Other; 2 Personal checks accepted; 3 Lunch available; 4 Dinner available; 5 Open all year;

Credit Cards: A, B, C, D, E
Notes: 2, 3, 4, 7, 8, 9, 10, 11, 12, 13, 14

DEWITT

Elaine's Bed and Breakfast Reservation Service

4987 Kingston Road, Elbridge, 13060
(315) 689-2082

A. A nice comfortable home in a well-established residential neighborhood, convenient to highways, shopping, restaurants, downtown Syracuse, Syracuse University, LeMoyne College, and the Medical Center. Three rooms available for guests: two have double beds and one has a single bed. One and one-half baths. Deck overlooks stream. Full breakfast. Hostess is antique dealer and home is furnished with antiques and original art works. Smoke-free home. Children and dogs welcome. Very flexible. DeWitt adjoins Syracuse on the east. $50.

B. Near Shoppington, this fine, older Colonial is warmly furnished with some antiques. A large front guest room has an antique double bed, and a den with a sofabed is available for families. $55.

DOLGEVILLE

Adrianna Bed and Breakfast

44 Stewart Street, 13329
(315) 429-3249

Adrianna

Adrianna is just off the New York Thruway at Exit 29A, amid glorious views of the Adirondack foothills. Just a short ride to Cooperstown, Saratoga, Syracuse, and Utica areas. A most cozy and hospitable bed and breakfast. Minimum stay weekends and holidays is two nights.

Host: Adrianna Naizby
Rooms: 3 (1 PB; 2 SB) $50-60
Full Breakfast
Credit Cards: None

DOVER PLAINS

Covered Bridge

P.O. Box 447 A, Norfolk, CT 06058
(203) 542-5944

1DPNY. Genuine old farmhouse with a large sitting porch on which to relax and admire the views of the Connecticut hills. Enjoy a full farm breakfast in the sunny dining room or on the porch. Four beautifully appointed guest rooms, one with private bath, are decorated with the owner's collection of antique linens. There are three doubles and one room with twin beds. There is also a pool for guests to enjoy. $65-95.

Nutmeg B&B Agency

P.O. Box 1117, West Hartford, CT 06107
(203) 236-6698

311. Tucked just over the border from Kent, Connecticut, is this charming "Eyebrow" Colonial built in 1850. Guests can use the living room with TV, warm up by the wood-burning stove, lounge on the large front porch complete with wicker furniture, and enjoy the pool. All four guest rooms are on the second floor. Three rooms share a bath. The room with a private bath has a handsome double sleigh bed. All rooms have spectacular views of the surrounding countryside, a foliage lover's delight. Full breakfast. Children are welcome. Pets in residence.

6 Pets welcome; 8 Children welcome; 9 Social drinking allowed; 10 Tennis available; 11 Swimming available; 12 Golf available; 13 Skiing available; 14 May be booked through travel agents.

Sarah's Dream

DRYDEN

Sarah's Dream

47-49 West Main Street, P.O. Box 1087, 13053
(607) 844-4321

Guests are personally welcomed by owners
Judi and Ken to "a place to be coddled." On
the National Register of Historic Places,
this antique-furnished circa 1828 Federal-
style homestead is subtly elegant yet unpretentious. Enjoy deluxe rooms and suites, air
conditioning, fireplace, porches, library,
TV, VCR, herb and flower gardens, afternoon tea, and beds and breakfast to make
guests sigh. At edge of the village. Convenient to Cortland, Ithaca, Cornell, wineries,
and Finger Lakes.

Hosts: Judi Williams and Ken Morusty
Rooms: 4 (PB) $55-120
Suites: 2 (PB)
Full Breakfast
Credit Cards: A, B, C, D, E
Notes: 2, 5, 8 (over 10), 9, 10, 11, 12, 13, 14

Serendipity
Bed and Breakfast

15 North Street, P.O. Box 287, 13053
(607) 844-9589; FAX (607) 844-8311

Circa 1834 village home features stained-
glass windows, queen-size brass beds, and
a superb full breakfast. In Dryden Village

minutes to Cornell University, Greek Peak
Ski area, and Suny Cortland in the heart of
the Finger Lakes Recreation area. Optional dinners. Children welcome. Smoking allowed in the common rooms.
Afternoon and evening snacks included.
Packages available.

Rooms: 4 (1 PB; 3 S2B) $59-105
Credit Cards: A, B, F (JCB)
Notes: 2, 3, 4, 5, 8, 9, 10, 11, 12, 13, 14

DURHAMVILLE

American
Country Collection

4 Greenwood Lane, Delmar, 12054
(518) 439-7001

166. Completely restored 1800s farmhouse
and barn on three tree-shaded acres. Decorated in a country motif and furnished with
solid cherry furnishings. Four rooms with
queen-size, double, or single beds and
shared baths. Full breakfast; children welcome. Resident barn cat. Smoking in common rooms. $40-50.

Elaine's Bed and Breakfast
Reservation Service

4987 Kingston Road, Elbridge, 13060
(315) 689-2082

This stately old farm Colonial sits on its
own quiet three acres in the country yet has
easy access to all activities in the Oneida
Valley: Sylvan Beach, Verona Beach, fishing, boating, Vernon Downs, antique shops
on Route 20, historic Fort Stanwix in
Rome, Charlestown outlet shopping in
Utica, and several nearby colleges. The interior is brand-new and carpeted throughout. Four guest rooms share two full baths
and have individual heat control. TV/VCR
in living room. Check in is after 5:00 P.M.
during the week as owner works in Rome.
MasterCard and Visa. Children under five
free. $45-65.

NOTES: Credit cards accepted: A MasterCard; B Visa; C American Express; D Discover Card; E Diner's
Club; F Other; 2 Personal checks accepted; 3 Lunch available; 4 Dinner available; 5 Open all year;

EAST CHATHAM

American Country Collection

4 Greenwood Lane, Delmar, 12054
(518) 439-7001

201. Two rural, all-season cottages nestled on the side of a quiet country road, shaded by large pine trees. Each one has fully equipped kitchen, private bath, hardwood floors, charcoal grill, and outside tables and chairs. Guests supply their own breakfast, lunch, and dinner. Only minutes away from Jiminy Peak Ski Center. Cottages are within driving distance of Lenox/Tanglewood, Massachusetts (12 miles); Stockbridge, Massachusetts (15 miles); Albany (35 miles), Old Chatham and the Shaker Museum (3 miles), and the Hudson/Olana Historic Site (20 miles). $99.

EAST HAMPTON

Mill House Inn

33 North Main Street, 11937
(516) 324-9766

A 1790 Colonial in "America's most beautiful village." Open all year so guests can enjoy lemonade while overlooking the Old Hook windmill or a restful nap in the back yard hammock. In the off-season, enjoy afternoon tea by the fireplace or a brisk walk to the beach.

Hosts: Daniel and Katherine Hartnett
Rooms: 8 (6 PB; 2 SB) $100-190
Full Breakfast
Credit Cards: A, B, C
Notes: 2, 5, 8, 10, 11, 12

Mill House Inn

EDEN

Eden Inn Bed and Breakfast

8362 North Main Street, 14057
(716) 992-4814

The Eden Inn was built in 1904 and is the largest home in Eden, New York. Seventeen miles southwest of Buffalo, just one hour from Niagara Falls. The inn is near tourist trains, wineries, Buffalo Raceway, and Erie County Fairgrounds. Each room at the Eden Inn is tastefully appointed with a theme in mind, including the Rose Suite with private whirlpool tub, the Amish Room, the Train Room, the Vineyard Suite, and the Bluhmen Suite (whirlpool bath). Child and cats in residence. No smoking. Whirlpool suites.

Hosts: Betsy and Chris Wahts
Rooms: 5 (3 PB; 2 SB) $50-95
Continental Breakfast weekdays
  Full Breakfast weekends
Credit Cards: C
Notes: 2, 5, 8, 9, 11, 12, 13, 14

EDMESTON

Elaine's Bed and Breakfast Reservation Service

4987 Kingston Road, Elbridge, 13060
(315) 689-2082

Six varied guest rooms, two baths, above a fine restaurant. Great location in a tiny village near Cooperstown, Baseball Hall of Fame, Farmers Museum, Otsego Lake, cruises, golf, good restaurants, art galleries, and Glimmerglass Opera.

6 Pets welcome; 8 Children welcome; 9 Social drinking allowed; 10 Tennis available; 11 Swimming available; 12 Golf available; 13 Skiing available; 14 May be booked through travel agents.

ELBRIDGE

Elaine's Bed and Breakfast Reservation Service

4987 Kingston Road, 13060
(315) 689-2082

A freshly remodeled and decorated Ranch-style home in the country on five acres, just 20 minutes west of Syracuse, seven minutes from downtown Skaneateles, and 12 minutes from Auburn. There are two guest rooms with good firm double beds sharing one and one-half baths. Quiet, peaceful, cozy, and comfortable. Smoke-free. Resident cat. Continental plus breakfast, more if required. Open year-round. Hostess runs Elaine's Bed and Breakfast Reserva-tion Service and buys and sells small antiques. Off Route 321 between Routes 5 and 20. From the west on Route 90, use Weedsport exit, from the east take 690 over Syracuse. Syracuse is the nearest large city. $45-50.

Fox Ridge Farm Bed and Breakfast

4786 Foster Road, 13060
(315) 673-4881

A large farmhouse in a picturesque setting with expansive lawns and flower gardens, on a quiet rural road. Hiking and cross-country ski trails wander through 120 acres of forests and meadows with sparkling streams and abundant wildlife. Guests enjoy a large family room with grand piano, wood-burning stove, TV, and books. Bedrooms are individually decorated with floral wallpaper and handmade quilts. A hearty full breakfast is served in a large country kitchen with a stone fireplace.

Hosts: Marge and Bob Sykes
Rooms: 3 (1 PB; 2 SB) $55-65
Full Breakfast
Credit Cards: None
Notes: 2, 5, 8, 10, 11, 12, 13

ELLICOTTVILLE

Ilex Inn

P.O. Box 1585, 14731
(716) 699-2002; FAX (716) 699-5539

A turn-of-the-century Victorian farmhouse furnished with antiques and period decor. Each guest room has a private bath. Guests may enjoy the hot tub or heated in-ground pool and are offered terry robes and Turkish towels. The elegant yet comfortable living room features a fireplace, cable TV, and video library. The upstairs sitting room and library-gallery has morning coffee, parlor games, and a lovely view. The innkeepers' double-smoked ham or freshly squeezed orange juice may accompany the pumpkin-ginger pancakes or fresh fruit fritters as samples of the plentiful daily fare. Golf or ski packages, canoe excursions, mountain bikes, feather beds, and other amenities such as flannel bed sheets are available upon request.

Hosts: Bill and M. J. Brown
Rooms: 5 (PB) $75-145
Full Breakfast
Credit Cards: A, B
Notes: 5, 8, 9, 10, 11, 12, 13

ELIZABETHTOWN

American Country Collection

4 Greenwood Lane, Delmar, 12054
(518) 439-7001

072. This bed and breakfast, circa 1775, was a sawmill, a "dine and dance," a resident summer art school and home of Wayman Adams, and since 1972 a summer residence for student classical musicians. It is on two and one-half acres bordered on two sides by the Bouquet River, a favorite fishing and swimming hole for the locals. Five guest rooms available, four with private bath. In summer, breakfast is served on the covered stone patio that overlooks the grounds. Small cottages also available. Children welcome. Resident pets. $66-78.

Stony Water Bed and Breakfast

Rural Route 1, Box 69, 12932
(518) 873-9125; (800) 995-7295

On 87 wooded acres tucked in a quiet valley between two running brooks, Stony Water provides a perfect refuge from the complexities of today's world. Two hours from Montreal and Albany, a half-hour from Lake Placid, and minutes from major Adirondack High Peaks' trailheads. This historic, restored Italianate house has strong ties to its literary and artistic past: Robert Frost, Louis Untermeyer, and Rockwell Kent. Four guest rooms, each with private baths, have views of the extensive perennial gardens and surrounding countryside. One room opens onto the in-ground swimming pool and woodlands beyond; one is a small cottage in the back garden. Dinner available except during July and August. Rated "excellent" by the ABBA.

Hosts: Winifred Thomas and Sandra Murphy
Rooms: 4 (PB) $75-85
Cottage: 1
Full Breakfast
Credit Cards: A, B, C
Notes: 2, 3, 4, 5, 8, 9, 10, 11, 12, 13, 14

ESSEX

American Country Collection

4 Greenwood Lane, Delmar, 12054
(518) 439-7001

183. Sitting atop a slight rise and well back from the road, this completely renovated 1836 Greek Revival home boasts spectacular views of Lake Champlain and the surrounding mountains. House is on the National Register of Historic Places. Guests can savor the solitude just by walking down to the lake through heirloom gardens. Fur-

nishings are a mix of antiques and modern pieces. Each of the two guest rooms has a queen-size bed, ceiling fan, sitting area, and private bath. Continental breakfast is served on the rear deck or in the breakfast room. Essex Ferry to Vermont is a quarter of a mile away. Ausable Chasm, horseback riding, and Elizabeth Museum are all only 10 miles; Westport Summer Theater is 12 miles away. $95.

189. Overlooking Lake Champlain, this charming, fully restored farmhouse dates back to the mid-1800s. The original buildings, surrounded by rolling fields and large locust trees, are on the National Register of Historic Places. Guests entering the home find themselves first in the common room, which contains comfortable chairs, sectional couch, and TV. Next comes the kitchen with its authentic working wood-burning stove. Beyond the kitchen is the formal dining room, where either a full country or Continental breakfast (guest's choice) is served. Adjacent to the dining room is the living room, containing piano, entertainment center, and large fieldstone fireplace. Four guest rooms boast hardwood floors, Oriental rugs, antique furnishings throughout, and lake or mountain views. Historic Essex and Essex Ferry to Vermont is only two miles away, while Westport Summer Theater and horseback riding are only eight miles farther. $50-75.

FAIR HAVEN

Brown's Village Inn Bed and Breakfast

Box 378, Stafford Street, 13064
(315) 947-5817

Traveling the Seaway Trail? For old-fashioned hospitality and a warm welcome, stop by and enjoy quality accommodations in a quiet and relaxing atmosphere. Minutes

6 Pets welcome; 8 Children welcome; 9 Social drinking allowed; 10 Tennis available; 11 Swimming available; 12 Golf available; 13 Skiing available; 14 May be booked through travel agents.

to shops, restaurants, and the beach. Guest cottage and antique shop on premises.

Host: Sally Brown
Rooms: 5 (1 PB; 4 SB) $50-65
Continental Breakfast
Credit Cards: A, B, D
Notes: 2, 5, 8, 9, 10, 11, 12, 13, 14

FAIRPORT

Woods-Edge

151 Bluhm Road, 14450
(716) 223-8877

Woods-Edge is in a quiet area surrounded with trees and wildlife. Near Exit 45 (NYS I-90) and only 20 minutes from downtown Rochester. The home is artistically decorated with barn beams and antique pine furnishings. Home has two guest rooms with private baths. The on-premises guest house is fully equipped, including large fireplace, for a private, hideaway weekend. Delicious home-cooked breakfasts. Reser-vations requested.

Hosts: Bill and Betty Kinsman
Rooms: 3 (PB) $65-95
Full Breakfast
Credit Cards: None
Notes: 2, 5, 8, 9, 10, 12, 13, 14

FAYETTEVILLE

Bed and Breakfast Leatherstocking

P.O. Box 53, Herkimer, 13350
(315) 733-0040; (800) 941-BEDS (2337)

003. This is an authentic antebellum home, large painted brick, in the historic section of a pretty suburban town. Only ten minutes from Syracuse University and Lemoyne College. Five miles from Green Lake State Park. Thirty minutes from Clinton. Walking distance to Fayetteville Mall. Three baths provide optional private bath possibilities to four bedrooms. Full breakfast served on weekends; Continental breakfast served on weekdays. $45-70.

Elaine's Bed and Breakfast Reservation Service

4987 Kingston Road, Elbridge, 13060
(315) 689-2082

Italianate brick built in 1830 and 1854. Many antiques, wide plank floors upstairs, main living room has original pier mirror, walnut valances, fireplace, light fixtures. First floor has room with double futon and private bath and new guest sitting room. Second floor has three guest rooms. Large room has antique double bed, smaller room has antique double bed, third room has two double beds. One bath upstairs at present, new bath being built soon. Fayetteville is a fine suburb about five miles east of Syracuse on Route 5. This bed and breakfast is in the historic preservation area. One can walk to restaurants and stores. $55-65.

FLEISCHMANNS

American Country Collection

4 Greenwood Lane, Delmar, 12054
(518) 439-7001

161. This 1867 classic Victorian summer retreat is at the entrance to the high peaks of the Catskill Mountains. A spacious late Victorian village cottage, its guest and common rooms are attractively furnished with select antiques, wicker, brass, and country chintz. Trout streams and well-marked hiking trails are all nearby. Skiing only five minutes away. Ten rooms, six with private baths, two with shared bath, and two efficiency apartments with private baths. Apartments are handicapped accessible. Smoking permitted. Children are welcome. Resident dog. $60-95.

NOTES: Credit cards accepted: A MasterCard; B Visa; C American Express; D Discover Card; E Diner's Club; F Other; 2 Personal checks accepted; 3 Lunch available; 4 Dinner available; 5 Open all year;

FLY CREEK

Bed and Breakfast Leatherstocking

P.O. Box 53, Herkimer, 13350
(315) 733-0040; (800) 941-BEDS (2337)

004. An old country farmhouse thoroughly inviting and updated, but unpretentious, homey, and clean. Only four miles from Cooperstown. Thirty minutes from Oneonta. Offers a rustic charm and low rates. Families are welcome. Single and double beds in three rooms. Shared baths. Crib available. Sits on 95 acres of rolling fields, wetlands, and woods. A Christian family endeavor, it welcomes all. Hearty country breakfast is served every day. Open May through October. $40.

FORESTBURGH

Inn at Lake Joseph

400 St. Joseph Road, 12777
(914) 791-9506

A quiet, secluded 125-year-old Queen Anne mansion surrounded by 2,000 acres of wildlife preserve and forest, with a 250-acre private lake. Once the vacation estate of Cardinals Hayes and Spellman, the mansion now offers fireplaces and Jacuzzis in the rooms, pool and lake swimming, boating, fishing, tennis, cross-country skiing, and more on the premises. Both breakfast and dinner are included in the daily rate.

Host: Ivan Weinger
Rooms: 10 (PB) $118-238
Full Breakfast
Credit Cards: A, B, C
Notes: 2, 3, 4, 5, 7, 8, 9, 10, 11, 12, 13, 14

FOSTERDALE

Fosterdale Heights House

205 Mueller Road, 12726
(914) 482-3369

Historic 1840 bed and breakfast on a Catskill mountaintop overlooks the scenic Delaware River Valley. A Victorian parlor with a grand piano, billiards, library, 20 acres of grounds, a pond, and a Christmas tree farm are surrounded by woodland. Canoeing and horseback riding are nearby, and a bountiful country breakfast is served each morning. Make new friends, or just relax alone together. A cool mountain breeze in the summer, exquisite fall foliage, warm and cozy by the stove in winter, and the mountain mist in the spring truly makes this a bed and breakfast for all seasons.

Host: Roy Singer
Rooms: 11 (5 PB; 6 SB) $58-117
Full Breakfast
Credit Cards: A, B
Notes: 2, 4, 5, 7, 9, 10, 11, 12, 13

The White Inn

FREDONIA

The White Inn

52 East Main Street, 14063
(716) 672-2103

Circa 1868. Built on the home site of the county's first physician, this elegant mansion features a 100-foot-long veranda where refreshments are served. Period antiques and reproductions are found in every bedroom. Guests and the public may enjoy gourmet meals at the inn, a charter member of the Duncan Hines "Family of Fine Restaurants." Antique shops, wineries, and the Chautauqua Institution are nearby.

Hosts: Robert Contiguglia and Kathleen Dennison
Rooms: 23 (PB) $59-159
Full Breakfast
Credit Cards: A, B, C, D, E
Notes: 2, 3, 4, 5, 7, 8, 9, 12, 13, 14

GALWAY

American Country Collection
4 Greenwood Lane, Delmar, 12054
(518) 439-7001

049. This was a stagecoach stop and tavern run by General E. Stimpson in the late 1700s. Local tradition indicates that it was a stopover for generals George Washington and Lafayette. In the 1960s, it housed famous and wealthy visitors to Saratoga Springs. This Center Hall Colonial is on three acres of tree-shaded lawns. The three guest rooms have private baths and Colonial decor, including some four-poster beds, comfortable chairs, and fresh flowers. Guests may use the in-ground pool. Smoking permitted in common areas only. Well-behaved children welcome. Pets in residence. A fully furnished cottage with bed loft, TV, wood-burning stove, and kitchen is available for weekly and monthly rental. $65-105.

GARRISON

The Bird and Bottle Inn
Rural Route 9, Old Albany Post Road, 10524
(914) 424-3000

Originally known as Warren's Tavern in 1761, this building was a stagecoach stop along the Albany Post Road. It is a perfect spot to stay overnight in one of the three rooms in the main building, each with a private bath, working fireplace, air conditioning, and canopied bed. A cottage steps away from the main building offers the same appointments. Near West Point, Boscobel Restoration, antiquing, and hiking. Price includes gourmet dinner and full breakfast Wednesday through Sunday. On Mondays and Tuesdays, a Continental breakfast is served. Closed the first two weeks of January. Member Independent Innkeepers of America.

Host: Ira Boyar
Rooms: 4 (PB) $195-215
Full Breakfast
Credit Cards: A, B, C, E
Notes: 3, 4, 5, 7 (limited), 9, 11, 12, 13, 14

Conesus Lake Bed and Breakfast

GENESEO

Conesus Lake Bed and Breakfast
2388 East Lake Road, 14435
(716) 346-6526; (800) 724-4841

On beautiful Conesus Lake near Route 390. Unique European styling with private balconies and flower boxes. Relaxing resort atmosphere includes large private dock, picnic pavilion, boat rentals, and overnight boat docking with mooring whips. Each attractive bedroom has queen-size bed and cable TV. Private bathroom and double whirlpool tub are available. Near excellent restaurants. Reservations suggested.

Hosts: Dale and Virginia Esse
Rooms: 3 (1 PB; 2 SB) $60-85
Full Breakfast
Credit Cards: A, B, D
Notes: 2, 5, 9, 11, 12, 13

GENEVA

Elaine's Bed and Breakfast Reservation Service

4987 Kingston Road, Elbridge, 13060
(315) 689-2082

A freshly decorated, comfortable, clean, and convenient brick Federalist house offers first-floor room with private bath and double bed. Upstairs there are two additional guest rooms, one with a queen-size bed and the other with a double. These rooms share a bath. Near historic Main Street, colleges, Cornell Experimental Agriculture Center, State Park on Seneca Lake. $50-75.

Geneva on the Lake

1001 Lochland Road, P.O. Box 929, 14456
(315) 789-7190; (800) 3GENEVA

Geneva on the Lake is an elegant, small resort on Seneca Lake in the Finger Lakes wine district. An Italian Renaissance villa offering luxurious suites overlooking a furnished terrace, formal gardens, pool, and lake. "The food is extraordinarily good," writes *Bon Appetit*. Friendly, attentive staff. Awarded AAA four diamonds for the twelfth consecutive year. Suite rates include Continental breakfast; complimentary bottle of wine, fresh fruit, and flowers on arrival; a wine and cheese party on Friday evenings; and a daily copy of the *New York Times* is provided. Lunch available July and August. Dinner available weekends only.

Host: William J. Schickel
Suites: 29 (PB) $113-440
Continental and Full Breakfast
Credit Cards: A, B, C, D
Notes: 2, 3 , 4 , 5, 7, 8, 9, 10, 11, 12, 14

99 William Street

99 William Street, 14456
(315) 789-1273

99 William Street is a pre-Civil War home that lends itself to gracious hospitality in these modern hectic times. In Geneva, New York, in the heart of the Finger Lakes region. Deep in history and rich with natural beauty, the inn is within a day's drive to wineries, state parks, and lakes, as well as Rochester, Ithaca, and Syracuse. Offered are two bedrooms with private baths and the privacy that guests expect and require. Reservations requested.

Hosts: Christopher M. Lang and David B. Gallipeau
Rooms: 2 (PB) $65
Continental or Full Breakfast
Credit Cards: None
Notes: 2, 5, 9, 10, 11, 12, 13

Virginia Deane's Bed and Breakfast

168 Hamilton Street, Routes 5 and 20, 14456
(315) 789-6152

Enjoy a little history in this antique-filled Colonial home in the 200-year-old city of Geneva. Next to Hobart and William Smith colleges. Choose from five rooms, each offering a different kind of charm. Minnie's Room is a combination bedroom and sitting

Virginia Deane's

room with a double bed, sofa, chairs, TV, and private bath. The Victorian Room has a separate entrance, private bath, TV, Victorian decor including a four-poster bed, and a marble-top vanity and dresser. Dolly's Bedroom is large and bright with rock maple beds and dresser, TV, and shared bath. The Brass Room has an antique brass bed surrounded by brass accessories, TV, and shared bath. The Little Penthouse has a living room, private bath, and TV.

Host: Deane V. Cunningham
Rooms: 5 (2 PB; 3 SB) $50-80
Continental Breakfast
Credit Cards: None
Notes: 2, 5, 7, 8, 9, 10, 11, 12, 13

GERMANTOWN

American Country Collection

4 Greenwood Lane, Delmar, 12054
(518) 439-7001

102. Built by Peter Rockefeller around 1807, this Center Hall Colonial was a roadside tavern and dance hall, then a fox farm until World War II. It features post-and-beam construction, oak-pinned rafters, hand-hewn timbers, and poured-glass windows. Four guest rooms, all with private baths, have air conditioning. Children over nine welcome. Smoking permitted on the first floor only. No pets. Full country breakfast. $75.

113. Wonderful views of the Catskill Mountains and the Hudson Valley can be had from this 18-year-old home. The guest quarters include two bedrooms and a private bath. There is a family room with fireplace, piano, and TV. Breakfast is served on the porch or in the dining room. Guests are welcome to use the in-ground swimming pool. Smoking outdoors only. Children welcome. Crib available. No pets allowed. Full breakfast served on weekends; Conti-

nental breakfast served Tuesday through Thursday. $60-65.

144. This cozy loft apartment is nestled on the eastern banks of the Hudson River among the gently rolling hills of Columbia County. There is a sitting room and eating area with ceiling fan, skylight, and fully equipped kitchen with sliding glass doors leading to the deck. The bedroom has a double bed and full shower bath. Everything is set up for guests to relax and enjoy. $95.

GHENT

American Country Collection

4 Greenwood Lane, Delmar, 12054
(518) 439-7001

082. This early 19th-century farmhouse on ten scenic acres of open fields is perfect for walking and picnicking. There is also a private one-acre pond for fishing and paddle-boating and a miniature horse farm. The guest rooms on the second floor are air-conditioned and have a TV and private bath. The two-room suite on the third floor is air-conditioned and has a TV. Smoking outdoors only. Children welcome. $65-70.

GLEN HAVEN

Elaine's Bed and Breakfast Reservation Service

4987 Kingston Road, Elbridge, 13060
(315) 689-2082

An entire new ranch-style house offers four bedrooms with individual heat, two bathrooms, living room, family room, dining room, and fully equipped kitchen. Deck and hot tub are outside. House is available as entire house or by the room as bed and breakfast. Also three rooms in owner's

NOTES: Credit cards accepted: A MasterCard; B Visa; C American Express; D Discover Card; E Diner's Club; F Other; 2 Personal checks accepted; 3 Lunch available; 4 Dinner available; 5 Open all year;

house for bed and breakfast. Property is on 28 acres of lawn, orchard, woods, and even a fishing pond. Two boat launches nearby. Restaurants and golf courses an easy drive away. Close to Homer, SUNY at Courtland, Ithaca, Syracuse, Skaneateles, and the Finger Lake area. Visa and MasterCard accepted. Well-behaved children welcome. Full breakfast. Hostess does catering. At south end of Skaneateles Lake. Between Routes 41 and 41A. Not on most road maps. $45-200.

GORHAM

Elaine's Bed and Breakfast Reservation Service

4987 Kingston Road, Elbridge, 13060
(315) 689-2082

This 14-room country Colonial-style farmhouse was built before the turn of the century and is decorated with many family treasures and special "finds." Take the opportunity to walk the five acres, enjoying the many wildflowers, fruit trees, berry bushes, and the owner's herb garden, or relax on one of the three porches. Choice of double or queen-size beds. The master bedroom suite has a king-size waterbed, sitting room, spacious private bath, whirlpool, and a wicker settee. Full breakfast on weekends and Continental breakfast weekdays. Two children over ten welcome. No pets, but there is a boarding kennel nearby.

GOWANDA

The Teepee

14396 Four Mile Level Road, 14070-9796
(716) 532-2168

This bed and breakfast is operated by Seneca Indians on the Cattaraugus Indian Reservation near Gowanda. Tours of the reservation and the Amish community nearby are available.

Hosts: Maxwell and Phyllis Lay
Rooms: 3 (SB) $45
Full Breakfast
Credit Cards: None
Notes: 2, 5, 6, 7, 8, 9, 10, 11, 12

GRAFTON

American Country Collection

4 Greenwood Lane, Delmar, 12054
(518) 439-7001

145. Step back in time into this quaint country inn in eastern Rensselaer County where the Green Mountains, the Berkshires, and the Taconic Valley come together. Relax and unwind in the common room furnished with period antiques, paintings, and prints, or sit by the warm double-sided fireplace. The five bedrooms offer oak furnishings, braided rugs, antiques, and a collection of period pieces, along with mints on the pillow each evening. Guests share two baths. Skiing, fishing, and hiking are nearby. Full breakfast Open April 15 through January 15. Children are welcome. Smoking on the first floor only. $45-55.

GREENFIELD

American Country Collection

4 Greenwood Lane, Delmar, 12054
(518) 439-7001

112. It was an inn for British officers during the War of 1812, then a stagecoach stop in the 1820s before serving as part of the Underground Railroad before the Civil War. A rich sense of history is enhanced by Oriental rugs and fine antiques from Europe and the Middle and Far East. Five guest rooms, three with private baths. One room has a Jacuzzi. Smoking outdoors and on the patio. Children over 11 welcome. Pets outside. $60-125.

6 Pets welcome; 8 Children welcome; 9 Social drinking allowed; 10 Tennis available; 11 Swimming available; 12 Golf available; 13 Skiing available; 14 May be booked through travel agents.

GREENVILLE

Balsam Shade

Rural Delivery 2, Box 114, Route 32, 12083-9505
(518) 966-5315

Balsam Shade is a home away from home with 60 years of family operation, proving it a lasting, quality vacation spot. Eighty acres of prime property with a beautiful view of the northern Catskill Mountains. Tall Balsam Fir trees and great bushy maples provide comfort and shade on a hot summer day. Beautiful flowers and 30 acres of lawns add to the natural beauty here. Three meals served daily. Seventy-five-foot swimming pool, tennis, game room, nightly entertainment, and playground for tots.

Hosts: Len and Jyl DeGiovine and children
Rooms: 60 (45 PB; 15 SB) $60-80
Full Breakfast
Credit Cards: None
Notes: 2, 3, 4, 8, 9, 10, 11

Greenville Arms

Greenville Arms

P.O. Box 659, 12083
(518) 966-5219

A historic Victorian inn in the Hudson River Valley, featuring 14 unique guest rooms, six acres of lush lawns, gardens, shade trees, and a 50-foot pool. Golf and tennis nearby. Catskill Mountain sightsee-ing and hiking. Original art, antiques, and fireplaces add warmth and grace to the din-ing rooms where guests enjoy famous coun-try breakfasts. Elegant country dining in the Vanderbilt Room on weekends.

Hosts: Eliot and Letitia Dalton
Rooms: 14 (PB) $110-125
Full Breakfast
Credit Cards: A, B, D
Notes: 2, 3, 4, 5, 9, 10, 12, 13, 14

GROTON

Elaine's Bed and Breakfast Reservation Service

4987 Kingston Road, Elbridge, 13060
(315) 689-2082

This charming 1867 Victorian in the coun-try has three guest rooms plus a single-size pull-out bed in the TV den upstairs. All guest rooms are large, bright, and individu-ally decorated. Rear room has an authentic antique three-quarter-size bed, heirloom quilt on the wall, and other family antique decorations. There are two sunny front rooms: one has a double bed, the other has two twin beds. Full country breakfast on weekends and Continental on weekdays. Family room with TV and wood-burning stove. Children over five years old are wel-come. $35-55.

HADLEY

American Country Collection

4 Greenwood Lane, Delmar, 12054
(518) 439-7001

135. Built in the late 1800s and purchased in 1988 by the present owners, this restored Victorian country inn is in the southern Adirondacks within easy driving distance to Saratoga, Glens Falls, and Lake George. Five distinctive guest rooms, all with pri-vate baths, are individually decorated and named and offer their own special amenities; two have Jacuzzis and one has a fireplace. Private dinners and breakfasts can be arranged in the three larger rooms. A gourmet breakfast served each morning may include Grand Marnier French toast or eggs Anthony, home-baked muffins, juice, coffee, or tea. Packages available. $80-145.

Saratoga Rose

Saratoga Rose

4174 Rockwell Street, 12835
(518) 696-2861; (800) 942-5025

Romantic Victorian inn in southern Adirondacks near Saratoga Springs and Lake George. Swimming, boating, outlet shopping, skiing, rafting, antiquing, golf, and tennis. Comfortable rooms with private baths. Fireplace room and room with private outside deck and Jacuzzi. Full gourmet breakfast included. Packages available. The candlelit restaurant offers specialties prepared by chef/owner Anthony Merlino.

Hosts: Anthony and Nancy Merlino
Rooms: 4 (PB) $75-140
Full Breakfast
Credit Cards: A, B, D
Notes: 2, 3, 4, 5, 9, 10, 11, 12, 13, 14

HAGUE

American Country Collection

4 Greenwood Lane, Delmar, 12054
(518) 439-7001

137. Rustic elegance with an Adirondack feel and 400 feet of sandy beachfront on the shore of Lake George describes the atmosphere of this bed and breakfast. Perfect as a romantic getaway or for families, there are eight cabins that can each accommodate up to six people and offer their own private baths, two with jet tubs. Five rooms in the lodge are also available, and there are two rooms that have one single and one double bed and share a bath. Children are welcome. Cottages available by the week only during July and August. Two-night minimum on weekends. $45-245.

198. Perched on a ledge above Lake George, this luxurious fieldstone home, circa 1900, boasts a panoramic view of the lake and the surrounding Adirondack Mountains. A full breakfast is served in the dining room with a 180-degree view of the lake or on the front porch facing the lake. Living room includes Oriental rugs, marble chess and backgammon set, grand piano, and a small library. Four guest rooms take up the whole second floor, all furnished with antiques and carpets. Spacious bathrooms convey an aura of Victorian grace and elegance. There are hiking trails, a swimming beach, boat launch, and horseback riding within five miles of the house. Lake George Village is 22 miles away. $90-125.

HAMILTON

Colgate Inn

On the Green, 13346
(315) 824-2300

---

6 Pets welcome; 8 Children welcome; 9 Social drinking allowed; 10 Tennis available; 11 Swimming available; 12 Golf available; 13 Skiing available; 14 May be booked through travel agents.

Whatever reason guests may have for visiting the area, they will find the atmosphere at the Colgate Inn relaxed and casual. The charm experienced upon entrance extends to the 43 guest rooms. Personal attention is a Marriott hallmark, and is especially true at this inn. Conferences, special events, elegant evenings, or casual nights out are all accommodated. The Salmagundi Dining Room is patterned after the Wayside Inn, home of 19th-century poet Henry Wadsworth Longfellow. Guests can also relax with friends in the 1840 tap room, order a light meal, or top off the stay with a nightcap before a restful evening.

Host: Doug Rusch
Rooms: 43 (PB) $55-85
Full Breakfast
Credit Cards: A, B, C, E
Notes: 2, 3, 4, 5, 8, 9, 10, 11, 12, 13, 14

HAMLIN

The International Bed and Breakfast Club, Inc.

504 Amherst Street, Buffalo, NY 14207
(800) 723-4262; FAX (716) 873-4462

NY7528PP. This 1910 English Tudor, placed amidst six wooded acres and perennial gardens, features natural woodwork, stained-glass windows, feather pillows, and Amish quilts recalling a bygone era. Three guest rooms with two shared baths are available. Full breakfasts include fresh fruit and homemade breads. It is a short stroll to Sandy Creek, and Hamlin Beach is just minutes away. Rochester is within 30 minutes, and Niagara Falls less than an 90-minute drive. Smoking in permitted areas only. No pets. $40-50.

HAMMONDSPORT

Blushing Rosé Bed and Breakfast

11 William Street, 14840
(607) 569-3402; (607) 569-3483

The Blushing Rosé has served as a pleasant hideaway for honeymooners, anniversary celebraters, and romantic trysters alike. Whether spending the day driving, hiking, biking, or just relaxing, this is the ideal haven in which to end the day and a great place to start the day with a copious specialty breakfast. The village has shopping, dining, and great walking. Keuka Lake is just a few doors away; wineries are nearby, as is the Corning Glass and Watkins Glen.

Hosts: The Laufersweilers
Rooms: 4 (PB) $65-85
Full or Continental Breakfast
Credit Cards: F
Notes: 2, 9, 10, 11, 12, 13

HAMPTON BAYS

House on the Water

P.O. Box 106, 11946
(516) 728-3560

Ranch house with two acres of garden on Shinnecock Bay. Quiet location. One mile to village, train, and bus. Seven miles to Southampton and Westhampton. Two miles to ocean beaches. Bicycles, windsurfers, pedal boat, barbecue, beach lounges, and umbrellas. German, Spanish, and French spoken. Kitchen facilities available. Closed November 1 through May 1.

Host: Mrs. Ute
Rooms: 2 (PB) $75-95
Full Breakfast
Credit Cards: None
Notes: 2, 9, 10, 11, 12, 14

House on the Water

HANCOCK

The Cranberry Inn Bed and Breakfast

38 West Main Street, 13783
(607) 637-2788

"Where you come as a guest, you leave as a friend." Built in 1894, this stately, turn-of-the-century Victorian is enveloped by the glorious Upper Catskill Mountains, the famous Delaware River, and a great front porch. Inside, enjoy a romantic fireplace, antique and Art Deco design, adorned in fine woodwork and old-style architecture. The inn offers warmth, charm, and hospitality. Come fish and canoe the rivers, bicycle and hike the miles of country roads, or shop for antiques. Seasonal packages are available.

Hosts: Lorene and George Bang
Rooms: 4 (2 PB; 2 SB) $55-75
Full Breakfast
Credit Cards: A, B, D
Notes: 2, 3, 4, 5, 7, 8, 9, 11, 12, 13, 14

HARTFORD

American Country Collection

4 Greenwood Lane, Delmar, 12054
(518) 439-7001

160. Within a short drive of both Saratoga Springs and Lake George, this historic Colonial tavern offers a relaxed country atmosphere in a quiet, rural setting. A history buff's delight, this restored home was built in 1802 and "remodeled" in 1878. Three second-floor rooms and one first-floor room are available for guests and offer both private and shared baths. A bountiful, full breakfast is served each morning in the dining room and includes juices and cereals, homemade rolls, breads, and muffins, eggs, bacon or sausage, and coffee and tea. $45-60.

Country Life

HEMPSTEAD (GARDEN CITY BORDER)

Country Life Bed and Breakfast

237 Cathedral Avenue, 11550
(516) 292-9219

Gracious old Dutch Colonial, near airports, beaches, train to Manhattan. Decorated with antiques and reproductions, the home has been featured on two house tours. Each room has air conditioning, color TV, and special charm: hand-crocheted spreads, marble top antique dresser, teddy bears, or other stuffed animals. Sightseeing, beaches, three universities nearby. Breakfast is served in a sunny, plant-filled room and consists of baked French toast, puff pancakes, or banana cheese toasties.

Hosts: Richard and Wendy Duvall
Rooms: 4 (PB) $60.05
Full Breakfast
Credit Cards: A, B
Notes: 2 (deposit), 4, 5, 8, 9, 10, 11, 12, 14

HILLSDALE

American Country Collection

4 Greenwood Lane, Delmar, 12054
(518) 439-7001

106. This inn is surrounded by 100 acres of meadows, woodlands, and an ancient ceme-

6 Pets welcome; 8 Children welcome; 9 Social drinking allowed; 10 Tennis available; 11 Swimming available; 12 Golf available; 13 Skiing available; 14 May be booked through travel agents.

tery. Built as a farmhouse around 1830, it was formerly the parsonage to the old church next door, then an inn with a somewhat dubious reputation during Prohibition. Four guest rooms, two with private baths. Smoking outdoors only. Breakfast is served on the screened porch or in the candlelit dining room. Children over 11 welcome. Two-night minimum stay in-season weekends; three-night minimum stay holiday weekends. $55-105.

199. Built in 1850, this historic Colonial cottage with gingerbread trim sits on a half-acre on the main street of Hillsdale. Just eight miles from the Massachusetts border, it is convenient to restaurants, shopping, and all the cultural attractions of Columbia County, and the Berkshires: Lenox, Tanglewood, Stockbridge, and Great Barrington. Entrance to guest room is private, and there is a color TV and air conditioning. Outside the rear door is a garden and an outside deck. Ski Catamount (four miles away) or Butternut (ten miles). Norman Rockwell Museum in Stockbridge is a 25-minute drive, and the Shaker Museum and Mac-Hyden Theater are each 15 miles. $65.

HOBART

Breezy Acres Farm Bed and Breakfast

Rural Delivery 1, Box 191, 13788
(607) 538-9338

"Better than home" reads one entry in the guest book. That's because the hosts strive for excellence in every area. Individually decorated rooms, each with private, squeaky-clean bath. Bountiful, homemade breakfast. Folders with menus, clippings about local events and activities. Spa, fireplace, pond for fishing and swimming, hunting, 300 acres for hiking, deck surrounded by beautiful flower gardens, shady porch for relaxing.

Hosts: Joyce and David Barber
Rooms: 3 (PB) $50-60
Full Breakfast
Credit Cards: A, B, C
Notes: 2, 5, 9, 10, 11, 12, 13

HOMER

Elaine's Bed and Breakfast Reservation Service

4987 Kingston Road, Elbridge, 13060
(315) 689-2082

Built in 1834, this village home was the first brick house in the quaint picturesque village of Homer. Guests may use both living rooms and piano. Breakfast served in dining room. Four guest rooms. Children welcome. This is a smoke-free bed and breakfast. It is furnished with pretty antiques and has wide plank floors. It is easy to find and guests can walk to Main Street. Homer is just north of Courtland and about halfway between Ithaca and Syracuse. Close to I-81. It is a lovely scenic drive along Skaneateles Lake to the village of Skaneateles, which takes about 30 minutes. The view from the lake road is breathtaking. $60-70.

HOPEWELL JUNCTION

Covered Bridge

P.O. Box 447 A, Norfolk, CT 06058
(203) 542-5944

1HJNY. This 1841 Georgian Colonial built for a prominent Dutch silversmith is set on six acres that include lovely perennial gardens and a pool. The house has six fireplaces with double living rooms that are adorned with large, imported crystal chandeliers and a fabulous sunroom that overlooks the grounds. The common rooms and the four guest rooms are all beautifully decorated with antiques, some of which the owners collected when they lived in France. A full country breakfast is served by the hostess, who attended the Culinary Institute of America. $95-140.

NOTES: Credit cards accepted: A MasterCard; B Visa; C American Express; D Discover Card; E Diner's Club; F Other; 2 Personal checks accepted; 3 Lunch available; 4 Dinner available; 5 Open all year;

Nutmeg B&B Agency

P.O. Box 1117, West Hartford, CT 06107
(203) 236-6698

342. This 14-room Georgian Colonial was built in 1841. There are six fireplaces, a formal dining room, and a sunroom overlooking two acres of lawn, a perennial flower garden, and swimming pool. The guest rooms feature queen-size beds, private baths, and each offers a Jacuzzi or working fireplace. Full gourmet breakfast. No children. No smoking.

ILION

Bed and Breakfast Leatherstocking

P.O. Box 53, Herkimer, 13350
(315) 733-0040; (800) 941-BEDS (2337)

005. Here is that fabled Victorian mansion with 14-foot ceilings and a wheeled ladder in the library, authentic furnishings, huge chandeliers and staircase, hangings, objets d'art, and other period artifacts. Four guest rooms on the second floor with private and shared baths. Canopied beds, sleigh beds, a feather bed, and fireplaces. $25-50.

ITHACA

The Federal House

P.O. Box 4914, 14852-4914
(607) 533-7362; 800-533-7362

A gracious circa 1815 inn featuring spacious rooms, exquisitely furnished with antiques and hand-carved mantels in the parlor and Seward Suite. The inn is in the heart of the Finger Lakes, just 15 minutes from Cornell and Ithaca colleges, downtown, wineries, state parks, and less than two miles from Cayuga Lake. The landscaped grounds, with gardens and gazebo, border the Salmon Creek and Falls, a wonderful, relaxing fishing and biking area. Full breakfast served. AAA approved.

Host: Diane Carroll
Rooms: 3 (PB) $65-130
Full Breakfast
Credit Cards: A, B, C, D
Notes: 2, 5, 9, 10, 11, 12, 13, 14

Hanshaw House Bed and Breakfast

15 Sapsucker Woods Road, 14850
(607) 257-1437; 800-257-1437

Framed by a white picket fence, this 1830s farmhouse is comfortable and elegant. Nestled serenely overlooking a pond and woods, rooms are furnished with antiques and colorful chintzes in a country English decor. Birds and wildlife complete the view. Scrumptious breakfasts are served in an elegant new dining room added on in the style of the 1830s house. Guests are invited to enjoy gardens and the patio in warmer weather. Private baths, goose-down comforters and pillows, and air conditioning make this a pleasant place to stay. Conveniently near colleges, state parks, skiing, fine restaurants, and vineyards.

Host: Helen Scoones
Rooms: 4 (PB) $68-110
Full Breakfast
Credit Cards: A, B, C
Notes: 2, 5, 8, 9, 10, 11, 12, 13

La Tourelle

1150 Danby Road, 96 B, 14850
(607) 273-2734; FAX (607) 273-4821
(800) 765-1492 Reservations

La Tourelle

---

6 Pets welcome; 8 Children welcome; 9 Social drinking allowed; 10 Tennis available; 11 Swimming available; 12 Golf available; 13 Skiing available; 14 May be booked through travel agents.

Rated highly by AAA and Mobil travel guides, La Tourelle is the perfect blend of Old World charm and contemporary comfort. Next to John Thomas Steakhouse. The beautifully appointed guest rooms are reminiscent of the delightful country hotels of Europe, each with private bath, air conditioning, TV, and telephone. Choose one of the king- or queen-size bedrooms or indulge in the Fireplace Suite or romantically exciting Tower Room.

Host: Leslie Leonard
Rooms: 35 (PB) $87-135
Continental Breakfast
Credit Cards: A, B, C
Notes: 4, 5, 6, 7, 8, 9, 10, 11, 12, 13, 14

Log Country Inn

Box 581, 14851
(607) 589-4771; (800) 274-4771

Enjoy the rustic charm of a log house at the edge of a 7,000-acre state forest. Modern accommodation in the spirit of international hospitality. European country breakfast, afternoon tea. Hiking, skiing, and sauna available. Convenient to Ithaca College, Cornell, Corning Glass, wineries, and antique shopping.

Host: Wanda Grunberg
Rooms: 3 (1 PB; 2 SB) $45-65
Full Breakfast
Credit Cards: A, B
Notes: 2, 4, 5, 6, 7, 8, 10, 11, 13

Peregrine House Victorian Inn

140 College Avenue, 14850
(607) 272-0919

An 1874 brick home with sloping lawns and pretty gardens, just three blocks from Cornell University. Down pillows, fine linens, and air-conditioned bedrooms with Victorian decor. In the center of Ithaca, one mile from Cayuga Lake, with its boating, swimming, summer theater, and wineries. Wonderful breakfasts, free snacks.

Host: Nancy Falconer
Rooms: 8 (PB) $69-99
Full Breakfast
Credit Cards: A, B, D
Notes: 2, 5, 8 (over 8), 9, 10, 11, 12, 13, 14

Rose Inn

Route 34 North, Box 6576, 14851-6576
(607) 533-7905; FAX (607) 533-7908

An elegant 1840s Italianate mansion on 20 landscaped acres. Fabulous circular staircase of Honduran mahogany. *Prix fixe* dinner served with advance reservations. Close to Cornell University. Twice selected by Uncle Ben's as one of the Ten Best Inns in America. Mobil four-star rated; AAA, four diamonds.

Hosts: Sherry and Charles Rosemann
Rooms: 15 (PB) $100-160
Suites: $185-250
Full Breakfast
Credit Cards: A, B
Notes: 2, 4, 5, 8 (over 10), 9, 10, 11, 12, 13, 14

JAMESVILLE

Elaine's Bed and Breakfast Reservation Service

4987 Kingston Road, Elbridge, 13060
(315) 689-2082

Country atmosphere. High on a hill, with a view for 35 miles, including three lakes, this owner-designed contemporary home offers the ultimate in peace and quiet, though only 15 minutes from downtown Syracuse or the university. Unique solarium full of plants and casual seating; rear deck with picnic table offers marvelous view. Guest room has private bath and queen-size bed. Resident cat. $60.

NOTES: Credit cards accepted: A MasterCard; B Visa; C American Express; D Discover Card; E Diner's Club; F Other; 2 Personal checks accepted; 3 Lunch available; 4 Dinner available; 5 Open all year;

JAY

The Book and Blanket Bed and Breakfast

P.O. Box 164, Route 9N, 12941-9998
(518) 946-8323

This charming, 100-year-old Greek Revival is nestled in the quaint hamlet of Jay, just seven miles from Whiteface Mountain and less than 20 minutes from Lake Placid. View of the Covered Bridge, and fishing and swimming in the Ausable River. The living room features a large fireplace, and an extra large porch is available for guests to enjoy. A booklover's dream, three guest rooms honor Jane Austen, F. Scott Fitzgerald, and Jack London, with their works well represented. Borrowers and browsers welcome. Full breakfast.

Hosts: Kathy, Fred, and Daisy the Basset Hound
Rooms: 3 (1 PB; 2 SB) $45-65
Full Breakfast
Credit Cards: C
Notes: 2, 5, 9, 11, 13

JEFFERSONVILLE

The Griffin House

Rural Delivery 1, Box 178, Maple Avenue, 12748
(914) 482-3371

Come home to history and hospitality at the Griffin House. Beginning in 1895, ten master carpenters worked five years with American Chestnut to create this masterpiece of woodwork. On a quiet estate, and nestled in the village of Jeffersonville, within walking distance of shops and restaurants. In this exquisite home, guests will enjoy fine antiques, spacious bedrooms, and a full cooked breakfast with the hosts, Irene and Paul. The original settlement home (circa 1840) occupies a wooded setting beneath majestic hemlocks and radiant maples, while Laundry Creek contributes a comforting symphony of sounds and a kaleidoscope of colors.

Hosts: Irene and Paul Griffin
Rooms: 4 (2 PB; 2 SB) $75-95
Full Breakfast
Credit Cards: None
Notes: 2, 5, 9, 10, 11, 12, 13, 14

JOHNSTOWN

American Country Collection

4 Greenwood Lane, Delmar, 12054
(518) 439-7001

099. This 100-year-old in-town home is on one-half acre of manicured lawns vegetable and flower gardens, with an above-ground swimming pool. Two guest rooms, one bath shared with owners. Rooms are normally rented to one party traveling together. The bedrooms have lots of natural light and cross ventilation. There's a TV in the living room and den. No smoking in bedrooms. No pets. Children over two are welcome. $40.

KATONAH

American Country Collection

4 Greenwood Lane, Delmar, 12054
(518) 439-7001

155. Dream away in this 16th-century Dutch Colonial farmhouse on four acres of woods, gardens, and maple sugar bush. A short climb up four steps brings guests to

6 Pets welcome; 8 Children welcome; 9 Social drinking allowed; 10 Tennis available; 11 Swimming available; 12 Golf available; 13 Skiing available; 14 May be booked through travel agents.

the master bedroom, which has a brass bed, free-standing fireplace, and private, hand-painted Portuguese tile bath. A small study with a desk and library connects to the bedroom and a common room. The third floor has two more bedrooms that share a bath. Across the street is a lovely pond for trout fishing or swimming. A full breakfast is served each morning. No smoking. $60-80.

KEENE VALLEY

High Peaks Inn
Route 73, P.O. Box 701, 12943
(518) 576-2003

A 1910 Adirondack lodge with wraparound porch with swing, living room with granite fireplace and piano, TV parlor, lots of books and board games, pool table, and grill on patio; all surrounded by mountain views. The inn offers small-town charm and tranquility, but it is still close to Lake Placid/Olympic region attractions including cross-country and downhill skiing at Whiteface Mountain, rock and ice climbing, hiking, and fishing and canoeing the Ausable River. Afternoon snacks provided.

Hosts: Jerry and Linda Limpert
Rooms: 8 (3 PB; 5 S2B) $65-80
Full Breakfast
Credit Cards: A, B
Notes: 2, 3, 5, 8, 9, 11, 12, 13

KENMORE

The International Bed and Breakfast Club, Inc.
504 Amherst Street, Buffalo, NY 14207
(800) 723-4262; FAX (716) 873-4462

NY5860PP. Casual country ambience awaits the traveler in this nicely appointed inn. Two rooms with shared bath in hall are available. Hosts are well-versed regarding golf and entertainment in the Buffalo area. Full breakfast. $45-50.

KINGSTON

Rondout Bed and Breakfast
88 West Chester Street, 12401
(914) 331-2369

Spacious and gracious 1905 mansion on two acres in a quiet neighborhood near the Hudson River and the Catskill Mountains. Hearty breakfasts, evening refreshments, hospitable and knowledgeable hosts. Excellent restaurants, cruises, antiques, museums, galleries, theaters, and five colleges are nearby. Kingston, rich in history and architectural variety, is an urban cultural park.

Hosts: Adele and Ralph Calcavecchio
Rooms: 4 (SB) $65-85
Full Breakfast
Credit Cards: A, B, C
Notes: 2, 5, 8, 9, 10, 11, 12, 14

LAKE LUZERNE

American Country Collection
4 Greenwood Lane, Delmar, 12054
(518) 439-7001

159. Imagine stepping back 100 years into a grand Victorian summer in Lake Luzerne. Carefully restored by the present owners, this inn has a genuinely warm, comfortable atmosphere characterized by a lot of personal service and attention. Ten rooms, with either a double or queen-size bed, offer private baths, in-room fireplaces, and two of the rooms have an additional single bed. Breakfast is served on a large sun porch each morning and consists of fruit, cakes, granola, waffles, French toast, crepes, omelets, sausage and homefries, coffee, or tea. $70-140.

The Lamplight Inn Bed and Breakfast
2129 Lake Avenue, Box 70, 12846
(518) 696-5294

NOTES: Credit cards accepted: A MasterCard; B Visa; C American Express; D Discover Card; E Diner's Club; F Other; 2 Personal checks accepted; 3 Lunch available; 4 Dinner available; 5 Open all year;

The Lamplight Inn

Award-winning 1992 "Inn of the Year."
Romantic 1890 Victorian estate nestled in
the Adirondacks across from a crystal clear
lake. Mountain-view rooms with fireplaces,
and memorable breakfast served on the picturesque sun porch.

Hosts: Gene and Linda Merlino
Rooms: 10 (PB) $80-140
Full Breakfast
Credit Cards: A, B, C
Notes: 2, 3, 5, 7 (limited), 8 (over 12), 9, 10, 11, 12,
13, 14

LAKE PLACID

Blackberry Inn

59 Sentinel Road, 12946
(518) 523-3419

This Colonial home, built in 1915, is one
mile from the center of the village on Route
73. Four guest rooms offer country flair.
Convenient to all major Olympic sites; surrounded by the Adirondack Parks. Nearby
recreation includes skiing, skating, hiking,
golf, and fishing. Home-baked breakfasts.

Hosts: Bill and Gail Billerman
Rooms: 4 (PB) $50-70
Full Breakfast
Credit Cards: None
Notes: 2, 5, 7, 8, 9, 10, 11, 12, 13

Highland House Inn

3 Highland Place, 12946
(518) 523-2377

Peaceful central location in the village of
Lake Placid. Lovely Adirondack decor
throughout. Year-round dining in the glass-
enclosed garden dining room. Full breakfast
including blueberry pancakes, always! All
rooms have TVs and ceiling fans. Hot tub
spa on the deck amidst the trees and always
at peak temperature throughout the year.
Fully efficient cottage with fireplace available, next to the inn.

Hosts: Teddy and Cathy Blazer
Rooms: 7 (PB) $65-75
Cottage: $80-105
Full Breakfast
Credit Cards: A, B
Notes: 2, 5, 7, 8, 9, 10, 11, 12, 13, 14

Interlaken Inn and Restaurant

15 Interlaken Avenue, 12946
(518) 523-3180

A Victorian inn in the heart of Lake Placid
featuring a gourmet restaurant and 12
uniquely decorated rooms. The inn has tin
ceilings, a cozy fireplace in the living
room, lots of lace and charm. Nearby
guests can enjoy golf, skiing, or any of the
pleasures of the Adirondacks. Modified
American Plan. Bed and Breakfast available April and November.

Interlaken Inn

6 Pets welcome; 8 Children welcome; 9 Social drinking allowed; 10 Tennis available; 11 Swimming available;
12 Golf available; 13 Skiing available; 14 May be booked through travel agents.

Hosts: Roy and Carol Johnson
Rooms: 11 (PB) $50-170
Full Breakfast
Credit Cards: A, B, C
Notes: 2, 4, 5, 7, 9, 10, 11, 12, 13, 14

South Meadow Farm Lodge

HCR 1 Box 44, Cascade Road, 12946
(800) 523-9369

Small farm on 75 acres, bordered by state land in the heart of the Adirondack High Peaks. Ski out the back door onto 50 kilometers of Olympic cross-country trails. Family-style lodging with full, hearty meals. Come any time of the year and share the lodge, the view, and the Adirondack hospitality.

Hosts: Tony and Nancy Corwin
Rooms: 5 (SB) $70-90
Full Breakfast
Credit Cards: A, B
Notes: 2, 3, 4, 5, 8, 9, 10, 11, 12, 13, 14

Spruce Lodge Bed and Breakfast

31 Sentinel Road, 12946
(800) 258-9350

Spruce Lodge has been in the Wescott family since 1949. The buildings were erected in the early 1900s. Large lawns extend down to a pond where guests can picnic or fish. Inside Lake Placid and close to all area activities. There is a view of the Sentinel Range and Whiteface from the back of the property.

Rooms: 7 (2 PB; 5 SB) $45-99
Cottage: 1
Continental Breakfast
Credit Cards: A, B
Notes: 2, 5, 8, 9, 10, 11, 12, 13

Stagecoach Inn

370 Old Military Road, 12946
(518) 523-9474

An Adirondack experience since 1833. Quiet, convenient location, close to winter and summer recreation, restaurants, sightseeing, and shopping. Rooms lovingly dec-

orated with quilts, wicker, and antiques. Outstanding great room and a front porch with rockers and a swing. Two-room family suites available. Fireplaces.

Host: Peter Moreau
Rooms: 9 (5 PB; 4 SB) $55-80
Full Breakfast
Credit Cards: A, B
Notes: 2, 5, 7, 8, 9, 10, 11, 12, 13, 14

LEWISTON

The International Bed and Breakfast Club, Inc.

504 Amherst Street, Buffalo, NY 14207
(800) 723-4262; FAX (716) 873-4462

NY8598PP. This renovated 1850s Colonial home is in a quiet residential area on the east bank of the Niagara River. It is only a few minutes from Fort Niagara and Niagara Falls. Four rooms are available: the master suite with queen-size bed, color TV with cable, ensuite bath, and dressing room; a four-poster bed and private ensuite bath; a queen-size bed; and a two-bedroom loft suite with double and twin beds. An extra single roll away is also available. Baths include three private and one shared facility. A full breakfast is served. No smoking except in designated area. $60-85.

LITTLE FALLS

Bed and Breakfast Leatherstocking

P.O. Box 53, Herkimer, 13350
(315) 733-0040; (800) 941-BEDS (2337)

006. White wooden Ionic columns decorate this 17-room wood-frame Victorian inside and out. Two grand pianos are in the music salon, and original art hangs in the art salon. Breakfast in the solarium, on the huge wraparound porch, or on the rear sun deck. Bookstore and art studio on the premises. Rail lift available on the main staircase.

NOTES: Credit cards accepted: A MasterCard; B Visa; C American Express; D Discover Card; E Diner's Club; F Other; 2 Personal checks accepted; 3 Lunch available; 4 Dinner available; 5 Open all year;

Three beautiful rooms with private and shared baths. Full breakfast served. $50-65.

LITTLE VALLEY

The Napoli Log Homestead

4748 Allegany Road, 14755
(716) 938-6755; (716) 358-3926

This cedar log home was built in 1988. It is furnished with Early American pieces handed down from five generations. Two rooms upstairs share a bath, and one room downstairs has a private bath. There is a cozy Victorian sitting room upstairs. The full breakfast of waffles and sausage, served with pure maple syrup or bacon and eggs, is included in the room rate. A convenient 20 minutes from Holiday Valley, Cockaigne, Allegheny State Park, Chautauqua Lake, and Amish settlement.

Hosts: Dean and Annette Waite
Rooms: 3 (1 PB; 2 SB) $40-50
Full Breakfast
Credit Cards: None
Notes: 2, 5, 8, 9, 10, 11, 12, 13

LIVERPOOL

Elaine's Bed and Breakfast Reservation Service

4987 Kingston Road, Elbridge, 13060
(315) 689-2082

Victorian house filled with country charm and antiques. A 100-year-old, three story house overlooking the Yacht Club on Onondaga Lake. Conveniently next to antique and craft center. Walk everywhere: restaurants, shops, library, prize-winning Johnson Park, grocery, just one-half block to Onondaga Lake Park. Only five minutes from NYS Thruway (I-90), Exit 38, and only five minutes to downtown Syracuse. One large guest room with a four-poster bed and bay window alcove with table and chairs for private morning coffee before going downstairs to a full country breakfast. The room is fresh, bright, and beautifully decorated. Another guest room features a maple and pine antique bed with matching chests and collections of powder boxes and dresser jars. These rooms share a lovely modern tub and shower bath. Smoking in designated areas. Ideal for a party of four. $45-65.

LIVINGSTON MANOR

Clarke's Place in the Country

811 Shandelee Road, 12758
(914) 439-5442

A unique contemporary rustic home on three acres in the heart of the Catskills. White pine interior throughout with great room that features a 20-foot cathedral ceiling and wood stove. On premises is a deep water, spring-fed stocked pond for year-round recreation, and a Hot Spring Spa has been added for under-the-stars tubbing! Minutes from downhill and cross-country skiing and some of the finest golfing anywhere. Certified executive chef serves a gourmet breakfast in the new solarium. Fine food, live entertainment, terrific antiques, and auctions only moments away. The world's best trout fishing. Ask about the weekend gourmet cooking class!

Hosts: Bob, Nan, and Josh Clarke
Rooms: 3 (PB) $70-80
Full Breakfast
Credit Cards: A, B
Notes: 2, 5, 8, 9, 10, 11, 12, 13

LOCKPORT

Hambleton House

130 Pine Street, 14094
(716) 439-9507; (716) 634-3650

Charm and hospitality in this historic Lockport home, circa 1850. Each room has a delicate blending of past and present. A grand staircase leads to two guest rooms along

6 Pets welcome; 8 Children welcome; 9 Social drinking allowed; 10 Tennis available; 11 Swimming available; 12 Golf available; 13 Skiing available; 14 May be booked through travel agents.

Hambleton House

with private guest parlor and dining room. The third and largest guest room is on the first floor. Guest rooms are air conditioned. Walking distance to historic Erie Barge Canal Locks. Short driving trips to many other places of interest including Niagara Falls and Old Fort Niagara.

Hosts: The Hambleton Family
Rooms: 3 (PB) $55-75
Continental Breakfast
Credit Cards: None
Notes: 5, 9, 14

The International Bed and Breakfast Club, Inc.

504 Amherst Street, Buffalo, NY 14207
(800) 723-4262; FAX (716) 873-4462

NY3502PP. This former produce farm is in historic Niagara County. Four large guest rooms on the second floor include a four-poster queen-size, a full-size sleigh bed and twin beds, and another full-size bed and twin bed for a child. There are two shared baths. A family-style breakfast is served with varying menus. Guests may dine in a formal dining room, country kitchen, or breakfast room. $55

NY9507PP. This historic home is within walking distance of historic Erie Barge Canal and the city's main street. Five rooms are available with private and semi-private

baths. The largest bedroom has a double bed, a day bed that sleeps two, and a private bath. A Continental plus breakfast is served. $55-75.

LYONS

Elaine's Bed and Breakfast Reservation Service

4987 Kingston Road, Elbridge, 13060
(315) 689-2082

Convenient to the popular Finger Lakes region, halfway between Rochester and Syracuse and Lake Ontario and Seneca Lake, this charmingly decorated brick Greek Revival was built in the mid 1840s. It was remodeled in the 1880s with Victorian touches. Three guest rooms share two-and-a-half baths and are named for roses, some of which can be found on the rose lawn or in the garden behind the house. Sweet Briar has skylights and stenciled walls and is furnished in golden oak that dates from the early 1900s. Garden Party has a skylight and is furnished with an antique iron and brass bed and wicker chairs. Rubaiyat has an antique mahogany bed, damask wallpaper, and lace curtains. $50-60.

The International Bed and Breakfast Club, Inc.

504 Amherst Street, Buffalo, NY 14207
(800) 723-4262; FAX (716) 873-4462

NY4218PP. This mid-1840s Greek Revival home was remodeled during the 1880s with Victorian touches. Each of the three guest rooms (which share a bath) is named for a type of rose; their namesakes may be found on the rose lawn or back garden, where Jackson and Perkins roses in the preliminary marketing stage are grown. Full gourmet breakfast on weekends, Continental only on weekdays; served in the garden or on the porch, weather-permitting. Other features include a music room with organ, a fireplace and an upstairs sitting room. Only a one-hour drive to Rochester to the west or Syracuse to the east; 20 minutes to Seneca Lake or Lake Ontario. Smoking is restricted. $60.

MARCELLUS

The Debevic Homested

2527 West Seneca Turnpike, 13108
(315) 673-9447

This old house has a wooded area for guests to stroll through. Rooms furnished in antiques, antique shop in house, and artist in residence. Close to great fishing, state fairgrounds, Finger Lakes attractions, Copperstown, New York state wineries, colleges, and cultural events in Skaneateles and Syracuse. Basket lunches provided at an additional cost. Artist weekends with workshops may be arranged.

Hosts: Frank and Jan Debevic
Rooms: 2 (SB) $40-55
Continental Breakfast
Credit Cards: None
Notes: 2, 3, 8, 9, 10, 11, 12

MAYVILLE

The Village Inn

111 South Erie Street, Route 394, 14757
(716) 753-3583

Spend restful nights in a turn-of-the-century Victorian near the shores of lakes Chautauqua and Erie. The home is furnished with antiques and trimmed in woodwork crafted by European artisans. Near the Chautauqua Institution, antique shops, wineries, swimming, golf, biking, arts and crafts, gliding, and water, downhill and cross-country skiing.

Host: Dean Hanby
Rooms: 3 (SB) $50
Full Breakfast
Credit Cards: C
Notes: 2, 5, 6, 7, 8, 9, 10, 11, 12, 13, 14

MOHAWK

Bed and Breakfast Leatherstocking

P.O. Box 53, Herkimer, 13350
(315) 733-0040; (800) 941-BEDS (2337)

008. This 1860s restored and refurbished Victorian farmhouse sits high on a hill on several acres of lawn and woodland overlooking the beautiful Mohawk Valley. Two private suites with fully equipped modern kitchenettes and private baths are offered. Full breakfasts are served year-round in owners' dining room. Extended stays considered. Close to Utica, Cooperstown, and environs. $55-80.

MONTGOMERY

American Country Collection

4 Greenwood Lane, Delmar, 12054
(518) 439-7001

182. This Center Hall Colonial inn was built in stages beginning around 1790. Recently completely renovated, it has the original wide board oak floors, now covered discreetly with Oriental rugs. Decor is French Country, and furnishings are a mix of contemporary and antique. The common room has couches, fireplace, and piano, while the dining room, also with fireplace, is dominated by a gigantic antique French armoire. The five guest rooms are all large, with private bath, sitting area, TV, and air conditioning. Continental or full breakfast (guest's choice) is served in the room, on the rear deck, or in the main dining room. Three miles to horseback riding, four to hiking, tennis, boating, swimming, and golf, and 10 to 15 to wineries and SUNY at New Paltz. $85.

6 Pets welcome; 8 Children welcome; 9 Social drinking allowed; 10 Tennis available; 11 Swimming available; 12 Golf available; 13 Skiing available; 14 May be booked through travel agents.

MUMFORD/ROCHESTER

Genesee Country Inn

948 George Street, Box 340, 14511-0340
(716) 538-2500; FAX (716) 538-4565

Historic stone mill on eight quiet acres of woods and waterfalls. Lovingly restored, with all timely conveniences, individually decorated guest rooms. Tea and full breakfast. Trout fishing. Nearby is Genesee Museum, fine restaurants, Rochester, and Letchworth State Park. Niagara Falls is one hour away. Chosen by *Country Inns* magazine as one of the 12 best inns in the USA. AAA, Mobil, CIBR.

Proprietor: Glenda Barklow
Innkeeper: Kim Rasmussen
Rooms: 9 (PB) $80-125
Full Breakfast
Credit Cards: A, B
Notes: 2, 9, 10, 11, 12, 13, 14

NAPLES

Elaine's Bed and Breakfast Reservation Service

4987 Kingston Road, Elbridge, 13060
(315) 689-2082

This big, rambling 1830s house in a country setting has a spectacular view of Canandaigua Lake. Enjoy a congenial Bavarian atmosphere, full breakfast, complimentary candy, outdoor recreations, spacious picnic grounds, gazebo, and patios. Quiet library, TV, and VCR. Marble fireplace. Separate smoking room. Accessible to the physically challenged. Just 13 miles from antique centers, the Finger Lake's Performing Arts Center, Finger Lakes Raceway, and Sonnenberg Gardens. Even closer to Bristol Mountain ski area, Bristol Valley Playhouse, wineries, and fishing swimming, and boating. Golf nearby. Discounts for private groups or seniors or extended stays. Open year-round. $60.

The International Bed and Breakfast Club, Inc.

504 Amherst Street, Buffalo, NY 14207
(800) 723-4262; FAX (716) 873-4462

This inn offers escape and serenity on a mountain in upstate New York. Several rooms are available. Guests may choose a suite with private deck and porch, king-size bed, two sitting areas, TV/VCR, and a private bath with Jacuzzi. Another suite has a queen-size bed, fireplace, sitting area, and private bath with hot tub. A third room has a king-size bed, dining table, small refrigerator, microwave, stone fireplace, private bath, and hot tub spa. A full gourmet breakfast is served. $80-175.

NELLISTON

Bed and Breakfast Leatherstocking

P.O. Box 53, Herkimer, 13350
(315) 733-0040; (800) 941-BEDS (2337)

009. Here is a lovingly restored limestone from the 1850s Federalist period, on the National Register of Historic Places. Fifty-foot sun deck at the rear overlooks the shores of the Mohawk and farmlands. Parking and turn-around available. Near Cooperstown and Howe Caves. Just a stone's throw to the capital district. Three rooms available to guests. All shared baths. $40-55.

NEW BALTIMORE

American Country Collection

4 Greenwood Lane, Delmar, 12054
(518) 439-7001

089. Originally a farmhouse in the early 1800s, this Victorian home was enlarged during the 1860s in Italianate style. Three guest rooms with private baths. One room has a working fireplace and air conditioning. The suite is air-conditioned as well. The living room has a piano and fireplace; the library has a TV and Victorian gas stove. Breakfast is served in front of the fire in the kitchen, in the dining room, or on the porch or terrace. It's an easy walk to the historic hamlet with its marina, old mill stream, and early cemetery. Smoking permitted. Children accepted occasionally. $65-75.

NEWBURGH

American Country Collection

4 Greenwood Lane, Delmar, 12054
(518) 439-7001

156. Come and visit this fully restored Queen Anne Victorian mansion, listed on the National Register of Historic Places, in the heart of the historic district. Enjoy a full breakfast served either in front of a 12-foot ceiling grand parlor fireplace with a crackling fire, or on a cabana-like sun porch with panoramic views of the majestic Hudson River and mountains. Both guest rooms are on the second floor and are furnished with antiques. One has a fireplace, air conditioning, and semi-private bath, and the other has a shared bath. Two apartments for long- or short-term rental also available. $65-75.

The International Bed and Breakfast Club, Inc.

504 Amherst Street, Buffalo, NY 14207
(800) 723-4262; FAX (716) 873-4462

NY1715PP. This fully restored New York Central Railroad caboose features a magnificent Hudson River view. It has a living room with fireplace and a complete galley; private twin platform beds and an upper cupola bunk provide sleeping space for up to three guests. Private shower, TV, full

heat and air conditioning. Pool privileges. Continental breakfast. Ideal for West Point and Hudson Valley lovers. $85.

NEW LEBANON

American Country Collection

4 Greenwood Lane, Delmar, 12054
(518) 439-7001

132. This historic Colonial was built in 1797 for a preacher and his family. Nestled on 18 acres just outside of town, this country inn is convenient to Lenox, the Berkshires, the Capital District, and major ski areas. There is a suite on the first floor with a leather mattress, day bed with a trundle, and a private bath, and four bedrooms on the second floor: two with private baths; the other two form a suite with a common sitting room and bath. Rooms are light and airy with homemade quilts and period Colonial furniture. A full country breakfast is served each morning. Smoking outside only. $65-90.

Covered Bridge

P.O. Box 447, Norfolk, CT 06058
(203) 542-5944

This 1797 Colonial farmhouse set on 18 acres offers a quiet country retreat but is close to all of the activities offered in the Berkshires. Guests may relax beside the fireplace in the living room, or enjoy the beautiful front porch with a view of the Taconic Hills. A full country breakfast is served in the dining room. There is a first-floor suite with a private bath, two guest rooms on the second floor that share a bath, and a two-bedroom suite with a private bath. $75-100.

---

6 Pets welcome; 8 Children welcome; 9 Social drinking allowed; 10 Tennis available; 11 Swimming available; 12 Golf available; 13 Skiing available; 14 May be booked through travel agents.

Elaine's Bed and Breakfast Reservation Service

4987 Kingston Road, Elbridge, 13060
(315) 689-2082

A cozy home filled with antiques, this rambling farmhouse on 50 acres lies in the heart of Shaker country. It has wide-plank floors, five delightful guest rooms, and three baths. The original house dates back to 1836. Share the relaxed country atmosphere with other interesting guests, a dog, and the cat family. Children and pets are welcome. A spacious new three-room contemporary apartment in an adjacent building is available. Moderate rates.

NEW PALTZ

American Country Collection

4 Greenwood Lane, Delmar, 12054
(518) 439-7001

116. Rejuvenating one's mind and body can be as simple as strolling through the apple, pear, and quince orchards on a warm summer day, or as fascinating as a session on stress management and holistic health offered by the host. Four guest rooms, two private baths, two shared baths. One room has a double Murphy bed, working fireplace, air conditioning, and private bath. All rooms have air conditioning. A healthful gourmet breakfast is served in the light and airy country kitchen. Smoking in guest rooms and outdoors. Children under seven stay for free. No pets. $78-89

117. Plan the day from the rambling lemonade porch of this immaculate Queen Anne Victorian in this tiny village near the Shawangunk Mountains. Three guest rooms, all with private baths. Guests in the master bedroom have a view of the solarium and the gardens from their indoor balcony. Smoking is allowed outdoors only.

Children over ten are welcome. There are two cats in residence. $85-95.

NEWPORT

Bed and Breakfast Leatherstocking

P.O. Box 53, Herkimer, 13350
(315) 733-0040; (800) 941-BEDS (2337)

010. This huge Georgian four-square limestone built around 1812 sits far back and high up on a groomed lawn in this pretty little village. All modern conveniences, networked security system, common rooms, and fireplaces; all rooms lovingly decorated. Two rooms: one double, one twin, both with private baths. Full breakfast is served. $40-55.

NEW ROCHELLE

Rose Hill Guest House

44 Rose Hill Avenue, 10804
(914) 632-6464

The hostess at this beautiful, intimate French Normandy home is a real estate agent and bridge Life Master. Weather permitting, enjoy breakfast on the flower patio or in the chandeliered library/dining room. Thirty minutes to Manhattan by train or car. Safe parking behind house. Two-night minimum stay required for holidays.

Host: Marilou Mayetta
Rooms: 2 (SB) $48.50-69.65
Continental Breakfast
Credit Cards: C
Notes: 2, 5, 6 (call), 7, 8, 9, 10, 12, 14

NEW WINDSOR

American Country Collection

4 Greenwood Lane, Delmar, 12054
(518) 439-7001

197. A nice combination of country, romance, and coziness awaits guests at the contemporary trilevel home. It sits on a slight rise, surrounded by 165 acres of lawn, fields, and woods where guests are free to wander. Furnishings are a mixture of traditional pieces and family antiques, each with its own history. There is a common living room, screened side porch, and TV room with wood-burning stove. The three guest rooms are decorated in country-Victorian ambience. Continental breakfast is served during the week, full breakfast on weekends. West Point, cross-country skiing, and Sugar Loaf Craft Village and Museum are each only 12 to 15 miles away. Even closer are the Brotherhood Winery and Crestview Lake for swimming and fishing. $43-65.

NEW YORK

Bed and Breakfast (& Books)

35 West 92nd Street, 10025
(212) 865 8740

Sample listings: Beautifully renovated townhouse on quiet tree-lined street near Central Park offers one double-bed room with private bath. Convenient to museums, theaters, shopping, and all transportation. Children welcome in loft areas. $80. Working artist's loft in the heart of Soho has comfortable twin-bed room, sitting area, and bath ensuite. Convenient to Soho galleries, shops, and restaurants. Sofa opens to sleep two. $92.50.

Host: Judith Goldberg
Rooms: 50 (45 PB; 5 SB) $70-90
Continental Breakfast
Credit Cards: None
Notes: 5, 14

Bed and Breakfast Network of New York

134 West 32nd Street, Suite 602, 10001
(212) 645-8134; (800) 900-8134

A reservation service for New York City, mostly Manhattan. Accommodations are in some of the most exciting parts of town: Greenwich Village, Midtown, Upper East and West sides, etc. Range from modest to luxurious, from townhouse to lofts to million dollar hi-rise condos. Weekly and monthly rates available. Also represent unhosted furnished apartments and studios ranging from $80-300.

Rooms: 300 (100 PB; 100 SB) $80-90
Continental Breakfast
Credit Cards: None
Notes: 2 (for deposit), 5, 6 (call), 8 (call), 14

Urban Ventures, Inc.

38 West 32, #1412, 10001
(212) 594-5650; FAX (212) 947-9320

Established in 1979, Urban Ventures has about 600 accommodations. Each has been inspected by Urban Ventures. A range of fifth-floor walk-ups to a three-bedroom house in center city. This service can provide unhosted apartments and bed and breakfast in every area of the city. Guests need only express their needs and they will find them met. In peak seasons, book at least three weeks prior to arrival. Brochure is free. The capable staff has been with this service for years.

Rooms: 300 (PB and SB) $65-95
Continental Breakfast
Credit Cards: A, B, C, D, E
Notes: 2, 5, 8, 9, 14

NIAGARA FALLS

The Cameo Inn

4710 Lower River Road, Route 18F, 14092
(716) 745-3034

This stately Queen Anne Victorian commands a majestic view of the lower Niagara River and Canadian shoreline. Lovingly furnished with period antiques and family heirlooms, the Cameo will charm guests with its quiet elegance. Here one can enjoy the ambience of days past in a peaceful set-

6 Pets welcome; 8 Children welcome; 9 Social drinking allowed; 10 Tennis available; 11 Swimming available; 12 Golf available; 13 Skiing available; 14 May be booked through travel agents.

ting far from the bustle of everyday life. Three guest rooms with private or shared baths are available, as well as a three-room private suite that overlooks the river.

Hosts: Greg and Carolyn Fisher
Rooms: 4 (2 PB; 2 SB) $65-115
Full Breakfast
Credit Cards: A, B, D
Notes: 5, 9, 10, 11, 12, 13, 14

The International Bed and Breakfast Club, Inc.

504 Amherst Street, Buffalo, NY 14207
(800) 723-4262; FAX (716) 873-4462

NY2144PP. Spend some quality time in this tastefully restored inn, small enough to guarantee that guests don't get lost in the crowd. The personal attention guests deserve at a price that makes sense. Enjoy old-fashioned hospitality in a convenient setting. Four guest rooms, some with private baths, some shared. Full breakfast is served. Plenty of off-street parking. Within walking distance of many Niagara Falls sights and sounds. $70.

NY4626PP. A beautifully restored turn-of-the-century home with outstanding architectural detailing. Queen-size, double, and twin beds in four guest rooms, with both private and shared baths. Full breakfast and afternoon tea served. Within walking distance of the falls and many popular tourist attractions. $50-75.

NORTH RIVER

Highwinds Inn

Barton Mines Road, P.O. Box 70, 12856
(518) 251-3760

At an elevation of 2,500 feet on 1,600 acres of land in the middle of a garnet mine. All guest rooms and the dining area have a spectacular view to the west. On the property there is mountain biking, canoeing,

hiking to several peaks and ponds, garnet mine tours, gardens, cross-country ski touring, tennis, swimming, and guided summer and winter midweek trips available. Nearby spring rafting on the Hudson; Lake George; Octoberfest. Picnic lunches can be arranged for guests. Closed April through June and November through Christmas.

Host: Kim Repscha
Rooms: 4 (PB) $100
Full Breakfast
Credit Cards: A, B
Notes: 2, 3, 4, 6, 8 (over 12), 9, 10, 11, 12, 13

NORTH TONAWANDA

The International Bed and Breakfast Club, Inc.

504 Amherst Street, Buffalo, NY 14207
(800) 723-4262; FAX (716) 873-4462

NY6119PP. Relax and enjoy the view from the veranda porch of this countryside setting overlooking the historic canal. One king-size room with private bath, warmly decorated with family antiques and a lovely view of the gardens. Continental plus breakfast served. Minutes to entertainment, restaurants, shopping and biking/hiking paths. Friendly hospitable hosts invite guests to enjoy the Niagara Frontier from Buffalo to Niagara Falls. $60.

NORTHVILLE

American Country Collection

4 Greenwood Lane, Delmar, 12054
(518) 439-7001

175. In the foothills of the Adirondacks, on the shores of the Great Sacandaga Lake, lies this charming lakefront Victorian inn where visitors can relax in the timely elegance of years gone by. There is a large common room with mahogany staircase, cable TV, comfortable sofa, chairs, and

---

NOTES: Credit cards accepted: A MasterCard; B Visa; C American Express; D Discover Card; E Diner's Club; F Other; 2 Personal checks accepted; 3 Lunch available; 4 Dinner available; 5 Open all year;

fireplace. Breakfast is available each morning in an adjacent dining room with guest refrigerator. Complimentary refreshments are served in the afternoon. Docking space is free in season. Arrangements can be made for small private parties, weddings, and business meetings. Six rooms, five on the second floor and one on the first floor, all with private baths. Smoking outside only. Well-behaved children are welcome; children under 12 must room with their parents. $65-75.

Bayside Guest House

OLCOTT

Bayside Guest House

1572 Lockport Olcott Road
(State Road 78), 14126-0034
(716) 778-7767; (800) 438-2192

Overlooking the harbor and marina, near Lake Ontario, this country-style Victorian home offers fishermen and travelers a comfortable, relaxed stay. Antiques and collectibles furnish this guest house. Great fishing, a county park, and many new shops within walking distance. Plenty of restaurants. One-half hour from Niagara Falls, one hour from Buffalo. Smoke free.

Host: Jane M. Voelpel
Rooms: 5 (SB) $30

Continental Breakfast
Credit Cards: None
Notes: 2, 5, 6, 8, 9, 10, 12

OLD CHATHAM

American Country Collection

4 Greenwood Lane, Delmar, 12054
(518) 439-7001

037. Wildflowers and birds, stone walls, and lawns beckon the guest to sit back and enjoy a simpler lifestyle in this 175-year-old Greek Revival private home on one-half acre. The home features a collection of antiques from the late 1700s that has been handed down from generation to generation. One second-floor guest room with private hall bath. Breakfast can be served on the patio in nice weather. Smoking limited to first floor. Adults only. No pets. $45.

OLIVEREA

Slide Mountain Forest House

805 Oliverea Road, 12410
(914) 254-5365; (914) 254-4269

Nestled in the Catskill Mountains State Park, this inn offers the flavor and charm of the old country. Come and enjoy the beautiful country setting, superb lodging, fine dining, and chalet rentals. Having run this bed and breakfast for more than 60 years, the hosts strive to give guests a pleasant and enjoyable stay. German and Continental cuisine, a bar and lounge, pool, tennis, hiking, fishing, antiquing, and more are available for guests' pleasure.

Hosts: Ursula and Ralph Combe
Rooms: 21 (17 PB; 4 SB) $50-70
Full Breakfast
Credit Cards: A, B, D
Notes: 2, 3, 4, 5 (chalets), 7, 8, 9, 10, 11, 12, 13

6 Pets welcome; 8 Children welcome; 9 Social drinking allowed; 10 Tennis available; 11 Swimming available; 12 Golf available; 13 Skiing available; 14 May be booked through travel agents.

ONTARIO

The Tummonds House

5392 Walworth/Ontario Road, 14519
(315) 524-5381

Fully restored 1897 Queen Anne Victorian home in a quiet country setting. Private guest entrance, living room with TV, and baby grand piano. Spacious bedrooms with king-size and double beds, all with wall-to-wall carpet. Full country breakfast served 5:00 A.M. to 9:00 A.M. Conveniently between NYS Thruway and Seaway Trail.

Hosts: James and Judith Steensma
Rooms: 4 (2 PB; 2 SB) $40-50
Full Breakfast
Credit Cards: None
Notes: 2, 5, 9, 12, 13

OTTO

The International Bed and Breakfast Club, Inc.

504 Amherst Street, Buffalo, NY 14207
(800) 723-4262; FAX (716) 873-4462

NY5140PP. This charming turn-of-the-century farmhouse is nestled among the old willow trees overlooking Cattaraugus Creek. Five rooms are available with shared baths. Guests may enjoy the spa on the terrace and a variety of seasonal activities: rafting, fishing, swimming, hiking, horseback riding, cross-country skiing, snowmobiling, ice skating, and tobogganing. New York's finest downhill skiing is nearby. A full breakfast is served, as well as other meals, featuring natural foods. $65.

PALENVILLE

American Country Collection

4 Greenwood Lane, Delmar, 12054
(518) 439-7001

031. This large old Victorian with wraparound porch is nestled along the creek by the scenic mountain road that leads to Tannersville. Leaf peepers, creek swimmers, waterfall seekers, hikers, and nature lovers will find this area exciting. One first-floor guest room with double bed and private bath. Four second-floor rooms share two baths. The living room has a fireplace, TV, and piano. Smoking limited. Children welcome. Pets in residence. Full breakfast served. $40-60.

The Kenmore Country Bed and Breakfast

The Kenmore Country Bed and Breakfast

Malden Avenue, 12463
(518) 678-3494

This quaint country home was built in the late 1800s and is nestled at the bottom of Hunter Mountain. Spend the night in one of the three cozy bedrooms. Enjoy the day relaxing in the large living room or screened porch. Close to many attractions. Cottage rental also available, but breakfast is not included.

Hosts: John and Lauren Hanzl
Rooms: 3 (1 PB; 2 SB) $50-60
Full Breakfast
Credit Cards: A, B, D
Notes: 5, 6 and 7 (limited), 9, 11, 12, 13

PENFIELD

Strawberry Castle

1883 Penfield Road, 14526
(716) 385-3266

NOTES: Credit cards accepted: A MasterCard; B Visa; C American Express; D Discover Card; E Diner's Club; F Other; 2 Personal checks accepted; 3 Lunch available; 4 Dinner available; 5 Open all year;

In suburban Rochester, this 1875 landmark Victorian Italianate villa combines the historic charm of yesteryear with the pleasures of a private luxury pool and patio on three acres of grounds. Brass or Empire beds in large, air-conditioned rooms. Fine restaurants and golf courses nearby. Turn this trip into a special memory.

Hosts: Anne Felker and Robert Houle
Rooms: 3 (PB) $75-95
Full Breakfast
Credit Cards: A, B, C
Notes: 2, 5, 9, 10, 11, 12, 14

PENN YAN

Finton's Landing

661 East Lake Road, 14527
(315) 536-3146

A secluded lakeside lawn leads to Finton's Landing where steamboats loaded grapes at harvest along 165 feet of private beach. A full breakfast is relished in two sunny dining areas or on the romantic porch. The parlor and living room, with fireplace, are filled with warmth and memories of a home more than 100 years old. Join the hosts and escape to countryside, fine waterfront restaurants, antique shops, and vineyard wine tastings.

Hosts: Doug and Arianne Tepper
Rooms: 4 (PB) $79
Full Breakfast
Credit Cards: A, B
Notes: 2, 5, 10, 11, 12, 13

The Wagener Estate Bed and Breakfast

351 Elm Street, 14527
(315) 536-4591

Centrally in the Finger Lakes, this bed and breakfast is in a historic 1796 home furnished with antiques and nestled on four acres. Hospitality, country charm, comfort, and an elegant breakfast await.

Hosts: Norm and Evie Worth
Rooms: 5 (3 PB; 2 SB) $55-70
Full Breakfast

Credit Cards: A, B, C
Notes: 2, 9, 10, 11, 12

PHILMONT

American Country Collection

4 Greenwood Lane, Delmar, 12054
(518) 439-7001

066. Set back from the country road, this spacious lodge-style bed and breakfast is enveloped in eight acres of woods but is just one mile from the Taconic Parkway and 30 minutes from Tanglewood, Massachusetts. Two air-conditioned guest rooms, each with private baths. No smoking. Children welcome. Full breakfast served in the kitchen, living room, sunroom, decks, or the patio in summer. $75.

PHOENIX

Elaine's Bed and Breakfast Reservation Service

4987 Kingston Road, Elbridge, 13060
(315) 689-2082

A stately Queen Anne-style 1850s home in a village nestled along the curving shoreline of the Oswego River and the old Erie Canal in north central New York. Arduously restored over several years by its present owners, it now offers three lovely guest rooms. They feature brass and iron beds, sumptuous down comforters, original and antique artwork, and turn-of-the-century oak furniture. Owner is an antique dealer. Phoenix is on Route 57 halfway between Syracuse and Oswego, right off 481. It is about 20 minutes to either city. Very easy to find. $50-75.

PINE HILL

Birchcreek Inn

Route 28, P.O. Box 583, 12465
(914) 254-5222

6 Pets welcome; 8 Children welcome; 9 Social drinking allowed; 10 Tennis available; 11 Swimming available; 12 Golf available; 13 Skiing available; 14 May be booked through travel agents.

A century-old estate on 23 wooded acres in the heart of the Catskill Mountains. Well known for extensive, delicious breakfasts. All guest rooms are beautifully decorated and have private baths. Close to hiking, downhill and cross-country skiing, auctions, antiques, fly fishing, horseback riding, and snowmobiling.

Hosts: Julie and Ron Odato
Rooms: 6 (PB) $50-75
Full Breakfast
Credit Cards: A, B, C
Notes: 2, 5, 6, 8, 9, 10, 11, 12, 13, 14

PINE PLAINS

Nutmeg Bed and Breakfast Agency

P.O. Box 1117, West Hartford, CT 06127-1117
(203) 236-6698; (800) 727-7592

Beautifully restored 23-room Victorian mansion with six antique-furnished guest rooms, some with private baths. One suite with sitting room and lovely view. Four porches for relaxing. Continental breakfast. Children over 12. Smoking allowed.

PITTSTOWN

Maggie Towne's Bed and Breakfast

Rural Delivery 2, Box 82, Valley Falls, 12185
(518) 663-8369; (518) 686-7331

An old Colonial amid beautiful lawns and trees, 14 miles east of Troy on NY Route 7. Enjoy tea or wine before the fireplace in the family room. Use the music room or read on the screened porch. The hostess will prepare lunch for guests to take on tour or enjoy at the house. It's 20 miles to historic Bennington, Vermont, and 30 to Saratoga Springs.

Host: Maggie Towne
Rooms: 3 (SB) $35-45
Full Breakfast
Credit Cards: None
Notes: 2, 3, 5, 8, 9, 10, 11, 12, 13, 14

POMPEY

Elaine's Bed and Breakfast Reservation Service

4987 Kingston Road, Elbridge, 13060
(315) 689-2082

Charming, well-furnished, sparkling ranch on two acres with a view of a sculpture garden. Guests may have the entire main floor. Two double bedrooms. Master bedroom opens to another room with a sleeper sofa for a family suite. One and one-half baths. Southeast of Syracuse in the country. Just north of Route 20. Less than 30 minutes from Syracuse. Moderate rates.

PORT JEFFERSON

Compass Rose Bed and Breakfast

415 West Broadway, 11777
(516) 474-1111

Dating from the 1820s, this home and barn of a ship's captain are above the busy harbor of Port Jefferson with its ferry to Connecticut. Beautiful Port Jefferson is a restored whaling village with unique shops and fine restaurants. Although modernized with new baths and central air conditioning, the home is decorated with antiques and country furnishings. Breakfast specialties of homemade breads, jams, freshly ground coffee, teas, and cereals are served each morning in the Rose Parlor.

Host: Kathleen Burk
Rooms: 4 (2 PB; 2 SB) $58-125
Continental Breakfast
Credit Cards: A, B, C, D
Notes: 2, 5, 7, 8, 9, 10, 11, 12, 14

PORT ONTARIO

Elaine's Bed and Breakfast Reservation Service

4987 Kingston Road, Elbridge, 13060
(315) 689-2082

NOTES: Credit cards accepted: A MasterCard; B Visa; C American Express; D Discover Card; E Diner's Club; F Other; 2 Personal checks accepted; 3 Lunch available; 4 Dinner available; 5 Open all year;

An authentic stone lighthouse built in 1838 to help guide shipping on Lake Ontario, is now completely furnished for nightly or weekly rental. First floor has large kitchen complete with kitchenwares for cooking, living room with fireplace, two bedrooms, and a bath. Second floor has two bedrooms and sitting room or third bedroom. There is a glassed-in cupola that may be accessed by a steel ladder. There are also three housekeeping cabins with three bedrooms each on this six-acre property. They have color cable TV and new rustic furniture. Two twin beds in each bedroom. There is also a marina. Port Ontario is just three miles west of Pulaski and I-81. $100-700.

POUGHKEEPSIE

Inn at the Falls

50 Red Oaks Mill Road, 12603
(914) 462-5770; (800) 344-1466

Inn at the Falls in Dutchess County combines the most luxurious elements of a modern hotel with the ambience and personal attention of a country home. Complimentary European-style breakfast is delivered to guest's room each morning. Twenty-two hotel rooms and 14 suites are all individually decorated for those who demand the finest in overnight accommodations.

Host: Arnold Sheer
Rooms: 22 (PB) $110-150
Suites: 14
Continental Breakfast
Credit Cards: A, B, C, D, E
Notes: 5, 8, 9, 10, 11, 12, 13, 14

PULASKI

Elaine's Bed and Breakfast Reservation Service

4987 Kingston Road, Elbridge, 13060
(315) 689-2082

A. On the banks of Salmon River is this executive-type house that is now a bed and breakfast and fisherman's lodge. On the first floor, with a separate entrance, there is a guest room with a double bed and two twins. The second-floor guest rooms can accommodate three, four, and five people. The basement has a large lounge with billiard table, a tackle shop, mud room, and full bath. Continental plus breakfast is served. Well-behaved children over five are welcome. Pets are welcome. Full meal plans and boxed lunches are available for a moderate price. $20-31.

B. A great stopping-off place on I-80 between Syracuse and Watertown, this original large brick Victorian sits back splendidly from the main street. Recently purchased by new owners, it has been refurbished where necessary yet reflects its origins via its great front porch and tall, mature trees in the front yard. There is a study where guests may watch cable TV or play table games. Elegantly furnished with antiques, the main house has four spacious guest rooms individually decorated with private baths, and two rear rooms share a bath. The gracious dining room has a fireplace with lovely gilded mirror above. Living room decor is Victorian. In addition to the main house, there are several efficiency cabins on the property. MasterCard, Visa, and Discover Cards accepted. Moderate rates.

QUEENSBURY

American Country Collection

4 Greenwood Lane, Delmar, 12054
(518) 439-7001

126. Original gingerbread accents this 100-year-old farmhouse on a working berry farm. There's a comfortable country feeling here with family furnishings and mementos, patchwork quilts, and oak furnishings. Two guest rooms with private baths. One room has a whirlpool tub. Excellent location for

outlet shopping, hot air balloon festival, Great Escape Amusement Park, and Lake George. Smoking outdoors only. Children over six welcome. Cat in residence. $60-70.

Crislip's Bed and Breakfast

693 Ridge Road, 12804
(518) 793-6869

Just minutes from Saratoga Springs and Lake George, this landmark Federal home provides spacious accommodations, complete with period antiques, four-poster beds, and down comforters. The country breakfast menu features buttermilk pancakes, scrambled eggs, and sausages. The hosts invite guests to relax on the porches and enjoy the beautiful mountain view of Vermont.

Hosts: Ned and Joyce Crislip
Rooms: 3 (PB) $55-75
Full Breakfast
Credit Cards: A, B
Notes: 2, 5, 8, 9, 10, 11, 12, 13

RED HOOK

American Country Collection

4 Greenwood Lane, Delmar, 12054
(518) 439-7001

115. This home, built in 1821 in the Federal-style and restored in 1988, offers a ground-level suite with private entrance and bath, non working fireplace, antique table and chairs, microwave, coffee maker, and small refrigerator. Smoking outdoors only. Children welcome. Port-a-crib available. No pets. Breakfast, made with only the freshest organic ingredients, is served at the table in front of the two deep-silled windows that look out to two acres of trees, and vegetable and flower gardens. Add $10 for one-night stays. $95.

REMSEN

Bed and Breakfast Leatherstocking

P.O. Box 53, Herkimer, 13350
(315) 733-0040; (800) 941-BEDS (2337)

013. A rare Welsh Barngarten greets the traveler, inviting the guest to sit among its array of blossoming plants, while the house, an old Victorian farmhouse with Welsh motif throughout, provides a secluded shelter in the foothills of the Adirondacks. The Victorian sitting room, with harmonium and old lithographs, is prologue to the three comfortably furnished rooms upstairs. Full breakfast. $55-60.

Tibbitts House Inn

RENSSELAER

Tibbitts House Inn

100 Columbia Turnpike, 12144
(518) 472-1348

This is a 136-year-old farmhouse acquainted with country living. The old house has an 84-foot windowed porch on which breakfast is served in season. Rooms are papered in cheerful patterns with braided and rag rugs on polished fir floors. Handmade quilts top crisp bed linens. Antiques abound. Two miles from Albany and the state capitol, museums, convention center, the new Knickerbocker Arena, and Hudson River boat launch.

Host: Claire E. Rufleth
Rooms: 5 (1 PB; 4 SB) $48-55

NOTES: Credit cards accepted: A MasterCard; B Visa; C American Express; D Discover Card; E Diner's Club; F Other; 2 Personal checks accepted; 3 Lunch available; 4 Dinner available; 5 Open all year;

Full and Continental Breakfast
Credit Cards: None
Notes: 2, 5, 7, 8, 10, 11, 12

REXFORD

American Country Collection

4 Greenwood Lane, Delmar, 12054
(518) 439-7001

042. This Queen Anne Victorian manor house had a humble beginning in 1763 as a cabin, grew to a farmhouse in the early 19th century, and in 1883 took on its present elegant form. Air-conditioned. One suite on the second floor has two bedrooms, a sitting room with TV, and a private bath. Two first-floor rooms with TV and private entrances. An English country buffet breakfast is served in the dining room or on the terrace. The Mohawk River, a yacht club, two golf courses, and a bicycle path are within walking distance. Smoking permitted with consideration for other guests. Children welcome. Two dogs in residence. $85-130.

123. An idyllic landscape of rolling hills, grassy fields, woodlands, and flowers surround this private suite set 800 feet back from a cul-de-sac on seven country acres. The suite includes a private bath, kitchenette, and separate entrance. No smoking. Children school age and over welcome. No pets. Arrangements for guest dog may be made occasionally. Fixings for breakfast provided in kitchenette for leisurely breakfast at guests' convenience. Weekly and monthly rates available. $65-85.

RHINEBECK

American Country Collection

4 Greenwood Lane, Delmar, 12054
(518) 439-7001

060. Skilled local craftsmen have painstakingly restored this 1860 Victorian in the heart of a historic village filled with antique and specialty shops, art galleries, and fine restaurants. The Aerodrome and Roosevelt and Vanderbilt mansions are just a short drive away. A gourmet breakfast is served at small tables in the fireplaced oak dining room. Five guest rooms with private baths. One room has a working fireplace. Guests may choose from brass, canopied, or carved Victorian beds. Smoking limited to parlor. Children over 16 welcome. No pets. $175-275.

192. A rambling contemporary home filled with light from large windows and sliding glass doors, overlooking 15 acres of rolling private countryside. House is furnished with an interesting combination of contemporary, antique, and modern pieces. Dining/breakfast room has an antique Spanish oak table, which seats 10, and an ornate crystal chandelier. Full gourmet breakfast served. All guest rooms are air-conditioned, and all baths have a skylight. Cross-country skiing, horseback riding, golf, tennis, and sailing, and the town of Rhinebeck are all less than six miles away. $75-175.

Village Victorian Inn

Village Victorian Inn

31 Center Street, 12572
(914) 876-8345

A seductive retreat filled with antiques, canopied beds, fine linens, and laces. In the heart of historic Rhinebeck Village and close to fine dining, historic mansions, the Hudson River, and antiquing.

Hosts: Judy and Richard Kohler
Rooms: 5 (PB) $175-250
Full Breakfast
Credit Cards: A, B, C
Notes: 5, 8, 10, 11, 12, 13

RICHFIELD SPRINGS _____

Bed and Breakfast Leatherstocking

P.O. Box 53, Herkimer, 13350
(315) 733-0040; (800) 941-BEDS (2337)

014. There is no pretension here with glorifying antiques. Instead an invitingly clean, comfortable, homey atmosphere suitable for large family gatherings awaits the traveler. A 14-room former railroad hotel and general store has been converted to a fine family dwelling with modern sun deck and turn-around, a family suite, or three immaculate guest rooms, with private and shared baths offered. Children welcome. $35-80.

015. Listed on the National Register of Historic Places, this spacious Victorian offers a full gourmet breakfast, cozy rooms with both private and shared baths, and a tasteful decor aimed at the comfort of the guests. Just minutes away from the Glimmerglass State Opera and the Baseball Hall of Fame. Three acres of trees for relaxing, and quiet common rooms for sitting and reading or TV watching. $60-75.

Country Spread Bed and Breakfast

23 Prospect Street, P.O. Box 1863, 13439
(315) 858-1870

Built in 1893 within the village limits, directly on New York State Route 28. Enjoy the many central Leatherstocking attractions including antiquing, opera, Cooperstown, swimming, and boating. Guest rooms have a country decorated flair. Breakfast offers many delicious choices from Karen's kitchen. Families welcome. The hosts have two well-behaved children. A casual respite with genuine and sincere hospitality. Rated and approved by the ABBA.

Hosts: Karen and Bruce Watson
Rooms: 2 (PB) $50-75
Full Breakfast
Credit Cards: A, B
Notes: 2, 5, 8, 9, 10, 11, 12, 14

RICHMONDVILLE _____

American Country Collection

4 Greenwood Lane, Delmar, 12054
(518) 439-7001

125. This renovated Federal-style home is on 23 acres of scenic pastures and pines. Three guest rooms have private baths and shared baths. In addition, there is a studio apartment suite and two cottages. There is a large living room with fireplace, light and airy dining room, and a deck. Special treats include fresh fruit at night and gifts at breakfast table on holidays. Smoking permitted. Resident dog. Guest pets accepted with $15 deposit. Children welcome. Crib available. $60-135.

ROCHESTER _____

Dartmouth House Bed and Breakfast

215 Dartmouth Street, 14607
(716) 271-7872

Enjoy 1905 Edwardian charm, antiques, cozy window seats, grand piano, and fireplace. Stroll through this quiet, architecturally fascinating neighborhood to the George Eastman Mansion and International

Museum of Photography. Just a mile from downtown, in the heart of the Cultural Park/East Avenue area, it's an easy walk to Rochester's largest collection of antique shops, bookstores, and trendy or formal restaurants. Breakfast? Full gourmet and served by candlelight, using owners' Depression glass collection. Dress code? Be comfy! Phones in rooms and air conditioning. Smoking outside.

Hosts: Ellie and Bill Klein
Rooms: 4 (2 PB; 2 SB) $50-110
Full Breakfast
Credit Cards: A, B, C
Notes: 2, 5, 9, 10, 11, 12, 14

The International Bed and Breakfast Club, Inc.

501 Amherst Street, Buffalo, NY 14207
(800) 723-4262; FAX (716) 873-4462

Built in the 1920s, this ten-room white frame house is just two minutes from the expressway serving Rochester's downtown and cultural district. The second-floor wing has two guest bedrooms that share a common sitting room and bath. Breakfast is served in the dining room or on the patio, weather permitting. Resident dog and cat. No smoking. $70.

ROME

Elaine's Bed and Breakfast Reservation Service

1987 Kingston Road, Elbridge, 13060
(315) 689-2082

A. On six acres near state thruway, this 1840 Cape saltbox is warmly furnished with many antiques and crafts made by the hostess. Full country breakfast of guests' choice. Suite features double bed, sitting area, and private bath. Two other rooms with one double bed each share main bath. Cot available. Perfect stop-off from Route 90 about halfway between Boston and Toronto. $45-60.

B. This brick Victorian farmhouse built in 1857 features complete antique furnishings. Three guest rooms are upstairs; one room offers a double and single bed. Near Griffiss Air Force Base. Pool, 40 acres, gardens, hiking trails, cross-country skiing. Near downhill skiing area. Resident dog and cat.

The Little Schoolhouse

6905 Dix Road, 13440
(315) 336-4474

A warm and welcoming 1840 Colonial saltbox on six private, quiet acres. Furnished in Early American with handcrafts throughout. Quick access to I-90, airport, and recreational facilities. Near Hamilton College. Enjoy breakfast in the summer kitchen or cozy dining room with homemade pastries and jellies always on the menu. Then take a tour of the Little Schoolhouse in the back yard, authentically furnished for the period 1900-1920.

Host: Beverly Zingerline
Rooms: 3 (1 PB; 2 SB) $50-60
Full Breakfast
Credit Cards: A, B
Notes: 2, 5, 8, 12, 14

ROSCOE

Huff House

100 Lake Anawanda Road, 12776
(800) 358-5012

In the renowned trout-fishing Catskills. Beautiful old Victorian inn on 188 acres of secluded mountains, just two hours from New York City. Golf and fly fishing school starting in May. Trout pond, golf, heated pool, and tennis available. Excellent dining and wine cellar. Closed November through April.

Hosts: Joseph and Joanne Forness
Rooms: 24 (PB) $105-140
Full Breakfast
Credit Cards: A, B, C
Notes: 2, 3, 4, 6 (limited), 7, 8, 9, 10, 11, 12, 14

6 Pets welcome; 8 Children welcome; 9 Social drinking allowed; 10 Tennis available; 11 Swimming available; 12 Golf available; 13 Skiing available; 14 May be booked through travel agents.

SANBORN

The International Bed and Breakfast Club, Inc.

504 Amherst Street, Buffalo, NY 14207
(800) 723-4262; FAX (716) 873-4462

NY3693PP. This chalet-style home is nestled in an apple orchard, set back from the road in the country, yet conveniently near shopping and historic sites of Niagara County. Historic Pekin United Methodist Church and the regionally renowned Schimschack's Restaurant, where Joe DiMaggio once dined with Marilyn Monroe, are both nearby. Guests will also enjoy hiking. Two rooms with shared bath are available. A full country breakfast may be enjoyed on the deck or in the dining room. $50.

SANDY CREEK

Tug Hill Lodge

8091 Salisbury Street, 13145
(315) 387-5326

Built in 1872. Italianate-style home is comfortably old-fashioned. In a garden, Tug Hill offers five guest rooms, all with double beds. Between Syracuse and Watertown on Route 81, Exit 37. A full breakfast is served.

Rooms: 5 (SB) $30
Full Breakfast
Credit Cards: None
Notes: 2, 5, 6 (call), 8, 9, 10, 11, 12, 13

SARANAC LAKE

Elaine's Bed and Breakfast Reservation Service

4987 Kingston Road, Elbridge, 13060
(315) 689-2082

A. On eight acres in the country is a delightfully decorated, cozy, rustic ranch with family room filled with country antiques, baskets, and dried flowers. Many books about the Adirondacks are available for guests to read. The skylight brightens the room and the fireplace warms guests on cool fall nights. Hearty mountain breakfasts are served. This bed and breakfast is on the St. Regis canoe carry. There is swimming at Hole Pond, and it is only about 20 minutes to Lake Placid, the site of the 1980 Winter Olympics. Three comfortable guest rooms, each with one double bed, share the modern shower bath. Easy to find on Route 30 near nice golf course. Saranac Lake is in the central-northern Adirondacks. Open year-round. $45.

Fogarty's Bed and Breakfast

37 Riverside Drive, 12983
(518) 891-3755; (800) 525-3755

Fogarty's is high on a hill overlooking Lake Flower and mountains Baker, McKenzie, and Pisgah, but only three minutes from the center of town. The bed and breakfast porches, wide doors, and call buttons attest to its past as a cure cottage. The living room and dining room are decorated with handsome woodwork, and the bathrooms have original 1910 fixtures. Swimmers and boaters can use Fogarty's dock, and cross-country skiers will find trails within a mile. More ambitious athletes should take a brief drive to Lake Placid's Olympic course or the slopes of Whiteface.

Hosts: Jack and Emily Fogarty
Rooms: 5 (SB) $45
Full Breakfast
Credit Cards: None
Notes: 2, 5, 7, 8, 9, 10, 11, 12, 13

SARATOGA SPRINGS

Adelphi Hotel

365 Broadway, 12866
(518) 587-4688

NOTES: Credit cards accepted: A MasterCard; B Visa; C American Express; D Discover Card; E Diner's Club; F Other; 2 Personal checks accepted; 3 Lunch available; 4 Dinner available; 5 Open all year;

Charming Victorian hotel built in 1877 in historic downtown Saratoga Springs. The Adelphi has 35 guest rooms lavishly decorated with period artwork, antiques, and wall coverings. These spacious rooms are air-conditioned, have private baths, cable TV, and direct-dial phones. A delightful complimentary Continental breakfast is served in the morning to the guest's room, parlor, or piazza overlooking Broadway. A beautifully landscaped outdoor pool is available to guests. The Adelphi Cafe offers a full bar, desserts, and special coffees throughout the entire season; dinner served in July and August only.

Hosts: Sheila Parkert and Gregg Siefker
Rooms: 35 (PB) $80-290
Continental Breakfast
Credit Cards: A, B, C
Notes: 2, 4, 8, 9, 11, 12, 14

American Country Collection

4 Greenwood Lane, Delmar, 12054
(518) 439-7001

105. The friendly atmosphere of this working organic farm is a delight for children and adults. The Victorian farmhouse and barns have been restored to offer seven air-conditioned guest rooms, all with private baths. One room has two double beds, private bath, TV, wood-burning stove, and private deck. A gourmet breakfast is served in the Florida room amid flowering plants and the hot tub/Jacuzzi. The Saratoga Performing Arts Center and racetrack are two miles away. Smoking permitted. Children welcome. $100.

107. This cozy, restored Victorian cottage with gingerbread millwork was probably the caretaker's home for one of the nearby mansions on North Broadway. It is within walking distance of the downtown shops and Skidmore College. Two guest rooms share one bath with the owner. Rooms are comfortable and immaculately clean. No smoking allowed. Cat in residence. Children are welcome. $55-95.

136. This "mini-suite" in a 140-year-old historic Federal-period brick home in town, offers two private apartment/suites that include a sitting room, refrigerator, microwave, coffee maker, porch, color TV, and antique furnishings. Its spacious front porch with wicker furniture and flower boxes invites guests to sit and enjoy the beauty of an evening sunset or a refreshing glass of lemonade. A Continental plus breakfast and a daily newspaper are delivered to the door each morning, and two ten-speed bikes are available to guests. $100.

139. This in-town historic home is only three blocks from the Saratoga Racetrack. Built in 1868 by a Civil War captain, it offers a front porch with white wicker furniture and a porch rocker and a side lawn with a patio, a picnic table, and an outdoor grill. Furnishings include a mix of antiques, floral print wallpaper, lace curtains, and fresh and dried arrangements. One first-floor room with a double bed and shared bath, one-second floor room with queen-size, double, and single beds and a private bath, two second-floor rooms with double beds and shared bath, and one second-floor room with a double bed, private side porch, and a shared bath. An apartment with full kitchen, microwave, cable TV, air conditioning, a double bed, and a private bath. Full breakfast. $65-125.

141. Capture the peace and charm of Saratoga in this warm and inviting 100-year-old Queen Anne-style home restored to its original elegance by its owners. Across the street from the Saratoga Racetrack, this bed and breakfast is minutes from the harness track and the Saratoga Performing Arts Center. Three rooms share one large bath with a double sink and vanity; two rooms have double beds; and a

6 Pets welcome; 8 Children welcome; 9 Social drinking allowed; 10 Tennis available; 11 Swimming available; 12 Golf available; 13 Skiing available; 14 May be booked through travel agents.

third room has two single beds. Bedrooms are light and airy, and all three rooms are air-conditioned in the summer. Full breakfast. $65-110.

180. This Colonial-style cobblestone home is just minutes from Victorian Round Lake and Saratoga. Guests are welcomed with gracious hospitality and casual elegance. There are four guest rooms on the second floor all with luxury linens, firm mattresses, ceiling fans, and fresh flowers. Breakfast is served fireside in the spacious dining room, or in the summer months on the deck surrounded by fragrant flowers. Wake-up coffee is available for early risers, and refreshments are served in the afternoons. Smoking permitted on the deck or porch only. No children. $70-95.

The Clarion Inn at Saratoga

231 Broadway, 12866
(518) 583-1890

A turn-of-the-century, fully restored historic inn in the heart of Saratoga, offering delightful atmosphere and cozy surroundings. Enjoy the intimate cocktail lounge and sample a special selection offered nightly in the Victorian appointed dining room, complete with a fireplace. Oversized rooms echo the Victorian era, and many overlook an English garden. Nearby are several quaint shops and boutiques, as well as outlet malls. Near the world-famous Saratoga thoroughbred track and historic mineral baths.

Rooms: 38 (PB) $39-300
Continental Breakfast
Credit Cards: A, B, C, D, E, F
Notes: 2, 4, 5, 7, 8, 9, 10, 11, 12, 13, 14

The Inn on Bacon Hill

P.O. Box 1462, 12866
(518) 695-3693

The Inn on Bacon Hill

A peaceful alternative where guests come as strangers and leave as friends, just ten minutes east of Saratoga Springs. This 1862 Victorian is in a quiet, pastoral setting with four air-conditioned bedrooms. Enjoy beautiful gardens and gazebo, explore country lanes, or relax in comfortable guest parlor with an extensive library. Baby grand piano adorns a Victorian parlor suite. Innkeeping courses offered. Full country breakfasts included.

Host: Andrea Collins-Breslin
Rooms: 4 (PB) $65-135
Full Breakfast
Credit Cards: A, B
Notes: 2, 5, 9, 10, 11, 12, 13, 14

Lombardi Farm Bed and Breakfast

41 Locust Grove Road, 12866
(518) 587-2074

A restored Victorian farm, two miles from the center of historic Saratoga Springs. Air-conditioned, private baths, and gourmet breakfast served in the Florida room. Hot tub/Jacuzzi. A peaceful country setting within two miles of the National Museum of Dance, National Museum of Racing, Thoroughbred Racetrack, Harness Track, Polo Club, Skidmore College, Yaddo Artists Retreat and Gardens, and famous Saratoga Mineral Baths. Open year-round. Member of Bed and Breakfast Association of Saratoga, Lake George and Gore Mountain, and American Automobile Association.

Hosts: Vincent and Kathleen Lombardi
Rooms: 4 (PB) $100
Full Breakfast

NOTES: Credit cards accepted: A MasterCard; B Visa; C American Express; D Discover Card; E Diner's Club; F Other; 2 Personal checks accepted; 3 Lunch available; 4 Dinner available; 5 Open all year;

Credit Cards: None
Notes: 2, 5, 7, 9, 10, 11, 12, 14

Six Sisters
Bed and Breakfast

149 Union Avenue, 12866
(518) 583-1173

This beautifully appointed 1880 Victorian is on a historic, flower-laden boulevard in the heart of Saratoga Springs. Luxurious, immaculate rooms and suites offer king-size beds, private baths, and air conditioning. Antiques, Oriental carpets, hardwood floors, and Italian marble create a resplendent decor. The inn is close to Skidmore College, Convention Center, the racetracks, SPAC, downtown, museums, spa, antiques, and restaurants. SPAC discounts. The owner is a native of Saratoga eager to share local information. Recommended by *Gourmet* and *Country Folk Art*.

Hosts: Kate Benton and Steve Ramirez
Rooms: 4 (PB) $70-110
Full Breakfast
Credit Cards: A, B
Notes: 2, 5, 8 (over 10), 9, 10, 11, 12, 13, 14

The Westchester House

102 Lincoln Avenue, Box 944, 12866
(518) 587-7613

The Westchester House

This gracious 1885 award-winning Queen Anne Victorian inn features elaborate chestnut moldings, antique furnishings, and up-to-date comforts. Enjoy the extensive library or play the baby grand piano. The charm and excitement, museums and racetracks, boutiques and restaurants of historic Saratoga are an easy walk from the Westchester House. After a busy day sampling the delights of Saratoga, relax on the wrap-around porch, in the old-fashioned gardens, or in the double Victorian parlors and enjoy a refreshing glass of lemonade. Rates higher during racing season. Two-night minimum stay is required for weekends and holidays. AAA three-diamonds approved.

Hosts: Bob and Stephanie Melvin
Rooms: 7 (PB) $70-125
Continental Breakfast
Credit Cards: A, B, C
Notes: 2, 5, 8 (over 12), 9, 10, 11, 12, 13, 14

SCHENECTADY

American Country Collection

4 Greenwood Lane, Delmar, 12054
(518) 439-7001

043. This bed and breakfast, formerly a tavern, is in the heart of the city's historic Stockade district. The entire house can be rented for overnight lodging, weddings, or long-term stays. Three second-floor guest rooms, each with a TV, share one and one-half baths. One has a working fireplace, and two are air-conditioned. The luxurious bath has a Jacuzzi and a separate shower. One two-room suite also with double bed and private bath. All are air-conditioned. Breakfast is served in the dining room or in the breakfast room that looks out into the gardens and terrace. Within walking distance to theaters, shopping, restaurants, bike trail, train station, and Union College. Smoking limited. Children welcome. No pets. $95.

6 Pets welcome; 8 Children welcome; 9 Social drinking allowed; 10 Tennis available; 11 Swimming available; 12 Golf available; 13 Skiing available; 14 May be booked through travel agents.

172. Set in the heart of historic Schenectady, this late Victorian-style home has been meticulously restored to its former charm and grace. Antiques of maple, cherry, and walnut. All hardwood floors. Guest rooms are air-conditioned. There is a separate guest sitting room that overlooks the garden. It has a TV, ceiling fan, and rattan rocking chairs. There is a half-bath on the first floor and full bath with extra-large tub on the second floor. Before retiring, guests fill out an individual menu request card for breakfast. Wake-up coffee available. Smoking in garden only. Children are welcome; no provisions for infants. Resident cat. $50-55.

196. This modern raised ranch is in a quiet residential area surrounded by a half-acre of lawn and trees. All rooms are carpeted and modestly decorated, each with telephone, central air conditioning, refrigerator, coffeemaker, microwave, and private bath. The two-room, ground-level suite has a private entrance, queen-size bed, and softside Jacuzzi; a second room includes a queen-size sofabed and a private deck. A two-room, second-floor suite includes a sitting room with couch and recliner, twin beds, and a jet-tub bath. A washer and dryer are also available for guest use. Breakfast-tray delivered by pre-arrangement. Smoking is permitted. Convenient to NY Thruway, Union College, Schenectady, and Capital District shopping areas. Well-suited for business travelers and long-term stays, as well as overnight or weekend accommodations. Children welcome, though no cribs are available. $55-65.

SCHUYLERVILLE (SARATOGA SPRINGS) ___

American Country Collection
4 Greenwood Lane, Delmar, 12054
(518) 439-7001

124. Built in 1770, this home is in the midst of an apple orchard on an elevation overlooking the Hudson River. The mantel holds cannonballs that American troops fired at the house when it served as a hospital for British and Hessian troops during the Revolutionary War. In the main house, there are three guest rooms with shared bath and a two-room suite with a double bed and private bath. The Apple Cottage offers one bedroom, one and one-half baths, living room with fireplace, kitchen, and sitting area with fireplace. The Island Cottage offers two bedrooms, bath, loft, living room/kitchen with fireplace, and screened porch. Smoking in common areas only. Children welcome in the Island Cottage. They are welcome at the main house and Apple Cottage when the pool is not open. Pets in residence. Full and Continental breakfast offered. $65-175.

SHELDRAKE ___

Elaine's Bed and Breakfast Reservation Service
4987 Kingston Road, Elbridge, 13060
(315) 689-2082

This 145-year-old Queen Anne house on Cayuga Lake is a destination in itself. Completely renovated in 1993, including new private baths. Two rooms have Jacuzzis and fireplaces, and two have private balconies. All four rooms have queen-size beds. A fifth guest room has two twin beds and shared bath. There are ceiling fans in all rooms. There is private lake frontage for swimming and boating. Complimentary rowboats and bikes for guests. Hiking and cycling. Golf and wineries are nearby. Gourmet breakfast. Infants and children over 12 are welcome. Off-season rates available. $65-125.

SHELTER ISLAND ___

The Bayberry Bed and Breakfast
36 South Menantic Road, P.O. Box 538, 11964
(516) 749-3375

NOTES: Credit cards accepted: A MasterCard; B Visa; C American Express; D Discover Card; E Diner's Club; F Other; 2 Personal checks accepted; 3 Lunch available; 4 Dinner available; 5 Open all year;

Experience an island accessible only by ferry with a simple, peaceful lifestyle, and a third of it is a nature conservancy. Activities include hiking, bird watching, biking, beaches, boating, fishing, winery tours, and antiquing. This home is in a setting abounding with wildlife, furnished with antiques, has an exceptionally large king-size bedroom, hammocks, swimming pool, and a cozy living room with a fireplace and a piano. Off-season rates are available.

Hosts: Suzanne and Richard Boland
Rooms: 2 (PB) $90-125
Credit Cards: None
Notes: 2, 5, 8 (over 14), 9, 10, 11, 12

SKANEATELES

Elaine's Bed and Breakfast Reservation Service

4987 Kingston Road, Elbridge, 13060
(315) 689-2082

A. New, custom-designed country ranch-style home with a view of drumlins. Two bedrooms, each with separate entrance and double bed. Full country breakfast. Several fine restaurants, boutiques, gift and antique shops, and art galleries in nearby village of Skaneateles, as well as an old-fashioned "five and dime." Also convenient to the Schweinfuth Art Center and Cayuga Museum of History, Seward House and Harriet Tubman House (a few minutes away in Auburn). Seasonal or Sunday schedulings of antique shows, the Syracuse Symphony, the Merry-Go-Round Playhouse, polo matches, and the Skaneateles Music Festival.

B. Nestled against a wooded hillside on a picturesque quiet country road, this remodeled farmhouse offers three freshly decorated guest rooms and two modern baths. One room has a double and single bed; one has two twins; and one has a double bed. Roll away and a chair bed are also available. A large family room with grand piano,

large color TV, VCR, and stereo is also available for guests' use on the same level. A Continental plus breakfast featuring homemade breads, muffins, and jams is served in the roomy country kitchen with custom-built stone fireplace. A larger hot breakfast is available for a nominal fee. There are hiking and cross-country ski trails on the 100-acre property. Children over ten preferred. This is a smoke-free house. Five miles north of Skaneateles Village, 14 miles west of Syracuse. $55-65.

C. A beautifully remodeled executive ranch nicely furnished with good traditional furniture, Oriental pieces, and antiques. Offers a guest room with a new queen-size antique iron bed with good firm bedding, new wallpaper and matching carpet, antique chest, and sparkling new private bath. No smoking. Hide-a-bed available in den if necessary for other people in the same guest party. Full breakfast. Hostess is active in Skaneateles Art Guild. Needlepoint, hand made quilts, and art decorate this lovely home. Resident cat. $70.

D. Cute, clean, comfortable, convenient, cozy, congenial, casual country atmosphere in a newly remodeled ranch on five acres. Adults preferred. Two modest guest rooms, each with a firm double bed, share a new bathroom. The hostess can direct guests to almost any place in Onondaga County including Syracuse (12 miles), Auburn (nine miles), Skaneateles Village (four miles). No smoking. Resident cat. $40-50.

E. Just three and one-half miles from the village is this new, custom-designed country ranch-style house with a view of drumlins. Guest bedroom wing is separate with its own shiny shower bath, plus a surprise. Full country breakfast. Easy to find; only seven country miles from the New York State Thruway (Interstate 90) at Weedsport.

6 Pets welcome; 8 Children welcome; 9 Social drinking allowed; 10 Tennis available; 11 Swimming available; 12 Golf available; 13 Skiing available; 14 May be booked through travel agents.

SODUS BAY

Elaine's Bed and Breakfast Reservation Service

4987 Kingston Road, Elbridge, 13060
(315) 689-2082

This turn-of-the-century waterfront home with expansive lawns and mature trees is on the east side of Sodus Bay. Three large guest rooms, each with private bath, TV, radio, and king- or queen-size beds, occupy the main house. A suite overlooking the bay has a full kitchen, living-dining room, king-size bed, private bath, TV, radio, and cassette player. Two guest cottages are also available: Guests may choose the Summer House with queen-size and double beds, private baths, a balcony, and porch; or the Caretaker's House, with living room, TV sleeper sofa, full kitchen, dining area, bath, and two bedrooms with two double or queen-size beds. A roll-away bed is also available. Parking area also accommodates boat and trailer. Full gourmet breakfast is served. Smoking allowed outside only. Resident cat.

SOUTHAMPTON

The New York Bed and Breakfast Reservation Center

P.O. Box 2646, 11969-2646
(212) 577-3512

Wide range of inns in New York City and surrounding areas. Hosted and unhosted accommodations available. The majority of accommodations are in doormen security buildings, others are in townhouses. Apartments by the month also available. $80-90.

The Old Post House Inn

136 Main Street, 11968
(516) 283-1717

The Old Post House, a small, charming country inn, was built in 1684 and is listed on the National Register of Historic Places. All rooms have private baths and air conditioning. Continental breakfast is included. Close to boutiques and Saks Fifth Avenue.

Hosts: Cecile and Ed Courville
Rooms: 7 (PB) $80-170
Continental Breakfast
Credit Cards: A, B, C
Notes: 3, 4, 5, 7, 8 (over 12), 9, 10, 11, 12

Village Latch Inn Resort

101 Hill Street, 11968
(516) 283-2160

Village Latch Inn is known internationally for its charming ambience. A 40-room Gatsby mansion on five acres, yet in town near beach. Antiques to modern duplexes. Number-one choice in 50 inn books from Frommer's to Fodor's. Also the mansion is available for celebrations, corporate outings, and weddings. Minimum stay weekends is two nights.

Hosts: Marta and Martin White
Rooms: 70 (PB) $85-195
Continental Breakfast
Credit Cards: A, B, C, D, E
Notes: 5, 6, 7, 8, 10, 11, 14

SOUTH OTSELIC

Bed and Breakfast Leatherstocking

P.O. Box 53, Herkimer, 13350
(315) 733-0040; (800) 941-BEDS (2337)

018. Surrounded by a picket fence, bordering state-owned hunting and fishing tracts with stocked trout streams, here is the ideal getaway for hiking, fishing, hunting, and skiing. Twenty-five minutes from SUNY Cortland and 30 minutes from Colgate. Huge kitchen with potbelly stove completes the country setting. Four guest rooms with two shared baths. Full country breakfasts served year-round. $30-55.

NOTES: Credit cards accepted: A MasterCard; B Visa; C American Express; D Discover Card; E Diner's Club; F Other; 2 Personal checks accepted; 3 Lunch available; 4 Dinner available; 5 Open all year;

SPENCER

Elaine's Bed and Breakfast Reservation Services

4987 Kingston Road, Elbridge, 13060
(315) 689-2082

This large updated farmhouse is just 20 minutes south of Ithaca and also convenient to Binghamton, Endicott, Elmira, and Watkins Glen. Across the road are five acres next to a quiet stream where the hostess allows tenting and picnics. She also arranges bike tours with or without lunch. There are hiking trails and cross-country skiing. Children over 12 are welcome. There are outside kennels for roving with rover. No pets inside. A full hearty country breakfast is served including delicious homemade breads and muffins and jams. This is a smoke-free bed and breakfast. Open year-round.

STANFORDVILLE

Lakehouse Inn on Golden Pond

Shelley Hill Road 12581
(914) 266-8093

The most enchanting lakefront sanctuary in the Hudson River Valley, this inn offers swimming, fishing, boating, suites with private Jacuzzi for two, wood-burning fireplaces, private decks, and stunning views of the lakes and woods. Gourmet breakfasts and afternoon appetizers. A unique private inn where guests are free to enjoy a special time in splendid circumstances. Just 90 minutes from Manhattan.

Hosts: Judy and Rich Kohler
Rooms: 8 (PB) $175-425
Full Breakfast
Credit Cards: A, B, C
Notes: 5, 8, 10, 11, 12, 13

STILLWATER

American Country Collection

4 Greenwood Lane, Delmar, 12054
(518) 439-7001

005. This is a quiet retreat on 100 acres of rolling countryside, complete with mountain vistas. The circa 1800 barn has been transformed into an exquisite home. It is conveniently between Saratoga Lake and Saratoga National Historical Park. Two rooms and two second-floor suites, each with private bath. Breakfast is served in the dining room or on the deck overlooking the countryside. Smoking outdoors only. Children over nine welcome. Dog in residence. $10 charge for one night stays. $85-135.

SYRACUSE (ELBRIDGE/JAMESVILLE)

Elaine's Bed and Breakfast Reservation Service

4987 Kingston Road, Elbridge, 13060
(315) 689-2082

A. Convenient to Syracuse University and LeMoyne College, this delightful knotty pine basement apartment can sleep two and has a completely furnished eat-in kitchen and attractive shower-bath with many built-ins. The living-bedroom includes color TV, desk, easy chairs, game table, and much more. Patio and yard. Quiet dead-end street with a great view. Use of laundry for long-term guests. Long-term rates available. $65-75.

B. This spacious Tudor built in 1920 offers three beautifully decorated guest rooms. An Art Deco room features a queen-size bed and private bath. A Victorian room has a double bed and shares a spacious vintage bath with a more traditional room that has a pair of twin beds, a sitting area, and TV. $60-70.

C. In the Eastside area near LeMoyne College and Syracuse University, this cute, customized Cape Cod has a newly redecorated first floor-guest room with a double bed, handmade chest, rocker, window seat, and private bath. An adjacent TV den can be a second guest room with a sofa bed. Both rooms are in a separate, rear wing of the house. $75.

6. On the western edge of the city, this three-year-young contemporary Cape is set on three acres. The guest room has a double bed and private bath. The property is a designated wildlife habitat. Peaceful, quiet setting, yet quite handy to shopping, state fair, zoo, restaurants, Onondaga Community College, highways, and Syracuse University. $45-60.

Pandora's Getaway

83 Oswego Street, 13027
(315) 635-9571

This restored Greek Revival home with sloping lawns is listed on the National Register of Historic Places and is 20 minutes from Syracuse. Easy access to thruway, NYS fairgrounds, Syracuse University, and Oswego. Relax on the front porch or in front of a fire in the living room. Various decors and amenities.

Host: Sandy Wheeler
Rooms: 4 (2 PB; 2 SB) $50-80
Full Breakfast
Credit Cards: A, B
Notes: 2, 5, 8, 10, 11, 12, 13, 14

THENDARA

Moose River House Bed and Breakfast

12 Birch Street, P.O. Box 184, 13472
(315) 369-3104

Back in the 19th century Moose River House was accessible only by the *Fawn*, a tiny side-wheeler that steamed upstream from Minnehaha, where New York's only wooden train rails terminated. Today, there are several routes to this northern Adirondack inn. However guests choose to arrive, they will not want to leave. From cross-country and downhill skiing in the winter, to hiking, horseback riding, and canoeing in the summer, the recreational options are vast. The adjacent town of Old Forge has a wealth of shops, restaurants, and recreational fun.

Hosts: Kate and Bill Labbate
Rooms: 4 (2 PB; 2 SB) $65-85
Full Breakfast
Credit Cards: A, B
Notes: 2, 5, 8 (over 12), 9, 10, 11, 12, 13

TROY

American Country Collection

4 Greenwood Lane, Delmar, 12054
(518) 439-7001

158. This unique Victorian farmhouse, circa 1849, is above Troy and set back 300 feet from the road with a long circular drive. It is near Rensselaer Polytechnical Institute, the Emma Willard School, Russell Sage College, and the Hudson Valley Community College. Four second-floor guest rooms share two full baths, and full country breakfast is served each morning. Smoking is allowed in designated areas only. $40-50.

TULLY-VESPER

Elaine's Bed and Breakfast Reservation Service

4987 Kingston Road, Elbridge, 13060
(315) 689-2082

Just four scenic miles from Route 81, on Route 80, this custom-built raised ranch offers two double bedrooms with a shared bath and a master bedroom with private bath. Well furnished and in a very quiet location at the rear of the home. Full country breakfast included. Very close to Song Mountain downhill ski area and a short drive to Labrador and Toggenburg ski areas. After skiing, guests may relax in front of the Pennsylvania bluestone fireplace. Take a pretty country drive to Cazenovia and Bouckville on Route 20 for the annual antique show and sale held in August. Open year-round. $55-65.

UTICA

Bed and Breakfast Leatherstocking

P.O. Box 53, Herkimer, 13350
(315) 733-0040; (800) 941-BEDS (2337)

019. Elegant brick Federalist-period home built around 1826 and on the National Register of Historic Places. Prearranged private dining and picnic lunches available. There are five guest rooms in the house with queen-size or single beds. Private and shared baths. Full breakfast served daily. Lots of history on a quiet street in a busy city in the center of New York state. $45-75.

020. Country charm in the city. Relax in this antique-filled, stenciled home year-round, enjoying breakfast on the porch in summer with herbs and vegetables fresh from the garden. A glass of mulled cider and a roaring fire greet guests in the fall and winter months. In an ideal location in south Utica. Just minutes from museums, shops, theaters, colleges, and restaurants. Single, double, and family suite available. $50-75.

The Iris Stonehouse Bed and Breakfast

16 Derbyshire Place, 13501-4706
(315) 732-6720; (800) 446-1456

In town, close to everything, this stately stone house with leaded-glass windows, listed on the local register of historic places. A separate guest sitting room, and guest rooms with private and shared baths. Full breakfast from the daily menu, central air, three miles from I-90, Exit 31 (NYS Thruway), one block off Genesee Street, three blocks from the North/South arterial and Routes 5, 8, and 12. No smoking.

Hosts: Shirley and Roy Kilgore
Rooms: 3 (1 PB; 2 SB) $45-60
Full Breakfast
Credit Cards: A, B, C
Notes: 2, 5, 9, 10, 12, 13, 14

VERNON

Bed and Breakfast Leatherstocking

P.O. Box 53, Herkimer, 13350
(315) 733-0040; (800) 941-BEDS (2337)

021. Steeped in history, this 18th-century inn has been restored, providing a clean, well-dressed bed and breakfast, close to cultural centers, antique centers, and universities. Three private bath suites and full breakfast. Also available are dried flower arrangements, quilts, crafts, and weavings, all homemade on the premises by the owners. $55-85.

Elaine's Bed and Breakfast Reservation Service

4987 Kingston Road, Elbridge, 13060
(315) 689-2082

A marvelous sprawling Victorian-Italianate manor house atop a knoll on seven acres. Filled with antiques, this home has been featured in several local history books and is a must-see for architectural and history buffs. There are five guest rooms. Children and well-behaved pets welcome. Full breakfast. No smoking allowed in the bedrooms. $60-70.

6 Pets welcome; 8 Children welcome; 9 Social drinking allowed; 10 Tennis available; 11 Swimming available; 12 Golf available; 13 Skiing available; 14 May be booked through travel agents.

Golden Rule Bed and Breakfast

VICTOR

Golden Rule Bed and Breakfast

6934 Rice Road, 14564
(716) 924-0610

This completely renovated and enlarged 1865 country schoolhouse is at the gateway to the Finger Lakes region of New York state. Two beautifully decorated large bedrooms containing antiques and offering panoramic views of the beautiful Bristol Hills. A complete gourmet breakfast is included in addition to afternoon tea.

Hosts: Karen and Dick de Mauriac
Rooms: 2 (SB) $55-75
Full Breakfast
Credit Cards: None
Notes: 2, 5, 9, 11, 12, 13

WARRENSBURG

American Country Collection

4 Greenwood Lane, Delmar, 12054
(518) 439-7001

067. This 1850 Greek Revival inn has a new guest house featuring ten rooms and a Jacuzzi in a plant-filled solarium. In the center of an old-fashioned Adirondack village that features bandstand concerts in the summer. The inn itself has a public restaurant, a cozy fireplace tavern, and a common room with TV. Ten rooms and one family suite with private baths, air conditioning, fireplace, queen-, king-size, or two twin beds. Handicapped access. Smoking permitted with consideration for nonsmokers. No pets. Children over 11 welcome. Minimum stay of two nights on holiday weekends and on July and August weekends. $95-160.

Country Road Lodge

HCR 1, Box 227, Hickory Hill Road, 12885
(518) 623-2207

With a view of the Adirondack Mountain and the Hudson River and minutes from Lake George, the lodge has offered seclusion and casual comfort since 1974. Homemade bread, hiking, skiing, horseshoes, badminton, books, board games. Fine restaurants and antiquing nearby.

Hosts: Steve and Sandi Parisi
Rooms: 4 (2 PB; 2 SB) $52-65
Full Breakfast
Credit Cards: None
Notes: 2, 5, 7, 9, 10, 11, 12, 13, 14

Country Road Lodge

The Merrill Magee House

2 Hudson Street, 12885
(518) 623-2449

NOTES: Credit cards accepted: A MasterCard; B Visa; C American Express; D Discover Card; E Diner's Club; F Other; 2 Personal checks accepted; 3 Lunch available; 4 Dinner available; 5 Open all year;

From the inviting wicker chairs on the porch to the elegant candlelit dining rooms, this inn offers the romance of a visit to a country estate. Guest rooms abound with 19th-century charm and 20th-century comforts. Guests can relax in the inn's secluded gardens, enjoy the outdoor pool, or shop for antiques in the village. In the Adirondack Park, all outdoor activities are minutes away.

Hosts: Ken and Florence Carrington
Rooms: 10 (PB) $85-105
Suite: 1
Full Breakfast
Credit Cards: A, B, C, D, E
Notes: 3, 4, 5, 7, 9, 10, 11, 12, 13, 14

White House Lodge

53 Main Street, 12885
(518) 623-3640

An 1847 Victorian in the heart of the Adirondacks. The home is furnished with many antiques. Only five minutes to Lake George Village, historic Fort William Henry, and Great Escape Amusement Park. Walk to restaurants, antique shops, and shopping areas. Enjoy the comfort of the air-conditioned TV lounge or rock on the front porch. Only 20 minutes to Gore Mountain Ski Lodge and the Adirondack Balloon Festival. Smoking allowed in TV lounge only.

Hosts: James and Ruth Gibson
Rooms: 3 (SB) $85
Continental Breakfast
Credit Cards: A, B
Notes: 5, 7 (limited), 8 (over 7), 10, 11, 12, 13

WATERLOO

Elaine's Bed and Breakfast Reservation Service

4987 Kingston Road, Elbridge, 13060
(315) 689-2082

A wonderful Federal brick Colonial built in 1833. The house is furnished with antiques that guests are welcome to purchase. There is also an antique shop on the first floor. This great old home is delightful with its fire-warmed dining room with wide plank and so much more to see! Full American breakfasts of choice. Restaurants, shops, and historic homes are within walking distance. Children over ten are welcome. Well-behaved dogs are also welcome; there is a resident Shih Tzu. $50-75.

The Front Porch

1248 Waterloo-Geneva Road, 13165
(315) 539-8329; (800) 231-8407

Old-fashioned charm beckons guests to this 1848 Victorian home, where they can relax amid period furnishings or wander outside through the ever-changing garden. Be pampered by modern conveniences such as queen-size beds, well-lit bathrooms, and air conditioning. Central to wine country between Syracuse, Rochester, and Ithaca. The area also offers the Cayuga Wine Trail, the Finger Lakes Antique Trail, historical homes and museums, and much more.

Hosts: Linda and John DeCicco
Rooms: 3 (1 PB; 2 SB) $55-65
Full Breakfast
Credit Cards: None
Notes: 2, 5, 9, 10, 11, 12

General Dobbin Bed and Breakfast

0089 Packwood Road, 13165
(315) 789-0580

This bed and breakfast was built in a country setting of meadows and woods in 1823. Tennis court and antique shop on the premises. Five miles to Seneca Lake and Geneva. Air-conditioned suite and room with private bath. Three and one-half miles south of Thruway Exit 42, off Route 14, within three miles of Routes 5 and 20.

Host: Betty Waldman
Rooms: 2 (PB) $65-75
Full Breakfast
Credit Cards: A, B
Notes: 2, 5, 9, 10, 11, 12, 13

6 Pets welcome; 8 Children welcome; 9 Social drinking allowed; 10 Tennis available; 11 Swimming available; 12 Golf available; 13 Skiing available; 14 May be booked through travel agents.

WATERVILLE

Bed and Breakfast Leatherstocking

P.O. Box 53, Herkimer, 13350
(315) 733-0040; (800) 941-BEDS (2337)

022. Consummate privacy and convenience embodied here in a newly renovated modern suite that features a fully equipped kitchen, queen suite, private bath, living room with queen-size sofa bed, TV, stereo, and solarium. Only minutes from Utica, Colgate, Hamilton, Bouckville, golf courses, fishing, hiking, riding, shopping, and fine dining. Easy parking. No pets. Continental breakfast. Can accommodate up to four adults; children 12 and older. $75-115.

Bed and Breakfast of Waterville

211 White Street, 13480
(315) 841-8295

This Victorian home in a historic area is close to Utica, Hamilton College, Colgate University, antique shops. One block from Route 12, and one mile from Route 20. Accommodations include a triple with private bath, triple and double rooms with shared bath. Experienced, enthusiastic hosts are a retired utility manager and a quilt maker.

Hosts: Carol and Stanley Sambora
Rooms: 3 (1 PB; 2 SB) $35-65
Full Breakfast
Credit Cards: A, B
Notes: 2, 5, 8, 9, 10, 12, 13, 14

WATKINS GLEN

Clarke House Bed and Breakfast

102 Durland Place, 14891
(607) 535-7965

Charming English Tudor home, circa 1920, in the lovely village of Watkins Glen. Walk to the famous gorge, restaurants, and activities at Seneca Lake. Short drive to Watkins Glen International Raceway, famous wineries, and Corning Glass. Immaculate bedrooms feature antique decor and twin, double, or queen-size beds. Hearty breakfast graciously served in the formal dining room, with high tea served at 4:00 P.M. Guest living room with fireplace. Central air conditioning.

Hosts: Jack and Carolyn Clarke
Rooms: 4 (2 PB; 2 SB) $55-65
Full Breakfast
Credit Cards: B
Notes: 2, 5, 9, 11, 12, 14

WESTHAMPTON BEACH

1880 House

2 Seafield Lane, 11978
(800) 346-3290

This 100-year-old country retreat is only 90 minutes from Manhattan on Westhampton Beach's exclusive Seafield Lane. A swimming pool and tennis court are on the premises, and it's only a short walk to the beach. The Hamptons offer numerous outstanding restaurants and shops. Indoor tennis is available locally, as is a health spa at Montauk Point. Minimum stay is two nights.

Host: Elsie Pardee Collins
Rooms: 2 (PB) $100-200
Full Breakfast
Credit Cards: A, B, C
Notes: 2, 5, 8, 9, 10, 11, 12, 14

WEST KILL

Marie's Dream House

Route 42, 12492
(518) 989-6565; (800) 336-9792

Set on 40 mountain acres secluded in the heart of the Catskill Mountains. Marie's Dream House offers year-round accommodations for skiers, hikers, fishermen, fall foliage lovers, and hunters. Bicycle routes

NOTES: Credit cards accepted: A MasterCard; B Visa; C American Express; D Discover Card; E Diner's Club; F Other; 2 Personal checks accepted; 3 Lunch available; 4 Dinner available; 5 Open all year;

from the door for all levels of riders. Special "Quilt Inn" week-long quilting seminars. On-premises restaurant serving Austrian and German cuisine family-style and homemade pastries in the Viennese Coffee Garden. Near Hunter Mountain Festivals and all Catskill ski areas.

Hosts: Marie Anders and Family
Rooms: 12 (PB) $40-85
Full Breakfast
Credit Cards: A, B, D
Notes: 2, 3, 4, 5, 8, 9, 11, 12, 13, 14

WESTPORT

The Inn on the Library Lawn, Inc.

1 Washington Street, 12993
(518) 962-8666

Restored 1875 Victorian inn overlooks Lake Champlain's northwest bay and the Green Mountains of Vermont. Walk to marina, beach, yacht club, 18-hole golf course and country club, summer concerts, and theater. Spacious rooms with private baths, air conditioning, and lake views. Full breakfast served on the outside deck or in the fireplaced lounge. Browse the resident antique shop and art gallery or the other fine shops and historical sites in the area.

Hosts: Ron and Liz Van Nostrand
Rooms: 10 (PB) $65-95
Full Breakfast
Credit Cards: A, B, C
Notes: 2, 8, 9, 10, 11, 12, 14

WEST WINFIELD

Bed and Breakfast Leatherstocking

P.O. Box 53, Herkimer, 13350
(315) 733-0040; (800) 941-BEDS (2337)

023. Here is an antique and stencil-laden Victorian frame house with deep front porch and common rooms. Gracious hospitality and service await guests in this beautifully furnished home, resplendent with craft items made on the premises. Near Bouckville and Hamilton. Bridal suite available with private bath and Jacuzzi spa tub and color TV. Great for getaways. Other rooms have shared baths and TV. $59-95.

WEVERTOWN

Mountainaire Adventures

Route 28, Box A, 12886
(800) 950-2194

Renovated private lodge and deluxe three-bedroom, handicapped-accessible chalet in the Adirondack Park, near Lake George and Gore Mountain Ski Center. Jacuzzi, sauna, beer and wine, hikes, and canoes. Custom adventure trips, such as white-water rafting and camping, are available. Ideal for private meetings or romantic getaways!

Host: Douglas Cole
Rooms: 8 (6 PB; 2 SB) $64.50-80.25
Full Breakfast
Credit Cards: A, B
Notes: 2, 4, 5, 6, 7, 8, 9, 10, 11, 12, 13, 14

WILLET

Woven Waters

HC 73, Box 193E, Cincinnatus Lake, 13863
(607) 656-8672

A beautifully renovated 100-year-old barn on the shores of a lovely private lake in south central New York. The rustic interior is accented with antiques and imported laces. Relax in the large, comfortable living room with beamed cathedral ceiling and massive stone fireplace, or on one of the porches overlooking the lake (one open, one enclosed).

Hosts: Erika and John
Rooms: 4 (SB) $58
Full Breakfast
Credit Cards: A, B, D
Notes: 5, 9, 13, 14

6 Pets welcome; 8 Children welcome; 9 Social drinking allowed; 10 Tennis available; 11 Swimming available; 12 Golf available; 13 Skiing available; 14 May be booked through travel agents.

WILSON

The International Bed and Breakfast Club, Inc.

504 Amherst Street, Buffalo, NY 14207
(800) 723-4262; FAX (716) 873-4462

NY6906PP. Enjoy spectacular Lake Ontario sunsets at this lakeside inn, in a casual countryside family-like atmosphere with friendly hosts. Four beautifully appointed rooms, some with private baths, along with a private sitting room exclusively for guests. Full breakfast served. Near Niagara Falls, Canada, and the Seaway Trail of New York state. $55-60.

WINDSOR

Country Haven

66 Garrett Road, 13865
(607) 655-1204

A restored 1800s farmhouse in a quiet country setting on 350 acres. A haven for the weary traveler. A weekend hideaway where warm hospitality awaits. Craft shop on premises. There is an 11K Volkssport hiking trail. One mile from Route 17 east, Exit 78; 12 miles east of Binghamton; and seven miles from Route 81.

Hosts: Rita and Doug Saunders
Rooms: 4 (1 PB; 3 SB) $45-55
Full Breakfast
Credit Cards: D
Notes: 2, 5, 8, 11, 12

WOODSTOCK

Mt. Tremper Inn

Box 51, Route 212 and Wittenberg Road, 12457
(914) 688-5329

Victorian hospitality and elegant antiques await guests in this 23-room mansion built in 1850 in the Catskill Mountains. Large parlor with fireplace, library/game room, classical music at breakfast. Outdoor dining in season. Near Woodstock, all ski slopes, historic Kingston, and Rhinebeck.

Host: Lou Caselli
Rooms: 12 (2 PB; 10 SB) $65-95
Full Breakfast
Credit Cards: A, B
Notes: 5, 7 (limited), 9, 10, 11, 13

YOUNGSTOWN

The International Bed and Breakfast Club, Inc.

504 Amherst Street, Buffalo, NY 14207
(800) 723-4262; FAX (716) 873-4462

NY4085PP. Large, comfortable country home built in 1880 offers three charming guest rooms with double beds and shared bath. Continental breakfast served in the Wagner Dining Room or on the covered porch in season. Only minutes away: historic Fort Niagara, sailing and sport fishing on Lake Ontario, and the lower Niagara. Also convenient to Niagara Falls, the beautiful nature trails of the Niagara River Gorge, and the nearby bridges to Canada, Niagara on the Lake and the Shaw festival. Smoking not permitted in the house. Open year-round. $55.

NY7052PP. This country home inn features three rooms, two with double beds and one with a single, sharing one bath. Guests enjoy the player-piano and traditional Irish guitar-music. 5:00 A.M. breakfast for fishermen or for those attending mass at the world-famous Lady of Fatima Shrine, a mile away. Special breakfast for children; full breakfast served daily. Convenient to Niagara Falls, Lewiston and Youngstown; Artpark, Lewiston Art Festival, Fort Niagara, and the fishing derby are among the nearby attractions. $40-60.

NOTES: Credit cards accepted: A MasterCard; B Visa; C American Express; D Discover Card; E Diner's Club; F Other; 2 Personal checks accepted; 3 Lunch available; 4 Dinner available; 5 Open all year;

North Carolina

Blake House Inn

ARDEN

Blake House Inn

150 Royal Pines Drive, 28704
(704) 684-1847

Built in 1847, Blake House Inn is one of the area's finest surviving examples of French Gothic architecture. The house served as a field hospital for Confederate armies still active in western North Carolina near the close of the war. The Blake House offers spacious bedrooms, all elegantly decorated with country antiques and family heirlooms. Minutes to Biltmore Estate, the Blue Ridge Parkway, and other area attractions. Fireside dining Wednesday through Saturday and brunch on Sunday.

Hosts: Bob, Eloise, and Pati Roesler
Rooms: 5 (PB) $70-90
Full Breakfast
Credit Cards: A, B
Notes: 2, 3, 4, 5, 8 (over 12), 10, 11, 12, 13

ASHEBORO

The Doctor's Inn

716 South Park Street, 27203
(910) 625-4916; (910) 625-4822

The Doctor's Inn is a home filled with antiques. It offers its guests the utmost in personal accommodations. Amenities include a gourmet breakfast served on fine china and silver, fresh flowers, terry-cloth robes and slippers, homemade "goodies," and a refrigerator stocked with soft drinks, juices, and ice cream parfaits. Nearby are 60 potteries and the North Carolina Zoo.

Hosts: Marion and Beth Griffin
Rooms: 2 (1 PB; 1 SB) $50 75
Full Breakfast
Credit Cards: None
Notes: 2, 5, 9, 10, 12

ASHEVILLE

Aberdeen Inn

64 Linden Avenue, 28801
(704) 254-9336

A 1908 Colonial with a wraparound porch for summer eating and rocking. Antiques, working fireplace, books, and a large sunroom for winter dining. Private grounds with century-old trees. Just six blocks to downtown and three miles to the Biltmore Estate. Welcome!

Host: Eleanor Smith
Rooms: 5 (PB) $70-80
Full Breakfast
Credit Cards: A, B
Notes: 2, 5, 7 (limited), 8 (over 12), 9, 14

---

6 Pets welcome; 7 Smoking allowed; 8 Children welcome; 9 Social drinking allowed; 10 Tennis available; 11 Swimming available; 12 Golf available; 13 Skiing available; 14 May be booked through travel agents.

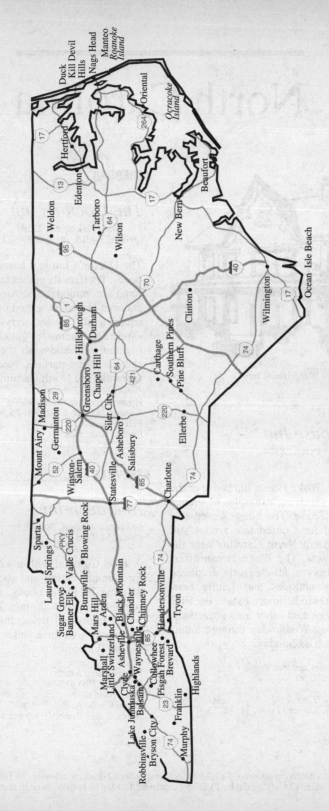

North Carolina

Acorn Cottage

25 Saint Dunstans Circle, 28803
(704) 253-0609

An English country cottage in the heart of
Asheville. The four guest rooms feature
queen-size beds, fine linens, air conditioning, and private baths. Come relax in this
1925 architecturally designed home built of
North Carolina granite, maple hardwood
floors, and a beautiful stone fireplace.
Acorn Cottage is in a natural woodland setting, yet in the heart of Asheville, only one-
quarter mile from the Biltmore Estate.

Host: Connie Stahl
Rooms: 4 (PB) $75-90
Full Breakfast
Credit Cards: A, B, D
Notes: 2, 5, 8, 9, 10, 12, 13, 14

Albemarle Inn

Albemarle Inn

86 Edgemont Road, 28801-1544
(704) 255-0027

Unmatched hospitality in a distinguished
Greek Revival mansion with exquisite
carved oak staircase, balcony, paneling, and
high ceilings. In a beautiful residential area.
On the National Register of Historic Places.
Eleven spacious and tastefully decorated
guest rooms with TV, telephones, air conditioning, and private baths with claw-foot

tubs and showers. Delicious breakfast
served in the dining room and sun porch.
Swimming pool.

Hosts: Dick and Kathy Hemes
Rooms: 11 (PB) $75-130
Full Breakfast
Credit Cards: A, B, D
Notes: 2, 5, 8 (over 13), 9, 10, 11, 12, 14

Applewood Manor

62 Cumberland Circle, 28801
(704) 254-2244

A fine, turn-of-the-century Colonial Revival manor set on two acres of rolling lawn
and woods in Asheville's historic Montford
District. Within 15 minutes of the finest
restaurants, antique shops, and area attractions, including the Biltmore Estate.
Amenities include private baths, queen-size
beds, fireplaces, balconies, full gourmet
breakfasts, and afternoon tea. Bikes, badminton, croquet, and complimentary fitness
club passes are available.

Hosts: Maryanne Young and Susan Poole
Rooms: 4 (PB) $85-115
Cottage: 1
Full Breakfast
Credit Cards: A, B
Notes: 2, 5, 9, 10, 11, 14

Beaufort House Victorian Bed and Breakfast

61 North Liberty Street, 28801
(704) 254-8334

Built in 1894, Beaufort House stands today
as an eloquent testimony to the gentle style
of living prevalent at the turn of the century.
Encompassing romance, history, and elegance, Beaufort House offers guests the
comforts of modern luxuries such as central
air conditioning, TVs, VCRs, telephones,
Jacuzzis, fitness facility, and bicycles. The
Beaufort House is listed on the National
Register of Historic Places and was previ-
ously featured in National Geographic's
Traveller magazine.

NOTES: Credit cards accepted: A MasterCard; B Visa; C American Express; D Discover Card; E Diner's Club;
F Other; 2 Personal checks accepted; 3 Lunch available; 4 Dinner available; 5 Open all year; 6 Pets welcome; 7
Smoking allowed; 8 Children welcome; 9 Social drinking allowed; 10 Tennis available; 11 Swimming avail-
able; 12 Golf available; 13 Skiing available; 14 May be booked through travel agents.

Hosts: Robert and Jacqueline Glasgow
Rooms: 6 (PB) $85-195
Full Breakfast
Credit Cards: A, B
Notes: 2, 5, 8, 9, 10, 11, 12, 13, 14

The Black Walnut Bed and Breakfast Inn

288 Montford Avenue, 28801
(704) 254-3878

The Black Walnut is a turn-of-the-century shingle-style home in the heart of the Montford historic district just minutes from downtown Asheville and the Biltmore Estate. The inn is decorated with a blend of antiques and traditional furniture. Amenities include large guest rooms with fireplaces, TV, full breakfast featuring homemade breads and preserves, welcoming refreshments, use of all common areas, the grand piano, and air conditioning. Weekly and monthly rentals also available.

Host: Jeanette Syprzak
Rooms: 6 (PB) $80-130
Full Breakfast
Credit Cards: A, B, C, D
Notes: 2, 5, 8, 9, 10, 11, 12, 13, 14

Blake House Inn

150 Royal Pines Drive, 28704
(704) 684-1847

Built in 1847, Blake House Inn is one of the area's finest surviving examples of French Gothic architecture. The house served as a field hospital for Confederate armies still active in western North Carolina near the close of the war. The Blake House offers spacious bedrooms, all elegantly decorated with country antiques and family heirlooms. Full breakfast. Minutes to Biltmore Estate, the Blue Ridge Parkway, and other area attractions. Fireside dining Wednesday through Saturday and brunch on Sunday.

Hosts: Bob, Eloise, and Pati Roesler
Rooms: 5 (PB) $70-90
Full Breakfast
Credit Cards: A, B, D
Notes: 2, 3, 4, 5, 8 (over 12), 10, 11, 12, 13

Cairn Brae

217 Patton Mountain Road, 28804
(704) 252-9219

Cairn Brae is in the mountains above Asheville. Very private, on three acres of woods, but only 12 minutes from downtown. Guests have private entrance to living room with fireplace. Complimentary snacks are served on the terrace overlooking Beaverdam Valley. Beautiful views. Woodsy trails. Quiet and secluded. Closed December 1 through March 31.

Hosts: Milli and Ed Adams
Rooms: 3 (PB) $85-100
Full Breakfast
Credit Cards: A, B, D
Notes: 2, 8 (over 10), 9, 10, 11, 12, 14

Carolina Bed and Breakfast

177 Cumberland Avenue, 28801
(704) 254-3608

Comfortable turn-of-the-century home on an acre of beautiful gardens in the historic Montford district. Charming guest rooms, four with fireplaces, have antiques and collectibles, as well as private baths. Convenient to downtown shopping, galleries, restaurants, and the Biltmore Estate. A quiet, relaxing getaway in the heart of the city.

Hosts: Sam and Karin Fain
Rooms: 5 (PB) $65-90
Full Breakfast
Credit Cards: A, B, D
Notes: 2, 5, 7 (limited), 8 (over 12), 9, 10, 12, 14

Cedar Crest Victorian Inn

674 Biltmore Avenue, 28803
(704) 252-1389

An 1890 Queen Anne mansion listed on the National Register of Historic Places. Lavish interior features carved oak paneling, ornate glasswork, authentic Victorian decor with period antiques, and romantic guest rooms. Croquet court, fireplaces, and English gardens. One-quarter mile from the entrance to the Biltmore Estate and four miles from the Blue Ridge Parkway.

NOTES: Credit cards accepted: A MasterCard; B Visa; C American Express; D Discover Card; E Diner's Club; F Other; 2 Personal checks accepted; 3 Lunch available; 4 Dinner available; 5 Open all year;

Hosts: Jack and Barbara McEwan
Rooms: 9; 2 suites $115-150
Continental Breakfast
Credit Cards: A, B, C, D, E
Notes: 2, 5, 7, 8 (over 12), 9, 10, 12, 14

The Colby House

230 Pearson Drive, 28801
(704) 253-5644; (800) 982-2118

This elegant and charming Dutch-Tudor house in the Montford historic district is known as "a special place." There are beautiful gardens, an outdoor porch, and inviting fireplaces. The home has four guest rooms, each with individual decor, queen-size beds, and private baths. A full breakfast is varied daily. Southern hospitality abounds in the host's personal attention to every guest's needs.

Hosts: Everett and Ann Colby
Rooms: 4 (PB) $75-95
Full Breakfast
Credit Cards: A, B, C
Notes: 2, 5, 9, 10, 11, 12, 13

Corner Oak Manor

53 Saint Dunstans Road, 28803
(704) 253-3525

This lovely English Tudor home is just minutes away from the famed Biltmore Estate and Gardens. Antiques, handmade

Corner Oak Manor

wreaths, weavings, and stitchery complement the restored elegance of this home. Breakfast specialties include orange French toast, blueberry-ricotta pancakes, or four-cheese herb quiche. A living room with fireplace and baby grand piano, and outdoor deck with Jacuzzi are among the gracious amenities.

Hosts: Karen and Andy Spradley
Rooms: 4 (PB) $85-100
Full Breakfast
Credit Cards: A, B, C, D
Notes: 2, 5, 8, 9, 14

Dry Ridge Inn

26 Brown Street, Weaverville, 28787
(704) 658-3899

This casually elegant bed and breakfast is quietly removed 10 minutes north of Asheville's many attractions. Country-style antiques and contemporary art enhance this unique 1800s village farmhouse. A full breakfast is served with individual seating. Relax in the outdoor spa or with quality reading after enjoying a day of mountain adventure. Minimum stay fall weekends and holidays: two nights.

Hosts: Paul and Mary Lou Gibson
Rooms: 7 (PB) $65-85
Full Breakfast
Credit Cards: A, B, C, D
Notes: 2, 5, 8, 9, 12, 13, 14

Flint Street Inns

100 and 116 Flint Street, 28801
(704) 253-6723

Two lovely old homes on an acre lot with century-old trees. Comfortable walking distance to town. Guest rooms, furnished with antiques and collectibles, have air conditioning, and some have fireplaces. The inns provide complimentary beverages, bicycles, and restaurant menus. Breakfast is full Southern-style, featuring home-baked breads and iron-skillet biscuits.

Hosts: Rick, Lynne, and Marion Vogel
Rooms: 8 (PB) $85

6 Pets welcome; 8 Children welcome; 9 Social drinking allowed; 10 Tennis available; 11 Swimming available; 12 Golf available; 13 Skiing available; 14 May be booked through travel agents.

Full Breakfast
Credit Cards: A, B, C, D
Notes: 2, 5, 7 (limited), 9, 12, 14

The Inn on Montford

296 Montford Avenue, 28801
(704) 254-9569

A turn-of-the-century Arts and Crafts home by Asheville's most famous architect. Filled with light, it is a perfect setting for the owners' fine collection of antiques, porcelains, and Oriental rugs. Fireplaces in all rooms, whirlpools in several, a wide front porch, boxwood garden with an arbor behind the house. The inn is in the Montford historic district, close to downtown and a ten-minute drive from the Biltmore Estate.

Hosts: Ripley Hotch and Owen Sullivan
Rooms: 4 (PB) $90-120
Full Breakfast
Credit Cards: A, B, C, D
Notes: 2, 5, 10, 12, 13, 14

Mountain Springs Cabins/Chalets

P.O. Box 2, Candler, 28715
(704) 665-1004

Enjoy the serenity of the mountain-fed stream and rolling mountains. Three miles from the foot of Mt. Pisgah and the Blue Ridge Parkway; there are numerous hiking trails, waterfalls, Sliding Rock, a mountaintop restaurant, and horseback riding. Visit the Biltmore House, Cherokee Indian Reservation, Chimney Rock Park, Mt. Mitchell, Great Smoky Mountains National Park, and the Blue Ridge Parkway. All cottages have kitchens, living rooms, one or two bedrooms, bath, porch, color TV, picnic table, and grill. Kitchens are fully equipped. Towels, linens, and blankets are provided.

Hosts: Sara and John Peltier
Rooms: 12 (PB) $80
Credit Cards: A, B
Notes: 5, 7, 9, 11, 12, 13

The Old Reynolds Mansion

The Old Reynolds Mansion

100 Reynolds Heights, 28804
(704) 254-0496

Bed and breakfast in an antebellum mansion listed on the National Register of Historic Places. Beautifully restored with furnishings from a bygone era. In a country setting with acres of trees, mountain views from all rooms. Wood-burning fireplaces, two-story verandas, and pool. Minimum stay weekends and holidays: two nights. Open weekends only January through March.

Hosts: Fred and Helen Faber
Rooms: 10 (8 PB; 2 SB) $55-95
Cottage: $120
Continental Breakfast
Credit Cards: None
Notes: 2, 7, 8 (over 11), 9, 10, 11, 12

Reed House

119 Dodge Street, 28803
(704) 274-1604

Come stay in this comfortable Victorian home built in 1892. Near Biltmore Estate. Breakfast, featuring homemade low-sodium muffins, is served on the wraparound porch. Relaxing rocking chairs everywhere. Furnished in period decor. On the National Register of Historic Places and a local historic property. Closed November 1 through May 1.

Host: Marge Turcot
Rooms: 3 (1 PB; 2 SB) $50-70
Cottage: $95
Continental Breakfast

NOTES: Credit cards accepted: A MasterCard; B Visa; C American Express; D Discover Card; E Diner's Club; F Other; 2 Personal checks accepted; 3 Lunch available; 4 Dinner available; 5 Open all year;

Credit Cards: A, B
Notes: 2, 7, 8, 9, 10, 11, 12

Richmond Hill Inn

87 Richmond Hill Drive, 28806
(800) 545-9238; FAX (704) 252-8726

Historic Victorian mansion built in 1889 overlooking the Blue Ridge Mountains and the Asheville skyline. Listed on the National Register of Historic Places. Magnificently restored mansion elegantly furnished with antiques, this AAA four-diamond inn features 36 guest rooms, all with private bath and many with a fireplace. Fine dining in the AAA four-diamond gourmet restaurant with mountain view. Croquet lawn and extensive library. Close to the Blue Ridge Parkway and Biltmore Estate.

Host: Susan Michel
Rooms: 36 (PB) $130-325
Full Breakfast
Credit Cards: A, B, C
Notes: 2, 4, 5, 7 (limited), 8, 9, 14

The Wright Inn and Carriage House

235 Pearson Drive, 28801
(704) 251-0789; (800) 552 5724

Elegantly restored Queen Anne Victorian inn in the Montford historic district. The main house offers eight guest rooms with telephones and cable TV. One suite, one

The Wright Inn

guest room, parlor, and drawing room all have fireplaces. Full breakfast served in the formal dining room. A three-bedroom carriage house with two baths is also available; breakfast not included.

Hosts: Carol and Art Wenczel
Rooms: 9 (PB) $75-110
Full Breakfast
Credit Cards: A, B
Notes: 2, 5, 9, 10, 11, 12, 13

BALSAM

Balsam Mountain Inn

P.O. Box 40, 28707
(704) 456-9498

Nestled among lofty peaks in the Great Smoky Mountains and just off the Blue Ridge Parkway, this historic inn was built in 1908 to serve the highest railroad depot in the east. The inn was restored in 1991, and now offers 34 cheerful rooms, two 100-foot porches with rockers and a view, a 2,000 volume library, and gracious dining. Plump pillows and soft comforters inspire pleasant dreams! Hiking, biking, relaxing, rafting, rail excursions, and shopping abound. Lunch is available June–October. Box lunches all year.

Hosts: Merrily Teasley and Bill Graham
Rooms: 34 (PB) $75-150
Full Breakfast
Credit Cards: A, B, D
Notes: 2, 3 (limited), 4, 5, 8, 9, 10, 11, 12, 13, 14

BANNER ELK

The Banner Elk Inn Bed and Breakfast

Highway 194 North (Main Street), Route 3, Box 1134, 28604
(704) 898-6223

The Banner Elk Inn Bed and Breakfast is a charmingly restored cozy little inn in town, population approximately 800, close to fine restaurants and the major attractions of Grandfather Mountain, Valle Crucis, Sugar

6 Pets welcome; 8 Children welcome; 9 Social drinking allowed; 10 Tennis available; 11 Swimming available; 12 Golf available; 13 Skiing available; 14 May be booked through travel agents.

and Beech Mountain ski resorts, and the nearby towns of Boone and Blowing Rock. There are four guest rooms, two with private large baths and two sharing baths for a four-person suite. Furnished with antiques and paintings collected from around the world. There is a wonderful great room, cable TV, stereo, and fireplace with a long walnut breakfast table set elegantly with fine china. Gourmet full breakfasts. English garden overlooking a restored splashing fountain.

Host: Beverly Lait
Rooms: 4 (2 PB; 2 SB) $70-95
Full Breakfast
Credit Cards: A, B
Notes: 2, 5 (for reservations), 6, 8 (over six), 9, 10, 12, 13, 14

Delamar Inn

BEAUFORT

Delamar Inn

217 Turner Street, 28516
(919) 728-4300

Enjoy the Scottish hospitality of this Civil War home in the heart of Beaufort's historic district. The inn offers three guest rooms with antique furnishings and private bath. After a delightful breakfast, enjoy a stroll to the waterfront, specialty shops, or historic sites. Borrow the hosts' bicycles or beach chairs, and upon return, guests will

find soft drinks, cookies, and a smile waiting. The hosts are pleased to have been selected for Beaufort's 1991–92 historic homes tour.

Hosts: Mabel and Tom Steepy
Rooms: 3 (PB) $58-88
Continental Breakfast
Credit Cards: A, B
Notes: 2, 5, 7 (limited), 8 (over 10), 9, 10, 11, 12

Langdon House Bed and Breakfast

135 Craven Street, 28516
(919) 728-5499

A step into history; a residence for discerning guests, and an experience akin to visiting friends. The art of innkeeping is practiced in this restored Colonial home. A good time is the "bottom line." Guest satisfaction is the hosts' priority. Fine breakfasts pique the senses. Special diets accommodated with advance notice. The mood is tempered by Vivaldi, Mozart, Windham Hill, and Irish folk music. Hosts want to take care of guests and be a resource regarding the area.

Host: Jim Prest, Owner/Innkeeper
Rooms: 4 (PB) $75-115
Full Breakfast
Credit Cards: None
Notes: 2, 5, 9, 10, 11, 12

Pecan Tree Inn

116 Queen Street, 28516
(919) 728-6733

A gracious 1866 Victorian home filled with antiques, one-half block from the waterfront in Beaufort's Historic District. Relax on one of the three porches or stroll through the large English garden. There are seven air-conditioned rooms, all with private baths. The bridal suite features a Jacuzzi tub for two and a king-size canopied bed. Guests will enjoy the hostesses' freshly baked homemade muffins, breakfast cakes, and breads, along with a choice of fruit, cereal, and beverages for breakfast. Only a few blocks to wonderful restaurants and quaint shops.

Hosts: Susan and Joe Johnson
Rooms: 7 (PB) $65-120
Continental Breakfast
Credit Cards: A, B, D
Notes: 2, 5, 8 (over 12), 9, 10, 11, 12, 14

BLACK MOUNTAIN

Black Mountain Inn
718 West Old Highway. 70, 28711
(704) 669-6528

Discover a peaceful retreat for body and soul. Built 150 years ago, this lovingly restored inn is cloaked in a long and colorful history. Once a studio and haven for artists, this small and intimate inn embraces its guests with long forgotten hospitality and charm. With seven comfortable guest rooms, each decorated with casual country decor, and with private bath.

Host: June Bergern Colbert
Rooms: 7 (PB) $60-65
Full Breakfast
Credit Cards. None
Notes: 2, 9, 10, 11, 12, 14

BLOWING ROCK

Hound Ears Club and Lodge
P.O. Box 188, 28605
(704) 963-4321

Luxury four-star resort in the heart of the Blue Ridge Mountains. Amenities include golf, tennis, swimming, fishing, and snow skiing, as well as excellent dining in the clubhouse. The 28 guest rooms are all centrally situated and entitle guests and club members to exclusive use of the facilities. Long-term and seasonal rentals available. Rate per person with two people per room. Modified American Plan.

Host: Lillian Smith
Rooms: 28 (PB) $110-140

Full Breakfast
Credit Cards: A, B, C
Notes: 3, 4, 5, 8, 9, 10, 11, 12, 13, 14

Maple Lodge
Box 1236, Sunset Drive, 28605
(704) 295-3331

A village inn since 1946, furnished in country antiques, goose-down comforters and handmade quilts. Relax in two warmly paneled parlors, one with a lovely stone fireplace. For breakfast, choose a cozy table warmed by the woodstove or overlooking a wildflower garden. In the heart of the village, one mile from the Blue Ridge Parkway. Hiking, antiquing, crafts nearby.

Hosts: Marilyn and David Bateman
Rooms: 10 (PB) $65-92
Full Breakfast
Credit Cards: A, B, D
Notes: 2, 5, 9, 10, 11, 12, 13, 14

Ragged Garden Inn
Box 1927 Sunset Drive, 28605
(704) 295-9703

Ragged Garden Inn, built at the turn of the century as a summer home, is surrounded by roses, rhododendrons, dogwoods, and azaleas. The building has a stone-columned entrance and its exterior is covered with chestnut bark slabs. It has an unusual slate and stone staircase. The common room has pre-blight chestnut paneling. The guest

Ragged Garden Inn

rooms are cozy with comforters, papered walls, and contrasting trim. The open-air porch overlooking the garden is used for breakfast. Pre-arranged dinner parties of eight or more can be accommodated.

Hosts: Joyce and Joe Villani
Rooms: 7 (PB) $55-90
Full Breakfast
Credit Cards: A, B
Notes: 2, 7 (limited), 8 (over 12), 9, 10, 11, 12, 13

Rocking Horse Inn

P.O. Box 629, 28605
(704) 295-3311

High in the North Carolina mountains, this country home is surrounded by the Moses Cone National Park. Quietly secluded but with easy access to the Blue Ridge Parkway with hiking and horse-back riding trails nearby. Seven guest rooms. Separate cottage for families. Afternoon refreshments on the porch, deck, or lawn are enticing, but the new Southern breakfast is a real treat.

Hosts: Bill and Glenda Howard
Room: 7 (PB) $65-80
Full Breakfast
Credit Cards: None
Notes: 2, 5, 8 (over 14), 10, 11, 12, 13

Stone Pillar Bed and Breakfast

144 Pine Street, P.O. Box 1881
(704) 295-4141

Nestled in the mountains, Blowing Rock is home to Stone Pillar Bed and Breakfast. On Pine Street, a half block from Main, the Stone Pillar offers a relaxing homelike atmosphere. There are six guest rooms, all with private baths. Guests have the chance to meet and swap experiences while enjoying a full, family-style breakfast. As one guest stated, "It's so easy to stay here, I feel as if I belong." The hosts hope all guests can stay with them and feel as if they belong.

Hosts: George Van Nuys and Ron Tharp
Rooms: 6 (PB) $50-90
Full Breakfast

Credit Cards: A, B
Notes: 2, 5, 8, 9, 10, 11, 12, 13

BREVARD

The Inn at Brevard

410 East Main Street, 28712
(704) 884-2105

Listed on the National Register of Historic Places, this inn hosted a reunion dinner for Stonewall Jackson's troops in 1911. Beautifully restored in 1984 with a European flavor throughout. Just minutes from Brevard Music Center, Blue Ridge Parkway, and Pisgah National Forest.

Hosts: Eileen and Bertrand Bourget
Rooms: 15 (14 PB; 1 SB) $69-125
Full Breakfast
Credit Cards: A, B
Notes: 2, 4, 8 (limited), 9, 10, 11, 12

The Red House Inn

412 West Probart Street, 28712
(704) 884-9349

The Red House was built in 1851 in the Blue Ridge Mountains, and has been lovingly restored and furnished in turn-of-the-century period antiques. Enjoy the wonderful Brevard Music Center performances every night during the summer and beautiful mountain colors in the fall. Come sit on the porch. Closed November 30 through April 1.

Hosts: Lynne Ong and Mary MacGillycuddy
Rooms: 6 (PB and SB) $45-79
Full Breakfast
Credit Cards: A, B
Notes: 2, 9, 10, 11, 12, 14

Womble Inn

301 West Main, 28712
(704) 884-4770

Two blocks from the center of Brevard, the Womble Inn invites guests to relax in a welcoming, comfortable atmosphere. Each of the six guest rooms is especially furnished

NOTES: Credit cards accepted: A MasterCard; B Visa; C American Express; D Discover Card; E Diner's Club; F Other; 2 Personal checks accepted; 3 Lunch available; 4 Dinner available; 5 Open all year;

in antiques. All of the guest rooms have private baths and air conditioning. After a sound sleep, guests will be served breakfast on a silver tray, or guests may prefer to be seated in the dining room. Full breakfast is an option.

Hosts: Steve and Beth Womble
Rooms: 6 (PB) $48-58
Continental Breakfast
Credit Cards: A, B
Notes: 2, 5, 8, 9, 10, 11, 12

BRYSON CITY

Fryemont Inn

Box 459, 28713
(704) 488-2159; (800) 845-4879

This inn overlooks the Great Smoky Mountains National Park. All rooms have private bath. Dinner and breakfast are included in the daily rate, and the inn is on the National Register of Historic Places. Featured in *Bon Appetit*. Guest rooms closed November through mid-April. Cottage suites open year-round.

Hosts: Sue and George Brown
Rooms: 39 (PB) $63-166
Full Breakfast
Credit Cards: A, B, D
Notes: 2, 3, 4, 5, 7, 8, 9, 10, 11, 12

Hamrick Inn

BURNSVILLE

Hamrick Inn
Bed and Breakfast

7787 Highway 80 South, 28714
(704) 675-5251

This charming three-story Colonial-style stone inn is nestled at the foot of Mt. Mitchell, highest mountain east of the Mississippi. Much of the lovely furniture was built by the hosts. There is a private porch off each guest room, where the view and cool mountain breezes may be enjoyed. Golf, hiking, fishing, rock hounding, and craft shopping are local activities. Near the Blue Ridge Parkway. Open April 1 through October 31.

Hosts: Neal and June Jerome
Rooms: 4 (PB) $50-60
Full Breakfast
Credit Cards: A, B
Notes: 2, 8, 9, 10, 11, 12, 13

Nu-Wray Inn

Town Square, P.O. Box 156, 28714
(704) 682-2329; (800) 3NUWRAY

Historic country inn since 1833. Nestled in the Blue Ridge Mountains in a quaint town-square setting. Thirty miles northeast of Asheville. Close to Blue Ridge Parkway, Mt. Mitchell, Grandfather Mountain, golf, antiques, crafts, hiking, fishing, or just relax on the porch. Room rates include hearty country sideboard breakfast and afternoon refreshments. Famous family-style dinners.

Hosts: Chris and Pam Strickland
Rooms: 26 (PB) $70-110
Full Breakfast
Credit Cards: A, B, C
Notes: 2, 4, 5, 8, 10, 11, 12, 13, 14

CANDLER

Glory Ridge
Bed and Breakfast

101 Glory Ridge Trail, 28715
(704) 667-2023

Step back in time over 100 years and rent a room or a cabin here at Glory Ridge. Feast on a country breakfast, then sit and rock on the porches while gazing at unspoiled mountain scenery, dream in front of a cozy fireplace, splash in the creek, walk the mountain trails, or hunt native wildflowers and fern. Glory Ridge is 30 minutes from the Blue Ridge Parkway, the Biltmore House, or downtown Asheville. Open May 1 through October 31 or by special arrangement.

Hosts: Ray and Celeste Rast
Rooms: 3 (PB) $55
Credit Cards: None
Notes: 2, 8

CARTHAGE

The Blacksmith Inn

703 McReynolds Street, 28327
(910) 947-1692; (800) 284-4515

This beautiful example of 1870 southern architecture has been lovingly restored and is the former home of the blacksmith for the Tyson and Jones Buggy Factory. Four spacious, tastefully decorated rooms are available, with a fireplace in each room. Just 12 minutes from Pinehurst (the golf capital of the world), 20 minutes from Seagrove (the pottery center of North Carolina), and Cameron and Aberdeen's antique shops and historic districts. On the National Register of Historic Places.

Hosts: Gary and Shawna Smith
Rooms: 4 (2 PB; 2 SB) $50
Full Breakfast
Credit Cards: None
Notes: 2, 5, 8, 12, 14

CHAPEL HILL

The Fearrington House Inn

2000 Fearrington Village Center, Pittsboro, 27312
(919) 542-2121

In a cluster of low, attractive buildings grouped around a courtyard and surrounded by gardens and rolling countryside, this elegant inn offers luxurious quarters in a country setting. A member of Relais et Chateaux. The restaurant's sophisticated regional cuisine prepared in the classical techniques has received national acclaim, including AAA's four diamond award.

Hosts: Jenny and R. B. Fitch
Rooms: 23 (PB) $150-230
Full Breakfast
Credit Cards: A, B
Notes: 2, 3, 4, 5, 9, 10, 11, 12, 14

The Elizabeth

CHARLOTTE

The Elizabeth
Bed and Breakfast

2145 East Fifth Street, 28204
(704) 358-1368

This 1927 lavender "lady" is in historic Elizabeth, Charlotte's second-oldest neighborhood. European country-style rooms are beautifully appointed with antiques, ceiling fans, decorator linens, and unique collections. A guest cottage offers a private retreat in elegant Southwestern style. All rooms have central air, private baths; some have television and telephones. Enjoy a generous Continental breakfast, then relax in the garden coutyard, complete with charming gazebo, or stroll beneath giant oaks trees to convenient restaurants and shopping.

Host: Joan Mastny
Rooms: 3 (PB) $58-88

NOTES: Credit cards accepted: A MasterCard; B Visa; C American Express; D Discover Card; E Diner's Club; F Other; 2 Personal checks accepted; 3 Lunch available; 4 Dinner available; 5 Open all year;

Cottage: 1 (PB)
Continental Breakfast
Credit Cards: A, B
Notes: 2, 5, 9, 11, 14

The Homeplace

5901 Sardis Road, 28270
(704) 365-1936

Restored 1902 Country Victorian with wraparound porch and tin roof, nestled amid two and one-half wooded acres. Secluded "cottage-style" gardens with a gazebo, brick walkways, and a 1930s log barn further enhance this nostalgic oasis in southeast Charlotte. Experienced innkeepers offer four guest rooms, a full breakfast, and a Victorian garden room for small meetings and special occasions. Opened in 1984, The Homeplace is "a reflection of the true bed and breakfast experience."

Hosts: Peggy and Frank Dearien
Rooms: 4 (2 PB; 2 SB) $68-88
Full Breakfast
Credit Cards. A, B, C
Notes: 2, 5, 8 (over 12), 14

The Inn Uptown

129 North Poplar Street, 28202
(704) 342-2800; (800) 959-1990

Constructed in 1890 and historically listed as the Bagley-Mullen House, this chateauesque home has been restored into "an elegant alternative in uptown hospitality." Convenient for both corporate and leisure travelers. Each of the six beautifully appointed rooms features a private bath, complimentary wine, remote control cable TV, telephone, and nightly turndown service. A complimentary full breakfast features specialities from the inn's kitchen and is served in the dining room. Approved for three-diamond AAA rating. Corporate rates are available.

Host: Elizabeth J. Rich
Rooms: 6 (PB) $89-149
Full Breakfast
Credit Cards: A, B, C, D, E
Notes: 2, 5, 9, 14

Still Waters

6221 Amos Smith Road, 28214
(704) 399-6299

A log resort home on two wooded acres overlooking the Catawba River at the upper end of Lake Wylie; within 15 minutes of downtown Charlotte. Full breakfast is served on glassed-in porch overlooking the lake. Enjoy the sportcourt, the garden, swimming, boating, fishing, or sitting in the lakeside gazebo. Convenient to I-85, airport, and Billy Graham Parkway.

Hosts: Janet and Rob Dyer
Rooms: 3 (PB) $55-85
Full Breakfast
Credit Cards: A, B, E
Notes: 2, 5, 8, 9, 10, 11, 12

CHIMNEY ROCK

Esmeralda Inn and Restaurant

P.O. Box 57, Highway 74, 28720
(704) 625-9105

Built in 1890, this three-story inn is surrounded by tall trees and within sight of the Chimney Rock Park. A great getaway, just 22 miles from Asheville. Come relax or dine on the open-air porches or dining room. Dinner served nightly; lunch is avail-

Esmeralda Inn

able six days a week. Thirteen bedrooms are available. Open mid-March to mid-December.

Hosts: Ackie and Joanne Okpych
Rooms: 13 (7 PB; 6 SB) $50-75
Continental Breakfast
Credit Cards: A, B, C, D
Notes : 3, 4, 9, 10, 11, 12

CHIMNEY ROCK VILLAGE

The Dogwood Inn

P.O. Box 159, Highway 64-74, 28720
(704) 625-4403

A charming white two-story European-style bed and breakfast. Come enjoy the five porches that grace this wonderful early 1900s inn on the banks of the peaceful Rocky Broad River. Massive Chimney Rock Mountain can be seen from any of the porches. A full buffet breakfast is served each morning. Children over 12 are welcome. Come rest a while. The river is calling.

Hosts: Marsha and Mark Reynolds
Rooms: 10 (2 PB; 8 SB) $65-80
Full Breakfast
Credit Cards: A, B, C, D
Notes: 2, 9, 10, 11, 12, 14

CLINTON

The Shield House Inn, Inc.

216 Sampson Street, 28328
(910) 592-3933; (800) 463-9817 reservations

These lodgings consist of two estates and a duplex bungalow. The Shield House Inn, Inc. is reminiscent of *Gone With the Wind* and the Courthouse Inn is a recently renovated courthouse. Both are listed on the National Register of Historic Places. These inns have wraparound porches and many dramatic features. Spacious bedrooms are decorated with period antiques, many marble-topped. Lounging areas available. In-room private baths, remote control TV. Some refrigerators. Bungalow has kitchen.

Hosts: Juanita McLamb and Anita Green
Rooms: 17 (PB) $50-100
Continental Breakfast
Credit Cards: A, B, C, D, E
Notes: 2, 5, 7 (limited), 8 (by arrangement), 9, 10, 12, 14

Windsong

CLYDE

Windsong: A Mountain Inn

120 Ferguson Ridge, 28721
(704) 627-6111

Enjoy a secluded, romantic interlude at this contemporary log inn high in the breathtaking Smoky Mountains. Though the inn is small and intimate, the rooms are large and bright, with high-beamed ceilings, pine log walls, and Mexican tile floors. Each room has a fireplace, oversize tub, separate shower, and private deck or patio. Guest lounge with billiards and wet bar. Full breakfast included. On 25 acres, with pool, tennis, hiking, and lovable llamas. Newly added is the Pond House, a separate two-bedroom log guest house with full kitchen. Near Maggie Valley. Llama trekking in national forest available. Closed mid- December to mid-February.

Hosts: Donna and Gale Livengood
Rooms: 5 (PB) $90-95
Full Breakfast
Credit Cards: A, B
Notes: 2, 9, 10, 11, 12, 14

CULLOWHEE

Cullowhee Bed and Breakfast

150 Ledbetter Road, 28723
(704) 293-5447

On a hillside among pines, oaks, and maples, this bed and breakfast offers the relaxing atmosphere of an immaculate country home and a beautiful view of the mountains. All bedrooms are comfortably furnished with queen- or king-size beds. The coffee pot starts at dawn for early risers, and a special treat awaits at breakfast with full country fare and hot muffins.

Hosts: Charles and Janet Moore
Rooms: 3 (PB) $55-65
Full Breakfast
Credit Cards: None
Notes: 2, 5, 11, 12, 13

DUCK

The Sanderling Inn Resort

1461 Duck Road, 27949
(919) 261-4111; (800) 701-4111

Year-round oceanfront resort (1985) only five miles from town—all rooms with bath, color cable TV, and private porch. Some with kitchen, wet bar, and refrigerator. Wheelchair accessible. Restaurant and bar, meeting rooms for 100 people. Health club with sauna, pools, hot tub, and tennis courts. Private beach. Non-smoking rooms, massage therapy, private conference center, off-season packages available.

Manager: Christine Berger
Rooms: 87 (PB) $110-350
Continental Breakfast
Credit Cards: A, B, C, D
Notes: 2, 3, 4, 5, 7, 8, 9, 10, 11, 12, 14

Arrowhead Inn

DURHAM

Arrowhead Inn

106 Mason Road, 27712
(919) 477-8430; (800) 528-2207

This restored 1775 manor house on four rural acres offers homey hospitality in an atmosphere that evokes Colonial Carolina. But along with 18th-century architecture, decor, and furnishings, the inn features contemporary comfort, sparkling housekeeping, and bounteous home-cooked breakfasts. Open year-round. Mentioned in *Food and Wine*, *USA Today*, and many metro newspapers.

Hosts: Jerry, Barbara, and Cathy Ryan
Rooms: 8 (6 PB; 2 SB) $72.15-155.40
Full Breakfast
Credit Cards: A, B, C, D, E
Notes: 2, 5, 8, 9, 10, 11, 12, 14

The Blooming Garden Inn

513 Holloway Street, 27701
(919) 687-0801

An unexpected use of color transforms this restored 1892 Queen Anne-style home into a cozy, pleasant retreat in downtown historic Durham. Exquisite antiques, stained glass, and craft/art treasures from around the world add to the visiting pleasure. In addition to three guest rooms, two spacious luxury suites with Jacuzzis for two are available. Extra person in room $20. Full gourmet breakfasts vary daily; e.g., walnut crepes with ricotta cheese filling topped by a raspberry sauce. Dolly's famous "five-minute tour" of nearby shop and restaurant locations—as well as the Duke University campus—is gladly offered to guests who desire a more personal introduction to Durham.

Hosts: Dolly and Frank Pokrass
Rooms: 5 (PB) $85-150
Full Breakfast
Credit Cards: A, B, C, D, E
Notes: 2, 5, 8, 9, 10, 14

The Lords Proprietors' Inn

EDENTON

The Lords Proprietors' Inn

300 North Broad Street, 27932
(919) 482-3641

Establishing a reputation for the finest accommodations in North Carolina, the inn offers 20 elegantly appointed rooms with private baths and spacious parlors for gathering for afternoon tea by the fire. A four-course dinner is served Tuesday through Saturday by reservation. MAP rates Tuesday to Saturday.

Hosts: Arch and Jane Edwards
Rooms: 20 (PB) $105-215
Full Breakfast
Credit Cards: None
Notes: 2, 4, 5, 7 (restricted), 8, 9, 10, 11, 12

The Trestle House Inn

Route 4, Box 370, 27932
(919) 482-2282

South of Albemarle's Colonial capital, off Route 32 and Soundside Road. Luxurious, immaculate accommodations include private baths, HBO, exercise room with steam bath, game room with billiards and shuffleboard, sun deck, and private 15-acre fishing lake. Overlooks a 60-acre wildlife preserve.

Hosts: Willie and Carol Brothers
Rooms: 4 (PB) $55-70
Full Breakfast
Credit Cards: A, B, C
Notes: 2, 5, 7 (limited), 8, 9, 10, 11, 12

ELLERBE

Ellerbe Springs Inn

2537 N. Hwy. 220, 28338
(910) 652-5600; (800) 248-6467

Ellerbe Springs Inn is a beautiful, historic resort nestled in nearly 50 acres of rolling hills and lush greenery. Established in 1857, the pre-Civil War manor has been completely renovated and redecorated as of 1988. Each of the 14 charming guest rooms features antique furniture and Oriental carpets. Private bathrooms and color cable TV are also available. Enjoy delectable Southern cooking in the gracious first-floor dining room, open seven days serving breakfast, lunch, and dinner. It's an easy drive from Charlotte, Greensboro, Raleigh, and Myrtle Beach. Family owned and operated. Listed in the National Register of Historic Places.

Host: Beth Cadieu-Diaz
Rooms: 14 (PB) $54-74
Full Breakfast
Credit Cards: A, B, C, D
Notes: 2, 3, 4, 5, 8, 9, 10, 12, 14

FRANKLIN

Buttonwood Inn

190 Georgia Road, 28734
(704) 369-8985

NOTES: Credit cards accepted: A MasterCard; B Visa; C American Express; D Discover Card; E Diner's Club; F Other; 2 Personal checks accepted; 3 Lunch available; 4 Dinner available; 5 Open all year;

A quaint, small mountain inn awaits those who prefer a cozy country atmosphere. Before hiking, golf, gem mining, or horseback riding, enjoy a breakfast of puffy scrambled eggs and apple sausage ring or eggs Benedict, Dutch babies, blintz soufflé, strawberry omelet, or stuffed French toast. Closed December through March.

Host: Liz Oehser
Rooms: 4 (2 PB; 2 SB) $54.50-65.40
Full Breakfast
Credit Cards: None
Notes: 2, 9, 10, 11, 12, 14

Country Time Bed and Breakfast

506 Potts Branch Drive, 28734
(704) 369-3648

A family farmhouse set in a valley surrounded by mountains. Each room is named after a set of the hosts' grandparents and decorated in their tastes with antique and reproduction furniture. The hosts are natives to the area and provide guests with a homey, Southern atmosphere. This home is a quiet, cheerful getaway from the rat-race, but only minutes from shopping and restaurants. Close by attractions include Appalachian Trail, waterfalls, Great Smokies Railway, and Biltmore House and Gardens.

Hosts: Greg and Darlene Kimsey
Rooms: 4 (PB) $50
Full Breakfast
Credit Cards: A, B
Notes: 2, 5, 8 (over 5), 9, 12, 13

The Franklin Terrace

67 Harrison Avenue, 28734
(704) 524-7907; (800) 633-2431

The Franklin Terrace, built as a school in 1887, is listed in the National Register of Historic Places. Wide porches and large guest rooms filled with period antiques will carry guests to a time gone by, when Southern hospitality was at its best. Antiques, crafts, and gifts are for sale on the main floor. Within walking distance of Franklin's

famous gem shops, clothing boutiques, and fine restaurants. Air conditioning. Private baths in all rooms. Open April 1 through November 15.

Hosts: Ed and Helen Henson
Rooms: 9 (PB) $52-65
Full Breakfast
Credit Cards: A, B, C, D
Notes: 8 (over 3), 9, 10, 11, 12, 14

GERMANTON

MeadowHaven Bed and Breakfast

NC Highway 8, P.O. Box 222, 27019
(910) 593-3996

A contemporary retreat on 25 country acres along Sauratown Mountain. Sixteen miles north of Winston-Salem and ten minutes from Hanging Rock State Park and the Dan River. Heated indoor pool, hot tub, game room, guest pantry, fishing pond, fireplaces, TV/VCR and movies. "Luv Tubs" for two and sauna available. Hiking, canoeing, horseback riding, golf, winery, art gallery, fresco, dining nearby. Plan a "lovebirds' retreat" to MeadowHaven.

Hosts: Samuel and Darlene Fain
Rooms: 3 (PB) $60-90
Luxury Cabin: $125-175
Full Breakfast
Credit Cards: A, B, C
Notes: 2, 5, 10, 11, 12, 14

MeadowHaven

Greenwood

GREENSBORO

Greenwood

205 North Park Drive, 27401
(919) 274-6350

Enjoy the warm hospitality of this 1910 home in the park in the historic district of Greensboro. Three minutes from downtown; three miles from I-85 and I-40. Air conditioning, two fireplaces in living rooms, swimming pool, TV room, and guest kitchen. Hearty continental breakfast is served. Minimum stay Southern Furniture Market: three nights.

Host: Jo Anne Green
Rooms: 3 plus suite (PB) $64-95
Continental Breakfast
Credit Cards: A, B, C, D
Notes: 2, 5, 7, 8 (over 4), 9, 10, 11, 12, 14

HENDERSONVILLE

Claddagh Inn

755 North Main Street, 28792
(704) 697-7778; (800) 225-4700

The Claddagh Inn is in downtown Hendersonville, just two blocks from the beautiful Main Street Shopping Promenade. The inn has undergone extensive remodeling. The guest rooms have private bath, telephone, and air conditioning. TV available. Guests

awake to a delicious full country breakfast. AAA approved. Listed on the National Register of Historic Places.

Hosts: Vickie and Dennis Pacilio
Rooms: 14 (PB) $63-89
Full Breakfast
Credit Cards: A, B, C, D
Notes: 2, 5, 7, 8, 9, 10, 11, 12, 14

Mountain Home Bed and Breakfast

10 Courtland Boulevard, P.O. Box 234, 28758
(704) 697-9090; (800) 396-0077 reservations only

Between Asheville and Hendersonville, near airport. Antiques and Oriental rugs grace this English-style home. Tennessee pink marble porch and rocking chairs to relax the day or night away. Cable TV and telephones in all rooms. Guest kitchen and laundry. Some rooms with private entrance. Full candlelight breakfast. Convenient to Biltmore Estate (on their preferred lodging list), Chimney Rock, Pisgah National Forest, Carl Sandburg Home and much more.

Hosts: Bob and Donna Marriott
Rooms: 7 (5 PB; 2SB) $70-95
Full Breakfast
Credit Cards: A, B, C, D
Notes: 2, 5, 8, 9, 10, 12, 13, 14

The Waverly Inn

783 North Main Street, 28792
(704) 693-9193; (800) 537-8195

Listed in the National Register of Historic Places, this is the oldest inn in Hendersonville. The recently renovated inn has something for everyone, including claw-foot tubs and king- and queen-size four-poster canopied beds. Convenient to restaurants, shopping, Biltmore Estate, Carl Sandburg home, Blue Ridge Parkway, and Flat Rock Playhouse. AAA approved. Member of NCBBI and IIA.

Hosts: John and Diane Sheiry
Rooms: 15 (PB) $79-109
Full Breakfast
Credit Cards: A, B, C, D
Notes: 2, 5, 8, 9, 10, 11, 12, 14

NOTES: Credit cards accepted: A MasterCard; B Visa; C American Express; D Discover Card; E Diner's Club; F Other; 2 Personal checks accepted; 3 Lunch available; 4 Dinner available; 5 Open all year;

HERTFORD

Gingerbread Inn and Bakery

103 South Church Street, 27944
(919) 426-5809

This beautifully restored turn-of-the-century home is on the local historic tour and boasts a wraparound porch with paired columns. The comfortably furnished rooms are spacious, with queen- or king-size beds and plush carpeting. All rooms are centrally air-conditioned and have color cable TV. The aroma of freshly baked gingerbread from the bakery entices guests during their stay, and guests are offered a gingerbread boy or girl for the ride home.

Host: Jenny Harnisch
Rooms: 3 (PB) $47.70
Full Breakfast
Credit Cards: A, B
Notes: 2, 5, 8, 9, 12

HIGHLANDS

Colonial Pines Inn

Route 1, Box 22B, 28741
(704) 526-2060

A quiet country guest house with lovely mountain view. Comfortably furnished with antiques and many fine accessories. One-half mile from Highlands' fine dining and shopping area. Full breakfast includes egg dishes, homemade breads, fresh fruit, coffee, and juice. A separate two-bedroom guest house with kitchen is great for small families.

Hosts: Chris and Donna Alley
Rooms: 6 (PB) $65-95
Guest House: $75-85
Full Breakfast
Credit Cards: A, B
Notes: 2, 5, 10, 11

The Laurels: Freda's Bed and Breakfast

Route 2, Box 102, 28741
(704) 526-2091

The Laurels, a unique bed and breakfast, is in historic Horse Cove, two and one-half miles outside of Highlands. It is on seven acres. Come in the afternoon and have an English tea. Two cozy fireplaces warm the cool evenings. The large English country breakfast features fresh fruit, bacon, ham, and eggs any way guests want them. The hosts grind their own whole-wheat flour and make crunchy toast, "from scratch" pancakes, homemade jams and a lemon curd specialty. Fish the half-acre pond stocked with rainbow trout. No smoking.

Hosts: Warren and Freda Lorenz
Rooms: 5 (PB) $60-70
Full Breakfast
Credit Cards: None
Notes: 2, 8, 9, 11, 12

The Laurels

Long House Bed and Breakfast

Highway 64E, P.O. Box 2078, 28741
(704) 526-4394; (800) 833-0020

Long House Bed and Breakfast offers a comfortable retreat in the scenic mountains of western North Carolina. Any time of the year guests can enjoy the beauty and charm of this quaint town and the scenic wonders of the Nantahala National Forest. The rustic mountain bed and breakfast offers country charm and warm hospitality. A hearty breakfast is served family-style and is usually the highlight of everyone's visit.

6 Pets welcome; 8 Children welcome; 9 Social drinking allowed; 10 Tennis available; 11 Swimming available; 12 Golf available; 13 Skiing available; 14 May be booked through travel agents.

Hosts: Lynn and Valerie Long
Rooms: 4 (PB) $55-95
Full Breakfast
Credit Cards: A, B
Notes: 2, 5, 8, 9

Ye Olde Stone House Bed and Breakfast

Route 2, Box 7, 28741
(704) 526-5911

This house built of stone is a mile from town. Rooms are bright, cheerful, and comfortably furnished. Perfect places for relaxing include a sunroom, porch, 30-foot deck, and attached year-round gazebo all with view. Two fireplaces provide gathering spots. After a restful night's sleep, rise to the smell of fresh brewed coffee and a full country breakfast. Separate, completely furnished chalet with fireplace and meadow view that sleeps four.

Hosts: Jim and Rene Ramsdell
Rooms: 4 (PB) $50-85
Full Breakfast
Credit Cards: A, B
Notes: 2, 5, 8, 9, 10, 11, 12, 13

HILLSBOROUGH

The Hillsborough House Inn

209 East Tryon Street, P.O. Box 880, 27278
(919) 644-1600

Italianate mansion and local landmark, circa 1790 and 1853 (completely renovated), on seven acres in a historic district. The inn has sweeping lawn, huge trees, gardens, landscaped swimming pool, fish pond, 80-foot veranda with rockers, family antiques, original art, whimsical sculpture, extensive library, and fireplaces. The splendid large five bedrooms have embroidered linens. Guests can enjoy the hammock, antique shops, historic sights, and nature areas. One suite with private Jacuzzi bath. Meeting rooms and wedding facilities also available.

Host: Katherine Webb
Rooms: 6 (PB) $95-105

Suite: 1 (PB) $165
Continental Breakfast
Credit Cards: A, B
Notes: 2, 5, 9, 11, 12, 14

Cherokee Inn

KILL DEVIL HILLS

Cherokee Inn

500 North Virginia Dare Trail, 27948
(919) 441-6127

This large beach house with cypress-wood interior is five hundred feet from ocean beach. Quiet and restful. Ideal for relaxing and romance. Close to fine restaurants, golf, hang gliding, scuba diving, wind surfing, deep-sea fishing, and shopping. Three-night minimum stay required for holidays. Closed October through April.

Hosts: Bob and Kaye Combs
Rooms: 6 (PB) $65-95
Continental Breakfast
Credit Cards: A, B, C
Notes: 2, 9, 10, 11, 12, 14

LAKE JUNALUSKA

Providence Lodge

207 Atkins Loop, 28745
(704) 456-6486

Providence Lodge is near the Blue Ridge Parkway and is an easy drive from the Cherokee Indian Reservation, Great Smoky Mountains National Park, or the Biltmore Estate in Asheville. Rustic, with period fur-

NOTES: Credit cards accepted: A MasterCard; B Visa; C American Express; D Discover Card; E Diner's Club; F Other; 2 Personal checks accepted; 3 Lunch available; 4 Dinner available; 5 Open all year;

niture, comfortable beds, claw-foot tubs, and big porches. Delicious family-style meals feature the best in country cooking. Closed September through May.

Hosts: Ben and Wilma Cato
Rooms: 16 (8 PB; 8 SB) $60-75
Credit Cards: None
Notes: 2, 4, 8, 9, 10, 11, 12

LAUREL SPRINGS

Burgiss Farm Bed and Breakfast

Route 1, Box 300, 28644
(919) 359-2995; (800) Bed-1505

Honeymooners love Burgiss Farm! This 1897 farmhouse, high in the mountains, has privacy with lots of spaces. Lots of action—mountain music and dancing, hiking, golfing, biking, lawn croquet, and canoeing and additional golfing nearby. Mountain crafts all over this area. Full breakfast from six different selections with Kona coffee. Guests decide what time to be served! By reservation only. Call for directions, questions, and reservations. Best time to call is 10:00 P.M.

Hosts: Tom and Nancy Burgiss
Rooms: 2 (PB) $75
Full Breakfast
Credit Cards: A, B
Notes: 2, 5, 8, 9, 10, 12, 13 (cross-country), 14 (up to 6 percent)

LITTLE SWITZERLAND

Alpine Inn

Highway 226 A, P.O. Box 477, 28749
(704) 765-5380

Alpine Inn is a small, quaint establishment with rustic mountain charm. An excellent view, from all rooms, of mountain ranges and valleys. One mile from the Blue Ridge Parkway. Guest rooms are cozy and comfortable with a home-like atmosphere. There is a variety of accommodations from a one bedroom to a full apartment. Break-

fasts, which are optional, are hearty and healthy, and range from $1-5. Full vegetarian breakfast available. Breakfast is served on the main balcony. Commune with nature's sunrises!

Hosts: Sharon E. Smith and William M. Cox
Rooms: 14 (PB) $36-60
Full and Continental Breakfast
Credit Cards: A, B
Notes: 2, 7, 8, 9, 10, 11, 12, 13

MADISON

The Boxley Bed and Breakfast Inn

117 East Hunter Street, 27025
(800) 429-3516

The Greek, Federal-style plantation home, built in 1825 on over an acre, is in the historic district of Madison. Boxwoods adorn the long front walk and the gardens in the rear. The porch connecting the main house to the dining room and kitchen is wonderful to sit and relax and enjoy the peacefulness and serenity of the 19th-century setting. The hosts want guests to make themselves at home.

Hosts: JoAnn and Monte McIntosh
Rooms: 4 (PB) $60
Full Breakfast
Credit Cards: A, B
Notes: 2, 5, 7, 9, 10, 12

MANTEO

The Roanoke Island Inn

305 Fernando Street, P.O. Box 1891, 27954
(919) 473-5511

Since 1937, island folks have welcomed visitors into their homes. In that tradition, the Roanoke Island Inn welcomes its guests! The Roanoke represents well over a hundred years of construction and additions to a waterfront family homeplace. This inn offers its guests the privacy of outside entrances, the comfort of a lobby, and the indulgence of a well-stocked innkeeper's pantry. A second-

6 Pets welcome; 8 Children welcome; 9 Social drinking allowed; 10 Tennis available; 11 Swimming available; 12 Golf available; 13 Skiing available; 14 May be booked through travel agents.

floor porch overlooks Manteo's acclaimed waterfront where visitors can stroll along the boardwalk to shops, restaurants, charter boats, and the movie theater. Bikes are available. The beaches, lighthouses, and sun-filled activities of the Outer Banks are just across the causeway.

Host: Ada Hadley
Rooms: 8 (PB) $78-108
Continental Breakfast
Credit Cards: A, B
Notes: 8, 9, 10, 11, 12

Tranquil House Inn

405 Queen Elizabeth Street, P.O. Box 2045, 27954
(800) 458-7069

In a charming waterfront village only minutes from the fabled Outer Banks beaches, a million miles from the rat race. Have the complimentary continental breakfast and coffee or evening wine on the breezy deck, or relax there after a day of touring the area's historic sites. Attractions include the Lost Colony outdoor drama, Elizabethan Gardens, Elizabeth II sailing vessel, and Wright Brothers Museum. Enjoy dinner at the restaurant, 1587, where guests will experience the ultimate in culinary vision and gracious hospitality. Complimentary bikes. Canoeing and kayaking available nearby.

Hosts: Don and Lauri Just
Rooms: 25 (PB) $79-159
Continental Breakfast
Credit Cards: A, B, C, D
Notes: 4, 5, 8, 9, 10, 11, 12, 14

MARSHALL

Marshall House Bed and Breakfast Inn

5 Hill Street, P.O. Box 865, 28753
(704) 649-9205; (800) 562-9258
FAX (704) 649-2999

Truly in the mountains, overlooking the quaint town of Marshall, the French Broad River, and the mountains, this 1903 house is decorated with fancy chandeliers, mirrors, and lots of antiques. Resident cats add extra charm, and the porch is for rocking in this very relaxed atmosphere. Listed on the National Register of Historic Places, the house welcomes all in an atmosphere of bygone days.

Hosts: Ruth and Jim Boylan
Rooms: 9 (2 PB; 7 SB) $39-75
Continental Breakfast
Credit Cards: A, B, C, D, E, F
Notes: 5, 6, 7, 8, 9, 11, 12, 13, 14

MARS HILL

Baird House, Ltd.

41 South Main Street, 28754
(704) 689-5722

Five guest rooms—two with a working fireplace, two with private bath—are featured in an old brick, antique-filled bed and breakfast inn that once was the grandest house in this pastoral corner of the western North Carolina mountains. Eighteen miles north of Asheville. Closed December.

Host: Yvette Wessel
Rooms: 5 (2 PB; 3 SB) $42.40-53
Full Breakfast
Credit Cards: C
Notes: 2, 8, 9, 10, 11, 12, 13, 14

MOUNT AIRY

Pine Ridge Inn

2893 West Pine Street, 27030
(919) 789-5034

Built in 1948, this Southern mansion offers private bedroom suites, swimming pool with sun deck, horseback riding, and golf nearby.

Hosts: Ellen and Manford Haxton
Rooms: 6 (PB) $60-100
Full or Continental Breakfast
Credit Cards: A, B, C
Notes: 2, 3, 4, 5, 7, 8, 9, 10, 11, 12, 14

MURPHY

Hill Top House

104 Campbell Street, 28906
(704) 837-8661

NOTES: Credit cards accepted: A MasterCard; B Visa; C American Express; D Discover Card; E Diner's Club; F Other; 2 Personal checks accepted; 3 Lunch available; 4 Dinner available; 5 Open all year;

Hill Top House is a step back into a turn-of-the-century home. Built around 1902, the house has been modernized only in the kitchen and plumbing. Each room has been tastefully decorated in period pieces and antiques. A full breakfast featuring homemade breads is served in the spacious dining room, and the hosts gladly cater to individual diet needs. Three rooms are available for reservations, all with queen-size or twin beds.

Hosts: Don and Jacqueline Heinze
Rooms: 3 (1 PB; 2 SB) $45-50
Full Breakfast
Credit Cards: None
Notes: 2, 5, 8, 9, 10, 11, 12

Huntington Hall Bed and Breakfast

500 Valley River Avenue, 28906
(704) 837-9567; (800) 824-6189

Ginger-peach crepes, English ivy, and low stone walls await. Five guest rooms with private baths. Wonderful breakfasts served on the sun porch overlooked by 100-year-old maple trees. This former mayor's home is warm and comfortable. Circa 1881. Here in the mountains of western North Carolina, guests can hike, whitewater raft, ride the Great Smoky Mountains Railway, visit the John C. Campbell Folk School, or just relax on the porch and smell the mountain breeze. Murder mystery weekends available.

Hosts: Bob and Katie DeLong
Rooms: 5 (PB) $49-85
Full Breakfast
Credit Cards: A, B, C, D, E
Notes: 2, 5, 8, 9, 10, 11, 12, 14

NAGS HEAD

First Colony Inn

6720 South Virginia Dare Trail, 27959
(919) 441-2343; (800) 368-9390 reservations
FAX (919) 441-9234

Enjoy Southern hospitality at the Outer Banks' only historic bed and breakfast inn

(National Register). Private beach access, pool, continuous wraparound verandas with rockers, elegant library, antique-filled rooms with private tiled bath, heated towel bars, Jacuzzis, wet bars with microwave ovens or kitchenettes, and remote-controlled heat pumps. Enjoy the complimentary continental breakfast buffet and afternoon tea in the sunny breakfast room. See the Lost Colony and Wright Brothers Memorial, fish, windsurf, hang glide, or stroll the beach. Honeymoons, anniversaries, weddings, and small conferences are specialties.

Hosts: The Lawrences
Rooms: 26 (PB) $75-225 seasonal
Continental Breakfast
Credit Cards: A, B, D
Notes: 2 (for deposit only), 5, 8, 9, 10, 11, 12, 14

The Aerie

NEW BERN

The Aerie

509 Pollock Street, 28560
(919) 636-5553; (800) 849-5553

A Victorian inn one block from Tryon Palace. Individually decorated rooms are furnished with antiques and reproductions; sitting room with player piano. Complimentary wine and beer. Choice of three breakfast entrees each morning.

Hosts: Howard and Dee Smith
Rooms: 7 (PB) $79-99

6 Pets welcome; 8 Children welcome; 9 Social drinking allowed; 10 Tennis available; 11 Swimming available; 12 Golf available; 13 Skiing available; 14 May be booked through travel agents.

Full Breakfast
Credit Cards: A, B, C
Notes: 2, 5, 7, 8, 9, 12, 14

Harmony House Inn

215 Pollock Street, 28560
(919) 636-3810; (800) 636-3113

This circa 1850 Greek Revival inn provides comfortable elegance in the historic district. Unusual spaciousness, antiques, a guest parlor, rocking chairs and swings on the front porch, and parking area add to guests' enjoyment. Complimentary soft drinks. Near Tryon Palace, restaurants, and shops.

Hosts: Ed and Sooki Kirpatrick
Rooms: 9 (PB) $85
Full Breakfast
Credit Cards: A, B, C, D
Notes: 2, 5, 8, 9, 10, 12, 14

Kings Arms Inn

Kings Arms Inn

212 Pollock Street, 28560
(919) 638-4409; (800) 872-9306

The King's Arms Inn, named for an old New Bern tavern reputed to have hosted members of the First Continental Congress, upholds a heritage of hospitality and graciousness as New Bern's "first and foremost" in bed and breakfast accommodations. Spacious rooms with comfortable four-poster, canopied, or brass beds; private baths; and elegant decor harbor travelers who want to escape the present and steep themselves in colonial history. Home-baked breakfasts consist of fresh home-baked muffins, including ham and cheese, blueberry, currant or cranberry; fresh fruit; juice; and cinnamon coffee or tea—all delivered to the room with a morning paper.

Hosts: Richard and Pat Gulley
Rooms: 10 (8-PB; 2-SB) $55-76
Continental Breakfast
Credit Cards: A, B, C
Notes: 2, 5, 8, 9, 10, 11, 12

New Berne House Inn

709 Broad Street, 28560
(800) 842-7688

Listed on the National Register of Historic Places and one block from Tryon Palace, New Berne House offers the charm and ambience of English country house decor. Guest rooms all have private baths, some with claw-foot tubs and pedestal sinks. Antique beds piled with pillows; crisp eyelet sheets; fireplaces in some rooms. The inn is noted for its fine breakfasts, including Southern specialties such as pralines'n'cream waffles and peach French toast. Special packages and rates, including mystery weekends, are available.

Hosts: Marcia Drum and Howard Bronson
Rooms: 7 (PB) $60-80
Full Breakfast
Credit Cards: A, B, C
Notes: 2, 5, 9, 10, 11, 12, 14

OCEAN ISLE BEACH

The Winds-Clarion Carriage House Inn

310 East First Street, 28469
(800) 334-3581 (US and Canada)

This delightful inn, surrounded by palm trees and lush subtropical landscaping, is on the oceanfront on an island beach just 20 minutes from North Myrtle Beach, South Carolina. The Winds features oceanfront two- and three-room suites and studios with

NOTES: Credit cards accepted: A MasterCard; B Visa; C American Express; D Discover Card; E Diner's Club; F Other; 2 Personal checks accepted; 3 Lunch available; 4 Dinner available; 5 Open all year;

full kitchens or kitchenettes and seaside balconies. Amenities include daily housekeeping, a heated pool, whirlpool, sauna, beach volleyball, fitness room, rental bicycles, sailboats, golf on 80 courses, and free tennis on the island. There are several restaurants on the island and nearby Myrtle Beach offers many more.

Hosts: Miller and Helen Pope
Rooms: 73 (PB) $53-174
Continental Breakfast
Credit Cards: A, B, C, D, E
Notes: 5, 7, 8, 9, 10, 11, 12, 14

OCRACOKE ISLAND

Oscar's House

Route 12, Box 206, 27960
(919) 928-1311

Oscar's House offers friendly accommodations in a comfortable 1940s home on Ocracoke Island. The home is one block from the harbor and one mile from the Atlantic Ocean, within easy walking distance of shops, restaurants, and historic sites. The full breakfast is healthy, and special diets are accommodated. Closed November through early April.

Host: Ann Ehringhaus
Rooms: 4 (2 SB) $53-59
Full Breakfast
Credit Cards: A, B
Notes: 2, 7 (limited), 8 (over 3), 9, 11

ORIENTAL

The Tar Heel Inn

Box 176, 205 Church Street, 28571
(919) 249-1078

This circa 1890 Inn has been restored to capture the feeling of an old English country inn. The garden and patio are for the guests to enjoy. Bikes are available for guests to pedal around town. Oriental is a quiet fishing village on the Neuse River and Pamlico Sount. It is known as the sailing capital of the Carolinas. Excellent restaurants and shops, sailing, golf, tennis, and fishing are within walking or biking distance.

Hosts: Shawna and Robert Hyde.
Rooms: 8 (PB) $60-85
Full Breakfast
Credit Cards: A, B
Notes: 2, 5. 8, 9, 10, 11, 12, 14

PINEBLUFF

Pine Cone Manor Bed and Breakfast

450 East Philadelphia Avenue, 28373
(919) 281-5307

Nestled in the charming village of Pinebluff (Pinehurst Resort area), this beautiful home was built in the early 1900s. Guests are invited to relax on the lovely porches or take a stroll along pine needle paths among many flowering trees and shrubs. Tee times can be arranged.

Host: Virginia H. Keith
Rooms: 4 (3 PB; 1 SB) $45-55
Continental Breakfast
Credit Cards: A, B
Notes: 2, 5, 7, 9, 10, 11, 12

Pine Cone Manor

PISGAH FOREST

The Pines Country Inn

719 Hart Road, 28768
(704) 877-3131

The Pines Country Inn is in the Blue Ridge Mountains overlooking a beautiful valley. Truly a country inn, where guests are treated like family at Grandma's house. Available by day, week, or month. Between Brevard and Hendersonville.

Hosts: Tom and Mary McEntire
Rooms: 18 (16 PB; 2 SB) $55-65
Full Breakfast
Credit Cards: None
Notes: 2, 4, 8, 11, 12

ROBBINSVILLE

Blue Boar Lodge

200 Santeetlah Road, 28771
(704) 479-8126

Secluded mountain retreat cooled by mountain breezes. Hiking, fishing, hunting, bird watching, and canoeing are all very close by. Rustic but modern house. Meals served family-style on the lazy Susan table. Away from all city traffic, ten miles northwest of Robbinsville. Quiet and peaceful. Rate includes breakfast and dinner. Open April 1 through mid-October.

Hosts: Roy and Kathy Wilson
Rooms: 7 (PB) $90
Full Breakfast
Credit Cards: A, B
Notes: 4, 7, 8, 11

SALISBURY

Rowan Oak House

208 South Fulton Street, 28144
(704) 633-2086; (800) 786-0437

Romantic and lavish describes this Queen Anne Victorian mansion: wraparound porch, rocking chairs, elaborate woodwork, stained glass, and original fixtures. Bedrooms are enormous with air conditioning, English and American antiques, fruit, and flowers. One room has Jacuzzi and gas log fireplace. A full gourmet breakfast will be served with silver, crystal, and Queen Louise china. In the heart of the historic district, one mile from I-85, Exit 76B.

Hosts: Bill and Ruth Ann Coffey
Rooms: 4 (2 PB; 2 SB) $65-95
Full Breakfast
Credit Cards: A, B, D
Notes: 2, 5, 7 (limited), 8 (over 10), 9, 10, 11, 12, 14

Rowan Oak House

SILER CITY

Bed and Breakfast at Laurel Ridge

Route 1, Box 116, 27344
(919) 742-6049; (800) 742-6049

In the heart of North Carolina, Laurel Ridge is a ten-year-old post and beam country home with an eclectic collection of antique and traditional furniture. The house sits on a ridge, overlooking the rocky river surrounded by one of the largest natural stands of mountain laurel east of the mountains. The setting is captivating with English country gardens, nature trails, and wildlife. The innkeeper is one of the area's most respected chefs.

Hosts: David J. Simmons and Lisa Reynolds
Rooms: 3 (1 PB; 2 SB) $45-95
Full Breakfast
Credit Cards: A, B, C
Notes: 2, 5, 7, 8, 9, 10, 11, 12, 14

SOUTHERN PINES

Knollwood House

1495 West Connecticut Avenue, 28387
(919) 692-9390

NOTES: Credit cards accepted: A MasterCard; B Visa; C American Express; D Discover Card; E Diner's Club; F Other; 2 Personal checks accepted; 3 Lunch available; 4 Dinner available; 5 Open all year;

A luxurious English manor house appointed with 18th-century antiques combined with contemporary comforts. The house stands on three acres of long leaf pines, dogwoods, magnolias, holly trees, and hundreds of flowering shrubs. From the back terrace, it is less than 100 feet to the 15th fairway of a championship golf course. And there are more than 30 courses just minutes away. Tennis, swimming, and riding too! Full and continental breakfast. Two suites, two guest rooms all with private baths. Meeting rooms, wedding facilities, and catering available.

Hosts: Mimi and Dick Beatty
Rooms: 4 (PB) $80-115
Continental and Full Breakfast
Credit Cards: A, B
Notes: 2, 5, 7 (limited), 8 (over 10), 9, 10, 11, 12, 14

Knollwood House

SPARTA

Turby-villa

Highway 18 North, Star Route 1, Box 48, 28675
(910) 372-8490

The Turby-villa is on 20 acres of beautiful mountain farmland. Breakfast is selected from a menu and served on a glassed-in porch with a beautiful view of the mountains. The bed and breakfast is ten miles from the Blue Ridge Parkway, which is maintained by the National Park Service, on Highway 18, two miles from Sparta.

Host: Maybelline Turbiville
Rooms: 3 (PB) $53

Full Breakfast
Credit Cards: None
Notes: 2, 5, 7, 8, 9, 10, 12

STATESVILLE

Cedar Hill Farm Bed and Breakfast

778 Elmwood Road, 28677
(704) 873-4332; (800) 484-8457 ext. 1254

An 1840 farmhouse and private cottage on a 32-acre sheep farm in the rolling hills of North Carolina. Antique furnishings, air conditioning, color cable TV, and telephones in rooms. After a full country breakfast, swim, play badminton, or relax in a porch rocker or hammock. For a busier day, visit two lovely towns with historic districts, Old Salem, or two large cities in a 45-mile radius. Convenient to restaurants, shopping, and three interstate highways.

Hosts: Jim and Brenda Vernon
Rooms: 2 (PB) $55-70
Full Breakfast
Credit Cards: A, B
Notes: 2, 5, 7 (limited), 8, 9, 11, 14

Madelyn's Bed and Breakfast

514 Carroll Street, 28677
(704) 872-3973

Fresh flowers and homemade cookies await guests' arrival at Statesville's first bed and breakfast. It is a charming 1940s brick home filled with unique collections of family antiques, Raggedy Anns, iron dogs, and bottles. There are three lovely bedrooms with private baths. Each has a different size bed to suit any traveler's needs. A full gourmet breakfast includes a choice of juice, fresh or baked fruit, bread, and entree. The house has central air conditioning. No smoking.

Hosts: Madelyn and John Hill
Rooms: 3 (PB) $65-75
Full Breakfast
Credit Cards: A, B
Notes: 2, 5, 9, 10, 11, 12, 14

6 Pets welcome; 8 Children welcome; 9 Social drinking allowed; 10 Tennis available; 11 Swimming available; 12 Golf available; 13 Skiing available; 14 May be booked through travel agents.

Willow Oaks

Willow Oaks

348 North Center Street, 28677
(704) 878-8632; (704) 872-0304 (evenings)

Enjoy luxurious accommodations in an elegant Southern home. Guest suite includes a bedroom with a queen-size four-poster bed, sunny sitting room with fireplace, and private bath with large soaking tub and shower. Guests may prefer accommodations in a single room with high ceilings, handsome woodwork, and a private bath. It is just a leisurely walk to downtown shops and restaurants, and has easy access to I-40 and I-77. Stop, relax, and discover Statesville's rich architectural heritage and small-town charm.

Hosts: Brenda and Jim Falter
Rooms: 2 (PB) $52-65
Full Breakfast
Credit Cards: None
Notes: 2, 5, 8, 9, 10, 12

SUGAR GROVE

Galloway's Rivendell Lodge

P.O. Box 211, 28679
(704) 297-1685

Secluded mountainside setting overlooking Watauga River rapids. Easy trail to the river. Guests have seen deer, beavers, rabbits, chipmunks, red-tailed hawks, herons, and humming birds on or near the property. Most guest rooms have down comforters and mountain views. Spacious great room

with fireplace and library; multi-level decks and picnic/grill facilities outside. Twenty-five miles from Blue Ridge Parkway (Blowing Rock exit).

Hosts: Sandy and Gary Galloway
Rooms: 4 (2-4 PB; 2 SB) $65-75
Full Breakfast
Credit Cards: None
Notes: 2, 5, 14

TARBORO

Little Warren

304 East Park Avenue, 27886
(919) 823-1314

Established in 1984, the Little Warren is a large, gracious Edwardian family home, renovated and modernized, in a quiet neighborhood in the historic district. Furnished with family English and American antiques and collectibles the house has a fireplaced common room and a deeply set wraparound front porch that overlooks the Town Common, one of two originally chartered commons remaining in the United States. Antiques available.

Hosts: Patsy and Tom Miller
Rooms: 3 (PB) $68.90
Continental and Full Breakfast
Credit Cards: A, B, C, D
Notes: 2, 5, 7, 8 (over 6), 9, 10, 14

TRYON

Fox Trot Inn

800 Lynn Road, Route 108, P.O. Box 1561, 28782
(704) 859-9706

An elegant retreat on eight wooded acres in the heart of Tryon. This large, graciously proportioned inn features four bedrooms, two of which are suites. All rooms have private baths. Wine and hors d'oeuvres each evening. Air conditioning. Heated swimming pool. Also available is a fully furnished guest house with hanging deck, mountain view, and cable TV. House rates are weekly; monthly rates are available.

NOTES: Credit cards accepted: A MasterCard; B Visa; C American Express; D Discover Card; E Diner's Club; F Other; 2 Personal checks accepted; 3 Lunch available; 4 Dinner available; 5 Open all year;

Guests may use the inn's pool. Closed December 15 through March 14.

Hosts: Mimi Colby and Betty Daugherty
Rooms: 4 (PB) $60-95
House: (PB) $350-450
Full Breakfast
Credit Cards: None
Notes: 2, 7, 9, 10, 11, 12

Pine Crest Inn

Pine Crest Inn

200 Pine Crest Lane, 28782
(704) 859-9135; (800) 633-3001

The four diamond Pine Crest Inn is nestled in the foothills of the Blue Ridge Mountains. Listed on the National Register of Historic Places, the inn has 30 private rooms, suites, or cottages. The gourmet restaurant, fireplaces, wide porches, and beautiful grounds create a casual elegance and relaxing atmosphere. Nearby attractions include the Blue Ridge Parkway and the famous Biltmore Estate and Gardens.

Hosts: Jeremy and Jennifer Wainwright
Rooms: 30 (PB) $125-150
Continental Breakfast
Credit Cards: A, B, C, D
Notes: 2, 4, 5, 7, 8, 9, 10, 11, 12, 14

Stone Hedge Inn

Box 366, 28782
(704) 859-9114

Grand old estate on 28 acres at the base of Tryon Mountain. Lodging in the main building, cottage, and guest house. Private baths, TV, antiques, and wonderful views.

Some rooms have kitchens and some have fireplaces. A full breakfast is served in the dining room by the picture windows. The restaurant features fine continental cuisine.

Hosts: Ray and Anneliese Weingartner
Rooms: 6 (PB) $65-85
Full Breakfast
Credit Cards: A, B
Notes: 2, 4, 5, 7, 8 (over 6), 9, 10, 11, 12, 14

VALLE CRUCIS

Mast Farm Inn

Box 704, 28691
(704) 963-5857

Recently restored 12-room inn on the National Register of Historic Places. Vegetables and berries for the dining room are grown on the 18-acre farm in North Carolina's high country near the Blue Ridge Parkway. Country cooking with a gourmet touch. Golf, hiking, swimming, fishing, and skiing are nearby. Breakfast and dinner are included. Rates quoted are Modified American Plan rates. Closed March 6 through April 25 and November 6 through December 26.

Hosts: Sibyl and Francis Pressly
Rooms: 12 (10 PB; 2 SB) $90-165
Continental Breakfast
Credit Cards: A, B
Notes: 2, 4, 9, 10, 11, 12, 13, 14

Mast Farm Inn

WAYNESVILLE

Grandview Lodge

809 Valley View Circle Road, 28786
(704) 456-5212; (800) 255-7826

A country inn in the western North Carolina mountains; open all year. Southern home cooking, with breakfast featuring homemade breads, jams, and jellies. Dinner includes fresh vegetables, freshly baked breads, and desserts. Meals, served family-style, are included in the rates. Private bath and cable TV. Reser-vations required.

Hosts: Stan and Linda Arnold
Rooms: 11 (PB) $95-110
Full Breakfast
Credit Cards: None
Notes: 2, 4, 5, 8, 9, 10, 11, 12, 13, 14

Hallcrest Inn

299 Halltop Circle, 28786
(704) 456-6457; (800) 334-6457

The homelike atmosphere here encourages a relaxing stay at this 1880s farmhouse on a mountaintop. Southern-style meals are served around large, lazy susan tables. All rooms have private baths. There's a beautiful view from the front porch, where rocking chairs await. The daily rate includes both breakfast and dinner. Closed December through April.

Hosts: Martin and Tesa Burson; David and Catherine Mitchell
Rooms: 12 (PB) $75-90
Full Breakfast
Credit Cards: A, B, D
Notes: 2, 4, 7, 8, 9 (limited), 10, 11, 12, 14

Haywood Street House Bed and Breakfast

409 South Haywood Street, 28786
(704) 456-9831

Built at the turn of the century, this historic home is graced with antique furnishings, beautiful oak paneling, cabinets, and mantels. Enjoy the cozy library for books and games, or great conversation in the parlor. A large veranda with rockers offers a panoramic view of the mountains. Walk to Main Street's shops and restaurants. Four charming guest rooms. Home-baked breakfast is served in the lovely dining room. A perfect home for small groups of family or friends.

Hosts: Lynn and Chris Sylvester
Rooms: 4 (2 SB) $50-55
Full Breakfast
Credit Cards: None
Notes: 2, 5, 9, 12, 13

Heath Lodge Mountain Inn

900 Dolan Road, 28786
(704) 456-3333; (800) 432-8499

Shaded by majestic oaks, this mountain inn is a rustic, secluded getaway 3,200 feet up in the North Carolina Smokies. The rustic mountain atmosphere belies the comfortably furnished and renovated 18 guest rooms and four suites, all with private baths and color cable TV. A massive stone fireplace dominates the picturesque dining room where the inn's famous bountiful mountain breakfasts and country American dinners are served. Two guest lounges, over 400 feet of porches with rockers, aid in an exceptional mountain inn experience. Close to horseback riding, whitewater rafting, spectacular golf courses, mountain trails, and within walking distance of the charming shops of Waynesville.

Hosts: Robert and Cindy Zinser
Rooms: 18 (PB) $65-95
Suites: 4 (PB)
Full Breakfast
Credit Cards: A, B, D
Notes: 2, 4, 5, 7, 8, 9, 10, 11, 12, 13, 14

The Palmer House

108 Pigeon Street, 28786
(704) 456-7521

Built before the turn-of-the-century, the Palmer House is one of the last of Waynesville's once numerous tourist homes. Within one block of Main Street. Relaxing

NOTES: Credit cards accepted: A MasterCard; B Visa; C American Express; D Discover Card; E Diner's Club; F Other; 2 Personal checks accepted; 3 Lunch available; 4 Dinner available; 5 Open all year;

environment, beautiful mountains, and good food. Guests also enjoy a ten percent discount at the hosts' bookshop on Main Street. A home away from home.

Hosts: Jeff Minick and Kris Gillet
Rooms: 7 (PB) $50-60
Full Breakfast
Credit Cards: A, B, C, D
Notes: 2, 5, 8, 9, 10, 11, 12, 13, 14

WELDON

Weldon Place Inn
500 Washington Avenue, 27890
(919) 536-4582; (800) 831-4470

This Home Away From Home is only two miles off I-95, Exit 173, halfway between New York and Florida. Sleep in a canopied bed, wake to singing sparrows, stroll through the cozy historic hometown and savor a gourmet breakfast. At the Weldon Place Inn the guest's peace of mind begins with antiques and country elegance. Personal attention is provided to insure the guest the ultimate in solitude and relaxation. Local attractions include state historic site, early canal system and railroad.

Hosts: Angel and Andy Whitby
Rooms: 4 (PB) $60-85
Full Breakfast
Credit Cards: A, B
Notes: 5, 7, 10, 14

Weldon Place Inn

WILMINGTON

Anderson Guest House
520 Orange Street, 28401
(919) 343-8128

An 1851 Italianate townhouse with separate guest quarters overlooking the private garden. Furnished with antiques, ceiling fans, and working fireplaces. Drinks on arrival. A delightful gourmet breakfast is served.

Hosts: Landon and Connie Anderson
Rooms: 2 (PB) $60-75
Full Breakfast
Credit Cards: None
Notes: 2, 5, 6, 7 (limited), 8, 9, 10, 11, 12

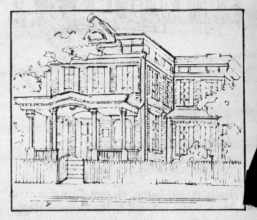

The Inn on Orange

The Inn on Orange
410 Orange Street, 28401
(910) 815-0035; (800) 381-4666

The Inn on Orange offers bedrooms with private baths, a comfortable living room and dining room (both with fireplaces), as well as a lovely bricked courtyard with a small swimming pool. A full breakfast is served each morning and guests may dine on the front porch, around the pool, or in the dining room. Complimentary coffee and cold beverages are always available. In the historic district and just a short walk to the

6 Pets welcome; 8 Children welcome; 9 Social drinking allowed; 10 Tennis available; 11 Swimming available; 12 Golf available; 13 Skiing available; 14 May be booked through travel agents.

Cape Fear River and Wilmington's better restaurants and night spots. Special rates can be arranged for extended stays by business people and the film industry.

Hosts: Paul Marston and Thomas Renner
Rooms: 4 (PB) $55-95
Full Breakfast
Credit Cards: A, B
Notes: 2, 5, 7, 9, 10, 11, 12, 14

Market Street

Market Street Bed and Breakfast

1704 Market Street, 28403
(910) 763-5442; (800) 242-5442

Built in 1917, this elegant Georgian-style brick house is listed on the National Register of Historic Places but has modern conveniences, including central air conditioning and paved off-street parking. Furnished with antiques and reproductions with a piano for guests' use. On U.S. Highways 17 and 74, with beaches, restaurants, and shopping nearby.

Hosts: Jo Anne and Bob Jarrett
Rooms: 2 (PB) $75
Suite: 1 (PB) $90
Full Breakfast
Credit Cards: A, B
Notes: 2, 5, 9, 10, 11, 12

The Worth House

412 South Third Street, 28401
(919) 762-8562

Elegantly restored Victorian inn is in historic Wilmington. Five spacious guest rooms/suites all with private bath and fireplace. Antiques, hardwood floors, fresh flowers, and romance surround guests. Full breakfast served in the privacy of guests' room, in the formal dining room, on the veranda, or in the garden. Telephones in each room; TV.

Hosts: Sharon and Dale Smith
Rooms: 5 (PB) $82-98
Full Breakfast
Credit Cards: A, B
Notes: 2, 5, 9, 10, 11, 12

WILSON

Miss Betty's Bed and Breakfast Inn

600 West Nash Street, 27893-3045
(919) 243-4447; (800) 258-2058 reservations only

Selected as one of the "Best Places To Stay In The South," Miss Betty's is comprised of four beautifully restored historic homes. In a gracious setting in the downtown historic section, where quiet Victorian elegance and charm abound in an atmosphere of all modern-day conveniences. Guests may browse for antiques at Miss Betty's or in any of the numerous antique shops that have given Wilson the title of "Antique Capital of North Carolina." A quiet eastern North Carolina town also known for its famous Eastern Carolina barbecue, Wilson features four beautiful golf courses, numerous tennis courts, and Olympic-size pool. Midway between Maine and Florida, along the main North-South Route I-95.

Hosts: Betty and Fred Spitz
Rooms: 10 (PB) $60-75
Full Breakfast
Credit Cards: A, B, C, D, E, F
Notes: 2, 5, 7, 9, 10, 11, 12

WINSTON-SALEM

Brookstown Inn

200 Brookstown Avenue, 27101
(910) 725-1120

NOTES: Credit cards accepted: A MasterCard; B Visa; C American Express; D Discover Card; E Diner's Club; F Other; 2 Personal checks accepted; 3 Lunch available; 4 Dinner available; 5 Open all year;

Travel back in time at the historic Brookstown Inn. Built in 1837 as a textile mill, the building was recently converted to a cozy inn with much of the original structure carefully preserved. Where young girls once carded and wove raw wool into cloth, today, the Brookstown Inn's Southern hospitality and authentic Early American decor let guests escape to the charm of yesteryear. The Brookstown Inn is in the National Register of Historic Places and is rated a AAA four-diamond inn.

Host: Deborah J. Bumgardner, CHA, General
  Manager
Rooms: 71 (PB) $99-135
Continental Breakfast
Credit Cards: A, B, C, F
Notes: 2, 5, 7, 8, 12, 14

Colonel Ludlow Inn

Summit and West Fifth, 27101
(910) 777-1887; (800) 301-1887

Two adjacent houses from the late 1800s listed on the National Register of Historic Places have been converted into a luxurious inn. The unique guest rooms (each with private deluxe bath and most with two-person whirlpool tubs) are furnished with beautiful period antiques. All rooms have telephones, stereo and tapes, cable TV and VCR with free movies, mini refrigerators, and coffee/tea makers. Some rooms feature fireplaces. Gourmet restaurants, cafes, shops, and parks are within easy walking distance.

Host: Ken Land
Rooms: 13 (PB) $72-189
Full Breakfast
Credit Cards: A, B, C, D
Notes: 2, 4, 5, 7, 9, 10, 11, 12, 14

Colonel Ludlow Inn

Lady Anne's Victorian Bed and Breakfast

612 Summit Street, 27101
(919) 724-1074

Warm Southern hospitality surrounds guests in this 1890 historic Victorian. An aura of romance touches every suite and room, all of which are individually decorated with period antiques and treasures, while skillfully including modern luxuries, such as private baths, whirlpools, balconies, porches, cable TV with HBO, stereo with music and tapes, and telephones. An evening dessert/tea tray and a delicious full breakfast are served on fine china and lace. Near downtown attractions, performances, restaurants, and shops. Near Old Salem Historic Village.

Host: Shelley Kirley
Rooms/Suites: 5 (PB) $55-145
Full Breakfast
Credit Cards: A, B, C
Notes: 5, 9, 10, 11, 12

Mickle House Bed and Breakfast

927 West Fifth Street, 27101
(919) 722-9045

Step back in time to a quaint 1892 Victorian cottage. A gracious welcome, lovely antiques, restful canopied and poster beds, and a delicious breakfast served in the spacious dining room or on the brick patio. The old-fashioned rocking chairs and swing on the porch and the boxwood gardens offer guests a respite from all cares. In the picturesque National Historic District of West End, it is only five minutes from Old Salem, the Medical Center, and the downtown/ convention center. Walk to fine restaurants, parks, shops, the YMCA, churches, and library. Golf, tennis, and swimming nearby.

Host: Barbara Garrison
Rooms: 2 (PB) $65
Full Breakfast
Credit Cards: A, B
Notes: 2, 5, 9, 10, 11, 12, 14

6 Pets welcome; 8 Children welcome; 9 Social drinking allowed; 10 Tennis available; 11 Swimming available; 12 Golf available; 13 Skiing available; 14 May be booked through travel agents.

Wachovia Bed and Breakfast, Inc.

513 Wachovia Street, 27101
(919) 777-0332

Lovely rose and white Victorian cottage on a quiet street, within walking distance of city center, Old Salem Historia, antique shops, and gourmet restaurants. A Euro-pean-style bed and breakfast, with flexible check-in/check-out. No rigid breakfast schedule. Expanded breakfast. Complimentary wine. No smoking.

Host: Susan Bunting
Rooms: 6 (2 PB; 3 SB) $45-65
Full Breakfast
Credit Cards: A, B
Notes: 2, 5, 8, 9, 10, 12

North Dakota

JAMESTOWN

Old West Bed and Breakfast

Box 211, Regent, 58650
(701) 563-4542

Country Charm. A farm home from the 1920s with cozy rooms decorated with antiques, collectibles, and handcrafted quilts. Two bedrooms share a bath; one has a private bath. $35.

LIDGERWOOD

Old West Bed and Breakfast

Box 211, Regent, 58650
(701) 563-4542

A comfortable older home with a choice of bedrooms on the second floor and a private bath. Children are welcome and a pet can be accommodated. $35.

LUVERNE

Volden Farm Bed and Breakfast

Rural Route 2, Box 50, 58056
(701) 769-2275

A retreat in the most real sense of the word. Peace, quiet, beauty, good books, art, nature, and animals join with home comforts, good food, great coffee, and conversation for an ideal stay on the Volden farm. Four guest rooms available with shared and private baths. Outdoor smoking permitted.

Hosts: Jim and JoAnne Wold
Rooms: 4 (1 PB; 3 SB) $50-75
Full Breakfast
Credit Cards: None
Notes: 2, 4, 5, 6 and 7 (limited), 8, 9, 10, 11, 12, 13, 14

Volden Farm

MCCLUSKY

Midstate Bed and Breakfast

Route 3, P.O. Box 28, 58463
(701) 363-2520

Country "peace and quiet" prevail at this easy-to-find location alongside Highway 200. This newer home is on a working grain and livestock farm. The house features a private entrance to the guests' lower level, which includes a bedroom, private bath, large TV lounge with fireplace, and a kitchenette. Upper level bedrooms share a bath. Guests may breakfast in a choice of locations, including the plant-filled atrium. For hunting enthusiasts, over 4,500 acres are reserved for guests to experience excellent hunting of upland game, water fowl, and deer. Hunting parties qualify for special rates.

Hosts: Grace and Allen Faul
Rooms: 4 (1 PB; 3 SB) $30
Full Breakfast

---

6 Pets welcome; 7 Smoking allowed; 8 Children welcome; 9 Social drinking allowed; 10 Tennis available; 11 Swimming available; 12 Golf available; 13 Skiing available; 14 May be booked through travel agents.

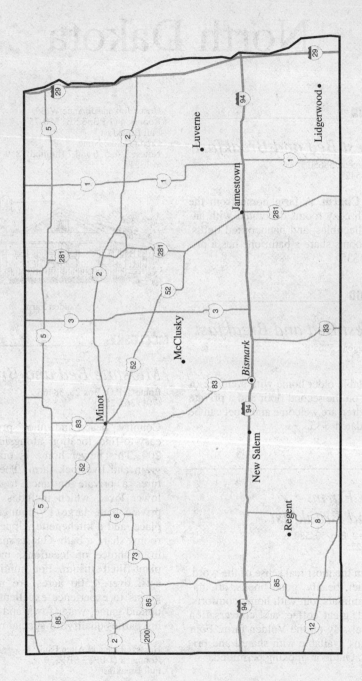

North Dakota

Credit Cards: None
Notes: 2, 4, 5, 6 and 7 (limited), 8, 9, 10, 11

MINOT

Old West Bed and Breakfast

Box 211, Regent, 58650
(701) 563-4542

Second-floor bedrooms offer complete privacy. Just a few blocks from Minot State College. The home is air-conditioned. Children are welcome. Smoking is permitted except in bedrooms. $35.

NEW SALEM

Old West Bed and Breakfast

Box 211, Regent, 58650
(701) 563-4542

Prairie View Bed and Breakfast. Scandinavian-style log home built by Finnish craftsmen in a quiet country setting. Four miles off I-94, 40 minutes from Bismarck and 100 miles from the Badlands. Guest rooms consist of one large bedroom with queen-size bed and private bath, and a family room with fireplace, wet bar, refrigerator, TV, full bed, and private entrance. Also, one large room upstairs with two full beds and a half-bath. Children welcome. Smoking is permitted in the family room. Continental breakfast. $35-50.

REGENT

Old West Bed and Breakfast

Box 211, 58650
(701) 563-4542

Not far from Medora and the Badlands. Outdoor heated swimming pool available in summer. Two bedrooms with double beds. No smoking. Children over 12 welcome. $40; rates not applicable during hunting season.

Prairie Vista

101 Rural Avenue SW, 58650
(701) 563-4542

One-story brick house on seven acres. Heated indoor pool, pool table, and shuffleboard. Seventy miles from Theodore Roosevelt National Park; two hours to state capital or casino. Three guest rooms with shared baths. Full breakfast served. Children over 12. No smoking.

Host: Marlys Prince
Rooms: 3 (SB) $50
Full Breakfast
Credit Cards: None
Notes: 2, 3, 4, 5, 9, 10, 12

NOTES: Credit cards accepted: A MasterCard; B Visa; C American Express; D Discover Card; E Diner's Club; F Other; 2 Personal checks accepted; 3 Lunch available; 4 Dinner available; 5 Open all year; 6 Pets welcome; 7 Smoking allowed; 8 Children welcome; 9 Social drinking allowed; 10 Tennis available; 11 Swimming available; 12 Golf available; 13 Skiing available; 14 May be booked through travel agents.

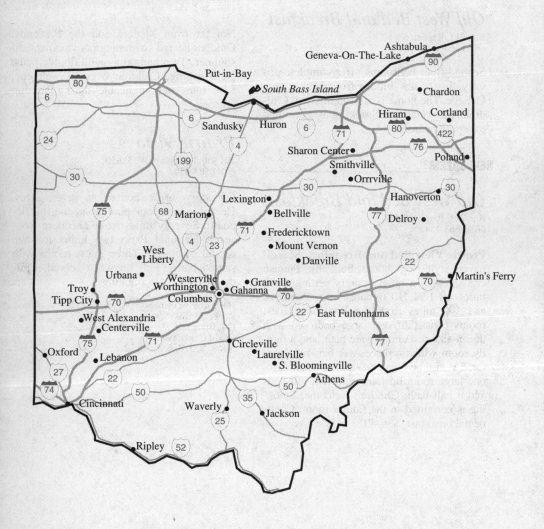

Ashtabula
Geneva-On-The-Lake
90
Put-in-Bay
Chardon
South Bass Island
80
6
Hiram
Cortland
6
Sandusky
Huron
80
422
24
4
6
71
76
Poland
199
Sharon Center
Smithville
30
Orrrville
30
75
30
Lexington
Hanoverton
68
Marion
Bellville
77
Delroy
71
Fredericktown
4
23
Mount Vernon
West
Liberty
Danville
22
Urbana
70
Martin's Ferry
Westerville
Granville
Troy
Worthington
Gahanna
70
Tipp City
70
Columbus
22
East Fultonhams
West Alexandria
Centerville
77
71
Circleville
Oxford
Lebanon
Laurelville
27
22
S. Bloomingville
50
Athens
74
50
50
Cincinnati
Waverly
35
Jackson
25
Ripley
52

Ohio

Ohio

ASHTABULA

Michael Cahill Bed and Breakfast

1106 Walnut Boulevard, 44004
(216) 964-8449

Large 1887 stick-style Victorian home on the National Register of Historic Places. It is a short walk to Lake Erie beach, marine museum, and charter boat fishing. This bed and breakfast overlooks the center of the harbor historic district. Large parlors, open porches, and convenience kitchen for guests. Ten minutes from I-90.

Hosts: Paul and Pat Goode
Rooms: 4 (2 PB; 2 SB) $45-55
Full Breakfast
Credit Cards: None
Notes: 2, 5, 8, 9, 10, 11, 12

ATHENS

The Albany House

9 Clinton Street, 45710
(614) 698-6311; (800) 600-4941

Enjoy today's comfort in yesterday's atmosphere at The Albany House, a charming 150-year-old bed and breakfast in the village of Albany, seven miles west of Athens and Ohio University. A historic house featuring antiques, quilts, Oriental rugs, and family heirlooms plus the modern amenities of air conditioning, indoor pool, fireplace, and guest living room with TV and VCR. Resident cat. Afternoon or evening beverages.

The Albany House

Hosts: Sarah and Ted Hutchins
Rooms: 7 (6 PB; 1 SB) $65-90
Continental Breakfast
Credit Cards: None
Notes: 2, 5, 7, 9, 10, 11, 12, 14

BELLVILLE

The Frederick Fitting House

72 Fitting Avenue, 44813
(419) 886-2863

An 1863 Victorian home in a quaint country village between Columbus and Cleveland. Gourmet breakfast served in hand-stenciled dining room, garden gazebo, or country kitchen. Near Mohican and Malabar Farm state parks, downhill and cross-country skiing, canoeing, and Kenyon and Wooster colleges. Closed Thanksgiving and Christmas.

Hosts: Ramon and Suzanne Wilson
Rooms: 3 (PB) $48-72
Full Breakfast

NOTES: Credit cards accepted: A MasterCard; B Visa; C American Express; D Discover Card; E Diner's Club; F Other; 2 Personal checks accepted; 3 Lunch available; 4 Dinner available; 5 Open all year; 6 Pets welcome; 7 Smoking allowed; 8 Children welcome; 9 Social drinking allowed; 10 Tennis available; 11 Swimming available; 12 Golf available; 13 Skiing available; 14 May be booked through travel agents.

Credit Cards: None
Notes: 2, 4, 7, 8 (over 7), 9, 10, 11, 12, 13

Yesterday Bed and Breakfast

CENTERVILLE

Yesterday Bed and Breakfast

39 South Main Street, 45458
(513) 433-0785; (800) 225-0485

Ten miles south of the center of Dayton, in the heart of the Centerville historic district, this house adjoins a group of fine antique shops. The Lavender and Old Lace Shop features fine bath products and vintage linens. The house was built in 1882 and is tastefully furnished with antiques. Near restaurants and two museums. Within easy driving distance of the Air Force Museum in Dayton, Kings Island Amusement Park, and historic Lebanon and Waynesville, both major antique centers. The University of Dayton and Wright State University are 15 to 20 minutes away. Discount for stay of three or more nights.

Host: Barbara
Rooms: 3 (PB) $65-70
Continental Breakfast
Credit Cards: None
Notes: 2, 8 (over 12), 9, 12, 14 (weekdays)

CHARDON

Bass Lake Inn

426 South Street, 44024
(216) 285-3100

Twelve tastefully decorated rooms provide guests with a queen-size bed, TV, gas log fireplace, kitchenette with refrigerator, microwave, and coffee maker, relaxing Jacuzzi, and spectacular view of the lake and golf course. Adjacent to the inn is Bass Lake Tavern, where guests can enjoy comfortable dining at the fireside or al fresco. Call for price information.

Host: Badge Siler
Rooms: 12 (PB)
Continental Breakfast
Credit Cards: A, B, C
Notes: 2, 3, 4, 5, 7, 9, 12, 13

CINCINNATI

Prospect Hill Bed and Breakfast

408 Boal Street, 45210
(513) 421-4408

Nestled into a wooded hillside, this Italianate Victorian townhouse was built in 1867 on Prospect Hill, Cincinnati's first suburb and now a national historic district. The bed and breakfast has been restored, keeping original woodwork, doors, hardware, and light fixtures. Each room is furnished with period antiques and offers fireplaces, skeleton keys, and spectacular views. A Continental plus buffet breakfast is served. Hot tub. Ample free parking. The only bed and breakfast downtown. Sixteen blocks to Convention Center.

Host: Gary Hackney
Rooms: 4 (2 PB; 2 SB) $79-109
Continental Breakfast
Credit Cards: A, B, C, D
Notes: 2, 5, 9, 11

The Victoria Inn of Hyde Park

3567 Shaw Avenue, 45208
(513) 321-3567; FAX (513) 321-3147

The Victoria Inn of Hyde Park is an elegantly comfortable bed and breakfast in the

NOTES: Credit cards accepted: A MasterCard; B Visa; C American Express; D Discover Card; E Diner's Club; F Other; 2 Personal checks accepted; 3 Lunch available; 4 Dinner available; 5 Open all year;

heart of Cincinnati's most charming neighborhoods. The inn received a *Better Homes & Gardens* award for outstanding renovation. Perfect for business or romantic getaway. Fifteen minutes to downtown, the Riverfront, zoo, and local universities. The only area bed and breakfast with private phones, fax, copier, and in-ground pool. Voted "Best B&B," *Cincinnati Magazine,* October 1993.

Hosts: Tom Possert and Debra Moore
Rooms: 3 (PB) $69-129
Full Breakfast
Credit Cards: A, B, C
Notes: 2, 5, 9, 10, 11, 12

CIRCLEVILLE

Castle Inn

610 South Court Street, 43113
(614) 477-3986; (800) 477-1541

Arches, battlements, towers, and plenty of stained glass adorn this romantic medieval "castle" completed in 1899 for a beautiful bride. All rooms feature Victorian antiques. Breakfast is served on English china in a museum-quality dining room overlooking the walled Shakespeare Garden. Murder mysteries arranged. Walk to good restaurants and antique and craft stores.

Hosts: Jim and Sue Maxwell
Rooms: 4 (PB) $65-85
Full Breakfast
Credit Cards: A, B, C
Notes: 2, 5, 8 (over 6), 10, 11, 12, 14

CLEVELAND

The Baricelli Inn

2203 Cornell Road, 44106-3805
(216) 791-6500; FAX (216) 791-9131

The turn-of-the-century brownstone is on the corner of Murray Hill and Cornell roads in the historic Little Italy area of Cleveland. By staying at the inn, guests are within walking distance of Case Western, university hospitals, and world-class museums. The seven European-styled guest rooms are comfortably furnished, and each features a private bath. Morning begins with a Continental breakfast featuring fresh fruits and sumptuous homemade pastries.

Host: Paul Minnillo
Rooms: 7 (PB) $100-130
Continental Breakfast
Credit Cards: A, B, C
Notes: 2, 4, 5, 7, 9

The Baricelli Inn

Private Lodgings, Inc. A-1

P.O. Box 18590, 44118
(216) 321-3213

A variety of accommodations including houses and apartments for rent in the greater Cleveland area. They are near the Cleveland Clinic, Case Western Reserve University, major museums and galleries, Metro park system, downtown Cleveland business district, and some are near or on Lake Erie. No credit cards. $45-125.

Notre Maison. A lovely French chateau not far from the university hospitals and museums. Two guest rooms with private bath or a carriage house with private bath are available. $65-75.

6 Pets welcome; 8 Children welcome; 9 Social drinking allowed; 10 Tennis available; 11 Swimming available; 12 Golf available; 13 Skiing available; 14 May be booked through travel agents.

COLUMBUS

50 Lincoln – A Very Small Hotel

50 East Lincoln Street, 43215
(614) 291-5056; (800) 750-5056
FAX (614) 291-4924

Gracious, comfortable, and friendly accommodations for discerning visitors to downtown businesses, the Ohio State University campus, and the arts. Eight guest rooms with queen-size beds, private full baths, telephone, and cable TV eclectically furnished to create a harmonious, relaxing atmosphere. Overnight guests enjoy a full gourmet breakfast: fresh fruit, a variety of entrees, homemade breads, specially blended coffee and teas. Perfect for small business meetings, retreats, and social functions. On-site catering services, with customized menus. One mile from downtown center and O.S.U. Short walk to fine restaurants, art galleries, shops, pubs, and parks.

Hosts: Jeffrey and Kelly Wilson
Rooms: 8 (PB); $89-119
Full Breakfast
Cards: A, B, C
Notes: 2, 3, 4, 5, 7, 8, 9, 10, 11, 14

Lansing Street Bed and Breakfast

180 Lansing, 43206
(614) 444-8488; (800) 383-7839

This bed and breakfast is found in a quaint and popular German village, near downtown. Charming shops and fun restaurants are within an easy walk. Two large suites offer all the desired amenities including private baths. Guests enjoy the carefully selected artwork in the front parlor, a great room with fireplace and a courtyard abounding with birds and windchimes. The hostess loves to cook, so gourmet breakfasts greet guests every morning.

Host: Marcia A. Barck
Rooms: 2 (PB) $70

Full Breakfast
Credit Cards: None
Notes: 2, 5, 6, 8, 9, 10

CORTLAND

The Old Mill Art Gallery Bed and Breakfast

114 South High Street (by the Waterfall), 44410
(216) 637-1187

A Georgian-style building overlooking the waterfall of Walnut Run Creek in the midst of two acres of scenic splendor. Four great rooms in the gallery are furnished with antiques, 18th-century furniture, and artwork. One room has a queen-size bed, and two rooms boast two double beds each. Every room has its own adjoining half-bath. The shower is shared. A beautifully furnished and appointed sitting room, and large inviting dining room, where complimentary evening desserts and Continental breakfast are served.

Hosts: Dick and Joyce Masters
Rooms: 4 (PB) $42.50
Continental Breakfast
Credit Cards: A, B, C, D
Notes: 2, 5, 8, 9, 10, 11, 12, 14

DANVILLE

The White Oak Inn

29683 Walhonding Road, 43014
(614) 599-6107

The White Oak Inn

This turn-of-the-century farmhouse in a rolling wooded countryside features antiques and hand-stitched quilts. Guests read, play board games, or socialize in the common room with a fireplace, or relax on the 50-foot-long front porch. An outdoor enthusiast's haven. Three rooms have fireplaces. Near the world's largest Amish population and historic Roscoe Village.

Hosts: Yvonne and Ian Martin
Rooms: 10 (PB) $70-140
Full Breakfast
Credit Cards: A, B, D
Notes: 2, 4, 5, 9, 10, 11, 12, 13, 14

DE GRAFF

Rollicking Hills

2 Rollicking Hills Lane, 43318
(513) 585-5161

This is a 160-acre farm in scenic hills. The homestead began as an Indian trading post in the late 1700s on a path that became the county stagecoach road. Remodeling in 1825 and an eight-room addition by the host's grandfather in 1865 are part of the home's five-generation history. Hiking, horseback riding, a natural peat bog left by a glacier, and farm animals including llamas. Lake well stocked with blue gill and large-mouth bass. Canoe to a bullfrog chorus. Spartan in-ground pool, cross-country skiing, beech-maple climax woods. No smoking. No alcohol or drugs. No pets.

Hosts: Susanne and Robert Smithers and family
Rooms: 4 (1 PB; 3 SB) $32-60
Full Breakfast
Credit Cards: None
Notes: 2, 3, 4, 5, 8

DELLROY

Whispering Pines Bed and Breakfast

P.O. Box 340, 44620
(216) 735-2824

Come to this 1880 Victorian home overlooking Atwood Lake. Filled with elegant antiques of the period, each guest room has a breathtaking view of the lake and a private bath. One room has a wood-burning fireplace. Our new Honeymoon Suite features a two-person spa, balcony, king-size bed, and wood-burning fireplace. Central air. Gift and antique gallery on premises. A scrumptious breakfast served on the enclosed porch makes this a perfect romantic getaway. The pontoon is available for rental. Golf, boating, and special events packages are also available.

Hosts: Bill and Linda Horn
Rooms: 5 (PB) $90
Honeymoon Suite: $150
Full Breakfast
Credit Cards: A, B
Notes: 2, 5, 9, 10, 11, 12

EAST FULTONHAM

Hill View Acres

7320 Old Town Road, 43735
(614) 849-2728

Ten miles southwest of Zanesville off US 22 West. Spacious home on 21 acres with pond. Enjoy the pool, year-round spa, or relax in the family room by the fireplace. Country cooking is a specialty. The area is popular for antiquing, pottery, and outdoor activities.

Hosts: Jim and Dawn Graham
Rooms: 2 (SB) $37.30-42.60
Full Breakfast (weekends)
Credit Cards: A, B
Notes: 2, 3, 4, 5, 7, 8, 9, 10, 11, 12

FREDERICKTOWN

Heartland Country Resort

2994 Township Road 190, 43019
(800) 230-7030

The Heartland Country Resort is a beautifully restored, spacious 1878 farmhouse with scenic views of rolling fields, pastures, and woods. There are a variety of things to do, including horseback riding on wooded trails with streams and hills or riding in one

6 Pets welcome; 8 Children welcome; 9 Social drinking allowed; 10 Tennis available; 11 Swimming available; 12 Golf available; 13 Skiing available; 14 May be booked through travel agents.

of the arenas. Guests can go swimming in the heated pool in the summer, go skiing in the winter, play pool in the large recreation room, or just relax on the comfortable screened porch or deck. Continental plus breakfast served.

Host: Dorene Henschen
Rooms: 4 (2 PB; 2 SB) $55-85
Continental Breakfast
Credit Cards: A, B
Notes: 2, 3 and 4 (by arrangement), 5, 6 (horses), 8, 9, 11, 12, 13, 14

GAHANNA

Shamrock Bed and Breakfast

5657 Sunbury Road, 43230-1147
(614) 337-9849

The Shamrock is a brick split-level ranch on over an acre of professionally landscaped grounds with perennial beds, roses, grape arbor, and flowering bushes. Guests enjoy the entire first floor, which has a fireplace, Florida room, and patio with gas grill. All rooms are furnished with original art and antiques. Large library; CDs and videos are available. Easy freeway access to most attractions. Traditional large Irish breakfast. Generally handicapped accessible.

Host: Tom McLaughlin
Rooms: 2 (1-1/2 PB) $50-55
Full Breakfast
Credit Cards: None
Notes: 2, 3, 5, 7, 8, 10, 11, 12, 13

GENEVA-ON-THE-LAKE

The Otto Court Bed and Breakfast

5653 Lake Road, 44041
(216) 466-8668

Hotel and cottage complex overlooking Lake Erie. Within walking distance of the famous Geneva-on-the-Lake amusement center, Geneva State Park and Marina, and the Old Firehouse Winery. Near the historic Ashtabula Harbor area and 13 covered bridges. Minimum stay weekends and holidays: two nights.

Host: C. Joyce Otto
Rooms: 12 (8 PB; 4 SB) $38-50
Full Breakfast
Credit Cards: A, B, D, F
Notes: 2, 4, 5, 7, 8, 9, 10, 11, 12, 13, 14

GRANVILLE

The Follett Wright House

403 East Broadway, 43023
(614) 587-0941

Built in 1860 and listed on the National Register of Historic Places, this gracious bed and breakfast overlooks the historic village of Granville. Within walking distance of Dennison University, shopping, and restaurants. Breakfast consists of homemade Danish rolls and other delicious specialties.

Hosts: Kirsten and Jurgen Pape
Rooms: 2 (PB) $60
Full Breakfast
Credit Cards: None
Notes: 2, 5, 6, 8, 9, 10, 11, 12

The Follett Wright House

HANOVERTON

The Spread Eagle Tavern

10150 Plymouth Street, P.O. Box 277, 44423
(216) 223-1583

NOTES: Credit cards accepted: A MasterCard; B Visa; C American Express; D Discover Card; E Diner's Club; F Other; 2 Personal checks accepted; 3 Lunch available; 4 Dinner available; 5 Open all year;

The Spread Eagle Tavern

The Spread Eagle Tavern is an artfully restored Federal-style three-story historic brick inn that features a gourmet restaurant, a unique rathskeller, seven dining rooms, and six guest rooms for overnight lodging. All rooms are tastefully decorated with antiques that give insight into Ohio's canal period history. Listed on the National Register of Historic Places. Quiet, romantic, and unique.

Hosts: Peter and Jean Johnson
Rooms: 6 (4 PB; 2 SB) $75-125
Continental Breakfast
Credit Cards: A, B, D
Notes: 3, 4, 5, 7, 8, 9, 12

HIRAM

The Lily Ponds

6720 Route 82, 44234
(216) 569-3222; (800) 325-5087

This spacious, lovely home in a quiet country setting is surrounded by woods and ponds. Five-minute walk to Hiram College campus; 15-minute drive to SeaWorld, Geauga Lake, and Aurora Farms; 45 minutes to Cleveland, Akron, and Youngstown. Charming guest rooms with private baths. Central air conditioning. The owner is a world traveler.

Host: Marilane Spencer
Rooms: 3 (PB) $55-75
Full Breakfast
Credit Cards: None
Notes: 2, 5, 8, 9, 10, 11, 12, 13, 14

HURON

Captain Montague's A Bed and Breakfast of Distinction

229 Center Street, 44839
(419) 433-4756

The Captain's is that perfect romantic retreat in a stately Southern Colonial manor that radiates Victorian charm. Experience a bygone era of lace, luster, and love. Nestled in the heart of vacation land on the shores of Lake Erie, The Captain's is within minutes of golf courses, estuaries, boating, and shopping. Cedar Point and the Lake Erie Islands are nearby. Enjoy the in-ground swimming pool and impeccable gardens. The Captain's is truly in the "heart" of Ohio. Minimum holiday weekend stay is two nights. Closed December 15 through April 1.

Hosts: Judy and Mike Tann
Rooms: 7 (PB) $68-105
Continental Breakfast
Credit Cards: None
Notes: 2, 5, 9, 10, 11, 12, 13 (cross-country)

JACKSON

The Maples

14701 State Route 93, 45640
(614) 286-6067

This 1907 farmhouse is on two acres and is surrounded by maple trees. The house boasts five fireplaces, massive oak pocket doors, and leaded-glass windows. Guest rooms are furnished in antiques and handmade quilts, and the house is fully air-conditioned for year-round comfort. A hearty full breakfast is served in the dining room, but guests may wish to dine on the screened porch or the patio in the rose garden. Enjoy gracious hospitality and country comfort at The Maples.

Hosts: Maria and Tony De Castro
Rooms: 4 (2 PB; 2 SB) $45-55
Full Breakfast
Credit Cards: A, B, C, D
Notes: 2, 5, 8, 12, 14

6 Pets welcome; 8 Children welcome; 9 Social drinking allowed; 10 Tennis available; 11 Swimming available; 12 Golf available; 13 Skiing available; 14 May be booked through travel agents.

LAURELVILLE

Hocking House Bed and Breakfast

18597 Laurel Street, P.O. Box 118, 43113
(614) 332-1655

The beautiful Hocking Hills region beckons. Caves, waterfalls, and forests—spectacular scenery abounds. All rooms feature private baths, antique furnishings, quilts, and handcrafted accessories made by the local artisans. Walk to restaurants and more in this friendly little village in the hills of scenic southeast Ohio. Inquire about seasonal discount.

Hosts: Max and Evelyn England, and Jim and Sue
  Maxwell
Rooms: 4 (PB) $45-65
Full Breakfast
Credit Cards: A, B
Notes: 2, 5, 8 (over 6), 11, 14

LEBANON

White Tor

1620 Oregonia Road, 45036
(513) 932-5892

White Tor is a farmhouse built in 1862. The well appointed two-room suite with queen-size bed and private bath is air conditioned. The English hosts offer a smoke-free environment, seven acres of tranquility, and garden beds ablaze with color. Just a 30-minute drive to Cincinnati, and a few minutes to Kings Island, the beach waterpark, and a wealth of antique malls. Come and enjoy!

Hosts: Eric and Margaret Johnson
Suite: 1 (PB) $70
Full Breakfast
Credit Cards: None
Notes: 2, 5, 9, 10, 11, 12

LEXINGTON

White Fence Inn

8842 Denman Road, 44904
(419) 884-2356

A breathtaking country retreat is on 73 acres, with gardens, apple orchard, grapevines, fishing pond, and fields. Breakfast is delectable and includes homemade granola, homemade jams, grape juice, pastries, and farm-fresh eggs. Dine in the large country dining room or out on the porch. Two large sitting rooms with fireplaces, games, TV, and spectacular views from every window. Special wedding or anniversary baskets available, and dessert bar Saturday nights for all guests, in season. The largest guest room boasts a king-size four-poster bed, cathedral wood ceiling, sunken tub, fireplace, and private deck.

Hosts: Bill and Ellen Hiser
Rooms: 6 (4 PB; 2 SB) $60-105
Full Breakfast
Credit Cards: None
Notes: 2, 5, 6, 8, 9, 10, 12, 13

MARION

Olde Towne Manor

245 St. James Street, 43302
(614) 382-2402

This elegant stone home is on a beautiful acre of land on a quiet street in Marion's historic district. Enjoy a quiet setting in the gazebo, or relax while reading from more than 1,000 books available in the library. A leisurely stroll will take guests to the home of President Warren G. Harding and the

Olde Towne Manor

NOTES: Credit cards accepted: A MasterCard; B Visa; C American Express; D Discover Card; E Diner's Club; F Other; 2 Personal checks accepted; 3 Lunch available; 4 Dinner available; 5 Open all year;

Harding Memorial. A quiet, relaxed, and elegant atmosphere for a stay. Awarded the 1990 Marion Beautification Award for Most Attractive Building.

Host: Mary Louisa Rimbach
Rooms: 4 (PB) $55-65
Full Breakfast
Credit Cards: A, B, C
Notes: 2, 5, 7 (limited), 8 (over 12), 10, 12

Mulberry Inn

MARTIN'S FERRY

Mulberry Inn
Bed and Breakfast

53 North Fourth Street, 43935
(614) 633-6058

This Victorian house built in 1868 by Dr. Ong features four period rooms with antiques, paintings, and quilts. Guests have a beautiful parlor to relax in, and a private dining room in which to enjoy the sumptuous Continental plus breakfast. Visit the oldest organized settlement in Ohio and Walnut Grove Cemetery (in which lies Betty Zane, who saved Fort Henry in the last battle of the Revolutionary War). This bed and breakfast is within walking distance of the Ohio River, museums, and shops. Wheeling, West Virginia, is five minutes away, where guests can visit Oglebay Park, Festival of Lights, Jamboree USA, dog races, many golf courses, and ice skating rinks. The inn is air-conditioned in the summer and has a beautiful wood-burning fireplace in the parlor.

Hosts: Shirley and Charlie Probst
Rooms: 4 (2 PB; 2 SB) $35-45
Full Breakfast
Credit Cards: A, B, D
Notes: 2, 5, 7, 8, 9, 10, 12, 13

MOUNT VERNON

The Russell-Cooper House

115 E. Gambier Street, 43050
(614) 397-8638

Ohio's only four-time national award winning bed and breakfast inn! History lives in this national register Inn, and all around Mount Vernon—"America's Hometown." Grand and comfortable, The Russell-Cooper House will refresh the spirit, ease the mind, stimulate the curiosity, and generally warm the cockles of the heart. Private baths, full delicious candlelit breakfasts, and a friendly "welcome home" will make a visit a memory guests will always cherish.

Hosts: Maureen and Tim Tyler
Rooms: 6 (PB) $55–75
Full Breakfast
Credit Cards: A, B, C
Notes: 2, 5, 7 (limited), 8 (over 12), 9, 10, 11, 12, 13, 14

ORRVILLE

Grandma's House
Bed and Breakfast

5598 Chippewa Road, 44667
(216) 682-5112

Peace and quiet prevail on this 1860s farm home with comfortable beds, antiques, and handmade quilts. In the heart of Wayne County's rolling farmland, planted in alter-

6 Pets welcome; 8 Children welcome; 9 Social drinking allowed; 10 Tennis available; 11 Swimming available; 12 Golf available; 13 Skiing available; 14 May be booked through travel agents.

nating strips of corn, soybeans, and wheat. Several hiking trails meander through the large woods on the hill. Hickory rockers grace the front porch for relaxing. Just a few minutes from Amish country.

Hosts: Marilyn and Dave Farver
Rooms: 5 (3 PB; 2 SB) $55-90
Continental Breakfast
Credit Cards: None
Notes: 2, 5, 8, 9, 11, 12

OXFORD

The Duck Pond

6391 Morning Sun Road
State Road 732 North, 45056
(513) 523-8914

An 1863 Civil War farmhouse on five and one-half acres. Furnished in country antiques and collectibles. Full country-style breakfast, including such specialties as Hawaiian French toast, German pancakes, and cheese blintzes. Three miles north of Miami University, two miles south of Hueston Woods State Park with golf, nature trails, boating, swimming, and fishing. Enjoy antiquing in Fairhaven on weekends, seven miles north, and in several other nearby towns during the week. Cat in residence. Ten-dollar charge for extra person in room. Closed Christmas.

Hosts: Don and Toni Kohlstedt
Rooms: 4 (1 PB; 3 SB) $50-70
Full Breakfast
Credit Cards: None
Notes: 2, 5, 9, 10, 11, 12

POLAND

Inn at the Green

500 South Main Street, 44514
(216) 757-4688

A classically proportioned Victorian townhouse on the south end of the green in preserved Connecticut Western Reserve Village. Featuring large moldings, 12-foot ceilings, five working Italian marble fire-

places, original poplar floors, interior-shuttered windows, and patio garden.

Hosts: Ginny and Steve Meloy
Rooms: 4 (PB) $45-50
Continental Breakfast
Credit Cards: A, B
Notes: 2, 5, 7, 8 (over 7), 9, 10, 11, 12, 14

PUT-IN BAY

Gayle's Guest House

Box 564 Tri Motor Drive, 43456
(419) 285-7181

On the south shore of South Bass Island, Put-In Bay, Ohio, Gayle's Guest House has been in operation for 11 years. All rooms are air-conditioned in the summer. Guests can cool off in the small pool after a day of biking or walking to see the island sights. Attractions include the Perry Memorial Monument, natural caves, and local wineries. Open in the winter for ice fishing. A full country breakfast is served.

Hosts: Gayle and Henry Polcyn
Rooms: 4 (PB) $75-85
Full Breakfast
Credit Cards: A, B
Notes: 2, 9, 11

RIPLEY

The Signal House

234 North Front Street, 45167
(513) 392-1640

Share historic charm and hospitality while visiting this 1830s home on the scenic Ohio River. View spectacular sunsets from three porches or elegant parlors. Enjoy spacious rooms furnished with family antiques. The area offers antiques and craft shops, restaurants, winery, herb farms, covered bridges, history (early pioneers and the Underground Railroad), and lots of friendly people. Pick-up provided from local marinas.

Hosts: Vic and Betsy Billingsley
Rooms: 2 (SB) $65-75

NOTES: Credit cards accepted: A MasterCard; B Visa; C American Express; D Discover Card; E Diner's Club; F Other; 2 Personal checks accepted; 3 Lunch available; 4 Dinner available; 5 Open all year;

The Signal House

Full Breakfast
Credit Cards: None
Notes: 2, 5, 9, 10, 11 (river), 12, 13 (water), 14

SANDUSKY

1890 Queen Anne Bed and Breakfast

714 Wayne Street, 44870-3507
(419) 626-0391

A family home for 30 years, the hosts have enjoyed sharing this home and community with guests. Three bedrooms furnished with family antiques and a lovely porch overlooking gardens and patio for breakfast in the warm months make a stay here unforgettable. Close to ferries for Cedar Point and Lake Erie Islands. Air conditioning.

Hosts: Joan and Robert Kromer
Rooms: 3 (2 PB; 1 SB) $70-80
Continental Breakfast
Credit Cards: A, B, D
Notes: 2, 5

The Red Gables Bed and Breakfast

421 Wayne Street, 44870
(419) 625-1189

A lovely old Tudor Revival home finished in 1907, The Red Gables is in the historic Old Plat District. Guests are welcomed into the great room, which features a massive fireplace and a large bay window where breakfast is served. The home features many interesting architectural details, including lots of oak woodwork. The Red Gables is decorated in an eclectic style from Oriental artifacts in the great room to flowered chintz in the bedrooms. The rooms are filled with handmade slipcovers, curtains, and comforters made by the innkeeper, who is a semiretired costume-maker. The guest rooms are light and airy, and have access to a wicker-filled sitting area, refrigerator, coffee maker, and tea kettle. Guests have said, "It's like going to Grandma's house!"

Host: Jo Ellen Cuthbertson
Rooms: 4 (2 PB; 2 SB) $50-90
Continental Breakfast
Credit Cards: A, B
Notes: 2, 5, 8 (limited Sunday-Thursday), 9, 10, 11, 12

The Red Gables

Wagner's 1844 Inn

230 East Washington Street, 44870
(419) 626-1726

Elegantly restored, antique-filled Victorian home. Built in 1844 and listed on the National Register of Historic Places. Features a Victorian parlor with antique Steinway

6 Pets welcome; 8 Children welcome; 9 Social drinking allowed; 10 Tennis available; 11 Swimming available; 12 Golf available; 13 Skiing available; 14 May be booked through travel agents.

piano, living room with wood-burning fireplace, billiard room, screened porch, and enclosed courtyard. Bedrooms are air-conditioned. In downtown Sandusky within walking distance of parks, historic buildings, antique shops, museums, and ferries to Cedar Point and Lake Erie Islands.

Hosts: Walt and Barb Wagner
Rooms: 3 (PB) $50-80
Continental Breakfast
Credit Cards: A, B, D
Notes: 5, 9, 10, 11, 12

SHARON CENTER

Hart and Mather Guest House

1343 Sharon Copley Road, P.O. Box 93, 44274
(216) 239-2801; (800) 352-2584

This 1840s home and the Sharon Center Circle where it sits are both on the National Register of Historic Places. Furnished with both traditional antiques and reproductions, Hart and Mather offers three guest rooms with private baths, one suite with an adjoining room, fireplace, and private bath. All rooms have color TV with VCR and full cable. Common living room with fireplace is available for guests' use, and a delicious breakfast comes from the in-house kitchen. Conference rooms available. Gift shop and cake shop open to the public.

Hosts: Thomas and Sally Thompson
Rooms: 4 (PB) $69-119
Continental Breakfast
Credit Cards: A, B, C, D
Notes: 2, 5, 7, 12, 13, 14

SMITHVILLE

The Smithville Bed and Breakfast

171 West Main Street, P.O. Box 142, 44677
(216) 669-3333; (800) 869-6425

Turn-of-the-century simple elegance. Enjoy breakfast in a solid cherry dining room. Breakfast features homegrown blueberry

specialties. An ideal stopping place while visiting the College of Wooster or Amish country. Three-room cottage suites available with special rates for weekly, monthly, and yearly options. Famous restaurants are nearby, as well as gift, craft, and antique shops. On State Road 585 just five miles northeast of Wooster.

Hosts: Jim and Lori Kubik
Rooms: 5 (PB) $52-62
Full Breakfast
Credit Cards: A, B, D
Notes: 2, 5, 8

Steep Woods

SOUTH BLOOMINGVILLE

Steep Woods

24830 State Route 56, 43152
(614) 332-6084; (800) 900-2954

This new log home on a wooded hillside is in the beautiful Hocking Hills, 60 miles southeast of Columbus. Nearby is the Hocking State Park with its famous recessed caves, waterfalls, and unusual rock formations. Available in the area are hiking, swimming, canoeing, fishing, horseback riding, and the Hocking Valley Scenic Railroad.

Hosts: Barbara and Brad Holt
Rooms: 2 (SB) $40
Full Breakfast
Credit Cards: None
Notes: 2, 5, 7, 9

NOTES: Credit cards accepted: A MasterCard; B Visa; C American Express; D Discover Card; E Diner's Club; F Other; 2 Personal checks accepted; 3 Lunch available; 4 Dinner available; 5 Open all year;

TIPP CITY

Willow Tree Inn

1900 West Street, Route 571, 45371
(513) 667-2957

Restored 1830 Federal manor home with four fireplaces. Pond, ducks, original 1830 barn on the premises, working springhouse and smokehouse, and beautiful gardens. Just minutes north of Dayton in a quiet location with attentive personal service.

Hosts: Tom and Peggy Nordquist
Rooms: 4 (1 PB; 3 SB) $48-68
Full Breakfast
Credit Cards: A, B
Notes: 2, 5, 7 (restricted), 8 (over 8), 9, 10, 11, 12

TROY

Allen Villa
Bed and Breakfast

434 South Market Street, 45373
(513) 335-1181

This bed and breakfast has seven fireplaces and is decorated in Victorian antiques. Each room has a private bath, TV, telephone, and central air conditioning. Both king- and queen-size beds are available. A self-serve snack bar is for guests' evening pleasure, and a bountiful breakfast is served on the 15-foot antique dining room table that seats 12 guests. Two furnished kitchenettes are available monthly. Walking distance to three fine restaurants.

Allen Villa

Hosts: Robert and June Smith
Rooms: 4 (PB) $54-74
Full Breakfast
Credit Cards: A, B, C, D
Notes: 2, 5, 7, 9, 10, 11, 12

URBANA

At Home in Urbana

301 Scioto Street, 43078-2129
(513) 653-8595; (800) 800-0970

At Home in Urbana is a restored 1842 home in a National Register historic district at the center of the Simon Kenton Historical Corridor along US Route 36. Guest rooms on the first and second floors await the traveler who wishes to step back in history among period pieces and family antiques. The historic, residential, and business districts, quaint shops, restaurants, movie theaters, and county library that contains genealogical records from 1805 are within easy walking distance.

Hosts: Grant and Shirley Ingersoll
Rooms: 3 (PB) $60-90
Suite: 1 (PB)
Full Breakfast
Credit Cards: A, B, C, D
Notes: 2, 5, 8 (over 12), 12, 13

WAVERLY

Governor's Lodge

171 Gregg Road, 45690
(614) 947-2266

Governor's Lodge is a place like no other. Imagine a beautiful, shimmering lake, an iridescent sunset, and a quiet calm. A friendly atmosphere in an eight-room bed and breakfast that is open year-round and in Lake White describes this bed and breakfast. Magnificent views can be enjoyed from every room. An affiliate of Bristol Village Retirement Community, it offers a meeting room and group rates for gatherings using the whole lodge.

6 Pets welcome; 8 Children welcome; 9 Social drinking allowed; 10 Tennis available; 11 Swimming available; 12 Golf available; 13 Skiing available; 14 May be booked through travel agents.

Hosts: David and Jeannie James
Rooms: 8 (PB) $53.70-68.20
Continental Breakfast
Credit Cards: A, B, C, E
Notes: 2, 5, 7, 8

Hosts: Dr. Mark and Carolyn Ulrich
Rooms: 2 (PB) $59
Full Breakfast
Credit Cards: A, B, C
Notes: 2, 5, 8, 12

WEST ALEXANDRIA

Twin Creek Country Bed and Breakfast

5353 Enterprise Road, 45381
(513) 787-3990; (513) 787-4264; (513) 787-3279

This 1830s farmhouse has been remodeled to offer a quiet getaway. The entire house, upper or lower level, or an individual room is available. There are three bedrooms, two bathrooms, furnished kitchen, and a living room. The owners live 100 yards away. Guests can roam 170 acres, which include 50 acres of woods. Restaurants, deli foods, and antique shops are a short distance away. Local catering available. Suitable for two families at once. Close to the I-70/I-75 interchange.

Hosts: Dr. Mark and Carolyn Ulrich
Rooms: 3 (1 PB; 2 SB) $59-79
Full Breakfast
Credit Cards: A, B, C
Notes: 2, 5, 8, 11, 12

Twin Creek Towne House Bed and Breakfast

19 East Dayton Street, 45381
(513) 787-3990; (513) 787-4264
(513) 787-3279

This Italianate Victorian home, built in 1875, offers two guest rooms on the upper level, furnished in antiques, with TV and air conditioning. The home has beautiful butternut woodwork. The Twin Creek Towne House Tea Room is on the lower level and is open for lunch on Wednesday, Thursday, and Friday from 11:00 A.M. to 2:00 P.M. Roll away beds are available, and a sitting parlor gives guests extra room to relax. Easily accessible from I-70, close to I-70/I-75 interchange.

WESTERVILLE

Priscilla's Bed and Breakfast

5 South West Street, 43081
(614) 882-3910

Priscilla's

Priscilla's 1854 home is surrounded by a one-half acre of white picket fence. Lovely perennial gardens, bird feeders, and birdbaths accompany the one-time log cabin in the historic setting adjacent to Otterbein College. Borrow bicycles, cook on the patio, and enjoy the water garden and adjoining Alum Creek Park. Leisurely browse through 35 shops. At the rear of the house, Priscilla operates a miniature dollhouse shop. Robes are provided. Two miles north of Columbus. Free airport pickup is available.

Host: Priscilla H. Curtiss
Rooms: 3 (1 PB; 2 SB) $45-60
Continental Breakfast
Credit Cards: None
Notes: 2, 5, 7 and 8 (limited), 9, 10, 11, 12

WEST LIBERTY

Liberty House Bed and Breakfast

208 North Detroit Street, 43357-0673
(800) 437-8109

NOTES: Credit cards accepted: A MasterCard; B Visa; C American Express; D Discover Card; E Diner's Club; F Other; 2 Personal checks accepted; 3 Lunch available; 4 Dinner available; 5 Open all year;

Built in the early 1900s, Liberty House has patterned oak floors and woodwork, Oriental rugs, antique furnishings, and three spacious air-conditioned bedrooms with private baths. Colorful gardens and a wrap-around porch with an old-fashioned swing beckon guests into Liberty House. AAA approved.

Hosts: Sue and Russ Peterson
Rooms: 3 (PB) $55-70
Full Breakfast
Credit Cards: A, B, D
Notes: 2, 4 (reservation), 5, 8, 9, 12, 13

WORTHINGTON

A.M. House
Bed and Breakfast

556 High Street, 43085
(614) 885-5580; (614) 885-5579

A restored turn-of-the-century Queen Anne home in the heart of Old Worthington, within walking distance of shops, restaurants, and New England-style village green. A.M. House has easy access to Columbus events and walking paths along the Olentangy River. Varied breakfast menus with special dietary needs considered. Enjoy porches and garden; TV in parlor. Discount for longer stay. Smoke-free and pet-free environment.

Hosts: Colin and Robin Buford Wigney; Doug and Lee Buford
Rooms: 4 (2 PB; 2 SB) $60-70
Full Breakfast
Credit Cards: None
Notes: 2, 5, 10

The Worthington Inn

649 High Street, 43085
(614) 885-2600

Historical inn, built in 1831 and refurbished in 1983 and 1990. Ohio's second oldest inn. Four-star Mobil rating. Has 26 exquisitely appointed hotel suites furnished with stunning period antiques. Highly acclaimed restaurant featuring regional American cuisine. Banquet facilities accommodating 150 guests. Stay includes Continental breakfast and champagne turndown. Details large and small taken care of professionally and personally. One mile south of I-270 at the corner of High and New England.

Host: Michael W. Murphy
Rooms: 26 (PB) $105-170
Continental Breakfast
Credit Cards: A, B, C, D, E
Notes: 2, 3, 4, 5, 7, 8, 9, 10, 11, 12, 13, 14

---

6 Pets welcome; 8 Children welcome; 9 Social drinking allowed; 10 Tennis available; 11 Swimming available; 12 Golf available; 13 Skiing available; 14 May be booked through travel agents.

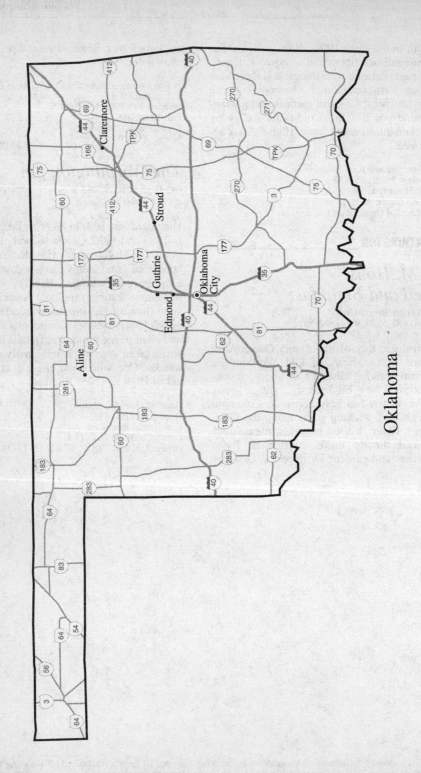

Oklahoma

ALINE

Heritage Manor

Rural Route 3, Box 33, 73716
(405) 463-2563; (405) 463-2566

Heritage Manor is a country getaway on 80 acres that was settled in the Land Run of 1893 in northwest Oklahoma. Two prestatehood homes have been joined together and restored by the innkeepers using a Victorian theme. Beautiful sunrises, sunsets, and stargazing from the rooftop deck. Guests can relax in the hot tub or read a book from the 5,000-volume library. Ostriches, donkeys, and Scotch Highland cattle roam a fenced area. Close to Homesteaders 1894 Sod House, Selenite Crystal digging area, and several other attractions.

Hosts: A. J. and Carolyn Rexroat
Rooms: 4 (S3B) $50
Full Breakfast
Credit Cards: None
Notes: 2, 3 (reservation), 4 (reservation), 6 (prior arrangement), 8, 10, 11, 13

CLAREMORE

Country Inn Bed and Breakfast

Route 3, Box 1925, 74017
(918) 342-1894

Leland and Kay invite guests to this country retreat. Stay in the charming barn-style guest quarters, separate from the main house. Enjoy the swimming pool, horse shoes, country walks, and bicycles or just relax country style. Guests may want to visit the numerous antique shops or take in the history of the J. M. Davis Gun Museum and Will Rogers Museum/Memorial while in Claremore.

Hosts: Leland and Kay Jenkins
Rooms: 2 (PB) $52
Suite: 1 (PB) $62
Full Breakfast
Credit Cards: None
Notes: 2, 5, 9, 11, 12

The Arcadian Inn

EDMOND

The Arcadian Inn Bed and Breakfast

328 East First Street, 73034
(405) 348-6347; (800) 299-6347

Grand wraparound front porch beckons to an old-fashioned intimate retreat. Luxurious Victorian bed and breakfast offers romantic packages, corporate accommodations, and family getaways. Special guest rooms fulfill dreams of yesterday. Private Jacuzzis and garden spa available. Enjoy Edmond's antique tours, tea rooms, and fine restaurants as well as Oklahoma City and Guthrie attractions.

Hosts: Martha and Gary Hall
Rooms: 5 (PB) $65-120
Full Breakfast
Credit Cards: A, B, C, D
Notes: 2, 4 (by reservation), 5, 10, 11, 12, 14

GUTHRIE

Harrison House Inn

124 West Harrison, 73044
(405) 282-1000

Thirty-five rooms furnished Victorian-style with antiques and quilts. All have private baths and central heat and air. Next door to the theater in central downtown Guthrie. Featured in *Glamour, Innsider,* and *Southern Living.*

Hosts: Jane and Claude Thomas
Rooms: 35 (PB) $57-87
Continental Breakfast
Credit Cards: A, B, C, D, E
Notes: 2, 5, 7, 8, 9, 10, 11, 12, 14

OKLAHOMA CITY

Flora's Bed and Breakfast

2312 Northwest 46th, 73112
(405) 840-3157

In a quiet neighborhood, this home is furnished with antiques and collectibles, and includes an elevator. Guests may relax in front of the large wood-burning fireplace, or enjoy the outdoors on a 1,500-square-foot balcony with a large spa. There is covered parking, and the hosts enjoy square dancing. Easy access to Cowboy Hall of Fame, Remington Park Race Track, Omniplex, and other points of interest. Many good eating places in the vicinity.

Hosts: Newton W. and Joann Flora
Rooms: 2 (PB) $50-55
Continental Breakfast
Credit Cards: None
Notes: 2, 5, 7, 8 (over 11), 9, 10, 12, 14

The Grandison Inn

The Grandison Inn

1841 Northwest 15th, 73106
(405) 521-0011

This country Victorian, circa 1896, has all of its original stained glass and brass lighting fixtures. The private suite with fireplace and Jacuzzi covers the entire third floor. Honeymoon and anniversary packages are available, as well as breakfast in bed and other room services. Enjoy the beautiful gazebo among fruit trees and gardens, relax on the rocker-lined front porch, or just spend time in the Victorian parlor. Convenient to downtown and I-35 and I-40.

Hosts: Claudia and Bob Wright
Rooms: 5 (PB) $55-125
Full Breakfast
Credit Cards: A, B, C, D
Notes: 2, 3, 4, 5, 6, 7, 9, 14

Willow Way

27 Oakwood Drive, 73121-5410
(405) 427-2133

Willow Way is a wooded town retreat in English Tudor style with antique decor and genuine charm. The den, with lofty beamed ceiling, fireplace, and picture window, is the guests' favorite place for bird watching and breakfast. Comfortable and safe with off-street parking. Quiet, near the race track, Cowboy Hall of Fame, and other area attractions. Three rooms with private baths. Full breakfast served.

NOTES: Credit cards accepted: A MasterCard; B Visa; C American Express; D Discover Card; E Diner's Club; F Other; 2 Personal checks accepted; 3 Lunch available; 4 Dinner available; 5 Open all year;

Hosts: Johnita and Lionel Turner
Rooms: 3 (2 PB; 1 SB) $50-80
Full Breakfast
Credit Cards: A, B
Notes: 2, 5, 8, 9, 12

STROUD

The International Bed and Breakfast Club, Inc.

504 Amherst Street, Buffalo, NY 14207
(800) 723-4262; FAX (716) 873-4462

OK 2978 PP. Midway between Oklahoma City and Tulsa, Stroud is the home of the region's largest factory direct outlet fashion mall, Tanger Mall, with more than 40 major outlets. Just two miles from the mall and one block off Stroud's main street, this bed and breakfast is listed on the National Registery of Historic Places and is the ancestral home of the town founder. Built in 1900, this two-story Victorian beauty retains its turn-of-the-century charm with the added comforts of modern life. Fresh flowers, green plants, decorator linens, window treatments, fresh fruit, bottled water, and their famous cookies are a few of the amenities.

6 Pets welcome; 8 Children welcome; 9 Social drinking allowed; 10 Tennis available; 11 Swimming available; 12 Golf available; 13 Skiing available; 14 May be booked through travel agents.

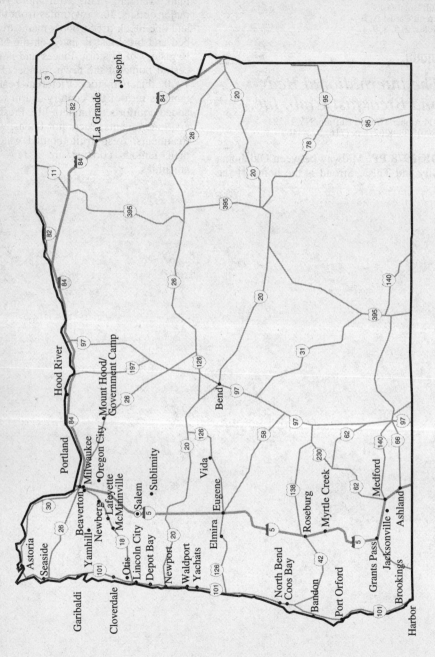

Oregon

Oregon

ASHLAND

Adams Cottage
Bed and Breakfast

737 Siskiyou Boulevard, 97520
(503) 488-5405; (800) 345-2570

Adams Cottage, built in 1900, offers picket-fence country charm with beautiful grounds surrounding the two-story house and secluded carriage house. Queen-size and twin beds, private bath, air conditioning, antiques, and gourmet breakfast. Short walk to shops, theater, SOSC, and museum of natural history. ABBN member.

Host: Jeff von Hauf
Rooms: 4 (PB) $59-110
Full Breakfast
Credit Cards: None
Notes: 2, 5, 8, 9, 10, 11, 12, 13, 14

Ashland's Victory House

271 Beach Street, 97520
(503) 488-4428

Celebrate the 1940s in this charming Tudor with eclectic furnishings that can accommodate couples or a group of 12 comfortably. Enjoy the USO den with a jukebox, piano, classical movies, and memorabilia. Soak in FDR's Hot Springs Spa on the deck. Full nutritious vegetarian breakfasts provided. Ashland offers Oregon Shakespeare Festival, art, music, and museum of natural history. Rogue River, Crater Lake, and Mount Ashland provide nearby rafting, hiking, fishing, and skiing.

Host: Dale Swire
Rooms: 5 (PB) $59-95
Full Breakfast
Credit Cards: None
Notes: 2, 5, 7 (limited), 8 (limited), 9, 10, 11, 12, 13, 14

Chanticleer Inn

120 Gresham Street, 97520
(800) 898-1950

Romantic and elegant restored 1920s Craftsman-style home on a third of an acre of beautiful grounds in a quiet residential neighborhood. Decor is country-French. Just a few-minutes' walk from the main shopping area, center of town, theaters, and restaurants. Full gourmet breakfasts served. Complimentary wine and refreshments. Corporate rates available as well as off-season specials including ski packages. Private parking. Groups and children welcome.

Host: Pebby Kuan
Rooms: 6 (PB) $90-160
Full Breakfast
Credit Cards: A, B
Notes: 2, 5, 8, 9, 10, 11, 12, 13, 14

Country Willows
Bed and Breakfast Inn

"Ashland's Country Inn"
1313 Clay Street, 97520
(503) 488-1590; (800) WILLOWS
FAX (503) 488-1611

Combine Ashland's theatrical attractions with a peaceful rural setting at this restored 1896 farmhouse on five acres. Guest rooms have views of the surround ing Siskiyou and Cascade mountains. Hiking trails are accessible from the grounds. Guests can relax in the Jacuzzi, the heated swimming pool, or on the inn porches, where the country quiet is disturbed only by the occasional honks of ducks and geese. Rooms are in the main house, a separate cottage, and the barn. Private baths and air conditioning. Bicycles are available to guests. Full gourmet breakfasts.

Host: Dan Durant
Suite: 1 (PB) $90-165
Full Breakfast
Credit Cards: A, B
Notes: 2, 5, 9, 10, 11, 12, 13, 14

Cowslip's Belle Bed and Breakfast

159 North Main Street, 97520
(503) 488-2901; (800) 888-6819

Teddy bears, chocolate truffles, sweet dreams, and scrumptious breakfasts can be enjoyed here. Just three blocks to the heart of town. Beautiful 1913 Craftsman bungalow and carriage house. Four queen/twin rooms with private baths and entrances. Featured in *Weekends for Two in the Pacific Northwest-50 Romantic Getaways, Best Places to Kiss in the Northwest,* and *Northwest Best Places.*

Hosts: Jon and Carmen Reinhardt
Rooms: 4 (PB) $75-115
Full Breakfast
Credit Cards: A, B
Notes: 2, 5, 9, 10, 11, 12, 13, 14

Cowslip's Belle

Hersey House

451 North Main Street, 97520
(503) 482-4563

Gracious living in an elegantly restored Victorian with a colorful English country garden. Also, a separate bungalow for families or groups that sleeps two to six. Sumptuous breakfasts. Central air conditioning. Walk to plaza and three Shakespeare theaters. Nearby, guests will find white-water rafting on the Rogue and Klamath rivers, Crater Lake National Park, Britt Music Festival, Jacksonville National Historic District, and Oregon wineries.

Hosts: Gail Orell and Lynn Savage
Rooms: 4 (PB) $94-104
Bungalow: 1 (PB) $120-180
Full Breakfast
Credit Cards: A, B
Notes: 2, 8 (limited), 9, 10, 11, 12, 13, 14

The Iris Inn

59 Manzanita Street, 97520
(503) 488-2286

A 1905 Victorian furnished with antiques. Elegant breakfasts feature eggs Benedict and cheese-baked eggs. Mountain views, quiet neighborhood. Near the Oregon Shakespeare Theater and the Rogue River for rafting. Cross-country and downhill skiing is also nearby. The Oregon Cabaret Theater operates year-round, and the Britt Music Festival is enjoyed during the summer in Jacksonville.

Host: Vicki Lamb
Rooms: 5 (PB) $95
Full Breakfast
Credit Cards: A, B
Notes: 2, 5, 8 (over 7), 10, 11, 12, 13

The Morical House

668 North Main Street, 97520
(503) 482-2254; (800) 208-0960

On one and one-half acres of beautifully landscaped grounds, this superbly restored 1880s farmhouse offers 18th-century hospitality with 20th-century comfort. The

NOTES: Credit cards accepted: A MasterCard; B Visa; C American Express; D Discover Card; E Diner's Club; F Other; 2 Personal checks accepted; 3 Lunch available; 4 Dinner available; 5 Open all year;

Morical House features five gracious, air-conditioned guest rooms, a bountiful breakfast menu that changes daily, afternoon refreshments, a putting green, and an unobstructed view of the Rouge Valley and Cascade Mountains.

Hosts: Gary and Sandye Moore
Rooms: 5 (PB) $85-115
Full Breakfast
Credit Cards: A, B
Notes: 2, 5, 8 (over 12), 9, 10, 11, 12, 13, 14

The Morical House

Mount Ashland Inn

550 Mount Ashland Road, 97520
(503) 482-8707

Enjoy mountain serenity and spectacular views from this beautifully handcrafted log inn 16 miles from Ashland. Relax in comfortable, welcoming surroundings accented by the sunny deck, rock fireplace, stained glass, hand carvings, Oriental rugs, and antiques. Hike and cross-country ski from the door; closest lodging to downhill ski area. AAA and Mobil recommended. Member of the Oregon Bed and Breakfast Guild and the Professional Association of Innkeepers International.

Hosts: Jerry and Elaine Shanafelt
Rooms: 5 (PB) $85-130
Full Breakfast
Credit Cards: A, B
Notes: 2, 5, 8 (over 9), 9, 10, 12, 13, 14

Pinehurst Inn at Jenny Creek

17250 Highway 66, 97520
(503) 488-1002

A true country inn, this historic 1920 roadhouse has been restored as a bed and breakfast/dinner house. The inn is on scenic and historic Highway 66, 23 miles east of Ashland and 39 miles west of Klamath Falls, on Jenny Creek in the beautiful Cascade Mountains. Each room is decorated with antique furniture and custom-made quilts. Our restaurant serves breakfast, lunch, and dinner to guests and the public.

Hosts: Mike and Mary Jo Moloney
Rooms: 4 (PB) $75-95
Suites: 2 (PB)
Full Breakfast
Credit Cards: A, B, D
Notes: 2, 3, 4, 5, 9, 13

The Queen Anne Bed and Breakfast

125 North Main Street, 97520
(503) 482-0220

This elegant 1880 Victorian home is furnished with antiques and vintage quilts. Splendid rose gardens and an exquisite English flower garden with a waterfall, gazebo, and spacious deck to enjoy. Two blocks away from the Shakespeare theaters and downtown. Full country breakfasts served in the morning.

Host: Elaine Martens
Rooms: 3 (PB) $75-125 in season
Full Breakfast
Credit Cards: None
Notes: 2, 5, 10, 12, 13

Redwing

115 North Main Street, 97520
(503) 482-1807

This 1911 Craftsman-style home, with its original lighting fixtures and beautiful woodwork, is nestled in Ashland's charming historic district. Each guest room enjoys

6 Pets welcome; 8 Children welcome; 9 Social drinking allowed; 10 Tennis available; 11 Swimming available; 12 Golf available; 13 Skiing available; 14 May be booked through travel agents.

its own distinctive intimacy and private bath. Guests can relax on the front porch swing and view the Cascade Mountains, or walk two blocks to Lithia Park, shops, or the nationally acclaimed Shakespearean Festival. In addition, downhill and cross-country skiing, river rafting, and salmon and steelhead fishing are all nearby.

Hosts: Mike and Judi Cook
Rooms: 3 (PB) $95
Full Breakfast
Credit Cards: None
Notes: 2, 5, 12, 13

Romeo Inn

Romeo Inn

295 Idaho Street, 97520
(503) 488-0884

Mobil gives this inn a three-star rating. A quiet, elegant, lovely Cape Cod amid pines with a valley view. Four spacious rooms with central air conditioning. Some rooms have fireplaces. Two luxurious suites with fireplaces; one has a whirlpool tub. There's a spa and pool, beautiful gardens, and gourmet breakfasts. Walk to the Oregon Shakespeare theaters and town. Member of the Oregon Bed and Breakfast Guild; AAA-rated three diamonds.

Hosts: Margaret and Bruce Halverson
Rooms: 6 (PB) $105-175
Full Breakfast
Credit Cards: A, B
Notes: 2, 5, 9, 10, 11, 12, 13, 14

The Wood's House
Bed Breakfast Inn

333 North Main Street, 97520
(503) 488-1598; (800) 435-8260

In the historic district of Ashland four blocks from the Shakespearean theaters, 100-acre Lithia Park, restaurants, and shops, this 1908 Craftsman-style home offers six sunny and spacious guest rooms. Simple furnishings of warm woods, antique furniture, fine linens, watercolors, Oriental carpets, lace, leather books, and private-label amenities invite guests to relax in this comfortable, yet elegant, home. The one-half-acre terraced English gardens provide many areas for guests to relax, read, and socialize. Golf, swimming, hiking, biking, rafting, and hot air ballooning nearby.

Hosts: Françoise and Lester Roddy
Rooms: 6 (PB) $65-112
Full Breakfast
Credit Cards: A, B
Notes: 2, 5, 8, 9, 10, 11, 12, 13, 14

ASTORIA

Astoria Inn
Bed and Breakfast

3391 Irving Avenue, 97103
(503) 325-8153

Relax and be pampered in the comfort of an 1890s Victorian. Magnificent views of the Columbia River. Hiking trails in the forest behind the inn. Beautifully decorated guest rooms with private baths. Full breakfast and daily snacks in rooms. Beautiful, quiet residential neighborhood just three minutes from shopping and restaurants.

Host: Mickey Cox
Rooms: 3 (PB) $60-85
Full Breakfast
Credit Cards: A, B
Notes: None

Columbia River Inn
Bed and Breakfast

1681 Franklin Avenue, 97103
(503) 325-5044; (800) 953-5044

A five-star Victorian charmer. Guests note an elegant "Painted Lady" when they enter the Columbia River Inn Bed and Breakfast,

NOTES: Credit cards accepted: A MasterCard; B Visa; C American Express; D Discover Card; E Diner's Club; F Other; 2 Personal checks accepted; 3 Lunch available; 4 Dinner available; 5 Open all year;

Columbia River Inn

built in the late 1870s. Nearby guests will find the Columbia River Maritime Museum and Captain George Flavel House. The ocean is five miles away. Full breakfast, and a gift shop on the premises; river view; off-street parking. "Come enjoy the new Stairway to the Stars, a unique terraced garden view of the celebrated Columbia River." Gazebo available for outdoor weddings and parties; write and ask for details and prices. During the summer and holidays, a minimum two-night stay is required. Closed Thanksgiving and Christmas day.

Host: Karen N. Nelson
Rooms: 5 (PB) $70-85 in season
Full Breakfast
Credit Cards: A, B
Notes: 2, 5, 8, 9, 12

Franklin Street Station Bed and Breakfast

1140 Franklin Street, 97103
(503) 325-4314; (800) 448-1098

This Victorian home is rated one of the finest bed and breakfast establishments in many publications. Six rooms, all with private baths (three suites), and three rooms with views of the Columbia River. Try the "Captain's Quarters," with a fabulous view, wet bar, fireplace, TV, VCR, stereo, and luxurious bath. Full breakfast. Close to downtown and within walking distance of museums. Make reservations in advance if possible.

Host: Renee Caldwell
Rooms: 6 (PB) $63-115
Full Breakfast
Credit Cards: A, B
Notes: 2, 5, 8, 9, 10, 11, 12, 14

Grandview Bed and Breakfast

1574 Grand Avenue, 97103
(503) 325-5555; (800) 488-3250

Wonderful views of the Columbia River; close to the best maritime museum on the West Coast and other museums, churches, and Victorian homes. Domestic and foreign ships in port. Light, airy three-story Victorian with hardwood floors. Guest rooms and two-bedroom suites available.

Host: Charleen Maxwell
Rooms: 3 (PB) $39-92
Suites: 3 (2 bedrooms, PB) $85-110
Full Breakfast
Credit Cards: A, B, D
Notes: 2, 5, 8 (over 10), 10, 11, 12, 14

Windover House Bed and Breakfast

550 West Lexington Avenue, 97103
(503) 325-8093

Windover House is in the historic town of Astoria, the first settlement west of the Mississippi in 1844. Enjoy the panoramic view of the mouth of the Columbia River and the Port of Astoria. The rooms are decorated with some family antiques, and a large Danish porcelain collection is displayed. A Danish breakfast is one of the breakfasts served.

Host: Coralie F. Smith
Rooms: 3 (PB) $60-70
Full Breakfast
Credit Cards: A, B, E
Notes: 7 (limited), 8 (over seven), 14

6 Pets welcome; 8 Children welcome; 9 Social drinking allowed; 10 Tennis available; 11 Swimming available; 12 Golf available; 13 Skiing available; 14 May be booked through travel agents.

BANDON

Sea Star Guesthouse

370 First Street, 97411
(503) 347-9632

This guest house is a comfortable, romantic
coastal getaway with European ambience. It
is on the harbor and provides harbor, river,
and ocean views. The shops, galleries, theater, and other sights of Old Town are just a
step away. The newly decorated rooms
offer a warm, private retreat. Some rooms
have skylights and open-beam ceilings; all
have decks. Prices include wine and breakfast served from the menu of Sea Star's
own charming bistro.

Hosts: David and Monica Jennings
Rooms: 4 (PB) $60-100
Full Breakfast
Credit Cards: A, B, C
Notes: 3, 4, 5, 8, 9, 12

BEAVERTON

The Yankee Tinker
Bed and Breakfast

5480 Southwest 183rd Avenue, 97007
(503) 649-0932

Suburban convenience close to Washington
County wineries, farms, and orchards, as
well as high-tech Sunset Corridor. Ten miles
west of Portland, midway between the coast
and the mountains. Windsurf, fish, boat, or
canoe on Hagg Lake, or canoe the lazy Tu-
alatin River. Canoe available. Private yard
with gardens and deck. Washington County
wines offered from 4:00-6:00 P.M. Comfortable rooms are furnished with family heirlooms, antiques, cozy quilts, and garden
flowers. The acclaimed breakfast often includes the Yankee tradition of pie.

Hosts: Jan and Ralph Wadleigh
Rooms: 3 (2 PB; 1 SB) $60-70
Full Breakfast
Credit Cards: A, B, C, E
Notes: 2, 5, 9, 14

BEND

Farewell Bend
Bed and Breakfast

29 Northwest Greeley, 97701
(503) 382-4374

Restored 70-year-old Dutch Colonial
house. Four blocks from downtown shopping, restaurants, and Drake Park on the
Deschutes River. In winter, ski Mount
Bachelor. In summer, golf, white-water
raft, fish, and hike. Complimentary wine or
sherry. King-size beds, down comforters,
handmade quilts, and terry-cloth robes.

Host: M. Lorene Bateman
Rooms: 2 (PB) $65
Full Breakfast
Credit Cards: C
Notes: 2, 5, 9, 10, 11, 12, 13, 14

BROOKINGS

Chetco River Inn

21202 High Prairie Road, 97415
(503) 469-8128
(800) 327-2688 Pelican Bay Travel

Relax in the peaceful seclusion of 35
forested acres. Only a short distance from
the seacoast town of Brookings. The inn is

Chetco River Inn

NOTES: Credit cards accepted: A MasterCard; B Visa; C American Express; D Discover Card; E Diner's
Club; F Other; 2 Personal checks accepted; 3 Lunch available; 4 Dinner available; 5 Open all year;

small, so guest numbers are limited. Surrounded on three sides by the lovely Chetco River, the inn uses alternative energy, but it will offer guests all the modern conveniences. Delicious big meals. River fishing, swimming, hiking, horseshoes, darts, croquet, and badminton for diversions.

Host: Sandra Brugger
Rooms: 4 (3 PB; 1 SB) $85
Full Breakfast
Credit Cards: A, B
Notes: 2, 4, 5, 7 (limited), 9, 11 (river)

Holmes Sea Cove Bed and Breakfast

17350 Holmes Drive, 97415
(503) 469-3025

A delightful seacoast hideaway with a spectacular ocean view, a trail to the beach, private guest entrances, and a tasty, expanded Continental breakfast served in the guest rooms. Enjoy beachcombing and whale watching.

Hosts: Jack and Lorene Holmes
Rooms: 3 (PB) $80-95
Continental Breakfast
Credit Cards: A, B
Notes: 2, 5, 10, 11, 14

The South Coast Inn

516 Redwood Street, 97415
(503) 469-5557; (800) 525-9273
FAX (503) 469-6615

A 1917 vintage home built in the Craftsman-style architecture by William Ward. Restored and furnished with antiques and treasures, this home has a happy, warm feeling that makes guests feel right at home. Large parlor, hot tub/sauna, spacious bedrooms upstairs. Ocean view; just a few blocks from the river and harbor. Gourmet breakfast, including Norwegian waffles. A private garden cottage is also available.

Hosts: Ken and Keith
Rooms: 3 (PB) $69-89
Full Breakfast
Credit Cards: A, B, C, D
Notes: 2, 5, 8 (over 12), 9, 10, 11, 12, 14

CANNON BEACH

Tern Inn

3663 South Hemlock, Box 952, 97110
(503) 436-1528

This European-style bed and breakfast has an ocean view. Light goose-down quilts for year-round comfort, private bath, and color TV. Fresh, home-baked goods are served, including vegetarian and low-cholesterol foods. Rooms are suitable for up to four adults, or they may be combined for seven adults. Special off-season and weekly rates available. Gift certificates. Six-percent lodging tax. Two-night minimum stay required Memorial Day through October 1.

Hosts: Chris and Enken Friedrichsen
Rooms: 2 (PB) $85-$105
Full Breakfast
Credit Cards: None
Notes: 2, 9, 10, 11, 12, 14

Sandlake Country Inn

CLOVERDALE (PACIFIC CITY)

Sandlake Country Inn

8505 Galloway Road, 97112
(503) 965-6745

Sshhh…it's a secret hideaway on the awesome Oregon coast—a private, peaceful place for making marriage memories. This 1894 shipwreck-timbered farmhouse on the

Oregon historic registry is tucked into a bower of old roses. Hummingbirds, Mozart, cookies at midnight, marble fireplaces, whirlpools for two, bikes, honeymoon cottage, breakfast "ensuite," vintage movies, "green" rooms, no smoking, wheelchair accessible, closed-caption TV. "Togetherness Baskets" available.

Hosts: Margo and Charles Underwood
Rooms: 4 (PB) $70-115
Full Breakfast
Credit Cards: A, B, D
Notes: 2, 3, 4, 14

Blackberry Inn

COOS BAY

Blackberry Inn Bed and Breakfast

843 Central, 97420
(503) 267-6951

On the southern Oregon coast, this charming bed and breakfast offers the elegant atmosphere of an old Victorian home. Since the inn is separate from the hosts' residence, guests can enjoy the hospitality and have privacy, too. A quick walk to several restaurants, stores, a theater, an art museum, and the city park, with its lovely Japanese gardens, tennis courts, and picnic areas.

Hosts: John and Louise Duncan
Rooms: 4 (3 PB; 1 SB) $35-50
Continental Breakfast
Credit Cards: A, B
Notes: 2, 5, 8, 9, 10, 11, 12

DEPOE BAY

Gracie's Landing

235 Bayview Avenue, P.O. Box 29, 97341
(503) 765-2322; (800) 228-0448 (reservations)

This Cape Cod-style Oregon coast inn is charming and relaxing. Parlor with baby grand piano; dining room with teas and coffees and homemade cookies available; and library/game room with fireplace. Fireplaces and whirlpool bathtubs lend romance to the rooms. Ocean fishing and whale watching tours add adventure. All rooms have TV/VCR, telephone, and "fishing village" view of the harbor. Receptions, retreats, and reunions welcome. Hors d'oeuvres, luncheons, or culinary extravaganzas can be arranged.

Hosts: Dale and LaRona ("Lee") Hoehne
Rooms: 13 (PB) $80-110
Full Breakfast
Credit Cards: A, B, C, D, E
Notes: 2, 5, 7, 9, 10, 12

ELMIRA

McGillivray's Log Home Bed and Breakfast

88680 Evers Road, 97437
(503) 935-3564

West of Eugene, Oregon, guests will find the best of yesterday with the comforts of today. Situated on five wooded acres, this air-conditioned home has wheelchair access. The hearty breakfasts are often prepared on an antique wood-burning cook stove.

Host: Evelyn R. McGillivray
Rooms: 2 (PB) $50-70
Full Breakfast
Credit Cards: A, B
Notes: 2, 5, 9

EUGENE

Atherton Place Bed and Breakfast

690 West Broadway, 97402
(503) 683-2674

NOTES: Credit cards accepted: A MasterCard; B Visa; C American Express; D Discover Card; E Diner's Club; F Other; 2 Personal checks accepted; 3 Lunch available; 4 Dinner available; 5 Open all year;

Close to downtown and University of Oregon on a tree-lined residential street is a quiet 1928 Dutch Colonial home featuring ceiling fans, antiques, French doors, and original crown molding. Each guest room has a firm queen-size bed; one room has a twin bed also. A three-course breakfast is creatively prepared and served. Amenities include upstairs sitting room with cable TV, early morning freshly ground coffee, and sweet dreams tea at bedtime.

Host: Marne Krozek
Rooms: 3 (1 PB; 2 SB) $50-80
Full Breakfast
Credit Cards: None
Notes: 2, 5, 10, 11, 12, 13

Kjaer's House in the Woods

814 Lorane Highway, 97405
(503) 343-3234

A 1910 Craftsman-style home in a peaceful setting on a quiet, countrylike road ideal for walking, jogging, hiking, or deer and bird watching. Antiques, Oriental carpets, and square grand piano available for guests. Member of the Oregon Bed and Breakfast Guild. "Urban convenience/suburban tranquility."

Hosts: George and Eunice Kjaer
Rooms: 2 (PB) $40-75
Full Breakfast
Credit Cards: None
Notes: 2, 5, 8 (limited), 9, 10, 11, 12, 13, 14

Kjaer's House in the Woods

The Oval Door

988 Lawrence at Tenth, 97401
(503) 683-3160; FAX (503) 485-5339

Newly built as a bed and breakfast inn, this 1920s-style home in the heart of Eugene has a wraparound porch and an inviting front door with an oval glass. Guest rooms are spacious and comfortable, each with large private bathroom. The Tub Room with Jacuzzi for two is a relaxing haven with bubbles, candle, and music. Hearty breakfast with homemade specialities. Guests love the porch swing and cozy library.

Hosts: Judity McLane and Dianne Feist
Rooms: 4 (PB) $65-90
Full Breakfast
Credit Cards: A, B, C
Notes: 2, 5, 8, 9, 12, 13, 14

Pookie's Bed 'n' Breakfast on College Hill

2013 Charnelton Street, 97405
(503) 343-0383;(800) 558-0383
FAX (503) 343-0383

This restored Craftsman home built in 1918 offers distinctive rooms with many antiques. The two rooms with queen-size bed and twin beds are upstairs and share a cozy sitting room. In a quiet, older neighborhood close to the University of Oregon, downtown, shopping, and fine restaurants. The hosts pamper their guests with a full breakfast served in the formal dining room at guests' convenience. Beautiful grounds with rose garden and wonderful yard where guests can relax. This is a nonsmoking facility; smoking permitted outside.

Hosts: Pookie and Doug Walling
Rooms: 2 (1 PB; 2 SB) $65-80
Full Breakfast
Credit Cards: None
Notes: 2, 5, 8, 9, 10, 11, 12, 13

GARIBALDI

No-How Inn

119 East Driftwood, P.O. Box 220, 97118
(503) 322-3369

6 Pets welcome; 8 Children welcome; 9 Social drinking allowed; 10 Tennis available; 11 Swimming available; 12 Golf available; 13 Skiing available; 14 May be booked through travel agents.

No-How Inn and Fishing Guide Service is quiet and secluded. It has a scenic view of the bay and hillside. Minutes away from chartered fishing boats, beaches, and golf. Bedrooms are beautifully decorated with ruffled curtains, each furnished in the past and present. King- and queen-size beds. Guests share bathroom. Full complimentary breakfast. Fishing guide service costs $75 or more.

Host: Norma Hanke
Rooms: 3 (SB) $75 or more
Full Breakfast
Credit Cards: B
Notes: 2, 7, 9, 12

GRANTS PASS

AHLF House Inn Bed and Breakfast

762 Northwest Sixth Street, 97526
(503) 474-1374

"The Jewel" of Grants Pass, this 1902 Queen Anne Victorian is the town's largest historic residence. Completely remodeled, this beautifully appointed home offers travelers pleasing accommodations. Featured on the walking tour of National Historic Buildings. A full breakfast and evening dessert and beverage are served. Rooms are spacious and comfortable with private baths; Jacuzzi available.

Hosts: Kenneth and Cathy Neuschafer
Rooms: 4 (PB) $55-75
Full Breakfast
Credit Cards: A, B
Notes: 2, 5, 9, 12, 14

Clemens House Bed and Breakfast Inn

612 Northwest Third Street, 97526
(503) 476-5564; (800) 344-2820

Down-home hospitality is plentiful and makes guests feel at ease in the elegant surroundings of this historic home. Antiques and family treasures are found throughout.

Clemens House

Guest rooms have private baths, queen-size beds, and air conditioning. One suite is extra spacious and has a small kitchenette, while another has a fireplace and can be made into a two-bedroom suite when the adjoining bedroom is included. The full breakfast is sure to please.

Hosts: Gerry and Maureen Clark
Rooms: 3 (PB) $60-80
Full Breakfast
Credit Cards: A, B
Notes: 2, 5, 8, 10, 11, 12, 14

Home Farm Bed and Breakfast

157 Savage Creek Road, 97527
(503) 582-0980

This 1944 farmhouse bed and breakfast with comfy decor invites guests to make their stay here. Doze in the country air, feast on hearty breakfasts, play checkers, or pitch horseshoes. There are two lovely guest rooms in the main house and two guest suites in the "bunkhouse"—one with a Western motif that is wheelchair accessible and one with an American flavor. All rooms are furnished with queen- or king-size beds and have private baths. Sailing and water sports available nearby.

Hosts: Cheri and Bill Murray
Rooms: 4 (PB) $50-70
Full Breakfast
Credit Cards: None
Notes: 2, 5, 8 (limited), 11, 12

NOTES: Credit cards accepted: A MasterCard; B Visa; C American Express; D Discover Card; E Diner's Club; F Other; 2 Personal checks accepted; 3 Lunch available; 4 Dinner available; 5 Open all year;

Pine Meadow Inn

1000 Crow Road, Merlin, 97532
(503) 471-6277

A distinctive country retreat on nine acres of meadow and woods at the gateway to the wild and scenic area of the Rogue River. Enjoy nearby white-water rafting, Shakespeare Festival, historic Jacksonville, and California redwoods. Wraparound porch with wicker furniture, English cutting and herb gardens, a hot tub under the pines, Koi pond. All guest rooms are sunny and well lit for reading, with queen-size, pillow-top mattresses, private baths, window seats, and sitting area. Turn-of the century antiques. Delicious, healthy breakfasts. Central air.

Hosts: Maloy and Nancy Murdock
Rooms: 3 (PB) $95-110
Full Breakfast
Credit Cards: None
Notes: 2, 5, 8 (over 8), 9, 12

Pine Meadow Inn

The Washington Inn

1002 Washington Boulevard, 97526
(503) 476-1131

The Washington Inn is a charming Victorian listed on the National Register of Historic Places. Each guest room is named for one of the Thompsons' three children and offers individual charms. Linda's is a suite

with fireplace, queen-size bed, private bath, and balcony; Pattie's Parlor is a red room with fireplace and large private bath with claw-foot tub; Sally's Sunny View overlooks the mountains, has a canopied bed, and is decorated in delicate pink. Many interesting shops and restaurants are within walking distance. Fishing, rafting, and jet-boat rides can be enjoyed on the Rogue River.

Host: Bill Thompson
Rooms: 3 (2 PB; 1 SB) $40-65
Continental Breakfast
Credit Cards: None
Notes: 2, 5, 9, 10, 12, 13, 14

HARBOR

Oceancrest House

15510 Pedrioli Drive, 97415
(800) 769-9200

Escape from the ordinary! Oceancrest House, on the Oregon coast three and one half miles north of the California border, offers a private place to relax, a panoramic view of the bay, and stairs to a beautiful secluded beach. Hosts pamper guests with luxurious furnishings and delicious baked goodies. Breakfast is served in guests' room for privacy and maximum relaxation. Enjoy watching the whales and pelicans, walking on the beach, or visiting the nearby redwood forests.

Hosts: Georgine Paulin and Ronya Robinson
Rooms: 1 (PB) $79-89
Continental Breakfast
Credit Cards: A, B, D
Notes: 2, 5, 9, 10, 12, 14

HOOD RIVER

Brown's Bed and Breakfast

3000 Reed Road, 97031
(503) 386-1545

This house is a functioning farmhouse built in the early 1930s and remodeled in 1985. It

6 Pets welcome; 8 Children welcome; 9 Social drinking allowed; 10 Tennis available; 11 Swimming available; 12 Golf available; 13 Skiing available; 14 May be booked through travel agents.

has a modern kitchen where the large farm-style breakfasts are prepared and a new bathroom that is shared by the two bedrooms. One bedroom has twin beds and overlooks beautiful Mount Hood, the other bedroom has a double bed and overlooks the orchard. Nestled in the forest and at the end of the road; the only noise to be heard is that of birds chirping. There are nature trails for either hiking or jogging.

Hosts: Al and Marian Brown
Rooms: 2 (SB) $60
Full Breakfast
Credit Cards: A, B
Notes: 2, 5, 8, 10, 12, 13

State Street Inn
Bed and Breakfast

1005 State Street, 97031
(503) 386-1899

Circa 1932. This traditionally styled English house with gabled roof and leaded-glass windows overlooks the Columbia River and Mt. Adams. Each of the four guest rooms is decorated in a different style: Colorado Old West, Massachusetts Colonial, California Sunshine, and Southern Maryland. Guests may sample wines at nearby wineries, try the local brew pub, or take a scenic train ride through local orchards.

Hosts: Mac and Amy Lee
Rooms: 4 (SB) $55-75
Full Breakfast
Credit Cards: A, B
Notes: 2, 5, 9, 10, 11, 12, 13, 14

JACKSONVILLE

Jacksonville Inn

175 East California Street, 97530
(503) 899-1900; (800) 321-9344

Jacksonville Inn offers eight air-conditioned rooms furnished with restored antiques and a historic honeymoon cottage furnished with everything imaginable. A lovely breakfast is provided. An award-winning dinner house featuring

gourmet dining and more than 1,000 wines is in the 1861 vintage building.

Hosts: Jerry and Linda Evans
Rooms: 9 (PB) $80-175
Full Breakfast
Credit Cards: A, B, C, D, E
Notes: 2, 3, 4, 5, 8, 9, 10, 11, 12, 13, 14

Orth House
Bed and Breakfast

105 West Main Street, P.O. Box 1437, 97530
(503) 899-8665

In the historic corridor of Jacksonville, this house was built in 1880 and is listed on the National Register of Historic Places. Featured on TV and in magazines for its unique restoration with hidden electronic wizardry. One block from Britt Music Pavilion, 16 miles to ski slopes. Senior discount rates.

Hosts: The Jays
Rooms: 3 (PB) $95-175
Full Breakfast
Credit Cards: None
Notes: 2, 5, 12, 13, 14

Orth House

Reames House 1868

540 East California Street, P.O. Box 128, 97530
(503) 899-1868

Built by one of Jacksonville's early sheriffs and prosperous merchants, this inn is on the

Reames House 1868

National Register of Historic Places. Victorian elegance—lace, climbing roses, and potpourri. Surrounded by spacious lawns and beautiful perennial gardens. Four guest rooms with period decor, two with private bath share a bright sitting room furnished with white wicker, plants, and twining rose stenciling. Breakfast dishes include Oregon's bounty of fruits, berries, and home-baked goods. Three blocks from the center of town.

Hosts: George and Charlotte Harrington-Winsley
Rooms: 4 (2 PB; 2 SB) $80-90
Full Breakfast
Credit Cards: None
Notes: 2, 5, 9, 10, 11, 12, 13, 14

JOSEPH

Chandlers' Bed, Bread and Trail Inn

700 Main Street, P.O. Box 639, 97246
(503) 432-9765; (800) 452-3781

The Chandlers' post and beam inn offers warm hospitality. At the base of the Wallowa Mountains, it provides a home base as guests explore the Eagle Cap wilderness, visit bronze casting foundries, galleries, or swim and fish at nearby Wallowa Lake. In the winter, Nordic skiing and snowmobiling are popular activities.

Hosts: Ethel and Jim Chandler
Rooms: 5 (SB) $60
Full Breakfast
Credit Cards: A, B
Notes: 2, 12, 13

Wallowa Lake Lodge

60060 Wallowa Lake Highway, 97846
(503) 432-9821

On the south shore of Wallowa Lake, the Wallowa Lake Lodge is one of the last authentic country inns of the 1920s. The lodge offers a homey atmosphere where guests can relax. Near the jagged, snow-capped peaks of the Eagle Cap Wilderness and within easy reach of Hell's Canyon Recreation Area. The art community of Joseph is six miles north. Plenty to do here at the lake: hiking, horseback riding, boat rentals, or taking an evening stroll among the towering pines. For breakfast or dinner the Camas Room Restaurant features homestyle dishes served with warm hospitality and professional service.

Hosts: Roxanne and Angela
Rooms: 22 (PB) $64.50-114
Full Breakfast
Credit Cards: A, B, D
Notes: 2, 4, 5, 8, 9, 10, 11, 12, 13, 14

LAFAYETTE

Kelty Estate Bed and Breakfast

675 Third Street, P.O. Box 817, 97127
(503) 864-3740

Built in 1872 in historic Lafayette, this early Colonial-style home is listed on the National Register of Historic Places. In the heart of Oregon Wine Country, Kelty Estate is perfect for visiting the entire Willamette Valley. After enjoying a breakfast featuring Oregon-grown products, guests may stroll across the street to browse at the antique mall, or visit the county museum or one of the many nearby wineries. Less than an hour's drive to the state capitol,

6 Pets welcome; 8 Children welcome; 9 Social drinking allowed; 10 Tennis available; 11 Swimming available; 12 Golf available; 13 Skiing available; 14 May be booked through travel agents.

Salem, or to the many attractions of Portland. Within two hours' drive of scenic Mount Hood, the Columbia River Gorge, or the colorful Oregon coast.

Hosts: Ron and JoAnn Ross
Rooms: 2 (PB) $55-65
Full Breakfast
Credit Cards: None
Notes: 2, 5, 8, 9, 12

LA GRANDE

Pitcher Inn
Bed and Breakfast

608 "N" Avenue, 97850
(503) 963-9152

The host and hostess lay out the welcome mat for guests at this recently remodeled Georgian home. The Pitchers have redecorated this 1925 home to give it its original feel. The homey dining room with oak floor and table welcomes guests in the morning for a full breakfast. Four guest rooms are available, and each room mingles a touch of romance with a different color theme and accents of roses, bows, and pitchers. Guests are welcome to enjoy the privacy of their room or join others downstairs in the living room. No smoking. Children over 12 allowed. Closed January 2 through 15.

Hosts: Carl and Deanna Pitcher
Rooms: 4 (1 PB; 3 SB) $55-95
Full Breakfast
Credit Cards: A, B
Notes: 2, 5, 8 (over 12), 10, 12, 13, 14

Stang Manor Inn

1612 Walnut Street, 97850
(503) 963-2400

Open the doors of this elegant old mansion and be surrounded by warm hospitality and the graciousness of the 1920s. Built by lumber baron August Stange, this Georgian Colonial home is in the beautifulGrande Ronde Valley of northeastern Oregon on the Oregon Trail, one mile from I-84. Afternoon tea and a sumptuous breakfast are served.

Stang Manor Inn

Hosts: Pat and Marjorie McClure
Rooms: 5 (PB) $70-90
Full Breakfast
Credit Cards: A, B
Notes: 2, 5, 9, 10, 11, 12, 13

LINCOLN CITY

Brey House Ocean View
Bed and Breakfast Inn

3725 Northwest Keel Avenue, 97367
(503) 994-7123

This three-story Cape Cod-style house has a nautical theme that shows throughout the home. Across the street from the ocean, guests are a short walk to shops and restaurants. Queen-size beds are in all the rooms, and guests can use the hot tub under the stars. Close to sea lion caves and the world's smallest harbor. Lincoln City is also the kite capital of the world. Enjoy watching the ocean while eating a fantastic breakfast served by the hosts.

Hosts: Milt and Shirley Brey
Rooms: 4 (PB) $65-85
Full Breakfast
Credit Cards: A, B, D
Notes: 5, 7, 9, 10, 11, 12, 14

McMINNVILLE

Steiger Haus

360 Wilson Street, 97128
(503) 472-0821

An architecturally delightful classic inn with Old World character and a lovely wooded garden setting. Within walking distance to Linfield College, downtown restaurants, and shops. Regional wine trips and Northwest Oregon day trips inspire countless return visits. Named the number two inn in America in 1991 by *The Inn Times*. Listed in *Northwest Best Places* and *Fodor's West Coast B&Bs*. Member Oregon Lodging Association and Professional Association of Innkeepers International. No smoking; no pets.

Hosts: Doris and Lynn Steiger
Rooms: 5 (PB) $65-90
Full Breakfast
Credit Cards: A, B
Notes: 2, 5, 8 (over 10), 14

MEDFORD

Waverly Cottage and Associated Bed and Breakfast

305 North Grape, 97501
(503) 772-1841

A state historic preservation officer describes Waverly Cottage as the most ornate Queen Anne-style cottage still standing in south Oregon. Fifteen years of authentic restoration by innkeeper. Guests may reserve the whole cottage for one low price. Three other adjacent historic properties. Full kitchens, and private baths and entrances. Firm queen- and king-size beds available. Award-winning roses. Color cable TV, VCR, and private cordless phones. Within walking distance of a dozen restaurants. Home away from home.

Host: David Fisse
Rooms: 11 (PB) $35-125
Continental Breakfast
Credit Cards: A, B, C, E, F (SOTA)
Notes: 2, 5, 6, 8, 9, 10, 11, 12, 13, 14

MILWAUKIE

Historic Broetje House

3101 Southeast Courtney, 97222
(503) 659-8860

An 1890 Queen Anne estate with 40-foot water tower nestled in quiet residential area 15 minutes from downtown Portland. Approximately two acres of lovely gardens, gazebo, and 100-year-old redwood trees. House and grounds used for weddings and receptions. Antique-filled rooms and country decor lend a warm, cozy atmosphere. Close to shopping and restaurants.

Hosts: Lorraine Hubbard and Lois Bain
Rooms: 3 (1 PB; 2 SB) $45-85
Full Breakfast
Credit Cards: A, B, C
Notes: 2, 5, 8, 9, 10, 11, 12, 13, 14

Historic Broetje House

MOUNT HOOD AREA

Falcon's Crest Inn

P.O. Box 185, 87287 Government Camp Loop Highway, 97028
(503) 272-3403; (800) 624-7384

Elegance "Mount Hood-style" features three rooms and two suites with private baths. Individually decorated with family heirlooms, in-room telephones, bed turndown service, morning refreshment tray. A full breakfast is served in the morning. Situated in the heart of a year-round recreation area, skiing, hiking, fishing, and horseback riding are all nearby. Corporate, private, and mystery parties. Holiday and ski packages are a specialty. Fine evening dining and spirits available.

6 Pets welcome; 8 Children welcome; 9 Social drinking allowed; 10 Tennis available; 11 Swimming available; 12 Golf available; 13 Skiing available; 14 May be booked through travel agents.

Hosts: Melody and Bob Johnson
Rooms: 5 (PB) $85-169
Full Breakfast
Credit Cards: A, B, C, D
Notes: 2, 4, 5, 9, 11, 12, 13, 14

MYRTLE CREEK

Sonka's Sheep Station Inn

901 Northwest Chadwick Lane, 97457
(503) 863-5168

The Sonka Ranch covers 400 acres along the picturesque South Umpqua River. This working ranch raises purebred Dorset sheep and markets fat lambs from 800 commercial ewes. Depending on the time of the year, guests can share ranch activities such as lambing, shearing, and haying. The working border collies always give demonstrations. Enjoy rural relaxing or visit local points of interest. More than just a bed and breakfast, this inn promises a memorable stay. Closed during the Christmas holidays.

Hosts: Louis and Evelyn Sonka
Rooms: 4 (3 PB; 1 SB) $50-60
Full Breakfast
Credit Cards: None
Notes: 2, 8, 9, 14

NEWBERG

Secluded Bed and Breakfast

19719 Northeast Williamson Road, 97132
(503) 538-2635

Beautiful country home on ten acres. The ideal retreat in the woods for hiking, country walks, and observing wildlife. Ten minutes' drive to several wineries; about one hour to the coast. Breakfast is a special occasion. Many antiques in the home. Situated near George Fox College and Linfield College.

Hosts: Durell and Del Belanger
Rooms: 2 (1 PB; 1 SB) $40-50
Full Breakfast
Credit Cards: None
Notes: 2, 5, 8, 10, 11, 12, 14

Spring Creek Llama Ranch Bed and Breakfast

14700 Northeast Spring Creek Lane, 97132
(503) 538-5717 (same for FAX)

"Quiet, peaceful, relaxing, beautiful setting, lovely home, wonderful hospitality . . ." That's how guests describe their stay at the llama ranch. Spacious and immaculate inside, this enormous home is nestled in the midst of 24 acres of rolling pasture and forest. Artifacts and llamas accent the rooms. Friendly llamas and contented barn cats love visitors. Spring is baby time. In the wine country of Yamhill County, Oregon, just 25 minutes from downtown Portland. Air-conditioned.

Hosts: Dave and Melinda Van Bossuyt
Rooms: 2 (PB) $55-65
Full Breakfast
Credit Cards: None
Notes: 2, 5, 8, 10, 11, 12, 14

NEWPORT

Oar House

520 Southwest Second Street, 97365
(503) 265-9571

Oar House, a Lincoln County historic landmark in the picturesque Nye Beach area of Newport, has offered comfort and conviviality to guests since the early 1900s. Origi-

nally a boarding house, later a bordello, and now a bed and breakfast, Oar House continues to attract visitors to its history, mystery, ghost, nautical theme, and hospitality. Each guest room has a queen-size bed, new furnishings, and a view of the ocean. The lighthouse tower provides 360-degree views from Yaquina Head to Yaquina Bay.

Host: Jan LeBrun
Rooms: 4 (PB) $80-120
Full Breakfast
Credit Cards: A, B
Notes: 2, 5, 9, 10, 11, 12

Ocean House Bed and Breakfast

4920 N.W. Woody Way, 97365
(503) 265-6158; (800) 56 BANDB

Ocean House at beautiful Agate Beach has guest rooms that overlook gardens and the surf. A private trail leads to beach and tidepools, and nearby attractions include the lighthouse, aquarium, marine science center, and bay front, with restaurants and galleries. Storm and whale watching lure winter guests, and the spacious great room is just the place to gather. Morning coffee for early birds is followed by breakfast in the sunroom. Special winter rates and gift certificates are available.

Hosts: Rob and Bette Garrard
Rooms: 4 (PB) $70-115
Full Breakfast
Credit Cards: A, B
Notes: 2, 5, 8 (over 14), 9, 12

Sylvia Beach Hotel

267 Northwest Cliff, 97365
(503) 265-5428

Oceanfront bed and breakfast for book lovers. Each room is named after a different author and decorated individually. Some have fireplaces. Hot spiced wine is served in the library at 10:00 P.M. Dinner served nightly. Not suitable for young children. No smoking.

Hosts: Goody Cable and Sally Ford
Rooms: 20 (PB) $61-129
Full Breakfast
Credit Cards: A, B, C
Notes: 2, 4, 5, 9, 10, 11, 12

Highlands Bed and Breakfast

NORTH BEND

Highlands Bed and Breakfast

608 Ridge Road, 97459
(503) 756-0300

Unbelievable panoramic views from this tranquil 3,000-square-foot cedar home on six secluded acres. Guests have a separate ground-floor entrance to their own family room with wood-burning stove, completely equipped kitchen, two beautifully appointed bedrooms (one with whirlpool tub), and a romantic spa on secluded deck. Private telephones, VCR. Full breakfast served on expansive deck.

Hosts: Tim and Marilyn Dow
Rooms: 2 (PB) $65-75
Full Breakfast
Credit Cards: A, B
Notes: 2, 5, 7 (limited), 8 (over 10), 9, 10, 11, 12, 14

OREGON CITY

Inn of the Oregon Trail

416 South McLoughlin, 97045
(503) 656-2089

---

6 Pets welcome; 8 Children welcome; 9 Social drinking allowed; 10 Tennis available; 11 Swimming available; 12 Golf available; 13 Skiing available; 14 May be booked through travel agents.

Enjoy Gothic Revitalization! Our Gothic Revival-style home built in 1867 by E.B. Fellow has three tastefully appointed guest rooms on the third floor overlooking landscaped gardens. An additional room on the bottom floor offers a private entrance, bath, fireplace, and wet bar. The main floor houses the Fellows House Restaurant, open to the public weekdays 11:00 A.M. to 3:00 P.M. Private dinners for inn guests are available with prior notice. Discover historic Oregon City, the end of the Oregon Trail. Just nine miles east of Portland on 99 East.

Hosts: Mary and Tom DeHaven
Rooms: 4 (PB) $47.50-85.00
Full Breakfast
Credit Cards: A, B
Notes: 2, 3, 4, 5, 9, 12, 13

OTIS

Salmon River Bed and Breakfast

5622 Salmon River Highway (Highway 18), 97368
(503) 994-2639

Rooms have TV and VCR. Rooms with private baths are off a main sitting room with fireplace and private entry. Decks and a covered patio with chairs provide places for smokers. One room has twin beds. This and one other room can accommodate a cot or crib, which hosts can provide at an additional charge of $15. Lady guests receive a craft choice from the greeter's basket. Newlyweds booking two or more nights receive a special gift. Emphasis on hospitality and low rates. Eight miles from Lincoln City and Coast. Hosts have traveled all 50 states, plus Canada, Mexico, Australia, and the "Kiwi" land.

Hosts: Marvin and Pawnee Pegg
Rooms: 4 (2 PB; 2 SB) $50-60
Full Breakfast
Credit Cards: A, B, D
Notes: 2, 5, 8, 10, 11, 12, 14

General Hooker's

PORTLAND

General Hooker's Bed and Breakfast

125 Southwest Hooker, 97201
(503) 222-4435; (800) 745-4135
FAX (503) 295-6727
E-MAIL 74227.414 @ COMPUSERVE.COM

In a quiet historic district and within walking distance of downtown, General Hooker's is a casually elegant Victorian townhouse that combines the best of two centuries: the mellow charm of family heirlooms from the 19th-century, and the comfort and convenience of the 20th-century. Eclectic in ambience, the house features a restrained use of Victorian detail, an interesting collection of Northwest art (some done by artists in the host's family), comfortable, tasteful furniture, and the music of Bach and Vivaldi playing throughout. Knowledgable host is a fourth-generation Portlander and a charter member of Oregon's Bed & Breakfast Guild. Sociable Abyssinian cat in residence. Wine and beer sold on premises. Two-night minimum stay required for holidays.

Host: Lori Hall
Rooms: 4 (2 PB; 2 SB) $70-105
Continental Breakfast
Credit Cards: A, B, C
Notes: 2, 5, 8 (over 10), 9, 10, 11, 12, 14

NOTES: Credit cards accepted: A MasterCard; B Visa; C American Express; D Discover Card; E Diner's Club; F Other; 2 Personal checks accepted; 3 Lunch available; 4 Dinner available; 5 Open all year;

John Palmer House

4314 North Mississippi Avenue, 97217
(503) 284-5893

Just 45 minutes from Columbia Gorge, Mount Hood, and wine country. One hour from the Pacific Ocean. This beautiful, historic Victorian can be guests' home away from home. Award-winning decor. Gourmet chef; the dinner-for-two is a not-to-be-missed experience. Kitchen units available for families. Day, weekly, and monthly rates available.

Hosts: Mary and Richard Sauter
Rooms: 7 (2 PB; 5 SB) $40-125
Full Breakfast
Credit Cards: A, B (6% service charge), C, D
Notes: 2, 4 (call), 5, 8, 9, 14

Pittock Acres Bed and Breakfast

103 NW Pittock Avenue, 97210
(503) 226-1163

This lovely 20-year-old contemporary with traditional, Victorian, and country furnishings is on a quiet country lane just five minutes from downtown Portland and within easy access to the historic Pittock Mansion. From the mansion grounds, walk beautiful forested trails to the zoo, Hoyt Arboretum, Washington Park, and the beautiful Japanese and rose gardens. Bus service is close by, as are fine restaurants, art galleries, and all major attractions and transportation.

Hosts: Linda and Richard Matson
Rooms: 3 (2 PB; 1 SB) $70-80
Full Breakfast
Credit Cards: A, B, C, D
Notes: 2, 5, 8 (over 13), 14

Portland Guest House

1720 Northeast Fifteenth Street, 97212
(503) 282-1402

Portland's most convenient address. A Victorian jewel in the historic Irvington neighborhood, this guest house is the closest bed and breakfast to the convention center, Coliseum, Lloyd Center, and public transit, including MAX line. Numerous coffeeshops, restaurants, shops and bookstores around the corner and down the street. Exquisite accommodations: great beds, vintage linens, private telephones, spacious suites, and luscious breakfasts. Stroll through herb, vegetable, and flower gardens. No smoking. Excellent value.

Host: Susan Gisvold
Rooms: 7 (5 PB; 2 SB) $55-85
Full Breakfast
Credit Cards: A, B, C
Notes: 2, 5, 9, 10, 11, 14

PORT ORFORD

Home by the Sea Bed and Breakfast

P.O. Box 606, 97465-0606
(503) 332-2855; Compuserve ID 72672, 1072

The hosts built this contemporary wood home on a spit of land overlooking a stretch of Oregon coast that takes one's breath away. Queen-size Oregon myrtle wood beds and cable TV are featured in both accommodations, which make ideal quarters for two couples traveling together. It's a short walk to restaurants, public beaches, historic Battle Rock Park, and the town's harbor. Amenities include a dramatic ocean view, direct beach access, smoke-free environment, full breakfast, laundry privileges, cable TV, and telephone jacks in the rooms. No pets. No children. Brochure available. Macintosh spoken.

Hosts: Alan and Brenda Mitchell
Rooms: 2 (PB) $75-85
Full Breakfast
Credit Cards: A, B
Notes: 2, 5, 9, 10, 12

ROSEBURG

The Woods

430 Oakview Drive, 97470
(503) 672-2927

6 Pets welcome; 8 Children welcome; 9 Social drinking allowed; 10 Tennis available; 11 Swimming available; 12 Golf available; 13 Skiing available; 14 May be booked through travel agents.

The Woods welcomes guests to air-conditioned comfort with two designated non-smoking contemporary country guest rooms. Queen-size beds, luxurious mattresses, and down bedding assure a restful night. The guest wing, with its microwave oven, refrigerator, two baths, and study with cable TV, VCR, and telephone is a private getaway. Deck and pond access from one bedroom. Open all year. First night's deposit will hold a reservation. Please call 48 hours in advance to cancel for refund.

Hosts: Wiley and Judy Wood
Rooms: 2 (PB) $65-75
Full Breakfast
Credit Cards: None
Notes: 2, 5, 8, 10, 11, 12

SALEM

Hampshire House Bed and Breakfast

975 "D" Street Northeast, 97301
(503) 370-7181

A 1920s Craftsman-style private home. Located at the foot of the Capital Mall. Within walking distance of all the government buildings, downtown, and Willamette University. There are two guest rooms available with shared bath. One room is decorated in wicker with a queen-size bed and the other in antiques with a full bed. Both are air-conditioned and have cable TV and radios. A hot breakfast is served in the dining room. Coffee or tea anytime.

Hosts: Michael and Audie Hampshire
Rooms: 2 (SB) $48
Full Breakfast
Credit Cards: A, B, D
Notes: 2, 5

SEASIDE

Gilbert Inn Bed and Breakfast

341 Beach Drive, 97138
(503) 738-9770

Gilbert Inn

The Gilbert Inn, Seaside's only Queen Anne Victorian, was built in the late 1800s. Today the inn features ten guest rooms, all with private baths, plush carpeting, antiques, and down quilts. The past has been left intact and modern comforts have been added. The house features 1892 natural tongue-and-groove fir ceilings and walls on the first two floors. The parlor features a large fireplace and is filled with flowery country French furniture and antiques. The Gilbert Inn is a wonderful escape to the past and guests can walk to everything—one block from the ocean and one block to Broadway. Gilbert Gardens, four luxury condonmiums, fully furnished, sleeps up to four. $10 per additional person. Closed January.

Hosts: Dick and Carole Rees
Rooms: 10 (PB) $69-95
Full Breakfast
Credit Cards: A, B, D
Notes: 2, 8, 9

SUBLIMITY

Silver Mountain Bed and Breakfast

4672 Drift Creek Road SE, 97385
(503) 769-7127

Visit a working farm in the Cascade foothills near Salem. Stay in the modernized "barn" with hot tub, sauna, pool table, Ping Pong, TV/VCR, fireplace, and kitchen. Join in the farm chores or relax by the swimming pool. Five minutes to Silver Falls State Park for biking, hiking, and picnicking. Fishing, hiking, white-water rafting, and float trips available on the nearby Santiam River. One hour from the ocean, mountains, or Portland. Open March through October.

Hosts: Jim and Shirley Heater
Rooms: 2 (SB) $60-75
Full Breakfast
Credit Cards: None
Notes: 2, 6, 8, 10, 11, 12

VIDA

McKenzie River Inn

49164 McKenzie Highway, 97488
(503) 822-6260

Nestled among stately fir and cedar trees on the bank of the world-famous McKenzie River in the Cascade Mountains 34.5 miles east of Eugene, Oregon and 87 miles west of Bend, Oregon. For those who enjoy fishing, hiking, rafting, golfing, photography, or just relaxing. Cozy one-bedroom housekeeping cottage with twin beds; guests do own cooking. Also available is a three-bedroom inn with twin or queen-size bed where full breakfast is served. All rooms overlook the McKenzie River.

Hosts: Hazel Brabham and Barbara Cochrane
Rooms: 4 (PB) $47.80-54
Full Breakfast
Credit Cards: F (travelers checks)
Notes: 2, 5, 10, 11, 12

WALDPORT

Cliff House

1450 Adahi Street-Yaquina John Point, Box 436, 97394
(503) 563-2506

"Pampered elegance by the sea." Each room is uniquely decorated with antiques, chandeliers, carpeting, remote control color TV; all have private cedar baths and balconies. Elegant lodging coupled with mag-

nificent panoramic ocean view. Deep-sea fishing, river fishing, crabbing, golf club (one-half mile), and croquet. Close to horseback riding. Massage by appointment. Minimum-stay requirements for weekends and holidays. Closed October 15 through March 31.

Host: Gabrielle Duvall
Rooms: 5 (PB) $95-225
Full Breakfast
Credit Cards: A, B
Notes: 2, 9, 10, 11, 12

YACHATS

The Kittiwake Bed and Breakfast

95368 Highway 101 South, 97498
(503) 547-4470
Compuserve 70413,3636

A calm ambience of personal relaxation and restoration permeates this romantic, two-story, 4000-square-foot contemporary home on the ocean at Ten Mile Creek. Two guest rooms with breathtaking ocean views. Conveniently between Yachats and Florence. Restaurants, shopping, sightseeing, sports, and other recreation areas within easy driving distance. Full breakfast is usually served; Continental breakfast is served on Wednesdays and upon request.

Hosts: Brigitte and Joseph Szewc
Rooms: 2 (PB) $100-115
Full Breakfast
Credit Cards: A, B, C
Notes: 5, 9, 12, 14

The Sanderling Bed and Breakfast

7304 Southwest Pacific Coast Highway, Milepost 160, 97498
(503) 563-4752

Large guest rooms, dining, and viewing room are all ocean front. Private baths, two-person Jacuzzi, and showers. Feather mattress and comforters. Full breakfast and special treats are often offered in evening.

6 Pets welcome; 8 Children welcome; 9 Social drinking allowed; 10 Tennis available; 11 Swimming available; 12 Golf available; 13 Skiing available; 14 May be booked through travel agents.

Early morning beverage of choice outside room. Smoke free. Miles of easy walking sandy beach. Inside lockup for cycles. Books, games, puzzles, and kites. The uncrowded Oregon beach provides beauty year-round. Breathtaking sunsets and dramatic winter storms. Discount rates for two or more nights.

Hosts: Ernie and Pat Swinn
Rooms: 4 (PB) $100-130
Full Breakfast
Credit Cards: A, B, C, D
Notes: 2, 5, 9, 12

Serenity Bed and Breakfast

5985 Yachats River Road, 97498
(503) 547-3813

Wholesome retreat nestled in the lush Yachats Valley. Gentle place to relax after countryside, forest, and tide pool explorations or bird watching. Minutes from Cape Perpetua, Sea Lion Caves, and the Oregon Coast Aquarium. Elegant European comfort with private two-person Jacuzzi tubs. Convenient to both Newport and Florence, Yachats is the gem of the Oregon coast. German cooking at its best.

Hosts: Sam and Baerbel Morgan
Rooms: 4 (PB) $69-145
Full Breakfast
Credit Cards: A, B
Notes: 2, 5, 11, 12, 14

Ziggurat

95330 Highway 101, P.O. Box 757, 97498
(503) 547-3925

Ziggurat means "terraced pyramid," and this one is a spectacular, contemporary, four-story sculpture by the sea. Guests have the privacy of the entire first floor where there are large, well-furnished suites and a library/living room equipped with refrigerator and microwave oven. The view continues with glass-enclosed decks where, on the second floor, superb food is served. Coastal activities are nearby. Closed Christmas and Thanksgiving

Hosts: Mary Lou Cavendish and Irv Tebor
Rooms: 3 (PB) $95-110
Full Breakfast
Credit Cards: None
Notes: 2, 8 (over 14), 9, 12, 14

YAMHILL

Flying M Ranch

23029 Northwest Flying M Road, 97148
(503) 662-3222; FAX (503) 662-3202

The bounty of Yamhill County's wine country joins with the coastal mountains to harbor the Flying M's spectacular log lodge. Delectable cuisine, year-round horseback riding, and limitless outdoor activities. Full-service restaurant, lounge, airstrip, gift shop, primitive camping, fishing, and dancing on Friday and Saturday evenings.

Hosts: Bryce and Barbara Mitchell
Rooms: 35 (PB) $50-150
Full Breakfast
Credit Cards: A, B, C, E
Notes: 2, 3, 4, 5, 6, 7, 8, 9, 10, 11, 14

NOTES: Credit cards accepted: A MasterCard; B Visa; C American Express; D Discover Card; E Diner's Club; F Other; 2 Personal checks accepted; 3 Lunch available; 4 Dinner available; 5 Open all year;

Pennsylvania

Adamstown Inn

ADAMSTOWN

Adamstown Inn

62 West Main Street, 19501
(717) 484-0800; (800) 594-4808

Experience the simple elegance of the Adamstown Inn, a Victorian bed and breakfast resplendent with leaded-glass windows and doors, magnificent chestnut woodwork, and Oriental rugs. All four guest rooms are decorated with family heirlooms, handmade quilts, lace curtains, fresh flowers, and many distinctive touches that make any stay special The accommodations range from antique to king-size beds. All rooms have private baths (two rooms feature two-person Jacuzzis). The Adamstown Inn is in the heart of the antique district and only minutes from the Reading Outlet Centers and Lancaster. Come experience the joy and magic of yesteryear.

Hosts: Tom and Wanda Berman
Rooms: 4 (PB) $65-105
Continental Breakfast

Credit Cards: A, B
Notes: 2, 5, 7 (limited), 8 (over 12), 9, 10, 11, 12, 14

ADAMSTOWN (REINHOLDS)

Bed and Breakfast Adventures

Suite 132, 2310 Central Avenue, North Wildwood, NJ 08260
(606) 522-4000; (800) 992-2632

PA703. Springwoods is a Civil War-era frame farmhouse that has been added to and tastefully restored. Accommodations include three guest rooms: one has a double bed and a private bath ensuite; another features brass twin beds, a queen-size sofa bed, sitting area, and detached bath; the third room with its double bed shares the bath when guests are traveling together. All rooms share a guest parlor with TV. Guests may swim in the pool, hike through the hillside, use the nearby public golf course, or shop at the Reading outlets. Lancaster Amish country and the Adamstown antique emporiums are both also nearby. Nonsmokers and children are welcome. $75.

AIRVILLE

Spring House

Muddy Creek Forks, 17302
(717) 927-6906

Built in 1798 of fieldstone, the house is named for the pure spring it protects in the tranquil pre-Revolutionary War river valley village. The village and house are on the National Register of Historic Places. Lov-

6 Pets welcome; 7 Smoking allowed; 8 Children welcome; 9 Social drinking allowed; 10 Tennis available; 11 Swimming available; 12 Golf available; 13 Skiing available; 14 May be booked through travel agents.

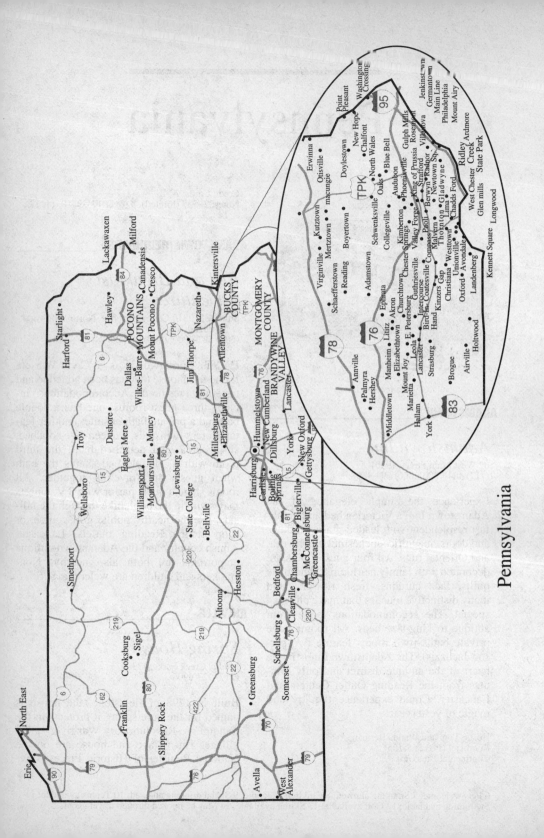

Pennsylvania

ingly restored to stenciled whitewashed walls, furnished with antiques and art, the inn offers full breakfast of local specialties, wine by the fire or on the front porch, Amish-made cheese, and caring hospitality. Horseback riding, scenic railroad, wineries, hiking, and trout fishing in immediate area. Near Amish community. Minimum stay weekends and holidays: two nights

Host: Ray Constance Hearne
Rooms: 5 (3 PB; 2 SB) $52-85
Full Breakfast
Credit Cards: None
Notes: 2, 5, 8, 9, 11, 12, 14

Spring House

AKRON

Boxwood Inn

Corner Diamond Street and Tobacco Road, P.O.
    Box 203, 17501
(800) 238-3466

Relax in the comfort of a newly renovated and professionally decorated 1768 stone farmhouse filled with quiet country charm. Hosts offer large common rooms and spacious grounds. Afternoon tea is served in the garden room. In addition to the guest rooms in the main house, there is a separate carriage house with fireplace, Jacuzzi, and balcony. Enjoy biking, walking, or driving

through Amish farm country. Visit quaint shops.

Hosts: June and Dick Klemm
Rooms: 5 (PB) $75-125
Full Breakfast
Credit Cards: A, B
Notes: 2, 14

ALLENTOWN

Bed and Breakfast of Valley Forge

P.O. Box 562, Valley Forge, 19481-0562
(215) 783-7838; (800) 344-0123

1201. A circa 1835 stone farmhouse bed and breakfast set amid nine huge sycamore trees. The inn is decorated in antiques. Guests are welcome to sit by the fire in the parlor, play games or cards, watch the cable TV or VCR. There are five guest rooms. The Gentlemen's Room sports a male look; however, female guests love it as well. It features an oak bed and writing desk. The Oak Room features an oak antique bed with matching washstand. The Ashley Room is decorated in Victorian and features a queen-size bed with an antique Victorian headboard and gorgeous late 1800s settee. The Victorian Room is decorated fully Victorian with an iron and brass queen-size bed and comfortable fainting couch. The Primitive Room is decorated with primitive country antiques. This room features a private out-house bath. $80.

Coachaus—The City Inn

107-111 North Eighth Street, 18101
(215) 821-4854; (800) 762-8680
FAX (215) 821-6862

Five gracious, century-old, lovingly restored brownstones provide a center-city oasis from which to explore antique shops, historic sites, museums, fine dining, golf, hiking, skiing, and professional theater. The rooms, apartments, and townhouses all have a

NOTES: Credit cards accepted: A MasterCard; B Visa; C American Express; D Discover Card; E Diner's Club; F Other; 2 Personal checks accepted; 3 Lunch available; 4 Dinner available; 5 Open all year; 6 Pets welcome; 7 Smoking allowed; 8 Children welcome; 9 Social drinking allowed; 10 Tennis available; 11 Swimming available; 12 Golf available; 13 Skiing available; 14 May be booked through travel agents.

unique charm and are fully equipped with the finest amenities for relaxation.

Host: Barbara Kocher
Rooms: 24 (PB) $78-185
Full Breakfast
Credit Cards: A, B, C, D, E
Notes: 2, 5, 6 (limited), 7, 8 (limited) , 9, 10, 11, 12, 13, 14

ALTOONA

Hoenstine's Bed and Breakfast

418 Montgomery Street, Hollidaysburg, 16648
(814) 695-0632

Antique lover's dream in an elegant 1839 townhouse in downtown registered historic Hollidaysburg. Next door to private historical and genealogical library. Hearty breakfast is at the whimsy of the host and the area's seasonal ingredients. Ask about children and pets. Three miles to Altoona. Near antique shops and parks in beautiful section of Pennsylvania. Protected by attack cats and standard poodle.

Host: Barbara Hoenstine
Rooms: 3 (1 PB; 2 SB) $50-60
Full Breakfast
Credit Cards: A, B
Notes: 2, 5, 9, 10, 11, 12, 13

ANNVILLE

Hershey Bed and Breakfast Reservation Service

P.O. Box 208, Hershey, 17033-0208
(717) 533-2928

Victorian mansion built in 1860, 10 miles from Hershey, 18 miles from Harrisburg, and two miles from Indiantown Gap. All queen-size beds in ten guest rooms. Four of the rooms can accommodate four people. Children welcome. Full breakfast. Air conditioning; private bath. No smoking. $50-75.

Swatara Creek Inn

Swatara Creek Inn

Box 692, Rural Delivery 2, 17003
(717) 865-3259

An 1860 Victorian mansion in a country setting near Hershey and featuring ten rooms with private baths, air conditioning, queen-size canopied beds, and a full breakfast served in the dining room. Sitting room and gift shop on the first floor. Restaurant within walking distance. Near Amish, Hershey, outlet shops, and Renaissance Faire at Mount Hope Winery. Handicapped accessible; AAA approved. No pets. No smoking.

Rooms: 10 (PB) $50-70
Full Breakfast
Credit Cards: A, B, C, D, E
Notes: 2, 5, 8, 9, 10, 11, 12, 14

ARDMORE

Bed and Breakfast of Philadelphia

1616 Walnut Street, Suite 1120,
  Philadelphia, 19103
(215) 735-1917; (800) 220-1917
FAX (215) 735-1905

Ardmore Bon Vivant. This attractively decorated suburban home is on a tree-lined street and offers a second-story sitting room

NOTES: Credit cards accepted: A MasterCard; B Visa; C American Express; D Discover Card; E Diner's Club; F Other; 2 Personal checks accepted; 3 Lunch available; 4 Dinner available; 5 Open all year;

with TV and wicker furniture for guest relaxation. All rooms have their own private baths. $50-60.

AUDUBON

Bed and Breakfast of Valley Forge

P.O. Box 562, Valley Forge, 19481-0562
(215) 783-7838; (800) 344-0123

1311. Blue Bonnet Farm Bed and Breakfast. An old country farmhouse, circa 1700s, sitting on several acres. It is very comfortably furnished with country antiques. There is an outdoor Jacuzzi built into the deck that leads through the garden walk, creating a most relaxing atmosphere so that guests may wind down after a busy day. Full breakfast every morning to start the day. Host is an artist, herbalist, and a Reiki practitioner. $55-85.

AVELLA

Weatherbury Farm

Rural Delivery 1, Box 250, 15312
(412) 587-3763

One hundred acres of meadows, gardens, fields, and valleys create a tranquil setting at the Tudor's bed and breakfast, the perfect getaway from everyday pressures. Guest rooms at this 1860s farmhouse are lovingly furnished with old-fashioned country charm. Awake to a bountiful farm breakfast. Later, get acquainted with the sheep, cattle, and chickens. Opportunities for golfing, fishing, boating, hiking, bicycling, and antiquing abound. Visit historic Meadowcroft Village, Starlake Amphitheater, and panhandle West Virginia. Convenient to Pittsburgh. Picnic lunches are available from a local source. Two additional rooms will be available June 1995.

Hosts: Dale, Marcy, and Nigel Tudor
Rooms: 2 (PB) $60

Full Breakfast
Credit Cards: A, B
Notes: 2, 5, 8, 9, 10, 11, 12, 14

AVONDALE

Association of Bed and Breakfasts in Philadelphia, Valley Forge, Brandywine

P.O. Box 562, Valley Forge, 19481-0562
(215) 783-7838; (800) 344-0123

500. The Hepburn Farm. Now reduced to three acres, was built in 1890 and occupied by Katherine Hepburn's grandparents. It has been totally renovated and centrally air-conditioned. Guests have a choice of two rooms or two suites. Each has a queen-size bed and a private bath. Breakfasts are full and hearty. Within the common room, guests will find a fireplace, TV, VCR, and a stationary bike (which will get the rider nowhere). Walk or jog down a quiet road, ride a 10-speed bike, pitch horse shoes, or just relax on the veranda. All of the Brandywine Valley attractions are within a 20-minute drive. No, pets. No children under 12 years. $80-90.

The International Bed and Breakfast Club, Inc.

504 Amherst Street, Buffalo, NY 14207
(800) 723-4262; FAX (716) 873-4462

This 1844 mill house overlooks horses grazing in a meadow in the heart of the Brandywine Valley, midpoint between historic Philadelphia and quaint Lancaster County. Three rooms are offered including a canopied double bed, a Victorian wicker single, and a wing with twin beds. Guests enjoy a hot tub and TV. Full breakfast with homemade breads is included. Rooms share a bath. $75.

6 Pets welcome; 8 Children welcome; 9 Social drinking allowed; 10 Tennis available; 11 Swimming available; 12 Golf available; 13 Skiing available; 14 May be booked through travel agents.

BALLY

Guesthouses, Inc.
P.O. Box 2137, West Chester, 19380
(215) 692-4575

006. A two-story Cotswold cottage charmingly furnished with antiques and handmade pieces. Meant just for two. Downstairs there is a living room with antique wood-burning stove and an efficiency kitchen. The bedroom with full-size bed and bath is upstairs. The kitchen can be stocked for breakfast or guests may have breakfast served in the nearby Wood cutter's House before an open fire or alfresco, depending on the season. $80.

BEDFORD

Bedford's Covered Bridge Inn
Rural Delivery 1, Box 196, 15559
(814) 733-4093

Delightful countryside accommodations in a historic home near a covered bridge afford guests full breakfasts and private baths amid a picturebook setting. Hiking, biking, antiquing, fishing, bird watching, and cross-country skiing are available from the door. Old Bedford Village, Blue Knoll ski resort, Shawnee State Park, Coral Caverns, and many covered bridges are nearby. Eight miles from Exit 11, I-76.

Rooms: 6 (PB) $65-85
Full Breakfast
Credit Cards: A, B, C, D
Notes: 2, 5, 8 (over 12), 9, 10, 11, 12, 13, 14

BELLEVILLE

Hickory Grove Bed and Breakfast
Rural Delivery 1, Box 281, 17004
(717) 935-5289

Charming country style in the heart of Amish country describes this bed and breakfast, which is only 30 minutes from Penn State University. Other nearby attractions include state parks, the Big Valley Auction and Flea Market, crafts, antiques, gift and quilt shops, plus a craft shop on the premises. Enjoy the flower and vegetable gardens, swing under the grape arbor, picnic on the patio. Homemade muffins and fruit cobbler made from fresh berries raised at Hickory Grove grace the breakfast table. Private entrance, fireplace, and family room.

Hosts: Caleb and Bertha Peachey
Rooms: 5 (1 PB; 4 SB) $40-45
Continental Breakfast
Credit Cards: None
Notes: 2, 5, 8

BERWYN

Bed and Breakfast of Valley Forge
P.O. Box 562, Valley Forge, 19481-0562
(215) 783-7838; (800) 344-0123

1770 Country Farmhouse. This farmhouse features beamed ceilings, hand-stenciled walls, antique country furnishings, samplers, and local quilts. The oldest part is a restored 1770 tenant house. Set on five acres, there are pastoral views from every room. Guest rooms may have a canopied bed and fireplace, or a private stairway to the cozy den with fireplace. A hearty country breakfast will be served in a brick-floored sunroom overlooking the gardens. Minutes from tennis and swimming. Resident Pomeranian. Three guest rooms with private bath. $85-110.

Hilltop Privacy. This home is in a quiet wooded area. The guest quarters occupy the entire downstairs and include two bedrooms, family room with fireplace, hot tub solarium, and bar area with private entrance off the gardens. Other amenities include cable TV, refrigerator, telephone, air conditioning, laundry facilities, use of the kitchen, and a breathtaking setting. Ingredients for breakfast are provided; self-serve at guests' leisure. Basic French and Dutch spoken. Weekly and monthly rates upon request.

BIGLERVILLE

Amanda's Bed and Breakfast

1428 Park Avenue, Baltimore, MD, 21217
(410) 225-0001; (800) 899-7533
FAX (410) 728-8957

324. Near Gettysburg, a log home; cozy and very inviting. Rural setting with deer, chipmunks, and a variety of birds. Hike along the Appalachian Trail. Spacious room with queen-size bed, private bath, and woodburning stove. Full breakfast. $85.

Mulberry Farm Bed and Breakfast

616 Flohrs Church Road, 17307
(717) 334-5827

Mulberry Farm Bed and Breakfast is a retreat from Gettysburg, Pennsylvania. An 1817 brick formal farmhouse, eight miles west of the battlefield, feels much more serene than the in-town spots. A fenced-in perennial garden and four acres of ground are enjoyed by guests. It's not a working farm, just here for guests to rest and relax. The owners have owned two other bed and breakfasts and love greeting, hosting, and helping guests get to know the area. Aside from the battlefield, the hosts are experts on the surrounding area that includes hiking, biking, and summer theater.

Host: Mimi Agard
Rooms: 4 (PB) $100-125
Full Breakfast
Credit Cards: A, B
Notes: 2, 5, 8, 9, 10, 11, 12, 13, 14

The Village Inn

BIRD-IN-HAND

The Village Inn of Bird-in-Hand

Box 253, 2695 Old Philadelphia Pike, 17505
(717) 293-8369

The historic Village Inn of Bird-in-Hand was originally built in 1734. It is listed on the National Register of Historic Places. The innkeepers reside in the inn and provide guests with the finest hospitality. It is in the heart of the Pennsylvania Dutch country. Each morning a Continental breakfast including fresh fruits, pastries, and cereals is served. All guests enjoy free use of the indoor and outdoor swimming pools and tennis courts within walking distance. A complimentary tour of the surrounding Amish farmlands is offered daily, except Sunday.

Hosts: Richmond and Janice Young
Rooms: 11 (PB) $75-139
Continental Breakfast
Credit Cards: A, B, C, D
Notes: 2, 5, 7, 8, 10, 11

BLUE BELL

Bed and Breakfast of Valley Forge

P.O. Box 562, Valley Forge, 19481-0562
(215) 783-7838; (800) 344-0123

6 Pets welcome; 8 Children welcome; 9 Social drinking allowed; 10 Tennis available; 11 Swimming available; 12 Golf available; 13 Skiing available; 14 May be booked through travel agents.

1106. Picture this 19th-century farmhouse with original, broad-beamed pine floors, thick stone walls with traditional curved windows, a cozy fireplace stove, and varied views of landscape and wildlife. This home is open to guests in the tradition of country hospitality, offering a home away from home in the privacy of two large, beautiful double rooms with private baths. Both rooms are furnished with antiques and traditional and contemporary artwork. Each room has a telephone. Breakfast is served. $65-75.

Stoney Creek. Guest quarters are reached through a private entrance from a garden walkway and have a fully equipped kitchen, cozy parlor, bedroom, and bath. Breakfast foods are provided in the kitchen. Enjoy 15 acres with bank barn, springhouse, orchard, stream, and swimming pool. Lots of room to roam, relax, and enjoy! $75. Weekly and monthly rates available.

BOILING SPRINGS

The Garmanhaus
217 Front Street, Box 307, 17007
(717) 258-3980

By the lake in the historic village of Boiling Springs, this gracious Victorian house has

The Garmanhaus

four guest rooms of double occupancy. Sitting room, where breakfast is served, overlooks lake. For the fisherman, world famous for its fly fishing is Yellow Breeches—a five-minute walk. Antique shops in nearby Carlisle. Excellent gourmet restaurant with an impressive wine list is a two-minute walk. The hosts promise a warm and charming time for all who stay.

Hosts: John and Molly Garman
Rooms: 4 (SB) $50
Continental Breakfast
Credit Cards: None
Notes: 2, 5, 9, 10, 11, 12, 13

The Enchanted Cottage

BOYERTOWN

The Enchanted Cottage
22 Deer Run Road, 19512
(610) 845-8845

Be the only guests in this rustic, romantic, one and one-half story Cotswold-style stone cottage nestled among rolling, wooded acres. Gourmet breakfasts are served in the main house beside the garden or before a blazing fire. Fine restaurant within walking distance. Close to historic sites, country auctions, Amish area, antiques, retail outlets, and flea markets. With fresh flowers and complimentary wine and cheese, this wonderful bed and breakfast offers an in-

NOTES: Credit cards accepted: A MasterCard; B Visa; C American Express; D Discover Card; E Diner's Club; F Other; 2 Personal checks accepted; 3 Lunch available; 4 Dinner available; 5 Open all year;

formal but gracious lifestyle in a storybook atmosphere.

Hosts: Peg and Richard Groff
Room: 1 (PB) $80
Full Breakfast
Credit Cards: None
Notes: 2, 3, 4, 5, 7, 9, 10, 12, 13, 14

BRANDYWINE

Bed and Breakfast Connections

P.O. Box 21, Devon, 19333
(215) 687-3565; (800) 448-3619 (outside PA)

G-04. Discover this tucked-away, quietly elegant manor house near the heart of the Brandywine Valley. With 36 acres, historic buildings, gardens, paths, and trails, each season is special at this bed and breakfast. Well-appointed rooms offer canopied king-size beds, queen-size, doubles, twins, suites, and five large country baths with showers. All rooms have TV, and most have private baths. A full country breakfast with homemade breads, muffins, croissants, and other goodies is served each morning. Concierge services are offered, and arrangements can be made for local activities. $85-120.

BRANDYWINE VALLEY

Hamanassett

P.O. Box 12, Lima, 19037
(610) 459-3000

Enjoy an elegantly quiet getaway at this private estate and magnificent 19th-century country mansion with 48 secluded acres of woodlands, gardens, fields, and trails. Near Pennsylvania/Delaware's beautiful Brandywine Valley attractions, including Longwood Gardens, Winterthur, Nemours, Hagley, etc. Excellent local dining. Rooms have king-size, queen-size, double, and twin beds; large, full private baths; TV; and amenities. Brochure available.

Host: Evelene Dohan
Rooms: 8 (7 PB; 1 SB)
Full Breakfast
Credit Cards: None
Notes: 2, 5, 9, 10, 12, 14

BROGUE

Bed and Breakfast Connections

P.O. Box 21, Devon, 19333
(215) 687-3565; (800) 448-3619 (outside PA)

H-11. Lovingly restored, this late 1800s six-room guest house is nestled in the woods beside a meandering stream. Relax on the screen porch and take in the beauty and serenity of this magnificent Susquehanna River estate that once was the home of Benjamin Franklin's grandson. Fish in the stream, swim in the old-fashioned swimming hole, bike or jog on the country roads, or wander through the grist mill that is being restored. Fine restaurants and a winery are nearby. Lancaster County attractions are within an easy drive. This is an ideal spot for business meetings with telephone and fax available. $95.

BUCKS COUNTY

Bed and Breakfast of Philadelphia

1616 Walnut Street, Suite 1120, Philadelphia, 19103
(215) 735-1917; (800) 220-1917
FAX (215) 735-1905

1819 Farmhouse. Step through the door of this Bucks County farmhouse and go back a century in time. Country crafts and antique farm implements, five fireplaces, and a Franklin stove, wide-plank floors and trestle tables all seduce guests into believing they have been lost in time. The two bedrooms on the second floor share a bath, and feature working fireplaces for cool nights and four-poster beds. Breakfasts are a treat and could include such Pennsylvania spe-

6 Pets welcome; 8 Children welcome; 9 Social drinking allowed; 10 Tennis available; 11 Swimming available; 12 Golf available; 13 Skiing available; 14 May be booked through travel agents.

cialities as shoofly pie or homemade scrapple. Children welcome. Smoking allowed. Pets allowed for an extra charge. $75-85.

Mill Creek Farm. On 14 beautiful acres in Bucks County, this host raises Thoroughbred horses on this classical Colonial farmstead. The original part of the stone house was built in 1750, and the second section was added before 1800. Three guest rooms, all with private baths, are available. A full breakfast is served each morning. Children welcome. No smoking. $115-125.

Bed and Breakfast of Valley Forge

P.O. Box 562, Valley Forge, 19481-0562
(215) 783-7838; (800) 344-0123

1804. A small inn, Federal-style of the early 1800s, on four landscaped acres. There are four tastefully appointed guest rooms, all with private baths. A full gourmet breakfast is served, and in pleasant weather, breakfast may be served on the outdoor patio. Guests are welcome to enjoy the in-ground pool. There are many nearby tourist sights including a winery, lake with sailboats, the Pearl Buck estate, Michener Art Museum, Mercer Museum, Peddler's Village, New Hope, etc. Excellent restaurants in the area. $75-110.

2003. Guest suites consist of bedroom, sitting room, bath, and balcony on a knoll overlooking fields and creek. Color TV, stereo, microwave oven, an open woodburning stove, and VCR for guests' use. Guest quarters may be entered from the main floor or by climbing one flight of stairs to use the private entrance from outside. Air-conditioned. Full breakfast is served all mornings except Sunday. Another small room is available for children only. $50-65.

Upper Black Eddy B&B. Welcome to peace and serenity in this 1820 farmhouse on 26 acres surrounded by hundreds of acres of wildlife preserve. Within minutes of the finest restaurants along the Delaware, and just 20 minutes to New Hope. Three antique-filled guest rooms. $115-135.

CANADENSIS

Brookview Manor Bed and Breakfast Inn

Rural Route 1, Box 365, 18325
(717) 595-2451

On four picturesque acres in the Pocono Mountains, Brookview Manor offers eight guest rooms and suites uniquely appointed with country and antique furnishings. Enjoy the wraparound porch, hiking trails, fishing, and nearby skiing, golf, tennis, boating, and antiquing. A delicious full breakfast, afternoon refreshments, and warm hospitality are all included.

Hosts: Lee and Nancie Cabana
Rooms: 8 (6 PB; 2 SB) $70-145
Full Breakfast
Credit Cards: A, B, C, D, E
Notes: 2, 5, 8 (over 12), 9, 10, 11, 12, 13, 14

Dreamy Acres

Box 7, 18325
(717) 595-7115

Dreamy Acres is in the heart of the Pocono Mountains vacationland on three acres of land with a stream flowing into a small pond. The house is 500 feet back from the highway, giving a pleasing, quiet atmosphere. Minimum stay weekends: two nights; holidays: three nights. Closed Christmas.

Hosts: Esther and Bill Pickett
Rooms: 6 (4 PB; 2 SB) $36-50
Continental Breakfast (May-October)
Credit Cards: None
Notes: 2, 7, 8 (12 and over), 9, 10, 11, 12, 13

NOTES: Credit cards accepted: A MasterCard; B Visa; C American Express; D Discover Card; E Diner's Club; F Other; 2 Personal checks accepted; 3 Lunch available; 4 Dinner available; 5 Open all year;

The Pine Knob Inn

P.O. Box 295, 18325
(717) 595-2532

Step back into yesteryear. Experience the atmosphere of years gone by in this 1840s inn on six and one-half acres abounding with antiques and art. Enjoy gourmet dining. Wine and spirits available. Guests gather on the veranda on summer evenings or by the fireplace after a day on the slopes. Come enjoy area hiking, biking, fishing, and fall foliage. Daily rate includes breakfast and dinner. Perfect place for a wedding.

Hosts: Dick and Charlotte Dornich
Rooms: 27 (21 PB; 6 SB) $150
Full Breakfast
Credit Cards: A, B
Notes: 2, 4, 5, 7, 8 (over 5), 9, 10, 11, 12, 13, 14

CARLISLE

Line Limousin Farmhouse Bed and Breakfast

2070 Ritner Highway, 17013
(717) 243-1281

This 110-acre homestead has an 11-room brick-and-stone home. It is only one and one-half miles from Exit 12 of I-81 and within close proximity to Dickinson College and many fine restaurants. Carlisle Fairgrounds, home of many fine automobile shows, is nearby. Furnishings inside the inn

Line Limousin Farmhouse

include antiques and a player piano that guests will enjoy pumping. Hosts raise Limousin beef cattle, and guests may play croquet, Bocce ball, or drive golf balls on farm or two of the golf courses that border the farm. No smoking.

Hosts: Robert and Joan Line
Rooms: 4 (2 PB; 2 SB) $50-75
Full Breakfast
Credit Cards: None
Notes: 2, 5, 8, 9, 12

CHADDS FORD

Association of Bed and Breakfasts in Philadelphia, Valley Forge, Brandywine

P.O. Box 562, Valley Forge, 19481-0562
(215) 783-7838; (800) 344-0123

1902. Relax at this bed and breakfast in an atmosphere of days gone by, circa 1740. County and township historic register. The master suite with private bath encompasses the entire top floor of the bed and breakfast, which was once a gristmill, creamery, U.S. Post Office, and a saw mill. There is one room with the original water wheel that powered the mill. History abounds! Enjoy a yummy country breakfast. $50-65.

CHALFONT

Bed and Breakfast Connections

P.O. Box 21, 19333
(215) 687-3565; (800) 448-3619

C-06. Nestled in beautiful central Bucks County, this inn offers comfortable lodging on more than four handsomely landscaped acres. Thoughtful improvements by each successive owner have enhanced the property to its present state. Each room is tastefully furnished with period pieces reflecting a warm and relaxing atmosphere. There is a cozy fireplace to enjoy in the winter, and a

6 Pets welcome; 8 Children welcome; 9 Social drinking allowed; 10 Tennis available; 11 Swimming available; 12 Golf available; 13 Skiing available; 14 May be booked through travel agents.

patio and swimming pool to enjoy in the summer. Sleep in the luxury of a queen-size spindle post bed, or choose the cozy twin-bed room. Private and semi-private baths. A full gourmet breakfast is served in the dining room. $75-95.

CHAMBERSBURG

Falling Spring Inn

1838 Falling Spring Road, 17201
(717) 267-3654

Enjoy country life in a mid-19th-century Pennsylvania stone farmhouse. Falling Spring Inn is two miles south of Exit 6 off I-81 and Route 30 in Chambersburg. The inn takes its name from the Falling Spring, a nationally renowned freshwater trout stream that moves slowly through inn property. The stream, a large pond, lawns, meadows, and wooded areas make for a pleasant overnight stay.

Hosts: Adin and Janet L. Frey
Rooms: 5 (PB) $49-69
Full Breakfast
Credit Cards: A, B
Notes: 2, 5, 8, 10, 11, 12, 13

CHESTER SPRINGS

Bed and Breakfast Connections

P.O. Box 21, Devon, 19333
(215) 687-3565; (800) 448-3619 (outside PA)

F-08. Complimentary wine or sparkling water await guests upon arrival at this lovely 1830s farmhouse with classic mid-century features. Two spacious guest rooms share a hall bath. While visiting, guests are invited to jog or walk a meandering trail or relax by the stream on this quiet ten-acre country retreat. A Continental plus breakfast is served in the dining room in front of the original fireplace and beehive oven. No smoking. Resident cat. $65.

Bed and Breakfast of Valley Forge

P.O. Box 562, Valley Forge, 19481-0562
(215) 783-7838; (800) 344-0123

0604. This Colonial stone inn in fox-hunt country is in a national register historic district 20 minutes west of Valley Forge National Historic Park. There is also a full-service restaurant. For guests planning a day in the country or Valley Forge Park, a stocked picnic basket for two can be prepared for an additional cost. Reception, business meetings, luncheons, and special occasions are welcome. There are stalls that will hold three guest horses. Each guest room has a different theme—nautical, safari, Jessica, and French suite. $55-125.

Springdale Farm. A circa 1840 farmhouse on ten acres of lawns and woods perfect for biking, jogging, hiking, or just appreciating. Good location for Longwood Gardens and Brandywine area. An expanded Continental breakfast is served in the formal dining room, with random-width flooring, fireplace, and beehive oven. Guests may choose to stay in the Blue Room with a reading corner and windows on three sides, or in Grandmother's Room with Early American pine furniture and rope bed. Enjoy fireplaces, porches, barbecue, patio, and chairs by the stream. $65-75.

CHRISTIANA

The Georgetown

1222 Georgetown Road, 17509
(717) 786-4570

Once a miller's home, the original structure was converted to a bed and breakfast for the enjoyment of guests in a relaxing home away from home. Entrance to the house is by a brick walkway. The herb garden on the left lets guests smell the lavender and mint that are just two of the herbs used to garnish morning breakfasts. There is a choice of three bedrooms decorated with antiques and collectibles. Lancaster County Amish, a unique group of people who travel in horse-drawn carriages, pass in front of The Georgetown. Visit the local Strasburg Train Museum.

Host: Doris W. Woerth
Rooms: 3 (1 PB; 2 SB) $40
Full Breakfast
Credit Cards: None
Notes: 2, 5, 11, 12

CHURCHTOWN

The Inn at Twin Linden

2029 Main Street, Narvon 17555
(215) 445-7619

This bed and breakfast is a perfect getaway in Pennsylvania Dutch country. Elegant restored historic estate with six guest rooms and one deluxe suite, private baths, queen-size canopied beds, air conditioning, unsurpassed gourmet breakfast, and outdoor Jacuzzi. On two acres of beautifully landscaped grounds and Amish farm views. A renowned candlelight dinner is served on the weekends. Intimate romantic setting with wicker-filled porches and private gardens. Afternoon tea and sherry included.

The Inn at Twin Linden

Hosts: Bob and Donna Leahy
Rooms: 6 (PB) $90-132
Suite: 1 (PB) $212
Full Breakfast
Credit Cards: A, B, C, D
Notes: 2, 4 (weekends), 5, 9

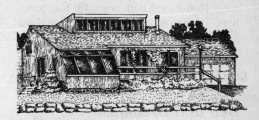

Conifer Ridge Farm

CLEARVILLE (BEDFORD)

Conifer Ridge Farm

Rural Route 2, Box 202A, 15535
(814) 784-3342

A beautiful, contemporary, passive solar home with a rustic exterior and an interior of exceptional design beauty. The 125-acre farm features a wading stream, a lake for swimming, fishing, boating, woodlands and mountains for hiking, Christmas trees, and grazing cattle. The Granary is a cabin that sleeps four. Day trips to Bedford Village, Raystown Lake, country auctions, and historic Bedford.

Rooms: 2 (PB) $55
Cabin: 1 (PB) $30
Full Breakfast
Credit Cards: None
Notes: 2, 4, 5, 6 (restricted), 7 (limited), 8, 11, 12, 13

COATESVILLE

Guesthouses, Inc.

P.O. Box 2137, West Chester, 19380
(215) 692-4575

096. Four guest houses. These newly restored guest house accommodations are in the small town of Coatesville, within 15 minutes of West Chester, Unionville,

---

6 Pets welcome; 8 Children welcome; 9 Social drinking allowed; 10 Tennis available; 11 Swimming available; 12 Golf available; 13 Skiing available; 14 May be booked through travel agents.

Exton, and on the eastern edge of Amish country. Each has complete facilities for two. The Victorian is elegantly decorated in antiques with some reproductions of the late 1800s era; the Stable is a charming country cottage adaptation; and the Carriage Houses are both beautiful interpretations of European modern functionalism. $80-90.

COLLEGEVILLE

Bed and Breakfast of Valley Forge

P.O. Box 562, Valley Forge, 19481-0562
(215) 783-7838; (800) 344-0123

Fircroft. Near Ursinas College. In 1838, this spacious Federal-style home with wraparound porch was built around the original 1769 homestead. The country kitchen has beamed ceiling and stained glass. A full country breakfast is served in the large formal dining room. Guest quarters are private and appealing. The bath has a flowered pedestal sink with gold fixtures and a claw-foot tub. $65.

Victorian Elegance. Skilled European and American craftsmen fashioned this 22-room Victorian mansion in 1897. Stained glass and fireplaces abound. A three-story winding chestnut staircase leads to the air-conditioned guest rooms, which offer such touches as marble lavatory, ornate medicine cabinet, and built-in armoire of exotic woods. A full breakfast is served in the dining room. This elegant mansion is renowned for year-round house tours, weddings both in the mansion and in the gardens, small corporate meetings, dinners in the dining room, and the perfect setting for wedding pictures. Seven guest rooms, each with private bath. $75-85.

COMPASS

Guesthouses, Inc.

P.O. Box 2137, West Chester, 19380
(215) 692-4575

775. This circa 1960 Victorian manor house is in the heart of Amish country. The downstairs common rooms are decorated in period furniture and include a large living room with fireplace, formal dining room where breakfast is served, and a light and sunny small conservatory where a welcoming refreshment is served. There are four large corner bedrooms. A full country breakfast is served. $65-85.

COOKSBURG

Clarion River Lodge

River Road-Cook Forest, 16217
(800) 648-6743

Nestled in northwestern Pennsylvania's great forest beside the gentle Clarion River, the 20-room Clarion River Lodge, featuring one of the finest dining rooms in western Pennsylvania, is a great place for romantic getaways. Chef-prepared entrees are complemented with a fine wine list. All rooms have private bath, air conditioning, and TV. Spectacular natural setting. Great canoeing and hiking. AAA three diamonds.

Host: Ellen O'Day
Rooms: 20 (PB) $89-129
Continental Breakfast
Credit Cards: A, B, C
Notes: 3, 4, 5, 7, 9, 11, 14

Gateway Lodge and Cabins

Route 36, Box 125, 16217
(814) 744-8017

Experience gracious hospitality at an authentic, rustic log cabin country inn that has been chosen as one of *Money* magasine's

'94 travel destinations. In William Penn's forest primeval, it offers cozy cottages with fireplaces, and an antique-filled lodge that are open year-round. Indoor heated pool, sauna, teatime, and planned activities available for lodge and cottage guests. On-premise gift shop and restaurant. Activities abound. Call or write for a free brochure.

Hosts: Joe and Linda Burney
Rooms: 16 (11 PB; l.5 SB) $55-164
Full Breakfast
Credit Cards: A, B, C, D
Notes: 2, 3, 4, 5, 8 (over 8), 9, 10, 11, 12, 13

Gateway Lodge

CRESCO

LaAnna Guest House

Rural Delivery 2, Box 1051, 18326
(717) 676-4225

Built in the 1870s, this Victorian home welcomes guests with large rooms that are furnished in Empire and Victorian antiques. In a quiet mountain village with waterfalls, mountain views, and outdoor activities.

Host: Kay Swingle
Rooms: 2 (SB) $25-30
Continental Breakfast
Credit Cards: None
Notes: 2, 5, 7, 9, 10, 11, 12, 13

DALLAS

The International Bed and Breakfast Club, Inc.

504 Amherst Street, Buffalo, NY 14207
(800) 723-4262; FAX (716) 873-4462

This inn is in the scenic Endless Mountains of northeast Pennsylvania. Each room has a private bath. Guest rooms include twin, double, king-size, and bunk beds. Suites are available, and the entire home is available to guests. Outdoor activities include canoeing, swimming, volleyball, cross-country skiing, ice skating, and tobogganing. A hearty farm breakfast is served. Children are welcome. No smoking in the inn or other buildings on the farm. $55-75.

Ponda-Rowland Bed and Breakfast Inn and Farm Vacations

Rural Route 1, Box 349, 18612
(717) 639-3245; (800) 854-3286
FAX (717) 639-5531

Large, scenic farm in the mountains. Farm animals. This 30-acre wildlife refuge offers ponds, hiking, canoeing, swimming, pony rides, cross-country skiing, and ice skating. State park, game land, fishing, horseback riding, antiquing, restaurants, skiing, and county fairs nearby. Museum-quality country antiques. Large stone fireplace. Circa 1850 timberframe (post-and-beam) double-plank construction. Rooms with fireplaces. Satellite TV. Awarded Gold Seal of Approval by Bed and Breakfast Worldwide. Featured in B&B/Unique Inns of Pennsylvania. Member of ABBA and PAII. AAA approved.

Hosts: Jeanette and Clifford Rowland
Rooms: 5 (PB) $65-95
Full Breakfast
Credit Cards: A, B, C, D
Notes: 2, 5, 8, 9, 11, 12, 13, 14

6 Pets welcome; 8 Children welcome; 9 Social drinking allowed; 10 Tennis available; 11 Swimming available; 12 Golf available; 13 Skiing available; 14 May be booked through travel agents.

DILLSBURG

Guesthouses, Inc.

P.O. Box 2137, West Chester, 19380
(215) 692-4575

163. A lovely historic manor house. All rooms and outbuildings are furnished with antiques. There are two bedrooms with fireplaces and one full bath for parties or families traveling together; downstairs there is a one-bedroom suite guest house-type facility with kitchen, bath, sitting room with fireplace, and bedroom with fireplace. There is also the Wash House that has a kitchen and sitting room downstairs, bedroom, and bath with shower on second floor. Full country breakfast in the main house or have the kitchen stocked for an extensive Continental breakfast. $100-170.

The Peter Wolford House

440 Franklin Church Road, 17019
(717) 432-0757

Beautifully restored historic 1800s farmhouse on ten country acres. The Federal-era brick home has six working fireplaces and is completely furnished with American antiques, quilts, and stenciling. The home retains its original pine floors, moldings, paneled doors, and hardware. Two bedrooms have fireplaces and double beds; the third, a queen-size bed and private porch. Unique brick-end barn and beautiful garden enhance the property. Adjacent to state game lands, midway between Harrisburg and Gettysburg. Come, relax, and enjoy!

Hosts: Ted and Loretta Pesano
Rooms: 3 (S2B) $60-65
Full Breakfast
Credit Cards: None
Notes: 2, 5 (except Christmas and New Year), 9, 12, 13

DILWORTHTOWN

Guesthouses, Inc.

P.O. Box 2137, West Chester, 19380
(215) 692-4575

168. Charming early 19th-century house surrounded by open fields where wildlife is appreciated. The English antique-furnished guest rooms are on the second floor, with a cozy downstairs common room with fireplace in the original section of the house. Central air conditioning assisted by fans in the bedrooms. A full country breakfast is served with homemade biscuits and lemon curd. $80-140.

DOYLESTOWN

Bed and Breakfast of Valley Forge

P.O. Box 562 Valley Forge, 19481-0562
(215) 783-7838; (800) 344-0123

The Butler's House. The original owners came to the unsettled wilderness of Bucks County in 1720 and built a stone dwelling to which a main formal house was added in 1840. A magnificent walk-in fireplace greets arriving guests. After a full day, guests can relax next to a fire in the living room or library. The country kitchen has rustic stone walls, beehive oven, and hand-hewn beams. Seven guest rooms, all with private baths. $95-100.

Highland Farms

70 East Road, 18901
(215) 340-1354

The famous country estate of lyricist Oscar Hammerstein, this bed and breakfast is on five acres, with a stone home, carriage house, and wine cellar all built in 1740. A 60-foot pool, tennis, video library, four-course breakfast, and afternoon refreshments are part of the amenities offered. Listed on the National Register of Historic Places, the beautifully decorated rooms are named after Hammerstein's Broadway musicals. Featured on CBS radio, ABC News, "Jeopardy" game show, and in *Gourmet* magazine.

NOTES: Credit cards accepted: A MasterCard; B Visa; C American Express; D Discover Card; E Diner's Club; F Other; 2 Personal checks accepted; 3 Lunch available; 4 Dinner available; 5 Open all year;

Highland Farms

Hosts: Mary and John Schnitzer
Rooms: 4 (2 PB; 2 SB) $100-175
Full Breakfast
Credit Cards: A, B, C
Notes: 2, 5, 7, 10, 11, 12, 13, 14

The Inn at Fordhook Farm

105 New Britain Road, 18901
(215) 345-1766

For more than 100 years Fordhook Farm has been the private home of W. Atlee Burpee, founder of the Burpee Seed Company, and his family. Nine major historic buildings constitute Fordhook Farm. Three of these are used for the inn: the main house, which began as a typical mid-18th-century Pennsylvania fieldstone farmhouse; the two-story carriage house, built in 1868 and converted into a private library in 1915 (it features a Gothic-style great room with exposed beams and rafters and chestnut paneling); and the converted Bucks County-style barn. Guest rooms and common areas are filled with family antiques, furnishings, and mementos. There are 60 acres of meadows, woodlands, gardens, and seed-development trial grounds to explore.

Hosts: Elizabeth Romanella and
   Blanche Burpee Dohan
Rooms: 7 (4 PB; 3 SB) $93-175
Full Breakfast
Credit Cards: A, B, C
Notes: 2, 5, 9, 11, 12, 14

Sign of the Sorrel Horse

4424 Old Easton Road, 18901
(215) 230-9999; (800) BUCK-CTY
FAX (215) 230-8053

Built in 1714 as a Gristmill, in the historical village of Dyerstown near New Hope, in the heart of Bucks County. The old mill supplied flour to Washington's troops and provided lodging for Lafayette and his officers during the Revolution. Converted into one of the most gracious inns and awarded "Best Inn Dining of the Year" for 1993-94 by *Country Inns Bed and Breakfast Magazine,* DiRoNA Award 1993-94, AAA three star rated. Fine gourmet dining in the Escoffier Room, and New American/Continental Cuisine in the New York-Paris Cafe. Garden weddings are the specialty of this bed and breakfast.

Hosts: Monique Gaumont-Lanvin and Jon Atkin
Rooms: 5 (PB) $85-125
Continental Breakfast
Credit Cards: A, B, C, E
Notes: 2, 4, 7 (limited), 9, 10, 11, 12, 13

DUSHORE

Cherry Mills Lodge

Rural Route 1, Route 87 South, 18614
(717) 928-8978

This historic inn, circa 1865, is in the scenic Endless Mountains near two beautiful state parks, covered bridges, and many waterfalls. Furnished with antiques, the lodge welcomes guests year-round. Relax with reading, fishing at the creek, and taking country walks in

Cherry Mills Lodge

6 Pets welcome; 8 Children welcome; 9 Social drinking allowed; 10 Tennis available; 11 Swimming available; 12 Golf available; 13 Skiing available; 14 May be booked through travel agents.

the beautiful valley, once an 1800s logging village. There is mountain biking, hiking, nearby cross-country skiing, tobogganing, hunting, swimming, canoeing, golf, and antiquing. Visit the Victorian town of Eagles Mere.

Hosts: Florence and Julio
Rooms: 8 (1 PB; 7 SB) $55-75
Full Breakfast
Credit Cards: None
Notes: 2, 7, 8, 9, 10, 11, 12, 13, 14

EAGLES MERE

Crestmont Inn

Crestmont Drive, P.O. Box 55, 17731
(717) 525-3519; (800) 522-8767

Perched high in the endless mountains of Sullivan County, Pennsylvania, is this vintage 1920s resort country inn. Each season provides an array of outdoor recreational activities in the refreshing and nostalgic setting of beautiful Eagles Mere—"The town that time forgot." Wonderful hiking and cross-country ski trails abound directly off the inn's grounds. The inn is surrounded by nature conservancy and is a short walk to the pristine Eagles Mere Lake. It promises comfortable lodging, fine dining, and warm hospitality. Thirty-three miles northeast of Williamsport.

Hosts: John and Jane Wiley
Rooms: 18 (PB) $118-178
Apartment: (EP)
Full Breakfast
Credit Cards: A, B
Notes: 2, 4, 5, 7, 8, 9, 10, 11, 12, 13, 14

Shady Lane: A Bed and Breakfast Inn

Allegheny Avenue, P.O. Box 314, 17731
(717) 525-3394; (800) 524-1248

A picturesque mountaintop resort close to excellent hiking, swimming, and fishing. In a quiet Victorian town high in the Endless Mountains, the charming seven-bedroom inn offers all the conveniences and ameni-

ties of a home away from home. Explore the laurel path that surrounds the crystal-clear lake. Take a step back in time to the Eagles Mere gaslight-era village shops. In winter, enjoy the famous Eagles Mere toboggan slide or some of the finest cross-country skiing. Mystery weekends. AAA and ABBA approved.

Hosts: Pat and Dennis Dougherty
Rooms: 8 (PB) $65-100
Full Breakfast
Credit Cards: None
Notes: 2, 5, 8, 9, 10, 11, 12, 13, 14

EAST PETERSBURG

Red Door Studio Bed and Breakfast Home

6485 Lemon Street, 17520
(717) 569-2909

In a small town surrounded by beautiful Amish farms and away from commercialism, an artist has opened her home to visitors of this lovely area. The private home is filled with paintings from a solo show of her trip to Africa and of Native Americans and canyons of the Southwest. Decorated with artifacts from around the world. For relaxing and picnicking there is a large landscaped yard with many private areas. Each room has color TV.

Host: Mary Elizabeth Patton
Rooms: 3 (1 PB; 2 SB) $40-45
Continental Breakfast
Credit Cards: None
Notes: 2, 5, 8, 9, 11

ELIZABETHTOWN

Hershey Bed and Breakfast Reservation Service

P.O. Box 208, Hershey, 17033-0208
(717) 533-2928

A luxurious getaway at a beautiful country estate home. Hobby farm with horses, Angus cattle, two fishing ponds, tennis

---

NOTES: Credit cards accepted: A MasterCard; B Visa; C American Express; D Discover Card; E Diner's Club; F Other; 2 Personal checks accepted; 3 Lunch available; 4 Dinner available; 5 Open all year;

court. Health room with hot tub. Full breakfast. Eight rooms and two suites with private baths. $60-100.

West Ridge Guest House

1285 West Ridge Road, 17022
(717) 367-7783

Tucked midway between Harrisburg and Lancaster, this European-type manor can be found four miles off Route 283 at the Rheems-Elizabethtown Exit. Nine guest rooms, four in the main house and five in a separate guest house that offers complete privacy. Three rooms with fireplace, two with Jacuzzi, four rooms feature decks, and all rooms have a telephone, TV, and VCR. Private baths. Each room decorated to reflect a different historical style. Exercise room with hot tub, large social room, and dining area. Fish in one of two ponds, or travel 20 to 40 minutes to local attractions, such as Hershey Park, Lancaster County Amish farms, outlet shopping, Masonic homes, or Gettysburg. Full breakfast. No smoking. Handicapped accessible.

Host: Alice P. Heisey
Rooms: 9 (PB) $60-85
Full Breakfast
Credit Cards: A, B, C, D
Notes: 2, 5, 8, 12, 14

ELIZABETHVILLE

Inn at Elizabethville

30 West Main Street, 17023
(717) 362-3476

In the heart of central Pennsylvania, the Inn at Elizabethville serves business and leisure travelers to northern Dauphin County. Built in 1883 and furnished in Mission Oak/Arts and Crafts style, the inn has seven guest rooms with private baths. Convenient to superb hiking, fishing, hunting, golf, and country auctions. A conference room, FAX, telephone, and copy service cater to business clients.

Inn at Elizabethville

Host: Jim Facinelli
Rooms: 7 (PB)
Continental Breakfast
Credit Cards: A, B
Notes: 2, 5, 8, 9, 11, 12, 14

EPHRATA

Clearview Farm Bed and Breakfast

355 Clearview Road, 17522
(717) 733-6333

A beautiful limestone farmhouse built in 1814, this bed and breakfast overlooks a large pond with a pair of swans. Beautifully restored and lovingly redecorated, it is surrounded by a well-kept lawn on 200 acres of peaceful farmland. A touch of elegance in Pennsylvania Dutch country, it was featured in *Country Decorating Ideas.* Rated four diamonds by AAA.

Hosts: Glenn and Mildred Wissler
Rooms: 5 (PB) $95
Full Breakfast
Credit Cards: D
Notes: 2, 5, 9, 10, 12

Hackman's Country Inn Bed and Breakfast

140 Hackman Road, 17522
(717) 733-3498

Hackman's Country Inn is an 1857 farmhouse on a 90-acre working farm in Lan-

6 Pets welcome; 8 Children welcome; 9 Social drinking allowed; 10 Tennis available; 11 Swimming available; 12 Golf available; 13 Skiing available; 14 May be booked through travel agents.

caster County. Shaded lawns and a porch provide a peaceful retreat on hot summer days. The inn features spacious, air-conditioned rooms with bubble-glass windows and patchwork quilts. Breakfast is served in the keeping room by the walk-in fireplace. Shop the nearby antique malls and outlets. Tour beautiful Amish country.

Host: Kathryn H. Hackman
Rooms: 4 (2 PB; 2 SB) $60-70
Full Breakfast
Credit Cards: A, B
Notes: 2, 5, 8, 9, 11, 12

The Historic Smithton Inn

The Historic Smithton Inn

900 West Main Street, 17522
(717) 733-6094

A romantic 1763 stone inn with fireplaces in every room, canopied beds, easy chairs, quilts, candles, down pillows, nightshirts, flowers, chamber music, and feather beds. Parlor, library, and Smithton's dahlia gardens are all open for guests to enjoy. Lancaster County is an antique and crafts area settled by the Pennsylvania Dutch, Mennonite, and Amish.

Host: Dorothy Graybill
Rooms: 8 (PB) $65-135
Full Breakfast
Credit Cards: A, B, C
Notes: 2, 5, 6, 8, 9, 10, 11, 12

The Inns at Doneckers

318-324 North State Street, 17522
(717) 738-9502

Experience Doneckers' warm hospitality in the picturesque setting of historic Lancaster County. Four inn properties surround the Doneckers Community, each within walking distance of Doneckers Fashion Stores for the family and home, and a gourmet restaurant. Artworks complex of more than 40 studios and galleries of fine art, quilts and designer crafts, and farmers' market. Each of the 40 rooms is appointed in fine antiques, hand-stenciled walls, some suites with fireplace and Jacuzzi. Choose from The Guesthouse, historic 1777 House, Homestead and Gerhart House. Closed Christmas Day.

Host: H. William Donecker
Rooms: 40 (38 PB; 2 SB) $59-175
Continental Breakfast
Credit Cards: A, B, C, D, E, F
Notes: 2, 3, 4, 5, 7, 8. 10, 11, 12, 14

ERIE

Historic Zion's Hill

8951 Miller Road, Erie, 16410
(814) 774-2971

Built in 1830, this Colonial home welcomes guests with five cozy rooms furnished with beautiful antiques. On a knoll surrounded by 100 acres of scenic hiking trails and a bird sanctuary, it was once the home and winter quarters of Dan Rice, model for America's

Historic Zion's Hill

Uncle Sam (1868). Convenient to beaches, Presque Isle State Park, fishing, and skiing.

Hosts: John and Kathy Byrne
Rooms: 5 (3 PB; 2 SB) $50–75
Continental Breakfast
Credit Cards: None
Notes: 2 (advance notice), 5, 8, 10, 11, 12, 13 , 14

Spencer House
Bed and Breakfast

519 West Sixth Street, 16507
(814) 454-5984; (800) 890-7263
FAX (814) 456-5091

A unique Victorian mansion in the heart of Erie with 12-foot ceilings and a large front porch. Hike or bike to Presque Isle. Near regional wineries, malls, and fine restaurants. Each of the five rooms has its own individual ambience and charm; all rooms have private baths, cable TV, telephone, and air conditioning; some have fireplaces and canopied beds. A full delicious breakfast is served. There is also a small gift shop and other amenities.

Hosts: Pat and Keith Hagenbuch
Rooms: 5 (PB) $75-110
Full Breakfast
Credit Cards: A, B, C, D
Notes: 2, 5, 8, 9, 10, 11, 12, 13, 14

ERWINNA

Evermay-on-the-Delaware

River Road, 18920
(215) 294-9100

Lodging is available in manor house and carriage house. Liquor license. Parlor with fireplace. A significant, distinguished country retreat on 25 acres of gardens, woodland paths, and pastures between the Delaware River and canal. Dinner served Friday, Saturday, Sunday, and holidays. Minimum stay weekends: two nights.

Hosts: Ron Strouse and Fred Cresson
Rooms: 16 (PB) $90-170
Continental Breakfast
Credit Cards: A, B

Closed December 24
Notes: 2, 4, 5, 7, 8 (over 12), 9, 14

Golden Pheasant Inn

Golden Pheasant Inn

River Road, 18920
(215) 294-9595

This 1857 fieldstone inn is between the Delaware River and the Pennsylvania Canal. Six intimate guest rooms feature four-poster, queen-size canopied beds. Three romantic dining rooms, including a candlelit greenhouse overlooking the canal. Masterful classical French cuisine by chef/owner Michel Faure. Extensive wine selections. Dinner served Tuesday through Sunday. Sunday Brunch is from 11:00 A.M. to 3:00 P.M. Minimum stay weekends: two nights; holidays: three nights.

Hosts: Michel and Barbara Faure
Rooms: 6 (PB) $110-135
Continental Breakfast
Credit Cards: A, B, E
Notes: 2, 4, 5, 6, 9, 11

FRANKLIN

Quo Vadis
Bed and Breakfast

1501 Liberty Street, 16323
(814) 432-4208; (800) 360-6598

Quo Vadis Bed and Breakfast "Whither Goest Thou?" A stately brick home,

6 Pets welcome; 8 Children welcome; 9 Social drinking allowed; 10 Tennis available; 11 Swimming available; 12 Golf available; 13 Skiing available; 14 May be booked through travel agents.

accented with terra cotta tile, Quo Vadis is an eclectic Queen Anne structure built in 1867. Spacious rooms with high ceilings, parquet floors, detailed woodworking, moldings, and friezes are hallmarks of Victorian elegance. The furnishings are heirloom antiques from four generations of the same family. The quilts and embroidery are the handiwork of two beloved ladies. Quo Vadis is in an architecturally prominent historic district listed in the National Register with a walking tour of the beautiful Allegheny Valley. Quo Vadis is on Pennsylvania Route 8 and US 62 near the junction of US 322. From I-80, Exit 3, 14 miles north on Pennsylvania Route 8.

Hosts: Kristal and Stanton Bowmer-Vath
Rooms: 6 (PB) $60-80
Full Breakfast
Credit Cards: A, B, C
Notes: 2, 5, 8 (limited), 9 (with discretion), 14

Fassitt Mansion

and enjoy the glow of one of six fireplaces. A full country breakfast is served in the cheerful dining room.

Hosts: Tara and Ed Golish
Rooms: 4 (PB) $75-110
Full Breakfast
Credit Cards: A, B
Notes: 2, 5, 7 (limited), 8, 9, 10, 12

GERMANTOWN

Bed and Breakfast of Philadelphia

1616 Walnut Street, Suite 1120, Philadelphia, 19103
(215) 735-1917; (800) 220-1917
FAX (215) 735-1905

"Ka Bob." This rambling house in a beautiful secluded property is near Fairmont Park. Wood paneling, six large fireplaces, and large bedrooms reflect Civil War suburbia. King-size, twins, or double bed. $40-50.

Quo Vadis

GAP

Fassitt Mansion

6051 Old Philadelphia Pike,
   Route 340, White Horse, 17527
(717) 442-3139; (800) 653-4139

In the rolling hills of Pennsylvania Dutch country, this restored 1845 country home combines charm with modern conveniences. Beautifully appointed rooms with locally made, hand-stitched Amish quilts. In winter, snuggle under down comforters

GETTYSBURG

Amanda's Bed and Breakfast

1428 Park Avenue, Annapolis, MD 21217
(301) 225-0001; (301) 383-1274

125. On Oak Ridge, this restored Colonial offers a splendid view of the town. Enjoy the charm of a bygone era with the comforts of home-cooked breakfasts, cozy quilts, and country antiques. Rooms are decorated with Civil War accents. Nine rooms have both private and shared baths. $79-99.

345. A quiet off-the-beaten-path, woodsy setting. The oldest part of the house served as a field hospital during the War Between the States. New additions enhance the former residence. Each room has a private bath. Several new rooms with fireplaces. Small conference facilities available. Full country breakfast. $68-89.

Baladerry Inn at Gettysburg

40 Hospital Road, 17325
(717) 337-1342

Baladerry Inn is on four secluded acres at the edge of the Gettysburg battlefield. The original brick Federal-style home, circa 1812, served as a hospital during the War Between the States. A large two-story great room dominated by a massive brick fireplace serves as both a dining and gathering area. A brick terrace provides an outdoor area for socializing, while a gazebo affords a private place of tranquility. Guest rooms in the carriage house, newly renovated in 1994, have fireplaces or a private brick patio plus a common area with fireplace, sunroom, and brick patio. Horseback riding nearby.

Hosts: Tom and Caryl O'Gara
Rooms: 8 (PB) $75-95
Full Breakfast
Credit Cards: A, B, C, E
Notes: 2, 5, 9, 10 (on premises), 11, 12, 13, 14

Beechmont Inn

315 Broadway, 17331
(800) 553-7009

An elegant 1834 Federal-period inn with seven guest rooms, private baths, fireplaces, air conditioning, afternoon refreshments,

and gourmet breakfast. One large suite has a private whirlpool tub, canopied bed, and fireplace. Gettysburg battlefield, Lake Marburg, golf, and great antiquing nearby. Convenient location for visits to Hershey, York, or Lancaster. Weekend packages and romantic honeymoon or anniversary packages offered. Picnic baskets available. Great area for biking and hiking. AAA and Mobil approved.

Hosts: Susan and William Day
Doubles: 7 (PB) $80-135
Full Breakfast
Credit Cards: A, B, C
Notes: 2, 5, 7 (limited), 8 (over 12), 9, 10, 11, 12, 13, 14

The Brafferton Inn

The Brafferton Inn

44 York Street, 17325
(717) 337-3423

Enjoy the grace and charm of the oldest house in historic downtown Gettysburg. This 1786 fieldstone home, recently updated, is listed on the National Register of Historic Places. Antiques and stenciling throughout. Featured in the February 1988 issue of *Country Living* magazine.

Hosts: Jane and Sam Back
Rooms: 10 (PB) $70-110
Suites: 2 (PB) $100-125
Full Breakfast
Credit Cards: A, B
Notes: 2, 5, 7, 8 (over 8), 9, 10, 12, 13, 14

6 Pets welcome; 8 Children welcome; 9 Social drinking allowed; 10 Tennis available; 11 Swimming available; 12 Golf available; 13 Skiing available; 14 May be booked through travel agents.

Brierfield
Bed and Breakfast

240 Baltimore Street, 17325
(717) 334-8725

In historic Gettysburg. Two blocks from Lincoln Square. Walking distance to fine restaurants and major historic attractions. The Brierfield is furnished with antiques, private baths, air conditioning, and shady porches. Full breakfast. Hot and cold beverages are available any time. Come and enjoy.

Host: Nancy Rice
Rooms: 5 (PB) $65-80
Full Breakfast
Credit Cards: None
Notes: 2, 5, 8, 9, 10, 12, 13, 14

Hickory Bridge Farm

96 Hickory Bridge Road, 17353
(717) 642-5261

At the edge of the mountains just eight miles west of Gettysburg. Country cottages in a quiet, wooded area by a pure mountain stream. Dinners are offered Friday, Saturday, and Sunday in a restored barn furnished with fine antiques. Family-owned and operated for 15 years. Reservations appreciated.

Hosts: Dr. and Mrs. James Hammett; Mary Lynn and Robert Martin
Rooms: 4 (PB) $45-85
Full Breakfast
Credit Cards: A, B
Notes: 2, 4, 5, 7, 8, 9, 11, 12, 13

Keystone Inn

231 Hanover Street, 17325
(717) 337-3888

Keystone Inn is a large late-Victorian brick house filled with lots of natural woodwork. The guest rooms are bright, cheerful, and air-conditioned. The soft pastels and ruffles give guests a warm welcome. Each room has a reading nook and writing desk. Relax

Keystone Inn

with a book in Aunt Weasie's Library. Choose a breakfast from the full menu.

Hosts: Wilmer and Doris Martin
Rooms: 4 (2 PB; 2 SB) $59-75
Full Breakfast
Credit Cards: A, B
Notes: 2, 5, 8, 10, 11, 12, 13

The Old Appleford Inn

218 Carlisle Street, 17325
(717) 337-1711

This elegant three-story Victorian mansion, built in 1867, has 12 antique-filled guest rooms, each with private bath and air conditioning. The living room features high ceilings, baby grand piano, and complimentary sherry. The Lincoln Library features many unique collections, books, and solitude. There's a plant-filled sunroom with white wicker and afternoon beverages. The apple-stenciled dining room is where the sumptuous breakfasts are served. Surrounded by history, this inn is on the Historic Pathway. Antiquing and sports nearby. Gettysburg College within walking distance. New carriage house offers accommodations for honeymooners. AAA-rated three diamonds.

Hosts: Maribeth and Frank Skradski
Rooms: 12 (PB) $93-138
Full Breakfast
Credit Cards: A, B, C, D
Notes: 2, 5, 8 (over 14), 9, 10, 12, 13, 14

NOTES: Credit cards accepted: A MasterCard; B Visa; C American Express; D Discover Card; E Diner's Club; F Other; 2 Personal checks accepted; 3 Lunch available; 4 Dinner available; 5 Open all year;

GETTYSBURG BATTLEFIELD

The Doubleday Inn

104 Doubleday Avenue, 17325
(717) 334-9119

Directly on the Gettysburg battlefield, this Colonial inn is beautifully restored with Civil War accents, comfortable antiques, and central air conditioning. Enjoy afternoon tea and a candlelight country breakfast in the morning. Roam the lovely grounds and enjoy the splendid views, overlooking historic Gettysburg and the National Military Park. On selected evenings, participate in a discussion with a Civil War historian who brings the battle alive with accurate accounts, authentic memorabilia, and weaponry.

Hosts: Charles and Ruth Anne Wilcox
Rooms: 9 (5 PB; 4 SB) $79-100
Full Breakfast
Credit Cards: A, B
Notes: 2, 5, 9, 10, 11, 12, 13, 14

The Doubleday Inn

GLADWYNE

Association of Bed and Breakfasts in Philadelphia, Valley Forge, Brandywine

P.O. Box 562, Valley Forge, 19481-0562
(215) 783-7838; (800) 344-0123
FAX (215) 783-7783

Glad Haven. This spacious, air-conditioned Cape Cod Colonial home is on a large wooded lot. Fine furnishings, collectibles, art, and expanses of windows all contribute to the sunlit, cheerful atmosphere. The gourmet country breakfasts are served in the formal dining room or in the sunroom with its wicker and foliage. The adjoining terrace, gardens, lawn, reflecting pool, and fountain enhance the feeling of privacy and rest. Private baths. $55.

0602. Gladwyne. In one of the prettiest rural areas on the Main Line, yet only 20 minutes from Philadelphia or King of Prussia and Route 202 on a beautiful acre opposite a golf course. Pre-World War II stone colonial is built in Pennsylvania Dutch farmhouse style. Second-floor double bedroom has privacy and the option of an additional single room should a two-room suite be required. Bath adjoins the suite. The third-floor accommodation consists of one double bedroom and bath. Guests are welcome to use the grounds, living room, kitchen, and eat-in screened porch. $75.

Bed and Breakfast of Philadelphia

1616 Walnut Street, Suite 1120, Philadelphia, 19103
(215) 735-1917; (800) 220-1917
FAX (215) 735-1905

Gladwyn Invitation. This comfortable ranch-style suburban home with nice sun porch and gardens offers a room with a double bed and private bath, and a room with a single bed and a shared bath. Host and hostess are widely traveled medical professionals. $40-60.

GLEN MILLS

Crier in the Country Restaurant and Guest House

Route 1, 19342
(610) 358-2411

6 Pets welcome; 8 Children welcome; 9 Social drinking allowed; 10 Tennis available; 11 Swimming available; 12 Golf available; 13 Skiing available; 14 May be booked through travel agents.

The charm of the building's history greets guests the moment they walk through the doors of this 18th-century country mansion. The addition of the guest rooms now gives The Crier in the Country true bed and breakfast ambience. Comfortable four-poster beds and authentic period furnishings grace every room. The deluxe suite offers the convenience of kitchen facilities as well as a separate conversation area. Dine comfortably in either of two grand parlors, each alive with the warm glow of candlelight and the soft shimmer of sparking crystal.

Rooms: 8 (PB) $65-100
Continental Breakfast
Credit Cards: A, B, C, D, E, F
Notes: 2, 4, 5, 7, 8, 9

Guesthouses, Inc.

P.O. Box 2137, West Chester, 19380
(215) 692-4575

838. Surrounded by 55 acres of fields and woods, Sweetwater Farm, circa 1734, is the quintessential American bed and breakfast. The four corner bedrooms of the main house all contain working fireplaces, four-poster or canopied queen-size beds, high ceilings, beautifully carved woodwork, and tall windows overlooking two sides of the countryside. Three of these rooms share a large hall bath. The Lafayette room has a new private bath. Two rooms with queen-size beds, and another with two beds, all with private adjoining baths, in the tavern wing of the main house. There are also five guest houses with one or two bedrooms. Full, hearty farm breakfast served. Swimming pool. Children and pets are welcome. $145-225.

GLEN ROCK

Dogwood House at Spoutwood Herb and Flower Farm

Rural Delivery 3, Box 66, 17327
(717) 235-6610

This antique-furnished private cottage sits on a peaceful 19th-century Pennsylvania German farm among rolling hills and streams. Fifteen percent guest discount on classes in gardening, cooking, healing with herbs, and dried flower design (call for schedule). Enjoy the gardens and the hot tub in season. Well-equipped kitchen. Close to hiking, swimming, boating, antiquing, Gettysburg, Lancaster, and Baltimore. More than double occupancy: $20 each additional person, $12.50 children under 10, children under 2 free.

Hosts: Rob and Lucy Wood
Cottage: 1 (PB) $70
Full Breakfast
Credit Cards: A, B
Notes: 2, 5, 8, 9, 11, 12, 14

Glen Rock Mill Inn

Glen Rock Mill Inn

50 Water Street, 17327
(717) 235-5918

An old mill built in 1837 has been transformed into an inn that offers cozy rooms furnished with comfortable antiques. The inn also operates as a restaurant featuring casual and fine dining. American breakfast and Sunday brunch are served. The restaurant has a waterfall in one dining room. The Mill Inn is in the gentle rolling green hills of Southern York County, close to antique shops, wineries, golf, and within an easy drive of Baltimore and Washington, D.C.

NOTES: Credit cards accepted: A MasterCard; B Visa; C American Express; D Discover Card; E Diner's Club; F Other; 2 Personal checks accepted; 3 Lunch available; 4 Dinner available; 5 Open all year;

Hosts: Tom and Bette Ranc
Rooms: 14 (PB) $55-155
American Breakfast
Credit Cards: A, B, C
Notes: 2, 3, 4, 5, 7, 8, 9, 12, 13, 14

GREENCASTLE

Welsh Run Inn
Bed and Breakfast

11299 Welsh Run Road, 17225
(717) 328-9506

Stately turn-of-the-century farmhome in the historic village of Welsh Run in a rural setting. Friendly, casual atmosphere. A wonderful full-course breakfast is served by candlelight in the formal dining room. Lovely hand-stenciled bedrooms. Antiquers will enjoy the many shops and malls the area has to offer. Only minutes from I-81, Whitetail Ski area, Greencastle Grump Golf Course, historic Mercersburg, and Hagerstown, Maryland; one hour to Gettysburg and Harpers Ferry; and one and one-half hours to Washington, D.C., Baltimore, or Harrisburg.

Hosts: Bob and Ellie Neff
Rooms: 3 (1 PB; 2 SB) $55-65
Full Breakfast
Credit Cards: A, B, C
Notes: 2, 5, 8, 9, 11, 12, 13, 14

GREENSBURG

Huntland Farm
Bed and Breakfast

Rural Delivery 9, Box 21, 15601
(412) 834-8483

The 100-acre Huntland Farm is three miles northeast of Greensburg, a convenient halfway stop between the East Coast and the Midwest. From Pennsylvania Turnpike, exit at New Stanton (east) or Monroeville (west). Circa 1848 house in scenic, historical Laurel Highlands of western Pennsylvania. Four corner bedrooms, two shared baths. Living

areas furnished with antiques. Good restaurants and antique shops nearby. Full country breakfast.

Hosts: Robert and Elizabeth Weidlein
Rooms: 4 (SB) $50-70
Full Breakfast
Credit Cards: C
Notes: 2, 5, 7, 9, 14

GULPH MILLS

Bed and Breakfast
of Valley Forge

P.O. Box 562, Valley Forge, 19481-0562
(215) 783-7838; (800) 344-0123

The Barn at Rebel Hill. A home made from a barn, this fabulous, luxury barn offers an atmosphere of quiet taste to highlight any visit to this historic area. All guest rooms are off the spacious entrance hall. A full breakfast is served in the parlor or in the great room with a fireplace and antiques. In warm weather, lounge or dine on the upper deck overlooking the enclosed stone paddock, the rolling green hills, and pond. Close to Valley Forge and Philadelphia. An easy drive to Brandywine and Amish areas. Three guest rooms, each with a private bath. $85-95.

GUTHRIESVILLE

Bed and Breakfast
of Valley Forge

P.O. Box 562, Valley Forge, 19481-0562
(215) 783-7838; (800) 344-0123

1503. Hosts invite guests to share the special warmth and serenity of this lovely example of an early 19th-century Pennsylvania farmhouse and experience the seclusion and relaxation offered. Enjoy the antiques throughout the bed and breakfast, the private porch and lawn area with lovely view of the surrounding countryside. Walk

---

6 Pets welcome; 8 Children welcome; 9 Social drinking allowed; 10 Tennis available; 11 Swimming available; 12 Golf available; 13 Skiing available; 14 May be booked through travel agents.

about eight acres of hills, meadow, and hedgerow. View the amazing abundance of plant and wildlife that live in the small marshland. Accommodations include two rooms, each with private bath, double bed, telephone, TV, and air conditioning. A third room is available that is suitable for children and has a double bed and single bed. $55-75.

Burns 1805 Bed and Breakfast. Lovely example of an early 19th-century Pennsylvania farmhouse overlooking a panoramic view of farm and woodland. It has been on Chester County day tours for many years. Share the special warmth and serenity of this lovely old house. Walk about on eight acres of hill, meadow, and hedgerow, or just enjoy the views from the porch. Close to the Amish/Lancaster area and the Brandywine Longwood Garden area. Two guest rooms, each with a private bath. $45-75.

HALLAM

Bed and Breakfast Connections
P.O. Box 21, Devon, 19333
(215) 687-3565; (800) 448-3619

H-09. After enjoying the attractions of York County, retreat to the quiet elegance of this lovely 1836 Colonial home appointed with a blend of antiques and authentic reproductions. On arrival, chat with the host in the comfortable living room to learn the history of the house, and then discover three tastefully decorated second-floor rooms, each with its own unique charm and decor. These three rooms share two full baths. A full gourmet breakfast, including dessert, is served in the large country dining room. The host will gladly help plan trips in the area, whether guests choose to go to York County, Amish country, Baltimore's inner harbor, or Gettysburg. Resident cat and smoker. $60.

HARFORD

Bed and Breakfast Adventures
Suite 132, 2310 Central Avenue, North Wildwood, NJ 08260
(606) 522-4000; (800) 992-2632

PA715. This country bed and breakfast is named after the settlement of nine pioneers who lived here more than 200 years ago. Its symmetrical floor plan and Colonial facade with nine narrow windows recalls the 18th-century Massachusetts homes those pioneers left behind. There are double, queen-, and twin-size bedrooms, each with a private bath and fireplace. A Continental plus breakfast featuring a hot entree is served daily. Skiing, hiking, cycling, antique shops, and quaint historic exhibits are nearby. $85.

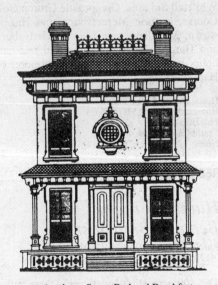

Academy Street Bed and Breakfast

HAWLEY

Academy Street Bed and Breakfast
528 Academy Street, 18428
(717) 226-3430; (201) 316-8148 (winter)

Outstanding historic 1863 Italianate Victorian built by a Civil War hero, the first sheriff of Wayne County. Near the largest and most beautiful recreational lake in the state, with all activities. Convenient to I-84. Lovely furnished inn; full gourmet breakfast and afternoon tea. Air-conditioned rooms. Cable TV. Closed November through April.

Host: Judith Lazan
Rooms: 7 (3 PB; 4 SB) $65-75
Full Breakfast
Credit Cards: A, B
Notes: 7, 9, 10, 11, 12

HERSHEY

Hershey Bed and Breakfast Reservation Service

P.O. Box 208, 17033-0208
(717) 533-2928

1. Lovely home near the Hershey Medical Center. One guest room with a private bath is offered. Choice of full or Continental breakfast is included. Air conditioning. Dog in residence. No smoking allowed. $50.

2. A former Milton Hershey Boys School, this large brick home is convenient to Hershey museums, park, rose gardens, Chocolate World, sports arena and stadium, theater, and outdoor recreations. Twelve guest rooms, one room with private bath, three shared bathrooms on the second level and one on the first floor. Continental breakfast. Resident cat. Handicapped-accessible. Air conditioning. No smoking. Children $5 with parents in same room. Extra adults $10. $59-69.

5. This home near the Hershey Motor Lodge offers three guest rooms with shared bath, plus a new suite with a private bath. A full breakfast is served. Children are welcome. $55-75

Pinehurst Inn Bed and Breakfast

50 Northeast Drive, 17033
(717) 533-2603

Spacious brick home surrounded by lawns. Warm, welcoming, many-windowed living room. Large porch with an old-fashioned porch swing. Within walking distance of all Hershey's attractions: Hershey Museum and Rose Gardens, Hershey Park, Chocolate World, and many golf courses. Less than one hour's drive to Lancaster and Gettysburg. Each room has a queen-size bed and a Hershey Kiss on each pillow.

Hosts: Roger and Phyllis Ingold
Rooms: 15 (1 PB; 13 SB) $45-67
Full Breakfast
Credit Cards: A, B
Notes: 2, 5, 8, 11, 12

HESSTON

Aunt Susie's Country Vacations

Rural Delivery 1, Box 225, 16647
(814) 658-3638

Experience country living in a warm, friendly Victorian parsonage or a renovated country store and post office. All rooms furnished with antiques and oil paintings. Raystown Lake is nearby; boating, swimming, and fishing are within three miles. Bring the family to the country.

Host: John Wilson
Rooms: 8 (2 PB; 6 SB) $50-55
Continental Breakfast
Credit Cards: None
Notes: 2, 5, 8, 9, 10, 11, 12

HOLTWOOD

Bed and Breakfast Adventures

Suite 132, 2310 Central Avenue, North Wildwood, NJ 08260
(606) 522-4000; (800) 992-2632

6 Pets welcome; 8 Children welcome; 9 Social drinking allowed; 10 Tennis available; 11 Swimming available; 12 Golf available; 13 Skiing available; 14 May be booked through travel agents.

PA705. This unique country cottage, all one floor, features two bedrooms: one is entered through the bathroom with shower and has a double bed; the other room is glass-enclosed and has a queen-size bed. Guests have access to a TV and VCR in the living room and a complete kitchen off of the dining room. A Continental breakfast is brought to the cottage each morning. The air-conditioned cottage can hold up to ten people, and is ideal for a family or group traveling together. Couples, children, and pets are welcome. $100.

Carriage Corner

HUMMELSTOWN

The Tea Cozy Bed and Breakfast

213 East Main Street, 17036
(717) 566-9976; (717) 566-1658

Charming bed and breakfast and tearoom, five minutes from Hershey and 30 minutes from Lancaster County. This historic Federal-style home, built in 1829, features rooms decorated with a delightful country decor. Breakfast in the tearoom or outdoor patio. Full breakfast available on Sunday morning. Guest rooms have queen-size beds, paddle fans, and air conditioning. Children welcome. No smoking.

Hosts: Sherry and Bill Aldinger
Rooms: 3 (1 PB; 2 SB) $55-70
Continental Breakfast
Credit Cards: None
Notes: 2, 3, 5, 8

INTERCOURSE (LANCASTER CO.)

Carriage Corner Bed and Breakfast

3705 East Newport Road, P.O. Box 371, 17534-0371
(717) 768-3059

With tasteful, handcrafted touches of folk art, this inn offers a relaxing country atmosphere. A five-minute walk takes visitors to Intercourse, which is a bustling village from yesteryear with Amish buggies converging. The inn overlooks the Stoltzfus Farm and accompanying family restaurant. In town, Kitchen Kettle Village lures all visitors to its unique shops. The surrounding area, in the heart of Amish farmlands, has a myriad of attractions and historic sites. Amish dinners arranged.

Hosts: The Schuit family
Rooms: 4 (2 PB; 2 SB) $55-65
Full Breakfast
Credit Cards: A, B
Notes: 2, 5, 8, 12

JENKINSTOWN

Bed and Breakfast of Philadelphia

1616 Walnut Street, Suite 1120, Philadelphia, 19103
(215) 735-1917; (800) 220-1917
FAX (215) 735-1905

Jenkinstown Victorian. Just off Jenkinstown's main thoroughfare on a quiet street sits this statuesque stone Victorian home. From the large porch, guests walk through double ruby-glass doors into a large foyer with a staircase that ascends all the way to the second-floor bedroom, which has a double bed, recliner/rocker, TV/AM radio, private bath, sitting room with two sofas, comfortable chairs, and reading lamps. Children over six are welcome. No smoking allowed. $40-50.

JIM THORPE

The Harry Packer Mansion

Packer Hill, P.O. Box 458, 18229
(717) 325-8566

This 1874 Second Empire mansion features original appointments and Victorian decor. Completely restored for tours, bed and breakfast, fabulous mystery weekends, and a host of other activities. The adjoining carriage house is decorated in a hunt motif.

Hosts: Bob and Patricia Handwerk
Rooms: 13 (9 PB; 4 SB) $75-110
Full Breakfast
Credit Cards: A, B
Notes: 2, 5, 9, 10, 11, 12, 13

The Harry Packer Mansion

The Inn at Jim Thorpe

4 Broadway, 18229
(717) 325-2599; FAX (717) 325-9145

The Inn at Jim Thorpe rests in a lovely setting in the heart of this historic town. The elegant, restored guest rooms are complete with private baths, remote cable TV, and air conditioning. While in town, take a historic walking tour of Millionaire's Row; shop in 50 quaint shops and galleries; go mountain biking on the Northeast's best trails; raft the turbulent Lehigh River. It's all right outside the door.

Host: David Drury
Rooms: 22 (PB) $65-100
Continental Breakfast
Credit Cards: A, B, C, D, E
Notes: 3, 4, 5, 7 (limited), 8, 11, 12, 13, 14

Victoria Ann's Bed and Breakfast

68 Broadway, 18229
(717) 325-8107

Built in 1860, this Victorian townhouse is a step back in time with the charm of antiques, lace, and elegant chandeliers from days gone by. Close to shops, ski resorts and white-water rafting, the house is in the heart of the historical district and offers spacious rooms, Victorian porches, and garden terraces.

Host: Louise Ogilvie
Rooms: 8 (1 PB; 7 SB) $65-145
Full and Continental Breakfast
Credit Cards: A, B, C
Notes: 2, 5, 9, 11, 12, 13, 14

KENNETT SQUARE

Association of Bed and Breakfasts in Philadelphia, Valley Forge, Brandywine

P.O. Box 562, Valley Forge, 19481-0562
(215) 783-7838; (800) 344-0123

0302. This circa 1704 Chester County solid fieldstone farmhouse sits on 20 acres of rolling farmland. Special amenities include pool, hot tub, and two rooms with a fireplace. The six guest rooms are furnished for guests' comfort and can accommodate up to six people in the suite. There is an array of beds such as a spool bed, rope bed, and crocheted canopied four-poster. A full breakfast is served. Near Valley Forge, Lancaster, Philadelphia, and Wilmington. Small conference meetings, weddings, and rental of entire house welcome (rates upon request). $95-168.50.

6 Pets welcome; 8 Children welcome; 9 Social drinking allowed; 10 Tennis available; 11 Swimming available; 12 Golf available; 13 Skiing available; 14 May be booked through travel agents.

2001. A full suite with private entrance adjoins this brick ranch home in the Brandywine Valley. Queen-size bedroom, TV, private bath, kitchen, and private entrance are surrounded by magnificent landscaping. The deck and grill are also available. In the main house, hosts offer a twin bedroom with private bath. A full, hot, and hearty breakfast. Winterthur, Longwood Gardens, Brandywine River Museum, Kennett Square, and Wilmington within minutes. Central air conditioning.

Bed and Breakfast of Chester County: A Reservation Service

P.O. Box 825, 19348
(610) 444-1367

This reservation service offers fine accommodations in the Brandywine Valley, an area that includes Pennsylvania and northern Delaware. Local attractions include Longwood Gardens, Winterthur, Brandywine River Museum of Chadd's Ford, Hagley Museum, Nemours, Valley Forge, Pennsylvania Dutch country, and the sights of Philadelphia and Wilmington, Delaware.

Owner: James R. Buckler
40 guest homes (85% PB; 15% SB) $45 and up
Continental and Full Breakfast
Notes: 2, 5, 7, 8, 9, 10, 11, 12

Bed and Breakfast at Walnut Hill

541 Chandler's Mill Road, Avondale, 19311
(610) 444-3703

This 1840 antique-filled mill house with warm country charm is on a crooked country road facing a horse-filled meadow and stream. Walnut Hill is only minutes from Longwood Gardens, Winterthur, and the Brandywine River Museum. The hosts enjoy discussing local lore, mapping out tours and points of interest, and making reservations. A gourmet country breakfast

will start guests on their way. Guests may enjoy the hot tub for relaxing moments. Canoeing nearby. Guests say they came as strangers, left as friends.

Hosts: Tom and Sandy Mills
Rooms: 2 (SB) $80
Full Breakfast
Credit Cards: None
Notes: 2, 5, 7, 8, 9, 10, 11, 12, 14

The Flower Farm

453 Bayard Road, 19348
(610) 444-5659; (800) 422-6320

The host of this 1828 stone farmhouse was the founding director of horticulture for the Smithsonian Institution, Washington, D.C., and is always willing to share his experiences from his worldwide travels with his guests. The house is filled with beautiful antiques and decorative arts collected all over the world. Guests are able to enjoy eight acres of terraced lawns and gardens and savor afternoon tea with homemade cakes, cookies, and pies as well as a complete country breakfast each morning. Several bedrooms are complete with working fireplaces. The Flower Farm was featured on national public television in 1994 as "Flower Beds and Breakfast" and is only minutes from renowned Longwood Gardens, Winterthur Museum and Gardens, the Brandywine River Museum, and many other attractions the Brandywine Valley has to offer.

Host: James R. Buckler
Rooms: 4(3PB) $75-$125
Cottage: (PB) $150-$250.
Full Breakfast
Credit Cards: A, B, C, D
Notes: 2, 4, 5, 6 (cottage only), 7 (limited), 8, 9, 14

Meadow Spring Farm

201 East Street Road, 19348
(215) 444-3903

The hosts of this 1836 farmhouse on a working farm with animals invite guests to participate in gathering eggs for breakfast.

NOTES: Credit cards accepted: A MasterCard; B Visa; C American Express; D Discover Card; E Diner's Club; F Other; 2 Personal checks accepted; 3 Lunch available; 4 Dinner available; 5 Open all year;

The house is filled with family antiques, Amish quilts, fine linens, and a doll collection, including Santas and cows. The hosts will prepare a gourmet breakfast for guests before they start their day touring the area. Guests are welcome to enjoy the pool, hot tub, game room, and solarium. This bed and breakfast has been featured in *Country Inns, New York Times*, and the Washington's Channel 7 television.

Hosts: Anne Hicks and Debbie Axelrod
Rooms: 7 (5 PB; 2 SB) $55-75
Full Breakfast
Credit Cards: None
Notes: 2, 5, 7, 8, 9, 10, 11, 12, 14

KIMBERTON

Bed and Breakfast of Valley Forge

P.O. Box 562, Valley Forge, 19481-0562
(215) 783-7838; (800) 344-0123

0705. Guests are invited to walk, pat the horses, or sit on the veranda and enjoy the view at this circa 1780 eight-acre farm. There is a private-entrance guest cottage that has a full kitchen, fireplace, bedroom, and bath. Fresh pastries are left in the kitchen along with fruit, juice, and coffee. Have a leisurely morning and a late breakfast. $100.

KING OF PRUSSIA

Bed and Breakfast of Valley Forge

P.O. Box 562, Valley Forge, 19481-0562
(215) 783-7838; (800) 344-0123

Tranquil Haven. This home is set in a peaceful, heavily wooded neighborhood and is decorated with both antique and modern furnishings. Sitting room with fireplace and color cable TV, laundry facilities, and in-ground pool. Gourmet breakfasts are served in the dining room or on the spacious screened porch overlooking the garden. Some French spoken. Two cats in residence. Three guest rooms with private baths. $45-60.

The Bucksville House

KINTNERSVILLE

The Bucksville House

Route 412 and Buck Drive
4501 Durham Road, 18930-1610
(610) 847-8948

Country charm and a friendly atmosphere await guests at this 1795 Bucks County registered historic landmark. Offering beautifully decorated rooms with many quilts, baskets, antiques, and handmade reproductions. Enjoy the seven fireplaces, air conditioning, gazebo, pond, herb garden, and brick courtyard. Near New Hope, Peddler's Village, and Nockamixon State Park.

Hosts: Barbara and Joe Szollosi
Rooms: 5 (PB) $95-130
Full Breakfast
Credit Cards: A, B, C, D
Notes: 2, 5, 9, 10, 11

6 Pets welcome; 8 Children welcome; 9 Social drinking allowed; 10 Tennis available; 11 Swimming available; 12 Golf available; 13 Skiing available; 14 May be booked through travel agents.

KINZERS

Sycamore Haven Farm
35 South Kinzer Road, 17535
(717) 442-4901

This dairy farm is 15 miles east of Lancaster, right in Pennsylvania Dutch country. The rooms are newly papered and painted, and there is a porch in the back of the house with a lovely swing. There is also a balcony with lounge chairs. Forty dairy cows are milked morning and evening. The children will really enjoy the numerous kittens, who like a lot of attention, and the lawn.

Hosts: Charles and Janet Groff
Rooms: 3 (SB) $30
Continental Breakfast
Credit Cards: None
Notes: 2, 5, 6, 8, 10, 11

KUTZTOWN

Around the World Bed and Breakfast
30 South Whiteoak Street, 18066
(610) 683-8885; FAX (610) 298-8414

This is a truly unique bed and breakfast decorated with artifacts from various regions of the world. There are two spacious private rooms and two lovely suites; all have their own private baths, luxurious queen-size beds, and are fully air-conditioned. A delicious country-style breakfast is served daily. Guests will find the conveniences of a hotel with the personality, comfort, and ambience of visiting an old friend. Fifteen minutes from Reading, Pennsylvania, the outlet shopping capital of the world.

Host: Jean F. Billig
Rooms: 2 (PB) $55-124
Suites: 2 (PB)
Full Breakfast
Credit Cards: A, B, D
Notes: 2, 5, 10, 11, 12, 13, 14

LACKAWAXEN

Roebling Inn on the Delaware

Roebling Inn on the Delaware
Scenic Drive, P.O. Box 31, 18435
(717) 685-7900

Featured in *New York* magazine, this classic inn is on the majestic upper Delaware River. With surrounding mountains, this is a great place to unwind. Old World charm plus private baths, TV, air conditioning, and queen-size beds. Walk to canoeing, hiking, rafting, fishing, tennis, historic sites. Five miles to skiing. Midweek specials. Minimum stay holidays is two or three nights. Closed Christmas.

Hosts: Donald and JoAnn Jahn
Rooms: 5 (PB) $49-95
Full Breakfast
Credit Cards: A, B, C
Notes: 2, 5, 7 (restricted), 8, 9, 10, 11, 12, 13, 14

LANCASTER

Bed and Breakfast: The Manor Inn
830 Village Road, Route 741,
   P.O. Box 416, Lampeter, 17537
(717) 464-9564

This cozy farmhouse is just minutes away from historic sights and attractions. Guests delight in Mary Lou's delicious breakfasts, featuring gourmet treats such as eggs Mornay, crepes or strata, apple cobbler, and homemade jams and breads. A swim in the pool or a nap under one of the many shade

NOTES: Credit cards accepted: A MasterCard; B Visa; C American Express; D Discover Card; E Diner's Club; F Other; 2 Personal checks accepted; 3 Lunch available; 4 Dinner available; 5 Open all year;

trees is the perfect way to cap a day of touring. Amish dinners can be arranged. Groups welcome.

Hosts: Mary Lou Paolini and Jackie Curtis
Rooms: 6 (4 PB; 2 SB) $75-99
Full Breakfast
Credit Cards: A, B
Notes: 2, 3, 4, 5, 8, 10, 11, 12

Bed and Breakfast of Philadelphia

1616 Walnut Street, Suite 1120, Philadelphia, 19103
(215) 735-1917; (800) 220-1917
FAX (215) 735-1905

John Hayes House. The John Hayes House is a working dairy farm surrounded by Amish farms. The house was built from bricks used as ballast in ships arriving from England in the late 1700s. There are three large comfortable bedrooms on the second floor that share a bath. All bedrooms are air-conditioned and a color TV is available. Breakfast is served in the sunny, antique-filled dining room only steps away from a genuine country kitchen with a lovely fireplace. Being a working farm, there are plenty of cows, cats, and dogs; only 20 minutes from Amish country, 25 minutes from Brandywine River area, and horseback riding with advance notice. No pets. Children over 12 welcome. Smoking outside only. $50-60.

Mennonite Farm. This is a simple, cozy farm owned by two remarkable, likable people who go out of their way to make their guests at home. Hannah's farm breakfasts are enormous, and what guests say about their visit here indicate that it is a very special place. Two second-floor guest rooms, one of which has a double bed and the other a twin bed, share a bath with a tub and shower. Children welcome. No smoking. $40-50. $5 additional charge for pets.

Sunny Acres. This country home is in a peaceful setting surrounded by Amish farms. A comfortable ranch house with a large sunroom to enjoy a full breakfast. There are two guest rooms on the ground level that share a bath. The location is ideal for touring Pennsylvania Dutch country, 20 minutes from Lancaster, and 12 minutes from Longwood Gardens and Winterthur. A special attraction for golf enthusiasts is the 18-hole golf course at Moccasin Run only a mile away. $45-55.

The Columbian

360 Chestnut Street, 17512
(717) 684-5869; (800) 422-5869 Reservations

This restored turn-of-the-century mansion is a splendid example of Colonial Revival architecture, complete with unique wrap-around sun porches, ornate stained-glass window, and magnificent tiered staircase. Decorated with antiques in Victorian and country style, large air-conditioned rooms offer queen-size beds and private baths. The hearty country breakfast consists of a variety of fresh fruit, hot main dishes, and homemade breads.

Hosts: Becky and Chris Will
Rooms: 6 (PB) $70-85
Full Breakfast
Credit Cards: A, B
Notes: 2, 5, 8, 9, 10, 11, 12, 13

Gardens of Eden Bed and Breakfast

1894 Eden Road, 17601
(717) 393-5179

Victorian iron master's home built circa 1860 on the banks of the Conestoga River is three miles northeast of Lancaster. Antiques and family collections of quilts and coverlets fill the four guest rooms, two with private bath. The adjoining guest cottage (restored summer kitchen) features a walk-in fireplace, bedroom, and bath on second floor. Marilyn's floral designs and friends' crafts are for sale. The three acres of gardens feature herbs, perennials, and wildflowers among the woodsy trails. Local attractions are personalized by a tour guide service and dinner in a young Amish couple's home. Canoe and rowboat available. Two bike trails pass the house.

Hosts: Marilyn and Bill Ebel
Rooms: 4 (2 PB; 2 SB) $65-110
Full Breakfast
Credit Cards: A, B, C (guaranty)
Notes: 2, 5, 10, 11, 12

Guesthouses, Inc.

P.O. Box 2137, West Chester, 19380
(215) 692-4575

151. In the quiet historic district of town and on the walking tour, this historic house-in-town raises its three-story brick face before a town park and hides a delightful small walled garden in back. The entire house is elegantly yet whimsically furnished, decorated, and designed. There is a new garden room where it is especially pleasant to dine in the morning. The guest room with private hall bath on the second floor is furnished in antiques of the 1800s period. $80-130.

Hershey Bed and Breakfast Reservation Service

P.O. Box 208, Hershey, 17033-0208
(717) 533-2928

1. Country farmhouse, circa 1817, on a working dairy farm near Hershey, Lancaster, and Harrisburg at Exit 20. Two guest rooms with shared bath, plus a cottage that sleeps four with private bath. Full breakfast. No smoking. $55.

2. Farmhouse inn, circa 1738, nestled on 12 acres of farmland in Lancaster County. Just off Route 283 between Lancaster and Harrisburg. Three guest rooms with private or shared bath. Continental breakfast. Resident cat. No smoking. $75-95.

3. Historic Civil War brick house near Routes 30 and 501. Seven guest rooms, including family suites, with private or shared bath. Continental breakfast. No smoking. $75-85; $95 for family of four with private bath.

Hollinger House

Hollinger House Bed and Breakfast

2336 Hollinger Road, 17602-4728
(717) 464-3050

Natural, friendly, romantic, comfortable—Hollinger House. A three-story Adams period brick home built in 1870 on more than five and one half acres with woodland stream and grazing sheep. Original hardwood floors, fireplaces, high ceilings, and large wraparound porch. The rooms have king- or queen-size beds, private baths, and air conditioning. Welcoming snacks are served. Minutes from downtown Lancaster, shopping outlets, historic attractions, farmers' markets, and Amish country.

Hosts: Gina and Jeff Trost
Rooms: 7 (5 PB; 2 SB) $85-95
Full Breakfast
Credit Cards: A, B, D
Notes: 2, 3, 4, 5, 8 (over 12), 9, 10, 11, 12

Homestead Lodging

184 East Brook Road, Smoketown, 17576
(717) 393-6927

Come to this beautiful Lancaster County setting, where guests hear the clippity-clop of Amish buggies going by and can experi-

---

NOTES: Credit cards accepted: A MasterCard; B Visa; C American Express; D Discover Card; E Diner's Club; F Other; 2 Personal checks accepted; 3 Lunch available; 4 Dinner available; 5 Open all year;

ence the sights and freshness of the farm-lands. The clean country rooms provide a homey atmosphere, and an Amish farm is adjacent to the property. There is a large grassy area and a creek to enjoy. Within walking distance of restaurants and within minutes of farmers' markets, quilts, an-tiques and craft shops, outlets, auctions, and museums.

Hosts: Robert and Lori Kepiro
Rooms: 5 (PB) $33-56
Continental Breakfast
Credit Cards: A, B
Notes: 2, 5, 7, 8, 9, 10, 11, 12

The King's Cottage, A Bed and Breakfast Inn

1049 East King Street, 17602
(800) 747-8717

Traditionally styled elegance, modern com-fort, and warm hospitality in Amish coun-try. King and queen-size beds, gourmet breakfasts, and personal service create a friendly atmosphere at this award-winning Spanish-style mansion. Relax by the fire and enjoy afternoon tea in the library while chatting with innkeepers about directions to restaurants and attractions. Special Amish dinners or personal tours arranged. Near farmers' markets, Gettysburg, and Hershey. Listed on the National Register of Historic Places. AAA- and Mobil-listed excellent.

Hosts: Karen and Jim Owens
Rooms: 8 (PB) $80-135
Full Breakfast
Credit Cards: A, B, D
Notes: 2, 5, 9, 10, 11, 12, 14

Lincoln Haus Inn Bed and Breakfast

1687 Lincoln Highway East, 17602
(717) 392-9412

A suburban home, built in 1915, with dis-tinctive hip roofs in Lancaster County. Front porch for sitting and double lawn swings for relaxing. Inside are natural oak woodwork and gleaming hardwood floors. Antique fur-

niture and rugs are throughout the house. Mary, a member of the Old Order Amish church, serves a full breakfast family-style in her shining, homey dining room. Her spe-cialty is to be a great hostess.

Host: Mary K. Zook
Rooms: 5 (PB) $48-75
Apartment: (PB)
Full Breakfast
Credit Cards: None
Notes: 2, 4 (with prior notice), 5, 8, 10, 11, 12, 14

Meadowview Guest House

2169 New Holland Pike, Route 23, 17601
(717) 299-4017

In the heart of the Pennsylvania Dutch area, close to historic sites, antiques, farmers' and flea markets, and excellent restaurants. Large air-conditioned rooms, and guest kitchen with coffee and tea. To help guests enjoy the beautiful county, personalized maps are provided.

Hosts: Ed and Sheila Christie
Rooms: 3 (1 PB; 2 SB) $30-50
Continental Breakfast
Credit Cards: None
Notes: 2, 5, 8 (over 6), 9, 10, 11, 12

Patchwork Inn

Patchwork Inn

2319 Old Philadelphia Pike, 17602
(717) 293-9078; (800) 584-5776

Patchwork Inn is a 19th-century farmhouse furnished throughout with antique oak. The inn is decorated with more than 70 new and

---

6 Pets welcome; 8 Children welcome; 9 Social drinking allowed; 10 Tennis available; 11 Swimming available; 12 Golf available; 13 Skiing available; 14 May be booked through travel agents.

antique quilts from all parts of the USA. The queen-size beds are covered with handmade quilts, and other private collections include 25 old telephones and an extensive Delft china collection. Reading material abounds, and bike storage and routes are available. Patchwork Inn is east of Lancaster, across the street from a working Amish farm.

Hosts: Lee and Anne Martin
Rooms: 4 (2 PB; 2 SB) $60-80
Full Breakfast
Credit Cards: A, B, D
Notes: 2, 5, 9

The Walkabout Inn

837 Village Road, Lampeter, 17537
(717) 464-0707

The Walkabout Inn is an authentic Australian-style bed and breakfast in the heart of Amish country, convenient to all major attractions. The house is a 22-room brick 1925 Mennonite farmhouse with wraparound porches. Australian-born Richard and his wife, Maggie, serve a full five-course candlelight breakfast. Guest rooms have private baths, canopied and/or queen-size beds, antiques, and cable TV, fireplaces and Jacuzzis. Ask about the $99 mid-week specials, which include an Amish dinner and tour. Anniversary and honeymoon specials available. Inn is AAA-rated three diamonds.

Hosts: Richard and Margaret Mason
Rooms: 5 (PB) $79-99
Suites: 2 (PB) $149
Full Breakfast
Credit Cards: A, B, C
Notes: 2, 4, 5, 8 (over 9), 9, 10, 11, 12, 14

Witmer's Tavern— Historic 1725 Inn

2014 Old Philadelphia Pike, 17602
(717) 299-5305

Lancaster's only pre-Revolutionary War inn still lodging travelers. Restored to the simple, authentic, pioneer style that was familiar to European immigrants who joined the Conestoga wagon trains being provisioned at the inn for the western and southern treks into the wilderness areas. Fresh flowers, working fireplaces, antique quilts, and antiques in all the romantic rooms. Pandora's Antique Shop is on the premises. Bird-in-Hand and Intercourse villages, other antique shops, and auctions just beyond. Valley Forge, Hershey, Gettysburg, Winterthur, Chadds Ford, and New Hope, all within a 90-minute drive. On the National Register of Historic Places and a national landmark.

Host: Brant Hartung
Rooms: 7 (2 PB; 5 SB) $60-90
Continental Breakfast
Credit Cards: None
Notes: 2, 5, 7, 8, 9, 10, 11, 12, 13, 14

Witmer's Tavern

Ye Olde Bank Bed and Breakfast

29 North Prince Street, 17603
(717) 393-7774

In the heart of downtown Lancaster within walking distance of the Farmers' Market, the Fulton Theatre, and a variety of shops and restaurants. Enjoy the delightful Continental plus breakfast, downy robes, and relaxing in a private bath.

Host: Nina Balgar
Rooms: 2 (PB) $75-105
Continental Breakfast
Credit Cards: None
Notes: 2, 5, 8, 9 12, 13, 14

NOTES: Credit cards accepted: A MasterCard; B Visa; C American Express; D Discover Card; E Diner's Club; F Other; 2 Personal checks accepted; 3 Lunch available; 4 Dinner available; 5 Open all year;

Bed and Breakfast of Valley Forge

P.O. Box 562, Valley Forge, 19481-0562
(215) 783-7838; (800) 344-0123

0303. A circa 1735 inn in the heart of Pennsylvania Dutch country. An intimate inn for all seasons. Historic, affordable, and highly recommended. The inn is a splendid fieldstone mansion overlooking picture-postcard fields and farms, and just minutes from all the attractions of Lancaster County. The inn features a full complimentary breakfast, lovely Victorian parlors, nine elegant but cozy bedrooms, six private and two shared baths, queen-size and single beds, air conditioning, TV, carriage rides, barbecues, mystery weekends, dinner at an Amish home, and special holiday packages. $54-140.

0704. A restored 1845 country home, surrounded by farmland and in the rolling hills of Pennsylvania, that combines Old-World charms with all modern conveniences. Guest rooms are beautifully appointed in a setting that includes genuine friendliness and hospitality. A full country breakfast is a delightful repast, including home-baked breads, rolls, and muffins. Breakfast is served in the cheerful dining room or on the front porch. Maps for bike tours are available. $60-100.

1307. This bed and breakfast was completed in 1919. The focal point is an elaborate leaded-glass doorway. The bed and breakfast has been kept in its original state throughout and has been furnished and decorated with antiques, Amish quilts, and crafts. $60.

LANDENBERG

Cornerstone Bed and Breakfast

Rural Delivery 1, Box 155, 19350
(215) 274-2143

To understand history is to live it. Charming 18th-century country inn with canopied beds, fireplaces in bedrooms, private baths, and antiques galore. Just minutes from Brandywine Valley museums and gardens: Longwood, Winterthur, and Hagley.

Hosts: Linda and Marty
Rooms: 5 (PB) $85-125
Full Breakfast
Credit Cards: A, B, C
Notes: 2, 5, 8, 9, 11, 12

LEOLA

Turtle Hill Road Bed and Breakfast

111 Turtle Hill Road, 17540
(717) 656-6163

Split-level home one mile off routes 272 and 222, between Ephrata and Lancaster in Lancaster County. Rural area, overlooks the Conestoga River, near an old mill and waterfall. Very scenic, quiet, and peaceful. A photographer's paradise!

Host: Jean W. Parmer
Rooms: 2 (SB) $50
Full Breakfast
Credit Cards: None
Notes: 2, 8, 10, 11, 12

LEWISBURG

Blue Ridge Bed and Breakfast

Route 2, Box 3895, 22611
(703) 955-1246; (800) 296-1246

Beautifully restored German stone home of the Federal period built in 1810. Thirty-three acres of rolling countryside in the tranquil Susquehanna Valley. Five bedrooms, all with private baths. Walking and cross-country skiing on premises; golfing and all water sports arranged by owners. Dinner is available by prior reservation. $65-75.

LIMA

Amanda's Bed and Breakfast

1428 Park Avenue, Annapolis, MD 21217
(301) 225-0001; (301) 383-1274

279. This bed and breakfast is a large 19th-century country manor house. Built in 1856, it has been on the National Register of Historic Places since 1971. More than three-fourths of the land is covered with luxuriant growth. Eight guest rooms, all with private baths, are available. $85-125.

Alden House

LITITZ

Alden House

62 East Main Street, 17543
(717) 627-3363; (800) 584-0753

Fully restored 1850 brick Victorian in the heart of the town's historic district. All local attractions are within walking distance. Relax at the end of the day on one of three spacious porches and watch Amish buggies or experience a whiff of fresh chocolate from the local candy factory. Home of the nation's oldest pretzel bakery. Family suites, off-street parking, and bicycle storage available. Antiques abound in this area as well as local handmade quilts. Enjoy old-fashioned hospitality.

Host: Fletcher and Joy Coleman
Rooms: 6 (PB) $65-100
Full Breakfast
Credit Cards: A, B
Notes: 2, 5, 8 (over 6), 9, 12, 14

Swiss Woods Bed and Breakfast

500 Blantz Road, 17543
(717) 627-3358; (800) 594-8018

Surrounded by meadows and colorful gardens, Swiss Woods, where the atmosphere is reminiscent of Switzerland, is a quiet retreat in Lancaster's Amish country. Visit local farmers' markets, bike through beautiful farmland, or ride the roller coaster at Hershey Park. All rooms feature patios or balconies. Wake up to the smell of the hosts' own blend of freshly brewed coffee. Breakfast is a highlight, receiving rave reviews from all. German spoken.

Hosts: Werner and Debrah Mosimann
Rooms: 7 (PB) $75-130
Full Breakfast
Credit Cards: A, B, D
Notes: 2, 5, 11, 12, 14

LONGWOOD

Guesthouses, Inc.

P.O. Box 2137, West Chester, 19380
(215) 692-4575

721. The guest entrance into the lofty guest living room with fieldstone fireplace is by way of a flagstone terrace enclosed by a screened porch. There are two bedrooms; one with full-size double bed, the other with twin beds, opposite a bath for both rooms.

NOTES: Credit cards accepted: A MasterCard; B Visa; C American Express; D Discover Card; E Diner's Club; F Other; 2 Personal checks accepted; 3 Lunch available; 4 Dinner available; 5 Open all year;

At the end of the great room is a kitchenette where guests may store cold drinks and such. A full country breakfast is served. $75-150.

MACUNGIE

Sycamore Inn
Bed and Breakfast

165 East Main Street, Route 100, 18062
(215) 966-5177

Kick-off-shoes comfort, hearty breakfast, personable hosts, and plenty of hospitality is what guests will find at this bed and breakfast. Look for a circa 1835 stone farmhouse with two houses in one. The quiet back house is the very cozy inn. Offering guest rooms furnished by antique theme, common room with walk-in fireplace, and enclosed porch surrounded by windows. There is also a "live in" antique shop for guests' enjoyment. Easy to find; lots to do.

Hosts: Mark and Randie Levisky
Rooms: 5 (3 PB; 2 SB) $70-80
Full Breakfast
Credit Cards: A, B
Notes: 2, 5, 7 (limited), 8 (over 12), 9, 10, 11, 12, 13

MAIN LINE

Guesthouses, Inc.

P.O. Box 2137, West Chester, 19380
(215) 692-4575

505. The house has been built entirely within a grand old bank barn. The guest floor is on the level of the main entrance and consists of a large open hall with entrance doors to the guest rooms. The suite consists of an oversized bedroom with sitting area and bar, furnished with antiques and a king-size or twin beds, and attached private bath. The other two guest rooms each have attached private baths, are generously furnished with creature comforts, and have queen- and king-size or twin beds. The guest level has its own elegant living room, complete with concert grand. A full country breakfast is served downstairs by candlelight in the large formal dining room. Fully air-conditioned. $90-95.

MALVERN

Bed and Breakfast
of Valley Forge

P.O. Box 562, Valley Forge, 19481-0562
(215) 783-7838; (800) 344-0123

Eaglesmere. This 21-sided contemporary home is nestled on a wooded cul-de-sac. It boasts three cathedral ceilings, exposed beams, and walls of windows overlooking Great Valley and Valley Forge Mountain. A gourmet breakfast is served in the dining room or on one of four decks. The enormous lower level contains the guest quarters. Preheated beds, bath gels, bathroom toe warmers, and thick terry-cloth robes are provided for guests' pleasure. Two guest rooms with private bath. $75.

Pickering Bend Bed and Breakfast. Bank house, circa 1790, offers the most bucolic atmosphere in Valley Forge country. This bed and breakfast is in the historic village of Charlestown; about six miles from the Valley Forge National Historic Park. Guests are invited to walk the grounds and enjoy the gazebo. The private entrance guest suite consists of patio, two bedrooms—one single bed and one queen-size bed—full kitchen, private bath, and bar area. The guest's quarters have a phone,

6 Pets welcome; 8 Children welcome; 9 Social drinking allowed; 10 Tennis available; 11 Swimming available; 12 Golf available; 13 Skiing available; 14 May be booked through travel agents.

A/C, color TV, VCR, fireplace, sofa and desk. Breakfast foods are self serve and provided in the guest's kitchen. Decor is country comfortable. $85-$100.

The Great Valley House of Valley Forge

110 Swedesford Road, Rural Delivery 3, 19355
(215) 644-6759

This historic 1690 stone farmhouse has rooms filled with antiques and lovely hand-stenciled walls. On four acres with swimming pool and walking trails for guests, this old farmhouse is ideal for a quiet getaway. A full breakfast is served in the pre-Revolutionary kitchen in front of a 14-foot walk-in fireplace. Just a short drive from Philadelphia, Lancaster, and Brandywine Valley. The Great Valley House has been featured in the *Philadelphia Inquirer* and the *Washington Post.*

Rooms: 3 (2 PB; 1 SB) $70-85
Full Breakfast
Credit Cards: None
Notes: 2, 3, 5, 7, 8, 9, 11, 14

Guesthouses, Inc.

P.O. Box 2137, West Chester, 19380
(215) 692-4575

198. A historic Sugartown, scene of the Radnor Hunt, this present-day stone house, next to fields that are home to deer and foxes, offers a very comfortable guest arrangement with a first-floor small private hall to the sunny corner guest room with king-size or twin beds, study area, and bath. The house has central air-conditioning. $70.

MANHEIM

Herr Farmhouse Inn

2256 Huber Drive, 17545
(717) 653-9852

Lancaster County Pennsylvania (Amish). Completely restored 1750 stone plantation home on eleven and one-half scenic acres. Inn includes all original woodwork, flooring, and cabinets. Take a step into yesteryear amidst antiques and reproductions of Colonial furnishings. The farm is intact with all outbuildings but is nonworking with the exception of one piece of livestock, a house cat named Clyde. Enjoy the six working fireplaces as well as Amish dining and other fine restaurants, indoor bicycle storage, central air, antiques, and historic attractions nearby. A Continental plus breakfast is served.

Host: Barry A. Herr
Rooms: 4 (2 PB; 2 SB) $70-95
Suite: $75-100
Continental Breakfast
Credit Cards: A, B
Notes: 2, 5, 7 (limited), 8 (over 12), 9, 10, 11, 12

Herr Farmhouse Inn

Stone Haus Farm

360 South Esbenshade Road, 17545
(717) 653-5819

In the country, this cozy bed and breakfast offers a relaxing environment for guests. Close to Lancaster Amish country, Hershey, Gettysburg, and a popular Mennonite restaurant. Guests are welcome to join hosts during their Mennonite church services. The hostess makes quilts and wall hangings.

Hosts: Henry and Irene Shenk
Rooms: 6 (SB) $29-40
Full Breakfast
Credit Cards: None
Notes: 2, 5, 8, 10

MARIETTA

The River Inn

258 West Front Street, 17547
(717) 426-2290

Restored home, circa 1790, in National Historic District of Marietta. Along Susquehanna River, near Lancaster, York, and Hershey attractions. Decorated with antiques and reproductions, this home offers three cozy guest rooms. When weather permits, breakfast is served on the screened porch. In the winter, warm the body with the six fireplaces throughout the home. Enjoy the herb and flower gardens. Owner can provide guided boat fishing on river. Air conditioning; cable TV.

Hosts: Joyce and Bob Heiserman
Rooms: 3 (PB) $60-70
Full Breakfast
Credit Cards: A, B, D, E
Notes: 2, 5, 9, 14

Vogt Farm Bed and Breakfast

1225 Colebrook Road, 17547
(717) 653-4810; (800) 854-0399

Vogt Farm guests are treated like friends by the hosts of this bed and breakfast. The guest rooms are decorated with antiques and other family treasures. Guests are welcome to enjoy the fireplace in the family room, cozy porches, and air conditioning. Breakfast is served at 8:30 A.M. weekdays, and 8:00 A.M. on Sunday in the large farm kitchen. Air-conditioned, spacious yard, three porches, and animals. Terry-cloth robes.

Rooms: 3 (SB) $55
Full Breakfast
Credit Cards: A, B, C, D
Notes: 2, 5, 8, 10, 12

McCONNELLSBURG

Market Street Inn

131 West Market Street, 17233
(717) 485-5495

In the green mountains 90 miles north of Washington, D.C., Market Street Inn offers canopied beds, toasty rooms, and private baths in a quiet McConnellsburg Historic District neighborhood. Gourmet breakfasts feature Burnt Cabins Grist Mill pancakes, locally smoked sausages, and seasonally stirred apple butter. Weekend antique and estate sales common. Minutes from Whitetail Ski Resort, Cowans Gap State Park (lake swimming and picnicking), Buchanan State Forest (mountain biking, cross-country skiing, and hiking), dinner theater, and great fishing holes. Inquire about the 1995 Victorian Christmas dinners. Air-conditioned. Close to I-70 and I-81, and Exit 13 of the Pennsylvania Turnpike.

Hosts: Margaret and Timothy Taylor
Rooms: 3 (PB) $55
Full Breakfast
Credit Cards: A, B
Notes: 2, 5, 8, 9, 10, 11, 12, 13, 14

MERTZTOWN

Longswamp Bed and Breakfast

Rural Delivery 2, Box 26, 19539
(215) 682-6197

This 200-year-old home, furnished with antiques and every comfort, is set in gorgeous countryside, yet is close to Reading, Kutztown, Allentown, and Amish country. Delicious, bountiful breakfasts draw raves from guests.

Hosts: Elsa and Dean Dimick
Rooms: 10 (6 PB; 4 SB) $63-79.50
Full Breakfast
Credit Cards: A, B
Notes: 2, 5, 8, 9, 10, 11, 12, 13

6 Pets welcome; 8 Children welcome; 9 Social drinking allowed; 10 Tennis available; 11 Swimming available; 12 Golf available; 13 Skiing available; 14 May be booked through travel agents.

MIDDLETOWN

Hershey Bed and Breakfast Reservation Service

P.O. Box 208, Hershey, 17033-0208
(717) 533-2928

Gracious home set on nine acres of land with a deck facing the woods. Ten minutes from Hershey Park and local attractions. Two guest bedrooms with shared bath. Full breakfast. No smoking. $50.

MILFORD

Black Walnut Bed and Breakfast Inn

Rural Delivery 2, Box 9285, 18337
(717) 296-6322

Tudor-style stone house with historic marble fireplace and 12 charming guest rooms plus one suite with antiques and brass beds. A 160-acre estate, it is quiet and peaceful and convenient to horseback riding, antiquing, golf, skiing, rafting, and canoeing on the Delaware River. Serving the finest cuisine and cocktails in a beautiful country setting overlooking a five-acre lake just outside of Milford.

Hosts: Robert Bateman and Cheryl Anderson
Rooms: 12 (8 PB; 4 SB) $60-150
Full Breakfast
Credit Cards: A, B, C
Notes: 2, 4, 5, 9, 11, 12, 13

Cliff Park Inn and Golf Course

Rural Route 4, Box 7200, 18337-9708
(717) 296-6491; (800) 225-6535 (out of state)

Historic country inn surrounded by long-established golf course with cliffs overlooking the Delaware River. Inn and restaurant rated three stars by Mobil. Fine dining. Rooms with fireplaces available. Modified American Plan or bed and breakfast plan available. Golf

Cliff Park Inn

school. Inn/golf packages. Cross-country skiing in winter. Golf and ski equipment rentals. Conferences. Country weddings. Ninety minutes from New York City. Brochures by FAX.

Hosts: The Buchanan family
Rooms: 18 (PB) $85-155
Full Breakfast
Credit Cards: A, B, C, D, E
Notes: 2, 3, 4, 5, 7, 8, 9, 11, 12, 13, 14

MILLERSBURG

Victorian Manor Inn

312 Market Street, 17061
(717) 692-3511

Victorian Manor Inn is on Route 147 between Harrisburg and Sunbury, one block from the picturesque Susquehanna River and historic Millersburg Ferry. The elegantly restored Second Empire home is furnished with period antiques and collectibles. Enjoy wicker-filled porches, gazebo, and courtyard, or relax in the spacious parlor. Whether visiting during the holiday season amid the exquisite Christmas decorations or in the summer with the quaint gardens in bloom, breakfast is always a treat.

Hosts: Skip and Sue Wingard
Rooms: 3 (1 PB; 2 SB) $ 50-75
Full Breakfast
Credit Cards: A, B, C
Notes: 2, 5, 9, 10, 11, 12

NOTES: Credit cards accepted: A MasterCard; B Visa; C American Express; D Discover Card; E Diner's Club; F Other; 2 Personal checks accepted; 3 Lunch available; 4 Dinner available; 5 Open all year;

MONTGOMERY COUNTY

Bed and Breakfast of Philadelphia

1616 Walnut Street, Suite 1120, Philadelphia, 19103
(215) 735-1917; (800) 220-1917
FAX (215) 735-1905

Blue Bell Artist's Roots. Stately brick posts guard the driveway of this solid, turn-of-the-century home. Inside guests will find a cozy, clean, country atmosphere. The hostess invites guests to share this hospitality, comfortable home, and, in the summer, the swimming pool and spacious grounds. One guest room is on the second floor and offers twin beds and a private bath. Children are welcome. Smoking is allowed. $30-40.

Shirl's Shed. Tucked away in a corner of this large, forest-rimmed back lawn of a comfortable suburban home is a small cottage with an attached greenhouse. The room includes a queen-size bed and private bath that is a greenhouse, walled and curtained with white boards and ruffled green calico for privacy, but open to the sun and moon and treetop vistas. Firewood is provided for the stove, and a generous breakfast basket filled with a Continental assortment is left at guests' doorstep to enjoy at leisure. Children welcome. Smoking allowed. $85.

MONTOURSVILLE

The Carriage House at Stonegate

Rural Delivery 1, Box 11 A, 17754
(717) 433-4340

Nestled in the lower Loyalsock Creek Valley on one of the oldest farms in the valley, the Carriage House offers its guests a unique concept in the bed and breakfast world. President Herbert Hoover was a descendant of the original settlers of the farm.

The converted carriage house provides visitors with total privacy and 1,400-square feet of space on two floors. The Carriage House is furnished in antiques and period reproductions. Two bedrooms and a bath upstairs, with a fully equipped kitchen, half-bath, and living/dining area downstairs.

Hosts: Harold and Dena Mesaris
Rooms: 2 (SB) $50
Continental Breakfast
Credit Cards: None
Notes: 2, 5, 6, 7, 8, 9, 10, 11, 12, 13, 14

MOUNT AIRY

Bed and Breakfast of Philadelphia

1616 Walnut Street, Suite 1120, Philadelphia, 19103
(215) 735-1917; (800) 220-1917
FAX (215) 735-1905

"Eyrie." This historically certified townhouse was built circa 1900 and is furnished in Victorian style with many antiques. On the third floor there is a room with a double bed and shared bath, and on the fourth floor there is a double bed with a shared bath, and a room with a pair of twins and a shared bath. $50-65.

Mount Airy Home. This spacious suburban home is set high above the street in a lovely garden. A three-minute walk from commuter rail and bus. Queen-size bed with a private bath, a pair of twins with a shared bath, and a double bed with a shared bath. $40-50.

MOUNT JOY

Cedar Hill Farm

305 Longenecker Road, 17552
(717) 653-4655

This 1817 stone farmhouse sits in a quiet area overlooking a stream. The charming bedrooms have private baths and are centrally

6 Pets welcome; 8 Children welcome; 9 Social drinking allowed; 10 Tennis available; 11 Swimming available; 12 Golf available; 13 Skiing available; 14 May be booked through travel agents.

air-conditioned. The working farm is near Amish farms and Hershey. Other attractions are nearby farmers' markets, antique shops, and interesting country villages.

Hosts: Russel and Gladys Swarr
Rooms: 5 (PB) $65-70
Continental Breakfast
Credit Cards: A, B, C, D
Notes: 2, 5, 8, 9, 10, 11, 12

Farmhouse Bed and Breakfast

MOUNT POCONO

Farmhouse Bed and Breakfast

HCR 1, Box 6 B, 18344
(717) 839-0796

An 1850 homestead on six manicured acres. Separate cottage and four suites, all with fireplace. Farm-style breakfast complete with original country recipes prepared by the host, a professional chef. Enjoy bedtime snacks freshly baked each day. Antiques adorn each room, with cleanliness being the order of the day. Accommodations have private baths, queen-size beds, TV, telephones, VCR, and air conditioning. Nonsmokers only.

Hosts: Jack and Donna Asure
Rooms: 5 (PB) $85-105
Full Breakfast

Credit Cards: A, B, D
Notes: 5, 9, 10, 11, 12, 13

MUNCY

The Bodine House

307 South Main Street, 17756
(717) 546-8949

Built in 1805 and in the national historic district of Muncy, the Bodine House offers guests the opportunity to enjoy the atmosphere of an earlier age. The comfortable rooms are furnished with antiques, and candlelight is used in the living room by the fireplace, where guests enjoy refreshments. Three blocks from town center, movies, restaurants, library, and shops.

Hosts: David and Marie Louise Smith
Rooms: 4 (PB) $50-75
Full Breakfast
Credit Cards: A, B, C
Notes: 2, 5, 8 (over 6), 9, 10, 11, 12, 13, 14

NAZARETH

Classic Victorian Bed and Breakfast

35 North New Street, 18064
(610) 759-8276

Come to the historic district of the quaint Moravian settlement of Nazareth established in 1740, and enjoy the feeling of being relaxed and pampered in this classic Victorian bed and breakfast. A turn-of-the-century Colonial Revival is a wonderful mix of Victorian and 18th-century traditional furnishings accented with lace, Oriental rugs, stained glass, and chestnut woodwork. A full candlelight breakfast complemented with Wedgewood and fine flatware and linens may be served in the formal dining room, sweeping front veranda, or second-floor balcony. The classic Victorian is 12 minutes from Bethlehem, 15 minutes away from the Bach Festival in May, skiing, major colleges, universities, and music festival in August.

NOTES: Credit cards accepted: A MasterCard; B Visa; C American Express; D Discover Card; E Diner's Club; F Other; 2 Personal checks accepted; 3 Lunch available; 4 Dinner available; 5 Open all year;

Classic Victorian

Hosts: Irene and Dan Sokolowski
Rooms: 3 (1 PB; 2 SB) $65-85
Full Breakfast
Credit Cards: A, B, C
Notes: 2, 5, 7, 8, 9, 12, 13

NEW CUMBERLAND

Hershey Bed and Breakfast Reservation Service

P.O. Box 208, Hershey, 17033-0208
(717) 533-2928

An 11-room limestone farmhouse that sits on three acres high on a hill overlooking Yellow Breeches Creek. Legend has it that this house was part of the Underground Railroad. Each guest room has a double bed and comfortable seating with good lighting. One room has a private bath; two rooms share a bath. Two rooms have large porches to enjoy in good weather. Antique furnishings throughout. Full breakfast. $65-110; $15 per additional person.

NEW HOPE (WRIGHTSTOWN)

Backstreet Inn of New Hope

144 Old York Road, 18938
(215) 862-9571

The Backstreet Inn of New Hope offers the comfort and serenity of a small inn in the town of New Hope, Bucks County. It is in a quiet, tucked-away street, yet within walking distance of the center of town. Minimum-stay requirements for weekends and holidays.

Hosts: Bob Puccio and John Hein
Rooms: 7 (PB) $78-120
Full Breakfast
Credit Cards: B, C
Notes: 2, 5, 7, 8, 10, 11, 12, 13, 14

Centre Bridge Inn

River Road, 18938
(215) 862-9139

A romantic country inn overlooking the Delaware River in historic Bucks County, featuring canopied beds and river views. Fine restaurant serving French Continental cuisine and spirits in an Old World-style dining room with fireplace. Minimum-stay requirements for weekends and holidays. Dining alfresco available in season.

Host: Stephen R. Dugan
Rooms: 9 (PB) $60-135
Continental Breakfast
Credit Cards: A, B, C
Notes: 2, 4, 5, 7, 8 (over 8), 9, 10, 11, 12

Hollileif Bed and Breakfast Establishment

677 Durham Road (Route 413), 18940
(215) 598-3100

Hollileif

6 Pets welcome; 8 Children welcome; 9 Social drinking allowed; 10 Tennis available; 11 Swimming available; 12 Golf available; 13 Skiing available; 14 May be booked through travel agents.

An 18th-century farmhouse on five and one-half acres of Bucks County countryside with romantic ambience, gourmet breakfasts, fireplaces, central air conditioning, and private baths. Gracious service is combined with attention to detail. Each guest room is beautifully appointed with antiques and country furnishings. Enjoy afternoon refreshments by the fireside or on the arbor-covered patio. Relax in a hammock in the meadow overlooking a peaceful stream. View a vibrant sunset and wildlife. Close to New Hope. AAA and Mobil rated.

Hosts: Ellen and Richard Butkus
Rooms: 5 (PB) $80-120
Full Breakfast
Credit Cards: A, B, C, D
Notes: 2, 5, 9, 10, 11, 12, 13, 14

Holly Hedge Estate

6987 Upper York Road, 18938
(215) 862-3136

This gracious stone manor home, on 20 serene, hillside acres, is surrounded by English country gardens, stone outbuildings, and a stream trickling down green lawns to a natural pond. There are 15 guest rooms with private baths. Several rooms have fireplaces, and a few have private entrances and kitchen facilities. Rooms are furnished with tasteful French, American, and English antiques and collectibles that produce a sophisticated, but warm, informal ambience. Expect such delicious specialities as fresh-fruit crepes, puffy frittatas, homemade breads and muffins, and selected coffees and imported teas for breakfast. Boating, tubing, tennis, swimming, antiquing, museums, galleries, and restaurants are nearby.

Rooms: 15 (PB) $65-150
Full Breakfast
Credit Cards: A, B, C, E
Notes: 2, 5, 8, 9, 10, 11, 12, 14

The Inn at Phillips Mill

North River Road, 18938
(215) 862-2984

Country French cuisine in a renovated 18th-century stone barn. Candlelit dining by the fire in winters and on the flower-filled patio in summers. Five cozy guest rooms decorated with antiques, each with private bath. Closed January.

Hosts: Brooks and Joyce Kaufman
Rooms: 5 (PB) $75-85
Continental Breakfast
Credit Cards: None
Notes: 2, 4, 7, 8 (over 10), 9, 11

Tattersall Inn

Box 569, Point Pleasant, 18950
(215) 297-8233

Overlooking a river village, this Bucks County manor house dates to the 18th century and features broad porches for relaxation and a walk-in fireplace for cool evenings. Continental-plus breakfast in the dining room, in the guests' room, or on the veranda. Enjoy the antique-furnished rooms and collection of vintage phonographs. Close to New Hope. AAA three diamonds, Mobil two-star rated.

Hosts: Gerry and Herb Moss
Rooms: 6 (PB) $70-109
Continental Breakfast
Credit Cards: A, B, C, D
Notes: 2, 5, 7 (limited), 8, 9, 10, 11, 13 (cross-country), 14

Tattersall Inn

NOTES: Credit cards accepted: A MasterCard; B Visa; C American Express; D Discover Card; E Diner's Club; F Other; 2 Personal checks accepted; 3 Lunch available; 4 Dinner available; 5 Open all year;

Wedgwood Inn of New Hope

111 West Bridge Street, 18938-1401
(215) 862-2570; FAX (215) 862-2570

Voted "Inn of the Year" by readers of inn guidebooks, this historic inn on two acres of landscaped grounds is steps from the village center. Antiques, fresh flowers, and Wedgwood china are the rule at the inn, where guests are treated like royalty. AAA three diamonds. Innkeeping seminars are offered.

Hosts: Carl A. Glassman and Nadine Silnutzer
Rooms: 12 (PB) $70-190
Continental Breakfast
Credit Cards: A, B, C
Notes: 2, 5, 8, 9, 10, 11, 12, 13, 14

NEW OXFORD

Guesthouses, Inc.

P.O. Box 2137, West Chester, 19380
(215) 692-4575

164. The main house, furnished with antiques, offers three accommodations for guests on the two upper floors. The guest house, a reconstruction of the carriage house, has a living room, dining room, kitchen, laundry, and large bath on the first floor, and two bedrooms and lavatory sink on the second floor. There is more than one-half mile of river frontage. Guests are welcome to use the rowboat or ice skate in season. $95-1,800.

NEWTOWN SQUARE

Bed and Breakfast Connections

P.O. Box 21, Devon, 19333
(215) 687-3565; (800) 448-3619 (outside PA)

G-08. A pre-Revolutionary farmhouse, 1715, overlooking Ridley Creek State Park. The old hearth and bake oven are still in use, as well as a restored fireplace with a mantel of orange chestnut. There are three cheerful second-floor guest rooms. The largest guest room has a canopied double bed, working fireplace, and private bath. A large spinning wheel occupies the corner of the pleasant twin-bedded room. The light and airy double-bedded room has built-in desk. These two rooms share a hall bath. No smoking. Resident cat. $70-105.

Guesthouses, Inc.

P.O. Box 2137, West Chester, 19380
(215) 692-4575

177. These rooms are on the first floor of a six-story architect-builder's home on a wide bend of the Crum Creek, home to woodchucks, foxes, and deer, as well as many native and migrating birds and waterfowl. Within 20 minutes of the Philadelphia International Airport, this modern guest accommodation has living room, kitchen/dining area, bedroom and bath, and deck overlooking the swimming pool that is available for use in season. Centrally air-conditioned. Two-night minimum stay. $110.

NORTH EAST

Grape Arbor Inn

51 East Main Street, 16428
(814) 725-5522; FAX (814) 725-8471

This beautifully restored 1832 brick Federal-style inn in the historic village of North East on Lake Erie once served as a stagecoach stop and an underground railroad station. After extensive renovation, the inn now serves as a vintage bed and breakfast in Pennsylvania Wine Country with local wineries offering wine tasting and tours. Guests enjoy a variety of activities including antiquing, biking, skiing, or a visit to the nearby Chautauqua Institute. Take a step back in time and experience a bygone era.

Hosts: Debra and Michael Ducato
Rooms: 4 (PB) $75-105

6 Pets welcome; 8 Children welcome; 9 Social drinking allowed; 10 Tennis available; 11 Swimming available; 12 Golf available; 13 Skiing available; 14 May be booked through travel agents.

Full Breakfast
Credit Cards: A, B, C
Notes: 2, 5, 8 (over ten), 9, 10, 11, 12, 13, 14

NORTH WALES

Joseph Ambler Inn

1005 Horsham Road, 19454
(215) 362-7500

As guests make their approach up the long
winding drive, they are struck at once by the
peaceful, historic setting of this fine country
inn. Nestled on 12 acres of picturesque lawns
and gardens, the inn features 28 delightful
guest rooms in three buildings with the outstanding Colonial restaurant in the Pennsylvania fieldstone barn. The guest rooms are
furnished with antiques and reproductions,
and each has a private bath, telephone, air
conditioning, and TV. Meeting and conference facilities are available for up to 50 people. Banquets, parties, and weddings may be
held for up to 120 people.

Hosts: Terry and Steve Kratz
Rooms: 28 (PB) $95-140
Full Breakfast
Credit Cards: A, B, C, D, E
Notes: 2, 4, 5, 7, 8, 9, 11, 12, 14

OAKS

Bed and Breakfast of Valley Forge

P.O. Box 562, Valley Forge, 19481-0562
(215) 783-7838; (800) 344-0123

Circa 1833 Stone Farmhouse. This is an
ongoing restoration of a Federal-style,
pointed-stone farmhouse built in 1833.
Highlights include five fireplaces, some of
which work, original woodwork, stenciling,
and antique furnishings. Breakfast is served
in the keeping room in front of a working
"walk-in" fireplace. Fragrances from the
herb garden are an aromatic delight in
spring and summer. The farmhouse is in a
small suburb close to Valley Forge and
Amish country, and an easy drive to the
Brandywine area. Two guest rooms are
available. $75-85.

OTTISVILLE

Auldridge Mead

523 Geigel Hill Road, 18942
(610) 847-5842; (800) 344-4171

Relax in a gorgeous 18th-century stone
farmhouse on 14 pastoral acres. Repose
amidst a virtual gallery of art and antiques;
ramble along scenic country roads; or relax
by the pool and watch the sailplanes fly
overhead. Be pampered with amenities
from almond soap to fresh roasted coffee by
the guest's door before breakfast, prepared
by a seasoned gourmet chef. Rooms and
suites. Swimming, tennis, golf, and skiing
nearby. Pets welcome. Children welcome.
Smoking downstairs only.

Hosts: Karyn Coigne and Craig Mattoli
Rooms: 5 (2 PB; 3 SB) $105-195
Full Breakfast
Credit Cards: C
Notes: 2, 5, 6, 7 (limited), 8, 9, 10, 11, 12, 13, 14

OXFORD

Association of Bed and Breakfasts in Philadelphia, Valley Forge, Brandywine

P.O. Box 562, Valley Forge, 19481-0562
(215) 783-7838; (800) 344-0123

NOTES: Credit cards accepted: A MasterCard; B Visa; C American Express; D Discover Card; E Diner's
Club; F Other; 2 Personal checks accepted; 3 Lunch available; 4 Dinner available; 5 Open all year;

0802. This modern log house is in a quiet wooded area away from all traffic noises. Families with children are welcome. There is one wheelchair/handicap-accessible guest room. Complimentary beverages and snacks are offered, and each morning a full hot breakfast is served. The decor is comfortable, well-lighted, relaxing, and livable. $40-50.

Bed and Breakfast Connections

P.O. Box 21, Devon, 19333
(215) 687-3565; (800) 448-3619 (outside PA)

H-01. This historic 18th-century house, once a stagecoach stop, is on a working dairy farm surrounded by Amish farms. The three-story home is a showcase for Colonial period furniture and local crafts, including salt-glazed "Bennington" pottery, hand-dipped scented candles with handmade tin holders, stenciled walls, and dried flower arrangements. There are three large comfortable guest bedrooms on the second floor that share a bath. All bedrooms are air-conditioned and a color TV is available. A full, country breakfast, served in the sunny, antique-filled sitting room/dining room, may include homemade breads, muffins, or sticky buns. Being a working farm, there are cows, dogs, and cats. Twenty minutes to Amish country, 25 minutes to the Brandywine River area. A Scottish golf course is within a few miles and, if given advance notice, the hostess will arrange for horseback riding or horse-drawn buggy rides. $60-80.

Hershey's Log House Bed and Breakfast

15225 Limestone Road, 19363
(215) 932-9257

Chester County quiet country farm. Wooded area, away from city and traffic noises. Midway between Lancaster (Amish country), Philadelphia, and Wilmington. Visit gardens, museums, and battlefields. Rooms have air conditioning, TV, and telephone for guests' convenience. Family room is also available; children are welcome. No smoking.

Hosts: E. E. and Arlene Hershey
Rooms: 3 (PB) $45-55
Full Breakfast
Credit Cards: None
Notes: 2, 5, 8, 10, 11, 12

PALMYRA

Hershey Bed and Breakfast Reservation Service

P.O. Box 208, Hershey, 17033-0208
(717) 533-2928

On the edge of town surrounded by one acre of country pleasures is this circa 1825 Georgian-style farmhouse. A warm "down home" atmosphere prevails throughout, offering simple hospitality and comfort away from the hustle and bustle of the city. The six air-conditioned rooms offer private baths and cozy, informal comfort. A full breakfast is served from 8:00 to 9:30 A.M., and afternoon or early evening refreshments provide a relaxing break from the day's activities. $65.

PAOLI

Bed and Breakfast of Valley Forge

P.O. Box 562, Valley Forge, 19481-0562
(215) 783-7838; (800) 344-0123

The General's Inn. This inn has been in service since 1745. It is authentically restored and furnished; air-conditioned. Eight complete suites, three with fireplaces and one with Jacuzzi. The first floor is an upscale restaurant and lounge open to the public for lunch and dinner. A Continental breakfast is served in the dining room. No pets; no children under 12. $85-135.

6 Pets welcome; 8 Children welcome; 9 Social drinking allowed; 10 Tennis available; 11 Swimming available; 12 Golf available; 13 Skiing available; 14 May be booked through travel agents.

The Great Valley House. On four acres, this 15-room stone farmhouse, built in 1692, is the second oldest in the state. It is one of the 100 oldest in the country. The original flooring, exposed beams, hand-wrought hinges, and fireplaces add to the charm. An English breakfast is served in front of the walk-in fireplace in the kitchen. Each of the three guest rooms is hand-stenciled, accented with handmade quilts, air-conditioned, furnished with antiques, TV, and radio. Refrigerator, coffee pot, and microwave are provided for guests. Swimming pool. $70-80.

Guesthouses, Inc.

P.O. Box 2137, West Chester, 19380
(215) 692-4575

557. Large three-story stucco-over-stone house built before the 18th century. Guest rooms on the third floor are air-conditioned and comfortably decorated with antiques. There is a room with queen-size bed and single bed, with bath, and a room with queen-size bed with a semi-private hall bath. On the second floor there is a large guest room with double bed and sitting area with either a private or semi-private bath. A full hearty breakfast is served in the old kitchen with its walk-in fireplace and open hearth fires. Guests are invited to enjoy the pool in season. $75-110.

PHILADELPHIA

Association of Bed and Breakfasts in Philadelphia, Valley Forge, Brandywine

P.O. Box 562, Valley Forge, 19481-0562
(215) 783-7838; (800) 344-0123

0211. This bed and breakfast, a circa 1850 Philadelphia row house, welcomes guests to a quiet, friendly neighborhood. The four-poster double bedroom has a private bath and air conditioning; if needed, a Port-a-crib and a double futon are available. Full breakfast is served in the morning. Close to the Italian Market, South Street, Antique Row, Independence Hall, and Penn's Landing. There is a private parking space for guests' car. $50-65.

1308. Guests are offered bed and breakfast in this cozy 150-year-old row house with hospitality that is memorable. The two third-floor rooms share a shower-bath, and one room has a private roof deck. Air conditioning in the double room. Breakfast is full, hot, and hearty, and is served in the airy breakfast room. Nearby parking lots and street parking. Close to the Art Museum, Please Touch Museum, Rodin Museum, Franklin Institute, and the Academy of Natural Sciences. No smoking. $32-42.

1602. Pleasant and comfortable accommodations in a 150-year-old townhouse in Center City Philadelphia. Each room has books, magazines, color cable TV, and air conditioning. Cultural attractions as well as the business district are within walking distance. A telefax and copier are available for the business guest. Full breakfast is served to guests. The private-entrance suite with fully equipped kitchen is entered by going down the spiral staircase to a lower level in the suite. $45-65.

1911. Philadelphia's famous Italian market offers a wonderful experience in delicious tastes and smells. It is truly an attraction that no visitor to Philadelphia should miss. Location affords guests easy access to the historical district of Philadelphia as well. $40-50.

1905. These guest accommodations consist of a spacious entire second floor that includes a bedroom with four-poster double bed, a private bath, and an adjoining sitting

NOTES: Credit cards accepted: A MasterCard; B Visa; C American Express; D Discover Card; E Diner's Club; F Other; 2 Personal checks accepted; 3 Lunch available; 4 Dinner available; 5 Open all year;

room with color cable TV. Hospitality, charm, and a delicious breakfast are offered. $70-85.

B 'n' B at 19th Street (1205). A recently restored 145-year-old townhouse just south of Rittenhouse Square. In good weather, breakfast is served in the minigarden or on the private deck of the third-floor suite. Afternoon tea and scones or a glass of wine can be enjoyed. Films on the VCR and popcorn in the parlor. A 20-minute walk to the Academy of Music, the Curtis Institute of Music, the University of the Arts, the Civil War and Rosenbach Rare Book museums, and theaters. $65-85.

Chestnut Hill Bed and Breakfast (1907). This home is a lovely renovated old stone schoolhouse. The atmosphere exudes the warmth and welcome of a cozy fire on a cold day. Its location in the historic area of Chestnut Hill in Philadelphia reminds one of the early days of this great nation. $65.

Country Inn the City (0206). This 12 room country inn in the historic area of Philadelphia is a restored, circa 1769, guest house within Independence National Historic Park. All rooms are individually decorated and have private baths, telephones, TV, and period furniture. An enclosed parking garage is next door. Continental breakfast is served weekdays and a full breakfast on weekends. Walk to restaurants and the major historic sites in Philadelphia. $95-140.

Historic Philadelphia Bed and Break-fast (2203). This circa 1811 certified historic home is near Society Hill. Guests have access to the city while also enjoying a historic atmosphere. Two guest rooms with private bath. Very comfortable. $65-70.

Marietta's Bed and Breakfast (1401). This turn-of-the-century elegant townhouse has high ceilings and is furnished throughout with antiques and artwork. Easy access to Center City, Rittenhouse Square, and an elegant shopping area. Good restaurants abound. $75-80.

Mount Vernon House. This is a recently renovated, three-story, brick, historical dwelling that is large and spacious with balconies and an atrium. The living room serves as a common room for the guest's use. A full, hot, hearty breakfast is served. There are several good restaurants within walking distance. The Art Museum, Boathouse Row, Fels Planetarium, Academy of Science, and the old Eastern State Penitentiary (now a historical landmark) are all within reasonable walking distance. Two bedrooms, one with a queen-size bed and the other with twins, share a bath when both are occupied. $60-70.

Society Hill Bed and Breakfast (0104). This townhouse was built about 1805 and renovated in the Federal style during the post-Civil War era. Four guest rooms with individual thermostat control for heat and air conditioning, and TV. Full breakfast. During warm weather, breakfast may be served on the patio. One and one-half blocks to Independence Hall. If guests stay over a Saturday night, there is a two-night minimum. $80.

The Spite House (0801). This historically certified home is associated with the Museum Council of Philadelphia and Delaware Valley, and the Historical Society of Pennsylvania. This is one of the "spite houses," so-called because it was built, according to legend, with its back to its neighbors. Full breakfast served. The first floor houses the kitchen, with its Victorian oak oval table and washstand. The second level features

6 Pets welcome; 8 Children welcome; 9 Social drinking allowed; 10 Tennis available; 11 Swimming available; 12 Golf available; 13 Skiing available; 14 May be booked through travel agents.

the parlor with grand piano, dining room, and butler's pantry, with original soapstone sink and dumbwaiter. In Mount Airy amid the Lutheran Seminary, Spring Garden College, and the Coombs College of Music. Near train station. $60-70.

Spruce Garden Bed and Breakfast (0205). Guest quarters are a private first-floor suite in an 1840 townhouse in Center City Philadelphia. A full breakfast is served in the second-floor dining area. The guest suite consists of two bedrooms, two bathrooms, and a sitting room for reading, TV, cards, or sipping sherry. If both rooms are rented at the same time, the occupants must be relatives or good friends, as one must pass through one bedroom to get out or enter the other. $60-70.

Trade Winds Bed and Breakfast (0101). This historically certified townhouse was built in 1790. Two third-floor guest rooms are elegantly appointed with collectibles and Old World antiques. Each room has color cable TV, telephone, and central air conditioning. The twin room has a refrigerator. A full breakfast is served on the French Empire table in the dining area. For special occasions, guests may consider a very large second-floor guest room with antique brass bed, fireplace, color cable TV, telephone, private bath, and air conditioning. On the Washington Square/Society Hill border. Six blocks to Independence Hall and one block to South Street. Public tennis courts across the street. $65-70 for rooms; $100 for suite.

Trinity Bed and Breakfast (2101). This home is one of four in a small court in the lovely and quiet Rittenhouse Square section within the bustle of the city. Guests have access to all the attractions of the city and can still enjoy a private retreat after a day of sightseeing. $75-85.

Washington Square B&B (1601). Built in the 1830s, this three-story Colonial townhouse is on one of Society Hill's narrow, cobblestone streets just blocks from Independence Hall. A wisteria-covered patio with a bubbling fountain welcomes guests in the summer. In the winter, a Franklin stove in the guests' parlor warms them. $60-65.

Bed and Breakfast Connections
P.O. Box 21, Devon, 19333
(215) 687-3565; (800) 448-3619 (outside PA)

A-01. Built between 1805 and 1810 and redone after the Civil War in Federalist style, this charming Society Hill townhouse saw further renovation when its current owners bought it as a shell some 20 years ago. This creative host has done much of the renovation himself, finding unusual artifacts in old churches and homes in the city that have created a unique and inviting atmosphere. The second-floor bedroom offers a color TV, telephone jack, and individual thermostat with a private hall bath. On the third floor there are two more rooms, one with a trundle bed and a queen-size bed and the other with a double bed. All rooms have an individual thermostat, TV, and private bath. Continental breakfast is served in the pleasant kitchen in the winter or on the patio in the warm months. Two-night minimum stay on weekends. $80.

A-09. This 1828 Federal-style home has been thoroughly renovated with the guest in mind. It is within an easy walk of the historic district. The guest is greeted in the magnificent two-story foyer with palladium window. Just off the foyer, there is a small library with shelves lined with books and movies for the guest's enjoyment. A full breakfast is served in the ground-floor kitchen/dining room. Each of the three guest rooms with contemporary cosmopoli-

NOTES: Credit cards accepted: A MasterCard; B Visa; C American Express; D Discover Card; E Diner's Club; F Other; 2 Personal checks accepted; 3 Lunch available; 4 Dinner available; 5 Open all year;

tan decor, offer queen-size beds, fireplace, private bath, and TV/VCR. No smoking permitted. $125.

A-11. Just two blocks from the Italian Market and two blocks from Antique Row, this home offers private third-floor accommodations. The double-bedded guest room furnished with antiques and collectibles has a sitting room and a private attached bath. A large collection of books is available for guests to enjoy during their stay, and the hosts are fluent in Portuguese and French and have a deep interest in music. Breakfast is a hearty Continental with delicious pastries, fresh fruit, and coffees and teas from nearby bakeries and markets. No smoking. $50-60.

A-12. Gaskill House. Though recently thoroughly renovated, this 1828 Federal-style home has always been a private residence. Just a block off South Street within an easy walk of the historic district, this distinctive bed and breakfast is infused with quiet elegance and charm. Guests are greeted in the magnificent two-story foyer with palladium window, then shown to the well-stocked library and large living room. A full breakfast is served in the ground-floor kitchen-dining room. Each of the three contemporary cosmopolitan bedrooms offers queen-size beds, fireplace, private bath, and TV/VCR. No smoking. $125.

B-09. The Gables. This 16-room mid-Victorian home, offers the guest a quiet retreat and the elegance of a Queen Ann Victorian home. Surrounded by the original iron fence and tall hedge, the 1889 home is sheltered by mature species gardens that create a natural seclusion from the bustle. The eight magnificently appointed second- and third-floor guest rooms are furnished in period antiques. Most rooms have private baths and some have working fireplaces.

Fifteen to twenty minute drive to Center City Philadelphia. $60-80.

B-11. This historic registered row home provides generous third-floor guest quarters and is close to the University of Pennsylvania, Drexel University, the Civic Center, and Children's Hospital. At one end of the third floor, guests will find a bedroom that can accommodate a family with its two twin beds and a double. The sitting room is at the opposite end of the hall and is perfect for relaxing in front of the TV or curling up with a book. Private bath. Laundry facilities and refrigerator space are available. $45-55.

2304. This 1830 historic townhouse is near the famous Delancey Street in Philadelphia. Walk to the university, the art museum, academy of music, the civic center in just 20 minutes or drive in eight minutes. Collector of antiques and art. House has central air conditioning, color cable TV, VCR, and wood-burning stove. Breakfast foods provided with kitchen privileges. $50-70.

Bed and Breakfast of Philadelphia

1616 Walnut Street, Suite 1120, 19103
(800) 220-1917; (215) 735- 1917; FAX (215) 735-1905

Cromwell House. The Cromwell House is an 1850 Victorian townhouse on "Architect's Row" in the art museum section of the city. The guest quarters, on the air-conditioned third floor, are a self-contained suite with private bath. It is furnished in the Queen Anne style with matching walnut twin beds and dressers. A writing desk is provided for those addicted to writing postcards to the folks back home. The full English breakfast may be served in the sunny kitchen greenhouse or in the city garden. $55-65.

6 Pets welcome; 8 Children welcome; 9 Social drinking allowed; 10 Tennis available; 11 Swimming available; 12 Golf available; 13 Skiing available; 14 May be booked through travel agents.

Logan Square Townhouse. This townhouse is near the Franklin Institute, Museum of Natural History, and the Moore College of Art. The third-floor bedrooms share the bathroom and its old-fashioned claw-foot tub with the hosts. One room offers a double bed and air conditioning for the summer nights. The other has a single bed and is fan-cooled. $32-42.

Modern Antique. This attractive, spacious 19th-century townhouse is in the Society Hill section of Philadelphia. It is within walking distance of Independence Hall and the historic area of Philadelphia. The living room opens onto the south-facing city patio/garden. The three bedrooms are spacious, comfortable, and air-conditioned. A full breakfast is served and low cholesterol diets can be accommodated. $65-80.

New Market Surprise. This historic 1811 Philadelphia brick townhouse was transformed from a dilapidated shell into a comfortable, attractive home with a modern interior. The two air-conditioned bedrooms on the second floor are simply furnished with a double bed in each room, private baths, and TV. There is a working fireplace on the third floor for guests' enjoyment. A full breakfast is served to guests willing to rise early on weekdays, and at a more leisurely hour on weekends. $60-65.

Olde City Inn. This lovely inn in Olde City Philadelphia overlooks Penn's Landing on the Delaware River on a historic street. The bed and breakfast inn offers elegance in a distinguished setting. Each of the 20 rooms is designed to cater to the guests' comfort and features exquisite furnishings and modern amenities. The Premium rooms have both fireplaces and Jacuzzi tubs. The suite consists of two spacious bedrooms and a parlor with a fireplace and a private kitchen. $150-200.

Rodman Renaissance. This hostess will provide guests with a warm welcome to this 90-year-old townhouse which has been lovingly restored and furnished with selected antiques suggesting the ambience of an earlier era. This three-story home offers a living room with fireplace, dining area, and kitchen on the first floor. On the third floor is a cozy, secluded double bedroom with adjacent, private powder room. $35-50.

Victoria Galerie. In one of center city Philadelphia's most desirable neighborhoods, with its high ceilings and large windows, Victoria Galerie reflects a bygone era. Guests will feel transported back to the 19th-century as they climb the winding stairs to private quarters. The large room is furnished with an antique Victorian headboard and inlaid-walnut closets and includes a private bath. $75.

Germantown Bed and Breakfast

5925 Wayne Avenue, 19144
(215) 848-1375

This cozy 1900s oak bedroom in a 100-year-old house has cable TV and a private tiled bath. This is a homestay with a family with four children. Twenty minutes to Independence Hall; walk to other historic sites, restaurants, and conveniences. Call for a detailed brochure.

Hosts: Molly and Jeff Smith
Room: 1 (PB) $40-45
Continental Breakfast
Credit Cards: None
Notes: 2, 5, 8, 9, 12, 14

The International Bed and Breakfast Club, Inc.

504 Amherst Street, Buffalo, NY 14207
(800) 723-4262; FAX (716) 873-4462

PA7349PP. Built in the 1830s, and lovingly renovated in the 1970s, this bed and breakfast is not just a home, but an experience: a medium red brick townhouse, set on the side of a narrow stone street, it is filled with the silent stories of the lady who once lived there. Just a block away is Washington Square Park, set aside by William Penn, who believed each citizen should have a patch of grass to call his own. Two rooms, shared bath. Full breakfast. $65.

The Thomas Bond House Bed and Breakfast

129 South Second Street, 19106
(215) 923-8523; (800) 845-BOND
FAX (215) 923-8504

An elegantly restored, circa 1769, prominent physician's home in Independence National Historic Park and Old City. Twelve guest rooms each with private bath, telephone, TV, period furniture, and individually controlled heat and air conditioning.

The Thomas Bond House

Suites have whirlpool tubs and fireplaces. Rates include breakfast, evening wine and cheese, turndown service, and beverages. Parking next door. Rated by AAA, Mobil, government, and AARP. Cookies baked fresh daily.

Host: Thomas Lantry
Rooms: 12 (PB) $80-150
Continental Breakfast weekdays; Full Breakfast
  weekends
Credit Cards: A, B, C, E
Notes: 2, 5, 7, 8, 9, 10, 11, 12, 14

PHOENIXVILLE

Bed and Breakfast Connections

P.O. Box 21, Devon, 19333
(215) 687-3565; (800) 448-3619 (outside PA)

F-01. Dating back to the 1860s, this former general store has been converted to a charming bed and breakfast with touches of the Netherlands. Three European-style guest rooms are on the second floor. The first is a large room with platform queen-size bed, private bath, and private deck. The other two rooms have queen-size or twin beds (which could be made into a king-size bed) and attached sitting rooms. These two rooms share a bath. Breakfast includes choice of American style or house special Dutch West Indies. No smoking. Resident cat and dog in owner's quarters only. $55-75.

Bed and Breakfast of Valley Forge

P.O. Box 562, Valley Forge, 19481-0562
(215) 783-7838; (800) 344-0123

1803. Accommodations consist of seven upscale efficiencies (each with full kitchen, bath, cable TV, and private entrance). Breakfast foods are provided in the kitchen and are

6 Pets welcome; 8 Children welcome; 9 Social drinking allowed; 10 Tennis available; 11 Swimming available; 12 Golf available; 13 Skiing available; 14 May be booked through travel agents.

self-serve. Nightly, weekly, and monthly stays are welcome. $100.

1910. Federal House Bed and Breakfast.

This three-story brick Italianate home was built in 1867 on land purchased from the Phoenix Iron Company in historic Chester County. From the stars on the ceiling to the faux marbled foyer, the interior of this home is decorated with period pieces from the 1800s to the 1930s, pulled together with an artistic 1990s flair. Enjoy the large living room, formal dining room, privately enclosed patio, and use of the Jacuzzi, which is open all year and is large enough to comfortably seat eight adults. Full breakfast including fruit, juices, hot beverage, and a choice of breakfast entree. The guest rooms have queen-size beds, private bath, TV, and air conditioning. $65-75.

Manor House. Built in 1928 by a British executive, this English Tudor home stands on a lovely sycamore-lined street. It boasts a massive slate roof and original red oak flooring and stairway. The spacious living room and cozy den both have fireplaces. Gourmet breakfasts are served in the formal dining room or on the brick-floored screened porch overlooking the garden. Complimentary bedtime beverage and snack in the room. Five guest rooms with private bath. $45-70.

Tinker Hill. This contemporary house on two and one-half acres is in a private, wooded area. Two-story glass-walled living room. Guest rooms are separated from the suite and overlook the woods. Hot tub on the deck; swimming pool. Full breakfast. $60-65.

POCONO MOUNTAINS

Nearbrook Bed and Breakfast

Rural Delivery 1, Box 630, Canadensis, 18325
(717) 595-3152

Meander through rock garden paths and enjoy the roses, woods, and stream at Nearbrook. A hearty breakfast is served on the outdoor porch. The hosts will join guests for morning conversation to help find trails for good hiking and describe other areas of interest. A contagious informality encourages guests to play the upright piano and enjoy the many games. Restaurant menus, maps, and art lessons are available.

Hosts: Barbara and Dick Robinson
Rooms: 3 (1 PB; 2 SB) $45
Full Breakfast
Credit Cards: None
Notes: 2, 5, 8, 10, 11, 12, 13, 14

POINT PLEASANT

Guesthouses, Inc.

P.O. Box 2137, West Chester, 19380
(215) 692-4575

174. A beautiful 40-acre country estate. The main house is spacious, airy, and modern. The three suite occupants are encouraged to use the main floor's great room with its comfortable reading areas by the two-story fireplace. Each suite has a queen-size bed and is decorated on a theme. The stone carriage house has a main room with a two-story fireplace, upstairs bedroom with a queen-size bed and a lovely peaked ceiling, kitchen, and firewood at door. Breakfast is served in the main house. The carriage house kitchen is left stocked for breakfast. $135-175.

RADNOR

Bed and Breakfast Connections

P.O. Box 21, Devon, 19333
(215) 687-3565; (800) 448-3619 (outside PA)

E-13. This home within a barn offers private quarters that provide more than a refreshing night's sleep and a delicious breakfast. The two-story entrance hall and stairway welcome guests to this 19th-century bank barn. There are three guest rooms with private baths. The first, a large king-size bedded room with a table and four chairs. For guests preferring a queen-size bed, there is a large sunny corner room. Both rooms have a small refrigerator. The third room offers twin or king-size sleigh bed accommodations, whichever guests prefer, and a sitting area. Breakfast is served either in guest room or in the two-story great room with a fireplace or, in warm weather, on the upper deck. $90-110.

Bed and Breakfast of Valley Forge

P.O. Box 562, Valley Forge, 19481-0562
(215) 783-7838; (800) 344-0123

Main Line Estate. This expansive English Tudor, built in 1969, is surrounded by three and one-half acres of original grounds belonging to two estates owned by brothers who made a local German beer. The spacious guest rooms can be reached privately by a back staircase. A full breakfast is served in the country French kitchen. Greenhouse, swimming pool, cabana, and tennis court. Washer/dryer, baby equipment, and cable TV available. $70.

READING

Bed and Breakfast Adventures

Suite 132, 2310 Central Avenue,
    North Wildwood, NJ 08260
(606) 522-4000; (800) 992-2632

PA704. Nestled along the banks of the picturesque Schuylkill River, within the sound of the waterfalls, this enchanting old 1700s farmhouse is rich in history and natural beauty. The upstairs has a Victorian decor, with one queen-size bedroom and a private bath with oversized Jacuzzi; the double-bed suite has an adjoining sitting area and private bath. Both have air conditioning, TV, and refreshments. Hosts offer a full-course Pennsylvania Dutch-style breakfast. Close to Reading outlets, Penn State, other campuses, and the Berks Jazz Fest (in March). Nonsmokers and couples are welcome. $75-85.

RIDLEY CREEK STATE PARK

Guesthouses, Inc.

P.O. Box 2137, West Chester, 19380
(215) 692-4575

125. The main house was built in the mid-1800s, and all the rooms are decorated with antique furnishings and decorative objects appropriate to the house. The guest wing is newly built and is separate from the rest of the house. The bedroom is large and sunny with a king-size bed and sitting area; the large bath is luxuriously appointed. Breakfast is served in the new garden room and kitchen. When the weather is mild, guests can take a swim and have breakfast served by the formal garden swimming pool. Fully air-conditioned. $100.

ROSEMONT

Bed and Breakfast of Valley Forge

P.O. Box 562, Valley Forge, 19481-0562
(215) 783-7838; (800) 344-0123

Conestoga. The hosts of this bed and breakfast inherited the home they were raised in. Guests have the privilege of the entire house. The interior of this 1890 home has been restored and furnished. Fully equipped kitchen, living room, dining room, sunroom, two bedrooms, and bath. On-site parking, TV, grill, and furnished patio. The kitchen is stocked with breakfast foods. Special rates for four people available. $100-150.

6 Pets welcome; 8 Children welcome; 9 Social drinking allowed; 10 Tennis available; 11 Swimming available; 12 Golf available; 13 Skiing available; 14 May be booked through travel agents.

SCHAEFFERSTOWN

The Franklin House

Main and Market Streets, 17088
(717) 949-3398

Beautiful limestone building, 1746, it is the oldest inn-hotel in Lebanon County. Locally grown fruits, vegetables, and private herb garden are featured. Lunch and dinner are available except on Mondays. Guest rooms are on the third floor. Rooms are small, but charming with a double bed, air conditioner, electric heat, and shared bath, which is on the second floor. Thirty minutes from Hershey, Lancaster, and Reading.

Hosts: Dottie and Lee Backenstose
Rooms: 5 (SB) $35
Continental Breakfast
Credit Cards: A, B, C
Notes: 2, 3 and 4 (limited), 5, 9, 11

SCHELLSBURG (BEDFORD AREA)

Amanda's Bed and Breakfast

1428 Park Avenue, Baltimore, MD, 21217
(410) 225-001; (800) 899-7533
FAX (410) 728-8957

130. A farmhouse with historic credentials, now a lovely bed and breakfast with modern touches. A trout stream and covered bridge, state park, plus other historic, scenic attractions abound. One hour to Falling Water, a home designed by Frank Lloyd Wright. Full breakfast. $75.

SCHWENKSVILLE

Bed and Breakfast of Valley Forge

P.O. Box 562, Valley Forge, 19481-0562
(215) 783-7838; (800) 344-0123

Highpoint Victoriana. Dutch Colonial Victorian five-acre farmette consists of a barn with vintage cars and fields that serve as a Christmas tree farm. The house has been carefully restored and modernized in authentic keeping with the Victorian atmosphere. It is filled with lovely antiques. Enjoy a lovely wraparound porch to cool guests in the summer, and a wood-burning stove to warm guests in the winter. Four guest rooms. $50-70.

SIGEL

Discoveries Bed and Breakfast

Rural Delivery 1, Box 42, 15860
(814) 752-2632

This Victorian house has four bedrooms and three baths. It has an ambience of country elegance—the bedrooms are beautifully decorated and furnished in antiques. Breakfast is served on a spacious enclosed front porch. Included in the meal are home-cured meats and home-baked breads and rolls. Adjacent to the house is a finished crafts and antique shop offering fine Victorian

Discoveries Bed and Breakfast

NOTES: Credit cards accepted: A MasterCard; B Visa; C American Express; D Discover Card; E Diner's Club; F Other; 2 Personal checks accepted; 3 Lunch available; 4 Dinner available; 5 Open all year;

furniture and handcrafted items of the highest quality. Six miles from Cook Forest State Park and three miles from Clear Creek State Park.

Hosts: Pat and Bruce MacBeth
Rooms: 4 (1 PB; 3 SB) $50-60
Full Breakfast
Credit Cards: None
Notes: 2, 11, 12

Applebutter Inn

SLIPPERY ROCK

Applebutter Inn

152 Applewood Lane, 16057
(412) 794-1844

Nestled in the rolling green meadows of rural western Pennsylvania, Applebutter Inn offers a window to the past. All eleven guest rooms contain private bath, color cable TV, and telephone. Full gourmet breakfast is included in the tariff and served at the adjacent Wolf Creek School Cafe, serving lunch and dinner to the public. Conference/meeting room available at the inn to accommodate 14-16 people, equipped with TV, VCR, telephone, and computer modem.

Hosts: Gary and Sandra McKnight
Rooms: 11 (PB) $69-115
Full Breakfast
Credit Cards: A, B, C
Notes: 2, 3, 4, 5, 8, 10, 11, 12, 13

SMETHPORT

Blackberry Inn Bed and Breakfast

820 West Main Street (US 6 and Highway 59), 16749-1039
(814) 887-7777

A Victorian home built in 1881 and restored in 1988-89. Guest parlor with TV. Guest telephone. Two large open porches. Breakfast is served at time guest desires. Friendly small-town atmosphere. Near Kinzua Bridge State Park and Allegheny National Forest. Wonderful area for hiking, biking, fishing, fall foliage tours, festivals, or just relaxing.

Hosts: Marilyn and Arnie Bolin
Rooms: 5 (S2B) $45-50
Full Breakfast
Credit Cards: None
Notes: 2, 5, 8, 11, 12, 13

SOMERSET

Bayberry Inn Bed and Breakfast

611 North Center Avenue, Route 601, 15501
(814) 445-8471

A romantic, friendly, comfortable inn that pays attention to detail, offering all non-smoking rooms with private baths. Homemade baked goods served at a lovely table for two. Near Exit 10 of the Pennsylvania Turnpike. Close to Seven Springs and Hidden Valley resorts, Frank Lloyd Wright's Falling Water, Ohiopyle white-water rafting, state parks, antique shops, and outlet malls.

Hosts: Marilyn and Robert Lohr
Rooms: 11 (PB) $45-55
Continental Breakfast
Credit Cards: A, B, C, D
Notes: 2, 5, 8 (over 11), 9, 10, 11, 12, 13, 14

6 Pets welcome; 8 Children welcome; 9 Social drinking allowed; 10 Tennis available; 11 Swimming available; 12 Golf available; 13 Skiing available; 14 May be booked through travel agents.

H. B.'s Cottage

231 West Church Street, 15501-1941
(814) 443-1204; FAX (814) 443-4313

Exclusive and elegant bed and breakfast in a stone-and-frame 1920s cottage with oversize fireplace in the living room. Furnished in traditional manner with accent pieces from overseas travels by the innkeepers, and collectible teddy bears from the hostess' collection. Guest room warmly and romantically decorated with a private porch. Downhill and cross-country skiing, biking, and tennis are specialties of hosts. Close to Seven Springs, Falling Water, biking and hiking trails, and white water.

Hosts: Hank and Phillis Vogt
Room: 1 (PB) $65
Full Breakfast
Credit Cards: A, B
Notes: 2, 5, 6, 9, 10, 11, 12, 13

SPLIT ROCK

Guesthouses, Inc.

P.O. Box 2137, West Chester, 19380
(215) 692-4575

031. This large, privately owned lodge is within an exclusive luxury resort on a large lake with every imaginable recreational facility available, including some of the area's finest skiing. The lodge is on two levels with decks all around on both levels: top floor has living, dining area, kitchen, bedroom, and bath. The lower floor has living, dining area, two bedrooms, and bath. There are fireplaces for seasonal use.

STARLIGHT

The Inn at Starlight Lake

Box 27, 18461
(717) 798-2519; (800) 248-2519
FAX (717) 798-2672

A classic country inn since 1909 on a clear lake in the rolling hills of northeast Pennsylvania, with activities for all seasons from swimming to cross-country skiing. Near the Delaware River for canoeing and fly fishing. Excellent food and spirits, convivial atmosphere. Modified American Plan.

Hosts: Jack and Judy McMahon
Rooms: 26 (20 PB; 6 SB) $110-154
Suite $170-200
Full Breakfast
Credit Cards: A, B
Notes: 2, 3, 4, 5, 7 (limited), 8, 9, 10, 11, 12, 13, 14

STATE COLLEGE (PINE GROVE MILLS)

Split-Pine Farmhouse Bed and Breakfast

347 West Pine Grove Road, P.O. Box 326, 16868
(814) 238-2028

Split-Pine is a vintage farmhouse, circa 1830-60, six miles from Penn State University. Ideal for university parents, business travelers to this dynamic area, antiquers, nature lovers enjoying the lovely countryside, water sportsmen, festival goers in summer, and Victorian and Colonial celebrations in the winter. Spacious rooms overlook charming grounds and country vistas. Sumptuous breakfasts. Private and shared baths. Minutes from the heart of things—miles and miles from concerns. Three crowns rating from the ABBA.

Host: Mae McQuade
Rooms: 3 (2 PB; 1 SB) $65-100
Suite: 1 $130
Full Breakfast
Credit Cards: A, B, D
Notes: 2, 5, 8 (over 12), 9, 10, 11, 12, 13, 14

STRAFFORD

Bed and Breakfast of Philadelphia

1616 Walnut Street, Suite 1120,
  Philadelphia, 19103
(215) 735-1917; (800) 220-1917
FAX (215) 735-1905

Stratford Village Home. Comfortable, attractive, Colonial-style surburban home

---

NOTES: Credit cards accepted: A MasterCard; B Visa; C American Express; D Discover Card; E Diner's Club; F Other; 2 Personal checks accepted; 3 Lunch available; 4 Dinner available; 5 Open all year;

with a pristine interior. Summer breakfasts under a yellow umbrella in the garden. Double bed with private bath available. $35-45.

STRASBURG (LANCASTER COUNTY)

The Decoy Bed and Breakfast

958 Eisenberger Road, 17579
(717) 687-8585; (800) 726-2287

The Decoy is in a quiet rural location with a spectacular view. A former Amish home, it has five rooms with private baths. Double, queen-, and king-size beds are available. Breakfasts are an adventure, with wonderful recipes gleaned from the large collection of cookbooks. The hostess is an avid quilter. Bicyclists are welcome, and hosts can help guests in planning their tours. Two resident cats also make guests feel welcome.

Hosts: Debby and Hap Joy
Rooms: 5 (PB) $47.70-63.60
Full Breakfast
Credit Cards: None
Notes: 2, 5, 8, 9, 12

THORNTON

Pace One Restaurant and Country Inn

Box 108, 19373
(215) 459-3702

Pace One is a renovated 250-year-old stone barn with rooms on the upper three levels. The ground floor is a restaurant and bar. Beautiful hand-hewn wood beams, old wood floors, and deep-set windows establish a charming rustic atmosphere.

Host: Ted Pace
Rooms: 6 (PB) $65-85
Continental Breakfast
Credit Cards: A, B, C, E
Notes: 2, 3, 4, 5, 7, 8, 9, 10, 11, 12

TROY

Silver Oak Leaf Bed and Breakfast

196 Canton Street, 16947
(717) 297-4315; (800) 326-9834

Silver Oak Leaf Bed and Breakfast is in the heart of the Endless Mountains. The house is a 90-year-old Victorian that has great charm. There is a great deal to do and see: antiques, auctions, fishing, hunting, or just relaxing. Gourmet breakfasts; wine served in the evening.

Hosts: Steve and June Bahr
Rooms: 4 (1 PB; 3 SB) $40-50
Full Breakfast
Credit Cards: None
Notes: 2, 5, 9, 10, 11, 12, 13

UNIONVILLE

Guesthouses, Inc.

P.O. Box 2137, West Chester, 19380
(215) 692-4575

194. The main house is a typical Pennsylvania stone long farmhouse built in the 18th century. A gem of a country estate and horse breeding farm, decorated with walls of paintings and rooms of comfortable antiques, here visitors will find repose and serenity. The guest rooms are on the second floor and overlook the terraces, extensive lawns, gardens, ponds, and swimming pool, which guests are welcome to enjoy seasonally. A healthful California menu breakfast is served in the breakfast room or on the terrace. $50-125.

VALLEY FORGE

Bed and Breakfast Connections

P.O. Box 21, Devon, 1933
(215) 687-3565; (800) 448-3619 (outside PA)

F-04. Enjoy the charm of this historic home convenient to the Valley Forge area. The

---

6 Pets welcome; 8 Children welcome; 9 Social drinking allowed; 10 Tennis available; 11 Swimming available; 12 Golf available; 13 Skiing available; 14 May be booked through travel agents.

original part of the house was built sometime before 1700, and two additions, each more than 200 years old, were constructed in the traditional Colonial style. Two third-floor rooms offer guests spacious privacy and the convenience of a small refrigerator, microwave oven, and telephone on the landing. A large, inviting second-floor room has an antique double bed and a sitting area with a camelback, and queen-size sofa bed. All rooms have private or semi-private baths. A full English-style breakfast is served in the oldest part of the house in front of the fireplace with its huge mantle and eight-foot-wide hearth. Resident dog and smoker. $60-85.

Bed and Breakfast of Philadelphia

1616 Walnut Street, Suite 1120, Philadelphia, 19103
(215) 735-1917; (800) 220-1917
FAX (215) 735-1905

Deer Run. Deer Run is an original farmhouse dating back to the 1880s. The home appears on survey maps from the 1740s and is an original William Penn land-grant property. The two guest rooms are decorated in period style. One has its original fireplace, pine random-width floors, and an original "rope" cannonball bed with a feather down mattress, and air conditioning. The second bedroom is decorated in Laura Ashley prints, and furniture includes an iron-and-brass bed and an oak dresser with an interesting French provincial sideboard and long chest. The two rooms share a bath. Children over 12 welcome. Limited smoking. $70-80.

Great Valley House. The title documents for this beautiful old stone house trace back to a grant from William Penn in 1681. This stone farmhouse has 15 rooms, which was built in three phases, and the latest phase was completed more than 200 years ago. Two guest rooms on the third floor are air-conditioned for summer comfort. Both

rooms have private baths. A full country breakfast is served before a warming fire in the 1690 kitchen or on the terrace under ancient trees in summer. Children welcome. Queen-size and double beds are available. $80-85.

Oak Haven. Oak Haven is a 1791 white southern Colonial set in a large yard with its own stream and cottage with Valley Forge National Park as a nearby neighbor. Close to King of Prussia, guests are near local attractions such as the Devon Horse Show. Three third-floor guest rooms are available with a variety of beds. Children over ten years old welcome. No smoking. $60-80.

Valley Forge Garden Spot. Lush greenery greets the eyes if guests arrive in spring or summer. This two-story Colonial-style house is nestled on a hillside bordered by flowering shrubs and trees. The hostess is a college professor and knowledgeable about many cultural and human service organizations. Breakfast is guests' preference. Three rooms, one with a pair of twin beds and a private bath, another with a pair of twin beds and shared bath, and a third with one single bed and shared bath. Children welcome. No smoking. $30-60.

Bed and Breakfast of Valley Forge

P.O. Box 562, 19481-0562
(215) 783-7838; (800) 344-0123

1400. Treetops Bed and Breakfast. Private, cozy guest cottage accommodating up to four people consists of a living room with TV and queen-size sofa bed, full kitchen stocked with goodies, full private bath, deck, and queen-size bedroom. Close to Valley Forge National Historic Park, as well as hiking and biking trails, tennis, golf, skiing, horseback riding, live theater, antiquing, shopping malls, and great restaurants. $90-115.

1909. Behind this ivy-covered circa 1770 house and beyond the barn is the guest cottage. Enter through the screened porch, furnished in wicker. Inside, the main floor includes a guest living room, dining area, fully equipped kitchen, and washer and dryer. Air-conditioned and comfortably furnished. Upstairs is the spacious queen-size bedroom, bath, and study. From this cottage the Valley Forge National Historical Park, horses, visiting deer, and fox. Cable TV and swimming pool. Weekly housekeeping. A two-room suite with private bath and fireplace is available in the main house. Stalls are available for guest horses. A honeymooner's delight! $85-100.

Country Charm. This Colonial farmhouse is on three acres of an original William Penn land grant and dates from the 1700s. The outbuildings include a smokehouse, springhouse, and outhouse. The home is cozy, comfortable, and furnished in traditional country style appropriate to the home's age, complete with antiques, quilts, and hand stenciling. A full breakfast is served in the cheerful dining room. $60-65.

Deep Well Farm. This 18th-century fieldstone farmhouse has 16-inch-thick walls and exposed beams overhead. Originally it was part of Gen. Anthony Wayne's estate. The two and one-half acres accommodate a horse barn and a pond where geese gather. The bedrooms are spacious and comfortable, cooled by ceiling fans. A full breakfast is served in the country dining room or kitchen. A parrot and two horses reside. One mile to Valley Forge Park; one-half mile to Valley Forge Music Fair. $60-70.

Guesthouses, Inc.

P.O. Box 2137, West Chester, 19380
(215) 692-4575

085. This beautiful historic property is on Valley Forge Mountain, within minutes of access to all major roads of the area. Behind a duck pond, with a deck overlooking pastures for sheep and horses. The second-floor, newly reconstructed guest accommodation is air-conditioned and charmingly furnished in country antiques, pastel chintzes, and dhurrie rugs. The kitchen is stocked for breakfast on bed and breakfast stays. Guests are invited to enjoy the outdoor pool in season. $120.

Valley Forge Mountain Bed and Breakfast

Box 562, 19481
(215) 783-7838; (800) 344-0123
FAX (215) 783-7783

George Washington had headquarters here. Between Philadelphia, Lancaster County, Reading outlets, and Brandywine Valley. French Colonial on three wooded acres adjacent to Valley Forge Park. Air conditioning, complimentary breakfast, guest room telephone, TV, VCR, computer, printer, FAX, two fireplaces. Bridle and hiking trail. Fine shopping, antiquing, restaurants, cross-country skiing, horseback riding, and golf within minutes. California king-size and California decor single with sitting room with private bath. Victorian decor double with sitting room with private bath. Jacuzzi on outdoor deck.

Host: Carolyn Williams
Rooms: 2 (PB) $45-65
Full Breakfast
Credit Cards: A, B, C, E
Notes: 2, 5, 7 (limited), 8, 9, 10, 11, 12, 14

VILLANOVA

Bed and Breakfast Connections

P.O. Box 21, Devon, 19333
(215) 687-3565; (800) 448-3619 (outside PA)

E-12. Elegant accommodations in this gracious 40-year-old English Regency-style home. Traditional and antique furniture

6 Pets welcome; 8 Children welcome; 9 Social drinking allowed; 10 Tennis available; 11 Swimming available; 12 Golf available; 13 Skiing available; 14 May be booked through travel agents.

grace the two second-floor guest rooms. Both provide double-bed accommodations and are attractively decorated with floral wallpaper reminiscent of the French country-side. Each room has a private bath. A full breakfast is served in the conservatory over-looking the English gardens and tennis court, weather permitting, or in the formal dining room in the winter months. Feel free to relax with a book in the conservatory or in the first-floor library. Two resident dogs. No smoking. $60-70.

Bed and Breakfast of Valley Forge

P.O. Box 562, Valley Forge, 19481-0562
(215) 783-7838; (800) 344-0123

English Regency. This home, featured on house tours, is on one and one-half acres in an elegant, quiet, wooded area. It is fur-nished with antiques, art, and Oriental rugs. The guest room is beautifully appointed and includes a graceful canopied bed and leather wing chair. Weekdays, breakfast is self-serve Continental. On weekends, a full breakfast is served. Central air condition-ing. $70-75.

VIRGINVILLE (KUTZTOWN) _____

Bed and Breakfast Adventures

Suite 132, 2310 Central Avenue, North Wildwood, NJ 08260
(606) 522-4000; (800) 992-2632

PA701. Nestled in the rolling hills of Berks County, this country cottage is separate from the main house. The bathroom with shower is on the first floor; the large up-stairs bedroom includes a swooning couch. The hostess brings breakfast over daily. Close to Kutztown State University, antique shopping and the Reading outlets. Non-smokers and children welcome. $85.

WASHINGTON CROSSING _____

Inn to the Woods

150 Glenwood Drive, 18977
(215) 493-1974; (800) 982-7619

Secluded elegance in historic Bucks County. This European-style bed and breakfast inn will enchant guests with ten acres of forest crisscrossed with deer paths and hiking trails. Deluxe accommodations include private bath, individually controlled heat and air conditioning, color TV, clock radio, hair dryer, and other amenities. Guests will enjoy the owner's worldwide collection of art and antiques, including a morning quiz on Victoriana during a gourmet breakfast and champagne brunch on Sundays. Continental breakfast is served midweek. Afternoon tea and hors d'oeu-vres, evening sherry. Guests love relaxing in the great room with raised hearth fire-place, atrium, and indoor fishpond. Just minutes from New Hope, and one mile from I-95.

Hosts: Barry and Rosemary Rein
Rooms: 7 (PB) $95-135
Full and Continental Breakfast
Credit Cards: A, B, C
Notes: 2, 5, 9, 14

WAYNE _____

Bed and Breakfast of Valley Forge

P.O. Box 562, Valley Forge, 19481-0562
(215) 783-7838; (800) 344-0123

Fox Knoll. Completely private accommo-dations in this 12-room old stone Colonial filled with antiques and country comfort. The guest entrance leads from the terrace to a spacious room with areas for eating, sit-ting, and sleeping. The kitchenette is fully equipped and stocked for breakfast, or join the hosts in the country dining room. The stone terrace with grill and umbrella are for guest use. Other amenities include a large stone fireplace, TV, and stereo. A cheerful bedroom with sitting room in the main house is also available. $55-90.

Woodwinds. Newly remodeled home on two acres on a quiet, wooded street, surrounded by gardens, lawns, and trees. The light, comfortable guest room is up a short, private flight of stairs separated from the hosts' quarters. Continental breakfast served in the formal dining room or on the terrace. One-half block from the main line train station and the Paoli local to Philadelphia. $55-65.

WELLSBORO

Kaltenbach's Bed and Breakfast Inn

Rural Delivery 6, Box 106 A, Kelsey Street Stony
   Fork Road, 16901
(717) 724-4954; (800) 722-4954

Nestled on 72 beautiful acres, Kaltenbach's Bed and Breakfast Inn features a view of the countryside unequaled in north central Pennsylvania. All-you-can-eat country-style breakfasts featuring homemade jellies, jams, and blueberry muffins. Spacious guest rooms with queen- and king-size beds. Accommodations for 32 guests. Cable TV in rooms; telephones available. Honeymoon suites with tub for two. Hiking, bicycling, horseback riding, and picnicking in summer. In winter, cross-country skiing and snowmobiling are nearby. Golf packages are available. Penna Grand Canyon.

Host: Lee Kaltenbach
Rooms: 11 (4 PB; 7 SB) $50-100
Full Breakfast
Credit Cards: A, B
Notes: 2, 3, 4, 5, 8, 9, 10, 11, 12, 13, 14

WEST ALEXANDER

Saint's Rest Bed and Breakfast

77 Main Street, P.O. Box 15, 15376
(412) 484-7950

Earl and Myrna invite guests to visit this beautiful gingerbread-style Victorian home one minute from Interstate 70 east or west. Fifteen minutes from Oglebay Park, Jamboree USA, and Wheeling Downs dog track. Saint's Rest stands on Old National Road. Fresh flowers, homemade muffins, a welcome-in drink, and good beds are just some of the guests' comments about this friendly home away from home.

Hosts: Myrna and Earl Lewis
Rooms: 2 (PB) $60
Full Breakfast
Credit Cards: None
Notes: 2, 5, 8, 9

Saint's Rest

WEST CHESTER

Association of Bed and Breakfasts in Philadelphia, Valley Forge, Brandywine

P.O. Box 562, Valley Forge, 19481-0562
(215) 783-7838; (800) 344-0123

0800. Circa 1755 historic farm bed and breakfast that has been recognized by the local historic society. Standing on wooded acres, surrounded by meadowland, pastureland, hunt country, and dirt roads. Children are welcome! Enjoy TV, VCR, games, and cards, and the wood-burning stove in the

---

6 Pets welcome; 8 Children welcome; 9 Social drinking allowed; 10 Tennis available; 11 Swimming available;
12 Golf available; 13 Skiing available; 14 May be booked through travel agents.

parlor. Fish, hike, or throw horseshoes outdoors. Continental breakfast is served in the morning. $60-65.

1103. This bed and breakfast is a one-of-a-kind custom reproduction Pennsylvania farmhouse sitting on three acres overlooking hills and meadows. Very quiet area, no bright lights. Guests are invited to sit by the wood-burning stove in the winter or on the patio in the summer. There are five guest rooms available; four on the second floor, and one on the third floor with a private bath. There is bumper pool in the game room. Breakfast here is famous for the sweet Swedish rolls. $60-95.

1802. This house, built in 1890, is on the National Register of Historic Places and is nestled among eight wooded acres. There are 17 rooms plus three full baths and two powder rooms. Much of the house, including two bedrooms, one bath, and one powder room, has been restored for guests. Restoration of two additional bedrooms and baths is in progress. Guests may enjoy walking the trails or simply observing beautiful sunsets, fall foliage, snow drifts, and animals. $65-75. Ten percent discount for weekly stays.

Bingham House. This modern farmhouse on property deeded from William Penn is furnished with Early American furnishings and antiques collected and inherited over the years. In West Chester, one-half hour to Brandywine Valley, Valley Forge, and Amish country, as well as all businesses along the Route 202 corridor from King of Prussia to Wilmington. Guests have access to refrigerator, microwave, grill, washer and dryer, telephone, TV, and VCR. $55-65.

The Bankhouse
Bed and Breakfast

875 Hillsdale Road, 19382
(610) 344-7388

An 18th-century "bankhouse" nestled in a quiet country setting with view of pond and horse farm. Rooms are charmingly decorated with country antiques and stenciling. Offers a great deal of privacy, including private entrance, porch, sitting room/library, and air conditioning. Near Longwood Gardens, Brandywine River Museum, and Winterthur. Easy drive to Valley Forge, Lancaster, and Philadelphia. Canoeing, horseback riding, biking, and walking/jogging trails offered in the area. Also, luscious country breakfast and afternoon snacks.

Hosts: Diana and Michael Bove
Rooms: 2 (1 PB; 1SB) $65-85
Full Breakfast
Credit Cards: None
Notes: 2, 5, 9, 12, 13

The Bankhouse

Bed and Breakfast
of Philadelphia

1616 Walnut Street, Suite 1120, Philadelphia, 19103
(215) 735-1917; (800) 220-1917
FAX (215) 735-1905

Hamanassett. This elegant manor house of a gentle country estate is tucked away on 36 acres of the Bradywine Valley. There are eight well-appointed rooms, all with private baths. When the cold winds blow, guests can relax before the large Federal fireplace in the grand living room, and a library with more than 2,000 volumes is available for guests to enjoy. Children over 12 welcome. Smoking outdoors only. $80-210.

Pheasant Hollow. This rural homestead of the 1800s sits quietly and majestically in the hills of Chester County. Set on three wooded acres, amidst neighboring horse farms, the first-floor guest rooms share a bath and are well-appointed with antiques and working fireplaces. A full country breakfast will satisfy any appetite for the better part of the day. Children are welcome. No smoking. $55-75.

West Chester Victorian Home. On a quiet knoll curved round by a country road, this gracious, former summer home is sheltered by ancient trees. It, and its equally gracious host, welcome the traveler to rooms with high ceilings and tall windows, warm breezes in the summer, and a crackling fire in the winter. The atrium is on ground level, just off the pool, with its queen-size double beds and private bath. A guest room with two twin beds, private bath, and fireplace is on the second floor. A third floor offers two rooms with double beds, one with a pair of twins; both share a bath. Children are welcome. Smoking is allowed. $40-60.

The Crooked Windsor

109 South Church Street, 19302
(215) 692-4896

Charming Victorian home in West Chester and completely furnished with fine antiques. Full breakfast served, along with teatime and refreshments for those who so desire. Also, pool and garden in season. Points of interest are within easy driving distance.

Host: Winifred Rupp
Rooms: 4 (SB) $65
Full Breakfast
Credit Cards: None
Notes: 2, 5, 8, 9, 11

Guesthouses, Inc.

P.O. Box 2137, West Chester, 19380
(215) 692-4575

093. Air-conditioned guest house offers a pleasant, comfortable, and convenient spot to use as a quiet retreat after a day's touring. The grounds have shade and foliaged privacy from the few houses that line this quiet dead-end street at the south edge of the borough. The main room is large and sunny and furnished in traditional oak with a queen-size bed, sitting area, dining and work area, and full bath. $75.

105. The guest house, a former carriage house, has been newly reconstructed and air-conditioned. There are two separate sections: one a first-floor apartment with fireplace, the other, on the up side of the building, has a living room with a clear view and a night telescope. There is a dining area and a kitchen that is stocked with breakfast treats. Bedroom is furnished with either twins or king-size bed with a festoon of dried spring flowers. $90-140.

627. The house is lovingly furnished with old Pennsylvanian family antiques and treasures. A quaint common room with modern entertainment is for guest use. The guest bedrooms are two to a floor in the front wing of the house; all large corner rooms, with tall ceilings and cross ventilation, and all are furnished with antique canopied high-post double-size beds. Country breakfast is served in the breakfast room or formal dining room. There is an outdoor swimming pool with spa. $75-110.

6 Pets welcome; 8 Children welcome; 9 Social drinking allowed; 10 Tennis available; 11 Swimming available; 12 Golf available; 13 Skiing available; 14 May be booked through travel agents.

707. The Valentine is newly restored and furnished to its original grandeur. The public rooms on the first floor are very elegant with high ceilings, carved woodwork, plaster ornamentation, gleaming hardwood floors, and tall Jefferson windows that open out to the loggia. Guest rooms are on the second and third floors. All are furnished in the Victorian Romantic-style and all have antique full-size beds. There are two additional bedrooms on the second floor that share a large hall bath. The top floor has four bedrooms that share a large hall bath. A full breakfast is served in the formal dining room. $65-110.

Monument House

1311 Birmingham Road, 19382
(610) 793-2986

Monument House is an early 19th-century clapboard house overlooking rolling farmland in the heart of Wyeth country, where the battle of the Brandywine was fought in 1777. Guests use the private first floor of the old part of the house, where there are two attractive double rooms with shared bathroom. Guests are also encouraged to make themselves at home in any other part of the house or grounds, as they wish.

Hosts: Maureen and Richard Brockman
Rooms: 2 (SB) $70
Full Breakfast
Credit Cards: None
Notes: 2, 5, 8, 9, 10, 11, 12, 14

WESTTOWN

Guesthouses, Inc.

P.O. Box 2137, West Chester, 19380
(215) 692-4575

110. On the outskirts of the rolling hills of Westtown, the beautifully preserved historic three-and-one-half-story stone farmhouse has been featured on Chester County Day. The interior is warm and inviting, generously furnished with antiques of the period and decorated with colors, fabrics, and objects of historical integrity. There is a

choice of two lovely second-floor, air-conditioned guest rooms; one with a full-size bed and one with twin beds. A country breakfast is served by the fire in the kitchen or in the sunroom, depending on season. $80-140.

WILKES-BARRE

The Weeping Willow Inn

Rural Delivery 7, Box 254, Tunkhannoch, 18657
(717) 836-5877

This comfortable Colonial home, circa 1840, has been lovingly restored, and the hosts cordially invite guests to experience its warmth and rich history. Three graciously appointed rooms furnished with a mixture of family treasures and antiques. A hearty country breakfast is served by candlelight. The hosts promise that a visit here will be one guests will never forget. Tunkhannoch abounds in scenic views, beautiful farmland, lovely lakes, and sleepy villages. Within 30 minutes of Wilkes-Barre and Scranton. Come relax, enjoy, and experience yesterday.

Hosts: Patty and Randy Ehrengeller
Rooms: 3 (PB) $60-70
Credit Cards: None
Notes: 2, 5, 8, 9, 10, 11, 12, 13

WILLIAMSPORT

The Reighard House

1323 East Third Street, 17701
(717) 326-3593; FAX (717) 323-4734

Built in 1905, the house is stone and brick. It has a formal parlor, a music room with grand piano, a library, and a formal oak-paneled dining room. Up the open oak staircase are six bedrooms, each with private bath, color TV, telephone, carpeting, and air conditioning. The old-fashioned front porch is perfect for relaxing.

Hosts: Bill and Sue Reighard
Rooms: 6 (PB) $68-88

NOTES: Credit cards accepted: A MasterCard; B Visa; C American Express; D Discover Card; E Diner's Club; F Other; 2 Personal checks accepted; 3 Lunch available; 4 Dinner available; 5 Open all year;

Full Breakfast
Credit Cards: A, B, C, E, F
Notes: 2, 5, 7, 8, 9, 10, 11, 12, 13, 14

YORK

Amanda's Bed and Breakfast

1428 Park Avenue, Annapolis, MD 21217
(301) 225-0001; (301) 383-1274

105. This 1836 restored brick Colonial is on three acres of manicured lawns with trees, shrubs, and flowers. This farmhouse with a fireplace has an antique shop on the premises. Three guest rooms with two shared baths. Just 20 minutes from Lancaster and a little more than an hour from Baltimore. $65.

Briarwold Bed and Breakfast

5400 Lincoln Highway, 17406
(717) 252-4619

Large, circa 1836, Colonial brick house, sitting in the middle of three acres of manicured lawn and many large trees. The three large bedrooms are furnished with country antiques, as are the other rooms of the house. Air conditioning.

Host: Marion Bischoff
Rooms: 3 (SB) $60
Full Breakfast
Credit Cards: None
Notes: 2, 5, 8, 12, 13

Smyser-Bair House Bed and Breakfast

30 South Beaver Street, 17401
(717) 854-3411

A magnificent 12-room Italianate townhouse in the historic district, this home is rich in architectural detail and contains stained-glass windows, pier mirrors, and ceiling medallions. There are three antique-filled guest rooms and a two-room suite. Enjoy the warm hospitality, walk to the farmers' market, historic sites, and antique shops. Eight blocks to the York Fairgrounds; near Lancaster and Gettysburg.

Hosts: The King family
Rooms: 4 (1 PB; 3 SB) $60-80
Full Breakfast
Credit Cards: A, B
Notes: 2, 5, 8, 9, 12, 13, 14

6 Pets welcome; 8 Children welcome; 9 Social drinking allowed; 10 Tennis available; 11 Swimming available; 12 Golf available; 13 Skiing available; 14 May be booked through travel agents.

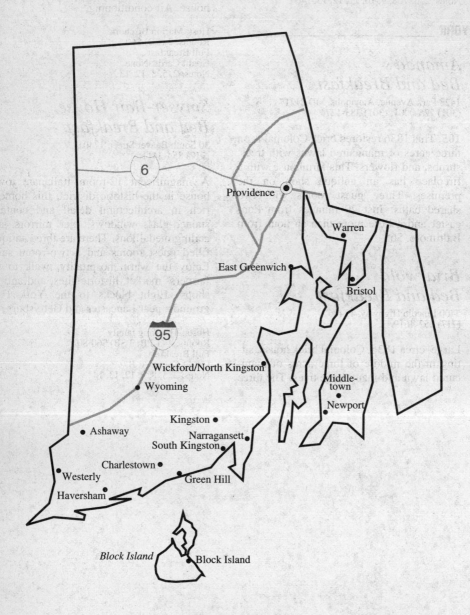

Providence

Warren

East Greenwich

Bristol

Wickford/North Kingston

Middle-
town

Wyoming

Newport

Kingston

Ashaway

Narragansett
South Kingston

Charlestown

Westerly

Green Hill

Haversham

Block Island
Block Island

Rhode Island

Rhode Island

Nutmeg B&B Agency

P.O. Box 1117, West Hartford, CT 06107
(203) 236-6698

514. Set on a knoll, this Colonial home is surrounded by trees and has a large yard, two patios, a screen house, and a pool. The three guest rooms share one bath on the second floor. There is a TV in the living room for guest use. A roll away bed is available. The home is convenient to Mystic, as well as the Coast Guard Academy, the University of Rhode Island, Newport, and Brown University. Continental breakfast. Smoking in designated areas. Children under six welcome. Pets in residence.

The Adrian

Old Town Road, 02807
(401) 466-2693; (800) 595-2693

This grand Victorian is now listed on the National Register of Historic Places. Cool, quiet location with scenic ocean views from lawns, porches, and decks, and a five-minute walk to the Atlantic Ocean and Old Harbor Village. Each of the ten rooms is furnished with antiques and has a private bath. Homemade Continental breakfast is included.

Host: Douglas Langdon
Rooms: 10 (PB) $75-175
Continental Breakfast
Credit Cards: None
Notes: 2, 8, 9, 11, 12

The Barrington Inn

Beach and Ocean Avenues, P.O. Box 397, 02807
(401) 466-5510

This recently renovated century-old farmhouse-turned-inn on beautiful Block Island has a warm, friendly atmosphere, and bright, cheerful rooms. Indescribable views await guests' visit. Watch the sunset from the private guest deck. Enjoy a peaceful, quiet setting. Walk to the beach, shops, and restaurants. Two-bedroom housekeeping apartments also available. Open April through October. Off-season rates. Brochure available.

Hosts: Joan and Howard Ballard
Rooms: 6 (PB) $45-145
Apartments: 2
Continental Breakfast
Credit Cards: A, B
Notes: 2, 8 (over 12), 9, 10, 11

The Blue Dory Inn

Box 488, 02807
(401) 466-5891; (800) 992-7290

The Victorian age is alive and well at the Blue Dory. On Crescent Beach, this delightful year-round inn offers an opportunity to revisit a period of time that has long since gone by. The inn is filled with antiques and turn-of-the-century decor, yet has all the modern comforts.

Host: Ann Loedy
Rooms: 14 (PB) $65-245
Continental Breakfast
Credit Cards: A, B, C, F
Notes: 2, 5, 7, 8, 9, 10, 11

NOTES: Credit cards accepted: A MasterCard; B Visa; C American Express; D Discover Card; E Diner's Club; F Other; 2 Personal checks accepted; 3 Lunch available; 4 Dinner available; 5 Open all year; 6 Pets welcome; 7 Smoking allowed; 8 Children welcome; 9 Social drinking allowed; 10 Tennis available; 11 Swimming available; 12 Golf available; 13 Skiing available; 14 May be booked through travel agents.

The Continental Inn
Box 575, 02807
(401) 466-5136

The Continental is in the historic district, within easy walking distance of the ferry landing, the beach, and all the shops and restaurants of the town. Bed and breakfast are provided in a home-like atmosphere at reasonable rates. It is one of Block Island's smallest inns, with a beautiful view of Continental Pond, home to ducks and geese in a very tranquil country setting.

Host: Lila Clerk
Rooms: 2 (SB) $65-115
Full Breakfast
Credit Cards: None
Notes: 2, 5, 7, 9, 10, 11

Harborside Inn
Water Street, 02807
(401) 466-5504

Escape from the 20th-century stress and strain to victorian-style peace and tranquility at Harborside Inn. As visitors sail into Old Harbor, they are welcomed by a harbor-view terrace decorated with window boxes ablaze with fresh red geraniums. On Water Street, it's a pleasant stroll to the stretching beaches, quaint shops, and breathtaking bluffs. At the end of the day, visit the festive and unusual sidewalk restaurant and bar, and enjoy cocktails, dinner, and Harborside hospitality.

Host: Christopher Sereno
Rooms: 35 (22 PB; 13 SB) $65-145
Full Breakfast
Credit Cards: A, B, C
Notes: 2, 3, 4, 7, 8, 9

Hotel Manisses
Spring Street, 02807
(401) 466-2421; (401) 466-2063

Step into 19th-century yesteryear with a stay at this romantic Victorian hotel featuring 17 meticulously appointed rooms with private baths and authentic Victorian furni-

Hotel Manisses

ture. Some rooms have Jacuzzis. The award-winning dining room serves dinner every evening. Sample delicious selections from the widely varied menu as featured in *Gourmet* magazine. Tableside flaming coffees, after dinner drinks, and desserts served nightly in the Upstairs Parlors. The petting zoo has llamas, Sicilian donkeys, Nubian, Pygmy, and fainting goats, and other wonderful animals.

Hosts: The Abrams family
Rooms: 17 (PB) $65-300
Full Breakfast
Credit Cards: A, B, C
Notes: 2, 4, 5, 7, 8 (over 10), 9, 10, 11, 14

Old Town Inn
P.O. Box 351, 02807
(401) 466-5958

The Old Town Inn is at the junction of Old Town Road and Center Road, about one mile from the ferry landing. Ten guest rooms; four in the old section featuring antique furniture and six in the new east wing featuring queen-size beds, full bath, refrigerator, etc. Breakfasts, served in the 19th-century dining rooms, are the best on the island. On about four acres of landscaped area.

Hosts: Ralph, Monica, and David Gunter
Rooms: 10 (8 PB; 2 SB) $80-120
Full Breakfast
Credit Cards: A, B
Notes: 2

NOTES: Credit cards accepted: A MasterCard; B Visa; C American Express; D Discover Card; E Diner's Club; F Other; 2 Personal checks accepted; 3 Lunch available; 4 Dinner available; 5 Open all year;

Rose Farm Inn

Roslyn Road, Box 3, 02807
(401) 466-2021

Experience the romance of the Victorian era. Guests can treat themselves to a romantic room beautifully furnished with antiques and king-size canopied bed or queen-size bed. Enjoy the peaceful tranquility of the farm from shaded decks cooled by gentle ocean breezes. Gaze at the ocean from the guest room window or share a whirlpool bath for two. Awaken to a light buffet breakfast served in the charming porch dining room with an ocean view. Bicycle rentals available. Closed November through April.

Hosts: Robert and Judith Rose
Rooms: 19 (17 PB; 2 SB) $90-175
Continental Breakfast
Credit Cards: A, B, C, D
Notes: 2, 7 (limited), 8 (over 12), 9, 10, 11, 14

The Sheffield House Bed and Breakfast

High Street, P.O. Box C-2, 02807
(401) 466-2494; FAX (401) 466-5067

The Sheffield House, an 1888 Queen Anne Victorian, is set amidst perennial gardens, a five-minute walk from beaches, shops, and restaurants. The seven guest rooms are individually decorated with antiques and family pieces for the comfort of the guests. Rocking chairs on the porch, a country kitchen, and quiet private garden ensure a tranquil getaway.

Hosts: Steve and Claire McQueeny and family
Rooms: 7 (5 PB; 2 SB) $50-140
Continental Breakfast
Credit Cards: A, B, C
Notes: 2, 5, 9, 10, 11, 14

1661 Inn Guest House and Nicholas Ball Cottage

Spring Street, 02807
(401) 466-2421; (401) 466-2063

Enjoy the spectacular ocean views and authentic New England decor of The 1661 Inn. Most rooms feature an ocean view, private deck, and Jacuzzi; some rooms feature fireplaces. Marvel at the spectacular views of the Atlantic Ocean from the canopy-covered deck while enjoying a full buffet breakfast and lunch menu. The Nicholas Ball Cottage has three luxurious rooms with fireplaces and Jacuzzis. Guest house open all year. There is a petting zoo with llamas, Sicilian donkeys, Nubian, Pygmy, and fainting goats, plus other wonderful animals.

Hosts: Joan and Justin Abrams; Steve and Rita Draper
Rooms: 19 (14 PB; 5 SB) $65-300
Full Breakfast
Credit Cards: A, B, C
Notes: 2, 3, 4, 5, 7, 8, 9, 10, 11, 14

The White House

Spring Street, 02807
(401) 466-2653

Large island manor house with two bedrooms and two baths. French Provincial antique furnishings. Notable collection of presidential autographs and documents. Full breakfast. All kinds of in-house services and amenities.

Host: J.V. Connolly
Rooms: 2 (SB) $100-120
Full Breakfast
Credit Cards: A, B, C
Notes: 2, 5, 7, 9, 10, 11

BRISTOL

Joseph Reynolds House

956 Hope Street, Route 114, P.O. Box 5, 02809
(401) 254-0230; (800) 754-0230
FAX (401) 253-1082

National Historic Landmark home (circa 1695) in an old New England seaport on Narragansett Bay. Close to new 13-mile bike path. The town has seven museums, including the America's Cup Hall of Fame.

---

6 Pets welcome; 8 Children welcome; 9 Social drinking allowed; 10 Tennis available; 11 Swimming available; 12 Golf available; 13 Skiing available; 14 May be booked through travel agents.

Host: Wendy Anderson
Rooms: 7 (4 SB) $75-85
Full Breakfast
Credit Cards: A, B, C
Notes: 2, 3 (boxed), 4, 5, 6, 8 (over 10), 9, 10, 11, 12, 14

William's Grant Inn

154 High Street, 02809
(401) 253-4222

Just two blocks from Bristol's harbor is William's Grant Inn, circa 1808. The home of a sea captain, this five-bay high-style Federal house is now a gracious inn for guests to enjoy. It is a showcase for traditional and whimsical artwork throughout. The eclectic full breakfasts are always a treat with chefs Mary and Mike! A central location to Boston, Providence, and Newport. Seven museums and a 30-mile bike path within two miles of the inn.

Hosts: Mary and Mike Rose
Rooms: 5 (3 PB; 2 SB) $65-95
Full Breakfast
Credit Cards: A, B, C, E, F
Notes: 2, 5, 7 (limited), 8 (over 12), 9, 10, 11, 12, 14

William's Grant Inn

CHARLESTOWN

One Willow by the Sea

1 Willow Road, 02813
(401) 364-0802

Enjoy hospitality year-round in a peaceful, rural home. South County shoreline community, where guest comfort is a priority. Wake to birds, sunshine, and sea breezes. Delicious gourmet breakfast is served in summer on the sun deck. Explore the miles of beautiful sandy beaches, salt ponds, and wildlife refuges. Restaurants, theaters, live music, antique shows, craft fairs, historic New England, and Narragansett Indian landmarks nearby. Providence, Newport, Block Island, and Mystic are short drives away. Host speaks French.

Host: Denise Dillon Fuge
Rooms: 4 (SB) $55-75
Full Breakfast
Credit Cards: None
Notes: 2, 5, 8, 10, 11, 12, 14

EAST GREENWICH

Anna's Victorian Connection

5 Fowler Avenue, Newport, RI 02840
(401) 849-2489

0017. The host, a retired executive and town councilman, welcomes travelers to his home with every comfort he ever wished for in his own years of travel. His quiet home in East Greenwich has been designed with guests' privacy in mind. Both guest rooms have king-size beds, convertible to twin, and private baths. Unwind by shooting pool in the pool room, or relax on the deck overlooking a former cranberry bog. $55-85.

GREEN HILL

Fairfield by the Sea

527 Green Hill Beach Road, 02879
(401) 789-4717

On four secluded acres, this Contemporary house with cathedral ceilings, spiral staircase, and lots of windows offers a casual friendly atmosphere. Beach is a short walk or bike ride away. Excellent golfing, the-

NOTES: Credit cards accepted: A MasterCard; B Visa; C American Express; D Discover Card; E Diner's Club; F Other; 2 Personal checks accepted; 3 Lunch available; 4 Dinner available; 5 Open all year;

ater, wildlife refuge. URI, Mystic, Block Island, and Newport are nearby. Perfect for biking, walking, and in-line skating. Delicious breakfasts lovingly prepared by hosts. One is a culinary graduate of Johnson-Wales and the other is a catering specialist. In residence, "Maxine," a five-pound dog that loves to play fetch and make new friends.

Hosts: Kit Lewis Reilly and Russell Reilly
Rooms: 2 (SB) $50-65
Full Breakfast
Credit Cards: C
Notes: 2, 5, 8, 10, 11, 12

HAVERSHAM

Covered Bridge

P.O. Box 447A, Norfolk, CT 06058
(203) 542-5944

1HR1. Early 1900s beach home the artist/architect owner has redone to create a spectacular home in a secluded setting overlooking a saltwater pond with a view of the ocean. There are two guest rooms in the main house, one with a balcony, which are decorated with antiques and paintings done by the owner. There are also two cottages on the grounds. A Continental plus breakfast is served in the dining room or on the terrace overlooking the water. $95-150.

KINGSTON

Anna's Victorian Connection

5 Fowler Avenue, Newport, RI 02840
(401) 849-2489

0014. This circa 1875 Victorian home is on a portion of land known as Brown's Corner, in the historic village of Kingston. It remained in the Brown family until 1992, when it was meticulously restored to its former beauty. King-size, queen-size, and double bedrooms are available, with private and shared baths, and gracious sitting rooms. A full breakfast is served in the ele-

gant dining room. The University of Rhode Island is a short walk away; saltwater beaches, the attractions of Newport, summer theater, antiques, and art are only a few minutes' drive. $45-80.

The Farmer Brown House

2492 Kingston Road, 02881
(401) 783-5477

Meticulously restored Victorian home in the historic village of Kingston. Two blocks from the University of Rhode Island; minutes from beaches, summer theater, antiques, art centers, and Newport's many attractions. Ten air-conditioned rooms, most with private baths. Gracious sitting room and full breakfast in elegant dining room with fireplace. Tennis, swimming, and golf nearby. No children. No smoking.

Host: Denise M. Cheltra
Rooms: 10 (8 PB; 2 SB) $75-120
Full Breakfast
Credit Cards: None
Notes: 2, 9, 10, 11, 12

MIDDLETOWN

Anna's Victorian Connection

5 Fowler Avenue, Newport, RI 02840
(401) 849-2489

0004. This small Victorian farmhouse has been completely restored by its owner to an airy country decor. Two twin rooms and a double room share two bathrooms—one is a "country bath," reminiscent of Saturday nights in a big steaming tub; the other is a modern bath with shower. Only two miles from Newport, this charming home offers easy access to beaches, a bird sanctuary, and St. George's School. $65–75.

0005. Dating from 1732, the living room of this ten-room, red-shingled farmhouse was once a plantation blacksmith's shop. The fireplace, granite walls, original wood ceiling, and hand-hewn beams provide authen-

6 Pets welcome; 8 Children welcome; 9 Social drinking allowed; 10 Tennis available; 11 Swimming available; 12 Golf available; 13 Skiing available; 14 May be booked through travel agents.

tic Colonial atmosphere. The Yellow and Peach Rooms share a bath, but each has a private lavatory. One has a queen-size bed; the other, twin four-posters. The Green Room sleeps four in king-size and double beds, with private bath. There is also a swimming pool. No smoking. Children over five welcome. $50-95.

The Briar Patch

42 Briarwood Avenue, 02842
(401) 841-5824

The Briar Patch is a small homestay inn featuring personal attention; bright, flowery decor; and ocean views. A four-minute walk from Newport Beach and famous Cliffwalk, with restaurants and clubs also within walking distance. Tennis, swimming, and golf nearby.

Host: Maureen McCracken
Rooms: 2 (2 PB) $95
Full Breakfast
Credit Cards: None
Notes: 2, 5, 8 (over 12), 9, 10, 11, 12

The Country Goose

563 Greenend Avenue, 02842
(401) 846-6308)

This charming country farmhouse, built in 1898, is the original farmhouse used for three generations. Guests receive complimentary wine and cheese upon arrival. Breakfast is served in surroundings of traditional country decor of family heirlooms and antiques. Guests may play softball, croquet, and volleyball. If requested, hosts can provide lounge chairs, a picnic table, and grills for cookouts. Just minutes from beaches, mansions, shopping, Tennis Hall of Fame, Norman Bird Sanctuary, and Yachting Center.

Hostess: Paula Kelley
Rooms: 3 (SB) $55-85
Full and Continental Breakfasts
Credit Cards: A, B
Notes: 2, 5, 7 (limited), 8, 9, 10, 11, 12

Finnegan's Inn at Shadow Lawn

120 Miantonomi Avenue, 02842
(401) 849-1298; (800) 828-0000
FAX (401) 849-1306

Finnegan's Inn at Shadow Lawn, one of Newport County's finest bed and breakfast inns, is on two acres of beautifully landscaped lawns and gardens. This 1850s Victorian mansion, with its crystal chandeliers and stained-glass windows, has eight large bedrooms, each with private bath, television, refrigerator, and air conditioning. Five rooms also have attached kitchens. Come and enjoy a complimentary bottle of wine, and join the hosts daily from 3:00 to 5:00 P.M. for a glass of sherry.

Hosts: Randy and Selma Fabricant
Rooms: 8 (PB) $65-130
Continental Breakfast
Credit Cards: A, B
Notes: 5, 8 (12 and older), 9, 10, 11, 12

Lindsey's Guest House

6 James Street, 02840
(401) 846-9386

One mile to Newport's famous mansions, Cliff Walk, and the Tennis Hall of Fame. Lindsey's is a split-level home with a large yard, deck, Continental plus breakfast, and off-street parking. Ten-minute walk to beaches and Norman Bird Sanctuary.

Host: Anne
Rooms: 3 (1 PB; 2 SB) $40-80
Continental Breakfast
Credit Cards: A, B
Notes: 2, 5, 8, 9, 10, 11, 12, 14

NARRAGANSETT

Bed and Breakfast Inns of New England

128 South Hoop Pole Road, Guilford, CT 06437
(800) 582-0853; (203) 457-0042

RI-905. Enjoy the elegance of a circa 1884 oceanfront Victorian summer estate on the

National Register of Historic Places. Overlooking the ocean and set on two acres, guests may explore the grounds, play croquet, sunbathe, swim in the ocean, and relax on the sun porch or patio. The eight guest rooms have a variety of bed sizes, and are furnished with antiques and collectibles. Many have ocean views, and all rooms have private baths. Children over ten are welcome. Resident dog, but no guest pets. No smoking. $60-125.

Four Gables

12 South Pier Road, 02882
(401) 789-6948

Built by an architect in 1898, this charming home has many interesting features. It is furnished with antiques and unique handcrafted items and offers an extensive library, especially in needlework and gardening. Fishing equipment and advice available. Breakfast is served in the dining room overlooking the ocean, or guests may choose to enjoy the veranda with its spectacular views. Within walking distance of the beach, restaurants, and shops, and within a short drive to many attractions.

Hosts: Terry and Barbara Higgins
Rooms: 2 (SB) $60-85
Full Breakfast
Credit Cards: A, B
Notes: 2, 5, 8 (over 12), 9, 10, 11, 12

1900 House

50 Kingstown Road, 02882
(401) 789-7971

Restored Victorian, circa 1900, with antique furniture, quiet street, lavender front door, and pretty gardens. Each room is unique, but all include country antiques, wooden bed frames, canopied bed, thick Oriental rugs, and small special touches such as the original owners' marriage certificate. Beach is a five-minute walk. Guests have use of a porch, which has cool sea breezes. Full gourmet breakfast served.

Hosts: Bill and Sandra Panzeri
Rooms: 3 (1 PB; 2 SB) $55-75
Full Breakfast
Credit Cards: None
Notes: 2, 5, 10, 11, 12

The Old Clerk House

49 Narrangansett Avenue, 02882
(401) 783-8008

Enjoy English country comfort in this Victorian home. Twin, double, and king-size beds with private baths, color TV, VCR, and air conditioning available. Full home-cooked breakfast is served in plant-filled sunroom. Only one block from beautiful beach, movie theater, library, and fine restaurants. Tennis three blocks away. Ten minutes to Block Island Ferry; 18 miles from Newport. Guest living room. Twenty minutes to golfing. Off-street parking. No smoking.

Host: Patricia Watkins
Rooms: 2 (PB) $65-85
Full Breakfast
Credit Cards: None
Notes: 2, 5, 9, 10, 11, 12, 14

Pleasant Cottage

104 Robinson Street, 02882
(401) 783-6895

This charming cottage is on a half-acre of woods and gardens. A quiet serene atmosphere awaits guests just blocks from lovely Narragansett Beach. Enclosed outdoor shower. Relax on large screened porch. Bedrooms with shared bath, or private bath and private entrance. Full breakfast served, including a treat for coffee lovers. Reservations and advance deposit required.

Hosts: Fred and Terry Sepp
Rooms: 3 (1 PB; 2 SB) $55-65
Full Breakfast
Credit Cards: None
Notes: 2, 9, 10, 11, 12

The Richards

144 Gibson Avenue, 02882
(401) 789-7746

6 Pets welcome; 8 Children welcome; 9 Social drinking allowed; 10 Tennis available; 11 Swimming available; 12 Golf available; 13 Skiing available; 14 May be booked through travel agents.

Gracious accommodations in an 1884 historic manse. Relax by the fire in the library or in the guest room with fireplace. Enjoy a leisurely full breakfast with homemade muffins, strudels, and blintzes. The hostess' special touches will spoil anyone—down comforters, canopied beds, and flowers from the gardens. Minimum-stay requirements for weekends and holidays. Special suite rates available for couples traveling together.

Hosts: Steven and Nancy Richards
Rooms: 4 (2 PB; 2 SB) $60-85
Suite: (PB) $10
Full Breakfast
Credit Cards: None
Notes: 2, 5, 9, 10, 11, 12

Seafield Cottage

110 Boon Street, 02882
(401) 783-2432

A 17-room, 100-year-old Cape Anne furnished with lace and full of charming ambience. Bedrooms with canopied beds, down comforters and pillows, and a swooner couch. Semi-private baths. Continental breakfast includes unlimited freshly ground imported coffee, capuccino, juice, fruit compote, breakfast calzones, Belgian waffles, Scotch scones, or coffeecake. One block from the ocean; 15 minutes from Newport.

Hosts: Carl and Anne Cottle
Rooms: 3 (S2B) $50
Continental Breakfast
Credit Cards: None
Notes: 2, 5, 9, 11, 12

The Wishing Well Bed and Breakfast

191 Ocean Road, 02882
(401) 782-6138

This Dutch Colonial, circa 1880, boasts breathtaking views of the Atlantic Ocean. Beaches, restaurants, and shops are within walking distance. Newport, casinos, and Block Island Ferry are a short drive. The house is decorated in a country Victorian-style with a romantic flair. Luxurious, private suite accommodations are offered; one with fireplace and private balcony. Each suite is equipped with radio, television, and VCR. Return to old world romance and relaxation at The Wishing Well.

Suites: 2 (PB) $85
Full Breakfast
Credit Cards: None
Notes: 2, 5, 10, 11, 12, 14

NEWPORT

Admiral Benbow Inn

93 Pelham Street, 02840
(401) 846-4256; (800) 343-2863
FAX (401) 846-4289

Built as an inn in 1855 and listed on the National Register of Historic Places, this Italianate Victorian is on a tree lined street in walking distance to all Newport has to offer. Beautifully decorated and accommodating. Room 12 has a spectacular view of Newport Harbor. Open all year; 15 rooms with private baths, telephones, AC, parking complimentary. Expanded Continental breakfast.

Host: Cathy Darigan
Rooms: 15 (PB) $98-125
Continental Breakfast
Credit Cards: A, B, C, E
Notes: 5, 8 (over 12), 9, 14

Admiral Farragut Inn

31 Clarke Street, 02840
(401) 846-4256; (800) 343-2863
FAX (401) 846-4289

The Admiral Farragut Inn, circa 1702, is a classic American Colonial. Exclusive and charming on a quiet gas lamp-lit street. Living history in authentic period antiques and handmade pencil post beds with comfortable duvets. Ideal for a winter getaway. Close to America's first synagogue, First Free Black Church, First Baptist Church, First Unitarian Church. Also near 1638 Trinity Church, The First Quaker Meeting

House, and The Friends Museum. A true experience. Sailing nearby.

Host: Mary Ann Brett
Rooms: 10 (PB) $55-135
Full Breakfast
Credit Cards: A, B, C, E
Notes: 1, 7, 8, 9

The Admiral Fitzroy Inn

398 Thames Street, 02840
(401) 848-8000; (800) 343-2863
FAX (401) 846-4289

This inn is in the heart of Newport's yachting district, central to all that Newport has to offer. The inn is decorated in its own distinctive style, artfully conceived, and a showcase for fine craftsmanship. Sleigh and brass beds, lace linens, and plush duvets are part of each room's individual decor, and each room has glazed finished walls, handpainted with pleasing designs and crisp flower motifs. Hidden away within the handmade Swedish cupboards, guests will find a TV with cable, a small refrigerator, electric tea kettle, and fixings. Also, in each room, there is a private bath with a tub, telephone, heat and cool controls, and a hair dryer. Complimentary full breakfast can be enjoyed downstairs, in the guests' own room, or on the deck overlooking Newport Harbor.

Host: Holly Eastman
Rooms: 18 (PB) $85-150
Full and Continental Breakfasts
Credit Cards: A, B, C, D, E
Notes: 2, 5, 7, 8, 9, 10, 11, 12. 14

Anna's Victorian Connection

5 Fowler Avenue, Newport, RI 02840
(401) 849-2489

0001. A beautiful 1883 Dutch Colonial revival house with terrific views of Newport's Easton Beach. Now retired, the hosts have two very graciously appointed suites, for two to four guests each, with private baths, telephone, and TV. A crib, playpen, and highchair are also available to accommodate children of all ages. Breakfast is served in the dining room, and in warmer months on a sun porch with water view. Smoking is permitted. A cat is in residence. $75-175.

0002. Husband and wife psychologists have turned the third floor of their Victorian home into a comfortable bed and breakfast. The "Blue Room" has a pop-up trundle bed, which becomes a double bed for couples or a pair of twins for others; the "Yellow Room" has a king-size bed and room for a third person or child; the "Peach Room" is the sitting room. All are air-conditioned and share a bath. There is also a "Toy Room," where visiting children are welcome to play. In the heart of downtown Newport, with off street parking, this home is an easy walk from restaurants and shopping. Dog and cat in residence. $50-85.

0003. An elegant Greek Revival "cottage" in a quiet, downtown Newport neighborhood, this private home offers truly exquisite decor, with a crackling fire in the living room in winter, and a screened porch furnished with wicker in the summer. Antiques and beautiful collections abound throughout. The guest rooms have canopied beds in both double- and twin-bedded rooms; there are also two guest sitting rooms. $95-150.

0006. Escape via launch from Newport or guests can bring their own boats to this classic 1869 lighthouse on a one-and-a-half acre island in Narragansett Bay. A museum and two guest rooms share the first floor; the lighthouse keeper's apartment is on the second. The rooms feature authentic period furnishings, and the view of the water and sky is unbeatable! No smoking. $50-115.

0008. This exquisite Empire Victorian house, built in 1873, is in the historic Point section of Newport. Luxury accommodations are available in rooms furnished with

6 Pets welcome; 8 Children welcome; 9 Social drinking allowed; 10 Tennis available; 11 Swimming available; 12 Golf available; 13 Skiing available; 14 May be booked through travel agents.

antiques, cable TV, and private baths. Many have spectacular views of Newport Harbor and the city. Full breakfast is served in the dining room, on the front porch, or in the garden, depending on the season. Off-street parking is available, so that guests may walk into downtown Newport and its attractions. $85-150.

0010. Built around the turn-of-the-century on the grounds of Newport's famous Ocean House, a favored resort of 19th-century society, this charming Victorian has been restored to its former elegance with a delightful mix of antiques and Shaker-style furniture. Each guest room features a queen-size bed, hand-stenciled walls, private bath, air conditioning, and TV. Full breakfast is served in the dining room or on the porch overlooking the garden. No smoking allowed. Children over six are welcome. $55-125.

0013. When this villa, designed by William Ralph Emerson, was built in 1869, the *Boston Journal* said, "The most elegantly finished house ever built in Newport is that of Mr. M.H. Sanford, just completed...." This magnificent home, the last remaining example of its style, has been in the hosts' family since 1895, and they take pride in offering extraordinary accommodations. Sit on the waterfront porch and watch the boats sail by, enjoy the pool and spa (by arrangement), or stroll into downtown Newport. $65-250.

0016. This elegant and historic Newport inn was built in 1760 for Colonel Francis Malbone, a wealthy shipping merchant. Seized by the British during the Revolutionary War, it was used to store gold, giving it the nickname, "Treasure House." Painstakingly restored and proudly listed on the National Register of Historic Places, the inn offers period charm and comfort in guest rooms and suites with private baths, elegant sitting

and dining rooms, and beautifully landscaped gardens. Children over 12 welcome. $85-225.

Brinley Victorian Inn

23 Brinley Street, 02840
(401) 849-7645

Romantic year-round, the inn becomes a Victorian Christmas dream come true. Comfortable antiques and fresh flowers fill every room. Friendly, unpretentious service and attention to detail will make this inn a traveler's haven in Newport. Park and walk everywhere. AAA approved. Minimum stay on weekends is two nights and on holidays is three nights.

Hosts: John and Jennifer Sweetman
Rooms: 17 (13 PB; 4 SB) $55-145
Continental Breakfast
Credit Cards: A, B
Notes: 2, 5, 7, 8 (over 12), 9, 10, 11, 12, 14

Cliffside Inn

2 Seaview Avenue, 02840
(401) 845-1811

An elegant Victorian Inn near the beginning of Newport's famous Cliffwalk and the beach. Built in 1880 by Governor Thomas Swann of Maryland as a summer residence, the house became the first location of St. George's School in 1897 and was later owned by Newport artist Beatrice Turner. In addition to a full breakfast, host serves appetizers. Guest rooms have private baths, some with whirlpool or steam baths. Some rooms have fireplaces. Air conditioning, cable TV, and telephones. Conference facilities are also available. "One of Newport's best kept secrets...," *Bed and Breakfast in New England.*

Host: Stephan Nicolas
Rooms: 12 (PB) $135-325
Full Breakfast
Credit Cards: A, B, C, D, E
Notes: 2, 5, 9, 10, 11, 14

NOTES: Credit cards accepted: A MasterCard; B Visa; C American Express; D Discover Card; E Diner's Club; F Other; 2 Personal checks accepted; 3 Lunch available; 4 Dinner available; 5 Open all year;

Cliff View Guest House

4 Cliff Terrace, 02840
(401) 846-0885

A two-story 1870 Victorian on a quiet dead-end street leading to the beautiful Cliff Walk, a three-mile path bordering the ocean. Five-minute walk to beach; 15-minute walk to downtown harbor area. Ten-room house with four guest bedrooms; two share a bath and have view of ocean; two have private baths, but no ocean view. Air conditioner can be installed for extra charge upon advance notice. The hostess' French-speaking grandson is on the premises June through September.

Host: Pauline Shea
Rooms: 4 (2 PB; 2 SB) $55-75
Continental Breakfast
Credit Cards: A, B
Notes: 2, 9, 10, 11, 12, 14

DESTINNATIONS
New England

P.O. Box 1173, Osterville, MA 02655
(508) 428-5600; Reservations (800) 333-4667
FAX (508) 420-0565

7455. In the heart of Newport, this collection of three fine inns, each different, offers traditional New England hospitality with today's amenities. One inn, with 15 individually decorated rooms, has private baths, telephone, and air conditioning; a gourmet Continental breakfast is served each morning. A second inn, circa 1702, has nine rooms with Colonial themes, a full breakfast is served each morning. The third inn, circa 1854, features 18 hand-painted guest rooms with private bath, telephone, air conditioning, refrigerator, and tea kettle (with fixings); there is a European-style elevator for easy access, and a full breakfast is served daily. A fourth building has nine rooms, each with private bath, TV, small refrigerator, and telephone; this building has no on-site innkeeper. Conference facilities available. Children over 12; no pets. Smoking restricted to certain buildings. Open year-round. $80-150.

The 1855 Marshall Slocum Guest House

29 Kay Street, 02840
(401) 841-5120

The house is comfortably furnished with a mixture of antiques, collectibles, and family treasures. Guests enjoy the floor-to-ceiling-mirrored foyer leading upstairs to the five bedrooms; two with private half baths, and three full baths. Hosts share the parlor, TV/reading room, and dining room where a full breakfast is served each morning. The spacious back yard and deck or the front porch with rockers are lovely places to breakfast, plan the day's activities, or take some sun and relax.

Host: Joan Wilson
Rooms: 5 (2 PB; 3 SB) $70-120
Full Breakfast
Credit Cards: A, B, C, D, E
Notes: 2, 3, 4, 5, 9, 10, 11, 12, 14

Finnegan's Inn at Shadow Lawn

120 Miantonomi Avenue, 02842
(401) 849-1298; (800) 828-0000
FAX (401) 849-1306

One of Newport County's finest inns, on two acres of beautifully landscaped lawns and gardens. This 1850s Victorian mansion, with its crystal chandeliers and stained-glass windows, has eight large bedrooms. Each with private bathroom, television, refrigerator, and air conditioning. Five rooms also have attached kitchens. Enjoy a bottle of complimentary wine. Join the hosts from 3:00 to 5:00 P.M. daily for a glass of sherry.

Hosts: Randy and Selma Fabricant
Rooms: 8 (PB) $95-130
Continental Breakfast
Credit Cards: A, B, C
Notes: 5, 9, 10, 12

The Francis Malbone House

392 Thames Street, 02840
(401) 846-0392

6 Pets welcome; 8 Children welcome; 9 Social drinking allowed; 10 Tennis available; 11 Swimming available; 12 Golf available; 13 Skiing available; 14 May be booked through travel agents.

This historic inn was built in 1760 for Colonel Francis Malbone, who made his fortune as a shipping merchant. The design of the house is attributed to Peter Harrison, the architect responsible for Touro Synagogue and the Redwood Library. Guests will enjoy the comfortable elegance of the Francis Malbone House, which is proudly listed on the National Register of Historic Places. The inn offers a downtown harbor location, private baths, full breakfast, fireplaces, corporate packages, and gracious rooms and gardens for elegant entertaining.

Host: Will Dewey
Rooms: 9 (PB) $105-295
Full Breakfast
Credit Cards: A, B, C
Notes: 2 , 5, 11, 14

Hydrangea House Inn

16 Bellevue Avenue, 02840
(800) 945-4667

In the heart of Newport's walking district, the inn's six guest rooms are sumptuously decorated with fine antiques, fine fabrics, and original works of art. All guest rooms have private baths, are air-conditioned, and are nonsmoking. All rates quoted include a gratifying three-course buffet breakfast each morning that is served in the inn's contemporary fine art gallery. The inn has been inspected and approved by AAA.

Host: Grant Edmondson
Rooms: 6 (PB) $59-139
Full Breakfast
Credit Cards: A, B
Notes: 2, 5, 8, 9, 10, 11, 12, 14

Jenkins Guest House

206 South Rhode Island Avenue, 02840
(401) 847-6801

The hosts built this Cape Cod when they were married. Since their eight children who were raised in this house are now grown and on their own, the hosts have been using the extra rooms for guests since 1978. Having lived in Newport all their lives, they have interesting stories to tell from a local viewpoint

Jenkins Guest House

and can provide helpful information about restaurants and places to visit. On a quiet little street just a three-minute walk from the beach or a ten-minute walk to the mansions or the harbor, with plenty of parking on the grounds. Enjoy the homemade muffins for breakfast in a country-in-the-city atmosphere. Air-conditioned.

Hosts: David and Sally Jenkins
Rooms: 3 (1 PB; 2SB) $65
Continental Breakfast
Credit Cards: None
Notes: 2, 8, 9, 10, 11

La Forge Cottage

96 Pelham Street, 02840
(401) 847-4400

A Victorian bed and breakfast in the heart of Newport's Historic Hill area. Close to beaches and downtown. All rooms have private baths, TVs, telephones, air conditioning, refrigerators, and full breakfast room service. French, Spanish, and German spoken. Reservations suggested. Minimum stay on weekends is two nights and on holidays is three nights.

Hosts: Louis and Margot Droual
Rooms: 6 (PB) $56-134.40
Suites: 4 (PB) $67.20-162.40
Full Breakfast
Credit Cards: A, B, C, D
Notes: 2, 5, 7, 8, 9, 10, 11, 12, 14

The Melville House

39 Clark Street, 02840
(401) 847-0640

Step back into the past and stay at a Colonial inn, built circa 1750, "where the past is present." The Melville House is on the National Register of Historic Places, and is in the heart of Newport's historic district. Walk around the corner to the Brick Market and the wharves. Enjoy a leisurely home-made breakfast in the morning, and join the hosts for complimentary tea and sherry before dinner. Off-street parking.

Hosts: Vince DeRico and David Horan
Rooms: 7 (5 PB; 2 SB) $50-125
Continental Breakfast
Credit Cards: A, B, C
Notes: 2, 3, 5, 9, 10, 11, 12, 14

Pilgrim House Inn

123 Spring Street, 02840
(401) 846-0040; (800) 525-8373

This Victorian inn, with its comforts and elegance, is two blocks from the harbor in the midst of the historic district. A living room with fireplace, immaculate rooms, and wonderful atmosphere await guests. Breakfast on the deck overlooking Newport's harbor. Just outside the door are the mansions, shops, and restaurants. Closed during the month of January.

Hosts: Pam and Bruce Bayuk
Rooms: 10 (8 PB; 2 SB) $49.50-137.50
Continental Breakfast
Credit Cards: A, B
Notes: 2, 8 (over 12), 9, 10, 11, 12, 14

Pilgrim House Inn

Polly's Place

349 Valley Road, Route 214, 02840
(401) 847-2160

A quiet retreat one mile from Newport's harbor, historic homes, and sandy beaches. Polly is a longtime Newport resident willing to give helpful advice to travelers interested in the area. Rooms are large, clean, and very attractive. Breakfast is served in the dining room with a lovely view of wildlife and birds of the area. The hostess also offers a one-bedroom apartment that is available by the week and completely equipped for reasonable rates. This bed and breakfast has been inspected and approved for cleanliness and quality.

Host: Polly Canning
Rooms: 4 (1 PB; 4 SB) $80
Apartment: 1
Full Breakfast
Credit Cards: None
Notes: 2, 9, 10, 11, 12, 14

Spring Street Inn

353 Spring Street, 02840
(401) 847-4767

An Empire Victorian, circa 1858, with seven double rooms and one apartment, all with private baths. Guest sitting room. Walk to all Newport highlights. Off-street parking. Harborview suite with balcony sleeps two to four people. Extensive full breakfast.

Host: Parvin Latimore
Rooms: 6 (PB) $50-140
Full Breakfast
Credit Cards: A, B
Notes: 2, 3, 4, 5, 8 (over 11), 9, 10, 14

Stella Maris Inn

91 Washington Street, 02840
(401) 849-2862

Elegant, romantic 1861 Victorian mansion completely restored in 1990. Some rooms with water view and fireplaces, all tastefully furnished with antiques. Large wraparound front porch with water view.

6 Pets welcome; 8 Children welcome; 9 Social drinking allowed; 10 Tennis available; 11 Swimming available; 12 Golf available; 13 Skiing available; 14 May be booked through travel agents.

Spacious gardens and tennis court. Hearty Continental breakfast featuring homemade muffins and breads. Walking distance to town. Parking on premises.

Hosts: Dorothy and Ed Madden
Rooms: 8 (PB) $65-150
Continental Breakfast
Credit Cards: None
Notes: 2, 5, 10, 11, 12

Villa Liberté

22 Liberty Street, 02840
(401) 846-7444; (800) 392-3717

Enjoy quiet and private luxury with contemporary European decor in the heart of Newport. Deluxe suites, queen rooms, and suites with kitchens are designed with hues of seafoam green and peach. Dramatic black and white tile baths feature pedestal sinks and arched alcoves. The Villa's ideal location is just a walk from the mansions, Newport's beaches, brick marketplace, and the wharf area. All accommodations have private baths, air conditioning, TVs, and telephones. Complimentary Continental breakfast is served on the sun deck.

Host: Leigh Anne Mosco
Rooms: 15 (PB) $59-175
Continental Breakfast
Credit Cards: A, B
Notes: 7, 8, 10, 11, 12

The Willows of Newport, "A Romantic Inn"

8 and 10 Willow Street, Historic Point, 02840
(401) 846-5486

In the historic section of Newport, The Willows pampers guests with "Secret Gardens," solid brass canopied beds, fresh flowers, mints on pillows, champagne glasses and silver ice bucket, and the lights on dim. Breakfast in bed on bone china and silver service. Three blocks from downtown and the waterfront. Parking and air conditioning. Open April 1 through November; closed December through March. Mobil three-star award.

Host: Patricia Murphy
Rooms: 5 (PB) $88-185
Continental Breakfast
Credit Cards: None
Notes: 2, 9, 10, 11, 12, 14

The Willows of Newport

NORTH KINGSTON

Fifty-Seven Bed and Breakfast

57 Thomas Street, 02852
(401) 294-7201

Enjoy a comfortable contemporary Cape cottage in a peaceful woodland setting. Three minutes from Wickford's Historic District, harbor, and shopping center. Guest bedroom and private bath have access to large outdoor pool and enclosed landscaped garden. No children. No smoking. Full or Continental breakfast included.

Host: Audrey Ebrahim
Room: 1 (1 PB) $75
Full or Continental Breakfast
Credit Cards: None
Notes: 2, 5, 11, 12

PROVIDENCE

Anna's Victorian Connection

5 Fowler Avenue, Newport, RI 02840
(401) 849-2489

NOTES: Credit cards accepted: A MasterCard; B Visa; C American Express; D Discover Card; E Diner's Club; F Other; 2 Personal checks accepted; 3 Lunch available; 4 Dinner available; 5 Open all year;

0009. This restored Federalist-style house, built in the heart of Providence in 1890, has the comfort and charm of a bed and breakfast, plus the privacy of a hotel. Ten guest rooms, each with private bath, pamper guests with canopied beds and fireplaces, air conditioning and TV, and a full breakfast. Close to the Rhode Island State capitol and government buildings, the inn is just a five-minute walk from the Amtrak station, while historic Benefit Street is only ten minutes away. No smoking. Children welcome. $69-99.

0011. Built in 1905 by a prosperous lumber dealer, this shingled Victorian house is listed by the Rhode Island Historic Preservation Commission. Its Art Nouveau stained-glass window is glorious! The college-professor host welcomes guests with comfortable beds, fireplace, and rocking chairs. This quiet home on Providence's East Side is close to Brown University and Rhode Island School of Design, yet within an hour of Newport, Cape Cod, Mystic Seaport, and Boston. No smoking. Children welcome. $45-75.

Old Court
Bed and Breakfast

144 Benefit Street, 02903
(401) 757-2002

In the heart of Providence's historic Benefit Street area, guests will find the Old Court, where tradition is combined with contemporary standards of luxury. The Old Court was built in 1863 and reflects early Victorian styles. In rooms that overlook downtown Providence and Brown University, ...feel as if they have entered a more

State House Inn

43 Jewett Street, 02908
(401) 351-6111

In the center of a quiet and quaint neighborhood, the State House Inn is a 100-year-old building newly restored and renovated into a country bed and breakfast. Minutes from downtown Providence and the many local colleges and universities. Brings country living to the big city.

Hosts: Frank and Monica Hopton
Rooms: 10 (PB) $75-105
Full Breakfast
Credit Cards: A, B, C
Notes: 5, 8, 9, 14

SOUTH KINGSTON

Bed and Breakfast
Inns of New England

128 South Hoop Pole Road, Guilford, CT 06437
(800) 582 0853; (203) 457-0042

910. The past comes alive in this 1898 Victorian that has been lovingly restored and furnished with antiques in the Victorian style. Only one block from an ocean beach, A Continental breakfast is served at the family-style table in a large dining room complete with a charming tiled fireplace. Guest rooms are as varied as they are appealing. Each room is furnished in a different representative period. Some have a view of the ocean and others are tucked among the caves. All have a warmth and charm to please almost everyone. Supervised children over ten are welcome. Limited smoking. Resident dogs and cats; no guest pets. $60-125.

The Gardner House

629 Main Street, 02879
(401) 789-1250

This 1818 Federal home was featured in *Country Interiors* in 1992. Immaculate rooms filled with antiques, private baths off

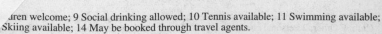

...dren welcome; 9 Social drinking allowed; 10 Tennis available; 11 Swimming available; ...Skiing available; 14 May be booked through travel agents.

each bedroom, gourmet breakfast served in the dining room, music, and candlelight set the mood for a memorable stay. Flowers and two acres of gardens and woodlands surround a huge pool and add an ambience of beauty. This historic area is near the University of Rhode Island, Theatre-by-the-Sea, beaches, fishing, Block Island, Newport, Mystic whaling village, bird and wildlife sanctuary, special restaurants, and superb scenery.

Hosts: Will and Nan Gardner
Rooms: 3 (PB) $65-85
Full Breakfast
Credit Cards: None
Notes: 2, 5, 8, 9, 10, 11, 12

Larchwood Inn

Larchwood Inn

521 Main Street, 02879
(401) 783-5454

The Larchwood Inn is a family-run country inn that has kept pace with the 20th century without sacrificing its rural beauty. Holly House, across the front lawn from the main inn, offers additional lodging. Most rooms have private baths, and all guests are encouraged to use the services of the main inn, which includes three restaurants (all of which serve three meals daily) and a cocktail lounge (with lunch and happy hour daily, and live music on the weekends).

Near beaches, boating, hiking, horseback and bike riding, and skiing. Breakfast not included in rates.

Host: Francis and Diann Browning
Rooms: 20 (12 PB; 8 SB) $40-90
Credit Cards: A, B, C, D, E
Notes: 2, 3, 4, 5, 6, 7, 8, 9, 10, 11, 12, 13, 14

WARREN

Nathaniel Porter Inn

125 Water Street, 02885
(401) 245-6622

Carefully restored 1750/1795 sea captain's home on the National Register of Historic Places in the historic section one block from harbor. Antique furnishings throughout building including two canopied beds. Fireplaces in each of the nine rooms. Antique shopping and a bike path nearby. Three-star award-winning restaurant for dinner, plus Sunday champagne buffet brunch. Featured in *Colonial Home* and *Country Living* magazines. Dinner for two available for additional cost of $29.

Hosts: Robert and Viola Lynch
Rooms: 3 (PB) $70
Continental Breakfast
Credit Cards: A, B, C, D
Notes: 2, 4, 5, 9, 11

WESTERLY

Anna's Victorian Connection

5 Fowler Avenue, Newport, RI 02840
(401) 849-2489

0015. Minutes from Rhode Island's lovely ocean beaches, this deluxe European-style bed and breakfast offers seven uniquely decorated units in a private, relaxing atmosphere. The lovely gardens and grounds include a Mediterranean pool and Jacuzzi on a private terrace. An ideal setting for wed' dings, honeymoons, or rekindling romar.' $75-175.

Grandview Bed and Breakfast

212 Shore Road, 02891
(401) 596-6384; (800) 447-6384

Stately turn-of-the-century home with splendid ocean view. Hearty Continental breakfast served on cheery breakfast porch. Large comfortable living room with stone fireplace. Walk to tennis and golf. A short drive to beaches, Mystic Seaport, Newport mansions, Watch Hill shopping, and the Foxwoods Casino.

Host: Pat Grande
Rooms: 12 (2 PB; 10 SB) $65-90
Continental Breakfast
Credit Cards: A, B, C
Notes: 2, 5, 8, 10, 11, 12, 14

Nutmeg B&B Agency

P.O. Box 1117, West Hartford, CT 06107
(203) 236-6698

504. Savor the splendid views from the wraparound stone porch of this turn of the century bed and breakfast. There are 12 guest rooms, two with private baths. The home has a large family room equipped with a player piano, cable TV, games, and variety of reading material. Pick-up available from local train station or airport. If guests love the beach, this home is a perfect base for enjoying the five Rhode Island beaches nearby. Only minutes from Mystic, Connecticut. Continental breakfast. Limited smoking. Children welcome. Pets in residence.

507. Five minutes from the beach, this renovated 1920 summer home is by a saltwater pond that looks out to the ocean. Originally a working farm, it provides the perfect quiet getaway. One guest room has two double beds, many windows, and a private bath with shower. The second guest room has a canopied double bed, private deck with a view of the water, and a private bath with a tub. For the family getaway, there are also two summer cottages available, one with three bedrooms and the other with six. Continental breakfast. No smoking. Children welcome. Pets in residence.

Shelter Harbor Inn

Shelter Harbor Inn

10 Wagner Road, 02891
(401) 322-8883

Originally a farm established in the early 1800s, the property is now a comfortable, unpretentious country inn. Numerous decks and terraces overlook beautiful fields and gardens bordered by stone walls. The inn is just a short drive from the gorgeous private beach and includes a hot tub overlooking Block Island, two paddle tennis courts, and a professional croquet court. Open daily, year-round for breakfast, lunch, and dinner.

Hosts: Jim and Debbye Dey
Rooms: 23 (PB) $82-116
Full Breakfast
Credit Cards: A, B, C, D, E
Notes: 2, 3, 4, 5, 7, 8, 9, 10, 11, 12, 14

The Villa

190 Shore Road, 02891
(401) 596-1054; (800) 722-9240

Escape to this hideaway of flower gardens, Italian porticoes, and verandas. Open year-round, The Villa is the ideal setting for weddings, honeymoons, and rekindling romances. Imagine being in a private suite in the winter, gazing at the hypnotic flames of a sensuous crackling fire. Summers here are warm and golden with cool ocean breezes. Some suites offer fireplaces and Jacuzzis, and all have color cable television and air

6 Pets welcome; 8 Children welcome; 9 Social drinking allowed; 10 Tennis available; 11 Swimming available; 12 Golf available; 13 Skiing available; 14 May be booked through travel agents.

conditioning. A pleasing, complimentary buffet breakfast is served in the dining room, poolside, or in private room. The romance of Italy awaits.

Host: Jerry Maiorano
Rooms: 7 (PB) $75-175
Credit Cards: A, B, C
Notes: 2, 5, 6, 7, 9, 10, 11, 12, 14

Woody Hill
Bed and Breakfast

149 South Woody Hill Road, 02891
(401) 322-0452

The hostess, a high school English teacher, invites guests to share this reproduction Colonial home with antiques and gardens. Snuggle under quilts, relax on the porch swing, visit nearby Newport and Mystic, and swim in the pool or at beautiful ocean beaches. Westerly has it all! Closed one week in February.

Host: Dr. Ellen L. Madison
Rooms: 4 (3 PB or SB) $60-105
Full Breakfast
Credit Cards: None
Notes: 2, 5, 8, 9, 10, 11, 12

WICKFORD

The Narragansett House

71 Main Street, 02852
(401) 294-3593; FAX (401) 294-6267

Come journey back to the 18th-century. This historic 1773 home was built as a Colonial tavern, where Revolutionary soldiers were mustered and boarded. Sunny, two-story guest suite with private entrance, surrounded by perennial gardens and private terrace for guests. The guest suite is fully applianced, and furnished in contemporary decor, with queen-size bed. An adjoining single bedroom is also available. A gourmet heart-healthy breakfast is served in guest suite or on the private garden terrace. Wickford is just a short distance from Newport, Block Island, Mystic, and Providence, making it an ideal location for lodging. Children over eight are welcome.

Hosts: Joyce and Paul Dodson
Room: 1 suite $95-115
Full Breakfast
Credit Cards: None
Notes: 2, 5, 8, 10, 11, 12

WYOMING

Anna's Victorian Connection

5 Fowler Avenue, Newport, RI 02840
(401) 849-2489

0007. One of the oldest wooden houses still standing in the United States, this three-story mansion built in 1698 has a center hall, double parlors, and double chimneys. The Marquis de Lafayette, George Washington, and Thomas Jefferson were among its notable guests. Later, it was a haven for escaping slaves on the pre-Civil War "underground railroad." Hosts love sharing their home's history over breakfast in the dining room. (Rumor has it that there may be a ghost or two still lurking around.) The seven guest rooms share baths. Twenty minutes from Newport and Providence. $40-95.

The Cookie Jar
Bed and Breakfast

64 Kingstown Road, (Just off I-95), 02898
(401) 539-2680; (800) 767-4262

The heart of this home, the living room, was built in 1732 as a blacksmith's shop. The original ceiling, handhewn beams, and granite walls remain today. The country property includes a barn, a swimming pool, 50 fruit trees, grapevines, a flower garden, and an acre of grass. The hosts offer friendly homestyle living just a short drive from the beaches, Newport, the University of Rhode Island, Foxwoods Casino, Mystic, and Providence.

Hosts: Dick and Madelein Sohl
Rooms: 3 (1 PB; 2 SB) $60-65
Full Breakfast
Credit Cards: None
Notes: 2, 5, 8, 9, 10, 11, 12, 14

NOTES: Credit cards accepted: A MasterCard; B Visa; C American Express; D Discover Card; E Diner's Club; F Other; 2 Personal checks accepted; 3 Lunch available; 4 Dinner available; 5 Open all year;

South Carolina

AIKEN

New Berry Inn

240 Newberry Street Southwest, 29801
(803) 649-2935

The New Berry Inn is a two-story Dutch
Colonial home, furnished with antiques, in
a parklike surrounding. Guests start their
day with a full breakfast, visit the antique
shops or the historical district of Old Aiken,
golf, horseback ride, and finish the evening
with dinner at one of the fine restaurants
near the inn.

Hosts: Mary Ann and Hal Mackey
Rooms: 5 (PB) $50-75
Full Breakfast
Credit Cards: A, B, C, D, E
Notes: 5, 10, 12, 14

ANDERSON

Evergreen Inn

1103 South Main Street, 29621
(803) 225-1109

Two historic mansions on the national register, with on-premises restaurant. The inn
has seven guest rooms, six baths, and eight
fireplaces; there is also a honeymoon suite
done in pink and rose velvet with satin and
lace. Just 20 minutes from three lakes, each
with more than 1,000 miles of shoreline and
public parks. Antique shops and the downtown area are within walking distance.
Halfway between Charlotte and Atlanta, the
inn is an excellent stopping place for a quiet
dinner and enjoyable stay.

Hosts: Peter and Myrna Ryter
Rooms: 7 (6 PB; 1 SB) $65

Continental Breakfast
Credit Cards: A, B, C, E
Notes: 4, 5, 9, 10, 11, 12, 14

River Inn

612 East River Street, 29624
(803) 226-1431

River Inn is constructed of heart-pine and
was completed in 1914 by Dr. Archer
LeRoy Smethers, founder of one of Ander
son's first hospitals. It is in the first estab
lished residential area in Anderson and
features ten-foot ceilings and the warmth of
beautiful walnut-stained woodwork. Each
bedroom has a private bath and working
fireplace. A full breakfast is served. There
is a large side porch with swing and rockers
for guests' enjoyment and a hot tub in the
spacious backyard for relaxation.

Hosts: Pat Clark and Wayne Hollingsworth
Rooms: 3 (PB) $50-75
Full Breakfast
Credit Cards: A, B, C
Notes: 2, 4, 5, 7, 8, 9, 11, 12, 13 (water), 14

River Inn

6 Pets welcome; 7 Smoking allowed; 8 Children welcome; 9 Social drinking allowed; 10 Tennis available; 11
Swimming available; 12 Golf available; 13 Skiing available; 14 May be booked through travel agents.

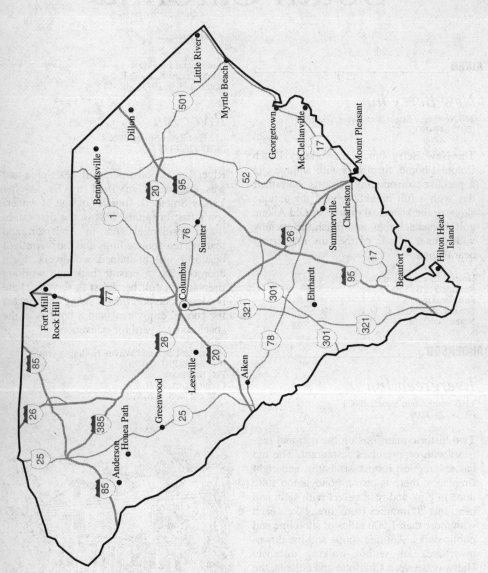

South Carolina

BEAUFORT

Bay Street Inn

601 Bay Street, 29902
(803) 522-0050

A restored antebellum home in coastal Beaufort, between Savannah and Charleston, filming site for *The Prince of Tides*. In the heart of the historic district directly facing the Intracoastal Waterway, the inn offers six antique-filled guest rooms, each with unobstructed river views, fireplaces, and private baths. Relax in the book-lined library, linger in the gracious living room, or enjoy the tranquil breezes on one of the three picturesque porches.

Hosts: Jeff and Leslee Pell
Rooms: 8 (PB) $95-155
Full Breakfast
Credit Cards: A, B, C, D
Notes: 2, 5, 8, 9, 10, 11, 12, 14

TwoSuns Inn Bed and Breakfast

1705 Bay Street, 29902
(803) 522-1122; (800) 532-4244
FAX (803) 522-1122

A prince of an inn in an antebellum brigadoon. Southern charm abounds in historic Beaufort, the film site for *Prince of Tides* and *Forrest Gump*. Informal elegance characterizes this 1917 grand home right on the bay. Visit quaint downtown, enjoy a carriage ride, or bicycle through the historic waterfront community. Relax in this newly restored home, complete with the hostess' weavings, period decor, collectibles, full handicapped facilities, and business amenities.

Hosts: Carrol and Ron Kay
Rooms: 5 (PB) $98-122
Full Breakfast
Credit Cards: A, B, C
Notes: 2, 5, 9, 10, 11, 12, 14

The Breeden Inn

BENNETTSVILLE

The Breeden Inn and Carriage House

404 East Main Street, 29512
(803) 479-3665

Built in 1886, the romantic Breeden Inn is a beautifully restored Southern mansion. On two acres in the historic district, well-preserved architectural delights highlight the interior. Provides very comfortable and livable surroundings that capture interest and inspire imagination. Listed on the National Register of Historic Places, the inn is 20 minutes off I-95. A great halfway point be-

TwoSuns Inn

NOTES: Credit cards accepted: A MasterCard; B Visa; C American Express; D Discover Card; E Diner's Club; F Other; 2 Personal checks accepted; 3 Lunch available; 4 Dinner available; 5 Open all year; 6 Pets welcome; 7 Smoking allowed; 8 Children welcome; 9 Social drinking allowed; 10 Tennis available; 11 Swimming available; 12 Golf available; 13 Skiing available; 14 May be booked through travel agents.

tween Florida and New York. The gathering room in the Carriage House and the great country kitchen, verandas, porticos and grounds—truly a Southern tradition—can be enjoyed at both houses. Beautiful antique decor, pool, cable TV in each room, phone in most rooms. A haven for antique lovers, runners, and walkers.

Hosts: Wesley and Bonnie Park
Rooms: 7 (PB) $55-65
Full Breakfast
Credit Cards: A, B, D
Notes: 2, 5, 8, 11, 12, 14

CHARLESTON

Ann Harper's Bed and Breakfast

56 Smith Street, 29401
(803) 723-3947

This circa 1870 home is in Charleston's historic district. Two rooms with connecting bath and sitting area with TV. The owner is a retired medical technologist and enjoys serving a full breakfast. Two-night minimum stay requested. Extra charge for single night.

Host: Ann D. Harper
Rooms: 2 (PB) $60-75
Full Breakfast
Credit Cards: None
Notes: 2, 5, 7 (limited), 8 (over 10), 9, 10, 11, 12

The Barksdale House Inn

27 George Street, 29401
(803) 577-4800

One of Charleston's most luxurious 13-room inns. A 215-year-old home featuring individually designed rooms; five with whirlpool tubs and fireplaces. Flowers, daily newspaper, wine, champagne, tea, sherry, fountain in the courtyard, and off-street parking. Guests can enjoy a Continental breakfast served on silver in the privacy of their rooms or in the courtyard.

Hosts: George and Peggy Sloan
Rooms: 13 (PB) $79-150
Continental Breakfast
Credit Cards: A, B
Notes: 2, 5, 7, 8 (over 7), 9, 10, 12, 14

The Battery Carriage House Inn (1843)

20 South Battery, 29401
(800) 775-5575

Stay in the carriage house of this landmark antebellum mansion at White Point Gardens (on the waterfront), the most elegant residential district of old and historic Charleston. Eleven rooms. Ample street parking. Silver tray Continental breakfast in room or garden. Fluffy robes and towels. Turndown service. Afternoon refreshments. Quiet garden. Cable TV and HBO. Private steambaths. Whirlpool tubs. Friendly, professional staff. Described as "Simply the best," "European," "Romantic," and "An unforgettable Charleston experience." Highly recommended.

Host: Katharine Hastie
Rooms: 11 (PB) $79-199
Continental Breakfast
Credit Cards: A, B, C, D
Notes: 2, 9, 10, 11, 12, 14

The Battery Carriage

The Belvedere

The Belvedere

40 Rutledge Avenue, 29401
(803) 722-0973

A Colonial Revival mansion built in 1900 with an exquisite Adamesque interior taken from the circa 1800 Belvedere Plantation house. In the downtown historic district, on Colonial Lake, within walking distance of historical points of interest, restaurants, and shopping. Guests are welcome to use the public areas and piazzas in this romantic, beautifully restored and refurbished mansion. Closed December 1 to February 10.

Hosts: David S. Spell and Rick Zender
Rooms: 3 (PB) $110
Continental Breakfast
Credit Cards: None
Notes: 2, 9, 10, 11, 12

Brasington House Bed and Breakfast

328 East Bay Street, 29401
(803) 722-1274

Elegant accommodations in a splendidly restored Greek Revival Charleston single house, furnished with antiques, in Charleston's beautiful historic district. Four lovely, well-appointed guest rooms with central heat and air conditioning include private baths, telephones, cable TV, and tea-making services. King-, queen-, and twin-size beds available. Included is a bountiful family-style breakfast, wine and cheese served in the living room, liqueurs and chocolates available in the evening. Off-street parking.

Host: Dalton K. Brasinton
Rooms: 4 (PB) $89-109
Full Breakfast
Credit Cards: A, B
Notes: 2, 5, 9, 10, 11, 12

Country Victorian Bed and Breakfast

105 Tradd Street, 29401-2422
(803) 577-0682

Rooms have private entrances and contain antique iron and brass beds, old quilts, oak and wicker antique furniture, and braided rugs over the heart-of-pine floors. Homemade cookies will be waiting. The house, built in 1820, is within walking distance of restaurants, antique shops, churches, art galleries, museums, and all points of historical interest. Parking and bicycles are available. Many extras.

Host: Diane Deardurff Weed
Rooms: 2 (PB) $70-95
Continental Breakfast
Credit Cards: None
Notes: 2, 5, 8 (over 10), 9, 10, 11, 12

1837 Bed and Breakfast and Tea Room

126 Wentworth Street, 29401
(803) 723-7166

Accommodations in a wealthy cotton planter's home and brick carriage house, now owned by two artists. In the center of the historic district, within walking distance of boat tours, old market, antique shops, restaurants, and main attractions. Full gourmet breakfast is served in the formal dining room or on the outside piazzas. Visit with others while enjoying such specialties as sausage pie, eggs Benedict, ham omelets, and home-baked breads (lemon, apple spice, banana, and cinnamon swirl). Afternoon tea

6 Pets welcome; 8 Children welcome; 9 Social drinking allowed; 10 Tennis available; 11 Swimming available; 12 Golf available; 13 Skiing available; 14 May be booked through travel agents.

is served. Canopied poster rice beds, verandas, rockers, and Southern hospitality.

Hosts: Sherri Weaver and Richard Dunn
Rooms: 8 (PB) $59-99
Full Breakfast
Credit Cards: A, B, C
Notes: 2, 5, 7 (limited), 9, 10

Fulton Lane Inn

202 King Street, 29401
(803) 720-2600; (800) 720-2688

The Fulton Lane Inn is quietly set off King Street on a pedestrian lane in the heart of the antique and historic district. Many rooms have cathedral ceilings or fireplaces, canopied beds, and large whirlpool baths to give a special romantic feeling of a bygone era. The gracious Southern hospitality includes a silver-service breakfast, wine and sherry, turndown with chocolates, and a newspaper. AAA four diamonds. Free parking. No smoking.

Host: Larry Spelts
Rooms: 27 (PB) $ 100-140
Continental Breakfast
Credit Cards: A, B
Notes: 2, 5, 8, 9, 10, 11, 12, 14

The Hayne House

30 King Street, 29401
(803) 577-2633

The Hayne House, circa 1755, is in the heart of the Charleston historic district one block from the Battery, which overlooks Charleston Harbor and Fort Sumter. A treasury of good books, art, and antiques provides guests all they need to step back in time. No TV. Parlor grand in living room, sherry on the piano, fireplaces throughout, Charleston garden, rockers, swing. Sea kayak, mountain biking, plantation natural history and birding excursions available on request. Smoking allowed on the back porch.

Rooms: 5 (3 PB; 2 SB) $50-110
Continental Breakfast
Credit Cards: A, B
Notes: 2, 5, 9, 10, 12, 14

Historic Charleston Bed and Breakfast

60 Broad Street, 29401
(803) 722-6606; (800) 743-3583

A reservation service for private historic homes, carriage houses, mansions, plantations in or near Charleston. This port city is one of the most historic in the United States, with many cultural activities offered. All bed and breakfasts offered have private baths, TV, and air conditioning. Many have lovely gardens, patios, or porches. Most locations are within walking distance of restaurants, shops, museums, and other historic sites. Beaches are ten miles away. $60-140

John Rutledge House Inn

116 Broad Street, 29401
(803) 723-7999; (800) 476-9741

This national landmark was built in 1763 by John Rutledge, co-author and signer of the U.S. Constitution. Large rooms and suites in the main and carriage houses offer the ambience of historic Charleston. Rates include wine and sherry upon arrival, turndown service with brandy and chocolate, and breakfast with newspaper delivered to guests' room. Free parking. AAA-rated four diamonds. Historic Hotels of America.

Rooms: 19 (PB) $130-285
Continental Breakfast
Credit Cards: A, B, C
Notes: 5, 7, 8, 9, 10, 12, 14

King Charles Inn

237 Meeting Street, 29401
(803) 723-7451

The King Charles is a 91-room inn providing an intimate setting in the center of the historic district. The inn has a quaint dining room, which serves low-country cooking for breakfast daily. Guests can enjoy strolling through the famous market area, which is filled with shops, restaurants, and outdoor vendors. Historic homes and famous churches are all within walking distance.

Host: Irene Morrison
Rooms: 91 (PB) $69-139
Full Breakfast
Credit Cards: A, B, C, D, E
Notes: 2, 5, 7, 8, 9, 10, 11, 12 ,14

King George Inn and Guests

32 George Street, 29401
(803) 723-9339

The King George Inn is a 200-year-old historic house in the downtown historic district. The inn is a Federal-style home with a Greek Revival parapet-style roofline. There are four stories in all, with three levels of lovely Charleston porches. All rooms have fireplaces, ten- to twelve-foot ceilings, and six-foot windows. All rooms have original lovely wide-planked hardwood floors, original eight-foot oak doors, old furnishings, and many antiques. Breakfast is seasonal. One-minute walk to King Street shopping and restaurants and a five-minute walk to the historic market. Maps and brochures of historic sights and dining information are available. On-site parking. Come visit the past!

Hosts: B. J., Mike and Deb
Rooms: 8 (PB) $70-110
Continental Breakfast
Credit Cards: A, B
Notes: 2, 5, 6 (limited), 7 (limited), 8, 9, 10, 11, 12, 13 (water), 14 (limited)

Kings Courtyard Inn

198 King Street, 29401
(803) 723-7000; (800) 845-0688

Kings Courtyard Inn, circa 1853, is in the heart of the antique and historic district. Convenient to attractions, shops, and restaurants. Rate includes Continental breakfast and newspaper, and wine and sherry served in the lobby. Turndown service with chocolate and brandy. Free parking. AAA four diamonds. Historic Hotels of

America. Double, king-, and queen-size beds and suites are available.

Host: Laura Howard
Rooms: 44 (PB) $100-200
Continental Breakfast
Credit Cards: A, B, C
Notes: 2, 5, 7, 8, 9, 10, 11, 12, 14

King's Inn

136 Tradd Street, 29401
(803) 577-3683

Iin the heart of the historic district, this private home includes two bed and breakfast units with separate entrances. One has a full kitchen. The waterfront, antique shops, and house museums are minutes away. The entire historic area can be covered on foot. Enjoy blooming gardens and magnificent house tours in April, the international arts festival—Spoleto—in May, and warm beaches in June. The hostess is a registered tour guide for Charleston.

Host: Hazel King
Rooms: 2 (PB) $90-100
Continental Breakfast
Credit Cards: None
Notes: 2, 5, 7, 8, 9

The Kitchen House (Circa 1732)

126 Tradd Street, 29401
(803) 577-6362

Nestled in the heart of the historic district, The Kitchen House is a completely restored 18th-century dwelling. Southern hospitality and a decanter of sherry await guests' arrival. The refrigerator and pantry are stocked for breakfast. Absolute privacy, cozy fireplaces, antiques, patio, and Colonial herb gardens. This pre-Revolutionary home was featured in *Colonial Homes* magazine and the *New York Times*. Complete concierge services.

Host: Lois Evans
Rooms: 3 (1 PB; 2 SB) $100-195
Full Breakfast
Credit Cards: A, B
Notes: 2, 5, 7, 8, 9, 10, 11, 12, 14

6 Pets welcome; 8 Children welcome; 9 Social drinking allowed; 10 Tennis available; 11 Swimming available; 12 Golf available; 13 Skiing available; 14 May be booked through travel agents.

The Kitchen House

Maison Du Pré

317 East Bay Street, 29401
(803) 723-8691; (800) 844-INNS

Three restored Charleston "single houses" and two carriage houses constitute Maison Du Pré, originally built in 1804. The inn features period furniture and antiques and is in the historic Ansonborough district. Complimentary Continental breakfast and a Low Country tea party are served. "Maison Du Pré, with its faded stucco, pink brick, and gray shutters is one of the city's best-looking small inns"—*New York Times*.

Hosts: Lucille, Bob, and Mark Mulholland
Rooms: 15 (PB) $98-200
Continental Breakfast
Credit Cards: A, B, C
Notes: 2, 5, 8, 9, 10, 11, 12, 14

The Planters Inn

112 North Market Street, 29401
(803) 722-2345; (800) 577-2125

The Planters Inn is in the center of Charleston's 800-acre historic district, steps away from landmark houses, gardens, and the waterfront park. The newly renovated inn has 41 spacious rooms and suites featuring high ceilings, oversized private baths, and large closets. Guests are treated to a silver-service Continental breakfast, refreshments each afternoon in the lobby, and turndown service every night.

Host: Bill McDonald
Rooms: 41 (PB) $89-149
Continental Breakfast
Credit Cards: A, B, C, D, E
Notes: 2, 5, 7, 8, 9, 12, 14

Rutledge Victorian Inn

114 Rutledge Avenue, 29401
(803) 722-7551

A century-old Italianate, very rare and decorative style, Victorian house in Charleston's downtown historic district. The house is quaint but elegant: a beautiful round decorative porch, 12-foot ceilings, eight- to ten-foot oak doors, hardwood floors, Oriental rugs, beautiful antiques, ten-foot windows, and fireplaces in every room. Private or shared baths are modern. Parking, air conditioning, and TV. Just a 20-minute walk to all tours and historic sites. Help with tours. Come and "set a spell" on an old rocker and feel the history.

Hosts: Lynn, B. J., and Mike
Rooms: 10 (7 PB; 3 SB) $55-110
Continental Breakfast
Credit Cards: A, B
Notes: 2, 5, 6 (limited), 7 (limited), 8, 9, 10, 11, 12

Rutledge Victorian Inn

NOTES: Credit cards accepted: A MasterCard; B Visa; C American Express; D Discover Card; E Diner's Club; F Other; 2 Personal checks accepted; 3 Lunch available; 4 Dinner available; 5 Open all year;

65 Radliffe Bed and Breakfast

65 Radcliffe Street, 29403
(803) 577-6183

On the northern edge of the historic district, convenient to historic sites, restaurants, and night life. Beaches, gardens, and plantations are less than a half-hour drive. Beautifully furnished room with antique cherry double bed in a simple-styled Charleston single house, circa 1880. Continental breakfast in formal dining room. Private balcony. Cable TV, coffee, and small refrigerator in room. Friendly, congenial host will help make a stay enjoyable.

Host: Doug Ludlum
Room: 1 (PB) $65-75
Continental Breakfast
Credit Cards: None
Notes: 2, 8, 9, 10, 11, 12

Thirty-Six Meeting Street

36 Meeting Street, 29401
(803) 722-1034

Built in 1740, this pre-Revolutionary War single house offers three elegant suites in the heart of the historic district a block and a half from the Battery. Each suite is elegantly furnished with rice beds, kitchenette, and private bath. Guests can enjoy the private walled garden for breakfast or after a day of sightseeing. Continental breakfast and bicycles available for guests.

Host: Anne Brandt
Rooms: 3 (PB) $75-125
Continental Breakfast
Credit Cards: A, B
Notes: 2, 5, 8, 9, 10, 11, 12, 14

Two Meeting Street Inn

2 Meeting Street, 29401
(803) 723-7322

"The Belle of Charleston's bed and breakfasts." This Queen Anne Victorian mansion, circa 1890-92, has welcomed guests for

Two Meeting Street Inn

more than 50 years. In the historic district overlooking the Battery, the inn charms its visitors with exquisite Tiffany windows, canopied beds, Oriental rugs, and English antiques. The day starts with freshly baked muffins served in the oak-covered courtyard, and ends with evening sherry on the wraparound piazza. The epitome of Southern hospitality and turn-of-the-century luxury. Two-night minimum stay requested for weekends and holidays.

Hosts: The Spell Family
Rooms: 9 (PB) $120-205
Continental Breakfast
Credit Cards: None
Notes: 2, 5

Victoria House Inn

208 King Street, 29401
(803) 720-2944; (800) 933-5464

Built in 1889, this Romanesque-style building has 16 elegantly renovated guest rooms. Modern amenities are provided in every room, including a stocked refrigerator. Guests receive evening turndown service, wine and sherry served in the lobby; Continental breakfast and newspaper delivered to the room each morning. Free on-site parking. AAA four diamonds.

Host: Randall Felkel
Rooms: 16 (PB) $115-150
Continental Breakfast
Credit Cards: A, B
Notes: 5, 7, 8, 9, 10, 12, 14

6 Pets welcome; 8 Children welcome; 9 Social drinking allowed; 10 Tennis available; 11 Swimming available; 12 Golf available; 13 Skiing available; 14 May be booked through travel agents.

Villa de La Fontaine Bed and Breakfast

138 Wentworth Street, 29401
(803) 577-7709

Villa de La Fontaine is a columned Greek Revival mansion in the heart of the historic district. It was built in 1838 and boasts a three-quarter-acre garden with fountain and terraces. Restored to impeccable condition, it is furnished with museum-quality furniture and accessories. The hosts are retired ASID interior designers and have decorated the rooms with 18th-century American antiques. Several of the rooms feature canopied beds. Breakfast is prepared by a master chef who prides himself on serving a different menu every day. Off-street parking. Minimum-stay requirements for weekends and holidays. The inn offers guests a choice between its four rooms and two suites.

Hosts: William Fontaine and Aubrey Hancock
Rooms: 6 (PB) $120-175
Full Breakfast
Credit Cards: A, B
Notes: 2, 5, 9, 10, 11, 12

COLUMBIA

Claussen's Inn

2003 Greene Street, 29205
(803) 765-0440; (800) 622-3382

Restored bakery, circa 1928, listed on the National Register of Historic Places and within walking distance of shopping, restaurants, and entertainment. Luxurious rooms with private baths, outdoor Jacuzzi, and four-poster beds. Rates include a Continental breakfast delivered to the room, complimentary wine and sherry, turndown service with chocolates and brandy, and a newspaper.

Host: Dan O. Vance
Rooms: 29 (PB) $105-120
Continental Breakfast
Credit Cards: A, B, C
Notes: 5, 7, 8, 9, 10, 12, 14

DILLON

Magnolia Inn Bed and Breakfast

601 East Main Street, Highway 9, 29536
(803) 774-0679

Southern hospitality abounds as guests enter the Magnolia Inn's magnificent foyer. Guests may relax and make themselves at home in the "duck" library or Victorian parlor. Mornings are filled with the savory aromas of breads, pastries, pecan-apple pancakes, breakfast casseroles, fresh fruits, coffee, or tea. Breakfast is served in the formal dining room or on the second-floor garden porch. Four guest rooms are available—the Azalea, the Camellia, the Dogwood, and the Jessamine. The Magnolia Inn is easily accessible from I-95. Business rates are available.

Hosts: Jim and Pam Lannoo
Rooms: 4 (PB) $45-55
Full Breakfast
Credit Cards: A, B, C
Notes: 2, 5, 8, 9, 11, 12, 14

EHRHARDT

Broxton Bridge Bed and Breakfast

Highway 601, 29081
(803) 267-3882; (800) 437-4868

This bed and breakfast offers five distinctive bedrooms. The Mallard Room on the ground floor has a queen-size bed and private bath. This room connects to the Dove Room, which is small and cozy with one twin-size bed and assigned bath. The Black Lab Room, also on the first floor, has two twin-size beds and an assigned bath. Upstairs, in addition to a beautiful view of the lake and woods, there are two beautiful bedrooms, the Pheasant and the Quail rooms, each featuring a queen-size brass bed, fireplace, and assigned baths.

NOTES: Credit cards accepted: A MasterCard; B Visa; C American Express; D Discover Card; E Diner's Club; F Other; 2 Personal checks accepted; 3 Lunch available; 4 Dinner available; 5 Open all year;

Host: Gwen Varn
Rooms: 5 (4 PB; 1 SB) $50
Continental Breakfast
Credit Cards: A, B, C
Notes: 2, 3, 4, 5, 8, 9, 10, 11 (on site), 12, 14

Ehrhardt Hall Bed and Breakfast Inn

South Broadway, 29081
(803) 267-2020

A stay at the Ehrhardt Hall is a return to the elegance of yesterday. The inn has been restored to its original grandeur with large windows and Old World appointments, all reminiscent of an era when graciousness and thoughtfulness were a way of life. All rooms are oversized with ceiling fans, armoires, sitting areas, private baths, color TV, fireplaces, and central heat and air conditioning. Indoor pool, large spa, gym, and dry sauna available. Tennis and golf nearby. No children. No smoking.

Host: Gwen Varn
Rooms: 6 (PB) $50-90
Continental Breakfast
Credit Cards: A, B, C
Notes: 5, 10, 11, 12, 14

FORT MILL

Pleasant Valley Bed and Breakfast Inn

P.O. Box 446, 29715
(803) 547-7551

Nestled in the beautiful Old English District, the inn is in the wooded, peaceful countryside. Built in 1874, it has been restored and furnished with antiques. Each guest room has its own bath and TV. After breakfast, take a stroll in the shade of 100-year-old oaks. Equipped with facilities for the disabled. The house is convenient to Carowinds Theme Park, Rock Hill, Lancaster, South Carolina, and Charlotte, North Carolina. Ten percent senior citizen discount. Close to Heritage, U.S.A. Closed December 15 to January 1.

Pleasant Valley Inn

Host: Anita Lawrence
Rooms: 5 (PB) $48-78
Continental Breakfast
Credit Cards: None
Notes: 2, 8, 10, 11, 12, 14

GEORGETOWN

Five Thirty Prince Street

530 Prince Street, 29440
(803) 527-1114

Innovatively decorated, light, airy 75-year-old home nestled in a charming circa 1725 historic district. Guests will enjoy happy colors, antiques and wicker, high ceilings with fans, an eclectic art collection, fireplaces, gardened patio, rocker-lined front porch, a complimentary libation, and full gourmet breakfasts. Stroll to shops, excellent restaurants, and the harbor walk. Short drive to nearby beaches. Golf, boat tram, carriage, and walking tours available. Enjoy the Low Country's finest. One hour to Charleston and Myrtle Beach.

Host: Nancy Bazemore
Rooms: 3 (2 PB; 1 SB) $70
Full Breakfast
Credit Cards: None
Notes: 2, 5, 6, 7, 9, 10, 11, 12, 14

6 Pets welcome; 8 Children welcome; 9 Social drinking allowed; 10 Tennis available; 11 Swimming available; 12 Golf available; 13 Skiing available; 14 May be booked through travel agents.

The International Bed and Breakfast Club, Inc.

504 Amherst Street, Buffalo, NY 14207
(800) 723-4262; FAX (716) 873-4462

This West Indies-style home was built in 1790 in the historic district of Georgetown. Quality craftsmanship and elegant furnishings. Public rooms include a large drawing room with fireplace, a parlor/game room, a beautiful dining room, and a wraparound veranda facing gardens and historic homes. All guest rooms feature early Colonial furnishings and private baths. Cottage with Jacuzzi. Available for meetings and social gatherings. Gourmet breakfast and evening refreshments served. Smoking permitted on veranda and patio. Special rates and discounts available. $70-115.

1790 House

630 Highmarket Street, 29440
(803) 546-4821

Meticulously restored, this 200-year-old plantation-style inn is in the heart of historic Georgetown. Spacious, luxurious rooms with fireplaces and central heat and air. Stay in the the Rice Planters Room, the beautiful honeymoon cottage with Jacuzzi tub, or one of the other lovely rooms. Walk to shops, restaurants, and historic sights. Just a short drive to Myrtle Beach and Grand Strand—a golfer's paradise.

Hosts: John and Patricia Wiley
Rooms: 6 (PB) $70-115
Full Breakfast
Credit Cards: A, B, C, D
Notes: 2, 5, 8, 9, 10, 12, 14

The Shaw House

613 Cypress Court, 29440
(803) 546-9663

Lovely view overlooking Willowbank Marsh; wonderful bird watching. Many antiques throughout the house; rocking chairs on porch. Within walking distance of the historic district and many wonderful restaurants. Fresh fruits and Southern breakfast. One-hour drive to Myrtle Beach or Charleston.

Hosts: Mary and Joe Shaw
Rooms: 3 (PB) $60
Full Breakfast
Credit Cards: C
Notes: 2, 5, 7, 8, 9, 10, 11, 12

The Shaw House

"ShipWright's"

609 Cypress Court, 29440
(803) 527-4475

Serving tourists or boaters. Transportation from intracoastal waterways provided. Quiet, spacious with a tasteful decor of heirlooms and antiques. Experience the breathtaking view of the Avenue of Live Oaks and the Alive Marshes of the Black River while rocking on the large porch or gazing out the great room window. Taste Grandma Eicher's pancakes, freshly ground coffee, and fresh fruit. Guests say, "I feel like I just visited my best friend." AAA approved.

Host: Leatrice Wright
Rooms: 2 (PB) $55
Full Breakfast
Credit Cards: None
Notes: 2, 5, 7, 8, 9, 10, 11, 12

NOTES: Credit cards accepted: A MasterCard; B Visa; C American Express; D Discover Card; E Diner's Club; F Other; 2 Personal checks accepted; 3 Lunch available; 4 Dinner available; 5 Open all year;

GREENWOOD

Inn on the Square
104 Court Street, 29646
(803) 223-4488

Greenwood's premier hotel combines great service with elegant surroundings to create an atmosphere of total comfort for the guest. The rooms are spacious and are furnished with beautiful reproductions typical of the period. Accent pieces in each room include mahogany rice-carved beds, Chippendale, or pencil posts-writing desks with Martha Washington chairs, and brass nightstands. They have custom-made solid mahogany armoires cleverly hiding a TV and closets for full length hanging items. The inn combines the style and elegance of turn-of-the-century architecture with such modern amenities as a three-story skylit atrium, beautifully appointed dining room, Charleston courtyard with pool, and an English-style pub (the Polo Club lounge). Full breakfast served on weekdays only.

Rooms: 48 (PB) $70-80
Full and Continental Breakfast
Credit Cards: A, B, C, D, E
Notes: 3, 4, 5, 7, 8, 10, 12, 14

HILTON HEAD ISLAND

Ambiance
8 Wren Drive, 29928
(803) 671-4981

Marny welcomes guests to sunny Hilton Head Island. This cypress home, nestled in subtropical surroundings, is in Sea Pines Plantation. Ambiance reflects the hostess's interior decorating business by the same name. All the amenities of Hilton Head are offered in a contemporary, congenial atmosphere. The climate is favorable year-round for all sports. Ambiance is across the street from a beautiful beach and the Atlantic Ocean.

Host: Marny Kridel Daubenspeck
Rooms: 2 (PB) $65-75
Continental Breakfast
Credit Cards: None
Notes: 2, 5, 7, 8 (over 12), 9, 10, 11, 12

A Home Away
3 Pender Lane, 29926
(803) 671-5578

Walk from this lovely home through the beautiful Forest Preserve or to the beaches of the Atlantic Ocean. Bikes are available to ride the many local bike paths. Charming setting in Sea Pines Plantation offers one comfortable guest room with TV and connecting private bath.

Host: Beverly D. Jones
Room: 1 (PB) $65-75
Continental Breakfast
Credit Cards: None
Notes: 2, 5, 9, 10, 11, 12

HONEA PATH

Sugarfoot Castle's Bed and Breakfast
211 South Main Street, 29654
(803) 369-6565

Enormous trees umbrella this circa-1880 brick Victorian home. Fresh flowers grace the 14-inch-thick walled rooms furnished with family heirlooms. Enjoy the living room's interesting collection or the library's comfy chairs, TV, VCR, books, fireplace, desk, and game table. Upon rising, guests will find coffee outside their doors, followed by a breakfast of fresh fruit, cereal, hot breads, and beverages served in the dining room by candlelight. Rock away the world's cares on the screened porch overlooking peaceful gardens.

Hosts: Cecil and Gale Evans
Rooms: 3 (SB) $48-51
Continental Breakfast
Credit Cards: A, B
Notes: 2, 5, 8 (over 10), 9, 10, 11, 12

6 Pets welcome; 8 Children welcome; 9 Social drinking allowed; 10 Tennis available; 11 Swimming available; 12 Golf available; 13 Skiing available; 14 May be booked through travel agents.

Able House Inn

LEESVILLE

Able House Inn

244 West Church Street, 29072
(803) 532-2763

Chateau estate, ten miles from I-20 on Route 1, 30 minutes from Columbia. Choose from five guest rooms, each with private bath. Living room, sunroom, swimming pool, and patio are available to guests. Fresh popcorn and soft drinks each evening.

Hosts: Annabelle and Jack Wright
Rooms: 5 (PB) $55-60
Continental Breakfast
Credit Cards: A, B
Notes: 2, 5, 7 (limited), 8, 9, 11, 12

LITTLE RIVER

Stella's Guest Home

P.O. Box 564, Highway 17, 29566
(803) 249-1871

Sometimes something different can be best, and when planning a trip to South Carolina's Grand Strand, guests are invited to stay with Stella. All of the guest rooms and suites are charmingly, tastefully, and luxuriously decorated and offer private baths, entrances, and color cable TV. Guests will find Stella's Guest Home to be genuinely convivial and welcoming. The hosts consider each guest a visiting friend and take a personal interest in their enjoyment.

Hosts: Mr. and Mrs. Lamb
Suites: 3 (PB) $30-50
No Breakfast
Credit Cards: None
Notes: 2, 5, 12

McCLELLANVILLE

Laurel Hill Plantation

8913 North Highway 17, P.O. Box 190, 29458
(803) 887-3708

Laurel Hill faces the Intracoastal Waterway and the Atlantic Ocean. Porches provide a scenic view of marshes and creeks. The house is furnished in country and primitive antiques that reflect the Low Country lifestyle. Thirty miles north of Charleston, 60 miles south of Myrtle Beach.

Hosts: Jackie and Lee Morrison
Rooms: 4 (PB) $65-85
Full Breakfast
Credit Cards: A, B
Notes: 2, 5, 9, 10, 11, 12, 14

Laurel Hill Plantation

MOUNT PLEASANT

Guilds Inn

101 Pitt Street, 29464
(803) 881-0510; (800) 331-0510

A six-room inn. All rooms have private baths with whirlpool tubs. In a historic

NOTES: Credit cards accepted: A MasterCard; B Visa; C American Express; D Discover Card; E Diner's Club; F Other; 2 Personal checks accepted; 3 Lunch available; 4 Dinner available; 5 Open all year;

neighborhood five miles from historic Charleston and four miles from the beaches of Sullivan's Island and Isle of Palms.

Hosts: Guilds and Joyce Hollowell
Rooms: 6 (PB) $75-125
Continental Breakfast
Credit Cards: A, B, C
Notes: 2, 3, 4, 5, 7, 8, 9, 10, 11, 12

Shem Creek Inn

1401 Shrimp Boat Lane, 29464
(803) 881-1000

The inn is on beautiful Shem Creek, just moments from Patriot's Point. It offers luxurious rooms with private balconies, spectacular marsh and creek views, and a sparkling pool overlooking the water. Dining is available at 11 superb restaurants, and a wonderful Continental breakfast is served in the lobby. Tennis, golf, and swimming nearby. Children welcome. Smoking permitted.

Host: Kay Hudson
Rooms: 50 (PB) $59-125
Continental Breakfast
Credit Cards: None
Notes: 2, 5, 7, 8, 9, 10, 11, 12, 14

MYRTLE BEACH

Brustman House Bed and Breakfast

400 25th Avenue South, 29577-4718
(803) 448-7699; (800) 448-7699

Quiet wooded setting, two minutes from beach, yet close to tennis, golf, amusement park, and discount shopping malls. Four luxurious rooms with private baths; one suite with kitchen and private entry sleeps three to eight. Scandinavian classic furniture; comfortable beds with Laura Ashley or down comforters. Landscaped estate grounds with badminton, croquet, and rose garden. Ten-grain buttermilk pancakes a breakfast specialty. Afternoon tea with wine and sweets. Children welcome.

Host: Dr. Wendell C. Brustman
Rooms: 5 (PB) $65-85
Full Breakfast
Credit Cards: None
Notes: 2, 5, 8, 9, 10, 11, 12, 14

Serendipity

407 71st Avenue North, 29572
(803) 449-5268

Award-winning Mission-style inn, one and one-half blocks from the beach. Pool, Jacuzzi, shuffleboard, and Ping Pong. Near 70 golf courses, tennis, pier, and deep-sea fishing. Guests have their choice of two rooms, four suites, and four efficiencies. Air conditioning, TVs, refrigerators, and private baths in all rooms. Historic Charleston 90 miles; great shopping and restaurants are nearby. Close to all country music theaters.

Hosts: Terry and Sheila Johnson
Rooms: 10 (PB) $45-110
Continental Breakfast
Credit Cards: A, B, C
Notes: 5, 7, 8, 9, 10, 11, 12, 14

ROCK HILL

East Main Guest House

600 East Main Street, 29730
(803) 366-1161

In the downtown historic district, this Craftsman-style bungalow has been completely renovated and beautifully decorated. Guest rooms include private baths, cable TV, telephones, fireplaces, and queen-size beds. The Honeymoon Suite has a canopied bed and a whirlpool tub. A TV/sitting/game room is provided, and breakfast is served in the beautifully appointed dining room or under the patio pergola. AAA three-diamond rated.

Hosts: Jerry and Melba Peterson
Rooms: 3 (PB) $59-79
Continental Breakfast
Credit Cards: A, B
Notes: 2, 5, 9, 10, 11, 12, 14

6 Pets welcome; 8 Children welcome; 9 Social drinking allowed; 10 Tennis available; 11 Swimming available; 12 Golf available; 13 Skiing available; 14 May be booked through travel agents.

SUMMERVILLE

Bed and Breakfast of Summerville

304 South Hampton Street, 29483
(803) 871-5275

Slaves' quarters of a restored 1865 house on the National Register of Historic Places in a quiet setting. Winter breakfast is self-prepared from stocked refrigerator. At other times, there is the option of being served in the greenhouse. Queen-size bed, telephone, TV, kitchenette, bath with shower, bikes, and pool are available. Winter monthly rental by reservation. Advance reservation a must.

Hosts: Dusty and Emmagene Rhodes
Room: 1 (PB) $45-50
Continental Breakfast
Credit Cards: None
Notes: 2, 5, 7, 8 (over 11), 9, 10, 11, 12

SUMTER

Bed and Breakfast of Sumter

6 Park Avenue, 29150
(803) 773-2903

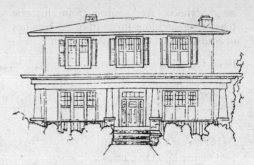

Bed and Breakfast of Sumter

Featured in the *New York Times* and *Sandlapper* magazine, this restored 1896 Prairie-style home sits in the heart of Sumter's historic district across from Memorial Park. Large front porch with swings and rocking chairs. Gracious guest rooms with antiques, fireplaces, all private baths. Formal Victorian parlor and TV sitting room. Cable. FAX. Gourmet breakfast (fruit, entree, home-baked breads). Antique shops, Swan Lake, and golf courses close.

Hosts: Jess and Suzanne Begley
Rooms: 5 (PB) $55-65
Full Breakfast
Credit Cards: A, B
Notes: 2, 5, 9, 10, 12, 14

NOTES: Credit cards accepted: A MasterCard; B Visa; C American Express; D Discover Card; E Diner's Club; F Other; 2 Personal checks accepted; 3 Lunch available; 4 Dinner available; 5 Open all year;

South Dakota

BRUCE

The International Bed and Breakfast Club, Inc.

504 Amherst Street,Buffalo, NY 14207
(800) 723-4262; FAX (716) 873-4462

Quiet country atmosphere. Built in 1908 in rural Brookings County in east central South Dakota. A home away from home for travelers, hunters, and fishermen. Four comfortable rooms, shared baths, and complete breakfasts provided. The inn also features a TV/game room and on-site laundry facilities. Convenient to the Laura Ingalls Wilder Museum and Pageant, the Summer Arts Festival at Brookings, and South Dakota State University. In addition to the full breakfast included in the room rate, other meals are available. Children are welcome. $35.

CANOVA

Skoglund Farm

Route 1, Box 45, 57021
(605) 247-3445

Enjoy the prairie: cattle, fowl, peacocks, a home-cooked evening meal, and full breakfast. Visit nearby attractions: Little House on the Prairie, Corn Palace, Doll House, Prairie Village, or just relax, hike, and enjoy a family farm. Rate includes evening meal and breakfast: $30 for adults; $20 for teens; $15 for children; children five and under free.

Hosts: Alden and Delores Skoglund
Rooms: 5 (SB) $30
Full Breakfast
Credit Cards: None
Notes: 2, 3, 4, 5, 6, 7, 8, 9, 10, 11, 12, 14

CHAMBERLAIN

Riverview Ridge

HC69 Box 82A, 57325
(605) 734-6084

Contemporary home built on a bluff overlooking a scenic bend in the Missouri River. King- and queen-size beds, full breakfast, secluded country peace and quiet. Just three and one-half miles north of downtown Chamberlain on Highway 50. Enjoy outdoor recreation, visit museums, Indian reservations and casinos, or just make this home away from home.

Hosts: Frank and Alta Cable
Rooms: 3 (1 PB; 2 SB) $50-60
Full Breakfast
Credit Cards: None
Notes: 2, 5, 8, 9, 11, 12

CUSTER

Custer Mansion Bed and Breakfast

35 Centennial Drive, 57730
(605) 673-3333

Historic 1891 Victorian Gothic home listed on the National Register of Historic Places. Features a blend of Victorian elegance and country charm with western hospitality. Clean, quiet accommodations and delicious

6 Pets welcome; 7 Smoking allowed; 8 Children welcome; 9 Social drinking allowed; 10 Tennis available; 11 Swimming available; 12 Golf available; 13 Skiing available; 14 May be booked through travel agents.

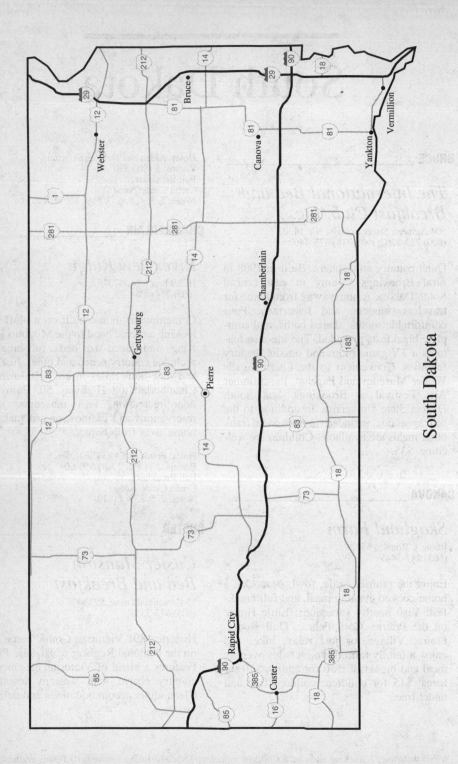

South Dakota

home-cooked breakfasts. Central to all of the Black Hills attractions, such as Mount Rushmore, Custer State Park, Crazy Horse Memorial. Recommended by *Bon Appétit*, and Mobil travel guide.

Hosts: Mill and Carole Seaman
Rooms: 6 (2 PB; 2 SB) $47.50-72.50
Full Breakfast
Credit Cards: None
Notes: 2, 5, 8, 10, 12, 13, 14

Custer Mansion

GETTYSBURG

Harer Lodge
Bed and Breakfast

Rural Route 1, P.O. Box 87A, 57442
(605) 765-2167; (800) 283-3356

Set in a prairie where buffalo once roamed, this modern cedar lodge has a miniature golf course, miniature horses, farm animals, and five lovely guest rooms, all with private baths. Enjoy the recreation room, reading room, fresh flowers in every room, and coffee and cookies when guests arrive. An authentic Native American tepee is available for campers, and a separate honeymoon cottage, done in romantic wispy white with an oversized Jacuzzi set in the floor, is available for newlyweds and anniversaries. The

honeymoon suite has sliding glass doors leading from the bathroom to a small private garden, complete with a porch swing and lots of privacy. Lunch and beverage served by candlelight, and breakfast is served in the cottage. Country store with South Dakota crafts, antiques, and a sweet shop is in a cream station/store restored on premises.

Hosts: Norma and Don Harer
Rooms: 5 (PB) $45-65
Cottage: 1 (PB) $75
Full Breakfast
Credit Cards: None
Notes: 2, 3, 4, 5, 8, 9, 12

RAPID CITY

Abend Haus Cottage and
Audrie's Cranbury Corner
Bed and Breakfast

23029 Thunderhead Falls Road, 57702-8524
(605) 342-7788

The Black Hills "inn place." Ultimate in charm and Old World hospitality, this country home and five-acre estate is surrounded by thousands of acres of national forest. Thirty miles from Mount Rushmore and seven miles from Rapid City. Each quiet, comfortable suite and cottage has a private entrance, private bath, hot tub, patio, cable TV, and refrigerator. Free trout fishing, biking, and hiking on property. Full breakfast served.

Hosts: Hank and Audry Kuhnhauser
Rooms: 6 (PB) $85
Full Breakfast
Credit Cards: None
Notes: 2, 5, 9, 10, 11, 12, 13

Betty Blount's
Domivara Lodge

Betty Blount's Bed and Breakfast
12760 Domivara Road, 57702
(605) 574-4207

NOTES: Credit cards accepted: A MasterCard; B Visa; C American Express; D Discover Card; E Diner's Club; F Other; 2 Personal checks accepted; 3 Lunch available; 4 Dinner available; 5 Open all year; 6 Pets welcome; 7 Smoking allowed; 8 Children welcome; 9 Social drinking allowed; 10 Tennis available; 11 Swimming available; 12 Golf available; 13 Skiing available; 14 May be booked through travel agents.

A unique log home off Highway 385 between two major recreational lakes: Pactola and Sheridan. Along with the breathtaking scenery laced with ponderosa pine, guests can spend time exploring, sightseeing, swimming, boating, hiking, etc. Dessert and coffee are served. A full breakfast of a variety of foods to please everyone's appetite may include broiled mountain trout, sourdough pancakes, Mexican egg baked dish, omelets, orange juice, tomato juice, fresh fruit (in season), rolls, French toast, scrambled eggs, bacon, or ham...whatever guests prefer!

Host: Betty Blount
Rooms: 3 (PB) $70-75
Full Breakfast
Credit Cards: None
Notes: 2, 5, 6, 7, 8, 9, 11, 12, 13

The Carriage House

721 West Boulevard, 57701
(605) 343-6415

This stately, three-story pillared Colonial house is on a historic, tree-lined boulevard of Rapid City. The English country decor creates an ambience of elegance, refinement, and relaxed charm. Gourmet breakfasts are served in the formal dining room. Scenic Mount Rushmore is only 26 miles away.

Hosts: Betty and Joel King
Rooms: 5 (2 PB; 3 SB) $59-89
Full Breakfast
Credit Cards: A, B
Notes: 2, 5, 9, 10, 11, 12, 13

Hotel Alex Johnson

523 6th Street, 57701
(800) 888-2539

Visit the Hotel Alex Johnson and stay at a historic landmark. There are 141 newly restored guest rooms. Old-World charm combined with award-winning hospitality, this legend offers a piece of Old West history in the heart of downtown Rapid City. Listed on the National Register of Historic Places.

Rooms: 141 (PB) $58-88
Full Breakfast
Credit Cards: A, B, C, D, E
Notes: 2, 3, 4, 5, 8, 9, 10, 12, 13, 14

Willow Springs Cabins

11515 Sheridan Lake Road, 57702
(605) 342-3665

Private one-room log cabins in the beautiful Black Hills National Forest. This secluded setting offers privacy like no other retreat. Each cabin is charmingly decorated with many antique treasures and extras. Breakfast is wonderful, featuring freshly ground coffee, juices, baked goods, and egg dishes served in the privacy of the cabin. Hiking, swimming, private hot tub, and fishing abound. Featured in *Country Living* magazine, October 1993.

Hosts: Joyce and Russell Payton
Cabins: 2 (PB) $90-100
Full Breakfast
Credit Cards: A, B
Notes: 2, 5, 8, 9, 10, 11, 12, 13, 14

VERMILLION

The Goebel House
Bed and Breakfast

102 Franklin, 57069
(605) 624-6691

A friendly old home built in 1916 and furnished with antiques and collectibles. Vermillion is home of the nationally known Shrine to Music Museum and the University of South Dakota. Four bedrooms grace the upper chambers and have both private and shared baths. Each room is individually decorated with furniture and mementos of the past.

Hosts: Don and Pat Goebel
Rooms: 4 (2 PB; 2 SB) $45
Full Breakfast
Credit Cards: None
Notes: 2, 5, 9, 10, 11, 12

NOTES: Credit cards accepted: A MasterCard; B Visa; C American Express; D Discover Card; E Diner's Club; F Other; 2 Personal checks accepted; 3 Lunch available; 4 Dinner available; 5 Open all year;

WEBSTER

Lakeside Farm Bed and Breakfast

Rural Route 2, Box 52, 57274
(605) 486-4430

Guests are invited to sample a bit of country life at Lakeside Farm. Feel free to explore the grove, barns, and pastures, or just relax with a cup of tea in the farmhouse. Accommodations for four to five guests on the second floor. The second-floor bathroom and shower serve both guest rooms. Children welcome. In northeastern South Dakota with museums featuring pioneer and Native American culture. Fort Sisseton nearby. No smoking or alcoholic beverages.

Hosts: Glenn and Joy Hagen
Rooms: 2 (SB) $40
Full Breakfast
Credit Cards: None
Notes: 2, 5, 8, 11, 12

YANKTON

Mulberry Inn

512 Mulberry Street, 57078
(605) 665-7116

This beautiful inn was built in 1873 and offers the ultimate in comfortable lodging with historic charm. Included in the National Register of Historic Places. Features parquet floors, six guest rooms furnished with antiques, two parlors with marble fireplaces, and a large porch for evening relaxation. In a quiet residential area, and within walking distance to the Missouri River, downtown, and fine restaurants. Only minutes from the beautiful Lewis and Clark Lake and Gavins Point Dam. Full breakfast at additional cost.

Hosts: Millie and Garrald Cameron
Rooms: 6 (2 PB; 4 SB) $35-51
Continental Breakfast
Credit Cards: A, B, C
Notes: 5, 8, 10, 11, 12, 13

Mulberry Inn

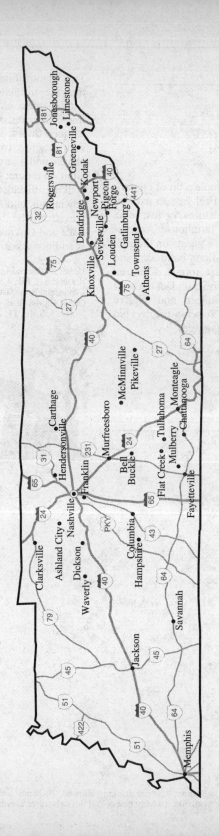

Tennessee

Jonesborough
Limestone
181

Greeneville
Kodak
81
Newport
Rogersville
Dandridge
Pigeon
32
Sevierville
Forge
40
Knoxville
Louden
Gatlinburg
441
75
Townsend
75
Athens
27
40
27
64
McMinnville
Pikeville
Carthage
Monteagle
Chattanooga
Hendersonville
Murfreesboro
31
24
Tullahoma
231
Mulberry
65
Franklin
Bell
Flat Creek
Buckle
Clarksville
24
65
Fayetteville
Nashville
Ashland City
PKY
Dickson
Columbia
43
40
Hampshire
64
Waverly
79
Savannah
Jackson
45
45
51
40
64
422
Memphis
51

Tennessee

ALLARDT

The Little Red Schoolhouse

P.O. Box 115, 38504-0115
(615) 879-8056

High upon the Cumberland Plateau, the old Allardt schoolhouse has been restored for guests' lodging pleasure. The schoolhouse features two bedrooms and two baths. Furnished in elegant antiques, complete with fireplace, and fully equipped kitchen. The area abounds in history, from the English colony of Rugby to Jamestown, home to the World War I hero, Sergeant Alvin York, as well as Mark Twain's parents. Allardt is a quaint German community settled in 1880 by the host's grandfather. Big South Fork National Park and Pickett State Park are a scenic 30-minute drive away.

Hosts: Charles and Lowanda Gernt
Rooms: 2 (PB) $65-75
Continental Breakfast
Credit Cards: None
Notes: 2, 5, 9, 12

ASHLAND CITY

Bird Song Country Inn Bed and Breakfast

Sycamore Mill, 1306 Highway 49 East, 37015
(615) 792-4005; FAX (615) 729-4005

Built in 1910 by the Cheek family of Maxwell House Coffee fame, this cedar lodge is listed on the National Register of Historic Places. An extensive collection of art and antiques brings the rooms to life.

Each one offers its own delights, from the large sunny guest rooms with adjoining bath to the masterful, yet cozy, great room, and the screened porch that overlooks sweeping lawns, English perennial gardens, and Sycamore Valley. Natural surroundings provide beautiful ways to relax. Stroll in the woods along Sycamore Creek; soak in the heated spa on the flagstone patio; enjoy a good book, a nap, or relax in the hammocks under stately trees. Trail rides available. Near Nashville 200, Beach Haven Winery, antiques shops, and fish restaurants on the river. Nashville is 20 minutes away.

Hosts: Anne and Brooks Parker
Rooms: 3 (PB) $80-100
Suite: 1 (PB)
Continental Breakfast
Credit Cards: A, B, C, D
Notes: 2, 5, 6, 7, 8, 9, 10, 11, 12, 14

ATHENS

Woodlawn

110 Keith Lane, 37303
(615) 745-8211; (615) 745-6029

Woodlawn is a beautiful antebellum mansion on five acres in historic downtown Athens. Built in 1858 by Mr. and Mrs. Alexander Hume Keith, it is listed on the National Register of Historic Places. The home was also used as a hospital during the Civil War and features 14 1/2-foot ceilings, antiques, and reproductions. The original smokehouse still stands on the grounds. Golf and white-water rafting on the Ocoee River are nearby. Off I-75 halfway between Chattanooga and Knoxville.

NOTES: Credit cards accepted: A MasterCard; B Visa; C American Express; D Discover Card; E Diner's Club; F Other; 2 Personal checks accepted; 3 Lunch available; 4 Dinner available; 5 Open all year; 6 Pets welcome; 7 Smoking allowed; 8 Children welcome; 9 Social drinking allowed; 10 Tennis available; 11 Swimming available; 12 Golf available; 13 Skiing available; 14 May be booked through travel agents.

Hosts: Barry and Susan Willis
Rooms: 4 (PB) $75-90
Full Breakfast
Credit Cards: A, B
Notes: 2, 5, 8 (over 9), 9, 10, 12, 14

BELL BUCKLE

Bed and Breakfast
About Tennessee

P.O. Box 110227, Nashville, 37222-0027
(615) 331-5244; FAX (615) 833-7701

Three double rooms, one room with two double beds, one room with a double and single. $50.

CARTHAGE

Bed and Breakfast
About Tennessee

P.O. Box 110227, Nashville, TN 37222-0227
(615) 331-5244: FAX (615) 833-7701

Southern hospitality in Vice President Gore's hometown. Charming hosts welcome the guest with tips on local area points-of-interest. Deluxe Continental breakfast served. $50.

CHATTANOOGA

Alford House
Bed and Breakfast

5515 Alford Hill Drive, 37419
(615) 821-7625; (800) 817-7625

This family owned and operated, three-story home, built in 1940, is filled with the charm of the Victorian era, and offers a Christian atmosphere. A wonderful collection of glass baskets are displayed for guests' enjoyment; some antiques are for sale. Within ten minutes of all attractions including the Tennessee Aquarium. Coffee is served early, and if desired, guests can enjoy the Continental plus breakfast in the gazebo, where mountain views can be seen.

Host: Rhoda Alford
Rooms: 4 (1 PB; 3 SB) $60-75
Continental Breakfast
Credit Cards: B
Notes: 2, 5, 8, 12, 14

Bed and Breakfast
About Tennessee

P.O. Box 110227, Nashville, TN 37222-0227
(615) 331-5244: FAX (615) 833-7701

The Charlet House. A quiet retreat on Signal Mountain, large trees, sidewalks, and 20 minutes from Chattanooga's riverfront attractions and restaurants. Two luxury suites with king-size beds and kitchenettes. Master suite has Jacuzzi and balcony. Large screened porch, deck area with grill overlooking pool. $85-95.

Colonial Revival House. A landmark classic in Chattanooga's Fort Wood area. Circular stairway with three bedrooms furnished in 19th-century elegance, each with private bath. Recent designer showcase house; beautifully decorated. $75-85.

Hilltop Country Victorian. Surrounded by porches. Excellent view of Lookout Mountain. Convenient to Chickamauga, Pigeon Mountains, Rock City, and other popular attractions. Four bedroom, three baths. $45-50.

Near Ocoee River and Deer Park. Hunting and fishing nearby. One double and one single room, private/shared bath, one single room with bath, one single room with shared bath. $26-40.

Rambling Tudor House. On Signal Mountain. Nine miles to downtown and convenient to tourist attractions. King-size room with private bath. Twin room with shared bath. $50-70.

NOTES: Credit cards accepted: A MasterCard; B Visa; C American Express; D Discover Card; E Diner's Club; F Other; 2 Personal checks accepted; 3 Lunch available; 4 Dinner available; 5 Open all year;

Restored Museum House. Fifteen minutes from Chattanooga near Chickamauga Battlefield Park. This antebellum plantation house features four rooms and three baths and a two-bedroom suite with bath and kitchen. Guest house also available. $55-125.

View of Lake. Near public access to lake for boating and fishing, public swimming, and picnic area. Food is provided, guests prepare own breakfast. Private twin suite with living room and kitchen. Near attractions, Lookout Mountain, Interstates 24 and 75. $50.

Tennessee Aquarium. Visitors to the new aquarium will want to see this nearby suite; queen-size bedroom with private bath, sitting room, and small kitchen. Swimming pool on premises. Three miles from University of Tennessee-Chattanooga; eight miles from airport. Children welcome. $85-100.

Captain's Quarters Bed and Breakfast

13 Barnhardt Circle, 30742
(706) 858-0624

Built in 1902, this home has been completely restored. Great attention has been paid to detail to retain the charm of yesterday and add the convenience of today. Adjacent to Chickamauga-Chattanooga Military Park and only 20 minutes from all the attractions in downtown, including the new Tennessee Aquarium. This quiet haven is convenient to many tourist attractions but restful when the day of sightseeing is done.

Hosts: Pam Humphrey and Ann Gilbert
Rooms: 7 (PB) $60-85
Full Breakfast
Credit Cards: A, B, C, D
Notes: 2, 5, 14

Chanticleer Inn

1300 Mockingbird Lane
Lookout Mountain, GA 37350
(706) 820-2015

Unique mountain stone buildings offer king- and queen-size, double, and twin rooms, some of which have antiques and fireplaces. Suites, cable TV, and a pool are all available in a quiet atmosphere. Great for honeymoons, families, reunions, or weekends. Only one block from Rock City Gardens and 15 minutes from the Tennessee Aquarium. AAA approved. Senior discounts. No pets.

Host: Gloria Horton
Rooms: 16 (PB) $40-86
Continental Breakfast
Credit Cards: A, B, C
Notes: 5, 7, 8, 9, 11

The Milton House Bed and Breakfast

508 Fort Wood Place, 37403
(615) 265-2800

This beautifully restored Southern mansion promises the perfect lodging experience for a wonderful stay in Chattanooga. Relive the past, yet still enjoy the luxuries and amenities of today in one of these elegant rooms furnished with period antiques. A sampling of the amenities includes a Jacuzzi, fireplaces, balcony, day room, antique roll-top desk, and claw-foot tubs. Listed on the national and local historic registers. In the downtown historic district of Fort Wood. A full home-cooked breakfast awaits guests each morning.

Host: Susan Mehlen
Rooms: 4 (3 PB; 1 SB) $65-175
Full Breakfast
Credit Cards: None
Notes: 2, 5, 8, 9, 10, 11, 12, 14

6 Pets welcome; 8 Children welcome; 9 Social drinking allowed; 10 Tennis available; 11 Swimming available; 12 Golf available; 13 Skiing available; 14 May be booked through travel agents.

CLARKSVILLE

Bed and Breakfast About Tennessee

P.O. Box 110227, Nashville, TN 37222-0227
(615) 331-5244: FAX (615) 833-7701

Beautiful property with wedding chapel on site and dining room supervised by internationally known chef. Excellent for weddings, family reunions, and anniversaries. Three log guest houses, circa 1790, accommodate from two to four couples. Meals available in nationally known dining room adjoining guest houses. Meals served at extra cost. $65.

COLUMBIA

Natchez Trace Reservation Service

P.O. Box 193, Hampshire, TN 38461
(615) 285-2777; (800) 377-2770

CUL-01 Milepost 409. Thirteen miles from Columbia and just five miles from Interstate 65, this 1901 farmhouse has been newly restored to elegant perfection. Double wraparound porch provides view of the Middle Tennessee countryside. The Columbia area is the antebellum home capital of Tennessee. A gourmet breakfast is served on fine linens and china. $80-95.

COL-01 Milepost 409. Thirteen miles from the trace, near Columbia, Tennessee, this log cabin inn was built in the early 1800s and boasts a kitchen and living room, as well as claw-foot bathtubs, fireplaces, and a balcony that offers a panoramic view of the countryside. Pieces of the hosts' artwork are in the inn. Rates include access to the grounds and tennis court. Luxury suite in main house. Cabin available. $85-130.

DANDRIDGE

Mill Dale Farm Bed and Breakfast

140 Mill Dale Road, 37725
(615) 397-3470; (800) 767-3471

This 19th-century farmhouse is in Tennessee's second oldest town. Three beautifully decorated guest rooms, all with private baths, are available to guests. The house is furnished with antiques, and the common rooms and kitchen have large stone fireplaces. One mile off I-40 with easy access to Gatlinburg, Pigeon Forge, and the Great Smoky Mountains. A delicious country breakfast is served.

Hosts: Lucy C. and Hood Franklin
Rooms: 3 (PB) $65
Full Breakfast
Credit Cards: None
Notes: 2, 5, 8, 10, 11, 12

Sugar Fork

Sugar Fork Bed and Breakfast

743 Garrett Road, 37725
(615) 397-7327; (800) 487-5634

Guests will appreciate the tranquil setting of Sugar Fork Bed and Breakfast on Dou-

---

NOTES: Credit cards accepted: A MasterCard; B Visa; C American Express; D Discover Card; E Diner's Club; F Other; 2 Personal checks accepted; 3 Lunch available; 4 Dinner available; 5 Open all year;

glas Lake in the foothills of the Great Smoky Mountains. Private access and floating dock. Enjoy warm-weather water sports and fishing year-round. Fireplace in common room, guest kitchenette, wraparound deck, swings, and park bench by the lake. A hearty breakfast is served family-style in the dining room or on the deck.

Hosts: Mary and Sam Price
Rooms: 3 (2 PB; 1 SB) $55-65
Full Breakfast
Credit Cards: A, B
Notes: 2, 5, 7, 8, 9, 10, 11, 12, 13

Sweet Basil and Thyme

P.O. Box 1132, 102 West Meeting Street, 37725
(800) 227-7128

This historically registered Victorian home, built circa 1830, is surrounded by rose gardens and furnished with antiques while reflecting the ambience of the past. A full gourmet breakfast is served, possibly in the garden, weather permitting. Dinner is available with advance reservations. Relax in the parlor or library, or simply stroll among the gardens. Within easy driving distance of Gatlinburg, Dollywood, Great Smoky Mountain National Park, and the University of Tennessee. Smoking is not allowed in the guest rooms.

Hosts: Dolores and Bill Pudifin
Rooms: 3 (1 PB; 2 SB) $50-65
Full Breakfast
Credit Cards: None
Notes: 5, 7 (limited), 8, 9, 12, 13

DICKSON

Bed and Breakfast About Tennessee

P.O. Box 110227, Nashville, TN 37222-0227
(615) 331-5244: FAX (615) 833-7701

Beautiful home filled with antiques. Experience the traditions, food, and customs of a contemporary Tennessee family in a small town near two state parks. Two rooms available with canopied bed or king-size waterbed. $45-55.

FAYETTEVILLE

The Heritage House

315 East College Street, 37334
(615) 433-9238

Visit this charming antebellum brick Colonial-style home with high ceilings, thick walls, and pocket doors. Relax in comfortably furnished rooms with cable TV, refrigerator, and antiques. Guests are welcome to enjoy the swing on the balcony or wicker chairs on the long front porch. Within walking distance of churches, movie theaters, restaurant, historical district, museum, and gift and antique shops. Other points of interest include Tims Ford Lake, Space and Rocket Center, canoe rental, and the Jack Daniel's Distillery.

Rooms: 2 (PB) $50
Continental Breakfast
Credit Cards: None
Notes: 2, 5, 8, 9

FLAT CREEK (SHELBYVILLE)

Bottle Hollow Lodge

111 Gobbler Ridge Road, 37160
(615) 695-5253

Nestled high in the rolling hills of Middle Tennessee, Bottle Hollow Lodge occupies 68 acres of beautiful countryside and magnificent views. The ultimate in peace, quiet, and solitude, this inn is just minutes from Lynchburg's Jack Daniel's Distillery and the site of the Tennessee Walking Horse National Celebration in Shelbyville. Bottle Hollow Lodge, with its inviting rockers on the front porch and plush sofas in front of the large stone fireplace, will add to the enjoyment of activities in the area.

6 Pets welcome; 8 Children welcome; 9 Social drinking allowed; 10 Tennis available; 11 Swimming available; 12 Golf available; 13 Skiing available; 14 May be booked through travel agents.

Hosts: Pat Whiteside
Rooms: 5 (PB) $85-150
Full Breakfast
Credit Cards: A, B
Notes: 2, 3 and 4 (by reservation), 5, 9, 12, 14

FRANKLIN

Natchez Trace Bed and Breakfast Reservation Service

P.O. Box 193, Hampshire, TN 38461
(615) 285-2777; (800) 377-2770

LEI-01 Milepost 436. Set in the lovely
Leipers Creek Valley near the village of
Leiper's Fork, this country home is only
two and one-half miles from the Natchez
Trace. There are facilities for horses; the
trail along the trace is just minutes away.
Large guest rooms with private baths.
Enjoy a full breakfast, and look out over the
peaceful setting. Swimming pool, exercise
room available. $65-85.

St. Mary of Magdala Country Bed and Breakfast

4673 Peytonsville Road, 37064
(615) 794-9861

Large log home furnished in Victorian
country-style. Three and one-half miles east
from I-65; ten minutes from historic Franklin,
and 30 minutes from Nashville. The serene
country setting includes a nearby church, and
nature trails with abundant wildlife and birds.
A favorite spot is the shaded porch with
swing and rocking chair. Special family suite
includes three bedrooms, sitting area, private
bath, and entrance. Lovely Southern breakfast served in the great room with a beautiful
stone fireplace.

Host: Mary Sue Walker
Rooms: 3 (1 PB; 2 SB) $45-125
Credit Cards: A, B
Notes: 2, 3, 4, 5, 8, 9

GATLINBURG

Bed and Breakfast About Tennessee

P.O. Box 110227, Nashville, TN 37222-0227
(615) 331-5244: FAX (615) 833-7701

Browse through an art gallery filled with
original works of art and works of local
craftsmen. Take in the expansive view of the
Smokey Mountains or take the Arts and
Crafts Tour Road. Near Cades Cove and
Dollywood. One mile from Pigeon Forge
and all the sights. One queen-size room with
brass bed and private bath. One room with
two double beds and private bath. $60-70.

Grandma's House. Two doubles with
private bath; or suite of rooms featuring
two bedrooms. Featuring Mystery Weekends. $55-75.

1865 Antebellum Plantation. Home has
grand entrance, nine working fireplaces,
listed with National Registry of Historic
Places, and overlooking the Tennessee
River. Beautiful swimming pool, gazebo,
and arbor. Five bedrooms with private
baths. Generous breakfast served. $115.

High on a hilltop above Gatlinburg. Hiking,
skiing, horseback riding, ice skating all
nearby. Antiques, cable TV, four rooms
with private baths. View Mount LeConte
from deck. $100.

Large Log Home. On one of the largest
golf courses in the area. Four bedrooms
with private baths, one with two double
beds. Great room with fireplace. Log
gazebo with Jacuzzi, tennis courts, and a
deck overlooking mountain streams. Full
breakfast served. $90.

NOTES: Credit cards accepted: A MasterCard; B Visa; C American Express; D Discover Card; E Diner's
Club; F Other; 2 Personal checks accepted; 3 Lunch available; 4 Dinner available; 5 Open all year;

Buckhorn Inn

2140 Tudor Mountain Road, 37738
(615) 436-4668

A unique country inn offering peaceful seclusion with the feeling and tradition of early Gatlinburg. Established in 1938, Buckhorn Inn is on a hillside facing magnificent views of Mount LeConte. There are 35 acres of woodland, meadows, and quiet walkways, including a self-guiding nature trail. Six miles northeast of Gatlinburg near the Greenbriar entrance to the Great Smoky Mountains National Park. Closed over Christmas.

Hosts: John and Connie Burns
Rooms: 12 (PB) $95-250
Full Breakfast
Credit Cards: A, B
Notes: 2, 4, 5, 9, 10, 11, 12, 13

Butcher House

Butcher House in the Mountains

1520 Garrett Lane, 37738
(615) 436-9457

Just 2,800 feet above the main street of Gatlinburg and the main entrance to the Smokey Mountain National Park, Butcher House in the Mountains offers seclusion as well as convenience. The large, spacious home is graced by Victorian, French, Queen Anne, and American country furniture. Antiques are tastefully placed throughout the house, and a downstairs kitchen is available for a before-bed dessert. The color coordination throughout is a delight to the senses with navy, blue, rose, and cremes being the predominant hues.

Hosts: Hugh and Gloria Butcher
Rooms: 5 (PB) $79-109
Full Breakfast
Credit Cards: A, B, C
Notes: 2, 5, 9, 10, 11, 12, 13

Eight Gables

219 North Mountain Trail, 37738
(615) 430-3344

Guests of this new bed and breakfast are welcomed by a peaceful mountain setting. Near the trolley stop, it features a unique design and decor. Comfort is assured in the spacious guest rooms, each decorated with an individual theme and style. Each first-floor guest room has a private entrance, and all of the second-floor guest rooms are graced with cathedral ceilings and arched windows. There is a "gathering room" for relaxing, a lounge for viewing TV. Full sit-

Eight Gables

down breakfast. Dramatic surroundings inside and out. Everything a guest might need marks this tribute to Southern hospitality. AAA-four diamond rated.

Host: Helen W. Smith
Rooms: 10 (PB) $89-110
Full Breakfast
Credit Cards: A, B
Notes: 2, 5, 9, 10, 11, 12, 13, 14

"7th Heaven" Log Inn

3944 Castle Road, 37738
(615) 430-5000; (800) 248-2923

On the 7th green of a golf resort, but guests don't have to play golf to enjoy sitting on the deck or in the log-gazebo Jacuzzi overlooking the creek, quiet pond, and beautiful, lush golf course. Gaze at the wonders of the Great Smoky Mountains National Park just across the road. Fully equipped guest kitchen, large game room with pool tables, and stone fireplace. Close to Dollywood, craft, antique, and outlet shopping. ABBA rated "excellent."

Hosts: Cherl and Don Roese
Rooms: 5 (PB) $77-125
Full Breakfast
Credit Cards: A, B
Notes: 2, 4, 5, 7, 9, 10, 11, 12, 13, 14

GREENEVILLE

Bed and Breakfast About Tennessee

P.O. Box 110227, Nashville, TN 37222-0227
(615) 331-5244; FAX (615) 833-7701

Restored Victorian. In historic district. Porches, stained-glass windows. Grand entrance hall. Five rooms, four baths. Full breakfast. Dinner available by appointment. $55-75.

Hilltop House

Rural Route 7, Box 180, 37743
(615) 639-8202

Come and experience the serenity of a 1920s manor house overlooking the Nolichucky River Valley and Appalachian Mountains in the background. All three guest rooms have private baths and spectacular mountain views, and two have their own verandas. Enjoy afternoon tea at 4:00 P.M. each day and sumptuous breakfasts. Nearby golf, mountain hiking, trout fishing, white-water rafting, mountain biking, or antiquing. The house is beautifully furnished with Oriental rugs, English antiques, and reproduction pieces.

Host: Denise M. Ashworth
Rooms: 3 (PB) $70-75
Full Breakfast
Credit Cards: A, B, C
Notes: 2, 3, 4, 5, 8 (over 3), 9, 11, 12, 14

HAMPSHIRE

Natchez Trace Bed and Breakfast Reservation Service

P.O. Box 193, Hampshire, 38461
(615) 285-2777; (800) 377-2770

HAM-01 Milepost 392. Contemporary cedar home furnished with antiques, set on 170 acres of wooded hills near the village of Hampshire, between Columbia and Hohenwald. Picture windows look out over the woods; have coffee on the spacious deck. Clear streams, a waterfall, birds, and wildflowers. Near Meriwether Lewis Park, Metal Ford, and Jackson Falls on the Trace. The hosts are experts on local wildflowers. Full breakfast. Guest room in home. Private cottage is also available for up to four people. $65-80.

HENDERSONVILLE

Monthaven

1154 Main Street West, 37075
(615) 824-6319

NOTES: Credit cards accepted: A MasterCard; B Visa; C American Express; D Discover Card; E Diner's Club; F Other; 2 Personal checks accepted; 3 Lunch available; 4 Dinner available; 5 Open all year;

On the National Register of Historic Places, Monthaven offers both a heritage of nearly 200 years, and a 75-acre estate for the enjoyment of visitors to Nashville and Middle Tennessee. The main house served as a field hospital during the Civil War. Log cabin, built in 1938 from 200-year-old timber, is available.

Hosts: Hugh Waddell and Alan Waddell
Rooms: 3 (PB) $75
Log Cabin: (PB) $85
Continental Breakfast
Credit Cards: Major
Notes: 2, 3, 4, 5, 6, 7, 8, 9, 10, 11, 12, 14

JACKSON

Bed and Breakfast About Tennessee

P.O. Box 110227, Nashville, TN 37222-0227
(615) 331-5244: FAX (615) 833-7701

A stately home of distinct charm, offering comfortable accommodations and Southern hospitality. Full breakfast served. One double bed with antiques and private bath. Room with two double beds, antiques, and shared bath. $50-60.

Jonesborough

JONESBOROUGH

Jonesborough Bed and Breakfast

100 Woodrow Avenue, P.O. Box 722, 37659
(615) 753-9223

This beautifully restored home was built in 1848 and is in Jonesborough's historic district. All restaurants and shops are within easy walking distance. To make a visit memorable, guests will find robes, high beds, antique furnishings, fireplaces, large porch with rocking chairs, secluded terrace, air conditioning, and a big breakfast. Private baths upon request. Rates are seasonal.

Host: Tobie Bledsoe
Rooms: 5 (PB/SB) $54-99
Full Breakfast
Credit Cards: None
Notes: 2, 5, 8, 9, 11, 12

KNOXVILLE

Bed and Breakfast About Tennessee

P.O. Box 110227, Nashville, TN 37222-0227
(615) 331-5244: FAX (615) 833-7701

Near University. Rooms with private baths, some with Jacuzzi. Penthouse room available. $75-150.

Maryville. Two rooms with shared bath. Restaurant on site. $45-50.

Restored 1900s Home. In quiet neighborhood, has antiques, and beautiful decor. Four miles from University of Tennessee and near Smokey Mountain sites. Breakfast served, other meals by appointment with host. Twin room and double room with shared bath. $45-60.

Middleton House Bed and Breakfast

800 West Hill Avenue, 37902
(615) 524-8100

Built in 1918 as a single-family home on the Tennessee River, adjacent to the University of Tennessee. In 1979, the Middleton House was converted into a bed and breakfast inn. It

6 Pets welcome; 8 Children welcome; 9 Social drinking allowed; 10 Tennis available; 11 Swimming available; 12 Golf available; 13 Skiing available; 14 May be booked through travel agents.

remains the exquisite inn for the special guests in Knoxville's quietest and most peaceful Maplehurst Park. Penthouse honeymoon suite, anniversary suite, and the loft suite all have Jacuzzis and king-size beds. Other rooms with sunken bathtubs, fireplace, or two double beds. Breakfast is served in bed each morning, and a high tea hour is offered most evenings.

Host: Michael Zwayyed
Rooms: 15 (PB) $44-195
Full Breakfast
Credit Cards: A, B, C, D, E, F
Notes: 2, 5, 8, 9, 10, 11, 12, 14

Mitchell's

1031 West Park Drive, 37909
(615) 690-1488

This bed and breakfast offers a comfortable room in a private home in a pleasant tree-shaded neighborhood near fine shops and restaurants. Parking at a private entrance, double bed, TV, refrigerator, and microwave; roll-away bed and crib available. It is 45 minutes to the Smoky Mountains, 25 minutes to Oak Ridge, one and one-half miles to I-75/I-40, and eight miles to downtown Knoxville.

Host: Mary M. Mitchell
Room: 1 (PB) $40
Continental Breakfast
Credit Cards: None
Notes: 2, 5, 6, 7, 8, 9

KODAK

Lincoln, Ltd.
Bed and Breakfast

P.O. Box 3479, Meridian, MS 39303
(601) 482-5483 information; (601) 633-MISS
  reservations;
FAX (601) 693-7447

64. Enjoy Southern hospitality and down-home friendliness in this charming inn.

Enjoy the beautiful handmade quilts, antique furniture, and family heirlooms. Southern farm-style breakfast served with

Snapp Inn

fresh-brewed coffee, homemade jams and jelly, and all the fixin's. Three rooms. $65.

LIMESTONE

Snapp Inn
Bed and Breakfast

1990 Davy Crockett Park Road, 37681
(615) 257-2482

These hosts will welcome guests into this gracious 1815 Federal home furnished with antiques and set in farm country. Enjoy the mountain view from the full back porch or play a game of pool or horseshoes. Close to Davy Crockett Birthplace Park; 15-minute drive to historic Jonesborough or Greeneville. Third person in room at no extra charge.

Hosts: Dan and Ruth Dorgan
Rooms: 2 (PB) $50
Full Breakfast
Credit Cards: None
Notes: 2, 5, 6, 8 (one child only), 9, 11, 12, 14

NOTES: Credit cards accepted: A MasterCard; B Visa; C American Express; D Discover Card; E Diner's Club; F Other; 2 Personal checks accepted; 3 Lunch available; 4 Dinner available; 5 Open all year;

LOUDON (KNOXVILLE) _____

The Mason Place
Bed and Breakfast

600 Commerce Street, 37774
(615) 458-3921

The Mason Place, in a quaint Civil War town along the Tennessee River, is a lovely, impeccably restored plantation home, circa 1865. Tastefully decorated throughout with comfortable period antiques, original chandeliers, delightful feather beds, and ten working fireplaces. Candlelight breakfast served in the dining room. Three acres of lawn and gardens, swimming pool, gazebo, and wisteria-covered arbor. Overflowing with charm and character, the home is near Knoxville, the Smoky Mountains, I-75, and I-40.

Hosts: Bob and Donna Siewert
Rooms: 5 (PB) $88-96
Full Breakfast
Credit Cards: A, B
Notes: 2, 5, 9, 10, 11, 12

McMINNVILLE _____

Falcon Manor
Bed and Breakfast

2645 Faulkner Springs Road, 37110
(615) 668-4444

Escape to the peaceful romance of the 1890s in one of the South's finest Victorian mansions. Rock on gingerbread verandas, shaded by giant trees. Indulge in the luxury of museum-quality antiques. Enjoy stories about the mansion's history and the innkeepers' adventures in restoring it. An ideal base for a Tennessee vacation, Falcon Manor is near the center of the Nashville-Chattanooga-Knoxville triangle. Easy access from I-24 and I-40. Country setting just minutes from town.

Rooms: 5 (1 PB; 4 SB) $75
Full Breakfast
Credit Cards: A, B
Notes: 2, 5, 8 (over 12), 9, 10, 11, 12, 14

MEMPHIS _____

Bed and Breakfast
About Tennessee

P.O. Box 110227, Nashville, TN 37222-0227
(615) 331-5244; FAX (615) 833-7701

Guest House. With twin beds, kitchenette, Hide-a-bed. Breakfast served at guest's leisure. $45-55.

Overton Park Area. Beautiful restored home furnished in antiques with swimming pool on site. Pool house available. Twin room with antique East Lake furnishings; Queen-size room with canopied bed and antiques; four-poster canopied bed with private bath. $90-100.

Twenty-five Minutes from Downtown. Three rooms with private baths, beautifully appointed, generous breakfast, genial hosts, picturesque surroundings. The surprise is the enormous enclosed room with a heated pool, waterfalls, sprays, flora, and large hot tub. Breakfast can be served in this surrounding if desired. $90.

Bed and Breakfast
in Memphis

P.O. Box 41621, 38174-1621
(901) 726-5920; (800) 336-2087 (reservations only)
FAX (901) 725-0194

D-0302. Gracious Southern living on the mighty Mississippi epitomizes this open and airy garden condo beautifully decorated with antiques and Oriental rugs. Two guest rooms, each with its own private bath, Continental breakfast served in full view of the river, and a thoroughly engaging Southern hostess all take guests back to a more gentle time of grace and elegance. The Wonders Series world-class exhibitions are within walking distance; great jazz and blues on famous Beale Street. Smoking outside only. $115.

D-0303. Magnificent sunsets. Romantic riverboats and city lights from a private balcony of this gorgeous unhosted condominium on the river. Spacious living room, dining room seating six, bedroom with king-size bed, Jacuzzi, and fully equipped kitchen with microwave. Private indoor parking, indoor and outdoor pools, spa, sauna, tennis courts, racquetball courts, and 24-hour security. Five-night minimum stay. Smoking on the balcony only. Unhosted. Weekly and monthly rates available. $155.

D-7369. Retreat to a nearby Arkansas working farm and Southern mansion just 30 minutes from downtown Memphis. Tour the farm and cotton gins, enjoy complimentary tea on the veranda each evening, and country breakfast each morning. Poke around antique shops, and eat some of the best catfish ever caught in nearby smaller towns. Take a jaunt into Memphis for nightlife, or bring a book and just relax. Three handsome guest rooms, two guest baths in the upstairs wing; TV in rooms. Resident dog. $95

E-1706. Leave cares behind and retreat to this beautiful private suite in elegant east location. Bright and cheery library opens to guest bedroom, with four-poster double bed, and private bath with Jacuzzi. Hosted. Dogs in residence. $85.

G-1900. This friendly host couple travels extensively in bed and breakfasts. Guests will enjoy breakfast on the screened porch in fashionable Germantown. Spacious guest room with antique pineapple twin beds, private bath, and use of office area for business travelers. Privacy, comfort, and congeniality for only $65.

M-0400. Say good-bye to expensive hotel rates and living out of a suitcase. For anyone forced to be away from loved ones, this is the next best thing. Charming one-bedroom apartment in award-winning midtown highrise offers large living room with Stearnes and Foster queen-size sleeper, dining and work area, full bath with shower, fully equipped kitchen with microwave, and ample closet space. Cable TV, VCR, and one complimentary video. FAX and secretarial services available. Unhosted. Minimums may apply. Weekly and monthly rates available. $125.

M-0404. Enjoy gracious hospitality that would make even Martha Stewart ask for entertaining tips. Exceptionally interesting host couple opens their beautiful home to guests! Two upstairs guest rooms with private guest bath. Quiet and elegant midtown neighborhood conveniently to all areas of the city. Visit Dixon Gallery and Gardens; the majestic Orpheum Theatre for Broadway hits, opera, and ballet; Memphis Brooks Museum of Art; and Beale Street for hot jazz and blues. No smoking. $75.

M-1200. Lovely gardens, lush trees, and scampering squirrels are all right in the heart of the city. Professionally decorated host home in the historic Hein Park near Rhodes College and the zoo. Choice of upstairs suite (double and single beds) with shower and wet bar, or downstairs guest room with king-size bed, cable TV, VCR, and private bath. Popular hostess teaches English at a local college and travels extensively. $75.

NOTES: Credit cards accepted: A MasterCard; B Visa; C American Express; D Discover Card; E Diner's Club; F Other; 2 Personal checks accepted; 3 Lunch available; 4 Dinner available; 5 Open all year;

Lowenstein-Long House

217 North Waldran, 38105
(901) 527-7174

This beautifully restored Victorian mansion near downtown is listed on the National Register of Historic Places. Convenient to all major attractions, such as the Mississippi River, Graceland, Beale Street, the Memphis Zoo, Brooks Museum, and the Victorian Village. Free off-street parking.

Hosts: Col. Charles and Margaret Long
Rooms: 4 (PB) $50-80
Full Breakfast
Credit Cards: None
Notes: 2, 5, 8, 9

North Gate Inn

MONTEAGLE

North Gate Inn

Monteagle Assembly 103, 37356
(615) 924-2799

The bright blue awning of this former 1890s boarding house welcomes guests to warm hospitality and sumptuous breakfasts. Attractive common areas include two inviting porches; one with a blue enamel wood stove for winter use. Original iron beds, custom mattresses, antique quilts, and ceiling fans in each charming guest room. Two-bedroom cottage also available. Close to hiking trails, waterfalls, caves, mountain vistas, antiques, and crafts. Explore the grounds of the historic Chautauqua of the South, Monteagle Assembly, or rock a while on the porch.

Hosts: Nancy and Henry Crais
Rooms: 7 (PB) $65-80
Cottage: $100-150
Full Breakfast
Credit Cards: None
Notes: 2, 5, 8, 9, 10, 11, 12, 14

MULBERRY

Mulberry House Bed and Breakfast

8 Old Lynchburg Highway, 37359
(615) 433-8461

This 110-year-old home in Mulberry, where Davy Crockett spent a winter, is nestled in the hills of Middle Tennessee, only seven miles from Lynchburg, home of Jack Daniel's Tennessee whiskey. Only 45 minutes from Huntsville, Alabama. There are many craft and antique shops to visit.

Host: Candy Richard
Rooms: 2 (PB) $40
Continental Breakfast
Credit Cards: A, B
Notes: 2, 5, 8, 9

MURFREESBORO

Bed and Breakfast About Tennessee

P.O. Box 110227, Nashville, 37222-0027
(615) 331-5244; FAX (615) 833-7701

Beautiful View. Spacious new inn with large pretty rooms, private baths. Master suite sleeps four, vaulted ceiling, with stove fireplace, sitting area with recliners. Ten miles from Shelbyville, Lynchburg, Tullahoma, and 15 miles from Fayetteville. Children over 12 accepted. No smoking except on porches and patios. Dinner by reservation. $75-150.

Historic Log House. One large room, private bath. Good kitchen facilities with food provided for breakfast. Room has private balcony overlooking the pool. $50.

Clardy's Guest House

Clardy's Guest House

435 East Main Street, 37130
(615) 893-6030

In the historic district, this 20-room Victorian Romanesque home is filled with antiques and features ornate woodwork and fireplaces. An eight-by-eight-foot stained-glass window overlooks the magnificent staircase. The area has much to offer history buffs and antique shoppers. Thirty miles from Nashville, just two miles off I-24.

Hosts: Robert and Barbara Deaton
Rooms: 3 (2 PB; 1 SB) $37-47
Continental Breakfast
Credit Cards: None
Notes: 2, 5, 7, 8, 9, 10, 11, 12, 14

NASHVILLE

Bed and Breakfast Adventures

P.O. Box 150586, 37215
(615) 383-6611; (800) 947-7404

Bed and Breakfast Adventures is a reservation service representing homestays and inns personally visited and approved by this establishment. Choose from historic or contemporary homes, romantic inns, condos, guest houses, log cabins, lake or mountain retreats, or working farms. Convenience, reason for visit, interests, etc. are carefully considered, then several hosts are selected for guests to choose from, so the stay will be a truly memorable, pleasant experience. $50-195.

Bed and Breakfast About Tennessee

P.O. Box 110227, Nashville, TN 37222-0227
(615) 331-5244: FAX (615) 833-7701

Antiques Shopping. Nineteen miles from Nashville. A Cape Cod-style guest house with fully equipped kitchen, king-size bedroom with Jacuzzi tub, double sink, and separate shower. $100.

Belle Meade Area. Private suite, including queen-size bed, living room with fireplace, kitchenette, full bath, hot tub, and TV. No children. No pets. No smoking. $100.

Blue "Old Saltbox" House. Surrounded by wooded hills just 20 minutes from downtown Nashville. House is decorated with woodcrafts by hosts. Breakfast, accompanied by homemade jam, is served in the sunny kitchen. Guests are welcome to tea in the Japanese garden or on the patio. One child on folding cot. No pets. No smoking. $45-60.

Built in Mid 1800s. On the site of Indian camping grounds is this beautiful Greek Revival with Victorian decorative elements. Served as a hospital during the Civil War. This home is 15 minutes from Nashville. Log guest house and main house are furnished in antiques. $75-85.

NOTES: Credit cards accepted: A MasterCard; B Visa; C American Express; D Discover Card; E Diner's Club; F Other; 2 Personal checks accepted; 3 Lunch available; 4 Dinner available; 5 Open all year;

Chalet Style. Two-story home with deck overlooking brook. Nestled in a forest of weeping willows, lush greenery, and gardens. Interior designer has filled home with wicker and color. Oriental rugs and antiques blend perfectly. One double and one twin room with a private/shared bath. Near Belle Meade Mansion and Cheekwood. Only 30 minutes to airport and Opryland. Swimming pool, playground, and tennis. Children over two years of age. No pets. No smoking. $50-60.

Congenial Hosts/Contemporary Home. Two rooms, one twin, one double, private/shared baths. $45-50.

Drake Farm. Creekside antebellum farm house, circa 1850. Children, pets, fireplace, country-style breakfast in dining room. Business travelers welcome. $45-60.

1800s Restored Stagecoach Inn. Ten miles from interstate near Brentwood. Resplendent with antiques. Downstairs has one double room with canopied bed, private bath, fireplace, and garden view. Upstairs features two double rooms with canopied beds, private/shared bath, antique vanities in each room. Creekside gingerbread cottage also available. Twenty minutes from Nashville. $65-75.

English-Style Cottage. Including living room, fireplace, kitchen loft, and master bedroom. One block from bus. $75-85.

Guest House. Three-room guest house with swimming pool. Large rooms, bath, kitchen. French doors open onto pool. $100.

Historic District of Nashville. This restored Victorian was built in 1902 by then-mayor of Nashville. Recently restored by an interior designer, the bedroom is furnished with antiques and features a huge adjoining bath. Across the street is a 100-year-old Catholic church. $55.

House of the Lake. Beautifully appointed home with three bedrooms with private baths, kitchen, and living room. $125.

Insurance Broker and nurse have one double and one twin room near major interstates and convenient to area colleges. $45-50.

Large Rural Estate. Very scenic and private. Ten rooms, each with double and single, half bath, rustic decor. Large baths in hall. Thirteen miles from Nashville. Perfect for corporate retreats, family reunions, and large groups. Parklike setting with picnic area, three swimming pools, on beautiful creek, near lake. $55.

Log Lodge. Near Opryland. Home features antiques, comfortable sitting area, and TV. Double room with private bath. Swimming pool in summer. No children. No pets. $75.

Music Row. All suite property with limited access door. Full suites, beautifully furnished. Swimming pool on property. $90-125.

Near Downtown. Beautiful older home has collections displayed throughout the house. Grand staircase to bed and breakfast rooms. One double with private bath; two doubles with shared bath; suite with small kitchen, and sitting room. $80-100.

6 Pets welcome; 8 Children welcome; 9 Social drinking allowed; 10 Tennis available; 11 Swimming available; 12 Golf available; 13 Skiing available; 14 May be booked through travel agents.

Near I-65 South. One king-size room, one queen-size room, one double room with private/shared bath. Host is a teacher who loves music. Prefers no smoking. $45-50.

Near Maryland Farms. Side entrance, deck, queen-size room with antiques, and private bath. Two single rooms upstairs with shared bath. $30-50.

Near Vanderbilt. Restored 1900s house has two suites. Suite one has double bed and adjoining Florida room with lots of windows and private bath. Suite two has double bed, private bath, and fireplace. Near interstates, downtown, antiques mall, and universities. $75-90.

On Old Hickory Lake. Handsome lakeside house on shore of lake. Views from all rooms. Afternoon sherry, Jacuzzis, fireplaces, canopied beds. Two-night minimum. $90-150.

Oldest House in Downtown. Built in 1859, this home features 12-foot ceilings and fireplaces. First floor is tea room where guests have breakfast. One block from Nashville Convention Center; fifteen minutes from Opryland. Rooms furnished in antiques. Private/shared baths. $55-75.

One block from Lipscomb University. This home has two double rooms and private baths. Recording artist and counselor enjoy people and are interested in country music. $45-50.

Overlooking the Cumberland River. Professionally decorated log house with fireplace, screened porch, and full kitchen. Two bedroom, two baths, and cable TV. Professional chef available. $95-150.

Pleasant Home on Wooded Lot. Three bedrooms, two baths, near major thoroughfares and airport. Host smokes. Children welcome. $45-50.

Quiet, Secluded Poolside Guest House. With twin beds and private bath. Close to I-40. Eight miles to downtown Nashville. Near good fishing. Adjoins 24-foot aboveground pool. $45-60.

Relax in Peace. Privacy and comfort at a cedar log lodge in the beautiful Tennessee hills, just 20 minutes from Nashville. Built in 1910 by the Cheek family of Maxwell House Coffee fame and listed on the National Register. Bird Song offers lazy hammocks and woodsy creekside beauty; lovely gardens and fascinating art. Three bedrooms with private baths; suite available. Deluxe Continental breakfast served. $85-100.

Restored 1900s. Minutes from downtown area in beautiful older neighborhood. Two double rooms with shared bath. No Smoking. $60-67.50.

King-size Room. With TV. Also one double room with private bath ensuite. Near bus and shopping. Three miles to Opryland. $45-50.

Small Apartment. Living room, large bedroom with double and single bed, private bath. Equipped kitchen, TV, and private entrance. $55-100.

Suite of Rooms. Lakeside home with beautiful gardens, boat dock, and lake swimming. Near homes of country music stars. Two-night minimum. $100.

Terrawin. Rock on the front porch, watch the cows, or lie in the hammock and enjoy the parklike grounds. Minutes from Opryland, the largest shopping district in Nashville, downtown, I-65 and I-40. Upstairs large room with queen-size bed, another large room with twin bed, and bath. Large suite with twin beds, and sleeper sofas. Room for sleeping bags. Fireplace and pool table. Continental breakfast is served. $50-55.

Two Bedrooms. With private/shared bath, hostess who loves people. Near all major interstates, airport, six minutes from downtown, bus nearby. Enjoy patio and hospitality. $45-50

Two Efficiency Apartments. Near downtown, refrigerator, stove, and microwave. Living room couch makes a bed, laundry, double bedroom, and private bath. Maximum five persons. $40-70.

Vanderbilt Area. Double room with beautiful antique bed, comfortable mattress, sitting room with desk, and private bath. Lovely antiques throughout the house. $60.

Natchez Trace Bed and Breakfast Reservation Service

P.O. Box 193, Hampshire, 38461
(615) 285-2777; (800) 377-2770

ASH-01 Milepost 450. Built in 1920 by the Cheek family of Maxwell House Coffee fame, this cedar log lodge is listed on the National Register of Historic Places. Extensive collection of art and antiques, large sunny guest room, masterful yet cozy great room, screened porch, and heated spa. Stroll along the creek or enjoy a nap in a hammock under stately trees; tennis and swimming nearby. A pleasant 20-minute drive to Nashville. Hosts have borrowed the

best ideas from country inns on several continents to make this a unique and wonderful place. $75-95.

NAS-01 Milepost 450. This large stone Georgian-style Nashville home was built in the 1920s by the owner of a local stone quarry. It is close to Vanderbilt University and all Nashville activity, as well as being a starting point for Natchez Trace travelers. There is a cottage with a queen-size bed and daybed behind the main house. Two guest rooms are available in the main house. $85.

Ms. Rickie's Bed and Breakfast

1614 19th Avenue South, 37212
(615) 269-3850

Whether line dancing at the Wildhorse Saloon, attending that important meeting, or enjoying the sights of the city, make a Nashville experience complete with a stay at Ms. Rickie's Bed and Breakfast. In a convenient setting, this historic Georgian home, with its private English-styled stone guest cottage, offers comfort, privacy, and those little added touches that let guests know they are special. Full gourmet breakfast served.

Hosts: Rickie and Chris Gantry
Rooms: 3 (PB) $75-100
Full Breakfast
Notes: 2, 5, 10, 11, 12, 14

Woodshire Bed and Breakfast

600 Woodshire Drive, Goodlettsville, 37072
(615) 859-7369

Family antiques, homemade preserves, and Southern hospitality—all just 15 to 20 minutes from Nashville's universities, museums, Parthenon, Opryland, and many country music attractions. Private entrance, use of screened porch, and Continental

6 Pets welcome; 8 Children welcome; 9 Social drinking allowed; 10 Tennis available; 11 Swimming available; 12 Golf available; 13 Skiing available; 14 May be booked through travel agents.

breakfast. Country atmosphere with urban conveniences. A mid-1800s reconstructed log cabin is also available.

Hosts: John and Beverly Grayson
Rooms: 2 (PB) $40-50
Log Cabin: $60-70
Continental Breakfast
Credit Cards: None
Notes: 2, 8, 14

NEWPORT

Christopher Place Country Inn

1500 Pinnacles Way, 37821
(615) 623-6555

Surrounded by expansive mountain views, this premier Southern estate includes over 200 acres to explore, with a pool, tennis court, and sauna. Relax by the marble fireplace in the library, retreat to the game room, or enjoy a hearty mountain meal in the restaurant. Romantic rooms are available with a hot tub or fireplace. Off I-40 at Exit 435, just 32 scenic miles from Gatlinburg and Pigeon Forge. Handicapped accessible. Opening spring 1995.

Host: Drew Ogle
Rooms: 10 (PB) $75-150
Full Breakfast
Credit Cards: A, B
Notes: 2, 3, 4, 5, 9, 10, 11, 12, 14

PIGEON FORGE

Hilton's Bluff Bed and Breakfast

2654 Valley Heights Drive, 37863
(615) 428-9765

Romantic hilltop hideaway. Beautiful two-story cedar inn with covered decks, oak rockers, and nature's ever-changing views. Decorated with country quilts and lace. There are ten guest rooms: executive, deluxe, and honeymoon, featuring king-size beds, waterbeds, and heart-shaped Jacuzzis. Den with stone fireplace, game room, and meeting

room. Southern gourmet breakfast. Elegant country living, minutes from the heart of Pigeon Forge and the Great Smoky Mountains National Park. Smoking restricted. No pets.

Hosts: Jack and Norma Hilton
Rooms: 10 (PB)$79-109
Full Breakfast
Credit Cards: A, B, C
Notes: 5, 9, 10, 11, 12, 13, 14

PIKEVILLE

Fall Creek Falls Bed and Breakfast

Route 3, Box 298B, 37367
(615) 881-5494

Enjoy the relaxing atmosphere of a country manor home on 40 acres of rolling hillside one mile from the nationally acclaimed Fall Creek Falls Resort Park. Beautiful accommodations have a common sitting area with TV. Lodging includes a full breakfast served in a cozy country kitchen, an elegant dining room, or a sunny Florida room with a magnificent view. Assistance with touring, dining, and shopping information. Off-season rates. AAA rated.

Hosts: Doug and Rita Pruett
Rooms: 8 (6 PB; 2 SB) $50-75
Full Breakfast
Credit Cards: A, B
Notes: 2, 3, 9, 10, 11, 12, 14

ROGERSVILLE

Hale Springs Inn

110 West Main Street, 37857
(615) 272-5171

This elegant, three-story Federal brick building, built in 1824, is the oldest continuously run inn in Tennessee. Beautifully furnished with antiques from the period. Some of the rooms feature four-poster canopied beds, and all rooms have working fireplaces. Air conditioning. Guests may bring their own wine. Candlelight dining.

NOTES: Credit cards accepted: A MasterCard; B Visa; C American Express; D Discover Card; E Diner's Club; F Other; 2 Personal checks accepted; 3 Lunch available; 4 Dinner available; 5 Open all year;

Host: Ed Pace
Rooms: 9 (PB) $45-75
Continental Breakfast
Credit Cards: A, B, C
Notes: 4, 5, 7, 8, 9, 10, 11, 12

Hale Springs Inn

RUGBY

Grey Gables
Bed 'n' Breakfast Inn

Highway 52, P.O. Box 5252, 37733
(615) 628-5252

Nestled on the outskirts of the 1880s English village of Rugby, Grey Gables offers the best of the Victorian English and Tennessee Country heritage, creatively blending Victorian and country antiques. Fare includes lodging, evening meal, and country breakfast. Visit the beautiful Cumberland Plateau, historic Rugby, and Grey Gables. In the tradition of the forebears, guests will receive a hearty welcome, a restful bed, and a full table. Reservations required.

Hosts: Bill and Linda Brooks Jones
Rooms: 8 (4 PB; 4 SB) $90
Full Breakfast
Credit Cards: A, B
Notes: 2, 3 (by reservation), 4, 5, 9, 11, 12, 14

Newbury House
at Historic Rugby

P.O. Box 8, Highway 52, 37733
(615) 628-2441; (615) 628-2430

Newbury House was the Rugby colony's first boarding house, established in 1880. Sash and pulley cords on the windows reveal an 1879 patent date. Board and batten siding, a lovely front porch, mansard roof, and dormer windows are all hallmarks of this beautifully restored, Victorian-furnished bed and breakfast. Newbury House lodged both visitors and incoming settlers, as well as British author Thomas Hughes's utopian colony. In a nationally registered village with historic building tours, museum stores, specialty restaurant, and river gorge hiking trails. Victorian cottages also available.

Host: Historic Rugby
Rooms: 5 (3 PB; 2 SB) $60-70
Full Breakfast
Credit Cards: A, B
Notes: 2, 3, 4, 5, 9, 11, 12

SAVANNAH

Bed and Breakfast
About Tennessee

P.O. Box 110227, Nashville, 37222-0027
(615) 331-5244; FAX (615) 833-7701

Comfortable home on Tennessee River. Family home furnished in antiques. Near Shiloh battlefield, a nice getaway from the city. All water sports are available. Will include dinner at extra cost. $70.

SEVIERVILLE

Huckleberry Inn

1754 Sandstone Way, 37867
(615) 428-2475

Huckleberry Inn is an authentic mountain log home on 25 acres, just behind Dolly-

6 Pets welcome; 8 Children welcome; 9 Social drinking allowed; 10 Tennis available; 11 Swimming available; 12 Golf available; 13 Skiing available; 14 May be booked through travel agents.

wood and surrounded by Pigeon Forge, Gatlinburg, and Sevierville. There are four guest rooms, all with private whirlpool baths; two with fireplaces. Enjoy a full country breakfast on the screened porch, or eat in the kitchen by the stone fireplace. Relax on the high back porch, and enjoy beautiful mountain views. Take a walk down to the spring or hike up the mountain. It's all here.

Hosts: Rich and Barb Thomas
Rooms: 4 (PB) $69-79
Full Breakfast
Credit Cards: A, B
Notes: 2, 3, 4, 5, 8, 9, 12, 13, 14

Von-Bryan Inn

2402 Hatcher Mountain Road, 37862
(615) 453-9832; (800) 633-1459

The Von-Bryan Inn is a magnificent log home with beautiful views from every window and every relaxing spot on the grounds. The inn is on top of a 2,100-foot mountain, and the views are almost breathtaking. No wonder most of the guests find it hard to break away long enough to take in the amusement parks and outlet malls. Rooms of cottages available.

Hosts: Joann and D. J. Vaughn and sons Patrick
    and David
Rooms: 10 (PB) $80-125
Full Breakfast
Credit Cards: A, B, C, D
Notes: 2, 5, 11, 12, 13

TOWNSEND

Richmont Inn

220 Winterberry Lane, 37882
(615) 448-6751

This lovely inn can be found on the "peaceful side of the Smokies." This Appalachian barn is beautifully furnished with 18th-century English antiques and French paintings in both the living and dining rooms. Enjoy the breathtaking mountain views. Graciously appointed rooms with sitting areas,

king-size beds, wood-burning fireplaces, spa tubs for two, and private balconies. French and Swiss cuisine are served at breakfast with flavored coffees. Special gourmet desserts are offered by evening candlelight. Featured in *Country Inns* magazine as a "sweet rendezvous," and awarded grand prize for dessert by *Gourmet Magazine*. Ten minutes away from the Great Smoky Mountains arts and craft shops and historic Cades Cove is nearby.

Hosts: Susan and Jim Hind
Rooms: 10 (PB) $90-135
Full Breakfast
Credit Cards: None
Notes: 2, 5, 9, 12, 14

Richmont Inn

TULLAHOMA

Ledford Mill

P.O. Route 2, Box 152, Wartrace 37183
(615) 455-2546

A totally private hideaway where the guests are the only ones in this cozy, open suite with kitchenette. Spend the night in a 19th-century grist mill, listening to the waterfalls and murmuring waters of Shippmans Creek.

Hosts: Norma and Bill Rigler
Room: 1 (PB) $70
Continental Breakfast
Credit Cards: A, B, C, D
Notes: 2, 5, 6, 7, 8, 9

NOTES: Credit cards accepted: A MasterCard; B Visa; C American Express; D Discover Card; E Diner's Club; F Other; 2 Personal checks accepted; 3 Lunch available; 4 Dinner available; 5 Open all year;

WAVERLY

The Nolan House Inn

Route 4, Box 164, Highway 13 North, 37185
(609) 234-2987

The Nolan House is an 1870 Victorian cottage. It has porches on all sides for relaxing, and a souvenir shop for browsing. It is furnished with Victorian furniture collected from the local antique shops. There is a large meeting room with adjoining kitchen for weddings, receptions, business meetings, etc. Every Saturday morning a hot breakfast is served in the large meeting room. Loretta Lynn's Dude Ranch is only seven miles down the road.

Host: La Verne Turner
Rooms: $30-35; $10 to add day bed
Credit Cards: None
Notes: 2, 5, 8

6 Pets welcome; 8 Children welcome; 9 Social drinking allowed; 10 Tennis available; 11 Swimming available; 12 Golf available; 13 Skiing available; 14 May be booked through travel agents.

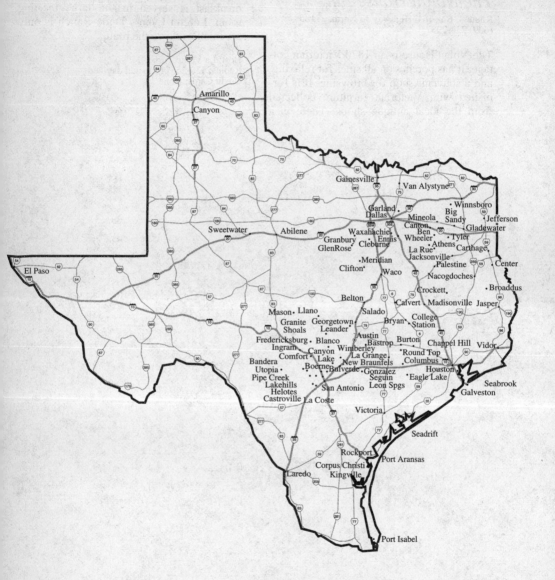

Texas

Texas

ABILENE

Bolin's Prairie House Bed and Breakfast

508 Mulberry, 79601
(915) 675-5855

Nestled in the heart of Abilene is a 1902 home furnished with antiques and modern luxuries combined to create a warm, homelike atmosphere. Downstairs, there are high ceilings, hardwood floors, and a woodburning stove. Upstairs are four unique bedrooms (Love, Joy, Peace, and Patience), each beautifully decorated. Breakfast of special baked-egg dishes, fruit, and homemade bread is served in the dining room that is decorated with a collection of cobalt glass and blue and white china.

Hosts: Sam and Ginny Bolin
Rooms: 4 (2 PB; 2 SB) $50-60
Full Breakfast
Credit Cards: A, B, C
Notes: 2, 5

AMARILLO

Parkview House

1311 South Jefferson, 79101
(806) 373-9464

This turn-of-the-century Prairie Victorian in the heart of the Texas Panhandle has been lovingly restored by the present owners to capture its original charm. Furnished with antiques and comfortably updated, it has a large family TV room and parlor for reading or listening to music. Convenient to biking, jogging, hiking, and the prize- winning musical drama *Texas* in Palo Duro State Park. Near the Panhandle Historical Museum, Lake Meredith, Alibates Quarries, and Route 66.

Hosts: Nabil and Carol Dia
Rooms: 5 (3 PB; 2 SB) $65-85
Suite: 1 (PB) $75
Continental Breakfast
Credit Cards: A, B, C
Notes: 2, 5, 8 (by arrangement), 9, 10, 14

ATHENS

Bed and Breakfast Texas Style

4224 West Red Bird Lane, Dallas, 75237
(214) 298-8586

New York Texas Cheesecake. This wonderful two-story farmhouse overlooks about 25 acres of a peaceful meadow and a well-stocked bass lake. The new inn has four upstairs guest bedrooms; two bedrooms have private baths, and two bedrooms share a hall bath. The host is famous for New York Texas Cheesecake, which is offered to all who come through the door. The inn provides a library, formal dining room, wonderful veranda with big rocking chairs, and rooms filled with antiques that are for sale. Breakfast will be a bonanza of ham or sausage, buttered new potatoes, and eggs with mushroom-and-onion sauce. Children and pets are welcome. Smokers are welcome to smoke on the porch. $79.

NOTES: Credit cards accepted: A MasterCard; B Visa; C American Express; D Discover Card; E Diner's Club; F Other; 2 Personal checks accepted; 3 Lunch available; 4 Dinner available; 5 Open all year; 6 Pets welcome; 7 Smoking allowed; 8 Children welcome; 9 Social drinking allowed; 10 Tennis available; 11 Swimming available; 12 Golf available; 13 Skiing available; 14 May be booked through travel agents.

AUSTIN

Austin's Wildflower Inn

1200 West 22½ Street, 78705
(512) 477-9639

Austin's Wildflower Inn is a carefully restored New England country-style bed and breakfast. Each room is furnished with antiques, all windows are filled with lace or embroidered curtains, and antiques and handmade quilts fill an antique captain's chest. A hearty full breakfast is served in the dining room or on the beautiful bilevel deck in the back garden. Tennis and trails for hiking and biking are nearby. Business rates available.

Host: Kay Jackson
Rooms: 4 (2 PB; 2 SB) $59-75
Credit Cards: A, B, C
Notes: 2, 5, 9, 10, 11, 12

Bed and Breakfast Hosts of San Antonio and South Texas

1777 N.E. Loop 410, Suite 600, San Antonio, 78217
(210) 824-8036; (800) 356-1605 (reservations)
FAX (210) 271-9145

701. This bed and breakfast is a quiet haven in a natural setting. It is furnished in family antiques, quilts, and collectibles. Leslie's Room has a double Victorian Murphy bed; Timary's Room has a brass double bed; they share a bath. The attic common room has TV, VCR, and telephone. Large decks, pool, pond, and patio table with chairs. Washer/dryer available. Fifteen minutes from downtown. $65.

Bed and Breakfast Texas Style

4224 West Red Bird Lane, Dallas, 75237
(214) 298-8586

Cliffside Guesthouse. The beautiful view and the large greenbelt area keep folks coming back to this cozy guest house with kitchenette. High above Barton Springs Creek, there is a queen-size Hide-a-bed and private bath. Breakfast goodies are placed in the small refrigerator for guests to prepare at their leisure. Smoking is permitted outside only. Two-night minimum stay. $65.

Tarrytown. This private residence in an older, affluent area of the city is perfect for business men and women who need to be near the heart of the city. The guest bedroom has a double bed and private bath. The home has many lovely antiques as well as contemporary furnishings. Breakfast will be Continental, served in the cozy breakfast nook. No smoking. Cat in residence. $60.

Carrington's Bluff

Carrington's Bluff Bed and Breakfast

1900 David Street, 78705
(512) 479-0638

Carrington's Bluff is in the heart of Austin on an acre of tree-covered bluff. Choose from an 1877 farmhouse, 1897 neo-classical Victorian, or 1910 country cottage. A collection of historic houses in the downtown area, just blocks from the University of Texas and state capitol grounds. Each has been transformed into an inviting bed and breakfast in the English country tradition. Antique-filled rooms and the sweet smell of potpourri await. Breakfast begins with gourmet coffee, fresh fruit, and homemade granola served on fine English china. Homemade muffins, breads, and a house specialty ensure guests won't go away hungry.

Hosts: Gwen and David Fullbrook
Rooms: 16 (14 PB; 2 SB) $60-99
Full Breakfast
Credit Cards: A, B, C, E
Notes: 2, 5, 8 (over 10), 9, 10, 11, 12, 14

Fairview—A Bed and Breakfast Establishment

1304 Newning Avenue, 78704
(512) 444-4746; (800) 310-4746

Surrounded by huge live oak trees on an acre of landscaped grounds, this turn-of-the-century Colonial Revival Austin historic landmark offers gracious accommodations. Carefully selected antique furnishings give each room its own unique style and romance. Fairview's six rooms range from luxury suites to elegant retreats. The gardens are a wonderful place to relax after a busy day. "Fairview is probably the grandest bed and breakfast in Austin (and one of the top two or three in the state)," *Texas Monthly*, August 1993.

Hosts: Duke and Nancy Waggoner
Rooms: 6 (PB) $89-129
Full Breakfast
Credit Cards: A, B, C, E
Notes: 2, 5, 9, 10, 11, 12, 14

The McCallum House

613 West 32nd Street, 78705
(512) 451-6744 (phone and FAX)

The historic McCallum House, an Austin landmark with a Texas historical marker, is six blocks north of the University of Texas-Austin and 20 blocks north of the Texas capitol and downtown. All rooms and suites have private baths, period Victorian furnishings, private telephones, kitchen facili-

ties, sitting areas, and color TVs. Four have private porches. Owner-occupant innkeepers are the hosts. Easy access to state capitol, LBJ Library, Highland Lakes, Zilker Park, Mount Bonnell, and lots more. $15 per night discount Sunday to Thursday with two nights or more. Two-night minimum stay on weekends.

Hosts: Nancy and Roger Danley
Rooms: 5 (PB) $85-105
Full Breakfast
Credit Cards: A, B
Notes: 2, 5, 9, 10, 11, 12

The McCallum House

Peaceful Hill Bed and Breakfast

10817 Ranch Road 2222, 78730-1102
(512) 338-1817

Deer watch as guests arrive at this small country bed and breakfast on ranch land high in the beautiful rolling hills just 15 minutes from the city. Only five minutes to Lake Travis and The Oasis. In the springtime, rock in the rocking chairs, swing on the porch swing, sip coffee or lemon-tea punch, breakfast on the big, round table, and admire the view of city and countryside—all from the south porch. In the cold of winter, sit by the grand stone fireplace and its crackling fire, while the south glass wall shows off views of the countryside and city. In the lazy summer, relax in the ham-

6 Pets welcome; 8 Children welcome; 9 Social drinking allowed; 10 Tennis available; 11 Swimming available; 12 Golf available; 13 Skiing available; 14 May be booked through travel agents.

mock built for two in the treed yard, go hiking, bicycling, and swimming, or play golf and tennis. All this and a home-cooked breakfast, too. Come and make Peaceful Hill home away from home—warm and friendly and comfortable. Peaceful is its name and peaceful is the game.

Host: Mrs. Peninnah Thurmond
Rooms: 2 (PB) $60
Full Breakfast
Credit Cards: A, B, C (corporate)
Notes: 2, 5, 7 (limited), 8, 9, 10, 11, 12, 13

Woodburn House Bed and Breakfast

4401 Avenue D, 78751
(512) 458-4335

This lovely 1909 Victorian landmark with porches front and side is nestled among 100-year-old trees in the historic Hyde Park neighborhood, a national register district. Four spacious rooms are available. Full formal breakfasts, antique furnishings, tree-lined streets, and luxurious linens provide the right environment for a truly pleasant stay. A mile and one-half from the University of Texas. Discounts for singles and longer stays.

Hosts: Herb and Sandra Dickson
Rooms: 4 (PB) $72-82
Full Breakfast
Cards: None
Notes: 2, 5, 8 (over 7), 9, 10, 11, 12

BANDERA

Bed and Breakfast Hosts of San Antonio and South Texas

1777 N.E. Loop 410, Suite 600, San Antonio, 78217
(210) 824-8036; (800) 356-1605 (reservations)
FAX (210) 271-9145

601. This dude ranch in the beautiful Texas hill country is "home on the range." Experience a real Texas ranch with a bed and breakfast package that includes a hayride on arrival (late afternoon), a great home-cooked dinner, comfortable cottage lodgings, full country breakfast, and a morning horseback trail ride—all for one modest daily price. Large pool, lounge with fireplace, and dining room at headquarters. Open seven days a week during the summer months. Three meals included. Two-day minimum. $75.

602. This inn, only six miles from Bandera Downs racetrack, is an early "no-frills" motel converted to real western bed and breakfast hospitality. Seven rooms with an assortment of all bed sizes, private baths, black-and-white TV, and clock radios. Breakfast, cooked to order, is served in the small adjoining cafe. Early coffee can be brought to the guests' room. Picnic and horseshoe facilities are available. $45.

The Historic Pfeiffer House

BASTROP

The Historic Pfeiffer House

1802 Main Street, 78602
(512) 321-2100

The Pfeiffer House is one of Bastrop's 25 Texas Historic Homes and is listed on the National Register of Historic Places. Each room is tastefully decorated with antiques, offering guests relaxation free from TV and telephone. A full breakfast is served formally in the dining room. The three upstairs bedrooms are charmingly decorated to give each room a warm, welcome feeling. Two porches invite guests to "sit a spell" and relax.

Hosts: Charles and Marilyn C. Whites
Rooms: 3 (SB) $66
Full Breakfast
Credit Cards: None
Notes: 2, 5, 10, 11, 12

BELTON

Bed and Breakfast Texas Style

4224 West Red Bird Lane, Dallas, 75237
(214) 298-8586

The Belle of Belton. A beautiful antebellum home right in town with five bedrooms to charm and pamper guests. The rooms are named after the four seasons: Spring, with twin four-poster beds and claw-foot tub across the hall; Summer, with king-size bed, white wicker furniture, and shared bath; Fall, with brass bed, rocking chairs in the triple window, and private bath with shower; Winter, with a corner cupola where poinsettias are displayed, queen-size bed, and private bath. Continental breakfast includes quiche or croissants, fresh fruit, and specially blended coffees or teas. $40-50.

BEN WHEELER

Bed and Breakfast Texas Style

4224 West Red Bird Lane, Dallas, 75237
(214) 298-8586

The Arc Ridge Guest Ranch. This 600-acre ranch in east Texas near Canton and Tyler has its own lake. The guest house has two bedrooms, living room, complete kitchen, and shower. Fishing and paddleboats are available. No hunters allowed in this environmentally protected area. Breakfast will be left in the refrigerator for guests to prepare themselves. Family rates will be considered. $75-250.

BIG SANDY

Bed and Breakfast Texas Style

4224 West Red Bird Lane, Dallas, 75237
(214) 298-8586

Annie's Bed and Breakfast. Take a step back in time at this fascinating inn that has 13 bedrooms, each with small refrigerator for soft drinks and fruit. Breakfast is served in Annie's Tea Room, a historical home that has been converted into a charming restaurant. Tyler is only 10-15 minutes away; Jefferson is 90 minutes away. Call early since rooms are booked far in advance. No smoking. $115-173.

BLANCO

Bed and Breakfast Hosts of San Antonio and South Texas

1777 N.E. Loop 410, Suite 600, San Antonio, 78217
(210) 824-8036; (800) 356-1605 (reservations)
FAX (210) 271-9145

603. A charming little four-room cottage on a large lot overlooking the beautiful Blanco River and Blanco State Park. Accommodates up to four persons, and has a fully equipped kitchen with breakfast provided. Walk to restaurants and shops, fishing and swim-

6 Pets welcome; 8 Children welcome; 9 Social drinking allowed; 10 Tennis available; 11 Swimming available; 12 Golf available; 13 Skiing available; 14 May be booked through travel agents.

ming; or just sit on the porch swing and enjoy the breeze and restful view. $50-65.

BOERNE

Bed and Breakfast Hosts of San Antonio and South Texas

1777 N.E. Loop 410, Suite 600, San Antonio, 78217
(210) 824-8036; (800) 356-1605 (reservations)
FAX (210) 271-9145

604. This bed and breakfast and guest house has three properties. The 1200-square-foot Guest House is romantic and secluded, overlooking lily ponds. Queen-size bed, single bed, single sleeper-sofa, kitchen, two baths, TV, telephone, and stereo. The Artist Studio has a panoramic view of the Hill Country. Table for games and cards, library, private bath, cable TV, and sitting area. The main house has two fireplaces, Italian marble floors, and picture windows that reveal the beauty of the countryside and the swimming pool. $85-125.

Borgman's Sunday House

Borgman's Sunday House Bed and Breakfast Inn

911 South Main, 78006
(210) 249-9563; (800) 633-7339

In a quaint and appealing setting in the beautiful Texas Hill Country. Each room is unique and most are furnished with antiques. All guest rooms are delightfully decorated, cozy, and immaculate. A bountiful breakfast is served in the restored German Sunday House. Close to antique and craft shops. Twenty-five miles from San Antonio and Sea World. Fifteen miles from Fiesta Texas theme park.

Hosts: Mike and Mary Jewell
Owners: Lou and Mary Lou Borgman
Rooms: 13 (PB) $45-70
Full Breakfast
Credit Cards: A, B, C, D, E
Notes: 2, 5, 7 (limited), 8 (limited), 11, 12, 14

BRENHAM

Captain Clay Home

Route 5, P.O. Box 149, 77833
(409) 836-1916

This early Texas home, circa 1852, is on a hilltop overlooking beautiful rolling countryside. Enjoy the peaceful porches, watching miniature horses frolic in the pastures, a walk to the creek, or a visit to the nearby Antique Rose Emporium. Air conditioning for summer and a big, cozy fireplace for winter make this a place to stay for all seasons. A private spa is available for year-round pleasure.

Host: Thelma Zwiener
Rooms: 4 (2 PB; 2 SB) $50-65
Full Breakfast
Credit Cards: None
Notes: 2, 5, 7 (outdoors), 8, 9, 11, 12

BROADDUS

Sam Rayburn Bed and Breakfast: The Cole House

Woodvillage Addition, Route 1,
   P.O. Box 258, 75929
(409) 872-3666

NOTES: Credit cards accepted: A MasterCard; B Visa; C American Express; D Discover Card; E Diner's Club; F Other; 2 Personal checks accepted; 3 Lunch available; 4 Dinner available; 5 Open all year;

In the piney woods of the Angelina National Forest is a peaceful little getaway on Sam Rayburn Lake. Not a traditional bed and breakfast, this is a cozy little guest house that will sleep nine adults. The setting would delight Thoreau himself, with the peaceful waters of the lake and tall, shady oak and pine trees, and absolute seclusion. Thirty years of antique collecting fill this five-room cottage on the lake. Fully central air conditioning. All-electric kitchen. Everything is furnished for a peaceful, relaxing stay.

Hosts: Gene and Jean Cole
Cottage: 2 (SB) $55
Continental Breakfast
Credit Cards: None
Notes: 2, 5, 9, 11, 13 (water), 14

BRYAN

Bed and Breakfast Texas Style

4224 West Red Bird Lane, Dallas, 75237
(214) 298-8586

Creekway. A contemporary home right in the middle of town, just ten minutes from Texas A&M University. Three guest rooms share a bath. Continental breakfast consists of sausage kolaches (Czech), fresh fruit platter, cereal assortment, and coffee or tea. Cats in residence. Smoking permitted outside only. $60.

BULVERDE

Bed and Breakfast Hosts of San Antonio and South Texas

1777 N.E. Loop 410, Suite 600, San Antonio, 78217
(210) 824-8036; (800) 356-1605 (reservations)
FAX (210) 271-9145

651. This bed and breakfast is in the heart of a 300-acre working ranch. This house has many antiques from the original owners, and their descendants are the hosts. Accommodates two to six guests. $65-125.

BURTON

Knittel Homestead Inn

520 Main Street, 77835
(409) 289-5102

This fully restored Queen Anne Victorian home resembles a Mississippi steamboat with wrapping porches. Beautifully furnished with antiques and country furniture, the home features three spacious bedrooms each with a private bath. Guests are treated to a delicious, all-you-can-eat country breakfast, and complimentary sodas, juices, and snacks. The home is listed on the National Register of Historic Places, and numerous local historic sites are within walking distance.

Hosts: Steve and Cynthia Miller
Rooms: 3 (PB) $75-100
Full Breakfast
Credit Cards: None
Notes: 2, 5, 8 (over 12), 9

CALVERT

Bed and Breakfast Texas Style

4224 West Red Bird Lane, Dallas, 75237
(214) 298-8586

Our House. The town of Calvert is a gem, with almost all its buildings on the National Register of Historic Places. This home offers five guest rooms and two baths in the hall. Breakfast is a gourmet treat, with Belgian waffles, ham and cheese omelets, fresh fruit, and beverage. Children welcome. The location is convenient to Bryan-College Station and all Aggie events. No smoking. $75.

CANTON

Bed and Breakfast Country Style

149 East Tyler Street, P.O. Box 1101, 75103
(903) 567-2899; (800) 725-2899

6 Pets welcome; 8 Children welcome; 9 Social drinking allowed; 10 Tennis available; 11 Swimming available; 12 Golf available; 13 Skiing available; 14 May be booked through travel agents.

A reservation service offering gracious hospitality in the true European lodging tradition in favored private homes in and near Canton. Personalized service and distinguished accommodations fit guests' needs and budget whether a single traveler, couple, family, or group. Full and Continental breakfasts. Close to Heritage Park. Group destination plans and charges available upon request. There are 40 guest rooms available through this service. $50-85.

Heavenly Acres Bed and Breakfast Guest Ranch

Route 3, Box 470, Mabank, 75147
(800) 283-0341; FAX (903) 887-6108

Heavenly Acres, 12 miles southwest of Canton, offers separate and private guest houses with a total guest capacity of 40 people. Each accommodation has TV/VCR with video library. All houses provide full kitchens, with microwaves, coffee makers, etc., and are stocked with country-breakfast grocery items and a variety of gourmet coffees, teas, and creamers. Snack baskets are provided. There are two private lakes with small fishing boats and paddle boats. Petting zoo with barnyard animals, trails, gazebo, and picnic areas. Children welcome. Pets allowed with prior approval. Smoking outside only. No minimum night stay required. $10 extra per additional person.

Host: Vickie J. Ragle
Houses: 4 (PB) $75
Full or Continental Breakfast
Credit Cards: A, B, C, D
Notes: 2, 3, 4, 5, 6, 8, 9, 10, 11, 12, 14

CANYON

Hudspeth House

1905 Fourth Avenue, 79015
(806) 655-9800

This historic bed and breakfast is on the road to and only 20 minutes from Palo Duro Canyon, home of the famous *Texas* musical drama. The facilities offer beautiful accommodations, good ol' American breakfasts. Take a stroll to the Panhandle Plains Museum or just relax and enjoy the warm hospitality.

Hosts: Mark and Mary Clark
Rooms: 9 (6 PB; 3 SB) $55-110
Full Breakfast
Credit Cards: A, B, C, D
Notes: 2, 3 (by reservation), 4 (by reservation), 5, 8, 9, 12, 14

CANYON LAKE

Bed and Breakfast Hosts of San Antonio and South Texas

1777 N.E. Loop 410, Suite 600, San Antonio, 78217
(210) 824-8036; (800) 356-1605 (reservations)
FAX (210) 271-9145

606. This private hilltop cottage sits on 4 acres. Two rooms, one with private bath and one with shared bath. King-size suite with private deck and great view. $65-125.

607. This large three-bedroom, two-bath house, is comfortably furnished, with large kitchen, microwave, fireplace, TV with VCR, stereo, washer, and dryer. Large deck overlooking lake. Forty minutes from downtown San Antonio. Special weekly and monthly rates available. Three-night minimum rate $295.

Aunt Nora's. Near Canyon Lake and New Braunfels on four acres in a restful setting. Rooms with private and shared baths. King-size suite has private deck with great view. $65-125.

CARTHAGE

Bed and Breakfast Texas Style

4224 West Red Bird Lane, Dallas, 75237
(214) 298-8586

NOTES: Credit cards accepted: A MasterCard; B Visa; C American Express; D Discover Card; E Diner's Club; F Other; 2 Personal checks accepted; 3 Lunch available; 4 Dinner available; 5 Open all year;

Best Little Horse House. Completely renovated, this carriage house was originally a stable that the host had moved to a beautiful spot surrounded by tall pines. Collectibles and fine antiques are attractively displayed in this getaway cottage. Breakfast may be delivered to the cottage in the morning or guests are invited into the main home for an exquisite meal. $75.

CASTROVILLE

Bed and Breakfast Hosts of San Antonio and South Texas

1777 N.E. Loop 410, Suite 600, San Antonio, 78217
(210) 824-8036; (800) 356-1605 (reservations)
FAX (210) 271-9145

505. This guest house is on the grounds of the 150-year-old Henri Castro Homestead. It is 20 minutes from Sea World of Texas, 30 minutes from the San Antonio Riverwalk, and 45 minutes from Fiesta Texas. Guest house includes king-size bed, double bed, twin bed, kitchen, barbecue pit on patio, and color TV with cable. $75.

506. This guest house in historic Castroville has queen-size bed, sofa that converts into a queen-size Hide-a-bed, and roll away double bed. Full bath and kitchen. A Continental breakfast is provided for guests to enjoy at their leisure. Walking distance to shops, churches, bakery, and restaurants. $75.

507. Antique shopping and bed and breakfast lodging for a couple or family of seven. Sofa bed in spacious living and dining area. Three bedrooms; queen-size, double, and single beds. Kitchen, bath, Continental or full breakfast. Children welcome. Pets welcome. $75.

CENTER

Pine Colony Inn

500 Shelbyville Street, 75935
(409) 598-7700

In a quiet East Texas town, this inn sits just west of the Sabine River, which runs between Texas and Louisiana. Only a few miles from Toledo Bend, it is a popular spot for bass fishing. Group gatherings welcome.

Hosts: Regina Wright and Marcille Hughes
Rooms: 12 (8 PB; 4 SB) $27-55
Full Breakfast
Credit Cards: A, B
Notes: 2, 5, 8, 9, 10, 11, 12, 14

Pine Colony Inn

CHAPPELL HILL

Stagecoach Inn

Main at Chestnut, P.O. Box 339, 77426
(409) 836-9515

The inn, built in 1850 by Jacob and Mary Haller, the founders of Chappell Hill, was a favorite stopping place for many notable Texans traveling from Houston to Austin or Waco over the first stagecoach line organized in Texas in 1841 by Smith and Jones. The inn, listed on the National Register of Historic Places, is a 14-room Greek Revival structure with six fireplaces, on three beautifully landscaped acres. A country breakfast is served.

Hosts: Elizabeth and Harvin Moore
Rooms: 6 (5 PB; 1 SB) $90
Full Breakfast
Credit Cards: None
Notes: 2, 5, 9, 12

6 Pets welcome; 8 Children welcome; 9 Social drinking allowed; 10 Tennis available; 11 Swimming available; 12 Golf available; 13 Skiing available; 14 May be booked through travel agents.

CLEBURNE

Bed and Breakfast Texas Style

4224 West Red Bird Lane, Dallas, 75237
(214) 298-8586

Anglin Queen Anne. Fine architecture, a magnificent collection of antiques, and genuine hospitality make a stay in this inn a memorable experience. There are five guest rooms, three with private baths. The bridal suite upstairs has two rooms. The sitting area has a working fireplace, and the bedroom has a double bed with matched bird's eye maple furniture including armoire and washstand. Four other rooms available. A full breakfast is served in the formal dining room or the big kitchen. The inn may be reserved for corporate meetings, weddings, teas, and other social events. Handicap access. No smoking. No pets. Bridal suite. $59-149.

CLIFTON

Bed and Breakfast Texas Style

4224 West Red Bird Lane, Dallas, 75237
(214) 298-8586

The Sweetheart Cottage. A historical home, once damaged in a tornado, now restored for a perfect weekend getaway. A loft room has a king-size bed, and a pull-out sofa is available downstairs. Country breakfast fare is left in the complete kitchen for the guests to prepare. No smoking. Two- night minimum stay required. $70.

COLLEGE STATION

Bed and Breakfast Texas Style

4224 West Red Bird Lane, Dallas, 75237
(214) 298-8586

Country Gardens. A sense of peace and tranquility will descend on guests as they enter this little country hideaway on four acres. Stroll through the wooded glen, fruit orchard, grapevines, and berry patches and enjoy the birds and wildflowers. The hosts will prepare a delicious breakfast of wheat pancakes or homemade bread, coffee, tea or milk, and fruit in season. Call for rates.

COLUMBUS

Raumonda Bed and Breakfast

1100 Bowie Street, P.O. Box 112, 78934
(409) 732-2190; FAX (409) 732-8730

Raumonda is an elegant bed and breakfast where guests step back to the Victorian era. Sleeps eight in three rooms, with two private baths and one shared bath. An enhanced Continental breakfast is served in the glassed gallery, on the balcony or pool gazebo, or in the breakfast room. Coffee, tea, juice, soft drinks, and ice are available during the evening hours. The host family will greet guests with warmth and offer hospitality reminiscent of the Old South. Learn about the history of Raumonda and the town of Columbus, and tour the historic sites. Children 12 and older welcome. No pets. Smoking in designated areas only.

Host: R. F. "Buddy" Rau
Rooms: 3 (2 PB; 1 SB) $80-140
Continental Breakfast
Credit Cards: None
Notes: 2, 5, 9, 10, 11, 12

COMFORT

Bed and Breakfast Hosts of San Antonio and South Texas

1777 N.E. Loop 410, Suite 600, San Antonio, 78217
(210) 824-8036; (800) 356-1605 (reservations)
FAX (210) 271-9145

608. This bed and breakfast lodge has tennis courts, swimming pool, hiking trail, and

---

NOTES: Credit cards accepted: A MasterCard; B Visa; C American Express; D Discover Card; E Diner's Club; F Other; 2 Personal checks accepted; 3 Lunch available; 4 Dinner available; 5 Open all year;

the Guadalupe River for rafting. Available for small or large groups. A home-style breakfast is served in the main lodge or provided in the guests' cottage. Two houses with three bedrooms each are offered for large groups. The Artist Cottage and the Lighthouse Cottage each have kitchenette and bath. The master bedroom in the main lodge has a private bath. Complimentary wine on arrival. $93.

The Comfort Common

The Comfort Common

818 High Street, P.O. Box 539, 78013
(512) 995-3030

Historic limestone hotel, circa 1880, listed on the National Register of Historic Places. Rooms and suites are furnished with antiques. The downstairs of the hotel features numerous shops filled with American antiques. A stay at the Comfort Common will put guests in the heart of the Texas Hill Country with Fredericksburg, Kerrville, Boerne, Bandera, and San Antonio all a brief 15-30 minutes away. Fiesta Texas theme park is only 20 minutes away.

Hosts: Jim Lord and Bobby Dent
Rooms: 6 (PB) $55-90
Full Breakfast
Credit Cards: A, B, C, D
Notes: 2, 5, 9, 12

CORPUS CHRISTI

Sand Dollar Hospitality

3605 Mendenhall, 78415
(512) 853-1222

Bay Breeze. This Texas Colonial home is truly charming. There are two guest rooms with private baths. One guest room has hunter decor, and the other is decorated with family heirlooms. There is also a "tree house" in the rear of the premises. It is fully furnished with a freestanding fireplace, and a picture window overlooking the bay. Guests are invited to enjoy the porch swing while relaxing or socializing. A full breakfast is served to guests. $60-85.

Driftwood. A great place for families or small groups. Near the bay, the Naval Air Station, and Corpus Christi State University, this home offers four spacious second-floor bedrooms that share a lounge area with refrigerator and TV. There are three full baths upstairs. A patio hot tub is available. A public golf course and fishing pier are nearby. Children welcome. Bus service nearby. No pets. Smoking on patio only. $54-60.

Park View. This contemporary one-story brick home is just across from a well-maintained city park and just two minutes from Padre Island Drive, which leads to Padre Island and numerous gulf beaches. The guest bedroom is decorated in Southwestern touches with a queen-size bed and private bath. Continental breakfast is served during the week and full breakfast on weekends. $51-54.

Sand Piper. Guests will feel at home in this attractive brick home on a quiet street in one of the city's nicer neighborhoods. There are two bedrooms available: one with a king-size bed and private bath; one with a double bed. Weather permitting, breakfast may be served on the lovely, plant-filled, covered patio. $51-54.

Seagull. New England and Old World decor add to the charm and homey atmosphere of this host home. When guests are done sightseeing or have had enough of the beach and sun, feel free to turn on the TV or curl up in one of the oversized chairs in the living room. There are two guest rooms available with a shared bath. $51-54.

Sea Secret. A light and airy second-floor apartment is just three blocks from the beach and offers two guest bedrooms. One has a queen-size bed; the other a single bed. Guest's quarters are downstairs. Older children are welcome. Full breakfast. $90.

CROCKETT

Bed and Breakfast Texas Style

4224 West Red Bird Lane, Dallas, 75237
(214) 298-8586

The Arledge House. This wonderful historic two-story home built in 1895 is on a spacious corner lot and is surrounded by large pecan trees. The bedrooms have king-size beds and private baths, TVs, and collectible items from the hosts' family. For breakfast the hosts will prepare a Mexican buffet or homemade cinnamon rolls with fresh fruit and coffee. $85.

DALLAS

Bed and Breakfast Texas Style

4224 West Red Bird Lane, 75237
(214) 298-8586

Artist's Haven. This private home offers two upstairs guest rooms with shared bath.

Each room has twin beds and lovely amenities. Breakfast is Continental plus, with fruit, pastries, and beverages. Cat in residence. No smoking. Children are welcome. $60.

The Cloisters. This lovely home is one block from White Rock Lake in a secluded area of Dallas. There are two guest rooms, each with a private bath. Both rooms have double beds, one with an antique Mexican headboard that is a conversation piece. Breakfast will be lots of protein, eggs, and/or blueberry pancakes. A bicycle is available for riding around the lake. No smoking. $75.

Coral Cove. Spacious home near Olla Podrida and Richardson has three bedrooms. One is a sitting room combination with private bath and cable TV. The other two share a bath and can accommodate families or couples traveling together. A welcoming glass of iced tea or cup of hot coffee is served upon arrival. Breakfast is full or Continental, guests' choice. Smoking permitted. Cats in residence. $50.

Executive Condo. This completely furnished condo in North Dallas is within walking distance of the Valley View shopping mall and five minutes from Galleria Mall. Visitors to this condo will be met by the owners and given a key. Breakfast fixings are left in the kitchen and guests may use the facility to prepare other meals as well. Murphy bed, TV available. Bath is full and private. No children. A pool and hot tub are available in the apartment complex. Smokers welcome. $60.

Fan Room. The antique fan displayed in this lovely twin bedroom is the focal point and was the start of a large collection of fans. The home is near Prestonwood, Marshall Fields, and the Galleria Mall. Southfork Ranch is a 15-minute drive north. A full country breakfast includes jalapeño muffins for first-time Texas visitors. There is a second bedroom near the kitchen with a double bed and private bath. $50.

Province. This private home offers a double bed and private bath. The hosts are health food enthusiasts and will serve fresh carrot juice to those who desire to try it. The conventional fare of toast, coffee, and fresh fruit is served as well. It is 25 minutes to downtown Dallas, the market, and convention center. Two blocks to the public bus line. No smoking; no children. $50.

The Rose. This historical home was built in 1901 and has three guest bedrooms, each with a private bath. Guests are treated to special breakfasts on the weekends, Continental during the week. Children over 12 welcome. Smoking permitted. $85.

Tudor Mansion. Built in 1933 in an exclusive neighborhood in the shadow of downtown, this Tudor-style mansion offers queen-size bed and private bath. A full gourmet breakfast of cheddar on toast, Texas-style creamed eggs with jalapeño, or fresh vegetable omelet is served. The bus line is three blocks away. Spanish and French are spoken. Three miles from downtown. Close to public golf course. $80.

Mansion on Main

802 Main Street, 75501
(903) 792-1835

"Twice As Nice," the motto of Texarkana (Texas and Arkansas) USA, is standard practice at the Mansion on Main. The 1895 Neoclassical Colonial, surrounded by 14 tall columns, was recently restored by the owners of the McKay House, a popular bed and breakfast in nearby Jefferson. Six bed chambers vary from the Governor's Suite to the Butler's Garret. Business and leisure guests enjoy Southern hospitality, period

furnishings, and a full gentleman's breakfast. Just 30 miles from the town of Hope, the birthplace of President Bill Clinton. Rated by AAA.

Hosts: Kay and Jack Roberts
Owners: Peggy and Tom Taylor
Rooms: 6 (PB) $55–110
Full Breakfast
Credit Cards: A, B, C
Notes: 2, 5, 12, 14

McKay House
Bed and Breakfast Inn

306 East Delta Street, 75657
(903) 665-7322; (903) 348-1929 (Dallas)

Jefferson is a riverport town from the frontier days of the Republic of Texas. It has historical mule-drawn tours, 30 antique shops, boat rides on the river, and a narrow-gauge train. The McKay House, an 1851 Greek Revival cottage, offers period furnishings, cool lemonade, porch swings, and fireplaces. Seven rooms that vary from the Keeping Room to the Garden Suite with two antique footed tubs. A full gentleman's breakfast is served in the Garden Observatory. Hospitality abounds, and Victorian nightclothes are provided. VIP guests have included Lady Bird Johnson and Alex Haley. Mobil travel guide.

Owner: Peggy Taylor
Innkeeper: Alma Anne Parker
Rooms: 7 (PB) $75-125
Full Breakfast
Credit Cards: A, B, C
Notes: 2, 5, 12, 14

EAGLE LAKE

Bed and Breakfast
Texas Style

4224 West Red Bird Lane, Dallas, 75237
(214) 298-8586

Eagle Hill Retreat. A historical mansion, circa 1936, and adjoining estate, 75 minutes from Houston and 90 minutes from San Antonio, offers an Olympic-size pool, wet and

6 Pets welcome; 8 Children welcome; 9 Social drinking allowed; 10 Tennis available; 11 Swimming available; 12 Golf available; 13 Skiing available; 14 May be booked through travel agents.

dry saunas, lighted tennis courts, two guest houses, and six bedrooms upstairs in the main home. Most rooms have two double beds and private baths, but the bridal suite has a four-poster king-size bed and fireplace. The guest houses have three bedrooms each and shared baths. Breakfast is served in the large dining room and is full Texas-style buffet. Nearby national wildlife refuge protects the Attwater's prairie chicken, which has been on the endangered species list. Children are welcome. Smoking is permitted in designated areas. Visitors may choose the guest house or the main house. A bridal suite is available. $65-150.

EL PASO

Bed and Breakfast Hosts of San Antonio and South Texas

1777 N.E. Loop 410, Suite 600, San Antonio, 78217
(210) 824-8036; (800) 356-1605 (reservations)
FAX (210) 271-9145

702. A bed and breakfast in the historical district downtown, beautifully landscaped, with two giant palm trees near the swimming pool and Jacuzzi. The three-story Victorian boasts original Tiffany doors and chandeliers. Rates include full breakfast, American or Mexican. Enjoy hors d'oeuvres by the pool. Gourmet dinners served with reservations made 24 hours in advance. Bridal suite with king-size bed, fireplace, and marble bath with Jacuzzi. The Rendezvous Room, with queen-size bed and private bath. The Spa Room with queen-size bed and seven foot claw-foot tub. The Pool View Room with double bed. $50-150.

Sunset Heights Bed and Breakfast Inn

717 West Yandell Avenue, 79902
(915) 544-1743; (800) 767-8513
FAX (915) 544-5119

National historic home offers restored Victorian elegance. Built in 1905, architectural

details feature Tiffany doors, windows, chandeliers, and stained-glass windows. Elegance surrounds guests inside and out. Palm trees, pool with Jacuzzi. All rooms have an individual motif. Marble baths and balcony baths. Antiques. Security. Catering to the carriage trade. Mature adults will appreciate gourmet French and Continental foods. Breakfast is three to eight courses. Dinner is six to twelve courses. Reservations required.

Hosts: R. Barnett and R. Martinez
Rooms: 6 (PB) $70-165
Full Breakfast
Credit Cards: A, B, C, D
Notes: 2, 3, 4, 5, 9, 11, 12, 14

Raphael House

ENNIS

Raphael House

500 West Ennis Avenue, 75119
(214) 875-1555

These six exquisite bedrooms with private baths are set in a beautifully restored 1906 Neo-classical mansion appointed with original antiques, rich wall coverings, and luxurious fabrics. Amenities include oversize beds with down comforters and pillows, claw-foot tubs with imported toiletries, afternoon refreshments, and turndown service. A full breakfast is served on the weekends, and a Continental breakfast on weekdays. In a national register historic district just 35 minutes from Dallas and 15 minutes from Waxahachie. Antiques, shopping, museums.

Host: Danna Cody Wolf
Rooms: 6 (PB) $65-100
Full and Continental Breakfasts
Credit Cards: A, B, C, D, E
Notes: 2, 5, 9, 10, 11, 12, 14

FREDERICKSBURG

The Austin Street Retreat

408 West Austin, 78624
(210) 997-5612

Sophisticated, worldly decor in this historic home. Originally a log and rock settlers' cabin, this luxurious villa now offers five suites. Each has private bath with whirlpool tubs, private outdoor terrace space, and luscious surroundings. Four suites have one bedroom with king-size bed and fireplace. One suite has two bedrooms with two queen-size beds. All suites have a small refrigerator, microwave, and coffee pot. A Continental breakfast is brought to guest's room.

Credit Cards: A, B, D
Notes: 2, 5, 8, 9, 10, 11, 12, 14

Das College Haus

106 West College, 78624
(210) 997-9047; (800) 654-2802

Visit historic Fredericksburg and stay at Das College Haus, just three blocks from downtown. Spacious rooms with private baths; all have access to the porches and balcony with porch swing and wicker rockers, where guests can relax and visit. Das College Haus is beautifully appointed with comfortable period furniture and original art and a wonderful "at home" atmosphere. After a delicious breakfast, guests may visit famed artist Tim Saska in his restored barn studio. Central heat and air, cable TV, VCR, and a collection of classic movies.

Hosts: Tim and Myrna Saska
Rooms: 3 (PB) $70-85
Full Breakfast
Credit Cards: None
Notes: 2, 5, 8, 9, 10, 11, 12, 14

Country Cottage Inn

Country Cottage Inn— Nimitz Birthplace

249 East Main Street, 78624
(210) 997-8549

Fredericksburg's two most historic homes (the Chester Nimitz Birthplace and Kiehne House) form this inn. Thick limestone walls, handcut beams and woodwork, and mellow stone fireplaces are in both homes. Both are on the National Register of Historic Places. Enjoy complimentary wine, Laura Ashley linens, king size beds, old fans, room refrigerators, microwaves, bathrobes, giant whirlpool tubs, tubside candles, and wood burning fireplaces.

Host: Jeffrey Ann Webb
Rooms: 7 (PB) $75-110
Full Breakfast
Credit Cards: A, B
Notes: 2, 5, 8, 9, 10, 11, 12

Magnolia House

101 East Hackberry, 78624
(210) 997-0306

Built circa 1923 and restored in 1991, this inn exudes Southern hospitality in a grand and gracious manner. Outside, magnolias and a bubbling fishpond and waterfall set a soothing mood. Inside, beautiful living room and formal dining room provide areas for guests to mingle. Four romantic rooms and two beautiful suites have been thoughtfully planned, decorated with antiques. Southern-style breakfast and complimentary wine cap a memorable experience.

6 Pets welcome; 8 Children welcome; 9 Social drinking allowed; 10 Tennis available; 11 Swimming available; 12 Golf available; 13 Skiing available; 14 May be booked through travel agents.

Hosts: Joyce and Patrick Kennard
Rooms: 6 (4 PB; 2 SB) $80-110
Full Breakfast
Credit Cards: None
Notes: 2, 5, 10, 11, 12

Schmidt Barn

231 West Main Street, 78624
(210) 997-5612

This guest house bed and breakfast is a renovated 1860s limestone barn (next door to the hosts' home) one and one-half miles from historic Fredericksburg. A loft bedroom with queen-size bed overlooks the living room below. Small kitchen and bath. All decorated with antiques. Featured in *Country Living* and *Travel & Leisure*.

Hosts: Charles and Loretta Schmidt
Room: 1 (PB) $75
Continental Breakfast
Credit Cards: A, B, D
Notes: 2, 5, 7, 8, 9, 14

GAINESVILLE

Alexander Bed and Breakfast Acres

Route 7, Box 788, 76240
(903) 564-7440; (800) 887-8794

Three-story Queen Anne Victorian home on 65 peaceful acres. Large wraparound porch for lounging; walking trails; near two large lakes, antiques, country farms, golfing, and zoo. Each bedroom decorated with different theme: cowboy quarters, antique, Oriental, or Amish. Separate conference room and extra lodging on third floor. Guest cottage with three bedrooms, one and one-half bath, kitchen, laundry, and living area. Full breakfast included. Lunch and dinner by reservation. Children welcome.

Hosts: Pamela and Jim Alexander
Rooms: 8 (5 PB; 3 SB) $45-120
Full Breakfast
Credit Cards: None
Notes: 2, 3 (by arrangement), 4 (by arrangement), 5, 8, 12, 13

GALVESTON

The 1887 Coppersmith Inn

1914 Avenue M, 77550
(409) 763-7004; (713) 965-7273

Beautiful and historical Queen Anne Victorian is complete with gingerbread trim, double veranda, and turret corners with bay windows. An elaborate staircase, built-in china cabinet and ornate woodwork are among the outstanding features. The home was renovated using many interesting faux painting art forms and is filled with period antiques. Beach, Strand Historical District, live theater, fine restaurants, and tour mansions nearby. Breakfast catered to guests' schedule. Children over five welcome. No smoking.

Host: Lisa Hering
Rooms: 4 (1 PB; 3 SB) $85-135
Full or Continental Breakfast
Credit Cards: A, B, C
Notes: 2, 5, 8 (over 5), 9, 11, 14

Madame Dyer's Bed and Breakfast

1720 Postoffice Street, 77550
(409) 765-5692

From the moment guests enter this carefully restored turn-of-the-century Victorian home built in 1889, they will be entranced by such period details as wraparound porches, high airy ceilings, wooden floors, and lace curtains. Each room is furnished with delightful antiques that bring back memories of days gone by. In the mornings, guests will awaken to a coffee tray outside their door. Breakfast is a special treat, served abundantly in the dining room. Come as a guest to Madame Dyer's and leave as a friend. Stay here and experience the splendor of the Victorian era on historic Galveston Island.

Hosts: Linda and Larry Bonnin
Rooms: 3 (PB) $100-125
Full Breakfast

NOTES: Credit cards accepted: A MasterCard; B Visa; C American Express; D Discover Card; E Diner's Club; F Other; 2 Personal checks accepted; 3 Lunch available; 4 Dinner available; 5 Open all year;

Credit Cards: A, B
Notes: 2, 5, 7 (limited), 8 (over 12), 9, 11, 12, 13

The Queen Anne Bed and Breakfast

1915 Sealy Avenue, 77550-2312
(409) 763-7088; (800) 472-0930

This home is a four-story Queen Anne Victorian built in 1905. Stained-glass windows, beautiful floors, large rooms, pocket doors, and 12-foot ceilings with transom doors; beautifully redecorated in 1991. Walk to historic shopping district, restaurants, 1886 opera house, museums, and the historic homes district. A short drive to the beach. A visit to Queen Anne is to be anticipated, relished, and remembered.

Hosts: John McWilliams and Earl French
Rooms: 4 (SB) $85-125
Full Breakfast
Credit Cards: A, B
Notes: 2, 5, 9, 11, 12, 13

Trube Castle Inn

1627 Sealy Avenue, 77550
(800) 662-9647

This remarkable castle, built in 1890, has been completely restored and is listed on the National Register of Historic Places. Offering just two exclusive suites, this 27-room mansion is furnished throughout with period antiques. Accommodations include private baths, private living rooms, porches,

Trube Castle Inn

stereo systems, TV, VCR, and in-room refrigerators. Within walking distance of historic Strand and beaches, "Texas' most fantastic Victorian home" replicates the Danish royal castle of the period and offers a unique opportunity to sample 1890s wealth and extravagance.

Host: Nonette O'Donnell
Suites: 2 (PB) $125-195
Full Breakfast
Credit Cards: A, B, C, D
Notes: 2, 5, 7 (limited), 9, 10, 11, 12, 14

The Victorian Inn

The Victorian Inn

511 Seventeenth Street, 77550
(409) 762-3235

Massive Italian villa built in 1899. Spacious guest rooms are romantically decorated with king-size beds and antiques. The four rooms on the second floor have balconies. Third-floor suite has a private bath and two bedrooms. The inn is within walking distance of historic Strand: restaurants, shops, and boats. Less than one mile to the beach.

Host: Marcy Hanson
Rooms: 6 (2 PB; 4 SB) $85-150
Continental Breakfast
Credit Cards: A, B, C
Notes: 2, 5, 7 (limited), 8 (over 12), 9, 11, 12, 14

GARLAND

Bed and Breakfast Texas Style

4224 West Red Bird Lane, Dallas, 75237
(214) 298-8586

6 Pets welcome; 8 Children welcome; 9 Social drinking allowed; 10 Tennis available; 11 Swimming available; 12 Golf available; 13 Skiing available; 14 May be booked through travel agents.

Catnip Creek. Right on Spring Creek, the hot tub on the deck overlooks a wooded creek. The guest room has a queen-size bed, private bath, and private entrance. Breakfast has granola and cinnamon-raisin biscuits or other homemade muffins and breads. Weekend guests are treated to a healthy quiche or pancakes. Herbal teas and special blended coffees are offered. Bicycles are provided. Just 30 minutes from downtown Dallas and very near Hypermart, the newest tourist attraction of the Metroplex. Also near South-fork Ranch. $45.

GEORGETOWN

Bed and Breakfast Texas Style

4224 West Red Bird Lane, Dallas, 75237
(214) 298-8586

Page House. This Queen Anne-style house, perched on top of a grassy knoll overlooking the banks of the South San Gabriel River, was built in 1903. Guests have a choice of four bedrooms, three upstairs and one downstairs, all with private baths. Lovely family treasures and antiques are throughout the home. Many items in the rooms may be purchased. The Tea Room, known for its delicious lunches, will be used for breakfast by guests. Dinner theatre in the barn at the back of the property. Smoking outdoors only. $85.

GLADEWATER

Rose Cottage Bed and Breakfast by the Lake

1620 West Lake Drive, 75647
(903) 845-6777; (903) 758-2290 reservations

A lovely brick two-bedroom cottage on a small lake. Completely remodeled in 1993 with pastel colors and attractive decor. Large patio, swing, picnic table, and large carport. Nice pier to swim off or tie boat to. Large fenced yard on ski water. Public beach one block away. All amenities of home with privacy and relaxation. Full breakfast or fixings provided. Gladewater noted antique shops. In city limits.

Hosts: Dell and Ernie Bunata
Cottage: 1 (PB) $85-95
Full Breakfast
Credit Cards: F
Notes: 5, 8, 9, 10, 11, 12, 14

GLEN ROSE

The Lodge at Fossil Rim

P.O. Box 2189, Route 1, Box 210, 76043
(817) 897-7452

In a secluded area, this Austin stone-and-cedar lodge offers luxurious accommodations surrounded by beautiful vistas and the abundant wildlife of Fossil Rim Wildlife Center. Pamper yourself with a choice of five spacious and uniquely furnished bedrooms, including private fireplaces, Jacuzzis, patios, and a generous multi-course breakfast prepared to taste. Fill the day with sunbathing by a spring-fed pool while enjoying the stunning view from the wraparound deck or discovering some of the world's most endangered wildlife. Only 75 miles southwest of Dallas.

Rooms: 5 (3 PB; 2 SB) $125-185
Full Breakfast
Credit Cards: A, B, C, D
Notes: 2, 7, 8, 9, 11, 12

GONZALEZ

Bed and Breakfast Hosts of San Antonio and South Texas

1777 N.E. Loop 410, Suite 600, San Antonio, 78217
(210) 824-8036; (800) 356-1605 (reservations)
FAX (210) 271-9145

609. This inn is a Greek Revival home built in 1914. Only one hour from San Antonio, Austin, and Victoria, it has three rooms that can serve as a weekend getaway or an oasis for business travelers. For breakfast, enjoy fruit, fresh pastries, homemade jams, juices,

NOTES: Credit cards accepted: A MasterCard; B Visa; C American Express; D Discover Card; E Diner's Club; F Other; 2 Personal checks accepted; 3 Lunch available; 4 Dinner available; 5 Open all year;

and other gourmet surprises with fresh brewed coffee or tea. Each room is unique with antiques and fresh flowers; there are porches to enjoy the breeze, church bells, and birds. Children over 12. No pets. No smoking. $65.

St. James Inn

723 St. James, 78629
(210) 672-7066

A former cattle baron's mansion. This bed and breakfast is a welcome respite from the busy life. Furnished with antiques, colorful collections, and warm hospitality. The rural area offers a fun opportunity for hiking, biking, antiquing, and roaming. The inn has cold lemonade on the front porch or spiced tea in front of a fire.

Hosts: Ann and J. R. Covert
Rooms: 5 (4 PB; 1 SB) $65-150
Full Breakfast
Credit Cards: A, B, C, D
Notes: 2, 3, 4, 5, 9, 10, 11, 12

GRANBURY

Dabney House Bed and Breakfast

106 South Jones, 76048
(817) 579-1260; (817) 823-6867 (evening)

Craftsman-style home built in 1907 boasts its original hardwood floors, ceiling beams, stained and beveled glass, and fixtures. Long-term business rates available per request as well as a whole house rental discount. Hosts offer a candlelight romantic dinner or group lunches per reservation only. Custom special occasion baskets available by advance order only. Special discounts for certified peace officers and firefighters.

Hosts: John and Gwen Hurley
Rooms: 4 (PB) $60-105
Full Breakfast
Credit Cards: A, B, C
Notes: 2, 3, 4, 5, 10, 11, 12, 14

The Doyle House Bed and Breakfast

205 West Doyle, 76048
(817) 573-6492

Experience the charm and atmosphere of The Doyle House Bed and Breakfast, a beautifully updated estate, circa 1880, on the banks of Granbury Lake. Ideal for a comfortable getaway, visiting Granbury's historic town square and courthouse, or activities around the pool, boathouse, or fishing platform. A full breakfast is served on the weekends, and a Continental breakfast on weekdays. The Doyle House provides guests with accommodations designed to make guests' visit one to remember—the hosts want guests to come back.

Hosts: Patrick and Linda Stoll
Rooms: 3 (PB) $75-115
Full and Continental Breakfast
Credit Cards: A, B, C, D, E
Notes: 2, 5, 8, 9, 10, 11, 12, 14

Log Cabin Inn

301 North Crockett, P.O. Box 343, 76048
(817) 579-9813

This rustic log cabin is on a large tree-shaded lot and 300 feet of waterfront on Lake Granbury, one block from the town's historic square. Two bedrooms are decorated with antiques, with one queen-size and one king-size bed. A queen-size couch is also available. Only leased to one party for privacy. Full kitchen and large den with TV. Very private. Swimming, golf, and skiing nearby. Children welcome. No smoking.

Host: Don Eichler
Rooms: 2 (PB) $85
Full or Continental Breakfast
Credit Cards: A, B
Notes: 2, 5, 8, 9, 11, 12, 13, 14

Pearl Street Inn Bed and Breakfast

319 West Pearl Street, 76048
(817) 279-PINK

6 Pets welcome; 8 Children welcome; 9 Social drinking allowed; 10 Tennis available; 11 Swimming available; 12 Golf available; 13 Skiing available; 14 May be booked through travel agents.

Relax and reminisce in the stately, stylish comfort of a 1912 prairie-style home. Three blocks from Granbury's historic square, this tastefully restored historical home features antique furnishings, two porches, cast-iron tubs, pocket doors, and scrumptious breakfasts. Indulge in live theater, state parks, drive-in movies, antique shopping, or festivals in a charming country setting, 30 miles south of the Dallas/Fort Worth metroplex. Guests may also simply stay in and enjoy a delightful stay where days move gently in all seasons.

Hosts: Danette D. Hebda
Rooms: 4 (PB) $59-98
Full Breakfast
Credit Cards: None
Notes: 2, 5, 9, 10, 11, 12, 14

GRANITE SHOALS

La Casita

1908 Redwood Drive, 78654
(210) 598-6443

Nestled 50 feet behind the main house, this private cottage is rustic and Texan on the outside, yet thoroughly modern inside with a queen-size bed. Native Texan hosts can suggest Highland Lakes parks, wineries, and river cruises. However, relaxing and bird watching in a country setting are the main attractions here. Guests choose an entrée with a full breakfast. Ideal location for small weddings, anniversaries, and birthdays. Laundry facilities available. Brochure available.

Hosts: Joanne and Roger Scarborough
Cottage: 1 (PB) $65
Full Breakfast
Credit Cards: None
Notes: 2, 5, 8, 9, 11, 12

HELOTES

Bed and Breakfast Hosts of San Antonio and South Texas

1777 N.E. Loop 410, Suite 600, San Antonio, 78217

(210) 824-8036; (800) 356-1605 (reservations)
FAX (210) 271-9145

501. This two-story rock home on three acres is a short distance from the famous Floore's Country Store dance hall. All rooms have twin or king-size beds and shared baths. There is one private bath. Within 20 minutes of Sea World, Fiesta Texas, Bandera Downs racetrack, golf courses, and downtown San Antonio. San Antonio VIA bus line stops in front of house. $55-70.

HOUSTON

The Highlander

607 Highland Avenue, 77009
(713) 861-6110; (800) 807-6110

This romantic 1922 four-square sits in a tranquil wildlife garden, yet is only five minutes from downtown. Between I-10W and I-45N and one block to Metro line, the location is convenient to everything. As longtime residents of Houston, hosts can help in planning intineraries. Amenities include fresh flowers, robes, telephones, turndown service, bedside snacks, and lovely full breakfast, along with Southern charm and Christian hospitality. Ask about Enchanted Evenings. FAX service available. Amtrak pickup free.

Hosts: Arlen and Georgie McIrvin
Rooms: 4 (2 PB; 2 SB) $75
Full Breakfast
Credit Cards: A, B, C, D
Notes: 2, 5, 10, 11, 12, 14

Patrician Bed and Breakfast Inn

1200 Southmore Avenue, 77004-5826
(713) 523-1114; (800) 553-5797
FAX (713) 523-0790

There will always be fresh flowers and a full breakfast at this 1919 three-story Colonial Revival mansion. Queen-size beds and private baths. Several rooms have adjoining sitting rooms, and some baths have clawfoot tubs and shower contraptions. Between

---

NOTES: Credit cards accepted: A MasterCard; B Visa; C American Express; D Discover Card; E Diner's Club; F Other; 2 Personal checks accepted; 3 Lunch available; 4 Dinner available; 5 Open all year;

downtown Houston and the Texas Medical Center. Walk to Houston Zoological Gardens, Hermann Park, and the Museum of Fine Arts. Excellent dining nearby.

Host: Pat Thomas
Rooms: 5 (PB) $70-90
Full Breakfast
Credit Cards: A, B, C, D, E
Notes: 2, 5, 9, 10, 12, 14

Robin's Nest

4104 Greeley, 77006
(713) 528-5821; (800) 622-8343

Historic, circa 1897, Queen Anne was originally a dairy farm. Feather beds atop fine mattresses, convenience of central location, and taste (buds) make the stay worthwhile. The rooms are spacious, furnished in eclectic Victorian with custom-made drapes, bed covers, etc. Robin's Nest is decoratively painted in concert with her sister "Painted Ladies." In the museum and arts district, surrounded by museums, art galleries, excellent restaurants, downtown, and the theater district.

Host: Robin Smith
Rooms: 4 (PB) $65-95
Full Breakfast
Credit Cards: A, B, C, D, E
Notes: 2, 5, 9, 10, 11, 12, 14

Sara's Bed and Breakfast Inn

941 Heights Boulevard, 77008
(713) 868-1130; (800) 593-1130

This Queen Anne Victorian is in Houston Heights, a neighborhood of historic homes, many of which are on the National Register of Historic Places. Each bedroom is uniquely furnished, having either single, double, queen-, or king-size beds. The balcony suite consists of two bedrooms, two baths, kitchen, living area, and balcony. The sights and sounds of downtown are only four miles away.

Hosts: Donna and Tillman Arledge
Rooms: 14 (12 PB; 2 SB) $55-150

Continental Breakfast
Credit Cards: A, B, C, D, E, F
Notes: 2, 5, 8, 9, 10, 11, 14

Webber House

Webber House Bed and Breakfast

1011 Heights Boulevard, 77008
(713) 864-9472

Built in 1907 by brickmason Samuel Webber, this red brick Queen Anne home is on the National Register of Historic Places. It features leaded and stained glass, curved oriel windows, beautiful cypress wood work, and venetian glass chandeliers. Accommodations range from a tall mahogany rice bed to an antique iron bed, all king- or queen-size. Private baths. The Webber House is in the middle of Historic Heights with antique shopping and dining nearby.

Host: Joann Jackson
Rooms: 3 (PB) $65-110
Continental Breakfast
Credit Cards: A, B, C, D
Notes: 2, 5, 9, 14

INGRAM

Bed and Breakfast Texas Style

4224 West Red Bird Lane, Dallas, 75237
(214) 298-8586

6 Pets welcome; 8 Children welcome; 9 Social drinking allowed; 10 Tennis available; 11 Swimming available; 12 Golf available; 13 Skiing available; 14 May be booked through travel agents.

Guadalupe Retreat. Swimming, tubing, or canoeing in the river is the fun and excitement at this bed and breakfast near Kerrville approximatcly onc hour from San Antonio. The mansion has a complete apartment with kitchen, two bedrooms, and bath. A delicious breakfast of blueberry muffins and poppy seed bread with a fruit plate, eggs, and bacon will be the fare. Smoking permitted. Children welcome. $75.

JACKSONVILLE

Bed and Breakfast Texas Style

4224 West Red Bird Lane, Dallas, 75237
(214) 298-8586

English Hearth. Right in Jacksonville, this Tudor mansion was built by a local lumber baron in the 1920s. Amenities include a 200-year-old grandfather clock, an olive wood dining room set, and other fine antiques. There are three guest bedrooms. The honeymoon suite has a private bath right in the room. Two bedrooms upstairs share a hall bath. Breakfast is Texas-style, with biscuits or croissants, eggs, choice of meats, fresh fruit or juice, and coffee. $65-85.

JASPER

The Belle-Jim Hotel

160 North Austin, 75951
(409) 384-6923

The Belle-Jim Hotel sits in the heart of the lakes of Deep East Texas, offering bed and breakfast accommodations in a turn-of-the-century atmosphere. Eight spacious guest rooms, decorated in period furnishings, helping to cross the threshold of time to the tranquility of a bygone era. All rooms have private baths and are air-conditioned. Full breakfast provided. Golf nearby. Children welcome.

Hosts: Pat and David Stiles
Rooms: 8 (PB) $50
Full Breakfast
Credit Cards: A, B, C
Notes: 2, 3, 5, 8, 12, 14

JEFFERSON

Pride House

409 Broadway, 75657
(903) 665-2675; (800) 894-3526

The first bed and breakfast in the state of Texas, Pride House offers ten rooms, all with private baths and inherited family Victorian antiques. Porches with rockers and swings, footed tubs, showers for two, and fireplaces. Large, sunny breakfast room that is used for small business conferences is where a full breakfast, made from Ruthmary's famous recipes, is served. Luxurious amenities and luscious interiors. The morning sun shines through original stained-glass windows of this 1888 Victorian mansion. King- and queen-size beds. Telephones and TVs by request.

Hosts: Carol and Lois
Rooms: 10 (PB) $65-100
Full Breakfast
Credit Cards: A, B
Notes: 2, 5, 8, 9, 12, 14

Wise Manor

312 Houston Street, 75657
(903) 665-2386

A gem of a Victorian home that looks as if it has just stepped out of a fairy tale. This little two-story cottage is painted in salmon tones with black gingerbread trim. Surrounded by large pecan trees, it peers out from behind a wrought-iron fence. It is furnished with Victorian pieces, marble-top tables, and ruffled curtains at the windows. Antique white bedspreads and folded appliquéd quilts adorn the ornate walnut beds.

Host: Katherine Ramsay Wise
Rooms: 3 (2 PB; 1 SB) $30-55
No Breakfast

NOTES: Credit cards accepted: A MasterCard; B Visa; C American Express; D Discover Card; E Diner's Club; F Other; 2 Personal checks accepted; 3 Lunch available; 4 Dinner available; 5 Open all year;

Credit Cards: A, B
Notes: 2, 5, 7, 8, 9, 12, 14

KINGSVILLE

Bed and Breakfast Hosts of San Antonio and South Texas

1777 N.E. Loop 410, Suite 600, San Antonio, 78217
(210) 824-8036; (800) 356-1605 (reservations)
FAX (210) 271-9145

610. A western resort near the famed King Ranch with private baths, a pool, conference facilities, and bird hunting (in season). Minutes from Baffin Bay fishing. Children over 12. From $50.

LA COSTE

Bed and Breakfast Hosts of San Antonio and South Texas

1777 N.E. Loop 410, Suite 600, San Antonio, 78217
(210) 824-8036; (800) 356-1605 (reservations)
FAX (210) 271-9145

502. This country inn is a small historic hotel including a swimming pool, spa, sauna, and Nordic Track. There are long porches where guests may train-watch or sunbathe. Rates include three meals daily, exercise, and group discussion classes. Shared and private baths. No children. $55-95.

Bed and Breakfast Texas Style

4224 West Red Bird Lane, Dallas, 75237
(214) 298-8586

Swan and Railway Inn. At one time it was known as the City Hotel and had only three guest bedrooms. It now has five, three with private bath. A separate historical building was added behind the new pool and contains a therapeutic hot tub, a Scandinavian sauna, exercise equipment, and room for aerobics classes. Breakfast may be yogurt and granola or bran muffins, fruit, and herb teas. About 18–20 minutes from San Antonio; ten minutes from Sea World. La Coste was a French settlement, and nearby Castroville has German roots. $55-65.

LA GRANGE

Meerscheidt Haus

(La Grange Bed and Breakfast)
458 North Monroe Street, 78945
(409) 968-9569

Built in the 1880s, this gracious Victorian home offers four bedrooms, each with private bath, all furnished with period antiques that are available to guests for purchase. The living room features games, puzzles, and relaxing music. The porch swing invites sunset watching. Breakfast in the formal dining room features German and Czech pastries, homemade breads and granola, and seasonal fruits. Meerscheidt Haus offers a retreat from the everyday. Come experience a return to the grace and elegance of yesteryear!

Hosts: Elva and Royce Keilers
Rooms: 4 (PB) $40-85
Full Breakfast
Credit Cards: A, B
Notes: 2, 5, 9, 10, 11, 12

LAKEHILLS

Bed and Breakfast Hosts of San Antonio and South Texas

1777 N.E. Loop 410, Suite 600, San Antonio, 78217
(210) 824-8036; (800) 356-1605 (reservations)
FAX (210) 271-9145

Wandering Aengus Cottage. Complete and separate hideaway in scenic area. Great getaway. $60-90.

6 Pets welcome; 8 Children welcome; 9 Social drinking allowed; 10 Tennis available; 11 Swimming available; 12 Golf available; 13 Skiing available; 14 May be booked through travel agents.

LAREDO

Bed and Breakfast Hosts of San Antonio and South Texas

1777 N.E. Loop 410, Suite 600, San Antonio, 78217
(210) 824-8036; (800) 356-1605 (reservations)
FAX (210) 271-9145

The Allen House Bed and Breakfast.
Only a five-minute drive from Mexico, this
beautifully decorated bed and breakfast is
furnished with family heirlooms, antiques,
and treasured collectibles. There are four
guest rooms, two with private baths and two
sharing a bath. Guests are encouraged to
make themselves at home in the sitting
room and the parlor with a baby grand
piano. The breakfast menu varies but always includes homemade breads, an abundance of fresh fruit, and homemade
granola. $50-95.

LA RUE

Dunsavage Farms

Route 2, Box 220, 75770
(800) 225-6982

In Athens, Texas, this country retreat is on a
picturesque hill with vistas seven miles in
all directions. Quiet home of the New York
Texas Cheesecake. Open pantry. Antiques,
library, and two fireplaces. Close to Canton
and Tyler lakes. Wildflowers and fall colors. Gourmet dinners Saturday nights. Huge
country gourmet breakfast. Accoladed in
Southern Living, Texas Highways, and
other national publications.

Host: Lyn Dunsavage
Rooms: 3 (PB) $79.95
Full Breakfast
Credit Cards: A, B, C
Notes: 2, 4, 5, 6, 7 (limited), 8, 9, 10, 11, 12, 14

LEANDER

Trails End Bed and Breakfast

12223 Trails End Road, 7, 78641
(512) 267-2901

Trails End Bed and Breakfast is a six-acre
scenic, restful, romantic setting in the Texas
Hill Country. The main house is a two-story
Colonial-type with fireplace, two wraparound porches, and observation deck with
a panoramic view of the Hill Country and
Lake Travis. The main house has architectural fixtures from 1920s through 1950s
with mahogany furniture throughout. Full
breakfast served in the dining room. Gift
shop for guests, swimming pool, gazebo,
bicycles, gardens and benches to enjoy the
outdoors. Guest house sleeps up to six and
has decks and patios to enjoy.

Hosts: JoAnn and Tom Patty
Rooms: 2 (PB) plus guest house $65-95
Full Breakfast
Credit Cards: A, B, C
Notes: 2, 4, 5, 8, 9, 10, 11, 12, 13 (water), 14

Trails End

LEON SPRINGS

Bed and Breakfast Hosts of San Antonio and South Texas

1777 N.E. Loop 410, Suite 600, San Antonio, 78217
(210) 824-8036; (800) 356-1605 (reservations)
FAX (210) 271-9145

504. A large country estate on 3.4 acres of wooded land with swimming pool. Beautiful Hill Country view. Three bedrooms, one with private bath. $65-90.

Miss Margaret's. Just 25 minutes from downtown San Antonio and ten minutes from Fiesta Texas. On nearly three and one-half acres of wooded land with swimming pool. $65-80.

LLANO

Bed and Breakfast Hosts of San Antonio and South Texas

1777 N.E. Loop 410, Suite 600, San Antonio, 78217
(210) 824-8036; (800) 356-1605 (reservations)
FAX (210) 271-9145

611. This inn is an elegantly restored and furnished Greek revival solid granite home. The rock was quarried nearby and transported to the site by mule-drawn wagons. A full breakfast is prepared each morning. Snacks are served on the patio in the evening where guests may purchase beer or wine. Biking, tennis, fishing, golf, and swimming are nearby. Choose from the Green Room or the West Room with private baths, the Rose Room with lavatory and tub, or the East Room with full bath just down the hall. $75.

Bed and Breakfast Texas Style

4224 West Red Bird Lane, Dallas, 75237
(214) 298-8586

Fraser House. Enjoy the four upstairs guest bedrooms of this 1900 solid granite house in the middle of town. The bedrooms have private baths with claw-foot tubs, a sleigh bed, a Jenny Lind bed, and iron beds. A ham and quiche breakfast along with complimentary mimosas will be served. $85.

MADISONVILLE

Bed and Breakfast Texas Style

4224 West Red Bird Lane, Dallas, 75237
(214) 298-8586

Ranch 102. This charming log home was built by the hosts as a getaway home about eight years ago. Ranch 102 is heated by a Ben Franklin stove that produces ample heat for the loft and three rooms downstairs. The full, well-stocked kitchen includes a microwave. TV, VCR, and lots of movies are provided for guests. Guests are invited to fish in the seven-acre lake and to walk around the farm. The hosts serve a full breakfast. $95.

MASON

Bed and Breakfast Hosts of San Antonio and South Texas

1777 N.E. Loop 410, Suite 600, San Antonio, 78217
(210) 824-8036; (800) 356-1605 (reservations)
FAX (210) 271-9145

612. This property is listed in the National Register of Historic Places. Discover scenery and people who reflect much of Texas's early history on this 320-acre working ranch. Deer, quail, wild turkey, and feral hogs are common sights. The two-story house has two bedrooms and two baths, living room, dining area, and modern kitchen with wood-burning stove. Children over 12 welcome. Special weekly and monthly rates available. $100.

6 Pets welcome; 8 Children welcome; 9 Social drinking allowed; 10 Tennis available; 11 Swimming available; 12 Golf available; 13 Skiing available; 14 May be booked through travel agents.

613. This bed and breakfast, on the second floor of a typical commercial building on the courthouse square, dates from 1879. Each of the four guest rooms features antique furniture and private baths. Enjoy a quiet stroll into the past around the square. Generous Continental breakfast is served, and guests may also use the fully equipped kitchen in the common area. No smoking. $45-60.

MERIDIAN

Bed and Breakfast Texas Style

4224 West Red Bird Lane, Dallas, 75237
(214) 298-8586

The Hastings House. This charming older home is on a farm near Meridian, just south of Fort Worth and Dallas. Close to Lake Whitney. The farmhouse is about 60 years old and has a large front porch, three bedrooms, living room, breakfast nook, and kitchen. There is a large bath. Breakfast is left in the refrigerator for guests to prepare. Local attractions include the Safari in nearby Clifton, the Dinosaur Tracks Park in Glenrose, and the pageant *The Promise* in Glenrose on weekends. $65.

MINEOLA

Munzesheimer Manor Bed and Breakfast Inn

202 North Newsom, 75773
(903) 569-6634

An 1898 country Victorian in a small town with a population of 5,000. Totally restored in 1987, the inn has central heat and air, and antique furnishings. Fresh flowers, chilled cider, Victorian nightshirts, candy mint sticks, full gourmet breakfast, and fresh ground coffee. Wraparound porches. Private baths. Some rooms have fireplaces. Country club golf and swimming nearby.

Antique shopping and fun places to eat in town and in the country. Regular craft and music festivals in the area.

Hosts: Bob and Sherry Murray
Rooms: 7 (PB) $65-90
Full Breakfast
Credit Cards: A, B, D, E
Notes: 2, 5, 10, 11, 12, 14

NACOGDOCHES

Hardeman Guest House

316 North Church Street, 75961
(409) 569-1947

This beautiful late-Victorian house listed on the National Register of Historic Places is in the heart of the oldest town in Texas. English, Oriental, French, and American rooms, furnished with antiques, quilts, original art, and owner's collections of American art pottery and Oriental porcelain. Home-baked breakfast breads and homemade jams and jellies highlight delicious breakfasts served on fine china, crystal, and silver. Furniture, paintings, collectibles, and crafts available. Special weekday business travel rates.

Host: Lea Smith
Rooms: 4 (PB) $65-80
Full Breakfast
Credit Cards: A, B
Notes: 2, 5, 6, 8, 9

PineCreek Lodge Bed and BreakfastCountry Inn

Route 3, Box 1238, 75964
(409) 560-6282

On a peaceful 140-acre wooded property near a flowing creek. Acres of beautiful grounds and flowers. Miles of surrounding country roads for driving and hiking enjoyment. Special features include large decks with swings and rocking chairs, hammock, pool, spa, fishing pond, and hiking trail. Each room has a private bath and deck with swing, air conditioning, ceiling fans, TV/VCR, refrigerator, phone, mono-

NOTES: Credit cards accepted: A MasterCard; B Visa; C American Express; D Discover Card; E Diner's Club; F Other; 2 Personal checks accepted; 3 Lunch available; 4 Dinner available; 5 Open all year;

grammed robes, and fresh flowers. Refreshments at check-in. No pets allowed. Smoking permitted outside only.

Hosts: Elmer and Edna Pitts
Rooms: 3 (PB) $65
Full Breakfast
Credit Cards: A, B, C
Notes: 2, 3, 4, 5, 8, 11 (on premises), 12, 13 (water)

NEW BRAUNFELS

Bed and Breakfast Hosts of San Antonio and South Texas

1777 N.E. Loop 410, Suite 600, San Antonio, 78217
(210) 824-8036; (800) 356-1605 (reservations)
FAX (210) 271-9145

614. A very large, luxurious home in a country setting within minutes of all San Antonio and New Braunfels attractions. Two upstairs suites; one double bed and one king-size bed with connecting bath and veranda. Full breakfast. Outside smoking only. Special weekday rates are available. $65-110.

615. A 144-year-old German pioneer farm house on 43 acres. Andrea's and Katherine's attic is a family suite of two bedrooms with a private bath. Hillside hideaway is a large bedroom with private porch. Rhapsody in Blue suite with sitting room and private work area. There are two whirlpool baths in Waldrip Haus. Danville School (circa 1900) is a one-room school restored with full kitchen and bath plus three bedrooms with private baths and a huge porch overlooking the pasture. Bring a horse, there's plenty of stable room. The "school" will accommodate 14 persons; the house 10-12 persons. Full breakfast. $85-125.

616. This historic inn has eight rooms with private baths and two suites. Wolfgang's Keller fine restaurant and piano bar downstairs; courtyard for special events. Landa Park, 18-hole municipal golf course, an-

tiquing, and Comal River nearby. Special weekday rates. $60-100.

Prince Solms Inn

295 East San Antonio Street, 78130
(210) 625-9169

Historic landmark in the heart of the Texas Hill Country. Built as a hotel in 1898, it is the oldest continuous business in the state of Texas. New Braunfels is well known for its rich German heritage; the inn is named after Prince Carl Solms von Braunfels, Germany. It is also the home of the world famous Wurstfest celebrated annually during October and November. All rooms furnished with Victorian-style antiques, each done differently. In historic downtown area, one block from the newly opened Hummel Museum.

Hosts: Robert and Pat Brent
Rooms: 10 (PB) $70-150
Continental Breakfast
Credit Cards: A, B, D
Notes: 2, 4, 5, 7, 9, 10, 11, 12, 14

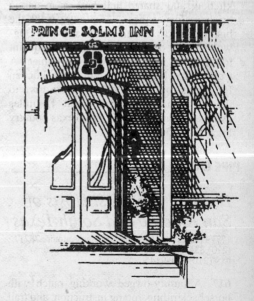

Prince Solms Inn

PALESTINE

Bed and Breakfast Texas Style

4224 West Red Bird Lane, Dallas, 75237
(214) 298-8586

Grandma's House. Nestled in the heart of East Texas is a country Christmas tree farm with a guest house furnished with twin beds and private bath. Relax on the front porch, stroll among the Christmas trees, or ride a paddleboat around the pond. Hearty breakfast of homemade bread, jellies, fresh farm eggs, quail, and gravy. Convenient to antique shopping, historical sites, spring dogwood trails, and fall foliage. Just 30 minutes to the East Texas Historical Train Ride at Palestine or Rusk, Canton's First Monday Trade Day, and Athens Black-eyed Pea Jamboree. $50.

The Sunday House. A charming duplex with two bedrooms, large parlor, full kitchen, and shared hall bath is a classic brick residence near downtown. Near the historic Texas Steam Train and the Dogwood Trails in spring, Palestine is a quaint town filled with many historic homes. A Continental breakfast is left in the kitchen for guests to prepare, or they may drive to the Christmas tree farm about 12 miles away and partake of the full Texas country breakfast. $50.

PIPE CREEK

Bed and Breakfast Hosts of San Antonio and South Texas

1777 N.E. Loop 410, Suite 600, San Antonio, 78217
(210) 824-8036; (800) 356-1605 (reservations)
FAX (210) 271-9145

617. A family-owned working ranch with horseback riding, roping instruction, and trail rides available at an extra charge. Horses for every experience level. There is a blacksmith

shop where the wranglers make craft items from horseshoes. Three guest houses, each with private bath: one large with two bedrooms, living area, kitchen, and deck; one medium; and one small with one bedroom. Swimming pool. $70-80.

PORT ARANSAS

Bed and Breakfast Hosts of San Antonio and South Texas

1777 N.E. Loop 410, Suite 600, San Antonio, 78217
(210) 824-8036; (800) 356-1605 (reservations)
FAX (210) 271-9145

618. Just steps from the beach, this inn also has a swimming pool, hot tubs, and guest rooms decorated in themes from around the world. Two honeymoon suites. Coffee in the lobby; no breakfast servic. Available local activities include windsurfing, deep sea fishing, and helicopter rides. $39-79.

Sand Dollar Hospitality

3605 Mendenhall, Corpus Christi, 78415
(512) 853-1222

Harbor View Bed and Breakfast. This three-story Mediterranean-style home on the Port Aransas Municipal Harbor offers three large bedrooms with private baths and a third-floor suite. On each of the three levels the decks and balconies afford a beautiful, unobstructed view of the harbor. The inn is within convenient walking distance of restaurants, shops, charter boats, and fishing operations. On-site mooring facilities are available for craft up to 50 feet in length. $70-90.

Sea Song. When being right on the water is a must, this is the host home for you. On the sandy shores of the Gulf of Mexico, this charming two-story home offers the discriminating guest all the amenities plus a full-course gourmet breakfast. A private entrance to the ground-level apartment opens into a spacious hall and living room with wet bar. There are three guest bedrooms and private baths. Two of the rooms have queen-size beds; the third has a double bed. A large deck off the living room faces the water. Two-night minimum. Children half-price (must be under one year or over twelve). $90.

PORT ISABEL

Yacht Club Hotel and Restaurant

700 Yturria Street, 78578
(512) 943-1301

Since 1926, the Yacht Club Hotel and Restaurant has provided its guests with fine dining in the casual atmosphere of the 1920s and 1930s. There are 24 cozy rooms that overlook the harbor. Come fish, beachcomb, visit Mexico, or relax and sip margaritas on the veranda. The award-winning chef serves fresh seafood, steaks, and pasta.

Host: Lynn Speter
Rooms: 24 (PB) $30-69
Continental Breakfast
Credit Cards: A, B, C, F.
Notes: 4, 5, 8, 9, 11, 14

RIO MEDINA

Bed and Breakfast Hosts of San Antonio and South Texas

1777 N.E. Loop 410, Suite 600, San Antonio, 78217
(210) 824-8036; (800) 356-1605 (reservations)
FAX (210) 271-0116

619. This inn is a restored two-story farmhouse in a beautiful rural setting. It has three bedrooms, bath, living room with sleeper-sofa, dining room, and kitchen. Adults only. $65.

Haby Settlement Inn. Cottage in beautiful rural setting lovingly restored has one bedroom, bath, living room with sleeper sofa, dining room, and kitchen. Adults only. $65.

ROCKPORT

Bed and Breakfast Hosts of San Antonio and South Texas

1777 N.E. Loop 410, Suite 600, San Antonio, 78217
(210) 824-8036; (800) 356-1605 (reservations)
FAX (210) 271-9145

620. This cottage has a queen-size bedroom and a double bed in the living room, one bath, and kitchen with microwave. Interesting shops on nearby downtown Main Street. Great fishing and all water sports available. Separate main house is also available for meetings. $70

Primrose Cottage. Victorian charm teamed with the amenities of the 1990s make this fully furnished cottage a truly special place. Sleeping accomodations consist of one queen-size bed and one double. Breakfast vouchers may be provided. Rockport, just one-half mile north of Corpus Christi on the Gulf of Mexico, is the art colony of the Texas Gulf Coast. $75-90.

ROUND TOP

Broomfields

419 North Nassau Road, 78954
(409) 249-3706; FAX (409) 249-3706

Country retreat five miles from Round Top on 40 acres of meadowland with wooded tracts and stocked pond. Historic restorations, classical music, and semiannual antique shows nearby. Spectacular displays of wildflowers in spring and foliage in fall. An 1800s Texas-vernacular modern home built with 100-year-old barn beams and furnished with selected European and American antiques. Comfortable, well appointed rooms and baths. Suppers and picnic lunches may be booked in advance. Antiques and decorative arts gallery on the premises.

Hosts: Julia and Bill Bishop
Rooms: 3 (1 PB; 2 SB) $70-95

6 Pets welcome; 8 Children welcome; 9 Social drinking allowed; 10 Tennis available; 11 Swimming available; 12 Golf available; 13 Skiing available; 14 May be booked through travel agents.

Full Breakfast
Credit Cards: None
Notes: 2, 3, 4, 5, 9, 10, 12

SALADO

The Rose Mansion and The Inn at Salado

P.O. Box 500, 76571
(817) 947-8200

The Rose Mansion. Nestled among towering oaks, elms, and persimmon trees, this traditional Greek Revival-style mansion and additional complimentary cottages are on four acres of landscaping and surrounded by a white picket fence. The main home, built in 1870 by Maj. A. J. Rose, has four bedrooms (three with fireplaces), a grand parlor, an elegant dining room, and a cozy country kitchen. There are two beautifully restored log cabins, a summer kitchen cottage, and a larger Greek Revival cottage. The mansion contains Rose family memorabilia and authentic antiques. A windmill with a cypress storage tank, a rock smokehouse, and an old wagon are nostalgic reminders of the past.

The Inn at Salado. Salado's first bed and breakfast is in the heart of the historic district. Restored to its original 1872 splendor, the inn was once the home of early Texas statesman Col. James Norton. Within walking distance of Salado's finest shops and restaurants. The inn offers nine rooms, all with private baths and most with fireplaces. Its decor and ambience is enhanced with numerous antiques and six covered porches that beckon guests to relax and linger awhile.

Hosts: Mansion—Lori Long; Inn—Gabriele Oborski
Rooms: Mansion—11; Inn—9
Full Breakfast
Credit Cards: A, B, C, D
Notes: 2, 4 (limited), 5, 8, 10, 11, 12

SAN ANTONIO

Adelynne's Summit Haus and Summit Haus II

427 West Summit, 78212
(210) 736-6272; (800) 972-7266

Two elegant 1920s residences in the heart of San Antonio, five minutes from downtown and Riverwalk. The main house is furnished with rare Biedermeier antiques. The cottage is furnished with 18th- and 19th-century French and English antiques. It is ideal for those who prefer an entire house to themselves. All rooms have TV, telephone, and refrigerator with complimentary beverages. Central heat and air, fireplaces, tree-shaded decks, and off-street parking. Personal service from people who care.

Host: Adelynne H. Whitaker
Rooms: 5 (3 PB; 2 SB) $75-95
Full Breakfast
Credit Cards: A, B, C
Notes: 2, 5, 8 (over ten), 9, 10, 11, 12, 14

Beckmann Inn

Beckmann Inn and Carriage House

222 East Guenther Street, 78204
(210) 229-1449

This elegant Victorian inn is in the heart of San Antonio in the King William historic district. The beautiful wraparound porch welcomes guests to this beautiful home. All rooms are colorfully decorated featuring ornately carved Victorian queen-size beds, antiques, and private baths. Ride the trolley or take the Riverwalk to the Alamo, restaurants, shops, Mexican Market, and much more. Guests receive gracious and warm hospitality during their stay.

Hosts: Betty Jo and Don Schwartz
Rooms: 5 (PB) $80-120
Full Breakfast
Credit Cards: A, B, C, E
Notes: 2, 5, 8 (over 12) 9, 12, 14

Bed and Breakfast Hosts of San Antonio and South Texas

1777 N.E. Loop 410, Suite 600, San Antonio, 78217
(210) 824-8036; (800) 356-1605 (reservations)
FAX (210) 271 9145

101. On the slopes of the San Antonio River near the downtown area, this bed and breakfast offers seven bedrooms with private bath. Enclosed porches overlooking the river provide a restful atmosphere. Spas are available at additional charge. $99-119.

102. Sitting atop a quiet legal office in the heart of downtown near the river, this bed and breakfast offers all the amenities with Southwest decor plus the use of office facilities by special arrangement. $85-99.

103. Near the Municipal Auditorium. Two suites, one is overlooking the river. There is also one other room. Private baths and Continental breakfast. $89-105.

201. This family home is near all downtown San Antonio attractions. They have an upstairs bedroom with double bed and a twin trundle; a private bath in the hallway. Airport transportation upon request. $42-60.

202. Infants and children 12 or older are most welcome at this 100-year-old, completely restored Victorian treasure of a home. Polished guest bedroom with double bed and shared bath in hallway. Additional guest room with double bed has many windows that provide a nice view of the garden in the back yard. Both rooms have TV and telephone. Continental breakfast is served in the dining room at whatever time the guests request. $47-60.

203. This lovely restored Victorian home has five rooms with private entrances and private baths. Four rooms are available with queen-size beds, and the bridal suite has a king-size bed, decorated in white. Baths may included footed tub with shower or shower only; one room has a kitchenette. Full breakfast is served in the dining room or on the veranda. $95-105.

204. This charming Victorian home built in 1910 has hardwood floors and furnishings appropriate to the era. Rooms include one downstairs with queen-size bed and private entrance and bath; upstairs rooms have queen-size beds and private baths, one with twin bed in an alcove. Breakfast is served by choice in the dining room, on shaded backyard deck, or on the spacious front porch. Laundry facilities available. Children over seven welcome. $85.

205. This carriage house is furnished in Victorian antiques. The spacious living area has queen-size sofa Hide-a-bed, fireplace, and access to patio with swimming pool and spa. Full kitchen with microwave, telephone, cable TV, separate bedroom with queen-size brass bed, and a white marble bath with claw-foot tub and shower are all downstairs. Upstairs accommodations include two bedrooms, queen-size beds, private baths, and fireplaces. Common area has living and dining area, kitchen, and

6 Pets welcome; 8 Children welcome; 9 Social drinking allowed; 10 Tennis available; 11 Swimming available; 12 Golf available; 13 Skiing available; 14 May be booked through travel agents.

Bed and Breakfast Hosts of San Antonio and South Texas (continued)

queen-size sleeper-sofa. Continental breakfast is provided at guests' leisure. Outdoor smoking only. $95-110.

206. Built in 1857 and recently restored, this former home of a pioneer Texas Ranger and cattle rancher is part of the historic district. The inn sits on spacious, beautifully landscaped grounds within a five-block stroll along the Riverwalk to all downtown attractions. Each of the five rooms and five suites is elegantly decorated with period antiques and has a private bath. Breakfast is served at private tables in the formal dining room or on the veranda. No children. No pets. Outside smoking only. $125-195.

207. This lovely home is listed on the National Register of Historic Places and is opposite the river and Guenther Mill. Accommodations include three rooms, one suite, and one carriage house. Baths may be attached with Continental shower tub or shower only. Rooms have impressive Victorian furniture, including queen-size beds. Full breakfast is included. Reduced rates Monday through Thursday. $90-130.

208. This elegant Victorian home with wicker-filled verandas has four rooms and one suite, all with private baths. Decor is thematic with queen-size beds, a fainting sofa, and the options of private entrances, kitchen facilities, adjoining veranda, outdoor sitting area, and footed tubs and/or showers. Older children welcome. $85-125.

209. Five beautifully restored bedrooms in this home have antiques and thematic decor. Options include queen-size beds, double-size sleigh bed, twin four-poster beds, queen-size sleeper sofa, and private baths either in hall-

way or attached. Full breakfast included with regular rate. Reduced rates Monday through Thursday. $90-125.

210. Built in 1900 by San Antonio mercantilist Alexander Joske, this restored two-story home has beautiful woodwork, an ornate stairway, stained-glass windows, antique furnishings, and large porches. Accommodations include three individually decorated rooms with an 1860s half-tester bed, a king-size bed, a private porch, and private baths with antique tub and/or shower. Riverwalk is only five blocks away. Outside smoking only. $90-105.

211. This carriage house has two individually decorated suites with antiques, wicker, and Victorian touches. One suite has a cathedral ceiling. Designer linens, fine toiletries, telephones, TV, fresh flowers, sitting area, full kitchen, and private bath are available in both suites. $125.

212. This guest house has a comfortable loft bedroom with a king-size bed. The downstairs has a double bed, a sitting room with queen-size Hide-a-bed, full kitchen, and dining area. $75.

213. This unique, romantic guest house has eclectic furnishings from around the world. The upstairs bedroom has an Indonesian throne converted to a bed and has a private bath. Downstairs living area has TV and refrigerator. The Ten Cent Trolley stops at the door. Continental breakfast served. Two-night minimum. Outside smoking only. $90.

301. This elegant mansion has three second-floor bedrooms. Guests may choose a double bed, queen-size bed, twin beds, or the Persian suite with king-size bed. All have private baths. Continental breakfast is served in the sunroom. Older children welcome. No smoking. $100-150.

NOTES: Credit cards accepted: A MasterCard; B Visa; C American Express; D Discover Card; E Diner's Club; F Other; 2 Personal checks accepted; 3 Lunch available; 4 Dinner available; 5 Open all year;

302. This garden villa has a variety of rooms and a bridal suite, all beautifully furnished including private baths. The suite has a king-size bed, fireplace, Jacuzzi tub, and shower. A swimming pool and roof garden are available, as well as FAX and secretarial services with adequate notice. Continental plus breakfast is served with weekend specialties. No children. Outside smoking only. Discounts for extended stays and weekdays. $75-95.

303. This large three-story home has 11-foot, heavy-beamed ceilings and three fireplaces. Guests may choose from three rooms and an upstairs cottage. Accommodations include a king-size bed, queen-size beds, a twin bed alcove, TV, and private baths. The cottage also has a refrigerator, a queen-size bed and a sofa Hide-a-bed. Full breakfast is included. Children welcome. Reduced rates Monday through Thursday. $75-100.

401. This home has four second-floor bedrooms, some with verandas, all with adjoining private baths and TV. Guests may choose from queen-size beds, a double bed with twin roll away, a king-size bed, or a full bed with a twin trundle bed in an alcove. Guests are two blocks from the Ten Cent Trolley to downtown. Continental breakfast is served in the coffee room. Two-day minimum on weekends. Children welcome. No smoking. $60-70.

402. After restoration, this home has become a "grand lady." Five rooms have antique beds, some with fireplace and private beaches overlooking the park. All have private baths with shower tub. The suite has a fireplace, veranda, and period antiques. Teatime occurs from 4:00 to 6:00 P.M. daily. Full breakfast is included. $80-90.

403. This spacious guest cottage has two bedrooms. One has twin beds and a beautifully furnished adjoining bath; the other has a double bed and sitting area with a bath in the hallway. A fully equipped kitchen, a game room with pool table, and extensive playground equipment for children of all ages. Accommodations are ideal for a family or couple. No smoking. $130.

404. This guest house is near McNay Art Museum. It is furnished in Cape Cod Colonial antiques with a tile-fronted fireplace in the sitting area, a canopied queen-size bed in the sleeping area, and a redwood deck overlooking the pool and hot tub. Full kitchen and bath included. Two-night minimum. No smoking. $107.

405. This Mexican/Southwest-style garden cottage is in a quiet residential area five minutes from downtown. A large room with cathedral ceiling, Saltillo tile floor, two twin beds, and a futon sofa. There is a fully equipped kitchenette, bathroom, and sliding doors to private patio and garden. Telephone and cable TV. Owner, originally from Germany, is an art educator at a number of cultural institutes in San Antonio. Ideal for monthly booking. $625 monthly.

406. This elegant and affordable inn is within a Texas historic landmark. Spacious guest rooms, fireplaces, and pool. Ideal for weddings, receptions, and conferences, One room with private bath, six rooms with shared bath. Continental breakfast, Children welcome. $59.

503. This is a modern upstairs guest house on two acres just 30 minutes from downtown. Living room, bedroom, kitchen, dinette, full bath, with one double bed and a trundle day bed. Children are welcome with

6 Pets welcome; 8 Children welcome; 9 Social drinking allowed; 10 Tennis available; 11 Swimming available; 12 Golf available; 13 Skiing available; 14 May be booked through travel agents.

Bed and Breakfast Hosts of San Antonio and South Texas (continued)

playground equipment and outdoor spa available. Breakfast is provided for guests to enjoy at their leisure. Ten minutes to Fiesta Texas, 25 minutes to Sea World. $60-75.

Alan's Guest House. In the King William area, Alan's Guest House has all the modern conveniences. Loft bedroom with twin beds, downstairs bedroom with double bed and private bath. Sofa bed in living room and full kitchen with Continental breakfast provided. Original portion of home was built in 1871. Two bicycles are available. $70-100.

Beauregard House Bed and Breakfast. Charming Victorian home built in 1910, with hardwood floors and period furnishings. Two downstairs rooms with queen-size beds share a bath. One of these rooms has a separate kitchen and private entrance. The upstairs room has twin beds and a private bath. Breakfast is served in the dining room, tree-shaded back yard deck, or spacious front porch. Laundry facilities available.

Bed and Breakfast on the River. Restored Victorian right on the river in downtown. All rooms feature queen-size beds and private baths. Some rooms have adjoining sitting room overlooking the river. Special Continental breakfast is provided. The host is a licensed hot-air balloon pilot and can arrange a charter flight for guests or anyone visiting San Antonio. $99.

The Bonner Garden. This bed and breakfast is a large Italian-style villa in the Monte Vista area. Stroll in the garden, relax on the rooftop, or swim in the beautiful pool surrounded by flowers and shrubs in full bloom. Three guest rooms with private bath in the main house and a private detached studio. This was the home of Mary Bonner, renowned artist. Call for current rates.

Buttercup Bed and Breakfast. Spacious guest cottage on one acre in a quiet Alamo Heights neighborhood. Two blocks to shopping center, VIA bus to downtown in minutes. Airport transportation provided. Landscaped grounds and extensive playground equipment make this home ideal for children of all ages. Private cottage consists of one bedroom with twin beds and adjoining bath, and a second bedroom with double bed and sitting area. Private bath in hallway. Hosts provide a special breakfast in the cottage kitchen for guests to serve themselves. Guests may use the kitchen and game room with pool table. No smoking. $115.

Cross Mountain Ranch. This modern upstairs guest house in the northwest hills of San Antonio set on 2.2 acres of land provides a living room, bedroom, kitchen, dinette, and full bath. Central heat and air conditioning. Children are welcome. Pets permitted outside. $60.

The Gatlin House. This beautifully restored turn-of-the-century Victorian home is furnished with lovely antiques. The first upstairs bedroom has a queen-size bed and adjoining private bath; the second has a double bed and private hallway bath. Each bedroom opens onto its own private porch. Continental breakfast. One-half block from Ten Cent Trolley and VIA bus. $55-65.

Joske House. The original owner of this beautiful house was an owner of the famed Joske's department stores of Texas. The present owner has two bedrooms with private baths for bed and breakfast. The staircase has magnificent stained glass two stories high. $90-105.

Linden House. Twelve blocks north of downtown, this house was built in 1902 by Judge Linden, a colorful character with a peg leg who rode posse with the best of them to pursue notorious criminals and bandits in South Texas. The present owners offer four second-floor bedrooms, each with adjacent private bath. A generous Continental breakfast is served in the coffee room. TV is available. Airport transportation. Convenient to downtown, only two blocks from the Ten Cent Trolley. No smoking. Older children welcome. $60.

Nunez Home. The Nunez Home is near all downtown San Antonio attractions. European guests have been very appreciative of this charming couple's knowledge of San Antonio and enjoy being welcomed as true friends into this restored family Victorian home. There is an upstairs bedroom with a double bed and a single bed with a private bath in the hallway. Airport transportation upon request. $35-45.

On the Riverwalk. On the slopes of the San Antonio River near the downtown area, this bed and breakfast offers seven bedrooms with private baths. The enclosed porches overlooking the river provide a restful atmosphere. Spas are available at an additional charge. $99-119.

River Haus. Sitting atop a quiet legal office in the heart of downtown near the river, this bed and breakfast offers all the amenities with Southwest decor, plus use of office facilities by arrangement. $99.

Royal Swan. Elegant Victorian home with five beautifully decorated bedrooms, private baths, and wicker-filled verandas. $80-125.

Summit Haus I and II. These two renovated 1920s residences–side by side–are in the historic Monte Vista area. The main residence provides a suite with king-size bed and a full bath, with a double bed in the adjoining sunroom. The cottage has two large bedrooms, one with a king-size bed and the other with a double bed. Summit Haus I is furnished with German Biedermier antiques, crystal, linens, porcelains, and antique Persian and Turkish rugs. Summit Haus II is furnished with French and English antiques. $70.

Terrell Castle Bed and Breakfast. This multi-story home boasts nine unique rooms and suites, all fully air-conditioned and heated. Antique furnishings in maple and walnut, fireplaces, TVs, private and shared baths are available. Two accommodations have hexagonal rooms. Twin, king-, and queen-size beds are available in various combinations. Full gourmet breakfast, telephone and FAX service, and crib are included. No charge for children under six. $70-190.

Utopia Bluebird Hill. Bird watcher's heaven! Stay in main house or cabin, which can sleep up to six people. $50-75.

Yellow Rose. Beautifully restored with five bedrooms and private baths. Lovely antiques grace each room. $90-125.

Bed and Breakfast Texas Style

4224 West Red Bird Lane, Dallas, 75237
(214) 298-8586

Romantic Hideaway. In a secluded area just 20-30 minutes west of San Antonio in the Hill Country lies this separate apartment that is perfect for a getaway from the city. There are two single beds, one double bed,

---

6 Pets welcome; 8 Children welcome; 9 Social drinking allowed; 10 Tennis available; 11 Swimming available; 12 Golf available; 13 Skiing available; 14 May be booked through travel agents.

and a private bath. Breakfast fixings are left in the refrigerator in the well-stocked kitchen. The hosts will escort guests to Sea World and provide discount fares. Smoking outside only. Pets welcome but must be restrained as there are dogs in residence. Children are welcome if families want to take advantage of this special offer. Nightly and weekly rates. $60-250.

The Belle of Monte Vista

505 Belknap Place, 78212
(210) 732-4006

J. Riely Gordon designed this Queen Anne-style Victorian as a model house. Built in 1890 with limestone, the house has been beautifully restored and is in the elegant Monte Vista historic district. Inside, guests will find eight fireplaces, stained-glass windows, a hand-carved oak staircase, and Victorian furnishings. Jim, JoAnn, and David serve a full Southern breakfast and will help guests plan the day.

Hosts: Jim Davis, JoAnn, and David Bell
Rooms: 5 (4S2B) $60
Full Breakfast
Credit Cards: None
Notes: 2, 5, 8, 9, 10, 12

Bonner Garden

145 East Agarita, 78212
(800) 396-4222

This historic, award-winning Italian villa was built in 1910 for Mary Bonner, an internationally famous artist and print maker. Totally restored in 1985, the villa is surrounded by lush gardens and an Olympic-size pool. The rooftop patio overlooks San Antonio. Rooms are comfortably furnished with either queen- or king-size beds. All rooms have TVs, telephones, and VCRs. A film library is available for relaxation enjoyment.

Hosts: Jan and Noel Stenoien
Rooms: 5 (PB) $75-95

Full Breakfast
Credit Cards: A, B, C, D
Notes: 2, 5, 9, 10, 11, 12, 14

Brookhaven Bed and Breakfast

128 West Mistletoe, 78212
(210) 733-3939; (800) 851-3666

A beautiful Queen Anne home built in 1914 in the heart of the Monte Vista historic district of San Antonio. The home is decorated with beautiful antiques and furniture of the 1914 style. A lovely wraparound porch furnished with beautiful plants and wicker furniture is available for guests' enjoyment. Only five minutes from the Riverwalk, Alamo, and other local attractions.

Hosts: Gene and Henna Siler
Rooms: 4 (PB) $65-85
Full Breakfast
Credit Cards: C, D
Notes: 2, 5, 7, 8, 9, 10, 12

Brookhaven

Chabot Reed House

403 Madison, 78204
(512) 223-8697

The Chabot Reed House is an 1876 Victorian house one block from the Riverwalk in the King William historic district in downtown San Antonio. A special treat is staying in the two guest suites in the carriage house. Luxurious, yet comfortable; bold and colorful with an appropriate sense of history and sophistication. Private and romantic, the carriage house is on lovely landscaped grounds to the side of the main house. Guests are welcomed in the manor house as well.

Hosts: Sister and Peter Reed
Rooms: 5 (4 PB; 1 SB) $125
Full Breakfast
Credit Cards: None
Notes: 2, 5, 8, 9, 12, 14

The Columns on Alamo

1037 South Alamo, 78210
(800) 233-3364

Resident innkeepers welcome guests to their gracious 1892 Greek Revival home and guest house in the historic King William area. Blocks from the river, restaurants, shopping, convention center, and Alamo; short drive to Sea World and Fiesta Texas. Furnished with comfortable antiques and period reproductions, queen-size beds, telephones, TVs, large common areas and verandas, and off-street parking. Generous Continental breakfast, buffet style, is served in the main house. The inn is smoke-free except for verandas and outdoors. Two-night minimum stay on weekends.

Hosts: Ellenor and Art Link
Rooms: 11 (PB) $85-135
Continental Breakfast
Credit Cards: A, B, C
Notes: 2, 5, 9, 12, 14

Falling Pines Inn

300 West French Place, 78212
(210) 733-1998

Falling Pines is in the Monte Vista historic district one mile north of downtown. Construction of the home began in 1911 under the direction of famed architect Atlee Ayres. Pine trees, not native to San Antonio, tower over the mansion on a one-acre parklike setting. Brick and limestone construction, a green tiled roof, and shuttered windows enhance a magnificent limestone archway entry and veranda on the front fa-

Falling Pines Inn

cade. The guest rooms are on the second level. The entire third floor is the Persian Suite and commands a grand view of downtown San Antonio. Fully restored, the mansion is furnished with traditional and antique furniture.

Hosts: Grace and Bob Daubert
Rooms: 4 (PB) $100-150
Full Breakfast
Credit Cards: A, B, C
Notes: 2, 5, 8 (over 10), 9, 10, 12, 14

Norton Brackenridge House

230 Madison, 78204
(210) 271-3442

This is a 90-year-old fully restored home in the King William historic district, the oldest historic district in Texas. It is a two-story house with Corinthian columns and verandas on the front and back. Decorated with Victorian antiques, it has private entrances and baths, central air and heat, and fans in all rooms. A full gourmet breakfast is served on the veranda or in the dining room.

Host: Frances Bochat
Rooms: 5 (PB) $90-115
Full Breakfast
Credit Cards: A, B, C, D
Notes: 2, 5, 7 (limited), 9, 12, 14

The Ogé House on the Riverwalk

209 Washington Street, 78204
(800) 242-2770; FAX (210) 226-5812

6 Pets welcome; 8 Children welcome; 9 Social drinking allowed; 10 Tennis available; 11 Swimming available; 12 Golf available; 13 Skiing available; 14 May be booked through travel agents.

Step back to an era of elegance and romance in this historic antebellum mansion shaded by massive pecans and oaks, on one and one-half landscaped acres along the banks of the famous San Antonio Riverwalk. The inn, beautifully decorated with antiques, has large verandas and a grand foyer. All rooms have either queen- or king-size beds, private baths, air conditioning, telephones, and TVs. Dining, entertainment, convention centers, trolley, and the Alamo are steps away.

Hosts: Patrick and Sharrie Magatagan
Rooms: 10 (PB) $125-195
Continental Breakfast
Credit Cards: A, B, C, D, E
Notes: 2, 5, 7 (limited), 9, 10, 12

Riverwalk Inn

329 Old Gailbeau Road, 78204
(210) 212-8300; (800) 254-4444
FAX (210) 289-9422

The Riverwalk Inn is comprised of five two-story log homes, circa 1840, that have been restored on the San Antonio Riverwalk and tastefully decorated in period antiques. Amenities include fireplaces, refrigerators, private baths, telephones, balconies, 80-foot porch, and conference area. Expanded Continental breakfasts and desserts served. Swimming nearby. Smoking permitted. No children.

Hosts: Johnny Halpenny; Jan and Tracy Hammer
Rooms: 11 (PB) $89-135
Continental Breakfast
Credit Cards: A, B, C, D
Notes: 2, 5, 8, 11, 14

San Antonio Yellow Rose

229 Madison, 78204
(210) 229-9903; (800) 950-9903

The 1879 home built by Charles Mueller, a German immigrant, is a brick Victorian with a mansard roof and large porches. The home has five bedrooms distinctively decorated with antiques, each with a private bathroom and television. A large living and dining room in 18th-century furnishings provide space to get comfortable. The bed and breakfast offers a full breakfast and off-street parking. In the King William historic district, just two blocks from the Riverwalk.

Hosts: Jennifer and Cliff Tice
Rooms: 5 (PB) $85-120
Full Breakfast
Credit Cards: A, B, C, D
Notes: 2, 5, 8, 9, 10, 12, 14

The Victorian Lady Inn

421 Howard Street, 78212
(210) 224-2524; (800) 879-7116

In a perfect area, this 1898 historic mansion carries guests back to all the splendor of the antebellum era. The spacious guest room offers antique furnishings, fireplaces, verandas, claw-foot tubs, and high-back beds. Delicious full breakfasts and afternoon teatime are served in the dining room. Just steps away are the Alamo, Riverwalk, Convention Center, and Ten Cent Trolley. Make a getaway special—experience true elegance at The Victorian Lady Inn.

Hosts: Joe and Kathleen Bowski
Rooms: 6 (PB) $65-140
Full Breakfast
Credit Cards: A, B, C, D
Notes: 2, 5, 8 (over 12), 9, 10, 11, 12, 14

SEABROOK

Bed and Breakfast Texas Style

4224 West Red Bird Lane, Dallas, 75237
(214) 298-8586

High Tide. Right on Galveston Bay at the channel where shrimp boats and ocean liners go in and out, this Cape Cod-style cottage is available for families or romantic getaways. It will sleep seven to nine people

---

NOTES: Credit cards accepted: A MasterCard; B Visa; C American Express; D Discover Card; E Diner's Club; F Other; 2 Personal checks accepted; 3 Lunch available; 4 Dinner available; 5 Open all year;

with two bedrooms downstairs, each with a private bath. A loft room upstairs with two double beds and a twin bed has a half-bath. A large deck with chairs is perfect for sunning and watching birds and boats. Continental breakfast. $65.

SEADRIFT

Hotel Lafitte

302 Bay Avenue, 77983
(512) 785-2319

A unique bed and breakfast on San Antonio Bay. Built in 1909 and fully restored in 1988. Furnished in antique Victorian style. In Seadrift, Texas, 30 miles south of Victoria on Highway 185.

Hosts: Frances and Weyman Harding
Rooms: 10 (4 PB; 6 SB) $60-115
Full Breakfast
Credit Cards: A, B, C
Notes: 2, 5, 7, 9, 11

SEGUIN

Bed and Breakfast Hosts of San Antonio and South Texas

1777 N.E. Loop 410, Suite 600, San Antonio, 78217
(210) 824-8036; (800) 356-1605 (reservations)
FAX (210) 271-9145

621. This historic Victorian home, built in the 1890s, has four bedrooms: Senator's Suite has a king-size brass bed, fireplace, screened sun porch, and private bath. Tanta Clara's Room has a white iron queen-size bed, fireplace, and a sunny and elegant shared bath. Kathinka's Quarters has a king-size bed and shared bath with antique footed tub. Ella's Chambers has mahogany twins, side yard, grape arbor, and private bath. Gourmet breakfast. Weekend and weekly rates available. $60-95.

SWEETWATER

Mulberry Manor

1400 Sam Houston, 79556
(915) 235-3811; (800) 235-3811

Come and be pampered in this beautifully restored 1913 mansion that was designed by John Young, father of actress Loretta Young. Large snack tray and beverage welcome guests upon arrival; they may be enjoyed in the atrium or in one of the large suites in front of a fireplace. Two of the baths feature oval and round 90-gallon marble tubs. Romantic candlelight dinners can be provided with special arrangement. Enjoy a delicious four-course breakfast served in the guest's room, or in one of the three dining rooms. Mulberry Manor is 250 miles west of Dallas and 400 miles east of El Paso on I-20.

Hosts: Raymond and Beverley Stone
Rooms: 4 (PB) $55-195
Full Breakfast
Credit Cards: A, B, C, D, E
Notes: 2, 3, 4, 5, 6, 8, 9, 10, 12, 14

TYLER

Bed and Breakfast Texas Style

4224 West Red Bird Lane, Dallas, 75237
(214) 298-8586

Vintage Farm Home. This newly renovated, circa 1836-1864 home, once an original dogtrot plantation home, sits in the piney woods of East Texas. Catch the morning sun or evening breeze on the large veranda where rocking chairs and a swing invite relaxation. Take a stroll through the trails during dogwood season or fall foliage. The guest room has a king-size bed and private bath. Breakfast is served downstairs in the cozy nook. $75-85.

6 Pets welcome; 8 Children welcome; 9 Social drinking allowed; 10 Tennis available; 11 Swimming available; 12 Golf available; 13 Skiing available; 14 May be booked through travel agents.

Mary's Attic
Bed and Breakfast

413 South College, 75702
(903) 592-5181; FAX (903) 592-3846

A two-bedroom, two-bath 1920 bungalow restored and furnished with English and American antiques on the brick streets in the historic part of Tyler. The Continental breakfast features homemade sweet rolls and breads. Refrigerator stocked with complimentary cold drinks, juice, and fresh fruit tray. No smoking. No pets. No children.

Rooms: 2 (PB) $75
Continental Breakfast
Credit Cards: A, B, D
Notes: 5, 9, 12

Rosevine Inn
Bed and Breakfast

415 South Vine, 75702
(903) 592-2221

Rosevine Inn is in the historic Brick Street Shoppes area of Tyler. There are several shops within walking distance and a lovely courtyard with fountain and fireplace. There is also an outdoor hot tub and game room complete with billiards for guests' enjoyment. A delectable breakfast awaits in the morning. The hosts welcome guests to Tyler, "Rose Capital of the World."

Hosts: Bert and Rebecca Powell
Rooms: 5 (PB) $65-75
Full Breakfast
Credit Cards: A, B, C, D, E
Notes: 2, 5, 8 (Call), 9, 10, 12, 14

The Woldert-Spence Manor

611 West Woldert Street, 75702
(903) 533-9057; (800) WOLDERT

This beautifully restored, two-story Queen Anne home is in the historic brick street district of Tyler. It has a historical designation, with roots that go back to the 1850s.

The original hardwood floors and stained-glass windows have been restored, and the home is decorated in antiques and collectibles. Rooms available with fireplace, private balcony or screened porch, and baths with restored claw-foot tubs. Covered spa available under the large shade trees in the rear garden, which also has a fish bowl with fountain and covered wishing well. An all-you-can-eat hearty breakfast is served on antique china with crystal in the formal dining room downstairs. A great place for that special getaway or for business. Walking distance to antique shops and minutes for Tyler Rose Garden, museums, lakes, and Caldwell Zoo. No pets. No minimum stay required.

Hosts: Richards and Patricia Heaton
Rooms: 5 (PB) $70-90
Full Breakfast
Credit Cards: A, B, C, D
Notes: 2, 5, 7 (limited), 8 (limited), 9, 10, 11, 12

UTOPIA

Bed and Breakfast Hosts of
San Antonio and South Texas

1777 N.E. Loop 410, Suite 600, San Antonio, 78217
(210) 824-8036; (800) 356-1605 (reservations)
FAX (210) 271-9145

622. This property on Indian Blanket Ranch is a bird watchers haven. Main house offers guest room with queen-size bed, access to the garden room with hot tub, and use of living room and fireplace. Second-floor suit sleeps five with a king-size bed, a sofa bed, and a single bed; kitchenette and deck. Also early Texas hideaway cabin with full kitchen and hot tub. $65-75.

Bed and Breakfast
Texas Style

4224 West Red Bird Lane, Dallas, 75237
(214) 298-8586

Bluebird Hill Ranch. A private cabin on a creek in a secluded corner of this 260-acre ranch home is now available for guests. Breakfast will be left in the refrigerator in the complete kitchen. The cabin will accommodate six people. Near Garner State Park and the Frio River, one hour to San Antonio. Two-night minimum stay. Smoking outside. $75.

Little Creek Lodge

P.O. Box 276, 78884
(210) 966-3765

A Hill Country hideaway that allows guests to leave the hustle and bustle of everyday life behind. Guests can relax on the 1,264 acres of peace and quiet. Enjoy an eight-bedroom, air-conditioned log lodge nestled atop a knoll overlooking a live creek. Bird watching and wildlife area on premises. Picnic, swimming, playground, and fishing are available. A weekend of fun and relaxation guests will not soon forget.

Hosts: Chris and Judy Ramsey
Rooms: 8 (PB) $65
Full Breakfast
Credit Cards: A, B
Notes: 2, 5, 7, 8, 9, 10, 11

VAN ALYSTYNE

Bed and Breakfast Texas Style

4224 West Red Bird Lane, Dallas, 75237
(214) 298-8586

The Durning House. Historic home that was an antique shop in the past and is now a bed and breakfast with two guest rooms. The owners welcome guests and then leave them with complete privacy. Breakfast is homemade cinnamon rolls, juice, and coffee. The room upstairs has a double bed and a small rocking cradle at the foot of the bed.

The downstairs room has an antique headboard almost to the ceiling and a double bed. One bath with claw-foot tub. Comfortable parlor and dining area downstairs. Hosts will only rent to one couple at a time unless they are a family or two couples traveling together so the bath can be private. $60-80.

VICTORIA

Friendly Oaks Bed and Breakfast

210 East Juan Linn Street, 77901
(512) 575-0000

In the shelter of ancient live oaks, history comes alive at the Friendly Oaks Bed and Breakfast in a preservation area of 80 restored Victorian homes. Each of the four rentable rooms has a private bath, its own brand of individualized decor, and reflects the preservation efforts of Victoria, Texas. The scrumptious gourmet breakfasts feature local produce. Whether guests are looking for a getaway weekend, a calm retreat for off-duty interim business time, or a honeymoon suite, the Friendly Oaks Bed and Breakfast can fill their hospitality needs. In addition, a conference room provides a quiet setting for retreats, meetings, seminars, parties, showers, and small weddings.

Hosts: Bill and Cee Bee McLeod
Rooms: 4 (PB) $65-85
Full Breakfast
Credit Cards: A, B
Notes: 2, 5, 8 (over ten), 10, 11, 12

VIDOR

Bed and Breakfast Texas Style

4224 West Red Bird Lane, Dallas, 75237
(214) 298-8586

6 Pets welcome; 8 Children welcome; 9 Social drinking allowed; 10 Tennis available; 11 Swimming available; 12 Golf available; 13 Skiing available; 14 May be booked through travel agents.

Poppa Bear's House. A warm and loving home near the Louisiana border and Beaumont. Teddy bears are displayed throughout the home. There is a pool for summer fun, fireplace for cozy visiting in winter. Breakfast will be Czech kolaches, homemade cinnamon rolls, juice or fruit, and coffee or tea. Visit the downs in Louisiana or the beach just south of Beaumont. Two rooms have queen-size beds, one with private bath. There is one room with a double. No smoking. Children welcome. $55.

WACO

Thornton's Bed and Breakfast

908 Speight, 76706
(817) 756-0273

Beautiful Texas Hill Country art and English antiques give this 1920s home a distinctive look. One block from Baylor University, this unique bed and breakfast features comfortable bedrooms, all with private baths. The fireplace makes the living room a delightful place to enjoy one of the many good books or periodicals from the library. Afternoon tea is served to arriving guests. A full breakfast is served each morning. Special dietary needs are considered.

Hosts: Davis and Jenifer Thornton
Rooms: 5 (PB) $75-95
Full Breakfast
Credit Cards: None
Notes: 2, 5, 12, 13 (water), 14

WAXAHACHIE

Bed and Breakfast Texas Style

4224 West Red Bird Lane, Dallas, 75237
(214) 298-8586

Millie's Victorian. This beautiful Queen Anne-style mansion filled with antiques has a guest bedroom downstairs with private entrance and private bath with a claw-foot tub. Enjoy a full breakfast in the dining room. Another guest area is a private gingerbread cottage behind the main home. Breakfast will be left in the kitchen of the private cottage. Nonsmokers. $75-150.

BonnyNook Inn

414 West Main, 75165
(214) 938-7207; (800) 486-5936

This bed and breakfast is in the historic district of the picturesque town of Waxahachie. There are four bedrooms upstairs with private baths. All rooms have antique double beds. One room has a lovely sleigh bed set. Jacuzzis available in two rooms. A Pennsylvania Dutch breakfast including shoofly pie and crepes will be served in the formal dining room. Lunch and dinner are available at an extra charge. Scarborough Fair is popular in the spring.

Hosts: Bonnie and Vaughn Franks
Rooms: 4 (PB) $70-95
Full Breakfast
Credit Cards: A, B, C, D, E
Notes: 2, 5, 8, 9, 12, 14

WIMBERLEY

Bed and Breakfast Hosts of San Antonio and South Texas

1777 N.E. Loop 410, Suite 600, San Antonio, 78217
(210) 824-8036; (800) 356-1605 (reservations)
FAX (210) 271-9145

623. An early Texas hillside retreat with all modern conveniences. Porches with rocking chairs, fireplaces in common room with books and games for relaxation. Two bedrooms: Zephyr with queen-size bed and twin trundle; Cat's Paw with queen-size bed. Upstairs suite, Spirit Wind, has fireplace, king-size bed, and sleeper-sofa. All have private bathrooms. Hot tub available. $70-80.

Bed and Breakfast of Wimberley

P.O. Box 589, 78676
(512) 847-9666; (512) 847-2837

Coleman Canyon Ranch. Relax on the front porch swing or hike over this Hill Country ranch, find fossils in the creek bed, or watch deer from the rear deck. Two bedrooms, two baths, living room, dining room, kitchen, and library. Four miles north of Wimberley Square. Full breakfast included. Two-night minimum stay holiday and Market Day weekends. Smoking outdoors only. No pets. Special dietary requirements can be met with advance notice. $100.

Dancing Water Inn. Step into a magical, relaxing environment of lush, green meadows painted with wildflowers. Experience the pure blue waters of Jacob's Well. Two native stone homes have been transformed to offer primitive folk art, handcrafted furniture, and exquisite textiles. Four private bedrooms, four fireplaces, four baths, conference room, hot tub, and massage therapy by appointment. A full kitchen provides a bountiful breakfast. Gourmet candlelight dinner by reservation. Swimming, hiking, biking, tennis, golf, sailing, water skiing, and horseback riding nearby. $65. Group rates available.

Delafield's Delight. This one-bedroom home in Eagle Rock has a large bedroom with a double bed and a trundle bed that sleeps two. Private bath and full kitchen. Relax in front of the wood-burning fireplace. Swimming, paddle boats, horseback riding, fishing, and golf are available nearby. Cook out on an old stone fireplace. $65.

The Homestead Bed and Breakfast. The Homestead guest cottages are on Cypress Creek, which is six miles long and fed from Jacob's Well. An abundance of wildlife lives in the area. The cottages can accommodate up to eight adults and are complete with full kitchens, telephone, cable, fireplace, microwave, air-conditioning, heat, and reading material. Continental breakfast is provided. From $75.

J. R. Dobie House. This restored, historic cottage is furnished with comfortable antiques: 1890s charm combined with 1990s comfort. Enjoy the wood-burning fireplace with the wood provided by the hosts. Cable TV, telephone, full kitchen, private bath, central air and heat, and picnic facilities are provided. $85.

Mountaintop Villa. Hilltop home with breathtaking views, indoor swimming pool, 225-square feet of decks on seven and one-half acres of beautiful Texas Hill Country. The house has more than 3,000-square feet and can sleep six people. $125 nightly Sunday through Thursday; $150 nightly Friday and Saturday; $800 weekly.

Singing Cypress Gardens Bed and Breakfast. This private estate is at the end of Mill Race Lane on Cypress Creek among trees and 600 feet of rolling creek property. Guests enjoy hand-laid rock steps into the creek and the picnic area. Visitors will also

6 Pets welcome; 8 Children welcome; 9 Social drinking allowed; 10 Tennis available; 11 Swimming available; 12 Golf available; 13 Skiing available; 14 May be booked through travel agents.

enjoy the view of 2,000-year-old cypress trees with beautiful Blue Hole Dam and waterfall just off to the left. Linens and kitchen items provided. Continental breakfast and wine are provided in the evening so guests won't be disturbed in the morning. Seven guest rooms, some with child and pet restrictions. $65-150.

Wide Horizon. On Ranch Road 12, south of the Blanco River, this bilevel home offers two very private accommodations, each with private entrance and private bath. The Southwest Suite has a wet bar, color TV, and king-size bed. The Antique Suite has a private sitting room with a Hide-a-bed and a large bedroom with antique double beds. Relax on the large deck that spans the width of the house. No smokers or pets. $90.

Blair House

1 Spoke Hill, Route 1, Box 122, 78676
(512) 847-8828

The Blair House, created to provide guests the ultimate inn experience, is nestled on 85 acres of beautiful Texas Hill Country, 45 minutes from Austin and San Antonio. Six rooms with private baths and Jacuzzi tubs are gracefully decorated to provide guests every comfort. Each room has a CD player, fresh flowers, and chocolates. The library has CDs, books, periodicals, TV, and movies. Three dining rooms, a large living room with fireplace, sauna, massage room, rocking chairs, hammocks, and swings await guests. Fine cuisine; all breads, pastries, and desserts are made in the kitchen daily. Full gourmet breakfasts with fresh ground French roast coffee starts the day; it ends with irresistible desserts. Saturday evening dining is unforgettable. Special

events, weddings, seminars, and business retreats are tailored to fit guests needs.

Host: Jonnie Stansbury
Rooms: 6 (PB) $100-125
Full Breakfast
Credit Cards: A, B, D
Notes: 2, 3, 4, 5, 9, 10, 11, 12, 14

Old Oaks Ranch

Old Oaks Ranch Bed and Breakfast

P.O. Box 912, 78676
(512) 847-9374

This bed and breakfast offers the warmth of the Texas Hill Country. There are three unique cottages here: the Chicken House, one bedroom with queen-size bed; the Storehouse, two bedrooms with king-size and two double beds, fireplace; and the Barn, with a queen-size bed and sitting room with fireplace. Furnished with comfortable antiques and bent willow, Old Oaks is the perfect escape from the hectic pace of the city.

Hosts: Susan and Bill Holt
Rooms: 4 (2 PB; 2 SB) $65-85
Full Breakfast
Credit Cards: A, B
Notes: 2, 5, 9, 10, 12, 14

NOTES: Credit cards accepted: A MasterCard; B Visa; C American Express; D Discover Card; E Diner's Club; F Other; 2 Personal checks accepted; 3 Lunch available; 4 Dinner available; 5 Open all year;

WINNSBORO _____

Thee Hubbell House

307 West Elm Street, 75494
(903) 342-5629

Thee Hubbell House bed and breakfast is in beautiful northeast Texas just 90 miles east of Dallas on a two-acre landscaped estate. A 105-year-old Colonial two-story with twelve bedrooms and suites, all with private baths. Common areas include a Jacuzzi and candlelight dining by reservation, two verandas, gallery, patio, parlor, garden room, and three dining rooms. Accessible to ten lakes, seven golf courses, more than 100 antique/arts and crafts shops. Southern hospitality at its best.

Hosts: Dan and Laurel Hubbell
Rooms: 12 (PB) $75-175
Full and Continental Breakfasts
Credit Cards: A, B, C, D, E, F
Notes: 2, 4, 5, 9, 10, 11, 12, 14

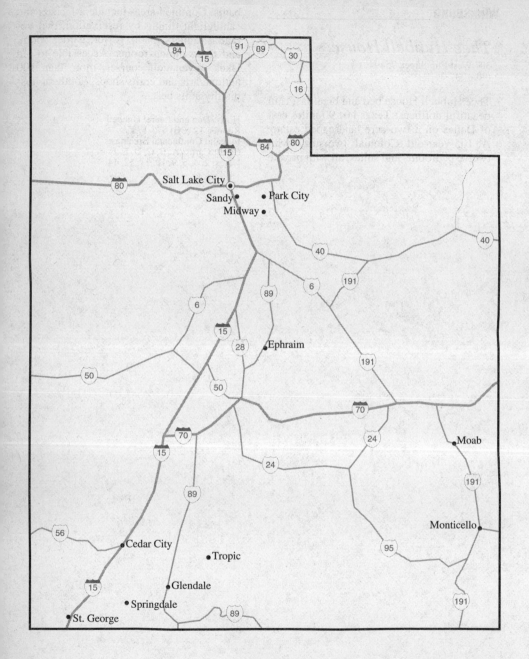

Utah

Utah

CEDAR CITY

Bed and Breakfast Rocky Mountains

906 South Pearl Street, Denver, CO 80209
(303) 744-8415; (800) 733-8415

The Paxman Summer House. A turn-of-the-century Victorian on a quiet street two blocks from the Shakespeare Festival. Tastefully decorated with antiques, it is a short drive to Cedar Mountain, Brian Head Ski Resort, Zion National Park, and Bryce Canyon National Park. Local golf course, pool, and tennis courts are nearby. The four rooms all have private baths. Smoking permitted outside.

EPHRAIM

Ephraim Homestead Bed and Breakfast

135 West 100 North (43-2), 84627
(801) 283-6367

Ephraim Homestead offers lodging in a pioneer log cabin or a rustic bar. The hosts' Victorian cottage is also occasionally available. All are furnished with antiques and surrounded by old-fashioned gardens under a canopy of trees. Breakfast is cooked on a century-old Monarch stove and served privately to guests in the cabin; others are served in the hosts' dining room or outdoors. A delicious nighttime treat is also provided. Truly a unique and memorable experience.

Hosts: Sherron and McKay Andreasen
Log Cabin: 1 (PB) $75
Barn: 2 (SB) $45-55
Full Breakfast
Credit Cards: None
Notes: 2, 5, 8, 10, 11, 12, 13 (cross-country)

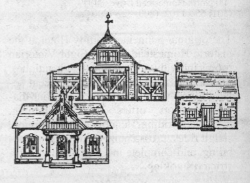

Ephraim Homestead

GLENDALE

Smith Hotel

Highway 89, P.O. Box 106, 84729
(801) 648-2156

This historic hotel/boarding house was built in 1927 by Mormon settlers. Enjoy western charm; screened porch overlooking the hills of southern Utah's beautiful Long Valley. Close to the scenic wonders of Zion, Bryce, and Grand Canyon national parks and the recreational facilities of Lake Powell. All rooms have private baths. Late 1800s private family cemetery on property. Continental plus breakfast served in family

NOTES: Credit cards accepted: A MasterCard; B Visa; C American Express; D Discover Card; E Diner's Club; F Other; 2 Personal checks accepted; 3 Lunch available; 4 Dinner available; 5 Open all year; 6 Pets welcome; 7 Smoking allowed; 8 Children welcome; 9 Social drinking allowed; 10 Tennis available; 11 Swimming available; 12 Golf available; 13 Skiing available; 14 May be booked through travel agents.

dining room. Meet other guests from all over the world. Hotel is nonsmoking.

Host: Shirley Phelan
Rooms: 7 (PB) $40-60
Continental Breakfast
Credit Cards: A, B
Notes: 9, 12

MIDWAY

Schneitter Family Hotel at the Homestead Resort

700 North Homestead Drive, 84049
(801) 654-1102; (800) 327-7220

The original Schneitter Family Hotel at the historic Homestead Resort. Eight Victorian rooms individually appointed with antiques, linens, and special amenities. Adjacent solarium and whirlpool. This AAA four-diamond resort offers golf, swimming, horseback riding, tennis, elegant dining, sleigh rides, cross-country skiing, snowmobiling, and complete meeting facilities. Restricted smoking.

Host: Britt Mathwich
Rooms: 8 (PB) $89-105
Continental Breakfast
Credit Cards: A, B, C, D, E
Notes: 2, 3, 4, 5, 8, 9, 10, 11, 12, 13, 14

MOAB

Castle Valley Inn

CVSR Box 2602, 424 Amber Lane, 84532
(801) 259-6012

Castle Valley Inn offers guests sophisticated comfort in the rugged canyonlands of southeast Utah. Its 11 acres of orchards, lawns, and fields feature 360-degree red-rock-to-mountaintop views. Visitors enjoy the outdoor Grandview hot tub. The inn offers full meal service to registered guests, with a complete gourmet breakfast included in room rates. No TV; VCRs and film library available. Close to Arches and

Canyonlands national parks. Five minutes to Colorado River Canyon.

Hosts: Eric and Lynn Thomson
Rooms: 8 (PB) $65-110
Full Breakfast
Credit Cards: A, B
Notes: 2, 3, 4, 5, 12, 14

Mi Casa Su Casa Bed and Breakfast

P.O. Box 950, Tempe, AZ 85281
(602) 990-0682

1101. The casual atmosphere of a ranch-style home nestled between the snow-capped La Sal Mountains and the red-rock canyons of the Colorado River. Mountain biking, whitewater challenging, and downhill or cross-country skiing are nearby. This home is a perfect place to relax at the end of the day. Four rooms with queen-size beds have private baths. One room with twin beds shares a bath. Hot tub. Maximum 14 guests. Full breakfast. Resident cats. No smoking. Children six and older are welcome. Roll away beds are available. $59-87.

MONTICELLO

The Grist Mill Inn

64 South 300 East; P.O. Box 156, 84535
(801) 587-2597; (800) 645-3762

Beautiful suites each with private bath and television. Enjoy a library with a view of the Blue Mountains for a quiet moment. Rise each morning to a full breakfast surrounded by original mill equipment and antiques. The Grist Mill is a nonsmoking establishment. Well-behaved children are welcome. Ask about the newest suite—The Caboose. It has the charms of a time past, with modern day luxury.

Hosts: Rye and Deanne Nellson
Rooms: 10 (PB) $56
Full Breakfast
Credit Cards: A, B, C, D, E
Notes: 2, 5, 8, 10, 11, 12, 13

NOTES: Credit cards accepted: A MasterCard; B Visa; C American Express; D Discover Card; E Diner's Club; F Other; 2 Personal checks accepted; 3 Lunch available; 4 Dinner available; 5 Open all year;

PARK CITY

Bed and Breakfast Rocky Mountains

906 South Pearl Street, Denver, CO 80209
(303) 744-8415; (800) 733-8415

Snowed Inn. Beautiful surroundings, comfort, and Victorian elegance describe this ten-room country inn situated outside of Park City. Each room offers a private bath with a soaking tub, as well as color TV. This is an excellent location for family reunions, weddings, receptions, and business functions. Continental breakfast. No pets. Moderate-luxury rates.

The Blue Church Lodge

424 Park Avenue, P.O. Box 1720, 84060
(801) 649-8009; (800) 626-5467;
FAX (801) 649-0686

Listed on both the Utah and National registers of Historic Places, the church was originally built in 1897. It was structurally rebuilt and remodeled in 1983, then redecorated in 1994. A unique Victorian era church on the outside, inside the lodge houses seven charmingly quaint and cozy, distinctively different, condominiums, ranging from a room with private bath up to a four-bedroom suite. Amenities include indoor spa, gameroom, laundry, private phones, color cable TV, private parking, ski lockers, maid service, gas burning fireplaces and continental breakfast. Children welcome. No smoking.

Host: Nancy Schmidt
Rooms: 7 (PB) $90-275
Continental Breakfast
Credit Cards: A, B
Notes: 2, 8, 9, 13, 14

The Old Miners' Lodge

615 Woodside Avenue, Box 2639, 84060
(801) 645-8068; (800) 648-8068
FAX (801) 645-7420

A restored 1889 miners' boarding house in the national historic district of Park City, within ten individually decorated rooms filled with antiques and older pieces. Close to historic Main Street, with the Park City ski area in its back yard, the lodge is "more like staying with friends than at a hotel!" A nonsmoking inn. Minimum-stay requirements Christmas and some special events.

Hosts: Hugh Daniels and Susan Wynne
Rooms: 10 (PB) $50-195
Full Breakfast
Credit Cards: A, B, C, D
Notes: 2, 5, 8, 9, 10, 11, 12, 13, 14

Old Town Guest House

Old Town Guest House

1011 Empire Avenue, Box 162, 84060
(801) 649-2642

This beautiful home on the historic register is the perfect place for active skiers, hikers, and bikers. Guests may enjoy all the conveniences of Park City, such as the state's largest ski area and the well preserved Main Street with all its shops and restaurants. This small charming inn has four rooms, each furnished with lodgepole-pine furnishings. A hearty mountain breakfast is served each morning.

Hosts: Debbie Lovci and John Hughes
Rooms: 4 (2 PB; 2 SB) $50-175
Full Breakfast
Credit Cards: None
Notes: 2, 3, 4, 5, 6, 8, 9, 12, 13, 14

6 Pets welcome; 8 Children welcome; 9 Social drinking allowed; 10 Tennis available; 11 Swimming available; 12 Golf available; 13 Skiing available; 14 May be booked through travel agents.

Washington School Inn

P.O. Box 536, 84060
(801) 649-3800; (800) 824-1672

Historic restoration of an old schoolhouse, decorated with modified Victorian furnishings. Hot tub and sauna on the property. Full breakfast and afternoon tea service included in rates. In downtown historic Park City, close to Salt Lake area airport (45 minutes) and some of the best skiing in the world.

Hosts: Nancy Beaufait and Delphine Covington
Rooms: 15 (PB) $75-225
Full Breakfast
Credit Cards: A, B, C, D, F
Notes: 5, 9, 10, 11, 12, 13, 14

SAINT GEORGE

Aunt Annie's Inn

139 North 100 West, 84770
(801) 673-5504; (800) 257-5504 (UT)

Aunt Annie's Inn is established in a quaint two-story 1890s adobe home nestled in the heart of historic St. George. It has a spacious parlor and dining area available to guests. The guest rooms are decorated with colorful wallpaper, antique furniture, and homemade quilts. Each room has a private bath, most of which have unique old-fashioned fixtures. Many shops and restaurants are within walking distance of the inn. National parks, golf, and skiing are only a few miles away.

Hosts: Bob and Claudia Tribe
Rooms: 5 (PB) $45-75
Full Breakfast
Credit Cards: A, B, C
Notes: 2, 5, 8, 10, 11, 12, 13, 14

Greene Gate Village

76 West Tabernacle Street, 84770
(801) 628-6999; (800) 350-6999

Step back in time behind the green gates, where nine beautifully restored homes provide modern comfort in pioneer elegance. Guests love the nostalgic charm of the Bentley House and its elegant Victorian

decor, or the quaint Trolley House. The Grainery sleeps three, in rooms where early settlers loaded supplies for their trek to California. The Orson Pratt home, built by another early Mormon leader, is on the National Register of Historic Places. Green Hedge, with one of the village's two bridal suites, was originally built in another part of town but was moved to Greene Gate Village in 1991. The Greenehouse, built in 1872, has all the modern conveniences of a full kitchen, swimming pool and tennis court (breakfast not included).

Hosts: John and Barbara Greene
Rooms: 18 (PB) $50-110
Full Breakfast
Credit Cards: A, B, C
Notes: 2, 4, 5, 8, 10, 11, 12, 13, 14

Penny Farthing Inn Bed and Breakfast

278 North 100 West, 84770
(801) 673-7755

Built in the 1870s, this traditional pioneer Victorian was built with 12-inch adobe handmade brick and a lava foundation. In the historical district on a quiet residential street. Five theme-decorated rooms done in antiques, collectibles, and handmade quilts. Honeymoon suite with queen-size brass bed done in whites, mauve, and lace, pull-chain water closet, and whirlpool. The Sir Winston, has the typical English motif, pull-chain water closet, and claw-foot tub. The Betsy Ross' decor is in Americana motif with complete bath. The Sego Lily has pioneer style and complete bath. The Morning Dove has a Southwest theme. Disabled accessible.

Hosts: Alan and Jacquie Capon, and the "Madam"
Rooms: 5 (PB) $55-110
Full Breakfast
Credit Cards: A, B
Notes: 2, 5, 8, 10, 11, 12, 13

Seven Wives Inn

217 North 100 West, 84770
(801) 628-3737; (800) 600-3737

NOTES: Credit cards accepted: A MasterCard; B Visa; C American Express; D Discover Card; E Diner's Club; F Other; 2 Personal checks accepted; 3 Lunch available; 4 Dinner available; 5 Open all year;

The inn consists of two adjacent pioneer adobe homes with massive hand-grained moldings, framing windows, and doors. Bedrooms are furnished with period antiques and handmade quilts. Some rooms have fireplaces; two have whirlpool tubs. Swimming pool on premises.

Hosts: Donna and Jay Curtis; Alison and Jon Bowcutt
Rooms: 12 (PB) $65-125
Full Breakfast
Credit Cards: A, B, C, D, E
Notes: 2, 5, 8, 9, 10, 11, 12, 14

Seven Wives Inn

SALT LAKE CITY

The Anton Boxrud Bed and Breakfast

57 South 600 East, 84102
(801) 363-8035; (800) 524-5511
FAX (801) 596-1316

The Anton Boxrud Bed and Breakfast is a charming, restored Victorian inn in a historic district of Salt Lake City and just one-half block from the governor's mansion. A hearty breakfast, and guests are on their way to Utah's many cultural events and world-renowned outdoor activities. During summer months the hosts welcome guests to join them on the veranda for great evening conversation.

Hosts: Mark A. Brown and Keith Lewis
Rooms: 6 (3 PB; 3 SB) $55-119
Full Breakfast
Credit Cards: A, B, C
Notes: 2, 5, 8, 9, 10, 11, 12, 13, 14

Bed and Breakfast Rocky Mountains

906 South Pearl Street, Denver, CO 80209
(303) 744-8415; (800) 733-8415

The National Historic Bed and Breakfast. This lovely 100-year-old home is one of the few original Perkins edition structures in the area. Only a 25-minute drive from some of the most beautiful canyons in the Wasatch Range. There are many state parks with well-maintained hiking trails close by, not to mention great skiing. Full gourmet breakfast. No smoking. Moderate-luxury rates.

Peery Hotel. Relax and enjoy this hotel in downtown Salt Lake City. The Peery offers a unique blend of elegance and the architectural atmosphere of a bygone era. Within walking distance of the Mormon Temple, seven theaters, 25 restaurants, clubs, and taverns. No pets. Continental plus breakfast. Moderate-luxury, seasonal rates.

Saltair Bed and Breakfast. Sunny, cozy, and restful! Guests will feel right at home in the warmth of this historic five-bedroom manor house. The handsome antiques, fine woodwork, and unique light fixtures give a turn-of-the-century appeal. Large cut-glass windows let in sunlight from the east and west, keeping the parlor and rooms bright all day. Brass and oak beds covered with Amish quilts add to restful nights. Full breakfast. No smoking. No pets. Well-mannered children only. Moderate rates.

Brigham Street Inn

1135 East South Temple, 84102
(801) 364-4461; FAX (801) 521-3201

Brigham Street Inn is a Victorian mansion built in 1896, done in both traditional and contemporary design. Minutes away from

Brigham Street Inn

Temple Square, downtown, and the University of Utah. Also minutes away from all outdoor activities: hiking, skiing, tennis, and golf.

Host: Nancy Pace
Rooms: 9 (PB) $75-175
Continental Breakfast
Credit Cards: A, B, C, D, E
Notes: 2, 5, 7, 9, 10, 11, 12, 13, 14

Mi Casa Su Casa Bed and Breakfast

P.O. Box 950, Tempe, AZ 85281
(602) 990-0682

1095. The Salt Lake City Historic Society has recognized this two-and-one-half-story brick house as one of Salt Lake's "Grand Old Homes." The beveled-glass windows and beautiful woodwork have been carefully restored according to the original 1901 plans. Rooms are furnished with antiques, including a hand-carved German dining table where a full breakfast is served. Close to the governor's mansion, downtown, University of Utah, and Temple Square. Five guest rooms on the second floor have queen-size or double beds, private and shared baths. Hot tub. Smoking allowed outside. Full breakfast. $45-109.

Saltair Bed and Breakfast

164 South 900 East, 84102
(801) 533-8184; (800) 733-8184

Antiques and charm complement queen-size brass beds, Amish quilts, and period lamps. A full breakfast featuring house juice and wake up favorites such as pumpkin/walnut waffles and saltair muffins greet each guest. Hospitality offered by innkeepers includes snacks, and use of parlor, dining room, TV and phone rooms. Close to the University of Utah, historic downtown, skiing, canyons, and seasonal recreation.

Hosts: Jan Bartlett and Nancy Saxton
Rooms: 7 (4 PB; 3 SB) $55-139
Full Breakfast
Credit Cards: A, B, C, E
Notes: 2, 5, 8, 9, 10, 11, 12, 13, 14

Wildflowers, A Bed and Breakfast

936 East, 1700 South, 84105
(801) 466-0600

Wildflowers is an 1891 Victorian home surrounded by quaking aspen, blue spruce and an abundance of wildflowers. Listed on the National Register of Historic Places, it sits amid homes of old Salt Lake. Five minutes from downtown, and 30 minutes from skiing (seven areas to choose from). In their careful restoration, the owners have kept the delights of the past and added the comforts of the present, including air conditioning. Hand-carved staircases, stained glass windows, claw-foot bathtubs, original chandeliers, Oriental rugs, antiques, private baths, a deck and a reading room make up the present Wildflowers. Guests will be warmly welcomed by owners and hosts who will serve a gourmet breakfast. Suite available with balcony and view of mountains.

Hosts: Cill Sparks and Jeri Parker
Rooms: 4 (PB) $60-125
Full Breakfast
Credit Cards: A, B
Notes: 2, 5, 8, 9, 10, 11, 12, 13, 14

NOTES: Credit cards accepted: A MasterCard; B Visa; C American Express; D Discover Card; E Diner's Club; F Other; 2 Personal checks accepted; 3 Lunch available; 4 Dinner available; 5 Open all year;

SANDY/SALT LAKE CITY

Mountain Hollow Inn Bed and Breakfast

10209 South Dimple Dell Road, 84092
(801) 942-3428

Mountain Hollow is nestled at the base of Little Cottonwood Canyon, close to major ski resorts, mountain biking areas, and the metropolitan night life of Salt Lake City. Twenty-five miles from Salt Lake International Airport. On a two-acre estate with trees, a creek, and a restful atmosphere. Each guest room is decorated with antique Victorian or country furniture. Complimentary beverages and treats available all the time. Come to relax and unwind in this country atmosphere.

Hosts: Doug and Kathy Larson
Rooms: 10 (1 PB; 9 SB) $62-150
Continental Breakfast
Credit Cards: A, B, C, D
Notes: 2, 5, 10, 11, 12, 13, 14

Mountain Hollow Inn

SPRINGDALE

Mi Casa Su Casa Bed and Breakfast

P.O. Box 950, Tempe, AZ 85281
(602) 990-0682

1098. Built in 1988 in a contemporary pioneer ranch style, this two-story inn is on a quiet dead-end street less than one mile from the south entrance to Zion National Park. Comfortable, clean, and bright with a contemporary interior, original artwork, and collectibles. One room is on the first floor with queen-size bed and private bath. Three rooms on the second floor all have queen-size beds and private baths. Children are welcome by prior arrangement. No smoking. Complimentary beverages. Breakfast is a culinary event! Hot tub. Visa and MasterCard are accepted. $70-85.

TROPIC

Mi Casa Su Casa Bed and Breakfast

P.O. Box 950, Tempe, AZ 85281
(602) 990-0682

1099. In tiny picturesque Tropic, this bed and breakfast is within walking distance of Bryce Canyon National Park's western boundary. The house was built in the early 1930s and a two-story addition was built in 1990. Come and go without entering the common rooms, or guests are welcome to share the living room with other guests. There are wraparound decks with spectacular views where guests can watch the sunset play upon the hoodoos of Bryce Canyon, as they turn from orange to pink to lavender. Five spacious guest rooms, each with queen-size bed, private bath, and picture windows. Children are welcome. Full breakfast. No smoking. $10 for additional person in room. $60-65.

1105. This bed and breakfast is a modern log home with flower gardens on a ten-acre working farm which produces grain and hay. The host couple is knowledgeable about area activities and sights. The three rooms all have private baths. Room one is on the first floor. Room two has a queen-size and a double bed, and TV. Room three has a queen-size bed and TV. Children are welcome. Full breakfast. Smoking allowed outside. Roll away beds available. Handicapped possible. $65.

6 Pets welcome; 8 Children welcome; 9 Social drinking allowed; 10 Tennis available; 11 Swimming available; 12 Golf available; 13 Skiing available; 14 May be booked through travel agents.

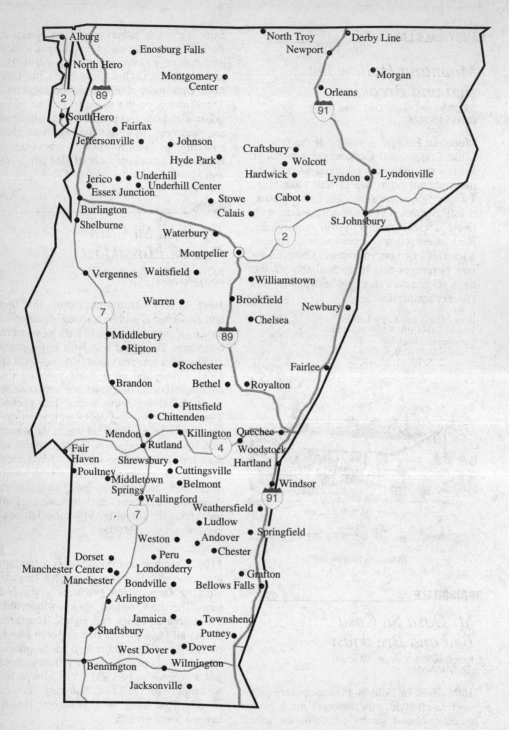

Alburg
Enosburg Falls
North Hero
Montgomery
Center
2   89
SouthHero
Fairfax
Jeffersonville
Johnson
Craftsbury
Hyde Park   Wolcott
Jerico   Underhill   Hardwick   Lyndon   Lyndonville
Essex Junction   Underhill Center
Stowe   Cabot
Burlington   Calais   St.Johnsbury
Shelburne
Waterbury   2
Montpelier
Vergennes   Waitsfield
Williamstown
Warren   Brookfield
Chelsea   Newbury
7
89
Middlebury
Ripton
Rochester   Fairlee
Brandon   Bethel   Royalton
Pittsfield
Chittenden
Mendon   Killington   Quechee
Fair   Rutland   4   Woodstock
Haven   Shrewsbury   Hartland
Poultney
Middletown   Cuttingsville
Springs   Belmont   Windsor
Wallingford   91
Weathersfield
7   Ludlow
Weston   Andover   Springfield
Chester
Dorset   Peru
Manchester Center   Londonderry
Manchester   Bondville   Grafton
Arlington   Bellows Falls
Jamaica   Townshend
Shaftsbury   Putney
West Dover   Dover
Bennington   Wilmington
Jacksonville

North Troy   Derby Line
Newport
Morgan
Orleans
91

Vermont

Vermont

ALBURG

Auberge Alburg

Rural Delivery 1, Box 3
South Main Street, 05440
(802) 796-3169

The Auberge—meaning *inn* in French—is a cozy, cosmopolitan, and multilingual bed and breakfast overlooking Lake Champlain. The ambience includes music, books, good conversation, espresso on the porch, and fresh-baked croissants for breakfast. There are guest rooms in both the main house and the renovated barn, which also has dormitory space for bikers and others. On the Vermont/New York/Quebec border, one hour from Montreal. Swimming and golf nearby. Pets welcome. Children welcome. No smoking.

Hosts: Gabrielle Tyrnauer and Charles Stastny
Rooms: 5 (1 PB; 4 SB) $50-75
Continental Breakfast
Credit Cards: None
Notes: 2, 3, 4, 6, 8, 9, 11, 12

Thomas Mott Bed and Breakfast

Blue Rock Road, Route 2, Box 149B, 05440-9620
(802) 796-3736; (800) 348-0843 (out of state)

Open all year and hosted by Patrick J. Schallert Sr., this completely restored 1838 farmhouse offers five rooms, all with private baths, which overlook Lake Champlain. A full view of the Green Mountains can be enjoyed from this beautifully restored bed and breakfast, and it is less than one hour to Burlington or the Islands of

Thomas Mott Bed and Breakfast

Montreal. Lake activities for all seasons; Sno-Springers and Vast; game room with bumper pool and darts. Approved AAA, ABBA, *Yankee* magazine, Mobil, and the National Bed and Breakfast Association. Complimentary Ben & Jerry's ice cream. Lawn games and rest and relaxation. Gourmet dinners with advance notice. Access Prodigy for more information.

Host: Patrick J. Schallert Sr.
Rooms: 5 (PB) $55-70
Full Breakfast
Credit Cards: A, B, D
Notes: 2, 4, 5, 8 (over 6), 9, 10, 11, 12, 13, 14

ANDOVER

Inn at HighView

Rural Route 1, Box 201A, 05143
(802) 875-2724

Vermont the way guests always dreamed it would be, but the way they've never found it. Secluded and relaxed elegance; breathtaking views of countryside from overlook gazebo and screened porch. Classically restored 18th-century farmhouse comfortably furnished. Warm conversation by a blazing fire, hearty breakfasts, and gourmet dinners.

All rooms with private baths. Cross-country skiing/hiking trails on 72 acres. Rock garden, swimming pool, and sauna. Ten minutes from Okemo Mountain, Weston, and Chester. Conference facilities and planning services available. Golf and tennis nearby.

Hosts: Greg Bohan and Sal Massaro
Rooms: 8 (PB) $80-125
Full Breakfast
Credit Cards: A, B
Notes: 2, 3, 4, 5, 6 (limited), 8, 9, 10, 11, 12, 13, 14

ARLINGTON

The Arlington Inn

Historic Route 7A, 05250
(800) 443-9442

A stately Greek Revival mansion set on lushly landscaped lawns offers elegantly appointed rooms filled with antiques and amenities. All rooms have private baths, air conditioning, and include breakfast. Between Bennington and Manchester. Antique shops, boutiques, museums, skiing, hiking, biking, canoeing, fly fishing, golfing, and many other outdoor activities are nearby. Tennis on the private court. Outstanding cuisine is served by romantic candlelight in the fireplaced, award-winning dining room with superb service. No smoking. AAA three-diamond rating, and Mobil three-stars rating.

Hosts: Deborah and Mark Gagnon
Rooms: 13 (PB) $65-175
Full Breakfast
Credit Cards: A, B, C, D, E
Notes: 4, 5, 8, 9, 10, 11, 12, 13, 14

The Evergreen Inn

Sandgate Road, Box 2480, 05250
(802) 375-2272

Country inn, family owned and operated since 1934. In a beautiful mountain valley by a stream. Friendly informal atmosphere. Home cooking and baking. Close to art centers, concerts, summer theaters, antiques, auctions, fairs, golf courses, and

The Evergreen Inn

discount stores. Hiking, cycling, canoeing, and swimming. Lunch available in July and August. Closed October 30 to May 1. Send for brochure.

Hosts: Mathilda and Kathleen Kenny
Rooms: 19 (PB and SB) $50-70
Full Breakfast
Credit Cards: None
Notes: 2, 3, 4, 6, 8, 9, 10, 11, 12

Hill Farm Inn

Rural Route 2, Box 2015, 05250
(802) 375-2269; (800) 882-2545

Visit one of Vermont's original farmsteads that has been an inn since 1905. Stay in a 1790 or 1830 farmhouse and enjoy hearty home cooking and mountain views. Nestled at the foot of Mount Equinox and surrounded by 50 acres of farmland with the Battenkill River bordering the lower pasture. Two-day minimum stay required for weekends, three-nights for holidays.

Hosts: Regan and John Chichester
Rooms: 13 (8 PB; 5 SB) $70-110
Full Breakfast
Credit Cards: A, B, C, D
Notes: 2, 4, 5, 8, 9, 10, 11, 12, 13, 14

Ira Allen House

Rural Delivery 2, Box 2485, 05250
(802) 362-2284

Vermont State Historic Site, home of Ira Allen (Ethan's brother, who lived here with him). Norman Rockwell Museum, Robert Todd Lincoln's Hildene, hiking, canoeing, biking, skiing, and antiques. Enjoy the unique experience of a relaxing stay at this historic inn on the Battenkill River along with a bountiful home-cooked breakfast. Dinner available on Saturdays during the winter.

Hosts: Rowland and Sally Bryant
Rooms: 9 (4 PB; 5 SB) $55-70
Full Breakfast
Credit Cards: A, B, C
Notes: 2, 4, 8 (over 10), 9, 10, 11, 12, 13

Shenandoah Farm

Battenkill Drive, 05250
(802) 375-6372

This Colonial home near the Battenkill River is five miles from Route 7A on Route 313. Close to Norman Rockwell Museum and recreational activities. Five antique-filled guest rooms are offered with private or shared baths.

Host: Woody Masterson
Rooms: 5 (3 PB; 2 SB) $60-75
Full Breakfast
Credit Cards: A, B
Notes: 2, 5, 8, 9, 10, 12, 13, 14

West Mountain Inn

West Mountain Inn

West Mountain Road, 05250
(802) 375-6516

Nestled on a mountainside, this century-old, seven-gable inn invites guests to dis-

cover its many treasures. Distinctively decorated guest rooms, comfortable common areas, 150 woodland acres with wildflowers, a bird sanctuary, and llamas provide space to relax and rejuvenate the body and spirit. Miles of wilderness, skiing, or hiking trails and the Battenkill River provide opportunities for seasonal outdoor activities. A hearty breakfast and a savory country dinner in front of an open hearth complement any stay.

Hosts: Wes and Mary Ann Carlson
Rooms: 15 (PB) $152-179
Full Breakfast
Credit Cards: A, B, C, D
Notes: 2, 4, 5, 8, 9, 10, 11, 12, 13, 14

Willow Bed and Breakfast

Historic Route 7A, 05250
(802) 375-9773

A picturesque 1850 Vermont farmhouse decorated with early American antiques. Nestled on the banks of the Battenkill River with a magnificent view of the mountains. Come and share a "touch of Vermont."

Host: Jean Parsell
Rooms: 3 (1 PB; 2 SB) $50-60
Full Breakfast
Credit Cards: A, B
Notes: 2, 5, 8, 10, 11, 12, 13

BELLOWS FALLS _____

Blue Haven Christian Bed and Breakfast

227 Westminster Road, 05101
(802) 463-9008; (800) 228-9008

This 1830 schoolhouse offers warm, cheery ambience. Far from the hustle-and-bustle world, tucked securely into a lush mountainside, Blue Haven is peaceful and protected. Canopy beds amid hand-painted vintage furnishings make this a retreat back to gentler times. Colorful antique glassware and crisp linens set the tone in this large farm kitchen, heady with irresistible aromas. The common room's ancient rock-

6 Pets welcome; 8 Children welcome; 9 Social drinking allowed; 10 Tennis available; 11 Swimming available; 12 Golf available; 13 Skiing available; 14 May be booked through travel agents.

ing chairs flank an old stone fireplace. Guests will have the feeling of visiting an old friend. French spoken. Full breakfast offered on weekends; Continental on weekdays.

Host: Helene A. Champagne
Rooms: 6 (5 PB; 1 SB) $45-80
Full and Continental Breakfast
Credit Cards: A, B, C
Notes: 2, 5, 8, 9, 10, 11, 12, 13, 14

The Leslie Place

BELMONT

The Leslie Place

P.O. Box 62, 05730
(802) 259-2903; (800) 352-7439

Peacefully set on 100 acres near Weston, this restored 1840 farmhouse is close to major ski areas, restaurants, theaters, and shops. Surrounded by mountain views and meadows, guests will find comfortably spacious rooms creating a welcome retreat.

Host: Mary K. Gorman
Rooms: 4 (PB) $60-80
Full Breakfast
Credit Cards: A, B
Notes: 2, 5, 8, 9, 10, 11, 12, 13

BENNINGTON

American Country Collection

4 Greenwood Lane, Delmar, NY 12054
(518) 439-7001

041. This carefully landscaped Victorian has a stream on the back property and a large front porch for rocking. There's a wood-burning stove on the brick hearth in the first-floor common room. Braided rugs cover wide-plank pine floors. Six guest rooms, two with private baths, and one cottage with king-size bed and private bath with Jacuzzi. Full gourmet breakfast includes pancakes, French toast, eggs, Belgian waffles, blintzes, or quiche. Smoking outdoors only. Children over 11 welcome. Ten percent gratuity. $65-140.

Molly Stark Inn

1067 East Main Street, 05201
(800) 356-3076

A true country inn with an intimate atmosphere, this 1890 Victorian home is on the main road through a historic town in southwestern Vermont and welcomes visitors year-round. Decorated and tastefully furnished with antiques, country collectibles, braided rugs on gleaming hardwood floors, and patchwork quilts on the beds. Private guest cottage with king-size brass bed, Jacuzzi, and woodstove. Guests are invited to use the wraparound front porch with rocking chairs, and the den and parlor with wood-burning stoves are most inviting on those cool Vermont nights. Clean, affordable, no smoking. Champagne dinner packages available.

Host: Reed Fendler
Rooms: 6 (2 PB; 4 SB) $60-80
Full Breakfast
Credit Cards: A, B, C, D
Notes: 2, 4, 5, 8, 9, 14

NOTES: Credit cards accepted: A MasterCard; B Visa; C American Express; D Discover Card; E Diner's Club; F Other; 2 Personal checks accepted; 3 Lunch available; 4 Dinner available; 5 Open all year;

South Shire Inn

124 Elm Street, 05201
(802) 447-3839

The South Shire Inn combines Old World charm and New World luxury to let guests experience bed and breakfast in an elegant tradition in this exquisite turn-of-the-century Victorian inn. All rooms have private baths, air conditioning, and telephones. Seven rooms have working fireplaces; four have Jacuzzi baths. The perfect stay for business or pleasure. Close to downtown.

Hosts: Kristina and Tim Mast
Rooms: 9 (PB) $80-165
Full Breakfast
Credit Cards: A, B, C
Notes: 2, 5, 10, 11, 12, 13

BETHEL

Greenhurst Inn

Rural Delivery 2, Box 60, 05032-9404
(802) 234-9474

Queen Anne Victorian mansion listed on the National Register of Historic Places. In central Vermont near I-89, halfway between Boston and Montreal. Mints on the pillows, Perrier in the rooms, and a library of 3,000 volumes. The inn was featured in the *New York Times* on March 3, 1991.

Host: Lyle Wolf
Rooms: 13 (7 PB; 6 SB) $50-100
Continental Breakfast
Credit Cards: A, B, D
Notes: 2, 5, 6 (limited), 7, 8, 9, 11, 12, 13, 14

Greenhurst Inn

Poplar Manor Bed and Breakfast

Rural Delivery 2, Box 136, Combined Routes 107 and 12, 05032
(802) 234-5426

In a beautiful setting in central Vermont, this 1810 Federal home offers friendly hospitality and quiet comfort. The rooms are decorated with antiques and homey collectibles. Guests are welcome to all indoor and outdoor areas. Many attractions nearby. Continental plus breakfast.

Host: Carmen E. Jaynes
Rooms: 3 (SB) $36-38
Continental Breakfast
Credit Cards: None
Notes: 2, 5, 6, 8, 9, 10, 11, 12, 13, 14

BONDVILLE

Alpenrose Inn

Winhall Hollow Road, 05340
(802) 297-2750

Small country inn on a quiet road. All rooms are furnished with antiques, some with canopied beds. Cozy lounge with large fireplace. Free tennis to house guests, golf, horseback riding, and fishing are minutes away. Near ski lifts and the Appalachian Trail.

Host: Rosemarie Strine
Rooms: 7 (PB) $65-115
Full Breakfast
Credit Cards: A, B, C
Notes: 2, 7 (limited), 9, 10, 11, 12, 13

BRANDON

American Country Collection

4 Greenwood Lane, Delmar, NY 12054
(518) 439-7001

177. This restored 1860s three-story manor offers travelers a truly Victorian experience. The owners painstakingly gathered

6 Pets welcome; 8 Children welcome; 9 Social drinking allowed; 10 Tennis available; 11 Swimming available; 12 Golf available; 13 Skiing available; 14 May be booked through travel agents.

authentic Victorian furnishings that make the intimacy of the inn more than just a notion. The elegant breakfast and common room are comfortably arranged for socializing or just relaxing before the fireplace with a good book. Guests may enjoy the wicker rockers on the porch, or stroll through the gardens and enjoy the hummingbirds and butterflies. Four guest rooms with private and shared baths are on the second floor; two with queen-size beds, one with twin, and one with double. Two additional guest rooms with private baths are on the third floor; one with twin bed and one with queen-size bed. Full breakfast is served. Children 12 and over welcome. Smoking permitted outside only. $50-85

Rosebelle's Victorian Inn

Rosebelle's Victorian Inn

P.O. Box 370, Route 7, 05733
(802) 247-0098

Charming "nonsmoking" 1839 Victorian mansard listed on National Register of Historic Places. Six guest rooms with semi- and private baths, antiques, full gourmet breakfast, and afternoon tea. Dinner is available on Friday and Saturday evenings by reservation during the peak season only. Open year-round with hiking, biking, golf, and spectacular foliage. Swimming is available at the state park 15 miles from the inn. Nordic and Alpine skiing nearby. Visit museums and antique shops, or read a good book. Only minutes from Middlebury Col-

lege. Not suggested for children under 12. Special packages and gift certificates available. Ici on parle français.

Hosts: Ginette and Norm Milot
Rooms: 6 (2 PB; 4 SB) $65-85
Full Breakfast
Credit Cards: A, B
Notes: 2, 4, 5, 9, 10, 11, 12, 13, 14

BROOKFIELD

Green Trails Country Inn

By the Floating Bridge, 05036
(802) 276-3412; (800) 243-3412

Cozy, relaxing, informal, like going home to Grandma's. Home-cooked meals at hearthside, guest rooms decorated with quilts and antiques. Swim, canoe, and fish in the pond. Hiking and biking, with breathtaking vistas. In winter, enjoy horse-drawn sleigh rides, cross-country skiing (34K tracked trails), and fireside friendship. "The epitome of a country inn"—NBC's "Today." Bed and breakfast or Modifed American Plan available. Closed April.

Hosts: Pat and Peter Simpson
Rooms: 15 (9 PB; 6 SB) $68-80
Credit Cards: None
Notes: 2, 4, 8, 9, 10, 11, 12, 13, 14

BURLINGTON

American Country Collection

4 Greenwood Lane, Delmar, NY 12054
(518) 439-7001

073. Guests find this turn-of-the-century farmhouse down a country lane on ten acres of locust and maple trees, gardens, woods, and pastures. Pillars and three porches emphasize the Victorian structure. Guests have a private entrance via a large porch with rockers. Guest refrigerator, dining room, and living room with fireplace, TV, VCR, stereo, and pool table. Three immaculate guest rooms, one single, are furnished with

antiques. Two share a bath. Smoking in the living room only. Children over 16 welcome. $50-85.

Howden Cottage Bed and Breakfast

32 North Champlain Street, 05401
(802) 864-7198

Howden Cottage offers cozy lodging and warm hospitality in the home of a local artist. In downtown Burlington, the house is convenient to shopping, Lake Champlain, movies, night spots, churches, and some of Burlington's best restaurants.

Host: Bruce Howden
Rooms: 3 (1 PB; 2 SB) $35-75
Continental Breakfast
Credit Cards: A, B
Notes: 2, 5, 9, 10, 11, 12, 13

CABOT

Creamery Inn Bed and Breakfast

P.O. Box 187, 05647
(802) 563-2819

This spacious and comfortable home, circa 1835, is picturesquely set only a mile from the Cabot Creamery. Guests may walk the country roads, enjoy ponds and waterfalls,

Creamery Inn

drive to Burke Mountain or Stowe for skiing, or just relax. Enjoy the full, homemade breakfast, featuring Finnish pancakes, muffins, and more. Special rates for stays of more than two nights.

Host: Dan Lloyd
Rooms: 4 (2 PB; 2 SB) $50-65
Full Breakfast
Credit Cards: None
Notes: 2, 4, 5, 8, 9, 11, 13

CALAIS

Evergreen's Chalet

HC 32, Box 41, 05648-7701
(802) 223-5156

Charming, nature lover's paradise on 140 acres. Dining/living room, full kitchen, three bedrooms, two baths, large deck/gas grille, carport, TV, VCR, phone, library, and games. Miles of nature trails/cross-country skiing. VAST snowmobile trail access on property. Full Continental breakfast available. No smoking or pets. Brochure available. Free guided nature tours available. Cross-country and alpine skiing. Daily, weekly, or monthly rates on request.

Hosts: Elizabeth and Wayne Morse
Rooms: 3 (1 PB; 2 SB)
Continental Breakfast
Credit Cards: A, B
Notes: 2, 5, 8, 11, 12, 13

CHELSEA

Shire Inn

8 Main Street, 05038
(802) 685-3031

An 1832 historic brick Federal, "Very Vermont" inn. Enjoy 18th-century accommodations with 20th-century bathrooms. Small and intimate; some rooms have working fireplaces. Chef-owned and operated, with five-course dining available. Just 30 miles north of Woodstock and Quechee; 34 miles to Hanover and Dartmouth; 30 miles south

6 Pets welcome; 8 Children welcome; 9 Social drinking allowed; 10 Tennis available; 11 Swimming available; 12 Golf available; 13 Skiing available; 14 May be booked through travel agents.

of Montpelier. Two-night minimum stay required for weekends and holidays.

Hosts: Jay and Karen Keller
Rooms: 6 (PB) $85-158
Full Breakfast
Credit Cards: A, B, C, D
Notes: 2, 4, 5, 8 (over 6), 9, 10, 11, 12, 13

CHESTER

Greenleaf Inn

Depot Street, Box 188, 05143
(802) 875-3171

Lovely 1880s home, now a comfortable village inn facing an expansive lawn. Five charming rooms, each with private baths. Walk to antiques and village green attractions. Bicycle tourists welcome. Full breakfast in the sunny dining room or enjoy a "breakfast basket" delivered to the room.

Hosts: Jerry and Robin Szawerda
Rooms: 5 (PB) $65-95
Full Breakfast
Credit Cards: A, B, C
Notes: 2, 4, 5, 8 (over 12), 9, 10, 11, 12, 13

Greenleaf Inn

Henry Farm Inn

P.O. Box 646, Green Mountain Turnpike, 05143
(802) 875-2674

The Henry Farm Inn provides the beauty of Vermont with old-time simplicity. Nestled on 50 acres of rolling hills and meadows, as-

suring peace and quiet. Spacious rooms, private baths, country sitting rooms, kitchen, and sunny dining room guarantee a feeling of home. Come visit for a day or more.

Host: J. B. Tanch
Rooms: 7 (PB) $50-90
Full Breakfast
Credit Cards: A, B, C
Notes: 2, 5, 8, 9, 12, 13, 14

CHESTER

The Hugging Bear Inn and Shoppe

Main Street, 05143
(802) 875-2412; (800) 325-0519

Bed, breakfast, and bears. Charming Victorian home on the village green. The shop has more than 3,500 bears, and guests may "adopt" a bear for the night as long as he's back to work in the shop by 9:00 A.M. the next morning. Puppet show often performed at breakfast; breakfast music provided by an 1890 music box. Two lovable cats in residence. A magical place to visit! Two-night minimum stay required for weekends; holidays two to three nights.

Hosts: The Thomases
Rooms: 6 (PB) $75-95
Full Breakfast
Credit Cards: A, B, C, D
Notes: 2, 5, 6 (call), 8, 9, 10, 11, 12, 13

The Inn at Long Last

Main Street, P.O. Box 589, 05143
(802) 875-2444

A warm and welcoming inn where all the rooms have individual themes, where the decor is highly personal, and where the staff hospitality is exceptional. Gardens, tennis courts, food, and theme weekends draw raves. Modified American Plan meals.

Host: Jack Coleman
Rooms: 30 (25 PB; 5 SB) $160
Full Breakfast
Credit Cards: A, B
Notes: 2, 4, 8, 9, 10, 12, 13, 14

NOTES: Credit cards accepted: A MasterCard; B Visa; C American Express; D Discover Card; E Diner's Club; F Other; 2 Personal checks accepted; 3 Lunch available; 4 Dinner available; 5 Open all year;

Inn Victoria and Teapot Shoppe

On the Green, P.O. Box 788, 05143
(802) 875-4288; (800) 732-4288

"The most romantic inn in southern Vermont"—*Vermont Guide*. Inn Victoria offers the perfect getaway. Start the day with a sumptuous country breakfast. Relax in a bubble tub for two. Nap in the queen-size beds littered with embroidered pillows. Enjoy an elegant afternoon tea. There are one- and two-bedroom suites, all with private baths. Be sure to visit Inn Victoria's Teapot Shoppe. Walk to shops and restaurants on the Chester Green. Enjoy summer theater, polo, concerts, art shows, craft shows, and country fairs. Go antiquing at the Four Centers in town. There is golf, boating, hiking, biking, and fishing. There are also three major ski areas nearby.

Hosts: K.C. and Tom Lanagan
Rooms: 7 (5 PB; 2 SB) $85-110
Full Breakfast
Credit Cards: A, B
Notes: 2, 4, 5, 7, 9, 10, 11, 12, 13, 14

Old Town Farm Inn

Rural Route 4, 05143
(802) 875-2346

Built in 1861, the inn has 11 acres with a spring-fed pond for swimming and ice-skating. Ten minutes from Okemo Mountain ski area and 30 minutes from Killington ski area. Cross-country skiing is also available. Foliage season, with its beautiful colors and crisp New England air, beckons people from all over the world. Rent a bike and see the countryside. "Country Inn Spring Water," which was started in 1984, is served and distributed exclusively from the inn.

Hosts: Fred and Jan Baldwin
Rooms: 11 (4 PB; 7 SB) $54-64
Full Breakfast
Credit Cards: A, B, E, F
Notes: 2, 8 (over 5), 9, 10, 11, 12, 13

Mountain Top Inn

CHITTENDEN

Mountain Top Inn

Mountain Top Road, 05737
(802) 483-2311; (800) 445-2100

Nestled amid the picturesque Green Mountains of central Vermont and secluded on a 1,000-acre estate, Mountain Top Inn commands a spectacular view of the lake and surrounding mountains. This warm New England country inn is steeped in the area's finest tradition and has been referred to as "Vermont's best kept secret." Fine dining and recreational facilities, including boating, sailing, windsurfing, canoeing, lake and fly fishing, trapshooting, horseback riding, golf school, 5-hole par-3 golf course, putting green, tennis, mountain biking, heated pool, cross-country skiing (110K), ice skating, horse-drawn sleigh rides, and winter horseback riding are available on premises.

Host: William Wolfe
Rooms: 35 (PB) $116-320
Full Breakfast
Credit Cards: A, B, C
Notes: 2, 3, 4, 5, 7, 8, 9, 12, 13, 14

CRAFTSBURY

Finchingfield Farm Bed and Breakfast

Rural Route 1, Box 1195
East Craftsbury Road, 05826
(802) 586-7763

This elegant, turn-of-the-century country house is set in the tranquil, picturesque vil-

6 Pets welcome; 8 Children welcome; 9 Social drinking allowed; 10 Tennis available; 11 Swimming available; 12 Golf available; 13 Skiing available; 14 May be booked through travel agents.

Finchingfield Farm

lage of East Craftsbury. Guest facilities include a library, cozy sitting room, four large, bright bedrooms (two with private baths), down comforters, and English-style antique furniture. The decor and service are distinctively British.

Hosts: Janet and Bob Meyer
Rooms: 4 (2 PB; 2 SB) $60-80
Full Breakfast
Credit Cards: A, B
Notes: 2, 5, 8, 11, 12, 13

CUTTINGSVILLE (SHREWSBURY)

Maple Crest Farm

Lincoln Hill Road, Box 120, 05738
(802) 492-3367

High in the Green Mountains, ten miles south of Rutland and 12 miles north of Ludlow, this 1808 27-room historic home has been lovingly preserved for five generations. Cross-country skiing and hiking are offered on the farm. Close to major ski areas, Rutland, and places of historic interest. A real taste of old Vermont hospitality. Maple syrup made on the premises. This year marks 24 years in business for this bed-and-breakfast home.

Hosts: William and Donna Smith
Rooms: 6 (1 PB; 5 SB) $50
Full Breakfast
Credit Cards: None
Notes: 2, 5, 8, 9, 10, 11, 12, 13, 14

DANBY

Quails Nest Bed and Breakfast Inn

Box 221, 05739
(802) 293-5099

Nestled in a quiet mountain village, the inn offers its guests friendly conversation around the fireplace, rooms filled with cozy quilts and antiques, tips about local attractions, and a hearty home-cooked breakfast in the morning.

Hosts: Nancy and Greg Diaz
Rooms: 6 (4 PB; 2 SB) $60-85
Full Breakfast
Credit Cards: A, B
Notes: 2, 5, 8 (over 8), 9, 10, 11, 12, 13

Silas Griffith Inn

South Main Street, 05739
(802) 293-5567

Built in 1891 by Vermont's first millionaire, now a lovingly restored Victorian mansion and carriage house. Relax in antique-filled guest rooms with spectacular Green Mountain views. Dinner is also available. Two-night minimum stay required over holidays.

Hosts: Paul and Lois Dansereau
Rooms: 17 (14 PB; 3 SB) $69-86
Full Breakfast
Credit Cards: A, B, C
Notes: 2, 4, 5, 8, 9, 11, 14

DERBY LINE

The Birchwood Bed and Breakfast

48 Main Street, P.O. Box 550, 05830
(802) 873-9104

A 1920 lovingly restored home in a charming village in the Northeast Kingdom at the Canadian border. Three individually decorated, antique-filled bedrooms include private bathrooms. A full breakfast is served each morning in the sunlit dining room. The region offers miles of unspoiled scenery. Enjoy the beauty of the area as well as the comfort and spaciousness of this home. A warm welcome awaits guests at the Birchwood Bed and Breakfast.

Hosts: Betty and Dick Fletcher
Rooms: 3 (PB) $55-60
Full Breakfast
Credit Cards: A, B
Notes: 2, 5, 10, 11, 12, 13

Derby Village Inn

46 Main Street, 05830
(802) 873-3604

A charming old Victorian mansion in the quiet village of Derby Line. Five charming rooms, each with private bath. Nestled within walking distance of the Canadian border and the world's only international library and opera house. The nearby countryside offers year-round recreation: downhill and cross-country skiing, water sports, cycling, fishing, hiking, golf, snowmobiling, sleigh rides, antiquing, and most of all, peace and tranquility. No smoking.

Hosts: Tom and Phyllis Moreau
Rooms: 5 (PB) $55-65
Full Breakfast
Credit Cards: A, B, D
Notes: 2, 5, 8, 9, 10, 11, 12, 13

DORSET

Barrows House

Route 30, 05251
(802) 867-4455; (800) 639-1620 (out of state)

The Barrows House is a collection of white clapboard buildings on 11 acres in the heart of a small picturebook Vermont town. Guests have a choice of 28 accommodations in eight different buildings (21 rooms and 7 suites), all with a history and style of their own. Dining is an informal and delicious adventure in American regional cuisine (offering a four-course country dinner with an elegant flair), which is included in

the rate. The complex offers tennis courts, outdoor heated pool, bicycles, sauna, and cross-country ski shop. Children welcome. Modified American Plan.

Hosts: Linda and Jim McGinnis
Rooms: 28 (PB) $180-230
Full Breakfast
Credit Cards: A, B, C, D, E
Notes: 2, 4, 5, 6, 8, 10, 11, 12, 13, 14

Barrows House

Marble West Inn

Dorset West Road, 05251
(800) 453-7629

Find peace and serenity in a restored 1840 Greek Revival country home with an elegant atmosphere that is graced with polished dark hardwood floors, Oriental rugs, a grand piano, library, and fireplaces. Two acres of land contain herb and flower gardens and trout ponds, providing panoramic views of the Dorset mountains. Afternoon refreshments. Special packages are available. No smoking.

Hosts: June and Wayne Erla
Rooms: 8 (PB) $90-130
Full Breakfast
Credit Cards: A, B, C
Notes: 2, 4, 5, 9, 10, 11, 12, 13, 14

EAST DOVER

Cooper Hill Inn

Cooper Hill Road, Box 146, 05341
(802) 348-6333

6 Pets welcome; 8 Children welcome; 9 Social drinking allowed; 10 Tennis available; 11 Swimming available; 12 Golf available; 13 Skiing available; 14 May be booked through travel agents.

Cooper Hill Inn

Informal and cozy hilltop inn with "one of the most spectacular mountain panoramas in all New England." Quiet country road location. Hearty home-cooked meals are a tradition here. Seven double rooms and three family suites all feature private baths. Breakfast included in the daily rate. Closed for one week in April and November.

Hosts: Pat and Marilyn Hunt
Rooms: 10 (PB) $72-120
Full Breakfast
Credit Cards: A, B, D
Notes: 2, 4, 8, 9, 10, 11, 12, 13, 14

ENOSBURG FALLS

Berkson Farms

Rural Delivery 1, Route 108, 05450
(802) 933-2522

A homey, relaxed atmosphere in this century-old restored farmhouse on a 600-acre working dairy farm. Surrounded by a large variety of animals and all the simple, wonderful joys of nature and life itself. Warm hospitality and country home cooking.

Hosts: Terry and Susan Spoonire
Rooms: 4 (1 PB; 3 SB) $58.85-69.55

Full Breakfast
Credit Cards: None
Notes: 2, 3, 4, 5, 6, 7, 8, 9, 10, 11, 12, 13

ESSEX JUNCTION

Country Comfort Bed and Breakfast

36 Old Stage Road, 05452
(802) 878-2589

Country charm near city sights, on a grassy plateau with distant mountain views creating a feeling of peace and space. Each room decorated with its name in mind (Country, Jenny Lind, Victorian, New England) with hand-picked antiques and collectibles. Guest living room with fireplace and TV. Full Vermont breakfast served in guest dining room. Grazing sheep and clucking hens complete the tranquil theme. "Guests arrive as strangers and depart as friends." Only nine miles from Burlington.

Hosts: Ed and Eva Blake
Rooms: 4 (2 PB; 2 SB) $50-65
Full Breakfast
Credit Cards: A, B
Notes: 2, 5, 8, 9, 10, 11, 12, 13, 14

FAIRFAX

American Country Collection

4 Greenwood Lane, Delmar, NY 12054
(518) 439-7001

149. Imagine being in a completely renovated New England carriage house in the year 1790, and begin the jouney through this inn with original exposed beams and wood-burning stove. Four rooms are available for guests. Two rooms on the second floor share a bath, and two rooms on the first floor share another bath and a Jacuzzi. Snacks, wine, beer, and soft drinks are available to guests, and a FAX machine, Macintosh computer, copier, and antique and gift shop are on premises. In the spring, enjoy watching maple syrup being made. Breakfast is served from 8:00-9:00 A.M. $48-78.

The Inn at Buck Hollow Farm

Rural Route 1, Box 680, 05454
(802) 849-2400

The Inn at Buck Hollow Farm is a small country inn nestled on 400 spectacular acres. It features canopied beds, beamed ceilings, sunroom with fireplace, and antique decor. The guests enjoy a heated pool, hot tub/spa, Jacuzzi, cross-country skiing, and an antique shop. With Burlington's famed marketplace and major ski resorts only minutes away, the Inn at Buck Hollow Farm is truly a four-season retreat.

Hosts: Dody Young and Brad Schwartz
Rooms: 4 (SB) $55-75
Full Breakfast
Credit Cards: A, D, C, D
Notes: 2, 5, 8, 9, 11, 13, 14

The Inn at Buck Hollow Farm

FAIR HAVEN

Bed and Breakfast Inns of New England

128 S. Hoop Pole Road, Guilford, CT 06437
(203) 457-0042; (800) 582-0853

713. A beautifully restored 1843 Greek Revival-style home. Savor the delicious, bountiful, expanded Continental breakfasts. Relax and enjoy the Keeping Room with cable TV and enjoy a crackling fire. The Gathering Room is wonderful for reading or board games. The Parlor provides a sedate atmosphere to enjoy a delicious liqueur from the complimentary cordial bar. Five elegant guest rooms, each with its own charm and personality. All double rooms have seating areas and private baths. Suites have a full living room, large bedroom, and private bath. Most rooms and all suites have air conditioning. Children over five are welcome. Limited smoking, but no cigars or pipes. No guest pets, please. $65-180. $20 for third person in room.

Maplewood Inn and Antiques

Route 22A South, 05743
(802) 265-8039; (800) 253-7729 (out of state)

Romantic, historic 1843 Greek Revival inn offering exquisitely appointed guest rooms and suites with private baths, antiques, working fireplaces, in-room color cable TV, radio, telephones, and air conditioning. Common rooms include keeping room with fireplace, gathering room/library, BYOB tavern, and parlor with games and complimentary cordial bar. Bikes, canoe, and antique shop on-site. Near lakes, skiing, restaurants, and many other attractions. Three-star Mobil, Three-diamond AAA.

Hosts: Cindy and Doug Baird
Rooms: 5 (PB) $70-105
Continental Breakfast
Credit Cards: A, B, D, E, F (Carte Blanche)
Notes: 2, 5, 7, 8 (limited), 9, 10, 11, 12, 13, 14

FAIRLEE

Silver Maple Lodge and Cottages

Route 5, 05045
(802) 333-4326; (800) 666-1946

Historic bed and breakfast country inn. Cozy rooms with antiques or knotty pine cottages, some with fireplaces. Enjoy the beach, boating, fishing, and swimming at

6 Pets welcome; 8 Children welcome; 9 Social drinking allowed; 10 Tennis available; 11 Swimming available; 12 Golf available; 13 Skiing available; 14 May be booked through travel agents.

Silver Maple Lodge

Lake Morey, one mile away. Golf, tennis, skiing, and hot-air balloon rides nearby. Dartmouth College is 17 miles away. Walk to restaurants. Two-night minimum stay required for holidays. Closed Christmas Eve.

Hosts: Scott and Sharon Wright
Rooms: 16 (14 PB; 2 SB) $48-72
Continental Breakfast
Credit Cards: A, B, C, D
Notes: 2, 5, 6, 7, 8, 9, 10, 11, 12, 13, 14

GRAFTON

Fitch Hill Inn

Rural Free Delivery, Box 1879
Fitch Hill Road, 05655
(802) 888-5941; (800) 639-2903

Affordable elegance on a hilltop overlooking Vermont's highest mountain in the beautiful Lamoille River Valley. Ten miles north of famous Stowe, the historic Fitch Hill Inn, circa 1795, offers four tastefully antique-decorated rooms, all of which have views, and a two-bedroom suite. There are four common living room areas and more than 300 video movies for guests to enjoy. Three porches offer spectacular views; rest and relax in our beautiful gardens. A full gourmet breakfast is served, and dinners are available at a modest price. Bedrooms include one with king-size bed. Packages available.

Host: Richard A. Pugliese
Rooms: 4 (SB) $59-105
Full Breakfast

Credit Cards: A, B
Notes: 2, 4, 5, 8, 9, 10, 11, 12, 13, 14

HARDWICK

Somerset House Bed and Breakfast

24 Highland Avenue, 05843
(80) 472-5484

Four pretty bedrooms are offered in this comfortable 1894 house where a gracious and elegant setting combines with a relaxing, friendly atmosphere. On a quiet maple-lined street near the village theater. Start the day with a good breakfast featuring quality homemade dishes, then explore the hidden perennial garden, the village, and the unspoiled countryside beyond.

Hosts: Ruth and David Gaillard
Rooms: 4 (SB) $65-75
Full Breakfast
Credit Cards: A, B
Notes: 2, 5, 8, 9, 10, 11, 12, 13

HARTLAND

American Country Collection

4 Greenwood Lane, Delmar, NY 12054
(518) 439-7001

163. Modern home in a rural farm setting. Guests have the privacy of the entire first floor, including private entrance, if desired. Mostly new and modern furnishings. Continental breakfast. Two rooms, one with twin beds and one with a double bed; each has a private bath. Resident cat. Children welcome. No smoking. $55-65.

JACKSONVILLE

American Country Collection

4 Greenwood Lane, Delmar, NY 12054
(518) 439-7001

NOTES: Credit cards accepted: A MasterCard; B Visa; C American Express; D Discover Card; E Diner's Club; F Other; 2 Personal checks accepted; 3 Lunch available; 4 Dinner available; 5 Open all year;

165. Victorian country home built in 1840. Queen Anne Colonial furnishings and in-ground pool. Dining room with fireplace, living room, and sitting room with TV. Three guest rooms with private and shared baths. Full breakfast. Children welcome. Smoking outside. $45-65.

JAMAICA

Three Mountain Inn
P.O. Box 180 A, 05343
(802) 874-4140

Small, romantic 1780s authentic country inn. Fine food and comfortable rooms. Many original details can be found, including three wood-burning fireplaces on the main floor, and several guests rooms also boast original fireplaces. In a historic village, just four blocks to hiking in the state park and cross-country skiing. Ten minutes to Stratton. The innkeepers plan special day trips with detailed local maps of the area. Special midweek rates. Honeymoon suites available. Small weddings, reunions, meetings. Bed and Breakfast and Modified American Plan available.

Hosts: Charles and Elaine Murray
Rooms: 16 (14 PB; 2 SB) $75-180
Full Breakfast
Credit Cards: A, B, C, D
Notes: 2, 4, 9, 10, 11, 12, 13, 14

JEFFERSONVILLE

Jefferson House Bed and Breakfast
Main Street, P.O. Box 288, 05464
(802) 644-2030

Enjoy the picturesque beauty of this turn-of-the-century Victorian home in historic Jeffersonville. It features a large wrap-around porch; a warm, friendly atmosphere; attractive, comfortable rooms; and a hearty, home-cooked breakfast. In spring and summer bike the country roads, hike the Long

Trail or Mount Mansfield. Autumn's foliage is a sight to behold. In the winter, nearby Smuggler's Notch offers great skiing while other activities are only minutes away.

Hosts: Dick and Joan Walker
Rooms: 3 (SB) $40-45
Full Breakfast
Credit Cards: None
Notes: 2, 5, 8, 12, 13

Mannsview Inn
Rural Route 2, Box 4319, Route 108 South, 05464
(802) 644-8321; (800) 937-6266 (reservations)

Mannsview Inn, circa 1875, is a Colonial-style home with a Victorian flair. Completely restored, it offers queen-size, high-poster beds, a library, parlor, fireplace, cable TV, and home-cooked breads and muffins with a full breakfast. At the base of Mount Mansfield in the heart of Vermont's number-one resort area, guests are surrounded by breathtaking mountain views, pastures, and trout streams. On the premises guests will also find a 10,000-square-foot antique center, canoe touring, skiing, hiking, and canoeing packages available. Kennels on premises.

Hosts: Bette and Kelley Mann
Rooms: 6 (2 PB; 4 SB) $50-70
Full Breakfast
Credit Cards: A, B, C, F
Notes: 2, 3, 5, 6, 8 (over 10), 9, 10, 11, 12, 13, 14

Windridge Inn
Main Street, P.O. Box 426, 05464
(802) 644-5556

Some of the more attractive elements of this Early American-style inn are antique furniture, old wood or slate floors, solid wide pine boards, and stenciled walls. This rusticity is balanced by the comfort of the king-size beds and silent air conditioning. The inn is renowned for its restaurant, Le Cheval d'Or, which features Vermont or New England products prepared in the French manner. Dinner is served by candle-

6 Pets welcome; 8 Children welcome; 9 Social drinking allowed; 10 Tennis available; 11 Swimming available; 12 Golf available; 13 Skiing available; 14 May be booked through travel agents.

light. There is a full bar and an excellent wine cellar. The inn and most of the village are on the National Register of Historic Places. Breakfast is not available at the inn but is served next door.

Host: Yves Labbé
Rooms: 4 (PB) $49-75
Credit Cards: A, B, C
Notes: 3, 4, 5, 7, 9, 10, 11, 13, 14

HYDE PARK

Bed and Breakfast Inns of New England

128 S. Hoop Pole Road, Guilford, CT 06437
(203) 457-0042; (800) 582-0853

VT 725. In the lovely Lamoille River Valley on a hill overlooking the magnificent Green Mountains, this inn, circa 1794, offers a special opportunity to enjoy a true Vermont experience. Set on four acres of woodland and central to Vermont's all-season vacation country, guests can choose from any number of activities: skiing, fishing, hiking, biking, canoeing, tennis, golf, auctions, and antique shopping. The inn is only 10 minutes from Stowe, one hour from Burlington Airport, and two hours from Montreal. A full gourmet breakfast is included, and dinners are available. Five tastefully decorated guest rooms, a Colonial dining room, a Federalist-style living room, and a comfortable library full of videotapes and books are available to guests. Private and shared baths. Children over nine welcome. No smoking. $50-75.

JERICHO

Henry M. Field House Bed and Breakfast

Rural Route 2, Box 395, 05465
(802) 899-3984

Henry M. Field House is near skiing, cycling, hiking, swimming, and golf. The house is convenient to Burlington area col-

Henry M. Field House

leges and shops. The Italianate Victorian was built in 1875 and features tall ceilings, wood floors, etched glass, and period decor including antique furniture and lighting. Vegetable crepes with a mushroom sauce, banana French toast, and a variety of home-baked items are specialties of the house. Children are welcome, but must be in another rented room.

Hosts: Mary Beth and Terrence Horan
Rooms: 3 (PB) $65-75
Full Breakfast
Credit Cards: A, B
Notes: 2, 5, 9, 10, 11, 12, 13

Homeplace

Rural Route 2, Box 367, 05465
(802) 899-4694

Homeplace is a quiet spot in a 100-acre wood. Perennial garden and friendly house and barn animals add to the relaxing atmosphere.

Hosts: Hans and Mariot Huessy
Rooms: 3 (1 PB; 2 SB) $55
Full Breakfast
Credit Cards: None
Notes: 2, 5, 8, 11, 12, 13, 14

NOTES: Credit cards accepted: A MasterCard; B Visa; C American Express; D Discover Card; E Diner's Club; F Other; 2 Personal checks accepted; 3 Lunch available; 4 Dinner available; 5 Open all year;

JOHNSON

The Homestead Bed and Breakfast

Rural Route 2, Box 623, 05656
(802) 635-7354

The quiet beauty of Vermont's countryside surrounds this circa 1830 brick Colonial farmhouse. A hearty breakfast starts guests on the way to enjoying the many activities offered in the area: canoeing, hiking, fishing, biking, antiquing, and skiing.

Hosts: Erwin and Ella May Speer
Rooms: 4 (SB) $40-50
Full Breakfast
Credit Cards: A, B
Notes: 2, 3, 4, 5, 8, 10, 11, 12, 13

KILLINGTON

Grey Bonnet Inn

Route 100 North, 05751
(802) 775-2537; (800) 342-2086

Romantic, antique filled mountain inn on 25 acres with indoor and outdoor pools, tennis, whirlpool, sauna, and game and exercise rooms. Library and cozy pub. Relax in front of the fire in the living room. All rooms have private baths, TVs, and telephones. Award-winning dining, piano entertainment, and ski movies. Indoor and outdoor pools. Cross-country skiing out the back door. AAA three-diamond and Mobil three-star rated. Closed April 15 to June 1 and October 22 to Thanksgiving.

Hosts: Barbara and Bill Flohr
Rooms: 40 (PB) $54-125
Full Breakfast
Credit Cards: A, B, C, D
Notes: 2, 4, 7, 8, 9, 10, 11, 12, 13, 14

Mountain Meadows Lodge

Thundering Brook Road, Rural Route 1
Box 4080, 05751
(802) 775-1010; (800) 370-4567

Settle into Mountain Meadows and enjoy the warmth and hospitality of this relaxed country inn. On the edge of Kent Lake, amid meadows, woods, and the rolling Green Mountains. Eighteen spacious guest rooms, all with private baths, are ideal for families and groups. Comfortable accommodations, roaring fireplaces, hand-hewn beams, high quality, hearty country breakfasts and superb dinners to satisfy guests with outdoors appetites. Sitting room/library with color TV and VCR, game room, outdoor hot tub, sauna, BYOB fireplace lounge. Complete ski touring center with 40K of groomed trails. Full breakfast and dinner included in rate. BP also available. Children of all ages welcome.

Hosts: Scott and Jane Stevens
Rooms: 18 (18 PB) $39-50
Full Breakfast
Credit Cards: A, B
Notes: 2, 4, 8, 9, 10, 11, 12, 13, 14

LONDONDERRY

The Highland House

Route 100, 05148
(802) 824-3019

This 1842 inn, with swimming pool and tennis court, set on 32 acres, offers 17 rooms, 15 with private bath. Classic candlelight dining with homemade soups, breads, and desserts. Within minutes of skiing, hiking, horseback riding, golf, shopping, and points of interest. Two-day, two-night minimum stay required on weekends and three-night stay on holidays. Closed one week in November and three weeks in April and May.

Hosts: Mike and Laurie Gayda
Rooms: 17 (15 PB; 2 SB) $75-103
Full Breakfast
Credit Cards: A, B, C
Notes: 2, 4, 7, 8 (over 5), 9, 10, 11, 12, 13

Swiss Inn

Route 11, Rural Route 1, Box 140, 05148
(802) 824-3442; (800) 847-9477

The Swiss Inn is in the heart of the Green Mountains with spectacular views of the

6 Pets welcome; 8 Children welcome; 9 Social drinking allowed; 10 Tennis available; 11 Swimming available; 12 Golf available; 13 Skiing available; 14 May be booked through travel agents.

surrounding area. These cozy, comfortable rooms all feature cable color TV, telephones, and private baths. Full Vermont breakfast is served daily. Two fireside sitting rooms, game room, and library are available for guests to enjoy. Restaurant on premises featuring Swiss specialties. Both downhill and cross-country skiing nearby in the winter. Shopping, antiques, golf, summer theater, and fall foliage at its best.

Hosts: Joe and Pat Donahue
Rooms: 18 (PB) $50-89
Full Breakfast
Credit Cards: A, B, C
Notes: 2, 4, 5, 7, 8, 9, 10, 11, 12, 13, 14

LUDLOW

American Country Collection

4 Greenwood Lane, Delmar, NY 12054
(518) 439-7001

134. Choose from a private cottage, chalet, or condominium nestled in the village of Okemo, on one of the surrounding lakes, in the country, or right on Okemo Mountain. Each home is distinctive in character and location, and generally sleeps four to six people. Over 30 rentals to choose from, each with fully equipped kitchen, living room (many with fireplace), bedrooms, and one or two baths. Several feature hot tubs. Breakfast is not provided. Children welcome. Smoking permitted. Quiet pets are also permitted at some. Call for rates.

The Andrie Rose Inn

13 Pleasant Street, 05149
(802) 228-4846; (800) 223-4846

Elegant circa 1829 country village inn at the base of Okemo Ski Resort. Enjoy fireside cocktails with complimentary hors d'oeuvres. Ten lavishly appointed, antique-filled guest rooms, all with private baths, fine linens, and down comforters. Some rooms boast whirlpool tubs and skylights.

Indulge the senses in one of the luxury suites featuring marble fireplaces, canopied beds, and oversize whirlpool tubs. Family suites also available. Savor delectable breakfasts and epicurean dinners. Use inn bikes to tour back roads. Minutes from lakes, theaters, golf, tennis, hiking, and downhill and cross-country skiing. Dinner served weekends and holidays.

Hosts: Jack and Ellen Fisher
Rooms: 10 (PB) $95-250
Full Breakfast
Credit Cards: A, B, C, D
Notes: 2, 4, 5, 10, 11, 12, 13, 14

The Andrie Rose Inn

Black River Inn

100 Main Street, 05149
(802) 228-5585

Rated "outstanding," a charming 1835 country inn on the bank of the Black River at the base of Okemo Mountain. Ten antique furnished guest rooms, eight with private baths. A variety of antique beds with down comforters and feather pillows, including a 1794 walnut four-poster that Abraham Lincoln slept in. Full country breakfast, fireside cocktails, dinners available. Near downhill and cross-country skiing, bicycle rentals, golf, hiking, swimming, and fishing.

Hosts: Rick and Cheryl DelMastro
Rooms: 10 (8 PB; 2 SB) $75-120
Full Breakfast
Credit Cards: A, B, C
Notes: 2, 4, 5, 7, 8 (over 12), 9, 10, 11, 12, 13, 14

NOTES: Credit cards accepted: A MasterCard; B Visa; C American Express; D Discover Card; E Diner's Club; F Other; 2 Personal checks accepted; 3 Lunch available; 4 Dinner available; 5 Open all year;

The Combes Family Inn

Rural Free Delivery 1, Box 275, 05149
(802) 228-8799

Bring the family to the Combes Family Inn in Vermont. The inn, a century-old farmhouse on a country backroad, offers a quiet respite from the hustle and bustle of today's hectic lifestyle! Relax and socialize (BYOB) in the Vermont Barnboard "keeping room," furnished with turn-of-the-century oak. Sample Bill's country breakfasts and Ruth's delicious home cooking. Lush Green Mountains invite a relaxing, casual vacation. Eleven cozy, country-inspired guest rooms—all with private baths. Minimum-stay requirements for fall and winter weekends and for holidays. Closed April 15 through May 15.

Hosts: Ruth and Bill Combes
Rooms: 11 (PB) $78-90
Full Breakfast
Credit Cards: A, B, C, D
Notes: 2, 4, 6, 7, 8, 9, 10, 11, 12, 13, 14

Echo Lake Inn

P.O. Box 154, 05149
(800) 356-6844

Year-round country inn and resort built in 1840. One of six inns in Vermont originally built as an inn. In beautiful lakes region, minutes to ski areas and golf. Tennis, pool, boating, fishing. Full breakfast and dinner, porch dining. Cocktail lounge, tavern, game room, steam bath, and Jacuzzi. Homemade desserts by the hostess. Lunch is seasonal. Dinner included in the rates. Menu according to season: homemade pasta, venison, and other game dishes, always fresh fish. Close to many points of interest such as the birthplace of President Calvin Coolidge and the cheese factory. On Route 100, five miles north of Ludlow. Closed April. Modified American Plan available.

Hosts: John and Yvonne Pardieu, Chip Connelly
Rooms: 26 (12 PB; 14 SB) $84-178
Full Breakfast
Credit Cards: A, B, C, D
Notes: 2, 3, 4, 7 (limited), 8 (over 5), 9, 10, 11, 12, 13, 14

Branch Brook Bed and Breakfast

LYNDON

Branch Brook Bed and Breakfast

South Wheelock Road, P.O. Box 143, 05849
(802) 626-8316; (800) 572-7712

This restored 1850 house in northeast Vermont has an attractive living room, dining room, and library all available for guests' use. Five guest rooms, three with private baths. One half mile off I-91 at exit 23. Burke Mountain ski area is eight miles away and provides both downhill and cross-country skiing. Hiking, biking, and swimming available. A complete breakfast prepared on an English AGA cooker is served in the dining room. AAA.

Hosts: Ted and Ann Tolman
Rooms: 5 (3 PB; 2 SB) $55-70
Full Breakfast
Credit Cards: A, B
Notes: 2, 5, 8, 9, 11, 12, 13

LYNDONVILLE

The Wildflower Inn

Darling Hill Road, 05851
(800) 627-8310

A perfect spot for a family getaway. The innkeepers and their warmhearted staff invite guests to enjoy each season's offering: nature trails, spectacular heated pool, and delightful gardens in summer; wildflowers and fishing in spring; excellent alpine and

---

6 Pets welcome; 8 Children welcome; 9 Social drinking allowed; 10 Tennis available; 11 Swimming available; 12 Golf available; 13 Skiing available; 14 May be booked through travel agents.

cross-country skiing in winter. Breathtaking views, great meals, teddybear pancakes, petting barn, and much more all year-round. Known as Vermont's best family inn. Rates include breakfast and snack. Off-season discount rates available.

Hosts: Jim and Mary O'Reilly
Rooms: 22 (20 PB; 2 SB) $89-135
Full Breakfast
Credit Cards: A, B
Notes: 2, 4, 5, 8, 9, 10, 11, 12, 13

MANCHESTER

American Country Collection

4 Greenwood Lane, Delmar, NY 12054
(518) 439-7001

080. Guests will find tranquility in this 1890 tenant farmer's house on a five-acre plot at the foot of the Green Mountains. Two cozy guest rooms are decorated in country pastels and prints. Each room has a magnificent view and private bath. Guests may enjoy tea on the deck by the brook, by the wood-burning stove in the dining room, or by the fireplace in the living room. Continental breakfast can be served in the dining room or on the deck. Smoking permitted, but not in the guest rooms. Children over 12 welcome. Dog in residence. $60.

Birch Hill Inn

P.O. Box 346, 05254
(802) 362-2761

Quiet country inn away from busy streets. Panoramic views, swimming pool, trout pond, and walking trails on premises. Golf, antiquing, biking, tennis, and hiking nearby. Birch Hill Inn has been selected for The Innkeepers Register. Closed November 1 through December 26 and April 5 through Memorial Day.

Hosts: Jim and Pat Lee
Rooms: 6 (PB) $105-130
Full Breakfast
Credit Cards: A, B, C
Notes: 2, 7 (limited), 10, 12, 13

1811 House

1811 House

Box 39, 05254
(802) 362-1811

This classic Vermont inn offers guests the warmth and comfort of their own home. Built in the 1770s, the house has operated as an inn since 1811 except for one brief period when it was the residence of Abraham Lincoln's granddaughter. All guest rooms have private baths; some have fireplaces, Oriental rugs, fine paintings, and canopied beds. More than three acres of lawn contain flower gardens, a trout pond, and offer an exceptional view of the Green Mountains. Walk to golf and tennis, near skiing, fishing, canoeing, and all sports.

Hosts: Marnie and Bruce Duff
Rooms: 14 (PB) $110-180
Full Breakfast
Credit Cards: A, B, C, D
Notes: 2, 5, 7 (limited), 8 (over 16), 9, 10, 11, 12, 13, 14

The Inn at Manchester

Historic Route 7A, Box 41, 05254-0041
(802) 362-1793

Beautifully restored turn-of-the-century Victorian set on four acres in the picture-book village of Manchester. Elegant rooms with bay windows, brass beds, antiques, and an extensive art collection. Luscious full country breakfast. Secluded pool, skiing, shops, and theater in the area. Come for peace, pancakes, and pampering. Guests can choose between 14 rooms and 4 suites.

Hosts: Stan and Harriet Rosenberg
Rooms: 18 (PB) $80-130

NOTES: Credit cards accepted: A MasterCard; B Visa; C American Express; D Discover Card; E Diner's Club; F Other; 2 Personal checks accepted; 3 Lunch available; 4 Dinner available; 5 Open all year;

Full Breakfast
Credit Cards: A, B, C, D
Notes: 2, 5, 7 (limited), 8 (over 8), 9, 10, 11, 12, 13, 14

Manchester Highlands Inn

Box 1754 AD, Highland Avenue, 05255
(802) 362-4565

Discover Manchester's first painted lady, a graceful Queen Anne Victorian inn on a hilltop overlooking town. Front porch with rocking chairs, large outdoor pool, game room, and pub with stone fireplace. Rooms individually decorated with feather beds, down comforters, and lace curtains. Gourmet country breakfast and afternoon snacks are served.

Hosts: Robert and Patricia Eichorn
Rooms: 15 (PB) $85-125
Full Breakfast
Credit Cards: A, B, C, D
Notes: 2, 5, 7 (limited), 8, 9, 10, 11, 12, 13, 14

Manchester Highlands Inn

Seth Warner Inn

Historic Route 7A, P.O Box 281, 05255
(802) 362-3830

This imposing, vintage 1800 Colonial inn is nestled between two mountain ranges. Carefully restored with open beams and stenciling. Furnished in antiques and offering guests rooms with country quilts and private bath. Guests enjoy complimentary wine in the parlor and a small library to browse. Candlelight country breakfast. Pond and garden. Air conditioning.

Hosts: Lee and Stasia Tetreault
Rooms: 5 (PB) $80-95
Full Breakfast
Credit Cards: A, B
Notes: 2, 5, 8 (over 12), 9, 10, 11, 12, 13

MANCHESTER CENTER

Brook-n-Hearth Inn

State Route 11 and 30, Box 508, 05255
(802) 362-3604

Homey Colonial-style inn one mile east of US 7 on Routes 11 and 30. Features full breakfast, cozy rooms with air conditioning, private baths, family suite, cable TV, lounge, BYOB, recreation rooms, outdoor heated swimming pool, and walking trails near a brook. Two-night minimum stay required over holidays. Closed from early November. to early May.

Hosts: Larry and Terry Greene
Rooms: 3 (PB) $54-80
Full Breakfast
Credit Cards: A, B, C, D
Notes: 2, 8, 9, 10, 11, 12, 13

The Inn at Ormsby Hill

Historic Route 7A, Rural Route 2
P.O. Box 3264 05255
(802) 362-1163

This splendid, restored manor house is on two and one-half acres overlooking the Green Mountains. Listed on Vermont's Register of Historic Places, the inn offers six guest rooms, all with private baths, four with fireplaces and whirlpools. Rates include full breakfast. Many excellent places for lunch and dinner nearby. Manchester is a four-season resort community with a full assortment of sports and cultural activities.

Hosts: Nancy and Don Burd
Rooms: 6 (PB) $90-160
Full Breakfast
Credit Cards: A, B, C
Notes: 2, 9, 10, 11, 12, 13, 14

6 Pets welcome; 8 Children welcome; 9 Social drinking allowed; 10 Tennis available; 11 Swimming available; 12 Golf available; 13 Skiing available; 14 May be booked through travel agents.

River Meadow Farm

P.O. Box 822, 05255
(802) 362-1602

Secluded farm at the end of a country lane
with beautiful views of the surrounding
countryside. The remodeled farmhouse was
built just prior to 1800. Five guest bedrooms sharing two and one-half baths, large
country kitchen with a fireplace and adjoining screen/glassed-in porch, pleasant dining
room, living room with baby grand piano,
and den with TV. Seventy acres to hike or
cross-country ski, bordered by the famous
Battenkill River.

Host: Patricia J. Dupree
Rooms: 5 (SB) $25/person
Full Breakfast
Credit Cards: None
Notes: 2, 5, 8, 9

MANCHESTER VILLAGE

The Battenkill Inn

Box 948, 05254
(800) 441-1628

Guests are invited to share the hospitable
warmth of a bygone era in an exquisite Victorian setting. Fine antiques and heavenly
breakfasts are enjoyed amid the painterly
beauty of the Battenkill River Valley. Play
afternoon croquet on sweeping lawns and
delight in evening hors d'oeuvres by a marble mantled fire. Alpine and cross-country
skiing, antiquing, golfing, canoeing, and
discount shopping are all nearby. Air-conditioned rooms with private baths.

Hosts: Ramsay and Mary Jo Gourd
Rooms: 10 (PB) $75-165
Full Breakfast
Credit Cards: A, B, C
Notes: 5, 8 (limited), 9, 10, 11, 12, 13, 14

The Reluctant Panther
Inn and Restaurant

West Road, P.O. Box 678, 05254-0678
(800) 822-2331

Relax and forget the world in individually
decorated, quiet guest rooms or suites. All
rooms offer private baths, telephones, air
conditioning, cable TVs, and some have
wood-burning fireplaces and Jacuzzis.
Enjoy a drink at the Panther Bar or the tree-
shaded patio, and experience an extraodi-
nary candlelight dinner at the
award-winning restaurant. House guests
enjoy priority for the fireplace or solarium
tables.

Hosts: Maye and Robert Bachofen
Rooms: 16 (PB) $160-300
Full Breakfast
Credit Cards: A, B, C
Notes: 2, 4, 5, 9, 10, 11, 12, 13, 14

MENDON

Red Clover Inn

Woodward Road, 05701
(802) 775-2290; (800) 752-0571

Down a winding country road, amid 13
acres, Red Clover Inn offers guests warmth,
pampering, and exceptional gourmet fare.
From enticing rooms with handmade quilts,
antiques, some whirlpools, and cozy fires to
sumptuous breakfasts and candlelit dining
with soft music, the atmosphere is relaxed
and peaceful. An added treat is Gruffy, a
carrot-loving pony, and Minnie, his lovable
miniature horse companion. Pool on
premises. A stay at this inn turns guests into
friends who cannot wait to return. Closed
from mid-April to Memorial Day.

Hosts: Sue and Harris Zuckerman
Rooms: 12 (PB) $90-195
Full Breakfast
Credit Cards: A, B
Notes: 2, 5, 6 (limited), 8 (over 8), 9, 10, 11, 12, 13,
14

MIDDLEBURY

The Annex

Route 125, 05740
(802) 388-3233

This 1830 Greek Revival home was originally built as an annex to the Bob Newhart

The Annex

"Stratford Inn." The annex features six rooms decorated in a blend of country, antiques, and homemade quilts. The nearby national forest provides hiking, skiing, and biking trails. Visit the UVM Morgan Horse Farm and the Shelburne Museum while in the area.

Host: T. D. Hutchins
Rooms: 6 (4 PB; 2 SB) $50-75
Continental Breakfast
Credit Cards: None
Notes: 2, 5, 8, 9, 10, 11, 12, 13

Bed and Breakfast Marblehead and North Shore

P.O. Box 35, Newtonville, MA 02160
(617) 964-1606; (800) 832-2632
FAX (617) 332-8572

19th-Century Farmhouse. Built in 1879, this beautiful country farmhouse is off a quiet country road on 20 acres of meadowland, surrounded by spacious lawns and lovely gardens. There are two beautifully decorated guest rooms and a two-bedroom suite that sleeps up to four. All rooms have private baths. Full country breakfast in the morning and complimentary wine and cheese in the evenings. This bed and breakfast is close to Middlebury College, many wonderful tourist attractions, and downhill and cross-country skiing areas. No smoking. Children over eight are welcome. Open year-round. Minimum stay of two nights required. $80-150.

The Middlebury Inn

Courthouse Square, 05753
(802) 388-4961; (800) 842-4666

Elegantly restored 1827 village inn in the historic district of a lovely college town. Guest rooms have private baths, telephones, and TVs. Formal or informal dining; afternoon tea served daily. Museums, unique shops, and historic sites to explore. Swimming, golf, hiking, boating, downhill and cross-country skiing are nearby. Special packages are available. Breakfast not included in the rates.

Hosts: Frank and Jane Emanuel
Rooms: 75 (PB) $80-170
Credit Cards: A, B, C, D
Notes: 2, 3, 4, 5, 6 (limited), 7 (limited), 8, 9, 10, 11, 12, 13, 14

The Middlebury Inn

A Point of View

Rural Delivery 3, Box 2675, 05753
(802) 388-7205

This country bed and breakfast, with fantastic views of the valley and Green Mountains, offers excellent beds in comfortable air-conditioned rooms. The living room has a large cable TV. The game room includes a pool table. This is a warm, friendly atmosphere where each guest is treated specially. Hostess prides herself on serving a Vermont-style breakfast featuring seasonal fruits and generous entrées. Area attractions

6 Pets welcome; 8 Children welcome; 9 Social drinking allowed; 10 Tennis available; 11 Swimming available; 12 Golf available; 13 Skiing available; 14 May be booked through travel agents.

include the Morgan Horse Farm, museums, and crafts center.

Host: Marie Highter
Rooms: 2 (1 PB; 1 SB) $45-50
Full Breakfast
Credit Cards: None
Notes: 2, 5, 7 (limited), 8, 9, 10, 12, 13

MIDDLETOWN SPRINGS

American Country Collection

4 Greenwood Lane, Delmar, NY 12054
(518) 439-7001

147. There is a treat waiting for guests as they step back 100 years in time to an age of elegance in this rural New England village. Listed on the National Register of Historic Places, this historic home is filled with antiques and a large music box collection. Near Lake St. Catherine for boating and picnicking. Fishermen will love the trout that can be caught in a stream bordering the property. Eight guest rooms are available, all with private baths, and a full breakfast is served daily. Dinner available nightly. $55-65.

MONTGOMERY CENTER

The Inn on Trout River

P.O. Box 76, The Main Street, 05471
(802) 326-4391; (800) 338-7049

Surrounded by magnificent mountain ranges in a quaint Currier and Ives-style village, this 100-year-old country Victorian inn features private baths, queen-size beds, down comforters, feather pillows, flannel sheets, cozy fireplaces, antiques, gourmet restaurant, a pub, and game room. Close to summer and winter sports, covered bridges, and shopping. A full menu at breakfast is always included. AAA three-diamond Historic Country Inn.

Hosts: Michael and Lee Forman
Rooms: 10 (PB) $86-103

The Inn on Trout River

Full Breakfast
Credit Cards: A, B, D
Notes: 2, 4, 5, 7, 8, 9, 10, 11, 12, 13, 14

Phineas Swann Bed and Breakfast

Main Street, Box 43, 05471
(802) 326-4306

A charming Victorian home with a country flavor, Phineas Swann has an enclosed porch and lots of gingerbread trim. Three large, cozy guest rooms. The nearby Green Mountains and Jay Peak provide plenty of hiking, skiing, and biking. Within walking distance of shops and restaurants. Awake to a hearty candlelight breakfast.

Hosts: Glen Bartolomeo and Michael Bindler
Rooms: 4 (1 PB; 3 SB) $55-70
Full Breakfast
Credit Cards: A, B
Notes: 2, 5, 8, 9, 11, 12, 13, 14

MONTPELIER

Betsy's Bed and Breakfast

74 East State Street, 05602
(802) 229-0466

Betsy's Bed and Breakfast is a warm and inviting Queen Anne home in the nation's smallest capital. The rooms are lavishly furnished with period antiques. Guests are invited to linger over a cup of coffee in the sun-filled dining room, chat with the own-

NOTES: Credit cards accepted: A MasterCard; B Visa; C American Express; D Discover Card; E Diner's Club; F Other; 2 Personal checks accepted; 3 Lunch available; 4 Dinner available; 5 Open all year;

ers by a crackling fire in the formal parlor, lift weights or cycle in the exercise room, rock on the front porch, hot tub under the stars, or hide away in their room and enjoy the peace and quiet.

Hosts: Jon and Betsy Anderson
Rooms: 4 (PB) $50-105
Full Breakfast
Credit Cards: A, B
Notes: 2, 3, 5, 8, 9, 10, 11, 12, 13, 14

MORGAN

Hunts Hideaway

Rural Route 1, Box 570, West Charleston, 05872
(802) 895-4432; (802) 334-8322

Contemporary split-level on 100 acres: brook, pond, and a 44-foot in-ground pool. In Morgan, six miles from I-91, near the Canadian border. Guests may use kitchen and laundry facilities. Lake Seymour is two miles away; 18-hole golf courses at Newport and Orleans; bicycling, jogging, skiing at Jay Peak and Burke Mountain, antiquing, bird watching, and fishing.

Host: Pat Hunt
Rooms: 3 (SB) $35
Full Breakfast
Credit Cards: None
Notes: 2, 5, 6, 7, 8, 9, 10, 11, 12, 13

NEWBURY

A Century Past

Box 186, Route 5, 05051
(802) 866-3358

A charming, historic house dating back to 1790, nestled in the tranquility of a quaint Vermont village. A cozy sitting room with fireplace; chat with newfound friends or curl up with a good book. Wake up to freshly baked muffins, hot coffee or tea, great French toast—all served in a comfortable dining room. Activities include walking, biking, and canoeing. Closed December and January.

Host: Patricia Smith
Rooms: 4 (2 SB) $58
Full Breakfast
Credit Cards: A, B
Notes: 2, 8 (over 12), 9, 10, 11, 12, 13

NEWPORT

American Country Collection

4 Greenwood Lane, Delmar, NY 12054
(518) 439-7001

148. With views of Lake Memphremogog, this charming Cape Cod set on a hillside in northeastern Vermont affords travelers of every taste a secluded retreat. Two second-floor rooms share one bath. One room has a double bed, one single bed, and a feather bed. The second room has a sofa that folds out into a double bed. (The second room is only rented to travelers who are with those in the first party.) Breakfast of juice, fresh blueberry pancakes, sausage or bacon, homemade corn muffins, and coffee or tea will satisfy guests for most of the day. $50.

NORTH HERO

Charlie's Northland Lodge

Rural Route 1, Box 88, U.S. Route 2, 05474
(802) 372-8822

Early 1800s guest house in a quiet village setting on North Hero Island overlooking Lake Champlain. Three guest rooms furnished with country antiques share a modern bath, private entrance, and living room. A place to fish, sail, canoe, bike, or just plain relax. In winter, guests may ice fish and cross-country ski.

Hosts: Dorice and Charlie Clark
Rooms: 3 (SB) $50-55
Continental Breakfast
Credit Cards: A, B, D
Notes: 2, 5, 9, 11, 12, 13

---

6 Pets welcome; 8 Children welcome; 9 Social drinking allowed; 10 Tennis available; 11 Swimming available; 12 Golf available; 13 Skiing available; 14 May be booked through travel agents.

NORTH TROY

American Country Collection

4 Greenwood Lane, Delmar, NY 12054
(518) 439-7001

193. Rural farmhouse on 52 acres with fields, woods, and panoramic view of Canadian mountains. A farm homestay that is very restful and quiet. Common room with parlor stove, TV, and piano. Three guest rooms: one double bed with private bath, and two rooms with double and single beds in each with a shared bath. Full breakfast. Children over six welcome. No smoking allowed. $35-60.

Bed and Breakfast Inns of New England

128 S. Hoop Pole Road, Guilford, CT 06437
(203) 457-0042; (800) 582-0853

VT740. Enjoy this bed and breakfast farm with 52 acres of fields and woods and panoramic views of the Canadian Sutton Range and Jay Peak. There is nearby fishing, tennis, and golf; however, guests are welcome to stay around the farm and relax. Breakfast is full in the winter and Continental in the summer. Three guest rooms: one with a double bed and private bath; one with double bed and shared bath with bedroom with twin bed. Children over 12 are welcome. No smoking. Resident dog and cat; no guest pets. $35-52. $20 for additional adult. $15 for children.

Bed and Breakfast Marblehead and North Shore

P.O. Box 35, Newtonville, MA 02160
(617) 964-1606; (800) 832-2632
FAX (617) 332-8572

Canadian Border Guesthouse. In northern Vermont, close to the Canadian border, this wonderful old farmhouse sits on 52 acres and offers panoramic views of the Sutton Range and Jay Peak. Acres of woodlands and fields provide outdoor enthusiasts with options for hiking, cross-country or downhill skiing, snowshoeing, fishing, and horseback riding. Guest accommodations include two rooms with shared bath, one room with private bath, a cozy living room with a parlor stove, TV, and piano. A country breakfast is included. $45-100.

ORLEANS

Valley House Inn

4 Memorial Square, 05860
(802) 754-6665; (800) 545-9711

One-quarter mile from Exit 26 off I-91. An 1800s country inn in a small village in the center of the Northeast Kingdom's lake region. Step back to the turn of the century in the grand lobby with its pressed metal ceiling and walls and half-moon front desk. Restaurant and cocktail lounge on premises. One mile from top 18-hole golf course. Downhill and cross-country skiing nearby. "A stay at a nice Vermont country inn doesn't have to be expensive."

Hosts: David and Louise Bolduc
Rooms: 22 (PB) $35-60
Full Breakfast
Credit Cards: A, B, C, D
Notes: 2, 3, 4, 5, 7, 8, 9, 10, 11, 12, 13, 14

ORWELL

Historic Brookside Farms

Route 22A, 05760
(802) 948-2727

In 1989, The Farms celebrated their 200th anniversary. This 300-acre estate with its Greek Revival mansion offers rooms furnished with antiques, which, as part of the antique shop, are for sale. On the premises are cross-country skiing, hiking, boating, and fishing; golf and tennis are nearby. Lunch and five-course dinners are available.

Rooms: 7 (4 PB; 3 SB) $85-150
Full Breakfast
Credit Cards: None
Notes: 2, 3, 4, 5, 7, 8, 9, 13, 14

PERU

Johnny Seesaw's

Route 11, Box 68, 05152
(802) 824-5533

The essential Vermont experience. Elegantly rustic lodge with cozy rooms and suites. Two-bedroom cottages with fireplaces. Extraordinary candlelit dinners. Red-clay tennis court and pool. Minutes to skiing or golf, horseback riding, and shopping in Manchester's discount outlets. Kids welcome and pets selectively permitted.

Hosts: Gary and Nancy Okun
Rooms: 21 (PB) $74-170
Full Breakfast
Credit Cards: A, B
Notes: 2, 3, 4, 6, 7, 8, 9, 10, 11, 12, 13, 14

PITTSFIELD

Swiss Farm Lodge

Route 100, 05762
(802) 746-8341; (800) 245-5726

A homey, comfortable, and attractive lodge nestled in a beautiful valley surrounded by mountains. Delight in the ambience of a working farm, producing the hosts' own polled Hereford Beef. Maple syrup is made from the trees on the farm. Convenient to major downhill and cross-country ski areas. Anything guests may desire is nearby. All meals are home-cooked and served in a large pleasant dining room.

Hosts: Mark and Sandy Begin and family
Rooms: 17 (14 PB; 3 SB) $40-50
Full Breakfast
Credit Cards: A, B
Notes: 5, 8, 9, 10, 11, 12, 13

POULTNEY

Bed and Breakfast Inns of New England

128 S. Hoop Pole Road, Guilford, CT 06437
(203) 457-0042; (800) 582-0853

VT712. This bed and breakfast is a 100-year-old beautifully restored Queen Anne Victorian. A wraparound porch and tower make this inn distinctive. Three guest rooms welcome guests with brass beds, antique oak, stenciling, and gorgeous views. An expanded Continental breakfast is served each morning, and all guests receive a loaf of "parting bread" when they leave. Lake St. Catherine is only three miles away, and five ski areas are within 20 miles. Private and shared baths. Children over eight are welcome. Smoking permitted. Resident dog and cats, but no guest pets, please. $55-60.

Lake Saint Catherine Inn

Cones Point Road, 05764
(802) 287-9347; (800) 626-LSCI (reservations)

Rural country resort on crystal-clear Lake Saint Catherine. Relaxation and wholesome dining. Families welcome. AAA approved. Rates include use of aluminum boats, canoes, paddleboats, and sailboats. Breakfast, dinner, and all gratuities are included in the daily rate. One housekeeping cottage sleeps six and is available with weekly rates. Many specials available throughout the season. Modified American Plan available. Open mid-May to mid-October.

Hosts: Patricia and Raymond Endlich
Rooms: 35 (PB) $128-825
Credit Cards: None
Notes: 2, 4, 7, 8, 9, 10, 11, 12

Stonebridge Inn

3 Beaman Street, Route 30, 05764
(802) 287-9849

6 Pets welcome; 8 Children welcome; 9 Social drinking allowed; 10 Tennis available; 11 Swimming available; 12 Golf available; 13 Skiing available; 14 May be booked through travel agents.

The Stonebridge Inn is in the village of Poultney, which dates back to 1761. Green Mountain College, a small, private four-year college, is within walking distance. The inn occupies one of Poultney's most opulent buildings, sitting on a knoll overlooking Main Street. Stonebridge Inn is ideal for year-round activities. In winter, ski Killington and Pico. At other times, enjoy swimming, fishing, and boating in one of the nearby lakes. Golf is minutes away, and hiking trips for all ability levels can be arranged at the inn.

Rooms: 6 (3 PB; 3 SB) $64-84
Credit Cards: A, B
Notes: 2, 4, 5, 8, 9, 10, 11, 12, 13

PUTNEY

Misty Meadow Bed and Breakfast

Rural Delivery 1, Box 458, 05346
(800) 56MISTY

High on a hillside overlooking the Connecticut River Valley, Misty Meadow is surrounded by acres of meadows, woodlands, and old stone walls. Relax and enjoy the views from the gazebo or take a leisurely stroll through the herb and perennial gardens. A full country breakfast, complete with homemade muffins and jams, is served fireside in the winter or on the patio in summer. Plenty of games and books available for the guests' enjoyment.

Hosts: Jane and Dave Savage
Rooms: 3 (PB) $55-85
Full Breakfast
Credit Cards: None
Notes: 2, 5, 8, 11, 12, 13, 14

American Country Collection

4 Greenwood Lane, Delmar, NY 12054
(518) 439-7001

176. Just imagine ten acres of rolling hills, fields, and meadows mingled with a view

that invites lingering and relaxation from a rear, three-tiered deck with gazebo. A very private setting in a rural farm area, yet only 15 minutes' driving time from Brattleboro. A contemporary center chimney Cape, with hardwood floors, Oriental rugs, wing-back chairs, and wonderful views all around. There are a living room and dining room, where a full breakfast is served each morning. Each bedroom has a full private bath, ceiling fan, large closet, antique furniture and fixtures, eyelet sheets, and colorful coverlets and quilts. Children are welcome. Smoking is permitted outside only. There are five resident cats, which are not allowed in the guest rooms, and two outside dogs. $55-75.

QUECHEE

Parker House Inn

16 Main Street, 05059
(802) 295-6077

The host family welcomes guests to an authentic village inn experience. The Parker House is a classic 19th-century Vermont inn, so each charming room's furnishings reflect that era. Dine on cuisine best described as American comfort food. Enjoy full privileges at the Quechee Club for golf, swimming, tennis, skiing, and fitness. In the heart of the Green Mountains with spectacular fall foliage, summer and winter sports, and the Quechee Gorge all nearby.

Hosts: Barbara and Walt Forrester
Rooms: 7 (PB) $95-125
Full Breakfast
Credit Cards: A, B
Notes: 2, 3, 4, 5, 7 (limited), 8, 9, 10, 11, 12, 13

The Quechee Inn at Marshland Farm

Clubhouse Road, 05059
(800) 235-3133

This 1793 farmstead overlooks the Ottauquechee River and Dewey's Pond. Seven miles to Hanover, New Hampshire (home of

NOTES: Credit cards accepted: A MasterCard; B Visa; C American Express; D Discover Card; E Diner's Club; F Other; 2 Personal checks accepted; 3 Lunch available; 4 Dinner available; 5 Open all year;

Dartmouth College) and Woodstock. Twenty-four guest rooms with Queen Anne-style furnishings with private bath. On-premises bicycle and canoe rentals. Home of the Vermont Fly-fishing School. Full weekend and weekday guest privileges at the nearby Quechee Golf Club. Fine dining with the menu featuring Vermont products. All rooms are air-conditioned.

Host: Hal Lothrop
Rooms: 24 (PB) $88-148
Continental Breakfast
Credit Cards: A, B, C, D, E
Notes: 2, 4, 5, 8, 9, 10, 11, 12, 13, 14

RIPTON

The Chipman Inn

Route 125, 05766
(802) 388-2390

A traditional Vermont inn built in 1828, in the Green Mountain National Forest. Fine food, wine, and spirits for guests. Nine rooms, all with private bath. Fully licensed bar and large fireplace. Closed November 15 to December 26 and April 1 to May 15.

Hosts: Joyce Henderson and Bill Pierce
Rooms: 9 (PB) $80-108
Full Breakfast
Credit Cards: A, B, C
Notes: 2, 4, 7, 8 (over 12), 9, 12, 13

ROCHESTER

Liberty Hill Farm

Rural Route 1, Box 158, 05767
(802) 767-3926

Liberty Hill Farm is a family dairy farm where guests can relax and enjoy the countryside and help with farm chores, if they desire. Meals—breakfast and dinner—are served family-style. There are seven guest rooms and four shared baths. Plenty of recreational activity nearby including tennis, swimming, golf and skiing. Children welcome. Modified American Plan.

Hosts: Bob and Beth Kennett
Rooms: 7 (4 SB) $100
Full Breakfast
Credit Cards: None
Notes: 2, 4, 5, 8, 10, 11, 12, 13

Fox Stand Inn

ROYALTON

Fox Stand Inn

Route 14, 05068
(802) 763-8437

Built in 1818 as a stagecoach stop. On the banks of the White River, the dining room and tavern are open to the public and offer international creations. The inn's second-floor has five comfortably furnished guest rooms. Nestled in the center of one of Vermont's acclaimed recreation regions. Swimming, canoeing, tubing, bicycling, hiking, and fishing are readily at hand. Antique shops, auctions, flea markets, and horse shows are found throughout the countryside.

Hosts: Jean and Gary Curbery
Rooms: 5 (SB) $50-60
Full Breakfast
Credit Cards: A, B
Notes: 2, 4, 5, 7, 9, 10, 11, 12, 13

RUTLAND

The Inn at Rutland

70 North Main Street, Route 7, 05701
(802) 773-0575

6 Pets welcome; 8 Children welcome; 9 Social drinking allowed; 10 Tennis available; 11 Swimming available; 12 Golf available; 13 Skiing available; 14 May be booked through travel agents.

The Inn at Rutland is an 1890s Victorian mansion restored to its original condition. Guest rooms have been tastefully decorated to recreate the past while maintaining modern comforts. All rooms have private bathrooms, telephones, and color cable TV. A large, gourmet Continental plus breakfast is served. The common rooms offer a comfortable atmosphere for conversation, reading by the fireplace, watching movies, or just relaxing. Carriage house for ski or bike storage, with some mountain bikes available for guests.

Hosts: Bob and Tanya Liberman
Rooms: 10 (PB) $49-139
Continental Breakfast
Credit Cards: A, B
Notes: 5, 8 (over 8), 9, 10, 11, 12, 13, 14

ST. JOHNSBURY

The Looking Glass Inn

Rural Free Delivery 3, Box 199, 05819
(802) 748-3052

The Looking Glass Inn welcomes guests to a relaxed world of warmth and comfort. Each of the six individually decorated rooms is furnished with an antique double bed. There are three large baths. Each morning a hearty country breakfast is served in the dining room at guests' leisure. Relax in the afternoon with tea or a warming glass of sherry. A candlelight dinner, by special request, adds a romantic touch to an evening. Curl up by the parlor stove with a good book or good friends. Vermont has it all, whether guests seek the advantages of the great outdoors or desire pure serenity. The entire inn is available for special occasions.

Host: Barbara Haas
Rooms: 6 (2 PB; 4 SB) $60-80
Full Breakfast
Credit Cards: A, B
Notes: 2, 4 (call), 5, 9, 10, 11, 12, 13, 14

SHAFTSBURG

Covered Bridge

P.O. Box 447A, Norfolk, CT 06058
(203) 542-5944

1SHUT. An 1890 Colonial in a charming village setting close to Williamstown, Massachusetts, and Bennington, Vermont. The three guest rooms, all decorated with antiques, share a bath. A full gourmet breakfast is served. $50-65.

SHELBURNE

The Inn at Shelburne Farms

Shelburne Farms, 05482
(802) 985-8498

The Inn at Shelburne Farms offers turn-of-the-century elegance, contemporary cuisine, and some of the most beautiful lake and mountain views anywhere in the world. Original furnishings and decor in its 24 bedrooms and spacious common rooms recall the grandeur and gracious hospitality of another era. Explore walking trails through the 1,000-acre property, stroll through the formal perennial gardens or curl up by a fire in the library. Enjoy breakfast and dinner, at an additional fee, in the midst of a spectacular country setting. Box lunches also available.

Rooms: 24 (17 PB; 7 SB) $100-230
Full Breakfast
Credit Cards: A, B, C, D, E
Notes: 2, 3, 4, 7, 8, 9, 10, 11, 12, 13

SHREWSBURY

Buckmaster Inn

Rural Route 1, Box 118, Lincoln Hill Road, 05738
(802) 492-3485

This historic country inn was originally a stagecoach stop and stands on a knoll overlooking a typical red barn scene and picturesque valley. The charm of a center hall, grand staircase, and wide-pine floors show-off family antiques. The wood-burning fireplaces, library, huge porches, dining room, and country kitchen with wood-burning stove are special favorites of guests. Near ski areas, eight miles southeast of Rutland near Cuttingsville.

Hosts: Sam and Grace Husselman
Rooms: 4 (2 PB; 2 SB) $50-65
Full Breakfast
Credit Cards: None
Notes: 2, 5, 8, 10, 11, 12, 13

SOUTH HERO

American Country Collection

4 Greenwood Lane, Delmar, NY 12054
(518) 439-7001

179. A quiet, secluded retreat on 10-plus acres with panoramic views of the Green Mountains and Lake Champlain. On a hill overlooking the surrounding countryside is a three-room studio suite with private entrance, patio, and landscaped garden. Furnished with modern pieces, it is a complete living unit. Included is a bedroom with a double bed, kitchen, large bath, washer and dryer, and a living room with TV, VCR, sofa, easy chairs, and wood stove. Sliding glass doors off the living room provide access to the outdoor patio. Smoking outside only. Extra fee for each extra adult and child over three. $60-80.

SPRINGFIELD

Hartness House Inn

30 Orchard Street, 05156
(802) 885-2115; (800) 732-4789

This beautiful 1903 inn is listed on the National Register of Historic Places. Once the home of Gov. James Hartness, this inn invites guests to step back in time to a setting of gracious living, with carved beams, majestic fireplaces, and a grand staircase leading up to 11 beautifully decorated rooms. Guests may also choose from 29 modern rooms in the annex. Enjoy swimming, tennis, gracious dining, and a unique feature: a 1910 tracking telescope and a small underground museum reached via a 240-foot tunnel.

Host: Eileen Gennette-Coughlin
Rooms: 40 (PB) $80-130
Full Breakfast
Credit Cards: A, B, C
Notes: 2, 3, 4, 5, 7 (limited), 8, 9, 10, 11, 12, 13

HARTNESS HOUSE
A COUNTRY INN

STOWE

American Country Collection

4 Greenwood Lane, Delmar, NY 12054
(518) 439-7001

074. Drive over the wood bridge that crosses the brook and up the long drive to the white Colonial set amid tall pine trees.

6 Pets welcome; 8 Children welcome; 9 Social drinking allowed; 10 Tennis available; 11 Swimming available; 12 Golf available; 13 Skiing available; 14 May be booked through travel agents.

The inn operates as a bed and breakfast from spring until the end of autumn. For the remainder of the year, the Modified American Plan is honored. The five guest rooms are large and sleep three or four people. Four rooms have private baths. Guests may use the living room/lounge with stone fireplace, game room, and workshop, where guests repair and sharpen skis. Easy access to antiquing, biking, hiking, canoeing, and leaf peeking. Smoking permitted. Full breakfast is offered. $63-113.

091. Contemporary alpine-style private home nestled into the side of the Worcester Mountain Range just six miles from Stowe. The second floor is entirely for guests' use. The two guest rooms share a bath. One room may be rented with private bath. Breakfast is served in the elegant country kitchen in front of the wood-burning stove. No smoking. Couples only. Two-night minimum stay during foliage season. $65-95.

190. Set on a knoll above a two-acre pond stocked with trout and on 21 acres of rolling meadows and forest is this cozy eight-year-old Colonial-style farmhouse. Upstairs are two guest rooms, each with private bath and sitting area. One room with double bed and one room with queen-size bed and up to two additional single beds. First-floor bath has full Jacuzzi. Breakfast served at guest's request. Children welcome. Outside smoking only. $70-80.

Andersen Lodge— an Austrian Inn

3430 Mountain Road, 05672
(802) 253-7336; (800) 336-7336

A small, friendly Tyrolean inn in a quiet setting. Heated swimming pool, tennis court, living rooms with fireplaces, TV, and air conditioning. Near a major ski area, 18-hole golf course, riding, hiking, and fishing. Recreational path close by. Sauna

and Jacuzzi. Closed April 10 to June 1 and October 25 to December 10.

Hosts: Dietmar and Trude Heiss
Rooms: 78 (PB) $78-98
Full Breakfast
Credit Cards: A, B, C
Notes: 2, 4, 8, 9, 10, 12, 13, 14

Bed and Breakfast Inns of New England

128 S. Hoop Pole Road, Guilford, CT 06437
(203) 457-0042; (800) 582-0853

720. An old-fashioned inn on 28 acres, with a big fieldstone fireplace, knotty pine walls, and a Ping-Pong table. In 1991, this inn celebrated its 50th anniversary as Stowe's very first ski lodge. A Continental breakfast is served each morning in summer months. Ten large rooms on two floors, each with a double and a single bed. Some rooms have private full baths. Children over five are welcome. Guest pets are sometimes allowed. Smoking allowed. $25-75. $15 for additional adult.

Brass Lantern Inn

717 Maple Street, 05672
(802) 253-2229; (800) 729-2980

A traditional Vermont bed and breakfast inn in the heart of Stowe. Award-winning restoration of an 1810 farmhouse and carriage barn overlooking Mount Mansfield, Vermont's most prominent mountain. The inn features period antiques, air conditioning, handmade quilts, and planked floors. Some rooms have whirlpools or fireplaces and most have views. An intimate spot for house guests only. AAA three-diamond inn. Special packages include honeymoon, adventure, skiing, golf, air travel, sleigh and surrey rides, and more.

Hosts: Dustin and Andy Aldrich
Rooms: 9 (PB) $70-150
Full Breakfast
Credit Cards: A, B, C
Notes: 2, 5, 9, 10, 11, 12, 13, 14

NOTES: Credit cards accepted: A MasterCard; B Visa; C American Express; D Discover Card; E Diner's Club; F Other; 2 Personal checks accepted; 3 Lunch available; 4 Dinner available; 5 Open all year;

Butternut Inn at Stowe

2309 Mountain Road, 05672
(800) 3 BUTTER

Award-winning inn on eight acres of beautifully landscaped grounds alongside a mountain stream. Cottage gardens, pool, antiques,
afternoon tea, and collectibles. All rooms
have private baths. Close to sleigh rides,
downhill and cross-country skiing, summer
hiking, golf, tennis, horseback riding. Highlighted as one of the "best bed and breakfasts in the northeast" by *Skiing* magazine.
Honeymoon and anniversary packages
available. Enjoy real "Texas" hospitality in
Vermont. No smoking.

Hosts: Jim and Deborah Wimberly
Rooms: 18 (PB) $90-140
Full Breakfast
Credit Cards: A, B
Notes: 9, 10, 11, 12, 13, 14

The Gables Inn

1457 Mountain Road, 05672
(802) 253-7730; (800) GABLES-1

A classic country inn with 19 beautifully
appointed rooms in an 1860s farmhouse.
New carriage house suites have queen-size
beds, fireplaces, Jacuzzis, and TVs. Out
door hot tub and pool, sitting room, and
den. Hearty country breakfasts. and summer garden lunch. Lunch is available during
the summer, and dinner during the winter.
Minutes from seasonal attractions and
Stowe Village. No smoking. Candlelight
dining in winter.

Hosts: Soi and Lynn Baumrind
Rooms: 19 (PB) $60-200
Full Breakfast
Credit Cards: A, B, C, D
Notes: 2, 3, 4, 5, 8, 9, 10, 11, 12, 13, 14

Green Mountain Inn

Main Street, P.O. Box 60, 05672
(802) 253-7301; (800) STOWE-INN (U.S.
and eastern Canada)

Beautifully renovated 1833 country inn
listed on the National Register of Historic

Places and a member of Historic Hotels of
America. There are 64 antique-furnished
rooms, cozy sitting areas, two restaurants
and bars, complimentary health club,
beauty salon, and shops. In the heart of
Stowe Village, close to area attractions:
alpine and Nordic skiing, hiking, biking,
tennis, golf, horseback riding, and antiquing. AAA and Mobil approved. Full
breakfast is available at extra cost.

Host: Patti Clark
Rooms: 64 (PB) $89-200
Credit Cards: A, B, C
Notes: 3, 4, 5, 6, 7, 8, 9, 10, 11, 12, 13, 14

Green Mountain Inn

Guest House Christel Horman

4583 Mountain Road, 05672
(802) 253-4846; (800) 821-7891

Small, cozy bed and breakfast offers eight
large double rooms with full private baths.
Guest living room with color TV, VCR,
hearthstone fireplace, and many books and
magazines. Rates include full country
breakfast. One and one-half miles to
downhill and cross-country skiing. Ski
week rate available.

Hosts: Christel and Jim Horman
Rooms: 8 (PB) $56-60
Full Breakfast
Credit Cards: A, B
Notes: 2, 5, 7, 8 (over 10), 9, 10, 11, 12, 13, 14

6 Pets welcome; 8 Children welcome; 9 Social drinking allowed; 10 Tennis available; 11 Swimming available;
12 Golf available; 13 Skiing available; 14 May be booked through travel agents.

Logwood Inn and Chalet

199 Edson Hill Road, 05672
(802) 253-7354; (800) 426-6697

Handsome main lodge offers 18 guest rooms and one fully equipped chalet. Large, quiet living room with a massive fieldstone fireplace, TV room, swimming pool, and tennis are amenities guests are welcome to use. Five private acres with trees and flowers in abundance, and many bedrooms have private balconies. Near golf course, riding, biking, and restaurants.

Hosts: Sheila and Len Shetler
Rooms: 26 (20 PB; 6 SB) $65-85
Full Breakfast
Credit Cards: A, B
Notes: 2, 5, 7, 8, 9, 10, 11, 12, 13, 14

The Raspberry Patch

606 Randolph Road, 05672
(802) 253-4145; (800) 624-0639

Country elegance, breathtaking views, and a warm, cheery welcome invite guests to enjoy the peaceful, friendly atmosphere. Rooms are beautifully decorated with down comforters and antiques. A great breakfast is served until 10:30 A.M. Sitting room with TV, games, and fireplace. Air conditioning. Minutes to restaurants.

Host: Linda V. Jones
Rooms: 4 (PB) $50-100
Full Breakfast
Credit Cards: A, B
Notes: 2, 5, 6, 8, 9, 10, 11, 12, 13, 14

The Siebeness

3681 Mountain Road, 05672
(802) 253-8942; (800) 426-9001

A warm welcome awaits guests at this charming country inn. Antiques, private baths, homemade quilts, and air conditioning. Fireplace lounge, BYOB bar, hot tub, pool with beautiful mountain views. Famous for outstanding food. Dinner available in fall and winter. Adjacent to Stowe's famous recreation path. Honeymoon, golf, and ski packages available.

Hosts: Nils and Sue Andersen
Rooms: 10 (PB) $60-95
Full Breakfast
Credit Cards: A, B, C, D, E
Notes: 2, 4, 5, 8, 9, 10, 11, 12, 13, 14

Ski Inn

Route 108, 05672
(802) 253-4050

This comfortable inn, noted for good food and good conversation, is a great gathering place for interesting people. Guests enjoy themselves and others. Nearest lodge to all Stowe ski lifts, with miles of cross-country trails at the door. Cool and quiet in the summer. Rooms are large and colorful, each with a double and single bed. Evening meal available during ski season. A minimum two-day, three-night stay is required over holidays.

Host: Harriet Heyer
Rooms: 10 (5 PB; 5 SB) $40-60
Full and Continental Breakfast
Credit Cards: C
Notes: 2, 4, 5, 8, 9, 10, 11, 12, 13, 14

Ski Inn

Stowe-Bound Lodge

673 South Main Street, 05672
(802) 253-4515

A small guest house on a sheep farm in the beautiful Green Mountains. Downhill and cross-country skiing in the winter. Hiking and biking in summer. Meals are plentiful. Anyone desiring to exchange the fast pace of city life for some relaxation and slower pace of country life will find Stowe, sometimes called the Ski Capital of the East, a refreshing change. Why not be Stowe-bound?

Hosts: Dick and Erika Brackenbury
Rooms: 12 (4 PB; 8 SB) $40-80
Full Breakfast
Credit Cards: None
Notes: 2, 5, 6, 7, 8, 9, 14

Timberholm Inn

452 Cottage Club Road, 05672
(802) 253-7603; (800) 753-7603
FAX (802) 253-8559

Nestled in the woods, this ten-room bed and breakfast is friendly, romantic, and comfortable. A large, airy common room has a fieldstone fireplace. Enjoy mountain views from the deck. Guests are also invited to enjoy the outdoor hot tub. Two-bedroom suites are ideal for families. Near skiing, golf, hiking, tennis, and bike trails. Feast on a Vermont country buffet breakfast. Game room. No smoking.

Hosts: Louise and Pete Hunter
Rooms: 10 (PB) $60-100
Full Breakfast
Credit Cards: A, B
Notes: 2, 5, 8, 9, 10, 11, 12, 13, 14

TOWNSHEND

Boardman House Bed and Breakfast

Box 112, 05353
(802) 365-4086

A 19th-century farmhouse set on the Village Green next to the most photographed church in Vermont. This is a prime foliage and antiquing area. Direct access to state routes 30 and 35 allows guests to pursue other interests from cross-country and downhill skiing to canoeing on the West River. Guests may choose between five rooms and one suite. Gourmet breakfasts feature pear pancakes, individual souffles, hot fruit compotes, homemade muffins, and more.

Hosts: Sarah Mesenger and Paul Weber
Rooms: 6 (5 PB; 1 SB) $65-85
Full Breakfast
Credit Cards: None
Notes: 2, 5, 6 (limited), 7 (limited), 8, 11, 12, 13

Sinclair Inn

UNDERHILL

Sinclair Inn Bed and Breakfast

Rural Route 2, Box 35, 05489
(802) 899-2234; (800) 433-4658

A showcase of builder Edward Sinclair's craftsmanship and fully restored in 1989, this 1890 Queen Anne Victorian has been described as "a study in architectural styles, incorporating features such as towers, gables, turrets, colored glass, and an intricately carved fretwork valance across the living room and stairway." Halfway between Burlington and Smuggler's Notch. Enjoy the nearby hiking, boating, sailing, biking, festivals, and shows. Discount ski lift tickets available. One room with fireplace. Handicap bathroom. No smoking.

Hosts: Jeanne and Andy Buchanan
Rooms: 6 (PB) $55-95
Full Breakfast
Credit Cards: A, B
Notes: 2, 5, 8 (over 12), 10, 11, 12, 13

6 Pets welcome; 8 Children welcome; 9 Social drinking allowed; 10 Tennis available; 11 Swimming available; 12 Golf available; 13 Skiing available; 14 May be booked through travel agents.

UNDERHILL CENTER

American Country Collection

186. A contemporary home on a hillside overlooking a stream-fed pond stocked with trout. The living room has a cathedral ceiling with floor-to-ceiling windows, a gas-log fireplace, and comfortable seating. Breakfast is served either in the dining room, on an outdoor deck, or on the enclosed side porch, all commanding a view of the pond and mountain. The inn offers four rooms, all with views of the mountain. Two rooms are on the first level, joined by a common room with wood-burning fireplace, TV, shared bath, and a kitchen, with access to a patio with a grill. The other rooms are on the second and third level and have private baths. Furnishings are a mix of antiques and contemporary. The inn is close to Burlington, Underhill State Park, St. Michael's College, the University of Vermont, and Trinity College. Smuggler's Notch offers both cross-country and downhill skiing. No smoking. Children welcome. Two cats in residence. $55-120.

VERGENNES

Emerson's Guest House

82 Main Street, 05491
(802) 877-3293

Emerson's Guest House

Experience fine Vermont hospitality in this 1850 Victorian home surrounded by spacious lawns, flowers, and vegetable gardens. Relax in the gracious living quarters or on the porch. Enjoy a full breakfast, which includes homemade breads, muffins, jams, and jellies. Visit nearby Shelburne Museum, Morgan Horse Farm, and Kennedy Brothers Marketplace. Area recreation includes fishing, boating, canoeing, hiking, and bicycling.

Hosts: Jeannette and Donald Michalets
Rooms: 6 (2 PB; 4 SB) $50-75
Full Breakfast
Credit Cards: A, B
Notes: 2, 5, 9, 10, 11, 12, 13

Strong House Inn

Strong House Inn

82 West Main Street, 05491
(802) 877-3337

Comfortable, elegant lodging in an 1834 Federal-style home listed on the National Register of Historic Places. In the heart of the Lake Champlain Valley, with fine views of the Green Mountains and Adirondack ranges, the area offers some of the finest cycling in Vermont. Nearby lake, hiking, golf, and Shelburne. The air-conditioned inn offers seven rooms, five with private baths and two with working fireplaces. A full country breakfast is included, and dinner is available upon request.

Host: Mary Bargiel
Rooms: 7 (5 PB; 2 SB) $65-140
Full Breakfast
Credit Cards: A, B, C
Notes: 2, 4, 5, 8, 9, 11, 12, 13, 14

NOTES: Credit cards accepted: A MasterCard; B Visa; C American Express; D Discover Card; E Diner's Club; F Other; 2 Personal checks accepted; 3 Lunch available; 4 Dinner available; 5 Open all year;

WAITSFIELD

Bed and Breakfast Inns of New England

128 S. Hoop Pole Road, Guilford, CT 06437
(203) 457-0042; (800) 582-0853

716. This inn, tucked alongside picturesque Route 100, is remarkable for not just one, but three reasons. The first is the wonderful full gourmet breakfast. The second is the inn itself, which is a piece of Vermont history. The third is the variety of attractions and activities its convenient location affords. All six bedrooms have private baths. Two-night minimum stay required during the fall and on weekends. Children over six are welcome. No smoking, please. Resident dog and horses. $75-115. $20 for third person.

Hyde Away Inn

Route 17, Rural Route 1, Box 65, 05673
(802) 496-2322; (800) 777-HYDE

A comfortable and casual, circa 1820 inn, less than five minutes from Sugarbush and Mad River Glen Ski areas, hiking and biking trails, and historic Waitsfield Village. Fourteen rooms (private and semi-private baths), common area with TV, and children's toy area. Public restaurant with delicious and affordable American cuisine: steaks, fresh seafood, and pastas. Rustic tavern with tavern menu. Package and group rates available. Ideal for groups and family gatherings.

Hosts: Bruce and Margaret
Rooms: 14 (4 PB; 10 SB) $49-80
Continental Breakfast
Credit Cards: A, B, C
Notes: 4, 5, 6 (limited), 8, 9, 10, 11, 12, 13, 14

Knoll Farm Guest House

Bragg Hill Road, 05673
(802) 496-3527; (802) 496-3939

This unique combination of inn and farm sits beautifully high in Green Mountains with spectacular views, rural setting, Scotch Highland cattle, and horses. Organic gardens, and abundant farm-fresh meals. Comfortable 1800s farmhouse with sunny bedrooms and family heirloom furniture. Expansive lawn, hammocks, swings, and nature paths. A special place since 1950s for rest, peaceful atmosphere, simple country living, beauty, and spiritual renewal. Guests have returned for more than thirty years.

Hosts: Ann Day
Rooms: 4 (SB) $70-90
Full Breakfast
Credit Cards: None
Notes: 2, 4, 7 (limited), 9, 10, 11, 12

Lareau Farm Country Inn

Box 563, Route 100, 05673
(802) 496-4949

Nestled in an open meadow near the Mad River, this 1832 Greek Revival farmhouse is only minutes from skiing, shopping, dining, soaring, and golf. Sleigh rides, cross-country skiing, and swimming on the premises. When guests come, they feel at home and relaxed. Hospitality is the inn's specialty. "One of the top 50 inns in America"—*Inn Times.*

Hosts: Dan and Susan Easley
Rooms: 13 (11 PB; 2 SB) $60-125
Full Breakfast
Credit Cards: A, B
Notes: 2, 5, 8, 11, 12, 13, 14

Millbrook Inn

Route 17, Rural Free Delivery, Box 62, 05673
(802) 496-2405; (800) 477-2809 (reservations)

Relax in the friendly, unhurried atmosphere of this cozy 1850s inn. Seven guest rooms are decorated with hand stenciling, antique bedsteads, and handmade quilts. Breakfast and dinner included in the daily rate. Dine in the romantic, small restaurant that features hand-rolled pasta, fresh fish, veal, shrimp, and homemade desserts from a varied menu. Full breakfast is available during the summer only; Modified American Plan during winter and fall. Two-day minimum

6 Pets welcome; 8 Children welcome; 9 Social drinking allowed; 10 Tennis available; 11 Swimming available;
12 Golf available; 13 Skiing available; 14 May be booked through travel agents.

stay required for weekends, three-nights for holidays. Closed from April 5 to June 10 and October 25 to Thanksgiving.

Hosts: Joan and Thom Gorman
Rooms: 7 (4 PB; 3 SB) $50-140
Credit Cards: A, B, C
Notes: 2, 4, 6 (limited), 8 (over 6), 9, 10, 11, 12, 13

Mountain View Inn

Rural Free Delivery, Box 69, Route 17, 05673
(802) 496-2426

This small country inn (circa 1826) has seven guest rooms, each with private bath, accommodating two people. The rooms are decorated with stenciling, quilts, braided rugs, and antique furniture. Meals are served family-style around an antique harvest table. Good fellowship is enjoyed around the wood-burning fireplace in the living room. Two-night minimum stay required on weekends.

Hosts: Fred and Susan Spencer
Rooms: 7 (PB) $37.80-70.20
Full Breakfast
Credit Cards: None
Notes: 2, 4, 5, 7 (limited), 8, 9, 10, 11, 12, 13, 14

Newtons' 1824 House Inn

Newtons' 1824 House Inn

Route 100, Box 159, 05673
(802) 496-7555

Enjoy relaxed elegance in a perfect country setting. Six beautiful guest rooms, all with private baths. Classical music, Oriental rugs, fireplaces, and a sun porch. Gourmet breakfast with breakfast souffles and freshly squeezed orange juice. Stroll on 52 acres on the Mad River. Even a private swimming hole! Featured in the *Los Angeles Times*, *Glamour* magazine, and *Travel*

& Leisure. Rated three diamonds by AAA and two stars by Mobil.

Hosts: Nick and Joyce Newton
Rooms: 7 (PB) $75-125
Full Breakfast
Credit Cards: A, B, D
Notes: 2, 5, 9, 10, 11, 12, 13, 14

The Waitsfield Inn

Route 100, Box 969, 05673
(802) 496-3979

This gracious 1820s restored Colonial inn is in the heart of the beautiful Mad River Valley. The inn, just minutes from Sugarbush, offers spectacular skiing and wonderful hiking, shopping, antiquing, and much more. Relax in one of the 14 rooms, all of which are beautifully appointed with antiques, quilts, and private baths. Enjoy a full breakfast and let the "innspired" hosts make every stay a memorable one.

Hosts: Steve and Ruth Lacey
Rooms: 14 (PB) $65-115
Full Breakfast
Credit Cards: A, B, C, D
Notes: 2, 5, 8, 9, 10, 11, 12, 13, 14

WALLINGFORD

American Country Collection

4 Greenwood Lane, Delmar, NY 12054
(518) 439-7001

055. This restored 1840 Colonial farmhouse, listed on the National Register of Historic Places, is on 20 acres of pasture and woods. The Gothic-style barn, a Vermont landmark, is often painted by artists. Swimming, fishing, and canoeing on the premises; golf, tennis, and horseback riding nearby. Four guest rooms, all with private baths. No smoking. Children over ten welcome. Pets in residence. Also, one fully equipped cottage with king-size bed and jet tub. Breakfast is $10 extra for cottage guests. Rates slightly higher during foliage season. Two-night minimum stay during foliage season. $70-140.

White Rocks Inn

Rural Route 1, Box 297, 05773
(802) 446-2077

Circa 1840s farmhouse inn, listed on the National Register of Historic Places, beautifully furnished with antiques, Oriental rugs, and canopied beds. All five rooms have private baths. Charming cottage with slate roof and cupola is also available. Cathedral ceiling in living area, loft bedroom, whirlpool bath, kitchenette, and deck overlooking pastures. Close to four major ski areas, hiking, horseback riding, canoeing, summer theater, and good restaurants. No smoking. Minimum-stay requirements for weekends and holidays. Closed November.

Hosts: June and Alfred Matthews
Rooms: 5 (PB) $60-95
Cottage: 1 (PB) $260 EP
Full Breakfast
Credit Cards: A, B, C
Notes: 2 (deposit), 8 (over 10), 9, 10, 11, 12, 13

WARREN

Beaver Pond Farm Inn

Rural Delivery Box 306, Golf Course Road, 05674
(802) 583-2861; FAX (802) 583-2860

Beaver Pond Farm is an elegantly restored Vermont farmhouse on a quiet country meadow with spectacular views of the nearby Green Mountains. It is adjacent to the Sugarbush Golf Course and 40K of groomed cross-country ski trails. One mile from downhill trails of Sugarbush. Hearty breakfasts, snacks, hors d'oeuvres, and setups. Prix fixe dinners are available three times a week during winter season. Package plans are available, including skiing in winter and golf in summer. Closed April 15 to May 25.

Hosts: Bob and Betty Hansen
Rooms: 6 (4 PB; 2 SB) $32-65
Full Breakfast
Credit Cards: A, B, C
Notes: 2, 4, 8 (over 6), 9, 10, 11, 12, 13, 14

West Hill House

West Hill House Bed and Breakfast

West Hill Road, Rural Route 1, Box 292, 05674
(802) 496-7162

Up a quiet country lane on nine acres, this 1860s farmhouse features gardens, pond, apple orchard, and fantastic views. One mile from Sugarbush Ski Resort, adjacent to championship golf course and cross-country ski trails. Extraordinary hiking, cycling, canoeing, and fishing. Near fine restaurants, covered bridges, quaint villages, and shops. Enjoy the comfortable front porch, fireplace, eclectic library, Oriental rugs, original art, and antiques. Bedrooms feature premium linens, down comforters, and good reading lights. Guest pantry with BYOB wet bar. Memorable breakfasts, afternoon and bedtime snacks, and picnic lunches.

Hosts: Dotty Kyle and Eric Brattstrom
Rooms: 5 (PB) $75-95
Full Breakfast
Credit Cards: A, B, C
Notes: 2, 3, 4 (call) 5, 8 (over 10), 9, 10, 11, 12, 13, 14

WATERBURY

American Country Collection

4 Greenwood Lane, Delmar, NY 12054
(518) 439-7001

039. This 1790 Cape Cod was once a stagecoach stop and is now a haven for modern-day travelers seeking country comfort and hospitality. The six guest rooms are filled with country antiques. One room has a working fireplace. Two have private baths. The inn has a library, living room, dining room, large porch, and country kitchen, where a full breakfast is served at the long trestle table next to the brick hearth overlooking the Green Mountains. Smoking in common areas only. Children over six are welcome. Three-night minimum stay over holiday weekends. $65-115.

Bed and Breakfast Inns of New England

128 S. Hoop Pole Road, Guilford, CT 06437
(203) 457-0042; (800) 582-0853

VT717. Come enjoy the wonderful comfort of this restored 1832 farmhouse. The front porch, furnished with wicker chairs and flowers, is an inviting spot to relax, watch the sun go down, or enjoy a glass of wine. The sunny common rooms are large but cozy. Each of the six guest rooms has a private bath and individually controlled heat and air conditioning. A full breakfast of homemade sweetbreads, muffins, raspberry and blueberry pancakes, eggs, juices, and coffee is served each morning. The neighborhood offers downhill and cross-country skiing, snowmobile rides, and the inn's big screen TV and VCR. Children over six are welcome. No guest pets, please. No smoking. $65-95.

VT718. This three-story Austrian chalet is a classic example of Tyrolean architecture, complete with intricately carved balconies. The stenciled booths in the BYOB pub are perfect for a game of backgammon or checkers, and the adjacent Austrian dining room is set for memorable, musical breakfasts. Ten second-floor guest rooms overflow with antiques, comforters, and quilts. Each room opens to a balcony that surrounds the bed and breakfast and provides relaxing views of the Green Mountains. Pri-

vate and shared baths. Children of all ages welcome. Two resident cats, but no guest pets, please. No smoking. $35-75.

Grünberg Haus Bed and Breakfast

Rural Route 2, Box 1595 AD, Route 100 S, 05676
(802) 244-7726; (800) 800-7760

Romantic Austrian chalet on a quiet mountainside, hand-built of native timber and fieldstone. Gorgeous guest rooms, secluded cabins, and spectacular carriage house. Warm-weather Jacuzzi, cold-weather sauna, ski center and walking trails, tennis court, year-round fireplace and BYOB pub. Savor our memorable breakfast feasts. In Ben & Jerry's hometown, between Stowe and Sugarbush ski resorts. "Home of hospitable innkeepers, chickens, and teddy bears." Central to Stowe, Burlington, Montpelier, covered bridges, and waterfalls.

Hosts: Christopher Sellers and Mark Frohman
Rooms: 10 (5 PB; 5 SB) $55-75
Full Breakfast
Credit Cards: A, B, C, D, F
Notes: 2, 3, 4, 5, 8, 9, 10, 11, 12, 13, 14

Grünberg Haus

Inn at Blush Hill

Blush Hill Road, Box 1266, 05676
(802) 244-7529; (800) 736-7522

A circa 1790 restored Cape on five acres with beautiful mountain views. The inn has four fireplaces, a large sitting room, fireplaced guest room, canopied bed, down comforters, and lots of antiques. Across from a golf course, and all summer sports are nearby. Enjoy skiing at Stowe, Sugarbush, and Bolton Valley. Packages available. AAA and Mobil rated.

Hosts: Gary and Pam Gosselin
Rooms: 6 (2 PB; 4 SB) $50-115
Full Breakfast
Credit Cards: A, B, C, D
Notes: 2, 5, 8 (over 6), 9, 10, 11, 12, 13, 14

The Old Stagecoach Inn

18 North Main Street, 05676
(802) 244-5056; (800) 262-2206

A historic village inn one-half mile from I-85 on scenic route 100. Built in 1826 as a stagecoach stop, the inn has been meticulously restored to its original Victorian elegance. With its central location in the heart of the Winooski River Valley and accessibility to world-class skiing, hiking, and water sports, amid 4,000 foot peaks and quaint villages, the Old Stagecoach Inn offers a world of pleasure in the atmosphere of a bygone era. No smoking.

Hosts: Jack and John Barwick
Rooms: 10 (7 PB; 3 SB) $35-110
Full Breakfast
Credit Cards: A, B
Notes 2, 4, 5, 8, 9, 10, 11, 12, 13

Thatcher Brook Inn

P.O. Box 490, Route 100 North, 05676
(802) 244-5911; (800) 292-5911

This faithfully restored Victorian mansion is listed on the Vermont Register of Historic Buildings. The guest rooms all have private baths; some have fireplaces, and others whirlpool tubs. Enjoy French country cuisine in the main restaurant or light fare in the Newsroom Bar and Grill. Near Ben & Jerry's Ice Cream factory, Cold Hollow Cider Mill, and Shelburne Museum.

Hosts: Kelly and Peter Varty
Rooms: 24 (PB) $75-175
Full Breakfast

Thatcher Brook Inn

Credit Cards: A, B, C, D, E
Notes: 2, 4, 5, 7 (limited), 8, 9, 10, 11, 12, 13, 14

WEATHERSFIELD

American Country Collection

4 Greenwood Lane, Delmar, NY 12054
(518) 370-4948

076. This gracious inn was once a farmhouse that served as a stagecoach stop, part of the Underground Railroad, and a summer estate. Ten guest rooms and two suites, all with private baths. Most rooms have working fireplaces. Handicapped accessible. Guests can relax in the conservatory or work out in the exercise room complete with Finnish sauna and pool table. A four-course breakfast begins the day. English high tea is served each afternoon, and a gourmet dinner is prepared each evening. Smoking in designated areas. Well-behaved children over eight welcome. Rates include breakfast, tea, and dinner. Two-night minimum stay on weekends; three nights on holidays. $175-205.

WEST DOVER

Austin Hill Inn

Route 100, 05356
(800) 332-RELAX

Escape to timeless relaxation just before the historic village of West Dover. Enjoy complimentary wine by crackling fireplaces, peacefulness, pampering, and pancakes. Guests rave about the special spot and luscious meals. Twelve antique-filled guest rooms, all with private baths. Heated outdoor pool. Minutes to golfing, skiing, craft and outlet shopping, museums, and galleries. Special Murder Mystery weekends.

Host: Robbie Sweeney
Rooms: 12 (PB) $80-125
Full Breakfast
Credit Cards: A, B, C, D
Notes: 2, 5, 8 (over 7), 9, 10, 11, 12, 13

Deerhill Inn

Deerhill Inn and Restaurant

Box 136, Valleyview Road, 05356-0136
(802) 464-3100; (800) 626-5674

A gracious English country house with mountain views, candlelight dining, superb cuisine, spacious sitting rooms, fine English and American antiques, afternoon tea, a licensed lounge, private baths, some rooms with canopied beds, lovely grounds, swimming pool, and tennis court. In Mount Snow area. Alpine and Nordic skiing, mountain biking, two championship golf courses, golf school, walking, fishing, boating, antiquing, shopping, craft fairs, Marlboro Music Festival, and just plain relaxing. Open from Thanksgiving to March 31 and Memorial Day through October.

Hosts: Robert and Joan Ritchie
Rooms: 17 (15 PB; 2 SB) $99-130
Full Breakfast

Credit Cards: A, B, C, E
Notes: 2, 4, 8 (over 8), 9, 10, 11, 12, 13, 14

West Dover Inn

P.O. Box 506, Route 100, 05356
(802) 464-5207

This historic old inn, circa 1846, in the foothills of the Green Mountains features elegant rooms, all with private baths, and luxurious fireplace suites with whirlpool tubs. Elegant dining in the Capstone Restaurant, featuring tableside cooking and an extensive wine list. Full bar and lounge. Minutes to golf, skiing, tennis, and swimming. AAA three-diamond rated.

Hosts: Don and Madeline Mitchell
Rooms: 12 (PB) $80-195
Full Breakfast
Credit Cards: A, B, C
Notes: 2, 4, 7, 8 (over 8), 9, 10, 11, 12, 13, 14

WESTON

Bed and Breakfast Inns of New England

128 S. Hoop Pole Road, Guilford, CT 06437
(203) 457-0042; (800) 582-0853

700. "Vermont's favorite breakfast," said the *Yankee Travel Guide* about this early American, circa 1790, Colonial-style bed and breakfast. The hosts hope that beginning the day with a hearty old-fashioned breakfast will set the proper tone for a very enjoyable day in Vermont. Guests can enjoy the large common room with woodstove, books, board games, TV, and large solar sun room area. Each room is decorated with antique furnishings and heavy quilts and comforters. There are eight guest rooms available with double or twin beds and shared baths. Six larger rooms have private baths and TV. Children are welcome. No smoking, please. No guest pets. $55-85.

NOTES: Credit cards accepted: A MasterCard; B Visa; C American Express; D Discover Card; E Diner's Club; F Other; 2 Personal checks accepted; 3 Lunch available; 4 Dinner available; 5 Open all year;

Inn at Weston

P.O. Box 56, 05161
(802) 824-5804

Enjoy beautifully appointed guest rooms and continental cuisine served in gracious style in this historic country inn. Nestled in the Green Mountains in the heart of the picturebook village of Weston, the inn was recently featured in *Gourmet* magazine. A pleasant walk to the Weston Playhouse, shops, and galleries. Dining rooms open to the public for dinner. Golf, tennis, downhill and cross-country skiing, and other activities close by.

Hosts: Bob and Jeanne Wilder
Rooms: 19 (12 PB; 7 SB) $66-111
Full Breakfast
Credit Cards: A, B, C, D
Notes: 2, 4, 5, 9, 10, 11, 12, 13

The Wilder Homestead Inn and 1827 Craft Shoppe

25 Lawrence Hill Road, 05161
(802) 824-8172

An 1827 brick home listed on the National Register of Historic Places. Walk to shops, museums, and summer theater. Crackling fires in common rooms, canopied beds, and down comforters. Rooms have original Moses Eaton stenciling and are furnished with antiques and reproductions. Weston Priory nearby. Minimum-stay requirements

The Wilder Homestead

August through October, during winter, and for holidays.

Hosts: Peggy and Roy Varner
Rooms: 7 (5 PB; 2 SB) $60-95
Full Breakfast
Credit Cards: A, B
Notes: 2, 5, 8 (over 6), 9, 10, 11, 12, 13

WILLIAMSTOWN

The Autumn Crest Inn

Rural Free Delivery 1, Box 1540, 05679
(802) 433-6627; (800) 339-6627

The Autumn Crest Inn is a fully restored farmstead over 180 years old, nestled on 46 lush acres of fields and forest overlooking the spectacular Williamstown Valley. Enjoy a cozy fireplaced living room and sleigh rides in the winter. In summer, relax on the wraparound front porch. Outstanding dinners by candlelight in a world-class setting. A robust breakfast is served each morning. This is a true country inn. AAA three diamonds.

Rooms: 18 (PB) $98-150
Full Breakfast
Credit Cards: A, B, C, E
Notes: 2, 4, 5, 6, 7, 10, 11, 12, 13, 14

WILMINGTON

The Inn at Quail Run

HCR 63, P.O. Box 28, Smith Road, 05363
(802) 464-3362; (800) 34 ESCAPE

Enjoy pristine mountain views, comfortable large rooms, a full country breakfast, and après ski snacks. On a quiet country road away from traffic, the entire inn is nonsmoking. In winter, enjoy cross-country trails, and in summer, enjoy the heated pool. Amenities include large sauna, TV room, library, exercise room, game room, and antique store. A charming and romantic getaway.

Hosts: Tom, Marie, and Molly Martin
Rooms: 15 (14 PB; 1 SB) $80-125
Full Breakfast
Credit Cards: A, B, C, D
Notes: 2, 5, 8, 9, 10, 11, 12, 13, 14

6 Pets welcome; 8 Children welcome; 9 Social drinking allowed; 10 Tennis available; 11 Swimming available; 12 Golf available; 13 Skiing available; 14 May be booked through travel agents.

Misty Mountain Lodge

326 Stowe Hill Road, Box 114, 05363
(802) 464-3961

A small family inn built in 1803, with a beautiful view of the Green Mountains. The lodge can accommodate 16 people. Home-cooked meals are prepared by the owners. The cozy living room has a large fireplace where guests gather to visit, read, or join in a hearty sing-along with the hosts. Summer walking trails. Close to major southern Vermont ski areas and Marlboro Music for summer enjoyment.

Hosts: Buzz and Elizabeth Cole
Rooms: 8 (1 PB; 7 SB) $60-105
Full Breakfast
Credit Cards: A, B, D
Notes: 2, 4, 5, 8, 9, 10, 11, 12, 13, 14

Nordic Hills Lodge

179 Coldbrook Road, 05363
(800) 326-5130

Become spoiled at Nordic Hills, where one of the family members will serve a choice-of-menu breakfast to start the day. This lodge offers the nostalgia of a country inn, with the relaxing qualities of modern amenities including a Jacuzzi, sauna, outdoor pool, game room, and in-room TV. For the more active, skiing, championship golf, tennis, and horseback riding are within minutes. Dinner available during the winter. Two-diamond AAA rating.

Hosts: George and Sandy Molner and
    Marianne Coppola
Rooms: 27 (PB) $70-130
Full Breakfast
Credit Cards: A, B, C, D, E
Notes: 2, 4, 7, 8, 9, 10, 11, 12, 13, 14

The Red Shutter Inn

Route 9 West, Box 636, 05363
(802) 464-3768; (800) 845-7548

This 1894 nine-room Colonial inn with fireplace suites sits on a hillside within walking distance of the town of Wilmington. Tucked behind the inn is the renovated carriage house with four rooms, one a two-room fireplace suite with a two-person whirlpool bath. A renowned restaurant with candlelight dining (alfresco dining on an awning-covered porch in the summertime). Championship golf (golf packages), skiing at Mount Snow and Haystack, cross-country skiing, hiking, boating, and antiquing are minutes away. Experience the congenial atmosphere of country inn life. Closed April.

Hosts: Max and Carolyn Hopkins
Rooms: 9 (PB) $90-165
Full Breakfast
Credit Cards: A, B, C, D
Notes: 2, 4, 7, 8 (over 12), 9, 10, 11, 12, 13

Shearer Hill Farm Bed and Breakfast

P.O. Box 1453, 05363
(802) 464-3253; (800) 437-3104

Pristine farm setting on country road, five miles from center of Wilmington. Large rooms with private baths. Delicious Vermont breakfast. Near downhill skiing, groomed cross-country skiing trails on property, swimming, hiking, boating, shopping, Marlboro Music Festival, horseback riding, and many fine restaurants.

Hosts: Bill and Patti Pusey
Rooms: 4 (PB) $80
Continental Breakfast
Credit Cards: A, B, D
Notes: 2, 5, 10, 11, 12, 13, 14

Trail's End—A Country Inn

Smith Road, 05363
(802) 464-2727; (800) 859-2585

A unique country inn tucked away on ten acres with flower gardens, a clay tennis court, heated outdoor pool, and a stocked pond. Selected by guests as "One of the Top 50 Inns in America" in *Inn Times*. Fifteen delightful rooms, all with private baths, including fireplace rooms and fireplace suites with canopied beds and whirlpool tubs. Full breakfast menu and afternoon tea. Warm

NOTES: Credit cards accepted: A MasterCard; B Visa; C American Express; D Discover Card; E Diner's Club; F Other; 2 Personal checks accepted; 3 Lunch available; 4 Dinner available; 5 Open all year;

Trail's End

hospitality and attention to detail are the hosts' specialties. Mobil two-star rated and the ABBA three-crown excellence. Closed mid-April through mid-May.

Hosts: Bill and Mary Kilburn
Rooms: 15 (PB) $90-150
Suites: $140-170
Full Breakfast
Credit Cards: A, B, C
Notes: 2, 7, 8, 9, 10, 11, 12, 13

WINDSOR

Juniper Hill Inn

Rural Route 1, Box 79, 05089
(802) 674-5273; (800) 359-2541

This elegant but informal inn allows guests to pamper themselves. Antique furnished guest rooms with private baths, many with working fireplaces. Marvelous views. Sumptuous candlelight dinners and hearty full breakfasts. Cool off in the outdoor pool, canoe, bike, hike, visit antique and craft shops, covered bridges, and museums. Twenty minutes to Woodstock and Quechee in Vermont and Hanover, New Hampshire. A perfectly romantic inn. Mobil and AAA rated. Closed April.

Hosts: Rob and Susanne Pearl
Rooms: 16 (PB) $85-125
Full Breakfast
Credit Cards: A, B
Notes: 2, 4, 9, 10, 11, 12, 13, 14

WOLCOTT VILLAGE

American Country Collection

4 Greenwood Lane, Delmar, NY 12054
(518) 439-7001

130. Twelve miles north of Stowe, this Greek Revival-style three-bedroom inn is bordered by the LaMoille River and offers guests authentically appointed rooms and spacious bed chambers. Guest rooms are decorated according to themes, and breakfast features fresh fruit, cereal, French toast or baked eggs, scones or hot muffins, locally made preserves, and coffee or tea. $59-74.

WOODSTOCK

Canterbury House

43 Pleasant Street, 05091
(802) 457-3077

A 115 year-old village townhome just east of the village green. This bed and breakfast, furnished with authentic Victorian antiques, has eight rooms with private baths. Living room with TV and stereo. Within walking distance of shops, the historic district, and restaurants. A full gourmet breakfast is served in the dining room. Guest rooms have air conditioning and fresh flowers. Bicycles provided summer and fall. Described as elegant but comfortable.

Hosts: The Holdens
Rooms: 7 (PB) $85-140
Full Breakfast
Credit Cards: A, B, C
Notes: 2, 5, 8, 9, 10, 11, 12, 13, 14

The Charleston House

21 Pleasant Street, 05091
(802) 457-3843

This circa 1835 Greek Revival home has been authentically restored. Listed on the National Register of Historic Places, it is

The Charleston House

furnished with antiques, combined with a hospitality reminiscent of a family homecoming. In the picturesque village of Woodstock, "one of the most beautiful villages in America."

Hosts: Barb and Bill Hough
Rooms: 7 (PB) $90-150
Full Breakfast
Credit Cards: A, B, C
Notes: 2, 5, 8 (over 9), 9, 10, 11, 12, 13, 14

Kedron Valley Inn

Route 106, 05071
(802) 457-1473

Historic inn with Victorian charm, canopied beds, fireplaces, and antique quilts. Award-winning cuisine. Casual dress. Voted "Inn of the Year" by inngoers. Featured in *Country Living*, *Yankee*, and *Country Home*. Swimming lake with beach. Trail rides, golf, tennis, and downhill and cross-country skiing nearby. Discounts for midweek stays.

Hosts: Max and Merrily Comins
Rooms: 27 (PB) $114-182
Full Breakfast
Credit Cards: A, B, C, D
Notes: 2, 4, 10, 11, 12, 13

The Woodstocker Bed and Breakfast

Route 4, 61 River Street, 05091
(802) 457-3896

At the foot of Mount Tom in the picturesque village of Woodstock, this romantic 1830s inn offers nine large, elegantly decorated, air-conditioned rooms with private baths. Bed chambers are appointed with queen-size or full beds as well as FM/cassette/CD stereos. A sumptuous four-course gourmet breakfast begins everyday. Afternoon refreshments are served. A short stroll over a covered bridge brings you to fine dining and shopping.

Hosts: Jerry and JaNoel Lowe
Rooms: 9 (PB) $90-125
Full Breakfast
Credit Cards: A, B
Notes: 2, 5, 9, 10, 11, 12, 13, 14

WOODSTOCK (TAFTSVILLE)

Applebutter Inn

Happy Valley Road, 05091
(802) 457-4158

The Applebutter Inn is a spacious, country elegant Federal home with six guest rooms on five acres in Taftsville, a historic hamlet of Woodstock, Vermont. Guests enjoy quality and comfort, warm hospitality and a full natural-foods breakfast (Beverlee's own applebutter). Fine linens and down comforters on 18th-century comfortable beds. Formal parlor and two sitting rooms with fireplaces induce ultimate relaxation.

Hosts: Andrew and Beverlee Cook
Rooms: 6 (2 PB; 4 SB) $65-95
Full Breakfast
Credit Cards: A, B
Notes: 2, 5, 8, 9, 10, 11, 12, 13, 14

NOTES: Credit cards accepted: A MasterCard; B Visa; C American Express; D Discover Card; E Diner's Club; F Other; 2 Personal checks accepted; 3 Lunch available; 4 Dinner available; 5 Open all year;

Virginia

Inn on Town Creek

ABINGDON

Inn on Town Creek

P.O. Box 1745, 445 East Valley Street, 24212-1745
(703) 628-4560; FAX (703) 628-9611

A historic creek is the theme of this bed and breakfast on four acres of beautifully land-scaped property. Multi-level brick patios and rock gardens provide tranquil privacy; air-conditioned, antique-filled rooms and the cordiality of the innkeepers offer a peaceful getaway to the discerning guest. Near fine dining, entertainment. Ample parking.

Hosts: Dr. and Mrs. Roger D. Neal
Rooms: 5 (4 PB; 1 SB) $75-150
Continental Breakfast
Credit Cards: None
Notes: 2, 4, 5, 8 (over 10), 9, 10, 11, 12, 14

River Garden
Bed and Breakfast

19080 North Fork River Road, 24210-4560
(703) 676-0335; (800) 952-4296

River Garden is nestled in the foothills of the Clinch Mountains, on the bank of the north fork of the Holston River outside historic Abingdon. Furnished with traditional, antique, and period furniture, each room has its own riverside deck overlooking the gentle rapids. Private exterior entrance, full, queen-, or king-size bed, full bath, and central heat and air. Guests are also granted kitchen privileges. Common areas include living room, den, dining room, and recreation room.

Hosts: Carol and Bill Crump
Rooms: 4 (PB) $60-65
Full Breakfast
Credit Cards: None
Notes: 2, 5, 9, 11, 12, 13, 14

Summerfield Inn

101 West Valley Street, 24210
(703) 628-5905

Summerfield Inn is in the Abingdon historic district, just two blocks from the world-famous Barter Theatre. Near the Appalachian Trail, Mount Rogers National Recreation Area, South Holston Lake, the Blue Ridge Parkway, Virginia Creeper Trail, excellent restaurants, and marvelous shops. Just off I-81 at Exit 17. Skiing an hour and one half away.

Hosts: Champe and Don Hyatt
Rooms: 4 (PB) $70-75
Full Breakfast
Credit Cards: A, B, C
Notes: 2, 7 (limited), 8 (over 12), 9, 10, 12, 14

6 Pets welcome; 7 Smoking allowed; 8 Children welcome; 9 Social drinking allowed; 10 Tennis available; 11 Swimming available; 12 Golf available; 13 Skiing available; 14 May be booked through travel agents.

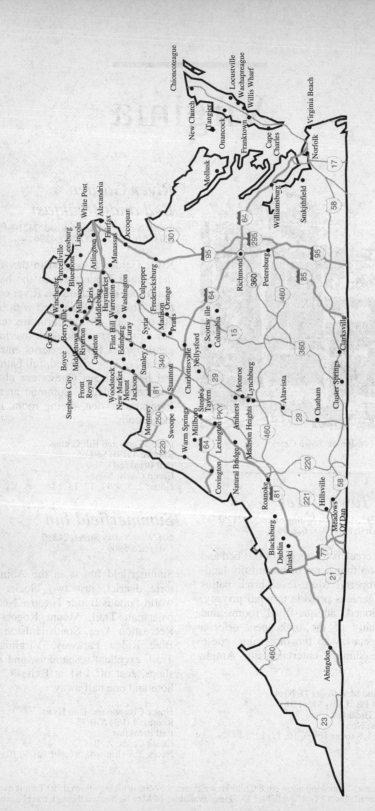

ALEXANDRIA

Amanda's Bed and Breakfast

1428 Park Avenue, Baltimore, MD 21217
(410) 225-0001; (800) 899-7533
FAX (410) 728-8957

183. Historic Old Town Alexandria. Four blocks to stores, restaurants, and historic sites. One room with double bed and private bath. Continental breakfast. $85.

Morrison House

116 South Alfred Street, 22314
(703) 838-8000

Centrally in Old Town Alexandria, Morrison House is a stroll from historic landmarks, quaint boutiques, and international dining. Downtown Washington, D.C. is less than ten minutes away, national airport is only three miles. Built in the style of an 18th-century manor house, Morrison House offers 45 elegantly appointed guest rooms, including three suites. All guest rooms are enhanced by fine Federal-period reproductions including mahogany four-poster beds, brass chandeliers, decorative fireplaces, and Italian marble baths. Services offered include 24-hour butler, concierge and room service, indoor valet parking, specialized laundry and valet services, shoe shine and newspaper delivery each morning, nightly turndown service with chocolates, and health club privileges. Complementary morning coffee in the parlor; afternoon tea is served daily from 3:00-5:00 P.M. in the parlor.

Hosts: Mr. and Mrs. Robert E. Morrison
Rooms: 45 (PB) $205-295
Credit Cards: A, B, C, E, F (Carte Blanche)
Notes: 2, 3, 4, 5, 8, 9, 10, 11, 12, 14

Princely Bed and Breakfast, Ltd.

819 Prince Street, 22314
(703) 683-2159

Thirty-three historic (1750-1875) homes in Old Town Alexandria. Most are furnished with antiques, many of which are museum quality. Breakfasts are Continental plus. Walk to all restaurants, shops, and monuments. Metro subway is a fast 15 minutes to the White House and frequents ten major universities within ten miles. Mount Vernon is seven miles away. Call 10:00 A.M. to 6:00 P.M., Monday through Friday. $75-100.

Host: E.T. Mansmann
Homes: 37 (PB and SB) From $75
Continental Plus Breakfast
Credit Cards: None
Notes: 2, 5, 7, 8, 9, 10, 12

ALTAVISTA

Castle to Country House

1010 Main Street, 24517
(804) 369-4911

Three luxurious, beautifully furnished guest rooms with access to a large living room with a fireplace, formal dining room, sitting room with color TV and VCR, and a sun porch. All rooms are equipped with color cable TV, telephones, queen-size beds, and private baths. Central heat and air conditioning. Guests may choose either a Continental or a full country breakfast. Whether traveling on business or vacationing for a week or a weekend, all are welcome.

Host: Christine Critchley
Rooms: 3 (PB) $50-60
Full Breakfast
Credit Cards: A, B, C, D
Notes: 2, 4, 5, 14

AMHERST

Dulwich Manor Bed and Breakfast

Route 5, Box 173 A, 24521
(804) 946-7207

Gracious country lodging in an elegant English-style manor house with views of the Blue Ridge Mountains. Six beautifully appointed bed chambers with fireplaces; windowseats or whirlpool tub; canopied, brass, and antique beds. Enjoy the hot tub in the Victorian gazebo. Surrounded by 85 acres of natural beauty at the end of a country lane. This perfect romantic getaway is convenient to Richmond, Charlottesville, Lynchburg, and Washington, D.C. A sumptuous country breakfast is served. Mobil three-star rating.

Hosts: Bob and Judy Reilly
Rooms: 6 (4 PB; 2 SB) $69-89
Full Breakfast
Credit Cards: None
Notes: 2, 5, 7 (restricted), 8, 9, 10, 12, 14

ARLINGTON

Amanda's Bed and Breakfast

1428 Park Avenue, Baltimore, MD 21217
(410) 225-0001; (800) 899-7533
FAX (410) 728-8957

189. Victorian built in 1899. All exterior gingerbread is original except for the gable trim. Period antiques and lovely decor. Metro is one block away. One room with double bed and private half-bath. Continental breakfast. $75-85.

BERRYVILLE

Blue Ridge Bed and Breakfast

Route 2, Box 3895, 22611
(703) 955-1246; (800) 296-1246

A. Colonial Williamsburg reproduction furnished with lovely antiques; near the Shenandoah River on 11 acres complete with Christmas trees. Perfect getaway; ideal for weekend bikers and hikers. Only 90 minutes from Washington, D. C. $55-95.

BLACKSBURG

L'Arche Bed and Breakfast

301 Wall Street, 24060
(703) 951-1808

An oasis of tranquility just one block from the Virginia Tech campus, L'Arche Bed and Breakfast is an elegant turn-of-the-century Federal Revival home situated among terraced gardens in downtown Blacksburg. Spacious rooms have traditional antiques, family heirlooms, hand-made quilts, and private baths. Delicious full breakfasts feature homemade breads, cakes, jams, and jellies.

Host: Vera G. Good
Rooms: 5 (PB) $80
Full Breakfast
Credit Cards: A, B
Notes: 2, 5, 10, 12, 13

L'Arche

Per Diem Bed and Breakfast

401 Clay Street Southwest, 24060
(703) 953-2604; (800) 272-4707

A unique cluster of three houses in downtown Blacksburg, Per Diem is one block from Virginia Tech's campus and the Huckleberry Trail. The main house, built in 1929, reflects traditional and Southwestern styles. The guest houses have complete kitchens

Per Diem

and living areas and are connected by wood decks to the main house, covered patio and heated swimming pool. All houses have cable TV, telephones, and antiques.

Host: Joanne Anderson
Rooms: 3 (PB); Suites: 4 (PB) $75-85
Full Breakfast
Credit Cards: A, B
Notes: 2, 5, 8 (over 12), 10, 11, 12

Sycamore Tree
Bed and Breakfast Inn

P.O. Box 10937, 24062-0937
(703) 381-1597

The romantic, luxurious vacation on a picturesque mountain meadow, in a custom-built bed and breakfast where guests will be pampered, enjoy wildlife from the porches, sip tea by the fire, or hike over 126 acres. The six guest rooms have private baths and central heat and air. Nearby are excellent restaurants, antique shops, golf courses, swimming, and university activities. Come be a part of the magic of the mountains.

Hosts: Charles and Gilda Caines
Rooms: 6 (PB) $85-110
Full Breakfast
Credit Cards: A, B
Notes: 2, 5, 8 (over 12), 10, 11, 12

BLUEMONT

Blue Ridge
Bed and Breakfast

Route 2, Box 3895, Berryville, 22611
(703) 955-1246; (800) 296-1246

A. Perfect for hiking the Appalachian Trail or biking. This retreat on the Shenandoah River 50 miles west of Washington, D.C., is a restful stopover for a bed and meals. From $30.

BOYCE

Blue Ridge
Bed and Breakfast

Route 2, Box 3895, Berryville, 22611
(703) 955-1246; (800) 296-1246

A. In the heart of fox hunt country. Lovely modern stone and clapboard house has a true western ranch house feel. Complete fox hunting arrangements available seven days a week for experienced riders, including complete care for horse and tack. Groom quarters available. Indoor ring. In the middle of 60 acres with beautiful views of mountains, a swimming pool, stable house, and kennel. $75-100.

B. Historic estate built in 1748 is graced by a lovely English hostess. On the National Register of Historic Places and featured in major books and the *Washington Post*. Over 1,000 spring bulbs, wicker-filled porch, acreage to hike, in-ground pool, and two lakes on property. George Washington really did sleep here, as well as Col. John S. Mosby. $90.

C. Beautiful view of the Blue Ridge to enjoy. Guests might even get a ride in a horse and buggy in this farm country. Less than two hours from the nation's capitol. $55.

The River House

Route 1, Box 135, 22620
(703) 837-1476; FAX (703) 837-2399

A rural getaway on the Shenandoah River, built in 1780 and 1820. Sixty miles east of Washington, D.C., convenient to scenic, historic, and recreational areas, the house offers

6 Pets welcome; 8 Children welcome; 9 Social drinking allowed; 10 Tennis available; 11 Swimming available; 12 Golf available; 13 Skiing available; 14 May be booked through travel agents.

special features and programs for house parties, small workshops, and family reunions. Accommodations are available for small, two- or three-day business conferences, and executive retreats during the week. Relaxing, book-filled bed/sitting rooms have fireplaces, air conditioning, and private baths. AAA-rated three diamonds.

Host: Cornelia S. Niemann
Rooms: 5 (PB) $80-115
Full Breakfast/Brunch
Credit Cards: A, B
Notes: 2, 3 and 4 (by arrangement), 5, 7, 8, 9, 10, 11, 12, 14

CAPE CHARLES

Amanda's Bed and Breakfast

1428 Park Avenue, Baltimore, MD 21217
(410) 225-0001; (800) 899-7533
FAX (410) 728-8957

122. Lovely, quiet, rural setting along the Chesapeake Bay featuring unspoiled land, abundant wildlife, game birds, miles of private beach, and nature's most fabulous sunsets. This two-story brick home has a great view of the bay and is decorated with antiques, reproductions, and collectibles. Three rooms with private baths. Full breakfast. $85.

138. Restored 1910 Colonial Revival. Just steps from a public beach on the bay. Relax on one of the porches, sample the cool breezes off the bay, or bike through the historic town. Guests set their own pace and explore. Four guest rooms and one cottage. Full breakfast. $70-80.

Pickett's Harbor

P.O. Box 97 AA, 23310
(804) 331-2212

Guests, seagulls, pelicans, and herons all love this secluded, marvelous, and wide beach nestled in pines and dogwoods on 27 acres. A

Colonial home (big house, little house, and kitchen) with cupboards, doors, and floors made from old barn rafters. Fireplaces, antiques, and reproductions. All rooms and the porch face the Chesapeake Bay. Country breakfast served overlooking the bay. Late afternoon beverage. Central air.

Hosts: Sara and Cooke Goffigon
Rooms: 6 (2 PB; 4 SB) $65-125
Full Breakfast
Credit Cards: None
Notes: 2, 5, 8, 10, 11, 12, 14

Pickett's Harbor

CASTLETON

Blue Knoll Farm

Route 1, Box 141, 22716
(703) 937-5234

This lovingly restored 19th-century farmhouse is in the foothills of the Blue Ridge Mountains. The original house was built before the Civil War. Four guest rooms with private baths are open to guests. Blue Knoll provides a charming, rural retreat minutes from a renowned five-star restaurant, the Inn at Little Washington, and other fine dining. Near Shenandoah National Park and Skyline Drive.

Hosts: Gil and Mary Carlson
Rooms: 4 (PB) $95-125
Full Breakfast
Credit Cards: A, B
Notes: 2, 5, 9

NOTES: Credit cards accepted: A MasterCard; B Visa; C American Express; D Discover Card; E Diner's Club; F Other; 2 Personal checks accepted; 3 Lunch available; 4 Dinner available; 5 Open all year;

Blue Ridge Bed and Breakfast

Route 2, Box 3895, 22611
(703) 955-1246; (800) 296-1246

A. Fabulous pre-Civil War house built in 1850, in a lovely country setting in the middle of five and one-half acres with small pond. Close to Thornton River, Inn at Little Washington, and Skyline Drive. Lovely mountain views. Two bedrooms and a suite with Jacuzzi are available. $95-125.

CHARLOTTESVILLE

Clifton—The Country Inn

Route 13, Box 26, 22901
(804) 971-1800

A Virginia historic landmark, Clifton is among the few remaining large plantation properties in Albermarle County. On 40 secluded acres with walking trails, private lake, spring-fed pool with waterfall, heated spa, tennis courts, and croquet pitch. Guest rooms feature wood-burning fireplaces, private baths, sitting areas, and canopied or four-poster beds. Only five miles to Charlottesville and Monticello.

Hosts: Craig and Donna Hartman
Rooms: 14 (PB) $155-198
Full Breakfast
Credit Cards: A, B, C, E
Notes: 2, 4, 5, 8, 9, 10, 11, 12, 13, 14

Guesthouses Bed and Breakfast

P.O. Box 5737, 22905
(804) 979-7264; FAX (804) 293-7791

Afton House. A mountain retreat with panoramic views east to valleys and hills, this spacious home is on the old road up the mountain pass. There are four bedrooms, mostly furnished with antiques. One has a private adjoining bath, and three share two hall baths. Full breakfast is served. Antique

shop on the premises and others in the village. $75-80.

Alderman House. This large, formal Georgian home is authentic in style and elegant in decor. It was built by the widow of the first president of the University of Virginia in the early 1900s and is about one mile from the university. Breakfast is served with true Southern hospitality. Guests may choose a room with a four-poster bed or one with twin beds, each with adjoining private bath. Air-conditioning. No smoking in the house. $80-86.

Ammonette Farm. This 110-year-old restored farmhouse is on a small farm with a pastoral setting and beautiful views. The guest room has three large windows, bright cheery colors, and private bath. Go hiking, enjoy the scenery, or just sit! Only 20 minutes to Charlottesville, 30 to Wintergreen. This farmhouse is ideal for families, as additional bedrooms are usually available for children. $68-80.

Auburn Hill. An antebellum cottage on a scenic farm that was part of the original Jefferson plantation. The main house was built by Jefferson for one of his overseers. It is convenient to Monticello and Ash Lawn, just six miles east of the city. The cottage has a sitting room with fireplace, bedroom with four-poster queen-size bed, and connecting bath and shower. Guests may use the pool in summer. Scenic trails, walks, and views. Air conditioning. No smoking. Supplies provided for guests to prepare breakfast. $100-125. Weekly rates available.

Balla Machree. A deluxe separate suite in a contemporary home, this superb lakefront location offers complete privacy for guests. The suite is ten miles west of Charlottesville and overlooks a 250-acre lake with excellent fishing. The cozy quarters have a private en-

6 Pets welcome; 8 Children welcome; 9 Social drinking allowed; 10 Tennis available; 11 Swimming available; 12 Golf available; 13 Skiing available; 14 May be booked through travel agents.

Guesthouses
Bed and Breakfast
(continued)

trance, large brick fireplace, and comfortable bedroom with iron frame double bed and private adjoining bath. Tennis is available on new courts, but please bring proper shoes. Golf, riding, hiking, fishing, and canoeing are nearby. Continental breakfast supplies left in the suite for guests to prepare. Air conditioning. $100-125.

Belleview. This contemporary frame guest cottage offering complete privacy to guests five miles west of Charlottesville, in the Farmington Hunt country. These lovely quarters include living room with fireplace, Pullman kitchen, two bedrooms (one with twin beds, one with double tester bed), and full bath. A flagstone terrace off the living room offers privacy and mountain views. Air conditioning. Supplies provided for guests to prepare breakfast. $125-200.

Bollingwood. A lovely home in a convenient neighborhood with a private "city" garden featured on the spring 1988 Friendly Garden Tour, this guest house is within walking distance of the University of Virginia, restaurants, and shops. One guest room with twin canopied beds has a hall bath. The second room has a double canopied bed, a three-quarter bed, and an adjacent bath. Air conditioning. $68-88.

Boxwood Lane Farm. Virginia country living at its best describes this lovely bed and breakfast. A boxwood-lined path leads to the gracious front door of this 19th-century manor house just 15 miles south of Charlottesville and 15 miles from the Blue Ridge Parkway. There is a fine collection of contemporary paintings in this tastefully appointed home of a designer and an architect. This home has lovely surroundings, country walks past gardens with ponds and unusual plantings, and a pool is available for summer enjoyment. There are two large guest rooms, one with a queen-size bed and wood-burning fireplace, and the other with a double bed. Both rooms offer private baths, air conditioning, and full breakfast. Smoking outside only. $80-100.

Carrsbrook. Peter Carr built this estate home in 1798 using many of the architectural innovations of his uncle and guardian, Thomas Jefferson, including 15-foot ceilings and Jefferson's characteristic way of hiding stairways. Private entrance to the suite is from a large patio overlooking a formal boxwood garden with the deepest hand-dug well in Albermarle County. Downstairs is the sitting room with a pull-out sofa, adjacent bath, and small refrigerator. Upstairs is a bedroom with a king-size bed. Listed on the National Register of Historic Places. Air conditioning. No smoking. $68-100.

Chathill. A delightful country house in a rural setting only a few minutes' drive from Charlottesville and the University of Virginia. Accommodations consist of a large paneled room with fireplace and sofa bed in the sitting area, a queen-size bed, and adjoining bath. During the summer, visitors enjoy the swimming pool and the informal gardens. No smoking in the house. Air conditioning. $80-100.

Clover Green Farm. This farm is in beautiful rolling country in the foothills of the Blue Ridge Mountains. Guests are welcome to sit by the fire in the living room or enjoy the spectacular views from the sunroom. The first-floor guest room with double bed is a large, sunny room furnished with Victorian family pieces. It has an adjoining bath with a shower stall. Smokers welcome. $68-100.

Coleman Cottage. A late 19th-century servant's house on Seven Oaks Farm, an antebellum estate 15 miles west of Charlottesville. Sitting below Afton Mountain, it offers guests splendid mountain views and spacious grounds. The cottage has three bedrooms (two with double, one with twin), living and dining rooms, kitchen, bath, and two porches. Convenient to Wintergreen ski resort 20 miles away. Air conditioning. Supplies provided for guests to prepare breakfast. $150-200.

Copps Hill Farm. This ranch home is set on a small horse farm seven miles northwest of Charlottesville. Guests may enter through private lower-level entrance, where they have the seclusion of their own suite, a family room with TV and sofa bed, and two bedrooms with adjoining bath. A full farm-style breakfast is served in the dining room or on the sun porch overlooking rolling pastures. Air conditioning. $68-80.

Cottage Grove. This quaint country cottage offers beautiful views from two porches. The cozy guest room has an antique double bed and private hall bath. Another bedroom with a queen-size bed and private adjacent bath is available for a minimum of two nights. No air conditioning. No smoking. $60-80.

Cross Creek. A spectacular wood, stone, and glass cottage on a hilltop nine miles west of Charlottesville, Cross Creek is a perennial favorite. The living room, dining room, half-bath, and kitchen are built around a massive central stone fireplace. A deck provides a wonderful wooded view. Two bedrooms (one double, one king) are on the lower level with a full bath across the hall. Air conditioning. Supplies provided for guests to prepare breakfast. $125-200.

Farmington Heights. Gracious living just off the Farmington Country Club back nine. This lovely home has wonderful views of pastures and hills. One guest room has a queen-size bed and adjoining bath; a second room has twin beds and private adjoining bath. This second room has a two-night minimum stay. In warmer weather, guests may enjoy the pool. Air conditioning. $72-100.

Fox Lane Farm. Lovely new home in the Victorian style built in beautiful Keswick hunt country. The guest quarters offer complete privacy in a large room with cathedral ceiling and many Victorian pieces. An old quilt hangs behind the brass double bed. There is a private entrance from a lovely deck overlooking the woods and garden. There is an adjoining full bath and a pullman kitchen where breakfast supplies will be left for guests. No smoking. Air conditioning. $80-100.

Indian Springs. This new cottage with a rustic feel is in a lovely wooded setting on a private lake. The lake is stocked and has a small dock for fishing, basking in the sun, or swimming at guests' own risk. There is a large main room with a king-size bed, a sitting area with a queen-size sofa bed, dining area, kitchen, and bath. This cottage has complete privacy. TV, air conditioning. Supplies are provided for guests to prepare breakfast. $125-200.

Ingleside. A farm that has been in the same family for several generations, Ingleside lies on 1,250 acres of rolling pasture backed by steep, wooded mountains. The house was built around 1840 of bricks made from the farm's red clay. Accommodations consist of a large, antique-furnished room with double bed, fireplace, and adjacent bath. A tennis court is available for guest use. Air conditioning. $72-80.

6 Pets welcome; 8 Children welcome; 9 Social drinking allowed; 10 Tennis available; 11 Swimming available; 12 Golf available; 13 Skiing available; 14 May be booked through travel agents.

Guesthouses
Bed and Breakfast
(continued)

Ingwood. In a lovely villa on six wooded acres in one of Charlottesville's most prestigious neighborhoods, Ingwood is an elegant, separate-level suite with its own drive and private entrance. The bedroom is appointed with antiques, queen-size bed, and adjoining bath. The sitting room includes a fireplace, Pullman kitchen, and sofa for an extra person. A second bedroom with twin beds and private bath is also available. Sliding glass doors open to a secluded terrace with a view of the woods. Air conditioning. Breakfast supplies are left in the suite for guests to prepare. $80-100.

Maho-Nayama. Attention to detail is evident in the landscaping and furnishings of this beautiful Japanese-style home. The large master bedroom has a king-size bed with custom furnishings. The master bath has a sunken tub. Two rooms with double beds share a connecting bath. A private tennis court is available with advance notice and a service fee. Maho-Nayama is in a rural wooded area six miles northeast of town. Air conditioning. $80-100.

Meadow Run. Enjoy relaxed rural living in this new Contemporary/Classical home six miles west of Charlottesville. Guest rooms have either a double bed or twin beds and share a bath. Guests are welcome to browse in the boat lover's library, play the grand piano, or lounge in the living room. Many windows offer bucolic vistas of the southwest range. Fireplaces in the kitchen and living room add to the homey, friendly feel. Air conditioning. $68-80.

Meander Inn. A 75-year-old Victorian farmhouse on 50 acres of pasture and woods skirted by hiking trails and traversed by the Rockfish River. The inn offers five twin or queen-size bedrooms, some with private bath. A full country breakfast is served. Guests may enjoy the hot tub, wood-burning stove, player piano, deck, or front porch. Wintergreen Resort and Stoney Creek golf and tennis facilities are available to guests. Smoking permitted outdoors only. Air conditioning. $60-90.

Millstream. A lovely, large house about 20 minutes north of Charlottesville up a long driveway lined with old box bushes. The house, with a brick English basement, was built before the Civil War and enlarged in 1866. There are two guest rooms, each with private bath. Guests may enjoy the fireplace in the library or the mountain views from the living room. A full breakfast is served in the kitchen, which has hand-hewn exposed beams. No smoking. Air conditioning. $80-100.

Nicola Log Cabin. This is a romantic, 200-year-old log cabin on a 150-acre farm in historic Ivy eight miles west of Charlottesville, and has spectacular views of the Blue Ridge Mountains. The one-room cabin has a double bed, sleeper sofa, a new bath with shower, microwave oven, refrigerator, and wood-burning stove. Children's playset and tennis court available. Supplies provided for guests to prepare breakfast. $100-150.

Northfields. This gracious home is on the northern edge of Charlottesville. The guest room is furnished with twin beds and has a TV, private bath, and air conditioning. There is another bedroom available with a double four-poster bed and private hall bath. A full gourmet breakfast is served. No smoking. $60-68.

Park Street Victorian. This late Victorian mansion is one of the largest homes in the downtown historical district. Surrounded by a large lawn and gardens, this accommodation offers a two-room suite with fireplace. Antique furnishings feature a stately high-back double bed. Private bath with shower adjoins the guest room. A Continental breakfast is served in a beautiful formal dining room. Air conditioning. $80-100.

Polaris Farm. In the middle of rolling farm land dotted with horses and cattle, this architect-designed brick home offers guests an atmosphere of casual elegance. The accommodations consist of a ground floor room with twin beds and adjoining bath, and two upstairs rooms with twin beds and shared bath. There are gardens and terraces where one can view the Blue Ridge Mountains; a spring-fed pond for swimming, boating, and fishing; miles of trails for walking or horseback riding (mounts available at nearby stables). Air conditioning. $68-100.

Recoletta. Recoletta is an older Mediterranean-style house built with flair and imagination. The red tile roof, walled gardens with fountain, and artistic design create the impression of a secluded Italian villa within walking distance of the University of Virginia, shopping, and restaurants. Many of the antique furnishings are from Central America and Europe. The charming guest room has a beautiful brass double bed and a private hall bath with shower. Air conditioning. $72-80.

The Rectory. This charming home in a small village five miles west of Charlottesville was a church rectory. It is furnished with lovely antiques and has an English garden in the back. The guest room overlooking the formal rose garden has its own entrance, twin beds, and adjoining full bath. Air conditioning. No smoking. $72-80.

Rolling Acres Farm. A lovely brick Colonial home in a wooded setting on a small farm, this guest house has two bedrooms with a hall bath upstairs. One room has a double bed and the other has twin beds. The house is furnished with many Victorian pieces. No smoking. Air conditioning. $68-72.

Upstairs Slave Quarters. A fascinating place to stay if guests want interesting decor with the privacy of their own entrance. There is a harmonious mixture of antiques and art objects. The guest suite consists of a sitting room with a fireplace and two bedrooms (king and single) with bath (tub only). A couch in the sitting room opens to a double bed for extra guests. Adjacent to the University of Virginia and fraternity row, it is especially convenient for university guests. Air conditioning. $80-100.

Wayside. A one-story brick Colonial furnished with Early American antiques, this well kept home is on an elegant private street near the University of Virginia. Guests may use a single or a double room with hall bath, or a twin room with adjoining bath and private entrance. Two-night minimum stay for the twin room. Air conditioning and ceiling fans. $60-80.

Westbury. Built around 1820, this antebellum plantation home is a beautiful reminder of what country living and Southern hospitality are all about. Once a carriage stop between the James River and the Shenandoah Valley, Westbury now returns to the old tradition of welcoming travelers. In Batesville, a tiny community southwest of Charlottesville with a genuine country store, Westbury is only 20 minutes from Skyline Drive and the Appalachian Trail. A comfortable double four-poster bed awaits in the guest room. Private hall bath. No air conditioning. $60-72.

6 Pets welcome; 8 Children welcome; 9 Social drinking allowed; 10 Tennis available; 11 Swimming available; 12 Golf available; 13 Skiing available; 14 May be booked through travel agents.

Winston. This quaint Cape Cod brick home is on a quiet side street in an academic neighborhood near the University of Virginia. The private upstairs guest room offers twin beds and an adjoining bath. A home-style breakfast is served. Air conditioning. $52-60.

Winton on Pantops. A brick Colonial east of town on Pantops Mountain overlooking the city of Charlottesville. The home offers two double bedrooms. One room also has a single bed, and both rooms share a hall bath. Full breakfast is served. There are resident cats. No air conditioning. $52-60.

High Meadows— Virginia's Vineyard Inn

Route 4, Box 6, Route 20 South, 24590
(804) 286-2218

Enchanting 19th-century European-style auberge with tastefully appointed, spacious guest rooms, private baths, and period antiques. Two-room suites available. Several common rooms, fireplaces, and tranquility. Pastoral setting on 50 acres. Privacy, relaxing walks, and gourmet picnics. Virginia wine tasting and romantic candlelight dining nightly. Virginia Architectural Landmark. National Register of Historic Places.

High Meadows

Hosts: Peter, Sushka, and Mary Jae Abbitt
Rooms: 12 (PB) $90.52-172.42
Full Breakfast
Minimum stay weekends and holidays: 2 nights
Credit Cards: A, B
Closed December 24-25
Notes: 2, 4, 6, 8, 9, 10, 11, 13, 14

The Inn at the Crossroads

Route 2, Box 6, North Garden, 22959
(804) 979-6452

Built in 1820 as a tavern on the historic James River Turnpike, the inn continues its long tradition, offering a quiet respite for the weary traveler. A four-story brick building with a long front porch, it is on five acres overlooking pastures and the foothills of the Blue Ridge Mountains, and is convenient to Monticello and Charlottesville, as well as the James River and Skyline Drive.

Host: Lynn L. Neville
Rooms: 5 (SB) $65-75
Full Breakfast
Credit Cards: A, B
Notes: 2, 5, 9, 10, 11, 12, 13, 14

The Mark Addy

Route 1, Box 375, Nellysford, 22958
(804) 361-1101; (800) 278-2154

Dr. Everett's "most commanding estate in Nelson County" has been beautifully restored and lovingly appointed. The charming rooms and luxurious suites enjoy magnificent views. The Mark Addy is located the beauty of the Blue Ridge Mountains, between Charlottesville and Wintergreen Resort, to encourage either relaxation or adventure. Become surrounded by 12.5 acres of serenity and the romance of a bygone era. The elegant and imaginative "cuisine de grandmére" will delight all tastes. Dinner available on weekends.

Rooms: 9 (PB) $90-125
Full Breakfast
Credit Cards: A, B
Notes: 2, 4, 5, 9, 10, 11, 12, 13, 14

Mountain Meadows Bed and Breakfast

P.O. Box 4, Ivy, 22945
(804) 977-6855 day; (804) 296-2934 evenings

A charming bedroom suite with a private entrance and bath built in a converted creamery. In a peaceful country setting with spectacular views of the Blue Ridge Mountains. A short drive to Charlottesville, the University of Virginia, Monticello, Ash Lawn, vineyards, and Wintergreen ski resort. Go to sleep to the sound of the soft bleating of the sheep and wake to a breakfast of farm eggs, laid by the happy hens.

Host: Sarah Churchill
Room: 1 (PB) $50-65
Full and Continental Breakfast
Credit Cards: F
Notes: 2, 5, 10, 12, 13

Silver Thatch Inn

3001 Hollymead Drive, 22901
(804) 978-4686

Silver Thatch Inn is a rambling white clapboard home that dates from 1780. With three dining rooms and seven guest rooms, it is a sophisticated retreat on the outskirts of Charlottesville. Silver Thatch's modern American cuisine uses the freshest of ingredients, and all sauces are prepared with fruits and vegetables. The menu features grilled meats, poultry, game in season, and there are always vegetarian selections. The inn provides a wonderful respite for the sophisticated traveler who enjoys fine food and a quiet, caring atmosphere.

Hosts: Vince and Rita Scoffone
Rooms: 7 (PB) $110-125
Continental Breakfast
Credit Cards: A, B, C, E
Notes: 2, 4, 5, 8, 9, 10, 11, 12, 14

200 South Street Inn

200 South Street, 22902
(800) 964-7008

Lovely restored inn, garden terrace, sweeping veranda, in historic downtown Charlottesville, with English and Belgian antiques, six Jacuzzis, 11 fireplaces, and canopied and four-poster beds. Continental breakfast and afternoon tea (with wine) and canapés. Just four miles to Monticello and one mile to the University of Virginia.

Host: Brendan Clancy
Rooms: 20 (PB) $98-185
Continental Breakfast
Credit Cards: A, B, C
Notes: 2, 4, 5, 7, 8, 9, 10, 11, 12, 13, 14

Eldon

CHATHAM

Eldon—The Inn at Chatham

Route 1, Box 254B, State Road 685, 24531
(804) 432-0935

Classically restored 1835 historic plantation manor home. One-half mile from Chatham, "Virginia's prettiest town." Five guest rooms, private baths, and full gourmet country breakfast. Formal garden, wooded country setting with original dependencies (smokehouse, ice house, stable, and servants' cottage). Intimate gourmet restaurant with a Culinary Institute of America graduate as the chef and pastry chef. Former home of Virginia's governor and Secretary of the Navy, Claude A. Swanson. Member BBAV.

Hosts: Joy and Bob Lemm
Rooms: 5 (4 PB; 2 SB) $55-120
Full Breakfast
Credit Cards: A, B
Notes: 2, 3, 4, 5, 7 (limited), 9, 10, 12

6 Pets welcome; 8 Children welcome; 9 Social drinking allowed; 10 Tennis available; 11 Swimming available; 12 Golf available; 13 Skiing available; 14 May be booked through travel agents.

House of Laird Bed and Breakfast

335 South Main Street, P.O. Box 1131, 24531
(804) 432-2523

Built in 1880, this Greek Revival house has been totally, lovingly restored and professionally decorated. The house sits in a garden surrounded by 200-year-old oaks. Famous for its Library Suite, two working fireplaces, antiques, Oriental rugs, Irish-estate canopied bed, roses, chocolates, bath with heated towels, cable TV, and gourmet breakfast in front of fire. Luxurious and private. This quiet setting is a short distance from historical houses and battlefields, vineyards, seasonal festivals, antique auctions, fine dining, scenic mountain drives, horseback riding, hiking, and boating.

Hosts: Mr. and Mrs. Ed Laird
Rooms: 4 (PB) $75-109
Full Breakfast
Credit Cards: A, B, C
Notes: 2, 5, 9, 12, 14

CHINCOTEAGUE

The Garden and the Sea Inn

Virginia Eastern Shore, Route 710,
 P. O. Box 275, New Church, 23415
(804) 824-0672

Elegant European-style country inn with French-style gourmet dining. Near beautiful beach and Wildlife Refuge at Chincoteague. Large, luxurious rooms, beautifully designed with custom canopied beds, designer fabrics, Victorian detail, stained glass, Oriental rugs, bay windows, and skylights. Spacious private baths with whirlpool tubs. Hearty Continental breakfast. Gourmet dining on premises, candlelight. Romantic escape package available. Beach, wildlife refuge, boating, tennis, and golf are nearby. Mobil three-star and AAA three-diamond ratings.

Hosts: Tom and Sara Baker
Rooms: 5 (PB) $110-150
Continental Breakfast
Credit Cards: A, B, C
Notes: 2, 4, 6, 7 (limited), 8, 9, 10, 11, 12, 14

Island Manor House

4160 Main Street, 23336
(804) 336-5436; (800) 852-1505 (reservations)

Gracious and romantic, this beautifully furnished antebellum home is filled with Federal-style antiques. A garden sitting room with a fireplace opening onto a private brick courtyard with a fountain and rose garden is inviting to sit in, and all rooms are air-conditioned. Delicious homemade breakfast and afternoon tea specialties. Four minutes from Chincoteague Wildlife Refuge (with over 300 species), and a beautiful beach. Bicycling, hiking, swimming, antiquing, and canoeing nearby. Ideal for small weddings, parties, and meetings.

Hosts: Charles D. Kalmykow and Carol W. Rogers
Rooms: 8 (4 PB; 4 SB) $65-120
Full Breakfast
Credit Cards: A, B
Notes: 2, 5, 7 (limited), 9, 11, 14 (off-season)

Island Manor House

Miss Molly's Inn

4141 Main Street, 23336
(804) 336-6686; (800) 221-5620

A charming Victorian inn on the bay. Close to Chincoteague National Wildlife Refuge and Assateague National Seashore. All rooms are air-conditioned and furnished with period antiques. Room rate incudes full

Miss Molly's Inn

breakfast and a traditional English afternoon tea. Marguerite Henry stayed here while writing Misty of Chincoteague. Closed early January–mid-February.

Hosts: Barbara and David Wiedenheft
Rooms: 7 (5 PB; 2 SB) $69-135
Full Breakfast
Credit Cards: None
Notes: 2, 8 (over 8), 9, 11, 12, 14

The Watson House

4240 North Main Street, 23336
(804) 336-1564

The Watson House has been tastefully restored with Victorian charm. Nestled in the heart of Chincoteague, the house is within walking distance of shops and restaurants. Each room has been comfortably decorated, including air conditioning, private baths, and antiques. A full, hearty breakfast and afternoon tea are served in the dining room or on the veranda. Enjoy free use of bicycles to tour the island. Chincoteague National Wildlife Refuge and Beach is two minutes away, offering nature trails, surf, and Chincoteague's famous wild ponies. AAA rated three diamonds.

Hosts: David and Jo Anne Snead;
   Tom and Jacque Derrickson
Rooms: 6 (PB) $65-105
Full Breakfast
Credit Cards: A, B
Notes: 2, 7 (limited), 9, 10, 11, 12

Buckhorn Inn

HCR 33, Box 139, 24421
(703) 337-6900; (800) 693-4242

A 180-year-old country inn nestled in the heart of the George Washington State Forest, just 12 miles west of Staunton on scenic Route 250. Comfortable rooms all with private baths provide a relaxed get-away-from-it-all atmosphere. The inn also provides grand buffets and family-style meals, and is featured in both the Uncle Ben's Country Inn brand rice national advertising program and the publication Virginia's Historic Restaurants. Bring an appetite.

Host: Garland Foster
Rooms: 6 (PB) $45-65
Full Breakfast
Credit Cards: A, B, D
Notes: 2, 3, 4, 5, 8, 9, 10, 11, 12, 13, 14

CLARKSVILLE

Needmoor Inn

801 Virginia Avenue, P.O. Box 629, 23927
(804) 374-2866

Needmoor Inn, circa 1889, a Victorian bed and breakfast in the heart of the beautiful Kerr Lake. The inn stands amid one and one-fourth acres of stately shade and fruit trees and a large herb garden. Enjoy comfortable antiques, private baths, gourmet breakfasts, complimentary bicycles, and a therapeutic massage. Activities in the area include water sports, excellent bass fishing, Occoneechee State Park, and Prestwould Plantation.

Hosts: Lucy and Buddy Hairston
Rooms: 3 (PB) $45-65
Full Breakfast
Credit Cards: None
Notes: 2, 5, 8, 9, 10, 11, 12

CLUSTER SPRINGS

Oak Grove Plantation

P.O. Box 45, 24535
(804) 575-7137

6 Pets welcome; 8 Children welcome; 9 Social drinking allowed; 10 Tennis available; 11 Swimming available; 12 Golf available; 13 Skiing available; 14 May be booked through travel agents.

Operated from May to September, by descendants of the family who built the house in 1820. Full country breakfast in the Victorian dining room. Hiking, biking, and birdwatching on 400 acres of grounds. Near Buggs Island for swimming, boating, and fishing; Danville to tour the last capital of the Confederacy; and Appomattox. One hour north of Raleigh-Durham.

Host: Pickett Craddock
Rooms: 2 (SB) $50
Full Breakfast
Credit Cards: None
Notes: 2, 4, 8, 9, 10, 11, 12, 14

COLUMBIA _____

Upper Byrd Farm Bed and Breakfast

6452 River Road West, 23038
(804) 842-2240

A turn-of-the-century farmhouse nestled in the Virginia countryside on 26 acres overlooking the James River. Enjoy fishing or tubing. Canoe rentals available. Visit Ashlawn and Monticello plantations. See the state's capitol or simply relax by the fire surrounded by antiques and original art from around the world. Breakfast is special.

Hosts: Ivona Kaz-Jespen and Maya Laurinaitis
Rooms: 4 (SB) $70
Full Breakfast
Credit Cards: None
Notes: 2, 5, 11, 14

COVINGTON _____

Milton Hall Bed and Breakfast Inn

207 Thorny Lane, 24426
(703) 965-0196

Milton Hall Bed and Breakfast Inn is a Virginia Historic Landmark, listed on the National Register of Historic Places. This country manor house, built by English nobility in 1874, is on 44 acres adjoining the George Washington National Forest and one mile from I-64, Exit 10. Spacious rooms are decorated in the style of the period and furnished with a combination of antiques, period reproductions, and unique pieces collected from various locations across the USA and overseas. Guest rooms feature queen-size beds, private baths, and sitting areas. All guest rooms, as well as common rooms, have fireplaces for guests' enjoyment.

Hosts: John and Vera Eckert
Rooms: 6 (PB) $75-140
Full Breakfast
Credit Cards: A, B
Notes: 2, 3, 4, 5, 6, 7, 8, 9, 10, 11, 12, 13, 14

Milton Hall

CULPEPER _____

Fountain Hall Bed and Breakfast

609 South East Street, 22701-3222
(703) 825-8200; (800) 476-2944

Built in 1859, this grand bed and breakfast is within walking distance of historic downtown Culpeper. The inn is furnished with antiques and warmly welcomes business and leisure travelers. Five guest rooms are offered, each with private bath. Breakfast is Continental plus. Area activities and attractions include wineries, historic battlefields, antique shops, Skyline Drive, Montpelier, and restaurants. Daily Amtrak stops, conve-

---

NOTES: Credit cards accepted: A MasterCard; B Visa; C American Express; D Discover Card; E Diner's Club; F Other; 2 Personal checks accepted; 3 Lunch available; 4 Dinner available; 5 Open all year;

nient to major airports. No smoking. AAA, Mobil, and BBAV inspections.

Hosts: Steve, Kathi, and Leah-Marie Walker
Rooms: 5 (PB) $75-115
Continental Breakfast
Credit Cards: A, B, C, D, E, F (Carte Blanche)
Notes: 2, 5, 8 (call), 9, 10, 11, 12, 13, 14

DRAPER

Claytor Lake Homestead Inn

P.O. Box 7, 24324
(703) 980-6777; (800) 676-LAKE

The inn is on the shores of Claytor Lake. Guests are greeted on the wraparound porch, then tour the 1800s farmhouse with its antiques, reproductions, and items from the old Hotel Roanoke. A gourmet country breakfast is served in the lakeview dining room featuring homemade muffins, Virginia ham, sausage, and other Southern foods. Swim or sun on the private beach. Boats, too! Blue Ridge Parkway, historic Newbern, and antique mall nearby.

Hosts: Judy and Don Taylor
Rooms: 5 (1 PB; 4 SD) $70
Full Breakfast
Credit Cards: A, B, C
Notes: 2, 5, 8, 12

DUBLIN

Bell's Bed and Breakfast

P.O. Box 405, 13 Giles Avenue, 24084
(703) 674-6331; (800) 437-0575

In the beautiful New River Valley of Southwestern Virginia, convenient to Radford University, Virginia Tech, New River Community College, Claytor Lake State Park, the historic Newbern community. Brick turn-of-the-century Victorian home on large, shady lawn. Available to guests downstairs are living room, wide porch, parlor with fireplace, and a formal dining room where breakfast is served. Upstairs are five guest rooms, four with fireplaces,

Bell's

private or shared baths, a sun porch, sitting room, and kitchen. Hosts are conversant in German and English.

Hosts: Helga and David Bell
Rooms: 5 (1 PB; 4 S3B) $45-65
Full Breakfast
Credit Cards: B
Notes: 2, 6 (call), 8, 9, 10, 12

EDINBURG

Edinburg Inn Bed and Breakfast, Ltd.

218 South Main Street, Route 2, Box 4, 22824
(703) 984-8286

This Victorian inn is in the heart of the Shenandoah Valley on the edge of town next to Stoney Creek and the Edinburg Mill Restaurant. Close to vineyards, antique shops, hiking, fishing, caverns, and other points of interest. The inn is reminiscent of grandma's country home, with a full breakfast.

Hosts: Judy and Clyde Beachy
Rooms: 3 (PB) $70-75
Full Breakfast
Credit Cards: A, B
Notes: 2, 4, 5, 8, 9, 10, 11, 12, 13

6 Pets welcome; 8 Children welcome; 9 Social drinking allowed; 10 Tennis available; 11 Swimming available; 12 Golf available; 13 Skiing available; 14 May be booked through travel agents.

FAIRFAX

The Bailiwick Inn

4023 Chain Bridge Road, 22030
(703) 691-2266; (800) 366-7666

In the heart of the historic city of Fairfax, 15 miles west of the nation's capital. George Mason University is just down the street, and Mount Vernon and Civil War battlefields are nearby. On the National Register of Historic Places. Fourteen rooms with queen-size feather beds and private baths, fireplaces, Jacuzzis, and bridal suite. Afternoon tea. Candlelight dinner served by reservation. Small meetings and weddings.

Hosts: Anne and Ray Smith
Rooms: 14 (PB) $105-225
Full Breakfast
Credit Cards: A, B, C
Notes: 2, 4, 5, 8, 11, 12, 14

FLINT HILL

Blue Ridge Bed and Breakfast

Route 2, Box 3895, Berryville, 22611
(703) 955-1246; (800) 296-1246

A. Lovely stone home built in 1812 with working fireplaces in bedrooms; a working cattle farm adjacent to Shenandoah National Park. With Virginia's Blue Ridge Mountains in the background, this inn offers guests a beautiful setting. Scenic pasture lands are surrounded by stone fences. Close to Inn at Little Washington and Old Rag Mountain. Private dining by appointment. $70-100.

B. Charming old schoolhouse completely renovated into a lovely restaurant and inn. Bedrooms are very spacious with queen-size beds and private baths. Lovely area with great hiking. Close to northern entrance to Skyline Drive. $125.

FRANKTOWN

Amanda's Bed and Breakfast

1428 Park Avenue, Baltimore, MD 21217
(410) 225-0001; (800) 899-7533
FAX (410) 728-8957

150. This charming 1895 Victorian home is in a setting of old maples, loblolly, white pines, dogwood, magnolia, and azaleas. The library is filled with volumes of books, many of them historical. Guests may also use the piano. Afternoon tea is served. Two rooms with private baths. Full breakfast. $75-85.

FREDERICKSBURG

Kenmore Inn

1200 Princess Anne Street, 22401
(540) 371-7622

Elegant inn built in the late 1700s. On the historical walking tour, near shops and the river. Grand dining and a relaxing pub

Kenmore Inn

NOTES: Credit cards accepted: A MasterCard; B Visa; C American Express; D Discover Card; E Diner's Club; F Other; 2 Personal checks accepted; 3 Lunch available; 4 Dinner available; 5 Open all year;

for enjoyment. Serving lunch and dinner six days.

Host: Alice Bannan
Rooms: 13 (PB) $85-150
Continental Breakfast
Credit Cards: A, B, C, E
Notes: 2, 3, 4, 5, 7, 9, 10, 11, 12, 14

La Vista Plantation

La Vista Plantation

4420 Guinea Station Road, 22408
(540) 898-8444

This lovely 1838 Classical Revival home is just outside historic Fredricksburg. On ten quiet acres, the grounds present a fine balance of mature trees, flowers, shrubs, and farm fields. The pond is stocked with bass. Choose from a spacious apartment that sleeps six with a kitchen and a fireplace, or a formal room with a king-size mahogany rice-carved four poster bed, fireplace, and Empire furniture. Homemade jams and farm-fresh eggs for breakfast.

Hosts: Michele and Edward Schiesser
Rooms: 2 (PB) $85
Full Breakfast
Credit Cards: A, B
Notes: 2, 5, 8, 9, 10, 12, 14

The Spooner House Bed and Breakfast

1300 Caroline Street, 22401
(540) 371-1267

A lovely two-room suite with private bath and private entrance in a 1794 Federal-style home in the town's national historic district. Continental plus breakfast brought with a morning newspaper at the guests' convenience to their private quarters. Complimentary tour of the Rising Sun Tavern next door to the Spooner House. Within walking distance of attractions, museums, restaurants, Amtrak, and shopping.

Hosts: Peggy and John Roethel
Room: 1 suite (PB) $85
Continental Breakfast Plus
Credit Cards: None
Notes: 2, 5, 9

FRONT ROYAL

Blue Ridge Bed and Breakfast

Route 2, Box 3895, Berryville, 22611
(703) 955-1246; (800) 296-1246

A. Gorgeous Georgian mansion in the heart of scenic Front Royal. Furnished with fabulous antiques. Close to Skyline Caverns and Skyline Drive. Many antique shops nearby. $70-95

Chester House

43 Chester Street, 22630
(703) 635-3937; (800) 621-0441

A stately Georgian mansion with extensive formal gardens on two acres in Front Royal's historic district. Quiet, relaxed atmosphere in elegant surroundings, often described as an oasis in the heart of town. Easy walking distance to antique and gift shops and historic attractions; a short drive to Skyline Caverns, Skyline Drive, Shenandoah River, golf, tennis, hiking, skiing, horseback riding, fine wineries, and excellent restaurants.

Hosts: Bill and Ann Wilson
Rooms: 6 (4 PB; 2 SB) $65-110
Continental Breakfast
Credit Cards: A, B, C
Notes: 2, 5, 9, 10, 11, 12, 13, 14

---

6 Pets welcome; 8 Children welcome; 9 Social drinking allowed; 10 Tennis available; 11 Swimming available; 12 Golf available; 13 Skiing available; 14 May be booked through travel agents.

Killahevlin

Killahevlin

1401 North Royal Avenue, 22630
(703) 636-7335; (800) 847-6132
FAX (703) 636-8694

Historic Edwardian mansion with spectacular views. Spacious bedrooms, professionally designed and restored with working fireplaces, private baths, and Jacuzzis. Private Irish pub for guests. Complimentary beer and wine. Close to Skyline Drive, Shenandoah National Park, hiking, golf, canoeing, horseback riding, antiquing, fine dining, wineries, and live theater. Property was built in 1905 for William E. Carson, father of Skyline Drive. National Register of Historic Places and Virginia Landmarks Register.

Hosts: Susan and John Lang
Rooms: 6 (PB) $85-145
Full Breakfast
Credit Cards: A, B
Notes: 2, 5, 9, 10, 11, 12, 13, 14

GORE

Blue Ridge Bed and Breakfast

Route 2, Box 3895, Berryville, 22611
(703) 955-1246; (800) 296-1246

A. Breathtaking view of Blue Ridge Mountains on top of Timber Ridge, Great North Mountain. Twenty acres for cross-country skiing; close to Skyline Drive and Capon Bridge. Stocked trout fishing. $50.

HAYMARKET

Blue Ridge Bed and Breakfast

Route 2, Box 3895, Berryville, 22611
(703) 955-1246; (800) 296-1246

A. Lovely home in middle of one and one-fourth acres. Fabulous views of Bull Run Mountain. Ten minutes from Manassas battleground. In-ground pool, handmade quilts. Hostess has worked for U.S. presidents. $55-65.

HILLSVILLE

Bray's Manor Bed and Breakfast

P. O. Box 385, 24343
(703) 728-7901

Bray's Manor is just off US 58, four miles east of I-77 at Exit 14. The porch and two decks offer cool breezes and lovely views of the surrounding countryside. The sitting room provides TV, VCR, and books before a warm fire in season. Large air-conditioned guest rooms, each featuring a queen-size bed, sitting area, private bath, and TV. Full country breakfast served from 7:00 to 10:00 A.M.

Hosts: Dick and Helen Bray
Rooms: 2 (PB) $65
Full Breakfast
Credit Cards: A, B, D
Notes: 2, 5, 8, 9, 10, 12, 14

LEESBURG

Fleetwood Farm Bed and Breakfast

Route 1, Box 306-A, 22075
(703) 327-4325; FAX (703) 777-8236

NOTES: Credit cards accepted: A MasterCard; B Visa; C American Express; D Discover Card; E Diner's Club; F Other; 2 Personal checks accepted; 3 Lunch available; 4 Dinner available; 5 Open all year;

Beautiful 1745 plantation manor house in the Hunt Country, a Virginia Historic Landmark. On the National Register of Historic Places. Fireplaces, air conditioning, private baths (one with large Jacuzzi), full country breakfast, cookout facilities, horseshoes, croquet, canoe, and fishing equipment. Riding stables nearby. Lovely gardens. Working sheep farm. Near Middleburg, Manassas battlefield, Harpers Ferry, and Wolftrap; 40 miles to Washington, D.C. Member of the BBAV; AAA rated three diamonds.

Hosts: Bill and Carol Chamberlain
Rooms: 2 (PB) $110-135
Full Breakfast
Credit Cards: None
Notes: 2, 5, 7 (outside), 8 (over 12), 9, 10, 11, 12, 14

The Norris House Inn

The Norris House Inn

108 Loudoun Street, SW, 22075
(703) 777-1806; (800) 644-1806
FAX (703) 771-8051

Elegant accommodations in the heart of Historic Leesburg. Six guest rooms, all furnished with antiques, and three with working fireplaces. Full country breakfasts served by candlelight and evening libations. Convenient in-town location with several restaurants nearby. Only an hour's drive to Washington, D.C. In the heart of the Virginia Hunt Country, rich in Colonial and Civil War history. Lots of antiquing and

wineries. Perfect for romantic getaways, small meetings, and weddings. Open daily by reservation.

Hosts: Pam and Don McMurray
Rooms: 6 (SB) $75-140
Full Breakfast
Credit Cards: A, B, C, D, E
Notes: 2, 5, 8 (over 12), 9, 10, 11, 12, 14

LEXINGTON

Historic Country Inns of Lexington

11 North Main Street, 24450
(703) 463-2044

Historic Country Inns of Lexington consists of three beautifully restored historic homes: Alexander-Withrow House and McCampbell Inn in the historic district, and Maple Hall, six miles north of Lexington, offering elegant lodging, intimate dining, fireplaces, fishing, swimming, tennis, historic touring, hiking, shopping, and relaxation. Wedding parties, honeymooners, small conferences, and family reunions, as well as travelers, enjoy the facilities. Come discover Lexington.

Owners: Peter M. Meredith family
Innkeeper: Don Fredenburg
Rooms: 43 (PB) $95-150
Continental Breakfast
Credit Cards: A, B, D
Notes: 2, 4, 5, 7 (limited), 8, 9, 10, 11, 14

The Hummingbird Inn

Wood Lane P.O.Box 147, Goshen, 24439
(800) 397-3214; (703) 997-9065

On a tranquil acre of landscaped grounds, the Hummingbird Inn, a unique Carpenter Gothic villa, offers accommodations in an early Victorian setting. Comfortable rooms are furnished with antiques and combine an old fashion ambience with modern convenience. Architectural features include wraparound verandas on the first and second floors, original pine floors of varying widths, a charming rustic den dating from

6 Pets welcome; 8 Children welcome; 9 Social drinking allowed; 10 Tennis available; 11 Swimming available; 12 Golf available; 13 Skiing available; 14 May be booked through travel agents.

the early 1800s, and a solarium. A wide trout stream defines one of the property lines, and the old red barn was once the town livery. Full breakfasts include country bacon, ham, or sausage, homemade bread, and unique area recipes.

Hosts: Diana and Jerry Robinson
Rooms: 4 (PB) $70-95
Full Breakfast
Credit Cards: A, B, C
Notes: 2, 4, 5, 9, 13, 14

Llewellyn Lodge at Lexington

603 South Main Street, 24450
(703) 463-3235; (800) 882-1145

A warm and friendly atmosphere awaits guests at this lovely brick Colonial. Upon arrival, receive a welcome with refreshments. A hearty gourmet breakfast is served that includes omelets, Belgian waffles, sausage, bacon, and homemade muffins. The decor combines traditional and antique furnishings. Within walking distance of the Lee Chapel, Stonewall Jackson House, Washington and Lee University, and Virginia Military Institute.

Hosts: Ellen and John Roberts
Rooms: 6 (PB) $70-85
Full Breakfast
Credit Cards: A, B, C
Notes: 2, 5, 9, 10, 11, 12, 14

LINCOLN

Springdale Country Inn

Lincoln, 22078
(703) 338-1832; (800) 388-1832

Restored historic landmark 45 miles west of Washington, D.C. This inn is on six acres of secluded terrain with a babbling brook, walking bridges, and terraced gardens. Full meal service available to groups; breakfast is included in room price. Fully air-conditioned.

Host: Nancy Fones
Rooms: 9 (3 PB; 6 SB) $95-125

Full Breakfast
Credit Cards: A, B
Notes: 2, 5, 8, 14

LOCUSTVILLE

Amanda's Bed and Breakfast

1428 Park Avenue, Baltimore, MD 21217
(410) 225-0001; (800) 899-7533
FAX (410) 728-8957

143. This 18th-century Colonial is near Wachapreague and just one mile from the ocean. Quiet and comfortable. Water sports nearby. One room with double bed and private bath. Continental breakfast. $75.

LOVE

Blue Ridge Bed and Breakfast

Route 2, Box 3895, Berryville, 22611
(703) 955-1246; (800) 296-1246

A. Cozy country room with private bath, private entrance, and sunny French doors that lead out to a large deck. Overlooks a quiet mountain stream. $65.

LURAY

Blue Ridge Bed and Breakfast

Route 2, Box 3895, Berryville, 22611
(703) 955-1246; (800) 296-1246

A. Fabulous mansion built in 1739. Eighteen acres with ponds, in-ground pool, great mountain views, and antique furnishings. Two separate cottages are also available. $85-150.

Shenandoah River Roost

Route 3, Box 566, 22835
(703) 743-3467

NOTES: Credit cards accepted: A MasterCard; B Visa; C American Express; D Discover Card; E Diner's Club; F Other; 2 Personal checks accepted; 3 Lunch available; 4 Dinner available; 5 Open all year;

Country log home facing the Shenandoah River. Three miles from famous Luray Caverns, ten minutes from Skyline Drive, fishing, swimming, tubing, and hiking. Close to two golf courses and horseback riding. No smoking.

Hosts: Gerry and Rubin McNab
Rooms: 2 (SB) $65
Full Breakfast
Credit Cards: None
Closed November 1-May 1
Notes: 2, 8 (over 12), 9, 10, 11, 12

The Woodruff House Bed and Breakfast

330 Mechanic Street, 22835
(703) 743-1494

This 1882 fairy-tale Victorian is beautifully appointed with period antiques, hallmarked silver, and fine china. Each room includes working fireplace and private bathroom. Escape from reality, come into this fairytale where the ambience never ends! Awaken to a choice of freshly brewed coffees (22 blends) delivered to guests' room door; a gourmet candlelit breakfast follows. Sumptuous candlelit high tea buffet dinner included. Relax in the fireside candlelit garden spa. Complimentary canoes and bicycles.

Hosts: Lucas and Deborah Woodruff
Rooms: 3 (PB) $85-145
Full Breakfast
Credit Cards: A, B, D
Notes: 2, 3, 4, 5, 8 (call), 9, 10, 11, 12, 13, 14

LYNCHBURG

Blue Ridge Bed and Breakfast

Route 2, Box 3895, Berryville, 22611
(703) 955-1246; (800) 296-1246

A. Built in 1874, this fabulous Victorian home is on the National Register of Historic Places, and has received the Merit Award from the Lynchburg Historic Association for outstanding exterior renovation. Near

Blue Ridge Parkway and Appomattox battleground. $65-70.

Lynchburg Mansion Inn Bed and Breakfast

405 Madison Street, 24504
(804) 528-5400; (800) 352-1199

Luxury accommodations in a 9,000-square-foot Spanish Georgian mansion in a residential downtown historic district. On the National Register of Historic Places. The street is still paved in turn-of-the-century brick. Known for attention to detail and quality of service. Remarkable interior cherry columns and wainscoting. Amenities include king- and queen-size beds, private ensuite bathrooms, fireplaces, TV with HBO, 200-thread-count sheets, turndown with chocolates, and hot tub. Full sumptuous breakfast is served in the formal dining room on antique china with fine silver and crystal. Two of the rooms are suites. Well-supervised children welcome. Skiing one hour away.

Hosts: Bob and Mauranna Sherman
Rooms: 4 (PB) $89-119
Full Breakfast
Credit Cards: A, B, C, E
Notes: 2, 5, 8, 10, 11, 12, 14

The Madison House Bed and Breakfast

413 Madison Street, 24504
(804) 528-1503; (800) 828-6422

Lynchburg's finest Victorian bed and breakfast (1880) boasts a magnificent, authentic interior decor. Spacious, elegantly appointed guest rooms graced with antiques, private baths, plush robes and linens. Full breakfast served on antique Limoges and Wedgwood china; afternoon tea included. Central air; in-room telephones; off-street parking. Near colleges, Appomattox, Thomas Jefferson's Poplar Forest, and fine restaurants.

6 Pets welcome; 8 Children welcome; 9 Social drinking allowed; 10 Tennis available; 11 Swimming available; 12 Golf available; 13 Skiing available; 14 May be booked through travel agents.

Hosts: Irene and Dale Smith
Rooms: 3 and 1 suite (PB) $70-109
Full Breakfast
Credit Cards: A, B, C
Notes: 2, 4, 5, 9, 10, 11, 12, 14

MADISON

Guesthouses Bed and Breakfast

P.O. Box 5737, Charlottesville, 22905
(804) 979-7264

Laurel Run. A recently built cottage in the woods of Madison County, 30 miles north of Charlottesville. This private cabin offers a great room, kitchen, dining area, and two bedrooms on the first floor. The loft has a double bed and cot. The broad, screened porch offers views of a stream, fields, and woods. Hiking, fishing, and riding are available in nearby Shenandoah National Park. Breakfast supplies are included for the first morning of guests' stay. $60-100.

MADISON HEIGHTS

Blue Ridge Bed and Breakfast

Route 2, Box 3895, Berryville, 22611
(703) 955-1246; (800) 296-1246

A. This 80-year-old grand Southern Colonial mansion is in the middle of 14 acres with fabulous views of Blue Ridge Mountains. Just minutes from Blue Ridge Parkway. Fishing on the James River. Near Appomattox battleground. $49-59.

Winridge

Route 1, Box 362, 24572
(804) 384-7220

Come and share this grand Southern Colonial home on a 14-acre country estate with views of the mountains. Enjoy the birds, flowers, and shade trees. Relax on the large, inviting porches. Warm, casual, and family atmosphere. Hot, hearty breakfasts are served in the dining room. Greenhouse and gardens for the guests' strolling pleasure. Close to Blue Ridge Parkway and Lynchburg.

Hosts: LoisAnn and Ed Pfister
Rooms: 3 (1 PB; 2 SB) $65-79
Full Breakfast
Credit Cards: None
Notes: 2, 5, 8, 10, 12, 13, 14

Winridge

MANASSAS

Blue Ridge Bed and Breakfast

Route 2, Box 3895, Berryville, 22611
(703) 955-1246; (800) 296-1246

A. In Manassas battlefields, this beautiful restored farmhouse was built upon General McDowell's campsite. Just five miles from I-66 and 35 minutes from Washington, D.C. Antiques, fireplaces, stone walls, barn and livestock, and old gas lamps throughout make this a special treat. $65.

MEADOWS OF DAN

Spangler's Bed and Breakfast

Route 2, Box 108, 24120
(703) 952-2454

NOTES: Credit cards accepted: A MasterCard; B Visa; C American Express; D Discover Card; E Diner's Club; F Other; 2 Personal checks accepted; 3 Lunch available; 4 Dinner available; 5 Open all year;

On Country Road 602 within view of the Blue Ridge Parkway at milepost 180, four miles from Mabry Mill, this 1904 farmhouse has a kitchen with fireplace, piano, and four porches. There is also an 1826 private log cabin perfect for one couple. An additional 1987 log cabin has two bedrooms, complete kitchen, and wraparound porch. Fishing in the lake, swimming, three boats, bikes, horseshoes, and volleyball.

Hosts: Harold and Trudy Spangler
Rooms: 7 (2 PB; 5 SB) $50-60
Full Breakfast
Credit Cards: None
Notes: 2, 5, 8, 9, 10, 11, 12

MIDDLEBURG

Amanda's Bed and Breakfast

1428 Park Avenue, Baltimore, MD 21217
(410) 225-0001; (800) 899-7533
FAX (410) 728-8957

126. Federal home, circa 1824, with high ceilings, seven working fireplaces, and a private garden. Three dining rooms, all with fireplaces and quiet music. Four guest rooms with private baths. A romantic retreat in Virginia's horse country. Continental breakfast. $125-225.

Blue Ridge Bed and Breakfast

Route 2, Box 3895, Berryville, 22611
(703) 955-1246; (800) 296-1246

A. Two-hundred-year-old cozy commercial inn in the heart of Middleburg with working fireplaces in all bedrooms. Complete facilities for dinner. Accessible to quaint shops and eateries. $95.

Welbourne

Middleburg, 22117
(703) 687-3201

A seven-generation, antebellum plantation home in the middle of Virginia's fox-hunting country. On a 600-acre working farm. Full Southern breakfasts, working fireplaces, and cottages of faded elegance. On the National Register of Historic Places.

Hosts: Nat and Sherry Morison
Rooms: 10 (PB) $64-96
Full Breakfast
Credit Cards: None
Notes: 2, 5, 6, 7, 8, 9

MIDDLETOWN

Blue Ridge Bed and Breakfast

Route 2, Box 3895, Berryville, 22611
(703) 955-1246; (800) 296-1246

A. Historic Victorian home on Main Street close to famous restaurant and theater. All period furniture. Minutes from many antique shops, Passion Play, and small lake with beach. $65.

Fort Lewis Lodge

MILLBORO

Fort Lewis Lodge

HCR 3, Box 21A, 24460
(703) 925-2314

Forests teaming with deer and wild turkey. A glistening river running cool and clear.

These are the gifts nature has bestowed on this historic 3,200-acre mountain farm. The lodge's large gathering room, 13 guest rooms, and two log cabins are decorated with wildlife art and handcrafted furniture. For dinner and breakfast guests will feast on meals of homemade everything in a magnificently restored 19th-century Lewis grist mill.

Hosts: John and Caryl Cowden
Rooms: 13 (PB) $130-180 Modified American Plan
Cabins: 2 (PB)
Full Breakfast
Credit Cards: A, B
Notes: 2, 3, 4, 8, 9, 11, 12, 14

MILLWOOD

Blue Ridge
Bed and Breakfast

Route 2, Box 3895, Berryville, 22611
(703) 955-1246; (800) 296-1246

A. Guests in the 1780s section of this stone mansion can enjoy huge fireplaces in every room. There is easy access through a separate entrance to the Shenandoah River. Easy drive to and from Washington, D.C., which is just an hour away. $70-108.

MOLLUSK

Guesthouses
on the Water at Greenvale

Route 354, Box 70, 22517
(804) 462-5995

Two separate and private guesthouses on 13 acres on the Rappahannock River and Greenvale Creek. Pool, dock, private beach, and bicycles. Each house is furnished with antiques and reproductions, and has two bedrooms, two baths, living room, kitchen, and deck. Air-conditioned. Enjoy sweeping water views, sunsets, and relax in peaceful tranquility. Weekly rates available.

Hosts: Pam and Walt Smith

Guest houses: 2 (PB) $85-125
Continental Breakfast
Credit Cards: A, B
Notes: 2, 5, 7, 9, 10, 11, 12

MONROE

Blue Ridge
Bed and Breakfast

Route 2, Box 3895, Berryville, 22611
(703) 955-1246; (800) 296-1246

A. Unique retreat with 200-year-old chestnut beams, vaulted ceilings, and colorful antiques. Sitting on 300 historic acres with a creek, lake, pond, and fields with splendid views of High Peak Mountains. Minutes off Blue Ridge Parkway and Appomattox battleground. Hosts are a retired educator and World War II British war bride who offer scrumptious breakfasts on English china and linens. $55.

MONTEREY

Highland Inn

Main Street, 24465
(703) 468-2143

Classic Victorian inn listed on the National Register of Historic Places. Tranquil location in the picturesque village of Monterey, nestled in the foothills of the Allegheny Mountains. There are 17 individually decorated

Highland Inn

rooms furnished with antiques and collectibles, each with private bath. Full-service dining room offers Continental cuisine for dinner Wednesday through Saturday and Sunday brunch. Antiquing, hiking, fishing, golf, and mineral baths are nearby.

Hosts: Michael Strand and Cynthia Peel
Rooms: 17 (PB) $49-69
Continental Breakfast
Credit Cards: A, B
Notes: 2, 4, 5, 7, 8, 9, 11, 12, 14

MOUNT JACKSON

Amanda's Bed and Breakfast

1428 Park Avenue, Baltimore, MD 21217
(410) 225-0001; (800) 899-7533
FAX (410) 728-8957

181. An 1830 Colonial homestead on seven acres overlooking the George Washington Mountains. Some bedrooms have wood burning fireplaces, and the antique furniture is for sale. Pool on premises. Area activities include craft fairs, hiking, fishing, tennis, and horseback riding. Five rooms with private baths. Two guest cottages. Full breakfast. $65-85.

Blue Ridge Bed and Breakfast

Route 2, Box 3895, Berryville, 22611
(703) 955-1246; (800) 296-1246

A. This 1830 stately Colonial is near George Washington Parkway, ten miles from Bryce. Six bedrooms with working fireplaces. There is also a cozy two and one-half room cottage separate from the main house. Pool and full breakfast. $65-90.

The Widow Kip's Shenandoah Inn

Route 1, Box 117, 22842
(703) 477-2400

A stately 1830 Colonial on seven rural acres in the Shenandoah Valley overlooking the mountains. Friendly rooms filled with family photographs, bric-a-brac, and antiques. Each bedroom has a working fireplace, canopied, sleigh or Lincoln bed. Two cozy cottages are also available. Pool on premises; nearby battlefields to explore, caverns, canoeing, hiking, or downhill skiing. Bicycles, picnics, and grill available. Holiday stay is a minimum of two nights.

Host: Betty Luse
Rooms: 7 (PB) $65-85
Full Breakfast
Credit Cards: A, B
Notes: 2, 5, 6 (call), 8 (call), 10, 11, 12, 13, 14

NATURAL BRIDGE

Burger's Country Inn

Route 2, Box 564, 24578
(703) 291-2464

This historic inn is furnished with antiques and country collectibles. The rambling farmhouse with wraparound porch and large columns is on ten wooded acres. Four guest rooms and three baths are available. Enjoy croquet in summer and relax by the fire in winter. Special Continental breakfast is included. Visit the Natural Bridge and historic Lexington. Beautiful Blue Ridge Parkway nearby. Call or write for brochure/reservations.

Host: Frances B. Burger
Rooms: 4 (2 PB, 2 SB) $45-50
Continental Breakfast
Credit Cards: None
Notes: 2, 5, 6, 7 (restricted), 8, 9, 12, 14

NELLYSFORD

Acorn Inn, Inc.

P.O. Box 431, 22958
(804) 361-9357

European-style inn with Dutch cyclist and American artist as hosts. Ten cozy guest rooms in a renovated horse stable. The ren-

6 Pets welcome; 8 Children welcome; 9 Social drinking allowed; 10 Tennis available; 11 Swimming available; 12 Golf available; 13 Skiing available; 14 May be booked through travel agents.

ovated stable has a center lounge with Finnish soapstone fireplace, striking photographs and woodcut prints, and artistic, friendly, contemporary atmosphere. There is also a charming cottage available. Delicious homemade breads and fruit cobbler are also available for guests' enjoyment. Close to Wintergreen Ski/Golf Resort, Blue Ridge Parkway, Appalachian Trail, and waterfalls. Continental plus breakfast.

Hosts: Kathy and Martin Versluys
Rooms: 10 (SB) $47
Cottage: 1 (PB) $95
Continental Breakfast
Credit Cards: A, B
Notes: 2, 5, 8, 10, 12, 13

NEW CHURCH

Amanda's Bed and Breakfast

1428 Park Avenue, Baltimore, MD 21217
(410) 225-0001; (800) 899-7533;
FAX (410) 728-8957

210. Twenty minutes from the most beautiful beaches on the east coast and a star-rated restaurant. Elegant lodging with gourmet candlelight dining. Five rooms, some complete with Jacuzzi and canopied beds. Breakfast served in pleasant dining room. $85-135.

NEW MARKET

Blue Ridge Bed and Breakfast

Route 2, Box 3895, Berryville, 22611
(703) 955-1246; (800) 296-1246

A. Beautiful Colonial house built in 1790 on 20 acres with fabulous view of Massanetta Mountains, and a fishing creek. Franklin D. Roosevelt slept here in 1936. Ski resort is only 15 miles away. $55-65.

B. Beautiful carriage house built in 1873 offers two rooms in the main house. There is a

cottage on the premises that offers two rooms decorated with lovely country decor and many oak and wicker antiques. In the heart of a busy Civil War town within easy walking distance of many quaint country shops and restaurants. $60-65.

A Touch of Country

A Touch of Country

9329 Congress Street, 22844
(703) 740-8030

Come relax at this restored 1870s home where a warm, friendly, atmosphere awaits. Daydream on the porch swings or stroll through town, with its antique shops, gift shops, and restaurants. Rest in one of six bedrooms decorated with a country flavor. In the morning enjoy a down-home country breakfast. Near caverns and battlefields.

Hosts: Jean Schoellig and Dawn Kason
Rooms: 6 (PB) $60-75
Full Breakfast
Credit Cards: A, B, D
Notes: 2, 5, 8 (over 12), 9, 10, 11, 12, 13, 14

NORFOLK

Page House Inn

323 Fairfax Avenue, 23507
(804) 625-5033

The restoration of the Page House Inn is a work of art, and a stay here is an experience not to be missed. This three-story Georgian Revival in-town mansion, made of brick laid in a Flemish bond pattern, underwent an award-winning rehabilitation, completed in 1991. The award was given by the city of Norfolk to the present owners for the quality of the workmanship and the attention paid to historic detail. The interior is picture perfect and has been featured in *Country Inns* magazine, April 1993, and chosen one of that publication's "Best Inns" for 1993 (February 1994). Highly rated by AAA, Mobil, and Frommer's, as well as by several other well-known guides, a stay at the Page House is like a step back in time to a place where guests are warmly received and well fed— almost like going to grandma's! Walk to all of the best cultural and tourist attractions as well as to the area's finest restaurants from the inn's central location in the Ghent historic district.

Hosts: Stephanie and Ezio DiBelardino
Rooms: 4 (PB) $75-120
Suites: 2 (PB) $130-145
Continental Breakfast
Credit Cards: A, B
Notes: 2, 5, 9, 11, 12, 14

Page House Inn

OCCOQUAN

Rockledge Mansion

410 Mill Street, 22125
(703) 690-3377

National historic landmark built in 1758, this stone house is less than a mile from I-95 and is 30 minutes from Washington, D.C. Working fireplaces, antiques, oversized Jacuzzis, and kitchenettes in accessory buildings. Walk

to the river, shops, art galleries, restaurants. Very quiet and private on two acres in the center of town. No meals on premises.

Hosts: Joy and Ron Houghton
Suites: 4 (PB) $75-120
Continental Breakfast
Credit Cards: None
Notes: 2, 5, 8, 9, 10, 11, 12, 14

ONANCOCK

The Spinning Wheel Bed and Breakfast

31 North Street, 23417
(804) 787-7311

An 1890s Folk Victorian home with antiques and spinning wheels throughout. Waterfront town listed on the National Register of Historic Places. Calm eastern shore getaway from D.C., Virginia, Maryland, Delaware, and New Jersey. Full breakfast. All rooms with private bath, queen-size bed, and air conditioning. Walk to restaurants, shops, and deep-water harbor. Golf and tennis available at private club. Near beach, bay, and ocean. Bicycles, antiques, museums, festivals, fishing, wildlife refuge, and Tangier Island cruise. Open May through October. AAA approved.

Hosts: Karen and David Tweedie
Rooms: 5 (PB) $85-95
Full Breakfast
Credit Cards: A, B
Notes: 2, 9, 10, 11, 12, 14

ORANGE

Hidden Inn

249 Caroline Street, 22960
(703) 672-3625; (800) 841-1253

A romantic Victorian featuring ten guest rooms, each with private bath. Jacuzzis, working fireplaces, and private verandas are available. Wicker and rocking chairs on the wraparound verandas; handmade quilts and canopied beds enhance the Victorian flavor. Full country breakfast, afternoon tea, and gourmet dinners are served. Minutes from Monticello, Montpelier, and Virginia wineries.

Hosts: Ray and Barbara Lonick
Rooms: 10 (PB) $79-159
Full Breakfast
Credit Cards: A, B
Notes: 2, 4, 5, 8, 9, 10, 12, 14

The Holladay House

The Holladay House

155 West Main Street, 22960
(703) 672-4893

The Holladay House, circa 1830, is a restored Federal-style home that has been in the Holladay family since 1899. The large, comfortable rooms are furnished with family pieces and each one features its own sitting area. Breakfast is normally served to guests in their own rooms. Surrounded by a residential neighborhood on three sides, the Holladay House is two blocks from the center of the historic town of Orange and just 90 minutes from Richmond or Washington, D.C.

Hosts: Pete and Phebe Holladay
Rooms: 6 (4 PB; 2 SB) $75-120
Full Breakfast
Credit Cards: A, B
Notes: 2, 5, 7 (limited), 8, 9, 10, 12, 14

PARIS

The Ashby Inn and Restaurant

Route 1, Box 2A, 22130
(703) 592-3900

In the quiet 18th-century village of Paris, just 12 miles west of Middleburg. Selected by the *Washington Post* in 1993 as one of "North America's 20 Most Romantic Hideaways." Stunning views of the Blue Ridge and ten guest rooms, five with fireplaces, reflect their early 19th-century origins. A first-rate restaurant, whose daily menu is guided more by tradition than trend. Midweek conferences. Antiquing, vineyards, riding, and golf. Sunday brunch.

Hosts: John and Roma Sherman
Rooms: 10 (8 PB; 2 SB) $80-175
Full Breakfast
Credit Cards: A, B
Notes: 2, 3, 4, 5, 7, 9, 10, 12

PETERSBURG

Mayfield Inn

3348 West Washington Street, 23804
(804) 733-0866; (804) 861-6775

Mayfield Inn is a 1750 manor house listed on the National Register of Historic Places. It was authentically restored and won the Virginia APVA Award in 1987. Guest accommodations are luxuriously appointed with Oriental carpets, pine floors, antiques, period reproductions, and private baths. Situated on four acres of grounds, with a 40-foot outdoor swimming pool.

Hosts: Jamie and Dot Caudle, and Cherry Turner
Rooms: 4 (PB) $65-90
Full Breakfast
Credit Cards: A, B
Notes: 2, 5, 7, 8, 9, 11, 12, 14

Mayfield Inn

NOTES: Credit cards accepted: A MasterCard; B Visa; C American Express; D Discover Card; E Diner's Club; F Other; 2 Personal checks accepted; 3 Lunch available; 4 Dinner available; 5 Open all year;

PRATTS

Blue Ridge
Bed and Breakfast

Route 2, Box 3895, Berryville, 22611
(703) 955-1246; (800) 296-1246

A. Lovely historic home built in 1870, tucked away on seven and one-half acres. Rooms have king- or queen-size beds and working fireplaces. Furnished with lovely antiques and reproductions. $45-75.

PULASKI

The Count Pulaski Bed and Breakfast and Gardens

821 North Jefferson Avenue, 24301
(703) 980-1163

In a mountain village in southwest Virginia at the major north-south artery I-81. Comfortable, spacious 80-year-old house furnished with family antiques, the owner's paintings, and items collected from living and traveling around the world. It is softly carpeted, with king- or queen-size beds, private baths, dimmer lights, ceiling fans, air conditioning, and three fireplaces. Gourmet breakfast is served elegantly by candlelight on a 150-year-old table. Nearby are antique shops, a variety of restaurants, hiking/biking trails, and water sports on the New River and Claytor Lake. A restful, relaxing getaway or travel stopover.

Host: Flo Stevenson
Rooms: 3 (PB) $75
Full Breakfast
Credit Cards: A, B
Notes: 2, 5, 12, 14

PURCELLVILLE

Blue Ridge
Bed and Breakfast

Route 2, Box 3895, Berryville, 22611
(703) 955-1246; (800) 296-1246

A. Lovely Victorian cottage, circa 1850, one hour from the nation's capitol. Authentically furnished in period antiques, down to rope beds. Extensive gardens with lovely view of the Blue Ridge Mountains. $80.

RICHMOND

Amanda's
Bed and Breakfast

1428 Park Avenue, Baltimore, MD 21217
(410) 225-0001; (800) 899-7533
FAX (410) 728-8957

271. Antiques, family heirlooms, and working fireplaces await guests at this bed and breakfast. Situated in the historic Church Hill district. Beautiful period furniture, canopied beds, large armoires, crystal chandeliers, and hospitality that will make any stay most pleasant. Five rooms with private and shared baths. Full breakfast, $75-160.

The Emmanuel Hutzler
House

2036 Monument Avenue, 23220
(804) 355-4885/353-6900

This large Italian Renaissance-style inn has been totally renovated in the past three years and offers leaded-glass windows, coffered ceilings, and natural mahogany raised paneling throughout the downstairs, as well as a large living room with marble fireplace for guests' enjoyment. There are four guest rooms on the second floor, each with private bath. One suite has a four-poster queen-size bed, love seat, and wing chair. The two queen-size rooms have a sitting area and private baths. The largest suite has a marble fireplace, four-poster mahogany bed, antique sofa, dresser, and a private bath with shower and Jacuzzi. Full breakfast served on the weekends. Breakfast is Continental plus weekdays.

Hosts: Lyn M. Benson and John E. Richardson
Rooms: 4 (PB) $89-135
Continental and Full Breakfasts

6 Pets welcome; 8 Children welcome; 9 Social drinking allowed; 10 Tennis available; 11 Swimming available; 12 Golf available; 13 Skiing available; 14 May be booked through travel agents.

Credit Cards: A, B, C, D
Notes: 2, 5, 9, 12, 14

West-Bocock House

1107 Grove Avenue, 23220
(804) 358-6174

Circa 1817 historic house in the heart of Richmond offers elegant guest rooms with private baths, French linens, fresh flowers, full breakfast, and off-street parking. Convenient to museums, historic sites, restaurants, shopping, and Capitol Square. The Wests invite visitors to sample true Southern hospitality.

Host: Billie Rees West
Rooms: 3 (PB) $65-75
Full Breakfast
Credit Cards: None
Notes: 2, 5, 9, 12, 14

The William Catlin House

2304 East Broad Street, 23223
(804) 780-3746

Antiques, family heirlooms, and working fireplaces await at the William Catlin House, Richmond's first and oldest bed and breakfast. In the historic district of Church

The William Catlin House

Hill, the house was built in 1845. The luxury of bedroom fireplaces, goose down pillows, and sherry promises a restful night. Each morning a delicious full breakfast and endless pots of coffee or tea await guests in the elegant dining room. While in the area, be sure to visit some of the numerous nearby historic sites. As seen in *Colonial Homes*, *Southern Living*, and *Mid-Atlantic* magazines.

Hosts: Robert and Josephine Martin
Rooms: 5 (3 PB; 2 SB) $70-89.50
Full Breakfast
Credit Cards: A, B, D
Notes: 2, 5, 7, 8, 9, 14

RIVERTON

Blue Ridge Bed and Breakfast

Route 2, Box 3895, Berryville, 22611
(703) 955-1246; (800) 296-1246

A. Lovely brick mansion built in 1876 in the middle of three and one-half acres. Porch filled with wicker, ceiling fans, seven lovely bedrooms (including waterbed with Soma Flotation System), and gorgeous antiques. Hundreds of videos are available for guests' use. Close to the north entrance of Skyline Drive. $65-120.

ROANOKE

The Manor at Taylor's Store

Route 1, Box 533, Wirtz, 24184
(703) 721-3951; (800) 248-6267

Explore this secluded, historic 120-acre estate convenient to Smith Mountain Lake, Roanoke, and the Blue Ridge Parkway. The manor has six guest suites with extraordinary antiques and Oriental rugs. Guests enjoy all luxury amenities, including central air conditioning, hot tub, fireplaces, private porches, billiard room, exercise room, guest kitchen, movies, and six private, spring-fed ponds for swimming, fishing, and canoeing. A lovely gazebo overlooks the ponds for picnics. A full "heart healthy" gourmet breakfast is served in the dining room with panoramic views of the countryside.

Hosts: Lee and Mary Lynn Tucker
Rooms: 6 (4 PB; 2 SB) $80-125
Cottage: 1 (PB)
Full Breakfast
Credit Cards: A, B
Notes: 2, 3, 5, 7 (limited), 8, 9, 10, 11, 12, 13, 14

The Mary Bladon House

381 Washington Avenue Southwest, 24016
(703) 344-5361

A lovely 1890s Victorian house in the historic Old Southwest neighborhood. Spacious rooms, tastefully decorated with crafts and period antiques to capture the charm of a time when elegant comfort was a way of life. A step back in time for the young and the young at heart.

Hosts: Bill and Sheri Bestpitch
Rooms: 2 (PB) $80
Suite: 1 (PB) $110
Full Breakfast
Credit Cards: A, B
Notes: 2, 5, 8, 9, 10, 11, 12, 14

The Mary Bladon House

SCOTTSVILLE

Guesthouses Bed and Breakfast

P.O. Box 5737, 22905
(804) 979-7264

Chester. This charming large country home in Scottsville, 25 minutes south of Charlottsville, was built in 1825 through 1875; lots of history and beautiful trees are on the grounds. Five guest rooms make this a great retreat for a large group, or come with a smaller group and meet fellow guests. Accommodations have bed sizes from a twin to a queen, and the house is furnished with an interesting and eclectic collection of pieces from the owner's travels. Several porches provide a pleasant place to sit at night. Full breakfast is served in the morning, and dinner is available by reservation. $80-100.

The Prodigal. On the site of an old summer kitchen, this cottage sits behind a farmhouse built around 1830. It features a large fireplace, sleeper-sofa, Pullman kitchen, full bath downstairs, and a room with a double bed upstairs. Fish in the pond, swim nearby in the Hardware River swimming hole, or rent a tube or canoe on the James River. Guests can even bring their horses. There are extra stalls and wooded trails. Air conditioning. Supplies provided for guests to prepare breakfast. $80-125.

SMITHFIELD

Isle of Wight Inn

1607 South Church Street, 23430
(804) 357-3176

This luxurious Colonial bed and breakfast inn is found in a delightful historic river port town. Several suites with fireplaces and Jacuzzis. Antique shop featuring tall-case clocks and period furniture. More than 60 old homes in town dating from 1750. Just 30 minutes and a ferry ride from Williamsburg and Jamestown; less than an hour from James River plantations, Norfolk, Hampton, and Virginia Beach.

Hosts: The Harts and the Earls
Rooms: 10 (PB) $49-79
Full Breakfast
Credit Cards: A, B, C, D
Notes: 2, 5, 7 (limited), 8, 9, 10, 11, 12, 14

Jordan Hollow Farm Inn

TANLEY

Jordan Hollow Farm Inn

Route 2, Box 375, 22851
(703) 778-2285; FAX (703) 778-1759

A restored Colonial horse farm featuring 21 rooms with private baths, several with fireplaces and whirlpool baths. Full-service restaurant and pub. Horseback riding, English and western. In the Shenandoah Valley just ten miles from Skyline Drive and six miles from Luray Caverns. Box lunches available. Full dinner provided in addition to a full breakfast under the Modified American Plan. Member IIA.

Hosts: Jetze and Marley Beers
Rooms: 21 (PB) $140-180
Full Breakfast

Credit Cards: A, B, D, E
Notes: 2, 3, 4, 5, 7, 8, 9, 10, 11, 12, 13, 14

STAUNTON

Ashton Country House

1205 Middlebrook Avenue, 24401
(703) 885-7819; (800) 296-7819

Ashton Country House, circa 1860, is a Greek Revival brick home on 20 peaceful acres on the outskirts of Staunton, yet only a five-minute drive into town. Each of the five spacious guest rooms features a private bath and a queen-size or double bed and air conditioning. Mornings begin with a hearty breakfast, which is often accompanied by live piano music. Convenient to historic attractions and fine restaurants.

Hosts: Sheila Kennedy and Stanley Polanski
Rooms: 5 (PB) $75-90
Full Breakfast
Credit Cards: None
Notes: 2, 5, 9, 10, 11, 12, 13

Frederick House

28 North New Street, P.O. Box 1387, 24402-1387
(800) 334-5575

A small hotel and Chumley's tearoom in the European tradition. Large, comfortable rooms or suites. Private baths, air conditioning, TV, telephones, robes, private entrances, and antique furnishings. Some balconies or fireplaces. Gourmet breakfast, delicious dining. Award-winning restoration and gardens. Listed in the National Register of Historic Places. Across from Mary Baldwin College. In historic district near shops, restaurants, and the Woodrow Wilson birthplace. In Central Shenandoah Valley near Skyline Drive and Blue Ridge Parkway.

Hosts: Joe and Evy Harman
Rooms: 14 (PB) $65-95
Full Breakfast
Credit Cards: A, B, C, D, E
Notes: 2, 3, 4, 5, 8, 9, 10, 11, 12, 13, 14

NOTES: Credit cards accepted: A MasterCard; B Visa; C American Express; D Discover Card; E Diner's Club; F Other; 2 Personal checks accepted; 3 Lunch available; 4 Dinner available; 5 Open all year;

Kenwood

235 East Beverley Street, 24401
(703) 886-0524

Spacious, restored 1910 Colonial Revival brick home adjacent to Woodrow Wilson Birthplace and Museum. Filled with period furniture and antiques, Kenwood offers comfortable accommodations in a relaxed atmosphere. Two miles west of the I-81 and I-64 intersection, near the Museum of American Frontier Culture, Skyline Drive, Blue Ridge Parkway, Statler Brothers Museum, and Monticello. Four guest rooms with queen-size beds, private baths, air conditioning, and full breakfast.

Hosts: Liz and Ed Kennedy
Rooms: 4 (PB) $70
Full Breakfast
Credit Cards: A, B
Notes: 2, 5, 8, 9, 10, 11, 12

The Sampson Eagon Inn

The Sampson Eagon Inn

238 East Beverley Street, 24401
(703) 886-8200; (800) 597-9722

In the Virginia historic landmark district of Gospel Hill, this gracious, circa 1840, town residence has been thoughtfully restored and transformed into a unique inn offering affordable luxury and personal service in an intimate, inviting atmosphere. Each elegant, spacious, air-conditioned room and suite features private bath, sitting area, canopied queen-size bed, and antique furnishings. Adjacent to the Woodrow Wilson Birthplace and Mary Baldwin College, the inn is within two blocks of downtown dining and attractions.

Hosts: Laura and Frank Mattingly
Rooms: 5 (PB) $80-95
Full Breakfast
Credit Cards: None
Notes: 2, 5, 9, 10, 11, 12, 13, 14

Thornrose House at Gypsy Hill

531 Thornrose Avenue, 24401
(703) 885-7026

A wraparound veranda and Greek colonnades distinguish this turn-of-the-century Georgian residence. Family antiques, a grand piano, and fireplaces create an elegant, restful atmosphere. Breakfast specialties served in a formal dining room energize guests for sightseeing in the beautiful Shenandoah Valley. Beside a 300-acre park with golf, tennis, swimming, and trails. Other attractions include Woodrow Wilson's birthplace, the Museum of American Frontier Culture, and the nearby Skyline Drive and Blue Ridge Parkway.

Hosts: Suzanne and Otis Huston
Rooms: 5 (PB) $55-75
Full Breakfast
Credit Cards: None
Notes: 2, 5, 8, 9, 10, 11, 12, 13

STEELE'S TAVERN

Amanda's Bed and Breakfast

1428 Park Avenue, Baltimore, MD, 21217
(410) 225-0001; (800) 899-7533
FAX (410) 728-8957

340. Explore historic towns of Virginia including Lexington, Charlottesville, Appomattox, and Monticello, or explore along the back roads. Enjoy Goshen Pass, Natural Bridge, antique shops, and crafts. Enjoy the sunsets in the mountains. Eleven rooms, each with private bath and wood-burning fireplaces. Full breakfast. $85-110.

6 Pets welcome; 8 Children welcome; 9 Social drinking allowed; 10 Tennis available; 11 Swimming available; 12 Golf available; 13 Skiing available; 14 May be booked through travel agents.

The Osceola Mill Country Inn

State Route 56, 24476
(703) 377-6455; (800) 242-7352
FAX (703) 377-6455

Get away to the hills of the Blue Ridge for a special retreat in the Mill Store cottage, the rustic rooms of the Mill House, or the elegant splendor of the Mangus House. Guests are treated to elegant regional dining amongst chestnut timbers and the millstones of the original milling rooms of this restored 19th-century grist mill. Group luncheons, retreats, meeting rooms, and small weddings are mong the offerings. Assistance available to plan hiking, biking, and group tours.

Host: Philip Clayton
Rooms: 12 (PB) $89-109: $139-169 cottage
Full Breakfast
Credit Cards: A. B
Notes: 2, 3, 4, 5, 8, 11, 12, 13, 14

STEPHENS CITY _____

Blue Ridge Bed and Breakfast

Route 2, Box 3895, Berryville, 22611
(703) 955-1246; (800) 296-1246

A. Lovely brick home built in 1819. Served as a tavern for 100 years. In a beautiful historic district. Decor includes lovely antiques, Oriental rugs, and beautiful old woodwork. Minutes from Belle Grove Plantation, Wayside Theater, and Skyline Drive. $55-65.

SWOOPE _____

Lambsgate Bed and Breakfast

Route 1, Box 63, 24479
(703) 337-6929

Six miles west of Staunton on Routes 254 and 833. Restored 1816 farmhouse and

Lambsgate

working sheep farm in the historic Shenandoah Valley. Relaxing country setting with hiking and biking nearby. Central for visiting historic sites, national park, and forests. Minimum stay over July 4 holiday is two nights.

Hosts: Dan and Elizabeth Fannon
Rooms: 3 (SB) $47.33
Full Breakfast
Credit Cards: None
Notes: 2, 5, 8, 9

SYRIA _____

Graves' Mountain Lodge

Route 670, 22743
(703) 923-4231

This peaceful lodge is on a large cattle and fruit farm in the shadow of the Blue Ridge Mountains next to the Shenandoah National Park. Guests enjoy three meals a day on the American Plan while getting rest and relaxation during their visit. Rooms, cabins, and cottages to choose from. Trout stream and farm ponds are available for fishing. Hiking trails and horseback riding are also available for guests' enjoyment. Open mid-March through November. Seasonal rates available.

Hosts: Rachel and Jim Graves
Rooms: 45 (38 PB; 7 SB) $60.35-74.35
Cottages: 9 (PB) $55.40-84.25

NOTES: Credit cards accepted: A MasterCard; B Visa; C American Express; D Discover Card; E Diner's Club; F Other; 2 Personal checks accepted; 3 Lunch available; 4 Dinner available; 5 Open all year;

Full Breakfast
Credit Cards: A, B
Notes: 2, 3, 4, 6, 7, 8, 9, 10, 11

TANGIER

Sunset Inn

Box 156, 23440
(804) 891-2535

The Soft Crab Capital of the nation, Tangier is a romantic destination for those who would see a largely unspoiled fishing village with quaint narrow streets. The inn offers nine rooms. All have air conditioning and private baths. There is a deck and cable TV. Guests enjoy a wonderful view of the bay. One half-block from the beach. Continental breakfast is served.

Hosts: Grace and Jim Brown
Rooms: 9 (PB) $60
Continental Breakfast
Credit Cards: None
Notes: 2, 5, 8, 9, 11

VIRGINIA BEACH

Barclay Cottage

400 16th Street, 23451
(804) 422-1956

Casual sophistication for adults, in a warm, historic, inn-like atmosphere. Two blocks from the beach and in the heart of the Vir-

Barclay Cottage

ginia Beach recreational area, the Barclay Cottage has been decorated in turn-of-the-century-style with antique furniture. The hosts welcome guests to the Barclay Cottage where their theme is, "We go where our dreams take us." Open May through October.

Hosts: Peter and Claire
Rooms: 6 (3 PB; 3 SB) $65-80
Full Breakfast
Credit Cards: A, B, C
Notes: 10, 11, 14

The Picket Fence

209 43rd Street, 23451
(804) 428-8861

The furnishings in this comfortable Colonial home glow with the patina of loving care. The beach is just one block away, and beach chairs and umbrellas are provided for comfort. Near the new Marine Science Museum. One room and a suite are available year-round. A guest cottage is open May through October.

Host: Kathleen J. Hall
Room: 1 (SB) $50-85
Suite: 1 (PB)
Cottage: 1 (PB)
Full Breakfast
Credit Cards: None
Notes: 2, 5, 9, 10, 11, 12

WACHAPREAGUE

Amanda's Bed and Breakfast

1428 Park Avenue, Baltimore, MD 21217
(410) 225-0001; (800) 899-7533
FAX (410) 728-8957

267. Lovely Victorian, circa 1875, in a quaint fishing village. Four bedrooms, two full baths, contemporary kitchen, living room, dining room, fireplace, central heat and air, cable TV, and stereo. Self-catered breakfast. Whole house rental. $500/week.

---

6 Pets welcome; 8 Children welcome; 9 Social drinking allowed; 10 Tennis available; 11 Swimming available; 12 Golf available; 13 Skiing available; 14 May be booked through travel agents.

The Burton House

The Burton House

11 Brooklyn Street, 23480
(804) 787-4560

The Burton House is composed of two side-by-side Victorian houses in a seaside fishing village. Both are fully air-conditioned when needed. Guests can enjoy biking, birding, and boating. Bikes are provided and rental boats are available. Generous country breakfast and afternoon tea or coffee. Quiet, affordable elegance. Cottages are also available. Marina is very close; guests should feel free to bring their own boats.

Hosts: Pat and Tom Hart
Rooms: 10 (PB) $65-85
Cabins: 4 (PB) $40-50
Full Breakfast
Credit Cards: A, B
Notes: 2, 5, 7 (porches), 8 (over 12), 10, 11, 12, 14

WARM SPRINGS

Blue Ridge Bed and Breakfast

Route 2, Box 3895, Berryville, 22611
(703) 955-1246; (800) 296-1246

A. This rambling old house was originally an 18th-century tavern and is within ten minutes of the famous Homestead Ski Resort, and five minutes from George Washington National Forest in the Allegheny Mountains. The home has gorgeous antiques, and suites and rooms (one with pri-

vate fireplace). Only a few doors away from famous warm pools bubbling up at 98° F. $55-90.

Meadow Lane Lodge

Route 1, Box 110, 24484
(703) 839-5959

A little jewel of a country inn, set in meadows and mountains on a 1,600-acre estate. Surrounded by bountiful resources for tennis, golf, swimming, riding, trout fishing, bird watching, botanizing, hiking, walking, and creative loafing. Wake to the sounds of roosters crowing in the barn and the smells of what will be a memorable breakfast.

Hosts: Cheryl and Steve Hooley
Rooms: 11 (PB) $100-140
Full Breakfast
Credit Cards: A, B, C
Notes: 2, 3, 4, 5, 8, 9, 10, 11, 12, 13

WARRENTON

The Black Horse Inn

Route 3, Box 240, 22186
(703) 349-4020

Rosemont is a beautiful Southern Colonial estate just one and one-half miles from historic Warrenton in the heart of some of Virginia's finest horse country. The original part of this lovely old home was built prior to the Civil War; the remainder was constructed approximately 80 years ago. Legend has it that Rosemont was used as a hospital after the Civil War, and was the first courthouse of Fauquier County. Rosemont is a gracious, comfortable country home with rooms of generous proportions. Fox hunting is available; hunter stable can accommodate equine guests. Golf nearby. Only 45 minutes from Washington, D.C.

Hosts: Lynn A. Pirozzoli, and Franklin P. Williams
Rooms: 9 (PB) $85-125
Credit Cards: A, B C
Notes: 2, 5, 8, 9, 12

NOTES: Credit cards accepted: A MasterCard; B Visa; C American Express; D Discover Card; E Diner's Club; F Other; 2 Personal checks accepted; 3 Lunch available; 4 Dinner available; 5 Open all year;

WASHINGTON

Blue Ridge Bed and Breakfast

Route 2, Box 3895, Berryville, 22611
(703) 955-1246; (800) 296-1246

A. Lovely 1850s house on quiet street with great views of mountains. Easy walk to Inn at Little Washington and local theater. House has lovely antiques including Rose Kennedy chaise lounge and working fireplace in bedroom. $80-125.

B. In quaint village close to world renowned cuisine and many charming antique shops. Turn-of-the-century home offers lovely garden, two bedrooms, and one full suite. Children welcome. Close to Old Rag Mountain and Little and Big Devil's Staircase, hiking trails, as well as trout fishing. $85 125.

Caledonia Farm—1812

Route 1, Box 2080, Flint Hill, 22627
(703) 675-3693; (800) BNB-1812

Beautifully restored 1812 stone home and romantic guest house on a farm adjacent to Shenandoah National Park. This landmark, listed on the National Register of Historic Places, offers splendor for all seasons in Virginia's Blue Ridge Mountains. Skyline Drive, wineries, caves, historic sites, and superb dining. Fireplaces, air conditioning, and bicycles. Only 68 miles to Washington, D.C. AAA-rated three diamonds.

Host: Phil Irwin
Rooms: 2 plus suite (1 PB; 2 SB) $80-140
Full Breakfast
Credit Cards: A, B, D
Notes: 2, 5, 8 (over 12), 9, 10, 11, 12, 13, 14

The Foster-Harris House

Main Street, Box 333, 22747
(703) 675-3757

A turn-of-the-century home in a historic village nestled in the foothills of the Blue Ridge Mountains, with country antiques, fresh flowers, and outstanding mountain views near Shenandoah National Park. Five-star restaurant in town. All rooms feature private baths and central air conditioning.

Host: Phyllis Marriott
Rooms: 4 (PB) $85-110
Full Breakfast
Credit Cards: A, B, C, D
Notes: 2, 5, 9, 10, 11, 12, 14

Heritage House

Heritage House

P.O. Box 427, 22747
(703) 675-3207

This 1837 manor house is in Little Washington, a picturesque village originally surveyed by George Washington. Guests are invited to enjoy heirloom antiques, international collectibles, gourmet breakfasts, and gorgeous panoramic views. Central to fine dining, antiquing, hiking, horseback riding, historic attractions, wineries, and the joys of Skyline Drive and the Shenandoah National Park. AAA three-diamond approved.

Hosts: Jean and Frank Scott
Rooms: 4 (PB) $95-125
Full Breakfast
Credit Cards: A, B
Notes: 2, 5, 9, 10, 12, 14

WHITE POST

L'Auberge Provencale

P.O. Box 119, 22663
(703) 837-1375; FAX (703) 837-2004

---

6 Pets welcome; 8 Children welcome; 9 Social drinking allowed; 10 Tennis available; 11 Swimming available; 12 Golf available; 13 Skiing available; 14 May be booked through travel agents.

Elegant overnight accommodations, with romantic dining and the breakfast of one's dreams. L'Auberge Provençale offers the perfect getaway for pleasure or business. Superb French cuisine moderne is created by Master Chef Alain. Chosen by the James Beard Foundation Great Country Inn Series; four-diamond rating. L'Auberge Provençale has recreated an inn of the south of France. Country charm, city sophistication—"Where great expectations are quietly met."

Hosts: Alain and Celeste Borel
Rooms: 10 (PB) $145-205
Full Breakfast
Credit Cards: A, B, C, E
Notes: 2, 4, 5, 9, 10, 11, 12, 14

WILLIAMSBURG

Amanda's Bed and Breakfast

1428 Park Avenue, Baltimore, MD 21217
(410) 225-0001; (800) 899-7533
FAX (410) 728-8957

253. This Flemish-bond brick home was one of the first homes built on Richmond Road after the restoration of Colonial Williamsburg began in the late 1920s. The house features 18th-century decor, and the owner's apple collection is evident throughout. Four rooms with private baths. Continental plus breakfast. $70-110.

Applewood Colonial

605 Richmond Road, 23185
(804) 229-0205; (800) 899-2753

Circa 1921, this Flemish-bond brick home was built during the restoration of Colonial Williamsburg. The inn's parlor is decorated Colonial style and features dentil crown molding. A crystal chandelier hangs above the dining table where breakfast is served. The Colonel Vaughn Suite boasts private entrance, fireplace, and queen-size canopied bed.

Host: Fred Strout
Rooms: 4 (PB) $75-120
Full Breakfast
Credit Cards: A, B
Notes: 2, 5, 8, 9, 10, 12, 14

Candlewick Bed and Breakfast

706 Richmond Road, 23185
(804) 253-8693; (800) 418-4949

This wonderful country home looks as though it jumped off the pages of *Country Living* magazine. A charming blend of 18th century, country, elegant bedrooms with canopied beds, and private baths. One bedroom can sleep three. Within walking distance of historic area and William and Mary College. Complimentary bicycles.

Host: Mary Peters
Rooms: 3 (PB) $75-95
Full Breakfast
Credit Cards: A, B
Notes: 2, 5, 8 (over 10), 9, 10, 11, 12, 14

The Cedars

616 Jamestown Road, 23185
(804) 229-3591; (800) 296-3591

Across the street from the College of William and Mary and a 10-minute walk to Colonial Williamsburg, The Cedars offers traditional colonial elegance, comfort, and hospitality. The three-story brick Georgian is the oldest and largest bed and breakfast in Williamsburg. Scrumptious full breakfasts are served by candlelight from a hand-hewn huntboard on the tavern porch. In the evening, the porch serves as a meeting place for cards, chess, or other diversions. On cool evenings, the fireplace in the sitting room invites relaxation and conversation. Each guest room has a unique personality. Four-poster and canopied beds abound. Offstreet parking.

Hosts: Carol, Jim, and Brona Malecha
Rooms: 9 (PB) $95-135
Cottage: 1 (PB) $150
Full Breakfast
Credit Cards: A, B
Notes: 2, 5, 8, 9, 14

NOTES: Credit cards accepted: A MasterCard; B Visa; C American Express; D Discover Card; E Diner's Club; F Other; 2 Personal checks accepted; 3 Lunch available; 4 Dinner available; 5 Open all year;

Colonial Capital

Colonial Capital
Bed and Breakfast

501 Richmond Road, 23185
(804) 229-0233; (800) 776-0570
FAX (804) 253-7667

Only three blocks from the historic area, this charming Colonial Revival home, circa 1926, and its gracious hosts welcome guests. Enjoy spring gardens, summer festivities, autumn colors, and Colonial Christmastide. Antique furnishings blend charm and elegance from the large parlor with wood-burning fireplace to the airy guest rooms, each with canopied bed and private bath. Full breakfast with a gourmet touch and afternoon tea and wine. ABC licensed, bikes, and free off-street parking. Gift certificates available. FAX can receive 24 hours a day. Special rates available January through March.

Hosts: Barbara and Phil Craig
Rooms: 5 (PB) $95-135
Full Breakfast
Credit Cards: A, B, C, D
Notes: 2, 5, 7, 8 (over 6), 9, 10, 12, 14

For Cant Hill Guest Home

4 Canterbury Lane, 23185
(804) 229-6623

This home is only a few blocks from the restored area of Williamsburg, yet very secluded and quiet in a lovely wooded setting overlooking a lake that joins the College of William and Mary campus. The rooms are beautifully decorated, and the hosts are happy to make dinner reservations for guests and provide helpful information on the many area attractions. Large Continental breakfast served in the guests' room.

Hosts: Martha and Hugh Easler
Rooms: 2 (PB) $65-75
Continental Breakfast
Credit Cards: None
Notes: 2, 5, 8 (over 10), 9, 10, 11, 12, 14

Governor's Trace

303 Capitol Landing Road, 23185
(804) 229-7552; (800) 303-7552

Reminisce and rekindle romance as the blaze in the bedroom fireplace radiates its warmth, and antique furnishings glow in the soft illumination. The scent of freshly cut flowers wafts from a nearby nook, where tomorrow morning a private candlelit Continental plus breakfast will be served. But for now, the covers on the Colonial canopied bed are turned down, and romance dances in the shadows. This bed and breakfast treasure, a perfect getaway to make new memories, is but a stone's throw from historic 18th-century Colonial Williamsburg, just one door away!

Hosts: Sue and Dick Lake
Room: 3 (PB) $95-115
Continental Breakfast
Credit Cards: A, B
Notes: 2, 5, 9, 10, 11, 12, 14

Hite's Bed and Breakfast

704 Monumental Avenue, 23185
(804) 229-4814

Attractive Cape Cod offering large rooms cleverly furnished with antiques and collectibles. Each room has a TV, telephone, radio, coffee maker, robes, and private baths. Guests will especially like the suite with its large sitting room and old-fashioned bathroom with claw-foot tub. In the parlor for guests' enjoyment is an antique pump organ and hand crank victrola. Guests can swing in the back yard and enjoy the squirrels, birds, and gold fish pond. Just a seven-minute walk to Colonial Williamsburg.

6 Pets welcome; 8 Children welcome; 9 Social drinking allowed; 10 Tennis available; 11 Swimming available; 12 Golf available; 13 Skiing available; 14 May be booked through travel agents.

Hosts: Mr. and Mrs. James Hite
Rooms: 2 (PB) $65-75
Suites: 1 (PB)
Continental Breakfast
Credit Cards: None
Notes: 2, 5, 8, 12

The Homestay
Bed and Breakfast

517 Richmond Road, 23185
(804) 229-7468 information; (800) 836-7468 reservations

Cozy and convenient. Enjoy the comfort of a lovely Colonial Revival home, furnished with turn-of-the-century family antiques and country charm. It is only four blocks to Colonial Williamsburg, and just minutes away from Jamestown, Yorktown, and other local attractions. Adjacent to the College of William and Mary. A full breakfast featuring homemade breads and a delicious hot dish is served in the formal dining room. Complimentary bicycles available.

Hosts: Barbara and Jim Thomassen
Rooms: 3 (PB) $70-85
Full Breakfast
Credit Cards: A, B
Notes: 2, 5, 8 (over 10), 9, 12, 14

Indian Springs
Bed and Breakfast

330 Indian Springs Road, 23185
(800) 262-9165

In a quiet, wooded setting downtown, Indian Springs offers a delightful retreat for guests after a day of sightseeing. Charming suites include king-size feather beds, private baths and private entrances. Veranda overlooking shady ravine is bird watchers' haven. A hearty breakfast is always on the menu. Cozy cottage available.

Hosts: Kelly and Paul Supplee
Rooms: 4 (PB) $75-110
Full Breakfast
Credit Cards: None
Notes: 2, 5, 9, 10, 11, 12, 14

Liberty Rose

1022 Jamestown Road, 23185
(804) 253-1260

Liberty Rose offers guests enchanting decor and delightful hospitality when visiting this bed and breakfast. This is a wonderful old Williamsburg home showcased on wooded hilltops near historic area. For lovers of exquisite queen-size beds, claw-foot bathtubs, marble showers, papered walls, 18th-century country French and Victorian antiques, fireplaces, chocolate chip cookies, in-room TV and VCR, and a big, scrumptious breakfast. "You'll love it!"

Hosts: Brad and Sandi Hirz
Rooms: 4 (PB) $100-165
Full Breakfast
Credit Cards: A, B
Notes: 2, 5, 10, 12, 14

Piney Grove
at Southall's Plantation

P.O. Box 1359, 23187-1359
(804) 829-2480

Piney Grove is 20 miles west of Williamsburg in the James River plantation country, among working farms, country stores, and historic churches. The elegant accommodations at this National Register of Historic Places property are in two restored antebellum homes (1800 and 1857). Guests are welcomed to enjoy the parlor-library, pool, nature trail, farm animals, or a game of croquet or badminton. Upon arrival, guests are served mint juleps and Virginia wine.

Hosts: Brian and Cindy, Joan, and Joseph Gordineer
Rooms: 5 (PB) $125-150
Full Breakfast
Credit Cards: None
Notes: 2, 5, 8, 9, 11, 12, 14

Spiggle Guest Home

720 College Terrace, 23185
(804) 253-0202

NOTES: Credit cards accepted: A MasterCard; B Visa; C American Express; D Discover Card; E Diner's Club; F Other; 2 Personal checks accepted; 3 Lunch available; 4 Dinner available; 5 Open all year;

Spend the night with these gracious hosts in this cozy 6,000-square-foot brick Colonial home on a beautiful, quiet residential street. Guests will see all of Williamsburg from this convenient location. A few minutes' walk to the restored area of Williamsburg and a ten-minute drive to shopping centers, Busch Gardens, and the Pottery Factory. Guest rooms are comfortably furnished, some with family antiques, and all include wall-to-wall carpeting, in-room refrigerators, coffee and tea makers, telephone jacks, TV, private baths, air conditioning, and choice of queen-size, double, or twin beds.

Hosts: Phil and Dottie Spiggle
Rooms: 4 (PB) $35-50
No Breakfast
Credit Cards: None
Notes: 2, 5, 9, 12

The Travel Tree

P.O. Box 838, 23187
(800) 989-1571

3. Historic estate on 45 acres of land offers four guest rooms and a guest cottage. Outdoor pool and pool house for warmer weather. Across the York River in Gloucester, 25 miles from historic area. Nonsmoking. $85-100.

9. Four-poster queen-bedded room with sitting area and private bath. Add the adjoining room with antique double bed for a family suite and enjoy all that Williams-burg has to offer. Near Busch Gardens, four miles from historic area. Nonsmoking. $75-130.

10. Rest safe and secure tucked under the eaves of a story-and-a-half cottage in a charming, wooded setting. Sleep upstairs in queen-size bed; relax downstairs in the sitting room with fireplace and Pullman kitchen. With sofa bed downstairs, accommodates four, and one and one-half baths. One mile from historic area. Nonsmoking. $100-140.

99. At the end of a long day, it is a pleasure to retreat to the charm of this guest room with fireplace, sitting area, and private bath. Climbing the stairs to the third floor in this reproduction 18th-century Connecticut tavern provides the transition to a luxurious rest. Expanded Continental breakfast greets guests in the morning in the formal dining room. One mile from Colonial Williamsburg. Nonsmoking. $90.

133. Luxury in home away from home in a spacious room complete with king-size bed, dining alcove, private bath, and private entrance. Or select the economical queen-bedded room with lovely wooded view, or twin-bedded room furnished with Oriental accents, adjacent shared bath. Three miles from historic area. Nonsmoking. $50-75.

133A. Be treated to the privacy of this refreshing, spacious room with king-size bed, breakfast area, and private bath and entrance. Enjoy breakfast at desired time and experience a relaxed pace on a Williamsburg holiday. Microwave, refrigerator, and coffee maker make a visit comfortable for a day or a week. Three miles from Colonial Williamsburg. Nonsmoking. $75.

133B. If guests prefer to be more in the midst of things, the hosts offer a queen-size room with lovely wooded view or a twin room furnished with Oriental accents and private bath. Have breakfast with the family in the dining room or on their screened deck in good weather. Three miles from Colonial Williamsburg. Nonsmoking. $60.

139. Relax in an airy, inviting room with private entrance, private bath, kitchenette, and patio doors leading to the lawn. Or choose the gracious suite furnished with 18th- and 19th-century antiques, a four-poster double bed, sitting area with fireplace, breakfast room, and private bath.

6 Pets welcome; 8 Children welcome; 9 Social drinking allowed; 10 Tennis available; 11 Swimming available; 12 Golf available; 13 Skiing available; 14 May be booked through travel agents.

One mile from historic area. Nonsmoking. $65-95.

139A. Savor the special ambience of Williamsburg in a suite furnished with 18th- and 19th-century antiques. Guests will have a bed/sitting room with poster bed and fireplace, breakfast room, dressing room, and bath. Cable TV, telephone, small refrigerator, coffee maker, and wet bar make it all seem like home. Wooded residential community offers peace and quiet. One mile from Colonial Williamsburg. Nonsmoking. $90.

139B. Relax in an inviting bed/sitting room with patio doors opening onto the lawn and woods. One wall is all glass for that outdoor feeling. Private entrance, bath, and kitchenette complete this home away from home. Cable TV and telephone add to the convenience. Hosts prepare breakfast and bring it to guests' room. One mile from Colonial Williamsburg. Nonsmoking. $75.

330. Only blocks from the visitor area but off the beaten path for a real sample of Williamsburg living. Guest room, two guest suites, and a guest cottage, each with private entrance. Seven blocks from historic area. Nonsmoking. $75-105.

501. Bike lovely streets of Williamsburg, returning in time for afternoon tea and wine in the parlor. Choose from five rooms, each charmingly furnished in the Colonial-style, with canopied or four-poster beds, and private baths. Four blocks from historic area. Smoking in parlor only. $95-155.

517. Enjoy the ambience of a lovely Colonial Revival home furnished with turn-of-the-century antiques and country charm.

Double, twin, or king-size beds available. Four blocks from Williamsburg's restored area. Nonsmoking. $70-85.

600. Colonial ambience in a stately brick home offering five guest rooms and a full breakfast prepared by a professional chef. Dinner is offered at an additional charge and is available with advance reservation only. Five blocks from the historic area. Nonsmoking. $90-150.

605. Walk to the historic area after starting the day with the companionship of fellow guests at breakfast. The lovely guest rooms, each in Colonial decor, will charm guests, from the first floor suite with fireplace to the quaint third floor dormered room. All have queen-size beds and private baths. Five blocks from historic area. Nonsmoking. $70-125.

706. Old World charm! Two guest rooms with private baths and a common sitting area provided by European hosts add a special touch to guests' visit. Seven blocks from the historic area. Nonsmoking. $85-95.

War Hill Inn

4560 Long Hill Road, 23188
(804) 565-0248; (800) 743-0248

This replica of an 18th-century home sits on a 32-acre farm three miles off Route 60. Close to the College of William and Mary, Colonial Williamsburg, Busch Gardens, and shopping outlets. Seven antique-furnished guest rooms with private baths. Cable TV. Country breakfast.

Hosts: Shirley, Bill, Cherie, and Will Lee
Rooms: 7 (PB) $65-85
Suites: 2
Cottage: 1 (PB) $110
Full Breakfast
Credit Cards: A, B, C
Notes: 2, 5, 8, 9, 14

NOTES: Credit cards accepted: A MasterCard; B Visa; C American Express; D Discover Card; E Diner's Club; F Other; 2 Personal checks accepted; 3 Lunch available; 4 Dinner available; 5 Open all year;

Williamsburg Manor
Bed and Breakfast

600 Richmond Road, 23185
(804) 220-8011; (800) 422-8011

This 1927 Georgian home was built during the reconstruction of historic Colonial Williamsburg. Recently restored to its original elegance and furnished with exquisite pieces including antiques and collectibles. Five well-appointed guest rooms with private bath, TV, and central air conditioning. Guests are treated to a lavish fireside breakfast prepared by the executive chef. Home is available for weddings, private parties, dinners, and meetings. Ideal location within walking distance of the historic area. On-site parking.

Hosts: Laura and Mickael Macknight
Rooms: 5 (PB) $90-150
Full Breakfast
Credit Cards: None
Notes: 2, 4, 5, 9, 10, 11, 12, 14

Williamsburg Sampler
Bed and Breakfast

922 Jamestown Road, 23185
(804) 253-0398; (800) 722-1169

This bed and breakfast is an elegant plantation-style, six-bedroom brick Colonial, richly furnished with antiques, pewter, and samplers. Internationally known as a favorite for honeymoons, anniversaries, or romantic getaways. The hosts return guests to an era when hospitality was a matter of pride and fine living was an art. Lovely rooms with four-poster king/queen-size beds plus private baths. Skip-lunch breakfast. Close to all major attractions. Personalized gift certificates available. AAA-rated three diamonds. Appeared on "CBS This Morning."

Hosts: Helen and Ike Sisane
Rooms: 4 (PB) $90-100
Full Breakfast
Credit Cards: A, B
Notes: 2, 5, 9, 10, 11, 12, 14

WILLIS WHARF

Amanda's
Bed and Breakfast

1428 Park Avenue, Baltimore, MD 21217
(410) 225-0001; (800) 899-7533
FAX (410) 728-8957

145. Eighty-year-old country farmhouse with wraparound porch and gazebo by a stream. Near freshwater pond, bird watching, photographic scenes, and guided tours. Amenities include outside swings, hammock, play gym, and bicycles. Relaxed family atmosphere. Four rooms with shared and private baths. Full breakfast. $60-75.

WINCHESTER

Blue Ridge
Bed and Breakfast

Route 2, Box 3895, Berryville, 22611
(703) 955-1246; (800) 296-1246

A. In urban Winchester, this lovely Dutch Colonial reproduction filled with Oriental antiques from all over the world is just seconds from I-81 and Shenandoah University. Easy drive to northern entrance of Skyline Drive. Outstanding cuisine and unique antique shops. Noted for delicious

Williamsburg Sampler

country breakfasts. Less than an acre of land is lusciously decorated with gorgeous gardens. $75.

WOODSTOCK

Azalea House

551 South Main Street, 22664
(703) 459-3500

The Azalea House dates back 100 years when it was built in the Victorian tradition and used as a church manse. The guest rooms are pleasing and comfortable, with antique furnishings and mountain views. Situated in the rolling hills of the Shenandoah Valley near fine restaurants, vineyards, shops, caverns, Civil War sites, hiking, and fishing. A great place to relax!

Hosts: Margaret and Price McDonald
Rooms: 2 (PB) $45-70
Suite: 1
Full Breakfast
Credit Cards: A, B, C
Notes: 2, 5, 9, 10, 11, 12, 13

Blue Ridge Bed and Breakfast

Route 2, Box 3895, Berryville, 22611
(703) 955-1246; (800) 296-1246

A. Quaint turn-of-the-century house built in 1885 offers casual country hospitality, many games, hiking, cycling, and antiquing. Close to military academy, Skyline Drive, and skiing. $45-60.

B. Lovely home in quaint town is on the National Register of Historic Places. Built in 1840, log house was the Toll Gate House. Has 21 boxwoods and over 1,000 spring bulbs. Furnished with New England antiques. $45-55.

C. Gorgeous mansion built in 1892 filled with antiques and hand-stenciled rooms. Hundreds of azaleas. In-ground swimming pool. $45-65

D. Beautiful farmhouse on 17 acres built in the 1880s. Completely refurbished and has huge deck overlooking Blue Ridge Mountains. Hosts welcome guests to share traditional Jewish Sabbath meals and customs. $40-55.

The Inn at Narrow Passage

US 11 South, 22664
(703) 459-8000

Historic log inn with five acres on the Shenandoah River. Colonial-style rooms, most with private baths and working fireplaces. Once the site of Indian attacks and Stonewall Jackson's headquarters, it is now a cozy spot in winter with large fireplaces in the common living and dining rooms. In spring and summer, fishing and rafting are at the back door. Fall brings the foliage festivals and hiking in the national forest a few miles away. Nearby are vineyards, caverns, historic sites, and fine restaurants. Washington, D.C., is 90 miles away.

Hosts: Ellen and Ed Markel
Rooms: 12 (10 PB; 2 SB) $55-95
Full Breakfast
Credit Cards: A, B
Notes: 2, 5, 8, 9, 10, 11, 12, 13, 1

The Inn at Narrow Passage

Washington

Albatross Bed and Breakfast

5708 Kingsway West, 98221
(206) 293-0677; (800) 484-9507 (Code 5840)

Across from the Skyline Marina, this 1927 Cape Cod-style home features full breakfasts, king- and queen-size beds, private baths, fine art, antiques, and island views. The marina offers charter boats, a deli, and fine dining. Nearby are the Washington Park and ferries to the San Juan Islands and Victoria, British Columbia. Sightseeing cruises aboard host's 46-foot sailboat are available. AAA approved.

Hosts: Barbie and Ken
Rooms: 4 (PB) $75-95
Full Breakfast
Credit Cards. A, B, C
Notes: 2, 5, 8, 9, 10, 11, 12, 13, 14

Channel House Bed and Breakfast

2902 Oakes Avenue, 98221
(360) 293-9382; (800) 238-4353

A classic island home built in 1902, the Channel House offers large, comfortable rooms, two with fireplaces, and lovely water and island views. The outdoor hot tub is a treat after a busy day of hiking or biking on the islands. Pat's oatmeal-raisin cookies are baked fresh every day. Anacortes is the beginning of the San Juan Island and Sydney, British Columbia ferry routes and a center for chartering sail- and power boats for wonderful vacation trips.

Hosts: Dennis and Patricia McIntyre
Rooms: 6 (PB) $69-95
Full Breakfast
Credit Cards: A, B, C, D
Notes: 2, 5, 9,12, 14

Channel House

Hasty Pudding House Bed and Breakfast

1312 Eighth Street, 98221
(206) 293-5773; (800) 368-5588

Celebrate romance in this delightful 1913 heritage home. A wonderful example of Craftsman-style architecture, this home is filled with Victorian antiques, fresh flowers, window seats, and wonderful private rooms, all with turn-of-the-century charm and comfort guests will enjoy. Snuggle in king-size, queen-size, and twin top-of-the-line beds that grandmother would envy. Melinda's luscious breakfasts and table setting will begin this Anacortes adventure each day of guests' stay.

Hosts: Mikel and Melinda Hasty
Rooms: 4 (2 PB; 2 SB) $65-85

6 Pets welcome; 7 Smoking allowed; 8 Children welcome; 9 Social drinking allowed; 10 Tennis available; 11 Swimming available; 12 Golf available; 13 Skiing available; 14 May be booked through travel agents.

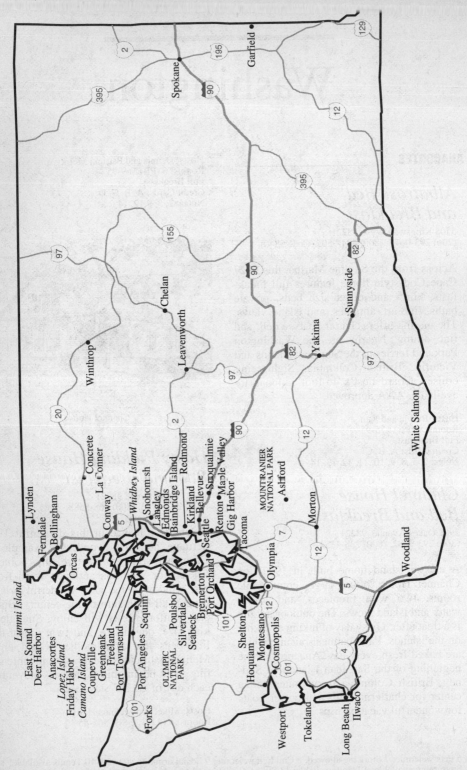

Washington

Full Breakfast
Credit Cards: A, B, C, D
Notes: 2, 5, 9, 10, 11, 12, 13, 14

A Pacific Reservation Service

701 Northwest 60th Street, Seattle, 98107
(206) 784-0539

Anacortes. This restored Victorian turn-of-the-century home features fine antiques, Oriental carpets, a library, colorful flower gardens, three fireplaces, and an outdoor hot tub. Wonderful views of Puget Sound can be seen from two of the guest rooms and the shared bathrooms. Intimate in size with warm hospitality. $69-125.

Sunset Beach Bed and Breakfast

100 Sunset Beach, 98221
(206) 293-5428

On the exciting Rosario Strait overlooking seven San Juan islands, this bed and breakfast invites guests to enjoy the water scenery that includes water birds, deer, fishing boats, and more. Take a stroll and enjoy the scenic view of the Olympic Mountains, or amble down the beach. Close to the ferry, marina, and excellent restaurants, and adjacent to Washington Park. Full breakfasts, queen-size beds, and private bath. Hot tub on request.

Hosts: Joann and Hal Harbei
Rooms: 3 (1 PB; 2 SB) $69
Full Breakfast
Credit Cards: A, B
Notes: 2, 5, 9, 11, 12, 14

ASHFORD

Growly Bear Bed and Breakfast

37311 State Road 706, 98304
(800) 700-2339

Experience a bit of history and enjoy a mountain stay at a rustic homestead house built in 1890. Hike in nearby Mount Rainier National Park. Dine at unique restaurants within walking distance of guest room. Be lulled to sleep by the whispering sounds of Goat Creek just outside the window. Awake in the morning to the aroma of freshly baked bread. Indulge in a basket of warm pastries from nearby Sweet Peaks Bakery.

Host: Susan Jenny
Rooms: 2 (1 PB; 1 SB) $70-90
Full Breakfast
Credit Cards: A, B, C
Notes: 2, 5, 9, 13, 14

Mountain Meadows Inn

28912 State Road 706 East, 98304
(206) 569-2788

Gracious hospitality, unique, quiet country atmosphere. Relax while absorbing nature's colors and sounds from the full porch overlooking the pond. Evening campfires. Nearby Mount Rainier National Park offers all-season recreation. Model trains are on display. Listed in *Northwest Best Places.* Two-night minimum stay during holidays.

Host: Chad Darrah
Rooms: 5 (PB) $65-95
Full Breakfast
Credit Cards: A, B
Notes: 2, 5, 7 (limited), 8 (over ten), 9, 12, 13, 14

BAINBRIDGE ISLAND

Bombay House

8490 Beck Road, 98110
(206) 842-3926; (800) 598-3926

The Bombay House is a spectacular 35-minute ferry ride from downtown Seattle. The house was built in 1907 and sits high on a hillside in the country overlooking Rich Passage. Widow's walk; rustic, rough-cedar gazebo; masses of gardens exploding with seasonal color. Watch the ferry pass and see the lights of Bremerton in the distance. Just a

NOTES: Credit cards accepted: A MasterCard; B Visa; C American Express; D Discover Card; E Diner's Club; F Other; 2 Personal checks accepted; 3 Lunch available; 4 Dinner available; 5 Open all year; 6 Pets welcome; 7 Smoking allowed; 8 Children welcome; 9 Social drinking allowed; 10 Tennis available; 11 Swimming available; 12 Golf available; 13 Skiing available; 14 May be booked through travel agents.

Bombay House

few blocks from the beach, a country theater, and fine dining. A great spot for the Seattle business traveler or vacationer.

Hosts: Bunny Cameron and Roger Kanchuk
Rooms: 5 (3 PB; 2 SB) $55-125
Continental Breakfast
Credit Cards: A, B, C
Notes: 2, 5, 9, 10, 11, 12, 14

A Pacific
Reservation Service

701 Northwest 60th Street, Seattle, 98107
(206) 784-0539

Bainbridge Island-1. This special country inn invites guests to sit on the wraparound porch, enjoy the beautiful flower gardens, the gazebo, or snuggle up by the crackling fire in the fireplace. A stay here will renew and refresh spirits. Built for a ship's captain, this lovely bed and breakfast offers nice views over the water, three bedrooms with private baths, and two bedrooms that share a bath. Legendary country breakfast. $65-95.

Bainbridge Island-2. This Bainbridge accommodation is on a beautifully landscaped acre enclosed by a forest on both sides. Guests can relax on comfortable wicker furniture and look out at the rose garden after a day of sightseeing or exploration. Perfect for honeymooners and couples. The cookie jar here is always deep, a new snack is served on the table next to the sofa every day, and the bedroom has a queen-size bed with a wonderful new mattress and a private bath. $85.

BELLEVUE

Bellevue Bed
and Breakfast

830 100th Avenue S.E., 98004-6746
(206) 453-1048

Hilltop, city, and mountain views. Private suite or single room with private bath and entrance. Full breakfast featuring gourmet coffee, central location, complimentary extras, and reasonable rates. Listed in "Seattle Best Places."

Hosts: Carol and Cy Garnett
Rooms: 2 (PB) $55
Full Breakfast
Credit Cards: A, B
Notes: 2, 3, 4, 5, 10, 11, 12, 13, 14

Petersen Bed
and Breakfast

10228 Southeast Eighth, 98004
(206) 454-9334

Petersen Bed and Breakfast is in a well-established neighborhood five minutes from the Bellevue Shopping Square and 20 minutes from Seattle. It offers two rooms, one with a queen-size waterbed, and a spa on the deck off the atrium kitchen. Homestyle breakfast.

Hosts: Eunice and Carl Petersen
Rooms: 2 (SB) $50-55
Full Breakfast
Credit Cards: None
Notes: 5, 8

BELLINGHAM

Bed and Breakfast Guild
of Whatcom County

2610 Eldridge Avenue, 98225
(206) 676-4560

NOTES: Credit cards accepted: A MasterCard; B Visa; C American Express; D Discover Card; E Diner's Club; F Other; 2 Personal checks accepted; 3 Lunch available; 4 Dinner available; 5 Open all year;

1. Elegant 1897 Queen Anne with sweeping view of bay and islands. Near the university. Ten guest rooms. Sumptuous breakfasts served. $55-75.

2. This charming home, surrounded by giant trees, overlooks sparkling Lake Whatcom. Guest rooms are spacious, comfortable, and gaily decorated. Homemade breakfasts are an adventure. Smoking porch, RV parking, private baths, and queen-size feather beds. Home away from home. $60-90.

4. Charming, elegant turn-of-the-century home with magnificent sunset views overlooking Bellingham Bay. Central location on two and one-half acres of mature gardens. Rose Room suite and Blue Room double are romantically decorated. Both rooms have private baths. Deliciously generous breakfasts. Hosts, Susan and Ernie, welcome guests. Winter weekly rates available. $50-95.

6. Victorian home in historic neighborhood overlooking bay and islands. Friendly hosts, Van and Barbara, offer local insights and a game of pool in the parlor. Guest rooms feature private baths and family heirlooms. Breakfast will help guests start the day with a smile. $45-70.

11. On 65 secluded acres. Enjoy wilderness trails, indoor swimming pool, sauna, full breakfast, six luxurious rooms, and conference space. A central location for snow skiing, shopping, dining, bicycling, hiking, and boating activities. Visa and MasterCard accepted. $65-95.

12. An 1892 Victorian home surrounded by 330 acres of woods, trails, and pastures on a working farm. Five miles from busy shopping centers. A hearty breakfast served by friendly farm folks. Children are welcome. $45-55.

13. This modern A-frame has two suites plus a honeymoon cottage set amid tall evergreens overlooking Lake Whatcom. All the amenities: hot tub, jacuzzi, tennis courts, and gourmet breakfast. $100-170.

De Cann House Bed and Breakfast

2610 Eldridge Avenue, 98225
(206) 734-9172

Victorian home in historic neighborhood overlooking bay and islands. Friendly hosts offer local insights and a game of pool in the parlor. Guest rooms feature private baths and family heirlooms. A complete breakfast starts every guest's day with a smile. In operation since 1986 with reasonable rates and treasures with stories attached.

Hosts: Barbara and Van Hudson
Rooms: 2 (PB) $50-70
Full Breakfast
Credit Cards: None
Notes: 2, 5, 9, 10, 11, 12, 13

A Pacific Reservation Service

701 Northwest 60th Street, Seattle, 98107
(206) 784-0539

Bellingham. Decorated with stained glass and etchings crafted by the hostess, this restored Victorian overlooking the bay is a great getaway spot. The two guest rooms have private baths. The hosts will be more than happy to give advice to sightseers if needed. Guests are assured a warm, friendly welcome at this bed and breakfast. $59.

Schnauzer Crossing

4421 Lakeway Drive, 98226
(360) 733-0055; (800) 562-2808; FAX (360) 734-2808

Schnauzer Crossing is a luxury bed and breakfast between Seattle and Vancouver, British Columbia. Enjoy this destination bed and breakfast, with its lakeside ambience, outdoor hot tub, and its master suite with fireplace and

6 Pets welcome; 8 Children welcome; 9 Social drinking allowed; 10 Tennis available; 11 Swimming available; 12 Golf available; 13 Skiing available; 14 May be booked through travel agents.

Jacuzzi. There is also a new cottage. Sail in the San Juan Islands or climb 10,000-foot Mount Baker. Experience Washington state!

Hosts: Vermont and Donna McAllister
Rooms: 3 (PB) $110-180
Full Breakfast
Credit Cards: A, B, D
Notes: 2, 5, 7 (limited), 8, 9, 10, 11, 12, 13

BREMERTON

Willcox House

2390 Tekiu Road, Northwest, 98312
(360) 830-4492

Overlooking Hood Canal and the Olympic Mountains is a place where time rests. Life is paced by the slow, steady hand of nature. It is quiet enough to hear the birds sing. Deer amble through the gardens. Saltwater beaches and good books wait for quiet companions. Willcox House is an elegant 10,000-square-foot mansion built in 1936 with landscaped grounds, private pier, and beach. Five guest rooms, all with private baths and magnificent views of Hood Canal and Olympic Mountains.

Hosts: Cecilia and Phillip Hughes
Rooms: 5 (PB) $110-165
Full Breakfast
Credit Cards: A, B
Notes: 2, 3, 4, 5, 9, 14

Willcox House

CAMANO ISLAND

Willcox House Bed and Breakfast

1462 Larkspur Lane, 98292
(206) 629-4746

Built in 1985, this two-story house with a wraparound covered porch is furnished with family antiques and named for an early 1900s children's illustrator, Jessie Willcox Smith, a relative. The rooms overlook the Puget Sound where snow geese and trumpet swans migrate each fall. Mount Baker looms in the distance. Gourmet breakfasts are served in a peaceful country setting. The house is on an island one hour north of Seattle connected by bridge to the mainland, close to picturesque towns and Canada.

Host: Esther Harmon
Rooms: 4 (PB) $55-65
Full Breakfast
Credit Cards: A, B
Notes: 2, 5, 8, 9, 10, 11, 12, 13

CASHMERE

Cashmere Country Inn

5801 Pioneer Drive, 98815
(509) 782-4212

This delightful 1907 farmhouse with five bedrooms welcomes guests with charm and hospitality. Every effort has been made to make each stay memorable. Among many outstanding features, the food is superb— prepared skillfully and presented beautifully. There is a pool and hot tub, and for flower lovers, the well-kept grounds boast country rose and herb gardens. Looking for that extra-special inn that defines a bed and breakfast? Guests will be pleased to discover Cashmere Country Inn.

Hosts: Patti and Dale Swanson
Rooms: 5 (PB) $75
Full Breakfast
Credit Cards: A, B, C
Notes: 2, 4, 5, 11, 12, 13, 14

NOTES: Credit cards accepted: A MasterCard; B Visa; C American Express; D Discover Card; E Diner's Club; F Other; 2 Personal checks accepted; 3 Lunch available; 4 Dinner available; 5 Open all year;

CHELAN

The Brick House Inn

304 Wapato Avenue, 98816
(509) 682-2233; (800) 799-2332

Built in 1910, this three-story Victorian boasts casual elegance, blending old with new. Stress-free relaxation in the heart of the city entices both the young and the young-at-heart! The wraparound porch and ample lawn invite outdoor comfort all year round. Group rates available. Completely nonsmoking inside. Whether a party of two or twelve, the hosts go out of their way to make guests' stay one of a kind!

Hosts: Mike, Debbie, and Amy Mack
Rooms: 6 (1 PB; 5 SB) $63-80
Continental Breakfast
Credit Cards: A, B, D
Notes: 2, 5, 8, 9, 10, 11, 12, 13

CONCRETE-BIRDSVIEW

Cascade Mountain Inn

3840 Pioneer Lane, 98237
(206) 826-4333; (800) 826-0015

This inn is close to the Skagit River, Baker Lake, and the North Cascades National Park, just off Highway 20 in a pastoral setting. One of the best in the Pacific Northwest, this inn has easy access to hiking, fishing, and sightseeing in one of the nation's most scenic mountain areas. Country breakfast. AAA rated three diamonds.

Hosts: Ingrid and Gerhard Meyer
Rooms: 6 (PB) $89-110
Full Breakfast
Credit Cards: A, B
Notes: 2, 5, 8 (over 10), 9, 14

CONWAY

South Fork Moorage

2187 Mann Road, 98238
(206) 445-4803

Floating in a quiet cove on a bend in the Skagit River, the Karma is the Northwest's most unique guest houseboat. Wake up on this cozy houseboat and share morning coffee with a neighboring eagle, curl up in the sleeping loft, and gaze at the stars. Enjoy a roaring fire in the forward cabin and candlelit stained glass windows. Sixty miles north of Seattle; 80 miles from Vancouver, British Columbia.

Host: J. R. Demick
Rooms: 4 (2 PB) $95-115
Credit Cards: None
Notes: 2, 6 (call), 9, 10, 11, 12, 13

Cooney Mansion

COSMOPOLIS

Cooney Mansion

1705 Fifth Street, 98537
(206) 533-0602

This historic register Arts and Crafts style lumber baron's retreat features original furniture and private baths. Relax in the Jacuzzi, exercise room, or sauna. Play golf, tennis, or curl up with a book from the extensive library. Sit in the rose garden or amble through Mill Creek Park with its bridges and waterfalls. The Cooney Mansion exudes an old-fashioned warmth and relaxed atmosphere. Two minutes' drive from Aberdeen and Hoquiam. The ballroom is perfect for retreats and weddings. Close to beaches, museums, antique shops, and historic seaport.

6 Pets welcome; 8 Children welcome; 9 Social drinking allowed; 10 Tennis available; 11 Swimming available;
12 Golf available; 13 Skiing available; 14 May be booked through travel agents.

Hosts: Judi and Jim Lohr
Rooms: 8 (5 PB; 3 SB) $55-115
Full Breakfast
Credit Cards: A, B, D, E
Notes: 5, 10, 12

The Colonel Crockett Farm

COUPEVILLE

The Colonel Crockett Farm Bed and Breakfast Inn

1012 South Fort Casey Road, 98239
(206) 678-3711

The inn offers 140 years of Victorian/ Edwardian serenity in a farm-quiet island setting with pastoral and marine views. Period antiques enhance three large bed/sitting rooms and two smaller bedrooms, all with private baths. Common areas include an oak-paneled library, a wicker-furnished solarium, and a dining room featuring individual tables. Full hot breakfast is served each morning, and the owners live in a separate apartment. This 1855 Victorian farmhouse is on the National Register of Historic Places. Extensive grounds, walkways, and flower beds. No smoking.

Hosts: Robert and Beulah Whitlow
Rooms: 5 (PB) $65-95
Full Breakfast
Credit Cards: A, B
Notes: 2, 5, 8 (over 14), 14

The Inn at Penn Cove

702 North Main Street, P.O. Box 85, 98239
(206) 678-8000; (800) 688-COVE

Two restored Victorian homes (one on the National Register of Historic Places, the other built for the daughter of Captain Coupe) in one of Washington's most historic towns. Walking distance to restaurants, shops, and museum. Within 20 miles of Deception Pass; even closer to Forts Casey and Ebey. All guest rooms have water views (five face Mount Baker). Private baths include one with spa tub, two with antique claw-foot tubs. Antique decor, music box, pump organ, VCR in lounge, afternoon tea.

Hosts: Gladys and Mitchell Howard
Rooms: 6 (4 PB; 2 SB) $60-125
Full Breakfast
Credit Cards: A, B, C, D
Notes: 2, 5, 8, 10, 12, 14

DEER HARBOR (ORCAS ISLAND)

Palmer's Chart House

Box 51, 98243
(206) 376-4231

The first bed and breakfast on Orcas Island (since 1975) with a magnificent water view. The 33-foot private yacht *Amante* is available for a minimal fee with Skipper Don. Low-key, private, personal attention makes this bed and breakfast unique and attractive. Well-traveled hosts speak Spanish.

Hosts: Majean and Donald Palmer
Rooms: 2 (PB) $45-60
Full Breakfast
Credit Cards: None
Notes: 2, 4 (call), 5, 8 (over 10), 9, 10, 11, 12, 14

Palmer's Chart House

NOTES: Credit cards accepted: A MasterCard; B Visa; C American Express; D Discover Card; E Diner's Club; F Other; 2 Personal checks accepted; 3 Lunch available; 4 Dinner available; 5 Open all year;

EASTSOUND (ORCAS ISLAND)

Kangaroo House

Box 334, 98245
(206) 376-2175

A 1907 Craftsman-style home on Orcas Island, gem of the San Juans. Period furnishings, large guest sitting room with stone fireplace, extensive lawns, and flower gardens. Smashing gourmet breakfasts. Walk to village shops, galleries, and restaurants. Panoramic view of the islands from Moran State Park.

Hosts: Jan and Mike Russillo
Rooms: 5 (2 PB; 3 SB) $65-100
Full Breakfast
Credit Cards: A, B
Notes: 2, 5, 8, 9, 10, 11, 12, 14

Outlook Inn on Orcas Island

P.O. Box 210, Main Street, 98245
(206) 376-2200; FAX (206) 376-2256

This remodeled turn-of-the-century country inn is on the gem of the San Juan Islands in Washington State. Rustic Victoriana with English and American antiques can be found throughout the house; handcrafted beds, marble-topped dresser, and period memorabilia are scattered through this lovely bed and breakfast. A conference room is available for banquets or will seat 75 people theater-style. Rooms are clean and comfortable, with colors inspired by the sea and influenced by nature. Gardens and ponds are available for guests to enjoy, and the inn offers a convenient central location. Breakfast, lunch, and dinner served during the high season. Continental breakfast served from November to April. Make reservations early.

Hosts: Carol Cheney and Jeanine McConnaughey
Rooms: 29 (11 PB; 18 SB) $35-94
Continental Breakfast
Credit Cards: A, B, C
Notes: 3, 5, 7, 8, 10, 12, 14

Turtleback Farm Inn

Route 1, Box 650 (Crow Valley Road), 98243
(206) 376-4914

This meticulously restored farmhouse has been described as a "marvel of bed and breakfastmanship decorated with country finesse and a sophisticated sense of the right antiques." Seven bedrooms with private baths. Award-winning breakfasts.

Hosts: William and Susan Fletcher
Rooms: 7 (PB) $75-125
Full Breakfast
Credit Cards: A, B
Notes: 2, 5, 9, 10, 11 (nearby), 12, 14

Whale Watch House

P.O. Box 729, 98245
(206) 376-4793

Watch the sunrise and spectacular sunsets over the Canadian Islands form the private beach front studio apartment on the north side of Orcas Island in the San Juan Islands. Quiet and peaceful. See whales, eagles, otters, and other wildlife. Beach access. Private bath. Color TV. Walking distance to town. Boating, fishing, kayaking, and bike rentals nearby. Pick up at ferry or airport available. Continental breakfast, and minor cooking facilities available.

Hosts: Joyce Colton
Room: 1 (PB) $65-85
Continental Breakfast
Credit Cards: None
Notes: 2, 5, 9, 10, 12, 14

EDMONDS

Harrison House

210 Sunset Avenue, 98020
(206) 776-4748

New waterfront home with sweeping view of Puget Sound and the Olympic Mountains. Many fine restaurants within walking distance. Spacious rooms have private bath, private deck, TV, wet bar, telephone,

6 Pets welcome; 8 Children welcome; 9 Social drinking allowed; 10 Tennis available; 11 Swimming available; 12 Golf available; 13 Skiing available; 14 May be booked through travel agents.

and king-size bed. University of Washington is nearby.

Hosts: Jody and Harve Harrison
Rooms: 2 (PB) $35-65
Continental Breakfast
Credit Cards: None
Notes: 2, 5, 9, 10, 11, 12, 13

Hudgens Haven

9313 190 Southwest, 98020
(206) 776-2202

Built in 1922, this restored farmhouse is nestled in former lumber town Edmonds, Washington. Just a few miles north of downtown Seattle. The ferry boat to the Olympic Peninsula departs from Edmonds. Guests may drive aboard or go as walk-on passengers for the short trip to Kingston across Puget Sound. The hosts offer a large guest room, handsomely furnished in Colonial-style antiques and a queen-size bed. Private bath and den with TV are at guests' disposal. Full breakfast for additional charge of $3.50. View of the Olympic Mountains and Puget Sound from the west windows, weather permitting.

Hosts: Edward and Lorna Hudgens
Room: 1 (PB) $45
Continental Breakfast
Credit Cards: None
Notes: 2, 5, 6 (dogs only), 10, 11, 12

FERNDALE

Slater Heritage House Bed and Breakfast

1371 West Axton Road, 98248
(206) 384-4273; (800) 815-4275

Step back a century, slow down, and breathe an atmosphere of forgotten elegance. This beautifully restored Victorian home is less than one mile off I-5. Close to the largest shopping mall in the Pacific Northwest, guests have easy access to mountains, water, or golf. Only 12 miles from Canada. Offering four lovely bedrooms with queen-size beds and private

baths. After a restful night's sleep, enjoy a leisurely breakfast prepared with special attention to quality and nutrition.

Hosts: the Armitage family
Rooms: 4 (PB) $60-85
Full Breakfast
Credit Cards: A, B
Notes: 2, 5, 8, 9, 10, 11, 12, 13

FORKS

Misty Valley Inn Bed and Breakfast

P.O. Box 2239, 194894 Highway 101, 98331
(206) 374-9389

This 6,000-square-foot stone and cedar home is nestled on a ridge in the rain forest and offers a magnificent view of Sol Duc River Valley. Antique furniture and collectibles are set off by rubbed natural woods and unusual lighting. Individualized wake-up and breakfast service times. A three-course breakfast is served in the main dining room or on the decks. Afternoon tea service and evening pastry treats. Queen-size brass beds with custom linens. Hot tub and air conditioning.

Hosts: Rachel and Jim Bennett
Rooms: 4 (1 PB; 3 SB) $55-70
Full Breakfast
Credit Cards: A, B
Notes: 5, 9

FREELAND

Cliff House

5440 Windmill Road, 98249
(360) 331-1566

On Whidbey Island, a setting so unique there is nothing anywhere quite like Cliff House. In a private world of luxury, this stunning home is the guests' alone. Secluded in a forest on the edge of Puget Sound, the views are breathtaking. Stone fireplace, spa, and miles of driftwood beach. King-size feather bed and gourmet kitchen. Also the Snug and Enchanting Seacliff cottage. Two-night minimum stay required.

NOTES: Credit cards accepted: A MasterCard; B Visa; C American Express; D Discover Card; E Diner's Club; F Other; 2 Personal checks accepted; 3 Lunch available; 4 Dinner available; 5 Open all year;

Hosts: Peggy Moore and Walter O'Toole
Rooms: 2 (PB) $155-310
Continental Breakfast
Credit Cards: B
Notes: 2, 5, 8 (over 14), 9, 12

FRIDAY HARBOR

Argyle House

685 Argyle Avenue, 98250
(206) 378-4084

Argyle House was built in 1910. It is a craftsman design and still retains its original charm and character. Each room has a private bath, down comforters, and a light and airy feeling. There is a nice hot tub and deck where guests can often see deer and eagles. There is also a basketball court and badminton for guests' enjoyment. Over an acre of beautiful grounds with flower gardens and fruit trees. Two blocks from downtown Friday Harbor.

Hosts: Bill and Chris Carli
Rooms: 3 (PB) $80-100
Full Breakfast
Credit Cards: A, B
Notes: 2, 5, 10, 12

States Inn

2039 West Valley Road, 98250
(206) 378-6240

A nine-bedroom country inn setting on 44 pastoral acres with a breathtaking valley

States Inn

view. Sleep under down comforters and wake to a delicious full breakfast. Also an horse ranch, now offering trail rides and boarding. AAA three-diamond rated.

Hosts: Kip and Linda Taylor
Rooms: 9 (PB) $80-110
Full Breakfast
Credit Cards: A, B
Notes: 2, 5, 8, 14

Tucker House Bed and Breakfast

260 B Street, 98250
(206) 378-2783; (800) 742-8210; FAX (206) 378-6437

A Victorian home, circa 1898, with two upstairs bedrooms, queen-size beds, and a shared bath. The property is surrounded with flowers, stately trees, and a white picket fence. The outside hot tub is available to all guests. There are three cottages on the property, each having a queen-size bed, private bath, woodstove, TV, and kitchenette, with room for additional guests. Two blocks from the ferry terminal and the heart of picturesque Friday Harbor. Tennis, swimming, and golf nearby. Pets welcome. Children welcome in the cottages. No smoking.

Hosts: Skip and Annette Metzger
Rooms: 5 (3 PB; 2 SB) $75-125
Full Breakfast
Credit Cards: A, B, C, D
Notes: 2, 5, 6, 8, 9, 10, 11, 12, 14

Wharfside Bed and Breakfast on Board the Jacquelyn

P.O. Box 1212, 98250
(206) 378-5661

A romantic winter retreat or challenging summer adventure—aboard the *Jacquelyn,* the West Coast's original floating bed and breakfast. This elegantly restored 60-foot traditional sailing vessel offers two spacious, private guest staterooms with private half-baths, a main salon replete with antiques, art, and artifacts, as well as a

6 Pets welcome; 8 Children welcome; 9 Social drinking allowed; 10 Tennis available; 11 Swimming available; 12 Golf available; 13 Skiing available; 14 May be booked through travel agents.

wood-burning stove for cozy evenings. Bask on deck while enjoying a sumptuous and hearty breakfast. Take a spin in the rowing gig.

Hosts: Clyde and Bette Rice
Rooms: 2 (SB) $80-85
Full Breakfast
Credit Cards: A, B
Notes: 2, 5, 6, 8, 9, 10, 11, 12, 14

GARFIELD

A Pacific Reservation Service

701 Northwest 60th Street, Seattle, 98107
(206) 784-0539

Garfield. This beautiful guest home was built as a Classical Revival house in 1898 and offers two guest rooms, one with a double bed and the other with two twin beds. There is a large shared bathroom with a huge claw-foot soaking tub. Breakfast might include juices, flapjacks with local organic red wheat, homemade jams, maple syrup, home-baked breads, and other delights prepared on an old-fashioned wood-burning stove. $75.

GIG HARBOR

A Pacific Reservation Service

701 Northwest 60th Street, Seattle, 98107
(206) 784-0539

Orchard. This lovely bed and breakfast was built in 1984 on three acres of rural land between Gig Harbor and Bremerton, 90 minutes from Seattle. The large guest room features a double bed and a private bath, and welcomes guests to relax in the two-person whirlpool tub. Views of Mount Rainier can be seen from the living and dining rooms. What a perfect spot for a quiet country getaway! $60-75.

Guest House Cottages

GREENBANK

Guest House Cottages

3366 South Highway 525, Whidbey Island, 98253
(206) 678-3115

A couple's romantic retreat, this AAA four-diamond-rated bed and breakfast hideaway offers storybook cottages in cozy settings on 25 acres. Fireplaces, VCRs, more than 300 complimentary movies, in-room Jacuzzis, kitchens, feather beds, country antiques, and wildlife pond are all amenities guests can enjoy. Continental plus breakfast. Pool, spa, peace, and pampering. Voted "Best Place to Kiss in the Northwest." Near the winery. Special midweek rates October 31 through March 15. Minimum-stay requirements for weekends and holidays.

Hosts: Don and Mary Jane Creger
Rooms: 6 (PB) $135-285
Continental Breakfast
Credit Cards: A, B, C, D
Notes: 2, 5, 9, 12, 14

HOOD CANAL

A Pacific Reservation Service

701 Northwest 60th Street, Seattle, 98107
(206) 784-0539

NOTES: Credit cards accepted: A MasterCard; B Visa; C American Express; D Discover Card; E Diner's Club; F Other; 2 Personal checks accepted; 3 Lunch available; 4 Dinner available; 5 Open all year;

Hood Canal Waterfront Victorian. This bed and breakfast offers three guest rooms, a charming atmosphere of genteel living, and sloping grounds leading to the beach. Enjoy a home-cooked breakfast and a relaxed friendly environment just right for getaways. $55-65.

Waterfront Hood Canal. This cozy bed and breakfast offers guests total privacy. There are two bedrooms, one with queen-size bed and the other with a double bed; both share a bath. A wall of windows allows guests to take in the ever-changing view. Guests can snuggle up in front of the tall stone fireplace or take the elevator to a private beach where oysters can be gathered. Hosts are not on location to serve breakfast; the full kitchen will have everything that is needed. $125 plus.

Waterfront Hood Canal Cottage. Guests can enjoy this private waterfront hideaway in an atmosphere of serenity; the sunsets are magnificent. The cottage and the two guest rooms are decorated in a quaint fashion with antiques, ruffles, and collectible memorabilia. The honeymoon cottage features its own hot tub and deck. A delicious light breakfast is brought to guests' rooms in the morning for private dining. $75-115.

Waterfront Mansion Hood Canal. Experience the grandeur of a bygone time and the opulence of the rich and famous in the 1930s at this premier bed and breakfast inn. Built in 1936, this inn is on several acres of waterfront property and features a combination of Art Deco and the architecture of northern China, seasoned with Northwestern flair. There are five guest rooms with private baths, towel warmers, clothes steamers, down comforters, and hair dryers. $105-165.

HOQUIAM

A Pacific Reservation Service

701 Northwest 60th Street, Seattle, 98107
(206) 784-0539

HO-1. A historic 20-room mansion is offered to guests on the southern tip of the Olympic Peninsula only two hours from Seattle and minutes to the Pacific Ocean. The mansion is filled with a fascinating array of antiques. Five bedrooms with queen-size beds share three baths. A full and delicious breakfast is served in the large, formal dining room. Recommended by the *Los Angeles Times*. $75.

ILWACO

Inn at Ilwaco

120 Williams Street NE, 98624-0922
(206) 642-8686

The inn, a 1928 New England/Georgian-style church lovingly transformed into a gracious bed and breakfast with a 120-seat wedding chapel/playhouse. Cozy guest rooms nestled under eaves and dormers. Generous and informal parlor with library. Eclectically furnished, some old, some new, some antiques, and country touches. Occupies hillside site overlooking historic port town where the Columbia River meets the ocean. Nearby are 28 miles of sandy beach, working lighthouses, museums, and three nationally acclaimed restaurants.

Host: John E. Attebery
Rooms: 9 (7 PB; 2 SB) $55-80
Full Breakfast
Credit Cards: A, B
Notes: 2, 5, 8, 9, 10, 12, 14

KIRKLAND

Shumway Mansion

11410 99th Place Northeast, 98033
(206) 823-2303

6 Pets welcome; 8 Children welcome; 9 Social drinking allowed; 10 Tennis available; 11 Swimming available; 12 Golf available; 13 Skiing available; 14 May be booked through travel agents.

Shumway Mansion

Overlook Lake Washington from this award-winning, 23-room mansion dating from 1909. Eight individually decorated guest rooms with private baths. Variety-filled breakfast. Complimentary use of athletic club. Short distance to all forms of shopping; 20 minutes to downtown Seattle. Water and snow recreation close at hand.

Hosts: Richard and Salli Harris
Rooms: 8 (PB) $65-95
Full Breakfast
Credit Cards: A, B, C
Notes: 2, 5, 8 (over 12), 9, 10, 11, 12, 13, 14

LA CONNER

Benson Farmstead

1009 Avon-Allen Road, Bow, 98232
(206) 757-0578

The Benson Farmstead is a 1914 restored 17-room farmhouse filled with antiques, quilts, and a cozy decor. It is surrounded by flower gardens and farmland and is just off I-5 near LaConner, Burlington, Chuckanut Drive, and the tulip fields. Third-generation Skagit Valley farmers, Jerry and Sharon are friendly hosts who serve a full country breakfast every morning and dessert and coffee in the evening.

Hosts: Jerry and Sharon Benson
Rooms: 4 (2 PB; 2 SB) $65-75
Full Breakfast
Credit Cards: A, B
Notes: 2, 5, 6 (call), 7 (limited), 8, 9, 10, 11, 12, 13

Heather House

505 Maple Street, 98257
(206) 466-4675

Three-bedroom, two-bath Cape Cod home in downtown La Conner. Easy walk to shopping and dining. Hosts live next door, so guests can enjoy freedom and privacy. View of farm, Cascade Mountains, and Mount Baker. Halfway between Seattle and Vancouver, British Columbia. Near ferry to the San Juan Islands.

Hosts: Wayne and Bev Everton
Rooms: 3 (SB) $50-70
Continental Breakfast
Credit Cards: A, B
Notes: 2, 5, 9, 10, 11, 12, 14

A Pacific Reservation Service

701 Northwest 60th Street, Seattle, 98107
(206) 784-0539

LA-1. This charming house was built in 1979 as a replica circa 1900 home. Three guest rooms offer guests total privacy. The host lives next door and comes over every morning to prepare breakfast. Enjoy the lovely views over the fields, meadows, and mountains. $50-75.

LA-2. Guests can relax and enjoy themselves in this beautiful Victorian-style country inn. The hosts offer ten guest rooms with private baths, telephone, TV, and some with fireplaces and wonderful views. The honeymoon suite features a Jacuzzi. Guests are invited to enjoy the outdoor hot tub. $55-150.

Ridgeway Farm Bed and Breakfast

1292 McLean Road, P.O. Box 475, 98257
(206) 428-8068; (800) 428-8068

The perfect getaway in the heart of the Skagit Valley tulip fields. Come enjoy the

---

NOTES: Credit cards accepted: A MasterCard; B Visa; C American Express; D Discover Card; E Diner's Club; F Other; 2 Personal checks accepted; 3 Lunch available; 4 Dinner available; 5 Open all year;

unique feeling of this 1928 yellow brick Dutch Colonial farmhouse on a "Ridgeway" out of the historic waterfront town of La Conner. Large windows offer an open, airy feeling, with views of the mountains and farms. Homemade desserts served by the fireplace in the evenings. Wake up to coffee, tea, or hot chocolate to sharpen the appetite for a hearty breakfast. Lilacs, rhododendrons, azaleas, roses, and thousands of tulips and daffodils. Flat terrain will delight bicycle fans. The hosts can fly guests on a scenic flight to the San Juan Islands. Glider or balloon flights can also be arranged.

Hosts: Louise and John Kelly
Rooms: 5 (2 PB; 3 SB) $75-95
Full Breakfast
Credit Cards: A, B, C, D
Notes: 2, 5, 9, 11, 12, 13

The White Swan Guest House

1388 Moore Road, Mount Vernon, 98273
(360) 445-6805

The White Swan is a "storybook" farmhouse six miles from the historic waterfront town of La Conner. Fine restaurants, great antiquing, and interesting shops in Washington's favorite artist community. Just an hour north of Seattle and 90 miles south of Vancouver. Separate honeymoon cottage. Gardens seen in *Country Home* magazine. Two stars in *Northwest Best Places*.

Host: Peter Goldfarb
Rooms: 4 (1 PB; 3 SB) $65-75; Cottage: $125
Continental Breakfast
Credit Cards: A, B
Notes: 2, 5, 8, 9, 12, 14

LANGLEY

Country Cottage of Langley

215 6th Street, 98260
(206) 221-8709

This restored farmhouse plus separate cottages on two beautiful acres with views of Puget Sound and Cascades is in a lovely country setting in Langley. All accommodations have private baths. Two blocks to the water and downtown Langley, antique and art capital of Whidbey Island. Fabulous four-course gourmet breakfast.

Hosts: Bob and Mary Decelles
Rooms: 5 (PB) $85-110
Full Breakfast
Credit Cards: A, B
Notes: 2, 5, 9, 10, 12, 14

Eagles Nest Inn

Eagles Nest Inn

3236 East Saratoga, 98260
(360) 221-5331

The inn's rural setting on Whidbey Island offers a sweeping view of Saratoga Passage and Mount Baker. Casual elegance and natural splendor abound. Relax and enjoy the wood stove, spa, library, and bottomless chocolate chip cookie jar. Canoeing available. Write or call for brochure. Two-night minimum stay requirement for holiday weekends.

Hosts: Joanne and Jerry Lechner
Rooms: 4 (PB) $95-115
Full Breakfast
Credit Cards: A, B, D
Notes: 2, 5, 8 (over 12), 14

Log Castle

3273 East Saratoga Road, 98260
(360) 221-5483

6 Pets welcome; 8 Children welcome; 9 Social drinking allowed; 10 Tennis available; 11 Swimming available; 12 Golf available; 13 Skiing available; 14 May be booked through travel agents.

On Whidbey Island, 30 miles north of Seattle. Log lodge on secluded beach. Big stone fireplace, turret bedrooms, panoramic views of Puget Sound and the Cascade Mountains. Norma's breakfast is a legend. Watch for bald eagles and Orca whales from the widow's walk. Two-night minimum stay required for holidays.

Hosts: Senator Jack and Norma Metcalf
Rooms: 4 (PB) $80-105
Full Breakfast
Credit Cards: A, B, D
Notes: 2, 5, 8 (over 10), 10, 12, 14

Lone Lake Cottages and Breakfast

5206 South Bayview Road, 98260
(206) 321-5325

Whidbey's Shangri-la. Enjoy privacy in the waterfront cottages or in a sternwheel houseboat. All are decorated with touches of the Orient. View, fireplace, kitchen, TV/VCR, Jacuzzi, canoes, fishing, and bicycles.

Host: Dolores Meeks
Rooms: 3 (PB) $110
Continental Breakfast
Credit Cards: None
Notes: 2, 5, 9, 10, 11, 12

The Whidbey Inn

106 First Street, P.O. Box 156, 98260
(206) 221-7115

Perched on a bluff, this bed and breakfast offers a dramatic view of the Saratoga Passage Waterway, the Cascade Mountains, and Camano Island from each room. When guests arrive, the hosts will greet them warmly, and encourage them to take a moment and relax over a glass of sherry and an appetizer. Each of the romantic rooms is decorated with antiques and offers a private bath with English amenities and Swiss chocolates on the pillows. The Whidbey Inn is a perfect setting for romance.

Host: Gretchen Bower
Rooms: 6 (PB) $95-150
Full Breakfast

Credit Cards: A, B, C
Notes: 2, 5

LEAVENWORTH

All Seasons River Inn Bed and Breakfast

P.O. Box 788, 8751 Icicle Road, 98826
(509) 548-1425; (800) 254-0555

A magical and enchanting place, the All Seasons River Inn is unique in that it was built as a bed and breakfast but offers the warm hospitality of home. Nestled in the evergreens overlooking the Wenatchee River, all rooms are spacious with antique decor, private baths, and riverfront decks. Some are available with Jacuzzis and fireplaces. The hosts invite guests to enjoy an evening in the guest living room, game room, and TV room, or listen to the relaxing sounds of the water below the decks. Guests will awaken to a hearty breakfast that will last them through the day. Hiking, biking, rafting, fishing, or cross-country skiing are all less than a mile from the door. Once guests have visited, they want to return again and again!

Hosts: Kathy and Jeff Falconer
Rooms: 5 (PB) $95-125
Full Breakfast
Credit Cards: A, B
Notes: 2, 5, 9, 10, 11, 12, 13, 14

Edel Haus Inn

320 Ninth Street, 98826
(509) 548-4412

Overlooking the Wenatchee River and just one half-block from downtown Leavenworth sits this classic and elegant old home. Lodging accommodations feature private baths, queen-size beds, outdoor hot tub, and cable TV in each room. Cottage suite offers Jacuzzi room with double tub and gas fireplace. Torch-lit outdoor patio and indoor dining nightly. Breakfast is not served. Northwest cuisine includes mesquite-grilled fish and beef, fresh pastas, homemade pizza, meatless entrees, and fabulous desserts. Guests receive a 50 percent discount on dinner.

Hosts: Gary Singer and Lorraine Craft
Rooms: 4 (PB) $70-95
Credit Cards: A, B
Notes: 2, 3, 4, 5, 8, 9, 10, 11, 12, 13, 14

A Pacific Reservation Service

701 Northwest 60th Street, Seattle, 98107
(206) 784-0539

This peaceful country inn is in a town that has taken on a Bavarian atmosphere with German stores, shops, restaurants, and flowers everywhere. Enjoy the wonderful views, hot tub, pool, and the Continental breakfast. Some rooms have private baths. $55-145.

Run of the River Bed and Breakfast

9308 East Leavenworth Road
P.O. Box 285, 98826
(509) 548-7171; (800) 288-6491

Imagine a quintessential Northwest log bed and breakfast inn. Rooms feature handhewn log beds and furniture, with a spectacular panorama of the river, bird refuge, and mountains that tower above. Leavenworth, a Bavarian village in the heart of the Cascade Loop, offers ample opportunity to enjoy the outdoors the way it should be: with lots of fun, lots of scenery and wildlife, and not many other folks to get in the way of those special moments. Great hikes start a short distance from the inn, or use complimentary mountain bikes for a rousing trail ride. The inn is an ideal base for sidetrips to Winthrop, Lake Chelan, and Grand Coulee. Very quiet, relaxing, and smoke-free. The perfect spot for a Northwest adventure.

Hosts: Monty and Karen Turner
Rooms: 5 (PB) $90-145
Full Breakfast
Credit Cards: A, B, C, D
Notes: 2, 5, 9, 10, 11, 12, 13, 14

LONG BEACH

A Pacific Reservation Service

701 Northwest 60th Street, Seattle, 98107
(206) 784-0539

LB-1. A three- to four-hour drive will take guests to this lovely but often undiscovered spot of the state where the Columbia River meets the Pacific Ocean. The best beachcombing, clam digging, salmon fishing, and relaxation can be found here. This historic inn offers 12 rooms that are furnished in antiques as a reminder of a gentler time. Five rooms have private baths. $60-145.

LOPEZ ISLAND

Aleck Bay Inn

Route 1, Box 1920, 98261
(206) 468-3535

The inn has seven acres bounded by the beaches and off-shore islands at the south end of Lopez Island. Enjoy a sun deck with hot tub overlooking the Strait of San Juan de Fuca. An absolute artist paradise. Full breakfast is served in the solarium beside the bay. All rooms have private bath, queen-size bed, Victorian canopies, floral linens, etc. Two with Jacuzzi tub. Guests may enjoy the TV/VCR, table tennis, billiards, piano, violin, and all kinds of games. Bike rental is available.

Host: David S. May
Rooms: 3 (PB) $85-139
Credit Cards: A, B, C, E
Notes: 2, 4, 5, 8 (call), 10, 12, 14

Edenwild Inn

Box 271, 98261
(206) 468-3238

This elegant country inn in Lopez Village, within walking distance of shops and restaurants, offers eight large, comfortable guest rooms, each of which has its own private bath, some with fireplaces, and some with water or garden views. There are facilities for children and a room designed for the handicapped. Included with the room is a full family-style breakfast served in the dining room or in the guests' room upon request, and an afternoon apéritif. If guests have any allergies or diet restrictions, just let the hosts know, as they hope to make every stay a pleasant one. For the comfort of the guests, this is a nonsmoking establishment. Ferry landing, sea plane, or airport pickup is available.

Host: Sue Aran
Rooms: 8 (PB) $85-140
Full Breakfast
Credit Cards: A, B
Notes: 2, 3, 4, 5, 8, 9, 12, 14

Inn at Swifts Bay

Route 2, Box 3402, 98261
(206) 468-3636

On Lopez Island, in the San Juans of Washington state, the Inn at Swifts Bay occupies three wooded acres. Five guest rooms, three with private bath. Fireplaces in common areas, hot tub on deck, private beach, award-winning breakfasts. A designated three-star Northwest Best Place, AAA, Mobil.

Hosts: Robert Herrmann and Christopher Brandmeir
Rooms: 5 (3 PB; 2 SB) $75-140
Full Breakfast
Credit Cards: A, B, C, D
Notes: 2, 5, 9, 10, 11, 12, 14

MacKaye Harbor Inn

Route 1, Box 1940, 98261
(206) 468-2253

The ideal beachfront getaway. Lopez's only bed and breakfast on a low-bank sandy beach. Kayak and mountain bike rentals and/or instruction. This 1927 Victorian home has been painstakingly restored. Guests are pampered in comfortable elegance. Eagles, deer, seals, and otters frequent this Cape Cod of the Northwest. Commendations from *Sunset*, *Pacific*

Northwest magazine, the *Los Angeles Times*, and *Northwest Best Places*.

Hosts: Brooks and Sharon Broberg
Rooms: 5 (1 PB; 4 SB) $69-130
Full Breakfast
Credit Cards: A, B
Notes: 2, 5, 9, 12, 14

A Pacific Reservation Service

701 Northwest 60th Street, Seattle, 98107
(206) 784-0539

LI-1. At the first stop by the ferry, relax at this Victorian waterfront inn with lovely antiques, a restaurant on the premises, and all the charm of a tranquil setting. Grand sunsets, sandy beaches, tidal pools, and beachcombing. Watching the eagles and other wildlife will keep guests busy. Bring a kayak, bicycles, windsurfing, or fishing gear. Five guest rooms, one with private bath. $75-115.

LUMMI ISLAND

Bed and Breakfast Guild of Whatcom County

2610 Eldridge Avenue, Bellingham, WA 98225
(206) 676-4560

1. Built by the town's first banker, this 1890s home has view rooms and suites, private and shared baths, with full Northwest breakfast. $50-80.

2. Completely restored Victorian close to golfing, mountains, water, and shopping. Only 12 miles to Canadian border. Four lovely rooms with private baths. $55-77.

7. Only 17 minutes from Bellingham to the ferry, then a five-minute ferry ride. Loganita, a lovely white villa, commands a breathtaking 180° marine view. Magnificent sandy beach! Beautiful sunsets. Luxurious suites, rooms, cottage (weekly rates), out-

NOTES: Credit cards accepted: A MasterCard; B Visa; C American Express; D Discover Card; E Diner's Club; F Other; 2 Personal checks accepted; 3 Lunch available; 4 Dinner available; 5 Open all year;

door spa, fireplaces. Visa and MasterCard accepted. No smoking. $75-165.

West Shore Farm Bed and Breakfast

2781 West Shore Drive, 98262
(206) 758-2600

Unique octagonal owner-built home with 180° view of islands, passing boats, sunsets, eagles, seals, and Canadian mountains on the northern horizon. The quiet natural beach, garden, orchard with resident poultry, stock of books, maps, bicycles, and natural gourmet food are rejuvenating.

Hosts: Carl and Polly Hanson
Rooms: 2 (PB) $90
Full Breakfast
Credit Cards: A, B
Notes: 2, 4, 5, 8, 9

The Willows Inn

2579 West Shore Drive, 98262
(360) 758- 2620

Established in 1911 by Victoria's grandparents, The Willows is an island landmark. On the sunset side of the island, it boasts a private beach and a spectacular view of the San Juan Islands. Noted for its fine dining and award-winning gardens, The Willows is a most peaceful and romantic destination. Ten minutes from I-5 near Bellingham and a seven-minute ferry ride brings guests to this quiet little island.

Hosts: Victoria and Gary
Rooms: 7 (PB) $95-135
Full Breakfast
Credit Cards: A, B
Notes: 2, 4, 9, 11

LYNDEN

Bed and Breakfast Guild of Whatcom County

2610 Eldridge Avenue, Bellingham, WA 98225
(206) 676-4560

10. Come feel the quiet, peaceful, Victorian elegance of this beautifully restored century-old home. At the edge of Lynden, a quaint Dutch village. Enjoy the third floor Century Tower Suite or second floor garden view rooms. Breakfast is the specialty here. Come and enjoy. $50-75.

Dutch Village Inn

655 Front Street, 98264
(206) 354-4440

This is a unique hotel built under a windmill in the charming Dutch community. Each room is individually decorated with antiques and is representative of a Dutch province. Continental breakfast served on Sundays.

Hosts: Elaine and Deena
Rooms: 6 (PB) $65-95
Full and Continental Breakfast
Credit Cards: A, B
Notes: 2, 5, 8, 9, 10, 11, 12, 13, 14

Dutch Village Inn

MAPLE VALLEY

Maple Valley Bed and Breakfast

20020 Southeast 228, 98038
(206) 432-1409

Welcome to this warm cedar home in the wooded Northwest. Spacious grounds, wildlife pond, and fine feathered friends. Experience the "Good Morning" rooster, hootenanny pancakes, "hot babies," and gracious family hospitality. Crest Airpark is just minutes away. Be special. Be a guest at Maple Valley.

Hosts: Jayne and Clarke Hurlbut
Rooms: 2 (SB) $50-65
Full Breakfast
Credit Cards: None
Notes: 2, 5, 8, 9, 10, 11, 12, 13, 14

Maple Valley

MERCER ISLAND

A Travellers Bed and Breakfast Reservation Service

P.O. Box 492, 98040
(206) 232-2345; FAX (206) 679-2345

This reservation service represents guest homes, inns, private residences, and cottages. More than 200 accommodations in the Pacific Northwest, including Vancouver and Victoria, British Columbia and Oregon coast. Assists in personal itineraries including ferries and car rental. All lodgings personally inspected and meet this company's high standards. In business since 1981. For reservations call Monday through Friday from 9:00 A.M. through 5:00 P.M. $50-175.

MONTESANO

Sylvan Haus—Murphy Bed and Breakfast

417 Wilder Hill Drive
P.O. Box 416, 98563
(206) 249-3453

A gracious, three-story family home surrounded by towering evergreens at the top of Wilder Hill Drive. Watch the changing seasons while breakfasting at the old round oak dining table. Grays Harbor, Sea-Tac Airport, Olympic Peninsula, and Lake Quinalt Rain Forest; 30 minutes to ocean beaches.

Hosts: Mike and JoAnne Murphy
Rooms: 3 (1 PB; 2 SB) $65
Full Breakfast
Credit Cards: None
Notes: 2, 5, 8 (over 14), 11, 12

MORTON

St. Helens Manorhouse Bed and Breakfast

7476 Highway 12, 98356
(206) 498-5243; (800) 551-3290

St. Helens Manorhouse, built in 1910, maintains its original woodwork and glass with loved antiques. Come to this countryside haven in the middle of Mount Rainier and St. Helens. Next to lake with fishing and windsurfing. Come sit on one of the porches and watch hang gliders or perhaps some eagles.

Hosts: Susyn Dragness and Baxter (kitty)
Rooms: 4 (2 PB; 2 SB) $59-89
Full Breakfast
Credit Cards: None
Notes: 2, 3, 5, 10, 11, 12, 13, 14

MOUNT RAINIER AREA

A Pacific Reservation Service

701 Northwest 60th Street, Seattle, 98107
(206) 784-0539

NOTES: Credit cards accepted: A MasterCard; B Visa; C American Express; D Discover Card; E Diner's Club; F Other; 2 Personal checks accepted; 3 Lunch available; 4 Dinner available; 5 Open all year;

Country Inn. Originally built in 1912, this inn was restored in 1984 and features 11 guest rooms with queen-size beds. The handmade quilts, antiques, tiffany lamps, and stained-glass windows all add to the comfort of this bed and breakfast. There is also a critically acclaimed restaurant that serves delicious food in a relaxed, genteel fashion by a big stone fireplace. $65-105.

OLYMPIA

The Cinnamon Rabbit

1304 Seventh Avenue Southwest, 98502
(206) 357-5520

This is an older home (1935) in a quiet neighborhood, just a 20-minute walk from downtown Olympia, Capitol Lake, and Budd Bay Inlet. There is a big front porch with wicker chairs, a real "cinnamon" rabbit, and a large gray cat. Guests enjoy a queen-size bed, the run of the living/ TV/music room, and the hot tub. Hosts are professional bakers so breakfast is always good! Hosts offer discounts for cash payment.

Hosts: Penny and Bob Williams-Young
Room: 1 (PB) $56.10-61.50
Full Breakfast
Credit Cards: A, B
Notes: 2, 5, 8, 9, 10, 11, 12

Harbinger Inn

1136 East Bay Drive, 98506
(206) 754 0380

Completely restored national historic landmark. View of East Bay marina, the capitol, and Olympic Mountains. Ideal setting for boating, bicycling, jogging, fine dining, and business ventures. A Northwest Best Place.

Hosts: Marisa and Terrell Williams
Rooms: 4 (1 PB; 3 SB) $60-90
Continental Breakfast
Credit Cards: A, B, C
Notes: 2, 5, 8 (over 12), 9

Puget View Guest House

7924 61st Avenue Northeast, 98516
(360) 459-1676

Classic Puget Sound. Quaint waterfront guest cottage suite that sleeps four, on the shore of Puget Sound next to host's log home. Expansive marine-mountain view. Breakfast is served privately in the cottage. Great honeymoon/romantic retreat. Near Tolmie State Park, five minutes off I-5, just north of downtown Olympia.

Hosts: the Yunkers
Cottage: 1 (PB) $89
Continental Breakfast
Credit Cards: A, B
Notes: 2, 5, 6, 7, 8, 9, 11

OLYMPIC

A Pacific Reservation Service

701 Northwest 60th Street, Seattle, 98107
(206) 784-0539

Olympic-1. With an unobstructed view over the water, this private two-bedroom cottage with double and twin beds invites guests to linger. Adjacent to a state park, one can rent a boat and enjoy the lovely water, or relax in the privacy of the cottage, which is nicely furnished and decorated in country-style. Breakfast will be served in the morning on a tray, to eat outside or in, depending on the weather. Minimum stay of two nights on the weekends. $85.

OLYMPIC PENINSULA

A Pacific Reservation Service

701 Northwest 60th Street, Seattle, 98107
(206) 784-0539

Olympic Peninsula-1. A splendid historic lodge. In a picturesque setting with the finest views ever offered from a lodge, the gravel lobby of this home with its imposing

6 Pets welcome; 8 Children welcome; 9 Social drinking allowed; 10 Tennis available; 11 Swimming available; 12 Golf available; 13 Skiing available; 14 May be booked through travel agents.

stone fireplaces offers the quiet elegance and charm of yesteryear. Cocktails by the fire, an elegant dinner in the restaurant, and a refreshing dip in an indoor pool add up to a great vacation experience. European-style bath in the lodge. Two-night minimum stay on weekends. $55.

ORCAS

A Pacific Reservation Service

701 Northwest 60th Street, Seattle, 98107
(206) 784-0539

OI-1. A large two-story log inn welcomes guests with seven bedrooms, all with private baths. Most of the rooms have views of the water. Rustic and comfortable, this inn is newly built and has a restaurant on the premises. Breakfast will be delivered in a basket to enjoy in the privacy of guests' own room. Seasonal rates. $65.

PORT ANGELES

Domaine Madeleine

146 Wildflower Lane, 98362
(206) 457-4174

Secluded, elegant, five-acre waterfront estate with water and mountain views. Three rooms with Jacuzzis. All rooms have fireplaces. Monet garden replica. Lawn games; whale, eagle, and deer watching; golf and skiing nearby. Breakfast so good that the inn pays if guests have lunch before 2:00 P.M. Practice languages or cooking with the hostess. No smoking.

Hosts: Madeleine and John Chambers
Rooms: 4 (PB) $95-165
Full Breakfast
Credit Cards: A, B
Notes: 2, 5, 9, 12, 13

A Pacific Reservation Service

701 Northwest 60th Street, Seattle, 98107
(206) 784-0539

Port Angeles-1. Uniquely European in style, this comfortable and magnificent English-style Tudor house was built in 1910 and restored to serve as an inn. Five guest rooms with a view of the water are available. Full breakfast. Wonderful antiques are throughout this lovely old house. Two-night minimum stay on weekends. Two blocks to downtown and restaurants. $55-85.

Tudor Inn

1108 South Oak, 98362
(206) 452-3138

Between the mountains and the sea, this half-timbered Tudor home was built by an Englishman in 1910 and has been tastefully restored and furnished with European antiques and an English garden. Two-night minimum stay required for weekends in July through September and for holidays.

Hosts: Jane and Jerry Glass
Rooms: 5 (2 PB; 3 SB) $55-85
Full Breakfast
Credit Cards: A, B
Notes: 2, 5, 9, 10, 11, 12, 13, 14

PORT ORCHARD

Reflections— A Bed and Breakfast Inn

3878 Reflection Lane, East, 98366
(206) 871-5582

Reflections is a Colonial home filled with New England antiques. Four rooms, each with a gorgeous view of Puget Sound. Relax in the hot tub, or enjoy the view from the gazebo on two and one-half acres of landscaped grounds. Gateway to the Olympic Peninsula; scenic ferry ride to Seattle. Full gourmet breakfast is served.

NOTES: Credit cards accepted: A MasterCard; B Visa; C American Express; D Discover Card; E Diner's Club; F Other; 2 Personal checks accepted; 3 Lunch available; 4 Dinner available; 5 Open all year;

Antique shopping in Port Orchard. Quality golf courses nearby.

Hosts: Jim and Cathy Hall
Rooms: 4 (2 PB; 2 SB) $55-90
Full Breakfast
Credit Cards: A, B
Notes: 2, 5, 9, 12

PORT TOWNSEND

Ann Starrett Mansion Bed and Breakfast Inn

744 Clay Street, 98368
(206) 385-3205; (800) 321-0644

Victorian Mansion, circa 1889, epitomizes the heart and soul of this Victorian seaport community. Internationally renowned for its classical architecture, antiques, and excellent service and food. In a quiet residential area within walking distance to town, theater, restaurants, beach, and ferry. Tennis, swimming, golf, and skiing nearby. Jacuzzi and fireplace. Full breakfast served. No children. No smoking.

Hosts: Edel and Bob Sokol
Rooms: 11 (9 PB; 2 SB) $65-185
Full Breakfast
Credit Cards: A, B, C, D
Notes: 2, 5, 9, 10, 11, 12, 13, 14

Chanticleer Inn

1208 Franklin Street, 98368
(800) 858-9421

Welcome to Port Townsend, Victorian seaport on the majestic Olympic Peninsula, gateway to the spectacular San Juan Islands and beautiful Victoria/Vancouver, British Columbia. The innkeepers invite guests to join them in their restored 1876 Victorian home set high above the water. Enjoy fine, crisp linen, fluffy duvets, and a creative breakfast beside a crackling fire, garnished by the sounds of live classical harp music.

Hosts: David and Susan Ross
Rooms: 5 (3 PB; 2 SB) $60-100
Full Breakfast

Credit Cards: A, B
Notes: 2, 8 (call), 14

The English Inn

718 F Street, 98368
(206) 385-5302

This 1885 Italianate-style Victorian house has five large sunny bedrooms. Two of the guest rooms have views of the nearby Olympic Mountains. The English Inn serves the best scones in the Northwest! The large garden offers a gazebo to linger in and a hot tub where guests can relax. Fifty miles from Seattle, Port Townsend is a Victorian seaport providing visitors with quaint shops, fine restaurants, and cultural events.

Hosts: Juliette and John Swenson
Rooms: 5 (PB) $65-95
Full Breakfast
Credit Cards: A, B
Notes: 2, 8 (over 12), 9, 10, 12, 14

Heritage House

305 Pierce Street, 98368-8131
(206) 386-6800

Featuring the finest collection of Victorian antiques on the Olympic Peninsula, this national historic landmark, circa 1880, offers spectacular water and mountain views from

Heritage House

---

6 Pets welcome; 8 Children welcome; 9 Social drinking allowed; 10 Tennis available; 11 Swimming available; 12 Golf available; 13 Skiing available; 14 May be booked through travel agents.

atop the bluff. Warm hospitality and comfort. Marvelous breakfasts, too.

Hosts: Kathryn, Gary, and Shanon Hambley
Rooms: 6 (4 PB; 2 SB) $55-125
Full Breakfast
Credit Cards: A, B, C, D
Notes: 2, 5, 8 (over 12), 9, 10, 11, 12, 14

Holly Hill House Bed and Breakfast

611 Polk, 98368
(206) 385-5619

Built in 1872, this home was a private residence until 1988. Well-preserved and graciously furnished, it feels like home. Queen-size beds in four rooms, and a king-size bed in the suite ensure comfort. Views of Admiralty Inlet and the Cascades can be enjoyed from many windows of this lovely home. All rooms have a large private bath, and a bountiful full breakfast is served. In historic Uptown, six blocks from downtown.

Host: Lynne Sterling
Rooms: 5 (PB) $76-130
Full Breakfast
Credit Cards: A, B
Notes: 2, 5, 9, 10, 12

Holly Hill House

The James House

1238 Washington Street, 98368
(206) 385-1238; (800) 385-1238

The first bed and breakfast in the Northwest, the James House is on the bluff overlooking this charming Victorian seaport town. With unobstructed views of Puget Sound, Mount Rainier, the Olympic and Cascade mountain ranges, the James House offers 12 rooms, including a cottage and a lovely two-bedroom suite. A full breakfast, afternoon sherry, homemade cookies, and lovely gardens are just a few of the amenities at this beautiful inn.

Hosts: Carol McGough and Anne Tiernan
Rooms: 12 (4 PB; 8 SB) $65-145
Full Breakfast
Credit Cards: A, B, C
Notes: 2, 5, 9, 10, 11, 12

Lizzie's Victorian Bed and Breakfast

731 Pierce Street, 98368
(206) 385-4168

An 1888 Victorian mansion within walking distance of shops and restaurants. The inn is decorated in antiques and some original wallpaper. Parlors are comfortable retreats for reading or conversation. Gateway to the Olympic Mountains, San Juan Islands, and Victoria. Wonderful breakfasts!

Hosts: Bill and Patti Wickline
Rooms: 8 (5 PB; 3 SB) $58-105
Full Breakfast
Credit Cards: A, B, D
Notes: 2, 5, 8 (over 10), 9, 10, 11, 12

Manresa Castle

Seventh and Sheridan, P.O. Box 564, 98368
(206) 385-5750; (800) 732-1281 (WA only)

This historic landmark, listed on the National Register of Historic Places, now houses 40 Victorian-style guest rooms, an elegant dining room, and an Edwardian-style lounge. Set atop Castle Hill, almost all rooms, including the dining room and lounge, have spectacular views of the town, harbor, marina, and/or Olympic Mountains. The guest rooms offer private baths, direct dial telephones, TV, and Continental breakfast.

Hosts: Lena and Vernon Humber
Rooms: 40 (PB) $64-175

NOTES: Credit cards accepted: A MasterCard; B Visa; C American Express; D Discover Card; E Diner's Club; F Other; 2 Personal checks accepted; 3 Lunch available; 4 Dinner available; 5 Open all year;

Continental Breakfast
Credit Cards: A, B
Notes: 4, 5, 7, 8, 9, 10, 11, 12, 14

A Pacific Reservation Service

701 Northwest 60th Street, Seattle, 98107
(206) 784-0539

1892 Castle. The castle sits on a hill with commanding marina views. It features rooms with private baths and Victorian decor, and lovely gardens. The landmark mansion is on the National Register of Historic Places and was totally restored in 1973. Enjoy splendid luxury while in Port Townsend. Continental breakfast. $75-150.

The Grand Dame. The most photographed house in Port Townsend, this great Victorian was built in 1889 by a wealthy contractor for his wife as a wedding present. It features a spiral freestanding staircase that is one of the finest in existence. Special frescoes in the dome will delight guests. Most of the rooms on the second floor have a wonderful view of the water and the mountains. Five bedrooms on the second floor, and four bedrooms on the carriage level. Both shared and private bath. Healthy breakfast is served on fine china. $60.

Sequim Victorian. A fine bed and breakfast inn, one-half mile from the beach, on Dungeness Spit, a quiet, peaceful area, yet only minutes from Port Townsend, Port Angeles, or the Victoria ferry. Remember that this area is the "Banana Belt" of the region, with less rainfall. Guests' favorite beverage and morning paper is delivered to their doors in the morning. A full breakfast is served downstairs. Four bedrooms, two that share a bath, and two that offer private baths, are available. $55-85.

The Palace Hotel

1004 Water Street, 98368
(206) 385-0773; (800) 962-0741 (WA only)

The Palace Hotel on Water Street is a beautifully restored Victorian hotel in the heart of Port Townsend's historic district. Close to galleries and shops, it offers convenient off-street parking and is within blocks of ferry and bus services. Accommodations range from Continental-style bedrooms with a shared bath to multi-room suites with kitchens and luxurious private baths. Any stay at the Palace includes a complimentary Continental breakfast. All rooms have cable TV, coffee, and tea. Many nonsmoking rooms are available, and children are welcome. Off-season discounts offered during the winter.

Rooms: 15 (12 PB; 3 SB) $55-100
Continental Breakfast
Credit Cards: A, B, C, D
Notes: 2, 3, 4, 5, 8, 10, 11, 12, 13, 14

Quimper Inn

Quimper Inn

1306 Franklin Street, 98368
(206) 385-1060

This 1886 mansion in the historic uptown district offers lovely water and mountain views. Four comfortable bedrooms, plus a two-room suite with a sitting room and bath. Antique period furniture, lots of books, and two porches for relaxation. A short walk to historic downtown with its many shops and restaurants. A wonderful breakfast is served.

Hosts: Ron and Sue Ramage
Rooms: 5 (3 PB; 2 SB) $65-130
Full Breakfast
Credit Cards: A, B
Notes: 2, 5, 9, 10, 12

6 Pets welcome; 8 Children welcome; 9 Social drinking allowed; 10 Tennis available; 11 Swimming available; 12 Golf available; 13 Skiing available; 14 May be booked through travel agents.

Ravenscroft Inn

Ravenscroft Inn

533 Quincy Street, 98368
(206) 385-2784; FAX (206) 385-6724

This classic seaport inn, built in the Colonial style, offers warm hospitality and scrumptious gourmet breakfasts served to morning piano concerts. Explore the great Olympic Peninsula, and stay where short stays are turned into lasting memories. From the bluffs of this historic Victorian town, there are panoramic views of the Olympic and Cascade mountains. Suite with soaking tub is also available. "The definitive B&B," says the *Los Angeles Times,* October 1993.

Hosts: Leah Hammer and John Ranney
Rooms: 8 (PB) $65-165
Full Breakfast
Credit Cards: A, B, C, D
Notes: 2, 5, 9, 10, 11, 12, 13, 14

POULSBO

Edgewater Beach Bed and Breakfast

26818 Edgewater Boulevard, 98370
(206) 779-2525; (800) 641-0955

Edgewater Beach Bed and Breakfast is a restful retreat on the banks of Hood Canal, the incredibly scenic fjord of Washington's Olympic mountains. Breakfast of smoked salmon and turkey, fruit, and freshly baked muffins tops a stay in the antique-filled cottage set in the midst of English cottage gardens. The friendly Edgewater Beach Bed and Breakfast hosts and their dog, cat, and parrot welcome guests to their wonderful accommodations at reasonable rates.

Hosts: Don Bell and Sandra Lee
Rooms: 3 (PB) $75-125
Full Breakfast
Credit Cards: A, B, C, D
Notes: 2, 5, 8, 9, 12, 14

PUGET SOUND INLET

A Pacific Reservation Service

701 Northwest 60th Street, Seattle, 98107
(206) 784-0539

Puget Sound Inlet-1. On the water, this bed and breakfast offers a delightful Victorian farmhouse with a rolling lawn down to the water's edge. Furnished with antiques and three bedrooms to choose from, this is a favorite of weekenders. A great breakfast is served in the morning. Shared bath. $60-75.

REDMOND

Lilac Lea Christian Bed and Breakfast

21008 Northeast 117th Street, 98053-5309
(206) 861-1898

Rural and secluded custom-built three-year-old Dutch Colonial just 17 miles from downtown Seattle. Features a second-floor suite with private entrance and bath, and decorated with antique furniture. Hosts are happy to help coordinate travel plans. Adjacent to an 800-acre park, near hiking and biking trails, antique shops, malls, and several national parks. No children. No pets. Alcohol and smoke free.

NOTES: Credit cards accepted: A MasterCard; B Visa; C American Express; D Discover Card; E Diner's Club; F Other; 2 Personal checks accepted; 3 Lunch available; 4 Dinner available; 5 Open all year;

Hosts: Chandler Haight and Ruthanne Hayes Haight
Room: 1 suite (PB) $65-85
Continental Breakfast
Credit Cards: None
Notes: 2, 5, 10, 11, 12, 13

RENTON

Holly Hedge House

908 Grant Avenue South, 98055
(206) 226-2555

Experience the ultimate in pampering and privacy in this meticulously restored 1900 scenic hilltop retreat. This unique lodging facility reserves the entire house to one couple to indulge in the beauty and affordable luxury. Landscaped grounds, wood deck with hot tub, swimming pool, stocked gourmet kitchen, whirlpool tub, CD, video, reading library, fireplace, and glassed-in veranda. Ten minutes from Sea-Tac International Airport, 20 minutes from Seattle, and five minutes from Lake Washington. A vacation, honeymoon, or corporate travel getaway. Ask about the Spirit Package.

Hosts: Lynn and Marian Thrasher
House: 1 (PB) $110
Full Breakfast
Credit Cards: A, B
Notes: 2, 5, 9, 10, 11, 12, 13

SAN JUAN ISLANDS

A Pacific Reservation Service

701 Northwest 60th Street, Seattle, 98107
(206) 784-0539

Friday Harbor. A floating inn designed from a restored 60-foot wooden sailboat offers guests two staterooms, one with a queen-size bed and private bath, the other with a double bed, two bunk beds, and shared bath. The hosts will provide a full seaman's breakfast that might be served on the deck in fair weather or in front of a roaring fire in the parlor. Have a totally different experience here! $85.

Orcas Island Country Inn. This is a beautiful country inn nestled in a valley with fine views of meadows and mountains. The inn offers eight guest rooms, all with private baths with claw-foot tubs, and antique furnishings. Guests can enjoy a gourmet breakfast in a charming, elegant atmosphere. $65-135.

Waterfront Country Inn. Built before 1888, this inn has been used as a town meeting hall, a barber shop, a general store, a post office, and a jail. Now as a popular getaway, it offers guest rooms with and without private baths, hand-carved beds, marble-topped dressers, and a collection of period memorabilia. No pets please. $60.

SEABECK

Summer Song

Box 82, 98380
(206) 830-5089

The majestic Olympic Mountains reflecting on Hood Canal provide a quiet, spectacular setting for this private waterfront cottage with its gentle touch of country comfort. The cottage will accommodate up to four guests and features a bedroom, living room, kitchen, bath, fireplace, TV, and VCR. A perfect place to relax, swim, boat, fish, or hike.

Hosts: Ron and Sharon Barney
Cottage: 1 (PB) $69
Full Breakfast
Credit Cards: A, B
Notes: 2, 5, 7, 9, 11, 14

SEATTLE

Alexis Hotel

1007 First Avenue at Madison, 98104
(206) 624-4844; (800) 426-7033 (reservations)

The elegant Alexis Hotel is snuggled in the heart of downtown Seattle, between colorful Pike Place Market and historic Pioneer

6 Pets welcome; 8 Children welcome; 9 Social drinking allowed; 10 Tennis available; 11 Swimming available; 12 Golf available; 13 Skiing available; 14 May be booked through travel agents.

Square. Just a block from the waterfront and financial district, the Alexis is ideal for business and leisure travelers. Luxury amenities offered: complimentary continental breakfast, evening turndown, welcome sherry, morning newspaper, overnight shoe shine service, 24-hour room service and concierge, and use of the private steamroom. The hotel has a strict no-tipping policy for the staff. Enjoy the three restaurants. For those who prefer more room, ask about the condominium-style rooms, the Arlington Suites.

Host: Stan Kott
Rooms: 54 (PB) $185-350
Continental Breakfast
Credit Cards: A, B, C, D, E, F
Notes: 2, 3, 4, 5, 6, 8, 9, 14

Bacon Mansion/ Broadway Guest House

959 Broadway East, 98102
(206) 329-1864; (800) 240-1864; FAX (206) 860-9025

One of Seattle's gracious mansions within two blocks of the Broadway shopping district, the Bacon Mansion is in the Harvard-Belmont historic district. Most rooms have

Bacon Mansion

private baths. Grand staircase, turn-of-the-century library; breakfast in the formal dining room.

Hosts: Daryl King and Tim Stiles
Rooms: 8 (6 PB; 2 SB) $65-125
Continental Breakfast
Credit Cards: A, B, C
Notes: 2, 5, 8, 9, 10, 14

Beech Tree Manor

1405 Queen Anne Avenue, North, 98109
(206) 281-7037

Wood paneling, English wallpaper, and matching fabrics create the ambience of an English country home. Decorated with original art, Oriental rugs, and antique beds. The innkeeper is also a chef.

Host: Virginia Lucero
Rooms: 6 (3 PB; 3 SB) $49-82
Full Breakfast
Credit Cards: A, B
Notes: 2, 5, 6, 8, 14

Bellevue Place Bed and Breakfast on Capitol Hill in Seattle

1111 Bellevue Place East, 98102
(206) 325-9253; (800) 325-9253; FAX (206) 455-0785

Bellevue Place is in the Landmark District of Capitol Hill. This 1905 storybook house with leaded glass and Victorian charm is close to Broadway restaurants and stores, Volunteer Park, and a 20 to 25-minute walk to downtown Seattle. Pressed cotton sheets and queen-size beds.

Hosts: Gunner Johnson and Joseph C. Pruett
Rooms: 3 (SB) $75-85
Full Breakfast
Credit Cards: A, B, C, D
Notes: 5, 10, 13, 14

B. Williams House Bed and Breakfast

1505 Fourth Avenue North, 98109
(206) 285-0810; (800) 880-0810; FAX (206) 285-8526

NOTES: Credit cards accepted: A MasterCard; B Visa; C American Express; D Discover Card; E Diner's Club; F Other; 2 Personal checks accepted; 3 Lunch available; 4 Dinner available; 5 Open all year;

A family bed and breakfast in an Edwardian home with much of the original woodwork and original gaslight fixtures. Decorated with antiques, most guest rooms have views of Seattle, the mountains, or the water. A sunny enclosed porch is shared by all. Beautiful gardens! Close to downtown, the Space Needle, and public market. Public transportation available.

Hosts: the Williams family
Rooms: 5 (2 PB; 3 SB) $70-99
Full Breakfast
Credit Cards: A, B, C, E
Notes: 2, 5, 7 (limited), 8 (call), 10, 11, 12

Chambered Nautilus

5005 22nd Avenue Northeast, 98105
(206) 522-2536

Seattle's finest, a gracious 1915 Georgian Colonial nestled high on a hill. This famous hospitable inn is furnished with a mixture of American and English antiques and reproductions, Persian rugs, a grand piano, and a 2,000-plus volume library. It offers national award-winning breakfasts, plus excellent access to Seattle's fine restaurants, theaters, shopping, public transportation, bike and jogging trails, tennis, golf, and the nearby University of Washington campus.

Hosts: Bunny and Bill Hagemeyer
Rooms: 6 (4 PB; 2 SB) $79-105
Full Breakfast
Credit Cards: A, B, C, E, F
Notes: 2, 5, 9, 10, 11, 12, 13, 14

Chelsea Station Bed and Breakfast Inn

4915 Linden Avenue North, 98103
(206) 547-6077

For a quiet, comfortable, and private accommodation, nothing beats Chelsea Station. With Seattle's rose gardens at the doorstep, guests can breathe in the restorative calm. Walk Greenlake's exceptional wooded pathways, then try a soothing cup of tea or a nap in the afternoon. That's the style at Chelsea Station, and guests are welcome to enjoy it. Member Washington Bed and Breakfast Guild. Three-night minimum stay over holidays.

Hosts: Dick and Marylou Jones
Rooms: 6 (PB) $69-104
Full Breakfast
Credit Cards: A, B, C, D, E, F
Notes: 2, 5, 8 (over 11), 9, 10, 11, 12, 14

Gaslight Inn

1727 15th Avenue, 98122
(206) 325-3654

This beautifully restored turn-of-the-century home is on Capitol Hill in downtown Seattle. Oak paneling, fireplaces, decks, and a heated in-ground pool make the Gaslight a very special place for the guests, whether they are visiting for pleasure or business. Guests may choose between nine rooms and five suites.

Hosts: Steve Bennett and Trevor Logan
Rooms: 14 (11 PB; 3 SB) $68-98
Continental Breakfast
Credit Cards: A, B, C
Notes: 2, 5, 7, 11

Gaslight Inn

Green Gables Guesthouse

1503 Second Avenue West, 98119
(206) 282-6863

A tranquil in-city retreat on historic Queen Anne Hill, just three blocks from Kerry Park and offering a commanding view of Seattle. Walk to many restaurants, shops, the Space Needle, and performing arts. Built in 1904, this home is filled with antiques, costumes,

6 Pets welcome; 8 Children welcome; 9 Social drinking allowed; 10 Tennis available; 11 Swimming available; 12 Golf available; 13 Skiing available; 14 May be booked through travel agents.

and family heirlooms. Spectacular box-beam ceilings and leaded glass windows make for a truly vintage setting. A private garden leads to Mercer House, which is designed for longer stays. Guests are served generous farm-style breakfasts.

Hosts: David and Lila Chapman
Rooms: 4 (2 PB; 2 SB) $75-125
House: 1 3-bedroom (2 PB; 1 SB)
Full Breakfast
Credit Cards: None
Notes: 2, 5, 8, 11, 14

Mildred's Bed and Breakfast

1202 15th Avenue East, 98112
(206) 325-6072

A traditional 1890 Victorian gem in an elegant style. Old-fashioned hospitality awaits. Red carpets, lace curtains, fireplace, grand piano, and wraparound porch. Across the street is the Seattle Art Museum, Flower Conservatory, and historic 44-acre Volunteer Park. Electric trolley at the front door. Minutes to city center, freeways, and all points of interest.

Host: Mildred Sarver
Rooms: 3 (PB) $75-85
Full Breakfast
Credit Cards: A, B, C, D, E
Notes: 2, 5, 8, 9, 10, 11, 12, 14

Mildred's

A Pacific Reservation Service

701 Northwest 60th Street, 98107
(206) 784-0539

The Downtown Hotel. Built in 1928 and recently remodeled, this lovely European-style hotel offers guests comfortable rooms with double or twin beds. Walk to the waterfront, scores of fine restaurants, Pike Place Market, the Kingdome, Amtrak station, and the convention center. Many of the original fixtures, such as the mahogany door and tiling, were left. Personal service, friendly staff, and professional help is at guests' beck and call. Continental breakfast. Parking available. $68.

BA-1. Here is the private apartment with everything: private entrance, living room with TV, phone, private bath, queen-size bed, and equipped kitchen. Maid service, chocolates on the pillow, fresh flowers, and a warm welcome. One block to bus lines and a 15-minute ride to downtown. Close to University of Washington area. $45.

BA-2. All the comforts of home can be found in this two-bedroom cottage in a quiet neighborhood. One bedroom features a 1925 antique bedroom set, and the second room offers twin beds. The cottage sleeps up to six, and is comfortably furnished with brass and oak accents. Close to Greenlake, the university, parks, the zoo, beaches, marinas, shops, and restaurants. Children welcome. No smoking. Monthly rates available. $85.

BA-4. A brand new home, Northwest style, offers a private suite of two rooms with sliding glass doors to a private patio. Private bath and queen-size bed. Kitchenette with breakfast supplies provided. Occasionally breakfast is served upstairs in the dining room. Close to Greenlake and restaurants. $55.

NOTES: Credit cards accepted: A MasterCard; B Visa; C American Express; D Discover Card; E Diner's Club; F Other; 2 Personal checks accepted; 3 Lunch available; 4 Dinner available; 5 Open all year;

BA-5. For families or business groups, nothing compares to the comfort of one's own house. Guests may take over the entire house or rent just one room, but will always receive a great value staying here. Close to Greenlake, shops, restaurants, and only minutes from downtown via the freeway. Two bedrooms are available, but sleeping accommodations can be made for up to ten guests. No smoking. No pets. Free off-street parking. $45.

BE-1. This large family home on Beacon Hill was built in 1910 with fine woodwork, beamed ceilings, built-ins, a tiled fireplace in the parlor, huge windows, and decks that take advantage of the wonderful views of Elliott Bay, the Olympic Mountains, and the skyline. Four guest rooms and two large bathrooms are offered. Fine antiques, Navajo weavings, and artwork from Latin American countries will delight. At breakfast time, enjoy the specialties of this inn: Mexican and Latin American dishes, or American, if desired. $35-45.

Bellevue-1. This wonderful contemporary home offers a private suite with two bedrooms, a living room, one full bath, and a private entrance. Have a full breakfast served upstairs in the dining room. Guests are also welcome to use the hot tub in the back. An urban oasis at its finest. One mile from the center of Bellevue, this guest home will be a comfortable retreat after a day of sightseeing or business. $50-55.

Bellevue-2. Hospitable retired hosts offer guests two bedrooms, with a living room, private bath, kitchenette, private entrance, and a tasty breakfast. Handy location. Fine views of the lake. $50-55.

CH-2. Here is a true Victorian built in 1890 with stained-glass windows, fine period furniture, original woodwork, and an ambi-

ence that is unequaled. The hostess makes everyone feel right at home. All the little touches that provide that special bed and breakfast experience are here. Breakfasts are legendary. $85.

CH-4. An elegantly furnished traditional brick house with a lovely garden and covered patio is on a tree-lined street in an exclusive, residential neighborhood. Within a few minutes from the University of Washington, downtown, theaters, shopping, and the convention center. On the bus lines. Breakfast is served in the formal dining room. Children welcome.

CH-5. A large turn of the century home that looks like a castle has been lovingly restored. The location is handy to everything in the city, only 12 blocks from downtown. The guest rooms are on the first floor and have private baths. The library with a wonderful window seat is available to lounge, read, watch TV, or sit and plan the day's activities. $45-55.

CH-6. A spacious Victorian greets its visitors with warm hospitality. From the second floor guests will have a great view of the city, the Space Needle, the Sound, and the Olympic Mountains. Walk to restaurants, shops, action on Broadway, and art museum. Two guest rooms share a bath. Home-cooked breakfast served in the dining room by an experienced hostess. Some Spanish, Norwegian, and Indonesian spoken. $55-65.

CH-10. A gracious brick building in the Georgian style welcomes guests in a convenient location on Capitol Hill. Walk to restaurants, bus lines, a fine city park, and other attractions. Spacious rooms on the first floor with sitting areas and queen-size beds. Enjoy breakfast on the patio or in the dining room. $79-92.

6 Pets welcome; 8 Children welcome; 9 Social drinking allowed; 10 Tennis available; 11 Swimming available; 12 Golf available; 13 Skiing available; 14 May be booked through travel agents.

A Pacific Reservation Service (continued)

CH-12. Private entrance, private bath, and double bedroom, all in this wonderful brick home. Guests may have as much privacy as they want. Self-catered breakfast is in the refrigerator. Visiting relatives love this spot, because of its convenience to the city, 15 minutes to downtown, or the bus lines. The hosts are young professionals, most interested in making guests' stay as pleasant as possible. So close to the University of Washington, one could even walk there. A fine garden is available for guests to enjoy. $65.

MAG-2. Two miles northwest of downtown, this bed and breakfast offers a quiet street and a private bedroom with a double bed, a single bed, and a private bath. Full breakfast is served, and guests have a lovely view of Seattle from the patio where breakfast is served. $65.

QA-1. A beautiful professional facility in an impressively restored building with a comfortable, relaxed atmosphere. Guests wish they could stay longer to enjoy the proximity to downtown, the fine antiques, the window seat, the wicker furniture, and great breakfasts that are served in the formal dining room. Four bedrooms, some with private baths. $65-75.

QA-6. On lower Queen Anne, only two blocks from the Seattle Center and all the restaurants and shops there, this bed and breakfast offers a delightful alternative to motels. Stay in these fine studio apartments, with queen-size beds, TV, telephones, and kitchenettes. $50-60.

QA-10. In a private home atmosphere, guests will enjoy a cozy one-bedroom suite on the second floor, private entrance, phone, TV, full kitchen. The inn is on a bus line. See the downtown skyscrapers from the bedroom windows and enjoy a lovely view of Capitol Hill. A second suite is on the garden level, with a private entrance, full bath, and kitchen. No breakfast is served. No smoking. $45-50.

QA-12. If there ever was the ultimate lodging for travelers, this must be it. The setting is Queen Anne Hill, the most desirable location in the city. Private suite with private bath, a European kitchen, private entrance, TV, phone, queen-size bed, and security system. The large deck lets one drink in the great view of Puget Sound and the Olympic Mountains. Ideal for honeymooners, business travelers, and visiting relatives. $75.

UD-3. A greenbelt with a creek through the adjacent property sets the tone for this stunning, architecturally designed, traditional home. Skylights, bright and airy, a sun deck, two double bedrooms, each of which is individually decorated, one of which has a full bath, and a private living room all add up to a great bed and breakfast experience. Add a home-cooked breakfast with great flair, and guests will never want to leave. $55-75.

Wallingford. Private suite with a queen-size bed, private entrance, living room, and kitchen in a private home, which is on the bus line. Guests are only a short three miles from the downtown core of the city and conveniently near the University of Washington and the people-oriented university district. This home is ideal for longer stays for the person who is looking for comfortable private lodgings. $60.

NOTES: Credit cards accepted: A MasterCard; B Visa; C American Express; D Discover Card; E Diner's Club; F Other; 2 Personal checks accepted; 3 Lunch available; 4 Dinner available; 5 Open all year;

Prince of Wales

Prince of Wales
Bed and Breakfast

133 13th Avenue East, 98102
(206) 325-9692; (800) 327-9692; FAX (206) 322-6402

Convenient to the business and convention traveler. Within walking distance of or a short bus ride to downtown Seattle and the Washington State Convention and Trade Center. A charming turn-of-the-century bed and breakfast on scenic Capitol Hill. Rooms include a romantic attic hideaway with private deck and panoramic view of the city skyline, Puget Sound, and Olympic Mountains. Restaurants and shops nearby. Great breakfasts! No smoking.

Hosts: Carol Norton and Chuck Morgan
Rooms: 4 (2 PB; 2 SB) $65-95
Full Breakfast
Credit Cards: A, B, C, D
Notes: 2, 5, 8, 9, 10, 11, 12

Queen Anne Hill
Bed and Breakfast

1835 7th West, 98119
(206) 284-9779

Picturesque view of the Olympic Mountains and Puget Sound. Beautiful art, unique collectibles, and antiques are accented by hardwood floors and Oriental carpets. Close to the Seattle Center, downtown, and historic Pike Place Market. Breakfast includes home-baked goods, fresh fruit, and made-to-order items.

Hosts: Mary and Chuck McGrew
Rooms: 5 (2 PB; 3 SB) $55-75
Full Breakfast
Credit Cards: A, B
Notes: 2, 5, 8, 9, 10, 11, 12, 14

Salisbury House

750 16th Avenue East, 98112
(206) 328-8682

An elegant turn-of-the-century home on Capitol Hill, just minutes from Seattle's cultural and business activities. Gracious guest rooms with private baths. A well-stocked library and wraparound porch invite relaxation. In a historic neighborhood with parks, shops, and restaurants.

Hosts: Mary and Cathryn Wiese
Rooms: 4 (PB) $72-93
Full Breakfast
Credit Cards: A, D, C, E
Notes: 2, 5, 8 (over 12), 9, 10, 11, 12

Salisbury House

6 Pets welcome; 8 Children welcome; 9 Social drinking allowed; 10 Tennis available; 11 Swimming available; 12 Golf available; 13 Skiing available; 14 May be booked through travel agents.

Shafer-Baillie Mansion Bed and Breakfast

907 14th Avenue East, 98112
(206) 322-4654; FAX (206) 329-4654

A quiet and livable atmosphere, Shafer-Baillie Mansion is the largest estate on historic Millionaire's Row on Seattle's Capitol Hill. This bed and breakfast has recently undergone a facelift, and guests will enjoy new luxury services and surroundings that are second to none. Entirely smokeless, but smoking is allowed on porches and balconies. A TV and refrigerator are in every room, and a gourmet Continental breakfast is served between 8:30 and 9:30 A.M. with the morning newspaper. Offering 13 suites, most with private baths. Telephone in most rooms.

Host: Erv Olssen
Rooms: 13 (10 PB; 3 SB) $65-115
Continental Breakfast
Credit Cards: C, D
Notes: 2, 5, 11, 12, 13, 14

Tugboat Challenger

1001 Fairview Avenue North, 98109
(206) 340-1201

Restored 1944 tugboat downtown. Carpeted, granite fireplace; laundry. Refrigerators, TV, phone, VCR, sinks, and sprinkler system, and private entrance for each room. Restaurants, bars, classic and modern sail boats, power boats, row boats, and kayak rentals. Featured in *Travel & Leisure*, *Cosmopolitan*, and many major papers. Two-night minimum stay on weekends and holidays.

Hosts: Jerry and Buff Brown
Full Breakfast
Credit Cards: A, B, C, D, E
Notes: 2, 5, 9, 14

Villa Heidelberg

4845 45th Avenue Southwest, 98116
(206) 938-3658

Historic 1909 vintage country home in the heart of West Seattle, 10 minutes to downtown, and 20 minutes to airport. Leaded glass, beamed ceilings, fireplaces, wraparound porch, lovely gardens, and view of Puget Sound and Olympic Mountains. Elegant breakfast.

Hosts: Barbara, John, and David Thompson
Rooms: 4 (SB) $55-85
Full Breakfast
Credit Cards: A, B, C
Notes: 2, 5

SEQUIM

Greywolf Inn

395 Keeler Road, 98382
(206) 683-5889

Enjoy a scenic drive from Seattle to Greywolf Inn, a five-acre country estate at the edge of nature's playground; the ideal starting point for light adventure on the Olympic Peninsula. Enjoy nearby bird watching, boating, or golfing, or head for the woods. Choices include Olympic National Park, Hurricane Ridge, the Hoh Rain Forest, and Sequim's own Dungeness Spit and Wildlife Refuge. A steaming hot tub, a good night's sleep, and plenty of pampering are waiting for guests at Greywolf. Join the hosts for fine food and good cheer at their splendid country inn.

Hosts: Peggy and Bill Melang
Rooms: 5 (PB) $65-98
Full Breakfast
Credit Cards: A, B, C
Notes: 2, 5, 9, 10, 11, 12, 13, 14

Margie's Inn on the Bay

120 Forrest Road, 98382
(360) 683-7011

A spacious, contemporary ranch home on beautiful Sequim Bay. Margie's is Sequim's only waterfront bed and breakfast. Margie's offers five well-appointed rooms, each with its own distinctive personality and private bath. King-size, queen-size, and twin beds are available. Relax in the evening with a good book, a movie in the

TV room, or a chat with the two Persian cats and an African gray parrot. Come and see the many attractions around Sequim.

Hosts: Margie and Don Vorhies
Rooms: 5 (PB) $69-125
Full Breakfast
Credit Cards: A, B
Notes: 2, 5, 8 (over 12), 9, 11, 12, 13, 14

SHELTON

Twin River Ranch Bed and Breakfast

5730 Highway 3, 98584
(360) 426-1023

Rural 1918 manor house is on the Olympic Peninsula. Stone fireplace, antiques, and granny rooms tucked under the eaves overlooking the garden and stream. Black Angus cattle graze on 140 acres of pasture surrounded by old-growth trees. Puget Sound laps the marsh, and gulls, blue heron, and eagles circle overhead in season. By advance reservation only.

Hosts: Phlorence and Ted Rohde
Rooms: 2 (SB) $60
Full Breakfast
Credit Cards: A, B
Notes: 2, 11, 12, 14

SILVERDALE

Seabreeze Beach Cottage

16609 Olympic View Road Northwest, 98383
(200) 092-4048

Seabreeze Beach Cottage

Challenged by lapping waves at high tide, this private retreat will awaken the five senses with the smell of salty air, a taste of fresh oysters and clams, views of the Olympic Mountains, the exhilaration of sun, surf, and sand. Spa at water's edge.

Host: Dennis Fulton
Rooms: 2 (PB) $119-149
Continental Breakfast
Credit Cards: A, B
Notes: 2, 5, 6, 8, 9, 11, 12, 14

SNOHOMISH

Countryman Bed and Breakfast

119 Cedar Street, 98290
(206) 568-9622

An 1896 landmark Queen Anne Victorian with all the extras. Near 250 antique shops. Fireplace, jetted Greek tub, art gallery. Complimentary tour of the historic district. Private parking and private airport nearby.

Hosts: Larry and Sandy Countryman
Rooms: 3 (PB) $65
Full Breakfast
Credit Cards: A, B, D
Notes: 2, 5, 6, 8, 10, 11, 12, 13, 14

A Pacific Reservation Service

701 Northwest 60th Street, Seattle, 98107
(206) 784-0539

SNO 1. This beautifully restored Victorian country estate was built in 1884. Crowning the crest of a hill overlooking Snohomish, with a panoramic view of the Cascades, Mount Rainier, and the Olympics, the accommodation offers a quiet serenity and relaxed atmosphere. Guests are encouraged to linger in the sun-filled parlors, stroll the beautiful gardens, or just relax and swim in the heated pool. Guest rooms are tastefully decorated with antiques, handmade quilts, and unique beds. $55-65.

6 Pets welcome; 8 Children welcome; 9 Social drinking allowed; 10 Tennis available; 11 Swimming available; 12 Golf available; 13 Skiing available; 14 May be booked through travel agents.

SNOQUALMIE

The Old Honey Farm Country Inn

8910 384 Avenue Southeast, 98065
(206) 888-9399; (800) 826-9077

Within the 35-acre historic Honey Farm with spectacular Cascade Mountain views from rooms, dining, and deck areas. Thirty minutes from Seattle and Snoqualmie Pass ski resorts; 45 minutes from Sea-Tac International Airport. Chef's choice dinners on weekends. Service bar. Snoqualmie Falls, shopping, fishing, swimming, hiking, and five public golf courses nearby. Smoke free. One room is wheelchair accessible.

Hosts: LeRoy, Scott, and Helen Gmazel
Rooms: 10 (PB) $75-135
Full Breakfast
Credit Cards: A, B, D
Notes: 3, 5, 8, 9, 10, 11, 12, 13

A Pacific Reservation Service

701 Northwest 60th Street, Seattle, 98107
(206) 784-0539

At the side of the spectacular Snoqualmie Falls, this new inn offers guests unequaled comfort, privacy, and style in each of the 90-plus rooms. Curl up in front of the wood-burning fireplace or relax in a personal spa. Each room has a private bath. A library, country store, and fine restaurant await guests. Hiking, biking, skiing, golf, wineries, and fishing are nearby. $150-450.

SPOKANE

Hillside House

1729 East 18th, 99203
(509) 535-1893 (day); (509) 534-1426 (night)

Charming guest house, built in the 1930s and enlarged through several additions, offers country decor and exquisite hospitality.

On a quiet residential street on a hillside overlooking the city and mountains. Hosts love to cook and share their knowledge of the community.

Hosts: Jo Ann and Bud
Rooms: 2 (SB) $50-55
Full Breakfast
Credit Cards: A, B
Notes: 2, 5, 10, 11, 12, 13, 14

Marianna Stoltz House

East 427 Indiana, 99207
(509) 483-4316

American four-square classic historic home is five minutes from downtown Spokane. Furnished with antiques, old quilts, and lace, the hosts offer a wraparound veranda, sitting room, and parlor, which provide relaxation and privacy. King-size, queen-size, or single beds, with private or semi-private baths, air conditioning and TV. A tantalizing, unique, and hearty breakfast is prepared fresh every day. Close to the Opera House, Convention Center, and Riverfront Park.

Host: Phyllis Magune
Rooms: 4 (2 PB; 2 SB) $59

Marianna Stoltz House

NOTES: Credit cards accepted: A MasterCard; B Visa; C American Express; D Discover Card; E Diner's Club; F Other; 2 Personal checks accepted; 3 Lunch available; 4 Dinner available; 5 Open all year;

Full Breakfast
Credit Cards: A, B, C, E
Notes: 2, 5, 8 (over 12), 9, 11, 12, 14

A Pacific Reservation Service

701 Northwest 60th Street, Seattle, 98107
(206) 784-0539

Spokane-1. Enjoy this fine, restored 1891 Victorian featuring hand-carved woodwork, tin ceilings, and an open, curved staircase. A cheerful fire in the parlor will warm guests in the winter, while the wraparound porch is a nice place to relax on a warm day. Period furniture decorates the guest rooms, and a wonderful home-cooked breakfast is served in the mornings. The host will gladly assist and advise sightseers. $45-55.

Spokane-2. This bed and breakfast is in an attractive suburb and offers guests a quiet, relaxing place to unwind and enjoy. This home features a living room bedroom combination, queen-size bed, private bath, TV, and a private deck overlooking a picturesque garden. A gourmet breakfast is served with the morning news. Golf course and shops are nearby. $45-55.

Spokane Bed and Breakfast Reservation Service

East 627-25th, 99203
(509) 624-3776

This reservation service covers Washington, northern Idaho, and British Columbia. Included are Colonial, authentic Victorian, and spacious contemporary homes. They are just blocks from city center activities, at lakeside, or at a winter ski resort. This is a free service designed to find the bed and breakfast specifically suited to the tastes and needs of visitors to these areas. $45-92.

SUNNYSIDE

Sunnyside Inn Bed and Breakfast

800 East Edison Avenue, 98944
(509) 839-5557; (800) 221-4195

Eight luxurious rooms all with private baths, many with private entrances, two with fireplaces. King- and queen-size beds, telephones, and cable TV. Seven rooms have double Jacuzzi tubs. In the heart of Washington wine country, near more than 26 wineries and tasting rooms. Business and government rates available.

Hosts: James and Geri Graves
Rooms: 8 (PB) $45-75
Full Breakfast
Credit Cards: A, B, C, D
Notes: 2, 3, 4, 5, 8, 9, 10, 11, 12, 14

TACOMA

Commencement Bay Bed and Breakfast

3312 North Union Avenue, 98407
(206) 752-8175

From its elevated perch above the scenic waterfront, this stately Colonial home affords breathtaking views of Mount Rainier, Commencement Bay, and the Cascades. Three elegantly appointed guest rooms with private bath. A variety of common areas offer a fireplace, hot tub, game room, and outdoor deck An office area with FAX and modem hookup awaits business travelers. Full and Continental breakfast provided. Tennis, swimming, and golf nearby. The hosts are knowledgeable of the historical, cultural, and natural aspects of the Tacoma area. No smoking. Special rates for summer and winter. AAA approved.

Hosts: Bill and Sharon Kaufmann
Rooms: 3 (PB) $75-105
Full and Continental Breakfast
Credit Cards: A, B, C
Notes: 2, 5, 8 (over 12), 10, 11, 12, 14

6 Pets welcome; 8 Children welcome; 9 Social drinking allowed; 10 Tennis available; 11 Swimming available; 12 Golf available; 13 Skiing available; 14 May be booked through travel agents.

Keenan House

2610 North Warner, 98407
(206) 752-0702

The Keenan House offers clean, attractively decorated rooms and a full breakfast, featuring freshly baked breads and rolls. Just seven blocks from the University of Puget Sound, ten minutes by car from Point Defiance Park and Vashon Island ferry and one and 90 minutes from Paradise Resort at Mount Rainier.

Host: Lenore Keenan
Rooms: 6 (2 PB; 4 SB) $45-65
Full Breakfast
Credit Cards: None
Notes: 2, 5, 8, 9, 12, 14

A Pacific Reservation Service

701 Northwest 60th Street, Seattle, 98107
(206) 784-0539

Cottage in the Woods. Standing on 15 forested acres, this hidden cottage will be equally suitable for long or short stays, honeymoons, anniversaries, or getaways. Overlooking a salmon stream and next to a golf course, it affords guests total privacy. Hosts live on the property and are available to assist guests with sightseeing plans, but will honor the privacy guests seek. One room has a freestanding fireplace on a hearth, brass bed, and kitchenette where breakfast is self-catered. $75.

Tacoma Tudor. This cozy bed and breakfast is next door to the Victorian Guesthouse. Enjoy friendly hospitality and comfort in this home with country-style decor. Guests should allow themselves to be pampered here. $45-55.

Victorian Guesthouse. This lovely guesthouse is near the university on a tree-lined street, away from the busyness of downtown. Mount Rainier and Commencement Bay are nearby. While relaxing in the parlor, the innkeeper can help guests with sightseeing plans. The Guesthouse offers clean, comfortable guest rooms furnished with country antiques. $40-50.

TOKELAND

Tokeland Hotel

100 Hotel Road, 98590
(206) 267-7006

A national historic landmark, the Tokeland Hotel is on a peninsula bordering Washington's Willapa Bay and the Pacific Ocean.

Host: Erin Radke
Rooms: 18 (SB) $43.50-95
Full Breakfast
Credit Cards: A, B, D
Notes: 2, 3, 4, 5, 7 (limited), 8, 9, 11, 14

Tokeland Hotel

WESTPORT

A Pacific Reservation Service

701 Northwest 60th Street, Seattle, 98107
(206) 784-0539

WE-1. A small, lovely town on the ocean where the salmon fishing is the greatest. If guests are not into fishing, there are many other activities to enjoy. This historic man-

---

NOTES: Credit cards accepted: A MasterCard; B Visa; C American Express; D Discover Card; E Diner's Club; F Other; 2 Personal checks accepted; 3 Lunch available; 4 Dinner available; 5 Open all year;

sion occupies eight acres, two blocks from the ocean, and possesses the peacefulness one desires. Choose from five bedrooms, all with private baths, with lace curtains, antiques, and fine period furnishings. Don't forget to take a long soak in the large hot tub on the grand cedar deck under the gazebo. Also enjoy the barbecue and picnic areas, badminton, volleyball, and horseshoes. $65.

WHIDBEY ISLAND

A Pacific Reservation Service

701 Northwest 60th Street, Seattle, 98107
(206) 784-0539

Oak Harbor. At this bed and breakfast guests can enjoy a fresh complete Northwest breakfast, including salmon or mussels prepared in the hostess' sunlit kitchen. Spend the day searching out the treasures of Whidbey Island, and spend the evening refreshing in the hot tub while enjoying the outside view. The hosts offer three wonderful, cozy rooms to guests when they are ready to retire for the evening. $65-95.

Whidbey-3. On a quiet cove along wooded shores, this turn-of-the-century country inn offers guests the charm and comfort of rooms and cottages. Some guest rooms are furnished with antiques. The cottages with kitchenettes are suitable for family getaways. Guests are invited to enjoy the charm of the big stone fireplace in the parlor and the breathtaking views over the water. $55-95.

Whidbey-4. This new and splendidly built waterfront inn offers a great getaway location. All rooms have lanais, queen-size beds, whirlpool bath for two, wood-burning fireplaces, and are beautifully decorated. Restaurant with award-winning cuisine is on the premises. $165.

Whidbey-5. This bed and breakfast is a spacious, modern beach home decorated with comfortable homey antiques, including a beautiful diamond-tufted leather love seat with matching wing-backed chairs. Guests can sit back, enjoy a warm, crackling fire, watch the 52-inch TV, or enjoy a game of pool. The breathtaking view of the Olympic Mountains, Puget Sound, and the San Juan Islands will encourage visitors to linger and sip freshly ground coffee while savoring the view. $65-95.

WHITE SALMON

The Inn of the White Salmon

172 West Jewett, P.O. Box 1549, 98672
(800) 972-5226

The inn, built as a small hotel in 1937, is now a bed and breakfast providing both privacy and an intimate atmosphere. Explore the Columbia River Gorge. The inn is just 65 miles east of Portland, Oregon. Enjoy elegant antiques, a cozy parlor, room or suite with private bath, a soak in the hot tub. Indulge in a lavish breakfast of more than 20 pastries and breads, and choose from among six breakfast entrees.

Rooms: 16 (PB) $89-115
Continental Breakfast
Credit Cards: A, B, C, E
Notes: 2, 5, 6, 8, 10, 11, 12, 13, 14

Llama Ranch Bed and Breakfast

1980 Highway 141, 98672
(509) 395-2786; (800) 800-LAMA

This inn stands between two snow-capped mountains. The hosts offer hands-on experience with llamas, including guided llama walks through the woods. Get better acquainted with these beautiful, intelligent animals. The bedrooms have queen-size beds and spectacular views in every direction of refreshing waterfalls and natural lava

6 Pets welcome; 8 Children welcome; 9 Social drinking allowed; 10 Tennis available; 11 Swimming available; 12 Golf available; 13 Skiing available; 14 May be booked through travel agents.

bridges. Nearby activities include white-water rafting, golf, plane trips over Mount St. Helens, fishing, hunting, hiking, cave exploration, and huckleberry picking. Cross-country skiing and snowmobiling in the winter. Close to nice restaurants.

Hosts: Jerry and Rebeka Stone
Rooms: 7 (2 PB; 5 SB) $55-75
Full Breakfast
Credit Cards: A, B, D
Notes: 2, 5, 8, 9, 12, 14

WINTHROP

Dommann's Bed and Breakfast

716 Highway 20, 98862
(509) 996-2484; (800) 423-0040

These antique-filled guest rooms are on the banks of the Methow River. Hosts offer a recreation room and piano. No smoking. The valley is a recreation paradise for photography, seasonal hunting, fishing, hiking, camping, and skiing. Eight lakes within six to eight miles; right at the foot of the Cascade Mountains.

Hosts: Hank and Jean Dommann
Rooms: 2 (1 PB; 1 SB) $55
Continental Breakfast
Credit Cards: None
Notes: 2, 5, 9, 10, 11, 12, 13

WOODLAND

Grandma's House

4551 Lewis River Road, 98674-9305
(206) 225-7002

Bed and breakfast featuring country charm in a three-bedroom 1917 farmhouse on 35 secluded acres overlooking the north fork of the Lewis River. Relax on the deck and view the river and occasional deer and eagle. Private boat launch. Good salmon and steelhead fishing. Eight miles east of Woodland and I-5 and 20 miles west of Cougar on Highway 503, scenic route to Mount St. Helen's National Monument. Full country breakfast. AAA approved.

Hosts: Warren and Louise Moir
Rooms: 2 (SB) $55-64
Full Breakfast
Credit Cards: A, B
Notes: 2, 5, 8, 9, 11, 12

YAKIMA

A Pacific Reservation Service

701 Northwest 60th Street, Seattle, 98107
(206) 784-0539

This stately English Tudor mansion was built in 1929 and is surrounded by beautiful grounds, formal hedges, a variety of trees, flowers, and a garden pool. Each room is furnished with antiques from the early 1800s and has a color TV. The bridal suite features a king-size bed, private bath, bar with refrigerator, microwave oven, and a bottle of champagne. $65-125.

West Virginia

BERKELEY SPRINGS

Amanda's
Bed and Breakfast

1428 Park Avenue, Baltimore, MD 21217
(410) 225-0001; (800) 899-7533
FAX (410) 728-8957

336. A four-season resort with mountains, lakes, pool, tennis, hiking, fishing, cross-country skiing, sauna, and spa. Chalets. Surrounded by natural beauty. Get pampered. Wood-burning fire stoves add to enjoyment.

Blue Ridge
Bed and Breakfast

Route 2, Box 3895, Berryville, VA 22611
(703) 955-1246; (800) 296-1246

A. Two houses; eight rooms completely redone. Close to mineral waters, a castle, Roman Bath and Massage, stocked fish ponds, health resort, golf, and horseback riding. $50-65.

B. Lovely Second Empire Victorian home built 110 years ago. On the National Register of Historic Places. Close to antique shops, horseback riding, swimming, fishing, boating, and tennis. $85-120.

The Country Inn

207 South Washington Street, 25411
(304) 258-2210; (800) 822-6630
FAX (304) 258-3986

Just over the mountain, the inn offers distinctive accommodations, 70 rooms, an art gallery, a lounge, gift shop, air conditioning, color cable TV, nonsmoking rooms, handicapped facilities, room service, and complimentary afternoon tea. Enjoy superb dining in one of two dining rooms, serving breakfast, lunch, and dinner. Table-side cooking, live entertainment on Saturday nights. Conference center for up to 60 people. Renaissance Spa, featuring whirlpool mineral baths, facials, massages, manicures, pedicures, and waxing.

Rooms: 70 (59 PB; 11 SB) $35-145
Full or Continental Breakfast
Credit Cards: A, B, C, D, E
Notes: 3, 4, 5, 7, 8, 10, 11, 12, 13, 14

CAIRO

Blue Ridge
Bed and Breakfast

Route 2, Box 3895, Berryville, VA 22611
(703) 955-1246; (800) 296-1246

Spectacular log guest house built in the early 1800s offers total privacy. In the middle of 430 acres this property includes two ponds for swimming or fishing and three creeks. Outstanding hiking and walking trails. Home of the American oil business—oil and gas wells on premises. Close to North Bend State Park, as well as glass, marble, and clothing outlets. $48-54.

CHARLESTON

Brass Pineapple
Bed and Breakfast

1611 Virginia Street East, 25311
(304) 344-0748; (800) CALL WVA

6 Pets welcome; 7 Smoking allowed; 8 Children welcome; 9 Social drinking allowed; 10 Tennis available; 11 Swimming available; 12 Golf available; 13 Skiing available; 14 May be booked through travel agents.

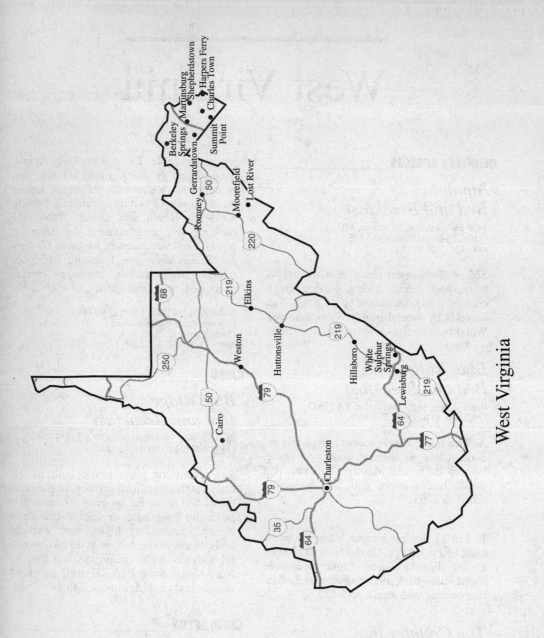

West Virginia

Harpers Ferry
Charles Town
Shepherdstown
Martinsburg
Summit
Point
Berkeley
Springs
Gerrardstown
Romney
Moorefield
Lost River
50
220
68
219
250
Elkins
Weston
Huttonsville
219
Hillsboro
White
Sulphur
Springs
Lewisburg
219
50
79
64
77
Cairo
Charleston
79
35
64

This cozy but elegant 1910 brick home is in Charleston's historic district. The house has been carefully restored to its original grandeur, with antiques throughout, lots of stained glass, and original oak woodwork. Guest rooms are furnished in elegant style with private baths, phones, and cable TV. Catering to business travelers, this bed and breakfast has two business-plan rooms offering phones with data jacks to accommodate laptop PCs, computer tables, and unlimited coffee, tea, and sodas. A small copier and FAX are on the first floor. Mints on pillows, fluffy robes, and turndown service add that special touch. Candlelight breakfast is accented with crystal and silver, and may be had alfresco in the petite rose garden in season.

Host: Sue Pepper
Rooms: 6 (PB) $75-95
Continental and Full Breakfasts
Credit Cards: A, B, C
Notes: 2, 5, 7 (limited), 9, 10, 11, 12, 14

CHARLES TOWN

Blue Ridge Bed and Breakfast

Route 2, Box 3895, 22611
(703) 955-1246; (800) 296-1246

Seventeen acres of formal and wild gardens. This 1923-1927 Tudor manor house is full of pure luxury and antiques, rare art, history, and gourmet cooking. Feather beds and down comforters. Private dining by appointment. Over 2,100 panes of glass in the house. Working fireplaces. $190 per person.

Cottonwood Inn

Route 2, Box 61-S
Kabletown Road and Mill Lane, 25414
(304) 725-3371

The Cottonwood Inn offers bed and breakfast accommodations in a restored Georgian farmhouse (circa 1800). The inn is on Bullskin Run in the historic Shenandoah Valley, near Harpers Ferry and Charles Town, and is furnished with antiques and period reproductions. Fireplaces in the dining room, parlor/ library, and one guest room. Guests are invited to enjoy the inn's peaceful, secluded acres, memorable country breakfasts, and warm hospitality. Seasonal rates are available.

Hosts: Colin and Eleanor Simpson
Rooms: 7 (PB) $75-105
Full Breakfast
Credit Cards: A, B, C, D
Notes: 2, 5, 7, 8, 9, 10, 11, 12, 13 (cross-country), 14

Cottonwood Inn

Gilbert House Bed and Breakfast

P O Box 1104, 25414
(304) 725-0637

Near Harpers Ferry and Antietam Battlefield. Experience a touch of class in the country. Enjoy the magnificent stone house, circa 1760, listed on the National Register and the Historic American Building Survey (1938), offering outstanding hospitality. Spacious and romantic rooms with working fireplaces and air conditioning. The Bridal Suite has curtains around the bed, claw-foot tub, etc. The house is filled with European treasures, some from royal families. In the Middleway historic district, an area of unsurpassed countryside and historic sites. The village is one of the first European settlements in the Shenadoah Valley and is on the original settlers' trail. Many colonial era mill sites in the immediate area. Local activities include theater at the Old Opera House,

NOTES: Credit cards accepted: A MasterCard; B Visa; C American Express; D Discover Card; E Diner's Club; F Other; 2 Personal checks accepted; 3 Lunch available; 4 Dinner available; 5 Open all year; 6 Pets welcome; 7 Smoking allowed; 8 Children welcome; 9 Social drinking allowed; 10 Tennis available; 11 Swimming available; 12 Golf available; 13 Skiing available; 14 May be booked through travel agents.

horse/auto races, shooting clubs, rafting, and outlet shopping. Village ghost.

Host: Bernie Heiler
Rooms: 3 (PB) $80-140
Full Breakfast
Credit Cards: A, B, C
Notes: 2, 5, 9, 12, 14

Hillbrook Inn

Route 2, Box 152 25414
(304) 725-4223

A true country inn with sweeping lawns, still-wild woods, meandering streams, tranquil duck ponds, and boxwood groves with beckoning benches. Perennial gardens burst with color, playing host to hummingbirds. Race horses, peach orchards, and herds of Angus are the only neighbors. This quintessential English country manor house is full of a wonderfully eclectic collection of antiques and objets d'art gathered over years of travel. Flemish oils, contemporary ceramics, African sculpture, and modern photography challenge the eye and mind. Books abound, and comfortable chairs encourage a good read in front of the fire. A seven-course dinner with wines and a full country breakfast are included. English high tea is available by reservation from November through April.

Host: Gretchen Carroll
Rooms: 6 (PB) $240-380
Full Breakfast and Dinner
Credit Cards: A, B, D
Notes: 2, 3 (by reservation), 4, 5, 7 (limited), 9, 12, 14

ELKINS

Tunnel Mountain Bed and Breakfast

Route 1, Box 59-1, 26241
(304) 636-1684

This charming, three-story fieldstone home is nestled on the side of Tunnel Mountain on five private, wooded acres, surrounded by scenic mountains, lush forests, and

sparkling rivers. The interior is finished in pine and rare wormy chestnut woodwork. Tastefully decorated throughout with antiques, collectibles, and crafts, it extends a warm and friendly atmosphere to guests.

Hosts: Anne and Paul Beardslee
Rooms: 3 (PB) $55-65
Full Breakfast
Credit Cards: None
Notes: 2, 5, 7, 9, 10, 11, 12, 13

GERRARDSTOWN

Gerrardstown's Prospect Hill Farm

Box 135, 25420
(304) 229-3346

Gerrardstown's Prospect Hill is a Georgian mansion set on 225 acres and listed on the National Register of Historic Places. Once a well-to-do gentleman's home, it has a permanent Franklin fireplace, antiques, and a hall mural depicting life in the early republic. Guests may choose one of the beautifully appointed rooms in the main house or the former slave quarters, where rooms are complete with country kitchen and fireplace. There is much to do on this working farm near Harpers Ferry, Martinsburg, and Winchester.

Hosts: Charles and Hazel Hudock
Rooms and Cottage: (PB) $85-95
Full Breakfast
Credit Cards: A, B
Notes: 2, 5, 7, 8 (in cottage), 9, 10, 11, 12

Prospect Hill Farm

HARPERS FERRY

Fillmore Street Bed and Breakfast

Fillmore Street, 25425
(304) 535-2619; (410) 321-5634

With a clear mountain view, this antique-furnished Victorian home is known for its hospitality, service, and gourmet breakfast. Private accommodations and baths, TVs, air conditioning, complimentary sherry and tea, and a blazing fire on cool mornings. Closed Thanksgiving, Christmas, and New Year's days.

Hosts: Alden and James Addy
Rooms: 2 (PB) $70-75
Full Breakfast
Credit Cards: None
Notes: 2, 5, 7, 8 (over 12), 9

HILLSBORO

The Current Bed and Breakfast

HC 64, Box 135, 24946
(304) 653-4722

This restored 1904 farmhouse rests in a high river valley surrounded by the Allegheny Mountains. Nearby the Greenbrier River Trail, Cranberry Wilderness, and many state and national forests and parks offer solitude and abundant wildlife. A cozy, relaxed atmosphere prevails. Antiques, quilts, and out door hot tub.

Hosts: Leslee McCarty and John Walkup
Rooms: 5 (1 PB; 4 SB) $50-75
Full Breakfast
Credit Cards: A, B
Notes: 2, 5, 8, 9, 12

HUTTONSVILLE

Hutton House

General Delivery, P.O. Box 88, 26273
(304) 335-6701

Enjoy the relaxed atmosphere of this historically registered and antique-filled Queen Anne Victorian. Guest rooms are individually styled, and each guest has his/her own personal favorite. Breakfast varies from gourmet to hearty. Sometimes it is served at a specific time, while at other times it is served at guests' leisure. Children can play games on the lawn. Guests can lose themselves in the beauty of the Laurel Mountains from the wraparound porch.

Hosts: Dean Ahren and Loretta Murray
Rooms: 6 (PB) $60-70
Full Breakfast
Credit Cards: A, B
Notes: 2, 5, 8, 9, 12, 13, 14

LEWISBURG

General Lewis Inn

301 East Washington Street, 24901
(304) 645-2600; (800) 628-4454

The General Lewis Inn is one of 54 historic buildings in the National Historic District of Lewisburg. It was created in 1929 by adding to an 1834 home. All rooms are furnished with antiques. The dining room serves a delicious selection of meals. A pond and garden, a living room with books, puzzles, and fireplace, and a wide veranda for rocking encourage relaxing. Two blocks away are shops for antiques, gifts, and clothing. Full breakfast at extra cost.

Hosts: Mary Noel Hock Morgan and Jim Morgan
Rooms: 25 (PB) $60-88
Full Breakfast
Credit Cards: A, B, C
Notes: 2, 3, 4, 5, 6, 7, 8, 9, 10, 11, 12, 14

LOST RIVER

Blue Ridge Bed and Breakfast

Route 2, Box 3895, Berryville, VA 22611
(703) 955-1246; (800) 296-1246

Outstanding log house complete with conference rooms, hot tub room, swimming pool,

6 Pets welcome; 8 Children welcome; 9 Social drinking allowed; 10 Tennis available; 11 Swimming available; 12 Golf available; 13 Skiing available; 14 May be booked through travel agents.

washer-dryer, Jacuzzi, six bedrooms with cable TV, and private baths. Fabulous view of Allegheny Mountains. Land borders George Washington National Forest. $82.

MARTINSBURG

Amanda's Bed and Breakfast

1428 Park Avenue, Baltimore, MD 21217
(410) 225-0001; (800) 899-7533
FAX (410) 728-8957

282. Restored 19th-century Federal-style stone farmhouse surrounded by acres of rolling pasture and woods. Seven-foot windows provide lots of cheery light and give each room a remarkable view. Visit nearby Harpers Ferry, Antietam Battlefield, and more. Three guest rooms with private and shared baths. Full breakfast. $85-100.

Aspen Hall Inn

405 Boyd Avenue, 25401
(304) 263-4385

This majestic 18th-century limestone mansion is surrounded by several acres of lawn and woods. An evening stroll will lead to a footbridge crossing the Tuscarora Creek. Stop by the gazebo to enjoy a cool drink and watch the ducks. Then explore the recently restored 1757 private fort. Five antique furnished queen-size guest rooms are air-conditioned. Fireplace and extra beds available. After a delicious country breakfast, there is outlet shopping and Harpers Ferry nearby.

Hosts: Gordon and LouAnne Claucherty
Rooms: 5 (PB) $95
Full Breakfast
Credit Cards: A, B
Notes: 2, 9, 10, 11, 12

Pulpit & Palette Inn

516 West John Street, 25401
(304) 263-7012

Oriental ambiance in a Victorian home. Two bedrooms sharing bath. Morning coffee/tea with shortbread and newspaper served in bed. Full breakfast, afternoon tea, evening drinks and hors d'oeuvres. Fifty-store outlet one block away. Other attractions and golf nearby. No children. No smoking.

Hosts: Bill and Janet Starr
Rooms: 2 (SB) $75
Full Breakfast
Credit Cards: A, B, D
Notes: 2, 9, 12

MIDDLEWAY

Blue Ridge Bed and Breakfast

Route 2, Box 3895, Berryville, VA 22611
(703) 955-1246; (800) 296-1246

Beautiful stone mansion built in 1760 in an 18th-century village. Close to Harpers Ferry. Romantic rooms and suite. Working fireplaces in bedrooms. Great hospitality. Walking tours and lectures given. On the National Register of Historic Places. $90-150.

MOOREFIELD

McMechen House Inn Bed and Breakfast

109 North Main Street, 26836
(304) 538-7173; (800) 2 WVA INN (reservations)

Return to the mid-1800s and imagine a time of delicate antebellum grace backdropped against roaring political activity. This Greek Revival home, circa 1853, is in historic Moorefield, and served as Civil War headquarters to both Union and Confederate forces as military control of this lovely valley changed hands many times. Here guests will find excellent food, spacious rooms, friendship, and generous hospitality. Hiking, golfing, train excursions, and wineries nearby. Lunch and dinner

NOTES: Credit cards accepted: A MasterCard; B Visa; C American Express; D Discover Card; E Diner's Club; F Other; 2 Personal checks accepted; 3 Lunch available; 4 Dinner available; 5 Open all year;

available on the weekends. Licensed to serve West Virginia wines. Potomac Highlands area.

Hosts: Linda, Bob, and Larry Curtis
Rooms: 7 (4 PB; 3 SB) $60-85
Full Breakfast
Credit Cards: A, B, C, E
Notes: 2, 3, 4, 5, 7 (limited), 9, 10, 11, 12

ROMNEY

Hampshire House 1884

165 North Grafton Street, 26757
(304) 822-7171

Completely renovated 1884 brick home. Period furniture, fireplaces, and air conditioning; quiet. Private baths and garden The charm of the 1880s with the comforts of today in a sleepy small town on the beautiful south branch of the Potomac River. Therapeutic massage available. No smoking.

Hosts: Jane and Scott Simmons
Rooms: 5 (PB) $65-85
Full Breakfast
Credit Cards: A, B, C, D, E
Notes: 2, 5, 9, 14

SHEPHERDSTOWN

Stonebrake Cottage

P.O. Box 1612, Shepherd Grade Road, 25443
(304) 876-6607

Stonebrake Cottage offers a private getaway near historic Shepherdstown on a 145-acre farm. The Victorian cottage furnished with antiques has a fully equipped kitchen, two bathrooms, three bedrooms, and central air. It is within minutes of the C&O Canal Tow Path, Harpers Ferry, Antietam Battlefields, Blue Ridge outlet center, and the Charles Town race track. Golf and horseback riding are available nearby. Discount available for one-week stays.

Host: Anne Small
Rooms: 3 (2 PB; 1 SB) $80-90
Full Breakfast
Credit Cards: A, B
Notes: 2, 5, 8, 9, 10, 12, 13, 14

Thomas Shepherd Inn

Box 1162, 25443
(304) 876-3715

Small, charming inn in a quaint, historic Civil War town that offers that special hospitality of the past. Guests find fresh flowers at their bedsides, fluffy towels and special soaps in their baths, complimentary beverage by the fireside, memorable breakfasts. Picnics available.

Host: Margaret Perry
Rooms: 6 (PB) $55-125
Full Breakfast
Credit Cards: A, B, C, D
Notes: 2, 5, 7 (limited), 8 (over 12), 9, 10, 12, 13

Thomas Shepherd Inn

SUMMIT POINT

Amanda's Bed and Breakfast

1428 Park Avenue, Baltimore, MD 21217
(410) 225-0001; (800) 899-7533
FAX (410) 728-8957

114. In the quaint village of Summit Point near Harpers Ferry. Decorated with cheery mixture of old and new. Old-fashioned hospitality for the crowd-weary traveler. Many activities in the area, including hiking, bicycling, and sightseeing. Two rooms with private baths. Continental breakfast. $70.

Blue Ridge Bed and Breakfast

Route 2, Box 3895, Berryville, VA 22611
(703) 955-1246; (800) 296-1246

6 Pets welcome; 8 Children welcome; 9 Social drinking allowed; 10 Tennis available; 11 Swimming available; 12 Golf available; 13 Skiing available; 14 May be booked through travel agents.

Small bed and breakfast inn between Harpers Ferry and Winchester, Virginia. Tucked away on a lovely tree-lined side street in quaint rural village. Decorated with a charming mixture of old and new collectibles, baskets, and quilts. Old-fashioned hospitality welcomes the crowd-weary traveler. $60.

VALLEY CHAPEL/WESTON

Ingeberg Acres Bed and Breakfast

Millstone Road, P.O. Box 199, 26446
(304) 269-2834

Guests can have a unique experience at this scenic 450-acre horse and cattle farm seven miles from Weston. The three air-conditioned guest rooms have shared bath. Enjoy patio, deck, and pool. Casual atmosphere, private pond for fishing, seasonal hunting, hiking, and bird watching. Full breakfast. No smoking.

Hosts: Inge and John Mann
Rooms: 3 (SB) $59
Full Breakfast
Credit Cards: None
Notes: 2, 5, 8, 9, 11, 12

WHITE SULPHUR SPRINGS

Blue Ridge Bed and Breakfast

Route 2, Box 3895, Berryville, VA 22611
(703) 955-1246; (800) 296-1246

Mansion built in 1819 just three blocks from famous Greenbrier resort and spa. Outside Greenbrier State Forest. Close to National Fish Hatchery. Trout-stocked rivers. Skiing and white-water rafting. $65-90.

The James Wylie House Bed and Breakfast

208 East Main Street, 24986
(304) 536-9444; (800) 870-1613

Circa 1819 Georgian Colonial house, this bed and breakfast is in a small-town setting ten blocks from the Greenbrier Resort and nine miles from historic Lewisburg. Large, spacious rooms offer comfort in this historic home. A family suite and log cabin guest house offer accommodations as well. The Wylie House has been given excellent reviews in a national golf magazine, *Mid-Atlantic Country* magazine, and statewide newspapers.

Hosts: Cheryl and Joe Griffith
Rooms: 4 (PB) $65-120
Full Breakfast
Credit Cards: A, B, C
Notes: 2, 5, 8, 9, 10, 11, 12, 13

The James Wylie House

NOTES: Credit cards accepted: A MasterCard; B Visa; C American Express; D Discover Card; E Diner's Club; F Other; 2 Personal checks accepted; 3 Lunch available; 4 Dinner available; 5 Open all year;

Wisconsin

Albany Guest House

405 South Mill Street, 53502
(608) 862-3636

Enjoy a restored, spacious block house in the heart of south central Wisconsin's Swiss communities. The refinished wood floors support Oriental carpets, king- and queen-size beds, antiques, and interesting pieces. Swing or rock among the flowers on the front porch, or stroll the two acres of lawn and gardens. Light the master bedroom fireplace or hike the Sugar River Trail.

Hosts: Bob and Sally Braem
Rooms: 4 (PB) $55-68
Full Breakfast
Credit Cards: None
Notes: 2, 5, 8, 9, 11, 12, 13

ALGOMA

Amberwood Beach Inn

N7136 Highway 42 Lakeshore Drive, 54201
(414) 487-3471; (602) 968-2850 (winter)

Lake Michigan beachfront. Private wooded acreage on the shores of Lake Michigan, less than ten miles from Door County. Large luxury suites, each with private bath and double French doors with private decks opening to the beach. Whirlpool tub, wet bars, refrigerators, Finnish sauna, and hot tub. Sleep to the sound of the waves, awaken to a sunrise over the water. Call for rates.

Hosts: Jan and George
Rooms: 5 (PB)
Full Breakfast

Credit Cards: A, B
Notes: 2, 8, 9, 11, 12

ALMA

The Gallery House

215 North Main Street, 54610
(608) 685-4975

Historic charm and a gourmet breakfast in the hosts' 1861 mercantile building. Three guest rooms with air conditioning. Visit the Gallery and Spice Shop for sculpture, photography, watercolors, herbs, spices, and gift items. Call for rates.

Hosts: Jan and Joe Hopkins
Rooms: 3 (1 PB; 2 SB)
Full Breakfast
Credit Cards: A, B
Notes: 2, 5, 9, 10, 11, 12, 13

Laue House Inn

Box 176, 54610
(608) 685-4923

The Laue House Inn is the best remaining example of domestic Italianate architecture in Buffalo County. Placed on the National Register of Historic Places in 1979. Step back in time and enjoy the moderately priced rooms of one of Alma's oldest and most elegant houses. There are six guest rooms with TV, air conditioning, and coffee. Fish cleaning facilities, gas grill for a picnic, canoe rental, bike rental, and public beach with tennis courts are also available. Basketball, hiking trails, and golf course are nearby.

Rooms: 6 (SB) $25-38
Continental Breakfast
Credit Cards: None
Notes: 2, 6, 8, 9, 10, 11, 12

6 Pets welcome; 7 Smoking allowed; 8 Children welcome; 9 Social drinking allowed; 10 Tennis available; 11 Swimming available; 12 Golf available; 13 Skiing available; 14 May be booked through travel agents.

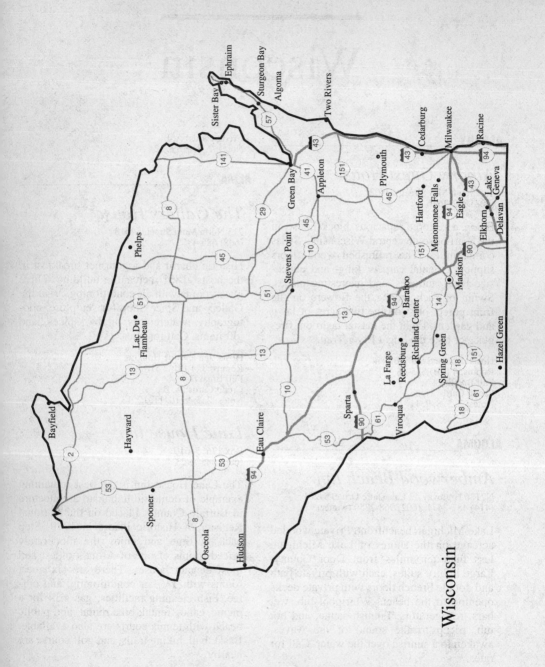

Wisconsin

APPLETON

The Queen Anne Bed and Breakfast

837 East College Avenue, 54911
(414) 739-7966

This three-story Queen Anne-style home has lovely oak trim, oak and maple floors, exquisite beveled and stained-glass windows, and fine period antique furnishings. Air-conditioned sleeping rooms with queen-size beds. Full breakfast is served on weekends; Continental on weekdays.Gracious hosts invite guests to relax and enjoy the nostalgia of times gone by. Within walking distance of Lawrence University. Visit the Houdini collection and the world's first hydroelectrically lighted home.

Hosts: Susan and Larry Bogenschutz
Rooms: 3 (1 PB; 2 SB) $60-85
Full or Continental Breakfast
Credit Cards: None
Notes: 2, 5, 10, 11, 12, 13

BARABOO

Baraboo's Gollmar Guest House

422 Third Street, 53913
(608) 356-9432

Elegant, 1889 Victorian Circus home. Original furniture, antiques, chandeliers, hand-painted murals, and beveled glass. Oak and maple wood floors. Untouched beaded oak woodwork, charming guest parlor library. Romantic guest rooms, queen-size beds, and private baths. Full outdoor patio, picnic areas, and gardens on grounds. Central air conditioning. Four blocks from downtown Baraboo and Circus World Museum, five minutes from the Crane Foundation and Devils Lake State Park, and ten minutes from the Delton/Dells area. Rates are subject to change

Hosts: Tom and Linda Luck
Rooms: 4 (2-3 PB; 1-2 SB) $50-65
Full Breakfast
Credit Cards: A, B
Notes: 2, 5, 8 (over 7), 9, 10, 11, 12, 13

Pinehaven Bed and Breakfast

E13083 Highway 33, 53913
(608) 356-3489

This chalet-style inn overlooks a scenic valley and small private lake. Each distinctly different guest room has a queen-size or twin beds; some have wicker furniture or antiques. The common room has a fireplace, TV/VCR, game table, and baby grand piano. Take a stroll in this inviting setting. Ask about the private guest house. Area activities include Devils Lake State Park, Circus World Museum, Wisconsin Dells International Crane Foundation, and ski resorts. Excellent restaurants nearby.

Hosts: Lyle and Marge Getschman
Rooms: 4 (PB) $65-95
Full Breakfast
Credit Cards: A, B
Notes: 2, 5, 8 (over 5), 9, 10, 11, 12, 13

BAYFIELD

The Old Rittenhouse Inn

301 Rittenhouse Avenue, 54814
(715) 779-5111

Elegant accommodations in the quaint village of Bayfield, the gateway to the Apostle Islands. Three Victorian homes are graced with lovely antiques and accented with fresh flowers and holiday adornments. All guest rooms are furnished with wood-burning fireplaces and private baths. Six-course, fixed-price dinners, featured in *Gourmet* magazine, change daily to utilize the area's fresh fruits and fish. Summer theater, sailing, and skiing nearby. Holiday dinner concerts, getaways, and other special events. Free brochure. Open year-round.

NOTES: Credit cards accepted: A MasterCard; B Visa; C American Express; D Discover Card; E Diner's Club; F Other; 2 Personal checks accepted; 3 Lunch available; 4 Dinner available; 5 Open all year; 6 Pets welcome; 7 Smoking allowed; 8 Children welcome; 9 Social drinking allowed; 10 Tennis available; 11 Swimming available; 12 Golf available; 13 Skiing available; 14 May be booked through travel agents.

Hosts: Mary and Jerry Phillips
Rooms: 20 (PB) $99-199
Continental Breakfast
Credit Cards: A, B
Notes: 2, 3, 4, 5, 8, 10, 11, 12, 13

BELLEVILLE

Abendruh
Bed and Breakfast
Swiss Style

7019 Gehin Road, 53508
(608) 424-3808

Abendruh stands for peaceful and relaxing lodging. Guest rooms are large, uniquely decorated, cool and relaxing in the summer, and warm and cozy in the winter. Take a leisurely walk or sit by a crackling fire. Enjoy Swiss and Norwegian settlements in neighboring villages. Visit many cultural events in the capital city of Wisconsin. Shopping, biking, and cross-country ski trails and parks are nearby. Featured as an exceptional bed and breakfast in *Wisconsin*, January 1992.

Host: Mathilde Jaggi
Rooms: 2 (PB) $45-65
Full Breakfast
Credit Cards: A, B
Notes: 2, 5, 10, 11, 12, 13

CEDARBURG

Stagecoach Inn

West 61 North 520, Washington Avenue, 53012
(414) 375-0208

The Stagecoach Inn is a historic, restored 1853 stone building of Greek Revival style. Its 12 cozy rooms feature stenciled walls and Laura Ashley comforters, central air conditioning, and private baths. Six suites with large whirlpool baths are available. In the heart of historic Cedarburg, the inn also features an on-premises pub with a 100-year-old bar and a chocolate shop. Restaurants, antique shops, and winery within walking distance.

Hosts: Liz and Brook Brown
Rooms: 13 (PB) $65-95
Continental Breakfast
Credit Cards: A, B, C, D, E
Notes: 2, 5, 9, 10, 11, 12, 13, 14

The Washington House Inn

West 62 North, 573 Washington Avenue, 53012
(414) 375-3550; (800) 554-4717

Built in 1884 and listed on the national registry, the Washington House Inn is in the heart of the Cedarburg historic district. Rooms feature antique furnishings, whirlpool baths, and fireplaces. Walking distance to Cedar Creek Settlement, antique shops, and fine dining.

Host: Wendy Porterfield
Rooms: 34 (PB) $61.95-167.75
Continental Breakfast
Credit Cards: A, B, C, D, E, F
Notes: 2, 5, 7, 8, 9, 10, 11, 12, 13, 14

CHETEK

Canoe Bay
Inn and Cottages

W16065 Hogback Road, 54728
(800) 568-1995

Wisconsin's ultimate getaway destination. Share the seclusion of this special hideaway with guests who want the very best! The inn is built in the grand tradition of northern lodges with a huge fieldstone fireplace and soaring cedar ceilings. Suites have oversized whirlpools. The lodge sits on the shore of a 50-acre crystal-clear, spring-fed private lake. Cottages are ultra-luxurious with fireplaces and private decks! The grounds include a 280-acre private forest of aspen, oak, and maple. Falls are brilliant with color. Winter sports of every type are available. Simply the best!

Hosts: Dan and Lisa Dobrowolski
Rooms: 4 (PB) $89-189
Cottages: 4 (PB)
Full Breakfast
Credit Cards: A, B, D
Notes: 5, 11, 12, 13

NOTES: Credit cards accepted: A MasterCard; B Visa; C American Express; D Discover Card; E Diner's Club; F Other; 2 Personal checks accepted; 3 Lunch available; 4 Dinner available; 5 Open all year;

Allyn Mansion

DELAVAN

Allyn Mansion Inn

511 East Walworth Avenue, 53115
(414) 728-9090

This meticulously restored 1885 national register mansion, in Wisconsin's Southern Gateways region, offers an authentic Victorian setting. Guests are encouraged to enjoy the entire house with its spacious rooms and fine antique furnishings. Read by one of the ten marble fireplaces, play the grand piano, peruse the collections of Victoriana, have a good soak in a copper bathtub, or swap stories with the hosts on restoration or antiquing.

Hosts: Joe Johnson and Ron Markwell
Rooms: 8 (S6B) $80-90
Full Breakfast
Credit Cards: A, B
Notes: 2, 5, 9, 10, 11, 12, 13, 14 (weekdays only)

EAGLE

Eagle Centre House

W370 S9590 Highway 67, 53119
(414) 363-4700

A replicated 1846 Greek Revival stagecoach inn decorated with authentic antiques on 20 secluded acres in the southern Kettle

Morraine Forest. Five large chambers with private baths, two with whirlpools. Near "Old World Wisconsin," the State of Wisconsin's Outdoor Living History Museum. Ski, bike, hike, shop, golf, swim, fish, or go horseback riding.

Hosts: Riene Wells (Herriges) and Dean Herriges
Rooms: 5 (PB) $85-125
Full Breakfast
Credit Cards: A, B, C
Notes: 2, 5, 9, 11, 12, 13, 14

EAU CLAIRE

Otter Creek Inn

2536 Highway 12, 54701
(715) 832-2945

Enjoy romantic double whirlpools, breakfast in bed, warm hospitality, and a crackling fire in the great room. This spacious three-story inn with country Victorian decor is nestled on one wooded acre. Relax amid the magnificent ambience of area antiques, and watch the deer and other wildlife saunter by on their way to the creek. Imagine all this country charm less than three minutes from numerous restaurants, shops, and museums.

Hosts: Randy and Shelley Hansen
Rooms: 5 (PB) $59-129
Continental Breakfast
Credit Cards: A, B, C, D
Notes: 2, 5, 9, 10, 11, 12, 13

Otter Creek Inn

6 Pets welcome; 8 Children welcome; 9 Social drinking allowed; 10 Tennis available; 11 Swimming available; 12 Golf available; 13 Skiing available; 14 May be booked through travel agents.

ELKHORN

Ye Olde Manor House

N7622, St. Rd. 12, 53121
(414) 742-2450

Country manor house, circa 1905, in a secluded setting overlooking a hillside and
Lauderdale Lakes. The suite features a private bath and sleeps up to five. The hosts
invite guests to relax and socialize in the
spacious living room or on the sun porch.
Sumptuous breakfast of home-baked goodies; special diets are honored. Enjoy hiking
or biking on the quiet country roads. In winter, skiing is available.

Hosts: Babette and Marvin Henschel
Rooms: 4 (2 PB; 2 SB) $50-90
Full Breakfast
Credit Cards: A, B, C, D
Notes: 2, 5, 8, 11, 12, 13, 14

EPHRAIM

Eagle Harbor Inn

9914 Water Street, Box 72, 54211
(414) 854-2121

Nestled in the heart of historic Ephraim,
Door County, Eagle Harbor is a gracious,
antique-filled country inn. This bed and
breakfast is across from the lake, and close
to the boat ramp, golf course, park, beach,
and cross-country ski trails.

Hosts: Ronald and Barbara Schultz
Rooms: 9 (PB) $70-135
Full Breakfast
Credit Cards: A, B
Notes: 2, 5, 9, 10, 11, 12, 13, 14

Hillside Hotel

9980 Highway 42, 54211
(414) 854-2417; (800) 423-7023

Our beautifully restored 1890s country-
Victorian inn overlooks Eagle Harbor on
Green Bay. Special to this inn are the full,
delightful breakfasts and afternoon teas;
feather beds; a spectacular view from the
100-foot veranda and most guest rooms;
antique furnishings; and a large, private
beach. The hosts also have two deluxe
housekeeping cottages. Near galleries,
shops, water sports, cultural events. Hillside is listed in the National Register of
Historic Places.

Rooms: 12 (SB) $68-89
Full Breakfast
Credit Cards: A, B, D
Notes: 2, 5, 8, 10, 11, 12, 13

GREEN BAY

The Astor House

637 South Monroe Avenue, 54301
(414) 432-3585

Rooms in five decorative motifs indulge
guests: restful Victorian London Room;
country French Marseilles Garden; expansive third-floor Hong Kong retreat; the contemporary surprise of New York loft; and
desert-palate of Laredo. Private baths,
whirlpools, fireplaces, refrigerators, cable
TV, telephone. Stereos, videos, and CDs
provide first-class comfort. Outstanding
bakery, fruit, and gourmet coffee greet the
guests each morning. Ideal choice for business or vacation. Tennis and golf nearby.
Children welcome.

Hosts: Doug Landwehr and Nan Nelson
Rooms: 5 (PB) $72-150
Continental Breakfast
Credit Cards: A, B, C
Notes: 2, 5, 8, 9, 10, 12, 14

HARTFORD

Jordan House

81 South Main Street, 53027
(414) 673-5643

This warm and comfortable Victorian
home, furnished with period antiques, is
forty miles from Milwaukee. Near Majestic
Holy Hill Shrine, Horicon Wildlife Refuge,
and Pike Lake State Park. Walk to state's
largest antique auto museum featuring

Kissel automobiles, antique shops, and downtown shopping.

Rooms: 4 (1 PB; 3 SB) $55-65
Full Breakfast
Credit Cards: A, B
Notes: 2, 5, 8, 10, 11, 12, 13

HAYWARD

Mustard Seed

205 California Avenue, 54843
(715) 634-2908

Relax in the indoor private spas or the outdoor massaging hot tub. Light a fire on a cold night or enjoy the air conditioning on a hot day. Enjoy a complimentary glass of wine on the glider in the private garden/yard. The hosts have five totally different bedrooms and one suite. Two have cable TV. Let the hosts' 100-year-old home offer a respite after a day of skiing, hiking, biking, boating, shopping, or reading. Feed the ducks and picnic at the pond. Come and be pampered.

Hosts: Marty and Mary Gervais
Rooms: 5 (PB) $60-85
Full Breakfast
Credit Cards: A, B, D
Notes: 2, 5, 8, 9, 10, 11, 12, 13

HAZEL GREEN

DeWinters of Hazel Green

2225 Main Street, P.O. Box 384, 53811
(608) 854-2768

DeWinters of Hazel Green is housed in a Federal and Greek Revival-style building, built of brick 145 years ago for John Faherty's home and store. By the end of the century, the building was a hotel hosting up to 45 people a night. The property was purchased by Edward Simison in 1946, and his son, Don, started renovation of DeWinters in 1984. The store and the house are furnished with heirlooms from the Simison family. Come, enjoy a quiet mining town, close to Galena, Illinois, and Dubuque,

Iowa, the Point of Beginning, and the cutest little gal in southwest Wisconsin.

Hosts: Don and Cari Simison
Rooms: 3 (1 PB; 2 SB) $45-75
Full Breakfast
Credit Cards: None
Notes: 2, 5, 8 (call), 11, 12, 13

Wisconsin House Stage Coach Inn

2105 Main Street, 53811-0071
(608) 854-2233

The inn is a historic, country-furnished bed and breakfast. Built in 1846 as a stagecoach inn, it now offers six guest rooms and two guest suites. Just 10 minutes from Galena, 12 minutes from Dubuque, and 15 minutes from Platteville. The inn is convenient to all the attractions of the tri-state area.

Hosts: Ken and Pat Disch
Rooms: 8 (6 PB; 2 SB) $60-110
Full Breakfast
Credit Cards: A, B
Notes: 2, 4, 5, 8, 9, 11, 12, 13, 14

HUDSON

Jefferson-Day House

1109 Third Street, 54016
(715) 386-7111

This 1857 home offers antique collections, air-conditioned rooms, double whirlpools, gas fireplaces, and three-course fireside breakfasts. The pleasing decor and friendly

Jefferson-Day House

atmosphere will relax guests, while the nearby St. Croix River, Octagon House Museum, and Phipps Theatre for the Arts will bring enjoyment.

Hosts: Sharon and Wally Miller
Rooms: 4 (PB) $79-159
Full Breakfast weekends
Continental Breakfast weekdays
Credit Cards: A, B, C, D
Notes: 2, 5, 8 (over 9), 9, 11, 12, 13, 14

Phipps Inn

Phipps Inn

1005 Third Street, 54016
(715) 386-0800

Described as the "Grand Dame" of Queen Anne houses in historic Hudson, this 1884 Victorian mansion offers authentic furnishings and cozy suites, some with fireplaces and whirlpools. Guests enjoy three parlors, two porches, a baby grand piano, and lavish and leisurely breakfasts in bed or in the elegant dining room. Only 30 minutes from Minneapolis/St. Paul. A romantic retreat.

Hosts: Cyndi and John Berglund
Rooms: 6 (PB) $89-159
Full Breakfast
Credit Cards: A, B
Notes: 2, 5, 9, 10, 11, 12, 13, 14

LAC DU FLAMBEAU

Ty-Bach

3104 Simpson Lane, 54538
(715) 588-7851

For a relaxing getaway anytime of the year, share this modern home on the shore of a tranquil northwoods lake with 80 acres of woods to explore. Guest quarters include a large living area and a deck overlooking "Golden Pond." Visit the area attractions: the cranberry marshes, the Native American Museum, pow-wows, professional theater, wilderness cruises, and more. Golf is 12 miles away. Guests are pampered with delicious country breakfasts served at flexible times.

Hosts: Kermit and Janet Bekkum
Rooms: 2 (PB) $50-60
Full Breakfast
Credit Cards: None
Notes: 2, 5, 6, 9, 11, 12, 13

LA FARGE

Trillium

Route 2, Box 121, 54639
(608) 625-4492

One's own private cottage on this farm amid 85 acres of fields and woods near a tree-lined brook. Experience Wisconsin in a thriving Amish farm community just 35 miles southeast of La Crosse. Children under 12 stay free.

Host: Rosanne Boyett
Cottage: 1 (PB) $65-70
Full Breakfast
Credit Cards: None
Notes: 2, 5, 8, 9, 10, 11, 12, 13

LAKE GENEVA

Eleven Gables Inn on the Lakes

493 Wrigley Drive, 53147
(414) 248-8393

Nestled in evergreen amid giant oaks in the Edgewater historical district, this quaint lakeside Carpenter's Gothic inn offers privacy in a prime area. Romantic bedrooms, bridal chamber, and unique country cottages all have fireplaces, down comforters, baths, TVs, and wet bars or cocktail refrigerators. Some have lattice courtyards, balconies, and private entrances. A private pier provides exclusive water activities. Bike rentals are available. This charming "Newport of the Midwest" community provides fine dining, boutiques, and entertainment year-round. Call for rates and packages

Host: A. Milliette
Rooms: 12 (PB)
Full Breakfast weekends
Continental Breakfast midweek
Credit Cards: A, B, C, E
Notes: 5, 7, 8, 9, 10, 11, 12, 13, 14

T. C. Smith Inn
Historic Bed and Breakfast

865 Main Street, 53147
(414) 248-1097; (800) 423-0233

Experience and recapture the majesty of 19th-century ambience at the downtown T. C. Smith Inn (circa 1845), complete with Oriental carpets, fine period antiques, and European paintings. Traditional to the grand Victorian era, the inn offers eight elegant, spacious, and bright guest chambers with a lake view and romantic surroundings. Buffet breakfast is served in the grand parlor under a crystal chandelier before the marble fireplace hearth. A garden and waterfall in the midst of new classic statues grace the large courtyard.

Hosts: The Marks family
Rooms: 8 (PB) $65-275
Full Breakfast
Credit Cards: A, B, C, D, E
Notes: 2, 5, 6, 7, 8, 9, 10, 11, 12, 13, 14

MADISON

Annie's Bed and Breakfast

2117 Sheridan Drive, 53704
(608) 244-2224

When guests want the world to go away, they come to Annie's Bed and Breakfast. This quiet little inn on Warner Park offers a beautiful view and deluxe accommodations. Enjoy the romantic gazebo surrounded by butterfly gardens or the lily pond by the terrace for morning coffee, followed by a sumptuous breakfast. The two-room suites are cozy with antiques, gorgeous quilts, and down comforters. Double Jacuzzi is available. Convenient to everything.

Hosts: Anne and Larry Stuart
Suites: 4 (PB) $84-100
Full Breakfast
Credit Cards: A, B, C
Notes: 2, 5, 8 (over 10), 9, 10, 11, 12, 13

Arbor House
An Environmental Inn

3402 Monroe Street, 53711
(608) 238-2981

Across the street from the UW Arboretum with its 1,200 acres ideal for biking, walking, and bird watching, Arbor House is on a large landscaped lot with native gardens and an abundance of trees. While preserving the charm of this nationally registered historic home, the inn is evolving into a model for urban ecology. The original wood floors, natural stone fireplaces, and sunny breakfast room are admired by visitors. Whirlpools and televisions in some rooms. A full gourmet breakfast is served weekends. Weekdays, breakfast is Continental plus. Guests are treated to a Gehl's Iced Cappuccino welcome beverage, a canoeing pass and Aveda and The Body Shop personal care products. Corporate lodging rate and meeting space are available.

Hosts: John and Cathie Imes
Rooms: 5 (PB) $69-115
Credit Cards: A, B, C
Notes: 2, 5, 8, 9, 10, 11, 12, 13

Canterbury Inn

315 West Gorham, 53703
(608) 283-2541; (800) 838-3850
FAX (608) 283-2541

Canterbury Inn is a literary bed and breakfast directly above what has become a Madison classic, Canterbury Booksellers

6 Pets welcome; 8 Children welcome; 9 Social drinking allowed; 10 Tennis available; 11 Swimming available; 12 Golf available; 13 Skiing available; 14 May be booked through travel agents.

Coffeehouse. Each of the inn's six rooms is decorated with murals depicting an individual story from Chaucer's *Canterbury Tales*. The rooms also hold bookshelves brimming with old and new titles for guests to enjoy, and a complimentary book and breakfast are provided with each stay. An intimate environment of another age, along with the most contemporary amenities including valet parking, whirlpools, VCRs, microwave ovens, and afternoon wine and cheese. The inn also has in-room FAX machine access, a conference room, and corporate discount plan that, along with its central location in downtown Madison, make it the ideal place for all travelers.

Hosts: Trudy and Harvey Barash
Rooms: 6 (PB) $100-250
Continental Breakfast
Credit Cards: A, B
Notes: 2, 3, 4, 5, 8, 9

MENOMONEE FALLS

Dorshel's Bed and Breakfast Guest House

W140 N7616 Lilly Road, 53051
(414) 255-7866

Contemporary home decorated with beautiful antiques and in a lovely wooded residential area. Enjoy breakfast on a screened porch or in the formal dining room. Play a game of pool or watch the wildlife feast at special feeders. Two fireplaces offer cozy warmth. Only 20 minutes from Milwaukee. Full Continental breakfast always includes Wisconsin's finest cheese, fresh fruits of the season, and special breads and pastries.

Hosts: Dorothy and Sheldon Waggoner
Rooms: 3 (2 PB; 1 SB) $45-60
Continental Breakfast
Credit Cards: None
Notes: 2, 5, 7, 9, 12, 13

MILWAUKEE

Marie's Bed and Breakfast

346 East Wilson Street, 53207
(414) 483-1512

Handsome 1896 Victorian home in historic Bay View district. Six minutes from downtown and seven minutes from the airport. Furnished with heirlooms, collectibles, and original artwork. Full breakfast served in the Fan Room or the garden. Off-street parking provided. Central air conditioning. Please write or call for a brochure.

Host: Marie M. Mahan
Rooms: 4 (S2B) $55-70
Full Breakfast
Credit Cards: A, B
Notes: 2, 5, 8, 9, 10, 11, 12

OSCEOLA

St. Croix River Inn

305 River Street, 54020
(715) 294-4248; (800) 645-8820

A meticulously restored 80-year-old stone home nestled in one of the region's finest recreational areas. Ski at Wild Mountain or Trollhaugen. Canoe or fish in the lovely St. Croix River. Then relax in a suite, some with fireplaces, all with Jacuzzi whirlpool baths. Breakfast served in room.

Host: Bev Johnson
Rooms: 7 (PB) $85-200
Full Breakfast
Credit Cards: A, B, C
Notes: 9, 10

PHELPS

Limberlost Inn

2483 Highway 17, 54554
(715) 545-2685

Modern log home with rustic northwoods charm surrounded by acres of national for-

---

NOTES: Credit cards accepted: A MasterCard; B Visa; C American Express; D Discover Card; E Diner's Club; F Other; 2 Personal checks accepted; 3 Lunch available; 4 Dinner available; 5 Open all year;

est and lakes. Relax on the porch swing, in the hammock, or in the sauna before retiring to the comfort of down pillows and handmade quilts. Enjoy the screened porch, decks, or VCR and movie collection in the living room. Full breakfast is served in front of the fieldstone fireplace in the dining room.

Hosts: Bill and Phoebe McElroy
Rooms: 2 (SB) $55
Full Breakfast
Credit Cards: None
Notes: 2, 5, 9, 11, 12, 13

PLYMOUTH

52 Stafford,
An Irish Guest House

52 Stafford Street, 53073
(414) 893-0552; (800) 421-4667

Listed on the National Register of Historic Places, this inn has 20 rooms, 17 of which have whirlpool baths and cable TV. 52 Stafford features one of the most beautiful pubs in America, serves lunch daily and dinner seven nights a week. Also features a full-time pastry chef. There are 35,000 acres of public recreation land nearby; cross-country skiing, hiking, biking, sports fishing, boating, swimming, and golf. Crystal-clear lakes and beautiful fall colors.

Hosts: Rip and Christine O'Dwanny
Rooms: 20 (PB) $69-99
Full Breakfast weekends
Continental Breakfast weekdays
Credit Cards: A, B, C, D, E
Notes: 2, 3, 4, 5, 6, 7, 8, 9, 10, 11, 12, 13, 14

RACINE

Lochnaiar Inn, Ltd.

1121 Lake Avenue, 53403
(414) 633-3300

On a hill overlooking Lake Michigan, the Lochnaiar Inn is truly exceptional. Six fireplaces and magnificent lake views set this English Tudor a step above the ordinary. Featured in the May 1992 issue of *Chicago* magazine as one of the eight best in the Midwest, Lochnaiar Inn features all private baths, whirlpool and deep empress tubs, suites with fireplaces, cable TV, small meeting rooms, and more. Preferred by Racine's major corporations for their special guests. Guests can be assured of a comfortable and relaxing stay. Fishing and sailing charters available. Full breakfast served weekends; Continental weekdays.

Hosts: Dawn and Jennifer Weisbrod
Rooms: 8 (PB) $75-175
Full and Continental Breakfasts
Credit Cards: A, B, C, D
Notes: 2, 5, 7 (limited), 8, 9, 10, 11, 12, 13

REEDSBURG

Parkview
Bed and Breakfast

211 North Park Street, 53959
(608) 524-4333

In Reedsburg's historic district, this 1895 Queen Anne Victorian home has fish ponds, a windmill, and playhouse enhanc-

Parkview

ing the grounds. Across from City Park and one block from downtown. Discover the original woodwork and hardware, tray ceilings, suitor's window, and built-in buffet inside this cozy home. Wisconsin Dells, Baraboo, and Spring Green are nearby.

Hosts: Tom and Donna Hofmann
Rooms: 4 (2 PB; 2 SB) $55
Full Breakfast
Credit Cards: A, B, C
Notes: 2, 5, 8, 9, 11, 12, 13

RICHLAND CENTER

The Mansion

323 South Central, 53581
(608) 647-2808

This 19-room brick mansion was built in the early 1900s by a lumberman and is just around the corner from the Frank Lloyd Wright Warehouse/Museum in the city of Wright's birth. Quarter-sawn oak woodwork and parquet floors of oak, walnut, and maple. Quietly elegant, but affordable. Air-conditioned, but no TV.

Hosts: Beth Caulkins and Harvey Glanzer
Rooms: 5 (S2B) $25-55
Continental Breakfast
Credit Cards: None
Notes: 2, 5, 6 (call), 7, 8 (over 12), 10, 11, 13

SISTER BAY

Church Hill Inn

425 Gateway Drive, 54234
(414) 854-4885; (800) 422-4906

Door County's only three-star hotel (Mobil Guide 1994). Charming European atmosphere, English antiques in individually decorated rooms—many with double whirlpools. Suites with whirlpools and fireplaces. Common areas with fireplaces, exercise room, sauna, and whirlpool. Includes fabulous breakfast buffet and complimentary hors d'oeuvres. Enjoy the outdoor heated pool in the summer. From November to June, the third night is free.

Hosts: Paul and Joyce Crittenden
Rooms: 34 (PB) $114-169
Full Breakfast
Credit Cards: A, B
Notes: 2, 4 (call), 5, 7 (limited), 8 (over 8), 9, 10, 11, 12, 13

SPARTA

Just-N-Trails Bed and Breakfast Farm Vacation

Route 1, Box 274, 54656
(608) 269-4522; (800) 488-4521

A bed and breakfast specializing in recreation, relaxation, and romance. Separate buildings: Paul Bunyan log cabin, with two bedrooms, whirlpool in the atrium, and a fireplace. The Granary, a perfect playhouse for two, features a whirlpool and fireplace. Little House on the Prairie log cabin with whirlpool and fireplace. Five rooms in 1920 farmhouse on active dairy farm. Laura Ashley linens. Four-course breakfasts. Near famous Elroy-Sparta Bike Trail. Skiing on premises.

Hosts: Donna and Don Justin
Rooms: 8 (7 PB; 1 SB) $65-195
Full Breakfast
Credit Cards: A, B, C, D
Notes: 2, 5, 8, 13, 14

SPOONER

Aunt Martha's Guest House Bed and Breakfast

1602 County Road A, HCR 59, 54801
(715) 635-6857

Guests enjoy many country activities, year-round. Hosts serve a hearty Continental breakfast each morning that features home-baked goods, fresh fruit, and fresh ground coffee and/or herbal teas. The structure was built in 1927 by a logger named Glen Marsh and restored to a country atmosphere with antiques and collectibles. Surrounded by beautiful lakes; just a short

---

NOTES: Credit cards accepted: A MasterCard; B Visa; C American Express; D Discover Card; E Diner's Club; F Other; 2 Personal checks accepted; 3 Lunch available; 4 Dinner available; 5 Open all year;

distance from lake activities. Guests may choose to simply enjoy the peace and quiet of the country.

Hosts: Robert M. Johnson and Mary C. Askov
Rooms: 3 (1 PB; 2 SB) $45-55
Continental Breakfast
Credit Cards: None
Notes: 2, 5, 8, 9, 10, 11, 12, 13

SPRING GREEN

Bettinger House Bed and Breakfast

Highway 23, 53577
(608) 546-2951

This 1904 brick home, once owned by the host's midwife grandmother, is near the world famous House on a Rock, Frank Lloyd Wright's Taliesin, and the American Players Theatre. A home-cooked full breakfast is served every morning.

Hosts: Marie and Jim Neider
Rooms: 6 (2 PB; 4 SB) $45-55
Full Breakfast
Credit Cards: A, B
Notes: 2, 5, 7, 8, 9, 10, 11, 12, 13, 14

STEVENS POINT

Dreams of Yesteryear Bed and Breakfast

1100 Brawley Street, 54481
(715) 341-4525

Dreams of Yesteryear

Designed by J. H. Jeffers, this bed and breakfast was built in 1901 and is lavish in Victorian detail. Period furniture is evident throughout. The hosts love to visit with guests and talk about this cozy home and its furnishings. The home is listed on the National Register of Historic Places, and its restoration was featured in *Victorian Homes* magazine.

Hosts: Bonnie and Bill Maher
Rooms: 5 (PB) $55-105
Full Breakfast
Credit Cards: A, B, D
Notes: 2, 5, 8 (over 12), 9, 10, 11, 12, 13, 14

Victorian Swan on Water

1716 Water Street, 54481
(715) 345-0595

This 1889 home creates happy memories with a timeless and contented elegance. A variety of woods in Victorian architecture, crown moldings, fireplaces, a secret Roman bath with a whirlpool, and quiet garden settings invite a gentle relaxation. Near a historic downtown district, river walks, ski trails, golf courses, and forest preserves. Bountiful breakfasts, TV room, meeting room, and air conditioning complete the guests' comfort.

Host: Joan Ouellette
Rooms: 4 (PB) $55-120
Full Breakfast
Credit Cards: A, B, C, D
Notes: 2, 5, 9, 10, 11, 12, 13, 14

STURGEON BAY

Inn at Cedar Crossing

336 Louisiana Street, 54235
(414) 743-4200

Warm hospitality, elegant antique-filled guest rooms, and creative regional cuisine are a tradition at this most intimate Door County inn listed on the National Register of Historic Places. Luxurious whirlpool tubs, cozy fireplaces, and evening refreshments await pampered travelers. Exquisite dining

6 Pets welcome; 8 Children welcome; 9 Social drinking allowed; 10 Tennis available; 11 Swimming available; 12 Golf available; 13 Skiing available; 14 May be booked through travel agents.

(breakfast, lunch, and dinner) features fresh regional ingredients, scratch bakery, fine wines, and libations. Set in the beauty and culture of Wisconsin's Door Peninsula.

Host: Terry Wulf
Rooms: 9 (PB) $79-135
Continental Breakfast
Credit Cards: A, B, D
Notes: 2, 3, 4, 5, 7 (limited), 8 (call), 9, 10, 11, 12, 13

The Scofield House Bed and Breakfast

908 Michigan Street, P.O. Box 761, 54235
(414) 743-7727

Described as "Door County's most elegant bed and breakfast." Authentic bed and breakfast in turn-of-the-century restored Victorian Queen Anne house, circa 1902. Prominent home of Sturgeon Bay Mayor Bert Scofield. Very ornate interior with in-laid floors and ornamented woodwork. Six guest rooms, each with private bath some with double whirlpool, fireplaces, color TV/cable, and VCR/stereo. Free movie library. High Victorian decor throughout with fine antiques. Air-conditioned. Full gourmet breakfast and afternoon complimentary sweet treats and teas. Call or write for brochure. Mobil Three-Star.

Hosts: Bill and Fran Cecil
Rooms: 6 (PB) $75-185
Full Breakfast
Credit Cards: None
Notes: 2, 5, 9, 10, 11, 12, 13

The Scofield House

White Lace Inn

White Lace Inn

16 North Fifth Avenue, 54235
(414) 743-1105

The White Lace Inn is a romantic getaway featuring three restored turn-of-the-century homes surrounding lovely gardens and a gazebo. The 15 wonderfully inviting guest rooms are furnished with antiques, four-poster and Victorian beds, in-room fire-places in some rooms, and double whirlpool tubs in others.

Hosts: Bonnie and Dennis Statz
Rooms: 15 (PB) $49-160
Continental Breakfast
Credit Cards: A, B, C, D
Notes: 2, 5, 9, 10, 11, 12, 13

TWO RIVERS

Red Forest Bed and Breakfast

1421 25th Street, 54241
(414) 793-1794

The Red Forest Bed and Breakfast is on Wisconsin's east coast. Minutes from Manitowoc, Wisconsin's port city of the Lake Michigan car ferry. Also midway from Chicago and the Door County Pe-ninsula. The hosts invite guests to step back in time to 1907 and enjoy the gra-cious three-story, shingle-style home.

Highlighted with stained-glass windows and heirloom antiques.

Hosts: Kay and Alan Rodewald
Rooms: 4 (2 PB; 2 SB) $60-75
Full Breakfast
Credit Cards: A, B, C
Notes: 2, 5, 8 (call), 9, 10, 11, 12, 13, 14

VIROQUA

Viroqua Heritage Inn Bed and Breakfast

220 East Jefferson Street, 54665
(608) 637-3306

Viroqua Heritage Inn

Memories are made at this elegant and romantic, warm and comfortable 1890 Queen Anne Victorian home complete with antiques, grand piano, fireplace, original gasolier chandeliers, and furnishings. Gorgeous bedrooms, plush robes, and guest concession area. Full breakfast graciously served. The inn is a perfect place for escaping or a great place to start an exploration of beautiful southwest Wisconsin. Amish nearby. Inn-to-inn bicycling and world-class bike routes. Murder mystery weekends. As seen in the April 1993 issue of *Reader's Digest* and the October 1992 *Smithsonian* magazine.

Hosts: Don and Nancy Seevers
Rooms: 4 (2 PB; 2 S1.5B)) $50-75
Full Breakfast
Credit Cards: A, B, C, D
Notes: 2, 5, 8, 9, 10, 11, 12, 13, 14

6 Pets welcome; 8 Children welcome; 9 Social drinking allowed; 10 Tennis available; 11 Swimming available; 12 Golf available; 13 Skiing available; 14 May be booked through travel agents.

Wyoming

Wyoming

BIG HORN

Spahn's Bighorn Mountain Bed and Breakfast

Box 579, 82833
(307) 674-8150

Towering log home and secluded guest cabins on the mountainside in whispering pines. Borders one million acres of public forest with deer and moose. Gracious mountain breakfast served on the deck with binoculars to enjoy the 100-mile view. Owner was a Yellowstone Ranger. Just 15 minutes from Sheridan and I-90.

Hosts: Ron and Bobbie Spahn
Rooms: 4 (PB) $65-100
Full Breakfast
Credit Cards: A, B
Notes: 4, 5, 8, 9, 13

CASPER

Durbin Street Inn Bed and Breakfast

843 South Durbin Street, 82601
(307) 577-5774; FAX (307) 266-5441

Whether traveling for business or pleasure, guests will feel right at home at the Durbin Street Inn. The 1917-built house is furnished mostly with antiques and tastefully decorated to provide a warm, relaxed atmosphere. Full breakfast is included, and other meals are available. Food is plentiful and very good. Within walking distance of downtown Casper, in the "Big Tree" area. Enquire about the Lodging Plus packages.

Hosts: Don and Sherry Frigon
Rooms: 5 (1-PB; 4-SB) $48.15-74.90
Full Breakfast
Credit Cards: A, B, C, D, E
Notes: 3, 4, 5, 7 (limited), 9, 11, 12, 13, 14

CHEYENNE

A. Drummond's Ranch Bed and Breakfast

399 Happy Jack Road, Route 210, 82007
(307) 634-6042

Quiet, gracious retreat conveniently between Cheyenne and Laramie in the Laramie Range, the scenic by-pass for I-80. Adjacent to a state park and five miles to a national forest; mountain biking, fishing, hiking, rock climbing, and cross-country skiing. Bring a horse or mountain bicycle and train at 7,500 feet. Boarding for horses and family pets. Soft Adventure two and three-night packages available. Outdoor hot tub. Added touches: flowers in room, terry-cloth robes for guests during stay; beverages, fresh fruit, and homemade snacks always available. No smoking. Reservations required. AAA rated three diamonds.

Host: Taydie Drummond
Rooms: 3 (1 PB; 2 SB) $60-80
Full Breakfast
Credit Cards: A, B
Notes: 2, 3 and 4 (call), 5, 6, 8, 9, 12, 13, 14

The Howdy Pardner

1920 Tranquility Road, 82009
(307) 634-6493; (307) 637-2702 office

A big Wyoming welcome awaits guests in a relaxed country setting. This very Western

---

NOTES: Credit cards accepted: A MasterCard; B Visa; C American Express; D Discover Card; E Diner's Club; F Other; 2 Personal checks accepted; 3 Lunch available; 4 Dinner available; 5 Open all year; 6 Pets welcome; 7 Smoking allowed; 8 Children welcome; 9 Social drinking allowed; 10 Tennis available; 11 Swimming available; 12 Golf available; 13 Skiing available; 14 May be booked through travel agents.

but modern, secluded ranch home on ten country acres is perched high on a hill, with views all around that invite walkabouts, yet is only ten minutes from Frontier Park, the airport, I-25, and I-80. Area attractions include the Old West Museum, Terry Bison Ranch, Laramie-Fox Park Excursion Trainride, Old Fort Laramie, Oregon Trail Wagon Ruts, Signature Cliff, and Frontier Days "Daddy of 'Em All" rodeos, and night shows during the last full week of July.

Host: Jan Peterson
Rooms: 3 (1 PB; 2 SB) $50-65
Full Breakfast
Credit Cards: A, B
Notes: 2, 5, 6, 8, 9, 10, 11, 12, 13, 14

CODY

Hunter Peak Ranch

Box 1731, Painter Route, 82414
(307) 587-3711

Hunter Peak Ranch, at a 6,700-foot elevation, is in the Shoshone National Forest, with access to North Absaroka and Beartooth Wilderness Areas and Yellowstone National Park. Come enjoy the area's photographic opportunities, hiking, fishing, horseback riding, and pack trips. Closed December 15 through May 15. Minimum stay of three nights.

Hosts: Louis and Shelley Cary
Rooms: 8 (PB) $63.80
Full Breakfast
Credit Cards: None
Notes: 2 (deposit), 3, 4, 7, 8, 9, 11, 14

The Lockhart Inn Bed and Breakfast

109 West Yellowstone Avenue, 82414
(307) 587-6074

The historic home of famous Cody author Caroline Lockhart. Built in the 1890s and refurbished from 1985 to 1991. Seven guest rooms, all with private baths, are decorated in turn-of-the-century style with modern conveniences. Enjoy breakfast in the dining

area where coffee, tea, cider, and brandy are always available. Wood-burning stove in parlor with piano. Within walking distance of Buffalo Bill Historical Center, Cody Nite Rodeo, Old Trail Town, and river rafting.

Host: Cindy Baldwin
Rooms: 7 (PB) $55-75
Full Breakfast
Credit Cards: A, B, D
Notes: 2, 3, 5, 8, 9, 10, 11, 12, 13, 14

Trout Creek Inn

Yellowstone Highway 14, 16, 20 West, 82414
(307) 587-6288

Imagine basking in the morning sunshine, a sumptuous breakfast on a lawn table, and scenic mountains all around (unless guests would prefer to be served in their rooms). This bed and breakfast is in the valley Theodore Roosevelt called the "world's most scenic." Private trout fishing, swimming, horseback riding, and picture taking. Four kitchenettes available; accessible to the handicapped. Lunch and dinner nearby. Tennis and golf is 15 miles away.

Hosts: Bert and Norma Sowerwine
Rooms: 21 (PB) $31.50-73.00
Continental Breakfast
Credit Cards: A, B, C, D, F
Notes: 2, 5, 6, 7, 8, 9, 11, 13

ENCAMPMENT

Platt's Rustic Mountain Lodge

Star Route 49, 82352
(307) 327-5539

A peaceful mountain view on a working ranch and wholesome country atmosphere. Lots of western hospitality. Horseback riding, pack trips, youth programs, photographic safaris, fishing, hiking, and rock hounding; fully guided wilderness tours available to ranch recreational activities and scenic mountain areas. Cattle drives, Indian tepee, private fishing ponds and streams with cabin rental. Enjoy the flora and fauna,

NOTES: Credit cards accepted: A MasterCard; B Visa; C American Express; D Discover Card; E Diner's Club; F Other; 2 Personal checks accepted; 3 Lunch available; 4 Dinner available; 5 Open all year;

historic trails, and old mining camps, plus snowmobiling and cross-country skiing in the winter. By reservation only. Lodge room and quiet atmosphere for workshops. Private cabin rentals available. Closed Thanksgiving and Christmas.

Hosts: Mayvon and Ron Platt
Rooms: 3 (SB) $55-65
Full or Continental Breakfast
Credit Cards: None
Notes: 2 (for deposit), 3, 4, 6, 8, 9, 10, 11, 12, 13

The Wildflower Inn

JACKSON

The Wildflower Inn

P.O. Box 3724, 83001
(307) 733-4710

A lovely log home with five sunny guest rooms, this bed and breakfast is on three acres of land only five minutes from the Jackson Hole Ski Area, 10 minutes from the town of Jackson, and 30 minutes from Grand Teton.

Hosts: Ken and Sherrie Jern
Rooms: 5 (PB) $110-130
Full Breakfast
Credit Cards: A, B
Notes: 2, 5, 8, 9, 10, 11, 12, 13

LANDER

Country Fare Bed and Breakfast

904 Main Street, 82520
(307) 332-5906

Country Fare is an adventure in old-fashioned charm. Enjoy the delicious English breakfasts, antique-filled bedrooms, and warm hospitality. Lander is the sports enthusiast's dream: hunting, fishing, hiking, snow sports, and more. On direct route to Yellowstone.

Hosts: A. R. and Mary Ann Hoyt
Rooms: 2 (SB) $60
Continental Breakfast
Credit Cards: A, B
Notes: 2, 5, 9, 10, 11, 12, 13, 14

LARAMIE

Annie Moore's Guest House

819 University Avenue, 82070
(307) 721-4177; (800) 552-8992

Restored Queen Anne home with six individually decorated guest rooms, four with sinks. Large, sunny, common living rooms, second-story sun deck. Across the street from the University of Wyoming; two blocks from the Laramie Plains Museum; six blocks from downtown shops, galleries, and restaurants. Just 15 minutes from skiing, camping, biking, and fishing in uncrowded wilderness areas.

Hosts: Ann Acuff and Joe Bundy
Rooms: 6 (SB) $50-60

Annie Moore's Guest House

6 Pets welcome; 8 Children welcome; 9 Social drinking allowed; 10 Tennis available; 11 Swimming available; 12 Golf available; 13 Skiing available; 14 May be booked through travel agents.

Continental Breakfast
Credit Cards: A, B, C, D
Notes: 2, 5, 9, 12, 13

NEWCASTLE

4W Ranch Recreation

1162 Lynch Road, 82701
(307) 746-2815

Looking for the unbeaten path? Spend a
few days on this working cattle ranch with
20,000 acres of diversified rangeland to
explore at leisure. Rates include three
meals a day.

Hosts: Bob and Jean Harshbarger
Rooms: 2 (SB) $60-100 (American Plan)
Full Breakfast
Credit Cards: None
Notes: 2, 3, 4, 5, 7, 8, 9

PINEDALE

Pole Creek Ranch

Box 278, 82941
(307) 367-4433

Relive the charm of the Old West in a rustic
log home overlooking a peaceful meadow
and the spectacular Wind River Mountains.
Pole Creek Ranch features horseback riding, wagon and sleigh rides, wild horse
tours on the Oregon Trail, and a hot tub.
Fishing, hunting, backpacking, white-water
rafting, snowmobiling, skiing, and historic
museums are all close by. Long-term family
stays are welcome.

Hosts: Dexter and Carole Smith
Rooms: 2 (SB) $50
Full Breakfast
Credit Cards: None
Notes: 2, 4, 5, 6, 8, 11, 12, 13

Window on the Winds

10151 Highway 191, Box 135, 82941
(307) 367-2600

The McKays invite guests to this rustic
home. The hosts offer lodge pole pine queen-
size beds, a large common room, all decorated in Western and Plains Indian decor.
Enjoy the breathtaking view of "the Winds"
or relax in the hot tub. Only minutes from
year-round mountain adventures (hiking,
fishing, skiing, and snowmobiling), and less
than two hours from Jackson and Yellowstone. Window on the Winds is the perfect
base for a western Wyoming vacation.

Hosts: Leanne McClain and Doug McKay
Rooms: 4 (SB) $52-60
Full Breakfast
Credit Cards: A, B
Notes: 2, 3, 4, 5, 6, 8, 9, 12, 13, 14

SARATOGA

Hotel Wolf

Box 1298, 82331
(307) 326-5525

The historic Hotel Wolf, built in 1893,
served as a stagecoach stop. During its early
years, the hotel was the hub of the community and noted for its fine food and convivial atmosphere. The same holds true
today. The dining room is acclaimed as one
of the finest in the region. AAA-rated
restaurant. Nearby is a mineral hot springs
and excellent fishing.

Hosts: Doug and Kathleen Campbell
Rooms: 6 (PB) $24-35
Suites: 3 (PB) $55-75
Credit Cards: A, B, C, E
Notes: 2, 3, 4, 5, 7, 8, 9, 10, 11, 12

WHEATLAND

The Blackbird Inn

1101 Eleventh, 82201
(307) 322-4540

This elegant three-story brick home has
four bedrooms and one suite sharing three
baths. Each bedroom has a different decorating theme. The Blackbird Inn is noted for
its wonderful front porch, complete with
swing, wicker furniture, and lemonade in
the summer. On chilly days, sit by the fireplace and sip a cup of herbal tea or hot
chocolate. Great biking, fishing, and bird

NOTES: Credit cards accepted: A MasterCard; B Visa; C American Express; D Discover Card; E Diner's
Club; F Other; 2 Personal checks accepted; 3 Lunch available; 4 Dinner available; 5 Open all year;

The Blackbird Inn

watching nearby. Thirty minutes from the mountains and the Oregon Trail.

Host: Dan Brecht
Rooms: 5 (SB) $35-50
Full Breakfast
Credit Cards: None
Notes: 2, 5, 6, 8, 9, 10, 11, 12, 14

WILSON (JACKSON HOLE)

Teton Tree House

Box 550, 83014
(307) 733-3233

This secluded but convenient mountain lodge is a classic bed and breakfast inn with warm, on-premises hosts. All rooms have private baths, excellent beds, and most have decks and wonderful views. The great room has a fireplace, piano, and walls of books. Breakfast is a low-cholesterol feast featuring huckleberry pancakes, coffee cakes, yeast breads, and other homemade treats. It is only eight miles from Grand Teton National Park, mountain climbing, and the rodeo. The hosts are 30-year locals who delight in sharing information with guests.

Hosts: Chris and Denny Becker
Rooms: 6 (PB) $95-125
Full Breakfast
Credit Cards: A, B, D
Notes: 2, 5, 8, 9, 10, 11, 12, 13

Teton View Bed and Breakfast

2136 Coyote Loop, Box 652, 83014
(307) 733-7954

Rooms all have mountain views, cozy country decor, private entrance, private deck overlooking Teton Mountain range, and comfortable lounge area with books and refrigerator. Convenient location to Yellowstone and Grand Teton national parks.

Hosts: John and Jo Engelhart
Rooms: 3 (1 PB; 2 SB) $60-90
Full Breakfast
Credit Cards: A, B
Notes: 2, 6 (call), 8, 9, 10, 11, 12, 13, 14

6 Pets welcome; 8 Children welcome; 9 Social drinking allowed; 10 Tennis available; 11 Swimming available; 12 Golf available; 13 Skiing available; 14 May be booked through travel agents.

Canada

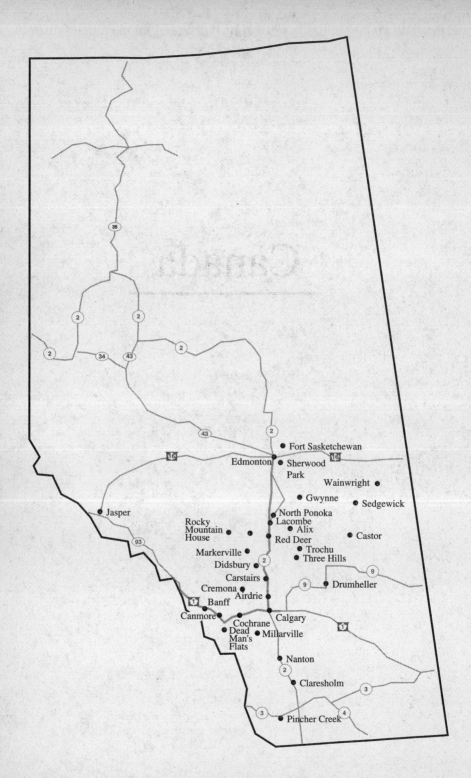

- 35
- 2
- 2
- 2
- 34
- 43
- 2
- 43
- 2
- 16
- 16
- ● Fort Sasketchewan
- Edmonton ● ● Sherwood Park
- ● Gwynne
- Wainwright ●
- ● Sedgewick
- Jasper ●
- Rocky Mountain House ●
- ● North Ponoka
- ● Lacombe
- ● Alix
- ● Red Deer
- ● Castor
- 93
- Markerville ●
- ● Trochu
- ● Three Hills
- Didsbury ●
- 2
- 9
- Carstairs ●
- 9 ● Drumheller
- Cremona ●
- ● Airdrie
- 1
- Banff ●
- Canmore ●
- ● Calgary
- Cochrane ●
- 1
- Dead Man's Flats ●
- ● Millarville
- ● Nanton
- 2
- ● Claresholm
- 3
- 3
- 4
- ● Pincher Creek

Alberta

Alberta

AIRDRIE

Bed and Breakfast
Wild Rose Country
(403) 337-3192

1. Golden Rod Bed and Breakfast is on a working cattle ranch. Three-year-old home with suite in walk-out basement for guest view. One queen size, two singles. Great mountain view. Golf, swimming, and theaters nearby. $35-50.

ALIX

Bed and Breakfast
Wild Rose Country
(403) 337-3192

2. Take a break in peaceful countryside within walking distance of Wildlife Habitat area. Reflexology, rejuvenate in the hot tub, bicycles, cross-country skis all available to guests. One double room and two singles. $30-40.

BANFF

Alberta and Pacific
Bed and Breakfast
P.O. Box 15477, MPO, Vancouver, BC V6B 5B2
(604) 944-1793

This home has three guest rooms on the main floor; one queen-size, one double, and one twin. Each room with private bath.

Visit unforgettable Lake Louise, Banff Centre within walking distance, and see the beauty of the Canadian Rocky Mountains.

Blue Mountain Lodge
Box 2763, T0L 0C0
(403) 762-5134; FAX (403) 762-8081

One block from Banff Avenue, minutes from shopping, restaurants, and hiking trails. Rooms and cabins are unique, and feature spectacular mountain views and period decor, with private or shared bath. Kitchen facilities, full Continental breakfast, complimentary tea, and coffee, sun decks with barbecue. Tennis, swimming, golf, and skiing nearby. No smoking.

Hosts: Hugh and Irene Simpson
Rooms: 12 (7 PB; 5 SB) $55-85
Continental Breakfast
Credit Cards: A, B
Notes: 5, 8, 9, 10, 11, 12, 13

Brewster's Kananaskis
Guest Ranch
Box 964, T0L 0C0
(403) 673-3737; FAX (403) 762-3953

The original Brewster Homestead offers cabin and chalet accommodations featuring antique furnishings, cedar interiors, and private shower baths. On the shores of the Bow River, the guest ranch also has a licensed dining room and cocktail lounge, whirlpool, trail riding, and western barbecues. Golf, white-water rafting, hiking, and mountain biking opportunities are also available. Just 45 minutes west of Calgary; 30 minutes east of Banff.

NOTES: Credit cards accepted: A MasterCard; B Visa; C American Express; D Discover Card; E Diner's Club; F Other; 2 Personal checks accepted; 3 Lunch available; 4 Dinner available; 5 Open all year; 6 Pets welcome; 7 Smoking allowed; 8 Children welcome; 9 Social drinking allowed; 10 Tennis available; 11 Swimming available; 12 Golf available; 13 Skiing available; 14 May be booked through travel agents.

Hosts: The Brewster family
Rooms: 33 (PB) $90
Full Breakfast
Credit Cards: A, B
Notes: 3, 4, 7, 8, 9, 11, 12, 14

CALGARY

Alberta and Pacific Bed and Breakfast

P.O. Box 15477, MPO, Vancouver, BC V6B5B2
(604) 944-1793

Modern, older home, pre-1919, has three upstairs spacious guest rooms; one "honeymoon" room with queen-size bed and ensuite bath; one with twin beds plus a single for king-size bed and ensuite private bath; one with double bed and ensuite private bath.

Barb's Bed and Breakfast

1308 Carlyle Road S.W., T2V 2T8
(403) 255-6596

A quiet spacious home in a well-treed residential area, close to Heritage Park, and minutes from downtown and transit. An easy 80-minute drive to Banff. Small kitchen, TV, sitting area, and private entrance. Full Continental breakfast at the guest's leisure. Queen-size and double rooms. Tennis, golf, and skiing nearby.

Host: Barbara I. Cook
Rooms: 2 (SB) $35-55
Continental Breakfast
Credit Cards: None
Notes: 2, 5, 7 (limited), 9, 10, 12, 13

Harrison's Bed and Breakfast Home

6016 Thornburn Drive N.W., T2K 3P7
(403) 274-7281

Harrison's is a cozy bungalow in a well-treed, quiet residential area of Calgary, where birds and squirrels are regular visitors. Guest's share the comfortable living room and sheltered patio. Breakfast is served overlooking the front garden. Swimming nearby.

Host: Susan Harrison
Rooms: 2 (SB) $50
Full Breakfast
Credit Cards: None
Notes: 2, 5, 9, 11, 13, 14

The Robin's Nest

Box 2, Site 7, Rural Route 8, T2J 2T9
(403) 931-3514

Guests are treated to new luxurious cedar cabins with panoramic mountain views. Succulent rainbow trout, freshly milled whole grain breads, and Saskatoon berries from the farm orchard grace the breakfast table. Sheep, highland cattle, and fjord ponies graze the hillside pastures. Walk the interpretive nature trails through the private wildlife sanctuary. Twenty minutes southwest of Calgary. Experience the serenity and romance of yesteryear on this century-old Jackson family homestead.

Hosts: Bill and Dorothy Jackson
Rooms: 3 (2 PB; 1 SB) $60-80
Full Breakfast
Credit Cards: None
Notes: 5, 8, 9, 10, 11, 12, 13

CANMORE

Alberta and Pacific Bed and Breakfast

P.O. Box 15477, MPO, Vancouver, BC V6B 5B2
(604) 944-1793

Hosts will welcome the guests to their lovely new home 22 kilometers from Banff National Park. The Canmore Nordic Center, site of the 1988 Winter Olympic Nordic Events, is minutes away. Breakfast is homemade and features European and Canadian cuisine. On the second floor one guest room with queen-size bed, one with twin bed. Both rooms have mountain views and full, ensuite bath. On the main floor one guest room with handicapped facilities, double bed and shared bath.

Cougar Creek Inn

P.O. Box 1162, T0L 0M0
(403) 678-4751

Quiet, rustic cedar chalet with mountain views in every direction. Grounds border on Cougar Creek. Land reserve with hiking trails borders property. Hostess is an outdoor enthusiast with a strong love for mountains and can assist guests' plans for local hiking, skiing, canoeing, mountain biking, and backpacking. Bonfire pit, private entrance, fireplace, sitting room with TV, games, private dining, serving area, and sauna.

Host: Patricia Doucette
Rooms: 4 (S2B) $55-60
Full Breakfast
Credit Cards: None
Notes: 2 (for deposit), 3, 5, 8, 9, 10, 11, 12, 13

The Georgetown Inn

1101 Bow Valley Trail; P.O. Box 3327, T0L 0M0
(403) 678-3439

At the gateway to Banff National Park, the Georgetown Inn offers all the comforts of a bed and breakfast and the privacy of an old fashioned inn. The inn is furnished with antiques. All fourteen rooms are individually decorated, have down duvets, and antique dressers. Small English pub serves home-cooked meals by the fireplace, or enjoy English afternoon tea in the summer months. Full breakfast is provided. Smoking only in pub.

Hosts: Barry and Doreen Jones and Family
Rooms: 14 (PB) $75-95
Full Breakfast
Credit Cards: A, B, C
Notes: 2, 4, 5, 7 (limited), 8, 9, 10, 11, 12, 13, 14

Spring Creek
Bed and Breakfast

Box 172; 1002 Third Avenue, T0L 0M0
(403) 678-6726

Adult home on Spring Creek in quiet corner of Canmore under picturesque Three Sisters Mountain near Banff National Park. Spa-

cious rooms with private baths. Views from each window. Full home-cooked breakfast. Guest sitting room. Wildlife nearby. Request slippers or socks worn indoors. Minimum stay two nights. No smoking.

Hosts: Dora and Frank Guy
Rooms: 2 (PB) $75-80
Full Breakfast
Credit Cards: None
Notes: 2, 5, 9, 10, 11, 12, 13

CARSTAIRS

Bed and Breakfast
Wild Rose Country

(403) 337-3192

3. Return to a simpler era in the romantic and comfortable luxury of a Victorian farmhouse among some of the best agricultural farmland in Alberta. One hour from Banff. Two queen-size rooms; two singles. Full breakfast provided. Workshops and retreats welcome. $50-65.

4. Enjoy the country inn atmosphere of an old English Tudor home. Excellent 18-hole golf course, tennis courts, and shale walking paths nearby. Three double rooms available. Full breakfast served in large spacious dining room or sunroom. Well-maintained lawns or gardens. Open May 1 to October 1. $40-50.

CASTOR

Bed and Breakfast
Wild Rose Country

(403) 337-3192

5. Country location offers a variety of recreational opportunities limited only by the imagination. Spend a peaceful afternoon bird watching or enjoy miles of trails perfect for walking, cycling, or cross-country skiing. One queen-size room; one dou-

---

6 Pets welcome; 8 Children welcome; 9 Social drinking allowed; 10 Tennis available; 11 Swimming available; 12 Golf available; 13 Skiing available; 14 May be booked through travel agents.

ble; two singles. Home-cooked breakfasts. $38-45.

CLARESHOLM

Anola's Bed and Breakfast

Box 340, T0L 0T0
(403) 625-4389

Experience the solitude of the prairies on this 3,800 acre grain farm, 30 minutes from Head Smashed in Buffalo Jump, a United Nations World Heritage site. Tea and muffins served on arrival. Private cottage decorated with quilts and antiques including a wood burning stove. Explore granddad's museum, a collection of western Canadian memorabilia, or tour the farms and learn the story of how wheat becomes bread and pasta.

Hosts: Anola and Gordon Laing
Rooms: 3 (1 PB; 2 SB) $50-95
Full Breakfast
Credit Cards: None
Notes: 2, 10, 11, 12

COCHRANE

Bed and Breakfast Wild Rose Country

(403) 337-3192

6. Angle Acres Bed and Breakfast is on a farm outside of Cochrane, just 20 minutes from the Calgary city limits and 90 minutes from Banff National Park. Two queen-size rooms and two single rooms are available. A full breakfast and evening tea is served. Plenty of area for hiking, or just relaxing and enjoying the quiet country. Open May 15 to October 1. $35-45.

7. Burke's Bed and Breakfast is open year-round. Comfortable, attractive guest rooms with double bed. Delicious home-made breakfast fare and afternoon tea. Close to town and country shopping,

restaurants, and activities. No smoking. Pets welcome. $30-45.

8. Cape Cod-style home nestled in forest 18 minutes northwest of Cochrane. Two bedrooms: one queen-size, one double. Shared bath. Library room and family room. Full country breakfast served on front porch or rear deck on warm sunny mornings. Two golf courses nearby. $40-50.

CREMONA

Bed and Breakfast Wild Rose Country

(403) 337-3192

9. Private ground-level entrance for guests. One separate cabin. Private bathrooms, coffee stations. Five rooms with variety of queen-size, double, and single beds. Relaxing, quiet country location on paved road. German spoken. Hearty breakfast. No smoking. $30-50.

DEAD MAN'S FLAT

Alberta and Pacific Bed and Breakfast

P.O. Box 15477, MPO, Vancouver, BC V6B 5B2
(604) 944-1793

Twenty miles from Banff, 20 minutes to Kananaskis Village, this large room offers three spacious, beautifully appointed and decorated guest rooms, each with queen-size bed and seating area, each with private bath.

DIDSBURY

Bed and Breakfast Wild Rose Country

(403) 337-3192

NOTES: Credit cards accepted: A MasterCard; B Visa; C American Express; D Discover Card; E Diner's Club; F Other; 2 Personal checks accepted; 3 Lunch available; 4 Dinner available; 5 Open all year;

10. Experience farm life with a stay on a working family farm. Unique country suite with a beautiful view of Rosebud Coulee. Scenic and peaceful. Suite furnished with TV, piano, and gas fireplace. Ideal for families. Farmyard and coulee provide for outdoor activities. Raspberry picking in season. Home-cooked breakfast. Closed May and September. $40-50.

11. Pengary House features three rooms: one with queen-size bed; second with double bed; and third with two singles. On 3/4 acre in the town of Didsbury, within walking distance of shopping, swimming pool, curling rink, and skating. Private sitting room for guests. Tea Room open daily from 2:00-5:00 P.M. Open Victoria Day weekend through Labour Day. $40-55.

12. Large, comfortable, two-story Cape Cod-style home, 45 minutes from Calgary. Country setting: walk trails, self-guided tours. Two large rooms with queen-size beds, reading nooks, antiques, shared bath. Outdoor barbecue, deck, gazebo, and hot tub. Breakfast served. $45-65.

Bed and Breakfast Wild Rose Country Association

c/o Bev Ausenhus, Rural Route 2
Didsbury, ALB T0M 0W0
(403) 335-4736

A cooperative association of more than 20 bed and breakfasts in central Alberta. They range from city to rural; small home stays to larger inns. All serve full breakfasts included with the accommodations. $30-75.

DRUMHELLER

Bed and Breakfast Wild Rose Country

(403) 337-3192

13. Enjoy a stay in a turn-of-the-century Victorian home. Sitting room with fireplace, antiques, piano, and TV. Large yard. One block from swimming pool, waterpark, river, restaurants, and shopping. Home-cooked breakfasts served in sunny breakfast room. Five guest rooms. $50-60.

EDMONTON

Alberta and Pacific Bed and Breakfast

P.O. Box 15477, MPO, Vancouver, BC V6B 5B2
(604) 944-1793

This home is a short drive to famous West Edmonton Mall, largest entertainment and shopping mall ever built. Two guest rooms are offered, one queen-size, one twin, and one guest bath. A full English breakfast is served or join the hosts for a weight-control breakfast.

FORT SASKATCHEWAN

Bed and Breakfast Wild Rose Country

(403) 337-3192

14. Bed and breakfast is on 20 acres of aspen park land, 4 kilometers from Elk Island National Park. The guests have their own private accommodation with cooking facilities and refrigerator. The Bird's Nest is a relaxing cozy hideaway with a private bath. A full breakfast is served in the bright sunny kitchen. One queen-size bed, one single available. $50-65.

GWYNNE

Gwynalta Farm

T0C 1L0
(403) 352-3587

Gwynalta is a lovely 400-acre farm in central Alberta. The farm has a natural valley

6 Pets welcome; 8 Children welcome; 9 Social drinking allowed; 10 Tennis available; 11 Swimming available; 12 Golf available; 13 Skiing available; 14 May be booked through travel agents.

and a mile of rugged lakeshore, with areas for bird watching, walking, and biking. Home-cooked meals and plenty of coffee and chatter. Experience the quiet serenity of a rural setting and the warm friendly atmosphere of a farm home. Home-cooked meals and plenty of coffee and chatter.

Host: Mabel Glaser
Rooms: 2 (SB) $30-60
Full Breakfast
Credit Cards: None
Notes: 3, 5, 7, 8, 10, 11, 12, 13

JASPER

Alberta and Pacific Bed and Breakfast

P.O. Box 15477, MPO, Vancouver, BC V6B 5B2
(604) 944-1793

Private entrance to newly furnished and decorated suite, living room with queen-size Hide-a-bed, cable TV, bedroom with queen-size bed, kitchenette has microwave and refrigerator, and private bath. A separate small bedroom is also available in the same area with double bed, TV, and private bath.

LACOMBE

Bed and Breakfast Wild Rose Country

(403) 337-3192

15. This 1903 Victorian farm home offers a friendly atmosphere where the guest can wake to the aroma of a fresh cup of coffee and warm muffins. Three golf courses are available for the guest's use. Four rooms with variety of bed sizes. $40-65.

16. Sunset Country is in a quiet rural setting with a split-level home surrounded by retreat garden areas. One queen-size size, one double, and two singles are available. Tasty

western breakfast around large country dining table. Open March 1 through November 15. $30-50.

MARKERVILLE

Bed and Breakfast Wild Rose Country

(403) 337-3192

17. Rooms decorated with handcrafted furnishings and antiques, private entrance. Rosewood cottage—detached. Music room, sauna, formal dining, or casual mountain view veranda for breakfast. Rolling hills and open meadows, much wildlife, and many birds. Five minutes to historic sites. One king-size, one double, and two single accommodations. $35-50.

MILLARVILLE

Hilltop Bed and Breakfast

Rural Route 1, T0L 1K0
(403) 931-3356

Enjoy the magnificent view of the Rockies just west of Millarville. Quiet, relaxing atmosphere. Two attractive guest rooms (one double, one queen-size) on the main floor with a full bath shared only by guests. Choice of breakfast including home baking, home preserves, and their own high-country honey.

Hosts: Bob and Lill Tedrick
Rooms: 2 (SB) $60
Full Breakfast
Credit Cards: None
Notes: 2, 5, 8 (over 9), 9, 12, 13

NANTON

Broadway Farm Bed and Breakfast

Box 294, T0L 1R0
(403) 646-5502

NOTES: Credit cards accepted: A MasterCard; B Visa; C American Express; D Discover Card; E Diner's Club; F Other; 2 Personal checks accepted; 3 Lunch available; 4 Dinner available; 5 Open all year;

In the beautiful and spacious prairies of south Alberta with a panaromic view of the Rocky Mountains and lovely sunsets. Full breakfast served in the atrium with beautiful plants. Three guest rooms with shared bath. Families welcome. Restricted smoking. Hosts offer pig roasts for group functions.

Hosts: Bill and Mary Gelden
Rooms: 4 (SB) $50
Full Breakfast
Credit Cards: None
Notes: 3, 4, 5, 8, 9, 10, 11, 12

Timber Ridge Homestead

P.O. Box 94, T0L 1R0
(403) 646-5683; (403) 646-2480 (winter)

Timber Ridge Homestead is a rustic establishment in the beautiful foothills of ranching country and lies about 70 miles southwest of Calgary. There are good, quiet horses to help guests explore the abundant wildflowers, wildlife, and wonderful views of the Rockies. Good, plain cooking.

Hosts: Bridget Jones and family
Rooms: 3 (SB) $25
Full Breakfast
Credit Cards: None
Notes: 2, 3, 4, 8, 9

NORTH PONOKA

Bed and Breakfast
Wild Rose Country

(403) 337-3192

18. Mid-century home provides second-story accommodations with a sitting room, deck for relaxing, and lots of outdoor activities. Wake up to fresh baked muffins and coffee or relax in the evening with the family favorites…popcorn. One double, three single accommodations. $35-45.

PINCHER CREEK

Allison House

1108 Hewetson Avenue; Box 1351, T0M 1W0
(403) 627-3739

Allison House is an Alberta-registered Heritage House in beautiful southwestern Alberta. Built in 1911 by early pioneers, it maintains the original floor plan and features stained-glass art designed by the owner. Easy access to Waterton National Park, Head Smashed in Buffalo Jump, World Heritage Site, and fishing in the Crowsnest Pass. Sporting facilities are on the nearby Oldman River Dam. Home to the Annual Cowboy Poetry and Western Art Show in June.

Hosts: Suzanne and Csaba Lorinczl
Rooms: 2 (1 PB; 1 SB) $35-55, Cash Only.
Full Breakfast
Credit Cards: None
Notes: 10, 11, 12, 13

RED DEER

Bed and Breakfast
Wild Rose Country

(403) 337-3192

19. Eighty-five-year-old home close to downtown. Open year-round. Spa facilities and treatments available for a peaceful escape with a personal touch. Relax and rejuvenate. One king-size, one double, and three singles. $45-55.

20. Open year-round. Come and enjoy a peaceful, quiet country setting with warm hospitality, farm-style breakfast, and homey atmosphere. Guest lounge, TV, laundry, and private entrance. Three double bed accommodations. $30-50.

6 Pets welcome; 8 Children welcome; 9 Social drinking allowed; 10 Tennis available; 11 Swimming available; 12 Golf available; 13 Skiing available; 14 May be booked through travel agents.

21. The McIntosh Tea House Bed and Breakfast is a historic house in the city of Red Deer. The home is completely restored and furnished with antiques. Guests may enjoy a private sitting room, three double guest rooms with private baths. $50-65.

ROCKY MOUNTAIN HOUSE

Bed and Breakfast
Wild Rose Country
(403) 337-3192

22. Quiet neighborhood with park across back alley. Close to cycling/walking trails, swimming pool, and other recreational facilities. Host enjoys music and wood carving. Hostess enjoys people and cooking. Open year-round. One queen-size, two doubles. $40-50.

SEDGEWICK

Bed and Breakfast
Wild Rose Country
(403) 337-3192

23. Large dining room, common living room complete with fireplace and hot tub. Tastefully decorated rooms with private baths in 1912-era house. Landscaping featuring natural prairie grasses, trees, and flowers. Guests treated to down-home country atmosphere and food. $45-55.

SHERWOOD PARK

Bed and Breakfast
Wild Rose Country
(403) 337-3192

24. Expect good Scottish hospitality at this new acreage home beside Cooking Lake, natural trails, and first-class bird watching.

Enjoy a lounge, kitchen, and whirlpool bath. One queen-size, one double, and one youth accommodation. $35-45.

SYLVAN LAKE

Bed and Breakfast
Wild Rose Country
(403) 337-3192

25. Enjoy a stay in a modern, clean, comfortable home. Guests are invited to sit on the patio and enjoy the nice yard. The friendly hosts are from Switzerland and offer homemade bread for breakfast. Nearby beach, shopping, and entertainment. $35-45.

THREE HILLS

Bed and Breakfast
Wild Rose Country
(403) 337-3192

26. Farm home offering quiet retreat in a picnic setting with great view. Hike the coulee, rejuvenate in the hot tub, enjoy outside fire pit and lawn swing, or barbecue on deck. One queen-size, one double, shared bath. $35-50.

TROCHU

Bed and Breakfast
Wild Rose Country
(403) 337-3192

27. St. Ann Ranch is open year-round and ideal for a peaceful or romantic getaway. Rooms furnished with period antiques, private guest entrance, library, TV room, breakfast room, patio, and parlor with fireplace. $45-75.

NOTES: Credit cards accepted: A MasterCard; B Visa; C American Express; D Discover Card; E Diner's Club; F Other; 2 Personal checks accepted; 3 Lunch available; 4 Dinner available; 5 Open all year;

WAINWRIGHT _____

Bed and Breakfast
Wild Rose Country
(403) 337-3192

28. Comfortable 1910-built home, newly renovated in a Victorian early-Canadian style. Private baths; Alberta Best, three-star Canada Select accommodation. Hosts are active in the hospitality industry. Several restaurants, shopping, indoor pool, and theater within walking distance. French and English spoken. $45-65.

6 Pets welcome; 8 Children welcome; 9 Social drinking allowed; 10 Tennis available; 11 Swimming available; 12 Golf available; 13 Skiing available; 14 May be booked through travel agents.

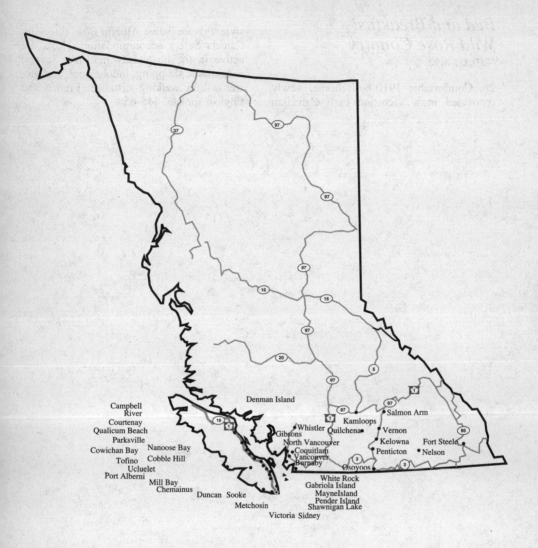

Campbell
River
Courtenay
Qualicum Beach
Parksville
Cowichan Bay   Nanoose Bay
Tofino   Cobble Hill
Ucluelet
Port Alberni
Mill Bay
Chemainus
Duncan   Sooke
Metchosin
Victoria Sidney

Denman Island

Whistler   Quilchena
Gibsons
North Vancouver
Coquitlam
Vancouver
Burnaby

Kamloops   Salmon Arm

Vernon
Kelowna
Penticton

Osoyoos

White Rock
Gabriola Island
MayneIsland
Pender Island
Shawnigan Lake

Fort Steele
Nelson

37
97
97
97
16   16
20
97
5
97
19
1
1
1
3   3
95

British Columbia

British Columbia

A B and C Bed and Breakfast of Vancouver

4390 Frances Street, V5C 2R3
(604) 263-5595; (800) 488-1941
FAX (604) 298-5917

Single to king-size beds, private and shared baths, suites, cabins to mansions, Jacuzzis, pool, and full to gourmet breakfasts included. Covering North and West Vancouver, Vancouver, Victoria, Parksville, Whistler, Richmond, Surrey, White Rock, and others. Car rentals and sightseeing tours arranged, with weekly and off-season rates. Wheelchair accessible. $75-150.

Born Free Bed and Breakfast of British Columbia, Ltd.

4390 Frances Street, V5C 2R3
(604) 298-8815; (800) 488-1941
FAX (604) 298-5917

This reservation service will help the guest find a home away from home in clean, comfortable homes with superfriendly hosts and hostesses. From modest to average to luxurious accommodations, all needs are considered. There are also accommodations for film crews, students, and those with long-stay and special requirements. Covering Vancouver, Victoria, and throughout British Columbia.

English Garden Bed and Breakfast

4390 Frances Street, V5C 2R3
(604) 298-8815; (800) 488-1941
FAX (604) 298-5917

Offering self-contained suites, private and shared baths, cabins, and mansion, full and gourmet breakfast included. This reservation services covers Gibsons, Victoria, Great Vancouver, and Nanaimo. Car rentals and sightseeing tours arranged. Wheelchair accessible. $75-150.

CAMPBELL RIVER

All Seasons Bed and Breakfast Agency

P.O. Box 5511, Station B, Victoria, V8R 6S4
(604) 655-7173

The Grey Mouse. Welcoming seaside home on a sandy beach. Sport court for tennis, volleyball, basketball, and shuffleboard. Hot tub. Nature trails and golf course in immediate area, and beachcombing on the doorstep. Nordic and alpine skiing 45 minutes away. Full breakfast served in the dining room. $55.

Campbell River Lodge and Fishing Resort

1760 Island Highway, V9W 2E7
(604) 287-7446

Small intimate fishing lodge on the banks of the famous Campbell River. Originally

NOTES: Credit cards accepted: A MasterCard; B Visa; C American Express; D Discover Card; E Diner's Club; F Other; 2 Personal checks accepted; 3 Lunch available; 4 Dinner available; 5 Open all year; 6 Pets welcome; 7 Smoking allowed; 8 Children welcome; 9 Social drinking allowed; 10 Tennis available; 11 Swimming available; 12 Golf available; 13 Skiing available; 14 May be booked through travel agents.

constructed of logs in 1948, the lodge is the oldest and most unique in the area. Offers old world charm and modern conveniences. Dine in the gourmet dining room or English-style pub. Relaxing outdoor hot tub overlooking Campbell River. Continental breakfast served daily.

Host: Brian Clarkson
Rooms: 28 (PB) $49-93
Continental Breakfast
Cards: A, B
Notes: 3, 4, 5, 6, 7, 8, 9, 10 ,11, 12, 14

CHEMAINUS

Garden City Bed and Breakfast Reservation Service

660 Jones Terrace, Victoria, V82 2L7
(604) 479-1986; FAX (604) 479-9999

K-12. Warm hospitality awaits guests at this modern, cozy home on a quiet road. Five-minute walk to beach. There are lovely sunsets, golf courses, restaurants, village, and marina. Fishing trips can be arranged. Walk to bus for skiing at Mount Washington. Guest room with queen-size bed and private bath overlooks the English garden. Fresh-ground coffee and delicious breakfast served inside or on patio. From $65.

Little Inn on Willow

9849 Willow Street, Box 958, V0R 1K0
(604) 246-4987

Imagine booking an entire luxury hotel for an evening! The entire property consists of one tiny fairy cottage, carefully crafted by local artisans to capture the romance that this seaside village is famous for. Features a fireplace, jet tub for two, TV/VCR, chilled champagne, and orange juice. Guests can also book a private steam and massage for an extra cost. Tennis, swimming, and golf nearby. The Continental breakfast is a Belgium waffle and coffee at Billy's Delight.

Little Inn on Willow

Hosts: Dave and Sonia Haberman
Room: 1 (PB) $150
Continental Breakfast
Credit Cards: A
Notes: 5, 9, 10, 11, 12

Pacific Shores All-Suite Inn

9847 Willow Street, Box 958, V0R 1K0
(604) 246-4987

Quaint European-style inn blended with all the amenities of a North American all-suite hotel. Features three tastefully decorated suites with handmade feather duvets, kitchens, cable TV, and VCR. Each suite has its own individual decor. The King-size Suite is a spacious one bedroom with a queen-size bed and double foldout bed in the living room. The Duchess is done with antiques, including a very comfortable turn-of-the-century queen-size bed and private library. The Princess is a bright cheery suite with the early morning sun shining through its corner turret. Continental breakfast is served. Tennis, swimming, and golf nearby. The Continental breakfast is a Belgium waffle and coffee at Billy's Delight.

Hosts: Dave and Sonia Haberman
Rooms: 3 (PB) $75-95
Continental Breakfast
Credit Cards: A
Notes: 5, 8, 9, 10, 11, 12

NOTES: Credit cards accepted: A MasterCard; B Visa; C American Express; D Discover Card; E Diner's Club; F Other; 2 Personal checks accepted; 3 Lunch available; 4 Dinner available; 5 Open all year;

Sea-Breeze Tourist Home

2912 Esplanade Street, P.O. Box 1362, V0R 1K0
(604) 246-4593

Turn-of-the-century home just steps from the beach and boat ramp in picturesque Chemainus. Play park and picnic area at the beach. Beautiful views from every room. Lighthouse and island view. Full breakfast is served on linen with silver and candles. English and German spoken. Smoking in designated areas only.

Hosts: John and Christa Stegemann
Rooms: 4 (2 PB; 2 SB) $45-55
Full Breakfast
Credit Cards: None
Notes: 5, 7 (limited), 8, 10, 11, 12

COBBLE HILL (VANCOUVER ISLAND)

Garden City
Bed and Breakfast
Reservation Service

660 Jones Terrace, Victoria, V8Z 2L7
(604) 479-1986; FAX (604) 479-9999

K-2. Just a 15-minute ferry ride from Campbell River sets this waterfront home with everchanging views of Inside Passage to Alaska. Rooms with queen-size or double beds with shared bath. A fully contained suite with queen-size bed, sofa bed, kitchen, bath, and private entrance is also available for a three-day minimum stay. Explore trails, canoe and kayak the waterways, visit native museum, and discover beach petroglyphs. From $55.

COLWOOD (VANCOUVER ISLAND)

Garden City
Bed and Breakfast
Reservation Service

660 Jones Terrace, Victoria, V82 2L7
(604) 479-1986; FAX (604) 479-9999

L-4. A solid cedar home nestled among fir trees with views overlooking Juan de Fuca Straits, city of Victoria, and the Olympic Mountains. Private baths and queen-size or double beds. Excellent home-cooked breakfast served each morning in dining room or solarium where guests can enjoy the unequaled view. Just 20 minutes from city centre, and very close to numerous golf courses, fishing, parks, hiking, etc. From $60.

COQUITLAM

Green Gables
Bed and Breakfast

2242 Park Crescent, V3J 6T2
(604) 469-7105

Private suite with fireplace, comfortable king-size bed, and private bath. Lovely home 30 minutes from Vancouver in very quiet location. Gourmet breakfast provided. Hosts are happy to assist with directions and information. English and German spoken.

Host: Gabriela Butz
Room: 1 (PB) $70
Full Breakfast
Credit Cards: None
Notes: 5, 8, 9, 10, 11, 12, 14

COURTENAY

Greystone Manor

4014 Haas Road, Rural Route 6,
   Site 684-C2, V9N 8H9
(604) 338-1422

A lovely view across Comox Bay to the mainland British Columbian coast mountains and one and a half acres of beautiful English gardens are the setting for Greystone Manor. Built in 1918, the manor is one of the oldest homes in the area. The guest sitting room has a wood fireplace and baby grand piano. Hosts originally from Bath, England.

6 Pets welcome; 8 Children welcome; 9 Social drinking allowed; 10 Tennis available; 11 Swimming available; 12 Golf available; 13 Skiing available; 14 May be booked through travel agents.

Hosts: Mike and Maureen Shipton
Rooms: 4 (SB) $60-70
Full Breakfast
Credit Cards: A, B
Notes: 5, 8 (over 12), 9, 11, 12, 13

COWICHAN BAY

All Seasons Bed and Breakfast Agency

Box 5511, Station B, Victoria, V8R 6S4
(604) 655-7173

Old Farm Bed and Breakfast. Originally a farmhouse, circa 1900, overlooking the Cowichan Estuary in the small fishing village of Cowichan Bay, one hour's drive north of Victoria. Ideal for biking the back roads to Chemainus, sailing, or playing tennis at one of North America's oldest courts. Excellent restaurants nearby. Spacious bedrooms, queen-size beds, private baths, and water views. Ideal for families or a getaway weekend. Resident dogs and cat; no guest pets. $65-75.

DENMAN ISLAND

Denman Island Guest House

3806 Denman Road, V0R 1T0
(206) 335-2688

Enjoy bed and breakfast accommodations in a turn-of-the-century farmhouse on Denman Island. The small farm has a beautiful mountain view with glimmers of the Strait of Georgia. Great location near the ocean and beaches. There are all the attractions of shore and water to enjoy. Hiking, cycling, and beachcombing are popular activities on the island as well as exploring the many craft stores. Fully licensed dining facilities feature hearty, country breakfasts and seafood dinners. Antique furniture complements the traditional farmhouse.

Host: Bob Okrainec
Rooms: 5 (SB) $50

Full Breakfast
Credit Cards: None
Notes: 4, 5, 7, 8, 9, 10, 11, 14

DUNCAN

Country Gardens Bed and Breakfast

1665 Grant Road, V9L 4T6
(604) 748-5865

Country charm in a lovely cedar log home on a private acreage overlooking beautiful Quamichan Lake. Home-cooked breakfast served on patio overlooking the lake or the tranquil garden with lily ponds. Resident Briard dog. Dutch spoken.

Host: Marjorie Gunnlaugson
Rooms: 2 (PB) $60-70
Full Breakfast
Credit Cards: None
Notes: 2, 5, 12

Grove Hall Estate Bed and Breakfast

6159 Lakes Road, V9L 4J6
(604) 746-6152

Take a scenic drive 36 miles north of Victoria and discover this historic Edwardian tudor mansion, hidden away on 17 tranquil lakefront acres. Magnificent antiques throughout. Exotic and romantic theme rooms highlighted by ornate Chinese Wedding Bed in the Singapore Room; Balinese art and batiks in the Indonesian Suite; flavors of Bangkok enhancing the Siamese Room. There is also a one-bedroom cottage available. Relax on the veranda while sipping tea and watching the graceful swans on the lake. Enjoy tennis or billiards. Close to Chemainus, sailing, golfing, and hiking. Minimum stay of two nights.

Host: Judy Oliver
Rooms: 3 (SB) $120-145
Cottage: $125
Full Breakfast
Cards: None
Notes: 2, 5, 9, 10, 11, 12, 14

NOTES: Credit cards accepted: A MasterCard; B Visa; C American Express; D Discover Card; E Diner's Club; F Other; 2 Personal checks accepted; 3 Lunch available; 4 Dinner available; 5 Open all year;

DUNCAN (VANCOUVER ISLAND)

Garden City
Bed and Breakfast
Reservation Service

660 Jones Terrace, Victoria, V82 2L7
(604) 479-1986; FAX (604) 479-9999

K-18. This century-old home offers quiet seclusion on two and one-half acres with formal gardens and beautiful views. Gourmet breakfast; chocolates, fruit, and flowers in room; lovely shops on premises. Afternoon tea on arrival. Hiking, birding, Native Heritage Centre, Forestry Museum, Chemainus murals, sailing, and golf. Queen-size and twin beds; shared bath. From $85.

FORT STEELE

Wild Horse Farm

Box 7, V0B 1N0
(604) 426-6000

Wild Horse Farm is a log-faced, two-story manor house built in 1929 by a nephew of John Jacob Astor IV. It is set against a Canadian Rockies backdrop, surrounded by 80 acres of meadows, woodlands, pastures, and gardens. Highland cows and assorted fowl keep an eye on guests playing croquet, lawn bowling, or relaxing on the grounds and screened veranda. Furnishings range from Tiffany lamps to bearskin rugs. Memorable breakfasts incorporate farm produce in vegetable fritattas, puffy oven pancakes, and fruit muffins served with homemade jams and fruit syrups.

Hosts: Bob and Orma Termuende
Rooms: 4 (2 PB; 2 SB) $58-93
Full Breakfast
Credit Cards: B
Notes: 2, 5, 7 (limited), 8, 9, 10, 11, 12, 13, 14
  (10%)

GABRIOLA ISLAND

Surf Lodge

885 Berry Point Road, Rural Route 1, Site 1,
  V0R 1X0
(604) 247-8940

On ten acres on the northwest shore of Gariola Island, facing the Georgia Strait and Vancouver Island and mainland mountains, Surf Lodge offers a relaxed atmosphere in a quiet setting. There are nine rooms in the main lodge and nine cabins, all with private paths, some with kitchenettes. Sunset watching from the dining room, deck, or licensed lounge. Seawater pool and other outdoor recreation facilities. Golf, tennis, scuba, and fishing charters nearby. Continental breakfast served, dinner available.

Host: Brian Colby
Rooms: 9 (PB) $55-78
Cabins: 9 (PB)
Continental Breakfast
Credit Cards: A, B
Notes: 2, 4, 5, 7, 8, 9, 10, 11, 12, 14

GALIANO ISLAND

Garden City
Bed and Breakfast
Reservation Service

660 Jones Terrace, Victoria, V8Z 2L7
(604) 479-1986; FAX (604) 479-9999

K-20. On over five acres of natural forest, this spacious home offers queen-size or twin beds, hot tub, sauna, and bicycles. There's even an opportunity to watch deer wander and eagles soar while enjoying a delicious breakfast or while exploring the scenic Gulf islands and beaches. Bordering Bluff Park, guests are close to golf courses, shops, and pubs. From $65.

GANGES

Hastings House

160 Upper Ganges Road, P.O. Box 111, V0S 1E0
(604) 537-2362

In a uniquely pastoral setting, Hastings House is a tranquil retreat for the discriminating guest who seeks and appreciates a tasteful difference in resort destinations. Enjoy a five-course dinner in the dining room prepared by Hastings House award winning chef. Nearby golf, sea-kayaking, bird watching, and fishing round out a perfect vacation. If coming to the island for the day, come to the Hastings House for Sunday brunch served from 11:00 A.M. to 1:00 ʾ.M. for $18.95 per person, reservations recommended.

Hosts: Catl Simpson and Ian Cowley
Rooms: 12 (PB) $220-420
Full and Continental Breakfast
Credit Cards: A, B
Notes: 4, 7, 10, 12, 14

GIBSONS

Ocean-View Cottage Bed and Breakfast

Rural Route 2, S46-C10, 1927 Grandview Road,
V0N 1V0
(604) 886-7943

A short cruise from Vancouver to this home and spacious self-contained cottage overlooking the Strait of Georgia and Vancouver Island. Queen-size and twin bedrooms with ensuite, private entrances, and sundeck. Hearty breakfast served. Close to shops, attractions, and fine dining. Self-contained cottage with one bedroom, sleeper-sofa, cot, and futon is also available. Sleeps six.

Hosts: Dianne and Bert Verzyl
Rooms: 3 (PB) $55-80
Full Breakfast
Credit Cards: A, B
Notes: 2, 5, 8, 9, 10, 11, 12, 13

KAMLOOPS

Alberta and Pacific Bed and Breakfast Agency

P.O. Box 15477, MPO, Vancouver, V6B 5B2
(604) 944-1793

9. Lakefront property with beautiful view of Paul Lake and the mountains. There is a private dock for swimming, fishing, and windsurfing, as well as hiking, walking, and biking trails. Three guest rooms, one with queen-size bed, TV and full private bath; one with double bed and private bath; one with single bed and shared bath.

Park Place Bed and Breakfast

720 Yates Road, V2B 6C9
(604) 554-2179

Delightful riverfront home on two acres with large swimming pool and breakfast solarium with a view. Full or Continental breakfast. Air-conditioned. Hosts' motto, "Come as a guest, leave as a friend."

Hosts: Lynn and Trevor Bentz
Rooms: 3 (1 PB; 2 SB) $50-60
Full Breakfast
Credit Cards: None
Notes: 2, 5, 9, 10, 11, 12, 13

KELOWNA

The Gables Country Inn

Box 1153, 2405 Bering Road, V1Y 7P8
(604) 768-4468

Discover the elegance and romance of yesteryear at the Okanagan's only Heritage Award-winning bed and breakfast. Lovely antique furnishings grace each unique upstairs bedroom. Linger through a delicious breakfast of freshly baked scones and muffins, homemade jams, and fresh, ground coffee on the old-fashioned covered verandah. Enjoy a crackling fire in the spacious

---

NOTES: Credit cards accepted: A MasterCard; B Visa; C American Express; D Discover Card; E Diner's Club; F Other; 2 Personal checks accepted; 3 Lunch available; 4 Dinner available; 5 Open all year;

sitting room or a dip in the swimming pool set in the secluded sunken garden. Near orchards and wineries, The Gables is open all year offering a smoke-free environment in which to relax.

Hosts: Brenda and Kik Clark
Rooms: 4 (SB) $55-65
Full Breakfast
Credit Cards: None
Notes: 5, 9, 10, 11, 12, 13

A View to Remember Bed and Breakfast

1090 Trevor Drive, V1Z 2J8
(604) 769-4028

For a romantic getaway holiday, relaxing business trip, or restful weekend, this gracious home is brimming with charm, antiques, attractive flower gardens, and a truly spectacular view. In a quiet area minutes to downtown, golfing, beaches, and tourist attractions. Deluxe accommodations include elegant, spacious guest rooms, cool in summer, each with private bath. Gourmet breakfast served on the patio in summer. Business services available.

Hosts: Celia and Robin Jarman
Rooms: 3 (PB) $55-70
Full Breakfast
Credit Cards: A
Notes: 2, 5, 8, 10, 11, 12, 13

MAYNE ISLAND

Garden City Bed and Breakfast Reservation Service

660 Jones Terrace, Victoria, V8Z 2L7
(604) 479-1986; FAX (604) 479-9999

K-25. Near Miner's Bay and village, this retreat is one of the most colorful and whimsical buildings on the island. Wonderful gardens of edible and medicinal herbs, flowers, and fruit trees, spacious decks, and magnificent views await. Guests can bicycle, drive, ramble through idyllic landscapes and marine scenery, or spend time on the water. Groups and families are welcome. From $60.

Oceanwood Country Inn

Oceanwood Country Inn

630 Dinner Bay Road, V0N 2J0
(604) 539-5074; FAX (604) 539-3002

Overlooking the water, Oceanwood has eight individually decorated guest rooms with private bath, plus a comfortable living room, well-stocked library, and cozy game room. The intimate 30-seat restaurant, open for dinner every day, serves Pacific Northwest cuisine. The extensive wine list features the best from British Columbia, Washington, Oregon, and California. There's a large hot tub in the waterfront terrace and a sauna. Breakfast and afternoon tea provided. Closed December to February. Limited smoking allowed.

Hosts: Marilyn and Jonathan Chilvers
Rooms: 8 (PB) $120-200
Full Breakfast
Credit Cards: A, B
Notes: 4, 7 (limited), 9, 10, 11, 12, 14

METCHOSIN (VANCOUVER ISLAND)

Garden City Bed and Breakfast Reservation Service

660 Jones Terrace, Victoria, V8Z 2L7
(604) 479-1986; FAX (604) 479-9999

6 Pets welcome; 8 Children welcome; 9 Social drinking allowed; 10 Tennis available; 11 Swimming available; 12 Golf available; 13 Skiing available; 14 May be booked through travel agents.

L-5. This five-acre farm is in a peaceful setting 25 minutes from Victoria. Complimentary tea, coffee, and biscuits. Spectacular mountain and sea views. Trails, beaches, parks, and wildlife. Charming, romantic suite with private entrance, queen-size bed, and ensuite bath and kitchnette. There is also an upstairs suite with queen-size and twin beds, private bath, and ocean view. Families welcome. Resident dogs. Ask about the romantic weekend champagne breakfast. From $75.

L-8. Enjoy this log home and unique country charm on over three acres of forest. Complete privacy including private hot tub. Queen-size bed, cozy down duvets, and ensuite bath. Close to city centre, Sooke, and lower Vancouver Island. Parks, trails, beaches, fishing, golf, plus a touch of wilderness. From $85.

L-12. This six and one-half acre minifarm is just a 45-minute drive from Victoria. A quiet setting with sheep, chickens, and organic fruit and vegetables. Dramatic views of Olympic National Park mountains. Comfortable rooms. Hearty breakfast includes homemade breads, preserves, and free-range eggs. Golf, Sooke Potholes, Sooke museum, biking, beach walking, fish charters, forestry tours, and whale watching. On city bus route. School-age children welcome. Maximum of five people. From $45.

L-18. It's time to smell the roses, breathe fresh sea air, and relax. Enjoy strolls in woods, on sandy beaches, and in sanctuaries, or play golf. Just 25 minutes from city centre or west to Sooke, China Beach, Port Renfrew Botannical Gardens (undersea). Adult oriented. Twin, queen-, and king-size beds; ensuite or shared baths. Delicious and healthy breakfasts. From $60.

MILL BAY (VANCOUVER ISLAND)

Garden City Bed and Breakfast Reservation Service

660 Jones Terrace, Victoria, V8Z 2L7
(604) 479-1986; FAX (604) 479-9999

K-3. A waterfront home 35 minutes from Victoria and 55 minutes from Nanaimo. Sweeping views of Saltspring Island, ocean, etc. Beach offers shell, driftwood, and rock collecting, swimming, canoeing, walking, and sunning. Golf courses, fishing charters, hiking, craft and art shows year-round, and a country music festival at the end of May. A fishing derby is in mid-August. Children welcome. Wheelchair accessible. Weekly rates available. From $55.

K-16. Contemporary Mill Bay home on one-half acre surrounded by ornamental trees and many flowers. Steps to the beach transport guests into a spectacular world overlooking the Saanich Peninsula and snowcapped Mount Baker. Experience unforgettable sunrises across the brilliant water. Suite with sofa, TV, table and chairs, ocean view, queen-size bed, and ensuite bath. There is also a twin-bedded room on the upper level with shared bath. From $45.

Pine Lodge Farm Bed and Breakfast

3191 Mutter Road, V0R 2P0
(604) 743-4083

A charming pine lodge built on a 30-acre farm overlooking ocean and islands. Walking trails, farm animals, deer, and magnificent Arbutus trees and to the paradiselike setting. Antique-filled lodge with stained-glass windows features cozy bedrooms with private baths, furnished with beautiful antiques. Enjoy a full breakfast with homemade jams, and then browse through a

NOTES: Credit cards accepted: A MasterCard; B Visa; C American Express; D Discover Card; E Diner's Club; F Other; 2 Personal checks accepted; 3 Lunch available; 4 Dinner available; 5 Open all year;

spectacular collection of antiques. Featured in *Country Living* and on CBS-TV.

Hosts: Cliff and Barbara Clarke
Rooms: 8 (PB) $65-95
Full Breakfast
Credit Cards: A, B
Notes: 2, 9, 12, 14

NANOOSE BAY

All Seasons Bed and Breakfast Agency

Box 5511, Station B, Victoria, V8R 6S4
(604) 655-7173

Madrona Point. Unrivaled West Coast beauty. Walk-on beach. Unwind and relax, this is paradise. Only minutes from Parksville and Rathtrevor Beach. Join over 90 percent of the guests who rate it a ten out of ten. Great swimming and some of British Columbia's best scuba diving year-round. Large suite with fireplace, private bath, private entrance, and hot tub outside the door—very romantic. Another guest room has a private bath, private entrance, and deck. Breakfast is served in room or on the patio. $75-95.

Somerville's by the Sea. Beautiful contemporary home on the Strait of Georgia. Explore the tidal pools below the separate suite that contains a queen-size bedroom, sitting room with TV, private bath, deck, and entrance. Two single sofa beds complete the scene. Another suite is also available. There is a wood-burning fireplace where guests can cook up a steak or a salmon. Horseback riding nearby, as are Fairwinds Golf Course and Schooner Cove Marina. Enjoy a "melt-in-your-mouth" breakfast. $75-85.

The Brown House

Box 62 Park Place Rural Route 2;
3020 Dolphin Drive, V0R 2R0
(604) 468-7804

Self-contained suite with private entrance, living room with TV and fireplace, bathroom with shower, Colonial bedroom with double bed. Peek-a-boo view of the Straits of Georgia. Four golf courses, three marinas, Rath Trevor Beach, horseback riding, nature trails, and many types of restaurants in the area. Fifteen miles north of Nanaimo, five miles south of Parksville, and a two-hour drive to Tofino.

Hosts: Edith and Ern Deadman
Rooms: 1 (PB) $60
Full Breakfast
Credit cards: None
Notes: 2, 5, 9, 10, 11, 12, 13

Garden City Bed and Breakfast Reservation Service

660 Jones Terrace, Victoria, V8Z 2L7
(604) 479-1986; FAX (604) 479-9999

K-19. A fully furnished, self-contained two-bedroom suite with kitchen, air conditioning, gas fireplace, and cable TV. Unique setting in Nanoose Bay across from waterfront and beach access. Private entrance, ground-level deck, fruit orchard, private patio, and fish pond. Close to regional park, golfing, horseback riding, fishing, sailing, and wildlife watching. Children welcome. No pets. From $75.

The Lookout at Schooner Cove

3381 Dolphin Drive, V0R 2R0
(604) 468-9796 (FAX and Phone)

Halfway between Victoria and Tofino, this cedar home is set in tall evergreens, with a 180-degree view of the Georgia Strait and the majestic mountains beyond. Relax on the wraparound deck in this little bit of heaven and enjoy the passing boats, Alaskan cruise ships, eagles, and whales. Fairwinds Golf Course and Schooner Cove Marina and Resort are within one-half

6 Pets welcome; 8 Children welcome; 9 Social drinking allowed; 10 Tennis available; 11 Swimming available; 12 Golf available; 13 Skiing available; 14 May be booked through travel agents.

mile. Hearty breakfast is served on the deck or in dining room at guests' convenience.

Hosts: Marj and Herb Wilkie
Rooms: 3 (2 PB; 1 SB) $55-75
Full Breakfast
Credit Cards: None
Notes: 8 (over 10), 9, 10, 11, 12, 13, 14

NELSON

Alberta and Pacific Bed and Breakfast Agency

P.O. Box 15477, MPO, Vancouver, V6B 5B2
(604) 944-1793

12. This British Columbia city has turn-of-the-century architecture with Victorian homes. A 1926 character home in the downtown area. Decorated with antiques. Four guest rooms. Ground-level guest rooms with queen-size-and twin beds with view of lake have one guest bath. Upstairs guest rooms each have queen-size beds, one with double Hide-a-bed, and seating area, each with private bath. Host is a chef from Vancouver and offers a full gourmet breakfast as well as vegetarian or low-sodium breakfasts if requested. A 10 percent discount is offered to seniors.

This magnificent house was built for a retired British army officer in 1920. Generous in proportion, the lodge has large rooms, wood paneling, grand fireplaces and stunning views of Kootenay Lake. Guests awake to the delicious aromas of homemade muffins and enjoy a full breakfast on the porch. There are walking trails in the forest above the lodge, a hot tub in the garden, and world-class recreation in the surrounding mountains and valleys.

Hosts Alan and Sue Dodsworth
Rooms: 6 (PB) $75-125
Full Breakfast
Credit Cards: A, B
Notes: 5, 8, 11, 12, 13

Helen's

Willow Point Lodge

Willow Point Lodge

Rural Route 1 S-21 C-31;
 2211 Taylor Drive, V1L 5P4
(604) 825-9411; FAX (604) 825-3432

NORTH VANCOUVER

Helen's Bed and Breakfast

302 East Fifth Street, V7L 1L9
(604) 985-4869

Welcome to this old Victorian home, its charm and comfort enhanced by antiques, wonderful views, and color cable TV in each room. Five blocks to the Pacific; 20 minutes to the Horseshoe Bay ferries to Victoria; minutes to Grouse Mountain Sky Ride, Whistler Ski Resort, restaurants, and shopping. Gourmet breakfast served in the citizen elegant dining room. Ten percent senior discount; ten percent discount from November through April. Member of the

NOTES: Credit cards accepted: A MasterCard; B Visa; C American Express; D Discover Card; E Diner's Club; F Other; 2 Personal checks accepted; 3 Lunch available; 4 Dinner available; 5 Open all year;

North Vancouver Chamber of Commerce. No GST.

Host: Helen Boire
Rooms: 3 (1 PB; 2 SB) $65 plus
Full Breakfast
Credit Cards: B
Closed Christmas
Notes: 2, 5, 7, 9, 11, 12, 13

Laburnum Cottage Bed and Breakfast

1388 Terrace Avenue, V7R 1B4
(604) 988-4877

Set on one-half acre of award-winning English garden, nestled against a forest, yet only 15 minutes from downtown. Each of the upstairs guest rooms in the main house has its own decor, featuring delicate wallpapers, stunning antiques, and invitingly warm colors complemented by magnificent garden views. Breakfasts are jolly occasions in the big country house-style kitchen near the cozy aga cooker, where all can enjoy a full three- or four-course meal.

Hosts: Delphine and Margot Masterton
Rooms: 3 (PB) $115 150 Canadian
Cottages: 2
Full Breakfast
Credit Cards: A, B
Notes: 2, 5, 8, 9, 10, 11, 12, 13, 14

Laburnum Cottage

Norgate Park House Bed and Breakfast

1226 Silverwood Crescent V7P 1J3
(604) 986-5069; FAX (604) 986-8810

This cedar-sided rancher has had an architect's hand in its renovations. Its intriguing nooks and crannies are filled with statues, wall hangings, and interesting knick-knacks from around the world. Two of the guest rooms open onto an unexpected large West Coast garden that includes more than 1,000 square feet of patio decking. The third room has its own private patio tucked off in a corner of the yard. The garden is both lush and green with ferns and rhododendrons. While sitting on the patio in the morning and having breakfast, it is hard to imagine it is only a 12-minute drive to the center of downtown Vancouver.

Hosts: Vicki Tyndall and Bill Girard
Rooms: 3 (SB) $70-80
Full Breakfast
Credit Cards: A, B
Notes: 5, 10, 11, 12, 13, 14

Old English Bed and Breakfast Registry

1226 Silverwood Crescent, V7P 1J3
(604) 986-5069; FAX (604) 986-8810

1. Lie back and enjoy tranquility at the end of the day in this elegant bed and breakfast. The guest rooms are built into the rocky evergreen slopes and look out through tall cedar and fir to the Pacific, sailing ships, and tiny islands. Guests will find the suites lovingly decorated with an assortment of finery that reflects both Canada and the Orient. Just 20 minutes from downtown Vancouver. Elizabeth has two rooms available; one is a queen-bed sitting room with private bath, fireplace, and, of course, a private patio deck to enjoy the view. The second room has a very large king-size bed, sitting room with a private bath, and private patio deck as well. $105-125.

6 Pets welcome; 8 Children welcome; 9 Social drinking allowed; 10 Tennis available; 11 Swimming available; 12 Golf available; 13 Skiing available; 14 May be booked through travel agents.

2. Jane pampers guests year-round in their own private garden suite in North Vancouver. Tastefully decorated with fine antiques, the suite is very cozy and romantic. It is complete in every detail, including fireplace, TV, stereo, and private patio. Prepare for the memorable gourmet breakfast that awaits each morning in this first-class accommodation. Close to beaches mountains, and only 20 minutes to downtown Vancouver. Children welcome. $95.

3. Guests will receive the royal treatment at Giselle's Bed and Breakfast in North Vancouver. This bed and breakfast is nestled on a very large lot that has a natural, parklike setting. Accommodations consist of three rooms. One room with a queen-size bed is tucked off to the side and has a private bath with a Jacuzzi for two. One of the upstairs rooms has a queen-size bed and its own patio deck. The other room is huge, with a sitting area, a king-size bed, and its own deck. Each room is equipped with TV and telephone. Giselle will bring coffee and the morning paper to start the day before breakfast is served. Near public transportation and 20 minutes from downtown. $75-85.

A Pacific Reservation Service

701 Northwest 60th Street, Seattle, WA 98107
(206) 784-0539

NVAN-1. One acre of seclusion. A short ten-minute ride over the Lions Gate Bridge from downtown. At the end of a dead-end street with a creek running through the award-winning English gardens and a fountain. This Tudor house is furnished with antiques of a distinctly British influence, and offers guests a queen-size room with private bath, a twin room with shared bath, and two private cottages. Breakfast is served in the oversized kitchen around a big table and will surely include some special surprises and a different elegant setting every morning. German and French spoken. From $85-105.

Sue's Victorian Guest House

Sue's Victorian Guest House—Circa 1904

152 East Third, V7L 1E6
(604) 985-1523

This lovely, restored 1904 nonsmoking home is just four blocks from the harbor, seabus terminal, and Quay market. Close to restaurants, shops, and transportation. The decor is ideal for those who appreciate that loving-hand touch, Victorian soaker baths (no showers), and are happy to remove outdoor shoes at the door to help maintain cleanliness. Each room is individually keyed and offers a TV, a short local-call phone, fan, and video player. Minimum stay is three nights during busy seasons; long-term stays encouraged. Cats in residence. Third person is $25 extra.

Host: Sue Chalmers
Rooms: 3 (1 PB; 2 SB) $50-60
No Breakfast
Credit Cards: B (deposit only)
Notes: 2 (for deposit), 5

OSOYOOS

Haynes Point Lakeside Guest House

3619 87th Street, V0H 1V0
(604) 495-7443

This bed and breakfast, overlooking Os-oyoos Lake, has three bedrooms: "Honeymoon," Oriental, and antique decors. All on the main floor. Guests may use living room, spacious deck, hammock, and large outdoor campfire. A marvelous breakfast is served on fine china as guests relax in air-conditioned comfort. Enjoy a walk around Haynes Point Provincial Park. Golf at six courses, all water sports, tennis, biking, horseback riding, and winery tours are available. Hosts enjoy pampering so their visitors have an unforgettable Okanagan holiday.

Hosts: John and June Wallace
Rooms: 3 (1 PB; 2 SB) $60-75
Full Breakfast
Credit Cards: None
Notes: 5, 7 (limited), 8 (by arrangement), 9, 10, 11, 12, 13

PARKSVILLE

All Seasons Bed and Breakfast Agency

P.O. Box 5511, Station B, Victoria, V8R 6S4
(604) 655-7173

Loon Watch. A gracious welcome awaits on Columbia Beach, close to Parksville or Qualicum. Fishermen will delight in local salmon fishing. Beachcomb or visit the many local artists and craftspeople. Cathedral Grove, with its 500-year-old trees, is a treat. Watch ships going up the Inside Passage to Alaska while lying in bed or relaxing on a private deck. Full breakfast. $45-75.

PENDER ISLAND

Hummingbird Hollow Bed and Breakfast

Rural Route 1; 36125 Galleon Way, V0N 2M0
(604) 629-6392

In the beautiful Gulf Islands near Victoria, British Columbia, Hummingbird Hollow is a tranquil lakeside retreat. Share the natural surroundings and eclectic garden with many species of birds, ducks, and deer. Spend leisurely days exploring the many beaches and hidden coves around the island. Spacious suites have refrigerators, queen-size beds, and private sunrooms. Canoe and rowboat available.

Hosts: Doreen Ball and Chuck Harris
Rooms: 3 (PB) $70-90
Full Breakfast
Credit Cards: None
Notes 2, 5, 9, 10, 11, 12

PENTICTON

Paradise Cove Bed and Breakfast

Box 699 Penticton; 3129 Hayman Road, Naramata, V3A 6P1
(604) 496-5896

Deluxe adult-oriented accommodations in this modern home in rolling orchard country overlooking Lake Okanagan. Panoramic lake, orchard, beach view. Clean, very quiet, friendly and comfortable. One full suite with kitchen, laundry, full bath, hot tub room, fireplace. Three queen-size rooms, two with private baths and lakeview decks. All rooms have phones and cable TV. Complimentary beverage service in each room. No pets.

Hostess: Ruth Buchanan
Rooms: 4 (3 PB; 1 SB) $70-95
Full breakfast
Credit Cards: None
Notes: 2, 5, 7 (limited), 8 (limited), 9, 11, 12, 13

PORT ALBERNI

Lakewoods Bed and Breakfast

9778 Stirling Arm Cr. Suite 339 C5 Rural Route 3 V9Y 7L7
(604) 723-2310

This bed and breakfast overlooks beautiful Sproat Lake and welcomes adult travelers to a peaceful waterfront home in a garden

6 Pets welcome; 8 Children welcome; 9 Social drinking allowed; 10 Tennis available; 11 Swimming available; 12 Golf available; 13 Skiing available; 14 May be booked through travel agents.

Lakewoods

setting. Have a swim before turning in or before the hosts serve a homemade breakfast. The hosts enjoy having coffee with their guests in the evenings. Dutch as well as English is spoken.

Hosts: Dick and Jane Visee
Rooms: 3 (1 PB; 2 SB) $55-70
Full Breakfast
Credit Cards: None
Notes: 2, 5, 9, 10, 11, 12, 13

QUILCHENA

Quilchena Hotel

V0E 2R0
(604) 378-2611

Break away from the fast lane. Come and partake of turn-of-the-century charm and down-home hospitality in Quilchena. Established by pioneer Joseph Guichon during the heyday of ranching, Quilchena offers history, recreation, and tranquility on one of British Columbia's largest working cattle ranches. Set against the backdrop of gently rolling range country, overlooking Nicola Lake, and offering a unique experience to people who appreciate fine food, friendly surroundings, leisure activities, and golf. Breakfast not included in rates.

Rooms: 16 (SB) $64-70
Full and Continental Breakfast
Credit Cards: A, B
Notes: 3, 4, 8, 9, 10, 11, 12

QUALICUM BEACH

All Seasons Bed and Breakfast Agency

Box 5511, Station B, Victoria, V8R 6S4
(604) 655-7173

Horse and Pheasant Farm. A warm welcome to this 24-acre horse farm with loads of walking and riding trails. Five minutes west of Parksville, close to Coombs market. Separate cottage (bedroom, bathroom, kitchen, and deck) suitable for two to four people. Bed and breakfast for horses too! (Horse rental nearby.) No pets. No smoking. Wholesome breakfasts suited to individual appetites delivered to the cottage. $69.

Qualicum Bay Bed and Breakfast. Spacious contemporary home on water's edge, 45 minutes north of Nanaimo. Rooms have ensuite bathrooms. Games area, cable TV and more than 50 movies to choose from. Self-contained cottage suitable for two to four people, all amenities. No pets. No smoking. No children under twelve. Full breakfasts served on patio or basket breakfast delivered to cottage. $75-110.

QUALICUM BEACH (VANCOUVER ISLAND)

Garden City Bed and Breakfast Reservation Service

660 Jones Terrace, Victoria, V8Z 2L7
(604) 479-1986; FAX (604) 479-9999

K-24. Rest and repast while visiting this bed and breakfast on seven acres overlooking the Georgia Strait and the Northern Gulf Islands, watch sea lions and seals bask, shuck oysters on beach, or walk the philosopher's path. All attractions are a day-trip or less away. Elderdowns on king-, queen-size, double, or twin beds; all ensuite baths. A two-bedroom, fully equipped suite with ocean view is also available. From $75.

SALMON ARM

Alberta and Pacific Bed and Breakfast Agency

P.O. Box 15477, MPO, Vancouver, V6B 5B2
(604) 944-1793

11. Enjoy the uniqueness of a log home in country tradition, overlooking a wild bird sanctuary on picturesque Shuswap Lake, a ten-minute walk to beautiful Margaret Falls and Herald Park, fifteen minutes by car from Salmon Arm. This home offers a private entrance to ground level walk-out, spacious self-contained guest suite with French doors overlooking garden and lake view, with double bed, seating area, dining area, kitchen, and private bath. On the main floor are two guest rooms, each with double bed and one guest bath.

The Silvercreek Guesthouse

The Silvercreek Guesthouse

6820-30th Avenue S.W. V1E 4M1
(604) 832-8870

This loghouse is on an acreage in a picturesque setting, with a view of the surrounding mountains and the Salmon River Valley. The Shuswap Lake, with 1,000 kilometers of shoreline, provides a variety of water-related activities. Salmon Arm is at the north end of the Okanagan Valley, which is famous for its fruit orchards and vineyards. The Silvercreek serves a full country breakfast with farm-fresh eggs and homemade jams.

Hostess: Gisela Bodnar
Rooms: 4 (1 PB; 3 SB) $35-40
Full Breakfast
Credit Cards: None
Notes: 5, 8, 9, 10, 11, 12, 13

SALT SPRING ISLAND

All Seasons Bed and Breakfast Agency

Box 5511, Station B, Victoria, V8R 6S4
(604) 655-7173

Joha's Eagleview. A 12-minute ferry ride from Campbell River to Quathiaski Cove on Quadra Island. Beautiful contemporary home with deck overlooking the Inside Passage to Alaska. Kayaking in salt or freshwater, shore diving possible from dock at Eagleview. Garden suite with ocean view, suits two to four people. Three-day minimum. Rooms with ocean or garden view. Children over 11. No pets. No smoking. $60-75.

Captain's Passage

1510 Beddis Road, V8K 2E3
(604) 537-9469

Hospitality, comfort, and privacy in a sea-view setting. Five-minute walk to beach, ten-minute drive to town. First-class rooms with wonderful ocean view of other islands and marine traffic. Delicious, full breakfasts with fresh produce and home baking.

Hosts: Bob and Lauretta Wilson
Rooms: 2 (PB) $75

6 Pets welcome; 8 Children welcome; 9 Social drinking allowed; 10 Tennis available; 11 Swimming available; 12 Golf available; 13 Skiing available; 14 May be booked through travel agents.

Captain's Passage

Full Breakfast
Credit Cards: A, B, C
Notes: 2, 5, 9, 10, 11, 12, 14

Cranberry Ridge
Bed and Breakfast

269 Don Ore Drive, V8K 2H5
(604) 537-4854

New home especially designed for bed and breakfast. Two kilometers south of Ganges, the main village on the island, on the route to Mount Maxwell Park. Fantastic view of the Gulf Islands and Georgia Strait from the Sunshine Coast of British Columbia to Mount Vernon in Washington State. Three bed and breakfast rooms with private entrances to each room. The Twig Room has a fireplace. Two rooms have Jaccuzi baths and showers. Large hot tub on the deck overlooking the view. All rooms face the view. "The Best of the Best on Salt Spring."

Hosts: Gloria and Rodger Lutz
Rooms: 3 (PB) $90-125
Full Breakfast
Credit Cards: A, B
Notes: 5, 7 (limited), 8 (over 16), 9, 10, 11, 12, 14

Garden City
Bed and Breakfast
Reservation Service

660 Jones Terrace, Victoria, V8Z 2L7
(604) 479-1986; FAX (604) 479-9999

K-23. On six-acres overlooking ocean and snowcapped mountains, this bed and breakfast offers a king-size bed with private bath, deck, and entrance. Fresh home baking, delicious breakfast, and will cater to vegetarians. From $65.

Weston Lake Inn
Bed and Breakfast

813 Beaver Point Road, V8K 1X9
(604) 653-4311

Nestled on a knoll of flowering trees and shrubs overlooking beautiful Weston Lake, this exquisite country bed and breakfast is a serene adult getaway. Down quilts, fresh bouquets, a fireside lounge, hot tub, wonderful breakfasts, and warm hospitality. Recommended in *Northwest Best Places*, the *Vancouver Sun*, and the *Seattle Times*. Salt Spring Island, near Victoria, has a mild climate, exceptional beauty, and a large population of artists and artisans. Hosts also offer skippered sailing charters in the beautiful waters of the Gulf Islands on a 36-foot boat.

Hosts: Susan Evans and Ted Harrison
Rooms: 3 (PB) $85-105
Full Breakfast
Credit Cards: A, B, C
Notes: 2, 5, 9, 10, 11, 12, 14

SHAWNIGAN LAKE (VANCOUVER ISLAND)__

Garden City
Bed and Breakfast
Reservation Service

660 Jones Terrace, Victoria, V8Z 2L7
(604) 479-1986; FAX (604) 479-9999

K-4. This lovely old home with a country atmosphere is between Victoria and Nanaimo. Just a five-minute walk to beach and lake. Queen-size and twin beds upstairs; shared bath. Main floor offers double bed with semi-private bath. Hearty country breakfast. From $55.

K-30. Peaceful country acreage. Just five minutes to beach, 45 minutes to Victoria, and near water sports, hiking, fishing, and golf. Enjoy home-cooked waffles, omelets, fresh fruite, etc. Queen-size, double, twin beds, ensuite and shared baths. From $55.

SIDNEY (VANCOUVER ISLAND)

All Seasons Bed and Breakfast Agency

Box 5511, Station B, Victoria, V8R 6S4
(604) 655-7173

Wind in the Willows. Quiet southwest exposure boasts terrific views of the Saanich Inlet. Close to airport, ferries, golf, sailing, Butchart Gardens. No children. No pets. No smoking. Full breakfast. $75-85.

SOOKE (VANCOUVER ISLAND)

Garden City Bed and Breakfast Reservation Service

660 Jones Terrace, Victoria, V8Z 2L7
(604) 479-1986; FAX (604) 479-9999

L-17. Two acres of incredible waterfront property overlooking a large estuary that attracts swans, geese, eagles, herons, etc. Watch the sunset or beachcomb. Private ensuite bath has a sauna, a six-foot Jacuzzi tub, separate shower, etc. Four-poster queen-size bed. Full breakfast served. Friendly dog in residence, so no guest pets. Ask about the new, beautiful family suite. From $95.

Ocean Wilderness

109 West Coast Road, Rural Route 2, V0S 1N0
(604) 646-2116

Ocean Wilderness offers five peaceful forested acres with beach; a natural haven for romantics. Watch for whales and eagles from the hot tub tucked in the Japanese gazebo. The large luxurious rooms with private entrances are furnished with antiques and canopied beds. Plant a "memory tree" after a multi-course breakfast served in the rustic log dining room.

Host: Marion Rolston
Rooms: 7 (PB) $75-150
Full Breakfast
Credit Cards: A, B
Notes: 2, 4 (by arrangement), 5, 6 and 8
  (by arrangement), 9, 12, 14

Ocean Wilderness

Sooke Harbour House

1528 Whiffen Spit Road, Rural Route 4, V0S 1N0
(604) 642-3421; FAX (604) 642-6988

Thirteen romantic guest rooms have fireplaces and breathtaking water views, some offering Jacuzzi tubs for two or hot tubs on private decks. Internationally renowned restaurant offers fresh local fish and shellfish, organic vegetables, salad greens, and edible flowers that are grown in the gardens, on nearby organic farms or harvested in the wilds around Sooke. This romantic inn is right on the water, 45 minutes Southwest of Victoria, on Vancouver Island.

Hosts: Sinclair and Frederique Philip
Rooms: 13 (PB) $155-275
Full Breakfast and Lunch
Credit Cards: A, B, C
Notes: 2, 4, 5, 6, 8, 9, 10, 11, 12, 14

6 Pets welcome; 8 Children welcome; 9 Social drinking allowed; 10 Tennis available; 11 Swimming available; 12 Golf available; 13 Skiing available; 14 May be booked through travel agents.

TOFINO

Silver Cloud

Box 188, V0R 2Z0
(604) 725-3998

Large waterfront property nestled in the quiet privacy of woods with two acres of spectacular gardens encircling the house and along the water. Bald eagles, otters, seals; excellent birding spot. Romantic, tastefully appointed queen-size rooms and private baths with view. Continental breakfast served on fine china in solarium overlooking water. Lower deck with ramp to beach. Gas barbeque. Nonview full apartment galley and bath also available. Sleeps two to four.

Host: Olivia Mae
Rooms: 3 (PB) $80-150
Continental Breakfast
Credit Cards: None
Notes: 5, 7, 9 (limited), 10, 11, 12

UCLUELET

All Seasons Bed and Breakfast Agency

Box 5511, Station B, Victoria, V8R 6S4
(604) 655-7173

Sheila's Bed and Breakfast. Quiet, friendly country setting off the Pacific Rim Highway a few minutes from Wikininish and Long Beach. Visit Hot Springs Cove or go fishing or whale watching. Tofino is home to the Longhouse Gallery of Canadian artist Roy Vickers. Comfortable rooms and cheery breakfasts. Adults only. No smoking. No pets. $45-55.

Burley's

1078 Helen Road, Box 550, V0R 3A0
(604) 726-4444

A waterfront home on a small drive-to island at the harbor mouth, offering single, double, and queen-size water- and regular

Burley's

beds, and TV in friendly Ucluelet. Enjoy the open ocean, sandy beaches, lighthouse lookout, nature walks, charter fishing, diving, fisherman's wharves, whale watching and sightseeing cruises, or later, the exhilarating winter storms. A view from every window. No pets; no smoking. Adult oriented. French spoken.

Hosts: Ron and Micheline Burley
Rooms: 6 (S4B) $40-65
Full Breakfast
Credit Cards: A, B
Notes: 10, 11, 12

VANCOUVER

Alberta and Pacific Bed and Breakfast Agency

P.O. Box 15477, MPO, V6B 5B2
(604) 944-1793

7. This Heritage Home is a short distance by car to downtown, Stanley Park, and Granville Island. The newly renovated suite of three rooms with private entrance, ground floor level, has one guest room with queen-size bed and sitting area, one with twin beds, guest lounge, and one guest bath.

NOTES: Credit cards accepted: A MasterCard; B Visa; C American Express; D Discover Card; E Diner's Club; F Other; 2 Personal checks accepted; 3 Lunch available; 4 Dinner available; 5 Open all year;

Albion Guest House Bed and Breakfast

592 W. 19th Avenue, U5Z-1W6
(604) 873-2287

This restored 1906 character home is on a quiet, tree-lined residential street in the city. Within walking distance of restaurants, speciality coffee shops, delicatessens, parks, theaters, shopping, a gambling casino, beaches, boating, parasailing, and windsurfing activities. Free bicycle rentals. The three guest rooms have thick feather mattresses, fine cotton linens, and down-filled duvets. The guests enjoy complimentary aperitifs, refreshments, and a gourmet breakfast. Nonsmoking establishment. Reservations recommended.

Hosts: Bill, Howard, Joyce and Guller
Rooms: 3 (1 PB, 2 SB) $85-120
Full Gourmet Breakfast
Credit Cards: A, B
Notes: 9, 10, 11, 12, 13, 14

All Seasons Bed and Breakfast Agency

Box 5511, Station B, Victoria, V8R 6S4
(604) 655-7173

Jane's Gourmet Bed and Breakfast. Private suite with queen-size bed, private bath, fireplace, TV, stereo, and antiques. Unwind and relax in a quiet residential area of North Vancouver, only 20 minutes from downtown. Close to the beach, mountains, and Horseshoe Bay ferry. Memorable full breakfasts. $85.

Laburnum Cottage. This charming home with beautifully appointed rooms is set on one-half acre of award-winning English country gardens. Featured in *Country Inns* magazine June 1992. All private bathrooms and queen-size beds. Superb full breakfasts. Check-in flexible. No smoking. No pets. $100.

Beautiful Bed and Breakfast

428 W 40th Avenue, V5Y 2R4
(604) 327-1102

Relax in elegance in this gorgeous, clean new Colonial home with antiques, fresh flowers, views, and quiet. Great central location five minutes from downtown. Walk to tennis, golf, Queen Elizabeth Park, VanDusen Gardens, YMCA/YWCA, three cinemas, shopping center, and fine restaurants. Three-quarters of a block from bus to downtown, airport, ferries, and UBC. Breakfast in formal dining room with linens, silver, fresh flowers. Friendly helpful host will assist the guest with travel plans. Nonsmoking. No pets. No children.

Hosts: Ian and Corinne Sanderson
Rooms: 6 (2 PB; 4 SB) $70-150
Full Breakfast
Credit Cards: None
Notes: 10, 12

Delta Place Hotel

645 Howe Street, V6C 2Y9
(604) 687-1122

The Delta Place Hotel is downtown Vancouver's full-service boutique hotel. With 197 superbly furnished rooms and suites, the Delta Place is a tranquil retreat in the heart of downtown Vancouver. With its central location, most things are within easy walking distance of the hotel, including great restaurants, museums, and the theatre, as well as the 195 shops of Pacific Centre directly across the street. Experienced leisure travelers will appreciate the friendly and knowledgeable staff, well-equipped health club, and superb cuisine.

Host: Marc Armstrong, General Manager
Rooms: 197 (PB) $99-240
Credit Cards: A, B, C, D, E, F
Notes: 2, 3, 4, 5, 6, 7, 8, 9, 11, 13, 14

Diana's Luxury Bed and Breakfast

1019 East 38 Avenue, V5W 1J4
(604) 321-2855

---

6 Pets welcome; 8 Children welcome; 9 Social drinking allowed; 10 Tennis available; 11 Swimming available; 12 Golf available; 13 Skiing available; 14 May be booked through travel agents.

This bed and breakfast is ten minutes from the airport and ten minutes from downtown Vancouver. Open year-round, it is close to shopping, restaurants, Stanley Park, Whistler ski area, and theaters. Guest accommodations include four guest rooms with shared bath, common living room with TV; a honeymoon suite with private bath, TV, Jacuzzi, and phone; and a self-contained one-bedroom apartment. Reservations with a one-night deposit required.

Hosts: Diana and Danny
Rooms: 6 (2 PB; 4 SB) $60
Full Breakfast
Credit Cards: A, B
Notes: 5, 7, 8, 9, 10, 11, 12, 13, 14

An English Garden Bed and Breakfast

4390 Frances Street, V5C 2R3
(604) 298-8815; Message (800) 488-1914;
FAX (604) 298-5917

White-stucco bungalow ten minutes from the top of Burnaby Mountain with its view of Vancouver, Grouse and Seymour Mountains, and Burrard Inlet. Two guest rooms, each with TV; one room has a view of the mountains. No pets; the hosts have a cat. A quick phone call in advance is appreciated.

Host: Norma McCurrach
Rooms: 2 (1 PB; 1 SB) $45-75
Full Breakfast
Credit Cards: A, B
Notes: 5, 10, 11, 12, 13, 14

Green Gables

628 Union Street, V6A 2B9
(604) 253-6230

Receive a warm welcome and friendly hospitality at Green Gables. Recently renovated, this 1898 Heritage Home is only one block from public transport or ten minutes' walk to downtown. The twin rooms are bright and comfortable, and guests are encouraged to feel at home in the dining and living areas, as well as the back sundeck overlooking the colorful garden. Over a de-

Green Gables

licious breakfast, plans are made for the day, and the well-traveled hosts are glad to help with tourist information.

Hosts: Carl and Mariko Shepherd
Rooms: 7 (SB) $40-59
Full Breakfast
Credit Cards: None
Notes: 5, 8, 9, 10, 13

Johnson House Bed and Breakfast

2278 W. 34th Avenue, V6M 1G6
(604) 266-4175

Wonderful restored Craftsman-style home is furnished with Canadiana antique furniture, carousel horses, and comfy brass and

Johnson House

iron beds. Full breakfasts including a main course, fresh fruit, and homemade muffins and jams. The friendly hosts invite guests to stay in one of Vancouver's finest and safest city neighborhoods. The house is a six-minute drive to downtown or the university and is close to fine restaurants, services, and tourist attractions. Fifteen minutes from the airport.

Hosts: Sandy and Ron Johnson
Rooms: 3 (2 PB; 1 SB) $65-105
Full Breakfast
Credit Cards: None
Notes: 2, 5, 9, 10, 11, 12, 13, 14

Kenya Court Guest House

2230 Cornwall Avenue, V6K 1B5
(604) 738-7085

Oceanview suites on the waterfront in a gracious heritage building minutes from downtown Vancouver. Across the street are tennis courts, a large heated saltwater pool, and walking and jogging paths along the water's edge. It's an easy walk to Granville Island, the planetarium, and interesting shops and restaurants. All the suites are large and tastefully furnished. Breakfast is served in a glass solarium with a spectacular view of English Bay.

Host: D.M. Williams
Suites: 4 (PB) From $85
Full Breakfast
Credit Cards: F
Notes: 2, 5, 9, 10, 11, 13

Lakewood House Bed and Breakfast

2118 East 10th Avenue, V5N 1Y1
(604) 251-2242; FAX (604) 253-7971

Lakewood House is a very convenient and quiet location. A short walk of three blocks to a Skytrain station, a beautiful lake, park, many restaurants and coffee houses. It is a newly constructed inn with great care and attention given to details that guests appreciate. The guest rooms have cable TV, private sink and mirror; with and without

private bath. Guests have access to a fully equipped guest kitchen with an adjoining laundry facility. The hosts take great pride in creating a comfortable atmosphere for their guests. They give careful attention to providing a generous and balanced breakfast for each guest at a time that is convenient.

Host: Alois Jauk
Rooms: $60-80
Continental Breakfast
Credit Cards: None
Notes: 6, 7, 8, 10, 11

The Manor Guest House

345 W. 13th Avenue, V5Y 1W2
(604) 876-5703

The Manor Guest House, an Edwardian Heritage mansion, is one of Vancouver's finest bed and breakfasts. Choose from nine spacious high-ceilinged rooms, most with king-size or twin beds and private bath. The self-contained penthouse suite has a loft, kitchen, and private deck, which offers a spectacular, unobstructed view of the city. The manor is in the heart of the city, a block from city hall and close to everything the guest would want to do in Vancouver. Generous healthful breakfast, featuring fresh daily baking.

The Manor Guest House

---

6 Pets welcome; 8 Children welcome; 9 Social drinking allowed; 10 Tennis available; 11 Swimming available; 12 Golf available; 13 Skiing available; 14 May be booked through travel agents.

Host: Brenda Rabkin
Rooms: 10 (6 PB; 4 SB) $55-95
Full Breakfast
Credit Cards: A, B
Notes: 5, 8, 9, 10, 11, 12, 13, 14

Nelson House

Nelson House

977 Broughton Street, V6G 2A4
(604) 684-9793

Nelson House is a large, 1907 Edwardian on a quiet, residential street, only minutes' walk from downtown, Stanley Park, and the beaches. Glowing fireplaces and a happy springer spaniel assure a warm welcome. The hosts are travelers, too, and each guest room suggests a different itinerary. Euro-style rooms that share the "loo" have a private washbasin. The "Studio," however, has it all—fireplace, kitchen, deck, Jacuzzi, and romantic Asian ambience.

Hosts: David Ritchie and O'Neal Williamson
Rooms: 5 (1 PB; 4 SB) $68-140
Full Breakfast
Credit Cards: A, B
Notes: 5, 9, 10, 11, 13, 14

Olde English Bed and Breakfast

1226 Silver Crescent, North Vancouver, V7P 1J3
(604) 986-5069; FAX (604) 986-8810

4. Near Stanley Park, this cedar-sided rancher has had an architect's hand in its renovations. The home is only 12 minutes from the center of downtown Vancouver. One guest room has a queen-size bed; another has twin beds; a third accommodates a single person. The three rooms share a bath. There is a sitting room with TV in the same wing. No smoking. No pets; resident cats. Not suitable for toddlers. $70.

5. This original Kitsilano Mansion has been completely remodeled while preserving its uniqueness. Each of the three guest rooms is thematically decorated with paintings and artwork. The Master Room contains a king-size bed, toilet, and sink. The other two rooms are queen-size; one includes a fireplace and French doors leading to a patio. There are two shared baths. Common areas include a steam room/sauna, full kitchen and sitting area with TV and a patio. No smoking. No pets. $85-95.

6. The Cliffridge is a one-level home decorated with a mixture of elegance and rattan. The guest area is a very private wing consisting of two bedrooms, a full shared bath, a living room with fireplace and a dining area. The queen-size bedroom opens onto a sunny garden; the other has a double bed, used only for family or traveling companions. Close to Grouse Mountain, Capilano Canyon Suspension Bridge, Cleveland Dam, hiking trails, and bus transportation to the city. $85.

7. The Roberts' Bed and Breakfast is high on the hill overlooking Horseshoe Bay, where many ferries come and go. Guests have a very private king-size bedroom with private bath and shower. The sitting room includes TV, stereo, and fireplace and opens onto a patio. Downtown Vancouver is 30 minutes away; Whistler only 75 minutes. No smoking. Not suitable for small children. No pets. $95.

NOTES: Credit cards accepted: A MasterCard; B Visa; C American Express; D Discover Card; E Diner's Club; F Other; 2 Personal checks accepted; 3 Lunch available; 4 Dinner available; 5 Open all year;

A Pacific Reservation Service

701 Northwest 60th Street, Seattle, WA 98107
(206) 784-0539

VAN-3. This Tudor house is furnished with antiques of a distinctly British influence and offers guests a room with a queen-size bed and a private bath, or one with twin and double beds, as well as two private cottages. Breakfast is served in the oversized kitchen and will include some special surprises and a different elegant setting every morning. Grouse Mountain and other attractions are nearby. $65-75.

VAN-4. This cozy, country heritage guest home features three private rooms with sitting area, cable TV, and private bath. Enjoy the full farm breakfasts in the morning, and take a dip in the large outdoor heated pool or soak in the whirlpool. $40-55.

Town and Country Bed and Breakfast in British Columbia

P.O. Box 74542
2803 West Fourth Avenue V6K 1K2
(604) 731-5942

Offering bed and breakfast homes in residential areas of Vancouver and Victoria, and the listings include some small inns. A few of the listings have waterfront or special views. Private and shared baths available. Some have from one to three guest rooms. Some character homes, some West Coast-style homes or townhouse accommodations. Usually within 15-20 minutes to city centre.

1. This comfortable, newly decorated home is in a quiet, central neighborhood. The hospitable hosts speak French and Ukrainian and enjoy sharing helpful information on the city. Close to restaurants, shops, parks, and major bus lines. Two guest rooms. Full breakfast. From $65.

2. Rest and relax in this home away from home. Guests have a choice of three lock-and-keyed bedrooms, each with a unique character. Antiques and collectibles from around the world are found throughout the house. A hearty breakfast featuring pancakes, eggs cooked any style, cereals, fresh fruits and juices, muffins, and wild oak porridge topped with fruit, nuts, sunflower seeds, and brown sugar. In the City Hall Heritage area. $75-135.

3. This modern home, directly across from the beach and park has a magnificent view of sea and mountains. German is a second language. Bus stops in front; 15 minutes to downtown and 10 minutes to UBC. Restricted smoking. No pets as there is a cat and dog on premises. Swimming, sailing, tennis, Jericho Nature Park are all five minutes away. Guest rooms have queen-size or double bed. Shared bathrooms. Breakfast served from 7:30 to 9:30 A.M. $75-95.

4. North Vancouver. Restful, peaceful seclusion. This charming home, with a Victorian air and antiques, is set on a half-acre of beautifully kept, award-winning English garden and surrounded by virgin forest. Only 15 minutes from downtown Vancouver and Horseshoe Bay; 5 minutes from Grouse Mountain and other North Shore attractions. Delphine and family offer beautifully appointed guest rooms, a choice of single, twin, or queen-sized beds. The Summer Cottage in the garden is a perfect honeymoon hideaway! Relax on the patio or in the cool of the garden with its little meandering creek. Everyone enjoys Delphine's great breakfasts with homemade jams, muffins, and blueberry pancakes made on the Aga stove. Only two blocks from major bus routes, lots of parking. German and French are spoken here. No smoking. $115-145.

6 Pets welcome; 8 Children welcome; 9 Social drinking allowed; 10 Tennis available; 11 Swimming available; 12 Golf available; 13 Skiing available; 14 May be booked through travel agents.

5. Not the usual bed and breakfast, this is a private suite one block from bus line, terrific view of mountains, sea, city. Fifteen minutes to downtown. Bedroom with queen-size bed, sitting room with Queen-size sofa bed, TV, also kitchen facilities. Suitable for three or four traveling together. No children. $85.

The Wedgewood Hotel

845 Hornby Street, V6Z 1V1
(604) 689-7777; (800) 663-0666

In the heart of downtown Vancouver across from the Court House, Art Gallery, and Robson Square, this four-star boutique hotel offers 93 luxurious guest rooms and suites, fine Italian restaurant with dancing to live entertainment, a popular piano lounge, coffee shop, health club, meeting and banquet facilities, valet parking, and more.

Hosts: Eleni Skalbania and Joanna Tsaparas
Rooms: 93 (PB) $180-420
Full or Continental Breakfast
Credit Cards: A, B, C, D, E, F
Notes: 3, 4, 5, 7, 8, 9, 14

The West End Guest House

1362 Hard Street, V6E 1G2
(604) 681-2889; FAX (604) 688-8812

This Heritage House was constructed in 1906 and occupied by one of the city's first photographers. Today, the West End Guest House offers the informal ambience of a fine country inn, the amenities of a small luxury hotel, and the excitement of its surroundings, such as shopping on Robson Street, a walk in Stanley Park, a peak at the zoo, possibly a splash at the Whale Show, or a romantic gaze at a sunset on English Bay. Rooms include a bathroom, TV, telephone, off-street parking, bathrobes and slippers, full breakfast, use of two bikes, and a sun deck with wicker furniture where, on a hot summer day, iced tea is served. Sherry is provided year-round in front of the fireplace.

Rooms: 7 (PB) $100-195
Full Breakfast
Credit Cards: A, B, C, D
Notes: 2, 5, 10, 11, 12, 13, 14

VERNON

The Falcon Nest Lodge

Rural Route 8, Site 7A, Comp. 1, V1T 8L6
((604) 545-1759; FAX (604) 545-1759

Exceptional comfort, attentive hospitality, and international cuisine at a vantage point high above the Okanagan Valley, Lake Okanagan, and the city of Vernon. The Falcon Nest is Emmy Kennedy's winning creation—a large, contemporary wood home with a variety of accommodations to suite most any travel need, from a family outing to a romantic escape. The interior is in perfect keeping with the magnificent view. Rooms are spacious, open, and beautifully appointed. Generous breakfasts with a European flair are served in three areas, so that different groups can gather as they wish. The living room has a fireplace and inviting places to sit, relax, visit, or read; while an adjoining room has a carpeted conversation pit in front of another fireplace. Accommodations, which are well spread out in this rambling home, are quite varied, yet Emmy's high standards of comfort and aesthetics remain constant. The host is an artist and an adventurer; she takes no shortcuts where her guests are concerned. Smoking outside only; full breakfast, game room; solarium with hot tub; TV in living room; Room D is a family accommodation for up to four people; hot springs, skiing, hiking, fishing, golfing, and horseback riding nearby. German and Italian spoken. Off-street parking. Honeymoon suite with Jacuzzi tub also available. Brochure available.

Host: Emmy Kennedy
Rooms: 7 (3 PB; 4 SB) $50-60, Suites from $85
Full Breakfast
Credit Cards: B
Notes: 4, 5, 6 (limited), 7 (limited), 8 (by arrangement), 9, 10, 11, 12, 13, 14

NOTES: Credit cards accepted: A MasterCard; B Visa; C American Express; D Discover Card; E Diner's Club; F Other; 2 Personal checks accepted; 3 Lunch available; 4 Dinner available; 5 Open all year;

Quail Bay

7603 West Kal Road, V1B 1Y4
(604) 542-3021

Lakefront turn-of-the-century cottage decorated in Victorian antiques and family heirlooms. Enjoy a full breakfast on the veranda
as the ducks swim by. Canoe and experience the serenity of the beautiful lake. A romantic get away. Cozy and private. The
mascot Bailey will wag her tail in greeting.

Host: Samantha Kosty
Rooms: 2
Cottage: 1 (PB) $65-90
Full Breakfast
Credit Cards: None
Notes: 6 (limited), 8, 9, 10, 11, 12, 13

The Schroth Farm

S6 C25 Rural Route 8, V1T 8L6
(604) 545-0010

Enjoy the farm. Only one mile from Vernon. This cozy, clean, vintage home offers a
self-contained guest room with adjoining
family room. Twin beds and double beds.
Private entrance, private bath. Single and
double rooms with private bath. The guest
rooms have their own VCR, cable TV, and
big refrigerator. Large patio for relaxing
hours, while watching the cattle and miniature goats on green pastures against a
mountain backdrop. Plenty of room, bring
the children. Winter skiing, sandy beaches,
excellent golf courses, trail riding, water
slide, mountain chair lift, and more in the
area. Canada's Playland.

Hosts: Fred and Helen Schroth
Rooms: 2 (PB) $45-55
Full Breakfast
Credit Cards: None
Notes: 5, 8, 9, 10, 11, 12, 13

Windmill House

5672 Learmouth Road; Rural Route 1, V1T 6L4
(604) 549-2804

Very unique windmill-shaped house in a
valley between low mountains. All-wood
interior and large living room give the

Windmill House

Windmill House a lodge-type atmosphere.
Three choices of full cooked breakfasts and
homemade muffins and jams await the
guest in the morning.

Hosts: Cor and Mary Manders
Rooms: 5 (2 PB; 3 SB) $46-70
Full Breakfast
Credit Cards: A, B
Notes: 3, 4, 5, 6, 8, 9, 10, 11, 12, 13

VICTORIA

Abigail's Bed and Breakfast Inn

906 McClure Street, V8V 3E7
(604) 388-5363; FAX (604) 361-1905

A short walk away from Victoria's main
attractions and fabulous shopping is Abigail's, a handsome Tudor building described as all gables and gardens and
crystal chandeliers. Inside, not a lavish detail is missed. Guest rooms are tastefully
decorated and have all been updated. A
number of rooms have private Jaccuzi
baths and wood-burning fireplaces. Abigail's offers a warm welcoming staff, a full
gourmet breakfast, and an evening sherry
hour for its guests.

6 Pets welcome; 8 Children welcome; 9 Social drinking allowed; 10 Tennis available; 11 Swimming available;
12 Golf available; 13 Skiing available; 14 May be booked through travel agents.

Host: Julie Usher
Rooms: 16 (PB) $112-215
Full Breakfast
Credit Cards: A, B
Notes: 5, 8, 9, 14

Alberta and Pacific Bed and Breakfast Agency

P.O. Box 15477, MPO, Vancouver, V6B 5B2
(604) 944-1793

8. Chalet, German-style home is opposite Swan Lake and within walking distance of Swan Lake Nature Sanctuary, restaurants, a pub; buses to the university, downtown, and Butchart Gardens. Spacious guest room has two double beds, seating area with TV, sliding glass doors to upper deck with panoramic view, and private ensuite bath. Second guest room is Victorian style with queen-size bed and private ensuite bath. Third guest room is on the main floor with double bed and shared bath and a Jacuzzi. Fourth guest room has twin beds, shared bath, Jacuzzi, available August only.

All Seasons Bed and Breakfast Agency

P.O. Box 5511, Station B, V8R 6S4
(604) 655-7173

Arundel Manor. Gracious Heritage Home on one-half acre of lawns and gardens, a short drive from city centre. The property slopes to an inlet. Superb sunset views. Full breakfast served in the handsome dining room or on the veranda. All rooms have private baths. Two rooms have balconies overlooking the water. Special gatherings or small weddings can be arranged. Honeymoons are special. $95-110.

Banavern. Splendid 1908 Edwardian home built by Samuel Maclure in an area of tall trees and mansion homes. A short walk to Government House, Craigdarrouch Castle, and Antique Row. Large rooms with private baths and fireplaces. Warm and friendly atmosphere with many extras. Full breakfast. Children and pets are welcome by prior arrangement. Check-in between 4:00 and 6:00 P.M. $75.

Bowden House. Built in 1913, this quiet, comfortable character home has been personally restored by the owners. It has high ceilings and the relaxed charm and ambience of the traditional bed and breakfast. Wake up to the aroma of fresh coffee and a hearty English breakfast. Stroll through Banfield Park overlooking the Seilerk Water. Guest rooms share bathrooms. $45-60.

Cadboro Bay. Lovely modern home is close to picturesque Cadboro Bay Village and the University of Victoria; only minutes from a sandy beach. Quiet secluded garden patio. Two rooms with brass beds are decorated in English country style with shared bath. There is also a detached cottage in the garden surrounded by flowers and containing a queen-size bed, private bath, kitchenette with microwave oven, and offers total privacy. Gourmet breakfasts. No smoking. No pets. $60-70.

Cedar Shade. Enjoy the quiet and comfort of this home with its herb garden, cedar-shaded pond, and lantern-lit patio. Quiet slumber under goose-down quilts. Ideal for families. Close to Butchart Gardens. Vegetarian or Continental fare. Check-in between 4:00 and 6:00 P.M. Hosts speak Ukranian. Nonsmoking. Queen-size or twin beds, shared bath. $60.

Ease Mate. Welcoming contemporary home in Cape Cod-style with extensive grounds. Antique pine furnishings and comfortable beds. Enjoy the stay with hosts who are keenly interested in the visual arts. Close to Butchart Gardens, the British Columbia Ferry Terminal at Swartz Bay, and a five-minute drive to Sidney or the airport. Full breakfast. Children welcome. Ask about pets. Considerate smokers. $35-75.

Fanny Davis Bed and Breakfast. Step back in time when staying in this 1910 Edwardian home with beamed ceilings and stained-glass windows, set in a flowery English-style garden in quiet Fairfield. Period furniture, queen-size beds, and down comforters. Three-course breakfast served on Wedgwood china. Close to Craigdarroch Castle, Victoria Art Gallery, Antique Row, and the seafront at Clover Point. Well-behaved pets are welcome by prior arrangement. $75-85.

French Beach Retreat. Secluded oceanfront retreat. A complete three-bedroom house with a wraparound balcony and view of the Strait of Juan de Fuca and Olympic Mountains. TV, stereo, VCR, fireplace, library, full kitchen, barbecue, microwave, and dishwasher. Walk to French Beach five minutes away or sit on a quiet cliff bench and watch the whales, eagles, and sea lions. Breakfast supplies and a complimentary bottle of wine provided. Stay a day or a month. $125-$1,200.

Gracefield Manor. Restored Plantation Colonial on 11 acres with breathtaking views of the Olympic Mountains and the sea. Endless opportunities for hikers, beachcombers, photographers, naturalists, and artists. Enjoy gracious living and antique furnishings, private baths, and full breakfasts. No smoking. No pets. $55-100.

Grahams Cedar House. Spectacular West Coast home in a woodsy setting where it is possible to listen to the peace and quiet. The town of Sidney is seven minutes away. Close to the Stone House Pub and the ferry terminal. The romantic master suite looks out on the deck and garden. The two-bedroom suite with full kitchen, bath, pri-

vate entrance, and patio accommodates up to six people. Full and healthy breakfasts and delicious baked goods often served on the sunny deck. It is a treat. No smoking. No pets. Air conditioning. $75-85.

Island View Bed and Breakfast. Spacious contemporary home overlooking quiet farmland with a great view of Mount Baker in Washington State. Island View Beach is just a short drive away. Dutch and German spoken. Air exchange system. $60-65.

Maridou House. Edwardian home close to the waterfront. Quiet, sunny rooms with many special touches to make guests feel at home. The McFarland Room (the Honeymoon Suite) boasts a lace-covered canopied bed and ensuite bathroom. Champagne and roses upon request! The rooms are named for the Scottish heritage of the owners. Full breakfast. No smoking. No pets. Check-in between 3:00 and 6:00 P.M.

Mulberry Manor. A jewel of the post-Victorian era, one of the last great houses designed by the renowed architect Samuel Maclure. Close to Oak Bay and surrounded by delightful landscaped gardens. Most rooms have balconies. This elegant home is superbly decorated, and was featured in the *House and Gardens* tour of Victoria in May 1993. All private baths. Truly special. Check-in by arrangement. $95-150.

Myllford Haven House. Enjoy this cottage-style, early 1900s bungalow where visitors to Victoria may enjoy Canadian hospitality. Begin the day with a hearty breakfast served in the bright and cheerful dining room, and finish the day by relaxing in the cozy parlor or garden. Queen-size beds and private baths. No children. No smoking. No pets. $62.50-75.

6 Pets welcome; 8 Children welcome; 9 Social drinking allowed; 10 Tennis available; 11 Swimming available; 12 Golf available; 13 Skiing available; 14 May be booked through travel agents.

Orchard House. Original farmhouse owned by the family who gave the land to Sidney to develop the town. Built in 1914, it retains many original features while offering total comfort. A five-minute walk from the Anacortes ferry, also within walking distance of the beach, tennis, shops, and restaurants. A favorite with those traveling by bicycle. Full breakfast served in the paneled dining room. Shared baths. Open year-round. No smoking. No pets. $45-69.

Prior House. Elegant English mansion built in 1912 for the King's representative in British Columbia. Enjoy the relaxed ambience of days gone by. Canopied beds, down comforters, private baths, and working fireplaces in every room. Breakfast is served in the paneled dining room overlooking the large garden terrace. Afternoon tea in the parlor. $110-190.

Raven Tree Gardens. Tudor style house on ten acres of garden and woodland, renowned iris gardens blooming in May and June. Quiet and secluded, afternoon tea served on the terrace overlooking the trout pond or in the guest lounge. Close to Sooke and the West Coast beaches. Close to historic 17 Mile House Pub. Children under 12 are welcome. Restricted smoking allowed. No pets. $75-90.

The Weekender. Open only on weekends from October to May. Open full time from June to September. Lovely home in South Fairfield area, just 200 feet from the ocean. Ideal for walkers and joggers. A short walk to Beacon Hill Park and Cook Street Village. Two large guest rooms with ensuite baths; one has a balcony with ocean views. Continental breakfast. Check-in from 4:00 to 6:00 P.M. No smoking. No pets. $70-90.

West Wind. The West Wind is on two acres of wooded privacy, just north of Pacific Rim National Park. Relax and unwind in beautiful surroundings in this home away from home. With one queen-size bed, one double bed, and a Hide-a-bed, it is ideal for a quiet retreat to a maximum of six people. Imagine a deluxe guest house with a fully equipped kitchen and a five-minute walk to Chesterman's Beach, Tofino's best-kept secret! Experience the serenity, the seclusion, and the solitude.

Wintercott. Traditional country house close to Butchart Gardens, 15-minute drive from Victoria. All rooms have private baths, four-poster beds, TV. Hot tub indoors. Weekend packages available. English cooked breakfasts, homemade bread, jams, and muffins. Afternoon tea in the atrium or on the deck. $85.

Ambleside Bed and Breakfast

1121 Faithful Street, V8V 2R5
(604) 383-9948; FAX (604) 383-3647

Ambleside offers traditional bed and breakfast hospitality in a freshly decorated 1920 Craftsman home in one of downtown Victoria's most scenic, walkable, and tranquil heritage neighborhoods. Delightful easy stroll to Inner Harbor through Beacon Hill Park or along panoramic oceanside pathways. Guest rooms feature Edwardian antique beds with eiderdown comforters and excellent mattresses. King-, queen-size, and

Ambleside

NOTES: Credit cards accepted: A MasterCard; B Visa; C American Express; D Discover Card; E Diner's Club; F Other; 2 Personal checks accepted; 3 Lunch available; 4 Dinner available; 5 Open all year;

twin beds available. A full home-cooked breakfast is served in the sunny dining room and always includes fresh fruit and a special hot entrée.

Hosts: Marilyn and Gordon Banta-Jessen
Rooms: 3 (1 PB; 2 SB) $65-90
Full Breakfast
Credit Cards: A, B
Notes: 2, 5, 8 (over 14), 10, 11, 12, 14

Beaconsfield Inn

998 Humboldt Street, V8V 2Z8
(604) 384-4044

Heritage 1905 English Manor, award-winning restoration, 11 guest rooms with private bathrooms, antiques, mahogany floors, fireplaces, Jacuzzis, claw-foots, stained glass, down comforters. Gourmet breakfast, tea, and sherry. Guest library, sunroom, dining room. Three blocks to downtown and the waterfront. Quiet. Adult-oriented. No pets. No smoking. Cottage garden. Complimentary parking. Highly rated by *Best Places to Kiss in the Northwest,* Fodors, AAA, *Special Places,* and *Northwest Best Places.*

Hosts: Con and Jodi Sollid
Rooms: 11 (PB) $90-195
Full Breakfast
Notes: 5, 10

The Bedford Regency Hotel

1110 Government Street, V8W 1Y2
(604) 384-6835; (800) 665-6500 (reservations)
FAX (604) 386-8930

The Bedford Regency Hotel is in the heart of Victoria, just steps away from the Inner Harbour. The Bedford embodies Old World charm and understated elegance. Luxurious and beautifully appointed rooms, wood-burning fireplaces, goose-down comforters, and oversized bath towels; some have Jacuzzi bathtubs. The guest services include morning coffee, a newspaper delivered to the room in the morning, evening turndown service,

and complimentary buffet European-style breakfast. Rooms have one queen-size bed.

Rooms: 40 (PB) $135-200
Full Breakfast
Credit Cards: A, B
Notes: 3, 4, 5, 7, 10, 11, 12, 14

Blenkinsop Bed and Breakfast

4049 Century Road, V8X 2E5
(604) 477-5195

Tastefully decorated new bungalow overlooking the pastoral Blenkinsop Valley. Gourmet and heart-smart breakfasts. Warm and congenial hosts serve complimentary afternoon sherry and evening tea and snack. Large family room has TV and VCR. Quiet cul-de-sac offers peaceful hours on the deck to enjoy the Valley scenes. Hosts are "travel wise." Close to University of Victoria. Three miles to downtown. Hosts are knowledgeable of what Victoria and Island have to offer.

Hosts: Charlie and Diana Shnider
Rooms: 3 (1 PB; 2 SB) $75-90
Full Breakfast
Credit Cards: None
Notes: 5, 9, 10, 11, 12, 14

The Captain's Palace White House Inn

309 Belleville Street, V8V 1X2
(604) 388-9191; (800) 563-9656

Unique accommodations in three Heritage mansions overlooking Victoria's Inner Harbour. A five-minute walk to parks, shopping, galleries, and entertainment, yet peacefully quiet for a good night's sleep in true-to-the-period (1897) four-poster beds, canopied beds, and wicker. A welcoming libation, coffee in guests' room, a full Canadian breakfast of choice, and free parking are included in the accommodation rate.

Hosts: Flos Prior and Helen Beirnes
Rooms: 19 (PB) $65-225 seasonal
Full Breakfast

6 Pets welcome; 8 Children welcome; 9 Social drinking allowed; 10 Tennis available; 11 Swimming available; 12 Golf available; 13 Skiing available; 14 May be booked through travel agents.

Credit Cards: A, B, C, E, F
Notes: 3, 4, 5, 6, 7, 8, 9, 10, 11, 12, 13, 14

Cherry Bank Hotel

825 Burdett Avenue, V8W 1B3
(604) 385-5380

First established in 1897, the Cherry Bank Hotel offers an Old World atmosphere in a quiet residential area two blocks from the center of town, Beacon Hill Park, the Royal British Columbia Museum, and much more. No TVs or telephones in the rooms—just old-fashioned, honest value. Enjoy comfort and charm at a reasonable price. Our rates include a full English breakfast served in the original guest dining room which houses the now-famous Spare Rib House.

Rooms: 26 (19 PB; 7 SB) $51-71
Full Breakfast
Credit Cards: A, B, C
Notes: 3, 4, 5, 7, 8, 9, 10

Crow's Nest

71 Linden Avenue, V8V 4C9
(604) 383-4492; FAX (604) 383-3140

1911 Heritage House with large bright rooms. Twenty-minute walk to downtown. Bus stop at corner. Close to Beacon Hill Park and moments to the ocean with unrestricted views of the Olympic Mountains. Three blocks to "The Village" with neighborhood pub, tearooms, and interesting restaurants and shops.

Hosts: Kit and Dene Mainguy
Rooms: 3 (1 PB; 2 SB) $65-85
Full Breakfast
Credit Cards: A, B
Notes: 2, 5, 9, 10, 14

Dashwood Seaside Manor

One Cook Street, V8V 3W6
(800) 667-5517

Victoria's Edwardian Inn by the Sea offers a welcome to all visitors. This 1912 Heritage mansion has 14 elegant suites. Close to town, next to lovely Beacon Hill Park,

on Victoria's enchanting Marine Drive. Breathtaking views, Old World charm. Some fireplaces, balconies, Jacuzzis.

Hosts: Derek Dashwood, family, and staff
Rooms: 14 (PB) $63-218 U.S.
Full Breakfast
Credit Cards: A, B, C, E
Notes: 2, 5, 6, 8, 9, 10, 11, 12, 14

Elk Lake Lodge Bed and Breakfast

5259 Pat Bay Highway (Route 17), V8Y 1S8
(604) 658-8879; FAX (604) 658-8879

Originally built in 1910 as a country chapel, Elk Lake Lodge has been beautifully restored, offering guests four comfortable rooms, a magnificent lounge, outdoor hot tub and patio, and delicious full breakfasts including home-baked goods and local produce. Just steps to lovely Elk Lake for swimming, picnicking, fishing, sailing, and windsurfing. Minutes from Butchart Gardens and golf courses. Minimum two-night stay during summer months.

Hosts: Marty and Ivan Musar
Rooms: 4 (2 PB; 2 SB) $70-90
Full Breakfast
Credit Cards: A, B, C
Notes: 8 (over 12), 9, 10, 11, 12, 14

Garden City Bed and Breakfast Reservation Service

660 Jones Terrace, V8Z 2L7
(604) 479-1986; FAX (604) 479-9999

A-2. This bed and breakfast is perfect for a retreat, private convention, family reunion, or wedding. Both singles and couples welcome. Relax and enjoy a country home with good food, a weight room, a swimming pool, parklike grounds, and much more. Close to Butchart Gardens, Brentwood Village, Swartz Bay ferries, aiport, city centre, and Sidney. $65.

NOTES: Credit cards accepted: A MasterCard; B Visa; C American Express; D Discover Card; E Diner's Club; F Other; 2 Personal checks accepted; 3 Lunch available; 4 Dinner available; 5 Open all year;

F-6. This 1910 Heritage Home is furnished with very fine antiques, etc. Bedrooms feature down-filled quilts and queen-size beds. Private and shared baths. Beautiful English-style garden; 25-minute walk to city centre. From $75.

F-7. The historic neighborhood of Rockland, nestled among Heritage home, Craigdarroch Castle, Lt. Governor's House, and public gardens. Hosts offer information and a hearty breakfast to make stays enjoyable. English and Japanese spoken. Ensuite baths. From $60.

F-14. Edwardian-style mansion in exclusive Rockland district. Close to buses, a 15-minute walk to town, and five-minute walk to the Lt. Governor's Residence and Craigdarroch Castle. Most rooms are large and have fireplaces, queen-size beds, and private baths. Gourmet breakfasts served. Children and pets welcome. From $65.

I-1. This 1912 Heritage Home on one-half acre of ocean inlet is just a ten-minute drive from city centre and the Inner Harbour. Large rooms with king- or queen-size beds, reflect the charm of the old with handsome antiques and collectibles, but also the new, with the comforts being so important. Each room has private ensuite bath. French doors in king-size rooms open to balconies overlooking the bird sanctuary and superb sunsets. From $85.

I-2. A lovingly restored 1913 home, especially for the bed and breakfast guest. Choose queen-, double-, twin-, or single-beds; each two guest rooms sharing a bath. Delightfully and personally furnished. Complimentary tea and fresh baked goodies greet guests on arrival, and breakfast is guests' choice from a great menu. Five-minute drive to downtown or take the bus from the corner. Overlooking a small park, a few steps to an ocean inlet. From $50.

J-2. This 1908 Character home in a quiet neighborhood is within walking distance of city centre, Inner Harbour, museum, etc. Warm, friendly atmosphere. Delicious breakfast. Near ocean with views of Olympic Mountains. Enjoy feeding ducks at Beacon Hill Park or explore many fine shops and restaurants. Double and queen-size beds, ensuite baths, and cable TV. No resident pet. From $60.

S-2. This bed and breakfast offers three cozy guest rooms with double beds and shared baths. Great breakfast and friendly hosts. Between Butchart Gardens and Empress Hotel on good bus line. Children welcome. From $55.

S-23. A cozy bungalow with gorgeous gardens. After a good night's sleep, guests will enjoy a wonderful breakfast in the antique-furnished dining room. Guests may enjoy that last cup of coffee out on the patio where they can enjoy the flowers, shrubs, and trees. From $55.

Gracefield Manor

3816 Duke Road, Rural Route 4, V9B 5T8
(604) 478-2459

Commanding home (captivating landmark) on a large acreage has recently been fully restored, recapturing the plantation-inspired feel of the Old South. Walk into the past

Gracefield Manor

---

6 Pets welcome; 8 Children welcome; 9 Social drinking allowed; 10 Tennis available; 11 Swimming available; 12 Golf available; 13 Skiing available; 14 May be booked through travel agents.

and enjoy peaceful ambience, antique furnishings, and the charm of an era of elegant
living. Retreat to the serenity of the countryside with water and mountain views and
sheep in the pasture. Abundance of fresh
air, beaches, parks, and golf courses. Only
20 minutes to Victoria.

Host: Shirley Wilde
Rooms: 3 (PB) $85-100
Full Breakfast
Credit Cards: B
Notes: 2, 5, 12

Graham's Cedar House Bed and Breakfast

1825 Lands End Road, Sidney, V8L 5J2
(604) 655-3699; FAX (604) 655-1422

Modern air-conditioned chalet home nestled in a six-acre wooded country estate
where tall douglas firs sprinkle sunlight
over lush fern beds. Stretch out in spacious
beautifully appointed one- or two-bedroom
suites with king- or queen-size beds. Private
patio deck entrances overlook natural
strolling gardens featuring statuary, fountains, and benches. Explore the forest, walk
to beach, marinas, or British-style pub.
Breakfast served at the guest's convenience. Close to Victoria, Butchart Gardens, USA/Canadian ferries.

Hosts: Dennis and Kay Graham
Suites: 2 (PB) $65-110
Full Breakfast
Credit Cards: A, B
Notes: 2, 5, 9, 10, 11, 12, 14

Gregory's Guest House

5373 Patricia Bay Highway, V8Y 1S9
(604) 658-8404; FAX (604) 658-4604

Early 1900s farmstead overlooking Elk
Lake, enjoy the farm animals, gardens and
country setting. Only 10 kilometers (6 miles)
from downtown. Bountiful complimentay
breakfast, cozy parlor with fireplace and antique furnishings. Convenient to ferries, airport and Butchart Gardens, nonsmoking.

Hosts: Paul and Elizabeth Gregory
Rooms: 3 (PB) $60-85
Full Breakfast
Credit Cards: A, B
Notes: 2, 8, 9, 10, 11, 12, 14

Heritage House Bed and Breakfast

3808 Heritage Lane, V8Z 7A7
(604) 479-0892

Beautiful 1910 Character home on three-
quarters of an acre in a country setting.
Quiet and secluded with a lounging veranda. Large rooms, guest parlor with fireplace, and library-den. Private parking.
Convenient to ferries, downtown, and all
highways. Reservations suggested. Two-
day minimum stay. No pets. No smoking.

Hosts: Larry and Sandra Gray
Guests: 4 (SB) $75-95
Full Breakfast
Credit Cards: A, B
Notes: 5, 9, 10, 11, 12

Holland House Inn

595 Michigan Street, V8V 1S7
(604) 384-6644; FAX (604) 384-6117

The Holland House Inn is a unique small
hotel where fine art and unequaled comfort
are combined to create an atmosphere of casual elegance for guests' enjoyment. Only
two blocks from Victoria's Inner Harbour
and the Seattle and Port Angeles ferry ter-
minals. Walking or jogging in the beauty of
Beacon Hill Park are just minutes away.
Downtown shopping, Parliament buildings,
and the British Columbia Provincial Museum are all within easy walking distance.
The bright and lovely accommodations—
some with fireplaces, all with private
baths—have queen-size beds, goose-down
duvets, antique furnishings, and delightful
small balconies. A full gourmet breakfast is
included and may be taken in either the
guest room or in the lounge.

Hosts: Robin Birsner and Lance Olsen
Rooms: 10 (PB) $80-210 (seasonal)
Full Breakfast

NOTES: Credit cards accepted: A MasterCard; B Visa; C American Express; D Discover Card; E Diner's
Club; F Other; 2 Personal checks accepted; 3 Lunch available; 4 Dinner available; 5 Open all year;

Credit Cards: A, B, C, E
Notes: 2, 5, 8, 9, 10, 11, 12, 14

Maridou House Bed and Breakfast

116 Eberts Street, V8S 3H7
(604) 360-0747

Gracious Edwardian home one-half block from seafront. Sightings of Orca whales not uncommon. Large home with three bedrooms available. One room has ensuite bathroom with Jacuzzi tub and canopied beds. Rooms named after family Scottish clan names. On direct bus route. Ten minutes from heart of downtown. Full breakfast served. Quiet residential area. Off-street parking. No pets or children under 12.

Hosts: Marilyn and Douglas Allison
Rooms: $45-95
Credit Cards: A, B

Mulberry Manor

Mulberry Manor

611 Foul Bay Road, V8S 1H2
(604) 370-1918

In almost an acre of beautiful landscaped gardens, Mulberry Manor was the last mansion designed by Samuel McClure. The ambience of each room is enhanced by elegant decor and complemented by luxurious furnishings to create the idyllic retreat for the discerning traveler. Sumptuous breakfasts served in the formal dining room provide the perfect start for a day's sightseeing around the provincial capital.

Host: Susan Temple
Rooms: 4 (PB) $80-120
Full Breakfast
Credit Cards: A, B
Notes: 2, 9, 10, 11, 12, 14

Mylfford Haven House

1239 Pandora Avenue, V8V 3R3
(604) 383-0699

Mylfford Haven House is a Heritage (restored) Home built in 1915 where the guests may enjoy legendary Canadian hospitality. A hearty breakfast is served in the bright and cheerful dining room after a quiet and restful night in one of the period bedrooms with queen-size beds. Then visit the many interesting historic and tourist sites that are within walking distance or a short drive. Bus service is also convenient. Afterward relax in the cozy parlor or private garden.

Hosts: Harold and Elizabeth Thomas
Rooms: 2 (PB) $75-85
Full Breakfast
Credit Cards: A, B
Notes: 5, 9, 10, 11, 12, 14

Oak Bay Guest House

1052 Newport Avenue, V8S 5E3
(604) 598-3812

This classic 1912 inn, established in 1922, has guests' comfort and pleasure at heart. Enjoy the peaceful location and scenic walks one block from the ocean. All rooms have private baths. There are two guest sitting rooms with antiques, library, and log fire. Wonderful home-cooked breakfast. Golf, village shopping, and dining. City bus at the door and minutes from downtown. Come and enjoy.

Hosts: Dave and Pam
Rooms: 11 (PB) $79-165
Full Breakfast
Credit Cards: A, B
Notes: 5, 7 (restricted), 9, 11, 12

Our Home on the Hill

Our Home on the Hill Bed and Breakfast

546 Delora Drive, V9C 3R8
(604) 474-4507

A warm welcome, as well as peace and quiet, awaits guests just 20 minutes from downtown Victoria. Enjoy the seclusion of the yard, relax amid the yesteryear charm of the antique-accented home, stroll along the ocean just moments away, or take a dip in the sheltered hot tub. A guest sitting room is available. A hearty breakfast includes special homemade jams, fresh muffins, and a hot entree.

Hosts: Grace and Arnie Holman
Rooms: 3 (1 PB; 2 SB) $60-65
Full Breakfast
Credit Cards: None
Notes: 2, 5, 8, 9, 10, 11, 12, 14

A Pacific Reservation Service

701 Northwest 60th Street, Seattle, WA, 98107
(206) 784-0539

VIC-A. A turn-of-the-century home one block from the beach and a grand beach walk. It offers three bedrooms, one with a private bath and fireplace, favorite with honeymooners. The spacious living room and dining room welcome guests to sit back and relax with the German hostess. She will fix a memorable breakfast. Discover the wonderful Beacon Hill Park close by. On a bus line. $60.

VIC-B. An elegant, refined small inn with ten bedrooms. Two blocks to the harbor and within walking distance of everything. All rooms have private baths and decks. The breakfasts are either served in the dining room or in the guests' own room. Ideal for a honeymoon, anniversary, or that special weekend. Unequalled comfort and charm with original art by the premier artists of Victoria. $100-160.

VIC-C. Here is luxury at a modest cost. This lodge features oversized rooms with private baths, refrigerators, and TV. Some rooms have kitchenettes. This residential area is 15 minutes from Victoria and close to Butchart Gardens, airport, and ferries. A delicious full breakfast is served. Golf, skiing, water skiing, fresh and saltwater fishing, swimming, and walking are just some of the activities. $55-75.

VIC-D. Turn-of-the-century mansion on 17 acres with frontage on a large lake. Built by prominent architect Samuel McClure, this special guest home features waterfront garden paths to enjoy while watching the graceful swans. Tennis court and billiard room with a magnificent antique table. Visit the famous Forest Open Air Museum. Three distinctively decorated guest rooms share a bath. From $95.

VIC-E. A truly fine mansion reflecting the Edwardian Tudor Revival style popular in British Columbia in the early years of the century. Minutes away from the inner harbor and the many attractions of Victoria. Most of the 14 rooms have oceanviews and others have a garden view. All suites are self-contained with private baths and full kitchens. Breakfast supplies are stocked in each refrigerator. $75-135.

VIC-F. An exceptional house on half an acre overlooking Portage Inlet. This house is three miles from the inner harbor and is

NOTES: Credit cards accepted: A MasterCard; B Visa; C American Express; D Discover Card; E Diner's Club; F Other; 2 Personal checks accepted; 3 Lunch available; 4 Dinner available; 5 Open all year;

furnished with antiques. Many views are available in this guest home featuring five bedrooms. Two rooms have private balconies, and all rooms have private baths. A sumptuous gourmet breakfast is provided to start the day's activities. $80-100.

VIC-2. The hostess of this wonderful bed and breakfast is dedicated to guests and shows this dedication in everything she does, from the welcome drink to the delicious breakfasts. This two-story house, built in 1885, features a high ceiling, fireplaces, charm, and fine antiques. One room has a private bath, the others share a bath. Breakfast will be served on fine china in the formal dining room. $65-100.

VIC-4. This guest home was built in 1899. It is now restored and offers three bedrooms with shared bath. Antiques fill the house and compliment the original woodwork fireplaces, floors, and fittings. A memorable full breakfast changes from day to day. $70-80.

Portage Inlet House, Bed and Breakfast

993 Portage Road, V8Z 1K9
(604) 479-4594

A delightful waterfront home ten minutes from downtown Victoria. Guests are welcome to stroll the "Acre of Paradise" overlooking beautiful Portage Inlet and observe the eagles, herons, swans, and ducks; in the autumn, see the Coho salmon run. All guests have their own bathrooms, entrances, TVs, and off-street parking spaces. The hosts raise much of the food themselves and purchase the balance from local farmers who are also "organically minded."

Hosts: Jim and Pat Baillie
Rooms: 4 (3 PB; 1 SB) $75-115
Full Breakfast
Credit Cards: A, B
Notes: 5, 8, 9

Prior House Bed and Breakfast Inn

620 St. Charles Street, V8S 3N7
(604) 592-8847

Formerly a private residence of the English Crown, this grand bed and breakfast inn has all the amenities of the finest European inn, featuring rooms with fireplaces, onyx marble whirlpool tubs, ocean and mountain views, sumptuous breakfasts and delicious afternoon teas. Heritage in a large garden setting. Rated outstanding by Northwest, Best Places, and AAA. Special private suite available for families.

Host: Candis Cooperrider
Rooms: 7 (PB) $100-260
Full Breakfast
Credit Cards: A, B
Notes: 5, 8 (limited), 10, 11, 12

Raven Tree Iris Gardens Bed and Breakfast

1853 Connie Road, Rural Route 2, V9B 5B4
(604) 642-5248

Gracious English Tudor mansion set in ten acres of landscaped gardens and woodland paths. Twenty-five minutes west of Victoria on the way to spectacular West Coast beaches. Thirty-five-mile bike trail and 3,500-acre hiking park nearby. Full breakfast and afternoon tea.

Rooms: 3 (PB) $75-95
Full Breakfast
Credit Card: A, B
Notes: 2, 9, 10, 11, 12, 14

The Sea Rose

1250 Dallas Road, V8V 1C4
(604) 381-7932

The Sea Rose is an oceanfront 1921-built Victorian-character home that was completely renovated in 1987 and redecorated in 1994. It is on Victoria's famous seafront and enjoys uninterrupted sea and mountain views. Just steps from Beacon Hill Park,

6 Pets welcome; 8 Children welcome; 9 Social drinking allowed; 10 Tennis available; 11 Swimming available; 12 Golf available; 13 Skiing available; 14 May be booked through travel agents.

The Sea Rose

bus routes, and the beach, The Sea Rose is in a perfect position to access all of the attractions for which Victoria is so famous. All suites have their own ensuite bathrooms and are tastefully furnished; most have oceanviews. Guests are served a hot, full breakfast in the original 1921 dining room with its stunning views of ocean, park, and mountains, as well as occasional glimpses of the famous Orca whales from the breakfast table. Nonsmoking building. No pets. Check in between 2:00 and 6:00 P.M. or phone, please. Check out by 11:00 A.M.

Hosts: Gail and Herman Hamhuis
Rooms: 4 (PB) $69-105
Full Breakfast
Credit Cards: A, B, C
Notes: 5, 8, 9, 12, 14

Sonia's Bed and Breakfast By the Sea

175 Bushby Street, V8S 1B5
(604) 385-2700; (800) 667-4489

Walk along the ocean to the Inner Harbor. Guest rooms have king- and queen-size beds. A penthouse has a large private sundeck overlooking the Straits of Juan de Fuca and will accommodate five people comfortably. The hosts were both born in Victoria and like to lay a map out to show their guests what to see and do. They have owned and operated Sonia's Bed and Breakfast for 10 years. Large hot breakfast.

Hosts: Sonia and Brian McMillan
Rooms: 3 (PB) $55-75 U.S.
Suite: $100-150 U.S.

Full Breakfast
Credit Cards: None
Notes: 2, 9, 10, 11, 12

Swallow Hill Farm Bed and Breakfast

4910 William Head Road, Rural Route 1,
V9B 5T7
(604) 474-4042

Small working farm near Victoria in peaceful country setting with pasture, pond, and orchard. Spectacular mountain and sea views. Abundant wildlife: deer, eagles, seals, otters, birds. Two comfortable suites, one with separate entrance. Queen-size and single beds, private baths, decks. Delicious breakfasts and friendly conversation. Enjoy favorite outdoor activities, see the sights, curl up with book, or just sit and watch nature unfolding. Whale watching, hiking, swimming, fishing, diving. So peaceful guests never want to leave.

Hosts: Gini and Peter Walsh
Rooms: 2 (PB) $65-75
Full or Continental Breakfast
Credit Cards: A, B, C
Notes: 5, 10, 11, 12

Swallow Hill Farm

Town and Country Bed and Breakfast in British Columbia

P.O. Box 74542
2803 West Fourth Avenue V6K 1K2
(604) 731-5942

NOTES: Credit cards accepted: A MasterCard; B Visa; C American Express; D Discover Card; E Diner's Club; F Other; 2 Personal checks accepted; 3 Lunch available; 4 Dinner available; 5 Open all year;

1. Beautiful Edwardian home one block to waterfront road, 10-minute drive to city centre. Three rooms, one with private bath, and two that share a bathroom. Furnished with antiques and other special touches. Some sea views. $75-115.

2. A delightful waterfront home overlooking Portage Inlet, with an acre of garden. Each guest has a comfortable king-size bed or twin bed, and each room has a private entrance, TV, and bathroom. Only 10 minutes from downtown Victoria and its many attractions. Within easy access to all the ferries that service Victoria. An abundance of wildlife resides on or visits the property, such as swans, Canada geese, pheasants, eagles, and ducks. Guests are welcome to enjoy the acre of "paradise." Breakfast specializes in organic home-grown food: home-grown fruit and juices, homemade jams, jellies, and ketchup. This inn grinds flour from wheat to make bread, scones, and pancakes. Heated with wood in the winter and utilizes solar panels for hot water in summer. No pets. $75-115.

3. The guests are special at Arundel Manor, a 1912 heritage home on a half-acre of land sloping to Portage Inlet, a bird sanctuary with stunning sunset views. The four large bedrooms, decorated with an eclectic mix of antiques, collectibles, and family heirlooms, have private ensuite bathrooms, and two have spacious balconies overlooking the water. The fifth room has twin beds and a private bathroom. A full home-cooked breakfast is served in the elegant dining room. A cheerful, welcoming lounge with fireplace awaits the guests. Check in between 2:00 and 4:00 P.M.; check out 11:00 A.M. No smoking. Not suitable for pets. $95-125.

4. New and unique, this lovely home with a Dutch atmosphere is in a truly beautiful scenic setting. Views of farmland, the Gulf Islands, and Mount Baker are there to enjoy. Only five minutes from sandy ocean beaches, 10 minutes from Butchart Gardens, and 25 minutes from the city centre. Share the living areas and pickup from ferry or airport are available. Dutch and German are second languages. No pets please. Full breakfast is served from 7 to 10 A.M. $75-95.

Wellington Bed and Breakfast

66 Wellington Avenue, V8V 4H5
(604) 383-5976; FAX (604) 385-0477

Just one-half block from the scenic Pacific Ocean, bordered by a panoramic walkway, three blocks from beautiful Beacon Hill Park, this 1912 inn offers guests a taste of true Victorian hospitality. All rooms have private baths, walk-in closets, large windows, king- or queen-size beds, and are wonderfully appointed. The quiet, tree-lined street allows for the most restful sleep, and the breakfasts are a delight.

Hosts: Inge and Sue Ranzinger
Rooms: 3 (PB) $55-75
Full Breakfast
Credit Cards: A, F
Notes: 2, 5, 8 (over 12), 9, 10, 11, 12, 14

Wooded Acres Bed and Breakfast

4907 Rocky Point Road, Rural Route 2, V9B 5B4
(604) 474-8959; (604) 478-8172

Country-style hospitality welcomes the guest to more than three acres of forest in the Victoria countryside. Bedrooms are decorated with antiques, queen-size beds, and cozy down-filled duvets. Special touches everywhere. Enjoy old-fashioned candlelight and soaking in the private hot tub spa. Full breakfast is a feast of specialties baked fresh every day and served at the guest's convenience. Special diets prepared on request. Brochure available. Two private suites.

6 Pets welcome; 8 Children welcome; 9 Social drinking allowed; 10 Tennis available; 11 Swimming available; 12 Golf available; 13 Skiing available; 14 May be booked through travel agents.

Hosts: Elva and Skip Kennedy
Rooms: 2 (PB) $110
Full Breakfast
Credit Cards: None
Notes: 2, 5, 7 (limited), 9, 10, 11, 12, 14

WEST VANCOUVER

Beachside Bed and Breakfast

4208 Evergreen Avenue, V7V 1H1
(604) 922-7773; (800) 563-3311
FAX (604) 926-8073

Stay in a quiet, beautiful, waterfront home in one of the finest areas in Vancouver. A lovely beach is at the doorstep. Minutes from downtown, Stanley Park, Horseshoe Bay ferries, and North Shore attractions. Its southern exposure affords a panoramic view of the city, harbor, and Alaska Cruise ships. A hearty home-baked breakfast is served in the seaside dining room. Close to fishing, sailing, wilderness hiking, skiing, antiques, shopping, and great restaurants.

Hosts: Gordon and Joan Gibbs
Rooms: 3 (PB) $95-150 Canadian
Full Breakfast
Credit Cards: A, B
Notes: 2, 5, 9, 10, 11, 12, 13, 14

Creekside Bed and Breakfast

1515 Palmerston Avenue, V7V 4S9
(604) 926-1861; (604) 328-9400 (cellular)
FAX (604) 926-7545

Quiet, romantic parklike casual setting with a creek flowing through this natural garden property. "All-you-can-eat" home-baked breakfast. Luxurious ensuite bath with two-person Jacuzzi in a glass-roofed bathroom. The second bath also has a Jacuzzi tub and skylights. In-room TVs with remotes, stocked mini-fridge, and coffee makers. Complimentary wines, beverages, snacks, toiletries, and robes. Ideal honeymoon setting. Commissionable. 50 percent deposit required. Half-price coupons available for

entertainment and dining. Two-day minimum stay.

Hosts: John Boden and Donna Hawrelko
Rooms: 2 (PB) $100-135
Full Breakfast
Credit Cards: A, B
Notes: 5, 6 (by arrangement), 7 (limited) 9, 10, 11, 12, 13, 14

WHISTLER

Alberta and Pacific Bed and Breakfast Agency

P.O. Box 15477, MPO, Vancouver, V6B 5B2
(604) 944-1793

13. European hospitality is offered at this chalet by French and German hosts. Enjoy the guest sitting room with wood stove, sun deck with view of Whistler and Blackcomb Mountains. Wake to a delicious Continental breakfast and the aroma of home-baked croissants and rolls. Whistler is building a reputation as a year-round resort. In summer there is hiking, horseback riding, swimming, biking, golf, tennis, canoeing, fishing, and windsurfing. In winter take in two of the most superb ski areas in North America, Whistler and Blackcomb Mountains. There is ski storage and a sauna for the guest's use. Winter ski packages are available. Six guest rooms, double or twin beds with down comforters, each guest room with its own private bath.

Golden Dreams Bed and Breakfast

6412 Easy Street, V0N 1B6
(604) 932-2667; FAX (604) 932-7055

Maximize a holiday and stay with locals! Uniquely decorated theme rooms feature sherry decanter and cozy duvets. Relax in a luxurious private Jacuzzi and awaken to nutritious vegetarian breakfast. Large sun deck with great views. Excellent trailside location to lake sports, village shops and restaurants, mountain biking, alpine hiking,

---

NOTES: Credit cards accepted: A MasterCard; B Visa; C American Express; D Discover Card; E Diner's Club; F Other; 2 Personal checks accepted; 3 Lunch available; 4 Dinner available; 5 Open all year;

horseback riding, rollerblading, and more! Golden Dreams is the inside edge at Whistler. Families welcome!

Hosts: Ann and Terry Spence
Rooms: 3 (1 PB; 2 SB) $65-95
Full Breakfast
Credit Cards: A, B
Notes: 2, 5, 8, 9, 10, 11, 12, 13

WHITE ROCK

Alberta and Pacific Bed and Breakfast Agency

P.O. Box 15477, MPO, Vancouver, V6B 5B2
(604) 944-1793

10. A traditional style residence, this very large home offers its guests comfortable rooms, a separate private lounge with log-burning fireplace, TV and stereo, piano and library, refrigerator, and hearty cooked breakfasts. It is three minutes from the U.S. border; 40 minutes from downtown Vancouver; 30 minutes from the international airport, and 20 minutes from the Victoria ferries. It is close to the finest of sailing, fishing, riding, and championship golf courses. Three guest rooms; the Eastlake furnished with a 19th-century Eastlake double bed and full ensuite bath; the Washington furnished with a 19th-century Colonial mahogany twin bedded suite with full private bath, and the Les Rideaux, decorated colorfully au Provincial with double bed, private balcony, and shared full bath.

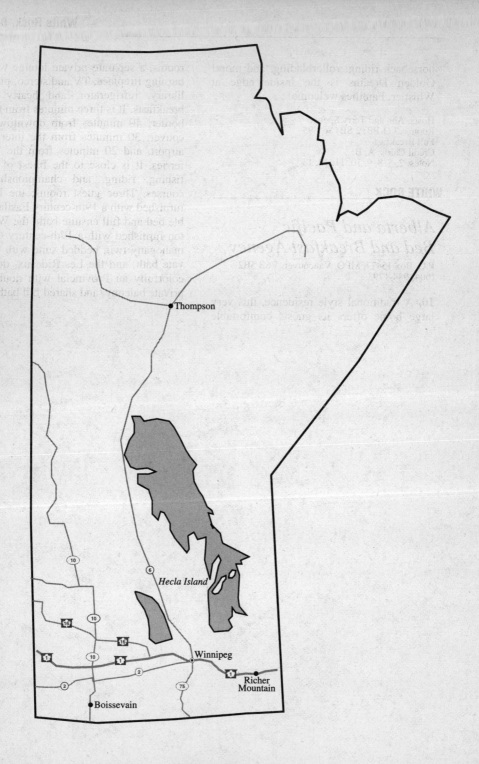

Manitoba

Manitoba

BOISSEVAIN

Dueck's Cedar Chalet

Box 362, R0K 0E0
(204) 534-6019

One mile east and three-fourths of a mile north of the town of Boissevain, Cedar Chalet offers accommodations with complete privacy, including Jacuzzi, color TV, refrigerator, and coffee percolator. Also offered is a motor home, which is air-conditioned, fully equipped to sleep six, and allows guests to sightsee in the area for $50 plus 12 cents a mile. Car rental is also available. Extra meals by prearrangement. English and German spoken. Boissevain is the home of the Canadian Turtle Derby. The chalet is near the golf course and offers a heated outdoor swimming pool, playground, Turtle Mountain Provincial Park, lake fishing, nature trails, horseback riding, and the International Peace Gardens.

Hosts: Hilda and Henry Dueck
Rooms: 4 (SB) $40-50
Full Breakfast
Credit Cards: None
Notes: 2, 3, 4, 5, 6, 8, 10, 11, 12, 13, 14

HECLA ISLAND

Solmundson Gesta Hus

Box 76 Hecla Provincial Park, R0C 2R0
(204) 279-2088

The guest house is within Hecla Provincial Park on 43 acres of private property. Enjoy luxurious European-style hospitality in a newly renovated and completely modern, comfortable home in an original Icelandic settlement. Relax on the veranda and enjoy the beautiful view of Lake Winnipeg. Enjoy the tranquil and peaceful atmosphere while petting the dogs and cats or feeding the ducks. The host is a commercial fisherman, so feast on the catch of the day along with garden fresh vegetables.

Hosts: Dave and Sharon Holtz
Rooms: 4 (1 PB; 3 SB) $45-75
Full Breakfast
Credit Cards:
Notes: 2, 4, 5, 6, 8, 9, 10, 11, 12, 13, 14

RICHER MOUNTAIN

Geppetto's

Box 2A, Rural Route 1, R0E 1S0
(807) 422-8809

Country-style hospitality in an attractive modern home, 40 minutes east of Winnipeg on Highway 1. Complimentary homemade beer and wine. Visit the 1200-square-foot craft shop where Geppetto makes wooden toys. Outdoor activities include bird watching, horse-shoe pits, cross-country skiing, snowmobiling, and hiking. Two golf courses within five minutes; four more within 20 minutes. Three rooms with shared bath.

Hosts: John and Sandy Cotie
Rooms: 3 (SB) $45
Full Breakfast
Credit Cards: B
Notes: 2, 3, 4, 5, 9, 12, 13

NOTES: Credit cards accepted: A MasterCard; B Visa; C American Express; D Discover Card; E Diner's Club; F Other; 2 Personal checks accepted; 3 Lunch available; 4 Dinner available; 5 Open all year; 6 Pets welcome; 7 Smoking allowed; 8 Children welcome; 9 Social drinking allowed; 10 Tennis available; 11 Swimming available; 12 Golf available; 13 Skiing available; 14 May be booked through travel agents.

IPSON

ed and Breakfast
Manitoba

Healy Crescent, Winnipeg, R2N 2S2
04) 256-6151

nna's Bed and Breakfast. Open year-
und, Anna and Robert invite guests to
are this comfortable home and warm
utch hospitality. Pickup at airport and
iin station. Completely private quarters
d private bath. Come and enjoy the heart
the north! $30-45.

NIPEG

ed and Breakfast
of Manitoba

)3 Healy Crescent, R2N 2S2
(204) 256-6151

Bannerman East. Come and enjoy this lovely Georgian home, evening tea, and quiet walks in St. Johns Park or along the Red River. Close to Seven Oaks Museum, the planetarium, concert hall, and Rainbow Stage. $40.

Belanger. Enjoy the relaxing atmosphere in this special home built in 1900. Sitting room adjacent to guest bedroom. Can accommodate a family of four. $40.

Drenker. Enjoy a private and pleasant stay in this quiet, neat home. In old St. Boniface, it is within walking distance of the Forks, the St. Boniface Hospital, and downtown. Near museum, Manitoba Theatre Centre, concert hall, and paddlewheel boats. $45.

Ellie. This downtown accommodation in a peaceful neighborhood is near bus service, two major hospitals, the zoo, convention center, concert hall, museums, theatre cen-

tre, the planetarium, the Forks, bus depot, and Via Rail. $45-47.

Fillion. In a nice community close to the Trans-Canada Highway city route. Nearby attractions include the mint, St. Vital Mall, Fun Mountain Waterslide, Tinkertown, outdoor pool, and bicycle path. $40.

Hawchuk. On the banks of the Red River, this beautiful Tudor home has English gardens and a riverbank walkway. Top off the day with a paddlewheel boat dinner cruise. English, German, and French spoken. Full-course dinner is available at an additional charge. $69.

Hillman. Cozy private sitting room and a full breakfast of guests' choice. Downtown, close to bus route, airport, Polo Park, planetarium, concert hall, and theatre centre. $45.

Johnson. In a quiet residential area with a very private yard for sunbathing. Private kitchen available. Near two public swimming pools, Assiniboia Downs Racetrack, shopping centres, and Living Prairie Museum. Children welcome. $40.

Mitchell/Cruickshank. Lovely old Winnipeg home on a quiet tree-lined street. Air-conditioned. Close to public transportation, shopping, theatres, museums, and city centre. Easy access to Assinboine Downs. $35-45.

Narvey. This quiet, attractive, comfortable home in the River Heights area offers a family room, garden, and good hospitality. Excellent city-wide bus service. Close to downtown, Assinboine Park and Zoo, the Forks, Grant Park, and Polo Park shopping malls. $32-42

NOTES: Credit cards accepted: A MasterCard; B Visa; C American Express; D Discover Card; E Diner's Club; F Other; 2 Personal checks accepted; 3 Lunch available; 4 Dinner available; 5 Open all year;

Paulley. Quiet, comfortable, relaxing, and within walking distance of the Convention Center, Manitoba Archives, tourist bureau, shopping, direct bus route to the Via Rail, the historic Forks site, and three hospitals. One block south of the Trans-Canadian Highway. $30-40.

Preweda. Enjoy complete privacy in lower level with a spacious and attractive sitting lounge. Excellent transit service and public library. Quick access to the mint, the Forks, downtown, Osborne Village, and St. Boniface Hospital. $45.

Rand. Location of convenience. Close to golf, parks, shopping, and downtown. Finest accommodations with truly knowledgeable, warm, friendly hospitality. The best brownie cake anywhere! $40-55.

Sclci. Very private facilities in this private home can accommodate a family of four. A warm welcome to guests, and quick access to the Trans-Canada Highway. $30-40.

Siemens. Warm hospitality and quiet relaxation! Can accommodate a family of five. Close to the express bus route, Unicity Mall, Assiniboina Downs, shopping, restaurants, and recreation. $38-40.

Tidmarsh. This attractive older home is in the quiet, tree-lined River Heights area. Guest sitting room on mezzanine floor with tea- and coffee-making facilities. Choose breakfast from an ample menu. Close to Polo Park shopping centre, the Forks, and the casino. Enjoy English-style hospitality. $40-42.

Zonneveld. Enjoy a relaxed atmosphere in this unique three-story home with a beautiful oak interior. Excellent transit service, near downtown, will pick up at the airport. Quick access to the Forks, zoo, hospital, and Dainavert Museum. $30-40.

Bright Oakes Bed and Breakfast

137 Woodlawn Avenue, R2M 2P5
(204) 256-9789

Guests can relax in comfortable, spacious bedrooms, play a tune on the grand piano, or swing in a hammock in the back yard. The four-level split home with many antique furnishings is on a half-acre of landscaped grounds near the river, the university, and many restaurants, with quick and easy access to St. Boniface and downtown attractions. A full breakfast can be enjoyed on the patio overlooking the gardens.

Hosts: Francis and Anya Lobreau
Rooms: 3 (1 PB; 2 SB) $40-45
Full Breakfast
Credit Cards: None
Notes: 5, 8, 10, 11, 12

Casa Antigua

209 Chestnut Street, R3G 1R8
(204) 775-9708

Casa Antigua is in a quiet, tree-lined neighborhood close to the heart of downtown Winnipeg. This home, built in 1906, is lovingly furnished with antiques. Nearby biking paths and walking trails. Full, homemade breakfast is served. Spanish and English spoken. Four guest rooms with shared baths. Smoking in designated areas only. Access to cross-country skiing.

Hosts: Marcial Hinojosa and Elvera Watson
Rooms: 4 (SB) $50
Full Breakfast
Credit Cards: A
Notes: 4, 5, 7 (limited), 8, 9, 11, 12, 13

6 Pets welcome; 8 Children welcome; 9 Social drinking allowed; 10 Tennis available; 11 Swimming available; 12 Golf available; 13 Skiing available; 14 May be booked through travel agents.

Cozy Cove Bed & Breakfast

13 Nichol Avenue, R2M 1V6
(204) 256-4430

Fifteen minutes from downtown Winnipeg. Complete privacy in the lower level featuring an attractive sitting lounge. Air-conditioned. Can accommodate a family of five. Bikes and cross country skis are available. Delicious breakfast is served in sunny dining room.

Hosts: Larry and Delann Preweda
Rooms: 2 (1 PB; 1 SB) $45
Full Breakfast
Credit Cards: A, B
Notes: 3, 4, 5, 6, 8, 9, 10, 11, 12, 13

Ellie's Bed and Breakfast

77 Middle Gate, R3C 2C5
(204) 772-5832; (204) 783-1462

Enjoy a stay in historic "Armstrong's Point" in the heart of Winnipeg. Nicely treed and peaceful. Hosts are well-traveled and love to cook. Known for their superb omelet, home-baked bread, scones, and muffins. Jams and jellies made in their own kitchen. Airport and train pickup available for an additional charge.

Hosts: Peter and Eugenia Ellie
Rooms: 3 (1 PB; 2 SB) $50-52
Full Breakfast
Credit Cards: None
Notes: 3, 4, 5, 8, 9

Mary Jane's Place

144 Yale Avenue, R3M 0L7
(204) 453-8104

Unique three-story Georgian-style home with a beautiful oak interior, nestled in the historic Crescentwood area of Winnipeg. Close to cultural and historic locations, airport, and highways. Dutch and English spoken. Four guest rooms with private and shared baths. Full or Continental breakfast served.

Hosts: Jack and Mary Jane
Rooms: 4 (1 PB; 3 SB) $40-42
Full and Continental Breakfast
Credit Cards: A, B
Notes: 2, 5, 8, 9, 11, 12

Prairie Charm Bed and Breakfast

Box 124 St Germain, R0G 2A0
(204) 253-3636

Prairie Charm offers gracious country living on a small acreage within city limits. Home is on private, parklike grounds. Antiques and family heirlooms add to the charm of this modern, split-level home. Three guest rooms with private and shared baths. Convenient to travelers arriving from the east, west, or south.

Hosts: Ray and Ann Ingalls
Rooms: 3 (1 PB; 2 SB) $40
Continental Breakfast
Credit Cards: None
Notes: 2, 5, 6, 8, 11, 12

Riverview

291 Oakwood Avenue, R3L 1E8
(204) 475-1291

Older home in a lovely, heavily treed residential area, near main highway and close to downtown Winnipeg. Bus service is excellent. Main bedroom has an adjoining sitting room. Single room also available with shared bath. Full, varied breakfast served featuring blueberry or strawberry waffles. Six restaurants within two blocks for lunch and dinner.

Hosts: Dennis and Colleen Belanger
Room: 1 (PB) $40
Full Breakfast
Credit Cards: None
Notes: 2, 5, 7, 9, 10, 11, 12

NOTES: Credit cards accepted: A MasterCard; B Visa; C American Express; D Discover Card; E Diner's Club; F Other; 2 Personal checks accepted; 3 Lunch available; 4 Dinner available; 5 Open all year;

West Gate Manor

71 West Gate, R3C 2C9
(204) 772-9788

In picturesque, historic Armstrong Point area of Winnipeg. Large living room is decorated in Victorian era splendor. Each bedroom reflects its own period and theme. One room has its own private sitting room. Sunroom with TV off the dining and living rooms. Guests receive discounts at local restaurants. Walking distance to downtown, restaurants, shopping, and cultural facilities.

Hosts: John and Louise Clark
Rooms: 6 (SB) $50-55
Full Breakfast
Credit Cards: A, B
Notes: 2, 5, 8 (over 10), 14

6 Pets welcome; 8 Children welcome; 9 Social drinking allowed; 10 Tennis available; 11 Swimming available; 12 Golf available; 13 Skiing available; 14 May be booked through travel agents.

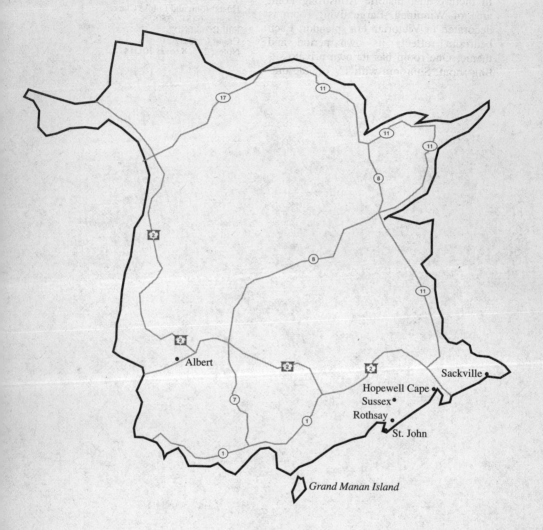

New Brunswick

New Brunswick

ALBERT

Florentine Manor

On Route 915 at Harvey, Rural Route 2, E0A 1A0
(506) 882-2271; FAX (506) 882-2271

While visiting Canada's East Coast, experience country living in a perfectly natural setting in this 1860 manor. The rooms are decorated with antiques of the Victorian era. All eight rooms are nonsmoking with private baths. Prime opportunity for viewing waterfowl, woodland birds, Fundy National Park, Hopewell Rocks Provincial Park, and spectacular shorebird migration. Within walking distance of Mary's Point, Canada's first hemispheric shorebird reserve. Hospitality is the hosts' way of life so come experience that down-home feeling. Exceptional hiking opportunities.

Host: Mary Tingley
Rooms: 8 (PB) $60-85
Full Breakfast
Credit Cards: A, B
Notes: 2, 3, 4, 5, 9, 10, 11, 12, 13, 14

GRAND MANAN ISLAND

Compass Rose

North Head, E0G 2M0
(506) 662-8570

Two small turn-of-the-century houses overlooking the Fisherman's Wharf at North Head. The ferry docks at adjoining wharf. Bedrooms are furnished simply with mostly pine. The dining room—serving breakfast, lunch, afternoon tea, and dinner—opens to a long deck that is an excellent vantage point for watching harbor activities and bird watching. Evening conversations and early morning plans are made in the sitting rooms around Franklin stoves.

Host: Cecilia Bowden
Rooms: 9 (SB) $55
Full Breakfast
Credit Cards: A, B
Notes: 2, 3, 4, 6, 8, 9, 10, 11, 12

HOPEWELL CAPE

Dutch Treat Farm

Rural Route 1, Hopewell Cape (Shepody), E0A 1Y0
(506) 882-2552

Come stay in this century-old country farmhouse overlooking Grindstone Island on Shepody Bay. Hosts look forward to sharing their home with those who want to discover the legacy, history, and beauty of Albert County. All-purpose trails lead from the farm to the hills, and to the Salt Marsh with its remnants of 18th-century Acadian agriculture. Close to Fundy National Park, the Rocks Provincial Park, Mary's Point, and the Shepody National Wildlife Area. Truly a haven for bird watchers and nature lovers. Special breakfast of pancakes and hosts' own maple syrup is designed to get guests ready for a day of traveling or exploring.

Hosts: Marla and Eric Rossiter
Rooms: 3 (SB) $30-35
Full Breakfast
Credit Cards: None
Notes: 2, 3 (call), 4 (call) 5, 6, 7 (limited), 8, 9, 10, 11, 12, 13

NOTES: Credit cards accepted: A MasterCard; B Visa; C American Express; D Discover Card; E Diner's Club; F Other; 2 Personal checks accepted; 3 Lunch available; 4 Dinner available; 5 Open all year; 6 Pets welcome; 7 Smoking allowed; 8 Children welcome; 9 Social drinking allowed; 10 Tennis available; 11 Swimming available; 12 Golf available; 13 Skiing available; 14 May be booked through travel agents.

ROTHESAY

Shadow Lawn Inn

3180 Rothesay Road, E2E 5A3
(506) 847-7539; FAX (506) 849-9238

Shadow Lawn, a four-star inn, is an ideal setting to host a variety of events, from a wedding reception, garden party, business luncheon, or a romantic dinner for two. In the typical countryside town of Rothesay, with many recreational facilities nearby, including an 18-hole golf course, tennis courts, and mooring facilities at the Rothesay Yacht Club. Shadow Lawn has nine guest rooms and two executive suites that have been richly decorated and lovingly restored. Dinner is served by reservation.

Hosts: Mr. and Mrs. Patrick Gallagher
Rooms: 9 (PB) $69-125
Continental Breakfast
Credit Cards: A, B, C, D, E, F
Notes: 2, 3, 4, 5, 7, 8, 9, 10, 11, 12, 13, 14

Shadow Lawn Inn

SACKVILLE

The Different Drummer

P.O. Box 188, 82 West Main Street, E0A 3C0
(506) 536-1291

Welcome to the Different Drummer Bed and Breakfast. Here guests can enjoy the

The Different Drummer

comforts and conveniences of modern living in a restful and homey atmosphere. Attractive bedrooms are furnished much as they would have been at the turn of the century, and they all have private baths. In the large parlor and adjacent sunroom guests can chat, browse through a well-stocked library, watch color TV, or just relax. Breakfast is served each morning; enjoy home-baked bread, muffins, local honey, freshly ground coffee, and berries in season.

Hosts: Georgette and Richard Hanrahan
Rooms: 8 (PB) $40-51
Continental Breakfast
Credit Cards: A, B
Notes: 5, 8, 9, 10, 11, 12, 14

Marshlands Inn

59 Bridge Street, P.O. Box 1440, E0A 3C0
(506) 536-0170; FAX (506) 536-0721

Inviting 1850 Victorian inn, formerly a private residence. Comfortably appointed guest rooms with antique furnishings and cozy living rooms with fireplaces. More than an inn, Marshlands is two stately manors plus a coach house with names like Hanson House, Stonehaven, and, of course, Marshlands. Offering 12 rooms in the main inn and 9 in Stonehaven, all feature magnificent oak floors and polished antiques. Private or shared bath facilities, parlors, a licensed dining room, gardens, and lawns.

Host: Peter and Diane Weeden
Rooms: 21 (17 PB; 4 SB) $53-89
Full Breakfast

NOTES: Credit cards accepted: A MasterCard; B Visa; C American Express; D Discover Card; E Diner's Club; F Other; 2 Personal checks accepted; 3 Lunch available; 4 Dinner available; 5 Open all year;

Credit Cards: A, B, C, D, E
Notes: 3, 4, 5, 7, 10, 11, 12, 14

SAINT JOHN

Five Chimneys Bed and Breakfast

238 Charlotte Street West, E2M 1Y3
(506) 635-1888; FAX (506) 635-8402

In Canada's oldest incorporated city, this 1855 Greek Revival home is near the Reversing Falls and the Digby Ferry. Three guest rooms with private and shared baths are available. Full breakfast includes whole-wheat and oatmeal pancakes, a cheesy egg dish, and oatmeal porridge, as well as homemade bread and jam. A warm welcome awaits all guests.

Host: Linda Gates
Rooms: 3 (1 PB; 2 SB) $45-55
Full Breakfast
Credit Cards: A, B
Notes: 2, 5, 8, 9, 10, 11, 12

Parkerhouse Inn

71 Sydney Street, E2L 2L5
(506) 652-5054; FAX (506) 636-8076

Built in 1891, this wonderful Victorian inn offers nine bedrooms, all with private baths. The bedrooms are warm and cozy decorated with antiques, plush linens, plants, and treasures. A careful restoration has preserved the original woodwork, stained-glass windows, a curved staircase, fireplaces, six-inch brass hinges on the doors, and a circular solarium. Wake up each morning to the aroma of freshly brewed coffee and homemade breads and muffins with freezer jams. Fresh fruit, bacon, sausage, eggs, and home fries are a welcome start to the day. The solarium is perfect for relaxing with a second cup of coffee and the morning paper.

Host: Pam Vincent
Rooms: 9 (PB) $79-95
Full Breakfast
Credit Cards: A, B, C, E
Notes: 4, 5, 7, 9, 11, 12, 14

SUSSEX

Stark's Hillside

Waterford, Rural Route 4, E0E 1P0
(506) 433-3764

Be together. Escape to a country dream with a spectacular view, rock water gardens, and hummingbirds. Relax or hike with Ginger. Easy access to the sights of Southern New Brunswick, find the 17 kissing bridges, visit Fundy National Park or the beautiful Saint John River. Special two-day packages available.

Hosts: Peter and Elizabeth Stark
Rooms: 2 (PB) $60
Full Breakfast
Credit Cards: B
Notes: 4 (call), 5, 12, 13, 14

---

6 Pets welcome; 8 Children welcome; 9 Social drinking allowed; 10 Tennis available; 11 Swimming available; 12 Golf available; 13 Skiing available; 14 May be booked through travel agents.

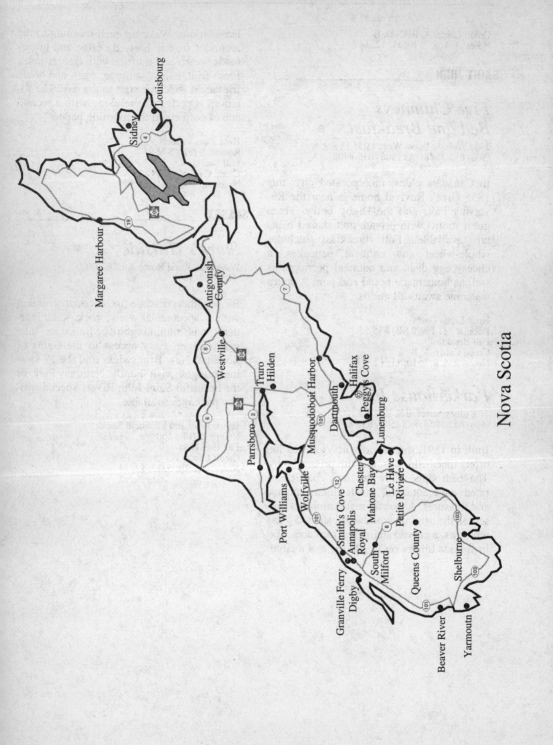

Nova Scotia

Louisbourg
Sidney
4
Margaree Harbour
19

Antigonish
County
7
6
Westville
Truro
Hilden
Parrsboro
2
6
Musquodoboit Harbor
Dartmouth
Halifax
Peggy's Cove
Lunenburg
Wolfville
12
Chester
Mahone Bay
Le Have
Petite Rivière
Port Williams
101
Smith's Cove
Annapolis
Royal
8
Granville Ferry
Digby
South
Milford
Queens County
103
Shelburne
Beaver River
Yarmouth
101
103

Nova Scotia

The King George Inn

548 Upper St. George Street, B0S 1A0
(902) 532-5286

Grand Victorian sea captain's home, furnished completely in period antiques. In historic Annapolis Royal (Canada's oldest settlement). A short walk from all major attractions. Inn features large, bright rooms with tall ceilings, cove moldings, leaded glass, rare carved woods, fireplaces, parquet floors, and legendary Nova Scotian hospitality. Family and honeymoon suites available.

Hosts: Michael and Donna Susnick
Rooms: 6 (2 PB; 4 SB) $45-52
Full Breakfast
Credit Cards: A, B
Notes: 6, 8, 9, 10, 11, 12, 14

The Poplars
Bed and Breakfast

124 Victorian Street, Box 277, B0S 1A0
(902) 532-7936

This restored Victorian home is in the heart of Canada's oldest permanent European settlement. A Registered Heritage site, it is shaded by huge 300-year-old poplars. Color cable TV in the family room, evening coffee and conversation. Two blocks from other amenities.

Host: Iris Williams
Rooms: 9 (6 PB; 3 SB) $35-49
Continental Breakfast
Credit Cards: B
Notes: 8, 9

Chestnut Corner
Bed and Breakfast

Rural Route 1, Afton, B0H 1A0
(902) 386-2403; Canada (800) 565-0000;
USA (800) 341-6096

Chestnut Corner is a relaxing country environment on Highway 4, 12.4 miles east of Antigonish town and 20 miles west of Cape Breton Island. Three tastefully decorated rooms provide single, twin, and queen-size accommodations. Clock radio and fan in each room. TV, VCR, and piano in lounges. Hiking trail on property. Nearby sandy beaches.

Hosts: Gordon and Joan Randall
Rooms: 3 (SD) $35-40
Full Breakfast
Credit Cards: None
Notes: 3, 6, 8, 9, 10, 11, 12

Green Haven Bed
and Breakfast

27 Greening Drive, B2G 1R1
(902) 863-2884; (902) 867-5059

Split-level residence with patio. Quiet wooded area within walking distance of university, live theater. Homemade breakfast featuring jams and oven-fresh muffins. Well-traveled hosts speak Polish, Russian, German, Spanish, English, and French. Den with cable TV, lots of books, and fireplaces.

Hosts: Martha and Al Balawyder
Rooms: 3 (1 PB; 2 SB) $38.85-55.50
Full Breakfast

NOTES: Credit cards accepted: A MasterCard; B Visa; C American Express; D Discover Card; E Diner's Club; F Other; 2 Personal checks accepted; 3 Lunch available; 4 Dinner available; 5 Open all year; 6 Pets welcome; 7 Smoking allowed; 8 Children welcome; 9 Social drinking allowed; 10 Tennis available; 11 Swimming available; 12 Golf available; 13 Skiing available; 14 May be booked through travel agents.

Credit Cards: None
Notes: 2, 3 (call), 4 (call), 5, 8, 9, 10, 11, 12, 13

LaBelle's

Frankville, B0H 1K0
(902) 234-2322

LaBelle's is a large, beautiful country home on acres of farmland and in view of the ocean. Quiet, homey atmosphere. Fresh toasted, homemade bread and muffins are served as part of a Continental breakfast. Three guest rooms with shared bath.

Hosts: Isabel and Elmer Fougere
Rooms: 3 (SB) $30-45
Continental Breakfast
Credit Cards: None
Notes: 8, 11, 12

BEAVER RIVER

Duck Pond Inn

Rural Route 1, Box 2495
Yarmouth County, B5A 4A5
(902) 649-2249; FAX (902) 649-2421

Elegantly restored and appointed sea captain's home. New queen-size four-poster beds, sparkling oversized bath, private lounge with TV. Full gourmet breakfast and complimentary tour of unique space museum operated by host. Beautiful rural setting yet convenient to Yarmouth and Digby ferries. Fine beach within short walk. Inn has won several awards. Reservations required.

Hosts: Tina and Harry Taylor
Rooms: 3 (1PB; 2 SB) $55-100
Full Breakfast
Credit Cards: None
Notes: 2, 4, 9, 11, 12

CHESTER

Haddon Hall Inn

67 Haddon Hill Road, B0J 1J0
(902) 275-3577; (902) 275-3578; FAX (902) 275-5159

Haddon Hall, one of Chester's renowned summer estates, was built in 1905 by Vernon Woolrich. On top of Haddon Hill, the residence offers a spectacular view of Mahone Bay and the town of Chester. This elegant country inn offers four beautiful guest rooms furnished in period furnishings, working fireplaces, private baths, TV, and telephones. Guests are invited to swim in the indoor pool or relax on the broad veranda. In the evening sit in front of a warm cracking fire in the Moose Room or in the library mezzanine.

Host: Linda Formosa
Rooms: 4 (PB) $90-125
Continental Breakfast
Credit Cards: A, B, C
Notes: 5, 10, 11, 12, 13

Mecklenburgh Inn

Mecklenburgh Inn

78 Queen Street, B0J 1J0
(902) 275-4638

A welcoming bed and breakfast in the heart of Chester, renowned seaside village/resort area. Rooms are spacious and comfortably appointed. Gourmet breakfasts are served around the big dining table before a crackling wood fire. The perfect home base from which to explore the area, browse the shops, or relax after a sail on the bay or a round of golf.

Host: Sue Fraser
Rooms: 4 (SB) $50-59
Full Breakfast
Credit Cards: B
Notes: 3, 8, 9, 10, 11, 12, 14

NOTES: Credit cards accepted: A MasterCard; B Visa; C American Express; D Discover Card; E Diner's Club; F Other; 2 Personal checks accepted; 3 Lunch available; 4 Dinner available; 5 Open all year;

Stoney Brook Bed and Breakfast

Box 716, B0J 1J0
(902) 275-2342

Charming 1860s home on large, landscaped property is a welcoming haven to visitors. A veranda offers comfortable chairs for relaxing. The back yard flower gardens and babbling brook offer a peaceful place for reading and enjoying nature. Five guest rooms with shared baths.

Hosts: Ned and Jeanne Nash
Rooms: 5 (3 PB; 2 SB) $50-53
Full Breakfast
Credit Cards: B
Notes: 2, 11, 12

DARTMOUTH

Riverdell Estate

68 Ross Road, Rural Route 3, B2W 5N7
(902) 434-7880

Nestled among the trees, beside a babbling brook, Riverdell offers executive country surroundings within minutes of Halifax and Dartmouth. Each day begins in the huge sun room where guests can bird watch while enjoying a hearty homemade breakfast. Browse among the collectibles, quilts, and antiques. Converse with knowledgeable, friendly hosts. Six rooms with private and shared baths. Suites have two-person whirlpools, fireplace, and feather bed.

Hosts: Clare and Isabel Christie
Rooms: 6 (4 PB; 2 SB) $65-140
Full Breakfast
Credit Cards: B, C
Notes: 5, 9, 10, 11, 12, 14

Stern's Mansion Inn Bed and Breakfast

17 Tulip Street, B3A 2S5
(902) 465-7414; (800) 565-3885
FAX (902) 466-2152

Restored century home with antique bedroom furnishings. Five rooms, private and shared baths, two with Jacuzzi spas, cable TV, VCR, telephone, and player piano. Four-course breakfast, evening tea and sweets. Honeymoon and special packages available.

Host: Bill deMolitor
Rooms: 5 (PB) $55-110
Full Breakfast
Credit Cards: A, B
Notes: 2, 5, 10, 11, 12, 14

DIGBY

Westway Inn

Plympton, B0W 2R0
(902) 837-7335; (902) 837-7276

The Westway Inn looks out over beautiful St. Mary's Bay. On the historic Evangeline Trail, it is conveniently on the corner of Highway 101 and French Road. Built in 1798, this 18th-century stagecoach stop boasts six rooms with private and shared baths, color TV, radio, two lounges, and a library. Antique furnishings with modern conveniences ensure a pleasant stay. Access to cross-country skiing.

Host: Alma Havenga
Rooms: 6 (1 PB; 5 SB) $36-45
Full Breakfast
Credit Cards: B
Notes: 5, 6, 7, 8, 9, 11, 12, 13

GRANVILLE FERRY

Nightingale's Landing Bed and Breakfast

P.O. Box 30; 5305 Granville Street, B0S 1K0
(902) 532-7615

Much-photographed 1870 Victorian gingerbread bed and breakfast overlooking the Annapolis River offers three comfortable bedrooms furnished in period antiques. Guests also enjoy the collection of antiques and family heirlooms in common rooms with high ceilings, antique chandeliers, marble fireplaces, and original wood moldings. A hearty gourmet breakfast is served in the dining room overlooking the river. After a day

6 Pets welcome; 8 Children welcome; 9 Social drinking allowed; 10 Tennis available; 11 Swimming available; 12 Golf available; 13 Skiing available; 14 May be booked through travel agents.

of touring, guests relax on the veranda or in the back yard glider and enjoy the peace and quiet of elegant country living.

Hosts: Sandy and Jim Nightingale
Rooms: 3 (1 PB; 2 SB) $45-55
Full Breakfast
Credit Cards: B
Notes: 2, 8 (over 7), 9, 10, 11, 12, 14

HALIFAX

Fresh Start Bed and Breakfast

2720 Gottingen Street, B3K 3C7
(902) 453-6616

Modest Victorian mansion with an informal atmosphere. Less than one mile from Citadel Hill, the public gardens, and other historic properties. Guests enjoy breakfast at their convenience, flexible check-out times, laundry service, and complimentary refreshments. On-site parking.

Hosts: Innis and Sheila MacDonald
Rooms: 6 (2 PB; 4 SB) $45-70
Full Breakfast
Credit Cards: A, B, C, E
Notes: 5, 6, 8, 9, 10, 11

Halliburton House Inn

5184 Morris Street, B3J 1B3
(902) 420-0658; FAX (902) 423-2324

Halliburton House Inn is a four-star registered Heritage property and is home to one of Halifax's finest restaurants. The inn's 28 comfortable guest rooms are tastefully furnished with period antiques. All have private bath, as well as the modern amenities expected by today's guests. Two suites have working fireplaces. The restaurant offers a relaxed, elegant setting for lunches and dinner. The menu specializes in seafood and wild game. On-site parking.

Host: Dr. Bruce Pretty
Rooms: 28 (PB) $110-135
Continental Breakfast
Credit Cards: A, B, C, D, E
Notes: 3, 4, 5, 7, 8, 9, 11, 12, 14

Prospect Bed and Breakfast

Box 68 Prospect Village, B0J 2V0
(902) 852-4493; (800) SALT-SEA

Pleasant informal atmosphere in a unique restored century-old convent. Canoe and rowboat for guest use. Small sand beach overlooking scenic Prospect Bay. Magnificent walking trails. Free boat tour with five-night stay. Near Peggy's Cove and Halifax. This bed and breakfast is at the end of the point; visitors can't go past it without getting wet.

Hosts: Helena and Stephen O'Leary
Rooms: 4 (SB) $50
Continental Breakfast
Cards: A, B
Notes: 2, 5, 8, 9, 10, 11, 12, 14

Salmon River House Country Inn

Head Jeddore, B0J 1P0
(902) 889-3353; (800) 565-3353

Circa 1855 inn is nestled in a beautiful panorama of wood, hills, and water. Thirty-five minutes from Dartmouth/Halifax. Six comfortable guest rooms, all with private baths. Wheelchair accessible. Honeymoon suite features whirlpool bath. Dining room, craft shop, and deck overlooking the water. Ask for Romantic Getaway, Canoe Adventure, or Sailboat Cruise packages. No smoking.

Hosts: Norma and Adrien Blanchette
Rooms: 6 (PB) $65-95
Credit Cards: A, B, E
Notes: 2, 3, 4, 5, 8, 9, 11, 12, 14

Virginia Kinfolks

1722 Robie Street, B3H 3E8
(902) 423-6687; (800) 668-STAY

A little bit of Virginia in Nova Scotia. Antique furnishings throughout including canopied beds. Full country-style breakfast. Convenient to downtown and all Halifax attractions including the waterfront. Discounts available for seniors and stay of three nights or more. Friendly atmosphere at a reasonable price.

Hosts: Dick and Lucy Russell
Rooms: 3 (1 PB; 2 SB) $45-60
Full Breakfast
Credit Cards: None
Notes: 2, 5, 6, 9, 10, 11, 12, 13

West Dover Seaside Cottages

7029 West Dover
c/o Box 68, Prospect Village, B0J 2V0
(902) 823-2652; (800) SALT-SEA

Verandas overlooking the ocean and quaint fishing village. Amenities include barbecue pits, picnic tables, ocean and lake swimming, boating, pier fishing, and the province's best hiking trails. Deep-sea fishing, boat tours, and water skiing arranged. Boat tour free with five nights accommodation. Modern cottages with full bath/shower and kitchen facilities. Each cottage has two or three bedrooms. All linens and towels provided. Convenient for day trips. Forty minutes to Halifax. One and a half miles to Peggy's Cove. Country store and Antique Folk Art store on site. Cable TV.

Hosts: John and Karen White
Cottages: 8 (PB) $60-80
Full Breakfast
Credit Cards: A, B
Notes: 2, 5, 7, 8, 9, 11, 12, 14

HILDEN

Ann's Farmhouse Bed and Breakfast

2627 Irwin Lake Road, B0N 1C0
(902) 897-0300

Pleasant old farmhouse surrounded by rolling pastures and woods. Lots of sheep and birds. A great place to walk or relax and yet only 15 minutes from downtown Truro with its shops and restaurants. Three guest rooms with shared bath facilities. Full

breakfast and evening snacks provided. No smoking or pets.

Hosts: David and Ann Pullen
Rooms: 3 (SB) $40-45
Full Breakfast
Credit Cards: B
Notes: 8, 12

LA HAVE

Goode's Landing Bed and Breakfast

Box 33; House 3384, Route 331 South, B0R 1C0
(902) 688-2161

Experience true down-home hospitality and comfort in this turn-of-the-century home furnished with some interesting antiques and collectibles. Relax on the veranda and watch the boats of the LaHave, the Rhine of Nova Scotia. Enjoy the private sunny patio, cast for mackerel off the wharf, stroll to Fort Point (first settled in 1632), and drop in at the famous LaHave Bakery for a snack. This artist's and bird watcher's paradise, with excellent windsurfing and cycling, is also near beaches. A short ferry ride delivers guests within minutes of Lunenburg and Mahone Bay. Two charming bedrooms each with double bed. Shared guest-only bath. Comfortable smoke-free environment. Start each day with a hearty captain's breakfast. Ici on parle francais.

Hosts: Michael and Darby Goode
Rooms: 2 (SB) $40-45
Full Breakfast
Credit Cards: B
Notes: 11, 12

LOUISBOURG

Greta Cross Bed and Breakfast

81 Pepperell Street, B0A 1M0
(902) 733-2833

An older home off Main Street on a hill overlooking the harbor and the Fortress of

6 Pets welcome; 8 Children welcome; 9 Social drinking allowed; 10 Tennis available; 11 Swimming available; 12 Golf available; 13 Skiing available; 14 May be booked through travel agents.

Greta Cross

Louisbourg. In a quiet area, it offers guests kitchen privileges and a baby-sitting service. Home-baked breads, muffins, oatcakes, and jams are provided for breakfast, and a snack is served on arrival if desired. Rated 2-1/2 stars Canada Select.

Host: Greta Cross
Rooms: 3 (SB) $35-40
Full Breakfast
Credit Cards: C
Notes: 2, 6, 8, 9, 10, 11

LUNENBURG

Blue Rocks Road Bed and Breakfast

579 Blue Rocks Road, Rural Route 1, B0J 2C0
(902) 634-3426

Comfortable home with veranda overlooking Lunenburg Bay, one hour from Halifax and close to beautiful unspoiled beaches. Friendly, relaxed atmosphere and great breakfasts including farm-fresh eggs. Also home of The Lunenburg Cyclist with everything for the cyclist. Quality bike rentals. Great cycling country! German and English spoken. No smoking.

Hosts: Al and Merrill Heubach
Rooms: 3 (1 PB; 2 SB) $55-65
Full Breakfast
Credit Cards: A, B
Notes: 8, 9, 10, 11, 12

Kaulbach House Historic Inn

75 Pelham Street, B0J 2C0
(902) 634-8818

In the heart of the National Historic District and overlooking the waterfront, this registered Heritage Inn, circa 1880, offers elegant accommodation in a gracious Victorian atmosphere. Each of the eight beautifully appointed guest rooms has color TV and six of the rooms have private baths. An elaborate three-course breakfast is served each morning. The entree changes daily with specialities like Cheese Strata and Maple Sugar Pears, or Quiche Lorraine and Strawberry Creme Brulee. Fully licensed dining is offered exclusively to the guests.

Hosts: Karen and Enzo Padovani
Rooms: 8 (6 PB; 2 SB) $55-85
Full Breakfast
Credit Cards: A, B, C
Notes: 4, 5, 9, 10, 11, 12, 14

The Lamb and Lobster Bed and Breakfast

619 Blue Rocks Road, B0J 2C0
(902) 634-4833

A working sheep farm with beautiful ocean views. Enjoy a walk in the pastures while the sheep graze. Fishing, scuba diving, and whale-watching tours available. Three rooms, two with queen-size beds, one with twin beds. Shared' bath facilities. Full home-cooked breakfast made with fresh farm eggs. Older children welcome.

Hosts: William and Hilary Flower
Rooms: 3 (SB) $50
Full Breakfast
Credit Cards: B
Notes: 8 (call), 10, 11, 12

South Shore Country Inn

Broad Cove, B0J 2H0
(902) 677-2042

Renovated, beautifully decorated century-plus old home with modern conveniences. Rooms are uniquely individual. Licensed dining room serves home-made English and Nova Scotian fare in elegant but comfortable surroundings. In a small scenic village.

This is an ideal spot for a getaway or rest and relaxation.

Host: Avril Betts
Rooms: 6 (2 PB; 4 SB) $60-95
Full and Continental Breakfast
Credit Cards: A, B, C, D, E
Notes: 3, 4, 6, 7, 9, 11, 14

MAHONE BAY

Sou'Wester Inn Bed and Breakfast

788 Main Street; Highway 3, Box 146, B0J 2E0
(902) 624-9296

Fine Victorian seaside shipbuilder's home with friendly and gracious accommodations. Enjoy evening tea, relax on the veranda, or sit by the water overlooking the beautiful bay. There are books, parlor games, and a piano for lazy days. Collectors, see the fine whale sculptures, antique and period furnishings. This bed and breakfast is on Nova Scotia's beautiful South Shore. Maps are available for scenic drives or quiet shoreline walks. Exquisite dining nearby.

Hosts: Ron and Mabel Redden
Rooms: 4 (PB) $65-70
Full Breakfast
Credit Cards: A, B
Notes: 9, 10, 11, 12, 14

Three Buoys House

Indian Point, Rural Route 2, B0J 2E0
(902) 624-6375

Relax on the deck overlooking the ocean in a quiet fishing settlement. Older home is in Indian Point, five miles east of Mahone Bay. Afternoon tea and breakfast are served on the deck. Boats swing on their moorings in the cove. Drop anchor for a few days and get to know the area. Many attractions and wonderful food are close by. Hosts are world travelers and chose Indian Point as their home. The hosts also love children so they are welcome at this bed and breakfast.

Hosts: Julia and Malcolm Stick
Rooms: 3 (1 PB; 2 SB) $45-50
Continental Breakfast
Credit Cards: None
Notes: 5, 8, 9, 10, 11, 12

MARGAREE HARBOUR

Harbour View Inn Bed and Breakfast

B0E 2B0
(902) 235-2314

Started in the early 1920s, the Harbour View Inn is an older home with a fantastic view of the Margaree Highland Mountains and a long wooden bridge where the famous salmon-fishing Margaree River begins. Three beaches just minutes away. There is a general store, whale cruises, deep-sea fishing, a large gift shop, and historic boats close by. Lounge with cable TV and VCR. Reading room. Hosts serve home-cooked meals including lobster, crab, and other seafood. Guests are allowed use of the kitchen.

Hosts: Connie and Glenn Jennex
Rooms: 3 (SB) $40-55
Full Breakfast
Credit Cards: A, B, C
Notes: 2, 3, 4, 6, 7, 8, 9, 10, 11, 12

MASSTOWN

Shady Maple Bed and Breakfast

Rural Route 1, B0M 1G0
(902) 662-3565

Restored century home and operating farm. Upstairs balcony affords a view of Cobequid Bay. Full four-course breakfast by candlelight. Evening snacks provided. Enjoy the heated outdoor pool and year-round spa, or sit by the fireplace in the den. Six miles from Tidal Bore look-off.

Hosts: Jim and Ellen Eisses
Rooms: 4 (SB) $40-65

6 Pets welcome; 8 Children welcome; 9 Social drinking allowed; 10 Tennis available; 11 Swimming available; 12 Golf available; 13 Skiing available; 14 May be booked through travel agents.

Full Breakfast
Credit Cards: B
Notes: 2, 5, 6, 8, 9, 11, 13, 14

MUSQUODOBOIT

Wayward Goose Inn Bed and Breakfast

343 West Petpeswick Road, B0J 2L0
(902) 889-3654

The Wayward Inn is a quiet inn where deer and loons visit regularly. One half-hour from Halifax-Dartmouth, the Wayward Goose blends the best of urban convenience with rural charm. The area offers the best of crafts, museums, and breathtaking scenery. Hike or ski the trails, swim off the dock, sail in the daysailer, paddle a canoe, row a rowboat, skate on the inlet, relax in the private living room with fireplace, stereo, cable TV, VCR, or play billiards in the game room. Rooms are tastefully appointed with private baths and other features. Honeymoon suite features a whirlpool bath for two. Packages are available. No smoking or pets.

Hosts: Randy and Judy Skaling
Rooms: 3 (PB) $45-65
Full Breakfast
Credit Cards: B
Notes: 2, 5, 8, 9, 11, 12, 14

MUSQUODOBOIT HARBOR

The International Bed & Breakfast Club, Inc.

504 Amherst Street, Buffalo, NY 14207
(800) 723-4262; FAX (716) 873-4462

NS3684PP. This quiet inn overlooks Petpeswick Inlet only half an hour from the twin cities of Halifax and Dartmouth. Three rooms are available with private baths. A luxury suite has a whirlpool bath, private living room, stereo, fireplace, TV, and VCR. Full breakfast, candlelight dinner, and a picnic basket available. $45-65.

PARRSBORO

Spencer's Island Inn

Rural Route 3, B0M 1S0
(902) 392-2721

Step back into the house of a shipbuilder of the famous mystery ship, Mary Celeste, in the seaside village of Spencer's Island. Comb the nearby tidal beach for odd and interesting rocks or visit the lighthouse. Open June through August. Take Route 209 to Spencer's Island, turn off at Spencer's Beach sign.

Hosts: Margaret Griebel
Rooms: 3 (1 PB; 2 SB) $35
Full Breakfast
Credit Cards: None
Notes: 2, 8

PEGGY'S COVE

Peggy's Cove Bed and Breakfast

19 Church Road, B0J 2N0
(902) 823-2265

Overlooking beautiful Peggy's Cove. Large comfortable rooms; friendly informal atmosphere. Two rooms feature patio doors opening onto a large shared balcony over the cove. Third room provides view of the mouth of the cove, St. Margaret's Bay, the church, and the Barrens. Experience life in this world-renowned little fishing village within easy walking distance of all Cove attractions and activities—lighthouse, fish houses, gift shops, and restaurant.

Hosts: Audrey O'Leary and
  Anne and Doug O'Hearn
Rooms: 3 (SB) $60
Full Breakfast
Credit Cards: A, B, C
Notes: 9, 11, 12, 14

PETITE RIVIERE

Little River Bed and Breakfast

5666 Route 331, B0J 2P0
(902) 688-1339

European-style dwelling offers peace and tranquility with ample parking for car or boat. Large deck equipped with a barbecue and picnic tables. Three rooms with private and shared bath. Full breakfast served. Cable TV, VCR, music, and piano in living room. Near beaches, nature walks, artists, swimming, and golf. Honeymoon packages available. No smoking.

Hosts: Joan and Tanya Patterson
Rooms: 3 (1 PB; 2 SB) $50-65
Full Breakfast
Credit Cards: B
Notes: 2, 3, 4, 5, 9, 11, 12, 14

PORT WILLIAMS

The Old Rectory Bed and Breakfast

1519 Highway 358, Rural Route 1, B0P 1T0
(902) 542-1815

Recently renovated Victorian home with gardens and orchard. (U-Pick and cider making in season.) Evening tea. Field trips available. Hike to Cape Split, visit historic Prescott House and Grand Pre Park. Local art galleries and cultural events in university town.

Hosts: Ron and Carol Buckley
Rooms: 3 (1 PB; 2 SB) $50-60
Full Breakfast
Credit Cards: None
Notes: 2, 8, 11, 12, 14

QUEENS COUNTY

River View Lodge

Box 129, Greenfield, B0T 1E0
(902) 685-2376; (902) 685-2423

Rustic five-bedroom lodge with a fireplace, TV/VCR in the living room. Dining room overlooks the scenic Medway River, which is great for its spring run of trout and Atlantic Salmon. Close to shopping mall, historical sites, and museums.

Hosts: Suzette and Moyal Conrad
Rooms: 5 (SB) $45
Full Breakfast
Credit Cards: B
Notes: 2, 3 (call), 4 (call), 6, 7, 8, 9, 11, 12

SHELBURNE

Ankriston Villa

Rural Route 3, B0T 1W0
(902) 637-3005 (Phone/FAX)

Overlooking the River Clyde, this elegant restored brick estate house offers superior accommodations in a scenic setting just minutes from the highway on Nova Scotia's South Shore. The comfortable patio area overlooks the river where sportsmen can fish for salmon. The hosts offer one double and one twin bedroom with private bath. The spacious drawing room and dining room, both with fireplaces, encourage guests to relax in comfort. Horseback riding nearby. Exit 28 Port Clyde, 2 miles from Highway 103.

Hosts: Starr and Don Nelson
Rooms: 2 (PB) $35-45
Full Breakfast
Credit Cards: None
Notes: 8, 9, 11, 12

Cooper's Inn and Restaurant

Box 959, 36 Dock Street, B0T 1W0
(902) 875-4656

In the historic waterfront area of the Loyalist town of Shelburne, the Cooper's Inn offers quality accommodations with private baths right on Shelburne Harbour. Within easy reach of fine beaches, sailing and boating facilities, the Roseway River sys-

---

6 Pets welcome; 8 Children welcome; 9 Social drinking allowed; 10 Tennis available; 11 Swimming available; 12 Golf available; 13 Skiing available; 14 May be booked through travel agents.

tem, riverside golf course, and the Shelburne historical museum complex. Full dining facilities feature regional cuisine and fresh local produce.

Hosts: Allan and Joan Redmond
Rooms: 5 (PB) $56-75
Continental Breakfast
Credit Cards: A, B, C
Notes: 3, 4, 11, 12, 14

Harbour House Bed and Breakfast

187 Water Street, Box 362, B0T 1W0
(902) 875-2074; (800) 565-0000

A 200-year-old Loyalist home, Harbour House offers a comfortable friendly atmosphere in a scenic location overlooking the beautiful Shelburne Harbour and Island's Park. Within walking distance of historic waterfront museum, park, harbor, stores, cinema, bank, post office, restaurants, and tourist bureau. Coffee and tea offered in the evening. English and German spoken. Free parking. No smoking.

Host: Wolfgang Schricker
Rooms: 3 (SB) $45
Full Breakfast
Credit Cards: B
Notes: 2, 8, 10, 11, 12, 14

SMITH'S COVE

Harbourview Inn

P.O. Box 39, B0S 1S0
(902) 245-5686

A turn-of-the-century village inn overlooking the tidal waters of the beautiful Annapolis Basin, the inn is furnished in Victorian country fashion and has welcomed summer guests since the 1890s. Harbourview offers guests a freshwater pool, tennis court, and an ocean beach for clamming, rock hounding, and viewing the world's most dramatic tides. Meals are served daily in a fully licensed dining room. Fresh local seafoods are featured.

Harbourview Inn

Hosts: Mona and Phillip Webb
Rooms: 12 (PB) $55-75
Full Breakfast
Credit Cards: A, B
Notes: 2, 4, 7, 8, 9, 10, 11, 12, 14

SOUTH MILFORD

Milford House

Box 521 Annapolis Royal, B0S 1A0
(902) 532-2617

Milford House is a rustic wilderness resort dating back to the 1860s with all accommodations in cabins dotted around the shores of two lakes. Each cabin has two to five bedrooms, bathroom, living room, veranda, and dock. There are no radios or TV. The main lodge features the dining room, living rooms, library, and children's game room. Tennis courts and croquet lawn available. Rates include breakfast and dinner.

Host: Maggie Nickerson
Cabins: 27 (PB) $137-149
Full Breakfast and Dinner
Credit Cards: B
Notes: 2, 4, 6, 7 (limited), 8, 9 (limited), 10, 11, 12, 14

SYDNEY

Park Place Bed and Breakfast

169 Park Street, B1P 4W7
(902) 562-3518

NOTES: Credit cards accepted: A MasterCard; B Visa; C American Express; D Discover Card; E Diner's Club; F Other; 2 Personal checks accepted; 3 Lunch available; 4 Dinner available; 5 Open all year;

Victorian-style house built for the steel plant circa 1901. Unique feature of curved walls in living room and hall. Near downtown. Close to Louisbourg and Miner's Museum.

Host: Ev McEwen
Rooms: 3 (SB) $40
Full Breakfast
Credit Cards: B
Notes: 5, 8, 9, 10, 11, 12, 13, 14

TRURO

The Silver Firs Bed and Breakfast

397 Prince Street, B2N 1E6
(902) 897 1900

This gracious 78-year-old traditionally furnished home is central with three elegant air-conditioned rooms, each with clock radio, TV, and private bath. Tea served upon arrival and bedtime snack. Gratifying breakfast served from 8:00 to 9:30 A.M. in attractive dining room. Library facilities, game room with pool table, games, puzzles, VCR. Open from May 15 to October 15; other times by request. Hosts happily meet airport, train, and bus arrivals and assist with itineraries. Children over 12. No smoking. No pets.

Hosts: Beverley and Grant Richardson
Rooms: 3 (PB) $75-95
Full Breakfast
Credit Cards: B
Notes: 8 (over 12), 9, 10, 11, 12, 13

WESTVILLE

Pinehedge Bed and Breakfast

Rural Route 1, B0K 2A0
(902) 396-5726

Three rooms with shared shower bath. Clock radio, TV, telephone, and hair dryers in all rooms. Cable TV in living room. Full breakfast featuring homemade bread and muffins. Close to beaches, golf, shopping,

PEI ferry, and Fun Park. Air-conditioned. Available May through October; other times by request.

Hosts: Theresa and John Patton
Rooms: 3 (SB) $40
Full Breakfast
Credit Cards: None
Notes: 2, 8, 9, 10, 11, 12

Stoneycombe Lounge

Rural Route 3, B0K 2A0
(902) 396-3954

Modern house with heated outdoor pool for relaxation. Set in the heart of the province with easy access to beaches, festivals, and the airport. Take day trips to many areas of interest and return for a late snack in the evening. Their three-star rating means that guests will be well looked after. Off-season rates are in effect for fall foliage days in glorious technicolor!

Hosts: Keith and Edith Selwyn-Smith
Rooms: 3 (PB) $45-55
Full Breakfast
Credit Cards: B
Notes: 2, 5, 8, 9, 11, 12, 14

WOLFVILLE

The Gingerbread House Inn Bed and Breakfast

8 Robie Tufts Drive; P.O. Box 819, B0P 1X0
(902) 542-1458

Restored 1893 carriage house has five masterfully decorated bedrooms all with private bath, entrances, and color TV. A candlelight full breakfast is included in the room price. The Garden Suite boasts a 21-foot tower, in-floor spa, fireplace, and wet bar. Available from May 1 to November 1.

Hosts: Ron and Doreen Cook
Rooms: 5 (PB) $59-125
Full Candlelight Breakfast
Credit Cards: None
Notes: 2, 8 (over 5), 9, 10, 11, 12, 13, 14

6 Pets welcome; 8 Children welcome; 9 Social drinking allowed; 10 Tennis available; 11 Swimming available; 12 Golf available; 13 Skiing available; 14 May be booked through travel agents.

Tattingstone Inn

434 Main Street, P.O. Box 98, B0P 1X0
(902) 542-7696

Enjoy fine country dining prepared by an award-winning chef. Whether guests choose to dine overlooking the garden or by the fireplace, each evening will be memorable. The inn features ten beautifully appointed rooms with private baths. Most have queen-size beds. Antiques and original art are featured throughout. All rooms and dining areas are air-conditioned and no smoking. Tennis courts and swimming pool are on site.

Host: Betsey Harwood
Rooms: 10 (PB) $78-138
Credit Cards: A, B, C
Notes: 4, 5, 10, 11, 12, 13, 14

YARMOUTH

Churchill Mansion Inn

Rural Route 1, B5A 4A5
(902) 649-2818

A truly unique mansion on top of a hill overlooking two lakes and the Bay of Fundy. Original light fixtures and carpets. Breakfast room overlooks Darling Lake. Widow's walk on top. Miles of sandy beach nearby. Canoe available in lake. Seafood buffet available nightly.

Host: Bob Benson
Rooms: 9 (PB) $39-59
Full Breakfast
Credit Cards: A, B, D
Notes: 3, 4, 6, 7, 8, 9, 11, 12, 14

Murray Manor Bed and Breakfast

225 Main Street, B5A 1C6
(902) 742-9625

Beautiful, well-maintained English home in the Gothic style was built in the 1820s by an Englishman named Bond. The house has a bell-cast roof, a five-bay facade with pointed Gothic windows. The three bedrooms are attractive and comfortable. Each have "prayer" windows (one must kneel in order to see out).

Hosts: George and Joan Semple
Rooms: 3 (SB) $55
Full Breakfast
Credit Cards: B
Notes: 5, 8 (older), 9, 10, 11, 12, 14

Victorian Vogue Bed and Breakfast

109 Brunswick Street, B5A 2H2
(902) 742-6398

Historic Queen Anne Revival has all the richness and charm guests will enjoy. Fireplaces, pocket doors, wainscoting, and stained-glass windows are just a few of the features gracing this beautiful sea captain's home. Tea, coffee, and desserts are available in the parlor each afternoon. Yarmouth is a wonderful historic seaport to explore. Magnificent home and scenic locations abound.

Host: Dawn-Marie Skjelmose
Rooms: 6 (1PB; 5 SB) $45-60
Full Breakfast
Credit Cards: A, B
Notes: 2, 5, 8, 9, 14

NOTES: Credit cards accepted: A MasterCard; B Visa; C American Express; D Discover Card; E Diner's Club; F Other; 2 Personal checks accepted; 3 Lunch available; 4 Dinner available; 5 Open all year;

Ontario

Squirrels Bed and Breakfast

Box 72; 190 Parkview Drive K0A 1A0
(613) 256-2995

Unique spacious home in the style of a German chalet. Full breakfast, with homemade bread and marmalade served in the sunroom overlooking the garden. Two double rooms with king-size bed or two single beds; one single room. Shared bath. Plenty of privacy. Hosts are world travelers and enjoy sharing experiences with their guests. Nonsmokers only. Reasonable rates.

Hosts: Pat and Ian Matheson
Rooms: 3 (SB) $45
Full Breakfast
Credit Cards: None
Notes: 2, 5, 8, 9, 10, 12, 13

Tackaberry's Grant

Rural Route 2, K0A 1A0
(613) 256-1481

Beautiful parklike setting in rolling farmland, 10 minutes southwest of Almonte and 40 minutes from downtown Ottawa. Two rooms, one with queen-size bed, one with two singles, with shared bath, in a charming, renovated 150-year-old farmhouse. Relax in the large in-ground pool or stroll the grounds, which include an apple orchard and pond. Friendly family dog will be delighted to accompany guests! Hearty full breakfast included. No smoking. No pets. Reservations recommended.

Hosts: Jack and Orchid Reid
Rooms: 2 (SB) $40
Full Breakfast
Credit Cards: None
Notes: 2, 5, 8, 9, 11, 12, 13

Ottawa Bed and Breakfast

488 Cooper Street, Ottawa, K1R 5H9
(613) 563-0161

1. Very large modern home. Two guest rooms with shared bath and sitting room with TV. One bedroom has twin beds, the other has a queen-size bed. Resident cat. No smoking. $55-73.

2. Large bungalow on a wooded lot in a nice residential area of Ottawa. Choose from two guest rooms —one with double bed, the second with twin beds, shared bath. Photographs of the home have been featured in a major magazine because of the extensive restoration work hosts have done. Enjoy the lovely garden. Parliament buildings are only a few minutes' drive by car or by bus, which is available nearby. Families welcome. Hosts speak French. $55-73.

Northridge Farm

Rural Route 2, N0B 1G0
(519) 634-8595

Enjoy the quiet space, comfort, and hospitality of 86 acres of rolling farmland, just 10 minutes west of Kitchener-Waterloo and 25 minutes east of Stratford. Three guest rooms, one with double and single beds, one with twin beds, one a single. Within an easy drive of Mennonite country, shopping outlets and farmers' markets. Visit the horses; farm has a complete equestrian fa-

6 Pets welcome; 7 Smoking allowed; 8 Children welcome; 9 Social drinking allowed; 10 Tennis available; 11 Swimming available; 12 Golf available; 13 Skiing available; 14 May be booked through travel agents.

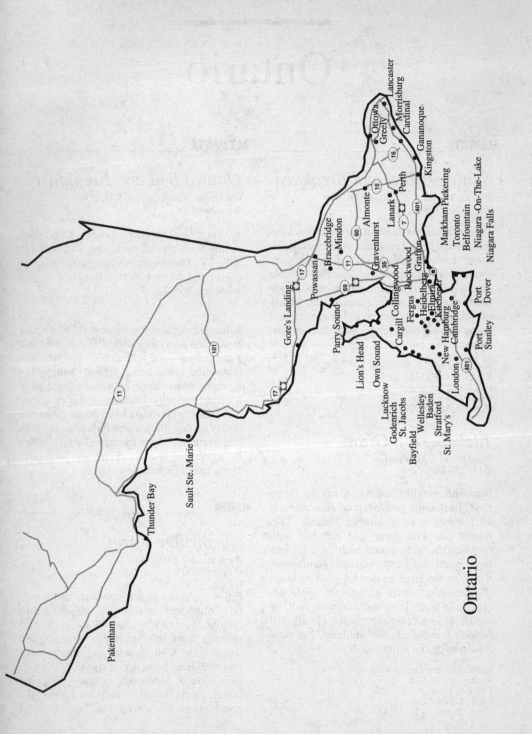

Lancaster
Morrisburg
Cardinal
Ottawa
Greely
Gananoque
16
Kingston
Perth
15
Lanark
Almonte
401
Pickering
Markham
Niagara -On-The-Lake
7
Mindon
Bracebridge
60
Belfountain
Toronto
Niagara Falls
Gravenhurst
11
Rockwood
Grafton
Port
17
35
Collingwood
Heidelberg
Dover
Powassan
Fergus
Elmira
Kitchener
69
Cargill
New Hamburg
Port
Gore's Landing
Cambridge
Stanley
Parry Sound
London
101
Lion's Head
401
Own Sound
11
Lucknow
Godenrich
St. Jacobs
Bayfield
Wellesley
17
Baden
Stratford
Sault Ste. Marie
St. Mary's

Thunder Bay

Pakenham

Ontario

cility. English lessons are available. No pets, please.

Hosts: Sarah Banbury and son, Michael
Rooms: 3 (SB) $55
Continental Breakfast
Notes: 2, 5, 7 (limited), 8 (over six), 9, 12, 13

BAYFIELD

The Little Inn of Bayfield

Main Street,;P.O. Box 100, N0M 1G0
(519) 565-2611; (800) 565-1832

Originally a stagecoach stop, the inn has been welcoming guests to this picturesque lakeside village since the 1830s. This designated Heritage Inn is replete with fireplaces, ensuite whirlpools, sauna, games, and books. Fine dining has long been a tradition, with superb meals and imaginative menus. Guests have a perfect base from which to explore the countryside and attend the Stratford and Blyth festivals. There is much to do any time of the year.

Hosts: Patrick and Gayle Waters
Rooms: 31 (PB) $80-190
Full and Continental Breakfasts
Cards: A, B, C, E
Notes: 2, 3, 4, 5, 6, 7, 8, 9, 10, 11, 12, 13, 14

BELFOUNTAIN

Cedarbrook

402 Bush Street, L0N 1B0
(519) 927-5559

Relax in this spacious air-conditioned country home and conference center overlooking rolling acres on the Credit River. Panoramic views, cathedral ceilings, fireplaces and guest rooms with ensuite bathrooms. Minutes from Forks of the Credit, Bruce Trail, Cataract falls, ski center and nature park. Close to Brampton, Missisauga and Guelph. Enjoy hiking, skiing, golf, hotair ballooning, bird watching, and antique and craft browsing. Home-baked break-

fasts. Dinner on request. TV room and laundry. No smoking. No pets.

Hosts: Gord and Ginny Edwards
Rooms: 6 (PB) $80-90
Full Breakfast
Credit Cards: A, B
Notes: 2, 4, 5, 9, 10, 12, 13

BLACKSTOCK

Landfall Farm

3120 Highway 7A, Rural Route 1, L0B 1B0
(905) 986-5588

An 1868 stone farmhouse in south central Ontario amidst crop fields and large, inviting lawns. Landfall Farms is a designated Heritage Site of architectural and historic significance. Its features include air conditioning, an antique shop, a living room with fieldstone fireplace, and a screened dining patio. There is also a landscaped swimming pool and a separate enchanting and peaceful pond area. The inn is near the charming lakefront town of Port Perry, a tourist shoppers'paradise. Perry offers golf, tennis, fishing, boating, and canoeing, as well as the outstanding feature of an outdoor groomed ice-skating rink on Lake Scugog. Cross-country and downhill skiing are also nearby.

Hosts: Mrs. Merle Heintzman
Rooms: 3 (SB) $60
Full Breakfast
Credit Cards: None
Notes: 2, 5, 6, 7 (limited), 8, 9, 10, 11, 12, 13

BRACEBRIDGE

Century House Bed and Breakfast

155 Dill Street, P1L 1E5
(705) 645-9903

These hosts invite guests to their charming, air-conditioned, restored century-old home in the province's premier recreational lake dis-

Century House

trict, a two-hour drive north of Toronto. Sandy's breakfasts are creative and generous. Waffles with local maple syrup are a specialty. Century House is close to shopping, beaches, and many craft studios and galleries. Enjoy the sparkling lakes, fall colors, studio tours, and winter cross-country skiing. A friendly dog is in residence.

Hosts: Norman Yan and Sandy Yudin
Rooms: 3 (SB) $55-60
Full Breakfast
Credit Cards: None
Notes: 2, 5, 7 (limited), 8, 10, 11, 12, 13, 14

CAMBRIDGE

Langdon Hall Country House Hotel

Rural Route 33, N3H 4RH
(519) 740-2100

This elegant and comfortable accommodation will provide guests with a home away from home. The Country House atmosphere is typified by the peaceful reading rooms and intimate paneled lounges and bar. All guest rooms are carefully furnished, each one different; most sitting areas are warmed by open fireplaces. Indoor recreational facilities include billiard and card rooms, whirlpools, saunas, and exercise rooms. Outdoors there are croquet and tennis courts and a heated swimming pool. Langdon Hall offers a quality of ser-

vice and courtesy that puts guests at their ease, secure in the knowledge that they will be well attended.

Hosts: William Bennett and Mary Beaton
Rooms: 41 (PB) $175-290
Continental Breakfast
Credit Cards: A, B, C, E
Notes: 3, 4, 5, 8, 9, 10, 11, 12, 13, 14

Red Door Bed and Breakfast

754 Queenston Road, N3H 3K3
(519) 653-9767

A warm welcome awaits every guest at the Red Door. Relax in the century home on a quiet tree-lined street in the heart of Preston, an area of Cambridge. Enjoy a leisurely breakfast in the family dining room. From this central location visit farmers' markets, factory outlets, Lion Safari, or Pioneer Sportsworld.

Hosts: Clare and Janet Bauman
Rooms: 2 (1 PB; 2 SB) $50
Full Breakfast
Credit Cards: None
Notes: 2, 5, 9, 10, 12

CARDINAL

Roduner Farm

Rural Route 1, K0E 1E0
(613) 657-4830

To this active dairy farm, the hosts have been welcoming guests for many years. Children like to gather the eggs and observe the milking. Relax on the shaded lawn or in this comfortable home. Close to Upper Canada Village, Thousand Islands, or the locks at Iroquois. Only a one-hour drive to Ottawa. Schweizerdeutsch and a little French are spoken. Cross-country skiing in area.

Hosts: Walter and Margareta Roduner
Rooms: 2 (1 PB; 1 SB) $40
Full Breakfast
Credit Cards: None
Notes: 2, 4 (call), 5, 6, 7, 8, 9, 11, 12, 13

NOTES: Credit cards accepted: A MasterCard; B Visa; C American Express; D Discover Card; E Diner's Club; F Other; 2 Personal checks accepted; 3 Lunch available; 4 Dinner available; 5 Open all year;

CARGILL

Cornerbrook Bed and Breakfast

Rural Rou; 2, N0G 1J0
(519) 366-2629

A warm welcome and relaxed atmosphere await in this modernized century-old brick home completely restored with two open staircases, carpet throughout, a few hand-quilted quilts, and a smattering of antiques to add a flavor of the past. Relax on the well-shaded lawn and enjoy the flower gardens. Convenient to Walkerton, Paisley, and the beaches at Kincardine and Port Elgin. Canoe and fish on the Saugeen River. Enjoy Lake Huron sunsets. Three attractive guest rooms, one with twin beds. Good home-cooked meals. Smoking allowed on the patio.

Hosts: Elaine and John Moffatt
Rooms: 4 (2 SB) $40
Full Breakfast
Credit Cards: None
Notes: 3, 4, 5, 8, 11, 12, 13

Beild House Country Inn

COLLINGWOOD

Beild House Country Inn

64 Third Street, L9Y 1K5
(705) 444-1522

This turn-of-the-century home has been meticulously converted into an elegant country inn. It features a five-course breakfast of guests' choice, picnic lunches, and afternoon teas, with a selection of hot and cold hors d'oeuvres offered each evening. Marvelous five-course gourmet dinners are also available. Discover the beauty of Georgian Bay and the Blue Mountains at Beild House Country Inn.

Hosts: Bill and Stephanie Barclay
Rooms: 17 (7 PB; 10 SB) $80-125
Full Breakfast
Credit Cards: A, B
Notes: 2, 3, 4, 5, 6, 7, 8, 9, 10, 11, 12, 13, 14

ELMIRA

Birdland Bed and Breakfast

1 Grey Owl Drive, N3B 1S2
(519) 669-1900

Come and enjoy hospitality in a chalet-style home in a quiet area of town, right in the heart of Ontario's Mennonite country. The guest rooms feature queen-size beds with private baths; one room even has a private sauna. Enjoy Elmira's unique craft and gift shops, or take a drive to Elora's scenic gorge. Close to an old covered bridge, the Factory Outlet Mall, and farmers' markets. The old-fashioned town of St. Jacobs is only minutes away. No smoking please.

Hosts: Robert and Alice Martin
Rooms: 2 (PB) $40-50
Full Breakfast
Credit Cards: None
Notes: 2, 5, 11, 12

The Evergreens

Rural Route 1, N3B 2Z1
(519) 669-2471

Welcome to a quiet bed and breakfast nestled among the evergreens. Enjoy long walks through the forest, swimming in the pool, or cross-country skiing in winter. Two comfortable bedrooms with two guest bathrooms, and breakfast with homemade baking and preserves. In Mennonite country, with Elmira, St. Jacobs, and Elora all nearby. North of Elmira, east off Regional Road 21 on Woolrich Road 2. Children

---

6 Pets welcome; 8 Children welcome; 9 Social drinking allowed; 10 Tennis available; 11 Swimming available; 12 Golf available; 13 Skiing available; 14 May be booked through travel agents.

welcome. No smoking in home. Open year-round.

Hosts: Rodger and Doris Milliken
Rooms: 2 (SB) $45
Full Breakfast
Credit Cards: None
Notes: 2, 5, 6, 7 (limited), 8, 9, 11, 12, 13

Teddy Bear Inn

Teddy Bear Bed and Breakfast Inn

Rural Route 1, N3B 2Z1
(519) 669-2379

Relax and enjoy the hospitality of this gracious and elegant inn, enhanced with Canadiana and quilts. In the Old Order Mennonite countryside close to St. Jacobs, Kitchener-Waterloo's markets, museums, Stratford, Elora, Fergus, and Guelph. Spacious deluxe bedrooms, private or shared bathrooms, TV lounge, and craft shop. Cross-country skiing, golf, boating, hiking, tours, and more nearby. Sumptuous Continental breakfast or full breakfast on request. Seminar and private dining facilities are available.

Hosts: Vivian and Gerrie Smith
Rooms: 3 (PB) $65
Full and Continental Breakfast
Credit Cards: A, B
Notes: 5, 12, 13, 14

FERGUS

The Breadalbane Inn

487 St. Andrew Street West, N1M 1P2
(519) 843-4770

This historic inn was built in 1860 by the founder of the town of Fergus. It boasts six tastefully decorated and comfortable bedrooms, each with ensuite washroom. The inn also features four dining rooms, two main and two private, seating 75. It has been recommended by the Epicure of *Toronto Life* magazine every year since 1984. Lunch is available Tuesday through Friday. Dinner is available Tuesday through Sunday. Cross-country skiing in area.

Hosts: Jean and Phil Cardinal
Rooms: 6 (PB) $60-85
Credit Cards: A, B
Notes: 2, 3, 4, 5, 7 (limited), 8, 9, 10, 11, 12, 13

GANANOQUE

The Victoria Rose Inn

279 King Street West, K7G 2G7
(613) 382-3368

This stately mansion, with a commanding central tower, was built by the first mayor in 1872. Seven elegant guest rooms with private bath and air conditioning. The honeymoon suite has a marble fireplace and Jacuzzi. Breakfasts are served in the formal dining room. Guests are welcome to enjoy the parlor, veranda, and two acres of garden. The ballroom is an ideal location for a family reunion, special party, or business meeting. The Rose Garden Tea Room is open in the summer for lunch and afternoon tea. Close to an excellent selection of restaurants, the summer playhouse, boat tours, and interesting shopping. Cross-country skiing in area.

Hosts: Liz and Ric Austin
Rooms: 7 (PB) $75-125
Full Breakfast
Credit Cards: A, B
Notes: 3, 5, 10, 11, 12, 13

GLEBE

Ottawa Bed and Breakfast

488 Cooper Street, Ottawa, K1R 5H9
(613) 563-0161

NOTES: Credit cards accepted: A MasterCard; B Visa; C American Express; D Discover Card; E Diner's Club; F Other; 2 Personal checks accepted; 3 Lunch available; 4 Dinner available; 5 Open all year;

1. Cottagelike home. Double bedroom with TV and desk. Shared bath. Resident cat and dog. No smoking. Hosts speaks French. $55-73.

GODERICH

Käthi's Guesthouse

Rural Route 4, N7A 3Y1
(519) 524-8587

This farm is set amid the rolling hills, near Lake Huron and 12 kilometers east of Goderich. Enjoy the privacy of the Guesthouse, with its two bedrooms and ensuite baths. A nice place for two couples traveling together or for young families with children. A crib is available. The hosts provide full country-style breakfast. Friendly pets. English and German are spoken here. Open year-round. Reservations preferred. Deposit required. Special rates for longer stays.

Hosts: Fritz and Käthi Beyerlein
Rooms: 2 (PB) $50
Full Breakfast
Credit Cards: None
Notes: 2, 5, 7, 8, 11

GORE'S LANDING

The Victoria Inn

Harewood Road, K0K 2E0
(905) 342-3261

This lakefront Victorian home on two acres of lawn overlooks three islands with a stupendous view and sunsets. The inn is open year-round, offering medium-priced accommodations and country home-cooking, specializing in local meat, fish, and vegetables. Nine bedrooms have been renovated, preserving the original windows and Art Nouveau and Arts and Crafts period woodwork. Facilities are available for group luncheons, business meetings, workshops, and receptions to 50 people. Close to fishing, skiing, antiques, concerts, golf, and curling.

Hosts: Donald and Donna Cane
Rooms: 9 (PB) $95-115
Full Breakfast
Credit Cards: A, B
Notes: 3, 4, 5, 9, 10, 11, 12, 13, 14

GRAFTON

Frome Farm

Rural Route 1, K0K 2G0
(905) 349-2815

This 120-year-old country house, set on an active 150-acre farm, has been comfortably modernized for guests' comfort and enjoyment. The house is in the rolling Northumberland Hills, near Lake Ontario and the historic towns of Cobourg and Port Hope. Full breakfast served daily; dinner on request. Home cooking, baking, jams, and preserves. Smoke-free environment. No children or pets, please.

Hosts: Phillippa W. Wilmer
Rooms: 2 (PB) $85
Full Breakfast
Credit Cards: None
Notes: 2, 3, 4, 5, 9, 10, 11, 12

GRAVENHURST

Cunningham's Bed and Breakfast

175 Clairmont Road, P1P 1H9
(705) 687-4511

Enjoy gracious living in an English garden setting, in this modern home on a quiet cul-de-sac at the edge of town. Friendly family room with fireplace and TV. Enjoy home baking and preserves, afternoon tea or evening snack in the sunny Muskoka Room. It is a short walk to Segwun Steamboat Tours, Bethune House, theatre, restaurants, shops, and parks. Off Bay Street, five blocks west of the post office.

Hosts: Leona (Lee) and David Cunningham
Rooms: 3 (1 PB; 2 SB) $50-60
Full Breakfast
Credit Cards: None
Notes: 2, 5, 8, 9, 10, 11, 12, 13

6 Pets welcome; 8 Children welcome; 9 Social drinking allowed; 10 Tennis available; 11 Swimming available; 12 Golf available; 13 Skiing available; 14 May be booked through travel agents.

GREELY

Patterson Place

6327 Emerald Links Drive, K4P 1M4
(613) 822-0280

Patterson Place is a Tudor-style home, overlooking the tenth fairway of a beautiful 18-hole golf course, and only 20 minutes outside of Ottawa. Guests can enjoy both the attractions of the nation's capitol and the serenity of the home's location in the country. Seasonal activities include skating on the canal or skiing in the Gatemans in the winter, or a round of golf, a leisurely stroll, or a bike ride in the summer.

Host: Jill M. Patterson
Rooms: 4 (1 PB; 3 SB) $45-69
Full Breakfast
Credit Cards: None
Notes: 2, 5, 8, 9, 12, 13

HEIDELBERG

Evergreen Lawns

64 Hilltop Court, Box 155, N0B 1Y0
(519) 699-4453

Welcome to Evergreen Lawns Bed and Breakfast in the quiet village of Heidelberg. In the hub of Mennonite country, just minutes away from the renowned farmers' markets and tourist attractions of St. Jacobs and Elmira. Close to the first outlet mall in Ontario, which opened in July 1994. Come experience another way of life in a unique country setting! Hosts are retired farmers living in this new split-level house on a large lot built mostly by themselves. They enjoy traveling and meeting people.

Hosts: Henry and Edna Shantz
Rooms: 2 (SB) $40-50
Full Breakfast
Credit Cards: None
Notes: 5

ILDERTON

Town & Country Bed and Breakfast in British Columbia

P.O. Box 74542, 2803 W. Fourth Avenue V6K 1K2
(604) 731-5942

18. Corsaut. Quiet, tree-shaded farm home just six miles north of the city offers two attractive rooms; one with a double bed and one with a single. Guests may enjoy the ponies and view antique John Deere tractors. Nonsmokers preferred. Air-conditioned. $35.

KINGSTON

Hotel Belvedere

141 King Street East, K7L 2Z9
(800) 559-0584

A collection of twenty unique rooms, each freshly decorated in period style, all with private bathrooms. Very central location. Continental breakfast brought to the guest room or served on the lovely terrace. Walking distance to the university, downtown retail shops, Lake Ontario, and the Thousand Island Boat Tours.

Rooms: 20 (PB) $79-149
Continental Breakfast
Credit Cards: A, B, C, E, F (En Route)
Notes: 2, 5, 7, 8, 9, 11

The Prince George Hotel

200 Ontario Street, K7K 3E9
(613) 547-4451; FAX (613) 547-9128

Built in 1809, the inn overlooks Lake Ontario and the park. Downtown, close to shopping, museums, cruise lines, farmers' market, and city hall. Decorated in Victorian style, either pine or mahogany. Old World pub, espresso and cappucino bar. Mediterranean bistro with open kitchen. Continental breakfast offered in spring and summer. Busiest outdoor patio in downtown Kingston!

Hosts: Phil Reid and Susan James
Rooms: 24 (24 PB) $50-115
Continental Breakfast
Credit Cards: A, B, C, E

KIRKFIELD

Metropolitan Bed and Breakfast Registry of Toronto

Suite 269, 615 Mount Pleasant Road
Toronto, Ontario M4S 3C5
(416) 964-2566; FAX (416) 537-0233

Sir William MacKenzie Inn. This grand 35-room mansion was built in 1888. On 13 acres of beautiful woods and lawns, it offers visitors the opportunity of going back to an era when leisure, grace, and beauty symbolized the good life. The inn features several comfortable lounge areas, a homey breakfast room, a large game room, video and book library, and a separate restaurant. Six large guest bedrooms all have ensuite bathrooms. Enjoy the fresh country air on the spacious veranda. Family-style dinners are available on request. A hot English-style gourmet breakfast is served each morning. $75-90.

KITCHENER

Austrian Home

90 Franklin Street North, N2A 1X9
(519) 893-4056

Enjoy this bed and breakfast in an Austrian-style home, 7.5 kilometers from the 401. Kitchener Transit is close by. The Austrian Home offers neat and friendly bedrooms with guest bathroom and European-style breakfast. Enjoy the garden and picnic area, as well as the many historic and cultural attractions in the area. Hosts speak English and German. No smoking.

Hosts: Frank and Maria Holl
Rooms: 2 (SB) $45
Full Breakfast
Credit Cards: None
Notes: 2, 5, 8, 9, 10, 11, 12, 13

Roots and Wings

11 Sunbridge Crescent, N2K 1T4
(519) 743-4557; FAX (519) 743-4166

Quiet street offers country living in the city with Jacuzzi, pool, and walking trails. Choose twin, queen-size, or double beds. Full breakfast is included. From charming and unique shopping and sumptuous hearty meals, to delightful country sightseeing, spend time and ride on horse-drawn trolleys to the heart of Mennonite country. Quaint villages and historic sights abound. A 30-minute drive to Stratford and Shakespearean plays, or a 90-minute drive to Niagara Falls. The hosts will help with guests' plans so as to not miss exciting new experiences.

Hosts: Ken Aram and Fay Teal-Aram
Rooms: 3 (1 PB; 2 SB) $50
Full Breakfast
Credit Cards: A
Notes: 5, 6, 7, 8, 9, 11

Why Not Bed and Breakfast

34 Amherst Drive, N2P 1C9
(519) 748-4577

Relax in this friendly hospitable home in a quiet area, only two minutes from Highway 401 and 20 minutes from downtown. Two comfortable guest bedrooms with five-piece guest bathroom. Delicious breakfast menu. Complimentary evening beverages available. Within a five-minute walk of beautiful forest trails, Grand River, art gallery, golf course, tennis, and indoor skating; restaurants and tourist attractions also close by. No smoking, please.

Hosts: Paula and David Farmer
Rooms: 2 (SB) $45-50
Full and Continental Breakfast
Notes: 2 (for deposit), 5, 8 (call), 9, 10, 10, 11, 12, 13

6 Pets welcome; 8 Children welcome; 9 Social drinking allowed; 10 Tennis available; 11 Swimming available; 12 Golf available; 13 Skiing available; 14 May be booked through travel agents.

LANARK

Red Eagle Guest House

Rural Route 3, K0G 1K0
(613) 259-3058

Relax and enjoy a full breakfast at this inn. For the budget-minded, guests have access to the fully equipped kitchen. Mingle in the four-bedroom guest house and hike the inn's 187 acres. For a real retreat, try the log cabin in the bush; no hydro guarantees a back-to-nature vacation. Family/group and weekly rates. Host speaks Polish, English, and French. Pets welcome.

Hosts: Donna A. and Jacques Rubacha
Rooms: 4 (SB) $45-55
Full Breakfast
Credit Cards: None
Notes: 2, 3, 4, 5, 6, 7, 8, 9, 10, 11, 12, 13

LANCASTER

MacPine Farms

Box 51, K0C 1N0
(613) 347-2003

Welcome to MacPine Holstein Farm on the shores of the St. Lawrence River, just south of the 401, a half-mile east of the Lancaster exit, and ten miles from the Quebec border. Enjoy this modernized century home, with comfortable new beds. Shaded by large old pine trees. A five-minute walk to the cottage on the river, where guests can swim, paddleboat, fish for Lancaster Perch, or relax and watch the boats go by. Area attractions include golf, fishing, boating, and craft and antique shops. Visit Upper Canada Village or the Highland Games. Go sightseeing or shopping in Montreal, Cornwall, or Ottawa. Enjoy breakfast in the new sunroom. Smoke-free home.

Hosts: Guelda and Robert MacRae
Rooms: 3 (SB) $40
Full Breakfast
Credit Cards: None
Notes: 2, 5, 8, 9, 11, 12, 13

LION'S HEAD

Steinwald Bed and Breakfast

Rural Route 4, N0H 1W0
(519) 795-7894

Experience a stay at one of the Bruce Peninsula's original log homes surrounded by a nature-lover's paradise. Amiable hosts are eager to share the pleasures of their charming home and property. Full breakfast is served in the cozy "keeping room," around the pioneer fireplace. In fine weather, guests have the option of being served on the patio overlooking the garden, which slopes down to the Stokes River.

Hosts: Don and Vonnie Robinson
Rooms: 3 (SB) $50-55
Full Breakfast
Credit Cards: None
Notes: 2, 3, 5, 7 (limited), 9, 10, 11, 12

LONDON

Clermont Place

679 Clermont Avenue, N5X 1N3
(519) 672-0767; FAX (519) 672-2449

A modern home in a parklike setting with its own heated outdoor pool. Central air conditioning, three attractive bedrooms sharing a four-piece bath. A full Canadian breakfast is served in the dining room or by the pool or gardens. Four free tennis courts behind the house; two public golf courses five minutes away. Forty minutes from the Stratford Shakespeare Festival. Close to the University of Western Ontario and University Hospital in North East London. Cross-country skiing in area.

Hosts: Doug and Jacki McAndless
Rooms: 3 (SB) $45-50
Full Breakfast
Credit Cards: B
Notes: 2, 3, 4, 5, 9, 10, 11, 12, 13

NOTES: Credit cards accepted: A MasterCard; B Visa; C American Express; D Discover Card; E Diner's Club; F Other; 2 Personal checks accepted; 3 Lunch available; 4 Dinner available; 5 Open all year;

Hilltop

82 Compton Crescent, N6C 4G1
(519) 681-7841

Modern air-conditioned home on a quiet crescent in south London, with easy access to Highway 401 and downtown London. Offers twin and double rooms, each with private bath. Dining room overlooks city and outdoor pool, which is available to guests. Nonsmoking adults. No pets.

Hosts: Beverley and Douglas Thomson
Rooms: 2 (PB) $55
Full Breakfast
Credit Cards: None
Notes: 5

Overdale Bed and Breakfast

2 Normandy Gardens, N6H 4A9
(519) 641-0236

Overdale is a contemporary home in northwest London. It is air-conditioned, comfortable, and quiet on a large lot with many flowers, trees, birds, and squirrels. Although almost in the country, it is just a 12-minute drive from downtown and 9 minutes from the University of Western Ontario. There is a guest sitting room with TV, etc. The hosts pride themselves on providing full gourmet breakfasts; special diets can also be accommodated.

Hosts: Bill and Jessica Mann
Rooms: 3 (1 PB; 2 SB) $46-55
Full Breakfast
Credit Cards: None
Notes: 5, 8, 9, 12

The Rose House

526 Dufferin Avenue, N6B 2A2
(519) 433-9978

The Rose House is a centrally air-conditioned, 125-year-old home on a fine residential street adjacent to downtown. This area has many historically designated homes. Within 15 minutes of the University of Western Ontario, all hospitals, major malls, and recreational facilities. It is a comfortable walk to live theatre, museums, art galleries, and fine restaurants. Breakfast is a full nutritional meal served family-style. No smoking. No small children. No federal or provincial taxes. Free parking. Reservations recommended.

Hosts: Betty and Douglas Rose
Rooms: 3 (1 PB; 2 SB) $40-55
Full Breakfast
Credit Cards: None
Notes: 5, 9, 10, 11, 12, 13

Serena's Place

720 Headley Drive, N6H 3V6
(519) 471-6228

Air-conditioned home in prestigious residential area of West London. Three bedrooms and full bath. Sunroom for relaxation. Near Springbank Park and Thames Valley Golf Course. Skiing nearby. Fifteen minutes from Theatre London. Bus service at the door. Open year-round.

Host: Serena Warren
Rooms: 3 (SB) $25-45
Credit Cards: None
Notes: 5, 12

Town & Country Bed and Breakfast

P.O. Box 74542, 2803 West 4th Avenue V6K 1K2
(604) 731-5942

1. Dorita Anderson's Place. Comfortable air-conditioned home in quiet and mature residential Orchard Park. Very convenient location: 15-minute scenic walk through Brescia College and 5-minute drive to UWO and University Hospital. Tennis courts, bus at the door. Rooms available include one with three-piece ensuite. English and Spanish spoken. Nonsmoking guests preferred. $42-47.

2. Chamberlain, Chiron House. Recall the comfort and elegance of an earlier time in this turn-of-the-century home, lovingly maintained and furnished in period an-

6 Pets welcome; 8 Children welcome; 9 Social drinking allowed; 10 Tennis available; 11 Swimming available; 12 Golf available; 13 Skiing available; 14 May be booked through travel agents.

Town & Country Bed and Breakfast
(continued)

tiques with modern amenities discreetly added. Within walking distance of theatre, restaurants, and shopping. Convenient to UWO and airport. Suite with whirlpool available. Free parking. $55.

3. Dillon's Place. This peaceful 1917 home in Old South has comfortable people and a large friendly Labrador. The second floor, which is for guests, has three attractive rooms and full bath. Central air for summer comfort, fireplace for cozy winter evenings. Nonsmoking adult guests are welcome. Nutritious breakfasts served. $40.

4. Cozy Corners. This 1871 Victorian style home is in the core area of London. It has been lovingly restored to maintain the warm glow of wood and stained glass. Guests have the use of two bedrooms, kitchenette, and bathroom. English and French spoken. Full breakfast served. $40.

5. Annigan's. Owned by an interior designer, this turn-of-the-century house, featuring a turret, fireplace, and fine architectural details, offers double and twin bedrooms; full bath, powder room, TV and smoking lounge. Downtown, Grand Theatre, UWO bus routes, antique stores close by. No pets please. Adults preferred. Reservations recommended, long-term rates available. Tenth anniversary! $50.

6. James. Completely redecorated home in beautiful Sherwood Forest. Five-minute drive from the university, 15 minutes from downtown. Cross-country skiing and nature walk at bottom of street. Central air, queen-size beds, shared bath. $42.

7. Halina Koch Bed and Breakfast. Share an artist's home featuring whitewashed walls, beamed ceilings, elegant living room with fireplace and TV, picturesque patio and garden, luxurious bathroom, air conditioning, welcoming refreshments, and other individual touches. The university, university hospital, and St. Joseph's Hospital are within walking distance. Downtown is five minutes by car or 10 minutes by bus. Languages: Spanish, Polish, plus some French and Italian. $35-45.

8. The Guest Suite. Charmingly furnished, private main-floor apartment in Old North London home. Suite includes sitting room with sofa bed, bedroom with three-piece ensuite, and kitchenette. Separate entrance from garden patio and spacious deck. Within walking distance to St. Joseph's and University Hospitals and the University of Western Ontario. Laundry, dry cleaning service at extra charge. Welcome nonsmokers, adults, no pets. Reservations recommended. Self-serve Continental breakfast. $50-65.

9. Overdale. Quiet, air-conditioned home in mature residential West London. Near parks and golf courses. Easily accessible to UWO and downtown by bus or car. King-size or twin beds. Rooms include one with three-piece ensuite. Special diets accommodated. Long-term rates available. $42-50.

10. Clermont Place. Air-conditioned home, in a parklike setting, recreational facilities near by. Close to highway 22 and 126 in Northeast London. Each room has a double bed, one with a waterbed. Gourmet meals, served by a cozy fireside, are available upon request. Nonsmoking adults preferred. $45.

11. JB's Place. Newer, air-conditioned home in North London, within walking distance of Mansonville Mall, restaurants, and city buses. Close to university, queen- or twin-size beds with shared bath, use of patio and BBQ. Airport pickup. Nonsmokers. No pets please. $50.

12. The Rose House. Comfortable central air-conditioned accommodations in an area of historic London. Enjoy a short stroll down tree-lined streets to shopping, Grand Theatre, and fine restaurants. Convenient to the University of Western Ontario, Fanshawe College, the airport, and the hospitals. Private four-piece bath or shared bath. Parking. Reservations recommended. No smoking. $30-50.

13. Hilltop. Modern air-conditioned home on quiet crescent in South London, with easy access to Highway 401, Victoria Hospital, and downtown, offers twin and double rooms, each with private bath. Dining room overlooks the city and outdoor pool which is available to guests. Nonsmoking adults. No pets. $55.

14. Vail. Modern, air-conditioned home one block north of St. Joseph's Hospital offers two bedrooms with double beds in a relaxing atmosphere. Television available. Ample parking, on bus routes, close to downtown or university hospital. $40.

15. Serena's Place. Air-conditioned home in prestigious residential area of West London. Three bedrooms and full bath. Sunroom for relaxation. Near Springbank Park and Thames Valley Golf Course. Ten minutes from Theatre London. Bus service at door. $25-45.

16. McLellan Place. Three houses West of Wellington on Baseline. Lovely air-conditioned home on bus route at the south edge of city, minutes from downtown, Storybook Gardens, miniature golf, waterslides. On bus route. Three large bedrooms,

two baths, TV available. Nonsmoking guests. No pets please. $45.

17. Regent Manor Bed and Breakfast. Traditional home in Old North, Regent Manor has queen-size luxury firm beds. Share a shower or soak in the ensuite tub. Great cooks serving full breakfast complete with cappuccino. Shop, take a bus, meditate at church or the synagogue, walk to UWO or the Merla Mae ice cream shop. Central air. Baby-sitting with notice. $40-60.

LUCKNOW

Perennial Pleasures Guesthome

Box 304, 558 Rose Street, N0G 2H0
(519) 528-3601

A friendly welcome awaits. Three bedrooms, each attractively decorated and equipped with a comfortable double bed (two with desks). Enjoy living room, dining room, deck and large colorful garden. One-story modern home. Enjoy walking, shopping, and antiquing in the nearby village. Lake Huron is 15 minutes away. Blythe Summer Theatre is 30 minutes. Many conservation areas offer cross-country skiing, snowmobiling, hiking, fishing, and boating.

Host: Joan Martin
Rooms: 3 (SB) $35
Full Breakfast
Credit Cards: None
Notes: 2, 3, 4, 5, 8, 9, 11, 12

MANSFIELD

Windborn Cottage

Rural Route 3, L0N 1M0
(705) 435-5324; FAX (705) 435-0943

Artist hosts in spacious home offering a blend of preconfederation antiquity and handcrafted comfort. The home is filled

6 Pets welcome; 8 Children welcome; 9 Social drinking allowed; 10 Tennis available; 11 Swimming available; 12 Golf available; 13 Skiing available; 14 May be booked through travel agents.

with works by the host and decorated with flair by the hostess. Bring a favorite beverage and share fireside, music, books, games, and lively conversation. Fall asleep to the sounds of the babbling trout stream.

Hosts: Allan and Lynn Ryan
Rooms: 2 (PB) $85-190 Canadian
Full Breakfast
Credit Cards: B
Notes: 2, 3 (call), 4 (call), 5, 8, 9, 11, 12, 13

MARKHAM

Metropolitan Bed and Breakfast Registry of Toronto

Suite 269, 615 Mount Pleasant Road
Toronto, Ontario M4S 3C5
(416) 964-2566; FAX (416) 537-0233

Valleyview. A 1950s style home down an apple tree lane in this town just north of Toronto. The house is furnished in a Traditional style and the hostess' needlepoint chairs accent the living room. Relax under the old willow tree by the babbling brook. The separate guest level has its own entrance, is roomy and inviting, and has a private bath. There is a guest refrigerator and tea-making facilities. Enjoy breakfast in the Canadiana dinning room or, weather permitting, on the private deck. $55.

MILFORD

Jackson's Falls Schoolhouse (1870) Bed and Breakfast Inn

Rural Route 2, County Road 17, K0K 2P0
(613) 476-8576

This 1870 schoolhouse operated as a school until 1960. Now it serves as breakfast, dinner room, and lounge for guests. The schoolroom is adjoined by four large guest rooms, all with private facilities. The inn is built in the style of an old Ontario establish-

ment. Room are furnished with antiques. Close to beaches and sand dunes, natural beauty, surrounded by Lake Ontario.

Hosts: Pete and Nancy Fleck
Rooms: 6 (4 PB; 2 SB) $55-75
Full Breakfast
Credit Cards: None
Notes: 2, 4, 5, 7 (limited), 9, 10, 11, 12

MINDEN

The Stone House

Rural Route 2, K0M 2K0
(705) 286-1250

Rustic elegance in secluded, mature woods. Four styles of accommodation, each offering full privacy. The Stone House has two bedrooms with king-size and twin beds, kitchen, and full bath. Large fieldstone fireplace in living room. The Roof Garden is an airy chalet-style studio with two sun decks, double and single beds, full bath, and kitchen. The Gingerbread Cottage has a twin/double bed, full bath, and a screened porch. The Sugar Cabin has single and queen-size beds, bath, and screened porch. Laundry facilities available, and coffee and tea are always on tap. Swimming, boating, and white-water rafting in lake or river within one mile. Just two hours from Toronto. Open from July 1 through August 31.

Host: Phyllis Howarth
Rooms: 2 (SB) $40-75
Cabin, Apartment, Trailer
Continental Breakfast
Credit Cards: None
Notes: 8, 9, 11, 12

MORRISBURG

Upper Canada Bed and Breakfast

P.O. Box 436, K0C 1X0
(613) 543-3336

This home overlooks the St. Lawrence Seaway in the peaceful outskirts of Morrisburg. Although in the country, it is less than 15

NOTES: Credit cards accepted: A MasterCard; B Visa; C American Express; D Discover Card; E Diner's Club; F Other; 2 Personal checks accepted; 3 Lunch available; 4 Dinner available; 5 Open all year;

minutes to Upper Canada Village, golf courses, the Playhouse, Queen's Gardens, nature trails, and the Seaway locks. Always lots to see and do nearby. It is only one hour to Ottawa and 90 minutes to Montréal. Down-home hospitality and good food are this bed and breakfast's trademarks.

Hosts: Nancy and George Davies
Rooms: 4 (SB) $50
Full Breakfast
Credit Cards: None
Notes: 7 (limited), 8, 9, 11, 12

NEW HAMBURG

Glenalby Dairy Farms

Rural Route 1, N0B 2G0
(519) 625-8353

Down-on-the-farm hospitality. Scenic, award-winning sixth generation farm. Lassie collies, English-style flower gardens, woodland and bluebird trails. Reserve afternoon tea, country suppers of cabbage rolls, oven-fresh bread, and wild berry pie. Early Canadian brass or pine beds topped with handmade quilts. Jams, jellies, and quilts for sale. Ten minutes to Stratford Theater, Amish-Mennonite area and their farmers' market, or Shakespeare's antique shops. Children welcome. Central air.

Host: Mrs. Ruby McMillan
Rooms: 4 (1 PB; 3 SB) $50-70
Full and Continental Breakfast
Credit Cards: None
Notes: 3, 4, 8, 10 ,11, 12, 13

The Pines

124 Shade Street, N0B 2G0
(519) 662-3525

Minutes from the Stratford Shakespeare Festival and a pleasant drive to Toronto, guests are welcomed to this century home in New Hamburg. Nestled beside a river, beneath towering pines, guest rooms are furnished with antiques. A double Jacuzzi is also available.

Hosts: Malcolm and Winsome Aird
Rooms: 3 (SB) $55-65
Full Breakfast
Credit Cards: None
Notes: 2, 5, 8, 9, 10, 12, 13

The Waterlot

17 Huron Street, N0B 2G0
(519) 662-2020

The Waterlot opened in the fall of 1974 and from the onset it has been committed to quality of ambience and service. Two large and comfortably appointed rooms share a memorable marbled shower, bidet, water closet, wet vanity, and sitting area. The inn is one of Ontario's finest dining establishments. This bed and breakfast offers quality and service in a memorable lodging.

Rooms: 3 (1 PB; 2 SB) $65-85
Continental Breakfast
Credit Cards: A, B, C
Notes: 2, 3, 4, 5, 9, 10, 11, 12, 13

The Waterlot

NIAGARA FALLS

Gretna Green

5077 River Road, L2E 3G7
(905) 357-2081

This tourist home offers bright, comfortable rooms with ensuite bathrooms; all guest rooms are air-conditioned and have TV. Families are welcome. This is like "a home away from home" where guests are treated to

6 Pets welcome; 8 Children welcome; 9 Social drinking allowed; 10 Tennis available; 11 Swimming available; 12 Golf available; 13 Skiing available; 14 May be booked through travel agents.

a full, home-cooked breakfast that includes homemade muffins, scones, jams, and jellies. Niagara has much to offer tourists—the falls, Skylow Tower, IMAX Theatre, the Floral Clock, the Rose Gardens, and museums. Bike rentals available.

Hosts: Stan and Marg Gardiner
Rooms: 4 (PB) $45-65
Full Breakfast
Credit Cards: None
Notes: 5, 7 (limited), 8, 9, 12

Gretna Green

The International Bed & Breakfast Club, Inc.

504 Amherst Street, Buffalo, NY 14207
(800) 723-4262; FAX (716) 873-4462

ON2803PP. Canadian Villa overlooking the Niagara River in Niagara Falls, Ontario and walking distance to the falls. Rooms include air conditioning, cable, and color TV. Three guest rooms include a double and two queen-size bedded rooms with ensuite private shower and baths. Guests enjoy the setting and the view overlooking the Niagara River. Ample parking. Continental breakfast. $55-65.

ON4744PP. This inn is on the Niagara's most scenic drive overlooking the river and only four blocks from the American and Canadian falls and Queen Victoria Park. The inn is distinguished by Strauss crystal

chandeliers, and guests will find Old World charm and hospitality. Five rooms with bath ensuite are available. The George Bernard Shaw Theatre is only 20 minutes away on the scenic Niagara Parkway. Gourmet breakfast and afternoon tea are available. Guests have ample free parking on the premises. $85-129.

NIAGARA-ON-THE-LAKE

Hiebert's Guest House

P.O. Box 1371, 275 John Street West, L0S 1J0
(905) 468-3687

Enjoy a peaceful setting in a quaint, historic town 20 minutes north of Niagara Falls, Ontario. Attend the Shaw Festival Theatre, browse through the many shops, or relax at the waterfront. Guest rooms offer queen-size and twin beds. Warm hospitality in air-conditioned comfort. Brochure available.

Hosts: Otto and Marlene Hiebert
Rooms: 3 (PB) $55-85
Full Breakfast
Credit Cards: None
Notes: 2, 5, 8, 10, 11, 12

The International Bed & Breakfast Club, Inc.

504 Amherst Street, Buffalo, NY 14207
(800) 723-4262; FAX (716) 873-4462

ON6865PP. This inn is on an acre of private lawns and mature trees on the outskirts of Niagara-on-the-Lake. Three rooms have either private or shared baths. Guests may use a whirlpool and sauna or swim in the indoor pool that is heated during the summer months. Enjoy browsing downtown for a wealth of fine quality clothes, antiques, and crafts. Plays written during the time of George Bernard Shaw are performed on three stages from spring through fall. Guests will enjoy driving or cycling along the picturesque parkway along the Niagara River. Full breakfast available. $95.

The Kiely Inn

209 Queen Street, L0S 1J0
(416) 468-4588

Elegant Georgian residence on one acre of
landscaped garden overlooking golf course
and Lake Ontario. Many verandas and
porches. Eleven guest rooms with ensuite
bathrooms and telephones. Six rooms with
fireplaces. Guest parlor. Inn furnished with
antiques and decorated in period style.
Sixty-seat, full-service dining room. Continental plus breakfast included in room rate.
Ample on-site parking.

Hosts: Ray and Heather Pettit
Rooms: 11 (PB) $75-168
Continental Breakfast
Credit Cards: A, B, C
Notes: 2, 3, 4, 5, 7, 9, 10, 11, 12, 14

Wren House

278 Regent Street, Box 311, L0S 1J0
(905) 468-4361

Historic home, circa 1838, in the heart of
historic Niagara-on-the-Lake. Quaint shops,
festival theaters, dining, and historic sites
within walking distance. Breakfast is an assortment of special dishes and baked goods.
Wineries, fruit orchards, Niagara Falls, and
many other attractions are nearby. Central
air-conditioning. No smoking.

Hosts: Barbara and Warren Aldridge
Rooms: 3 (PB) $80-90
Full Breakfast
Credit Cards: None
Notes: 2, 5, 9, 10, 12

OTTAWA

Albert House

478 Albert Street, K1R 5B5
(613) 236-4479; (800) 267-1982

Gracious Victorian home built in 1875 by a
noted Canadian architect. Each room is individually decorated and has private facilities,
telephone, TV, and air conditioning. Guest
lounge with fireplace. Famous Albert House

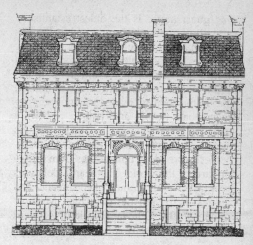

Albert House

breakfast. Parking is available, but within
walking distance to most attractions. There
are two large friendly dogs in the house.

Hosts: Cathy and John Delroy
Rooms: 17 (PB) $68-90
Full Breakfast
Credit Cards: A, B, C, E
Notes: 5, 7, 9, 14

Auberge McGee's Inn

185 Daly Avenue, K1N 6E8
(613) 237-6089; FAX (613) 237-6201

Fourteen-room historic Victorian Inn,
downtown on a quiet avenue. Within walking distance of excellent restaurants, museums, Parliament, Rideau Canal, and
University of Ottawa. Ten guest rooms with
private baths, four with shared baths. Cable
TV, telephone, Jacuzzi ensuites. Kitchenette facilities for longer stays. Complimentary full breakfast. No smoking.
Reservations recommended.

Hosts: Anne Schutte and Mary Unger
Rooms: 14 (10 PB; 4 SB) $58-150
Full Breakfast
Credit Cards: A, B
Notes: 5, 8 (call), 9 (limited), 10, 11, 12, 13

Australis Guest House

35 Marlborough Avenue, K1N 8E6
(613) 235-8461

6 Pets welcome; 8 Children welcome; 9 Social drinking allowed; 10 Tennis available; 11 Swimming available;
12 Golf available; 13 Skiing available; 14 May be booked through travel agents.

This guest house is the oldest established and still operating bed and breakfast in Ottawa. On a quiet, tree-lined street one block from the Rideau River, with its ducks and swans, and Strathcona Park, it is a 20-minute walk to the Parliament buildings. The home boasts leaded windows, fireplaces, oak floors, and unique eight-foot stained-glass windows. The spacious rooms, including one with private bathroom, feature many collectibles from different parts of the world. The hearty, delicious breakfasts, with home-baked breads and pastries, help start the day right. Multiple winner of the Ottawa Hospitality Award and recommended by *Newsweek*.

Hosts: Brian and Carol Waters
Rooms: 3 (1 PB; 2 SB) $45-65
Full Breakfast
Credit Cards: None
Notes: 5, 7, 10, 11, 12, 13

Australis Guest House

Beatrice Lyon Guest House

479 Slater Street, K1R 5C2
(613) 236-3904

This is an old-fashioned family home surrounded by large trees. The place is within walking distance of the Parliament buildings, the Museum of Man, the National Archives, Byward Market, Rideau Canal, and Hull, Quebec. Children are welcome,

and baby-sitting can be arranged. The host is a member of the Downtown Bed and Breakfast Association.

Host: Beatrice Lyon
Rooms: 3 (SB) $45
Full Breakfast
Credit Cards: None
Notes: 2, 5, 7, 8, 9, 10, 11, 12, 13

Blue Spruces

187 Glebe Avenue, K1S 2C6
(613) 236-8521

Edwardian home, furnished with fine Victorian English and Canadian pine antiques, in Ottawa's downtown core. Minutes from Parliament. Delicious full breakfast, including fresh ground coffee, is served in the elegant dining room.

Hosts: Patricia and John Hunter
Rooms: 3 (PB) $65-70
Full Breakfast
Credit Cards: A, B
Notes: 5, 9, 13

By-The-Way

310 First Avenue, K1S 2G8
(613) 232-6840

Modern, comfortable, and elegant, By-The-Way Bed and Breakfast offers all the conveniences and is close to downtown Ottawa and many interesting attractions. A few minutes' walking distance from interesting boutiques, shops, and restaurants. The host is happy to guide first-time visitors to Ottawa. Central air-conditioned, smoke and pollen-free.

Hosts: Krystyna, Rafal, and Adam
Rooms: 3 (1 PB; 2 SB) $50-70
Full Breakfast
Credit Cards: A
Notes: 5, 10, 11, 12, 13, 14

Gasthaus Switzerland Inn

89 Daly Avenue, K1N 6E6
(613) 237-0335; (800) 267-8788;FAX (613) 594-3327

Gasthaus Switzerland is a charming, affordable three-star inn in downtown Ottawa. All

NOTES: Credit cards accepted: A MasterCard; B Visa; C American Express; D Discover Card; E Diner's Club; F Other; 2 Personal checks accepted; 3 Lunch available; 4 Dinner available; 5 Open all year;

rooms feature comfortable, cozy Swiss-style beds covered with handmade duvets, air-conditioned, smoke-free, direct-dial telephone, modem, and full cable TV. Traditional Swiss hospitality in the heart of Canada's capital! Recommended by CAA, AAA, Canada Select, and Tourism of Ontario.

Hosts: Josef and Sabina Sauter
Rooms: 25 (21 PB; 4 SB) $64-88
Full Breakfast
Credit Cards: A, B, C, E, F
Notes: 5, 9, 10, 11, 12, 13, 14

Haydon House

18 The Driveway, K2P 1C6
(613) 230-2697

Haydon House is a completely renovated and modernized Victorian-era mansion that offers rest and comfort. It is air-conditioned, has a private outdoor portico sitting area, spacious bedrooms, and modern facilities embellished with traditional Canadian pine decor. Ensuite, large room with double bed and two single beds, private bath. Haydon House is nestled in a tranquil residential area beside the historic and picturesque Rideau Canal and scenic parkway. All important points of interest, such as the Parliament buildings, museums, and National Art Gallery, are within a short and easy walk.

Host: Mary Haydon
Rooms: 3 (1 PB; 2 SB) $65-85
Continental Breakfast
Credit Cards: None
Notes: 2, 5, 7, 8, 9, 10, 11, 12, 13

Ottawa Bed and Breakfast

488 Cooper Street, K1R 5H9
(613) 563-0161

1. Large, elegant Heritage Home within walking distance of Parliament Hills and museums. Choose from three guest rooms, one with queen-size brass bed, private en-suite bath, sitting area, stained-glass window, and balcony. The other two rooms, each with a double bed, share a five-piece

bath. This century-old home is full of interesting furniture, the dining room chairs are antique church chairs. Resident cat. This home has been featured many times on television and articles in magazines and newspapers. $55-73.

2. Edwardian manor-type home on a fine residential street in Ottawa's West End. Choose from three guest rooms, one with king-size bed, one with twin beds, and one with single bed, share a bath. Enjoy the patio gardens, close to downtown Ottawa. No smoking. Hosts speak French. $55-73.

3. Contemporary brick home in the suburbs of Ottawa. Choose from three guest rooms—large room (a triple) with double and single beds, a twin bedroom, and a single bedroom, with shared baths. Hostess has an interesting collection of artwork. Walk to a large outdoor swimming pool. Families welcome. $55-73.

4. A 150-acre grain farm with a beautiful home built in 1867. Kitchen and dining room a joy to look at. Two rooms—one has a very large bedroom with a double and single bed. Full bath on the same floor. Lovely garden plus in-ground swimming pool. $55-73.

OWEN SOUND

Moses' Sunset Farms Bend and Breakfast

Rural Route 6, Twp Box S578
20th Avenue East, N4K 5N8
(519) 371-4559

Well-traveled hosts own and operate Owen Sound's longest established bed and breakfast. Forty picturesque acres just five minutes from city's center. Ideal for day trips to Manitoulin Island, around Georgian Bay and Bruce Trail. Gorgeous during autumn.

6 Pets welcome; 8 Children welcome; 9 Social drinking allowed; 10 Tennis available; 11 Swimming available; 12 Golf available; 13 Skiing available; 14 May be booked through travel agents.

Beautiful antique furnishings. Gardens, patio, and pond for outdoor enjoyment. Host hobby is beekeeping. Hostess is gourmet cooking teacher. Special classes offered for groups. Inquire regarding children. No smoking.

Hosts: Bill and Cecilie Moses
Rooms: 4 (1 PB; 3 SB) $45-75
Full Breakfast
Credit Cards: None
Notes: 5, 9, 10, 11, 12, 13, 14

Owen Sound Country Homes Bed and Breakfast Association

Rural Route 6, N4K 5N8
(519) 371-4559; (519) 538-2803

Quality, clean, nonsmoking, charming homes within 15 miles of Owen Sound. The homes are all in the country but are not generally farms. A participating member places guests according to their tastes and home availability. Homes feature great breakfasts, interesting hosts, and travel information for local day tripping. Five separate homes and hosts form this association. $45-79.

PAKENHAM

Stonebridge Bed and Breakfast

Rural Route 4, K0A 2X0
(613) 624-5431

Gracing a high bluff of stately shade trees and sweeping lawns, Stonebridge overlooks the Village of Pakenham, the gently flowing Mississippi River, and North America's only five-span stone bridge. Large and gracious family home with comfortable bed-sitting rooms, a formal dining room, home-cooked meals, a fireside lounge, a solarium, large summer room, shaded veranda, and ample parking. Candlelight group dinners by reservation; a tea room from May to October; and services for seminars, recep-

tions, and weddings. Lunch is available from May to October. No smoking.

Hosts: Thora and Bob Pugh
Rooms: 3 (SB) $50
Full Breakfast
Credit Cards: B
Notes: 2, 3 (call), 5, 8 (over 12), 9, 11, 12, 13

PALGRAVE

Country Host

Rural Route 1, L0N 1P0
(519) 941-7633

Country Host reservation service was organized in 1980 and represents fine guest homes in some of Ontario's most picturesque areas. Tucked away in the countryside, with a few in the villages, these homes continue the European tradition of lodging in comfortable privacy at reasonable cost. Country Host homes have particular appeal to Bruce Trail hikers, naturalists, bird watchers, and nature lovers. Locations include Niagara Escarpment close to Bruce Trail, Mount St. Louis-Horseshoe Valley, Sundridge, Lake Nipissing, Point Pelee National Park, Bolton, Palgrave, Mono Mills, and Orangeville. Rates range from $35-40 for singles and $45-60 for doubles. A hearty breakfast is included, and family rates are available. Plan early.

PARRY SOUND

Belvedere Bed and Breakfast

18 Belvedere Avenue, P2A 2A1
(705) 746-8372

Grand three-story Edwardian-style home surrounded by century-old oak trees in older part of town with lovely bay view. Three guest rooms offer a view of the bay, one with private balcony, one with private bath. Breakfast served on screened porch. Within walking distance of major points of interest. No smoking.

NOTES: Credit cards accepted: A MasterCard; B Visa; C American Express; D Discover Card; E Diner's Club; F Other; 2 Personal checks accepted; 3 Lunch available; 4 Dinner available; 5 Open all year;

Hosts: David and Joanne Brunton
Rooms: 3 (1 PB; 2 SB)
Full Breakfast
Credit Cards: None
Notes: 5, 8, 10, 11, 12, 13

Blackwater Lake
Bed and Breakfast

Rural Route 1, Blackwater Lake Road, P2A 2W7
(705) 389-3746; FAX (705) 389-3746

Cozy Chalet-style home offers comfort and relaxation. Seven acres on the shore of Blackwater Lake just 35 minutes from Parry Sound. Enjoy fishing, swimming, boating, skiing, hiking, and hunting at the doorstep. Two guest rooms with balconies. No smoking.

Host: Trudy Wissel
Rooms: 3 (SB) $50-85
Credit Cards: None
Notes: 3, 4, 5, 9, 10, 11, 13

Cascade 40
Bed and Breakfast

40 Cascade Street, P2A 1J9
(705) 746-8917

Wooden doorknobs, wooden deck chairs and wooden shingles are only a few of the interesting things in this designated Heritage Home. Close to Festival of the Sound, Rainbow Theater, 30,000 Island Cruise, town beach, and hiking trails. Hosts offer accommodation on second floor as well as air-conditioned third-floor suite with private bath and kitchenette. No pets. Outside smoking only.

Hosts: Rick and Sally Coomber
Rooms: 4 (1 PB; 3 SB) $50
Full and Continental Breakfast
Credit Cards: None
Notes: 5, 8, 9, 10, 11, 12, 13

Evergreen

P.O. Box 223, P2A 2X3
(705) 389-3554

Elegant cedar log home. Spacious cedar decks overlooking lovely parklike grounds on the shore of Lake Manitouwabing. Comfortable guest lounge with TV and reading material. Take the spiral staircase down to the billiard room with professional-size table and game table. Enjoy a hearty breakfast served on the screened summer porch. Swim at the beach or fish from the dock. Canoe available for rent.

Hosts: Shirley and Andres Wallenius
Rooms: 4 (SB) $46
Full Breakfast
Credit Cards: None
Notes: 2, 7, 8, 9, 10, 11, 12

Jantje Manor

43 Church Street, P2A 1Y6
(705) 746-5399

Beautifully restored Victorian home in the heart of Parry Sound. Entering the front door it is like a step back in time. The front parlor entices guests to sit and visit. The library, with its fireplace, invites guests to curl up with a good book. The bedrooms are tastefully decorated and furnished with antiques. In the summer, the verandas and the screened porch offer a pleasant place to sit and relax. A full breakfast is served in the dining room. Cross-country skiing in area.

Hosts: Jean Weening
Rooms: 4 (1 PB, 3 SB) $45-75
Full Breakfast
Credit Cards: None
Notes: 5, 11, 13

Quilt Patch
Bed and Breakfast

Rural Route 2, P2A 2W8
(705) 378-5279

This new home is in a quiet country setting with a cozy family room and two adjoining guest bedrooms. The parklike setting is overlooking the woods. Within walking distance of the sand beach on Little Otter Lake. Good swimming. Home-cooked breakfast

6 Pets welcome; 8 Children welcome; 9 Social drinking allowed; 10 Tennis available; 11 Swimming available;
12 Golf available; 13 Skiing available; 14 May be booked through travel agents.

included. English and German spoken. No smoking or pets please.

Hosts: Mary and Lorne Steckley
Rooms: 2 (SB) $45-55
Full and Continental Breakfast
Credit Cards: None
Notes: 8, 11

PERTH

House on the Corner

53 Wilson Street West, K7H 2N3
(613) 264-0901

Tastefully decorated century Victorian brick home in the heart of historic Perth. Air-conditioned, Jacuzzi, two sitting rooms, TV room with fireplace, garden deck overlooking watergarden. Perth boasts many heritage buildings, the oldest golf club in Canada, museum, antique shops and parks. Many organized special events from the Maple Festival to Theatre Festivals and sports tournaments. Sumptuous full breakfast served. Other meals and special picnic baskets are available by prior arrangement. No smoking. Cross-country skiing in area.

Hosts: Fran and Sam Bonner
Rooms: 3 (SB) $45-60
Full Breakfast
Credit Cards: None
Notes: 2, 3 (call), 4 (call), 11, 12, 13

Perth Manor Heritage Inn

23 Drummound Street West, K7H 2S6
(613) 264-0050; FAX (613) 264-0051

Old mansion built in 1878. Tapestry in dining room. Eight guest rooms in the main house, two in carriage house, with private and shared baths. Solarium, bar, patio overlooking lily ponds and large perennial garden. Library, antique furniture, fireplaces, and chandeliers. Smoking in designated areas only.

Hosts: Gisela and Phil Aston
Rooms: 10 (1 PB; 9 SB) $70-135
Full Breakfast-Summer
Continental Breakfast-Winter
Credit Cards: A, B, C
Notes: 2, 3, 4, 5, 6, 7 (limited), 8 (call), 9, 10, 11, 12, 13, 14

PICKERING

Metropolitan Bed and Breakfast Registry of Toronto

Suite 269, 615 Mount Pleasant Road
Toronto M4S 3C5
(416) 964-2566; FAX (416) 537-0233

Rouge River Bed and Breakfast. A modern home in a country setting is offered at this bed and breakfast on the Pickering border. The hosts are friendly and attentive and will help with sightseeing suggestions for attractions in the area. The guest bedroom is bright and cheery and the bathroom can be private if guests wish. $55.

PORT DOVER

Bed and Breakfast by the Lake

30 Elm Park, N0A 1N0
(519) 583-1010

Port Dover is a pleasant small town on the north shore of Lake Erie, a good base for exploring Long Point Bird Observatory, strolling around Port Dover Harbor's craft shops, and experiencing excellent summer theater at Lighthouse Theater. Home is bright, open, and airy ranch, graciously furnished with antiques and art. Attractive brick patio and garden provide lovely view of Lake Erie and easy access to sandy beach.

Hosts: Christine and Peter Ivey
Rooms: 2 (SB) $55
Full Breakfast
Credit Cards: None
Notes: 2, 5, 7, 9, 11, 12

PORT STANLEY

Great Lakes Farms Guest House

Rural Route 1, Union, N0L 2L0
(519) 633-2390; (519) 631-2171
FAX (519) 633-4807

NOTES: Credit cards accepted: A MasterCard; B Visa; C American Express; D Discover Card; E Diner's Club; F Other; 2 Personal checks accepted; 3 Lunch available; 4 Dinner available; 5 Open all year;

This century-old home is amid apple trees on a 250-acre farm. Rent one room or rent the whole house for a night, a weekend, or longer. Enjoy TV, a pool table, whirlpool, Continental breakfast, and the warmth of this country retreat, just five minutes from Port Stanley.

Hosts: Bob and Marge Thomas
Rooms: 3 (SB) $45-55
Continental Breakfast
Credit Cards: None
Notes: 2, 5, 8, 9, 11, 12, 13, 14

POWASSAN

Satis House
Bed and Breakfast

Rural Route 2, P0H 1Z0
(705) 724-2187

Satis House is a large home featuring Georgian and Victorian architecture. It is approximately three and one-half hours south of Toronto between Trout Creek and Powassan. On a gorgeous property with 100 acres providing soothing, beautiful views in all seasons. Guests return for the comfort and excellent full breakfast served. Outside smoking only.

Host: Jo-Anne Hynd
Rooms: 3 (SB) $50
Full Breakfast
Credit Cards: B
Notes: 3, 4, 5, 6, 7 (limited), 9, 10, 11, 12, 13, 14

RIDEAU CANAL

Ottawa Bed and Breakfast

488 Cooper Street, Ottawa, K1R 5H9
(613) 563-0161

1. A beautiful 19th-century home on Queen Elizabeth Driveway in a prestigious neighborhood facing Rideau Canal. Two guest rooms on the third floor, one with double bed, the other with twin beds, share a bath and have views of the canal or Brown's Inlet. Walk to fine restaurants and book and antique shops. No smoking. $55-73.

2. Three-story older home overlooking Rideau Canal. Twin bedroom off the sunroom. Breakfast served in the beautiful miniature garden. Resident cat. No smoking. Hosts speak French. $55-73.

ROCKWOOD

Blue Heron
Bed and Breakfast

106 John Street, N0B 2K0
(519) 856-2275

In the cozy village of Rockwood, the Blue Heron has luxurious accommodations in a modern, air-conditioned home shared with a friendly St. Bernard named Friar Tuck. Sumptuous full breakfast is included. Sit and relax in the private Oriental garden. Nearby are quality golf courses, unique conservation area, antique and craft markets, and harness racing.

Hosts: Bob and Pauline Dahlke
Rooms: 2 (SB) $60
Full Breakfast
Credit Cards: None
Notes: 2, 5, 9, 11, 12, 13, 14

The International Bed & Breakfast Club, Inc.

504 Amherst Street, Buffalo, NY 14207
(800) 723-4262; FAX (716) 873-4462

ON2275PP. A modern comfortable home in the village of Rockwood with a unique Oriental garden for guests to relax in and enjoy. Two spacious, well-decorated rooms share a bath; the smaller bedroom has a romantic theme, the large bedroom accommodates a sitting room with a view overlooking the garden. Nearby attractions include the Rockwood Conservation area, unique and very picturesque; Blue Springs Golf Club, home of the Canadian PGA; Radial Railway Museum of Guelph Line; Niagara Escarpment hiking. Adults only. No smoking. Full breakfast. $55.

6 Pets welcome; 8 Children welcome; 9 Social drinking allowed; 10 Tennis available; 11 Swimming available; 12 Golf available; 13 Skiing available; 14 May be booked through travel agents.

Jakobstettel Guest House

ST. JACOBS

Jakobstettel Guest House, Inc.

16 Isabella Street, N0B 2N0
(519) 664-2208; fax (519) 664-1326

Turn-of-the-century completed renovated estate Victorian home has 12 individually decorated guest rooms with private baths. Library, lounge for all guests, and open kitchen all day and evening for coffee, tea, juice, and cookies. Outdoor pool, tennis court, horseshoe pits, bikes, and walking trail. Within a few blocks of more than 80 retail shops, this is a shopper's delight.

Host: Elle Burbacher
Rooms: 12 (PB) $105-150
Continental Breakfast
Credit Cards: A, B, C
Notes: 2, 5, 10, 11, 14

ST. MARY'S

Westover Inn

300 Thomas Street, N4X 1B1
(519) 284-2977

The Westover Inn, built in 1867, began as a limestone Victorian mansion and now offers 22 guest rooms set among 19 acres of landscaped grounds. There are three buildings now available to guests. The original Manor boasts five charming second-floor guest rooms and one luxurious suite complete with whirlpool. All rooms in the Manor are different shapes with original moldings and 11-foot ceilings. The Manor also houses the inn's dining room, lounge, meeting room, a comfortable common room and registration desk. The Terrace sits on a gentle rise overlooking the Manor and holds 12 guest rooms. Finally, the Thames Cottage is nestled in the trees and offers privacy and luxury in its two-bedroom suites with living room. All these suites overlook the Teahouse with its surrounding gardens. Outdoor swimming pool and licensed patio on the premises. Hiking and cross-country skiing trails, boating, two golf courses, and unique country shopping are within a few minutes' drive.

Host: Julie Docker
Rooms: 22 (PB) $95-200
Full Breakfast
Credit Cards: A, B, C, E
Notes: 3, 4, 5, 7, 8, 9, 10, 11, 12, 13, 14

SAULT STE. MARIE

Hillsview Bed and Breakfast

406 Old Garden River Road, P6B 5A8
(705) 759-8819; FAX (705) 945-1253

Enjoy country living in the city. Convenient to Agawa Canyon Train Tour Station, the International Bridge, and Highway 17. Near groomed cross-country and hiking trails, downhill skiing, shopping, and restaurants. Three guest rooms with shared bath, featuring queen-size and full-size beds. Clean, comfortable surroundings featuring a fireplace in winter and patio in summer. Continental breakfast is served from 6:30 to 7:15 A.M. and a full breakfast is served including homemade jams and preserves from 7:15 to 9:00 A.M.

Hosts: Joe and Helen Douville
Rooms: 3 (SB) $40
Full and Continental Breakfast
Credit Cards: None
Notes: 2, 5, 8, 10, 11, 12, 13

NOTES: Credit cards accepted: A MasterCard; B Visa; C American Express; D Discover Card; E Diner's Club; F Other; 2 Personal checks accepted; 3 Lunch available; 4 Dinner available; 5 Open all year;

STRATFORD

Burnside Guest Home

139 William Street, N5A 4X9
(519) 271-7076

Burnside is an ancestral, turn-of-the-century home featuring many family antiques and heirlooms. Recently redecorated in light, airy colors. Host is a horticultural instructor and an authority on local and Canadian genealogy. Stratford Theater, Avon Theater, and Tom Patterson Theater only minutes away. Interesting shops and restaurants are also a short walk away. The Avon Trail, part of a network of hiking and cross-country skiing trails that can connect London, Ontario, to the Niagara Escarpment, is nearby. Four guest rooms feature a variety of bed sizes and shared baths. Full, home-cooked breakfast served to guests.

Host: Lester (Les) J. Wilker
Rooms: 4 (SB) $55-65
Full Breakfast
Credit Cards: A
Notes: 2, 5, 8 (call), 9, 10, 11, 12, 13

The Stone Maiden Inn

123 Church Street, N5A 2R3
(519) 271-7129

Named after the stone maiden heads that grace the front hallway, The Stone Maiden offers quiet Victorian elegance with superior accommodations and the utmost in personal service. Handmade quilts, ensuite bathrooms, and handsome antiques grace the 14 air-conditioned guest rooms. Some rooms have canopied beds, fireplaces, and whirlpool tubs. Generous breakfast and afternoon refreshments. Visit Stratford during May to October for the world-renowned Shakespearean Festival. Close to city center and three theaters. Private parking.

Hosts: Barb and Len Woodward
Rooms: 14 (PB) $85-160
Full Breakfast
Credit Cards: A, B
Notes: 2, 7, 9, 10, 11, 12, 14

Woods Villa

62 John Street North, N5A 6K7
(519) 271-4576

Woods Villa combines Victorian elegance with modern comfort. Most of the five large bedrooms have fireplaces and all have TVs. There is a large heated pool with terrace, and ample off-street parking. Breakfast is served in the dining room. Woods Villa features a sizable collection of automatic musical instruments, player pianos, and juke boxes ready to play for guests. An easy 10-minute stroll from downtown Stratford.

Host: Ken Vinen
Rooms: 5 (SB) $80
Full Breakfast
Credit Cards: A, B
Notes: 5, 9, 10, 11, 12, 13

Burken Guest House

322 Palmerston Boulevard, M6G 2N6
(416) 920-7842; FAX (416) 960-9529

In a charming residential neighborhood adjacent to downtown. Eight tastefully appointed rooms with washbasins, private

Burken Guest House

telephones, and ceiling fans; shared baths. European-style atmosphere. Limited free parking on premises; public transportation nearby. Friendly, capable service.

Hosts: Burke and Ken
Rooms: 8 (SB) $60-65
Continental Breakfast
Credit Cards: A, B
Notes: 5, 8, 9, 14

THORNDALE

Town & Country Bed and Breakfast in British Columbia

P.O. Box 74542, 2803 West Fourth Avenue V6K 1K2
(604) 731-5942

19. Cove Bed and Breakfast. Enjoy a hearty country breakfast in this modern country home on a paved road five minutes northeast of London. It is a 25-minute drive to Stratford theatres, five minutes to Kilbyrne farm, London Archery, hiking, and cross-country skiing. There is a grass airstrip close by, and the gliding club is 15 minutes east. Enjoy a complimentary late evening snack. Fireplace, TV, swimming pool. No smoking. $45.

THUNDER BAY

Unicorn Inn

Rural Route 1, South Gillies, P0T 2V0
(807) 475-4200

Intimate, widely acclaimed serenity of country-elegant accommodations and superb dining. Restaurant rated among top 57 in Canada by *Where to Eat in Canada 1994*. Nestled in the heart of a hidden rock valley on 640 acres of spectacular fields, forests, and mountains. Bright cozy rooms with oak floors and handcrafted pine furniture; exquisite honeymoon cottage with bay windows and view.

Hosts: David and Arlan Nobel
Rooms: 4 (1 PB; 3 SB) $59-89
Full Breakfast
Credit Cards: A, B, E
Notes: 2, 4, 5, 8, 9, 11, 13, 14

TORONTO

Beaconsfield Bed and Breakfast

38 Beaconsfield Avenue, M6J 3H9
(416) 535-3338

Colorful, unpretentious 1882 Victorian home full of fun and sun, art and heart. In a quiet, downtown, multi-cultural neighborhood just west of the commercial core, it's a short trolley ride to major theaters and sites along Queen Street. Choose between imaginatively decorated rooms or the very private "San Miguel" Mexican honeymoon suite with tree-top terrace. All have top-of-the-line beds. Creative breakfasts musically served in eclectic dining room. Great location. Parking. Information galore.

Hosts: Bernie and Katya McLoughlin
Rooms: 4 (1 PB; 3 SB) $65-95
Full Breakfast
Credit Cards: None
Notes: 2, 5, 8, 9

Broadleaves

67 Orchard View Boulevard, M4R 1C1
(416) 486-5252

Uptown home surrounded by maple, linden, and ash trees. Convenient to the Yonge-Eglinton area. Fine restaurants, specialty shops, cinemas, dinner theaters, and parks nearby. Two guest rooms available, one featuring a double bed with original oak trim and working fireplace. Second room features a twin bed with French doors leading to the sunroom. Guest accommodations are separate from hosts' with exclusive use of treetop deck and separate kitchen for light snacks.

Hosts: Cavelle and Peter Davis
Rooms: 2 (SB) $60-65

NOTES: Credit cards accepted: A MasterCard; B Visa; C American Express; D Discover Card; E Diner's Club; F Other; 2 Personal checks accepted; 3 Lunch available; 4 Dinner available; 5 Open all year;

Continental Breakfast
Credit Cards: None
Notes: 5

The International Bed & Breakfast Club, Inc.

504 Amherst Street, Buffalo, NY 14207
(800) 723-4262; FAX (716) 873-4462

ON1455PP. This fully restored Heritage Mansion was built in 1891. The Victorian style private home is on a lovely tree-lined residential boulevard in Toronto's oldest historic village. The mansion is within walking distance of transportation, minutes to major downtown attractions, theaters, and museums. This "home away from home" has fourteen large, bright rooms tastefully furnished with antiques. The four guest accommodations have private and shared bath arrangements. A Continental plus breakfast is served and is special when guests indulge in hot-from-the-oven home-made muffins, tea biscuits, Danish, corn bread, and the hosts' famous Sunday brunch. $50-95.

Metropolitan Bed and Breakfast Registry of Toronto

Suite 269, 615 Mount Pleasant Road
Toronto, M4S 3C5
(416) 964-2566; FAX (416) 537-0233

The Admiral St. George. This beautiful turn-of-the-century home offers every comfort in a friendly atmosphere. Open fireplaces in the dining room, living room, and some bedrooms add to the warmth. The house is furnished with antiques, surrounded by trees, and has a guest kitchen and private parking. Most of the spacious, elegant guest bedrooms feature either fireplace, bay corner window, or a deck, with private or shared bath. Minutes to the subway. It is the perfect location for business or holiday travelers; just a short walk to the museum, art gallery, university, theatres,

fashionable Yorkville, and many fine restaurants. English and French are spoken. No smoking. $65-75.

Al's Place. This quiet suburban home is close to restaurants and shops in the North End of Toronto. Fairview Shopping Mall is within walking distance. Easy access to other parts of Toronto, the downtown area, and out of town. The host is a retired engineer who loves meeting people from other places. Al speaks fluent Hungarian in addition to English. Air-conditioned. No smoking. Al serves a full breakfast that includes homemade grape or other gourmet jams. $55.

Bain House. Close to the lively Greek neighborhood in Toronto's East End, this restored three-story Victorian home offers memorabilia from the fifties era that the hostess has collected. Some of the furnishings are also "early fifties style." The bustling neighborhood has great shopping, sidewalk fruit markets, open cafés, and all the great aromas of yummy shish kebab and other Greek specialties. After a full day of taking in the sights, guests may relax on the outside deck. Ten-minute walk to subway; easy access to all of Toronto's tourist attractions. Two guest accommodations, one with queen-size bed and one with twin bed, share a bath. Off-street parking available. Nonsmokers only. $50.

Bed and Breakfast at Bayview. This grand modern house is exquisitely decorated and furnished and has a wonderful Oriental flavor. The hosts speak Dutch, German, Indonesian, and English. The spacious lower level offers total privacy. It has a large bedroom, separate sitting room featuring a fireplace, color TV and VCR, private bath, as well as a dining area and kitchenette with a microwave oven. The pretty blue room upstairs has a queen-size bed and a full bath with Jacuzzi. The hostess, a registered

6 Pets welcome; 8 Children welcome; 9 Social drinking allowed; 10 Tennis available; 11 Swimming available; 12 Golf available; 13 Skiing available; 14 May be booked through travel agents.

Metropolitan Bed and Breakfast Registry of Toronto (*continued*)

nurse, caters to special dietary needs on request. Nonsmokers only. $65-80.

Bonnie's Bungalow. Enjoy birds? Watch them feed and bathe through the large living room picture window or while sitting on the spacious veranda. Make yourself at home in Bonnie's comfortable bungalow, which she shares with her dog, Rebel. The guest bedroom is well appointed with a queen-size bed and sitting area. It is on the main floor and has a shared bath. This well-kept home is fully air-conditioned and offers a Jacuzzi. $55

Brain. This friendly family is interested in music, art, and travel. In fact, interesting artifacts from all over the world decorate this very convenient home in North Toronto. They love meeting people from other parts of the world. The hostess is a very fine sculptress and has won awards for her work. The house is just a few steps to the Lawrence subway station for a fast run downtown. Walk a very short distance to Yonge Street and visit the stores, cafés, night clubs, and restaurants. There is parking and air conditioning. The dining room overlooks the garden. The two guest rooms, one with a double bed and one with a twin bed, share a bath. Nonsmokers only. Full, hot breakfast is served. $52.

Clair on the Square. Built in the mid 1850s, this classic Victorian yellow-brick home is on a half-acre of land on the west side of Clan Gregor Square in picturesque Bayfield Village. This bed and breakfast has been tastefully restored and furnished with antiques, art, and chintz. It has the original pine and ash floors. The guest bedrooms are pretty and comfortable. Each is appointed with traditional furniture, lots of personal touches, and has either a shared or private bath. No smoking. Delicious full breakfasts with home baking, Clair's preserves, and often fruit from the garden are served at the harvest table in the spacious dining room. $75-110.

Cuddle Close. On the eastern boundary of Toronto, this modern, if unusual, house backs onto Canada's largest urban park, home to much wildlife, while being convenient to Canada's largest highway. As new gardeners the hosts are eager to discuss their developing garden and their "backs of steel—with trap doors." Allison can describe the current community theatre productions—and may even be working on one—while John can discuss celestial navigation on a cloudy night with traveling sailors! Ballroom dancers will learn of the places to strut their telemarks, corta jacas, etc. Air-conditioned. Nonsmokers please. $55-65.

Gingerbread House. This fine old house is surrounded by trees and shrubs that give it a country feeling year-round. From the outside this lovely home is more like a cottage than a house. But inside are spacious, comfortable rooms, with 1920s period furnishings and private baths. Perfect for the business traveler, downtown and airport are minutes away. Pickup at the airport available by special request. FAX service available. Two blocks from the subway and GO transit. Fully air-conditioned. No smoking please. There are two resident cats, three fireplaces, and a warm, friendly atmosphere. In summer, breakfast is sometimes served in the spectacular back yard. $60-75.

Joan's Bed and Breakfast. This neat suburban bungalow is in Toronto's East End, within walking distance of the subway for a

NOTES: Credit cards accepted: A MasterCard; B Visa; C American Express; D Discover Card; E Diner's Club; F Other; 2 Personal checks accepted; 3 Lunch available; 4 Dinner available; 5 Open all year;

quick trip downtown. Visitors are a short bus ride from the Metro Zoo, the Science Centre, and a major shopping mall. The pretty guest bedroom is decorated in a Canadian East Coast theme and has a shared bath. Air-conditioned. $50.

Kent House. This airy, modernized, three-story midtown home, historic in nature because of its Edwardian heritage, is in a quiet area, one and one-half blocks from Summerhill subway station. This house is furnished in eclectic style, combining the richness of tribal rugs with contemporary and antique furniture and art. Excellent restaurants and shopping are a 10-minute walk away. A short stroll toward downtown Toronto will bring guests to the internationally known Yorkville area and the Royal Ontario Museum. The cozy guest room is tastefully decorated and overlooks a quiet city garden. There is a private four-piece bath for the exclusive use of the guests. Parking is available. Fully air-conditioned. Nonsmokers only. A full English-style breakfast is served, and in good weather can be enjoyed on the open-air deck. $75.

Little Italy. Enjoy the inner-city neighborhood with its Cappuccino bars and cafes, gourmet pizza, Italian bakery, and authentic restaurants. The hostess lives in a Victorian row house built in 1905 and completely renovated to the open-plan look with oak floors throughout. The house is decorated with Asian art and artifacts brought back from world travels. Join the hostess in discussing theatre, jazz clubs, wine tasting, and gourmet cooking. A piano and exercise bike are available. House is fully air-conditioned. The two guest accommodations have double beds and a shared bath. Nonsmokers only, please. $55-60.

Mayfair. Elegant 1910 Edwardian home furnished with antiques and Persian carpets featuring many leaded and stained-glass windows and beautiful oak paneling. In a quiet residential area, the inn is adjacent to a 400-acre park. Private off-street parking. Each suite has an ensuite four-piece bathroom, private sitting room, and color, cable TV. Congenial, well-traveled hosts enjoy helping guests with plans. No smoking, please. There is a dog and cat in host quarters only. English and French spoken. Subway at the corner (three-minute walk). Air-conditioned. $65-70.

Midtown. This is the perfect home for visitors unfamiliar with Toronto, for the well-traveled host knows her city well and thoroughly enjoys advising her guests on what to see and do and how best to get there. A walk of just a block and a half along a gracious tree-lined street brings guests to a handy little bus that takes them to a subway stop and downtown in minutes. The peaceful neighborhood is one of Toronto's oldest and most distinguished. The home is tastefully appointed. The furniture is teak, and the colors are warm. The walls hold many pictures and souvenirs of the host's world travels. The comfortable guest bedroom is on the main floor and has a shared bath. Parking for one car. No smokers please. Breakfast is served in the large formal dining room. $65.

Riverbridge. This airy, interesting home is perched high on the west bank of the Credit River west of Toronto. Once an inn, the house is set facing the river amid towering trees on half an acre of lush greenery. From the pool deck, guests can glimpse Olympic-style canoeists and scullers on the river, and excellent walks and parks are nearby. In winter, the fireplace crackles nightly. The hosts, an international photographer and a business communicator, are well traveled and speak several languages. Business facilities are available. Atmosphere is calm, relaxed, and

6 Pets welcome; 8 Children welcome; 9 Social drinking allowed; 10 Tennis available; 11 Swimming available; 12 Golf available; 13 Skiing available; 14 May be booked through travel agents.

Metropolitan Bed and Breakfast Registry of Toronto (continued)

friendly. The guest room has a queen-size bed and private bath. Air-conditioned. Ample free off-street parking. $60.

Seasons. The decor of this modern, spacious home is contemporary with a few antiques to add interest. The two guest rooms on the upper level are inviting and tastefully decorated: the Spring Room with twin beds in daffodil yellow and the Autumn Room with a king-size bed in warm shades of brown and gold. They share a bath. The host, Douglas, will be delighted to discuss amateur theatre, in which he is involved, or perhaps play a selection on the grand piano. Sing along or lounge on the bench in the bay window overlooking the crystal waters of the pool. Parking. Swimming. No smoking. Cat, Fluffy, in residence. Air-conditioned. A full breakfast is served in the dining room and features such delights as coddled eggs, home baking, or Linda's famous peach pancakes, together with fresh fruit, juices, and cereals. $60.

Seaton Pretty. Nestled in Toronto's historic "Cabbagetown" lies the Edwardian home of Seaton Pretty. Charmed with interesting and unusual artifacts, this tastefully appointed home is within walking distance to the best of Toronto's attractions, shopping, theatre district, and nightlife. The three guest accommodations have double or queen-size beds and share a bath. The hosts are caterers by trade. Wafting smells of fine cuisine and a unique coffee mug collection make breakfast a delightful event. Bike rentals available. $60-65.

Sunnyside House. This charming Victorian mansion makes a wonderful getaway. The guest suite with a queen-size bed features antiques, a superb sitting room, private bath, and balcony. The hostess is an antique dealer, and her good taste in furnishings is reflected throughout this bed and breakfast home. Breakfast is self-serve. Coffee, juice, fruit, cereal, and muffins are provided. $75.

Villa McNab. Come and stay at luxurious, Spanish-style Villa NcNab, a unique bed and breakfast experience. Enjoy imaginative breakfasts by the large, indoor pool, with its tropical plants and pool-side bar (BYOB). Laze in the Jacuzzi or sauna, or just relax in the room with TV and private facilities. In winter, enjoy the sitting room with a blazing log fire. After caring for guests in a stately home in England for 11 years, the hosts know how to pamper their guests. $95.

Wilkie House. This large executive home in the Burlington core is just a walk away from Spencer Smith Park on the shores of Lake Ontario, the Joseph Brant Museum, or the Burlington Art Centre. Shoppers will enjoy the boutiques of Village Square and the new Mapleview Mall. A nearby bus connects to GO Transit/Toronto. It is less than an hour's drive to Niagara, Kitchener's Mennonite country, Rockton Lion Safari, and the Mountsberg Wildlife Centre. The guest bedroom features two antique spool beds with quilts, private bath, cable TV, and VCR. Off-street parking available. In residence is a tabby cat and a golden retriever, named Tara. Air-conditioned. Breakfast is served in the bright formal dining room. $60.

The Yellow Door. This lovely, traditional townhouse is on a quiet street overlooking a small park. This home is furnished with English antiques and is friendly and comfortable. The cheerful guest bedroom is well appointed and offers a private bath. The hosts, Pat and Terry, are originally from England and know how to make a visit a pleasant and memorable experience. Nonsmokers only. Air-conditioned. In fine weather guests may wish to enjoy breakfast in the quiet courtyard. $75.

Orchard View

92 Orchard View Boulevard, M4R 1C2
(416) 488-6826

Spacious 1911 home is uniquely decorated for the 1990s. Choose between the double bed with private ensuite bath or the twin room with sitting area and separate entrance to the main bath. Full breakfast served, Close to subway, shops, and restaurants.

Hosts: Donna andKen Ketchen
Rooms: 2 (1 PB; 1 SB) $60-65
Full Breakfast
Credit Cards: None
Notes: 5, 9 ,10, 11, 14

Terrace House

52 Austin Terrace, M5R 1Y6
(416) 537-8093

Lovely residence built in 1913 is in the historic Casa Loma neighborhood of downtown Toronto. House features the original stained glass and leaded windows, and the living room has a beautiful scrolled ceiling. The dining room is rich with wood beams and oak trim. A full hot breakfast is served. The Skylight Room features a large skylight set in a sloped ceiling above the queen-size bed. The Tulip Room is blooming with tulips. It offers twin beds, a private sun porch, and a sitting room. The Peach Room is cozy with white eyelet and wicker. It has a queen-size bed and private bath with shower. All are air-conditioned. No smoking.

Host: Judy Carr
Rooms: 3 (1 PB; 2 SB) $65-80
Full Breakfast
Credit Cards: A
Notes: 5, 9, 10, 12, 14

Toronto Bed and Breakfast Inc.

Box 69, 235 College Street, M5T 1R5
(416) 596-1118; (416) 588-8800
FAX (416) 977-2601

Amblecote. This bed and breakfast provides the ambience of a large Edwardian home in an elegant residential neighborhood. Within walking distance of downtown Toronto, Casa Loma, shopping, museums, and restaurants. Bedrooms are beautifully appointed with period furniture and single, double, or queen-size beds and share a bath. The single guest room, named the Kelmscott Room, features an antique Eastlake-style bed, and a double room, the Willow Room, is distinguished by its four-poster bed. The drawing room features a grand piano. No smoking. Parking. Cat in residence. The distinctive and varied breakfasts are served in the formal dining room and, in the winter, often beside a cozy fire. $61-66.

Beachview. This bed and breakfast is a lakefront property in Toronto's Beaches neighborhood. The clean and comfortable rooms have a direct view of the lake. Relax with access to TV or enjoy the sun porch, which also has a view of Lake Ontario. Steps away from the lake boardwalk, restaurants, shopping, municipal pool, and Greenwood Racetrack. Nonsmoking preferred. Ceiling fans. 70-pound lap dog named Virgil. Full breakfast. $66.

Birchcroft. A quiet and friendly contemporary home in the airport area. Hosts have extensive travel knowledge and can assist visitors in their stay. Pickup at the airport can be provided if arranged in advance. Olympic swimming pool, mini-golf, Centennial Park, and airport hotel strip are minutes away. Two guest rooms with single or queen-size beds have private and shared baths. Recreation room privileges. TV. Large back yard. Parking. Nonsmoking preferred. Cat, Marmalade, in residence. Full

6 Pets welcome; 8 Children welcome; 9 Social drinking allowed; 10 Tennis available; 11 Swimming available; 12 Golf available; 13 Skiing available; 14 May be booked through travel agents.

Toronto Bed and Breakfast Inc. (continued)

breakfast. Low-salt diet breakfast also available. Seasonal operation only. $56.

Cabbagetown. This new elegantly decorated home in the heart of old Cabbagetown, the first established community in Toronto, within walking distance to Eaton Centre, theatres, and many dining establishments. The host has lived in Toronto for years and can discuss the history as well as make recommendations on a variety of local events and attractions to see. The guest rooms have twin, single, double, or queen-size beds and private and shared baths. Other amenities include air conditioning, parking, TV, and pure-water system. Lap dog in residence. Enjoy breakfast in the atrium dining room or on a private deck. $50-75.

Castleview. Welcome to the Victorian charm of Castleview Guest House. It is a few blocks north of the University of Toronto in the beautiful historic Annex community. The magnificent castle, Casa Loma, is within walking distance. Castleview is half a block from a subway terminal. Bloor Street, with its dozens of shops and restaurants, is only two blocks away. Guests will certainly enjoy their time at Castleview with its beautiful woodwork, old fireplaces, and friendly, gracious hostess. The guest rooms have twin, single, double, and queen-size beds and private and shared baths. $51-70.

Donna's. Set in a quiet residential area on a large corner lot, this home is close to the subway, Yorkdale Shopping Centre, Pioneer Village, and many other attractions. The bathroom is shared between the two guest rooms with twin beds, and the large, treed garden beckons guests to relax. The

host also speaks Latvian and German. Pick up at the Glencairn subway can be arranged. Air-conditioned. Parking. Smoking. A delightful variety of breakfasts will be served in the family dining room. $58.

Downtowner. A quiet contemporary home in the downtown core. Steps away from Yonge Street, north of the famous Eaton Centre. Church Street Village, theatres, restaurants, major hospitals, and the University of Toronto are always in walking distance. The subway system is just steps away. Guests' comfort and needs are a priority, and they are encouraged to enjoy the extensive library. The guest room has a queen-size bed and shared bath. The amenities include air-conditioning, pool, gym, whirlpool, sauna, laundry facilities, private phone, and TV. Attention paid to special diets and guests' choice of breakfast served. $65.

The Garden House. This Victorian home combines Old-World charm with modern conveniences. Within walking distance of the university and several hospitals. Subway, buses, and streetcars are only a few minutes away. Stroll along colorful Bloor Street and Markham Village, see the museums and galleries, dine at ethnic restaurants and cafés, or take the subway to Harbourfront. The hosts have a selection of guidebooks and tourist information. The inn offers nicely furnished, air-conditioned rooms with a large semi-private bath. In summer, relax in the garden. Long-term guests can be accommodated at special rates. No smoking. Children welcome. Cat and lap dog in residence. Enjoy a delicious full breakfast in the dining room. The hosts will do their best to observe special diet needs. $56.

Lionsgate. Why not stay in the heart of Toronto? Nestled in a quiet neighborhood and with walking distance of Yonge Street, "Yorkville," and major attractions, this inn is

NOTES: Credit cards accepted: A MasterCard; B Visa; C American Express; D Discover Card; E Diner's Club; F Other; 2 Personal checks accepted; 3 Lunch available; 4 Dinner available; 5 Open all year;

less than a three-minute walk from the subway line. Guest accommodations have double and queen-size beds with private and shared baths. Air-conditioned. Limited private parking. TV. Cats in residence. No smoking. No children under 12. Enjoy breakfast in a delightful setting. $60-95.

Mabel's Bed and Breakfast. Contemporary home with a spacious patio and back garden on a quiet residential street. Broadview subway station is around the corner and a mere five minutes from downtown. The Broadview-Danforth area is well know for its colorful ethnic restaurants, cafés, and shops. Nearby parks beckon for a walk along beautifully wooded trails. All in all, an ideal location from which a visitor can experience the many and varied pleasures Toronto has to offer. The guest accommodation has a double and private bath. Parking. Fans. No smoking. $70.

Old Cabbagetown. Charmingly restored Victorian family home in a renovated and gentrified part of Cabbagetown. Room has view of CN Tower. Delightful historical walking tour (self-guided tour brochures available). Riverdale Farm, an old-fashioned farm complete with cows, horses, and chickens, is a five-minute walk. Minutes to subway or a brisk walk to either Yorkville or the Eaton Centre. A variety of restaurants are close by. Parking. Air-conditioned guest room. TV. Families welcome! No smoking. Cat in residence. The hosts cater to special dietary needs with breakfast being served either in the antique dining room or on the outdoor deck. $60.

Valleyview. This new home combines the best of the old—a Victorian courtyard and antiques—with the new. Come for the convenience, steps from the Broadview subway station and streetcars downtown, the view of the ravine and the city skyline from a private deck, the comfort of an ensuite Jacuzzi,

complete with terry-cloth robes, an eiderdown on the queen-size bed, and a private bathroom. Air-conditioned with ceiling fans. Parking. No smoking. Coffee in room and a wide choice of breakfast treats. A favorite choice for special occasions. $85.

UNIONVILLE

Metropolitan Bed and Breakfast Registry of Toronto

Suite 269, 615 Mount Pleasant Road
Toronto, M4S 3C5
(416) 964-2566; FAX (416) 537-0233

River Run. This lovely modern home in the country just north of Toronto offers the best of both worlds. The village Main Street is just a short walk from the house and features many interesting shops and restaurants. Guests seeking solitude can walk from the back yard of this home through a ravine setting to a parkland area with its own pond, where they can have a picnic lunch or just enjoy the sights and sounds of nature. The hostess is an accomplished artist. Many of her interesting watercolors and glass pieces are displayed. She will be happy to describe the various works, which are available for purchase. The house is air-conditioned. Parking is provided. The guest suite has a king-size bed, large sitting room, and private bath. $60.

WELLESLEY

Firella Creek Farm

Rural Route 2, N0B 2T0
(519) 656-2974

Retreat to nature in the heart of Mennonite farming area. Full country breakfast with a view of the trout pond, stream, and orchard. Relax beside the fireplace; hike or cross-country ski through the forest where wildlife abounds. German and Canadian

6 Pets welcome; 8 Children welcome; 9 Social drinking allowed; 10 Tennis available; 11 Swimming available; 12 Golf available; 13 Skiing available; 14 May be booked through travel agents.

meals. Local tours of the cider mill and points of interest are available upon request. On Regional Road 5 between Wellesley and Crosshill. No smoking.

Hosts: Adolph and Emily Hafemann
Rooms: 3 (1 PB; 2 SB) $40-45
Full Breakfast
Credit Cards: None
Notes: 2, 3, 4, 5, 8, 9, 10, 11, 12

Paradise Farm

Rural Route 3, N0B 2T0
(519) 699-4871; FAX (519) 699-4872

Welcome to this sheep farm for a first-class bed and breakfast on a beautiful 63 acres with rolling hills, forest, and a designated building of historic significance, close by Waterloo and Kitchener. Enjoy the sights and sounds of the country with breakfast on the sun deck, and relax beside the fireplace or around a campfire and watch spectacular sunsets after busy days! Enjoy the trails for nature hikes, animal watching, or jogging and a large pond for swimming!

Hosts: Olena and Friedrick Kirebart
Rooms: 2 (SB) $52
Full Breakfast
Credit Cards: None
Notes: 2, 4, 6, 8, 9, 11

ZEPHYR

High Fields Ranch

11570 Concession 3, Rural Route 1, L0E 1T0
(905) 473-6132; FAX (905) 473-1044

Enjoy a relaxed and informal atmosphere in a very private country setting with a peaceful panoramic view. The inn holdings include 175 acres of groomed trails for hiking, snow-mobiling, cross-country skiing, and horse-back riding. Aromatherapy massage and aesthetic services available on premises. Golfing, tennis, swimming, skiing very near. All meals available with advance notice. Reservation and deposit required. Credit cards accepted. A brochure is available.

Hosts: Norma and John Daniel
Rooms 3 (2 PB; 1 SB) $60-70
Full Breakfast
Credit Cards: A, B, C
Notes: 2, 3, 4, 5, 9, 10, 11, 12, 13, 14

Prince Edward Island

CHARLOTTETOWN

Dunstaffnage Heights Bed and Breakfast

Rural Route 3, C1A 7J7
(902) 628-1715

Charming country heritage home, ten kilometers from Charlottetown in Dunstaffnage, Highway 2 East. Quiet parklike setting close to beaches, golf, and other attractions. Five guest rooms, antique motif. Full bath on each floor. Reasonable rates include gourmet breakfast. Vegetarians welcomed. Laundry facilities. Picnic and barbeque, recreation room with fireplace, TV, reading and games area, piano. Complimentary coffee, tea, wine. Separate two-bedroom, six-person cottage. No smoking accommodation.

Hosts: Sol and Evelyn Feldstein
Rooms: 5 (SB) $40-45
Full Breakfast
Credit Cards: None
Notes: 2, 8, 9, 10, 11, 12, 14

An Island Rose

285 Kinlock Road, Rural Route 1, C1A 7J6
(902) 569-5030

Our three-star home has a rural ocean setting with a superb view of Northumberland Strait. Seven minutes from downtown, on beautiful Bellevue Cove with its beaches and clam digging. Three tastefully decorated rooms, one with a queen-size bed, half-bath, and balcony, one with a queen-size bed, and one with twins. Guest lounge with a balcony. A two-bedroom self-contained apartment is also available.

Hosts: Nora and Steve Stephenson
Rooms: 3 (1.5 PB; 2 SB) $45-55
Apartment: $400 per week
Continental Breakfast
Credit Cards: A
Notes: 2, 9, 10, 11, 12

Campbells Maple Bed and Breakfast

28 Maple Avenue, C1A 6E3
(902) 896-4488

This bed and breakfast is in suburban Charlottetown, just 10 miles from the North Shore Beach and National Park. Is a 10-minute drive to downtown Charlottestown, and a 5-minute drive to airport. Full breakfast with fruit and muffins. Visitors will find a friendly welcome with local information provided. Living room and large garden available to guests.

Rooms: 4 (S2B) $40-45
Full Breakfast
Credit Cards: None
Notes: 2, 3, 4, 5, 6, 7, 8, 9, 10, 11, 12, 13, 14

MURRAY RIVER

Bayberry Cliff Inn Bed and Breakfast

Rural Route 4, Little Sands, C0A 1W0
(902) 962-3395

On the edge of a 40-foot cliff, the inn consists of two converted post-and-beam barns decorated with antiques and marine art. Stairs to the shore allow for swimming, tubing, snorkeling, and beachcombing. Seal boat tours and bird watching tours nearby, as well as fine restaurants and craft shops.

---

6 Pets welcome; 7 Smoking allowed; 8 Children welcome; 9 Social drinking allowed; 10 Tennis available; 11 Swimming available; 12 Golf available; 13 Skiing available; 14 May be booked through travel agents.

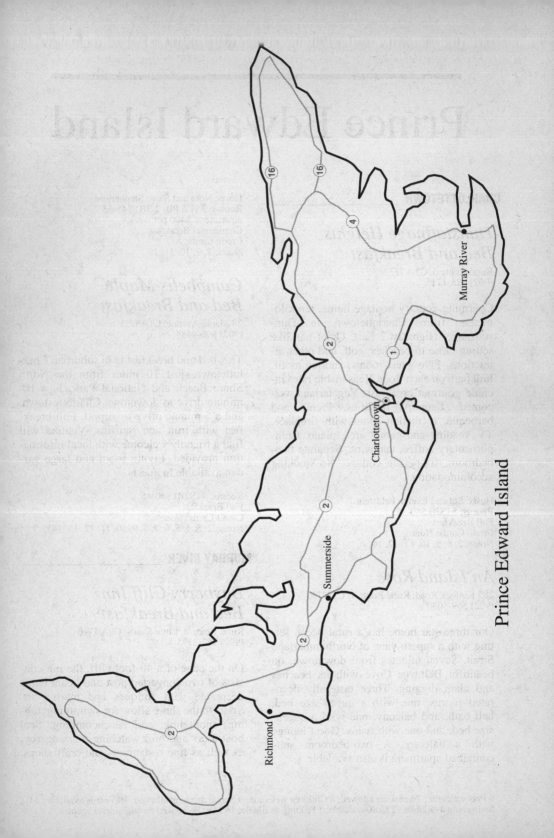

Prince Edward Island

A honeymoon suite with private bath is available. Closed from October 1 to May 1.

Hosts: Nancy and Don Perkins
Rooms: 8 (3 PB; 5 SB) $45-75
Full Breakfast
Credit Cards: A, B
Notes: 2, 8, 9, 11, 12, 14

RICHMOND

Mom's Bed 'n' Breakfast

C0B 1Y0
(902) 854-2419

In a quiet village in unspoiled Prince County. One hour from Charlottetown. 1875 Heritage home, modern comfort, cherished past. Four rooms: three with double beds, one has private bath; one with two doubles and powder room. Parlor with piano. Private dining area, two verandas. Short drive to sandy beaches, Mill River Golf, village store, service station, crafts. Smoking on veranda. No pets. Reservations recommended. Bicycle storage. Visa accepted. Open from May to October 15. Off-season rates before June 28 and after September 6. Weekly rates on request. Full breakfast included.

Hostess: Erma Gaudet-MacArthur
Rooms: 5 (1PB; 4 SB) $35-65
Full Breakfast
Credit Cards: B
Notes: 2, 8, 9, 10, 11, 12

Silver Fox Inn

SUMMERSIDE

Silver Fox Inn

61 Granville Street, C1N 2Z3
(902) 436-4033

For more than a century, proud owners have carefully preserved the beauty of these spacious rooms with their fireplaces and fine woodwork. Combining modern comfort with the cherished past, the Silver Fox Inn offers accommodations for 12 guests. Its six bedrooms, each with private bath, feature period furnishings.

Host: Julie Simmons
Rooms: 6 (PB) $60-75
Continental Breakfast
Credit Cards: A, B, C
Notes: 5, 9, 10, 11, 12, 13, 14

NOTES: Credit cards accepted: A MasterCard; B Visa; C American Express; D Discover Card; E Diner's Club; F Other; 2 Personal checks accepted; 3 Lunch available; 4 Dinner available; 5 Open all year; 6 Pets welcome; 7 Smoking allowed; 8 Children welcome; 9 Social drinking allowed; 10 Tennis available; 11 Swimming available; 12 Golf available; 13 Skiing available; 14 May be booked through travel agents.

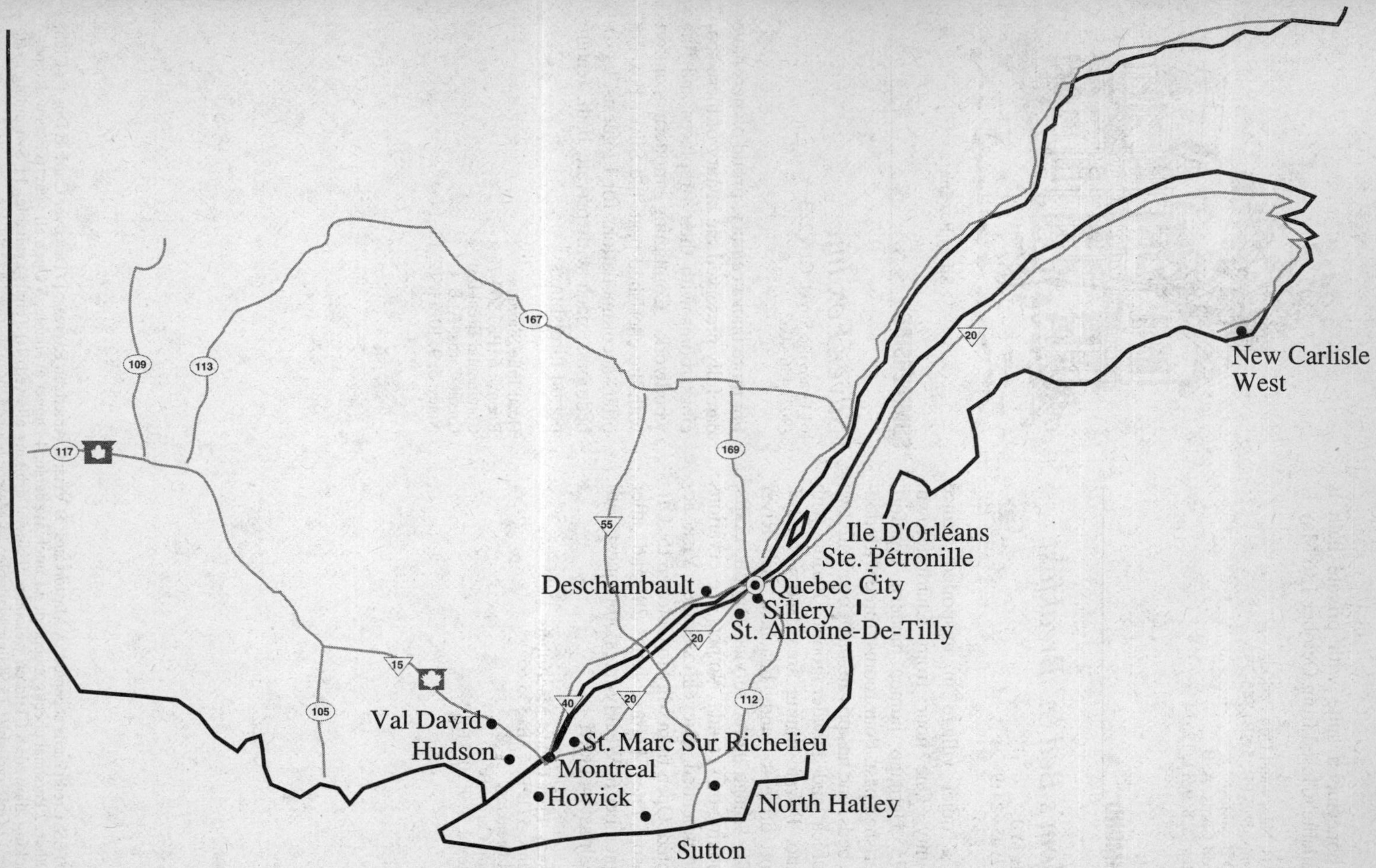

New Carlisle
West

20

Ile D'Orléans
Ste. Pétronille
Quebec City
Sillery
St. Antoine-De-Tilly

112

St. Marc Sur Richelieu

North Hatley

Sutton

169

Deschambault

20

20

55

St. Marc Sur Richelieu
Montreal
Howick

40

167

Val David
Hudson

15

105

113

109

117

Quebec

Quebec

DESCHAMBAULT

Auberge Chemin Du Roy

106 St. Laurent, G0A 1S0
(418) 286-6958

Only 40 minutes from Québec, the town of Deschambault invites guests to discover its historic past by staying at this Victorian inn. The antiques evoke a feeling of serenity and romance near the fireplace. Guests can also relax with the murmuring waterfall front the house and the St. Lawrence River breezes.

Hosts: Francine Bouthat and Gilles Laberge
Rooms: 8 (4 PB; 4 SB) $59-74
Full Breakfast
Credit Cards: D
Notes: 4, 5, 7, 8, 9, 10, 11, 12

HOWICK

Hazelbrae Farm

1650 English River Road, J0S 1G0
(514) 825-2390

Come and savor the peaceful surroundings in a spacious comfortable fifth-generation dairy farmhouse. Homemade specialties for

Hazelbrae Farm

breakfast. Enjoy in-ground pool or visiting by back yard campfire. Less than one hour from Montréal and close to New York state border. The hosts have been welcoming guests for more than ten years.

Hosts: John and Gloria Peddie
Rooms: 4 (1 PB; 3 SB) $50
Full Breakfast
Credit Cards: None
Notes: 2, 3, 4, 5, 8, 11, 12

HUDSON

Riversmead Bed and Breakfast

245 Main Road, J0P 1H0
(514) 458-5053

Riversmead is a fine century-old Georgian brick home set on large grounds with a swimming pool. This quiet and beautiful village on the shores of the Ottawa River offers fine restaurants, antique stores, excellent shopping, bicycle routes, and easy access to Montréal or Ottawa. Riversmead was built in 1850 by host Fred Henshaw's great-grandfather, who was a riverboat ship owner and local businessman. Delicious breakfasts and warm hospitality are offered either on the sunny porch or in the Victorian dining room.

Hosts: Naomi and Fred Henshaw
Rooms: 5 (SB) $60
Full Breakfast
Credit Cards: None
Notes: 2, 5, 12, 13

NOTES: Credit cards accepted: A MasterCard; B Visa; C American Express; D Discover Card; E Diner's Club; F Other; 2 Personal checks accepted; 3 Lunch available; 4 Dinner available; 5 Open all year; 6 Pets welcome; 7 Smoking allowed; 8 Children welcome; 9 Social drinking allowed; 10 Tennis available; 11 Swimming available; 12 Golf available; 13 Skiing available; 14 May be booked through travel agents.

ILE D'ORLÉANS

La Maison Sous les Arbres au Bord de L'eau

1415 Chemin Royal, St. Laurent, G0A 3Z0
(418) 828-9442; FAX (418) 828-9442

This home is ten minutes from Old Quebec and close to the St. Lawrence River. Very quiet. Enjoy the wildlife during vacation in this home. The pool is open after 5:00 P.M. Enjoy breakfast in the "Glass House," which faces the garden and river. Each room has a private entrance and gallery. No smoking. Cats in residence.

Hosts: Germaine and Louis Dumas
Rooms: 3 (1 PB; 2 SB) $60
Full Breakfast
Credit Cards: None
Notes: 5, 8, 10, 11, 12, 13

La Maison Sous les Arbres

Le Mas de L'Isle

155 Chemin Royal, St. Jean, G0A 3W0
(418) 829-1213

Le Mas de L'Isle is on the beautiful Île d'Orléans on a little cliff in the peaceful village of St. Jean. French and English are spoken. The breakfast is unforgettable, and the view of the St. Laurent River is breathtaking. Guests can relax, read, or listen to music in the family room. Cat (Cannelle) on the premises. Only a 30-minute drive to Quebec City and "La Joie de Vivre" of French Canada.

Hosts: Yolande and Claude Dumesnil
Rooms: 3 (2 SB) $55
Full Breakfast
Credit Cards: B
Notes: 4 (call), 5, 8, 11, 12, 13

MONTRÉAL

Armor Inn

151 Sherbrooke Est., H2X 1C7
(516) 285-0140

Armor Inn is a little European-style hotel in the heart of downtown Montréal, near Prince Arthur and St. Denis Streets. Just a 15-minute walk from Old Montréal, the Palais des Congrès, or shopping in Montréal's network of underground shopping malls. Warm family atmosphere. Room rate includes breakfast. Parking available.

Host: Annick Morvan
Rooms: 15 (7 PB; 8 SB) $38-75
Continental Breakfast
Credit Cards: A, B
Notes: 5, 7, 8

A Bed and Breakfast—A Downtown Network

3458 Laval Avenue, H2X 3C8
(514) 289-9749; (800) 267-5180
FAX (514) 287-7387

1. Downtown, turn-of-the-century home. This restored Victorian home features a marble fireplace, original hardwood floors, and a skylight. The host offers two charmingly decorated double rooms and grandma's quilts in the winter. Guests can bird watch on the balcony or have a challenging game of Trivial Pursuit in the evening. Full breakfast. $35-55.

2. Be in the heart of everything! The big bay window of Bob's 90-year-old restored home overlooks the city's most historic park. Original woodwork and detail add to the charm of this nine-room home, where a double and triple are offered. The neighborhood is famous for excellent "bring your

own wine" restaurants, and the host knows them all. Full breakfast. $35-75.

3. Downtown double off Sherbrooke Street. This antique-filled apartment on Drummond Street is tastefully decorated and only two minutes from the Museum of Fine Arts and all shopping. Mount Royal Park is nearby, and McGill University is just two blocks away. The hosts pamper guests with a gourmet breakfast and invite them for a sherry in the evening. One double room, shared bath. $55.

4. Downtown, in the heart of the Latin Quarter. Enjoy the superb location of this restored traditional Québecoise home. The host, active in the restaurant business, offers two sunlit doubles and one triple with a bay window opening onto a typical Montreal scene. The privacy of this tastefully furnished home is perfect for first or second honeymoons. Shared bath, full breakfast. $55-75.

6. When traveling to Quebec City, stop at this landmark home built in 1671 facing the beautiful St. Lawrence River. The hostess, a blue-ribbon chef, offers a memorable breakfast featuring Quiche Floriane. For an unforgettable stay, guests are invited to experience the warmth and hospitality of a typical Québecoise home. Two enchanting doubles. Full breakfast. $55.

7. This Old Montreal landmark offers eight guest rooms and one suite. Decorated with a combination of antiques and contemporary pieces, the guest rooms are spacious and air-conditioned. All have private baths in marble, some with Jacuzzi. In winter, snuggle before a crackling fire with a good book. Within strolling distance of Notre Dame church, fine restaurants, shops, and museums. Enjoy the richness of Montreal's heritage. Full gourmet breakfast. $75-95.

Auberge de la Fontaine

1301 East Rachel Street, H2J 2K1
(514) 597-0166; (800) 597-0597

Guests will be warmly welcomed in this charming bed and breakfast inn, in front of Parc la Fontaine, an 84-acre park close to the downtown area. The 21 air-conditioned rooms and suites, some with whirlpool bath, others with terrace or balcony, are beautiful, comfortable, and will make guests feel at home. Enjoy a generous Continental buffet and free access to the kitchen for snacks. Take this opportunity to discover the exclusive shops, restaurants, and art galleries of the Plateau Mont-Royal, typical of French Montreal.

Hosts: Céline Boudreau and Jean Lamothe
Rooms: 21 (PB) $99 175
Continental Breakfast
Credit Cards: A, B, C, E, F
Notes: 5, 7, 8, 10, 11, 14

Bed and Breakfast à Montréal

P.O. Box 575, Snowdon Station, H3X 3T8
(514) 738-9410; FAX (514) 735-7493

These bed and breakfasts are in the finest private homes and condo apartments, carefully selected for their comfort, cleanliness, and convenient locations. Many are within walking distance of Old Montreal and the Convention Centre. All of the hosts are fluent in English and will enhance visit with suggestions, outgoing personalities, and delicious breakfasts. Stay long enough to visit Old Montreal, the lively Latin Quarter, the Underground City, Botanical Gardens, Mount Royal Park, and St. Joseph's Oratory, among other sights. Visits can also arranged to Quebec City. Coordinator: Marian Kahn.

Brigette's Bed and Breakfast. Brigette's love of art and antiques is obvious in this fabulous three-story townhouse. Fireplace, cozy living room, and a view of the city's most historic park all add to the charm of

6 Pets welcome; 8 Children welcome; 9 Social drinking allowed; 10 Tennis available; 11 Swimming available; 12 Golf available; 13 Skiing available; 14 May be booked through travel agents.

this home. One double with brass bed, duvet, antique pieces, and guests' own bathroom. Experience nearby "bring your own wine" restaurants. $50-70.

Jacky's Bed and Breakfast. This interior designer-hostess has created warmth and charm in this elegant downtown condo, with treasures collected from India and New Mexico. The guest room has a queen-size bed and private bathroom facilities. Sherbrooke Street, the Museum of Fine Arts, and the city's best shopping are all just two minutes away. $65-85.

Johanna's Bed and Breakfast. This elegant hostess invites guests to this bright, airy, two-story home filled with European style. An avid gardener, she is pleased to share the joys of the garden with guests. This Westmount home is just five minutes from downtown. One double with a private bathroom is offered. $60-70.

Manoir Ambrose. On the quiet and restful slope of beautiful Mont-Royal. Within walking distance of Montréal's many restaurants, theaters, shopping districts, and metro system.

Marian's Bed and Breakfast. Stay in this 14th-floor apartment and enjoy magnificent views of St. Joseph's Oratory and Mount Royal Park. Guests delight in the host's special pelican collection and the textile hangings collected during international travels. One charming double room with private bath is available. Downtown is just five minutes away. $45-65.

Martha's Bed and Breakfast. Guests can walk from Martha's house to Montreal's hockey arena, the Forum, or the city's most elegant shopping complex, Westmount Square. Stenciled glass windows, original woodwork and detail, and smart period furnishings are just some of the features of this bed and breakfast. $50-70.

A Quebec City Choice. Enjoy the beauty of the St. Lawrence River and the Laurentian Mountains from this Quebec City condo complex, just five minutes from Old Quebec. The enthusiastic hostess, fluent in English, will guide guests well during their stay. One guest room with private bath is offered here. $60-80.

Downtown Montreal Bed and Breakfast and Apartments

3523 Jeanne-Mance, H2X 2K2
(514) 845-0431

In the heart of downtown, close to all festivals, and the convention center. Color TV, radio, delicious full breakfast. Access to a different kitchen for guests. The number-one place to stay. Limited parking available. Also, beautiful downtown apartments, all furnished for short or long rentals. Open year-round. Recommended by the French guide *Le Routard*, "...certainly one of our best address."

Host: Bruno Bernard
Rooms: 7 (4PB; 3SB) $60-70
Full Breakfast
Credit Cards: A, B, C
Notes: 5, 7, 8, 14

La Maison de Grand Pré

4660 rue de Grand-Pré, H2T 2H7
(514) 843-6458; FAX (514) 843-8691

Built in 1865, this house has maple trees out front and a small park behind. Four double rooms have fans. Guests share two large bathrooms that have showers and old-fashioned tubs. A balcony and reading/smoking room are also available. The breakfast includes hot breads and croissants fresh daily from the neighborhood bakery, fruits from the open market, homemade crepes, French toast, omelets, and espresso coffee. Tea, cookies, and fruit are served as a welcome snack. The metro station is four minutes' walking distance from the house, and the boutiques, outdoor cafés, and restaurants of St. Denis Street are one block away. The host, a former university professor, is bilingual.

Host: Jean-Paul Lauzon
Rooms: 4 (2 SB) $45-65
Full Breakfast
Credit Cards: None
Notes: 2, 5, 7, 8, 9, 11, 14

A Montréal Oasis Bed and Breakfast

3000 Chemin de Breslay, H3Y 2G7
(514) 935-2312

This spacious home is in what is known as the Priest Farm District (once a holiday resort for priests). With original lead windows and slanted ceilings on the third floor. In a beautiful downtown neighborhood with large trees and pretty gardens. Swedish hostess is world traveled, loves all kinds of music and African art. Friendly blue cream Siamese cat in residence. Hostess also operates a small bed and breakfast network of homes in downtown, Old Montréal, and the Latin Quarter.

Hostess: Lena Blondel
Rooms: 30 (5 PB; 25 SB) $40-90
Full Breakfast
Credit Cards: None
Notes: 5, 14

NEW CARLISLE WEST

Bay View Farm

Box 21, 337 Main Highway, Route 132, G0C 1Z0
(418) 752-2725; (418) 752-6718

Between New Carlisle and Bonaventure on the rugged and beautiful Baie de Chaleur coastline of Quebec's Gaspé Peninsula on Route 132. Seaside accommodations include five comfortable guest rooms. Full country breakfast is made from fresh farm

Bay View Farm

and garden products. Additional light meals by arrangement. Handicrafts on display. August Bay View Folk Festival, museums, historic sites, Fauvel Golf Course, beaches, lighthouse, hiking, bird watching. Breathtakingly beautiful panoramic seascapes. Tranquil and restful environment. Also available is a fully equipped seaside country house for $350 per week.

Host: Helen Sawyer
Rooms: 5 (1PB, 4SB) $35
Country House: $350
Full Breakfast
Credit Cards: None
Notes: 3, 4, 5, 8, 10, 11, 12, 13

NORTH HATLEY

Cedar Gables

4080 Magog Road; Box 355, J0B 2C0
(819) 842-4120

Established in 1985 as the area's premiere bed and breakfast, Cedar Gables is a large, tastefully decorated home, circa 1890s, at the lakeside on Lake Massawippi in the heart of Québec's eastern townships. Easily accessible, the inn is 10 minutes from the U.S./Canada I-91/Autoroute 55 northeast corridor. The five guest rooms have private baths ensuite. Four rooms have king-size beds and the fifth, a canopied double. It is a five-minute walk to a unique resort village where shopping, browsing,

6 Pets welcome; 8 Children welcome; 9 Social drinking allowed; 10 Tennis available; 11 Swimming available; 12 Golf available; 13 Skiing available; 14 May be booked through travel agents.

Cedar Gables

and a full range of dining is available. Detailed brochure available.

Hosts: Ann and Don Fleischer
Rooms: 5 (PB) $76-99
Full Breakfast
Credit Cards: A, B, C
Notes: 2, 5, 6, 7 (limited), 8 (over 12), 9, 10, 11, 12, 13, 14

QUEBEC CITY

Le Chateau de Pierre

17 Avenue Sainte Genevieve, G1R 4A8
(418) 694-0429

This old English mansion is in the heart of this historic city. Very comfortable rooms have private baths and are nicely decorated. Near all historical activities. Open year-round.

Hosts: Richard and Lily Couturier
Rooms: 16 (PB) $65-105
Continental Breakfast
Credit Cards: A, B
Notes: 2, 5, 7, 8, 13

Hayden's Wexford House

450 Rue Champlain, G1K 4J3
(418) 524-0525

Ancestral home built in the beginning of the 18th-century at the heart of the Heritage and near Old Quebec City. Near many points of interest. In summer, relax in the little flower garden and in the winter by the fireside. Enjoy breakfast in a warm decor and relaxed atmosphere. Enjoy the river view from guest rooms. Open year-round.

Host: Michelle Paquet Rivière
Rooms: 3 (SB) $60-65
Full Breakfast
Credit Cards: B
Notes: 2, 5, 8, 9, 10, 11, 12, 13

Hôtel Marie Rollet

81 Rue Sainte Anne, G1R 3X4
(418) 694-9271

Built in 1876 by the Ursulines Order, the Marie Rollet House offers the ancestral charm of a turn-of-the-century European manor. Guests will be captivated by its warm woodwork, its tranquility and serenity. Area attractions can be reached on foot. Two rooms offer a working fireplace and most have air-conditioning. A rooftop terrace with a garden view gives guests an opportunity to relax in a calm environment.

Hosts: Gerald Giroux and Diane Chouinard
Rooms: 10 (PB) $55-95
No Breakfast
Credit Cards: A, B
Notes: 5, 7, 8, 10, 11, 12, 13, 14

Hôtel Marie Rollet

NOTES: Credit cards accepted: A MasterCard; B Visa; C American Express; D Discover Card; E Diner's Club; F Other; 2 Personal checks accepted; 3 Lunch available; 4 Dinner available; 5 Open all year;

Au Manoir Ste. Geneviève

13 Avenue Sainte Geneviève, G1R 4A7
(418) 694-1666; FAX (418) 694-1666

Enjoy a stay in this Victorian stone mansion furnished with antiques. Conveniently across from Governor's Park. View of Chateau Frontenac and St. Lawrence River. Next door to U.S. consulate. Recommended by AAA and the *New York Times*. Modern facilities. Some efficiencies.

Rooms: 10 (PB) $85-100
Credit Cards: A, B
Notes: 5, 7, 8, 14

Au Petit Hotel

Au Petit Hotel

3 Ruelle des Ursulines, G1R 3Y6
(418) 694-0965; FAX (418) 692-4320

In the heart of Old Quebec, Au Petit Hotel offers quiet surroundings with a warm and hospitable atmosphere, such as the Ursulines convent, the Citadel, and the Chateau Frontenac. Discriminating gourmets will have no trouble finding neighborhood restaurants, smart boutiques, and all kinds of entertainment.

Host: The Tim Family
Rooms: 16 (PB) $45-70
Continental Breakfast
Credit Cards: A, B, C
Notes: 5, 7, 8

Tim House

84 Rue Saint-Louis, G1R 3Z5
(418) 694-0776

Built in 1900 on what is now one of Québec City's main streets, Tim House offers guests the luxury and charm of its Victorian architecture, which is complemented by its convenience to area attractions. All guests have access to the family room on the second floor of the house. Breakfast is served between 8:00 and 10:00 A.M. in a beautiful dining room, also on the second floor. All taxes are included in rates. Free parking available.

Host: Tim Supheavy
Rooms: 3 (1PB; 2 SB) $44-70
Continental Breakfast
Credit Cards: A, B, C
Notes: 2, 5, 8, 9, 13

ST. ANTOINE-DE-TILLY

Auberge Manoir de Tilly

3854 Chemin de Tilly, G0S 2C0
(418) 886-2407

Manoir de Tilly dates from 1786 and is an authentic manor built by one of the king's representatives. The chef offers a highly praised cuisine, where regional farm and sea products are lovingly prepared for guests. In 1990 a 32-room pavilion was added, as well as a health center and conference facilities. The rooms are lovingly decorated and offer calm and tranquility. The manor is only a few kilometers from historic Quebec City. Golf and tennis courts nearby.

Host: Jocelyne Gagnon
Rooms: 32 (PB) Call for price information
Full Breakfast
Credit Cards: A, B, C
Notes: 4, 5, 7, 8, 9, 10, 11, 12, 14

6 Pets welcome; 8 Children welcome; 9 Social drinking allowed; 10 Tennis available; 11 Swimming available; 12 Golf available; 13 Skiing available; 14 May be booked through travel agents.

SAINTE-PÉTRONILLE

Auberge la Goéliche Inn

22 Chemin du Quai, G0A 4C0
(418) 828-2248; FAX (418) 692-1742

Overhanging the St. Lawrence River, this castlelike inn offers a breathtaking view of Quebec City, a 15-minute drive away. It is also close to famous Mont Ste. Anne ski center. Its 24 rooms are warmly decorated in rustic French-Canadian style. Outdoor swimming pool. English and Continental breakfasts. Guided tours of historic surroundings available.

Hosts: Janet Duplain, Andrée Marchand,
  and Alain Turgeon
Rooms: 24 (PB) $80-130
Full or Continental Breakfast
Credit Cards: A, B, C
Notes: 3, 4, 5, 7, 8, 9, 10, 11, 12, 13, 14

ST. MARC SUR RICHELIEU

Auberge Handfield

555 Richelieu, J0L 2E0
(514) 584-2226

This quintessentially French inn is on the Richelieu River in an ancient French-Canadian village where French is universally spoken. The somewhat rustic decor of this venerable 150-year-old mansion is complemented by antiques and locally crafted furnishings. A marina and other resort facilities, including a health club and, outstanding French cuisine, make this a most enjoyable holiday experience.

Host: Conrad Handfield
Rooms: 53 (PB) $75-105
Full Breakfast
Credit Cards: A, B, C, D, E
Notes: 3, 4, 5, 7, 8, 9, 10, 11, 12, 13, 14

Hostellerie les Trois Tilleuls

290 Rue Richelieu, J0L 2E0
(514) 584-2231

The Hostellerie les Trois Tilleuls is a charming inn on the banks of the Richelieu River, a short 30 minutes from Montreal. The 24 rooms with balconies overlook the Richelieu River. The dining room features authentic French cuisine with an extensive wine list of exceptional vintages.

Host: Michel Aubriot
Rooms: 24 (PB) $84-145
Full Breakfast
Credit Cards: A, B, C, D, E
Notes: 3, 4, 5, 7, 8, 9, 10, 11, 12, 14

SILLERY

Fernlea

2156 Rue Dickson, G1T 1C9
(418) 683-3847

Comfortable English-style home and decor, with a fireplace that is especially nice after a day of skiing in the winter. In warm weather the beautiful English garden is a welcome sight, with a patio to relax on after spending a pleasant day in the city. Attractive residential neighborhood where guests may walk, bike, or jog. Québec, with hundreds of wonderful restaurants, is also a city of history. Plan to spend several days— there is so much to see and do. Tours can be arranged with pickup at the house.

Hostess: Joyce Butler-Coutts
Rooms: 3 (SB) $45-65
Full Breakfast
Credit Cards: None
Notes: 2, 5, 8, 9, 10, 11, 12, 13, 14

SUTTON

Auberge Schweizer

357 Schweizer Road, J0E 2K0
(514) 538-2129

Established by a Swiss-German family in 1938, this 130-acre estate overlooks Sutton Valley, 19 kilometers from the Vermont border. The family provides a personal atmosphere, serving garden-grown vegetables, home-baked bread, and meats from the farm. A classical piano recital is part of every week. Many hiking trails, two idyllic ponds, and beautiful sunsets make a stay an unforgettable experience. Comfortable rooms and chalets.

Hosts: Pauline and Heidi Schweizer
Rooms: 14 (5 PB; 9 SB) $50-80
Full Breakfast
Credits Cards: B
Notes: 2, 4, 5, 8, 9, 11, 12, 13

VAL DAVID

Auberge Charme de Suisse

1459 Rue Merette, J0T 2N0
(819) 322-3434

This inn has beautiful and quiet surroundings in the midst of various activities: golf, skiing, swimming, and an outdoor heated swimming pool on the premises. Each room has a private bath and balcony. The host is from Switzerland. Inquire for directions.

Host: Alfred Giger
Rooms: 10 (PB) $65-85
Full Breakfast
Credit Cards: A, B
Notes: 4, 5, 7, 8, 11, 12, 13, 14

6 Pets welcome; 8 Children welcome; 9 Social drinking allowed; 10 Tennis available; 11 Swimming available; 12 Golf available; 13 Skiing available; 14 May be booked through travel agents.

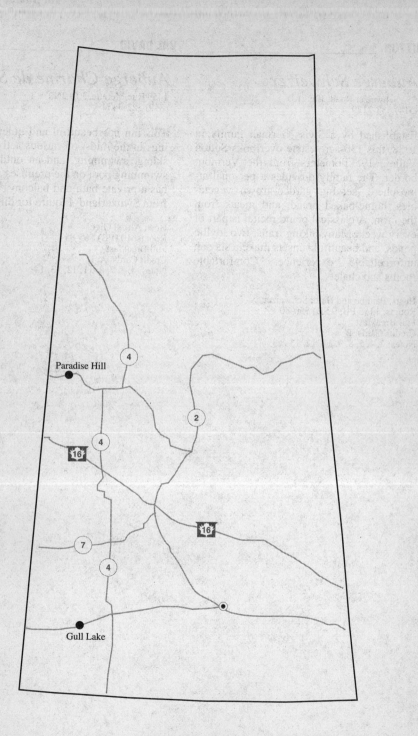

Paradise Hill

④ 4

② 2

④ 4

🛡16

🛡16

⑦ 7

④ 4

Gull Lake

Saskatchewan

Saskatchewan

GULL LAKE

Magee's Farm

Box 428, S0N 1A0
(306) 672-3970

Mixed working farm for four generations. Home cooking with their own produce. Photography is one of the host's hobbies. In southwest Saskatchewan. Hosts are interested in conservation and people. They share their yard with grandchildren and other small animals.

Hosts: Beatrice and Tom Magee
Cottage: 4 (PB) $40
Full Breakfast
Credit Cards: D, E
Notes: 2, 3, 4, 5, 6, 7, 9, 11, 12

PARADISE HILL

Country Cottage
All Season Vacation Farm
Bed and Breakfast

Box 126, S0M 2G0
(306) 344-2137

In home loghouse accommodation or guest cottage for up to five people. Quiet, relaxing rural setting, lots of trees, bushes, wild flowers, berries, farm animals, and birds. Badminton, table tennis, scenic hiking, lakes, swimming pool, historic sites, and skiing nearby. Home baking and organic homegrown produce used. RV, tenters, hunters, cross-country skiers, and snow mobilers welcome. Families with children welcome.

Hosts: Robert and Marla Rauser
Rooms: 2 (PB) $35
Credit Cards: None
Notes: 2, 3, 4, 5, 6, 7 (limited), 8, 9, 10, 11, 12, 13, 14

NOTES: Credit cards accepted: A MasterCard; B Visa; C American Express; D Discover Card; E Diner's Club; F Other; 2 Personal checks accepted; 3 Lunch available; 4 Dinner available; 5 Open all year; 6 Pets welcome; 7 Smoking allowed; 8 Children welcome; 9 Social drinking allowed; 10 Tennis available; 11 Swimming available; 12 Golf available; 13 Skiing available; 14 May be booked through travel agents.

Puerto Rico
Virgin Islands

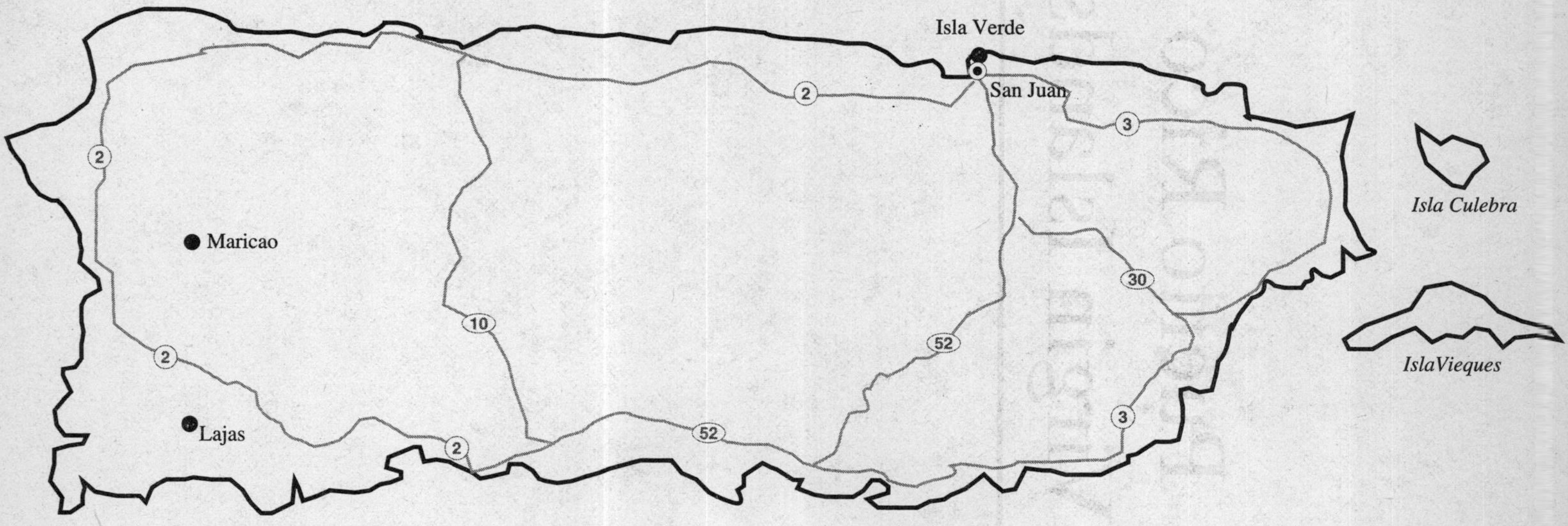

Isla Culebra

IslaVieques

Puerto Rico

3

30

3

Isla Verde

San Juan

52

2

52

10

2

Maricao

2

Lajas

2

Puerto Rico

CABO ROJO

Parador Perichi's

Road 102, KM 14.3, Piaya Joyuda, 00623
(809) 851-3131 (0590, 0560, 0620)
FAX (809) 851-0590

Parador Perichi's Hotel, Restaurant, and Cocktail Lounge in Joyuda, site of Puerto Rico's resorts on the west. Excellence has distinguished Perichi's in its 12 years of hospitality and service. Thirty air-conditioned rooms are furnished with wall-to-wall carpeting, private baths and balconies, color TV, and telephones. Perichi's award-winning restaurant features the finest foods. After sunset, meet friends in the well-stocked and cozy lounge. Live music on weekends at the pool area. Comfortable banquet room can accommodate 300 people—for those who like to combine business with pleasure.

Rooms: 30 (PB) $69.15-79.45
Full Breakfast
Credit Cards: A, B, C, D, E, F
Notes: 3, 4, 5, 7, 8, 9, 10, 11, 12, 13, 14

CULEBRA

Villa Arynar

Box 744, 00775
(809) 742-3145

Villa Arynar is a new waterfront home on Puerto Rico's offshore island, Culebra. It is easily and inexpensively accessible by direct flights from San Juan. The island features the Caribbean's most beautiful and unspoiled beaches, incredible snorkeling and scuba diving, wildlife preserves and a friendly and unhurried way of life. At Villa Arynar luxuriate on the hugh decks while watching boats go by and let the peace and tranquility make this a vacation to remember.

Hosts: Francette and Bernie Roeder
Rooms: 2 (SB) $60-65
Full Breakfast
Credit Cards: A, B, C, D
Notes: 9, 11

ISLA VERDE

The Duffys' Inn

9 Isla Verde Road, 00979
(809) 726-1415; (800) 221-3917

The Duffys', established in 1947 from an old Spanish hacienda with lush tropical plants in the courtyard, is open 24 hours. A full-menu restaurant operates from 7:30 A.M. until midnight. Across the street from the ocean and near the airport. Casinos, golf, tennis, water sports, and other dining facilities are nearby. Comfortable rooms include air conditioning, ceiling fans, cable TV, and telephones.

Host: Madeline Weihe
Rooms: 10 (PB) $55-75
Full Breakfast
Credit Cards: A, B, C
Notes: 3, 4, 5, 7, 9, 10, 11, 12, 14

LAJAS

Parador Villa Parguera

P.O. Box 273, 00667
(809) 899-7777

NOTES: Credit cards accepted: A MasterCard; B Visa; C American Express; D Discover Card; E Diner's Club; F Other; 2 Personal checks accepted; 3 Lunch available; 4 Dinner available; 5 Open all year; 6 Pets welcome; 7 Smoking allowed; 8 Children welcome; 9 Social drinking allowed; 10 Tennis available; 11 Swimming available; 12 Golf available; 13 Skiing available; 14 May be booked through travel agents.

Parador Villa Parguera is on the southwest coast of Puerto Rico in the fishing village of La Parguera, near the famous Phosphorescent Bay. Facilities include a restaurant, bar, and saltwater swimming pool. All rooms have private baths, air conditioning, color TVs, and telephones. Trips may also be arranged for snorkeling and diving, or to the channels and the island of Mata La Gata.

Rooms: 62 (PB) $75
Continental Breakfast
Credit Cards: A, B, C, E
Notes: 3, 4, 5, 7, 8, 9, 11, 13, 14

MARICAO

La Hacienda Juanita

Road 105, KM 23.5, Box 777, 00606
(809) 838-2550

Built 160 years ago as the main lodge of a coffee plantation, this bed and breakfast offers lush tropical vegetation and verdant views of the mountains. Caressed by the scent of orange, grapefruit, and guava, and kissed by the bright starlight of the mountain elevation. Songs of tropical birds, wide verandas with wicker furniture, and rocking chairs invite lazy siestas.

Host: Luis Rivera-Lugo
Rooms: 21 (PB) $69.55-90.95
Full Breakfast
Credit Cards: A, B, C
Notes: 2, 3, 4, 5, 7, 8, 9, 10, 11, 14

OLD SAN JOSÉ

Casa San José

159 San José Street, 00901
(809) 723-1212

The beautiful mansion of Casa San José has old marble floors throughout three floors and the mezzanine and possesses one of the few elevators to be found in a historic building. There are four one-bedroom suites, one two-bedroom suite, and four double rooms, all furnished comfortably and elegantly with antiques and an eclectic

mixture of beautiful furnishings. Balconies surround the interior patio, a quiet green place with the sound of water in the fountain. Particularly special is the Salón Grande on the second floor. It is a lovely place to enjoy afternoon tea, cocktails, or to sit and enjoy a book. Breakfast and a light lunch are served.

Rooms: 10 (PB) $170-700
Continental Breakfast
Credit Cards: A, B, C, E
Notes: 5, 7, 9, 10, 11, 14

El Canario Inn

SAN JUAN

El Canario Inn

1317 Ashford Avenue, Condado, 00907
(809) 722-3861; (800) 533-2649

San Juan's most historic and unique bed and breakfast. All 25 guest rooms are air-conditioned, with private bath, telephone, and cable TV. Beautiful tropical patio areas for relaxation. Only one block to beautiful Condado Beach, casinos, boutiques, and many fine restaurants. El Canario is perhaps the best deal for the vacation dollar in the Caribbean. Higher rates apply when booked through 800-number reservation service.

Hosts: Jude and Keith Olson
Rooms: 25 (PB) $65-90
Continental Breakfast

NOTES: Credit cards accepted: A MasterCard; B Visa; C American Express; D Discover Card; E Diner's Club; F Other; 2 Personal checks accepted; 3 Lunch available; 4 Dinner available; 5 Open all year;

Credit Cards: A, B, C, D, E
Notes: 5, 7, 8, 9, 14

El Prado Inn

1350 Calle Luchetti, 00907
(809) 728-5925; (800) 468-4521

In the most elegant section of San Juan, this small, exclusive inn is perfect for a tour base in San Juan. Continental breakfast is served by the Spanish-style patio and the pool. A three-minute walk to major hotels, bars, discos, casinos, and restaurants. All rooms with private baths, cable TV, air conditioners, and fans.

Host: Chris Teseo
Rooms: 22 (PB) $49-89
Continental Breakfast
Credit Cards: A, B, C, D, E
Notes: 5, 6, 7, 8, 9, 10, 11, 14

Tres Palmas Guest House

2212 Park Boulevard, 00979
(809) 727-4617; FAX (809) 727-5434

This impeccably neat, gray Spanish-style house with tile roof is locked behind a wrought-iron gate. The petite hacienda beckons a small group of guests who delight in its intimacy as well as outstanding unobstructed views of the Atlantic just across the roadway. The pleasant and modest guest accommodations boast little touches such as attractive wall coverings, mirrors over the beds, and modern, private baths. All guest rooms boast air conditioning, clock radios, and separate outside entrances. There are also two efficiency apartments in a neighboring building.

Host: Eric Torres
Rooms: 10 (9 PB; 1 SB) $55-100
Continental Breakfast
Credit Cards: A, B, C
Notes: None

VIEQUES

Villa Esperanza Beach Hotel

P.O. Box 1569, 00765
(809) 741-8675; FAX (809) 741-1313

This inn is on the southern side of the picturesque island of Vieques, 16 miles off the eastern coast of Puerto Rico. A stroll through the lovely gardens takes guests directly to the tropical, aquamarine waters of the Caribbean Sea. Enjoy kayaking, snorkeling, swimming, fishing, scuba diving, water biking, and sailing. Some of the guest rooms can accommodate a family of four. Excellent restaurant with a veranda overlooking the sea, where the Beach Bar opens at 11:30 A.M. and serves a light lunch.

Hosts: Sally Acevedo and Carlos Ruiz-Cox
Rooms: 20 (PB) $76-96
Continental Breakfast
Credit Cards: A, B, C
Notes: 2, 3, 4, 5, 6, 7, 8, 9, 10, 11

6 Pets welcome; 8 Children welcome; 9 Social drinking allowed; 10 Tennis available; 11 Swimming available; 12 Golf available; 13 Skiing available; 14 May be booked through travel agents.

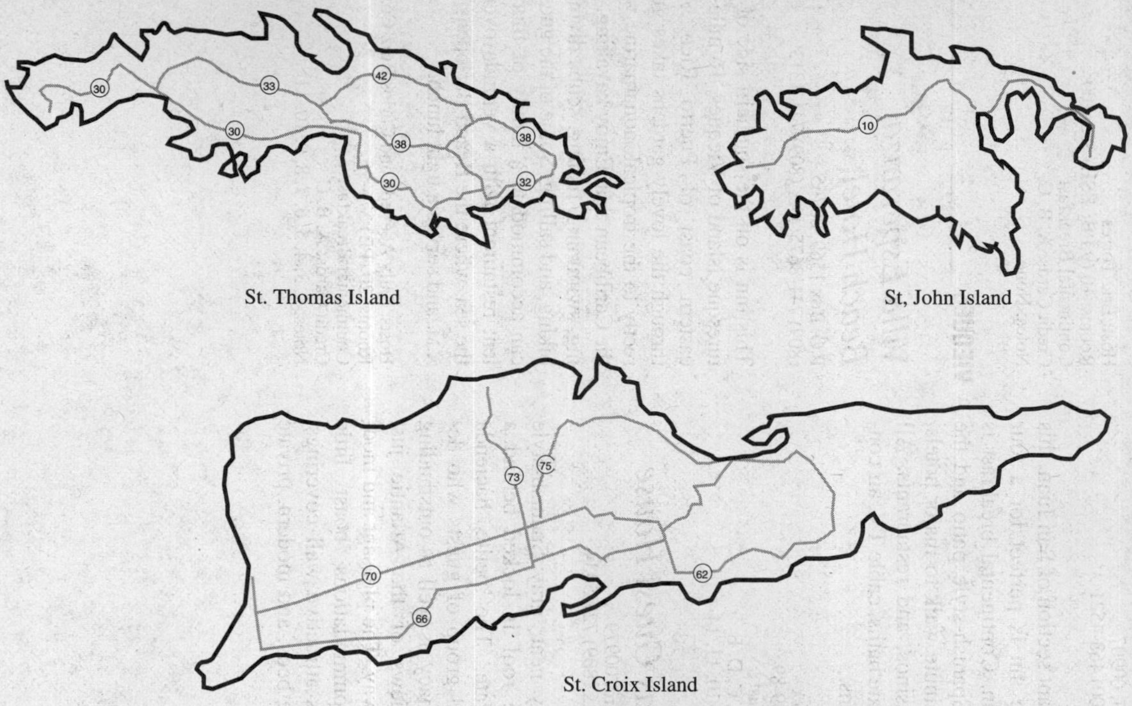

St. John Island

St. Croix Island

St. Thomas Island

Virgin Islands

Virgin Islands

ST. CROIX

Pink Fancy Inn

27 Prince Street, 00820
(809) 773-8460; (800) 524-2045
FAX (809) 773-6448

A small, uniquely private inn is in downtown Christiansted in St. Croix, this historic
landmark was built in 1780 and 1880 and
completely remodeled in 1990. Guests will
find a pool, courtyard, garden, hardwood
floors, air conditioning, cable TV, telephone, clock radio, plus a ceiling fan, a large
room, and friendly and helpful staff. Room
rates include Continental breakfast, an
honor bar open 24 hours a day, and the inn is
within walking distance of restaurants and
duty-free shopping. Arrangements made for
water sports, an island tour, and wedding
and honeymoon packages.

Host: Dixie Ann Tang Yuk
Rooms: 12 (PB) $75-125
Continental Breakfast
Credit Cards: A, B, C
Notes: 5, 7, 8, 9, 10 11, 12 (call), 14

ST. JOHN

The Cruz Inn

Box 566, Cruz Bay, 00831
(809) 693-8688; (800) 666-7688

Charming West Indian-style inn with sunset
bar and view of water and islands. Guest
rooms with shared bath and efficiency and
one-bedroom apartments with bath and
kitchen. Some accommodations have air
conditioning. Just ten minutes from the
dock at Cruz Bay. Personalized service.
Weekly entertainment. Continental breakfast served. Children welcome in apartments only.

Host: Gayle Gosselin
Rooms: 14 (5 PB; 9 SB) $50-95
Continental Breakfast
Credit Cards: A, B, C, D
Notes: 5, 7, 8 (limited), 9, 10, 11, 14

ST. THOMAS

American Country Collection

4 Greenwood Lane, Delmar, NY 12054
(518) 439-7001

Pink Fancy Inn

401. This bed and breakfast is in town and offers rooms and family suites with kitchenette, air conditioning, TV, and telephone in guests' rooms. Minutes from shopping and restaurants. Dinner is available and a full breakfast is served. Double beds in the rooms, and four double beds in the suites. No pets. Smoking allowed. Ten percent gratuity. $60-120.

402. This small bed and breakfast hotel is representative of Spanish Colonial architecture, 800 feet above Charlotte Amalie, the capital of the Virgin Islands. Minisuites and rooms with air conditioning and private baths are available. Suites also have cable TV. A full-service restaurant is on premises, and a Continental breakfast and pool with a snack bar are available for guests to enjoy. Smoking permitted. Free transportation to Magens Bay Beach daily. Ten percent gratuity. $60-135.

404. Spacious and luxurious guest rooms, all with either king- or queen-size bed, cable TV, ceiling fan, air conditioning, and private bath, are what guests will find in this lovely bed and breakfast. A large, luxurious pool overlooks Charlotte Amalie Harbor. Continental breakfast is served daily, and a gourmet restaurant serving Continental cuisine with West Indian flair is on the premises. Piano lounge with outdoor terrace for dancing. No pets. Smoking permitted. Ten percent gratuity. $95-190.

Danish Chalet Inn

P.O. Box 4319, 00803
(809) 774-5764; (800) 635-1531
FAX (809) 777-4886

Family-operated 13-room inn overlooking beautiful Charlotte Amalie Harbor with cool harbor and mountain breezes. Ten minutes from the airport and a five-minute walk to the center of town for duty-free shopping, fine restaurants, and waterfront activities; 15 minutes to world-famous beaches. In-room telephones, sun deck, Jacuzzi, honor bar, free beach towels, and welcoming beverage. Congenial family atmosphere. Dinner restaurant two minutes away. Minimart and laundromat a block away.

Hosts: Frank and Mary Davis
Rooms: 13 (5 PB; 8 SB) $60-95
Continental Breakfast
Credit Cards: A, B
Notes: 5, 7, 8, 9, 10, 11, 12, 14

Galleon House

Box 6577, 00804
(809) 774-6952; (800) 524-2052
FAX (809) 774-6952

Lovely 14-room small hotel in a historic district one block from town. Fantastic harbor view. Warm, hospitable inn with delightful home-cooked breakfast. Freshwater pool, easy walk to shopping and restaurants. Air-conditioned rooms with private balconies, cable TVs, telephones, and guest refrigerators. Call or write for color brochure.

Host: John Slone
Rooms: 14 (12 PB; 2 SB) $49-119
Continental Breakfast
Credit Cards: A, B, C, D
Notes: 5, 7, 8, 9, 11, 12, 14

The Heritage Manor

P.O. Box 90, 00804
(809) 774-3003; (800) 828-0757
FAX (809) 776-9585

Beautifully restored 19th-century mansion boasts European country charm and is very clean. All rooms feature air conditioning, fans, refrigerators, and some have kitchens. Enjoy the pool, sundeck, and courtyard. Only five minutes to shops, restaurants, the harbor, ferries, and downtown. Continental breakfast available December through April.

Host: Susan Murphy
Rooms: 8 (4 PB; 4 SB) $50-130
Continental Breakfast
Credit Cards: A, B, C
Notes: 5, 7, 9, 11, 12, 14

NOTES: Credit cards accepted: A MasterCard; B Visa; C American Express; D Discover Card; E Diner's Club; F Other; 2 Personal checks accepted; 3 Lunch available; 4 Dinner available; 5 Open all year;

Bed and Breakfast
Recommendation Form

As *The Annual Directory of American and Canadian Bed & Breakfasts* gains approval from the traveling public, more and more inns ask to be included on our mailing list. If you know of another bed and breakfast which may not be on our list, give them a great business-boosting opportunity by providing us with the following information:

B&B Name _____

Address _____

City _____ State _____ Zip Code _____

Telephone _____

Name of Hosts _____

B&B Name _____

Address _____

City _____ State _____ Zip Code _____

Telephone _____

Name of Hosts _____

B&B Name _____

Address _____

City _____ State _____ Zip Code _____

Telephone _____

Name of Hosts _____

◆

Please send this form to:
The Annual Directory of American and Canadian Bed & Breakfasts
211 Seventh Avenue North
Nashville, TN 37219

Notes

Notes

Notes

Notes

Notes

Notes

Notes

Notes

Notes

Notes

Notes

Notes

Notes

Notes

Notes

Notes

Notes

Notes

Notes